The **Rough Guide** to

Australia

written and researched by

Margo Daly, Anne Dehne, David Leffman and Chris Scott

with additional contributions by

Chris Canty, Tim Dub, Simon Foster, Helen Marsden, Suzanne Morton-Taylor and Ian Osborn

NEW YORK • LONDON • DELHI

www.roughguides.com

Contents

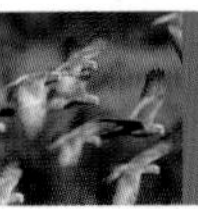

Australian wildlife colour section following p.312

The great outdoors colour section following p.592

Food and drink colour section following p.872

◀◀ Swimmers at Noosa, Queensland ◀ Great Barrier Reef

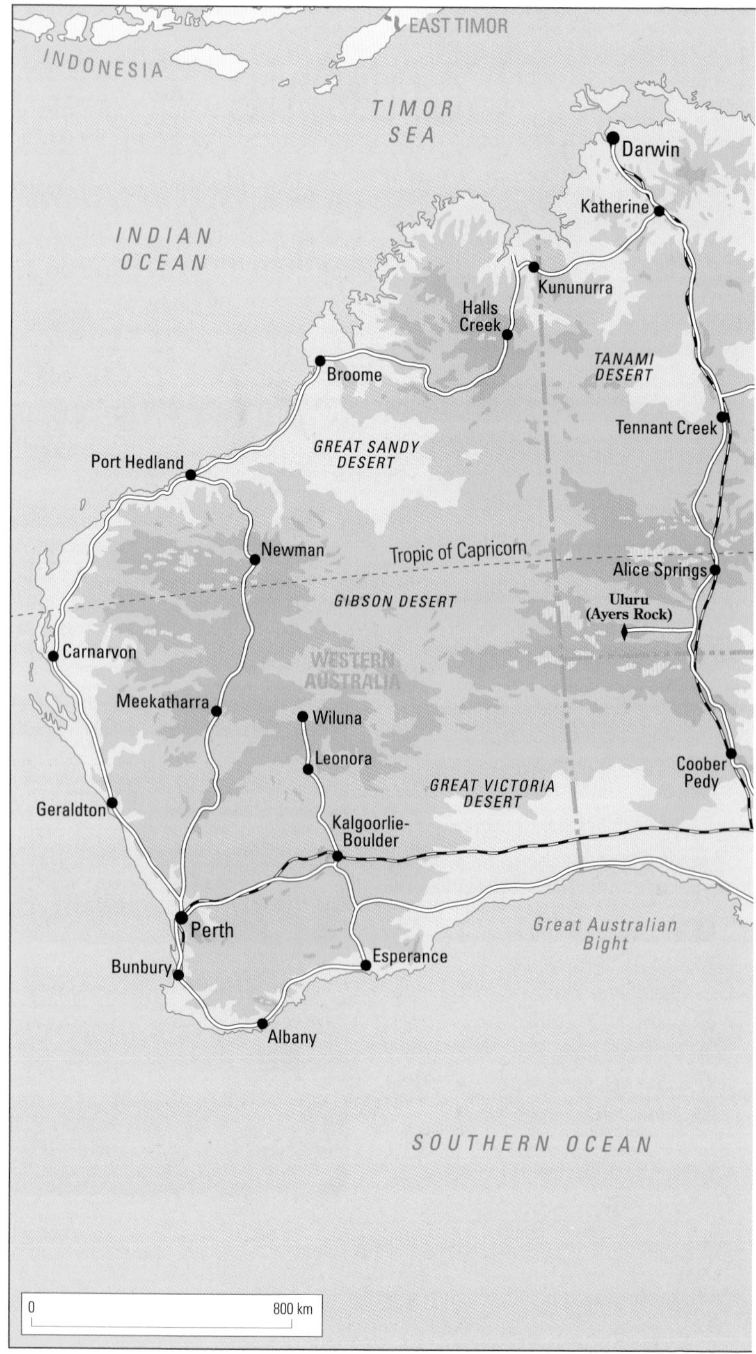
EAST TIMOR
INDONESIA
TIMOR SEA
INDIAN OCEAN
Darwin
Katherine
Kununurra
Halls Creek
TANAMI DESERT
Broome
Tennant Creek
GREAT SANDY DESERT
Port Hedland
Newman
Tropic of Capricorn
Alice Springs
GIBSON DESERT
Uluru (Ayers Rock)
Carnarvon
WESTERN AUSTRALIA
Meekatharra
Wiluna
Leonora
Coober Pedy
GREAT VICTORIA DESERT
Geraldton
Kalgoorlie-Boulder
Perth
Great Australian Bight
Bunbury
Esperance
Albany
SOUTHERN OCEAN
0
800 km

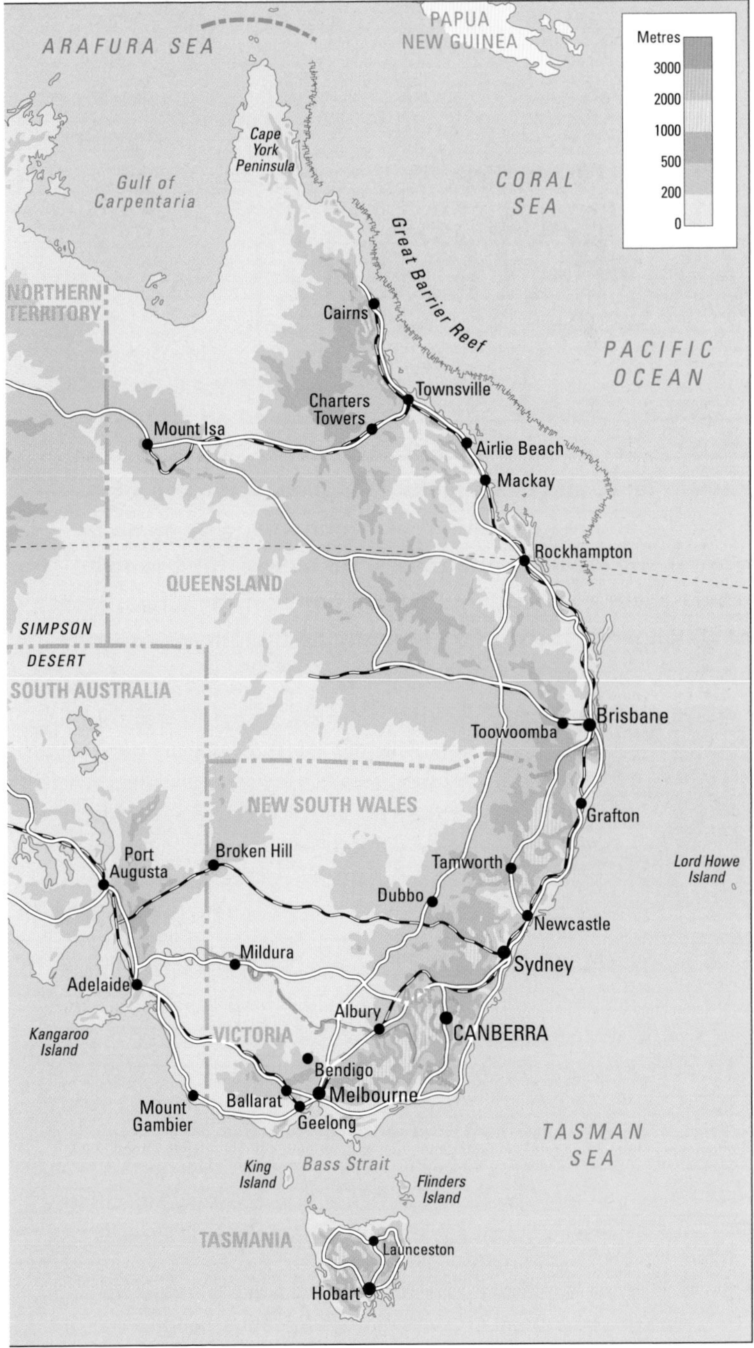

ARAFURA SEA
PAPUA NEW GUINEA
Metres
3000
2000
1000
500
200
0
Cape York Peninsula
Gulf of Carpentaria
CORAL SEA
Great Barrier Reef
NORTHERN TERRITORY
Cairns
PACIFIC OCEAN
Townsville
Charters Towers
Mount Isa
Airlie Beach
Mackay
Rockhampton
QUEENSLAND
SIMPSON DESERT
SOUTH AUSTRALIA
Brisbane
Toowoomba
NEW SOUTH WALES
Grafton
Port Augusta
Broken Hill
Tamworth
Lord Howe Island
Dubbo
Newcastle
Mildura
Sydney
Adelaide
Albury
CANBERRA
Kangaroo Island
VICTORIA
Bendigo
Melbourne
Ballarat
Mount Gambier
Geelong
TASMAN SEA
King Island
Bass Strait
Flinders Island
TASMANIA
Launceston
Hobart

Introduction to Australia

Australia is massive, and sparsely peopled: in size, it rivals the USA, yet its population is just twenty million. It is an ancient land, and often looks it: in places, it's the most eroded, denuded and driest of continents, with much of central and western Australia – the bulk of the country – overwhelmingly arid and flat. In contrast, its cities, most of which were founded as recently as the mid-nineteenth century, express a youthful energy.

The most memorable scenery is in the Outback, the vast desert in the interior of the country west of the Great Dividing Range. Here, vivid blue skies, cinnamon-red earth, deserted gorges and other striking geological features – as well as bizarre wildlife – comprise a unique ecology, one that has played host to the oldest surviving human culture for up to 70,000 years (just 10,000 years after *Homo sapiens* is thought to have emerged from Africa).

This harsh interior has forced modern Australia to become a **coastal country**. Most of the population lives within 20km of the ocean, occupying a suburban, southeastern arc extending from southern Queensland to Adelaide. These urban Australians celebrate the typical New World values of material self-improvement through hard work and hard play, with an easy-going vitality that visitors, especially Europeans, often find refreshingly hedonistic. A sunny climate also contributes to this exuberance, with an outdoor life in which a thriving beach culture and the congenial backyard "barbie" are central.

While visitors might eventually find this *Home and Away* lifestyle rather prosaic, there are opportunities – particularly in the Northern Territory – to gain some experience of **Australia's indigenous peoples** and their

▶ The Great Ocean Road, Victoria

culture, through visiting ancient art sites, taking tours and, less easily, making personal contact. Many Aboriginal people – especially in central Australia – have managed to maintain a traditional lifestyle (albeit with modern accoutrements), speaking their own languages and living according to their law. Conversely, most Aboriginal people you'll come across in country towns and cities are victims of what is scathingly referred to as "welfare colonialism" – a disempowering consequence of dole cheques and other subsidies combined with little chance of meaningful employment, often resulting in a destructive cycle of poverty, ill health and substance abuse. There's still a long way to go before black and white people in Australia can exist on genuinely equal terms.

Where to go

For visitors, deciding where to go can mean juggling with distance, money and time. You could spend months driving around the Outback, exploring the national parks, or hanging out at beaches; or you could take an all-in two-week "Reef, Rock and Harbour" package, encompassing Australia's outstanding trinity of "must-sees".

Fact file

- With an area of eight million square kilometres, Australia is the **sixth largest country** in the world.
- The **population** stands at just twenty million, of whom some 85 percent live in urban areas, mainly along the coast. About 92 percent of the population are of European origin, 2 percent Aboriginal, and around 6 percent Asian and Middle Eastern.
- Much of Australia is arid and flat. One third is **desert** and another third steppe or semi-desert. Only six percent of the country rises above 600m in elevation, and its **tallest peak**, Mount Kosciuszko, is just 2228m high.
- Australia's main **exports** are fossil fuels, minerals, metals, cotton, wool, wine and beef, and its most important **trading partners** are Japan, China and the US.
- Australia is a **federal parliamentary state** (formally a constitutional monarchy) with two legislative houses, the Senate and the House of Representatives. The chief of state is the British Monarch, represented by the Governor-General, while the head of government is the Prime Minister.

Outdoor activities

Though there's fun to be had in the cities, it's really the **great outdoors** that makes Australia such a special place. Its multitude of national parks – around a thousand in total – embrace everything from isolated beaches and tropical rainforest to the vast wildernesses of the bush and the Outback. Visitors are spoilt for choice when it comes to getting out and about, with a huge range of outdoor pursuits on offer – everything from diving off the Great Barrier Reef or white-water rafting Tasmania's Franklin River to hot-air ballooning over Alice Springs or even skiing in the Australian Alps. Perhaps the best way to see something of the great outdoors, and certainly the cheapest and the most popular, is bushwalking – you'll find trails marked in every national park. For more, see p.64 and *The great outdoors* colour section.

Both options provide thoroughly Australian experiences, but neither will leave you with a feeling of having more than scraped the surface of this vast country. The two big natural attractions are the two-thousand-kilometre-long **Great Barrier Reef** off the Queensland coast, with its complex of islands and underwater splendour, and the brooding monolith of **Uluru** (Ayers Rock), in the Northern Territory's Red Centre. You should certainly try to see them, although exploration of other parts of the country will bring you into contact with more subtle but equally rewarding sights and opportunities.

The **cities** are surprisingly cosmopolitan: waves of postwar immigrants from southern Europe and, more recently, Southeast Asia have done much to erode Australia's Anglocentrism. Each Australian state has a capital stamped with its own personality, and nowhere is this more apparent than

▲ Luna Park, Sydney

in New South Wales, where glamorous Sydney has the iconic landmarks of the Opera House and Harbour Bridge. Elsewhere, the sophisticated café society of Melbourne (Victoria) contrasts with the vitality of Brisbane (Queensland). Adelaide, in South Australia, has a human scale and old-fashioned charm, while Perth, in Western Australia, camouflages its isolation with a leisure-oriented urbanity. In Hobart, the capital of Tasmania, you'll encounter fine heritage streetscapes and get a distinct maritime feel. The purpose-built administrative centre of Canberra, in the Australian Capital Territory, often fails to grip visitors, but Darwin's continuing revival enlivens an exploration of the distinctive "Territory".

Away from the suburbs, with their vast shopping malls and quarter-acre residential blocks, is the transitional "bush", and beyond that the wilderness of the **Outback** – the quintessential Australian environment. Protected from the arid interior, the **east coast** has the pick of the country's greenery and scenery, from the north's tropical rainforests and the Great Barrier Reef to the surf-lined beaches further south. The east coast is backed by the Great Dividing Range, which steadily decreases in elevation as it extends from Mount Kosciuszko (2228m) in New South Wales north into tropical Queensland. If you have time to spare, a trip to often-overlooked **Tasmania**, across the Bass Strait, is worthwhile: you'll be rewarded with vast tracts of wilderness as well as landscapes almost English in their bucolic qualities.

◀ Camp breakfast in the Outback

When to go

Australia's **climate** has become less predictable in recent times, although like the rest of the planet the country has rarely had stable weather patterns over the last few thousand years. Recently observed phenomena, such as an extended drought in the eastern Outback, the cyclic El Niño effect, and even the hole in the ozone layer – which is disturbingly close to the country – are probably part of a long-term pattern.

Visitors from the northern hemisphere should remember that, as early colonials observed, in Australia "nature is horribly reversed": when it's winter or summer in the northern hemisphere, the opposite season prevails Down Under, a principle that becomes harder to apply to the transitional seasons of spring and autumn. To confuse things further, the four seasons only really exist in the **southern half of the country** outside of the tropics. Here, you'll find reliably warm summers at the coast with regular, but thankfully brief, heatwaves in excess of 40°C. Head inland, and the temperatures rise further. Winters, on the other hand, can be miserable, particularly in Victoria, where the short days add to the gloom. Tasmania's highlands make for unpredictable weather all year round, although summer is the best time to explore the island's outdoor attractions.

In the **coastal tropics**, weather basically falls into two seasons. The best time to visit is during the hot and cloudless Dry (from April to November), with moderate coastal humidity maintaining a pleasant temperature day and night and cooler nights inland. In contrast, the Wet – particularly the "Build Up" in November or December before the rains commence – can

▼ Federation Square, Melbourne

▲ Customized surfboard, Sydney

be very uncomfortable, with stifling, near-total humidity. As storm clouds gather, rising temperatures, humidity and tension can provoke irrational behaviour in the psychologically unacclimatized – something known as "going troppo". Nevertheless, the mid-Wet's daily downpours and enervating mugginess can be quite intoxicating, compelling a hyper-relaxed inactivity for which these regions are known; furthermore, the countryside – if you can reach it – looks its best at this time.

Australia's **interior** is an arid semi-desert with very little rain, high summer temperatures and occasionally freezing winter nights. Unless you're properly equipped to cope with these extremes, you'd be better off coming here during the transitional seasons between April and June, or October and November.

Aboriginal art

Aboriginal art has grown into a million-dollar industry since the first canvas **dot paintings** of the central deserts emerged in the 1970s. Though seemingly abstract, early canvases are said to replicate ceremonial sand paintings – temporary "maps" fleetingly revealed to depict sacred knowledge. In the tropics, figurative **bark** and **cave paintings** are less enigmatic but much older, though until recently they were ceremonially repainted. The unusual **x-ray style** found in the Top End details the internal structure of animals. The Northern Territory – and Alice Springs, in particular – are the best places to look; for tips on buying Aboriginal art as well as didgeridoos, see pp.601–602.

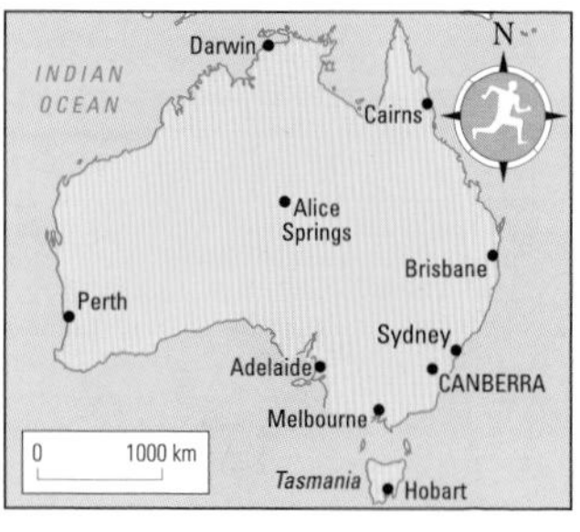

In general, the **best time to visit** the south is during the Australian summer, from December to March, though long summer holidays from Christmas through January mean that prices are higher and beaches more crowded at this time. In the tropical north, the best months are from May to October, while in the Centre they are from October to November and from March to May. If you want to tour extensively, keep to the southern coasts in summer and head north for the winter.

Average temperatures (°C) and rainfall (mm)

	Jan/Feb		Mar/Apr		May/Jun		July/Aug		Sept/Oct		Nov/Dec	
Adelaide												
Av. temp. (°C)	28	27	25	22	18	16	14	15	17	21	22	25
Av. rainfall (mm)	20	20	25	45	65	70	65	60	55	40	25	20
Alice Springs												
Av. temp. (°C)	36	35	32	27	22	21	19	21	25	30	32	35
Av. rainfall (mm)	35	40	25	20	25	25	20	20	10	25	30	35
Brisbane												
Av. temp. (°C)	27	27	26	25	23	21	23	22	24	25	26	27
Av. rainfall (mm)	160	160	150	80	70	60	55	50	50	75	100	140
Cairns												
Av. temp. (°C)	31	31	30	29	28	25	25	27	27	28	30	31
Av. rainfall (mm)	400	440	450	180	100	50	30	25	35	35	90	160
Canberra												
Av. temp. (°C)	27	25	23	20	15	13	12	13	15	18	22	25
Av. rainfall (mm)	55	50	50	45	50	30	30	50	50	70	65	65
Darwin												
Av. temp. (°C)	31	30	31	32	31	30	30	31	32	32	33	32
Av. rainfall (mm)	400	430	435	75	50	10	5	10	15	70	110	310
Hobart												
Av. temp. (°C)	21	21	20	17	14	12	11	12	15	18	19	20
Av. rainfall (mm)	50	45	50	55	50	45	50	50	55	55	50	50
Melbourne												
Av. temp. (°C)	26	26	24	21	16	15	14	15	17	19	21	20
Av. rainfall (mm)	45	50	55	60	55	50	50	50	55	65	55	55
Perth												
Av. temp. (°C)	30	30	28	25	22	20	19	19	20	22	25	28
Av. rainfall (mm)	10	15	25	50	125	185	175	145	80	75	25	20
Sydney												
Av. temp. (°C)	25	25	24	23	20	17	16	17	19	22	23	24
Av. rainfall (mm)	100	105	125	130	125	130	110	75	60	75	70	75

All temperatures are in Centigrade: to convert to Fahrenheit multiply by 9/5 and add 32.

things not to miss

It's not possible to see everything that Australia has to offer in one trip – and we don't suggest you try. What follows, in no particular order, is a selective taste of the country's highlights: beautiful beaches, outstanding national parks, spectacular wildlife and lively festivals. They're arranged in five colour-coded categories, which you can browse through to find the very best things to see and experience. All highlights have a page reference to take you straight into the Guide, where you can find out more.

01 Sailing in the Whitsundays (Qld) Page **434** • There's fantastic sailing and diving – and whale watching in season – in the idyllic white-sand Whitsunday Islands.

02 Blue Mountains (NSW) Page **204** • World Heritage–listed, the Blue Mountains, just west of Sydney, get their name from the blue mist of fragrant eucalyptus oil hanging in the air all year round.

03 Coober Pedy (SA) Page **798** • The underground homes, shops and churches of Coober Pedy – where temperatures soar to over 50˚C in summer – are the most enduring symbol of the harshness of Australia's Outback.

04 Beer Can Regatta, Darwin (NT) Page **563** • Wacky boat races in sea craft made entirely from beer cans, held in early August.

05 Skiing in the Snowy Mountains (NSW) Page **253** • The Snowy Mountains have the best skiing in Australia.

06 Humpback whales (Qld) Page **407** • Saved from extinction by a ban on whaling, humpback whales migrate up the Queensland coast between June and October to calve around the Whitsundays' warm tropical waters.

07 Overland Track in Cradle Mountain-Lake St Clair National Park (Tas) Page **1068** • The eighty-kilometre Overland Track is Australia's greatest extended bushwalk, spread over five or more mud- and leech-filled days of physical, exhilarating exhaustion.

09 Diving at the Great Barrier Reef (Qld) Page **418** • Come face-to-face with stunning coral and shoals of curious fish.

08 Melbourne Cup (Vic) Page **61** • Melbourne's venerable horse race brings the entire country to a standstill around the radio or TV.

10 Bushtucker Page **54** • Witchetty grubs and wattle seeds, possum-tail soup and rooburgers – a few restaurants around the country are now experimenting with bushtucker.

11 Fraser Island (Qld) Page **409** • The giant dunes, freshwater lakes and sculpted, coloured sands of the world's largest sand island form the backdrop to exciting 4WD safaris.

12 Climbing Sydney Harbour Bridge (NSW) Page **113** • Scale the bridge for adrenaline thrills and great vistas – or walk or cycle across it for free.

13 The Franklin River (Tas) Page **1071** • Whitewater rafting is the only way to explore the wild Franklin River, one of the great rivers of Australia.

14 Kangaroo Island (SA) Page **765** • Unspoilt Kangaroo Island boasts fantastic coastal scenery and excellent wildlife-spotting opportunities.

15 Sydney Opera House (NSW) Page **111** • Take in a performance at one of the world's busiest performing-arts centres – interval drinks certainly don't have such spectacular harbour views anywhere else in the world.

16 Kakadu National Park (NT) Page **566** • Australia's largest national park is a vast World Heritage–listed wilderness with an amazing diversity of wildlife.

17 Crocodiles (NT) Page **566** • Head up north to see the Territory's growing population of fearsome crocs.

18 Canoeing up the Katherine Gorge (NT) Page **583** • Hop on a cruise or paddle a canoe through the dramatic orange cliffs of the Katherine Gorge – you won't have it to yourself, but it's still hugely enjoyable.

19 Boating on the Murray River (SA) Page **782** • By far the best way to see the great brown Murray River is to get out on the water – hop on a paddle steamer, splash about in a canoe or rent a houseboat.

20 Giant termite mounds (NT) Page **577** • These impressively huge towers – up to 4m tall – are a regular feature of the Top End.

21 Barossa Valley wineries (SA) Page **751** • Australia's premier wine-producing region, just 50km from Adelaide, is a great place to stop over and unwind.

22 Watching a match at the MCG (Vic) Page **838** • Taking in a game of cricket or, even better, Aussie Rules football at the venerable Melbourne Cricket Ground (MCG) is a must for sports fans.

23 The Kimberley (WA) Page **706** • Regarded as Australia's last frontier, the Kimberley is a sparsely populated, untamed wilderness that contains some stunning landscapes.

24 Mardi Gras (NSW) Page **170** • The irreverent Oxford Street parade, from "dykes on bikes" to the "Melbourne marching boys", ends the summer season.

25 Kings Canyon in Watarrka National Park (NT) Page **615** • The hike around the canyon's rim takes you past exposed lookouts, domed outcrops, and a secluded waterhole that's great for a dip on a hot day.

26 Wilpena Pound (SA) Page **806** • Fantastic hikes amid spectacular scenery at the famous elevated basin of Wilpena Pound in the Flinders Ranges National Park.

27 Manly Ferry (NSW) Page **95** • The short ferry trip from Circular Quay to the surfing Mecca of Manly takes in picture-postcard views of Sydney Harbour.

28 Mutawintji National Park (NSW) Page **355** • Red, barren earth laced with ancient galleries of Aboriginal rock art, secluded gorges and quiet waterholes.

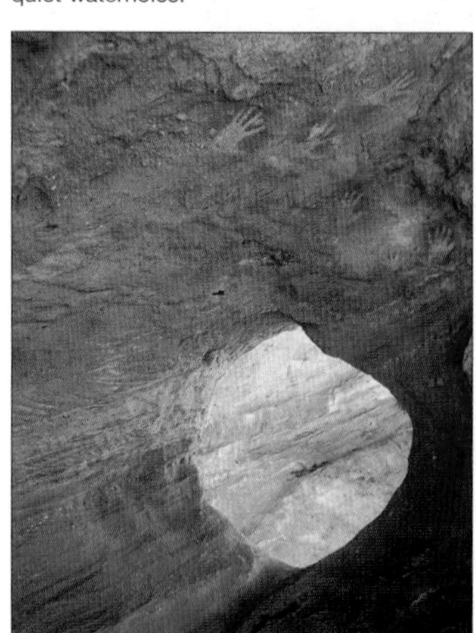

29 Lake Eyre (SA) Page **810** • This massive saline lake, topped by a glaring salt crust and walled by red dunes, creates a harsh, unforgettable landscape.

30 Aboriginal Dance Festival at Laura (Qld) Page **489** • Electrifying celebration of Aboriginal culture, held in June in odd-numbered years.

31 Hiking through Carnarvon Gorge (Qld) Page **509** • With its Aboriginal art sites and magical scenery, a day-hike into the Carnarvon Gorge takes some beating.

32 Karijini National Park (WA) Page **694** • The water-carved gorges of the Karijini National Park make a dramatic backdrop for challenging canyoneering adventures.

34 Tall Timber Country (WA) Page **657** • The primeval karri forests of the so-called Tall Timber Country are one of WA's greatest natural sights. Get a bird's-eye view from the Tree Top Walk.

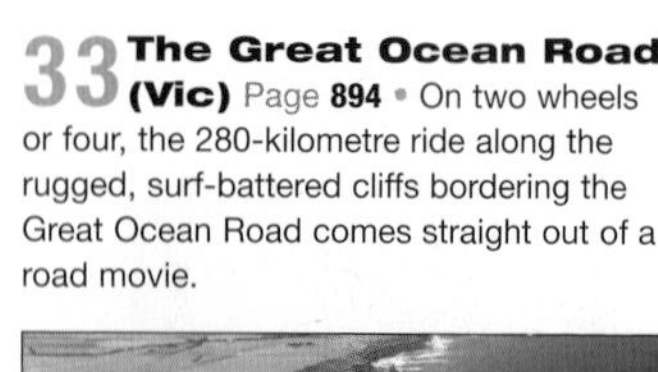

33 The Great Ocean Road (Vic) Page **894** • On two wheels or four, the 280-kilometre ride along the rugged, surf-battered cliffs bordering the Great Ocean Road comes straight out of a road movie.

35 Broken Hill (NSW) Page **346** • Pay a visit to the Royal Flying Doctor Service and the School of the Air headquarters at NSW's historic Outback mining town and thriving arts centre.

36 Rent a four-wheel-drive Page **40** • Adventure off-road from Queensland's Cape York (p.485) to the Territory's Central Deserts (p.706) or WA's Kimberley (p.612).

37 Bondi Beach (NSW) Page **146** • Beach, surf and café culture: Sydney's famous beach has something for everyone.

38 Wilsons Promontory National Park (Vic) Page **947** • Victoria's most popular national park, "The Prom" boasts some superb coastal scenery and bushwalks.

39 Birdsville Races (Qld) Page **515** • Birdsville Hotel is the focus for the annual Birdsville Races, when five thousand people descend on the tiny desert township in Queensland's Outback for a weekend of drinking, horse racing and mayhem.

40 Atherton Tablelands (Qld) Page **473** • With its majestic rainforest, crater lakes and abundant wildlife, you could spend days exploring the Atherton Tablelands.

41 Uluru (NT) Page **620** • Uluru, otherwise known as Ayers Rock, is a sacred site for Aboriginal people, and a magnet for tourists the world over.

Basics

Basics

Getting there

Few will be surprised to learn that flying is the main way of getting to Australia. You can fly pretty much every day to the main east-coast cities from Europe, North America and Southeast Asia. Airfares always depend on the season, with the highest fares being the two weeks either side of Christmas, when the weather is best in the main tourist areas. Fares drop during the "shoulder" seasons – mid-January to March and mid-August to November – and you'll get the best prices during the low season, April to June. Because of the distance from most popular departure points, flying on weekends does not alter the price.

To cut costs, use a **specialist flight agent** or a discount agent, who may also offer special student and youth fares as well as travel insurance, rail passes, car rental, tours and the like. If Australia is only one stop on a longer journey, you might want to consider buying a Round-the-World (RTW) ticket (see below). Some travel agents sell pre-packaged RTW tickets that will have you touching down in about half a dozen cities, and Australia is frequently part of the regular eastbound RTW loop from Europe.

Flights from the UK and Ireland

The north Australian coast is just fifteen hours' **flying** time from London; though in practice the journey to Sydney or the other eastern cities takes a minimum of 21 hours including stopovers. If you break the trip in Southeast Asia or North America, getting to Australia need not be the tedious, seat-bound slog you may have imagined. Note there are no direct flights from Ireland.

Sydney and Melbourne are served by the greatest number of airlines, and carriers such as Qantas charge the same price to fly to any east-coast city between Cairns and Adelaide; flights to Darwin and Perth are around £100 cheaper, but you'll spend at least that much on the overland journey to the east coast. An **open-jaw ticket** (flying into one city and out from another) usually costs no more than an ordinary return.

Direct scheduled flights depart from London's Heathrow airport, although Singapore Airlines has flights from Manchester to Singapore that connect with onward flights to Sydney. With Qantas you can fly from regional airports at Aberdeen, Belfast, Edinburgh, Glasgow, Manchester or Newcastle to connect with your international flight at Heathrow.

Tourists and those on one-year working visas are generally required by Australian immigration to arrive with a ticket out of the country, so **one-way tickets** are really only viable for Australian and New Zealand residents.

The cheapest **fare** you're likely to find is around £550 return, available during the low-season months of April to June, though special offers can go as low as £450; if you insist on flying with Qantas, BA or Singapore Airlines, expect to pay from around £800 for a flight in this off-peak period with special offers sometimes taking prices down to £600. The **most expensive time** to fly is in the two weeks before Christmas, when you'd be lucky to find anything for less than £1000 return: to stand a chance of getting one of the cheaper tickets, book at least six months in advance. Prices also go up from mid-June or the beginning of July to mid-August coinciding with the peak European holiday period. In between times (the shoulder seasons of mid-Aug to Nov and mid-Jan to March) you should expect to pay around £700 (or up to £950 with one of the prestige airlines).

An excellent alternative to a long direct flight is a **multi-stopover ticket**, which can cost the same or just a little more than the price of an ordinary return; check airlines for routings. Unusual routes are inevitably more expensive, but it's possible to fly via South America with

Fly less – stay longer! Travel and climate change

Climate change is the single biggest issue facing our planet. It is caused by a build-up in the atmosphere of carbon dioxide and other greenhouse gases, which are emitted by many sources – including planes. Already, flights account for around 3–4 percent of human-induced global warming: that figure may sound small, but it is rising year on year and threatens to counteract the progress made by reducing greenhouse emissions in other areas.

Rough Guides regard travel, overall, as a global benefit, and feel strongly that the advantages to developing economies are important, as are the opportunities for greater contact and awareness among peoples. But we all have a responsibility to limit our personal "carbon footprint". That means giving thought to how often we fly and what we can do to redress the harm that our trips create.

Flying and climate change

Pretty much every form of motorized travel generates CO_2, but planes are particularly bad offenders, releasing large volumes of greenhouse gases at altitudes where their impact is far more harmful. Flying also allows us to travel much further than we would contemplate doing by road or rail, so the emissions attributable to each passenger become truly shocking. For example, one person taking a return flight between Europe and California produces the equivalent impact of 2.5 tonnes of CO_2 – similar to the yearly output of the average UK car.

Less harmful planes may evolve but it will be decades before they replace the current fleet – which could be too late for avoiding climate chaos. In the meantime, there are limited options for concerned travellers: to reduce the amount we travel by air (take fewer trips, stay longer!), to avoid night flights (when plane contrails trap heat from Earth but can't reflect sunlight back to space), and to make the trips we do take "climate neutral" via a carbon offset scheme.

Carbon offset schemes

Offset schemes run by **climatecare.org**, **carbonneutral.com** and others allow you to "neutralize" the greenhouse gases that you are responsible for releasing. Their websites have simple calculators that let you work out the impact of any flight. Once that's done, you can pay to fund projects that will reduce future carbon emissions by an equivalent amount (such the distribution of low-energy lightbulbs and cooking stoves in developing countries). Please take the time to visit our website and make your trip climate neutral.

www.roughguides.com/climatechange

Aerolineas Argentinas, which offers stops in Buenos Aires and Auckland return.

If you're considering booking a return ticket with Qantas or British Airways and are thinking of heading over to New Zealand or the South Pacific in between, you might want to consider buying a **Boomerang Pass**; see p.35 for more details.

Most of the routings **from Ireland** involve a stopover in London and transfer to one of the airlines listed on p.30. Fares in low-season are usually around the €950 mark, and €1300 in high season. There are often good deals on Olympic Airways from Dublin via Greece. Singapore Airlines has flights ticketed through from Dublin, Shannon or Cork via London to Singapore and Sydney, while Malaysian Airlines also goes from all three Irish airports via Kuala Lumpur. The three airports are also served by the affiliated British Airways and Qantas: all their flights to Australia have a Dublin–London add-on included in the price. For youth and student discount fares, the best first stop is Usit (see p.33).

RTW tickets

Round-the-World (RTW) tickets incorporating Australia provide a chance to see the world on your way to and from Down Under; RTW flights come pre-packaged in a tantalizing variety of permutations, with stopovers chiefly in Asia, the Pacific and North America, but you can pretty much devise your fantasy itinerary and get it priced. A good agent should be able to piece together sector fares from various airlines: providing you keep your itinerary down to three continents, prices range from around £850 for a simple London–Bangkok–Sydney–LA–London deal to well over £1000 for more complicated routings.

Getting there from the US and Canada

From Los Angeles it's possible to **fly non-stop** to Sydney in fourteen and a half hours. Qantas, United, Air Canada and Air New Zealand all operate direct to the east coast of Australia. Flying on a national Asian airline will most likely involve a stop in their capital city (Singapore, Tokyo, Hong Kong, etc), and if you're travelling from the west coast of North America to the east coast of Australia you'll probably find their fares on the Pacific route somewhat higher than their American and Australian competitors. However, if you're flying from the east coast of North America to, say, Perth, a carrier such as Singapore Airlines or Malaysia Airlines with a transatlantic routing may offer the best value.

Many of the major airlines offer deals whereby you can make stopovers either at **Pacific Rim destinations** such as Tokyo, Honolulu or Kuala Lumpur or at a number of exotic South Pacific locations. Either there will be a flat surcharge on your ticket or they may offer you a higher-priced ticket allowing you to make as many stops as you like, within certain parameters, over a fixed period of time.

Sample lowest standard scheduled **fares** for low/high seasons are approximately as follows: to Sydney or Melbourne from Chicago or New York (US$1550/1950); Los Angeles or San Francisco (US$1150/1800); Montréal or Toronto (CDN$1500/2500); Vancouver (CDN$1400/2450); to Perth from New York, Los Angeles or San Francisco (US$1950/2400); Vancouver, Toronto or Montréal (CDN$2100/3100). The price of an **open-jaw ticket** (flying into one city and returning from another) should be approximately the average of the return fares to the two cities. If you plan on flying around Australia, it may be more cost effective to buy a Qantas AirPass (see p.35).

RTW or Circle Pacific tickets

The best deal, if you don't mind planning your itinerary in advance, will most likely be a Round-the-World (RTW) ticket or a Circle Pacific, which has stopoffs in Australia and New Zealand from North America.

A sample **RTW itinerary** would be: Los Angeles–Sydney–Singapore–Bangkok–Delhi–London–Los Angeles (US$4220). While a sample **Circle Pacific route** is New York–Hong Kong–Bangkok–Bandar Seri Begawan (Brunei)–Perth–Kuala Lumpur–New York (US$3921).

Getting there from New Zealand and South Africa

New Zealand–Australia routes are busy and competition is fierce, resulting in an ever-changing range of deals and special offers; your best bet is to check the latest with a specialist travel agent (see p.32) or the relevant airlines' websites. The recent influx of low-cost, **no-frills airlines** has meant a further price drop, with the likes of Virgin Blue, Virgin's low-cost Pacific subsidiary, offering special "Happy Hour" fares daily, from one dollar plus tax. It's a relatively short hop across the Tasman Sea: **flying time** from Auckland to Sydney is around three and a half hours.

All the **fares** quoted below include tax and are for travel during low or shoulder seasons; flying at peak times (primarily Dec to mid-Jan) can add substantially to these prices. Ultimately, the price you pay for your flight will depend on how much flexibility you want; many of the cheapest deals are hedged with restrictions – typically, a maximum stay of thirty days and a fourteen-day advance-purchase requirement. The New Zealand, Web-based Freedom Air specializes in no-frills, low-cost trans-Tasman air travel, with return flights from Auckland, Christchurch, Dunedin, Palmerston North and Wellington starting from around NZ$480. Pacific Blue flies from Christchurch and Wellington from around NZ$500 return. The cheapest regular return fare from Auckland to Sydney is usually with Aerolineas Argentinas (also to Melbourne) for around NZ$380–$500, but flights tend to be heavily booked.

Flying **from South Africa**, the journey time is around twelve hours, travelling from

Johannesburg to Sydney. The main carriers are Qantas and South African Airways, which both offer ten flights a week from around ZAR7800 in low season and ZAR11,800 in high season.

Getting there from Southeast Asia

This is a very popular route for travellers en route to Australia from Europe, or vice versa, especially Australian backpackers heading in the other direction at the start of their trip. Travelling **overland through Southeast Asia** is a bit more demanding than Australia, but it's a fascinating region and is unlikely to make a big dent in your budget. It also shouldn't make too much of a difference to the price of your plane ticket, since many Asian airlines stop in Bangkok, Singapore, Jakarta, Denpasar or Kuala Lumpur on the way to Australia, and breaking your journey is either free or possible for a small extra charge. If you want to go overland on the route detailed below between Bangkok and Bali, rather than just stop over, you could buy a Round-the-World ticket with an overland component. If you do buy a one-way ticket from Bali, you will still need to be in possession of a return ticket out of Australia to get through immigration, probably best routed via Bangkok.

Overland from Bangkok to Bali

Bangkok is a popular starting point for an overland route, with return flights available from around £380–450 in the UK and US$800 in the US. From Bangkok an inexpensive bus service leaves twice daily for the 2000-kilometre ride to Singapore, though it's a gruelling 48-hour trip unless you make a stop or two along the way; a more comfortable option is the International Express train from Bangkok to Butterworth, in Malaysia (21hr), then an overnight train to Kuala Lumpur (9hr), and another train to Singapore (8hr); you will usually need to stay overnight in Butterworth or Penang to connect with the train to KL, but at least a few days is recommended. Book both journeys a day or two in advance to be sure of a seat; the combined price for first class is UK£33/US$50, but considerably cheaper second- and third-class fares are available. Of course, you could instead go in luxury on the *Eastern and Oriental Express* (Ⓦwww.orient-express.com), modelled on the original *Orient Express*; the 41-hour journey via Kuala Lumpur costs from UK£1330/US$1860 per person.

From Singapore, you can cross to the **Indonesian islands** of Sumatra or Kalimantan (Indonesian Borneo) and from there island-hop via local buses and ferries southeast through to Java and Bali, from where you can take a short flight to Darwin in Australia's Northern Territory.

Allow at least a month travelling overland from Bangkok to Bali, but be aware that there is still **political and social unrest** right through Indonesia, including Bali, and travel through some of these regions may not be wise or even possible. Check your country's Department of Foreign Affairs website (see p.80) for the latest information.

Airlines, agents and tour operators

Travel websites and the airlines' own websites offer the best deals and cut out the cost of agents and middlemen. If your time is short and you're reasonably sure of what you want to do, it may not be a bad idea to pre-book some of your accommodation and tours. See below for a list of operators and Australian tour specialists.

Online booking

Ⓦ**www.expedia.co.uk** (in UK), Ⓦ**www.expedia.com** (in US),
Ⓦ**www.expedia.ca** (in Canada)
Ⓦ**www.lastminute.com** (in UK)
Ⓦ**www.opodo.co.uk** (in UK)
Ⓦ**www.orbitz.com** (in US)
Ⓦ**www.travelocity.co.uk** (in UK), Ⓦ**www.travelocity.com** (in US), Ⓦ**www.travelocity.ca** (in Canada)
Ⓦ**www.zuji.com.au** (in Australia), Ⓦ**www.zuji.co.nz** (in New Zealand)
Ⓦ**www.travelshop.com.au** (in Australia)

Airlines

Aerolineas Argentinas UK ⓣ0800/096 9747, US ⓣ1-800/333-0276, Canada ⓣ1-800/688-0008, Ⓦwww.aerolineasargentinas.com.
Air China UK ⓣ020/7744 0800, US ⓣ212-371-9898, Canada ⓣ416-581-8833, Australia ⓣ02/9232 7277, Ⓦwww.air-china.co.uk, Ⓦwww.airchina.com.cn.

Air New Zealand Australia ⓣ13 24 76, NZ ⓣ0800/737 000, ⓦwww.airnz.co.nz.
Air Pacific UK ⓣ0870/572 6827, US ⓣ1-800/227-4446, Australia ⓣ1800 230 150, NZ ⓣ0800 800 178, ⓦwww.airpacific.com.
All Nippon Airways (ANA) UK ⓣ0870/837 8866, Republic of Ireland ⓣ1850/200 058, US & Canada ⓣ1-800/235-9262, ⓦwww.anaskyweb.com.
American Airlines UK ⓣ0845/7789 789, Republic of Ireland ⓣ01/602 0550, US ⓣ1-800/433-7300, Australia ⓣ1300 650 747, NZ ⓣ0800 887 997, ⓦwww.aa.com.
British Airways UK ⓣ0870/850 9850, Republic of Ireland ⓣ1890/626 747, US & Canada ⓣ1-800/AIRWAYS, Australia ⓣ1300 767 177, NZ ⓣ09/966 9777, ⓦwww.ba.com.
Cathay Pacific UK ⓣ020/8834 8888, US ⓣ1-800/233-2742, Australia ⓣ13 17 47, NZ ⓣ09/379 0861, ⓦwww.cathaypacific.com.
China Airlines UK ⓣ020/7436 9001, US ⓣ1-917/368-2003, Australia ⓣ02/9231 5588, NZ ⓣ09/308 3364, ⓦwww.china-airlines.com.
Emirates UK ⓣ0870/243 2222, US ⓣ1-800/777-3999, Australia ⓣ02/9290 9700, NZ ⓣ09/968 2200, ⓦwww.emirates.com.
Freedom Air Australia ⓣ1800 122 000, NZ ⓣ0800 600 500, ⓦwww.freedomair.com/en.
Garuda Indonesia UK ⓣ020/7467 8600, US ⓣ1-212/279-0756, Australia ⓣ1300 365 330 or 02/9334 9944, NZ ⓣ09/366 1862, ⓦwww.garuda-indonesia.com.
JAL (Japan Air Lines) UK ⓣ0845/774 7700, Republic of Ireland ⓣ01/408 3757, US & Canada ⓣ1-800/525-3663, Australia ⓣ02/9272 1111, NZ ⓣ09/379 9906, ⓦwww.jal.com or ⓦwww.japanair.com
KLM (Royal Dutch Airlines) UK ⓣ0870/507 4074, Republic of Ireland ⓣ1850/747 400, US ⓣ1-800/225-2525, Australia ⓣ1300 303 747, NZ ⓣ09/921 6040, SA ⓣ11/961 6767, ⓦwww.klm.com.
Korean Air UK ⓣ0800/413 000, Republic of Ireland ⓣ01/799 7990, US & Canada ⓣ1-800/438-5000, Australia ⓣ02/9262 6000, NZ ⓣ09/914 2000, ⓦwww.koreanair.com.
Malaysia Airlines UK ⓣ0870/607 9090, Republic of Ireland ⓣ01/676 2131, US ⓣ1-212/697-8994, Australia ⓣ13 26 27, NZ ⓣ0800 777 747, ⓦwww.malaysia-airlines.com.
Olympic Airways UK ⓣ0870/606 0460, US ⓣ1-800/223-1226, Canada ⓣ1-416/964-2720, Australia ⓣ02/9251 2044, ⓦwww.olympic-airways.com.
Qantas Airways UK ⓣ0845/774 7767, Republic of Ireland ⓣ01/407 3278, US & Canada ⓣ1-800/227-4500, Australia ⓣ13 13 13, NZ ⓣ0800 808 767 or 09/357 8900, SA ⓣ11/441 8550, ⓦwww.qantas.com.
Pacific Blue NZ ⓣ0800/670 000, outside NZ ⓣ07/3295 2284, ⓦwww.flypacificblue.com.
Royal Brunei UK ⓣ020/7584 6660, Australia ⓣ1300 721 271, NZ ⓣ09/977 2209, ⓦwww.bruneiair.com.
Singapore Airlines UK ⓣ0844/800 2380, Republic of Ireland ⓣ01/671 0722, US ⓣ1-800/742-3333, Canada ⓣ1-800/663-3046, Australia ⓣ13 10 11, NZ ⓣ0800 808 909, SA ⓣ11/880 8560 or 11/880 8566, ⓦwww.singaporeair.com.
South African Airways UK ⓣ0870/747 1111, US & Canada ⓣ1-800/722-9675, Australia ⓣ1800 221 699, NZ ⓣ09/977 2237, SA ⓣ11/978 1111, ⓦwww.flysaa.com.
Thai Airways UK ⓣ0870/606 0911, US ⓣ1-212/949-8424, Canada ⓣ1-416/971-5181, Australia ⓣ1300 651 960, NZ ⓣ09/377 3886; ⓦwww.thaiair.com.
United Airlines UK ⓣ0845/844 4777, US ⓣ1-800/UNITED-1, Australia ⓣ13 17 77, ⓦwww.united.com.
Virgin Atlantic UK ⓣ0870/380 2007, US ⓣ1-800/821-5438, Australia ⓣ1300 727 340, SA ⓣ11/340 3400, ⓦwww.virgin-atlantic.com.
Virgin Blue Australia ⓣ13 67 89, outside Australia ⓣ07/3295 2296, ⓦwww.virginblue.com.au.

Agents and tour operators

AAT Kings UK ⓣ0870/240 2440, US & Canada ⓣ1-800/353-4525, Australia ⓣ1300 556 100, NZ ⓣ0800 500 146, ⓦwww.aatkings.com. Long-established Australian coach-tour operator that offers a wide selection of escorted and independent tours, the best of which are 4WD Wilderness Safari tours and camping adventures.

Abercrombie and Kent US ⓣ1-800/554-7016, ⓦwww.abercrombiekent.com. Offers 8- to 21-day high-end tours, ranging from basic trips (including Sydney, Melbourne and the Great Barrier Reef) to more extensive ones (including Tasmania and the Outback). Also specializes in family tours and customized itineraries. Extensions available to Papua New Guinea, New Zealand and Fiji.

Air Brokers International US ⓣ1-800/883-3273, ⓦwww.airbrokers.com. US consolidator and specialist in RTW and Circle Pacific tickets.

Airtreks.com US & Canada ⓣ1-877/AIRTREKS or 415/977-7100, ⓦwww.airtreks.com. RTW and Circle Pacific tickets for North Americans. The website features an interactive database that lets you build and price your own round-the-world itinerary.

Asia Transpacific Journeys US ⓣ1-800/642-2742, ⓦwww.asiatranspacific.com. Long-established outfit with a wide range of customized itineraries and group tours including nature, adventure and Aboriginal rock art.

ATS Tours US ⓣ1-888/781 5170, ⓦwww.atstours.com. Huge Australian and New Zealand specialist; dive deals, fly-drives, city stopovers, rail/bus passes, motel vouchers and other add-ons.

Australia Travel Centre Republic of Ireland ⓣ01/804 7188, ⓦwww.australia.ie. Specialists in long-haul flights.

Australian Pacific Touring UK ⓣ020/8879 7444, US & Canada ⓣ1-800/290 8687, Australia ⓣ1300 655 965, NZ ⓣ0800-APTOURS, ⓦwww.aptours.com. Comprehensive range of Australia-wide coach tours including a 28-day "Rock, Kakadu, Reef" tour for £4940 per person twin share, including meals and accommodation, plus fully escorted trips from North America.

Austravel UK ⓣ0870/166 2020, Republic of Ireland ⓣ01/642 7009, ⓦwww.austravel.net. Specialists for flights and tours to Australia. Issues ETAs (see p.33) and traditional visas for an administration fee of £17.

Contiki UK ⓣ020/8290 6422, ⓦwww.contiki.com. Big-group, countrywide bus and 4WD tours for fun-loving 18- to 35-year-olds. All transport (excluding flights to Australia) and most meals covered; plenty of additional excursions (climbing, diving, etc) at extra cost. From £105 for a 4-day Sydney and around, to a 25-day Sydney to Darwin via the east coast from £1395.

ebookers UK ⓣ0800/082 3000, Republic of Ireland ⓣ01/488 3507, ⓦwww.ebookers.com. Low fares on an extensive selection of scheduled flights and package deals.

Explore UK ⓣ0870/333 4001, Republic of Ireland ⓣ01/677 9479, ⓦwww.explore.co.uk. Bus and 4WD tours ranging from an 18-day Outback Adventure (£1899) to a 31-day Australia Adventure for £2625 – and all with flights from the UK.

Flight Centre UK ⓣ0870/499 0040, US ⓣ1-866/967-5351, Canada ⓣ1-877/967-5302, Australia ⓣ13 31 33, NZ ⓣ0800 243 544, SA ⓣ0860/400 727, ⓦwww.flightcentre.com. Competitive discounts on airfares and a wide range of package holidays and adventure tours.

Holiday Shoppe NZ ⓣ0800 808 480, ⓦwww.holidayshoppe.co.nz. One of New Zealand's largest travel agencies. Good for budget airfares and accommodation packages.

Lee's Travel UK ⓣ0870/027 3338, ⓦwww.leestravel.com. Good deals from the UK, especially on Southeast Asian airlines.

North South Travel UK ⓣ01245/608 291, ⓦwww.northsouthtravel.co.uk. Friendly, competitive travel agency, offering discounted fares worldwide. Profits are used to support projects in the developing world, especially the promotion of sustainable tourism.

Quest Travel UK ⓣ0871/423 0135, ⓦwww.questtravel.com. UK specialists in RTW and Australian discount fares.
STA Travel UK ⓣ0870/1630 026, Australia ⓣ1300 733 035, US ⓣ1-800/781-4040, Canada ⓣ1-888/427-5639, NZ ⓣ0508/782 872, SA ⓣ0861/781 781; ⓦwww.statravel.com. Worldwide specialists in independent travel; also student IDs, travel insurance, car rental, rail passes, and more. Good discounts for students and under-26s.
Student Universe US & Canada ⓣ1-800/272-9676, ⓦwww.studentuniverse.com. Competitive student-travel specialists for North Americans; no card or membership required.
Swain Australia Tours US ⓣ1-800/227-9246, ⓦwww.swainaustralia.com. Excellent range of customized tours to meet individual travel needs and budgets, from a five-day Sydney Sampler (US$395) to a twelve-day Ultimate Outback (US$9720), including tours specifically designed for families.
Trailfinders UK ⓣ0845/058 5858, Republic of Ireland ⓣ01/677 7888, Australia ⓣ1300 780 212, ⓦwww.trailfinders.com. One of the best-informed and most efficient agents for independent travellers.
Travelbag UK ⓣ0800/082 5000, ⓦwww.travelbag.co.uk. Specialists in RTW tickets, many with Australian components, with good deals aimed at the backpacker market. Plus car and campervan rental, farmstays, coach and 4WD tours.
Travel Cuts US ⓣ1-800/592-2887, Canada ⓣ1-866/246-9762, ⓦwww.travelcuts.com. Canadian student-travel organization with offices in many North American cities.
Usit Republic of Ireland ⓣ01/602 1904, ⓦwww.usit.ie. Student and youth specialists for flights, accommodation and transport.
World Expeditions UK ⓣ0800/074 4135, US ⓣ1-888/464-8735, Canada ⓣ 1-800/567-2216, Australia ⓣ1300 720 000, NZ ⓣ 09/ 368 4161, ⓦwww.worldexpeditions.co.uk. Australian-owned adventure company; small-group active wilderness holidays; cycling, canoeing, rafting, 4WD excursions, walking and camping. All expeditions are graded according to difficulty.

Entry requirements

All visitors to Australia, except New Zealanders, require a visa or Electronic Travel Authority (ETA) to enter the country; if you're heading overland, you'll obviously also need to check visa requirements for the countries en route. You can get visa application forms from the Australian high commissions, embassies or consulates listed below.

The easiest option for nationals of the UK, Ireland, the US, Canada, Malaysia, Singapore, Japan and most European countries who intend to stay for less than three months is to get an **ETA**, valid for multiple entry over one year. Applied for online or from travel agents and airlines at the same time as you book your flight, it replaces the visa stamp in your passport (ETAs are computerized) and saves the hassle of queuing or sending off your passport. ETAs can be applied for on the Web with a credit card for AUS$20 (see the Australian government websites below or go directly to ⓦwww.eta.immi.gov.au). In this case, an additional fee may be levied on top of the cost of your ETA – in the UK around £20.

Citizens of other countries and visitors who intend to stay for longer than three months should apply for a **visitor visa**, valid for three to six months. You'll need to complete an application form and lodge it either in person or by post to the embassy or consulate. It costs AUS$70 (or the equivalent in your country) and takes up to three weeks to process. If you think you might stay more than three months, it's best to get the longer visa before departure, because once you get to Australia extensions cost AUS$205. Once issued, a visa usually allows multiple entries, so long as your passport is valid.

An important condition for all holiday visa applications is that you have **adequate funds** both to support yourself during your stay – at least AUS$1000 a month – and eventually to get yourself home again.

Twelve-month **working holiday visas** are available to citizens of Britain, Ireland, Belgium, Denmark, Finland, Italy, Estonia, France, Taiwan, Malta, Sweden, Norway, Canada, the Netherlands, Germany, Japan and Korea, aged 18–30. The stress is on casual employment: you are meant to work for no more than six months at any one job. You must arrange the visa several months in advance of you arriving in Australia. Working visas cost AUS$185; some travel agents such as STA Travel in the UK (see p.33) can arrange them for you.

Young American citizens wishing to work in Australia might consider the **Special Youth Program**, designed to allow people aged 18–30 to holiday while working in short-term employment over a four-month period. See BUNAC (Ⓦwww.bunac.com), Camp Counselors (Ⓦwww.ccusa.com) or Council/CIEE (Ⓦwww.ciee.org) for more information.

Australia has strict **quarantine laws** that apply to bringing fruit, vegetables, fresh and packaged food, seed and some animal products, into the country, and when travelling interstate (see p.39); there are also strict laws prohibiting drugs, steroids, firearms, protected wildlife and associated products. You are allowed AUS$900 worth of goods, including gifts and souvenirs, while those over 18 can take advantage of a duty-free allowance on entry of 2.25 litres of alcohol and 250 cigarettes or 250g of tobacco.

Australian embassies and consulates abroad

Canada

Ottawa Australian High Commission, Suite 710, 50 O'Connor St, Ottawa, ON K1P 6L2 Ⓣ613/236-0841, Ⓦwww.ahc-ottawa.org.

Indonesia

Bali Australian Consulate, Australian Consulate-General, Jalan Hayam Wuruk No 88B, Tanjung Bungkak, Denpasar, Bali 80234 Ⓣ0361/241 118, Ⓦwww.dfat.gov.au/bali.
Jakarta Australian Embassy, Jalan HR Rasuna Said Kav C15–16, Jakarta Selatan 12940 Ⓣ021/2550 5555, Ⓦwww.austembjak.or.id.

Malaysia

Kuala Lumpur Australian High Commission, 6 Jalan Yap Kwan Seng, Kuala Lumpur Ⓣ2146 5555, Ⓦwww.australia.org.my.

Netherlands

The Hague Australian Embassy, Carnegielaan 4, 2517 KH The Hague Ⓣ070/310 8200, Ⓦwww.australian-embassy.nl.

New Zealand

Auckland Australian Consulate-General, Level 7, Price WaterHouse Coopers Tower, 188 Quay St, Auckland Ⓣ09/921 8800, Ⓦwww.australia.org.nz. Also 72–76 Hobson St, Thorndon, Wellington Ⓣ04/473 6411.

Republic of Ireland

Dublin Australian Embassy, 7th Floor, Fitzwilton House, Wilton Terrace, Dublin 2 Ⓣ01/ 664 5300, Ⓦwww.australianembassy.ie.

Singapore

Australian High Commission, 25 Napier Rd, Singapore Ⓣ065/6836 4100, Ⓦwww.singapore.embassy.gov.au.

South Africa

Pretoria Australian High Commission, 292 Orient St, Arcadia, Pretoria Ⓣ12/423 6000, Ⓦwww.australia.co.za.

Thailand

Bangkok Australian Embassy, 37 South Sathorn Rd, Bangkok Ⓣ02/344 6593, Ⓦwww.austembassy.or.th.

UK

London Australian High Commission, Australia House, Strand, London WC2B 4LA Ⓣ020/7379 4334, Ⓦwww.australia.org.uk.

US

Washington Australian Embassy, 1601 Massachusetts Ave NW, Washington, DC 20036-2273 Ⓣ202/797-3000, Ⓦwww.austemb.org.

Getting around

Australia's vastness makes the distances, and how you cover them, a major feature of any stay in the country. In general, public transport will take you only along the major highways to capital cities, the bigger towns between them, and popular tourist destinations; to get off the beaten track you'll have to consider driving, either by buying or renting your own vehicle. Frequencies and journey times of long-distance bus, train and plane services can be found under "Travel details" at the end of each chapter, with local buses and trains covered in the main text.

If you're travelling by road, check out the route on a map first, as it's very easy to underestimate **distances and conditions** – you may well be letting yourself in for a three-day bus journey, or planning to drive 500km on bad roads. Bear in mind what the **weather** will be doing, too; you don't necessarily want to head into central Australia in a battered old car during the summer, or into the northern tropics in the wet season.

By plane

Flying between major destinations, your main choice of airlines is between Qantas, Jetstar and Virgin Blue; a typical one-way flight from Sydney to Adelaide with Jetstar costs from around AUS$114, from Perth to Darwin with Virgin Blue AUS$285, and Cairns to Melbourne with Qantas AUS$198. Elsewhere, **regional routes** are served by smaller airlines such as Regional Express (Rex), which covers New South Wales, Victoria and South Australia; and state-based companies such as Skywest in Western Australia and Airnorth (part of Regional Link) in the Northern Territory. It's worth checking websites for their latest deals, which are often very good, especially when you consider the time and money you'd otherwise spend on a long bus or train journey.

If you're flying from Britain or Ireland and want to include a trip to New Zealand or the South Pacific on your itinerary you could save money by booking a **Qantas Boomerang Pass**, which must be purchased before arrival. The pass divides these areas into three zones based on distance and you are required to book at least two flights costing from £65 for single-zone, £120 for two-zone, or £146 for three-zone flights. You pay according to how many zones your flight crosses. Note, though, that the Boomerang Pass is not always as good value as it sounds: check Qantas Internet rates first, as well as current deals with other domestic airlines. For those travelling from North America, the **Qantas Aussie AirPass** offers similar internal-flight discounts if purchased with the return airfare, starting from US$1099/CDN$1499 for three domestic flights.

Another type of flight offered all over Australia is brief **sightseeing** or joyrides. Everything is covered, from biplane spins above cities to excursions to the Great Barrier Reef and flights over well-known landscapes. A good example is a flight from Alice Springs to Uluru in a small plane, which enables you to visit the Rock in a day, but also observe the impressive central Australian landforms from the air. Bill Peach Journeys (Ⓣ02/9693 2233, Ⓦwww.aircruising.com.au) offers a twelve-day Outback tour by air that flies from Sydney and takes in the main sights and cities, including Darwin, Broome, Kakadu, Alice Springs and Uluru, from AUS$12,395 and includes absolutely everything.

Domestic airlines

Jetstar Ⓣ13 15 38, Ⓦwww.jetstar.com.au.
Qantas Ⓣ13 13 13, Ⓦwww.qantas.com.au.
Regional Express Ⓣ13 17 13, Ⓦwww.rex.com.au.
Regional Link Ⓣ1800 627 474, Ⓦwww.regionallink.com.au.
Skywest Ⓣ1300 660 088, Ⓦwww.skywest.com.au.
Virgin Blue Ⓣ13 67 89, Ⓦwww.virginblue.com.au.

Mileage chart

	Adelaide	Alice Springs	Brisbane	Broken Hill	Broome	Cairns
Adelaide	x	1533	2045	508	3235	3143
Alice Springs	1533	x	3106	1599	2580	2200
Brisbane	2045	3106	x	1600	4250	1718
Broken Hill	508	1599	1600	x	3350	2324
Broome	3235	2580	4250	3350	x	3426
Cairns	3143	2200	1718	2324	3426	x
Canberra	1210	2650	1345	929	4260	3010
Darwin	3025	1489	3500	3135	1868	2610
Melbourne	731	2181	1674	865	3958	3410
Perth	2690	3542	4375	2990	2264	6010
Sydney	1421	2815	940	1160	5502	2135
Townsville	2490	1773	1361	1980	3325	348
Uluru	1600	457	2996	1690	2150	2419

By train

The populous southeast has a reasonably comprehensive service: interstate railways link the entire east coast from Cairns to Sydney, and on to Melbourne and Adelaide. Each state operates its own rail network. The two great (or perhaps just long) journeys are the twice-weekly **Indian Pacific** (Perth–Sydney; 66hr; one-way, seat only AUS$590; sleeper AUS$1320; luxury sleeper with meals AUS$1720), across the Nullarbor Plain, and the seasonally twice-weekly **Ghan** (Adelaide–Darwin; 47hr; one-way, seat only AUS$555; sleeper AUS$1490; luxury sleeper with meals AUS$1920). Services are operated by Great Southern Railway (Ⓣ13 21 47, Ⓦwww.gsr.com.au), who offer concessionary fares for students and YHA/Backpacker cardholders (see p.51), which work out only around fifteen percent more than a bus. Remember though, this is not a European-style high-speed network; journey times are similar to those of buses.

On the overnight Ghan and Indian–Pacific, a twin-share "Red Kangaroo" sleeper service provides washing facilities and converts from a day lounge into a sleeper, while "Gold Kangaroo" lays on a luxury en-suite cabin and all meals for the full "Orient Express" treatment. Either of these options is well worth considering for the full two-and-a-half day trawl from Sydney to Perth if you have something against flying. The seat-only option is a reclining chair with generous legroom and a reading light, with access to a lounge and buffet, DVDs and showers. With a pair of Gold Kangaroo tickets between capitals and/or Alice, you get the offer of motorail car transportation for just AUS$99 – something that's really caught on with southerners wanting to tour the Centre or Top End with their own vehicles, but enjoy the train ride there. Great Southern Railway also runs an overland interstate service between Melbourne and Adelaide (11hr; AUS$78–167).

Other than these, there are a couple of inland tracks in Queensland – to Mount Isa, Longreach and Charleville, plus the rustic

Canberra	Darwin	Melbourne	Perth	Sydney	Townsville	Uluru
1210	3025	731	2690	1421	2490	1600
2650	1489	2181	3542	2815	1773	457
1345	3500	1674	4375	940	1361	2996
929	3135	865	2990	1160	1980	1690
4260	1868	3958	2264	5502	3325	2150
3010	2610	3410	6010	2135	348	2419
x	3925	648	3959	286	2286	2612
3925	x	3790	4019	3995	2509	1946
648	3790	x	3392	1002	2507	2310
3959	4019	3392	x	4110	4265	2062
286	3995	1002	4110	x	2110	2950
2286	2509	2507	4265	2110	x	2210
2612	1946	2310	2062	2950	2210	x

Cairns–Forsayth run and isolated Croydon–Normanton stretch – and suburban networks around some of the major cities. Only around Sydney does this amount to much, with decent services to most of New South Wales. There are no passenger trains in Tasmania.

The advantages of travelling by train rather than bus are comfort and (usually) a bar; disadvantages are the slower pace, higher price and potential booking problems – Queensland trains, for example, travel at about 60kph and require a month's advance booking during the holiday season.

Rail Australia (Ⓦwww.railaustralia.com.au) offers a range of **rail passes**, including the Great Southern Railway Pass (AUS$590, AUS$690/conc), which must be bought before you arrive in Australia and lets you loose without limit on their routes described above for a six-month period. To be sure that you can make full use of your pass, it's advisable to book your route when you buy it. Western Australia, Victoria, New South Wales and Queensland also have their own passes available through main stations, but check any travel restrictions before buying – interstate routes do not overlap as far as passes are concerned.

By bus

Bus travel is almost certainly the cheapest way to get around, but it's also the most tiresome. Even though the bus network reaches much further than the train network, routes follow the main highways between cities, and may mean arriving or departing at smaller places in the middle of the night. And services are not daily as you might think, especially in Western Australia, where there's only one bus a week to Adelaide. The buses are about as comfortable as they can be, with reclining seats, air-con, toilets and DVDs. If possible, try and plan for a stopover after every twenty hours – if you try stoically to sit out a sixty-hour marathon trip, you'll need a day or more to get over it and the roadhouse food you'll have survived on. **Discounts** (ten percent, or fifteen percent if you buy your ticket before entering Australia) are available on many fares if you have a YHA, ISIC or recognized backpacker card such as VIP (see p.51), or if you are a pensioner.

The major **interstate bus company** on the mainland is Greyhound/McCafferty's (Ⓣ13 14 99, Ⓦwww.greyhound.com.au), which covers the entire country. Along the east coast, there's also Premier Motor Service (Ⓣ13 34 10, Ⓦwww.premierms.com.au), calling in everywhere along the highway between Melbourne and Cairns, plus Countrylink (Ⓣ13 22 32, Ⓦwww.countrylink.info), while in WA Integrity Coach lines (Ⓣ1800/226339, Ⓦwww.integritycoachlines.com.au) runs from Perth as far as Port Hedland. Firefly Express (Ⓣ1300 730 740, Ⓦwww.fireflyexpress.com.au) runs to Sydney, Melbourne and Adelaide and usually has the cheapest fares for these routes. Tasmania is thoroughly covered by Tasmanian Redline Coaches (Ⓣ1300 360 000, Ⓦwww.tasredline.com.au) and Tassielink (Ⓣ1300 300 520, Ⓦwww.tassielink.com.au).

Sample direct **one-way fares** from Sydney are: Adelaide AUS$159 (23hr), Alice Springs AUS$397 (47hr), Brisbane AUS$111 (17hr), Cairns AUS$336 (2 days), Darwin AUS$664 (3 days, 2hr), Melbourne AUS$67 (12hr) and Perth AUS$405 (3 days, 12 hrs). Return fares are, at best, only marginally cheaper than two singles.

A good-value option for bus travellers is to buy a **pass**, though bear in mind that you won't save money over shorter routes and that passes are non-refundable. Greyhound offers a range of over twenty passes lasting between one and twelve months covering preset routes, on which you can break your journey as often as you like and travel in any direction, but are not allowed to backtrack. Sample fares include the six-month Melbourne–Cairns "Western Explorer" pass for AUS$736, AUS$662/conc; a one-year "Best of the East", which circuits via everywhere between Adelaide, Uluru, Alice Springs, Mount Isa, Cairns, Sydney and Melbourne for AUS$1277, AUS$1149/conc; and the "All Australian" pass for AUS$2573, AUS$2315/conc. Year-long **kilometre passes** are more flexible, giving you unlimited travel up to 20,000 kilometres in any direction until you have used up the distance paid for – these work out around 8¢ per kilometre. Tasmania has its own passes starting from AUS$135 for seven days' travel within a ten-day period.

Driving interstate

When driving across state borders bear in mind that your car may be subject to a customs search by officers on the lookout for fruit and fresh produce, which often cannot be carried from one state, to minimize the spread of plant pests and viruses. You'll see large bins at the side of the road as you approach a state border line for this purpose: dump any perishables here before crossing; otherwise, you risk receiving a large fine if pulled over and caught with them.

By car

To fully explore Australia you'll **need your own vehicle**. This will enable you to get to the national parks, isolated beaches and ghost towns that aren't serviced by public transport and make the country such a special place. If your trip is a long one – three months or more – then **buying a vehicle** may well be the cheapest way of seeing Australia. On shorter trips you should consider **renting** – if not for the whole time then at least for short periods between bus rides, thereby allowing you to explore an area in depth.

Most foreign licences are valid for a year in Australia. An International Driving Permit (available from national motoring organizations) may be useful if you come from a non-English-speaking country. **Fuel** prices start at around $1 per litre for unleaded, with diesel about five percent more: prices increase by ten to fifteen percent along the Outback highways and can double at remote stations. The **rules of the road** are similar to those in the UK and US. Most importantly, drive on the left (as in the UK), remember that seatbelts are compulsory for all, and that the speed limit in all built-up areas is 50kph or less. Outside built-up areas, maximums are around 110kph on long, isolated stretches – except in the Northern Territory, where common sense is your only limit between towns. Whatever else you do in a vehicle, avoid driving when you are tired – get out of the car every two hours – and don't drink alcohol; random breath-tests are common even in rural areas, especially during the Christmas season and on Friday and Saturday nights. One rule that might catch you out in town is that **roadside parking** must be in the same direction as the traffic; in other words, don't cross oncoming traffic to park on the right.

Main **hazards** are boredom and fatigue, and animal collisions – a serious problem everywhere (not just in the Outback) at dawn, dusk and night-time. Driving in the Outback is by far the most dangerous tourist pursuit in Australia and every year several people get killed in single-vehicle rollovers or head-on collisions, particularly Europeans on short see-it-all holidays in cumbersome 4WDs or motor homes. Beware of fifty-metre-long **roadtrains**: these colossal trucks can't stop quickly or pull off the road safely, so if there's the slightest doubt, get out of their way; only overtake a roadtrain if you can see well ahead and are certain that your vehicle can manage it. On dirt roads be doubly cautious, or just pull over and let the roadtrain pass.

Roads, Outback driving and breakdowns

Around the cities the only problem you'll face is inept signposting, but the quality of interstate main roads – even Highway 1, which circles the country – isn't always great, and some of the minor routes are awful. **Conditions**, especially on unsealed roads, are unpredictable, and some roads will be impassable after a storm, so always seek reliable advice (from local police or a roadhouse) before starting out. Make it clear what sort of vehicle you're driving and remember that their idea of a "good" or "bad" road may be radically different from yours. Some so-called "4WD only" tracks are easily navigable in ordinary cars as long as you take it easy – high ground clearance, rather than four-driven wheels, is often the crucial factor.

Rain and flooding – particularly in the tropics and central Australia – can close roads to all vehicles within minutes, so driving through remote regions or even along the coastal highway in the wet season can be prone to delays. The stretches of highway between Broome and Kununurra and Cairns to Townsville are notorious for being cut by floods during the summer cyclone season.

Several remote and unsealed roads through central Australia (the Sandover and Plenty highways, the Oodnadatta, Birdsville and Tanami tracks, and others) are theoretically open to all vehicles in dry winter weather, but unless you're well equipped with a tough car, don't attempt a crossing during the summer, when extreme temperatures place extra strain on both driver and vehicle.

On **poor roads and dirt tracks**, the guidelines are to keep your speed down to 80kph, stick to the best section and never assume that the road is free from potholes and rocks. Long corrugated stretches can literally shake the vehicle apart – check radiators, fuel tanks and battery connections after rough stretches; reducing tyre pressures slightly softens the ride but can cause the tyres to overheat making them more prone to punctures. Windscreens are often shattered by flying stones from passing traffic, so slow down and pull over to the left.

At all times carry plenty of **drinking water** and **fuel**, and if you're heading Outback tell someone reliable your timetable, route and destination so that a rescue can be organized if you don't report in. Carry a detailed map, and don't count on finding regular signposts. In the event of a breakdown in the Outback, **always stay with your vehicle**: it's more visible to potential rescuers and you can use it for shade. If you're off a main track, as a last resort, burn a tyre or anything plastic – the black smoke will be distinctive from the average bushfire.

Car, 4WD and campervan rental

To **rent** a car you need a full, clean driver's licence and be at least 21 years old, rising to 25 for 4WDs and motorcycles (see below). Check on any mileage limits or other restrictions, extras, and what you're covered for in an accident, before signing. The multinational operators Hertz, Budget, Avis and Thrifty have offices in the major cities, but outside of these, lack of competition makes their standard **rates** expensive at AUS$70–90 a day for a small car. Local firms – of which there are many in the cities – are almost always better value. A city-based non-multinational rental agency will supply new cars for around AUS$45 a day with unlimited kilometres. One-way rental might appear handy, but is usually very expensive: at least AUS$200 extra for the drop-off fee.

Four-wheel drives are best used for specific areas rather than long term, as rental and fuel costs are steep, starting at around AUS$120 a day. Some 4WD agents actually don't allow their vehicles to be driven off sealed roads, so check the fine print first. **Campervans** and **motor homes** cost from AUS$50 a day for a two-berth campervan in low season (up to AUS$175 high season) with unlimited kilometres – amazing value when you consider the independence, comfort and the saving on accommodation costs: plus one-way rental is possible. Like cars, campervans can be limited to sealed roads, but they give you the chance to create your own tour of a lifetime across Australia. Remember, though, that the sleeping capacity stated is an absolute maximum, which you wouldn't want to endure for too long. Furthermore, in the tropics the interior will never really cool enough overnight unless you leave the doors open – which brings the bugs in. Consider sleeping outside under a mozzie dome or inner tent.

For **4WD campervans**, the high-roofed Toyota Troop Carriers used by Britz, Apollo and Kea, to name a few, are a tough all-terrain vehicle fitted with 180-litre fuel tanks that will only be stopped off-road by your experience or the height of the roof. With these models it's important to understand the operation of the free-wheeling hubs on the front axle to engage 4WD – many a Britz camper and the like has become bogged by tourists who didn't engage 4WD correctly. The only drawback with this popular model is the high fuel consumption of around 7kpl. Lighter 4WD utes fitted with a cabin and a pop-up roof can't really take the same hammering but will be more economical, while the large Isuzu-based six-berthers look chunky but would really be a handful off-road and use even more fuel. With all these 4WD campers it's vital to appreciate the altered driving dynamics of an already high vehicle fitted with a heavy body. In the hands of overseas renters they regularly topple when an inexperienced driver drifts off the road, overcompensates and rolls over.

Prices for 4WD campers start around AUS$150 a day in the low season up to

AUS$250 in the high season. In addition to the big companies listed below, several smaller or local outfits buy in high-mileage, ex-rental vehicles to rent out at low prices. Branches of the big rental chains and local firms for all types of vehicles are detailed in "Listings" sections throughout the Guide.

Car rental agencies

Avis UK ⓣ0870/606 0100, Republic of Ireland ⓣ021/428 1111, US ⓣ1-800/230-4898, Canada ⓣ1-800/272-5871, Australia ⓣ13 63 33 or 02/9353 9000, NZ ⓣ09/526 2847 or 0800 655 111, ⓦwww.avis.com.
Budget UK ⓣ0870/156 5656, US ⓣ1-800/527-0700, Canada ⓣ1-800/268-8900, Australia ⓣ1300 362 848, NZ ⓣ0800 283 438, ⓦwww.budget.com.
Europcar UK ⓣ0870/607 5000, Republic of Ireland ⓣ01/614 2800, US & Canada ⓣ1-877/940-6900, Australia ⓣ393/306 160, ⓦwww.europcar.com.
Hertz UK ⓣ020/7026 0077, Republic of Ireland ⓣ01/870 5777, US & Canada ⓣ1-800/654-3131, Australia ⓣ13 30 39, NZ ⓣ0800 654 321, ⓦwww.hertz.com.
Holiday Autos UK ⓣ0870/400 4461, Republic of Ireland ⓣ01/872 9366, Australia ⓣ1300 554 432, ⓦwww.holidayautos.co.uk. Part of lastminute.com.
National UK ⓣ0870/400 4581, US ⓣ1-800/CAR-RENT, Australia ⓣ0870/600 6666, NZ ⓣ03/366 5574, ⓦwww.nationalcar.com.
Thrifty UK ⓣ01494/751 540, Republic of Ireland ⓣ01/844 1950, US & Canada ⓣ1-800/847-4389, Australia ⓣ1300 367 227, NZ ⓣ09/256 1405, ⓦwww.thrifty.com.

Campervan and motor-home rental agencies

Apollo Motorhome Holidays ⓣ1800 777 779, ⓦwww.apollocamper.com.au.
Backpacker Campervans ⓣ1800 670 232, ⓦwww.backpackercampervans.com.
Britz ⓣ1800 331 454, ⓦwww.britz.com.
Maui ⓣ1300 363 800, ⓦwww.maui-rentals.com.
Kea Campers ⓣ1800 252 555, ⓦwww.keacampers.com.

Buying a car

Buying a used vehicle needn't be an expensive business and a well-kept car should resell at about two-thirds of the purchase price at the end of your trip. If you're lucky, or a skilful negotiator, you might

Best secondhand buys

Big-engined, mid-1980s **Holden Kingswood** or **Ford Falcon** station wagons are popular travellers' cars: cheap, roomy, reliable, mechanically simple and durable, with spares available in just about any city supermarket, roadhouse or wrecker's yard. At the bottom end, AUS$2000 plus a bit of luck should find you some kind of old car that runs reliably. Chances are, if a vehicle has survived this long, there's nothing seriously wrong with it and you should be able to nurse it through a bit further. Real bargains can also be secured from travellers desperate to get rid of their vehicle before flying out. Ideally, though, you should plan to pay at least AUS$4000 in total for a sound, and well-equipped vehicle. Manual transmission models are more economical than old automatics, with the four-speed versions superior to the awkward, three-speed, steering-column-mounted models. Smaller and less robust, but much more economical to run, are old Japanese station wagons or vans such as **Mazda L300s** (also in 4WD version), suitable for one or two people. Any city backpackers' notice-board will be covered in adverts of vehicles for sale.

Four-wheel drives are expensive and, with poor fuel economy and higher running costs, worth it only if you have some actual off-highway driving planned; to do that you can't buy an old wreck. **Toyota FJ** or **HJ Land Cruisers** are Outback legends, especially the long-wheelbase (LWB) models: tough, reliable and with plenty of new and used spares all over the country. If nothing goes wrong, a diesel (HJ) is preferable to a petrol (FJ) engine, being sturdier and more economical – although all Toyota engines, particularly the six-cylinder FJs, seem to keep on running, even if totally clapped out. The trouble with diesels is that problems, when they occur, tend to be serious and repairs expensive. Generally, you're looking at AUS$8000 for a 20-year-old model.

even make a profit. A good place to evaluate vehicle prices and availability online is at Ⓦwww.autotrader.com.au.

If you don't know your axle from your elbow but are not too gullible, **car yards** can provide some advice: in Sydney, they're the most common place to buy a used vehicle, and some even cater specifically to travellers (see p.207) – but don't forget you're dealing with used-car salesmen whose worldwide reputation precedes them; a buy-back guarantee offered by some car yards and dealers is usually a guarantee to pay you a fraction of the car's potential value. Assuming you have a little time and some mechanical knowledge, you'll save money by buying privately. **Backpackers' notice-boards** in main exit points from Australia are the best places to look. One of the great advantages of buying from a fellow traveller is that you may get all sorts of stuff thrown in – camping gear, eskies and many of the spares listed below. The disadvantage is that the car may have been maintained on a backpacker's budget.

A **thorough inspection** is essential. Rust is one thing to watch for, especially in the tropics where humidity and salt air will turn scratches to holes within weeks – look out for poorly patched bodywork. Take cars for a spin and check the engine, gearbox, clutch and brakes for operation, unusual noises, vibration and leaks; repairs on some of these parts can be costly. Don't expect perfection, though: worn brake-pads and tyres, grating wheel-bearings and defective batteries can be fixed inexpensively, and if repairs are needed, it gives you a good excuse to haggle over the price. All tyres should be the same type and size. If you lack faith in your own abilities, the various state automobile associations offer rigorous pre-purchase inspections for about AUS$100, which isn't much to pay if it saves you from buying a wreck – and plenty of people do.

Four-wheel driving: some hints

The Outback is not the place to learn how to handle a 4WD and yet this is exactly where many tourists attracted by driving a tough off-road vehicle do so. In late 2002, a solo German tourist was rescued by chance after waiting a week on the 1900-kilometre-long Canning Stock Route in WA, almost out of water and fuel. A novice four-wheel driver, he assumed his bushcamper was an unstoppable, all-terrain machine until he got bogged in a saltpan through lack of experience. Take all the spares listed on p.43, plus a shovel, hi-lift jack and gloves. In addition to the many "how to" manuals easily found in bookshops, if you're planning a long off-road tour, *Explore Australia by Four-Wheel Drive* (Viking) will suit recreational drivers. The following basic hints should help; see also the advice on creek crossings on p.492.

- Be aware of your limitations, and those of your vehicle.
- Know how to operate everything – including free-wheeling hubs (where present) and how to change a wheel – before you need it.
- Always cross deep water and very muddy sections on foot first.
- Don't persevere if you're stuck – avoid wheel spin (which will only dig you further in) and reverse out. Momentum is key on slippery surfaces such as mud, sand and snow – as long as you're moving forward, however slowly, resist the temptation to change gear, and so lose traction.
- Reducing tyre pressures down to 1 bar (15lb psi) dramatically increases traction in mud and sand, but causes tyre overheating, so keep speeds down. Carry a compressor or reinflate as soon as possible.
- If stuck, clear all the wheels with your hands or a shovel, create a shallow ramp (again, for all wheels), engage four-wheel drive, lower pressures if necessary, and drive or reverse out in low-range second.
- Keep to tracks – avoid unnecessary damage to the environment.
- Driving on beaches can be great fun, but is treacherous – observe other vehicles' tracks and be aware of tidal patterns.
- Consider a rented satellite phone for remote travel (see "Phones" on p.78).

If you're **buying privately** (or from a dealer), you should also check the requirements of the state transport department: in most states you'll need a roadworthiness certificate to have the vehicle transferred from its previous owner's name to yours. This means having a garage check it over; legally, the previous owner should do this, and theoretically it guarantees that the car is mechanically sound – but don't rely on it. You then proceed to the local Department of Transport with the certificate, a receipt of purchase, your driver's licence and passport; they charge a percentage of the price as stated on the receipt to register the vehicle in your name. WA-registered cars are a special case because a new roadworthy certificate is not necessary when the car is sold. This means that cars with WA plates are much easier to sell on wherever you are (as long as you keep the WA registration). You get some really clapped-out bangers still on the road in WA until the police slap an "unroadworthy" ticket on them.

If the annual **vehicle registration** is due, or you bought an interstate or deregistered vehicle ("as is", without number plates), you'll have to pay extra for registration, which is dependent on the engine size and runs into hundreds of dollars. Note that cars with interstate registration can be difficult to sell: if possible, go for a car with the registration of the state where you anticipate selling. Registration includes the legal minimum third-party personal **insurance**, but you might want to increase this cover to protect you against theft of the vehicle, or if you've bought something more flash go the whole way with comprehensive motor insurance. Joining one of the **automobile clubs** for another AUS$90 or so is well worth considering, as you'll get free roadside assistance (within certain limits), and discounts on road maps and other products. Each state has its own, but membership is reciprocal with overseas equivalents.

Equipping your car

Even if you expect to stick mostly to the main highways, you'll need to carry a fair number of **spares**: there are plenty of very isolated spots, even between Sydney and Melbourne. For ordinary cars, the cheapest place to buy spares is at a supermarket – head for the racks of any branch of K-Mart or Coles. A **towrope** is a good start; passing motorists are far cheaper than tow trucks. In addition – and especially if your vehicle is past its prime – you should have a set of spark plugs, points, fuses, fuel filters (for diesels), fan belt and radiator hoses – you need to check and maybe replace all these anyway. A selection of hose clamps, radiator sealant, water-dispersing spray, jump leads, tyre pump/compressor and a board to support the jack on soft ground will also come in handy. Again, if the car is old, establish its engine oil consumption early on; a car can carry on for thousands of kilometres guzzling oil at an alarming rate, but if the level drops too much the engine will cook itself. If you're confident, you might want to get hold of a Gregory's workshop manual for your vehicle; even if you're not, carry a copy and the above spares anyway – someone might help who knows how to use them. A ten-litre or bigger fuel container is also useful in case you run out.

Before you set off, check **battery** terminals for corrosion, and the battery for charge – buy a new one if necessary and don't risk money on a secondhand item. Carry two spare tyres. In fact, one of the best things you can do is start a long road trip with six new tyres, oil, filters, and radiator coolant, as well as points (if present) and plugs on a petrol engine. **Off-road** drivers in remote regions should add to the list a puncture repair kit, bead breaker and tubes – and know how to use them. Keeping tyres at the correct pressure and having a wheel balance/alignment will reduce wear.

By motorcycle

Motorcycles, especially large-capacity trail bikes, are ideal for the Australian climate, although long distances place a premium on their comfort and fuel range. Japanese trail bikes, such as Yamaha's XT600, sell for around AUS$4000 and allow 100kph on-road cruising, are manageable on dirt roads and have readily available spares. A bike like the Honda XL650V Transalp is heavier but has a much smoother engine and fairing, which add up to better long-range comfort and reasonable gravel manners.

If it's likely that you'll return to your starting point, look out for dealers offering buy-back options that guarantee a resale at the end of your trip; bikes can be more difficult to sell privately than cars. Whether you're planning to ride off or on the bitumen, plenty of water-carrying capacity is essential in the Outback. **Outback night-riding** carries risks from collisions with wildlife from which a rider always comes off badly; all you can do is make sure your lights and brakes are up to it and keep your speed down to under 100kph.

Motorcycle **rental** has become widely available from the main southern cities. All types of models are available but for extended touring you can't beat something like a BMW GS1150: comfortable, economical and a pleasure to ride loaded, two-up, day in, day out (although tyre choice will be critical for unsealed roads and it weighs a ton). Among other outlets, 1150s are available from ⓦwww.carconnection.com.au from around AUS$120 a day, or at a flat rate of AUS$5500 for three months (plus various deposits and bonds). *The Adventure Motorcycling Handbook* (Trailblazer) is a definitive manual for preparation and riding off the beaten track and includes a regional rundown of Australia's Outback tracks.

Hitching

The official advice for hitching in Australia is don't: with so many affordable forms of transport available, there's no real need to take the risk of jumping into a stranger's vehicle.

If you must do it, **never hitch alone**, and always avoid being dropped in the middle of nowhere between settlements. Remember that you don't have to get into a vehicle just because it stops: choose who to get in with and don't be afraid to ask questions before you do get in, making the arrangement clear from the start. Ask the driver where he or she is going rather than saying where you want to go. Try to keep your pack with you; having it locked in the boot makes a quick escape more difficult.

A much better method is lining up lifts through backpackers' notice-boards (though this means sharing fuel costs). This option gives you the chance to meet the driver in advance, and – as a fellow traveller – they will most likely be stopping to see many of the same sights along the way. In out-of-the-way locations, roadhouses are a good place to head, as the owners often know of people who'll be heading in the same direction as you.

The best way to ensure your safety, apart from exercising your judgement and common sense, is to make concrete arrangements before your departure and stick to them.

Health

Australia has high standards of hygiene, and there are few exceptional health hazards – at least in terms of disease. No vaccination certificates are required unless you've come from a yellow-fever zone within the past week. Standards in Australia's hospitals are also very high, and medical costs are reasonable in comparison to Europe and the US.

The national healthcare scheme, **Medicare**, offers a reciprocal arrangement – free essential healthcare – for citizens of the UK, Ireland, New Zealand, Italy, Malta, Finland, the Netherlands, Norway and Sweden. This free treatment is limited to public hospitals and casualty departments (though the ambulance ride to get you there isn't covered); at GPs, you pay up front (about AUS$40 minimum) with two-thirds of your fee reimbursed by Medicare (does not apply to citizens of New Zealand and Ireland).

Collect the reimbursement from a Medicare Centre (many branches) by presenting your doctor's bill together with a **Medicare Card**. This card is available from any Medicare Centre. Anyone eligible who's staying in Australia for a while – particularly those on extended working holidays – is advised to obtain one. Applicants need to bring their passport and the National Health documents of their country. Dental treatment is not included: if you find yourself in need of dental treatment in one of the larger cities, try the dental hospital, where dental students may treat you cheaply or for free.

The sun

Australia's biggest health problem is also one of its chief attractions: **sunshine**. A sunny day in London, Toronto or even Miami is not the same as a cloudless day in Cairns, and the intensity of the Australian sun's damaging ultraviolet rays is far greater. Whether this is because of Australia's proximity to the ozone hole is a matter of debate, but there's absolutely no doubt that the southern sun burns more fiercely than anything in the northern hemisphere, and you need to take extra care.

Australians of European origin, especially those of Anglo-Saxon or Celtic descent, could not be less suited to Australia's outdoor lifestyle, which is why two out of three Australians are statistically likely to develop **skin cancer** in their lifetime, the world's worst record. About five percent of these will develop potentially fatal melanomas, and about a thousand die each year. Looking at the ravaged complexions of some older Australians (who had prolonged exposure to the sun in the days before there was an awareness of the great dangers of skin cancer) should be enough to make you want to cover yourself with lashings of the highest factor **sun block** (SPF 35+), widely used and sold just about everywhere. Sunscreen should not be used on babies less than six months old: instead, keep them out of direct sunlight. What looks like war paint on the noses of surfers and small children is actually zinc cream; the thick, sticky waterproof cream, which comes in fun colours, provides a total blockout and is particularly useful when applied to protruding parts of the body, such as noses and shoulders.

These days, Australians are fully aware of the sun's dangers, and you're constantly reminded to **"Slip, Slop, Slap"**, the government-approved catch-phrase reminding you to slip on a T-shirt, slop on some sun block and slap on a hat – sound advice. Pay attention to any moles on your body: if you notice any changes, either during or after your trip, see a doctor; cancerous melanomas are generally easily removed if caught early. To prevent headaches and – in the long term – cataracts, it's a good idea to wear sunglasses; look for "UV block" ratings when you buy a pair.

The sun can also cause **heat exhaustion** and **sunstroke**, so in addition to keeping well covered up, stay in the shade if you can. Drink plenty of liquids: on hot days when walking, experts advise drinking a litre of water an hour – which is a lot to carry. Alcohol and sun don't mix well; when you're feeling particularly hot and thirsty, remember that a cold beer will actually dehydrate you.

Wildlife dangers

Although **mosquitoes** are found across the whole of the country, malaria is not endemic; however, in the tropical north there are regular outbreaks of similarly transmitted Ross River Fever and Dengue Fever, chronically debilitating viruses that are potentially fatal to children and the elderly. Outbreaks of Ross River Fever occur as far south as Tasmania, which is reason enough not to be too blasé about mozzie bites. Aeroguard and Rid are the most popular brands of insect repellent.

The danger from other **wildlife** is much overrated: snake and spider bites are an essential part of the perilous Outback myth, and crocodile and shark attacks are widely publicized – nonetheless, all are extremely rare.

The way to minimize danger from **saltwater crocodiles** (which actually range far inland; see p.566) is to keep your distance. If you're camping in the bush within 100km of the northern coast between Broome (WA) and Rockhampton (QLD), make sure your tent is at least 50m from waterholes or creeks, don't collect water at the same spot every day or leave any rubbish around, and always seek local advice before pitching up camp. Four-wheel drivers should take extra care when walking creeks prior to driving across.

Snakes almost always do their best to avoid people and you'll probably never see one. They're more likely to be active in hot weather, when you should be more careful. Treat them with respect, and it's unlikely you'll be bitten: most bites occur when people try to catch or kill snakes. Wear boots and long trousers when hiking through undergrowth, collect firewood carefully, and, in the event of a confrontation, back off. **Sea snakes** sometimes find divers intriguing, wrapping themselves around limbs or staring into masks, but they're seldom aggressive. If **bitten** by a snake, use a crepe bandage to bind the entire limb firmly and splint it, as if for a sprain; this slows the distribution of venom into the lymphatic system. Don't clean the bite area (venom around the bite can identify the species, making treatment easier), and don't slash the bite or apply a tourniquet. Treat all bites as if they were serious and always seek immediate medical attention, but remember: not all snakes are poisonous, not all poisonous snakes inject a lethal dose of venom every time they bite, and death from snakebite is rare.

Two **spiders** whose bites can be fatal are the funnel-web, a black, stocky creature found in the Sydney area, and the small redback, a relative of the notorious black widow of the Americas, usually found in dark, dry locations all over Australia (ie outdoor toilets, among shrubs, under rocks and timber logs), although they are less common in colder regions like Tasmania. Both are prolific in January and February, when there is the greatest danger of bites. Treat funnel-web bites as for snakebites, and apply ice to redback wounds to relieve pain; if bitten by either, get to a hospital – antivenins are available. Other spiders, centipedes and scorpions can deliver painful wounds but generally only cause serious problems if you have allergies.

Ticks, **mites** and **leeches** are the bane of bushwalkers, though spraying repellent over shoes and leggings will help keep these pests away in the first instance. **Ticks** are poisonous – spring is the time when they produce the most toxins during feeding – and attach themselves to long grass and bushes, often latching on to passing animals that brush against them. Ticks can cause paralysis and death in people, but the most common complaint to humans is local discomfort and allergic reactions. However, the Paralysis Tick, a native of Australia, can be found from Cairns to Lakes Entrance and is a life-threatening parasite of both man and animals. This tick is very common and regularly causes paralysis in dogs and cats.

Check yourself over after a hike: look for local stinging and swelling (usually just inside hairlines) and you'll find either a tiny black dot, or a pea-sized animal attached, depending on which species has bitten you. Use fine-pointed tweezers and grasp it as close to the skin as possible, and gently pull the tick out, trying to avoid squeezing the animal's body, which will inject more venom. Seek medical attention if you are not successful. A lot of bushwalkers advocate dabbing kerosene, alcohol or insect repellent on the ticks before pulling them out but the official medical advice is don't – it will cause the ticks to inject more toxins into the host's body. **Mites** cause an infuriating rash known as "scrub itch", which characteristically appears wherever your clothes are tightest, such as around the hips and ankles. Unfortunately, there's not much you can do except take antihistamines and wait a day or two for the itching to stop. **Leeches** are gruesome but harmless: insect repellent, fire or salt gets them off the skin, though bites will bleed heavily for some time.

More serious is the threat from various types of **jellyfish** (also known as stingers or sea wasps), which occur in coastal tropical waters through the summer months. Two to watch out for are the tiny irukandji and the saucer-sized box jellyfish, though both are virtually invisible in water. **Irukandji** have initially painless stings, but their venom causes "irukandji syndrome", which can be fatal. Its symptoms are somewhat similar to those of decompression illness: elevated heart rate and increased blood pressure; in addition to that, excruciating pain, anxiety and an overwhelming sense of doom and dread. **Box jellyfish** stings leave permanent red weals, and the venom can cause rapid unconsciousness and even kill, by paralyzing the heart muscles, if the weals cover more than half a limb. Treat stinger victims by dousing the sting area (front and back) with liberal amounts of vinegar – which you may find in small stands on affected beaches, such as North Queensland. Never rub with sand or towels, or attempt to remove tentacles from the skin – both could trigger the release of more venom; apply mouth-to-mouth resuscitation if needed, and get the victim to hospital for treatment. Whatever the locals are doing, don't risk swimming anywhere on tropical beaches during the stinger season (roughly Oct–May) – stinger nets don't offer any protection against the tiny irukandji that pass through the mesh designed to stop the box jellyfish. Specific **reef hazards** are covered at the start of the chapter on Queensland's tropical coast.

For more background on Australian fauna, see "Wildlife" on p.1100.

Other health hazards

One thing to watch out for in the hot and humid north is **tropical ear**, a very painful fungal infection of the ear canal. Treatment is with ear drops, and if you think you might be susceptible, use them anyway after getting wet.

Although you're unlikely to find yourself in the path of a raging **bushfire**, it helps to know how to survive one. If you're in a car, don't attempt to drive through smoke but park at the side of the road in the clearest spot, put on your headlights, wind up the windows and close the air vents. Although it seems to go against common sense – and your natural instincts – it's safer to stay inside the car. Lie on the floor and cover all exposed skin with a blanket or any covering at hand. The car won't explode or catch on fire, and a fast-moving wildfire will pass quickly overhead. If you smell or see smoke and fire while walking, find a cleared rocky outcrop or an open space: if you're trapped in the path of the fire and the terrain and time permits, dig a shallow trench – in any event, lie face down and cover all exposed skin.

Medical resources for travellers

UK and Republic of Ireland

British Airways Travel Clinics ⓣ0845/600 2236, ⓦwww.britishairways.com/travel/healthclinintro/public/en_gb for nearest clinic.
Hospital for Tropical Diseases Travel Clinic ⓣ0845/155 5000 or ⓣ020/7387 4411, ⓦwww.thehtd.org.
MASTA (Medical Advisory Service for Travellers Abroad) ⓣ0113/238 7575, ⓦwww.masta.org for information on clinics in the UK.
Tropical Medical Bureau Republic of Ireland ⓣ1850/487 674, ⓦwww.tmb.ie.

US and Canada

CDC ⓣ1-877/394-8747, ⓦwww.cdc.gov/travel. Official US government travel-health site.
International Society for Travel Medicine ⓣ1-770/736-7060, ⓦwww.istm.org. Has a full list of travel-health clinics.
Canadian Society for International Health ⓦwww.csih.org. Extensive list of travel-health centres.

Australia, New Zealand and South Africa

Travellers' Medical and Vaccination Centre ⓣ1300/658 844, ⓦwww.tmvc.com.au. Lists travel clinics in Australia, New Zealand and South Africa.

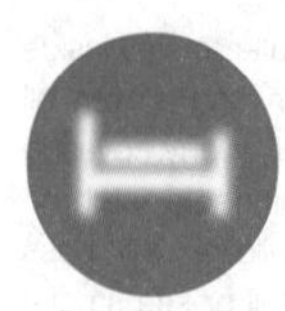

Accommodation

Finding somewhere to bed down is rarely a problem, even in the smallest of places. However, on the east coast it's a good idea to book ahead for Christmas, January and the Easter holidays, as well as for long weekends, especially when big sporting events are held (see "Festivals" on p.59).

Watch out for the term **"hotel"**, which in Australia means a pub or bar. Although they were once legally required to provide somewhere for customers to sleep off a skinful – and many still do provide accommodation – the facilities are by no means luxurious. Those highlighted in this Guide do offer decent rooms, though the majority of them are still primarily places to drink, can be loud, and are not usually enticing places to stay.

The flip side of this is that many places that would call themselves hotels anywhere else prefer to use another name – hence the reason for so many motels and resorts, and, in the cities, "private hotels" or (especially in Sydney and Melbourne) boutique hotels that tend to be smaller and run along guesthouse lines. There are also a growing number of B&Bs and farmstays where you can join in with farm life.

Australia caters extremely well for travellers, with a huge array of excellent hostels and "backpackers", and caravan parks that offer accommodation in the form of permanent on-site vans and cabins or chalets, as well as campervan facilities and tent spaces, and sometimes self-catering apartments.

Hotels and motels

Cheaper Australian **hotels** tend to be basic – no TV, and shared bathrooms and plain furnishings – and aren't always the best choice for peace and quiet. In country areas hotels are often the social centre of town, especially on Friday and Saturday nights. But with double rooms at around AUS$50–70 and singles from AUS$40 (often with breakfast included), they can be better value – and more private – than hostel accommodation. **Motels** are typically a comfortable, bland choice, often found en masse at the edge of town to catch weary drivers, and priced on average upwards of AUS$70 for a

Accommodation price codes

All the accommodation listed in this book has been categorized into one of eight **price codes**, as set out below. These represent the cost of the **cheapest** available **double** or twin room in **high season**; single rooms are generally about two-thirds the price of doubles. Hostels and backpackers' accommodation mainly have beds in dormitories. Where this is the case the price stated is in dollars per dorm bed per night in high season. However, in addition, they quite often provide single and double rooms, for which we have provided the price code. For units, cabins and caravans, the code covers the cost of the entire unit, which may sleep as many as six people.

In the lower categories, most rooms will be without private bath, though there's usually a washbasin in the room. From code ❹ upwards you'll most likely have private facilities. Remember that many of the cheaper places may also have more expensive rooms with en-suite facilities.

❶ Under $35
❷ $35–55
❸ $55–80
❹ $80–110
❺ $110–150
❻ $150–200
❼ $200–250
❽ $250 and upwards

double room with TV and bath, not including breakfast. They rarely have single rooms, but they may have larger units for families, often with basic cooking facilities.

In cities, you're far more likely to come across a hotel in the conventional sense. The cheaper of these may well describe themselves as "**private hotels**" to distinguish themselves from pubs. Some of these, especially in inner cities, can be rather sleazy, but others are very pleasant family-run guest-houses. Double rooms might cost anything from AUS$60 and up, and there are often singles available. More expensive hotels in the cities are standard places, aimed at the business community; in resorts and tourist areas they're more like upmarket motels. Prices are between AUS$150 to AUS$300 or more in five-star establishments: a typical city three-star will probably cost you above AUS$120. Similar places in a resort or country area charge AUS$100 or more.

There are numerous nationwide hotel and **motel chains** that give certain guarantees of standards, among them familiar names such as Best Western and Travelodge, as well as Australian ones such as Budget, Golden Chain and Flag. All have directories of their members, which you can use to plan ahead. While you might find it rather restrictive to use them for your whole stay, they offer dependable facilities and can be used to ensure that you have a reservation on arrival, or at anywhere else you know you'll be spending some time.

Resorts and self-catering apartments

You'll find establishments calling themselves **resorts** all over Australia, but the term is not a very clearly defined one. At the bottom end, price, appearance and facilities may be little different to those of a motel, while top-flight places can be exclusive hideaways costing hundreds of dollars a night. Originally, the name implied that the price was all-inclusive of accommodation, drinks, meals, sports and anything else on offer, but this isn't always the case. These places tend to be set in picturesque locations – the Barrier Reef islands swarm with them – and are often brilliant value if you can wangle a stand-by or off-season price.

Self-catering apartments or country cabins can be a very good deal for families and larger groups. The places themselves range from larger units at a motel to purpose-built apartment hotels, but are usually excellent value. Cooking facilities are variable, but there'll always be a TV and fridge; linen (generally not included) can sometimes be rented for a small extra charge.

Farmstays and B&Bs

Another option in rural areas are **farmstays** on working farms, and **B&Bs** or guesthouses; the last two are predominantly in the south and east and can be anything from someone's large home to your own colonial cottage – ask what the "breakfast" actually includes. Farmstays are even more variable, with some offering very upmarket comforts while at others you make do with the basic facilities in vacant shearers' quarters; their attraction is that they are always in out-of-the-way locations, and you'll often get a chance to participate in the working of the farm, or take advantage of guided tours around the property on horseback or by 4WD.

Hostels

There's a huge amount of budget accommodation in Australia, and though the more shambolic operations don't survive for long, standards are variable. Official **YHA youth hostels** (see p.51 for a list of associations) are pretty dependable – if often relatively expensive – and in most places their regimented rules and regulations have been dropped in the face of competition, especially from the firmly established **VIP Backpacker Card** network, whose membership card is as useful and widely known as the YHA. Another well-known network of backpacker hostels is **Nomads**, which also issues a membership card entitling holders to plenty of discounts.

At their best, hostels and backpackers' accommodation are excellent value and are good places to meet other travellers and get on the grapevine. There's often a choice of dormitories, double or family rooms, plus bike rental, kitchen, games room, TV, Internet access, a pool and help with finding work or organizing trips. Many have useful notice boards, organized activities and tours. At

their worst, their double rooms are poorer value than local hotel accommodation, and some are simply grubby, rapid-turnover dives – affiliation to an organization does not ensure quality. Hostels charge AUS$18–30 or more for a dormitory bed, with doubles – if available – from around AUS$50.

Most establishments prohibit the use of personal sleeping bags and instead provide all bedding needs, but it might be a good idea to carry at least a sheet sleeping-bag for the few hostels that still don't provide linen.

Youth hostel associations

The **International YHA card** (Ⓦwww.yha.com.au) is available through your national youth-hostel association before you leave home, or you can purchase a one-year Hostelling International card in Australia for AUS$37. YHA Membership and Travel Centres can be found in Sydney, Darwin, Brisbane, Cairns, Adelaide, Hobart, Melbourne and Perth, and at many YHA hostels. Australian YHA hostels number about 140, with thousands more worldwide.

UK and Republic of Ireland

Hostelling International Northern Ireland Ⓣ028/9032 4733, Ⓦwww.hini.org.uk.
Irish Youth Hostel Association Republic of Ireland Ⓣ01/830 4555, Ⓦwww.irelandyha.org.
Scottish Youth Hostel Association Ⓣ01786/891 400, Ⓦwww.syha.org.uk.
Youth Hostel Association (YHA) England and Wales Ⓣ0870/770 8868, Ⓦwww.yha.org.uk.

US and Canada

Hostelling International-American Youth Hostels US Ⓣ1-301/495-1240, Ⓦwww.hiayh.org.
Hostelling International Canada Ⓣ1-800/663-5777, Ⓦwww.hihostels.ca.

Australia and New Zealand

Australia Youth Hostels Association Australia Ⓣ02/9565 1699, Ⓦwww.yha.com.au.
Youth Hostelling Association NZ Ⓣ0800 278 299 or 03/379 9970, Ⓦwww.yha.co.nz.

Camping, caravan parks and roadhouses

Perhaps because Australian hostels are so widespread and inexpensive, simple tent **camping** is an option little used by foreign travellers. But don't let this put you off: national parks and nature reserves offer a host of camping grounds, which, depending on the location, will have an amenities block with flushing toilets, hot and cold showers, drinking water, plus a barbecue and picnic tables. Others, however, provide nothing at all, so come prepared, especially in national parks where **bushcamping** is often the only option for staying overnight. Vital equipment includes ground mats and a range of pegs – some wide (for sand), others narrow (for soil). A hatchet for splitting firewood is light to carry and doubles as a hammer. Fuel stoves are recommended, but if you do build a fire, make sure it doesn't get out of control – and always observe any fire bans. Prices depend on state

Hostel passes

If you're travelling on a budget, it's well worth laying your hands on at least one of the following **hostel passes**, which give you cheaper rates – around ten percent off – on accommodation at member hostels, and also entitle you to a wide range of other discounts on everything from bus tickets and tours to phone calls, museum entry fees and meals.

Probably of most use in Australia is a **VIP Backpacker Card** (Ⓦwww.vipbackpackers.com), which doubles as a rechargeable eKit phone card with a few dollars' worth of phone calls factored into the price of the card (AUS$43 for one year, AUS$57 for two years). At present, there are around 125 member hostels around the country, and your card will also be valid at one hundred more in New Zealand.

Nomads (Ⓦwww.nomadsworld.com) works along similar lines; their card, which also doubles as a rechargeable phone card, costs AUS$34 a year. Their network comprises about 70 hostels in Australia, many of them in old pubs, a few of them "working hostels" in country areas specializing in harvest work, and there are also affiliated hostels in New Zealand, Fiji, and a few other countries.

policy and site facilities, and you'll usually need a permit from the local NPWS (National Parks and Wildlife Service) office, details of which are given throughout the Guide. Payment will be either by self-registration (fill in a form, put it into an envelope together with the required money, and drop it off in a box on the camp ground), or a park ranger will do the rounds and collect the money.

Camping rough by the road is not a good idea, even if you take the usual precautions of setting up away from the roadside and avoiding dry riverbeds. If you have to do it, try and ensure you're not too visible: having a group of drunks pitch into your camp at midnight is not an enjoyable experience. Animals are unlikely to pose a threat, except to your food – keep it in your tent or a secure container, or be prepared to be woken by their nocturnal shenanigans.

All over Australia, **caravan parks** (sometimes called holiday parks) are usually extraordinarily well-equipped: in addition to an amenities block and a coin-operated laundry, very often you'll get an ironing board, a camp kitchen, a coin-operated barbecue, a kiosk and a swimming pool, maybe even a children's playground and a tennis court. If you are travelling without a tent, renting an on-site van (with cooking facilities but shared amenities) is a cheap, if somewhat basic, accommodation option, whereas cabins usually come with cooking facilities and an en-suite bathroom. In some upmarket caravan parks, cabins can even be slightly more expensive than a motel room, but as they are larger and better equipped, they are a good choice for families or groups travelling together.

Expect to pay AUS$10–18 per tent for an unpowered site, or AUS$36–90 for a van or cabin, depending on its location, age, size and equipment. Highway **roadhouses** are similar, combining a range of accommodation with fuel and restaurants for long-distance travellers.

Food and drink

Australia is almost two separate nations when it comes to food. In the cities of the southeast – especially Melbourne – there's a range of cosmopolitan and inexpensive restaurants and cafés featuring almost every imaginable cuisine. Here, there's an exceptionally high ratio of eating places to people, and they survive because people eat out so much – three times a week is not unusual. Remote country areas are the complete antithesis of this, where the only thing better than meat pies and microwaveable fast-food are the plain, straightforward counter meals served at the local hotel, or a slightly more upmarket bistro or basic Chinese restaurant.

Traditionally, Australian food found its roots in the English overcooked-meat-and-three-veg "common-sense cookery" mould. Two things have rescued the country from its culinary destitution: **immigration** and an extraordinary range of superb, locally produced fresh ingredients. Various ethnic cuisines are briefly discussed below, but in addition to introducing their own cuisine, immigrants have had at least as profound an effect on mainstream Australian food. "Contemporary Australian" cuisine is an exciting blend of tastes and influences from around the world – particularly Asia and the Mediterranean – and many not specifically "ethnic" restaurants will have a menu that includes properly prepared curry, dolmades and fettuccine alongside steak and prawns. This healthy, eclectic – and above all, fresh – cuisine has a lot in common with California cooking styles, and both go under the banner of "East meets West" or fusion cuisine.

Australian food

Meat is plentiful, cheap and excellent: steak forms the mainstay of the pub-counter meal and of the ubiquitous **barbie** – as Australian an institution as you could hope to find: free or coin-operated barbecues can be found in car parks, campsites and beauty spots all over the country. As well as beef and lamb, emu, buffalo, camel and witchetty grubs may be served, especially in more upmarket restaurants, but the two most common are kangaroo, a rich, tender and virtually fat-free meat, and crocodile, which tastes like a mix of chicken and pork and is at its best when simply grilled. At the coast, and elsewhere in specialist restaurants, there's tremendous **seafood**: prawns and oysters, mud crabs, Moreton Bay bugs (small crustaceans) and yabbies (sea- and freshwater crayfish), lobsters, and a wide variety of fresh- and seawater fish – barramundi has a reputation as one of the finest, but is easily beaten by sweetlips or coral trout.

Fruit is good, too, from Tasmanian apples and pears to tropical bananas, pawpaw (papaya), mangoes, avocados, citrus fruits, custard apples, lychees, pineapples, passion fruit, star fruit and coconuts – few of them native, but delicious nonetheless. **Vegetables** are also fresh, cheap and good, and include everything from European cauliflowers and potatoes to Chinese bok choy and Indian bitter gourds. Note that aubergine is known as eggplant, courgettes as zucchini and red or green peppers as capsicums.

Vegetarians might assume that they'll face a narrow choice of food in "meatocentric" Australia, and in the country areas that's probably true. But elsewhere, most restaurants will have one vegetarian option at least, and in the cities veggie cafés have cultivated a wholesome, trendy image that suits Australians' active, health-conscious nature.

Finally, a word on **eskies** – insulated food containers varying from handy "six-pack" sizes to cavernous sixty-litre trunks capable of refrigerating a weekend's worth of food or beer. No barbie or camping trip is complete without a couple of eskies. The brand name "Esky" has been adopted to describe all similar products.

Ethnic food

Since World War II, wave after wave of immigrants have brought a huge variety of ethnic cuisines to Australia: first North European, then Mediterranean and most recently Asian.

Chinese

Chinese restaurants were on the scene early in Australia – a result of post-goldrush Chinese enterprise – and Sydney, Melbourne and Darwin have Chinese connections dating back to the 1850s. The Chinese restaurants you'll find in most of the country tend to be rather old-fashioned and heavily reliant on MSG, but they're often the only alternative to Australian food. In contrast, the Chinatown area of big cities will provide a chance to sample some regional Chinese dishes as well as the usual Cantonese fare.

Two specialities served in Chinese restaurants are *yum cha* (or dim sum), lots of little titbits such as steamed buns and dumplings served from trolleys; and steamboat, an Asian version of fondue. Both are tasty and extremely good value for money – especially for a group.

Other Asian cuisines

Since the 1970s, a new wave of immigrants from Southeast Asia has further energized Australian cuisine. **Vietnamese** restaurants not only offer some of the cheapest meals anywhere, they also come with the freshest

Bushtucker

The first European colonists decided that the country was not "owned" by the **Aborigines** because they didn't systematically farm the land. As many frustrated pastoralists later came to realize, this was a direct response to Australia's erratic seasons, which don't lend themselves to European farming methods with any degree of long-term security. Instead, Aborigines followed a nomadic lifestyle within extensive tribal boundaries, following seasonal game and plants and promoting both by annually burning off grassland.

Along the coast, indigenous people speared turtles and dugong from outrigger canoes, caught **fish** in stone traps, piled emptied oyster shells into giant middens, and even cooperated with dolphins to herd fish into shallows. Other **animals** caught all over the country were possums, snakes (highly prized), goannas, emus and kangaroos. These animals were thrown straight onto a fire and cooked in their own juices, and sometimes their skin, bones and fat used as clothing, tools and ointment respectively. More meagre pickings were provided by honey and green ants, water-holding frogs, moths and various grubs – the witchetty (or *witjuti*) being the best known. Foot-long ooli worms were drawn out of rotten mangrove trunks, and tiny native bees were tagged with strands of spider web and then followed to their hives for honey; another sweet treat was mulga resin, picked off the tree trunk.

Plants, usually gathered by women, were used extensively and formed the bulk of the diet. The cabbage palm, sea almond, mangrove seeds, pandanus and dozens of fruits, including tropical coconuts, plums and figs, all grew along the coast. Inland were samphire bush, wild tomatoes and "citrus", grasstree hearts, cycad nuts (very toxic until washed, but high in starch), native millet, wattle seeds, waterlily tubers, nardoo seeds (a water fern), fungi, macadamia nuts, quandongs and bunya pine nuts – the last had great social importance in southern Queensland, where they were eaten at huge feasts. In Queensland's far north, meat and vegetables are wrapped in banana leaves (*kup maori*) and roasted in an underground oven; one of the Torres Strait Islanders' few surviving traditional styles of cooking.

It's tempting to taste some bushfoods, and a good few city **restaurants** are now experimenting with them as ingredients; otherwise, you'll need expert guidance, as many plants are poisonous. A few tours and safaris (particularly in the Northern Territory) give an introduction to living off the land; for further reading, try *Bush Tucker: Australia's Wild Food Harvest* by Tim Low.

of ingredients: accompanying most meals is a plate of red chillies, lemon wedges and beansprouts.

There are numerous **Malaysian** and **Indonesian** restaurants and market stalls, where hearty noodle soups and satays with hot peanut sauce are served up. Hawker-style stalls in city food-courts often serve *laksa*, a huge bowl of hot and spicy coconut-milk-based soup full of noodles, tofu and chicken or prawns.

The biggest success, however, are the **Thai** restaurants, and it's hard to believe that they've been around for less than twenty years. Dishes can be fiery, yet subtly flavoured, with ingredients such as basil, lemongrass, garlic, chilli and coriander.

Because so much fresh seafood is available in Australia, **Japanese** food is more accessible – and less expensive – than it is in many other countries. There may not be a large Japanese population, but there are a huge number of Japanese visitors, and plenty of places catering for them (you'll find lots on the Gold Coast and in Cairns, for example).

Mongolian barbecues are an unusual, fast and inexpensive complement to the already diverse Asian food culture. Thinly sliced meat or seafood is added to a selection of sliced vegetables and stir-fried in a soy-type sauce before your eyes on a giant wok – a Mongol warrior's shield is said to have been the original cooking utensil.

Italian – and coffee

The Italian influence on Australian cooking has been enormous. Second in number only to the English as an ethnic group, the Italians brought with them their love of food, which was a perfect complement to the Australian climate and way of life, and from the 1950s pizzerias, espresso and *gelati* bars, and the then-exotic taste of garlic, were conquering palates countrywide. One particularly Australian metamorphosis is **focaccia**, now a staple of every city café and even beginning to make an appearance in country towns.

Australia can also thank the Italians for elevating **coffee** to a pastime rather than just a hot drink. Nowadays, every suburban café has an espresso machine, and it's not just used to make cappuccino. Other styles of coffee have adopted uniquely Australian names: a "flat white" is a plain white coffee, a "café latte" is a milkier version usually served in a glass (like cappuccino without the froth), a "long black" is a regular cup of black coffee, and a "short black" is an espresso – transformed by a splash of milk into a macchiato. ("Espresso" is also a brand of instant coffee, so ask for a short black if you're after the genuine article.)

Other European and Middle Eastern cuisines

Melbourne is Australia's food capital, with its legendary **Greek** population among the many European influences in the city. As well as *taverna*-style Greek restaurants, *souvlaki* bars, with spiced lamb rotating on a spit, abound. **Turkish** and **Lebanese** takeaways, found throughout Australia, use a similar ingredient for their spicy filled rolls, while some Turkish places also offer *börek*, small, simple but spicy variants on a pizza. Lebanese restaurants are especially good for vegetarians, with falafel rolls (pitta bread stuffed with chickpea patties, hummus and *tabbouleh*) making an inexpensive, filling meal.

Central European influences are most obvious in baking, particularly in Melbourne, where there is a large **Jewish** community made up of immigrants from prewar Poland, and there are also a few **Polish** restaurants serving hearty, peasant-style dishes. **German** influences are most prominent around Adelaide – as well as at deli counters throughout the country, where you'll find an abundance of Australian-made small goods and sausages.

Eating out

Restaurants are astonishingly good value compared with Britain and North America, particularly as many restaurants are BYO (bring your own alcohol): you're rarely far from a bottle shop (the Australian term for an off-licence or liquor store). Corkage fee is around AUS$1–3. Some licensed restaurants also allow BYO wine, but if you add their steeper corkage fee to the price of your bottle, you might as well stick to their wine list. You should have no problem finding an excellent two-course meal in a BYO restaurant for AUS$25 or less, though a main course at a moderate restaurant is around AUS$17–24.

Infamous Australian foods

Chicko Roll Imagine a wrapper of stodgy dough covered in breadcrumbs, filled with a neutered mess of chicken, cabbage, thickeners and flavourings, and then deep-fried. You could only get away with it in Australia.

Damper Sounding positively wholesome in this company, "damper" is the swagman's staple – soda bread baked in a pot buried in the ashes of a fire. It's not hard to make after a few attempts – the secret is in the heat of the coals and a splash of beer.

Lamington A chocolate-coated sponge cube rolled in shredded coconut.

Pavlova ("pav"). A dessert concoction of meringue with layers of cream and fruit; named after the eminent Russian ballerina. Made properly with fresh fruit and minimum quantities of cream and sugar, it's not bad at all.

Pie floater The apotheosis of the meat pie; a "pie floater" is an inverted meat pie swamped in mashed green peas and tomato sauce; found especially in South Australia. Floaters can be surprisingly good, or horrible enough to put you off both pies and peas for life.

Vegemite Regarded by the English as an inferior form of Marmite and by almost every other nationality with total disgust, Vegemite is an Australian institution – a strong, dark, yeast spread for bread and toast.

Witchetty grubs (*witjuti*). About the size of your little finger, witchetty grubs are dug from the roots of mulga trees and are a well-known Australian bushtucker delicacy. Eating the plump, fawn-coloured caterpillars live (as is traditional) takes some nerve, so try giving them a brief roasting in embers. They're very tasty either way – reminiscent of peanut butter.

There are also lots of excellent **cafés** and **coffee shops**. In the cities and resorts, modern cafés are often the best places to go for a decent meal, and will be open from early in the morning until late at night, serving food all day; in the country, they may stick more or less to shop hours.

The **hotel** counter meal is another mainstay, and at times may be all that's available: if it is, make sure you get there in time – meals in pubs are generally served only from noon to 2pm and again from 6 to 8pm, and rarely at all on Sunday evening. The food – served at the bar – will be simple but substantial and inexpensive (usually around AUS$14 or less): steak, salad and chips, and variations on this theme. Slightly more upmarket is the hotel **bistro** or restaurant in a motel, where you sit down to be served much the same food; these places often have a help-yourself salad bar, too. Usually the most expensive thing on the menu is a huge steak for AUS$15–20.

In cities and bigger resorts, you'll find fantastic fast-food in **food courts**, often in the basements of office buildings or in shopping malls, where dozens of small stalls compete to offer Thai, Chinese, Japanese or Italian food as well as burgers, steaks and sandwiches. On the road, you may be reduced to what's available at the roadhouse, usually the lowest common denominator of reheated meat-pies and microwaved ready-meals.

Drink

Australians have a reputation for enjoying a drink, and **hotels** (also sometimes called taverns, inns, pubs and bars) are where it mostly takes place. Traditionally, public bars are male enclaves, the place where mates meet after work on their way home, with the emphasis more on the beer and banter than the surroundings. While changing attitudes have converted many city hotels into comfortable, relaxed bars, a lot of Outback pubs are still pretty spartan and daunting for strangers of either sex, but you'll find barriers will come down if you're prepared to join in the conversation.

Friday and Saturday are the serious party nights, when there's likely to be a band and – in the case of some Outback establishments – literally everybody for a hundred kilometres around jammed into the building. **Opening hours** vary from state to state; they're usually 11am to 11pm, but are often much later, with early closing on Sunday. Some places are also "early openers", with hours from 6am to 6pm.

For **takeout** sales (known in Australia as takeaway), liquor stores or off-licences are known as bottle shops. These are usually in a separate section attached to a pub or supermarket – in some states, you can't buy alcohol from supermarkets or grocery stores. There are also **drive-in** bottle shops attached to pubs where you can load bulk purchases directly into the boot of your car; these solve the question of parking, though aren't totally the lazy option as you normally have to get out of the car to make your selection. If you plan to visit **Aboriginal communities** in the Outback, bear in mind that some of them are "dry". Respect their regulations and don't take any alcohol with you, even if members of the communities ask you for "grog".

Beer

As anyone you ask will tell you, the proper way to drink **beer** in a hot country such as Australia is ice cold (the English can expect to be constantly berated for their warm beer preferences) and fast, from a small container so it doesn't heat up before you can down the contents. Tubular foam or polystyrene coolers are often supplied for **tinnies** (cans) or **stubbies** (short-necked bottles) to make sure they stay icy. Glasses are always on the small side, and are given confusingly different names state by state. The standard ten-ounce (half-pint) serving is known as a **pot** in Victoria and Queensland, and a **middie** in New South Wales and Western Australia, where the situation is further complicated by the presence of fifteen-ounce **schooners**. A **carton** or **slab** is a box of 24–30 tinnies or stubbies, bought in bulk from a bottle shop and always cheaper when not chilled (a "Darwin stubby", with typically Territorian eccentricity, is two litres of beer in an oversized bottle).

Australian beers are lager- or pilsner-style, and even the big mass-produced ones are pretty good – at least once you've worked up a thirst. They're considerably stronger than their US equivalents, and marginally stronger than the average British lager at just under five percent alcohol. Each state has its own **label** and there are fierce local loyalties, even though most are sold nationwide: Fourex (XXXX; see p.373) and Powers in Queensland; Swan in Western Australia; Coopers in South Australia; VB in Victoria; Tooheys in New South Wales; and Boags in Tasmania. Almost all of these companies produce more than one beer – usually a light low-alcohol version and a premium "gold" or bitter brew. There are also a number of smaller "boutique" breweries and specialist beermakers: Tasmania's Cascade, WA's Redback or Matilda Bay, Queensland's Cairns' Draught and Eumundi are more distinctive but harder to find. Fosters is treated as a joke in Australia, something that's fit only for export. Larger bottle shops might have imported beers, but outside cities (where Irish pubs serve surprisingly authentic-tasting Guinness) it's rare that you'll find anything foreign on tap.

Wines and spirits

Australian **wines** have long been appreciated at home, and it's not hard to see why; even an inexpensive bottle (around AUS$12) will be better than just drinkable, while pricier varieties compare favourably with fine French wines – though some critics complain that Australian reds have become a bit too "woody" in recent years. If you're new to Australian wines, you'll always find Yalumba, Lindemans and Wolf Blass will give satisfaction, but the secret is to be adventurous: you're extremely unlikely to be disappointed. Even the "chateau cardboard" four-litre bladders or wine casks that prevail at parties and barbecues are perfectly palatable. Whatever the colour, a mid-range bottle of wine will set you back about AUS$16.

The biggest wine-producing **regions** are the Hunter Valley in New South Wales and the Barossa Valley in South Australia, but you'll find smaller commercial vineyards from Kingaroy in Queensland to Margaret River in southwest Western Australia; all are detailed in the text of the Guide. If you buy at these places, you'll be able to sample in advance (see the box on "Wine-tasting tips" on p.752). Most bottle shops will, in any case, have a good range of very reasonably priced options. For more on Australian wines, check out Ⓦwww.boutiquewines.com.au, which has links to many vineyards; and Ⓦwww.australianwines.com.au, for maps and a description of the most important Australian wine regions, as well as FAQs about how to best serve and drink local wines.

The Australian wine industry also makes port and brandy as a sideline, though these are not up to international standards. Two excellent dark **rums** from Queensland's sugar belt are well worth tasting, however: the sweet, deliciously smoky Bundaberg (see p.415) and the more conventionally flavoured Beenleigh. They're of average strength, normally 33 percent alcohol, but beware of "overproof" variations, which will have you flat on your back if you try to drink them like ordinary spirits.

The media

Local papers are always a good source of listings, if not news. You should be able to track down some international papers, or their overseas editions – British, American, Asian and European – in the state capitals. Australian television isn't particularly exciting unless you're into sport, of which there's plenty, and commercial stations put on frequent advertising breaks throughout films.

Newspapers and magazines

The Murdoch-owned *Australian* (Ⓦwww.theaustralian.news.com.au) is the country's only national daily (that is, Monday to Saturday) newspaper; aimed mainly at the business community, it has good overseas coverage but local news is often built around statistics. Each state (or more properly, each state capital) has its own daily paper, the best of which are two Fairfax-owned papers, the *Sydney Morning Herald* (Ⓦwww.smh.com.au) and Melbourne's venerable *The Age* (Ⓦwww.theage.com.au) – both available across the southeast (the two papers share similar content in their weekend-edition magazines). If you're interested in wildlife, pick up a copy of the quarterly *Australian Geographic* (related only in name to the US magazine) for some superb photography and in-depth coverage of Australia's remoter corners, or the quarterly *Australian Wildlife* magazine published by the Wildlife Preservation Society. There are some excellent glossy Australian-focused adventure-travel magazines, too, such as the quarterly *Wild*, while the beautifully produced and written quarterly *40° South* concentrates on all things Tasmanian (it's hard to track down; see Ⓦwww.fortysouth.com.au for details). You'll find Australian versions of all the fashion mags, from *Vogue* to *Marie Claire*, plus enduring publications such as the *Australian Women's Weekly*. The excellent *Australian Gourmet Traveller* celebrates both fine food and travel. Gossipy magazines such as *Who Weekly* feature the lowdown on the antics of international and Australian celebs.

Television

Australia's first **television** station opened in 1956 and the country didn't get colour television until 1974 – both much later than other Westernized countries. It is governed by Australian content rulings, which means that there are a good amount of Australian dramas, series and soap operas, many of which go on to make it big overseas, from *Neighbours* and *Home and Away* to *The Secret Life of Us*. However, there's a predominance of American programmes and lots of repeats. Australian TV is also fairly permissive in terms of sexual content compared to the programming of Britain or

North America. There are three predictable commercial stations: Channel Seven; Channel Nine, which aims for an older market with more conservative programming; and Channel Ten, which tries to grab the younger market with some good comedy programmes. In addition, there is also the more serious ABC – a national, advertisement-free station still with a British bias, showing all the best British sitcoms and mini-series – and the livelier SBS, a government-sponsored, multicultural station, which has the best coverage of world news, as well as interesting current-affairs programmes and plenty of foreign-language films. In more remote areas you won't be able to access all five channels, and often only ABC and one commercial offering are receivable. There are over 35 pay-TV stations, though the pay-TV culture is not as firmly established yet as in other countries, and even expensive hotels often still only have terrestrial TV.

Radio

The best **radio** is on the various ABC stations, both local and national. ABC Radio National – broadcast all over Australia – offers a popular mix of arty intellectual topics, and another ABC station, 2JJJ ("Triple J"), a former Sydney-based alternative-rock station, is aimed at the nation's youth and is available across the country in watered-down form.

Festivals and major sporting events

The nationwide selection of festivals listed below all include, necessitate and are, in some cases, the imaginative product of prolonged beer-swilling. Why else would you drive to the edge of the Simpson Desert to watch a horse race? More seriously, each mainland capital tries to elevate its sophistication quotient with a regular celebration and showcase of art and culture, of which the biennial Adelaide Arts Festival is the best known.

Besides the major events listed below, there's a host of smaller, local events, many of which are detailed throughout the Guide. Also, all cities and towns have their own agricultural "shows", which are high points of the local calendar. The Christmas and Easter holiday periods, especially, are marked by celebrations at every turn, all over the country.

January

Sydney Festival NSW. Starts the first week. Three weeks of festivities take place all over the city – in parks, theatres and cinemas – with something for absolutely everyone, from new film and outdoor jazz to contemporary art and current-events lectures. Ⓦwww.sydneyfestival.com.au.

Tamworth Country Music Festival NSW. Third week. Ten days of Slim Dusty and his ilk, culminating in the Australian Country Music Awards. Ⓦwww.telstra.com/countrywide/countrymusic.

Big Days Out Various locations. Late Jan to early Feb. This event has got bigger and bigger since the first Big Day Out in Sydney over fifteen years ago and today is Australia and New Zealand's largest outdoor music festival, with over 250,000 people gathering at six different locations over successive weekends to see bands such as Muse, Jet and Kasabian. Kicks off in Auckland, then moves on to the Gold Coast, Sydney, Melbourne, Adelaide and finally Perth. Ⓦwww.bigdayout.com.

February

Sydney Gay and Lesbian Mardi Gras NSW. Early Feb to early March. Sydney's proud gay-community's festival runs throughofut February and culminates at the beginning of March with an extravagant parade and an all-night dance party. Ⓦwww.mardigras.org.au.

Perth International Arts Festival WA. Early February to early March. Australia's oldest and largest arts festival, attracting renowned international artists, performers and attendees to indoor and outdoor events all over the city. Ⓦ www.perthfestival.com.au.

March

Adelaide Arts Festival SA. First two weeks; held in even-numbered years. The country's best-known and most innovative biennial arts festival (next one in 2008), including one of the largest literary festivals in the world; not to be missed. Ⓦ www.adelaidefestival.org.au.
Womadelaide SA. First or second weekend. Part of the Womad festival circuit; three-day party featuring world music, folk, blues and jazz. Ⓦ www.womadelaide.com.au.
Australian Grand Prix Melbourne, VIC. First or second weekend. Formula One street racing that follows a week of partying; formerly held in Adelaide, now relocated to Albert Park in Melbourne. Ⓦ www.grandprix.com.au.
Moomba Waterfest VIC. Second weekend. A long weekend of partying in Melbourne, beginning and ending with fireworks, with lots of water-based fun on the Yarra River in between. Ⓦ www.melbourne.vi.gov.au.

April

Melbourne International Comedy Festival VIC. Starts first week. Comics from around the world gather at bars, halls and theatres across the city for three weeks. Ⓦ www.comedyfestival.com.au.

June

Sydney International Film Festival NSW. Mid-June. Important film festival, running for over two weeks and based at the glorious State Theatre. Ⓦ www.sydneyfilmfestival.org.
Barunga Cultural and Sports Festival NT. Mid-June. This three-day festival, held on Aboriginal land near Katherine, offers a rare and enjoyable opportunity to encounter Aboriginal culture in the NT. No alcohol. Entry fee.
Laura Dance and Cultural Festival Cape York, QLD. Third weekend; held in odd-numbered years. Three-day, alcohol-free celebration of authentic Aboriginal culture. Biennial (next one is 2007).

July

Imparja Camel Cup Alice Springs, NT. Second Saturday. Camel racing that first saw camels charging down the dry Todd River; the event is now held at Blatherskite Park, with free buses to the site. Ⓦ www.camelcup.com.au.
Brisbane Festival Brisbane, QLD. Mid-July; held in even years. Huge, biennial (the next one is 2008), seventeen-day festival featuring performing arts, food and drink, music, writing and children's events topped off with fireworks. Ⓦ www.brisbanefestival.com.au.
Darwin Beer Can Regatta NT. Third Sunday. Mindil Beach is the venue for the recycling of copious empties into a variety of "canstructed" seacraft. Also a thong-throwing contest; Territorian eccentricity personified. Ⓦ www.beercanregatta.org.au.
Melbourne International Film Festival VIC. End July to mid-August. The country's largest and most prestigious film festival, lasting for over a fortnight. Ⓦ www.melbournefilmfestival.com.au.

August

Isa Rodeo Mount Isa, QLD. Second or third weekend. Australia's largest rodeo – a gritty, down-to-earth encounter with bulls, horses and their riders. Ⓦ www.isarodeo.com.au.
Henley-on-Todd Regatta Alice Springs, NT. Third Saturday. Wacky races in bottomless boats running down the dry Todd River; the event is heavily insured against the river actually flowing. Ⓦ www.henleyontodd.com.au.
Shinju Matsuri Festival Broome, WA. End August. Probably the most remote big festival, but this doesn't stop the town packing out for WA's ten-day Oriental-themed pearl festival. Ⓦ www.shinjumatsuri.com.

September

Birdsville Races QLD. First weekend. Once a year, the remote Outback town of Birdsville (population approx 120) comes alive for a weekend (Fri and Sat) of drinking and horse racing – a well-known and definitive Australian oddity. Ⓦ www.birdsvilleraces.com.
AFL Grand Final Melbourne, VIC. Last Saturday. Huge, testosterone-charged sporting event. The Australian Football League final is held at Melbourne's MCG and is accompanied by lots of beer drinking and celebrating, depending on which team wins. Ⓦ www.afl.com.au.

October

Manly Jazz Festival Sydney, NSW. First weekend. Long-established, free three-day jazz festival featuring artists from all over the world.
Melbourne International Arts Festival VIC. Mid-Oct. Two-week celebration of visual, performing and written arts in venues all over the city; lots of international and Australian "big names". Ⓦ www.melbournefestival.com.au.

November

Melbourne Cup Flemington Racecourse, VIC. First Tuesday. Australia's Ascot, a 146-year-old horse race that brings the entire country to a standstill around the radio or TV. Ⓦ www.melbournecup.com.

December

Christmas Day Sydney, NSW. For travellers from the northern hemisphere, turkey on the beach is an awesome concept – on Sydney's Bondi Beach, it's coupled with a lot of alcohol, making this public holiday a raucous riot. Sadly, though, the days of free partying are long gone and the organized festivities are a ticket affair only.

New Year's Eve The fireworks display from Sydney Harbour Bridge is a grand show, and a fine example to the rest of the world of how to welcome the New Year. To get the best views along the water's edge, you'll need to get there when it's still light.

Sydney–Hobart Yacht Race Sydney, NSW. Crowds flock to the harbour to witness the start of this classic regatta, which departs Sydney at 1pm on Boxing Day and arrives in Hobart three days later. Ⓦ www.rolexsydneyhobart.com.

Sports and outdoor activities

Australians are sports mad, especially for the ostensibly passive spectator sports of cricket, Aussie Rules football, rugby (league or union), tennis or any type of racing, from cockroach to camel. No matter what it is, it'll draw a crowd – with thousands more watching on TV – and a crowd means a party. Even unpromising-sounding activities such as surf lifesaving and yacht racing (the start of the Sydney to Hobart race just after Christmas is a massive social event; see p.996) are tremendously popular.

Football

The wintertime football (**footy**) season in Australia lasts from March to September, and comes in several varieties. Before World War II, soccer was played by British immigrants, but with postwar immigration it was branded as "ethnic", as new clubs became based on the country of origin of the players: Australian Rules (see below) was considered the game "real Australians" played. Before the National Soccer League's (NSL) competition was disbanded in 2004, more than fifty percent of the former NSL's twelve clubs had evolved from communities of postwar immigrants – mainly Italians, Greeks and Yugoslavs. The former chairman of Soccer Australia (now rebranded Football Federation Australia), David Hill, believed that their fervent nationalism marginalized the game; his mid-1990s ban on clubs that included national flags in their logos won support as well as accusations of the pursuance of a policy of "ethnic cleansing". The new A-League competition, with eight teams from Australia and New Zealand, is the latest attempt to promote national rather than localized, politicized interest in the sport. The best players invariably head off to play overseas but can usually be seen in Australia's national team, the **Socceroos**, interest in which has increased significantly since their appearance at the 2006 World Cup – their first for thirty years – where they (controversially) lost to eventual champions Italy in the second round.

Australian Rules ("**Aussie Rules**") football dominates Victoria, Tasmania, South Australia and Western Australia. It's an extraordinary, anarchic, no-holds-barred, eighteen-a-side brawl, most closely related to Gaelic football and known dismissively north of the Victorian border as "aerial ping pong". The ball can be propelled by any means necessary, and the fact that players aren't sent off for miscon-duct ensures a lively, skilful and, above all, gladiatorial confrontation. Aussie Rules stars have delightful sobriquets such as "Tugger" and "Crackers", and their macho garb consists of tiny butt-hugging shorts and bicep-revealing tank tops. The game is mostly played on cricket grounds, with a ball similar to that used in rugby or American football. The aim is to get the ball through the central uprights for a goal (six points). There are four 25-minute quarters, plus lots of time added on for injury. Despite the violence on the pitch (or perhaps because of it), Aussie Rules fans tend to be loyal and well behaved. Victoria has traditionally been the home of the game, and Victorian sides are expected to win the AFL Flag, decided at the Grand Final in September (see p.60), as a matter of course.

Rugby

In New South Wales and Queensland, **Rugby League** attracts the fanatics, especially for the hard-fought State of Origin matches. The thirteen-a-side game is one at which the Australians – known as the **Kangeroos** – seem permanent world champions, despite having a relatively small professional league. Formerly run by the Australian Rugby League (ARL), the game was split down the middle in 1996, when Rupert Murdoch launched Super League in an attempt to gain ratings for his Foxtel TV station. It quickly became obvious that the game could not support two separate competitions, and in 1997 they united to form the National Rugby League (NRL).

Rugby League is the football code in Sydney, and the majority of the fifteen NRL teams are based there. One of the sadder consequences of this media-inspired revolution has been the loss of some of the traditional inner-city clubs through mergers. Many people also resent the way in which this one-time bastion of working-class culture has been coopted by pay TV.

Rugby Union is very much a minority interest domestically. However, the introduction of a Super 12 competition, involving teams from Australia, New Zealand and South Africa, has generated a much greater interest in what was formerly an elitist sport, and the national team, the **Wallabies**, are hugely popular.

Gambling

Australians are obsessive about gambling, though legalities vary from state to state. Even small towns have their own racetracks, and there are government TAB betting agencies everywhere; you can often bet in pubs, too. Many states have huge casinos and clubs, open to anyone, with wall-to-wall one-armed bandits (poker machines or "pokies"); there are also big state lotteries.

Cricket

In summer, **cricket** is played from October to March, and is a great spectator sport – for the crowd, the sunshine and the beer as much as the play. Every state is involved, and the three- or four-day Sheffield Shield matches of the interstate series are interspersed with one-day games and internationals, as well as full five-day international test matches.

The international competition that still arouses greatest interest is that between Australia and England – **The Ashes**. Having been around for over 120 years, this is perhaps the oldest rivalry between nations in international sport. The "trophy" competed for has an interesting provenance: in 1882, an Australian touring side defeated England at the Oval in South London by seven runs, and the *Sporting Times* was moved to report, in a mock obituary, that English cricket had "died at the Oval... deeply lamented by a large circle of sorrowing friends". The funeral ceremony involved the cremation of a set of bails, which were then preserved in a funerary urn. Each time the two countries compete, this is the trophy that is up for grabs (though the urn itself never actually leaves Lord's cricket ground in London) and a new crystal trophy goes to the winners. In 2006, Australia took the Ashes back Down Under after demolishing England in the first series whitewash since 1920.

Outdoor pursuits

Though the cities are fun, what really makes Australia special is the great outdoors: the vast and remote wilderness of the bush, the legendary Outback, and the thousands of kilometres of unspoilt coastline. There's tremendous potential here to indulge in a huge range of **outdoor pursuits** – hiking, fishing, surfing, diving, even skiing –

National parks

The Australian Government federal **Department of the Environment and Heritage** (DEH) is tasked with protecting and conserving the nation's natural environment (and aspects of its cultural heritage). Its mandate includes dealing with international problems such as whaling, and making decisions about the Australian Antarctic Division. Under the DEH, Parks Australia (itself under the Director of National Parks) manages Commonwealth reserves including six **Commonwealth national parks**, three of which are jointly managed by traditional Aboriginal owners – Booderee in Jervis Bay Territory, and in the Northern Territory, Uluru-Kata Tjuta and Kakadu – while the remaining three protect unique island ecosystems, including Norfolk Island National Park. The DEH also manages the Australian National Botanic Garden in Canberra and botanic gardens at Booderee and Norfolk Island, as well as a number of marine protected areas.

Each state and territory has their own protected area management authority; departmental names vary from state to state, but Australians tend to generically dub them as the **National Parks and Wildlife Service (NPWS)**, which is how we refer to them in the Guide.

The thousand-odd **national parks** range from suburban commons to the Great Barrier Reef, and from popular hiking areas within striking distance of the big cities to wilderness regions that require days in a 4WD simply to reach. They protect everything within their boundaries: flora, fauna and landforms as well as Aboriginal art and sacred sites, although not always to the exclusion of mineral exploitation, as in Karijini in WA or Kakadu in the Territory.

Entry and camping **fees** are variable. Some parks or states have no fees at all, some charge entry fees but often don't police the system, some charge for use of camping facilities, while others require permits bought in advance; each state or territory usually offers a pass – which makes it cheaper if you want to visit many national parks and for longer periods – but unfortunately no national pass is available. If you're camping you can usually pay on site, but booking ahead might be a good idea during the Christmas, Easter and school holidays. Some parks have cabin accommodation, either self-catering or bunk-style with a camp kitchen, but nearby resorts or alternative accommodation are always independently run. For details on the names and vagaries of each state or territory's system, consult the websites listed below.

Australian Capital Territory Environment ACT Ⓦwww.environment.act.gov.au

Commonwealth Department of the Environment and Heritage (DEH) Ⓦwww.deh.gov.au

New South Wales NSW National Parks and Wildlife Service (NPWS) Ⓦwww.nationalparks.nsw.gov.au

Northern Territory Parks and Wildlife Commission of the Northern Territory Ⓦwww.nt.gov.au/ipe/pwcnt

Queensland Environmental Protection Agency (EPA)/Queensland Parks and Wildlife Service Ⓦwww.epa.qld.gov.au

South Australia National Parks and Wildlife SA Ⓦwww.environment.sa.gov.au/parks

Tasmania Tasmania Parks and Wildlife Service Ⓦwww.parks.tas.gov.au

Victoria Parks Victoria Ⓦwww.parkweb.vic.gov.au

Western Australia Department of Conservation and Land Management (CALM) Ⓦwww.calm.wa.gov.au

especially in the multitude of national parks that cover the country. Further information on all of these is available from local tourist offices, which publicize what's available in their area: from **Parks Australia**, which has detailed maps of parks with walking trails, climbs, swimming holes and other activities, to specialist books. In addition, virtually any activity can be done as part of an organized excursion, often with all the gear supplied. If you want to go it alone, you'll find plenty of places ready to rent or sell you the necessary equipment. Before indulging in adventure activities, check your insurance cover (see "Travel essentials").

As with any wilderness area, the Australian interior does not suffer fools, and the coast conceals **dangers**, too: sunstroke and dehydration are risks everywhere, with riptides, currents and unexpectedly large waves to be wary of on exposed coasts. In the more remote regions, isolation and lack of surface water compromise energetic outdoor activities such as bushwalking or mountain biking, which are probably better practised in the cooler climes and more populated locations of the south.

Bushwalking

Bushwalking in Australia doesn't mean just a stroll in the bush, but refers to self-sufficient hikes, from a day to a week or longer. It's an increasingly popular activity nationwide, and you'll find trails marked in almost every national park, as well as local bushwalking clubs whose trips you may be able to join.

It's essential to be **properly equipped** for the conditions you'll encounter – and to know what those conditions are likely to be. Carry a map (often on hand at the ranger station in popular national parks), know how the trail is marked, and stay on the route. If your trip is a long one, let someone know where you're going, and confirm to them that you've arrived back safely – park rangers are useful contacts for this, and some will insist on it for overnight walks, which may require registration. One point worth noting is that in national park areas the estimated duration of a given walk is often exaggerated – certainly in the Territory and WA: you can comfortably divide the indicated time by half or more. On formed tracks a walking speed of 3 to 4kph is average. The essentials, even for a short walk, are adequate clothing including a wide-brimmed hat, enough food and, above all, water – and plenty of it (see p.66). Other useful items include a torch, matches or lighter, penknife, sun block, insect repellent, toilet paper, first-aid kit, and a whistle or mirror to attract attention if you get lost. A lot of this gear can be rented, or bought cheaply at disposal stores, which can often also put you in touch with local clubs or specialists.

Long-distance tracks exist mostly in the south of the country, with Tasmania's wilderness areas being perhaps the most rewarding bushwalking location; the eighty-kilometre Overland Track from Cradle Mountain to Lake St Clair is one of the country's best-known trails. On the mainland, the Blue Mountains, a two-hour train ride from Sydney, the Snowy Mountains further south, and Victoria's spectacular Grampians are all popular regions for longer, marked walks.

South Australia's **Flinders Ranges**, 300km north of Adelaide, are accessible along the Heysen Trail from the Fleurieu Peninsula, the walk into the thousand-metre-high natural basin of Wilpena Pound being the highlight. In temperate southwestern WA, the 960-kilometre **Bibbulmun Track**, an old Aboriginal trail passing through the region's giant eucalypt forests, was completed in 2002 from Albany to Kalamunda near Perth. In the same year the 220-kilometre Larapinta Trail, along the McDonnell Ranges west of Alice Springs was also completed: an initially strenuous hike out of Alice Springs that should only be attempted in winter. Queensland's rainforested coastal strip offers plenty more opportunities for walks, including the Lamington area in the south, and around northern Atherton Tablelands and Hinchinbrook Island.

Throughout the text of the Guide, we mention specialist bushwalking **guides and maps** that are relevant. Two of Australia's best-regarded bushwalkers are John Chapman and Tyrone T. Thomas, and both publish a range of walking guides. Try to get hold of the latest edition of Chapman's rigorously updated *Bushwalking in Australia*, which details the country's best bushwalks.

Watersports

The oceans and seas around Australia are a national playground and are not just for lying by or playing volleyball on the beach. Always take local advice on the waves, which must be treated with respect. If possible, **swim** from a patrolled beach, between the flags: raise one hand if you get into difficulty, and clear the water if a siren sounds – it could signal dangerous waves, a shark sighting or a swarm of bluebottles (stinging jellyfish).

Enjoying the water doesn't necessarily involve any special effort or equipment, but if you want it, there are plenty of activities on offer. Probably the easiest to get into is **surfing**, starting with bodysurfing and progressing to boogie-boards (small boards that you lie on) and then on to full-scale surfboards; seaside hostels often have boards that they loan out free. Surfing is popular everywhere, but don't expect the local surfie community to be too friendly at first – they're often very cliquey. Throughout the year, the country plays host to a number of high-profile competitions such as the Easter World Championships, held at Bell's Beach, southwest of Melbourne, and November's Margaret River Classic, south of Perth – both good opportunities to catch some wave-riding action. One peculiarly Australian institution is the **surf carnival**, when teams of volunteer lifesavers demonstrate their skills; it makes for a great day out on the beach. **Windsurfing** and **sailing** are also extremely popular, and you'll be able to rent equipment and get instruction in almost any resort, though some of the best sailing in the country can be found around Queensland's Whitsunday Islands or off WA's West Coast. Other **watersports** include white-water rafting, sea-kayaking and canoeing.

The Great Barrier Reef is one of the world's great **scuba-diving** Meccas, with some other lesser-known but excellent sites around the country – such as West Australia's Ningaloo Reef. Dive facilities in Australia are of a high standard, and scuba courses are not that expensive, though if you simply want to try it once there are plenty of people offering closely supervised "resort dives". Good rental gear is widely available, but if you're bringing your own, check for compatibility problems; yokes are the Australian norm, so if your first-stage fitting is DIN (likely in Europe and the UK), you'll need an

Bush essentials

Four things above all:

Fire The driest continent on earth is covered by vegetation that has evolved with regular conflagrations, and is always at risk from bushfires. At least three times in the last ten years Sydney has been ringed with burning bushland, and during the terrible bushfire season of 2002/2003 a large part of the Alpine region in Australia's southeast was ablaze for almost two months, wreaking havoc on bush and forests, animals and people. Only a few human lives were lost, however, mainly owing to the skills, resilience and determination of the fire fighters and local residents. Even in wet years, there's a constant red alert during summer months. Always use an established fireplace where available, or dig a shallow pit and ring it with stones. Keep fires small and make absolutely sure embers are smothered before going to sleep or moving on. Never discard burning cigarette butts from cars. Periodic total fire bans – announced in the local media when in effect – prohibit any fire in the open, including wood, gas or electric barbecues, with heavy fines for offenders.

Check on the local fire danger before you go bushwalking – some walking trails are closed in the riskiest periods (summer – Dec, Jan & Feb – in the south; the end of the dry season – Sept/Oct – in the north). If driving, carry blankets and a filled water container, listen to your car radio and watch out for roadside fire-danger indicators. See "Health" for potential bushwalking hazards and advice on how to deal with them – including ways to survive if caught in a bushfire.

Water Carry plenty with you and do not contaminate local water resources. In particular, soaps and detergents can render water undrinkable and kill livestock and wild animals. Avoid washing in standing water, especially tanks and small lakes or reservoirs.

Waste Take only photographs, leave only footprints. That means carrying all your rubbish out with you – never burn or bury it – and making sure you urinate (and bury your excrement) at least 50m from a campsite or water source.

Hypothermia In Tasmania, where the weather is notoriously changeable, even in summer, prepare as you would for a walk in Scotland.

adaptor. **Snorkelling** is the low-tech alternative, and still allows you to get dramatically close to the aquatic life around a reef.

Fishing is an Australian obsession, conducted on rivers and lakes, off piers or small boats ("tinnies"), or out at sea where – if your bank balance is up to the challenge – marlin and other game fish are caught. Again, all the equipment – even boats – can be rented in most good fishing areas. Barramundi, renowned for its fighting qualities, is the thing to go for up north. Bear in mind that recreational fishing licenses may be required depending on the state or territory.

Other pursuits

Alice Springs' wide-open spaces make it the country's **hot-air-ballooning** capital and also the main base for **camel treks** into the surrounding desert.

More regular **riding**, on horseback, is offered all over the country – anything from a gentle hour at walking pace to a serious cattle roundup. **Cycling** and mountain biking are tremendously popular, too, as well as being a good way of getting around resorts; just about all hostels rent out bikes, and we've listed other outlets throughout the Guide.

Australia's wilderness is an ideal venue for extended **off-road driving** and **motorbiking**, although permission may be needed to cross station- and Aboriginal-owned lands, and the fragile desert ecology should be respected at all times. Northern Queensland's Cape York and WA's Kimberley are the most adventurous destinations, 4WD-accessible in the dry season only. The great **Outback tracks** pushed out by explorers or drovers, such as the Warburton Road and Sandover Highway and the Tanami, Birdsville and Oodnadatta tracks, are actually two-wheel driveable in dry conditions, but can be hard on poorly prepared vehicles. Getting right to the tip of Queensland's eight-hundred-kilometre-long Cape York Peninsula will definitely require a 4WD or trail bike; while the Kimberley's notoriously corrugated Gibb River Road in WA is also popular in the Dry.

Finally, you may not associate Australia with **skiing**, but there's plenty of it in the

Australia's top dive-sites

Bougainville Reef Coral Sea, Great Barrier Reef, QLD. Exceptional in every way: kilometre-deep coral walls, clear water, and both reef and pelagic life in abundance. Liveaboard trips from Cairns and Port Douglas.

Cod Hole Far North Reef, Great Barrier Reef, QLD. Where the giant potato cod and divers meet. Liveaboard trips from Cairns.

Geographe Bay WA. The HMS *Swan* was sunk to make a recreational diving wreck just off Cape Naturaliste, a couple of hours south of Perth.

Lord Howe Island NSW. The world's southernmost reef surrounds one of the world's most beautiful islands. Flights from Brisbane and Sydney.

Ningaloo Reef WA. Whale sharks come through from April to June, but there's great diving all year, in places right off the beach. Tours from Exmouth or Coral Bay.

Port Lincoln SA. South Australian waters are one of the last bastions for the poorly understood great white shark. Shark-cage diving trips out from Port Lincoln.

Seal Rocks NSW. Hosts a great grey nurse convergence every so often, a chance to be surrounded by these fierce-looking but largely harmless sharks. Trips from Foster or Tuncurry.

Yongala Shipwreck QLD. Huge fish and the remains of a 100-metre-long passenger liner that went down in an early twentieth-century cyclone. Trips from Townsville and Cairns.

1500-metre-high Australian Alps on the border of Victoria and New South Wales, based around the winter resorts of Thredbo, Perisher, Falls Creek and Mount Hotham. Europeans tend to be sniffy about Australian skiing, and certainly it's limited, with a season that lasts barely two to three months – from the end of June until end of September, if you're lucky – and very few challenging runs. The one area where it does match up to Europe is in the prices. On the other hand, it's fun if you're here, and the relatively gentle slopes of the mountains are ideal for cross-country skiing, which is increasingly being developed alongside downhill.

Travelling with children

Australians have an easy-going attitude to children and in most places they are made welcome. With plenty of beautiful beaches, parks and playgrounds, travelling with children in Australia can be great fun.

Getting around

Most forms of **transport** within Australia offer child concessions. Throughout the country, metropolitan buses and trains give discounts of around fifty percent for children and many allow children under 4 or 5 to travel free. Most interstate buses offer around twenty percent off for children under the age of 14.

Long-distance train travel is limited in Australia. It's also a slower and more expensive option, but if you're travelling with small children it does have the advantage of sleepers and a bit more freedom of movement. Domestic airlines offer discounts of around fifty percent of the full adult fare for children between 2 and 11 years. However, it's worth checking for adult discount deals, which are likely to be even cheaper. Infants usually travel free of charge.

Otherwise, there's always the option of **self-drive**. Car rental is reasonably priced, and motor homes and campervans are also available for rental. They're an excellent way of seeing Australia and make it possible to camp rough in some spectacular national parks, as well as the many caravan parks, which offer power, amenities and often a pool and activities room. It's important to remember (especially when travelling with children) that Australia is a huge place and that driving outside of the major cities almost always involves long distances; you'll need to take more activities for the car – music, books, magnetic games, cards – than usual. Stop regularly for breaks: most towns in Australia have public playgrounds.

Accommodation

Many **motels** give discounts for children and some offer a baby-sitting service – it's worth checking when you book. If you like the idea of a quiet whinge-free bushwalk or cocktails by the pool, most resorts have kids' clubs, organized children's activities and baby-sitting services.

Although initially more expensive, **self-contained accommodation** can prove cheaper in the long run as it's possible to cook your own meals. These days, youth hostels are not exclusively for young backpackers and most provide affordable family rooms – some en suite. A few of the more modern hostels are positively luxurious, most are in fabulous locations, and in cities they're usually conveniently close to the city centre. They all have communal kitchens, lounge areas and television, and there are usually plenty of books and games.

Aside from camping, the most economical way to see the country is to stay in some of the thousands of **caravan parks**. Most have on-site vans or self-contained cabins at very reasonable rates for families. Check with information centres for caravan-park listings.

Eating out

Things have moved on in Australia and, in the cities especially, many of the more atmospheric upmarket **restaurants** are welcoming to children, often providing highchairs, toys, blackboards, drawing materials and a reasonable children's menu. Otherwise, there are still plenty of the standard fast-food outlets, which often have enclosed play areas, and children are allowed in the dining section of pubs for counter meals. Most country towns have pubs and some have RSL clubs (Returned Servicemen's League), which are a good cheap way to feed the family on basic pub food and make a welcome change from the greasy hamburgers, chips, meat pies and steak sandwiches sold practically everywhere.

Kids' gear

Car and van rental companies provide **child safety seats**. Taxis will also provide child seats if you request them when making a booking, although there may be a longer wait. Airlines will allow you to carry a pram or travel cot for free, and it's possible to rent baby equipment from some shops – check the local *Yellow Pages* for listings. When planning a sightseeing day that involves a lot of walking, check with the tourist attraction to see if they rent out pushchairs, as this can make the difference between a pleasant and an awful day out.

Activities

Most tours and entry fees for tourist destinations offer **concession rates** for children and many also offer family tickets. If you have two or more children these will usually work out substantially cheaper. Museums often have special children's areas, and during **school holidays** many run supervised activities, along with programmes that include storytelling and performances (check "Opening hours and public holidays" for school holiday dates). In most states, the National Parks and Wildlife Service (NPWS) runs entertaining and educational ranger-led walks and activities during the school holidays. The walks are free, but there's usually a park entrance fee. Check at information centres or with NPWS in each state for timetables and fees.

Sun care

The Australian **sun** is ferocious, making it essential to combine outdoor activities with sensible skin care. A broad-spectrum, water-resistant sunscreen (minimum SPF of 30) is essential; see "Health" for more on sunscreens. There's a "no hat, no play" policy in school playgrounds and most kids wear legionnaire-style caps, or broad-brimmed sun hats, which are cheap and easy to find in surf shops and department stores. All sunglasses in Australia are UV-rated and most kids also wear UV-resistant Lycra swim tops or wetsuit-style all-in-ones to the beach. The Cancer Council Australia has shops in most Australian cities selling a high-quality and colourful range of all these items; for locations, consult Ⓦwww.cancer.org.au.

Helpful publications

In Sydney, look for *Sydney's Child* (Ⓦwww.sydneyschild.com.au), a free monthly magazine listing kids' activities in and around the city and advertising a range of services including babysitting. Spin-offs *Canberra's Child* (Ⓦwww.canberraschild.com.au), *Melbourne's Child* (Ⓦwww.melbourneschild.com.au), *Brisbane's Child* (Ⓦwww.brisbaneschild.com.au) and *Adelaide's Child* (Ⓦwww.adelaideschild.com.au) have the same format and the websites include some of the content. All can be picked up at libraries and major museums. In other states, most tourist information centres will be able to help with suggestions for planning a child-friendly itinerary.

Working in Australia

Most visitors' visas clearly state that no employment of any kind is to be undertaken during a visit to Australia. However, if you're in possession of a Working Holiday Visa (see "Entry requirements") and are prepared to try anything – officially for no more than six months at a time – there are plenty of possibilities for finding work. There are also organized work programmes – both paid and voluntary (see p.71).

In practice, this means that the only jobs officially open to you are unskilled, temporary ones. The **National Harvest Hotline** (ⓣ1800 062 332, ⓦwww.jobsearch.gov.au/harvesttrail) has information about harvesting or farm-labouring jobs and will put you in touch with potential employers. Just remember that crop picking is hard work for low wages (usually paid on a commission basis). It's also worth noting that harvest work is often on farms or plantations that are quite some distance away from a town. In some cases, employers or a workers' hostel in a nearby town will provide transport to and from work – sometimes, but not always, free of charge. In other cases, you will be given some basic accommodation on the farm; or you may even be required to pitch your own tent. There is no centralized agency for casual work, such as bar or restaurant, construction and factory work. A good place to start searching, however, is **Travellers' Contact Point** (ⓣ1800 647 640, ⓦwww.travellers.com.au), which has a branch in most of the major cities. Services include a job notice-board, skills testing, CV updating and help with the required paperwork. You can view the jobs posted online by their recruitment agency, travellers@work at ⓦwww.taw.com.au. The travel centre **Backpackers World** also runs an employment agency (ⓣ1800 676 763, ⓦwww.backpackersworld.com.au), with branches all over Australia except South Australia and Tasmania. Quite a few hostels run their own employment agency or have a permanently staffed **employment desk**. Some charge a membership fee – about AUS$40 a year. All of these places will help with all aspects of working, from organizing tax file numbers to actually getting you jobs. In addition, more specialized **employment agencies** are worth a try in the cities if you have a marketable skill (computer training, accountancy, nursing, cooking and the like). They might have better, higher-paid jobs on their books, though they may be looking for full-time or at least longer-term commitment. **Newspaper job ads** are also worth checking out, especially in smaller local papers. One useful **website** is ⓦwww.mycareer.com.au, which is Australia's largest online job-search engine, and has links to the *Sydney Morning Herald* and Melbourne's *The Age* classified sections. And finally, fellow travellers, hostel staff in smaller hostels, and **notice boards** may be

Tax

In recent years, employers have been threatened with huge fines for offering cash-in-hand labour and, as a result, it's difficult to avoid paying income **tax**, which is levied at 29 percent for earnings under about $26,000 per annum and deducted at source. To become part of the system you'll need a **tax file number** (form available at post offices or taxation offices), which is pretty easy to obtain on presentation of a passport with relevant visa. Your employer will give you a couple of weeks' grace, but not much more – if you don't have a number, after that you'll be taxed at 49 percent. Nowadays, it's hard to claim a tax rebate, no matter how little you earn; however, it's worth a try, and possibly a visit to a tax adviser.

the best source of all, especially in remote areas. This is where you'll find out about local opportunities. The hostels themselves may occasionally offer free nights in lieu of cleaning work – or even pay you for jobs that involve a bit more skill. Some of the hostels in the big cities or in country towns where there is a lot of harvesting work also arrange employment.

Australia is becoming increasingly tough on people working either on tourist visas or on expired working visas. If you're caught **working illegally**, you will have any visa cancelled and will be asked to leave the country immediately; you may be taken into detention if immediate arrangements cannot be made. Furthermore, you will be forbidden to reapply for a working visa for three years, but even after this time period it is extremely unlikely that you would be granted another visa under normal circumstances. Employers can be fined up to AUS$10,000 for employing illegal workers, and are liable for prosecution.

Study and work programmes

AFS Intercultural Programs UK ⓣ0113/242 6136, US ⓣ1-800/AFS-INFO, Canada ⓣ1-800/361-7248 or 514/288-3282, Australia ⓣ1300 131 736, NZ ⓣ0800 600 300, SA ⓣ11/447 2673, international enquiries ⓣ1-212/807-8686, ⓦwww.afs.org. Intercultural exchange organization with programs in over 50 countries.

American Institute for Foreign Study ⓣ1-866/906-2437, ⓦwww.aifs.com. Language study and cultural immersion, as well as au pair and Camp America programs.

ATCV (Australian Trust for Conservation Volunteers) Australia ⓣ1800 032 501, ⓦwww.atcv.com.au. Volunteer work (unpaid) on conservation projects across Australia; about AUS$33 a day charged for food and accommodation. The projects are usually four to six weeks long.

BTCV (British Trust for Conservation Volunteers) ⓣ01302/572 244, ⓦwww.btcv.org.uk. One of the largest environmental charities in Britain, with a programme of national and international working holidays (as a paying volunteer).

BUNAC UK ⓣ020/7251 3472, US ⓣ1-800/GO-BUNAC, ⓦwww.bunac.org. Organizes working holidays in a range of destinations for students.

Camp America UK ⓣ020/7581 7373, Australia ⓣ03/9826 0111, NZ ⓣ09/416 5337, SA ⓣ021/419 5740, ⓦwww.campamerica.co.uk. Organizes cultural-exchange programmes all over the world.

Council on International Educational Exchange (CIEE) UK ⓣ020/8939 9057, US ⓣ1-800/40-STUDY or 1-207/533-7600, ⓦwww.ciee.org. Leading NGO offering study programmes and volunteer projects around the world.

Earthwatch Institute UK ⓣ01865/318 838, US ⓣ1-800/776-0188 or 978/461-0081, Australia ⓣ03/9682 6828, ⓦwww.earthwatch.org. Scientific expedition project that spans over 50 countries with environmental and archeological ventures worldwide.

Visitoz UK ⓣ01865/861 516, Australia ⓣ07/4168 6106, ⓦwww.visitoz.org. Provides work on farms and stations and rural hospitality for all those who would like to work in the bush and have the experience of a lifetime. Previous knowledge is not required. Participants must attend a four-day preparation and orientation course and during this period a job is chosen from a few suitable ones offered. Driving licences are necessary for most of the jobs.

Work Oz UK ⓣ0870/240 7367, ⓦwww.workoz.com. An organization owned and run by ex-Australian high-commission staff, designed to assist working-holiday-visa applicants with help in finding employment in Australia, pre-book hostel accommodation prior to arrival, arrange pick-ups from the airport and arrange travel insurance.

WWOOF (Willing Workers on Organic Farms) Australia ⓣ03/5155 0218, ⓦwww.wwoof.com.au. Woofing is a great way to experience a side of Australia that you'd never see if you just worked in an office and then beachbummed your way up the east coast. As you are not paid cash, a work visa is not required: you put in about half a day's work at your host's place in exchange for full board and lodging, and the rest of the time is yours to go exploring. You are expected to stay at least two nights; everything else is negotiable. The Australian WWOOF Book lists over 1000 organic farms and 100 non-farm hosts (such as organic nurseries and greengrocers, alternative schools). By ordering the book you become a member (AUS$55 single, AUS$65 for two people travelling together); the membership includes basic work-insurance for one year.

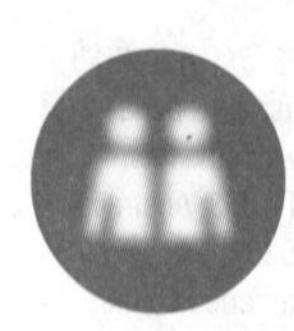

Gay and lesbian Australia

Australia is now well and truly planted on the Queer map as year after year the beautiful people flock Down Under, lured by the conducive climate and laid-back lifestyle and eager to hang out with the homeboys on balmy beaches and sun-kissed city streets. Sydney is Australia's gay-friendly capital, especially in March when hundreds of thousands of people flock to Oxford Street and Moore Park for the Sydney Gay & Lesbian Mardi Gras. Despite its reputation as a macho culture, the country revels in a large and active scene: you'll find an air of confidence and a sense of community that is often missing in other parts of the world.

The colonists transported English law to Australia, but in 1972 South Australia was the first state to enact **decriminalization**, followed the next year by the ACT and Northern Territory. Surprisingly, Victoria and New South Wales (generally thought of as liberal states) delayed similar legislation until the 1980s. Less surprisingly, Queensland took the plunge only in 1991, while it took a decade of constant petitioning from the Tasmanian Gay and Lesbian Rights Group, and pressure from the Federal Government and the UN Human Rights Committee for the law to change in Tasmania in 1997. In Western Australia, there's still an **age of consent** of 21, whereas the ages of consent in ACT and Victoria (both 16), SA and Tasmania (both 17), are the same as the heterosexual age. In the Northern Territory and NSW, the homosexual age of consent is 18. In Queensland, the age of consent for homosexuals depends on the sexual act practised, with anal sex outlawed until 18 but otherwise 16. Sex between women is either not mentioned in state laws or is covered by the heterosexual age. The foreign partner in a **de facto** gay relationship can apply to permanently reside in Australia, a much better situation than in many countries, but the current battle the gay and lesbian lobby groups are waging is to make same-sex relationships as completely equal in the eyes of the law as heterosexual ones, in terms of marriage, parenting, next-of-kin rights, superannuation and age of consent.

Today, Australia is testimony to the power of the **pink dollar**, and there's an abundance of gay venues, services, businesses, travel clubs, country retreats and the like. Given the climate, the scene obviously makes use of sun and sport, and while it's far from limited to the tan-and-toned muscle crowd, if you want to make the most of a thriving community, it's a good idea to pack your swimming, snorkelling and clubbing gear.

Australian dykes are refreshingly open and self-possessed – a relief after the more closed and cliquey scene in Europe. The flip side of their fearlessness is the predominance of S&M on the scene. Maybe the climate has something to do with it, but you'll see a good deal of tattoos and pierced flesh around. Dyke and gay scenes are nothing if not mercurial, and Australia is no exception. We've done our best to list bars, clubs and meeting places, but be warned that venues open, change their names, shut for refurbishment, get relaunched and finally go out of business with frightening rapidity.

Where and how to go

Sydney is the jewel in Australia's luscious navel. Firmly established as one of the world's great gay cities – only San Francisco can really rival it – it attracts lesbian and gay visitors from around the world. Melbourne closely follows the scene in Sydney, but for a change of pace, take a trip to Brisbane and the Gold Coast. Perth, Adelaide and Darwin all have smaller, quieter scenes.

Away from the cities, things get more discreet, but a lot of **country areas** do have very friendly local scenes – impossible to pinpoint, but easy to stumble across. Australians on the city scene are a friendly bunch, but in a small country town they get really friendly, so if there's anything going on you'll probably get invited along.

The **Outback** covers the vast majority of the Australian continent and is, in European terms, sparsely populated. Mining and cattle ranching are the primary employers and they help to create a culture not famed for its tolerance of homosexuality. Tread carefully: bear in mind that Uluru may be 2000km from Sydney as the crow flies, but in many ways it's a million miles away in terms of attitudes.

Each chapter of this Guide has specific gay and lesbian listings, with a wealth of information – see in particular the box on pp.170–171, which has all you need to know to join in Sydney's Mardi Gras celebrations.

Gay and lesbian contacts

Personal contacts

Pinkboard Ⓦwww.pinkboard.com.au. Popular, long-running Australian website featuring personal ads and classifieds sections with everything from houseshares, party tickets for sale, employment and a help-and-advice section. It's free to run your own personal or classified.

Press and multimedia

Each major capital has excellent free gay newspapers, such as the *Sydney Star Observer* (Ⓦwww.ssonet.com.au) and the *Melbourne Community Voice* (Ⓦwww.mcv.net.au), which give the local lowdown. Otherwise, check out:

ALSO Foundation Ⓦwww.also.org.au. Based in Victoria, they have a good website with an excellent nationwide business and community directory.

DNA Ⓦwww.dnamagazine.com.au. National glossy – an upmarket lifestyle magazine for gay men.

LOTL (Lesbians on the Loose) Ⓦwww.lotl.com. A monthly publication available at lesbian and gay venues.

The Pink Directory Ⓦwww.thepinkdirectory.com.au. Online directory of gay and lesbian business and community information.

Tourist services and travel agents

GALTA (Gay and Lesbian Tourism Australia) Ⓦwww.galta.com.au. An online resource and nonprofit organization set up to promote the gay and lesbian tourism industry. Website has links to accommodation, travel agents and tour operators, and gay and lesbian printed and online guides.

Gay Travel Ⓦwww.gaytravel.com. Online travel agent, concentrating mostly on accommodation.

International Gay and Lesbian Travel Association Ⓦwww.iglta.org. Trade group with lists of gay-owned or gay-friendly travel agents, accommodation and other travel businesses.

Q Beds Ⓦwww.qbeds.com. An online accommodation directory and booking service for gay- and lesbian-owned, -operated or -friendly businesses.

Travel essentials

Costs

If you've travelled down from Southeast Asia, you'll find Australia expensive on a day-to-day basis, but fresh from Europe or the US you'll find prices comparable or cheaper; note, though, that in Sydney the cost of living has crept up over the years, and any prolonged length of time spent in the city will quickly drain any savings you might have unless you have a contingency plan in place, such as finding work.

If you're prepared to camp, you might get by on a **daily budget** of AUS$50 (£20/US$49/€30, but you should count on around AUS$75 (£30/US$60/€45) a day for food, board and transport if you stay in hostels, travel on buses and eat and drink fairly frugally. Stay in motels and B&Bs (assuming you're sharing costs) and eat out regularly, and you'll need to budget AUS$115 (£45/US$90/€70) or more: extras such as scuba-diving courses, clubbing, car rental, petrol and tours will all add to your costs. A **Goods and Services Tax** (GST) of ten percent was introduced in 2000, and caused a general across-the-board price hike. Under the Tourist Refund Scheme (TRS), visitors can claim GST refunds for goods purchased in Australia as they clear customs (goods need to be taken within hand luggage), providing individual receipts exceed AUS$300, and the claim is made within thirty days of purchase.

Tipping is not customary in Australia, and cab drivers and bar staff don't generally expect anything – though they won't refuse it if offered. In cafés and restaurants, you might leave the change – only the more upmarket establishments expect ten percent.

Crime and personal safety

Australia today can pride itself on being a relatively safe country, although increasingly it is following the American trend in gun-related incidents. This is not to say there's no petty crime, or that you can leave normal caution behind, though you're more likely to fall victim to a fellow traveller or an opportunist: theft is not unusual in hostels and many therefore provide lockable boxes. But if you leave valuables lying around, or on view in cars, you can expect them to be stolen.

One place where violence is commonplace is at the ritual pub "blue" (fight), usually among known protagonists on a Friday or Saturday night in smaller, untouristed towns. Strangers are seldom involved without at least some provocation. Be aware also of drug- and drink-related crime, especially around known hotspots such as Kings Cross in Sydney. Exercise caution, don't forget common-sense, streetwise precautions, and you should be fine.

Travellers with Disabilities

The vast distances between Australia's cities and popular tourist resorts present visitors with mobility difficulties with a unique challenge but, overall, travel in Australia for people with disabilities is rather easier than it would be in, say, the UK and Europe.

The federal government provides information and various nationwide services through the National Information Communication Awareness Network (NICAN) and the Australian Council for the Rehabilitation of the Disabled (ACROD) – see below for contact details.

Much of Australia's tourist **accommodation** is well set-up for people with disabilities, because buildings tend to be built outwards rather than upwards; all new buildings in Australia must comply with a legal minimum accessibility standard.

Disability needn't interfere with your **sightseeing**: the attitude of the management at Australia's major tourist attractions is excellent, and they will provide assistance where they can. For example, you'll find you can view rock art at Kakadu National Park, do a tour around the base of Uluru, snorkel unhindered on the Great Barrier Reef, go on a cruise around Sydney Harbour, and see the penguins at Phillip Island.

For a good overview of accessible travel in Australia, *Easy Access Australia* (AUS$27.45) is a comprehensive guide written by the wheelchair-user Bruce Cameron for anyone with a mobility difficulty, and has information on all the states, with maps, and a separate section with floor plans of hotel rooms. See ⓦwww.easyaccessaustralia.com.au for details on how to get hold of a copy.

Useful contacts

ACROD (Australian Council for Rehabilitation of the Disabled) ⓣ02/6283 3200, ⓦwww.acrod.org.au. Regional offices provide lists of state-based help organizations, accommodation, travel agencies and tour operators.

NICAN (National Information Communication Awareness Network) ⓣ02/6241 1220 or 1800 806 769, ⓦwww.nican.com.au. A national, nonprofit, free information service on recreation, sport, tourism, the arts, and much more, for people with disabilities. Has a database of over 4500 organizations – such as wheelchair-accessible tourist accommodation venues, sports and recreation organizations, and rental companies who have accessible buses and vans.

Paraplegic and Quadriplegic Association ⓣ03/9415 1200, ⓦwww.paraquad.asn.au. Serves the interests of the spinally injured; offices in each state capital.

The number to call for **emergencies** – police, ambulance or fire brigade – is ⓣ000.

Ⓦ www.wheelabout.com and Ⓦ www.accessibility.com.au both have lists of accommodation and transport in Australia for people with disabilities, as well as Access Maps of major Australian cities.

Electricity

Australia's electrical current is 240/250v, 50Hz AC. British appliances will work with an adaptor for the Australian three-pin plug. American and Canadian 110v appliances will also need a transformer.

Insurance

Even if you're entitled to free emergency healthcare from Medicare (see "Health"), some form of travel insurance is essential to help plug the gaps and cover you in the event of losing your baggage, missing a plane and the like. A typical travel insurance policy usually provides cover for the loss of baggage, tickets and – up to a certain limit – cash and cheques, as well as cancellation or curtailment of your journey. If you're thinking of doing any "high-risk" activities such as scuba diving, skiing or even just hiking, you may need to pay an extra premium; check carefully before you take out any policy what exactly you are covered for in case of an accident. If you do take medical coverage, ascertain whether benefits will be paid as treatment proceeds or only after return home, and whether there is a 24-hour medical emergency number. When securing baggage cover, make sure that the per-article limit – typically under £500/US$1000 – will cover your most valuable possession. If you need to make a claim, you should keep receipts for medicines and medical treatment, and in the event you have anything stolen, you must obtain an official written statement from the police.

Internet

Internet access is widespread, easy and cheap across Australia. In the cities, Internet cafés are everywhere, typically charging AUS$3–6 an hour with concessions as well as "happy hours". Many places to stay – especially hostels – also provide terminals for their guests at similar rates (hotels will charge more), although some places still opt for the user-reviled coin-op booths, while at some places you buy a card that works like a phone card.

Out in the country, even the smallest one-horse town will have a Telecentre – a council- or privately-run outlet, although opening times can be pretty provincial, too. Throughout the Guide, you'll find Internet locations have been identified, where available.

Laundry

Known as **laundromats**, these are rare outside urban centres. Hostels always have a laundry with at least one coin-operated washing machine and a dryer, as do most caravan parks, holiday units and a lot of motels. Five-star hotels, of course, will do it for you.

Mail

Every town of any size will have a **post office**, or at least an Australia Post agency, usually at the general store. Post offices and agencies are officially open Monday to Friday

Rough Guides travel insurance

Rough Guides has teamed up with Columbus Direct to offer you **travel insurance** that can be tailored to suit your needs. Products include a low-cost **backpacker** option for long stays; a **short-break** option for city getaways; a typical **holiday-package** option; and others. There are also annual **multi-trip** policies for those who travel regularly. Different sports and activities (trekking, skiing, etc) can be usually covered if required.

See our website (Ⓦ www.roughguidesinsurance.com) for eligibility and purchasing options. Alternatively, UK residents should call ⓣ 0870/033 9988; Australians should call ⓣ 1300 669 999 and New Zealanders should call ⓣ 0800 55 9911. All other nationalities should call ⓣ +44 870/890 2843.

9am to 5pm; big city GPOs sometimes open late or on Saturday morning as well. Out in the country, it's rare to see post boxes.

Domestically, the **mail service** has a poor reputation, at least for long distances: it will take a week for a letter to get from Wittenoom (WA) to Wagga Wagga (NSW), though major cities have a guaranteed express-delivery service to other major cities – worth the expense for important packages. On the other hand, international mail is extremely efficient, taking four to five working days to the UK, four to six to the US and five to seven to Canada. **Stamps** are sold at post offices and agencies; most newsagencies sell them for standard local letters only. A standard letter or postcard within Australia costs 50¢; printed aerogrammes for international letters anywhere in the world cost 95¢; postcards cost AUS$1.10 and regular letters start at AUS$1.80 to Europe, the US or Canada. Large **parcels** are reasonably cheap to send home by surface mail, but it will take up to three months for them to get there. Economy Air is a good compromise for packages that you want to see again soon (up to 20kg) – expect a fortnight to Europe. To get more information on letter and parcel postage rates, and expected delivery waits, go to Ⓦwww.austpost.com.au and click on "postage calculator".

Maps

The Rough Guide **map of Australia** (1:4,500,000) is handily printed on rip- and waterproof paper. Also finely produced are GeoCenter (including NZ) and Nelles, both 1:4,000,000, with good topographical detail: the Nelles (printed in northern and southern halves on both sides of the sheet) includes additional detail of major city environs. The Bartholomew and the new Globetrotter (both 1:5,000,000) are the best of the rest.

In Australia, UBD (Ⓦwww.ubd.com.au), Gregory's (Ⓦwww.gregorys-online.com), HEMA Ⓣ(wwww.hemamaps.com.au), Westprint (Ⓦwww.westprint.com.au) and the state-produced AusMap publish national, regional and city maps of varying sizes and quality. HEMA produces scores of regional and themed maps and atlases covering the entire country many times over. Cities, states, national parks, fishing, hiking, 4WD and wine are some of the many themes covered. BP and the state motoring organizations have regularly updated touring guides to Australia, with regional maps, listings and details of things to see and do – something for the back shelf of the car rather than a backpack.

Money

Australia's **currency** is the Australian dollar, or "buck", written as AUS$ or $ – which is how we write it in the Guide – and divided into 100 cents. The colourful plastic notes with forgery-proof clear windows come in AUS$100, AUS$50, AUS$20, AUS$10 and AUS$5 denominations, along with AUS$2, AUS$1, 50¢, 20¢, 10¢ and 5¢ coins. There are no longer 1¢ or 2¢ coins so an irregular bill, such as $1.99 etc, will be rounded up or down to the closest denomination, which can be confusing at first.

At the time of writing, the Australian dollar has an **exchange rate** of AUS$2.50 for £1; AUS$1.25 for US$1; AUS$1.10 for CDN$1; AUS$0.90 for NZ$1; and AUS$0.20 for ZAR1. To check the latest exchange rate, log onto Ⓦwww.xe.com.

The unfortunate closure of local **banks** throughout much of Australia means you will no longer necessarily find a branch of one of the main banks in every town, though there will be a local agency that handles bank business – usually based at the general store, post office or roadhouse – though not necessarily a 24-hour **ATM** machine. The best policy is always make sure you have some cash on you before leaving the bigger towns, especially at weekends. The major banks, with branches countrywide, are Westpac (Ⓦwww.westpac.com.au), ANZ (Ⓦwww.anz.com.au), the Commonwealth (Ⓦwww.commbank.com.au) and the National Australia Bank (Ⓦwww.national.com.au); you can search their websites for branch locations. For banking hours, see "Opening hours and public holidays".

All **post offices** act as Commonwealth or National Australia Bank agents, which means there's a fair chance of changing money even in the smallest Outback settlements – withdrawals at these places are often limited by a lack of ready cash, however, though less remote post offices may have EFTPOS facilities (see opposite).

If you're spending some time in Australia, and plan to work or move around, it makes life a great deal easier if you **open a bank account**. To do this you'll need to take along every piece of ID documentation you own – a passport may not be enough, though a letter from your bank manager at home may help – but it's otherwise a fairly straightforward process. The Commonwealth Bank and Westpac are the most widespread options, and their keycards give you access not only to ATM machines but also anywhere that offers **EFTPOS** facilities (Electronic Funds Transfer at Point of Sale). This includes many Outback service stations and supermarkets, where you can use your card to pay directly for goods and to withdraw cash as well. Bear in mind that **bank fees** and charges are exorbitant in Australia; most banks allow only a few free withdrawal transactions per month (depending on who you bank with – it's well worth shopping around before you open an account), and there are even bigger charges for using a competitor's ATM machine, as well as monthly fees.

Discount cards soon pay for themselves in savings. If you're a full-time student, it's worth applying for an **International Student ID Card** (ISIC; Ⓦwww.isic.org), which entitles the bearer to special air, rail and bus fares and discounts at museums, theatres and other attractions. The card costs £7; US$22; CDN$16; NZ$20; and AUS$18 in Australia itself. If you're no longer a student, but are 26 or younger, you still qualify for the **International Youth Travel Card**, which costs the same price and carries the same benefits, while teachers qualify for the **International Teacher Card** (same price and some of the benefits). All these cards are available from the website above or branches of STA Travel.

Opening hours and public holidays

Shops and services are generally open Monday to Friday 9am to 5pm and until lunchtime on Saturday. In cities and larger towns, many shops stay open late on Thursday or Friday evening – usually until 9pm – and all day on Saturday, and shopping malls and department stores in major cities are now often open all day Sunday as well.

In remote country areas, **roadhouses** provide all the essential services for the traveller and, on the major highways, are generally open 24 hours a day. **Tourist offices** – even ones well off the beaten track – are often open every day or at least through the week plus weekend mornings; urban information centres are more likely to conform to normal shopping hours.

Tourist attractions such as museums, galleries and attended historic monuments are often open daily, though those in rural communities may have erratic opening hours. Practically without exception all are closed on Good Friday and Christmas Day. Specific opening hours are given throughout the Guide.

Banking hours are Monday to Thursday 9.30am to 4pm, Friday 9.30am to 5pm. A change in the law has made Saturday bank opening legal, though it's not yet fully in practice. In country areas, some banks may

Holidays

National holidays are New Year's Day, Australia Day (Jan 26), Good Friday, Easter Monday, Anzac Day (April 25), Queen's Birthday (June 10, except WA), Christmas Day and Boxing Day (except SA). Note, when a public holiday falls on a weekend, Australians tend to take the following Monday off. State holidays are listed in the capital city accounts of each state or territory. **School holidays** transform beaches into bucket-and-spade war zones, national park campsites are full to overflowing, and the roads are jammed. Dates vary from year to year and state to state but all schools (except Tasmania) have four terms. Generally, things start to get busy mid-December to the end of January or beginning of February (January is worst, as many people stay home until after Christmas), two weeks around Easter, another couple of weeks in late June to early July, and another two weeks in late September to early October. January and Easter are the **busiest periods** when you are likely to find accommodation booked out.

have more limited hours, such as lunchtime closures, or some agencies may be open later, and some big-city branches might also have extended hours. ATMs are generally open 24 hours. See "Mail" for post office opening hours.

Phones

Public telephones take coins or phone cards, which are sold through newsagents and other stores. Many bars, shops and restaurants have orange or blue payphones; watch out for these as they cost more than a regular call box. Whatever their type, payphones do not accept incoming calls.

Local calls are **untimed**, allowing you to talk for as long as you like; this costs around 17¢ on a domestic phone, though public phones may charge 50¢. Many businesses and services operate free call numbers, prefixed ⓣ1800, while others have six-digit numbers beginning ⓣ13 that are charged at the local-call rate – both can only be dialled from within Australia. Numbers starting ⓣ1900 are premium-rate private information services.

Phone cards are a cheap way to call cross-country or abroad. Various brands are available, but all require a minimum of 40¢ to call the local centre, after which you key in your scratch number and telephone number. Rates are incredible, from as low as 5¢ a minute.

It's also possible to pop into Woolworths and buy a **pre-paid mobile phone** for as little as AUS$99 with a pay-as-you-go SIM card. Or you can just buy the pre-paid SIM cards alone in various denominations for your own handset – CDMA and GSM are compatible. Telstra is the main provider and with the widest coverage, but does not include unpopulated areas in the north and west of the country. Vodafone is a long way behind on cross coverage but may work out cheaper solely for urban use.

As anywhere in the world, mobile phone reception will drop off in remote areas. A solution offering guaranteed reception (but at call rates several times higher) is a **satellite phone**. Little bigger than a conventional GSM, they can be rented from ⓦwww.rentasatphone.com.au from around AUS$21 per day and can run both GSM as well as the special satellite SIM cards.

Police and the law

Things to watch out for, most of all, are drugs. A lot of marijuana is grown and its use is widespread, but you'd be foolish to carry it when you travel, and crazy to carry any other illicit narcotic. Each state has its own penalties, and though a small amount of grass may mean no more than confiscation and an on-the-spot fine, they're generally pretty tough – especially in Queensland. Driving in general makes you more likely to have a confrontation of some kind, if only for a minor traffic infringement. Drunk driving is taken extremely seriously, so don't risk it – random breath tests are common around all cities and larger towns.

Making international calls

Calling Australia from home

Dial the relevant international access code + 61 + city code, omitting the initial zero.

The **international access code** for the UK, the Republic of Ireland, New Zealand and South Africa is ⓣ00; for the US and Canada ⓣ011.

Calling home from Australia

The **international access code** for Australia is ⓣ0011. Note that the initial zero is omitted from the area code when dialling the UK, the Republic of Ireland and New Zealand from abroad.

To the UK Australian international access code + 44 + city code.

To the Republic of Ireland Australian international access code + 353 + city code.

To the US and Canada Australian international access code + 1 + area code.

To New Zealand Australian international access code + 64 + city code.

To South Africa Australian international access code + 27 + city code.

Lesser potential problems are **alcohol** – there are all sorts of controls on where and when you can drink, and taking alcohol onto Aboriginal lands can be a serious offence; smoking, which is increasingly being banned in public places; and nude or topless sunbathing, which is quite acceptable in many places, but absolutely not in others – follow the locals' lead.

Seasons

In the southern hemisphere, the seasons are reversed: summer lasts from November to February, winter from June to September. But, of course, it's not that simple: in the tropical north, the important seasonal distinction is between the Wet (effectively summer) and the Dry (winter) – for more on their significance to travellers, see p.555.

Shopping

Australians love to shop, and you'll find plenty of outlets to tempt you to part with your cash, from designer boutiques to large department stores. Australians also do vintage very well, and there are some excellent thrift shops to be found, especially around Chapel Street in Melbourne and Paddington in Sydney. Worth a browse are the weekly markets that take place on any given day in most cities and resort towns, selling everything from secondhand clothes and new-age remedies to fresh seafood and mouthwatering delicacies; the most popular ones are Mindil Beach in Darwin (see p.563), Queen Victoria Market in Melbourne (see p.836) and, in Tasmania, Hobart's Salamanca Market (see p.989). In Sydney, Paddington Market is a great place to pick up one-off new designer clothes, while Glebe's Saturday market is the place to go for crystals, tie-dye and lava lamps. For souvenirs, there's no shortage of shops selling Australiana, mass-produced tat such as stuffed koalas, painted boomerangs and the like. If you're looking for something more authentic, there are a

Clothing and shoe sizes

Women's dresses and skirts

American	6	8	10	12	14	16	18		
Australian	8	10	12	14	16	18	20		
British	8	10	12	14	16	18	20		
Continental	36	38	40	42	44	46	48		

Women's shoes

American	5	6	7	8	9	10	11		
Australian	5	6	7	8	9	10	11		
British	3	4	5	6	7	8	9		
Continental	35	36	37	38	39	40	41		

Men's suits

American	44	46	48	50	52	54	56	58	
Australian	34	36	38	40	42	44	46	48	
British	34	36	38	40	42	44	46	48	
Continental	44	46	48	50	52	54	56	58	

Men's shirts

American	14	15	15.5	16	16.5	17	17.5	18	
Australian	36	38	39	41	42	43	44	45	
British	14	15	15.5	16	16.5	17	17.5	18	
Continental	36	38	39	41	42	43	44	45	

Men's shoes

American	7	7.5	8	8.5	9.5	10	10.5	11	11.5
Australian	6.5	7	7.5	8	9	9.5	10	10.5	11
British	6.5	7	7.5	8	9	9.5	10	10.5	11
Continental	39	40	41	42	43	44	44	45	46

number of good art and craft stores around The Rocks in Sydney, selling genuine opals and handcrafted didgeridoos. The best place to shop for Aboriginal art, however, is Alice Springs, where many galleries sell on behalf of the artist and the money goes back to the Aboriginal communities.

Gemstones such as the Australian opal are a popular purchase, though the quality and price varies from place to place so be sure to shop around before you buy; of course, you could always try fossiking for your own at one of the mining towns such as Coober Pedy in South Australia (see p.800). Broome in Western Australia has long been the "pearl capital" of Australia, and is a good place to pick up your very own cultured pearl plus all manner of mother-of-pearl trinkets. Note, if you purchase goods worth more than AUS$300 in one single transaction, you can claim the tax back under the Tourist Refund Scheme (see p.70).

Time

Australia has three time zones: Eastern Standard Time (QLD, NSW, VIC, TAS, VIC), Central Standard Time (NT, SA) and Western Standard Time (WA). Eastern Standard Time is ten hours ahead of GMT (Greenwich Mean Time) and fifteen hours ahead of US Eastern Time. (When it's 10pm in Sydney, it's noon in London, 7am in New York and 4am in Los Angeles – but don't forget daylight saving, which can affect this by one hour either way.) Central Standard Time is thirty minutes behind Eastern Standard, and Western Standard two hours behind Eastern. Daylight saving (Oct–March) is adopted everywhere except QLD, NT and WA; clocks are put forward one hour.

Tipping

Tipping is not customary in Australia, and cab drivers and bar staff don't generally expect anything. In fact cab drivers often round the fare down rather than bother with change. In cafés and restaurants, you might leave the change- only very fanay establishments expect ten percent.

Tourist information

Australian tourism abroad is represented by the Australian Tourist Commission, whose website Ⓦwww.australia.com has links to everything you need to start planning your trip.

More detailed information is available by the sackful once you're in the country. Each state or territory has its own **tourist authority**, which operates information offices throughout its own area and in major cities in other parts of Australia – some are even represented abroad (those with London offices are detailed below). A level below this are a host of regional and community-run visitors centres and information kiosks. Even the smallest Outback town has one – or at the very least an information board located at a rest spot at the side of the road.

Hostels are excellent places to pick up information, with notice boards where you'll often find offers of cheap excursions or ride shares, and comments and advice from people who've already passed that way.

Finally, most tourist hotspots will have a travellers' centre, such as Backpackers World Travel (Ⓦwww.backpackersworld.com.au), World Wide Workers (Ⓦwww.worldwideworkers.com) and Travellers Contact Point (Ⓦwww.travellers.com.au). Once you've signed up with them, they can help you find work and pre-book travel and accommodation as you move around; you also get discounted phone and Internet rates, cheap drinks at selected pubs, use of notice boards and help with work.

Tourist offices and government sites

Australian Department of Foreign Affairs Ⓦwww.dfat.gov.au, Ⓦwww.smartraveller.gov.au.
British Foreign & Commonwealth Office Ⓦwww.fco.gov.uk.
Canadian Department of Foreign Affairs Ⓦwww.dfait-maeci.gc.ca.
Irish Department of Foreign Affairs Ⓦwww.foreignaffairs.gov.ie.
New Zealand Ministry of Foreign Affairs Ⓦwww.mft.govt.nz.
South African Department of Foreign Affairs Ⓦwww.dfa.gov.za.
US State Department Ⓦwww.travel.state.gov.

Women and sexual harassment

The stereotyped image of the Aussie male is of a boozy bloke interested in sport, his car and his mates, with his wife or girlfriend a poor fourth. The Australian ethos of "mateship" traditionally excluded women – the hard, tough life of the early days of white settlement, when women were scarce, fostered a male culture that's to some extent still current. In the main cities, attitudes are generally enlightened, but in the more remote country and Outback areas the older attitudes are more tenacious and sexual harassment can be commonplace – if rarely threatening.

In public life, Australia has one of the best records for **sexual equality** in the world – it was the second country to give women the vote (after New Zealand in 1893). However, corresponding changes in attitudes have not always kept pace. Today, a woman can be served a drink anywhere in the country, but the way that some Australian pubs are set up – with two separate bars – continues to reflect the old bias; you'll still see signs saying "Ladies' Lounge". **Outback** and **country pubs** are still very much male bastions, though that doesn't mean you should avoid them altogether – many are frequented by decent salt-of-the-earth Aussie blokes, some of the nicest people you could wish to meet.

As always, common sense prevails: avoid travelling to remote areas on your own and don't walk home alone late at night. Recent high-profile backpacker murder cases prove that it's not only when travelling alone that **hitchhiking** is dangerous – and that even male company is no safeguard. If you must do it, never do it alone – and heed the general advice and warnings given in "Getting around".

Guide

Guide

1

Sydney and around

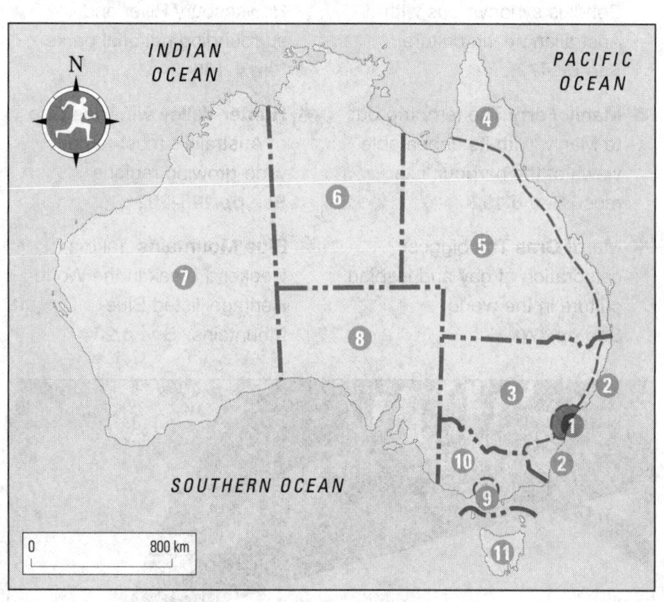

CHAPTER 1

Highlights

✱ **Opera House performance** Admire the stunning exterior of this Australian icon, or better still, take in a performance. See p.111

✱ **Climbing Sydney Harbour Bridge** Scale the famous coathanger for great harbour views. See p.113

✱ **Bondi Beach** Bold, brash Bondi is synonymous with Australian beach culture. See p.147

✱ **Manly Ferry** The ferry trip out to Manly, with its unbeatable views of the harbour, is a must. See p.152

✱ **Mardi Gras** The biggest celebration of gay and lesbian culture in the world. See pp.170–171

✱ **Oxford Street** Crammed with bars, clubs and restaurants, a night out on Oxford Street is essential. See p.177

✱ **Paddington Market** Visit Paddington on Saturday, when the famous market is in full swing. See p.179

✱ **Cruising on the Hawkesbury River** Explore the pretty Hawkesbury River and surrounding national parks. See p.189

✱ **Hunter Valley wineries** One of Australia's most famous wine-growing regions. See pp.196–202

✱ **Blue Mountains** Take a weekend break in the World Heritage–listed Blue Mountains. See p.204

△ Sydney Harbour Bridge

Sydney and around

Flying into **Sydney** provides the first snapshot of Australia for most overseas visitors: toy-sized images of the Harbour Bridge and the Opera House, tilting in a glittering expanse of blue water. The Aussie city par excellence, Sydney stands head and shoulders above any other in Australia. Taken together with its surrounds, it's in many ways a microcosm of Australia as a whole – if only in its ability to defy your expectations and prejudices as often as it confirms them. A thrusting, high-rise business centre, a high-profile gay community and inner-city deprivation of unexpected harshness are as much part of the scene as the beaches, the bodies and the sparkling harbour. Its sophistication, cosmopolitan population and exuberant nightlife are a long way from the Outback, and yet Sydney has the highest Aboriginal population of any Australian city, and bushfires are a constant threat.

The area around – everything in this chapter is within day-trip distance – offers a taste of virtually everything you'll find in the rest of the country, with the exception of desert. There are magnificent **national parks** – Ku-ring-gai Chase and Royal being the best known – and native wildlife, each a mere hour's drive from the centre of town; while further north stretch endless ocean **beaches**, great for surfers, and more enclosed waters for safer swimming and sailing. Inland, the Blue Mountains, with three more national parks, offer isolated bushwalking and scenic viewpoints. On the way are historic colonial towns that were among the earliest foundations in the country – Sydney itself, of course, was the very first. The commercial and industrial heart of the state of New South Wales, especially the central coastal region, is bordered by **Wollongong** in the south and **Newcastle** in the north. Both were synonymous with coal and steel, but the smokestack industries that supported them for decades are now in severe decline. This is far from an industrial wasteland, though: the heart of the coal-mining country is the **Hunter Valley**, northwest of Newcastle, but to visit it you'd never guess, because this is also Australia's oldest, and arguably its best-known, wine-growing region.

Sydney

The 2000 Olympics were a coming-of-age ceremony for **SYDNEY**. The impact on the city was all-embracing, with fifty years' worth of development

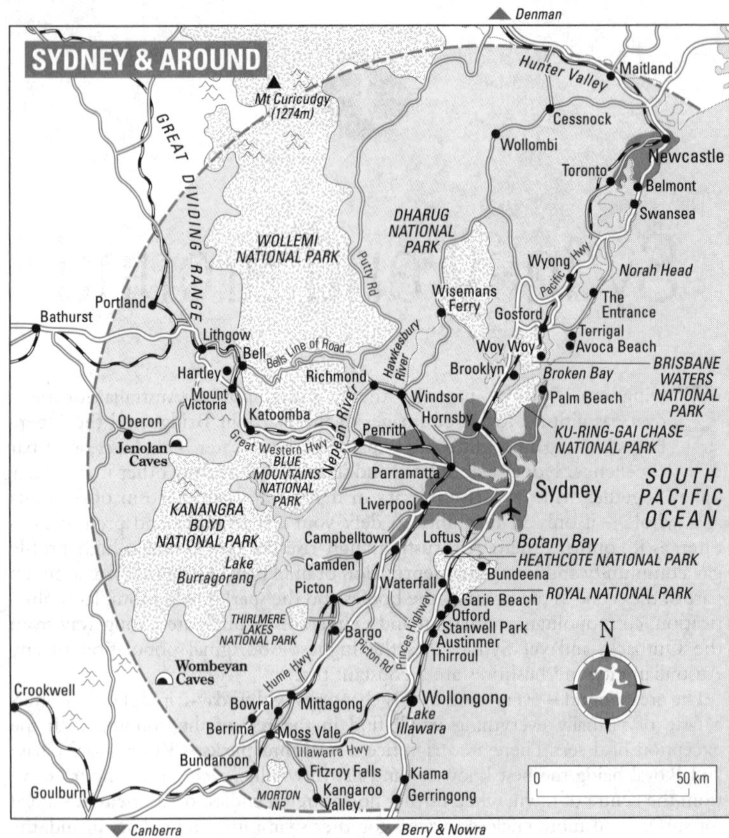

compressed into four years under the pressure of intense international scrutiny. Transport infrastructure was greatly improved and a rash of luxury hotels and waterside apartments added to the skyline. The City of Sydney Council spent $200 million to enhance and beautify the city streets, public squares and parks; and licensing laws changed, too, creating a European-style bar culture. Sydney now has all the vigour of a world-class city, with the reputation of its restaurants in particular turning the lingering cultural sneers to swoons. It seems to have the best of both worlds – twenty minutes from Circular Quay by bus, the high-rise office buildings and skyscrapers give way to colourful inner-city suburbs where you can get an eyeful of sky and watch the lemons ripening above the sidewalk, while to the centre's north and south are corridors of largely intact bushland where many have built their dream homes. During every heatwave, however, bushfires threaten the city, and sophisticated Sydney becomes closer to its roots than it sometimes feels. In the summer, the city's hot offices are abandoned for the remarkably unspoilt beaches strung along the eastern and northern suburbs.

It's also as beautiful a city as any in the world, with a **setting** that perhaps only Rio de Janeiro can rival: the water is what makes it so special, and no introduction to Sydney would be complete without paying tribute to one of the world's great **harbours**. Port Jackson is a sunken valley that twists inland to meet the fresh water of the Parramatta River; in the process it washes into a hundred coves and bays, winds around rocky points, flows past the small harbour islands, slips under bridges and laps at the foot of the Opera House. Sydney is seen at its gleaming best from the deck of a harbour ferry, especially at weekends when the harbour's jagged jaws fill with a flotilla of small vessels, racing yachts and cabin cruisers; getting away from the city centre and exploring them is an essential part of Sydney's pleasures.

It might seem surprising that Sydney is not Australia's capital: the creation of Canberra in 1927 – intended to stem the intense rivalry between Sydney and Melbourne – has not affected the view of many Sydneysiders that their city remains the true capital of Australia, and certainly in many ways it feels like it. The city has a tangible sense of history: the old stone walls and well-worn steps in the backstreets around The Rocks are an evocative reminder that Sydney has more than two hundred years of white history behind it.

Some history

The early history of Sydney is very much the history of white Australia, right from its founding as a penal colony, amid brutality, deprivation and despair. In January 1788, the **First Fleet**, carrying over a thousand people, 736 of them convicts, arrived at **Botany Bay** expecting the "fine meadows" that Captain James Cook had described eight years earlier. In fact, what greeted them was mostly swamp, scrub and sand dunes: a desolate sight even for sea-weary eyes. An unsuccessful scouting expedition prompted Commander Arthur Phillip to move the fleet a few kilometres north, to the well-wooded Port Jackson, where a stream of fresh water was found. Based around the less than satisfactory Tank Stream, the settlement was named **Sydney Cove** after Viscount Sydney, then Secretary of State in Great Britain. In the first three years of settlement, the new colony nearly starved to death several times; the land around Sydney Cove proved to be barren. When supply ships did arrive, they inevitably came with hundreds more convicts to further burden the colony. It was not until 1790, when land was successfully farmed further west at **Parramatta**, that the hunger began to abate. Measure this suffering with that of the original occupants, the **Eora Aborigines**: their land had been invaded, their people virtually wiped out by smallpox, and now they were stricken by hunger as the settlers shot at their game – and even, as they moved further inland, at the Eora themselves.

By the early 1800s, Sydney had become a stable colony and busy trading post. Army officers in charge of the colony, exploiting their access to free land and cheap labour, became rich farm-owners and virtually established a currency based on rum. The **military**, known as the New South Wales Corps (or more familiarly as "the rum corps"), became the supreme political force in the colony in 1809, even overthrowing the governor (mutiny-plagued Captain Bligh himself). This was the last straw for the government back home, and the rebellious officers were finally brought to heel when the reformist Governor **Lachlan Macquarie** arrived from England with forces of his own. He liberalized conditions, supported the prisoners' right to become citizens after they had served their time, and appointed several to public offices.

By the 1840s, the transportation of convicts to New South Wales had ended, the explorers Lawson and Blaxland had found a way through the Blue Mountains to the Western Plains, and **gold** had been struck in Bathurst. The population soared as free settlers arrived in ever-increasing numbers. In the Victorian era, Sydney's population became even more starkly divided into the **haves** and the **have-nots**: while the poor lived in slums where disease, crime, prostitution and alcoholism were rife, the genteel classes – self-consciously replicating life in the mother country – took tea on their verandas and erected grandiloquent monuments such as the Town Hall, the Strand Arcade and the Queen Victoria Building in homage to English architecture of the time. An outbreak of the plague in The Rocks at the beginning of the twentieth century made wholesale slum clearances inevitable, and with the demolitions came a change in attitudes. Strict new vice laws meant the end of the bad old days of backstreet knifings, drunk-filled taverns and makeshift brothels.

Over the next few decades, Sydney settled into comfortable **suburban living**. The metropolis sprawled westwards, creating a flat, unremarkable city with no real centre, an appropriate symbol for the era of shorts and knee socks and the stereotypical, barbecue-loving Bruce and Sheila – an international image that still plagues Australians. Sydney has come a long way since the parochialism of the 1950s, however: skyscrapers at the city's centre have rocketed heavenward and constructions such as the **Opera House** began to reflect the city's dynamism. The cultural clichés of cold tinnies of beer and meat pies with sauce have long been tossed out, giving way to a city confident in itself and its culinary attractions, too. Today, Sydney's citizens don't look inwards – and they certainly don't look towards England. Thousands of immigrants from around the globe have given Sydney a truly cosmopolitan air and it's a city as thrilling and alive as any.

Arrival

The dream way to **arrive** in Sydney is, of course, by ship, cruising in below the great coathanger of the Harbour Bridge to tie up at the Overseas Passenger Terminal alongside Circular Quay. The reality of the functional airport, bus and train stations is a good deal less romantic.

By air

Sydney's **Kingsford Smith Airport**, referred to as "Mascot" after the suburb where it's located, is 8km south of the city, near Botany Bay (international flight times Ⓣ13 12 23, Ⓦwww.sydneyairport.com.au). Domestic and international terminals are linked by a free shuttle bus if you're travelling with Qantas (every 30min), or you can take the KST-Bus ($5) or the **Airport Link** underground railway ($4.70), which also connects the airport to the City Circle train line in the heart of Sydney in around fifteen minutes (Mon–Fri every 10min, Sat & Sun every 15min; one way $13; to compete with taxis, there's a group fare for four people of $32 to City Circle line stations; Ⓦwww.airportlink.com.au). A return Airport Link transfer is included in the excellent-value Sydney Pass tourist transport package (see p.94), which you can buy from the Sydney Visitor Centre (see below). Buses run regularly into the city (see box opposite), while a **taxi** to the city centre or Kings Cross costs $32–36.

Bureau de change offices at both terminals are open daily from 5am until last arrival with rates comparable to major banks. On the ground floor (Arrivals) of the international terminal, the **Sydney Visitor Centre** (daily 5am until last arrival; Ⓣ02/9667 6050) can arrange car rental and onward travel – it's licensed to sell train and bus tickets – and **book hotels** anywhere in Sydney and New South Wales free of charge and at stand-by rates. Most hostels advertise on an adjacent notice board; there's a freephone line for reservations, and many of them will refund your bus fare; a few also do free airport pick-ups.

Airport buses

State Transit Authority (STA)

STA's daily east–west commuter route stops at the international and domestic terminals: the Metroline #400 & #401 go frequently to Bondi Junction via Maroubra and Randwick in one direction, and to Burwood in the other (tickets cost a maximum of $5.40).

Shuttle services – Sydney area

KST Sydney Transporter ⓣ02/9666 9988, ⓦwww.kst.com.au. Private bus service dropping off at hotels or hostels in the area bounded by Kings Cross and Darling Harbour. Service leaves when the bus is full ($10 one way, $18 return). Bookings three hours in advance for accommodation pick-up to the airport.

Super Shuttles ⓣ02/9311 3789, ⓦwww.supershuttle.com.au. Minibus service (quick call-out service) to and from the city and eastern beaches – Bondi, Coogee, Randwick, Clovelly and Bronte – and dropping off at all hostels, motels and hotels ($15 one way). Book accommodation pick-up 1hr in advance for airport transfers.

Coach and shuttle services – central coast and south coast

Aussie Shuttles ⓣ1300 130 557, ⓦwww.ben-air.com.au. Pre-booked door-to-door service to accommodation anywhere on the central coast ($60–75).

Premier Motor Service ⓣ13 34 10, for bookings outside Australia ⓣ02/4423 5233, ⓦwww.premierms.com.au. Departs daily at 9.30am and 3.30pm, from the domestic terminal, fifteen minutes later from the international terminal, to south-coast towns as far as Eden ($65). Bookings necessary.

By train and bus

All local and interstate **trains** arrive at **Central Station** on Eddy Avenue, just south of the city centre. There are no lockers at the station, but you can store your luggage at Wanderers' Travel, 810 George St, a three-minute walk around the block (daily 7am–8pm; $4 per day). From outside Central Station, and neighbouring **Railway Square**, you can hop onto nearly every major bus route, and from within Central Station you can take a CityRail train to any city or suburban station (see "City transport" on p.92).

All **buses** to Sydney arrive and depart from Eddy Avenue and Pitt Street, bordering Central Station. The area is well set up, with decent cafés, a 24-hour police station and a huge YHA hostel as well as the **Sydney Coach Terminal** (ⓣ02/9281 9366; Mon–Fri 6am–7.30pm, Sat & Sun 9am–6pm), which has a luggage-storage room ($5–15 per 24hr, depending on size) and can **book accommodation**, tours and all coach tickets and passes. Greyhound Australia has separate ticket offices/departure lounges also on Eddy Avenue.

Information

There are three **Sydney Visitor Centres** offering comprehensive information, free accommodation and tour-booking facilities, and selling tourist transport tickets and sightseeing passes. One is at the international airport terminal (see opposite); the others are centrally located at The Rocks, on the corner of Argyle and Playfair streets, and at Darling Harbour, beside the IMAX cinema (both daily 9.30am–5.30pm; ⓣ02/9240 8788 or 1800 067 676, ⓦwww.sydney visitorcentre.com). Free **maps** and brochures can be picked up at all three, including the very useful *Sydney: The Official Guide*. Tourism New South Wales (Tourist Information Line ⓣ13 20 77, ⓦwww.visitnsw.com.au) runs the **City Host information kiosks** (daily 9am–5pm) at Circular Quay (on the corner of Pitt and Alfred streets), Martin Place and Town Hall, providing brochures, maps and face-to-face information.

Several free **magazines** are worth picking up at tourist offices: the quarterly *This Week in Sydney* is best for general information; while *TNT Magazine* is the pick of an array of publications aimed at **backpackers**, giving the lowdown on Sydney on the cheap.

City transport

Sydney's **public transport network** is extremely good, though the system relies heavily on buses, and traffic jams can be a problem. **State Transit Authority (STA)** operate buses, trains and ferries – see box on pp.95–97 for information on the great-value Sydney Pass, which enables travel on all three – and there's also a privately run light rail and monorail system whizzing about the city centre, as well as plenty of licensed taxis. Trains stop around midnight, as do most regular buses, though several services towards the eastern and northern beaches, such as the #380 to Bondi Beach, the #372 and #373 to Coogee and the #151 to Manly, run through the night. Otherwise, a pretty good network of **Nightride buses** shadows the train routes to the suburbs, departing from Town Hall station (outside the Energy Australia Building on George Street) and stopping at train stations – where taxis wait at designated ranks. For all public transport information, routes and timetables, call ⓣ13 15 00 (daily 6am–10pm) or check ⓦwww.131500.info.

Buses

Within the central area, **buses** – hailed from yellow-signed bus stops – are the most convenient, widespread mode of transport, and cover more of the city than the trains. With few exceptions buses radiate from the centre, with major interchanges at Railway Square near Central Station (especially southwest routes), at Circular Quay (range of routes), from York and Carrington streets outside Wynyard station (North Shore), and Bondi Junction station (eastern suburbs and beaches). Single-ride **tickets** can be bought on board from the driver and cost from $1.70 for up to two distance-measured sections, with a maximum fare of $5.40; $2.80 (up to 5 sections) is the most typical fare. Substantial discounts are available with TravelTen tickets and other travel passes (see box on pp.94–95); these must be validated in the ticket reader by the front door. Bus **information**,

Smartvisit Card

All three Sydney Visitor Centres sell the **See Sydney & Beyond Smartvisit Card** (ⓣ1300 661 711, ⓦwww.seesydneycard.com), which comes in two-, three- and seven-day versions (to be used over consecutive days) with or without a transport option (two-day $119/$145, three-day $149/$205, seven-day $209/$275; cheaper children's passes are available) and includes admission to forty well-known attractions in Sydney and the Blue Mountains, as well as a range of discounts. If an action-packed, fast-paced itinerary is your thing, the card can be good value and it's certainly a convenient way to bypass the queues.

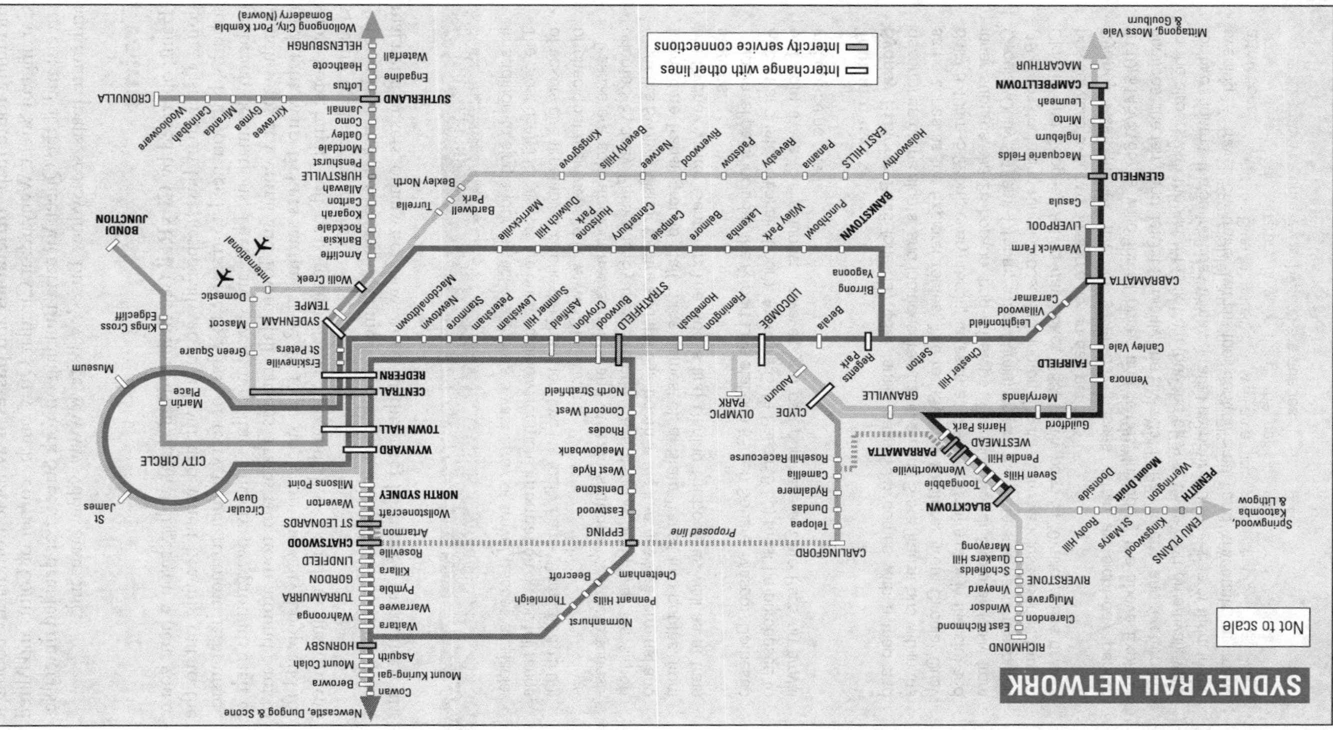

SYDNEY RAIL NETWORK
Not to scale
Interchange with other lines
Intercity service connections
Newcastle, Dungog & Scone
Cowan
Berowra
Mount Kuring-gai
Mount Colah
Asquith
HORNSBY
Waitara
Wahroonga
Warrawee
TURRAMURRA
Pymble
GORDON
Killara
LINDFIELD
Roseville
CHATSWOOD
Artarmon
ST LEONARDS
Wollstonecraft
Waverton
NORTH SYDNEY
Milsons Point
WYNYARD
TOWN HALL
CENTRAL
REDFERN
Circular Quay
St James
CITY CIRCLE
Museum
Martin Place
Kings Cross
Edgecliff
BONDI JUNCTION
Green Square
Mascot
Domestic
International
Erskineville
St Peters
SYDENHAM
TEMPE
Wolli Creek
Arncliffe
Banksia
Rockdale
Kogarah
Carlton
Allawah
HURSTVILLE
Penshurst
Mortdale
Oatley
Como
Jannali
SUTHERLAND
Loftus
Engadine
Heathcote
Waterfall
HELENSBURGH
Wollongong City, Port Kembla
Bomaderry (Nowra)
Kirrawee
Gymea
Miranda
Caringbah
Woolooware
CRONULLA
Turrella
Bardwell Park
Bexley North
Kingsgrove
Beverly Hills
Narwee
Riverwood
Padstow
Revesby
Panania
EAST HILLS
Holsworthy
Macdonaldtown
Newtown
Stanmore
Petersham
Lewisham
Summer Hill
Ashfield
Croydon
Burwood
STRATHFIELD
Homebush
Flemington
LIDCOMBE
Berala
Regents Park
Marrickville
Dulwich Hill
Hurlstone Park
Canterbury
Campsie
Belmore
Lakemba
Wiley Park
Punchbowl
BANKSTOWN
Birrong
Yagoona
Normanhurst
Thornleigh
Pennant Hills
Beecroft
Cheltenham
EPPING
Eastwood
Denistone
West Ryde
Meadowbank
Rhodes
Concord West
North Strathfield
Proposed line
OLYMPIC PARK
CARLINGFORD
Telopea
Dundas
Rydalmere
Camellia
Rosehill Racecourse
CLYDE
Auburn
GRANVILLE
PARRAMATTA
Harris Park
WESTMEAD
Pendle Hill
Wentworthville
Seven Hills
Toongabbie
BLACKTOWN
RICHMOND
East Richmond
Clarendon
Windsor
Mulgrave
Vineyard
RIVERSTONE
Schofields
Quakers Hill
Marayong
Doonside
Rooty Hill
Mount Druitt
St Marys
Werrington
Kingswood
PENRITH
EMU PLAINS
Springwood, Katoomba & Lithgow
Guildford
Merrylands
Yennora
FAIRFIELD
Canley Vale
Sefton
Chester Hill
Leightonfield
Villawood
Carramar
CABRAMATTA
Warwick Farm
LIVERPOOL
Casula
GLENFIELD
Macquarie Fields
Ingleburn
Minto
Leumeah
CAMPBELLTOWN
MACARTHUR
Mittagong, Moss Vale & Goulburn

including route maps, **timetables** and **passes**, is available from handy booths at Carrington Street, Wynyard; at Circular Quay on the corner of Loftus and Alfred streets; and at the Queen Victoria Building on York Street. For detailed timetables and route maps, see Sydney Buses' website ⓦwww.sydneybuses.info.

Trains

Trains, operated by **CityRail** (see Sydney Rail map), will get you where you're going faster than buses, especially at rush hour and when heading out to the suburbs, but you need to transfer to a bus or ferry to get to most harbourside or beach destinations. There are seven train lines, mostly overground, each of which stops at Central and Town Hall stations. Trains run from around 5am to midnight, with **tickets** starting at $2.40 for a single on the City Loop and for short hops; buying off-peak returns (after 9am and all weekend) means you can save up to thirty percent.

Automatic ticket-vending machines (which give change) and barriers (insert magnetic tickets; otherwise, show ticket at the gate) have been introduced just

Travel passes

In addition to single-journey tickets, there's a vast array of **travel passes** available. The most useful for visitors are outlined below; for more **information** on the full range of tickets and timetables, phone the Transport Infoline (daily 6am–10pm; ⓣ13 15 00) or check out their website (ⓦwww.131500.info).

Passes are sold at most **newsagents** and at **train stations**; the more tourist-oriented Sydney Pass and Sydney Explorer Pass can be bought at the airport (from the Sydney Visitor Centre and the STA booth in the international terminal and from State Transit ground staff in the domestic), at State Transit Info booths, from the Sydney Visitor Centre in The Rocks and Darling Harbour, as well as at train stations.

No travel pass includes the Airport Line stations (Green Square, Mascot, Domestic Airport and International Airport). An extra Gate Pass ($9.80) must be purchased to exit from these four stations; however, you can purchase a Gate Pass on arrival without being fined.

Tourist passes

Sydney Explorer Pass (one-day $39, family pass $97) comes with a map and description of the sights, and includes free travel on any State Transit bus within the same zones as the Explorer routes. The red **Sydney Explorer** (from Circular Quay daily 8.40am–5.22pm; every 18min) takes in all the important sights in the city and inner suburbs, via 26 hop-on, hop-off stops. The blue **Bondi Explorer** (daily from Circular Quay 9.15am–4.15pm; every 30min) covers the waterside eastern suburbs (19 stops, including Kings Cross, Paddington, Double Bay, Vaucluse, Bondi, Bronte, Clovelly and Coogee). A **two-day ticket** ($68, family pass $170) allows use of both bus services over two days in a seven-day period.

Sydney Pass (three-, five- or seven-day passes within an eight-day period; $110/$145/$165) is valid for all buses and ferries, including the above Explorer services, the ferry and JetCat to Manly, the RiverCat to Parramatta, and a return trip to the airport with the Airport Link train (buy the pass at the airport on arrival), valid for two months. It also includes three narrated harbour cruises – one of them in the evening – travel on trains within the central area, and discounts at many attractions.

about everywhere. On-the-spot fines for fare evasion start from $200, and transit officers patrol frequently. All platforms are painted with designated "nightsafe" waiting areas and all but two or three train carriages are closed after about 8pm, enforcing a cattle-like safety in numbers. Security guards also patrol trains at night; at other times, if the train is deserted, sit in the carriage nearest the guard – marked by a blue light.

Ferries

Sydney's distinctive green-and-yellow **ferries** are the fastest means of transport from Circular Quay to the North Shore, and, indeed, to most places around the harbour. Even if you don't want to go anywhere, a ferry ride is a must, a chance to get out on the water and see the city from the harbour. There's also a speedy **hydrofoil**, the JetCat, which reaches Manly in half the time, but with less charm.

Ferries chug off in various directions from the wharves at Circular Quay (see Sydney Ferries map); cruises depart from Jetty 6. The last fast JetCat service (takes 15min) from Circular Quay to Manly is at 8.20pm, after which time the

Bus, train and ferry passes

Travelpasses allow unlimited use of buses, trains and ferries and can begin on any day of the week. Most useful are the **Red Travelpass** ($33 a week), valid for the city and inner suburbs, and inner-harbour ferries (not the Manly Ferry or the RiverCat beyond Meadowbank); and the **Green Travelpass** ($41), which allows use of all ferries – except JetCats before 7pm. Passes covering a wider area cost between $45 and $55 a week, and monthly passes are also available.

DayTripper tickets ($15.40) are also available for unlimited travel on all services offered by CityRail, Sydney Buses and Sydney Ferries, and they can even be purchased on board buses and ferries.

Bus and ferry passes

The **Blue Travelpass** ($30 a week) gives unlimited travel on buses in the inner-city area and on inner-harbour ferries but cannot be used for Manly or beyond Meadowbank; the **Orange Travelpass** ($37 a week) gets you further on the buses and is valid on all ferries; and the **Pittwater Travelpass** ($51 a week) gives unlimited travel on all buses and ferries. These Travelpasses start with first-use rather than on the day of purchase.

Bus

TravelTen tickets represent a 20 percent saving over single fares by buying ten trips at once; they can be used over a space of time and for more than one person. The tickets are colour-coded according to how many sections they cover: the Brown TravelTen ($22.40), for example, is the choice for trips from Leichhardt to the city, while the Red TravelTen ($29.60) is the one to buy if you're staying at Bondi. In addition, there's a two-zone bus-only travel pass for $30.

Ferry

FerryTen tickets, valid for ten single trips, start at $32.50 for Inner Harbour Services, go up to $46.60 for the Manly Ferry, and peak at $65.70 for the JetCat services.

Train

Seven Day RailPass tickets allow unlimited travel between any two nominated stations and those in between, with savings of about twenty percent on the price of five return trips. For example, a pass between Bondi Junction and Town Hall would cost $23.

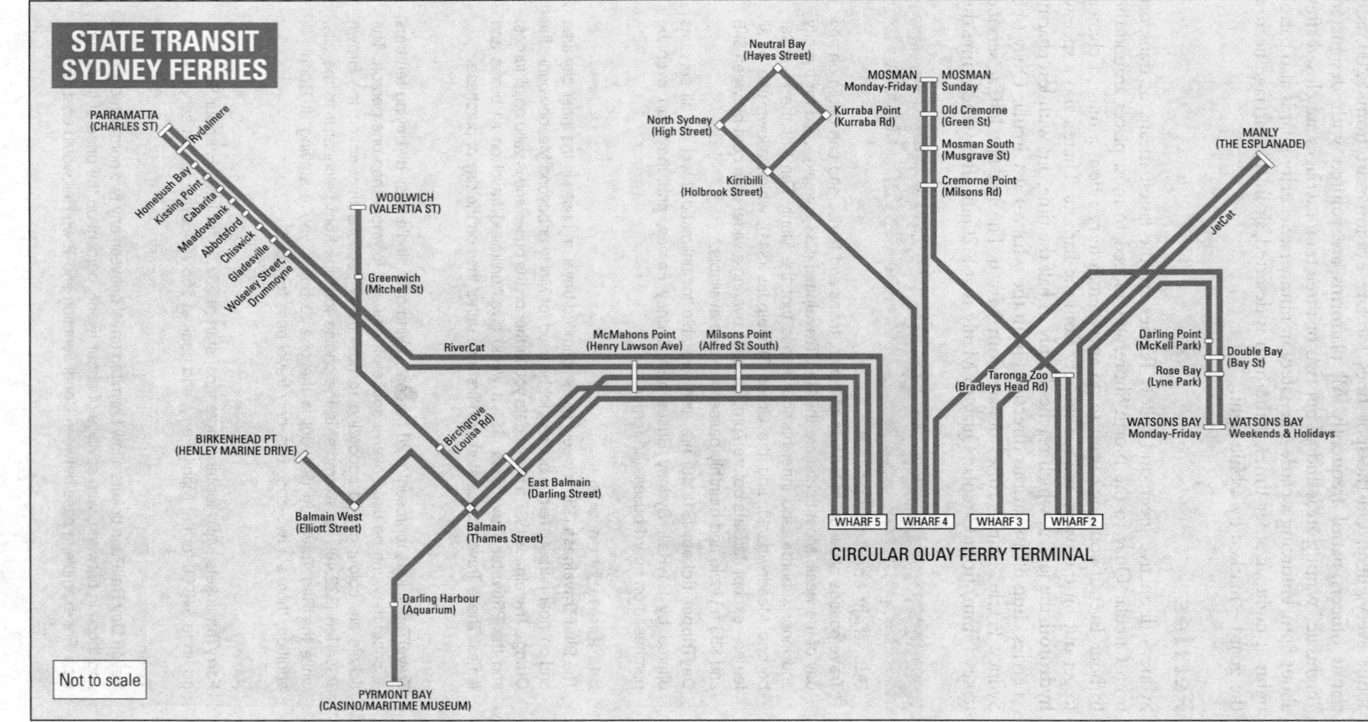
STATE TRANSIT SYDNEY FERRIES
PARRAMATTA (CHARLES ST)
Rydalmere
Homebush Bay
Kissing Point
Cabarita
Meadowbank
Abbotsford
Chiswick
Gladesville
Wolseley Street, Drummoyne
WOOLWICH (VALENTIA ST)
Greenwich (Mitchell St)
RiverCat
McMahons Point (Henry Lawson Ave)
Milsons Point (Alfred St South)
Neutral Bay (Hayes Street)
North Sydney (High Street)
Kurraba Point (Kurraba Rd)
Kirribilli (Holbrook Street)
MOSMAN Monday-Friday
MOSMAN Sunday
Old Cremorne (Green St)
Mosman South (Musgrave St)
Cremorne Point (Milsons Rd)
MANLY (THE ESPLANADE)
JetCat
Darling Point (McKell Park)
Double Bay (Bay St)
Rose Bay (Lyne Park)
Taronga Zoo (Bradleys Head Rd)
WATSONS BAY Monday-Friday
WATSONS BAY Weekends & Holidays
Birchgrove (Louisa Rd)
BIRKENHEAD PT (HENLEY MARINE DRIVE)
East Balmain (Darling Street)
Balmain West (Elliott Street)
Balmain (Thames Street)
Darling Harbour (Aquarium)
PYRMONT BAY (CASINO/MARITIME MUSEUM)
WHARF 5
WHARF 4
WHARF 3
WHARF 2
CIRCULAR QUAY FERRY TERMINAL
Not to scale

slower Manly Ferry (30min) operates until 11.45pm, 11pm on Sundays. Other ferry routes, such as those to Parramatta and Pyrmont Bay, operate only until early evening, while ferries to closer locations including Neutral Bay and Balmain continue to around 11.30pm. Except for the Manly Ferry, services on Sunday are greatly reduced and often finish earlier. Timetables for each route are available at Circular Quay and on the Sydney Ferries website Ⓦwww.sydneyferries.info.

One-way **fares** are $5 ($6.20 for the Manly Ferry); return fares are doubled. The pricier JetCat to Manly and RiverCat to Parramatta are $7.90 and $7.50 respectively. Travelpasses and FerryTen tickets can offer substantial savings – see box on p.95 for details.

Monorail and Light Rail

The city's monorail and the light rail system are run by **Metro Transport Sydney** (Ⓣ02/9285 5600, Ⓦwww.metromonorail.com.au; see the Central Sydney map for more details on routes).

△ The Metro Monorail

The **Metro Monorail** is essentially a tourist shuttle designed to loop around Darling Harbour every three to five minutes, connecting it with the city centre. Thundering along tracks set above the older city streets, the "monster rail" – as many locals know it – doesn't exactly blend in with its surroundings. Still, the elevated view of the city, particularly from Pyrmont Bridge, makes it worth investing $4.50 (day-pass $9) and ten minutes to do the whole eight-stop circuit (Mon–Thurs 7am–10pm, Fri & Sat 7am–midnight, Sun 8am–10pm).

Metro Light Rail (MLR) runs from Central Station to the Pyrmont Peninsula and on to Lilyfield in the inner west. There are fourteen stops on the route, which links Central Station with Chinatown, Darling Harbour, the fish markets at Pyrmont, Star City Casino, Wentworth Park's greyhound racecourse, Glebe (with stops near Pyrmont Bridge Road, at Jubilee Park, and at Rozelle Bay by Bicentennial Park) and Lilyfield, not far from Darling Street, Rozelle. The air-conditioned light rail vehicles can carry 200 passengers, and are fully accessible to disabled commuters. The service operates 24 hours every ten to fifteen minutes to the casino (every 30min midnight–6am) with reduced hours for stops beyond to Lilyfield (Mon–Thurs & Sun 6am–11pm, Fri & Sat 6am–midnight). There are two zones: zone 1 stations are Central to Convention Centre in Darling Harbour, and zone 2 is from Pyrmont Bay to Lilyfield. Tickets can be purchased at vending machines by the stops; singles cost $3/$4.20 for zone 1/zone 2, returns $4.60/$5.70, a day-pass costs $8.40 (family $20) and a weekly one $20. A TramLink ticket, available from any CityRail station, combines a rail ticket to Central Station with an MLR ticket.

If you plan on using the monorail and light rail a lot, it might be worth purchasing a **METROcard** ($18), which gives six rides on either the monorail or light rail; the card can then be topped up for subsequent rides at $2.50 per ride. STA travelpasses cannot be used on either system.

Taxis

Taxis are vacant if the rooftop light is on, though they are notoriously difficult to find at 3pm, when the shifts change over. The four major city **cab ranks** are outside the *Four Seasons Hotel* at the start of George Street, The Rocks; on Park Street outside Woolworths, opposite the Town Hall; outside David Jones department store on Market Street; and at the Pitt Street ("CountryLink") entrance to Central Station. Drivers don't expect a tip but often need directions – try to have some idea of where you're going. Check the correct tariff rate is displayed: tariff 2 (10pm–6am) is twenty percent more than tariff 1 (6am–10pm). See "Listings", p.182, for phone numbers.

Accommodation

There are a tremendous number of places to stay in Sydney, and fierce competition helps keep prices down. Finding somewhere to stay is usually only a problem just before Christmas and throughout January, in late February/early March during the Gay Mardi Gras, and at Easter: at these times, **book ahead**. All types of accommodation offer a (sometimes substantial) discount for **weekly bookings**, and may also cut prices considerably during the **low season** (from autumn to spring, school holidays excepted). Overall, weekend rates are often considerably more than weekday rates, especially at the boutique hotels, which get booked out in advance.

The larger **international hotels** in The Rocks and the Central Business District (CBD) charge $200 and upwards for a double room, although Internet specials are often posted. The least expensive hotels in the city centre, usually above **pubs**, and sharing bathrooms, start from $100. Rates in Kings Cross are much cheaper, with rooms in **private hotels** available for $70 (sharing a bathroom) and around $90 en suite, and around $120–180 in three- or four-star hotels. **Motels**, such as ones we've listed in Glebe and Surry Hills, charge around $100. An increasing number of mid-range boutique hotels and **guest-houses** are smaller, more characterful places to stay, charging upwards of $150. **Serviced holiday apartments** can be very good value for a group, but are heavily booked.

Despite the number of **hostels** all over Sydney and the rivalry between them, standards are variable and, in Kings Cross especially, can be very low. As the scene changes rapidly, it's worth getting the latest news from other travellers. Rates (which should include bedding) can range from $25 to $35 depending on the number of dorm beds, the hostel standard and location. Rates rise in summer and fall in winter. Doubles average around $65, and $85 for an ensuite; weekly rates usually save the cost of a night's stay. All hostels have a laundry, kitchen and common room with TV unless stated otherwise. Office hours are restricted, so it's best to arrange an arrival time.

For longer stays, a **flat-share** can be an alternative to hotels or hostels. Saturday's real-estate section of the *Sydney Morning Herald* is the first place to look, or try café notice boards, especially in King Street in Newtown, Glebe Point Road in Glebe, or Hall Street, Bondi Beach (the window of the health-food store at 29 Hall St is crammed with house-share notices aimed at travellers). The average shared-house room price is around $175 a week (usually two weeks in advance, plus a bond/deposit of four weeks' rent; you'll usually need to get hold of at least your own bedroom furniture and linen). Sleeping With The Enemy, 375 Bulwara Rd, Ultimo (Ⓣ02/9211 8878, Ⓦwww.sleepingwiththeenemy.com), organizes travellers' (aimed at under-28s) house-shares in fully equipped inner-city terraces but sharing a room with up to five others (from $120/week for a one-month stay).

The nearest **campsites** to the centre are in the suburbs of Rockdale, 13km south of the city, and North Ryde, 14km northwest (see box on p.100).

Where to stay

The listings below are arranged by area. For short visits, you'll want to stay in the **city centre** or the immediate vicinity: **The Rocks**, the **CBD** and **Darling Harbour** have the greatest concentration of expensive hotels and now also several backpackers' hostels, while the area around Central Station and Chinatown, known as **Haymarket**, has some cheaper, more downmarket places and an ever greater concentration of hostels, led by the huge YHA. **Kings Cross** has more backpackers' accommodation and cheaper hotels (some with a few dorm beds) than elsewhere – there are also some good upmarket choices, too – though the area is falling out of favour as travellers head for the newer hostels in town to avoid the sleaze and the all-night partying, concentrated on Darlinghurst Road, the hardcore red-light strip. Despite this, Kings Cross remains a lively and convenient base; it's only a ten-minute walk from the city and has its own train station, and the pleasant atmosphere of leafy Victoria Street and the backstreets seems a world away. The adjacent suburbs of **Woolloomooloo**, **Potts Point** and **Elizabeth Bay** move gradually upmarket – a little less accessible, but quieter. To the west, leafy and peaceful **Glebe** is another slice

Campsites around Sydney

The three caravan parks listed below are the closest sites to the centre. Camping rates rise in the peak season and cost from $25–40 for two people in an unpowered site to $35–50 for a powered site; expect to pay $10 less in low season.

Lakeside Caravan Park Lake Park Rd, Narrabeen, 26km north of the city ⓣ02/9913 7845, ⓦwww.sydneylakeside.com.au. Great spot by Narrabeen Lakes on Sydney's northern beaches. Free gas BBQs, camp kitchen and a nearby shop. Minimum two-night stay in a range of cabins and modern two-bedroom villas; all are en suite and linen is included. Bus #190 or #L90 from Wynyard station and then a ten-minute walk. Cabins ⑤, villas ⑥–⑦

Lane Cove River Tourist Park Plassey Rd, North Ryde, 14km northwest of the city ⓣ02/9888 9133, ⓦwww.lanecoverivertouristpark.com.au. Wonderful bush location beside Lane Cove National Park, right on the river, in Sydney's northern suburbs. Great facilities include a bush kitchen (with fridge), TV room and swimming pool. Train to Chatswood then bus #550 or #551. En-suite cabins ⑦

Sheralee Tourist Caravan Park 88 Bryant St, Rockdale, 13km south of the city ⓣ02/9567 7161. The cheapest and closest option to the centre. Small park with camp kitchen. Train to Rockdale station and then a ten-minute walk.

of prime travellers' territory, featuring several backpackers' and a number of small guesthouses.

For longer stays, consider somewhere further out, on the **North Shore**, where you'll get more for your money and more of a feel for Sydney as a city. **Kirribilli**, **Neutral Bay** or **Cremorne Point**, only a short ferry ride from Circular Quay, offer some serenity and affordable waterviews as well. Large old private hotels out this way are increasingly being converted into hostels, particularly on Carabella Street in Kirribilli. **Manly**, tucked away in the northeast corner of the harbour, is a seaside suburb with ocean and harbour beaches, just thirty minutes from Circular Quay by ferry. It has a concentration of hostels and also more upmarket accommodation; the beachside **eastern suburbs** of **Bondi** and **Coogee** offer similar places to stay and are closer to the city.

The Central Business District (CBD)

Hotels & B&Bs

Central Park 185 Castlereagh St, City ⓣ02/9283 5000, ⓦwww.centralpark.com.au. Small chic hotel in a great position in the midst of city bustle right near Town Hall and Hyde Park. Studios have king-size beds and smart and spacious bathrooms with bathtubs. Smaller standard rooms are still a good size although minus the tub; all come with sofa, desk, air-con and well-equipped kitchenette. Tiny daytime lobby café. 24hr reception. Rooms ⑧, studios ⑧

Grand Hotel 30 Hunter St, City ⓣ02/9232 3755, ⓦwww.merivale.com.au/thegrand. Close to Wynyard station, with several floors of accommodation above one of Sydney's oldest (but not necessarily nicest) pubs, which opens until midnight Thursday to Saturday. Rooms, sharing bathrooms, are fine – all brightly painted, with colourful bed covers, heating and ceiling fans. ④ includes continental breakfast.

Intercontinental 117 Macquarie St, City ⓣ02/9230 0200, ⓦwww.intercontinental.com. The old sandstone Treasury building forms the lower floors of this 31-storey, five-star property, with stunning views of the Botanic Gardens, Opera House and harbour. Pool and gym on the top floor. All this comes at a price, of course: $410 city view and $500 harbour view. ⑧

Travelodge Wynyard 7–9 York St, City ⓣ02/9274 1222. Central position for both the CBD and The Rocks. This 22-storey four-star hotel has the usual motel-style rooms but excels with its spacious studios, which come with kitchen area. Rooms ⑧, studios ⑧

Hostels

base Backpackers 477 Kent St, City ⓣ02/9267 7718, ⓦwww.basebackpackers.com. This huge

360-bed hostel is in a great location near Town Hall station. Single female travellers can enjoy the *base* "Sanctuary" concept; a women-only section featuring all the home comforts, from hairdryers in the bathrooms to free Aveda hair-care products and feather pillows. Well-furnished rooms and dorms (four-, six-, eight- and ten-bed) with shared bathrooms all have air-con. It's well set up with the usual facilities plus Internet access and a solarium for that all-year tan. Dorms $26–32, rooms ❺

Sydney Backpackers Victoria House, 7 Wilmot St, City ⓣ02/9267 7772 or 1800 88 77 66, ⓦwww.sydneybackpackers.com. Very central choice off the George Street cinema strip. Clean and spacious, although lacking a little in atmosphere. Six- and eight-bed dorms – one en-suite dorm on every floor – and spacious twins (no doubles); all rooms have air-con. Dorms $28–33, rooms ❺

The Rocks

Hotels & B&Bs

Lord Nelson Brewery Hotel Cnr Argyle and Kent streets, The Rocks ⓣ02/9251 4044, ⓦwww.lordnelson.com.au. This colonial-style B&B in a historic pub has nine cozy rooms. Price varies according to size and position: best is the corner room with views of Argyle St. Serves beer brewed on the premises, plus bar food daily and upmarket meals from its first-floor brasserie (lunch Wed–Fri, dinner Tues–Sat). ❼–❽ includes continental breakfast.

Mercantile 25 George St, The Rocks ⓣ02/9247 3570, ⓔmerc@tpg.com.au. High-spirited Irish pub; bistro meals served at outdoor tables that make a fine spot to watch the weekend market crowds. Has a stash of fab rooms upstairs, which are always booked out – get in early. Original features include huge fireplaces in several rooms, all furnished in colonial style. Several have bathrooms complete with spa baths. ❻–❼ includes cooked breakfast.

Old Sydney Holiday Inn 55 George St, The Rocks ⓣ02/9252 0524, ⓦwww.sydneyhotels.holiday-inn.com. Four-and-a-half star in a great location right in the heart of The Rocks, with impressive architecture: eight levels of rooms around a central atrium creates a remarkable feeling of space. The best rooms have harbour views, but the rooftop swimming pool (plus spa and sauna) also gives fantastic vistas. 24hr room service. Variable rates start from $260. ❽

The Russell 143A George St, The Rocks ⓣ02/9241 3543, ⓦwww.therussell.com.au. This small hotel has forever-popular shared-bathroom rooms. The priciest of the en-suite rooms have views of Circular Quay. Sunny central courtyard and a rooftop garden with small restaurant serving continental breakfast. ❼–❽

Darling Harbour and Ultimo

Glasgow Arms 527 Harris St, Ultimo, opposite the Powerhouse Museum ⓣ02/9211 2354. Close to Darling Harbour, the seven rooms are situated above a very pleasant pub with courtyard dining (Sat dinner only, closed Sun); double-glazed windows are handy now the bar closes at 3am. The high-ceilinged rooms – nicely decorated down to the polished floorboards – are good value, all with en suite, air-con and TV. ❼ includes continental breakfast.

Haymarket and around Central Station

Hotels

Aarons Hotel 37 Ultimo Rd, Haymarket ⓣ02/9281 5555, ⓦwww.aaronshotel.com.au. Large, three-star hotel right in the heart of Chinatown, with its own modern café downstairs, which does room service, too. Colourful feature-walls add a splash to comfortable en-suite rooms, all with TV, air-con and fridge. The least expensive are internal, small and box-like, with skylight only, while the pricier courtyard rooms have their own balconies. ❺–❼

Capitol Square Capitol Square, Campbell and George streets, Haymarket ⓣ02/9211 8633, ⓦwww.rydges.com.au. One of the city's most affordable chains right next to the Capitol Theatre and cafés, and across from Chinatown. Small enough not to feel impersonal, with modern – if a little chintzy – rooms. Parking $22. ❻–❼

Pensione Hotel 631–635 George St, Haymarket ⓣ02/9265 8888, ⓦwww.pensione.com.au. This stylish budget private hotel opposite Chinatown couldn't be more central. The

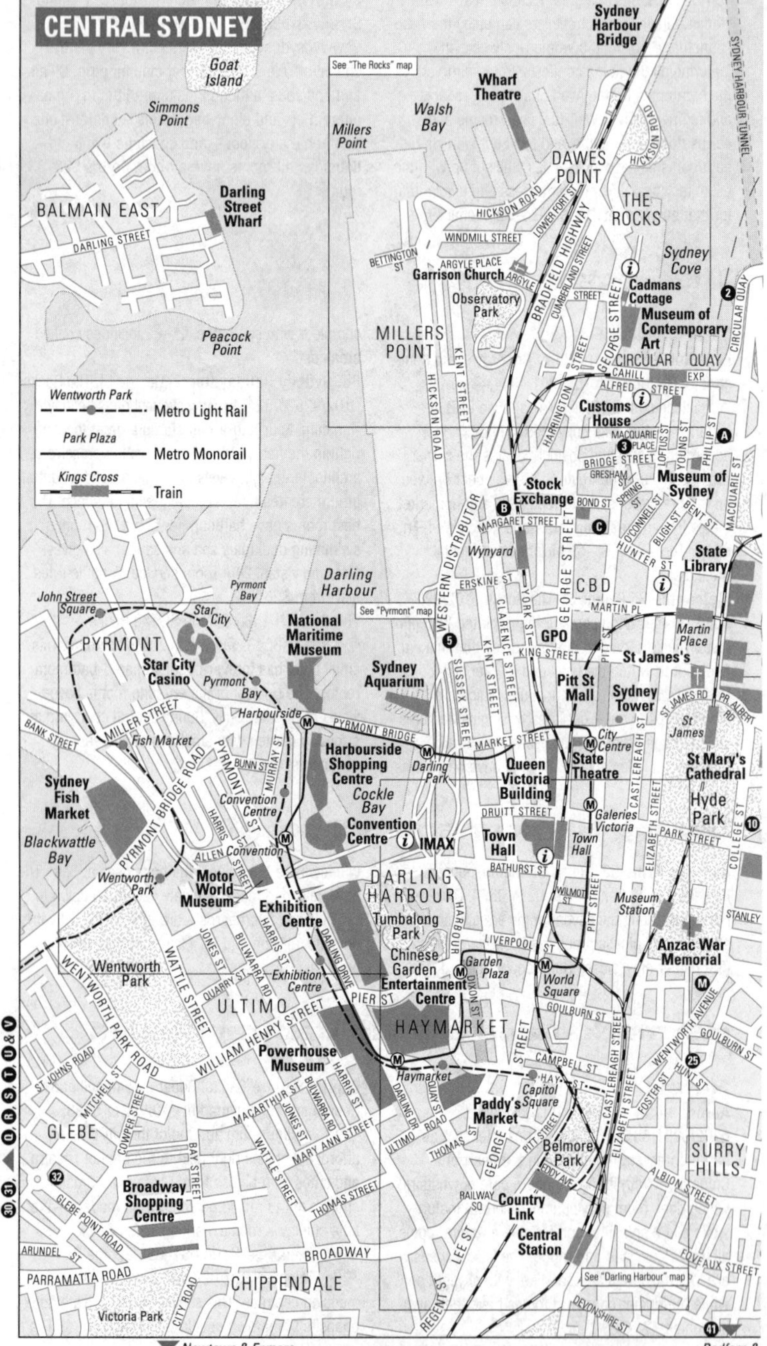
CENTRAL SYDNEY
Goat Island
Simmons Point
Balmain East
Darling Street
Darling Street Wharf
Peacock Point
See "The Rocks" map
Sydney Harbour Bridge
Wharf Theatre
Walsh Bay
Millers Point
Dawes Point
The Rocks
Hickson Road
Windmill Street
Lower Fort St
Bradfield Highway
Cumberland Street
Argyle Place
Garrison Church
Observatory Park
Cadmans Cottage
Museum of Contemporary Art
Sydney Cove
Circular Quay
Sydney Harbour Tunnel
Cahill Exp
Alfred Street
Customs House
Kent Street
Harrington Street
George Street
Macquarie Place
Bridge Street
Museum of Sydney
Stock Exchange
Margaret Street
Wynyard
Hunter St
State Library
Western Distributor
Erskine St
CBD
Martin Pl
Martin Place
GPO
King Street
St James's
Pitt St Mall
Sydney Tower
Sydney Aquarium
National Maritime Museum
Darling Harbour
Pyrmont Bay
Star City
Pyrmont
Star City Casino
John Street Square
Harbourside
Pyrmont Bridge
Miller Street
Fish Market
Bank Street
Pyrmont Bridge Road
Sydney Fish Market
Blackwattle Bay
Harbourside Shopping Centre
Darling Park
Market Street
City Centre
State Theatre
Queen Victoria Building
St James
St Mary's Cathedral
Hyde Park
Cockle Bay
Convention Centre
IMAX
Town Hall
Galeries Victoria
Druitt Street
Bathurst St
Park Street
College St
Wentworth Park
Motor World Museum
Exhibition Centre
Darling Harbour
Tumbalong Park
Chinese Garden
Museum Station
Anzac War Memorial
Liverpool St
Garden Plaza
World Square
Entertainment Centre
Haymarket
Ultimo
Wentworth Park
Wentworth Park Road
William Henry Street
Powerhouse Museum
Goulburn St
Campbell St
Hay St
Capitol Square
Paddy's Market
Belmore Park
Surry Hills
Glebe
Glebe Point Road
Broadway Shopping Centre
Broadway
Railway Sq
Country Link
Central Station
Parramatta Road
Chippendale
Victoria Park
City Road
Regent St
Lee St
Devonshire St
Foveaux Street
Albion Street
See "Darling Harbour" map
See "Pyrmont" map
Metro Light Rail
Metro Monorail
Train
Wentworth Park
Park Plaza
Kings Cross
Newtown & Enmore
Redfern &
30, 31, Q, R, S, T, U & V

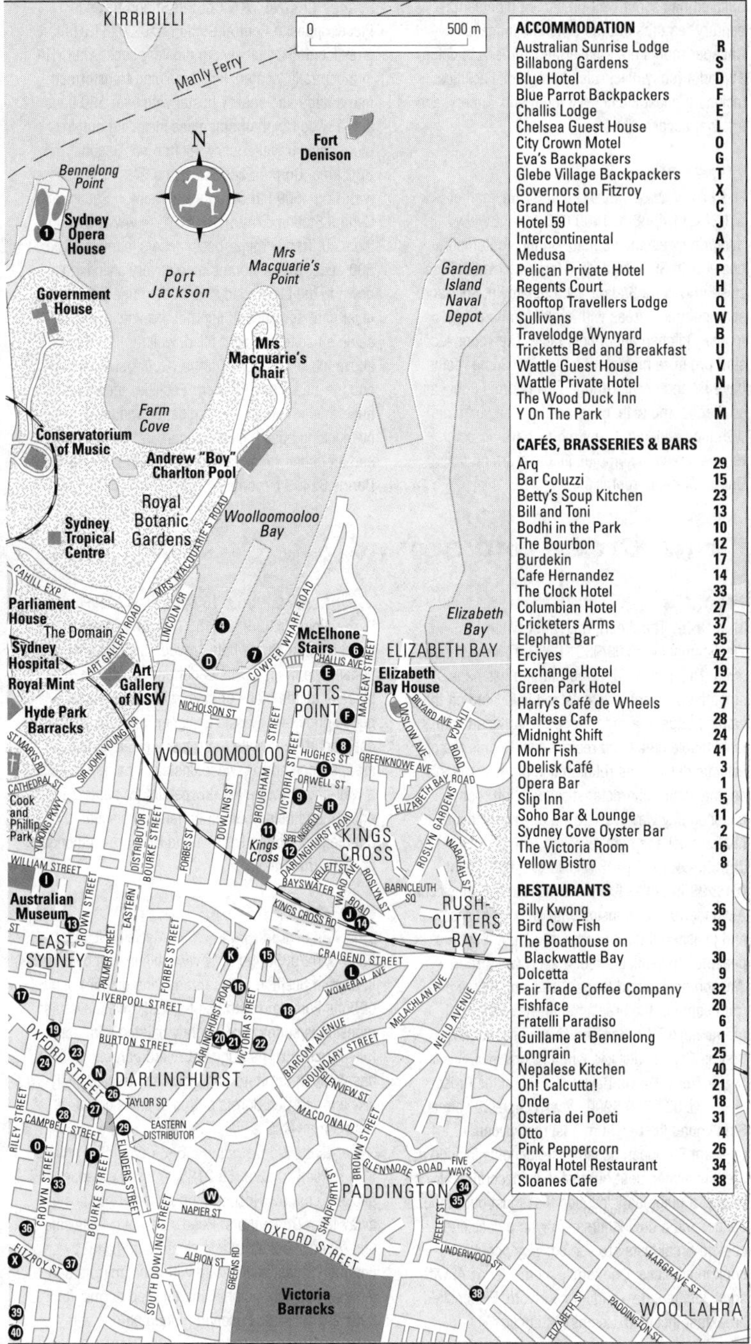
ACCOMMODATION
Australian Sunrise Lodge R
Billabong Gardens S
Blue Hotel D
Blue Parrot Backpackers F
Challis Lodge E
Chelsea Guest House L
City Crown Motel O
Eva's Backpackers G
Glebe Village Backpackers T
Governors on Fitzroy X
Grand Hotel C
Hotel 59 J
Intercontinental A
Medusa K
Pelican Private Hotel P
Regents Court H
Rooftop Travellers Lodge Q
Sullivans W
Travelodge Wynyard B
Tricketts Bed and Breakfast U
Wattle Guest House V
Wattle Private Hotel N
The Wood Duck Inn I
Y On The Park M
CAFÉS, BRASSERIES & BARS
Arq 29
Bar Coluzzi 15
Betty's Soup Kitchen 23
Bill and Toni 13
Bodhi in the Park 10
The Bourbon 12
Burdekin 17
Cafe Hernandez 14
The Clock Hotel 33
Columbian Hotel 27
Cricketers Arms 37
Elephant Bar 35
Erciyes 42
Exchange Hotel 19
Green Park Hotel 22
Harry's Café de Wheels 7
Maltese Cafe 28
Midnight Shift 24
Mohr Fish 41
Obelisk Café 3
Opera Bar 1
Slip Inn 5
Soho Bar & Lounge 11
Sydney Cove Oyster Bar 2
The Victoria Room 16
Yellow Bistro 8
RESTAURANTS
Billy Kwong 36
Bird Cow Fish 39
The Boathouse on Blackwattle Bay 30
Dolcetta 9
Fair Trade Coffee Company 32
Fishface 20
Fratelli Paradiso 6
Guillame at Bennelong 1
Longrain 25
Nepalese Kitchen 40
Oh! Calcutta! 21
Onde 18
Osteria dei Poeti 31
Otto 4
Pink Peppercorn 26
Royal Hotel Restaurant 34
Sloanes Cafe 38
0 500 m
N
KIRRIBILLI
Manly Ferry
Fort Denison
Bennelong Point
Sydney Opera House
Port Jackson
Mrs Macquarie's Point
Garden Island Naval Depot
Government House
Mrs Macquarie's Chair
Farm Cove
Conservatorium of Music
Andrew "Boy" Charlton Pool
Royal Botanic Gardens
Woolloomooloo Bay
Sydney Tropical Centre
CAHILL EXP
MRS MACQUARIE'S ROAD
Parliament House
The Domain
Sydney Hospital
Royal Mint
Hyde Park Barracks
ART GALLERY ROAD
Art Gallery of NSW
LINCOLN CR
COWPER WHARF ROAD
McElhone Stairs
CHALLIS AVE
ELIZABETH BAY
Elizabeth Bay
Elizabeth Bay House
POTTS POINT
MACLEAY STREET
NICHOLSON ST
WOOLLOOMOOLOO
SIR JOHN YOUNG CR
ST MARYS RD
CATHEDRAL ST
Cook and Phillip Park
YURONG PKWY
HUGHES ST
ORWELL ST
GREENKNOWE AVE
ELIZABETH BAY ROAD
ONSLOW AVE
ITHACA ROAD
BILYARD AVE
VICTORIA STREET
BROUGHAM STREET
DOWLING ST
FORBES ST
BOURKE STREET
DISTRIBUTOR
INGREAD AV
DARLINGHURST ROAD
Kings Cross
KINGS CROSS
ROSLYN GARDENS
WARATAH ST
WILLIAM STREET
Australian Museum
CROWN STREET
EASTERN
BAYSWATER
KELLETT ST
WARD AVE
ROSLYN ST
BARNCLEUTH SQ
RUSH-CUTTERS BAY
KINGS CROSS RD
EAST SYDNEY
FORBES STREET
PALMER STREET
CRAIGEND STREET
WOMERAH AVE
LIVERPOOL STREET
McLACHLAN AVE
NEILD AVENUE
DARLINGHURST ROAD
VICTORIA STREET
BARCOM AVENUE
BOUNDARY STREET
GLENVIEW ST
OXFORD STREET
BURTON STREET
DARLINGHURST
TAYLOR SQ
EASTERN DISTRIBUTOR
MACDONALD
BROWN STREET
RILEY STREET
CAMPBELL STREET
FLINDERS STREET
GLENMORE ROAD
FIVE WAYS
CROWN STREET
BOURKE STREET
SHADFORTH ST
PADDINGTON
NAPIER ST
SOUTH DOWLING STREET
OXFORD STREET
FEELEY ST
UNDERWOOD ST
HARGRAVE ST
FITZROY ST
ALBION ST
GREENS RD
Victoria Barracks
ELIZABETH ST
PADDINGTON ST
WOOLLAHRA
42 SCG
Bondi, Paddington Market & Centennial Parklands

building has some well-preserved nineteenth-century features but the style is minimalist. Cheaper rooms are smaller and come with cable TV and a funky black-tiled bathroom. Facilities include a guest kitchen/TV room and laundry, and Internet access. ❺–❻

Hostels

Footprints Westend 412 Pitt St, Haymarket ⓣ02/9211 4588 or 1800 013 186, ⓦwww.footprintswestend.com.au. Bright, contemporary hostel with 300+ beds in a large renovated hotel close to Central Station and Chinatown. Spic-and-span common areas with funky furniture, big modern kitchen and a pool table. The young local staff organize nights out and tours. Some rooms have TV and/or mini-fridge while dorms (four- and six-bed) come with lockers; all are en suite and with nice bedding. Many rooms have air-con: request these in summer, as there are no fans. Dorms $28–30, rooms ❺

Sydney Central YHA Cnr Pitt St and Rawson Place, opposite Central Station ⓣ02/9281 9111, ⓔsydcentral@yhansw.org.au. Very successful YHA in a centrally located, listed building transformed into a huge and snazzy hostel with over 550 beds and a wide range of amenities including employment desk, travel agency, rooftop pool, sauna and BBQ area. Dorms $28–34, rooms ❻

wake up! 509 Pitt St, opposite Railway Square and Central Station ⓣ02/9264 4121, ⓦwww.wakeup.com.au. Trendy mega-backpackers' complex (over 500 beds) with a vibrant interior. Very styled, right down to the black-clad staff in the huge intimidating foyer with its banks of Internet terminals. Rooms, some en suite, are light filled, well furnished and, above all, serviceable. Dorms – four-, six-, eight- and ten-bed – have lockers. Facilities include a huge modern kitchen with gigantic windows overlooking busy Railway Square, a streetside café and an underground late-opening bar and eatery. Dorms $24–34, rooms ❺–❻

Kings Cross and around

Hotels

Blue Hotel The Wharf, 6 Cowper Wharf Rd, Woolloomooloo ⓣ02/9331 9000, ⓦwww.tajhotels.com. This luxury Taj establishment has bags of smooth contemporary style and is located on the water's edge in a redeveloped wharf lined with fashionable cafés and restaurants. Rooms are of eclectic design and retain much of the building's original wharf characteristics, with loft rooms boasting city views. There's a day spa, indoor heated pool and gym. ❽

Challis Lodge 21–23 Challis Ave, Potts Point ⓣ02/9358 5422, ⓦwww.budgethotelssydney.com. A wonderful old mansion with sixty-eight rooms and polished timber floors throughout. Set on a peaceful, tree-filled street a short walk from Woolloomooloo and Kings Cross, and a step away from some of the area's trendiest eateries. All rooms have TV, fridge and sink; guest laundry. Rooms ❹, en suite ❺, with balcony ❻

Hotel 59 59 Bayswater Rd, Kings Cross ⓣ02/9360 5900, ⓦwww.hotel59.com.au. Small hotel (just eight rooms) reminiscent of a pleasant European guesthouse; benefits include a friendly owner, petit but tastefully decorated air-con rooms, a quiet leafy location that's just out of the bustle, and a downstairs café where delicious cooked breakfasts are served. Very popular, so book in advance. One family room (sleeps 4) with small kitchenette. Outdoor courtyard. Full cooked breakfast included. Rooms ❹, studio ❺

Regents Court 18 Springfield Ave, Potts Point ⓣ02/9358 1533, ⓦwww.regentscourt.com.au. Small hotel, raved about by international style mags for its decor and ambience, this place is a little piece of glam without an outrageous price tag. Classic designer furniture, and each apartment-style room has a sleek kitchen area, air-con and TV/video. Instead of a bar, there's a well-chosen wine list downstairs (at bottle-shop prices), and help-yourself coffee and biscotti. Small but elegant rooftop kitchen and BBQ area, amongst potted citrus trees. ❼

Hostels

Blue Parrot Backpackers 87 Macleay St, Potts Point ⓣ02/9356 4888, ⓦwww.blueparrot.com.au. In a great position in the trendy (and quieter) part of Potts Point and with helpful staff, this converted mansion is sunny, airy, brightly painted and tastefully furnished. The huge courtyard garden out back has wooden furniture and big shady trees. Mostly six- and ten-bed dorms but no doubles or twins. Dorms from $25.

Eva's Backpackers 6–8 Orwell St, Potts Point ⓣ02/9358 2185, ⓦwww.evasbackpackers.com.au. Recommended family-run hostel away from Darlinghurst Road's clamour; feels safe and friendly. Colourful and clean rooms and common areas, well set up with fans, mirrors and lamps. Four-, six-, eight- and ten-bed dorms; four-beds are en suite. Peaceful rooftop garden with table umbrellas, greenery, BBQ area and fantastic views over The Domain. The guest kitchen/dining room, positioned at street level, feels like a café and is conducive to socializing, though this isn't a "party" hostel. Dorms $26, rooms ❺

The Wood Duck Inn 49 William St, East Sydney ⓣ02/9358 5856 or 1800 110 025, ⓦwww.woodduckinn.com.au. Fun hostel with fine views overlooking Hyde Park run by two switched-on brothers who can help you kick-start a working holiday. Don't be put off by the dingy, endless flights of concrete steps: they emerge into the nerve centre, a sunny rooftop with fantastic city views and quirky surfboard tabletops. The spacious dorm-only accommodation below has polished floors, citrus-coloured walls, high ceilings, and fresh flowers in the hall. Dorms $22.

Surry Hills, Darlinghurst, Paddington and Woollahra

BIG 212 Elizabeth St, Surry Hills ⓣ02/9281 6030, ⓦwww.bighostel.com. Stylish 140-bed part-boutique hotel, part-hostel in a lousy location opposite the railway line but a five- to ten-minute walk to Central Station, Chinatown and Oxford Street. Sunny rooms have extra-thick glass to keep the noise pollution at bay, and air-con. An organic café serves breakfast through dinner (plus $5 specials). Dorms $24.50, rooms ❺

City Crown Motel 289 Crown St, cnr of Reservoir St, Surry Hills ⓣ02/9331 2433, ⓦwww.citycrownmotel.com.au. Ordinary-looking motel but with a fantastic location in the heart of the fashionable Surry Hills scene. The en-suite units are air-con with free in-house movies. Some parking space ($15 extra): enter on Reservoir St. Rooms ❻

Medusa 267 Darlinghurst Rd, Darlinghurst ⓣ02/9331 1000, ⓦwww.medusa.com.au. This boutique hotel is a modernist's dream, set in a grand heritage mansion and decorated with a mix of cutting-edge and dramatic furniture and fittings. The seventeen rooms all have a balcony, DVD player and microwave, with chaise longues, and

Gay and lesbian accommodation

You shouldn't encounter any problems booking into a regular hotel, but here are several places that cater to a gay clientele or are gay friendly. Other particularly welcoming places in our general listings include *BIG* (p.105), *Medusa* (p.105) and *Sullivans* (p.106).

Chelsea Guest House 49 Womerah Ave, Darlinghurst ⓣ02/9380 5994, ⓦwww.chelsea.citysearch.com.au. Tastefully decorated terrace-house in the quieter leafy backstreets of Darlinghurst. Standard en-suite doubles, plus deluxe rooms with king-sized beds including a couple of suites ($185–195); singles ($94) share bathrooms but have sinks. Light breakfast served in the courtyard. B&B from ❻

Governors on Fitzroy 64 Fitzroy St, Surry Hills ⓣ02/9331 4652, ⓦwww.governors.com.au. Long-established gay B&B in a restored Victorian terrace just a few blocks from Oxford Street. The six guest rooms – big and well appointed – share bathrooms but have their own basin. A full cooked breakfast is served in the dining room or the garden courtyard. Guests – mostly men – can also meet and mingle in the spa. B&B ❼

Pelican Private Hotel 411 Bourke St, Darlinghurst ⓣ02/9331 5344, ⓦwww.pelicanprivatehotel.iwarp.com. Comfortable budget accommodation in one of Sydney's oldest gay guesthouses, a short walk from Oxford Street. The mid-nineteenth-century sandstone building's tree-filled garden is an inner-city oasis and the communal kitchen (with help-yourself breakfast) here makes it even more sociable. Appealing, good-sized, well-furnished rooms have fans, TV and fridge, but share bathroom facilities. Extra $5 for a cooked breakfast in the hotel's street-front café. ❺

Wattle Private Hotel 108 Oxford St, cnr Palmer St, Darlinghurst ⓣ02/9332 4118, ⓦwww.sydneywattle.com. You can't get any closer to the action at this long-established gay-friendly hotel. The en-suite rooms have a contemporary feel – the best is on the roof, opening out to the rooftop garden with city and harbour views. From ❻

access to the stunning interior courtyard for the deluxe rooms. Glamorous and attentive staff. 8

Sullivans 21 Oxford St, Paddington ⓣ02/9361 0211, ⓦwww.sullivans.com.au. Medium-sized contemporary-style private hotel in a trendy location, run by staff tuned into the local scene (free guided walking tour of Paddington included). Comfortable, modern en-suite rooms with TV and telephones. Free (but limited) parking, swimming pool, free guest bicycles, fitness centre, and a café open for a huge and delicious breakfast. 8

Y On The Park 5–11 Wentworth Ave, Darlinghurst ⓣ02/9264 2451, ⓦwww.yhotel.com.au. Great location just off Oxford St near Hyde Park for this YWCA (both sexes welcome); the hostel is surprisingly stylish and caters to every level of traveller. En-suite, shared-bathroom or self-catering studios, and deluxe rooms even come with a pamper pack and plunger coffee. Good-value singles and four-bed dorms (made-up beds with towel, no bunks). Dorms $35, rooms 6–7

Inner west: Glebe and Newtown

Australian Sunrise Lodge 485 King St, Newtown ⓣ02/9550 4999, ⓦwww.australiansunriselodge.com. Inexpensive and well-managed small private hotel well positioned for King Street action but with good security. Single and double rooms, some en suite, come with TV, fridge and toaster. Ground-floor rooms are darker, smaller and cheaper – better options are the sunny rooms on the top two floors, all with cute balconies. En-suite family rooms also available. Rooms 5–6

Billabong Gardens 5–22 Egan St, off King St, Newtown ⓣ02/9550 3236, ⓦwww.billabonggardens.com.au. In a quiet street but close to the action, this long-running purpose-built hostel is arranged around a peaceful inner courtyard with swimming pool, and has excellent communal facilities. Clean dorms (four- to six-bed; some en suite), single ($49), twin and double rooms and motel-style en suites. Daily $5 charge for the popular undercover car-park. Dorms $25, rooms 4

Glebe Village Backpackers 256 Glebe Point Rd, Glebe ⓣ02/9660 8133 or 1800 801 983, ⓦwww.glebevillage.com. Three large old houses with a mellow, sociable atmosphere – the generally laid-back guests socialize in the leafy streetside fairy-lit garden. Staffed by young locals who know what's going on around town. Doubles and twins plus four, six-, ten- or twelve-bed dorms. Dorms $26–30, rooms 3

Rooftop Travellers Lodge 146 Glebe Point Rd, Glebe ⓣ02/9660 7711, ⓦwww.rooftoptravellerslodge.com. This excellent-value budget retreat for short and long stays is right in the heart of Glebe and has a large kitchen and fabulous city views from the rooftop. Rooms can sleep up to four people and have air-con, PC and free broadband. Parking included. 6

Tricketts Bed and Breakfast 270 Glebe Point Rd, Glebe ⓣ02/9552 1141, ⓦwww.tricketts.com.au. Luxury B&B in an 1880s mansion. Rooms – en suite – are furnished with antiques and Persian rugs, and the lounge, complete with a billiard table and leather armchairs, was originally a small ballroom. Also a self-contained one-bedroom garden apartment with its own veranda. Delicious, generous and sociable breakfast. 8

Wattle Guest House 44 Hereford St, Glebe ⓣ02/9552 4997, ⓦwww.wattlehouse.com.au. Top-class, small, cozy and clean Victorian residence on a quiet street with well-furnished doubles, all sharing bathroom. Pretty gardens and an outdoor eating area make staying here extra pleasant, and there's even a library room. Very popular, so book in advance. 5, includes breakfast.

Bondi Beach

Bondi Beachhouse YHA 63 Fletcher St, cnr Dellview St, Bondi ⓣ02/9365 2088, ⓔbondi@intercoast.com.au. Actually closer to Tamarama Beach than Bondi, in a former student boarding-house – international students still stay, hence the buffet-style breakfasts and dinners at cut-rate prices. Painted vibrant citrus colours and with a sunny internal courtyard with BBQ, and a rooftop deck with fabulous ocean views. The Art Deco building has spacious high-ceilinged dorms (four-, six- and eight-bed, with lockers) and rooms – some en suite, with fridges and kettles – all have ceiling fans. Bag one of the beach-view rooms, which go for the same price. Lots of local info; free surf talks. Dorms $29, rooms 4, en suite 5

Bondi Serviced Apartments 212 Bondi Rd, Bondi ⓣ02/8837 8000 or 1300 364 200, ⓦwww.bondi-serviced-apartments.com.au. Good-value serviced motel studio apartments halfway between Bondi Junction and Bondi Beach. Air-con units with clean modern furniture, TV, telephone, kitchen and a balcony with sea view. Cheaper, older-style

Holiday apartments

The following places rent out apartments, generally for a minimum of a week. All are completely furnished and equipped – though occasionally you're expected to provide linen and towels: check first. Many hotels (some called apartment hotels) and all hostels also have self-catering facilities – see main listings for details.

Enoch's Holiday Flats ⓣ02/9388 1477. One-, two- or three-bedroom apartments, all close to Bondi Beach, sleeping two to six people. $300–700 weekly, depending on the size, the season and how long you're renting for.

Manly National 22 Central Ave, Manly ⓣ02/9977 6469, ⓕ9977 3760. One- and two-bedroom holiday apartments for up to four people; swimming pool; linen not supplied. One-bedroom $700–1100 weekly, two-bedroom $980–1500.

Medina Executive Apartments Head office, Level 1, 355 Crown St, Surry Hills ⓣ02/9360 1699 or 1300 300 232, ⓦwww.medina.com.au. Upmarket studio or one-, two- and three-bedroom serviced apartments with resident managers and reception in salubrious locales. City locations – Lee St near Central Station, Kent St and Martin Place in the CBD, King St Wharf at Darling Harbour; inner city and eastern suburbs – Chippendale, Surry Hills, Paddington, Double Bay and Coogee; and lower North Shore – Crows Nest and North Ryde. All include undercover parking. From $850 weekly.

The Park Agency 190 Arden St, Coogee ⓣ02/9315 7777, ⓦwww.parkagency.com.au. Spacious, well-set-up studio and one-, two- and three-bedroom apartments near Coogee Beach. All fully furnished, including washing machine and linen. From $750 per week for the smaller units, $850–1500 per week for the larger properties. Cheaper quarterly leases available.

Sydney City Centre Serviced Apartments 7 Elizabeth St, Martin Place ⓣ02/9233 6677, ⓦwww.accommodationsydneycity.com.au. Fully equipped, open-plan studio apartments sleeping two; kitchenette, laundry, TV, video, fans; basic, but in an excellent location. A good choice for long-stayers, as they rent out for a minimum of thirteen weeks. $250–350 weekly.

apartments without views. Rooftop pool. Cheaper weekly or monthly rates. ❻–❼

Noah's Backpackers 2 Campbell Parade, Bondi Beach ⓣ02/9365 7100 or 1800 226 662, ⓦwww.noahsbondibeach.com. Huge hostel opposite the beach offering marvellous ocean views from the rooftop deck with a BBQ area and convenient kitchen. Beach-view rooms with sink, TV, fridge, fan and lockable cupboard plus four-, six- and eight-bed dorms. Clean, well run but with cramped bathrooms. Excellent security. Dorms $22–25, rooms ❹

Coogee

Coogee Bay Boutique Hotel 9 Vicar St, Coogee ⓣ02/9665 0000, ⓦwww.coogeebayhotel.com.au. Newer hotel attached to the rear of a pub, the older, sprawling *Coogee Bay Hotel*. Rooms – all with balconies, half with ocean views – look like something from *Vogue Interior*, luxurious touches include marble floors in the bathrooms. Cheaper rooms in the old hotel heritage wing are noisy at weekends but are just as stylish; several offer splendid water views. Parking included. 24hr reception. The pub, one of the busiest in Australia, has an excellent brasserie, several bars and a nightclub. ❻–❽

Dive Hotel 234 Arden St, Coogee Beach ⓣ02/9665 5538, ⓦwww.divehotel.com.au. A wonderful small hotel opposite the beach; features include Art Deco tiling and high, decorative-plaster ceilings. A pleasant, bamboo-fringed courtyard (with BBQ and discreet guest laundry) opens out from the spacious breakfast room for buffet-style breakfasts. Larger two rooms at the front have splendid ocean views; one at the back has its own balcony. All have funky little bathrooms, CD players, cable TV, queen-sized beds, and a handy kitchenette with microwave and crockery. ❻

Surfside Backpackers Coogee 186 Arden St, Coogee ⓣ02/9315 7888, ⓦwww.surfsidebackpackers.com.au. On Coogee's main drag, above *McDonald's* and opposite the beach, Coogee's largest hostel tends to attract a drinking, party crowd – try elsewhere for quiet. Modern facilities and great views from its high balconies, but a bit of a concrete tower-block feel, and not as clean as it should be. Mostly six-, eight- and ten-bed dorms. Doubles outside the peak periods only. Dorms $22–28, rooms ④

Wizard of Oz Backpackers 172 Coogee Bay Rd, Coogee ⓣ02/9315 7876, ⓦwww.wizardofoz.com.au. Top-class hostel run by a friendly local couple in a big and beautiful Californian-style house with a huge veranda and polished wooden floors. Spacious, vibrantly painted dorms with ceiling fans, and some well-set-up doubles. Big-screen TV, modern kitchen, good showers and big, pleasant backyard with BBQ. Same couple run the *Coogee Beachside Budget Accommodation* at 178 Coogee Bay Rd, which has one-bedroom apartments sleeping up to four with linen supplied. Dorms $27, rooms ⑤, apartments ④–⑥

North Shore

Cremorne Point Manor 6 Cremorne Rd, Cremorne Point ⓣ02/9953 7899, ⓦwww.cremornepointmanor.com.au. Huge, restored Federation-style villa. Nearly all rooms are en suite, except for a few good-value singles (from $66), which have their own toilet and sink, and all have TV and fridge; some pricier rooms have harbour views. One family room has its own kitchen. Guest balcony also has great views. Communal kitchen and laundry. ⑦–⑧ includes light breakfast.

Elite Private Hotel 133 Carabella St, Kirribilli ⓣ02/9929 6365, ⓦwww.elitehotel.com.au. Bright place offering good rooms with sink, TV, fridge and kettle; some dearer ones have a harbour view and most share bathrooms. Small, communal cooking facility and garden courtyard. Only minutes by ferry from the city (to Kirribilli Wharf) and near Milsons Point train station. Cheaper weekly rates. ④–⑤

Glenferrie Lodge 12A Carabella St, Kirribilli ⓣ02/9955 1685, ⓦwww.glenferrielodge.com. Another made-over Kirribilli mansion: clean, light and secure with 24hr reception. Three-share dorms and single, double or family rooms (all shared bathroom). Some pricier rooms have their own balcony and harbour glimpses but guests can also hang out in the garden and on the guest verandas. Ferry to Kirribilli Wharf or train to Milsons Point. Dorms $40, rooms ⑥–⑦ includes cooked buffet breakfast.

Manly and the northern beaches

Avalon Beach Hostel 59 Avalon Parade, Avalon ⓣ02/9918 9709, ⓔgunilla@avalonbeach.com.au. At one of Sydney's best – and most beautiful – surf beaches, this rather tired-looking hostel has an airy beach house feel with breezy balconies. Dorms (four- and six-bed) and rooms have storage area and fans but bathroom facilities are stretched at peak times. Boat trips on Pittwater can be organized; surfboard rental available. Dorms $20–22, rooms ②

Manly Backpackers Beachside 28 Raglan St, Manly ⓣ02/9977 3411, ⓦwww.manlybackpackers.com.au. A modern and purpose-built two-storey "hostel with lifestyle" one block from the surf. One of the few hostels in Manly that manages to be both clean and fun, with a spacious well-equipped kitchen and outside terrace with BBQ. Attracts long-stayers. Twin and double rooms – some en suite – plus small four-bed dorms (six-bed is largest). Best dorm at the front with a balcony. Dorms $26, rooms ④

Manly Pacific Sydney 55 North Steyne, Manly ⓣ02/9977 7666, ⓦwww.accorhotels.com. Beach-front, multi-storey, four-star hotel with 24hr reception, room service, spa, sauna, gym and heated rooftop pool. You pay well for it all, and more for an ocean view, which is spectacular. ⑦

Palm Beach Bed and Breakfast 122 Pacific Rd, Palm Beach ⓣ02/9974 1608, ⓦwww.palmbeachbandb.com.au. Incredibly friendly and slightly quirky B&B (antique cars are scattered about the front lawn). All rooms have balconies and water views of either Pittwater or the Pacific, and the emphasis is on relaxing and unwinding in this leafy setting. Four rooms – with French themes – have either en-suite or shared bathroom. Rooms ⑧

Periwinkle Guesthouse 18–19 East Esplanade, cnr Ashburner St, Manly ⓣ02/9977 4668, ⓔperiwinkle.manly@bigpond.com. Pleasant B&B in a charming restored 1895 villa on Manly Cove. Close to the ferry, shops and the harbour and perfect for swimming, sailing or just listening to the lorikeets chatter. Rooms have fridge and fans; several en suites and larger family rooms available. Communal kitchen, laundry, courtyard with BBQ, and car park. ⑦–⑧ includes light breakfast.

Cronulla Beach

Cronulla Beach YHA 40 Kingsway, Cronulla ⓣ02/9527 7772, ⓦwww.cronullabeachyha.com. No-fuss hostel in this unpretentious, surf-oriente… suburb, two minutes from the sand and ev… to the shops and restaurants of Cronulla … w… …d for day-trips to … live-in mana… …ger offers surf trips … to Watta… …the Royal National … …onulla. Dorms $26,

The City

Port Jackson carves Sydney in two … by the Harbour Bridge and Harbour Tunnel. The **South Shore** is t… activity, and it's here that you'll find the **city centre** and most of the thin… see and do. Many of the classic images of Sydney are within sight of **Circular Quay**, making this busy waterfront area on Sydney Cove a logical – and pleasurable – point to start discovering the city, with the **Sydney Opera House** and the expanse of the Royal Botanic Gardens to the east of Sydney Cove and the historic area of **The Rocks** to the west. By contrast, gleaming, slightly tawdry **Darling Harbour**, at the centre's western edge, is a shiny redeveloped tourist and entertainment area.

Circular Quay

At the southern end of Sydney Cove, **Circular Quay** is the launching pad for harbour and river ferries and sightseeing boats, the terminal for buses from the eastern and southern suburbs, and a major suburban train station to boot (some of the most fantastic views of the harbour can be seen from the above-ground station platforms). Circular Quay itself is always bustling with commuters during the week, and with people simply out to enjoy themselves at the weekend. Restaurants, cafés and fast-food outlets line the Quay, buskers entertain the crowds, and vendors of newspapers and trinkets add to the general hubbub. The sun reflecting on the water and its heave and splash as the ferries come and go make for a dreamy setting – best appreciated over an expensive beer at a waterfront bar. The inscribed bronze pavement-plaques of **Writers' Walk** beneath your feet as you stroll around the Circular Quay waterfront provide an introduction to the Australian literary canon. There are short biographies of writers ranging from Miles Franklin, author of *My Brilliant Career*, through Booker Prize–winner Peter Carey and Nobel Prize–awardee Patrick White, to the feminist Germaine Greer, and quotable quotes on what it means to be Australian. Notable literati who've visited Australia – including Joseph Conrad, Charles Darwin and Mark Twain – also feature.

Having dallied, read, and taken in the views, you could then embark on a sightseeing **cruise** or enjoy a ferry ride on the harbour (see box, p.110). Staying on dry land, you're only a short walk from most of the city-centre sights, along part of a continuous foreshore walkway beginning under the Harbour Bridge and passing through the historic area of Sydney's first settlement The Rocks, and extending beyond the Opera House to the Royal Botanic Gardens.

Besides ferries, Circular Quay still acts as a passenger terminal for ocean liners; head north past the Museum of Contemporary Art to Circular Quay West. It's a long time since the crowds waved their hankies regularly from the **Overseas Passenger Terminal**, looking for all the world like the deck of a ship itself, but you may still see an ocean liner docked here; even if there's no ship, take the escalator and the flight of stairs up for excellent views of the harbour. The rest

[illegible] ses

[illegible] choice of **harbour cruises**, almost all of them leaving from Jetty 6, [illegible] and the rest from Darling Harbour. Apart from the running commentary [illegible] e rather annoying), most offer nothing that you won't get on a regular [illegible] **y** for a lot less. The best of the ordinary trips is the thirty-minute ride to [illegible] **y**, but there's a ferry going somewhere at almost any time throughout the day. If you want to splash out, take a **water-taxi** ride – Circular Quay to Watsons Bay, for example, costs $54 for the first passenger and then an additional $9 for each extra person. Pick-ups are available from any wharf if booked in advance (try Water Taxis Combined on ⓣ02/9555 8888, ⓦwww.watertaxis.com.au). One water-taxi company, **Watertours**, located on Cockle Bay Wharf in Darling Harbour (ⓣ02/9211 7730, ⓦwww.watertours.com.au), even offer tours on their bright yellow taxis, from $12.50 for a speedy ten-minute, one-way spin under the Harbour Bridge to the Opera House (every 15min).

The **Australian Travel Specialists (ATS)** at Jetty 6, Circular Quay and the Harbourside Shopping Centre at Darling Harbour (ⓣ02/9211 3192, ⓦwww.atstravel.com.au) book all cruises; the majority are offered by **Captain Cook Cruises** and **Matilda**, although those offered by the State Transit Authority (STA) – **Harboursights Cruises** (ⓣ13 15 00, ⓦwww.sydneyferries.nsw.gov.au) – are the best value: choose between the Morning Harbour Cruise (daily 10.30am; 1hr; $18), the recommended Afternoon Harbour Cruise to Middle Harbour and back (Mon–Fri 1pm, Sat & Sun 12.30pm; 2hr 30min; $24), or the Evening Harbour Cruise (Mon–Sat 8pm; 1hr 30min; $22). Buy tickets at the Sydney Ferry ticket offices at Circular Quay. STA cruises are also included in a Sydney Pass – see p.94.

There are also a number of more romantic sailing options. **Svanen Charters'** (ⓣ02/9698 4456, ⓦwww.svanen.com.au) sailing ship, built in 1922, is moored at Campbells Cove, and runs harbour day-sails for $110, including morning tea and lunch, or longer overnight sails to Broken Bay, Port Hacking, Jervis Bay or Port Stephens (2 nights $297, 3 nights $396). Sydney's oldest sailing ship, the *James Craig*, an 1874 three-masted iron barque, is part of the **Sydney Heritage Fleet** based at Wharf 7, Pirrama Rd, Pyrmont, near Star City Casino, and does six-hour cruises on Saturdays or Sundays (ⓦwww.sydneyheritagefleet.com.au; 10.30am–5pm; $193; over-12s only; morning and afternoon tea and lunch provided). **Sydney by Sail** (ⓣ02/9280 1110, ⓦwww.sydneybysail.com) offers the popular small-group, three-hour Port Jackson Explorer cruise (daily 1pm; $130) on board a luxury Beneteau yacht, departing from the National Maritime Museum at Darling Harbour (free entry to the museum included).

There are several alternatives for more thrills (but noise pollution for the locals). **Ocean Extreme** (ⓣ1300 887 373, ⓦwww.oceanextreme.com.au) offers a hair-raising, forty-five minute, small-group (maximum ten) "Extreme Blast" (daily 11am & 1pm; $75) on an RIB (Rigid Inflatable Boat). At speeds of more than 100kph, the harbour scenery is mostly a blur. **Harbour Jet** (ⓣ1300 887 373, ⓦwww.harbourjet.com) runs the 35-minute "Jet Blast" (daily except Tues noon, 2 & 4pm from Convention Jetty, Darling Harbour; $60), on a boat that roars along at 75kph, accompanied by blasting music.

of the terminal is given over to swanky restaurants and bars with fabulous views – *Aria*, *Wildfire* and *Cruise Bar* among them.

Leading up to the Opera House is the once-controversial **Opera Quays** development, which runs the length of **East Circular Quay**. Since its opening, locals and tourists alike have flocked to promenade along the pleasant colonnaded lower level with its outdoor cafés, bars and bistros, upmarket shops and Dendy Cinema, all looking out to sublime harbour views. The distasteful apartment building above, dubbed "The Toaster" by locals and described by Robert Hughes, the famous expat Australian art critic and historian, as "that dull, brash, intrusive apartment block which now obscures the Opera House from three directions", caused massive protests, but went up anyway, opening in 1999.

Customs House

The railway and the ugly Cahill Expressway block views to the city from Circular Quay, cutting it off from Alfred Street immediately opposite, with its architectural gem, the sandstone and granite **Customs House**. First constructed in 1845, it was redesigned in 1885 by the colonial architect James Barnet to give it its current Classical Revival–style facade, and its interior revamped in 2005. On the ground floor a **City Exhibition Space** keeps pace with the development of Sydney with an up-to-the-minute detailed 500:1 scale model of the city set into the floor under glass and accompanied by a multimedia presentation. Sydney's premier **public library** (Mon–Fri 10am–7pm, Sat 11am–4pm, closed public holidays) is housed on the first three floors, whilst the top floor is the only reminder of the building's previous incarnation, a pricey contemporary brasserie, *Cafe Sydney* (see p.156), which comes with partial Harbour Bridge views.

Museum of Contemporary Art (MCA)

The **Museum of Contemporary Art** (**MCA**; daily 10am–5pm; free; free tours Mon–Fri 11am & 1pm, Sat & Sun noon & 1.30pm; ⓣ02/9252 2400 for details of special exhibitions and events; ⓦwww.mca.com.au), on the western side of Circular Quay with another entrance on George Street (no. 140), was developed out of a bequest by the art collector John Power in the 1940s to Sydney University to purchase international contemporary art. The growing collection finally found a permanent home in 1991 in the former Maritime Services Building, provided for peppercorn rent by the State Government. The striking Deco-style 1950s building is now dedicated to international twentieth-century art, with an eclectic approach encompassing lithographs, sculpture, film, video, drawings, paintings and Aboriginal art, shown in themed temporary exhibitions. The museum's superbly sited, if expensive, café has outdoor tables overlooking the waterfront and Opera House.

The Sydney Opera House

The **Sydney Opera House**, such an icon of Australiana that it almost seems kitsch, is just a short stroll from Circular Quay, by the water's edge on **Bennelong Point**. It's best seen in profile, when its high white roofs, at the same time evocative of full sails and white shells, give the building an almost ethereal quality. Some say the inspiration for the distinctive design came from the simple peeling of an orange into segments, though perhaps Danish architect **Jørn Utzon**'s childhood as the son of a yacht designer had something to do with their sail-like shape – he certainly envisaged a building that would appear to "float" on water. Despite its familiarity, or perhaps precisely because you already feel you know it so well, it's quite breathtaking at first sight. Close up, you can see that the shimmering effect is created by thousands of white tiles.

The feat of structural engineering required to bring to life Utzon's "sculpture", which he compared to a Gothic church and a Mayan temple, made the final price tag AUS$102 million, ten times original estimates. Now almost universally loved and admired, it's hard to believe quite how controversial a project this was during its long haul from plan – as a result of an international competition in the late 1950s – to completion in 1973. For sixteen years construction was plagued by quarrels and scandal, so much so that Utzon, who won the competition in 1957, was forced to resign in 1966. Some put it less kindly and say he was hounded out of the country by politicians – the newly elected Askin government disagreeing over his plans for the completion of the interior – and xenophobic local architects. Seven years and three Australian architects later the interior, which at completion never matched Utzon's vision, was finished: the focal Concert Hall, for instance, was designed by **Peter Hall** and his team. However, Utzon now has a chance to have final say: in 1999, he was appointed as a design consultant to prepare a Statement of Design Principles for the building, which will become the permanent reference for its conservation and development. At the time of writing, Utzon was continuing his consultancy with the Opera House and the first stage of the new masterplan, the **Reception Hall** opened to much acclaim in mid-2004. It represents the only space in the building ever built using the design of the original architect and is occasionally open to the public.

"Opera House" is actually a misnomer: it's really a performing-arts centre, one of the busiest in the world, with five performance venues inside its shells, plus restaurants, cafés and bars, and a stash of upmarket souvenir shops on the lower concourse. The building's initial impetus, in fact, was as a home for the Sydney Symphony Orchestra, and it was designed with the huge **Concert Hall**, seating 2690, as the focal point; the smaller **Opera Theatre** (1547 seats) is used as the Sydney performance base for Opera Australia (seasons June–Nov & Feb–March) and the Australian Ballet (mid-March to May & Nov–Dec). There are three theatrical venues: the **Drama Theatre**, used primarily by the Sydney Theatre Company; The Playhouse, used by travelling performers; and the more intimate **The Studio**. There's plenty of action outside the Opera House, too, with the use of the Mayan temple–inspired **Forecourt** and Monumental Steps as an amphitheatre for free and ticketed concerts – rock, jazz and classical, with a capacity for around five thousand people. Sunday is also a lively day on the forecourt, when the **Tarpeian Markets** (10am–4pm), with an emphasis on Australian crafts, are held.

If you're not content with gazing at the outside, **guided tours** are available from the booking office (discounts for booking online at Ⓦwww.sydneyoperahouse.com): the Front-of-House tour gives an overview of the site, looking at the public areas and discussing the unique architecture (daily 9am–5pm; every 30min; 1hr; $26), while early-morning backstage tours include access to the scenery docks, rehearsal rooms, technical areas and breakfast in the Greenroom (daily 7am; 2hr; $140; bookings on Ⓣ02/9250 7250). These tours also visit the foyer of The Playhouse where two original Utzon models of the Opera House are displayed, alongside a series of small oil paintings depicting the life of **Bennelong**, the Iora tribesman who was initially kidnapped as little more than an Aboriginal "specimen" but later became a much-loved addition to Governor Arthur Phillip's household; Phillip later built a hut for him on what is now the site of the Opera House.

The best way to appreciate the Opera House, of course, is to attend an evening **performance**: the building is particularly stunning when floodlit and, once you're inside, the huge windows come into their own as the dark harbour waters reflect a shimmering night-time city – interval drinks certainly aren't like this anywhere else in the world. You could choose to **eat** at what is considered to be one of Sydney's best restaurants, *Guillame at Bennelong* (see p.156) overlooking the city skyline or take a **drink** at the *Opera Bar* on the lower concourse with outside tables and an affordable all-day menu (see p.165), plus there's a sidewalk café, a bistro and several theatre bars. Good-value **packages**,

△ *The Opera Bar*, outside Sydney Opera House

which include tours, meals, drinks and performances, can be purchased over the Internet or on site (Ⓣ02/9250 7250, Ⓦwww.sydneyoperahouse.com).

The Harbour Bridge

The charismatic **Harbour Bridge**, northeast of Circular Quay, has straddled the channel dividing North and South Sydney since 1932; today, it makes the view from Circular Quay complete. The largest arch bridge in the world when it was built, its construction costs weren't paid off until 1988. There's still a toll ($3) to drive across, payable only when heading south; you can walk or cycle it for free. Pedestrians should head up the steps to the bridge from Cumberland Street, opposite the *Glenmore Hotel* in The Rocks, and walk along the eastern side for fabulous views of the harbour and Opera House (cyclists keep to the western side).

The bridge demands full-time maintenance, protected from rust by continuous painting in trademark steel-grey. Comedian Paul Hogan, of *Crocodile Dundee* fame, worked as a rigger on "the coathanger" before being rescued by a New Faces talent quest in the 1970s. To check out Hoge's vista, you can follow a rigger's route and climb the bridge with **Bridge Climb**, who take specially equipped groups (maximum 12) to the top of the bridge from sunrise until after dark (minimum age 10 and 1.2 metres in height; twilight climbs $249, Mon–Fri day or night climbs $169, Sat–Sun day or night climbs $189; booking advised, particularly for weekends, on Ⓣ02/8274 7777 or Ⓦwww.bridgeclimb.com). Though the experience takes three and a half hours, only two hours is spent on the bridge, gradually ascending and pausing while the guide points out landmarks and offers interesting background snippets. The hour spent checking in and getting kitted up at the "Base" at 5 Cumberland St, The Rocks, and the grey *Star Trek–style* suits designed to blend in with the bridge, make you feel as if you're preparing to go into outer space. It's really not as scary as it looks – harnessed into a cable system, there's no way you can fall off. So that nothing can be dropped onto cars or people below, cameras cannot be taken on the walk (only your glasses are allowed, attached by special cords), limiting scope for one of the world's greatest photo opportunities. Though one group photo on top of the bridge is included in the climb price, the jolly strangers, arms akimbo, crowd out the background. To get a good shot showing yourself with the splendours of the harbour behind, taken by the guide, you'll need to fork out another $16.

If you can't stomach (or afford) the climb, there's a **lookout point** (daily 10am–5pm; $9; Ⓦwww.pylonlookout.com.au; 5min walk from Cumberland St then 200 steps) actually inside the bridge's southeastern pylon where, as well as gazing out across the harbour, you can study a photo exhibition on the bridge's history.

The Rocks

The Rocks, immediately beneath the bridge, is the heart of historic Sydney. On this rocky outcrop between Sydney Cove and Walsh Bay, Captain Arthur Phillip proclaimed the establishment of Sydney Town in 1788, the first permanent European settlement in Australia. Within decades, the area had degenerated into little more than a slum of dingy dwellings, narrow alleys and dubious taverns and brothels. In the 1830s and 1840s, merchants began building fine stone warehouses here, but as the focus for Sydney's shipping industry moved from Circular Quay, the area fell into decline. By the 1870s and 1880s, the notorious Rocks "pushes", gangs of "larrikins" (louts), mugged passers-by and brawled with each other: the narrow street named **Suez Canal** was a favourite place to hide in wait. Some say the name is a shortening of Sewers' Canal, and indeed the area was so filthy that whole streetfronts had to be torn down in 1900 to contain an outbreak of the bubonic plague. It remained a run-down, depressed and depressing quarter until the 1970s, when there were plans to raze the historic cottages, terraces and warehouses to make way for office towers. However, due to the foresight of a radical building-workers' union which opposed the demolition, the restored and renovated **historic quarter** is now one of Sydney's major tourist attractions and, despite a passing resemblance to a historic theme park, it's worth exploring. It's also the best place for souvenir shopping, especially at weekends when The Rocks Market (10am–5pm) takes over the northern end of George and Playfair streets.

There are times, though, when the old atmosphere still seems to prevail: Friday and Saturday nights in The Rocks can be thoroughly drunken, and New Year's Eve is also riotously celebrated here, to the backdrop of fireworks over the harbour. The best time to come for a drink is Sunday afternoon when many of the pubs here offer live jazz or folk music.

Information, tours and transport

The Rocks Discovery Museum (daily 10am–5pm; free) is a good starting point and offers background information and displays of its rich history, from the lives of the original Cadigal inhabitants to the 1970s protests that helped preserve the area from major redevelopment. The small museum is tucked away down Kendall Lane in a restored 1850s sandstone warehouse facing the Rocks Centre, a busy arcade of boutique shops and cafés. Above the arcade, on the corner of Argyle and Playfair streets, is the **Sydney Visitor Centre** (daily 9.30am–5.30pm; Ⓣ02/9240 8788, Ⓦwww.sydneyvisitorcentre.com); amongst the heaps of brochures on offer here, make sure you pick up *The Rocks Map*, essential material for finding your way around the meandering streets. Another great introduction to the area is the long-running **The Rocks Walking Tours**, starting from 23 Playfair St, Rocks Square (Mon–Fri 10.30am, 12.30pm & 2.30pm, Jan 10.30am & 2.30pm only, Sat & Sun 11.30am & 2pm; 1hr 30min; $19; Ⓣ02/9247 6678, Ⓦwww.rockswalkingtours.com.au).

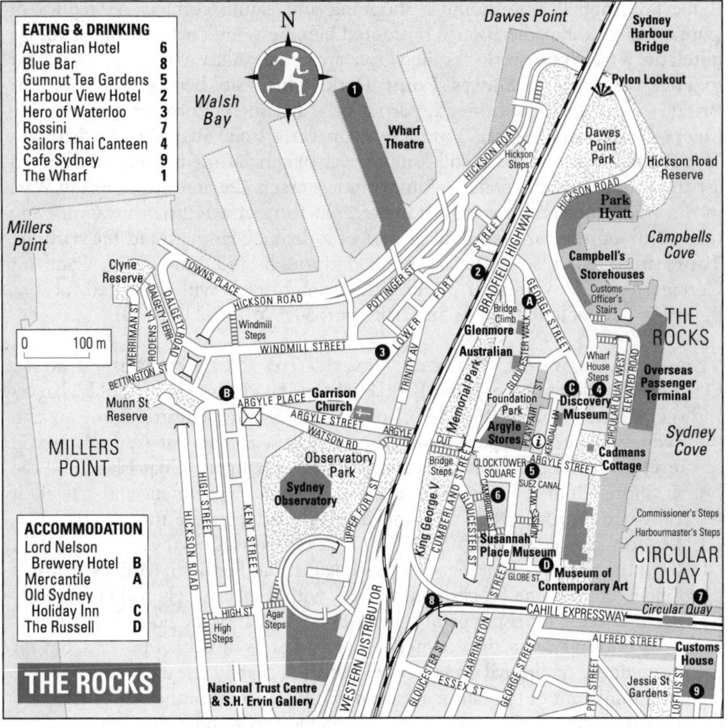

The corner of Argyle and Kent streets, Millers Point, is a terminus for several useful **bus routes**; aim to head here through The Rocks and then catch a bus back: routes #431–434 go along George Street to Railway Square and from there to various locations including Glebe and Balmain, while #339 goes to the eastern beaches suburb of Clovelly via George Street in the city and Surry Hills.

From Cadmans Cottage to Dawes Point Park

Exploring the narrow alleys and streets hewn out of the original rocky spur, which involves climbing and descending several stairs and cuts to different levels, is the area's chief delight. Across George Street from the Discovery Museum, in a small tree-filled reserve, is **Cadmans Cottage**, the oldest private house still standing in Sydney, built in 1816 for John Cadman, ex-convict and Government coxswain (Mon–Fri 9.30am–4.30pm, Sat & Sun 10am–4.30pm; free). You can poke around a few rooms to see how the original settlers lived. Also housed in the cottage is the **National Parks and Wildlife Service** bookshop and information centre (same hours; ⓣ02/9247 5033, ⓦwww.nationalparks.nsw.gov.au), providing information about the Sydney Harbour National Park and taking bookings for trips to Fort Denison and other harbour islands that are part of the park.

From the cottage, head north along the waterfront walkway past the Overseas Passenger Terminal to **Campbell's Cove**, where the beautifully restored 1830s **Campbell's Storehouses**, once part of the private wharf of the merchant

Robert Campbell, now house a shopping and eating complex. A replica of Captain Bligh's ship, the *Bounty*, is moored here between cruises, while a luxury hotel, the *Park Hyatt*, overlooks the whole area. The walkway continues adjacent to Hickson Road to **Dawes Point Park**, which sits beneath the Harbour Bridge offering fantastic views, particularly at sunset. Looking out past the Opera House, you can see **Fort Denison** on a small island in the harbour: "Pinchgut", as the island is still known, was originally used as a special prison for the tough nuts the penal colony couldn't crack. During the Crimean Wars in the mid-nineteenth century, however, old fears of a Russian invasion were rekindled and the fort was built as part of a defence ring around the harbour. **Tours** from Circular Quay are booked through, and leave from, Cadmans Cottage (daily 11.45am; 3hr 30min; $22; brunch tours with a cooked meal in the fort's café included, Sat & Sun 9am; 3hr; $47; ⓣ02/9247 5033).

The old wharves, Millers Point and Observatory Park

On the west side of Dawes Point Park, Hickson Road passes several old wharves and the **Wharf Theatre** (Pier 4/5), home to the Sydney Theatre Company and the Sydney Dance Company. From the restaurant and its bar (see p.173) you can revel in the sublime view across Walsh Bay to Balmain, Goat Island and the North Shore. Guided tours, including the costume department and a peek at set construction, run on the first and third Thursday of the month (10.30am; 1hr; $8; bookings essential; ⓣ02/9250 1777, ⓦwww.sydneytheatre.com.au).

Beyond the wharves, looking west towards Darling Harbour, **Millers Point** is a reminder of how The Rocks used to be – with a surprisingly real community feel so close to the tourist hype of The Rocks, as much of the housing is government- or housing association-owned. The area has its upmarket pockets, but for the moment the traditional street-corner pubs and shabby terraced houses on the hill are reminiscent of the raffish atmosphere once typical of the whole area, and the mostly peaceful residential streets are a delight to wander through.

You can reach the area through the Argyle Cut (see opposite) or from the end of George Street, heading onto Lower Fort Street, where you could stop for a drink at the **Hero of Waterloo** at no. 81 (see p.165), built from sandstone excavated from the Argyle Cut in 1844, before peeking in at the **Garrison Church** (daily 9am–5pm) on the corner of Argyle Street, the place of worship for the military stationed at Dawes Point fort (the fort was demolished in the 1920s to make way for the Harbour Bridge) from the 1840s. Beside the church, **Argyle Place** has some of the area's prettiest old terrace houses.

From here, walk up the steps on Argyle Street opposite the church to **Observatory Park** with its shady Moreton Bay figs, park benches and lawns, for a marvellous hilltop view over the whole harbour in all its different aspects – glitzy Darling Harbour, and the newer Anzac Bridge in one direction and the older Harbour Bridge, with gritty container terminals, and ferries gliding by, in the other; on a rainy day, you can enjoy it from the bandstand that dominates the park. It's also easy to reach the park from the **Bridge Stairs** off Cumberland Street by the Argyle Cut.

The Italianate-style **Sydney Observatory** from which the park takes its name marked the beginning of an accurate time standard for the city when it opened in 1858, calculating the correct time from the stars and signalling it to Martin Place's GPO and the ships in the harbour by the dropping of a time ball in its tower at 1pm every day – a custom that still continues. Set amongst some very pretty gardens, the Observatory is now a **museum of astronomy** (daily 10am–5pm; free; ⓦwww.sydneyobservatory.com.au). A large section is devoted to the Transit of Venus, a rare astronomical event occurring about twice every century; it was the observation of this that prompted Captain Cook's 1769 voyage. The extensive exhibition of astronomical equipment, both obsolete and high-tech, includes the (still-working) telescope installed under the copper dome to observe the 1874 Transit of Venus. Another highlight, in the "Stars of the Southern Sky" section, are three animated videos of Aboriginal creation stories, retellings of how the stars came to be, from the Milky Way to Orion. Every evening, you can view the sky through telescopes and learn about the Southern Cross and other southern constellations (times vary with season; 2hr tours include a lecture, film, exhibition, guided view of the telescopes and a look at the sky, weather permitting; $15; booking essential on ⓣ02/9217 0485, usually up to a week in advance); the small planetarium is only used during night visits when the sky is not clear enough for observation.

Argyle Cut and Gloucester Street

From the Observatory, head back to Argyle Street and walk under Bradfield Highway to the **Argyle Cut**, which slices through solid stone connecting Millers Point and Circular Quay. The cut took sixteen years to complete, carved first with chisel and hammer by convict chain-gangs who began the work in 1843; when transportation ended ten years later the tunnel was still unfinished, and it took hired hands to complete it in 1859.

Once you've passed through the cut, look out for the **Argyle Steps**, which lead back up to Cumberland Street. The Harbour Bridge is accessible by foot from here via the pylon staircase or you can sit back and enjoy the splendid views from a couple of fine old boozers, the *Glenmore* and the *Australian*. From the latter, head down **Gloucester Street**; at nos. 58–64 is the **Susannah Place Museum** (Jan daily 10am–5pm; Feb–Dec Sat & Sun 10am–5pm; $8; ⓦwww.hht.net.au), a row of four brick terraces built in 1844 and occupied by householders until 1990. It's now a "house museum" (including a re-created 1915 corner store), which conserves the domestic history of Sydney's working class. There's a fascinating archeological site seen as you exit the museum, which has been in excavation since 1994. The earliest buildings date back to 1795 and the site has revealed over three quarters of a million artefacts – the steps, paths and walls that the early colonizers carved out from the rock are clearly visible.

City Centre

From Circular Quay south as far as King Street is Sydney's **Central Business District**, often referred to as the **CBD**, with **Martin Place** as its commercial nerve-centre. A pedestrian mall stretching from George Street to Macquarie Street, lined with imposing banks and investment companies, Martin Place has its less serious moments at summer lunchtimes, when street performances are held at the little amphitheatre, and all-year-round stalls of flower- and fruit-sellers add some colour. The vast **General Post Office (GPO)**, built between 1865 and 1887 with its landmark clock-tower added in 1900, broods over the George Street end in all its Victorian-era pomp. The upper floors have been incorporated into part of a five-star luxury hotel, the *Westin Sydney*; the rest of the hotel resides in the 31-storey tower behind. The old building and the new tower meet in the grand Atrium Courtyard, on the lower ground floor, with its restaurants, bars, classy designer stores, and the **GPO Store**, a gastronome's delight featuring a butchers', fish shop, deli, cheese room, wine merchant and greengrocer. The other end of Martin Place emerges opposite the old civic buildings on lower Macquarie Street. The cramped streets of the CBD itself, overshadowed by office buildings, have little to offer as you stroll through, though a crowd often gathers outside the **Australian Stock Exchange**, opposite Australia Square at 20 Bond St, to gaze at the computerized display of stocks and shares through the glass of the ground floor.

Museum of Sydney

North of Martin Place, on the corner of Bridge and Phillip streets, stands the **Museum of Sydney** (daily 9.30am–5pm; $10; ⓣ02/9251 5988 for exhibition details, ⓦwww.hht.net.au). The site itself is the reason for the museum's existence, for here from 1983 a ten-year archeological dig unearthed the foundations of the first Government House built by Governor Phillip in 1788, which was home to eight subsequent governors of New South Wales before being demolished in 1846. The museum is totally original in its approach, presenting history in an interactive manner, through exhibitions, film, photography and multimedia. A key feature of the museum are the special exhibitions – about four each year – so it's worth finding out what's on before you go.

First Government Place, a public square in front of the museum, preserves the site of the original Government House: its foundations are marked out in different-coloured sandstone on the pavement. The site is best appreciated from the glass lookout on level 3 of the museum, which is also the logical place to start your tour. From up high, you'll notice 29 erect poles near the entrance, **The Edge of the Trees**, an emotive sculptural installation, which attempts to convey the complexity of a shared history that began in 1788. Each pole represents one of the original 29 clans that lived in the greater Sydney area, and you can't help but notice the symbolism of the poles, standing quietly to one side, overlooking the comings and goings of Government House. Beside the glass lookout on level 3 is a small but evocative gallery with Aboriginal artefacts, early European writings about their encounters, and a fascinating contemporary video by Aboriginal filmmaker Michael Riley reflecting the clan's own perspective of colonization. On the same level, a large area is devoted to some rather wonderful **panoramas** highlighting Sydney's evolution into a city. At the dark and creepy **Bond Store** on level 2, holographic "ghosts" relate tales of old Sydney as an ocean port.

There's also an excellent **gift shop** with a wide range of photos, artworks and books on Sydney and the expensive, licensed *MOS* **café** on First Government Place.

Sydney Architecture Walks offers various **walking tours**, led by young architects, leaving from here every Wednesday and Saturday at 10.30am (2hr; $25; bookings ⓣ02/8239 2211, ⓦwww.sydneyarchitecture.org).

Sydney Sculpture Walk

The specially commissioned artworks of the **Sydney Sculpture Walk** – a City of Sydney Council initiative for the 2000 Olympics and the 2001 Centenary of Federation – form a circuit from the Royal Botanic Gardens, through The Domain, Cook and Phillip Park, the streets of the CBD, Hyde Park and East Circular Quay. One of the most striking of the ten site-specific pieces is Anne Graham's *Passage*, at the eastern end of Martin Place. At timed intervals, a fine mist emerges from grilles marking the outlines of an early colonial home that once stood here, creating a ghostly house on still days. A map showing the sculpture sites is available from Sydney Town Hall (p.119) or the City Exhibition Space (p.111), or there are details at ⓦwww.cityofsydney.nsw.gov.au.

King Street to Liverpool Street

Further south from Martin Place, the streets get a little more interesting. The rectangle between Elizabeth, King, George and Park streets is Sydney's prime shopping area, with a number of beautifully restored **Victorian arcades** (the Imperial Arcade, Strand Arcade and Queen Victoria Building are all worth a look) and Sydney's two **department stores**, the very upmarket David Jones on the corner of Market and Elizabeth streets, established over 160 years ago, and Myers on Pitt Street Mall.

The landmark **Sydney Tower**, or "Centrepoint" as it is still known to the locals, on the corner of Market and Pitt streets, a giant golden gearstick thrusting up 305m, is the tallest poppy in the Sydney skyline. The 360-degree view from the top is especially fine at sunset, and on clear days you can even see the Blue Mountains, 100km away. There are three ways to enjoy the views: **Tower & OzTrek** (daily 9am–10.30pm, Sat until 11.30pm; $24; Ⓦwww.sydneytoweroztrek.com.au) combines entry to the glass-fronted observation level at the top of the tower with a tacky forty-minute "virtual ride" introduction to a clichéd Australia on entry level; **Skywalk** (daily 9am–10pm; day or night walk $109, dusk walk $139; Ⓦwww.skywalk.com.au) is a tamer but higher version of the Harbour Bridge walk where you venture out to two glass-floored platforms, harnessed to external walkways – unfortunately, cameras are not permitted for safety reasons; alternatively, you can see the same view, without the crowds and the entry ticket, at the **revolving restaurants** below the observation level; the tower revolution takes about seventy minutes and nearly all the tables are by the windows (bookings Ⓣ02/8223 3800; level 1 restaurant three-course dinner $75, Tues–Sat from 5.30pm; level 2 restaurant buffet, Mon–Sat lunch $42.50, Sun lunch $49.50, Mon–Sun dinner $52.50).

Nearby, several fine old buildings – the State Theatre, the Queen Victoria Building and the Town Hall – provide a pointed contrast. If heaven has a hallway, it surely must resemble that of the restored **State Theatre**, just across from the Pitt Street Mall at 49 Market St. Step inside and take a look at the ornate and glorious interior of this picture palace opened in 1929 – a lavishly painted, gilded and sculpted corridor leads to the lush, red and wood-panelled foyer. To see more of the interior, you'll need to attend the Sydney Film Festival (see p.174) or other events held here, such as concerts and drama, or you can take a guided tour (monthly 10.30am; 1hr 30 min; $15). Otherwise, pop into the beautiful little *Retro Cafe*, adjacent, for a coffee.

The stately **Queen Victoria Building** (abbreviated by locals to the QVB), taking up the block bounded by Market, Druitt, George and York streets, is another of Sydney's finest. Stern and matronly, a huge statue of Queen Victoria herself sits outside the magnificent building. Built as a market hall in 1898, two years before her death, the long-neglected building was beautifully restored and reborn in 1986 as an upmarket shopping mall with a focus on fashion: from the basement up, the four levels become progressively exclusive (shopping hours Mon–Sat 9am–6pm, Thurs until 9pm, Sun 11am–5pm; building open 24hr). The interior is magnificent, with its beautiful woodwork, gallery levels and antique lifts; Charles I is beheaded on the hour, every hour, by figurines on the ground-floor mechanical clock. From Town Hall station you can walk right through the basement level (mainly bustling food stalls) and continue via Sydney Central Plaza to Myers Department Store, emerging on Pitt Street without having to go outside.

In the realm of architectural excess, however, the **Town Hall** is king – you'll find it across from the QVB on the corner of George and Druitt streets. It was built during the boom years of the 1870s and 1880s as a homage to Victorian England; the huge organ inside its Centennial Hall gives it the air of a secular cathedral. Throughout the interior, different styles of ornamentation compete in a riot of colour and detail; the splendidly dignified toilets are a must-see. Concerts and theatre performances (see p.172) set off the splendiferous interior perfectly.

South to Chinatown

Between Town Hall and Central Station, **George Street** becomes increasingly downmarket, with sex shops side by side with discount stores. Along the way

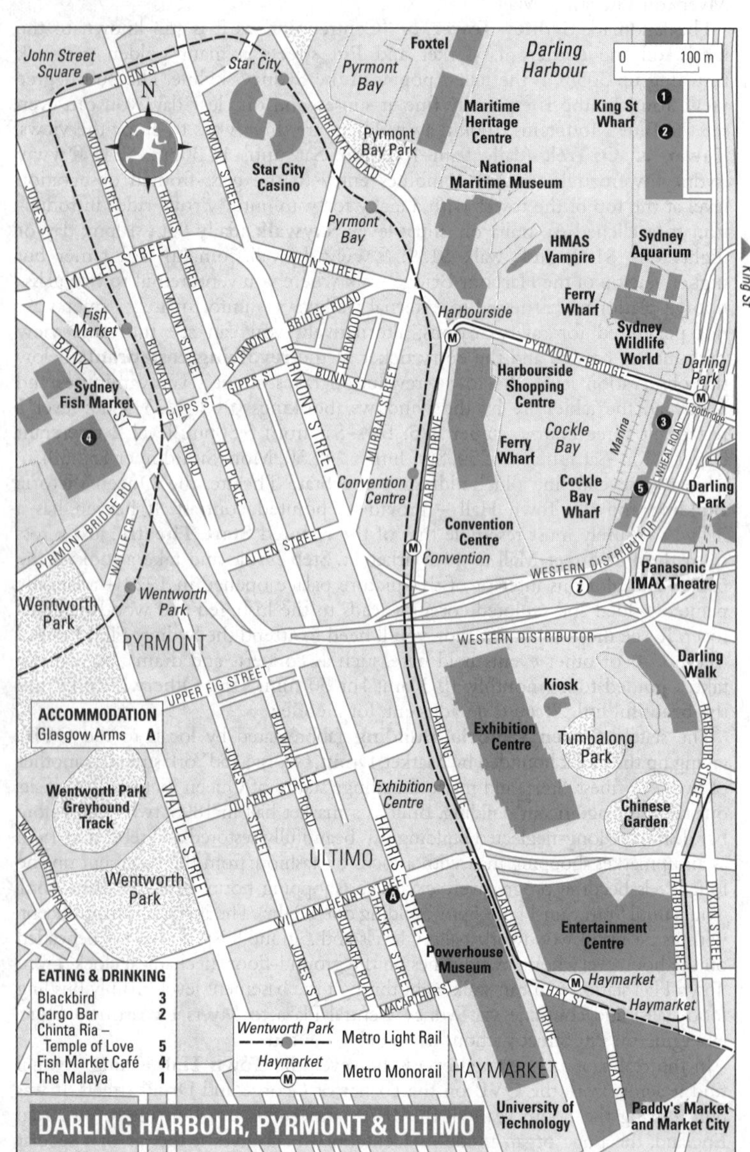

you'll pass Chinatown, in the area known as **Haymarket**, and a little further west is Darling Harbour. The short stretch between the Town Hall and Liverpool Street is for the most part teenage territory, a frenetic zone of **multi-screen cinemas**, pinball halls and fast-food joints, though the **Metro Theatre** is one of Sydney's best live-music venues (see p.167) and *Planet Hollywood* also attracts a keen stream of youngsters and tourists alike. The stretch is trouble-prone on Friday and Saturday nights when there are pleasanter places to catch a film (see cinema listings, p.173). Things change pace at Liverpool Street, where Sydney's **Spanish Corner** consists of a clutch of Spanish restaurants and the *Spanish Club*.

Sydney's **Chinatown** is a more full-blooded affair than Spanish Corner and probably the most active of the ethnic enclaves in the city. Through the ornate Chinese gates, **Dixon Street** is the main drag, buzzing day and night as people crowd into numerous restaurants, pubs, cafés, cinemas, food stalls and Asian grocery stores. Towards the end of January or in the first weeks of February, Chinese New Year is celebrated here with gusto: traditional dragon and lion dances, food festivals and musical entertainment compete with the noise and smoke from strings of Chinese crackers. Friday nights are also a good time to visit, when a **night market** takes over Dixon and Little Hay streets (6–11pm). For a calmer retreat, on the edge of Chinatown, at the southern fringes of Darling Harbour, is the serene **Chinese Garden** (see p.128).

The area immediately south of Chinatown is enlivened by Sydney's oldest market, bustling **Paddy's Market** (Thurs–Sun 9am–5pm), in its undercover home in between Thomas and Quay streets. It's a good place to buy cheap vegetables, seafood, clothes, cheap souvenirs and bric-a-brac. Above Paddy's, the multilevel **Market City Shopping Centre** has a very modern Asian feel as well as some excellent outlet stores for discounted fashion. There's also a first-rate Asian food court, on the top floor next to the Reading multiscreen cinema.

The historic precinct: Hyde Park, College Street and Macquarie Street

Lachlan Macquarie, reformist governor of New South Wales between 1809 and 1821, gave the early settlement its first imposing public buildings, clustered on the southern half of his namesake Macquarie Street. He had a vision of an elegant, prosperous city – although the Imperial Office in London didn't share his enthusiasm for expensive civic projects. Refused both money and expertise, Macquarie was forced to be resourceful: many of the city's finest buildings were designed by the ex-convict architect Francis Greenway and paid for with rum money, the proceeds of a monopoly on liquor sales. Hyde Park was fenced off by Governor Macquarie in 1810 to mark the outskirts of his township, and with its war memorials and church, and peripheral museum and Catholic cathedral, is still very much a formal city park.

Hyde Park

From the Town Hall, it's a short walk east to **Hyde Park** along Park Street, which divides the park into two sections, with the Anzac Memorial in the southern half, and the Sandringham Memorial Gardens and Archibald Fountain in the north, overlooked by St James's Church across the northern boundary. From Queens Square, **St James's Church** (daily 9am–5pm; Wednesday concert 1.15pm; $5) marks the entry to the park – the Anglican church, completed in 1824, is Sydney's oldest existing place of worship. It was one of Macquarie's schemes built to ex-convict Greenway's design, and the architect originally planned it as a courthouse – you can see how the simple design was converted into a graceful church. Pop into the crypt to see the richly coloured **Children's Chapel** mural painted in the 1930s. Behind St James train station, the **Archibald Fountain** commemorates the association of Australia and France during World War I; near here is a **giant chess set** where you can challenge the locals to a match. Further south near Park Street, the Sandringham Memorial Gardens also commemorate Australia's war dead, but the most potent of these monuments is the **Anzac War Memorial** at the southern end of the park (daily 9am–4.30pm; free). Fronted by the tree-lined Pool of Remembrance, the thirty-metre-high cenotaph, unveiled in 1934, is classic Art Deco right down to the detail of Raynor Hoff's stylized soldier figures solemnly decorating the exterior.

College Street: the Australian Museum and St Mary's Cathedral

Facing Hyde Park across College Street, at the junction of William Street as it heads up to Kings Cross, the **Australian Museum** (daily 9.30am–5pm; 45min tours 11am & 2pm; $10, special exhibitions extra; Ⓦwww.austmus.gov.au) is primarily a museum of natural history, with an interest in human evolution and Aboriginal culture and history. The collection was founded in 1827, but the actual building, a grand sandstone affair with a facade of Corinthian pillars, wasn't fully finished until the 1860s and was extended in the 1980s. The core of the old museum is the three levels of the **Long Gallery**, Australia's first exhibition gallery, opened in 1855 to a public keen to gawk at the colony's curiosities. Many of the classic displays of the following hundred years remain here, Heritage-listed, contrasting with a very modern approach in the rest of the museum.

On the **ground floor**, the impressive **Indigenous Australian** exhibition looks at the history of Australia's Aboriginal people from the Dreamtime to more contemporary issues of the "stolen generation" and the freedom rides, a series of protests that took place in 1965 by a bus full of protesters travelling around rural NSW towns highlighting the racial discrimination experienced by Aboriginal people. The ground-floor level houses the **Skeletons** exhibit, where you can see a skeletal human going through the motions of riding a bicycle, for example. Level 1 is devoted to **minerals**, but far more exciting are the disparate collections on level 2 – especially the **Birds** and **Insects** exhibit, which includes chilling contextual displays of dangerous spiders such as redbacks and funnel-webs. In the newer section, **Search and Discover** is aimed at both adults and children, a flora and fauna identification centre with Internet access and books to consult, while the **Human Evolution** gallery traces the development of fossil evidence worldwide and ends with an exploration of archeological evidence of Aboriginal occupation of Australia. A separate section, **More Than Dinosaurs**, deals with fossil skeletons of dinosaurs and giant marsupials: best of all is the model of the largest of Australia's megafauna, the wombat-like Diprotodon, which may have roamed the mainland as recently as ten thousand years ago.

Up College Street is Catholic **St Mary's Cathedral** (daily 6.30am–7.30pm, Sat 8am–6.30pm; free tours Sun noon; 1hr), overlooking the northeast corner of Hyde Park. The huge Gothic-style church opened in 1882, though the foundation stone was laid in 1821. In 1999, the cathedral at last gained the twin stone spires originally planned for the two southern towers by architect William Wardell in 1865. The cathedral also acquired an impressive new forecourt – a pedestrianized terrace with fountains and pools – with the consolidation of two traffic-isolated parks into the large **Cook and Phillip Park**. Its **recreation centre** (Mon–Fri 6am–10pm, Sat & Sun 7am–8pm; swim $6) has a fifty-metre swimming pool, gym and an excellent vegetarian restaurant. The remodelling also created a green link to The Domain.

Macquarie Street

Macquarie Street neatly divides business from pleasure, separating the office towers and cramped streets of the CBD from the open spaces of The Domain. The southern end of Governor Macquarie's namesake street is lined with the grand edifices that were the result of his dreams for a stately city: Hyde Park Barracks, Parliament House, the State Library, and the hospital he and his wife designed. The new Sydney – wealthy and international – shows itself on the corner of Bent and Macquarie streets in the curved glass sails of the 41-floor Aurora Place tower, designed by Italian architect Renzo Piano, co-creator of the extraordinary Georges Pompidou Centre in Paris.

At the southern end of the street, bordering Hyde Park, the **Hyde Park Barracks** (daily 9.30am–5pm; $10), designed as convict lodgings by ex-convict Francis Greenway, was built in 1816, again without permission from London, to house six hundred male convicts. Now a museum of the social and architectural history of Sydney, it's a great place to visit for a taste of convict life during the early years of the colony: start at the top floor, where you can swing in recreations of the prisoners' rough hammocks. Computer terminals allow you to search for information on a selection of convicts' history and background – several of those logged were American sailors nabbed for misdeeds while in Dublin or English ports (look up poor William Pink). After the Barracks closed in 1848, the building was used to house single immigrant women, many of them Irish, escaping the potato famine; an exhibition looks at their lives, and there's a moving monument in the grounds erected by the local Irish community. Look out, too, for the excellent temporary historical exhibitions (Ⓣ02/8239 2311 for details).

Next door, sandstone **Sydney Hospital**, the so-called "Rum Hospital", funded by liquor-trade profits, was Macquarie's first enterprise, commissioned in 1814 and therefore one of the oldest buildings in Australia. From here it's a short walk through the grounds to The Domain and across to the Art Gallery of New South Wales. One of the original wings of the hospital is now **NSW Parliament House** (Mon–Fri 9am–4pm; Ⓣ02/9230 2111 or Ⓦwww.parliament.nsw.gov.au to check for tour times), where as early as 1829 local councils called by the governor started to meet, making it by some way the oldest parliament building in Australia. Changing exhibitions in the foyer represent community or public-sector interests and range from painting, craft and sculpture to excellent photographic displays. You can listen in on Question Time (Tues–Thurs 2.15pm) when the parliament is sitting; book tickets in advance by telephone. The other wing was converted into a branch of the **Royal Mint** in response to the first Australian goldrush, and for some time served as a museum of gold mining; most of the building has now been taken over by NSW Historic Houses Trust offices, but a café (Mon–Fri 9am–4pm) extends onto the balcony overlooking Macquarie Street, and some interpretive boards detail the Mint's history.

The **State Library of New South Wales** (Mon–Fri 9am–9pm, Sat & Sun 11am–5pm, Mitchell Library closed Sun; free guided tours Tues 11am & Thurs 2pm) completes the row of public buildings on the eastern side of Macquarie Street. This complex of old and new edifices includes the 1906 sandstone **Mitchell Library**, with an imposing Neoclassical facade gazing across to the verdant Royal Botanic Gardens. Its archive of old maps, illustrations and records relating to the early days of white settlement and exploration in Australia includes the original **Tasman Map**, drawn by the Dutch explorer Abel Tasman in the 1640s. The floor-mosaic in the foyer replicates his curious map of the continent, still without an east coast, and its northern extremity joined to Papua New Guinea. A glass walkway links the library with the modern building housing the General Reference Library. Free exhibitions relating to Australian history, art, photography and literature are a common feature of its vestibules, while lectures, films and video shows take place regularly in the **Metcalfe Auditorium**, which holds free and ticketed events (ⓣ02/9273 1414 or ⓦwww.sl.nsw.gov.au for details and bookings). The glass-roofed **café** in the basement (Mon–Fri noon–3pm, Sat & Sun 11am–3.30pm) is a relaxing, inexpensive spot for lunch or just coffee and cake. It's also worth browsing in the library's **bookshop** on the ground floor for an impressive collection of Australia-related tomes.

The Domain and the Royal Botanic Gardens

The Cook and Phillip Park fills in the green gap between Hyde Park and **The Domain**, a much larger, plainer open space that stretches from behind the historic precinct on Macquarie Street to the waterfront, divided from the Botanic Gardens by the ugly Cahill Expressway and Mrs Macquarie's Road. In the early days of the settlement, The Domain was the governor's private park; now it's a popular place for a stroll or a picnic, with the Art Gallery of New South Wales, an outdoor swimming pool and Mrs Macquarie's Chair to provide distraction. On Sundays, assorted cranks and revolutionaries assemble here for Speakers' Corner, and every January thousands of people gather on the lawns to enjoy the free open-air concerts of the Sydney Festival (see p.176).

Art Gallery of New South Wales

Beyond St Mary's Cathedral, Art Gallery Road runs through The Domain to the **Art Gallery of New South Wales** (daily 10am–5pm, Wed till 9pm; free except for special exhibitions; free general tours Tues–Sun 11am, 1 & 2pm, Mon 1 & 2pm; ⓣ02/9225 1744 or ⓦwww.artgallery.nsw.gov.au), whose collection was established in 1874. The original part of the building (1897) is an imposing Neoclassical structure with a facade inscribed with the names of important Renaissance artists, and principally contains the large collection of European art dating from the eleventh century to the twentieth; extensions were added in 1988, doubling the gallery space and providing a home for mainly Australian art. On lower level 3 is the **Yiribana Gallery**, devoted to the art and cultural artefacts of Aboriginal and Torres Strait Islanders; one of the most striking exhibits is the **Pukumani Grave Posts**, carved by the Tiwi people of Melville Island. There's also a highly recommended free one-hour tour of the indigenous collection (Tues–Sun 11am). Other highlights include some classic **Australian paintings** on level 4: Tom Roberts' romanticized shearing-shed scene *The Golden Fleece* (1894) and an altogether less idyllic look at rural Australia in Russell Drysdale's *Sofala* (1947), a depressing vision of a drought-stricken town.

In addition to the galleries, there's an auditorium used for art lectures, an excellent bookshop, a coffee shop on level 2, and a restaurant on level 5 that attracts Sydneysiders for its food and atmosphere.

Mrs Macquarie's Chair and "The Boy"

Beyond the Art Gallery is the beginning of one of Sydney's most popular jogging routes – Mrs Macquarie's Road, built in 1816 at the urging of the governor's wife, Elizabeth. The road curves down from Art Gallery Road to Mrs

Macquarie's Point, which separates idyllic Farm Cove from the grittier Woolloomooloo Bay. At the end is the celebrated lookout point known as **Mrs Macquarie's Chair**, a seat fashioned out of the rock. From here, Elizabeth could admire her favourite view of the harbour on her daily walk in what was then the governor's private park. On the route down to the point, the **Andrew "Boy" Charlton Pool** is an open-air, chlorinated saltwater swimming pool safely isolated from the harbour waters (daily Sept–May 6am–8pm; $5.20) on the Woolloomooloo side of the promontory, with views across to the engrossingly functional Garden Island Naval Depot. "The Boy", as the locals fondly call it, was named after the gold-medal-winning Manly swimmer, who turned 17 during the 1924 Paris Olympics. It's a popular hangout for trendy Darlinghurst types and sun-worshipping gays.

The Royal Botanic Gardens

The **Royal Botanic Gardens** (daily 7am–sunset; free; ⓦ www.rbgsyd.nsw.gov.au), established in 1816, occupy the area between this strip of The Domain and the Sydney Opera House, around the headland on Farm Cove where the first white settlers struggled to grow vegetables for the hungry colony. While duck ponds, a romantic rose garden and fragrant herb garden strike a very English air, look out for native birds and, at dusk, the fruit bats flying overhead (hundreds of the giant bats hang by day in the Palm Grove area near the restaurant) as the nocturnal possums begin to stir. There are examples of trees and plants from all over the world, although it's the huge, gnarled native Moreton Bay figs that stand out. The gardens provide some of the most stunning **views** of Sydney Harbour, particularly the section between Mrs Macquarie's Point and Main Pond, and are always crowded with workers at lunchtime, picnickers on fine weekends, and lovers entwined beneath the trees.

Many **paths** run through the gardens. A popular and speedy route (roughly 15min) is to start at the northern gates near the Opera House and stroll along the waterfront path. Once you've passed through a second set of gates, walk up the **Fleet Steps** to Mrs Macquarie's Chair (see above) with fantastic views of the city skyline through trees. Within the northern boundaries of the park, the sandstone mansion glimpsed through a garden and enclosure is the **Government House** (built 1837–45), seat of the governor of New South Wales, and still used for official engagements by the governor, who now lives in a private residence. The stately interior has limited opening hours (free guided tour every half-hour Fri–Sun 10.30am–3pm; 45min; ⓣ 02/9931 5222 or ⓦ www.hht.net.au for more details) but you are free to roam the grounds (daily 10am–4pm). Further south, just inside the gardens at the end of Bridge Street, the **Conservatorium of Music** is housed in what was intended to be the servants' quarters and stables of Government House. Public opinion in 1821, however, deemed the imposing castellated building far too grand for such a purpose and a complete conversion, including the addition of a concert hall, gave it a loftier aim of training the colony's future musicians.

Below the Conservatorium, the remaining southern area of the gardens has a herb garden, the **Tropical Centre** (daily 10am–4.40pm; $2.20), where a striking glass pyramid and adjacent glass arc respectively house native tropical plants and exotics, a popular café at Palm Grove Centre and, next door, a small **visitor information outlet** (daily 10am–2.30pm) where free **guided tours** of the gardens commence (daily 10.30am; 1hr 30min; additional tours March–Nov 1pm; 1hr). If you're short of time, the **Trackless Train** runs through the gardens every thirty minutes (daily 9.30am–5pm; all-day hop-on-hop-off service $10) between the visitor centre and the entrance near the Opera House.

Darling Harbour and around

Darling Harbour, once a grimy industrial docks area, lay moribund until the 1980s, when the State Government chose to pump millions of dollars into the regeneration of this prime city real estate as part of the 1988 Bicentenary Project. The huge redevelopment scheme around Cockle Bay, which opened in 1988, included the building of the above-ground monorail – one of only a few

△ Darling Harbour

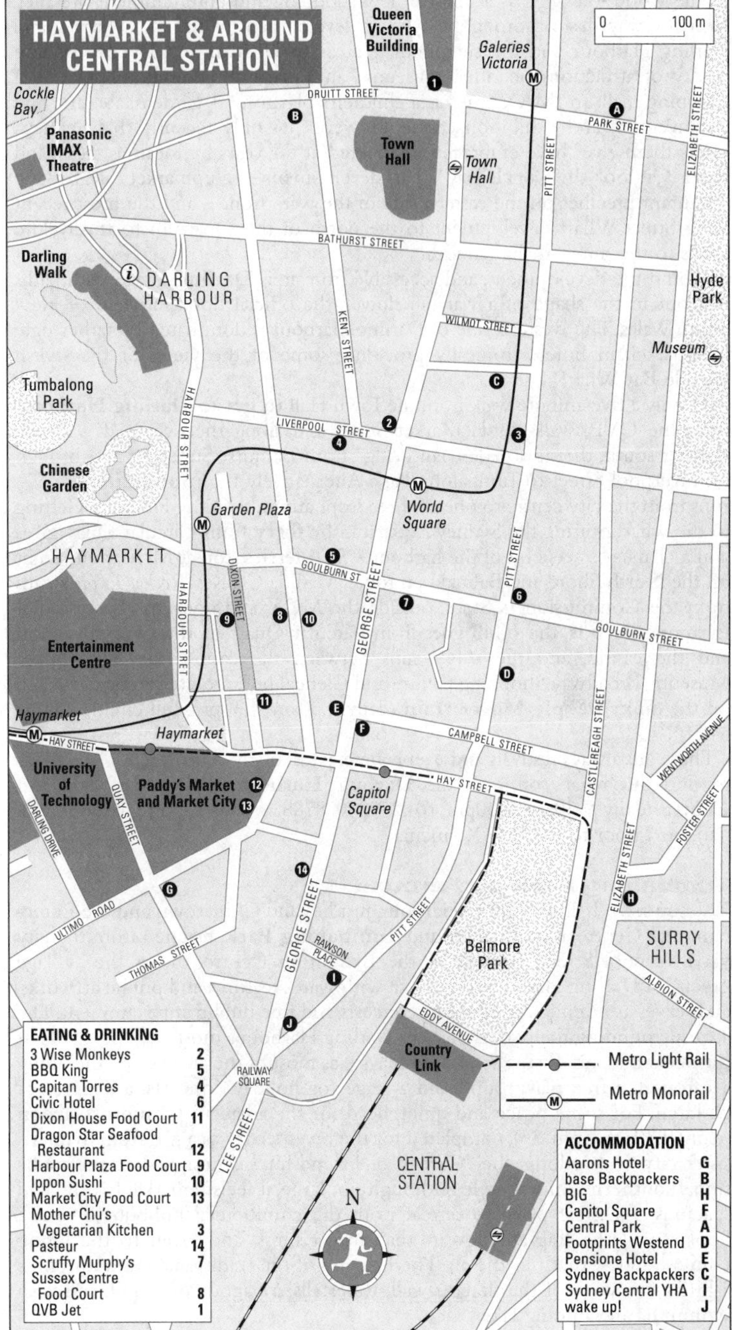

HAYMARKET & AROUND CENTRAL STATION
Queen Victoria Building
Galeries Victoria
0 100 m
Cockle Bay
Panasonic IMAX Theatre
DRUITT STREET
PARK STREET
Town Hall
Town Hall
PITT STREET
ELIZABETH STREET
BATHURST STREET
Darling Walk
DARLING HARBOUR
Hyde Park
KENT STREET
WILMOT STREET
Museum
Tumbalong Park
HARBOUR STREET
LIVERPOOL STREET
Chinese Garden
World Square
Garden Plaza
HAYMARKET
DIXON STREET
GOULBURN ST
GEORGE STREET
PITT STREET
GOULBURN STREET
Entertainment Centre
HARBOUR STREET
CASTLEREAGH STREET
Haymarket
Haymarket
HAY STREET
CAMPBELL STREET
WENTWORTH AVENUE
University of Technology
Paddy's Market and Market City
Capitol Square
HAY STREET
DARLING DRIVE
QUAY STREET
FOSTER STREET
ELIZABETH STREET
ULTIMO ROAD
GEORGE STREET
PITT STREET
RAWSON PLACE
Belmore Park
SURRY HILLS
THOMAS STREET
ALBION STREET
EDDY AVENUE
Country Link
RAILWAY SQUARE
Metro Light Rail
Metro Monorail
LEE STREET
CENTRAL STATION
N
EATING & DRINKING
3 Wise Monkeys 2
BBQ King 5
Capitan Torres 4
Civic Hotel 6
Dixon House Food Court 11
Dragon Star Seafood Restaurant 12
Harbour Plaza Food Court 9
Ippon Sushi 10
Market City Food Court 13
Mother Chu's Vegetarian Kitchen 3
Pasteur 14
Scruffy Murphy's 7
Sussex Centre Food Court 8
QVB Jet 1
ACCOMMODATION
Aarons Hotel G
base Backpackers B
BIG H
Capitol Square F
Central Park A
Footprints Westend D
Pensione Hotel E
Sydney Backpackers C
Sydney Central YHA I
wake up! J

in the world – as well as a massive new shopping and entertainment precinct. In many ways it's a thoroughly stylish redevelopment of the old wharves, and Darling Harbour and the surrounding areas of **Ultimo** and **Pyrmont** have plenty of attractions on offer: museums, an aquarium, entertainment areas, a shopping mall, an IMAX cinema, a children's playground, gardens, a casino and a convention and exhibition centre. However, it's only recently that Sydneysiders themselves have embraced it. Sneered at for years by locals as tacky and touristy, it took the Cockle Bay Wharf development – an upmarket café, bar and restaurant precinct on the eastern side of the waterfront – and the most recent King Street Wharf development to the north of the aquarium to finally lure locals to the much-maligned area.

Behind the development, and accessible from it, is **Darling Park**, with paths laid out in the shape of a waratah flower, the official floral emblem of New South Wales. The western side of Darling Harbour is dominated by rather ugly modern chain hotels, ironically providing some of the view for the stylish Cockle Bay Wharf diners.

It's only a five-minute walk from the Town Hall **to get to Darling Harbour**; from the QVB, walk down Market Street and along the overhead walkway. Further south, there's a pedestrian bridge from Bathurst Street, or cut through on Liverpool Street to Tumbalong Park. Alternatively, the **monorail** (see p.97) runs from the city centre to one of three stops around Darling Harbour. Getting to the wharf outside the Sydney Aquarium by **ferry** from Circular Quay gives you a chance to see a bit of the harbour – STA ferries stop at McMahons Point on the North Shore and Balmain en route. Matilda Cruises' *Rocket Express* runs from the Commissioners Steps, outside the MCA, and goes via the casino at Pyrmont. By **bus**, the #443 goes from Circular Quay via the QVB, Pyrmont and the casino, and the #449 runs between the casino, the Powerhouse Museum, Broadway Shopping Centre and Glebe. The large site can be navigated on the dinky **People Mover train** (daily 9.30am–4.30pm; full circuit 20min; $4.50).

There are always festivals and events here, particularly during school holidays; to find out what's on, visit the **Darling Harbour Visitor Information Centre** (daily 9.30am–5.30pm; ⓣ02/9240 8788, ⓦwww.darlingharbour.com.au), next door to the IMAX cinema.

Tumbalong Park and around

The southern half of Darling Harbour, just beyond Chinatown and the Entertainment Centre, is focused around **Tumbalong Park**, reached from the city via Liverpool Street. Backed by the Exhibition Centre, this is the "village green" of Darling Harbour, complete with water features and public artworks, and serves as a venue for open-air concerts and free public entertainment. The area surrounding the park is perhaps Darling Harbour's most frenetic – at least on weekends and during school holidays – as most of the attractions, including a carousel, a free playground and a stage for holiday concerts, are aimed at children. For some peace and quiet, head for the adjacent **Chinese Garden** (daily 9.30am–5pm; $6), completed for the bicentenary as a gift from Sydney's sister city Guangdong; the "Garden of Friendship" is designed in the traditional southern Chinese style. Although not large, it feels remarkably calm and spacious – a great place to retreat from the commercial hubbub to read a book, smell the fragrant flowers that attract birds, and listen to the lilting Chinese music that fills the air. The balcony of the traditional tearoom offers a bird's-eye view of the dragon wall, waterfalls, a pagoda on a hill, and carp swimming in winding lakes.

Beyond the children's playground, the Southern Promenade of Darling Harbour is dominated by the **Panasonic IMAX Theatre** (films hourly from 10am; 2D films $18, 3D $22.50; ⓣ02/9281 3300, ⓦwww.imax.com.au). Its giant, eight-storey-high cinema screen shows a constantly changing programme from their 100-film library, with an emphasis on scenic wonders, the animal kingdom and adventure sports.

Sydney Aquarium and Sydney WildlifeWorld

At the bottom of Market Street is **Pyrmont Bridge**, a pedestrian walkway across Cockle Bay, linking the two sides of the harbour. On the eastern side is the fantastic **Sydney Aquarium** (daily 9am–10pm; $27.50; ⓦwww.sydneyaquarium.com.au). If you're not going to get the chance to explore the Great Barrier Reef, the aquarium makes a surprisingly passable substitute. The entry level exhibits freshwater fish from the Murray Darling basin, Australia's biggest river system, but speed past these to get to the two underwater walkways, where you can wander in among sharks and watch gigantic stingrays gliding overhead. Another area features exotic species from the Barrier Reef, including a mass of glowing, pulsating Moon Jellyfish. Educational displays highlight the threats to the reef and its conservation. Alongside all the fish, there are also platypus, crocodiles, seals and Little Penguins in enclosures.

Next door is the equally impressive **Sydney WildlifeWorld** (daily 9am–10pm; $27.10; ⓦwww.sydneywildlifeworld.com.au), a mesh-domed centre with free-flying birds and a compact collection of over 130 species of animals found throughout Australia. The elegant glass displays are carefully thought out, giving a good impression of the natural environment the animals live in. Koalas and kangaroos are the inevitable highlights, but snakes, spiders and other creepy crawlies make interesting viewing and you might even get the chance to handle some nonpoisonous species.

The National Maritime Museum and around

On the western side of Pyrmont Bridge, the **National Maritime Museum** (daily 9.30am–5pm, Jan until 6pm; free entry to the museum, but you must purchase a $30 Big Ticket for guided tours of HMAS *Vampire*, the *James Craig* and HMAS *Onslow*; ⓦwww.anmm.gov.au), with its distinctive modern architecture topped by a wave-shaped roof, highlights the history of Australia as a seafaring nation, but goes beyond maritime interests to look at how the sea has shaped Australian life, covering everything from immigration to beach culture and Aboriginal fishing methods in seven core-themed exhibitions. Highlights include the "Merana Eora Nora – First People" exhibition, delving into indigenous culture, and "Navigators – Defining Australia", which focuses on the seventeenth-century Dutch explorers. Outside, several vessels are moored: the navy destroyer *Vampire*, and a submarine, HMAS *Onslow*, plus the beautifully restored 1874 square-rigger, the *James Craig*, are permanently on display, while a collection of historic vessels, including a 1970s Vietnamese refugee boat, are rotated. The pleasant alfresco café here, which you don't have to enter the museum to use, has views of the boats. The bronze **Welcome Wall** outside the museum pays honour to Australia's six million immigrants.

Included in the museum entry is a behind-the-scenes tour of the **Maritime Heritage Centre** at Wharf 7, just beyond the museum off Pirrama Road and beside Pyrmont Bay Park, where conservation and model-making work takes place and some of the collection is stored. Also at the wharf, the Sydney Heritage Fleet's collection of restored boats and ships is moored, the oldest of which was built in 1888. Slightly south, the two-level **Harbourside Shopping**

Centre provides opportunities for souvenir hunting: don't miss the first-floor **Gavala: Aboriginal Art & Cultural Education Centre** (daily 10am–9pm), the only fully Aboriginal-owned and -run store in Sydney (all profits go back to the artists), selling Aboriginal art, clothing, accessories and music.

Ultimo: the Powerhouse Museum and around

From Tumbalong Park, a signposted walkway leads to **Ultimo** and the **Powerhouse Museum** on Harris Street (daily 10am–5pm; $30, extra for special exhibitions; free 45min tour daily 11.30am, 12.30pm & 1.30pm; ⓦwww.powerhousemuseum.com). Located, as the name suggests, in a former power station, this is arguably the best museum in Sydney, an exciting place with fresh ideas, combining arts and sciences, design, pop culture and technology under the same roof. There are several big temporary exhibitions each year, with past popular themes as diverse as "The Lord of the Rings" and "The Great Wall of China". The permanent displays are varied, presented with an interactive approach that means you'll need hours to investigate the five-level museum properly. The entrance level is dominated by the huge **Boulton and Watt Steam Engine**, first put to use in 1875 in a British brewery; still operational, the engine is often loudly demonstrated. The **Kings Cinema** on level 3, with its original Art Deco fittings, suitably shows the sorts of newsreels and films a Sydneysider would have watched in the 1930s. Judging by the tears at closing time, the special **children's areas** are a great success. Level 4 houses a transport section brought to life by an impressive sound-and-light show.

Pyrmont: Star City Casino and the Sydney Fish Market

Frantic redevelopment is taking place at **Pyrmont**, which juts out into the water between Darling Harbour and Blackwattle Bay. The once dilapidated suburb was Sydney's answer to Ellis Island in the 1950s when thousands of immigrants disembarked at the city's main overseas passenger terminal, Pier 13. Today, the former industrial suburb, which had a population of only nine hundred in 1988, is being transformed into a residential suburb of twenty thousand, housed in modern units and groovy renovated warehouses, paid for with AUS$2 billion worth of investment. With the New South Wales government selling AUS$97 million worth of property, this has been one of the biggest concentrated sell-offs of land in Australia. The area has certainly become glitzier, with Sydney's casino, Star City, and two TV companies – Channel Ten and Foxtel – based here. Harris Street has filled up with new shops and cafés, and the area's old pubs have been given a new lease of life, attracting the young and mobile. The approach to the spectacularly cabled **Anzac Bridge** (complete with statue of an Australian and New Zealand Army Corps soldier) – Sydney's newest – cuts through Pyrmont and saves between fifteen and twenty minutes' travelling time to Sydney's inner west.

Beyond the Maritime Museum, on Pyrmont Bay, palm-fronted **Star City Casino** is the city's unashamedly tacky 24-hour gambling HQ. As well as the casino, the building houses two theatres, fourteen restaurants, cafés and theme bars, souvenir shops, a convenience store and a nightclub. The casino interior itself is a riot of giant palm sculptures, prize cars spinning on rotating bases, Aboriginal painting motifs on the ceiling, Australian critters scurrying across a red-desert-coloured carpet and an endless array of flashing poker machines. Dress code is smart casual. You can just wander in and have a look around or a drink, without betting. **To get to the casino**, hop on the Metro Light Rail (see p.97), which pulls in right underneath the casino; alternatively, bus #449 runs in a loop to and from Broadway in the city via the QVB to the casino and the Exhibition Centre in Darling Harbour, and the #443 runs from Circular Quay via Phillip and Market streets and the QVB.

The best reason to visit this area, though, is the **Sydney Fish Market**, on the corner of Pyrmont Bridge Road and Bank Street (daily 7am–4pm; Ⓦwww.sydneyfishmarket.com.au), only a ten-minute walk via Pyrmont Bridge Road from Darling Harbour. The market is the second-largest seafood market in the world for variety of fish, after the massive Tsukiji market in Tokyo. You need to visit early to see the **auctions** (Mon–Fri only, with the biggest auction floor on Fri; buyers begin viewing the fish at 4.30am, auctions begin 5.30am, public viewing platform opens 7am); buyers log into computer terminals to register their bids.

You can take away oysters, prawns and cooked seafood and eat picnic-style on waterfront tables while watching the boats come in. Everything is set up for throwing together an impromptu meal – there's a bakery, the Blackwattle Deli, with an extensive (and tempting) cheese selection, a bottle shop and a grocer. Alternatively, you can eat in at *Doyles*, the casual and slightly more affordable version of the famous *Doyles* fish restaurant at Watsons Bay; at the excellent sushi bar; or have dirt-cheap fish and chips at one of the bustling cafés (see p.162). Retail shops open at 7am. The increasingly popular **Sydney Seafood School** (Ⓣ02/9004 1111) offers seafood cookery lessons, from Thai-style to French provincial, plus a two-hour, early-morning tour of the selling floor departing from *Doyles* (Mon & Thurs 6.55am; $20).

To get to the fish market, take the Metro Light Rail from Central to Fish Market station on Miller Street, or take bus #443 from Circular Quay or the QVB and make the five-minute walk from the corner of Harris Street and Pyrmont Bridge Road.

The inner west

West of the centre, immediately beyond Darling Harbour, the inner-city areas of **Glebe** and **Newtown** surround Sydney University, their vibrant cultural mix enlivened by large student populations. On a peninsula north of Glebe and west of The Rocks, **Balmain** is a gentrified former working-class dock area popular for its village atmosphere, while en route **Leichhardt** is a focus for Sydney's Italian community.

Glebe

Right by Australia's oldest university, **Glebe** has gradually been evolving from a café-oriented student quarter to more upmarket thirty-something territory with a New Age slant. Indeed, it's very much the centre of alternative culture in Sydney, with its yoga schools, healing centres and organic food shops. **Glebe Point Road** is filled with a mix of cafés with trademark leafy courtyards, restaurants, bookshops and secondhand shops as it runs uphill from **Broadway**, becoming quietly residential as it slopes down towards the water of Rozelle Bay. The side streets are fringed with renovated two-storey terraced houses with white-iron lacework verandas. Not surprisingly, Glebe is popular with backpackers and offers several hostels (see "Accommodation", p.106). The **Broadway Shopping Centre** on nearby Broadway, but linked to Glebe by an overhead walkway from Glebe Point Road opposite one of the street's most popular cafés, *Badde Manors*, is handy if you're staying in the area, with its supermarkets, speciality food shops, huge food court, record, book and clothes shops and twelve-screen cinema.

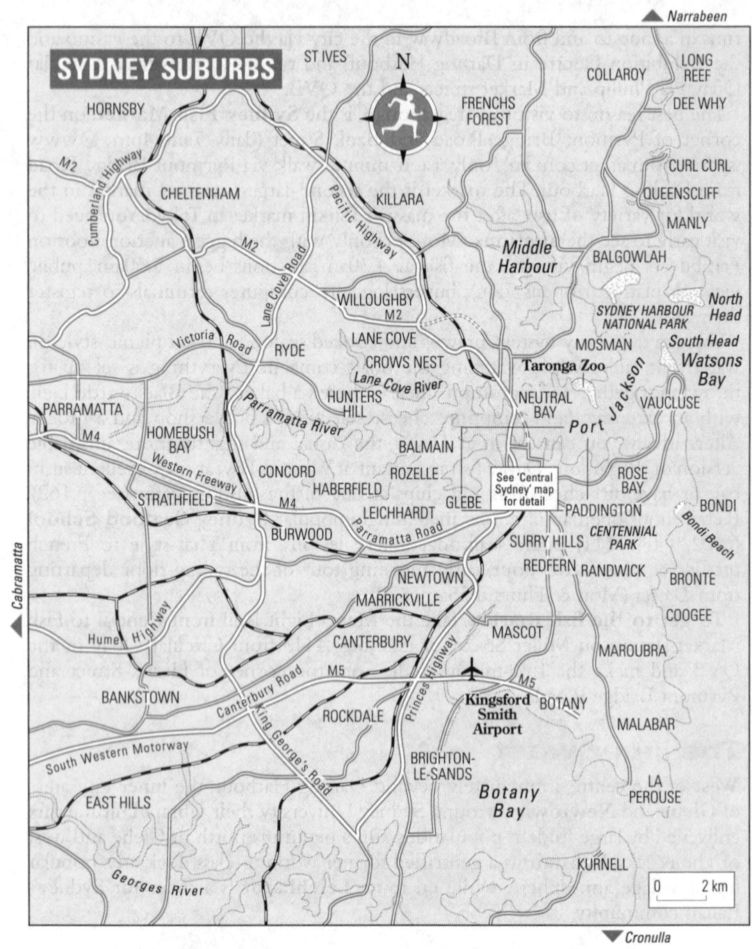

Just before the beginning of Glebe Point Road, on Broadway, **Victoria Park** has a pleasant, heated outdoor swimming pool (Mon–Fri 6am–7.15pm, Sat & Sun 7am–5.45pm; $4.20) with attached gym and a sophisticated café. From the park, a path and steps lead up into **Sydney University**, inaugurated in 1850; your gaze is led from the walkway up to the Main Quadrangle and its very Oxford-reminiscent clock tower and Great Hall. You're welcome to wander round the university grounds, and there are several free museums and galleries to visit. Glebe itself is at its best on Saturday, when **Glebe Market** (10am–4pm), which takes place on the shady primary-school playground on Glebe Point Road (opposite the GNC Live Well healthfood supermarket), is in full swing. On sale are mainly secondhand clothes and accessories, CDs, the inevitable crystals and a bit of bric-a-brac. At 49 Glebe Point Rd, you'll find the excellent **Gleebooks** – one of Sydney's best-loved bookshops. The original, now selling secondhand and children's books, is worth the trek further up to 191 Glebe Point Rd, past St Johns Road and Glebe's pretty park. A few blocks on from here, the action stops and Glebe Point Road trails off into a more residential area, petering out at **Jubilee Park**. The pleasantly landscaped waterfront park, complete with huge, shady Moreton Bay fig trees, a children's playground and its picturesque Harbour Foreshore Walk around Blackwattle Bay offers an unusual view of far-off Sydney Harbour Bridge framed within the cabled Anzac Bridge.

Buses #431, #433 and #434 run to Glebe from Millers Point, George Street and Central Station; #431 and #434 run right down the length of Glebe Point Road to Jubilee Park, with the #434 continuing on to Balmain, while the #433 runs half-way, turning at Wigram Road and heading on to Balmain. From Coogee beach, the #370 runs to Glebe via the University of NSW and Newtown. The Metro Monorail runs between Central Station and Rozelle stopping at the "Glebe" stop, just off Pyrmont Bridge Road, and the "Jubilee" stop at Jubilee Park. Otherwise, it's a fifteen-minute **walk** from Central Station up Broadway to the beginning of Glebe Point Road.

Newtown and around

Newtown, separated from Glebe by Sydney University and easily reached by train (to Newtown station), is a hip, inner-city neighbourhood. What was once a working-class district – a hotchpotch of derelict factories, junkyards and cheap accommodation – has transformed into a trendy, offbeat area where body piercing, shaved heads and weird fashions rule. Newtown is characterized by a large gay and lesbian population, and a rich cultural mix and healthy dose of students and lecturers from the nearby university. It also has an enviable number of great cafés and diverse restaurants, especially Thai. The Dendy Cinema complex is a central focus, more like a cultural centre than just a film theatre, with its attached bookshop, excellent record store, and streetfront café, all open daily and into the night.

The main drag, gritty, traffic-fumed and invariably pedestrian-laden **King Street**, is filled with unusual secondhand, funky fashion and speciality and homeware shops and a slew of bookshops, old and new. For two weeks in June, various shop windows are filled by irreverent and in-your-face art in the Walking the Street exhibition. The highlight of the year, however, is in November (second Sun) when the huge **Newtown Festival** takes over nearby Camperdown Memorial Park, with over 200 stalls and live music on three stages.

King Street becomes less crowded south of Newtown station as it heads for a kilometre towards St Peters train station, but it's well worth strolling down to look at the more unusual speciality shops (buttons, ribbons, vintage records, Chinese medicine), as well as some small art galleries and yet more retro and funky new clothes shops. It's also stacked with culturally diverse restaurants, including Singaporean, Japanese, Turkish and African, and closer to St Peters station are several colourful businesses aimed at the local Indian community.

Enmore Road stretching west from King Street, opposite Newtown station, is a similar mix of speciality shops and evidence of a migrant population – such as the African International Market at no. 2 and Amera's Palace Bellydancing Boutique at no. 83. It's generally much quieter than King Street, except when a big-name band or comedian is playing at the Art Deco **Enmore Theatre**, at no. 130. Beyond here, the very multicultural, lively but down-at-heel **Marrickville** stretches out, known for its Vietnamese and Greek restaurants.

Erskineville Road, extending from the eastern side of King Street, marks the beginning of the adjoining suburb of **Erskineville**, a favourite gay address; the *Imperial Hotel* at 35 Erskineville Rd (see p.169), has long hosted popular drag shows, and is famous as the starting point of the gang in the 1994 hit film *The Adventures of Priscilla, Queen of the Desert.*

Buses #422, #423, #426 and #428 run to Newtown from Circular Quay via Castlereagh Street, Railway Square and City Road. They go down King Street as far as Newtown station, where the #422 continues to St Peters whilst the others turn off to Enmore and Marrickville. From Coogee beach, take the #370 bus to Glebe, which goes via Newtown. Alternatively, catch a **train** to Newtown, St Peters or Erskineville stations.

Leichhardt, Rozelle and Balmain

It takes half an hour on the #440 bus to get from The Rocks to **Leichhardt**, Sydney's "Little Italy", where the famous **Norton Street** strip of cafés and restaurants runs off unattractive, traffic-jammed **Parramatta Road** (buses #436, #437 and #438 from George Street in the city will also take you here). Leichhardt is very much up and coming – shiny, trendy, Italian cafés keep popping up all along the strip, though its focus is the upmarket cinema complex, The Palace (which hosts a two-week Italian film festival in late Oct), with its attached record store, bookshop and Internet café and nearby shopping mall. Closer to Parramatta Road is the **Italian Forum**, an upmarket shopping and dining centre and showcase for all things Italian. However, the lively, much-loved and enduring *Bar Italia*, a ten-minute walk further down Norton, is still the best Italian café in Leichhardt (see p.160 for more details on cafés and restaurants in this area).

From Leichhardt, the #445 bus runs along Rozelle High Street and down the hill to Balmain's waterfront. **Rozelle**, once very much the down-at-heel, poorer sister to Balmain, has emerged as a fully-fledged trendy area, with the Sydney College of the Arts and the Sydney Writers' Centre now based here, in the grounds of the 61-hectare waterfront **Callan Park** on Balmain Road. Darling Street has a string of cafés, bookshops, speciality shops, gourmet grocers, restaurants, made-over pubs, and designer home-goods stores, and is at its liveliest on the weekend, when a huge **flea market** (Sat & Sun 9am–4pm) takes over the grounds of Rozelle Primary School, near the Victoria Road end.

Balmain, directly north of Glebe, is less than 2km from the Opera House, by ferry from Circular Quay to Darling Street Wharf, but stuck out on a spur in the harbour and kept apart from the centre by Darling Harbour and Johnston's Bay, it has a degree of separation that has helped it retain its village-like atmosphere and made it the favoured abode of many writers and filmmakers. Like better-known Paddington, Balmain was once a working-class quarter of terraced houses that has gradually been gentrified. Although the docks at White Bay no longer

Goat Island

Just across the water from Balmain East, **Goat Island** is the site of a well-preserved gunpowder-magazine complex. The sandstone buildings, including a barracks, were built by two hundred convicts between 1833 and 1839. Treatment of the convicts was harsh: 18-year-old Charles Anderson, a mentally impaired convict with a wild, seemingly untameable temper who made several escape attempts, received over twelve hundred lashes in 1835 and was sentenced to be chained to a rock for two years, a cruel punishment even by the standards of the day. Tethered to the rock, which you can still see, his unhealed back crawling with maggots, he slept in a cavity hewn into the sandstone "couch". Eventually, Anderson ended up on Norfolk Island (see p.296), where under the humane prisoner-reform experiments of Alexander Maconochie, the feral 24-year-old made a startling transformation.

At the time of writing, the island was closed and awaiting a major conservation face-lift by the NPWS to make the buildings more accessible to the public.

operate, the pubs that used to fuel the dockworkers still abound, and **Darling Street** and the surrounding backstreets are blessed with enough watering holes to warrant a pub crawl – two classics are the *London Hotel* on Darling Street and the *Exchange Hotel* on Beattie Street. Darling Street also rewards a leisurely stroll, with a bit of browsing in its speciality shops (focused on clothes and gifts), and grazing in its restaurants and cafés. The best time to come is on Saturday, when the lively **Balmain Market** occupies the shady grounds of St Andrews Church (7.30am–4pm), on the corner opposite the *London Hotel*. An assortment of books, handmade jewellery, clothing and ceramics, antiques, home-made chocolates, cakes and gourmet foods and organic produce are on sale. The highlight is an eclectic array of food stalls in the church hall where you can snack your way from the Himalayas to Southern India.

For a **self-guided tour** of Balmain and Birchgrove, buy a *Balmain Walks* leaflet ($2.20) from Balmain Library, 370 Darling St, or the well-stocked Bray's Bookshop, at no. 268. The most pleasurable way **to get to Balmain** is to catch a ferry from Circular Quay to Darling Street Wharf in Balmain East, where the #442 bus waits to take you up Darling Street to Balmain proper (or it's about a ten-minute walk). Buses #432 and #433 run out to Balmain via George Street, Railway Square and Glebe Point Road and down Darling Street; faster is the #442 from the QVB, which crosses Anzac Bridge and heads to Balmain Wharf.

The inner east

To the **east**, **Surry Hills**, **Darlinghurst** and **Paddington**, once rather scruffy working-class suburbs, have long been taken over and revamped by the young, arty and upwardly mobile. **Kings Cross**, or "the Cross", is home to Sydney's red-light district as well as many of its tourists, while in adjacent **Woolloomooloo** container ships tie up at the docks in view of the newly renovated wharf. Further east, the Cross fades into the more elegant but tightly packed suburbs of **Potts Point** and **Elizabeth Bay**, which trade on their harbour views and proximity to the trendy restaurant province.

Surry Hills

Surry Hills, directly east of Central Station from Elizabeth Street, was traditionally the centre of the rag trade, which still finds its focus on Devonshire Street. Rows of tiny terraces once housed its original poor, working-class population, many of them of Irish origin. Considered a slum by the rest of Sydney, the dire and overcrowded conditions were given fictional life in Ruth Park's *The Harp in the South* trilogy (see "Books", p.1131), set in the Surry Hills of the 1940s. The area became something of a cultural melting pot with European postwar immigration, and doubled as a grungy, studenty, muso heartland in the 1980s, fuelled by cheap bars and cheaper rent. By the mid-1990s, however, the slickly fashionable scene of

Redfern

Just beyond Surry Hills, and only 2km from the glitter and sparkle of Darling Harbour, **Redfern** is Sydney's underbelly. Around the **Eveleigh Street** area, Australia's biggest urban Aboriginal community lives in "**the Block**", a squalid streetscape of derelict terrace houses and rubbish-strewn streets not far from Redfern train station – the closest Sydney has to a no-go zone. The Aboriginal Housing Company, set up as a co-operative in 1973, has had problems paying for repairs and renovation work. Recently, the company began knocking down derelict houses and relocating people, upsetting many residents who want to keep the community together.

neighbouring Darlinghurst and Paddington had finally taken over Surry Hills' twin focal points of parallel **Crown Street**, filled with cafés, swanky restaurants, funky clothes shops and designer galleries, and leafy **Bourke Street**, where a couple of Sydney's best cafés lurk among the trees. As rents have gone up, only **Cleveland Street**, running west to Redfern and east towards Moore Park and the Sydney Cricket Ground (see p.138), traffic-snarled and lined with cheap Lebanese, Turkish and Indian restaurants, retains its ethnically varied population.

Surry Hills is a short **walk** up a steep hill from Central Station (Devonshire St or Elizabeth St exit); take Fouveaux or Devonshire Street and you'll soon hit Crown, or it's an even quicker stroll from Oxford Street, Darlinghurst, heading south along Crown or Bourke streets.

A good time to visit the area is the first Saturday of the month when a lively **flea market**, complete with tempting food stalls, occupies the small Shannon Reserve, on the corner of Crown and Fouveaux streets, overlooked by the **Clock Hotel**. The hotel, which has expanded out of all recognition from its 1840s roots, is emblematic of the new Surry Hills, with its swish restaurant and bar. The area's artistic side can be experienced nearby at the **Brett Whiteley Studio** at 2 Raper St (Sat & Sun 10am–4pm; ⓣ02/9225 1881; $7); walk about three blocks further south down Crown Street, and it's off Davies Street. Whiteley was one of Australia's best-known contemporary painters with an international reputation by the time he died in 1992 of a heroin overdose at the age of 53; wild self-portraits and expressive female nudes were some of his subjects, but it is his sensual paintings of Sydney Harbour for which he is most well known, painted from his home in Lavender Bay. In 1986, Whiteley converted this one-time factory into a studio and living space, and since his death it has become a museum and gallery showing his paintings and memorabilia.

Darlinghurst, Paddington and Woollahra

Oxford Street, from Hyde Park to Paddington and beyond, is a major amusement strip. Waiting to be discovered, here and in the side streets, is an array of nightclubs, restaurants, cafés, pubs, cinemas and late-night bookshops. The Oxford Street shopping strip –– many would argue Sydney's best for labels and funky style – starts at the corner of Victoria Street in Darlinghurst and doesn't stop until the corner of Jersey Road in Woollahra. Around **Darlinghurst**, Oxford Street is the focus of Sydney's very active gay and lesbian movement. Hip and bohemian, Darlinghurst mingles seediness with a certain hedonistic style. There's another concentration of cafés, restaurants and fashion on Liverpool Street, while Victoria Street is a classic pose strip with the legendary, street-smart *Bar Coluzzi* (see p.161).

Paddington, a slum at the start of the twentieth century, became a popular hangout for hipsters during the late 1960s and 1970s. Since then, the young professionals have taken over and turned Paddington into the smart and fashionable suburb it is today: the Victorian-era terrace houses, with their iron-lace verandas reminiscent of New Orleans, have been beautifully restored. Many of the terraces were originally built in the 1840s to house the artisans who worked on the graceful, sandstone **Victoria Barracks** on the southern side of Oxford Street, its walls stretching seven blocks, from Greens Road to just before the Paddington Town Hall on Oatley Road. **Shadforth Street**, opposite the entrance gates, has many examples of the original artisans' homes. Though the barracks are still used by the army, there are free guided tours (Thurs 10am).

Crossing to the north side of Oxford Street, the small, winding, tree-lined streets running off it are a pleasant place for a stroll. Head via Underwood and Heeley streets to "**Five Ways**", where you'll find cafés, speciality shops and a

△ Victorian terrace houses, Paddington

typically gracious old boozer, the *Royal Hotel* (see p.162). Continuing east there are more shops along Elizabeth Street, while back on Oxford Street the main Paddington action of stylish boutiques and arty homeware stores attracts the "see and be seen" crowd. Always bustling, the area really comes alive on Saturdays, when everyone descends on **Paddington Market** (9am–4pm) in the church grounds at no. 395, opposite Elizabeth Street. The ever-expanding market sells everything from funky handmade jewellery to local artwork, as well as cheap fresh flowers and vintage clothes; you can even get a massage or a tarot reading between a cup of coffee and an organic sandwich.

Woollahra, along Oxford Street from Paddington, is even more moneyed but contrastingly staid, with expensive **antique shops** and **art galleries** along **Queen Street** replacing the fashion and trendy lifestyle focus of Paddington's shops. Leafy Moncur Street hides *jones the grocer* (at no. 68), where Woollahra locals gather for coffee at the long central table; it also sells stylishly packaged, outlandishly priced and utterly delicious groceries and gourmet treats.

Transport heading in this direction includes **buses** #380, #381 and #382 from Circular Quay, which both run up Elizabeth Street in the city and along Oxford Street to Bondi Junction. The #378, from Central Station, also heads along Oxford Street. Bus #389 from Circular Quay runs via Elizabeth and William streets in the city and along Glenmore Road and Hargrave Street, Paddington, to emerge on Oxford Street.

Centennial Parklands

South of Paddington and Woollahra lies the great green expanse of **Centennial Parklands** (daily sunrise to sunset; Ⓦwww.cp.nsw.gov.au), opened to the citizens of Sydney at the Centennial Festival in 1888. With its vast lawns, rose gardens and extensive network of ponds complete with ducks it resembles an

English country park, but is reclaimed at dawn and dusk by distinctly antipodean residents, including possums and flying foxes. The park is crisscrossed by walking paths and tracks for cycling, rollerblading, jogging and horse riding: you can rent a bike or rollerblades nearby (see p.181) or hire a horse from the adjacent equestrian centre and then recover from your exertions in the café with its popular outside tables or, in the finer months, stay on until dark and catch an outdoor film at the Moonlight Cinema (see p.173). Adjoining **Moore Park** is incorporated under the banner of Centennial Parklands and has facilities for tennis, golf, grass-skiing, bowling, cricket and hockey; it's also home to the Sydney Cricket Ground and the Entertainment Quarter (see below). Pick up a free map of the Centennial Parklands from gate entrances or at the Park Office (Mon–Fri 8.30am–5pm; ⓣ02/9339 6699), near the café and easily reached from the Paddington gates off Oxford Street (opposite Queen Street). To get to the park you can take a **bus** from Central Station (#372, #393 or #395) or from Elizabeth Street in the city, before Museum station (#L90, #391, #394 or #396; #394 and #396 extend to and from Circular Quay). Alternatively, you could take a bus to Oxford Street, Paddington, and then walk in via the Paddington gates or further along at the Woollahra gates (opposite Ocean Street).

The Sydney Cricket Ground (SCG)

The venerated institution of the **Sydney Cricket Ground (SCG)** earned its place in cricketing history for Don Bradman's score of 452 not out in 1929, and for the controversy over England's bodyline bowling techniques in 1932. Ideally, proceedings are observed from the lovely 1886 Members Stand, while sipping an icy gin and tonic – but unless you're invited by a member, you'll end up elsewhere, probably drinking beer from a plastic cup. Cricket spectators aren't a sedate lot in Sydney, and the noisiest barrackers will probably come from "the Hill" – or the Doug Walters Stand, as it's officially known. The Bill O'Reilly Stand gives comfortable viewing until the afternoon, when you'll be blinded by the sun, whereas the Brewongle Stand provides consistently good viewing. Best of all is the Bradman Stand, with a view directly behind the bowler's arm, and adjacent to the exclusive stand occupied by members, commentators and ex-players. The Test to see here is, of course, **The Ashes**; the Sydney leg of the five tests, each for five days, begins on New Year's Day. For information, scores, prices and times, call ⓣ02/9360 6601. You can buy tickets for all matches at the gates on the day subject to availability, or purchase them in advance from Ticketek (ⓣ02/9266 4800, ⓦwww.ticketek.com.au). Die-hard cricket fans can go on a **tour** of the SCG on non-match days (Mon–Fri 10am & 1pm, Sat 10am; 1hr 30min; $25; ⓣ1300 724 737, ⓦwww.scgt.nsw.gov.au), which also covers the **Aussie Stadium** next door, where the focus is on international and national rugby league and rugby union, and Aussie Rules football matches, when Sydneysiders come out to support their local team, The Swans.

Fox Studios and the Entertainment Quarter

Also within Moore Park, immediately southeast of the SCG, are the Murdoch-owned **Fox Studios** (ⓦwww.foxstudios.com.au), constructed at a cost of AUS$300 million within the old Agricultural Showgrounds site. The **Professional Studio**, opened in May 1998, takes up over half the site and has facilities for both film and television production, with six high-tech stages and industry tenants on site providing everything from casting services to stunt professionals. Films made here include *The Matrix* trilogy, *Mission Impossible II*, Baz Luhrmann's *Moulin Rouge*, and Episode I and II of the *Star Wars* saga. The **public areas** of the site are focused around a state-of-the-art, twelve-screen **cinema complex**, complete with digital surround-sound and VIP lounges, and a smaller four-screen arthouse cinema; international film premieres are sometimes held here.

The old Show Ring, on the south side of Fox Studios, once the preserve of wood-chopping competitions and rodeo events, is now known as the **Entertainment Quarter** (Ⓦ www.eqmoorepark.com.au) and is home to everything from open-air cinema and circuses to the weekend craft market (Sat & Sun 10am–6pm), as well as the International Food Market (Fri from 6pm) and the fresh-produce Farmers Market (Wed, Sat & Sun from 10am). The Show Ring is adjacent to the gleaming shops, cafés, restaurants and bars of pedestrianized **Bent Street**. There's a stand-up comedy venue, the *Comedy Store* (see p.173) and two music venues, City Live and the Hordern Pavilion (see p.167).

The theme-park area of Fox Studios, the Backlot, was a commercial failure, closing in 2001. However, there's still a lot to attract families including the mini-golf course by the old Backlot entrance (the film-themed murals are still there) and the indoor **Lollipops Playground** (daily 9.30am–6pm; 1–2 years $9, 3–12 years $12, adults $5 includes a coffee; Ⓣ 02/9331 0811), perfect for a rainy day. Just outside are two free playgrounds and a carousel ($2.50).

To get here, catch **buses** #339, #392, #394 or #396 from Central, Wynyard, or Town Hall.

Kings Cross and Potts Point

The preserve of Sydney's bohemians in the 1950s, **Kings Cross** became an R&R spot for American soldiers during the Vietnam War. Now Sydney's red-light district, it is still frequented by sailors from the ships docked in Woolloomooloo, and its streets are prowled by prostitutes, drug abusers, drunks and homeless teenagers. Despite this, it is also a bustling centre for backpackers and other travellers, especially around leafy and quieter Victoria Street, and there are lots of fashionable restaurants and cafés, particularly as you head north towards the harbour and the more upmarket Potts Point. The two sides of "the Cross" (as locals call it) coexist with little trouble, though some tourists seem a little surprised at where they've ended up, and it can be rather intimidating for lone women. However, the constant flow of people (and police officers) makes it relatively safe, and it's always lively, with bars and eating establishments open all hours.

Heading up **William Street** from Hyde Park and past Cook and Phillip Park and the Australian Museum, Kings Cross beckons with its giant neon Coca-Cola sign. By day, William Street looks quite grotty thanks to streams of fast and fumey traffic heading out of the city centre; at night, hardcore transvestite streetwalkers and kerb-crawling patrons go about their business. However, with the Cross City Tunnel easing traffic along here, there are long-term plans for William Street to become a European-style boulevard, tree-lined, traffic-calmed, and with wide pavements for café tables and strolling pedestrians. At the top of the hill, **Darlinghurst Road** is Kings Cross's "action zone". At weekends, an endless stream of suburban voyeurs emerge from Kings Cross station, near the beginning of the Darlinghurst Road "sin" strip, and trawl along the streets as touts try their best to haul them into tacky strip-joints and seedy nightclubs. The strippers and sleaze extend to the end of Darlinghurst Road at the El Alamein fountain in the paved Fitzroy Gardens, which though pleasant-looking, is the usual hangout of some fairly abusive drunks. It's much changed on Sundays, however, when it's taken over by a small arts and crafts market. Generally, Kings Cross is much more subdued during the day, with a slightly hungover feel to it: local residents emerge and it's a good time to hang out in the cafés.

From Fitzroy Gardens, **Macleay Street** runs through quieter **Potts Point**, an upmarket area of tree-lined streets, apartment blocks, classy boutique hotels, stylish restaurants, buzzy cafés and occasional harbour glimpses over wealthier Elizabeth Bay, just to the east; this is as close to European living as Sydney gets. The area was Sydney's first suburb, developed land granted to John Wylde in 1822 and Alexander Macleay in 1826. The grand villas of colonial bureaucrats gave way in the 1920s and 1930s to Art Deco residential apartments, and in the 1950s big, splendid hotels were added to the scene. The area is set to go more upmarket and more residential with the conversion of all the large hotels into luxury apartments.

You can get to Kings Cross by **train** or **bus** (#311 from Central Station #323–#326 from Circular Quay; #327 from Gresham St in the city), or it's not too far to walk; for a quieter route than William Street, you could head up from The Domain via Cowper Wharf Road in Woolloomooloo, and then up the McElhone Stairs to Victoria Street.

Woolloomooloo

North of William Street just below Kings Cross, **Woolloomooloo** occupies the old harbourside quarter between The Domain and the grey-painted fleet of the **Garden Island Naval Depot**. Once a narrow-streeted slum, Woolloomooloo is quickly being transformed, though its upmarket apartment developments sit uneasily side by side with problematic community housing, and you should still be careful in the backstreets at night. There are some lively pubs and some more old-fashioned quiet drinking holes, as well as the legendary **Harry's Café de Wheels** on Cowper Wharf Road, a 24-hour pie-cart operating since 1945 and popular nowadays with Sydney cabbies and hungry clubbers (see p.161).

Next door, the once picturesquely dilapidated **Woolloomooloo Finger Wharf**, dating from 1917, is now a posh complex comprising a marina, luxury residential apartments, the cool *Blue Hotel* and its funky *Water Bar*, and some slick restaurants offering alfresco dining. The general public are free to wander along the wharf and even go inside: there's a free exhibition space with a changing theme in the centre.

Woolloomooloo is best reached **on foot** from Kings Cross by taking the **McElhone Stairs** or the **Butlers Stairs** from Victoria Street; or from the Royal Botanic Gardens by walking south around the foreshore from Mrs Macquarie's Chair; alternatively, take **bus** #311 from Kings Cross, Circular Quay or Central Station.

The Harbour

Loftily flanking the mouth of Sydney Harbour are the rugged sandstone cliffs of North Head and South Head, providing spectacular viewing points across the calm water to the city 11km away, where the Harbour Bridge spans the sunken valley at its deepest point. The many coves, bays, points and headlands of Sydney Harbour, and their parks, bushland and swimmable beaches, are rewarding to explore. However, harbour beaches are not as clean as ocean ones, and after storms are often closed to swimmers (see p.146). Finding your way by ferry is the most pleasurable method: services run to much of the **North Shore** and to harbourfront areas of the **eastern suburbs**. The eastern shores are characterized by a certain glitziness and are the haunt of the nouveaux riches, while the leafy North Shore is very much old money. Both sides of the harbour have pockets of bushland that have been incorporated into **Sydney Harbour National Park**, along with five islands, two of which – Goat Island and Fort Denison – can be visited on tours (see p.134 and p.116); the other three – Shark Island,

Clark Island and Rodd Island – are bookable for picnics but you must provide your own transport. The NPWS publishes an excellent free map detailing the areas of the national park and its many walking tracks, available from Cadmans Cottage in The Rocks.

Elizabeth Bay to South Head

The suburbs on the hilly southeast shores of the harbour are rich and exclusive. The area around **Darling Point**, the enviable postcode 2027, is the wealthiest in Australia, supporting the lifestyle of waterfront mansions and yacht-club memberships enjoyed by some-time residents Nicole Kidman and Lachlan Murdoch. A couple of early nineteenth-century mansions, Elizabeth Bay House and Vaucluse House, are open to visitors, providing an insight into the life of the pioneering upper crust, while the ferry to **Rose Bay** gives a good view of the pricey contemporary real estate; the bay is close to beautiful **Nielson Park** and the surrounding chunk of Sydney Harbour National Park. At South Head, **Watsons Bay** was once a fishing village, and there are spectacular views from **The Gap** in another section of the national park. Woollahra Council (ⓦwww.woollahra.nsw.gov.au) has brochures detailing three **waterside walks**: the 5.5-kilometre (3hr) **Rushcutters Bay** to Rose Bay harbour walk, which can then be continued with the eight-kilometre (4.5hr) walk to Watsons Bay, and the fascinating five-kilometre cliffside walk from Christison Park in **Vaucluse** (off Old South Head Road) to Watsons Bay and **South Head**, with shipwreck sites, old lighthouses and military fortifications along the way.

Buses #324 and #325 from Circular Quay via Pitt Street, Kings Cross and Edgecliff cover the places listed below, heading to Watsons Bay via New South Head Road; #325 detours at Vaucluse for Nielson Park. Bus #327 runs between Martin Place and Bondi Junction stations via Edgecliff station and Darling Point.

Elizabeth Bay and Rushcutters Bay

Barely five minutes' walk northeast of Kings Cross, **Elizabeth Bay** is a well-heeled residential area, centred on **Elizabeth Bay House**, at 7 Onslow Ave (Tues–Sun 10am–4.30pm; $8; bus #311 from either Railway Square or Circular Quay, or walk from Kings Cross station), a grand Regency residence with fine harbour views, built in 1835. Heading southeast, you're only a few minutes' walk from **Rushcutters Bay Park**, wonderfully set against a backdrop of the yacht- and cruiser-packed marina in the bay; the marina was revamped for the 2000 Olympics sailing competition. You can take it all in from the tables outside the very popular Rushcutters Bay Kiosk.

Double Bay and Rose Bay

Continuing northeast to **Darling Point**, McKell Park provides a wonderful view across to **Clarke Island** and **Bradleys Head**, both part of Sydney Harbour National Park; follow Darling Point Road (bus #327 from Edgecliff station). Next port of call is **Double Bay**, dubbed "Double Pay" for obvious reasons. The noise and traffic of New South Head Road are redeemed by several excellent antiquarian and secondhand bookshops, while in the quieter "village", some of the most exclusive shops in Sydney are full of imported designer labels and expensive jewellery. Eastern-suburbs socialites meet on Cross Street, where the swanky pavement cafés are filled with well-groomed women in Armani outfits. Double Bay's hidden gem is **Redleaf Pool** (daily Sept–May dawn–dusk; free), a peaceful, shady harbour beach enclosed by a wooden pier you can dive off or just laze on; there's also an excellent café here. A ferry stops at both Darling Point and Double Bay; otherwise, catch buses #324, #325 or #327.

A ferry to **Rose Bay** from Circular Quay gives you a chance to check out the waterfront mansions of **Point Piper** as you skim past. Rose Bay itself is a haven of exclusivity, with the verdant expanse of the members-only Royal Sydney Golf Course. Directly across New South Head Road from the course, waterfront **Lyne Park**'s **seaplane** service has been based here since the 1930s. Rose Bay is also a popular **windsurfing** spot; you can rent equipment from Rose Bay Aquatic Hire (see p.183).

Nielson Park and Vaucluse

Sydney Harbour National Park emerges onto the waterfront at Bay View Hill, where the delightful 1.5-kilometre **Hermitage walking track** to Nielson Park begins; the starting point, Bay View Hill Road, is off South Head Road between the Kambala School and Rose Bay Convent (bus #324 or #325). The walk takes about an hour, with great views of the Opera House and Harbour Bridge, some lovely little coves to swim in, and a picnic ground and sandy beach at yacht-filled **Hermit Point**. Extensive, tree-filled **Nielson Park**, on Shark Bay, is one of Sydney's delights, a great place for a swim, a picnic, or refreshment at the popular café. The decorative Victorian-era mansion, **Greycliffe House**, built for William Wentworth's daughter in 1852 (see below), is now the headquarters of Sydney Harbour National Park (Mon–Fri 10am–noon; Ⓦ www.nationalparks.nsw.gov.au) and provides excellent information and maps on all waterfront walks. With views across the harbour to the city skyline, the park is a prime spot to watch both the New Year's Eve fireworks and the Sydney to Hobart yachts racing out through the heads on Boxing Day.

Beyond Shark Bay, Vaucluse Bay shelters the magnificent Gothic-style 1803 **Vaucluse House** and its large estate on Wentworth Road (Tues–Sun & public holiday Mondays 10am–4.30pm, grounds open daily 10am–4.30pm; $8), with tearooms in the grounds for refreshment. The house's original owner, explorer and reformer William Wentworth, was a member of the first party to cross the Blue Mountains. In 1831, he invited four thousand guests to Vaucluse House to celebrate the departure of the hated Governor Darling – the climax of the evening was a fireworks display that burned "Down with the Tyrant" into the night sky. To get here, walk from Nielson Park along Coolong Road (or take bus #325). Beyond Vaucluse Bay, narrow **Parsley Bay**'s shady finger of a park is a popular picnic and swimming spot, crossed by a picturesque pedestrian suspension bridge.

Watsons Bay and South Head

On the finger of land culminating in South Head, with an expansive sheltered harbour bay on its west side, and the treacherous cliffs of The Gap on its ocean side, **Watsons Bay** was one of the earliest settlements outside of Sydney Cove. In 1790, Robert Watson was one of the first signalmen to man the clifftop flagstaffs nearby, and by 1792 the bay was the focus of a successful fishing village; the quaint old wooden fishermen's cottages are still found on the tight streets around Camp Cove. It's an appropriate location for one of Sydney's longest-running fish restaurants, *Doyles*, by the old Fishermans Wharf, now the ferry terminal (accessible by ferry from Circular Quay, or Rocket Harbour Express Cruise from Darling Harbour – see box on p.110). In fact, *Doyles* has taken over the waterfront here, with two restaurants, a takeaway, and a seafood bistro in the bayfront beer-garden of *Doyles Palace Hotel*.

Spectacular ocean views are just a two-minute walk away through grassy Robertson Park, across Gap Road to **The Gap** (buses terminate just opposite – the #324, #325, and faster #L24 from Circular Quay, and the #L82 from

Circular Quay via Bondi Beach), whose high cliffs are notorious as a place to commit suicide. You can follow a walking **track** north from here to South Head through another chunk of Sydney Harbour National Park, past the HMAS *Watson* Military Reserve. The track heads back to the bay side, and onto Cliff Street, which leads to **Camp Cove**, a tiny palm-fronted harbour beach popular with families; a small kiosk provides refreshments.

Alternatively, reach Camp Cove by walking along the Watsons Bay beach and then along Pacific Street and through Green Point Reserve. From the northern end of Camp Cove, steps lead up to a boardwalk, which will take you to **South Head** (470m circuit), the lower jaw of the harbour mouth affording fantastic views of Port Jackson and the city, via Sydney's best-known **nudist beach**, Lady Jane (officially "Lady Bay"), a favourite gay haunt. It's not very private, however: a lookout point on the track provides full views, and ogling tour boats cruise past all weekend. From Lady Bay, it's a further fifteen minutes' walk along a boardwalked path to South Head itself, past nineteenth-century fortifications, lighthouse cottages, and the picturesquely red-and-white-striped Hornby Lighthouse.

The North Shore

The **North Shore** is generally more affluent than the South. **Mosman** and **Neutral Bay** in particular have some stunning waterfront real estate, priced to match. It's surprising just how much harbourside bushland remains intact here – "leafy" just doesn't do it justice – and superbly sited amongst it all is **Taronga Zoo**. A ride on any ferry lets you gaze at beaches, bush, yachts and swish harbourfront houses, and is one of the chief joys of this area.

North Sydney and around

North Sydney has been associated with "pure fun" since the 1930s – beside the Harbour Bridge on Lavender Bay at **Milsons Point**, you can't miss the huge laughing clown's face that belongs to **Luna Park**. Generations of Sydneysiders have walked through the grinning mouth, and the park's old rides and conserved 1930s fun hall, complete with period wall murals, slot machines, silly mirrors and giant slippery dips, have great nostalgia value for locals. Luna Park has had its ups and downs over the years, but in 2004 it reopened to its former glory (Mon–Thurs & Sun 11am–6pm, Fri 11am–10pm, Sat 10am–11pm, longer hours during school holidays; individual ride tickets $3–5, unlimited-ride day-pass $39). The ferry to Milsons Point Wharf from Circular Quay or Darling Harbour pulls up right outside (or train to Milsons Point station). Beyond the park, a boardwalk goes right around Lavender Bay offering spectacular views of the Harbour Bridge and Opera House, most notably from McMahons Point Wharf and the adjacent park at Blues Point – which is a photographer's delight.

Right next door to Luna Park is Sydney's most picturesquely sited public swimming pool, with terrific vistas of the Harbour Bridge – the heated **North Sydney Olympic Pool**, Alfred South Street (Mon–Fri 5.30am–9pm, Sat & Sun 7am–7pm; $4.70). There's an indoor 25-metre pool as well as a 50-metre outdoor pool, a gym, sauna, spa, café, and an expensive restaurant, *Aqua*, overlooking the pool.

Just east of the Harbour Bridge and immediately opposite the Opera House, **Kirribilli** and adjacent Neutral Bay are mainly residential areas, although Kirribilli hosts a great general **market** on the fourth Saturday of the month in Bradfield Park (7am–3pm), the best and biggest of several rotating markets on the North Shore (see "Markets"). On Kirribilli Point, the long-standing prime minister, native Sydneysider John Howard, lives in an official residence, **Kirribilli House**, snubbing Canberra, the usual PM's residence. Next door, Admiralty House is the Sydney home of the Governor General and where the British royal family stay when they're in town.

Following the harbour round you'll come to upmarket **Neutral Bay**. A five-minute walk from Neutral Bay ferry wharf via Hayes Street and Lower Wycombe Road is **Nutcote**, at 5 Wallaringa Ave (Wed–Sun 11am–3pm; $7), the former home for 45 years of May Gibbs, the author and illustrator of the famous Australian children's book, *Snugglepot and Cuddlepie*, about two little gumnuts who come to life; published in 1918, it's an enduring classic. Bush-covered **Cremorne Point**, which juts into the harbour here, is also worth a jaunt. Catching the ferry from Circular Quay brings you in by a quaint open-access sea pool; from here, you can walk right around the point to Mosman Bay (just under 2km), or in the other direction, past the pool, there's a very pretty walk along **Shell Cove** (1km).

Mosman Bay: Taronga Zoo

Mosman Bay's seclusion was first recognized as a virtue during its early days as a whaling station, since it kept the stench of rotting whale flesh from the Sydney Cove settlement. Now the seclusion is a corollary of wealth. The ferry ride into the narrow, yacht-filled bay is a choice one – get off at Mosman Wharf – and fittingly finished off with a beer at the unpretentious *Mosman Rowers' Club* (visitors welcome).

What Mosman is most famous for, though, is **Taronga Zoo** on Bradleys Head Road, with its superb hilltop position overlooking the city (daily 9am–5pm; $32, Zoo Pass including return ferry and entry $39; car park $10; Ⓦwww.zoo.nsw.gov.au). The wonderful views and the natural bush surrounds are as much an attraction as the chance to get up close to the animals. The zoo houses bounding Australian marsupials, native birds (including kookaburras, galahs and cockatoos), reptiles, and sea lions and seals from the sub-Antarctic region. You'll also find exotic beasts from around the world, including giraffes, gorillas and many a playful chimpanzee. The spectacular **Asian Rainforest** exhibit includes a long-awaited new home for Taronga's five Asian elephants.

You can get close to kangaroos and wallabies in the **Australian Walkabout** area, and the **koala house** gives you eye-level views; to get closer, arrange to have your photo taken next to a koala (daily 11am–2.45pm; $16.95). For a more **hands-on experience**, a VIP Aussie Gold Tour (daily 9.15am & 1.15pm; 1hr 30min–2hr; $77 includes zoo entry and koala picture; book 24hr in advance on Ⓣ02/9978 4782) will give you and a small group a session with a zookeeper, guiding you through the Australian animals, some of which can be handled. Keeper talks and feeding sessions – including a free-flight bird show and a seal show – run through the day; details are on the map handed out on arrival.

The zoo can be reached by **ferry** from Circular Quay to Taronga Zoo Wharf (every half-hour). Although there's a lower entrance near the wharf on Athol Road, it's best to start your visit from the upper entrance and spend several leisurely hours winding downhill to exit for the ferry. State Transit buses meet the ferries for the trip uphill, but a better option is to take the **Sky Safari** cable car included in the entry price. **Bus** #247 from Wynyard or the QVB also goes to the zoo.

Bradleys Head

Beyond the zoo, at the termination of **Bradleys Head Road**, Bradleys Head is marked by an enormous mast that once belonged to HMS *Sydney*, a victorious

World War II Royal Australian Navy battleship lost (with all 645 hands) in 1941 off Australia's west coast after sinking a German raider. The rocky point is a peaceful spot with a dinky lighthouse and, of course, a fabulous view back over the south shore. A colony of ringtailed possums nests here, and boisterous flocks of rainbow lorikeets visit. The headland comprises another large chunk of Sydney Harbour National Park: you can walk to Bradleys Head via the six-kilometre **Ashton Park walking track**, which starts near Taronga Zoo Wharf, and continues beyond the headland to Taylors Bay and Chowder Head, finishing at **Clifton Gardens**, where there's a jetty and sea baths on **Chowder Bay**. The now defunct military reserve that separates Chowder Bay from another chunk of Sydney Harbour National Park on Middle Head is open to the public (see below), reached by a boardwalk from the northern end of Clifton Gardens.

Middle Harbour

Middle Harbour is the largest inlet of Port Jackson, its two sides joined across the narrowest point at **The Spit**. The Spit Bridge opens regularly to let tall-masted yachts through – much the best way to explore its pretty, quiet coves and bays (see box p.110). Crossing the Spit Bridge, you can walk all the way to Manly Beach along the ten-kilometre Manly Scenic Walkway (see p.151). The area also hides some architectural gems: the mock-Gothic 1889 bridge leading to **Northbridge**, and the idyllic enclave of **Castlecrag**, which was designed in 1924 by **Walter Burley Griffin**, fresh from planning Canberra and intent on building an environmentally friendly suburb – free of the fences and the red-tiled roofs he hated – that would be "for ever part of the bush". Bus #144 runs to Spit Road from Manly Wharf, taking in a scenic route uphill overlooking the Spit marina. To get to Castlecrag, take bus #207 from Wynyard.

Between Clifton Gardens and Balmoral Beach, a military reserve and naval depot at **Chowder Bay** blocked coastal access to both **Georges Head** and the more spectacular **Middle Head** by foot for over a century. Since the military's 1997 withdrawal from the site, walkers can now trek all the way between Bradleys Head and Middle Head, with the most popular section being between the six-kilometre stretch between Taronga and Balmoral. The 1890s military settlement is open to visitors as a reserve, and NPWS offers tours exploring its underground fortifications (4th Sun of month Oct–May only, 10.30am; 2hr; $13.20). You can reach the military reserve entrance from the northern end of Clifton Gardens (see above) or walk from Balmoral Beach.

The bush of Middle Head provides a gorgeous backdrop to **Balmoral Beach** on Hunters Bay. The shady tree-lined harbour beach is very popular with families. Fronting the beach, there's something very Edwardian and genteel about palm-filled, grassy Hunters Park and its bandstand, which is still used for Sunday jazz concerts or Shakespeare recitals in summer. The antiquated air is added to by the pretty, white-painted **Bathers Pavilion** at the northern end, now converted into a restaurant and café (see p.164). There are two sections of beach at Balmoral, separated by **Rocky Point**, a noted picnicking spot. South of Rocky Point, the "baths" – actually a netted bit of beach with a boardwalk and lanes for swimming laps – have been here in one form or another since 1899; you can rent sailboards, catamarans, kayaks and canoes and take lessons from Balmoral Sailing Club at the southern end of the beach (see p.183).

On the Hunters Bay side of Middle Head, tiny **Cobblers Beach** is officially **nudist**, and is a much more peaceful, secluded option than the more famous Lady Jane at South Head. The hillside houses overlooking Balmoral have some of the highest price tags in Sydney: for a stroll through some prime real estate, head for **Chinamans Beach**, via Hopetoun Avenue and Rosherville Road. To get to Balmoral, catch a ferry to Taronga Zoo Wharf then bus #238 via Bradleys Head Road, or after 7pm Monday to Saturday the ferry to South Mosman (Musgrave Street) Wharf, then bus #233, or #257 via Military Road (#257 originates at Chatswood station).

Ocean beaches

Sydney's **beaches** are among its great natural joys. The water and sand seem remarkably clean – people actually fish in the harbour – and at Long Reef, just north of Manly, you can find rock pools teeming with starfish, anemones, sea-snails and crabs, and even a few shy moray eels. In recent years, whale populations have recovered to such an extent that humpback and southern right whales have been regularly sighted from the Sydney headlands in June and July on their migratory path from the Antarctic to the tropical waters of Queensland, and southern right whales even occasionally make an unusual appearance in Sydney Harbour itself – the three southern right whales frolicking under the Harbour Bridge in July 2002 caused a sensation. Don't be lulled into a false sense of security, however: the beaches do have **perils** as well as pleasures. Some beaches are protected by special shark nets, but they don't keep out stingers such as bluebottles, which can suddenly swamp an entire beach; listen for loudspeaker announcements that will summon you from the water in the event of shark sightings or other dangers. Pacific **currents** can be very strong indeed – inexperienced swimmers and those with small children would do better sticking to the sheltered **harbour beaches** or **sea pools** at the ocean beaches. Ocean beaches are generally patrolled by **surf lifesavers** during the day between October and April (all year at Bondi): red and yellow flags (generally up from 6am until 6 or 7pm) indicate the safe areas to swim, avoiding dangerous rips and undertows. It's hard not to be impressed as **surfers** paddle out on a seething ocean, but don't follow them unless you're confident you know what you're doing. Surf schools can teach the basic skills, surfing etiquette and lingo: see "Surfing" in the Listing section. You can check daily **surf reports** on Ⓦwww.realsurf.com.

The final hazard, despite the apparent cleanliness, is **pollution**. Monitoring shows that it is nearly always safe to swim at all of Sydney's beaches – except after storms, when storm water, currents and onshore breezes wash up sewage and other rubbish onto harbour beaches making them (as signs will indicate) unsuitable for swimming and surfing. To check pollution levels, consult the Beachwatch Bulletin (Ⓣ1800 036 677, Ⓦwww.epa.nsw.gov.au).

Topless bathing for women, while legal, is accepted on many beaches but frowned on at others, so if in doubt, do as the locals do. There are two official **nudist** beaches around the harbour (see p.143 and p.145).

Bondi and the eastern beaches

Sydney's eastern beaches stretch from Bondi down to Maroubra. Heading south from Bondi, you can walk right along the coast to its smaller, less brazen but very lively cousin **Coogee**, passing through gay-favourite **Tamarama**, family focused, café-cultured **Bronte**, narrow **Clovelly** and **Gordons Bay**, the latter with an underwater nature trail. Randwick Council has designed the Eastern Beaches Coast Walk from Clovelly to Coogee and beyond to more downmarket **Maroubra**, with stretches of boardwalk and interpretive boards detailing environmental features. Pick up a free guide-map detailing the walk from the council's Customer Service Office, 30 Francis St, Randwick (Ⓣ02/9344 7006,

Ⓦwww.randwickcitytourism.com.au), or from the beachfront Coogee Bay Kiosk, opposite *McDonald's* on Arden Street. It's also possible to walk north all the way from Bondi to South Head along the cliffs now that missing links in the pathway have been connected with bridges and boardwalk.

Bondi Beach

Bondi Beach is synonymous with Australian beach culture, and indeed the mile-long curve of golden sand must be one of the best-known beaches in the world. It's the closest ocean beach to the city centre; you can take a train to Bondi Junction and then a ten-minute bus ride, or drive there in twenty minutes. Big, brash and action-packed, it's probably not the best place for a quiet sunbathe and swim, but the sprawling sandy crescent really is spectacular.

Red-tiled houses and apartment buildings crowd in to catch the view, many of them erected in the 1920s when Bondi was a working-class suburb. Although still residential, it's long since become a popular gathering place for backpackers from around the world (see box below).

The beachfront **Campbell Parade** is both cosmopolitan and highly commercialized, lined with cafés and shops. For a gentler experience, explore some of the side streets, such as **Hall Street**, where an assortment of kosher bakeries and delis serve the area's Jewish community, and some of Bondi's best cafés are hidden. On Sunday, the **Bondi Beach markets** (10am–5pm), in the grounds of the primary school on the corner of Campbell Parade and Warners Avenue facing the northern end of the beach, place great emphasis on groovy fashion and jewellery. Between Campbell Parade and the beach, **Bondi Park** slopes down to the promenade, and is always full of sprawling bodies. The focus of the promenade is the arcaded, Spanish-style **Bondi Pavilion**, built in 1928 as a deluxe changing-room complex and converted into a community centre hosting an array of workshops, classes and events, from drama and comedy in the theatre and the Seagull Room (the former ballroom) to outdoor film festivals in the courtyard (programme details on Ⓣ02/8362 3400, Ⓦwww.waverley.nsw.gov.au). A community-access **art gallery** on the ground floor (daily 10am–5pm) features changing exhibitions by local artists. In September, the day-long Festival of the Winds, Australia's largest **kite festival**, takes over the beach.

Surfing is part of the Bondi legend, the big waves ensuring that there's always a pack of damp young things hanging around, bristling with surfboards. However, the beach is carefully delineated, with surfers using the southern end.

Christmas Day on Bondi

For years, backpackers and Bondi Beach on **Christmas Day** were synonymous. The beach was transformed into a drunken party scene, as those from colder climes lived out their fantasy of spending Christmas on the beach under a scorching sun. The behaviour and litter began getting out of control, and after riots in 1995, and a rubbish-strewn beach, the local council began strictly controlling the whole performance, with the idea of trying to keep a spirit of goodwill towards the travellers while also tempting local families back to the beach on what is regarded as a family day. Nowadays, alcohol is banned from the beach and surrounding vicinity on Christmas Day, and police enforce the rule with on-the-spot confiscations. However, a **party** is organized in the Pavilion, with a bar, DJs, food and entertainment running from 11am to 8pm. Around 3000 revellers cram into the Pavilion, while thousands of others – including a greater proportion of the desired family groups – enjoy the alcohol-free beach outside. In 2006, **tickets** for the Pavilion bash were $65 in advance from record stores or from Ticketek (Ⓣ02/9266 4800, Ⓦwww.ticketek.com.au).

Bondi's surf lifesavers

Surf lifesavers are what made Bondi famous; there's a bronze sculpture of one outside the Bondi Pavilion. The surf-lifesaving movement began in 1906 with the founding of the Bondi Surf Life Bathers' Lifesaving Club in response to the drownings that accompanied the increasing popularity of swimming. From the beginning of the colony, swimming was harshly discouraged as an unsuitable bare-fleshed activity. However, by the 1890s swimming in the ocean had become the latest fad, and a Pacific Islander introduced the concept of catching waves or **bodysurfing** that was to become an enduring national craze. Although "wowsers" (teetotal puritanical types) attempted to put a stop to it, by 1903 all-day swimming was every Sydneysider's right.

The bronzed and muscled surf lifesavers in their distinctive red-and-yellow caps are a highly photographed, world-famous Australian image. Surf lifesavers (members of what are now called Surf Life Saving Clubs, abbreviated to SLSC) are volunteers working the beach at weekends, so come then to watch their exploits – or look out for a surf carnival; lifeguards, on the other hand, are employed by the council and work all week during swimming season (year-round at Bondi).

There are two sets of flags for swimmers and boogie-boarders, with families congregating at the northern end near the sheltered saltwater pool (free), and everybody else using the middle flags. The beach is netted and there hasn't been a shark attack for over forty years. If the sea is too rough, or if you want to swim laps, there's a seawater swimming pool (plus gym, sauna, massage service and poolside café) at the southern end of the beach under the **Bondi Icebergs Club** on Notts Avenue (Mon–Fri 6am–6.30pm, Sat & Sun 6.30am–6.30pm; $4.50). Part of the Bondi legend since 1929, members must swim throughout the winter, and media coverage of their plunge, made truly wintry with the addition of huge chunks of ice, heralds the first day of winter. The recently rebuilt clubhouse is a great place for a drink (see p.167).

Topless bathing is condoned at Bondi – a long way from conditions right up to the late 1960s when stern beach inspectors were on the lookout for indecent exposure. If you want to join in the sun and splash but don't have the gear, Beached at Bondi, on the beach in front of the Pavilion, rents out everything from umbrellas, wetsuits, cozzies and towels to surfboards and boogie-boards, and has lockers for valuables.

Reach Bondi Beach on **bus** #380, #L82 or #389 from Circular Quay via Oxford Street and Bondi Junction, or take the train to Bondi Junction station, then transfer to these buses or to the #361, #381 and #382.

Tamarama to Gordons Bay

Many people find the smaller, quieter beaches to the south of Bondi more enticing, and the oceanfront and clifftop **walking track** to Clovelly (about 2hr) is popular – the track also includes a fitness circuit, so you'll see plenty of joggers en route. Walk past the Bondi Icebergs Club on Notts Avenue (see above), round Mackenzies Point and through Marks Park to the modest and secluded **Mackenzies Bay**. Next is **Tamarama Bay**, a deep, narrow beach favoured by the smart set and a hedonistic gay crowd ("Glamarama" to the locals), as well as surfers. Tamarama is a fifteen-minute walk from Bondi or a 300-metre walk from the #380 bus stop on Fletcher Street, or take bus #360 or #361 from Bondi Junction.

Walking through Tamarama's small park and following the oceanfront road for five minutes will bring you to the next beach along, **Bronte Beach** on Nelson

△ Sydney surfer

Bay. More of a family affair with a large green park, a popular café strip and sea baths, it's easily reached on bus #378 from Central Station via Oxford Street and Bondi Junction, where you can also catch #361. The **northern end** has inviting flat-rock platforms, popular as fishing and relaxation spots, and the beach here is cliff-backed, providing some shade. The **park** beyond is extensive with Norfolk Island Pines for shade, electric barbeques, a **mini-train ride** ($3), here since 1947, and an imaginative children's playground. The secluded and peaceful Bronte Gully lies to the rear where kookaburras are a common sight and brightly coloured lorikeets are often seen bathing in the waterfall. At the **southern end** of the beach, a natural rock enclosure, the "Bogey Hole", makes a calm area for kids to swim in, and there are rock ledges to lie on around the enclosed sea swimming pool known as **Bronte Baths** (open access; free). Nearby, palm trees give a suitably holiday feel as you relax at one of the outside tables of Bronte Road's wonderful café strip (eight to choose from, plus a fish-and-chip shop).

From Bronte, it's a pleasant five-minute walk past the baths to **Waverly Cemetery**, a fantastic spot to spend eternity. Established in 1877, it contains the graves of many famous Australians, with the bush-poet contingent well represented. **Henry Lawson**, described on his headstone as poet, journalist and patriot, languishes in section 3G 516, while **Dorothea Mackeller**, who penned the famous poem *I love a sunburnt country*, is in section 6 832–833. Beyond here – another five-minute walk – on the other side of Shark Point, is the channel-like **Clovelly Bay**, with concrete platforms on either side and several sets of steps leading into the very deep water. Rocks at the far end keep out the waves, and the sheltered bay is popular with lap-swimmers and snorkellers; you're almost certain to see one of the bay's famous blue groupers (snorkels can be rented up the road at Clovelly). There's also a free swimming pool. A grassy park with several terraces extends back from the beach and is a great place for a picnic. The divinely sited café is packed at weekends, and on Sunday afternoons and evenings the nearby *Clovelly Hotel* is a popular hangout, with free live music and a great bistro, or get rock-bottom-priced drinks and fab views at the *Clovelly Bowling Club*. To get to Clovelly, take **bus** #339 from Millers Point via

Central Station and Albion Street, Surry Hills; #360 from Bondi Junction; or the weekday peak-hour #X39 from Wynyard.

From Clovelly, it's best to stick to the road route along Cliffbrook Parade rather than rockhop around to equally narrow **Gordons Bay**. Unsupervised, undeveloped Gordons Bay itself is not a pretty beach, but another world exists beneath the sheltered water: the protected **underwater nature trail**, marked out for divers, is home to a range of sea creatures; diving and snorkelling gear can be rented at Clovelly. From here, a walkway leads around the waterfront to Major Street and then onto **Dunningham Reserve** overlooking the northern end of Coogee Beach; the walk to Coogee proper takes about fifteen minutes in all.

Coogee

While Coogee has a lively bar, café, restaurant and backpacker scene, and some big hotels, there's just something more laid-back, community oriented and friendlier about it than Bondi – and it's not totally teeming with trendies. With its hilly streets of Californian-style apartment blocks looking onto a compact, pretty beach enclosed by two cliffy, green-covered headlands, Coogee has a snugness that Bondi just can't match. Everything is close to hand: beachfront Arden Street has a down-to-earth strip of cafés that compete with each other to sell the cheapest cooked breakfast, while the main shopping street, Coogee Bay Road, running uphill from the beach, has a choice selection of coffee spots and eateries, plus a big supermarket.

The ugly high-rise *Holiday Inn* has spoilt the southern end of the beach, though its bar does have fabulous views over the water. Other 1990s developments were more aesthetically successful: the imaginatively modernized promenade is a great place to stroll and hang out. Between it and the medium-sized beach is a grassy park with free electric barbecues, picnic tables and shelters. The beach is popular with families (there's an excellent children's playground at the southern end) and travellers, as there's a stack of backpackers' hostels. However, one of Coogee's chief pleasures is its baths, beyond the southern end of the beach. The first, the secluded McIvers Baths, traditionally remains for women and children only and is known by locals as **Coogee Women's Pool** (noon–5pm; entry by donation). Just south of the women's pool, the unisex **Wylies Baths**, a saltwater pool on the edge of the sea, is at the end of Neptune Street (May–Sept 7am–5pm; Oct–April 7am–7pm; $3.00) with big decks to lie on, and solar-heated showers; it's a fine spot for the excellent coffee made at its kiosk.

Reach Coogee on **bus** #373 or #374 from Circular Quay via Randwick, or #372 from Central Station. There are also buses from Bondi Junction via Randwick – #313 and #314 – while the #370 runs from Leichhardt via Glebe and Newtown.

Immediately south of Wylies, **Trenerry Reserve** is a huge green park jutting out into the ocean; its spread of big, flat rocks offers tremendous views and makes a great place to chill out. Probably the most impressive section of Randwick Council's **Eastern Beaches Coast Walk** commences here. The walk, sometimes on boards, is accompanied by interpretive panels detailing the surrounding plant- and bird-life. Steps lead down to a rock platform full of teeming rock pools, and you can swim in a large tear-shaped pool. It's quite thrilling with the waves crashing over – but be careful of both the waves and the dangerous blue-ringed octopus that are found here. At low tide you can continue walking along the rocks around Lurline Bay; otherwise, you must follow the streets inland, rejoining the waterfront from Mermaid Avenue. Jack Vanny Memorial Park is fronted by the cliff-like rocks of Mistral Point, a great spot to sit and admire the ocean, and down by the water the **Mahon Pool**, a small, pleasant open-access sea pool, with waves crashing at its edge and surrounded by great boulders, has an unspoilt, secluded feel. The isolated *Pool Caffe* across the road on Marine Parade makes a wonderful lunch or coffee spot.

Manly and the northern beaches

Manly, just above North Head at the northern mouth of the harbour, is doubly blessed with both ocean and harbour beaches. When Captain Arthur Phillip, the commander of the First Fleet, was exploring Sydney Harbour in 1788, he saw a group of well-built Aboriginal men onshore, proclaimed them to be "manly" and named the cove in the process. During the Edwardian era it became fashionable as a recreational retreat from the city, with the promotional slogan "Manly – seven miles from Sydney, but a thousand miles from care". An excellent time to visit is over the Labour Day long weekend in early October, for the **Jazz Festival** with free outdoor concerts featuring musicians from around the world. Beyond Manly, the **northern beaches** continue for 30km up to the Barrenjoey Peninsula and **Palm Beach**. Pick up the excellent free *Sydney's Northern Beaches Map* from the Manly Visitor Centre (see below). The northern beaches can be reached by regular **bus** from various city bus terminals or from Manly Wharf; routes are detailed throughout the text below.

Manly

A day-trip to Manly, rounded off with a dinner of fish and chips, offers a classic taste of Sydney life. The ferry trip out here has always been half the fun: the legendary Manly Ferry service commenced in 1854, and the huge old boats come complete with snack bars selling the ubiquitous meat pie. Ferries terminate at **Manly Wharf** in Manly Cove, near a small section of calm harbour beach with a netted-off swimming area popular with families. Like a typical English seaside resort, Manly Wharf had always housed a tacky funfair until a few years ago; now the wharf is all grown up with a slew of cafés and brand shops, including multicultural food stalls and a very swish pub, the *Manly Wharf Hotel*. You'll also find the **Manly Visitor Information Centre** (summer daily 10am–5pm; winter Mon–Fri 9am–5pm, Sat & Sun 10am–4pm; ⓣ02/9977 1088, ⓦwww.manlytourism.com.au; lockers $2) out the front. The wharf is now a hub for adventure activity: three watersports companies based here offer parasailing, kayaking and rigid-inflatable-boat tours through crashing surf to North Head; ask at the tourist office for details.

From the wharf, walk along West Esplanade to **Oceanworld** (daily 10am–5.30pm; $17.95; ⓣ02/8251 7877, ⓦwww.oceanworld.com.au), where clear acrylic walls hold back the water so you can saunter along the harbour floor, gazing at huge sharks and stingrays. Divers hand-feed sharks three times weekly (11am

The Manly Scenic Walkway

The **Manly Scenic Walkway** follows the harbour shore inland from Manly Cove all the way back to Spit Bridge on Middle Harbour, where you can catch bus #180 back to Wynyard station in the city centre (20min). The wonderful eight-kilometre walk takes you through some of the area's more expensive neighbourhoods before heading into a section of **Sydney Harbour National Park**, past a number of small beaches and coves (perfect for stopping off for a dip), Aboriginal middens and some subtropical rainforest. The entire walk takes three to four hours but is broken up into six sections with obvious exit/entry points; pick up a **map** from the Manly Visitor Information Centre or NPWS offices (see p.182).

Mon, Wed & Fri) and there's always a range of shows and guided tours, including the Dangerous Australians show with local (and deadly) snakes and spiders. You can also dive amongst the **grey nurse sharks** – which can grow up to 160kg – with Shark Dive Xtreme (30min; qualified diver $175, unqualified diver $235; bookings ⓣ02/8251 7878). Opposite, the screams come from the three giant waterslides of **Manly Waterworks** (Oct to Easter Sat, Sun, school & public holidays 10am–5pm; 1hr $14.50, all day $19.50; height restriction 120cm or more). Between the slides and Oceanworld, the **Manly Art Gallery and Museum** (Tues–Sun 10am–5pm; $3.60) has a collection started in the 1920s of Australian paintings, drawings, prints and etchings, and a stash of beach memorabilia including huge, early wooden surfboards and old-fashioned swimming costumes.

Many visitors mistake Manly Cove for the ocean beach, which in fact lies on the other side of the isthmus, 500m down **The Corso**, Manly's busy pedestrianized main drag filled with surf shops, cafés, restaurants and pubs. The ocean beach, **South Steyne**, is characterized by the stands of Norfolk pine that line the shore. Every summer, a beach-hire concession rents out just about anything to make the beach more fun, from surfboards to snorkel sets, and they also have a bag-minding service. A six-kilometre-long shared pedestrian and **cycle path** begins at South Steyne and runs north to Seaforth, past North Steyne beach and Queenscliff. You can rent mountain bikes from Manly Cycles, a block back from the beach at 36 Pittwater Rd (ⓣ02/9977 1189; 1hr $12, all day $25). For a more idyllic beach, follow the footpath from the southern end of South Steyne around the headland to Cabbage Tree Bay, with two very pretty, protected green-backed beaches at either end: **Fairy Bower** to the west and **Shelley Beach** to the east.

Belgrave Street, running north from Manly Wharf, is Manly's alternative strip, with good cafés, interesting shops, yoga schools and the Manly Environment Centre at no. 41, whose aim is to educate the community about the local biodiversity and the issues affecting it.

Ferries leave Circular Quay for Manly twice an hour, between about 6am and 11.45pm (30min; $6.20). Faster JetCat catamarans ($7.90) operate in the morning and evening on weekdays (Mon–Fri 6–9.25am & 4.20–8.30pm) and during the day on weekends (Sat 6.10am–3.35pm, Sun 7.10am–3.35pm).

North Head

You can take in more of the Sydney Harbour National Park at **North Head**, the harbour mouth's upper jaw, where you can follow the short circuitous Fairfax Walking Track to three lookout points, including the **Fairfax Lookout**, for splendid views. A regular #135 **bus** leaves from Manly Wharf for Manly Hospital, from where it's a 25-minute walk through the national park to North Head lookout. Right in the middle of the park is a military reserve with its own **National Artillery Museum** (Wed, Sat & Sun 11am–4pm; $11) sited in the historic **North Fort**, a curious system of tunnels built into the headland – it takes up to two hours to wander through them with a requisite guided tour.

There's more history at the old **Quarantine Station**, on the harbour side of North Head, used from 1832 until 1984: arriving passengers or crew who had a contagious disease were set down at Spring Cove to serve a spell of isolation at the station, all at the shipping companies' expense. Sydney residents, too, were forced here, most memorably during the plague, which broke out in The Rocks in 1900, when 1828 people were quarantined (104 plague victims are buried in the grounds). The site, its buildings still intact, is now a tourist attraction, with **guided daytime tours** (Wed–Fri 3pm, Sat & Sun 10am & 3pm; 2hr; $25; ⓣ1 300 886 875, ⓦwww.q-station.com.au) and spookier **night-time tours** (Tues & Thurs 6.30pm, Wed–Sun 8pm, Fri & Sat also 9pm; 2–3hr; $34 includes light supper), giving an insight not only into Sydney's immigration history but the evolution of medical science in the last 170 years, often in gory detail. The tours provide the only opportunity to get out to this beautiful isolated harbour spot with its views across to Balmoral Beach. The daytime tours coordinate with the #135 bus from Manly Wharf (bus fare extra); no public transport is available for the night-time visits.

Freshwater to Palm Beach

Freshwater, just beyond Manly, sits snugly between two rocky headlands on Queenscliff Bay, and is one of the most picturesque of the northern beaches. There's plenty of surf culture around the headland at Curl Curl, and a walking track at its northern end, commencing from Huston Parade, will take you above the rocky coastline to the curve of **Dee Why Beach** (bus #136, #146, #152, #158 or #169 from Manly Wharf; bus #178 from outside the QVB in the city).

Several other picturesque beaches lie up the coast, including the long sweeping **Collaroy Beach**, family friendly **Mona Vale** and the unusual orange sands of **Bilgola Beach**, from where a trio of Sydney's best beaches, for both surf and scenery, run up the eastern fringe of the mushroom-shaped **Barrenjoey Peninsula**: Avalon and Whale beaches are popular surfie territory, while the more fashionable Palm Beach caters to visiting celebs and Sydney identities getting away from the city.

Backed by bush-covered hills (where koalas can still be found), and reached by 3km of winding road, smallish **Avalon Beach** has a suitably secluded feel and is indeed a slice of paradise on a summer's day. A pleasing set of shops and eateries run at right angles from the beach on Avalon Parade, location of the popular travellers' hangout, *Avalon Beach Hostel* (see p.108).

At the northern point of the peninsula is **Palm Beach**, a hangout for the rich and famous and a popular city escape. It's also the location of "Summer Bay" in the long-running Aussie soap *Home and Away*, with the picturesque Barrenjoey Lighthouse and bush-covered headland – part of **Ku-ring-gai Chase National Park** – regularly in shot. To blend right in, you can stay at the quirky *Palm Beach Bed and Breakfast* at 122 Pacific Rd (see p.108) with lovely views of the ocean. A steep walking path to the summit of Barrenjoey Headland from the car park at the base takes twenty to forty minutes, rewarded by a stunning panorama of Palm Beach, Pittwater and the Hawkesbury River. The NPWS offers weekend tours of the sandstone lighthouse, which dates from 1881 (Sun every 30min 11am–3pm; 30min; gold coin donation).

Buses #190 and #L90 run up the peninsula from Central via Wynyard to Avalon, continuing to Palm Beach via the Pittwater side; change at Avalon for bus #193 to Whale Beach. Buses #188 and #L88 go from Central and Wynyard to Avalon, and the #187 and #L87 run from The Rocks to Newport.

Botany Bay

The southern suburbs of Sydney, arranged around huge **Botany Bay**, are seen as the heartland of red-tiled-roof suburbia, a terracotta sea spied from above as the planes land at **Mascot**. Clive James, the area's most famous son, hails from Kogarah – described as a 1950s suburban wasteland in his tongue-in-cheek *Unreliable Memoirs*. The popular perception of Botany Bay is coloured by its proximity to an airport, a high-security prison (Long Bay), an oil refinery, a container terminal and a sewerage outlet. Yet the surprisingly clean-looking water is fringed by quiet, sandy beaches and the marshlands shelter a profusion of birdlife. Whole areas of the waterfront, at **La Perouse**, with its associations with eighteenth-century French exploration, and on the **Kurnell Peninsula** where Captain Cook first set anchor, are designated as part of **Botany Bay National Park**, and large stretches on either side of the Georges River form a State Recreation Area. **Brighton-Le-Sands**, the busy suburban strip on the west of the bay, is a hive of bars and restaurants and is something of a focus for Sydney's Greek community. Its long beach is also a popular spot for windsurfers and kite-surfers.

La Perouse

At least, is there any news of Monsieur de Laperouse?

Louis XVI, about to be guillotined, 1793

La Perouse, tucked into the northern shore of Botany Bay where it meets the Pacific Ocean, contains Sydney's oldest Aboriginal settlement, the legacy of a mission. The suburb took its name from the eighteenth-century French explorer, **Laperouse**, who set up camp here for six weeks, briefly and cordially meeting Captain Arthur Phillip, who was making his historic decision to forgo swampy Botany Bay and move on to Port Jackson. After leaving Botany Bay, the Laperouse expedition was never seen again.

A monument erected in 1825 and the excellent NPWS-run **La Perouse Museum** (Wed–Sun 10am–4pm; $5.50), which sits on a grassy headland between the pretty beaches of Congwong Bay and Frenchmans Bay, tell the whole fascinating story. There is also an exhibition that looks at the Aboriginal history and culture of the area.

The surrounding headlands and foreshore have been incorporated into the northern half of **Botany Bay National Park** (no entry fee; the other half is across Botany Bay on the Kurnell Peninsula). An **NPWS visitor centre** (ⓣ02/9311 3379) in the museum building provides details of walks including a fine one past Congwong Bay Beach to Henry Head and its lighthouse (5km round trip); ask about the "whale" Aboriginal rock carving. The idyllic veranda of the *Boatshed Cafe*, on the small headland between Congwong and Frenchmans bays, sits right over the water with pelicans floating about below. La Perouse is at its most lively on **Sunday** (and public holidays) when, following a tradition established at the start of the twentieth century, Aboriginal people come down to sell boomerangs and other crafts, and demonstrate snake-handling skills (from 1.30pm) and boomerang throwing. There are also tours of the nineteenth-century fortifications on **Bare Island** (Sat, Sun & public holidays 1.30pm & 2.30pm; $7.70; ⓣ02/9311 3379), joined to La Perouse by a thin walkway; the island was originally built amid fears of a Russian invasion and featured in *Mission Impossible II*.

To **get to La Perouse**, catch bus #394 or #399 from Circular Quay via Darlinghurst and Moore Park, or #393 from Railway Square via Surry Hills and Moore Park, or the #L94 express from Circular Quay.

The Kurnell Peninsula and Cronulla

From La Perouse, you can see across Botany Bay to Kurnell and the red buoy marking the spot where Captain James Cook and the crew of the *Endeavour* anchored on April 29, 1770, for an eight-day exploration. Back in England, many refused to believe that the uniquely Australian plants and animals they had recorded actually existed – the kangaroo and platypus in particular were thought to be a hoax. **Captain Cook's Landing Place** is now the south head of **Botany Bay National Park**, where the informative **NPWS Discovery Centre** (Mon–Fri 11am–3pm, Sat & Sun 10am–4.30pm; car fee $7; ⓣ02/9668 9111) looks at the wetlands ecology of the park and tells the story of Cook's visit and its implications for Aboriginal people. Indeed, the political sensitivity of the spot that effectively marks the beginning of the decline of an ancient culture has led to the planned renaming of the park to Kamay-Botany Bay National Park, "Kamay" being the original Dharawal people's name for the bay. Set aside as a public recreation area in 1899, the heath and woodland is unspoilt and there are some secluded beaches for swimming; you may even spot parrots and honeyeaters. To get here, take the train to Cronulla and then Kurnell Bus Services route #987 (ⓣ02/9524 8977).

On the ocean side of the **Kurnell Peninsula** sits Sydney's most southern beach suburb and its longest stretch of beach – just under 5km; the sandy stretch of Bate Bay begins at **Cronulla** and continues as deserted, dune-backed **Wanda Beach**. This is prime **surfing** territory – and the only Sydney beach accessible by train (40min from Central Station on the Sutherland line; surfboards carried free). Steeped in surf culture, everything about Cronulla centres on watersports and a laid-back beach lifestyle, from the multitude of surf shops on Cronulla Street (which becomes a pedestrianized mall between Kingsway and Purley Place), to the outdoor cafés on the beachfront and the surfrider clubs and boating facilities on the bay. Even the *Cronulla Beach YHA* at 40 Kingsway (see p.109) is aimed primarily at surfers with surf excursions to Garie and free use of boogie boards. Unfortunately, the ethnically charged **riots** in December 2005 did much to damage Cronulla's reputation as a chilled beach-resort destination, and tensions between local surfers and Middle Eastern youths from the western suburbs still exist.

Eating and drinking

If the way its chefs are regularly stolen to work overseas is any indication, Sydney has blossomed into one of the great restaurant capitals of the world, offering a fantastic range of cosmopolitan eateries, covering every imaginable cuisine. Quality is uniformly high, with the freshest produce, meat and seafood always on hand, and a culinary culture of discerning, well-informed diners. The restaurant scene is highly fashionable and businesses rise in favour, fall in popularity and close down or change names and style at an astonishing rate. For a comprehensive guide, consider investing in the latest edition of *Cheap Eats in Sydney* or the *Sydney Morning Herald Good Food Guide*. All New South Wales' restaurants are **nonsmoking**, except for reception areas and outside tables.

Sydney's fully fledged **café culture** can be found most notably in Potts Point, Darlinghurst, Surry Hills, Glebe, Newtown, Leichhardt and the eastern beaches of Bondi, Bronte and Coogee.

There are many fascinating **ethnic** enclaves, representing the city's diverse communities, where you can eat authentic cuisines including: Jewish on Hall Street, Bondi Beach; Chinese in Haymarket; Turkish and Indian on Cleveland Street, Surry Hills; Italian in East Sydney, Leichhardt and Haberfield; Portuguese on New Canterbury Road, Petersham; Greek in Marrickville and Brighton-Le-Sands; Indonesian on Anzac Parade, in Kingsford and Kensington. Much further out, reached by train, Cabramatta is very much a Little Vietnam.

All restaurants in the following listings are **open** daily for lunch and dinner, unless otherwise stated, and the more specific café times are given (many are open early for breakfast, one of Sydney's most popular meals).

The CBD and Circular Quay

The cafés and food stalls in the business and shopping districts of the CBD cater mainly for lunch-time crowds, and there are lots of **food courts** serving fast food and snacks. Check out the selection in the basements of the **QVB**, **Myers** department store on Pitt Street Mall, and the **MLC Centre** near Martin Place, and on the first floor of the **Hunter Connection** shopping arcade, 310 George St, opposite Wynyard station. The classiest is the foodie's paradise in the basement of the **David Jones** department store on Market Street. There are lots of great Italian espresso bars for quick coffee hits throughout the CBD. Many museums and tourist attractions also have surprisingly good **cafés** – notably the MCA, the Australian Museum, Hyde Park Barracks and the Art Gallery of New South Wales.

Cafés and brasseries

Obelisk Café Shop 1, 7 Macquarie Place, City. Fabulous outdoor spot on a historic square with big shady trees, close to Circular Quay. Attracts a working crowd who plunge in for great coffee, *pizzetta*, sandwiches and salads. Mon–Fri 6.30am–5pm, Sat 9am–2pm.

QVB Jet Cnr York and Druitt streets, City. Very lively Italian café-bar, on the corner of the QVB looking across to Town Hall, with big glass windows and outdoor seating providing people-watching opportunities. Coffee is predictably excellent, and the menu is big on breakfast. The rest of the day, choose from pasta, risotto, soups, salads and sandwiches. Licensed. Mon–Fri 7.30am–10.30pm, Sat 8.30am–10.30pm, Sun 9.30am–6pm.

Rossini Wharf 5, Circular Quay. Quality alfresco Italian fast food while you're waiting for a ferry or just watching the quay. *Panzerotto* – big, cinnamon-flavoured and ricotta-filled doughnuts – are a speciality. Pricey but excellent coffee. Licensed. Daily 7am–11pm.

Sydney Cove Oyster Bar Circular Quay East. En route to the Opera House, the quaint little building housing the bar and kitchen was once a public toilet, but don't let that put you off. The outdoor tables right on the water's edge provide a magical location to sample Sydney Rock Pacific oysters (around $17.50 for a half a dozen), or just come for coffee, cake and the view. Licensed. Daily 11am–11pm.

Restaurants

Cafe Sydney Level 5, Customs House, 31 Alfred St, Circular Quay ☎02/9251 8683. Though the wide-ranging food here – from a tandoori oven to French- and Italian-inspired dishes – has never been that highly rated, the views of the Harbour Bridge and Opera House from the balcony are jaw dropping, plus service is great and the atmosphere is fun (the Fri night jazz is popular). Very much on the tourist agenda. Mains start from $24. Licensed. Closed Sun dinner.

Guillaume at Bennelong Sydney Opera House, Bennelong Point ☎02/9241 1999. French chef Guillaume Brahimi has fused his name with the Opera House's top-notch restaurant, housed in one of the iconic building's smaller shells; the huge windows provide stunning harbour views. For one splash-out, romantic meal in Sydney, come here. With mains at around $45 (elegant modern French fare), it's not the most expensive place in town and if you can't afford it you can opt for a drink at the bar. Lunch Thurs & Fri, dinner Mon–Sat.

The Rocks

There are several good **pubs** in The Rocks (see p.165), many of which serve some kind of food, but for the most part the area around the harbour has a choice of expensive restaurants, popular for business lunches, or trading on fantastic views.

Restaurants

Gumnut Tea Gardens 28 Harrington St, The Rocks ☎02/9247 9591. Popular lunchtime venue in historic Reynolds Cottage. Munch on delicious gourmet meat-pies and ploughman's lunch in the serene leafy courtyard, or sip tea in the antiquated lounge. Live jazz on Fri night and Sun lunch. BYO. Daily 8am–5pm, dinner Wed–Fri.

Sailors Thai Canteen 106 George St, The Rocks. Cheaper version of the much-praised, pricey downstairs restaurant (bookings ☎02/9251 2466), housed in the restored Sailors' Home. The ground-level canteen with a long stainless-steel communal table looks onto an open kitchen, where the chefs chop away to produce simple one-bowl meals. Licensed. Closed Sun.

The Wharf Pier 4, Hickson Rd, The Rocks, next to the Wharf Theatre ⓣ02/9250 1761. Enterprising expensive modern food (lots of seafood), served up in an old dock building with heaps of raw charm and a harbour vista; bag the outside tables for the best views. Cocktail bar open from noon until end of evening performance. Closed Sun.

Darling Harbour

The Cockle Bay Wharf restaurant precinct harbours some excellent quality food. Beyond Darling Harbour, you can eat fantastically well at the Sydney Fish Market.

Restaurants

Blackbird Cockle Bay Wharf, Darling Harbour ⓣ02/9283 7835. Bar-restaurant with the feel of a funky American diner; sit on stools at the bar or couches out the back, or enjoy the water views from the terrace. Generous, good-value meals to suit all cravings – from dhal to spaghetti, noodles, salads and pizzas from a hot-stone oven – and breakfast until 4pm. Licensed. Daily 8–1am.

Chinta Ria – Temple of Love Roof Terrace, 201 Sussex St, Cockle Bay Wharf, Darling Harbour ⓣ02/9264 3211. People still queue to get in here (bookings lunch only) years after opening, as much for the fun atmosphere – a blues and jazz soundtrack, and decor that mixes a giant Buddha, a lotus pond and 50s-style furniture – as for the yummy Malaysian food. Moderate. Licensed & BYO.

Fish Market Cafe Sydney Fish Market, Pyrmont ⓣ02/9660 4280. Located on the left-hand side after the entrance of the undercover market, this is the pick of the hawkers for its excellent-value seafood platter with Kilpatrick oysters, lobster tails and steamed catch of the day. Mon–Fri 4am–4pm, Sat & Sun 5am–5pm.

The Malaya 39 Lime St, King Street Wharf, Darling Harbour ⓣ02/9279 1170. Popular, veteran Chinese–Malaysian place in swish water surrounds, serving some of the best and spiciest *laksa* in town. Mains from $20. Licensed.

Haymarket, Chinatown and around Central Station

The southern end of George Street and its backstreets have plenty of cheap restaurants, of variable quality. Chinatown around the corner is a better bet: many places here specialize in *yum cha* (or *dim sum* as it's also known), and there are several late-night eating options. Inexpensive licensed Asian **food courts**, serving everything from Japanese to Vietnamese, and, of course, Chinese food, can be found in the Sussex Centre (1st floor, 401 Sussex St; daily 10am–9.30pm); Dixon House (basement level, corner Little Hay and Dixon streets; daily 10.30am–8.30pm); the Harbour Plaza (basement level, corner Factory and Dixon streets; daily 10am–10pm); but the best is on the top floor of the Market City Shopping Centre, above Paddy's Market at the corner of Ultimo Road and Thomas Street (daily 8am–10pm). A few blocks from Chinatown back toward the city centre, there's a good array of Spanish eateries on Liverpool Street, almost all of them boisterous and lively.

Cafés and food courts

Ippon Sushi 404 Sussex St, Haymarket. Fun, inexpensive Japanese sushi train downstairs, with a revolving choice of delectable dishes from $2.50 to $5.50 (depending on plate colour), and a proper restaurant menu upstairs. Licensed & BYO. Daily noon–11pm.

Mother Chu's Vegetarian Kitchen 367 Pitt St, City. Taiwanese Buddhist cuisine in suitably plain surrounds, and true to its name, family run. Though onion and garlic aren't used, the eats here aren't bland. Inexpensive. Don't try to BYO – there's a no-alcohol policy. Closed Sun.

Pasteur 709 George St, Haymarket. Popular Vietnamese cheap-eat specializing in *pho*, a rice-noodle soup, served with fresh herbs, lemon and bean sprouts. Most noodles (mainly pork, chicken and beef) are $9, and there's nothing over $11.

Refreshing pot of jasmine tea included. BYO. Daily 10am–9pm.

Restaurants

BBQ King 18 Goulburn St, Haymarket ⓣ02/9267 2433. Late-night hangout of chefs, rock stars and students alike, this unprepossessing but always packed Chinese restaurant does a mean meat dish, as suggested by its name and the duck roasting in the window, but there's a big vegetarian menu, too. Communal tables. Inexpensive to moderate. Licensed. Daily 11.30am–2am (last orders 1.30am).

Capitan Torres 73 Liverpool St, Haymarket ⓣ02/9264 5574. Atmospheric and enduring Spanish place specializing in seafood. Freshly displayed catch of the day and an authentic tapas menu, plus great paella. Sit downstairs at the bar or upstairs in the restaurant. Inexpensive to moderate. Licensed.

Dragon Star Seafood Restaurant Level 3, Market City Shopping Centre, Hay Street, Haymarket ⓣ02/9211 8988. Sitting proudly aside from the food court, this 800-seater Cantonese establishment is officially Australia's largest restaurant. You can eat some of the best *yum cha* in Sydney here, and you'll still have to queue for it on the weekend if you haven't booked. Moderate to expensive. Licensed. Daily 10am–3pm.

Glebe

In Glebe, you'll find both cheap and upmarket restaurants, ethnic takeaways, delis and a string of good cafés. **Glebe Point Road** is dominated by cafés – with a cluster of particularly good places at the Broadway end. Also check pub listings (p.166) for cheap Italian food at the characterful *Friend in Hand Hotel*.

The Boathouse on Blackwattle Bay End of Ferry Rd, Glebe ⓣ02/9518 9011. Atmospheric restaurant located above Sydney Women's Rowing Club, with fantastic views across the bay to Anzac Bridge and the fishmarkets, opposite. Fittingly, seafood is the thing here (and this is one of the best places to sample some), from the six different kinds of oysters to the raved-about snapper pie. Expensive at around $45 for mains, but worth it. Licensed. Closed Mon.

Fair Trade Coffee Company 33 Glebe Point Rd, Glebe. Delightful ambience with funky music and dishes from around the world – Columbia, Morocco, Indonesia and the Middle East are all featured, with nothing over $12.50. Plenty of vegetarian options, and the all-day cooked breakfast is fantastic. Promotion of the FairTrade standards is a bonus. Daily 7am–9pm.

Osteria dei Poeti 73 Glebe Point Rd, Glebe ⓣ02/9571 8955. Lively Italian tavern specializing in classic regional dishes, hand-made cannelloni, and a selection of charming Italian wines. Prices are pretty reasonable, too. Licensed & BYO. Closed Sun.

Newtown

On the other side of Sydney University from Glebe, **King Street** in Newtown is lined with cafés, takeaways and restaurants of every ethnic persuasion, particularly Thai. For gorgeous courtyard Thai dining, check out also *Sumalee* at the *Bank Hotel* (see p.166).

Green Gourmet 115 King St, Newtown. Loud and busy Chinese vegan eatery, which always has plenty of Asian customers, including the odd Buddhist monk. The devout Buddhist owner's creativity is reflected in the divine tofu variations on offer. Order off the menu (mains around $15) or to get a taste of everything, there's a nightly buffet or *yum cha* at weekend lunch. The same owners run the excellent Vegan's Choice Grocery next door. Daily lunch and dinner.

Kilimanjaro 280 King St, Newtown. Long-running Senegalese-owned place serving authentic and simple dishes that span Africa – from West African marinated chicken to North African couscous.

Vegetarian eating

Vegetarians are well catered for on just about every café menu, and most contemporary restaurant menus, too. The following are specifically vegetarian: *Fair Trade Coffee Company* (see above), *Bodhi in the Park* (see p.161), *Green Gourmet* (see above) and *Mother Chu's Vegetarian Kitchen* (see p.157).

Casual and friendly atmosphere, with African art and craft adorning the walls. Inexpensive. BYO.

The Old Fish Cafe 239 King St, Newtown. This little corner place, decorated with strands of dried garlic and chilli, is pure Newtown: lots of shaven heads, body piercings, tattoos and bizarre fashions. Food is simple – mainly focaccia and mini pizzas – and the excellent raisinloaf goes

△ *The Old Fish Cafe*, Newtown

well with a coffee. Daily 6am–7pm, later in summer.

Thai Pothong 294 King St, Newtown ⓣ02/9550 6277. King Street's best and largest Thai; excellent service and moderate prices (mains around $20). Booking essential at the weekend. Closed Mon lunch.

Balmain and Leichhardt

Further west is **Leichhardt**, Sydney's "Little Italy", which has a concentration of cafés and restaurants on **Norton Street**; while the **Darling Street** strip of restaurants runs from Rozelle to upmarket **Balmain**.

Bar Italia 169 Norton St, Leichhardt. Like a community centre, with the day-long comings and goings of Leichhardt locals, and positively packed at night. The focaccia, served during the day, comes big and tasty, and coffee is spot-on. Some of the best *gelato* in Sydney; pasta from $11.50, and the extra night-time menu includes more substantial meat dishes. Shady courtyard out the back. BYO. Mon–Thurs 9am–11.30pm, Fri & Sat 9am–midnight.

Circa Café 344 Darling St, Balmain. Airy building with a shady front courtyard and lots of classic cinema posters plastered to the walls. Hearty breakfasts, home-made pies and delicious savoury crepes are its specialities. Mon–Sat 7am–4pm.

Surry Hills and Redfern

Just east of Central Station, **Cleveland Street** in Surry Hills, running down to Redfern, is lined with cheap Turkish, Lebanese and Indian restaurants, which are among the cheapest and most atmospheric in Sydney. **Crown Street** in Surry Hills is home to several funky cafés and some upmarket restaurants.

Cafés and pubs

Erciyes 409 Cleveland St, Redfern ⓣ02/9319 1309. Among the offerings of this busy family-run Turkish restaurant is delicious *pide* – a bit like pizza – available with 22 different types of toppings, many vegetarian; takeout section, too. Bellydancing Friday & Saturday nights when bookings are essential. Inexpensive. BYO. Daily 10am–midnight.

Maltese Cafe 310 Crown St, Surry Hills. Established in the early 1940s, this café is known for its delicious (and ridiculously cheap at $1.10) Maltese *pastizzi* – flaky pastry pockets of ricotta cheese, plain or with meat, spinach or peas – to eat in or take away. Inexpensive. Sun–Thurs 9am–9pm, Fri 9am–10pm, Sat 8am–9pm.

Mohr Fish 202 Devonshire St, Surry Hills. Tiny but stylish fish-and-chip bar on the street corner, with stools and tiled walls, which packs in the customers. The modern restaurant next door, owned by the same family, is equally excellent. Moderate. Licensed & BYO. Mon–Fri 11am–10pm, Sat & Sun 8am–11pm.

Restaurants

Billy Kwong 355 Crown St, Surry Hills. Traditional Chinese cooking gets a stylish slant at this restaurant owned by celebrity chef Kylie Kwong. The space itself – all dark polished wood and Chinese antiques but brightly lit and with contemporary fittings – complements the often adventurous combination of dishes and flavours. Mains start from $22. Moderate to expensive. Licensed & BYO. Dinner daily. No bookings, so you'll have to queue.

Bird Cow Fish 500 Crown St, Surry Hills ⓣ02/9380 4090. Stylish delicatessen cum bistro with a contemporary menu including kangaroo livers and fabulous cheese selections, but wines overly expensive. Usually packed, so book in advance. Mains start from $18. Licensed & BYO. Daily 8am–10pm.

Longrain 85 Commonwealth St, Surry Hills ⓣ02/9280 2888. Hip restaurant and bar housed in a converted warehouse in the rather subdued north side of Surry Hills off Wentworth Avenue. The contemporary Thai flavours are much raved about with dining on three long community-style wooden tables. Expensive. BYO. Closed Sun dinner.

Nepalese Kitchen 481 Crown St, Surry Hills ⓣ02/9319 4264. Peaceful establishment with cozy wooden furniture, religious wall hangings and traditional music. The speciality here is goat curry, served with freshly cooked relishes that traditionally accompany the mild Nepalese dishes, and simple but delicious *momos* (stuffed handmade dumplings). Vegetarian options, too. Lovely courtyard for warmer nights. Inexpensive. BYO. Dinner nightly.

Darlinghurst and East Sydney

Oxford Street is lined with restaurants and cafés from one end to the other. **Taylor Square** and its surroundings is a particularly busy area, with lots of ethnic restaurants and several pubs. **Victoria Street** in Darlinghurst has a thriving café scene. East Sydney, where Crown Street heads downhill from Oxford Street towards William Street, has some excellent Italian restaurants and coffee bars – particularly on **Stanley Street**.

Cafés and pubs

Bar Coluzzi 322 Victoria St, Darlinghurst. Veteran Italian café that's almost a Sydney legend: tiny and always packed with a diverse crew of regulars spilling out onto wooden stools on the pavement and partaking in the standard menu of focaccias, muffins, bagels and, of course, coffee. Daily 5am–6pm.

Betty's Soup Kitchen 84 Oxford St, Darlinghurst. Soup is obviously the thing here, with continually changing specials that make for a cheap but filling meal, served with damper, but there's also all the simple things your ideal granny might serve: stews, sausages or fish fingers with mash, pasta, salads and desserts. Delicious home-made ginger beer and lemonade. Nothing over $15. BYO. Daily noon–10.30pm, Fri & Sat to 11.30pm.

Bill and Toni 74 Stanley St, East Sydney. Cheap, atmospheric Italian, where it's worth the queue up the stairs for the huge servings of simple home-made pasta and sauces. The café downstairs serves tasty Italian sandwiches (daily 7am–10pm). Inexpensive. BYO. Breakfast, lunch and dinner daily.

Bodhi in the Park Cook and Phillip Park, College St, East Sydney ⓣ02/9281 6162; another branch at Capitol Square, 730–742 George St, Haymarket. Interesting Chinese vegetarian and vegan food, with the focus on delicious *yum cha*, which is served daily until 4pm. Well situated for the local galleries and museums or if you've been for a swim in the park's pool. Organic and biodynamic produce is used. Inexpensive. Licensed. Closed Mon dinner.

Restaurants

Fishface 132 Darlinghurst Rd, Darlinghurst ⓣ02/9332 4803. This is one place where size doesn't matter – it's tiny – and the excellent range of seafood and sushi speak for themselves. Everything is fresh: the fish and chips served in a paper cone, the pea soup with yabby tails or the sushi prepared before your eyes. Moderate–expensive. Licensed & BYO. Dinner Mon–Sat.

Oh! Calcutta! 251 Victoria St, Darlinghurst ⓣ02/9360 3650. Certainly not your grungy neighbourhood Indian: the interior was fitted out by a star interior decorator. *Oh! Calcutta!* keeps getting suitably exclamatory reviews for its authentic – and occasionally inventive – food. Dishes such as quail and goat regularly appear beside more mainstream fare. Try for a balcony table upstairs. Moderate. Licensed & BYO wine only. Dinner Mon–Sat.

Onde 346 Liverpool St, Darlinghurst. People keep returning to this French-owned restaurant, situated in a Darlinghurst side-street, which serves outstanding and very authentic bistro-style food: soups and patés to start, mains such as steak and frites or confit of duck, plus a fish dish. Portions are generous, service excellent and desserts decadent. Moderate. Licensed, and all wine is available by the glass. Dinner nightly.

Pink Peppercorn 122 Oxford St, Darlinghurst ⓣ02/9360 9922. A place that keeps springing up on critics' favourites lists, lured by the unusual Laotian-inspired cooking – including the signature dish: stir-fried king prawns and pink peppercorns. Moderate. Licensed & BYO. Dinner daily.

Kings Cross, Potts Point and Woolloomooloo

Many of the coffee shops and eateries in the "Cross" cater for the tastes (and wallets) of the area's backpackers, though there are also several stylish restaurants, particularly in Potts Point. Many are also open late.

Cafés and pubs

Cafe Hernandez 60 Kings Cross Rd, Kings Cross. Veteran Argentinian-run 24hr coffee shop. Relaxed and friendly with an old-time feel, you can dawdle here for ages and no one will make you feel unwelcome. Spanish food is served – *churros*, tortilla, *empanadas* and good pastries – but the coffee is the focus. Open daily.

Harry's Café de Wheels Cnr Cowper Wharf Rd and Dowling St, Woolloomooloo.

Sometimes, there's nothing like a good old-fashioned pie, and this little cart (open 24hr) has been serving them up for over sixty years. Some gourmet and vegetarian options have made it onto the menu but the standard meat pie with mashed peas and gravy is still the favourite.

Yellow Bistro 57 Macleay St, Potts Point ⓣ02/9357 1744. Quaint, village-style bistro extremely popular with locals. Delectable fluffy quiches and other mouthwatering savouries served on the ample terrace overlooking Macleay Street at lunch, simple but delicious contemporary meals in the cozy dining room at night. Breakfast and lunch daily, dinner Tues–Sat.

Restaurants

Dolcetta 165 Victoria St, Potts Point ⓣ02/9331 5899. Tiny, down-to-earth Italian restaurant with just four tables inside and two more on the street overlooking the fashionable *Dov* restaurant. All dishes under $15. BYO. Mon–Sat 6am–10pm, Sun 7am–4pm.

Fratelli Paradiso 12–16 Challis Ave, Potts Point ⓣ02/9357 1744. This place has everything, from gorgeous wallpaper and a dark furniture fit-out to flirty waiting staff and a diverse wine list. There's even an adjoining bakery, which runs out of stock before lunchtime most days. And the food's amazing, too – calamari, veal, pizzas and pastries – with a blackboard menu that changes daily. Moderate. Licensed. Breakfast and lunch daily, dinner Mon–Fri.

Otto The Wharf, 6 Cowper Wharf Rd, Woolloomooloo ⓣ02/9368 7488. *Otto* is the sort of restaurant where agents take actors and models out to lunch, or a well-known politician could be dining at the next table. Trendy and glamorous, with a location not just by the water but *on* the water. The exquisite Italian cuisine – very fresh seafood – coupled with friendly service and a lively atmosphere, is what keeps them coming back. Expensive. Licensed. Lunch and dinner daily.

Paddington

As **Oxford Street** continues through Paddington, it becomes gradually more upmarket; the majority of restaurants here are attached to gracious old pubs and most have had a complete culinary overhaul and now offer far more than the steak-and-three-veg option of times past.

Royal Hotel Restaurant *Royal Hotel*, 237 Glenmore Rd, off Five Ways, Paddington. Grand old triple-storey pub-restaurant serving some of the most mouthwatering steaks in Sydney, nonstop from noon to 11pm (9pm Sun). Eating on the veranda is a real treat, with views over the art gallery and Five Ways action below. Tables fill fast – no bookings. There's also the *Elephant Bar* upstairs (see p.167). Moderate.

Sloanes Cafe 312 Oxford St, Paddington. The emphasis in this veteran café is on good, unusual vegetarian food, moderately priced, but some meatier dishes have slipped onto the menu, including a BLT with guacamole to die for; the fresh juice bar has always been phenomenal. The stone-floored dining room opens onto the street to check out all the Saturday-market action, or for more peace eat out back under vines in the delightful courtyard. Breakfast and lunch served all day. BYO. Daily 6.30am–5pm.

Bondi and Watsons Bay

Bondi is a cosmopolitan centre with the area's many Eastern European and Jewish residents giving its cafés a continental flair; there are also some fantastic kosher restaurants, delis and cake shops. The Bondi Beach area is full of cheap takeaways, fish-and-chip shops and beer gardens, as well as some seriously trendy cafés and restaurants. To the north, **Watsons Bay** is known for its famous seafood restaurant, *Doyles*.

Bondi Social 1st Floor, 38 Campbell Parade, Bondi Beach ⓣ02/9365 1788. You could easily miss the sandwich-board sign pointing you to this hidden gem, but once found a million-dollar balcony view of the beach awaits those wanting to escape the mêlée of the Campbell Parade pavement. The wood interior is rich and dim-lit at night; the mood promises romance and an interesting dining experience with a worldwide influence. Tapas-style dishes $10–15. Licensed. Tues–Fri 6pm–midnight, Sat & Sun 8.30am–9pm.

Bondi Tratt 34B Campbell Parade, Bondi Beach ⓣ02/9365 4303. Considering the setting, with outdoor seating overlooking the beach, not at all expensive. Come here to take in the view and the invariably buzzing atmosphere over breakfast, lunch and dinner, or just a coffee. Serves contemporary Australian and Italian food – cheap pasta deals from 5–7pm. Licensed & BYO. Daily from 7am–10pm.

Doyles on the Beach 11 Marine Parade, Watsons Bay ☎02/9337 1350; also *Doyles Wharf Restaurant* ☎02/9337 1572. The former is the original of the long-running Sydney fish-restaurant institution, but both serve great if overpriced seafood (but without the flair and inspiration of newer places) and have views of the city across the water. The adjacent boozer serves pub-versions in its beer garden. A water taxi can transport you from Circular Quay to Watsons Bay. Expensive. Daily lunch and dinner.

Eggs 100 Brighton Boulevard, North Bondi. Groovy, relaxed little café tucked down a quiet residential street around the corner from the North Bondi set of shops. Locals straggle in all day long to lap up the three eggs cooked any style or hearty pancakes. Everything under $15. Daily 7 am–3pm.

Gertrude & Alice Cafe Bookstore 40 Hall St, cnr Consett Ave, Bondi Beach. Open daily from 9.30am until late into the night, it's hard to decide if *Gertrude & Alice* is more of a café or a secondhand literary bookshop. With small tables crammed into every available space, a big communal table and a comfy couch to lounge in, it can be tough going for browsers to get to the books at busy café times. A homely hangout with generous, affordable servings of Greek and Mediterranean food, great cakes, even greater coffee and lots of conversation.

Bronte, Clovelly and Coogee

South of Bondi, **Bronte**'s beachfront café strip is wonderfully laid back, and **Coogee** has a thriving café scene.

Barzura 62 Carr St, Coogee ☎02/9665 5546. Fantastic spot providing up-close ocean views. Both a café and a fully fledged restaurant, with wholesome breakfast until 1pm, snacks until 7pm, and restaurant meals – such as seafood spaghetti or grilled kangaroo rump – served at lunch and dinner. Unpretentious though stylish service encourages a large local crowd. Mains $14–26; pasta deals 5–7pm. Licensed & BYO. Daily 7am–10pm.

Jack & Jill's Fish Café 98 Beach St, Coogee ☎02/9665 8429. This down-to-earth fish restaurant on the north side of the beach is a local legend. Come here to enjoy delightfully cooked fish, from the basic battered variety to tasty tandoori perch. Mains $14–20. Tues–Sat from 5pm, Sun from noon.

Melonhead 256 Coogee Bay Rd, Coogee. The smell of fresh fruit wafts down the street from this fantastic juice bar. Apart from custom-made smoothies, crushes and milkshakes, there are enticing salads and Turkish rolls to choose from. Daily 6am–8pm.

Seasalt 1 Donnellan Circuit, Clovelly ☎02/9664 5344. Open-fronted café-restaurant, with fabulous views over the beach to cliffs, greenery and houses. *Seasalt* looks really smart, but it's the sort of casual beach joint where you can come in sand-covered and have just a coffee, as well as the place to head for a full meal with wine. Cuisine is fresh and modern with a seafood basis; lunch mains range from $22 to $27, and dinner (fully clothed and groomed) from $22 to $30. Sophisticated, extensive breakfast packs them in at weekends. Takeaways from the small kiosk. Licensed. Mon–Fri 9am–3.30pm, Sat & Sun 8.30am–4pm; dinner Fri & Sat 6–10pm summer only.

Swell Restaurant 465 Bronte Rd, Bronte ☎02/9386 5001. One of three Bronte café-restaurants to open in the evening down at the beach these days. Sit inside for the latest in sharp interiors, or out on the pavement for a delightful Bronte Beach view. There's plenty of competition alongside, so prices are very reasonable for what you're getting. Dinner mains all $28. Daily 7am–10pm.

North Shore and Manly

Military Road, running from Neutral Bay to Mosman, rivals and perhaps outdoes all the gourmet streets south of the harbour. The string of excellent restaurants tends to be expensive, but there are a number of tempting pastry shops and well-stocked delis. **Miller Street**, which runs from North Sydney, has a great range of eateries around **Cammeray**. **Manly** offers something for every taste and budget; there's an upmarket food hall and food stalls on Manly Wharf, and loads of good cafés and restaurants on **Belgrave Street**, **Darley Street** and along **South Steyne**.

The Bathers Pavilion 4 The Esplanade, Balmoral Beach ⓣ02/9969 5050. Indulgent beach-house-style dining in the former (1930s) changing rooms on Balmoral Beach. The very pricey restaurant-and-café double-act is presided over by one of Sydney's top chefs, Serge Dansereau. Fixed-price dinner menu in the restaurant is $120 for three courses (from $75 lunchtime). Weekend breakfast in the café is a North Shore ritual – expect to queue to get in (the restaurant has Sun breakfast only, for which you can book) – while the wood-fired pizzas are popular later in the day. Licensed. Café daily 7am–midnight, restaurant lunch and dinner daily.

Café Steyne Cnr South Steyne and Victoria Parade, Manly. The laid-back staff and customers epitomize the Manly vibe, and it's easy to spend time over the giant breakfast plates or tucking into the gourmet burgers. BYO. Mon & Tues 7.30am–4pm, Wed–Sun 7.30am–11pm.

Maisy's Cafe 164 Military Rd, Neutral Bay. Cool hangout on a hot day or night (open 24hr), with funky interior and music. Good for breakfast – from croissants to bacon and eggs – or delicious Maltese *pastizzi* plus soups, burgers, pasta and cakes. Not cheap, but servings are generous. BYO.

Pacific Thai Cuisine 2nd floor, 48 Victoria Parade, cnr South Steyne, Manly ⓣ02/9977 7220. With crisp decor and fantastic views of the beach from its upstairs location, this inexpensive Thai restaurant offers a variety of fresh favourites as well as chef's specials such as Chu Chi Curry (red curry with kaffir lime leaves). Vegetarian options, too. Inexpensive to moderate. Licensed & BYO.

Roger Fish Café Grill Shop 6, 2A Waters Rd, Neutral Bay ⓣ02/9953 6242. An interactive, fresh seafood experience: choose not only your preferred catch (from a changing menu of up to 23 choices) but also the cooking style, flavouring and even the thickness of the fillet. Personalised, yet still moderately priced, fish and chips. Licensed & BYO. Lunch and dinner daily.

Entertainment, nightlife and culture

To find out exactly **what's on** in Sydney, Friday's *Sydney Morning Herald* offers "Metro", a weekly entertainment lift-out, and the *Daily Telegraph* has the "Seven Days" pull-out every Thursday. In addition to these and the rather bland monthly programmes distributed by various tourist organizations (see p.91), there is a plethora of **free listings magazines** for more alternative goings-on – clubbing, bands, fashion, music and the like – which can be found lying around in the cafés, record shops and boutiques of Paddington, Darlinghurst, Glebe and Kings Cross: these include *The Brag* and *Drum Media*, with their weekly band listings and reviews, and *3D World* and *Beat* covering the club scene. *City Hub*, a politically aware, free, weekly newspaper, also has an excellent events listing section and *TNT Magazine* has a "What's On In Sydney" section. The Sydney Citysearch **website** (ⓦwww.sydney.citysearch.com.au) has listings of film, theatre and music events.

The two main **booking agencies** are Ticketek (bookings ⓣ02/9266 4800, ⓦwww.ticketek.com.au) and Ticketmaster7 (bookings ⓣ13 61 00, ⓦwww.ticketmaster7.com). Ticketek outlets are at 195 Elizabeth St (cnr Park St), the State Theatre and the Theatre Royal. Ticketmaster7 outlets include the Capitol Theatre and the Entertainment Quarter.

Pubs and bars

The differences between a restaurant, bar, pub and nightclub are often blurred in Sydney, and one establishment may be a combination of all these under one roof, with a place to suit any mood and taste. Sydney's bland pub wilderness has all but disappeared and you'll find a fashionable **bar** on almost every corner, offering everything from poetry readings and art classes to groovy Sunday afternoon jazz or DJ sessions. Not to be outdone, the traditional hotels are getting in renowned chefs and putting on food far beyond the old pub-grub fare. Sydney has many **Art Deco pubs**, a classic 1930s style notably seen in the tilework; we've mentioned some of the best below.

Legendary beer gardens

Many Sydney pubs have an outdoor drinking area, perfect for enjoying the sunny weather – the four listed below, however, are outright legends.

The Coogee Bay Hotel Arden Street, Coogee. Loud, rowdy and packed with backpackers, this enormous beer garden across from the beach is renowned in the eastern suburbs. The hotel has six bars in all, including a big-screen sports bar for all international sporting events. Revellers can buy jugs of beer and cook their own meat from 9.30am till late.

Doyles Palace Hotel 10 Marine Parade, Watsons Bay. Still known to locals as the Watson's Bay Hotel, the beer garden here gives uninterrupted views across the harbour, which you can enjoy with fresh fish and chips from the renowned *Doyles* kitchen or a steak from the outdoor BBQ.

Newport Arms Hotel 2 Kalinya St, Newport. Famous beer-garden pub established in 1880 with a huge deck looking out over Heron Cove at Pittwater. Good for families, with a children's play area. The bistro's Asian-influenced salads and big seafood servings complement a large wine list.

The Oaks Hotel 118 Military Rd, Neutral Bay. The North Shore's most popular pub takes its name from the huge oak tree that shades the entire beer garden. Cook your own (expensive) steak, or order a gourmet pizza from the restaurant inside.

The Rocks and CBD

Australian Hotel 100 Cumberland St, The Rocks. Convivial corner hotel seemingly always full of Brits. The crowded outside tables face towards a sports centre under the Harbour Bridge, but it's the veranda upstairs that gives sweeping vistas of Circular Quay and the Opera House. Inside, original fittings give a lovely old-pub feel. Known and loved for its Bavarian-style draught beer brewed in Picton, plus delicious gourmet pizzas with toppings that extend to native animals – emu, kangaroo and crocodile.

Blue Bar 36th Floor, *Shangri-La Hotel*, 176 Cumberland St, The Rocks. Top-floor bar of the five-star *Shangri-La Hotel* has a stunning 270-degree view – the Opera House, Darling Harbour, Middle Harbour and Homebush Bay to the Blue Mountains. Mega-expensive lounge is worth it for the view alone – dress smart to get in. Daily 5pm–1am (Sun until midnight).

Harbour View Hotel 18 Lower Fort St, The Rocks. Sibling to the stately *Exchange Hotel* in Balmain, this three-storey renovated gem puts you right under the bridge – and close enough from the top balcony cocktail bar to raise a glass to the grey-overall-clad bridge climbers making their way back from the summit. The crowd is mixed, and better for it although drinks are a little pricey. Exceptional upstairs restaurant.

Hero of Waterloo 81 Lower Fort St, Millers Point, The Rocks. One of Sydney's oldest pubs, built in 1843 from sandstone dug out from the Argyle Cut (see p.117), this place has plenty of atmosphere and oozes history. Open fireplaces make it a good choice for a winter drink, and it serves simple meals.

Opera Bar Lower Concourse Level, Sydney Opera House. In summer, you can't move for the people – a mix of concertgoers, tourists and office workers – but that's half the fun of this stunningly located bar with outside tables. Watch the ferries come in, and have a drink next to one of the world's greatest buildings. Jazz on Sun afternoons and a bar-snack menu.

Slip Inn 111 Sussex St. Now famous as the place where Mary Donaldson met her Prince Frederick of Denmark, this huge three-level place has several bars, a bistro and a nightclub, *The Chinese Laundry*, overlooking Darling Harbour. Front bars have a pool room, while downstairs a boisterous beer garden fills up on sultry nights, with the quieter, more sophisticated *Sand Bar* beside it. Excellent wine list, with lots available by the glass; bar food includes Thai and pizzas.

Darling Harbour, Haymarket and around

3 Wise Monkeys 555 George St, cnr Liverpool St. Good mix of Sydneysiders and travellers who come for the relaxed pub atmosphere, beers on tap, pool tables, live music and DJs to 3am.

Cargo Bar 52–60 The Promenade, King Street Wharf, Darling Harbour. Multi-level bar with plenty of outdoor seating downstairs and sofas and stools upstairs. Views of Darling Harbour are quite dazzling at night when the lights of the hotels and casino glitter off the water. Drinks are not cheap, but yummy pizzas are satisfying.

Civic Hotel 388 Pitt St, cnr Goulburn St, Haymarket ⓣ02/8267 3186. Beautiful 1940s Art Deco–style pub, its original features in great condition. Upstairs, there's a glamorous dining room and cocktail bar with performance spaces offered to young artistic talent. Handy meeting point for Chinatown and George Street cinema forays.

Scruffy Murphy's 43 Goulburn St. Rowdy, 24hr Irish pub with Guinness on tap, of course; phenomenally popular with travellers and expats, who come for some hearty home cooking, too. Just around the corner from Central Station.

Inner west: Glebe, Newtown and Balmain

Bank Hotel 324 King St, next to Newtown station. Smart-looking pub open late and always packed with local arty residents and visiting musos. Cocktail bar out back and a great Thai restaurant, *Sumalee*, in the leafy beer garden.

Exchange Hotel Cnr Beattie & Mullens sts, Balmain. Classic Balmain backstreet corner pub, built in 1885, with a vast wrought-iron balcony. There are four lively bars, live music in the adjoining nightclub and the *Bloody Mary Breakfast Club* on Saturday and Sunday mornings (10am–3pm).

Friend in Hand 58 Cowper St, cnr Queen St, Glebe ⓣ02/9660 2326. Character-filled pub in the leafy backstreets of Glebe, with all manner of curious objects dangling from the walls and ceilings of the public bar; a popular haunt for backpackers. Diverse entertainment in the upstairs bar (where you can also play pool), poetry, stand-up comedy and crab-racing nights – call to check what's on when. There's a good Italian restaurant serving pasta dishes from $10 (closed Sun lunch) and great-value $3 breakfasts from 7am.

Nag's Head Cnr Lodge St and St Johns Rd, off Glebe Point Rd, Glebe. Calling itself a "posh pub", this is a good place for a quiet drink. Decor and atmosphere is very much that of a British boozer: several imported beers on tap – Guinness, Boddingtons, Stella and Becks – and pints and half-pints available. Its bistro dishes up excellent steaks and other grills, and there's an extensive bar menu. Pool tables in the loft area upstairs.

Darlinghurst, Kings Cross and Woolloomooloo

The Bourbon 24 Darlinghurst Rd, Kings Cross. Established in 1968 when it was frequented by US soldiers on R&R, this infamous 24-hour Kings Cross restaurant and drinking hole has been given a swish new upgrade, which hasn't done much to deter some of its more colourful regulars. New terrace upstairs, a lounge bar out the back and the front opens up onto the street (bistro daily noon to 10pm). Bands on every night (usually covers) and DJs playing retro-80s disco four nights a week. There may be a cover charge at weekends depending on the night.

Burdekin 2 Oxford St, Darlinghurst. Well-preserved Art Deco pub with several trendy bars on four levels. The dimly-lit basement *Dug Out Bar* (from 5pm) is tiny and beautifully tiled, and has table service and generous cocktails, while the spacious, ground-level *Main Bar* sports dramatic columns and a huge round bar.

Green Park Hotel 360 Victoria St, Darlinghurst. A Darlinghurst stalwart, partly because of the stash of pool tables in the back room, but mainly because of the unpretentious vibe. The bar couldn't be more unassuming; there's nothing decorating the walls, and humble bar-tables with stools and a few lounges out the back accommodate the regular arty crowd.

Soho Bar & Lounge *Piccadilly Hotel*, 171 Victoria St, Kings Cross. Trendy, Art Deco pub on leafy Victoria Street. Ground-floor *Piccadilly* bar is the most Deco, but locals head for the upstairs *Leopard Lounge* bar (Fri & Sat nights) to hang out on the back balcony, play pool and sample the seasonally updated cocktail menu. The attached nightclub, *Yu*, runs on Fri, Sat & Sun nights from 10pm to sunrise.

The Victoria Room Level 1, 235 Victoria St, Darlinghurst. Atmospheric drawing room from the Colonial era with elegant sofas, a grand piano and chandeliers, yet a positively trendy atmosphere popular with the chill-out crowd. Tapas are served from the cocktail bar, and there's High Tea on Sat and Sun afternoons.

Surry Hills, Paddington and Woollahra

The Clock Hotel 470 Crown St, Surry Hills. This huge hotel has expanded out of touch with its 1840s roots (the landmark clock tower was only added in the 1960s). Upstairs, a swish restaurant and bar runs off the huge balcony; downstairs, the booths and tables fill up quickly for after-work drinks, and the four pool tables are ever popular.
Cricketers Arms 106 Fitzroy St, Surry Hills. Just down the road from the live-music scene at the *Hopetoun* (see p.168), the *Cricketers* has an equally dedicated clientele. A young, offbeat crowd – plenty of piercings and shaved heads – cram in and fall about the bar, pool room and tiny beer garden, and yell at each other over a funky soundtrack. Hearty bar snacks and a bistro (Tues–Sun 3–10pm).
Elephant Bar *Royal Hotel*, 237 Glenmore Rd, Paddington. The top-floor bar of this beautifully renovated, Victorian-era hotel has knockout views of the city, best appreciated at sunset (happy hour 5–6pm). The small interior is great, too, with its fireplaces, paintings and elephant prints. As it gets crowded later on, people pack onto the stairwell and it feels like a party.

Bondi and Coogee

Beach Palace Hotel 169 Dolphin St, Coogee. Home to a young and drunken crowd, made up of locals, beach babes and backpackers. Features seven bars, two restaurants and a great view of the beach from the balcony under the distinctive dome.
Beach Road Hotel 71 Beach Rd, Bondi Beach. Huge, stylishly decorated pub with a bewildering range of bars on two levels, and a beer garden. Popular with both travellers and locals for its good vibe. Entertainment, mostly free, comes from rock bands and DJs. Cheap Italian bistro, *No Names*, takes over the beer garden and has a set menu for $12; upmarket contemporary Australian restaurant upstairs.
Bondi Hotel 178 Campbell Parade, Bondi Beach. Huge pub dating from the 1920s, with many of its original features intact, seating outside and an open bar area where locals hang out with sand still on their feet. Sedate during the day but at night an over-the-top, late-night backpackers' hangout. Mon–Sat until 4am, Sun until midnight.
Bondi Icebergs Club 1 Notts Ave, Bondi Beach. Famous for its winter swimming club (see p.148), *Icebergs* is a fantastic place to sip a beer on the balcony and soak up the views and atmosphere of Bondi Beach. The *Sundeck Café* within the club offers Mediterranean-style light meals all day, but the seafood-inspired menu here is divine, though expensive.

Live music: jazz, blues and rock

The live-music scene in Sydney has passed its boom time, and pub venues keep closing down to make way for the dreaded poker machines. However, there are still enough venues to just barely nourish a steady stream of local, interstate and overseas acts passing through each month, peaking in summer with a well-established open-air festival circuit. Pub bands and clubs are often free, especially if you arrive early; door charge is usually from $5, with $25 the uppermost price for smaller international acts or the latest interstate sensation. Sunday afternoon and early evening is a mellow time to catch some music, particularly jazz, around town.

The **venues for major events**, with bookings direct or through Ticketek or Ticketmaster (see p.164), are the Entertainment Centre at Haymarket near Darling Harbour (enquiries and credit-card sales ⓣ02/9266 4800); The Hordern Pavilion at Driver Avenue, Entertainment Quarter, Moore Park (ⓣ02/8117 6700); the Capitol Theatre, 13 Campbell St, Haymarket (ⓣ02/9266 4800); the Enmore Theatre, 130 Enmore Rd, just up from Newtown (ⓣ02/9550 3666); the centrally located Metro Theatre, 624 George St (ⓣ02/9264 2666); and City Live (ⓣ02/9358 8000) at Fox Studios.

There are now several big outdoor rock concerts throughout spring and summer but Homebake and the Big Day Out are still the best. **Homebake** (around $80; ⓦwww.homebake.com.au) is a huge annual open-air festival in

The Domain in early December with food and market stalls, rides and a line-up of over fifty famous and underground Australian bands, from Spiderbait to Jet. The **Big Day Out**, on the Australia Day weekend (around $115; ⓦwww.bigdayout.com), at the Showground at Sydney Olympic Park, features big international names like The Streets, Muse and Scribe as well as big local talent like Something for Kate and The Drones. Also see "Festivals', p.177, for the Manly Jazz Festival.

The Basement 29 Reiby Place, Circular Quay ⓣ02/9251 2797. This dark and moody venue is an institution that attracts the great and rising names in jazz, acoustic and world music as well as a roster of the world's most renowned blues performers. To take in a show, book a table and dine in front of the low stage; otherwise, you'll have to stand all night at the bar at the back. Recorded broadcasts on the Internet on ⓦwww.thebasement.com.au.

Bridge Hotel 135 Victoria Rd, Rozelle ⓣ02/9810 1260. Legendary inner-west venue specializing in blues and pub rock, with some international but mostly local acts. Also good pub theatre and comedy nights.

Hopetoun Hotel 416 Bourke St, cnr of Fitzroy St, Surry Hills ⓣ02/9361 5257. One of Sydney's best venues for the indie band scene, "The Hoey" focuses on new young bands: local, interstate and international acts all play in the small and inevitably packed front bar (Mon–Sat from 7.30pm; cover charge depends on the act, though sometimes free), and on Sun there are DJs (5–10pm; $5). Popular pool room, drinking pit in the basement, and inexpensive little restaurant upstairs (meals from $5–10). Closes midnight.

Rose of Australia Hotel 1 Swanson St, Erskineville ⓣ02/9565 1441. Trendy inner-city types mix with Goths, locals and gays to sample some favourites of the pub circuit. Line-up changes regularly, and bands play Wed to Fri on a rotational basis, so you can catch anything from an original rock act through to a country-and-western cover band. Music is from 9pm (from 6.30pm Sun) and is always free.

Sandringham Hotel 387 King St, Newtown ⓣ02/9557 1254. "The Sando" features local and interstate indie bands, who play on the stage upstairs (Thurs–Sat 8.30pm–midnight, Sun 7–10pm; usually $8, more well-known bands $15).

Side On Cafe 83 Parramatta Rd, Annandale ⓣ02/9519 0055. Sydney's most interesting venue calls itself a "multi-arts complex" with a nightly programme running Thurs to Sun in an intimate café atmosphere. There's jazz (Fri & Sat) from popular trios to the latest experimental fusions; world music/Latin (Thurs) and cabaret (Sun). Also an art gallery and sometimes film screenings and script readings. Book if you want to dine (ⓣ02/9516 3077); mains such as steak with roasted vegetables cost around $20. Door charge $10–15.

Clubs

Many of Sydney's best clubs are at **gay** or **lesbian** venues, and although we've listed these separately opposite, the divisions are not always clear – many places have specific gay, lesbian and straight nights scheduled each week. A long strip of thriving clubs stretches from Kings Cross to Oxford Street and down towards Hyde Park. The scene can be pretty snobby, with door gorillas frequently vetting your style. Admission ranges from $5 to $30; many clubs stay open until 5am or 6am on Saturday and Sunday mornings. There are also good clubs attached to several of the drinking spots listed on pp.164–167. Below are the bigger venues or places with something unusual to offer.

Candy's Apartment 22 Bayswater Rd, Kings Cross. The most happening place in town, this music-portal transforms itself every night with the coolest DJs playing gigs early and then churning out fresh dance mixes as the night progresses. $20.

Club 77 77 William St, East Sydney. The big nights are Thurs to Sat at this intimate and relaxed club. Drinks are cheap and there's a swag of regulars who come here for the progressive and rare funk and house music. $10.

Havana Club 169 Oxford St, Darlinghurst. Alternating resident DJs and live musicians/percussionists ensure that there's always something new happening. The younger crowd comes on Fri for the high-octane beats, while Sat are predominantly 25- to 30-year-olds. Fri & Sat 10pm–6am. $15–25.

Home Cockle Bay Wharf, Darling Harbour. The first really big club venture in Sydney, lavish *Home* can cram 2000 punters into its cool, cavernous interior. Also a mezzanine, a chill-out room, and outdoor balconies. Decks are often manned by big-name DJs, drinks are expensive, and staff beautiful. Packed with a younger crowd on Fridays for its flagship night Sublime, with four musical styles across four levels. On Saturdays, Together at Home plays progressive and funky house. Fri & Sat from 11pm till late. $15–25.

Le Panic 20 Bayswater Rd, Kings Cross. This one-stop-shop for late-night partying has a sizeable dance floor surrounded by a swarthy bar and comfy booths. A private and exclusive lounge off to the side acts as a chill-out room. $10.

Tank 3 Bridge Lane, off George St, City. This is for the glamorous industry crowd – fashion, music and film aficionados. If you don't belong, the style police will spot you a mile away. All very "funky" – from the house music played by regular or guest DJs to the mirrors and wash basins in the toilets. Three amazing bars and a VIP section. Attire is smart casual to funky street wear, but attitude and good looks override the dress code. Fri & Sat 10pm–6am. $15–20.

The World Bar 24 Bayswater Rd, Kings Cross. With cheap drinks on Fri and Sat nights and a relatively relaxed door policy, *The World* is popular with a fun, party-loving crowd of travellers, who jive to a pleasing mix of funk and house grooves in a pleasant Victorian-era building with a big front balcony. Mon–Thurs & Sun noon–4am, Fri & Sat noon–6am. $15, free before midnight.

Gay and lesbian bars and clubs

The last few years have seen a quiet diminishing of specifically gay and lesbian bars, and due to Sydney's highly restrictive liquor-licensing laws, the smaller venues vanish and the large ones just get bigger. One of the best things about the city's gay and lesbian scene is that it's concentrated in two areas so it's easy to bar hop: in the inner east around Oxford Street, Darlinghurst, including Surry Hills and Kings Cross, and in the inner west in adjoining Newtown and Erskineville. Those wanting a comfortable place to drink with a mixed clientele should also check out pubs already listed such as the *Green Park Hotel* or the *Burdekin* (p.166). Entry is free unless otherwise indicated.

Arq 16 Flinders St, cnr Taylor Square, Darlinghurst. Huge nine-hundred-person capacity, state-of-the-art mainstream club with everything from DJs and drag shows to pool competitions. Two levels, each with a very different scene: the Arena, on the top floor, is mostly gay, while the ground-floor Vortex is a quieter, less crowded mix of gay and straight, with pool tables. Chill-out booths, laser lighting, viewing decks and fishtanks add to the fun, friendly atmosphere. Sun is the big night. Thurs–Sun from 9pm. Fri $10, Sat $20, Sun $5. Check website for specific events ⓦ www.arqsydney.com.au.

Columbian Hotel 117 Oxford St, cnr Crown St, Darlinghurst. Mixed-clientele bar where people come to get revved-up in the evenings and renew their energy the day after. The downstairs bar offers an airy, comfortable space to drink, bop and chat, with open windows onto the street. Upstairs (6pm–late) gets very crowded Thurs to Sun nights, attracting a hip and chilled crowd. The music is Hi-NRG upstairs, progressive house downstairs (Mon–Sun 10am till late).

Exchange Hotel 34 Oxford St, Darlinghurst. In the downstairs *Phoenix* bar, Saturday night's Crash underground "alternative" dance club is mostly gay shirtless men dancing en masse, but on Sun nights there's a happy mix of gays and dykes. After midnight, it's at its peak with a raunchier, bacchanalian crowd that you won't find anywhere else on the strip (Sat & Sun from 10pm; $10 Sat, $5 Sun).

Imperial Hotel 35 Erskineville Rd, Erskineville ⓣ 02/9519 9899. Late-night gay-and-lesbian venue, with four bars including a popular, hot and sweaty dance-floor in the basement (Fri & Sat progressive, commercial, Hi-NRG 11pm–6am for $5), and a riotous drag-show line-up in the *Cabaret Room* (Thurs–Sat; free; call for show times). Bingay (gay and lesbian bingo) is held Tuesdays 8.30pm. The film *The Adventures of Priscilla, Queen of the Desert* both started and ended here; it was the *Imperial*'s finest hour, and the memories are kept alive in the photo-lined cocktail bar, the *Priscilla Lounge* (cabaret Thurs–Sat 10.30pm; free). Pool tables and music videos in the public bar. Mon–Thurs 3pm–2/3am, Fri & Sat 1pm–7am, Sun 1pm–midnight.

Midnight Shift 85 Oxford St, Darlinghurst. "The Shift", running for over 25 years, is a veteran of the Oxford Street scene. The *Shift Video Bar* is a large drinking and cruising space to a music-video backdrop; pool tables out back. Upstairs, the weekend-only club is a massive space with drag

Gay and lesbian Sydney

Sydney is indisputably one of the world's great gay cities – indeed, many people think it capable of snatching San Francisco's crown as the Queen of them all. There's something for everyone – whether you want to lie on a beach during the warmer months (Oct–April) or party hard all year round. Gays and lesbians are pretty much accepted, particularly in the inner-city and eastern areas. They have to be – there's too many of them for anyone to argue. A big drawcard is the **Sydney Gay & Lesbian Mardi Gras**; the festival lasts for four weeks, starting the first week of **February**, kicking off with a launch in Hyde Park, followed two weeks later by a Fair Day in Victoria Park and culminating in the parade and party on the last weekend of February or the first weekend of March. The first parade was held in 1978 as a gay-rights protest and today it's the biggest celebration of gay and lesbian culture in the world. In 1992, an unprecedented crowd of 400,000, including a broad spectrum of straight society, turned up to watch the parade and two years later it began to be broadcast nationally on television. Mardi Gras turned 29 in 2007 but for a while it looked like it wouldn't make it. By 1999, the combined festival, parade and party was making the local economy $100 million dollars richer and the increasing commercialization of Mardi Gras was drawing criticism from the gay and lesbian community. Its bubble burst in 2002, after financial mismanagement saw the Mardi Gras organization in the red to the tune of $500,000. Instead of throwing in the towel, the fundraising organization was rebuilt as the "New Mardi Gras"; although less cash-rich, New Mardi Gras is drawing on the resources and creativity of its talented community along with the desire to keep the festival going in order to revive the old Mardi Gras spirit.

But don't despair if you can't be here for Mardi Gras or the Sleaze Ball (the annual Mardi Gras fundraiser in late Sept/early Oct). The city has much more to offer. **Oxford Street** is Sydney's official "pink strip" of gay restaurants, coffee shops, bookshops and bars, and here you'll find countless pairs of tight-T-shirted guys strolling hand-in-hand, or checking out the passing talent from hip, streetside cafés. However, the gay–straight divide in Sydney has less relevance for a new generation, perhaps ironically a result of Mardi Gras' mainstream success. Several of the long-running gay venues on and around Oxford Street have closed down and many remaining attract older customers, as younger gays and lesbians embrace inclusiveness and party with their straight friends and peers or choose to meet new friends on the Internet instead of in bars. **King Street**, Newtown, and nearby **Erskineville** are centres of gay culture, while lesbian communities have carved out territory of their own in **Leichhardt** (known affectionately as "Dykehart") and **Marrackville**. The bar and club listings have not been split into separate gay and lesbian listings, as the scene thankfully doesn't divide so neatly into "them and us", but weekly event listings are included in the free magazines (see below).

If you've come for the sun, popular **gay beaches** are Tamarama (see p.146), Bondi (see p.147), and "clothing-optional" Lady Jane, while pools of choice are Red Leaf harbour pool at Double Bay (see p.141) and the appropriately named Andrew "Boy" Charlton pool in The Domain (see p.125). The Coogee Women's Baths, at the southern end of Coogee Beach (see p.150), is popular with lesbians.

Mardi Gras, Sleaze and PRIDE

From a queer perspective, the best time of year to visit Sydney is still February, when the **Sydney Gay & Lesbian Mardi Gras** takes over the city. Four weeks of exhibitions, performances and other events – including the ten-day **Mardi Gras Film Festival** in mid-February, showcasing the latest in queer cinema – represent the largest gay-and-lesbian arts festival in the world, paving the way for the main event, an exuberant night-time parade down Oxford Street, when up to half-a-million gays and straights jostle for the best viewing positions, before the Dykes on Bikes, traditional leaders of the parade since 1988, roar into view. Participants devote months to the preparation of outlandish floats and outrageous costumes at Mardi Gras workshops, and even more time is devoted to the preparation of beautiful bodies in Sydney's packed gyms. The **parade** begins at 7.30pm (finishing around 10.30pm), but people line the barricades along Oxford Street from mid-morning (brandishing stolen milk crates to stand on for a better view). If you can't get to Oxford Street until late afternoon, your best chance of finding a spot is along Flinders Street near Moore Park Road, where the parade ends. Otherwise, AIDS charity The Bobby Goldsmith Foundation (ⓣ02/9283 8666, ⓦwww.bgf.org.au) has around 7000 grandstand ("Glamstand") seats on Flinders Street, at $110 each.

The all-night **dance party** that follows the parade attracts up to 25,000 people and is held in several differently-themed dance spaces at The Entertainment Quarter in Moore Park (including a women's space in the *Fuse Bar*). You may have to plan ahead if you want to get a **ticket**: party tickets ($125 in advance, or $140 at the gates) sometimes sell out by the end of January. The purchase of tickets used to be restricted to "Mardi Gras members" to keep the event queer, with special provisions for visitors from interstate and overseas, but as the New Mardi Gras is rebuilding the old memberships and procedures no longer exist, tickets can be bought from Ticketek (ⓣ02/9266 4800, ⓦwww.ticketek.com.au) or for general enquiries contact the **New Mardi Gras office** (ⓣ02/9568 8600, ⓦwww.mardigras.org.au). Your local gay-friendly travel agent can also organize tickets. The **Sydney Gay & Lesbian Mardi Gras Guide**, available from mid-December, can be picked up from bookshops, cafés and restaurants around Oxford Street or viewed online from their website.

Sydney just can't wait all year for Mardi Gras, so the **Sleaze Ball** is a very welcome stopgap in early October and acts as a fundraiser for the Mardi Gras organizers. Similar to the Mardi Gras party, it's held at The Entertainment Quarter, and goes on through the night. Tickets, which cost around $110, are organized by New Mardi Gras and sold through Ticketek. The community centre **PRIDE** (ⓣ02/9331 1333, ⓦwww.pridecentre.com.au) have been organizing a similarly priced and over-the-top **New Year's Eve party** for the past decade, usually also at The Entertainment Quarter.

For those who miss the parties themselves, the **recovery parties** the next day are nearly as good; virtually all the bars and clubs host all-day sessions after the parties, especially the lanes behind the *Flinders Bar*, which are packed with exhausted but deliriously happy party-people.

Groups and information

See also p.105 for gay- and lesbian-friendly **places to stay**, and pp.169–173 for a lowdown on the **club scene** and listings of specifically gay and lesbian venues.

Information The Bookshop, 207 Oxford St, Darlinghurst (ⓣ02/9331 1103), is a good starting point for getting to know gay Sydney, with a complete stock of gay- and lesbian-related books, cards and magazines. The staff are friendly and ready to help in any way they can. You can pick up the free gay and lesbian weeklies *Sydney Star Observer* (ⓦwww.ssonet.com.au) and *SX* (ⓦwww.sxnews.com.au) and the monthly lesbian-specific *LOTL* (*Lesbians on the Loose*; ⓦwww.lotl.com) from here and other venues and gay-friendly businesses in the eastern suburbs and inner west. These magazines will tell you where and when the weekly dance parties are being held, and where you can buy tickets.

Support networks Gay & Lesbian Counseling Service (daily 4pm–midnight; ⓣ02/8594 9596). AIDS Council of NSW (ACON), 9 Commonwealth St, Surry Hills ⓣ02/9206 2000. Albion Street Centre, 150–154 Albion St, Surry Hills ⓣ02/9332 1090; counseling, testing clinic, information and library. Anti-Discrimination Board ⓣ02/9268 5544.

shows, DJs and events; cover charge upwards of $15. Mainly men. Downstairs bar daily noon–6am, club Fri & Sat 11pm–7am. $20.

Taxi Club 40 Flinders St, Darlinghurst. A Sydney legend and famous (or notorious) for being the only place you can buy a drink after 10pm on Good Friday or Christmas Day, but don't bother before 2 or 3am, and you'll need to be suitably intoxicated to appreciate it fully. There's a strange blend of drag queens, taxi drivers, lesbians and boys (straight and gay) to observe, and the cheapest drinks in gay Sydney. An upstairs dance club (free) operates Friday and Saturday from 1am. Supposedly a members' club but bring ID to show you're from out of town. 24hr except for a clean-up from 6–9am.

Classical music, theatre and dance

Sydney's **arts scene** is vibrant and extensive. The Sydney Symphony Orchestra plays at the Town Hall, St James' Church or the Concert Hall at the Opera House, while the Australian Ballet performs at the Opera House and the Capitol Theatre. The free outdoor performances in The Domain, under the auspices of the Sydney Festival, are a highlight of the year, with crowds gathering to enjoy the music with a picnic.

Concert halls

City Recital Hall Angel Place, between George and Pitt streets, City ☎02/8256 2222. Opened in 1999, this classical-music venue right next to Martin Place was specifically designed for chamber music. Seats over 1200, but on three levels, giving it an intimate atmosphere.

Conservatorium of Music Royal Botanic Gardens, off Macquarie St, City ☎02/9351 1263. Students of the "Con" give free lunchtime recitals every Wednesday at 1.10pm during term time in Recital Hall West. Other concerts, both free and ticketed (anywhere from $10 up to around $35) are given by students and staff here and at venues around town; a programme is available from the concert department. See p.125 for more details.

St James' Church King St, beside Hyde Park, City ☎02/9232 3022. St James' highly acclaimed chamber choir, whose repertoire extends from Gregorian chant to more contemporary pieces, can be heard on Sundays at 11am (plus 4pm last Sun of the month). St James' music programme also includes a series of lunchtime concerts (Wed 1.15pm; 30min; $5 donation).

Sydney Opera House Bennelong Point ☎02/9250 7777. The Opera House is, of course, the place for the most prestigious performances in Sydney, hosting not just opera and classical music but also theatre and ballet in its many auditoriums. Forget quibbles about ticket prices (classical concerts from $50, ballet from $65, opera from $95) – it's worth going just to say you've been. See pp.111–113 for more details.

Town Hall Cnr Druitt and George streets, City ☎02/9265 9189. Centrally located concert hall (seats 2000) with a splendid high-Victorian interior – hosts everything from chamber orchestras to bush dances and public lectures.

Theatre and dance

Bangarra Dance Theatre Pier 4, Hickson Rd, Millers Point, The Rocks ☎02/9251 5333. Formed in 1989, Bangarra's innovative style fuses contemporary movement with the traditional dances and culture of the Yirrkala Community in the Northern Territory's Arnhem Land. Based at the same pier as the Wharf Theatre but performing at other venues in Sydney and touring nationally and internationally – call for the latest details.

Belvoir St Theatre 25 Belvoir St, Surry Hills ☎02/9699 3444. Highly regarded two-stage venue for a wide range of contemporary Australian and international theatre.

Ensemble Theatre 78 McDougall St, Milsons Point ☎02/9929 0644. Hosts Australian contemporary and classic plays.

The Footbridge Theatre Parramatta Rd, University of Sydney, Glebe ☎02/9692 9955. Rich and varied repertoire, from cabaret to Shakespeare.

Lyric Theatre Star City Casino, Pirrama Rd, Pyrmont ☎02/9657 9657. The place to see those big musical extravaganzas imported from the West End and Broadway. The casino's smaller theatre, the Star City Showroom, puts on more off-beat musicals – such as the *Rocky Horror Picture Show* – and comedy.

NAISDA Dance College 3 Cumberland St, The Rocks ⓣ02/9252 0199. Established in 1976, this famous training company for young Aboriginal and Islander dancers, based in The Rocks, puts on mid-year and end-of-year performances at the NAISDA Studios at the college; call for times.

The Playhouse, Drama Theatre and The Studio Sydney Opera House, Bennelong Point ⓣ02/9250 7777. The Playhouse and Drama Theatre show modern and traditional Australian and international plays mostly put on by the Sydney Theatre Company, while the Studio, the Opera House's smallest venue (with the most affordable ticket prices), is flexible in design with a theatre-in-the-round format, and offers an innovative and wide-ranging programme of contemporary performance: theatre, cabaret, dance, comedy, and hybrid works.

Wharf Theatre Pier 4/5, Hickson Rd, Millers Point, The Rocks ⓣ02/9250 1777. Home to the Sydney Dance Company and the highly regarded Sydney Theatre Company, producing Shakespeare and modern pieces. Atmospheric waterfront location, two performance spaces and a good restaurant (see p.157), bar and café.

Fringe theatre, comedy and cabaret

As well as the venues listed below, also see the *Bridge Hotel* (p.168), which has Monday comedy nights and Tuesday improv and cabaret runs, and *The Imperial* (p.169) for its brilliant, free drag shows.

New Theatre 542 King St, Newtown ⓣ02/9519 8958. Professional and amateur actors (all unpaid) perform contemporary dramas with socially relevant themes. Tickets $25.

NIDA 215 Anzac Parade, Kensington ⓣ02/9697 7613. Australia's premier dramatic training ground – the National Institute of Dramatic Art – where the likes of Mel Gibson, Judy Davis and Colin Friels started out, also offers student productions for talent-spotting. Tickets $25.

Stables Theatre 10 Nimrod St, Darlinghurst ⓣ02/9361 3817. Home theatre for the Griffin Theatre Company, whose mission is to develop and foster new Australian playwrights.

Sydney Comedy Store Entertainment Quarter, Driver Ave, Moore Park ⓣ02/9357 1419, ⓦwww.comedystore.com.au. International (often American) and Australian stand-up comics Tues to Sat; open-mic nights Tues and new comics Wed. Bar open from 7pm, show 8.30pm. Meals aren't available inside, but nearby restaurants offer meal discounts for *Comedy Store* ticket-holders. Bookings recommended. Entry Tues & Wed $15, Thurs $20, Fri $27.50, Sat $29.50.

Cinemas

The commercial movie centre of Sydney is two blocks south of the Town Hall at 505–525 George St where you'll find the two big chains, Hoyts (ⓣ02/9273 7431) and Greater Union (ⓣ02/9267 8666), under one roof. This is mainstream, fast-food, teenager territory and there are much nicer places to watch a film, especially at the locals in the list below. Other more pleasantly located Hoyts can be found at the Broadway Shopping Centre, on Broadway near Glebe (ⓣ02/9211 1911); and at the 12-screen complex at Entertainment Quarter (ⓣ02/9332 1300), where five of the screens have an upmarket La Premiere section aimed at couples with double seats (bookings ⓣ02/9332 1300 ext 5; $25–30 includes soft drinks and popcorn). Hoyts' art-house option, the four-screen Cinema Paris (ⓣ02/9332 1633), is also at the Entertainment Quarter. Another mainstream multiplex is bang in Chinatown – Reading Cinemas, at Level 3, Market City Shopping Centre, Haymarket (ⓣ02/9280 1202). Standard tickets cost around $15, but Tuesdays are reduced-price (around $10.50) at all of these cinemas and their suburban outlets, and Monday or Tuesday at most of the art-house and local cinemas listed below.

In the summer, there are two open-air cinemas: from November to the end of March, the **Moonlight Cinema**, in the Centennial Park Amphitheatre (Oxford Street, Woollahra entrance; Tues–Sun, films start 8.45pm, tickets from 7pm or bookings on ⓣ1300 551 908; $14.50), shows classic, art-house and cult films; and throughout January and February, the **Open Air Cinema** (tickets

Film festivals

The **Sydney Film Festival**, held annually for two weeks in **early June**, is an exciting programme of features, shorts, documentaries and retrospective screenings from Australia and around the world. Founded in 1954 by a group of film enthusiasts at Sydney University, the festival struggled with prudish censors and parochial attitudes until freedom from censorship for festival films was introduced in 1971. From the early, relaxed atmosphere of picnics on the lawns between screenings and hardy film-lovers crouching under blankets in freezing prefabricated sheds, it has gradually moved off-campus, to find a home from 1974 in the magnificent State Theatre (see p.119). Films are also shown at the wonderfully sited three-screen Dendy Quays in Circular Quay. The festival was once mainly sold on a subscription basis, but subscriptions now only apply to screenings at the State Theatre; the more provocative line-up of films at the Dendy Quays aims to attract a new, younger audience on a single-or packaged-ticket basis. Single **tickets** cost around $15, selected film packages of five to ten $12.50 each, eleven or more $11 each or, if you can't decide, there are 10- or 20-film Flexi Passes for $120/$200; **subscriptions** for the State Theatre programme start from $170 for one-week daytime-only unreserved stalls seating, and go up to $290 for two weeks' reserved dress-circle night-time screenings. For more information, call or drop into the festival office at Level 5, 414–418 Elizabeth St, Surry Hills (Mon–Fri 9am–5pm; ⓣ02/9280 0511; bookings ⓣ02/9280 0611 or via ⓦwww.sydneyfilmfestival.org).

There are also two short film festivals in the summer with the sort of irreverent approach that once fuelled the Sydney Film Festival. Stars above and the sound of waves accompany the week-long **Flickerfest International Short Film Festival** (single ticket $14, season pass $120; ⓣ02/9365 6888, ⓦwww.flickerfest.com.au), held in the amphitheatre of the Bondi Pavilion in early January, and showcasing foreign and Australian productions, including documentaries. The **Tropfest** (ⓣ02/9368 0434, ⓦwww.tropfest.com) is a competition festival for short films held annually around the end of February; its name comes from the *Tropicana Cafe* on Victoria Street, Darlinghurst, where the festival began almost by chance in 1993 when a young actor, John Polsen, forced his local coffee spot to show the short film he had made. He pushed other filmmakers to follow suit, and the following year a huge crowd of punters packed themselves into the café to watch around twenty films. These days, the entire street is closed to traffic to enable an outdoor screening, while cafés along the strip also screen the films inside. The festival has grown enormously over the years, and the focus of the event in Sydney has moved to The Domain, with huge crowds turning up to picnic and watch the free 8pm screening (plus live entertainment from 3pm), while outdoor screenings are held simultaneously in capital cities Australia-wide. The judges are often famous international actors, and Polsen himself, still the festival's director, has made it as a Hollywood director with his films *Swimfan* (2002) *Hide and Seek* (2005). Each state capital also screens the event simultaneously in venues ranging from cafés to parks. Films must be specifically produced for the festival and be up-to-the-minute – an item is announced a few months in advance of the entry date that must feature in the shorts. In 2007, it was "sneeze" – however you wanted to interpret it.

Other film festivals include the **World of Women (WOW) Film Festival** held over three days in late October at the Chauvel Cinema, Paddington (ⓦwww.FutureTrain.com.au/wift/wow); and a **gay and lesbian film festival** in late February as part of the Gay and Lesbian Mardi Gras.

from 6.30pm or bookings on ⓣ13 61 00; $19) is put up at Mrs Macquarie's Point in the Royal Botanic Gardens for a very picturesque film screening – mainly mainstream recent releases and some classics. See box above for details of Sydney's annual film festivals.

Chauvel Twin Cinema Paddington Town Hall, cnr Oatley Rd and Oxford St, Paddington ⓣ02/9361 5398. Varied programme of Australian and foreign films plus classics at this cinephile's cinema. Discount on Mon and Tues.
Cremorne Orpheum 380 Military Rd, Cremorne ⓣ02/9908 4344. Charming heritage-listed, six-screen cinema built in 1935, with a splendid Art Deco interior and old-fashioned friendly service. The main cinema has never dispensed with its Wurlitzer organ recitals preceding Sat night and Sun afternoon films. Mainstream, and foreign new releases. Discount on Tues.
Dendy 261 King St, Newtown ⓣ02/9550 5699. Trendy four-screen cinema complex with attached café, bar and bookshop, showing prestige new-release films. The newer, three-screen Dendy Opera Quays, 2 East Circular Quay (ⓣ02/9247 3800), is superbly sited. Discount on Mon.
Govinda's Movie Room 112 Darlinghurst Rd, Darlinghurst ⓣ02/9380 5155. Run by the Hare Krishnas (but definitely no indoctrination), Govinda's shows two films every night from a range of classics and recent releases in a pleasantly unorthodox cushion-room atmosphere. The movie-and-dinner deal (all-you-can-eat vegetarian buffet) is popular – $16.90 for the meal with an extra $7.90 to see a movie. Buy your film ticket after you've ordered your meal, or you may miss out on busy nights. Film only is $10.90 but diners are given preference.
Palace Cinemas Chain of inner-city cinemas showing foreign-language, art-house and new releases: Academy, 3A Oxford St, cnr South Dowling St, Paddington (ⓣ02/9361 4453); Verona, 17 Oxford St, cnr Verona St, Paddington (ⓣ02/9360 6099), with a bar; Norton, 99 Norton St, Leichhardt (ⓣ02/9550 0122), the newest with a bookshop and cybercafé. Discount Mon.
Panasonic IMAX Theatre Southern Promenade, Darling Harbour ⓣ02/9281 3300. State-of-the-art giant cinema screen showing a choice of four films designed to thrill your senses; $18 for 2D version, $17–22.50 for 3D. Screenings on the hour, 10am–10pm.

Art galleries and exhibitions

The Citysearch Sydney website (ⓦwww.sydney.citysearch.com.au) has comprehensive listings of art galleries and current exhibitions, while Friday's "Metro" section of the *Sydney Morning Herald* offers reviews of recently opened shows, or check out the useful *Artfind Guide* online (ⓦwww.artfind.com.au). Galleries tend to be concentrated in Paddington and Surry Hills, with a few smaller ones on King Street, Newtown.

Artspace The Gunnery Arts Centre, 43–51 Cowper Wharf Rd, Woolloomooloo ⓣ02/9356 0555. In a wonderful location, showing provocative young artists with a focus on installations and new media. Tues–Sat 11am–5pm.
Australian Centre for Photography 257 Oxford St, Paddington ⓣ02/9332 1455. Exhibitions of photo-based art from established and new international and Australian artists in two galleries. Emerging photographers are showcased on the Project Wall. There's a specialist bookshop, photography courses, and a dark room for hire, plus the very good French-style *Bistro Lulu*. Tues–Fri noon–7pm, Sat & Sun 10am–6pm.
Australian Galleries: Painting & Sculpture 15 Roylston St, Paddington ⓣ02/9360 5177. Serene gallery exhibiting and selling contemporary Australian art, including works by Gary Shead, Jeffrey Smart and John Coburn. Mon–Sat 10am–6pm.
Australian Galleries: Works on Paper 24 Glenmore Rd, Paddington ⓣ02/9380 8744. Works for sale here include drawings by William Robinson, Brett Whiteley and Arthur Boyd, as well as prints and sketches by young Australian artists. Mon–Sat 10am–6pm, Sun noon–5pm.
Hogarth Galleries Aboriginal Art Centre 7 Walker Lane, Paddington ⓣ02/9360 6839. Extensive collection of work by contemporary Aboriginal artists, both tribal and urban, and special exhibitions. Tues–Sat 10am–5pm.
Ivan Dougherty Gallery Cnr Albion Ave and Selwyn St, Paddington ⓣ02/9385 0726. This is the exhibition space for the College of Fine Arts (COFA), University of NSW. The ten shows per year focus on international contemporary art with accompanying forums, lectures and performances. Mon–Sat 10am–5pm (closed Jan).
Josef Lebovic Gallery 34 Paddington St, Paddington ⓣ02/9332 1840. Renowned print and graphic gallery specializing in Australian and international prints from the nineteenth, twentieth and twenty-first centuries, as well as vintage photography. Wed–Fri 1–6pm, Sat 11am–5pm.
Ray Hughes Gallery 270 Devonshire St, Surry Hills ⓣ02/9698 3200. Influential dealer with a stable of high-profile contemporary Australian and New Zealand artists. Openings monthly, with two artists per show. Tues–Sat 10am–6pm.

Festivals and events

The Sydney year is interspersed with festivals and events of various sorts that reach their peak in the summer. Check the City of Sydney Council's online "What's On" section (Ⓦwww.cityofsydney.nsw.gov.au) for details of events year-round, or its free weekly listings *City Life* which comes out Wednesday and is available at the Town Hall and tourist offices.

The **New Year** begins with a spectacular **fireworks** display from the Harbour Bridge and Darling Harbour. There's a brief hiatus of a week or so until the annual **Sydney Festival** (Ⓣ02/8248 6500, Ⓦwww.sydneyfestival.org.au), an exhaustive and exhausting arts event that lasts for most of **January** and ranges from concerts, plays and outdoor art installations to circus performances. About fifty percent of the events are free and are based around urban public spaces, focusing on Circular Quay, The Domain, Darling Harbour, and Sydney Olympic Park; the remainder – mostly international performances – can cost a packet. The general programme is usually printed in the *Sydney Morning Herald* in the previous October while a full eighty-plus-page programme is available nearer the time. From Boxing Day to the end of January, **Darling Harbour** hosts its own festival (see Ⓦwww.darlingharbour.com.au), linked with the Festival of Sydney. Most of the attractions are aimed at children, but the very lively **Bacardi Latino Festival** is perfect for a balmy evening.

Australia Day on January 26 is a huge celebration in Sydney, with activities focused on the water (see Australia Day Council of NSW; Ⓦwww.australiaday.com.au). Sydney's passenger ferries race from Fort Denison to the Harbour Bridge, there's the Tall Ships Race from Bradleys Head to the Harbour Bridge, a 21-gun salute fired from the Man O'War steps at the Opera House, and an aerial display of military planes. The **Australia Day Regatta** takes place in the afternoon, with hundreds of yachts racing all over the water, from Botany Bay to the Parramatta River. There are also free events at The Rocks, Hyde Park, and at Darling Harbour, where the day culminates at around 9pm with a fireworks display. In addition, many museums let visitors in for free. Besides all this, there are at least two outdoor rock concerts to choose from: **Yabun** (formerly "Survival"), which celebrates Aboriginal culture and acts as an antidote to the mainstream white Australia Day festivities, is held at Redfern Oval (free; no alcohol allowed; contact Koori Radio on Ⓣ02/9564 5904 or check Ⓦwww.gadigal.org.au); while the **Big Day Out** (see p.59) is usually held that day at the Showground at Sydney Olympic Park, featuring around sixty local and international bands and DJs.

Horse racing in Sydney

There are horse-racing meetings on Wednesday, Saturday and most public holidays throughout the year, but the best times to hit the track are during the **Spring and Autumn Carnivals** (Aug–Sept and March–April), when prize money rockets, and the quality of racing rivals the best in the world. The venues are well maintained, peopled with colourful racing characters and often massive crowds. Principal **racecourses** are: Royal Randwick (Alison Road, Randwick), which featured in *Mission Impossible II*; Rosehill Gardens (James Ruse Drive, Rosehill); and Canterbury Park (King Street, Canterbury; Ⓣ02/9930 4000), which has midweek racing, plus floodlit Thursday-night racing from September to March. Entry is around $12, or $20–25 on carnival days. Contact the Australian Jockey Club (Ⓣ02/9663 8400, Ⓦwww.ajc.org.au) for details of many other picturesque country venues to choose from. Every Friday, the *Sydney Morning Herald* publishes its racing guide, "The Form". Bets are placed at TAB shops; these are scattered throughout the city, and most pubs also have TAB access.

An entirely different side of Sydney life is on view at the impressive summer **surf carnivals**, staged regularly by local surf lifesaving clubs; contact Surf Life Saving NSW (Ⓣ02/9984 7188, Ⓦwww.surflifesaving.com.au) for details.

At the end of **February** the city is engulfed by the **Sydney Gay & Lesbian Mardi Gras** (see p.170). Another big event is the **Sydney Royal Easter Show** (Ⓦwww.eastershow.com.au), an agricultural and garden show in **late March/early April**, based at the Showground at Sydney Olympic Park. For twelve consecutive days (with the second weekend always the Easter weekend) the country comes to the city for a frantic array of amusement-park rides, fireworks, parades of prize animals, a rodeo, and wood-chopping displays. In **May**, the week-long **Sydney Writers Festival** (mostly free; Ⓦwww.swf.org.au) takes place in the very scenically located Wharf Theatre complex.

The **Sydney International Film Festival** takes over many of the city's screens in **June** (see box, p.174). Every even-numbered year, the **Biennale of Sydney** takes place over six weeks from early June until mid-August, with provocative contemporary art exhibitions at various venues and public spaces around town, and the **City to Surf Race**, a 14-kilometre fun run from the city to Bondi, happens every **August**. Labour Day weekend in early **October** is marked by the **Manly International Jazz Festival**, with several free outdoor, waterfront events and a few indoor concerts charging entry. This is followed by the very Italian **Blessing of the Fleet** at Darling Harbour. In **November**, the coast between Bondi and Tamarama is transformed for two weeks by the magical **Sculpture By The Sea** exhibition (Ⓦwww.sculpturebythesea.com). The year is brought to a close by the **Sydney to Hobart Yacht Race**, when it seems that half of the city turns up at or on the harbour on December 26 to cheer the start of this classic regatta and watch the colourful spectacle of two hundred or so yachts setting sail for a 630-nautical-mile slog.

Shopping

Sydney's main shopping focus is the city centre, in the stretch between Martin Place and the QVB. Apart from its charming old nineteenth-century arcades and two **department stores**, David Jones and Myers, the city centre also has several modern multi-level **shopping complexes** where you can hunt down clothes and accessories without raising a sweat, among them Skygarden (between Pitt and Castlereagh streets) and Centrepoint on Pitt Street Mall, on the corner of Market Street. Much of the area from the QVB to the mall is linked by underground arcades, which will also keep you cool.

Most stores are **open** Monday to Saturday 9am to 6pm, with Thursday late-night shopping until 9pm. Many of the larger shops and department stores in the city are also open on Sunday 10am to 5pm, as are shopping centres in tourist areas such as Darling Harbour. If you've run out of time to buy presents and souvenirs, don't worry: the revamped **Sydney Airport** is attached to one of the biggest shopping malls in Sydney, with outlets for everything from surfwear to R.M. Williams bush outfitters, at the same prices as the downtown stores. The Rocks is the best place for souvenir and duty- and GST-free shopping.

Fashion

Oxford Street in Paddington is the place to go for interesting fashion, with outlets of most Australian designers along the strip. You'll find more expensive designer gear in the city, at the Strand Arcade, 412 George St, and David Jones department store (see p.119). For striking street fashion, check out Crown Street in Surry Hills, with places such as Wheels & Doll Baby at no. 259, and King Street in Newtown running up to St Peters, where you'll also find cheaper styles, retro clothes and other interesting junk. To go with the outfits, funky Australian **jewellery** can be found in the Strand Arcade at Dinosaur Designs (also at 339 Oxford St, Paddington), and at Love and Hatred, both on Level 1.

The quality Australian **bush outfitters** R. M. Williams, with branches at no. 71 and no. 389 George Street, is great for moleskin trousers, Drizabone coats and Akubra hats. However, for an even wider range of Akubra **hats**, check out Strand Hatters on the ground floor of the Strand Arcade. If it's interesting **surfwear** you're after, head for Mambo at Market City, Hay St, Haymarket (also at 17 Oxford St, Paddington; 80 The Corso, Manly; and 80 Campbell Parade, Bondi Beach), and an array of surf shops at Manly and Bondi Beach.

Arts and crafts

The Rocks is heaving with **Australiana** and **arts and crafts** souvenirs, from opals to sheepskin – weekends are particularly busy when the open-air market takes over George Street. Tourists flock to Ken Done's emporium here at 123 George St and 1–5 Hickson Rd (in the restored Australian Steam and Navigation Building) to buy his colourful designs, which feature Sydney's harbour, boats and flowers; there's a Done Art & Design store at the airport, too, and another at the Market City Shopping Centre. The best place to buy **Aboriginal** art and crafts is the Aboriginal-owned and -run Gavala, in the Harbourside shopping centre in Darling Harbour.

Music and books

For a take-home sample of the **Australian music** scene in all its variety, from Aboriginal through to indie and jazz, head for the Australian Music Centre shop, Level 4, The Arts Exchange, 10 Hickson Rd, The Rocks, with very knowledgeable staff and a relaxed listen-before-you-buy policy.

One of the biggest **bookshops** in the city is the long-running, Australian-owned Dymocks, 428 George St, open daily, on several floors with an impressive Australian selection and a café. Book superstores include Kinokuniya in Galleries Victoria, on the corner of George and Park streets; Borders, 77 Castlereagh St, between King and Market streets; and Collins Superstore, Level 2, Broadway Shopping Centre near Glebe. Nearby, Gleebooks, 49 Glebe Point Rd, Glebe, is one of Australia's best bookshops, specializing in academic and alternative books, contemporary Australian and international literature, and is open daily until 9pm; book launches and other literary events are regularly held. Ariel has two large, lively and hip branches, one at 103 George St, The Rocks, and the other at 42 Oxford St, Paddington; both branches open daily until midnight. Macleay Bookshop, 103 Macleay St, Potts Point (daily until 7pm), is a tiny and peaceful choice. The **Travel Bookshop** at 175 Liverpool St, Darlinghurst (closed Sun), is the place to head for maps, guides and travel journals, plus a good selection of Australiana. **Secondhand books** can be found at Glebe and Paddington markets, at Gleebooks Second Hand Books, 191 Glebe Point Rd (daily until 9pm); upstairs at Lesley McKays Bookshop, 346 New South Head Rd, Double Bay (the ground level, for new books, is open until midnight); and in the secondhand bookshops on King Street, Newtown – in particular, check out the amazingly chaotic piles of books at Gould's Book Arcade, nos. 32–38 (daily 8am–midnight).

Food and drink

There are several handy **supermarkets** in the city centre with extended opening hours: one is in the basement of Woolworths on the corner of Park and George streets, above Town Hall station (Mon–Fri 6.30am–midnight, Sat & Sun 8am–midnight); and there are three small Coles supermarkets in the city – Wynyard station; 388 George St; and 580 George St in the Pavilion Central Shopping Centre (daily 6am–midnight) – while the larger Coles in Kings Cross, at 88 Darlinghurst Rd, and on Broadway near Glebe are both also handy for travellers (all daily 6am–midnight). In the suburbs, large supermarkets such as Coles stay open daily until about 10pm or midnight, and there are plenty of (albeit overpriced) 24-hour convenience stores in the inner city and suburbs, often attached to petrol stations. For **delicatessen** items, look no further than the splendid food hall at David Jones (see p.119). The **Australian Wine Centre**, corner of George and Alfred streets, Circular Quay (Mon–Sat 9.30am–6.30pm, Sun 11am–5pm), sells more than a thousand **wines** from around Australia and even has an in-house wine bar.

Markets

The two best **markets** are the Paddington Market (9am–4pm) and Balmain Market (7.30am–4pm), both on Saturday, while the relaxed Glebe Market (10am–4pm), also on a Saturday, and flea market at Rozelle (Sat & Sun 9am–4pm) are also worth a look. The Rocks Market on George Street (Sat & Sun 10am–5pm) is more touristy but good for a browse, while Paddy's Market, in Haymarket near Chinatown (Thurs–Sun 9am–5pm), is Sydney's oldest, selling fruit and veg, deli products, meat and fish, plus large quantities of bargain-basement clothes and toys. There's also a series of alternating Saturday markets on the North Shore; the scenically sited Kirribilli Market (fourth Sat of month) is the best known. Foodies should check out the series of **produce markets**: at Pyrmont Bay Park in front of the Star City Casino (first Sat of month 7–11am); at the Showring at The Entertainment Quarter in Moore Park (Wed & Sat 10am–4pm); and at Northside Produce Market at the Civic Centre, Miller Street, North Sydney, between Ridge and McClaren streets (third Sat of month 8am–noon).

Listings

Airlines (domestic) Aeropelican (☎02/4928 9600) to Inverell or Williamtown, both nr Newcastle; Qantas, see address below (☎13 13 13), Australia-wide including Albury, Armidale, Ballina, Coffs Harbour, Dubbo, Lord Howe Island, Moree, Narrabri, Newcastle, Norfolk Island, Port Macquarie, Tamworth and Wagga Wagga; Regional Express (REX; ☎13 17 13) to Albury, Ballina, Bathurst, Bourke, Broken Hill, Dubbo, Griffith, Lismore, Melbourne, Merimbula, Mildura, Moruya, Narrandera, Orange, Parkes, Taree and Wagga Wagga; Air Link (☎1300 662 823) to Bathurst, Bourke, Cobar, Coonamble, Dubbo, Lightning Ridge, Mudgee and Walgett; Jetstar (☎13 15 38) to Adelaide, Brisbane, Cairns, Gold Coast, Hamilton Island, Hobart, Launceston, Melbourne, Mackay, Rockhampton, Sunshine Coast, Townsville and Whitsunday Coast, Virgin Blue (☎13 67 89), Australia-wide to all state capitals as well as much of coastal Queensland, and Coffs Harbour.

Airlines (international) Aeroflot, Level 24, 44 Market St ☎02/9262 2233; Air Canada, Level 12, 92 Pitt St ☎02/9232 5222; Air New Zealand, Level 18, 264 George St ☎13 24 76; Air Pacific, Level 10, 403 George St ☎1800 230 150; Alitalia, 64 York St ☎02/9244 2400; British Airways, Level 19, AAP Centre, 259 George St ☎1300 767 177; Cathay Pacific, 8 Spring St ☎13 17 47; Continental, 64 York St ☎02/9244 2242; Delta, Level 9, 189 Kent St ☎02/9251 3211; Finnair, 64 York St ☎02/9244 2299; Garuda, 55 Hunter St ☎1300 365 330; Gulf Air, 12/403 George St ☎02/9244 2199; Japan

Cars: buying and selling

Sydney is the most popular place to buy a car or campervan in which to travel around Australia. The information below is specific to buying a car in NSW – for general background on buying and selling a car, see pp.41–42.

Before you start looking, it's a good idea to join the **NRMA motoring association**, 74 King St, City (ⓣ13 21 32, ⓦwww.mynrma.com.au; $55 joining fee plus $151.80 annual charge per vehicle; overseas motoring association members have reciprocal membership); membership entitles you to roadside assistance and a reduced rate for a vehicle inspection of a potential purchase ($199; bookings ⓣ13 11 22). The NRMA's website has an excellent "Motoring" section where you can find out market prices and cars for sale. The Office of Fair Trading's useful *The Car Buyers Handbook: Buying and Maintaining a Car in NSW* can be viewed online (ⓣ13 32 20, ⓦwww.fairtrading.nsw.gov.au). Thursday's *Weekly Trading Post* (or check ⓦwww.tradingpost.com.au) has a big secondhand-car section. The *Sydney Morning Herald*'s Friday "Drive" supplement has ads for secondhand dealers (most on Parramatta Road from Annandale onwards) and private used cars for sale at the pricier end of the market. Demand to see a "pink slip" (certificate of roadworthiness) that is less than 28 days old. If you're serious about buying, contact REVS (ⓣ02/9633 6333, ⓦwww.revs.nsw.gov.au) to check if there are any payments owing or unpaid parking fines and call the RTA (above) to check registration is still current.

Sydney is well equipped with dealerships who will arrange to **buy back** the vehicle they've sold you at the end of your trip – expect to get thirty to fifty percent back. The longest running is **Travellers Auto Barn**, 177 William St, Kings Cross (ⓣ02/9360 1500, ⓦwww.travellers-autobarn.com.au), with offices in Melbourne, Brisbane, Cairns, Perth and Darwin, or the more down-to-earth **Traveller's Mate** (ⓣ02/9556 2113, ⓦwww.travellersmate.com.au), in Arncliffe near Mascot airport.

The **Kings Cross Car Market**, Kings Cross Car Park, Level 2, Ward Ave (Mon–Thurs & Sun 9am–4.30pm, Fri & Sat 9am–3.30pm; ⓣ02/9358 5000 or 1800 808 188, ⓦwww.carmarket.com.au), is specifically aimed at travellers, with help with paperwork and contract exchange provided. It's also one of the few places where you will be able to sell a car registered in another state. Dealers are barred, and fees for sellers are $60–85 per week. Many of the vehicles come equipped with camping gear and other extras. Third-party property **insurance** ($260 for 3 months, $425 for 12 months) can be arranged – the NRMA often refuses to cover overseas travellers. It's worth checking the Car Market's website, where sellers can advertise for $30. **Paddy's Motor Market**, held on Sunday at Flemington Market opposite Flemington station, Austen Avenue entrance (10am–4pm; ⓣ1300 361 589, ⓦwww.paddysmotormarket.com.au; selling fees $55 for two Sundays), is better for buying than selling: if you're trying to sell a vehicle that's travelled around Australia, particularly if the clock is past 200,000km, local buyers won't be interested.

Airlines, Level 14, 201 Sussex St ⓣ02/9272 1111; KLM, 13th floor, 115 Pitt St ⓣ1300 303 747; Korean Air, Level 4, 333 George St ⓣ02/9262 6000; Luthansa, 143 Macquarie St ⓣ02/9367 3888; Malaysia Airlines, 16 Spring St ⓣ02/9364 3500; Olympic, 3rd Floor, 37–49 Pitt St ⓣ02/9251 1048; Qantas, 10 Bridge St ⓣ13 13 13; Scandinavian Airlines, Level 15, 31 Market St ⓣ1300 727 707; Singapore Airlines, 31 Market St ⓣ13 10 11; Thai Airways, 75 Pitt St ⓣ02/9251 1922; Virgin Atlantic, Level 8, 403 George St ⓣ02/9244 2747.

Banks and foreign exchange Head offices of banks are mostly in the CBD, around Martin Place; hours are Mon–Thurs 9.30am–4pm, Fri 9.30am–5pm, with some suburban branches open later and on Saturday. American Express outlets include 105 Pitt St (Mon–Fri 9am–5pm; ⓣ1300 139 060); 296 George St (daily 8.30am–5.30pm); *Quay Grand Hotel*, Circular Quay East (Mon–Fri 9am–5pm, Sat & Sun 11am–4pm); lost or stolen traveller's cheques ⓣ1800 251 902. Money can also be exchanged at Travelex bureaux de change at the airport and several city locations including 32 Martin Place and 37–49 Pitt St, near Central Station (Mon–Fri 9am–5.15pm, Sat 10am–2.45pm; ⓣ02/9241 5722). UAE Money Exchange, Shop 175

Harbourside shopping centre, Darling Harbour (daily 9.30am–9pm; ⓣ02/9212 7124).

Camping equipment and rental Kent Street in the city behind the Town Hall (and near YHA headquarters) is nicknamed "Adventure Alley" for its preponderance of outdoor equipment stores; the best known is the high-quality Paddy Pallin at no. 507. Cheaper options include army surplus stores at the downtown ends of George and Pitt streets near Central Station, and suburban K-Mart stores (closest stores to the city are at Spring Street, Bondi Junction, and at the Broadway Shopping Centre, Bay Street) or hostel notice boards. Only a few places rent gear, mostly based in the suburbs: try Alpsport, 1045 Victoria Rd, West Ryde (ⓣ02/9858 5844), with weekend rental of a backpack for around $32, sleeping bag from $27 and tent from $55.

Consulates Embassies are all in Canberra (see p.241), and it's usually easier to call them when in difficulty than to go to the consulates in Sydney: Canadian, Level 5, 111 Harrington St ⓣ02/9364 3000; New Zealand, Level 10, 55 Hunter St ⓣ02/8256 2000; UK, Level 16, Gateway Building, 1 Macquarie Place ⓣ02/9247 7521; US, Level 59, MLC Centre, 19–29 Martin Place ⓣ02/9373 9200. For visas for onward travel, consult "Consulates and Legations" in the *Yellow Pages*.

Cycling Bicycles are carried free on trains outside of peak hours (Mon–Fri 6–9am & 3.30–7.30pm) and on ferries at all times. The Roads and Traffic Authority (RTA; ⓣ1800 060 607, ⓦwww.rta.nsw.gov.au) produces a handy fold-out map, *Sydney Cycleways*, showing both off-road paths and suggested bicycle routes, which they will post out. The best source of information, however, is the organization Bicycle NSW, based at Level 5, 822 George St (Mon–Fri 9am–5.30pm; ⓣ02/9218 5400, ⓦwww.bicyclensw.org.au). Two useful publications are *Bike It Sydney* ($13), which has backstreet inner-city bike routes, and *Cycling Around Sydney* ($25), which details 25 of the best rides; they also have free council and RTA bike-route maps. Popular cycling spots are Centennial Park and the bike path that runs from Manly (see p.152). The international cycling activist group Critical Mass has a Sydney movement; on the last Friday of the month meet at the Archibald Fountain in Hyde Park for an hour-long mass ride through the city at 6pm. Recommended central bicycle shops include Clarence Street Cyclery, 104 Clarence St (ⓣ02/9299 4962); Woolys Wheels, 82 Oxford St, Paddington (ⓣ02/9331 2671); and Inner City Cycles, 151 Glebe Point Rd, Glebe (ⓣ02/9660 6605). Clarence Street Cyclery also rents mountain bikes ($50 per day), as does Inner City Cycles ($33 per 24hr, $55 per weekend). For a leisurely ride in the park, Centennial Park Cycles, 50 Clovelly Rd, Randwick (ⓣ02/9398 5027), rents bikes at hourly rates (mountain bikes $12 per hour, $40 per day; bikes for kids $10 per hour, $35 per day; tandems $20 hour, $65 day), as well as rollerblades ($18 per hour) and pedal cars ($25–35 per hour).

Disabled travellers See also "Travellers with Disabilities", p.74. Disability Australia, 52 Pitt St, Redfern, NSW 2016 ⓣ02/9319 6622. Spinal Cord Injuries Australia, PO Box 397, Matraville NSW 2036 (ⓣ02/9661 8855, ⓦwww.spinalcordinjuries.com.au), publishes the very useful *Access Sydney* ($10 plus postage). Most national parks have wheelchair-accessible walks; check ⓦwww.nationalparks.nsw.gov.au. Post-Olympic improvements include many wheelchair-accessible train stations; check ⓦwww.cityrail.nsw.gov.au. All taxi companies take bookings on behalf of Wheelchair Accessible Taxis; for numbers, see "Taxis" below.

Diving One of the best places to dive is at Gordon Bay in Clovelly, and off North and South heads. Nearby Pro Dive Coogee, 27 Alfreda St, Coogee (ⓣ02/9665 6333), offers boat and shore dives anywhere between Camp Cove (Watsons Bay) and La Perouse (4hr double boat dive from $199; double shore dive $105), plus dives all over Sydney. Aquatic Explorers, 40 Kingsway, under *Cronulla Beach YHA*, Cronulla (ⓣ02/9523 1518), does local weekend coordinated shore dives (free but gear rental costs $50–75 per day) and also organizes boat dives, night dives and weekends away up and down the New South Wales coast. Dive Centre Manly, 10 Belgrave St, Manly (ⓣ02/9977 4355), offers shore dives to Shelley Beach, Fairlight, and Little Manly, plus Harbord if conditions are good, and boat dives off North and South heads and Long Reef (boat dives 4 daily Fri–Sun; single boat dive $90, double $145; shore dives twice daily; single shore dive $75, double $90; rates include equipment). They also have a Bondi branch at 192 Bondi Rd (ⓣ02/9369 3855) offering shore dives at Camp Cove and North Bondi (double dive $95) and boat dives to South Head and Maroubra where there's a chance to see sharks. All of the above also offer dive courses.

Hospitals (with emergency departments) St Vincent's Hospital, cnr Victoria and Burton streets, Darlinghurst ⓣ02/8382 1111; Royal Prince Alfred, Missenden Rd, Camperdown ⓣ02/9515 6111; Prince of Wales, Barker St, Randwick ⓣ02/9382 2222.

Immigration Department of Immigration, 26 Lee St, near Central Station, City ⓣ13 18 81.

Internet access You can surf the Net for free at the State Library, Macquarie St, for up to an hour a day, but can't send emails. Global Gossip ($4 for 30min–1hr) has several offices including 790 George St, nr Central Station; 415 Pitt St, nr Chinatown (both daily 9am–11pm); 14 Wentworth Ave, next to Hyde Park (Mon–Fri 9am–6pm); 61 Darlinghurst Rd, Kings Cross (daily 8–1am); 37 Hall St, Bondi (Mon–Thurs 9am–midnight, Fri–Sun 9am–11pm) – they also offer cut-rate international calls and parcel post. Phone Net Cafe, 73–75 Hall St, Bondi (Mon–Fri 8am–10pm, Sat & Sun until 9pm; from $3.30 for 1hr), is a lively café haunt in its own right.

Left luggage There are lockers at Wanderers' Travel, 810 George St, close to Central Station (daily 7am–8pm; $4 per day). Also locker rooms at the airport and the Sydney Coach Terminal ($5–15 per 24hr).

Libraries See the State Library, p.123, and City of Sydney Library, p.111.

Maps Map World, 280 Pitt St (Ⓣ02/9261 3601, Ⓦwww.mapworld.net.au), has Sydney's biggest selection of maps and travel guides; see also "Parks and wildlife", below.

Medical centres Broadway Medical Centre, 185–211 Broadway, near Glebe (Ⓣ02/9281 5085), general practitioners open Mon–Fri 9am–7pm, Sat & Sun 11am–5pm, no appointment necessary; Skin Cancer Centre, 403 George St (Ⓣ02/9262 4877); Sydney Sexual Health Centre, Sydney Hospital, Macquarie St (Ⓣ02/9382 7440 or 1800 451 624); The Travel Doctor, 7th Floor, 428 George St (Ⓣ02/9221 7133, Ⓦwww.traveldoctor.com.au).

Parks and wildlife information The NPWS, Cadmans Cottage, 110 George St, The Rocks (Ⓣ02/9247 5033, Ⓦwww.nationalparks.nsw.gov.au), is the information centre for Sydney Harbour National Park and books tours to its islands; they do not arrange camping permits. For these and information on other national parks around Sydney, go to The National Parks Centre, 102 George St, The Rocks (Ⓣ02/9253 4600). The Sydney Map Shop, part of the Surveyor-General's Department, 22 Bridge St (Ⓣ02/9228 6111), sells detailed National Park, State Forest and bushwalking maps of New South Wales.

Pharmacy (late-night) Crest Hotel Pharmacy, 60A Darlinghurst Rd, Kings Cross (daily 8.30am–midnight; Ⓣ02/9358 1822).

Police Headquarters at 14 College St (Ⓣ02/9339 0277); emergency Ⓣ000.

Post office The General Post Office (GPO) is in Martin Place (Mon–Fri 8.15am–5.30pm, Sat 10am–2pm). Poste restante is located at the post office in the Hunter Connection shopping mall at 310 George St (Mon–Fri 8.15am–5.30pm), opposite Wynyard station. Log your name into the computer to see if you have any post before queueing. Poste Restante, Sydney GPO, Sydney, NSW 2000.

Public holidays In addition to the Australia-wide public holidays (see Basics, p.77), the following are celebrated only in New South Wales: Bank Holiday – first Mon in Aug; Labour Day – first Mon in Oct; Queen's Birthday – first Mon in June.

Scenic flights Sydney Harbour Seaplanes, Rose Bay (Ⓣ02/9388 1978), can take you on a 15min scenic flight over Sydney Harbour and Bondi Beach ($125 per person, min 2, max 8), or the harbour and the Northern beaches ($195), or drop you off for lunch at Palm Beach or one of the Hawkesbury River restaurants ($395 including lunch).

Surfing The two best surf schools in Sydney, offering both individual and group lessons, are Let's Go Surfing (Ⓣ02/9365 1800), which also has its own surf store renting and selling boards at 128 Ramsgate Ave, North Bondi; and Manly Surf School (Ⓣ02/9977 6977), which covers the northern beaches.

Swimming pools Most pools are outdoors and unheated, and open from the long weekend in Oct until Easter. Those detailed in the text, with times and prices given, are: Cook and Phillip Park Aquatic and Leisure Centre, near Hyde Park (p.122); Andrew "Boy" Charlton in The Domain (p.125); North Sydney Olympic Pool, North Sydney (p.143); Victoria Park, City Road, next to Sydney University (p.149); and the pool of champions, the Sydney International Aquatic Centre at Homebush Bay (p.203).

Taxis Legion Ⓣ13 14 51; Premier Ⓣ13 10 17; St George Ⓣ13 21 66; Taxis Combined Ⓣ13 33 00. For harbour water-taxis, call Taxis Afloat Ⓣ02/9955 3222.

Telephones The unattended Telstra Pay Phone Centre, 231 Elizabeth St, City (Mon–Fri 7am–11pm, Sat & Sun 7am–5pm), has private booths; BYO change or phonecard. Global Gossip (see "Internet access" above) offers discount-rate international calls, and Backpackers Travel Centre (see below) sells their own rechargeable discount phonecard.

Tennis Rushcutters Bay Tennis Centre, 7 Waratah St, Rushcutters Bay (Ⓣ02/9357 1675; daily 8am–11pm; courts $20 per hour, $24 after 4pm and on Sat & Sun; racket rental $3). If you don't have anyone to play, the managers will try to provide a partner for you.

Travel agents Backpackers World Travel, 234 Sussex St (Ⓣ02/8268 6001, Ⓦwww.backpackersworld.com.au), does everything from international flights to bus passes; offices also at 91 York St (Ⓣ02/8268 5000); at 488 Pitt St, near Central Station (Ⓣ02/9282 9711); 212 Victoria St, Kings Cross (Ⓣ02/9380 2700); and 2B Grosvenor St,

Bondi Junction (☎02/9369 2011). Flight Centre, 52 Martin Place (☎13 18 66), also at several other locations, offers cheap domestic and international air tickets. STA Travel has many branches, including Town Hall Square, 464 Kent St (☎02/9262 9763), or try Student Flights (☎1300 762 410), with several offices including 140 King St, Newtown; 50 Spring St, Bondi Junction; and 87 Glebe Point Rd, Glebe. Trailfinders is at 8 Spring St (☎1300 780 285). YHA Travel, 422 Kent St (☎02/9261 1111), is a full travel agent and also has a branch at *Sydney Central YHA*, 11 Rawson Place off Eddy Ave (☎02/9281 9444), and offers an excellent range of Sydney tours.

Watersports Rose Bay Aquatic Hire, just near the waterfront at 1 Vickery Ave, Rose Bay (☎02/9371 7036), rents out kayaks ($20 per hour single kayak, $30 double; Wed–Sun only) and motorboats ($80 for the first two hours, $15 for each subsequent hour; weekends only). Balmoral Windsurfing, Sailing and Kayaking School, at the Balmoral Sailing Club, southern end of the Esplanade (open Oct–April; ☎02/9960 5344), rents out sailboards (from $40–50 per hour), offers sailboarding and Hobiecat dinghy sailing courses (both 4hr over 2 days; $255), as well as five-day holiday courses for kids ($365). Northside Sailing School, Spit Bridge, Mosman (☎02/9969 3972), specializes in weekend dinghy sailing courses on Middle Harbour during the sailing season (Sept–April); tuition is one-on-one ($130 per 3hr lesson). Sydney by Sail, based at Darling Harbour (☎02/9280 1110), has Learn To Sail programmes for yacht sailing throughout the year, from a Level 1 Introductory Course (12-hour 2-day course; $425) to a Level 4 Inshore Skipper Course (3-day, 2-night live-aboard; $695). Experienced sailors can charter the yachts from $495 per half-day. For other sailing courses and yacht rental, contact the NSW Yachting Association (☎02/9660 1266, ⓦwww.nsw.yachting.org.au). Natural Wanders Sea Kayak Adventures (☎02/9899 1001) arrange sea-kayaking in the harbour: their most popular trip is the Berry Island Paddle (3hr 30min; $90) or for experienced kayakers there's the Bridge Paddle (3hr 30min; $90), from Lavender Bay near Luna Park, under the Harbour Bridge and exploring the North Shore; picnic brunch included.

Women Contact the Women's Information and Referral Service (Mon–Fri 9am–5pm; ☎1800 817 227) for information on International Women's Day events in March. For this and other women's organizations, services and referrals, also try The Women's Library, 8–10 Brown St, Newtown (Tues, Wed & Fri 11am–5pm, Thurs 11am–8pm, Sat & Sun noon–4pm), which lends feminist and lesbian literature. The Feminist Bookshop is in Orange Grove Plaza on Balmain Road, Lilyfield (☎02/9810 2666).

Work If you have a working holiday visa, you shouldn't have too much trouble finding some sort of work, particularly in hospitality or retail. Offices of the government-run Centrelink (☎13 28 50) have a database of jobs. Centrelink also refers jobseekers to several private "Job Network" agencies, including Employment National (☎13 34 44). The private agency Troys, at Level 11, 89 York St (☎02/9290 2955), specializes in the hospitality industry. If you have some office or professional skills, there are plenty of temp agencies that are more than keen to take on travellers: flick through "Employment Services" in the *Yellow Pages*. For a whole range of work, from unskilled to professional, the multinational Manpower is a good bet (☎13 25 02). Otherwise, scour hostel notice boards and the *Sydney Morning Herald*'s employment pages – Saturday's bumper edition is best.

Around Sydney

If life in the fast lane is taking its toll, Sydney's residents can easily get away from it all. Right on their doorstep, golden beaches and magnificent national parks beckon, interwoven with intricate waterways. Everything in this part of the chapter can be done as a day-trip from the city, although some require an overnight stay to explore more fully. See the box on p.185 for some of the huge variety of tours on offer.

North of Sydney, the Hawkesbury River flows into the jagged jaws of the aptly named **Broken Bay**. The entire area is surrounded by bush, with the huge spaces of the **Ku-ring-gai Chase National Park** in the south and the **Brisbane Waters National Park** in the north. Beyond Broken Bay, the **Central Coast** between Gosford and Newcastle is an ideal spot for a bit of fishing, sailing and lazing around. **Newcastle** is escaping its industrial-city tag and the attractive beach metropolis is coming up in the world, with a surfing, student, café and music culture all part of the mix. Immediately beyond are the wineries of the **Hunter Valley**.

Moving on from Sydney

Most **bus** services from Sydney depart from **Eddy Avenue**, alongside Central Station, and tickets can be bought from the Sydney Coach Terminal, cnr Eddy Ave and Pitt St (daily 6am–10pm; ⓣ02/9281 9366) or direct from bus companies. There are four **interstate services**: Greyhound Australia has Australia-wide services (ⓣ13 14 99, ⓦwww.greyhound.com.au); Firefly Express (ⓣ1300 730 740, ⓦwww.fireflyexpress.com.au), daily to Melbourne and connecting to Adelaide; Murray's (ⓣ13 22 51, ⓦwww.murrays.com.au; also from Strathfield station), to Canberra daily; while Premier Motor Service departs just around the corner at 490 Pitt St (ⓣ13 34 10, ⓦwww.premierms.com.au), heading to Cairns via the north coast, and to Melbourne via the south coast. Most bus services to **destinations within NSW** also depart from Eddy Avenue: Keans (ⓣ02/6543 1322), daily to the Lower and Upper Hunter Valley; Port Stephens Coaches (ⓣ02/4982 2940 or 1800 045 949, ⓦwww.pscoaches.com.au), daily to Port Stephens via Newcastle outskirts; Selwoods (ⓣ02/6362 7963, ⓦwww.selwoods.com.au), daily to Orange via the Blue Mountains, Lithgow and Bathurst; Premier Motor Service (ⓣ13 34 10, ⓦwww.premierms.com.au), daily to Bega via the south coast, with one service daily continuing on to Eden; Rover Coaches (ⓣ02/4990 1699, ⓦwww.rovercoaches.com.au; also from *Four Seasons Hotel*, The Rocks), daily to Cessnock and Hunter Valley resorts. Prior's Scenic Express departs from Parramatta, Liverpool and Campbelltown train stations (ⓣ02/4472 4040 or 1800 816 234), daily except Saturday to the Southern Highlands and Kangaroo Valley, thence to Moruya or Narooma via the south coast including Batemans Bay and Ulladulla.

All out-of-town trains depart from the **country trains terminal** of Central Station (information and booking from the Countrylink Travel Centre 6.30am–10pm; ⓣ13 22 32, ⓦwww.countrylink.nsw.gov.au). The *Indian Pacific*, the *Ghan* and the *Overland* are managed by Great Southern Railway (bookings ⓣ13 21 47, ⓦwww.gsr.com.au). Interstate trains should be booked as early as possible, especially the *Indian Pacific* and Brisbane–Cairns trains.

The *Spirit of Tasmania* **ferry** from Sydney to Devonport in Tasmania leaves from Darling Harbour; see p.128 for details.

The big four **car-rental companies**, with expensive new-model cars, charge from $50 per day for a small manual, with much cheaper rates for five- to seven-day and longer rentals: Avis, airport (ⓣ02/8374 2847) and 200 William St, Kings Cross (ⓣ02/9357 2000); Budget, airport (ⓣ02/9207 9165) and 93 William St, Kings Cross (ⓣ02/8255 9600); Hertz (ⓣ13 30 39), airport and cnr William and Riley streets, Kings Cross; Thrifty, airport (ⓣ1300 367 227) and 75 William St, Kings Cross. There are cheaper deals with the popular Bayswater, 180 William St, Kings Cross (ⓣ02/9360 3622), which has low rates but limited kilometres; Travellers Auto Barn, 177 William St, Kings Cross (ⓣ02/9360 1500 or 1800 674 374), does cheap one-way rentals to Melbourne, Brisbane or Cairns but with a minimum ten-day hire.

Tours from Sydney

Day-tours from Sydney range from a sedentary trip on a bus to a wildlife park to a day of canyoning in the Blue Mountains, and there are many overnight trips, too. You'll almost certainly have a better time with one of the outfits who specialize in small-group tours, quite often with an emphasis on physical activities such as bushwalking, horse riding, whitewater rafting or abseiling, as opposed to taking one of the commercial bus-tour operators such as AAT Kings. **One-way tours** can be the next best thing to going by car: small groups in minibuses travel from Sydney to Melbourne (for example), taking detours to attractions along the way that you'd never be able to reach on public transport.

As well as booking direct on the numbers given, most of the tours listed below can be booked through YHA Travel (ⓣ02/9261 1111, ⓦwww.yha.com.au).

Day- and overnight trips around Sydney

Oz Trek ⓣ02/9666 4262 or 1300 661 234, ⓦwww.oztrek.com.au. Recommended active full-day tours to the Blue Mountains ($54), with a choice of three bushwalks (30min–1hr 30min). Small groups (max 20). The trip can be extended to overnight packages with either horse riding ($239), abseiling ($239) or a Jenolan Caves visit ($209). City, Glebe, Kings Cross, Bondi and Coogee pick-ups.

Waves Surf School ⓣ02/9369 3010 or 1800 851 101, ⓦwww.wavessurfschool.com.au. One- or two-day "Learn To Surf" trips in the Royal National Park, learning surfing technique and etiquette and beach safety, and with a chance to spot wildlife (one day with lunch $75; two days with meals, bushwalking and camping or sleep-on-board bus $199; additional nights optional). City, Bondi and Coogee pick-ups.

Wildframe Ecotours ⓣ02/9440 9915, ⓦwww.wildframe.com. Two full-day tours to the Blue Mountains (both $85) and overnight tours starting at $136. The Grand Canyon Eco-tour is for fit walkers as it includes a small-group bushwalk (max 21) through the Grand Canyon (5km; 3hr); BYO lunch in Katoomba. The Blue Mountains Bush Tour is more relaxed with several short bushwalks and BYO lunch in Blackheath. Kangaroo spotting promised on both trips.

Extended and one-way tours

Ando's Outback Tours ⓣ02/6842 8286 or 1800 228 828, ⓦwww.outbacktours.com.au. Popular five-day tour from Sydney to Byron Bay but getting well off the beaten track inland via the Blue Mountains, the Warrumbungles, Coonabarabran and Lightning Ridge ($485 all-inclusive; departs Sydney every Sun); includes a stay on the rural property of the true-blue family who run the tours. Finding farm work is a common bonus.

Autopia Tours ⓣ03/9419 8878 or 1800 000 507, ⓦwww.autopiatours.com.au. This excellent, long-established Melbourne-based tour company has a four-day Sydney to Melbourne tour via the Blue Mountains, Jenolan Caves, Canberra, the Snowy Mountains and Victoria's Alpine Way ($395; includes meals, dorm accommodation). Small-seater buses with the driver acting as guide.

Oz Experience ⓣ02/9213 1766 or 1300 300 028, ⓦwww.ozexperience.com. A cross between transport and tours that go a little off the beaten track, with a hop-on, hop-off component lasting six months; accommodation and meals not included. Scheduled routes include Sydney to Cairns in nine days ($795); Sydney to Brisbane via the Warrumbungles and Byron Bay in four days ($380); and Sydney to Melbourne in three days via the south coast, Canberra and the Snowy Mountains ($300). There are also Sydney to Byron Bay options encompassing beach, surf and bush experiences.

There are many places renting **campervans** and **4WDs**. All Seasons Campervans, 77 Planthurst Rd, South Hurstville (Ⓣ02/9547 0100), offers a wide range of campervans and motorhomes with linen, sleeping bags and free delivery within the CBD. Britz Campervan Rentals, 653 Gardeners Rd, Mascot (Ⓣ02/9667 0402 or 1800 331 454), has campervans, 4WD campers and camping gear, available one-way to Adelaide, Alice Springs, Brisbane, Cairns, Darwin, Melbourne and Perth. Travel Car Centre, 26 Orchard Rd, Brookvale (Ⓣ02/9905 6928 or 1800 440 300), has been established for over twenty years and has hatchbacks, station wagons, campervans and 4WDs available for long- or short-term rental. Travellers Auto Barn (Ⓣ02/9360 1500; see above) offers budget campervan and 4WD bushcamper rentals.

For **motorbike** rental, there's Bikescape, 183 Parramatta Road, Annandale (Ⓣ1300 736 869, Ⓦwww.bikescape.com.au), with scooters from $80 per day and motorbikes from $115 (cheaper weekend and longer term rates available).

To the **west**, you escape suburbia to emerge at the foot of the beautiful World Heritage–listed **Blue Mountains**, while the scenic Hawkesbury–Nepean river valley is home to historic rural towns such as **Windsor**.

Heading **south**, the **Royal National Park** is an hour's drive away, while on the coast beyond are a string of small, laid-back towns – Waterfall, Stanwell Park, Wombarra – with beautiful, unspoilt **beaches**. The industrial city of **Wollongong** and neighbouring Port Kembla are impressively located between the Illawarra Escarpment and the sea, but of paltry interest to visitors, although more interesting spots cluster around. Inland, the **Southern Highlands** are covered with yet more national parks, punctuated by pleasing little towns such as **Bundanoon** and **Berrima**.

North

The **Hawkesbury River** widens and slows as it approaches the South Pacific, joining Berowra Creek, Cowan Creek, Pittwater and Brisbane Water in the system of flooded valleys that form **Broken Bay**. The bay and its inlets are a haven for anglers, sailors and windsurfers, while the adjoining bushland is virtually untouched. Two major **national parks** surround the Hawkesbury River: **Ku-ring-gai Chase** in the south and **Dharug**, inland to the west.

The **Pacific Highway** up here, partly supplanted by the **Sydney–Newcastle Freeway**, is fast and efficient, though not particularly attractive until you're approaching Ku-ring-gai Chase; if you want to detour into the national parks or towards Brooklyn, don't take the freeway. The **rail** lines follow the road almost as far as Broken Bay, before they take a scenic diversion through the **Central Coast**, passing Brooklyn, Brisbane Waters, Woy Woy and Gosford en route to **Newcastle**.

Ku-ring-gai Chase National Park

Only 24km from the centre of Sydney, **Ku-ring-gai Chase** is much the best known of New South Wales' national parks and, with the Pacific Highway running all the way up one side, is also the easiest to get to. The bushland scenery is crisscrossed by walking tracks, which you can explore to seek out Aboriginal rock carvings, or just to get away from it all and see the forest and its wildlife. Pick up information about walks in the park from the **Kalkari**

△ Ku-ring-gai Chase National Park

Visitor Centre (daily 9am–5pm), on the Ku-ring-gai Chase Road. There are four road entrances to the park and an $11 entrance fee for cars. Without your own transport, take a ferry or boat cruise to the Pittwater side from Palm Beach (see p.153), or a train to Turramurra station and then Shorelink Bus #577 (Ⓣ02/9457 8888 for times) to the Bobbin Head Road entrance.

At the northeastern corner of Ku-ring-gai Chase National Park, West Head juts into Broken Bay where it marks the entrance to **Pittwater**, a deep ten-kilometre-long sheltered waterway. From the West Head lookout, reached via West Head Road, there are superb views across to Barrenjoey Head and Barrenjoey Lighthouse at Palm Beach on the eastern shore of Pittwater. From West Head, the **Garigal Aboriginal Heritage Walk** (3.5km circuit) leads to the Aboriginal rock-engraving site, the most accessible Aboriginal art in the park.

The only place to **camp** is *The Basin* (Ⓣ02/9974 1011 for bookings; Ⓦwww.basincampground.com.au) on Pittwater, reached via the Palm Beach Ferry Service. Facilities at the site are minimal, so bring everything with you. If you want to stay in the park in rather more comfort, there's the very popular *Pittwater YHA* (Ⓣ02/9999 5748, Ⓔpittwater@yhansw.org.au; dorms $28, rooms ④; bookings essential and well in advance for weekends). The hostel is accessed by regular **ferry** from Church Point Wharf (last departure 7pm; Ⓣ02/9999 3492 for times; 15min; $10 return) or water taxi (free-phone at the wharf), alighting at Halls Wharf and walking 15 minutes up the hill. It's one of New South Wales' most scenically sited hostels – a rambling old house overlooking the water (kayaks available) and surrounded by spectacular bush walks. Bring supplies with you – the last food (and bottle) shop is at Church Point.

Two direct **buses** run to Church Point: #E86 from Central Station (weekdays only) or #156 from Manly Wharf.

Koala patting and other wildlife experiences

It is no longer legal to physically pick up and hold a koala in New South Wales' wildlife parks, but photo-opportunity "patting" sessions are still on offer. Below are several hands-on wildlife experiences around Sydney.

The **Koala Park Sanctuary** (daily 9am–5pm; $19; Ⓦwww.koalaparksanctuary.com.au) was established as a safe haven for koalas in 1935 and has since opened its gates to wombats, possums, kangaroos and native birds of all kinds. Koala-feeding sessions (daily 10.20am, 11.45am, 2pm & 3pm) are the patting and photo-opportunity times. Around 25km north of Sydney, not far from the Pacific Highway on Castle Hill Road, West Pennant Hills; train to Pennant Hills then bus #651 or #655 towards Glenorie (Mon–Sat).

One of Sydney's oldest wildlife reserves, **Waratah Park Earth Sanctuary** (Ⓣ02/9986 1788, Ⓦwww.waratahpark.com.au), sits in stunning bush scenery on the edge of Ku-ring-gai Chase National Park about 36km north of Sydney. Waratah is most famous as the home of Skippy the bush kangaroo, television's marsupial star. The sanctuary can only be seen on a ninety-minute guided spotlight tour (advance bookings essential; departs after sunset Thurs–Sun; $16.50). The park is reached via Mona Vale Road – it's signposted from Terrey Hills.

At **Featherdale Wildlife Park** (daily 9am–5pm; $19; Ⓦwww.featherdale.com.au), patting koalas is the special all-day attraction. Located at 217 Kildare Rd, Doonside, 30km west of Sydney off the M4 motorway between Parramatta and Penrith; train to Blacktown station, then bus #725.

The **Australian Reptile Park** (daily 9am–5pm; $20; Ⓦwww.reptilepark.com.au), 65km north of Sydney, just off the Pacific Highway before the Gosford turn-off, offers photographic opportunities with koalas, and has kangaroos roaming the park that you can tickle and hand-feed, though its real stars are the reptiles, with native Australian species well represented and visible all year round thanks to heat lamps in the enclosures. The highlights are Eric, New South Wales' largest saltwater crocodile, and the sizeable Perentie lizard of central Australia. Reptile shows twice a day. You can also watch snakes and funnel web spiders being milked for their venom for the Commonwealth Serum Laboratories. There's no public transport: eight companies offer day-tours, including Oz Trek (see p.185).

The Hawkesbury River

One of New South Wales' prettiest rivers, lined with sandstone cliffs and bush-covered banks for much of its course and with some interesting old settlements alongside, the **Hawkesbury River** has its source in the Great Dividing Range and flows out to sea at Broken Bay. For information about the many national parks along the river, contact the NPWS in Sydney (Ⓣ02/9247 5033) or at 370 Windsor Rd in Richmond (Ⓣ02/4588 5247). Short of chartering your own boat, the best way to explore the river system is to take a cruise (see box opposite); the River Boat Mail Run is the most interesting.

Upstream: Wisemans Ferry

WISEMAN'S FERRY is a popular recreational spot for day-trippers from Sydney – just a little over an hour from the city centre by car, and with access to the **Dharug National Park** over the river by a free 24-hour car ferry. Dharug's rugged sandstone cliffs and gullies shelter Aboriginal rock engravings, which can be visited only on ranger-led trips during school holidays; there's a camping area at Mill Creek (Gosford NPWS Ⓣ02/4320 4203 for details of walks and camping; bookings for both essential at weekends and holiday periods). Open to walkers, cyclists and horse riders but not vehicles,

Exploring the Hawkesbury River system

Brooklyn, just above the western mass of Ku-ring-gai Chase National Park, and easily reached by train to Brooklyn station from Central Station in Sydney and from Gosford, is the base for Hawkesbury River Ferries (ⓣ02/9985 7566), whose River Boat Mail Run still takes letters, as well as tourists, up and down the river. Departures are from Brooklyn Wharf on Dangar Road (Mon–Fri 9.30am excluding public holidays; 4hr; $45 including morning tea; booking essential).

Gosford's Public Wharf is the starting point for the MV *Lady Kendall* (ⓣ02/4323 1655, ⓦwww.starshipcruises.com.au), which cruises both Brisbane Waters and Broken Bay (Mon–Wed, Sat & Sun, daily during school & public holidays, 10.15am & 1pm; 2hr 30min; $24; bookings essential), and calls in at Woy Woy at 10.40am and 12.10pm.

Windsor is the base for the *Hawkesbury Paddlewheeler* (ⓣ02/4575 1171, ⓦwww.paddlewheeler.com.au), which has a good-value Sunday-afternoon Jazz Cruise: live jazz and a BBQ lunch for $30 (12.30–3pm; advance bookings essential).

Boat and houseboat rentals and fishing charter

Barrenjoey Boating Services at Governor Phillip Park, Palm Beach (ⓣ02/9974 4229), hires out **boats** that seat up to six people (2hr $50, 4hr $65, 8hr $110) and are perfect for fishing expeditions around the mouth of the Hawkesbury. The centre has a fishing shop and sells bait supplies and hires out rods. Otherwise, if you're keen to fish and can get four people together, you can charter a boat, including all the gear and bait, plus a skipper who knows exactly where to go, with Fishabout Tours (ⓣ02/9451 5420; $150 per person; 7hr), who have a great reputation on the Hawkesbury. **Houseboats** can be good value if you can get a group together, with prices starting from $590 for a weekend and $1100 for a week for four people. The Sydney Visitor Centre in Sydney (ⓣ02/9667 6050) has details of operators, or try Able Hawkesbury River Houseboats, on River Road in Wisemans Ferry (ⓣ1800 024 979, ⓦwww.hawkesburyhouseboats.com.au), or Ripples Houseboats, 87 Brooklyn Rd, Brooklyn (ⓣ02/9985 5534, ⓦwww.ripples.com.au).

the **Old Great North Road** was literally carved out of the rock by hundreds of convicts from 1829; you can camp en route at the *Ten Mile Hollow* camping area.

The settlement of Wisemans Ferry was based around ex-convict Solomon Wiseman's home, Cobham Hall, built in 1826. Much of the original building still exists in the blue-painted *Wisemans Ferry Inn* on the Old Great North Road (ⓣ02/4566 4301; motel ❸, pub ❸–❹), with character **rooms** upstairs sharing bathrooms, and en-suite, motel-style rooms outside at the back. Other accommodation in the surrounding area includes *Del Rio Riverside Resort* (ⓣ02/4566 4330, ⓦwww.delrioresort.com.au; en-suite cabins ❻), a campsite in Webbs Creek reached via the Webbs Creek car ferry, 3km south of Wisemans Ferry; facilities include a bistro, swimming pool, tennis court and golf course. *Rosevale Farm Resort*, 3km along Wisemans Ferry Road en route to Gosford (ⓣ02/4566 4207; vans ❷, motel ❸), has less expensive camping and motel units – cheaper weekdays – in extensive bushland close to Dharug National Park.

Taking the ferry across the river from Wisemans Ferry, it's then a scenic nineteen-kilometre river drive north along Settlers Road, another convict-built route, to **St Albans**, where you can partake of a cooling brew (or stay a while) at a pub built in 1836, the hewn sandstone *Settlers Arms Inn* (ⓣ02/4568 2111; en-suite rooms ❼). The pub is set on two and a half acres, and much of the vegetables and herbs for the delicious home-cooked food are organically grown on site (lunch daily, dinner Fri–Sun).

The Upper Hawkesbury: Windsor

About 50km inland from Sydney and reached easily by train from Central Station via Blacktown, **WINDSOR** is probably the best preserved of all the historic Hawkesbury towns, with a lively centre of narrow streets, spacious old pubs and numerous historic colonial buildings. It's terrifically popular on Sundays, when a **market** takes over the shady, tree-lined mall end of the main drag, George Street, and the *Macquarie Arms Hotel*, which claims to be the oldest pub in Australia, sponsors live rock'n'roll on the adjacent grassy village green. Next door to the pub, the **Hawkesbury River Museum and Tourist Information Centre** (daily 11am–3pm; museum $2.50; ⓣ02/4577 2310, ⓦwww.hawkesburyweb.com) doles out local information. From Windsor, Putty Road (Route 69) heads north through beautiful forest country, along the eastern edge of the Wollemi National Park, to Singleton in the Hunter Valley.

From Richmond, just 7km northwest of Windsor, the **Bells Line of Road** (Route 40) goes to Lithgow via Kurrajong and is a great scenic drive; all along the way are fruit stalls stacked with produce from the valley. There's a wonderful view of the Upper Hawkesbury Valley from the lookout point at **Kurrajong Heights**, on the edge of the Blue Mountains. Another scenic drive from Richmond to the Blue Mountains, emerging near Springwood (see p.205), is south along the Hawkesbury Road, with the **Hawkesbury Heights Lookout** halfway along providing panoramic views. Not far from the lookout, the modern solar-powered *Hawkesbury Heights YHA* (ⓣ02/4754 5621; rooms ❸) also has lovely views from its secluded bush setting.

The Central Coast

The shoreline between Broken Bay and Newcastle, known as the **Central Coast**, is characterized by large **coastal lakes** – saltwater lagoons almost entirely enclosed, but connected to the ocean by small waterways. The northernmost, **Lake Macquarie**, is the biggest saltwater lake in New South Wales. Most travellers bypass the Central Coast altogether on the Sydney–Newcastle Freeway, which runs some way inland, but to see a bit more of the coastal scenery and the lakes, stay on the older Pacific Highway, which heads to Newcastle via **Gosford**, home of the Australian Reptile Park (see p.188).

North of Gosford, Tuggerah and Munmorah lakes meet the sea at **THE ENTRANCE**, a favourite fishing spot with anglers – and with swarms of pelicans, which descend upon Memorial Park for the afternoon fish-feeds (3.30pm; free). The beaches and lakes along the coast from here to Newcastle are crowded with caravan parks, motels and outfits offering the opportunity to fish, windsurf, sail or water-ski: although less attractive than places further north, they make a great day-trip or weekend escape from Sydney. The **Entrance Visitors Centre**, Marine Parade (daily 9am–5pm; ⓣ02/4385 4430 or 1800 806 258, ⓦwww.cctourism.com.au), has a free accommodation booking service.

Central Coast Tourism (ⓣ1300 725 105, ⓦwww.cctourism.com.au) offers **tourist information** on the whole region and accommodation bookings. Within the Central Coast area there's a well-developed **bus service** run by the private Busways (ⓣ02/4392 6666) and Red Bus Services (ⓣ02/4332 8655).

Newcastle

NEWCASTLE was founded in 1804 for convicts too hard even for Sydney to cope with, but the river is the real reason for the city's existence: coal, which lies in great abundance beneath the Hunter Valley, was and still is ferried from the

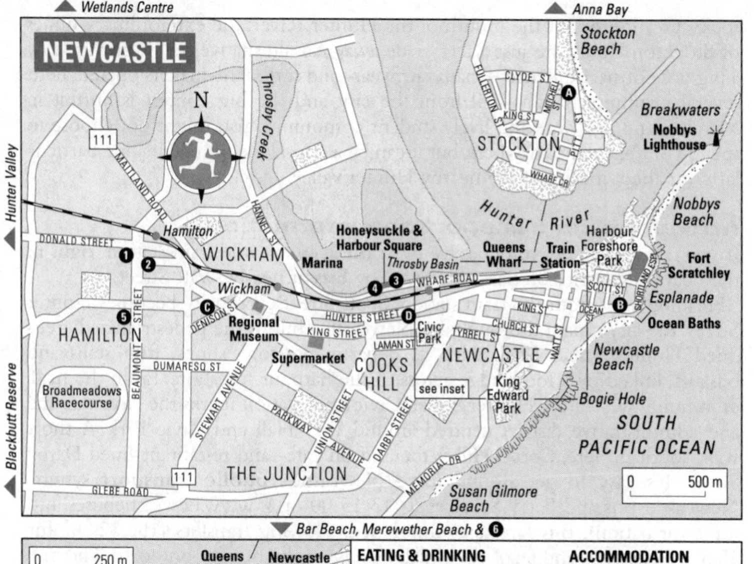

EATING & DRINKING

- Al-Oi-Thai 13
- The Beach Hotel 6
- The Brewery 8
- Brewery Restaurant 4
- Crown & Anchor 10
- Eurobar 5
- Finnegan's 11
- Goldbergs Coffee House 14
- Harry's Café de Wheels 7
- The Kent 2
- The Last Drop Espresso Bar 9
- Produce Café 3
- Supply 12
- Sydney Junction Hotel 1

ACCOMMODATION

- Clarendon Hotel D
- Newcastle Backpackers C
- Newcastle Beach YHA E
- Quality Hotel Noah's on the Beach B
- Stockton Beach Tourist Park A

countryside to be exported around the country and the world. The proximity of the mines encouraged the establishment of other **heavy industries**, though the production of steel here ceased in late 2000 and most of the slag heaps have been worked over, but the docks are still functional, particularly with the through traffic of coal from the Hunter Valley. Today, Newcastle remains the world's largest coal-exporting port, and there may be a couple of dozen bulk carriers queued off the beaches at any one time; ironically, the city also has a reputation as being one of the most environmentally progressive places on earth.

New South Wales' second city, with a population of over a quarter of a million, Newcastle has long suffered from comparison with nearby Sydney. However, for a former major industrial city, it's surprisingly attractive, a fact now being more widely recognized. The city is experiencing a **real-estate boom**: hundreds of apartments and hotels have gone up, and old icons are being redeveloped, such as the once grand *Great Northern Hotel* on Scott Street, first built in 1938 and with a $3 million facelift almost complete. Years of accumulated soot has been scraped off the city's stately buildings, riverside gardens have been created in front of the city centre, and a former goods yard has been converted into a waterside entertainment venue. The once blue-collar town is taking to tourism in a big way, trading particularly on its **waterside location** – the surf beaches are wonderful, and there are some more sheltered sandy beaches around the rocky promontory at the mouth of the Hunter River; the extraordinary dunes of Stockton Beach are just a ferry ride away. An alternative feel is provided by a big dose of **surf culture** – many surfwear- and surfboard-makers operate here, several champion surfers hail from the city, and the big contest is Surfest in March – and the large and lively student community. You might not choose to spend your entire holiday here, but it can be a good base for excursions, particularly for the wineries of the nearby Hunter Valley.

Arrival, public transport and information

If you're not driving, you'll arrive by **train** at Newcastle train station, right in the heart of the city on Scott Street, or by **bus** at nearby Watt Street.

Heading west from the train station, Scott Street eventually becomes Hunter Street, the city's main thoroughfare. Newcastle's hub is the pedestrianized, tree-lined Hunter Street Mall, with its department store, shops, fruit stalls and buskers, linked by a footbridge across to the harbour foreshore. From the mall, continuing west along Hunter Street, Civic train station marks the city's cultural and administrative district centred around City Hall and Civic Park. A short walk south of here, Cooks Hill is focused on café- and restaurant-lined Darby Street. It's easy to get around using Newcastle's **public transport** system, Newcastle Bus and Ferry Services (ⓣ13 15 00 or ⓦwww.newcastlebuses.info for information). Bus fares are time-based, allowing transfers (1hr $2.80; 4hr $5.50; all-day bus and ferry $8.40); all tickets can be bought on board. The one ferry operating goes to Stockton, departing from Queens Wharf (Mon–Sat 5.15am–midnight, Sun 8.30am–10pm; $2 one way). Two passenger-train lines have several suburban stops, the most useful heading towards Sydney, with handy stops at Civic for Darby Street and Hamilton for Beaumont Street (fares from $2.80 single).

You can familiarize yourself with the city sights on **Newcastle's Famous Tram** (Mon–Fri 11am & 1pm, hourly services 10am–1pm during school holidays; 45min; $12; ⓣ02/4963 7954), the usual twee coach-done-out-as-a-tram deal, departing from Newcastle station.

The very helpful **Newcastle Visitors Information Centre** (Mon–Fri 9am–5pm, Sat & Sun 9.30am–4.30pm; ⓣ02/4974 2999 or 1800 654 558, ⓦwww.visitnewcastle.com.au) at 361 Hunter St, opposite Civic station, can provide other local information and maps.

Accommodation

Clarendon Hotel 347 Hunter St ⓣ02/4927 0966, ⓦwww.clarendonhotel.com.au. This central 1930s Art Deco pub has been beautifully renovated and shows its original features in the bar downstairs. The stylish, vibrantly coloured rooms are totally contemporary and offer great value. A bright café-bistro with a huge courtyard does good-value meals from breakfast on. Free parking. ❼

Newcastle Backpackers 42 & 44 Denison St, Hamilton ⓣ02/4969 3436 or 1800 333 436, ⓦwww.newcastlebackpackers.com. An outstanding home-style hostel and guesthouse run by a friendly family with dorms and doubles set in three adjacent wooden bungalows with a heated swimming pool at the back. Located 3km from the city centre and beach but only a few minutes' walk from lively Beaumont Street; take the free bus running from the city centre to the museum, or call for a free pick-up. The owner runs people down to the beach most days and offers free surfing lessons (boogie-boards free, surfboards $20 per day). Dorms $21, rooms ❷–❸

Newcastle Beach YHA 30 Pacific St, cnr King St ⓣ02/4925 3544, ⓔnewcastle@yhansw.org.au. Fantastic hostel in an impressively restored, spacious old building complete with ballroom, huge staircases, a lounge with a fireplace and leather armchairs, a pool table and courtyard with BBQ, plus the usual facilities. Four-bed dorms, doubles, twins and family rooms. Just 50m from the surf and right in the centre of town; free boogie-boards, and surf boards to hire ($8 for 1hr). Dorms $29.50, rooms ❺

Quality Hotel Noah's on the Beach Cnr Shortland Esplanade and Zaara St ⓣ02/4929 5181, ⓦwww.noahsonthebeach.com.au. Upmarket, modern multi-storey motel right opposite Newcastle Beach. Most rooms have ocean views. Room service. ❽

Stockton Beach Tourist Park Pitt St, Stockton Beach ⓣ02/4928 1393. Picturesquely sited campground right on the extensive beach with a camp kitchen. Two-minute ferry ride from the city. Cabins ❹, en-suite cabins ❻

The City

Newcastle has whole streetscapes of beautiful **Victorian terraces** that put Sydney's to shame – pick up a free *Newcastle Visitor Guide* from the tourist office, to steer you around some of the old buildings. A couple of buildings in **Newcastle Harbour Foreshore Park** show the trend for the city's wealth of disused public architecture: on one corner of the park stands the beautiful Italianate brick **Customs House**, now a popular pub. Nearby is the wooden two-storey **Paymasters House**, where you can sit with a coffee in its fine veranda café and contemplate the water. The restored **Queens Wharf**, a landmark with its distinctive observation tower, is located on the south bank of the Hunter River. It's linked to the city centre by an elevated walkway from Hunter Street Mall and boasts *The Brewery*, a popular and stylish waterfront drinking spot (see p.195). Further along the foreshore is the new **Honeysuckle** development, an assortment of renovated rail sheds, wharves, pristine walkways and smart new apartments centring on Harbour Square. You'll find a string of stylish cafés and restaurants here, and on Sunday there's a produce and craft market boasting some interesting food alternatives such as gourmet *pizzetta*s.

Besides Newcastle's waterside attractions, the **Newcastle Regional Museum**, 787 Hunter St (Tues–Sun 10am–5pm, daily during school holidays; free), might be of interest. Housed in what began as a brewery in the 1870s, it focuses on the history of the mining and steel industries of the area; on the top floor is the Supernova hands-on science centre, much the best thing about the museum.

Beaches and wildlife reserves

The city centre, positioned on a narrow length of land between the Hunter River to the west and the Pacific Ocean to the east, has several popular and pleasantly low-key beaches close by. **Newcastle Beach**, only a few hundred metres from the city on Shortland Esplanade, has patrolled swimming between flags, a sandy saltwater pool perfect for children, shaded picnic tables and good surfing at its southern end. At the northern end, the beautifully painted Art Deco–style, free **Ocean Baths** houses the changing pavilions for the huge saltwater pool, which has its own diving board.

North of Newcastle Beach, beyond Fort Scratchley, is the long, uncrowded stretch of **Nobbys Beach**, with a lovely old beach pavilion. A walkway leads to Nobbys Head and its nineteenth-century lighthouse.

If you follow Shortland Esplanade south from Newcastle Beach, you'll come to the huge expanse of King Edward Park, with good walking paths and cliff views over this rocky stretch of waterfront. One section of the rock ledge holds Australia's first man-made ocean pool, the **Bogie Hole**, chiselled out of the rock by convicts in the early nineteenth century for the Military Commandant's personal bathing pleasure. The cliffs are momentarily intercepted by **Susan Gilmore Beach** – secluded enough to indulge in some nude bathing – then further around the rocks is **Bar Beach**, a popular surfing spot that's floodlit at night. The longer **Merewether Beach** next door has a fabulous ocean bath at its southern end and a separate children's pool; overlooking the beach is *The Beach Hotel*, a fine place for a drink.

Just two minutes by ferry from Queens Wharf across the Hunter River, the beachside suburb of **Stockton** is the starting point for the vast, extraordinary **Stockton Beach**, which extends 32km north to **Anna Bay**. Two kilometres wide at some points and covered in moving sand dunes, some of which are up to 30m high, Stockton Bight, as it's officially known, looks strikingly like a mini-desert and has been the location for a Bollywood film. It's become something of an adventure playground in recent years, with thrilling quad-bike tours offered by Sand Safaris (2hr; $139, pick-ups from Stockton ferry extra $10; ⓣ02/4965 0215, ⓦwww.sandsafaris.com.au), which also take in the 1974 shipwreck, the *Sygna Bergen*. You can sandboard down the dunes on the 4WD beach tours offered by Dawsons Scenic Tours (from $20; 1hr 30min tour; pick-ups from Anna Bay; ⓣ02/4982 0602, ⓦwww.portstephensadventure.com.au) or explore them on horseback with Horse Paradise Tours, based at Williamtown (from 1hr beginner, $40; ⓣ02/4965 1877, ⓦwww.users.bigpond.com/horseparadise).

Inland, **Blackbutt Reserve** is a large slab of bushland in the middle of Newcastle suburbia in New Lambton Heights about 10km southwest of the city (daily 9am–5pm; free; koala talks Sat & Sun 2.30pm, koala feeding daily 2–3pm); consisting of four valleys, it includes a remnant of rainforest, creeks, lakes and ponds and 20km of walking tracks to explore them. En route you'll see kangaroos, koalas, wombats, emus and other native animals in the reserve's wildlife enclosures. To get here from the city, take bus #222 or #224 to the Carnley Avenue entrance; for the entrances on Lookout Road, you can take bus #363; the tourist office produces a helpful free map. Northwest of the city, the **Wetlands Centre**, Sandgate Road, Shortland (daily 9am–5pm; $5; ⓣ02/4951 6466, ⓦwww.wetlands.org.au), is situated on the wetlands of Hexham Swamp by Ironbark Creek and is home to a mass of birdlife. There are walking and cycling trails here, and you can rent canoes from tourist information. Reach the Wetlands Centre by train from Newcastle to Sandgate, from where it's a ten-minute walk.

Eating

The two streets to head for are **Darby Street**, close to the city centre, which has a multicultural mix of restaurants and some very hip cafés, as well as some secondhand bookshops and retro clothes stores to browse in between coffees; and **Beaumont Street** in Hamilton, 3km northwest of the city centre (train to Hamilton station or bus #260), with a concentration of Italian places, as well as Turkish, Lebanese, Japanese and Indian; it's jam-packed Friday and Saturday nights. Another good spot in the city centre is Market Square Foodcourt, upstairs in the Hunter Street Mall, with a range of food bars. Newcastle has the only franchise of the Sydney legend, *Harry's Café de Wheels*, an all-day, **late-night** pie-cart (Mon, Tues & Sun to 11pm, Wed & Thurs to 1am, Sat & Sun to 4am) stationed on Wharf Road near *The Brewery* (see opposite).

Al-Oi-Thai 133 Darby St ⓣ02/4929 3610. Delicious, traditional Thai food served in stylish surrounds. Justifiably popular. Lunch Wed–Sat, dinner Tues–Sun; BYO. Another branch at 50 Beaumont St, Hamilton (ⓣ02/4969 1434).

Brewery Restaurant "The Boardwalk", 1 Honeysuckle Drive ⓣ02/4929 5792. Not to be confused with *The Brewery* at Queens Wharf. The best regarded of the contemporary restaurants at the new Honeysuckle development concentrates on fresh seafood and modern bistro-style dishes. Closed Sun dinner.

Eurobar 79 Beaumont St, Hamilton. Spacious (and very trendy) interior with outdoor tables to check out the busy street action, but it still gets packed: Italian risottos, Greek pastas and Kilpatrick oysters ensure a European flavour, with nothing over $20. Licensed & BYO. Daily 7.30am–11pm.

Goldbergs Coffee House 137 Darby St. This perennially popular Darby Street institution is big, buzzy and airy with modish green walls and polished wooden floors. The emphasis is on the excellent coffee, plus very reasonably priced eclectically modern meals. Also outside courtyard. Licensed. Daily 7am–midnight.

The Last Drop Espresso Bar 37 Hunter St. Great little café near the YHA, which serves excellent coffee, fresh juices, frappés and smoothies and tasty gourmet sandwiches. Mon–Fri 7am–4pm, plus Nov–Feb Sat & Sun 7am–3pm.

Produce Café Honeysuckle Railway Buildings, Merewether ⓣ02/4927 5366. Champion of the area's produce, this café uses local ducks, sourdough bread, organic milk and vegetables to rustle up gourmet breakfasts, sandwiches and delicious meals. Daily 7am–3pm.

Supply Cnr King & Watt sts, around the corner from the YHA. With a light, modern and airy interior and groovy music playing, this is a good place to clear a hangover. Breakfasts, pastas, salads and dinner served at very reasonable prices. Mon–Fri 7.30am–5pm, Sat & Sun 8.30am–4pm.

Entertainment and nightlife

The area known as "the cultural precinct", near Civic Park on King, Hunter and Auckland streets, is the location for two refurbished Art Deco venues; pick up a monthly calendar from the tourist office for details of what's on. At the **University Conservatorium of Music** on Auckland Street (ⓣ02/4921 8900), there are often free lunchtime concerts as well as evening performances, while the grand **City Hall**, 290 King St (ⓣ02/4974 2948), has occasional classical music events such as the Australian Chamber Orchestra. Mainstream **cinema** is on offer at the three-screen Greater Union, nearby at 183 King St ($9 discount Tues; ⓣ02/4926 2233). Both art-house and mainstream releases are shown around the corner at the three-screen Showcase City Cinemas, 31–33 Wolfe St, off Hunter Street Mall ($12.50; ⓣ02/4929 5019).

For **nightlife listings**, check out the supplement "TE" in Wednesday's *Post* or the fortnightly free music mag, *U Turn*. During term time, the students of Newcastle University add a lot of life to the city but there is always a thriving live-music scene. One of the best venues in town for live bands is the uni's **Bar on the Hill** at Callaghan, 12km west of the city (ⓣ02/4921 5000; bus #260 or train to Warabrook station), and the **Cambridge Hotel** at 789 Hunter St, West Newcastle (ⓣ02/4962 2459), is also a big venue for touring interstate and international bands. On Friday and Saturday nights, the city pubs on Hunter Street and parallel King Street are lively and there are a few **nightclubs** – *Surf City* on adjacent Watt Street has a young crowd and is very popular, while near the harbour, *Fanny's*, 311 Wharf Rd, has a wild reputation. The Newcastle Visitors Information on George Street hands out drink and door-admission coupons and has a good knowledge of what's going on.

Pubs and bars

The Beach Hotel Opposite Merewether Beach ⓣ02/4963 1574. With a huge beachfront beer garden, this is popular all weekend and is the place to go on Sun nights when there are live bands (free).

The Brewery Queens Wharf, 150 Wharf Rd. Popular waterfront drinking hole with three bars – grab tables right on the wharf or on the upstairs balcony. Food from the busy bistro can be eaten outside (weekend breakfasts, too). Live music or DJs Wed–Sun (free).

Crown & Anchor 189 Hunter St. Well-known city boozer, with outdoor tables alongside the classic, beautifully tiled exterior. Popular balcony upstairs, overlooking the street. The nightclub, *Frost Bites* (Wed–Sun; free), specializes in lethal sno-cone alcoholic drinks.

Finnegan's Cnr Darby and King streets. Newcastle's obligatory Irish theme pub. Inevitably lively and popular, especially with travellers, as they often put on free-food nights to pack them in.

The Kent 59 Beaumont St, cnr Cleary St, Hamilton ⓣ02/4961 3303. Beautifully renovated old pub and music venue, which is busy most nights – pool comps, quizzes, karaoke, a rock duo Fri to Sun nights, and Sun afternoon jazz (4.30–8.30pm) – but with several refuges, including a plant-filled beer garden and a great bistro. No cover charge.

Sydney Junction Hotel 8 Beaumont St, Hamilton ⓣ02/4961 2537. "SJs", as the locals call it, is a young and lively pub in an equally animated strip – open to 1am most nights and until 4am Fri and Sat. Bands – local and touring – and CD launches Thurs to Sat nights. Usually free but entry up to $15 for major gigs.

Listings

Banks and exchange American Express, 49 Hunter St ☎1300 139 060. Commonwealth Bank, 136 Hunter Street Mall (☎02/4927 2777), has foreign exchange.
Car rental A.R.A ☎02/4962 2488; Thrifty ☎02/4942 2266.
Internet access Battle Ground, 169 King St (daily 10am–10pm; $6 per hour).
Left luggage At the train station (daily 8am–5pm; $1.50 per article per day).
Post office Newcastle GPO, 96 Hunter St, NSW 2300 (Mon–Fri 8am–5pm).
Supermarket Coles, cnr King and National Park streets; open 24hr.
Taxi Taxi Services Co-Op ☎02/4979 3000.

The Hunter Valley

New South Wales' best-known wine region and Australia's oldest, the **Hunter Valley** is an area long synonymous with fine **wine** – in particular, its golden, citrusy **Sémillon** and soft and earthy **Shiraz**. The first vines were planted in 1828, and some still-existing wine-maker families, such as the Draytons, date back to the 1850s. In what seems a bizarre juxtaposition, this is also a very important **coal-mining region**, in the **Upper Hunter Valley** especially.

By far the best-known wine area, though, is the **Lower Hunter Valley**, nestled under the picturesque **Brokenback Range** around the main town of **CESSNOCK** – even the town's jail and high school have their own vineyards. The town itself is uninteresting, and surprisingly unsophisticated given the wine culture surrounding it, though the main drag, Vincent Street, has been landscaped in an attempt to improve things, and it features some big old country pubs that you can stay at or eat in for a taste of Australian rural life.

△ Winery, Hunter Valley

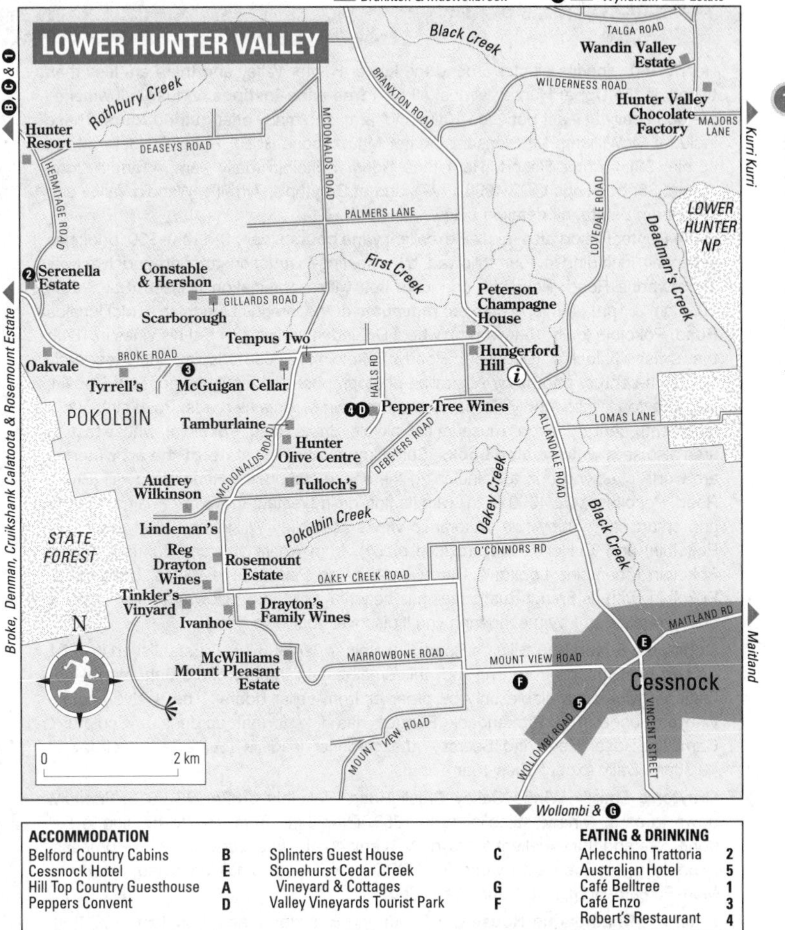

ACCOMMODATION				EATING & DRINKING	
Belford Country Cabins	B	Splinters Guest House	C	Arlecchino Trattoria	2
Cessnock Hotel	E	Stonehurst Cedar Creek Vineyard & Cottages	G	Australian Hotel	5
Hill Top Country Guesthouse	A	Valley Vineyards Tourist Park	F	Café Belltree	1
Peppers Convent	D			Café Enzo	3
				Robert's Restaurant	4

The wine-tasting area of **Pokolbin** is twelve to fifteen kilometres northwest, and has some very salubrious accommodation and a fine-dining scene, including the **Hunter Valley Gardens Village** on Broke Road in Pobolkin (Ⓣ02/4990 4477, gardens daily 9am–5pm, Dec & Jan to 8pm; $19.50; Ⓦwww.hvg.com.au), though it can seem like an exhausting winery-theme park, with its hot-air ballooning, horse-and-carriage rides, wall-to-wall B&Bs, resorts and shops, and wineries offering tours, tastings and wine courses, all screaming out their attractions. To experience the real appeal of the Hunter Valley wine country – its charming bush and farming feel and its vast vineyards seemingly lost among forested ridges, red-soiled dirt tracks, and paddocks with grazing cattle – take the **Lovedale/Wilderness Road area** north of Cessnock, or visit towns such as **Wollombi**, 28km southwest; **Broke**, 35km northwest; **Branxton**, 22km north; and the still unspoilt **Upper Hunter**, west of Muswellbrook, with its marvellous ridges and rocky outcrops.

Hunter Valley wineries

Nearly 150 wineries cluster around the Lower Hunter Valley and there are less than twenty in the Upper Hunter; almost all offer **free wine-tastings**. Virtually all wineries are open daily at least between 10am and 4pm, and many offer **guided tours**. These include: McWilliams Mt Pleasant Estate, Marrowbone Road, Pokolbin (daily 11am; 45min; $3); Hunter Resort, Hermitage Road, Pokolbin (daily 9am, 11am & 2pm; 45min; $5; bookings ⓣ02/4998 7777); and at Drayton's, Tyrrell's, Wandin Valley and Wyndham Estate, all detailed below.

The Hunter Resort also runs an excellent **wine course** (daily 9–11am; $30; bookings essential) including a tour followed by a tasting-instruction tutorial; and Ivanhoe, Marrowbone Road, Pokolbin, conducts free wine-appreciation classes (Sat & Sun 10.30am & 1pm; 45min). There are **museums** at the famous Lindeman's, McDonalds Road, Pokolbin (daily 10am–5pm), where Dr Lindeman first planted his vines in 1842; the swish Tulloch's (Debeyers Road, Pokolbin), whose display includes early twentieth-century photos by Australian photographer and family friend, Max Dupain; Reg Drayton Wines (cnr McDonalds and Pokolbin Mountains roads, Pokolbin); and a nineteenth-century "shop" museum at Oakvale (Broke Road, Pokolbin), whose tasting area also sells **wine-related books**. Some impressive new **state-of-the art wineries** are worth checking out, too, including the space-station-like Hungerford Hill (Broke Road, Pokolbin ⓣ02/4990 0711) with its fine-dining restaurant *Terroir* (mains $30–40) and smart café. Enjoy fine panoramic **views** at Audrey Wilkinson (Debeyers Road, Pokolbin) and Tinkler's Vineyard (see p.201), from where you can continue to the Pokolbin Mountains Lookout. The award-winning Pepper Tree Wines, Halls Road, Pokolbin, with its French-rustic feel, has beautiful **gardens**. Below are a few more of our favourites, but by meandering you'll discover your own gems.

Constable & Hershon Gillards Road, Pokolbin ⓣ02/4998 7887. Established in 1981 by two best friends from England, this small establishment offers unhurried wine-tastings (wine is available only by order or from cellar doors). The twelve-hectare vineyard under the Brokenback Ranges has five formal gardens - Sculpture, Camellia, Rose, Herb and Secret - the gardener leads a tour every weekday at 10.30am. Daily except Tues 10am–5pm.

Drayton's Family Wines Oakey Creek Road, Pokolbin ⓣ02/4998 7513. Friendly, down-to-earth winery, established in 1853. Everything from vine to bottling is still done here and the excellent tours (daily 11am; 45min; free) show the whole process. A pretty picnic area with wood-fired BBQ overlooks a small dam and vineyards. Mon–Fri 8am–5pm, Sat & Sun 10am–5pm.

Peterson Champagne House Cnr Broke and Branxton roads, Pokolbin ⓣ02/4998 7881. The only Hunter Valley winery to specialize in sparkling wines, they also use their *méthode champenoise* expertise to produce for other wineries. The pretty duck-pond stone-set building makes a pleasant tasting - and eating - spot: the *Magnum*

Pick up the excellent free *Hunter Valley Wine Country* guide with a handy pull-out map from the **Hunter Valley Wine Country Visitor Information Centre** (Mon–Fri 9am–5.30pm, Sat 9am–5pm, Sun 9am–4pm; ⓣ02/4990 4477, ⓦwww.winecountry.com.au), Main Road, Pokolbin, scenically sited amongst vineyards and with the pleasant, affordable *Wine Country Café*. If it's closed, you can still pick up the free guides from a rack outside. Try to tour the wineries during the week; at weekends, both the number of visitors and accommodation prices go up, and it can get booked out completely when there's a concert on in the valley. In late October, Wyndham Estate (see box above) hosts the night-time **Opera in the Vineyards** (bookings via Ticketek ⓣ13 28 49; tickets $70–160; ⓦwww.wyndhamestate.com) on the banks of the Hunter

Café's fantastic, well-priced cooked breakfast (daily 9–11am) can be teamed with some champers. For more indulgence, the Hunter Valley Chocolate Factory is right next door. Daily 9am–5pm.

Rosemount Estate McDonalds Road, Pokolbin ☎02/4998 6670. Occupying a converted blue church built in 1909, next to a delightful café and art gallery, this intimate cellar-only location offers some of Australia's best-known, award-winning wines grown at its famous vineyards in the Upper Hunter. Daily 10am–5pm.

Scarborough Gillards Road, Pokolbin ☎02/4998 7563. Small, friendly winery with a reputation for outstanding wines, specializing in Chardonnay and Pinot Noir. Pleasantly relaxed sit-down tastings are held in a small cottage with wonderful valley views. Daily 9am–5pm.

Tamburlaine Mcdonalds Road, Pokolbin ☎02/4998 7570. The jasmine-scented garden outside provides a hint of the flowery, elegant wines within. Tastings are well orchestrated and delivered with a heap of experience. Daily 9am–5pm.

Tempus Two Broke Road, Pokolbin. This huge, contemporary winery – all steel, glass and stone – has a high-tech urban-chic exterior. Owned by Lisa McGuigan, of the well-known wine-making family, whose unique-tasting wines are the result of using lesser-known varieties such as Pinot Gris, Viognier and Marsanne. The attached Japanese–Thai *Oishi* (☎02/4993 3999) has surprisingly moderate prices (noodle soups $8, mains $16.50), and there's a lounge area where you can relax over an espresso. Daily 9am–5pm.

Tyrrell's Broke Road, Pokolbin ☎02/4993 7000. The oldest independent family vineyards – and one of the best – producing consistently fine Sémillon wines. The tiny ironbark slab hut, where Edward Tyrrell lived when he began the winery in 1858, is still in the grounds, and the old winery with its cool earth floor is much as it was. Beautiful setting against the Brokenback Range. Mon–Sat 8.30am–5pm, with free tour 1.30pm.

Wandin Valley Estate Cnr Wilderness and Lovedale roads ☎02/4930 7317. Picturesquely sited on a hundred acres of vineyards, producing a variety of wines but best known for its hot-selling rosé. There are magnificent views across the Wategos and the Brokenback Range, especially from the balcony of the European-style *Bel Posto Café/Restaurant*: mains $25–35; cellar-door priced wine. Free tours on demand. Mon–Fri 9am–5pm, Sat & Sun 10am–5pm.

Wyndham Estate Dalwood Road, Dalwood. A scenic drive through the Dalwood Hills leads to the Lower Hunter's northern extent, where Englishman George Wyndham first planted Shiraz in 1828. Now owned by multinational Pernod Ricard, there's an excellent guided tour (daily 11am; free), which covers the vines and wine-making techniques and equipment, including the original basket press. The idyllic riverside setting – grassy lawns, free BBQs – makes a great spot for picnics and the annual opera concert. Restaurant (☎02/4938 3444) and outdoor café. Daily 10am–4.30pm.

River, followed a week later by a day of fine food, wine and music at **Jazz in the Vines** (tickets $45; ☎02/4930 9190, Ⓦwww.jazzinthevines.com.au) based at Tyrrell's Vineyard (see box above). In late November, January and February, Bimbadgen Estate hosts **A Day on the Green**, a sunset concert in their amphitheatre, featuring the likes of Chris Isaak and The Pretenders (tickets through Ticketek; $90; Ⓦwww.adayonthegreen.com.au).

Other Hunter Valley activities include **hot-air ballooning** – Balloon Aloft Australia offers sunrise champagne flights ($295; ☎02/4938 1955 or 1800 028 568, Ⓦwww.balloonaloft.com) – and cross-country **horse riding**, which *Hill Top Country Guesthouse* (see p.200) offer on their 300-acre property ($50; 1hr 30min).

Getting there and around

By car, the Lower Hunter Valley is two hours north of Sydney along the Pacific Highway (the F3), or for a more scenic route turn off the F3 towards Peats Ridge and drive via the **Wollombi Valley**. A meandering route from the Blue Mountains via **Putty Road** is popular with motorcyclists. Rover Coaches (ⓣ02/4990 1699, ⓦwww.rovercoaches.com.au) leave daily from Central Station and The Rocks travelling via Newcastle and Maitland to Cessnock and on to Pokolbin resorts. Keans (ⓣ02/6543 1322) goes from Central Station to Scone via the Hunter Valley (once daily except Sat); stops include Kurri Kurri, Neath, Cessnock, Pokolbin and Muswellbrook. For the Upper Hunter, take a train to Newcastle, where Sid Fogg's Coachlines (ⓣ02/4928 1088) heads to Maitland, Branxton, Singleton, Muswellbrook and Denman (Mon, Wed, Fri only).

Before you think about driving and wine tasting, consider the perils of drink-driving. Rover Coaches (above) offers a daily hop-on, hop-off **Wine Rover service**; stops include the tourist office, around eighteen wineries plus eating places (Mon–Fri $30; Sat & Sun $40). **Vineyard tours** are also an option, with a big range on offer. Many are exhausting return trips from Sydney (see box on p.185), but several local operators offer day-trips from within the valley. The excellent, long-established Hunter Valley Day Tours (ⓣ02/4951 4574) offers a wine-and-cheese tasting tour ($80 for Cessnock, Pokolbin and Maitland pick-ups; $95 from Newcastle; restaurant lunch included), with very informative commentary. The long-established, family-run Hunter Vineyard Tours (ⓣ02/4991 1659, ⓦwww.huntervineyardtours.com.au) visits five wineries (Cessnock pick-up $50, Newcastle or Maitland $55; restaurant lunch $25 extra). Also recommended are Trek About 4WD Tours (ⓣ02/4990 8277; $45) and Aussie Wine Tours (ⓣ02/4991 1074, ⓦwww.aussiewinetours.com.au; $45 mid-week, $50 weekend), both supportive of small local wineries and flexible. Otherwise, Hunter Valley Cycling, located in the Hunter Valley Gardens on the corner of McDonalds and Broke roads in Pokolbin, offer mountain **bikes** and tandems with free delivery and collection within the Hunter Valley (ⓣ04 1828 1480, ⓦwww.huntervalleycycling.com.au; from $30 per day), or you can hire a **taxi** (Cessnock RadioCabs ⓣ02/4990 1111).

Hunter Valley accommodation

Since the Hunter Valley is a popular weekend trip for Sydneysiders, accommodation **prices** rise on Friday and Saturday nights and most places only offer two-night deals; the price ranges below indicate the substantial mid-week to weekend variable. Advance **booking** is essential for weekends, and during the October and November string of events.

Belford Country Cabins 659 Hermitage Rd, Pokolbin ⓣ02/6574 7100, ⓦwww.belfordcabins.com.au. Family-run, fully equipped and excellent-value self-catering two- and four-bedroom wooden bungalows set in bushland. Comfy, spacious and clean cabins – renovated ones are quite stylish – each with its own barbecue. Games room with pool table, table tennis and TV; outdoor pool and playground. ❻

Cessnock Hotel 234 Wollombi Rd, Cessnock ⓣ02/4990 1002, ⓦwww.cessnockhotel.com.au. Renovated pub with a great bistro-cum-bar, the *Kurrajong Café*. Rooms all share bathrooms but they're huge with high ceilings, fans and really comfy beds. Big veranda to hang out on; cooked breakfast served in the café. ❸–❹

Hill Top Country Guesthouse 288 Talga Rd, Rothbury ⓣ02/4930 7111, ⓦwww.hilltopguesthouse.com.au. Rural retreat on 300 acres of the Molly Morgan range, with fantastic views. Explore the property by foot, horse, mountain bike ($16.50 half-day) or 4WD tour and then retreat for a massage. The family home, with six guest bedrooms on top of the ridge in wooded gardens, has the feel of an old-fashioned guesthouse, with a piano, billiard table and wood fire in the communal rooms. The new "Lovenest" villas on the valley floor offer modern rooms with en-suite bathrooms and unobstructed views of the Lower Hunter farmland from the balcony. Light breakfast included (lunch and dinner available). Rooms ⑤–⑥, villas ⑦–⑧

Peppers Convent Halls Road, Pokolbin ⓣ02/4998 7764, ⓦwww.peppers.com.au. The swankiest place to stay in the Hunter Valley, with a price to match (from $396 per night). The guesthouse, converted from an old convent, has heaps of cozy cachet, fireplaces and low beams. Part of the Pepper Tree Wines winery (see box p.198), with wine tasting there and fine dining at *Robert's Restaurant* (see p.202), just a stroll away. ⑧

Splinters Guest House 617 Hermitage Rd, Pokolbin ⓣ02/6574 7118, ⓦwww.splinters.com.au. Built and run by an affable former woodwork-teacher, the mezzanine-bedroomed cottages on this 25-acre property feature heaps of timber, slate floors, leadlight windows and New Guinea artefacts, and come with wood-combustion stove, leather armchairs and kitchen with espresso machine (cook-your-own breakfast supplied). Also en-suite rooms with a mini-espresso machine and an egg cooker (light breakfast included); everyone gets port and chocolate in their room. There's a covered BBQ area with fountain, a telescope, guest-lounge massage chairs, a practice golf green, gazebo, walking tracks, dogs and horses. Wineries and restaurant within wandering distance. Best value around, especially mid-week. Cottages ⑧, en-suite rooms ⑦–⑧

Stonehurst Cedar Creek Vineyard & Cottages Wollombi Rd, Cedar Creek, 10km northwest of Wollombi ⓣ02/4998 1576, ⓦwww.cedarcreekcottages.com.au. An idyllic choice away from the busy Pokolbin area on a 550-acre deer- and cattle-stocked farm. Run by the delightful Stonehurst Wines, whose tiny chapel-like tasting room, constructed from recycled materials, and wine from insecticide-free, handpicked, estate-grown grapes, illustrate the owners' philosophy. The self-catering cottages are made from recycled timber. Expect queen-sized beds, wood combustion stoves, ceiling fans, flowers on the table, TV, comfy lounges, stylish decor, and a BBQ outside. Breakfast hamper, port and chocolate included; civilized noon check-out. ⑦–⑧

Valley Vineyards Tourist Park 137 Mount View Rd, 2km west of Cessnock ⓣ02/4990 2573, ⓦwww.valleyvineyard.com.au. High-standard campsite with kitchen, BBQ area, pool and on-site Thai restaurant. Cabins (BYO linen) have external en-suites, cottages (linen included) internal. Cabins ③–④, cottages ④–⑤

Eating and drinking

Many of the Hunter's excellent (and pricey) **restaurants** are attached to wineries or are among vineyards rather than in the towns (see box on pp.198–199), while the Hunter's large old **pubs** dish out less fancy but more affordable grub; see the "Accommodation" section above for bistro options. Every year over a mid-May weekend, around eight wineries along and around the scenic Lovedale and Wilderness roads team up with local restaurants to host the **Lovedale Long Lunch** (ⓣ02/4930 7611, ⓦwww.lovedalelonglunch.com.au). The Hunter olive-growing industry has also taken off: check out the Hunter Olive Centre (Pokolbin Estate Vineyard, McDonalds Road, Pokolbin; ⓣ02/4998 7524), where you can sample different olives from around the valley and enquire about the weekend-long **The Feast of the Olive Festival** in late September. Other places where you can taste the local wares include The Hunter Valley Cheese Company at the McGuigan Cellar, Broke Road; the newer Binnorie Dairy, just across the road from the Hunter Resort, which specializes in soft fresh cheeses; fresh farm produce at Tinkler's Vineyard, Pokolbin Mountains Road; delicious fudge made behind a glass viewing window at The Chocolate Factory on Lovedale Road; or you can drink local-brewed beer at the Blue Tongue Brewery at the Hunter Resort (daily 7.30am–midnight). Just about every winery and accommodation place in the valley has a BBQ, so for picnic or self-catering supplies there's the large Coles supermarket in Cessnock, at 1 North Ave (Mon–Sat 6am–midnight, Sun 8am–8pm), or the small **supermarket** in the Hunter Valley Gardens Village. You can also get deli supplies from the Australian Regional Food Store at the Small Winemakers Centre on McDonalds Road.

Arlecchino Trattoria Serenella Estate, Hermitage Road, Pokolbin ☎02/4998 7120. Stylish interpretation of a trattoria, attached to the Cecchini-family-established winery. The wood-fired pizza ($10.50–18) is worth the drive out here; a small but delicious menu includes pasta and risotto ($17), a few meaty mains ($24) and *gelato*. The dining room, with cool stone floors and crisp white tablecloths, overlooks a dam and vineyards from windows on three sides. Lunch Wed–Sun, dinner Wed–Sat.

Australian Hotel 136 Wollombi Rd, Cessnock. The excellent bistro at *The Australian* is popular with the locals, and the pub showcases the Hunter's coal-mining roots with mining paraphernalia and related art. Though some steaks hit the $25 mark, mains average between $15 and $19, and the menu encompasses stir-fries, gourmet salads and vegetarian dishes.

Café Belltree Margan Family Winegrowers, 266 Hermitage Rd, Pokolbin ☎02/6574 7216. Experienced wine-maker Andrew Margan turns out some tasty wines, and the attached Mediterranean-influenced eatery is pretty good, too. Dishes use seasonal, local produce, and a changing blackboard menu of share plates (around $20; wines served with a $5 corkage) adds to the convivial atmosphere. Most lunchtimes it's crowded and lively, and you'll need to book, despite the café appellation. The deck is a great spot to hang out and soak up the isolated bush feel with a cake teamed with a Toby's Estate Coffee in the quieter morning or afternoon. Daily 10am–5pm.

Café Enzo Peppers Creek Antiques, Broke Road, Pokolbin. Relaxing courtyard café that feels like it's been lifted from the south of France; light Mediterranean menu ($21–27) and excellent Italian-style coffee, or start the day here with a cooked breakfast. Though it's pricey, the spot is worth it. Daily 9am–5pm.

Robert's Restaurant Pepper Tree Wines, Halls Road, Pokolbin ☎02/4998 7330. *Robert's* is a long-established Hunter Valley fine-dining institution, as much for the setting in a charming 1876 wooden farmhouse filled with flowers and antiques, and shaded by a huge peppertree, as for the French rustic-style food, cooked in a wood-fired oven. Mains average $38.

West

For over sixty years, Sydney has slid ever westwards in a monotonous sprawl of shopping centres, brick-veneer homes and fast-food chains, along the way swallowing up towns and villages, some dating back to colonial times. The first settlers to explore inland found well-watered, fertile river flats, and quickly established agricultural outposts to support the fledgling colony. **Parramatta**, **Liverpool**, **Penrith** and **Campbelltown**, once separate communities, are now satellite towns inside Sydney's commuter belt. Yet, despite Sydney's advance, bushwalkers will find there's still plenty of wild west to explore in the beauty of the **Blue Mountains**. Heading west, however, now starts for many travellers with a visit to the Olympic site at **Homebush Bay**.

Parramatta and Penrith

Situated on the Parramatta River, a little over 20km upstream from the harbour mouth, **PARRAMATTA** was the first of Sydney's rural satellites – the first farm settlement in Australia, in fact. The fertile soil of "Rosehill", as it was originally called, saved the fledgling colony from starvation with its first wheat crop of 1789. It's hard to believe today, but dotted here and there among the malls and busy roads are a few remnants from that time – eighteenth-century public buildings and original settlers' dwellings that warrant a visit if you're interested in Australian history.

It's a thirty-minute train ride from Central Station to Parramatta, but the most enjoyable way to get here is on the sleek RiverCat ferry from Circular Quay up the Parramatta River (1hr; $7.50 one way). The wharf is on Phillip Street, a couple of blocks away from the helpful visitor centre within the **Parramatta Heritage Centre**, corner of Church and Market streets (daily 9am–5pm;

Sydney Olympic Park at Homebush Bay

The main focus of the 2000 Olympic events was **Sydney Olympic Park** at **Homebush Bay**. Virtually the geographical heart of the westward-sprawling city, Homebush Bay already had some heavy-duty sporting facilities – the State Sports Centre and the Aquatic Centre – in place. The **Sydney Olympic Park Authority (SOPA)** has turned Sydney Olympic Park into an entertainment and sporting complex with family-oriented recreation in mind, with events such as free outdoor movies, multicultural festivals and children's holiday activities. For details, check ⓦwww.sydneyolympicpark.nsw.gov.au.

The AUS$470-million Olympic site was centred around the 110,000-seat **Telstra Stadium**, the venue for the opening and closing ceremonies, track and field events, and marathon and soccer finals. And despite an AUS$68-million overhaul to reduce the number of seats to 83,500, it's still Sydney's largest stadium, though with a more realistic number for its use as an Australian Rules football, cricket, rugby league, rugby union, soccer and concert venue. Tours of the stadium, with commentary, are available daily (every half-hour 10.30am–4pm; 1hr tour $27.50; check it's a non-event day first by contacting ⓣ02/8765 2300 or ⓦwww.telstrastadium.com.au).

Opposite the Olympic site is the huge **Bicentennial Park**, opened in 1988; more than half is conservation wetlands – a boardwalk explores the mangroves and you can observe the profusion of native birds from a bird hide. There are around 8km of cycling and walking tracks, and the Parklands Express Train Shuttle tours the wetlands on Sundays (12.30pm, 1.15pm, 2.15pm, 3pm & 3.45pm; 45min; $4.40), with four hop-on-hop-off stops. Further north, the green-friendly Athletes' Village is now a solar-powered suburb, **Newington**.

To get an overview of the site, there's an **observation centre** on the 17th floor of the *Novotel Hotel* (daily 10am–4pm; $4), on Olympic Boulevard between the Telstra Stadium and the Aquatic Centre. The *Novotel* is Olympic Park's social focus, with several places to eat and drink, including the popular *Homebush Bay Brewery*.

Visiting the venues

The best way to get out to Olympic Park is to take a ferry up the Parramatta River: the **RiverCat** from Circular Quay ($7.50 one way to Homebush Bay) stops off frequently en route to Parramatta. Otherwise, a direct **train** from Central to Olympic Park station runs four times daily weekdays (otherwise and at weekends change at Lidcombe station from where trains depart every 10min). You can get to some venues directly by **bus** from Strathfield train station: #401–404 run regularly to the Homebush Bay Olympic Centre, the State Sports Centre and the Athletic Centre via the Olympic Park ferry wharf. To get around the extensive site you can **hire bikes**, though on the weekend only ($12 hour, $22 half-day) from the **Sydney Olympic Park Visitor Gateway**, right next to Olympic Park station on the corner of Showground Road and Murray Rose Avenue (daily 9am–5pm; ⓣ02/9714 7888). The **Games Trail Tour**, a walking tour exploring the Olympic sites and stories, leaves from outside the information centre (daily noon, 1.30pm & 3pm; no booking necessary; $20; 1hr).

ⓣ02/8839 3311, ⓦwww.visitsydney.org/parramatta), by the convict-built Lennox Bridge. The centre hands out free walking-route maps detailing its many historical attractions. Parramatta's most important historic feature is the National Trust–owned **Old Government House** (Mon–Fri 10am–4pm, Sat & Sun 10.30am–4pm; $7) in **Parramatta Park** by the river. Entered through the 1885 gatehouse on O'Connell Street, the park – filled with native trees – rises up to the gracious old Georgian-style building, the oldest remaining public edifice in Australia. It was built between 1799 and 1816 and used as the Viceregal residence until 1855; one wing has been converted into a pleasant teahouse. History aside, Parrammata today is a modern multicultural suburban town with a wealth of international restaurants around Church and Phillip streets, and bargain shops and factory outlets on its outskirts.

Continuing west, the Western Highway and the rail lines head on to **PENRITH**, the most westerly of Sydney's satellite towns, in a curve of the Nepean River at the foot of the Blue Mountains (on the way out here you pass **Featherdale Wildlife Park**; see box on p.188). Penrith has an old-fashioned Aussie feel about it – a tight community that is immensely proud of the Panthers, its boisterous rugby-league team. The area is also the home of the extensive International Regatta Centre on Penrith Lakes, spreading between Castlereagh and Cranebrook roads north of the town centre, and used in the Olympics; at **Penrith Whitewater Stadium** you can go on a thrilling ninety-minute white-water rafting session ($72; bookings ⓣ02/4730 4333, ⓦwww.penrithwhitewater.com.au).

The Blue Mountains region

The section of the Great Dividing Range nearest Sydney gets its name from the blue mist that rises from millions of eucalyptus trees and hangs in the mountain air, tinting the sky and the range alike. In the colony's early days, the **Blue Mountains** were believed to be an insurmountable barrier to the west. The first expeditions followed the streams in the valleys until they were defeated by cliff faces rising vertically above them. Only in 1813, when the explorers Wentworth, Blaxland and Lawson followed the ridges instead of the valleys, were the "mountains" (actually a series of canyons) finally conquered, allowing the western plains to be opened up for settlement. The range is surmounted by a

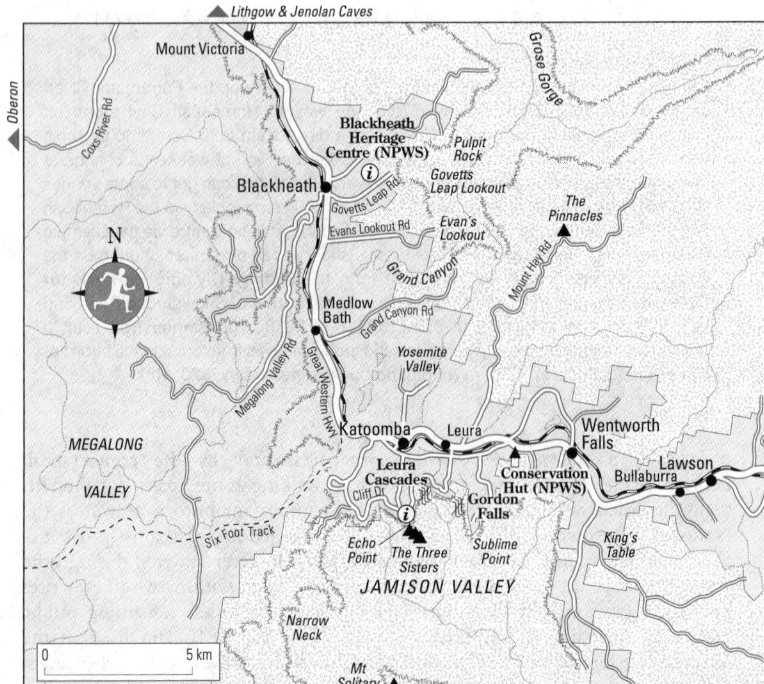

plateau at an altitude of more than 1000m where, over millions of years, rivers have carved deep valleys into the sandstone, and winds and driving rain have helped to deepen the ravines, creating a spectacular scenery of sheer precipices and walled canyons. Before white settlement, the Daruk Aborigines lived here, dressed in animal-skin cloaks to ward off the cold. An early coal-mining industry, based in Katoomba, was followed by tourism, which snowballed after the arrival of the railway in 1868; by 1900, the first three mountain stations of Wentworth Falls, Katoomba and Mount Victoria had been established as fashionable resorts, extolling the health-giving benefits of eucalyptus-tinged mountain air. In 2000, the Blue Mountains became a **UNESCO World Heritage Site**, joining the Great Barrier Reef; the listing came after abseiling was finally banned on the mountains' most famous scenic wonder, the **Three Sisters**, after forty years of clambering had caused significant erosion. The Blue Mountains stand out from other Australian forests, in particular for the **Wollemi Pine**, discovered in 1994 (see p.209), a "living fossil" that dates back to the dinosaur era.

All the villages and towns of the romantically dubbed "**City of the Blue Mountains**" – principally Glenbrook, Springwood, Wentworth Falls, Leura, Katoomba and Blackheath – lie on a ridge, connected by the Great Western Highway. Around them is the **Blue Mountains National Park**, the state's fourth-largest national park and to many minds the best. The region makes a great weekend break from the city, with stunning views and clean air complemented by a wide range of accommodation, cafés and restaurants. But be warned: at weekends, and during the summer holidays, Katoomba is thronged with escapees from the city, and prices escalate accordingly. Even at their most crowded, though, the Blue Mountains always offer somewhere where you can

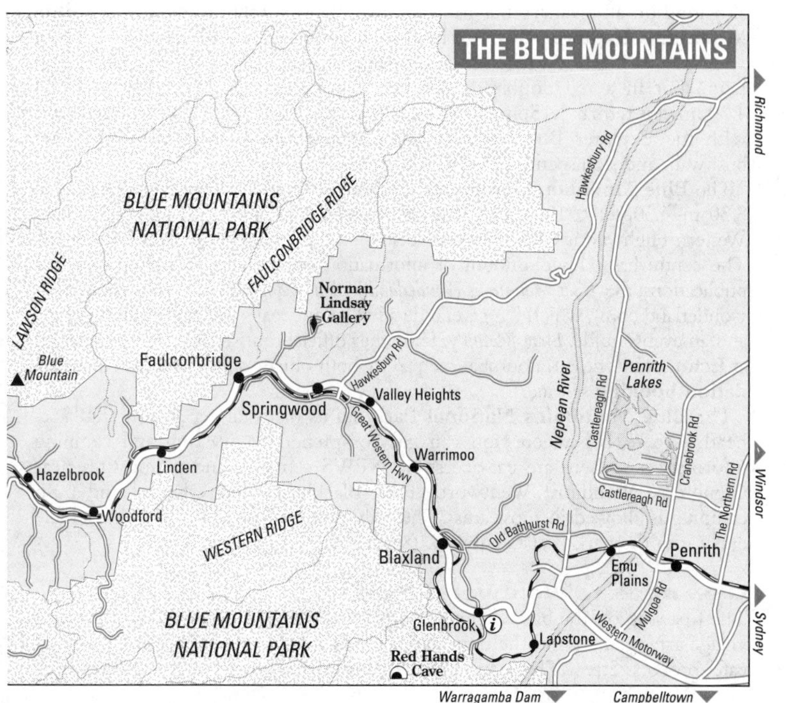

find peace and quiet, and even solitude – the deep gorges and high rocks make much of the terrain inaccessible except to bushwalkers and mountaineers. Climbing schools offer courses in rock-climbing, abseiling and canyoning for both beginners and experienced climbers, while Glenbrook is a popular mountain-biking spot.

Transport, tours and information

Public transport to the mountains is quite good but your own vehicle will give you much greater flexibility, allowing you to take detours to old mansions, cottage gardens and the lookout points scattered along the ridge. **Trains** leave from Central Station for Mount Victoria and/or Lithgow and follow the highway, stopping at all the major towns en route (frequent departures until about midnight; 2hr; $11.60 one way to Katoomba, $16.20 off-peak day return). If you're dependent on public transport, Katoomba makes the best base: facilities and services are concentrated here, and Blue Mountains Bus Co (ⓣ02/4751 1077, ⓦwww.mountainlink.com.au) has half-hourly **bus** services to Blackheath, Mount Victoria (no service weekends), Echo Point and the Scenic World complex, Leura, Wentworth Falls and North Katoomba. Buses leave from Katoomba Street outside the *Carrington Hotel*, and opposite the *Savoy*.

The two Katoomba-based, hop-on-hop-off tour buses have offices by the train station exit on Main Street; passes include discounts to some of the attractions en route. **Trolley Tours** (ⓣ02/4782 7999 or 1800 801 577, ⓦwww.trolleytours.com.au), run by Blue Mountains Bus Co, is a minibus decked out like a tram, which does a scenic circuit with commentary from Katoomba to Leura around Cliff Drive to the Three Sisters and back, taking in attractions along the way (departs Katoomba hourly 9.15am–4.15pm; $15 all-day pass is also valid on all ordinary bus routes, above). The slightly more extensive **Blue Mountains Explorer Bus**, run by Fantastic Aussie Tours (ⓣ02/4782 1866 or 1300 300 915, ⓦwww.fantastic-aussie-tours.com.au), also links Katoomba and Leura but in a red double-decker bus (departs Katoomba hourly 9.30am–4.30pm, last return 5.15pm; 30 stops; $29 all-day pass). There's no commentary with the Explorer Bus, but you get a 29-page guide with maps detailing bushwalk and sightseeing options.

The **Blue Mountains Information Centre** (Mon–Fri 9am–5pm, Sat & Sun 8.30am–4.30pm; ⓣ1300 653 408, ⓦwww.bluemts.com.au) is on the Great Western Highway at Glenbrook (see below), the gateway to the Blue Mountains. The centre has a huge amount of information on the area, including two free publications: the *Blue Mountains Wonderland Visitors Guide* (ⓦwww.bluemountainswonderland.com), which has several detailed colour maps and bushwalking notes, and an events guide, *Imag Monthly*. The other official tourist information centre is at **Echo Point**, near Katoomba (see p.208); both offices offer a **free accommodation booking** service.

The **Blue Mountains National Park** has its main ranger station at Blackheath (see p.210), where you can get comprehensive walking and camping information – there are car-accessible NPWS camping and picnic sites near Glenbrook, Woodford, Wentworth Falls, Blackheath and Oberon, and bush camping is allowed in most areas. The only point where you must pay vehicle entry into the park is at Glenbrook ($7).

Glenbrook to Wentworth Falls

The first stop off the busy highway from Sydney is **GLENBROOK**, a pleasant village arranged around the train station, with an adventure shop and a strip of cafés on Ross Street. The section of the **Blue Mountains National Park** here is popular for **mountain biking** along the **Oaks Fire Trail** (it's best to start the thirty-kilometre trail higher up the mountain in **WOODFORD** and head downhill, ending up in Glenbrook; bike rental is available at Katoomba, see p.214). Several bushwalks commence from the part-time NPWS office at the end of Bruce Road (Sat & Sun, public and school holidays 8.30am–4.30pm; ⓣ02/4739 2950). In summer, head for the swimmable **Blue Pool** and **Jellybean Pool**, an easy, one-kilometre walk away. One of the best hikes from here is to see the Aboriginal hand stencils on the walls of Red Hands Cave (6km; 3hr return; medium difficulty). With a car or bike you can get there via road and continue to the grassy creekside Eoroka picnic ground (also camping) where there are lots of eastern grey kangaroos.

The small town of **WENTWORTH FALLS**, 32km further west, was named after William Wentworth, one of the famous trio who conquered the mountains in 1813. A signposted road leads from the Great Western Highway to the **Wentworth Falls Reserve**, with superb views of the waterfall tumbling down into the Jamison Valley. You can reach this picnic area from Wentworth train station by following the easy creekside 2.5-kilometre **Darwin's Walk** – the route followed by the famous naturalist in 1836 to the cliff edge, where he described the view from the great precipice as one of the most stupendous he'd ever seen. Most of the other bushwalks in the area start from the national park's **Valley of the Waters Conservation Hut** (Mon–Fri 9am–4pm, Sat & Sun 9am–5pm; ⓣ02/4757 3827), about 3km from the railway station at the end of Fletcher Street. Blue Mountains Explorer Bus offers a once-daily shuttle bus to the national park at Wentworth Falls (departs Katoomba 9.15am, returning at 5.25pm) as part of their day-pass.

Leura

Just 2km west of Wentworth Falls, the wealthy **LEURA**, packed with cafés and antique stores, is a scenic spot with views across the Jamison Valley to the imposing plateau that is **Mount Solitary**. The main shopping strip, **Leura Mall**, has a wide nature strip lined with cherry trees and makes a popular picnicking spot. In fact, Leura is renowned for its beautiful gardens, and nine are open to the public during the **Leura Gardens Festival** (early to mid-Oct; $17.50 all gardens, or $5 per garden; ⓦwww.leuragardensfestival.com.au). Open all year round, though, is the beautiful National Trust–listed **Everglades Gardens** (daily 10am–5pm; $7) at 37 Everglades Ave, 2km southeast of the Mall. There are wonderful Jamison Valley views from its formal terraces, a colourful display of azaleas and rhododendrons, an arboretum, and a simple tearoom. Just over a kilometre south of the Mall is the Gordon Falls picnic area on Lone Pine Avenue, where Leura's mansions and gardens give way to the bush of the **Blue Mountains National Park**; it's an easy ten-minute return walk to the lookout over the falls or there's a canyon walk (2hr circuit; medium difficulty) via Lyre Bird Dell and the Pool of Siloam, which takes in some of the Blue Mountains' distinctive hanging swamps, an Aboriginal rock shelter and cooling rainforest. From Gordon Falls, a 45-minute bushwalk part-way along the Prince Henry Cliff Walk (see p.210) heads to **Leura Cascades** picnic area off **Cliff Drive** (the scenic route around the cliffs that extends from Leura to beyond Katoomba) where there are several bushwalks, including a two- to three-hour circuit walk to the base of the cascading **Bridal Veil Falls** (not to be confused with Bridal Veil Falls on the north side of Leura at Grose Valley (see p.211)). To the east of Gordon Falls, Sublime Point Road leads to the aptly named **Sublime Point** lookout, with panoramic views of the Jamison Valley.

Katoomba and around

KATOOMBA, 103km west of Sydney, is the biggest town in the Blue Mountains and the area's commercial heart; it's also the best located for the major sights of Echo Point and The Three Sisters. There's a lively café culture on **Katoomba Street**, which runs downhill from the train station; the street is also full of vintage and retro clothes shops, secondhand bookstores, antique dealers and giftshops. When the town was first discovered by fashionable city-dwellers in the late nineteenth century, the grandiose **Carrington Hotel**, prominently located at the top of Katoomba Street, was the height of elegance (an historian gives 1hr–1hr 30min tours of the hotel; $8; bookings ⓣ02/4754 5726). It's recently been returned to its former glory, with elegant sloping lawns running down to the street, half of which has been taken over by a new **town square**.

Across the railway line (use the foot-tunnel under the station and follow the signs), a stunning introduction to the ecology of the Blue Mountains can be had at the **Edge Maxvision Cinema**, at 225 Great Western Highway (ⓣ02/4782 8900, ⓦwww.edgecinema.com.au), a huge six-storey cinema screen created as a venue to show *The Edge Movie* (daily 10.20am, 11.05am, 12.10pm, 1.30pm,

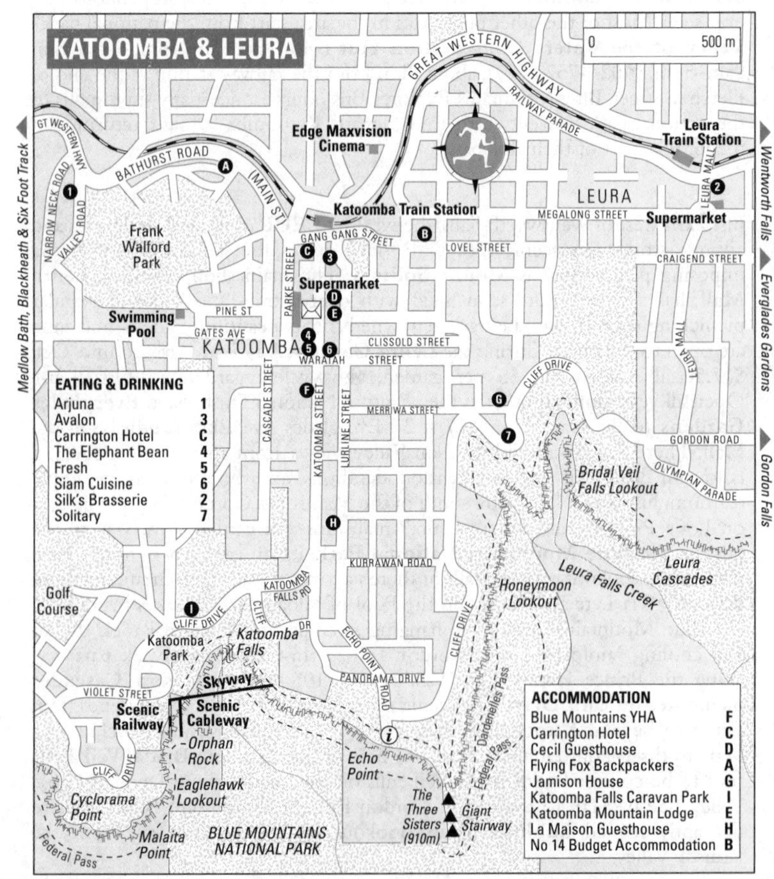

△Scenic Skyway and the Three Sisters

2.15pm & 5.30pm; $14.50). The highlight of the forty-minute film is the segment about the "dinosaur trees", a stand of thirty-metre-high **Wollemi Pine**, previously known only from fossil material over sixty million years old. The trees – miraculously still existing – survive deep within a sheltered rainforest gully in the **Wollemi National Park**, north of Katoomba, and they made headlines when they were first discovered in 1994 by a group of canyoners. Since the discovery, the first cultivated Wollemi Pine was planted in 1998 at Sydney's Royal Botanic Gardens.

A 25-minute walk south from the train station down Katoomba Street and along Lurline Street and Echo Point Road (or by tour or regular bus from outside the Savoy Theatre; see p.206) will bring you to **Echo Point**. From the projecting lookout platform between the **information centre** (daily 9am–5pm) and souvenir shops and eateries at the Three Sisters Heritage Plaza, breathtaking vistas take in the Kedumba and Jamison valleys, Mount Solitary, the Ruined Castle, Kings Tableland and the Blue Mountains' most famous landmark, the **Three Sisters** (910m). These three gnarled rocky points take their name from a – possibly apocryphal – Aboriginal Dreamtime story that relates how the Kedumba people were losing a battle against the rival Nepean people: the Kedumba leader, fearing that his three beautiful daughters would be carried off by the enemy, turned them to stone, but was tragically killed before

The Six Foot Track

Along the Great Western Highway, about 2.5km west of Katoomba train station, is the **Explorers Tree**, initialized by Blaxland, Lawson and Wentworth during their famous 1813 expedition. From Nellies Glen Road here is the start of the 42-kilometre **Six Foot Track** to the Jenolan Caves (2–3 days; carry plenty of water) and shorter walks to Pulpit Rock and Bonnie Doon Falls. There are four basic **campsites** along the way, plus well-equipped cabins at Binda Flats (see p.216). Blackheath NPWS can provide more bushwalking and camping information. Blue Mountains Guides (ⓣ02/4782 6109, ⓦwww.bluemountainsguides.com.au) offers a **guided walk** along the track (3-day $660; camping). Otherwise, Fantastic Aussie Tours (see p.206) provides a daily transfer service for bushwalkers from Katoomba to the start of the track and a return service a few days later from Jenolan Caves (2hr; $35). Tread Lightly Eco Tours (see p.215) run a popular morning Wilderness Walk ($30) that takes in some of the track. A more unusual way to do the track is to enter Australia's largest annual off-road marathon, the **Six Foot Track Marathon** held in March (more details at ⓦwww.coolrunning.com.au).

he could reverse his spell. The Three Sisters are at the top of the **Giant Stairway** (1hr 45min one way), the beginning of the very steep 800-step stairs into the 300-metre-deep **Jamison Valley** below, passing **Katoomba Falls** en route. There's a popular walking route, taking about two hours and graded medium, down the stairway and part-way along the **Federal Pass** to the **Landslide**, and then on to the Scenic Railway or Cableway (see below), either of which you can take back up to the ridge.

To spare yourself the trek down into the Jamison Valley or the walk back up, head for the very touristy **Scenic World complex** at the end of Violet Street off Cliff Drive. Apart from housing a small cinema showing a pictorial documentary of the area (free with purchase of any ticket), you can take a short and pricey glass-bottomed cable-car ride over the valley in the **Scenic Skyway**, or choose between two modes of transport to get to the valley floor: the original **Scenic Railway** or the modern **Scenic Cableway** (daily 9am–4.50pm; depart every 10min; $8 for one-way journey on each ride; ⓦwww.scenicworld.com.au). The Railway and Cableway offer steep descents to the valley floor with fantastic views of the Three Sisters along the way, and end up about 100 metres away from each other making it easy to go down by one and up by the other. Once at the bottom, a scenic two-kilometre boardwalk meanders through the rainforest with interpretative boards detailing natural features and history along the way. For the more energetic, there's a tranquil but moderately difficult twelve-kilometre return bushwalk to the Ruined Castle.

A short walk from the Scenic World complex along Cliff Drive is the **Katoomba Falls picnic area** in Katoomba Park, where there's a kiosk and several bushwalking options. The **Prince Henry Cliff Walk** (9km one way; 1hr 30min; easy) is a long, pleasant stroll along the plateau clifftop via Echo Point all the way to **Gordon Falls** (see p.210) with glorious lookouts along the way. A scenic drive following Cliff Drive southwest of Katoomba Falls leads to several other spectacular lookouts: Eaglehawk, the Landslide, and Narrow Neck – a great sunset spot, with views into both the Jamison and Megalong valleys.

Blackheath

Two train stops beyond Katoomba, and 11km further northwest along the Great Western Highway, there are more lookout points at **BLACKHEATH** – just as impressive as Echo Point and much less busy. One of the best is **Govetts Leap**, at the end of Govetts Leap Road (just over 2km east of the highway through the village centre), near the **Blackheath Heritage Centre** (daily 9am–4.30pm; ⓣ02/4787 8877), which acts as the **Blue Mountains National Park headquarters**. The two-kilometre **Fairfax Heritage Track** from the NPWS centre is wheelchair- and pram-accessible and takes in the Govetts Leap Lookout with its marvellous panorama of the **Grose Valley** and the much-photographed Bridal Veil Falls. Many walks start from the centre, but one of the most popular, **The Grand Canyon** (5km; 3hr 30min; medium difficulty), begins from **Evans Lookout Road** at the south end of town, west of the Great Western Highway.

Govetts Leap Road and its shady cross-street, Wentworth Street, have lots of antique and craft shops, an antiquarian bookshop, and great cafés and restaurants. Ten kilometres southwest of Blackheath, across the railway line, the beautiful unspoilt **Megalong Valley** is reached via winding Megalong Road; it's popular for **horse riding** (see "Listings" p.214), and there are creeks with swimmable waterholes.

Mount Victoria and around

At the top of the Blue Mountains, secluded and leafy **MOUNT VICTORIA**, 6km northwest of Blackheath along the Great Western Highway and the last mountain-settlement proper, is the only one with an authentic village feel. The great old pub, the *Imperial* (see below), is good for a drink or meal, and there's old-fashioned scones at the *Bay Tree Tea Shop* opposite. Worth a browse are several antique and secondhand bookshops. Some short **walks** start from the Fairy Bower picnic area, a ten-minute walk from the Great Western Highway via Mount Piddington Road.

Beyond Mount Victoria, drivers can circle back towards Sydney via the scenic **Bells Line of Road**, which heads east through the fruit- and vegetable-growing areas of Bilpin and Kurrajong to Richmond, with growers selling their produce at roadside stalls. On the way, **Mount Tomah Botanic Garden** (daily: April–Sept 10am–4pm; Oct–March 10am–5pm; $4.40; ⓦwww.rbgsyd.nsw.gov.au; no public transport) has been the cool-climate outpost of Sydney's Royal Botanic Gardens since 1987. The popular *Garden Restaurant* (lunch daily; licensed; ⓣ02/4567 2060; mains $35) with a pricey contemporary Australian menu has fantastic north-facing views over the gardens, Wollemi National Park and Bilbin orchards. Cheaper light lunches are also available and there's a kiosk, plus free electric barbecues and picnic tables. By car, you can continue west along the Bells Line of Road to the Zig Zag Railway at Clarence, just over 35km away (see p.215).

Accommodation in the Blue Mountains

Accommodation rates rise on Friday and Saturday nights – aim to visit on weekdays when it's quieter and cheaper. The tourist offices at Glenbrook and Echo Point can book accommodation. **Katoomba** is the obvious choice if arriving by train, particularly for those on a budget, since it has several **hostels** to choose from, but if you have your own transport you can indulge in some of the more unusual and characterful **guesthouses** in **Blackheath** and **Mount Victoria**. There are also many charming **holiday homes**: weekend rates average $300, but the weekly rate is often only $75 to $100 more (linen extra), so consider staying longer: contact Soper Bros, 173 The Mall, Leura (ⓣ02/4784 1633, ⓦwww.soperbros.com.au). There are two council-run **caravan parks**: *Katoomba Falls*, at Katoomba Falls Road (ⓣ02/4782 1835; en-suite cabins ③) and *Blackheath*, at Prince Edward Street (ⓣ02/4787 8101; cabins ②, en-suite ③); you can **camp** at both of these, as well as in the grounds of *Flying Fox Backpackers* (see below), and in the bush at several NPWS sites (see p.205).

Hostels

Blue Mountains YHA 207 Katoomba St, Katoomba ⓣ02/4782 1416, ⓔbluemountains@yhansw.org.au. Huge 200-bed YHA hostel right in the town centre. The former 1930s guesthouse has been modernized but retains its charming lead-lighted windows, Art Deco decor, huge ballroom and an old-fashioned mountain-retreat ambience, with an open fire in the reading room, separate games room (with pool table), Internet access and a pleasant courtyard. Most rooms and some of the four-bed dorms are en suite (also 8-bed dorms). A dedicated information room has topographic maps; friendly reception staff are very helpful. Dorms $27.50–29.50, rooms ❺

Flying Fox Backpackers 190 Bathurst Rd, Katoomba ⓣ02/4782 4226 or 1800 624 226, ⓦwww.theflyingfox.com.au. Colourfully painted, homely and comfortable bungalow near the station, with spacious seven-bed dorms and lovely laid-back doubles (no en suites). Outside, there's a courtyard and a popular "chill-out" hut with a fire, and a bush-outlook camping site ($13 per person). Camping gear is rented out at reasonable rates and the knowledgeable managers offer info on bushwalks and camping, and free transport to walks. Dorms $23, rooms with breakfast, ❹

No 14 Budget Accommodation 14 Lovel St, Katoomba ⓣ02/4782 7104, ⓦwww.numberfourteen.com. This relaxed hostel in a charming restored former guesthouse – polished floors, cozy fire, and original features – is like a home away from home, run by an informative, friendly young couple who put in a lot of effort. Mostly twin and double rooms, some en suite, plus four-share dorms with comfy beds instead of bunks; all centrally heated. Peaceful veranda surrounded by pretty plants and valley views. Dorms $22, rooms ❹

Hotels, motels and guesthouses

Carrington Hotel 15–47 Katoomba St, Katoomba ⓣ02/4782 1111, ⓦwww.thecarrington.com.au. When it opened in 1882, the *Carrington* was the region's finest. Now fully restored, original features include stained-glass windows, open fireplaces, a splendid dining room and ballroom, cocktail bar, snooker and games room, library and guest lounges. The spacious, well-aired en-suite rooms are beautifully decorated in rich heritage colours. Cheaper rooms share bathrooms. Buffet breakfast. Rooms ❼, en suite ❽

Cecil Guesthouse 108 Katoomba St, Katoomba ⓣ02/4782 1411, ⓦwww.ourguest.com.au. Very central choice, set back from the main street. There are great views over the town and Jamison Valley from the common areas and some bedrooms (these ones go first). Rather shabby but charming – an old-fashioned 1940s atmosphere with log fires, games room and tennis courts, plus modern touches such as the spa. Most rooms share bathrooms, but some are en suite. Light breakfast included. Rooms ❺, en suite ❻

Glenella 56 Govett's Leap Rd, Blackheath ⓣ02/4787 8352. Guesthouse in a charming 1905 homestead with antique-furnished rooms, most en suite, but there are slightly cheaper share-bathroom options. ❻

Imperial 1 Station Street, Mount Victoria ⓣ02/4787 1233, ⓦwww.hotelimperial.com.au. Nicely restored huge country pub with beautiful lead lighting. Good-value, filling and tasty bistro meals. There are en-suite rooms and spacious, pleasantly decorated guesthouse-style share-bathroom options, or more basic no-frills "pub" style rooms. Breakfast included. Basic ❺, en suite ❼

Jamison House 48 Merriwa St, cnr Cliff Drive, Katoomba ⓣ02/4782 1206, ⓦwww.jamisonhouse.com. Built as a guesthouse in 1903, this seriously charming place has amazing, unimpeded views across the Jamison Valley. The feel is of a small European hotel, added to by the French restaurant downstairs, *The Rooster*, in a gorgeous dining room full of original fixtures (dinner daily, lunch Sat & Sun; set-price menus: two-course $54, three-course $68) and with big picture windows. Upstairs, a breakfast room gives splendid views – provisions (and an egg cooker) come with the room – and there's a sitting room with a fireplace. All rooms en suite. ❼

Jemby-Rinjah Eco Lodge 336 Evans Lookout Rd, 4km from Blackheath ⓣ02/4787 7622, ⓦwww.jembyrinjahlodge.com.au. Accommodation in distinctive one- and two-bedroom timber cabins (with own wood fires) in tranquil bushland near the Grose Valley. There's a licensed common area whose focal point is the huge circular "fire pit"; a restaurant operates in here most Friday and Saturday nights. Bushwalks organized for guests. Cabins sleep two to six people. ❽

Katoomba Mountain Lodge 31 Lurline St, Katoomba ⓣ02/4782 3933, ⓦwww.katoombamountainlodge.com.au. Family-run, central accommodation with eighteen guestrooms on three floors and great views from its veranda. There's also a communal kitchen and dining room. ❹

La Maison Guesthouse 175–177 Lurline St, Katoomba ⓣ02/4782 4996, ⓦwww.lamaison.com.au. This modern place feels more like a small hotel than a guesthouse. With a four-star level of comfort in the spacious, conservatively decorated, well-furnished rooms (with bathtubs in the en suites), and very obliging management, it's one of the best-value places in Katoomba, and in a good spot between the town centre and Echo Point. Also a garden and deck, guest spa and sauna. ❻

Eating, drinking and nightlife

Cuisine in the Blue Mountains has gone way beyond the ubiquitous "Devonshire teas", with many well-regarded restaurants, and a real **café culture** in Katoomba and Leura. There are some great bakeries, too: top of the list is *Hominy*, 185 Katoomba St (daily 6am–5.30pm), with no eating area of its own, but the street's public picnic tables just outside. Also see p.207 for the *Conservation Hut Café* and accommodation listings for other eating options.

There are several **nightlife** options in Katoomba. The salubrious cocktail bar and cabaret room at *The Clarendon* hosts eclectic folk, blues, jazz, and world music (Thurs–Sat, sometimes Sun; $10–45; dinner plus show extra $20–25; bar 6pm, dinner 7pm, show 8.30pm). *Tris Elies Nightclub* beside the train station at 287 Bathurst Rd (☎02/4782 4026; Wed 9pm–midnight, Thurs–Sat 9pm–3am) puts on karaoke (Wed), jamming sessions (Thurs; $5), world, blues, rock music (Fri; $10), and eclectic club nights (Sat; $10–15), plus grill-style meals. On the other side of the tracks, opposite the station, the huge and now rather hip *Gearin Hotel* (☎02/4782 4395) is a hive of activity, with several bars where you can play pool, see touring bands (Fri & Sat nights) or boogie at the club nights ($10). There's more mainstream action at the *Carrington*, below.

Arjuna 16 Valley Rd, just off the Great Western Highway, Katoomba ☎02/4782 4662. Excellent, authentic Indian restaurant. A bit out of the way but positioned for spectacular sunset views, so get there early. Good veggie choices, too. BYO. Evenings from 6pm; closed Tues & Wed.

Avalon 18 Katoomba St ☎02/4782 5532. Stylish place with the ambience of a quirky café, in the dress circle of the old Savoy Theatre, with many Art Deco features intact. Beautiful views down the valley, too – turn up for lunch or early dinner to see them. Moderately expensive menu, but generous servings and to-die-for desserts – or come here just for a drink. BYO & licensed. Lunch & dinner Wed–Sun.

Carrington Hotel 15–47 Katoomba St, Katoomba ☎02/4782 1111. The *Carrington* has a host of bars in and around the grand old building. *Champagne Charlie's Cocktail Bar* has a decorative glass ceiling dome and chandeliers. You can order an understandably pricey drink and take it into one of the classic Kentia-palm-filled lounges or out onto the wonderful front veranda overlooking the lawns. Its really splendid Grand Dining Room has columns and decorative inlaid ceilings; the high-tea buffet here on Sun is a treat (3–5pm; $16.50), or for dinner, mains are around $33 (also Fri night seafood and carvery buffet; $55). Cheaper drinks and a livelier atmosphere are found in the modern annexe next door, the *Carrington Bar* (live music Wed–Fri includes a piano player on Thurs night; bistro above), and the down-to-earth public bar, with a separate entrance on Main Street opposite the train station; there's a nightclub above, *The Attic* (Fri & Sat 10.3–3am; $5).

The Elephant Bean 159 Katoomba St, Katoomba. Small, squeezy café that serves the best coffee in Katoomba – choose from lots of styles – and great all-day breakfasts with eggs every way (or there's even a big vegan breakfast for $10.95). Other choices include the popular burgers for veggies or carnivores and sourdough sandwiches (all $8.50) and salads ($8). Not the place for cakes though, with only a couple of choices.

Fresh 181 Katoomba St, Katoomba. Spacious goldfish-bowl at the bottom end of the main street, by the busy lane heading to the health-food co-op, post office and supermarket, is the most popular café with locals, from cops to arty types. With an open kitchen, wooden interior, good music, sunny tables outside and a big magazine stash. Superb gourmet pies, from Thai vegetable to *rogan josh* ($4.50 takeaway, $11.50 eat-in with salad), big fruit muffins, and great coffee. Extensive blackboard lunch for around $15.

Il Postino 13 Station St, opposite the train station, Wentworth Falls. Great relaxed café in the original old post office – the cracked walls have become part of an artfully distressed, light and airy interior; outside tables on a street-facing courtyard. Menu is Mediterranean- and Thai-slanted, with plenty for vegetarians (nothing over $14). Excellent all-day breakfast featuring many pancake variations. BYO. Daily 8.30am–6pm.

Siam Cuisine 172 Katoomba St, Katoomba ☎02/4782 5671. One of three much-of-a-muchness Thai restaurants interspersed along Katoomba Street. This one is popular, inexpensive, and offers cheap lunchtime specials. BYO. Closed Mon.

Silk's Brasserie 128 The Mall, Leura ☎02/4784 2534. Parisian-style bar with excellent service and well-priced food – lunch mains peak at $22. At dinner, the sophisticated European-style dishes, from confit of duck to Tasmanian salmon, range from $26–33. Licensed, with many wines available by the glass.

Solitary 90 Cliff Drive, Leura Falls ☎02/4782 1164. Perched on a hairpin bend on the mountains' scenic cliff-hugging road, the views of the Jamison Valley and Mount Solitary from this former kiosk, now modern Australian restaurant, are sublime. Expect beautifully laid tables, eager service, a well-chosen and reasonably priced wine list, jazz on the soundtrack, and fine food. There's a fireplace in the back room, and picnic tables outside, which are popular for the weekend breakfast. Moderate to expensive. Licensed. Lunch Sat & Sun, dinner Tues–Sat.

Victory Café 17 Govetts Leap Rd, Blackheath ☎02/4787 6777. A very pleasant space in the front of an old Art Deco theatre now converted into an antiques centre. Gourmet sandwiches ($8.90) and café favourites ($7–15) with an interesting spin; special mains such as Szechuan chicken, and all-day breakfast, with also plenty for vegetarians. Daily 8.30am–5pm.

Listings

Adventure activities Australian School of Mountaineering, at Paddy Pallin, 166 Katoomba St, Katoomba (☎02/4782 2014, ⓦwww.asmguides.com). Katoomba's original abseiling outfit offers daily day-long courses ($125), plus canyoning to Grand, Empress or Fortress canyons (Oct–May daily 9am; $145; also less frequent trips to other canyons), rock-climbing and bush-survival courses. Another long-established operator, High 'n' Wild Mountain Adventures, 3–5 Katoomba St, Katoomba (☎02/4782 6224, ⓦwww.high-n-wild.com.au), has a good reputation for its beginners' courses in abseiling (half-day $95, full day $135), canyoning (from $150), rock-climbing (half-day $119, full day $169), plus guided bushwalking and bushcraft courses. Both include lunch on full-day courses.

Bike rental The friendly Vélo Nova, 182 Katoomba St, Katoomba (☎02/4782 2800), has mountain bikes from $28 half-day, $50 full day.

Bus services See p.206.

Camping equipment Paddy Pallin, 166 Katoomba St, Katoomba (☎02/4782 4466), sells camping gear and a good range of topographic maps and bushwalking guides and supplies. For cheap gear, go to K-Mart (next door to Coles supermarket, Katoomba Street). *Flying Fox Backpackers* (p.212) rents gear to guests.

Car rental Redicar, 80 Megalong St, Leura ☎02/4784 3443, ⓦwww.redicar.com.au.

Festivals Blue Mountains Music Festival ⓦwww.bmff.org.au. Three-day mid-March festival of folk, roots and blues features Australian and international musicians on several indoor and outdoor stages ($160 whole weekend, $90 full-day ticket, $55–70 night ticket).

Horse riding Blue Mountains Horse Riding Adventures (☎02/4787 8688, ⓦwww.megalong.cc; pick-ups from Blackheath), escorted trail rides in the Megalong Valley and along the Coxs River; beginners' one-hour Wilderness Ride ($45), experienced riders' all-day adventure along the river ($165). Werriberri Trail Rides offer horse riding and overnight stays for all abilities in the Megalong Valley (☎02/4787 9171; 2hr ride, including Katoomba pick-up, $78; pony rides from $5.50 for 5min).

Hospital Blue Mountains District Anzac Memorial, Katoomba ☎02/4784 6500.

Internet Access Katoomba Book Exchange, 34 Katoomba St, Katoomba ($2.50 for 15min, $8 for 1hr; Mon, Tues & Fri 10am–6pm, Wed & Thurs 10.30am–5pm).

Laundry The Washing Well, K-Mart car park, Katoomba. Daily 7am–7pm.

Pharmacies Blooms Springwood Pharmacy, 161 Macquarie Rd, Springwood (Mon–Fri 8.30am–9pm, Sat & Sun 9am–7pm); Greenwell & Thomas, 145 Katoomba St, Katoomba (Mon–Fri 8.30am–7pm, Sat & Sun 9am–6pm).

Post office Katoomba Post Office, Pioneer Place, off Katoomba St, Katoomba, NSW 2780.

Supermarket Coles, Pioneer Place off Katoomba St, Katoomba (daily 6am–midnight).

Swimming pool Katoomba Aquatic Centre, Gates Ave, Katoomba (Mon–Fri 6am–8pm, Sat & Sun 8am–8pm, winter weekends closes 6.30pm; ☎02/4782 1748; swim $4.70), has outdoor and indoor complex with toddlers pool, sauna, spa and gym.

Taxis Taxis wait outside the main Blue Mountains train stations to meet arrivals; otherwise, for the upper mountains call Katoomba Radio Cabs

(☎02/4782 1311), or for the middle mountains call Blue Mountains Taxi Cab (☎02/4759 3000).
Tours Most tours of the Blue Mountains start from Sydney; see box on p.185. For the two hop-on hop-off tour services from Katoomba, see p.208. Fantastic Aussie Tours (see p.206) also do large-group coach tours to the Jenolan Caves: a day-tour (daily; $63–70 with one cave entry), or adventure caving ($100). The excellent Blue Mountains Walkabout (☎0408 443 822, Ⓦwww.bluemountainswalkabout.com) is an all-day (8hr), off-the-beaten-track bush roam (around 10km) between Faulconbridge and Springwood led by an Aboriginal guide; expect to look at Aboriginal rock carvings, taste bushtucker and swim in waterholes in summer ($95, BYO lunch; own train journey to Faulconbridge). Tread Lightly Eco Tours offer recommended small-group, expert-guided 2hr, half-day and full-day bushwalk and 4WD tours from Katoomba.
Trains Katoomba station general enquiries ☎02/4782 1902.

Lithgow and the Zig Zag Railway

En route to Bathurst and the Central West on the Great Western Highway, **Lithgow**, 21km northwest of Mount Victoria, is a coal-mining town nestled under bush-clad hills, with wide leafy streets, quaint mining cottages and some imposing old buildings. About 13km east of the town on the Bells Line of Road, by the small settlement of **Clarence**, is the **Zig Zag Railway**. In the 1860s, engineers were faced with the problem of how to get the main western railway line from the top of the Blue Mountains down the steep drop to the Lithgow Valley, so they came up with a series of zigzag ramps. These fell into disuse in the early twentieth century, but tracks were relaid by rail enthusiasts in the 1970s. Served by old steam trains, the picturesque line passes through two tunnels and over three viaducts. You can stop at points along the way and rejoin a later train. The Zig Zag Railway can be reached by ordinary State Rail train on the regular service between Sydney and Lithgow, by requesting the guard in advance to stop at the Zig Zag platform; you then walk across the line to Bottom Point platform at the base of the Lithgow Valley. To catch the Zig Zag Railway from Clarence, at the top of the valley, you'll need to have your own transport. Zig Zag trains depart from Clarence daily (11am, 1pm & 3pm; from the Zig Zag platform add 40min to these times; $20; no bookings required; ☎02/6353 1795, Ⓦwww.zigzagrailway.com.au). There are plenty of **motels** in and around Lithgow, especially on the Great Western Highway – and the **Lithgow Visitor Information Centre**, 1 Cooerwull Rd (daily 9am–5pm; ☎02/6353 1859, Ⓦwww.tourism.lithgow.com), can advise on other accommodations.

Kanangra Boyd National Park and the Jenolan Caves

Kanangra Boyd National Park shares a boundary with the Blue Mountains National Park. Further south than the latter, much of it is inaccessible, but you can explore the rugged beauty of **Kanangra Walls**, where the Boyd Plateau falls away to reveal a wilderness area of creeks, deep gorges and rivers below. Reached via Jenolan Caves, three **walks** leave from the car park at Kanangra Walls: a short lookout walk, a waterfall stroll and a longer plateau walk – contact the NPWS in **Oberon** for details (38 Ross St; ☎02/6336 1972). Vehicle entry to the park is $7. *Boyd River* and *Dingo Dell* camping grounds, both off Kanangra Walls Road, have **free bush camping** (pit toilets; limited drinking water at Dingo Dell).

The **Jenolan Caves** lie 30km southwest across the mountains from Katoomba on the far edge of the Kanangra Boyd National Park – over 80km by road – and contain New South Wales' most spectacular limestone formations. There are ten "show" caves, with daily guided tours at various times throughout the day

(9.30am–5.30pm; 2hr night tours depart 8pm on school holidays and Saturdays only). If you're coming for just a day, plan to see one or two caves: the best general cave is the Lucas Cave ($22; 1hr 30min), and a more spectacular one is the Temple of Baal ($30; 1hr 30min) while the extensive River Cave, with its tranquil Pool of Reflection, is the longest and priciest ($36; 2hr). The system of caves is surrounded by the **Jenolan Karst Conservation Reserve**, a fauna and flora sanctuary with picnic facilities and walking trails to small waterfalls and lookout points. It and the caves are administered by The Jenolan Caves Trust (Ⓣ02/6359 3311, Ⓦwww.jenolancaves.org.au), which also offers **adventure caving** in various other caves (2hr Plughole tour $58, 7hr Central River Adventure Cave tour $187.50).

The Jenolan Caves Trust also looks after several **places to stay** in the vicinity. The most central is *Jenolan Caves House* (en-suite rooms ❼, motel rooms ❺), a charming old hotel that found fame as a honeymoon destination in the 1920s. In the old hotel section, there's a good restaurant (mains from $20), a bar and a more casual bistro. About ten minutes by car from the caves in a secluded woodland setting are the *Jenolan Caves Cottages* at Binda Flats (sleeps 6; ❹–❺; BYO linen). Other places to stay in the area include *Jenolan Cabins*, 42 Edith Rd, 4km west on Porcupine Hill (Ⓣ02/6335 6239, Ⓦwww.jenolancabins.com.au; ❻), whose reasonably priced, well-equipped two-bedroom timber cabins with wood fires accommodate six (BYO linen) – all with magnificent views over the Blue Mountains and Kanangra Boyd national parks and the Jenolan Karst Conservation Reserve; 4WD tours of the area are also offered (from $80 half-day including lunch).

There's **transport** to Jenolan Caves with Fantastic Aussie Tours (see p.210; 1hr 30min; $35; departs Katoomba 11.15am; departs Jenolan Caves 3.45pm), designed as an overnight rather than a day-return service; otherwise, the same company offers day-tours from Katoomba, as do several other operators (see "Listings" p.215), or there are many tours from Sydney (see box p.185).

South

Once you escape Sydney's uninspiring outer suburbs, the journey south is very enjoyable. Beyond Botany Bay and Port Hacking, the Princes Highway and the Illawarra railway hug the edge of the **Royal National Park** for more than 20km. South of the park, the railway and the scenic Lawrence Hargrave Drive (Route 68) follow the coast to **Wollongong**. Between here and Nowra, the ocean beaches of the Leisure Coast are popular with local holidaymakers, while fishermen, windsurfers and yachtsmen gather at **Lake Illawarra**, a huge coastal lake near Port Kembla. A few kilometres further down the coast is the famous, and occasionally lethal, blowhole at **Kiama**.

Inland, southwest of Wollongong, the softly rolling hills of the **Southern Highlands** are dotted with old country towns such as **Berrima** and **Bundanoon**, the latter overlooking the wild and windswept crags of **Morton National Park**.

Transport down south is good, with a frequent train service operating between Sydney and Nowra, stopping at most of the coastal locations detailed below. The main bus service is Premier Motor Service, which stops at Wollongong and Kiama en route to Bega and Eden (Ⓣ13 34 10, Ⓦwww.premierms.com.au). Greyhound Australia (Ⓣ13 20 30) has a daily Sydney–Melbourne coastal route, which also stops at Wollongong and Kiama.

The Royal and Heathcote national parks

The **Royal National Park** is a huge nature reserve right on Sydney's doorstep, only 36km south of the city. Established in 1879, it was the second national park in the world (after Yellowstone in the USA). The railway between Sydney and Wollongong marks its western border, and from the train the scenery is fantastic – streams, waterfalls, rock formations and rainforest flora fly past the window. If you want to explore more closely, get off at one of the stations along the way – Loftus, Engadine, Heathcote, Waterfall or Otford – all starting points for walking trails into the park. On the eastern side, from Jibbon Head to Garie Beach, the park falls away abruptly to the ocean, creating a spectacular coastline of steep cliffs broken here and there by creeks cascading into the sea and little coves with fine sandy beaches; the remains of **Aboriginal rock carvings** are the only traces of the original Dharawal people.

You can also drive in at various points ($11 car entry; gates open 24hr except at Garie Beach and other picnic spots where gates close at 8.30pm). Coming in at the northern end, turning off the Princes Highway south of Loftus, you can visit the **NPWS Visitor Centre** (daily 9am–4.30pm; Ⓣ02/9542 0648, Ⓦwww.npws.nsw.gov.au), 2km from Loftus train station. The easy one-kilometre track from here to the Bungoona Lookout boasts panoramic views and is wheelchair-accessible. Cars are allowed right through the park, exiting at **Waterfall** on the Princes Highway or **Stanwell Park** on Lawrence Hargrave Drive. Not far south of the NPWS centre, **Audley** is a picturesque picnic ground on the Hacking River, where you can rent a bike or canoe and where you'll find another **NPWS Visitor Centre**. Deeper into the park, on the ocean shore, **Wattamolla** and **Garie beaches** have good surfing waves; the two beaches are connected by a walking track. There are kiosks at Audley, Wattamolla and Garie Beach.

There's a small, very basic but secluded YHA **youth hostel** inside the park, 1km from Garie Beach (bookings essential; Ⓣ02/9261 1111, Ⓔbookings@yhansw.org.au; key must be collected in advance; dorms $14, rooms ❷), with solar lights and cold-water showers. The **bushcamp** at North Era requires a permit from the visitor centre; often full weeks in advance on weekends, you'll need to book and the permit can be posted out to you (which can take up to 5 days), or you can purchase it before leaving Sydney at the NPWS centre at 102 George St, Sydney (see p.115).

Heathcote National Park, across the Princes Highway from the Royal National Park, is much smaller and quieter. This is a serious bushwalkers' park with no roads and a ban on trail bikes. The best **train** station for the park is Waterfall, from where you can follow a twelve-kilometre trail through the park, before catching a train back from Heathcote. On the way you pass through quite a variety of vegetation and alongside several swimmable pools, the carved sandstone of the **Kingfisher Pool** making it the most picturesque, and there is a small, six-site, very basic camping ground beside it (no drinking water), and another one at Mirang Pool. **Camping** permits and maps are available from the Royal National Park NPWS Visitor Centre (see above) or at The Rocks NPWS office in Sydney (see above). By **car**, you can reach the picnic area at Woronora Dam on the western edge of the park: turn east off the Princes Highway onto Woronora Road (free entry).

South down the coast

For a **scenic drive from Sydney** – bush, coast and cliff views and beautiful beaches – follow the Princes Highway south, exiting into the Royal National Park after Loftus onto Farnell Drive; the entry fee at the gate is waived if you are just driving through without stopping. The national park route emerges above the cliffs at **Otford**, beyond which the **Lawrence Hargrave Drive** (Route 68) continues to Thirroul.

A few kilometres from Otford is the impressive clifftop lookout on Bald Hill above **Stanwell Park**, where you're likely to see the breathtaking sight of **hang-gliders** taking off. The Sydney Hang Gliding Centre (Ⓣ0400 258 258, Ⓦwww.hanggliding.com.au) offers tandem flights with an instructor for around $180 during the week, $195 weekends; the centre also runs courses (from $195 per day). At **Clifton**, the *Imperial Hotel* is a must for an en-route drink, as it sits right on the cliff's edge. By the time you get to **AUSTINMER** you're at a break in the stunning cliffs and into some heavy surf territory. The down-to-earth town has a popular, very clean, patrolled surf beach that gets packed out on summer weekends.

There's impressive cliff scenery again as you pass through **Scarborough** (best seen from the historic *Scarborough Hotel*), **Wombarra** and **THIRROUL**. Thirroul is the spot where the English novelist D.H. Lawrence wrote *Kangaroo* during his short Australian interlude; the town and the surrounding area are a substantial part of the novel, though he renamed the then-sleepy village Mullumbimby. Thirroul is now gradually being swallowed up in the suburban sprawl of Wollongong; it's busy, with plenty of shops and cafés, including the excellent and appropriately literary *Oskar's Wild Bookstore & Coffee Bar* at 289 Lawrence Hargrave Drive. At the southern end of the beach, **Sandford Point**, as it's known (it's actually Bulli Point on maps) is a famous surf break. *Ryan's Hotel*, 138 Philip St (Ⓣ02/4267 1086; ⑤), has en-suite **rooms** with two restaurants – a Thai and an Italian – downstairs. Cheaper rooms are available at *The Beaches Hotel*, 272 Lawrence Hargrave Drive (Ⓣ02/4267 2288; ④), where you can barbecue your own steaks in the popular beer garden.

After Thirroul, Lawrence Hargrave Drive joins up with the Princes Highway going south into Wollongong (Route 60) or heading northwest, uphill to a section of the forested **Illawarra Escarpment** and the **Bulli Pass**. There are fantastic views from the Bulli Lookout, which has its own café, and further towards Sydney at the appropriately named **Sublime Point Lookout**. You can explore the escarpment using the **walking tracks** that start from the lookouts, and another extensive part of the **Illawarra Escarpment State Recreation Area**, about 10km west of Wollongong's city centre on Mount Kembla and Mount Keira.

Wollongong

Although it's New South Wales' third-largest city, **WOLLONGONG** has more of a country-town feel; the students of Wollongong University give it extra life in term time and it has a big dose of surf culture as the city centre is set right on the ocean. Eighty kilometres south of Sydney, it's essentially a working-class industrial centre – Australia's largest steelworks at nearby Port Kembla looms unattractively over Wollongong City Beach but the **Illawarra Escarpment** (see above) rises dramatically beyond the city and provides a lush backdrop.

There's not really much to see in the **city centre** itself (concentrated between Wollongong train station and the beach), which has been swallowed up by a giant shopping mall on **Crown Street**, but the regional art centre, the **Wollongong City Gallery**, on the corner of Kembla and Burelli streets (Tues–Fri 10am–5pm, Sat & Sun noon–4pm; free), shows changing exhibitions and has a permanent collection with an emphasis on contemporary Aboriginal and colonial Illawarra artists. If you continue east down Crown Street and cross Marine Drive, you'll hit **Wollongong City Beach**, a surf beach that stretches over 2km. Most locals choose the more salubrious **North Wollongong Beach** (bus #20 from the Crown Gateway bus interchange near City Mall). But in between the two beaches, sheltering beside Flagstaff Point, is the city's highlight, **Wollongong Harbour**, with its fishing fleet in Belmore Basin, a fish market, a few seafood restaurants, and a picturesque nineteenth-century lighthouse on the breakwater; there's also gentle swimming from its beach. At the end of October, the **Viva la Gong festival** spices up the city with a sculpture exhibition along the seafront and events every night including circus, dance, music and the like.

Away from the centre, science and religion provide the most interest. North of the city centre, near the University of Wollongong at the southern end of **Fairy Meadow Beach** and next to Brandon Park, is the $6 million **Science Centre** on Squires Way (daily 10am–4pm; $10; Ⓦsciencecentre.uow.edu.au; train to Fairy Meadow station, then a 10–15min walk); attractions include the state's best **planetarium** (daily shows noon & 3pm; 30min; laser concert Sat, Sun & school holidays 1pm; $2 extra per show; planetarium-only $6) and over a hundred themed kid-friendly hands-on exhibits. South of the centre, the vast **Nan Tien Buddhist Temple**, the largest in Australia, is on Berkeley Road, Berkeley, reached from Sydney by train to Unanderra station and a twenty-minute walk, or by bus from Wollongong train station with Premier (Ⓣ02/4229 4911). The Fo Guang Shan Buddhists welcome visitors to the temple (Tues–Sun 9am–5pm) and offer a good-value $9 vegetarian lunch, weekend meditation and Buddhist activity retreats in peaceful and surprisingly upmarket guesthouse accommodation (Ⓣ02/4272 0500, Ⓦwww.nantien.org.au; ❺).

Practicalities

The best and cheapest way to get to Wollongong from Sydney by public transport is the frequent **train** from Central Station, which hugs the coast and stops at most of the small towns en route; Wollongong station is right in the centre just off Crown Street. Pioneer Motor Service has three to four **bus** services on weekdays and two a day at weekends (see p.184). **Wollongong Tourist Information Centre**, near the mall at 93 Crown St (Mon–Fri 9am–5pm, Sat 9am–4pm, Sun 10am–4pm; Ⓣ02/4227 5545, Ⓦwww.tourismwollongong.com), provides information and can advise on **accommodation**. The central *Boat Harbour Motel*, on the corner of Campbell and Wilson streets (Ⓣ02/4228 9166, Ⓦwww.boatharbour-motel.com.au; ❼), has comfortable and spacious rooms with balconies, some with sea views; more upmarket, and also with water views, is Wollongong's four-and-a-half-star *Novotel Northbeach*, 2–14 Cliff Rd, North Wollongong (Ⓣ02/4226 3555, Ⓦwww.novotelnorthbeach.com; ❽). The colourful and home-like *Keiraleagh House*, 60 Kembla St (Ⓣ02/4228 6765, Ⓔkeiraleagh@backpack.net.au; dorms $20, rooms ❹), in an old converted mansion a few blocks back from the beach, has dorms (up to 6-bed) as well as singles, and doubles (some en suite); rooms are comfy and clean with desks and an armchair. A garden with a barbecue area makes for happy mingling between the students, surfers and travellers who all stay here. The **YHA hostel** at 75–79 Keira St, near the intersection with Smith Street (Ⓣ02/4229 1132; dorms $28.50, rooms ❻), is modern and lively with a central alfresco courtyard. The rather expensive rooms have the luxury of en-suite facilities and shared balconies. There's nowhere central to **camp**, but the two caravan parks to the north are right on the beach: *Corrimal Beach Tourist Park* is on Lake Parade in Corrimal, 6km north at the mouth of Towradgi Lagoon (Ⓣ02/4285 5688; en-suite cabins ❺); while *Bulli Beach Tourist Park* is 11km north of town on Farrell Road, Bulli (Ⓣ02/4285 5677; bungalows ❹, en-suite cabins ❺–❼).

Wollongong isn't renowned for its **food**, which can be a bit hit or miss. There's a concentration of cafés on Crown Street near the tourist office – *Flame Tree Music Café* at no. 89 is worth checking out. On Keira Street, well-regarded *Lorenzo's Diner* at no. 119 (Ⓣ02/4229 5633; lunch Thurs & Fri, dinner Tues–Sat; license) serves top-notch contemporary Italian food at surprisingly moderate prices, while *Monsoon* at no. 193 (Ⓣ02/4229 4588; lunch & dinner Tues–Sat) is a hip Vietnamese restaurant with an Australian slant. The front of the beachside Entertainment Centre is the setting for the *Five Islands Brewing Company*, where you can try at least ten delicious and varied ales with an imaginative bar menu.

Kiama and around

Of the coastal resorts south of Sydney, **KIAMA** is probably the most attractive – though if you want more than a day- or overnight trip to the beach, you'd be better off continuing down to Nowra and beyond. A large resort and fishing town, Kiama is famous for its star attraction, the **Blowhole**, a five-minute walk from the **railway station** on Blowhole Point. Stemming from a natural fault in the cliffs, the Blowhole explodes into a waterspout when a wave hits with sufficient force. It's impressive, but also potentially dangerous: freak waves can be thrown over 60m into the air and have swept several over-curious bystanders into the raging sea – so stand well back. The **Kiama Visitor Information Centre**, nearby on Blowhole Point Road (daily 9am–5pm; Ⓣ02/4232 3322, Ⓦwww.kiama.com.au), supplies details of other local attractions such as **Cathedral Rocks**, a few kilometres to the north, whose rocky outcrops drop abruptly to the ocean.

There's an abundance of B&Bs and motels along the Princes Highway; the tourist office (see above) has a comprehensive list and can book **accommodation** for free. Budget alternatives in Kiama include *Kiama Backpackers*, 31 Bong Bong St, very close to the train station and right near the beach (Ⓣ02/4233 1881; dorms $20, rooms ❸), though it sometimes closes down in winter; and the *Grand Hotel*, on the corner of Manning and Bong Bong streets (Ⓣ02/4232 1037; ❹), which has budget-priced, old-fashioned share-bathroom pub accommodation – the pub restaurant serves decent filling meals for lunch and dinner daily. The closest **campsite** to the centre is at *Blowhole Point Holiday Park* right near the Blowhole (Ⓣ02/4232 2707 or 1800 823 824, Ⓦwww.kiama.net/holiday/blowhole; en-suite cabins ❽). There are plenty of **places to eat** in Kiama – Thai, Chinese, Italian restaurants and lots of cafés – with a concentration on Manning and Terralong streets.

Gerringong, 10km south of Kiama, is wonderfully scenic, set against green hills with glorious sweeping views of **Seven Mile Beach**. You can camp beside the beach at *Seven Mile Beach Holiday Park* (Ⓣ02/4234 1340, Ⓦwww.kiama.net/holiday/sevenmile; bunkhouses ❹, safari tents ❺, en-suite cabins ❻), located beside Crooked River and within walking distance of Gerringong and its cafés.

West of Kiama, a steep road leads to **Mount Saddleback Lookout**, from where on a clear day you can get an incredible view of the entire coast – from the Royal National Park in the north to Jervis Bay in the south. Beyond the lookout, you can head north to join the Illawarra Highway, and follow that inland to **Macquarie Pass**, the gateway to the Southern Highlands. The **Macquarie Pass National Park** is one of the southernmost stands of Australia's subtropical rainforest; the **Minnamurra Rainforest Centre** on Jamberoo Mountain Pass Road (park daily 9am–5pm, centre and *Lyrebird Café* 9am–4pm; boardwalk closes 4pm, track closes 3pm; Ⓣ02/4236 0469; car entry $11), has a wheelchair-accessible elevated loop **boardwalk** from the centre (1.6km return; 30min–1hr) through subtropical and temperate rainforest – you'll see cabbage tree palms, staghorn ferns and impressive Illawarra fig trees – and a viewing platform to **Minnamurra Falls**. The impressive **Carrington Falls**, also within the park, are 8km east of Robertson by road, and are worth a detour: a turn-off from the Jamberoo Mountain Pass Road leads to lookout points over the waterfalls. Free **bushcamping** is possible in Macquarie Pass National Park.

Inland: the road to Canberra

If you want to take your time travelling from Sydney to Canberra, there are a number of convenient diversions off the speedy South Western Motorway (M5). About 40km south of Parramatta, the Camden Valley Way heads west from the motorway to **CAMDEN** on the Nepean River, where John Macarthur pioneered the breeding of merino sheep in 1805. The town still has a rural feel and several well-preserved nineteenth-century buildings, the oldest of which dates from 1816. En route, you'll pass **Mount Annan Botanical Garden** (daily: April–Sept 10am–4pm; Oct–March 10am–6pm; $4.40; Ⓦwww.rbgsyd.nsw.gov.au). Actually the native-plant section of the Royal Botanic Gardens in Sydney, this outstanding collection of flora is the largest of its kind in Australia. Within the grounds, you can eat well at the idyllically sited *Gardens Restaurant* at outside tables surrounded by trees. A major attraction, it makes sense to book if you intend to dine (Ⓣ02/4647 1363); there's also a kiosk in the park.

From Camden, Remembrance Drive passes through **Picton** and on to the **Wirrimbirra Sanctuary** at **Bargo** (Tues–Sun 9.30am–4.30pm; free; Ⓣ02/4684 1112, Ⓦwww.wirrimbirra.com.au), a peaceful bushland spot owned by the National Trust, with a field studies centre, a native-plant nursery, bushwalking trails and a visitor information centre (Tues–Sun 9am–4.30pm). You can stay over in the bunk-style cabins ($15 per person) or camp with the opportunity of spotting wallabies, kangaroos, wombats, brush-tailed possums and goannas, along with 150 different species of birds in the wild. Without your own **transport**, you can get here by train from Sydney to Bargo and then walk a couple of kilometres.

The Southern Highlands

From Bargo, you can detour onto the Old Hume Highway, through the picturesque **Southern Highlands**, a favourite weekend retreat for Sydneysiders since the 1920s; the pretty Highlands towns are full of cafés, restaurants, antique shops and secondhand bookstores and there's an emerging wine industry. The cooler-climate wines produced here are building a good reputation, and visiting the wineries – an excellent alternative to the better known Hunter Valley – is a great way to enjoy the beautiful countryside of the area; the information centre at Mittagong can provide a map of all the local cellar doors. The Southern Highlands is well served by **transport**, with a frequent train service between Sydney and Canberra stopping at Picton, Mittagong, Bowral, Moss Vale, Bundanoon and Goulburn. Berrima Coaches provides a local bus service (Ⓣ02/4871 3211).

Marking the beginning of the Highlands is **MITTAGONG**, a small agricultural and tourist town 110km south of Sydney, mostly visited on the way to the limestone, NPWS-run **Wombeyan Caves** (daily 9am–5pm; guided and self-guided tours: one-cave guided tour $16; two-cave Explorer Pass $28; 1hr 30min for each cave) in the nearby hills. The route to the five caves begins 4km south of the town off the highway and winds upwards for 65km on a partly unsealed road. The associated **campsite** near the caves (ⓣ02/4843 5976, ⓦwww .national parks.nsw.gov. au; cabins ❹, cottages ❻) is well run.

Neighbouring **BOWRAL**, 6km southwest, is a busy, well-to-do town; its main strip, Bong Bong Street, is full of upmarket clothes and homeware shops and it has a good bookstore and a cinema. It was also the birthplace of cricket legend Don Bradman and cricket fans should check out the **Bradman Museum** (daily 10am–5pm; $8.50), on Jude Street, in an idyllic spot between a leafy park and the well-used cricket oval and club.

The picturesque village of **BERRIMA** is 7km on from Bowral and boasts a complement of well-preserved and restored old buildings, including the *Surveyor General Inn*, which has been serving beer since 1835; you can stay in one of its four modest Victorian rooms with shared bathrooms (ⓣ02/4877 1226; ❹). Otherwise, visit the 1838 sandstone **courthouse**, on the corner of Argyle and Wiltshire streets (daily 10am–4pm; $6), adjacent to the **Berrima Visitor Centre** (same hours; ⓣ02/4877 1505). Across the road, the still-operational **Berrima Gaol** once held the infamous bushranger Thunderbolt – and also has the dubious distinction of being the first place in Australia where a woman was executed.

Five kilometres south of **Moss Vale** on the Old Hume Highway is the turn-off to **BUNDANOON**, famous for its April celebration of its Scottish heritage with the annual Highland Games – Aussie-style. Bundanoon is in an attractive spot set in hilly countryside scarred by deep gullies and with splendid views over the gorges and mountains of the huge **Morton National Park** (car fee $7), which extends east from Bundanoon to near Kangaroo Valley (see below). The park, and Bundanoon, have traditionally been a **cycling** Mecca, with the long-established Ye Olde Bicycle Shop renting out mountain bikes (Mon–Fri 9am–4.30pm, Sat & Sun 9am–5pm; $18.50 per hour, $28 half-day, $45 full day; ⓣ02/4883 6043). A recommended evening activity – set off at sunset, armed with a torch – is a visit to **Glow Worm Glen**; after dark, the small sandstone grotto is transformed by the naturally flickering lights of these tiny creatures. It's a 25-minute walk from town via the end of William Street, or an easy forty-minute signposted trek from Riverview Road in the park. The Bundanoon **YHA hostel**, on Railway Avenue (ⓣ02/4883 6010; dorms $24.50, rooms ❹), is a spacious Edwardian-era guesthouse complete with open fireplaces and an outdoor spa (extra charge), and set on extensive grounds where you can also camp. A good-value **motel** with great facilities is the central *Bundanoon Country Inn* on Anzac Parade (ⓣ02/4883 6068; ❺). For more style, the elegant, antique-furnished *Tree Tops Country Guesthouse*, 101 Railway Ave (ⓣ02/4883 6372, ⓦwww.treetopsguesthouse.com.au; ❽ includes breakfast), dates from 1910. Recommended **places to eat** are the *Bloomin' Café*, on Railway Avenue, which doubles as a modern Australian restaurant on Saturday nights (dinner bookings Fri & Sat only ⓣ02/4883 6354; otherwise, daily 9am–5pm) or pub grub at the *Bundanoon Hotel* on Erith Street (ⓣ02/4883 6005; closed Mon & Tues).

At the northeast edge of Morton National Park, 17km from Kangaroo Valley, **Fitzroy Falls** is a must-see. A short boardwalk from the car park takes you to the waterfall plunging 80m into the valley below, with glorious views of the Yarrunga Valley beyond. **The NPWS Visitor Centre** (daily 9am–5.30pm; entry fee $3) has a buffet-style café with a very pleasant outside deck. Detailed information about walking tracks and scenic drives in the surrounding area is available, and the office issues **camping** permits for the nearby bushcamp at Yarrunga Creek and the *Gambells Rest* camping ground (bookings essential ⓣ02/4887 7270) near Bundanoon, which has flush toilets and hot showers but no drinking water.

Kangaroo Valley

Between Moss Vale and Nowra on the coast, **Kangaroo Valley** is a popular spot for weekenders from Sydney – a lovely, hidden valley situated between the lush dairy country of Nowra and the Southern Highlands. Continuing along the highway, a kilometre before entering the village, the picturesque old sandstone Hampden Suspension Bridge crosses the Kangaroo River. Kangaroo Valley Safaris are based here for canoe hire; they also operate self-guided overnight canoe safaris along the Kangaroo River and Shoalhaven Gorge with a pick-up service at the end of your journey (ⓣ02/4465 1502, ⓦwww.kangaroovalleycanoes.com.au). You can stock up on supplies at the nearby service station. In **KANGAROO VALLEY** village itself, Moss Vale Road has several craft, antique and gift shops but is dominated by the characterful old pub, the *Friendly Inn Hotel* at no. 159, which is overflowing on weekends. The area is prime **B&B** territory and *Tall Trees Bed and Breakfast*, 8 Nugents Creek Rd, 1km east from the Kangaroo Valley village (ⓣ02/4465 1208, ⓦwww.talltreesbandb.com.au; ❼–❽), has log fires and great views across the valley from its patio; the self-contained studio has a spa, wood fire and kitchen. Leaving the village, the narrow and winding road climbs 700m up Cambewarra Mountain and then descends to the coast with superb panoramas all the way.

You can **get to Kangaroo Valley** daily except Saturday from Campbelltown train station on the outskirts of Sydney on Priors Scenic Express (ⓣ02/4472 4040 or 1800 816 234); a half-hour stop is scheduled at Fitzroy Falls (see opposite).

Travel details

Sydney is very much the centre of the Australian transport network, and you can get to virtually anywhere in the country from here on a variety of competing services. The following list represents a minimum; as well as the dedicated services listed below, many places will also be served by long-distance services stopping en route.

Trains

Sydney to: Adelaide (Indian Pacific; Sat & Wed 2.55pm; 24hr 10min); Brisbane (2 daily; 14hr 10min); Broken Hill (1 daily; 15hr); Canberra (2 daily; 4hr 15min); Dubbo (2 daily; 6hr 30min); Goulburn (4 daily; 2hr 45min); Katoomba (29 daily; 2hr 10min); Maitland (6 daily; 2hr 45min); Melbourne (2 daily; 11hr; plus daily bus/train Speedlink via Albury; 12–13hr); Murwillumbah (3 daily; 13hr 45min); Newcastle (28 daily; 2hr 45min); Perth (Indian Pacific; Sat & Wed 2.55pm; 67hr 45min); Richmond (14 daily; 2hr); Windsor (14 daily; 1hr 45min); Wollongong (32 daily; 1hr 30min).

Buses

Sydney to: Adelaide (3 daily; 22hr); Albury (4 daily; 8hr 30min); Armidale (2 daily; 8hr 30min); Batemans Bay (2 daily; 5hr 20min); Bathurst (1 daily; 3hr 15min); Bega (2 daily; 8hr); Brisbane (9 daily; 15–17hr, with connections to Cairns and Darwin); Broken Hill (1 daily; 15hr 40min); Byron Bay (7 daily; 13hr 15min); Canberra (11–14 daily; 4hr); Cessnock (1 daily; 2hr 30min); Coffs Harbour (7 daily; 9hr); Eden (2 daily; 8hr 30min–9hr 30min); Forster (1 daily; 6hr); Glen Innes (2 daily; 10hr); Grafton (3 daily; 10hr); Melbourne (6 daily; 12–18hr); Mildura (3 daily; 16hr); Mittagong (4 daily; 2hr 20min); Moss Vale (1 daily; 2hr 45min); Muswellbrook (1 daily; 3hr 30min); Narooma (2 daily; 8hr); Newcastle (8 daily; 3hr); Nowra (2 daily; 3hr–4hr 20min); Orange (1 daily; 4hr 15min); Perth (2–3 daily; 52–56hr); Port Macquarie (6 daily; 7hr); Port Stephens (1 daily; 3hr); Scone (1 daily; 6hr); Tamworth (1 daily; 7hr); Taree (2 daily; 6hr 30min); Tenterfield (1 daily; 12hr).

Flights

Sydney to: Adelaide (16 daily; 2hr 10min); Albury (8 daily; 1hr 20min); Alice Springs (1 daily; 3hr 15min); Armidale (4 daily; 1hr 10min); Ballina (4–7 daily; 1hr 40min); Bathurst (3 daily Mon–Fri;

40min); Bourke (1 daily except Sat; 3hr 10min); Brisbane (42 daily; 1hr 30min); Broken Hill (1 daily; 1hr 50min); Cairns (8 daily; 3hr 10min); Canberra (20–25 daily; 45min); Cobar (2 daily except Sat; 2hr 25min); Coffs Harbour (7 daily; 1hr 15min); Cooma (1–2 daily; 1hr); Darwin (1 daily; 4hr 25min); Dubbo (5–7 daily Mon–Fri; 1hr); Fraser Coast (1–2 daily; 1hr 40min); Gold Coast (17 daily; 1hr 20min); Grafton (1 daily; 2hr); Griffith (3–4 daily; 1hr 25min); Hamilton Island (2 daily; 2hr 25min); Hobart (8 daily; 1hr 50min); Inverell (1–2 daily; 1hr 55min); Launceston (2 daily; 1hr 40min); Lismore (3–4 daily; 1hr 35min); Lord Howe Island (1 daily; 1hr 50min); Melbourne (58 daily; 1hr 20min); Merimbula (3 daily; 1hr 35min); Mildura (1 daily; 2hr 40min); Moruya (2 daily; 50min); Mudgee (2 daily Mon–Fri, 1 daily Sat & Sun; 1hr); Narrandera (2 daily; 1hr 30min); Newcastle (1 daily except Sun; 40min); Norfolk Island (4 weekly; 2hr 20min); Orange (3–4 daily; 45min); Parkes (2–3 daily; 1hr); Perth (8 daily; 4hr 50min); Port Macquarie (6 daily; 1hr); Port Stephens (Mon–Fri 1 daily; 1hr); Prosperine (1 daily; 2hr 30min); Rockhampton (1 daily; 2hr); Sunshine Coast (4 daily; 1hr 30min); Tamworth (4 daily; 1hr); Taree (2–3 daily; 50min); Townsville (1 daily; 2hr 40min); Uluru (2 daily; 3hr 30min); Wagga Wagga (3–6 daily; 1hr 10min).

2

Coastal New South Wales and the ACT

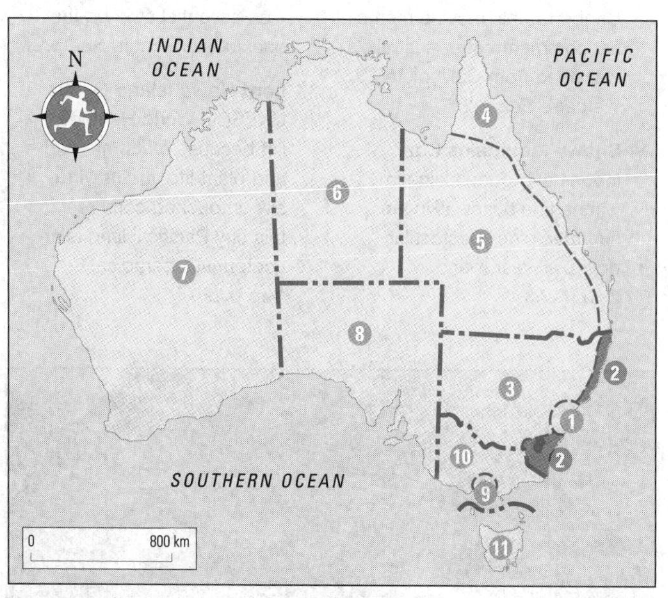

CHAPTER 2 Highlights

* **New Parliament House, Canberra** The stunning angular design of the New Parliament House is matched by its interior, which shows contemporary Australian design at its best. See p.235

* **Australian War Memorial** Located near the heart of Canberra, this moving memorial commemorates Australia's war dead from Gallipoli to Vietnam. See p.237

* **Snowy Mountains** Cozy lodges and good skiing in winter, fine bushwalking in summer, plus spectacular drives all year round. See p.253

* **Bellingen** Arty little town in the beautiful Bellinger Valley where everyone has a smile on their face – take a lazy canoe trip, drink great coffee at the enticing cafés and soak up the good vibes. See p.267

* **Byron Bay** New-Age Mecca with 30km of sandy beaches – an essential stop on the backpacker circuit. See p.277

* **Lord Howe Island** On the UNESCO World Heritage list because of its rare bird and plant life and its virtually untouched coral reef, this tiny Pacific island is an ecotourist's paradise. See p.290

△ Lord Howe Island

2

Coastal New South Wales and the ACT

New South Wales is Australia's premier state in more ways than one. The oldest of the five states, and also the most densely populated, its 6.7 million residents make up a third of the country's population. The vast majority occupy the urban and suburban sprawl which straggles along the state's thousand-plus kilometres of **Pacific coastline**, and the consistently mild climate and many beaches draw a fairly constant stream of visitors, especially during the summer holiday season, when thousands of Australians descend on the coast to enjoy the extensive surf beaches and other oceanside attractions.

South of Sydney, there's a string of low-key family resorts and fishing ports, good for watersports and idle pottering. To the **north** the climate gradually becomes warmer, and the coastline more popular – the series of big resorts up here includes **Port Macquarie** and **Coffs Harbour** – but there are plenty of tiny national parks and inland towns where you can escape it all. One of the

National parks in New South Wales

The **National Parks and Wildlife Service** (NPWS) charges **entrance fees** at many of its parks – usually $6–15 per car and $4 for motorcycles (often on an honour system). If you intend to "go bush" a lot in New South Wales you can buy an **annual pass** for $65, which includes all parks except Kosciuszko. Because of its popularity as a skiing destination, entrance to Kosciuszko is a steep $27 per car per day in winter and $16 per car per day in summer – if you plan on spending any length of time here, or are going to visit other parks as well, consider the $190 annual pass which covers entry to all parks, including Kosciuszko. Passes can be bought at NPWS offices and some park entry-stations, over the phone using a credit card (Ⓣ02/9585 6068 or 1300 361 967) or online (Ⓦwww.npws.nsw.gov.au).

You can **camp** in most national parks. Bushcamping is generally free, but where there is a ranger station and a designated campsite with facilities, fees are charged, usually around $6 per site. If the amenities are of a high standard, including hot showers and the like, or if the spot is just plain popular, fees can be as high as $25 per tent. There are often electric or gas barbecues on campsites, but you'll need a fuel stove for hard-core bushcamping. Open **fires** are banned in most parks and forbidden everywhere on days when there is high danger of fire – it's worth checking the NPWS for details of any current bushfires and park closures before you visit.

COASTAL NEW SOUTH WALES
QUEENSLAND
VICTORIA
SOUTH PACIFIC OCEAN
Coolangatta
Tweed Heads
Murwillumbah
Woodenbong
Nimbin
Byron Bay
Kyogle
Lismore
Lennox Head
Casino
Ballina
Bald Rock
Evans Head
Goondiwindi
Dumaresq
Mungindi
Tenterfield
Clarence
Pacific Hwy
Yamba
Moree
Warialda
Emmaville
Gwydir Hwy
Grafton
Glen Innes
Inverell
Bingara
Tingha
Ben Lomond
Newell Hwy
New England Hwy
Wee Waa
Walgett
Woolgoolga
Guyra
NEW ENGLAND NP
Dorrigo
Coffs Harbour
Narrabri
Namoi
NEW ENGLAND PLATEAU
Bellingen
Mylestom
Armidale
Uralla
Bowraville
Nambucca Heads
Manilla
Maclean
Walcha
Oxley Hwy
WARRUMBUNGLES
Gunnedah
Tamworth
Kempsey
Crescent Head
Coonabarabran
Nundle
Port Macquarie
Wauchope
Quirindi
Crowdy Head
Gilgandra
Coolah
BARRINGTON TOPS NP
Murrurundi
Wingham
Taree
Gloucester
Scone
Forster-Tuncurry
Merriwa
Wallis Lake
Muswellbrook
Dubbo
Gulgong
Bulahdelah
Seal Rocks
Myall Lake
Hunter
Singleton
Mudgee
Port Stephens
Maitland
Cessnock
Nelson Bay
Newcastle
Parkes
Orange
Bathurst
Lithgow
Forbes
Katoomba
Cowra
Sydney
Camden
Picton
Bargo
Young
Crookwell
Wollongong
Bowral
Boorowa
Moss Vale
Robertson
Bundanoon
Kiama
Cootamundra
Hume Hwy
Goulburn
Berry
Olympic Way
Murrumbidgee
Yass
MORTON NP
Nowra-Bomaderry
Barton Hwy
Jervis Bay
Gundagai
BOODEREE NP
Queanbeyan
Tumut
Snowy Mts Hwy
CANBERRA
Ulladulla
Braidwood
Princes Hwy
Tharwa
ACT
NAMADGI NP
Batemans Bay
Tumbarumba
DEUA NP
KOSCIUSZKO NP
Murray
Narooma
Cooma
WADBILLIGA NP
Tilba Tilba
Thredbo
Bermagui
Jindabyne
Monaro Hwy
Mt Kosciuszko (2228m)
Bega
Tathra
Candelo
Merimbula
Bombala
Eden
Snowy
BEN BOYD NP
N
0 100 km
Lord Howe Island (700km from Sydney) & Norfolk Island (1600km from Sydney)
0 3 km
Lord Howe Island
0 3 km
Norfolk Island

most enjoyable beach resorts in Australia is **Byron Bay**, which is just about managing to retain its slightly offbeat, alternative appeal, radiating from the still-thriving hippie communes of the lush, hilly **North Coast Hinterland**.

Just over 280km southwest of Sydney is the **Australian Capital Territory (ACT)**, which was carved out of New South Wales at the beginning of the twentieth century as an independent base for the new national capital, **Canberra**, a city struggling to shed its dull image. Canberra is also the gateway to the **Snowy Mountains**, where the Great Dividing Range builds to a crescendo at **Mount Kosciuszko** (Australia's highest at 2228m), marking the peak of the Australian Alps, which offer skiing in winter and glorious hiking in summer.

Also included in this chapter are the Pacific islands far off the north coast of New South Wales: subtropical **Lord Howe Island**, 700km northeast of Sydney, and **Norfolk Island**, 900km further northeast and actually closer to New Zealand, inhabited by the descendants of the *Bounty* mutineers.

Australian Capital Territory

The first European squatters settled in the valleys and plains north of the Snowy Mountains in the 1820s, though until 1900 this remained a remote rural area. When the Australian colonies united in the **Commonwealth of Australia** in 1901, a capital city had to be chosen, with Melbourne and Sydney the two obvious and eager rivals. After much wrangling, and partly in order to avoid having to decide on one of the two, it was agreed to establish a brand-new capital instead. In 1909, Limestone Plains, south of Yass, was chosen out of several possible sites as the future seat of the Australian government. An area of 2368 square kilometres was excised from the state of New South Wales and named the **Australian Capital Territory**, or **ACT**. The name for the future capital was supposedly taken from the language of local Aborigines: **Canberra** – the meeting place.

Canberra is situated on a high plain (600m above sea level). There's a predominatly dry, sunny climate, and daytime **temperatures** can reach 40°C in summer, though they're usually in the high twenties; in winter they drop to anything from 12°C to down below freezing. Spring and especially autumn – when the trees are dressed in exquisite reds and golds – can be really delightful, though. The mountain ranges to the west and south of the city rise to 1900m and are snow-covered in winter.

Canberra

In 1912 **Walter Burley Griffin**, an American landscape architect from Chicago, won the international competition for the design of the future Australian capital, **CANBERRA**. His plan envisaged a garden city for about 25,000 people based in five main centres, each with separate city functions, located on three axes: land, water and municipal. Roads were to be in concentric circles, with arcs linking the radiating design. Construction started in 1913, but political squabbling and the effects of World War I, the Depression and World War II prevented any real progress being made until 1958, when growth began in earnest. In 1963 the Molonglo River was dammed to form long, artificial **Lake Burley Griffin**; the city centre, **Civic**, coalesced along the north shore to face **parliamentary buildings** to the south; while a host of outlying **satellite suburbs**, each connected to Civic by a main road cutting through the intervening bushland, took shape. The population grew rapidly, from fifteen thousand in 1947 to over three hundred thousand today, completely outstripping Burley Griffin's original estimates – though Canberra's decentralised design means that the city never feels crowded.

Being such an overtly planned place populated by civil servants and politicians, Canberra is in many ways a city in search of a soul: while there are all the

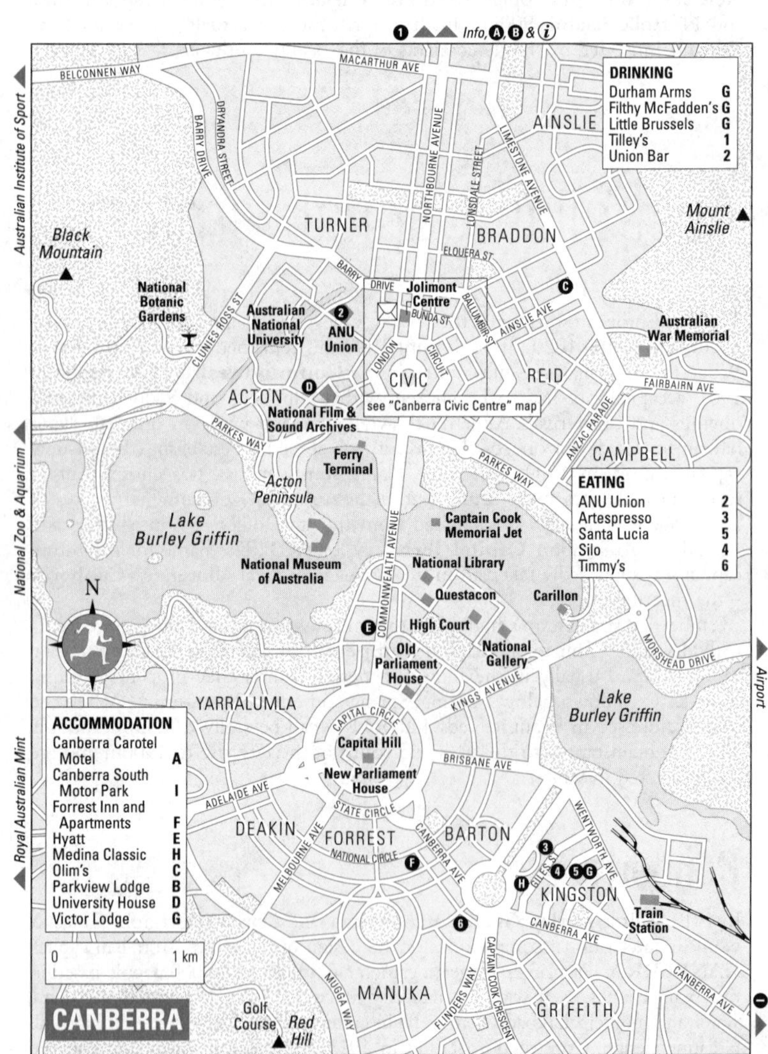

galleries, museums and attractions that there should be, many seem to exist simply because it would be ridiculous to have omitted them from a national capital. A few key sights are genuinely worth an overnight stay, however, namely the **War Memorial**; the extraordinary, partly subterranean **Parliament House**; and the **National Botanic Gardens**. The city's other main draw – that of being surrounded by the unspoilt wilderness of the **Brindabella Ranges** and the **Namadgi National Park** – took a severe battering in 2003, when seventy percent of rural ACT was destroyed in a terrible **bushfire**, which also gutted over five hundred homes. The forests were so badly burnt that they will take decades to recover, and are barely worth the effort to see at the present.

Canberra's **nightlife** – in term time at least – is alive and kicking. The two universities here (and the Duntroon Military Academy) mean there's a large and lively **student population** (good news for those who have student cards, as most attractions offer hefty discounts), and the city is also said to have more **restaurants** per capita than any other in Australia, which is saying something. Canberra also holds the dubious title of Australia's **porn capital**, due to its liberal licensing laws, which legalize and regulate the sex industry.

Arrival and information

Canberra's **airport**, 7km east of the city, handles domestic flights only. The Airliner Shuttle bus ($7 single, $12 return) runs from the airport to Civic every thirty minutes from about 6.30am to 7pm Monday to Friday, and 10.30am to 6pm Saturday to Sunday. The **train station** is located southeast of the centre, on Wentworth Avenue in Kingston; buses #35, #39 or #769 can get you to Civic, or Kingston accommodation is a short walk (or taxi ride) away. The **long-distance bus terminal** is in Civic at the **Jolimont Centre**, 65–67 Northbourne Ave; the centre has showers, lockers ($5), Internet kiosk, some **tourist information** and **ticket booking desks** for tours, trains and buses. There is a free direct telephone line to the tourist office (see below), to taxi companies and to accommodation.

The main tourist office, **Canberra Visitor Information Centre**, is inconveniently located 3km north of the centre at 330 Northbourne Ave (Mon–Fri 9am–5pm, Sat & Sun 9am–4pm; ⓣ02/6205 0044, ⓦwww.visitcanberra.com.au) – it's on the #51, #53 and #55 bus routes, amongst others. They also have a desk at the airport (ⓣ02/6205 0666), open Monday to Friday 8.30am to 5.30pm.

City transport

With Canberra's sights so spread out, you'd have to be very enthusiastic to consider walking everywhere. A good option is to rent a **bike** and take advantage of the city's excellent network of cycle paths (see "Listings" on p.240); when you get tired, city buses have special bike-racks on the front. If you're driving yourself, make sure you carry a good-quality **map** – Canberra's baffling concentric street plan can turn navigating the city's roads into a Kafka-esque nightmare.

City buses run by Action (timetables and information ⓣ13 17 10, ⓦwww.action.act.gov.au) operate daily from around 6.30am to 8pm or later, though weekend services are greatly reduced. Almost all services pass through the **City Bus Interchange** in Civic, a set of open-air bays around the eastern end of Alinga Street. **Tickets** are available from drivers, and cost $3 for a single journey, $4.40 for an off-peak pass (valid 9am–4.30pm and after 6pm) and $6.60 for an all-day pass. These two passes, plus bulk tickets (ten rides for $22) and weekly passes are also available from most newsagents. A more expensive option is the hop-on-hop-off **Explorer Bus** (ⓣ0418 455099, ⓦwww.canberradaytours.com.au; $50), which circuits the major sights around four times a day, with a pick-up from central accommodation.

For a different view of the place, **ballooning** is massively popular in Canberra, and you can make a dawn ascent above the city with either Dawn Drifters (ⓣ02/6285 4450, ⓦwww.dawndrifters.com.au) or Balloon Aloft (ⓣ02/6285 1540, ⓦwww.canberraballoon.com.au) – an hour-long flight and champagne breakfast costs from $235 per person.

Accommodation

Most of Canberra's **accommodation** is located either in Civic or south of the lake at Kingston, both on bus routes and within striking distance of sights and places to eat. **Rates** fall at weekends, when the city empties, but hotel rooms can become scarce during big **conferences**, which can happen at any time through the year. If you have trouble finding parking space in Civic, there's **24-hour parking** inside the Canberra Centre, accessed off Ballumbir Street.

Hotels, motels and guesthouses

Forrest Inn and Apartments 30 National Circuit, Forrest ⓣ02/6295 3433, ⓦwww.forrestinn.com.au. Next to the pretty Serbian church, this modern, clean and clinical motel is lacking in atmosphere, but professionally run. Bus #39. ❻

Hyatt Commonwealth Avenue, Yarralumla ⓣ02/6270 1234, ⓦwww.canberra.park.hyatt.com. Easily the most stylish (and most expensive) hotel in Canberra, set amongst lawn and gardens in a complex of low-set 1930s buildings. ❽

Medina Classic 11 Giles St, Kingston ⓣ02/6239 8100, ⓦwww.medina.com.au. Tasteful, upmarket one-, two- and three-bedroom, self-catering serviced apartments with fully equipped kitchens (except for a couple of smaller apartments). Facilities include laundry, swimming pool, spa, gym and undercover parking; bike rental available. Popular with families, and staff are friendly. Bus #39. ❻

Olim's cnr Ainslie and Limestone avenues, Braddon ⓣ02/6248 5511, ⓦwww.olimshotel.com. Close to the War Memorial, this is Canberra's least expensive "real" hotel, with a range of cheaper rooms in the older, National Trust–listed main building, and modern, self-contained apartments in a newer wing. Definitely needs to be booked ahead. Bus #33 or #40. Rooms ❺

Parkview Lodge 526 Northbourne Ave, Downer, 4km north ⓣ02/6249 8038, ⓦwww.mirandalodge.com.au. Good, nonsmoking B&B with off-street parking and en-suite rooms with TV and fridge (some also have spas). Bus #51, #53 or #56. ❺

Quest Canberra 28 West Row, Civic ⓣ02/6243 2222, ⓦwww.questapartments.com.au. Smart, self-contained apartments in the city centre, though kitchens in the cheaper Studio rooms are fairly basic. ❻

University House 1 Balmain Crescent, Acton ⓣ02/6125 5276, ⓦwww.anu.edu.au/unihouse. Excellent-value hotel run by the Australian National University on the edge of their huge, semi-rural campus, just a short way from the National Film Archive. Very popular with conference delegates and visiting lecturers – once again, book ahead. Bus #34. ❺

Hostels

Canberra City YHA 7 Akuna St, Civic ⓣ02/6257 3999, ⓦwww.yha.com.au. This cavernous, organized, centrally located hostel has a gym, bar, rooftop BBQ garden, laundry, Internet café, sauna, bike rental, cable TV, lockers in every room and 24hr check-in. Dorms $25, rooms ❸

City Walk Hotel 2 Mort St, Civic ⓣ02/6257 0124, ⓕ6257 0116. Not far from the bus station, this spic-and-span place has a very central location and a lively Irish bar downstairs (guests often get discounted beer). Facilities include a kitchen, Internet access and a common room with TV. Dorms $28, rooms ❹

Victor Lodge 29 Dawes St, Kingston, 4km southwest ⓣ02/6295 7777, ⓦwww.victorlodge.com.au. Small, friendly and very popular family-run hostel-cum-guesthouse, situated close to lots of good restaurants. The dorms are clean and bright, but the rooms are overpriced. Facilities include a well-equipped kitchen and BBQ area, laundry, TV room, Internet access and very reasonable bike rental, plus free city pick-ups and drop-offs. Bus #39, #80 or #84. Dorms $25, rooms ❹

Camping and caravan parks

Canberra Carotel Motel and Caravan Park Federal Highway, Watson, 7km north ⓣ02/6241 1377, ⓦwww.carotel.com.au. Caravan park with a swimming pool and café, plus camping space. Bus #36. Cabins ❸–❹

Canberra South Motor Park Canberra Ave, Symonstone, 4km southeast ⓣ02/6280 6176, ⓦwww.csmp.net.au. Well-equipped park on a little creek with air-con options and en-suite cabins. ❹

The City

North of Lake Burley Griffin, Civic's shops, restaurants, cafés and pubs sit immediately west of the **Australian National University (ANU)**, whose grounds house the National Film and Sound Archive. This in turn borders on to the lakeside **National Museum of Australia**, the **National Botanic Gardens** and the flanks of 806-metre-high **Black Mountain**, topped by the distinctive Telstra Tower. East of Civic is one of Canberra's key sights, the **Australian War Memorial**.

South of the lake, the main landmark is **Parliament House**, dug into the top of Capital Hill. This looks lakewards over the **old Parliament House**, and a clutch of cultural institutions, housed in interesting buildings: the **National**

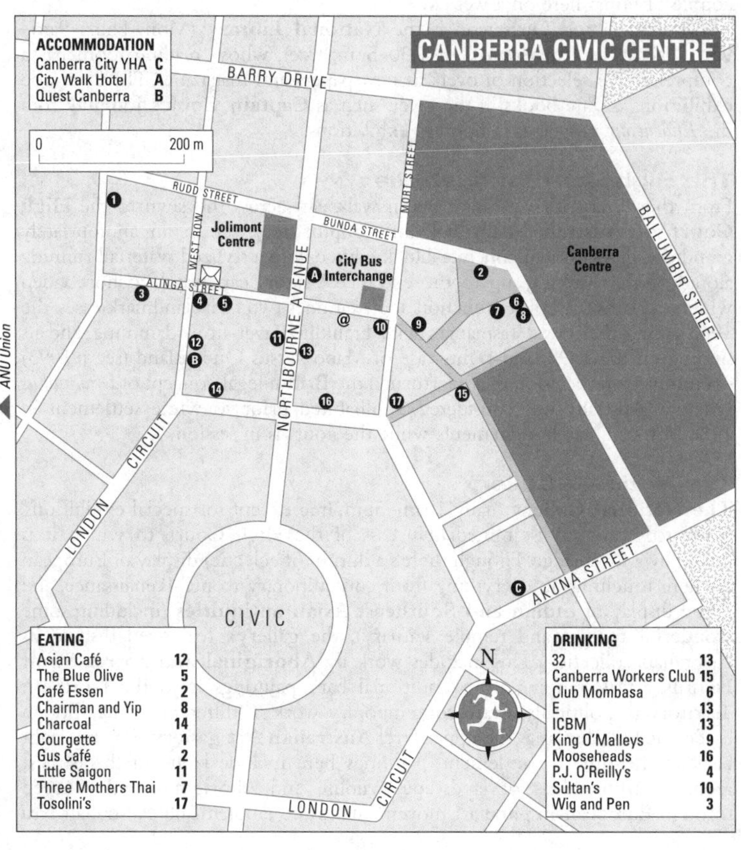

Library, **Questacon** (the National Science and Technology Centre), the **National Gallery** and the **High Court**. Most of the city's foreign **embassies** – intended to resemble the vernacular architecture of their home countries – cluster around Yarralumla and Forrest, on the far side of Capital Hill.

Many of the city's sights are within striking distance of **bus #34**, which runs Monday to Friday roughly every thirty minutes from 6.30am until 6.30pm, and then hourly until 10.30pm, with an hourly service at the weekends between 8am and 6pm. The only major attraction off its route is the War Memorial; catch bus #33 or #40 instead.

Questacon and the National Library

Crossing the lake south from Civic over Commonwealth Avenue Bridge, you turn left onto King Edward Terrace. The odd-shaped building before you with a truncated tower is **Questacon** (daily 9am–5pm; $15.50, children $9; Ⓦwww.questacon.edu.au), the hands-on National Science and Technology Centre. This is great fun, especially for children, with heaps of interactive exhibits explaining sound, light, geology and other bits of physics; favourites include a simulated earthquake, miniaturized but real tornadoes and lightning storms, a free-fall simulator and a "swinging" bridge which leaves you reeling out of the building (even though the swinging is all done with mirrors). You'll easily kill a couple of hours here on a wet day.

Looming behind Questacon is the **National Library** (Mon–Thurs 9am–9pm, Fri & Sat 9am–5pm, Sun 1.30–5pm; free), whose reading room has a comprehensive selection of overseas newspapers and magazines. There are also exhibitions of rare books in the foyer, such as **Captain Cook's journal** from the *Endeavour*, as well as temporary exhibitions.

The High Court of Australia

From the library, it's a pleasant 500m walk east across the lawn to the **High Court of Australia** (daily 9.45am–4.30pm; free), set in an appropriately grandiose, glass-fronted concrete-block edifice with a stylized waterfall running alongside the walkway up to the entrance. Visitors can watch a short video which explains the court's function and examines two of its landmark cases: the 1983 ruling that saved Tasmania's wild Franklin River from damming, and its finding on the 1992 land-rights case of Mabo versus Queensland (see p.1093) – a momentous decision that overturned the British legal concept of *terra nullius* whereby Australia was considered uninhabited prior to white settlement in 1788. You can watch judgements while the court is in session.

The National Gallery

The National Gallery (daily 10am–5pm, free except for special exhibitions; Ⓦwww.nga.gov.au) is immediately east of the High Court, to which it is linked by a footbridge. Though there's a dutiful (if eclectic) display of European art here touching on everything from contemporary to pre-Renaissance, and a fine display of **Indian and Southeast Asian antiquities** (including some wonderful textiles and temple statuary), the gallery's real strengths are its Australian collection. This includes work by **Aboriginal and Torres Strait Islands** artists, ranging from traditional bark paintings from the Northern Territory to politically aware contemporary work in different media, though by far the best display is the upper level **Australian Art gallery**. Starting right back at the time of settlement, paintings here include some of the earliest recorded impressions of landscape, wildlife and Aborigines, and proceed through European-inspired art movements to the emphatically Australian *Ned*

Kelly series by Sidney Nolan; while there are also some Brett Whiteleys, samples of the nightmarish work of Albert Tucker, and fine pieces by Arthur Boyde and the Aboriginal-influenced John Olson. Other works on permanent display include Russell Drysdale's *The Drover's Wife* (1945), probably his best-known painting.

Outside, the **Sculpture Garden** overlooking Lake Burley Griffin includes a dispersed version of Rodin's freestanding bronze statues *The Burghers of Calais*. Also visible and audible across the water from here is the **Carillon** stranded on Aspen Island, whose three elegant bell-towers and 53 bronze bells – ranging from tiny to huge – were a gift from the British government to mark Canberra's fiftieth birthday. It's pleasant to sit on the lawns under a shady tree by the lake and listen to the Carillon recitals (June–Aug Sun & Wed 12.30pm–1.20pm; Sept–May Mon, Wed, Fri & Sun 12.30pm–1.20pm). On summer evenings, concerts and other events, such as open-air film screenings, are sometimes held here to coincide with special exhibitions (ask at the tourist office for details).

The Old and New Parliament houses

Away from the lake and at the foot of Capital Hill, the **Old Parliament House** (daily 9am–5pm; $2; Ⓦwww.oph.gov.au) is a grand, white Neoclassical wedding-cake of a building, in use between 1927 and 1988. A **tour** – they run once an hour – shows just how crowded and inconvenient the building actually was, all imposingly gloomy, Victorian-style wood panelling and moulded plaster, though the leather seats in the old senate are pretty comfortable. Old Parliament House also houses the **National Portrait Gallery** – though this is due to move to a new building near the High Court – mostly comprising large portraits of prime ministers. Outside, you can wander in the adjacent **Senate Rose Garden**, or take a look at the so-called **Aboriginal Tent Embassy** on the lawn in front, which has been here, on and off, since 1972 and serves as a focus for the million-odd representatives of Australia's oldest culture – you'll be welcomed for a cup of tea and a (political) chat.

Behind Old Parliament House and built into the side of Capital Hill, (New) **Parliament House** (daily 9am–5pm; free; Ⓦwww.aph.gov.au) is an extraordinary construction, though only the landmark, four-piece **flagpole** is visible from the outside. Designed by the American-based architect Romaldo Giurgola and opened in May 1988, it's certainly impressive in scale and concept despite having numerous detractors – the former Prime Minister Malcolm Fraser, who commissioned the building, described it later as "an unmitigated disaster" and "my one very serious political mistake". Make sure you catch one of the free **guided tours**, which run every half-hour between 9am and 4pm.

Outside the ground-floor entrance level is a **mosaic** by the Aboriginal artist Michael Tjakamarra Nelson – a piece that conveys the idea of a sacred meeting place. Inside, the impressive **foyer** is dominated by marble staircases and over forty columns clad in grey-green and rose-pink marble, representing a eucalypt forest. The floors are made of native woods, and the walls feature marquetry panels detailing native plants. Beyond the foyer, the **Great Hall** sports a twenty-metre-high **tapestry** based on a painting by Arthur Boyd showing the opposing forces of life and death meeting in blackened trees set against a powerful sky (look for the cockatoo). Other chambers are adorned with paintings by artists such as Albert Tucker, Sidney Nolan and Ian Fairweather, as well as portraits of political figures, photographs and ceramics. Important documents in the country's political history are also displayed.

When Parliament is in session – usually from seventy to eighty days a year – you can sit in the **public galleries** and watch the proceedings in the House of

Representatives (the lower chamber of Parliament) or the Senate (the upper chamber of the legislature); Question Time in both chambers starts at 2pm, with the House of Representatives making for better viewing. To guarantee a seat at busy times (like budget day), book in advance on ⓣ02/6277 5399.

The diplomatic quarters and the mint

A trip among the upmarket suburban homes in Canberra's diplomatic quarters – **Yarralumla** and **Forrest** – completes the political sightseeing tour. The consuls and high commissions were asked to construct buildings that exemplified the typical architecture of the countries they represent – look out for the eye-catching embassies of Thailand, Indonesia (with a small cultural centre), China and Papua New Guinea.

At the **Royal Australian Mint** (Mon–Fri 9am–4pm, Sat & Sun 10am–4pm; free; ⓦwww.ramint.gov.au), a few kilometres to the southwest on Denison Street, Deakin, you can watch coins being made (Mon–Fri only) and even stamp out your own dollar coin (for twice the face value) – great entertainment for kids. There's also a small display of historic Australian currency, including gold bars and "holey" dollars.

Lake Burley Griffin and around

Canberra is oriented around **Lake Burley Griffin**, which stretches for eleven kilometres from west to east; **Black Mountain** sits just north of its mid-point. A **cycle track** circuits the entire lake; while **bus #81**, which runs from Civic at the weekends and daily during school holidays, links – or comes very close to – almost all of the following sights. You can also make **lake cruises** by arrangement from the Ferry Terminal in north-shore Acton (ⓣ0419 418 846, ⓦwww.lakecruises.com.au).

The **National Zoo and Aquarium** (daily 10am–5pm; $23.50, children $12.50; ⓦwww.nationalzoo.com.au) sits on the lake's far western shore on Lady Denman Drive. They've all the usual native suspects, but the best feature of this zoo are their **big cats**, which include tigers, lions, cheetahs and snow leopards. Their two-hour Zoo Venture **tour** (Mon–Fri $95, Sat & Sun $125) lets you hand-feed most of these, along with some of the native animals; while $150 gets you in to pet a cheetah for fifteen minutes – you need to book both in advance.

Moving eastwards around the lakeshore, the **National Museum of Australia** (daily 9am–5pm; free; ⓦwww.nma.gov.au) occupies the little Acton Peninsula about two kilometres from Civic. The unmistakable postmodern building, which looks like a giant skateboard loop painted black and orange, is considerably more interesting than the contents, which – despite a professional presentation – are barely more ambitious than the average provincial museum collection. Items include bottles, old photos, eccentric vehicles and a collection of skins, film and photographs which outline the sad decline of Tasmania's **thylacine**, or marsupial wolf, which became extinct in the 1920s; but politics have hamstrung any comprehensive attempt at portraying Aboriginal culture. The museum does host some good **temporary exhibitions** at intervals through the year (entrance fee payable) – check the website for details.

Black Mountain, or rather the **Telstra Tower** poking upwards from the summit, is like a two-hundred-metre-high homing beacon for the city, visible from miles away. Bus #81 goes up to the tower's base, and there are magnificent panoramic views of Canberra from the 66-metre-high viewing platform. There's also a walking track up here from the **National Botanic Gardens**

below on Clunies Ross Street (daily 8.30am–5pm; free; free guided tours daily at 11am & 2pm), which has done an amazing job recreating a wide swathe of native habitats, including rainforest, in what was a sheep paddock in the 1970s. You can spend a couple of tranquil hours here walking through the undergrowth and spotting reptiles and birds, including rare **gang-gang cockatoos**. Their outdoor **café** (same hours) is beautifully set amongst shaded fern-gardens and lawns.

The area between the gardens and Civic is filled by the green and spacious **ANU (Australian National University)** campus. On McCoy Circuit here, the **National Film and Sound Archives** (Mon–Fri 9am–5pm, Sat & Sun 10am–5pm; free) houses a comprehensive collection of Australian sound and screen recordings dating back to the 1890s. One of the Archives' gems is their reconstruction of the five surviving minutes of *The History of the Kelly Gang*, made in 1906 and quite possibly the world's first feature film.

Back on the lakeshore and just east of the Commonwealth Avenue Bridge, the **Captain Cook Memorial Jet** spurts a column of water 140m into the air (10am–noon & 2–4pm, also 7–9pm during daylight saving). It was built in 1970 to mark the bicentenary of Captain Cook's "discovery" of Australia. The park immediately behind it is the venue for all sorts of outdoor shows, from the springtime **Floriade** flower festival, to New Year's Eve firework displays.

The Australian War Memorial

Due east of Civic on Limestone Avenue, the **Australian War Memorial** (daily 10am–5pm; free) does a good job of positively commemorating Australia's war dead whilst avoiding any glorification of war itself – a notable achievement for a country that sees participation in world wars as the core of its identity. The centrepiece is the Byzantine-style, domed **Hall of Memory**, approached past

△ Australian War Memorial

The Anzacs

Travelling around Australia you'll notice that almost every town, large or small, has a war memorial dedicated to the memory of the Anzacs, the **Australia and New Zealand Army Corps**. When war erupted in Europe in 1914, Australia was overwhelmed by a wave of pro-British sentiment. On August 5, 1914, one day after Great Britain had declared war against Germany, the Australian prime minister summed up the feelings of his compatriots: "When the Empire is at war so Australia is at war." On November 1, 1914, a contingent of twenty thousand enthusiastic volunteers – the **Anzacs** – left from the port of Albany in Western Australia to assist the mother country in her struggle.

In Europe, Turkey had entered the war on the German side in October 1914. At the beginning of 1915, military planners in London (Winston Churchill prominent among them) came up with a plan to capture the strategically important Turkish peninsula of the Dardanelles with a surprise attack near **Gallipoli**, thus opening the way to the Black Sea. On April 25, 1915, sixteen thousand Australian soldiers landed at dawn in a small bay flanked by steep cliffs: by nightfall, two thousand men had died in a hail of Turkish bullets from above. The plan, whose one chance of success was surprise, had been signalled by troop and ship movements long in advance; by the time it was carried out, it was already doomed to failure. Nonetheless, Allied soldiers continued to lose their lives for another eight months without ever gaining more than a foothold. In December, London finally issued the order to withdraw. Eleven thousand Australians and New Zealanders had been killed, along with as many French and three times as many British troops. The Turks lost 86,000 men.

Official Australian historiography continues to mythologize the battle for Gallipoli, elevating it to the level of a national legend on which Australian identity is founded. From this point of view, in the war's baptism of fire, the Anzac soldiers proved themselves heroes who did the new nation proud, their loyalty and bravery evidence of how far Australia had developed. It was "the birth of a nation", and at the same time a loss of innocence, a national rite of passage – never again would Australians so unquestioningly involve themselves in foreign ventures. Today the legend is as fiercely defended as ever, the focal point of Australian national pride, commemorated each year on April 25, **Anzac Day**.

an eternal flame which rises from a rectangular pond. Look up at the ceiling to see mosaics depicting veterans of World War II, while the lovely blue stained-glass windows commemorate those who fought in World War I. In the centre is the tomb of the Unknown Australian Soldier, while over 100,000 names of the fallen are etched onto the walls outside. Wings either side house paintings by war artists, battle dioramas and military relics including huge naval guns and giant bombers, as well as countless films, and sound-and-light shows.

The Australian Institute of Sport

A couple of kilometres north of Black Mountain is the ultramodern **Australian Institute of Sport (AIS)**, on Leverrier Crescent in Bruce (daily 9am–5pm; tours 10am, 11.30am, 1pm & 2.30pm; ⓦwww.ausport.gov.au; bus #431). Founded to improve the national sports profile after Australia's dismal showing in the 1976 Olympics, AIS has since churned out world-beating athletes with such regularity that other countries now copy their training techniques. **Tours** ($13, children $7) are guided by athletes and last ninety minutes, and introduce you to their intensive schedules, while the **Sportex** interactive exhibition gives you the chance to test your prowess at various sports. For an extra charge you can use the heated pool, spa, sauna and tennis courts.

Eating

There are so many **cafés and restaurants** around Civic and Kingston (and nearby **Manuka**) that finding somewhere to eat is never a problem. The cafés all serve light meals, while the restaurants feature a definite bias towards Southeast Asian food. The following is only a tiny selection; there are also cafés at Parliament House, the National Gallery, Botanic Gardens and other sights to keep you topped up as you tour.

Cafés

The Blue Olive 56 Alinga St, Civic. Home-baked speciality breads and cakes, toasted Turkish sandwiches and ice-cold beer from the in-house bottle shop. Mon–Sat 7am–late.

Café Essen Garema Arcade, Civic. Long-standing and much-loved coffee house with enormous, cheap and unusual brunches, and all-day breakfasts. Daily from 7.30am.

Gus Café Bunda St, Civic. Canberra's best café, this place serves inexpensive light meals, good pasta and fresh soups, with lots of choice for vegetarians. It's popular with students and an arty crowd, and sports outside tables under vines. Daily 7.30am–10pm, later at the weekend.

Silo 36 Giles St, Kingston. Narrow and cramped, yet their excellent coffee and croissants are an institution with Canberra's smart set, who also buy wholemeal bread from their bakery. Expect weekend crowds and rude staff.

Restaurants

ANU Union Union Crescent, Acton. The students' union here has a super-cheap bistro upstairs offering basic, filling canteen food such as roast beef, peas, chips and gravy. Mon–Fri lunch and dinner.

Artespresso 31 Giles St, Kingston ⓣ02/6295 8055. Executives plot global domination over barramundi and duck in this swanky bar-restaurant, which also has fine artworks on periodic display. Tues–Sat, noon till late.

Asian Café 32 West Row, Civic ⓣ02/6262 6233. Extremely popular, inexpensive restaurant serving tasty versions of Malay and Chinese staples – fried noodles, sweet-and-sour and the rest. Mains around $15.

Chairman and Yip 108 Bunda St, Civic ⓣ02/6248 7109. This stylish and eccentric restaurant offers Eastern Chinese classics such as meltingly tender, aromatic Shandong Lamb. Not cheap at around $30 for a main, though they also offer early-evening set-meals from $35. Lunch Mon–Fri, dinner Mon–Sat.

Charcoal 61 London Circuit, Civic ⓣ02/6248 8015. Grilled steak, in shamelessly large servings, is the mainstay here, though they also offer grilled reef fish. Steaks around $30.

Courgette 54 Marcus Clarke St, Civic ⓣ02/6247 4042. Smart restaurant serving modern European cuisine – their venison with quince jam is fantastic. There's also an extensive wine cellar. Mon–Fri lunch, Mon–Sat dinner. Mains around $33.

Little Saigon Cnr Alinga St and Northbourne Ave, Civic ⓣ02/6230 5003. Large, busy, cheap and tasty Vietnamese restaurant, with dismal decor and $8 lunchtime specials (which can be taken out). Best to book at weekends. Daily 9am–3pm & 5–10.30pm.

Santa Lucia 21 Kennedy St, Kingston ⓣ02/6295 1813. Unpretentious, family-owned Italian trattoria that has been serving filling home-style meals for decades. Mains $20.

Three Mothers Thai 34 Garema Place, Civic ⓣ02/6249 8900. There are posher Thai restaurants than this one, but none to match the friendly staff, fast service and tasty, good-value menu. Mains around $15.

Timmy's just up from the cinema on Furneaux St, Manuka ⓣ02/6295 6537. This friendly and very popular Malay restaurant does good seafood. Mains around $15.

Tosolini's cnr East Row and London Circuit, Civic ⓣ02/6247 4317. Very popular, modern Australian-Italian eaterie with fantastic pastries. Tues–Sun noon–3pm & 6–10.30pm, plus weekend breakfast 8.30–11.30am.

Drinking, nightlife and entertainment

For **information** about upcoming events, the daily *Canberra Times* is your best bet; the most extensive listings are published every Thursday in the "Good Times" supplement. For details of gigs and club nights, pick up a copy – or check out the websites – of the free monthly music magazines *BMA* (ⓦwww.bmamag.com) or *3D World* (ⓦwww.threedworld.com.au) available from record shops, hostels and bars.

Drinking and nightlife

Civic's biggest **pubs** are *P.J. O'Reilly's*, at the corner of West Row and Alinga Street; *Mooseheads* on London Circuit; and *King O'Malleys*, at 131 City Walk, which all get loud and busy on Friday and Saturday nights. The **best beer**, however, is served at the *Wig and Pen* on Alinga Street, which brews its own excellent lager, ale and bitter on site. In Kingston, the main watering holes are the *Durham Arms* and *Filthy McFaddens*, both on Green Square, while (expensive) Belgian beers are served over the road at *Little Brussels*, 29 Jardine St.

Canberra's many **nightclubs** are mostly in Civic, and open Thursday to Saturday or Sunday from about 8pm. The most lively is *ICBM*, 50 Northbourne Ave, where a mix of students and civil servants let their hair down; nearby *E*, *32* and *Sultan's* all have DJs playing pop and house. *Club Mombasa*, on Bunda Street, plays more laid-back African, Latin and Pacific sounds to an older crowd.

For **live music**, the best bet in term time is the ANU's *Union Bar*, which features indie gigs, touring big-name bands and all-night raves (see Ⓦwww.anuunion.com.au for details). The *Canberra Workers Club* in Civic also hosts big touring bands, with cheap drinks until midnight. *Tilley's* is another good spot, a couple of kilometres northwest of Civic in Lyneham at the corner of Wattle and Brigalow streets, a restaurant-café-bar with live music – of varying types and quality – at weekends.

Theatre and cinema

The main **drama** venue in the capital is the Canberra Theatre Centre on London Circuit, whose several theatres host plays, concerts, dance performances and travelling shows. Less-mainstream options include The Street Theatre (Ⓣ02/6247 1519, Ⓦwww.thestreet.org.au), on the corner of Childers Street and University Avenue, and a number of active independent theatre groups based at the Gorman House Arts Centre on Ainslie Avenue, Braddon (Ⓣ02/6249 7377, Ⓦwww.gormanhouse.com.au). There's also inexpensive student theatre at the ANU Arts Centre, Union Court, ANU (Ⓣ02/6215 2419).

As for **cinemas**, big mainstream releases are shown at Greater Union, corner of Bunda and Mort streets in Civic (Ⓣ02/6247 5522), with another branch on the corner of Furneaux Street and Canberra Avenue in Manuka (Ⓣ02/6295 6042). The Dendy, upstairs in the Canberra Centre, Civic (Ⓣ02/6221 8900), is slightly less commercial, with a scattering of international and art-house films.

Listings

Airlines Qantas Ⓣ13 13 13, Ⓦwww.qantas.com.au; Virgin Blue Ⓣ13 67 89, Ⓦwww.virginblue.com.au.
Banks ANZ, Commonwealth, National Australia Bank and Westpac all have branches in the pedestrian area of Civic.

Bike rental For making the most of Canberra's cycle tracks, Mr Spokes Bike Hire (Ⓣ02/6257 1188) is located next to the ferry dock on the north side of the lake, and hires out bikes ($12 an hour, or $38 for the day),

Moving on from Canberra

Long-distance **bus services** use the Jollimont Centre terminal (see p.231); tickets are available here for direct services with Greyhound (Ⓣ13 14 99, Ⓦwww.greyhound.com.au) to Sydney, Brisbane, Melbourne and Adelaide; and Murrays Coaches (Ⓣ13 22 51, Ⓦwww.murrays.com.au) to Sydney, Bateman's Bay, Woolongong and, during winter, a Snow Express to Thredbo. There are also daily **trains** to Sydney from the train station in Kingston. There's a Countrylink desk in the Jollimont Centre for tickets, or book online at Ⓦwww.countrylink.info.

tandems ($24/$75) and pedal "cars" ($30 an hour).

Books Smiths Alternative Bookshop, opposite the Post Office on Alinga St, is a small but interesting independent book store; there's also a small second-hand store and a travel bookshop, next to the bus station in the Jollimont Centre.

Car rental Canberra is an expensive place to rent a car, but relatively good deals are available with Rumbles, 11 Paragon Mall, Gladstone St, Fyshwick (☎02/6280 7444). Others, with desks at the airport include: Avis ☎02/6249 1601; Budget ☎13 27 27; Hertz ☎02/6249 6211 or 13 30 39; and Thrifty ☎1300 367 227.

Embassies and high commissions There are over seventy in Canberra (all the following are in Yarralumla, unless otherwise stated): Britain, Commonwealth Ave ☎02/6270 6666; Canada, Commonwealth Ave ☎02/6270 4000; China, 15 Coronation Drive ☎02/6273 4780; Ireland, 20 Arkana St ☎02/6273 3022; Malaysia, 7 Perth Ave ☎02/6273 1543; New Zealand, Commonwealth Ave ☎02/6270 4211; Singapore, 17 Forster Crescent ☎02/6273 3944; Thailand, 111 Empire Circuit ☎02/6273 1149; USA, 21 Moonah Place ☎02/6214 5600.

Festivals The big event of the year is the Canberra Festival – the anniversary of the city's foundation – celebrated with concerts, theatre, exhibitions, street parades and fireworks for ten days from the beginning of March. The Royal Canberra Show is an agricultural fair lasting three days over the last weekend in February, while the Floriade is a spring festival marked by floral displays, theatre and music, from mid-September to mid-October. Even more popular, though less feted by the tourist board, is the annual Summernats Car Festival in January (details on ☎02/6241 8111 or at Ⓦwww.summernats.com.au), when revheads convene in Exhibition Park.

Gay and lesbian Canberra Gay Information and Support Service; daily 6–10pm ☎02/6247 2726.

Hospitals John James Memorial Hospital, Strickland Crescent, Deakin ☎02/6281 8100 (private); The Canberra Hospital, Yama Drive, Garran ☎02/6244 2222.

Internet access If your accommodation can't help out, there are some terminals at the bus station in Jollimont Centre, and a huge subterranean Net-bar near the Action bus stops in Civic.

Markets Gorman House Markets, Gorman House Arts Centre, Ainslie Ave, Braddon (Sat 10am–4pm; just up Ainslie Avenue from the Canberra Centre), is a community market where items such as pottery, hand-painted T-shirts, bric-a-brac and second-hand clothes are sold; Old Bus Depot Markets, Wentworth Ave, Kingston Foreshore (Sun 10am–4pm), is the big Sun market in town and the only one indoors – handicrafts, great food, musicians and other entertainment.

NRMA (National Roads and Motorists Association) 92 Northbourne Ave, Braddon, or Belconnen Mall, Belconnen ☎13 21 32. Publishes a very useful map of Canberra and the ACT, free to members.

Police ☎02/6256 7777.

Post office Alinga St, Canberra, ACT 2600 (Mon–Fri 9am–5pm; ☎02/6209 1680).

Shopping Shopping hours are Mon–Thurs 9am–5.30pm, Fri 9am–9pm, Sat 9am–4pm, Sun 10am–4pm. Civic's main option is the massive Canberra Centre mall, with similar shopping centres in most suburbs.

Taxis Canberra Cabs (☎13 10 08) can be booked; there's also a taxi rank on Bunda St, Civic, outside the cinema.

Tours Canberra has good connections to the winter snowfields at Thredbo and Perisher; contact Murrays Coaches or a travel agent for seasonal bus-ski-accommodation packages.

Travel agents Flight Centre, 111 Alinga St (☎02/6247 8199); STA Travel, near *Gus's Café*, 13 Garema Place, Civic (☎02/6247 8633).

Around Canberra

Canberra's reputation for being surrounded by attractively rugged countryside took a sad beating from the awful 2003 **bushfires** which burned out two thirds of the ACT. While Australian native vegetation is generally fire-tolerant, some species even needing annual conflagrations to pop open seed pods or encourage new growth, these fires were so intense that huge areas of forest were totally incinerated, and will take decades to recover. All the same, there are still a couple of picnic grounds, short walks and stands of regenerating woodland which make for a decent half-day out – just don't expect anything too dramatic.

South: Lanyon Homestead and Namadgi National Park

Leaving the city behind, the Tharwa Road follows the course of the **Murrumbidgee River**. Thirty-two kilometres from Canberra, at the southern end of the Tuggeranong Valley, the convict-built **Lanyon Homestead** (Tues–Sun 10am–4pm; $7, admission to grounds free) dates back to the earliest European settlement of the region. Thoroughly refurbished by the National Trust, it now houses a small display outlining the history of the area before Canberra existed, but the real reasons to come are the house itself and the **Sidney Nolan Gallery** (Tues–Fri 10am–4pm, Sat & Sun 10am–5pm; $3) next door, where you'll find works by the famous Australian painter, including some of his Kelly and Burke and Wills series, alongside changing exhibitions of contemporary Australian art. There's no public transport out here.

Namadgi National Park occupies almost half of the ACT, largely made up of wilderness areas in the west and southwest. Its mountain ranges and high plains, rising to 1900m, have a far more severe climate than low-lying Canberra and give rise to the Cotter River and many smaller streams. In the northwest, the Corin Road leads to **Corin Dam**, while in the south the partly surfaced Bobyan Road cuts right through the national park, emerging beneath the Snowy Mountains in the south. There are **picnic grounds** and bush campsites by the Orroral River and near Mount Clear in the south.

The **Namadgi Visitors Information Centre**, 3km south of **Tharwa** on the Naas Road (Mon–Fri 9am–4pm, Sat, Sun & public holidays 9am–4.30pm; ⓣ02/6207 2900, ⓦwww.environment.act.gov.au), has displays and videos about the park, and also provides guided tours on request, as well as detailed information on bushwalking tracks and emergency shelters in the remote areas.

West: Tidbinbilla Nature Reserve and Cotter Reserve

The small **Tidbinbilla Nature Reserve**, to the southwest of the city (daily 9am–6pm, 9am–8pm during daylight saving), is an enjoyable place with relatively easy walks and some wheelchair-accessible paths. The area around the park entrance and **information centre** (Mon–Fri 9am–4.30pm, Sat & Sun 9am–5.30pm; ⓣ02/6205 1233, ⓦwww.environment.act.gov.au) is home to kangaroos and wallabies in spacious bush enclosures, and you can also see koalas, lots of birds and **corroboree frogs**, an extremely rare alpine amphibian. Picnic grounds are dotted all along the sealed road leading through the reserve, and on long weekends and during the school holidays it's a busy place, especially popular with families.

The **Canberra Space Centre** on Discovery Drive in Tidbinbilla (visitors centre open daily 9am–5pm, till 8pm in summer; free; ⓦwww.cdscc.nasa.gov) sounds like every child's dream, though in fact the displays of spacecraft and highly sensitive communications equipment are not as exciting as you might have hoped. Operated in conjunction with NASA, the purpose of the station is to pick up even the most obscure signals from outer space; there are only two others in the world with the same range as Tidbinbilla – one near Madrid, the other in Goldstone, California.

Southwest of here, Corin Road turns off the Tidbinbilla Road towards the **Corin Forest** (Sat & Sun 10am–5pm, also weekdays during school holidays 10am–4pm; ⓦwww.corin.com.au) and reservoir, a popular recreation spot in the hills, with many walking trails, year-round bobsledding, picnic grounds and barbecue facilities. In winter you can ski on artificial snow and during school holidays special activities are organized for children.

The south coast and Snowy Mountains

The **south coast**, with its green dairylands and small fishing villages, is delightful in a quiet sort of way – an area for casting a rod, surfing or relaxing on the many stunning beaches – with no huge resorts or commercial developments. Inland are the **Snowy Mountains**, the Great Dividing Range's highest peaks, which have Australia's best skiing and, in summer, some fine bushwalking.

The direct route from Sydney to Melbourne via the inland **Hume Highway** (covered in Chapter 3) passes close to Canberra and the Snowy Mountains. The coastal route, the **Princes Highway**, is slightly longer but much more scenic. Give yourself four or more days if you want to appreciate the national parks, sandy beaches, mountains, valleys and forests that comprise this beautiful stretch of the coast.

The south coast

The **south coast** of New South Wales is all rather low-key and family-oriented, with a few wildlife and amusement parks to keep the children happy, and plenty of opportunities for traditional outdoor pursuits. Exposed parts on this stretch of the coast are perfect for **surfing**, while the numerous coastal lakes, bays and inlets are suited for **swimming**, windsurfing, sailing or canoeing. Away from the ocean there's some superb, rugged scenery, with some great **bushwalking** and **horse riding** in the forest-clad, mountainous hinterland. The stretch between **Jervis Bay** and **Batemans Bay** in particular can get busy during the summer months, especially from Christmas to the end of January.

Most of the way down the coast from Sydney, the **Princes Highway** runs a few kilometres inland. Away from the towns, apparently obscure turn-offs from the highway often lead to beautiful and secluded beaches – it's worth taking some time to make your own discoveries. From **Canberra** there are three main routes to the coast: through Kangaroo Valley, via Goulburn and Moss Vale; the Kings Highway to Batemans Bay; and the Monaro and Snowy Mountains highways to Bega via Cooma. **Transport** links to the south coast include **trains** from Sydney as far as Bomaderry, plus **bus** services along the Princes Highway from Sydney and Melbourne to Eden, and from Canberra to Eden via the Snowy Mountains (detailed within individual town accounts and on p.301).

Berry

Sixteen kilometres north of Nowra along the Princes Highway, **BERRY** is a pretty, historic town with many listed buildings, surrounded by dairy country and green hills. The main drag, **Queen Street,** is packed with upmarket homeware shops, little art galleries, cafés and restaurants, and is home to two country pubs. The town's popularity, enhanced by the proximity of **Kangaroo Valley** and the beach at **Gerringong**, means that Berry gets, unbearably crowded on fine weekends, especially when the monthly market (first Sun of month) is on. The *Berry Hotel* (see below) can arrange tours to the nearby chocolate factory and the many **wineries** in the region ($20); the Coolangatta Estate (daily 10am–5pm; ⓣ02/4448 7131, ⓦwww.coolangattaestate.com.au), just 5km out of Berry on Bolong Road, and the Silos Estate (Wed–Sun 10am–5pm; ⓣ02/4448 6082, ⓦwww.thesilos.com), at Jasper's Brush, are among the best.

Practicalities

Berry is easily reached by **train** on CityRail's South Coast Line from Sydney. The Shoalhaven **tourist office** (daily 9am–5pm; ⓣ02/4421 0778 or 1300 662 808, ⓦwww.shoalhavenholidays.com.au) can help you out with any queries and accommodation bookings – it's located on the Princes Highway, to the south of Berry just after the road bridge between Nowra and Bomaderry.

Accommodation

There are hundreds of rural B&Bs in the hills around town; check out the Shoalhaven tourist office's website for listings. Nearer to town, the Coolangatta and Silos estates (see below) offer luxury B&B (❻–❽).

The Berry Hotel 120 Queen St ⓣ02/4464 1011, ⓦwww.berryhotel.com.au. A really lovely old coach-house offering pretty, old-fashioned rooms, including a huge family flat that could happily sleep ten people. A full country breakfast is included in the (higher) price at weekends. Singles ❸, doubles ❹, family flat $60pp

The Bunyip Inn 122 Queen St ⓣ02/4464 2064. Upmarket option in an imposing National Trust-classified former bank, with a lovely leafy garden and swimming pool; some of the thirteen olde-worlde rooms have four-poster beds. ❺

Postman's Ghost Cnr Queen and Prince Alfred sts ⓣ02/4464 3379. Housed, not surprisingly, in the striking old post office, the four luxurious suites here are all strikingly decorated, with some featuring four-poster beds and others clawfoot baths. ❺–❼

Eating

The Berry Hotel 120 Queen St. This much-loved place boasts the best food in town, served in either the pub itself, the large courtyard at the back, or a cozy-cottage dining room with open fire. Food consists of posh pub tucker at lunch and affordable Mod Oz offerings in the evening, including the delicious cumin-spiced lamb rump with puy lentils, aubergine and yoghurt. Entertainment Saturday evenings.

Cuttlefish Queen St. Stylish pizza-bar located over the top of the *Hedgehog Café*, overlooking a beautiful nursery. Also serves modern Italian mains and desserts. Dinner from 6pm plus Fri–Sun 11.30am–3pm. Closed Tues.

Emporium Food Co. 127 Queen St. Opposite the *Berry Hotel*, this gourmet deli serves posh sandwiches, savoury pies, beautiful little cakes and excellent coffee – try and grab one of the little ornate tables at the front of the shop. Mon–Sat 9am–5pm, Sun 10am–4.30pm.

Silos Winery Princes Highway, Jaspers Bush ⓣ02/4448 6082, ⓦwww.thesilos.com. The finest dining in the area, with an eclectic, Asian-inspired Mod Oz menu, beautifully crafted desserts and idyllic views over the vineyard. Pricey. Wed–Sat lunch & dinner, Sun lunch.

Jervis Bay

Around 40km south of Berry, the sheltered waters of **Jervis Bay** are, by a political quirk, technically part of the ACT, in order to provide Canberra with access to the sea. The area attracts a lot of visitors due to its proximity to Sydney, and the delights of the nearby Booderee National Park.

The best place to base yourself if you don't fancy bushcamping is the small, slightly lacklustre town of **HUSKISSON**, at the mid-point of the bay, which has good **diving** in pristine waters – suprisingly enough, it's the second most popular dive spot in Australia after the Great Barrier Reef. For details of one-off dives, packages and snorkelling, contact Deep 6 Diving (ⓣ02/4441 5255, ⓦwww.deep6divingjervisbay.com.au), at 64 Owen St. **Sealife-watching tours** are available all year with Dolphin Watch Cruises (2hr; $22; ⓣ02/4441 6311 or 1800 246 010, ⓦwww.dolphinwatch.com.au), 50 Owen St, and Dolphin Explorer Cruises at no. 62 (2hr; $22; ⓣ02/4441 5455 or 1800 444 330, ⓦwww.dolphincruises.com.au); whales can be spotted from June to November. The beachfront *Husky Pub*, which has a good bistro and plenty of pool tables, is very much the focus of the town.

The beautiful coast of **Booderee National Park** ("bay of plenty", or "plenty of fish"), at the southern end of the bay, is very popular: rugged cliffs face the pounding ocean along its eastern boundary, while the park's northern side, within the confines of the bay, is marked by tranquil beaches of dazzling white sand and clear water. Inland, heaths, wetlands and forests offer strolls and bushwalks; there's also great snorkelling from the park and around nearby Bowen Island, with a chance of spotting a range of marine life including dolphins, stingrays and – around the island – a penguin colony. The park is jointly run by Wreck Bay Aboriginal Community and Environment Australia, and NPWS passes are not valid. The **Wreck Bay Aboriginal Community** organizes a summer cultural interpretation programme, Wreck Bay Walkabouts (bookings through the tourist office; free), which covers diet and medicines, archeology and wildlife; alternatively, try the highly recommended Barry's Bushtucker Tours (ⓣ02/4442 1168).

Booderee Botanic Gardens (daily 8am–6pm during DST; 9am–4pm rest of the year; free), on Cave Beach Road, focuses on regional coastal flora and has a number of pleasant walks with interpretative boards.

Practicalities

You'll need your own transport to explore Jervis Bay. The Shoalhaven **tourist office** has information on the area. Booderee National Park's visitor centre (daily 10am–4pm; ⓣ02/4443 0977, ⓦwww.booderee.gov.au) is at the entrance to the park on Jervis Bay Road; detailed walking maps are available, and you also pay the $10 entry fee here. They handle all bookings for the three insanely popular, unpowered **campsites** (up to $20 per site) in the park – a ballot is held in August for spots over the Christmas holiday period. The *Cave Beach* site is the most sought-after, despite its cold showers, but *Bristol Point* and *Green Patch* also get plenty of guests; the latter is the only one of the three suitable for campervans.

Bushy Tail Caravan Park 29 Deakin St, Erowal Bay ⓣ02/4443 0468. You feel like you're way out in the wilderness at this excellent caravan park, a short drive southwest of Huskisson just past Erowal Bay. It's an easy-going place set in thick forest and is literally hopping with 'roos – especially fun for kids. Sites $15–20, cabins ❷–❸

Huskisson B&B 12 Tomerong St, Huskisson ⓣ02/4441 7551, ⓦwww.huskissonb&b.com.au. Lovely, beachy B&B in a 1913 weatherboard cottage with well-decorated "shabby chic" rooms, nourishing breakfasts and multitude of home comforts. ❻

Jervis Bay Backpackers 16 Elizabeth Drive, Vincentia ⓣ02/4441 6880, ⓦwww.jervisbaybackpackers.com.au. Just south of Huskisson, this very homely and welcoming place offers the only budget accommodation in the area. Dorms $30, doubles ❸

Paper Bark Camp Woollamia Rd ⓣ02/4441 6066, ⓦwww.paperbarkcamp.com.au. Unusual luxury resort set in the middle of the bush, with accommodation in romantic en-suite safari tents on stilts, huge beds, private verandas, solar-powered lighting and a superb restaurant which is very inexpensive for what you get. Breakfast included. ❽

Ulladulla and around

ULLADULLA is a fairly uninspiring fishing port, unattractively arranged along the Princes Highway, whose saving grace is its small, pretty harbour. In terms of **activities**, there's swimming at the free seawater pool by the wharf (Nov–March 7–11am & 2–6pm; closed Tues), and scuba diving run by Ulladulla Dive & Adventure (ⓣ02/4455 3029, ⓦwww.ulladulladive.com.au), 211 Princes Highway. The local Budamurra Aboriginal community (ⓣ02/4455 5883, ⓦwww.budamurra.asn.au) has constructed an interesting cultural trail, "One track for all", at Ulladulla Head; turn off the highway at North Street and keep going. Guided tours ($10) are also offered by the Budamurra people, and include tips on boomerang throwing, didgeridoo playing and fire making, as well as some bushtucker.

The town is set within a beautiful area, dominated by the sandstone plateau of the **Morton National Park** to the west, one of the biggest and wildest national parks in NSW. The park presents a mostly inaccessible barrier, and although you can drive across it on horrifically corrugated dirt roads, it's strictly 4WD only in the wet. There's a good bushwalk to the top of the 720-metre **Pigeon House Mountain**, towards the south of the park in the Budawang Ranges, where there are also Aboriginal cave sites and numerous waterfalls. The marked trail takes about four hours return and is accessed from the Princes Highway, via the Wheelbarrow Road turn-off 8km south of Ulladulla.

There are attractive river mouths, beaches and lakes along the coast in both directions. Pretty **Lake Conjola** (10km to the north), **Lake Burrill** (5km to the south) and **Lake Tabourie** (13km to the south) are all popular with fishermen, canoeists and campers. A few kilometres further on, the village of **Milton** is more pleasant than it first appears as you speed through on the Princes Highway, and is home to numerous antique shops, craft shops and cafés.

Practicalities

Premier Motor Service and Transborder call at Ulladulla, connecting the town with the coastal towns and Canberra respectively. There's a **tourist office** (Mon–Fri 10am–6pm, Sat & Sun 9am–5pm; ⓣ02/4455 1269, ⓦwww.shoalhavenholidays.com.au) on the Princes Highway as it runs through Ulladulla, which has an activities and accommodation booking service.

Accommodation

Bannister's Point Lodge 191 Mitchell Parade, Mollymook ⓣ02/4455 3044, ⓦwww.bannisterspointlodge.com.au. Just south of Milton, the rooms in this designer place are all decorated to the highest specifications; all have balconies with sea views, huge rainforest showers, and some have outdoor plunge pools. A spectacular cliff-top infinity pool adjoins a Moroccan-style bar with Campari-bottle lamp shades; an award-winning if pricey restaurant, and indulgent day-spa are also on site. ❽

Traveller's Rest 63 Princes Highway ⓣ02/4454 0500, ⓦwww.southcoasttravellersrest.com. Small backpackers' with nice facilities, but quite unfriendly and included only because it's the only hostel for miles around. It's up for sale though, so fingers crossed the new owners will be a little more welcoming. Dorms $25, doubles ❸

Ulladulla Guesthouse Cnr Burrill and South sts ⓣ02/4455 1796, ⓦwww.guesthouse.com.au. This smart guesthouse is chintzy in a good way, and boasts fine, comfortable rooms, a palm-fringed swimming pool and an art gallery. The charming, traditional restaurant here serves top-notch French cuisine at far-less-than-Parisian prices (open for dinner Mon, Thurs, Fri & Sat). The cozy environment and extremely warm welcome make this a real charmer. ❼–❽

Ulladulla Headland Tourist Park South St ⓣ02/4455 2457. Superb cliff-top location overlooking the harbour plus excellent amenities, including a swimming pool, tennis court, children's playground and smart cabins. Sites $30–40, cabins ❸–❺

Eating

Bannister's Point Lodge 191 Mitchell Parade ⓣ02/4455 3044, ⓦwww.bannisterspointlodge.com.au. The restaurant at *Bannister's Point Lodge* (see opposite) is one of the best on the south coast, with award-winning food and a particularly good wine cellar. Open for dinner Tues–Sun.

Edge Café Cnr Boree and Green sts. The best lunch option in town, this spacious hideaway offers gourmet pizza, pasta, salads and lots of veggie plates, plus great brunches. BYO. Mon–Thurs 8am–5pm, Fri 8am–10pm, Sat 9am–10pm.

Millard's Cottage 81 Princes Highway ⓣ02/4455 3287. This striking pink building, just before you cross Millard's Creek, is one of Ulladulla's oldest. The interior is fairly traditional too, while the menu offers very fine dining with lots of wines by the glass and some pricey, unusual seafood and meat mains such as pork with strawberry-and-balsamic-vinegar sauce. Licensed and BYO. Mon–Sat from 6pm, plus noon–2pm Thurs–Sat.

Batemans Bay and around

At the mouth of the Clyde River and the end of the highway from Canberra, **BATEMANS BAY** is a favourite escape for the landlocked residents of the capital, just 152km away. It's not the most exciting place on the coast, but since it's a fair-sized resort, there's plenty to do. The town itself is focused around Clyde and Orient streets, which run into one another. Beach Road runs alongside the river to the pleasant marina, then southeast past a string of good beaches – the further you go, the nicer they get. You can take a **cruise** on the Clyde River with Merinda Cruises (3hr; $25; ⓣ02/4472 4052) whose trips include a stop at the pretty village of **Nelligen**, just upstream. Alternatively, Straight Up Kayaks (ⓣ0418 970 751, ⓦwww.straightupkayaks.com.au) offer dusk paddles and full-day tours to Nelligen.

There's a number of small zoos and theme parks around town; you can cuddle wombats, koalas and wallabies at the **Birdland Animal Park** (daily 9.30am–4pm; $16; ⓦwww.birdlandanimalpark.com.au), just south of town at 55 Beach Rd in Batehaven. In **MOGO**, 10km to the south, you can step back in time at the open-air **Old Mogo Town Goldrush Theme Park** (daily 10am–4pm; $14; ⓦwww.oldmogotown.com.au), a reconstruction of a mid-nineteenth-century goldrush town. Nearby **Mogo Zoo** (daily 9am–5pm; feeding at 10.30am & 1.30pm; $18.50; ⓦwww.mogozoo.com.au) began life as a small sanctuary, and has grown to something more akin to the Serengeti, housing snow leopards, giraffe, monkeys and lions.

Practicalities

Murray's Coaches, Transborder and Premier Motor Service all call at Batemans Bay. The **tourist office** (daily 9am–5pm; ⓣ02/4472 6900 or 1800 802 528, ⓦwww.naturecoast-tourism.com.au) is on Princes Highway, at the corner of Beach Road, and has details of all the motels and holiday units in town.

Accommodation

Accommodation consists mainly of motels and a wide range of holiday units; most of the latter require a minimum booking during peak times. There's good bushcamping just north of town in the Murramarang National Park, at Pebbly (ⓣ02/4478 6023), Pretty (ⓣ02/4457 2019) and Depot (ⓣ02/4478 6582) beaches (all $5–8 per adult); the coastal strip is popular not only with campers but also with kangaroos, which come here at dawn and dusk to frolic on the beach.

Batemans Bay Beach Resort 51 Beach Rd ⓣ02/4472 4541 or 1800 217 533, ⓦwww.beachresort.com.au. Smart, spacious resort with very plush beachfront cabins, some prime camping spots overlooking the water, and some reasonably priced lodgings. Sites $428–432, lodgings ❷, cabins ❻–❼

Batemans Bay YHA & Shady Willows Holiday Park ⓣ02/4472 4972, ⓦwww.shadywillows.com.au. Decent holiday park with pool and good facilities located close to town, though it's quite a walk to the beaches. There's a small YHA section here too, offering a rare chance to break out of the backpacker posse and mix it with some "outsiders". Dorms $25, doubles ❸, sites $20, cabins ❸–❹

Beechwood Court B&B 12 Beechwood Court, Batehaven ⓣ02/4472 9127. Beautiful waterfront setting at Sunshine Bay, just south of town. The modern, well-decorated rooms have king-sized beds and it's worth being first in line for breakfast in the morning. ❻

Clyde View B&B 17 Braidwood Rd, Nelligen, 15km north of Batemans Bay ⓣ02/4478 1019, ⓦwww.clydeviewbb-nelligen.com. Lovely B&B which strikes just the right balance between bright modern decor and traditional-style fixtures. You can breakfast on the patio overlooking the river. ❻

Eating

There's a number of decent **places to eat** in Batemans Bay, especially down Clyde and Orient streets and on the esplanade.

Good Food Café 45 Orient St. Cheap and healthy luncheon fare, plus great mugs of coffee, home-made savouries and cake.

On the Pier Old Punt Rd, just over the bridge to the north ⓣ02/4472 6405. The nicest restaurant in town by a stretch. It's a bright, breezy place with good lounging possibilities, a great Aussie wine list, and imaginative seafood mains. As promised, you can actually eat on the pier. Daily noon–2.30pm & 6–8.30pm.

Starfish Deli Next to the boatshed on Clyde Street. Trendy and popular place with river views and a modern menu, including a variety of wood-fired pizzas and posh burgers. Open daily for breakfast, lunch and dinner.

Naroomа

Surrounded on three sides by beautiful beaches, inlets and coastal lakes, **NAROOMA** is perfect for watery pursuits, and lies at the heart of an area famous for its succulent **freshwater oysters**. The town is rather spread out along the Princes Highway – first Wagonga then Campbell Street as it runs through the centre – with a marina down to the west and beaches to the east. Southern right and humpback whales migrate past the bay in June and July and from September to early November; there's also a decent chance of seeing seals from the lookout at the end of Bar Rocks Road, particularly in spring.

You can canoe on the **Wagonga Inlet** and sail to the town's star attraction, **Montague Island**, an offshore sanctuary for sea birds, seals and Little penguins 9km offshore; the Narooma Marina Centre (ⓣ02/4476 2126), on Riverside Drive, rents out kayaks and boats. If you want to actually disembark at the island, you'll have to go on a tour with Narooma Charters (3hr; $70; ⓣ0407 909 111, ⓦwww.naroomacharters.com.au; or book at the tourist office, see opposite), since it's a protected wildlife reserve. Morning tours include a nature walk on the island with an NPWS guide, whilst evening tours have time set aside to see the penguins come ashore (both $99/4hr). Scenic inlet cruises through the mangroves are available aboard the *Wagonga Princess* (Sun, Wed & Fri; 3hr; $30; ⓣ02/4476 2665, ⓦwww.wagongainletcruises.com; or book through the tourist office, see opposite), a charming little pine ferry very different from the usual glass-bottomed tourist hulks. **Diving** is available with several outfits, the best of which is Montague Island Diving (ⓣ02/4476 1741); you'll need to rent gear with Ocean Hut, 123 Princes Highway, if you don't have your own. If catching marine life is more your thing, try Island Charters (ⓣ02/4476 1047, ⓦwww.islandchartersnarooma.com) for reef and game fishing.

If you're in town around the end of September, don't miss the annual **Great Southern Blues and Rockabilly Festival** (ⓦwww.bluesfestival.tv).

Practicalities

Murray's Coaches and Transborder run to Narooma from Canberra and Batemans Bay, while Premier Motor Service buses stop here on their Sydney–Melbourne route. The **tourist office** (daily 9am–5pm; ⓣ02/4476 2881, ⓦwww.naturecoast-tourism.com.au) is on Campbell Street.

Accommodation

Ecotel 44 Princes Highway, on the northern side of the inlet ⓣ02/4476 2217, ⓦwww.ecotel.com.au. Good-value motel where everything is done with the environment in mind, so you can holiday and salve your conscience at the same time. ❸–❹

Narooma Surfbeach Resort Ballingalla St ⓣ02/4476 2275, ⓦwww.naroomagolf.com.au. Adjoins the much-celebrated Narooma Golf Club, the beach and a creek. It's spacious, well-situated, and far nicer than the caravan parks in town. Sites $25–30, cabins ❸–❻

Narooma YHA Backpackers On the Princes Highway south of town ⓣ02/4476 4440, ⓦwww.yha.com.au. A motel-style hostel offering dorms with a fridge, TV and kettle, plus a pleasant garden, sunny communal area and free bikes. Dorms $28, doubles $65

Pub Hill Farm Tourist Drive 4, just south of Narooma, then turn right onto Scenic Drive ⓣ02/4476 3177, ⓦwww.pubhillfarm.com. A further-flung option is this country-style B&B with four well-decorated en-suite rooms. It's extremely scenically situated, overlooking Mount Dromedary and Wagonga Inlet, and backs onto Punkallah Creek. ❹–❺

Eating

Casey's Café Cnr of Canty and Wagonga sts. A bright, cheery establishment, serving healthy, hearty food with many veggie options, giant smoothies and the best coffee in town. Daily 8am–4.30pm.

Lynch's Restaurant On the Princes Highway ⓣ02/4476 3002. Posh pub serving excellent contemporary Australian cuisine and local oysters. Daily from 6pm.

Pelicans Riverside Drive, by the marina ⓣ02/4476 2403. An upmarket, nautical-style option offering fancy breakfasts and lunches, plus excellent seafood in the evening, including Thai seafood lasagne and lemongrass swordfish. Tues–Thurs 8am–5pm, Fri & Sat 8am–late, Sun 8am–4pm.

Quarterdeck Marina Riverside Drive, by the marina ⓣ02/4476 2723. An eclectic and colourful restaurant with a great deck, good breakfast pancakes, and Oz-style tapas. Daily 8am–4pm.

Central Tilba and Tilba Tilba

Just off the highway 10km south of Narooma are the picturesque mountain villages of **CENTRAL TILBA** and **TILBA TILBA**. Central Tilba is by far the quaintest village on the south coast, set beautifully against the forested slopes of Mount Dromedary; with many an old timber shop selling art, fudge, jewellery and gourmet foodstuffs, it invariably gets packed at weekends. The area is also famous for its cheeses, and Central Tilba's hundred-year-old **ABC Cheese Factory** (daily 9am–5pm), on the main street, is open for visits and free tastings. The next logical step is some wine-tasting at **Tilba Valley Wines** (May–July & Sept Wed–Sun 11am–4pm; Oct–April daily 10am–5pm), signposted off the Princes Highway 5km north of Central Tilba on Tourist Drive 6; you can get to it via Central Tilba, but the road is unsealed and on the rough side. Situated on Corunna Lake, the winery provides an idyllic spot for a home-made lunch on the terrace, a game of croquet with the English owner, or to while away an evening listening to live jazz, soul and blues. If you're feeling energetic, follow the walking trail which starts from Pam's Store in Tilba Tilba, the smaller of the two villages but no less pretty. The track leads through a forest to the summit of **Mount Dromedary** (797m); the return walk is about 11km (allow 5–6hr).

The *Dromedary Hotel* (ⓣ02/4473 7223; ❸), on Bate Street in Central Tilba, is a historic pub with open fires; counter **meals** are served and **B&B** accommodation in plain, pretty rooms is available. *Two Story Bed and Breakfast* (ⓣ02/4473 7290, ⓦwww.tilbatwostory.com; ❹), also on Bate Street, is a delightful, deeply homely place, with tasteful chintzy decor and very friendly owners. A kilometre down Bate Street on the Tilba–Punkalla Road is *The Bryn* (ⓣ02/4473 7385,

ⓦ www.thebrynattilba.com.au; ⑤–⑥), a great B&B boasting bucolic views and a huge guest-lounge with a wood-burning stove. In Tilba Tilba, *Green Gables B&B* (ⓣ 02/4473 7435, ⓦ www.greengables.com.au; ⑤–⑥) is stylish, comfortable, and has gourmet breakfasts. Back on Bate Street, the *Rose & Sparrow Café* and *Tilba Teapot* offer scrumptious cream teas and light **meals**.

Wallaga Lake and around

Continuing south for a few kilometres along the main Princes Highway brings you to the turn-off to one of the best scenic detours along the coast, heading through Wallaga Lake to Tathra via **Bermagui**, 8km southeast from the highway. It's as pleasant a drive as you'll find in this area, crossing wooden bridges over pristine lagoons, traversing bush and beach. Nearby **Jingarra Trail Rides** (1hr for $30 or 4hr ride plus lunch $95; ⓣ 02/4473 7529, ⓦ www.jingarratrailrides.com), at the turn-off from the Princes Highway to Bermagui, run some excellent horse-riding trips.

Some 5km north of Bermagui on the road to Tathra lies **Wallaga Lake**, one of the largest saltwater lakes on the Australian coast. The area around the lake is home to a thriving local **Koorie** community, who run their own Umbarra Aboriginal Cultural Centre (Mon–Fri 9am–5pm, Sat & Sun 9am–4.30pm; free; ⓣ 02/4473 7232, ⓦ www.umbarra.com.au). The centre operates daily **tours** ($20–60) to local sacred sites, including Gulaga (Mount Dromedary) and Mystery Bay, with hands-on activities such as face painting with ochres, building bark huts, sampling bushtucker and traditional medicine ($7 per activity). They also run cruises on Wallaga Lake, a wild and lovely place where flocks of black swans and pelicans perch on the sand bars as the tide washes in and out. Further south on the road to Bermagui, in a terrific location backing onto the lake and 400m from the wild Camel Rock Beach is *Wallaga Lake Park* (ⓣ 02/6493 4655; sites $32–45, cabins ③–⑤). Not far south of Bermagui, unsealed tracks branch off the coast road to **Mimosa Rocks National Park**, where there are opportunities for bushwalking, camping and swimming – check the National Parks website (ⓦ www.nationalparks.nsw.gov.au) for details.

For a quieter alternative to the highway you can continue south along the coast road to Merimbula via the pleasant fishing village of **Tathra**, passing the coastal **Bournda National Park**, and many little art galleries and wineries en route.

Burnum Burnum: Aboriginal activist

Wallaga Lake is the birthplace of one of Australia's most important Aboriginal figureheads, the elder named **Burnum Burnum**, an ancestral name meaning "great warrior". He is best known for his flamboyant political stunts, which included planting the Aboriginal flag at Dover to claim England as Aboriginal territory in Australia's bicentennial year, in order to highlight the dispossession of his native country. He was born under a sacred tree by Wallaga Lake in January 1936. His mother died soon afterwards and he was taken by the Aborigines Protection Board and placed in a mission at Bomaderry, constituting one of the "stolen generation" of indigenous children removed from their families in this period. After graduating in law and playing professional rugby union for New South Wales, he became a prominent political activist in the 1970s. He was involved in various environmental and indigenous protests, including erecting the "tent embassy" outside the Federal Parliament in Canberra (see p.235), and standing twice, unsuccessfully, for the senate. Burnum Burnum died in August 1997 and his ashes were scattered near the tree where he was born.

Merimbula

The pretty town of **MERIMBULA** is surrounded by lagoons, lakes, rivers and ocean, making it ideal for watery endeavours or an evening stroll along the various shores. By day, you can explore Merimbula Lake (actually the wide mouth of the Merimbula River) and Pambula Lake with Merimbula Marina (Ⓣ02/6495 1686, Ⓦwww.merimbulamarina.com; or book through the tourist office, see p.249). They offer dolphin tours, boat rental, fishing charters, whale-watching tours (Sept–Nov & Feb–May) and cruises on *Sinbad* (2hr 30min; $25).

There are some good **dive** sites around town: the people to call are Merimbula Diver's Lodge (Ⓣ02/6495 3611, Ⓦwww.merimbuladiverslodge.com.au), who also run a comfy lodge at 15 Park St. You've a chance in a million of seeing a whale while you're under water, but it has happened. To see sharks and tropical fish that are firmly under control, check out the **aquarium** (daily 10am–5pm; $9.90; Ⓣ02/6495 4446, Ⓦwww.merimbulawharf.com.au) at the end of Lake Street.

Practicalities

You can get to Merimbula by **bus** on Premier Motor Service's Sydney–Eden run, and Countrylink, which links the town with Canberra, Cooma, Bega and Eden. The **tourist office** (daily 9am–5pm; Ⓣ02/6495 1129, Ⓦwww.sapphirecoast.com.au) on Beach Street can advise you of availability for all the accommodation in town.

Accommodation

There are dozens of **motels** (❹) and **holiday apartments** in Merimbula, all of which get booked up during the summer holidays, when many places hike their rates considerably and accept only weekly bookings.

Mandeni Resort Sapphire Coast Drive, 7km north from Merimbula on the road to Tathra Ⓣ02/6495 9644 or 1800 358 354, Ⓦwww.mandeni.com.au. Fully-equipped timber cottages in a bushland setting, sleeping up to six. Facilities include tennis courts, two swimming pools, a golf course, walking trails and, bizarrely, a needlecraft centre. Two-night minimum stay. ❺

Merimbula Beach Cabins 47–65 Short Point Rd Ⓣ02/6495 1216 or 1800 825 555, Ⓦwww.beachcabins.com.au. Spacious studios plus one- or two-bed cabins with inspiring ocean views, in a pleasant bushland setting overlooking Short Beach and Back Lake. Also has a pool and BBQ area. ❹–❺

Merimbula Beach Holiday Park 2 Short Point Rd Ⓣ02/6495 1269 or 1300 787 837, Ⓦwww.holidaypark.com.au. The nicest of several caravan parks in town, this one is scenically located in a breezy spot above the lovely Short Point Beach, and has a great pool. Good for families. Sites $28–32, cabins and villas. ❸–❽

Wandarrah Lodge YHA 8 Marine Parade Ⓣ02/6495 3503, Ⓦwww.yha.com.au. Modern, purpose-built youth hostel close to both the beach and lake, with good communal areas, ping pong, BBQ and bright, clean dorms. The very friendly owners take groups out to Ben Boyd National Park, or to see the 'roos at Pambula Beach on request. Dorms $29, doubles ❸

Eating

Limetree Café Just down from the tourist office. Funky joint serving good coffee and great lunchtime burgers, wraps and home-made cakes.

Sante Fe 23 Beach St. The chilli-fanatics here do Mexican-flavoured wood-fired pizzas and a few mains. Open daily for lunch & dinner.

Waterfront Café On the promenade by the tourist office. Smart place with good breakfasts and lunches, including the delicious coconut, lime and prawn salad.

Zanzibar Café Cnr of Market and Main sts Ⓣ02/6495 3636. Brand new restaurant in a very so-so location, but serving excellent Mod Oz food including the renowned Eden mussel chowder. Tues–Sat 6–9pm.

Eden and around

EDEN, on pretty Twofold Bay, is just about the last seaside stop before the Princes Highway heads south towards Victoria, and by far the nicest coastal village in the south. In 1818 the first **whaling station** on the Australian mainland was established here, and **whaling** remained a major industry until the 1920s. Today Eden is touristy in a quiet sort of way, with good fishing and plenty of reminders of the old days, including the excellent **Killer Whale Museum** (Mon–Sat 9.15am–3.45pm, Sun 11.15am–3.34pm; $6; Ⓦwww.killerwhalemuseum.com.au) on the main drag, Imlay Street. The star attraction is the huge skeleton of "Old Tom", who used to herd baleen whales into the bay then lead whaling boats towards the pods, in order to get his chops around the discarded bits of carcass. There's also plenty of old whale bones, boats, some interesting Aboriginal history, and a (literally) incredible account of a man being swallowed by a sperm whale and coming out alive fifteen hours later.

The busy main **wharf** in Snug Cove, at the bottom of Imlay Street, is a good place for a stroll, as are the two pretty **beaches**, Aslings and Cocora. Cat Balou Cruises (Ⓣ02/6496 2027, Ⓦwww.catbalou.com.au) is based at the main wharf, and offer two-hour dolphin-spotting tours ($30) plus whale-watching **cruises** (late Sept–late Nov; 3hr 30min; $65). Ocean Wilderness (Ⓣ02/6496 9066, Ⓦwww.oceanwilderness.com.au) run half-day **kayaking** adventures ($80), while Freedom Charters (Ⓣ02/6496 1209, Ⓦwww.freedomcharters.com.au) are the town's **fishing** specialists.

Heading south from Eden, you become increasingly surrounded by the vast temperate rainforests that characterize southeastern Australia. Roads lead off the highway to the east into the magnificent **Ben Boyd National Park**, which hugs the coast to the north and south of Eden, and offers good walking, beaches and bushcamping (bookings through Merimbula NPWS; Ⓣ02/6495 5000; $5 per adult per night). Inland, the summit of **Mount Imlay** can be reached via a walking track that starts at the picnic grounds on Burrawang Forest Road, 14km south of Eden (3hr return). The steep, strenuous ascent is rewarded by a panoramic view over the coast and across the dense forests of the hinterland onto the Monaro Plain.

Practicalities

Eden is easily accessible by **public transport**: Premier Motor Service's Sydney–Eden buses stop here, and Countrylink buses link the town with Canberra, Cooma, Bega and Merimbula. For information on the local area, or accommodation and activity bookings, call in at the **tourist office** (daily 9am–5pm; Ⓣ02/6496 1953, Ⓦwww.sapphirecoast.com.au) on the highway.

Accommodation

Cocora Cottage 2 Cocora St Ⓣ02/6496 1241, Ⓦwww.cocoracottage.com. Pretty, heritage-listed B&B with fine rooms, a cute garden bedecked with flowers, and a stunning sun-deck with views over the bay at the rear. 5–6

Crown & Anchor Inn 239 Imlay St Ⓣ02/6496 1017, Ⓦwww.crownandanchoreden.com.au. This little gem is the best B&B on the south coast, set in a beautiful, historic building packed with antique furniture. Most of the exceedingly comfy rooms have superlative ocean views, while breakfast is served on the back deck, overlooking the water. Complimentary champagne on arrival is offered by the lovely owners. 6

Eden Tourist Park Aslings Beach Rd Ⓣ02/6496 1139, Ⓦwww.edentouristpark.com.au. Peaceful, leafy park with Lake Curalo on one side, and Aslings Beach on the other. Sites $20–24, cabins 3–4

Heritage House Motel & Units 178 Imlay St Ⓣ02/6496 1657, Ⓦwww.heritagehouseunits.com. Pleasant motel rooms and one- or two-bed units right in the centre of Eden; it's all a cut above the usual motel fare, with some rooms boasting striking views over Twofold Bay. 5–6

Eating

All the good places to eat in Eden are down at the main wharf.

Snug Cove Café Good breakfasts plus focaccias, wraps and smoothies at lunchtime.
Taste of Eden Bright and breezy café serving breakfast and lunch at long wooden tables – seafood and mussels are a mainstay of the changing whiteboard menu.
Wharfside Café Great brekkies, including apple and banana fritters with ricotta and honey, as well as good coffee, gourmet salads and seafood lunches.
The Wheelhouse ⓣ02/6496 3392. An excellent, airy seafood restaurant which gets good reviews. Daily from 6pm.

The Snowy Mountains

The rounded, granite-strewn **Snowy Mountains** are just one section of the Australian Alps which sprawl from northeast Victoria via the Crackenback Range to the township of **Cooma**. Though it's a continuous massif, only the New South Wales section is strictly known as the Snowy Mountains. **Mount Kosciuszko**, at 2228m the highest mountain in Australia, is located close to the Victorian border in the far southeast – it was named in 1840 by the Polish-born explorer Paul Strzelecki, after the Polish freedom fighter General Tadeusz Kosciuszko. The **Kosciuszko National Park**, which surrounds the peak, includes most of the Snowy Mountains region and almost everything of interest.

Compared to the high mountain ranges of other continents, the "roof of Australia" is relatively low and, despite the name, the flattened mountaintops lie below the line of permanent snow. After heavy snowfalls in winter, however (roughly late June–early Oct), winter-sports fans congregate at the **ski resorts** in the Mount Kosciuszko area. The downhilling isn't world-class and the snow is rarely dry, but it's better than you might think, and if you're into back-country skiing, the Snowy Mountains offer a paradise of huge, empty valleys, snowgum forests and wildlife. In summer the towns and resorts are less crowded: Perisher and Mount Selwyn almost completely close down, but Thredbo operates ski-lifts throughout the year up to the mountaintops, from where you can bushwalk across the wildflower-covered high country. Other activities include mountain biking, horse trekking, fishing and white-water rafting in the crystal-clear mountain rivers.

△ Snowy Mountains

Skiing and snowboarding in the Snowy Mountains

The easiest option for **skiing in the Snowy Mountains** is to arrange a **ski package** departing from Sydney or Canberra – always check exactly what's included in the price. Be aware that snow conditions can let you down and that the resorts' interpretation of "good" conditions may not match yours, so check an independent source like the excellent Ⓦwww.ski.com.au (which also has links for accommodation) before you go.

Recommended operators include Ski One (Ⓣ02/6456 2022 or 1300 850 380, Ⓦwww.skione.net), who can put together a basic low-season weekend package, including transport by bus, national park entry, ski rental, lift pass and lessons, plus two nights' accommodation, dinner and breakfast for around $570; and Ski Kaos (Ⓣ02/9976 5555, Ⓦwww.skikaos.com.au) who offer weekend deals for $209 – you'll have to add food, lift pass and equipment onto this.

The longest **downhill runs** are at Thredbo, while the Perisher Valley/Mount Blue Cow/Smiggin Holes/Guthega complex (known as Perisher Blue; all one lift pass) is the largest and most varied; other resorts include Mount Selwyn and Charlotte Pass. If you have your own equipment and vehicle, and don't need a package, all the resorts have good websites detailing the myriad of lift pass prices and lift-and-lesson combos (Ⓦwww.thredbo.com.au, Ⓦwww.perisherblue.com.au, Ⓦwww.charlottepass.com.au and Ⓦwww.selwynsnow.com.au). Resorts are generally **child-friendly**, particularly at Charlotte Pass, where the homely and old-fashioned *Kosciuszko Chalet* (Ⓣ1800 026 369; ⑧) offers free childcare throughout the ski season. Paddy Pallin (Ⓣ02/6456 2922 or 1800 623 459), in Jindabyne, run all manner of cross-country ski trips, plus white-water rafting on the Murray River and mountain biking in summer.

Getting there and around

The **Snowy Mountains Highway** leads straight across the mountain ranges and through the national park from Cooma to Tumut. If you want to see more of the alpine scenery, head along the spectacular **Alpine Way**, turning off the highway at Kiandra in the heart of the park and heading via Khancoban to Thredbo. In winter, check road conditions before driving anywhere; **snow chains** must be carried by two-wheel drives between June and October, and roads might be closed altogether.

Bus services to and around the park are far more frequent in winter than in summer – a **rental car** is strongly recommended for summer sojourns or trips deep into the national park at any time of the year. Transborder Alpine Express links Canberra, Cooma, Jindabyne and Thredbo daily, while Greyhound run a similar service between June and late September. Additional winter-only bus services include the Adaminaby Bus Service shuttle between Cooma, Adaminaby and the Mount Selwyn ski resort. A number of small bus companies link Jindabyne and all the ski-fields in the winter – contact the tourist office in Jindabyne (see p.256) for details. Regional Express **flies** into the Snowy Mountains Airport at Cooma from Sydney.

Perisher Blue Skitube (Ⓣ02/6456 2010, Ⓦwww.perisherblue.com.au/winter/skitube; June to mid-Oct only; $25–53) is a **railway** under the mountains, linking the ski areas of Bullocks Flat, Perisher Valley and Mount Blue Cow. Autopia Tours (Ⓣ03/9419 8878 or 1800 000 507, Ⓦwww.autopiatours.com.au) operates a year-round Melbourne–Sydney four-day tour via the Alpine Way for $395.

Cooma

Although **COOMA** functions mainly as a service centre for skiers, it's a fairly attractive place in its own right, with a number of fine old buildings on Lambie and Vale streets in particular – the tourist office (see below) has a map of the "Lambie Town Walk", which takes you past places of note.

If you're interested in the history and technical details of the Snowy hydroelectric project, which utilizes the water of the area's rivers to provide electricity to the ACT, NSW and Victoria, check out the **Snowy Mountains Hydro Information Centre** (Mon–Fri 8am–5pm, Sat & Sun 9am–2pm; ⓦwww.snowyhydro.com.au), on the Monaro Highway in North Cooma. The long-established Yarramba Trail Rides (1hr; $40; ⓣ02/6453 7204, ⓦwww.yarramba.com.au) is located northwest of town on Dry Plains Road, on the way to Adaminaby.

Practicalities

The staff at the **tourist office** (daily 9am–5pm; ⓣ02/6450 1742 or 1800 636 525, ⓦwww.visitcooma.com.au) on the main road, Sharp Street, will just about vault over the counter in their eagerness to give you information about Kosciuszko National Park; they also offer an accommodation booking service and details of local farmstays, plus copies of the free monthly *Snowy Times*, which has detailed resort information, maps, and listings of skiing prices and packages.

Accommodation

Accommodation can be hard to come by during the ski season – try these places first.

Bunkhouse Motel 28–30 Soho St ⓣ02/6452 2983, ⓦwww.bunkhousemotel.com.au. Set around a pleasant central courtyard, this long-established, homely hostel and motel has a slightly Wild West feel to it. The wooden-walled dorms are chalet-cozy and the doubles adequate. Dorms $30, doubles ❸

Royal Hotel Cnr Lambie and Sharp sts ⓣ02/6552 2132. Fairly average rooms with shared bathrooms, most with French windows opening onto the pretty wrought-iron balcony. There's a bistro serving pub food attached. Singles ❶, doubles ❷

Snowtels Caravan Park 286 Sharp St ⓣ02/6452 1828, ⓦwww.snowtels.com.au. Probably the best of the town's campsites, but still fairly depressing. Sites $18–22, cabins ❷–❺

White Manor Motel 252 Sharp St ⓣ02/6452 1152, ⓦwww.whitemanor.com. Far pleasanter than the majority of motels, with large, bright rooms, an abundance of potted plants and a good helping of chintz. ❹–❺

Eating

The Lott 178 Sharp St. Bright, cushion-strewn café turning out good breakfasts and lunches.

Danielle's Above the tourist office. Colourful (some would say too much so) place doing light lunches plus pastas and Mod Oz mains in the evening. Tues–Sat lunch & dinner.

Rose's Lebanese Restaurant Massie St. Tasty, Middle Eastern food in slightly bland surrounds. Mon–Sat 11.30am–2.30pm & 6pm until late.

Thai Continental 76 Sharp St. Great-value $7 lunch specials and a long list of spicy Thai favourites in the evenings. Closed Mon.

Kosciuszko National Park and around

The largest national park in New South Wales, **Kosciuszko National Park** extends 200km north to south, encompassing an area of some 6500 square kilometres. The scenery includes ten peaks above 2100m, forested valleys and a beautiful plateau with glacial lakes and rivers. The main centres are the lakeside resort of **Jindabyne**, just outside the eastern boundary of the park, and the ski resort of **Thredbo**, 30km further west along the scenic Alpine Way and actually in the national park. The ski resorts of Perisher Valley and Mount Blue Cow can be reached via the Skitube from Bullocks Flat, roughly midway between Jindabyne and Thredbo, or you can get to them by driving round the slightly hairy Kosciuszko Road from Jindabyne, passing Smiggin Holes on the way and

Bushwalking in the park

Some of Australia's most interesting and beautiful **bushwalking tracks** pass through the area. You might see echidnas, wombats or even a heavyweight 'roo crashing through the powder, between beautiful snowgums with multicoloured bark in greens and yellows. One of the most accessible of routes is the walking trail to the top of **Mount Kosciuszko**. The **chairlift** from Thredbo (see below) will take you up to Crackenback Station on the edge of the plateau, where you begin the 6.5-kilometre walk to the summit, stopping at the **Mount Kosciuszko Lookout** after 2km for panoramic views – from here Australia's highest peak seems barely higher than the surrounding country. The **altitude** at the top of the chairlift will have you struggling to catch your breath for a moment, and it can be minus five up here even in summer, so check conditions at the bottom. Perhaps the best hike in the park is the main range walk from Charlotte Pass to the lovely Blue Lake, and then up Kosciuszko via more glacial lakes. Alternatively, take the **Skitube** from Bullocks Flat on the Alpine Way to Perisher Valley and Mount Blue Cow (which has a bistro and art gallery), where more fine trails await. For more ideas, check out the huge map outside the Valley Terminal at Thredbo.

finishing up at Charlotte Pass. To the north, the **Yarrangobilly Caves** are well worth the long drive.

The **entry fee** to the park is a hefty $27 per car per 24hr in winter, or $16 in summer; the recent price hike on the cost of an NSW annual park pass ($190) means it's only worth forking out for the yearly ticket if you intend to spend a good chunk of time here in the snow season. You can buy passes online, over the phone (see p.254 for both) or at the visitor entrance station on the Alpine Way between Jindabyne and Thredbo. Arriving by bus, you'll still have to make a one-off payment of $11.45 ($6.60 in summer). The **Snowy Region Visitor Centre** (daily: March–Nov 8.30am–5.30pm; Dec–Feb 8.30am–5pm; ⓣ02/6450 5600) in Jindabyne is the park's main tourist office, and has details of walking trails, ranger-guided tours and campsites, as well as a useful free map and a good café. There are also NPWS **ranger stations** at Perisher Valley (ⓣ02/6457 5214), Khancoban (ⓣ02/6076 9373), Yarrangobilly (ⓣ02/6454 9597) and Tumut (ⓣ02/6947 7025).

Jindabyne and Thredbo

A scenic settlement at the man-made lake of the same name, **JINDABYNE**, 63km west of Cooma, is the jumping-off point for the national park's ski resorts. The town itself is entirely new, having been relocated when the Snowy Mountains Scheme dammed the Snowy River and drowned the first settlement. There's good fishing on the lake and in summer you can also swim and sail – equipment is available to rent in the town.

From Jindabyne, the Alpine Way continues into the national park and runs through **THREDBO**, an attractive, bustling little village, squeezed into a narrow valley beside the road and the Crackenback River, with alpine-style houses huddled against the mountainside. Unlike the other resorts, it's also reasonably lively in summer and – with its Crackenback **chairlift** giving easy access to the high country – makes a good base for bushwalking. The chairlift (daily 8.30am–4pm; $26 return) originates in the Valley Terminal, which is also a one-stop shop for all the activities in town, including rock-climbing, golf, tennis, guided walks and bobsledding. **Mountain biking** down the ski runs is amazingly popular in summer, given the steepness of the slopes; if this need for speed afflicts you, Raw NRG (ⓣ02/6457 6282, ⓦwww.rawnrg.com.au), based at the Jindabyne end of the village, will be able to kit you out with bikes and body armour. Across the wooden footbridge from the Valley Terminal in the Village Square complex, the small **tourist office** (daily: winter 8.30am–6pm; summer 9am–5pm; ⓣ02/6459 4100, ⓦwww.thredbo.com.au) deals with enquiries – all the village's shops, eateries and services are clustered just behind here. There are several annual events in the Thredbo calendar. Musical highlights include the **Thredbo Blues Festival** (ⓦwww.thredboblues.com) in mid-January, the **Global Music Festival** in March, and the **Thredbo Jazz Festival** (ⓦwww.thredbojazz.com) in early May.

Yarrangobilly Caves

The **Yarrangobilly Caves**, a vast system of about sixty limestone caves at the edge of a rocky plateau surrounded by unspoiled bushland, are one of the few specific sights in the park; they're located 6.5km off the Snowy Mountains Highway near Kiandra, 109km northwest of Cooma and 77km south of Tumut. There are guided tours daily to the **Jersey** (1pm; $13) and **Jillabenan** (11am & 3pm; same price) **caves**. A third cave, the **South Glory Cave** (daily 9am–4pm; $10.50), can be explored on a self-guided tour. From walking trails along the edge of the rock plateau there are panoramic views of the Yarrangobilly Gorge, and a steep trail leads from the Glory Hole car park to a **thermal pool** at the bottom of the gorge near the Yarrangobilly River. The spring-fed pool, which you can swim in (free), has a constant year-round temperature of 27°C.

National Park accommodation

In winter **rooms** are almost impossible to come by without a reservation; minimum stays are enforced and **prices** more than double (all prices listed below are for this season). In summer the situation is less dire, and you should have little difficulty finding somewhere in one of the resorts, or at motels on the fringes of the park. Most accommodation in Thredbo can be **booked** through the Thredbo Resort Centre above the tourist office (same contact details, see above) or Thredbo Accommodation Services (ⓣ1300 801 982, ⓦwww.thredboproperties.com.au); the Snowy River Visitors Centre in Jindabyne (ⓣ02/6450 5600) also handles accommodation bookings. There's a couple of beautiful **bushcamping** sites at Thredbo Diggins and Ngarigo, between Thredbo and Jindabyne on the Alpine Way (contact the Snowy River Visitor Centre for details).

Budget

Kosciuszko Mountain Retreat Sawpit Creek, near the visitor entrance station on the Alpine Way ⓣ02/6456 2224, ⓦwww.kositreat.com.au. Beautiful, tranquil campsite set amongst a snowgum forest; kangaroos are regular visitors. Sites $25–35, cabins ❹–❻

Snowline Caravan Park Junction of Alpine Way and Kosciuszko Rd, Jindabyne ⓣ02/6456 2099, ⓦwww.snowline.com.au. Right on the lakeshore, this excellent campsite has the cheapest dorms in town, as well as a spa, sauna, European café-restaurant, tennis courts and boat rental. Dorms $28, sites $32–36, cabins ❸–❻

Snowy Mountain Backpackers 7–8 Gippsland St, Jindabyne ⓣ1800 333 468, ⓦwww.snowybackpackers.com.au. Pleasant hostel with clean, light dorms that's a good deal cheaper than the YHA in Thredbo. The kitchen and common area with comfy sofas are fantastic, and there's a good café, massage and full disabled access. Dorms $44, doubles ❺

Thredbo YHA Lodge 8 Jack Adams Pass, Thredbo ⓣ02/6457 6376, ⓦwww.yha.com.au. Central, purpose-built hostel with cozy open fires, comfy communal areas and great views across the mountains. Unfortunately for backpackers, in peak season this must be the most expensive hostel in Australia with room to spare. Dorms $75, doubles ❻

Moderate and expensive

Bimble Gumbie 942 Alpine Way, Crackenback, between Jindabyne and Thredbo ⓣ02/6456 2185, ⓦwww.bimblegumbie.com.au.

The most characterful place in the mountains by a very long way, a tranquil cluster of eclectically decorated farmhouses set in sculpture-filled bushland, overflowing with art from every continent and century. The shelves are full of books, you can bring your dog to the property and brekkie is included. Excellent value, and not to be missed. ❺–❽

Crackenback Farm Alpine Way, between Jindabyne and Thredbo ⓣ02/6456 2198, ⓦwww.crackenback.com.au. Plush loft rooms in a very cozy farmhouse with indoor pool, sauna, day-spa, full-sized billiard table and the obligatory roaring fires. The contemporary restaurant here is one of the best in the region, and the bar boasts Australia's largest collection of schnapps. ❻–❽

The Denman Diggings Terrace, Thredbo ⓣ02/6457 6222, ⓦwww.thedenman.com.au. Smart boutique hotel in the heart of the village with minimalist, upmarket rooms, a swanky cocktail bar, day-spa and *The Terrace*, an award-winning restaurant. Breakfast is included, and dinner packages are available. ❽

Kasees Lodge 4 Banjo Drive, Thredbo ⓣ02/6457 6370, ⓦwww.kasees.com.au. An excellent guesthouse centred around the very cozy, European-style guest lounge, which has a piano for après-ski singalongs. The eight large rooms have the best mountain views in town. ❽

The north coast

The coast from Sydney **north to Queensland** is more densely populated and much more touristy than its southern counterpart, with popular holiday destinations such as **Port Stephens**, **Port Macquarie**, and **Coffs Harbour** strung along the coast north of Newcastle. Since the 1970s, the area around **Byron Bay** has been a favoured destination for people seeking an alternative lifestyle; this movement has left in its wake not only disillusioned hippie farmers (as well as a few who've survived with their illusions intact), but also a firmly established artistic and alternative scene.

As in the south, the **coastline** consists of myriad inlets, bays and coastal lakes, interspersed by white, sandy beaches and rocky promontories. Parallel to the coast are the rocky plateaus of the **Great Dividing Range**, whose national parks provide bushwalkers with remote, rugged terrain to explore. Numerous streams tumble down from the escarpment in mighty waterfalls, creating fertile river valleys where the predominant agricultural activity is cattle breeding; in the north, subtropical and tropical agriculture takes over, especially the cultivation of bananas. In essence, the further you go, the better this coast gets.

Getting up the north coast is easy, with frequent **train** and **bus** services between Sydney and Brisbane, as well as a number of local bus services (detailed within individual town accounts and on p.301).

Port Stephens

Just north of Newcastle, the wide bay of **Port Stephens**, which extends inland for some 25km, offers calm waters and numerous coves ideal for swimming, watersports and fishing, while the ocean side has good surf and wide, sandy beaches. In January, thousands of families arrive to take their annual holiday in the area dubbed "Blue Water Paradise". The main township of **NELSON BAY** is perched at the tip of the bay's southern arm, together with the quieter settlements of Shoal Bay, Soldiers Point, Fingal Bay and Anna Bay. Stockton Beach, to the south, has the largest sand dunes in the eastern Australian mainland. Moonshadow 4WD Tours (ⓣ02/4984 4760, ⓦwww.moonshadow4wd.com.au), 35 Stockton St, Nelson Bay, run trips to the giant slopes – try sandboarding across or driving down in a 4WD; the black, metallic pyramids rising out of the sand (World War II anti-tank defences) give the experience a sci-fi twist.

From May to November you might see **whales** as they migrate first north then south, while **dolphin cruises** are available all year round; try Moonshadow Cruises (1hr 30min; $21; ⓣ02/4984 9388, ⓦwww.moonshadow.com.au;) in Nelson Bay or Simba II Cruises (3hr; $25; ⓣ02/4997 1084) at Tea Gardens, at the end of the bay's northern arm, who also run a ferry service across to Nelson Bay ($20 return). Much more satisfying than a motor cruise, though, are the eco-friendly trips aboard a fifteen-metre catamaran run by Imagine Cruises (dolphin cruise 1hr 30min, $22; whale-and-dolphin cruise in season 3hr, $55; ⓣ02/4984 9000, ⓦwww.imaginecruises.com.au) out of Nelson Bay. To get amongst the dolphins and other marine life contact Pro Dive (ⓣ02/4981 4331, ⓦwww.prodivenelsonbay.com) at the d'Albora Marina in Nelson Bay. You can **surf**, go **horse-trekking**, **parasail**, **sea-kayak** and rent jet skis all around the bay; contact the tourist office or look on their excellent website (see below) for details.

Practicalities

Getting around the bay is easiest if you have your own vehicle, though Busways call at Tea Gardens en route between Sydney and Taree, and Greyhound and Premier Motor Service stop at Karuah, midway around the bay. Port Stephens Coaches (ⓦwww.pscoaches.com.au) links all the smaller beach settlements with Nelson Bay, and runs an express service from Sydney and Newcastle. The **tourist office** (daily 9am–5pm; ⓣ02/4980 6900 or 1800 808 900, ⓦwww.portstephens.org.au) is at Victoria Parade in Nelson Bay, and offers an accommodation, tour and cruise booking service.

Accommodation-wise, there are scores of motels (❹-❺) and even more holiday apartments to choose from in the area, though many insist on weekly bookings during the holiday season – the tourist office will be able to help you out if you find yourself homeless.

Halifax Holiday Park Beach Rd, Little Beach, 2km east of Nelson Bay ⓣ02/4981 1522 or 1800 600 201, ⓦwww.beachsideholidays.com.au. A well-equipped beachside campsite with camp kitchen, BBQ area and kids activities. Sites $32, cabins ❹–❻

Melaleuca Surfside Backpackers 2 Koala Place, One Mile Beach ⓣ02/4982 1248, ⓦwww.melaleucabackpackers.com.au. Tree-house-style timber bungalows, camping and dorms set in tranquil bushland roamed by koalas and possums. A great option, especially as it's only minutes from an excellent surf beach. Sites $14pp, dorms $25, doubles ❸

Nelson Bay B&B 81 Stockton St, Nelson Bay ⓣ02/4984 3655, ⓦwww.nelsonbaybandb.com.au. Bright, architect-designed B&B with three good queen rooms, ten minutes' walk from town. ❺–❻

Samurai Beach Bungalows YHA Frost Rd, Anna Bay ⓣ02/4982 1921, ⓦwww.yha.com.au. Set in rainforest, this is the best budget option in the area, with four bungalows – and resident possum – arranged around an undercover "bush" kitchen. There are free boards and bikes, a nice pool and a BBQ area. Port Stephens Buses from Sydney stop outside. Dorms $26, doubles ❸–❹

Myall Lakes National Park and around

From Port Stephens the Pacific Highway continues north past the beautiful **Myall Lakes National Park**, which well rewards a day or so of exploration.

About 20km before the small town of **Bulahdelah**, turn right onto Tea Gardens Road for a heavenly drive to **Mungo Brush**, along the shores of Myall Lake. There are plenty of gentle walking tracks around here, while a more challenging 21-kilometre hike leads back to **Hawks Nest**, on Port Stephens Bay. Just after Mungo Brush, the charming Bombah Point Ferry takes you and your car over Myall Lake (daily 8am–6pm; every 30min; $4) and back to Bulahdelah and the highway via the unsealed Bombah Point Road.

Heading north again towards Forster–Tuncurry, you can turn east just after Bulahdelah onto the extremely scenic **Lakes Way** (tourist drive 6). A short distance away, at Bungwahl, a turn-off leads down mostly unsealed roads to **SEAL ROCKS**, a remote, unspoilt fishing village and the only settlement in the **national park**. The first beach you come to, the thoughtfully named Number One Beach, is truly beautiful, with crystal-clear waters marooned between two headlands. Two minutes to the south, there are great waves for surfing. **Sugar Loaf Point Lighthouse** is around ten minutes' walk up a steep path; the grounds offer fantastic 360-degree views, and the lookout below leads down to a deserted, rocky beach. Seal Rocks' seasonal agglomerations of nurse sharks make it one of the best **dive sites** in New South Wales; contact Forster Dive Centre (see below) to arrange a trip.

North of Seal Rocks, the exhilarating drive through the tiny **Booti Booti National Park** takes you through endless forests, over a narrow spit of land between Wallis Lake and Elizabeth Bay where it's hard to keep your eyes on the road, especially at sunset. Ten kilometres further north, a bridge connects the twin holiday towns of **FORSTER–TUNCURRY**, the former set on the strip of land separating **Wallis Lake** from the ocean. The lake is very pretty, but Forster itself decidedly isn't, being somewhat blighted by high-rise development. It's a good base for all manner of cruises and watersports though, and famous for its **oysters** and playful resident **dolphins** – Amaroo Cruises (2hr; $40; ⓣ0419 333 445, ⓦwww.amaroocruises.com.au), at the end of Memorial Drive, run daily dolphin-watching trips. Forster Dive Centre (ⓣ02/6555 4477, ⓦwww.forsterdivecentre.com.au), at 15 Little St, arrange **diving trips** at Seal Rocks, while the nearby Boatshed Number One (ⓣ02/6554 7733) rents out boats, canoes and wave skis. For non water-babies, Tobwabba Gallery (Mon–Fri 9am–5pm in theory if not always in practice; free; ⓦwww.tobwabba.com.au) on Breckenbridge Street has some great traditional art.

Practicalities

To explore the Myall Lakes National Park in your own time you really need a vehicle, although Busways runs along the Lake Way to Bungwahl. Greyhound and Premier Motor Service **buses** both serve Forster, with Greyhound also stopping at Bulahdelah. The well-organized **tourist office** (daily 9am–5pm; ⓣ02/6554 8799 or 1800 802 692, ⓦwww.greatlakes.org.au), on Little Street in Forster, is responsible for the Myall Lakes area and offers an accommodation booking service.

Wharf Street, the main strip in Forster, has numerous cafés, restaurants and takeaways; nearby on waterfront Memorial Drive is *Bella Bellissimo*, the best place to **eat** in town, offering gourmet pizza, pastas and risottos, and a buzzy atmosphere at both lunch and dinner. If you want to **stay** in the area overnight, bushcamping in the Myall Lakes is an attractive option; check the national parks website (ⓦwww.nationalparks.nsw.gov.au) for listings. There are scores of holiday apartments and motels (❹–❺) in Forster.

Forster Caravan Park Reserve Rd, Forster ⓣ02/6554 6269, ⓦwww.escapenorth.com.au/forstercaravanpark. Centrally located tourist park overlooking the marina, and less tacky than the ones on the southern approach to the town. Spotless amenities, playground and beach frontage. Sites $29, cabins ❸–❻

Forster YHA 43 Head St, Forster ⓣ02/6555 8155, ⓦwww.yha.com.au. This functional backpackers' isn't one of Australia's best but it's just three minutes' walk from the main beach, and has free boogie-boards and a BBQ area. Dorms $25, doubles ❸

Myall Shores Ecotourism Resort Right by the Bombah Point Ferry on the northern side of the lake (see opposite), 16km southeast of Bulahdelah ⓣ02/4997 4495, ⓦwww.myallshores.com.au. Beautifully located, tranquil resort boasting stylish waterfront villas, cabins, a few bunks, camping and a good café-restaurant, plus canoe and boat rental. The best option in the national park by far if you don't like to stay under canvas. Sites $26, bunks ❷, cabins and villas ❹–❽

Seal Rocks Camping Reserve Seal Rocks ⓣ02/4997 6164 or 1800 112 234, ⓦwww.sealrockscampingreserve.com.au. Glorious, unspoilt site right on the beautiful Number One Beach, with basic facilities. Although there's a small general store in the settlement, you should bring supplies in with you. *Treachery Camp* is a couple of minutes' drive around the headland if it's full here. Sites $22–25, cabins ❾–❺

Sundowner Tiona Tourist Park The Lakes Way, 19km south of Forster ⓣ1800 636 452, ⓦwww.sundownerholidays.com. Beautiful location right on Seven Mile Beach, in the Booti Booti National Park, plus good facilities, some backpacker accommodation and nice cabins. Sites $28–32, dorms $22.50, cabins ❹–❽

Barrington Tops and Ellenborough Falls

Heading from Forster–Tuncurry via Nabiac and Gloucester, you arrive at the World Heritage–listed **Barrington Tops National Park** (ⓦwww.barringtons.com.au). It's gentle, hilly farming country up to the country town of **Gloucester**; about 40km beyond here, unsealed roads lead through the park. The closest you'll get to the park with public transport is on the train from Sydney or Newcastle to Gloucester or Dungog; *The Barringtons Country Retreat* (see below) offers free pick-ups from the latter.

The Barrington Tops themselves are two high, cliff-ringed plateaus, **Barrington** and **Gloucester**, which rise steeply from the surrounding valleys. The changes in altitude within the park are so great – the highest point is 1586m – that within a few minutes you can pass from areas of subtropical rainforest to high, windswept plateaus covered with snow gums, meadows and subalpine bog. Up on the plateau, snow is common from the end of April to early October.

The **Great Lakes Visitors Centre** in Forster (see opposite) can help with specific routes or organized 4WD tours into the national park. There are plenty of picnic grounds, walking trails and scenic **lookouts** in the park. A 4WD is often required to access the many **campsites** (often free): check out the national parks website (ⓦwww.nationalparks.nsw.gov.au) or contact the NPWS in Gloucester (ⓣ02/ 6538 5300) or Scone (ⓣ02/6540 2300) for locations and advice. The other **accommodation** in the area is relatively pricey, but there are lots of options. One of the closest places to the park itself is *Salisbury Lodges* (ⓣ02/4995 3285, ⓦwww.salisburylodges.com.au; ❻), at 2930 Salisbury Rd in Salisbury, 40km northwest of Dungog. This wilderness retreat is perfect for a cozy country weekend and has lovely timber lodges, a great restaurant and a gorgeous rainforest setting. A slightly cheaper alternative is *The Barringtons Country Retreat* (ⓣ02/4995 9269, ⓦwww.thebarringtons.com.au; ❺–❽) on Chichester Dam Road, 23km north of Dungog, whose cabins and lodges boast log fires and corner spa baths.

Heading north to Port Macquarie via Gloucester and Wingham, you can call at the two-hundred-metre-high **Ellenborough Falls**, one of the most spectacular waterfalls on the whole coast; the falls are located near Elands on Bulga Forest Drive – unsealed for much of the way.

Port Macquarie and around

The fast-growing town of **PORT MACQUARIE**, at the mouth of the Hastings River, has a beautiful natural setting. Long, sandy **beaches** extend far along the coast, while the hinterland is dotted with forests, mountains and pretty towns. The town was established in 1821 as a place of secondary punishment

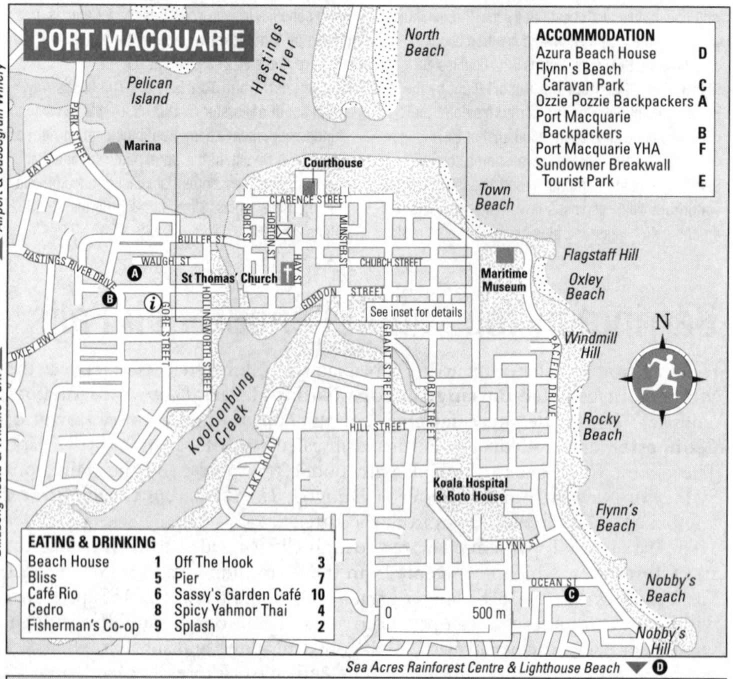

PORT MACQUARIE

ACCOMMODATION

Azura Beach House	D
Flynn's Beach Caravan Park	C
Ozzie Pozzie Backpackers	A
Port Macquarie Backpackers	B
Port Macquarie YHA	F
Sundowner Breakwall Tourist Park	E

EATING & DRINKING

Beach House	1	Off The Hook	3
Bliss	5	Pier	7
Café Rio	6	Sassy's Garden Café	10
Cedro	8	Spicy Yahmor Thai	4
Fisherman's Co-op	9	Splash	2

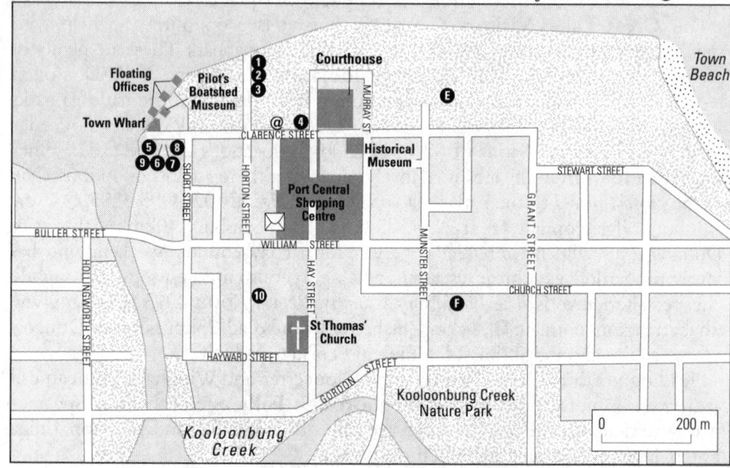

for convicts who continued their criminal ways after arrival in New South Wales, though by the late 1820s the **penal settlement** was closed and the area opened up to free settlers. An increasing number of backpackers call into "Port", but it remains primarily a family resort, albeit one which is pushing steadily upmarket. The **activities** on offer are really the thing here, with mini-zoos, nature parks, cruises on the Hastings River, horse riding and, above all, watersports and fishing outlets all vying for your attention.

Arrival and information

Greyhound and Premier Motor Service stop at Port Macquarie on their runs between Sydney and Brisbane, while Kean's run to Tamworth, Nambucca Heads and Coffs Harbour. **Buses** drop you in the centre of town on Hayward Street, although not all make the detour from the Pacific Highway, so check carefully. Countrylink **trains** stop in Wauchope, 22km to the west, from where there's a connecting bus service. You can **fly** to Port Macquarie from Sydney with Qantas; the airport is about 6km west of town.

Horton Street is the main downtown street, running north to the Hastings River. The helpful **tourist office** (Mon–Fri 8.30am–5pm, Sat & Sun 9am–4pm; ⓣ02/6581 8000 or 1300 303 155, ⓦwww.portmacquarieinfo.com.au), just out of the CBD on the corner of Gore and Gordon streets, can book rooms and activities. The town's attractions and beaches are far flung, and local transport isn't the best. You can **get around** much of town on Busways (ⓣ02/6583 2499, ⓦwww.busways.com.au), but the best option is **cycling** (see p.265).

Accommodation

Despite the huge number of motels and apartments in town, Port can still get booked out in the summer, so it's best to make reservations in advance – out of season, prices drop dramatically. The tourist office can book you an apartment, but the motels are all pretty similar, so outside peak time just cruise around town to see which takes your fancy. All three backpackers' do free pick-ups from the coach stop.

Azura Beach House 109 Pacific Drive ⓣ02/6582 2700, ⓦwww.azura.com.au. A truly lovely little B&B close to Shelly Beach. Four modern, stylish rooms with balconies, pool, BBQ and comfy guest-lounge fitted out with books and films. The very considerate hosts provide picnics on request and rustle up very nice breakfasts on the beautiful wooden veranda, overlooking rainforest. Complimentary travel transfers. ⑤

Flynn's Beach Caravan Park 22 Ocean St, 2.5km from the centre ⓣ02/6583 5754, ⓦwww.flynnsbeachcaravanpark.com.au. Excellent eco-friendly site just 200m from Flynn's Beach, with a range of cabins set in a forest of ferns and gum trees, pool and BBQ areas. Sites $31–38, cabins ⑤

Ozzie Pozzie Backpackers 36 Waugh St ⓣ02/6583 8133 or 1800 620 020, ⓦwww.ozziepozzie.com. Friendly, colourfully decorated place set around a small central courtyard, with standard dorms, free boogie-boards, bikes for $5, BBQ area and free muesli for breakfast. Dorm $26, doubles ③

Port Macquarie Backpackers 2 Hastings River Drive, cnr Gordon St ⓣ02/6583 1791 or 1800 688 882, ⓦwww.portmacquariebackpackers.com.au. Great hostel in an 1888 Victorian Gothic weather-boarded building, instantly recognizable by the globe outside. Colourful, comfy dorms, fine communal areas, pool and BBQ area, plus a fun atmosphere. The enthusiastic ex-backpacker owner runs kangaroo camping trips to the beautiful Crowdy Bay National Park, and there's free use of bikes, surfboards and fishing gear. Dorms $27, doubles ③

Port Macquarie YHA 40 Church St ⓣ02/6583 5512, ⓦwww.yha.com.au. Very compact and very yellow YHA in a quiet part of town, with an atmosphere to match. Nice dorms and ok communal areas are supplemented by free boogie-boards, bikes ($5), and a small outdoor area. Dorms $27, doubles ③, family rooms ④

Sundowner Breakwall Tourist Park 1 Munster St, on the riverfront ⓣ02/6583 2755 or 1800 636 452, ⓦwww.sundownerholidays.com. Right in the heart of town next to the river, this family-oriented site is superbly located and feels roomy despite the number of cottages and cabins packed into it. Lots of activities – including surf trips – are offered in case the pool and kids club lose their appeal. Dorms $25, sites $35–$42, cabins and cottages ⑤–⑧

The Town and around

Port Macquarie has a tendency to destroy reminders of its past, though a few early buildings survive (you can get a historic-walk leaflet at the tourist office). The **Historical Museum** (Mon–Sat 9.30am–4.30pm; $5), opposite the courthouse, illuminates early life in the penal settlement, and houses a rather gruesome convict whipping stool complete with fake blood that should frighten the kids into good behaviour. The main **Maritime Museum** (daily 10am–4pm; $4) at 6 William St contains the usual mix of nautical artefacts and model boats, while its outpost, the **Pilots Boatshed Museum** (Mon–Fri 10am–2pm), at the far western end of Clarence Street, can book cruises on the MV *Wentworth* (Tues & Thurs 10.30am/1pm; 1hr/2hr; $15/10).

The river foreshore, with its anglers and pelican colony, is a pleasant place for a peaceful sunset stroll or to grab some fish and chips. Floating offices where you can book anything from dolphin tours to seaplane flights are located along its western end, towards the town wharf (see "Listings", opposite). Midway down, near the northern end of Horton Street, you can step aboard the **Alma Doepel** (daily 9am–dusk; $3; ⓦwww.almadoepel.com.au), a wonderfully restored timber sailing ship.

Perhaps the best attraction in the town centre, however, is the **Kooloonbung Creek Nature Park**, a large bushland reserve remarkably close to the CBD. From the entrance at the corner of Horton and Gordon streets, you can step onto trails among casuarinas, eucalypts and swampy mangroves, visit a cemetery containing the graves of eminent early settlers, or sweat through a small patch of rainforest – were it not for the boardwalks and faint hum of traffic, it'd be amazingly easy to believe that you were lost in the bush.

A string of fine beaches run down the ocean-facing side of town (Town, Flynn's and Lighthouse are patrolled); perhaps the best way to spend a day in Port Macquarie is to rent a bike and explore the cliff-top paths and roads that link them all. You can call in at the **Sea Acres Rainforest Centre** (daily 9am–4.30pm; free guided walks at regular intervals; $6), south of the town on Pacific Drive, on the way – the impressive centre houses three different types of rainforest, which can be inspected at close quarters from a boardwalk.

Back towards the town centre on Lord Street, in the grounds of **Roto House**, is Australia's oldest **koala hospital** (daily 8am–4.30pm; free; guided tour 3pm; feeding times 8am & 3pm; ⓦwww.koalahospital.org) – you can even adopt one of the "patients" if you get particularly attached. For yet more cuddly creatures, the **Billabong Koala & Wildlife Park** (daily 9am–5pm; koala petting at 10.30am, 1.30 & 3.30pm; $15) at 61 Billabong Drive, off the Oxley Highway west of the town centre, has emu chicks, kangaroos, monkeys, koalas and an assortment of reptiles.

You'll find the **wines** produced at Cassegrain Winery (daily 9am–5pm; ⓦwww.cassegrain.com), on Fernbank Creek Road, off the Pacific Highway west of town, on many a wine list in the area; the award-winning restaurant here, *Ça Marche* (daily noon–3pm & Fri 6–9pm; ⓣ02/6582 8320, ⓦwww.camerche.com.au), is a great spot for a long lunch overlooking the vineyards.

Eating and drinking

There are a growing number of good, innovative places to **eat** in town. You can buy fresh fish and seafood for the BBQ from the **Fishermen's Co-op**, by the town wharf. Where a phone number is listed, it's best to book.

Beach House Horton St. Unquestionably the best location in town, this large bar is the perfect place for breakfast, a long lunch, or best of all, early-evening drinks that you can soak up with a gourmet pizza or pasta. The decor and ambience don't quite live up to the river views, but there aren't many complaints from the many punters who pack it out in summer.

Bliss 74 Clarence St ⓣ02/6584 1422, ⓦwww.blissrestaurant.com. The sunset views across the river at this stylish, upmarket eaterie are blissful indeed, and the imaginative Mod Oz and Southeast Asian fusion dishes only add to the effect. Daily from 6.30pm & Sun–Fri 11.30am–2.30pm.

Café Rio 74 Clarence St ⓣ02/6583 3933. Chilled by day, buzzing by night, this cheerfully decorated open-fronted café does wraps, burgers, pasta and sandwiches for lunch and more upmarket fare in the evening. Daily 10.30am–8.30pm.

Cedro Cnr Clarence and Short sts. The enticing breakfast menu here includes ricotta hotcakes with banana, walnuts and maple syrup, while at lunch Dr Seuss fans can enjoy green eggs and ham, the grassy hue in this case created by green chillis, peppers and coriander – you can eat in the minimalist interior, or at sunny outdoor tables. Daily 7.30am–2.30pm.

Off The Hook Horton St. Catchily named takeaway serving the best fish and chips in town, handily located thirty seconds from the river.

Pier 2/72 Clarence St. Large, airy bar with an impressive range of Belgian and European designer beers on tap, and filled with a young, trendy sort of crowd at night. The casual, attached café is open for breakfast, lunch and dinner.

Spicy Yahmor Thai Corner of Clarence and Hay sts ⓣ02/6583 9043. Busy local Thai serving good-value favourites including red, green and yellow curries, stir-fries and Thai salads. Daily from 5.30pm.

Splash 3/2 Horton St ⓣ02/6584 4027, ⓦwww.restaurantsplash.com. A new arrival and already established as one of Port's best restaurants, this upmarket place has a fresh blue interior and a large outdoor dining area overlooking the river. The delicious, Mod Oz menu is notable for its extensive range of oysters and a well-thought-out wine list. Mon–Fri lunch & Mon–Sat dinner.

Listings

Bike rental Graham Seers Cyclery, Shop 2 Port Marina, Bay St ⓣ02/6583 2333. $30/half-day or $40/full day.

Boat rental The Settlement Point Boatshed (ⓣ02/6583 6300), 2km north of the CBD next to the Settlement Point Ferry (follow Park St north over the road bridges), rents out canoes (singles $6/hr, doubles $10/hr) and a range of boats ($10/1hr up to $85/full day).

Camel safaris Port Macquarie Camel Safaris ⓣ02/6585 5996. Half-hour ($23) or hour-long rides ($45) from Lighthouse Beach (daily except Mon & Thurs). The longer ride needs to be pre-booked at least a day in advance.

Car rental Hertz, Gordon St ⓣ02/6583 6599; Thrifty, corner of Horton and Hayward sts ⓣ02/6584 2122.

Cruises Port Macquarie Cruise Adventures, river foreshore ⓣ02/6583 8483 or 1300 555 890, ⓦwww.cruiseadventures.com.au. Prices range from $15 for a short sunset cruise (1hr 30min) to $69 for a trip to the Everglades rainforest (5hr 30min).

Diving Rick's Dive School ⓣ02/6584 7759.

Fishing Ocean Star, Town Wharf ⓣ026584 6965 or 0416 240 877.

Horse riding Bellrowan Valley Horse Riding ⓣ02/6587 5227, ⓦwww.bellrowanvalley.com.au. Thirty-minute drive from Port Macquarie in beautiful bushland. Rides range from a one-hour trip ($50) to a two-day tour with overnight pub-stay ($299).

Hospital Port Macquarie Hospital, Wright's Rd ⓣ02/6581 2000.

Internet access Port Surf Hub, 57 Clarence St.

Police ⓣ02/6583 0199.

Post office Williams St.

Seaplane flights Akuna Seaplanes ⓣ07/5448 8699 or 1300 369 216, ⓦwww.akunaseaplanes.com.au. Flights range from $50 for twelve minutes up to $185 for longer jaunts. Minimum two people.

Surfing Port Macquarie Surf School ⓣ02/6585 5453, ⓦwww.portmacquariesurfschool.com.au.

Taxis Port Macquarie Taxicabs ⓣ02/6581 0081.

Watersports For parasailing and jet-skiing on the river and ocean, try Port Water Sports (ⓣ02/6582 4004) or Port Venture (ⓣ02/6583 3058 or 1300 7955 77, ⓦwww.portventure.com.au).

The coast north to Nambucca Heads

The coastline between Port Macquarie and Nambucca Heads, 115km to the north, has some magical spots. **KEMPSEY**, though not one of them, is a large service-town 49km from Port Macquarie, and home to a prominent Aboriginal population, the **Dunghutti** people. The Dunghutti's ability to demonstrate continuous links with their territory led in 1996 to a successful native title claim for a portion of land at **CRESCENT HEAD**, 21km southeast of Kempsey. The agreement was both the first recognition of native title by an Australian government on the mainland, and the first time that an Australian government negotiated an agreement with indigenous people to acquire their land. There are some wonderful waterfront **campsites** around Crescent Head, including the amusingly named *Delicate Nobby Camping Ground* (ⓣ02/6566 0144, ⓦwww.delicatenobby.com; sites $18 per adults) on Point Plomer Road, set in secluded bushland ten minutes' drive from the township.

Slightly further up the coast is **Hat Head National Park** and the small town of **SOUTH WEST ROCKS**, perched on a picturesque headland. The excellent *Hat Head Holiday Park* (ⓣ02/6567 7555, ⓦwww.4shoreholidayparks.com.au; sites $13.50–22, cabins ❸) is the best place to stay. Further north, back on the Pacific Highway, you'll pick up signs for **TAYLORS ARM** and its famous pub, **The Pub with No Beer**, which claims to have provided the inspiration for the popular Australian folk song of the same name, penned by Slim Dusty and Gordon Parsons.

Further north again is the laid-back holiday town of **NAMBUCCA HEADS**. There's some excellent **surf** on Main, Beilby's and Shelly beaches, and great **swimming** in the crystal-clear water at the extremely scenic rivermouth. Whales can be sighted from Scotts Head, a popular surfing spot to the south, during their southern migration (July–Oct). The town is on the main Sydney–Brisbane **bus** and **train** routes, with Greyhound, Premier Motor Service and Countrylink calling in. Busways also operate a daily service to Urunga, Coffs Harbour and Bellingen.

The best place to **stay** is *Beilby's Beach House* (ⓣ02/6568 6466, ⓦwww.beilbys.com.au; ❸–❹) at 1 Ocean St, a modern but homely B&B with a pool. Alternatively, the exceptionally well-located *White Albatross Holiday Resort* (ⓣ02/6568 6468 or 1800 152 505, ⓦwww.whitealbatross.com.au; sites $29–34, cabins and vans ❷–❻) is right on the lagoon and ocean beach; the attached *Bluewater Brasserie* (ⓣ02/6568 6344) serves good pub food on a veranda overlooking the lagoon. Upriver, *Matilda's* (Mon–Sat noon–2pm & 6pm–close; ⓣ02/6588 6024), on Wellington Drive, is a long-standing favourite with locals, serving up delicious Mod Oz food in a cute yet classy building.

The Bellinger Region

The **Bellinger Region** is a beautiful area just south of Coffs Harbour, which truly has something for everyone. It comprises the country village of Dorrigo and its spectacular plateau, the charming town of **Bellingen** and the Bellinger Valley, and the pristine seaboard around **Urunga** and **Mylestom**.

Urunga and Mylestom

URUNGA, 20km north from Nambucca Heads, is a small beachside town where the Bellinger and Kalang rivers meet the sea. Nearby **MYLESTOM**,

7km further down the highway, is an undeveloped backwater which occupies a stunningly beautiful spot on the wide Bellinger River. You can take advantage of its riverside setting at the **Alma Doepel Reserve**'s sheltered, sandy river beach. Two minutes' walk to the east is a gorgeous sweep of surf beach – often gloriously deserted. If you want to **stay** overnight, the *North Beach Caravan Park* is on Beach Parade in Mylestom (ⓣ02/6655 4250, ⓦwww.nbcp.net; sites $30–36, cabins ④), along with a couple of restaurants, but you're really better off just stopping by for a quick swim, then heading inland up into the valley.

Bellingen

Just after Urunga, a turn-off heads 12km west to the bewitching town of **BELLINGEN**, one of the prettiest and most characterful spots in New South Wales, with a strong alternative bent (you'll find colourful Tibetan prayer flags fluttering in the wind across town). It's full of arts and crafts, great cafés and thriving small businesses – most people come to "Bello" for a day-trip and end up staying a week. Just before town, the **Old Butter Factory**, a renovated dairy, contains a complex of art galleries and craft shops; massages are available if you call ahead (ⓣ0413 104 800; 2hr; $85) and there's also a pleasant café. Bellingen has an interesting monthly **market** (third Saturday of the month; 7am–2pm) in Bellingen Park, with buskers, crafts and organic food stalls; the predominantly foodie Growers' Market is held on the second and fourth Saturday. There's more shopping at the **Hammond and Wheatley Emporium** on Hyde Street, a glorious restored department store. At **Heartland Didgeridoos**, opposite the Shell garage, you can make your own didj, or try some out in front of the presumably long-suffering owner. For a cooling break from crafts and culture, walk for five minutes down Waterfall Way before hopping over a white gate and heading down to the river; the **rope swings** here are great fun, and you can **swim** back into town (or float if you're staying at the *YHA* and borrow one of their tubes).

Just east of town in Fernmount is the much-recommended **Bellingen Canoe Adventures** (ⓣ02/6655 9955, ⓦwww.canoeadventures.com.au), whose daily meanders down the tranquil Bellinger River bring sightings of koalas, eagles and the odd dolphin. Half-day tours cost $44, and sunset and full-moon trips with champagne are also available ($20). One of the town's more unusual sights is the fairy-lit **horse-drawn carriage** roaming the streets – thirty-minute rides cost $15 (ⓣ02/6655 0270, ⓦwww.fairytale tours.com.au).

Each year Bellingen hosts a lively **jazz festival** (ⓦwww.bellingenjazzfestival .com.au) over the third weekend in August, followed by the **Global Carnival** (ⓦwww.globalcarnival.com) of world music at the end of September. David Helfgott (whose life was dramatised in the 1996 film, *Shine*) lives nearby; if you're very lucky, you might catch one of his rare piano performances somewhere in town.

Practicalities

The **tourist office** (daily 9am–5pm; ⓣ02/6655 1522, ⓦwww.bellingermagic .com) is at the Old Butter Factory, and can book accommodation, activities and festival tickets. Busways operates a **bus** service from Coffs Harbour, Urunga, Mylestom and Nambucca Heads, while Kean's runs from Coffs, Armidale and Dorrigo three times a week – the bus stop is at the corner of Hyde and Church streets, by the mural.

Accommodation

Bellingen has lots of great places to rest your head. The creekfront *Bellingen YHA* (☎02/6655 1116, ⓦwww.bellingenyha.com.au; dorms $25, doubles ❸), at 2 Short St, is one of the best hostels in Australia. It's based in a beautiful two-storey timber house with a huge balcony facing Bellingen Island, which is full of jacaranda trees that come alive with fruit bats at dusk. If you don't want to sleep in one of the lovely dorms you can join the queue for the hammock or outdoor gazebo. By day, the owners run excursions to Dorrigo National Park ($25) and trips to the alternative, mostly nudist, community at Bundagen ($15). They also have bikes for rent, free tubes, pick-ups from Urunga, honesty-box cookies and a wall of nudey pics – join it if you dare. Another great option is the Federation-style *Rivendell Guesthouse* (☎02/6655 0060, ⓦwww.rivendell guesthouse.com.au; ❺), centrally located at 10–12 Hyde St. It boasts four beautifully decorated rooms with private verandas, and a pool; a full cooked breakfast plus after-dinner port and choccies are included. For something a bit different, the *Koompartoo Retreat* (☎02/6655 2326, ⓦwww.koompartoo.com .au; ❺), five minutes' walk from town on the corner of Rawson and Dudley streets, has four superb, architect-designed hardwood chalets with balconies, Moroccan-style bed linen and stained-glass windows, tucked away amongst five acres of rainforest rich in birdlife.

Eating and drinking

The town is full of great **cafés and restaurants**, making eating out a delight.

Bellingen Gelato Bar 101 Hyde St. Stylish *gelateria* with fifties-style decor, a cool old jukebox, funky lighting, delicious home-made cakes and mouthwatering ice cream – try the pistachio. Daily 10am–5pm.

Boiling Billy Church St. Cozy place serving good coffee, warming porridge, Turkish breakfasts and the predictably wholesome Bello Burger, made with lentils and brown rice. Closed Sun.

Federal Hotel Hyde St ☎02/6655 1003. This animated, heritage-listed pub is the only one in town, and Bello's social hub. There's excellent live music (check the board outside); *Relish*, an excellent brasserie; comfortable, good-value rooms (❸) and backpacker bunks ($25); and a breezy, lace-front veranda with battered brown-leather sofas and funky lighting.

Lodge 241 117–241 Hyde St. Standing alone at the end of town as you head up to Dorrigo, this striking, three-storey Federation-style building houses a fabulous café and gallery, and has bucolic views over hills and creeks. The big blackboard menus feature the likes of wild game pâté and baked cheesecake, and it's also home to the local chess club – you can have a game or peruse a newspaper while you wait. Daily 8am–5pm.

No. 2 Oak St ☎02/6695 5000. Locals get a glazed look in their eyes when you mention this one; the multiple award-winning restaurant is everyone's favourite, and rustles up some truly stunning contemporary Australian food in a cute heritage cottage – just go. It's best to book. Tues–Sat from 6.30pm.

Riverstone 105–109 Hyde St ☎02/6655 9099, ⓦwww.riverstonecafe.com.au. A newcomer in town but already well-loved, with organic brekkies and lunches, interesting beers and a short-but-sweet wine list. The coffee here is the best in town, which must be a relief to the owner, who took nine months to perfect the blend. The funky interior often hosts blues and roots music in the evening. Daily 8am–2pm, plus Fri 6–9pm.

Sis de Lane Church St. Funky new eaterie with fresh juices plus ricotta pancakes with grilled banana and honey for breakfast, quality antipasto at lunch, and amazing carrot cake for afternoon tea; you sit at a huge wooden table down the middle, allowing you to drool over everyone else's food.

Inland to Dorrigo

The Waterfall Way winds steeply from Bellingen up to **DORRIGO**, past some spectacular lookouts. **Dorrigo** is a quiet country town with sleepy, wide streets lined by plenty of little shops, art galleries and cafés, which, in combination with the natural attractions nearby, make it well worth a day or so of exploration. **Dorrigo National Park** should be first on your list of things to do: the protected area contains a startlingly beautiful remnant of World Heritage–listed rainforest in a region that was once heavily forested, due to the lure of the valuable Australian cedar or "red gold". The **Rainforest Centre** (daily 9am–4.30pm; free; ⓣ02/6657 2309), 2km east of town on Dome Road, is a great facility and makes the national park unusually accessible; it has interpretative displays on flora and fauna, a café and walking-trail maps. Several walks start right behind the centre: the boarded **Skywalk** is the most spectacular and also the least strenuous, extending high over the rainforest canopy for 200m. Other **trails** here range from the eight-hundred-metre Lyrebird Walk up to the Wonga Walk (6.6km return), which winds through the rainforest and underneath the Crystal Shower and Tristania falls. It's cool, misty and slightly eerie down on the forest floor, and easy to believe you're miles from anywhere as huge trees and vines soar overhead. All the walks starting behind the centre are open from 5am to 10pm daily, so visitors can observe the forest's nocturnal creatures. Wilder trails, with more majestic waterfalls and great escarpment views, begin from the Never Never Picnic Area, a further 10km down Dome Road. Aside from visiting the magnificent Dangar Falls, 2km north along Hickory Street, the main strip, there isn't much to do in town, although it's a pleasant little place. The **Dorrigo Folk and Bluegrass Festival** (ⓦwww.dorrigo.com/festival) is held at the end of October each year.

Practicalities

The only way to get to Dorrigo on **public transport** is with Kean's, which runs to the town from Coffs Harbour via Bellingen, and on up to Armidale three times a week – buses stop at the corner of Hickory and Cudgery streets. The **tourist office** (daily 10am–4pm; ⓣ02/6657 2486) at 36 Hickory St can advise you on the many **farmstays** in the area, but there's plenty of **accommodation** in town: for budget accommodation, head to the friendly *Beds on a Budget* (ⓣ02/6657 2431; singles $25, doubles ❷) at 14 Bielsdown St; it's like staying in someone's house, but a funky and chilled-out one at that. Nearer the park at 325 Dome Rd, *Gracemere Grange* (ⓣ02/6657 2630; backpackers $30, doubles ❸) is a comfortable guesthouse stuffed with trinkets from around the world – try to get the cute attic room.

For **eating**, *Fresh* (Tues–Fri 6am–5pm & Sat from 6pm; ⓣ02/6657 2356) is hard to beat. This funky, extremely flowery place at 18–20 Cudgery St has a changing daily menu featuring truly exquisite – and great-value -- quiches, gourmet sandwiches, risottos and Asian broths. Down on Hickory Street, *Misty's* (Wed–Sun from 6pm & Sun lunch from noon; ⓣ02/6657 2855) is another local favourite, housed in a charming 1920s weatherboard cottage with stained-glass windows, and serving gorgeous contemporary regional cuisine – rooms are also available (❹). The *Waterfall Winery* and attached *Lick the Spoon Café*, at 51–53 Hickory St, has a gourmet deli and lunches, home-made gluten-free cakes, and wines fermenting in vast steel drums out the back – persimmon and other fruity flavours are the house specialities (available for tasting Mon–Fri 10am–4pm & Sat 10am–noon).

Coffs Harbour

Back on the Pacific Highway, **COFFS HARBOUR** – or "Coffs" – is beautifully set at a point where the mountains of the Great Dividing Range fall almost

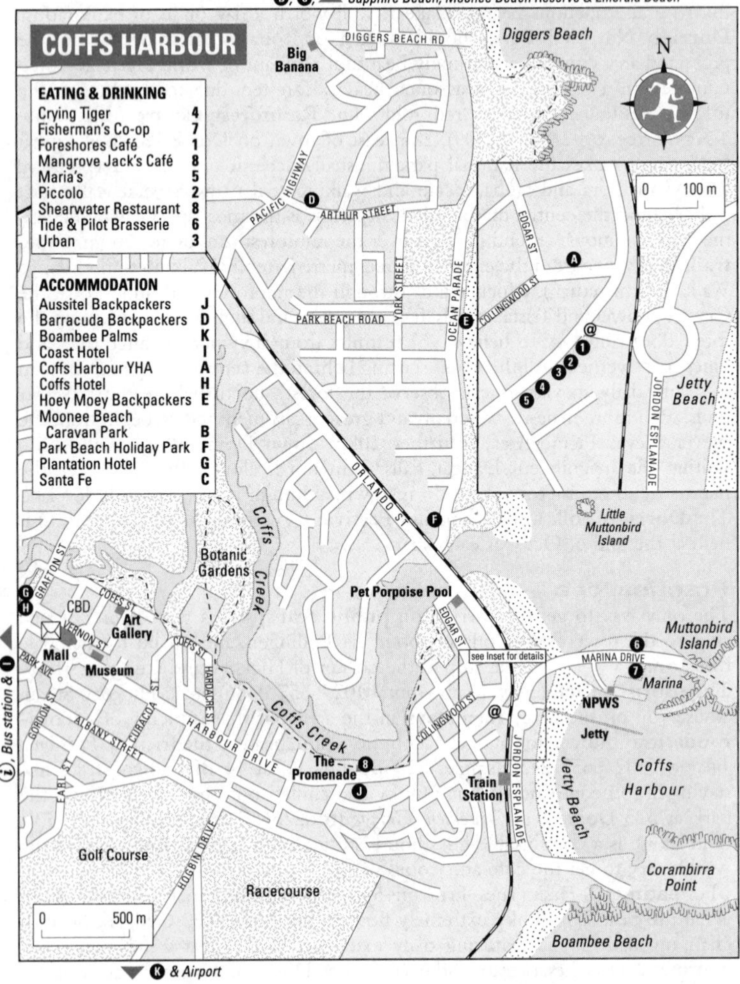

directly into the South Pacific Ocean, and boasts glorious expanses of whitesand to the north. The town is basically a lot of fun, with more activities than you can shake a stick at – in particular, the **Solitary Islands** just offshore are notable for diving, with fringing coral reefs, a plethora of fish, and migrating whales between late May and late November.

Arrival and information

All long-distance buses stop at the **bus station** on the corner of McLean Street and the Pacific Highway; the **train station** is by the harbour. Greyhound and Premier Motor Service stop here on their east-coast runs; Kean's link the town with Bellingen, Dorrigo, Armidale and Tamworth; Busways run to Bellingen, Urunga and Nambucca Heads; and Ryan's to Grafton. You can fly to Coffs with Qantas, Virgin Blue or Brindabella; the **airport** is about 5km south of town.

Coffs is rather spread out, and if you haven't rented a bike or car (see p.273) you'll have to use either taxis or the half-hourly **bus** (Busways ⓣ02/6583 2499, ⓦwww.busways.com.au) which runs between the town centre, Coffs Jetty and Park Beach.

The town is split into three distinct sections: the CBD and mall; the jetty, around 2km to the east; and Sapphire, Moonee and Emerald **beaches** to the north -- Ryan's run buses to all three from Monday to Saturday. The helpful **tourist office** (daily 9am–5pm; ⓣ02/6652 1522 or 1300 369 070, ⓦwww.coffscoast.com.au), next to the bus station, can book accommodation for you. The NPWS (ⓣ02/6652 0900) has an office down at the marina, and offers ranger tours of Muttonbird Island (Oct–Jan; $10; call to check the schedule).

Accommodation

Coffs gets packed out during the Christmas and Easter holidays, and weekly **bookings** are often compulsory. Motels are two a penny, particularly down Ocean Parade, and all fairly predictable – the tourist office can book you one, or just drive around and look for vacancies. All the hostels do free pick-ups on request.

Hostels

Aussitel Backpackers 312 Harbour Drive ⓣ02/6651 1871 or 1800 330 335, ⓦwww.aussitel.com. The best backpackers' in Coffs – very friendly and bursting with "all down the pub together" spirit. Good facilities, plus helpful management, heated pool, free canoes, fishing gear, boogie-boards and surfboards, bikes ($5) and lots of activities. Dorms $27, doubles ❸

Barracuda Backpackers 19 Arthur St ⓣ02/6651 3514, ⓦwww.backpackers.coffs.tv. Small, chilled-out place with homely communal area and good kitchen, pool, free use of fishing gear, boogie-boards and surfboards, plus heaps of organized activities. Dorms $24, doubles ❸

Coffs Harbour YHA 51 Collingwood St ⓣ02/6652 6462, ⓦwww.yha.com.au. This huge hostel has faultless facilities and very helpful staff who can sign you up for an avalanche of activities. Bikes are available to rent ($10) and there's a pleasant pool area. Dorms $27, doubles ❸

Hoey Moey Backpackers Ocean Parade ⓣ02/6651 7966, ⓦwww.hoeymoey.com.au. This motel-style hostel backing onto Park Beach is pretty much party central. The facilities aren't great though, and it's a long way from town. Free courtesy bus, plus pool competitions with free pizza, free beer on arrival, free use of boogie-boards and surfboards, and frequent live music. Dorms $26, doubles ❸, motel rooms ❸–❺

Guesthouses and holiday parks

Boambee Palms 5 Kasch Rd, Boambee ⓣ02/6658 4545, ⓦwww.boambeepalms.com.au. Luxury B&B just south of town, near the delightful village of Sawtell. The four suites here are very stylishly done out, and there's tennis, a pool and barbie, plus yummy breakfasts. ❻–❼

Moonee Beach Caravan Park Moonee Beach Rd, 12km north off the Pacific Highway ⓣ02/6653 6552. Magical camping-spot in bush surroundings, with beach, estuary and headlands to explore. Sites $23–32, vans ❸, cabins ❺–❻

Park Beach Holiday Park Ocean Parade ⓣ02/6648 4888 or 1800 200 111, ⓦwww.parkbeachholidaypark.com.au. Huge, well-ordered campsite, just across the road from the beach, with BBQ, pool and children's playground. Sites $26–$33, cabins and villas ❸–❻

Santa Fe 235 Mountain Way, Sapphire Beach ⓣ02/6653 7700, ⓦwww.santefe.net.au. Just west of the Pacific Highway, 9km north of town. This luxury B&B with a Mexican feel boasts three beautifully decorated guest-suites with private decks, lush gardens, a pool, hammocks and gourmet breakfasts – an extremely relaxing option, and a great place to spoil yourself. ❻–❽

The Town

The small **Historical Museum** (Tues–Sun 10am–4pm; $3), at 191A Harbour Drive, has an interesting collection of relics owned by early pioneers, as well as artefacts belonging to the **Gumbaingirr** people. The star exhibit is the original, Doctor Who–esque Solitary Islands lighthouse – ask for a demo.

The **CBD** and shopping mall, clustered around the western end of Harbour Drive and Grafton Street, is where the major shops and services are located. A charming **creek walk** and **cycle trail** begins on nearby Coffs Street and winds its way down the creek's southern bank to the sea; halfway along, on Hardacre Street, are the magnificent **Botanic Gardens** (daily 9am–5pm; donation). These delightfully tranquil subtropical gardens feature a mangrove boardwalk, sensory herb garden and a slice of rainforest; guided walks are available. A little further on is **The Promenade**, a breezy boutique shopping centre on Harbour Drive. Promenade Canoes (ⓣ02/6651 1032, ⓦwww.promenadecanoes.com.au), on the ground floor, rents out single canoes ($12/hr), doubles ($17/hr) and peddle boats ($15/30min).

The boat-filled **marina**, with its adjacent Jetty Beach and historic pier, is unquestionably the nicest part of town, and perfect for a pre-dinner sunset stroll. A fifteen-minute walk from here takes you to the top of **Muttonbird Island Nature Reserve**, offering fantastic views back over Coffs Harbour, its beaches and the Great Dividing Ranges beyond. Thousands of wedge-tailed shearwaters, or muttonbirds, travel to the island from Southeast Asia each year to breed (Aug–April). Partially visible to the north are the five islands and several islets making up the **Solitary Islands Marine Reserve**, the largest such preserved area in New South Wales; the mingling of tropical and temperate waters means that there's a huge variety of sealife – see p.274 for dive operators. Over Coffs Creek from the marina, Park Beach is a decent stretch of sand, as is Boambee Beach to the south and Digger's Beach around the headland to the north. Little Digger's Beach, to the north again, is the spot to get rid of your white bits.

Aside from the beaches, there are a couple of must-see family attractions in Coffs: the **Pet Porpoise Pool** (daily 9am–4pm; performances at 10am & 1pm;

△Big Banana

adults $26, kids $13; ⓦ www.petporpoisepool.com), on Orlando Street, is home to a number of rescued dolphins (which used to be known as porpoises, hence the misleading moniker), fairy penguins, seals, emu, kangaroo and sea lions. Fierce environmentalists might want to stay away.

The real biggie for many though is the **Big Banana** (daily 9am–5pm; free entry but charges for rides and shows; ⓦ www.bigbanana.com), a "horticultural theme park" 3km north of Coffs on the Pacific Highway, announced by a bright-yellow concrete banana. There's a show shedding light on the town's $70-million-a-year banana industry, but after you've seen it you're free to get down to the more serious business of tobogganing, taking a monorail tour, buying banana-related merchandise and eating chocolate-covered bananas – it's good for kids, but best avoided by theme-park phobics.

Eating, drinking and nightlife

The mall has a wealth of little cafés which are good for a lunchtime sandwich and a coffee, albeit in less-than-scenic surrounds. Much more relaxing is the marina end of Harbour Drive, filled with restaurants of all persuasions; it's hardly worth looking beyond this buzzy little stretch for your nightly feed – where a telephone number is listed, you might need to book. Nightlife is covered by the *Coast*, *Coffs* and *Plantation* hotels lined up along Grafton Street, which cater for classier punters, backpackers and locals respectively – all are pretty lively in summer, and between them you'll find live music most nights.

Crying Tiger Harbour Drive ⓣ 02/6650 0195. Contemporary Thai with a very zen interior. The sleek food is a little pricier than at your average local Thai, but the beautiful curries and stir-fries more than justify it. Daily from 5.30pm.

Fisherman's Co-op The Marina. Fish and chips to die for, for just $8; you can eat on the deck or take away. Fresh seafood is sold in the shop next door. Daily until early evening (shop closes 5.30pm).

Foreshores Café 394 Harbour Drive. Large, airy place whose burgers conform to the Australian standard that requires all meat patties to be embellished with beetroot and pineapple – these throw in egg, BBQ sauce, bacon, cheese and onion for good measure. Daily 7.30am–3pm & Wed–Sun dinner in high season.

Mangrove Jack's Café The Promenade ⓣ 02/6652 5517. The decor isn't quite as polished as at the *Shearwater* (see opposite), but there are the same fine creek views and slightly flashier, more expensive food. Daily from 7am for breakfast & lunch, Tues–Sat for dinner.

Maria's 368 Harbour Drive ⓣ 02/6651 3000. Traditional, bustling Italian with shouting and huge pepper-grinders. Daily from 5.45pm.

Piccolo 390 Harbour Drive ⓣ 02/6651 9599. Stylish Italian eaterie that wouldn't look out of place in Sydney or Melbourne. The low-level lighting, scarlet floor and cushion-stuffed window seats create an intimate atmosphere which is complemented by the delicious food. Mains $27. Tues–Sat from 6pm.

Shearwater Restaurant The Promenade ⓣ 02/6651 6053. Grab a veranda table overlooking Coffs Creek and feast on breakfast risotto or french toast, BBQ lamb kofta at lunch, or Mod Oz–style dishes in the evening. Mains $26. Daily 8am–late.

Tide & Pilot Brasserie Marina Drive ⓣ 02/6651 6888. Coffs' premier seafood restaurant is a classy place overlooking the ocean on one side, and the marina on the other. The stylish, breezy atmosphere, and excellent (if pricey) food conspire to produce a very nice night out. Daily noon–2.30pm & Mon–Sat from 6pm.

Urban 384A Harbour Drive. Extremely red, perfectly named, coffee lounge. The lattes, "mugachinos" and espressos are as good as you'd expect, and there are burgers, wraps and daily specials available at lunch.

Listings

Bike rental Bob Wallis Cycles, corner of Orlando and Collingwood sts ⓣ 02/6652 5102. $18/half-day, $25/full day, or $40/two days.

Car rental Europcar ⓣ 02/6651 8558; Hertz ⓣ 02/6651 1899; Thrifty ⓣ 02/6652 8622.

Cruises Spirit of Coffs Harbour Cruises, Marina Drive ⓣ02/6650 0155. Whale-watching trips (late May–late Nov; $39), dolphin cruises ($25) and lunch tours ($45). Pacific Explorer, in the yellow floating shed at the marina ⓣ02/6652 8988. Whale-watching trips only in season ($30).
Diving Jetty Dive Centre, 398 Harbour Drive ⓣ02/6651 1611, ⓦwww.jettydive.com.au. $55 per dive, $155 for a one-day Discover Scuba course (minimum two people), and Open Water courses from $295. Snorkelling and whale-watching trips also available.
Horse riding Valery Trails, Valery Rd, 20km southwest of Coffs off the Pacific Highway at Bonville ⓣ02/6653 4301, ⓦwww.valerytrails.com.au. One- or two-hour excursions ($40 or $45), breakfast or BBQ rides ($60) and two-day trips overnighting at the pub in Bellingen ($250).
Hospital 345 Pacific Highway ⓣ02/6656 7000.
Internet access Jetty Dive Centre, Harbour Drive.
Police 22 Moonee St ⓣ02/6652 0299.
Post office In the Palms Centre at the CBD end of Harbour Drive; there's a smaller branch at the marina end of the road, on the corner with Camperdown St.
Sky diving Coffs City Skydivers ⓣ02/6651 1167, ⓦwww.coffsskydivers.com.au. Tandem dives from 10,000ft for $325 or courses from $445.
Surfing East Coast Surf School, Digger's Beach ⓣ02/6651 5515, ⓦwww.eastcoastsurfschool.com.au. Two-hour introductory lessons ($50), five-lesson courses ($200) and overnight camps ($330).
Taxi ⓣ13 10 08.
Watersports Liquid Assets Adventure Tours, 38 Marina Drive ⓣ02/6658 0850, ⓦwww.surfrafting.com. Sea- and river-kayaking, surf rafting (all $50/half-day) and white-water rafting on the Goolang ($80/half-day) or Nymboida ($150/full day) rivers. Coffs Ocean Jet Ski Hire (ⓣ02/6651 3177 or 0418 665 656, ⓦwww.coffsjetskihire.com.au) rent out single ($90/half-hour) or double machines ($110/half-hour) from Park Beach.

Grafton and around

GRAFTON, 83km along the Pacific Highway from Coffs Harbour, is a pleasant district capital on a bend of the wide **Clarence River**, which almost encircles the city. Grafton is a genteel, old-fashioned town with wide, tree-lined avenues – head down Victoria and Fitzroy streets, lined with pretty, Federation-style houses, rather than the workaday main strip, Prince Street. The week-long **Jacaranda Festival** (late Oct–early Nov; ⓦwww.jacarandafestival.org.au) celebrates the town's jacaranda and flame trees, which come ablaze with purple, mauve and red blossoms in the spring. Out of festival time this is a quiet place, where the main attraction is cruising on the river or visiting some of the historic buildings preserved by the National Trust. **Schaeffer House** (Tues–Thurs & Sun 1–4pm; $3), at 190 Fitzroy St, has a collection of beautiful china, glassware and period furniture; on the same street at no. 158 is the **Grafton Regional Gallery** (Tues–Sun 10am–4pm), which has some fine temporary exhibitions and local artwork. In front of the *Crown Hotel-Motel*, on Prince Street, you can **cruise** down the river on *River Explorer II* with Great Time Cruises (2hr lunch trips $15, 2hr BBQ trips $22; ⓣ02/6642 3456, ⓦwww.greattimecruises.com.au).

Practicalities

The staff at the **tourist office** (daily 9am–5pm; ⓣ02/6642 4677, ⓦwww.clarencetourism.com), on the Pacific Highway at the corner of Spring Street in South Grafton, can give you information on scenic drives, river cruises and the national parks that surround the town. Countrylink **train** services along the north coast stop at Grafton station, close to the river crossing in South Grafton, while **long-distance buses** stop near the tourist office. Either way, it's a half-hour walk into the town proper, across a fine, split-level road-and-rail bridge. Grafton is on the main Sydney–Brisbane Greyhound and Premier Motor Service routes; Ryans's also run to Coffs Harbour, while Busways operate regular buses between the town and South Grafton.

There's some decent **accommodation** in Grafton, notably in the two old pubs: the *Roches Family Hotel* (ⓣ02/6642 2866; singles ❶, doubles ❷) at 85 Victoria St and the *Crown Hotel-Motel* (ⓣ02/6642 4000, ⓦwww.crownhotelmotel.com; singles ❶, doubles ❷–❸, motel rooms ❸–❹) at 1 Prince St both offer cheap rooms and good pub food. The food is better at the former, and the location, right next to the river, more pleasant at the latter. More in keeping with the town's style, *Arcola B&B* (ⓣ02/6643 1760, ⓦwww.arcola.com.au; ❻), at 150 Victoria St, is situated in a delightful heritage house on the banks of the river and serves delicious breakfasts.

The best place to **eat** is *Georgie's Café* (Tues–Sat 10am–2pm & 6pm–close, Sun 10am–2pm; book for dinner ⓣ02/6642 3177) at the Regional Art Gallery, which serves excellent sandwiches and light meals in a leafy courtyard or inside amongst the art. Smart, contemporary Australian cuisine is on the menu in the evenings.

Around Grafton

From Grafton it's 47km northeast to **Maclean**, a small delta town which proclaims its Scottish heritage with tartan lampposts and street signs in Gaelic – turn off the Pacific Highway at Cowper for a more scenic run into town along the Clarence River. Continuing east along the same road, you reach the twin settlements of **YAMBA** and **ILUKA** – two very pretty holiday villages facing each other across the mouth of the river. Yamba in particular is an up-and-coming little place, with a fresh, surfie vibe. Clarence River Ferries shuttle between the two communities (foot passengers only; 4 daily; $5.70; ⓣ02/6646 6423) and also cruise along the river. Busways run daily services to both settlements from Grafton.

In sun-drenched Yamba, far nicer than the many motels (❹–❺) is the idyllic *Calypso Holiday Park* (ⓣ02/6646 8847, ⓦwww.calypsoyamba.com.au; sites $23–28, cabins ❸–❺) on Harbour Street. The *Yamba Pacific Hotel* (ⓣ02/6646 2125, ⓦwww.pacifichotelyamba.com.au; dorms $50, doubles ❹, motel rooms ❺) commands a terrific location overlooking the picturesque Main Beach at 18 Pilot St, and has decent pub rooms, great live music (Thurs–Sat), and an excellent, inexpensive restaurant. This is also an outstanding place to **eat**; try the funky *Caper Berry Café* on the corner of Coldstream and Yamba streets for lunch, and *Sea Spray* or *Castalia*, located next door to each other on Clarence Street, for stylish food in the evening.

A few kilometres south of Yamba is **Yuraygir National Park**, with plenty of basic but attractive **bushcamping** (book via Grafton NPWS; ⓣ02/6441 1500; $5–8 per adult per night) and a spectacular strip of sand at Angourie Point, which became New South Wales' first **surfing reserve** in 2007. Eighty kilometres west of Grafton, the **Gwydir Highway** runs through the rugged and densely forested **Gibraltar Range** and **Washpool** national parks, both with walking tracks, bushcamping, lookout points and waterfalls galore.

Ballina and around

North of Grafton are **Ballina** and **Lennox Head**, the latter in particular worth a stop before the madness of Byron Bay. The old port of **BALLINA**, at the mouth of the Richmond River, is a quiet, undeveloped holiday town; it hasn't escaped the clutches of the "big things" though, with the **Big Prawn** marking the entrance to town on the highway from Grafton. Four kilometres north on

Gallans Road, east of the Pacific Highway, the tea trees of the **Thursday Plantation** (daily 9am–5pm; free; Ⓦwww.tphealth.com) produce the all-healing oil; the plantation – with a sculpture park and tea-tree maze in the grounds, and a shop full of soothing goodies – makes for an interesting visit. On Regatta Avenue by Las Balsas Plaza is the **Maritime Museum** (daily 9am–4pm; donation; Ⓦwww.ballinamaritimemuseum.org.au). Its star exhibit is a raft – with a sail some say was painted by Salvador Dalí – from the 1973 Las Balsas expedition, in which three vessels set sail from Ecuador in an aim to prove that ancient South American civilizations could have traversed the Pacific. A mere 179 days and nine thousand miles later the twelve-strong crew arrived in Ballina, sporting some choice facial hair. A few doors down is **Richmond River Cruises** (2hr; $24; Ⓣ02/6687 5688), who run trips downriver. To go it alone, call **Ballina Boat Hire** (Ⓣ00403 810 277), who rent out tinnies ($40/2hr).

Practicalities

You can **fly** to Ballina from Sydney with Virgin Blue, Regional Express or Jetstar, who also have flights from Melbourne. Greyhound and Premier Motor Service connect the town by **bus** to all stops between Sydney and Brisbane; Kirklands run to Byron Bay, Brisbane, Lismore and Lennox Head; while Blanch's operate services to and from the airport, and to Lennox Head and Byron Bay. To get around town, you can rent **bikes** from Jack Ransom Cycles (Ⓣ02/6685 3485) at 16 Cherry St. The **tourist office** (Mon–Fri 9am–5pm; Ⓣ02/6686 3484, Ⓦwww.discoverballina.com) is in Las Balsas Plaza, and can book accommodation, river cruises and other tours.

Accommodation

Ballina Lakeside Holiday Park North of the river on Fenwick Drive Ⓣ02/6686 3953 or 1800 888 268, Ⓦwww.ballinalakeside.com.au. Good holiday park, right next to the lagoon with plenty of good facilities. Sites $30–35, cabins and villas ❸–❻
Ballina Manor 25 Norton St Ⓣ02/6681 5888, Ⓦwww.ballinamanor.com.au. This very grand, very English place is the most upmarket option in town. ❻
Ballina YHA Travellers Lodge 36 Tamar St Ⓣ02/6686 6737, Ⓦwww.yha.com.au. Clean, motel-style place with a swimming pool, bikes for rent ($5) and free fishing rods, boogie-boards and snorkel gear. Dorms $27, doubles ❹
Brundah B&B 37 Norton St Ⓣ02/6686 8166, Ⓦwww.brundah.com.au. Boutique B&B set in a stunning heritage-listed Federation house amidst beautiful gardens. ❻
Flat Rock Tent Park Just off the coast road 5km northeast of town, on Flat Rock Rd Ⓣ02/6686 4848. This unspoilt, unpowered site is for tents only (although perhaps not for much longer) and set right on Angels Beach. Sites $19

Eating

For tasty alfresco **food**, *Shelly's on the Beach* has a variety of breakfasts and lunches, enticing cakes, and great views over Shelly's Beach – follow the bridge and sea wall 2km north of town. The owners of the *River Thai* (Tues–Sat from 6pm), on the corner of Norton and River streets, serve excellent curries, stir-fries and the like, while for very civilized, wood-panelled fine dining try the *Ballina Manor Restaurant*. *Sandbar* (Wed–Sat dinner and drinks, Sat & Sun breakfast and lunch), at 23 Compton Drive just over the river, is the first designer-style place to hit Ballina and an excellent spot for early-evening drinks.

Lennox Head

LENNOX HEAD, 11km north of Ballina, is a small, relaxed town with a surfie feel. At the southern end of the fabulous Seven-Mile Beach, The Point rates among the best **surfing** spots in the world, and professionals congregate here for the big waves in May, June and July. Adding to Lennox Head's appeal is the calm, fresh water of **Lake Ainsworth**; stained dark by the tea trees around its banks, it's a popular swimming spot for families seeking refuge from the crashing surf in the soft, practically medicinal water (it's effectively diluted tea-tree oil).

There are a couple of inexpensive places **to stay** in town. *Lennox Head Beach House YHA* (Ⓣ02/6687 7636, Ⓦwww.yha.com.au; dorms $24, rooms ❸), at 3 Ross St, is a great little hostel ideally situated between the lake and the beach; Reiki massage, reflexology and Bowen therapy are available in-house (free short sessions on Thurs), and there are boards, fishing gear, bikes, windsurfers (free lessons) and paddle-skis (all $5), plus a herb garden for creative cooks. The friendly owners do free pick-ups from Ballina. *Lake Ainsworth Caravan Park* (Ⓣ02/6687 7249, Ⓦwww.bscp.com.au/lakeains; sites $21–27, cabins ❸–❹), on Pacific Parade, is a fairly standard holiday park but superbly located right by the water. They might be doing away with tent sites though, so call first to check. *Randall's on Ross* (Ⓣ02/6687 7922; ❻) is a great B&B option at 9 Ross St, with excellent breakfasts and very comfy queen-sized beds.

As for **food**, there's *Lennox Head Pizza & Pasta* on Ballina Street (try the calzone) or *Mi Thai* (Wed–Sun from 6pm) a few doors down. *Seven Mile Café* (Wed–Sun from 6pm & Fri–Sun from noon; Ⓣ02/6687 6210) on Pacific Parade has great sea views, a very bright colour scheme and bold Mod Oz food to match. Before you hit the waves stop by the cute *Café de Mer*; the full Aussie breakfasts on Turkish bread should sort you out for the day, and don't miss the yummy home-made cakes. The *Lennox Point Hotel* serves excellent modern Australian food in its bistro, *Ruby's by the Sea*, while the pub itself is a convivial sort of place, with live music from Thursday to Sunday.

Since Lennox Head is off the Pacific Highway, no long-distance **bus** services call here; you can try and get picked up off the Greyhound and Premier Motor Service buses at Ballina, or jump on a local service from Byron Bay, Ballina, Lismore or Evans Head (Kirklands or Blanch's).

Byron Bay and around

Situated at the end of a long sweeping bay, the township of **BYRON BAY** boasts 30km of almost unbroken sandy beaches and is a "must do" on the backpacker circuit. What once made the place special – the small-community feel, the free-for-all atmosphere, the barefoot hippies and the herbalists – is fast disappearing. Byron these days is still beautiful and undeniably good fun, but the ever-encroaching chain stores and the profusion of competing tie-dye therapies combine to make it, in summertime at least, about as alternative as MTV.

Arrival and information

Trains no longer call into Byron, although Countrylink still operate a bus service to a large number of east-coast destinations. Greyhound and Premier Motor Service stop in town on their east-coast runs, and drop you at the bus stop on Jonson Street. Local bus services include Kirklands, which run to Brisbane, Surfers, Tweed Heads, Murwillumbah, Brunswick Heads, Lennox Head and Ballina; and Blanch's, which call at Ballina, Lennox Head and Mullumbimby. The closest **airport** is Ballina, 39km south, served by Jetstar, Virgin and Regional Express; Blanch's run a connecting bus service (3–7 daily). Brisbane 2 Byron (Ⓣ07/5429 8759 or 1800 626 222, Ⓦwww.brisbane2byron.com) serve Brisbane

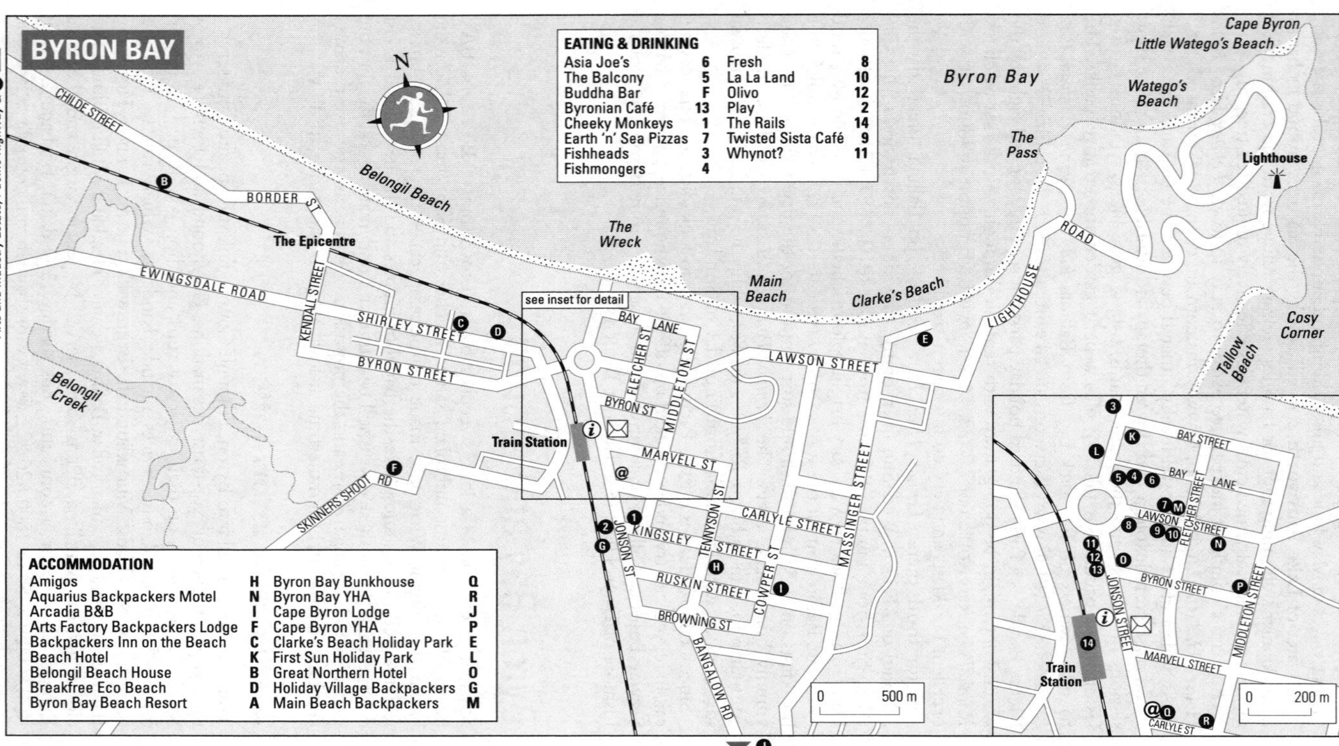
BYRON BAY
EATING & DRINKING
Asia Joe's 6
The Balcony 5
Buddha Bar F
Byronian Café 13
Cheeky Monkeys 1
Earth 'n' Sea Pizzas 7
Fishheads 3
Fishmongers 4
Fresh 8
La La Land 10
Olivo 12
Play 2
The Rails 14
Twisted Sista Café 9
Whynot? 11
ACCOMMODATION
Amigos H
Aquarius Backpackers Motel N
Arcadia B&B I
Arts Factory Backpackers Lodge F
Backpackers Inn on the Beach C
Beach Hotel K
Belongil Beach House B
Breakfree Eco Beach D
Byron Bay Beach Resort A
Byron Bay Bunkhouse Q
Byron Bay YHA R
Cape Byron Lodge J
Cape Byron YHA P
Clarke's Beach Holiday Park E
First Sun Holiday Park L
Great Northern Hotel O
Holiday Village Backpackers G
Main Beach Backpackers M
Arts and Industry Estate, Pacific Highway & A
N
Cape Byron
Little Watego's Beach
Watego's Beach
Byron Bay
The Pass
Lighthouse
Cosy Corner
Tallow Beach
Belongil Beach
The Wreck
Main Beach
Clarke's Beach
Belongil Creek
The Epicentre
Train Station
see inset for detail
CHILDE STREET
BORDER ST
EWINGSDALE ROAD
KENDALL STREET
SHIRLEY STREET
BYRON STREET
SKINNERS SHOOT RD
LIGHTHOUSE ROAD
LAWSON STREET
MASSINGER STREET
CARLYLE STREET
COWPER ST
TENNYSON ST
KINGSLEY STREET
RUSKIN STREET
BROWNING ST
BANGALOW RD
JONSON ST
MARVELL ST
MIDDLETON ST
FLETCHER ST
BAY LANE
BYRON ST
BAY STREET
LAWSON STREET
JONSON STREET
MARVELL STREET
MIDDLETON STREET
CARLYLE ST
0 500 m
0 200 m

airport daily ($32), and Kirklands run to the Gold Coast airport at Coolangatta (2–3 daily).

The helpful **tourist office** (daily 9am–5pm; ⓣ02/6680 9271, ⓦwww.visitbyronbay.com), at 80 Jonson St near the bus stop, has a huge range of printed information and activities. **Byron Bus & Backpacker Travel** (daily 7.30am–6.30pm; ⓣ02/6685 5517), a few doors down at no. 84, book all manner of tours, activities, travel tickets and cheap car rental, and also has Internet access. There are a plethora of other "information centres" along Jonson Street, but they're really geared up for selling adventure activities and tours.

Accommodation

During December and January especially, demand for accommodation in all categories far exceeds supply, and it's essential to book well in advance – think weeks rather than days for hostels, and months ahead for hotels and apartments; many places impose fairly draconian minimum stays. There's a dedicated **accommodation** desk in the tourist office (daily 9.30am–5pm; ⓣ02/6680 8666, ⓦwww.byronbayaccom.net), which books everything except hostels. The **backpackers'** in Byron Bay are among the liveliest in Australia, but prices and stress levels rise dramatically in summer due to overcrowding. If you're part of a group, **holiday apartments** (booked through the accommodation desk at the tourist office and real-estate agents in town) might be a more practical option. If all places in town are full, try **Brunswick Heads**, about 18km further up the coast, or Lennox Head, about 12km south.

Tours from Byron Bay

There are plenty of tours available to the rainforest, waterfalls and national parks in the hinterland around Byron Bay. All tours can be booked at Byron Bus & Backpacker Travel (see above). The following are some of the more specialist and unusual operators.

Byron Bay Wildlife Tours ⓣ0429 770 686, ⓦwww.byronbaywildlifetours.com. See 'roos, koalas, wallabies, flying foxes and parrots in the hills and on the coast near Byron ($40/5hr).

Cape Byron Kayaks ⓣ02/6680 955, ⓦwww.byron-bay.com/capebyronkayaks. Paddle with dolphins, turtles and get some free Tim Tams into the bargain ($60/3hr).

Green Triangle ⓣ1800 503 475, ⓦwww.greentriangle.com.au. Takes the scenic route to Brisbane, departing Byron Tuesday and Friday at midday, and stopping in Nimbin and Springbrooks National Park before arriving in Brisbane at 6.30pm ($54).

Jim's Alternative Tours ⓣ02/6685 7720, ⓦwww.jimsalternativetours.com. Jim's tours give a genuinely interesting insight into the hinterland's alternative way of life, en route to Nimbin, Minyon Falls, and The Channon Markets, all set to cool tunes ($35/full day); bear in mind a large proportion of the people who sign up only do so to buy dope in Nimbin.

Mountain Bike Tours ⓣ0429 122 504, ⓦwww.mountainbikestours.com.au. Tours through the rainforest that will satisfy both the casual cyclist and the rabid downhiller. Full-day tours in the Mount Jerusalem or Nightcap national parks ($99), or multi-day tours on the east coast ($1450).

Samudra Byron Bay Retreats ⓣ02/6685 5600, ⓦwww.samudra.com.au. Yoga in the morning, surfing in the afternoon, and vegetarian meals in between – a great, healthy way to relax. Weekends $630, three days $910, week $1740.

Surfari ⓣ02/6684 8111, ⓦwww.surfaris.com. If you really want to learn to surf, this is a great way of doing it. For $549 you'll spend five days living with gnarly wave-riders who'll chuck you in the water every day until you get it.

Motels, hotels, guesthouses and apartments

Amigos 32 Kingsley St ⓣ02/6680 8662, ⓦwww.amigosbb.com. Charming, peacefully located guesthouse just five minutes' walk from town. Latin-influenced rooms, polished wood floors, colourful Cuban artwork, a sunny kitchen/lounge, hammocks, newspapers and a tranquil garden make this the perfect haven. Shared bathroom 5, en suite 6

Arcadia B&B 48 Cowper St ⓣ02/6680 8699, ⓦwww.arcadiaguesthouse.com.au. Fresh, contemporary guesthouse in a Federation-era homestead; most of the brightly decorated rooms are en suite and have enticing spa- or clawfoot baths. Guests can use the funky pink bikes for free. 6

Belongil Beach House 25 Childe St ⓣ02/6685 7868, ⓦwww.belongilbeachouse.com. One of the best places in town, this Balinese-style complex has spacious timber cottages set around a landscaped garden. Accommodation ranges from en-suite dorms to self-contained apartments with stained-glass windows and mosaic floors. There's an excellent café, *Cicada*, next door. Dorms $33, doubles, studios and apartments 4–7

Breakfree Eco Beach 35–37 Shirley St ⓣ02/6639 5700, ⓦwww.ecobeachbyron.com.au. Clean, stylish motel free of the dreadful interior design tendencies that usual bedevil this type of place. Pristine pool, fresh, green paint jobs and BBQ area; all motels should be like this. 6

Byron Bay Beach Resort Bayshore Drive, 3km north on the road to the Pacific Highway (turn off at the Arts and Industry Estate) ⓣ02/6685 8000, ⓦwww.byronbaybeachresort.com.au. Lovely complex set in subtropical gardens and rainforest; accommodation is in wooden chalets, and there's also a great pool, bar, restaurant, tennis courts and golf course. 6–8

Great Northern Hotel Cnr Jonson and Byron sts ⓣ02/6685 6454. The clean, no-frills pub rooms here are right above the main street and amongst the cheapest in town; the noise from bands playing below makes it a place for confirmed night-owls only though. 2–3

Hostels

Aquarius Backpackers Motel 16 Lawson St ⓣ02/6685 7663 or 1800 029 909, ⓦwww.aquarius-backpackers.com.au. Excellent hostel boasting characterful, split-level en-suite dorms with fridge, motel rooms, and some cute apartments. There's also a small "beach", BBQ, tour desk, excellent communal areas, pool, and a bar with a daily happy hour. Dorms $30, doubles 3, motel rooms 4, apartments 5–6

Arts Factory Backpackers Lodge Skinners Shoot Rd ⓣ02/6685 7709, ⓦwww.artsfactory.com.au. In a bushland creek setting, this unusual place is a sprawling riot of sculpture, crafts and old buses – if you value a hippie atmosphere you'll love it, but the sheer number of backpackers wanting to stay here means it can be a bit of a scrum. You can sleep in a dorm, tepee, wagon or at the camping ground, and the undeniably great facilities include a pool, beach volleyball, ping pong, boards, bikes ($7), as well as poi-twirling classes and plenty of hammocks to lounge on. Dorms $36, doubles 4, chalets 6–7

Backpackers Inn on the Beach 29 Shirley St ⓣ02/6685 8231, ⓦwww.backpackersinnbyronbay.com.au. Sociable hostel with direct access to Belongil Beach, a cozy cushion-strewn lounge, large clean dorms, pool and – almost uniquely in backpacker territory – a bath. Dorms $32, doubles 4

Byron Bay Bunkhouse 1 Carlyle St ⓣ02/6685 8311 or 1800 241 600, ⓦwww.byronbaybunkhouse.com.au. Colourfully decorated hostel linked to a language school. Big veranda, clean kitchen and *Oska's Cafe* is just underneath for quick breakfast fixes; a good choice. Dorms $27.

Byron Bay YHA 7 Carlyle St ⓣ02/6685 8853, ⓦwww.yha.com.au. Bright, peaceful option with a BBQ area and pool, comfy dorms, plus free boogie-boards and bikes. An excellent choice if you're not that into Byron's party-hostel scene. Dorms $33, doubles 4

Cape Byron Lodge 78 Bangalow Rd ⓣ02/6685 6445 or 1800 111 030, ⓦwww.capebyronlodge.com. Simple, friendly place with the cheapest dorms in Byron, plus the usual bikes, boards and activities, though it's a bit out of town. Dorms $27, rooms 3–4

Cape Byron YHA Cnr Middleton and Byron sts ⓣ02/6685 8788, ⓦwww.yha.com.au. Relaxed hostel with a pleasant pool, games room, fairly standard dorms and overpriced doubles. BBQ once a week, plus free bikes and boogie-boards; a solid option. Dorms $32, doubles 5

Holiday Village Backpackers 116 Jonson St ⓣ02/6685 8888 or 1800 350 388, ⓦwww.byronbaybackpackers.com.au. Well-equipped, motel-style hostel with standard dorms, a pool, BBQ and free boards and bikes. Dorms $32, doubles 4

Main Beach Backpackers Cnr Lawson and Fletcher sts ⓣ02/6685 8695, ⓦwww.mainbeachbackpackers.com. Safe, pleasant hostel with standard dorms, a great sundeck, pool, free bikes and boogie-boards, a great BBQ two nights a week, and it's the best-located hostel in town to boot, just 100m from Main Beach. Dorms $30, doubles 3–4

Campsites

Broken Head Holiday Park Beach Rd, Broken Head, 6km south ⓣ02/6685 3245, ⓦwww.brokenhd.com.au. The best of the bay's holiday parks, this site has good facilities and gentle, wooded inclines that afford great sea views over the southern end of Tallow Beach and the aptly named Broken Head Rocks. Sites $30–33, cabins ❸–❻

Clarke's Beach Holiday Park Off Lighthouse Rd ⓣ02/6685 6496, ⓦwww.byroncoast.com.au/clarkes. Pleasant wooded site with standard amenities but a fantastic setting right on the fabulous Clarke's Beach. Sites $40–43, cabins ❺

First Sun Holiday Park Lawson St ⓣ02/6685 6544, ⓦwww.bshp.com.au/first. Excellent central location on Main Beach. Cabins range from basic to fully self-contained. Sites ❶, cabins ❸

The Town and around

There's plenty of opportunity to soak up the local atmosphere – and the often bizarre mix of countercultures as surfie meets soap starlet meets hippie – simply by wandering the streets. If you want to explore, one of the first places to visit is the

Alternative and artistic Byron Bay

Byron Bay offers a huge variety of alternative therapies, New Age bookshops, crystals, palmists and tarot readers – all with a good dose of capitalism, as prices are hiked up during the lucrative summer months. The alternative culture attracts artists and artisans in droves, and galleries and artists' studios abound.

Alternative therapies

Noticeboards around town advertise hundreds of conventional and slightly wackier therapies. At the rear of the *Belongil Beach House* on Childe Street, the **Relax Haven** (ⓣ02/6685 8304) has a flotation tank and massage (1hr float $35, 1hr massage $50, 2hr float and massage $65). **Quintessence** (ⓣ02/6685 5533, ⓦwww.quintessencebyron.com.au), Shop 8, 11 Fletcher St, is more for good old-fashioned pampering, with aromatherapy, massage and a range of indulgent packages ($95–$145). Heading off the deep end of the purple spectrum, the **Ambaji Wellness Centre** (ⓣ02/6685 6620, ⓦwww.ambaji.com.au) at 6 Marvel St is very New Age, and offers a wide range of treatments from massage and reflexology to tarot readings, crystal healing and chakra clearing. Get a copy of *Body & Soul* from the tourist office for the full gamut of good vibes.

Arts and crafts

Local arts and crafts are on display at the **Byron Bay market**, held on the first Sunday of each month on Butler Street, behind the train station. There are others at The Channon and Alstonville on the second Sunday, Mullumbimby on the third Saturday, Uki (north of Nimbin) and Ballina on the third Sunday, and at the showground at Bangalow, 13km southwest, on the fourth Sunday of each month. The **Arts Factory**, on Skinners Shoot Road, has an artist's workshop that you can visit (most days 9.30am–1pm; ⓣ0438 949 398, ⓦwww.byrontik.com), and the **Byron Craft Market** is held here every Saturday (8.30am–3pm) with a courtesy bus (8am–3pm) from the train station, just over the rails. **The Epicentre**, on Border Street near Belongil Beach, has a yoga studio and lots of resident artists and craftspeople. Beyond here, 3km west of town off Ewingsdale Road (the road to the Pacific Highway), the **Arts and Industry Estate** is a browser's dream, with over three hundred studios run by local artisans selling furniture, jewellery, art and glassware. Back in town, Jonson Street is lined with shops selling clothes and locally made crafts, particularly jewellery.

The **Byron Bay Writers' Festival** (ⓣ02/6685 5115, ⓦwww.byronbaywritersfestival.com.au) is held annually around the beginning of August; check the website for exact dates and details of readings, workshops and film screenings.

lighthouse on the rocky promontory of **Cape Byron.** The cape is the easternmost point of the Australian mainland and is a popular spot to greet the dawn (see p.285 for tours); with a bit of luck you'll see **dolphins**, who like to sport in the surf off the headland, or **humpback whales**, which pass this way heading north in June or July and again on their return south in September or October.

Main Beach in town is as good as any to swim from, and usually has relatively gentle surf. One reason why Byron Bay is so popular with surfers is because its beaches face in all directions, so there's almost always one with a good swell; conversely, you can usually find somewhere for a calmer swim. West of Main Beach, you can always find a spot to yourself on **Belongil Beach**, from where there's sand virtually all the way to **Brunswick Heads**.

To the east, Main Beach curves round towards Cape Byron to become **Clarke's Beach**; The Pass, a famous surfing spot, is at its eastern end. This and neighbouring **Watego's Beach** – beautifully framed between two rocky spurs – face north, and usually have the best surfing. On the far side of the cape, **Tallow Beach** extends towards the **Broken Head Nature Reserve**, 6km south of the town centre at Suffolk Park; there's good surf at Tallow just around the cape at Cosy Corner, and also at Broken Head. From the car park here, a short stroll through rainforest leads to the secluded, nudist **Kings Beach**.

The diversity of marine life in the waters of Byron Bay makes it a prime place to **dive**, though these are rock – rather than coral – reefs. Tropical marine life and creatures from warm temperate seas mingle at the granite outcrop of **Julian Rocks Aquatic Reserve**, 3km offshore; by far the most popular spot here is **Cod Hole**, an extensive underwater cave inhabited by large moray eels and other fish. Between April and June is the best time to dive, before the plankton bloom (see p.284 for dive operators).

Eating

Byron Bay is a great place to eat, with street food stalls, cafés, and restaurants galore sprinkled down Jonson Street and the roads leaving off it, although the alternative, vegetarian joints that once prevailed are being hustled out of town by upmarket delis and lunch spots.

Cafés and takeaways

Asia Joe's Bay Lane. Come early to snag one of the few tables at this popular, funky takeaway. Try Joe's famous *laksa* and other bargain stir-fries and noodles. BYO. Daily 5–9.30pm.

Byronian Café 58 Jonson St. A great vantage point from which to survey the madness of Jonson St over a coffee or mango *lassi*; the lunch menu ranges from scrummy roast veggies and tahini in pitta ($10) to blue-eyed cod with chilli, coriander and Thai salad ($21). Daily 6am–3pm.

Fishmongers Bay Lane, behind the *Beach Hotel*. Locals rave about this stylish little place, and justifiably so: $9.50 will get you delectably battered fish, hand-cut chips, kumara crisps, a wedge of lemon and a pot of tartare sauce. Daily noon–9.30pm.

Twisted Sista Café Lawson St. Unctuous banana smoothies and really quite gigantic cakes, plus the usual sandwiches, wraps and burgers. Daily 7am–4.30pm.

Restaurants

The Balcony Lawson St ⓣ02/6680 9666. An early-evening cocktail on the balcony of this beautiful, eclectically decorated bar-restaurant is the most relaxing way to kick off a night in Byron. Succulent food is served at breakfast, lunch and in the evening, when the style is Mod Oz with a Spanish twist. Booking essential, sometimes even for drinks. Daily 8–12.30am.

Buddha Bar At the Arts Factory, Skinners Shoot Rd ⓣ02/6685 5833. Excellent gourmet pub food in funky environs: eat in 1950s-style booths, cushion-stuffed conservatories, or on leather sofas, surrounded by artwork and hippies. BYO. Also a great drinking den, with frequent live music and fire-twirling galore. Mon–Sat 4pm–midnight, Sun 4–10pm.

Earth 'n' Sea Pizzas 11 Lawson St ⓣ02/6685 6029 or 6685 5011. The huge pizza menu at this perennially popular restaurant includes all the classics and some more off-the-wall combos such as the Beethoven, an alarming medley of prawn, banana and pineapple. BYO and licensed. Daily from 5.30pm.

Fishheads Right at the beach end of Jonson St ⓣ026680 7632, ⓦwww.fishheadsbyron.com.au. Seafood restaurant that would be entirely perfect were it not for its carpark views. Still, you can hear the sea from the sleek wooden deck, and the food's very good. BYO. Daily 7.30am–late.

Fresh 7 Jonson St ⓣ02/6685 7810. Fast becoming a Byron institution, this funky, eastern-inspired place caters for all your daily eating needs, from sweetcorn-fritter stacks and salsa at breakfast, to Bangalow pork ribs and jungle curry ($22) in the evening. Daily 7.30am–late.

Olivo 34 Jonson St ⓣ02/66857950. Dishes such as braised seafood stew with Lebanese couscous and walnut bread ($28) attract an upmarket clientele, who work their way through the local wine list in the cozy, brickwork interior. BYO and licensed. Daily from 6.30pm.

Whynot? 18 Jonson St ⓣ02/6680 7994. This acclaimed café-restaurant is an all-day kind of affair with Aussie-style tapas, cocktails (happy hour 5–7pm) and a great-value three-course Mod Oz evening menu ($30) served in the minimalist, art-cluttered interior or at outdoor tables. Daily 6am–midnight.

Entertainment and nightlife

The weekly free community newspaper, *The Byron Shire Echo*, has a comprehensive gig guide; many of the best are in tiny venues out in the hinterland. There's plenty of activity in summer: **New Year's Eve** is such a big event that the council has taken to closing the town off, so come early. The huge **Blues and Roots Festival** (ⓦwww.bluesfest.com.au) takes over Red Devil Park every Easter; check the website for exact dates and to book tickets. Similarly, the **Splendour in the Grass** music festival (ⓦwww.splendourinthegrass.com), usually held in late July, brings in huge crowds. In the Arts Factory complex, **The Lounge Cinema** (ⓣ02/6685 5828) would be up there in the world's coolest cinema competition. Pigskin-covered seats are sprinkled with light by a large disco ball, and three art-house or mainstream films are screened daily, at very reasonable prices. Get there early to slouch on one of the cushions at the front.

Beach Hotel Cnr Jonson and Bay sts ⓣ02/6685 6402. This huge bar, superbly sited right opposite Main Beach, has a large terrace and bistro, and attracts a cross-section of locals and visitors. There's live music every night in high season, including jazz sessions on Sunday afternoon.

Cheeky Monkeys 115 Jonson St ⓣ02/6685 5886. Renowned backpacker party zone, with loud music, lots of frolicking, and $2 meals from 7pm to see you through to closing time eight hours later. Closed Sun.

Great Northern Hotel Cnr Jonson and Byron sts ⓣ02/6685 6454. Huge and occasionally raucous Aussie pub with nightly live music in high season. The bistro does $10 pizza-and-pasta deals from Mon to Thurs. Closes anywhere between 1am and 3am, depending on the crowd.

La La Land Lawson St. The little sister of the Melbourne institution, this is the hippest nightspot in town, and a major stop on the international DJ circuit. The cavernous, chandelier-bedecked interior is fairly chilled until 10.30pm, after which it gets reliably rammed with locals and well-heeled backpackers. $10–25 cover, depending on the DJ. Mon–Sat 8pm–3am, Sun 8pm–midnight.

Play The Plaza ⓣ02/6685 8989, ⓦwww.playnightclub.com.au. Small, funky club that punches above its weight in attracting big-name DJs, with music ranging from electro house to drum 'n' bass. $5–$15 cover depending on DJ. Daily 10pm–3am.

The Rails At the old train station. Good local bands rock the mike at this busy place a few times a week, and with its covered outdoor area, it's a better bet than the pub.

Listings

Bike rental Most hostels have bikes which can either be used free or rented by guests; otherwise try Byron Bay Bicycles (ⓣ02/6685 6067, ⓦwww.byronbaybicycles.com.au), Shop 8 The Plaza, behind Woolworth's ($15/4hr or $22/8hr).

Car rental Jetset, Marvell St ⓣ02/6685 5517; Hertz, Marvel St ⓣ02/6680 7925; Thrifty, Shirley St ⓣ02/6685 7925.

Circus School Circus Arts (ⓣ02/6685 6566, ⓦwww.circusarts.com.au) will have you swinging from the chandeliers and generally clowning about in no time. Ninety-minute trapeze workshops ($45), and circus-skills taster courses from $25.

Diving Sundive, next door to *Cape Byron YHA* on Middleton St ⓣ02/6685 7755, ⓦwww.sundive.com.au. Byron's only five-star PADI centre offers Open Water courses ($375), a Discover Scuba taster ($160), dives at Julian Rocks ($85 first dive, $75 for subsequent dives) for qualified divers, plus snorkelling and whale-watching trips.

Hang-gliding Byron Airwaves Hang Gliding School ⓣ02/6629 0354, ⓦwww.byronair.cjb.net. Thirty-minute tandem flights cost $145.

△ Byron Bay Blues and Roots Festival

Horse riding Pegasus Park ⓣ02/6687 1446, ⓦwww.pegasuspark.com.au. Trot through the hinterland ($50/hr or $70/2hr) or fulfil that galloping-down-a-deserted-beach fantasy ($70/hr or $90/2hr).
Hospital Wordsworth St, off Shirley St ⓣ02/6685 6200.
Internet access You can't move on Jonson St for Internet cafés; the cheapest is at Peter Pan's, 87 Jonson St ($2/hr).
Left luggage Byron Bus & Backpacker Travel (see p.279) have storage lockers ($4/5hr or $8/24hr).
Police 2 Shirley St ⓣ02/6685 9499.
Post office 61 Jonson St.
Skydiving Skydive Byron Bay (ⓣ02/6684 1323, ⓦwww.skydivebyronbay.com) offer Australia's highest jump (14,000ft), with spectacular views over Cape Byron for $329.
Sunrise tours See the first rays to hit mainland Australia with Pioneering Spirit and finish up with coffee and cake ($15; ⓣ02/6685 7721). Of course, you could just walk up to the lighthouse yourself, but it's quite a trek, particularly at that time of the morning.
Surfing Black Dog Surfing, Shop 8, The Plaza ⓣ02/66809828, ⓦwww.blackdogsurfing.com. The best of many outlets offering gear hire and lessons; they guarantee you'll stand up on your first lesson, a bold claim worth testing out. One- to five-day courses range from $60 to $200.
Taxi Byron Bay Transport Services ⓣ02/6685 5008. There's a taxi rank on Jonson St, opposite the *Great Northern Hotel*.

Far north coast hinterland

The beautiful **far north coast hinterland** lies between the major service town of **Lismore**, in the fertile Richmond River valley to the south, and **Murwillumbah**, in the even lusher valley of the Tweed River near the Queensland border. Much of the area dances to a different tune, with hippies, craft markets, communes and Kombi vans very much the norm in this "Rainbow Region". The hinterland's three rainforest national parks and several reserves are World Heritage–listed: **Mount Warning National Park** rises in the middle of a massive caldera, on whose northwest and southern rims lie the **Border Ranges and Nightcap national parks**, the latter near countercultural **Nimbin** and **The Channon**, home to the largest and most colourful market in the area.

You need your own **vehicle** to get the best out of the area, particularly to complete one of the most **scenic drives** in New South Wales, the short round-trip over the mountainous, winding country roads north and northeast of Lismore to Nimbin, The Channon and Clunes, and then via Eltham and Bexhill, with superb views from the ridges and hilltops.

Nimbin and around

Fifty kilometres inland from Byron via Lismore is **NIMBIN**, site of the famed Aquarius Festival that launched Australian hippie culture in 1973; it's a friendly little place and synonymous with the country's alternative life. The surrounding rainforest is dotted with as many as fifty communes, while the town itself is famous for live music, crafts and New Age therapies, but mainly **marijuana**. Visitors are invariably offered dope as soon as they set foot in town and you'll see it smoked openly on the streets; however, that doesn't mean to say you can wave joints around and expect not to get arrested should the police make one of their infrequent visits. Try to time your visit to coincide with the annual **Mardi Grass and Cannabis Law Reform Rally** (ⓦwww.nimbinmardigrass.com), held on the first weekend in May, when the town becomes a tent city and a high proportion of the temporary population have dreadlocks – bong throwing, joint rolling and campaigning rallies are amongst the activities on offer. Alternatively, aim to make it here on a **market** day (third and fifth Sunday of the month), where you'll catch some music, crafts and great organic food.

The tiny centre of Nimbin is aglow with buildings painted in bright, psychedelic designs, while small stores sell health food and incense sticks; everything of interest is on the main strip, Cullen Street. The **Nimbin Museum** (daily 9am–5pm; gold-coin donation) is a weird and wonderful living museum run by hippies, with a Kombi van left where it was driven through the front wall, lots of way-out graffiti and a ceiling mobile made from hand whisks – it nevertheless manages to impart a message of sorts about the value of Bundjalung Aboriginal culture and the benefits of cannabis use. If you have Green leanings, the **Nimbin Environmental Centre** might be of interest – they campaign on environmental issues, and can arrange visits to the **Djanbung Gardens Permaculture Centre** (ⓦwww.permaculture.com.au), a showcase for a system of sustainable agriculture that is gaining ground worldwide. The **Hemp Embassy** (daily 10am–5pm; ⓦwww.hempembassy.net) too is worth a look; learn why the Hemp Party believe the herb should be legalized (you can even join if you want) and browse through some of their previous campaigns and press releases.

Practicalities

Nimbin has its own **tourist office** (daily 9am–5pm; ⓣ02/6689 1764) at 8 Cullen St. There's no regular public transport to the town: the **Nimbin Shuttle Bus** runs up from Byron (Mon–Sat; $25 return; ⓣ02/6680 9189, ⓦwww.nimbintours.com) but is really as much a day-tour as the other options running out of the bay (p.279).

Accommodation

There are a number of **places to stay** in and near Nimbin, though during Mardi Grass the place is booked up well in advance, so be prepared to **camp**; all the hostels have pitches available.

Granny's Farm Backpackers & Camping ⓣ02/6689 1333. In a peaceful farm setting a short walk from town, this extremely pretty little hostel has a converted old train carriage you can sleep in down by the creek, two pools, and a general emphasis on having a good time. Dorms $20, doubles ❷–❸

Grey Gum Lodge 2 High St ⓣ02/6689 1713. Right in town, this very comfortable and beautifully decorated guesthouse is about as smart as it gets hereabouts, with a saltwater swimming pool but no Nimbin vibe – a plus for some people. ❸

Nimbin Rox YHA 74 Thorburn St ⓣ02/6689 0022, ⓦwww.yha.com.au. The pick of the hostels, this friendly, well-managed place has a range of accommodation plus a pool, flotation tank and massage room in its fruit garden. It's set in a superb hilltop location just outside town and named after the huge sacred rock monoliths which it overlooks. Camping $12, dorms $24, canvas lodges, doubles and tepees ❷

Rainbow Retreat 75 Thorburn St ⓣ02/6689 1262, ⓦwww.rainbowretreat.net. The hippiest place in town, with accommodation either in a dorm, an old VW Kombi, a gypsy wagon or a cheap double, plus camping space. It shares a stretch of Goolmanger Creek with the resident platypus, while horses munch between the tent spaces. Camping $13, dorms $20, doubles ❷–❸

Eating, drinking and nightlife

Cullen Street is full of good **places to eat**, including the legendary *Rainbow Café*, which has a nice garden out the back and serves good coffee, all-day breakfasts, burgers and salads. The *Nimbin Retro Café* has lots of tasty munchies – yummy veggie fare, hot chocolate and cakes, while *Nimbin Pizza & Pasta* is a long-established favourite offering gargantuan pizzas topped with local organic produce. For **nightlife and entertainment** there's the *Nimbin Hotel*, which sees plenty of live music and some interesting local characters; the *Rainbow Retreat* (see above), with more live bands; and the *Hemp Bar*, next to the Hemp Embassy, a cozy, Amsterdam-esque drinking hole. *The Nimbin Bush Theatre*

(ⓣ02/6689 1111), located in an old butter factory over the bridge opposite *Granny's Farm Backpackers*, serves fabulous food and is home to a charming little cinema – call or check the notice boards in town for screenings.

The Channon and the Nightcap National Park

THE CHANNON, a 26-kilometre drive south of Nimbin, is a pretty village on the banks of **Terania Creek**. It's home to the **Channon Craft Market** (second Sunday of the month), the best – and the first – of its type in the Rainbow Region. Begun in 1976 to provide the rapidly starving hippies with some cash, the rule that you have to "make it or bake it" still holds fast – it's a colourful spectacle and well worth a trip. The funky, heritage-listed *Channon Tavern* is located within an old butter factory, and serves up hearty dinners and local gossip.

A fourteen-kilometre drive into the **Nightcap National Park**, along the unsealed Terania Creek Road, brings you to **Protestors Falls** and a rainforest valley filled with ancient brush box trees, saved by the 1979 protest which was the first successful anti-logging campaign in Australia. You can walk down to the bottom of the falls, named after the dispute, to the Terania Creek Picnic Area. Also within the park are the one-hundred-metre cascades of **Minyon Falls**, often more of a trickle in summer; a steep walk (2hr return) leads down to the base. You're allowed to **camp** at the *Rummery Park Camping Ground* ($3 per adult) in nearby **Whian Whian State Conservation Area**, 2km from Minyon Falls along Peates Mountain Road; for something more comfortable try the arty *Havan's Ecotourist Retreat* (ⓣ02/6688 6108, ⓦwww.rainbowregion.com/havan; ❺), just off Terania Creek Road on Lawler Road, overlooking the creek and rainforest.

Murwillumbah and around

MURWILLUMBAH is a quiet, inland town on a bend of the Tweed River, a little over 30km northwest of Byron Bay. It's a good base for exploring the beautiful Tweed Valley and the mountains that extend to the Queensland border. It's well worth dropping by the **Tweed River Regional Art Gallery** (Wed–Sun 10am–5pm; free), at the corner of Tweed Valley Way and Minstral Road, which displays the work of local artists and travelling exhibitions.

At the Murwillumbah exit on the Pacific Highway, the **Big Avocado** lures the visitor towards **Tropical Fruit World** (daily 10am–4.30pm; $32; ⓦwww.tropicalfruitworld.com.au), slightly to the south on Duranbah Road. A plantation which has been turned into a miniature theme park, it grows avocados, macadamia nuts and many kinds of tropical fruit; you can ride around in open-air buses and miniature trains, or cruise around on man-made "tropical canals". There are canoes and aqua-bikes for rent, as well as a fruit market selling plantation produce.

The **Tweed Valley** and the surrounding land close to the Queensland border are among the most beautiful areas of New South Wales, ringed by mountain ranges that are actually the remains of an extinct volcano. Some twenty million years ago a huge shield **volcano** spewed lava through a central vent onto the surrounding plain. Erosion carved out a vast bowl around the centre of the resultant mass of lava, while the more resistant rocks around the edges stood firm. Right at the bowl's heart is **Mount Warning** (1157m), or Wollumbin ("cloud catcher") to the local **Bundjalung** Aborigines, the original vent of the volcano, whose unmistakable, twisted profile rises like a sentinel from the Tweed Valley. The mountain is a place of great cultural significance to the Bundjalung, who believe that only expressly chosen people may attempt the steep three-hour path to the summit; however, as at Uluru, many visitors can't resist the dazzling views on offer.

North of Murwillumbah is Tourist Drive 40, a 57-kilometre **scenic drive** through the **Tweed Valley**, which takes in some of its best features en route from Murwillumbah up to Tweed Heads and the state border. Tours are given during the cane-harvesting season at **Condong Sugar Mill** (mid-June to Nov Tues–Thurs 9am–3pm; $7; ⓣ02/6670 1700), on the Tweed River about 5km north of Murwillumbah.

Practicalities

Greyhound and Premier Motor Service long-distances **buses** stop in town. The **tourist office** (Mon–Sat 9am–4.30pm, Sun 9.30am–4pm; ⓣ02/6672 1340, ⓦwww.tweed-coolangatta.com) is located in the Rainforest Heritage Centre on Alma Street, and has an accommodation booking service.

Places to stay in Murwillumbah include the Art Deco *Imperial Hotel* (ⓣ02/6672 1036; singles ❶, doubles ❷) at 115 Main St, a grand old building right in the centre of town, with good-value singles and doubles, an excellent bistro and local bands at weekends. *Mount Warning Riverside YHA Backpackers* (ⓣ02/6672 3763, ⓦwww.yha.com.au; dorms $25, doubles ❷), at 1 Tumbulgum Rd, is a truly wonderful find; a cozy hostel in a house leaning over the river, it has swimming, bikes for rent, free canoes and rowing boat, plus free ice cream every evening at 9pm – stay for two nights and you'll get a free trip to Mount Warning. Alternatively, make the most of the countryside by staying in rural accommodation: *Mount Warning Forest Hideaway* (ⓣ02/6679 7277, ⓦwww.foresthideaway.com.au; ❹–❺), on Byrill Creek Road near the village of Uki, southwest of town, occupies a hundred acres of lush forest and offers motel-style units with cooking facilities, plus a swimming pool.

Places to eat include the *Blue Frog*, on Wharf Street, for breakfast and lunch, and the *Imperial Hotel*, where you'll find the best bistro food in town.

Lord Howe and Norfolk islands

Lord Howe Island, 700km northeast of Sydney, and roughly in line with Port Macquarie, is technically a part of New South Wales, despite its distance from the mainland. Its nearest neighbour is **Norfolk Island**, 900km further northeast, an external independent territory of Australia, though geographically it's closer to New Zealand. The approach to tourism of the two subtropical islands couldn't be more different: Lord Howe is the perfect eco-destination, attracting outdoor types with its rugged beauty, while Norfolk Island receives fewer visitors, concentrating primarily on its status as a tax haven. Neither island caters to budget travellers.

Getting there

You can **fly to Lord Howe Island** with Qantas from Sydney (at least daily for most of the year), Brisbane (weekly) and Port Macquarie (once weekly in the summer) for about $800 return in peak season, or $600 return in the winter months. Overseas visitors can fly to Lord Howe as an add-on fare on an air pass (see p.35). Norfolk Air (Ⓣ1300 663 913, Ⓦwww.norfolkair.com) operate **flights to Norfolk Island** from Sydney (four per week), Brisbane (four per week) and Newcastle (one per week), while Air New Zealand fly to the island twice a week from Auckland – flights from Australia cost around $800 return, and those from New Zealand near to $550; all flights from Norfolk are subject to a $30 departure tax. There are no flights between the two islands.

On both islands, accommodation has to be arranged before you book your air travel, to limit the number of tourists staying each night. It's often much easier – and better value – to go on a **package tour**. Prices for seven nights range from around $990 in winter to $1400 in summer: try Oxley Travel (Ⓣ02/6583 1955 or 1800 671 546, Ⓦwww.oxleytravel.com.au) or Talpacific Holidays (Ⓣ1300 665 737, Ⓦwww.talpacific.com).

Lord Howe Island

I would strongly urge preserving this beautiful island from further intrusions of any kind...

Government Expedition, 1882

World Heritage–listed **LORD HOWE ISLAND** is a kind of Australian Galapagos, and a favourite destination for ecotourists. Just 11km long and 2.8km across at its widest point, the crescent-shaped island's only industry other than tourism is its plantations of **kentia palms** (see p.291) and two-thirds of the island is designated as Permanent Park Reserve. As you fly in, you'll get a stunning view of the whole of the volcanic island: the towering summits of rainforest-clad **Mount Gower** and **Mount Lidgbird** at the southern end; the narrow centre with its idyllic lagoon and a **coral reef** extending about 6km along the west coast; and a group of tiny islets off the lower northern end of the island providing sanctuary for the prolific **bird-life**.

The emphasis here is on tranquillity: there are only 350 islanders; no rowdy nightclubs spoiling the peace; no mobile-phone coverage; and most of the four hundred visitors allowed at any one time are couples and families. Even disregarding the island's ecological attractions, it's a fascinating place to stay: most visitors are intrigued by the small details of island life, such as how children are schooled and food is brought from the mainland, and are generally eager to sample life in this egalitarian paradise where no one locks their car (or even takes the key out of the ignition), bike or house. Though it's expensive to get to the island, once here you'll find that cruises, activities and bike rental are all relatively affordable – the same doesn't apply to eating out, unfortunately. The island's **climate** is subtropical, with temperatures rising from a mild 19°C in winter to 26°C in the summer, and an annual rainfall of 1650mm. It's cheaper to visit in the winter, though some places are closed.

Some history

Lord Howe Island was discovered in 1788 by Lieutenant Henry Lidgbird Ball (who named the island after the British admiral Richard Howe), commander of the First Fleet ship *Supply*, during a journey from Sydney to found a penal colony on Norfolk Island. The island wasn't inhabited for another 55 years, however; the first **settlers came** in 1833, and others followed in the 1840s. In 1853 two white men arrived with three women from the Gilbert Islands in the central Pacific, and

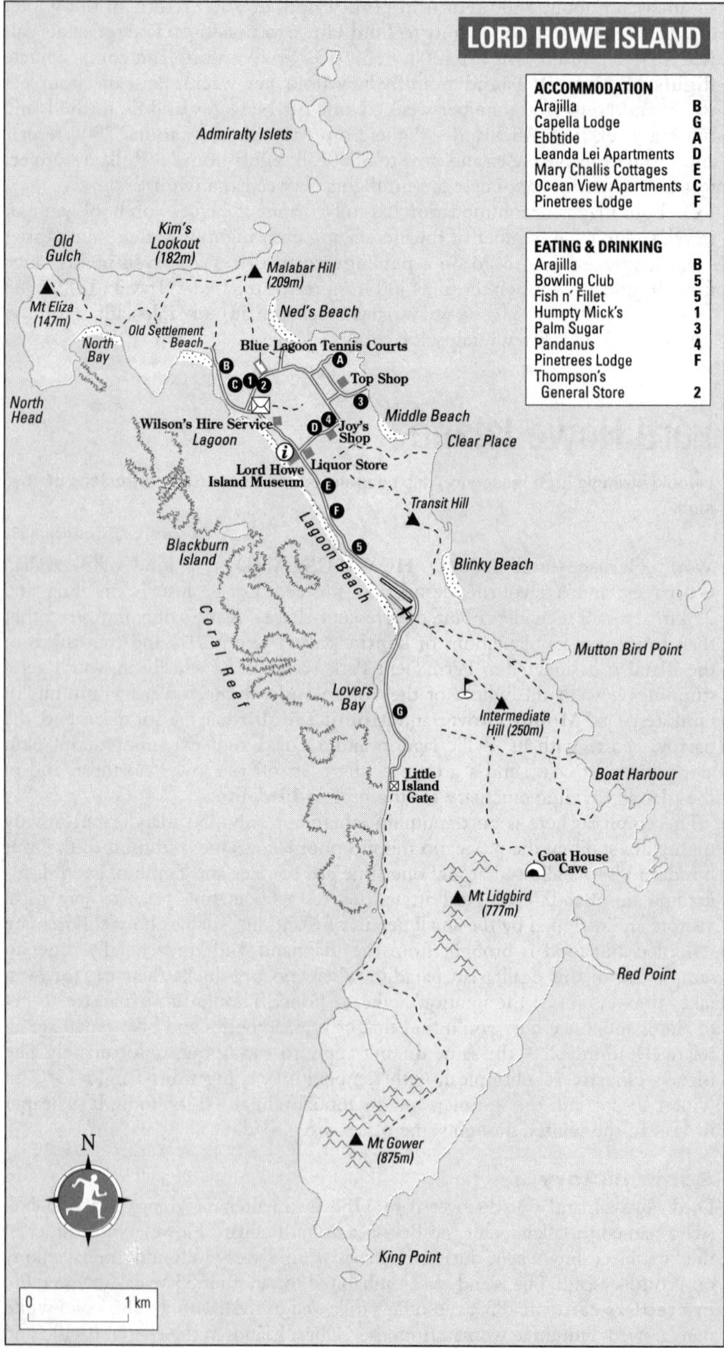

LORD HOWE ISLAND
ACCOMMODATION
Arajilla B
Capella Lodge G
Ebbtide A
Leanda Lei Apartments D
Mary Challis Cottages E
Ocean View Apartments C
Pinetrees Lodge F
EATING & DRINKING
Arajilla B
Bowling Club 5
Fish n' Fillet 5
Humpty Mick's 1
Palm Sugar 3
Pandanus 4
Pinetrees Lodge F
Thompson's General Store 2
Admiralty Islets
Kim's Lookout (182m)
Old Gulch
Malabar Hill (209m)
Mt Eliza (147m)
Ned's Beach
Old Settlement Beach
North Bay
Blue Lagoon Tennis Courts
Top Shop
North Head
Middle Beach
Wilson's Hire Service
Lagoon
Joy's Shop
Clear Place
Liquor Store
Lord Howe Island Museum
Transit Hill
Blackburn Island
Lagoon Beach
Blinky Beach
Coral Reef
Mutton Bird Point
Lovers Bay
Intermediate Hill (250m)
Little Island Gate
Boat Harbour
Goat House Cave
Mt Lidgbird (777m)
Red Point
N
Mt Gower (875m)
King Point
0
1 km
Ball's Pyramid (23km)

Lord Howe ecology

Seven million years ago, a volcanic eruption on the sea floor created Lord Howe Island and its 27 surrounding islets and outcrops – the island's boomerang shape is a mere remnant (around two percent) of its original form, mostly eroded by the sea. While much of the **flora** on the island is similar to that of Australia, New Zealand, New Caledonia and Norfolk Island, the island's relative isolation has led to the evolution of many **new species** – of the 241 native plants found here, 105 are endemic, including the important indigenous **kentia palm** (see below).

Similarly, until the arrival of settlers, fifteen species of flightless **land birds** (nine of which are now extinct) lived on the island, undisturbed by predators and coexisting with migrating sea birds, skinks, geckos, spiders, snails and the now-extinct giant horned turtle. However, in the nineteenth century Lord Howe became a port of call for ships en route to Norfolk Island, whose hungry crews eradicated the island's stocks of **white gallinule** and **white-throated pigeon**. The small, plump and flightless **woodhen** managed to survive, protected on Mount Gower, and an intensive captive breeding programme in the early 1980s saved the species (there are now about 350). About one million **sea birds** – fourteen species – nest on Lord Howe annually: it is one of the few known breeding-grounds of the providence petrel; has the world's largest colony of red-tailed tropic birds; and is the most southerly breeding location of the sooty tern, the noddy tern and the masked booby. Cats have now been eradicated from the island, as a result of which bird numbers have soared, and a plan to exterminate rats and mice is under way. Nervous travellers can rest in peace on Lord Howe, safe in the knowledge that there are none of the poisonous spiders and snakes that blight the mainland.

The cold waters of the **Tasman Sea**, which surround Lord Howe, host the world's southernmost **coral reef**, a tropical oddity which is sustained by the warm summer current sweeping in from the Great Barrier Reef. There are about sixty varieties of brilliantly coloured and fantastically shaped coral, and the meeting of warm and cold currents means that a huge variety of both **tropical and temperate fish** can be spotted in the crystal-clear waters. Some of the most colourful species include the yellow moon wrasse, parrotfish and the yellow-and-black banner fish. Unique to Lord Howe is the doubleheader, with its bizarre, bulbous forehead and fat lips. Beyond the lagoon, the water becomes very deep, with particularly good diving in the seas around the **Admiralty Islets**, which have sheer underwater precipices and chasms. The diving season lasts from May to November (for information on dive companies, see p.295).

it is from this small group that many of Lord Howe's present population are descended. In the 1840s and 1850s the island served as a stopover for **whaling ships** from the US and Britain, with as many as fifty ships a year passing through. In 1882, a government expedition from the mainland recommended that in order to preserve the island, no one other than the present "happy, industrious" leaseholders and their families be allowed to make permanent settlement.

With the decline of whaling, economic salvation came in the form of the "thatch" palm, one of the four endemic species of the **kentia palm**. Previously used as roofing for the islanders' homes, it began to be exported as a decorative interior plant, boosting the island's economy. The profits from the kentia trade were shared out equally amongst the Lord Howe residents, each of whom was in turn expected to take on an equal share of the (not overly hard) work on the kentia plantations. In 1918, however, the kentia industry was damaged by the appearance of **rats**, which escaped onto the island from a ship. **Tourism** was eventually to become the mainstay of the island – Lord Howe became a popular stopover on the cruise-ship circuit before World War II, and after the war it began to be visited by holiday-makers from Sydney, who came by seaplane.

△ Masked booby, Lord Howe Island

Today, rats still pose a hazard to the palms, but the **kentia industry** is nonetheless in resurgence, with profits going towards the preservation of the island's unique ecosystem. Seeds are no longer exported but instead cultivated in the Lord Howe Island Board's own **nursery**, which sells two and a half million plants annually; they also grow seedlings here for regeneration around the island. You can visit the nursery, as well as other parts of the island on guided walks with Ron's Rambles (ⓣ02/6563 2010 or book at Thompson's General Store – see opposite; $20). Ron will have you sniffing herbs, feeling rocks and believing some tall stories about the early islanders' bushcraft.

Arrival, information and transport

There's no official transport from the **airport**, located in the narrow central part of the island, but wherever you're staying, you'll be met on arrival by your lodge-owner. The island's **tourist office** (Mon–Fri 9.30am–3pm, Sun 9am–2pm; ⓣ02/6563 2114 or 1800 240 937, ⓦwww.lordhoweisland.info) is located inside the Lord Howe Island Museum at the junction of Lagoon and Middle

Beach roads: all tours and activities can be booked here, and the useful *Ramblers Guide to Lord Howe Island* ($9), which covers all the walks on the island in great detail, is also available.

Crossing the centre of the island to the north, Ned's Beach Road has a cluster of **shops** and **services**, including Thompson's General Store (daily 8am–6pm; ⓣ02/6563 2155), where you can book most activities, order roast chooks, and rent fishing or snorkelling gear. You'll also find a community hall-cum-summer cinema and a **post office** (Mon–Fri 10am–3pm) on this road. There are no ATMs on the island, although Larrup's beachwear shop on Ned's Beach Road and Joy's Shop (daily 9am–6.30pm), give $50–100 cash out on eftpos or credit cards to customers. Basically, it's a good idea to bring all the **cash** you'll need with you.

There are three places to buy **groceries** and sundries on the island: Thompson's General Store; Joy's Shop, opposite *Leanda Lei Apartments* on Middle Beach Road; and Top Shop (Mon–Fri 9am–12.30pm & 4.30–6pm, Sun 9am–12.30pm), tucked away on Skyline Street off Mutton Bird Drive, where you can buy fresh meat and vegetables. Inevitably, transport costs make things more expensive than on the mainland.

Transport

The island has few **roads** and only a small number of cars. There are sporadic streetlights down Lagoon Road, but you'll need to bring a torch with you, or buy one from one of the stores, if you want to venture far at night – in wet conditions, you might see some glow-in-the-dark funghi. The most common ways to get around are by **bicycle**, boat or on foot. Most lodges offer **bikes** to guests, but they don't have lights either, so if you want to ride at night attach a torch; if your lodge has exhausted its supply, then you can also rent cycles from Wilson's Hire Service (closed Sat; ⓣ02/6563 2045; $7), opposite Lagoon Beach. **Cars** can be rented at Wilson's ($55/day) and *Leanda Lei Apartments* ($66/day; ⓣ02/6563 2195); there are only a few available, so pre-booking is essential.

Accommodation

Most of the accommodation on Lord Howe Island is **self-catering** and of a good standard. All the lodges are centrally located, with the exception of *Capella Lodge*, where the privacy, views and air of luxury more than compensate.

Arajilla Lagoon Rd ⓣ02/6563 2002 or 1800 063 928, ⓦwww.arajilla.com.au. This chocolates-on-your-pillow kind of place nestles amongst kentia palms and banyan forest, a short hop away from Old Settlement Beach. The ten stylish suites and couple of two-bed apartments all have private decks, and the yurt (where you can do yoga and have a massage) is shortly to be transformed into a spa. Delicious meals are taken in the beautiful Balinese-style bar-restaurant. Full board only. Suites $528pp, two-bed apartments $1078–1155 per night. Closed June–Aug.

Capella Lodge Lagoon Rd ⓣ02/9544 2273, ⓦwww.lordhowe.com. Nestling under Mount Gower and Mount Lidgbird, this is the most luxurious place to stay on the island. The stunning bar, restaurant and infinity pool overlook the mountains, and the suites and loft apartments are all interior-designed to within an inch of their lives. Breakfast, sunset drinks and canapés, and contemporary fusion-style evening meals are included in the price. There's also an indulgent spa. The one niggle is that the restaurant isn't open to non-residents – it seems a shame not to share those views. Full board only, $490–690pp.

Ebbtide Muttonbird Drive ⓣ02/6563 2023, ⓦwww.ebbtide-lhi.com.au. Nestling up on the cliff by Searles Point, this very friendly place has simple, stylish apartments and cottages set in a tropical garden of pawpaw and banana (guests can help themselves). A private bush-track leads down to Ned's Beach. 7–8

Leanda Lei Apartments Middle Beach Rd ⓣ02/6563 2095, ⓦwww.leandalei.com.au. Smart, clean and run with friendly efficiency by the Riddle family. The studios and one- or two-bedroom apartments here are set in lush manicured grounds with BBQs, close to Lagoon Beach. ❼–❽

Mary Challis Cottages Lagoon Rd ⓣ02/6563 2076. Situated right by Lagoon Beach, these two cute cottages have everything you'll need, plus some home-baked goodies on arrival, and a couple of docile cows. ❻

Pinetrees Lodge Lagoon Rd ⓣ02/9262 6585, ⓦwww.pinetrees.com.au. The island's first guest-house is a family-friendly place, set in extensive, forested grounds and rigorously maintained by an army of staff. Accommodation is in motel-style units or newer "garden cottages" set around the original lodge, where everyone takes full advantage of the delicious meals included in the price. There's also a tennis court, and a boatshed over the road on Lagoon Beach, a delightful place for a sundowner from the honesty bar. Full board $240–400pp.

The island

A good way to kick off your island idyll is with a trip to the **Lord Howe Island Museum** (Mon–Fri 9am–3pm, Sat & Sun 9.30am–2pm), on the corner of Middle Beach and Lagoon roads, which goes a long way to answering all those "so who's related to who?" questions you inevitably bore your lodge-owner with. The museum hosts very good slide-shows on island history and ecology a few evenings a week, narrated by the island naturalist, Ian Hutton (days and times vary, check at the tourist office; $6), as well as irregular cultural nights.

Walking trails and activities

At the island's **northern end**, you can walk all the way from North Bay or Old Settlement Beach on the western side to Ned's Beach on the east, stopping at various lookout points – allow a good five hours. Relaxed, educational half-day **guided walks** are available for around $20 from personable local resident Ron (for a bit of folklore and local colour) or Ian Hutton (for an informed look at the island's ecology); book at Thompson's Store for either. If you simply want to take in the beautiful views, it's very easy to do it yourself. From the path behind **Old Settlement Beach**, it's a steep two-kilometre climb over a hill to **North Bay**, where there's a picnic area and BBQ; you start the twenty-minute trek to the summit of **Mount Eliza** (147m) from behind the huts here. It's worth taking a boat to **North Bay** with Islander Cruises (ⓣ02/6563 2021; $15) and beginning the walk from there, as the initial hike from Old Settlement Beach takes a lot out of you without giving a lot back. The summit of Mount Eliza is the most accessible place to see **sooty terns** in their southernmost breeding grounds. When the colony visits the island between September and March each female lays a single speckled egg on the bare ground, which means that the actual summit has to be closed for the birds' protection.

Back at the base at **North Bay**, a five-minute walk through forest leads to **Old Gulch**, a beach of boulders, where at low tide you can rock-hop to the **Herring Pools** at the base of the cliff front and examine the colourful marine life before returning to the picnic area. Walking back up the hill towards Old Settlement Beach you can take the path east to **Kim's Lookout** (182m), which provides a good view of the settlement and the lagoon beaches and islets. Heading along the cliff edge from here, you come to **Malabar Hill** (209m), which gives access to one of the world's largest nesting concentrations of **red-tailed tropic birds**, who between September and May make their homes in the crannies of the cliff face below, laying only one egg and looking after the chick for twelve weeks until it can fly. From the summit, you can just see Ball's Pyramid way down to the south around the corner of Mount Lidgbird. To complete the walk, you drop down to **Ned's Beach**, where you'll probably need a long drink. There are more walks in the centre of the island – maps are available from the tourist office and at your accommodation.

Slightly less energetic activities are available at the *Blue Lagoon Lodge*'s **tennis courts** on Ned's Beach Road (book at Thompson's General Store, balls and rackets are available to rent), and the nine-hole **golf course** near *Capella Lodge* ($20 with your own clubs, $30 with theirs; balls $1); there's a chicken race held here on Fridays at 2pm. For something even less strenuous, Whitfield's run a half-day tour of the island in their air-conditioned bus, with a tea break included ($28).

Mount Gower

The ultimate view on the island is at its **southern end**, where the lofty summit of **Mount Gower** (875m) gives vistas over the whole island and out to sea towards the world's tallest sea stack, **Balls Pyramid** (548m), a spike of volcanic rock which breaks dramatically up out of the ocean 23km from Lord Howe. Mount Gower is high enough to have a true **mist forest** on its summit, with a profusion of ferns, tree trunks and rocks covered in mosses. This extremely strenuous walk can be undertaken only with a licensed **guide** (Jack Shick is the most experienced; 8hr; $35, BYO lunch; booking essential ⓣ02/6563 2218) and is definitely not for the faint-hearted – one section of the walk runs precariously along a narrow cliff-face above the sea, and in parts the track is so steep that you have to pull yourself up the guide ropes. The path to the top was blazed by botanists in 1869, who took two days to get there, but they were rewarded with the discovery of a plant seen nowhere else on earth – the **pumpkin tree**, bearing fleshy orange flowers. You can see other rare endemic plants here, including the island apple and the blue plum, as well as birds such as the providence petrel and the woodhen.

To join the walk, you have to be at the Little Island Gate on the south of the island by 7.30am: you can get a lift there with Whitfield's Island Tours (ⓣ02/6563 2115; $6 return), or it's about a half-hour cycle ride from the north of the island.

Water-based activities

The island has some sensational swimming, snorkelling and diving sites, as well as a large number of boat trips. The beaches here are lovely, though the white sand isn't the soft, powdered stuff you find on the mainland, but rather rough little bits of broken-up coral. There's stunning snorkelling at **Sylphs Hole**, off Old Settlement Beach, and on the east side of the island at Ned's Beach, where corals lie only 10m from the shore. The combination of temperate and tropical waters make double-headed wrasse, lobsters and angelfish a common sight. **Snorkelling gear** and wetsuits can be borrowed cheaply from the hut at the back of Ned's Beach (put your money in the honesty box); sets are also available from most lodges and at Wilson's Hire Service ($4). Every day around an hour after low tide, Ned's Beach is the scene of a **fish-feeding** frenzy, when people gather to throw fish scraps into the water, attracting a throng of big trevally, kingfish and reef sharks.

If you want to **surf** on the island it's best to bring your own board (Qantas can accommodate them if you call in advance), although Larrup's have a few available for rent ($20/half-day, $30 full day). Blinky Beach is the best for surfing, although you can also paddle out 1500m into the lagoon to the break beyond the reef to catch a few waves with the locals.

Glass-bottom boat cruises over the beautiful reef are available from Lagoon Beach with Lord Howe Environmental Tours (ⓣ02/6563 2214; 2hr; $30), based on Lagoon Road. If you're interested in **diving**, **fishing**, **snorkelling tours**, **kayaking**, or any kind of **boat trip**, one of the two adjacent boatsheds on Lagoon Road will sort you out. **Busty's Boatshed** is a one-stop shop for Islander Cruises (ⓣ02/6563 2021, ⓔislandercruises@bigpond.com.au), the locally owned Howea Divers (ⓣ02/6563 2290, ⓔhoweadivers@bigpond.com.au), Lord Howe Nature Tours (ⓣ02/6563 2447) and Sea to Summit Expeditions (ⓣ02/6563 2218). The **Pro Dive Boatshed** next door is home to the Sydney-based dive outfit (ⓣ02/9281 5066 or 1800 820 820, ⓦwww.prodive.com.au), Marine Adventures (ⓣ02/6563 2195, ⓦwww.marineadventures.com.au) and Lulawai Cruises (same number). Both sheds offer a bewildering array of magical experiences, from North Bay barbecue trips and sunset tours in the lagoon, to snorkelling excursions, dive courses, leisurely fishing jaunts, and cruises around the awe-inspiring Ball's Pyramid.

Eating and drinking

Bookings are necessary at all **eating** places for evening meals (not much vegetarian food is available, so ask beforehand). The **Co-op** (closed Wed & Sat) on Ned's Beach Road, opened in an attempt to reduce the amount of packaging brought onto the island, is a great place to stock up on bulk items like muesli and pasta. There's no **pub** on Lord Howe; the closest thing to a **bar** is the *Bowling Club* (daily from 4.30pm), which also hosts a popular disco on Friday nights (8pm–midnight).

Arajilla Lagoon Rd ⓣ02/6563 2002. This luxury resort has an excellent restaurant serving delicious Australian cuisine in the evenings, although due to full board being offered to guests it rarely has space for non-residents.

Fish 'n' Fillet ⓣ02/6563 2208. These guys hold fish-fry nights at the bowling club on Tuesday and Thursday from 5.30pm. If you want to take the DIY option, they run a great scheme where you leave your seafood order in the boxes outside Humpty Mick's or Joy's Shop by 3pm, and the fish is delivered straight to your door between 5pm and 6.30pm – just leave the money on your table if you're out.

Humpty Mick's Ned's Beach Rd. An essential lunch or snack stop offering affordable salads, speciality burgers, focaccias and daily fish specials – it should reopen in October 2007 following renovations. Daily 8am–8.30pm

Palm Sugar Skyline Drive ⓣ02/6563 2120. Afternoon tea, amazing cakes, and some excellent evening meals are served on the colourful, tranquil veranda. Private lunches, beach picnics and BBQs are available on request. 2pm–close, closed Wed.

Pandanus Anderson Rd ⓣ02/6563 2240. This pleasant, minimalist restaurant has wooden floors, starchy white table linen and beachy artwork, and serves pizza, pasta and mains with an Italian flavour. Daily from 6.30pm & Thurs–Sat lunch.

Thompson's General Store Ned's Beach Rd. Inexpensive takeaway sandwiches, fish and beef burgers at lunchtime only.

Pinetrees Lodge Lagoon Rd ⓣ02/6563 2177. The Monday-night fish fry here is the best of several on the island; it's well worth booking for this quintessential Lord Howe experience, including as it does vast plates of sushi, fried kingfish, chips, salads and groaning tables of desserts. Go early and have a glass of wine over at the lodge's boatshed on the lagoon, where you can watch the often spectacular sunset.

Norfolk Island

Just 8km long and 5km wide, tiny, isolated **NORFOLK ISLAND** is an External Territory of Australia located 1456km east of Brisbane. The island has had an eventful history, being linked with early convict settlements and later with the descendants of Fletcher Christian and other "mutiny-on-the-*Bounty*" rebels. It's a unique place, forested with grand indigenous pine trees, and with a mild subtropical **climate** ranging between 12°C and 19°C in the winter and from 19°C to 28°C in the summer; Norfolk is also said to have the world's **cleanest air** after Antarctica. The island's **tax-haven** status makes it a refuge for millionaires, and most visitors spend a fortune in the island's numerous **duty-free stores**.

Norfolk mainly attracts honeymooners or retired Australians and New Zealanders (known as the "newly weds and nearly deads"). All visitors require a **passport** to visit the island, which has its own Legislative Assembly. A thirty-day **visitor permit**, extendable to 120 days, is granted automatically on arrival. The island has no income tax, finances being raised from sources such as departure tax ($30) and a road levy included in the price of petrol. Most of the 1900 local people remain unaffected by tourism, maintaining their friendly attitude, amusing nicknames (confusingly used in the island's telephone directory) and the remnants of their dialect, **Norfolk**, a mixture of old West Country English and Tahitian (see p.298). While the crime rate on Norfolk is for the most part very low, two **murders** in 2002 and 2004 (the second that of the Deputy Chief Minister) have subjected the island to unprecedented and unwelcome media attention.

Much of the land is cleared for cultivation, as islanders have to grow all their own fresh food; cattle roam freely on the green island and are given right of way, creating a positively bucolic atmosphere. At the centre of the island is its only significant settlement, **Burnt Pine** – on the south coast, picturesque **Kingston** is the sightseeing focus. Scenic winding roads provide access to the **Norfolk Island National Park** and the **Botanic Garden** in the northern half of the island, which together cover twenty percent of Norfolk's area with subtropical rainforest. Norfolk Island is also an ornithologist's paradise, with nine endemic **landbird** species, including the endangered **Norfolk Island green parrot**, with its distinctive chuckling call. The two small, uninhabited islands immediately south of Norfolk, **Nepean** and **Phillip** islands, are important **sea bird** nesting sites.

Some history

A violent **volcanic eruption** three million years ago produced the Norfolk Ridge, extending from New Zealand to New Caledonia (Norfolk Island's closest neighbour, 700km north), with only Norfolk, **Phillip** and **Nepean islands** remaining above sea level. **Captain Cook** "discovered" the islands in 1774, but it's now believed that migrating Polynesian people lived here in the fourteenth or fifteenth centuries – their main settlement at Emily Bay has been excavated and stone tools found. Cook thought the tall **Norfolk pines** would make fine ships' masts, with accompanying sails woven from the native flax. Norfolk Island was settled in 1788, only six weeks after Sydney. However, plans to use the fertile island as a base to grow food for the starving young colony of Australia floundered when, in 1790, a First Fleet ship, the *Sirius*, was wrecked on a reef off the island, highlighting the island's lack of a navigable harbour. This **first settlement** was proved unviable when the pines were found not to be strong enough for masts, and it was finally abandoned in 1814. Most of the buildings were destroyed to discourage settlement by other powers.

Norfolk's isolation was one of the major reasons for its **second settlement** as a **prison** (1825–55), described officially as "a place of the extremest punishment short of death"; up to two thousand convicts were held on Norfolk, overseen by sadistic commandants who had virtually unlimited power to run the settlement and inflict punishments as they saw fit. Some of the imposing stone buildings designed by Royal Engineers still stand in **Kingston**, on the southern coast of the island.

Norfolk Island was again abandoned in 1855, but this time the buildings remained and were used a year later during the **third settlement**, which consisted of 194 Pitcairn Islanders (the entire population of the island), who left behind their overcrowded conditions to establish a new life here. The new settlers had only eight family surnames among them – five of which (Christian, Quintal, Adams, McCoy and Young) were the names of the original mutineers of the *Bounty*. These names – especially Christian – are still common on the island, and today about one in three islanders can claim descent from the mutineers. These descendants still speak some of their original language to each other: listen for expressions such as 'Watawieh Yorlye?' (how are you?) and 'Si Yorlye Morla' (see you tomorrow). **Bounty Day**, the day the Pitcairners arrived, is celebrated in Kingston on June 8.

Information, transport and tours

The island's **airport** is on the western side of the island, just outside **Burnt Pine**, the main service centre; here you'll find the **tourist office** (Mon, Tues, Thurs & Fri 8.30am–5pm, Wed 8.30am–4pm, Sat 8.30am–3pm; ⓣ6723/22147, ⓦwww.norfolkisland.com), which books tours and activities; the liquor bond store, which sells discounted alcohol on production of your airline ticket; the **post office**; the Communications Centre, where you go to make international **phone calls**; and two banks, Westpac and Commonwealth (the latter has the island's only ATM).

There's no public transport on Norfolk Island and it's rather hilly, so getting around by **car** is much the best option. Many accommodation places offer a car as part of the package or give you a big discount on **car rental**. It's very cheap anyway, with rates between $20 and $25 per day – Aloha Rent A Car (ⓣ6723/22510) is based at the airport. No one bothers with seat belts or even driving mirrors, and the maximum speed limit is only 50kph (40kph in town). There are also a limited number of **bikes** for rent, which can be arranged through the tourist office or your accommodation.

Tours

Pinetree Tours (ⓣ6723/22424, ⓦwww.pinetreetours.com) has an office on the main street next to the Commonwealth Bank; they offer a slew of **tours**, including an introductory half-day bus trip around the island ($25), a convict tour ($25) and meals in islanders' homes ($50). Bounty Excursions (ⓣ6723/23693, ⓔbounty@norfolk.nf) also runs a range of cultural and historic trips, while Culla & Co (ⓣ6723/22312), on Rooty Hill Road, offers shire-horse-drawn carriage rides of the island.

The island is surrounded by a coral reef and pristine waters, so at least one waterborne tour is a must; the volcanic sea floor is full of caves and swim-throughs and the whole area is a marine reserve – commercial fishing is banned. There are several glass-bottomed **boat cruises** ($20) on Emily Bay, including on the *Bounty Glass Bottomed Boat* (ⓣ6723/22515) and *Christian's Glaas Bohtam Boet* (ⓣ6723/23258). For fishing trips, call Advance Fishing (ⓣ6723/23363, ⓦwww.nf/advancefishing). Bounty Divers (ⓣ6723/24375, ⓦwww.bountydivers.nf) runs PADI courses ($500) and has **dive** charters ($120 per dive, including gear), **snorkelling** and **diving** gear for rent, and guided reef-walks. Tropical Sea Kayaks (ⓣ6723/80508, ⓦwww.seakayaking.nf) runs an easy tour (1hr 30min; $25) and a beautiful, longer paddle taking in tall cliffs, tiny islands, sea stacks and arches before culminating in a swim in the tranquil lagoon ($45).

Accommodation

The island has lots of **accommodation** in comfortable 1970s-style motels; a central online **booking service** for these places is available at Ⓦwww.norfolk-islandaccommodation.com, or call Ⓣ6723/22255.

Anson Bay Lodge Ⓣ6723/22897, Ⓔansonbaylodge@norfolk.nf. Small, blue weatherboard cottage for two to four people, located on Bullock's Hut Road. One of the cheapest places on the island but not for people offended by pine furniture. ④

Christians of Bucks Point Ⓣ6723/23833, Ⓦwww.christians.nf. Frilly, historic property on the southeast coast, where much of the timber used is from original convict buildings. You can pick fruit in the orchard when it's in season. ⑧

Forrester Court Clifftop Cottages Ⓣ6723/22838, Ⓦwww.forrestercourt.com. Lovely boutique cottages with great views over Cascade Bay and a tennis court. Car rental and a breakfast basket is included in the price. ⑧

Shearwater Scenic Villas Ⓣ6723/22539, Ⓦwww.shearwater.nf. Self-contained accommodation in extensive grounds, with terrific water views over Bumbora Reserve. ⑧

Tintoela of Norfolk Ⓣ6723/22946, Ⓦwww.tintoela.nf. Large, luxury wooden house, and adjacent cottages sleeping up to ten, with panoramic views of Cockpit Valley and Cascade Bay. ⑧

Whispering Pines Mount Pitt Rd Ⓣ6723/22114, Ⓦwww.norfolk-pines-group.nf/whisper.html. Another place that won't break the bank, with charming, hexagonal timber cottages hidden in thickly wooded gardens. ⑤

The island

The island's main settlement, **BURNT PINE**, is a fairly modern affair crammed with shops selling everything from cosmetics to stereos, all at duty-free prices; most shops are closed on Wednesday and Saturday afternoons and all day Sunday. The island's ecotourism attraction, **A Walk in the Wild** (daily 2–5pm; free), is based here at Taylor's Road, educating visitors about the fragile, disappearing rainforest and its bird life.

KINGSTON is Norfolk's administrative centre, with the Legislative Assembly meeting in the military barracks, and the old colonial Government House now home to the island's Administrator. There's an excellent view from the **Queen Elizabeth Lookout** over the **Kingston and Arthur's Vale Historic Area** and the poignant seafront **cemetery**, containing a number of graves from the brutal second settlement and detailed interpretative boards. It's expensive to visit the remaining buildings and their museums: you can tour the buildings separately ($8) or with a combined ticket ($20), which allows multiple access to all sites spread over several days. **Quality Row** bears some of the world's most impressive examples of Georgian **military architecture**, and looking at the buildings now it's difficult to imagine the suffering that took place behind their walls. This is the place to come for a taste of Norfolk Island history: there are four museums housed under the umbrella of the **Norfolk Island Museum** (daily 11am–3pm; $8 per museum or $18 combined ticket; Ⓦwww.museums.gov.nf). The **Archeological Museum** is located in the basement of the former Commissariat, which was built in 1835; the upstairs was converted to the All Saints Church by the Pitcairners. Close by, in the **No. 10 House Museum**, there are examples of Norfolk pine furniture made by convicts.

The worthwhile **Social History Museum** is located in the pier store and outlines the story of the island through its three settlements. Perhaps most interesting, though, is the **Maritime Museum**, in what was once the Protestant chapel; various artefacts recovered from the 1790 wreck of the *Sirius* are on display, including its huge anchor, but more compelling is the *Bounty*-related paraphernalia brought here by Pitcairners, including the ship's cannon and even the kettle that was used on Pitcairn Island for everything from fermenting liquor to boiling sea water for salt. The Kingston area is also the site of the island's main swimming **beaches**, protected by a small reef. Immediately in front of the walls of the ruined barracks is **Slaughter Bay**, which has a sandy beach dotted with interestingly gnarled and eroded basalt rock formations; the small hard-coral reef is excellent for **snorkelling**. At low tide you can take a cruise in a glass-bottomed boat (see "Tours", p.298) from nearby Emily Bay, which is also a beautiful, safe swimming area backed by a large pine forest.

In **Bumbora Reserve**, just west of Kingston, reached by car via Bumbora Road, you can see the natural regrowth of Norfolk pines; from the reserve you can walk down to Bumbora Beach, a shady little strip of sand where you'll find some safe pools for children to swim in at low tide. There's another track down to **Crystal Pool**, which has more swimming and snorkelling.

The west coast

West of Burnt Pine, along Douglas Drive, you'll find the exquisite **St Barnabas Chapel**, once the property of the Melanesian Mission (Anglican), which relocated gradually here from New Zealand between 1866 and 1921. The chapel's rose window was designed by William Morris and some of the others by Sir Edward Burne-Jones; the altar was carved by Solomon Islanders – ancestral masters of the craft.

Further down the **west coast** there's a scenic picnic area with tables and barbecues high over **Anson Bay**, from where it's a satisfying walk down to the beach. Immediately north of here, the **national park** has 8km of walking trails, many of them old logging tracks. Many walks start from **Mount Pitt** (320m), a pleasing drive up a fairly narrow and winding sealed road surrounded by palms and trees – worth it for the panoramic views. The most enjoyable walk from here is the three-kilometre route to the **Captain Cook Memorial** (1hr 45min), which starts as a beautiful grassy path but soon becomes a downward-sloping dirt track with some steps. Just south of the national park, on Pitt Road, the tranquil rainforest of the **Botanic Gardens** is worth a stroll. Here you can observe the forty endemic plant species, including the pretty native hibiscus, the native palm, and the island's best-known symbol, the **Norfolk pine**, which can grow as high as 57m with a circumference of up to 11m. Camping isn't allowed in the national park or the gardens, although they're both open around the clock.

Eating, drinking and entertainment

Norfolk Island **food** is plain and fresh, with an emphasis on locally caught fish and home-grown seasonal produce. Tahitian influence remains in the tradition of big fish-fries, and in some novel ways of preparing bananas. As most accommodation is self-catering, you'll need to head to the Foodland Supermarket in Burnt Pine (daily to 6pm). On Sunday afternoon fresh fish is sold at the Kingston pier.

The best, and most expensive, **restaurant** is *Mariah's* (☎6723/22255), at *Hillcrest Gardens Hotel* on Taylor's Road, for à la carte dining with spectacular views of Phillip Island. *Dino's* (☎6723/24225), on Bumboras Road, is a quality licensed Italian place with a pleasant ambience, while the *South Pacific Resort* puts on big fish-fries, smorgasbord nights, carveries and musical shows at various times during the week; on other nights an ordinary brasserie menu is available from 5.30pm. A superb spot for **lunch** is the extremely popular *Café Pacifica* (☎6723/23210) on Cutters Corn Road, set in a leafy nursery and serving exquisite brunches and afternoon teas.

The **clubs** on the island provide good places to eat, drink and mingle with the locals. Facing each other across Burnt Pine's main street are the *Sports and Workers Club* and the *Norfolk Island Bowling Club*. The *Golf Club* in Kingston has a popular bar that also serves meals. The only **pub** is the *Brewery*, opposite the airport, with local ales such as "Bee Sting" and "Bligh's Revenge", pool tables and a rough, late-night crowd that can be a bit intimidating for single women.

Travel details

Most public transport in New South Wales originates in Sydney, and the main services are outlined in the "Travel details" section at the end of Chapter 1 on p.223; check individual town accounts in Chapter 2 to see which operator you need to contact.

Trains

All trains on the north coast, and most of the ones in the south, are run by Countrylink (Ⓣ13 22 32, Ⓦwww.countrylink.info), which extends its network with additional bus services from Transborder (Ⓣ02/6241 0033, Ⓦwww.transborderexpress.com.au) in the south and Sunstate in the north (Ⓣ07/3260 1666, Ⓦwww.sunstatecoaches.com.au). On the south coast, CityRail (Ⓣ13 15 00, Ⓦwww.cityrail.info) runs to **Berry** (change at Wollongong; 18 daily; 3hr).

Sydney–Brisbane direct (1 daily; 14hr 10min), with stops including Dungog (3hr 30min), Gloucester (4hr 15min), Wauchope (for Port Macquarie; 6hr 30min), Nambucca Heads (8hr), Urunga (8hr 15min), Sawtell (8hr 35min), Coffs Harbour (8hr 40min), Grafton (10hr) and Casino (11hr 15min), with buses meeting trains at Casino and continuing on to Brisbane via Lismore, Ballina, Lennox Head, Byron Bay, Murwillumbah and Tweed Heads (1–2 daily; pick-ups only on some routes).

Canberra–Sydney (2 daily; 4hr 20min).

Buses

Greyhound (Ⓣ13 14 99, Ⓦwww.greyhound.com.au) and Premier Motor Service (Ⓣ13 34 10, Ⓦwww.premierms.com.au) run frequent services along the east coast from Sydney to Brisbane, stopping many places en route. Other operators in NSW are Busways (Ⓦwww.busways.com.au), Kean's (Ⓣ02/6543 1322, Ⓦwww.keans.com.au), Blanche's (Ⓣ02/6686 2144, Ⓦwww.blanches.com.au), Ryan's (Ⓦwww.ryansbusservice.com.au), Kirklands (Ⓦwww.kirklands.com.au), Murray's (Ⓣ32 22 51, Ⓦwww.murrays.com.au), Deane's Buslines (Ⓦwww.deansbuslines.com.au), Tathra Bus Service (Ⓦwww.tathrabus.com.au) and Surfside (Ⓣ07/5574 5111, Ⓦwww.surfside.com.au).

Byron Bay to: Ballina (13–22 daily; 40min); Brisbane (9 daily; 2hr 30min); Buladelah (6 daily; 9hr 20min); Brunswick Heads (10–13 daily; 15min); Coffs Harbour (8 daily; 4hr); Forster (1 daily; 8hr 45min); Grafton (8 daily; 3hr); Karuah (7 daily; 9hr 45min); Lennox Head (8–12 daily; 25min); Lismore (6–10 daily; 2hr 5min); Maclean (5 daily; 2hr 15min); Murwillumbah (5 daily; 55min); Nambucca Heads (6 daily; 3hr 30min); Port Macquarie (5 daily; 8hr); Surfers Paradise (9 daily; 1hr 20min); Sydney (4 daily; 14hr 15min); Tweed Heads (4–5 daily; 1hr 20min); Urunga (6 daily; 3hr 20min).

Canberra to: Adelaide (3 daily; 19hr) Batemans Bay (2–3 daily; 2hr 25min); Bega (1 daily; 4hr 10min); Cooma (2 daily; 1hr 50min–2hr 10min); Eden (1 daily; 5hr); Jindabyne (1 daily; 2hr 40min); Melbourne (3 daily; 8hr 30min); Merimbula (1 daily; 4hr 35min); Narooma (1–2 daily; 4hr 30min); Sydney (16 daily; 3hr 30min); Thredbo (1 daily; 3hr 20min).

Coffs Harbour to: Bellingen (Mon–Fri 4–5 daily, Sun 1 daily; 1hr); Byron Bay (8 daily; 3hr 50min); Dorrigo (Tues, Thurs & Sun 1 daily; 1hr 10min); Grafton (8–12 daily; 1hr 10min); Nambucca Heads (6–11 daily; 1hr); Port Macquarie (6–7 daily; 2hr 40min); Urunga (6–11 daily; 40min).

Port Macquarie to: Ballina (5 daily; 6hr); Bellingen (Tues, Thurs & Sun; 3hr 15min); Byron Bay (6 daily; 7hr); Coffs Harbour (6 daily; 2hr 40min); Dorrigo (Tues, Thurs & Sun; 3hr 50min); Grafton (5 daily; 4hr 10min); Nambucca Heads; Wauchope (2–6 daily; 1hr).

Flights

Airlines operating in New South Wales include Qantas (Ⓣ13 13 13, Ⓦwww.qantas.com.au), Virgin

Blue (T 13 67 89 or 07/3295 2296, W www.virginblue.com.au), Jetstar (T 13 15 38 or 03/8341 4901, W www.jetstar.com), Regional Express (T 13 17 13 or 02/6393 5550, W www.regionalexpress.com.au) and Brindabella (T 02/6248 8711, W www.brindabellaairlines.com.au).

Ballina to: Melbourne (2–6 per week; 2hr 5min); Sydney (5 daily; 1hr 50min).

Canberra to: Brisbane (10 daily; 1h 55min); Melbourne 15 daily; 1hr); Sydney (25–28 daily; 35min).

Coffs Harbour to: Brisbane (1–2 daily; 1hr); Lord Howe Island (1 per week, summer only; 2hr) Port Macquarie (1–2 daily; 1hr 30min); Sydney (6–7 daily; 1hr 25min).

Lismore to: Sydney (3–4 daily; 1hr 50min).

Lord Howe Island to: Brisbane (1–2 per week; 1hr 35min); Port Macquarie (summer only; 1 per week; 1hr 20min); Sydney (1–3 daily; 1hr 30min).

Norfolk Island to: Brisbane (3–4 per week; 2hr 25min); Newcastle (1 per week); Sydney (4 per week; 2hr 30min).

Port Macquarie to: Coffs Harbour (1–2 daily; 30min); Lord Howe Island (summer only; 1 per week; 1hr 20min); Sydney (3–8 daily; 1hr).

3

Inland New South Wales

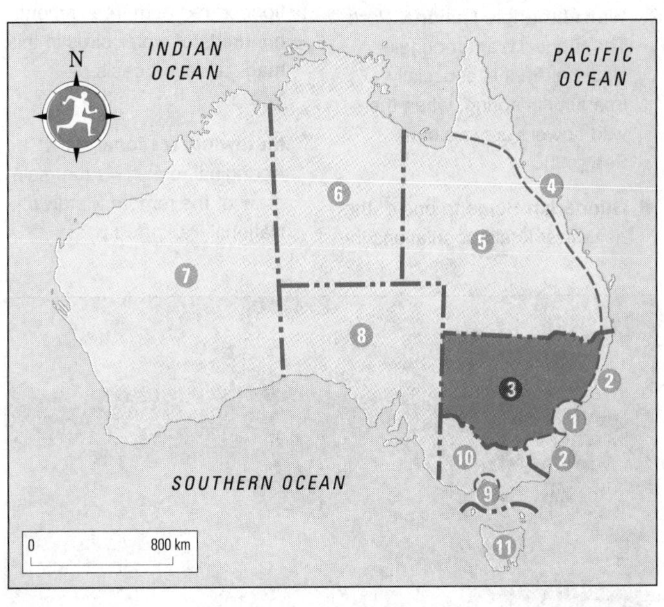

CHAPTER 3

Highlights

* **Tamworth Country Music Festival** Fans from all over the world descend on Tamworth for this famous annual festival. See p.330
* **Bald Rock** Climb one of the largest granite monoliths in the world for unbeatable views. See p.337
* **Warrumbungle National Park** The rugged Warrumbungle National Park is especially beautiful in spring, when the wild flowers are in bloom. See p.338
* **Gunnedah** Home to one of the healthiest koala populations in the state, and a good place to spot them in the wild. See p.340
* **Broken Hill** Take a mine tour, visit the Royal Flying Doctor Service or browse the art galleries of this gracious Outback town. See p.346
* **Menindee Lakes** Boat through flooded red gum trees among hundreds of water birds in this magical desert oasis. See p.354
* **Mutawintji National Park** Aboriginal rock art is the main draw of the remote Mutawintji National Park. See p.355

△ Bald Rock

3

Inland New South Wales

Inland New South Wales is a very different proposition from the populous coast, and although it's not a stand-alone holiday destination and it might strike you as boring at times, travelling here gives you a real insight into the Australian way of life. The region stretches inland for around a thousand kilometres, covering a strikingly wide range of landscapes, from the rugged slopes of the **Great Dividing Range** to the red-earth desert of the Outback, dotted with relatively small agricultural and mining communities. The Great Dividing Range itself runs parallel to the coast, splitting the state in two.

West of the range, towns such as **Bathurst** and **Dubbo** date back to the early days of Australian exploration, when the discovery of a passage through the Blue Mountains opened up the rolling plains of the west. Free (non-convict) settlers appropriated vast areas of rich pastureland here and made immense fortunes off the back of sheep farming, establishing the agricultural prosperity which continues to this day. When gold was discovered near Bathurst in 1851, and the first **goldrush** began, New South Wales' fortunes were assured. Although penal transportations ceased the following year, the population continued to increase rapidly and the economy boomed as fortune-seekers arrived in droves. At much the same time, Victoria broke off to form a separate colony, followed by Queensland in 1859.

Agriculture also dominates the southern section of the state, where the fertile **Riverina** occupies the area between the Murrumbidgee, Darling and Murray rivers (the last dividing New South Wales from Victoria). In the north, falling away from the Great Dividing Range, the gentle sheep- and cattle-farming tablelands of the **New England Plateau** extend from the northern end of the Hunter Valley to the border with Queensland.

Moving west away from the coast the land becomes increasingly desolate and arid as you head into the state's harsh **Outback** regions, where the mercury can climb well above the 40°C mark in summer and even places which look large on the map turn out to be tiny, isolated communities. The small town of **Bourke** is traditionally regarded as the beginning of the real Outback ("Back O'Bourke" is Australian slang for a remote place in the Outback); other destinations in the area include the opal-mining town of **Lightning Ridge** and, in the far west of the state almost at the South Australian border, the mining

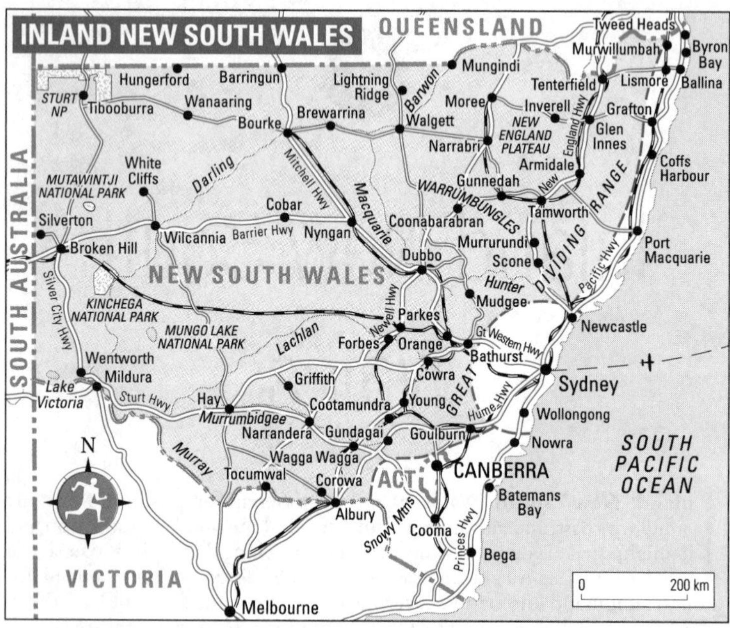

settlement of **Broken Hill**, a surprisingly gracious city surrounded by the desert landscape of *Mad Max*.

Out beyond the Blue Mountains, the **Great Western Highway** takes you as far as Bathurst; from there the **Mid-Western Highway** goes on to join the **Sturt Highway**, which heads, via Mildura on the Victorian border, to Adelaide. Any route west is eventually obliged to cross the **Newell Highway**, the direct route between Melbourne and Brisbane that cuts straight across the heart of central New South Wales.

Inland New South Wales still has a fairly extensive **rail** network, although the operator, Countrylink (Ⓣ13 22 32 for reservations, Ⓦwww.countrylink.info), has replaced many train services with buses. The train journey from Sydney to Broken Hill ($260 return; 13hr each way) is a great way to see the vast desert in air-conditioned comfort – if you're lucky the train will pass through one of the huge sand storms that ravage the region from time to time. A one-month Backtracker pass ($275) with Countrylink will get you just about anywhere in the state. Greyhound **buses** run through Scone, Tamworth, Armidale and Glen Innes en route between Sydney and Brisbane via the New England Highway, and Kean's Travel services Armidale, Uralla, Walcha and Tamworth on its way from Port Macquarie to Scone. For details of the **National Parks and Wildlife Service (NPWS)** in New South Wales, including park entry fees, see p.227.

The central west

The **central west** of New South Wales is rich farmland, and the undulating green hills provide both seasonal work and easy hiking tracks. Although **Dubbo** is the region's major hub, and home to a famous zoo, **Bathurst** is the most sophisticated town, attracting the Sydney crowds on weekends with fine architecture and numerous museums. **Cowra**'s fame derives from the breakout of Japanese prisoners here during World War II, while **Young** was the site of the Lambing Flat Riots against Chinese miners in 1861, both significant events in Australian history. Both towns lack major draws though, and could easily be overlooked. **Parkes**' only attraction is the observatory, although you have to be quite into astronomy to enjoy it. Don't expect culinary diversity in the central west; your best bet for gourmet food is **Orange**, which has developed a bit of a café society. Alternatively, you could lunch at one of the wineries around **Mudgee** and **Young**, which are gaining popularity and make a pleasant break from the road.

Bathurst and around

The pleasant city of **BATHURST**, elegantly situated on the western slopes of the Great Dividing Range 209km west of Sydney, is Australia's oldest inland settlement. Its beautifully preserved nineteenth-century architecture makes it worth a weekend visit from the capital, to browse the antique shops and mellow out in one of the city's many cafés. The settlement was founded by Governor Macquarie in 1815, but Bathurst remained nothing more than a small convict and military settlement for years, only slowly developing into the main supply centre for the rich surrounding pastoral area. It was the discovery of **gold** nearby at Lewis Ponds Creek at Ophir in 1851 (see p.310), and on the Turon River later the same year, which changed the life of the town and the colony forever. Soon rich fields of alluvial gold were discovered in every direction and, being the first town over the mountains for those on the way to the goldfields, Bathurst prospered and grew. The population increased dramatically: in 1885 Bathurst was proclaimed a city, and by the late 1890s it was even proposing itself as the site for the capital of the new Commonwealth of Australia.

Although there's still the odd speck of gold and a few gemstones (especially sapphires) to be found in the surrounding area, modern Bathurst has reverted to its role as the capital of one of the richest fruit- and grain-growing districts in Australia. The presence of the **Charles Sturt University**, one of Australia's leading institutes, gives the city an academic feel and adds to its liveliness. In October and November, rev-heads turn up for the big annual motor-racing meetings – centred on the famous **Bathurst 1000** endurance race – at the Mount Panorama Racing Circuit. If V8 supercars do it for you, this is the place to be.

Arrival, information and accommodation

Countrylink **trains** and long-distance **buses** run to Bathurst from Sydney, with onward services to Broken Hill. The **tourist office** is at 1 Kendall Ave (daily 9am–5pm; ⓣ02/6332 1444 or 1800 681 000, ⓦwww.bathurst.nsw.gov.au).

Accommodation

Accommodation is relatively expensive here, and if you visit on a race day prices rise by fifty percent and everywhere gets booked solid. There are a dozen or more motels along the highway, and camping 5km east of town on the highway in Kelso.

Bathurst Panorama Holiday Park Sydney Rd ⓣ02/6331 8286, ⓦwww.bathurstholidaypark.com.au. A spacious, well-kept park, with a tennis court and large swimming pool. Cabins ❸

Commercial Hotel 135 George St ⓣ02/6331 4109, ⓦwww.geocities.com/commercialhotelbathurst. Functional place with the cheapest rooms in town. Dorms $20, doubles ❷

Dinta Glen B&B 3 Strathmore Drive, Forest Grove ⓣ02/6332 6662. Tranquil and rustic B&B ten minutes' drive from the centre. ❹

Park Hotel 201 George St ⓣ02/6331 3399, ⓦwww.parkhotel.com.au. Comfortable rooms plus live music and karaoke on weekends. Breakfast is included. ❸

Royal Apartments 108 William St ⓣ02/6332 4920, ⓦwww.bathurstheritage.com.au. The town's jewel-in-the-crown heritage building, with tasteful, fully serviced antique apartments and two indoor restaurants. ❻

The Russells 286 William St ⓣ02/6332 4686, ⓦwww.therussells.com.au. Small family home offering four-star B&B rooms with log fires and generous cooked breakfasts. ❹

The City

Because of its cool climate – proximity to the mountains means it can be cold at night – and a scattering of grand nineteenth-century buildings, the city has a very different feel to anywhere on the baking plains further west. The **old courthouse** on Russell Street, built in 1880, makes a good place to start exploring; there's an interesting little **museum** tucked away in the east wing (Tues, Wed, Sat & Sun 10am–4pm; $3), which displays relics and archives of regional pioneer history along with some interesting Aboriginal artefacts.

The **Regional Art Gallery**, 70–78 Keppel St (Tues–Sat 10am–5pm, Sun 11am–2pm; free), houses a fine provincial art collection which has very good ceramics and paintings by Lloyd Rees (though not often on display), as well as regular special and travelling exhibitions. **Machattie Park**, further north at the corner of Keppel and William streets, offers a chance to relax amid landscaped Victorian-era gardens with duck ponds and spreading shady trees. Look out too for the well-preserved **Chifley Home** at 10 Busby St (Sat–Mon 11am–2pm; $6), once the residence of Ben Chifley, Bathurst's most famous son, who was born to a blacksmith here in 1885 and served as prime minister of Australia between 1945 and 1949.

The **Fossil and Mineral Museum** at 224 Howick St (Mon–Sat 10am–4pm, Sun 10am–2pm; $8) has some interesting crystals as well as Australia's only complete *tyrannosaurus rex* skeleton – a fearsome sight. Driving up William Street will lead you to **Mount Panorama** and its famous racing circuit, providing panoramic views of the city. The circuit is accessible by car, making every boy's dream of racing on an official circuit come true. The **National Motor-Racing Museum** (daily 9am–4.30pm; $7; ⓦwww.nmrm.com.au), at Murray's Corner at the beginning of the racing circuit, features famous racing cars and bikes, plus photographs and memorabilia from the races. The **Bathurst Sheep and Cattle Drome** on Limekilns Road, 8km northeast of the city, has an entertaining and educational show (call ⓣ02/6337 3634 for show times; $14, children $8.80; ⓦwww.bathurstsheepandcattledrome.com.au) covering everything you always wanted to know about sheep shearing and milking cows.

Eating, drinking and nightlife

There's a variety of **restaurants** in the city centre, offering Thai, Indian and modern Australian cuisine. Most of the town's **pubs** also serve counter meals or have bistros at the back. Due to the presence of so many students, Bathurst has a reasonable **nightlife**, centred mainly on pubs close to the university.

Annie's Old Fashioned Ice Cream Parlour Cnr Church and George sts. The best place in town if you're after ice cream. Also good for coffee.

Carrington 99 Keppel St ⓦwww.carringtonbathurst.com.au. A lively club with a *Moulin Rouge* feel featuring jazz, blues and folk; check the website to see what's on.

Cobblestone Lane 173 George St ⓣ02/6331 2202. The hottest pick in the town, located in the historic Webb building, and serving modern Australian cuisine with Mediterranean influences. Closed Mon.

Crowded House Café 1 Ribbon Gang Lane ⓣ02/6334 2300. Good lunches and great modern Australian cuisine in the evenings in the neo-Gothic Old School House; you can eat inside, or out in the leafy courtyard. Closed Sun.

Elie's Café 108 William St, in the *Royal Hotel*. A rather standard menu, but with a great covered terrace suitable for people spotting.

Lamplighters 126–130 William St ⓣ02/6331 1448. Superb à la carte dining, with blackboard specials of steak and seafood in a wood-panelled setting. Closed Sun.

Oxford Cnr William and Piper sts. Particularly popular amongst students, with a regular club night on Friday and a huge alfresco bar.

Around Bathurst

The area around Bathurst, heading towards the **Mudgee wine country**, is dotted with semi-derelict villages and ghost towns dating back to the goldrushes of the nineteenth century. A scenic drive via Peel and Wattle Flat leads to the tiny, picturesque village of **SOFALA**, 35km north of Bathurst on the Turon River, on the way to Mudgee. Gold was found in the river here in 1851, just three weeks after the first gold strikes in Australia, and today the narrow, winding main street still follows the course of the water. You can **stay** at the *Old Gaol* on Barkley Street (ⓣ02/6337 7064; ③), a rustic old hotel with a warm welcome and comfy beds. A good spot for a drink is the *Sofala Royal Hotel*, a very atmospheric, classic wooden pub with a big balcony; they also offer meals with a seasonal flavour.

From Sofala, a very narrow unsealed road follows the Turon River towards **HILL END**, an even more important goldrush town located on a plateau above the Turon Valley, 86km from Bathurst. In 1870, Hill End was the largest inland centre in New South Wales, a booming gold-mining town with a population of about twenty thousand, with 53 hotels and all the accoutrements of a wealthy settlement. Within ten years, however, gold production had faltered and Hill End became a virtual ghost town. It stayed that way until 1967, when the area was proclaimed a historic site and huge efforts were made to restore and preserve the town. You can pick up a leaflet at the **NPWS visitors centre** in the old hospital (daily 9.30am–12.30pm & 1.30–4.30pm; ⓣ02/6337 8206), where there's also a small **museum** ($2.20), and take a self-guided walk around the village, or rent some equipment and try your hand at panning or fossicking. There's an underground **mine tour** daily at 1pm ($6) and a gold-panning tour at 11am ($3). You can **stay** in the *Royal Hotel* here (ⓣ02/6337 8261, ⓕ6337 8393; ③) and **eat** in the restaurant. There's also the four-star *Cooke's Cottage B&B* (ⓣ02/6332 5832; ⑤), as well as camping areas run by the NPWS.

Another enjoyable excursion from Bathurst takes in the former gold-mining towns of **Rockley**, 35km to the south, and **Trunkey Creek**, before continuing to the spectacular **Abercrombie Caves**, 72km south of town in the middle of a large nature reserve. The principal and most impressive cavern, the **Grand Arch** (daily 9am–4pm; $13), is 221m long, about 39m wide at the north and south entrances, and in some places over 30m high – it's said to be the largest natural limestone arch in the southern hemisphere. More than eighty other caves are dotted around the reserve; more than a century ago, miners constructed a dance floor in one of them, and concerts and church services are still held here occasionally (see Ⓦwww.jenolancaves.org.au for details). Also within the reserve are old gold mines, and swimming holes in **Grove Creek**, which runs through the reserve, plunging 70m over the Grove Creek Falls at the southern edge. There's a **camping area** on the shore (Ⓣ02/6359 3911; cabins ❷).

Orange and around

ORANGE, on the Mitchell Highway en route from Bathurst to Dubbo, is a pretty town on the eastern slopes of Mount Canobolas; coming from Bathurst, the drive is a pleasant one through undulating countryside, with the valley opening up before you. As befits the town's juicy name, **fruit** is the major local industry, although it's apples rather than oranges which are the mainstay, based in the orchards southwest of the town. You can find apple-picking **work** here from late February or early March for a period of about six weeks, while cherry picking takes place from late November to early January – contact Ready Workforce (Ⓣ02/6360 3044). Many growers have rough accommodation on their properties but demand often outstrips supply, so bring a tent. If you want to sample the local produce rather than pick it, turn up for **Food Week** in April.

Practicalities

The **tourist office**, on Byng Street in Civic Square (daily 9am–5pm; Ⓣ02/6393 8226, Ⓦwww.orange-nsw.com), has information on local attractions including fossicking for gold in the **Ophir Reserve**. Countrylink has daily **train** services from Sydney and Dubbo and you can **fly** out with Regional Express.

An appealing place both to **stay** and eat is the *Metropolitan Hotel* at 107 Byng St (Ⓣ02/6362 1353; ❸–❹), just up from the tourist office. It's a huge, old-fashioned country pub built in 1872, with a wooden veranda. Hotel rooms have TV but no en-suite bathrooms; the more expensive motel suites come with all mod cons. The imposing *Duntryleague Guesthouse* (Ⓣ02/6362 3822, Ⓦwww.duntryleague.com; ❹) is a large, heritage-listed Federation Gothic mansion with modern rooms. There are lots of quality **B&Bs** around – one of the nicest central choices, located in an 1878 magistrate's home with high ceilings, is *Cotehele* (Ⓣ02/6361 2520, Ⓦwww.cotehele.com.au; ❺–❻). All rooms have a different feel and breakfast can be served in the shady yard. There are two **caravan parks**, both a few kilometres from the centre: the *Colour City Caravan Park*, to the north on Margaret Street (Ⓣ02/6362 7254; cabins ❷), is the best.

Orange prides itself on being rather cosmopolitan, and has quite a **café** society and some well-regarded **restaurants**. *Scottys on Summer*, at 202 Summer St, does gourmet sandwiches, while *Belgravia at Union Bank* at 84 Byng St is a wine cellar and bar which serves great antipasti in their cozy courtyard. The *Lakeside Café & Cellar* on Lake Canobolas Road (Ⓣ02/6365 3456) is a very pleasant spot for lunch and local wines, while *Selkirks* at 179 Anson St (Tues–Sat dinner; Ⓣ02/6361 1179) offers pricey but highly recommended modern Australian cuisine.

Forbes and Parkes

West of Orange are the important regional towns of Forbes and Parkes. **FORBES**, on the Lachlan River, is a graceful old place famous as the stomping ground of the nineteenth-century bushranger Ben Hall, who is buried in the town's cemetery. **PARKES**, 33km from Orange along the Newell Highway, is well known for its **Observatory**, whose 64-metre radio telescope was used during the Apollo 11 mission to the moon, as well as in the 2000 film *The Dish*. The observatory's visitor centre (daily 8.30am–4.15pm; free; Ⓦwww.parkes.atnf.csiro.au) has a 25-minute audiovisual presentation, **The Invisible Universe** (daily 8.30am–3.30pm; every 30min; $6.50), and a short 3D film. Both Forbes and Parkes are serviced from Sydney by Countrylink, with a changeover at Cootamundra, while Greyhound has a direct service to Melbourne and Brisbane.

Mudgee and the wine country

About 120km north of Bathurst, the large, old country town of **MUDGEE** (meaning "the nest in the hills" in the Kamilaroi language) is the centre of an often-overlooked wine region. The town is set along the lush banks of the Cugewong River, and the countryside appears to have more grazing cows and sheep than vineyards, though the wines have improved vastly since the days when they were referred to as "Mudgee mud". Mudgee itself is popular with the Sydney crowd, not least because of the many art galleries and local produce shops that dot the town. You can reach Mudgee via Hill End, but it's a bumpy unsealed route, and you're better off approaching via Sofala and Ilford on an 88-kilometre sealed road (except for a small section) – watch out for sheep.

Practicalities

Countrylink runs a **bus** and **train** service to Mudgee from Sydney, changing at Lithgow, just east of Bathurst. The useful **tourist office** is at 84 Market St (Mon–Fri 9am–5pm, Sat 9am–3.30pm, Sun 9.30am–2pm; Ⓣ02/6372 1020, Ⓦwww.visitmudgeeregion.com.au) and has detailed winery information and maps.

Accommodation

Mudgee's popularity and proximity to Sydney means that **accommodation** is booked out at weekends, when it's best to call in advance.

Bleak House 7 Lawson St Ⓣ02/6372 4888, Ⓦwww.geocities.com/bleakhousemudgee. 1860s heritage house with pool and private lace-ironwork verandas overlooking the Cugewong River. ⑥

Central Motel 120 Church St Ⓣ1800 457 222, Ⓔcentral@hwy.com.au. Inexpensive but well-equipped motel, with tidy if slightly clinical rooms. ③

Lauralla Historic Guesthouse Corner of Lewis and Mortimer sts Ⓣ02/6372 4480, Ⓦwww.lauralla.com.au. Classic, late Victorian-style home with quaint and cozy rooms. Their restaurant was closed at the time of writing. ⑥

Mudgee Riverside Caravan and Tourist Park 22 Short St Ⓣ02/6372 2531, Ⓦwww.mudgeeriverside.com.au. Shady caravan park with a children's playground, barbeque area and bike rental. Cabins ③

Wanderlight Motel 107 Market St Ⓣ02/6372 1088, Ⓦwww.wanderlight.bestwestern.com.au. Central three-star motel with a pool and spa. ④

Eating

Your best bet for a gourmet **meal** would be at one of the wineries; not all of them have a restaurant, but if they do it's generally of good quality. The award-winning *Blue Wren Winery* (Ⓣ02/6372 6205, Ⓦwww.bluewrenwines.com.au) is

Mudgee wineries: four of the best

Botolabar Botolabar Lane ⓣ02/6373 3840, ⓦwww.botobolar.com. Australia's first organic winery is known for its Marsanne, among others, with tastings on a shady terrace. There's also a picnic area and BBQs. Mon–Sat 10am–5pm, Sun 10am–3pm.

Huntington Estate Wines Cassilis Rd ⓣ02/6373 3825, ⓦwww.huntingtonestate.com.au. Huntington produces some of the region's most delicious wines. Particularly recommended are the young Semillons and the intense, heady Cabernet Sauvignon. An excellent annual chamber-music festival takes place here in November. Mon–Fri 9am–5pm, Sat 10am–5pm, Sun 10am–3pm.

Miramar Wines Henry Lawson Drive ⓣ02/6373 3874, ⓦwww.miramarwines.com.au. Established by respected wine-maker Ian MacRae in 1977, this winery specializes in delicious whites, with atmospheric tastings among old cobwebbed casks. For no apparent reason, prices here are lower than at most other places. Daily 9am–5pm.

Pieter Van Gent Black Springs Rd ⓣ02/6373 3030, ⓦwww.pvgwinery.com.au. Tastings in a delightful setting: beautiful nineteenth-century choir stalls on cool earth floors, overshadowed by huge old barrels salvaged from Penfolds Winery. Try their Pipeclay Port, a tawny specimen aged in wood. The wine maker is Dutch, and the herbs he uses in his traditional vermouth are specially imported from the Netherlands. Mon–Sat 9am–5pm, Sun 10.30am–4pm.

the best known, using mainly local produce and with great outdoor dining. For more down-to-earth food you can try the inexpensive *Soldiers Club* brasserie at 99 Mortimer St in town or the *Lawson Park Hotel*, a great old country pub on Church Street.

Dubbo

DUBBO, named after an Aboriginal word meaning "red earth", lies on the banks of the Macquarie River, 420km northwest of Sydney and about 200km from Bathurst. The regional capital for the west of the state, it supports many agricultural industries and is located at a vital crossroads where the Melbourne–Brisbane Newell Highway meets the Mitchell Highway and routes west to Bourke or Broken Hill.

As such, it's well used to people passing through, but not staying long. If you do stop the only real attraction is the open-range **Western Plains Zoo** on Obley Road, 5km south of town off the Newell Highway (daily 9am–5pm, ticket is valid for two consecutive days; $32; ⓦwww.zoo.nsw.gov.au). The vast zoo-cum-safari park features expansive landscaped habitats in which many Australian animals are allowed to roam; other animals such as the endangered black rhino or Sumatran tiger are kept in segregated enclosures. The zoo is crisscrossed by walking and cycling paths: it's best to start exploring early, as temperatures can become unbearable by noon and the animals sometimes slink off out of sight into the shade. Early birds can opt for the morning walk, which is a good opportunity to get close to the animals without the crowds (Wed, Fri, Sat & Sun 6.30am during school holidays). Even better is waking up with the sound of roaring lions, possible in the basic **tent camp** at the entrance to the park (ⓣ02/6881 1405; dinner, breakfast and walks included ⓻). There's no public transport to the zoo, so **cycling** there and around the zoo itself is a good option; Wheeler Cycles, 25 Bultje St (ⓣ02/6882 9899),

Australian wildlife

Since Australia broke away from the ancestral supercontinent Gondwana about ninety million years ago, its plants and animals have developed in splendid isolation from the rest of the world. Even though it shares the same latitude as South America and Africa, the country's wildlife is distinctly different: most of the few mammal species are marsupials but there is a great diversity of birdlife, reptiles, amphibians and fish.

◀ Kookaburra

Marsupials and monotremes

▲ Echidna

Seventy percent of all the world's **marsupials** are found in Australia. Probably best known are the members of the macropod ("big foot") family: the symbolic **kangaroo** (one of the two animals on Australia's coat of arms), and its more petite cousins, the **wallaby**, **wallaroo** and **pademelon**. The **red kangaroo**, standing up to 2m tall, bounds across the savannahs and deserts of the continent, whereas herds of the slightly smaller **Western** and **Eastern grey kangaroo** are a frequent sight in eucalypt forests, shrub- and grasslands. Another marsupial of iconic status is the cuddly, tree-hugging **koala** – found in Eastern and Southern Australia –, while the stiff-haired, tubby **wombat** lives a solitary life in burrows in the hilly forest country of Eastern Australia and Tasmania. The majority of the country's marsupials, however, are small, mouse- or cat-sized animals: **possums**, **bettongs**, **potoroos**, **numbats** and **gliders**.

Monotremes only occur in Australia and New Guinea. They exhibit some of the same characteristics as mammals (they are warm-blooded, have hair on their bodies, and produce milk to feed their offspring) but lay soft-shelled eggs and are similar to reptiles in that they have a single opening (cloaca) for excretion and the reproductive tract. With some luck, shy **platypuses** can be spotted at dusk or dawn at the edge of tropical to cool temperate rivers and freshwater lakes along the East Coast and in Tasmania. This creature, with its broad duck's bill, webbed feet and the body of an otter, seemed so improbable to nineteenth-century scientists that upon seeing the first stuffed specimen they believed it to be a hoax, assembled from parts of other animals. The slightly less bizarre long-nosed, spiky **echidna** resembles a big hedgehog and can be found all over Australia.

▼ Wombat

Dangers Down Under

▲ Redback spider

Australia has more than its fair share of deadly animals, some large and aggressive, others small but poisonous. Basking firmly in the former is the **estuarine crocodile**, a reptile not to be trifled with: sturdy and broad snouted, a mature male can measure up to 6m and weigh up to 100kg. Its commonly used name, the saltwater crocodile, is misleading, as "salties" can be found near the coast as well as in waterways up to 200km inland. They have no predators other than themselves (and man) and are opportunistic hunters, lying inert for weeks before suddenly attacking their prey, which, very occasionally, includes unwary humans – do not swim in rivers and waterholes in the tropical north unless they are confirmed safe by locals.

Australia is home to three quarters of the world's most venomous **snakes**, a long list that includes the death adder, copperhead, tiger snake, king brown and inland taipan, the deadliest land snake in the world. However, you're more likely to encounter **redback spiders**, which are very common in urban and suburban areas all over Australia. They love dry, sheltered areas such as sheds, logs and junk piles – take care when using an outdoor "dunny"! Similarly dangerous, **funnel-web spiders**, large, black, burrow-living creatures, occur in coastal and mountain regions in eastern Australia from Gladstone to southern Tasmania. They can inflict painful and potentially fatal bites. Particularly notorious for the toxicity of its venom is the Sydney funnel-web, but since the development of antivenoms, no deaths from spider bites have been recorded.

▼ Great white shark

The **great white shark**, much feared by surfers, inhabits the temperate coastal waters around the southern part of Australia. It is on the list of endangered animals, and despite the increase in people using coastal waters for recreation, the number of shark attacks per capita has not risen over a century. When Steve Irwin, the famous Australian environmentalist and TV personality, died in August 2006 after a stingray barb punctured his heart, **stingrays** replaced sharks as the object of the public's morbid fascination. However, an incident like this is extremely rare, as a stingray only lashes its tail with the venomous, jagged barb in self-defence – most stings are in the foot or leg and are sustained when wading in murky, very shallow waters.

Invasive species

Over the years, a number of species have been introduced to Australia, usually in order to control an indigenous pest – and often with spectacularly disastrous effects. **Camels** were introduced by Afghans in the 1840s and have done so well in the country's central deserts that they have now become a pest; while authorities have had to erect a 5400-kilometre-long fence to protect cattle from marauding **dingoes**, descended from dogs the Aborigines brought to Australia some 12,000 years ago. Most insidious of all, however, is the **cane toad**, an amphibian imported from Latin America in the 1930s in an unsuccessful attempt to control the cane beetle, an insect that was doing great damage to the sugar-cane fields of north Queensland. Unfortunately, the highly poisonous toads turned out to be huge pests themselves. Having no natural predators, they embarked on a relentless march down the East Coast and across the top of the continent, and have now reached the north coast of New South Wales and the lush floodplains of the Top End.

Birds

Groups of **emus** – the other animal on Australia's coat of arms – roam across all areas of mainland Australia except rainforest and very arid deserts. A flightless, drab bird, it can reach speeds of up to 60kph. In contrast, the similar-sized **cassowary**, a more colourful relative with blue-black plumage and a bright blue neck and head, wanders through pockets of rainforest in coastal far-northeast Queensland.

A lot of birds can be heard before they are seen: at dusk and dawn, **kookaburras** fill the bush with their raucous laughter, and many a camper is awoken by the screeching of **galahs** or **cockatoos**. The gregarious family of parrots to which they belong is particularly abundant in Australia; the 56 species found here range from large, impressive birds such as the **yellow-** or **red-tailed black cockatoo** to smaller, equally colourful **lorikeets**, **budgerigars** and **cockatiels**. **Little penguins**, the smallest in the world, are the only penguin species to breed on the Australian mainland.

▲ Flock of flaming galahs

rents out bikes for $15 per day, or electronic carts and bikes ($15 for 4hr) can be rented at the zoo itself.

The state's largest **Livestock Market**, 3km north of town on the Newell Highway, auctions sheep and cattle every Monday, Thursday and Friday (unloading from 8.30am). It's worth a visit just to see the local farmers decked out in their Akubra hats and Drizabone coats, and to inhale the authentic smell of country life. The YHA gives its guests lifts to the market on request.

In the centre of town, **Old Dubbo Gaol** on Macquarie Street (daily 9am–4.30pm; $12; ⓦwww.olddubbogaol.com.au) is worth an hour or so. A hundred years ago, this fortress-style building housed some of the west's most notorious criminals, and today it glories in the details of nineteenth-century prison life, giving loving attention to the macabre – the gallows, the hangman's kit and the careers of some of those who were executed here. Also worth a look-in is the National Trust property **Dundullimal Homestead** (Tues–Sun 10am–4pm; $8), 2km past the zoo on Obley Road. An 1840s slab house with stone stables, it now houses a craft shop and mini-farm.

The **Western Plains Cultural Centre** at 76 Wingewarra St (Wed–Mon 10am–4pm; free; ⓦwww.wpccdubbo.org.au) houses both the **Art Gallery**, which has regularly changing exhibitions, and the **Dubbo Regional Museum**, showing pastoral scenes of early settlers.

Practicalities

Dubbo's 24-hour **bus terminal**, at the junction of the Mitchell and Newell highways, is busy with daily connections to Brisbane, Sydney, Melbourne, Adelaide, Canberra, Newcastle and Port Stephens. Just across the railway line is the **train station**, terminal for the XPT (Express Passenger Train) to and from Sydney. Countrylink (ⓣ13 22 32, ⓦwww.countrylink.info) buses leave here for Bourke and Lightning Ridge. You can also **fly** to Dubbo daily with Regional Express (ⓣ13 17 13, ⓦwww.regionalexpress.com.au), Airlink (ⓣ1300 662 823, ⓦwww.airlinkairlines.com.au) and Qantaslink (ⓣ13 13 13, ⓦwww.qantas.com.au) from Sydney. Regional Express also flies to Broken Hill and Coolangatta from here. The tiny airport is 5km northwest of town; a taxi (ⓣ13 10 08) into the centre will set you back around $10. Thrifty (at the train station) **rents cars** from $77 a day. The **tourist office** (daily 9am–5pm; ⓣ02/6801 4450, ⓦwww.dubbotourism.com.au) is set in a riverside park at the corner of Erskine and Macquarie streets, just off the Newell Highway.

Accommodation

As you'd expect, there are plenty of **motels**, with the majority on the Mitchell Highway (Cobra Street as it passes through town). Unfortunately Dubbo has problems with theft, even from caravan parks, so keep an eye on your belongings at all time.

Amaroo Hotel 83 Macquarie St ⓣ02/6882 3533, ⓕ884 2601, ⓔamaroohotel@bigpond.com. The most salubrious pub-hotel in town, with large rooms and springy beds. Breakfast is included. ❸–❹

Castlereagh Hotel Cnr Brisbane and Tabralgar sts ⓣ02/6882 4877, ⓕ684 1520. This old hotel has the cheapest singles in town. The en-suite doubles aren't quite as good as you'd get in a motel, though they've got a lot more charm. ❸

De Russi Hotel 95 Cobra St ⓣ02/6882 7888, ⓦwww.derussihotels.com.au. The trendiest option of the lot, with stylish motel-style rooms, a pool and wireless Internet throughout. The restaurant serves modern Australian dishes. ❹

Dubbo Backpackers YHA 87 Brisbane St ⓣ02/6882 0922, ⓦwww.yha.com.au. The only hostel in town, this inviting family-run place is within walking distance of the train station and city centre. You can also camp in their small garden. Dorms $23, rooms ❷

Dubbo Cabin & Caravan Parklands ⓣ02/6884 8633, ⓦwww.dubboparkland.com.au. The best of the town's caravan parks, occupying a green spot right on the river, though the luxurious cabins (some even have spas) are expensive. Also has camping space. Cabins ❹

Mayfair Cottage 10 Baird St ⓣ02/6882 5226, ⓔdonjstephens@bigpond.com. Centrally located B&B with very comfortable and well-decorated rooms in a separate guest wing, plus a pool. ❹

Eating and drinking

Given its remoteness, the **café society** which Dubbo has recently developed comes as something of a surprise, with restaurants just as creative as the ones you'd find on the coast. For the less adventurous, there are decent pub meals in the many hotels.

Amaroo Hotel 83 Macquarie St. Your best bet if you crave the usual steak and veggies at rock-bottom prices.

Grapevine Café 144 Brisbane St. A low-key and relaxing place with a lovely, leafy courtyard and generous portions.

Sticks and Stones 215 Macquarie St ⓣ02/6885 4852. Gourmet pizzas, right at the bottom of the main shopping street. Daily from 6pm.

Two Doors Tapas and Wine Bar 215B Macquarie St ⓣ02/6885 2333. Wide selection of tasty hot and cold tapas in generous portions, but with a hefty price tag. Closed Sun.

Village Hot Bake Darling St, by the train station. The best place for fresh bread, cakes, pies, fries and pizzas.

Cowra

Nestled on the banks of the Lachlan River, 107km southwest of Bathurst along the Mid-Western Highway, **COWRA** is a green little town, though it doesn't invite to stay longer than necessary. Its only claim to fame is the **Cowra Breakout** of World War II. August 5, 1944, saw the escape of 378 Japanese prisoners of war armed with baseball bats, staves, home-made clubs and sharpened kitchen knives – those who were sick and remained behind hung or disembowelled themselves, unable to endure the disgrace of capture. It took nine days to recapture all the prisoners, during which four Australian soldiers and 231 Japanese died. The breakout was little known until the publication of Harry Gordon's excellent 1970s account *Die Like the Carp* (republished as *Voyage of Shame*).

You can see the site of the **POW camp**, now just ruins and fields, on Sakura Avenue on the northeast edge of town. The graves of the escapees, who were buried in Cowra, were well cared for by members of the local Returned Servicemen's League, a humanitarian gesture that touched Japanese embassy officials who then broached the idea of an official **Japanese War Cemetery**. Designed by Shigeru Yura, the tranquil burial ground lies north of the camp, on Doncaster Drive. The theme of Japanese–Australian friendship and reconciliation continued in Cowra with the establishment of the **Japanese Garden** (daily 8.30am–5pm; $8.50) in 1979, with funding from Japanese and Australian governments and companies. The large garden, designed to represent the landscape of Japan, is set on a hill overlooking the town, on a scenic drive running north off Kendal Street, the main thoroughfare. There's another antiwar symbol in the shape of the **World Peace Bell** on Civic Square, while an avenue of cherry trees connects the war cemeteries, the POW campsite and the Japanese Garden.

A holographic explanation of the breakout can be seen at the **tourist office** at the junction of the Olympic Highway, Laghlan Valley Way and Mid-Western

Highway (daily 9am–5pm; ⓣ02/6342 4333, ⓦwww.cowratourism.com.au), although its emphasis is more on the few Australian casualties than the Japanese prisoners who died.

Countrylink **buses** pass through town en route from Bathurst to Sydney and Melbourne (with a change at Cootamundra). If you want to taste the local **wine** (the region is best known for its Chardonnays) head for the *Quarry Cellar Door and Restaurant*, 4km from Cowra on Boorowa Road (cellar Tues–Sun 10am–4pm, Wed–Sun lunch, Fri & Sat dinner; ⓣ02/6342 3650, ⓦwww.cowraregionwines.com). If you're interested in some **grape-picking** work, contact Oz Jobs (see below).

Young

Seventy kilometres southwest of Cowra along the Olympic Highway and serviced four times a week by Countrylink, the hilly town of **YOUNG** is a good spot to pick up some **cherry-picking** work during the season (approximately six weeks from the first week of Nov); being monotonous rather than strenuous, the work is popular with retired Queenslanders. To just pick your own and have a look at some orchards and packing sheds, head to any one of a number of places on the way into town from Cowra; you could also contact Oz Jobs on Boorowa Street (ⓣ02/6382 4728). The long weekend in October generally coincides with the **cherry blossoms** being in full bloom – a glorious sight – and there's even an annual Cherry Festival (late Nov/early Dec) celebrating the harvest with games and competitions. There are also several vineyards on the slopes of the undulating area, which is becoming known as the **Hilltops wine region**. Two worth visiting are the small, family-run Lindsays Woodonga Hill Winery, 10km north of Young on Olympic Highway (daily 9am–5pm), and Chalkers Crossing winery on Grenfell Road (Mon–Fri 9.30am–4.30pm, Sat & Sun 11.30am-4.30pm; ⓦwww.chalkerscrossing.com.au), where they also produce olive oils.

A former gold-mining centre previously known as Lambing Flat, the town was the scene of racist violence – the notorious **Lambing Flat Riots** – against Chinese miners in June 1861. As the gold ran out, European miners resented what they saw as the greater success of the more industrious Chinese, and troops had to be called in when the Chinese were chased violently from the diggings and their property destroyed. Carried at the head of the mob was a flag made from a tent flysheet, with the Southern Cross in the centre and the slogan "Roll Up, Roll Up, No Chinese" painted on. Following the riots, the Chinese Immigration Restriction Act was passed, one of the first steps on the slippery slope towards the White Australia Policy of 1901. You can see the original flag, and other exhibits relating to the riots, in the **Lambing Flat Folk Museum** (daily 10am–4pm; $4) in the Community Arts Centre, Campbell Street. Apart from the museum and seasonal work, there's no real reason to make the detour to Young.

For more information, contact the **tourist office**, 2 Short St (Mon–Fri 9am–5pm, Sat & Sun 9.30am–4pm; ⓣ02/6382 3394, ⓦwww.visityoung.com.au). A recommended **farmstay** outside town on the Olympic Highway is *Old Nubba School House* (ⓣ02/6943 2513; ❹–❺), offering peaceful self-contained accommodation in the grounds of a friendly family farm. By far the most enjoyable spot for **lunch** is *Café Lunch A lot*, 67 Lynch St, with a tiny French terrace, creative salads and a vast selection of teas.

The Hume Highway and the Riverina

The rolling plains of southwestern New South Wales, spreading west from the Great Dividing Range, are bounded by two great rivers: the **Murrumbidgee** to the north and the **Murray** to the south, the latter forming the border with the state of Victoria. This area is now known as the **Riverina**.

The land the explorer John Oxley described as "uninhabitable and useless to civilized man", began its transformation to fertile fruit-bowl when the ambitious **Murrumbidgee Irrigation Scheme** was launched in 1907; the area around **Griffith** and **Leeton** now produces ninety percent of Australia's rice, most of its citrus fruits and twenty percent of its wine grapes, so if you're looking for work on the land, you've a reasonable chance of finding it here.

The capital of the central Riverina is **Wagga Wagga**, Australia's most populous inland city. Along the Upper Murray, the main towns are on the Victorian side of the river, but you may end up dropping into **Albury** en route between Melbourne and Sydney, or into **Wentworth** as a day-trip from Mildura or on the way to or from Broken Hill. There are several interesting **festivals** in the region, including the Wagga Wagga Jazz Festival in September (Ⓦwww.waggajazz.org.au) and the Festival of Griffith, an orgy of Aussie wine, food and culture held on Easter Saturday.

If you want a quick route to Melbourne from Sydney or vice versa, you'll inevitably end up on the rather tedious **Hume Highway**, which has improved over the years, but still narrows to one lane either way in parts. Choked with trucks, particularly at night, accidents are not infrequent, so keep your wits about you. While the highway itself may seem dreary, some of the nearby towns are truly and typically Australian – rich in food, wine, flora and fauna, and friendly locals.

Goulburn and beyond

GOULBURN, just off the Hume Highway, is a large regional centre and home to a quality **wool industry**, established in the 1820s. The town, with its wide streets, has a conservative country feel, but boasts some large and impressive public buildings. Goulburn's wool traditions have been immortalized by the **Big Merino** (daily 8am–8pm), a fifteen-metre-high sheep which stands proudly next to the Ampol service station on the Old Hume Highway; the first floor has a display on the industry, and on the third level you can look out over the town through the sheep's eyes. To get closer to the real thing and enjoy a glimpse into Australian country life, head for the long-established **Pelican Sheep Station** on Braidwood Road, 10km south of town (Ⓣ02/4821 4668, Ⓦwww.pelicansheepstation.com.au; bunkhouses ❷, cabins ❸, cottage ❹, plus camping), where tours include a shearing demonstration and the chance to see sheepdogs being put through their paces – kids can cuddle newborn lambs in April.

There are several historic places to visit in Goulburn, including the National Trust property **Riversdale**, an 1840 coaching inn on Maud Street (mid-Sept to mid-July Sat & Sun 10am–4.30pm, at other times by appointment on ⓣ02/4821 4741; $5), and the **Old Goulburn Brewery** on Bungonia Road (daily 11am–5pm; free), which has been brewing traditional ales and stouts since 1836. The **Cathedral of Saint Saviour**, completed in 1884, is one of the most attractive old churches in Australia, with some beautiful stained-glass and a fine organ.

Practicalities

Now bypassed by the Hume Highway, Goulburn is still the traditional stop-off point en route to Canberra from Sydney, with regular Countrylink and Greyhound **buses** passing by. You can get an informative pamphlet of walks and heritage buildings from the **tourist office** opposite the shady, flower-filled Belmore Park at 201 Sloane St (daily 9am–5pm; ⓣ02/4823 4492, ⓦwww.igoulburn.com).

The most intriguing place to **stay** in the area is at the *Gunningbar Yurt Farm*, 20km out of town on Grabben Gullen Road (ⓣ02/4829 2114; free as a helper with four hours' work per day – all meals included as part of a WWOOF placement, see p.71). Essentially a sheep property, the several yurts here provide an educational centre for groups of children to help them become more self-sufficient and environmentally aware. If you want to stay, you must call in advance; someone can pick you up if you don't have your own transport. In town, *Tattersalls Hotel*, 74 Auburn St (ⓣ02/4821 3088, ⓕ4822 3505; $22), is a hostel offering good and clean, if basic, dorm accommodation. The luxurious *Bentley Lodge B&B* on the edge of the town at 102 Clyde St (ⓣ02/4822 5135, ⓦwww.bentleylodge.com; ⑤) hires out classic sports-cars for a burn along the country lanes.

The best place to **eat** in Goulburn is the licenced *Paragon Café* at 174 Auburn St, where you can fill up with inexpensive breakfasts, hamburgers, steaks, fish and Italian fare. A host of other good, multi-ethnic eateries can be found close by on the same street.

The Bungonia State Recreation Area and the Wombeyan Caves

The **Bungonia State Recreation Area**, 35km east of Goulburn, covers a rugged strip of the Southern Tablelands containing some of the deepest **caves** in Australia, the spectacular limestone Bungonia Gorge and the Shoalhaven River. There are also plenty of bushwalking tracks with good river and canyon views, and a well-equipped **campground** near the entrance of the park (ⓣ02/4844 4277; $5 per person). About an hour north of Goulburn via Taralga are the huge and more accessible **Wombeyan Caves** (tours at 1pm & 2.30pm; $21; ⓦwww.jenolancaves.org.au), which you can tour with a guide.

Yass and the Burrinjuck Waters State Park

YASS, 87 kilometres west of Goulburn just off the Hume Highway, is an appealing little town with a rural feel, kept green by the Yass River. Both Countrylink and Greyhound pass through the town which, before European settlement, had a high Aboriginal population, who gave the town its name, "yharr", meaning running water. The famous explorer **Hamilton Hume** chose to retire here, the town's main claim to fame; the National Trust–owned **Cooma Cottage** (Mon & Thurs–Sun 10am–4pm; $4.40), a well-preserved nineteenth-century homestead, was his former home and now a museum, set in a hundred acres of rolling countryside and containing excellent material on Hume and his expeditions. Hume was different from many of his contemporaries in that he was born in Australia – in Parramatta, to free settlers in 1797 – and his explorations relied on his first-hand knowledge of the bush and of Aboriginal skills and languages. Hume's best-known exploration was when he paired with **Hovell**, an English sea captain, to head for Port Phillip Bay; you can follow in their footsteps on the Hume and Hovell Walking Track, which starts at Gunning, 50km east of Goulburn, and runs over 400km southwest to Albury (details from the tourist office). He also assisted Sturt in tracing the Murray and Darling rivers.

The **Yass and District Museum** on Comur Street (Sat & Sun 10am–4pm, weekdays when volunteers available; $3) contains displays on what the town looked like back in the 1890s. The **Yass Valley Festival** (second weekend in Nov) features food, wine and music, plus a flying dog competition where discs are thrown into the air and the dog has to 'fly' to catch it. About 20km along the road to Gundagai at Gap Range is the **gallery** of the internationally renowned glass sculptor Peter Crisp (ⓣ02/6227 6073, ⓦwww.petercrisp.com.au), whose exquisite work is available for sale – if you can afford it. This is also a good area for wine tours (ask at the tourist office).

The terrific **tourist office** in Coronation Park on Comur Street (Mon–Fri 9am–4.30pm, Sat & Sun 9am–4pm; ⓣ02/6226 2557, ⓦwww.yass.nsw.gov.au) has maps outlining a two-kilometre informative walk through town and can provide information on the Hume and Hovell Walking Track. There are some lovely **bed and breakfasts** in Yass. One of the best is *Kerrowgair*, an elegant historical residence at 24 Grampian St (ⓣ02/6226 4932, ⓦwww.kerrowgair.com.au; ❺). The *Australian Motel* at 180 Comur St (ⓣ02/6226 1744; ❸) is decent value, while at the bottom of the range is the cheap pub-style *Club House Hotel* at 190 Comur St (ⓣ02/6226 1042; ❷). *Yass Caravan Park* (ⓣ02/6226 1173; cabins ❷) is central though lacks character, and there are lots of places to **eat** on Comur Street.

Continuing for 27km along the Hume Highway towards Gundagai you'll reach a turn-off for the Burrinjuck Waters State Park. From here it's a 25-kilometre drive to the park, set around the gigantic (at 2.5 times the size of Sydney Harbour) **Burrinjuck Dam** ($7 per car per day), with camping (ⓣ02/6227 8114; cabins ❷, cottages ❸) and picnic areas filled with kangaroos and chirping rosellas. **WEE JASPER**, a picturesque village located on the backwaters of the dam, has basic campsites (ⓣ02/6227 9626, ⓦwww.weejasperreserves.com.au). From here you can visit **Carey's Caves** (tours Fri–Mon noon & 1.30pm, Sat & Sun also at 3pm; $11; ⓦwww.weejaspercaves.com), for a look at some of Australia's most spectacular limestone rock formations.

Turning off the Hume Highway at Bowning brings you to the peaceful village of **Binalong**. Australia's best-known poet, Banjo Patterson, spent much of his childhood here, attending the local school. Binalong railway station was used to transport gold from nearby Lambing Flat (Young), which made it a lucrative area for bushrangers; the grave of one of the most daring, "Flash" Johnny Gilbert, lies alongside the road to Harden. A Countrylink **coach** passes through Binalong on its way to Harden from Yass.

Gundagai and Holbrook

One hundred and four kilometres west of Yass, **GUNDAGAI** sits on the banks of the Murrumbidgee, at the foot of the rounded bump of Mount Parnassus. The town was once situated on the alluvial flats north of the river, despite warnings from local Aborigines that the area was prone to major flooding. Proving them correct, old Gundagai was the scene of Australia's worst flood disaster in 1852, when 89 people drowned. Gold was eventually discovered here in 1858, and by 1864 Gundagai had become a boom town, preyed upon by the romantically dubbed bushranger Captain Moonlight. The relocated town, on the main route between Sydney and Melbourne until bypassed by the Hume Highway, became a favoured overnight stopping-point amongst pioneers heading into the interior by bullock cart. A large punt was the only means of crossing the Murrumbidgee until the **Prince Alfred Bridge** was erected in 1867, a pretty wooden structure which can still be used by pedestrians.

Gundagai found immortality through a **Jack Moses** poem, in which "the dog sat on the tuckerbox, nine miles from Gundagai" and stubbornly refused to help its master pull the bogged bullock team from the creek. Somehow the image became elevated from that of a disobedient hound and a cursing teamster to a symbol of the pioneer with his faithful hound at his side. As a consequence, a statue of the dog was erected just outside town at **Five Mile Creek**, where pioneers used to camp overnight – it's still a very pleasant spot to take a break.

In the town itself, not much more than a tiny commercial centre which lacks character, the **tourist office** at 249 Sherridan St (Mon–Fri 8am–5pm, Sat & Sun 9am–noon & 1–5pm; ⓣ02/6944 0250, ⓦwww.gundagai.nsw.gov.au) can help with accommodation and also sells CDs of folk songs featuring Gundagai people. Countrylink and Greyhound **buses** both service the town on a regular basis. If you want to **stay**, the most luxurious option is the old convent at *Lanigan Abbey* (ⓣ02/6944 2852, ⓦwww.laniganabbey.com.au; ❻), complete with intact chapel behind St Patrick's church and an art gallery next door. Otherwise there are plenty of hotels along the main road.

The *Gundagai District Services Club* (daily noon–2pm & 5.30–9pm; ⓣ02/602944 1355) across the road from the tourist office has good Chinese and Aussie **food** but little ambience.

Wagga Wagga

WAGGA WAGGA, known simply as "Wagga" (and pronounced "Wogga"), is the most populous inland city in Australia and the capital of the Riverina region, with around 58,000 inhabitants, though despite its size it remains a green and pleasant place. Its curious name is thought to come from the Widadjuri, the largest of the New South Wales Aboriginal peoples: "wagga" means crow, and its repetition signifies the plural (though some claim it means "dancing men").

Wagga's main attractions are on the edge of the city. A half-hour walk to the south at the base of Willans Hill are the impressive **Botanic Gardens**, a huge place with attractions including a walk-through bird aviary (from where many birds escaped during a 2007 storm), a children's petting-zoo (daily 8am–4pm or 5pm in summer), bush trails and picnic areas. The **Museum of the Riverina** has two sites: one near the Botanic Gardens (Tues–Sat 10am–5pm, Sun noon–4pm; free) on Lord Baden Powell Drive, which hosts a hotchpotch collection of old farm machinery, printing presses and a display of over two hundred door-knockers; and the other back in town at the **historical council chamber** (same hours), which often hosts travelling exhibitions.

Also in the centre, the **Regional Art Gallery** on Baylis Street (Mon–Sat 10am–5pm, Sun noon–4pm; free; ⓦwww.waggaartgallery.org) is home to the **National Art Glass collection**, as well as touring exhibitions and over five hundred works by Australian printmakers from 1940 onwards.

On Sunday mornings a bit of life is sparked by the **market** (7.30am–noon) at the Myer car park on O'Reilly Street, which has secondhand clothes and books, crafts, local produce and cakes. A farmers' market at Wollundry lagoon near the tourist office is held on the second Saturday of each month. The city's **Charles Sturt University** boasts a well-regarded wine course and has its own on-campus **winery** (and cheesery) on Coolamon Road, both of which are open for tastings and sales (Mon–Fri 11am–5pm, Sat & Sun 11am–4pm; ⓣ02/6933 2435) – try the unusual lemon Myrtle cheese. Sweet teeth can tour the heavenly Green Grove Organics **liquorice and chocolate factory** at 8 Lord St in Junee, 50km away (daily tours 10am–4pm; $4; ⓦwww.greengroveorganics.com).

Practicalities

Roughly halfway between Sydney (470km) and Melbourne (435km), Wagga is just off the Sturt Highway, the main route between Adelaide and Sydney. Interstate Greyhound **buses** heading to and from Brisbane, Sydney, Adelaide, Melbourne and Canberra all pass through, stopping at the train station a little out of town. Countrylink **trains** run daily from Sydney and Melbourne. Baylis Street, the main strip (and Fitzmaurice Street, its continuation), extends from the train station to the bridge spanning the Murrumbidgee River.

The **tourist office**, on Tarcutta Street, close to the river (daily 9am–5pm; ⓣ1300 100 122, ⓦwww.visitwaggawagga.com.au), has local information and maps and also books **accommodation** in town and on local **farmstays**.

Accommodation

Lawson Motor Inn 117–121 Tarcutta St ⓣ02/6921 2200, ⓦwww.thelawson.com.au. Well-run four-star motel with spacious, well-furnished rooms with satellite TV and kitchenettes. ❺

The Manor 38 Morrow St ⓣ02/6921 5962, ⓦwww.themanor.com.au. Historic B&B next to the beautiful lagoon-front park, with heavy wooden furniture, old gramophones and pleasant communal areas. ❹–❻

Romano's Hotel Cnr Sturt and Fitzmaurice sts ⓣ02/6921 2013, ⓦwww.romanoshotel.com.au. Old hotel with a nineteenth-century feel and rather old-fashioned rooms (single rates available). ❷–❸

Victoria Hotel 55 Baylis St ⓣ02/6921 5233, ⓦwww.vichotel.net. Good doubles with shared bathrooms – but none of the character of *Romano's*. Singles ❶, doubles ❷

Wagga Beach Caravan Park 2 Johnston St ⓣ02/6931 0603, ⓦwww.wwbcp.com.au. The town's best-situated caravan park, this shady and tranquil place has a free gas barbecue right on the town beach, five minutes' walk from the main shops. En-suite cabins ❷–❸

Eating, drinking and nightlife

In the town centre, the Baylis/Fitzmaurice strip and its side streets provide fertile **eating** ground. Wagga also has several huge clubs – *Wagga RSL*, on the corner of Dobbs and Kincaid streets, has a Chinese restaurant and Friday-night piano bar. For **drinking** and **dancing**, the town's most popular spot is the lively *Victoria Hotel*, whilst *The Black Swan Hotel* (alias "The Muddy Duck") in North Wagga, close to the university, is eternally popular with the student population.

Creeds At *Romano's Hotel*. This hotel has a good modern restaurant with lots of seafood and other dishes, plus decent espresso and all-day breakfasts. Great terrace for summer eating.

Indian Tavern Tandoori Restaurant 81 Peter St ⓣ02/6921 3121. A popular spot with authentic tandoori dishes, though can be a bit liberal with the chilli sauce.

Montezuma's 85 Baylis St. Cosy wooden cantina where you can enjoy the best Mexican food in town, surrounded by kitschy relics. The friendly and exuberant owners add to the atmosphere. Wed–Sat lunch, Tues–Sun dinner.

Scribbles Café 22 Fitzmaurice St. An inviting spot to check your email and linger over a cup of coffee or snack. Daily from 8am, dinner Thurs–Sat.

Victoria Hotel 55 Baylis St. Good and extensive bistro menu with everything from avocado salad to rump steak; the upstairs balcony is open on Fri and Sat nights.

Wagga Wagga Winery Oura Rd, a fifteen-minute drive northeast of town ⓣ02/6922 1221, ⓦwww.waggawaggawinery.com.au. One of the best local places to eat. The wines themselves are nothing special, but the excellent local food (from $20 a head) and the setting, in an old pine-log building with a large veranda and a garden area, is very pleasant. Wed–Sun lunch, Fri & Sat dinner by appointment.

The Murrumbidgee Irrigation Area

Irrigation has transformed the area northwest of Albury, between the Lachlan and the Murrumbidgee rivers, into a fertile valley full of orchards, vineyards and rice paddies, cut through with irrigation canals. The **Murrumbidgee Irrigation Area** (or **MIA**) extends over two thousand square kilometres, a mostly flat and – from ground level at least – featureless landscape that is nonetheless responsible for producing enormous amounts of rice, wine grapes and citrus fruits.

Probably the main reason you'll visit this off-the-beaten-track area is to find **work**, with abundant fruit-picking available roughly between August and March. If you base yourself in **Griffith** or **Leeton** you'll need your own transport – if only a bicycle – since the orchards are up to 10km outside town. To avoid the possibility of a wasted trip due to a late season or a poor crop, it's essential to check with Ready Workforce (ⓣ02/6964 3232) or Summit Personnel (ⓣ02/6964 2718) before turning up.

Griffith

Citrus orchards line the way into **GRIFFITH**, with a range of low hills in the background. The major centre of the MIA, it's known for its large **Italian population**, the descendants of immigrants who came in the 1920s, having already tried mining in Broken Hill, and again after World War II. Needless to say, a string of excellent Italian cafés and restaurants line the tree-filled main street of Banna Avenue, and many **wineries** are run by Italian families. The city was designed by Walter Burley Griffin, the landscape architect from Chicago who was also responsible for Canberra's confusing layout; although Griffith suffers from a similar charm deficit, it does have a rather spacious feel.

The best way to get an overview of the area is to head for **Scenic Hill**, the escarpment that forms the northern boundary of the city, where the **Sir Dudley de Chair's Lookout** gives a panoramic view of the horticultural enterprises below. Immediately beneath this rocky outcrop is the **Hermit's Cave**, where Valerio Recetti, an Italian immigrant, lived alone and undetected for ten years, working only at night and early in the morning with stone-age tools to create a home in the caves. **Pioneer Park** (daily 9am–4.30pm; $9), in an extensive bushland setting 2km north from the city centre, has 36 buildings recreating the era of the early MIA, and also houses the **Italian Museum** (same hours and entrance fee), which gives an overview of early immigrants and their traditions.

There are seventeen **wineries** in the area surrounding Griffith, thirteen of which are open to the public (some by appointment only). The oldest winery, McWilliam's Hanwood Estate (Mon–Sat 9am–5pm; ⓦwww.mcwilliams.com.au), was established in 1913 and holds tastings in a building resembling a wine barrel; while one of the more celebrated vineyards is De Bortoli Wines (Mon–Sat 9am–5pm, Sun 9am–4pm; ⓦwww.debortoli.com.au) at De Bortoli Road, Bilbul, the birthplace of the sensational Noble One Botrytis Semillon dessert wine, which has raked in over three hundred gold medals across the world. For a complete overview of the wineries, head for the tourist office.

Practicalities

The **tourist office**, on the corner of Jondaryan and Banna avenues (Mon–Fri 9am–5pm; ⓣ02/6962 4145, ⓦwww.griffith.com.au), is a great source of information and hands out the *Self-drive Tour* brochure. Griffith is serviced daily by **bus** and **train** with Greyhound, Countrylink and V-Line.

Accommodation

For camping, there's the cheap and basic **campsite** at the showground on the edge of town; otherwise, head for the *Griffith Tourist Caravan Park*.

Griffith International Hostel 112 Binya St ⓣ02/6964 4236, ⓦwww.griffithinternational.com.au. Basic backpackers' with communal kitchen and living room but little vibe. More a functional place for fruitpickers than a fun place to hang out. Dorms $19–24, doubles ❷

Griffith Tourist Caravan Park 919 Willandra Ave, 2km south of the centre ⓣ02/6964 2144, ⓕ6964 1126. Popular with fruit-pickers and other labourers, with a large tennis court and well-kept amenities. Cabins ❷

Ingleden Park Cottage Coghlan Rd ⓣ02/6963 6527, ⓦwww.ingleden.com.au. One of the better local B&Bs, set on a working farm 15km from town, with modern rooms in a garden cottage. ❹–❺

Victoria Hotel 384 Banna Ave ⓣ02/6962 1299, ⓦwww.hotelvictoria.com.au. The best option in the centre of town, with basic rooms, a covered courtyard, and quality bistro meals downstairs. ❹

Eating and drinking

There's no shortage of good Italian places to **eat** and **drink** on Banna Avenue. For gourmet picnic supplies, Riverina Grove on Whybrow Street is a fantastic deli stocking a wide range of regional produce like plums in port, local salami and cheeses. For drinking, the town convenes at the *Gemini Hotel* on Banna Avenue, where you can sip a cocktail or down a schooner while listening to live music at the weekends.

Bertoldo's Pasticceria 324 Banna Ave. Cheap, bakery-style place with inexpensive and filling pasta dishes and wraps for lunch. Also has a superb selection of mouthwatering *gelati*.

Coro Club 20–26 Harward Rd. Large, cheap portions of Chinese food if you've had enough of all things Italian. Lunch and dinner from Wed–Sun.

Il Corso Café & Pizza 232 Banna Ave. Offers a range of Italian food beyond the familiar pasta options, including chicken and seafood dishes. Takeaway and BYO available.

Michelin 72 Banna Ave. Highbrow French cuisine in a contemporary setting with an industrial feel. The duck breast or fish of the day comes with a price tag. Also serves tapas and cocktails. Tues–Sat lunch & dinner.

Vita's 252–254 Banna Ave. One of the more upmarket Italian places, serving risotto, pasta and seafood – no pizza though. A good place for people-spotting on their covered terrace. Closed Sun.

Around Griffith

Twenty-five kilometres northeast of Griffith is the **Cocoparra National Park**, set in the wooded Cocoparra Range. The park has five different walking tracks ranging from easy to medium, and in winter heavy rainfall creates spectacular waterfalls. For information about camping and bushwalking ask at the NPWS office at 200 Yambil St in Griffith (ⓣ02/6966 8100). Much further away, on the flat plains 185km northwest of town, is **Willandra National Park**, reached via **Hillston** (64km from Griffith) on the unsealed Hillston–Mossgiel road. The park was created in 1971 from a section of the vast Big Willandra pastoral station, a famous stud-merino property founded in the 1860s. As well as allowing you to experience the semi-arid riverine plains country at close quarters, a visit to the 1918 **homestead** gives an insight into station life and the wool industry. Wet weather makes all the roads to Willandra impassable, so check before you head out with the **NPWS** in Griffith. They also handle **accommodation** bookings for shared rooms in the shearers' quarters ($25 per person); take extra supplies in case you get rained in. You'll need your own transport to get to both parks.

Fifty-nine kilometres southeast of Griffith and serviced from Sydney by both Greyhound and Countrylink, **LEETON** is the third-largest town in the MIA, with a quarter of its population of Italian extraction. There's little on offer for visitors not after fruit-picking work, but if you do happen to get stuck here, pay a visit to the **tourist office** at 10 Yanco Ave (Mon–Fri 9am–5pm, Sat & Sun 9.30am–12.30pm; ⓣ02/6953 6481, ⓦwww.leetontourism.com.au) for information on the area and details of visiting the town's rice mill. There are two **caravan parks**, both 2km southeast: the *Leeton Caravan Park*, on Yanco Avenue (ⓣ & ⓕ02/6953 3323), caters for fruit-pickers with basic bunkrooms ($11 per person) and also has en-suite cabins with TV (❷–❸), while *An Oasis Caravan Park* on Corbie Hill Road (ⓣ02/6953 3882, ⓕ6953 6256; cabins and spacious cottage ❷) caters more for tourists, with a better range of facilities.

Narrandera

Thirty kilometres southeast of Leeton, at the junction of the Sturt and Newell highways, **NARRANDERA** is a popular overnight stop en route from Adelaide to Sydney, or from Melbourne to Brisbane. It's a pleasant place to take a break, set on the **Murrumbidgee River** with streets lined with tall native trees; its white cedars, which blossom in November, are particularly beautiful. In mid-March the town hosts the **John O'Brien Festival** (ⓦwww.johnobrien.com.au), a commemoration of the famous poet-priest who lived here in the early 1900s, with bush poetry and Irish music.

A good place to cool down is **Lake Talbot**, a willow-fringed expanse of water flowing from the Murrumbidgee River. Right next to the lake are the Lake Talbot Pools (Nov–April Mon–Fri 6am–9pm; adults $2), a family-friendly complex with picnic areas, barbecues, water slides and an Olympic-sized swimming pool. Nearby, a reserve along the river has been declared a **koala** regeneration area for a disease-free colony of koalas; to get there, follow the Bundidgerry Walking Track around Lake Talbot and the Murrumbidgee River. Fishing fanatics could try out the lake or river for some Murray cod, yellowbelly and redfin.

Practicalities

Countrylink **buses** pass through town on their way from Griffith to Wagga Wagga, and a **train** runs to Sydney once a week. Greyhound stops at Narrandera South on route to Adelaide, Brisbane, Melbourne or Sydney. Free maps of the Bundidgerry track are available at the friendly **tourist office**, in Narrandera Park on the Newell Highway (daily 9am–5pm; ⓣ02/6959 1766 or 1800 672 392, ⓦwww.narrandera.visitnsw.com.au). The best place for a good **meal** is the reliable *Ex-Servicemen's Club*, opposite the tourist office on Bolton Street – don't expect a cozy atmosphere though. The *Murrumbidgee Hotel* also does good bistro meals.

Historic Star Lodge 64 Whitton St ⓣ02/6959 1768, ⓦwww.historicstarlodge.com.au. The best place to stay in Narrandera, this fine B&B boasts many original 1916 features, a huge balcony and friendly owners. Full breakfast is included. ❹

Lake Talbot Caravan Park Gordon St ⓣ02/6959 1302, ⓦwww.laketalbot.com. Quiet and shady caravan park, well positioned above the lake and pool, and with cabins. ❸

Mid Town Motor Inn Situated off the highway on the corner of East and Larmer sts ⓣ02/6959 2122,

Ⓕ6959 3271. Clean four-star motel with a Mediterranean feel in its modern rooms. They also have a swimming pool. ❸
Murrumbidgee Hotel 159 East St Ⓣ02/6959 2011. The most appealing of the various classic country hotels, complete with iron-lace balconies, which line East Street. The simple rooms are very good value. ❶
Narrandera Hotel 183 East St Ⓣ02/6952 2122. Another of the old East Street hotels, this large, rambling building oozes country charm, though it's not as cheap as the *Murrumbidgee Hotel.* ❷

Albury and around

The small city of **ALBURY**, a bustling place with a pleasant atmosphere, is a major stopover point en route between Sydney and Melbourne. The city is nestled against the Murray River and twinned with **Wodonga**, across the river in Victoria.

A good spot for a picnic is **Noreuil Park**, a peaceful place looking across to a bush-covered riverbank in Victoria. People lie about under the large gum trees here – one of which was marked by the explorer Hovell at the point where he and Hume crossed the Murray – and swim in the river. You can also take to the water with a **cruise** on a replica paddle-steamer (Ⓣ04/17 698 502; $16 or $20 at lunchtime); there are two or three departures a day depending on the water level and demand. For a more active way of exploring the river, hire a **canoe** (Ⓣ02/6041 1822; $25 half-day, $35 full day, $70 two-day camping trip), which is less reliant on water levels. Another green spot is the **Albury Botanical Gardens** at the Dean Street end of Wodonga Place. Established in 1877, the gardens house some impressive old trees, including a huge 41-metre Queensland kauri pine.

The excellent **Albury Regional Art Centre** (Mon–Fri 10.30am–5pm, Sat & Sun 10.30am–4pm; free; Ⓦwww.alburycity.nsw.gov.au/gallery), at 546 Dean St in the decorative old town hall, hosts periodic exhibitions and has a sizeable collection of sketches by Russell Drysdale (1912–81), who lived in the area in the 1920s and married into a local family. The **Albury Regional Museum** (Ⓦwww.alburycity.nsw.gov.au/museum) was closed at the time of writing but will be relocated to another part of town, together with the new library – ask at the tourist office.

Practicalities

Although Albury is the major centre, the principal **tourist office** is on the Wodonga side of the river on the Hume Highway (daily 9am–5pm; Ⓣ1300 796 222, Ⓦwww.destinationalburywodonga.com.au). Albury is serviced regularly by **bus** and **train** from Sydney, Melbourne, Canberra and Wagga Wagga by Countrylink, Greyhound and V-line.

Accommodation

Being a major stopover has contributed to the ridiculous number of **motels** in a city that can be explored within a day. The cheapest ones are along the highway, the truck noise being the only difference from the ones in the centre. Good options are the plush *Carlton Country Comfort*, at the corner of Dean and Elizabeth streets (Ⓣ02/6021 5366, Ⓦwww.countrycomfort.com.au; ❺), or the simple *New Albury Hotel* just off the highway at 491 Kiewa St, about 2km north of the bridge over the Murray (Ⓣ02/6021 3599; ❸), with its own Irish bar. **Campers** are catered for at *All Season Tourist Park*, 7km north on the highway (Ⓣ02/6025 1619, Ⓦwww.alburyallseasons.com.au; cabins ❸).

Eating, drinking and nightlife

Dean Street is the main street for food. If you are ravenous and broke, head for *The Commercial Club*, which serves up a cheap deal with all the pasta, steak, seafood and salad you can eat for $14. For something a little less functional, the retro *Electra Café* on the corner of Dean and Macauley streets serves a variety of internationally influenced meals on kitsch crockery (open daily for lunch & Mon–Sat for dinner), while the licensed *Thai Lotus Flower Restaurant*, 610 Dean St, is a popular dinner destination. A smarter option is *Canteen Cuisine* on the same strip at no.479, with all-day breakfasts on Sunday and a wide selection of wines.

Nightlife is better than you might think: *The Bended Elbow* at 480 Dean St is a lively pub, and *Roi Bar*, almost opposite (Ⓦwww.roibar.com.au), has DJs most Saturday nights. *The New Albury Hotel* has jazz on Friday nights.

The Upper Murray

Following the **Upper Murray River** between Albury and the South Australian border, there's little of interest on the New South Wales side until the old port town of **Wentworth** and its surrounding storehouse of ancient Aboriginal history around **Lake Victoria** and in the remote **Mungo National Park**. The main centres are on the Victorian side of the river, Mildura (see p.938) and Echuca (see p.943) chief among them, although the New South Wales riverside towns of **Tocumwal** and **Corowa**, not far from Albury, are pleasant enough.

Corowa and Tocumwal

It's 56km from Albury northwest to the pleasant town of **COROWA**, across the Murray from Victoria's Rutherglen wine region (see p.962). Blue flags flying all over town proclaim it to be the birthplace of **Federation**, since the Federation Conference of 1893 was held at Corowa's courthouse. The town also has the more dubious honour of being the largest pork producer in the southern hemisphere. You can reach Corowa from Albury using V-line or Countrylink buses.

The **tourist office** is at 88 Sanger St (Mon–Sat 10am–5pm, Sun 10am–1pm; Ⓣ02/6033 3221, Ⓦwww.corowa.nsw.gov.au). There are stacks of motels in town offering very reasonable **accommodation**, such as the three-star, riverside *Corowa Golf Club Motel* (Ⓣ02/6033 0634, Ⓦwww.corowagolfclubmotel.com.au; ❸). Campers could try the *Bindaree Motel and Caravan Park*, 454 Honour Ave (Ⓣ02/6033 2500; cabins ❹, motel rooms with kitchenette ❺–❻), which has riverside views. There are several places on the main street where you can get a **meal**, including the *Royal Hotel*, which serves up decent counter food, *D'Amico's* Italian restaurant (closed Wed), and the *Old Corowa Bakehouse*, a popular café-bakery that opens early.

TOCUMWAL ("Toc" to locals) is a small river-town: **Foreshore Park**, just behind the main street, is peaceful and shaded by large gum trees, and there's a sandy river beach only ten minutes' walk away which makes a welcome break. In front of the park is the **tourist office** (Mon–Fri 10am–5pm, Sat & Sun 10am–2pm; Ⓣ03/5874 2131 or 1800 677 271, Ⓦwww.toconthemurray.com.au), which provides information about the area including some fine wineries, walking tracks and river sports, and has cheap Internet access. Greyhound **buses** pass through en route from Brisbane to Melbourne, while V-line will get you as far as Griffith, and Countrylink will take you to Albury.

Tocumwal has some classic old **country hotels**, most notably the *Tocumwal Hotel* at 17–33 Deniliquin St (Ⓣ03/5874 2025, Ⓔpalmshotel@westnet.com.au; ❸), a

△ The Murray River

hospitable place built in 1861 with clean and simple self-contained motel units. Next door is *Central Store Antiques*, which has good tearooms serving reasonably priced sandwiches and light meals.

Wentworth and Lake Victoria

Once a thriving river-port, **WENTWORTH** is now a sleepy old town overshadowed by nearby Mildura, across the Murray River in Victoria. Located at the junction of the Murray and the Darling, the "two rivers" town was for seventy years the centre of river trade between New South Wales, Victoria and South Australia. The extension of the railway at the turn of the century bypassed Wentworth, however, and at the same time ended much of the river trade. To get to Wentworth you'll need to go via Mildura or Broken Hill, as there are no long-distance **buses** passing through.

Enquire at the **tourist office**, 66 Darling St (Mon–Fri 9am–5pm, Sat & Sun 10am–2pm; ⓣ03/5027 3624, ⓦwww.wentworth.nsw.gov.au), about river cruises departing from Mildura Wharf aboard a period paddle-steamer (or call direct on ⓣ03/5023 2200; $24). The **Old Wentworth Gaol** on Beverly Street (daily 10am–5pm; $6) was built of handmade bricks in 1879, and ghosts of former prisoners are believed to make the occasional appearance, leaving shades on pictures taken. Opposite, **Pioneer World** (daily 11am–4pm; $5) is a folk museum exhibiting items related to Aboriginal and European history of the area, and models of giant, but extinct, Australian animals. Perhaps the most interesting thing to do, however, is simply to drive down Old Renmark Road and have a look at the amazing, Sahara-like sand dunes.

Harry Nanya Tours (ⓣ03/5027 2076, ⓦwww.harrynanyatours.com.au) in Wentworth organizes visits to significant **Aboriginal sites** around Lake Victoria, and Mungo National Park (see below), accompanied by accredited Barkindji guides. In 1994, ancient Aboriginal graves were discovered at Lake Victoria, to the west of town, when the partial draining of the eleven-square-kilometre lake revealed skeletons buried side by side and in deep layers. Some of the estimated ten thousand graves (well-known to the Barkindji people) date back six thousand years, in what is believed to be Australia's largest pre-industrial burial site, surpassing any such finds in Europe, Asia or North and South America. The site also challenges the premise that Aboriginal lifestyles were solely nomadic, suggesting that here at least they lived in semi-permanent dwellings around the lake.

Among the various places to **stay** in Wentworth, the best waterfront choice is the *Willow Bend Caravan Park* on Darling Street (ⓣ03/5027 3213, ⓕ5027 3305; on-site vans ❷, cabins ❸), right near the shops but also at the confluence of the Darling and Murray rivers, where there are plenty of trees. Otherwise try the *Wentworth Grande Resort*, 61 Darling St (ⓣ03/5027 2225, ⓦwww.wentworthgranderesort.com.au; ❹), for more luxury with a pool and river views.

Mungo National Park

Mungo National Park, in the far southwest of New South Wales, is most easily reached from the river townships of Wentworth or Mildura (over the Victorian border about 110km away – see p.938); organized tours run to the park from both towns – if you want to tackle it on your own, you'll need a 4WD. The park is part of the dried-up **Willandra Lakes System**, which contains the longest continuous record of Aboriginal life in Australia, dating back more than forty thousand years. During the Ice Age the system formed a vast chain of freshwater lakes, teeming with fish and attracting waterbirds and mammals. Aborigines camped at the shores of the lake to fish and hunt, and buried their dead in the sand dunes. When the lakes started drying out fifteen thousand years ago, Aborigines continued to live near soaks along the old river channel. The park covers most of one of these dry lake-beds, and its dominant feature is a great, crescent-shaped dune, at the eastern edge of the lake, commonly referred to as the **Walls of China**.

There's an NPWS office (Ⓣ03/5021 8900) on the corner of the Sturt Highway at Buronga, near Mildura in Victoria, where you can book accommodation in the park. The official **visitors centre** is by the park's southwest entrance, and has a very informative display on its geological and Aboriginal history. Nearby, the impressive old **Mungo Woolshed** is open for inspection. From here it's a short drive to the lookout point on the rim of the lake, the former shore, from where you can look across the dry lake-bed to the Walls of China. A signposted track takes you on a return trip (1hr) across the lake floor to the dune, then over the top and on to the northwest part of the park. At sunset, or on nights with a full moon, the scenery takes on an eerie, otherworldly quality.

Beds in the former shearers' quarters and NPWS **campsites** in the park can be booked in advance through the NPWS office. Otherwise, try *Mungo Lodge* on the Mildura Road (Ⓣ03/5029 7297, Ⓦwww.mungolodge.com.au; ⑤), which has motel units and self-contained cottages, plus a licensed restaurant.

The New England Plateau

The **New England Plateau** rises parallel to the coast, extending from the northern end of the Hunter Valley, some 200km north of Sydney, all the way to the Queensland border. At the top it's between 1000m and 1400m above sea level, and on the eastern edge an escarpment falls away steeply towards the coast. This eastern rim consists of precipitous cliff-faces, deep gorges, thickly forested valleys, streams and mighty waterfalls, and because of its inaccessibility remains a largely undisturbed wilderness. On the plateau itself the scene is far more pastoral, as sheep and cattle graze on the undulating highland. Because of the altitude, the **climate** up here is fundamentally different from the subtropical coast, a mere 150km or so away: winters are cold and frosty, with very occasional snowfalls, while in summer the fresh, dry air can offer welcome relief after the heat and humidity of the coast. Even during a summer heatwave, when the daytime temperature might exceed 30°C, the nights will be pleasantly cool – perhaps attracting the mainly Scottish immigrants who, despite the name, transformed the New England highlands into pastures in the nineteenth century.

The **New England Highway**, one of the main links between Brisbane and Sydney, passes all the major towns – **Tamworth**, **Armidale**, **Glen Innes** and **Tenterfield** – from where scenic side-roads branch off towards the coast. Farms and stations all over the highlands provide farmstay accommodation, offering horse riding and other activities. The area is well served by **bus**: Greyhound Australia (Ⓣ13 20 30) has daily services between Sydney or Canberra and Brisbane and between Brisbane and Melbourne, both via New England. Keans Travel (Ⓣ02/6543 1322) runs between Port Macquarie and Scone via Nambucca Heads, Coffs Harbour, Bellingen, Dorrigo, Armidale, Uralla, Walcha and Tamworth.

The Upper Hunter Valley

The upper end of the **Hunter Valley** is Australia's main horse-breeding area – indeed it claims to deal in as much horseflesh as anywhere in the world – with at least thirty stud farms; sires are flown in from all over the world to breed with the local mares. There are cattle- and sheep-breeding stations up here too, while the fertile soils of the Upper Hunter also yield a harvest of cereals and fruits including, of course, grapes – see the box, pp.198–199 for a sampling of Hunter Valley wineries.

The pretty township of **SCONE** is at the centre of the Hunter Valley horse trade; you can get further details of the business from the **tourist office** on the corner of Susan and Kelly streets (daily 9am–5pm; ⓣ02/6545 1526, ⓦwww.horsecapital.com.au), which also has an excellent Internet café. The best time to visit is during the **Scone Horse Festival** – ten days in the middle of May – which features local prize specimens in horse shows, rodeos and races; book your accommodation in advance if you're planning to stay. At any time of year, ask at the tourist information centre about regular races held in the area.

Lake Glenbawn, 15km east of Scone, makes for a pleasant excursion. The dam holds back the waters of the Upper Hunter, storing up to 750 billion litres for irrigation purposes. Recreation facilities at the reserve here include a caravan park and boat rental: the lake is great for water-skiing, canoeing, sailing and fishing. You can continue past the dam and climb to the plateau of the Barrington Tops (see p.261) to the national park of the same name.

Northeast of Scone is polo country, the haunt of mega-rich Australians. If you fancy seeing the elitist sport in action, there are polo grounds at **Gundy** and at **Ellerston**. Heading on towards the heart of the New England Plateau you'll pass **Burning Mountain**, about 20km north of Scone, near the village of Wingen. The smoking vents don't indicate volcanic activity but rather a seam of coal burning 30m under the surface: the fire was ignited naturally, perhaps by a lightning strike or spontaneous combustion, over a thousand years ago. The area, protected as a nature reserve, can be reached via a signposted **walking trail** that starts at the picnic grounds at the foot of the hill, just off the New England Highway; pick up the informative NPWS guide to the area's walking tracks from any NPWS office; the nearest one is in Scone. You might also see aquatic fossils on your walk – this area was once under the ocean. Fourteen kilometres north of Wingen, **MURRURUNDI** marks the end of the Upper Hunter Valley. It's a pretty spot, enclosed by the Liverpool Ranges; the *Café Telegraph* here makes a cheerful refreshment stop, and has seats outside in the garden with the creek flowing past.

Practicalities

Countrylink **trains** run twice daily from Sydney to Scone; Greyhound **buses** stop at Murrurundi and Scone; and Kean's Travel call at Wingen. Places to **stay** in the area are widely scattered. By far the most enjoyable, located between Gundy and Ellerston is *Belltrees*; the family estate of the White family, who gave the world the Nobel Prize–winning novelist Patrick White. Belltrees Station is a collection of buildings, including the 1832 Semphill Cottage, set among pepper trees; there's even a small school, which was established in 1879. You can stay at the country house next door to the Whites' residence, or in the mountain retreat where Patrick White used to escape when he returned home to visit in later life; there are also a couple of cheaper self-contained **cottages** sleeping four people (prices from $110 to $250 per person, meals often included; ⓣ02/6546 1123, ⓦwww.belltrees.com), and polo tuition can be arranged.

Right in Scone, the *Royal Hotel-Motel* on St Aubins Street (ⓣ02/6545 1722; ❷–❸) offers simple pub accommodation and fancier motel units – it also serves good counter meals. Right at the lake, the *Lake Glenbawn Holiday Village* (ⓣ02/6543 7752, ⓦwww.lakeglenbawncottages.com.au; ❹–❺) has camping and three-bedroom cottages.

In nearby Aberdeen, a few kilometres south on the New England Highway, is *Segenhoe B&B*, at 55 Main Rd (ⓣ02/6543 7382, ⓦwww.segenhoeinn.com; ❻–❼), a charming sandstone residence from the early 1800s with large, period-style rooms; the staff can arrange a host of activities. Also recommended is the forested mountain-retreat *Craigmhor* (ⓣ02/6543 6394, ⓦwww.craigmhor.com.au; ❺), on Upper Rouchel Road in the foothills of the Barrington Tops, 48km east of Aberdeen.

If you're hungry for scones in Scone, head to *Asser House Café* on Kelly Street, where they also serve excellent tea and coffee; otherwise, the best **food** is at the modern-Australian *Quince*, 109 Susan St (ⓣ02/6545 2286).

Tamworth and around

TAMWORTH – on the New England Highway, 130km north of Scone – is also known as the "City of Lights" because they were the first in Australia to be fitted with electric street-lighting in 1888. To most Australians, however, Tamworth means **country music** – it's a sort of antipodean Nashville. The twelve-metre-high golden guitar in front of the **Golden Guitar Complex** (daily 9am–5pm; $8; ⓦwww.biggoldenguitar.com.au), on the southern edge of town, sums up the town's role as the country-and-western capital of Australasia. Inside the centre, you'll find waxwork figures of the great Australian country stars such as Chad Morgan, Buddy Williams, Smoky Dawson and his horse Flash, Slim Dusty, Reg Lindsay and Tex Morton. In the second half of January,

△ Tamworth Country Music Festival

the town is the focus of the annual, week-long **Tamworth Country Music Festival**, when fans from all over the world descend, packing out camping spots. Every pub, club and hall in town hosts gigs, record launches and bush poetry, culminating in the presentation of the Australian Country Music Awards – for further information and bookings, contact the tourist office (see below). There's more musical memorabilia at the corner of Brisbane Street and Kable Avenue, where the **Hands of Fame** cornerstone bears the palm-prints of various country greats.

Don't give up on Tamworth entirely if country music isn't your thing. The **Powerstation Museum** at 216 Peel St (Wed–Sat 9am–1pm; $3.50) celebrates those pioneering street-lights, and there are numerous **art galleries** and crafts studios around town – the **Tamworth Regional Gallery**, above the library at 466 Peel St (Tues–Sat 10am–5pm, Sun noon–4pm; free; ⓦwww.tamworth.nsw.gov.au/gallery), has frequently changing exhibitions, with good contemporary and Aboriginal art. Natural attractions include the **Oxley Lookout and Nature Reserve** at the end of White Street, with panoramic views of the city and the Peel River Valley; and Lake Keepit, 56km northwest of the city, where you can rent boats and mess about on the water.

The former gold-mining township of **NUNDLE** lies some 60km southeast of town in the "hills of gold" – people still visit with picks, shovels and sieves in the hope of striking it lucky. If you want to join them for a day, you no longer need to buy a fossicking licence but it's still worth dropping by the General Store on Jenkins Street; they'll point you in the right direction to start digging.

Practicalities

There's a daily **train** service between Sydney and Armidale via Tamworth, and both Greyhound and Kean's Travel **buses** pass through on a daily basis, the former en route between Sydney and Brisbane. The big, guitar-shaped **tourist office** (daily 9am–5pm; ⓣ02/6755 4300, ⓦwww.visittamworth.com) is on the corner of Peel and Murray streets, and can give you information on local bus services to Nundle.

Accommodation

There's a fair spread of **accommodation** in Tamworth, though you might have trouble finding a room during the festival, when you could try the string of **motels** on the New England Highway outside town.

Tamworth

Bunkhouse 118 New England Highway ⓣ02/6762 6300, ⓔbunkhouse@tpg.com.au. Spotless and inexpensive hostel with a/c, though a bit clinical. Dorms $20, rooms ❷

Paradise Caravan Park Peel St ⓣ & ⓕ02/6766 3120, ⓦwww.paradisetouristpark.com.au. The closest place to town for campers and caravaners, on the river about five minutes' walk from the centre. Cabins ❸

Quality Hotel Powerhouse Cnr East St and Armidale Rd ⓣ02/6766 7000, ⓦwww.qualityhotelpowerhouse.com.au. This smart motel has a corporate feel and five-star facilities, including room service, gym, swimming pool and sauna. ❻

Tamworth YHA 169 Marius St, opposite the train station ⓣ02/6761 2600, ⓦwww.yha.com.au. Slightly scruffy place with well maintained, if old, facilities. Dorms $21–23, rooms ❷

Around Tamworth

Austin Caravan Park 4km north of town off the New England Highway ⓣ02/6766 2380, ⓦwww.austintouristpark.com.au. Occupies a riverside spot with a postage-stamp of a pool and a children's playground. Cabins ❷

Jenkins St Guest House 85 Jenkins St, Nundle ⓣ & ⓕ02/6769 3239. Beautiful place with polished wood floors, fresh flowers in all rooms and an excellent local chef (dinner Fri & Sat, lunch Sat & Sun). ❺–❻

Leconfield 50km east of Tamworth ⓣ02/6769 4328, ⓦwww.leconfield.com. If you want a taste of Australian country living, this place offers a five-day residential Jackeroo and Jilleroo school ($550) where you learn to ride and groom horses, shear and throw fleeces, lasso, whip crack and go out mustering. They can arrange pick-ups from *Tamworth YHA*.

Peel Inn Jenkins St, Nundle ⓣ02/6769 3377, ⓕ6769 3307, ⓦwww.peelinn.com.au. Historic hotel with rooms and hearty meals; they also organize gold-panning. ❷

Eating, drinking and entertainment

Outside festival time, you'll be disappointed if you think the town's **clubs and pubs** constantly resound to country-and-western. Probably the biggest venue (with no country outside festival time, but bands from Wed to Sat) is the *Imperial Hotel* on the corner of Brisbane and Marius streets. The *Central Hotel*, on the corner of Peel and Brisbane streets, has bands from Thursday to Saturday and you can catch some acts on the first Friday and third Sunday of the month in the *West's Diggers*.

Inland Café 407 Peel St. A busy lunch spot with cakes, focaccia and pasta, plus good coffee.
Jack Style 15 Fitzroy St. Large and inexpensive Thai restaurant with Buddhas hanging on the wall.
Old Vic Café 261 Peel St. A good people-watching spot with an urban feel, serving fruit juices, pasta and pastries for lunch.
Quality Hotel Powerhouse Cnr East St and Armidale Rd. Good-quality modern Australian mains ($30) in a very genteel setting.
West's Diggers Club Cnr Bourke St and Kable Ave. Filling and inexpensive feeds of nachos, steak, chips and veggies in a pub-like environment.

Armidale and around

The city of **ARMIDALE** is home to the **University of New England**, which together with a couple of famous boarding schools, gives an unexpectedly academic feel to a place so far up-country. Australia's highest city at around 1000m, Armidale is cooler than the surrounding plains and is also a place of considerable natural beauty, especially in autumn, when its many parks are transformed into a sea of red and golden leaves.

The central pedestrian mall, **Beardy Street**, is flanked by quaint Australian country pubs with wide, iron-lace verandas – on the last Sunday of the month the street comes alive with an extensive **market** complete with buskers. The excellent **New England Regional Art Museum** on Kentucky Street (Tues–Fri 10am–5pm, Sat & Sun 9am–4pm; free; ⓦwww.neram.com.au) includes fine surrealist work by Clifford Bayliss among others, displays by Arthur Streeton and Tom Roberts, plus big-name temporary exhibits from Sydney. Next door, the arresting modern building with the distinctive ochre-coloured tin roof is the indigenous-run **Aboriginal Centre and Keeping Place** (Mon–Fri 9am–4pm; ⓣ02/6771 1242; free), an educational, visual and performing-arts centre which has displays of artefacts and interpretive material, plus special exhibitions. You might also want to visit the **Folk Museum**, at the corner of Rusden and Faulkner streets (daily 1–4pm; donation), which has a collection of artefacts from the New England region and displays on local history. There's more history at the **Saumarez Homestead** (daily 10am–4pm, closed mid-June to Sept; entry to homestead by guided tour only at 10:30am & 2pm daily, Sat & Sun also at 3pm & 4pm; $8) behind the airport, a perfectly preserved dwelling dating from the 1800s. A two-hour **free bus tour** of the city with Heritage Tours departs from the tourist office daily at 10am – otherwise, pick up the self-drive leaflet from the centre.

One of the best ways to get around town is by **bike**: there's a signposted city tour, as well as a bike path to the **university campus**, 5km northwest of the city. On the campus are two small specialized museums (Antiquity and Zoology; Mon–Fri 9am–4.30pm; both free), a kangaroo and deer park, and the historic Booloominbah homestead, built in the 1880s as a fashionable gentlemen's residence and now housing the university's principal administration office.

Practicalities

Armidale has a helpful **tourist office** at 82 Marsh St (daily 9am–5pm; ⓣ02/6772 4655, ⓦwww.armidaletourism.com.au), which has information on accommodation, local sites and the area's national parks. The **bus** terminal is nearby, from where Countrylink, Greyhound and Kean's Travel services depart. There's also a daily **train** from Sydney. Plenty of places offer car rental, among them Budget, 101 Barney St (ⓣ02/6772 4719), and Realistic Car Rentals, at Armidale Exhaust Centre on the corner of Rusden and Dangar streets (ⓣ02/6772 8078). Bikes can be rented from Armidale Bicycle Centre, 244 Beardy St (ⓣ02/6772 3718). For taxis, call Armidale Radio Taxis (ⓣ13 10 08).

Accommodation

Glenhope Homestead Red Gum Lane ⓣ02/6772 1940, ⓦwww.glenhopealpacas.com. For a real country feel, head 4km northwest of the city to this working alpaca farm. The self-contained doubles with kitchenette are modern, and boast a scenic location overlooking the farm. ❹–❺

Hideaway Motor Inn 70 Glen Innes Rd ⓣ02/6772 5177. Right in the centre of town, this clean motel is the cheapest of its kind, with small but well-furnished rooms. ❸

Lindsay House 128 Faulkner St ⓣ02/6771 4554, ⓦwww.lindsayhouse.com.au. This nineteenth-century residence is the nicest place to stay in Armidale, with large en-suite rooms, a bar and a garden. ❺

Pembroke Tourist and Leisure Park 39 Waterfall Way, 2km east of town ⓣ02/6772 6470, ⓦwww.pembroke.com.au. This leisure-park complex has good facilities including a swimming pool and tennis court, and is also home to a small *YHA* dormitory. Dorms $24–27, on-site vans ❷, cabins ❸

Poppy's Cottage Dangarsleigh Rd ⓣ02/6775 1277, ⓦwww.poppyscottage.com.au. B&B set in a farm cottage five minutes' drive from town and close to a local vineyard. ❺

Tattersalls Hotel 147 Beardy St ⓣ02/6772 2247. Inexpensive and good-value singles and doubles in a central, quiet location. ❷

Eating, drinking and nightlife

Armidale has an appealing range of **restaurants** to choose from, many of them around Beardy and March streets. *Jean Pierre's* on March Street lives up to its name, serving Chateaubriand and filet mignon, while *The Flying Duck*, on the same strip at no.130, is a candlelit Spanish tapas restaurant with a homely feel (both closed Sun & Mon). Good, inexpensive **counter meals** are served at many of the grand old pubs on Beardy Street, including the *New England Hotel* and the *Imperial*. Get the *Good Food Guide* from the tourist office for a complete list. For term-time **entertainment** (March–Nov) head to the *St Kilda*, *Tattersalls*, *New England* or *Wicklows* hotels in the centre for live music on Friday and Saturday nights.

Around Armidale

Armidale makes for a good staging-post north through the **New England Plains** or east to the coast through a hat full of Australia's most beautiful national parks. If you don't mind dirt roads (mostly fine for 2WD in the dry), you can get to Coffs Harbour via hundreds of kilometres of rainforest roads, waterfalls and lookouts (get a map from the tourist office). The exceptional **New England National Park**, 85km east on the Waterfall Way, and the several patchwork sections of the **Oxley Wild Rivers**, **Guy Fawkes River**, and **Cathedral Rock** national parks around it are full of ancient ferns, towering canopy trees, gorges and spectacular **waterfalls** (although the falls can diminish to a trickle during prolonged dry spells). The most impressive are the **Wollomombi Falls**, among the highest in Australia, plunging 225m into a gorge just over 40km east of Armidale, off the road to Dorrigo. Nearby are the **Chandler Falls**, while **Ebor Falls**, a stunning double drop of the Guy Fawkes River, can be viewed from platforms just off Waterfall Way, another 40km beyond Wollomombi. Between Wollomombi and Ebor, **Point Lookout** in the New England National Park offers a truly wonderful panoramic view across the forested ranges – you'd be forgiven for thinking you were in the middle of the Amazon. The road to the lookout is unsealed gravel, but is usually in reasonable condition, and there are simple **cabins** and bush **campsites** where you can stay overnight: phone the NPWS in Armidale (ⓣ02/6738 9100) for further information – advance booking is essential. The rest of the park is virtually inaccessible wilderness.

URALLA, 22km south of Armidale, is another old gold-town, though in this case the town has managed to hang on, with a population of a couple of thousand. The Historic Building Walk will take you past the town's highlights, including **McCrossin's Mill Museum** (daily noon–5pm; $4), an old three-storey flour mill on Salisbury Street. Fossicking is still possible at the old Rocky River diggings: enquire at the **tourist office** on the New England Highway (daily 9.30am–4.30pm; ⓣ02/6778 4496, ⓦwww.uralla.com).

Gold apart, Uralla's other claim to fame is **Captain Thunderbolt**, the bushranger who terrorized the gold-rich New England region in the nineteenth century when the town was on the major Sydney–Brisbane route. A charismatic fellow, he promised his Aboriginal wife never to shoot anyone, and he never did. The police, however, had made no such promises, and Thunderbolt was apparently killed here in 1870 – although the story that the corpse was actually his brother and that Thunderbolt was alive and well and plying his trade in California is supported by much more evidence. There's a bronze statue of the bushranger and his horse at the corner of Bridge and Salisbury streets.

South of Armidale towards Walcha is **Dangars Lagoon**, a wetland region visited by more than a hundred different kinds of bird; a hide is provided for spotters. **Dangars Falls** and a network of twenty walking tracks and lookouts around **Dangars Gorge** are only 22km from Armidale on a minor road. Beyond these, about 20km east of Walcha, a turn-off from the Oxley Highway leads to Apsley Gorge and two more waterfalls in another section of the Oxley Wild Rivers National Park. **WALCHA** itself, 65km southwest of Armidale, is surrounded by national parks, making it a great base for nature freaks. There are the usual pioneer museums in town, but more interesting is the **Amaroo Museum and Cultural Centre** on Derby Street (Mon–Fri 9am–5pm; donation), which displays arts and crafts made by local Aboriginal people. For more information on the area, head for the **tourist office** at 51 Fitzroy St (Mon–Fri 8.30am–4.30pm, Sat & Sun 9am–4pm; ⓣ02/6774 2460, ⓦwww.walchansw.com.au). West of Armidale, 27km along the Bundarra Road, is the **Mount Yarrowyck Nature Reserve**, where an Aboriginal cave-painting site can be accessed via a three-kilometre circuit walk.

Glen Innes and around

GLEN INNES, the next major stop north on the New England Highway, about 100km from Armidale, is another pleasant town in a beautiful setting. Although agriculture is still important up here, you begin to see more and more evidence of the gemfields – sapphires are big business, as, to a lesser extent, is tin mining. In the centre, on **Grey Street** especially, numerous century-old public buildings and parks have been renovated and spruced up, and there's some fine country architecture, including a couple of large corner pubs with iron-lace verandas.

The Land of the Beardies History House (Mon–Fri 10am–noon & 1–4pm, Sat & Sun 1–4pm; $6; Ⓦwww.beardieshistoryhouse.info), in the town's first hospital on the corner of Ferguson Street and West Avenue, displays pioneer relics, period room settings and a reconstructed slab hut. The name alludes to the two hairy stockmen who settled the area in the nineteenth century, and the Land of the Beardies title is one which the town is proud of; the **Land of the Beardies Festival** is held in early November, with everything from a beard-growing contest to dances, parades and arts-and-crafts exhibits. The **Scottish legacy** of the original settlers is reflected in the name of the town itself and in many of its streets, which are rendered in both English and Gaelic. The local granite **Australian Standing Stones** at Martins Lookout, Watsons Drive, are based on the Ring of Brodgar in Scotland and are intended to honour the "contribution of the Celtic races to Australia's development". The stones are the site of a **Celtic Festival** (Ⓦwww.australiancelticfestival.com) during the first weekend of May, when locals dust off their bagpipes, eat haggis, stage highland games and see the Celtic slaves take on the Roman legions.

While you're in the area, you might also consider a horseback pub-crawl with **Great Aussie Pub Crawls on Horseback** (Ⓣ02/6732 1599, Ⓦwww.pubcrawlsonhorseback.com.au), who run half-hour to four-day horse-riding adventures through the bush with overnight stops at traditional Aussie pubs – a weekend trip costs $375, all inclusive. You can also go fossicking (sieving river silt in the faint hope of finding a sapphire) here – ask at the tourist office.

Practicalities

Greyhound **buses** pass through town on their way from Sydney to Melbourne and you can get as far as Armidale and Tenterfield with Countrylink. The **tourist office** is at 152 Church St (Mon–Fri 9am–5pm, Sat & Sun 9am–3pm; Ⓣ02/6732 2400, Ⓦwww.gleninnestourism.com), as the New England Highway is called as it passes through town; they can help book **accommodation** and have a sapphire shop attached. Good accommodation options include the air-conditioned *Central Motel* on Meade Street (Ⓣ02/6732 2200; ❸–❹); the fancier (though without a/c) *Comfort Inn* on Church Street, 1km south of the centre (Ⓣ02/6732 2255, Ⓕ6732 1515; ❹), with a pool, spa and extensive landscaped grounds; and *Craigieburn Tourist Park*, 2km south of town off the New England Highway (Ⓣ02/6732 1283; cabins ❷–❸), set in lush forest and a great place for spotting wildlife. The nicest place by far, however, is the very welcoming 1920s *Mackenzie House* (Ⓣ02/6732 1679, Ⓦwww.mackenziehouse.com.au; ❺), quietly but conveniently situated right opposite the park in a lovely garden.

For **food**, try the *Tea and Coffee Shop* on Grey Street, a cozy tearoom with loads of pancakes, an array of interesting sandwiches, savoury croissants and hot breakfasts. Alternatively, there's modern Australian cuisine at the *Tasting Room*

The Myall Creek massacre

In the first decades of the nineteenth century, when European settlers started to move up to the highlands and to use Aboriginal-occupied land on the plateau as sheep and cattle pasture, many of the local Aborigines fought back. Time and again bloody skirmishes flared up, though most were never mentioned in pioneer circles and have subsequently been erased from public memory. The **Myall Creek massacre** is one of the few that has found a place in the history of white Australia.

For Aboriginal people, expulsion from the lands of their ancestors amounted to spiritual as well as physical dispossession, and they resisted as best they could: white stockmen staying in huts far away from pioneer townships or homesteads feared for their lives. In 1837 and 1838, Aborigines repeatedly ambushed and killed stockmen near the Gwydir and Namoi rivers. Then, during the absence of the overseer at Myall Creek Station, near present-day Inverell, twelve farm hands organized a raid in retribution, killing 28 Aborigines. In court, the farm hands were acquitted – public opinion saw nothing wrong with their deed, and neither did the jury. The case was later taken up again, however, and seven of the participants in the massacre were sentenced to death on the gallows.

(closed Mon & Sun) and hefty feeds with $7 specials at the *Imperial Hotel* on Grey Street.

Inverell

The area between Glen Innes and **INVERELL**, 67km to the west and serviced daily from Tamworth by Countrylink, is one huge gemfield. Industrial diamonds, garnets, topaz, zircons and over half the world's sapphires are mined in the area – Inverell is in fact known as "Sapphire City", and at the **Dejon Sapphire Centre**, on the Gwydir Highway 18km east of town, you can watch gems being mined, washed, sorted and cut (daily 9am–5pm, mine tours 10.30am & 3pm; free). The showroom has a display of sapphires in 155 colours, from pale blue and green to gold, lemon and pink.

If you want to try your own luck, you'll need to contact the **tourist office** on Campbell Street (Mon–Fri 9am–5pm, Sat 9am–1pm; ⓣ02/6728 8161, ⓦwww.inverell-online.com.au), which can direct you to the designated areas. If you decide to **stay**, try the *Royal Hotel*, 260 Byron St (ⓣ02/6722 2811; ❸), which has clean rooms with shared facilities, open fires, air conditioning and counter meals; or the quiet, leafy *Sapphire City Caravan Park* on Moore Street (ⓣ02/6722 1830; on-site vans ❷, cabins ❸).

Tenterfield and around

Less than 20km from the Queensland border, **TENTERFIELD** marks the northern end of the New England Plateau. From here you can go straight to Ballina on the coast or continue north on the New England Highway. Tenterfield is a lively town, and although only tiny, it has a confirmed place in Australian history, being the birthplace of the **Australian Federation**; in 2001 it played host to many centennial celebrations. Its title was earned when the Prime Minister of New South Wales, Sir Henry Parkes, made his famous Federation speech here in 1889, advocating the union of the Australian colonies; twelve years later the **Commonwealth of Australia** was inaugurated.

The **Sir Henry Parkes museum** (daily 10am–4pm; $5) recalls the occasion, and you'll still see the federation flag flown around town. Tenterfield's other claim to fame is as the birthplace of **Peter Allen**, the singer who penned the very popular *Tenterfield Saddler* (the saddlery is on High Street) and *I still call Australia home* (he moved to the USA).

Tenterfield's real attractions lie outside town. Just 30km to the northeast is **Bald Rock**, in the national park of the same name, which claims to be Australia's second-largest monolith after Uluru, but a grey-granite version, 213m high. You can walk up the northeast side to the summit, from where there are breathtaking panoramic views well into Queensland.

The excursion to Bald Rock combines nicely with a visit to the nearby 210-metre-high **Boonoo Boonoo Falls**, also set in a national park of the same name, which is home to endangered brush-tailed rock wallabies. The road is sealed as far as Bald Rock, but there's an unsealed road (passable in a 2WD) branching off before you reach the rock and running for around 12km to the falls. En route to Bald Rock on the left you'll pass **Thunderbolt's Hideout**, the rock shelter and stable of the bushranger Captain Thunderbolt (see p.334). Details are available from the **tourist office**, 157 Rouse St (Mon–Fri 9.30am–5pm, Sat 9.30am–4.30pm, Sun 9.30am–4pm; ⓣ02/6736 1082, ⓦwww.tenterfield.com). To get to Tenterfield, use Greyhound from Brisbane or Sydney or Countrylink from Armidale.

Accommodation in Tenterfield includes a wide range of motels and pubs. The *Telegraph Hotel/Motel* on Manners Street (ⓣ02/6736 2888; ❷) is central, clean and has good counter meals.

The northwest

From Dubbo, the **Newell Highway**, the main route from Melbourne to Brisbane, continues through the wheat plains of the northwest, their relentless flatness relieved by the ancient eroded mountain ranges of the **Warrumbungles**, near Coonabarabran, and **Mount Kaputar**, near Narrabri, with the Pillaga Scrub between the two towns. Clear skies and the lack of large towns make this an ideal area for stargazing, and large telescopes stare into space at both **Coonabarabran** and **Narrabri**. The thinly populated northwest is home to a relatively large number of Aborigines, peaking in the town of Moree, the area's largest. In 1971 Charles Perkins, an Aboriginal activist, led the **Freedom Ride**, a group of thirty people – mostly university students – who bussed through New South Wales on a mission to root out racism in the state. The biggest victory was in Moree itself when the riders, facing hostile townsfolk, broke the race bar by escorting Aboriginal children into the public swimming pool.

The **Namoi Valley** – extending from **Gunnedah**, just west of Tamworth, to Walgett – with its rich black soil is **cotton country**. Beyond Walgett, just off the Castlereagh Highway that runs from Dubbo, is **Lightning Ridge**, a scorching-hot, opal-mining town relieved by the hot artesian bore baths which are a feature of the northwest.

Coonabarabran and the Warrumbungles

COONABARABRAN is a touristy little town on the Castlereagh River, 160km north of Dubbo via the Newell Highway. People come here to **gaze at stars** in the clear skies, or for bushwalking and climbing in the spectacular **Warrumbungles**, an ancient mountain range 35km to the west.

By virtue of its proximity to the **Siding Spring Observatory Complex** (Mon–Fri 9.30am–4pm, Sat & Sun 10am–2pm; $16.50 including tour; ⓦwww.sidingspringexploratory.com.au), perched high above the township on the edge of Warrumbungle National Park, Coonabarabran considers itself the astronomy capital of Australia. The skies are exceptionally clear out here, due to the dry climate and a lack of pollution and population. The giant 3.9-metre optical telescope (one of the largest in the world) can be viewed close up from an observation gallery, and there's an astronomy exhibition, complemented by hands-on exhibits and a video show.

You can't actually view the stars at Siding Spring because, as a working observatory, it's closed at night. However, the **Skywatch Observatory** (daily 10.30am till late; $5, night show $15; book before dusk on ⓣ02/6842 3303, ⓦwww.skywatchobservatory.com), on Timor Road, 2km from town on the way to the Warrumbungles, has night viewing through its modern telescope, plus a planetarium, theatre, "pathway to the stars" space-simulation computer programme and even a Thai restaurant. On a different tack, Ukerbarley Tours (ⓣ02/6843 4446) runs cultural **tours** focusing on the Gamilaroi Aboriginal history of the region.

Warrumbungle National Park

The rugged **Warrumbungles** are ancient mountains of volcanic origin with jagged cliffs, rocky pinnacles and crags jutting from the western horizon. The dry western plains and the moister environment of the east coast meet at these ranges, with plant and animal species from both habitats coexisting in the park. Resident fauna include four species of kangaroo, plus koalas and a variety of birds including wedgetail eagles, superb blue wrens, eastern spinebills and mountain galaxies.

The **Warrumbungle National Park** ("crooked mountains") was once bordered by three different language groups – the Kamilaroi, the Weilwan and the Kawambarai – and evidence of past Aboriginal habitation here is common, with stone flakes used to make tools indicating old campsites. The Warrumbungle National Park is spectacular, especially in spring when the wild flowers in the sandstone areas are in bloom. Remember to bring plenty of water when walking in summer and a warm coat in winter as nights can be chilly and snow is not an uncommon sight.

The **National Park Visitors Centre**, in the park near the campground (daily 9am–4pm; ⓣ02/6825 4364, ⓦwww.nationalparks.nsw.gov.au), has hands-on displays and detailed maps of walking tracks. The wheelchair-accessible bitumen **Gurianawa Track** makes a short circuit around the centre and overlooks the flats where eastern grey kangaroos gather at dusk. Another good introduction to the park is the short **White Gum Lookout Walk** (1km), with panoramic views over the ranges – particularly dramatic at sunset. However, the ultimate – for the reasonably fit only – is the 14.5-kilometre (roughly 5hr) **Grand High Tops Trail** along the main ridge and back. The walk begins at the kangaroo-filled Camp Pincham and follows the flat floor of Spirey Creek through open forests full of colourful rosellas and lorikeets, and lizards basking on rocks. As the trail climbs, there are views of the three-hundred-metre-high Belougery Spire, and more scrambling gets you to the foot of the **Breadknife**, the park's most famous feature, a 2.5-metre-wide rock flake thrusting 90m up into the sky. From here the main track heads on to the rocky slabs of the Grand High Tops, with tremendous views of most of the surrounding peaks. Experienced walkers could carry on to climb Bluff Mountain and then head west for Mount Exmouth (1205m), the park's highest peak; both are great spots from which to watch the sunrise. The Warrumbungles are very popular with **rock climbers**, who are allowed to climb anywhere except the Breadknife; permits are required. There isn't any public transport to the Warrumbungles, so you'll need your own.

Practicalities

In addition to the National Park Visitors Centre, Coonabarabran has its own **tourist office** on the Newell Highway, or John Street as it's called as it passes through town (daily 9am–5pm; ⓣ02/6849 2144 or 1800 242 881, ⓦwww.coonabarabran.com). Inside there's a display of ancient megafauna – the large animals that used to roam the continent before human habitation – including a diprotodon, a wombat the size of a hippo. The only **bus** passing through town is the Greyhound service from Melbourne to Brisbane.

Good places to **eat** here include the wonderful *Woop Woop*, which has excellent modern cuisine in a cozy room of exposed brick and iron girders, situated in an alleyway just off John Street (closed Mon). Other establishments are all on John Street itself: the bright and airy *Jolly Cauli*, at no. 30, offers a wide choice of dishes, delicious coffee and home-made cakes, and also serves as the town's Internet café, although more terminals can be found at the community centre just across the road next to the post office. The *Imperial Hotel* has the best counter meals.

Accommodation

Accommodation in the national park itself is limited to **campsites** ($5 per person plus $7 per vehicle), some of which have hot showers, electric barbecues and fireplaces (note that wood is not supplied, and while plenty of places sell it, there's a fine for collecting it in the park), and *Balor Hut*, an eight-bunk hut adjacent to the Breadknife (mattresses aren't provided). Bookings aren't necessary for any of the sites, but you may need to book the hut; reservations can be made at the National Park Visitors Centre. Anyone planning to stay in the park will need to bring provisions. There are plenty of alternative **accommodation** options in town.

In the national park

Tibuc Farm Timor Rd, 16km from town ⓣ02/6842 1740, ⓦwww.coonabarabran.com/tibuc. Nestled under Bulleamble Mountain, with three self-contained cabins varying from the decently equipped to the extremely basic (cold water only and no power). If you're not bringing your own linen, mention it when booking. Sleeps four. ④

Warrumbungles Mountain Lodge Timor Rd, 9km from town en route to the park ⓣ02/6842 1832, ⓦwww.warrumbungle.com. Set in bushland on the Castlereagh River. Rooms (BYO linen) have extra bunks and kitchens, so are good for families and small groups; there's also a small saltwater pool and facilities for tennis and basketball. Dorms $19, cabins & motel ③

In town

All Travellers Motor Inn John St ⓣ02/6842 1133, ⓦwww.alltravellers.com.au. Three-and-a-half-star motel with air conditioning and wheelchair-accessible rooms. ④

El Paso Motel Newell Highway, 1km from the centre ⓣ02/6842 1722, ⓦwww.elpaso.com.au. One of the cheaper places to stay, but with good facilities including a large pool and licensed restaurant. ③

Imperial Hotel John St ⓣ02/6842 1023. Excellent hotel which has a guest lounge, kitchenette, very reasonable singles and doubles, and a huge veranda with tables and armchairs. ❶

John Oxley Caravan Park 1.5km along the Oxley Highway ⓣ02/6842 1635. Shady and relaxing caravan park, one of two in town. Cabins ❷

The Namoi Valley: Gunnedah and around

On the Oxley Highway, 76km west of Tamworth, **GUNNEDAH** is one of the largest towns in the northwest, although more a regional commercial centre than a place to visit. The town was the inspiration for the Australian poet **Dorothea MacKellar** (1885–1968) and her patriotic verse *My Country*, in which she pledged her undying love for what was then – and still remains – a drought-stricken land. The opening stanza is familiar to most Australians, who learn it by rote at school:

I love a sunburnt country
A land of sweeping plains
Of ragged mountain ranges
Of drought and flooding rains…

Gunnedah has one of the healthiest **koala populations** in the state, and there's a semi-permanent resident bear in a eucalypt opposite the **tourist office** (Mon–Fri 9am–5pm, Sat & Sun 10am–3pm; ⓣ02/6740 2230 or 1800 562 527, ⓦwww.infogunnedah.com.au) in Anzac Park on South Street. The staff put out a "koala today" sign when he's home and have accurate information on the whereabouts of the town's other bears. Otherwise, you have a good chance of seeing some on the **Bindea Walking Track**, a 7.4-kilometre walk from the tourist office, or a 4.5-kilometre trek through the bush from the car park at Porcupine's Lookout in the porcupine reserve, just southeast of the centre. Gunnedah is a major **beef cattle-selling** centre, with auctions on Tuesdays; there are also **markets** on the third Saturday of the month, at Wolseley Park in Conadilly Street. The **Waterways Wildlife Park** (daily 10am-4pm; $5), 7km west of Gunnedah on Mullaley Road (the Oxley Highway), is a green lakeside spot which makes for an inviting break from the highway and is home to emus, kangaroos, wombats, lizards and possums.

A daily Countrylink **train** stops in Gunnedah on its way from Sydney to Moree. Should you want to **stay** in Gunnedah, try the friendly *Regal Hotel* at 298 Conadilly St (ⓣ02/6742 2355; ❷), which has a guest lounge with an open fire and good bistro meals, or *Roseneath Manor* at 91 Maitland St (ⓣ02/6742 1906; ❸), a historic nineteenth-century B&B with three cozy rooms and a cooked breakfast. The nearest **caravan park** is 1km east of town on Henry Street (ⓣ02/6742 1372; cabins ❷). **Eating** out is confined to the usual pub meals; otherwise, head for Conadilly Street for a couple of decent coffee joints including the *Redgum Outdoor*, which is also good for cake and healthy luncheon fare.

Narrabri, Mount Kaputar National Park and Wee Waa

While Gunnedah does have some cotton crops, the slightly smaller town of **NARRABRI**, 97km northwest via the communities of Boggabri and Baan Baa, is recognized as the commercial centre of cotton growing. The **tourist office** is on the Newell Highway (Mon–Fri 9am–5pm, Sat & Sun 10am–2pm; ⓣ02/6799 6761, ⓦwww.visitnarrabri.com.au). The **Australia Telescope** complex lies

20km west on the Yarrie Lake road and consists of six antennas, five of which move along a three-kilometre railtrack. Opening times vary (ask at the tourist office), entry is free and there are lots of computer models to play with.

The other main attraction around Narrabri is **Mount Kaputar National Park**. The drive into the park to the 1524-metre-high **lookout** – with its panoramic views encompassing the vast Pillaga Scrub, the Warrumbungles and the New England Tablelands – is steep, narrow and partly unsealed. There are nine marked bushwalking trails in the park, with brochures available from the **NPWS office** at 100 Maitland St in Narrabri (Mon–Fri 8.30am–4.30pm; ⓣ02/6792 7300). The most striking geological feature of the park is **Sawn Rocks**, a basalt formation that looks like a series of organ pipes; it's reached via the northern end of the park on the unsealed road heading to Bingara. There are **camping** facilities at **Dawsons Spring**, with hot showers, and a couple of cabins sleeping a maximum of six, with bathroom, kitchen and wood stove (reservations via NPWS; cabins ❷–❸). If you want to **stay** in Narrabri itself, or grab something to **eat**, try the good-value *Tourist Hotel* at 142 Maitland St (ⓣ02/6792 2312; ❷), which offers homely and clean rooms, and has its own restaurant (Wed–Sat).

The drive from Narrabri to **WEE WAA**, roughly 40km west, is littered with shattered bottles (thrown from speeding cars), announcing your entry into redneck territory. Wee Waa was where the Namoi cotton industry began in the 1960s, and the large cotton "gins" or processing plants are located here. If you can stand the rather raw, dispirited town and the blazing summer heat, you could earn some cash from the **cotton-chipping** work that's available here in abundance in December and January; ask at one of the two pubs on Rose Street, the main drag, and someone will send you in the right direction. From Wee Waa you can head west to Walgett and on to Lightning Ridge.

Lightning Ridge

The population of **LIGHTNING RIDGE**, 74km north of Walgett on the Castlereagh Highway, is officially four thousand but unofficially it's reckoned to be nearer ten thousand. It's a transient place where people in their hordes pitch up, lured by the town's one attraction: **opal**. Amid this harsh landscape scarred by holes and slag heaps, Lightning Ridge's opal fields are the only place in the world where the extremely valuable black opal can consistently be found. This lone enticement is heavily exploited by the town's opal galleries and mines, among them the **Walk-in Mine**, 1 Bald Hill Rd (daily 9am–5pm; tours $5), which has tours to an underground mine and the opportunity to go fossicking. There's even an opal and gem **festival** in late July, which sees the population shoot up by another few thousand souls, plus the **Great Goat Race**, which is held down the main street over the Easter weekend. The effects of the opal obsession can also be seen in the gloriously crazy constructions of the few who have struck it lucky; check out the **Bottle House**, 60 Opal St (daily 9am–5pm; $8), a bizarrely beautiful cottage and dog kennel built entirely from wine bottles set in stone.

There are clearly demarcated **fossicking** areas where you can try your luck at finding opals – don't do it anywhere else, or you may stray onto others' claims (infringements are taken very seriously). Recover afterwards in the 42°C water of the hot **artesian bore baths** on Pandora Street (open 24hr; free); these tap into the great Artesian Basin, an underground lake of fresh water that's about the size of Queensland. More cooling is the Olympic Pool on Gem Street (late Sept to Easter daily 10am–8pm), particularly appealing in the scorching heat since parts of the pool are shaded from the sun. The **Goondee Aboriginal Keeping Place** on Pandora Street (call ⓣ02/6829 2001 for opening times) has Aboriginal artefacts and information on bushtucker.

Practicalities

Countrylink runs **buses** to Lightning Ridge from Sydney via Dubbo daily. The **tourist office** is in the Lions Park, on the Bill O'Brian Way (daily 9am–5pm; ⓣ02/6829 1670, ⓦwww.lightningridge.net.au), and has opal-buying rooms attached – ask for the useful *Lightning Ridge Walgett and District* brochure, which contains a handy guide to buying the stones. The centre can also fill you in on **accommodation** possibilities (all have rooms with a/c), which include the central *Black Opal Motel* on Opal Street (ⓣ & ⓕ 02/6829 0518; ❸), and *Lightning Ridge Hotel Motel & Caravan Park*, a friendly pub on Onyx Street (ⓣ02/6829 0304; ❸) which also has cabins (❷) and van and tent sites (❶). The best place to camp, though, is *Crocodile Caravan and Camping Park* on Morilla Street (ⓣ02/6829 0437, ⓕ6829 2049; vans ❶, cabins ❷), which has a pool, spa and air-cooled cabins.

Back O'Bourke: the Outback

Travelling beyond Dubbo into the northwest corner of New South Wales, the landscape transforms into an endless expanse of largely uninhabited red plain – the quintessential **Australian Outback**. The searing summer heat makes touring uncomfortable from December to February. Bourke, about 370km along the Mitchell Highway, is generally considered the turning point; venture further and you're into the land known as **"Back O'Bourke"** – the back of beyond.

En route to Bourke, the Mitchell passes through **Nyngan**, the geographical centre of New South Wales, where the Barrier Highway heads west for 584 sweltering kilometres, through **Cobar** and **Wilcannia**, to **Broken Hill**.

Bourke and around

BOURKE is mainly known for its remoteness, and this alone is enough to attract tourists; once you've crossed the North Bourke Bridge that spans the Darling River, you're officially "out back".

Bourke was a **bustling river port** from the 1860s to the 1930s, and there remain some fine examples of riverboat-era architecture, including the huge reconstructed wharf, from where a track winds along the magnificent, tree-lined river. Thanks to **irrigation** with Darling River water, crops as diverse as cotton, lucerne, citrus, grapes and sorghum are successfully grown here despite the 40°C summer heat, while Bourke is also the commercial centre for a vast sheep- and cattle-breeding area. River **cruises** are available aboard the old paddleboat *Jandra*, which operates between Easter and October (Mon–Sat 1hr $13; or Sun 2hr $2; – call the tourist office for bookings).

With a **population** of three thousand (approximately twenty-five percent Aboriginal), Bourke acts as a base for regional services and welfare. Unfortunately, there is sporadic trouble involving alcoholism and aimless youngsters, and after dark the atmosphere can be intimidating. Visitors are best off drinking in the *Port of Bourke Hotel*, the *Oxley Club* or *Bowling Club*, and avoiding the *Post Office Hotel*.

Practicalities

An ongoing project to seal the **roads** in this corner of New South Wales has made it much more accessible than previously, but many lesser-travelled routes remain little more than dirt tracks. The **tourist office**, inside the former train station on Anson Street (Easter–Oct daily 9am–5pm; Nov–Easter Mon–Fri 9am–5pm, Sat 9am–4pm; ⓣ02/6872 1222, ⓦwww.visitbourke.com), can provide "Mud Maps" – roughly drawn maps marking places of interest off the beaten track in the surrounding area, though bear in mind that these destinations can be as far as 200km away. Staff at the centre can arrange **tours** (Mon–Fri 2–5.30pm, Sat 9.30am–1pm; $22) covering orchards and vineyards in summer, and historical buildings and cotton farms in winter.

Countrylink **buses** arrive here from Dubbo four times weekly, and you can **fly** here with Airlink from Sydney via Dubbo (also four per week). **Accommodation** in town includes the pleasant *Port of Bourke Hotel* on Mitchell Street (ⓣ02/6872 2544; ❸), which has a restaurant and air-conditioned rooms, some sharing a bath, some en suite, but all opening out on to a sociable veranda. An ideal way to see how life is lived out here is to stay on an **Outback station**; the tourist office has details of those that welcome visitors, among them *Comeroo Camel Station* (ⓣ02/6874 7735, ⓦwww.comeroo.com; $77 per person dinner and bed & breakfast and $99 full-board in the homestead), a unique experience with artesian hot bores, river waterholes with yabbying and fishing opportunities, and resident buffalo and ostriches. For those interested in **employment** in Bourke – harvesting tomatoes, onions and grapes between November and February and cotton chipping between December and February – *Kidman's Camp Tourist Park* (ⓣ02/6872 1612, ⓕ6872 3107), 8km north of town on the Darling River, may be able to point you in the right direction.

The *Port of Bourke Hotel* is the best place in town for **food** and **drink**, with fresh and healthy bistro meals, or counter meals out in the shady beer garden. The *Bowling Club Restaurant*, on the corner of Richard and Mitchell streets, serves counter lunches and dinners, as well as Chinese food.

West and north of Bourke

West of Bourke, it's 193km to the small settlement of **WANAARING**, past a reconstruction of Fort Bourke, built by Major Mitchell in 1835 as a secure depot to protect his stocks from Aboriginal people while he explored the Darling River.

Northwest, the road runs 215km to **HUNGERFORD**, on the Queensland border, and the **Dingo Fence** (see p.1101). The state border bisects Hungerford, which consists of little more than a couple of houses, a post office and a pub but was made famous (amongst Australians) by poet Henry Lawson's short story, *Hungerford*. Make sure you shut the steel dingo-proof fence behind you when you drive through – there's a heavy fine if you don't.

Heading directly north from Bourke, the sealed Mitchell Highway goes right up to just past Charleville in Queensland (see p.512). If you're passing this way, **BARRINGUN**, on the border 135km from Bourke, is worth a stopoff just to have a drink at the remarkably genteel *Tattersalls Hotel*, set amid a flower-scented garden. Across the road and closer to the border is the painted tin shed that comprises the *Bush Tucker Inn* (Ⓣ02/6874 7584; ❶), which has meals, rooms, fuel and camping space.

South and east of Bourke

Amidst the empty, featureless plains, the elongated **Mount Gunderbooka** (498m), about 70km south of Bourke en route to Cobar, appears all the more striking. Likened to a mini-Uluru, the mountain was of similar cultural significance to the Aboriginal people of the area, with semi-permanent waterholes and caves where several cave paintings can be seen – contact the **NPWS** on Oxley Street in Bourke for details (Ⓣ02/6872 2744).

Twenty-eight kilometres east of Bourke, en route to Brewarrina, is a turn-off south to **Mount Oxley**, climbed by the explorers Sturt and Hume in 1829 to herald white settlement in the area. It's on private property, so you must first pick up a key from the tourist office in Bourke, which also organizes tours here. The town of **BREWARRINA** (locals call it "Bree"), 100km east of Bourke on the Barwon River, has a large Aboriginal population and is a very pleasant Outback town, rather than the collection of sheds in the desert you might expect out here. In the days of riverboats, this was an important outpost, and the abundant fish stocks in the river made the area a natural fishery for the original Aboriginal population. Their stone fish-traps – a labyrinth of large, partly submerged boulders – can still be seen in the river, where as many as five thousand Aborigines used to gather to catch fish. The excellent **Aboriginal Cultural Museum** (Mon–Fri 9am–5pm, Sat 10am–2pm; $6), located near the ancient fisheries in an earth-covered building similar to an Aboriginal shelter, explains the history of the area's Ngemba people and offers walkabout tours.

Cobar

Since copper was discovered here in 1869, **COBAR**, just under 160km south of Bourke and the first real stop on the Barrier Highway between Nyngan and Broken Hill, has experienced three mining booms. Today, it's home to the vast **CSA Mine**, said to be the most highly mechanized in Australia, extracting about 550,000 tonnes of copper every year. Earlier booms resulted in a number of impressive public buildings, among them the 1882 courthouse and the police station, as well as the *Great Western Hotel* on Marshall Street, whose iron-lace verandas are said to be the longest in the state. Most people only stop here to refuel before the monotonous 250-kilometre stretch to Wilcannia; there is, however, a lovely picnic spot in Drummond Park, just off the highway on Linsley Street.

For more about the town, head for the excellent **tourist office** (Mon–Fri 8.30am–5pm, Sat & Sun 9am–5pm; $6; Ⓣ02/6836 2448, Ⓦwww.cobar.nsw.gov.au) on Marshall Street. The attached **museum** has some great exhibits, like bush soap, made from kerosene, ashes and lard, and staff can tell you about above-ground tours of the CSA mine as well as provide Mud Maps showing places of interest around Cobar. Chief of these, and arguably one of the most significant Aboriginal rock-art locations in New South Wales, is the **Mount Grenfell Historic Site**, a 67-kilometre drive northwest of town (the last 27km are unsealed). The rocky ridge contains three art sites with over 1300 motifs – human and animal figures, including the emus that you're still likely to see around the site, plus abstract designs and hand stencils. Older layers are visible beneath the more recent pigments, but there's no way to tell exactly how old the art is. The adjacent semi-permanent waterhole explains the significance of the site for the Wongaibon people. The **NPWS** in Cobar, at 19 Barton St (ⓣ02/6836 2692), hands out a leaflet about the site, and the signposted walk to the top of the ridge (5km return). To reach the site, head west along the Barrier Highway for 40km, then take the signed turn-off 27km north along a gravel road past Mount Grenfell Homestead to the picnic site.

There are lots of **motels** along the highway in Cobar. The *Cross Roads Motel*, at the corner of Bourke and Louth roads (ⓣ & ⓕ02/6836 2711; ❸), has air conditioning and pools, while the *Cobar Caravan Park* (ⓣ02/6836 2425; cabins ❷–❸) has smart cabins and shady trees. You can also stay at the charismatic and inexpensive *Great Western Hotel* (ⓣ02/6836 2503; ❸), which has a good restaurant and all-you-can-eat breakfasts ($12). The tourist office can advise on **Outback bush-stays** such as *Trilby Station* (ⓣ02/6874 7420, ⓦwww.trilbystation.com.au; campsites ❶, bunks $30, doubles ❹), two hours' drive distant.

Wilcannia and around

The next major town on the Barrier Highway is **WILCANNIA**, 260km west of Cobar. The former "Queen City of the West" was founded in 1864 and until the early 1900s was a major port on the Darling River, from where produce was transported by paddle-steamers and barges down the Darling–Murray river system to Adelaide. Droughts, the advent of the railways and the motor car put an end to the river trade, and today the only reminders of that prosperous era are the ruins of the docks and the old lift-up bridge, along with a few impressive public buildings such as the post office, police station, courthouse, Catholic convent and Council Chambers on Reid Street, which houses the **tourist office** (daily 9am–5pm; ⓣ08/8091 5909). Nowadays Wilcannia survives as a service centre for a far-flung Outback population, with its banks, shops, motels and service stations, though problems with unemployment and alcoholism combine to give it a bit of a rough-town reputation.

Heading north or south of Wilcannia you can follow the river along one of Australia's last great 4WD adventures – the **Darling River Run** – 829km of Outback history, heritage and landscape running between Brewarrina and Wentworth. Further information on the run is available from the tourist office in Bourke (see p.342).

You can travel the Darling River upstream northwest of Wilcannia all the way to Bourke, just under 300km, on unsealed roads that closely follow the east and west banks – there are crossings at the settlements of Tilpa and Louth. Station properties dot the riverfront, including **Mount Murchinson Station**, on the west side of the river 30km northwest of Wilcannia, said to have once been managed by the son of Charles Dickens. At **TILPA**, 130km north of Wilcannia, there's a classic Outback pub, the 1890s *Tilpa Hotel* (ⓣ02/6837 3928, ⓦwww.tilpapub.com.au; ❷), which has meals (the steak sandwiches are huge), accommodation and fuel; for a $2 donation towards the Royal Flying Doctor Service, you can immortalize your name on the pub's tin wall. Ninety-three kilometres further on, at **LOUTH**, *Shindy's Inn* sells diesel and petrol, and has basic **accommodation** in miniature cabins (Ⓣ02/6874 7422; ❷).

White Cliffs

From Wilcannia, you can head north off the Barrier Highway to the opal fields at **WHITE CLIFFS**, 98km away. Four kangaroo shooters found opals here in 1889 and four thousand miners followed. Besides opals, White Cliffs is famous for its extraordinary summer heat, and many of the two hundred residents **live underground** in "dug-outs". There are all sorts of underground attractions, as well as a solar power station that looks like something out of a space odyssey. For the authentic underground experience, there are two places to **stay**: the original and very friendly *White Cliffs Underground Motel* (Ⓣ08/8091 6647 or 8091 6677, Ⓦwww.undergroundmotel.com.au; ❹), which comes complete with licensed restaurant and outdoor swimming pool; and the only subterranean B&B in the town, *PJs* (Ⓣ08/8091 6626, Ⓔpjsunderground@bigpond.com; ❺–❻), with its underground spa-bath and 64-million-year-old rock roof. Cheaper above-ground options include the *White Cliffs Hotel/Motel* (Ⓣ08/8091 6606; ❹) or, if you can bear the heat, **camping** (with hot showers) at *Opal Pioneer Reserve*, close to town (Ⓣ08/8091 6688). **Tourist information** is available on Keraro Road at the White Cliffs General Store (daily 7am–7pm; Ⓣ & Ⓕ08/8091 6611).

There are several **tours** to White Cliffs from Broken Hill, including Broken Hill's Outback Tours (Ⓣ08/8087 7800, Ⓦwww.outbacktours.net) or Tri-State Safari (Ⓣ08/8088 2389, Ⓦwww.tristate.com.au); otherwise, you'll need your own transport to get here. The only fuel stop between Wilcannia and Broken Hill is at the *Little Topar Hotel*, roughly halfway along the 195-kilometre stretch of the Barrier Highway.

Broken Hill and around

The ghosts of mining towns that died when the precious minerals ran out are scattered all over Australia. **BROKEN HILL**, on the other hand, celebrated its centenary in 1988, and its famous "Line of Lode", one of the world's major lead-silver-zinc ore bodies and the city's raison d'être, still has a little life left in it after being mined continuously for over 110 years.

Almost 1200km west of Sydney and about 500km east of Adelaide, this surprisingly gracious Outback mining-town – with a population of around 21,000 and a feel and architecture reminiscent of the South Australian capital – manages to create a welcome splash of green in the harsh desert landscape that surrounds it. Extensive revegetation schemes around Broken Hill have created grasslands that, apart from being visually pleasing, help contain the dust that used to make the residents' lives a misery. It's aided by a reliable water supply – secured for the first time only in 1953 – via a one-hundred-kilometre pipeline from the Darling River at Menindee.

Inevitably, Broken Hill revolves around the **mines**, but in the last decade it has also evolved into a thriving **arts centre**, thanks to the initiative of the **Brushmen of the Bush**, a painting school founded by local artists Hugh Schulz, Jack Absalom, John Pickup and the late Pro Hart and Eric Minchin. Diverse talents have been attracted to Broken Hill, and their works are displayed in galleries scattered all over town. Some may be a bit on the tacky side, but others are excellent, and it's well worth devoting some time to gallery browsing.

Remember to adjust your watch here: Broken Hill operates on **South Australian Central Standard Time**, half an hour behind the rest of New South Wales. All local transport schedules are in CST, but you should always check. The city is also a convenient base for touring far-northwest New South Wales and nearby areas in South Australia.

Arrival, information and getting around

The useful **tourist office**, at the corner of Bromide and Blende streets (daily 8.30am–5pm; ⓣ08/8088 9700, ⓦwww.visitbrokenhill.com.au), can give you a map ($2.20) for a self-guided heritage walk along Argent and Blende streets, or information on the guided walking tour which delves into the city's history (Mon, Wed, Fri 10am, no tours late Dec–early May; 1hr 30min–2hr; donation). The **bus terminal**, from where you can catch the Countrylink service to Dubbo or Buses R Us (ⓣ08/8285 6900) to Adelaide or Mildura, is behind the tourist office. The **train station** is on Crystal Street, a block below Argent Street, and from here the Indian Pacific or Countrylink will take you as far as Sydney and Perth. The **airport** is 5km south of town but there's no shuttle bus – either catch a taxi (around $15) or arrange to have a rental car waiting (see p.353). Murton's City Bus (ⓣ08/8087 3311) runs hourly or half-hourly along four routes through Broken Hill – the tourist office can provide a combined timetable and route map.

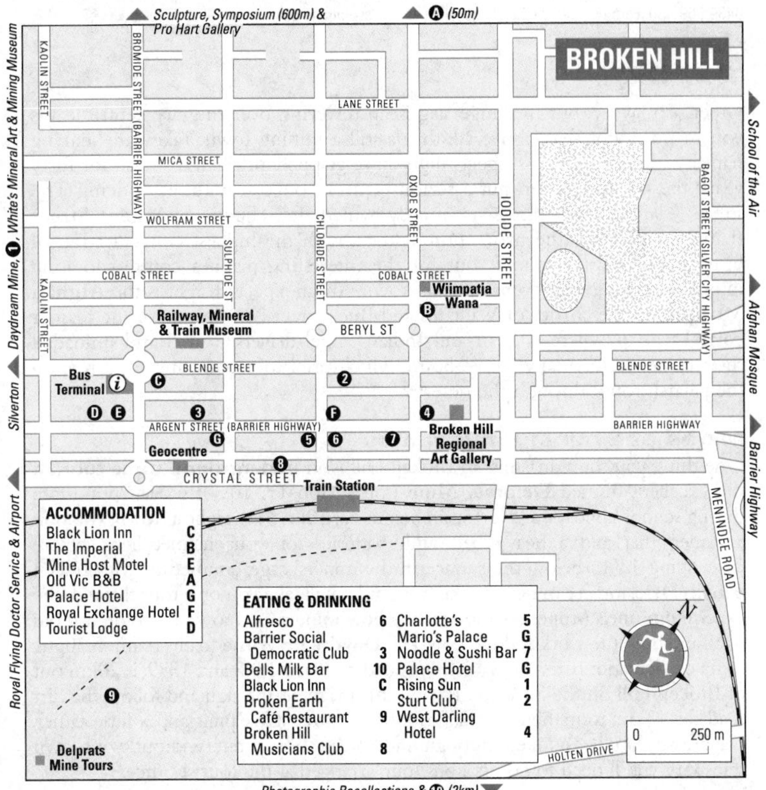

Accommodation

Black Lion Inn 34 Bromide St ⓣ08/8087 4801. Opposite the bus station. This is the town's cheapest but simplest pub, with quiet rooms including some singles ($24). ❶–❷

The Imperial 88 Oxide St ⓣ08/8087 7444, ⓦwww.imperialfineaccommodation.com. The pick of the crop: a classy, four-and-a-half-star in a beautiful old building with huge veranda. The five spacious rooms have all mod-cons, and there's also a kitchenette, free breakfast at any time, a billiard room, a guest lounge, pool and garden. Complimentary port in the lounge area. ❺

Lake View Caravan Park 1 Mann St, 3km northeast ⓣ & ⓕ08/8088 2250. A large site with disabled-access, en-suite cabins, a swimming pool and kiosk. On-site vans ❶–❷, cabins ❸

Mine Host Motel 120 Argent St ⓣ08/8088 4044, ⓔminehost@iinet.net.au. Clean and functional and with a small pool, but little character. Central location right near the bus station, and close to clubs and pubs. ❹

Old Vic B&B 230 Oxide St ⓣ08/8087 1169 or 0439 369 480. Farmhouse-style family guesthouse which is much cosier than it looks from the street. A good breakfast is included and all rooms share the bathroom. It's a 15min walk from the centre, though there are a couple of good pubs nearby for food. ❷–❸

Palace Hotel 227 Argent St ⓣ08/8088 1699. Corner pub with one of the largest hotel balconies in New South Wales and a profusion of murals on every available surface, including a Botticelli-style *Birth of Venus* (painted by Mario, the landlord) which featured to hilarious effect in the film *Priscilla, Queen of the Desert*. All rooms have a/c, phone and a sink, and some are en suite. ❸–❺

Royal Exchange Hotel 320 Argent St, cnr Chloride St ⓣ08/8087 2308, ⓦwww.royalexchangehotel.com. Plush, hotel-style ensuites with smart furnishings and Internet data-ports. ❻

Tourist Lodge 100 Argent St ⓣ08/8088 2086, ⓦwww.yha.com.au. Large YHA-affiliated hostel near the bus terminal – the only backpacker place in town. The shared kitchen/dining/TV room and common room are well equipped, and there's a swimming pool. Dorms $22, doubles ❷–❸

The City

Green it may be, but the huge slag heap towering over the city centre leaves you in no doubt that, above all, this is still a mining town. Take care shaking hands with anyone you suspect might have gripped a drill and shovel for forty years; the old-timers can put a serious squeeze on you without noticing. The streets – laid out in a grid – are mostly named after chemicals; **Argent Street** (Latin for silver) is the main thoroughfare, with the highest concentration of historic buildings, but look out for the interesting plaques commemorating important people and events all over town. An unexpected sight is the **Afghan Mosque** on the corner of Williams and Buck streets, on the site of the former **camel camp** where Afghan and Indian camel-drivers loaded and unloaded their camel teams (daily 9am—5pm), which used to accompany explorers on their harsh route through the desert.

Mines and mining museums

One thing you shouldn't miss in Broken Hill is an **underground mine tour**. At the excellent disused **Delprats Mine** (tours Mon–Fri 10.30am, Sat 2pm, more during school holidays, arrive 15min before start; 2hr; $44), right in town, you don a miner's hat and a heavy belt with batteries for your helmet light, before descending 130m below the surface in the miners' cage, jammed in with fifteen people. Here, former miners working as guides will take you on a tour through the system of tunnels (stopes), demonstrating how miners used to work in the bad old days, and how the work is done now. The **Daydream Mine** (daily 10am–3.30pm; tours on demand; 1hr; $16), which operated between 1882 and 1889, is 20km out of Broken Hill on the Silverton Road – turn right at the sign and follow the dirt road for 13km; tours here are half as long as those at Delprats and a little tamer. Daydream can be booked through the tourist office, but without your own transport, you'll need to go on a bus tour, arranged at the tourist office.

△ Mine, Broken Hill

There are three other mining-related attractions in the city. A visit to the bizarre but wonderful **White's Mineral Art and Mining Museum**, at 1 Allendale St off Silverton Road (daily 9am–5pm; $4), is the next best thing to going underground. The art section is pretty extraordinary, consisting mainly of collages of crushed minerals depicting Broken Hill scenes, and at the back there's a walk-in underground mine, recreated so convincingly that it genuinely looks and feels like the real thing. Inside, you're given an entertaining lecture, with videos and models, on the history of Broken Hill and its mines, while a shop at the front of the museum sells minerals, opals, jewellery and pottery.

The **Railway, Mineral and Train Museum** (daily 10am–3pm; $2.50), opposite the tourist office, features an extensive mineral collection as well as old railway machinery and memorabilia including the fittings from the bedroom of the *Maidens Hotel* in Menindee, where the explorers Burke and Wills stayed on their ill-fated expedition (see box, p.514). There are a few carriages and three glorious engines outside. Finally, the **Geocentre**, in a nineteenth-century bond store on the corner of Bromide and Crystal streets (Mon–Fri 10am–4.45pm, Sat & Sun 1–4.45pm; $3.50), looks at Broken Hill's geology, mineralogy and metallurgy. One of the highlights is the spectacular *Silver Tree*, a 68-centimetre-high figurine wrought of pure silver from the Broken Hill Mines, depicting five Aborigines, a drover on horseback, kangaroos, emus and sheep gathered under a tree.

Art galleries and sculpture parks

If you only go to one gallery in Broken Hill, make it the **Pro Hart Gallery** at 108 Wyman St (Mon–Sat 9am–5pm, Sun 1.30–5pm; $4; Ⓦ www.prohart.com.au). A recently deceased Broken Hill miner turned artist, Pro Hart's sculptures, etchings and prints typically depict Outback events and people such as race meetings, backyard barbecues and union leaders – look out for the fantastic ten-metre-long *History of Australia* showing scenes of Aboriginal life before the arrival of Captain Cook, the early pioneers, bush rangers and the founding of Broken Hill. The gallery's three levels are said to hold the largest **private art collection** in the southern hemisphere, with a truly astounding amount of the artist's own work as well as works by other Australian painters – Tom Roberts, Sidney Nolan, David Boyd and Albert Namatjira among them, as well as (amazingly) originals by Salvador Dalí, Picasso, Rembrandt, Turner, Constable and Monet. There's a collection of Hart's sculptures in a lot across the road which you can check out for free. If you're buying, you can get a print for $75; a small painting will set you back about $3500.

Broken Hill Regional Art Gallery, in Sully's Emporium at 408 Argent St (daily 10am–5pm; donation), has an excellent representative collection of artists from Broken Hill as well as Australian art in general. Established in 1904, it's the second-oldest gallery in the state – after the Art Gallery of New South Wales in Sydney – with a small collection of nineteenth- and early twentieth-century paintings including works by Sidney Nolan, John Olsen, and the "Brushmen of the Bush" (though these are sometimes moved to make way for special exhibitions). Also on display are temporary photography exhibitions and sculptures created by artists who participated in the 1993 Sculpture Symposium at The Living Desert (see below).

There's Aboriginal art – albeit with modern influence – at the **Thankakali Cultural Centre**, on the corner of Beryl and Buck streets (Mon–Thurs 8am–3pm, Fri 8am–noon; free), while **D'Art De Main Gallery**, at 233 Rowe St (daily 9am–5pm; free) has a good collection of sculptures, portraits and landscapes by Geoff De Main, who also painted many of the wall murals you'll see around town. **Photographic Recollections**, on Eyre Street (Mon–Fri 10am–4.30pm, Sat 1–4.30pm; $5), provides a pictorial history of Broken Hill, with over six hundred photographs accompanied by well-researched text that delves into mining, union and social history. The location itself, in the former **Central Power Station**, tells a story of the city's very Outback past; Broken Hill produced all its power here from the 1930s until as late as 1986, when it finally went onto the national grid.

Six kilometres out of town, the **Sculpture Symposium** in **The Living Desert Reserve** is the most dramatic of Broken Hill's art exhibits, a reserve in the eroded Barrier Ranges desert region containing a group of sculptures carved from Wilcannia sandstone boulders. The twelve artists involved in their creation were part of a sculpture symposium in 1993 and were drawn from diverse cultures – two from Mexico (including an Aztec Indian), two from Syria, three from Georgia (in the Caucasus), and five Australians, including two Bathurst Islanders – and this is reflected in the variety of their works. The pieces by the Georgian artists – Badri Sulushia's *Outback Madonna and Child*; Valerian Jiiya's Cubist interpretation; and Jumber Jikiya's horse's head, a tribute to the rare breed of Georgian horses slaughtered under Stalin's orders – are particularly fine. The best time to visit the sculptures is at sunset on a clear evening, when the light is magical and the rocks glow crimson. It's a pleasant fifteen-minute walk to the sculptures up the hill from the car park of the Living Desert Reserve. An **information brochure** ($1.10) about the sculptures is available from the tourist office.

The Royal Flying Doctor Service and the School of the Air

Broken Hill offers an excellent opportunity to visit two Australian Outback institutions: the Royal Flying Doctor Service (RFDS) and the School of the Air. The **Royal Flying Doctor Service**, at Broken Hill Airport, offers guided

Mining and unionism in Broken Hill

The story of Broken Hill began in 1883 when a German-born boundary rider from Mount Gipps Station, Charles Rasp, pegged out a forty-acre lease of a "broken hill" that he believed was tin. A syndicate of seven was formed, founding the **Broken Hill Proprietary (BHP)** to work what turned out to be rich silver, lead and zinc deposits. Broken Hill's mines, dominated by BHP until they withdrew operations in 1939, have contributed greatly to the wealth of Australia: the deposit, more than 7km long and up to 250m wide, is thought originally to have contained more than three hundred million tonnes of silver, zinc and lead ores. Even now there's said to be ten years left in the "Line of Lode" currently being worked by the Perilya and CBH companies.

In the early years, living and working **conditions** for the miners were atrocious. The climate was harsh, housing was poor and diseases such as typhoid, scarlet fever and dysentery – to say nothing of work-related illnesses such as lead poisoning and mining accidents – contributed to a death rate almost twice the New South Wales average; there have been around eight hundred deaths in mining accidents since operations began. The mine and the growing town rapidly stripped the landscape of timber, leaving the settlement surrounded by a vast, bleak plain and beleaguered by dust storms. Not surprisingly, perhaps, Broken Hill was at the forefront of **trade union** development in Australia, as the miners, many of them recent immigrants, fought to improve their living and working conditions. It was their ability to unite that ultimately won them their battles, above all in the Big Strike of 1919–20, when, after eighteen months of holding out against the police and strikebreakers, major concessions were won from BHP.

The unions typified the precious Australian concept of **mateship** – some miners literally died for each other, or worked for fifteen years side by side with the same partner. Not that the trade union movement at Broken Hill should be viewed through too-rosy glasses: the union, which effectively ran the town in conjunction with the mine companies, was also a bastion of racism and male supremacy – non-whites were not tolerated in town, nor were working women who happened to be married – and local attitudes remain strongly conservative.

Despite the life left in Broken Hill's mineral deposits, the **future** is none too certain. With modern mining technology the ore is removed faster, and the numbers employed are lower. Between 1970 and 1975, about four thousand people were employed in the mines. By the early 1980s this number had been reduced to 2500, and less than six hundred work there now. The population continues to decrease gradually and every few years another of the city's many pubs closes down.

tours (Mon–Fri 9am–5pm, Sat & Sun 11am–4pm; $5.50; ⓦwww.rfds.org.au) with an accompanying video and talk – it's best to buy your ticket in advance from the tourist office as places are limited. In the headquarters you'll see the radio room where calls from remote places in New South Wales, South Australia and Queensland are handled, before going out to the hangar to see the aircraft. The popularity of the tours is due to the Australian television series *The Flying Doctors*, which is shown worldwide, and since a third of their annual budget of $30 million has to come through fund-raising – the rest of the money is from the State and Federal governments – whatever you spend on the tour and at the souvenir shop here is going to a good cause.

In many ways the **School of the Air** on Lane Street is indebted to the RFDS: lessons for children in the Outback, in a transmission area of 1.8 million square kilometres, were formerly conducted via RFDS two-way radio (these days it's all by webcam). The radio service was established in 1956 to improve education for children in the isolated Outback, and you can still listen to the transmission in a schoolroom surrounded by children's artwork (Mon–Fri, term time only 8.20am; book in advance at the tourist office; $4.40). It's frighteningly like being back at school, with jolly primary-school teachers hosting singalongs; what comes out of the radio is a static squawk, but the children in the far-flung areas seem to enjoy it.

Eating, drinking and nightlife

Restaurants aren't really Broken Hill's style – the town is famous for its bad **food**, and if your meal looks like it was trucked a thousand kilometres through a sandstorm to get here, that's because it probably was. Broken Hill still has the proverbial pub on every corner, and most of them serve **counter meals**, though they're not the best. For grocery supplies, visit the late-opening IGM behind the police station on Blende Street, or the large supermarkets in out-of-town Westside Plaza, Galena Street (open daily 9am–9pm).

Eating

Alfresco 397 Argent St. Outdoor dining with a large selection of gourmet salads and pastas. Also good for fresh smoothies and milkshakes. Fully licensed.

The Barrier Social Democratic Club 214 Argent St. Edible salad bar plus good, inexpensive breakfasts between 7 and 9am.

Bell's Milk Bar 160 Patton St, south side of town. A great spot – a bit like a 1950s diner with a rock 'n' roll jukebox and vinyl booths. They specialize in spiders (soda ice-cream floats), milkshakes and smoothies, but there's no food.

Broken Earth Café Restaurant Federation Way (just past Delprats Mine). The place for smart dining, with a funky curved roof which is visible all over town. Great views and the modern Australian food and wine is ... better than elsewhere.

Charlotte's 317 Agent St. A cosy little place opposite the post office, with good coffee and a range of cakes, muffins and slices.

Noodle & Sushi Bar 351 Argent St. Something completely different, with everything from Mongolian to Singapore noodles as well as Japanese sushi.

Sturt Club Cnr Blende and Chloride sts. The best of the lot, with various fish, meat, pasta and nachos-type meals (daily noon–2pm & 6–9pm). Lunch will set you back $7–9.

West Darling Hotel Cnr Oxide and Argent sts. This hotel has the not-monumental honour of serving the town's best pub lunch, according to locals.

Drinking and nightlife

The city has always been a legendary **drinking hole**, and once had over seventy hotels. Many pubs have been converted for other uses, but there are still more than twenty licensed establishments and a pub crawl is highly recommended. Some places to include for an early drink are the kitsch-crammed

Palace Hotel, 227 Argent St, which memorably featured in *The Adventures of Priscilla, Queen of the Desert*; the *Rising Sun*, 2 Beryl St, popular with younger locals on Friday nights; the *Black Lion Inn*, 34 Bromide St, good any time but especially during happy hour (times vary) at the cocktail bar; and the *Mulga Hill Tavern*, on the corner of Oxide and Williams streets.

Another option is to sample the local culture at one of the numerous **clubs** which often host live entertainment on Friday and Saturday nights. *The Broken Hill Musicians Club* at 276 Crystal St has inherited Broken Hill's famous *Two Up School*, once an illegal back-lane gambling operation. The *Broken Hill* was immortalized by Kenneth Cook's 1961 novel (and later film), *Wake in Fright*. Try to make it here on Fridays and Saturdays, when the boys from the bush turn up in force to bet as much as $200 on one flip of a coin.

Listings

Airlines Qantas ⓣ13 13 13; Regional Express ⓣ13 17 13.
Bookshops ABC Centre, 309 Argent St (inside Cubans Radio), specializes in local history and the Outback. For secondhand books, try Browzers Bookshop at 345 Argent St.
Car rental Avis, 195 Argent St ⓣ08/8087 7532; Hertz, at the tourist office ⓣ08/8087 2719; Thrifty, 190 Argent St ⓣ08/8088 1928. All have desks at the airport too. You'll pay around $75/125 a day for a saloon car/4WD; small cars are nonexistent here – utes with giant roo-bars are the vehicle of choice.
Cinema Village Silver City Cinema, 41 Oxide St ⓣ08/8087 4569.
Hospital Broken Hill Base Hospital and Health Services, 176 Thomas St ⓣ08/8080 1333.
Internet City Internet, 78 Gypsum St (daily 9am–late; $8/hour). There's also free access at the library, on the corner of Blende and Chloride streets, but you have to book.
Laundry Oxide St Laundrette, 241 Oxide St ⓣ08/8088 2022. Service washes available, with free pick-up and delivery.
Pharmacies Amcal Chemist, Westside Plaza, Galena St, has an after-hours emergency number (ⓣ08/8088 4800), but the most central pharmacy is Peoples CP Chemist, 323 Argent St.
Post office Cnr Argent and Chloride sts.
Swimming pool North Pool, north of the centre on McCulloch St (open daily in theory, if not always in practice: April–Oct 6am–6pm; Nov–March 5.30–8pm; $2), is heated in winter.
Taxi Yellow Radio Cabs ⓣ13 10 08.

Around Broken Hill

The ghost town of **SILVERTON**, just 25km northwest of Broken Hill on a good road, makes a great day out. If the scene looks vaguely familiar, you've probably seen it before: parts of *Mad Max II* were shot around here, and the *Silverton Hotel* has appeared as the "Gamulla Hotel" in *Razorback*, "Hotel Australia" in *A Town Like Alice*, and "Juanita's Diner" in *Fiddlers Green* with Don Johnson. It also seems to star in just about every commercial – usually beer-related – that features an Outback scene. In the tradition of all Outback pubs, it has its own in-jokes; you'll find out what all the laughter is about if you ask to "take the test".

Taking the **Silverton Heritage Trail**, a two-hour stroll around town marked by white arrows, is a good way to work up a thirst, though it's far too hot to attempt in the summer. Along the way you'll pass the old **Silverton School Craft Centre** and the 1889 vintage **Silverton Gaol Museum** (daily 9.30am–4.30pm; $3), with the usual collection of relics from pioneer days and Outback stations, plus mining equipment. There's a burgeoning **art scene** here too, with four galleries to browse through. **Peter Browne's Gallery** (daily 9am–5pm; ⓦwww.outbackgalleries.com.au), in an 1884 house on a hill, is worth a look for its unique decoration and the humorous paintings of bush scenes, koala-shearing, kookaburras boiling the billy, and Browne's trademark emus with huge, saucer-shaped eyes.

One of the most enjoyable things to do in Silverton is to go on a camel tour. The Cannard family, who run the **Silverton Camel Farm** (daily 9am–4pm; ⓦwww.silvertoncamels.com), come from a long line of camel trainers and have forty working animals. You can't miss their farm on the way into Silverton, with the shapes of camels looming like desert mirages. You can hop on for half an hour ($15), or trot for an hour along the nearby creek ($25). There's also a great sunset trek (2hr; $50) to the Mundi Mundi Plain to look at the setting sun, and a return trip under the night stars accompanied by a pack of lively dogs.

Beyond Silverton, the road continues a further 14km to the **Umberumberka reservoir**, Broken Hill's only source of water until the Menindee Lakes Scheme was set up. A few kilometres further on you reach the **Mundi Mundi Plains Lookout**: here, the undulating plateau you have been driving across descends gradually to a vast plain, and on clear days you can see the blurred outline of the northern Flinders Ranges in South Australia in the distance (the lookout is the spot where, at the end of *Mad Max II*, Mel Gibson tipped the semi-trailer).

If you want to **stay** in Silverton, your only choice is to camp at Penrose Park, where there's a shower, toilets and barbecue – ask at the house there or call ⓣ08/8088 5307. Note that there's no **fuel** available at Silverton.

Kinchega National Park and the Menindee Lakes

Flat **Kinchega National Park** is situated among the beautiful Menindee Lakes, near the township of **MENINDEE**, southeast of Broken Hill in an area of great natural beauty. There's a sealed road for the 110km to Menindee and the park entrance, and dirt roads thereafter (usually no problem for 2WD in the dry). Before you go, visit the Broken Hill **NPWS** at 183 Argent St (ⓣ08/8080 3200) to check road conditions, or ask at the **tourist office** (daily 10am–2pm, longer during high season; ⓣ08/8091 4274), where you can get a free, detailed, hand-drawn "Mud Map" of the lakes area, showing areas of interest.

After the 110km drive through red desert from Broken Hill, the sight of the large red river gums on the creek bed, the spreading blue water, expanses of bright green grass in the flood plains and the bleached skeletons of old eucalypts in the lake is breathtaking. The Menindee "Lakes" are actually a series of flood plains fed by the Darling River, and the waters are a major habitat for **water birds**; there are over 210 species here in total, including numerous little black cormorants (shags), pelicans, ibis, white egrets and whistling kites. There's an **information shelter** 5km into the park and a normally unmanned visitor information centre about 10km further on near the historic and exceptionally well preserved **Kinchega Woolshed**, part of the Kinchega Station, one of the first pastoral settlements in the area when it was established in 1850, and which continued to operate until 1967; you can explore it by following the signposted **woolshed walk**.

Accommodation is available in shearers' sheds next to the old woolshed ($16.50 per adult; book at Broken Hill NPWS), and there are also 35 **campsites** scattered throughout the woodland along the river. Campsite No. 3 near Menindee Lake, right by the river amongst the gums, is the nicest unless the lake is dry, in which case head for Burke and Wills' old base camp (they stopped here from October 1860 until January 1861 – a tree marks the spot) by Wethell Lake. The camping areas have composting toilets and seats, but you'll have to purify the water.

Burke and Wills stayed in Menindee at the *Maidens Hotel*, Yartla Street (Ⓣ08/8091 4208; ❷–❸), on their ill-fated trip north in 1860 (see box on p.514). Unfortunately the room in which they stayed is now full of poker machines, but there is some interpretive material in the hotel (the room's fittings are now in the Railway Museum in Broken Hill; see p. 350), and the green courtyard is a good place for a drink or a counter meal. Otherwise, you can stay at the *Burke & Wills Motel* opposite (Ⓣ08/8091 4313, Ⓕ8091 4406; ❸), or camp in relative comfort at the *Menindee Lakes Park* on Lakes Shore Road, 5km northwest of town (Ⓣ08/8091 4315, Ⓕ8091 4325; on-site vans ❶). If you don't have transport, you can take a **day-tour** out here from Broken Hill with Tri-State Safari (Ⓣ08/8088 2389, Ⓦwww.tristate.com.au).

Mutawintji National Park

Mutawintji National Park, 130km northeast of Broken Hill in the Bynguano Ranges, has totally different and perhaps even more fascinating scenery to offer, with secluded gorges and quiet waterholes attracting a profusion of wildlife. The main highlights of the park are the ancient galleries of **Aboriginal rock art** in the caves and overhangs; you can only visit these accompanied by an Aboriginal tour guide (Wed & Sat 11am Eastern Standard Time; 3hr; $20; bookings required, contact the Broken Hill tourist office on Ⓣ08/8088 9700) – there are no tours in the hot summer months. While on the tour you get to visit the **Mutawintji Cultural Resource Centre**, an amazing multimedia collaboration between indigenous Australians and the NPWS which tells of tribal history and myth in sound and pictures. There's a **camping** area at Homestead Creek, among river red gums at the entrance to Homestead Gorge, and a number of **walking trails** (including the short wheelchair-accessible Thakaaltjika Mingkana Walk). Access to and within the park is via unsealed gravel roads, and you'll need to bring extra fuel as none is available here. It's normally fine for 2WD vehicles, but check locally, as the roads can quickly become impassable after even a light rain; bring extra food just in case. The NPWS office in Broken Hill can provide other information. You can also get here from Broken Hill with Tri-State Safari (Ⓣ08/8088 2389, Ⓦwww.tristate.com.au).

Travel details

Most public transport in New South Wales originates in Sydney, and the main services are outlined at the end of Chapter 1 on pp.223–224.

Trains

All trains are run by Countrylink, which extends its network with additional bus services. For full details, see Ⓦwww.countrylink.info or call Ⓣ13 22 32.

- Sydney–**Albury** (2 daily; 7hr 35min), via **Cootamundra** (5hr) and **Wagga Wagga** (6hr 10min).
- Sydney–**Armidale** (1 daily; 8hr 10min), via **Tamworth** (6hr 15min).
- Sydney–**Broken Hill** (2 daily; 13hr), via **Dubbo** (6hr 40min).
- Sydney–**Dubbo** (3 daily; 6hr 30min), via **Bathurst** (3hr 30min).
- Sydney–**Goulburn** (4 daily; 2hr 35min).
- Sydney–**Melbourne** (2 daily; 11hr), with stops at **Cootamundra** (5hr) and **Wagga Wagga** (6hr 10min).
- Sydney–**Moree** (1 daily; 9hr) via **Gunnedah** (6hr 20min) and **Narrabri** (7hr 45min).
- Sydney–**Scone** (2 daily; 4hr 20min).
- The New South Wales leg of the Indian Pacific linking Sydney and Perth via Adelaide takes in **Menindee** (16hr 10min) and **Broken Hill** (18hr 55min).

Buses

Albury to: Canberra (4 daily; 4hr 20min); Corowa (3 per week; 1hr); Melbourne (3 daily; 3hr 45min); Yass (3 daily; 4hr).
Armidale to: Brisbane (2 daily; 7hr 30min); Melbourne (1 daily; 18hr 45min); Port Macquarie (3 per week; 6hr 15min); Sydney (1 daily; 9hr); Tamworth (2 daily; 2hr 10min); Tenterfield (3 daily; 3hr).
Bourke to: Dubbo (4 per week; 4hr 45min).
Broken Hill to: Adelaide (3 per week; 7hr); Cobar (1 daily; 5hr 20min); Dubbo (1 daily; 9hr 30min); Mildura (3 per week; 4hr); Sydney (1 daily; 15hr 40min).
Coonabarabran to: Melbourne (1 daily; 7hr 30min).
Dubbo to: Bathurst (4 per week; 2hr 45min); Bourke (4 per week; 4hr 45min); Brisbane (1 daily; 11hr 30min); Broken Hill (1 daily; 9hr 30min); Cobar (1 daily; 3hr 40min); Coonabarabran (1 daily; 1hr 50min); Cootamundra (3 per week; 4hr 15min); Forbes (1 daily; 2hr 35min); Lightning Ridge (1 daily; 4hr 50min); Narrandera (1 daily; 5hr 15min); Orange (4 per week; 2hr 40min); Parkes (1 daily; 2hr 10min); Sydney (1 daily; 6hr 30min).
Griffith to: Canberra (2 daily; 6hr 35min); Cootamundra (1 daily; 2hr 35min); Hay (2 daily; 3hr 50min); Leeton (2 daily; 50min); Narrandera (2 daily; 1hr 15min); Wagga Wagga (2 daily; 2hr 40min).
Lithgow to: Bathurst (3–6 daily; 1hr); Coonabarabran (1 daily; 5hr 30min); Cowra (1 daily; 2hr 40min); Dubbo (4 per week; 4hr 35min); Mudgee (2 daily; 2hr 35min); Orange (2–5 daily; 1hr 45min–2hr).
Tamworth to: Armidale (1 daily; 2hr 10min); Dorrigo (1 daily; 4hr 10min); Port Macquarie (3 per week; 8hr 30min); Scone (1 per week; 2hr 15min); Tenterfield (1 daily; 4hr 30min).

Flights

Armidale to: Sydney (4 daily; 1hr 15min).
Broken Hill to: Adelaide (1–3 daily; 1hr 40min); Dubbo (1daily; 2hr); Sydney (2 daily; 3hr 45min).
Dubbo to: Broken Hill (1 daily; 2hr); Cobar (5 per week; 1hr); Lightning Ridge (5 per week; 1hr 40min); Sydney (10 daily; 1hr); Walgett (5 per week; 1hr 10min).

Coastal Queensland

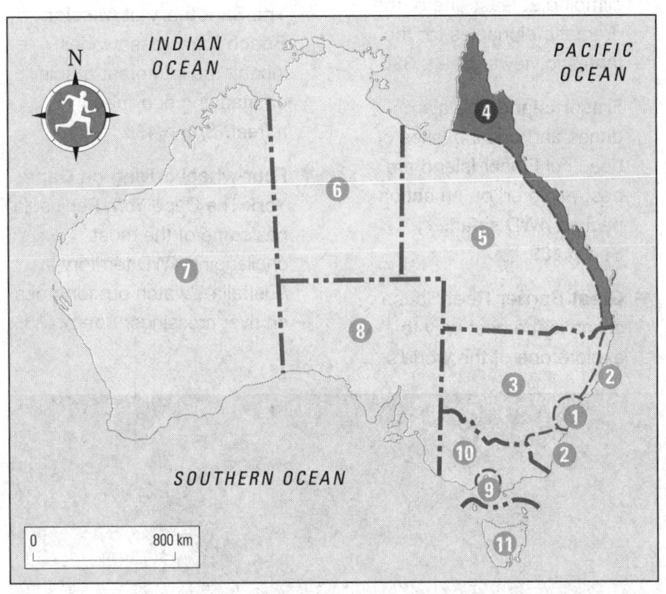

CHAPTER 4

Highlights

* **Gold Coast** The beaches, bars and theme parks of Australia's prime domestic holiday destination provide raucous thrills around the clock. See p.383

* **Glass House Mountains National Park** One of the few really special places on the Sunshine Coast; it's worth climbing at least one of the dramatic pinnacles for the fantastic views. See p.398

* **Fraser Island** The giant dunes and pristine lakes of beautiful Fraser Island are best explored on an action-packed 4WD safari. See p.409

* **Great Barrier Reef** Scuba diving is the best way to explore one of the world's most beautiful coral complexes. See p.418

* **The Whitsundays** Lying inside the Great Barrier Reef, the rainforested peaks and long white beaches of the Whitsunday Islands offer some of Australia's most picturesque cruising. See p.431

* **The Sanctuary at Mission Beach** Rare cassowaries inhabit the rainforest at this outstanding eco-friendly retreat. See p.455

* **Four-wheel driving on Cape York** The Cape York Peninsula has some of the most challenging 4WD territory in Australia – watch out for crocs on river crossings. See p.485

△ Sailing off the Whitsundays

4

Coastal Queensland

Running for over 2500 kilometres from the New South Wales border to Australia's northernmost tip at Cape York, **Coastal Queensland** contains almost everything that lures visitors to Australia. Set down in the more developed southeastern corner, the state capital **Brisbane** is a relaxed city with a lively social scene and good work possibilities. South between here and the border, the **Gold Coast** is Australia's prime holiday destination, with a reputation founded on some of the country's best surf – though this now takes second place to a belt of beach-front high-rises, theme parks, and the host of lively bars and nightclubs surrounding **Surfers Paradise**. An hour inland, the **Gold Coast Hinterland**'s green heights offer a chain of national parks packed with wildlife and stunning views. Heading north of Brisbane, fruit and vegetable plantations behind the gentle **Sunshine Coast** benefit from rich volcanic soils and a subtropical climate, overlooked by the spiky, isolated peaks of the **Glass House Mountains**. Down on the coast, **Noosa** is an up-and-coming resort town with more famous surf. Beyond looms **Fraser Island**, whose surrounding waters host an annual **whale migration** and where huge wooded dunes, freshwater lakes and sculpted coloured sands form the backdrop for exciting safaris.

North of Fraser the humidity and temperature begin to rise as you head **into the tropics**. Though there's still an ever-narrowing farming strip hugging the coast, the Great Dividing Range edges coastwards as it progresses north, dry at first, but gradually acquiring a green sward which culminates in the steamy, rainforest-draped scenery around **Cairns**. Along the way are scores of beaches, archipelagos of islands and a further wealth of national parks, some – such as **Hinchinbrook Island** – with superb walking trails. Those with work visas can also recharge their bank balances along the way by **fruit and vegetable picking** around the towns of **Bundaberg**, **Bowen**, **Ayr** and **Innisfail**. Moving north of Cairns, rainforested ranges ultimately give way to the savannah of the huge, triangular **Cape York Peninsula**, a sparsely populated setting for what is widely regarded as the most rugged 4WD adventure in the country.

Offshore, the tropical coast is marked by the appearance of the **Great Barrier Reef**, among the most extensive coral complexes in the world. The southern reaches out from Bundaberg and **1770** are peppered with sand islands or **cays**, while further north there's a wealth of beautiful granite islands between the coast and reef, covered in thick pine forests and fringed in white sand – the pick of which are the **Whitsundays** near **Airlie Beach** and **Magnetic Island** off Townsville. Many of these islands are accessible on day-trips, though some offer everything from campsites to luxury resorts if you fancy a change of pace from tearing up and down the coast. The reef itself can be explored from **boat**

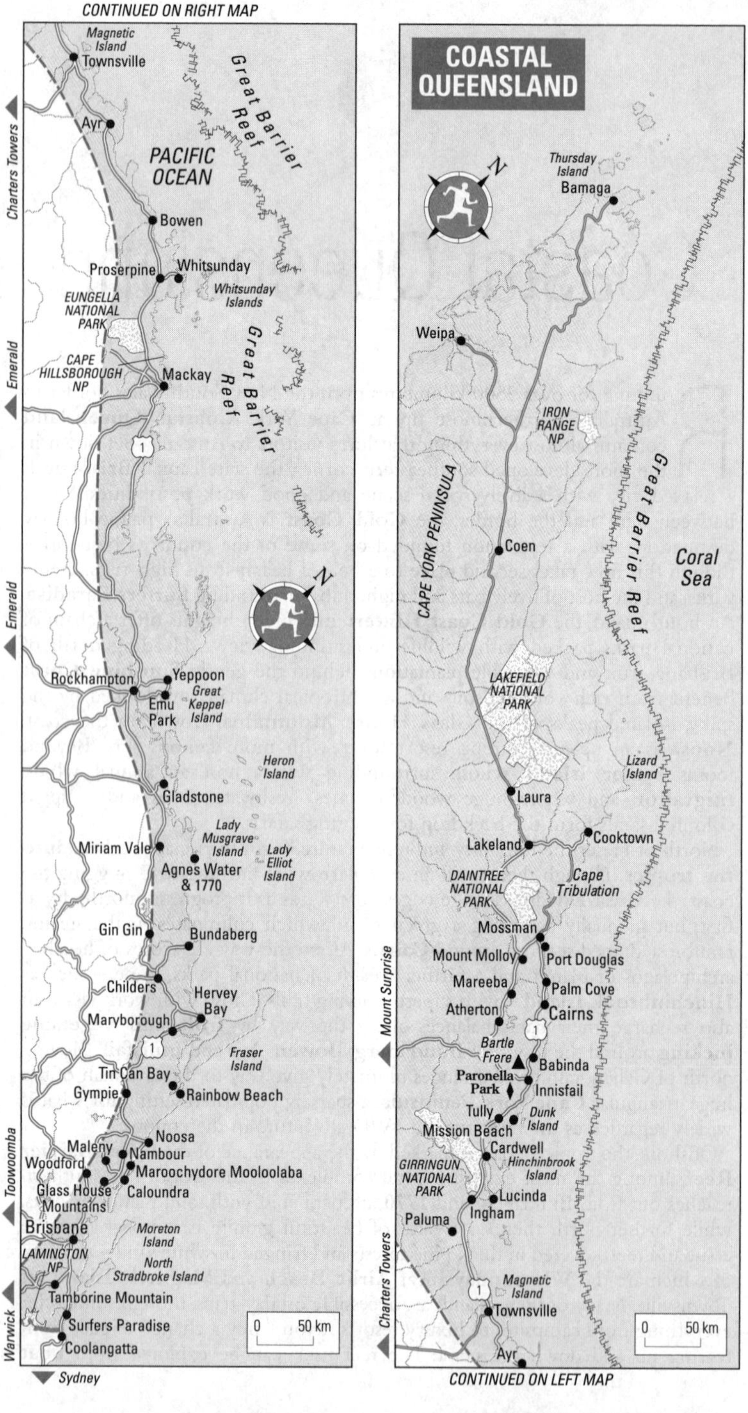

COASTAL QUEENSLAND

CONTINUED ON RIGHT MAP

Magnetic Island
Townsville
Ayr
Charters Towers
PACIFIC OCEAN
Great Barrier Reef
Bowen
Proserpine
Whitsunday
Whitsunday Islands
EUNGELLA NATIONAL PARK
CAPE HILLSBOROUGH NP
Emerald
Mackay
Great Barrier Reef
1
N
Emerald
Rockhampton
Yeppoon
Emu Park
Great Keppel Island
Heron Island
Gladstone
Lady Musgrave Island
Miriam Vale
Agnes Water & 1770
Lady Elliot Island
Gin Gin
Bundaberg
Childers
Hervey Bay
Maryborough
1
Fraser Island
Tin Can Bay
Gympie
Rainbow Beach
Toowoomba
Noosa
Maleny
Nambour
Woodford
Maroochydore Mooloolaba
Glass House Mountains
Caloundra
Brisbane
Moreton Island
LAMINGTON NP
North Stradbroke Island
Tamborine Mountain
Warwick
Surfers Paradise
Coolangatta
Sydney
0 50 km

Thursday Island
Bamaga
N
Weipa
IRON RANGE NP
CAPE YORK PENINSULA
Great Barrier Reef
Coen
Coral Sea
LAKEFIELD NATIONAL PARK
Lizard Island
Laura
Lakeland
Cooktown
DAINTREE NATIONAL PARK
Cape Tribulation
Mossman
Mount Surprise
Mount Molloy
Port Douglas
Mareeba
Palm Cove
Atherton
Cairns
1
Bartle Frere
Babinda
Paronella Park
Innisfail
Tully
Dunk Island
Mission Beach
Cardwell
Hinchinbrook Island
GIRRINGUN NATIONAL PARK
Lucinda
Ingham
Paluma
Charters Towers
Magnetic Island
1
Townsville
Ayr
0 50 km

CONTINUED ON LEFT MAP

excursions of between a few hours and several days' duration; **scuba divers** are well catered for, though the best of the coral is within easy snorkelling range of the surface.

As a prime tourist destination, Queensland's coast seldom presents **accommodation** problems, with a good range of everything from budget to upmarket options in just about every location. Just be aware that the Easter and Christmas holidays – or even just weekends – can see **room shortages** and price hikes at popular locations, including some national parks: booking in advance is wise, and may even get you discounted rates.

The **rail line** runs from Brisbane to Cairns (incredibly, there is no train between Byron Bay and Murwillumbah in New South Wales, and Brisbane – you have to bus between the two), while the main **road** is the more-or-less coastal Highway 1 to Cairns, with frequent long-distance **buses** serving all towns along the route. A few out-of-the-way spots are covered on local transport, but it's worth renting a car from time to time to reach some of the less accessible parks or beaches. **Driving**, Queensland's roadsigns are infuriatingly confusing and contradictory, and tailgating seems to be mandatory – have a good look at a detailed road **map** (those put out by the state automobile association, the RACQ, are the best) before setting out anywhere. From the Bundaberg area north, you also need to watch out for **cane trains** that cross roads during the sugar-crushing season (roughly June–Dec); crossings are usually marked by flashing red lights.

As for **weather**, winters are dry and pleasant throughout the region, but the summer climate (Dec–April) becomes more oppressive the further north you travel, with the possibility of cyclones bringing torrential rain and devastating storms to the entire tropical coast.

Some history

In a way, Queensland's popularity as a holiday hot-spot is surprising, as this is perhaps Australia's most **conservative** state, often lampooned as being slow and regressive. There are, however, very physical and **social divisions** between the densely settled, city-oriented southeastern corner and the large rural remainder, which is mostly given over to mining and farming. These divisions date back to when Brisbane was chosen as capital on Queensland's **separation** from New South Wales in 1859; the city proved an unpopular choice with the northern pioneers, who felt that the government was too far away to understand, or even care about, their needs. These needs centred around the north's **sugar plantations** and the use of Solomon Islanders for labour, a practice the government equated with **slavery** and finally banned in 1872. Ensuing demands for further separation, this time between tropical Queensland and the southeast, never bore fruit, but the remoteness of northern settlements from the capital led to local self-sufficiency, making Queensland far less homogenous than the other eastern states.

The darker side of this conservatism has seen Queensland endure more than its fair share of extreme or simply **dirty politics**. During the 1970s and early 1980s, the repressive stranglehold of a strongly conservative National Party government, led by the charismatic and slippery Sir Johannes Bjelke-Petersen (better known as "**Joh**"), did nothing to enhance the state's image. Despite a long-term Labor government since his time, state politics remain predominantly right-wing, as was seen in the late 1990s by the emergence from southeast Queensland of Pauline Hanson and her One Nation Party, whose shallow, racist outbursts won favour with a fair number of Australians who felt ignored by the main parties. The current Labor Premier, **Peter Beattie**, was elected for the third successive time in 2004, and was the first state premier to act on the Australia-wide **water**

shortage caused by a decade of poor rainfall, by implementing water-recycling measures for domestic, industrial and agricultural use in 2007.

Brisbane and around

By far the largest city in Queensland, **BRISBANE** is not quite what you'd expect from a state capital with over one and a half million residents. Although there is urban sprawl, high-rise buildings, slow-moving traffic, crowded streets and the other trappings of a business and trade centre, there's little of the pushiness that usually accompanies them. To urbanites used to a more aggressive approach, the atmosphere is slow, even backward (a reputation the city would be pleased to lose), but to others the languid pace is a welcome change and reflects relaxed rather than regressive attitudes.

Brisbane is an attractive enough place, with the typical features of any Australian city of a comparable age and size – a historic precinct, museums and botanic gardens – though there are no outstanding sights. It's a fairly easy place to find casual, short-term **employment** however, and there's a healthy, unpredictable social scene, tempting many travellers to spend longer here than they had planned. As for exploring further afield, you'll find empty beaches and surf on **North Stradbroke Island** and dolphins around **Moreton Island** – both easy to reach from the city.

Some history

In 1823, responding to political pressure to shift the "worst type of felons" away from Sydney, the New South Wales government sent Surveyor General **John Oxley** north to find a suitable site for a new prison colony. Sailing into **Moreton Bay**, he was shown a previously unknown river by three shipwrecked convicts who had been living with Aborigines. He explored it briefly, named it "Brisbane" after the governor, and the next year established a convict settlement at **Redcliffe** on the coast. This was immediately abandoned in favour of better anchorage further upstream, and by the end of 1824 today's city centre had become the site of Brisbane Town.

Twenty years on, a land shortage down south persuaded the government to move out the convicts and free up the Moreton Bay area to settlers. Immigrants on government-assisted passages poured in and Brisbane began to shape up as a busy **port** – an unattractive, awkward town of rutted streets and wooden shacks. As the largest regional settlement of the times, Brisbane was the obvious choice as capital of the new state of Queensland on its formation in 1859, though the city's first substantial buildings were constructed only in the late 1860s, after fire had destroyed the original centre and state bankruptcy was averted by Queensland's first gold strikes at Gympie. Even so, development was slow and uneven: new townships were founded around the centre at Fortitude Valley, Kangaroo Point and Breakfast Creek, gradually merging into a city.

After World War II, when General Douglas MacArthur used Brisbane as his headquarters to coordinate attacks on Japanese forces based throughout the Pacific, Brisbane stagnated, earning a reputation as a dull, underdeveloped backwater – not least thanks to the Bjelke-Petersen regime. Since his time,

Aboriginal Brisbane

John Oxley recorded that the **Brisbane Aborigines** were friendly; in the early days, they even rounded up and returned runaways from the settlement. In his orders to Oxley on how to deal with the indigenous peoples, Governor Brisbane admitted, though in a roundabout way, that the land belonged to them: "All uncivilized people have wants ... when treated justly they acquire many comforts by their union with the more civilized. This justifies our occupation of their lands."

But future governors were not so liberal, and things had soured long before the first squatters moved into the Brisbane area and began leaving out "gifts" of poisoned flour and calling in the Native Mounted Police to disperse local Aborigines – a euphemism for exterminating them. In the later part of the nineteenth century, survivors from these early days were dispossessed by the **Protection Act** (in force until the 1970s) which saw them rounded up and relocated onto special reserves away from traditional lands.

A trace of Brisbane's Aboriginal past is found at the Nudgee Bora Ring about 12km north of the centre at Nudgee Waterhole Reserve, at the junction of Nudgee and Childs roads. Last used in 1860, two low mounds where boys were initiated form little more than an icon today, and you'll probably feel that it's not worth the trip. More rewarding are the several Aboriginal walking trails at Mount Coot-tha; the City Hall information desk has leaflets on these which explain traditional uses of the area (see p.369).

escalating development has impressed upon the city's skyline and from 2001 until 2005 Brisbane boasted the country's highest internal=migration figures and a quarter of the national **population growth**, resulting in booming house prices and the redevelopment of the dilapidated Brisbane River foreshore into upmarket apartments.

Arrival, information and city transport

Brisbane Airport is located 9km northeast of the centre, at the end of Kingsford Smith Drive. You'll find banks, ATMs and luggage lockers at both the domestic and the international terminals. To get to the city from either terminal, there's the speedy **Airtrain** ($12 one way; ⓦ www.airtrain.com.au), which takes just twenty minutes to reach Brisbane's Transit Centre; or the **Skytrans bus** ($9 one way, $15 return; ⓦ www.coachtrans.com.au), which takes up to forty minutes but delivers direct to central accommodation as well as the Transit Centre. A **taxi** into the city costs around $35 for the half-hour trip. For the Gold Coast, Skytrans delivers direct to accommodation for $18.50 one way.

Long-distance buses and trains all end up at Brisbane's **Transit Centre**, located in the heart of the city on Roma Street. On the highest of the three levels are the **bus offices**, luggage lockers and a hostel information desk (daily 8am–5pm). The middle floor has fast-food joints, a bar, toilets and showers, a medical centre and ATMs, while on the ground floor is the arrival and departure point for local and interstate **trains**.

Major destinations along Australia's east coast between Sydney and Cairns, along with inland routes to Mount Isa, are serviced by Greyhound Australia (ⓣ 13 20 30) and Premier (ⓣ 13 34 10). Local buses to the Gold Coast include Kirkland's (ⓣ 1300 367 077) and Coachtrans (ⓣ 13 12 30); travelling north, Suncoast Pacific (ⓣ 07/3236 1901) cover all Sunshine Coast towns to Noosa; and heading westwards, Crisp's (ⓣ 07/4661 8333) runs daily to Warwick, Moree

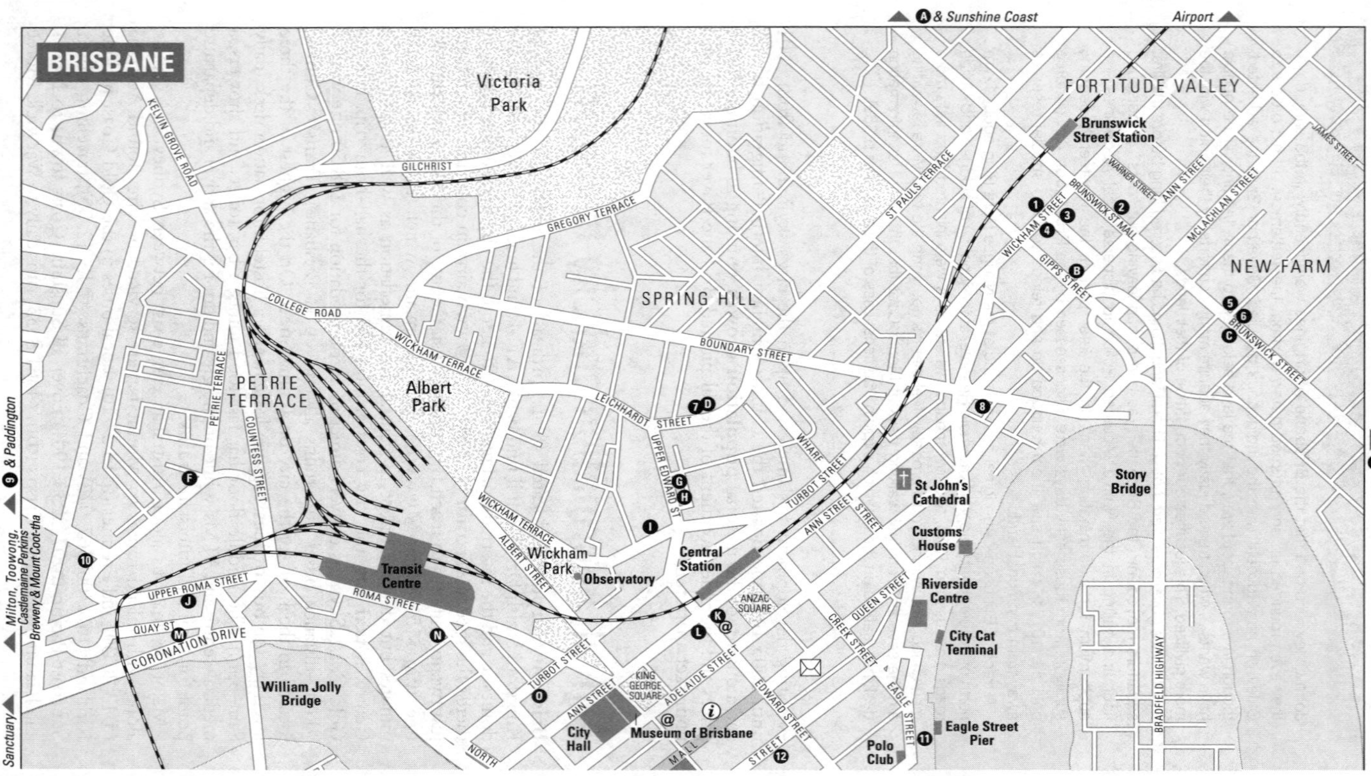
BRISBANE
A & Sunshine Coast
Airport
Victoria Park
FORTITUDE VALLEY
Brunswick Street Station
NEW FARM
SPRING HILL
PETRIE TERRACE
Albert Park
Wickham Park
Observatory
Central Station
Transit Centre
St John's Cathedral
Customs House
Riverside Centre
City Cat Terminal
Eagle Street Pier
Polo Club
Story Bridge
William Jolly Bridge
City Hall
Museum of Brisbane
ANZAC SQUARE
KING GEORGE SQUARE
KELVIN GROVE ROAD
GILCHRIST
GREGORY TERRACE
ST PAULS TERRACE
JAMES STREET
WARNER STREET
ANN STREET
MCLACHLAN STREET
BRUNSWICK ST MALL
WICKHAM STREET
GIPPS STREET
BRUNSWICK STREET
COLLEGE ROAD
WICKHAM TERRACE
BOUNDARY STREET
LEICHHARDT STREET
UPPER EDWARD ST
WHARF
TURBOT STREET
STREET
PETRIE TERRACE
COUNTESS STREET
ALBERT STREET
UPPER ROMA STREET
ROMA STREET
QUAY ST
CORONATION DRIVE
QUEEN STREET
CREEK STREET
EAGLE STREET
ADELAIDE STREET
EDWARD STREET
MALL
NORTH
BRADFIELD HIGHWAY
9 & Paddington
Milton, Toowong, Castlemaine Perkins Brewery & Mount Coot-tha
Sanctuary
E

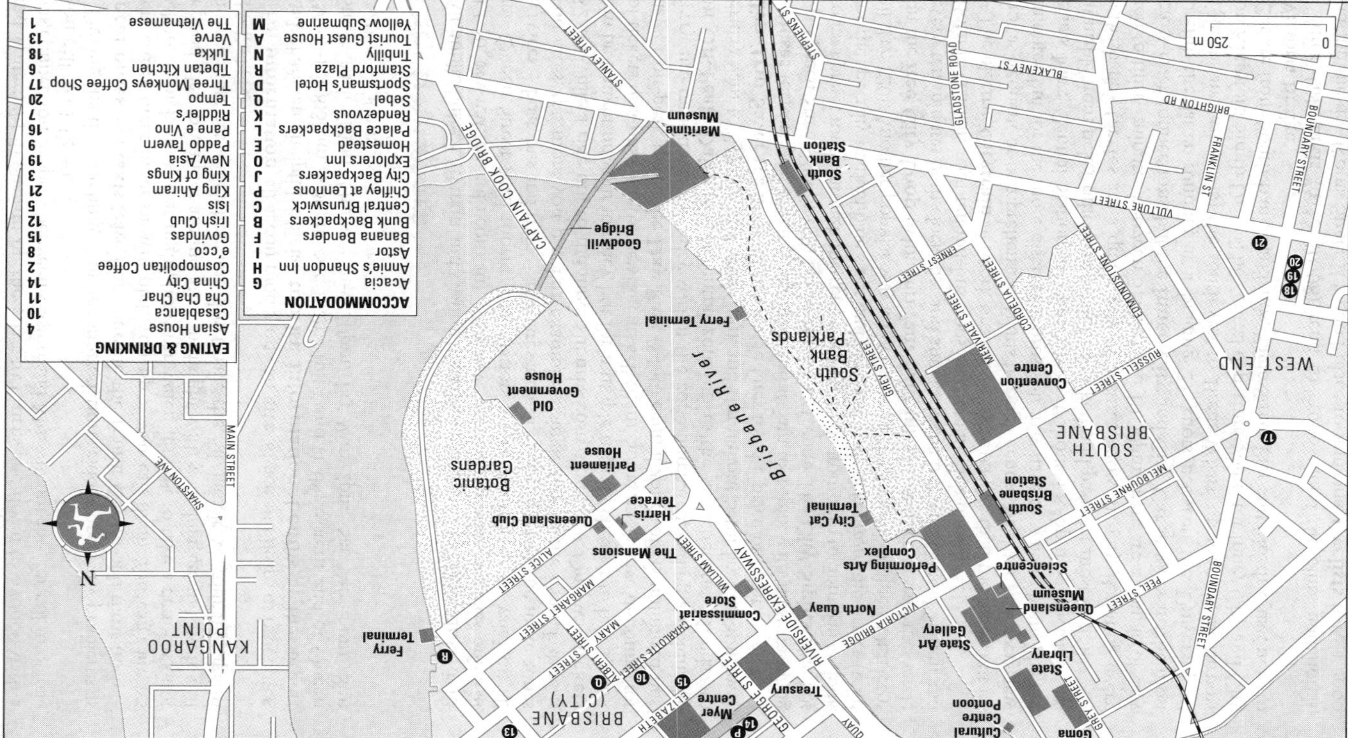
Ipswich
Gold Coast
ACCOMMODATION
Acacia G
Annie's Shandon Inn H
Astor I
Banana Benders F
Bunk Backpackers B
Central Brunswick C
Chifley at Lennons P
City Backpackers J
Explorers Inn O
Homestead E
Palace Backpackers L
Rendezvous K
Sebel Q
Sportsman's Hotel D
Stamford Plaza R
Tinbilly N
Tourist Guest House A
Yellow Submarine M
EATING & DRINKING
Asian House 4
Casablanca 10
Cha Cha Char 11
China City 14
Cosmopolitan Coffee 2
e'cco 8
Govindas 15
Irish Club 12
Isis 5
King Ahiram 21
King of Kings 3
New Asia 19
Paddo Tavern 9
Pane e Vino 16
Riddler's 7
Tempo 20
Three Monkeys Coffee Shop 17
Tibetan Kitchen 6
Tukka 18
Verve 13
The Vietnamese 1
N
KANGAROO POINT
SHAFSTON AVE
MAIN STREET
BRISBANE (CITY)
Ferry Terminal
Botanic Gardens
Old Government House
Parliament House
Queensland Club
The Mansions
Harris Terrace
Goodwill Bridge
CAPTAIN COOK BRIDGE
ALICE STREET
MARGARET STREET
MARY STREET
ALBERT STREET
CHARLOTTE STREET
ELIZABETH
GEORGE STREET
WILLIAM STREET
Myer Centre
Treasury
Commissariat Store
RIVERSIDE EXPRESSWAY
Brisbane River
Ferry Terminal
Maritime Museum
STANLEY STREET
South Bank Parklands
South Bank Station
STEPHENS ST
City Cat Terminal
North Quay
QUAY
VICTORIA BRIDGE
Performing Arts Complex
State Art Gallery
Cultural Centre Pontoon
Goma
GREY STREET
State Library
Queensland Museum
Sciencentre
South Brisbane Station
Convention Centre
GREY STREET
ERNEST STREET
MERIVALE STREET
CORDELIA STREET
GLADSTONE ROAD
BLAKENEY ST
SOUTH BRISBANE
PEEL STREET
MELBOURNE STREET
RUSSELL STREET
EDMONDSTONE STREET
VULTURE STREET
BRIGHTON RD
FRANKLIN ST
BOUNDARY STREET
BOUNDARY STREET
WEST END
0 250 m
Ipswich, St Lucia & Lone Pine

and Tenterfield. Trains run up the coast to Cairns and down to Sydney, with a bus connection to spots between Casino and Murwillumbah – for rail information call ⓣ13 12 30.

During the day, reaching your accommodation seldom poses any problems as **local buses** and **taxis** leave from outside the Transit Centre, and most hosteliers either meet buses or will pick you up if you call them. You can't always rely on a pick-up late at night, however, when it's best to take a taxi – it's not a good idea to wander around after midnight with your luggage in tow. If you simply must get somewhere and don't have the cab fare, leave your luggage in the lockers.

For **information**, all accommodation can give advice and heaps of brochures, and there are helpful official **tourist information booths** at the airport (Mon–Fri 8.30am–4.30pm, Sat 10am–1pm) and at the eastern end of Queen Street Mall (Mon–Thurs 9am–5.30pm, Fri 9am–7pm, Sat 9am–5pm, Sun 9.30am–4.30pm).

City transport

All public buses, Citytrain and Council ferries are operated by **Translink** (ⓣ13 12 30, ⓦwww.transinfo.com.au), who have a bookings and enquiries office at the Queen Street Mall tourist information booth. All tickets are valid on all services – boat, bus and train – and fares are calculated by zone: the more zones you cross, the more you pay. For example, a single fare in the central zone is $2.20, while a ride out to the inner suburbs costs around $4. One-way **tickets** can be bought on your journey, but for multiple trips it's cheaper to buy a book of tickets or a **pass** – most newsagents sell them. Some passes give discounts for day or off-peak travel: the **Day Pass** ($4.40 central zone) offers unlimited bus, ferry and train travel for a day within the zone purchased, ending at midnight; an **Off-Peak Daily** ($3.30 central zone) gives the same benefits Monday to Friday 9am to 3.30pm and after 7pm, and throughout Saturday and Sunday. A **Ten-Trip Saver** is a book of ten single fares for the price of eight.

Buses (drivers give change) run from about 5am to 11pm, with most travelling via Queen Street Bus Station below the Myer Centre. The **City Sights** blue bus tours a preset route through the centre with a guide from 9am to 5pm daily – look for the specially marked blue stops and purchase your ticket from the driver (valid all day; $20). Another popular way to get around the Central Business District is on the **free City Loop** (Mon–Fri 7am–5.50pm). The distinctive red buses circle every ten minutes both clockwise and anticlockwise between Central Station and Botanic Gardens with ten red-bus stops en route in each direction.

The electric **Citytrain** network provides a faster service than the buses, but it's not as frequent or comprehensive. Trains through central Brisbane run every few minutes, but for the more distant suburbs you may have to wait an hour. The last trains leave Central Station on Ann Street at about 11.45pm – timetables are available from ticket offices. You can buy tickets and passes at most stations.

Brisbane's **ferries** are a quick way of getting across the city. Running every ten to thirty minutes between 5.50am and 10.30pm, there are a couple of easy cross-river connections, but the **Inner City** and **City Cat** services are the most useful, the latter running at a bracing 27 knots between the University of Queensland campus in the southwest to Bretts Wharf, up towards the airport on Kingsford Smith Drive. The central departure points for Inner City and City Cat are from South Bank Parklands, Eagle Street Pier and North Quay, next to Victoria Bridge.

After dark, **taxis** (ⓣ13 10 08) tend to cruise round the clubs and hotels; during the day Roma Street is a good place to find one. **Cyclists** have a good number of bike routes from which to choose, with maps available from the tourist information booths and libraries. A few hostels **loan** bikes, or they can be easily rented elsewhere (see p.378).

Accommodation

Brisbane's inner-city accommodation is varied and excellent value, with a range of hostels, motels, boutique apartments and international hotel chains spread right across the city centre. Beds are scarce only during major sports events such as the annual Brisbane Cup horse race in June, and the Royal Queensland Show (the "Ekka") in August. Prices at more upmarket places may also drop at weekends and outside peak season, due to the scarcity of business customers and competition from the Gold Coast.

City centre

All the following are within a short walk of Central Station, on the Citytrain line.

Acacia 413 Upper Edward St ⓣ07/3832 1663. Don't be put off by the slightly austere brick exterior: this is a clean, orderly, motel-like B&B with shared and en-suite rooms. ❸

Annie's Shandon Inn 405 Upper Edward St ⓣ07/3831 8684, ⓦwww.anniesinn.net. A cozy, family-run B&B with single, double and en-suite rooms just five minutes' walk from the city centre. ❸

Astor 193 Wickham Terrace ⓣ07/3144 4000, ⓦwww.astorhotel.com.au. Boutique hotel in a smart, renovated nineteenth-century colonial building, with a range of en-suite rooms and fully serviced apartments. Doubles ❹, suites ❺, two-bedroom apartments ❻

Chifley at Lennons 66 Queen St Mall ⓣ07/3222 3222, ⓦwww.chifleyhotels.com. Bang in the city centre, this new place offers tidy, ordinary hotel rooms at a good price. ❻

Explorers Inn 63 Turbot St (cnr George St) ⓣ07/3211 3488, ⓦwww.explorers.com.au. Friendly budget hotel but without parking. Standard rooms are good for single travellers, while superior rooms have plenty of space – all rooms are non-smoking. ❹

Palace Backpackers Cnr Ann and Edward streets ⓣ1800 676 340, ⓦwww.palacebackpackers.com.au. Huge downtown hostel, purpose-built in 1911 but completely revamped (except for the ancient lift). The noise from the attached *Down Under Bar* prompts some travellers to move elsewhere for some sleep. Poky singles, high-ceilinged and spacious doubles, and three- to nine-bed dorms. Dorms $25–28, rooms ❸

Rendezvous 255 Ann St ⓣ07/3001 9888, ⓦwww.rendezvoushotels.com. Spacious hotel rooms and apartments with kitchen and laundry make this one of the best boutique options in town, often with substantial weekend or special package deals. ❻

Sebel Cnr Albert and Charlotte streets ⓣ07/3224 3500, ⓦwww.mirvachotels.com.au. Great views, a rooftop pool and large suites, though the basic studio rooms are not as good. Studio ❻, suites ❼

Sportsman's Hotel 130 Leichhardt St, Spring Hill ⓣ07/3831 2892, ⓦwww.sportsmanshotel.com.au. Gay-friendly pub with rooms; predominantly male clientele but both sexes welcome. ❸

Stamford Plaza Edward St ⓣ07/3221 1999, ⓦwww.stamford.com.au. Top-notch hotel with a grand mix of colonial and modern buildings overlooking the river and Botanic Gardens. ❽

Tinbilly Cnr George and Herschel streets ⓣ1800 446 646, ⓦwww.tinbilly.com. Modern party-hostel and bar almost directly opposite the Transit Centre; facilities are good though doubles are expensive and the noise level can build through the evening. Dorms $25, rooms ❹

Petrie Terrace

The following are a ten-minute walk west of Roma Street, or take bus #144 from opposite the Transit Centre.

Banana Benders 118 Petrie Terrace ⓣ07/3367 1157, ⓦwww.bananabenders.com.au. A small, friendly hostel with a homely, easy-going feel. There's a small kitchen and BBQ area, a casual TV-and-video lounge, deck-space for dining, and free entry to the local public pool. Dorms $23–25, rooms ❸

City Backpackers 380 Upper Roma St ⓣ07/3211 3221, ⓦwww.citybackpackers.com. One of Brisbane's biggest hostels, this busy, well-run place has clean facilities, fair-sized rooms, its own bar with budget meal deals and BBQ nights, swimming pool and free undercover parking. Dorms $21, en-suite rooms ❸

Yellow Submarine 66 Quay St ⓣ07/3211 3424. Small, comfortable hostel in a refurbished 1860s building with landscaped courtyard. Full kitchen facilities, laundry, BBQ and pool. The friendly owners put on free three-hour sailing trips every Wednesday around the bay and free BBQs at weekends, ensuring a sociable atmosphere. The staff can help out with work connections. Dorms $25, rooms ❸

Fortitude Valley and New Farm

The Valley's accommodation is well placed for clubs but the area can be seedy late at night. Most buses travelling up Adelaide Street pass through here, or you can take the Citytrain to Brunswick Street station. For New Farm, take a bus (#177, #178, #167 or #168) from Adelaide Street.

Bunk Backpackers Cnr Ann and Gipp streets ⓣ1800 682 865, ⓦwww.bunkbrisbane.com.au. From the outside, this place looks like a stark fortress badly located between two busy roads, but good-quality facilities including a pool and spa make this warehouse-sized backpackers' bearable. The attached nightclub-bar adds to the noise though. Dorms $23, doubles ❸, apartments ❺

Central Brunswick 455 Brunswick St, Fortitude Valley ⓣ07/3852 1411, ⓦwww.centralbrunswickhotel.com.au. Sparkling modern red-brick building with comfortable hotel rooms, all with own bath and TV, some apartment-style with kitchen facilities. Shared amenities include spa and gym. ❺

Homestead 57 Annie St, New Farm ⓣ07/3358 3538 or 1800 658 344. A large house converted to a hostel, with quiet atmosphere, a pool shaped like a shamrock and plenty of outdoor space. There are free bikes, and the hostel arranges trips to Mount Coot-tha. Dorms $21, rooms ❸

Tourist Guest House 555 Gregory Terrace, Fortitude Valley ⓣ1800 800 589, ⓦwww.touristguesthouse.com.au. This is a clean, quiet hostel with beautiful landscaping, some parking space, family rooms, laundry and kitchen. Dorms $25, rooms ❸

The City

The city is focused around the meandering loops of the **Brisbane River**, with the triangular wedge of the business centre on the north bank surrounded by community-oriented suburbs. At the city's heart are the busy, upmarket commercial and administrative precincts around Queen Street and George Street, an area of glass towers, cafés and century-old sandstone facades that extends southeast to the Botanic Gardens on the river. Radiating north, the polish gives way to less conservative shops, accommodation and eateries around Spring Hill, Fortitude Valley and New Farm, and the aspiring suburbs of Petrie Terrace and Paddington. To the west is a blaze of riverside homes at Milton and Toowong and the fringes of Mount Coot-tha. Across the river, the major landmarks are the South Bank Cultural Centre and South Bank Parklands, which stretch to Kangaroo Point. Beyond are the open, bustling streets of South Brisbane and the West End, more relaxed than their northern counterparts.

Downtown

Queen Street is Brisbane's oldest thoroughfare, the stretch between George and Edward streets a **pedestrian mall** flanked by multistorey shopping centres. The area is always busy with people running errands, eating at the many cafés, window shopping or just socializing, and there's usually some kind of entertainment too:

either informal efforts – acrobats, buskers and the occasional soap-box orator – or more organized events such as dancing or jazz sessions on the small stage about halfway down the street.

City Hall, Museum of Brisbane and Central Business District

North from the mall along Albert Street, you arrive at **King George Square**, with its fountains and bronze sculptures of swaggies, native wildlife and what look like large pieces of futuristic circuitry. Facing the square to the west is **City Hall**, a stately 1920s building ruined by an ugly clock tower. Inside, the **Museum of Brisbane** (daily 10am–5pm; free) has a smattering of paintings with regular exhibitions by prominent Australian artists, and a social history gallery which gives an uneventful account of Brisbane's past and its rather more exciting aspirations for the future. There's a huge satellite image of the "200km City" plus an eclectic mix of television displays, retro posters and antique icons. The **clock tower** is open, too, if you want a view of the city centre (Mon–Fri 10am–3pm, Sat 10am–2pm; $2); access is through the City Hall foyer.

Flanked by roads further up Albert Street, tiny **Wickham Park** is overlooked by the grey cone of Brisbane's oldest building, a windmill known locally as the **Observatory**, built by convicts in 1829 to grind corn for the early settlement. The original wooden sails were too heavy to turn but found use as a gallows until being pulled off in 1850, and all grinding was done by a treadmill – severe punishment for the convicts who had to work it. After the convict era the building became a signal station and now stands locked up and empty, held together with a cement glaze.

East between here and the river lies Brisbane's **Central Business District**, which was heavily developed in the 1990s and left with a legacy of glassy high-rises sprouting alongside the restaurants and shops of the Riverside Centre; the few surviving old buildings are hidden among the modern ones. The copper-domed **Customs House** (daily 10am–4pm; free) at the upper end of Queen Street, built in 1889, harbours a small collection of Chinese antiques and hosts free concerts given by the Queensland University Orchestra every month, while the neo-Gothic **St John's Cathedral** (daily 9.30am–4.30pm; donation) on Ann Street has some elegant stained-glass windows and the only fully stone-vaulted ceiling in Australia. Sunday morning is made lively by the Eagle Street Markets between the river and the road – too trendy for bargains, but not bad for jewellery and leatherwork, clothing and $25 massages.

The historic precinct

The area south between Queen Street and the Botanic Gardens contains some of Brisbane's finest architecture, dating from the earliest days of settlement until the late nineteenth century. Between Elizabeth and Queen streets, occupying an entire block, is the former **Treasury** with its classical facade. Built in the 1890s, its grandeur reflects the wealth of Queensland's gold mines (though by this point most were on the decline) and was a slap in the face to New South Wales, which had spitefully withdrawn all financial support from the fledgling state on separation some forty years previously, leaving it bankrupt. With irony typical of a state torn between conservatism and tourism, the building is now Brisbane's 24-hour **casino**.

South along William Street, the **Commissariat Store** is contemporary with the Observatory, though in considerably better shape. Originally a granary, it's now a museum (Tues–Sun 10am–4pm; $4) and headquarters of the Royal Historical Society of Queensland; the knowledgeable staff pep up an otherwise dusty collection of relics dating back to convict times. Further south along George Street you pass **Harris Terrace** and **The Mansions**, two of the city centre's last surviving rows of Victorian-era terraced houses, the latter guarded by stone cats on the parapet corners. Nearby, on the corner of George and Alice streets, the **Queensland Club** was founded in 1859, just four days before the separation of Queensland from New South Wales. Heavy walls, columns and spacious balconies evoke a tropical version of a traditional London club; entrance and membership – women are still not allowed to join – are by invitation only. Diagonally opposite, **Parliament House** (Mon–Fri 9.30am–4pm, Sat & Sun 10am–2pm; free guided tours when Parliament not in session) was built to a design by Charles Tiffin in 1868, in an appealingly compromised French Renaissance style which incorporates shuttered north windows, shaded colonnades and a high, arched roof to allow for the tropical climate. You can see the grand interior on an hour-long guided tour, and there's access to the chambers when there's no debate in progress.

South of Parliament House, George Street becomes a pedestrian lane along the western side of the Botanic Gardens and home to the Queensland University of Technology. Here you'll find **Old Government House** (Mon–Fri 10am–4pm; free), the official residence of Queensland's governors and premiers between 1862 and 1910. Another of Tiffin's designs, the building has been comprehensively restored to its stately, early twentieth-century condition, and is well worth a look for its furnishings.

The Botanic Gardens

Bordered by Alice Street, George Street and the river, Brisbane's **Botanic Gardens** overlook the cliffs of Kangaroo Point and, while more of a park than a botanic garden, provide a generous arrangement of flowers, shrubs, bamboo thickets and green grass for sprawling on, all offering an easy escape from city claustrophobia. Free **guided tours** (Mon–Sat 11am & 1pm except mid-Dec to Jan) leave from the rotunda, 100m inside the gardens' main entrance, halfway along Alice Street.

Once a vegetable patch cultivated by convicts, formal gardens were laid out in 1855 by Walter Hill, who experimented with local and imported plants to see which would grow well in Queensland's then untried climate. Some of his more successful efforts are the oversized **bunya pines** around the Edward Street entrance at the east end of Alice Street, planted in 1860, and a residual patch of the **rainforest** that once blanketed the area, at the southern end of the park. **Mangroves** along the river, accessible by a **boardwalk**, are another native species more recently protected. During the day, cyclists flock to the park, as it's at one end of a popular cycling and jogging track that follows the north bank of the river south to St Lucia and the University of Queensland. At the southern end of the gardens, classical music recitals are held on an open-air stage in the summer, beyond which the pedestrian **Goodwill Bridge** crosses over the river to South Bank Parklands.

The northern neighbourhoods

North of the river, just beyond Brisbane's central business district, are several former suburbs which have been absorbed by the city sprawl: **Paddington** and **Petrie Terrace** to the west, **Spring Hill** and **Fortitude Valley** to the north, and **New Farm** to the east. Houses in these areas are popular with Brisbane's aspiring professional class, and while office buildings and one-way streets are beginning to encroach, there's also an older character reflected in the many high-set, wooden-balconied and tin-roofed Queenslander houses still standing – some lovingly restored to original condition.

Fortitude Valley

While the other northern neighbourhoods are mainly residential, **Fortitude Valley** – better known as just "**the Valley**" – is a tangled mix of shops, restaurants, bars and clubs, comprising Brisbane's unofficial centre of artistic, gastronomic and alcoholic pursuits. An eclectic mix of the gay, the groovy and the grubby, the Valley is mostly focused along partially pedestrianized **Brunswick Street**, which sports a kilometre-long melange of nightclubs, an Irish pub, a compact Chinatown complete with the usual busy restaurants and stores, and a burgeoning European street-café scene. The area is in a state of inner-city gentrification, when the urban poor make way for hipsters, artists and students, though Brunswick Street itself has so far avoided the yuppies and smarmy wine-bars which have descended on parallel **James Street**, and remains a good spot to enjoy an evening out among Brisbane's young, fun and adventurous. It's best at weekends when cafés buzz and live musicians compete for your attention; on Saturday there's a secondhand market in the mall. After dark the Valley's streets can be somewhat sleazy, with an element of drug-related petty crime – if you've any distance to go on your own after the pubs close, take a taxi.

South Brisbane

Across the river from the city centre, the main points of interest are the **South Bank Cultural Centre** and the nearby **South Bank Parklands**, both of which lie either side of Victoria Bridge (a continuation of Queen Street). Both

The Brisbane River

The sluggish, meandering **Brisbane River** is, at four hundred million years old, one of the world's most ancient waterways. It flows from above Lake Wivenhoe – 55km inland – past farmland, into quiet suburbs and through the city before emptying 150km downstream into Moreton Bay. Once an essential trade and transport link with the rest of Australia and the world, it now seems to do little but separate the main part of the city from South Brisbane; though it's superficially active around the city centre, with ferries and dredgers keeping it navigable, most of the old wharves and shipyards now lie derelict or buried under parkland.

If the locals seem to have forgotten the river, it has a habit of reasserting its presence through **flooding**. In February 1893 cyclonic rains swelled the flow through downtown Brisbane, carrying off Victoria Bridge and scores of buildings: eyewitness accounts stated that "debris of all descriptions – whole houses, trees, cattle and homes – went floating past". This has since been repeated many times, notably in January 1974 when rains from **Cyclone Wanda** completely swamped the centre, swelling the river to a width of 3km at one stage. Despite reminders of this in brass plaques marking the depths of the worst floods at **Naldham House Polo Club** (at 1 Eagle St), some of Brisbane's poshest real estate flanks the river, with waterfront mansions at Yeerongpilly, Graceville and Chelmer, southwest of the centre. They're all banking on protection from the Lake Wivenhoe dam, completed in 1984, which should act as a buffer against future floods.

The most enjoyable and cheapest way to explore the downtown reaches of the river is simply to take a return ride on the **City Cat** (see p.366 for details); this popular, if unofficial, sightseeing trip means that the service can be severely overcrowded during holidays. You can also take **sightseeing cruises** with River City Cruises ($25; ⓣ0428 278 473, bookings essential) from the South Bank Cruise Terminal at South Bank Parklands; and **lunch and dinner cruises** aboard the *Kookaburra River Queen* (call ahead for bookings and prices; ⓣ07/3221 1300, ⓦwww.kookaburrariverqueens.com).

are easily reached by Citytrain to South Brisbane Station, while plenty of buses from all parts of the city stop outside the station on Melbourne Street.

Beyond here, the **West End** is South Brisbane's answer to Fortitude Valley, with no sights as such but popular for the escalating number of **restaurants and cafés** strung out along Boundary Street.

The South Bank Cultural Centre

The **South Bank Cultural Centre** comprises separate adjacent buildings between Grey Street and the river housing the Queensland Museum, Sciencentre, the State Art Gallery, State Library and Gallery of Modern Art (better known as GOMA). The buildings themselves are a mass of dull, 1980s-style concrete facades, but they hide some of Australia's better museum collections and are well worth a visit.

The **Queensland Museum** (daily 9.30am–5pm; free, except for special exhibitions) is essentially a natural history museum. It kicks off with full-scale models of a humpback-whale family suspended from the lobby ceiling, then takes you past displays of finds from the state's fossil sites, including a reconstruction of Queensland's own *Muttaburrasaurus*. There's also a little bit on the marine environment, particularly turtles, and the **Museum Zoo**, where hundreds of models, skeletons and remains of wildlife are arranged in a long conga line in order of size. The topmost floor has an exhibition on **Aboriginal Queensland**, with the usual cases of stone tools and boomerangs enlivened by photos, accounts by early settlers and Aboriginal elders, interactive videos and Dreamtime stories.

In the same building but with a separate entrance, the **Sciencentre** (daily 10am–5pm; $9.50) is good for those who prefer to prod and dismantle exhibits rather than peer at them through a protective glass case. It's great for children, with favourites including the "perception tunnel", which gives the impression of rotating although you remain stock still, and the "Thongophone", a set of giant pan pipes played by whacking the top with a flip-flop – all good rainy-day material.

The adjoining **State Art Gallery** (Mon–Fri 9am–5pm, Sat & Sun 10am–5pm; free, except for special exhibitions) houses a collection of Australian painting from the early days of local settlement up to the present, with most important artists represented. Top of the bill are astounding works by Sidney Nolan from his series on **Mrs Fraser** (of Fraser Island fame), watercolours by Aboriginal artists Albert Namatjira and Joe Rootsey, Ian Fairweather's abstract canvases and a nineteenth-century **stained-glass window** of a kangaroo hunt. The selection is broad enough to trace how Australian art began by aping European tastes and then, during the twentieth century, found its own style in the alienated works of Nolan, Boyd and Whiteley, who were all inspired by Australian landscape and legends.

A couple of blocks northwest, on Grey Street, **GOMA** (Gallery of Modern Art; daily 10am–5pm; free) is a huge, airy space with constantly changing exhibitions, many of them by Southeast Asian and Pacific artists as well as Australians – recent shows included work by the Chinese artist Fang Lijiu and an installation of clips from Jackie Chan films.

The South Bank Parklands

The **South Bank Parklands** date back to just 1988 but despite this are one of the nicest parts of the city – you can promenade under shady fig trees along the riverfront; **picnic** under rainforest plants and bamboo on lawns lining the banks of shallow, stone-lined "streams" (which are convincing enough to attract large, sunbathing water dragons and birds); or make use of the **artificial beach** and accompanying saltwater pool. **Bands** play most Saturday nights, either on the outdoor stage or at the *Plough Inn*, a restored, century-old pub on the cobbled high street; other attractions include the exhibits at the **Maritime Museum** (daily 9.30am–4.30pm; $7), where there's a 90-year-old Torres Strait pearling lugger and a World War II frigate, *Diamantina*, on show in the dry dock.

You can reach South Bank Parklands on Citytrain to **South Bank station**; by ferry or City Cat; or by taking the pedestrian Goodwill Bridge from the city Botanic Gardens to the Maritime Museum.

Southwest of the centre

A few worthwhile sights lie southwest of the city centre, some of which – such as Lone Pine Sanctuary – you can reach **by boat** along the Brisbane river, though all are also accessible by other forms of public transport.

The Castlemaine Perkins Brewery: XXXX

Just west from Petrie Terrace on Milton Road (take the Citytrain to Milton and it's just across the street), the **Castlemaine Perkins Brewery** (Ⓣ07/3361 7597, Ⓦwww.xxxx.com.au) has been making Queensland's own beer since 1878. Their famous yellow-and-red **XXXX** emblem is part of the Queensland landscape – it's splashed across T-shirts, the roofs of Outback hotels, and the labels of countless discarded bottles and cans littering everything from roadsides to the Great Barrier Reef. For enthusiasts, the adjacent **Alehouse Visitor Centre** runs tours (Mon–Fri 10am–4pm on the hour; $18; bookings essential and you must wear fully-enclosed shoes) which incorporate a one-hour overview of the brewing process and four free beers in the Ale House.

△ The Castlemaine Perkins Brewery

Drinks for women: the Regatta Hotel

Though Australian **pubs** still tend towards being all-male enclaves, women were once legally barred to "protect" them from the corrupting influence of foul language. On April 1, 1965, Merle Thornton (mother of the actress Sigrid Thornton) and her friend Rosalie Bogner chained themselves to the footrail of the **Regatta Hotel** bar at Toowong in protest; the movement they inspired led to the granting of "the right to drink alongside men" in the mid-1970s. The grand, pink-and-white colonial hotel, now a trendy place for a drink after work on Fridays, is on the west bank of the river along Coronation Drive, about 2km from the city centre towards St Lucia – catch the City Cat ferry to Regatta.

Mount Coot-tha

The lower slopes of **Mount Coot-tha**, about 5km from the city centre away from the river along Sir Samuel Griffith Drive (bus #471 from Adelaide St runs hourly 9.15am–3.15pm), are the setting for Brisbane's second **botanic gardens** (daily 8am–5pm; free). Sunday picnickers are a common sight in this leafy haven, where careful landscaping and the use of enclosures have created a variety of climates – dry pine and eucalypt groves, a cool subtropical rainforest complete with waterfalls and streams, and the elegant Japanese Gardens with bonsai and fern houses. The steamy **tropical plant dome** contains a pond stocked with lotus lilies and fish, overhung by lush greenery dripping with moisture. Informative **free guided walks** depart from the information kiosk at 11am and 1pm daily.

The other dome in the gardens does duty as a **planetarium** (Tues–Sun 10am–4.30pm, plus a late-night show Sat 7.30pm; $13; ⓣ07/3403 2578). While the foyer display is dated, the show itself, which you view lying back under the dome's ceiling, gives a unique perspective of the key features of Brisbane's night sky.

After visiting the botanic gardens most people head up the road to Mount Coot-tha's **summit** for panoramas of the city and, on a good day, the Moreton Bay islands. Walking tracks from here make for moderate hikes of an hour or two through dry gum woodland, and include several **Aboriginal trails** – the best of these branches off the Slaughter Falls track with informative signs pointing out plants and their uses. Pamphlets on the tracks are available from the botanical gardens or the information desk in the foyer of Brisbane's City Hall.

Lone Pine Sanctuary

Lone Pine Sanctuary, on Jesmond Road in Fig Tree Pocket (daily 8am–5pm; $22), has been a popular day-trip upstream since first opening its gates in 1927. Here you can see native Australian fauna in their natural state which, in the case of the sanctuary's hundred-odd koalas, means being asleep for eighteen hours a day. In nearby cages you'll find other slumbering animals, including Tasmanian devils, fruit bats, blue-tongued lizards and dingoes. Indeed, about the only lively creatures you'll see are birds and a colony of hyperactive sugar gliders in the nocturnal house. Alternatively, head for the outdoor paddock where tolerant wallabies and kangaroos allow themselves to be petted and fed by visitors.

You can catch **bus** #430 from outside the Myer Centre on Elizabeth Street to Lone Pine, but the best way of getting there is to take a ninety-minute **river cruise** past Brisbane's waterfront suburbs with Mirimar Cruises (daily 10am, returns to city 2.45pm; $48, including entry to Lone Pine; ⓣ1300 729 742), whose boats depart from the Cultural Centre Pontoon beside the State Library. Free pick-up from central accommodation is usually possible if you call ahead. Note that the City Cat and other public ferries do not go as far upstream as Lone Pine.

Eating

Brisbane has no gastronomic tradition to exploit, but there's a good variety of **cafés and restaurants** all over the city, with a trend towards "modern Australian" cuisine (creative use of local produce, with Asian and Mediterranean influences). Fortitude Valley has a dense grouping of Asian restaurants (and a fashionable café society), while South Brisbane's Boundary Street has more of a European flavour.

The **counter meals** offered by many downtown hotels (especially during the week) are the cheapest route to a full stomach – aim for lunch at around noon and dinner between 5 and 6pm – or try one of the scores of cafés and **food courts** in the centre catering to office workers. Restaurants **open** from around 11am to 2pm for lunch, and from 6 to 10pm or later for evening meals; many are closed for one day a week (often Monday).

City centre

Cha Cha Char Pier 1, Eagle St ⓣ3211 9944. With an owner who is well connected to the beef industry, steak is the thing to go for here, and around $35 will buy you one of the best you will ever eat. Also recommended for its wine selection and riverside location.

China City 76 Queen St Mall. Probably the most authentic Cantonese food in Brisbane – though also relatively expensive – especially good for its seafood and *yum cha* (dim sum) selection. Seafood mains from $19.

e'cco 100 Boundary St ⓣ07/3831 8344, ⓦwww.eccobistro.com. Boasts an impressive awards list, not to mention their own cookbook – you'll have to book here, and sometimes days ahead. Not cheap but good value, with all mains at $36. Open for lunch Tues–Fri, dinner Tues–Sat.

Govindas 1st floor, 99 Elizabeth St. Hare Krishna-run vegetarian food bar, with a $10 all-you-can-eat menu. There's also a $6 banquet every Sunday, but you'll have to sit through a lot of chanting before you actually get to eat. Mon–Thurs 11am–6.30pm, Fri 11am–8.30pm, Sat 11am–2.30pm, Sun 5–7pm.

Irish Club 171 Elizabeth St. Not a theme-bar clone but the genuine deal, with set pub lunches and dinners from $7.

Pane e Vino Cnr Charlotte and Albert streets. Likeable Italian café-restaurant with pavement tables, catering mainly to nearby office executives. Pre-order and finish lunch before 12.45pm Mon–Fri and get a fifteen percent discount; light meals from $12, otherwise main courses are around $25.

Riddler's 124 Leichhardt St. Cavernous, budget Italian restaurant with huge pizzas, small but filling pasta favourites and very average salads.

Verve 109 Edward St. Modern Italian in an ambient basement cellar with funky music and art. Pastas and risottos $11–16, mains under $20 and enticing blackboard specials such as goat's-cheese gnocchi. Closed Sun.

Petrie Terrace

Casablanca 52 Petrie Terrace. Inexpensive brasserie and café serving the young and pretentious. Tapas are served at the bar for around $15, and the food is excellent and mouthwateringly spicy, with leanings towards North African cuisine. R&B, hip-hop or live music provides atmosphere at weekends and there are Latin dance classes in the cellar Tues–Fri.

Paddo Tavern 186 Given Terrace (cnr Caxton St). Huge Irish pub with a dozen pool tables plus beer and steak for $8. Live comedy acts downstairs.

Fortitude Valley

Asian House 165 Wickham St. Good, filling Chinese food at very reasonable prices – most mains, such as roast pork or greens in oyster sauce, are under $15.

Cosmopolitan Coffee 322 Brunswick St Mall. This relaxed place is something of an institution with Brisbane's café society; it opens early for breakfast and is less pretentious than the surrounding competition.

Isis Cnr of Brunswick and Robertson streets ⓣ07/3852 1155. Smart, popular, long-running brasserie with a predominantly French-influenced menu and mains at around $35.

King of Kings 169 Wickham St. Two restaurants with separate entrances, in the same building: upstairs it's huge and tacky, but popular with the local Chinese community thanks to its fine late-morning *yum cha* tea selections – be prepared to queue at weekend lunchtimes. Open daily for lunch and dinner.

Tibetan Kitchen 454 Brunswick St ⓣ07/3358 5906. It's hard to resist any place that advertises "traditional Tibetan, Sherpa,

Nepalese foods", and luckily the stuff on offer here, including the Valley's best samosas and curries, is tasty, cheap, and served in a very attractive setting. Mains $15–18. Open daily for dinner only; booking advisable at weekends.

The Vietnamese 194 Wickham St ⓣ07/3252 4112. With an interior as plain and unassuming as the name over the door, this is no-frills, genuine Vietnamese food – the steamboat is excellent, as are the chicken salad and Vietnamese spring rolls (self-assembled using a boiled rice-noodle wrapper). Most mains cost around $12, and two can eat well for $30. You'll need to book at the weekend.

South Brisbane

King Ahiram 88 Vulture St. A long-running Lebanese takeaway and restaurant; not worth crossing town for, but good for kebabs and sticky Middle Eastern desserts if you're in the area.

New Asia 153 Boundary St. Forget the flashier Vietnamese restaurants in the neighbourhood, this is the best – prawns grilled on sugar cane, deep-fried quail, rice-noodle dishes – most for less than $10 a dish.

Tempo 181 Boundary St. Great Italian-style home cooking, with fresh salads and fine seafood pasta – even humble sandwiches come with a salad big enough to be a meal in itself. The most expensive dish costs around $15. Open Tues–Sun 9am–late.

Three Monkeys Coffee Shop 58 Mollison St. Decorated with a funky assortment of African oddments; serves average coffee, awesome cakes, and effortlessly achieves the sort of bohemian atmosphere most cohopffee ss merely aspire to. Greek-influenced menu with plenty of vegetarian options, and nothing over $15. Open daily 9am–late.

Tukka 145 Boundary St ⓣ07/3846 6333. Combines native fruits, seeds, herbs and meats with European-style cooking techniques for a genuinely Australian meal, loosely inspired by Aboriginal bushtucker. Mains around $28, with a $69 five-course set meal available. Booking essential.

Nightlife

The days when Brisbane nights were a byword for boredom have long gone, with the city enjoying a recent explosion of home-grown musical talent: **bands** such as Savage Garden, Regurgitator, Custard and Powderfinger have put Brisbane firmly on the Australian pop-culture map. While there are plenty of central places to fire up with a few drinks on Friday and Saturday nights, the big push is out to Fortitude Valley's **bars and clubs**. Live-music venues are very fluid and tend to open and close in the blink of an eye; places listed below should be here to stay, but check with **music stores** such as Rocking Horse, just off Queen Street Mall in Albert Street, or weekly **free magazines** for up-to-the-minute reviews and listings – *Rave* for general information, *Time Off* for rock and live bands, and *Scene* for dance. There's no standard charge for club entry, and many places offer free nights and special deals.

City centre

The Brew House 142 Albert St ⓣ07/3003 0098. Microbrewery producing British-style ale, bitter and stout as well as lager, plus a sports bar with live bands or DJ Fri and Sat nights. Call first to arrange a brewery tour.

Café Brussels Cnr of Mary and Edward streets. Ice-cold European beers served amongst century-old wooden panelling, tiles and light fittings.

Down Under Bar At *Palace Backpackers* (cnr Ann and Edward streets). Hugely popular and often overtly get-drunk-throw-up-and-fall-down venue for travellers.

Victory Hotel 127 Edward St. Nice beer garden with braziers taking the chill off in winter and live bands Wed–Sun.

Petrie Terrace and Spring Hill

The Living Room 2 Caxton St. The latest place to be seen, this is a modern hip-hop club with live bands and guest DJs on weekends, jazz every Wed and mellow acoustic shows on Sun.

Paddo Tavern 186 Given Terrace. Band and disco on Fri night and a sit-down comedy club most days of the week.

Sportsman's Hotel 130 Leichhardt St. Gay, lesbian and straight crowds fill the two floors, which have pool tables, pinball, bands, bottle shop and bistro. Fantastic drag nights Thurs–Sun.

Fortitude Valley and New Farm

Arena 201 Brunswick St ☎07/3252 5690. Long-established venue hosting popular DJs and dance parties as well as local and international touring bands. Call for listings.

The Beat 677 Ann St. Small, crowded and sweaty pub with a beer garden outside where you can recharge your batteries on bar food. The $10 cover charge is a bit off-putting, but it's one of the best techno/dance venues in town, and open until 5am. Upstairs is the *Cockatoo Club*, a stridently gay venue with both indoor and outdoor bars, and a penchant for commercial dance music. Open Wed–Sun.

Columbian Brand new, decidedly cool bar and live-music venue that's yet to find its feet as it experiments with everything from jazz to metal. Live bands at weekends, DJs most nights.

Dooley's Cnr Brunswick and McLachlan streets. Rowdy, popular Irish pub hosting bands of variable quality; territorial male behaviour is the norm in the big pool-hall upstairs.

Fringe bar Cnr of Ann and Constant streets. Funky dance club, with live bands Thurs and weekend.

GPO Ann St. Trendy dance-bar on two floors inside a beautiful nineteenth-century sandstone building – a bit too self-aware for its own good but shaping up to rival *The Press Club* for fashion-concious clientele.

The Press Club In the *Empire Hotel* (cnr Brunswick and Ann streets). Club with door gorillas, leather lounges, big cushions to rest your feet on and a huge glam/industrial fan as the centrepiece, all of it enveloped in a relaxed and funky dance beat. Rather a "fabulous" crowd, out to see and be seen, with drinks prices to match. Closed Mon.

Ric's Bar 321 Brunswick St. Narrow, crowded place and overtly pretentious – getting to the bar takes some effort. Nightly mix of live Aussie bands downstairs and DJ-driven techno upstairs at the *Upbar*.

Tivoli 52 Costin St. Originally an Art-Deco theatre, now one of Brisbane's most popular live venues for big-name domestic touring bands.

Troubadour 322 Brunswick St. Nightly live music, usually pub-style acoustic or rock – it's a bit of a low-key option, but you can at least have a conversation with your mates here.

Waterloo Hotel Cnr Ann St and Commercial Rd. Manages to attract some big-name Australian touring bands, but almost always has good local talent Fri and Sat nights.

The Wickham Hotel Cnr Wickham and Alden streets. Queensland's most popular gay pub. Drag show on Thurs and DJs every night.

Zoo 711 Ann St. One of the best clubs in the valley, offering a hectic night out featuring dub or local bands, and jazz every last Sun of the month. Wed–Sun 5pm–late.

Gay and lesbian Brisbane

Brisbane's gays and lesbians revel in a loud and energetic scene which gets better every year. In June the Pride Collective hosts the annual **Pride Festival** (🌐www.prideawards.org.au), a diverse three-week event with a street march, fair, art exhibitions, a film festival, sports events and general exhibitionism, culminating with a dance party – the Queen's Birthday Ball. At the **Sleaze Ball** in November there's another opportunity to indulge in hedonism of all kinds at this all-day party at the RNA Showgrounds.

The **gay scene** is largely clustered around the suburbs of Spring Hill, Fortitude Valley, New Valley, New Farm and Paddington. For up-to-the-moment information, listen to Queer Radio, Station ZZZ 102.1FM (Wed 6–9pm) or pick up a copy of the fortnightly *Qnews* (🌐www.qnews.com.au) or *Queensland Pride* from gay nightclubs, street distributors and some coffee shops.

For **gay-friendly accommodation**, try *Central Brunswick Apartment Hotel*, or the *Sportsman's Hotel* (see p.367); nightlife focuses on *Cockatoo Club* above *The Beat*, *The Wickham Hotel* and *Sportsman's Hotel* – all listed under "Nightlife" on opposite. Bent Books, on the corner of Vulture and Boundary streets in the West End, is the longest-established gay **bookshop** in Brisbane, and **medical advice** is available at the Brunswick Street Medical Centre, 665 Brunswick St, New Farm (☎07/3358 1977). Gay and lesbian health service, open Mon–Sat from 8am.

Listings

Airlines Air New Zealand, 243 Edward St ⓣ13 24 76, ⓦwww.airnewzealand.com.au; Air Niugini, 99 Creek St ⓣ13 13 30, ⓦwww.airniugini.com.pg; Air Vanuatu, Floor 5, 293 Queen St ⓣ07/3221 2566; British Airways, 313 Adelaide St ⓣ07/3238 2900; Cathay Pacific ⓣ07/3860 4455; Garuda, 340 Adelaide St ⓣ07/3210 0031; Japan Airlines, Level 14, 1 Waterfront Place, Eagle St ⓣ07/3229 9922; Jetstar ⓣ13 15 38; Korean Air, 400 Queen St ⓣ07/3226 6000; Malaysia Airlines, 17th Floor, 80 Albert St ⓣ13 26 27; Qantas, 247 Adelaide St domestic ⓣ13 13 13, international ⓣ07/3234 3747; Royal Brunei, 60 Edward St ⓣ1800/221 221; Singapore Airlines, 344 Queen St ⓣ13 10 11; Thai International, 145 Eagle St ⓣ07/3832 2778; Virgin Blue, 131 Barry Parade, Fortitude Valley ⓣ13 67 89, ⓦwww.virginblue.com.au.

Banks Queensland banking hours are Mon–Fri 9.30am–4pm; major branches in the centre are around Queen and Edward streets.

Bike rental Valet Cycle Hire (ⓣ0408 003 198, ⓦwww.cyclebrisbane.com) delivers bikes direct to your accommodation ($35 for one day, $50 for two and $100 for a week); their van is usually parked inside the Botanic Gardens off Alice Street.

Car rental You'll pay around $40 for a single-day's car rental; longer terms work out from $27 a day, while campervans start at $59 a day for long-term rental. Shop around and read rental conditions before signing; most places will deliver and the minimum age is 21. Abel (ⓣ13 14 29, ⓦwww.abel.com.au); East Coast (ⓣ1800 028 881, ⓦwww.eastcoastcarrentals.com.au); Ezy (ⓣ1300 661 938, ⓦwww.ezycarhire.com.au); Travellers Auto Barn (ⓣ1800/674 374, ⓦwww.travellers-autobarn.com.au) have campers for $60 a day and station wagons for $25 a day; Wicked (ⓣ1800 246 869, ⓦwww.wickedcampers.com.au) specializes in discount long-term campervan rentals.

Cinemas Dendy, 346 George St (ⓣ07/3211 3244, ⓦwww.dendy.com.au); Greater Union, inside the Myer Centre, Queen St Mall (ⓦwww.greaterunion.com.au); Moonlight (ⓦwww.moonlight.com.au) show outdoor screenings of current and classic films through the summer in public parks; Regent, Queen St Mall (ⓦwww.greaterunion.com.au).

Consulates Britain, Level 26, 1 Eagle St ⓣ07/3236 2575; Japan, 12 Creek St ⓣ07/3221 5188; Malaysia, 345 Ann St ⓣ07/3221 1199; Papua New Guinea, 320 Adelaide St ⓣ07/3221 7915; Philippines, 126 Wickham St, Fortitude Valley ⓣ07/3252 8215; Thailand, 87 Annerley Rd ⓣ07/3891 3111.

Hospitals/medical centres Royal Brisbane, Herston Rd, Herston (ⓣ07/3636 8111; buses #126, #144 or #172 from outside City Hall); Travellers' Medical Service, Level 1, 245 Albert St (Mon–Fri 7.30am–7pm, Sat 8.30am–5pm, Sun 9.30am–5pm; ⓣ07/3211 3611, ⓦwww.cbdmedical.com.au), for general services, vaccinations and women's health.

Internet Most hostels have terminals where you can log on from around $4 an hour; the IYHA store, near the *Tinbilly* hostel on George Street, charges just $3 an hour.

Left luggage None at the airport, but available at the Transit Centre for $6 per day per locker.

Markets Eagle St (Sun until 3pm) and Brunswick St Mall (Sat until 4pm) for bits and pieces; South Bank Parklands (Fri night, Sat & Sun until 5pm) for clothing, arts and crafts and a family atmosphere; King George Square Market in front of City Hall (Sun 8am–4pm) is small but has nice contemporary crafts; while the Riverside Centre (Sun) is more "arty" than the rest.

Pharmacies Transit Centre Pharmacy (daily 7am–6pm); Day & Night Pharmacy, Queen St Mall (Mon–Sat 8am–9pm, Sun 10am–5pm).

Police Queensland Police Headquarters is opposite the Transit Centre on Roma St ⓣ07/3364 6464.

Post office 261 Queen St (Mon–Fri 9am–5pm; ⓣ13 13 18 for poste restante; bring photo ID to collect).

Sport Queensland's sport is rugby league, and the Broncos' stomping ground is the Suncorp Stadium on Castlemain St, five minutes' walk west of the city (tickets cost $24–43 and are available from Ticketek outlets or ⓦwww.ticketek.com.au); the event of the year is the State of Origin series in May or June. Cricket matches are played at "The Gabba" on Vulture Street, 3km southeast of the City, and the Queensland Reds rugby union team play at Ballymore Stadium (tickets cost $25–55 available from Ticketmaster 7 outlets or ⓦwww.ticketmaster7.com).

Travel agents Backpackers World Travel, 131 Elizabeth St ⓣ1800 676 763; Flight Centre, 181 George St ⓣ07/3229 0150; STA, 111 Adelaide St ⓣ07/3221 5722; Student Flights, 126 Adelaide St ⓣ07/3229 8449; Trailfinders, 91 Elizabeth St ⓣ07/3229 0887; YHA, 154 Roma St, opposite the Transit Centre ⓣ07/3236 1680.

Work Brisbane offers fairly good employment prospects if you're not too choosy. Many hostels run effective ad hoc agencies for their guests, or for out-of-town work, try Brisbane's WWOOF office at *Banana Benders* backpackers' 118 Petrie Terrace (ⓣ07/3367 1165).

Tours from Brisbane

Most **tours** from Brisbane are pretty straightforward day-trips by bus to take in the highlights of Lamington, Tamborine Mountain, the Sunshine Coast or Gold Coast. Allstate Scenic Tours (☎07/3003 0700, Ⓦwww.daytours.com.au) has been running day-trips to Green Mountain at Lamington National Park for years (daily; $65), and you can arrange to be dropped off on one day and picked up another. Australian Day Tours (☎07/3236 4155, Ⓦwww.daytours.com.au) has a dozen or so day-tours to the Sunshine Coast, Gold Coast theme parks, or Lamington and Tamborine Mountain costing between $80 and $120. Coachliner (☎07/3236 1239) goes to Tamborine Mountain or the Sunshine Coast ($65–100); while Far Horizons (☎07/3284 5475) operates day-trips to Lamington, the Glass House Mountains, or Hinterland cattle stations from around $75.

If you want a bit more depth to your trips, or to visit more distant regions, try the highly recommended Bushwacker (☎1300 559 355, Ⓦwww.bushwacker-ecotours.com.au) for day-trips to various parts of the Gold Coast Hinterland and Glass House Mountains, featuring plenty of wildlife, rainforests, bushtucker and swimming holes ($65). Sunrover Expeditions (☎1800 353 717, Ⓦwww.sunrover.com.au) and Moreton Bay Escapes (☎1300 559 355, Ⓦwww.moretonbayescapes.com.au) offer one- to three-day 4WD safaris to Moreton, North Stradbroke and Fraser islands from around $119 and also get great reviews. Cat-o'-Nine-Tails (see p.380) run trips to St Helena Island.

The Moreton Bay Islands

Offshore from Brisbane are the shallow waters of **Moreton Bay**, famous throughout Australia as the home of the unfortunately named Moreton Bay Bug, which is actually a small, delicious lobster-like crustacean. The largest of the bay's islands, **Moreton** and **North Stradbroke**, are generously endowed with sand, and are just the right distance from the city to make their beaches accessible but seldom crowded. The island of **St Helena** is not somewhere you'd visit for sun and surf, but its prison ruins recall the convict era and make for an interesting day-trip. In the bay itself, look for dolphins, dugong (sea cows) and humpback whales, which pass by in winter en route to their calving grounds up north.

St Helena Island

Small, low and triangular, **St Helena Island** sits 8km from the mouth of the Brisbane River, and from the 1850s until the early twentieth century served as a **prison**. The government found it particularly useful for political trouble-makers, such as the leaders of the 1891 shearers' strike and, with more justice, a couple of slave-trading "Blackbirder" captains.

A tour of the penal settlement, tagged the "Hell Hole of the South Pacific" during its working life, leaves you thankful you missed out on the "good old days". Escape attempts (there were only ever three) were deterred by sharks, whose presence was actively encouraged around the island. Evidence of the prisoners' industry and self-sufficiency is still to be seen in the stone houses, as well as in the remains of a sugar mill, paddocks, wells, and an ingenious lime kiln built into the shoreline. The Deputy Superintendent's house has been turned into a bare **museum** (reached from the jetty on a mini-tramway), displaying a ball and chain lying in a corner and photographs from the prison era. Outside, the two cemeteries have been desecrated: many headstones were carried off as souvenir coffee-tables, and the corpses dug up and sold as medical specimens. The remaining stones comprise simple concrete crosses stamped with a number for the prisoners, or inscribed marble tablets for the warders and their children.

Cat-o'-Nine-Tails offers day-trips (Mon–Fri departing 9.30am and returning 2.15pm, Sat & Sun departing 11am and returning at 4pm; $69 including lunch; ⓣ07/3893 1240, ⓦwww.sthelenaisland.com.au) and **night tours** (departs some Friday and Saturday nights; $79 includes three-course meal), the latter including a theatrical sound-and-light show on the island. Advance bookings are essential. Boats leave around 15km east of the city from the public jetty in the suburb of **Manly**, a ten-minute walk from Manly train station – from Brisbane, you can reach Manly direct from Roma Street, Central and South Brisbane train stations.

Moreton Island

A 38-kilometre-long, narrow band of stabilized, partly wooded sand dunes, **Moreton Island**'s faultless beaches are distinctly underpopulated for much of the year, and perfect for lounging, surfing or fishing. Many people just come over for the day, but it's also possible to camp or stay in a resort, and even bring your own vehicle across – make sure it's a four-wheel drive, however.

The main arrival point on the island is **TANGALOOMA**, a small settlement of wooden houses and a few shops midway along Moreton's west coast. Offshore here are a set of wrecks, deliberately sunk to create an artificial reef, providing fine **snorkelling** at high tide. Nearby, *Tangalooma Wild Dolphin Resort* (ⓣ07/3268 6333, ⓦwww.tangalooma.com; ⑥) is a casual, upmarket affair with a range of rooms and units that incorporate parts of a former **whaling station**; they organize daily **dolphin feeding** for wild dolphins who rock up every evening for a handout, and a short 4WD tour and sand-tobogganing trip for $25. The resort is also the only place on the island that has a restaurant and serves cold drinks – tidy dress is required. There's a National Parks **campsite** nearby (with water, showers and toilets), which gets as crowded as anywhere on the island – permits are available from the ranger based at *Tangalooma Resort* (ⓣ07/3408 2710). A three-kilometre track heads south from Tangalooma to the **desert**, where the dunes are a great place to try **sand-tobogganing**.

With your own vehicle, or on foot if you don't mind hiking, you can take the ten-kilometre track from Tangalooma across to Moreton's more attractive eastern side, where the beach has good **surf** and it's less crowded. At **Eagers Creek**, at the end of the track, there's another campsite and a five-kilometre return trip up sandy **Mount Tempest**'s 280-metre peak – an exhausting climb. Head 10km north up the beach from Eagers Creek, and you'll find Blue Lagoon, the largest of the island's freshwater lakes, only 500m from the beach and adjacent to the smaller, picturesque **Honeyeater Lake**. Blessed with shady trees, the dunes behind the beach make an ideal place to camp, and the site is supplied with water, showers and toilets. Dolphins come in close to shore – a practice that Moreton's Aborigines turned to their advantage by using them to chase fish into the shallows. Writing in the 1870s about his life in Brisbane, Tom Petrie reported that the Ngugi men would beat the surf with their spears, and:

> **By and by, as in response, porpoises would be seen as they rose to the surface (…) making for the shore and in front of them schools of tailor fish. It may seem wonderful, but they were apparently driving the fish towards the land. When they came near, [the Ngugi] would run out into the surf, and with their spears would jab down here and there at the fish, at times even getting two on one spear, so plentiful were they.**

The north and south ends of the islands are only accessible from the Tangalooma area by four-wheel drive, though there are tiny settlements at both: **BULWER**, on the island's northeast corner, comprises a cluster of weatherboard "weekenders" and a store stocking fuel and beer and providing basic **accommodation** in six-person units (Ⓣ07/3203 6399; ⑤); while right at Moreton's southern tip, tiny **KOORINGAL** has a store offering fuel, supplies and drinks from their bar (daily 8am–midnight), as well as **holiday units** that sleep up to ten (Ⓣ07/3217 9965, Ⓔmoretonbeach@optusnet.com.au; ⑤).

Getting to Moreton

Tangalooma Wild Dolphin Resort operate **fast ferries** direct to the resort from their wharf, 8km out of the city at the end of Holt Street, off Kingsford Smith Drive at Pinkenba (daily at 8am, 10am and 5pm; $65 open return). For an extra $5 you can book a pick-up from the Transit Centre to the wharf when you make your booking.

The other main option is MiCat (Ⓣ07/3909 3333, Ⓦwww.micat.com.au), a huge modern catamaran crossing daily at 8.30am to the wrecks just north of *Tangalooma Wild Dolphin Resort* from their wharf at 14 Howard Smith Drive, Lytton – you can get here from Brisbane in an hour by catching the train to Wynnum Central from the Transit Centre, then a bus from outside the station on Andrew Street to the wharf. Fares for the catamaran are $44 for a day return or $30 each way; a four-wheel drive and two passengers cost $150 return.

Aside from **tours** listed in the box on p.379, MiCat also offers a range of day and overnight trips, including sandboarding and four-wheel-driving, and can also organize National Park **camping permits** at $4 a night. If you're planning to stay a while, note that there are **no banks** on the island, and that supplies are expensive – it's best to be self-sufficient and have enough water if you are camping. Before you go in the sea, remember that the beaches aren't patrolled and there are no shark nets. The worst times to visit are at Christmas and Easter, when up to a thousand vehicles crowd onto the island all at once.

North Stradbroke Island

North Stradbroke Island is, at 40km long, the largest and most established of the bay's islands, with sealed roads and the fully serviced townships of Dunwich, Amity and Point Lookout. Ninety percent of "**Straddie**" is given over to mining the island's titanium-rich sands, and the majority of the 3200 residents are employees of Consolidated Rutile Ltd. The mine sites south of Amity, and in the central west and south, are far from exhausted but their future is precarious, thanks to an oversupply on the world market. Other industries focus on timber, a by-product of preparing land for mining, and, increasingly, tourism.

Stradbroke's **diving** is renowned for congregations of the increasingly rare grey nurse shark, along with moray eels, dopey leopard sharks, and summertime manta rays. Courses, dives and accommodation can be arranged through *Manta Lodge* (see p.382)

Unless you need to fuel up or visit the bank, there's little to keep you at **Dunwich**, Straddie's ferry port. Two sealed roads head out of town, east through the island's centre towards Main Beach, or north to Amity and Point Lookout. The road through the centre passes two lakes – the second and smaller of these, **Blue Lake**, is a national park and source of fresh water for the island's wildlife, which is most visible early in the morning. Beyond Blue Lake you have to cross the **Eighteen Mile Swamp** to reach **Main Beach** and, though there's a causeway, the rest of the route is for 4WDs only. You can **camp** behind the beach anywhere south of the causeway (north of it is mining company land), but be prepared for the mosquitoes that swarm around the mangroves; the southernmost point is an angling and wildlife Mecca, with birdlife and kangaroos lounging around on the beaches.

Heading north from Dunwich, it's 11km to where the road forks left for a further 6km to **AMITY**, a sleepy place built around a jetty at the northwestern point of the island; there's a store, **campsite** and *Sea Shanties* at 9A Cook St (ⓣ07/3409 7161, ⓦwww.seashanties.com.au; ③), which offers low-key beachfront **accommodation** in self-contained cabins sleeping four (bring your own sleeping bag or bedding).

Point Lookout

Stay on the road from Dunwich past the Amity turn-off, and it's another 10km to **POINT LOOKOUT**, at Straddie's northeastern tip. The township spreads out around the island's single-rock headland, overlooking a string of beaches, a sports pub, a takeaway pizza place, a store, some cafés and various **places to stay**. Top of the range are *Straddie Views B&B* at 26 Cummings Parade (ⓣ07/3409 8875; ⑤), with a nice veranda offering ocean views; and *Samarinda* (ⓣ07/3409 8785, ⓦwww.samarinda.com.au; ⑤), with motel rooms and two-bedroom units. At the other end of the scale, *Manta Lodge*, at 1 Eastcoast Rd (ⓣ07/3409 8888, ⓦwww.stradbrokeislandscuba.com.au; dorms $27, rooms ④), offers budget rooms and has surfboards, bikes and fishing gear for rent; they also organize scuba diving, and 4WD, walking and trail-riding trips. *Stradbroke Tourist Park* (ⓣ07/3409 8127; four- to six-person cabins ⑤) is the best of the local caravan parks.

Point Lookout's **beaches** are picturesque, with shallow, protected swimming along the shore. Home and Cylinder beaches are both patrolled and, therefore, crowded during holiday weekends; if you don't mind swimming in unwatched waters, head for the more easterly Deadman's Beach or Frenchman's Bay. On the headland above the township, there are fine views and the chance to see loggerhead turtles and dolphins; from the walking track around North Gorge down to Main Beach you might see whales, if you have binoculars.

Getting to the island, and getting around

Island ferries leave from Toondah Harbour at **Cleveland** – take the train to Cleveland from Brisbane's Transit Centre, then catch the special red-and-yellow National Bus to the harbour ($2). Stradbroke Ferries ($17 return per person by water taxi, $112 return per car by barge; ⓣ07/3286 2666, ⓦwww.stradbrokeferries.com.au) and Sea Stradbroke ($10 return per person, $112 return per car; ⓣ07/3488 9777, ⓦwww.seastradbroke.com) cross to Dunwich around fourteen times daily between them.

To **get around** the island, the Dunwich–Point Lookout **bus** connects with all water taxis ($9.50 return), and various operators offer **4WD safaris**: Sunrover Expeditions (ⓣ07/3880 0719, ⓦwww.sunrover.com.au) and Straddie Kingfisher Tours (ⓣ07/3409 9502, ⓦwww.straddiekingfishertours.com.au) both come recommended. Some roads on Stradbroke are open to mining vehicles only, so drivers should look out for the signs. **Off-roading** through the centre on non-designated roads is not advised: quite apart from the damage caused to the dune systems, the sand is very soft and having your vehicle pulled out will be very expensive. Driving on the beach requires a 4WD and a **permit**, which can be obtained from Stradbroke Island Tourism on Junner Street in Dunwich ($15 for 48 hours; ⓣ07/3409 9555, ⓦwww.stradbroketourism.com).

The Gold Coast

Beneath a jagged skyline shaped by countless high-rise beach-front apartments, the **Gold Coast** is Australia's Miami Beach or Costa del Sol, a striking contrast to Brisbane, only an hour away to the north. Aggressively superficial, it's not the place to go if you're seeking peace and quiet, but its sheer brashness can be fun for a couple of days – perhaps as a weekend break from Brisbane. There's little variation on the beach and nightclub scene, however, and if you're concerned this will leave you jaded, bored or broke, you'd be better off avoiding this corner of the state altogether.

The coast forms a virtually unbroken beach 40km long, from **South Stradbroke Island** past **Surfers Paradise** and **Burleigh Heads** to the New South Wales border at **Coolangatta**. The **beaches**, nominally why everyone comes to the Gold Coast, swarm with bathers and board-riders all year round: **surfing** first blossomed here in the 1930s and the key surf beaches at Coolangatta, Burleigh Heads and South Stradbroke still pull daily crowds of veterans and novices. In the meantime, other attractions have sprung up, notably the **club and party** scene centred on Surfers Paradise, and several action-packed **theme parks**, domestic holiday blackspots mostly based about 15km northwest of the town.

With around three hundred days of sunshine each year there's little "off-season" as such. **Rain** can, however, fall at any time during the year, including midwinter – when it's usually dry in the rest of the state – but even if the crowds do thin out a little, they reappear in time for the **Gold Coast Indy** car race in October and then continue to swell, peaking over Christmas and New Year. The end of the school year in mid-November also heralds the phenomenon that is **Schoolies Week**, when thousands of high-school leavers from across the country ditch exam rooms and flock to Surfers for a few days of hard partying, a rite of passage which causes an annual budget-accommodation crisis.

Getting there and around

From Brisbane, local buses from Roma Street Transit Centre to the Gold Coast include Kirkland's (Ⓣ1300 367 077), which runs about eight times daily to Southport, Surfers, Burleigh Heads and Coolangatta; and Coachtrans (Ⓣ13 12 30), which runs three services daily to the same places. Coachtrans also organizes transfers direct **from Brisbane airport** to Gold Coast accommodation or theme parks; transport to the latter from central Brisbane accommodation can be arranged as well (all from $37). You can also get to the Gold Coast from Brisbane airport and the city by taking the **Citytrain** to Nerang station, where you pick up Surfside Bus connections on to Surfers Paradise – a total cost around $27.

From New South Wales, the coastal highway enters Queensland at Coolangatta, where you'll also find the **Gold Coast airport**. The Gold Coast Tourist Shuttle (Ⓣ07/5574 5111, Ⓦwww.gcshuttle.com.au) runs buses to all points between the airport and Surfers Paradise for $17 one way, while Con-X-ion (Ⓣ07/5556 9888, Ⓦwww.con-x-ion.com) offers theme-park transfers.

Getting around, Surfside Buses run a 24-hour bus service (up to six times hourly; timetables available from bus drivers, on Ⓣ13 12 30 or at Ⓦwww.surfside.com.au) along the Gold Coast Highway from Tweed Heads and

Coolangatta to Surfers Paradise and out to all the theme parks. Their various **passes** give unlimited travel for between three and fourteen days ($12–114). Otherwise, you'll need to take a **taxi** or rent a vehicle; there are more details in accounts of the individual resorts.

Surfers Paradise

Spiritually, if not geographically, **SURFERS PARADISE** is the heart of the Gold Coast, the place where its aims and aspirations are most evident. For the

△ Skyline, Surfers Paradise

residents, this involves making money by providing services and entertainment for tourists; visitors reciprocate by parting with their cash. All around and irrespective of what you're doing – sitting on the beach, **partying** in one of the frenetic nightclubs along Orchid or Cavill avenues, shopping for clothes or even finding a bed – the pace is brash and glib. Don't come here expecting to be allowed to relax; subtlety is nonexistent and you'll find that enjoying Surfers depends largely on how much it bothers you having the party mood rammed down your throat.

Surfers' **beaches** have been attracting tourists for over a century, though the town only started developing along commercial lines during the 1950s when the first multistorey beach-front apartments were built. The demand for views over the ocean led to ever-higher towers which began to encroach on the dunes; together with the sheer volume of people attracted here, this has caused **erosion** problems along the entire coast. But none of this really matters. Though Surfers Paradise is a firm tribute to the successful marketing of the ideal Aussie lifestyle as an eternal beach party, most people no longer come here for the sun and sand but simply because everyone else does.

Arrival and information

Surfers' **bus station** (6am–10pm) is on Beach Road on the corner of the highway, one street down from Cavill Avenue. Coachtrans run to Brisbane (Ⓣ13 12 30); Kirkland's to Brisbane, Byron Bay and Lismore (Ⓣ1300 367 077); and Greyhound Australia (Ⓣ13 20 30) and Premier (Ⓣ13 34 10) right down the east coast. At the bus station you'll find luggage lockers, bus-company desks and an accommodation information counter. The **tourist office** is in a booth on Cavill Avenue (Mon–Fri 8.30am–5.30pm, Sat 8.30am–5pm, Sun 9am–4pm; Ⓣ1300 309 440, Ⓦwww.verygc.com), but the accommodation desk is usually just as well-informed.

Security is worth bearing in mind: many people come here simply to prey on tourists, especially around Christmas and Easter, or on teenagers during Schoolies Week in November. Don't leave vehicles unlocked at any time, don't take valuables onto the beach, and don't wander alone at night; muggings are common, especially around nightclubs, so take advantage of the courtesy buses run by hostels.

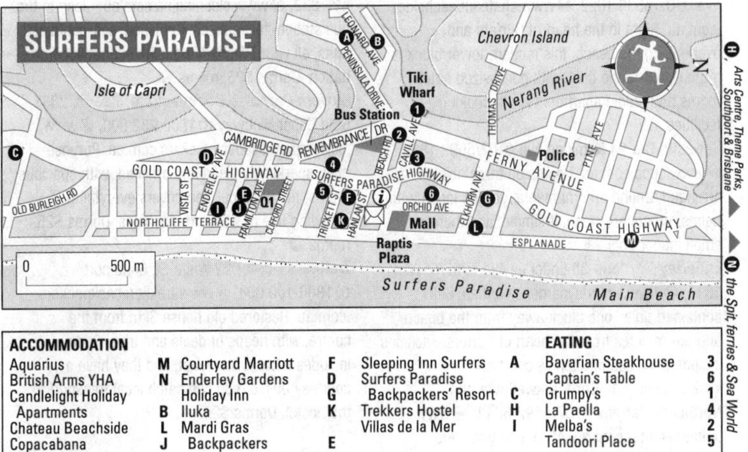

Accommodation

Surfers' **accommodation** is split between high-end, high-rise **hotels**; lower-rise **apartment blocks** that can be an excellent deal for a group, though you usually have to stay for a minimum of three nights; and **backpacker hostels**, which tend to be very hard-sell – don't expect any peace until you've signed up for trips to nightclubs, parties and beach events. Whatever you choose, **book in advance**. There are simply too many possibilities to give a comprehensive list; those below are central and good value. If you want to **camp**, you'll have to head south to the quieter sections of the Gold Coast, though all campsites get booked solid through the Christmas break.

Hotels

Courtyard Marriott Cnr Surfers Paradise Boulevard and Hanlan St ⓣ1800 074 317, ⓦwww.marriott.com.au/oolcy. Very flash, very central international chain offering a good deal if you're looking for something in this sort of market. ❼

Holiday Inn 22 View Ave ⓣ07/5579 1000, ⓦwww.holidayinnsurfersparadise.com.au. Another reliable big chain set just a short walk back from the beach, and offering online booking discounts. ❼

Iluka Cnr Hanlan St and Esplanade ⓣ07/5539 9155. Medium-sized tower with beach views from the front, offering hotel rooms and apartment units with kitchen. ❺

Motels and apartments

Candlelight Holiday Apartments 22–24 Leonard Ave ⓣ07/5538 1277, ⓦwww.candlelightholiday apartments.com.au. Very pleasant, self-contained one-bedroom units in a quiet street close to the bus station with very helpful and friendly owners. Minimum three-night stay. ❺

Chateau Beachside Cnr Esplanade and Elkhorn Ave ⓣ07/5538 1022, ⓦwww.chateaubeachside .com.au. Right in the heart of Surfers and overlooking the beach, this modern tower block is a great mid-range deal, with good-sized hotel rooms and studio apartments with cooking facilities. ❺

Copacabana 24 Hamilton Ave ⓣ07/5592 1866, ⓦwww.copa.com.au. Rooms on three levels arranged around an ornamental garden laden with palms; rooms are clean, if simple, and there's a small indoor pool. ❻

Enderley Gardens 38 Enderley Ave ⓣ07/5570 1511, ⓦwww.enderleygardens.com.au. Self-contained units, one block away from the beach and ten minutes from the heart of Surfers. Facilities include pool, spa and tennis court. ❻

Villas de la Mer Cnr Markwell Ave and Northcliffe Terrace ⓣ07/5592 6644, ⓦwww .villasdelamer.com.au. Attractive two- and three-bedroom apartments in a three-storey security complex. Simple but modern and well furnished. ❻

Hostels

Aquarius 44 Queen St, Southport ⓣ1800 229 955, ⓦwww.aquariusbackpackers.com.au. Offers a tiny TV lounge on each floor, pool and communal kitchen, plus a courtesy bus to and from Surfers. Small four- and six-bed dorms. Dorms $25, rooms ❸

British Arms YHA 70 Sea World Drive ⓣ07/5571 1776 or 1800 680 269, ⓦwww.yha .com.au. Well placed for Sea World, about 5km north of the centre. Good facilities, plus a lively English bar and grill serving up pub fare, occasional entertainment and a range of beers till late. Dorms $26, rooms ❸

Mardi Gras Backpackers 28 Hamilton Ave ⓣ1800 801 230, ⓦwww.goldcoastbackpackers .com.au. Secure, purpose-built hostel, with safe car park. Facilities include a small kitchen and a bar, but there's no pool and the place feels a bit sterile. Four-bed dorms $25, tiny doubles ❸

Sleeping Inn Surfers 26 Peninsula Drive ⓣ1800 817 832, ⓦwww.sleepinginn.com.au. Close to the bus station, these nicely furnished, self-contained units, all with TV, provide quality budget accommodation. Dorms $25, rooms ❸

Surfers Paradise Backpackers' Resort 2837 Gold Coast Highway ⓣ1800 282 800, ⓦwww .surfersparadisebackpackers.com.au. Purpose-built, sparklingly clean and efficient, with spacious rooms; the price per bed covers everything, including use of washing machines. Dorms $25, rooms ❸

Trekkers Hostel 22 White St, Southport ⓣ1800 100 004, ⓦwww.trekkersbackpackers .com.au. Restored old house 3km from the centre, with heaps of deals and trips. Price includes a basic breakfast, and they have a courtesy bus, or you can catch local transport to the hostel. Dorms $25.

The City

Downtown Surfers Paradise is a thin ribbon of partially reclaimed land between the ocean and the **Nerang River** which – as the Broadwater – flows north, parallel with the beach, past **the Spit** and South Stradbroke Island into the choked channels at the bottom end of Moreton Bay. Reclaimed land in the river forms islands whose names reflect the fantasies of their founders – Isle of Capri, Sorrento, Miami Keys – and which have become much-sought-after real estate.

From its dingiest club to its best restaurant, Surfers exudes entertainment, and at times – most notoriously at New Year and Christmas – you can spend 24 hours a day out on the town. Another thing you'll spend is money: the only free venue is the beach and with such a variety of distractions it can be financial suicide venturing out too early in the day – the city is full of tourists staggering around at noon with terrible hangovers and empty wallets, complaining how expensive their holiday has become. The area around **Orchid Avenue** and partially pedestrianized **Cavill Avenue** is a bustle of activity from early morning – when the first surfers head down to the beach and the shops open – to after midnight, when there's a constant exchange of bodies between the bars and nightclubs. If you spend any length of time in town, you'll get to know the district intimately.

Surfers' tower-block cityscape makes an immediate impression, but the stakes in who can build highest and so block their neighbours' view of the beach have recently been upped considerably: occupying an entire block on the highway between Clifford Street and Hamilton Avenue, **Q1** is – at 80 storeys and 322.5m high – the world's tallest residential building. You can ride the lift up 78 storeys in 42.7 seconds to the **observation deck** (Fri & Sat 8am–midnight, Sun–Thurs 8am–8.30pm; $17.50) for a drink at the bar and stupendous views down on the puny high-rises below, the endless strip of golden sand fringing the sea, and inland as far south as Mount Warning in New South Wales.

Surfing the Gold Coast

As locals will tell you, the Gold Coast has some of the best **surfing beaches** in the world. In terms of consistency this might be true – on any given day there will be good surf somewhere along the coast – with two-hundred-metre-long sand-bottom point breaks and rideable waves peaking at about four metres in prime conditions.

The coast is known for its **barrels**, particularly during the summer storm season when the winds shift around to the north; in winter the swell is smaller but more reliable, making it easier to learn to surf. A rule of thumb for finding the best surf is to **follow the wind**: head to the north end of the coast when the wind blows from the north, and the south when it comes from the south. Generally, you'll find the **best swell** along the southern beaches, and on South Stradbroke Island. Sea temperatures range between 26°C in December and 17°C in June, so a 2–3mm wetsuit is adequate. Hard-core surfies come for Christmas and the cyclone season, though spring is usually the busiest time. On the subject of **general safety**, all beaches as far north as Surfers are patrolled – look for the signs – and while sharks might worry you, more commonplace hostility is likely to come from the local surfies, who form tight-knit cliques with very protective attitudes towards their patches.

For expert **tuition**, **tours**, or **advice** anywhere on the Gold Coast, contact Go Ride a Wave (☎1300 132 441, Ⓦwww.gorideawave.com.au); beginners pay around $60 for a two-hour session. **Competitions** or events are held somewhere along the coast on most weekends, advertised through local surf shops. To try your hand at **kitesurfing**, another popular Gold Coast pastime, contact Pureaqua (☎07/5571 1622, Ⓦwww.pureaqua.com.au) on the Broadwater at Southport – beginners pay $185 for a three-hour intro package.

Across the Esplanade, the **beach** is all you could want as a place to recover from your night out; it runs 5km or more north from here via **Main Beach** to **the Spit**, so finding empty sand shouldn't be too difficult. If you're feeling energetic, seek out a game of volleyball or head for the surf: the swell here is good in a northerly wind, but most of the time it's better for boogie-boards.

The theme parks

All the theme parks are a bundle of fun, especially for children, and are easy to spend a full day at – Wet 'n' Wild takes some beating on a hot day though. All are located to the north of town on Surfside and Gold Coast Shuttle bus routes. Check out the park websites for the latest discounted deals on entry and **combination passes** to more than one park.

Around 5km north of Surfers at the Spit, **Sea World** (daily 10am–5pm; $64; access on the Surfside Bus from the highway; Ⓦwww.seaworld.com.au) is the longest running of the Gold Coast's theme parks. Besides various stomach-churning rides, the park features immaculately trained dolphins and killer whales, and helps rehabilitate stranded wild dolphins for later release.

Movie World (daily 10am–5pm; $64; Ⓦwww.movieworld.com.au), on the Pacific Highway 14km north of Surfers, is a slice of Hollywood featuring studio tours, Western shows and stunt demonstrations. Near Movie World, **Wet 'n' Wild** (daily 10am–4.30pm or later; $42; Ⓦwww.wetnwild.com.au) has a series of pools linked by vicious water slides – the back-breaking "twister" and the 25-metre-tall, high-speed slide alone are worth the entrance fee. **Dreamworld** (daily 10am–5pm; $64; Ⓦwww.dreamworld.com.au), also on the Pacific Highway at Coomera, 17km north of Surfers Paradise, has a violent double-loop roller-coaster and a fairground atmosphere, as well as a collection of hand-reared tigers in a large enclosure.

Although not strictly speaking a theme park, a themed show which gets great reviews is the **Australian Outback Spectacular**, located on the Pacific Highway between Wet 'n' Wild and Movie World (Tues–Sun; $89; bookings essential; Ⓣ13 33 86, Ⓦwww.outbackspectacular.com.au). This two-hour evening show features stunning demonstrations of horsemanship, camel races, a cattle round-up, plus a huge meal.

Eating

Surfers has somewhere to eat wherever you look, though most places are forgettable **snack bars and cafés**. In fact, there are surprisingly few **restaurants**, which have mostly migrated south to Broadbeach Mall or north to Broadwater and Southport, where there's usually a Porsche or two parked along Tedder Avenue's trendy café strip. For **supplies**, there's a supermarket downstairs in the Centro Centre (on Cavill Avenue) and a 24-hour Night Owl store on the highway near Trickett Street. If a phone number is listed, it's best to book.

Bavarian Steakhouse Cavill Ave, towards Tiki Wharf Ⓣ07/5531 7150. Wood-panelled theme restaurant on several floors, where you can wolf down steins of beer and plates of beef while staff dressed in leather and lace pump away on Bavarian brass instruments. Good fun if you're in the mood and fair value – about $28 for steak, salad and fries.

Captain's Table Upstairs at 26 Orchid Ave Ⓣ07/5531 5766. Award-winning restaurant with excellent seafood variations – the $22 plate of delicious barbecued Moreton Bay Bugs should not be missed. Get in before 6.30pm for a discount and table with a view.

Grumpy's Tiki Village, at the river end of Cavill Avenue Ⓣ07/5531 6177. Casual "Pacific Island"-style decor and views out over the Nerang River are a great setting for wolfing down seafood dishes from around the globe. Not cheap – even a plain grilled fish costs $30 – but large portions and good atmosphere.

La Paella 3114 Gold Coast Highway. Tiny yet lively Spanish restaurant with excellent tapas for $15, sangría by the bucket and sumptuous veal casserole for $25. Dinner only.

Melba's 46 Cavill Ave ☎07/5592 6922. Ambitious café-restaurant attached to the nightclub of the same name, with a mix of Mediterranean-style light meals and snacks served – unusually for Surfers – at pavement tables. The seafood fettuccine and Moroccan duck are the chef's specialities, with mains between $25 and $35. Daily 7am–5am.

Tandoori Place 7–9 Trickett St ☎07/5592 1004. Fast-food ambience, but actually better than first impressions would suggest; their sweet curries are tasty, and they have a limited vegetarian menu. Most main dishes cost around $20.

Nightlife and entertainment

Next to the beach, Surfers' **nightclubs** and **bars** – mostly located in Orchid Avenue – are its reason to be. Initially, particularly if you're staying at a hostel or have picked up a free pass somewhere, your choice will most likely be influenced by the various **deals** on entry and drinks. In addition, there are booze-cruise nightclub **tours** offered by various places for around $60, which includes transport and often a club pass valid for the rest of your stay. Opening times are from around 6pm to 3am or later; bars are open daily and clubs from Thursday to Sunday.

In addition to the nightspots below, the Gold Coast often hosts big **dance parties** and live **music festivals** (Good Vibrations, in February, is one of the biggest), usually held at outdoor venues such as Doug Jennings Park at the Spit. You can find out the latest in the free Brisbane **magazines** *Scene*, *Rave* and *Time Off* (see p.376) and also in the more locally-oriented *Tsunami*.

Cocktails and Dreams Orchid Ave. Nightly dance crowd in the late teen bracket, who party against a background of neon and disco lighting.

Fever 26 Orchid Ave. The best place for house and dance on the coast, with an ever-changing array of local and international DJs.

Howl at the Moon Upstairs at Centro Centre on Cavill Ave ☎07/5527 5522. Hugely popular restaurant, bar and nightclub with two live pianists performing their own sing-along renditions of popular hits. Daily 8pm–2am, bookings advisable.

Melba's 46 Cavill Ave. Big and relatively upmarket nightclub with a monstrous, atmospherically lit bar and powerful sound system – plus a noticeably older crowd than the rest of Surfers' clubs.

The Party At *The Mark*, Orchid Ave. Live rock bands on Friday and Sunday (with a variable cover charge); DJs for the rest of the week.

Rose and Crown Raptis Plaza, Cavill Ave. Despite the name, more a club than a pub, though it comes complete with a couple of pool tables and a long bar. It's a popular place to kick off the evening; entertainment varies from decent local bands to DJs and strip shows (male and female).

The Shack Orchid Ave. Popular for its pool tables, plus regular live bands, DJ sessions and regular drinks specials.

Shooters Orchid Ave, next to *Cocktails and Dreams*. Crowds heading for more serious dance spots start out here for a game of pool and a few drinks; a definite stop on the backpacker bar-crawl trail.

Surfers Beergarden Cavill Ave, opposite Orchid Ave. Good for live music, with local and interstate band talent on Thurs and Sat nights.

Troccadero 7–9 Trickett St ☎07/5570 2100. Surfers' live-music mainstay, often attracting major Australian touring bands. There's also a packed and sweaty nightclub here from Thurs to Sat, with a cover charge of $9.

Listings

Car rental CY Rent a Car, 9 Trickett St ⓦwww.cyrentacar.com.au; East Coast Car Rentals, 25 Elkhorn Ave ⓦwww.eastcoastcarrentals.com.au; Surfers Paradise Car Hire, inside the Transit Centre ⓦwww.surfersparadisecarhire.com; Red Back Rentals, inside the Transit Centre, Beach Rd ⓦwww.redbackrentals.com.au; Red Rocket, Centre Arcade, Orchid Ave ⓦwww.redrocketrentals.com.au.

Hospitals and medical centres Gold Coast Hospital, Nerang St, Southport ☎07/5571 8211; Gold Coast Medical Centre, Centro Centre, on Cavill Avenue ☎07/5538 8099.

Pharmacy Piaza Shopping Plaza, cnr Elkhorn Ave and Gold Coast Highway (daily 7am–midnight).

Post office The main post office is in the Centro Centre on Cavill Avenue.

Surf rental Surfworld, Centro Centre, on Cavill Avenue ☎07/5538 4825. Typical prices are $25 a day for board rental, plus credit-card deposit. For tuition, see the box on p.387.

Taxis ☎13 10 08.

Gold Coast tours and cruises

Land-based **day-trips** from the Gold Coast concentrate on various Hinterland national parks (see p.393). Bushwacker Ecotours (ⓣ07/3871 0057, ⓦwww.bushwacker-ecotours.com.au), Mountain Trek Adventures (ⓣ07/5578 3157) and Southern Cross (ⓣ1800 067 367, ⓦwww.sc4wd.com.au) are all in the adventurous bracket, with 4WD day-tours and night-time wildlife-spotting ventures ($85–125). Mountain Coach Company (ⓣ07/5524 4249) run up daily to O'Reilly's at Lamington ($48 return), and Scenic Hinterland Tours (ⓣ07/5531 5536, ⓦwww.hinterlandtours.com.au) do comfortable trips to almost all the Hinterland national parks (from around $55 return).

The following explore the Nerang River and seafront on one-hour to half-day **cruises**: Adventure Duck (ⓣ07/5528 4544), a unique amphibious bus, departs eight times daily from Orchid Avenue for an hour-long trip ($32); Bluefire (ⓣ07/5557 8888) offer an evening-meal cruise ($85 includes a seafood buffet); and Wyndham Cruises (ⓣ07/5539 9299) spend a couple of hours on the water for $39. See below for trips to South Stradbroke Island.

South Stradbroke Island

South Stradbroke Island is a twenty-kilometre-long, narrow strip of sand, separated from North Stradbroke Island by the 1896 cyclone and, as apartment buildings edge closer, doomed to become an extension of the Gold Coast. For now, though, South Stradbroke's relatively isolated and quiet beaches offer something of an escape from the mainland, though most day-trippers come over simply to get plastered in the bar at *South Stradbroke Island Resort* (ⓣ07/5577 3311, ⓦwww.ssir.com.au; rooms ❺; four-bed cabins ❻). Alternative accommodation is available at the new *Couran Cove Resort* (ⓣ07/5597 9000, ⓦwww.couran.com; cabins and rooms ❼), which offers a much more exclusive atmosphere, and doesn't welcome day-guests. There's also some of the coast's finest **surf** to ride along the southeast shore, though local surfies are notoriously protective.

Day-trippers can get to South Stradbroke on the *South Stradbroke Island Resort* fast **ferry** (daily 10.30am, return between 2.30pm and 5pm depending on the day; $25) from Runaway Bay Marina, 5km north of Surfers on Bayview Street – bookings (through the *Resort*) are essential.

Surfers Paradise to Currumbin

The central section of the Gold Coast lacks any real focus. Haphazardly developed and visually unattractive, it exists very much in the shadow of Surfers Paradise, but can't match its intensity. The highway is just a continuous maze of crowded, multi-lane traffic systems and drab buildings which lose momentum the further south you drive, but once you leave the road there are fine **beaches**, two **wildlife sanctuaries** and – unbelievably amidst all the commotion and noise – a tiny **national park**, which preserves the coast's original environment.

Burleigh Heads National Park and around

Around 7km south of Surfers, **Burleigh Heads** consists of a traffic bottleneck where the highway dodges between the beach and a rounded headland; there can be very good surf here but the rocks make it rough for novices. Sixty years ago, before the bitumen and paving took over, this was all dense eucalypt and vine forest, the last fragment of which survives as **Burleigh Head National Park**. Entrance is on foot from the car park on the Esplanade, or turn sharply at the lights below the hill just south of the headland for the **tourist office** (daily 10am–3pm).

Geologically, Burleigh Heads stems from the prehistoric eruptions of the Mount Warning volcano (p.287), 30km to the southwest. Lava surfaced through vents, cooling to tall hexagonal basalt columns, now mostly tumbled and covered in vines. Rainforest colonized the richer volcanic soils, while stands of red gum grew in weaker sandy loam; along the eastern seafront there's a patch of exposed heathland bordered by groups of pandanus, and a beach along the mouth of Tallebudgera Creek. This diversity is amazing considering the minimal space, but urban encroachment has seriously affected the **wildlife** – you can still see butterflies, scrub turkeys and sunbathing dragons though.

Less than 2km inland on West Burleigh Road, the **David Fleay Wildlife Park** (daily 9am–5pm; $15.40; take the Surfside Bus; ⓣ07/5576 2411) is an informal park with boardwalks through forest pens and plenty of rangers at hand to answer your questions. The late David Fleay was the first person to persuade platypus to breed in captivity and the park has a special section devoted to this curious animal, along with crocodiles, koalas, glider possums, and plenty of birds. They have various guided tours through the day, including through their **nocturnal house** – a chance to see normally somnambulant Australian wildlife in action.

Currumbin Beach and Sanctuary

A further 6km past Burleigh Heads, **Currumbin Beach** is a good, relatively undeveloped stretch of coast between Elephant Rock and Currumbin Point, and given a breeze there are usually some decent rollers to ride. Just to the north, **Palm Beach** is more sheltered. *Vikings*, in the surf-club building below Elephant Rock, serves Chinese **food**, or you can fill up on regular pub fare at the *Palm Beach Surf Club* along the beach front.

CURRUMBIN is a leftover from the days before high-density development, just a few streets of houses off the highway down a bumpy lane – though a major housing estate is on the drawing board. The focus is **Currumbin Sanctuary**, on Tomewin Street (daily 8am–5pm; $29.50; ⓦwww.currumbin-sanctuary.org.au), which was started in 1946 by Alex Griffiths, who developed this seventy-acre reserve of forest and water as a native wildlife refuge. There are the usual feeding times (throughout the day), shows and tame kangaroos but the park's strongest point is its beautiful natural surroundings, best experienced from the **elevated walkways** through the forest, where you'll see koalas, tree kangaroos and birds at eye-level. A Saturday morning **farmers' market** sets up opposite the sanctuary once or twice a month.

Coolangatta

On the Queensland–New South Wales border 10km south of Currumbin, **COOLANGATTA** merges seamlessly with Tweed Heads (in New South Wales) along Boundary Street. With only a giant concrete plinth just off the main road marking the border, you'll probably make the crossing between states without realizing it. Unless it's New Year, when everyone takes advantage of the one-hour time difference between the states to celebrate twice, most travellers bypass Coolangatta completely; in doing so, they miss some of the best surf, least crowded beaches and the only place along the Gold Coast which can boast a real "local" community. Even the motel towers on Point Danger are well spaced, and the general ambience is that of a small seaside town.

Arrival, information and accommodation

The **Gold Coast airport** is 3km west of Coolangatta – see p.383 for local buses and transfers. There are two **long-distance bus stops**: Premier set down in Bay Street, just over the border in Tweed Heads (and inside the NSW time zone); while Greyhound use a bus shelter at the corner of Warner and Chalk streets, in Coolangatta and Queensland. Coolangatta's helpful **tourist office** is about halfway down Griffith Street (Mon–Fri 8.30am–5.30pm, Sat 9am–4pm; ⓣ1300 309 440, ⓦwww.goldcoasttourism.com.au). **Taxis** can be booked on ⓣ13 10 08 while **car rental** is available through Coolangatta Car Rentals, inside the Coolangatta Place complex halfway down Griffith Street (ⓣ07/5536 9960); prices start at around $35 a day.

Accommodation

Accommodation is concentrated down towards the border, where apartment buildings overlook the sea on Marine Parade and Point Danger.

Calypso Plaza 97 Griffith St ⓣ07/4124 9943. Modern and expensive resort hotel, with suites and two-bedroom penthouse apartments, right across from Greenmount Beach. ❼

Kirra Beach Hotel Marine Parade, across from the beach at Kirra Point ⓣ07/5536 3411, ⓦwww.kirrabeachhotel.com.au. Ideal location for board-riders, although staff are indifferent. Some rooms are quite spacious, and all have bath, TV and fridge. Minimum 3-night stay for $175.

Kirra Tourist Park 1km west on Charlotte St, Kirra ⓣ07/5581 7744. Probably the cheapest bet in the area, with four- and two-person cabins and tent sites. Rates drop for longer stays. Camping $24, cabins ❷–❹

Sunset Strip Budget Resort 199 Boundary St ⓣ07/5599 5517, ⓦwww.sunsetstrip.com.au. Offers family rooms, singles and good facilities – there's a huge kitchen, living area (with three TVs), twenty-metre pool and sun deck. Basic twins ❸, self-contained flats ❼

YHA 3km up the coast at 230 Coolangatta Rd/Gold Coast Highway, Bilinga, near the airport ⓣ07/5536 7644, ⓦwww.coolangattayha.com. Helpful management and nicely located for the quieter beaches, though a bit far from Coolangatta itself. Dorms $25, rooms ❸

The Town

Coolangatta is set out one block back from **Greenmount Beach** along **Griffith Street**, where you'll find banks, shops and little in the way of high-density development. Running parallel, and connected by a handful of short streets, **Marine Parade** fronts the shore, the view north over sand and sea ending with the jagged teeth of the skyscrapers on the horizon at Surfers Paradise. The state border runs along Griffith Street and uphill to the east along its continuation, Boundary Street, up to Point Danger at the end of the small peninsula.

At **Point Danger**, the Captain Cook Memorial Lighthouse forms a shrine where pillars enclose a large bronze globe detailing Cook's peregrinations around the southern hemisphere (see also p.1083). Twenty-five metres below, surfers in their colourful wet suits make the most of **Flagstaff Beach**'s swell – at weekends this area is very crowded.

Other good spots to **surf** include the area between Point Danger and Kirra Point, to the west (the latter was nominated by world surfing champion Kelly Slater as his favourite break); Greenmount, which is fairly reliable and a good beach for beginners; and Snapper Rocks and Point Danger, at the end of the peninsula, for the more dedicated – exactly where depends on the wind. For sun worshippers, Coolangatta Beach, just west of Greenmount, is right in town, but the six-kilometre stretch of sand further west, beyond Kirra Point, is wider and less crowded. **Surfing gear and information** are available from Pipedream, Griffith Street (ⓣ07/5599 1164), and Mount Woodgee, 122 Griffith St (ⓣ07/5536 5937); surfboard and ski rental is around $20 a day plus credit-card deposit. All shops have decent secondhand boards for sale, though local boards tend to be too thin and lightweight to use elsewhere. For **tuition**, see the box on p.387.

Eating, drinking and nightlife

There are plenty of **snack bars** along Griffith Street, while the best deals on **restaurant meals** are at the *Surf Life Saving Club* and *Surf Club*, both along Marine Parade, where you can get huge counter lunches with sea views from about $15. At *Little Malaya*, at the western end of Marine Parade, you can get large noodle soups with chicken or seafood for $9, along with satays and curries for $17 or so. *L9One*, down near the border on Griffith Street, is a large bar-bistro complex with an expensive surf-and-turf menu and **live bands** most weekends – you can also catch bands at the *Coolangatta Hotel*'s **nightclub**, on the corner of Marine Parade and Warner Street. If you're doing your own cooking, there's a 24-hour Night Owl convenience store at the Showcase Shopping Centre beside the *Coolangatta Hotel*, and bigger **supermarkets** across the border at the main shopping centre on Wharf Street, in Tweed Heads.

The Gold Coast Hinterland

Beginning around 30km inland from the coast's jangling excesses, the **Gold Coast Hinterland** is a mountainous, rainforested plateau encompassing a series of beautifully wild **national parks**, all packed with scenery, animals and birds. The pick of the bunch is **Green Mountain** at **Lamington National Park**, with atmospheric **hiking trails** through beech forest and a stunning density of birdlife. **Tamborine Mountain**'s less rugged walking tracks and country "villages" also provide a relaxing weekend escape, while waterfalls in **Springbrook National Park** make for an easy day-trip. **Access** is by **tour bus** from Brisbane and the Gold Coast – see the boxes on p.379 and p.390 – but to explore to any degree you'll need your own vehicle, which will also work out the cheapest option for a group. If you're **driving**, carry a good road map, as **signposts** are few and far between – all places are reached off the Pacific Highway between Brisbane and the Gold Coast.

Weather ranges from very wet in summer (when there are leeches in abundance and some hiking trails are closed) to fairly cool and dry in winter, though **rain** is a year-round possibility. If you're planning to **hike**, you'll need good footwear for the slippery paths, although trails are well-marked. **Accommodation** is in resorts, motels and campsites, so if you're on a tight budget bring a **tent** – make sure you book all accommodation in advance. You'll need a **fuel stove** if you're camping, as collecting firewood in national parks is forbidden; barbecues and wood are often supplied on sites, however.

Tamborine Mountain

Tamborine Mountain is a volcanic plateau about 40km inland as the crow flies from the Gold Coast, whose remaining pockets of rainforest are interspersed with the little satellite suburbs of northerly **Eagle Heights**, adjoining **North Tamborine** and **Mount Tamborine**, about 5km south. Once the haunt of the Wangeriburra Aborigines, Tamborine Mountain's forests were targeted by the timber industry in the late nineteenth century until locals succeeded in getting the area declared Queensland's **first national park** in 1908. A trip here provides a pleasant escape from the city, with a surplus of tearooms, country accommodation and easy walking tracks through accessibly small, jungley stands of timber.

EAGLE HEIGHTS is the largest settlement, though it's not much more than a five-hundred-metre-long strip, **Gallery Road**, lined with cafés and craft showrooms. The **botanic gardens** (free), off Long Road, are very pretty, with small picnic lawns surrounding a pond overlooked by tall trees; for something a little more energetic, head to **Palm Grove Circuit** at the end of Palm Grove Avenue, a 2.5km-long mix of dry forest, a few small creeks, and a limpid, eerie gloom created by an extensive stand of elegant piccabean palms. Hidden 20m up in the canopy are elusive wompoo pigeons, often heard but seldom seen, despite their vivid purple-and-green plumage and onomatopoeic call.

A few kilometres west, **NORTH TAMBORINE** sports a **tourist office** at the junction of Western Road and Geissmann Drive (Sat 9.30am–3.30pm; Sun–Fri 10.30am–3.30pm; ⓣ07/5545 3200), a post office, ATMs, fuel stations and even more cafés. The best walk here is about a kilometre south down Western Road, where a three-kilometre track slaloms downhill through open scrub and rainforest to **Witches Falls**. The easy walk is more rewarding for the views off the plateau than for the falls themselves, which are only a trickle that disappears over a narrow ledge below the lookout. Far more impressive is **Cedar Creek Falls**, a good swimming spot a couple of kilometres north of North Tamborine along Geissmann Drive (the road to Brisbane). Finally, down near **Mount Tamborine** – which is otherwise purely residential – there's a stand of primitive, slow-growing cycads (see box on p.451) and a relatively dry climate at **Lepidozamia National Park** on Main Western Road.

Practicalities

Driving from the coast, turn off the Pacific Highway north of the theme parks at Oxenford and follow Route 95 up to Eagle Heights; from Brisbane, turn off the highway at Beenleigh and take Route 92 to North Tamborine.

The mountain's abundant **accommodation** is generally of a romantic-getaway nature, including cozy rooms at *The Polish Place*, 333 Main Western Rd, North Tamborine (ⓣ07/5545 1603, ⓦwww.polishplace.com.au; self-contained chalet ❼); or suites with four-poster beds, plus a pool and surrounding forest at *Ambience Retreat*, 25 Eagle Heights Rd, North Tamborine (ⓣ07/5545 1766, ⓦwww.mazsretreat.com; ❻). Alternatively, there's *The Cottages*, 23 Kootenai Drive, North Tamborine (ⓣ07/5545 2574, ⓦwww.thecottages.com.au; ❼), or the very stylish, wooden pole-frame buildings at *Pethers Rainforest Retreat* (ⓣ07/5545 4577, ⓦwww.pethers.com.au; ❼). The sole budget option is *Tamborine Mountain Caravan and Campsite* at Thunderbird Park, near Cedar Creek on Tamborine Mountain Road (ⓣ07/5545 0034; camping $18).

Springbrook National Park

At the edge of a plateau along the New South Wales border, **Springbrook National Park** comprises several separate fragments – the best of which are **Purling Brook Falls** and **Natural Bridge** – featuring abundant forest, waterfalls and swimming holes. To get there, turn off the Pacific Highway inland from Burleigh Heads at **Mudgeeraba** and then follow the twisty road 20km southwest to a junction, where Route 99 heads left to Purlingbrook, and Route 97 heads right to Natural Bridge.

Purling Brook Falls is about 8km south of the junction. The 109-metre falls are very impressive after rain has swollen the flow; a four-kilometre track zigzags down the escarpment and into the rainforest at the base of the falls before curving underneath the waterfall (expect a soaking from the spray) and going back up the other side. In the plunge pool at the foot of the falls, the force of the water is enough to push you under; swimming is more relaxed in a couple of pools downstream, picturesquely encircled by lianas and red cedar. There's a **campsite** outside the forest, near the top of the falls, with a **store** about 4km back along the main road.

A ten-kilometre drive beyond the falls brings you to **Best of All Lookout** and a broad vista south to Mount Warning. On the lookout road, *Mountain Lodge* **youth hostel** (☎07/5533 5366; dorms \$26, rooms ❸) has a ski-cabin design, a fireplace for cold winter nights, a big kitchen and a fair claim to being the first place in Australia to see the sun each day. Call in advance to book and arrange a **pick-up** from the Gold Coast (minimum of two people staying two nights; \$20 return per person), and bring all your own supplies.

Natural Bridge is about 24km from the Purlingbrook Falls junction. It's a dark, damp and hauntingly eerie place, where a collapsed cave ceiling beneath the riverbed has created a subterranean waterfall. You can walk in through the original cave-mouth some 50m downstream; from the back of the cave the forest outside frames the waterfall and blue plunge pool, surreally lit from above; **glow worms** illuminate the ceiling at night.

Lamington National Park

Lamington National Park occupies the northeastern rim of a vast 1156-metre-high caldera centred on Mount Warning, 15km away in New South Wales. An enthralling world of rainforest-flanked rivers, open heathland and ancient eucalypt woods, Lamington's position on a crossover zone between subtropical and temperate climes has made it home to a staggering variety of plants, animals and birds, with isolated populations of species found nowhere else in the world. There are two possible bases for exploring the park: **Binna Burra** on the drier northern edge, and **Green Mountain** (better known for the well-publicized **O'Reilly's Guesthouse**) in the thick of the forest, with a twenty-kilometre-long hiking track linking the two.

By road from Brisbane or the coast, it's simplest to first aim for **Nerang**, inland from Surfers Paradise on the Pacific Highway. From here, Binna Burra is 36km southwest via tiny **Beechmont**, while Green Mountain/*O'Reilly's* is about 65km away via **Canungra township**. If you don't have a car, accommodation might provide a **pick-up** from the coast, and some tour operators may be willing to take you up one day and pick you up on another if asked in advance.

Beechmont or Canungra are the last proper sources of **supplies**, fuel and cash, though there's resort and campsite **accommodation** at both Green Mountain and Binna Burra, which must be booked in advance. Once here, Lamington has to be explored on foot: most of the tracks described below are clearly signposted and **free maps** are available from local National Parks ranger stations.

Binna Burra

Binna Burra is a massive tract of highland forest where, overlooking the Numinbah Valley from woodland on the crown of Mount Roberts, you'll find **accommodation** at the upmarket *Binna Burra Mountain Lodge* (Ⓣ07/5533 3622, Ⓦwww.binnaburralodge.com.au; camping $11 per person, on-site tents ❸, cabins ❻). They offer wooden twin-share cabins with log fires, along with on-site tents and a campsite with hot showers; phone in advance to arrange a **pick-up** from the Gold Coast airport and Nerang station (to connect with the train from Brisbane airport). The *Lodge* also has an expensive **restaurant** and less formal café if you're not self-catering. Hikers can also **bushcamp** inside the national park between February and November; for details contact the ranger in Beechmont (daily 8am–4pm; Ⓣ07/5533 3584).

Of the **walks**, try the easy five-kilometre **Caves Circuit**, which follows the edge of the Coomera Valley past the white, wind-sculpted Talangai Caves to remains of Aboriginal camps, strands of *psilotum nudum* (a rootless ancestor of the ferns), and a hillside of strangler figs and red cedar. The **Ballunji Falls Track** is a little more demanding, with some vertical drops off the path; key features along the way include views of Egg Rock from **Bellbird Lookout**, at its most mysterious when shrouded in dawn mists, and a stand of majestic forty-metre-tall box brush trees. The trail can be extended out to **Ships Stern**, a tiring and dry 21-kilometre hike (8hr return), with some wonderful views off the escarpment. **Dave's Creek Circuit** is similar but about half as long, crossing bands of rainforest and sclerophyll before emerging onto heathland. Look for tiny clumps of red **sundew** plants along the track, which supplement their nitrogen intake by trapping insects in sticky globules of nectar.

By far the best of the longer tracks is the **Border Track**; a relatively easy 21-kilometre, nine-hour path (one way) through rainforest and beech groves linking Binna Burra with Green Mountain. If you need road transport between the two, the *Lodge* usually runs a free weekly service to *O'Reilly's* for its guests, and will often take others for a fee if there's room – departures depend on demand, so all arrangements have to be made on site.

Green Mountain

Green Mountain is Lamington at its best, a huge spread of cloud forest filled with ancient, moss-covered trees and a mass of wildlife including so many birds that you hardly know where to start looking. The road up from Canungra ends at ★ *O'Reilly's Guesthouse* (Ⓣ07/5544 0644, Ⓦwww.oreillys.com.au; ❽), a splendid and comfortable place opened in 1926; there's a limited **store** (with EFTPOS facilities) and a moderately priced **restaurant** here for meals and snacks throughout the day. An exposed **National Parks campsite** with showers (Ⓣ07/5544 0634 or Ⓦwww.epa.qld.gov.au for essential advance booking) is nearby. If you can't get in here, head back 7km towards Canungra and *Cainbable Mountain Lodge* (Ⓣ07/5544 9207, Ⓦwww.cainbable.com; ❻), whose modern, self-contained chalets sleep from four to eight people and have splendid views.

The **birdlife** around *O'Reilly's* is prolific and distracting: you can't miss the chattering swarms of crimson rosellas mingling with visitors on the lawn, and determined twitchers can clock up over fifty species without even reaching the forest – most spectacular is the black-and-gold regent bowerbird. But it's worth pushing on to the **treetop walk** just beyond the clearing, where a suspended walkway swings 15m above ground level. At the halfway anchor point you scale a narrow ladder to vertigo-inducing mesh platforms 30m up the trunk of a strangler fig to see the canopy at eye level. Soaking up the increased sunlight at this height above the forest floor, tree branches become miniature gardens of mosses, ferns and orchids. By night the walkway is the preserve of possums, leaf-tailed geckoes and weird stalking insects.

If you manage only one day-walk at Lamington, make it the exceptional fifteen-kilometre **Blue Pool–Canungra Creek** track (5hr return), which features all the jungle trimmings: fantastic trees, river crossings and countless opportunities to fall off slippery rocks and get soaked. The first hour is dry enough as you tramp downhill past some huge red cedars to Blue Pool, a deep, placid waterhole where platypuses are sometimes seen on winter mornings; this makes a good walk in itself. After a dip, head upstream along Canungra Creek; the path traverses the river a few times (there are no bridges, but occasionally a fallen tree conveniently spans the water) – look for yellow or red arrows painted on rocks that indicate where to cross. Seasonally, the creek can be almost dried up; if the water is more than knee-deep, you shouldn't attempt a crossing and will need to retrace your steps. Follow the creek as far as Elabana Falls and another swimming hole, or bypass the falls; either way, the path climbs back to the guesthouse.

Another excellent trail (17.5km return) takes six hours via **Box Creek Falls** to the eastern escarpment at **Toolona Lookout**, on the Border Track to Binna Burra; rewards are a half-dozen waterfalls, dramatic views into New South Wales, and encounters with clumps of moss-covered **Antarctic beech trees**, a Gondwanan relic also found in South America.

The Sunshine Coast

The **Sunshine Coast**, stretching north of Brisbane to Noosa, is a more pedestrian version of the Gold Coast, where largely domestic tourist development is tempered by, and sometimes combined with, agriculture. Much of the local character is due to the lack of death taxes in Queensland, something which, together with the mild climate, attracts retirees from all over Australia. The towns tend to be bland places, though there's striking scenery at the **Glass House Mountains**, good beaches and surf at **Maloolaba** and **Maroochydore**, and upmarket beach life at **Noosa**. Though you'll find the **hinterland** far tamer than that behind the Gold Coast, it still has some pleasant landscapes and scattered hamlets rife with Devonshire cream teas and weekend markets.

Without your own transport, the easiest way through the area is by **bus**, either with local transit or tour companies, or the national long-distance carriers. Brisbane's **Citytrain** network can also take you into the region, with stops at the Glass House Mountains, Woombye, Nambour and Eumundi, from where there's a connecting local bus to Noosa. There's also the **Sunshine Coast airport** just north of Maroochydore, serving Brisbane, Sydney and Melbourne.

Woodford, the Glass House Mountains and Australia Zoo

The unremarkable town of **Caboolture** marks the start of the Sunshine Coast, 40km north of Brisbane, though the first place of interest lies 20km northwest, where the two-street town of **WOODFORD** draws thousands for the annual folk festival in December (Ⓦwww.woodfordfolkfestival.com).

Route 60 runs thirty kilometres north from Caboolture to **Beerwah**, providing access to **Glass House Mountains National Park**: nine dramatic, isolated pinnacles jutting out of a flat plain, visible from as far away as Brisbane. To the Kabi Aborigines, the mountains are the petrified forms of a family fleeing the incoming tide, though their current name was bestowed by Captain Cook because of their "shape and elevation" – a resemblance that's obscure today. The peaks themselves vary enormously: some are rounded and fairly easy to scale, while a couple have vertical faces and sharp spires requiring competent climbing skills. It's worth conquering at least one of the easier peaks, as the views are superb: **Beerburrum**, overlooking the township of the same name, and **Ngungun**, near the Glass House Mountains township, are two of the easiest to climb, with well-used tracks which shouldn't take more than two hours return; the latter's views and scenery outclass some of the tougher peaks, though the lower parts of the track are steep and slippery. **Tibberoowuccum**, a small peak at 220m just outside the national-park boundary, must be climbed from the northwest, with access from the car park off Marsh's Road. The taller mountains – **Tibrogargan** and **Beerwah** (the highest at 556m) – are at best tricky, and **Coonowrin** should be attempted only by experienced climbers after contacting the National Parks office in Beerwah (Ⓣ07/5494 0150).

For maps of the region and local climbing conditions, ask the experienced volunteers at the **visitor tourist office** at the Matthew Flinders Park Rest Area, 2km north of **Beerburrum town** and about 20km north of Caboolture. The most convenient **accommodation** in the area is at *Glasshouse Mountains Holiday Village* (Ⓣ07/5496 9338; camping $18, cabins ❷), south of the Glass House Mountains township, 25km north of Caboolture at the foot of Mount Tibrogargan.

Australia Zoo

Australia Zoo (daily 9am–4.30pm; $46; Ⓣ07/5494 1134, Ⓦwww.crocodilehunter.com), just north of Beerwah, became famous through the antics of the late zoo director **Steve Irwin**, otherwise known for his "Crocodile Hunter" screen persona. Despite his tragic death in 2006, the staff here continue Irwin's tradition of exuberant exhibitionism, and it remains one of the largest and most enjoyable commercial zoos in Australia, with plenty of hands-on experience with both foreign and native animals. The best way into the area is up along Route 60 via Beerwah, or south along Route 6 from Landsborough; contact the zoo in advance for a **free pick-up** from Beerwah station (on the Citytrain network from Brisbane) and most places along the coast between Caloundra and Noosa. Otherwise, numerous **tours** run here from Brisbane.

Caloundra

On the coast 20km east of Landsborough – there's a local bus from Landsborough train station – **CALOUNDRA** just manages to hold on to its small seaside-town atmosphere, and as such is unique along the Sunshine Coast, where busy highways and beach-front overdevelopment have long since put paid to this elsewhere. Even so, there are plenty of towering apartment blocks, though central **Bulcock Street** has only low-rise buildings and is lined with trees. Caloundra's **beaches** are very pleasant: the closest is at Deepwater Point, just two streets south of Bulcock Street – Shelley Beach and Moffat Beach, about a kilometre distant, are much quieter. The **bus terminal** is on Cooma Terrace, one street south of Bulcock, where there's also **tourist office** (Mon–Fri 8.30am–5pm; Ⓣ07/5491 2555). For

△Steve Irwin at Australia Zoo

accommodation try *Caloundra City Backpackers*, 84 Omrah Ave (Ⓣ07/5499 7655; dorms $22, rooms ❷), which is clean, well run, and just two minutes from Deepwater Point. *Estoril*, at 38 McIlwraith St (Ⓣ07/5491 5988, Ⓦwww.estoril.com.au; ❼), offers self-catering apartments sleeping four in a high-rise block right next to Moffat Beach, and has a huge pool.

Mooloolaba

The coast north of Caloundra kicks off with **MOOLOOLABA**, a mess of high-rise units, boutiques and flashy, forgettable dining experiences – though the beaches are long, sandy and excellent for surfing. The town's sole land-based attraction is **Underwater World** on Parkyn Parade (daily 9am–6pm, last entry at 5pm; $25.50), with superb views of sharks, turtles and nonchalant freshwater crocodiles staring blankly at you through observation windows. For the real thing, Sunreef at 110 Brisbane Rd (Ⓣ07/5444 5656, Ⓦwww.sunreef.com.au) can take qualified **scuba divers** fifteen minutes offshore to where the HMAS *Brisbane* lies in 8–28m of water; the 133m-long destroyer was deliberately sunk as a dive site in 2005 and has already become home to a large array of marine life. It's an expensive trip, however – $210 plus gear rental for just two dives – and an unpleasant experience in heavy swell; if you're heading north, save your dollars for the *Yongala* (see p.440).

Buses set down on Smith Street, a short way back from shops and restaurants lining the hundred-metre-long, seafront Esplanade. The Esplanade has plenty of modern high-rise **holiday apartments** all charging around $250 and up for a two bedroom, self-contained unit: options include *Sirocco* (Ⓣ07/5444 1400, Ⓦwww.siroccoapartments.com.au) and *Peninsular* (Ⓣ07/5444 4477, Ⓦwww.peninsular.com.au). Alternatively, *Sandcastles*, on the corner of Esplanade and

Parkyn Parade (Ⓣ07/5478 0666, Ⓦwww.sandcastlesonthebeach.com.au; ❺) offers older rooms right next to the Surf Club, while *Mooloolaba Beach Backpackers* at 75 Brisbane Rd (Ⓣ5444 3399, Ⓦwww.mooloolababackpackers.com; dorms $25, rooms ❸) is a clean and friendly budget option where the price includes a free breakfast, bike, kayak and boogie-board loans, and barbecue nights. **Eating** options are everywhere, though the best deals and sea views are at *Mooloolaba Surf Club*'s smart café, bar and restaurant on the Esplanade (daily noon–2pm & 6pm–late, plus Sun from 8am). *Mooloolaba Hotel*, on the Esplanade, hosts rock bands every Friday and Saturday, and opens its doors as a **nightclub** on Sundays.

Maroochydore

Most of the other accommodation options for independent travellers are 3km north of Mooloolaba at **MAROOCHYDORE**. With a multi-lane highway tearing through the middle of the town this isn't an immediately attractive place, but away from the centre the beaches and surrounding streets are quiet, and the surf – as usual – is great. **Buses** set down outside a shopping mall on First Avenue, just a short walk from **accommodation** at *Cotton Tree Caravan Park* (Ⓣ1800 461 253, Ⓦwww.maroochypark.qld.gov.au; camping $23, four- to five-person cabins ❼), on Cotton Tree Parade right at the northern end of the beach. Just around the corner, *Cotton Tree Backpackers*, 15 Esplanade (Ⓣ07/5443 1755, Ⓦwww.cottontreebackpackers.com; dorms $23, rooms ❸), is a bright, airy place in an old beach house and hands out surfboards and kayaks. A final option is the hidden *Maroochydore Backpackers*, a kilometre from the bus and beach at 24 Schirrmann Drive (Ⓣ07/5443 3151, Ⓦwww.yhabackpackers.com.au; dorms $26, rooms ❸); they have rooms, dorms, tent sites and offer free pick-ups from Maroochydore. **Moving on**, Noosa is an easy 30km north of Maroochydore along the coastal David Low Way, or a little more along Route 70 to Tewantin.

Nambour, the hinterland, and on to Noosa

Bisected by tramways from surrounding sugar plantations, the functional town of **Nambour** sits 15km inland from Maroochydore on Highway 1 in the centre of the Sunshine Coast's farming region. There's not much in town to detain you, though five kilometres south between the highway and **Woombye** you'll find it hard not to at least pause and gawk at the renowned and ridiculous **Big Pineapple** which overshadows the eponymous plantation (daily 9am–5pm; free except tours and rides; Ⓣ07/5442 1333). Activities include trips around the plantation on a cane train and, of course, climbing the fibreglass fruit. Woombye is a stop on Brisbane's **Citytrain** network, or Sunshine Coast Coaches run here from Nambour.

A two-hour (90km) circuit drive from Nambour along the Blackall Range takes you into the **Sunshine Coast hinterland**, a rural English-style idyll with fields dotted by herds of pied dairy cattle, and occasional long views out to the coast. Several settlements – such as **Montville** and **Mapleton** – have dolled themselves up as "villages" and suffer from an overdose of potteries and twee tearooms, though it's worth stretching your legs to reach a couple of respectably sized **waterfalls** up here: Kondalilla, 3km north from Montville towards Nambour, with swimming holes along Obi Obi Creek; and Mapleton Falls, just west of Mapleton, where the river plunges over basalt cliffs.

A much more genuine place is **MALENY**, whose ageing hippy population, single street of cafés (the *Upfront Club* has good food with a healthy inclination and live bands at weekends), co-operative supermarket, and short river walk all create a pleasantly alternative atmosphere. About 5km south out of town, **Mary Cairncross Park** (winter 10am–4pm; summer 9am–5pm; donation) is a small patch of rainforest inhabited by snakes, wallabies and plenty of birds; there's a fantastic view south over the Glass House Mountains from the entrance. Maleny's many **accommodation** options include self-contained cabins at *Maleny Palms Tourist Park* on Macadamia Drive (ⓣ07/5494 2933, ⓦwww.malenypalms.com.au; cabins ④), 1km west of town; the friendly *Maleny Hills Motel* (ⓣ07/5494 2551, ⓦwww.malenyhills.com.au; ③), about 5km east of town on the Montville road; and *Lyndon Lodge B&B* (ⓣ07/5494 3307, ⓦwww.lyndonlodge.com; ⑤), also on the Maleny–Montville road, and with superb views and very helpful owners.

Back down near Nambour and heading north on Highway 1, you can reach Noosa by turning coastwards at **EUMUNDI**, a tiny town also on the Citytrain line and known for its Wednesday and Saturday **markets**, reputed to be the biggest and best in Australia. An appealing place to **stay overnight** here is *Hidden Valley B&B and Cookery School* (ⓣ07/5442 8685, ⓦwww.eumundibed.com; ⑦), an old Queenslander home with great decor set on four acres of land – one separate guest room is a beautifully renovated railway caboose.

Noosa

The exclusive end of the Sunshine Coast and an established celebrity "des-res" area, **NOOSA** is dominated by an enviably beautiful headland, defined by the mouth of the placid **Noosa River** and a strip of beach to the southeast. Popular since **surfers** first came in the 1960s to ride the fierce waves around the headland, the setting compensates for the density of cloned apartment boxes in "Mediterranean" colours around town. Beach and river aside, there's also a tiny national park where you'll almost certainly see **koalas**, and a couple of shallow **lakes** just north with good paddling potential.

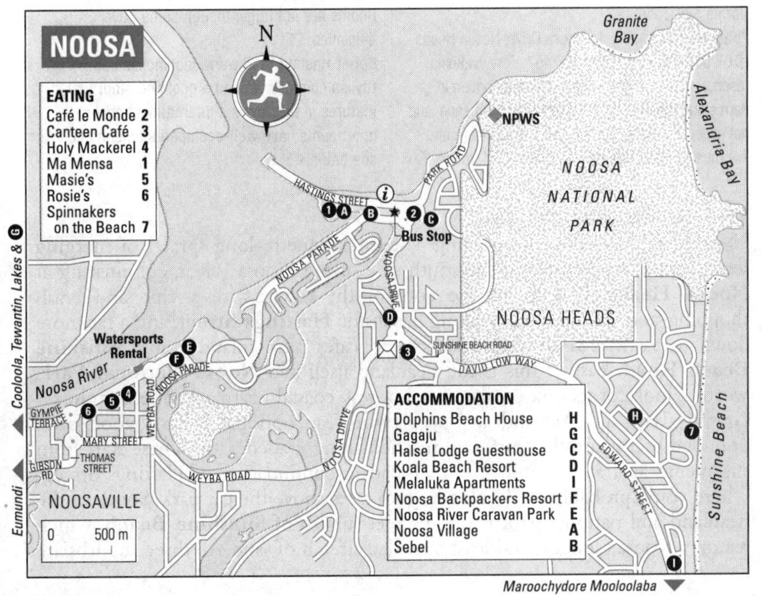

Information and accommodation

The long-distance "**Transit Centre**" – just a bus shelter – is at the junction of Noosa Parade and Noosa Drive. Avoid the commercially driven information booths scattered all over Noosa and head to the government-backed, volunteer-run **Noosa tourist office** by the roundabout on Hastings Street (daily 9am–5pm; ⓣ07/5447 4988).

All **accommodation** will help organize activities and tours, from surfing lessons to Fraser Island safaris. Van parks and a couple of hostels are the budget options; most places here are motels, apartments or expensive chain hotels. **Prices** double everywhere apart from the hostels during school holidays.

Dolphins Beach House 14 Duke St, Sunshine Beach ⓣ1800 454 456, ⓦwww.dolphinsbeachhouse.com. Self-contained units with a distinctly mellow, New Age feel and surfboards to rent, about five minutes' walk from the sea. ④

Gagaju Call ahead for directions or pick-up ⓣ07/5474 3522. An eco-friendly bush camp near the lakes north of Noosa, with recycled timber bunkhouses and space for campers. Canoes and camping equipment, advice on hikes and canoe trips, and fireside bush-poetry readings are among the attractions. Their three-day independent canoe trip is highly recommended. Dorms $15, camping $10.

Halse Lodge Guesthouse YHA 17 Noosa Drive, Noosa Heads ⓣ1800 242 567, ⓦwww.halselodge.com.au. Giant, sprawling, immaculate 1888 Queenslander building in large grounds close to Noosa Beach; there's a bit of a regimented atmosphere and it's not a place for partying. Often full despite the number of rooms, so book in advance. Dorms $26, rooms ③

Koala Beach Resort 44 Noosa Drive, Noosa Heads ⓣ07/5447 3355 or 1800 357 457, ⓦwww.koalaresort.com.au. Central budget accommodation in dorms and motel units. Nowhere near the beach, and not especially clean, but the party atmosphere and live music might compensate. Dorms $24, rooms ③

Melaluka Apartments 7 Selene St, Sunshine Beach ⓣ1800 003 663, ⓦwww.melaluka.com.au. A well-appointed high-rise development with excellent, self-contained apartment accommodation – one of the best deals in town. Dorms $23, apartments ④

Noosa Backpackers Resort 9 William St, Noosaville ⓣ1800 626 673, ⓦwww.noosabackpackers.com.au. Converted motel units with small dorms and basic rooms but close to the activities centre on Gympie Terrace and free use of boogie-boards and surfboards. Dorms $23, rooms ③

Noosa River Caravan Park Russell St, Noosaville ⓣ07/5449 7050. Large campsite and van park with splendid river views, but with no cabins or on-site vans. Sites $22.

Noosa Village 10 Hastings St ⓣ07/5447 5800, ⓦwww.noosavillage.com.au. Unpretentious, tidy motel that's an extraordinarily good deal given its location on Noosa's most glitzy, upmarket street. Rooms are not huge, though some have balconies. ⑥

Sebel Hasting St ⓦwww.sebelnoosa.com. Stylish comforts around a pool and other water features in this low-set international chain; apartments have well-equipped kitchens and spa baths. ⑧

The town and around

"Noosa" is a loose term covering a seven-kilometre-long sprawl of merging settlements stretched along the south side of the Noosa River, culminating at **Noosa Heads**. This forms the core of the town, with a chic and brash shopping-and-dining enclave along beachside **Hastings Street**, and a far more down-to-earth area of shops, banks and cafés 1km inland along **Sunshine Beach Road**. East of this is the headland itself and **Noosa National Park**, worth a look for its mix of mature rainforest, coastal heath and fine **beaches** – Granite Bay and Alexandria Bay ("swimwear optional") have good sand pounded by unpatrolled surf – all reached along graded paths. These start from the picnic area at the end of Park Road (a continuation of Hastings Street), where you'll probably see **koalas** in gum trees above the car park. South of the headland and national park is the discreet suburb of **Sunshine Beach**, which features Noosa's longest and least crowded stretch of sand. All three suburbs are connected by a **bus service** (Sunbus), which goes by every twenty minutes or so between 5am and 9pm, with service extended to midnight at weekends.

West from Noosa Heads, **Noosaville** is a mainly residential district along the riverfront. In the late afternoon, half of Noosa promenades along **Gympie Terrace** as the sinking sun colours a gentle tableau: mangroves on the opposite shore, pelicans eyeing anglers for scraps and landing clumsily midstream, and everything from cruise boats to windsurfers and kayaks out on the water. If you just want to take a quick ride along the river, hop on the **Noosa ferry**, which runs six times daily (10am–6pm) from the Sheraton Noosa Jetty off Hastings Street upstream to the suburb of **Tewantin**; it costs $12 for the hour-long return journey, or $17.50 for an all-day pass.

Eating

Noosa's **nightlife** is pretty tame, and eating out is the main pastime. Hastings Street has long been the place to dine and be seen in Noosa, but soaring rents have seen some excellent eateries relocate to Noosaville, where you'll now find lots of casual diners checking out the places clustered along Gympie Terrace and Thomas Street.

Café le Monde Hastings St, Noosa Heads ⓣ07/5449 2366. Slightly snobbish atmosphere and a mainly international menu – try the Le Monde salad at $18. Happy hour Mon–Fri 4–6pm and 9–10pm; live music Thurs–Sun.

Canteen Café Sunshine Beach Rd, Noosa Heads. Somewhere to slump over a big breakfast and good strong coffee, rather than be seen.

Holy Mackerel 187 Gympie Terrace, Noosaville. Unquestionably the place for fish and chips – try the sensational coconut prawns and handmade ice creams. Daily 10am–late.

Ma Mensa Hastings St, Noosa Heads. Obligatory Italian bistro with outdoor tables, which is inexpensive for the location. Very fine steamed mussels for $21, and lots of pasta dishes for around $17.

Noosa water activities

Noosa's original reason to be was the **surf**, and if you know what you're doing you'll find all the necessary gear at Surf World, 34 Sunshine Beach Rd, Noosa Heads (ⓣ07/5447 3538). The best surf is found around Noosa Heads; if you're a novice and put off by the crowds, try a lesson with Learn to Surf (ⓣ0418 787 577, ⓦwww.learntosurf.com.au) or Wavesense (ⓣ07/5474 9076, ⓦwww.wavesense.com.au); costs are around $55 for a two-hour introduction, up to $650 for a five-day intensive course.

Most other water activities, including the popular **river cruises**, are based to the west around Noosaville and Tewantin. Noosa River Cruises, on Gympie Terrace in Noosaville (ⓣ07/5449 7362), and Everglades Waterbus, Harbour Town Complex, Tewantin (ⓣ07/5447 1838, ⓦwww.evergladeswaterbus.com), have day-tours on the river and lakes for around $65. To get as far as Lake Cootharaba, Beyond (ⓣ1800 657 666, ⓦwww.beyondnoosa.com.au) has six-hour cruises upriver for $84 and full-day tours for $149, which includes a cruise and a 4WD run up the sands to Rainbow Beach.

For **watersports**, Pro Ski, on the river bank at Gympie Terrace in Noosaville (ⓣ07/5449 7740), has **water-skiing** ($90 for 30min or $140 for an hour including instruction) and **jet skis** ($65 for 30min); next door, Pelican Boat Hire (ⓣ07/5449 7239, ⓦwww.pelicanboathire.com.au) has small **outboard** boats for hire ($34 for the first hour and $12 for additional hours) as well as canoes and surf skis ($12 for the first hour and $6 for additional hours). Kingfisher Boat Hire (ⓣ07/5449 9353), at the Harbour Town Complex in Tewantin, rents out **fishing boats** with fuel, rods, bait pumps, crab pots, ice boxes and the rest, for around $35 an hour. Kayanu, at the Noosa River Shopping Centre on Gympie Terrace (ⓣ0438 788 573, ⓦwww.kite-surf.com.au), has two-hour **kite surfing courses** ($150), and also rents out kayaks.

Masie's 247 Gympie Terrace, Noosaville. Excellent steak and seafood dishes served in a rather formal and airy setting with some outside tables. Try the seafood pie or pan-fried veal – mains cost around $25. Closed Mon.

Rosie's Gympie Terrace, near the corner of Albert St, Noosaville ⓣ07/5449 7888. Tiny and intimate BYO place, with a new menu every week. It's popular with locals, with mains from around $24.

Spinnakers on the Beach Sunshine Beach Surf Club. Spacious bar and restaurant with unbeatable views. Big servings of seafood, steaks, pasta and salad, all in the $15–25 range. Courtesy bus from Noosa on Wed and Fri nights.

Around Noosa: lakes Cooroibah and Cootharaba

North of Noosa, a winding six-kilometre stretch of the Noosa River pools into lakes **Cooroibah** and **Cootharaba** as it nears Tewantin. Placid, and fringed with paperbarks and reedbeds, the lakes look their best at dawn before there's any traffic; they're saltwater and average just 1m in depth, subject to tides.

You can **cruise** the lakes from Noosa (see p.401), or drive up from Tewantin; turn off the main road onto Werin Street at the school – there is a sign, but it's easy to miss – then turn left again and follow the signposts. About 6km along is **Cooroibah township** on Cooroibah's western shore, where there's a boat ramp. It's 10km by water from here to Lake Cootharaba, or 17km by road to lakeshore **BOREEN POINT**, a small place with fuel, a general store and the low-slung, colonial-era wooden *Apollonian Hotel* (ⓣ07/5485 3100; ④), which oozes character and serves cold drinks and pub lunches; there's also a council-run **campsite** here. Another 4km and the road runs out at **Elanda Point** (where there's another small store) from where there's a footpath to Cootharaba's northernmost edge at **Kinaba**, basically a tourist office set where Kin Kin Creek and the Noosa River spill lazily into the lake through thickets of mangroves, hibiscus and tea trees – the so-called **Everglades**. A boardwalk from Kinaba leads to a hide where you can spy on birdlife, and the picnic area here is a former **corroboree ground**, which featured in the saga of Eliza Fraser (see p.410). **Canoes** and kayaks can be rented at all the townships from around $40 a day.

The Fraser Coast

The **Fraser Coast** covers over 190km of the coastline north from Noosa, forming a world of giant dunes, forests, coloured sands and freshwater lakes where fishing and four-wheel driving are the activities of preference. But it doesn't have to be a macho tangle with the elements: for once it's relatively easy and inexpensive to rent tents and a 4WD and set off to explore in some comfort. The main destination for all of this is **Fraser Island**, an enormous, elongated and largely forested sand island, which has just about enough room for the crowds of tourists who visit each year. On the way there, the small townships of **Rainbow Beach** and **Tin Can Bay**, on the mainland off Fraser's southernmost tip, offer a more laid-back view of the region, with another long strip of beach and the chance to come into contact with wild **dolphins**. You can catch a ferry to Fraser Island from the Rainbow Beach area, though the main access point is **Hervey Bay**, a tourist hub which also offers seasonal **whale-watching cruises**.

The Fraser Coast's abundant fresh water, seafood and plants must have supported a very healthy Aboriginal population; campfires along the beach allowed Matthew Flinders to navigate Fraser Island at night in 1802. The area was declared an Aboriginal reserve in the early 1860s but, with the discovery of **gold** at Gympie in 1867, Europeans flocked in thousands into the region. The subsequent economic boom sparked by the gold rush saved the fledgling Queensland from bankruptcy but the growth in white settlement saw the Aboriginal population cleared out so that the area could be opened up for recreation. More recently, the big issues here have been caused by the local logging, tourism and conservationist camps all struggling for control of resources: the balance between protection and "development" – a word with almost religious connotations in Queensland – is far from being established.

The main route into the area is off Highway 1, 60km north of Noosa at **Gympie** for Tin Can Bay and Rainbow Beach, or a further 85km north up the highway at **Maryborough** for Hervey Bay; **long-distance buses** serve all three towns daily. **Tours** around the region run from Noosa, Rainbow Beach and Hervey Bay (the best place to arrange self-drive 4WD expeditions); those from Noosa often zip straight up **Cooloola Beach** in a 4WD from Tewantin to Rainbow Beach, a forty-kilometre run of uninterrupted sand.

Tin Can Bay and Rainbow Beach

Tin Can Bay and **Rainbow Beach** are small, slowly developing coastal townships reached off Route 15 northeast of Gympie. Some 55km along, **TIN CAN BAY** occupies a long wooded spit jutting north into a convoluted inlet; the main drag, **Tin Can Bay Road**, runs for a couple of kilometres past a small shopping centre, post office and a few places to stay and eat before petering out at the Yacht Club. The reason to come here is to see – and even feed – the wild **indo-pacific dolphins** who pull in daily at **Barnacle Point** jetty, just short of the Yacht Club, but it's also just a nice place to kick back and do nothing for a day, though there's no beach.

Greyhound **buses** set down just off the main road in Bream Street at the *Sleepy Lagoon Motel* (Ⓣ07/5486 4124, Ⓦwww.tincanbay.gday.com.au; dorms $20, motel rooms ④), which is attached to the pub. A more upmarket alternative is *Seychelle Luxury Units* at 23 Bream St (Ⓣ07/5486 2056; ⑤), while *Kingfisher Caravan Park*, a little further up off Tin Can Bay Road (Ⓣ07/5486 4198; ③), is well-equipped and has camping and cabins. For **eating**, there are a couple of cafés and a pub, though *Barnacles*, at the dolphin feeding station at Barnacle Point, does great, inexpensive lunches.

Rainbow Beach

RAINBOW BEACH, 80km from Gympie and 48km from Tin Can Bay, is a very casual knot of streets set back from a fantastic **beach** facing into **Wide Bay**. The main recreations here are fishing, surfing and kite-boarding – there's almost always a moderate southeasterly blowing – but you can also take a 4WD (when the tide is right) or walk 10km south along the beach to the coloured sand cliffs at **Double Island Point**, whose streaks of red, orange and white are caused by minerals leaching down from the cliff-top. On the far side of the point lies the rusty frame of the *Cherry Venture* **shipwreck**, beached during a storm in 1973, then – for 4WDs only – it's a clear 40km run down the beach to Tewantin.

The township lies either side of **Rainbow Beach Road**, which ends above the surf at a small **shopping complex** housing a post office, service station and store – **buses** pull in nearby on Spectrum Street. **Accommodation** includes *Rainbow Beach Holiday Village*, at 13 Rainbow Beach Rd (ⓣ07/5486 3222, ⓦwww.beach-village.com.au; camping $22, self-contained units ④), and *Fraser's Backpackers*, 18 Spectrum St (ⓣ07/5486 8885, ⓦwww.rainbowbeachbackpackersresort.com.au; dorms $22, rooms ③). There's a lively **pub** on the main road serving huge steaks at around $20, while *Coloured Sands Café* in the shopping complex does good coffee and cooked breakfasts.

Heading to Fraser, the island is only accessible to 4WD vehicles (see pp.409–414 for full information). *Fraser's Backpackers* arrange an all-inclusive three-day, two-night **four-wheel-drive tour** for $175; you can also **rent** a vehicle with Safari (ⓣ1800 689 819, ⓦwww.safari4wdhire.com.au), who offer five-seater off-roaders from about $140 per day for a three-day rental, and can sort out **packages** including vehicle permits and National Park camping fees (the latter can also be booked at ⓦwww.epa.gov.qld.au).

Barges to Fraser leave from **Inskip Point**, 10km north of Rainbow Beach, for the fifteen-minute crossing to Hook Point on the island's south coast – be aware that this is a difficult landing, not for novice drivers. There are two **barge services**, both charging the same rates (pedestrians free, 4WDs $75 each way); the first barge leaves Inskip Point at 6.30am, while the last departs Fraser at 5.30pm. If you're driving your own vehicle over, you need to buy a **vehicle permit** and pay **camping fees** for the island – these can both be arranged through the backpackers or Safari.

Hervey Bay

Around 35km northeast of Maryborough along Route 57, **HERVEY BAY** is a rapidly expanding sprawl of coastal suburbs known locally as "God's Waiting Room" due to the large number of retirees living here. Though very spread out, it's in fact a straightforward enough place, somewhere to pull up for only as long as it takes to join the throng crossing to **Fraser Island**, or to venture into the bay to spot **whales** in the spring.

Pialba is Hervey Bay's commercial centre, an ugly blob of carparks, shopping malls and industrial estates where the road from Maryborough enters town. It's about 1km from here to the **Esplanade**, which forms a pleasant seven-kilometre string of motels and shops facing a wooded foreshore as it runs east through the conjoined suburbs of **Scarness** and **Torquay** to **Urangan**.

Practicalities

Buses wind up in Pialba at the Centro Shopping Complex, where there's a helpful **tourist office** (Mon–Fri 6am–5.30pm, Sat & Sun 6.30am–1pm; ⓣ07/4124 4000); your accommodation won't be short on advice either. The **airport** is about 5km south of Urangan off Booral Road. Hervey Bay has a decent **local bus** service, circuiting around town from Centro between about 6am and 6pm, though you'll need a taxi for the airport ($10–15; ⓣ13 10 08).

Before crossing **to Fraser Island**, remember that the island's roads are 4WD only – see pp.409–414 for the full island account. For a quick trip without a vehicle, there's a **passenger-only ferry** from Urangan harbour to the west-coast

Whale watching from Hervey Bay

Humpback whales are among the most exciting marine creatures you can encounter: growing to 16m long and weighing up to 36 tonnes, they make their presence known from a distance by their habit of "breaching" – making spectacular, crashing leaps out of the water – and expelling jets of spray as they exhale. Prior to 1952 an estimated ten thousand whales made the annual journey between the Antarctic and tropics to breed and give birth in shallow coastal waters; a decade later whaling had reduced the population to just two hundred. Now protected, their numbers have increased to over five thousand, many of which pass along the eastern coast of Australia on their annual migration. An estimated two thirds enter Hervey Bay, making it the best place to spot humpbacks in the country. The **whale-watching season** here lasts from August to November, a little later than northern waters because Fraser Island leans outwards, deflecting the creatures away from the bay as they migrate north, but funnelling them in to the constricted waters when returning south.

In the early months you're more likely to see mature **bulls** who, being inquisitive, swim directly under the boat and raise their heads out of the water, close enough to touch. You may even see them fighting over mating rights and hear their enchanting mating songs; of course you may also see and hear nothing at all. The later part of the season sees **mothers and playful calves** coming into the bay to rest before their great migration south, a good time to watch the humpbacks breaching. Whether all this voyeurism disturbs the animals is unclear, but they seem at least tolerant of the attention paid to them.

The town makes the most of their visit with an August **Whale Festival**, and operators are always searching for new gimmicks to promote day-cruises and flights. For **flights**, try Air Fraser Island (Ⓣ1800 247 992, Ⓦwww.airfraserisland.com.au), costing from $85 per person (depending on the number of passengers) for a thirty-minute buzz. **Cruises** last for a morning or a full day and cost around $95 per person; some boats can take up to 150 passengers but this doesn't necessarily mean they feel overcrowded – check the boat size, viewing space, speed of vessel and how many will be going before committing yourself. *Quick Cat* (Ⓣ07/4128 9611) works with a spotter plane to almost guarantee sightings; *Spirit of Hervey Bay* has underwater portals to view the whales if they come close; while Whalesong (Ⓣ1800 689 610, Ⓦwww.whalesong.com.au), Tasman Venture (Ⓣ07/4124 3222, Ⓦwww.tasmanventure.com.au) and the sailing catamaran *Blue Dolphin* (Ⓣ07/4124 9600, Ⓦwww.bluedolphintours.com.au) also come recommended.

Kingfisher Bay Resort six times a day ($50 return). **Vehicle barges to Fraser** – which also allow foot-passengers – cross to the island's west coast from Urangan harbour and River Heads, 17km south. Those **from Urangan** make for a very difficult landing at Moon Point, departing daily at 8.30am and 3.30pm, returning at 9.30am and 4.30pm. The **River Heads** barge crosses to Wangoolba Creek daily at 8.30am, 10.15am and 3.30pm, returning at 9.30am, 2.30pm and 4.30pm; this is the easiest place to land a vehicle on Fraser and is recommended if you haven't had much 4WD experience.

Unless on an organized tour, you need a **barge ticket** (returns are $130 for vehicle including driver and three passengers, $22 for pedestrians), **vehicle permit** for the island if driving ($33.45), plus you'll have to pay **camping fees** in advance for national-park sites if you're planning to camp ($4.50 per person per night; book at Ⓦwww.epa.qld.gov.au). All these can also be arranged where you rent your vehicle – and are usually covered in package deals – or from barge offices at Urangan and River Heads. It's essential to **pre-book barge services** (Ⓣ07/4125 4444, Ⓕ4125 4000). Note that you can use return tickets only on the same barge; if you're planning a different exit from the island, you'll have to buy two one-way tickets. For **tours of Fraser**, see the box on opposite.

Accommodation

Accommodation is packed during the whale-watching season and at Christmas and Easter, when motel prices can double. Most places will pick you up from the bus station, and all can organize tours to Fraser, with the hostels specializing in putting together budget self-drive packages. If you're **camping**, the best van parks are those fronting the beach on the Esplanade at Pialba (T07/4128 1399) and Scarness (T07/4128 1274).

Arlia Sands 13 Ann St, Torquay T07/4125 4360, Wwww.arliasands.com.au. Extremely comfortable, well-equipped apartments sleeping from two to four people in a quiet street off the Esplanade – an ideal family option. One- or two-bedroom apartments 5

Bayview Motel 399 Esplanade, Torquay T07/4128 1134, Wwww.thebayviewmotel.com.au. This historic guesthouse with wooden floors and colourful interior design boasts spotless rooms and friendly owners who can't do enough for you. 4

Beaches 195 Torquay Rd, Torquay T1800 655 501, Wwww.beaches.com.au. Busy party hostel with lively bar/bistro and cheerful staff, one street back from the Esplanade. Dorms $22, rooms 3

Fraser Roving 412 Esplanade, Torquay T07/4125 6386, Wwww.fraserroving.com. Barracks-like but clean and efficient backpackers with its own bar and pool, and specializing in Fraser trips. Dorms $20, rooms 3

Friendly Hostel 182 Torquay Rd, Scarness T1800 244 107, Wwww.thefriendlyhostel.com.au. Relaxed, intimate guesthouse, with comfy three-bed self-contained dorms and a nice, family atmosphere. Dorms $21, rooms 2, self-contained apartments sleeping six 5

Koala Backpackers 408 Esplanade, Torquay T1800 354 535, Wwww.koalaresort.com.au. Large hostel with party atmosphere in a great location close to shops, with its own fleet of 4WDs. Dorms $22, rooms 3

Mango Tourist Hostel 110 Torquay Rd, Torquay T07/4124 2832, Wwww.mangohostel.com. Delightful old Queenslander with polished floors and just three rooms. The hosts are extremely knowledgeable on Fraser Island and can organize alternative nature-based walking tours, ecotours or sailing trips. Dorms $19, rooms 2

Playa Concha 475 Esplanade, Torquay T07/4125 1544, Wwww.playaconcharesort.com. Comfortable Esplanade motel surrounded by palms and ferns, with a mix of single and double rooms and excellent-value, roomy apartments sleeping up to six people. 5

Eating and drinking

Apart from snack bars and fast-food joints in Pialba, most of the places to eat and spend the evening are along the Esplanade at Torquay.

Beachside Hotel Cnr Esplanade and Queens St, Scarness. Lively bar with retro furnishings and an open front for sea views. DJ Wed–Sat nights.

Black Dog Café Cnr Esplanade and Denman Camp Rd, Scarness. An odd name for what is actually a small, smart restaurant with heavy Asian leanings – mostly Japanese. Udon soup, sushi, and beef teriyaki sit strangely alongside Cajun fish and Caesar salad. Good value, with mains at $18–25.

Gringo's 449 Esplanade, Torquay. Good Mexican menu with enchiladas, chilli con carne and nachos, spiced to individual tolerances and with bean fillings as an alternative to meat. Main courses cost around $19. Daily from 5.30pm.

O'Reileys 446 Esplanade, Torquay. Savoury pizza, pasta and crepes, but best for fruit pancakes and cream. Open breakfast and dinner only; closed Mon.

Sails Cnr Fraser St and Esplanade, Torquay T07/4125 5170. Moderately upmarket Mediterranean/Asian brasserie, and a good place to splash out a little. Good choices are the Shanghai noodles and seafood risotto, and there are some decent vegetarian options too, along with good old Aussie steaks. Alternatively, just plump for their tapas platter and a cocktail. Daily 10am–midnight.

Thai Diamond 353 Esplanade, Scarness. Inexpensive yet filling dishes with cheerful service in an unassuming cafeteria-style setting. Licensed and BYO. Daily 10am–midnight.

Listings

Airlines Air Fraser Island (☎1800 247 992, Ⓦwww.airfraserisland.com.au) for whale spotting and flights to Fraser; Jetstar (Ⓦwww.jetstar.com.au) and Virgin Blue (Ⓦwww.virginblue.com.au) for intercity flights. For Lady Elliot Island, contact the resort direct (see p.417).
Banks Most banks are in Pialba, with a few scattered along the Esplanade at Torquay.
Camping equipment Some 4WD operators also rent camping equipment.
Car rental Nifty, 463 Esplanade (☎1800 627 583), has decent runarounds from $29 a day. For 4WD, Fraser Magic in Urangan (☎07/4125 6612, Ⓦwww.fraser-magic-4wdhire.com.au) has the lowest rates and has been going forever; Bay 4WD Centre, 54 Boat Harbour Drive, Pialba (☎1800 687 178, Ⓦwww.bay4wd.com.au), offers much the same deal. For more information about 4WD rental for Fraser Island, see the box on p.411.
Internet access Several hostels can oblige, as can the tourist office near the bus station at Pialba's Centro shopping complex ($4 an hour).
Pharmacy Day and Night Pharmacy, 418 Esplanade, Torquay (daily 8am–8pm).
Post office On the Esplanade, Torquay.
Taxi ☎13 10 08.
Watersports Torquay Beach Hire, 415 Esplanade at Torquay (☎07/4125 5528), offers surf skis, windsurfers and outboard-driven tinnies for a day's fishing.

Fraser Island

With a length of 123km, **Fraser Island** is the world's largest sand island, but this dry fact does little to prepare you for the experience. Accumulated from sediments swept north from New South Wales over the last two million years, the scenery ranges from silent forests and beaches sculpted by wind and surf to crystal-clear streams and dark, tannin-stained lakes. The east coast forms a ninety-kilometre razor-edge from which Fraser's tremendous scale can be absorbed as you travel its length; with the sea as a constant, the dunes along the edge seem to evolve before your eyes – in places low and soft, elsewhere hard and worn into intriguing canyons. By contrast, slower progress through the forests of the island's interior creates more subtle impressions of its age and permanence – a primal world predating European settlement – brought into question only when the view opens suddenly onto a lake or a bald blow. In 1992, the entire island was recognized as a UNESCO **World Heritage Site**,

Tours and cruises from Hervey Bay

Not surprisingly, all **tours from Hervey Bay** involve Fraser Island: day-trips start at around $100, overnight camping trips from $250 – all include guides. For **day-trips**, Fraser Island Co (☎1800 063 933, Ⓦwww.fraserislandco.com.au) is a little pricey at $135, but has an excellent BBQ lunch, new vehicles and first-rate guides – it also seems to work out of sync with rival tours' schedules, so you don't keep bumping into busloads of other visitors. Alternatively, Fraser Venture Tours (☎1800 249 122, Ⓦwww.fraser-is.com) does recommended **overnight trips** with accommodation at Eurong ($269). For **three-day all-inclusive packages** covering just about the whole island, the best is again offered by Fraser Island Co (see above; $400), along with the less expensive Cool Dingo ($369; ☎1800 072 555, Ⓦwww.cooldingotour.com) and Sand Island Safaris ($348; ☎1800 246 911, Ⓦwww.sandislandsafaris.com.au).

Cruises are offered by most of the boat operators outside the whale-watching season (see box on p.407) and spend about four hours searching for dolphins, turtles and – with real luck – dugongs (sea cows) at $95 per person. Alternatively, Krystal Clear (☎07/4124 0066) and Blue Horizon (☎1800 247 992) allow four to five hours for snorkelling, coral viewing, and a BBQ lunch for $70–80.

△ Four-wheel driving on Fraser Island

with all but a few pockets of freehold land and the tiny township of Eurong being national park.

Some history

To the Kabi Aborigines, Fraser Island is **K'gari**, a beautiful woman so taken with the earth that she stayed behind after creation, her eyes becoming lakes that mirrored the sky and teemed with wildlife so that she wouldn't be lonely. The story behind the European name is far less enchanting. In 1836, survivors of the wreck of the *Stirling Castle*, including the captain's wife **Eliza Fraser**, landed at Waddy Point. Though runaway convicts had already been welcomed into Kabi life, the castaways suffered "dreadful slavery, cruel toil and excruciating tortures", and two months after the captain's death Eliza was presented as a prize during a corroboree at Lake Cootharaba. She was rescued at this dramatic point by former convict John Graham, who had lived with the Kabi and was part of a search party alerted by three other survivors from the *Stirling Castle*. The exact details of Eliza's captivity remain obscure as she produced several conflicting accounts, but her role as an "anti-Crusoe" inspired the work of novelist Patrick White and artist Sidney Nolan.

Arrival, information and getting around

The easiest way to reach Fraser – albeit a very small fragment – is to take the daily fast **passenger ferry** from Hervey Bay to *Kingfisher Bay Resort* (p.412). Alternatively, guided **day-tours** from Hervey Bay whip around the main sights – usually some of the forest, a couple of lakes, and the beach as far as Indian Head – but the wildlife and overall feel of the area are elusive unless you get away from the more popular places, camp for the night and explore early on in the day. Again, you can take an overnight tour, but it's far cheaper to assemble a group and **rent a 4WD**, either independently or through accommodation, and then catch a **vehicle barge** from Rainbow Beach or Hervey Bay.

Once on the island, there are a couple of **safety points** to bear in mind. As there have never been domestic dogs on the island, Fraser's **dingoes** are considered to be Australia's purest strain, and they used to be a common sight. After one killed a child in 2000, however, dingoes which frequented public areas were culled and you'll probably not see many. If you do encounter some, keep your distance, back off rather than run if approached, and – despite their misleadingly scrawny appearance – **don't feed them**, as it's the expectation of hand-outs which makes them aggressive. You should also be aware that **sharks** and severe currents make Fraser a dangerous place to get in the sea; if you want to swim, stick to the freshwater lakes. Lastly, pack some powerful **insect repellent**.

For **supplies**, the east-coast settlements of Happy Valley and Eurong have stores, telephones, bars and fuel; there's another store at *Cathedral Beach Resort* but no shops or restaurant at Dilli. You'll save money by bringing whatever you need with you; and make sure you **take all garbage home** or place it in the large, wildlife-proof metal skips you'll find along the way.

Getting around

Driving on the island requires a **4WD vehicle**. The east beach serves as the main highway, with roads running inland to popular spots; make sure you pick up a **tide timetable** from barge operators, as parts of the beach are only reliably negotiable at low tide. Other tracks, always slower than the beach, crisscross the interior; the main tracks are often rough from heavy use, and minor roads tend to be in better shape. **General 4WD advice** is to lower your tyre pressure to around 12psi to increase traction on the sand, but this isn't generally necessary (if you get bogged, however, try it first before panicking). Rain and high tides harden sand surfaces, making driving easier. **Road rules** are the same as those on the mainland. Most **accidents** involve collisions on blind corners, rolling in soft sand (avoid hard braking or making sudden turns – you don't have to be

Renting a 4WD for Fraser Island

Fraser Island is simply too large and varied to appreciate fully on a day-trip, and with competition in Hervey Bay keeping prices to a minimum it's a great opportunity to learn how to handle a 4WD. See p.409 for some recommended outfits; a stipulation of the Fraser Coast 4 Hire Association is that the company should take time to protect both itself and you with a full briefing on the island and driving practicalities. Renting a 4WD over three days, expect to pay around $115 per day for two-seaters such as a Suzuki, up to $200 per day for an eight-seater Landrover Defender or Toyota Landcruiser, including insurance. Note that older ex-army Landrovers, while mechanically sound, are uncomfortable and best avoided unless you're trying to save money.

Conditions include a minimum driver age of 21 and a $500 deposit, payable in plastic or cash – note that advertised prices are normally for renting the vehicle only, so tents, food, fuel, and ferry and vehicle permit for the island are extra, available separately or as part of a package. Fuel surcharge is also a point of contention – most hostels currently charge $30 extra per person, expensive considering a three-day trip would commonly use less than $100 of fuel. To help cut costs, you'll want to form a group of five or six. All hostels naturally want to sell you their tour but will usually fill the car to capacity (usually eight) to maximize their profit, which can be very uncomfortable on the bumpy tracks around Fraser. A three-day, two-night trip works out to about $135 a person plus extras.

going very fast for your front wheels to dig in, turning you over), and trying to cross apparently insignificant creeks on the beach at 60kph – 4WDs are not invincible. Don't drive your vehicle into the surf; you'll probably get stuck and even if you don't, this much saltwater exposure will rust out the bodywork within days (something the rental company will notice and charge you for). Noise from the surf means that pedestrians can't hear vehicles on the beach and won't be aware of your presence until you barrel through from behind, so give them a wide berth.

Walking is an excellent way to see the island. There's only one established circuit, and even that is very under used, running from Central Station south past lakes Birrabeen and Boomanjin, then up the coast and back to Central Station via lakes Wabby and McKenzie; highlights are circumnavigating the lakes, chance encounters with goannas and dingoes, and the energetic burst up Wongi Blow for sweeping views out to sea. A good three-day hike that by each sundown renders you all but unconscious after all that walking across sand, it requires no special skills beyond endurance and the ability to set up camp before you pass out. If this is your thing, head to *Mango Tourist Hostel* (Ⓣ07/4124 2832) in Torquay for more details.

Accommodation

All **accommodation** needs to be booked in advance. Top of the range are the plush hotel rooms and self-contained villas at *Kingfisher Bay Resort* (Ⓣ07/4125 5511 or 1800 072 555, Ⓦwww.kingfisherbay.com; ❼) on the west coast; it's close to forest but 15km across the island to the beach. Most of the other options are along **Seventy-Five Mile Beach** on the east coast: the southernmost (and first if you're coming up from Rainbow Beach) is friendly and low-key *Dilli Village* (Ⓣ07/4127 9130, Ⓦwww.dillivillage.com; camping $10, bunkhouse ❷, cabins ❸), not far from Lake Boomanjin. Moving north up the beach, *Eurong Beach Resort* (Ⓣ07/4127 9122, Ⓦwww.eurongbeach.com; ❻) has motel-style rooms near the road exit from Central Station. From here, it's a good way up to *Yidney Rocks Beachside Apartments* (Ⓣ07/4125 2343; ❼), whose motel-like self-contained units are a little overpriced, and *Fraser Island Wilderness Retreat* at Happy Valley (Ⓣ07/4127 9144, Ⓦwww.fraserislandco.com.au; doubles ❻, five-bed lodge ❼), which provides comfortable cabins and good food.

With a National Parks **camping permit** (bookings Ⓣ13 13 04 or Ⓦwww.epa.qld.gov.au), you can **camp** anywhere along the eastern foreshore except where signs forbid, or if you need tank water, showers, toilets and barbecue areas, use the **National Park campsites** at Central Station, Lake Boomanjin or Lake Allom, Dundubara and Waddy Point on the east coast. There are also **privately run campsites** at *Cathedral Beach Resort* (Ⓣ07/4127 9177) and the nicer *Dilli Village* (see opposite).

Around Central Station

Most people get their bearings by making their first stop at **Central Station**, an old logging depot with campsite, telephone and information hut under some monstrous bunya pines in the middle of the island, halfway between the landing at Wanggoolba Creek and Eurong on the east coast. From the station, take a stroll along **Wanggoolba Creek**'s upper reaches, a magical, sandy-bottomed stream so clear that it's hard at first to see the water as it runs across the forest floor. It's a largely botanic walk from here to **Pile Valley**, where satinay trees humble you to insignificance as they reach 60m to the sky. The trees produce a very dense timber, durable enough to be used as sidings on the Suez Canal, and are consequently in such demand that the trees on Fraser have almost been logged out.

There are several **lakes** around Central Station, all close enough to walk to and all along main roads. A nine-kilometre track leads north to **Lake McKenzie**, the most popular on the island and often very crowded: ringed by white sand, with clear, tea-coloured water reflecting a blue sky, it's a wonderful place to spend the day. Eight kilometres to the south, **Birrabeen** is mostly hemmed in by trees, while **Boomanjin**, 8km further, is open and perched in a basin above the island's water-table – there's a National Parks campsite here, or it's not too far to the coast at *Dilli Village* if you want to spend the night in the area.

Seventy-Five Mile Beach

East-coast **Seventy-Five Mile Beach** is Fraser's main road and camping ground, and one of the busiest places on the island. Vehicles hurtle along, pedestrians and anglers hug the surf, and tents dot the foredunes; this is what beckons the crowds over from the mainland. Coming from Central Station, you exit onto the beach at **Eurong**, a complex of motel accommodation and shops; 6km north, **Hammerstone Blow** is slowly engulfing **Lake Wabby**, a small but deep patch of blue below the dunes with excellent swimming potential – another century and it will be gone. Another 10km along at **Rainbow Gorge**, a short trail runs between two blows, through a hot, silent desert landscape where sandblasted trees emerge denuded by their ordeal. Incredibly, a dismal spring seeps water into the valley where the sand swallows it up; "upstream" are the gorge's stubby, eroded red fingers.

Another five kilometres brings you to **Happy Valley**, another source of supplies and beds, and then after the same distance again you cross picturesque **Eli Creek**, where water splashes briskly between briefly verdant banks before spilling into the sea. Sand-filtered, it's the nicest swimming spot on the island, though icy-cold. Back on the beach, another 4km brings you to the *Maheno* **shipwreck**, beached in 1935 and now a skeleton almost consumed by the elements, and the start of a line of multicoloured sand cliffs known as the **Cathedrals**. About 5km up the beach from here is the **Dundubara campsite**, behind which is the tiring, hot four-kilometre walk up Wungul Sandblow through what may as well be the Sahara; turn around at the top, though, and the glaring grey dune-scape is set off by distant views of a rich blue sea.

Approximately 20km north from Dundubara, **Indian Head** is a rare – and pretty tall – rocky outcrop, the anchor around which the island probably formed originally. It's not a hard walk to the top, and on a sunny day the rewards are likely to include views down into the surf full of dolphins, sharks and other large fish chasing each other; in season you'll certainly see pods of whales too, breaching, blowing jets of spray, and just lying on their backs, slapping the water with outstretched fins. From here there's a tricky bit of soft sand to negotiate for a final nine-kilometre run around to **Champagne Pools**, a cluster of shallow, safe swimming pools right above the surf line, which mark as far north as vehicles are allowed to travel.

The interior, west coast and far north

Fraser's wooded **interior**, a real contrast to the busy coast and popular southern lakes, gets relatively few visitors. It encloses **Yidney Scrub**, the only major stand of rainforest left on the island, and although the name doesn't conjure up a very appealing image, the trees are majestic and include towering kauri pines. There's a circuit through Yidney from Happy Valley, taking in Boomerang and Allom **lakes** on the long way back to the beach near the *Maheno*. You can camp at Allom, a small lake surrounded by pines and cycads, and completely different in character from its flashy southern cousins. Further north, another road heads in from Dundubara township to **Lake Bowarrady**, a not particularly exciting body of water famed for turtles who pester you for bread – if you can't imagine being pestered by a turtle, try refusing to hand it over.

The island's **west coast** is a mix of mangrove swamp and treacherously soft beaches, both largely inaccessible to vehicles. Access is via rough tracks which cross the island via Lake Bowarrady and Happy Valley to where the Urangan barge lands at Moon Point, though there's a better road to *Kingfisher Bay Resort* from the Central Station area.

The Southern Reef

Sand carried north up the coast by ocean currents is swept out to sea by Fraser Island's massive outwards-leaning edge, eventually being deposited 80km offshore as a cluster of tiny, coral-fringed sand islands – **cays** – which mark the southernmost tip of Queensland's mighty **Great Barrier Reef**. The coastal settlements of **Bundaberg**, **1770** and **Gladstone** each offer access to a cay, either on day-trips or for an overnight stay in a resort; either way, there's the chance to do some excellent **scuba diving**. Bundaberg – along with the nearby hamlet of **Childers** – also lies at the heart of a rich sugar cane, fruit and vegetable farming area, and both are popular places to find short-term crop-picking **work**.

All the towns are either on, or accessed from, Highway 1 and are served by **long-distance buses**; Bundaberg and Gladstone are also on the **train line**.

Childers

About 60km up the highway from Hervey Bay, **CHILDERS** is a pretty, one-horse highway town, sadly known for the terrible **fire** which burned down the old *Palace Backpackers* in 2000, killing fifteen people. The town has moved on, however, and the site has been rebuilt as a tasteful, low-key memorial and **tourist office** (Mon–Fri 9am–4pm, Sat & Sun 9am–3pm; ⓣ07/4126 3886). Childers' core of old buildings offers an excuse to pull up and stretch your legs; these include the photogenic *Federal Hotel*, a wooden pub built in 1907, and the musty, bottle-filled and slightly dull **Childers Pharmaceutical Museum** (Mon–Fri 8.30am–4pm, Sat 8.30am–noon; $4). Just west of Childers, **Flying High** (daily 9am–4.30pm; $14.50) is a huge aviary with just about every type of Australian parrot and finch zipping around, squawking, or chewing the furnishings.

If you're after **farm work**, it's available from March to January; *Childers Lodge* on Churchill Street (ⓣ07/4126 2244, ⓦwww.childersbackpackers.com; $150 per week) has numerous contacts, and offers free transport to and from work, but is often full. *Hotel Childers*, on the same road (ⓣ07/4126 1719; ❸), is a great place to stay, with very cute "country-style" rooms, a spacious beer garden and the best **meals** in Childers – the *Laurel Tree Cottage*, on the main street at the Bundaberg end of town, comes a close second with traditional fare including delightful pies.

Bundaberg and around

Fifty kilometres off the highway from Childers, surrounded by canefields and fruit farms, **BUNDABERG** is famous for its **rum**, though the town is otherwise a humdrum place whose attractions are scarcely advertised. The adjacent coast is, however, an important place for **marine turtles**, who mass in huge numbers every summer to lay their eggs on the beaches, and those wanting **work** are virtually guaranteed seasonal employment (mostly Feb–Nov) picking avocados, tomatoes, snow peas and zucchini on farms in the area. You can also fly from town to the local Barrier Reef cay, **Lady Elliot Island**, which offers a basic resort and good scuba diving.

"**Bundie**" is synonymous with rum throughout Australia and if you believe their advertising pitch, the town's **rum distillery** on Whittered Street, about 2km east of the town centre along Bourbong Street (tours Mon–Fri 10am–3pm, Sat & Sun 10am–2pm; $9.90), accounts for half the rum consumed in the country each year. A distillery tour allows fans to wallow in the overpowering pungency of raw molasses and ends, of course, with a free sample – though you probably won't need to drink much after inhaling the fumes in the vat sheds, where electronic devices are prohibited in case a spark ignites the vapour.

Flying 1270km from Sydney to Bundaberg in 1921, **Bert Hinkler** set a world record for continuous flight in his flimsy wire-and-canvas Baby Avro, demonstrating its potential as transport for remote areas and so encouraging the formation of Qantas the following year (see p.523). In 1983, the house where Hinkler lived at the time of his death in England was transported to Bundaberg and rebuilt in the Botanic Gardens, 4km from the centre over the Burnett Bridge towards Gin Gin, sharing its desirable surroundings with a Sugar Museum, Historical Museum and a steam train (all daily 10am–4pm; $5 for the house). Outside the house, landscaped gardens flank ponds where Hinkler was supposedly inspired to design aircraft by watching ibises in flight.

△ Bundaberg Rum

Practicalities

Bundaberg lies along the south bank of the **Burnett River**, about 15km from the coast. **Bourbong Street**, the main thoroughfare, runs parallel to the river and is where you'll find banks, the post office, and Internet cafés. The **bus terminal** is on Targo Street, and the **train station** is 500m west on McLean Street. The **airport**, for departures to Lady Elliot Island amongst other places, is 4km from the centre on the Childers Road. The **tourist office** (daily 9am–5pm; ⓣ07/4153 8888, ⓦwww.bundabergregion.info) is at 271 Bourbong St. **Moving on**, trains and long-distance buses – Greyhound (ⓣ13 20 30) and Premier (ⓣ13 34 10) – head up the coast to Gladstone and down to Childers and beyond; Greyhound also runs to Agnes Water daily (for 1770).

Accommodation

The first two backpackers' listed can find you work. Most motels are west of the centre, and camping is also available at Mon Repos Beach – see opposite.

Alexandra Park Motor Inn 66 Quay St ⓣ07/4152 7255. A modern Queenslander-style place with huge rooms. ④

Backpackers & Travellers Lodge Opposite the bus terminal on Targo St ⓣ07/4152 2080. Central workers' hostel. Dorms $20.

City Centre Backpackers 216 Bourbong St, near the train station ⓣ07/4151 3501. Similar to the *Travellers Lodge*, and just as full of workers. Dorms $23, rooms ②

Feeding Grounds Backpackers North of the river on Hinkler St ⓣ07/4152 3659, ⓦwww.footprintsadventures.com.au. A much more relaxed place to stay than the other backpackers' in town. Dorms $20.

Finemore Caravan Park Quay St ⓣ07/4151 3663. Pleasant location overlooking the river. Cabins ③

Oscar Motel 252 Bourbong St ⓣ07/4152 3666, ⓦwww.oscarmotel.com.au. Motel just west of the centre, with a pool and barbecue area. Rooms and units ③–④

Eating

For **eating**, *JJ's Café* on Bourbong Street opens at 6.30am for big breakfasts, while the nearby *Club Hotel* serves filling counter meals for lunch and dinner, and sports a beer garden. For modern Italian, try *Statics*, on Targo Street.

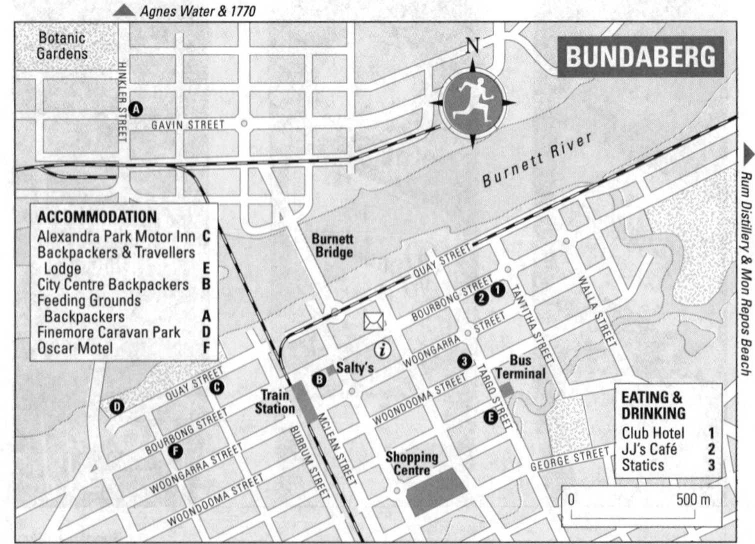

Mon Repos Beach and the turtle rookery

Mon Repos Beach is 15km east of Bundaberg, reached by initially following Bourbong Street out of town towards the port and looking out for small brown signposts for the beach (or larger ones for the *Turtle Sands Tourist Park*). Once the site of a French telegraph link to New Caledonia, today Mon Repos' reputation rests on being Australia's most accessible **loggerhead turtle rookery**. From October to March, female loggerheads clamber laboriously up the beaches after dark, excavate a pit with their hind flippers in the sand above the high-tide mark, and lay about a hundred parchment-shelled eggs. During the eight-week incubation period, the ambient temperature of the surrounding sand will determine the sex of the entire clutch; 28.5°C is the change-over point between male and female. On hatching, the endearing, rubbery-brown youngsters stay buried in the nest until after dark, when they dig themselves out en masse and head for the sea. In season, about a dozen turtles lay each night, and watching the young leave the nest and race towards the water like clockwork toys is both comical and touching – your chances of seeing both laying and hatching in one evening are best during January. The loggerhead's future doesn't look too bright at present: since 1980 Mon Repos' rookery population has halved, most likely due to net-trawling offshore.

The National Parks service runs nightly **guided tours** ($5.50) from November to March, when the beach is otherwise off limits between 6pm and 6am; most accommodation places can book you on a tour and transport package ($65). For **accommodation** at Mon Repos Beach, the first-rate *Turtle Sands Tourist Park* (☎07/4159 2340; cabins ③) is right next to the turtle rookery and a kilometre of beach.

Lady Elliot Island

The Great Barrier Reef's southernmost outpost, **Lady Elliot Island** is a two-kilometre-square patch of casuarina and pandanus trees stabilizing a bed of coral rubble, sand and – in common with all the southern cays – a thick layer of **guano**, courtesy of the generations of birds which have roosted here. The elegant **lighthouse** on Lady Elliot's west side was built in 1866 after an extraordinary number of wrecks on the reef; on average, one vessel a year still manages to come to grief here. Wailing shearwaters and the occasional suicide of lighthouse staff didn't endear Lady Elliot to early visitors, but a low-key **resort** and excellent reef have now turned the island into a popular escape.

Shearwaters aside, there's a good deal of **birdlife** on the island; residents include thousands of black noddies and bridled terns, along with much larger frigate birds and a few rare **red-tailed tropicbirds** – a white, gull-like bird with a red beak and wire-like tail – which nest under bushes on the foreshore. Both loggerhead and green **turtles** nest on the beaches too, and in a good summer there are scores laying their eggs here each night. The main reason to come to Lady Elliot, however, is to go **scuba diving**: the best spots for diving are out from the lighthouse, but check on daily currents with the dive staff at the resort before getting wet. The Blowhole is a favourite with divers, with a descent into a cavern (keep an eye out for the "gnomefish" here), and there's also the 1999 wreck of the yacht *Severence* to explore. You've a good chance of encountering harmless leopard sharks, sea snakes, barracuda, turtles and gigantic manta rays wherever you go. Shore dives cost $35 per person, while boat dives are $45 ($65 for night dives), plus gear rental.

Lady Elliot can only be reached **by air** on daily flights from Hervey Bay or Bundaberg (overnight return $195; book through the resort). **Accommodation**

The Great Barrier Reef

The **Great Barrier Reef** is to Australia what rolling savannahs and game parks are to Africa, and is equally subject to the corniest of representations. "Another world" is the commonest cliché, which, while being completely true, doesn't begin to describe the feeling of donning mask and fins and coming face to face with extraordinary animals, shapes and colours. There's so little relationship to life above the surface that distinctions normally taken for granted – such as that between animal, plant and plain rock – seem blurred, while the respective roles of observer and observed are constantly challenged by shoals of curious fish following you about.

Beginning with Lady Elliot Island, out from Bundaberg, and extending 2300km north to New Guinea, the Barrier Reef follows the outer edge of Australia's continental plate, running closer to land as it moves north: while it's 300km to the main body from Gladstone, Cairns is barely 50km distant from the reef. Far from being a continuous, unified structure, the nature of the reef varies along its length: the majority is made up by an intricate maze of individual, disconnected patch reefs, which – especially in the southern sections – sometimes act as anchors for the formation of low sand islands known as **cays**; continental islands everywhere become ringed by **fringing reefs**; and northern sections form long **ribbons**. All of it, however, was built by one animal: the tiny **coral polyp**. Simple organisms, related to sea anemones, polyps grow together like building blocks to create modular colonies – **corals** – which form the framework of the reef's ecology by providing food, shelter and hunting grounds for larger, more mobile species. Around their walls and canyons flow a bewildering assortment of creatures: large rays and turtles "fly" effortlessly by, fish dodge between caves and coral branches, snails sift the sand for edibles, and brightly coloured nudibranchs dance above rocks.

The reef is administered by the **Marine Parks Authority**, which battles against – or at least attempts to gauge – the effects of overfishing, pollution, agricultural runoff, environmental fluctuations and tourism. All these things are beginning to have a serious effect on the Reef, with many formerly colourful coral gardens reduced to weed-strewn rubble. Don't let this put you off going – the Reef is still unquestionably worth seeing, and if the government realizes how much tourism will be lost if the Reef dies, they may get more involved in protecting it. In order to **minimize damage**, visitors should never stand on or hold onto reefs when snorkelling or diving; even if you don't break off branches, you'll certainly crush the delicate polyps.

Diving and other ways of seeing the Reef

Scuba diving is the best way to get to grips with the Reef, and **dive courses** are on offer right along the coast. Five days is the minimum needed to safely cover the course work – three days pool and theory, two days at sea – and secure you the all-important C-card. The quality of training and the price you pay vary; before signing up, ask others who have taken courses about specific businesses' general attitude and whether they just seem concerned about processing as many students in as short a time as possible – you need to know that any problems you may encounter while training will be taken seriously. Another consideration is whether you ever plan to dive again: if this seems unlikely, **resort dives** (a single dive with an instructor) will set you back only $75 or so, and they're usually available on day-trips to the Reef and island

on the island is with the comfortable *Lady Elliot Island Resort* (Ⓣ1800 072 200, Ⓦwww.ladyelliot.com.au; ⑧), which has basic four-person tented cabins as well as motel-like suites with private bathrooms and ocean views. Breakfast and dinner (but not lunch or flights) are included in the rates, and it's worth enquiring about discounts for longer-term packages – if you're not interested in underwater activities, a day or two is ample time to see everything and unwind, though.

resorts. **Qualified divers** can save on rental costs by bringing some gear along; tanks and weightbelts are covered in dive packages but anything else is extra. You need an alternative air source, timer, C-card and log book to dive in Queensland (the last is often ignored, but some places insist, especially for deep or night-time dives).

Snorkelling is a good alternative to diving: you can pick up the basics in five minutes and with a little practice the only thing you sacrifice is the extended dive time that a tank allows. If you think you'll do a fair amount, buy your own mask and snorkel – they're not dramatically expensive – as rental gear nearly always leaks. Look for a silicone rubber and toughened glass mask and ask the shop staff to show you how to find a good fit. If getting wet just isn't for you, try **glass-bottomed boats** or "subs", which can still turn up everything from sharks to oysters.

Reef hazards

Stories of shark attacks, savage octopuses and giant clams all make good press, but are mostly the stuff of fiction. However, there are a few things at the Reef capable of putting a dampener on your holiday, and it makes sense to be careful. The best protection is simply to **look and not touch**, as nothing is actively out to harm you.

Seasickness and **sunburn** are the two most common problems to afflict visitors to the Reef, so take precautions. Coral and shell **cuts** become badly infected if not treated immediately by removing any fragments and dousing with antiseptic. Some corals can also give you a nasty **sting**, but this is more a warning to keep away in future than something to worry about seriously. Animals to avoid tend to be small. Some dangerous **jellyfish** (see p.46) are found at the Reef during summer – wear a protective Lycra "stinger suit" or full wetsuit with hood. Conical **cone shells** are home to a fish-eating snail armed with a poisonous barb which has caused fatalities. Don't pick them up: there is no "safe" end to hold them. Similarly, the shy, small, **blue-ringed octopus** has a fatal bite and should never be handled. **Stonefish** are camouflaged so that they're almost impossible to distinguish from a rock or lump of coral. They spend their days immobile, protected from attack by a series of poisonous spines along their back. If you tread on one, you'll end up in hospital – an excellent argument against reef-walking. Of the larger animals, **rays** are flattened fish with a sharp tail-spine capable of causing deep wounds – don't swim close over sandy floors where they hide. At the Reef, the most commonly encountered **sharks** are the black-tip and white-tip varieties, and the bottom-dwelling, aptly named carpet shark, or wobbegong – all of these are inoffensive unless hassled.

Reef tax

The Marine Parks Authority levies a fee commonly referred to as **reef tax** (currently $6 per person per day, though some tour operators add $5 extra for administration) to help fund monitoring and management of human impact on the Reef. On most tours and boat trips, you will be required to pay the reef tax in addition to the cost of the tour. You may feel a little annoyed at having to fork out the extra money, especially if you've already paid quite a lot for your trip, but this is simply a "user-pays" system to help ensure that the Reef is maintained for everyone to experience and enjoy.

Agnes Water, 1770 and around

On the coast 100km north of Bundaberg along the Rosedale road, the tiny settlements of **Agnes Water** and nearby **1770** mark the spot where Captain Cook first set foot in Queensland on May 24, 1770. It's a pretty area whose attractions include pockets of mangrove, fan palm and paperbark wetlands, and Queensland's northernmost **surf beach** at Agnes Water, while 1770 is the closest point on the mainland with boats out to **Lady Musgrave Island** and nearby reefs. Greyhound Australia operates a **daily bus** in both directions between Bundaberg and Agnes Water, stopping opposite *Cool Bananas Hostel* on Spring Road.

AGNES WATER consists of a service station, two shopping complexes, several large resort villages and the *Agnes Water Tavern* – which does excellent meals. The town is fronted by a stunning, sweeping **beach** backed by sand dunes, and there are some delightful coastal walks in the area, including the three-kilometre trail from Agnes Headland along the wooded ridge to Springs Beach, which is best reached from the Museum on Spring Road. **Accommodation** includes *1770 Getaway* (ⓣ07/4974 9323, ⓦwww.1770getaway.com.au; ❺) on Spring Road, featuring nicely designed apartments with balconies overlooking four acres of landscaped gardens; motel-like *Agnes Palms Beachside Apartments* (ⓣ07/4974 7200, ⓦwww.barrierreef.net; ❸), on the road to 1770 and fronted by tropical bush just two hundred metres from the beach; and *Cool Bananas Hostel* (ⓣ07/4974 7660, ⓦwww.coolbananas.biz.com; dorms $22) on Spring Road. Street Beat (ⓣ07/4974 7697), across the road, hires out scooters ($65 per day), cars ($55 per day) and 4WD vehicles ($105 per day).

1770 is even smaller, occupying the foreshore of a narrow promontory some 6km to the north. At the end of the road is windswept Round Hill, with exposed walking trails and coastal views, though the main reason to come here is to take a **day-trip to the reef**. Boats leave from the marina: *Reef Jet* ($140; ⓣ1800 177 011) runs day-trips to **Fitzroy Reef** lagoon, while *Spirit of 1770* ($145; ⓣ1800 631 770, ⓦwww.spiritof1770.com.au) visits **Lady Musgrave Island**. Snorkelling gear is included in the price, but **scuba diving** at either is about $50 extra. At 1770, **places to stay** include *The Beach Shacks* (ⓣ07/4974 9463, ⓦwww.1770beachshacks.com; ❻), which has four luxurious tropical pole homes facing the ocean; a budget alternative are the cabins and tent sites at *Captain Cook Holiday Village* (ⓣ07/4974 9219, ⓦwww.1770holidayvillage.com; camping $23, cabins ❹), which has a store, bar and bistro. For **eating**, *Saltwater Café* overlooks the ocean on Captain Cook Drive and does an excellent fish and chips – other mains cost around $20, and there's a lively **bar** next door.

Eurimbula National Park, on the west side of 1770 across Round Hill Creek, abounds with birdlife. You can **tour** the region aboard *The Larc* **amphibious bus** (ⓣ07/4974 9422; full day $115, sunset cruise $30), which spends the day exploring the remote coastline. For 4WD road access to the park, head 10.5km back towards Miriam Vale from Agnes Water, where you'll see the track and national-park sign to the north of the road. You can **bushcamp** about 15km inside the park in the dunes behind Bustard Beach, but beware of the prolific sand flies.

Lady Musgrave Island

Lady Musgrave Island is another tiny, low sand cay covered in soft-leaved **pisonia trees** which host the usual throng of roosting birdlife, ringed by a coral wall which forms a large turquoise **lagoon**. Diving inside the lagoon here is safe but pretty tame (though snorkelling is good); outside the wall is more exciting. Relatively easy, inexpensive access means that Lady Musgrave is the best of the southern cays on which to **camp**, though the island itself is off-limits during the tern nesting season (Oct–April); there are **no facilities** at all on the island, so make sure you bring absolutely everything you need with you, including all camping and cooking gear, a fuel stove, food and more water than you need (which is at least five litres a day).

The only way over to Lady Musgrave is from 1770 aboard *Spirit of 1770*, which runs out here daily for snorkelling and scuba diving in the lagoon (see opposite). The crew take out campers too, and will arrange for fresh provisions to be brought over if you're planning a long stay; National Park **camping permits** can also be organized, at $4.50 per person a day (or book them via Ⓦwww.epa.qld.gov.au).

Gladstone and Heron Island

Around 90km up Highway 1 from the Miriam Vale turn-off, **GLADSTONE** is a busy port, and also the site of the Boyne Island processing plant, which refines aluminium from ore mined at Weipa on the Cape York Peninsula. Glaringly hot, there's no reason to visit unless you're trying to reach **Heron Island**. If you've time to spare, the **Tondoon Botanic Gardens**, about 7km south of town, comprise a partly wild spread of wetlands, woodlands, forests and native shrubs, all expertly laid out – you'll probably clock up wallabies and birdlife here too.

The main strip is **Goondoon Street**, where there's a "mall" – just the usual high-street shops, post office and banks – plus a couple of hotels and motels. You'll find a helpful **tourist office** (Mon–Fri 8.30am–5pm, Sat & Sun 9am–5pm) inside the ferry terminal at the marina, about 2km north of the centre on Bryan Jordan Drive. *Gladstone Reef Hotel*, 38 Goondoon St (Ⓣ07/4972 1000; ④), has ordinary motel rooms and good views from a rooftop pool. Places to eat include *Swaggy's Australian Restaurant*, 56 Goondoon St, with typical Aussie grills, and *Scotties*, five buildings further down, which offers contemporary cuisine at gourmet prices.

Non-island-based **diving** can be arranged through Gladstone Dive Centre, 16 Goondoon St (Ⓣ07/4972 9185, Ⓦwww.gladstonedive.com.au), which runs regular trips to the southern cay islands – you need to arrange things with them before turning up.

Heron Island

Famous for its diving, **Heron Island** is small enough to walk around in an hour, with half the cay occupied by a comfortable **resort** and **research station**, and the rest covered in groves of pandanus, coconuts and shady pisonias. You can literally walk off the beach and into the reef's maze of coral, or swim along the shallow walls looking for action. The eastern edges of the lagoon are good for snorkelling at any time, but **scuba diving** must be arranged through the resort, which charges $50 for a standard dive and $75 to venture out at night; you can also spend a day touring some more isolated reefs for $300 a person – equipment is extra. A drift along the wall facing Wistari reef to Heron Bommie covers about everything you're likely to encounter. The coral isn't that good but the amount of life is astonishing: tiny boxfish hide under ledges; turtles, cowries, wobbegong, reef sharks, moray eels, butterfly cod and octopuses secrete themselves among the coral; manta rays soar majestically; and larger reef fish gape vacantly as you drift past. The bommie itself makes first-rate **snorkelling**, with an interesting swim-through if your lungs are up to it, while the Tenements along the reef's northern edge are good for bigger game – including sharks.

There's a price to pay for all this natural wonder, namely no day-trips and no camping. *Heron Island Resort* (reservations Ⓣ13 24 69, island reception Ⓣ07/4972 9055, Ⓦwww.heronisland.com; ⑧) is excellent, but its rates, coupled with the ferry charge ($200 return) are steep, even after taking advantage of the regular **Web specials** and packages. **Ferries** leave from Gladstone Marina daily at 11am, except at Christmas; there's a car lockup here ($12 a day) operated by the tackle shop (8am–5pm).

The tropics: Rockhampton to Cape York

The tropics kick in at **Rockhampton**, 100km north of Gladstone, but with the exception of the **Mackay region** – a splash of green with a couple of good national parks – it's not until you're well past the tropic line and north of **Townsville** that the tropical greenery associated with north Queensland finally appears. Then it comes in a rush, and by the time you've reached the tourist haven of **Cairns** there's no doubt that the area deserves its reputation: coastal ranges covered in rainforest and cloud descend right to the sea. **Islands** along the way lure you with good beaches, hiking tracks and opportunities for snorkelling and diving: Great Keppel near Rockhampton, the Whitsundays off **Airlie Beach**, Magnetic Island opposite Townsville, and Hinchinbrook and Dunk further north are all must-sees. **Cairns** itself serves as a base for exploring highland rainforest on the **Atherton Tablelands**, coastal jungles in the **Daintree** and, of course, for trips out to the most accessible sections of the Great Barrier Reef.

Until recently, the region's **weather** involved dry, relatively cool winters (June–Aug) and extremely humid summers (Dec–Feb) with torrential rainfall and devastating cyclones. As with everywhere else, the climate is less predictable these days, though the pattern still holds to some degree. All the main towns between Rockhampton and Cairns are on Highway 1, served by Greyhound and Premier long-distance **buses** and also the **train**.

Rockhampton

Straddling the Tropic of Capricorn, **ROCKHAMPTON** was founded after a false goldrush in 1858 left hundreds of miners stranded at a depot 40km inland on the banks of the sluggish **Fitzroy River**, and their rough camp was adopted by local stockmen as a convenient port. The iron trelliswork and sandstone buildings fronting the river recall the balmy 1890s, when money was pouring into the city from a prosperous cattle industry and nearby gold and copper mines; today Rockhampton feels a bit despondent – the mines have closed (though before they did, they managed to fund the fledgling BP company), the beef industry is down in the dumps and the summers, unrelieved by coastal breezes, are appallingly humid. Bearing this in mind, the city is best seen as a springboard for the adjacent Capricorn Coast.

Arrival, information and accommodation

Rockhampton is divided by the Fitzroy River, with all services clustered directly south of the **Fitzroy Bridge** along Quay and East streets; the Bruce Highway runs right through town past two pairs of fibreglass bulls (repeatedly "de-balled" by pranksters). Greyhound and Premier **buses** stop at the Mobil service station just north of the bridge on the highway; **local buses** to or from Yeppoon and the coast set down, amongst other places, along Bolsover Street. The **train station** is 1km south of the centre on Murray Street, and the **airport** is 4km to the west at the end of Hunter Street – Virgin and Qantas fly daily from Brisbane. **Banks**, the post office and other services are mostly along East Street, and there's an Internet bar at *Jungle* (see p.424). The **tourist office** is in the old riverside customs house on Quay Street (Mon–Fri 8.30am–4.30pm, Sat & Sun 9am–4pm; ⓣ07/4922 5339). Recent reports of nasty incidents involving gangs of Aboriginal teenagers are unfortunately too numerous to ignore; there's no need for paranoia, but do follow local advice and don't walk alone at night.

Accommodation

If your only reason for being in Rockhampton is to get to Great Keppel, there's little reason to stay over – catch a local bus to Rosslyn Bay or Yeppoon (see p.425).

The pick of the city's **accommodation** choices are the reasonably priced though often noisy suites above the pub at the historic *Criterion Hotel* on Quay Street (ⓣ07/4922 1225, ⓦwww.thecriterion.com.au; ③), which overlooks the river. Budget options include *River View Lodge* at 48 Victoria Parade (ⓣ07/4922 2077; ②), with shared facilities but in a pleasant and central location; the *YHA*'s well-appointed compound north of the river at 60 MacFarlane St, close to the

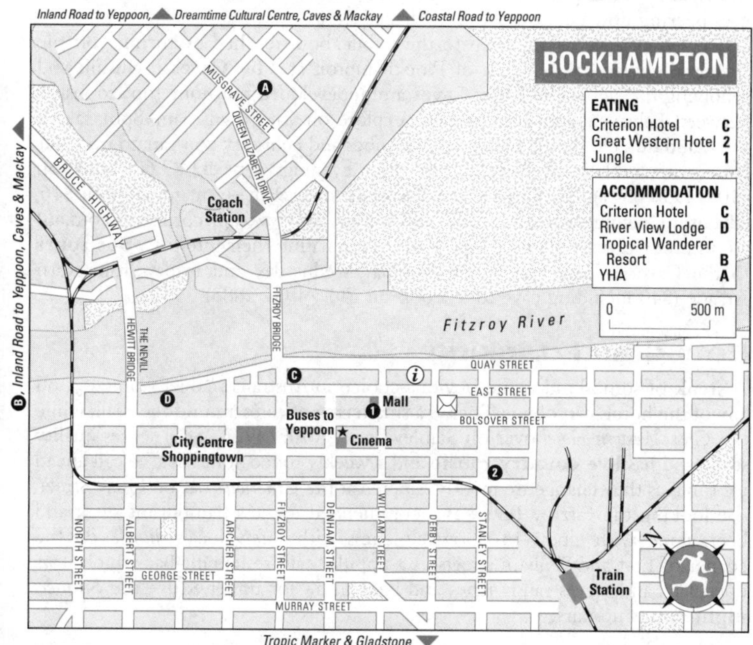

long-distance bus stop (ⓣ07/4927 5288, ⓦwww.yha.com.au; dorms $22); or the *Tropical Wanderer Resort*, on the highway 3km north of the river (ⓣ1800 815 563, ⓦwww.tropicalwanderer.com.au; cabins ❸, units ❹), with a restaurant and attractive gardens.

The City and around

It doesn't take long to look around the city. The **Tropic Marker**, 3km from the river at Rockhampton's southern entrance, is just a spire informing you of your position at 23° 26' 30" S. Apart from a riverside stroll to take in the early twentieth-century architecture or the brown-stained boulders midstream that gave the city its name, there's very little else to detain you.

About 5km north of town on the Bruce Highway, the **Dreamtime Cultural Centre** (Mon–Fri 10am–3.30pm; tours with an Aboriginal guide from 10.30am; $12.75) offers a good introduction to central Queensland's Aboriginal heritage. Inside, chronological and Dreamtime histories are intermingled, with a broad dissection of the archeology and mythology of Carnarvon Gorge (see p.509). Outside, surrounded by woodland, gunyahs (shelters of bark and branches) and stencil art, you'll find an unlikely walk-through dugong (sea cow), and the original stone rings of a **bora ground** which marked the main camp of the Darumbal, whose territory reached from the Keppel Bay coastline inland to Mount Morgan. The tour also discusses plant usage and introduces boomerang, dance and didgeridoo skills – audience participation is definitely encouraged.

The limestone hills north of Rockhampton are riddled with a **cave system**, thick with tree roots encased in stone after forcing their way down through rocks, "cave corals" and "frozen waterfalls" – minerals deposited by evaporation after annual floods. The **ghost bat** (Australia's only carnivorous species) and the **little bent-winged bat** – both now endangered – seasonally use the caves for roosts, and you might catch the odd group huddled together on the ceilings, eyes peering down at you over leaf-shaped noses.

Two sets of caverns are open to the public, both reached by turning off the Bruce Highway 25km north of Rockhampton at **The Caves** township and following the signs. The **Etna Caves** are undeveloped but none too extensive; between February and June you can explore on your own (6am–8pm; take a torch and durable shoes); between December and February you can go on a **bat tour** with a National Parks ranger (four evenings a week; $7.60; book on ⓣ07/4936 0511). The **Capricorn Caverns** (daily 9am–4pm; guided tour $16, adventure caving tour $60; ⓣ07/4934 2883, ⓦwww.capricorncaves.com.au) are impressive, with plenty of spotlights illuminating their interiors. **Bus tours** to the Caverns leave at 9am on Monday, Wednesday and Friday from Kern Arcade ($40 including cave tour; book on ⓣ07/4934 2883).

Eating and drinking

A **steak** of some kind is the obvious choice in Australia's "Beef Capital", and any of the hotels can oblige. There's a smattering of cafés around the mall, while the *Great Western Hotel* over on Stanley Street (ⓣ07/4922 3888) serves quality steak, and has **live country music** and a weekly rodeo "out back" – call ahead for times as they change frequently. A perch at the *Criterion*'s bar on Quay Street, overlooking the Fitzroy River, is recommended for less flamboyant steak and beer, along with elbow-to-elbow closeness with a few locals. *Jungle*, on the corner of East and William streets, is a popular café-restaurant-bar which stays open late, and serves sandwiches and light meals for under $10 – the *Strutters* **nightclub** is upstairs.

The Capricorn Coast

Views from the volcanic outcrops overlooking the **Capricorn Coast**, some 40km east of Rockhampton, stretch across graziers' estates and pineapple plantations to exposed headlands, estuarine mudflats and the Keppel Islands. The coastal townships of **Yeppoon** and **Emu Park**, 20km apart and settled by cattle barons in the 1860s, were soon adopted by Rockhampton's elite as places to beat the summer temperatures, and retain a pleasantly dated holiday atmosphere – besides being much nicer places to stay than Rockhampton. **Great Keppel Island** is the coast's main draw, however, accessed from **Rosslyn Bay**, just south of Yeppoon.

There are **two roads** to the coast from Rockhampton: on the north side of the river, turn east and it's 50km to Emu Park; or drive 5km further up Highway 1 and then turn coastwards for the 40km run to Yeppoon. Young's **buses** run from Rockhampton to Yeppoon, Emu Park and Rosslyn Bay (6–12 services daily from the stop beside the car park in Bolsover Street, near the junction with William; ⓣ07/4922 3813); if you're heading to Great Keppel, Rothery's Coaches (ⓣ07/4922 4320) offer a transfer from Rockhampton direct to the ferry terminal – call them to book.

Emu Park and Yeppoon

EMU PARK comprises a pleasant sandy beach and breezy hillside covered by scattered Queenslander houses, where the wind howls mournful tunes through the wires of the **Singing Ship**, a peculiar monument to Captain Cook. A decent, motel-like **place to stay** is *Endeavour Inn* on Hill Street (ⓣ07/4939 6777, ⓦwww.endeavourinn.com.au; ③); it's also worth checking on the status of *Emu Park Beach House*, 88 Pattison St (ⓣ1800 333 349, ⓦwww.emusbeachhouse.com), currently closed for renovations but a friendly and restful place in the past.

Heading north up the coast from here, it's 18km via **Rosslyn Bay** to **YEPPOON**'s quiet handful of streets, which face the Keppel Islands over a blustery expanse of sand and sea. All services are on **Normanby Street**, at right angles to the seafront Anzac Parade. **Buses** pull into the depot on Hill Street, which also runs off Anzac Parade parallel with Normanby. For **accommodation**, *Driftwood Motel*, about 2km north of town at 7 Todd Ave (ⓣ07/4939 2446, ⓦwww.driftwoodunits.com.au; ④), has straightforward but smartly equipped self-contained rooms overlooking the beach. There are basic dorm beds at *Yeppoon Backpackers*, 30 Queen St (ⓣ1800 636 828; $20), while the *Strand Hotel* (ⓣ07/4939 1301; ③), on the corner of Anzac Parade and James Street, offers basic, four-bed units. The *Poinciana Tourist Park* (ⓣ07/4939 1601, ⓦwww.poincianatouristpark.com; camping $19, cabins ③), just south of town off the Emu Park road, has inexpensive, self-contained cabins and shady tent sites.

Yeppoon prides itself on its fresh **fish**, and there are plenty of **restaurants** where you can sample it. The pick of the lot is *Seagulls Seafood* on Anzac Parade, which specializes in local Spanish Mackerel dishes, and its bucket of seafood is excellent value at $15. The nearby *Keppel Bay Sailing Club* has a cheaper bar with long views of the islands, while their restaurant offers budget all-you-can-eat lunches and dinners. For weekend **entertainment**, try *Bonkers Nightclub*, one road back from Anzac Parade on Hill Street.

Rosslyn Bay and Great Keppel Island

Great Keppel is the largest of the eighteen Keppel islands, a windswept hillock covered in casuarinas and ringed by white sand so fine that it squeaks when you walk through it, all surrounded by an invitingly clear blue sea – just the place for a few days of indolence. **Ferries** leave from **ROSSLYN BAY**, 5km south of Yeppoon: the *Freedom Fast Cat* departs from the marina three times daily at 9am, 11.30am and 4pm ($37 return; the last leaves Great Keppel at 5.00pm). There's exposed **free parking** at the harbour, though for protection from salt spray, leave your car undercover at Great Keppel Island Security Car Park ($9 a day; ⓣ07/4933 6670), opposite the Rosslyn Bay junction on the main road.

Great Keppel Island

Arriving at Great Keppel, the ferry leaves you on a spit near several **accommodation** choices; most offer packages or last-minute discounted packages if you ask for them. Near to the spit, *Great Keppel Island Holiday Village YHA* (ⓣ1800 180 235, ⓦwww.gkiholidayvillage.com.au; dorms $31, tent cabins ③, cabins ⑤) is spruce, very friendly, and has a first-rate kitchen. Along the beach, *Keppel Lodge* (ⓣ07/4939 4251, ⓦwww.keppellodge.com.au; ③) is a pleasant, motel-like affair; further down still you come to the *Great Keppel Island Resort* (ⓣ07/4939 5044, ⓦwww.greatkeppelresort.com.au; ⑧). This place changes its style on a regular basis; at present it's family-oriented for the most part, with a lively bar and pool which may be open to non-guests. For **food**, there's a tearoom at the Shell House boutique on Fisherman's Beach, and a late-opening pizza shack – much frequented after the bar closes.

Great Keppel's main **beaches**, Putney and Fisherman's, are remarkably pleasant considering the number of people lounging on them at any one time, but a half-hour walk will bring you to more secluded spots. Reached by a woodland path past the resort, Long Beach attracts sun-worshippers, while snorkellers make the short haul over sand dunes at the western end to shallow coral on Monkey Beach. **Middens** (shell mounds) on Monkey Beach were left by Woppaburra Aborigines, who were enslaved and forcibly removed to Fraser Island by early settlers.

Mackay and around

Some 360km north of Rockhampton along a famously unexciting stretch of Highway 1, the fertile Pioneer Valley makes the **MACKAY** area an appealing break from the otherwise dry country between Bundaberg and Townsville. Despite encounters with aggressive Juipera Aborigines, John Mackay was impressed enough to settle the valley in 1861, and within four years the city was founded and the first **sugar cane** plantations were established. Sugar remains the main industry today, though after years in the doldrums, Mackay is currently enjoying an economic boom, driven by the **coal mines** out west in the Bowen Basin, for which Mackay has become a dormitory town and service centre. Though the city itself has no specific sights and is barely geared up for tourism, Mackay's proximity to national parks at seafront **Cape Hillsborough** and rainforested **Eungella** – where you are almost certain to see platypus – makes it well worth a visit.

Practicalities

Mackay's centre straddles the crossroads of **Victoria** and **Sydney** streets, with the **bus station** – just a set-down point outside Mackay Travelworld – off Victoria on Macalister Street. Both **trains** (the station is on Connors Rd, 3km south off Milton St along Boundary Rd or Paradise St) and **planes** arrive south

Sugar cane on the Tropical Coast

Sugar cane, grown in an almost continuous belt between Bundaberg and Mossman, north of Cairns, is the Tropical Coast's economic pillar of strength. Introduced in the 1860s, the crop subtly undermined the racial ideals of British colonialists when farmers, planning a system along the lines of the southern United States, employed **Kanakas** – Solomon Islanders– to work the plantations. Though only indentured for a few years, and theoretically given wages and passage home when their term expired, Kanakas on plantations suffered greatly from unfamiliar diseases, while the recruiting methods used by "**Blackbirder**" traders were at best dubious and often slipped into wholesale kidnapping. Growing white unemployment and nationalism through the 1880s eventually forced the government to ban blackbirding and repatriate the islanders. Those allowed to stay were joined over the next fifty years by immigrants from Italy and Malta, who mostly settled in the far north and today form large communities scattered between Mackay and Cairns.

After cane has been planted in November, the land is quickly covered by a blanket of dusky green. Before cutting, seven months later, the fields are traditionally fired to burn off leaves and maximize sugar content – though the practice is dying out. Cane fires often take place at dusk and are as photogenic as they are brief; the best way to be at the right place at the right time is to ask at a mill. Cut cane is then transported to the mills along a rambling rail network. The mills themselves are incredible buildings, with machinery looming out of makeshift walls and giant pipes which belch out steam around the clock when the mill is in operation. Cane is juiced for raw sugar or molasses, as the market dictates; crushed fibre becomes fuel for the boilers that sustain the process; and ash is returned to the fields as fertilizer. **Farleigh Mill** (ⓣ07/4963 2700), north of Mackay, is open for **tours** (Mon–Fri 1pm; $17) during the crushing season (June–Nov); sturdy shoes, a long-sleeve shirt and long trousers are essential.

of town; a taxi into town from either terminal will set you back around $15. Virgin and Qantas have direct flights from Mackay to all the major cities between Cairns and Brisbane. Mackay Travelworld (Mon–Fri 7am–6pm, Sat 7am–2pm; ⓣ07/4944 2144) is the **ticket agent** for bus, train and air travel. The **tourist office** (ⓣ07/4952 2677) is badly informed and poorly located 3km south of town along the Nebo Road (Highway 1); you're better off consulting the staff at wherever you're staying.

Accommodation

It's sometimes hard to find a bed in Mackay, as many motels and van parks can be almost permanently full of mine workers – book ahead. There's also accommodation near the national parks – see pp.428–431.

Cool Palms Motel 4 Nebo Rd ⓣ07/4957 5477. The closest motel to town, quiet and inexpensive. ❷

El Toro Motor Inn 14 Nebo Rd ⓣ07/4951 2722. Not too far from the centre, with a friendly atmosphere and pool. ❹

Gecko's Rest 34 Sydney St ⓣ07/4944 1230, ⓦwww.geckosrest.com.au. This central, modern hostel, set in a converted shopping arcade, has spacious rooms with a/c as well as a large, well-equipped kitchen, but little natural light. Dorms $21, rooms ❷

Larrikin Lodge 32 Peel St ⓣ07/4951 3728. Low-set, comfortable Queenslander house with a laid-back feel, two-minutes' walk from the bus station. The staff are very knowledgeable about the region, and the lodge runs its own bus to Eungella National Park. Phone ahead to arrange check-in outside the office opening hours (7am–2pm & 5–8.30pm). Dorms $21, rooms ❷

The Park Nebo Rd ⓣ07/4952 1211. Two kilometres south from the centre, this is a tidy caravan park with self-contained units in a garden setting. ❷

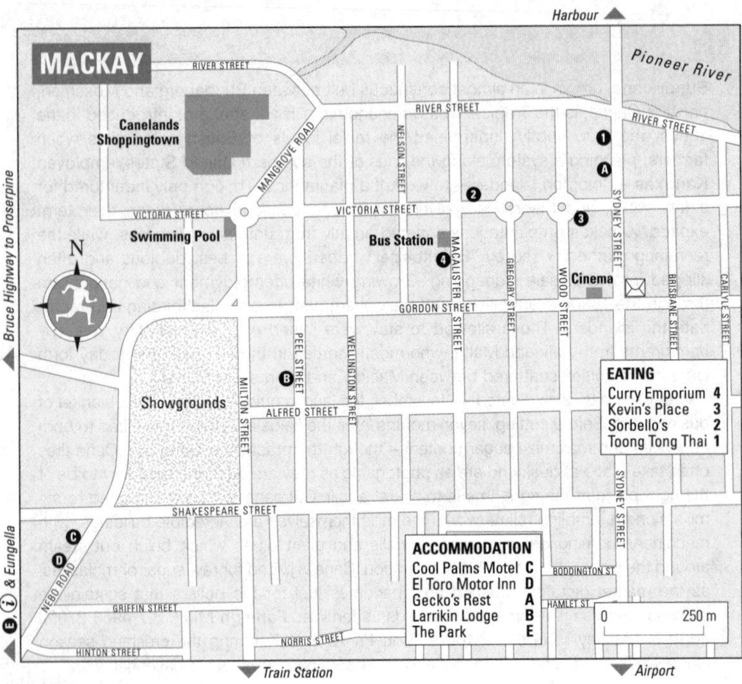

Eating

Aside from the following, several downtown pubs and restaurants also offer filling week-time lunch specials for $5–10.

Curry Emporium Macalister St, next to the bus stop. Delicious Indian dishes – try the Durban Maharajah lamb, on the bone and cooked in red curry – everything is under $20. Closed Sun & Mon.

Kevin's Place Cnr Wood and Victoria streets. Singaporean–Chinese restaurant with fixed-price lunches (try the *laksa* – a colossal bowl of noodles, seafood and spicy coconut soup) and à la carte dinners – around $22 – featuring five-spice squid and whole fried fish. Closed Sun evenings.

Sorbello's 166 Victoria St. Good choice for pastas and other Italian dishes for around $20 per person.

Toong Tong Thai 10 Sydney St. Long-established, cheerful Thai restaurant and takeaway with authentically hot and spicy food. There's a selection of appealing lunchtime specials, or it's around $25 a head for a full meal.

Cape Hillsborough National Park

Cape Hillsborough, about an hour's drive north of Mackay, is the site of a pretty beachfront national park; Reeforest Tours in Mackay (Ⓣ07/4959 8360, Ⓦwww.reeforest.com.au) sometimes run here, but you'll probably need your own vehicle to reach it. First head north up Highway 1 for about 20km and then take the signposted **Seaforth road**, past the inevitable canefields and the imposing bulk of Mount Jukes, for a further 30km to Cape Hillsborough.

The main area of the national park is set around a broad two-kilometre **beach**, backed by a good picnic area and framed by the beautifully wooded cliffs of Cape Hillsborough to the north and Andrews Point to the south; the shallow bay is good for swimming outside the stinger season. Hidden in bushland at the end of the road, the *Cape Hillsborough Resort* (Ⓣ07/4959 0152,

Ⓦ www.capehillsboroughresort.com.au; camping $20, cabins ❸) has a pool, basic store (which closes at 6pm) and restaurant. A good **walk** heads out 2km past here to **Hidden Valley**, a patch of cool, shady forest on a rocky beach where you'll find the outline of an Aboriginal fish trap; keep your eyes peeled for dolphins, turtles and pelicans out in the bay.

Five hundred metres back up the road towards Mackay, an excellent two-kilometre trail follows a **boardwalk** through coastal mangroves (bring insect repellent) and then snakes up to a ridge for views out over the area from open gum woodland peppered with grevillias, cycads (see box on p.451) and grasstrees – the latter identified by their tall, spear-like flower spike. There's also a huge **midden** up here, the remains of Aboriginal shellfish feasts, and plenty of reptiles sunning themselves around the edges of the path.

Eungella National Park

Some 80km west of Mackay, magical rainforest and rivers would make **Eungella National Park** (pronounced "young-g'lla) worth the journey even if you weren't almost guaranteed to see **platypuses**. There are two separate sections: lowland swimming holes and tropical rainforest at **Finch Hatton Gorge**, and highland rainforest at **Broken River**. The park's isolation has produced several unique species, including the Mackay tulip oak, the Eungella honeyeater and the much-discussed but probably extinct **gastric brooding frog**, known for incubating its young in its stomach.

Day-trips taking in both sections of the park can be arranged from Mackay with Reeforest Tours ($99; Ⓣ 1800 500 353, Ⓦ www.reeforest.com) or the *Larrikin Lodge* (see p.427; $65). Both run only if they have sufficient numbers – otherwise, you'll need your own vehicle. **From Mackay**, head south down the Nebo Road (Highway 1) to the city limits and follow signs initially west along the Peak Downs Highway; if you're coming south down the highway **from Proserpine**, follow the signs just south of tiny Kuttabul, around 30km north of Mackay.

△ Platypus, Eungella National Park

Finch Hatton Gorge

The Eungella road cuts through prime cane country and past several **sugar mills** as it runs the length of the Pioneer Valley, past the townships of **Marian** and **Mirani**. Some 60km from Mackay, signposts just before Finch Hatton township mark the turn-off to **Finch Hatton Gorge**, 12km from the main road across several fords – access depends on the season, though generally it's negotiable by all vehicles. Immediately across the first creek, *Platypus Bush Camp* (Ⓣ07/4958 3204, Ⓦwww.bushcamp.net; camping $7.50, dorms $20, cabins ❸) provides camping and basic cabin accommodation: mattress, pillow, amenities and kitchen are supplied; the rest (including food) is up to you. This is the most authentic rainforest experience you can have anywhere in Queensland: you'll see an astonishing array of bird- and animal-life (including the elusive platypus), sit by a fire under the stars, shower in the rainforest amidst fairy-like fireflies, and be lulled to sleep by a gurgling creek. About a kilometre and three creeks further on you'll find comfortable units at *Finch Hatton Gorge Cabins* (Ⓣ07/4958 3281, Ⓦwww.finchhattongorgecabins.com.au; dorms $16.50, cabins ❹) and a small **tearoom**. This is also the pick-up point for **Forest Flying** ($45; advance booking essential on Ⓣ07/4958 3359), which can take you for a ride 25m up through the tree tops (and a flying-fox colony) on a wire-and-sling affair – much more secure than it sounds, and offering as close a view of the forest canopy as you'll ever get.

Another kilometre past the tearoom, the road ends at a picnic area, from where graded **walking tracks** ascend through a hot jungle of palms, vines and creepers to where the gorge winds down the side of Mount Dalrymple as a rocky creek pocked with swimming holes. **Araluen Falls** (1.5km from the picnic area), a beautiful – if icy – pool and cascade, is the perfect place to spend a summer's day; further up (3km from the picnic area) is an even more attractive cascade at the **Wheel of Fire Falls**, where you can sit up to your neck in the water.

Eungella township and Broken River

About 15km past Finch Hatton township, the main road makes an unforgettably steep and twisting ascent up the range to **EUNGELLA**. This spread-out hamlet comprises a general store, fish-and-chip shop, a couple of cafés and the *Eungella Chalet* **hotel**, whose back-lawn beer garden and swimming pool sit just metres away from a seven-hundred-metre drop into the forest, with a fantastic panorama down the valley. The best **place to stay** here is the friendly *Eungella Holiday Park* (Ⓣ07/4958 4590; camping $20, cabins ❹) – take the first right at the top of the range – which has log cabins, units and campsites, more great views, plus its own store and an ATM.

A final 5km further from Eungella, through patches of forest and dairy pasture and beside a tiny bridge, **Broken River** is home to the usually unattended **National Parks office**, a bush **campsite** (book on Ⓣ13 13 04 or Ⓦwww.epa.qld.gov.au) with cold showers, a picnic area and the excellent *Broken River Mountain Resort* (Ⓣ07/4958 4528, Ⓦwww.brokenrivermr.com.au; doubles ❹, four-person self-contained cabins with fireplaces ❺). You can pick up free **maps** at the ranger's office, but the **kiosk** here is currently closed. Be prepared for **rain**: Eungella translates as "Land of Cloud".

The best vantage point for **platypus watching** is the purpose-built **platform** by the picnic area; normally fairly timid creatures, here they've become quite tolerant of people, and you can often see them right through the day. The real star of Broken River, though, is the **forest** itself, whose ancient trees with buttressed roots and immensely high canopies conceal a floor of rich rotting timber, ferns, palms and vines. Local cabbage palms, with their straight trunks and crown of large, fringed leaves; huge, scaly-barked Mackay cedar; and tulip oaks are all endemic – many other shrubs and trees here are otherwise only found further south, indicating that Eungella may have once been part of far more extensive forests. It can be difficult to see **animals** in the undergrowth, but the sun-splashed paths along riverbanks attract goannas and snakes, and you'll certainly hear plenty of birds. The best two **walking tracks** are either following the river upstream to Crediton and then returning along the road (16km return), or heading through the forest and down to *Eungella Chalet* (13km return). If you're not that dedicated, there's also an easy **forty-minute circuit** from the picnic grounds upstream to Crystal Cascades.

On to Whitsunday

PROSERPINE, 123km north of Mackay, is a small workaday sugar town on the turn-off from Highway 1 to Whitsunday, and site of the regional **train station** and **airport**, though there's another major airport on Hamilton Island. Arriving by **long-distance bus**, there's no need to get out here as all services continue to Airlie Beach. If you do wind up in town, Whitsunday Transit (ⓣ07/4946 1800) run a **local bus** six times daily between Proserpine and Whitsunday; contact them in advance to arrange train station and airport **pick-ups** (the airport is 10km south of town). Late arrivals can stay at the functional *Proserpine Motor Lodge*, 184 Main St (ⓣ07/4945 1788; ③), or the van park on Jupp Street.

Twenty kilometres east off the highway, **WHITSUNDAY** is the cover-all name for the sprawling communities of Cannonvale, Airlie Beach and Shutehaven (aka Shute Harbour), access points for the **Whitsunday Islands** (see p.434). Despite an attractive setting, nobody comes to Whitsunday to spend time in town, it's just a place to be while deciding which island to visit. **Cannonvale** and **Airlie Beach** are the service centres, while island ferries generally leave from **Shutehaven**, 10km on from Airlie past Cape Conway National Park. Other cruises leave from **Abel Point Marina**, just on the Cannonvale side of Airlie.

Cannonvale, Airlie Beach and Shutehaven

Coming from Proserpine, Whitsunday's first community is **CANNONVALE**, a scattering of modern buildings fringing the highway for about a kilometre or so, overlooked by luxury homes set higher up on the wooded slopes of the Conway Range. Just around the headland past Abel Point Marina, **AIRLIE BEACH** is nestled between the sea and a hillside covered in apartment blocks, with all services crammed into one short stretch of **Shute Harbour Road** and the hundred-metre-long **Esplanade**. Despite the name, Airlie Beach has only a couple of gritty stretches of sand, which get covered at high tide – though the view of the deep turquoise bay, dotted with yachts and cruisers, is gorgeous. To make up the shortfall, there's a free, open-air **landscaped pool** between Shute Harbour Road and the sea, complete with showers, changing rooms, picnic hotplates, benches and a little sand.

Airlie's main preoccupation is with **organizing cruises** (see box on p.438), but you can also rent **watersports gear** from the kiosk on the beach; organize half-day to six-day **sea-kayaking** expeditions with Salty Dog (ⓣ07/4946 1388, ⓦwww.saltydog.com.au); or visit **Bredl's Wildlife Park** (daily 9am–4.30pm; $25), a ten-acre bush-zoo 4km from Airlie Beach towards Shutehaven, which has an excellent reptile collection. A **flea market** is held near the long-distance bus stop on Saturday mornings, for local produce and souvenirs (8am–noon). Otherwise, **Conway National Park** comprises a mostly inaccessible stretch of forested mountains and mangroves facing the islands, but there's a small picnic area on the roadside about 7km from Airlie on Shute Harbour Road, from where an easy walking track climbs Mount Rooper to an observation platform giving views of the islands' white peaks jutting out of the unbelievably blue sea.

A final 3km on, **SHUTEHAVEN** (Shute Harbour) comprises a cluster of houses with stunning views overlooking the islands from wooded hills above **Coral Point**; it's one of Australia's busiest harbours, and most of the island ferries and bareboat charters depart from here.

Practicalities

Airlie's **long-distance bus terminal** is at the eastern end of town, off the Esplanade past the *Airlie Beach Hotel*. By **air**, island transfers are available with Air Whitsunday (Ⓣ07/4946 9111, Ⓦwww.airwhitsunday.com), and intercity flights with Virgin Blue (Ⓦwww.virginblue.com.au) and Jetstar (Ⓦwww.jetstar.com.au); long-distance flights use Proserpine or Hamilton Island, while local flights to or around the islands depart from Whitsunday Airport, about halfway between Airlie and Shutehaven. The Whitsunday Transit **bus** runs between Cannonvale, Airlie and Shutehaven roughly twice an hour from around 6am to 6pm, and around once an hour between Cannonvale and Airlie from 6pm until 10.30pm. Staff at the town's hotels, hostels and other places offer limitless **information**, though don't expect it to be unbiased; the information office, Whitsunday.com, up at the Cannonvale end of Airlie (Ⓣ07/4946 5299, Ⓦwww.airliebeach.com) is probably the most objective source, but it's a good idea to ask other visitors about which cruises they recommend before making a decision.

Accommodation

Unless you're in town during the September Whitsunday Fun Race, Christmas or New Year, you'll have little trouble finding **accommodation**, which is concentrated in Airlie Beach itself. **Hostels** are all cramped, but a pool and kitchen are standard amenities; **motels** and **resorts** often insist on minimum stays of three nights during Christmas and Easter, though might offer discounted rates at other times. All places act as booking agents for tours and transport.

Airlie Beach Hotel On the Esplanade near the bus station, Airlie Ⓣ07/4964 1999, Ⓦwww.airliebeachhotel.com.au. This formerly seedy motel is now one of the smartest places to stay in Airlie. Refurbished older motel rooms ❺, new beachfront hotel rooms ❻

Airlie Beach YHA 394 Shute Harbour Rd, Airlie Ⓣ07/4946 6312, Ⓦwww.yha.com.au. Generally busy and somewhat crowded, with tidy dorms and doubles. Dorms $23, rooms ❸

Airlie Cove Van Park 3km towards Shutehaven on Shute Harbour Rd Ⓣ07/4946 6727, Ⓦwww.airliecove.com.au. Try this place for camping and upmarket cabins. Camping $27, cabins ❺

Airlie Waterfront Backpackers Near the *Airlie Beach Hotel*, Airlie Ⓣ07/4948 1300, Ⓦwww.airliewaterfront.com. Six-person apartments above a boutique shopping complex with private bedrooms, shared bathrooms and kitchens; also has dorms and close to the bus stop. Dorms $20, rooms ❸

Airlie Waterfront Bed and Breakfast Cnr Broadwater and Mazlin streets, Airlie Ⓣ07/4946 7631, Ⓦwww.airliewaterfrontbnb.com.au. One- or two-bedroom serviced apartments in a modern timber house with fantastic bay views; rooms are comfortably furnished, and some have outdoor spa baths. ❽

Beaches 362 Shute Harbour Rd, Airlie Ⓣ07/4946 6244 or 1800 636 630. Brash backpackers' hostel, with plenty of bunks and double rooms available. Dorms $20, rooms ❸

Coral Point Lodge 54 Harbour Ave, Shute Harbour Ⓣ07/4946 9500, Ⓦwww.coralpointlodge.com.au. Delightful, excellent-value rooms and apartments with the best views in the Whitsundays. It's a bit hard to find – turn up the hill immediately after the Shell garage and keep going to the end. The attached café-restaurant is well worth a stop even if you're not staying here. ❺

Coral Sea Resort 25 Oceanview Ave, at the Cannonvale end of Airlie ⓣ07/4946 6458, ⓦwww.coralsearesort.com. Airlie Beach's only real full-blown resort; rooms (some with ocean views) are all very smart, and there's a private jetty, popular bar and pool area too. ❼

Koalas Shute Harbour Rd, at the Cannonvale end of Airlie ⓣ1800 466 444, ⓦwww.koaladventures.com. Basic six-bed dorms, each with bathroom and TV. Facilities include a communal kitchen, volleyball court and large pool in pleasant landscaped grounds; you can also camp here. Dorms $20, rooms ❸

Magnum's By the bridge on Shute Harbour Rd, Airlie ⓣ1800 624 634. Tidy cabins with en-suite bathrooms, pleasantly sheltered tropical lawns, and a loud bar and nightclub next door. Dorms $16, rooms ❸

On the Beach Shute Harbour Rd, Cannonvale end of Airlie ⓣ07/4946 6359. Unpretentious central motel with self-contained serviced units overlooking Airlie's artificial pool and the bay. ❹

Whitehaven Holiday Units 285 Shute Harbour Rd, Airlie ⓣ07/4946 5710, ⓔwhithavenunits@wilpat.com.au. Extraordinarily quiet, given its central location, with friendly staff. Rooms are simply furnished and face the sea. ❺

Eating and entertainment

As with the accommodation, the majority of **restaurants**, as well as the liveliest **nightclubs**, are in Airlie – there are also busy clubs at *Beaches* and *Magnum's* backpackers'.

Café Mykonos 287 Shute Harbour Rd, Airlie. Cheap and cheerful kebabs, souvlakia, dolmades and salads, with nothing over $12. Basically a takeaway, but there are a few tables and chairs if the nearby beach doesn't appeal.

Deja Vu 303 Shute Harbour Rd, Airlie. Award-winning BYO restaurant tucked away in a small courtyard, with a seasonal menu (around $35 per person). Tues–Sun dinner only.

Golden Temple 252 Shute Harbour Rd, Cannonvale. Popular and friendly Chinese restaurant with spacious dining and the usual takeaway menu – all mains are under $20.

Hog's Breath Café Shute Harbour Rd, Airlie. The original of this chain of Tex-Mex grill restaurants, still serving good grub. Main courses cost around $24.

Juice Bar Cannonvale end of Shute Harbour Rd. Nightly grind to loud music. Daily 10pm–late.

KC's 50 Shute Harbour Rd, Airlie. Blowout on chargrilled steak, kangaroo, croc and seafood in noisy comfort; this place stays open until 3am and often has live bands. Mains from $25.

Morocco's Shute Harbour Rd, at the Cannonvale end of Airlie. Lively bar with a huge video screen, party atmosphere, and cheap Mexican and Cajun dishes. Daily 3pm–2am.

Paddy Shenanigan's Below the *Juice Bar*. A popular place to down a few pints and set the mood before heading upstairs.

Sailing Club Up past the bus stop off the Esplanade. Bar and decent pub food from 10am until late, with views out over the bay.

Listings

Banks NAB and Commonwealth in Airlie, plus ANZ and Westpac in Cannonvale.

Boat charters Unless you know exactly what you want, bookings are best made through an agent. Bareboat charters should be undertaken by experienced sailors only: the average wind speed in the Whitsundays is 15–25 knots, which means serious sailing. Five-person yachts start at around $450 a day; add another $120 during holiday seasons. Whitsunday Rent-a-Yacht (ⓣ07/4946 9232, ⓦwww.rentayacht.com.au) and Queensland Yacht Charters (ⓣ07/4946 7400, ⓦwww.yachtcharters.com.au) have been going for years and are thoroughly reliable.

Car and scooter rental Cars cost around $50 a day and scooters from $35. Airlie Beach Budget Autos, 285 Shute Harbour Rd, Airlie ⓣ07/4948 0300; Fun Rentals, next to the Caltex fuel station at the Cannonvale end of Airlie ⓣ07/4948 0489; Tropic Car Hire, 15 Commercial Close, Airlie ⓣ07/4946 5216; We Do Scooters ⓣ07/4946 5425.

Car lockup There's limited parking space at Shutehaven; undercover facilities are available behind the Shell garage ($8 a day, or $14 for 24hr); there's an open-air grid at the harbour itself ($8 a day), and a free but unguarded area at the Lions Lookout up the hill from the Shell garage. Otherwise, contact Shute Harbour Secured Parking

(☎07/4946 9666) or Whitsunday Airport Secured Parking, midway between Airlie and Shutehaven (☎0419 790 995).

Diving The best of Airlie's limited scuba diving options is aboard *Fantasea* (☎07/4946 5111, ⓦwww.fantasea.com.au), which makes daily trips to the company's "Reef World" pontoon at Hardy Reef; from here, you take a smaller launch to various dive sites. Two dives cost $199; you must be certified already. Scuba is also often available on island cruises – see box on p.438. You might be asked to provide a dive medical certificate, especially if you are over 45 years old.

Doctor Opposite *McDonald's*, Shute Harbour Rd, Airlie (daily 8am–7pm; 24hr phoneline ☎07/4948 0900).

Internet If your accommodation can't help out, airliebeach.com, up near the *Hog's Breath Café* at the Cannonvale end of town, has a stack of terminals.

Joy flights Whitsunday Tigermoth Adventures (☎07/4946 9911, ⓦwww.tigermothadventures.com.au) take you on rides over the Whitsundays in a vintage biplane (10min–1hr; $99–360); Air Whitsunday (☎07/4946 9111, ⓦwww.airwhitsunday.com) offer flights out to the islands and Great Barrier Reef in a seaplane ($135–350); and Flying Tours (☎07/4946 9102, ⓦwww.avta.com.au) run light aircraft and helicopter tours of the reef and islands ($129–660).

Left luggage There's a set of lockers with 24hr access on the corner of Shute Harbour Rd and the Esplanade ($4–6 per day).

National Parks office Shute Harbour Rd, 3km out towards Shutehaven on the left of the road (Mon–Fri 9am–5pm; ☎07/4946 7022, ⓦwww.epa.qld.gov.au). Island camping permits and a small environmental display.

Pharmacy Airlie Day and Night Pharmacy (daily 8am–8pm).

Police Shute Harbour Rd, Cannonvale ☎07/4948 8888.

Post office In the centre of town, right behind *McDonald's*.

Supermarket The biggest is in Cannonvale, though Airlie has a well-stocked local food store about halfway through the town on Shute Harbour Road.

Taxi ☎13 10 08.

The Whitsundays

The **Whitsunday Islands** look just like the granite mountain peaks they once were before rising sea levels cut them off from the mainland six thousand years ago. They were seasonally inhabited by the Ngaro Aborigines when Captain Cook sailed through in 1770; he proceeded to name the area after the day he arrived, and various locations after his expedition's sponsors. Today, dense green pine forests, vivid blue water and roughly contoured coastlines give the islands instant appeal, and the surrounding seas bustle with yachts and cruisers. Resorts first opened here in the 1930s and now number eight, but the majority of islands are still undeveloped national parks, with campsites on thirteen of them. Resorts aside, the few islands left in private hands are mainly uninhabited and largely the domain of local yachties. Those covered below all have regular connections to the mainland.

There are two ways to explore the Whitsundays: staying on the islands or cruising around them. **Staying** allows you to choose between camping and resort facilities, with snorkelling, bushwalks and beach sports to pass the time. **Cruises** spend one or more days around the islands, perhaps putting ashore at times (check this, if it's the islands themselves you want to see) or diving and snorkelling. Don't miss the chance to do some **whale-watching** if you're here between June and September, when humpbacks (see p.407) arrive from their Antarctic wintering grounds to give birth and raise their calves before heading south again.

If you're planning to make use of the 34 island **campsites**, you'll first need to arrange transport, then obtain **permits** from the local National Parks office (see "Listings" above). At most, campsite facilities comprise a pit toilet, picnic tables and rainwater tanks, so take everything you'll need with you, especially insect repellent, a fuel stove (wood fires are prohibited) and **drinking water** – if you're planning a long stay, you can arrange for cruise boats to ferry in supplies. **Resorts** sometimes have a higher profile than the islands they're built on,

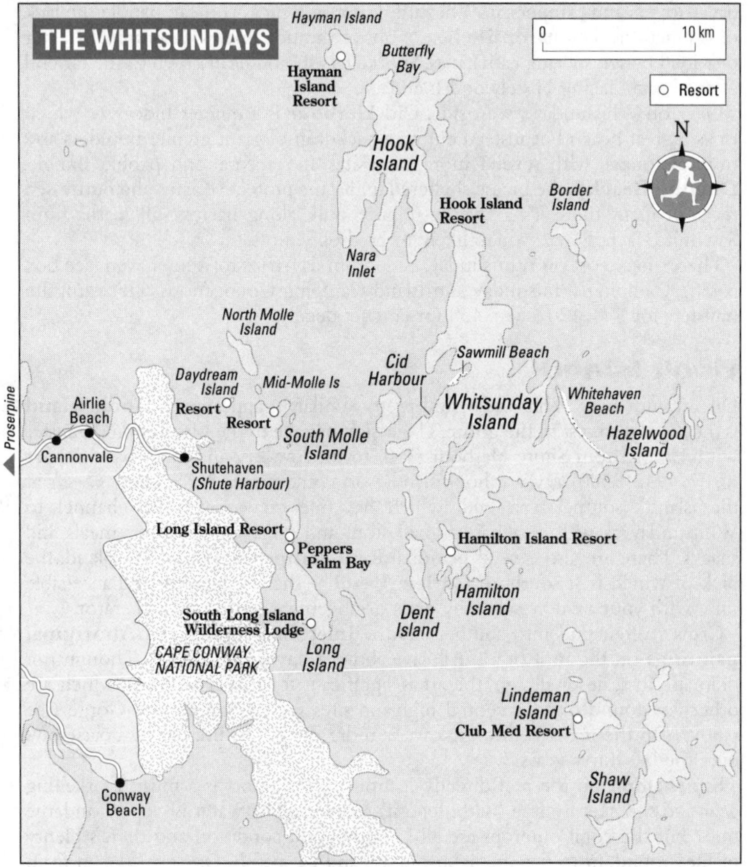

though staying at them is often beyond most budget travellers' means; stand-by deals can slash prices though, and polite bargaining is always worth a try. Most, in any case, allow day-trippers to use their facilities.

The resort islands all offer relatively expensive return **ferry transfers** to and from the mainland. If you'd like to see more than one island, or plan to camp away from a resort, it's cheaper to choose some sort of a **cruise** or **camping transfer** – for details, see the box on pp.438–439. Once you've arranged everything else, check your **departure points**; most cruises leave from Abel Point Marina, while resort ferries and island transfers tend to use Shutehaven – both stops on the Whitsunday Transit bus.

Whitsunday Island

The largest island in the group, National Parks–run **Whitsunday Island** is also one of the most enjoyable. Its east coast is home to **Whitehaven Beach**, easily the finest in all the islands, and on the agenda of just about every cruise boat in the region. Long, blindingly white, and still clean despite the numbers of day-trippers and campers, it's a beautiful spot so long as you can handle the lack of distractions. The **campsite** here is above the tide line, with minimal shelter provided by whispering casuarinas. Snorkellers should head down to the far end of the beach, facing Hazelwood Island.

Over on Whitsunday's west side, **Cid Harbour** is a quieter hideaway which lacks a great beach but instead enjoys a backdrop of giant granite boulders and tropical forests, with several more campsites above coral and pebble shingle. **Dugong Beach** is the nicest, sheltered under the protective arms and buttressed roots of giant trees; it's a twenty-minute walk along narrow hill paths from Sawmill Beach, where you're likely to be dropped off.

There's no resort on Whitsunday; aside from day-trips to Whitehaven (see box p.438), Camping Whitsunday and Island Camping Connections offer campsite transfers for $90–120 (see p.438 for contact details).

Hook Island

Directly north of Whitsunday, and pretty similar in appearance, **Hook Island** is the second largest in the group. The easiest passage to the island is on a transfer with *Voyager* from Shute Harbour ($50) to the low-key and fairly basic **resort** (Ⓣ07/4946 9380, Ⓦwww.hookislandresort.com; dorms $35, cabins ④–⑤) at the island's southeastern end, which has fine views over the channel to Whitsunday, as well as a bar, a small store and a cafeteria serving meals and snacks. There are also several National Parks **campsites** around the island, the pick of which is at southern **Curlew Beach** – sheltered, pretty and accessible only with your own vessel or by prior arrangement with a tour operator.

Cruises often pull into southern **Nara Inlet** for a look at the **Aboriginal paintings** on the roof of a small cave above a tiny shingle beach. Though not dramatic in scale or design, the art is significant for its net patterns, which are otherwise found only at central highland sites such as Carnarvon Gorge (see p.509). On the rocks below the cave is more recent graffiti, left by boat crews over the last thirty years.

Snorkelling on the reef directly in front of the resort is a must; snorkelling gear and surf skis are free (with deposit) to guests. The water is cloudy on large tides, but the coral outcrops are all in fairly good condition and there's plenty of life around, from flatworms to morays and parrotfish. Day-cruises run from Airlie to the snorkelling spots and visit the top-rate fringing coral at **Manta Ray Bay**, **Langford Reef** and **Butterfly Bay**, on the northern and north-eastern tips of the island – visibility can be poor here, but on a good day these sites offer some of the best diving in the Whitsundays.

Hayman Island

The extremely high price of accommodation at the *Hayman Island Resort* (Ⓣ07/4940 1244, Ⓦwww.hayman.com.au; ⑧) pales into insignificance when compared with the resort's building costs, which topped $300 million. Guests indulge in lush rooms with extravagant and genuine Baroque and Renaissance furnishings, and staff move about through underground tunnels so that they don't get in the way. Not surprisingly, day-trippers aren't allowed anywhere near the place, although cruises and some dive-trips stop off for a look at the coral off **Blue Pearl Bay** – which isn't actually that exciting – on the island's west coast.

The Molles and nearby islands

South Molle Island was a source of fine-grained stone for Ngaro Aborigines, a unique material for the tools that have been found on other islands and may help in mapping trade routes. The slightly shabby **resort** (Ⓣ07/4946 9433, Ⓦwww.southmolleisland.com.au; ⑤) in the north of the island offers heaps of extras – such as guided walks, and all sports and facilities – along with stand-by rates. **Walking tracks** from behind the golf course lead to gum trees and rainforest, encompassing vistas of the islands from the top of Spion Kop and Mount Jeffreys, and some quiet beaches at the south end.

South Molle's resort can sometimes organize a lift to the **campsite** on uninhabited **North Molle Island**, only 2km away (or contact Camping Whitsunday; see box on p.438); the beach here is made up of rough coral fragments, but the snorkelling is fairly good. There are another couple of campsites on **Mid-Molle Island**, joined to South Molle by a low-tide causeway about half a kilometre from the resort.

Daydream Island is little more than a tiny wooded rise between South Molle and the mainland, with a narrow beach running the length of the east side, and coral to snorkel over at the north end. The **resort** (Ⓣ07/4948 8488, Ⓦwww.daydreamisland.com; ⑧) offers fine food and hospitality, but its regimental lines dominate views of the island from the sea and detract from an otherwise very pretty scene. Fantasea (see p.438 for details) offers day-trips for $65, or $72 including lunch at the resort.

Tiny **Planton**, **Tancred** and **Denman** islands are just offshore from South Molle – with no facilities and limited camping at the National Parks sites here, they're about as isolated as you'll get in the Whitsundays. All three are surrounded by reef, but be careful of strong currents. Again, Camping Whitsunday and Island Camping Connections offer drop offs for $40–45 (see p.438).

Long Island

Long Island is exactly that, being not much more than a narrow, ten-kilometre ribbon almost within reach of the mainland forests. There are a few worthwhile hikes through the rainforest to **Sandy Bay** (where there's a National Parks campsite) or up **Humpy Point**, as well as **three resorts**. *Long Island Resort* at Happy Bay (Ⓣ07/4946 9400, Ⓦwww.clubcroc.com.au; packages including meals and transfers ⑥) is a family-oriented place with all sorts of entertainment on hand; Fantasea (see p.438) run a day-trip here for $59. *Peppers Palm Bay* (Ⓣ07/4946 9233, Ⓦwww.peppers.com.au; cabins and bungalows ⑧), half a kilometre south at the island's waist, is a more exclusive upmarket retreat, but for a real escape, head to *South Long Island Wilderness Lodge* (Ⓣ07/3221 7799, Ⓦwww.southlongisland.com; ⑧), whose self-contained waterfront cabins, superb food and attentive service are only accessible by helicopter.

Hamilton and Lindeman islands

The apartment buildings dominating the view on **Hamilton Island** are the Gold Coast revisited, and it's interesting to speculate about what will happen to them during the next big cyclone. An enormous colony of fruit bats lives in the trees behind the waterfront and, apart from the flocks of cockatoos, seems to be the only native wildlife here. The island is privately owned, and its businesses operate under a lease: development includes a quaint **colonial waterfront** with hotel, bakery and various other stores, the *Hamilton Island Resort* (Ⓣ13 73 33, Ⓦwww.hamiltonisland.com.au; ⑥), a small **zoo**, and so many restaurants, pools, gift shops and sports facilities that the original character of the island has long since vanished. The twin towers of the resort loom over the beach complex, and the best view of the whole area is from one of their **external glass lifts**, which run up to penthouse level. Fantasea (see p.438) runs a day-trip here for $83.

Getting around the Whitsundays

Island resort transfers to Hamilton, Daydream, *Long Island Resort* and South Molle are offered by Fantasea (Ⓣ07/4946 5111, Ⓦwww.fantasea.com.au) and Cruise Whitsundays (Ⓣ07/4946 4662, Ⓦwww.cruisewhitsundays.com.au); other resorts run their own transfers for guests only. Fantasea and Voyager (Ⓣ07/4946 5255, Ⓦwww.wiac.com.au) also offer **three-island day-cruises**: Voyager call in at Hook, Daydream and Whitehaven Beach on Whitsunday ($130 including lunch, glass-bottom boat tour and snorkelling gear) and Fantasea to *Long Island Resort*, Daydream and Hamilton ($75 boat only). For **camping transfers** to National Parks campsites, contact Island Camping Connections (Ⓣ07/4946 5255) or Camping Whitsunday (Ⓣ07/4946 9330, Ⓦwww.campingwhitsundays.com.au).

Day-cruises usually take in two or more islands, and offer the chance to experience the thrills of boom-netting – sitting in a large rope hammock stretched above the water at the front of the boat so that you can catch the full soaking force of the waves – and do some snorkelling; others may concentrate on a single theme, such as whale watching, fishing or lazing on Whitehaven Beach. **Multi-day cruises** cover much the same territory but at a slower pace, and may give sailing lessons. **Scuba diving** is also often available to certified divers on cruises, at wildly variable rates upwards of $60 a dive. Groups with yachting experience might consider a **bareboat charter** (see "Listings" on p.434 for operators).

The list below is not exhaustive; word of mouth is the best method of finding out about who is still in business, what the current deals are and if operators live up to their advertisements. Check the **length** of trips carefully – "three days" might mean one full day and two half-days – along with how much time is actually spent cruising and at the destination, how many other people will be on the cruise, and the size of the vessel. There are scores of beautiful boats, so you'll be swayed by your preference for a performance racing yacht or a fun trip with lots of deck space on which to lounge. Bear in mind that a cheerful (or jaded) crew can make all the difference, and that **weather conditions** can affect destinations offered. Many yachts also have poor environmental practices and pump waste directly into the sea, so it's wise to ask probing questions. Finally, if you want to save money, shop around as close to departure times as possible, when advertised prices tend to drop.

Day-trips: sailing

The following cost $95–120.

Illusions Ⓣ07/4946 5255, Ⓦwww.illusions.net.au. Catamaran trip to Hayman's Blue Pearl Bay includes snorkelling, boom-netting and lunch.

Maxi Ragamuffin Ⓣ1800 454 777, Ⓦwww.maxiaction.com.au. This 24-metre-long racer runs to Blue Pearl Bay (Mon, Wed & Sat) and Whitehaven Beach (Tues, Thurs & Sun), with snorkelling and diving available. Lunch included.

Day-trips: powered vessels

With the exception of *Ocean Rafting*, the following cost around $130, and include lunch unless otherwise stated.

Lindeman Island suffered as a victim of feral goats, though their eradication has seen native plants making a comeback in a small melaleuca swamp and on the wooded northeast side. **Mount Oldfield** offers panoramic views, while other walking tracks lead to swimming beaches on the north shore. The *Club Med* **resort** (Ⓣ1800 258 263, Ⓦwww.clubmed.com.au; ⑧), Australia's first, has all the services you'd expect and no day-trippers.

Mantaray ⓣ1800 816 365, ⓦwww.mantaraycharters.com. Fast and relatively roomy boat out to Whitehaven, where you spend around three hours at leisure before heading north to Mantaray Bay and some good snorkelling.

Ocean Rafting ⓣ07/4946 6848, ⓦwww.oceanrafting.com. Great-value, action-packed cruise on a zippy inflatable to Whitehaven Beach, with options to visit either Hill Inlet or the Aboriginal caves at Nara Inlet ($100). Maximum 25 passengers.

Reefjet ⓣ07/4946 5366, ⓦwww.reefjet.com.au. Fast run out to Whitehaven Beach and Hook Island for sand and snorkelling.

Whitehaven Express ⓣ07/4946 7172, ⓦwww.whitehavenexpress.com.au. Trips to Whitsunday Island, stopping for scenery at Hill Inlet before a snorkel and beach BBQ at Whitehaven.

Longer trips

The following cost $300–500 for two-night, three-day outings; trips depart at around 9am from Abel Point Marina, returning on day three about 4pm. The basic itinerary is to visit Hook Island via Nara Inlet, then move round to Whitehaven Beach on Whitsunday. There are two major sailboat companies in town, fronting for the majority of vessels: **Oz Adventure Sailing** (ⓣ1800 359 554, ⓦwww.ozsailing.com.au) specializes in classic tall and vintage-style ships, while **Southern Cross** (ⓣ1800 675 790, ⓦwww.soxsail.com.au) puts the emphasis on maxi-yacht racers. Another large stable is owned by **Tallarook** (ⓣ1800 331 316, ⓦwww.tallarookdive.com.au), whose varied bag of vessels get mixed reports, but offer diving for certified divers.

Anaconda III ⓣ1800 677 119, ⓦwww.airliebeach.com. The largest party yacht in the Whitsundays, taking up to fifty passengers, and fantastically comfortable. Relatively expensive, but you do get three full days and three nights aboard.

Derwent Hunter (Oz Adventure Sailing). Ninety-foot schooner built in 1945 and totally refitted with timber decking and fittings after years spent as a research vessel and a film set, and yet more time engaged in dubious activities in the South China Seas.

Dream Catcher (Oz Adventure Sailing). Beautiful, classic wooden ketch with modern furnishings and carrying just ten passengers.

Iceberg ⓣ07/4125 2343, ⓦwww.sailingwhitsundays.net. Modern, fifteen-metre cruising yacht with an enthusiastic crew, focusing on fun-filled adrenalin activities including kitesurfing. Maximum of thirteen passengers.

Siska (Southern Cross). A 25-metre ocean maxi-yacht with room for twenty passengers, and winner of races between the UK and Australia.

Southern Cross (Southern Cross). The company's flagship: a high-speed, 21-metre-long America's Cup challenger accommodating fourteen passengers, aimed at couples.

Waltzing Matilda (Oz Adventure Sailing). A more modern design than most of Oz Adventure Sailing's fleet, this eighteen-metre ketch is not that roomy, but has a great atmosphere.

Bowen and the route to Townsville

BOWEN, a quiet seafront settlement 60km northwest of Proserpine, was once under consideration as the site of the state capital, but it floundered after Townsville's foundation. Today, stark first impressions created by the sterile bulk of the saltworks on the highway are offset by a certain small-town charm and some pretty beaches just off to the north. The main attraction for travellers though is the prospect of seasonal **farm work**: Bowen's mangoes and tomatoes are famous throughout Queensland, and there's a large floating population of itinerant pickers in town between April and January. The backpackers hostels (see below) can help with finding work, though nothing is guaranteed.

Bowen's attractive **beaches** lie a couple of kilometres north of the town centre. **Queens Beach**, which faces north, is sheltered, long and has a stinger net for the jellyfish season, but the best is **Horseshoe Bay**, small, and hemmed in by some sizeable boulders, with good waters for a swim or snorkel – though the construction of an oversized resort nearby threatens to ruin the atmosphere.

With your own transport, it might be worth **skipping Bowen** in favour of the ranch-style *Bogie River Bush House* (ⓣ07/4785 3407, ⓦwww.bogiebushhouse.com.au; dorms $20, rooms ⑤), about 60km inland from town towards Collinsville. This splendid retreat has a pool and offers the chance to go horse riding, fishing, or to play with tame wildlife; you can also organize farm work here.

Bowen practicalities

Bowen's centre overlooks **Edgecumbe Bay**, with all the shops and services spaced out along broad but empty **Herbert Street**. The **train station** is a few kilometres west of town near the highway, while **buses** stop outside Bowen Travel (ⓣ07/4786 2835), just off Herbert on Williams Street, which can organize tickets for both.

Budget **accommodation** – which should be booked in advance and is usually offered at weekly rates only – consists of *Bowen Backpackers*, at the beach end of Herbert Street (ⓣ07/4786 3433, ⓔbowenbackpackers@bigpond.com; sometimes closes Jan–March; dorms $23.50, rooms ②), who have a huge pool out the back; and *Reefers by the Beach* at 93 Horseshoe Bay Rd (ⓣ07/4786 4199, ⓦwww.reefers.com.au; dorms $25, rooms ②), a spacious place with a pool located 3km from town near the beaches. **Mid-range** choices include *Castle Motor Lodge*, 6 Don St (ⓣ07/4786 1322, ⓦwww.caslemotorlodge.com.au; ④), about the closest option to the centre of town. You can **eat** at the *Grand View Hotel*, down near the Harbour Office on Herbert, or *McDee's Café*, on the corner of Herbert and George streets; alternatively, stock up at Magee's **supermarket** on Williams Street and at the town's numerous fruit and vegetable stalls.

The Burdekin River, Ayr and the Yongala

Further on up the highway, 115km past Bowen, are the towns of **Home Hill** and **Ayr**, separated by a mill, a few kilometres of canefields and the iron framework of the **Burdekin River Bridge**. The river, one of the north's most famous landmarks, is still liable to flood during severe wet seasons, despite having to fight its way across three weirs and a dam. On the northern side, **AYR** is a compact farming town fast becoming another popular stop on the **farm work** trail. The highway – which runs through town as Queen Street – is where you'll find the **bus stop** and all essential services, as well as two workers' hostels which can find you employment picking and packing capsicums, amongst other things – *Ayr Backpackers*, on Willmington Street (ⓣ07/4783 5837; phone in advance for pick-up; dorms $110 per week; single nights only available outside of the fruit-picking season and on special request), is definitely the better option.

Ayr's other attraction is easy access to the wreck of the **Yongala**, a 109m-long passenger ship which sank with all hands during a cyclone in 1911. It now lies intact and encrusted in coral in 18–30m of water, and is home to turtles, rays, moray eels and huge schools of barracuda, mackerel and trevally, making for a staggeringly good **wreck dive**. *Yongala Dive*, out from Ayr at 56 Narrah St,

Alva Beach (ⓣ07/4783 1519, ⓦwww.yongaladive.com.au; dorms $25, rooms ❸) run trips for **certified divers only** from $200, including all gear rental, pick-up from town, and two dives. They also have very comfortable **accommodation** if you plan to stay overnight. Be aware that the wreck is in an exposed location, and it's not much fun diving here if the weather is rough; this is also a demanding site – deep, with strong currents and startlingly big fish – and it's best not to go unless you've logged twenty dives or more.

Townsville

Hot and stuffy **TOWNSVILLE** sprawls around a broad spit of land between the isolated hump of Castle Hill and swampy Ross Creek. While its biggest attraction is **Magnetic Island**, just offshore, the city does have its moments: there's a visible maritime history; long sea views from the Strand promenade; and the muggy, salty evening air and old pile houses on the surrounding hills which mark out Townsville as the coast's first really tropical city.

Townsville was founded in 1864 by John Melton Black and Robert Towns, entrepreneurs who felt that a settlement was needed for northern stockmen who couldn't reach Bowen when the Burdekin River was in flood. Despite an inferior harbour, the town soon outstripped Bowen in terms of both size and prosperity, its growth accelerated by **gold** finds inland at Ravenswood and Charters Towers (see p.528). Today, it's the gateway to the far north and transit point for routes west to Mount Isa and the Northern Territory; it's also an important military centre, seat of a university and home to substantial Torres Strait Islander and Aboriginal communities.

Arrival and information

Townsville's roughly triangular city centre is hemmed in by Cleveland Bay to the north, Ross Creek to the south and Castle Hill to the west. Following the north bank of Ross Creek, **Flinders Street** is the main drag, sectioned into a downtown pedestrian mall before running its last five hundred metres as **Flinders Street East**. The **train station** is central, just southwest of the centre along Flinders Street; the **airport** is 5km northwest of town, served by a shuttle bus ($8 single, $14 return; book in advance on ⓣ07/4775 5544). Virgin Blue flies to town from Brisbane, and Jetstar and Qantas from everywhere else. At the moment there are **two long-distance bus stops**: Premier (ⓣ13 34 10) pull in on the south side of Ross Creek on Palmer Street, with a short walk across a bridge to the city centre; Greyhound (ⓣ13 14 19) stop north of the centre outside the Magnetic Island Breakwater ferry terminal on Sir Leslie Theiss Drive.

Public transport serves the suburbs rather than the sights, though much of what there is to see is central; some hostels have **bikes** available. A very helpful **information booth**, with a separate counter handling and booking diving, cruises and tours is located in Flinders Street Mall (daily 9am–5pm).

Accommodation

Lodgings are concentrated around the city centre and might collect you from transit points if you call ahead.

Civic Guesthouse 262 Walker St ⓣ1800 646 619, ⓦwww.civicguesthouse.com. Clean and helpful backpackers' with a well-equipped kitchen, spa pool and free Friday-night BBQs. Deals on dive courses with Ocean Dive next door. Dorms $24, rooms ❸

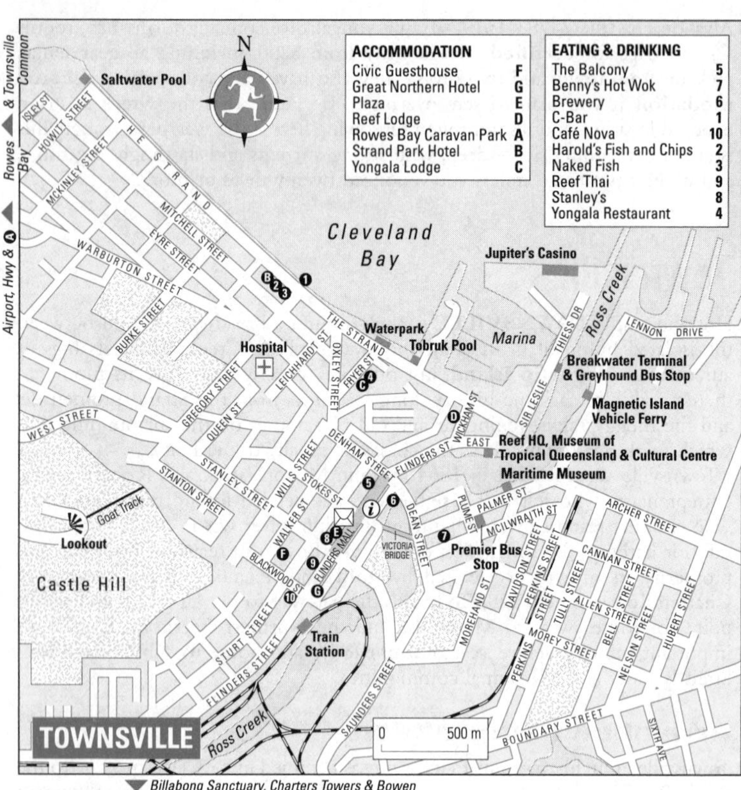

Great Northern Hotel Cnr Flinders and Blackwood streets ⓣ07/4771 6191. The downstairs bar in this Old Queenslander pub has lots of character, and serves huge meals from $12. Rooms have fan or a/c and shared facilities. ③

Plaza Cnr of Flinders and Stanley streets ⓣ07/4772 1888, ⓦwww.plazahotels.com.au. Downtown, motel-like apartments; modern, friendly and with a bit more panache than the average hotel. ⑤

Reef Lodge 4–6 Wickham St ⓣ07/4721 1112, ⓦwww.reeflodge.com.au. The cheapest place in town, and friendly enough with all facilities including a girls-only dorm, though a bit cramped. Dorms $22, rooms ③

Rowes Bay Caravan Park Heatley Parade ⓣ07/4771 3576, ⓦwww.rowesbaycp.com.au. Off The Strand, 3km north of the centre towards Pallarenda, overlooking Magnetic Island across the bay; take bus #7 from the mall. Very popular cabins and campsites, so worth booking in advance. Camping $20, cabins (with or without en suite) ③

Strand Park Hotel 59–60 The Strand ⓣ07/4750 7888, ⓦwww.jasons.com.au. Small boutique motel in Townsville's prettiest area, offering self-contained double rooms and suites with either garden or sea views. Rooms ⑤–⑥

Yongala Lodge 11 Fryer St ⓣ07/4772 4633, ⓦwww.historicyongala.com.au. A welcoming place, named after the city's most famous shipwreck, with spacious if slightly shabby motel rooms joined to a historic old Queenslander with original furnishings. ④

The City and around

Funded by inland gold mines during the late nineteenth century, some of Townsville's solid stone colonial buildings are quite imposing, especially along Flinders Street East. On the corner of the Mall and Denham Street, the **Perc**

Tucker Art Gallery (Mon–Fri 10am–5pm, Sat & Sun 10am–2pm; free) is another grand old building, featuring travelling exhibitions of mainly antique art. On Friday (6.30pm–9pm May–Dec) and Sunday (8.30am–1pm), the Mall itself hosts **Cotters Market**, which has good local produce and crafts.

Castle Hill looms over the city centre, an obvious target if you're after clear views of the region. There's a road to the top from Stanley Street; on foot, head along Gregory Street to Stanton Terrace and join a walking path of sorts that climbs to the lookout, for vistas over the city to the distant Hervey Range and Magnetic Island.

The Strand runs northwest along Cleveland Bay, lined with more old houses and fig trees looking out to Magnetic Island. The busy waterfront strip here is a beautiful stretch of palms, beach, shady lawns and free hotplates for picnics, plus cafés, a swimming pool and excellent **children's waterpark**, plus a specially built jetty for fishing. Off the eastern end of the road along Sir Leslie Theiss Drive, you'll find the Magnetic Island Breakwater ferry terminal, a **marina** (where most dive-trips depart) and the adjacent **Jupiter's Casino** – once the only legal gaming venue in Queensland.

The Reef HQ, Museum of Tropical Queensland and Cultural Centre

The **Reef HQ**, on Flinders Street East (daily 9.30am–5pm; aquarium $21.50, IMAX theatre $14), houses a terrific aquarium and **IMAX theatre** (hourly shows), which projects films with a popular science theme onto a domed ceiling to create an overwhelming, wraparound image. The huge live tanks in the **aquarium** contain recreations of the reef, where you can watch schools of fish drifting over coral, clown fish hiding inside anemones' tentacles and myopic turtles cruising past. Between the main tanks are smaller ones for oddities – sea snakes, deep-sea nautiluses, baby turtles and lobsters. Upstairs, videos about the reef are shown, and you can handle some inoffensive invertebrates including tiny clams, sea slugs and starfish.

Next door, an innovative building houses the **Museum of Tropical Queensland** (daily 9.30am–5pm; $12), which showcases the Queensland Museum's marine archeology collection. The centrepiece is a full-sized, cut-away replica – figurehead and all – of the front third of the **Pandora**, a British frigate tied up in the tale of the **Bounty mutiny**, which sank on the outer reef in 1791 (see box on p.444 for the full tale). Accompanying artefacts salvaged off the wreck since its discovery in 1977 include water jars and bottles, tankards owned by the crew, and the surgeon's pocket watch, with glass face and finely chased gold and silver mountings. Dioramas recreate life on board, with views into the cramped captain's cabin and a dramatic reconstruction of the sinking, while a life-sized blueprint of the *Pandora*'s upper deck is mapped out on the carpet. You can also join in the twice-daily "Running Out the Gun", the loading and mock firing of a replica cannon from the *Pandora*. Other sections of the museum cover Outback Queensland's extensive **fossil finds** (including several life-sized dinosaur models).

In the same building, the **Cultural Centre** hasn't really found its feet yet, but hopes to showcase Aboriginal and Torres Strait Island dance and music. Hour-long **performances** (Mon, Wed, Thurs & Fri 11am; $12) are scheduled for the near future.

Townsville Common and Billabong Sanctuary

The **Townsville Common Conservation Park** (daily 7.30am–7.30pm; free) is 6.5km north of the centre, on the coast at **Pallarenda**. The Bohle River pools into wetlands below the Many Peaks Range, a habitat perfect for wildfowl

The Bounty and the Pandora

In 1788, the British Admiralty vessel **Bounty** sailed from England to Tahiti, with a mission to collect **breadfruit** seedlings, intended to provide a cheap source of food for Britain's plantation slaves in the West Indies. But the stay in Tahiti's mellow climate proved so much better than life on board the *Bounty* that on the return journey in April 1789 the crew **mutinied**, led by the officer **Fletcher Christian**. Along with eighteen crew who refused to join in the mutiny, **Captain William Bligh** was set adrift in a longboat far out in the Pacific, while the mutineers returned to Tahiti, intending to settle there.

Things didn't go as planned, however. After an incredible feat of navigation over 3600 nautical miles of open sea, Bligh and all but one of his companions reached the Portuguese colony of Timor in June, emaciated but still alive, from where Bligh lost no time in catching a vessel back to England, arriving there in March 1790. His report on the mutiny immediately saw the Admiralty dispatch the frigate **Pandora** off to Tahiti under the cold-hearted **Captain Edwards**, with instructions to bring back the mutineers to stand trial in London.

Meanwhile in Tahiti, Christian and seven of the mutiny's ringleaders – knowing that sooner or later the Admiralty would try to find them – had, along with a group of Tahitians, taken the *Bounty* and sailed off into the Pacific. Fourteen of the *Bounty*'s crew stayed behind on Tahiti, however, and when the *Pandora* arrived there in March 1791, they were rounded up, clapped in chains and incarcerated in the ship's brig, a three-metre-long wooden cell known as **"Pandora's Box"**.

Having spent a fruitless few months island-hopping in search of the *Bounty*, Captain Edwards headed up the east coast of Australia where, on the night of August 29, the *Pandora* hit a northern section of the Great Barrier Reef. As waves began to break up the vessel on the following day, Edwards ordered the longboats to be loaded with supplies and abandoned the ship, leaving his prisoners still locked up on board; it was only thanks to one of the crew that ten of them managed to scramble out as the *Pandora* slid beneath the waves.

In a minor replay of Bligh's voyage, the *Pandora*'s survivors took three weeks to make it to Timor in their longboats, and arrived back in England the following year. Edwards was castigated for the heartless treatment of his prisoners, but otherwise held blameless for the wreck. The ten surviving mutineers were court-martialled: four were acquitted, three hanged, and three had their death sentences commuted. Captain Bligh was later made Governor of New South Wales, where he suffered another mutiny known as the **"Rum Rebellion"** (see "History", p.1084). To add insult to injury, the *Bounty*'s whole project proved a failure; when breadfruit trees were eventually introduced to the West Indies, the slaves refused to eat them.

Seventeen years later, the American vessel *Topaz* stopped mid-Pacific at the isolated rocky fastness of **Pitcairn Island** and, to the amazement of its crew, found it settled by a small colony of English-speaking people. These turned out to be the descendants of the *Bounty* mutineers, along with the last survivor, the elderly **John Adams** (also known as Alexander Smith). Adams told the *Topaz*'s crew that having settled Pitcairn and burned the *Bounty*, the mutineers had fought with the Tahitian men over the women, and that Christian and all the men – except Adams and three other mutineers – had been killed. The other three had since died, leaving only Adams, the women, and their children on the island. After Adams' death, Pitcairn's population was briefly moved to Norfolk Island in the 1850s (see p.296), where some settled, though many of their descendants returned and still live on Pitcairn.

including the brolga, the stately symbol of the northern marshes. Less popular – with rice farmers anyway – are the huge flocks of magpie geese that visit after rains and are a familiar sight over the city. You need a vehicle to reach the park, but once there you can get about on foot, although a car or bike makes short work of the less-interesting tracks between lagoons. Camouflaged **hides** at Long Swamp and Pink Lily Lagoon let you clock up a few of the hundred or more bird species in the park: egrets stalk frogs around waterlilies, ibises and spoonbills strain the water for edibles and geese honk at each other, undisturbed by the low-flying airport traffic – bring binoculars.

Seventeen kilometres south of Townsville on the highway, **Billabong Sanctuary** (daily 8am–5pm; $26; Ⓦ www.billabongsanctuary.com.au) is a well-kept collection of penned and wild Australian fauna laid out around a large waterhole. Amongst the free-ranging wildlife you'll find wallabies and flocks of demanding whistling ducks on the prowl for handouts; animals you'll probably be happier to see are caged include saltwater crocs, cassowaries (bred for release into the wild), dingoes, wedge-tailed eagles and snakes. A swimming pool and accompanying snack-bar make the sanctuary a fine place to spend a few hours, and you can also tour the grounds with an Aboriginal guide and get an introduction to bush foods.

Eating, drinking and entertainment

There are plenty of good **eating** options in Townsville, with restaurants grouped in three main areas: in the centre on Flinders Street; south on Palmer Street; and out along The Strand. For evening **entertainment**, many of the town's hotels cater to the sizeable military and student presence and have regular live music, for which you might have to pay a cover charge.

Cafés and restaurants

The Balcony Flinders St Mall. Mediterranean-style salads and grills, good coffee and cakes, and a great view over the mall from upper-storey balcony tables. Mains around $18.

Benny's Hot Wok Palmer St. Stylish and popular Singaporean and Asian café-restaurant, with tasty bowls of noodle soup for around $15, and Indonesian or Thai curries for about $21.

Brewery Cnr of Denham and Flinders streets. Café, bar and boutique brewery housed in the old post office building. The beer and ambience are good, though the outdoor tables are a bit noisy thanks to the adjacent main road.

C-Bar The Strand. One of several café-restaurants in the area, right on the seafront with outside tables and a bar overlooking Magnetic Island. Good for anything from a coffee or beer to succulent char-grilled steak or lamb kebabs and salad. Happy hour daily from 5 to 6pm, with live local bands on Sun evenings. Mains around $21.

Café Nova Cnr of Blackwood and Flinders streets, near the station. Long-running student venue, with generous helpings and meals, including tasty salads, for under $15. Tues–Fri 10.30am–midnight, Sat & Sun 6pm–midnight.

Harold's Fish and Chips The Strand, opposite *C-Bar*. If you can't catch your own from the nearby fishing jetty, console yourself with a takeaway from this excellent establishment.

Naked Fish Next door to *Harold's*. Upmarket modern seafood with mains from $20 to $30, excellent calamari and a broad wine list. Daily 5pm–late.

Reef Thai 455 Flinders St. Seafood green curry, satays and a chilli-packed beef dish known as "crying tiger". Mains around $17. Daily 5.30–10pm.

Stanley's Cnr Flinders and Stanley streets. Airy café and bistro serving early breakfasts, pasta, ornate sandwiches and grills.

Yongala Restaurant 11 Fryer St, in front of the *Yongala Lodge*. Historic, authentically furnished surroundings where you can enjoy live music and good, Greek-influenced food. Appropriately, the building's architect was on board the *Yongala* when it sank.

Pubs, bars and clubs

Bank Flinders St East. Drunken mix of military and locals can make this nightclub a hair-raising place to spend an evening.

Exchange Hotel Flinders St East. This pub is a real locals' watering-hole, with occasional live bands.

Mad Cow Flinders St East. Pool tables and dancing to cheesy pop – packed on weekends.

Molly Malones Flinders St East. Standard Irish bar with stout on tap. Happy hour Mon–Fri 5–6pm, live bands Wed & Sat, and Irish dancing on Sun evenings.

Diving and reef trips from Townsville

The main diving attraction out from Townsville is the *Yongala* shipwreck (see p.440), though there's also access to the local stretch of the Barrier Reef. For **reef day-trips**, the options are *Sunsea* (☎07/4772 7711, Ⓦwww.sunferries.com.au), a big tourist catamaran which runs to John Brewer Reef; or Tropical Dive (☎07/4771 6150, Ⓦwww.tropicaldiving.com.au), who visit Wheeler Cay in a more youth-oriented vessel – either option costs around $145, plus $75–$120 for two dives. For the **Yongala**, Adrenaline (☎07/4724 0600, Ⓦwww.adrenalinedive.com.au) runs day-trips ($179), while Prodive (☎07/4721 1760, Ⓦwww.prodivetownsville.com.au) offers three-day live-aboard trips including both the *Yongala* and Barrier Reef ($775).

Listings

Banks All located on Flinders St Mall, and there are ATMs in most pubs.
Bookshops Mary Who?, at 414 Flinders St, has a fine range of just about everything.
Car rental Independent (☎07/4725 2771, Ⓦwww.independentrentals.com.au) has basic models from $35 a day.
Hospital Townsville General Hospital, Eyre St ☎07/4781 9211.
Internet At Umbrella Gallery, 482 Flinders St ($3–4 per hour).
Police 30 Stanley St ☎07/4760 7777.
Post office Behind Flinders St Mall on Sturt St, near the junction with Stanley St.
Taxi There's a stand at Flinders St Mall ☎13 10 08.
Tours Detours (☎07/4728 5311, Ⓦwww.detourcoaches.com) run day-tours to the old gold-mining town of Charters Towers ($115) and rainforest at Paluma ($98); Ironbark Tours (☎0427 798 794, Ⓦwww.ironbarktours.com.au) also visit Paluma ($125), and more forest and waterfalls at Wallaman Falls ($140).

Magnetic Island

Another island named by Captain Cook in 1770 – after his compass played up as he sailed past – **Magnetic Island** is a beautiful triangular granite core 12km from Townsville. There's a lot to be said for a trip here: lounging on a beach, swimming over coral, bouncing around in a moke from one roadside lookout to another, and enjoying the sea breeze and the island's vivid colours. Small enough to drive around in half a day, but large enough to harbour several small settlements, Magnetic Island's accommodation and transfer costs are considerably lower than on many of Queensland's other islands, and if you've ever wanted to spot a **koala** in the wild, this could be your chance – they're often seen wedged into gum trees up in the northeast corner of the island.

Seen from the sea the island's apex, **Mount Cook**, hovers above eucalypt woods variegated with patches of darker green vine forest. The north and east coasts are pinched into shallow **sandy bays** punctuated by granite headlands and coral reefs, while the western part of the island is flatter and edged with mangroves. A little less than half the island is designated as national park, with the settlements of **Picnic Bay**, **Nelly Bay**, **Arcadia** and **Horseshoe Bay** dotted along the east coast. Shops and supplies are available on the island, so there's no need to bring anything with you.

Arrival and island transport

Two ferries operate between Townsville and Magnetic Island. **Sunferries** leaves from the Breakwater terminal on Sir Leslie Theiss Drive for the marina at Nelly Bay, midway along the east coast, at least ten times daily, with extra departures at weekends ($26 return; ⓣ07/4771 3855); pick up a **timetable** from any information booth. There's no need to book, just buy a ticket at the jetty and hop on board. The **Magnetic Island Car Ferry** ($144 return for a car and up to three passengers, pedestrians $22 return; ⓣ07/4772 5422, ⓦwww.magneticislandferry.com.au) operates to Geoffrey Bay, Arcadia, at least four times daily from Ross Street, at the end of Palmer Street on the south bank of the creek in Townsville.

Magnetic Island has 35km of road, including a dirt track to West Point and a sealed stretch between Picnic and Horseshoe bays. **Magnetic Island Bus Service** (ⓣ07/4778 5130) meets all Sunferries and runs between Picnic Bay and Horseshoe Bay more or less hourly between 6.45am and 8.55pm with late services to 11.40pm on weekends; their day-pass ($12) allows unlimited travel and can be purchased from the bus driver or at the tourist office in the Nelly Bay Ferry Terminal. For your **own transport**, Moke Magnetic at Nelly Bay Ferry Terminal (ⓣ07/4778 5377, ⓦwww.mokemagnetic.com) rents out fun mini-mokes for a flat $68 a day plus $200 deposit, while Tropical Topless (ⓣ07/4758 1111), across the car park from the same ferry terminal charge $60 a day plus fuel; both require a minimum driver age of 21, and ask that you stick to sealed roads. Some accommodation rent out **bicycles** for about $15 a day, as do Island Bike (ⓣ0425 244 193, ⓦwww.islandbike.com.au), who deliver anywhere on the island.

Accommodation

Magnetic Island's **accommodation** is ubiquitous, with options for all budgets. Most lodgings have Internet access, rent out snorkelling gear, bikes, beach gear and watersports equipment, can make tour bookings and might pick you up if you call in advance.

Nelly Bay

Base Backpackers 1 Nelly Bay Rd ⓣ1800 242 273, ⓦwww.basebackpackers.com. Large, modern backpackers' with a lively atmosphere, large pool, bar and DJ, situated at the secluded southern end of Nelly Beach. It has excellent facilities, and there's a restaurant serving cheap meals. Dorms $26, female-only dorm $30, doubles ❸

Beachside Palms 7 Esplanade ⓣ0419 660 078. Four clean and spacious one- and two-bed apartments facing the beach, with pool and laundry facilities. ❺

Magnetic Island Tropical Resort Yates St ⓣ1800 069 122, ⓦwww.magneticislandresort.com. Clean and comfortable chalet-style cabins with a/c and bathroom, in a lovely eight-acre bush

△Magnetic Island

setting attracting lots of birdlife. Reasonably priced evening steak-and-seafood restaurant and complimentary breakfast. 4

Segara Villas 20 Mango Parkway ☎07/4778 5151, ⓦwww.segara.com.au. Beautiful Balinese-style villas with polished wooden floors, set around a pool amidst tropical gardens. 6

Arcadia

Arcadia Beach Guest House 27 Marine Parade ☎07/4778 5668. Nautically-themed modern units with a slightly quirky touch; the pricier units are aimed at the "romantic-getaway" market. 3–5

Foresthaven 11–13 Cook Rd ☎07/4778 5153. Self-contained apartments with pool and tropical garden backing onto national park; they also offer dorms, though this is not primarily a backpackers'. Dorms $25, doubles 3

Marshall's 3 Endeavour Rd ☎07/4778 5112. Friendly, low-key B&B with a family atmosphere and quiet garden close to walking trails. Three-day discounts are available. 4

Horseshoe Bay

Bungalow Bay YHA 40 Horseshoe Bay Rd ☎07/4778 5577, ⓦwww.bungalowbay.com.au. Quiet retreat with cabin accommodation in a large wooded setting with pool, restaurant, large kitchen and a campsite. The owner feeds hundreds of wild lorikeets every afternoon. Dorms $21, rooms 3

Maggie's Beach House Pacific Drive ☎1800 001 544. Large, purpose-built backpackers' complex overlooking the sea, with its own pool, budget restaurant, Internet facilities and bar. There's too much bare concrete though, and you can't help feeling that this sort of high-density accommodation misses the whole point of Magnetic Island. Dorms $26, rooms 3

New Friends Bed & Breakfast Horseshoe Bay Rd ☎07/4758 1220. Spacious, well-furnished apartments in large grounds, five minutes' walk from the beach. 5

Sails 13 Pacific Drive ☎07/4778 5117, ⓦwww.sailsonhorshoe.com.au. Self-contained apartments with a full range of modern amenities, including pool and outdoor BBQ area, at the quiet end of Horseshoe Bay. One-bedroom apartments 6, villas 7

The island

Set on the southernmost tip of the island, **PICNIC BAY** is a languid spot, well shaded by surrounding gum woodland and beachfront fig trees, with a nice beach facing Townsville. Once the main ferry terminal (which has since relocated to Nelly Bay), this tiny settlement at the end of the sealed road is now facing an identity crisis, and there's not really much to do here.

Moving up the east coast, **NELLY BAY** is thriving thanks to the new marina complex and ferry terminal, and comprises a sprawl of houses fronted by a good beach, with a little reef some way out. Two streets back is a shopping complex with a supermarket and a couple of places to eat, while the **aquarium** (daily 9am–5pm; $2) just around the corner has tanks of giant clams – all part of a research project, and only open to the public as an afterthought. Alternatively, there's a **walking track to Arcadia** from here, though it can be hot work – start early and take plenty of water. A little further along the coast, **ARCADIA** surrounds Geoffrey Bay and counts the good-value *Banister's Seafood Restaurant* at 22 McCabe Crescent among its attractions. At Arcadia's northern end is the perfect swimming beach of **Alma Bay**, hemmed in by cliffs and boulders, and with good snorkelling over the coral just offshore. A **walking track** from the end of Cook Road leads towards Mount Cook and the track to Nelly Bay, or up to Sphinx Lookout for sea views. At dawn or dusk you might see the diminutive island **rock wallaby** on an outcrop or boulder near Arcadia's jetty.

North of Arcadia the road forks, with the right branch (prohibited to rental vehicles) leading via tiny **Florence Bay** – one of the prettiest on the island – to Radical Bay, and the main road carrying on to Horseshoe. Leave your car at the junction here and continue uphill on foot to **the Forts**, built during World War II to protect Townsville from attack by the Japanese. The walking track climbs gently for about 1.5km through gum-tree scenery to gun emplacements (now just deserted blockhouses) set one above the other among

Magnetic Island tours and excursions

For a **tour** of the island, plump for a day out in a 4WD with Tropicana ($159 if booked online; ⓣ07/4758 1800, ⓦwww.tropicanatours.com.au); the cost seems steep, but you'll be very well fed and looked after, plus you'll see just about all the island's beaches and bays. You could also spend a day **sailing** to hard-to-reach beaches and bays with Jazza ($95; ⓣ1800 808 002, ⓦwww.jazza.com.au), including snorkelling, lunch and afternoon tea; or try your hand at **sea-kayaking** with Magnetic Island Sea Kayaks ($59 including breakfast; ⓣ07/4778 5424, ⓦwww.seakayak.com.au).

Relatively murky waters don't make Magnetic Island the most dramatic place to learn to **scuba dive**, but with easy shore access it's very cheap – certification courses start at $299 – and on a good day there's some fair coral, a couple of small shipwrecks and decent fish-life. Pleasure Divers (ⓣ1800 797 797) run courses, dive around the island, and can also arrange dives to the *Yongala* for experienced divers (see p.440).

granite boulders and pine trees. The best views are from the slit windows at the command centre, right at the pinnacle of the hill. The woods below the Forts are the best place to see **koalas**, introduced to the island in 1930. They sleep during the day, so tracking them down involves plenty of wandering around – although if you hear ferocious pig-like grunts and squeals, then some lively koalas are not far away.

Horseshoe Bay and around

The road ends in the north at **HORSESHOE BAY** on the island's longest and busiest beach, half of which is developed and half of which remains blissfully secluded, with views north beyond the bobbing yachts to distant Palm Island. The cluster of shops at the road's eastern end features a general store and bakery. Places **to eat** include the quaint *Sandbar Restaurant*, which serves excellent seafood, and the more flamboyant *Marlin Bar and Grill* with cheap steaks, several beers on tap and cocktails by the jug. The beach, which is good for swimming most of the year, is also a great place for activities – several beach-front operators **rent** out jet skis, kayaks, surf skis and boats, and provide joyrides on inflated tubes and water skis. Other diversions include **horse rides** with the experienced Bluey's Horseshoe Ranch ($75 for the popular beach ride, $105 for a half-day ride; advance bookings necessary on ⓣ07/4778 5109). **Walking tracks** lead over the headland to Radical Bay by way of tiny **Balding Bay**, arguably the nicest on the island; you can spend a perfect day here snorkelling around the coral gardens just offshore and cooking on the hotplate provided. **Radical Bay** itself is another pretty spot, half a kilometre of sandy beach sandwiched between two huge, pine-covered granite fists.

Townsville to Cairns

Just an hour to the north of Townsville the arid landscape that has predominated since Bundaberg transforms into dark green plateaus shrouded in cloud. There's superlative scenery at **Wallaman Falls**, inland from **Ingham**, and also near Cairns as the slopes of the coastal mountains rise up to front the **Bellenden Ker Range**. Forests here once formed a continuous belt but, though logging has thinned them to a disjointed necklace of national parks, it still seems that almost every side-track off the highway leads to a waterhole or falls surrounded by jungle

– this is where it really pays to have your own vehicle. There's also a handful of **islands** to explore, including the wilds of **Hinchinbrook**, as well as the **Mission Beach** area between **Tully** and **Innisfail**, where you might find regular work on fruit plantations or further opportunities to slump on the sand.

Paluma and Jourama Falls

The change in climate starts some 60km north of Townsville, where the Mount Spec road turns west off the highway and climbs a crooked 21km into the hills to **Paluma** township. Halfway there, a solid stone bridge, built by relief labour during the Great Depression of the 1930s, spans **Little Crystal Creek**, with some picnic tables and barbecue hotplates by the road, and deep swimming holes overshadowed by rainforest just up from the bridge – beware of slippery rocks and potentially strong currents. Look out too for large, metallic-blue **Ulysses butterflies** bobbing around the canopy.

PALUMA itself consists of a handful of weatherboard cottages in the rainforest at the top of the range. A couple of **walking tracks** (from 500m to 2km in length) take you into the gloom, including a ridgetop track to Witt's Lookout. Keep your eyes open for **chowchillas**, plump little birds with a dark body and white front which forage by kicking the leaf litter sideways; you'll also hear whipbirds and the snarls of the black-and-blue **Victoria riflebird**, a bird of paradise – they're fairly common in highland rainforest between here and the Atherton Tablelands, but elusive. For a good glimpse of these head for *Ivy Cottage Tearooms* (Tues–Fri 10.30am–4pm, Sat & Sun 10am–5pm), whose garden and birdtable is the local riflebird population's favourite afternoon haunt – their Devonshire cream teas aren't bad either. They also offer B&B **accommodation** (Ⓣ07/4770 8533; ⑤); alternatives include self-contained cabins at *Misthaven Units* (Ⓣ07/4770 8607; ④) and *Paluma Rainforest Cottages* (Ⓣ07/4770 8520, Ⓦwww.palumarainforest.com.au; ⑤).

Past Paluma the range descends west, leaving the dark, wet coastal forest for open gum woodland. *Hidden Valley Cabins* (Ⓣ07/4770 8088, Ⓦwww.hiddenvalleycabins.com.au; ③–④), 24km beyond Paluma on a dirt road near Running River, provides a spa, pool, beer, meals and packed lunches. Nearby is **the Gorge**, a lively section of river with falls, rapids and pools – drive down in a 4WD or walk the last kilometre.

Back on the coastal highway heading north, you pass the **Frosty Mango roadhouse** (daily 8am–6pm), whose exotic fresh cakes and ice creams are made from locally grown fruit, before encountering more aquatic fun at **Jourama Falls**, accessed west off the highway down a six-kilometre part-asphalt road. This ends at a low-key **National Parks campsite** (book on Ⓣ13 13 04 or at Ⓦwww.epa.qld.gov.au) set amongst gum and wattle bushland peppered with huge **cycads**. From here an hour-long walking track follows chains across the rocky riverbed to more swimming holes surrounded by gigantic granite boulders and cliffs, finally winding up at the falls themselves – which are impressive in full flood but fairly insignificant by the end of the dry season.

Ingham and around

Home to Australia's largest Italian community, the small town of **INGHAM**, 110km north of Townsville, is well placed for trips inland to **Girringun National Park** – home to Australia's highest waterfall – and also gives access to the tiny port of **Lucinda**, the southern terminus for ferries to Hinchinbrook Island (p.452). Pasta and wine are to be had in abundance during the May **Italian Festival**, but the town is better known for events surrounding the

Cycads

Cycads are extremely slow-growing, fire-resistant plants found throughout the tropics, with tough, palm-like fronds – relics of the age of dinosaurs. Female plants produce large cones which break up into bright orange segments, each containing a seed; these are eaten (and so distributed) by emus, amongst other creatures. Despite being highly toxic to humans – almost every early Australian explorer made himself violently ill trying them – these seeds were a staple of Aborigines, who detoxified flour made from the nuts by prolonged washing. They also applied "fire-stick farming" techniques, encouraging groves to grow and seed by annual burning.

former *Day Dawn Hotel* (now *Lee's Hotel*) on Lannercost Street, the legendary "**Pub with No Beer**". During World War II, Ingham was the first stop for servicemen heading north from Townsville, and in 1941 they drank the bar dry, a momentous occasion recorded by local poet Dan Sheahan and later turned into a popular ballad – it's not the only pub in Australia which claims to be the inspiration for this ditty, however. If you've an hour to kill in town, there's a nice easy **walk** around the well-signposted **Tyto Wetlands** on the southern outskirts; it's under construction at the moment but aims to establish 90 hectares of wetlands, with bird hides and paths.

The highway curves through town as Herbert Street, though most services are located slightly to the west along **Lannercost Street**. Long-distance **buses** stop ten times daily just where the southern highway meets Lannercost Street; **trains** stop 1km east on Lynch Street – you can buy **tickets** from Ingham Travel at 28 Lannercost St. Information is available at the well-informed **Hinchinbrook Visitor Centre** (Mon–Fri 8.45am–5pm, Sat & Sun 9am–2pm; Ⓦwww.hinchinbrooknq.com.au), on the corner where the highway from Townsville meets Lannercost Street; they also stock brochures on local national parks.

Accommodation options include *Palm Tree Caravan Park* (Ⓣ07/4776 2403; cabins ❸), straightforward pub rooms at *Lee's Hotel* (Ⓣ07/4776 1503; ❸, including continental breakfast), or basic dorm beds at the *Royal Hotel* (Ⓣ07/4776 2024; $14) on Lannercost Street. *Lee's* does filling budget **meals** and the bar hasn't run out of beer since the 1940s. The *Olive Tree Coffee Lounge*, just a few doors along from the Visitor Centre, is a great Italian place, with home-made pizza and pasta.

Leaving, Highway 1 is well-marked, but for the various sections of Girringun National Park, turn west down Lannercost Street and follow the **Trebonne** road (lucidly signposted, "This road is not Route 1"); for Lucinda, follow the signs for Forest Beach and Halifax from the town centre.

Girringun National Park

Several disconnected areas of wilds west of Ingham together form **Girringun National Park**, named after a mythical storyteller from the local Aboriginal tribe. The road from Ingham divides 20km along at Trebonne, with separate routes from here to either Mount Fox or Wallaman Falls. For **Mount Fox**, stay on the road for 55km as it crosses cattle country to the base of this extinct volcanic cone; the last two kilometres are dirt and can be unstable. A rocky, unmarked path climbs to the crater rim through scanty forest; it's hot work, so start early. The crater itself is only about 10m deep, tangled in vine forest and open woodland. With prior permission, you might be able to camp at the nearby township's cricket grounds – either ask at the school, or call Ⓣ07/4777 5104.

The signposted 40km route to **Wallaman Falls** runs along a mostly sealed road up the tight and twisting range. Tunnelling through thick rainforest along the ridge (where cassowaries are commonly sighted), the road emerges at a bettong-infested National Parks **campsite** (bookings on ⓣ13 13 04 or ⓦwww.epa.qld.gov.au) before reaching a picnic area at the falls **lookout**. The falls – at 268m, Australia's highest – are spectacular, leaping in a thin ribbon over the sheer cliffs of the plateau opposite and appearing to vaporize by the time they reach the gorge floor. A walk down a narrow and slippery path from the lookout to the base dispels this impression, as the mist turns out to be from the force of water hitting the plunge pool. If you're staying the night, walk from the campsite along the adjacent quiet stretch of **Stoney Creek** at dawn or late afternoon to see platypuses.

Cardwell

Some 50km north from Ingham lies the modest little town of **CARDWELL** – just a quiet string of shops on one side of the highway, with the sea on the other. It's made attractive by the outline of **Hinchinbrook Island**, which hovers just offshore, so close that it almost seems to be part of the mainland. Access to the island is the main reason to stop here, though you can also buy very cheap **lychees** from roadside stalls in December.

Cardwell spreads for about 2km along the highway, with banks, the post office, supermarket and hotel all near or south of the **old jetty**, itself about halfway along the road. Just north of the jetty, the National Parks–run **Rainforest and Reef Centre** (daily 8am–4.30pm; free) has a walk-through rainforest and mangrove display, plus a ranger on hand to answer any questions. For island permits, see opposite.

If you'd like to spend a few days **cruising** around Hinchinbrook's crocodile- and dugong-infested coastline instead of hiking its trails, Hinchinbrook Rent a Yacht, based south of town at the Port Hinchinbrook Marina (ⓣ07/4066 8007, ⓦwww.hinchinbrookrentayacht.com.au) hire out bareboat **yachts** and **houseboats** sleeping from six to twelve people; prices work out at around $90 per person per day in a group of six for a minimum four-day charter.

Buses pull up beside the BP service station and *Seaview Café* at the "Transit Centre" – actually just an open-sided bus shelter; the **train station** is about 200m further back. You can buy **tickets** at *Seaview Café* (daily 8am until late).

Accommodation options include nice gardens and cute rooms at *Cardwell Bed & Breakfast*, two streets behind the bus stop at 18 Gregory St (ⓣ07/4066 8330, ⓦwww.cardwellhomestay.com.au; ④); self-contained, simple units at *Cardwell Beachfront Motel*, 1 Scott St (ⓣ07/4066 8776; ④); or *Kookaburra Holiday Park*, 175 Bruce Highway (ⓣ07/4066 8648, ⓦwww.kookaburraholidaypark.com.au; camping $11, dorms $18, cabins ③, motel rooms ④). For **food**, *Annie's Kitchen*, just up the highway from the bus stop, opens early and is the best of the town's numerous cafés; fish and chips can be had from *Seafood Fish & Chips* opposite the Rainforest Centre. If you're self-catering, head for the small supermarket on the north side of town.

Hinchinbrook Island

Across the channel from Cardwell, **Hinchinbrook Island** looms huge and green, with mangroves rising to forest along the mountain range that forms the island's spine, peaking at **Mount Bowen**. The island's drier east side, hidden behind the mountains, has long beaches separated by headlands and the occasional sluggish creek. This is Bandjin Aboriginal land, and though early

Europeans reported the people as friendly, attitudes later changed and nineteenth-century "dispersals" had the same effect here as elsewhere. The island was never subsequently occupied, and apart from a single resort, Hinchinbrook remains much as it was two hundred years ago. Today, the island's main attraction is the superb **Thorsborne Trail**, a moderately demanding hiking-track along the east coast which takes in forests, mangroves, waterfalls and beaches.

Practicalities

If you're not interested in a serious hike then Hinchinbrook Ferries (Ⓣ1800 777 021, Ⓦwww.hinchinbrookferries.com.au) offers an excellent **day-trip** ($90), departing daily at 9am from the marina at Cardwell, cruising after **dugong** and stopping for a three-kilometre beach and rainforest walk before winding up with a dip in the pool at the island's sole proper **accommodation**, *Hinchinbrook Island Wilderness Lodge* (Ⓣ1800 777 021, Ⓦwww.hinchinbrookresort.com.au; four-person cabins ❻, luxury treehouse doubles with all meals ❽). The lodge is set on Cape Richards at Hinchinbrook's northernmost tip and makes a comfortable retreat

The Thorsborne Trail needs some **advance planning**. The National Parks **campsites** charge $4.50 per person per night, and are best booked online at Ⓦwww.epa.qld.gov.au (where you can also read current warnings and download a **trail map**). Do this as far ahead as possible – visitor numbers on the island are restricted and the trail is usually booked solid. Next you need to book **ferry transfers**, though note there are **no ferries** in February and March, and different operators service the north and south ends of the island. For ferries to Ramsay Bay at Hinchinbrook's **north end**, contact Hinchinbrook Island Ferries at Cardwell's marina ($66 one way, $90 return; Ⓣ1800 777 021, Ⓦwww.hinchinbrookferries.com.au); for George Point at the **south end**, contact Hinchinbrook Wilderness Safaris in Lucinda ($66 one way, $77 return; Ⓣ07/4777 8307, Ⓦwww.hinchinbrookwildernesssafaris.com.au), who also offer transfers to Zoe Bay. You can book **buses** from Lucinda to Ingham or Cardwell for $25 per person with Ingham Travel (Ⓣ07/4776 5666).

The drier winter months (June–Oct) provide optimum **hiking conditions**, though it can rain throughout the year. **Hiking essentials** include water-resistant footgear, pack and tent, a lightweight raincoat and insect repellent. Wood fires are prohibited, so bring a **fuel stove**. *Kookabura Holiday Park* in Cardwell (see opposite) rents out camping gear. Although streams with **drinking water** are fairly evenly distributed, they might be dry by the end of winter, or only flowing upstream from the beach – collect from flowing sources only. As for **wildlife**, you need to beware of crocodiles in lowland creek systems. Less worrying are the white-tailed rats and marsupial mice that will gnaw through tents to reach food; there are metal food-stores at campsites, though hanging anything edible from a branch may foil their attempts.

The Thorsborne Trail

The 32-kilometre **Thorsborne Trail** is manageable in two days, though at that pace you won't see much. **Trailheads** are at Ramsay Bay in the north and George Point in the south, and the route is marked with orange triangles (north to south), or yellow triangles (south to north). The north to south route is considered slightly more forgiving as it eases into ascents, although the advantage of ending up in the north is that the pick-up with Hinchinbrook Ferries includes a welcome few hours unwinding at the *Hinchinbrook Island Wilderness Lodge*'s bar and pool.

Boats **from Cardwell** take you through the mangroves of Missionary Bay in the north to a boardwalk that crosses to the eastern side of the island at **Ramsay Bay**. The walk from here to **Nina Bay**, which takes a couple of hours, is along a fantastic stretch of coast with rainforest sweeping right down to the sand and Mount Bowen and Nina Peak as a backdrop. If long bushwalks don't appeal, you could spend a few days camped at the forest edge at Nina instead; a creek at the southern end provides drinking water and Nina Peak can be climbed in an hour or so. Otherwise, continue beyond a small cliff at the southern end of Nina, and walk for another two hours or so through a pine forest to **Little Ramsay Bay** (drinking water from Warrawilla Creek), which is about as far as you're likely to get on the first day.

Moving on, you scramble over boulders at the far end of the beach before crossing another creek (at low tide, as it gets fairly deep) and entering the forest beyond. From here to the next camp at **Zoe Bay** takes about five hours, following creek beds through lowland casuarina woods and rainforest, before exiting onto the beach near Cypress Pine waterhole. A clearing and pit toilets at the southern end of Zoe Bay marks the **campsite** – though you'll need to check with the National Parks service about the safest areas to camp, as **crocodiles** have recently been seen here. This is one of those places where you'll be very glad you brought insect repellent.

Next day, take the path to the base of **Zoe Falls** – the waterhole here is fabulous but not safe for swimming – then struggle straight up beside them to the cliff top, from where there are great vistas. Across the river, forest and heathland alternate: the hardest part is crossing **Diamantina Creek** – a fast-flowing river with huge, slippery granite boulders. **Mulligan Falls**, not much further on, is the last source of fresh water, with several rock ledges for sunbathing around a pool full of curious fish – stay off the dangerously slippery rocks above the falls. Zoe to Mulligan takes around four hours, and from here to George Point is only a couple more if you push it, but the falls are a better place to camp and give you the chance to backtrack a little to take a look at the beachside lagoon at **Sunken Reef Bay**.

The last leg to **George Point** is the least interesting: rainforest replaces the highland trees around the falls as the path crosses a final creek before arriving at unattractive Mulligan Bay. The campsite at George Point has a table and toilet in the shelter of a coconut grove but there's no fresh water, nothing to see except Lucinda's sugar terminal, and little to do except wait for your ferry.

Murray Falls and Tully

North of Cardwell up Highway 1, it's 20km to where a side road heads another 20km inland past banana plantations to attractive **Murray Falls**, right at the edge of the Cardwell Range. It's really just worth a look to break your journey, but there's a large **camping area** here (book online at Ⓦwww.epa.qld.gov.au) and tracks through the forest to permanent swimming holes and lookouts across the bowl of the valley. There's a basic store on the approach road, some distance from the falls, but it's best to stock up in Cardwell beforehand.

Some 45km north of Cardwell, **TULLY** lies to the left of the highway on the slopes of **Mount Tyson**, whose 450-centimetre annual rainfall is the highest in Australia. Chinese settlers pioneered banana plantations here at the beginning of the twentieth century, and it's now a stopover for **white-water rafting** day-trips out of Cairns and Mission Beach on the fierce and reliable Tully River, 45km inland. Otherwise the town is nothing special, a triangle of narrow streets with cultivated lawns and flowerbeds backing onto roaring jungle at the end of Brannigan Street, a constant reminder of the colonists' struggle to keep chaos at bay. Though most people drive the extra thirty minutes to Mission Beach, there's **accommodation** here at *Green Way Caravan Park* (Ⓣ07/4068 2055; cabins ③) or the well-managed *Banana Barracks* hostel at 50 Butler St (Ⓣ07/4068 0455, Ⓦwww.bananabarracks.com; dorms $22.50), which has excellent **farm work** connections, plus free weekend beach-trips and barbecues.

Mission Beach and around

After branching east off the Bruce Highway a couple of kilometres past Tully, a loop road runs 18km through canefields and patches of rainforest to **Mission Beach**, the collective name for four peaceful hamlets strung out along a fourteen-kilometre stretch of sand. The coastal forest is home to the largest surviving **cassowary** population in Australia, while not far offshore lies little **Dunk Island**, whose idyllic beaches and rainforest track make it a pleasant day-trip.

The area owes its name to the former Hull River Mission, destroyed by a savage **cyclone** in 1918. In 2006, **Cyclone Larry** stripped the rainforest canopy and flattened farms between here and Cairns, wiping out the entire year's banana crop – though the effects will be visible for years, the forest is already well on the way to recovery.

Arrival and information

From south to north, Mission Beach comprises the communities of **South Mission**, **Wongaling Beach**, **Mission Beach** and **Bingil Bay**, each around four or five kilometres from its neighbours. **Long-distance buses** set down outside the shopping-centre office at Wongaling Beach, from where your accommodation might collect you if forewarned. Alternatively, a **local bus** plies the route between South Mission and Bingil Bay (roughly eight per day Mon–Sat 8.30am–6pm; Ⓣ07/4068 7400, Ⓦwww.transnorthbus.com); for a taxi call Ⓣ07/4068 8155. The **tourist office** (Mon–Fri 9am–5pm) is just north of Mission Beach township along Porter Promenade; right behind it, the **Environmental Information Centre** (Mon–Fri 10am–5pm; free) has a display on local habitat, along with a nursery growing seeds collected from cassowary droppings, with the aim of safeguarding the food supply for future generations of this giant bird.

Accommodation

Accommodation is fairly evenly distributed along the coast and covers everything from camping to resorts. All can provide information and book you on white-water rafting trips and other tours in the area. **Campsites** include the tidy *Coconut Village Caravan Park* at South Mission (Ⓣ07/4068 8129, Ⓔbig4ccv@bigpond.com.au; units ③), and the *Hideaway Holiday Village* at Mission Beach (Ⓣ07/4068 7104; cabins ③).

Cassowaries

Aside from the lure of the beach, Mission's forests are a reliable place to spot **cassowaries**, a blue-headed and bone-crested rainforest version of the emu, whose survival is being threatened as their habitat is carved up – estimates suggest that there are only a couple of thousand birds left in tropical Queensland (though they are also found in New Guinea and parts of Indonesia). Many larger trees rely on the cassowary to eat their fruit and distribute their seeds, meaning that the very make-up of the forest hinges on the bird's presence. Unlike the emu, cassowaries are not at all timid and may attack if they feel threatened: if you see one, remain quiet and keep a safe distance.

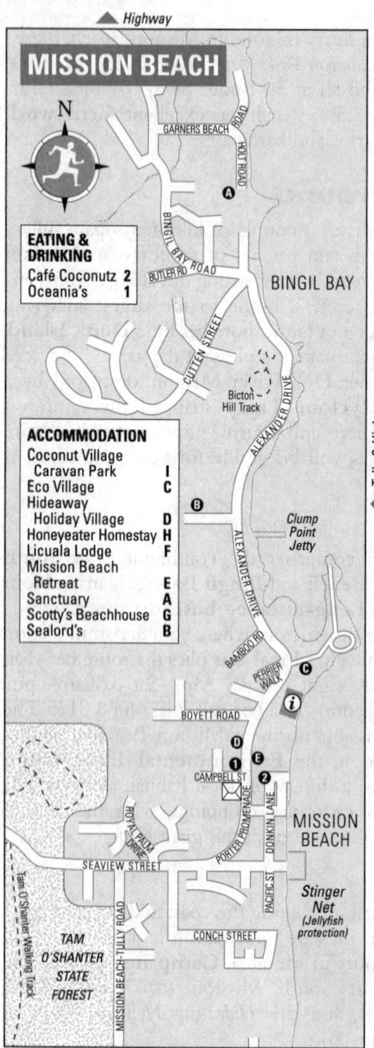

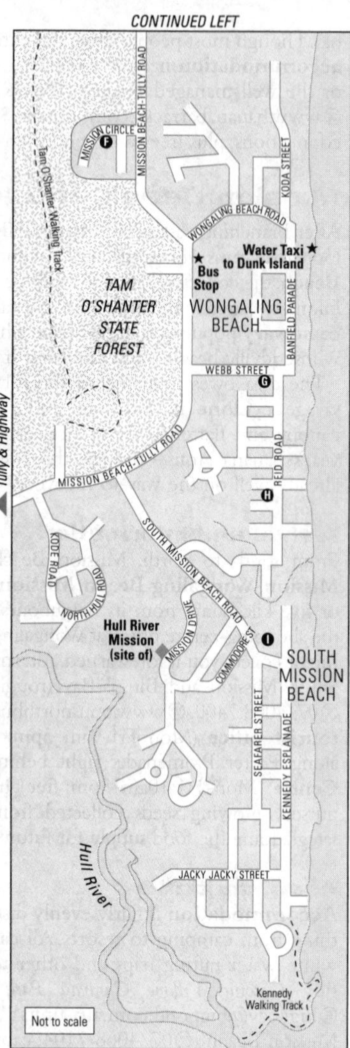

Eco Village Clump Point ⓣ07/4068 7534, ⓦwww.ecovillage.com.au. Smart motel accommodation set just back from the beach amongst pandanus, native nutmeg trees and tropical gardens with a natural rock pool. The luxury rooms all have a Jacuzzi. ❻

Honeyeater Homestay 53 Reid Rd, Wongaling ⓣ07/4068 8741, ⓦwww.honeyeater.com.au. Balinese-inspired house, whose lush tropical gardens surrounding the pool make the place look far larger and more secluded than it actually is. Takes a maximum of six people. ❺

Licuala Lodge 11 Mission Circle, Mission Beach ⓣ07/4068 8194, ⓦwww.licualalodge.com.au. Delightful tropical-style B&B with airy wooden verandas and traditional, high-ceilinged interior; the landscaped garden and pool are worth a stay in themselves, and the huge breakfast will keep you going all day. ❺

Mission Beach Retreat Mission Beach ⓣ1800 001 056, ⓦwww.missionbeachretreat.com.au. Conveniently located next to the shops in Mission Beach, close to the beach and with a small pool and laundry. Dorms $21, rooms ❷

Sanctuary Holt Rd, Bingil Bay ⓣ1800 777 012, ⓦwww.sanctuaryretreat.com.au. An outstanding operation set in fifty acres of thick rainforest. There's abundant wildlife – including cassowary – and a 700m forest track down to a beach. Huts are on stilts (and walled with fine-meshed netting, so you wake up surrounded by greenery), while cabins have verandas; there's also a bar, pool, yoga lessons and an excellent-value restaurant. Note that hut-access paths follow steep slopes, and some find the wildlife's proximity unsettling. Advance booking essential. Huts ❸, cabins ❺

Scotty's Beachhouse 167 Reid Rd, Wongaling ⓣ1800 665 567, ⓦwww.scottysbeachhouse.com.au. A popular party backpackers' near the bus stop and right across from the beach at Wongaling, with bunkhouses, a pool and a fine restaurant offering cheap meals. Dorms $22, rooms ❷

Sealord's 4 James Rd, Clump Point, Mission Beach ⓣ07/4088 6444, ⓦwww.sealords.com.au. Smart B&B just up the road from the Dunk Island jetty, with polished wooden floors and themed bedrooms. ❺

Mission Beach

Right down at the bottom end of the beach, **SOUTH MISSION** is a quiet, mostly residential spot, with a long, clean beach. Signposted off the main road on Mission Drive is a monument to the original site of the **Hull River Mission**; after the 1918 cyclone, the mission was relocated to safer surroundings on Palm Island. At the end of beach-front Kennedy Esplanade, the **Kennedy Walking Track** weaves through coastal swamp and forest for a couple of hours to the spot where Edmund Kennedy originally landed near the mouth of the Hull River – a good place to spot coastal birdlife and, quite likely, crocodiles.

Heading 4km north of South Mission takes you to **WONGALING BEACH**, a slowly expanding settlement based around a shopping centre and Mission's only **pub**. A further 4km lands you at **MISSION BEACH** itself, a cluster of shops, boutiques, restaurants, banks and a post office one block back from the beach on Porter Promenade. Inland between the two, a six-kilometre walking track weaves through **Tam O'Shanter State Forest**, a dense maze of muddy creeks, vine thickets and stands of licuala palms (identified by their frilly, saucer-shaped leaves). If you don't see **cassowaries** here – sometimes leading their knee-high, striped chicks through the undergrowth – you'd be very unlucky. Continuing 6km north of Mission township past **Clump Point** – a black basalt outcrop with views south down the beach sitting above **Clump Point Jetty** – the road winds along the coast to sleepy **BINGIL**

Tours from Mission Beach

Among the local tours worth seeking out, Raging Thunder's "Xtreme Team" (ⓣ1800 337 116, ⓦwww.rtextreme.com) is exclusive to Mission Beach and offers the best-value **river rafting** down the Tully River in small groups, getting to the river before the busloads arrive from Cairns – a full day costs $165. Skydive Mission (ⓣ1800 638 005, ⓦwww.jumpthebeach.com.au) can take you to three thousand metres for **freefall** fun ($219), and also offers skydiving over Dunk Island ($439). If it's riverine wildlife you're after, Hinchinbrook Explorer (ⓣ07/4088 6154, ⓦwww.hexplorer.com.au) runs four-hour croc-spotting trips with dinner thrown in ($50), or you can go paddling around Dunk Island for the day with Coral Sea Kayaking ($93; ⓣ07/4068 9154, ⓦwww.coralseakayaking.com). For **reef trips**, Quick Cat (ⓣ07/4068 7289, ⓦwww.quickcatcruises.com.au) run a passenger ferry daily to Beaver Cay on the Barrier Reef for coral viewing and snorkelling ($144), while Calypso II (ⓣ07/4068 8432, ⓦwww.calypsodive.com) caters more specifically to **scuba divers**, but is pretty pricey at $235 for a reef trip with two dives – you'll get a better deal out of Cairns.

BAY. Just before, there's a parking bay on the roadside for the excellent **Bicton Hill track**, a four-kilometre hilly walk through wet tropics forest where encounters with cassowaries are again likely. From here, the road continues inland alongside the **Clump Mountain National Park** and back to the main highway.

There are stores and **places to eat** at all four hamlets, though only Mission Beach has a comprehensive range – the best of the restaurants here are *Oceania's*, with an eclectic "Asian" menu, and *Café Coconutz*, which serves light meals and fresh juices, and also has a **bar**.

Dunk Island

In 1898 Edmund Banfield, a Townsville journalist who had been given only weeks to live, waded ashore on **Dunk Island**. He spent his remaining years – twenty-five of them – as Dunk's first European resident, crediting his unanticipated longevity to the relaxed island life. A tiny version of Hinchinbrook, Dunk attracts far more visitors to its resort and camping grounds. While there's a satisfying track over and around the island, it's more the kind of place where you make the most of the beach – as Banfield discovered.

Vessels from the Mission Beach area put ashore on or near the jetty, next to *BB's* **restaurant**, which sells sandwiches and hot meals; there's no store on the island. On the far side is the shady National Parks **campsite** (book online at Ⓦwww.epa.qld.gov.au), with toilets, showers and drinking water. Five minutes along the track is the **resort** (Ⓣ07/4068 8199, Ⓦwww.dunk-island.com; ❼), a low-key affair well hidden by vegetation; day-guests have to pay $40 to use the resort facilities, which includes lunch. The best places to relax are either on **Brammo Bay**, in front of the resort, or **Pallon Beach**, behind the campsite. Note that the beaches are narrow at high tide and the island is close enough to the coast to attract box jellyfish in season, but you can always retreat to the resort pool.

Before falling victim to incipient lethargy, head into the interior past the resort and **Banfield's grave** for a circuit of the island's west. The full nine-kilometre **trail** up Mount Cootaloo, down to Palm Valley and back along the coast is a three-hour rainforest trek, best tackled clockwise from the resort. You'll see green pigeons and yellow-footed scrubfowl foraging in leaf litter, vines, trunkless palms and, from the peak, a vivid blue sea dotted with hunch-backed islands.

Two **ferry** operators run to Dunk daily, costing $21 one way or $42 return; book directly or through your accommodation. Quick Cat (20min; Ⓣ07/4068 7289, Ⓦwww.quickcatcruises.com.au) departs from the Clump Point Jetty at 8.30am, 10am, 2pm and 4pm; the last ferry leaves Dunk at 4.30pm. Water Taxis (10min; Ⓣ07/4068 8310) leave from Wongaling Beach at 8.30am, 9.30am, 11am, 12.30pm, 2.30pm and 4.15pm, with the last boat leaving Dunk at 4.45pm. Phone operators to see if they offer bus transfers from your accommodation. The island is 5km and barely fifteen minutes offshore, but even so the tiny **water taxis** are not really suitable if you have much luggage. **Camping gear** can be rented from the complex next to the post office in Mission Beach; you can also leave surplus equipment with them.

Paronella Park, Innisfail and the Bellenden Ker Range

Back on the highway around 25km north of Tully, tiny **Silkwood** marks the turn inland for the 23-kilometre run through canefields to **Paronella Park**

Cane toads

Native to South America, the huge, charismatically ugly **cane toad** was recruited in 1932 to combat a plague of greyback beetles, whose larvae were wreaking havoc on Queensland's sugar cane. The industry was desperate – beetles had cut production by ninety percent in plague years – and resorted to seeding tadpoles in waterholes around Gordonvale. They thrived, but it soon became clear that toads couldn't reach the adult insects (who never landed on the ground), and they didn't burrow after the grubs. Instead they bred whenever possible, ate anything they could swallow, and killed potential predators with poisonous secretions from their neck glands. Native wildlife suffered: birds learned to eat nontoxic parts, but snake populations have been seriously affected. Judging from the quantity of flattened carcasses on summer roads (running them over is an unofficial sport), there must be millions lurking in the canefields, and they're gradually spreading into New South Wales and the Northern Territory – they arrived in Darwin, via Kakadu, in 2006. Given enough time, they seem certain to infiltrate most of the country.

The toad's outlaw character has generated a cult following, with its warty features and nature the subject of songs, toad races, T-shirt designs, a brand of beer and the award-winning **film** *Cane Toads: An Unnatural History* – worth seeing if you come across it on video. The record for the largest specimen goes to a 1.8-kilogram monster found in Mackay in 1988.

(daily 9.30am–5pm; $26; ⓣ07/4065 3225, ⓦwww.paronellapark.com.au). This extraordinary estate was laid out by **José Paronella**, a Spanish immigrant who settled here in 1929 and constructed a **castle** complete with florid staircases, water features and avenues of exotic kauri pines amongst the tropical forests. Left to moulder for twenty years, the park was reclaimed from the jungle and restored during the 1990s, and now forms a splendidly romantic theme park, with half-ruined buildings artfully part-covered in undergrowth, lush gardens and arrays of tinkling fountains – all gravity-fed from the adjacent Mena Creek. A former walk-through aquarium has become the roost of endangered little bent-winged bats, and native vegetation includes a bamboo forest and dozens of *angiopteris* ferns, rare elsewhere. Fifteen-minute indigenous cultural performances held four times a day and educational bush-tucker walking tours add to the park's appeal, so you'll need a good couple of hours to do the place justice; it's possible to **camp** here and explore after dark – phone ahead for details. There's a **restaurant** on site, or you can eat across Mena Creek at the old pub.

The Paronella Park road and highway converge again 25km on at **INNISFAIL**, a small but busy town on the Johnstone River and a good spot to find work **picking bananas**: the specialists here are *Innisfail Budget Backpackers*, on the highway just on the northern side of town (ⓣ07/4061 7833, ⓦwww.jobsforbackpackers.com.au; dorms $130 per week); and the much smarter *Codge Lodge*, near the pale-pink Catholic church on Rankin Street (ⓣ07/4061 8055; dorms $25 or $130 per week, rooms ❸). Innisfail is worth a quick stop anyway as a reminder that modern Australia was in no way built by the British alone: there's a sizeable **Italian community** here, represented by the handful of delicatessens displaying herb sausages and fresh pasta along central Edith Street. The tiny red **Lit Sin Gong temple** on Owen Street (and the huge longan tree next to it) was first established in the 1880s by migrant workers from southern China, who cleared scrub and created market gardens here; many of Innisfail's banana plantations have been bought up recently by **Hmong** immigrants from Vietnam.

The Bellenden Ker Range

Just north of Innisfail, the Palmerston Highway turns off Highway 1 for its ascent to the bottom end of the Atherton Tablelands (see p.473), and at about the same point you begin to see the **Bellenden Ker Range**, which dominates the remaining 80km to Cairns and includes Queensland's highest mountain, **Bartle Frere**. While the fifteen-kilometre, two-day return climb through **Wooroonooran National Park** to the 1600-metre summit is within the reach of any fit, well-prepared bushwalker, you should check the National Parks website first (Ⓦwww.epa.qld.gov.au) or contact the park ranger (Ⓣ07/4067 6304) for accurate information about the route. Peak climb or not, it's worth visiting **Josephine Falls**, at the start of the summit track, which forms wonderfully enclosed jungle waterslides: leave the highway 19km north of Ingham at one-house **Pawngilly** and continue for 8km via Bartle Frere township. The **summit track** itself – closed at the time of writing due to damage from the 2006 cyclone – is marked from here with orange triangles and passes through rainforest, over large granite boulders and out onto moorland with wind-stunted vegetation. Much of the summit is blinded by scrub and usually cloaked in rain, but there are great views of the tablelands and coast during the ascent.

Further along the highway, there's a detour at **BABINDA** township – dwarfed by a huge sugar mill – to another waterhole 7km inland at **the Boulders**, where an arm of Babinda Creek forms a wide pool before spilling down a collection of house-sized granite slabs. Cool and relatively shallow, the pale blue waterhole is an excellent place to swim, though several deaths have been caused by subtle undertows dragging people over the falls – be very careful and stay well clear of the falls side of the waterhole. You can also **camp** here for free.

Nearing the end of the range is **Gordonvale**, the place where the notorious **cane toad** was first introduced to Australia (see box on p.1102), from where the tortuous Gillies Highway climbs from the coast to lakes Barrine and Eacham on the Atherton Tablelands, sunday. Marking the turn-off is **Walsh's Pyramid**, a natural formation which really does look like an overgrown version of its Egyptian counterpart. From here, the last section of Highway 1 carries you – in thirty minutes – through the suburbs of Edmonton and White Rock to Cairns.

Cairns and around

CAIRNS was pegged out over the site of a sea-slug fishing camp when gold was found to the north in 1876, though it was the Atherton Tablelands' tin and timber resources that established the town and kept it ahead of its nearby rival, Port Douglas (see p.480). The harbour is the focus of the north's fish and prawn concerns, and tourism began modestly when marlin fishing became popular after World War II. But with the "discovery" of the reef in the 1970s and the appeal of the local climate, tourism snowballed, and high-profile development has now replaced the unspoiled, lazy tropical atmosphere that everyone originally came to Cairns to enjoy.

For many visitors primed by hype, the city falls far short of expectations. However, if you can accept the tourist industry's shocking intrusiveness and the fact that you're unlikely to escape the crowds, you'll find Cairns a convenient base with a great deal on offer, and easy access to the surrounding area – especially the Atherton Tablelands and, naturally, the **Great Barrier Reef** and islands.

Arrival and getting around

Downtown Cairns is the grid of streets behind the Esplanade, overlooking the harbour and Trinity Bay. **Long-distance buses** are operated by Greyhound Australia (Ⓣ13 20 30), which sets down and has an office at the Reef Fleet Terminal (office open Mon–Fri 8.30am–5.30pm, Sat & Sun 8.30am–3pm) and Premier (Ⓣ13 34 10), which sets down at the south end of Lake St. Whitecar Coaches (Ⓣ07/4091 1855) run daily to several Atherton Tablelands towns from their depot at 46 Spence St; Country Road Coachlines (Ⓣ07/4045 2794) run to Cooktown via Port Douglas and Cape Tribulation, or Mareeba and Lakeland Downs; Coral Reef Coaches (Ⓣ07/4098 2800) and Sun Palm Coaches (Ⓣ07/4084 2626) both operate a daily service to Cape Tribulation via Port Douglas. The **train station** is 750m from the main drag, under the Cairns Central development between Bunda and McLeod streets. Queensland Rail (Ⓣ13 22 32, Ⓦwww.qr.com.au) trains head south down the coast to Brisbane and up to Kuranda on the Atherton Tablelands, while the Savannah lander (Ⓣ4053 6848, Ⓦwww.savannahlander.com.au) runs west to Forsayth in the Gulf region (p.539). The **airport** is about 7km north along the Cook Highway; a taxi into Cairns costs around $15, or a **shuttle bus** ($11) connects with most flights and delivers to all central accommodation. Some accommodation also collects from arrival points if contacted in advance.

For **getting around**, Sunbus, the **local bus** service, is based at the Transit Mall on City Place (Lake St), and serves the city and Northern Beaches as far as Palm Cove; daily, weekly and monthly passes are available, and you can get **free timetables** from the driver. You may also be able to **rent bikes** at your accommodation, or check out the rental outfits on p.467. If you want to buy a **secondhand car**, try Travellers' Auto Barn at 123–125 Bunda St (Ⓣ07/4041 3732, Ⓦwww.travellers-autobarn.com), or check the classified ads in the Wednesday and Saturday editions of the local paper, the *Cairns Post*. Cars for sale are also advertised on notice boards outside *Johno*'s on the corner of Aplin and Abbott streets, and in an arcade beside the museum at City Place.

Information

Cairns' official **tourist office** is the Gateway Discovery Centre, housed in the old Shire Offices at 51 Esplanade (Ⓣ07/4041 3588, Ⓦwww.tropicalaustralia.com.au); though this promotes only those operators that pay to be featured, the staff are friendly and they have a wealth of brochures and flyers. Other places around town with prominent blue "i" signs, along with the backpacker agents on Shield Street, tend to focus on selling the tours that they'll make the most commission on – don't expect them to provide unbiased, informed opinions. One exception – though based out of town – is **Cairns Discount Tours** (Ⓣ07/4055 7158, Ⓔtours@iig.com.au), which specializes in last-minute deals and comes recommended for its honest approach and comprehensive knowledge of the local tour options.

Accommodation

Cairns has a prolific number of **places to stay** in every price bracket, and the following is just a selection. Most are pretty central, though there's a knot of backpacker hostels west of the train station, of which *Dreamtime* and *Tropic Days* are the pick. The nearest official **campsite** is the recently refurbished *City Holiday Park* at 12–30 Little St (Ⓣ07/4051 1467, Ⓦwww.cairnscamping.com.au; camping $20, cabins ③), with good amenities and a pool. If Cairns itself doesn't appeal but you want access to all its attractions, consider staying 15km north beyond the airport at the city's Northern Beaches (see p.468).

Expect seasonal **price fluctuations** at all accommodation, with Christmas and Easter being the busiest times, and February to March the quietest; **book ahead** but beware of committing yourself to a long-term deal until you've seen the room – you won't be able to get a refund. All hostels have kitchens, and most have a courtesy bus service, laundry and a pool. Hostels make most of their profits through commissions, not beds, so don't admit to making tour bookings elsewhere if you want your room to remain available.

For a change of pace, **farmstays** in the Cairns region include *Mount Mulligan Station* (ⓣ1800 359 798, ⓦwww.outbackfarmstay.com.au; three-day package $200 per person) and *Springmount Station* (ⓣ1800 333 004, ⓦwww.springmountstation.com; $240 for the same, plus horse riding), where you can horse ride, camp out under the stars, swim in bush waterways or bushwalk – both get good reviews and provide all meals plus free return transport from Cairns.

Hotels, motels and guesthouses

The Balinese 215 Lake St ⓣ07/4051 9922, ⓦwww.balinese.com.au. Slightly sterile but comfy motel with carved wooden doors, bamboo blinds and lots of tiling. There's a small pool, satellite TV, inclusive breakfast and airport courtesy bus. ④

Floriana 183 Esplanade ⓣ07/4051 7886, ⓦwww.florianaguesthouse.com. Amiable old guesthouse with sea views and Art Deco decor in the reception. Rooms overlooking the Esplanade are nice and airy, as are the self-contained flats;

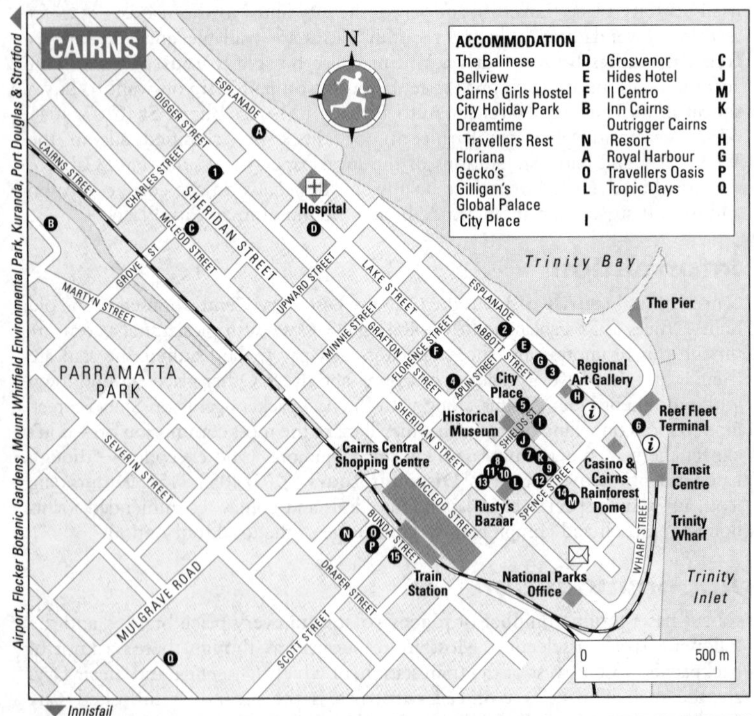

EATING & DRINKING

Adelfia	4	Cock & Bull	1	Green Ant	15	La Pizza	2	Swiss Cake and Coffee Shop	10	Woolshed	5
Café China	12	Curry Bowl	7	La Fettuccina	11	Red Ochre	13			Yacht Club	6
Chapel	3	Dundee's	14	Oliver's	9	Sushi Zipang	8				

the cheaper rooms have no windows and get pretty stuffy. ❸–❹

Grosvenor 188 McLeod St ⓣ1800 629 179, ⓦwww.grosvenorcairns.com.au. Bright and cheerful motel offering self-contained apartments and deluxe units; not very central but close to the highway. Apartments ❺, units ❻

Hides Hotel Cnr Lake and Shields streets ⓣ07/4051 1266, ⓦwww.clubcroc.com.au. One of the oldest hotels in town (and formerly the roughest), now under the *Club Crocodile* banner. The higher-priced motel rooms have been totally revamped; the cheaper hotel rooms are unadorned pub rooms, with original fittings. ❹

Il Centro 26–30 Sheridan St ⓣ07/4031 6699, ⓦwww.ilcentro.com.au. Modern and fairly spacious self-contained apartments with either pool or street views. ❺

Inn Cairns 71 Lake St ⓣ07/4041 2350, ⓦwww.inncairns.com.au. Smart boutique apartments slap in the centre of town, with pool and BBQ area, plus rooftop views out to sea. ❻

Outrigger Cairns Resort 53–57 Esplanade ⓣ07/4046 4141, ⓦwww.outrigger.com.au. Plush high-rise hotel in a prime location close to the casino, restaurants, shops and the "beach". ❼

Royal Harbour 73–75 Esplanade ⓣ07/5665 4450, ⓦwww.stellaresorts.com.au. Self-contained hotel apartments with sea views – it feels surprisingly secluded given the location. Minimum two-night stay. ❻

Hostels

Bellview 85 Esplanade ⓣ07/4031 4377, ⓦwww.bellviewcairns.com.au. Family-run hostel that has been around forever, though the site is being eyed by property speculators. Motel-like facilities and a range of rooms. Dorms $20, rooms ❷

Cairns' Girls Hostel 147 Lake St ⓣ07/4051 2016, ⓦwww.cairnsgirlshostel.com.au. Renovated 1930s Queenslander, with tidy rooms and secure feel. Can be hard to locate; look for the adjacent laundry. Dorms $18, rooms ❷

Dreamtime Travellers Rest 4 Terminus St, behind the train station ⓣ07/4031 6753, ⓦwww.dreamtimetravel.com.au. Small, friendly hostel with a keen owner and very relaxed tropical atmosphere about ten minutes' walk from the centre. There's also a great café run by the same family next door. Dorms $22, rooms ❷

Gecko's 187 Bunda St ⓣ1800 011 344, ⓦwww.geckosbackpackers.com.au. Overcrowded hostel in an old Queenslander, with wooden floors and period furnishings; staff are good but rooms are pretty airless and hot in the summer. Dorms $22, rooms ❷

Gilligan's 57–89 Grafton St ⓣ07/4041 6566, ⓦwww.gilligansbackpackers.com.au. Massive backpackers' resort with CCTV cameras, 24-hour reception and every conceivable facility – there's even a two-thousand-capacity bar hosting DJs and live bands. Not a bad choice if you're looking for security but very impersonal. Dorms $27, rooms ❺

Global Palace City Place, Lake St ⓣ07/4031 7921, ⓦwww.globalpalace.com.au. This large, modern backpackers' right in the centre of town has an industrial feel but is well organized and offers good facilities. Dorms $25, rooms ❸

Travellers Oasis 8 Scott St ⓣ1800 621 353, ⓦwww.travoasis.com.au. Very friendly old Queenslander, run by *Tropic Days* and with the same attention to easy comfort and detail, though not as spacious. Double rooms are particularly nice, and have balconies. Dorms $24, rooms ❸

Tropic Days 28 Bunting St ⓣ07/4041 1521, ⓦwww.tropicdays.com.au. Though a little bit out of town, this is one of the best hostels in Cairns, with a big pool, nice gardens, colourful rooms and a highly sociable atmosphere. There's a small campsite too, and a courtesy bus through the day. Camping $11 per person, dorms $24, rooms ❸

The City

Cairns' strength is in doing, not seeing: there are few monuments, natural or otherwise. This is partly because the Cape York goldfields were too far away and profits were channelled through Cooktown, and partly because Cairns was remote, lacking a rail link with Townsville until 1924; people came here to exploit resources, not to settle. Your best introduction to the region's heritage is at the **Cairns Historical Museum**, at the junction of Shields and Lake streets (Mon–Sat 10am–4pm; $5), which uses photos and trinkets to explore maritime history, the Tjapukai and Bama Aborigines of the tablelands, and Chinese involvement in the city and Palmer goldfields.

At **City Place**, the open-air pedestrian mall outside the museum, you'll find Cairns' souvenir-shopping centre, with a rash of cafés, and shops selling didgeridoos, T-shirts, paintings and cuddly toy koalas. Local performers do their best at the small **sound shell** here from time to time, and there are often more professional offerings in the evenings. Between Grafton and Sheridan streets, towards Spence Street, **Rusty's Bazaar markets** (Fri, Sat & Sun morning) sell a fantastic range of local produce from crafts to herbs, tropical fruit and veg, coffee and fish, with excellent deals on surplus produce around noon on Sunday.

Moving east, the seafront **Esplanade** is packed through the day and into the night with people cruising between accommodation, shops and restaurants. Grabbing an early-morning coffee here, you'll witness a quintessentially Cairns scene: fig trees framing the waterfront, with a couple of trawlers, cruise boats and seaplanes bobbing at anchor in the harbour. Joggers jog, and others promenade along the edge at low tide and watch birds feeding in the shallows – there's an identification chart in the park – while an excellent **skateboard park** is thoughtfully located up towards the hospital. In the opposite direction, Cairn's well-planned **artificial beach** actually sits way above the tide-line, but encloses five landscaped swimming lagoons which are packed at weekends. Facing the lagoon on the far end of the Esplanade is the glass-domed **casino** and Cairns Rainforest Dome (daily 7am–6pm; $25), an equally artificial replica, this time of the rainforest with caged birds and several depressed-looking crocodiles. Opposite, the **Reef Fleet Terminal** is where most day-cruises to the reef depart from, while **The Pier**, once a busy collection of boutique stores, is now a lifeless shopping plaza for the attached *Shangri-la* hotel.

The Esplanade's **night market** (daily 5pm until late) runs through to Abbott Street and has a mix of fast-food courts, trendy tack and good-quality souvenirs, plus a great location near plenty of bars. Just around the corner from the Esplanade on Shields Street, **Cairns Regional Art Gallery** (Mon–Fri 10am–5pm, Sat & Sun 1–5pm; $5) is worth a look if Cairns' crasser commercial side is beginning to grate; exhibitions include both local artists' work and travelling shows.

Heading out of the centre, the city's natural attractions include the wonderful **Flecker Botanic Gardens** (Mon–Fri 8.30am–5.30pm; free guided walks Mon–Fri 1pm) and adjacent **Mount Whitfield Environmental Park**, whose cool, tranquil rainforest is dense enough for wallabies. Both are accessed off Collins Avenue, west off the northern end of Sheridan Street; several buses run up here from the City Place Transit Mall, or it's a forty-minute walk. Also worth a look are the **mangrove walks** on the airport approach road nearby, whose boardwalks and hides give you a chance to see different varieties of mangrove trees, mudskippers and red-clawed, asymmetric fiddler crabs. Take some insect repellent or you'll end up giving the flies a free lunch. Alternatively, Habitat Cruises ($59; ⓣ07/4041 3851, ⓦwww.cairnshabitatcruises.com.au) explore the local mangrove creeks for birds and also work in a visit to a crocodile farm.

Activities

In addition to the tours covered in the box on opposite, several operators offer more activity-led excursions. For **bushwalking**, Wooroonooran Safaris (ⓣ1300 661 113, ⓦwww.wooroonooran-safaris.com.au) spends a moderately strenuous day hiking through thick rainforest just north of Bartle Frere, where you're guaranteed to see wildlife and get wet crossing creeks ($149 all-inclusive). **Wildlife-spotting tours** focus on the Atherton Tablelands' platypus, tree kangaroos and rare possums, and are run by Wildscapes Safaris (Ⓣ07/4057 6272, Ⓦwww.wildscapes-safaris.com.au), Wait-a-While Tours (Ⓣ07/4098 2422, Ⓦwww.waitawhile.com.au) and Currawong (Ⓣ07/4093 7287, Ⓦwww.australiawildlifetours.com); expect to pay in the region of $195 for an afternoon-to-night excursion. Wait-a-While also offer specialized **birding** trips, as does Cassowary Tours (Ⓣ07/4043 1202, Ⓦwww.cassowarytours.com.au), who can put together some week-long packages.

Bicycle tours around the Atherton Tablelands are on offer four times a week with Bandicoot ($99; Ⓣ07/4055 0155, Ⓦwww.bandicootbicycles.com), or you can get stuck into some moderate to extreme off-road biking around Cairns and Cape Tribulation with Dan's Mountain Biking ($75–135; Ⓣ07/4032 0066, Ⓦwww.cairns.aust.com/mtb); both come highly recommended. Cairns' **bungee-jumping** venue is a purpose-built platform surrounded by rainforest, in the hills off the coastal highway 8km north of Cairns; contact A.J. Hackett ($120; Ⓣ07/4057 7188), which offers heaps of combined package deals with other extreme-sport operators.

White-water rafting is organized on the reliable Tully River near Tully or the slightly less turbulent Barron River behind Cairns, and is wild fun despite being a conveyor-belt business: as you pick yourself out of the river, the raft is dragged back for the next busload. A "day" means around five hours rafting; a "half-day" about two. Agents include RnR (Ⓣ07/4041 9444, Ⓦwww.raft.com.au) and Raging Thunder (Ⓣ07/4030 7990, Ⓦwww.ragingthunder.com.au); day-trips with either company cost from $98 to $155 and multi-day expeditions from $735 to $1300, plus a compulsory rafting levy of $25 per day. For better value, consider the "Xtreme Team" packages available only from Mission Beach (see p.455), which gets you on the river before the Cairns day-trippers arrive and with smaller groups.

Finally, two places well worth looking into if you want to arrange a spot of small-scale **fishing** for barramundi and other estuary fish are Paradise Sportfishing (Ⓣ07/4055 6088) and All Tackle (Ⓣ07/4034 2550); both charge around $95 per person for a full day of shore-based fishing, or $160 from a boat.

For **diving**, see the box on pp.470–471.

Tours from Cairns

Before exploring locally or around the Atherton Tablelands, Port Douglas and Cape Tribulation, bear in mind that the cheapest day-tours will set you back $90 per person, while it costs as little as $55 per day to rent a four-seat car, plus perhaps a bit less for fuel – though of course you'll miss out on a tour guide's local knowledge.

For day-trips to the **Atherton Tablelands**, the **Daintree** and **Cape Tribulation**, the following come highly recommended in the $90 bracket: Uncle Brian Ⓣ07/4050 0615, Ⓦwww.unclebrian.com.au; Cape Trib Connections Ⓣ07/4053 3833, Ⓦwww.capetribconnections.com; and Trek North Safaris Ⓣ07/4051 4328, Ⓦwww.treknorth.com.au. Ranging further afield, Wilderness Challenge (Ⓣ07/4035 4488, Ⓦwww.wilderness-challenge.com.au) has day-trips to the Daintree, Cape Tribulation and **Mossman Gorge** ($145), and an overnight trip to Cooktown ($275) and the Aboriginal rock-art sites around **Laura** ($415). For **Cape York**, the following organize trips to the tip by 4WD, boat and plane, and enjoy reliable reputations; you're looking at $800–2200 for an all-inclusive, week-long trip, depending on the level of comfort offered: Heritage Tours Ⓣ07/4038 2628, Ⓦwww.heritagetours.com.au; Billy Tea Bush Safaris Ⓣ07/4032 0077, Ⓦwww.billytea.com.au; Exploring Oz Ⓣ13 00 888 112, Ⓦwww.exploring-oz.com.au. You can also **fly** with the mail to remote stations across Cape York from Monday to Friday with Aero-Tropics ($375–550 depending on destination; Ⓣ07/4040 1222, Ⓦwww.aero-tropics.com.au).

Eating and nightlife

Cairns has no shortage of places to **eat**. Least expensive are the Esplanade takeaways serving Chinese food, falafel, kebabs and pasta. Some, like *La Pizza* on the corner of Aplin Street, open early and close very late, switching from coffee and croissants at dawn to fast food during the day and evening. The night market also houses a fast-food plaza, with a choice ranging from fish and chips to pizza or sushi; alternatively, you can stock up at the **supermarkets** on Abbott Street or in Cairns Central.

Openly drinking on the streets is illegal in Cairns, but the **pub and club** culture thrives undaunted. Clubs open around 6pm, most charging $5 entry for the bar and disco, or more if there's a band playing. Many pubs also feature live music once a week – reviews and details are given in Cairns' free weekly **listings magazine**, *Time Out*; for some indigenous sounds, try to catch one of the up-and-coming local **Torres Strait Islander** performers, such as the Brisco Sisters. Try not to make yourself an obvious target for the **pickpockets** and bag-snatchers who work the nightclubs, though the steady reports of drink-spikings, rapes and muggings are more worrying – don't hang around outside venues, and get a taxi home.

Cafés and restaurants

Adelfia Cnr of Lake and Aplin streets. Lively Greek taverna with particularly tasty seafood and grills. Most main dishes around $27.

Café China Cnr of Spence and Grafton streets. Two sections here cater to an increasing number of Chinese visitors to Cairns: there's an inexpensive noodle house on Spence Street where most dishes are under $10, and a more sophisticated Cantonese restaurant on Grafton, with great roast meat or seafood dishes from $15, and daily *yum cha* sessions (best selection at weekends).

Chapel 94 Esplanade. Funky atmosphere with alternative music, al fresco café and a larger restaurant upstairs with a menu to please everyone except those paying. Mains around $30. Daily 7am–late.

Cock & Bull 6 Grove St, cnr Grafton St. Keg Guinness, hearty counter meals (from around $15) and a pleasant garden atmosphere.

Curry Bowl In Mainstreet Arcade between Grafton and Lake streets, just south of Shields St. Very ordinary-looking fast-food counter, but the portions of (mostly vegetarian) Sri Lankan dahls and curries are large, cheap and pretty authentic.

Dundee's 29 Spence St. Popular upmarket grill restaurant, with leanings towards native fauna – choose from kangaroo, emu or crocodile – and seafood. The best dishes are the kangaroo satay and seafood platter (includes crays and mud crab). Mains around $30.

Green Ant 83 Bunda St. Cheap, cheerful and tasty evening meals with unbeatable drink deals. Mains – such as spicy chicken salsa or meat grills served with rice or chips – go for around $12, while the burgers will remind you what burgers used to be like before fast-food versions appeared. Live bands at weekends. Daily 4pm–midnight.

La Fettuccina 41 Shields St ⓣ07/4031 5959. Superb home-made pasta and sauces for around $18, though it's very popular, so get in early or book – their "small" servings would be enough for most people.

Oliver's Boland Centre, Shield St. Australian game meats and seafood, perked up by using native herbs and flavourings (such as scallops steamed in paperbark). Mains around $35.

Red Ochre 43 Shields St. Long-running restaurant with Outback decor and a menu revolving around truly Australian ingredients such as kangaroo and crocodile – although emu meat seems to have been replaced by ostrich. Tasty, but some dishes are a bit overworked. Mains $28 and up.

Sushi Zipang 39 Shields St. The best place in town for sushi, which parades across a conveyor belt on colour-coded bowls, noodle soups or other Japanese light meals – popular with Japanese tourists. Most meals around $15.

Swiss Cake and Coffee Shop 93 Grafton St. Top-notch patisserie with crisp strudels, rich cakes and fine coffee.

Woolshed 22 Shields St. Budget backpackers' diner, with huge and inexpensive meals, beer by the jug and party fever. Hostels give out vouchers for various discount meal deals here; it's worth "upgrading" these for a couple more dollars and getting a full-blown feed.

Yacht Club Esplanade. Opens at 11am for drinks and enticing grill-and-salad meals at around $15; their "Sunset Special" (6.30–8.30pm) is a bucket of prawns and a beer.

Nightlife

Bassment Ground floor of the *Woolshed*, 22 Shields St. Fri-and Sat-night house and trance, with guest DJs from 11pm to 5am.
Casa De Meze Cnr Aplin St and the Esplanade. Week-time karaoke venue but perks up on Fri, when there are live bands, and Sat, when free salsa dance classes are held.
Club Nu Trix 53 Spence St. Cairns' only dedicated gay club, with drag/diva shows on Sat. Wed–Sun 9pm–late.
Inbox Café 119 Abbott St. Good place to check out the local music scene, with live gigs mixing with DJs at the weekend and special promotions throughout the week. Closed Mon.
Johno's Cnr Abbott and Aplin streets. Traditional backpackers' haunt, with a huge video screen and a youngish clientele. Live music, including international bands, most nights, and it's even worth catching Johno and the house band – they've been a Cairns' institution for decades.
P.J. O'Brien's City Place, next to *Hides Hotel*, Shields St. This Irish bar attracts a mix of locals and tourists, and hosts some big-name Queensland indie band nights. Best on Fri, Sat & Sun nights.
Shenanegins Cnr Shields St and Esplanade. Rowdy Irish bar with live bands from Thurs to Sun nights.

Listings

Airlines All of the following fly to Cairns: Air New Zealand ⓣ13 24 76, ⓦwww.airnz.com.au; Air Niugini ⓣ1300 361 380, ⓦwww.airniugini.com.pg; Cathay Pacific ⓣ13 17 47, ⓦwww.cathaypacific.com; Continental ⓣ1300 737 640, ⓦwww.continental.com; JAL ⓣ07/4031 1912, ⓦwww.jal.com; Jetstar ⓣ13 15 38, ⓦwww.jetstar.com; Qantas ⓣ13 13 13, ⓦwww.qantas.com.au; Virgin Blue ⓣ13 67 89, ⓦwww.virginblue.com.
Banks and exchange Banks are scattered throughout the city centre, mostly around the intersection of Shields and Abbott streets and in Cairns Central. Some booths around the Esplanade also offer bureau de change facilities, though rates are lower than at the banks.
Bike rentals Bandicoot Bicycle Hire & Tours, 59 Sheridan St ⓣ07/4055 0155; bike rental from $18 a day.
Books Exchange Book Shop, 78 Grafton St, has an excellent range of secondhand books to buy or exchange.
Camping equipment Adventure Equipment, 133 Grafton St (ⓣ07/4031 2669), stocks and rents out all types of outdoor gear and even kayaks; City Place Disposals, on the corner of Shields and Grafton streets, has more down-to-earth, non-brand-name equipment.
Car rental On a day-by-day basis you're looking at around $55 for a four-person runaround, though longer rentals might come in at only $45 a day. Four-wheel-drives are around $165 per day. A1 Car Rental, 141 Lake St ⓣ07/4031 1326; All Day, 151 Lake St ⓣ07/4031 3348, ⓦwww.cairns-car-rentals.com; Billabong, 134 Sheridan St ⓣ07/4051 4299, ⓦwww.billabongrentals.com.au; Integra Car, 131 Lake St ⓣ1800 067 414, ⓦwww.integracar.com.au; Minicar Rentals, 150 Sheridan St ⓣ07/4051 6288, ⓦwww.minicarrentals.com.au.
Cinemas There are multi-screens at BC City Cinemas, at 108 Grafton St and in Cairns Central.
Hospital and medical centres Cairns Medical Centre, on the corner of Florence and Grafton streets (ⓣ07/4052 1119) is open 24 hours for vaccinations and GP consultations (free if you have reciprocal national health cover). Hospitals include Base Hospital, at the northern end of the Esplanade (ⓣ07/4050 6333), or Cairns Private Hospital (ⓣ07/4052 5200) on the corner of Upward and Lake streets, if you have insurance.
Internet access If your accommodation isn't connected, try the backpacker places around the intersection of Shields and Abbot streets, or the more relaxed and friendly *Inbox Café* at 119 Abbott St ($3 per hour).
National Parks Office At the southern end of Sheridan, just past the police station – look for the building with green and yellow trim (Mon–Fri 8.30am–5pm; ⓣ07/4046 6600). Staff are very helpful, and have plenty of free brochures on regional parks, plus books for sale on wildlife and hiking.
Pharmacy Cairns Day and Night Pharmacy and Medical Centre, 29B Shields St (daily 8am–9pm).
Police 5 Sheridan St ⓣ07/4030 7000.
Post office 13 Grafton St, and upstairs in Orchid Plaza off the Transit Mall, Lake St.

Scenic flights Daintree Air Services (☎07/4034 9300, ⓦwww.daintreeair.com.au) charges $200 for a 1-hour flight over the reef; they also buzz up to Lizard Island (see p.489; $590) or Cape York ($990) for the day.
Taxis The main cab rank is on Lake St, west of City Place, or call ☎13 10 08.
Travel agents Flight Centre, 24 Spence St ☎07/4052 1077; STA, 9 Shields St ☎07/4031 4199; Trailfinders, next to *Hides Hotel*, Shields St ☎07/4041 1199.
Work The backpacker contact points along Shields St or your accommodation may be able to help out with WWOOF placements on the Atherton Tablelands.
Yacht Club 4 Esplanade ☎07/4031 2750. Worth contacting for hitching/crewing north to Cape York and the Torres Strait, south to the Whitsundays and beyond, and even to New Guinea and the Pacific.

Around Cairns

There's a fair amount to see and do **around Cairns** (unless otherwise stated, the areas below can be reached on Sunbus services from City Place; see p.464). About 12km northwest near Redlynch, **Crystal Cascades** (Wongalee Falls) is a narrow forest gorge gushing with rapids, small waterfalls and swimming opportunities – somewhere to picnic rather than explore. Don't leave valuables in your car, and heed warnings about the large, serrated, heart-shaped leaves of the stinging tree (also known locally as "Dead man's itch") found beside the paths here; the stories about this plant's sting may seem exaggerated, but if stung you'll believe them all. Backtracking through **Kamerunga** township – as far as you'll get on the bus – there's a marked, fairly steep track through the **Barron Gorge National Park** up through forests to Kuranda (see p.473).

Cairns' variously developed **Northern Beaches** all lie off the highway past the airport (which can make them slightly noisy places to stay). They offer a slower pace than the city, while still being close enough for easy access – all but distant Ellis are on bus routes. Around 8km north, **HOLLOWAYS BEACH** is a string of suburban streets fronting a long strip of sand, quiet except for the airport to the south; *Strait on the Beach* **café** has ordinary takeaway food but great views from its shaded terrace, while *Billabong B&B* on Caribbean Street (☎07/4037 0162, ⓦwww.cairns-bed-breakfast.com; ⑤) is a delightful and secluded spot set on a man-made island, surrounded by water and full of birdlife – the tariff includes a sumptuous gourmet breakfast. **YORKEYS KNOB**, 2km further up the highway, is one of the best **kite-surfing** beaches in Australia – Kiterite at 471 Varley St (☎07/4055 7918) offers three-hour introductory lessons for $130. *Villa Marine*, 8 Rutherford St (☎07/4055 7158, ⓦwww.villamarine.com.au; ④–⑤), has self-contained, spacious units set fifty metres back from the beach beside a cool patch of rainforest; the manager here is a mine of useful information about the Cairns region. You can **eat** at the popular and picturesque **marina**.

About 12km north of Cairns on the highway, the township of **Smithfield** marks the starting point for the Kennedy Highway's ascent to Kuranda, in the Atherton Tablelands. Shortly before, a large complex on the roadside houses both the **Kuranda Skyrail** cable-car terminus (see p.475) and the **Tjapukai Aboriginal Park** (daily 9am–5pm; various packages $31–105, plus transfers). The park's hefty admission price isn't bad value, as it includes entry to boomerang and didgeridoo displays, a fine museum, and three separate theatre shows featuring Dreamtime tales and dancing; it's not eye-opening stuff, but does offer a light-hearted and entertaining introduction to Aboriginal culture.

Up the highway beyond Smithfield are the more developed and upmarket tourist areas of **TRINITY BEACH** and **PALM COVE**, both with spotlessly clean, palm-fringed beaches and lots of luxury holiday apartments, beach resorts, cafés, boutique shops, restaurants and watersports. You can expect to pay from $150 per night at the resorts here, with minimum stays enforced during the high seasons. The *Sebel Reef House & Spa* at Palm Cove (Ⓣ07/4055 3633, Ⓦwww.reefhouse.com.au; ⑧) is the grandest of all the resorts along the coast, whilst the most exclusive is *Kewarra Beach Resort*, also at Palm Cove (Ⓣ07/4057 6666, Ⓦwww.kewarrabeachresort.com.au; ⑧), tucked away in a secluded patch of rainforest on the quietest stretch of beach. **Cairns Tropical Zoo** (daily 8.30am–5pm; $28), nearby on the main highway, offers close-up views of Australia's often-elusive fauna – their night tour (Mon–Thurs & Sat 7–10pm; $85 plus transfers) is particularly recommended.

If you want to really escape for a few days, however, you couldn't ask for a finer place to unwind than **ELLIS BEACH**, thirty minutes north of Cairns on the way to Port Douglas (and unfortunately beyond the reach of bus services) and nothing more than an endless strip of sand and coastal belt of trees beside *Ellis Beach Bungalows* (Ⓣ07/4055 3538, Ⓦwww.ellisbeach.com; camping $26, cabins ③, bungalows ⑤).

The Reef and diving

One of Cairns' major draws is the **Great Barrier Reef**, and there are so many cruise or dive options that making a choice can be very daunting. A lot of fuss is made about the differences between the **inner reef** (closer to the coast, and visited by slower boats), the **outer reef** (closest to the open sea and the target of most speedy operators) and **fringing reef** (surrounding Fitzroy and Green islands), but the coral and fishlife at any of them can be either excellent or tragic. The state of Cairns' **coral** is the subject of much debate: years of agricultural run-off and recent **coral-bleaching** events – not to mention the sheer number of visitors – has had a visibly detrimental effect in the most visited areas, though remoter sections tend to be in better condition. Having said that, almost everywhere is still packed with marine life, ranging from tiny gobies to squid, turtles, and big pelagic fish – only seasoned divers might come away disappointed.

Vessels to take you there range from old trawlers to racing yachts and high-speed cruisers; **cruises** and **dive trips** last from a day to over a week. All day-trip operators have **ticket desks** at, and depart from, the **Reef Fleet Terminal** at the end of Spence Street; you can also **book** through an agent, but either way need to do so at least a day in advance. One way to choose the

△ Aerial view of the Great Barrier Reef

Reef trips and dive schools

The **reef cruises** and **diving** listings given below are not mutually exclusive – most outfits offer diving, snorkelling (usually free) or just plain old sailing. **Prices** can come down by as much as thirty percent during the low seasons (Feb–April & Nov). All dive schools run trips in their own boats, primarily to take students on their certification dives – **experienced divers** may want to avoid these, and should always make their qualifications known to onboard dive staff, who might then be able to arrange something a bit more adventurous than simply joining the heavily-shepherded groups. Paddy Colwell, a **marine biologist** at Reef Teach (see p.469), can also organize a day-trip to the reef and accompany you on your dives (around $200 all inclusive); these come highly recommended. Beware of "**expenses only**" boat trips offered to backpackers, which usually end up in sexual harassment once out at sea. If in doubt, find out from any booking office in town if you're dealing with an authorized, registered operator.

Reef cruises

SAILBOATS

Day-trips $89–170; three days (two nights) $380–500.

Ocean Free ⓣ07/4041 1118, ⓦwww.oceanfree.com.au. Day-trips to the reef around Green Island, aboard a nineteen-metre rigged schooner.

Ocean Spirit Cruises ⓣ07/4031 2920, ⓦwww.oceanspirit.com.au. Large vessel that holds up to a hundred passengers – it sails out to Michaelmas Cay, reputed for its clams, and motors back, ensuring adequate time on the reef. Great presentation but one of the more expensive sailing trips.

Passions of Paradise ⓣ07/4050 0676, ⓦwww.passions.com.au. Popular with backpackers, this roomy and very stable sail-catamaran cruises out to Upolu Cay.

Santa Maria ⓣ07/4031 0558, ⓦwww.reefcharter.com. Twenty-metre, replica nineteenth-century rigged schooner with maximum of ten passengers for overnight trips to Thetford and Moore reefs.

POWERBOATS

$99–190 (day-trips only).

Great Adventures ⓣ1800 079 080, ⓦwww.greatadventures.com.au. Trips on a large, fast catamaran to a private reef pontoon via Green Island.

Osprey V ⓣ1800 079 099, ⓦwww.downunderdive.com.au. Speedy vessel which runs out to the outer Norman and Hastings reefs; comfortable boat, great crew and the best meals of any day-trip.

Quicksilver ⓣ07/4087 2100, ⓦwww.quicksilver-cruises.com. Probably the highest priced in this bracket, but also one of the largest, comfiest vessels, docking at its own stable pontoon mooring at Agincourt reef.

Reef Magic ⓣ1300 666 700, ⓦwww.reefmagiccruises.com. High-speed catamaran which spends five hours at the Marine World pontoon, on the outer reef, for snorkelling and glass-bottom-boat trips.

Reef Quest ⓣ07/4046 7333, ⓦwww.diversden.com. Stable, well-equipped catamaran which covers any number of sites depending on weather conditions.

Sunlover Cruises ⓣ1800 810 512, ⓦwww.sunlover.com.au. Fast catamaran to outer reefs of Moore and Arlington and Fitzroy Island; also offers packages including reef trips and overnight stays on Fitzroy.

Diving

DAY-TRIPS

$60–155; diving upwards of $50 for two dives, including gear rental.

Compass ⓣ1800 815 811, ⓦwww.reeftrip.com. Slow boat, not very stable in windy conditions but one of the cheapest, with boom-netting on the way out.

Noah's Ark Too ⓣ07/4050 0677. Real budget diving at Michaelmas Cay and Hastings Reef; great value, but don't expect many creature comforts.

Sea Quest ⓣ1800 612 223, ⓦwww.diversden.com.au. Very comfortable and speedy vessel running to Norman Reef with excellent crew.

Seastar II ⓣ07/4041 6218, ⓦwww.seastarcruises.com.au. Long-established family-run business with permits for some of the best sections of Hastings Reef and Michaelmas Cay – slow boat leaves at 7.45am to ensure adequate time on the reefs.

Silverswift ⓣ07/4044 9944, ⓦwww.silverseries.com.au. Large 24-metre catamaran whose speed means that you get longer at the reef – there's just enough time to get in three dives if you want.

Super Cat ⓣ1800 079 099, ⓦwww.downunderdive.com.au. Another well-organized budget option, though a faster, newer vessel than most in the price range.

Tusa ⓣ07/4031 1048, ⓦwww.tusadive.com. Purpose-built vessel holding a maximum of 28 passengers; a roving permit means each trip could go to any of ten separate reefs.

LIVE-ABOARDS

Live-aboard trips cater to more serious divers, last from three days upwards and cover the best of the reefs. **Prices** vary seasonally, with cheaper rates from February to June. All costs below include berth, meals and dives, but not gear rental. Remember that weather conditions can affect the destinations offered. For further information and **comparisons** of various operations, check out Diversion Travel (ⓣ07/4039 0200, ⓦwww.diversionoz.com).

Mike Ball ⓣ07/4053 0500, ⓦwww.mikeball.com. Luxury diving with one of Queensland's best-equipped and longest-running operations; venues include the Cod Hole and Coral Sea sites. From $1077.

Nimrod Explorer ⓣ07/4031 5566, ⓦwww.explorerventures.com. Motorized catamaran with basic or plush cabins; four- to eight-day Cod Hole and Coral Sea trips cost $1050–2775.

Spirit of Freedom ⓣ07/4047 9150, ⓦwww.spiritoffreedom.com.au. Huge 33-metre vessel with superlative facilities, sailing to Cod Hole, the Ribbons and Coral Sea. Three days from $1100, four days from $1375, seven days from $2325.

Taka ⓣ07/4051 8722, ⓦwww.takadive.com.au. Fast, thirty-metre vessel with four levels and onboard facilities including digital-photography equipment rental and computers. Four days at the Cod Hole and Ribbon reefs $1000; five days (including Coral Sea sites) $1180.

Undersea Explorer ⓣ07/4099 5911, ⓦwww.undersea.com.au. Scientific research vessel where guests are allowed to participate in ongoing projects; destinations include Osprey Reef, Cod Hole and the Ribbons, and occasional trips to the historic *Pandora* wreck (see p.444). Seven days $3000.

Vagabond ⓣ07/4059 0477, ⓦwww.vagabond-dive.com. Twenty-metre yacht with maximum of ten passengers and a roving permit to suit weather conditions. Two days from $230, dives $25 each.

DIVE SCHOOLS

Ask around about what each **dive school** offers, though training standards in Cairns are uniformly sound. You'll pay around $370 for a budget Open-Water Certification course, diving lesser reefs whilst training and returning to Cairns each night; and $500–650 for a four- or five-day course using better sites and staying on a live-aboard at the reef for a couple of days doing your certification. The following schools are long-established and have a solid reputation; certification dives are either made north at Norman, Hastings and Saxon reefs, or south at Flynn, Moore and Tetford.

CDC 121 Abbott St ⓣ07/4051 0294, ⓦwww.cairnsdive.com.au.

Deep Sea Divers Den 319 Draper St ⓣ07/4046 7333, ⓦwww.diversden.com.

Down Under Dive 287 Draper St ⓣ07/4052 8307, ⓦwww.downunderdive.com.au.

Pro-Dive Cnr Abbott and Shields streets ⓣ07/4031 5255, ⓦwww.prodivecairns .com.Lucky Dogs

right boat is simply to check out the **price**: small, cramped, slow tubs are the cheapest while roomy, faster catamarans are more expensive; to narrow things down further, find out which serves the best **food**. Before going to the reef (or even if you're not) take in the superb two-hour **Reef Teach** multimedia and interactive show in Cairns at the Bolands Centre, 14 Spence St (Mon–Sat 6.15pm; $13; Ⓦwww.reefteach.com.au), at which eccentric marine biologist Paddy Colwell gives more essential background than the dive schools and tour operators have time to impart – this is the most worthwhile thing you can do in Cairns.

Dive sites

The dozen or more **inner reef** sites are much of a muchness. Concentrated day-tripping means that you'll probably be sharing the experience with several other boatloads of people, with scores of divers in the water at once. On a good day, snorkelling over shallow outcrops is enjoyable; going deeper, the coral shows more damage, but there's plenty of patchily distributed marine life. **Michaelmas Cay**, a small, vegetated crescent of sand, is worth a visit: over thirty thousand sooty, common and crested terns roost on the island, while giant clams, sweetlips and reef sharks can be found in the surrounding waters. Nearby **Hastings Reef** has better coral, resident moray eel and bulky maori wrasse, as well as plenty of sea stars and snails in the sand beneath. The two are often included in dive- or reef-trip packages, providing shallow, easy and fun diving. Another favourite, **Norman Reef**, tends to have very clear water, and some sites preserve decent coral gardens with abundant marine life.

One of the cheaper options for diving the **outer reef** is to take an overnight trip (sleep on board) to nearby sections such as **Moore** or **Arlington** reefs, which take between ninety minutes and two hours to reach – it's rather generalized terrain, but the advantages over a simple day-excursion are that you get longer in the water plus the opportunity for night dives. **Longer trips** of three days or more venture further from Cairns into two areas: a circuit north to the Cod Hole and Ribbon reefs, or straight out into the Coral Sea. **The Cod Hole**, near Lizard Island (see p.489), has no coral but is justifiably famous for the mobs of hulking potato cod which rise from the depths to receive hand-outs; currents here are strong, but having these monsters come close enough to cuddle is awesome. **The Ribbons** are a two-hundred-kilometre string boasting relatively pristine locations and good visibility, as do the **Coral Sea** sites; these are isolated, vertically walled reefs some distance out from the main structure and surrounded by open water teeming with seasonal bundles of pelagic species including mantas, turtles and seasonal minke whales. The most-visited Coral Sea sites are **Osprey** and **Holmes** reefs, but try to get out to **Bougainville Reef**, home to everything from brightly coloured anthias fish to fast and powerful silvertip sharks.

Green Island and Fitzroy Island

Heart-shaped, tiny and sandy, **Green Island** is the easiest of any of the Barrier Reef's coral cays to reach, making it an accessible, if expensive, day-trip from Cairns. This, combined with the island's size, means that it can be difficult to escape other visitors, but you only need to put on some fins, visit the **underwater observatory** ($5; free admission with some ferry tickets) or go for a cruise in a glass-bottomed boat to see plentiful coral, fish and turtles. The five-star rooms at the *Green Island Resort* (Ⓣ07/4031 3300, Ⓦwww.greenislandresort.com.au; ⑦) attract long-term guests, and there's a restaurant and pool open to day-trippers, plus plenty of sand to laze on. **Daily ferries** from the Reef Fleet Terminal in Cairns include Big Cat ($62; ⓣ07/4051 0444, ⓦwww.bigcat-cruises.com.au), which departs at 9am, and Great Adventures ($60; ⓣ07/4044 9944), departing at 8.30am, 10.30am and 1pm from Trinity Wharf. Both run courtesy buses which will collect you from your accommodation. Day-trippers on a budget should bring their own lunches, as the resort's restaurant is very expensive. Alternatively, Ocean Free ($109; ⓣ07/4053 5888, ⓦwww.oceanfree.com.au) offers **sailing tours** to Green Island with offshore snorkelling.

Fitzroy Island is a continental island, not a cay like Green Island, and sports a **resort** which has undergone many makeovers recently and is currently in redevelopment limbo once again. Fitzroy is actually quite large and, away from the resort, there are some worthwhile walks through highland greenery where you can escape the sunbathing hordes, notably the two-hour trek to the Lighthouse for excellent views. Fitzroy Island Ferries (45min each way; $42 return; ⓣ07/4030 7907, ⓦwww.fitzroyisland.com.au) operates three **ferries** a day from Reef Fleet Terminal, and can also fill you in on the latest about the resort.

The Atherton Tablelands

The **Atherton Tablelands**, the highlands behind Cairns, are named after **John Atherton**, who made the tin deposits at Herberton accessible by opening a route to the coast in 1877. Dense forest covered these highlands before the majority was felled for timber and given over to dairy cattle, tobacco and grain. The remaining pockets of forest are magnificent, but it's the area's understated beauty that draws most visitors today, and though **Kuranda** and its markets pull in busloads from the coast, there are several quieter national parks brimming with rare species. You could spend days here, driving or hiking through rainforest to crater lakes and endless small waterfalls, or simply camp out for a night and search for wildlife with a torch. For a contrast, consider a trip west to the mining town of **Chillagoe**, whose dust, limestone caves and Aboriginal art place it firmly in the Outback.

Numerous **tours** run here from Cairns (see box on p.465), and there's a limited **bus service** with Whitecar Coaches (ⓣ07/4091 1855), who run from their Cairns depot at 46 Spence St to Kuranda, Mareeba, Atherton, Herberton and Ravenshoe twice a day from Monday to Friday, and once a day to Kuranda, Mareeba and Atherton at the weekend. You really need your own car to explore widely: **drivers** can reach the tablelands on the Palmerston Highway from Innisfail; the twisty Gillies Highway from Gordonvale; the Kennedy Highway from Smithfield to Kuranda; or Route 81 from Mossman to Mareeba. Two unforgettable alternatives are to ride up to the tablelands **by train** from Cairns to Kuranda, which winds through gorges and rainforest; or in the green gondolas of the **Kuranda Skyrail cable car**, with fantastic aerial views of the forest canopy en route between Smithfield and Kuranda – either method costs $37 one way or $54 return.

Kuranda and the Barron Gorge

A constant stream of visitors arriving from the coast has turned the formerly atavistic community of **KURANDA** into a stereotypical resort village, though it's still a pretty spot and good for a half-day excursion. Most people come for the much-hyped daily **markets**, best from 8.30am to 3pm on Wednesday, Friday and Sunday, though these are shrinking as less-regulated events at

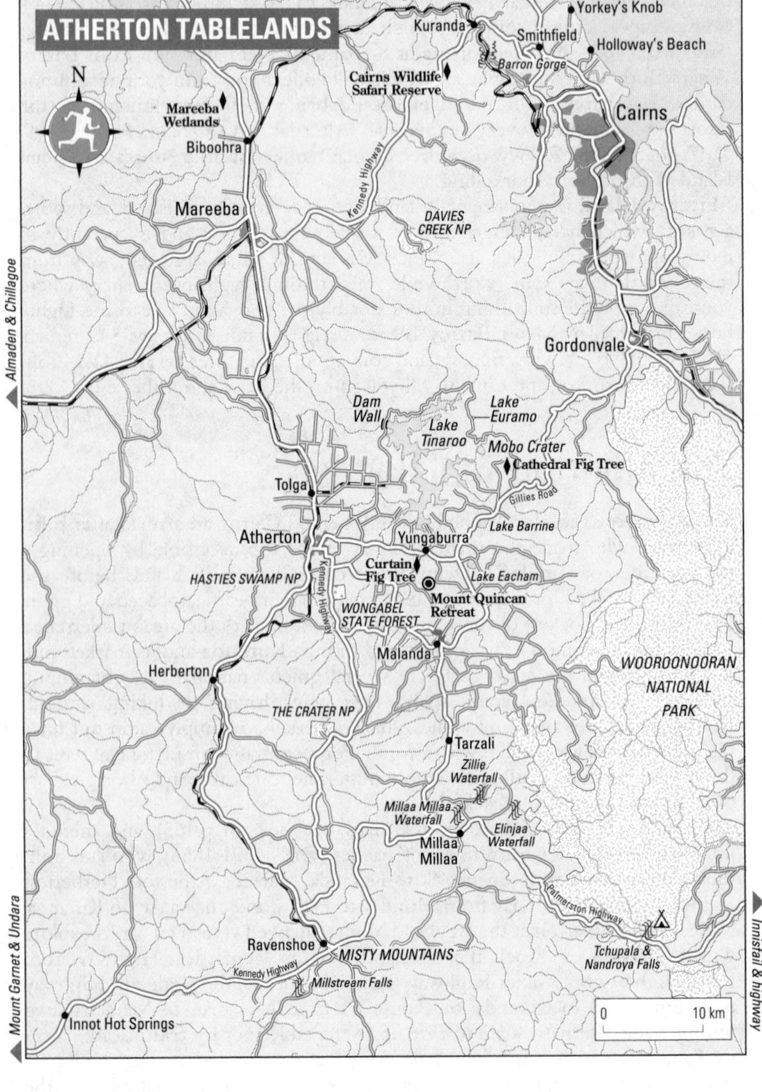

Yungaburra and Port Douglas gain momentum. There are also a number of good wildlife enclosures, notably the **Butterfly Sanctuary** (daily 9.45am–4pm; $14), a mix of streams and "feed trees" where giant ulysses and birdwing butterflies' numbers are being pumped up by a breeding programme; and **Birdworld** (daily 9am–4pm; $14), a superb aviary with realistically arranged vegetation and nothing between you and a host of native and exotic rarities. At the **Koala Gardens** (daily 9am–4pm; $33) next door you can cuddle koalas and see wallabies, wombats, snakes and crocodiles in a rather bland environment. Look out for discounted combined deals to all three attractions.

The wet tropics and World Heritage

Queensland's **wet tropics** – the coastal belt from the Paluma Range, near Townsville, to the Daintree north of Cairns – are **UNESCO World Heritage** listed, as they contain one of the oldest surviving tracts of rainforest anywhere on earth. Whether this listing has benefited the region is questionable, however; logging has slowed, but the tourist industry has vigorously exploited the area's status as an untouched wilderness, constantly pushing for more development so that a greater number of visitors can be accommodated. The clearing of mangroves for a marina and resort at Cardwell is a worst-case example; Kuranda's **Skyrail** was one of the few projects designed to lessen the ultimate impact (another highway – with more buses – was the alternative). Given the profits to be made, development is inevitable, but it's sad that a scheme designed to promote the region's unique beauty may accelerate its destruction.

Kuranda sits at the top of the **Barron Gorge**, spectacular in the wet season when the river rages down the falls, which are otherwise tamed by a hydroelectric dam upstream. Cross the rail bridge next to the station and take a path leading down to the river, where Smiley's Adventure Hire offers 45-minute **cruises** (five daily Wed–Sun; $14; ⓣ0412 775 184) or canoe rentals to explore the river at your leisure. On foot, a **walking track** descends to cold swimming spots along the railway and river from the lookout at the end of Barron Falls Road, 2km from town. Other trails follow the road beyond the falls through the Barron Gorge National Park and down to Kamerunga, near Cairns – see p.468 for details.

Just 9km from Kuranda down the Mareeba road, **Cairns Wildlife Safari Reserve** (daily 9am–4.30pm; $24; ⓣ07/4093 7777, ⓦwww.cairnswildlifesafarireserve.com.au) has a few native species but draws the crowds with Sumatran tigers, cheetahs, white rhinos and ring-tailed lemurs in pretty authentic, savannah surroundings – there are guided tours and feeding sessions throughout the day.

Practicalities

The road from Cairns comes in at the top of town, while trains and the Skyrail cable car arrive 500m downhill; **essential services** – post office, store (EFTPOS), bank, cafés – are laid out between them along Coondoo Street.

Given its accessibility from Cairns, Kuranda doesn't tempt many people to stay overnight; it's virtually a ghost town after the markets close, and there's little **accommodation**. Just up from the Skyrail terminus and orchid-shrouded train station, you'll find the quiet *Kuranda Backpackers' Hostel* at 6 Arara St (ⓣ07/4093 7355, ⓦwww.kurandabackpackershostel.com; dorms $19, rooms ❷), with a plentiful supply of bunks, large grounds, kitchen and laundry. Around the corner is *Kuranda Hotel* (ⓣ07/4093 7206; ❸), with motel rooms out the back of an incongruous Irish theme pub. The nearest **campsite** is just out of town across the Mareeba road at the pleasantly shaded *Kuranda Rainforest Accommodation Park* (ⓣ07/4093 7316, ⓦwww.kurandarainforestpark.com.au; camping $19, cabins ❷, bungalows ❹).

Cafés are legion, though pricey: *Annabel's Pie Shop*, across from the main markets, has excellent pasties and pies; while *Billy's* at the *Middle Pub* (halfway down Coondoo Street) does tasty charcoal grills and salads.

Mareeba and around

West of Kuranda, rainforest quickly gives way to dry woodland and tobacco plantations, quite a change from the coast's greenery. **MAREEBA**, 35km along,

Birding on the tablelands

The northern end of the Atherton Tablelands, as it slopes downhill between Mareeba and Mossman, encompasses a broad range of habitats, from dry gum woodland to highland rainforest, open farmland, lowland wetlands and the coast, and as such is one of the richest areas for **birding** in Australia, with over 350 species recorded, including thirteen endemics. Several places along the Mareeba–Mossman road have now set themselves up as **birdwatchers' retreats**, and can fill you in on places to improve your tallies: near the tiny hamlet of **Julatten**, about 50km north of Mareeba via Mount Molloy, *Kingfisher Park* (ⓣ07/4094 1263, ⓦwww.birdwatchers.com.au; ④) has very clued-up owners and a choice of old cabins or motel rooms. The retreat is within striking distance of fabled (in birding circles at least) **Mount Lewis**, and features in Sean Dooley's book *The Big Twitch*, a humourous insight into the obsessive world of serious birdwatching.

is a quiet place and the tablelands' oldest town, founded in the 1900s after the area was opened up for **tobacco** farming. **Coffee** has largely replaced this now – Coffee Works, on Mason Street at the southern end of town (daily 9am–4pm), is one of several places where you can take a tour ($6), buy fresh beans, or try a brew at their café. Fruit plantations have also become a profitable business, with several farms recently branching out into **tropical fruit wine** production and opening cellar doors to promote their mango wines, coffee liqueurs and banana brandy – try Golden Drop Winery (daily 8am–6.30pm), 10km north of Mareeba off the highway at Biboohra.

Just beyond Biboohra, the **Mareeba Wetlands** (Wed–Sun 10am–4pm, closed Jan–March; $10; ⓣ07/4093 2514, ⓦwww.mareebawetlands.com) is a stunning five-thousand-acre reserve of tropical savannah woodlands with grass-fringed lagoons that attract seasonal flocks of brolgas, jabiru storks and black cockatoos, along with resident wallabies and goannas. The wetlands are also part of a breeding programme for rainbow-coloured **gouldian finches**, a formerly common bird now virtually extinct in the wild, but which you can see in the aviary here. You can rent canoes or join a boat tour, book twilight ranger-led walks, or **stay** in tented cabins (④) at their **safari camp** when it's not being used by researchers – all of these need to be booked in advance.

Back in Mareeba, all the shops and banks can be found on Byrnes Street, with the **tourist office** (daily 8am–4.30pm) about a kilometre south of town along the Atherton road, marked by a memorial to James Venture Mulligan, the veteran prospector who discovered the Palmer River Goldfields. Just opposite, the *Jackaroo Motel* (ⓣ07/4092 2677, ⓦwww.jackaroomotel.com; ④) is one of Mareeba's better **places to stay**, or try the *Tropical Tablelands Caravan Park* (ⓣ07/4092 1158; cabins ③). The town is pretty seedy **after dark**, with plenty of drunks staggering around even early on. **Moving on**, Atherton is 30km south, while roads north head via the township of Mount Molloy to Cooktown or the coast at Mossman. For Chillagoe, follow signs from the northern end of town for Dimbulah.

West to Chillagoe

The 150-kilometre road to **Chillagoe** mysteriously alternates between corrugated gravel and isolated sections of bitumen, but poses no real problem during the dry season. Thirty kilometres before town, the *Almaden Hotel*'s cool, mirrored, well-supplied bar and beer garden are an incredible oasis in ramshackle, dilapidated **Almaden**.

CHILLAGOE dates from 1887, when enough copper ore was found to keep a smelter running until the 1950s; nowadays a gold mine 16km west at Mungana seems to keep the place ticking over. Red dust, hillocks, a service station, a general store and a single, short street of oversized hotels complete the picture. The main point of coming here is to see Chillagoe's **caves**, ancient limestone hillocks hollowed out by rain and half-buried in the scrub, explored on tours from the Hub (see below). The most interesting caves are **Royal Arch**, **Donna** and **Trezkinn**, full of natural sculptures including a few large **stalagmites**. Wildlife here includes grey swiftlets and agile pythons, which somehow manage to catch bats on the wing. A footpath leads through grassland between the caves, where you'll find echidnas, kangaroos, black cockatoos and frogmouths, the last being odd birds whose name fits them perfectly. **Balancing Rock** offers panoramic views, with Chillagoe hidden by low trees, while obscure Aboriginal paintings and engravings have been found near **the Arches**, west at Mungana.

The **Hub Tourist Information Centre** (ⓣ07/4094 7111) is on Queen Street, Chillagoe's main drag, and can arrange **tours** of three of the town's caves (daily 9am, 11am & 1.30pm; $11–13.75); check well in advance as the tours may not run during the wet season and numbers are limited. **Accommodation** is available at the *Chillagoe Caves Lodge* on King Street (ⓣ1800 446 375, ⓔcaveslodgechillgoe@bigpond.com; ④), which has a pool and serves meals, or at *Chillagoe Cabins*, at the Mareeba end of town (ⓣ07/4094 7206, ⓦwww.chillagoe.com; ④), with self-contained cabins and a pleasant garden atmosphere. **Heading west** from Chillagoe, the road continues 500km to Karumba and the Gulf of Carpentaria (see p.539), but it doesn't improve, and there's little fuel or help along the way.

Atherton and around

Thirty kilometres south of Mareeba and centrally placed for forays to most of the area's attractions, **ATHERTON** is the largest town in the tablelands. It was founded in part by Chinese miners who settled here in the 1880s after being chased off the goldfields: 2km south of the centre, the corrugated-iron **Hou Wang Temple** (daily 10am–4pm; $7) is the last surviving building of Atherton's old **Chinatown**, a once-busy enclave of market gardens and homes which was abandoned after the government gave the land to returning World War I servicemen. The temple was restored in 2000, with an accompanying museum containing photographs and artefacts found on site – the excellent **birds of prey show** is also held here (Mon, Thurs, Sat & Sun 11am & 2.30pm; $12).

The other reason to come to Atherton is to catch the authentically grubby 1920s **steam train** to Herberton, which leaves on Wednesday and Sunday from Platypus Park, just south of town (departs 10.30am, returns 3pm; $27.50); along the way you get to look at tunnels, forest and the pretty Carrington Falls, and then have an hour or so to look around Herberton (see p.479) before the return trip. Otherwise, you can clock up more local **birdlife** at **Hasties Swamp**, a big waterhole and two-storey observation hide about 5km south of town. While nothing astounding, it's a peaceful place populated by magpie geese, pink-eared ducks, swamp hens and assorted marsh tiggets.

Atherton's banks, shops and early-opening **cafés** – *Chatterbox* is the most lively – can be found along Main Street, with a supermarket right at the south end past the post office. There's a friendly **tourist office** (daily 9am–5pm; ⓣ07/4091 4222) just south of the centre. **Accommodation** includes green and spacious campsites at the *Woodlands Tourist Park*, just at the edge of town on Herberton Road (Ⓣ07/4091 1407, Ⓦwww.woodlandscp.com.au; cabins ③–④); the heavily tiled and hospitable *Atherton Travellers Lodge*, 37 Alice St, off Vernon Street (Ⓣ07/4091 3552, Ⓦwww.athertontravellerslodge.com.au; dorms $18, rooms ②), which specializes in finding farm work; and the very pleasant *Atherton Blue Gum* at 36 Twelfth Ave (Ⓣ07/4091 5149, Ⓦwww.atherton bluegum.com; ⑤), a modern, timber B&B which also runs regional tours.

Lake Tinaroo

At the village of **Tolga**, 5km north of Atherton, a turn-off leads to **Lake Tinaroo**, a convoluted reservoir formed by pooling the Barron River's headwaters. At the end of the fifteen-kilometre sealed road is the dam wall and nearby *Lake Tinaroo Holiday Park* (Ⓣ07/4095 8232, Ⓦwww.ltholidaypark.com .au; cabins ③), which also rents out canoes for $35 a day. Past here, a gravel road runs 25km around the lake to the Gillies Highway, 15km east of Yungaburra, passing five very cheap **campsites** on the north shore before cutting deep into native forests. It's worth stopping along the way for the short walks to bright-green **Mobo Crater**, spooky **Lake Euramo**, and the **Cathedral Fig**, a giant tree some 50m tall and 43m around the base; the thick mass of tendrils supporting the crown have fused together like molten wax.

Yungaburra and around

Just 13km east of Atherton at the start of the Gillies Highway to Gordonvale, the self-consciously pretty village of **YUNGABURRA**, consisting of the old wooden *Lake Eacham Hotel*, a store, a handful of houses and some quaint restaurants, makes an excellent base to explore the tablelands. The village is also the venue for a huge **market** held on the last Saturday of each month. Good places for wildlife spotting include a **platypus-viewing platform** on the river where the road from Atherton comes into town, and the **Curtain Fig Tree** (again signposted off the Atherton road), another extraordinarily big parasitic strangler fig whose base is entirely overhung by a stringy mass of aerial roots drooping off the higher branches. Informative **wildlife guides** can help you spot some of the rarer nocturnal marsupials around town; contact Alan's Wildlife Tours ($60; Ⓣ07/4095 3784, Ⓦwww.alanswildlifetours.com.au).

Considering its diminutive size, Yungaburra has plenty of **places to stay**. The pine-and-slate *On the Wallaby Hostel*, 37 Eacham Rd (Ⓣ07/4095 2031, Ⓦwww.onthewallaby.com; dorms $20, rooms ③), is an excellent budget option which organizes canoe and wildlife-spotting trips. The upmarket *Eden House* (Ⓣ07/4095 3355, Ⓦwww.edenhouse.com.au; ⑥) is another good bet. For a **romantic weekend**, though, the secluded, self-contained wooden-pole houses which overlook an extinct volcano crater at *Mt Quincan Crater Retreat*, on the Peeramon Road about 8km southeast of Yungaburra (Ⓣ07/4095 2255, Ⓦwww .mtquincan.com.au; ⑧), are absolutely unbeatable – and it's also infested with tree kangaroos. For **eating**, *Flynn's Café* does an excellent breakfast, or try the bratwurst and rosti at *Nick's Swiss Italian Restaurant* (closed Mon). *Eden House* has an "Australian contemporary" menu and inexpensive set dinners, while the popular *Burra Inn* (Ⓣ07/4095 3657) offers eclectic gourmet treats, from Tuscan lamb to kangaroo pie.

Lakes Eacham and Barrine

A few kilometres east of Yungaburra at the start of the Gillies Highway down to Gordonvale are the **crater lakes**, or "maars", of Barrine and Eacham – blue, still discs surrounded by thick rainforest (though parts of this were badly battered by **Cyclone Larry** in 2006). **Lake Eacham** has a picnic area and an easy four-kilometre trail around its shores, taking you past birds and insects foraging on the forest floor, and inoffensive **amethystine pythons** – Australia's largest snake – sunning themselves down by the water. There's **accommodation** near the lake at the cozy *Crater Lake Rainforest Cottages* (ⓣ07/4095 2322, ⓦwww.craterlakes.com.au; ⑦), with four self-contained themed cottages set in a forest clearing; and *Chambers Wildlife Lodges* (ⓣ07/4095 3754, ⓦwww.rainforest-australia.com; minimum three-night stay ⑧), something of a magnet for local birdlife and mammals.

For its part, **Lake Barrine** has a tearoom overlooking the water serving good cream teas and canteen-style meals, and a **cruise boat** (daily 10.15am, 11.30am, 1.30pm, 2.30pm & 3.30pm; $13) which spends an hour circuiting the lake. To get away from the crowds, head for the two enormous kauri pines which mark the start of an underused six-kilometre **walking track** around the lake; keep your eyes peeled for spiky-headed water dragons, more pythons and hordes of musky rat-kangaroos, which look exactly as you'd expect them to.

The Southern Tablelands

The Kennedy Highway continues 80km down from Atherton to Ravenshoe, the highlands' southernmost town, past easy walking tracks at first **Wongabel State Forest** and then **the Crater** at Mount Hypipamee, a 56-metre vertical rift formed by volcanic gases blowing through fractured granite that's now filled with deep, weed-covered water. There are picnic tables here but camping is prohibited. An alternative road south from Atherton – and the train (see p.477) – circles west via **HERBERTON**, a quaint, one-time timber town without a modern building in sight. During the 1880s there were thirty thousand people here (a century before Cairns' population numbered so many), and the railway from Atherton was built to service the town. If you happen to be in Herberton at lunchtime on Sunday, there are huge outdoor **barbecues** at the *Royal Hotel*'s beer garden.

RAVENSHOE is notable for the *Tully Falls Hotel*, Queensland's highest pub, and **Millstream Falls**, Australia's broadest waterfall, 5km southwest. There's also another **steam railway** here, with a train departing Saturday and Sunday at 2.30pm to the tiny siding of Tumoulin, Queensland's highest train station – call Ravenshoe's **Visitor Centre** (daily 9am–4pm; ⓣ07/4097 7700) for bookings. Southeast of town, a series of marked **hiking trails** through the **Misty Mountains**' forests and streams offer walks of between a day and a week in length, with campsites laid out at regular intervals – for practical information check out ⓦwww.mistymountains.com.au, or call the National Parks Service on ⓣ07/4046 6600.

For **accommodation** in Ravenshoe, try the *Old Convent B&B* (ⓣ07/4097 6454, ⓦwww.theoldconvent.com.au; ④) or *Tall Timbers Caravan Park* (ⓣ07/4097 6325; cabins ③). Southwest, the road drops off the tablelands past **Innot Hot Springs** – with its huge anthills and steamy upwellings behind the *Hot Springs Hotel* – and the township of **Mount Garnet**, to the start of the Gulf Developmental Road.

Malanda, Millaa Millaa and the Palmerston Highway

About 25km southeast of Atherton, the **dairy** at **MALANDA** provides milk and cheese for the whole of Queensland's far north, plus most of the Northern Territory and even New Guinea. In the centre of town, the *Malanda Hotel* (ⓣ07/4096 5488; ③) was built in 1911 to sleep three hundred people and claims to be the **largest wooden building** in the southern hemisphere; its old furnishings and excellent restaurant are worth a look even if you're not staying here, though the bar is so cavernous it always feels empty. Back less than a kilometre towards Atherton, there's a roadside swimming hole and short rainforest walk at **Malanda Falls Environmental Park**; the display at the **tourist office** here (daily 9.30am–4.30pm; $3) gives a rundown of the tablelands' geology and its Aboriginal and settler history. For **somewhere to stay**, *Fur 'n' Feathers*, about 7km south via Tarzali (Ⓣ07/4096 5364, Ⓦwww.rainforesttreehouses.com.au; ⑧), is another of the tablelands' superlative accommodation options, with wooden pole-frame treehouses set amongst a hundred acres of thick, wildlife-packed rainforest.

From Malanda it's about 20km south to **MILLAA MILLAA**, a quiet, five-hundred-metre street with the usual hotel and general store. A waterfall circuit starts 2km east of the town, where a fifteen-kilometre road passes three small cascades. There's a National Parks **campsite** about 27km southeast of Millaa Millaa, from where walking tracks lead to mossy **Tchupala Falls** and the impressive **Nandroya Falls**, before the Palmerston highway descends 40km to Innisfail and the coast.

Cairns to Cape Tribulation

Just a couple of hours' drive **north of Cairns** on the Cook Highway are the Daintree and Cape Tribulation, the tamed fringes of the Cape York Peninsula. The highway initially runs to **Port Douglas** and **Mossman**, a beautiful drive past isolated beaches where hang-gliders patrol the headlands. North of Mossman is **the Daintree**, Australia's largest and the world's oldest surviving stretch of tropical rainforest. World Heritage listing hasn't saved it from development: roads are being surfaced, land has been subdivided, and there's an ever-increasing number of services in place, undermining the wild and remote brochure image. While this disappoints some visitors, the majestic forest still descends thick and dark right to the sea around **Cape Tribulation**, and you can explore paths through the jungle, watch for wildlife, or just rest on the beach.

Tours from Cairns will show you the sights, but you really need longer to take in the rich scenery and atmosphere – without your own transport, Sun Palm Coaches (Ⓣ07/4084 2626, Ⓦwww.sunpalmtransport.com) and Coral Reef Coaches (Ⓣ07/4098 2800, Ⓦwww.coralreefcoaches.com.au) both run daily shuttle buses from Cairns to Cape Tribulation (about $65 single), via Port Douglas and Mossman.

Port Douglas and around

Massive development in recent years has seen the once pretty fishing village of **PORT DOUGLAS**, an hour north of Cairns, turned into an upmarket tourist hub, with a main street full of boutiques, shopping malls and holidaying hordes. However, the town does have a huge **beach**, along with plenty of distractions to keep you busy for a day or two, and it's getting to be as good a place as Cairns to pick up a regional tour or dive trip to the reef.

The town comprises a small grid of streets centred around Macrossan Street – which runs between Four Mile Beach and Anzac Park – with the **marina** a couple of blocks back. Between the end of Macrossan Street and the sea, **Anzac Park** is the scene of an increasingly busy Sunday-morning **market**, good for fruit, vegetables and souvenirs. Near the park's **jetty** you'll find the whitewashed timber church of **St Mary's by the Sea**, built after the 1911 cyclone carried off the previous structure.

Out to sea, the vegetated sand cays known as **the Low Isles** make a good day-trip, with fine snorkelling, a lighthouse and an interpretive centre; you can get there with *Wavedancer* ($132; ⓣ07/4087 2100, ⓦwww.quicksilver-cruises.com), *Sailaway* ($140; ⓣ07/4099 4772, ⓦwww.sailawayportdouglas.com) and *Shaolin* ($140; ⓣ07/4099 4772, ⓦwww.shaolinportdouglas.com), a romantic Chinese junk. **Reef trips** mostly head to Agincourt; Quicksilver's fast catamaran ($210; ⓣ07/4087 2100, ⓦwww.quicksilver-cruises.com) is best for a day-trip cruise, while **divers** should contact Poseidon, 34 Macrossan St ($210 for three dives; ⓣ07/4099 4772, ⓦwww.poseidon-cruises.com.au).

Practicalities

As in Cairns, a prolific number of businesses offer tourist information – the Port Douglas **tourist office** at 23 Macrossan St (daily 8.30am–5.30pm; ⓣ07/4099 5599) can sort out everything from Aboriginal-guided tours of Mossman Gorge to sailing trips and buses to the Daintree.

Accommodation

The most upmarket of the town's **accommodation** options is the huge *Mirage Resort* (ⓣ07/4099 5888, ⓦwww.sheraton-mirage.com; ❽), off Davidson Street on the way into town. There are a pack of more affordable apartments along Macrossan Street, all offering comfortable rooms and a pool, including *Macrossan House* at no. 19 (ⓣ07/4099 4366, ⓦwww.macrossanhouse-port-douglas.com.au; ❺) and *New Port* at no. 16 (ⓣ07/4099 5700, ⓦwww.thenewport.com.au; ❺). *Mango Tree Apartments*, 91 Davidson St (ⓣ07/4099 5677; ❺), is just back from Four Mile Beach, while the pleasant *Port O'Call Lodge*, about 1km from town on Port Street (ⓣ07/4099 5422, ⓦwww.portocall.com.au; dorms $25, rooms ❹), is the only real budget option.

Eating and drinking

Places to eat abound along Macrossan Street. Near the tourist office, *EJ Seamarket* is a licensed fish-and-chip shop, so you can grab a cold beer while waiting for your meal to crisp. The *Iron Bar* has rough-cut timber furniture and a mid-range surf 'n' turf menu; *Mango Jam Café* across the road opens late for wood-fired pizza; and the nearby *Star of Siam* has moderately priced Thai fare. *The Living Room*, around the corner on Wharf Street (Tues–Sun 6.30pm–late; ⓣ07/4099 4011), sports a huge outdoor deck leading into the cool interior of a renovated wooden Queenslander house; its Asian-fusion menu is thick with seafood specialities such as blue swimmer crab and tiger prawns (mains around $30). If it's just a cooling **drink** you're after, both the *Court House Hotel* and *Central Hotel* are old-style wooden pubs with plenty of local atmosphere.

Mossman

MOSSMAN, 14km past Port Douglas, is a quiet town which has hardly changed since the 1950s; rail lines between the canefields and mill still run along the main street. Ten minutes inland, **Mossman Gorge** looks like all rainforest rivers should; the boulder-strewn flow is good for messing around in on a quiet day, but attracts streams of tour buses and car break-ins in peak season. There are also plenty of **walking trails** taking in the gorge and rainforest, lasting from a few minutes to a couple of hours. **Kuku Yalanji**, the local Aboriginal

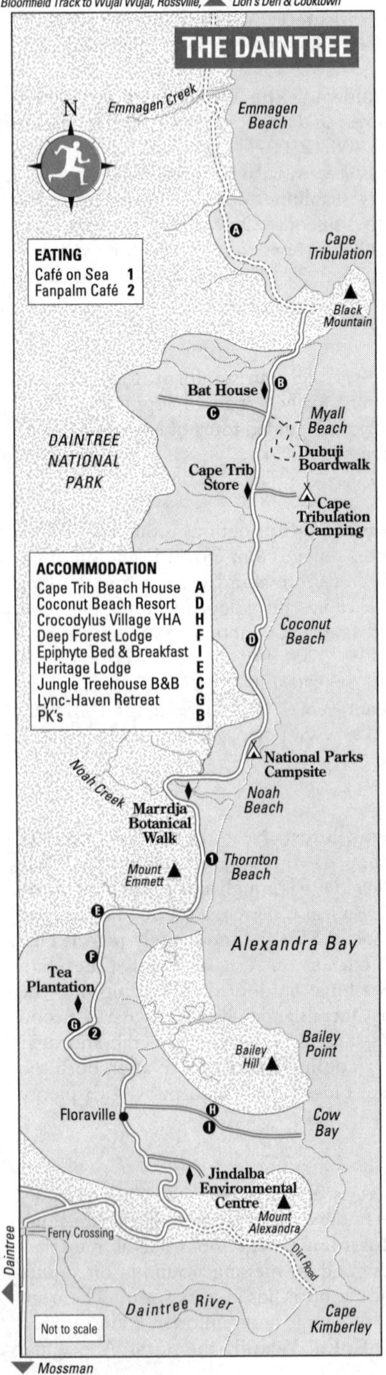

comm-unity, also conduct **tours** of the gorge explaining its history and local plant usage (Mon–Sat 9am, 11am, 1pm & 3pm; $25; bookings on ⓣ07/4098 2595, ⓦwww.yalanji.com.au). If you want to stay somewhere plush in the area, book in at the exclusive *Silky Oaks Lodge* (ⓣ1300 134 044, ⓦwww.silkyoakslodge.com.au; ⑧), 12km from town through the canefields; there's not much rainforest here, but you get very well looked after.

Continuing north, the road splits left to Daintree township or right for the Daintree Ferry to Cape Tribulation. Backtracking southeast, you leave the highway and climb to **Mount Molloy** and either Mareeba or the Peninsula Developmental Road – the easier, inland route to Cooktown.

The Daintree

Set off the Mossman to Cape Tribulation road, riverside **DAINTREE** township – a former timber camp – is now more or less just one big pub, a general store and a campground. Birders will want to contact Chris Dahlberg here (ⓣ07/4098 7997) for his exceptional two-hour dawn **birding tours** ($55), though most people bypass Daintree completely and instead follow the road to the **Daintree River Ferry** (6am–midnight; pedestrians $1 each way, vehicles $16 return) and the start of the Cape Tribulation road. The river crossing can be very busy, with the 25-vehicle-capacity cable ferry taking around fifteen minutes for the return trip.

The Cape Tribulation road

Across the river is the start of the **Daintree National Park** and the 35-kilometre scenic drive to the tiny settlement of Cape Tribulation, beyond which the sealed road ends and becomes a 4WD-only route to Cooktown. From the ferry crossing at Daintree River, it's 8km through rainforest over the convoluted Alexandra Range to the **Jindalba Environmental Centre** (daily 8.30am–5pm; $25), which features a five-level, 27-metre-high tower with identification charts for the plants and birds you're likely to see at each stage – the top also provides a fabulous view over the canopy. Just up the road, **Floraville** has the regional pub and a café; past here, a six-kilometre side road from the airstrip heads straight to the coast and **Cow Bay**'s excellent **beach**. **Accommodation** along the Cow Bay road includes the open-plan, laid-back *Epiphyte Bed and Breakfast*, off a short track about 4km along (Ⓣ07/4098 9039, Ⓦwww.rainforestbb.com; ③); and the jungle-clad cabins of *Crocodylus Village*, about 3km along (Ⓣ07/4098 9166, Ⓦwww.crocodyluscapetrib.com; dorms $23, rooms ③). Meals at the latter are healthy and inexpensive, and they arrange night walks, kayak trips to Snapper Island, and diving at the local reef.

Back on the Cape Tribulation road, another few kilometres lands you at *Fanpalm Café*, which marks the start of a **boardwalk** through a forest of fan palms, and the cabins, self-contained units and camping at *Lync-Haven Retreat* (Ⓣ07/4098 9155, Ⓦwww.lynchaven.com.au; ④). Moving on past a tea plantation and tiny **ALEXANDRA BAY** township, there's further **accommodation** up against the forest fence at *Deep Forest Lodge* (Ⓣ07/4098 9162, Ⓦwww.daintreedeepforestlodge.com.au; ⑤), which has well-furnished, self-contained cabins; and *Heritage Lodge*, inland off the main road (Ⓣ07/4098 9138, Ⓦwww.heritagelodge.net.au; ⑦), which has boutique cabins, a fancy restaurant and walking trails along **Cooper Creek**. The next stop is 4km on at sandy Thornton Beach, where you'll find a **licensed kiosk** at *Café on Sea*; from here it's another few kilometres to the **Marrdja Botanical Walk**, where concrete paths and boardwalks follow the creek through a mixture of forest to mangroves at the river mouth on **Noah Beach**. Look for spiky lawyer cane, lianas twisted into corkscrew shapes where they once surrounded a tree, and the spherical pods of the cannonball mangrove – dried and dismembered, they were used as puzzles

△ The Daintree National Park

by Aboriginal peoples, the object being to fit the irregular segments back together. There's a National Parks **campsite** (pre-book via ⓦwww.epa.qld.gov.au) in woodland behind the beach; it's big but prone to be muddy and is closed during the wet season.

Just up the road is the exclusive beachfront *Coconut Beach Resort* (ⓣ1300 144 044, ⓦwww.coconutbeach.com.au; ❽), with an extensive array of facilities including a huge A-frame restaurant where "smart tropical dress" is required. North of here, the **Cape Trib Store** has a café and supplies, with a natural swimming hole in the forest close by. The café is also the base for **Mason's Tours** (ⓣ07/4098 0070, ⓦwww.masonstours.com.au), which organizes 4WD safaris and local day and night walks – they also publish a very detailed map of the Bloomfield Track to Cooktown if you're heading that way. Opposite the store, a short road heads through thick forest to **Myall Beach** and *Cape Tribulation Camping* (ⓣ07/4098 0070, ⓦwww.capetribcamping.com.au; tent sites $24, safari tents ❸). Plants close in again a couple of kilometres up the main road at **Dubuji Boardwalk**, a 1.2-kilometre-long replay of Marrdja, though with a greater variety of forests.

Cape Tribulation

Cape Tribulation – a forty-minute drive from the ferry crossing – was named when Captain Cook's vessel hit a reef offshore in June 1770. The cleared area below the steep, forested slopes of **Mount Sorrow** has a café, store, ATM, pharmacy and a **Bat House** (Tues–Sun 10.30am–3.30pm; $2), worth a visit to handle tame, orphaned flying foxes. The beach here is attractive and accessed along a boardwalk from the township. Beds and camping are available at the often noisy and overcrowded *PK's* hostel (ⓣ1800 232 333, ⓦwww.pksjunglevillage.com; dorms $25, rooms ❹). Alternatively, there are comfy but rustic wooden cabins hidden in the forest at *Jungle Hideaway B&B* (ⓣ07/4099 5651, ⓦwww.rainforesthideaway.com; ❺), set 200m up in the hills, as well as the supremely idyllic jungle-beachfront *Cape Trib Beach House*, 2.5km north (ⓣ07/4098 0030, ⓦwww.capetribbeach.com.au; dorms $25, cabins ❺–❻). All can organize horse riding, sea-kayaking, guided forest walks and the exhilarating experience of abseiling through the canopy with Jungle Surfing Tours ($99; ⓣ07/4098 0040, ⓦwww.junglesurfingcanopytours.com).

The area is best explored on foot, for the simple pleasure of walking through the forest with the sea breaking on a beach not five minutes distant. A **path** runs out to the cape, where you may see brilliantly coloured pittas (small, tailless birds with a buff chest, green back and black-and-rust heads) bouncing around in the leaf litter, or even a crocodile sunning itself on the beach. One way to penetrate the undergrowth away from the paths is to follow small creeks: **Emmagen**, about 6km north, runs halfway up Mount Sorrow and is recommended for its safe swimming holes, but get advice on the route first from your accommodation.

The Bloomfield Track

Spanning 80km from Cape Tribulation to where it joins the Cooktown Road at Black Mountain, the **Bloomfield Track** is completely impassable after rain and otherwise requires a 4WD. If you don't have your own, the Country Road Coachlines **bus** (ⓣ07/4045 2794) runs up it three times per week on its Cairns–Cooktown run, weather permitting – contact them in advance for a pick-up anywhere along the Cape Tribulation road.

The Bloomfield Track's exciting section with virgin rainforest and drastic gradients lies below the halfway mark of the tidal **Bloomfield River**, which has to be crossed at low water. Beyond the **Wujal Wujal Aboriginal community** on the north side, the road flattens out to run past *Bloomfield Cabins and Camping* (Ⓣ07/4060 8207, Ⓦwww.bloomfieldcabins.com; ③), where there's plentiful camping space and three basic cabins. *Home Rule Rainforest Lodge*, at **ROSSVILLE** (Ⓣ07/4060 3925; ③), offers kitchen facilities and inexpensive meals; alternatively, you could fork out for the exclusive *Peppers Bloomfield Lodge* (Ⓣ07/4035 9166, Ⓦwww.bloomfieldlodge.com.au; ⑧). Moving on, it's not far now to the more down-to-earth *Lions Den* **pub** at Helenvale near **Black Mountain** (see p.487), about thirty minutes from Cooktown.

The Cape York Peninsula and Torres Strait Islands

The **Cape York Peninsula** points north towards the Torres Strait and New Guinea, and tackling the rugged tracks and hectic river crossings on the "Trip To The Tip" is an adventure in itself – besides being a means to reach **Australia's northernmost point** and the communities at **Bamaga** and **Thursday Island**, so different from anywhere else in Australia that they could easily be in another country. But it's not all four-wheel driving across the savannah: during the dry season the historic settlement of **Cooktown**, the wetlands at **Lakefield National Park** and **Laura**'s Aboriginal heritage are only a day's journey from Cairns in any decent vehicle. Given longer you might get as far as the mining company town of **Weipa**, but don't go further than this without off-road transport; while some have managed to reach the Tip in family sedans, most who try fail miserably.

With thousands making the overland journey between May and October, a **breakdown** won't necessarily leave you stranded, but the cost of repairs will make you regret it. **Bikers** should travel in groups and have off-roading experience. Those without their own vehicle can take **overland tours** right to the Tip (see box on p.465), or get as far as Cooktown with the Country Road Coachlines **bus**. It's also possible to **cruise** up to Thursday Island. **Airlines** servicing the Cape from Cairns include Aero-Tropics (Ⓣ07/4040 1222, Ⓦwww.aero-tropics.com.au), Skytrans (Ⓣ1800 818 405, Ⓦwww.skytrans.com.au) and Regional Pacific Airlines (Ⓣ07/4040 1400, Ⓦwww.regionalpacific.com.au).

You'll find a few roadhouses and motels along the way, but north of Weipa **accommodation** on the Cape is mostly limited to camping, and it's inevitable if you head right to the Tip that one night at least will be spent in the bush. Settlements also supply meals and provisions, but there won't be much on offer, so take all you can carry. Don't turn bush campsites into rubbish dumps: take a pack of bin liners and remove all your garbage. **Estuarine crocodiles** are present throughout the Cape: read the warning under "Wildlife dangers" in Basics (p.45) and see also p.566. There are few **banks**,

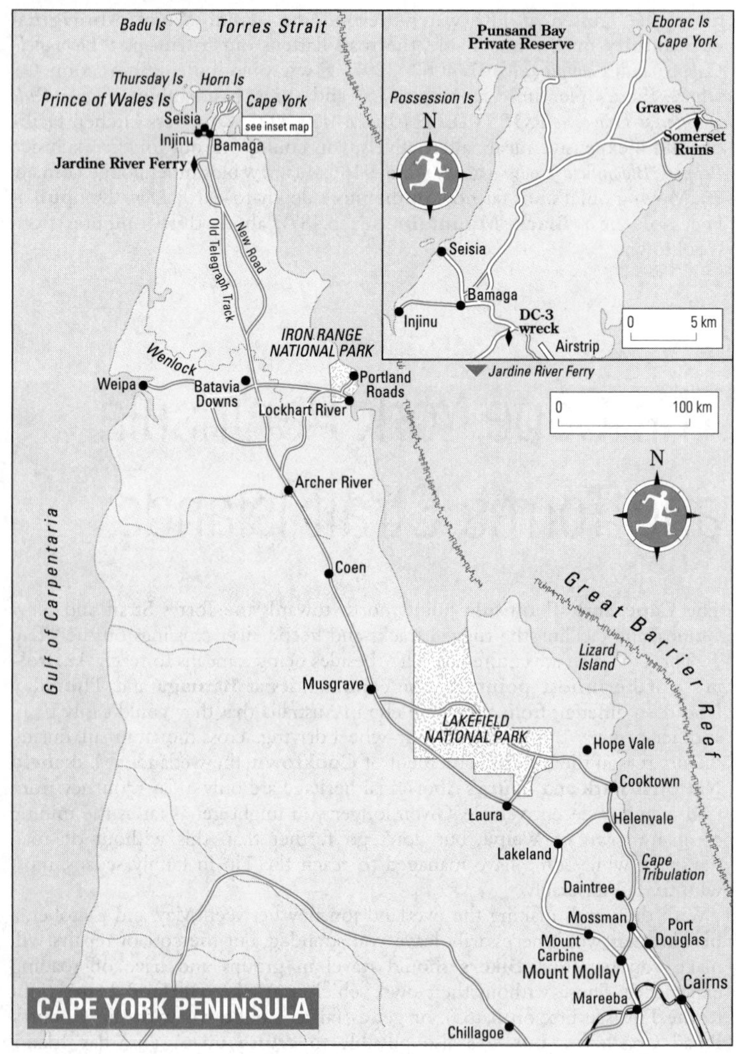

so take enough cash to carry you between points – some roadhouses accept plastic. In Cairns, the National Parks office stocks **maps** and brochures on the Cape's national parks, whilst the RACQ (Ⓦ www.racq.com) has up-to-date information regarding current road conditions. **Essential items** for any vehicles heading to the Tip include a first-aid kit, a comprehensive tool kit and spares, extra fuel cans and a tarpaulin for creek crossings. A winch, and equipment for removing, patching and inflating tyres may also come in handy.

Mossman to Cape York

Not as pretty as the coastal Bloomfield Track but considerably easier, the 260-kilometre inland road to Cooktown and points north leaves the Cook Highway just before Mossman and climbs to the drier scrub at **MOUNT CARBINE**, a former tungsten mine whose roadhouse and *Mt Carbine Hotel* (ⓣ07/4094 3108; ③), with simple but clean rooms, fulfil all functions. Next stop is **LAKELAND**, whose café, hotel and fuel stop marks the junction for routes north along the Peninsula Developmental Road to Laura. The road to Cooktown lies east, past cataracts at the **Annan River Gorge**, and the mysterious **Black Mountain**, two huge dark piles of lichen-covered granite boulders near the road. Aborigines reckon the formation to be the result of a building competition between two rivals fighting over a girl, and tell stories of people wandering into the eerie, whistling caverns, never to return.

At this point it's worth making the four-kilometre detour south along the Bloomfield Track to the *Lions Den* at **HELENVALE** (ⓣ07/4060 3911, ⓦwww.lionsdenhotel.com.au; safari tents ③). The *Den* is an old-style pub playing up for tourists during the day, but one hundred percent authentic at night, from the iron sheeting and beam decor to the nasty exhibits in glass bottles on the piano. Those with 4WD vehicles can follow the track south from Helenvale to Cape Tribulation (see p.484), while back on the main road it's another twenty minutes to Cooktown past the birdlife-filled waterholes of **Keatings Lagoon Conservation Park**, just 5km short of town.

Cooktown

After the *Endeavour* nearly sank at Cape Tribulation in 1770, Captain Cook landed at a natural harbour to the north, where he spent two months repairing the vessel, observing the "Genius, Temper, Disposition and Number of the Natives" and – legend has it – naming the kangaroo after an Aboriginal word for "I don't know". Tempers wore thin on occasion, as when the crew refused to share a catch of turtles with local Aborigines and Cook commented: "They seem'd to set no value upon any thing we gave them."

The site lay dormant until **gold** was discovered southwest on the Palmer River in 1873, and within months a harbour was being surveyed at the mouth of the **Endeavour River** for a tented camp known as **COOKTOWN**. A wild

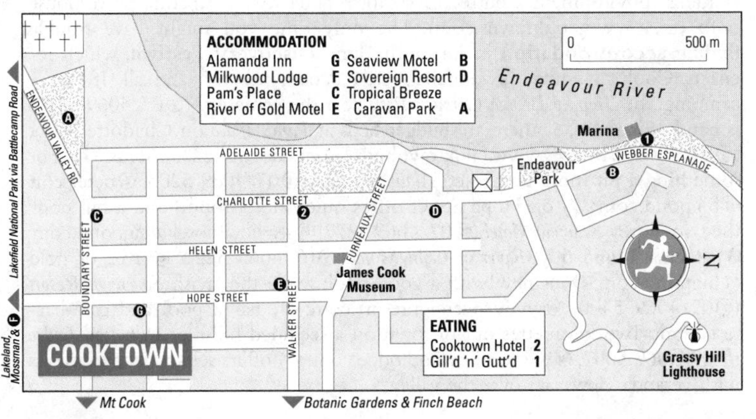

success while gold lasted, the settlement once boasted a main street alive with hotels and a busy port doing brisk trade with Asia through thousands of Chinese prospectors and merchants. But the reserves were soon exhausted and by 1910 Cooktown was on the decline. Today, the town's main drag, Charlotte Street, is neat but quiet, good for random wandering past the old wharves and **Endeavour Park**, the site of Cook's landing, now graced by a statue of the great navigator. Among monuments on the lawn are the remains of defences sent from Brisbane in the nineteenth century to ward off a threatened Russian invasion: one cannon, three cannonballs and two rifles. Just outside town, 500m along Endeavour Valley Road, Cooktown's half-wild **cemetery**, divided into Jewish, Chinese, Protestant and Catholic sections, suggests how cosmopolitan the town once was. The cemetery's most famous resident is **Mary Watson** of Lizard Island (see p.489), whose grave near the entrance is decorated with seashells and a painting of a pietà.

The best **views** of the town and river are from the top floor of the old Sisters of Mercy Convent, now the **James Cook Museum** (daily 9.30am–4pm; $9) containing a bit of everything: artefacts jettisoned from the *Endeavour*, a reconstructed joss house; a display on pearling around Thursday Island; and an account of the "hopelessly insolvent" Cooktown–Laura railway. There are more views of the district from the red-and-white, corrugated-iron cone of **Grassy Hill Lighthouse**, reached on a concrete track from the end of Hope Street. **Mount Cook** is a rather tougher proposition, a two-hour return hike through thick forest on meagre paths – follow the orange triangles from the nondescript starting point beyond Ida Street (you can pick up free maps of the route from the Council Offices next to the post office, open Mon–Fri 9am–4.30pm). At the end of Walker Street, the **Botanic Gardens** date back to the 1870s and house galleries of plant illustrations inside **Nature's Power House Environment Centre** ($3). The road past the gardens runs down to sandy **Finch Beach** on Cherry Tree Bay; although it's reputedly a safe swimming beach, you should heed the home-made warning signs saying "Dispela Stap Hia", with a picture of a croc underneath.

Practicalities

Country Road Coachlines **buses** (ⓣ07/4045 2794 for times and prices) run three times a week between Cairns and Cooktown, either along the coastal road via Cape Tribulation and the Bloomfield Track, or the inland road via Mount Molloy and Lakeland.

Cooktown's **tourist office**, with helpful, informed staff, is at the Botanic Gardens' Environment Centre (ⓣ07/4069 6004, ⓦwww.naturespowerhouse.info or ⓦwww.cooktowns.com). The only time you might have trouble finding **accommodation** is during the June **Discovery Festival**, which re-enacts Cook's landing – wooden boat, redcoats, muskets and all. If you're camping, the *Tropical Breeze Caravan Park* near the cemetery (ⓣ07/4069 5417) is handy for town, or there are budget beds at *Pam's Place* on Charlotte Street (ⓣ07/4069 5166, ⓦwww.cooktownhostel.com; dorms $23, rooms ❸). For something a bit more upmarket, *Alamanda Inn* (ⓣ07/4069 5203, ⓔpeterscott@bigpond.com; ❸) on Hope Street offers quiet motel rooms and a big pool; the two-storey *Seaview Motel* (ⓣ07/4069 5377, ⓔseaviewmotel@bigpond.com; ❹) is central and tidy; *River of Gold Motel* (ⓣ07/4069 5222, ⓔriver_of_gold@bigpond.com; ❺) is new with a good pool; while the lavish *Sovereign Resort* (ⓣ07/4069 5400, ⓦwww.sovereignresort.com; ❻) has a pool and café-bar-restaurant. Two kilometres out of town on a secluded hillside, *Milkwood Lodge* (ⓣ07/4069 5007, ⓦwww.milkwoodlodge.com; ❺) offers self-contained cabins with veranda views out over the valley.

For **eating**, there are riverside views from *Gill'd 'n' Gutt'd*, a chip shop at Fisherman's Wharf; restaurants at the motels; and the *Cooktown Hotel* (also known as the *Top Pub*) on the corner of Charlotte and Walker streets, the best spot for drink and bar meals. The **supermarket** is the last source of fresh provisions before Weipa, and the town's **bank** has an ATM.

Moving on, Country Road Coachlines (Ⓣ07/4045 2794) head back to Cairns three times a week, either via inland or coastal routes – this is a genuine bus service rather than a tour, so you can get off along the way. Those continuing **up Cape York** have two options: vehicles other than 4WDs have to head southwest to Lakeland for Laura and points north; stronger sets of wheels can reach Lakefield National Park more directly by heading towards the Hope Vale community and then taking the Battle Camp road. The **last fuel** this way until Musgrave is about 33km from Cooktown at the *Endeavour Falls Tourist Park* (Ⓣ07/4069 5431; self-contained units ❸), a nice spot in itself with a neighbouring waterfall, forest and an apparently croc-free swimming hole – though don't swim here without advice from the tourist park.

Lizard Island

Lizard Island is one of the most isolated resorts in Australia, a granite rise covered in stunted trees and heath, 90km north of Cooktown and 30km offshore within sight of the outer reef – **divers** rave about the fringing coral here. Shell middens show that Lizard was regularly visited by Aboriginal peoples, but the island was uninhabited when **Robert Watson** built a cottage and started a sea-slug processing operation here in the 1870s, accompanied by his wife **Mary** and two Chinese servants. Aborigines attacked the house while Robert was at sea in October 1881, killing one of the Chinese and forcing Mary, her baby and Ah Sam to flee in a water tank; they paddled west for five days before dying of thirst. Despite this sad story, there are far worse places to spend a few days than in the exclusive lodge here or even simply camped in a tent.

The only regular access is on **flights from Cairns** with Hinterland Aviation ($400 return; Ⓣ07/4035 9323) and Daintree Air Services ($600 return; Ⓣ07/4034 9300, Ⓦwww.daintreeair.com.au). Those unable to afford the swish but exorbitantly-priced *Voyages Lizard Island* **lodge** (Ⓣ1300 134 044, Ⓦwww.lizardisland.com.au; ❽) – which has a bar and restaurant – can use the **National Parks campsite** (permits from Cairns' National Parks office or book online at Ⓦwww.epa.qld.gov.au) down on Watson Beach. Campers should be self-sufficient in food and bring charcoal beads for cooking (gas cylinders and fuel are not allowed on the plane); the lodge is off-limits apart from in serious emergencies. The lodge can arrange diving for its guests.

Quinkan Country: Laura

Back on the now-unsealed Peninsula Road, 60km north of Lakeland, **LAURA**'s store-cum-post office and roadhouse support the two-day **Aboriginal Dance Festival** (Ⓦwww.laurafestival.tv), an electrifying assertion of Aboriginal identity held in June of odd-numbered years. At any time you can visit the sandstone caves and ridges covered in **Aboriginal art** at **Split Rock**, 13km south of town, where a steep track leads to a two-hour gallery circuit. Paintings depict animals, humans and startling spirit figures associated with sorcery: spidery, frightening **Quinkan** with pendulous earlobes, and dumpy **Anurra**, often with their legs twisted upwards. Other sites show scenes from post-Contact life, depicting horses, rifles and clothed figures; some caves here were probably in use until the 1930s. The **Quinkan and Regional Cultural Centre** (open daily, but irregular hours; ⓣ07/4060 3457, ⓦwww.quinkancc.com.au) organise guided rock-art **tours** and have current information on upcoming dance festivals.

Moving on, it's a straight 170km run up the Cape York road to **Musgrave** (not suitable for 2WD after rain), or – in the right vehicle – you can detour north to Musgrave via Lakefield National Park.

Lakefield National Park

Ideally you'd take at least a week to absorb **Lakefield National Park**'s fifty thousand square kilometres of savannah and riverine floodplain, but even a single night spent here will give you a feel for the Cape's most accessible wilderness area. Apart from the **Old Laura Homestead** – built between 1892 and 1940 and standing abandoned in the scrub on the **Laura River** – the park's pleasures revolve around outdoor pursuits, fishing and exploring lagoons for wildlife. Lakefield's **crocodile-conservation** programme means you might see both fresh- and saltwater types; birdlife is plentiful and plenty of kangaroos put in an appearance. **Magnetic anthills** are a common landmark: the ants build flattened towers aligned north to south to prevent overheating in the midday sun.

Four-wheel-drive vehicles are strongly recommended for all routes, though lesser vehicles can usually manage the rough **170-kilometre track** through the park between Laura and Musgrave Roadhouse if there hasn't been any rain for a good while. **Ranger stations**, where you pick up **camping permits**, are located at New Laura (ⓣ07/4060 3260), 50km from Laura at the southern end of the park, and at Lakefield (ⓣ07/4060 3271), 30km further on at the centre of the park. Pick of the many **campsites** are *Kalpowar Crossing* (near Lakefield, with showers and toilets); *Seven Mile Waterhole*, 13km west of Lakefield ranger station; and *Hann Crossing*, in the north of the park.

Laura to Iron Range and Weipa

Following the main road, the 300km that stretches between Laura and Archer River passes in a haze of dust, jolts and **roadhouses** supplying fuel, food, beds and drink. First on the list is **MUSGRAVE** (135km from Laura), a converted homestead where the track from Lakefield National Park joins the Cape York road; there's **accommodation** about 28km east towards the park at *Lotus Bird Lodge* (ⓣ07/4060 3400, ⓦwww.lotusbird.com.au; ⑧), whose spacious wooden cottages are surrounded by much the same scenery as you'll find in the national park. Back on the road north, the next two hours are a wild roller-coaster ride – look out for "Dip" signs warning of monster gullies – down to **COEN**, 107km from Musgrave. Coen's **Ambrust Store** handles camping, provisions, fuel, post-office business and has an ATM machine; the *Exchange Hotel* is the place to find bar **meals** and a cooling drink. The *Homestead Guest House*, on Regent Street, has **beds** (ⓣ07/4060 1157; ④).

Back on the main road north, it's 70km to the friendly **Archer River Roadhouse** (ⓣ07/4060 3266; ④), which has a campsite and accommodation in units, as well as the last reliable **fuel** on the main Cape York road before Bamaga, 400km away. Beyond are routes east to Iron Range (155km) and west to Weipa (190km), covered on opposite.

Iron Range

There's nothing else in Australia quite like the magnificent jungle at **Iron Range National Park**, a leftover from the Ice Age link to New Guinea, which hides fauna found nowhere else on the continent – the nocturnal **green python** and brilliant blue-and-red **eclectus parrot** are the best-known species. Three hours bouncing along a 110-kilometre 4WD track from the main road should bring you to a clearing where the army simulated a nuclear strike in the 1960s – fortunately using tons of conventional explosives instead of the real thing. Turning right at the junction here takes you past the **ranger station** (T07/4060 7170 – contact them about campsites and walking tracks in the park) to **LOCKHART RIVER**, an Aboriginal mission and fishing beach; supplies and fuel are sold here during weekday trading hours. The road left passes two bush campsites near the Claudie River and Gordon's Creek crossings, before winding up at **PORTLAND ROADS** and the remains of a harbour used by US forces in World War II – there are a few houses and beach **accommodation** here (T07/4060 7193, Wwww.portlandhouse.com.au; 5), though no stores or any public services. There's further **bush camping** a few kilometres back towards the junction at **Chili Beach**, a perpetually blustery, tropical setting backed by forest and coconut palms.

Next day, you have the chance to experience something unique on the mainland – seeing sunrise and sunset over different seas – by taking **Frenchman's Road** to Weipa. This runs northwest 30km back from the Lockhart/Portland junction, crosses the difficult Pascoe and Wenlock rivers, and emerges on the Peninsula Developmental Road, 2km north of **Batavia Downs**. Head through Batavia and cross more creeks – which look worse than they are – to the main Weipa road; the trip from coast to coast takes between six and eight hours.

Weipa

West-coast **WEIPA** is a company town of red clay and yellow mining trucks dealing in kaolin and bauxite. The area was one of the first in Australia to be described by Europeans: Willem Janz encountered "savage, cruel blacks" here in 1606, a report whose findings were subsequently reiterated by Jan Carstensz, who found nothing of interest and sailed off to chart the Gulf of Carpentaria instead. Apart from a mission built at **Mappoon** in the nineteenth century, little changed until aluminium ore was first mined here in the 1950s, and Comalco built the town and began mining.

All traffic in Weipa gives way to the gargantuan mine vehicles and stays out of the restricted areas. The town comprises mostly company housing, but does offer long-forgotten luxuries: you can pick up **vehicle spares** at the auto wreckers and service station on the way into town, and there's a **supermarket** and post office just in front of *Weipa Camping Ground* (T07/4069 7871, Wwww.campweipa.com; camping $20, units 4), a large campsite featuring hot showers and a laundry, where you can unwind and swap tales about the rigours of the trip. The *Albatross Hotel* (T07/4069 7314, Ealbatrosshotel@bigpond.com; 5) up the road has rooms and bungalows, and its beer deck looks out over the western sea.

Around town, the **library**'s Cape York Collection contains a unique collection of books and documents relating to the area, while the **Uningan Nature Reserve**, situated on the Mission River, preserves sixteen-metre-high middens composed entirely of shells left over from Aboriginal meals – some over 1600 years old. Driving is the only way to get here, and guidebooks are available from the campsite. Keep an eye out for crocs while walking around the reserve.

Moving on, a barge to Karumba and Normanton in the Gulf of Carpentaria departs every Thursday – contact Gulf Freight Services (☎07/4051 3411). Note that there is no reliable source of fuel between Weipa and Bamaga (340km).

North of the Wenlock River

The bridge over the seasonally deep, fast-flowing **Wenlock River**, an hour north of the Weipa junction on the main road up the Cape, marks the start of the most challenging part of the journey north, with road conditions changing every wet season. The road divides 42km further on, where die-hards follow the **Old Telegraph Track**, which has all the interesting scenery and creek crossings, though the telegraph lines have been dismantled, and many of the poles have been robbed of their ceramic caps by souvenir hunters. The first travellers of the year build simple rafts and log bridges to cross the creeks; as tracks dry and traffic increases, jarring corrugations and potholes are more likely to pose a problem, constituting a serious test of vehicle strength. There are some fine **creek crossings** on this route: **Bertie**'s potholes are large enough to submerge an entire vehicle; **Gunshot**'s three-metre vertical clay banks are a real test of skill (use low range first, and keep your foot off the brake); and the north exit at **Cockatoo** is deceptively sandy. Dozens wipe out on Gunshot every season; for the cautious there's a 24-kilometre detour via open scrub at Heathlands to the north side.

Those less certain of their abilities avoid the Old Telegraph Track and take the longer **New Road** to the east, consisting of 200km of loose gravel, bulldust and shocking **corrugations**. The two routes rejoin one another briefly after 75km, after which the New Road diverges left for 54km to the **Jardine River Ferry** crossing ($90 return, including use of the Injinu campsite at Bamaga), while the Old Telegraph Track ploughs on past beautiful clear green water and basalt formations at **Twin Falls**' safe swimming holes, through the deep **Nolans Brook**, before reaching the hundred-metre-wide **Jardine River** – the likelihood of crocodiles here only adds to the risks. However, it's worth the trip

Crossing creeks by 4WD

While Cape York's **crocodiles** make the standard 4WD procedure of walking creek crossings before driving them potentially dangerous, wherever possible you should make some effort to gauge the waters' depth and find the best route. *Never* blindly follow others across. Make sure all **rescue equipment** – shovel, winch, rope, etc – is easy to reach, outside the vehicle. **Electrics** on petrol engines need to be waterproofed. On deep crossings, block off air inlets to prevent water entering the engine, slacken off the fan belt and cover the radiator grille with a tarpaulin; this diverts water around the engine as long as the vehicle is moving. Select an appropriate **gear** (changing it in midstream will let water into the clutch) and drive through at walking speed; clear the opposite embankment before stopping again. In deep water, there's a chance the vehicle might float slightly, and so get pushed off-track by the current – though there's not much you can do about this. If you **stall**, switch off the ignition immediately, exit through windows, disconnect the battery (a short might restart the engine) and winch out. Don't restart the vehicle until you've made sure that water hasn't been sucked in through the air filter – which will destroy the engine. If you have severe problems, recovery will be very expensive; see Basics, p.40.

to camp (assuming you have enough fuel) before heading back via the ferry. From here, the last hour to Bamaga passes the remains of a **DC-3** that crashed just short of the airstrip in 1945.

Bamaga and around

BAMAGA, a community of stilt houses and banana palms founded by Saibai islanders in 1946, owes nothing to the rest of Australia's suburban values. Around the intersection you'll find a workshop and **service station** selling fuel (Mon–Fri 9am–5pm, Sat 9am–12.30pm, Sun 1.30–3pm), airline offices, a hotel and a **shopping centre** containing fresh veggies, a National Australia Bank agent, telephones, a café and post office. For **accommodation**, there's the central *Resort Bamaga* (Ⓣ07/4069 3050, Ⓦwww.resortbamaga.com.au; ❺), which has motel rooms, or turn left at the junction to **Injinu campsite** (Cowall Creek). Turning right past the shopping centre, you come to the coast at **SEISIA** (Red Island Point). There's another fuel station and well-stocked store here, and you can stay at the *Seisia Holiday Park* (Ⓣ07/4069 3243, Ⓦwww.seisiaholidaypark.com; camping $10, cabins ❺), under palms near the jetty, and take advantage of showers, laundry facilities, a canteen and **fishing safaris**. Peddell's **ferry** departs from Seisia to Thursday Island (see p.494).

Cape York and Somerset

To make local contacts, hang around Bamaga. To stay with the overland crowd, head 16km north to a road junction, then bear left for 11km to the idyllic beach at **Punsand Bay Camping Resort** (Ⓣ07/4069 1722, Ⓦwww.punsandbay.com.au; camping $10, cabins/prefab tents including three meals ❽), a just reward for the trials of the journey, with camping, cabins, prefab tents, a licensed restaurant and basic provisions. Around here you might spot the rare **palm cockatoo**, a huge, crested black parrot with a curved bill. You could spend a day recuperating on the beach, or return to the junction and take the seventeen-kilometre road to the very **tip of Cape York**, past the Somerset fork, to its end at another campsite (shower, water and kiosk). Follow the footpath through vine forest onto a rocky, barren headland and down to a turbulent sea opposite the lighthouse on Eborac Island, where a sign concreted into an oil drum marks the tip of mainland Australia and the end of the journey.

Somerset

Established on government orders in 1864 to balance the French naval station in New Caledonia, **Somerset** is known for one of its first settlers, **Frank Jardine**, whose legendary exploits assume larger-than-life proportions (fearless pioneer to some, brutal colonial to others). Though envisaged as a second Singapore, Somerset never amounted to more than a military outpost and in 1877, after the pearling trade in the Torres Strait erupted into lawlessness, the settlement was abandoned in favour of a seat of government closer to the problem at Thursday Island.

Today, only a few cannons, machine parts and mango trees testify to Somerset's former inhabitants; the buildings succumbed to white ants or were moved long ago. Frank and his wife Sana are buried on the beach directly below (standing up, say locals), next to a **Chinese cemetery** and traces of a jetty into the Adolphus Channel. Dogged exploration of the dense undergrowth above the beach to the left will uncover remains of a **sentry post** and a cave with stick-figure paintings, presumably Aboriginal.

Thursday Island and the Torres Strait

Just a short boat ride beyond Cape York, little **Thursday Island** is the administrative centre for the dozens of other populated specks of land which lie scattered across the two-hundred-kilometre-wide **Torres Strait**, which separates Australia from New Guinea. Thursday Island is easily reached from Cape York by ferry and from Cairns by air, and offers a fascinating glimpse into an all-but-forgotten corner of Australia, and one whose inhabitants, the **Torres Strait Islanders**, have a very different world view from the country's white population.

The strait is named after **Luís Vaez de Torres**, who navigated its waters in 1606; at this time, the different Torres Strait Islands existed in a complicated state of trade and warfare, which was brought to an end when the islanders enthusiastically embraced the arrival of Christianity – known here as the "**Coming of the Light**" – in 1871. **Pearling** (for mother of pearl) was the main source of employment here from this point until after WWII, when the advent of plastics saw the industry collapse and a mass migration of islanders to the Australian mainland. Those who chose to stay formed a movement to establish an Islander Nation, which bore its first fruit on June 3, 1992, when the **Mabo Decision** acknowledged the Merriam as traditional owners of easterly Murray Island, thereby setting a precedent for mainland Aboriginal claims and sending shock waves through the establishment.

Coming over by ferry from the mainland, you pass **Possession Island** and come within sight of a plaque commemorating James Cook's landing here on August 22, 1770, when he planted the flag for George III and Great Britain. Then it's into the shallow channel between Horn Island and **Prince of Wales Island**, the strait's largest, stocked with deer and settled by an overflow population unable to afford Thursday's exorbitant land premiums.

Thursday Island and around

A three-square-kilometre dot within sight of the mainland, **Thursday Island** wears a few aliases: known simply as "T. I." in day-to-day use, it was coined "Sink of the Pacific" for the variety of peoples who passed through in pearling days, and the local tag is Waiben or (very loosely) "Thirsty Island" – once a reference to the availability of drinking water and now a laconic aside on the quantity of beer consumed. The hotel clock with no hands hints at the pace of life and it's only for events like Christmas, when wall-to-wall aluminium punts from neighbouring islands make the harbour look like a maritime supermarket car-park, that things liven up. Other chances to catch Thursday in carnival spirit are during the annual **Coming of the Light festivities** on July 1, and the full-bore **Island of Origin** rugby-league matches later in the same month – in one year 25 players were hospitalized, and another killed.

In town there are traces of the **old Chinatown** district around Milman Street, and a reminder of Queensland's worst shipping disaster in the **Quetta Memorial Church**, way down Douglas Street, built after the ship hit an uncharted rock in the straits in 1890 and went down with virtually all the Europeans on board. The Aplin Road **cemetery**, where two of the victims are buried, has tiled Islander tombs and depressing numbers of **Japanese graves**, all victims of pearl diving during the early twentieth century. As a by-product of the industry, Japanese crews had accurately mapped the strait before World War II and it's no coincidence that the airstrip was **bombed** when hostilities were declared in 1942; fortifications are still in place on

Thursday's east coast. Bunkers and naval cannon at the **Old Fort** on the opposite side date from the 1890s.

The **Gab Titui Cultural Centre** across from the ferry terminal provides an interesting insight into island affairs and has a daily dance performance (Mon–Sat 9am–5pm, Sun 2–5pm, reduced opening times Jan–Feb; $6; Ⓣ07/4090 2130); the town's only **café** is inside.

Just a few minutes from Thursday's wharf by water taxi ($15), **Horn Island** is another small chunk of land surrounded by mangroves and coral, the site of an open-cut gold mine and the **regional airport** (with regular flights to and from Cairns). The main reason to take a trip across is to visit the **pearling museum**, run by an ex-diver and stocked with his memorabilia – including an old-fashioned bronze dive helmet. He also owns Horn's sole **place to stay** and eat, the *Gateway Torres Strait Resort* (Ⓣ07/4069 2222, Ⓦwww.torresstrait.com.au; ⑤).

Practicalities

Ferries to Thursday Island run from Seisia with Peddell's (June–Sept Mon–Sat; Oct–May Mon, Wed & Fri; $47 one way; Ⓣ07/4069 1551, Ⓦwww.peddellsferry.com.au). Between June and October, Peddell's Buses (Ⓣ07/4069 1551) meet incoming ferries for a ninety-minute **island tour** ($25). It's also possible to **cruise** up to Thursday Island. aboard the Trinity Bay passenger and car ferry (Ⓣ07/4035 1234, Ⓦwww.seaswift.com.au). The ferry departs Cairns at 2pm every Friday, arriving in Thursday Island approximately 6pm on Sunday. Accommodation is in air-conditioned four-bed cabins which cost $685 for one-person private use, or $410 per person if three or four people travel together; taking along a 4WD vehicle costs an additional $690.

Flying, Aero-Tropics (Ⓣ07/4040 1222, Ⓦwww.aero-tropics.com.au) and Regional Pacific Airlines (Ⓣ07/4040 1400, Ⓦwww.regionalpacific.com.au) both service the airport on Horn Island daily from Cairns via Bamaga, with water-taxi connections over to nearby Thursday Island.

Thursday's **wharf** sits below the colonial-style Customs House, a minute from the **town centre** on Douglas Street. Here you'll find a post office with payphones, a **bank** and two of the island's **hotels**: the *Torres* just beats the neighbouring *Royal* as Australia's northernmost bar. Facing the water on Victoria Parade, there are clean **lodgings** at the *Federal Hotel* (Ⓣ07/4069 1569, Ⓦwww.federalhotelti.com.au; ⑤), while on Douglas Street, *Mura Mudh* (Ⓣ07/4069 2050, Ⓕ4069 1311; ①) is a cheap and cheerful **hostel** run by Thursday Islanders.

Travel details

Trains

Brisbane to: Ayr (6 per week; 22hr); Bowen (6 per week; 20hr); Bundaberg (6 per week; 6hr); Caboolture (6 per week; 1hr); Cairns (5 per week; 31hr); Cardwell (5 per week; 26hr 30min); Gladstone (6 per week; 9hr); Ingham (5 per week; 25hr 30min); Innisfail (5 per week; 29hr); Mackay (6 per week; 17hr); Proserpine (6 per week; 19hr); Rockhampton (6 per week; 11hr 30min); Townsville (6 per week; 23hr); Tully (5 per week; 27hr 30min).

Bundaberg to: Ayr (6 per week; 9hr 30min); Bowen (6 per week; 14hr); Brisbane (6 per week; 6hr); Caboolture (6 per week; 5hr 45min); Cairns (5 per week; 24hr); Cardwell (5 per week; 19hr 30min); Gladstone (6 per week; 2hr 15min); Ingham (5 per week; 17hr 45min); Innisfail (5 per week; 23hr); Mackay (6 per week; 10hr 15min); Proserpine (6 per week; 12hr 15min); Rockhampton (6 per week; 4hr 15min); Townsville (6 per week; 17hr); Tully (5 per week; 21hr).

Cairns to: Ayr (5 per week; 9hr); Bowen (5 per week; 11hr); Brisbane (5 per week; 31hr); Bundaberg (5 per week; 24hr); Caboolture (5 per week; 30hr); Cardwell (5 per week; 4hr); Gladstone (5 per week; 22hr); Ingham (5 per week; 4hr); Innisfail (5 per week; 2hr); Kuranda (2 daily; 1hr 45min); Mackay (5 per week; 14hr); Proserpine (5 per week; 12hr); Rockhampton (5 per week; 8hr); Townsville (5 per week; 7hr); Tully (5 per week; 3hr).
Ingham to: Ayr (5 per week; 3hr 30min); Bowen (5 per week; 5hr 30min); Brisbane (5 per week; 25hr 30min); Bundaberg (5 per week; 17hr 45min); Caboolture (5 per week; 24hr 30min); Cairns (5 per week; 4hr); Cardwell (5 per week; 1hr); Gladstone (5 per week; 16hr 30min); Innisfail (5 per week; 3hr 15min); Mackay (5 per week; 8hr 45min); Proserpine (5 per week; 6hr 30min); Rockhampton (5 per week; 15hr); Townsville (5 per week; 2hr); Tully (5 per week; 1hr 45min).
Mackay to: Ayr (6 per week; 5hr); Bowen (6 per week; 3hr 30min); Brisbane (6 per week; 17hr); Bundaberg (6 per week; 10hr 15min); Caboolture (6 per week; 16hr); Cairns (5 per week; 14hr); Cardwell (5 per week; 10hr); Gladstone (6 per week; 8hr); Ingham (5 per week; 8hr 45min); Innisfail (5 per week; 12hr 30min); Proserpine (6 per week; 2hr); Rockhampton (6 per week; 6hr); Townsville (6 per week; 6hr 30min); Tully (5 per week; 10hr 30min).
Prosperpine to: Ayr (6 per week; 2hr 30min); Bowen (6 per week; 45min); Brisbane (6 per week; 19hr); Bundaberg (6 per week; 12hr 15min); Caboolture (6 per week; 18hr); Cairns 5 per week; 12hr); Cardwell (5 per week; 8hr); Gladstone (6 per week; 10hr); Ingham (5 per week; 6hr 30min); Innisfail (5 per week; 9hr 30min); Mackay (6 per week; 2hr); Rockhampton (6 per week; 8hr 30min); Townsville (6 per week; 4hr 30min); Tully (5 per week; 8hr 30min).
Rockhampton to: Ayr (5 per week; 11hr); Bowen (6 per week; 9hr 30min); Brisbane (6 per week; 11hr 30min); Bundaberg (6 per week; 4hr 15min); Caboolture (6 per week; 10hr 30min); Cairns (5 per week; 8hr); Cardwell (5 per week; 16hr 15min); Gladstone 6 per week; 2hr 30min); Ingham (5 per week; 15hr); Innisfail 5 per week; 18hr 15min); Mackay (6 per week; 6hr); Proserpine (6 per week; 8hr 30min); Townsville (6 per week; 12hr); Tully (5 per week; 16hr).
Townsville to: Ayr (6 per week; 1hr 30min); Bowen (6 per week; 3hr); Brisbane (6 per week; 23hr); Bundaberg (6 per week; 17hr); Caboolture (6 per week; 22hr); Cairns (5 per week; 7hr); Cardwell (5 per week; 3hr); Gladstone (6 per week; 14hr 30min); Ingham (5 per week; 2hr); Innisfail (5 per week; 5hr); Mackay (6 per week; 6hr 30min); Proserpine (6 per week; 4hr 30min); Rockhampton (6 per week; 12hr); Tully (5 per week; 4hr).

Buses

Airlie Beach to: Ayr (6 daily; 3hr 30min); Brisbane (5 daily; 18hr); Bundaberg (3 daily; 12hr 30min); Cairns (6 daily; 10hr); Cardwell (6 daily; 6hr 45min); Childers (5 daily; 13hr 15min); Hervey Bay (5 daily; 14hr); Ingham (6 daily; 6hr); Innisfail (6 daily; 9hr); Mackay (6 daily; 2hr 15min); Mission Beach (6 daily; 8hr); Mooloolaba (1 daily; 17hr 30min); Noosa (1 daily; 16hr 45min); Rockhampton (5 daily; 7hr 30min); Townsville (6 daily; 4hr); Tully (6 daily; 7hr 35min).
Brisbane to: Airlie Beach (5 daily; 18hr 30min); Ayr (5 daily; 22hr 30min); Agnes Water (1 daily; 11hr); Bowen (5 daily; 20hr 30min); Bundaberg (5 daily; 9hr); Burleigh Heads (6 daily; 1hr 30min); Byron Bay (10 daily; 4hr); Cairns (5 daily; 28hr 30min); Cardwell (6 daily; 26hr); Childers (5 daily; 8hr); Coolangatta (8 daily; 2hr 30min); Gladstone (4 daily; 11hr); Hervey Bay (7 daily; 5hr); Ingham (5 daily; 24hr); Innisfail (7 daily; 27hr); Mackay (8 daily; 15hr 30min); Mission Beach (5 daily; 26hr 25min); Mooloolaba (6 daily; 2hr 30min); Noosa (9 daily; 2hr 50min); Rockhampton (5 daily; 11hr 30min); Surfers Paradise (every 30min; 1hr 30min); Sydney (7 daily; 17hr 30min); Townsville (5 daily; 24hr); Tully (5 daily; 27hr).
Bundaberg to: Airlie Beach (5 daily; 10hr 30min); Agnes Water (1 daily; 1hr 30min); Ayr (5 daily; 14hr); Brisbane (5 daily; 6hr 30min); Cairns (6 daily; 20hr 30min); Cardwell (6 daily; 17hr); Childers (5 daily; 50min); Hervey Bay (5 daily; 1hr 45min); Ingham (5 daily; 19hr); Innisfail (5 daily; 3hr); Mackay (5 daily; 9hr); Mission Beach (5 daily; 20hr); Noosa (2 daily; 7hr); Rainbow Beach (1 daily; 4hr 30min); Rockhampton (5 daily; 3hr 30min); Townsville (5 daily; 15hr 30min); Tully (5 daily; 19hr 30min).
Cairns to: Airlie Beach (5 daily; 11hr); Atherton Tablelands (2 per day Mon–Fri); Ayr (5 daily; 7hr 30min); Brisbane (5 daily; 28hr 30min); Bundaberg (6 daily; 20hr 30min); Cape Tribulation (2 daily; 5hr); Cardwell (6 daily; 3hr); Childers (5 daily; 23hr); Cooktown (up to 6 per week; 12hr); Hervey Bay (5 daily; 24hr); Ingham (6 daily; 3hr 30min); Innisfail (6 daily; 1hr 15min); Mackay (5 daily; 13hr); Mission Beach (4 daily; 2hr 30min); Noosa (2 daily; 27hr 30min); Port Douglas (2 daily; 2hr); Rockhampton (5 daily; 17hr 30min); Townsville (6 daily; 6hr); Tully (6 daily; 2hr 45min).
Hervey Bay to: Airlie Beach (5 daily; 14hr); Agnes Water (1 daily; 4hr); Ayr (5 daily; 15hr 30min); Brisbane (7 daily; 5hr); Bundaberg (5 daily; 1hr 45min); Cairns (6 daily; 20hr 30min); Cardwell

(5 daily; 20hr); Childers (5 daily; 50min); Ingham (5 daily; 19hr); Innisfail (5 daily; 22hr); Mackay (5 daily; 10hr 30min); Mission Beach (5 daily; 21hr); Noosa (4 daily; 4hr); Rainbow Beach (1 daily; 2hr); Rockhampton (5 daily; 6hr); Townsville (5 daily; 19hr); Tully (5 daily; 20hr 30min).

Mackay to: Airlie Beach (6 daily; 2hr 15min); Ayr (6 daily; 5hr); Brisbane (8 daily; 15hr 30min); Bundaberg (5 daily; 9hr); Cairns (5 daily; 13hr); Cardwell (6 daily; 9hr); Childers (5 daily; 11hr); Hervey Bay (5 daily; 10hr 30min); Ingham (6 daily; 9hr); Innisfail (6 daily; 12hr); Mission Beach (6 daily; 10hr 30min); Noosa (2 daily; 14hr); Rockhampton (5 daily; 5hr); Townsville (6 daily; 6hr 30min); Tully (6 daily; 10hr).

Mission Beach to: Airlie Beach (6 daily; 8hr); Ayr (5 daily; 5hr 30min); Brisbane (5 daily; 26hr 25min); Bundaberg (5 daily; 20hr); Cairns (4 daily; 2hr 30min); Cardwell (5 daily; 1hr); Childers (4 daily; 21hr); Hervey Bay (5 daily; 21hr); Ingham (5 daily; 2hr); Innisfail (5 daily; 1hr); Mackay (6 daily; 10hr 30min); Noosa (2 daily; 25hr); Rockhampton (4 daily; 16hr); Townsville (5 daily; 3hr 30min); Tully (5 daily; 30min).

Noosa to: Airlie Beach (1 daily; 16hr 45min); Agnes Water (1 daily; 9hr); Ayr (1 daily; 20hr); Brisbane (9 daily; 2hr 50min); Bundaberg (2 daily; 7hr); Cairns (2 daily; 27hr 30min); Cardwell (2 daily; 24hr); Childers (2 daily; 5hr 30min); Hervey Bay (4 daily; 4hr); Ingham (2 daily; 23hr); Innisfail (2 daily; 26hr); Mackay (2 daily; 14hr); Mission Beach (2 daily; 25hr); Rainbow Beach (2 daily; 3hr); Rockhampton (2 daily; 10hr); Tin Can Bay (1 daily; 2hr 30min); Townsville (2 daily; 21hr); Tully (2 daily; 25hr).

Rockhampton to: Airlie Beach (5 daily; 7hr 30min); Ayr (5 daily; 10hr); Brisbane (5 daily; 11hr 30min); Bundaberg (5 daily; 3hr 30min); Cairns (5 daily; 17hr 30min); Cardwell (5 daily; 14hr); Childers (5 daily; 5hr); Hervey Bay (5 daily; 6hr); Ingham (5 daily; 11hr 30min); Innisfail (5 daily; 16hr); Mackay (5 daily; 5hr); Mission Beach (4 daily; 16hr); Noosa (2 daily; 10hr); Townsville (2 daily; 11hr); Tully (5 daily; 14hr).

Surfers Paradise to: Brisbane (every 30min; 1hr 30min); Burleigh Heads (every 10min; 30min); Byron Bay (10 daily; 3hr); Coolangatta (every 10min; 1hr); Sydney (7 daily; 15hr 30min).

Townsville to: Airlie Beach (6 daily; 4hr); Ayr (5 daily; 1hr); Brisbane (5 daily; 24hr); Bundaberg (5 daily; 15hr 30min); Cairns (6 daily; 6hr); Cardwell (5 daily; 2hr); Childers (5 daily; 18hr); Hervey Bay (5 daily; 19hr); Ingham (5 daily; 1hr 30min); Innisfail (5 daily; 4hr 30min); Mackay (6 daily; 6hr 30min); Mission Beach (5 daily; 3hr 30min); Noosa (2 daily; 17hr); Rockhampton (2 daily; 11hr); Tully (5 daily; 3hr).

Ferries

Airlie Beach/Shute Harbour to: Daydream Island (1–2 daily; 45min); Hamilton Island (1–3 daily; 1hr); Hook Island (1–2 daily; 1hr 30min); Lindeman Island (2 daily; 1hr 30min); South Molle Island (2 daily; 45min); Whitsunday Island (1 daily; 2hr).

Brisbane to: Moreton Island (2 daily; 2hr); North Stradbroke Island (11 daily; 30min); St Helena (3 or more per week; 2hr).

Cairns to: Thursday Island (1 per week; 36hr).

Cape York to: Thursday Island (Mon–Fri 2 daily; 1hr 15min–2hr).

Cardwell to: Hinchinbrook Island (2 daily; 1–2hr).

Hervey Bay to: Fraser Island (8 daily; 30min–1hr).

Mission Beach to: Dunk Island (10 or more daily; 15min).

Rosslyn Bay to: Great Keppel Island (3 daily; 45min–1hr).

Surfers Paradise to: South Stradbroke Island (3 or more daily; 30min).

Townsville to: Magnetic Island (10 or more daily; 45min).

Weipa to: Normanton (1 per week; 24hr).

Flights

Brisbane to: Adelaide (many daily; 3hr 30min); Alice Springs (2 daily; 4hr 30min); Bundaberg (2 daily; 50min); Cairns (many daily; 2hr 10min); Canberra (many daily; 2hr); Charleville (1 daily; 2hr); Darwin (2 daily; 3hr 40min); Emerald (2 daily; 1hr 40min); Gladstone (4 daily; 1hr 15min); Hervey Bay (2 daily; 1hr 15min); Hobart (many daily; 3hr 50min); Longreach (1 daily; 3hr); Mackay (9 daily; 3hr); Maroochydore–Sunshine Coast (many daily; 30min); Melbourne (many daily; 2hr 25min); Mount Isa (2 daily; 4hr); Norfolk Island (4 per week; 3hr 45min); Perth (many daily; 5hr); Proserpine (2 daily; 1hr 50min); Rockhampton (4 daily; 1hr 5min); Roma (1 daily; 1hr 10min); Sydney (many daily; 1hr 35min); Townsville (6 daily; 1hr 50min).

Bundaberg to: Brisbane (3 daily; 1hr); Cairns (2 daily; 4hr 50min); Gladstone (1 per week; 35min); Lady Elliot (1 daily; 45min); Mackay (1 daily; 2hr); Rockhampton (1 daily; 50min).

Cairns to: Bamaga (1 daily; 1hr 45min); Bundaberg (2 daily; 4hr 50min); Cooktown (1 daily; 45min); Dunk Island (1 daily; 45min); Lizard Island (2 daily; 1hr); Mackay (2 daily; 2hr 45min); Proserpine (6 per week; 2hr); Rockhampton (2 daily; 3hr); Thursday Island/Horn Island (1–2 daily; 2hr); Townsville (2 daily; 1hr); Weipa (1 daily; 1hr 15min).

Gladstone to: Bundaberg (1 per week; 35min); Rockhampton (5 per week; 25min).

Gold Coast–Coolangatta to: Adelaide (many daily; 3hr 35min); Canberra (12 daily; 2hr 40min); Melbourne (many daily; 3hr 35min); Sydney (many daily; 1hr 15min).
Mackay to: Cairns (2 daily; 2hr 45min); Rockhampton (2 daily; 45min); Townsville (4 daily; 1hr).
Rockhampton to: Cairns (2 daily; 3hr); Gladstone (5 per week; 25min); Great Keppel Island (3 daily; 25min); Mackay (2 daily; 45min); Townsville (2 daily; 1hr 50min).
Sunshine Coast–Maroochydore to: Brisbane (many daily; 30min); Melbourne (1 daily; 3hr); Sydney (1 daily; 1hr 45min).
Townsville to: Cairns (2 daily; 1hr); Mackay (4 daily; 1hr); Rockhampton (2 daily; 1hr 50min).

5

Outback Queensland

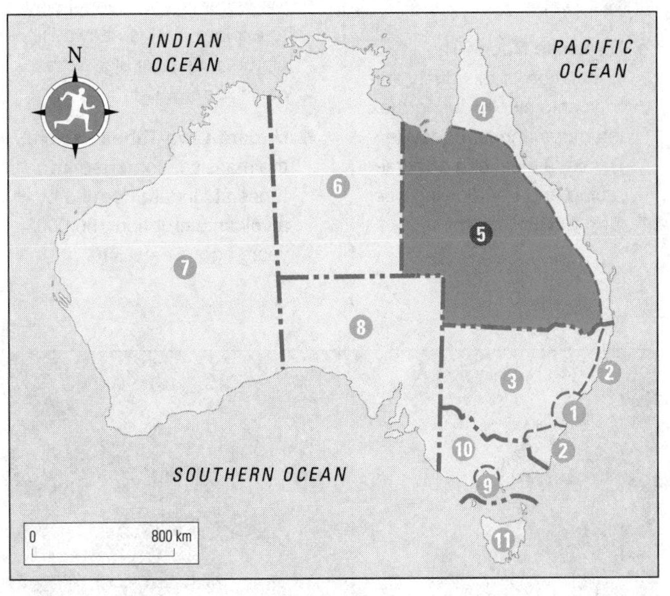

CHAPTER 5

Highlights

* **Artesian hot spa at Mitchell** The hot springs in single-street Mitchell make for an enjoyable wallow on a cold winter's morning. See p.508

* **Carnarvon Gorge** Reach fantastic Aboriginal art sites with a hike through the verdant Carnarvon Gorge. See p.509

* **Birdsville Races** The population of this dusty little township swells during the infamous annual Birdsville Races, a weekend of horse racing and free-flowing beer. See p.516

* **Crayfish Derby at Winton** The winner nets $1500 and the runner-up gets to eat all the competitors at the biennial Australian Crayfish Derby, held in September in the archetypal frontier town of Winton. See p.524

* **Lawn Hill Gorge** Taking to the water is a wonderful way to explore the lush Lawn Hill Gorge, a spectacular Outback oasis. See p.538

* **Undara Lava Tubes** Explore the massive, contorted lava tubes at Undara, formed by a volcanic eruption 190,000 years ago. See p.540

△ Canoeing through Lawn Hill Gorge

5

Outback Queensland

Outback Queensland, the west of the state, is thinly populated by tenacious farming communities swinging precariously between famine and survival, and seems hard to reconcile with Queensland's lush, wet tropics. The population is concentrated in the relatively fertile highlands along the Great Dividing Range, which run low behind the coast; on the far side, featureless plains slide over a hot horizon into the fringes of South Australia and the Northern Territory. Untouched by overseas visitors, the only places attracting tourists in any numbers are the Stockman's Hall of Fame at Longreach, the oases of Carnarvon Gorge in the Central Highlands and the northwest's Lawn Hill Gorge. But elsewhere the opportunities for exploration are immense, with precious stones, fossils, waterholes and Aboriginal art in abundance. The region is also responsible for producing two of Australia's best-known icons: Banjo Paterson first performed *Waltzing Matilda* in a hotel in Winton; and the same town tussles with nearby Longreach for the right to claim the honour of being the birth-place of Qantas airlines.

Choosing where to go is often determined by the most convenient starting point. **Main roads** and **trains** head west from the coast at Brisbane, Rockhampton, Townsville and Cairns; **buses** from Brisbane, Cairns and Townsville cross outback Queensland as they head interstate, but otherwise there's little in the way of public transport. If you're **driving**, your vehicle must be well maintained and you should carry essential spares, as even main centres often lack replacement parts.

Unless you're experienced and well equipped, you'll find that western summers effectively prohibit travel, as searing temperatures and violent flash floods can isolate areas (especially in the Channel Country on the far side of the Great Dividing Range) for days or weeks on end. Consequently, many tour companies, tourist offices and motels simply shut up shop between November and March, or at least during January and February. On the other hand, water revives dormant seeds and fast-growing desert flowers, which cover the ground to the horizon in good years. At other times, expect hot days and cool nights, plenty of dust and sparse landscapes.

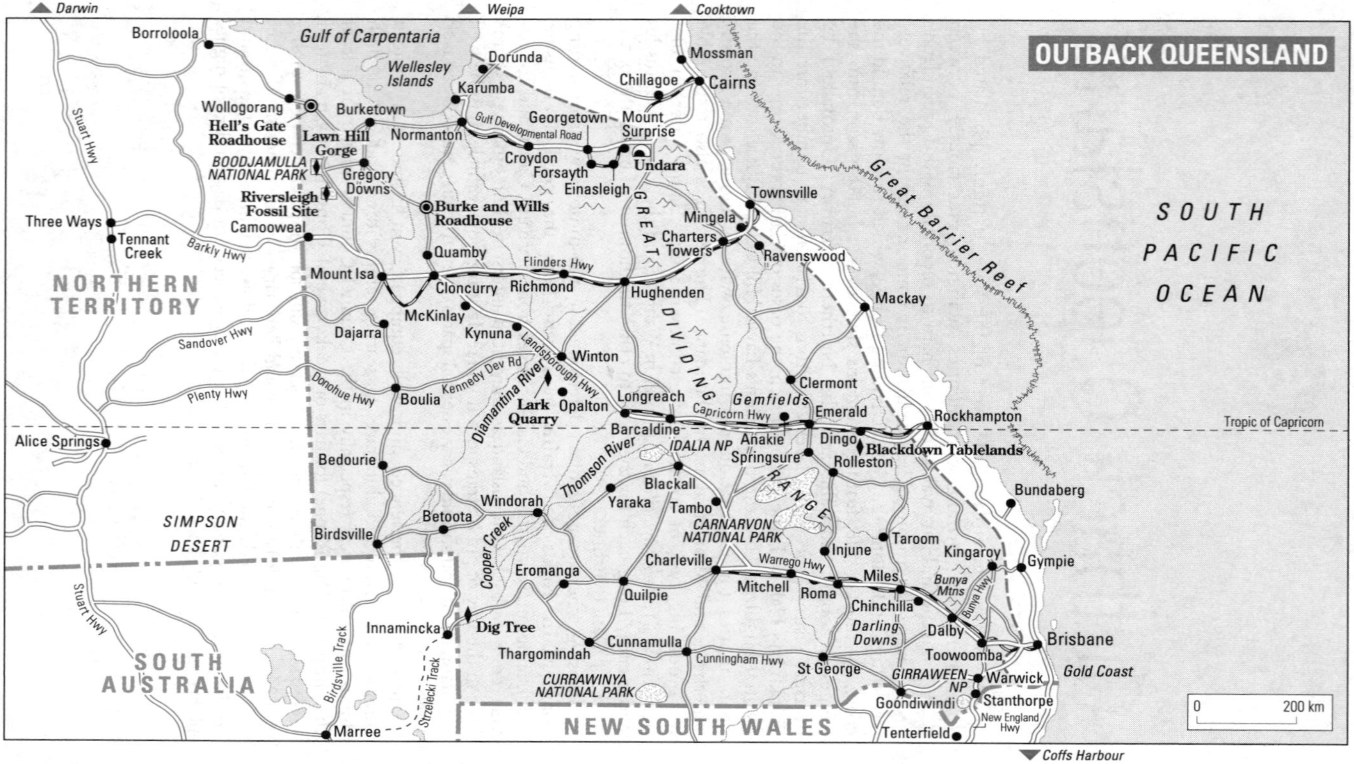

OUTBACK QUEENSLAND
Darwin
Weipa
Cooktown
Coffs Harbour
Gulf of Carpentaria
Wellesley Islands
SOUTH PACIFIC OCEAN
Great Barrier Reef
Tropic of Capricorn
0 200 km
NORTHERN TERRITORY
SOUTH AUSTRALIA
NEW SOUTH WALES
SIMPSON DESERT
GREAT DIVIDING RANGE
Borroloola
Dorunda
Mossman
Cairns
Chillagoe
Karumba
Wollogorang
Hell's Gate Roadhouse
Burketown
Lawn Hill Gorge
Normanton
Gulf Developmental Road
Georgetown
Mount Surprise
Croydon
Forsayth
Einasleigh
Undara
BOODJAMULLA NATIONAL PARK
Gregory Downs
Riversleigh Fossil Site
Burke and Wills Roadhouse
Townsville
Mingela
Charters Towers
Ravenswood
Three Ways
Tennant Creek
Barkly Hwy
Camooweal
Quamby
Stuart Hwy
Mount Isa
Cloncurry
Richmond
Flinders Hwy
Hughenden
Mackay
McKinlay
Kynuna
Dajarra
Sandover Hwy
Landsborough Hwy
Winton
Kennedy Dev Rd
Donohue Hwy
Plenty Hwy
Boulia
Diamantina River
Lark Quarry
Opalton
Longreach
Clermont
Gemfields
Capricorn Hwy
Emerald
Rockhampton
Barcaldine
Anakie
Dingo
Blackdown Tablelands
Alice Springs
IDALIA NP
Springsure
Rolleston
Thomson River
Bedourie
Blackall
Bundaberg
Yaraka
Tambo
Windorah
Betoota
CARNARVON NATIONAL PARK
Taroom
Birdsville
Cooper Creek
Injune
Kingaroy
Gympie
Charleville
Warrego Hwy
Eromanga
Mitchell
Roma
Miles
Bunya Mtns
Bunya Hwy
Quilpie
Chinchilla
Darling Downs
Dalby
Innamincka
Dig Tree
Birdsville Track
Strzelecki Track
Cunnamulla
Thargomindah
Cunningham Hwy
St George
Toowoomba
Brisbane
Gold Coast
GIRRAWEEN NP
Warwick
CURRAWINYA NATIONAL PARK
Goondiwindi
Stanthorpe
New England Hwy
Marree
Tenterfield

Brisbane to Cooper Creek and Birdsville

The thousand-plus-kilometre haul from the comforts of the coast to Queensland's remote southwestern corner dumps you tired and dusty on the South Australian border, with some exciting routes down the Birdsville and Strzelecki tracks or through the hostile red barrier of the Simpson Desert yet to come. There are two ultimate targets: the outpost of **Birdsville**, with its annual horse races, and the **Dig Tree** at Nappa Merrie on **Cooper Creek**, monument to the Burke and Wills tragedy (see box on p.514). The highway scenery is as bleak as you'd expect: after crossing the fertile disc of the **Darling Downs**, the country withers and dries, marooning communities in isolation and hardship. Detour north through Queensland's **Central Highlands** however, and you'll find a landscape peppered with forested sandstone gorges and the Aboriginal sites at **Carnarvon National Park** – worth the journey even if you don't go any further.

From Brisbane, the most practical route through the area is on the **Warrego Highway**, through Toowoomba, Roma and Charleville towards Quilpie. Roma is the jumping-off point for the highlands and from Quilpie there are largely unsurfaced roads to Birdsville and the Dig Tree. The twice-weekly Westlander **train** runs in this direction from Brisbane to Charleville, as do daily **buses** en route from Brisbane to Mount Isa. Alternatively, there's the southern **Cunningham Highway** via Warwick and Goondiwindi (the limit of bus services in this direction) to Cunnamulla, beyond which lesser roads head across oil, gas and opal fields towards the Dig Tree – you might need a four-wheel-drive vehicle to get this far.

The Darling Downs

The **Darling Downs**, a broad spread of prime agricultural land first explored by **Ludwig Leichhardt** in the 1840s, sprawl westwards from the back of the Great Dividing Range behind Brisbane. Settlements strung out along the main roads here are for the most part unadorned farming centres of little interest in themselves, though solid stone architecture lends some sense of style to the gateway towns of **Toowoomba** and **Warwick**. A far bigger draw is the scenery along the downs' fringes, particularly the **Bunya Mountains** between Toowoomba and Kingaroy in the north and around the southeasterly **Granite Belt** – where there are also wineries and the possibility of **farm work**. But even if you tear across the central downs without stopping, you'll notice that the flat grasslands provide clear evidence of Aboriginal custodial practices – created by controlled burning designed to clear woodland and increase grazing land for game, they perfectly suited European pastoral needs. The downs are relatively fertile and stud farms, dairy, cotton, wool and cereal farming have all been successfully tried at one time or another. Even unwanted plants thrive – during the 1920s millions of acres of land were infested by **prickly pear**, a South American cactus. It was finally brought to heel by the tiny parasitic *cactoblastis* moth in 1930 – a success story of biological control on a scale to match the later failure of the introduction of the cane toad (see box on p.459).

From Brisbane, the Warrego Highway climbs a steep escarpment to Toowoomba and the central downs – followed by long-distance **buses** – while the Cunningham Highway cuts through Cunningham's Gap to Warwick and the south.

Toowoomba

TOOWOOMBA, 160km west of Brisbane, is a stately but staid university city perched on the edge of a six-hundred-metre escarpment, its stylish houses and blaze of late nineteenth-century sandstone architecture along central Main and Ruthven streets a reminder of its former business wealth. However, the town is frankly dull, and a prolonged drought has limited the appeal of the September **flower festival**, when a select few gardens display prize blooms. At other times the main attraction is the **Cobb & Co. Museum**, 27 Lindsay St (daily 10am–4pm; $8), 500m northeast of the centre across spacious Queens Park, which recalls the period from the 1860s to 1924 when intrepid coaches bounced across the Outback delivering mail and passengers. Aside from an impressive collection of these vehicles, the museum also houses interactive exhibitions on local history and flora and fauna, along with a working smithy at the back. If you've any spare time, **Picnic Point** at the top of Tourist Road, 2.5km east of the centre, is a pleasant spot on a warm day, offering a café, bar and restaurant as well as a picnic space, all with splendid views off from the escarpment.

Downtown Toowoomba is a compact area based around the intersection of **Ruthven Street**, which runs north to south, and **Margaret Street**, which runs east to west. Around the intersection you'll find shops, restaurants, banks and a post office. The **bus station** is one block east of here along Neil Street; **trains** pull up 500m northwest on Railway Street. The **tourist office** is in James Street, south off Ruthven (daily 9am–5pm; ⓣ1800 331 1155, ⓦwww.toowoomba.qld.gov.au). **Accommodation** prospects include the *Jolly Swagman Caravan Park*, at 47 Kitchener Rd (ⓣ07/4632 8735; camping $15, cabins ❷), about 1km southeast of the centre; and the central *James Street Motor Inn* on the corner of James and Kitchener streets (ⓣ07/4639 0200, ⓦwww.jamesstmotorinn.com.au; ❹). For **food**, *Jilly's Café* on Ruthven Street has a varied menu which includes some vegetarian options – check for daily specials such as pumpkin and pine-nut risotto, or five-spice chicken.

Moving on from Toowoomba, Polleys Coaches (ⓣ07/5482 9455, ⓦwww.polleys.com.au) head north to Kingaroy; Greyhound Australia (ⓣ13 14 99, ⓦwww.greyhound.com.au) continue northwest on their Charleville to Mount Isa run; and Crisps (ⓣ07/3236 5266, ⓦwww.crisps.com.au) run south to Warwick, where you can connect with services to Brisbane, Stanthorpe and Goondiwindi.

Kingaroy and around: the Northern Downs

KINGAROY is a small town in the heart of peanut country on the very fringes of the downs, 120km north of Toowoomba. A cluster of castle-like peanut silos in the middle of town aptly symbolize the fame Kingaroy owes to the late **Johannes Bjelke-Petersen** – better known simply as "Joh" – who farmed nuts here before becoming Queensland Premier in 1968, an office he held for nineteen years. His equally charismatic wife, Flo, also attained fame, making it onto postcards with her pumpkin scone recipe. Joh passed away in April 2005, but remains in no danger of obscurity, with a dam, bridge, road and sportsground named after him, and his ominous catchphrase "Don't you worry about that" still on everyone's lips. To get in touch with what Kingaroy is all about, take the free fifty-minute tour at the **Kingaroy Toasted Peanut Factory** (Mon–Fri 10.30am), 1km south of the centre on Kingaroy Street. Here, the scent of roasting is so seductive that you'll want to head back to the **Peanut Van** outside Lions Park, between the factory and town, which sells roasted nuts by the kilo. The last few years has also seen a rash of **wineries** springing up around Kingaroy, most open for tasting – and, of course, buying – daily. Stuart Range Estates (tours daily 10am & 2pm; $2; ⓣ07/4162 3711), just northeast of the centre at the end of William Street, has definite potential, though at present the wine is still a little green.

Kingaroy's tiny centre is built around the intersection of Haly Street and parallel Youngman and Kingaroy streets, which run north to south through town. The peanut silos are to the east, just along Haly Street, facing the **tourist office** (Mon–Fri 9am–5pm, Sat & Sun 10am–4pm; ⓣ07/4162 3199), which hands out a wineries map. For **somewhere to stay**, *Kingaroy Holiday Park* (ⓣ07/4162 1808, ⓦwww.kingaroycaravanpark.com.au; camping $20, cabins ❸), 1km south near the peanut factory on Walter Road, has a variety of accommodation options in leafy surroundings. Otherwise, *Kingaroy Hotel-Motel* (ⓣ07/4162 1677; ❸) on the corner of Youngman and Haly streets, and the central *Club Hotel* (ⓣ07/4162 2204; ❸) on Kingaroy Street have good-value, similarly appointed rooms. The latter also offers occasional **live music**. Polleys Coaches (ⓣ07/5482 9455, ⓦwww.polleys.com.au) leave daily from Kingaroy to Gympie (on the coast) and Toowoomba, while drivers can also take the Bunya Highway to Dalby.

The Bunya Mountains

Southwest of Kingaroy, a sixty-kilometre section of road twists through the **Bunya Mountains** before you reach Dalby, back on the Warrego Highway. Among the mountains' general greenery and clusters of unlikely flowers, you'll find stands of enormous **bunya pines**, which once covered the mountains and whose seeds were a valuable food source for local Aborigines, who gathered seasonally to gorge themselves. On his trip across the downs in 1844, the indefatigable Ludwig Leichhardt witnessed the collection and roasting of nuts at such a feast and persuaded the government to make the area an Aboriginal reserve, free from logging or settlement. The decree was revoked in 1860, but today the Bunya Mountains still retain a significant stand of pines, along with orange-flowering silky oaks and ancient **grass trees**, with their three-metre-high, spear-like flower heads.

Two national parks run sites along the road at Burton's Well and Westcott make for good **bushcamping**, with another wallaby-infested site at the hamlet of Dandabah; the **ranger's office** here deals with enquiries on all three (daily 2–4pm; ⓣ07/4668 3127, ⓦwww.epa.qld.gov.au; advance booking essential during holiday periods; camping $4.50). Less frugal accommodation is on hand about 500m north along the main road at the cosy and fun *Rice's Log Cabins* (ⓣ07/4668 3133, ⓦwww.riceslogcabins.com.au; ❹), or you can find a **chalet rental** through ⓦwww.bunyamountains.com.au. Note that the mountains are generally several degrees cooler than the plains below, and it gets seriously cold in winter. Walking tracks between the three campsites lead through the forest to orchid-covered lookouts and waterfalls – **satin bowerbirds** and **paradise riflebirds**, with their deep blue-black plumage and long curved beaks, are both fairly common here.

The Granite Belt

The southeastern edge of the Darling Downs along the New South Wales border, known as Queensland's **Granite Belt**, is a major wine- and fruit-producing area, which regularly records the state's **coldest temperatures** – on a winter's night it drops well below freezing here. Heading south from Toowoomba, you pass through the one-horse town of **NOBBY**, whose former resident **Steele Rudd** created archetypal Australian country characters in his "Dad and Dave" tales – commemorated at the *Nobby Hotel* in paintings and farm bric-a-brac.

Around 85km south of Toowoomba, **WARWICK** makes a fine base for exploring the region, and is known across the state for its cheese. Services are centred around Grafton and Palmerin streets, where sandstone buildings date back to the time when Warwick graziers competed fiercely with Toowoomba's merchants to establish the downs' premier settlement. Warwick itself shouldn't tie you up for long, but it sits beside the **Condamine River**, which – though unimpressive where it flows through town – later joins the Murray/Darling river system, Australia's longest, before emptying into the ocean near Adelaide. At **Queen Mary Falls**, 43km east from Warwick beyond Killarney, a tributary exits the forest in a plunge off the top of the plateau. A two-kilometre-long track climbs to the escarpment at the head of the falls from the road, with a kiosk, accommodation and lunches provided by *Queen Mary Falls Tourist Park* (ⓣ07/4664 7151, ⓦwww.queenmaryfallscaravanpark.com.au; camping $18, cabins ❸); you need your own transport to get here.

Warwick's **tourist office** is on Albion Street (daily 8.30am–5pm; ⓣ07/4661 3122, ⓦwww.southerndownsholidays.com.au), while **buses** pull up on central Grafton Street. The **October rodeo** is about the only time you might experience trouble finding **accommodation** – try *Warwick Tourist Caravan Park*, 18 Palmer Ave (ⓣ07/4661 8335; camping $15, cabins ❸), 1.2km north of town on the highway, *Warwick Motor Inn*, 17 Albion St (ⓣ07/4661 1533; ❸), or *Country Rose Motel* (ⓣ07/4661 7700; ❹). **Heading on**, both Crisps Coaches (ⓣ07/4661 8333, ⓦwww.crisps.com.au) and Greyhound Australia (ⓣ13 14 99, ⓦwww.greyhound.com.au) run south to Stanthorpe along the New England Highway and southwest to Goondiwindi along the Cunningham Highway.

Stanthorpe

Sixty kilometres south of Warwick along the New England Highway, **STANTHORPE** was founded in the 1880s around a tin-mining operation on Quart Pot Creek, but really took off in the 1940s after Italian migrants started up the fruit farms and wineries that now throng the region. Today, it's a miniature version of Warwick: central Maryland Street sports a couple of sandstone facades while retiree bungalows sprout on the hills above; there are good opportunities for wine sampling and – in season – **fruit-picking work**.

To start a **wine tour**, Heritage Wines (daily 9am–5pm; ⓣ07/4685 2197, ⓦwww.heritagewines.com.au), 15km north on the New England Highway – worth a visit for its huge, antique-laden reception room alone – and Ballandean Estate (daily 8.30am–5pm; ⓣ07/4684 1226), the region's oldest vineyard, 20km southwest of town, both produce excellent wines. A full list of wineries – and advice on the best – is available at Stanthorpe's **tourist office** (daily 8.30am–5pm; ⓣ07/4681 2057), overlooking the river just south of the centre on Leslie Parade. Staff can also help if you want to try fossicking for **topaz** (a semiprecious stone found near tin deposits), 13km northwest of Stanthorpe at Swiper's Gully; permits are available from the *Blue Topaz Caravan Park*.

Stanthorpe has a good range of **accommodation**. For camping try *Blue Topaz Caravan Park* (Ⓣ07/4683 5279; cabins ❷; camping $15), 5km south along the highway, or the spacious *Top of Town* (Ⓣ07/4681 4888, Ⓦwww.topoftown.com.au; camping $15, cabins ❸), on the highway 2km north of Stanthorpe. There are hostel beds at the excellent *Backpackers of Queensland*, 80 High St (Ⓣ0429 810 998, Ⓦwww.backpackersofqueensland.com.au; dorms $150 per week), who also arrange **farm work**, while *Stannum Lodge Motor Inn* (Ⓣ07/4681 2000, Ⓦwww.stannumlodge.com.au; ❹) on Wallangarra Road is a central motel with good facilities, including a swimming pool.

Girraween National Park

The hills around Stanthorpe are granite, exposed as fantastic monoliths at **Girraween National Park**, 30km south down the New England Highway. There's a National Parks **campsite and ranger's office** here (Ⓣ07/4684 5157, Ⓦwww.epa.qld.gov.au; camping $4.50) with showers, toilets and the chance of seeing small, shy, active **sugar gliders** just after dark. Listen for claws clattering over bark and then shine your torch overhead to catch a set of glowing eyes in the spotlight.

With more energy than skill, you can climb several of the giant hills with little risk, as long as rain hasn't made them dangerously slippery – trails are well marked and **free maps** are available from the ranger's office. The **Castle Rock** track (2hr return) initially follows a gentle incline past lichen-covered boulders in the forest, then a dotted white line into a fissure – look up and you'll see loose rocks balanced above you – before emerging onto a thin ledge above the campsite. Follow this around to the north side and clamber to the very top for superb views of the Pyramids, the Sphinx and Mount Norman, the park's 1267-metre apex, poking rudely out of the woods. It's a further forty minutes' walk from the Castle Rock campsite to the Sphinx and Turtle Rock: **Sphinx** is a broad pillar topped by a boulder, while **Turtle Rock**'s more conventional shape means a scramble, with no handholds on the final stretch. Pat yourself on the back however, if you make it to the top of the completely bald **South Pyramid** (2hr return from Castle Rock) without resorting to hands and knees. At the top is Balancing Rock, an oval boulder teetering so precariously on its narrow end that you can see underneath to where the support is surely only a few years away from collapse. From here you can take a well-earned rest and look across to the unscaleable North Pyramid.

The Central Downs and around

To break the unexciting journey northwest across the downs from Toowoomba to Dalby, turn off the highway about 45km from Toowoomba at tiny Jondaryan township and head 3km south to the **Jondaryan Woolshed** (Wed–Sun 10am–4pm; $9, or $13 including tour; Ⓣ07/4692 2229, Ⓦwww.jondaryanwoolshed.com). This collection of old buildings – all relocated from elsewhere, with the exception of the shed itself – gives a glimpse of old-time life on the downs: exhibits worth a closer look include a document dating from 1880, which itemizes some of the schoolmistress's tasks – including splinting broken legs, wallpapering buildings to keep out snakes and being able to fight off "swaggies" (hobos, or drifters) trying to sleep in the schoolhouse. Make sure you catch one of the **tours** (Sat, Sun & holidays 10.30am & 1.30pm) when the smithy is working and you can watch sheep shearers at work in the vast woolshed, lit by a bare bulb – a very surreal tableau. They also offer basic **accommodation** ($10–16; meals by arrangement) either in safari tents or the bitterly cold shearers' quarters.

Stops over the next 200km include **Dalby**, **Chinchilla** and **Miles**, rural centres devoid of attractions but with the usual complement of services and places to stay. One place worth stopping at however, is *Possum Park* (ⓣ07/4627 1651, ⓦwww.possumpark.com.au; carriages ❸), some 20km north of Miles. A **motel** sited in World War II ammunition bunkers in prime bushland, accommodation here is in restored train carriages or your own tent – you'll need your own vehicle to get here, and bring your own food.

Roma and Mitchell

ROMA, 140km west of Miles, was founded by settlers eager to occupy country made available by the opening up of the Darling Downs in 1862. Today, the town thrives on farming, supplemented by the **oil and gas** fields which have been exploited intermittently since the 1900s. Roma was also the venue for the 1871 trial of the audacious **Captain Starlight** (also known as Harry Redford), who stole a thousand head of cattle from a nearby property and drove them down through the South Australian deserts to Adelaide for sale. An unusual white bull in the herd was recognized and Redford arrested, but his pioneering of a new stock route won such popular approval that the judge refused to convict him.

A useful place to stock up before heading north to Carnarvon National Park, Roma is a typical inland town – tidy, with streets lined with **bottle trees** (not only bottle-shaped but also full of sugary water for emergency stock-watering), and a slightly dated air lent by the iron decorations and wrapround balconies of its hotels. **Romavilla Winery** (Mon–Fri 8am–5pm, Sat 9am–noon & 2–4pm; ⓣ07/4622 1822, ⓦwww.romavilla.com) has been producing prize-winning wine since 1863; it's an eccentric, overgrown place about a kilometre north of town on the Carnarvon road, at Quintin Street.

The Warrego Highway runs through Roma as Bowen Street and it's here, on the eastern side of town, that you're greeted by the **Big Rig** (daily 9am–5pm; $10 or $15.50 with night show; ⓣ07/4622 4355, ⓦwww.thebigrig.com.au), originally a drilling tower left as a monument to the oil boom of the 1920s and now a $5 million complex exploring the history of Australia's oil and gas industry. It also doubles as the town's **tourist office**. Most of the town's shops, banks and businesses are one block north of Bowen Street, on parallel McDowall Street. Roma's **accommodation** choices include the *Starlight Motor Inn* (ⓣ07/4622 2666, ⓕ4622 2111; ❹), with standard motel beds, the less pricey *Bottle Tree Gardens* (ⓣ07/4622 6111, ⓕ4622 6499; ❹), on the corner of Bowen and Charles streets, and the *Big Rig Tourist Park*, 4 McDowall St (ⓣ07/4622 2538; camping $18, cabins ❸) near the Big Rig, which has bright modern cabins and hot showers, welcome during the sub-zero winter nights. **Restaurants** in Roma are fairly basic, though *Deano's*, at 77 Quintin St, does good steaks and *Golden Dragon* at 60–62 McDowall St serves reasonable Chinese food.

The **train station** is one block south of the highway at the corner of Station and Charles streets, and **buses** pull up along the highway at the more central of the two BP roadhouses. **Tickets** for both can be obtained from Harvey World Travel, 71 Arthur St (ⓣ07/4622 1416). **Heading on**, the Carnarvon Developmental Road (take Quintin St from the town centre) heads north for access to Carnarvon National Park; otherwise, the next stops west along the highway are Mitchell and Charleville.

Mitchell

MITCHELL is a delightful, single-street highway town 88km west of Roma right on the western rim of the Downs, beside the Maranoa River. As with Roma, Mitchell has its local outlaw legend; the protagonists this time were the two **Kenniff Brothers**, who raided the district for cattle and horses in the early 1900s. After killing a policeman during one arrest attempt, they were finally ambushed south of town and dragged off for trial in Brisbane; unlike Captain Starlight, they were sentenced to death, though one brother had this commuted to a prison term.

There are two reasons to pass through Mitchell – either to follow the two-hundred-kilometre track north to **Mount Moffat** in Carnarvon National Park, or to make use of the town's **hot artesian springs**, which have been thoughtfully channelled into an open-air swimming pool and spa (daily 8am–6pm; $6) in the grounds of the old **Kenniff Courthouse** – good, steamy fun on a cold winter's morning. The courthouse itself now houses a **tourist office** (daily 8am–6pm; ⓣ07/4623 8171), and also incorporates the *Healthy Byte Café*, an Internet terminal and a weekend cinema. For **somewhere to stay**, the excellent council-run campsite back across the Maranoa River allows you to pitch a tent free for two nights ($5.50 per tent per night thereafter); the *Mitchell Motel* (ⓣ07/4623 1355; ❸), on the western side of town, is one of the alternatives. Aside from the café in the courthouse, the central *Blue Pub* is a good place to **eat**.

Moving on, all transport and the Warrego Highway continue a further 180km west to Charleville. The **train station** is 500m from the courthouse at the western side of town, and the newsagent on the main street doubles as the bus agent.

Carnarvon National Park

North of Roma and Mitchell, Queensland's Central Highlands consist of a broad band of weathered sandstone plateaus, thickly wooded and spectacularly sculpted into sheer cliffs and pinnacles. It's an extraordinarily primeval landscape, and one still visibly central to Aboriginal culture, as poor pasture left the highlands relatively unscathed by European colonization. Covering a huge slice of the region, the fragmented sections of **Carnarvon National Park** include **Carnarvon Gorge** and **Mount Moffatt**: Carnarvon Gorge has the highest concentration of Aboriginal art and arguably the best scenery, while Mount Moffatt is harder to reach but wilder – it isn't possible to drive directly between the two sections, though you can hike with permission and advice from the rangers.

As there's **no public transport** to the park, you'll need your own vehicle: **access** to Carnarvon Gorge is from Roma to the south, or Emerald to the north, and to Mount Moffat from Roma or Mitchell. All these roads involve some stretches of dirt, making them impassable after heavy rain (most likely Nov–May). Always carry extra rations in case you get stranded for a while and – unless you're desperately short of supplies – stay put in wet weather: you'll only churn the road up and make it harder for others to use. Summer **temperatures** often reach 40°C, while winter nights can be below freezing. Gathering firewood is prohibited inside the park, so stop on the way in or bring a gas stove. For **information** and **campsite bookings** check out ⓦwww.epa.qld.gov.au.

Carnarvon Gorge

The partially sealed Carnarvon Gorge **access road** is reached off the Carnarvon Highway between Roma (200km) and Emerald (250km) and runs 45km west, past views of the Consuelo Tableland standing out magnificently above dark forests, to the park's edge at the mouth of the gorge. The **ranger station** here

△ The Carnarvon Gorge

(daily 8am–5pm; ⓣ07/4984 4505) has a payphone, an orientation model of the gorge, free maps and a library on the highlands and its wildlife.

Accommodation is best booked well in advance: nearby options are *Carnarvon Gorge Wilderness Lodge* (ⓣ1800 644 150, ⓦwww.carnarvon-gorge.com; ❽), 2km before the ranger station, where comfortable rooms are surrounded by a neat lawn and respectably sized cycad palms; or a further 2km away at the creekside *Takarakka Bush Resort* (ⓣ07/4984 4535, ⓦwww.takarakka.com.au; camping $12, canvas "cabins" ❹). The *Wilderness Lodge* also has a bar and a store selling basics, fuel and LP gas refills. If both of these are full, *Warremba Farmstay and Camping* (ⓣ07/4626 7175; ❸, camping $15) is back on the Carnarvon Highway 57km from the gorge, heading south to Roma, and offers homestay accommodation plus a campsite with hot showers, toilets, and big kitchen area.

Boomerangs

Curved **throwing sticks** were once found throughout the world. Several were discovered in Tutankhamun's tomb, Hopi Indians once used them and a 23,000-year-old example made from mammoth ivory was recently found in Poland. Since that time the invention of the bow and arrow superseded what Aborigines call a **boomerang** or *karli*, but their innovation of a stick that returns has kept the boomerang alive, not least in people's imaginations – they were originally used as children's toys but were then modified into decoys for hunting wildfowl. The non-returning types depicted in Carnarvon Gorge show how sophisticated they became as **hunting weapons**. Usually made from tough acacia wood, some are hooked like a pick, while others are designed to cartwheel along the ground to break the legs of game. Thus immobilized, one animal would be killed while another could be easily tracked to meet the same fate. Besides hunting, the boomerang was also used for digging, levering or cutting, as well as for musical or ceremonial accompaniment, when pairs would be banged together. At Carnarvon Gorge, the long, gently curved boomerangs stencilled on the walls in pairs are not repetitions but portraits of two weapons with identical flight paths; if the first missed through a gust of wind, for instance, the user could immediately throw the second, correcting his aim for the conditions.

Along the gorge

Carnarvon Creek's journey between the vertical faces of the gorge has created some magical scenery, where low cloud often blends with the cliffs, making them look infinitely tall. Before setting off between them, climb **Boolimba Bluff** from the *Takarakka* campsite for a rare chance to see the gorge system from above; it's a tiring climb but the views from the "Roof of Queensland" make the three-kilometre track worth the effort.

The **day-walk** (19km return from the ranger station) into the gorge takes some beating, featuring several intriguing side-gorges. The best of these contain the **Moss Garden** (3.5km), a vibrant green carpet of liverworts and ferns lapping up a spring as it seeps through the rockface, and **Alijon Falls** (5km), which conceal the enchanting Wards Canyon, where a remnant group of *angiopteris* ferns hang close to extinction in front of a second waterfall and gorge, complete with bats and blood-red river stones.

Carnarvon's two major **Aboriginal art sites** are the Gallery (5.6km) and Cathedral Cave (at the end of the trail, 9.3km from the *Takarakka* campsite), both on the gorge track, though if you keep your eyes open there are plenty more to be found. These are Queensland's most documented Aboriginal art sites, though the paintings themselves remain enigmatic. A rockface covered with engravings of vulvas lends a pornographic air to **the Gallery**, and other symbols include kangaroo, emu and human tracks. A long, wavy line here might represent the rainbow serpent, shaper of many Aboriginal landscapes. Overlaying the engravings are hundreds of coloured stencils, made by placing an object against the wall and spraying it with a mixture of ochre and water held in the mouth. Always personal and striking, hands – including children's – form the bulk of the designs, but there are also artefacts, boomerangs and complex crosses formed by four arms. Goannas and mysterious net patterns at the near end of the wall have been painted with a stick. **Cathedral Cave** is larger, with an even greater range of designs, including seashell pendant stencils – proof that trade networks reached from here to the sea – and engravings of animal tracks and emu eggs.

Mount Moffatt

Mount Moffatt is part of an open landscape of ridges and lightly wooded grassland, at the top of a plateau to the west of Carnarvon Gorge. The area was the Kenniff Brothers' stomping ground: it was here that they murdered a policeman and station manager in 1902, events which were to lead to their being run to ground by a group of vigilantes. Years later in 1960, archeological excavations at their hideout, **Kenniff Cave**, were the first to establish that Aboriginal occupation of Australia predated the last Ice Age, and – though the cave is closed due to instability – there's plenty of evidence of indigenous tenure throughout the area.

Access to this area of the park is from Roma via Injune (250km), or direct from Mitchell (220km). Although the park perimeter can often be reached in 2WD vehicles, you'll need a 4WD to get around once there. As there is **no fuel or supplies** of any kind available in the park, make sure you have enough before arrival – last sources for either are at Injune (150km) or Mitchell. There are four **bush campgrounds** in the park, two of which have drinking water; check out Ⓦwww.epa.qld.gov.au as you'll need to book in advance.

Mount Moffatt's attractions are spread out over an extensive area. At the southern entrance to the park, the **Chimneys** area has some interesting sandstone pinnacles and alcoves, which once housed bark burial-cylinders – look for the stencil of an entire body, arms spread-eagled. Around 6km on from here the road forks, and the right track continues 10km to the **ranger station** (Ⓣ07/4626 3581), where you can collect your map of the area and plan any bushwalking. The left track, meanwhile, runs 6km past *Dargonelly* campsite to **Marlong Arch**, a sandstone formation decorated with handprints and engravings. Five kilometres northeast from here, a trail leads to **Kookaburra Cave**, named after a weathered, bird-shaped hand stencil. A further 5km beyond the cave is **Marlong Plain**, a pretty expanse of blue grass surrounded by peaks, and another sandstone tower known as **Lot's Wife**. Ten kilometres north of Marlong Plain, a lesser track leads to several sites associated with the Kenniff legend, including the murder scene, and the rock where they are believed to have burned the evidence. Finally, for pure scenery, head 15km due east of Marlong Plain to the **Mahogany Forest**, a stand of giant stringybark trees.

Charleville to Cooper Creek and Birdsville

The last place of any size on the journey west from Roma is **CHARLEVILLE**, terminus for the **train** and – in this direction anyway – the **bus**. A walk around reveals a compact, busy country town with broad streets, shaded pavements and some solid buildings constructed when the town was a droving centre and staging post for Cobb & Co. It's well known as a victim of **contradictory weather** – in November 1947 a typical hot summer afternoon was interrupted for twenty minutes as the temperature plummeted and a blast of massive hailstones stripped trees, smashed windows and roofs and killed pets and poultry. In 1990 the town centre was struck by five-metre-deep floodwaters from the Warrego River – a dramatic end to years of drought. At the end of the nineteenth century, attempts were made to end another dry spell with **Stiger Vortex Guns**, giant conical contraptions supposed to seed rainclouds. During trials, two of the six guns exploded and the meteorologist who recommended them was run out of town. Only two have survived – one is in the Queensland Museum in Brisbane and the other is outside the **Scout Hut** on Sturt Street, heading south towards Cunnamulla.

The **National Parks Centre**, right on the Warrego Highway as you come in from Mitchell on the eastern side of town (Mon–Fri 9am–4pm; free), is dedicated to studying and breeding populations of regional rarities such as the absurdly cute **bilby** (for more on which see p.514) and the graceful **yellow-footed rock wallaby**, both of which are on show. Three kilometres south of town, on Qantas Drive (off the Matilda Highway), the **Cosmos Centre and Observatory** (April–Oct daily 10am–6pm, with night shows at 7.30pm; Nov–March daily except Sat 10am–5pm, with night shows Mon, Wed, Fri & Sat at 8pm; day/night shows $19/35; ⓣ07/4654 7771, ⓦwww.cosmoscentre.com) provides visitors with the opportunity to observe the night sky through powerful **Meade telescopes** – the lack of industrial light and pollution, combined with a low horizon, make the location ideal. During daylight hours, the centre has interactive displays and films explaining the history of astronomy and the formation of the universe. **Booking** is essential for night-time stargazing.

Charleville practicalities

The town is small but laid out in a confusing grid pattern, with the centre around the intersection of Wills and Galatea streets. Most services – banks, shops and post office – are along Wills, and transport also sets down here: **buses** outside the *Young Tiger* restaurant, and **trains** at the street's easternmost end. The **tourist office** (April–Sept daily 9am–5pm; Oct–March Mon–Fri 9am–5pm; ⓣ07/4654 3057) is a kilometre south of town on Sturt Street (the Mitchell Highway). **Rooms** can be found at the peaceful and modern *Charleville Motel* (ⓣ07/4654 1566; ❹), near the train station on King Street, or the town's historic *Corones Hotel* on Wills Street (ⓣ07/4654 1022, ⓦwww.hotelcorones.com.au; hotel rooms ❷, motel doubles ❸). To **camp**, head for *Bailey Bar Caravan Park*, on King Street (ⓣ07/4654 1744; camping $21, cabins ❸). For **meals**, there's Thai food at the *Young Tiger* on Wills Street and generous meals at the *Corones Hotel*, whose dining rooms have been refurbished to original 1925 condition.

Moving on from Charleville, roads head north to Blackall and Longreach (covered by Brisbane–Mount Isa buses), south via Cunnamulla to New South Wales, and further west to Quilpie. **Flights** to Brisbane leave from the tiny strip outside town. All transport **bookings** can be made with Western Travel Service at 37 Alfred St (ⓣ07/4654 1260).

Cunnamulla and Currawinya National Park

CUNNAMULLA, a nondescript handful of service stations and motels 200km south of Charleville, is a trucking stop on the long run down the Mitchell Highway to Bourke in New South Wales. There's a helpful **tourist office** (daily 9am–3pm; ⓣ07/4655 2481) in the old schoolhouse on central Jane Street, with **accommodation** just around the corner at the *Cunnamulla Hotel* (ⓣ07/4655 1102; ❸) on Stockyard Street, or a short way south at *Jack Tonkin Caravan Park* (ⓣ07/4655 1421; camping $15, cabins ❷). Cunnamulla's Council Offices (ⓣ07/4655 1131), on the corner of Stockyard and Louise streets, are the place to arrange a **fossicking licence** ($5.55, valid for a month) if you're planning to head 160km northwest to the **Yowah Opal Fields**, where shallow deposits yield much-sought-after opalized Yowah Nuts – the fields host a three-day **Opal Festival** in mid-July. At the fields, beware of unfenced vertical shafts, which are practically invisible until you're on your way down – always look where you're going and never step backwards. Yowah has bore water, fuel and a caravan park (Ⓣ07/4655 4953; camping $12, cabins ❷).

Two hundred kilometres southwest of Cunnamulla on minor roads, **Currawinya National Park** (Ⓦwww.epa.qld.gov.au) features mallee scrub, wetlands and associated wildlife, in contrast to the semi-arid land more typical of the region. One animal to benefit is the highly endangered **bilby**, which, with its long ears and nose, looks like a cross between a rabbit and a bandicoot. Feral cats, rabbits, and grazing cattle have brought the bilby close to extinction, but a recently completed **fence** at Currawinya will keep all these pests out, allowing the new bilby population – reintroduced from Charleville's National Parks Centre – to prosper. You can camp at Currawinya, but check on road conditions and practicalities with the National Parks ranger first (Ⓣ07/4655 4001). Past Currawinya is the tiny border town of **Hungerford**, where you can stock-up on fuel and groceries at the *Royal Mail Hotel*. From here it's a 200-kilometre run southeast on a largely unsealed road to Bourke.

Quilpie and the road to the Dig Tree

QUILPIE is a compact, dusty farming community 200km west of Charleville. The **tourist office** (Mon–Fri 8am–5pm, Sat & Sun 10am–4.30pm, closed Nov–March; Ⓣ07/4656 2166) is on Brolga Street, and other amenities include

The Burke and Wills saga

In 1860 the government of Victoria, then Australia's richest state, decided to sponsor a lavish expedition to make the first south to north **crossing** of the continent to the Gulf of Carpentaria. Eighteen men, twenty camels (shipped, along with their handlers, from Asia) and over twenty tons of provisions started out from Melbourne in August, led by **Robert O'Hara Burke** and **William John Wills**. It didn't take long for the leaders' personalities to cause problems, and by December, Burke had impatiently left the bulk of the expedition and supplies lagging behind and raced ahead with a handful of men to establish a base camp on **Cooper Creek**. Having built a stockade, Burke and Wills started north, along with two other members of their team (Gray and King), six camels, a couple of horses and food for three months. Four men remained at camp, led by William Brahe, waiting for the rest of the expedition to catch up. In fact, most of the supplies and camels were dithering halfway between Melbourne and Cooper Creek, unsure of what to do next.

As Burke and Wills failed to keep a regular diary, few details of the "**rush to the Gulf**" are known. They were seen by Kalkadoon Aborigines following the Corella River into the Gulf, where they found that vast salt marshes lay between them and the sea. Disappointed, they left the banks of the Bynoe (near present-day Normanton) on February 11, 1861, and headed back south. Their progress slowed by the wet season, they killed and ate the camels and horses as their food ran out. Gray died after being beaten by Burke for stealing flour; remorse was heightened when they staggered into the Cooper Creek stockade on April 21 to find that, having already waited an extra month for them to return, Brahe had decamped that morning. Too weak to follow him, they found supplies buried under a tree marked "**Dig**", but failed to change the sign when they moved on, which meant that when the first rescue teams arrived on the scene, they assumed the explorers had never returned from the Gulf. Trying to walk south, the three reached the Innamincka area, where Aborigines fed them fish and nardoo (water fern) seeds, but by the time a rescue party tracked them down in September, only King was still alive. The full, sad tale of their trek is expertly told by Alan Moorehead in his classic account *Cooper's Creek*, a book well worth tracking down in your library (see "Books").

a supermarket, bakery, butcher's and a fuel depot. The *Channel Country* **caravan park** is at 21 Chipu St (☎07/4656 2087; camping $15, cabins ❷) and there are also beds at the *Quilpie Motor Inn* (☎07/4656 1277; ❹). The *Imperial Hotel* serves evening meals between 6 and 7.30pm, and there are a couple of cafés in town, which close around 5.30pm.

As there are few signposts, a **map** is essential if you plan to follow the 490-kilometre, largely unsealed route from Quilpie to the Dig Tree at Nappa Merrie, just 30km from the South Australian border. The **last fuel** along the way lies an hour west of Quilpie at **EROMANGA**, a maintenance depot with a population of eighty souls whose ancient *Royal Hotel* (☎07/4656 4845; ❷) offers beer, food, information, and four motel rooms. From here you head across the stony plains above the huge gas and oil reserves of the **Cooper Basin**, past the cattle stations of Durham Downs and Karmona, lonely "nodding donkeys" and unaccountably healthy-looking droughtmaster cattle, to the **Dig Tree on Cooper Creek**.

The site of Burke and Wills' **stockade** (see box on opposite), Depot Camp 65, is a beautiful shaded river-bank alive with pelicans and parrots, and it's hard to believe that anyone could have starved to death nearby. The **Dig Tree** is still standing and protected by a walkway, but the three original blaze marks reading "BLXV, DIG 3FT NW, DEC 6 60-APR 21 61" have been cemented over to keep the tree alive. Burke's face was carved into the tree on the right by John Dickins in 1898, and is still clearly visible.

Pressing on, you'll be relieved to know that it's only 50km to **Innamincka**'s pub, at the top of the Strzelecki Track in South Australia.

Quilpie to Birdsville

The long road from Quilpie west to Birdsville is a relatively easy journey, manageable in good conditions without a 4WD, though depth markers along the road give an idea of how saturated this **Channel Country** becomes after rain. First stop is **WINDORAH**, a limp settlement of a dozen buildings offering fuel, a post office and an amazingly well-provisioned store. The *Western Star Hotel* (☎07/4656 3166; ❹) is hard to pass by for a cold drink and a look at its collection of old photos; they also have tidy air-conditioned **rooms** and might let you **camp** out the back. Windorah is the last place with **fuel** before Birdsville, 385km away.

The ruins of the John Costello hotel lie 80km further west, opposite a windmill. Tired of riding 30km every morning to round up his stockmen from the bar, the manager of a nearby station had the local liquor licence transferred from the JC to his homestead in the 1950s. He pulled the roof off the hotel for good measure, and there's now little left beyond the foundations and some posts. Another 140km brings you to more remains at **Betoota**, whose only building, the 1880s Betoota Hotel, was in business until 1997, when this was Australia's smallest town (population 1). Beyond here the country turns into a rocky, silent plain, with circling crows and wedge-tailed eagles the only signs of life, and it's hard to imagine what the occasional fenceline or grid is keeping apart. Driving can be hazardous here – you'll pass plenty of wrecks and shredded tyres – but with care (and good luck), the Diamantina River and Birdsville are just three hours away.

Birdsville and beyond

Famous for the **horse races** on the first weekend in September, when a few thousand beer-swilling spectators pack out the dusty little settlement, at other times **BIRDSVILLE** is something of an anticlimax, a handful of buildings where only the hotel and roadhouses seem to be doing business. But unless you've flown in, you'll probably be glad simply to have arrived intact. The misleadingly named **caravan park** (Ⓣ07/4656 3214; camping only $20) comprises a large patch of scrub and an amenities block by the creek, or you can **camp for free** outside town along the artesian overflow, where huge flocks of raucous corellas seem to justify the township's name – though it's actually a corruption of "Burt's Ville", after the first storekeeper. Given the lack of alternatives, don't be surprised to find the comfy accommodation at the *Birdsville Hotel* (Ⓣ07/4656 3244, Ⓦwww.theoutback.com.au; ④) full; during race weekend, all beds are reserved for the bar staff anyway, so you have to camp. For more on the **race weekend** check out Ⓦwww.birdsvilleraces.com, which gives a good breakdown of what to expect: alcohol and ponies, in that order – the hotel trades over 50,000 cans of beer in just two nights. **Provisions** and snacks can be bought from the general store. If you're organizing your own food, prepare the next day's meals after dark when the flies have settled down. You owe yourself at least one drink in the hotel's mighty bar; order by 5.30pm if you want a full evening meal – the "seven-course takeaway" is a pie and a six-pack.

The **Wirrarri Information Centre** (Mon–Fri 8.30am–4.30pm; Ⓣ07/4656 3300) on Billabong Boulevard will give you the lowdown on the state of the various Outback tracks if you're planning to use them, or ask at the fuel station (Ⓣ07/4656 3236) across from the hotel. The Information Centre can also direct you to another **tree** blazed by Burke and Wills across the Diamantina, otherwise hard to locate among the scrub, or to attractions in town such as the stone shell of the original 1923 **Australian Inland Mission**. The **Birdsville Working Museum** (daily 8am–6pm; $8; Ⓣ07/4656 3259), as its name suggests, is more than just a collection of old stuff: all the exhibits, from petrol pumps and farm machinery to a complete blacksmith's shop, are fully restored and regularly operated.

Outside Birdsville, 14km north on the Bedourie road, there's a stand of slow-growing, old and very rare **Waddi trees**. They're about five metres tall and resemble sparse conifers wrapped in prickly feather boas with warped, circular seed-pods; the wind blowing through the needles makes an eerie noise like the roar of a distant fire. For something more dramatic, head out west 33km to **Big Red**, at the start of the Simpson Desert crossing. Simpson's largest dune may seem unimpressive from below, but your opinion will change radically if you walk up or try to plant a 4WD on the top. If you're having a hard time getting up the long western face, there's a less steep track immediately on the right, which has a couple of quick turns near the summit. Two-wheel-drive vehicles can often reach the base (check with the fuel station before setting off) and it's worth it to see the dunes, flood plains and stony gibber country (red desert, covered with loose stone) on the way.

North of Birdsville, the next substantial settlement, Mount Isa, is a lonely 700km further on, with fuel available about every 200km. Those heading **west across the Simpson Desert** to Dalhousie Springs in South Australia need a Desert Parks Pass ($95), available online at Ⓦwww.parks.sa.gov.au, or from the Birdsville National Parks office on Jardine Street (Ⓣ07/4656 3272 or 4656 3249). Feasible in any sound vehicle during a dry winter, the 520-kilometre **Birdsville Track** heads from the racecourse down to Marree in South Australia (see p.810).

Rockhampton to Winton

Heading west from Rockhampton, the Capricorn and Landsborough highways run through the heart of **central Queensland** to Winton and ultimately Mount Isa. There's a lot to see here – just a couple of hours from the coast you'll find magical scenery atop the forested, sandstone plateau of the **Blackdown Tablelands**, while the town of **Emerald** offers the chance of seasonal farm work, and is also a gateway to the **Gemfields**' sapphire mines. Continuing inland, both **Barcaldine** and **Longreach** are historically important towns, the latter hosting the archetypal Outback museum in the **Stockman's Hall of Fame**. Further west, **Winton** sits surrounded by a timeless, harsh orange landscape, with close access to some remote bush, unexpectedly imprinted with a dramatic set of dinosaur footprints at **Lark Quarry**.

Buses run by Emerald Coaches (Ⓣ07/4982 4444, Ⓦwww.emeraldcoaches.com.au) connect Rockhampton, via all stops along the Capricorn Highway, with Barcaldine and Longreach, from either of which you can pick up a Greyhound service to Winton on their Brisbane–Mount Isa run. Alternatively, you can catch the twice-weekly *Spirit of the Outback* **train** from Rockhampton as far as Longreach.

Into the Northern Highlands

As you move inland, the coastal humidity is left behind and the gently undulating landscape becomes baked instead of steamed. The highway loops over low hills before adopting a pattern that becomes ever more familiar – straight for miles and then an unexpected bend. Bottle trees, with their bulbous, thick grey trunks and spindly, thinly leaved branches, herald the drier climate. Gradually, the deep-blue platform of the **Blackdown Tablelands** emerges from the horizon and, by the time you reach tiny Dingo, 150km from Rockhampton, dominates the landscape. **DINGO** is somewhere to stock up – the bus drops off here, there's a hotel, van park, fuel station and store, and a bronze monument to the town's namesake.

The Blackdown Tablelands

Floating 600m above the heat haze, the **Blackdown Tablelands**' gum forests, waterfalls and escarpments are a delight, and a scenic refuge from the dry, flat lands below. A corrugated, unsealed twenty-kilometre **access road** is signposted on the highway 11km west of Dingo, and runs flat through open scrub to the base of the range; the following ascent is steep, twisting and slippery, as "pea gravel" puts in an appearance. Views over a haze of eucalyptus woodland are generally blocked by the thicker forest at the top of the plateau, but at **Horseshoe Lookout** there's a fabulous view north and, after rain, **Two Mile Falls** rockets over the edge of the cliffs. From here the road runs past **Mimosa Creek campground**, an excellent spot shaded by massive stringybark trees, with tank water, tables, toilets, fire pits and a creek to bathe in. At night the air fills with the sharp scent of woodsmoke, and the occasional dingo howls in the distance – with a torch, you might see **greater**

gliders or the more active brushtail possum. Watch out for **currawongs** (crows) that raid unattended tables, tents and cars for anything, edible or not. Temperatures can reach 40°C on summer days, and drop below zero on winter nights.

Walks in the park include short marked trails from the campsite to **Officers Pocket**, a moist amphitheatre of ferns and palms with the facing cliffs picked out yellow and white in the late afternoon; and a circuit track along **Mimosa Creek**, past remains of cattle pens and stock huts to some beautifully clear ochre stencils of hands and weapons made by the Gungaloo people over a century ago. Blackdown's finest scenery, however, is at **Rainbow Falls**, at the end of the vehicle track 6km past the campsite. At their glorious best around dawn, the falls are surrounded by eerie gum forest; from the lookout above you can spy on birds in the rainforest below and hear the explosive thumps of rock wallabies tearing across ledges hardly big enough for a mouse. A long staircase descends into a cool world of spring-fed gardens, ending on a large shelf where the falls sprays from above into a wide pool of beautifully clear but paralysingly cold water.

Campsite bookings can be made through the National Parks office in Emerald (Ⓣ07/4982 4555), or with the special booking service (Ⓣ13 13 04). There's no public transport into the park, but call ahead and **Namoi Hills Cattle Station** (Ⓣ07/4935 9121, Ⓕ4935 9234; bunks $19, doubles ❷), set at the base of the tablelands, will pick you up at the drop-off point on the highway. They offer accommodation-and-meal packages, run tours round the station and onto the tablelands and regularly cater to the tour-bus crowd – phone ahead to check which days are booked if you want peace and quiet.

Emerald and around

The highway west of Dingo crosses the lower reaches of the **Bowen Basin coalfields** into cotton country, signalled by fluffy white tailings along the roadside. **EMERALD**, 125km along, is a misleadingly named place. This close to the Gemfield towns of Sapphire and Rubyvale, you'd think its origins could be traced to precious stones, but in fact the area was named by a surveyor who passed through after unusually heavy rains had greened the landscape. A dormitory town for nearby coal mines, and set at the junction of routes north to Mackay and south to Carnarvon Gorge, Emerald is a busy place at the heart of a soundly productive district: the rich soil supports sunflowers, citrus trees, grape vines, lychees and rock melons, all of which attract swarms of seasonal **fruit-pickers**. Despite being over a hundred years old, the town appears quite modern due to rebuilding after a series of disastrous fires in the 1950s.

Most essential services are on the Capricorn Highway, here called **Clermont Street**, where the main feature is the pristine **train station**, built in 1901 and restored in 1986. Emerald Coaches' **buses** (Ⓣ07/4982 4444) run to Longreach (twice weekly), Mackay and Rockhampton (both daily), and pull up at the east end of Clermont Street; at the west end, the **tourist office** (Mon–Sat 9am–5pm, Sun 10am–2pm; Ⓣ07/4982 4142, Ⓦwww.centralhighlandstourism.org.au) has leaflets on local attractions. **Accommodation** is plentiful, though during the April harvest or November cotton-chipping season there may be very little room available. The *Central Inn* (Ⓣ07/4982 0800; ❸), near the station on Clermont Street, has a big kitchen, simply furnished rooms, and offers good advice for either farm work or visiting the Gemfields; the *Meteor Motel* (ⓣ07/4982 1166, ⓦwww.emeraldmeteormotel.com.au; ❹) on the corner of Opal and Egerton streets has a pool and a good steak restaurant; and the *Explorers Inn Motel* (ⓣ07/4987 6222, ⓦwww.emeraldexplorersinn.com.au; ❺) is in a quiet spot at the edge of town – it's newer than the rest with comfortable, well-appointed rooms and a saltwater pool.

South to Springsure and Carnarvon Gorge

Carnarvon Gorge lies 200km or so south of Emerald via the town of **SPRINGSURE**, which is set below the dramatic orange cliffs of Mount Zamia, also known as Virgin Rock – though weathering since it was named means you can barely see the likeness of the Madonna and Child. If you wind up here for the night, the *Zamia Motel* (ⓣ07/4984 1455; ❸) has comfortable rooms and a café. It's worth pausing in the area to detour 10km southwest to **Rainworth Fort** (Mon–Wed & Fri 9am–2pm, Sat & Sun 9am–5pm; $6), to see how Aborigines put up a strong resistance to this district bein520g settled. The fort is a squat stockade of basalt blocks and corrugated iron built by settlers for protection after "**the Wills Massacre**", when on October 17, 1861, Kari Aboriginal forces stormed Cullin-la-ringo station and killed nineteen people in apparent retaliation for the slaughter of a dozen Aborigines by a local squatter. White response was savage, spurred on by vigilantes – newspapers reported that "a great massacre has been made among the blacks of the Nogoa [river district]". The fort, and newer structures of Cairdbeign School and Homestead at the same site, house a few relics of the period. Back on the Carnarvon road, it's 70km from Springsure to **Rolleston**, the last source of fuel, supplies and accommodation before Carnarvon Gorge.

The Gemfields

The country an hour west of Emerald is sparse and always hot, the scrub interrupted only by ugly cleared patches covered in rubble, from mining operations. This wasteland masks one of the world's richest **sapphire fields** and, with hard work, the chances of finding some are good – though you're unlikely to get rich. The easiest fields to reach are the **Anakie Fields**, with facilities at Anakie, Sapphire and Rubyvale; Anakie township is off the highway about 45km west of Emerald, Sapphire is 9km north of Anakie, and Rubyvale a further 8km north. Though well worked, the Anakie Fields are the best place for the newcomer to pick up tips; old hands proceed directly to the **Willows** (see p.520), 27km west of Anakie along the Capricorn Highway. There's **no transport** to the Anakie Fields, but through-buses heading west from Emerald can drop you at the Willows.

ANAKIE (a local Aboriginal word for "permanent water") has no gemfields itself, but gave its name to those at Sapphire and Rubyvale. Unusually pretty, it comprises a van park (ⓣ&ⓕ07/4985 4142; cabins ❷) with hot showers by the waterhole and a small shop (open daily), backing onto a pub, post office and store. The **Gemfields Information Centre** (daily 8am–6pm; ⓣ07/4985 4525, ⓦwww.bigsapphire.com.au) near the highway has fuel, licences, rough maps and advice.

In contrast, the country around **SAPPHIRE** looks like a war zone. You'll find a post office and houses scattered along the road and a section of Retreat Creek, where the first gems were found. *Sunrise Cabins* (ⓣ07/4985 4281; ❸) has cabins

△The Rubyvale Gem Gallery

and tent sites across the road from the medical centre, in sight of the creek. *Blue Gem Caravan Park* (Ⓣ07/4985 4162; ❷) has a store, fuel and fast food, or try a meal at *Thai & Chinese* next door. Towards Rubyvale is Pat's Gem Park (Ⓣ07/4985 4544) with a café, jewellery, craft displays and **fossicking lessons** for beginners. Forever Mine (Ⓣ07/4985 4616), a little further along Rubyvale Road, charges a seemingly steep $50 to fossick, though for this you get a tractor-scoop (about four buckets of wash) to pick through.

RUBYVALE itself has several shops, service stations and a few **exhibition mines** to look around. Tour groups tend to visit Miner's Heritage (daily 9am–5pm; $9), but equally interesting is Bobby Dazzler (daily 9am–5pm; $6), on the hill as you approach town. The ground beneath each new development here has to be mined first; outdoor tennis courts and the surfaced road were built only after years of wrangling over whether the ground had given up all its treasures. You'll hear plenty of tall stories during the annual **August Gemfest**, which includes a Wheelbarrow Race in odd-numbered years. Here, in imitation of the first pioneering miners, all-comers push their one-wheeled transport, laden with pick and shovel, up the seventeen-kilometre track from Anakie to Rubyvale, pausing only at Sapphire to take on board a bucket of dirt. Rubyvale's facilities include fuel, a general store, a **van park** with campsites and cabins (Ⓣ07/4985 4118; cabins ❷), and *Rubyvale Holiday Units* (Ⓣ07/4985 4518; ❸), which has very comfortable motel-style rooms. For **eating** there's the *New Royal Hotel*, a smart stone-and-timber building with a mighty fireplace and tasty food.

The **Willows Gemfield**, part mining camp, part township, is the most recent designated fossicking area and fair-sized gems are rumoured to have been found. The immaculate, well-shaded *Willows Caravan Park* (Ⓣ & Ⓕ07/4985 5128; cabins ❶) has wangled a liquor licence and acts as a bank agent as well as supplying fuel and digging equipment. The gemfields are just down the track from the park.

Gem mining

Gems were first discovered in 1870 near Anakie, but until Thai buyers came onto the scene a century later operations were low-key; even today there are still solo fossickers making a living from their claims, however. Formed by prehistoric volcanic actions and later dispersed along waterways and covered by sediment, the **zircons**, **rubies** and especially **sapphires** found here lie in a layer of gravel above the clay base of ancient riverbeds. This layer can be up to 15m down so gullies and dry rivers, where nature has already done some of the excavation for you, are good places to start digging.

Looking for surface gems, or **specking**, is best after rain, when a trained eye can see the stones sparkle in the mud. It's erratic but certainly easier than the alternative – **fossicking** – which requires a pick, shovel, sieve, washtub full of water and a canvas sack before even starting (this gear can be rented at all of the fields). Cut and polished, local zircons are pale yellow, sapphires pale green or yellow to deep blue, and rubies are light pink, but when they're covered in mud it's hard to tell them from gravel, which is where the washing comes in: the wet gems glitter like fragments of coloured glass.

You have to be extremely enthusiastic to spend a summer on the fields, as the mercury climbs steadily to 42°C, topsoil erodes and everything becomes coated in dust. The first rains bring floods as the sunbaked ground sheds water, and if you're here at this time you'll be treated to the sight of locals specking in the rain, dressed in Akubra hats and long Drizabone raincoats and shuffling around like mobile mushrooms. Conditions are best as soon after the wet season as possible (around May), when the ground is soft and fresh pickings have been uncovered – not surprisingly, this is also the busiest period.

If this all seems like too much hard work, try a **gem park** such as Pat's, where they've done all the digging for you and supply all the necessary gear for about $12. All you have to do is sieve the wash, flip it onto the canvas and check it for stones. There's an art to sieving and flipping, but you're pretty sure to find something, since park owners lace the wash with rejects. Gem parks will also value and cut stones for you. Another break from the business end of a pick is to pay $5, take a **mine tour**, and see if the professionals fare any better (contact Sapphire Safaris ⓣ07/4985 4388). In some ways they do – the chilled air 5m down is wonderful – but the main difference is one of scale rather than method or intent.

If you're still keen you'll need a **fossicker's licence**, available from shops and gem parks, which allows digging in areas set aside for the purpose or on no-man's-land. The $5.55 licence is valid for one month and gives you no rights at all other than to keep what you find and to camp at fossick grounds. To "stake a claim" – which gives you temporary ownership of the land to keep others away – you need a **Miner's Right** from the field officer in Emerald (Department of Minerals and Energy, Clerana Centre, Clermont St ⓣ07/4982 4011). This also carries obligations to restore the land to its original state and maintain it for two years after quitting the site.

Over the Range to Winton

Vistas from the rounded sandstone boulders at the top of the Great Dividing Range, west of the tiny railway stop of **Boguntungan**, reveal a dead-flat country beyond. Rivers flow to the Gulf of Carpentaria or towards the great dry lakes of South Australia, while unsealed roads run north to Clermont and south to Charleville.You'll notice an increase in temperature as flies appear from nowhere, tumbleweeds pile up on fences and trees never seem closer than the horizon. In terms of numbers, **sheep** are the dominant mammal in these parts, though there are some cattle and even a few people out here.The next stops on the road or rail line before Barcaldine are the townships of **Alpha**, where you can find fuel and a café or two, and **Jericho**, one of the last places in Queensland with a drive-in movie theatre, which shows films on Saturday nights.

Barcaldine, Blackall and around

The only place of any size on the way to Longreach is **BARCALDINE**, 300km west of Emerald, an unassuming grid of quiet streets belying an important niche in Australian history. It was near here during the 1885 drought that geologists first tapped Queensland's **artesian water**, revolutionizing Outback development. The town further secured its place in history during the 1891 **shearers' strike** which – though a failure itself – ultimately led to the formation of the **Australian Labor Party**. On the highway, outside the station which became the focus of the dispute, is a granite monument – sculpted to resemble the tips of a pair of shears – to shearers arrested during the strike. Right next to it, the sagging silver trunk of the **Tree of Knowledge**, a rallying point for shearers, struggles gamely to improve on its 180 years.

The town's only other sight as such is the **Australian Workers' Heritage Centre** (Mon–Sat 9am–5pm, Sun 10am–5pm; $12), unmissable underneath a yellow-and-blue marquee on Ash Street. With an expanding collection of displays concentrating on the history of the workers' movement after the shearers' strike, as well as videos, artefacts and plenty of sepia-tinted photos covering themes including Outback women and Aboriginal stockmen, the museum acts as a useful counterpart to Longreach's Stockman's Hall of Fame. On the highway, the **tourist office** (Mon–Fri 8.30am–4.30pm; ⓣ07/4651 1724) will direct you to other attractions such as **Mad Mick's Funny Farm** (open most mornings April–Sept, or by arrangement; adults $10, children $7; ⓣ07/4651 1172), which has been restored to its early twentieth-century condition and is inhabited by friendly, hand-reared animals; admission includes a ride in a Model-T Ford, and tea and damper. For a closer look at Outback caves, waterholes and **Aboriginal art** – much of it on private property – with a tall tale or two thrown in, contact Artesian Country Tours (ⓣ07/4651 2211, ⓦwww.artesiancountrytours.com.au); their day-long "Aramac & Graceville" tour (Wed & Sat; $145 including all transport, lunch and tea) is highly recommended.

Both Emerald Coaches and Greyhound **buses** stop in Barcaldine; banks and other **services** are mostly on Box Street, which runs south off the highway. **Accommodation** options include the *Ironbark Inn* (ⓣ07/4651 2311; ❸), an "Outback-style" motel with attached steakhouse, *Barcaldine Motel* (ⓣ07/4651 1244; ❸) and *Barcaldine Tourist Park* (ⓣ07/4651 6066; camping $12, cabins ❷), all on Box Street. Barcaldine has a disproportionate number of **bars**, probably due to the hot summers – the *Artesian*, *Commercial* and *Union* hotels are three highway establishments all offering cold drinks and pub meals.

Blackall and Idalia National Park

One hour south of Barcaldine on the Landsborough Highway, a sign at **BLACKALL** welcomes you to Merino Country. It was near here in 1892 that **Jackie Howe** fleeced 321 sheep in under eight hours using hand shears, a still-unbroken record. If you want to **visit a sheep station** to see modern shearers in action, it can be arranged by the tourist office (daily 9am–noon & 1–5pm; ⓣ07/4657 4637), just off Shamrock Street on Short Street. There's more on the industry at the steam-driven **woolscour** (the plant where the freshly sheared fleeces are vigorously washed and cleaned), built in 1908 and in operation for seventy years; it has been restored recently and has guides on hand to show you around (daily 8am–4pm; $9.90). You could also track down the famous **black stump**, a surveying point used in pinpointing Queensland's borders in the nineteenth century and now the butt of many jokes; the original stump has been replaced by a more interesting fossilized one. Otherwise, pass time at the new **artesian spa** (Mon–Fri 6–10am & 2.30–6pm, Sat & Sun 11–6pm; $1.50), a large pool along the line of Mitchell's, at the town's Aquatic Centre on Salvia Street.

The town sits on the banks of the often dry (but occasionally five-metre-deep) Barcoo River. Two-hundred-metre-long **Shamrock Street**, shaded by palms and bottle trees, is the main road on which you'll find banks, supplies and a few places **to eat** – if you're neatly dressed you can savour good food at the *Blackall Club*. The most central **places to stay** are the smart *Acacia Motor Inn* (☎07/4657 6022; ❹), on Shamrock Street, or at *Blackall Caravan Park* (☎07/4657 4816; camping $15, cabins ❷) on Hart Lane, where you can yarn with other travellers around a huge campfire and be fed communal pot roasts, billy tea and damper for an extra fee. Greyhound **buses** heading to Brisbane stop in town; tickets are available from Blackall Travel (☎07/4657 4422).

Around 155km southwest of Blackall, **Idalia National Park** preserves one of Queensland's last wild groups of **yellow-footed rock wallabies**, fantastically pretty animals with long, ringed tails (though these can be seen more easily at Charleville, if you're heading that way). You can generally get into the park in a normal vehicle with care, but for current **access details** contact the ranger on ☎07/4657 5033, or check out Ⓦwww.epa.qld.gov.au.

Longreach

LONGREACH, 110km west of Barcaldine and right on the Tropic of Capricorn, is different from other western towns – it's doing more than surviving. Today this is mainly due to the **Stockman's Hall of Fame**, an ambitious museum which pulls in busloads of tourists, but the town was also one of the first to realize the potential of tapping Queensland's artesian water reserves for stock farming, and was the original headquarters of **Qantas**.

On the highway 2km north of the town centre, the **Stockman's Hall of Fame** (daily 9am–5pm; $22.50; Ⓦwww.outbackheritage.com.au) is a masterpiece not just in architectural design – it's a blend of aircraft hangar and cathedral – but in being an encyclopedia of the Outback right in its heart. The display unashamedly romances the Outback through videos, slide shows, photographs and exhibits, but this isn't just another local museum where anything more than five years old is shown for its own sake. History starts in the Dreamtime and moves on to early explorers and pioneers (including a large

Qantas

There's always been contention between Longreach and Winton as to which was the birthplace of **Qantas** (the Queensland and Northern Territories Aerial Service). Though the company officially formed at Winton, the first joy-flights and taxi service actually flew from Longreach in 1921, pioneered by Hudson Fysh and Paul McGinness. Their idea – that an airline could play an important role by carrying mail and passengers, dropping supplies to remote districts and providing an emergency link into the Outback – inspired other projects such as the Flying Doctor Service. Though the company's headquarters moved to Brisbane in 1930, Qantas maintained their offices at Longreach until after World War II – during the war US Flying Fortresses were stationed here – by which time both the company and its planes had outgrown the town.

section on women in the Outback), before ending with personal accounts of life in the bush. Among more day-to-day features are some offbeat selections; if you thought barbed wire was just something to get stuck on, then check out the collection here, which has over a hundred types from the old hook design to modern razor wire. You'd be hard pushed not to find something of interest in the museum, be it boxing kangaroos, rodeos, bark huts or tall stories.

Adjacent to the Hall of Fame is the **Qantas Founders Outback Museum** (daily 9am–5pm; museum $18, 747 tour $15, combined ticket $30; Ⓦwww.qfom.com.au), whose prized possession is a decommissioned Qantas jumbo jet that can be viewed on a guided tour (booking advisable). An original 1922 hangar forms part of the exhibition, which also includes a beautiful collection of classic advertising posters.

Practicalities

Longreach is a more active version of Barcaldine, with plenty of spruce old buildings and a further abundance of watering holes. The main drag is south off the highway along **Eagle Street**, where you'll find hotels, cafés, banks, a cinema and a well-stocked supermarket. The **airport** is off the highway between town and the Hall of Fame, while **trains** terminate at the station at the junction of Galah Street and the highway. Greyhound and Emerald Coaches **buses** set down on Eagle Street at Longreach Outback Travel Centre (Ⓣ07/4658 1776, Ⓦwww.lotc.com.au), which can arrange tickets for onward travel, as well as **tours** of nearby sheep stations ($42), and waterway cruises on a paddle-boat ($46). The **tourist office** (April–Oct Mon–Fri 9am–5pm, Sat & Sun 9am–1pm; Nov–March Mon–Fri 9am–4.30pm, Sat & Sun 9am–noon; Ⓣ07/4658 3555) is in a replica of Qantas's original office, on the corner of Eagle and Duck streets opposite the post office.

A good **campsite** is *Gunnadoo Van Park* (Ⓣ07/4658 1781; camping $20, cabins ❶), on Thrush Road looking across to the Hall of Fame. Other **accommodation** includes the friendly B&B *Hallview Lodge*, 81 Wompoo St (Ⓣ07/4658 3777; ❸); the motel-style *Albert Park Motor Inn* on Hudson Fysh Drive (Ⓣ07/4658 2411; ❹); and *Longreach Motor Inn* on Galah Street (Ⓣ07/4658 2322; ❹). For meals, the *Longreach RSL Club* on Duck Street welcomes visitors, and the motels also have **restaurants**. You can try the *Lyceum* hotel for counter food, or *Starlight's Hideout Tavern* for meals and nightlife.

Winton and around

At the far end of a mind-numbingly bland 173-kilometre-long run northwest from Longreach across the Mitchell Plains, **WINTON** is a real frontier town, and an excellent base for exploring this corner of the Outback. Dust devils blow tumbleweeds down the streets, and the main change over the last fifty years is that 4WDs have superseded the horse as a means of getting around. As Queensland's largest cattle-trucking depot, Winton has a constant stream of roadtrains rumbling through it, and conversations in hotel bars tend to revolve around problems of stock management. Winton has its share of history too: Qantas was founded here in 1920 and **Waltzing Matilda**, that evergreen ballad, premiered at the *North Gregory Hotel*. The surrounding countryside is an eerie world of windswept plains and eroded **jump-ups** – flat-topped hills layered in orange, grey and red dust – complete with **opal deposits** at Opalton and a stunning set of **dinosaur footprints** at Lark Quarry.

Waltzing Matilda

The first public performance of "Banjo" Paterson's ballad **Waltzing Matilda** was held in April 1895 at Winton's *North Gregory Hotel*, and has stirred up gossip and speculation ever since. Legend has it that Christina MacPherson told Paterson the tale of a swagman's brush with the law at the Combo Waterhole, near Kynuna, while the poet was staying with her family at nearby Dagwood Station. Christina wrote the music to the ballad, a collaboration which so incensed Paterson's fiancée, Sarah Riley, that she broke off their engagement. While a straightforward "translation" of the poem is easy enough – "Waltzing Matilda" was contemporary slang for tramping (carrying a bedroll or swag from place to place), "jumbuck" for a sheep, and "squatters" refers to landowners – there is some contention as to what the poem actually describes. The most obvious interpretation is of a poor tramp, hounded to death by the law, but first drafts of the poem suggest that Paterson – generally known as a romantic rather than a social commentator – originally wrote the piece about the arrest of a union leader during the shearers' strike, and later toned it down. Either version would account for the popularity of the poem, which was once proposed as the national anthem – Australians readily identify with an underdog who dares to confront the system.

Winton's central drag is **Elderslie Street**, where you'll find banks, a post office and service stations. If there's a film on, treat yourself to a session in the **open-air cinema**, complete with canvas seats and original projector, at the corner of Elderslie and Cobb streets; the café here stays open until after dark. A few doors down, next to the *North Gregory Hotel*, the immense wooden **Corfield & Fitzmaurice building** (Mon–Fri 9am–5pm, Sat 9am–12.30pm; $4) opened as a store in 1916 and now houses a vast collection of rocks and fossils from around the world, along with a life-size diorama of the Lark Quarry dinosaurs – garbage bins around town are also shaped as dinosaur feet.

Further down Elderslie Street, opposite a tepid swimming pool and bronze statue of the jolly swagman, the **Waltzing Matilda Centre** (daily 8.30am–5pm; $17.50; ⓣ07/4657 1466, ⓦwww.matildacentre.com.au) has some unusual items, including an indoor billabong, a fine display of Aboriginal artefacts including an entire tree with a boomerang half-carved out of its trunk, and a bottle collection covering everything from poisons to schnapps. The centre also doubles as a **tourist office** and sorts out **tours** to local sights – check with them too about road conditions before visiting Opalton or Lark Quarry. For some really ludicrous fun, the **Australian Crayfish Derby**, part of the Outback Festival held in September in odd-numbered years, has to be worth a look; the owner of the winning crustacean nets $1500, and the runner-up gets to eat all the competitors. Every April the **Waltzing Matilda Festival** involves a rodeo and arts events, attracting bush poets to compete with "Banjo" Paterson.

Winton's **accommodation** prospects include the *Matilda Country Tourist Park* (ⓣ07/4657 1607; camping $15, cabins ❷) on Chirnside Street, about 700km from Elderslie Street where the Landsborough Highway kinks into town; the neat and trim *Banjo Holiday Units* (ⓣ07/4657 1213; ❸) on nearby Manuka Street; and the *North Gregory Hotel* (ⓣ07/4657 1375; hotel rooms ❷, motel rooms ❸), which has en-suite and shared bathrooms. The *North Gregory* is also one of the best places **to eat** in town, with the early-opening *Twilight Café* opposite. Alternatively, **Carisbrooke Station**, 85km southwest of Winton in the middle of some rugged scenery (ⓣ07/4657 3885, ⓦwww.carisbrooketours.com.au; ❸), offers beds and **tours**, including one out to Lark Quarry.

Moving on, Greyhound **buses** depart from the Matilda Centre once daily in each direction towards Mount Isa and Brisbane.

Opalton

South of Winton, a 120-kilometre-long unsealed road runs south down through the beautifully stark jump-ups and spinifex scrub to **OPALTON**, a multicultural shantytown where Yugoslav, Czech and Australian miners are reworking century-old **opal diggings** with Chinese and Korean finance. You need to be entirely self-sufficient here, as the only modern feature is a solar-powered telephone and there isn't any drinking water. During the summer there won't be any miners either – hotels in Winton are easily preferable to Opalton's 40°C-plus temperatures. Fossicking zones have been established where you can pick over old tailings for scraps. There is a **camping** and caravan area, washing water, and a small **store** that's open most days from 10am to 2pm – it doesn't sell fuel, however.

Lark Quarry

It takes about two hours to drive the 120km southwest on the Jundah Road from Winton to **Lark Quarry**, dodging kamikaze kangaroos and patches of bulldust. Once you've arrived there's no doubt that this is the rough heart of the Outback, and nor is it surprising to find **dinosaur** remains here: the place looks prehistoric, swarming with flies and surrounded by stubby hills where stunted trees and tufts of grass tussle with rocks for space. A hundred million years ago this was a shrinking waterhole across which a carnivorous dinosaur chased a group of various turkey-sized herbivores through the mud to a rockface where it caught and killed one as the others fled back past it. Over **three thousand footprints** have been found recording these few seconds of action, excavated in the 1970s and now protected by an awning and walkway around them maintained by the National Parks service. Indentations left by small, amazingly sharp, three-clawed feet – some very light as the prey panicked and ran on tiptoe – stream in all directions, while those left by the larger predator go only one way. Paths lead around to other, buried tracks where the chase ended.

Beyond Winton

From Winton, it's 340km northwest to Cloncurry (covered by the Greyhound bus). Some 165km along, the **Combo Waterhole** is a shaded, muddy soak just off the road which provided the inspiration for Banjo Paterson's classic ballad *Waltzing Matilda*. A shade further on, **KYNUNA's** low-slung *Blue Heeler Hotel* (☎07/4746 8650; ❸) is also worth a stop, not least for its ice-cold beer, as is the *Walkabout Creek Hotel* at **McKINLAY**, 75km past Kynuna, which you might recognize as the rowdy Outback pub in the film *Crocodile Dundee*.

West of Winton – there's no bus – it's 367km to Boulia through more stark landscape, with fuel available every 150km and the chance to see the enigmatic **Min Min Light**, an unexplained glowing oval reputedly seen bobbing around the bush at night. **BOULIA**'s services include **rooms** at the *Australian Hotel* (☎07/4746 3144; ❸), a van park, store and roadhouse; if you need a reason to visit, make it the **July camel races**, when the town gets lively and inordinate quantities of beer are consumed. At quieter times of the year, drop in to the **Min Min Encounter Centre** (Mon–Fri 8.30am–5pm, Sat & Sun 9am–5pm; $12), a cross between a museum and sound-and-light show. Boulia's **tourist office** (daily 8.30am–6pm; ☎07/4746 3386) is here too, along with *Encounter's Café*, which claims to serve the Outback's best cappuccino – there's certainly no competition for a good many miles around.

Moving on from Boulia, Mount Isa is 300km north on bitumen, and Birdsville is 400km south on a mostly reasonable road. If you're really enjoying the ride, Alice Springs is 800km west on the Donohue and Plenty "highways" – a long stretch of dust and gravel. There's fuel every 250km or so, and track conditions improve once you're over the border into the NT.

Townsville to the Territory

All the major settlements along the thousand-kilometre stretch between Townsville and the Northern Territory border are **mining** towns, spaced so far apart that precise names are redundant: **Mount Isa** becomes "the Isa", **Cloncurry** "the Curry", and **Charters Towers** "the Towers", as if nowhere else existed. It's a shame that most people see this vast area as something to be crossed as quickly as possible, because even if time is limited and you're relying on public transport, Charters Towers' century-old feel and Mount Isa's strange setting are worth a stopover. With the freedom of your own vehicle, there's untramped bush at **Porcupine Gorge**, north of Hughenden in the heart of **dinosaur country**, and the spectacular oasis of **Lawn Hill Gorge**, all a lifetime away from the coast's often banal spirit. The main route through into the Territory is along the Flinders and Barkly highways – covered daily by Greyhound **buses** – and there's also the twice-weekly Inlander **train** between Townsville and Mount Isa.

Gold country

There's little scenic variation over the two-hour journey from the coast to the heights of the inland range at the community of **Mingela**, but dry scrub at the top once covered seams of ore which had the streets of both **Charters Towers** and **Ravenswood** bustling with lucky-strike miners. Those times are long gone – though gold is still extracted from old tailings or sporadically panned from the creek beds – and the towns have survived at opposite extremes: connected by road and rail to Townsville, Charters Towers became a busy rural centre, while Ravenswood, half an hour south of Mingela, was just too far off the track and wasted to a shadow. Detours (ⓣ07/4728 5311) run **day-trips** from Townsville to one or the other for about $115.

Ravenswood

As the wind blows dust and dried grass around the streets between mine shafts and lonely old buildings, **RAVENSWOOD** fulfils ideas of what a ghost town should look like. Gold was discovered here in 1868 and within two years there were solid brick houses, a frenetic atmosphere and seven hundred miners on Elphinstone Creek working seams of gold, silver and lead ore. As one historian put it, "Every building on the main street was either a public house and dance house or a public house and general store."

The main attraction is to wander between the restored buildings, trying to imagine how the others must have looked. The curator of the **Court House Museum** (daily except Tues 10am–3pm; $2; ⓣ07/4770 2047 to book) gives entertaining tours of the museum, town and – with sufficient notice – current mining efforts. Built in 1879, the **post office** today doubles as the town's store and fuel supply. Unsurprisingly, the two most complete survivals are **hotels**, though how they both keep going with a scattered population of barely three hundred souls is anybody's guess. You'll probably end up in one as the day heats up, for a drink or a **meal**; the *Railway* (ⓣ07/4770 2144; ❷) seems to be the more popular, but though the *Imperial* (ⓣ07/4770 2131; ❷) looks the worse for wear, it has original wood panelling, mirrors and swing doors on the bar.

Charters Towers and around

Once Queensland's second-largest city, and often referred to in its heyday simply as "the World", **CHARTERS TOWERS** is a showcase of colonial-era architecture. An Aboriginal boy named **Jupiter Mosman** found gold here in 1871 and within twelve months three thousand prospectors had stripped the landscape of trees and covered it with shafts, chimneys and crushing mills. At first, little money was reinvested – the **cemetery** is a sad record of cholera and typhoid outbreaks from poor sanitation – but by 1900, despite diminishing returns, Charters Towers had become a prosperous centre. There's been minimal change since then and the population, now mainly sustained by cattle farming, has shrunk to about a third of what it was in its prime. Good times to visit are for the May Day weekend **Country Music Festival**, and the Easter **Rodeo**.

The town itself is worth about an hour of your time, with plenty of spruce old buildings along Gill and Mosman streets, including the pink-and-white headquarters of the *Northern Miner*, one of Queensland's oldest surviving

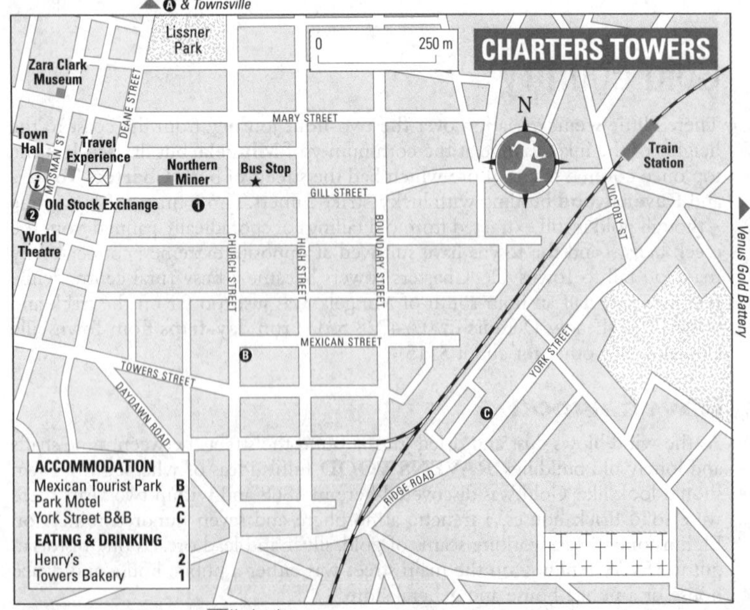

newspapers on Gill Street, the classical elegance of the post office and the **World Theatre**, and the shaded country arcades outside the stores. The courtyard and glass roof at the former **Stock Exchange** and **Assayer's Office** now front some quiet shops, while the adjacent, solid facade of the **town hall** betrays its original purpose as a bank, which stored gold bars smelted locally. Just down Mosman Street is the **Zara Clark Museum** (daily 10am–3pm; $4.40), housing an absorbing jumble of everything from old wagons to a set of silver tongs for eating frogs' legs. Further along the road there's plenty of shade under giant fig trees at **Lissner Park**, whose Boer War memorial recalls stories of **Breaker Morant**, a local soldier executed by the British after shooting a prisoner.

The **Venus Gold Battery** (daily 9.30am–3.30pm; guided tours every half-hour; $12), 4km out of town down Gill Street, is a fascinating illustration of the monumental efforts needed to separate gold from rock. Abandoned in 1972 after a century of operations, the battery is a huge, gloomy temple to the past, its machinery lying silent and piecemeal around the place. The intention is to restore it to full working order, presumably without recreating the actual conditions – it was a hideous place, a sweatbox filled with noxious mercury fumes and the noise of huge hammers smashing chucks of ore into a manageable size.

Practicalities

All essential services are along Gill and Mosman streets. **Trains** stop at the eastern end of Gill Street and **buses** halfway along by the Woolworths service station – **tickets** for either can be arranged through Travel Experience, 13 Gill St (Ⓣ07/4787 2622). The helpful tourist office at 74 Mosman St (daily 9am–5pm; Ⓣ07/4752 0314) has rough maps and advice on gold-panning tours in the area. For **accommodation**, the *Mexican Tourist Park* (Ⓣ07/4787 1161; camping $15, on-site vans and cabins ③), at the corner of Church and Mexican streets on the site of the once-busy Mexican Mine, is shaded and central. In tune with the local atmosphere is *York Street B&B* at 58 York St (Ⓣ07/4787 1028; dorms $17, doubles ③), a nicely restored, old timber building with wide verandas and a pool. The *Park Motel* (Ⓣ07/4787 1022; ④), on the corner of Mosman and Deane streets, is also central and comfortable. For **food**, the motel does cheap meals, while *Towers Bakery* at 114 Gill St has award-winning meat pies, and *Henry's Café and Restaurant*, next to the World Theatre on Mosman, is a pricey place with an eclectic, modern Australian menu.

Dinosaur country

HUGHENDEN, 245km west of Charters Towers along the highway, looks big compared with some of the places you pass on the way there. A dozen wide streets, a supermarket, a couple of hotels and banks all conspire to make you feel that you've arrived somewhere. There are two places to spend time – the **swimming pool** on Resolution Street and the **Dinosaur Museum and information centre** (daily 9am–5pm; $3; Ⓣ07/4741 1021) on Gray Street. The display at the latter focuses on the swamp-dwelling **Muttaburrasaurus**, bones of which were found south of town in 1963 and assembled into a ten-metre-long skeleton. Though this family of dinosaurs was formerly believed to be vegetarian, *Muttaburrasaurus*' needle-like teeth have prompted a rethink about their possible diet. For **accommodation**, *Wrights Motel* (Ⓣ07/4741 1677, Ⓕ07/4741 1170; ③) opposite the museum has reasonably priced rooms and a restaurant, and the *Rest Easi Motel* (Ⓣ & Ⓕ07/4741 1633; camping $15, rooms ③), on the Flinders Highway to the west of the town centre, is quiet and also has camping facilities. *Pete's Country Café*, before the tracks on the other side of town, has good **burgers** and doubles as the **bus stop**, while *FJ Holden's Café* at 55 Brodie St is a 1950s-style diner complete with gingham tablecloths and Elvis memorabilia. Routes head out of Hughenden in all directions – aside from the highway west, there's the road north to Porcupine Gorge, or long stretches south to Winton or Longreach. You should fuel up before leaving town.

Porcupine Gorge is 70km north of Hughenden along the partially surfaced Kennedy Developmental Road, accessible only if you have your own vehicle (you can usually get by without a 4WD). A deep gash, completely invisible among the drab brown scrub until you're virtually in it, it's best seen at the start of the dry season (May–July) before the **Flinders River** stops flowing, when good swimming holes, beautifully coloured cliffs, flowering bottlebrush and banksia trees reward the effort of getting here. A National Parks **campsite** (book on ⓣ13 13 04 or ⓦwww.epa.qld.gov.au) at the top of the gorge has limited cold water, toilets and nothing else. Look for wallabies on the walk into the gorge, which leads down steps from the campsite and becomes an increasingly steep, rough path carpeted in loose stones. The white riverbed has been moulded by water into soft, elongated forms, curving into a pool below the orange, yellow and white bands of **Pyramid Rock**. This is the bush at its best – sandstone glowing in the afternoon sun against a deep-blue sky, with animal calls echoing along the gorge as the shadow of the gorge wall creeps over distant woods.

Richmond

More of the regional fossil record is on show 115km west of Hughenden along the highway at **RICHMOND**, whose **Marine Fossil Museum** and **information centre** (daily 8.30am–4.45pm; $10; ⓣ07/4741 3429) displays the petrified remains of hundred-million-year-old fish, long-necked elasmosaurs, and models of a **kronosaur** excavated in the 1920s by a team from Harvard University and now on show in the USA. Pride of the collection are a complete skeleton of a seal-like **pliosaur** – the most intact vertebrate fossil ever found in Australia – and the **minmi ankylosaur**, with its armour-plated hide.

Not many people hang around in Richmond, though it's by no means an unpleasant place – just very small. A roadside park makes a good spot to stretch your legs, with an original Cobb & Co. coach and views out across the Flinders River. There's **accommodation** at the *Richmond Lake View Caravan Park* (ⓣ07/4741 3772; camping $12, bunkhouse and cabins ❷), or at *Ammonite Inn Motel*, 88 Goldring St (ⓣ07/4741 3932, ⓕ4741 3934; ❹). The museum's **café** is the only one in town – otherwise head to the old wooden *Federal Palace Hotel* or one of the service stations for a feed.

Cloncurry and around

CLONCURRY, 280km west of Richmond, is caught between two landscapes, where the flat eastern plains rise to a rough and rocky plateau. Besides being the place where Australia's **highest temperature** (53.1°C) was recorded, Cloncurry offers glimpses into the **mining history** that permeates the whole stretch west to larger Mount Isa. Copper was discovered here in 1867 but as the town lacked a rail link to the coast until 1908, profits were eroded by the necessity of transporting the ore by camel to Normanton, and Cloncurry, as a result, never reflected the quality of its mines. Even the current resurgence in mining hasn't had much effect, besides raising motel rates; miners are flown in from the coast to the mines, work their two-week shifts at their self-contained mine sites, then head home again, all without spending more than a couple of hours in the town itself.

Buildings at the **Mary Kathleen Memorial Park Museum** (Mon–Fri 7am–4pm, Sat & Sun 9am–3pm; $7.50; ⓣ07/4742 1361) were salvaged from Mary Kathleen, a short-lived uranium mining town between Cloncurry and Mount Isa. The museum is primarily of geological interest, a comprehensive catalogue of local ores, fossils and gemstones arranged in long cases, though Aboriginal tools and Burke's water bottle add some historical depth. The park also acts as an **information centre**, with good tips on where to go bush-bashing for gemstones in the area.

A positive side to Cloncurry's isolation is that it inspired the formation of the **Royal Flying Doctor Service**. Over on the corner of King and Daintree streets, **John Flynn Place** (Mon–Fri 8am–4.30pm, closed Dec–Feb; $8.50) is a monument to the man who pioneered the use of radio and plane to provide a "mantle of safety over the Outback". The exhibition explains how ideas progressed with technology, from pedal-powered radios to assistance from the young Qantas, resulting in the opening of the first Flying Doctor base in Cloncurry in 1928. A very different aspect of Cloncurry's past is also evident in the two foreign **cemeteries** on the outskirts of town. To the south of the highway, before you cross the creek on the way to Mount Isa, a hundred overgrown plots recall a brief nineteenth-century goldrush when the harsh conditions took a terrible toll on **Chinese** prospectors. Equally neglected are the unnamed graves of **Afghanis** at the north end of Henry Street, all aligned with Mecca. Afghanis were vital to Cloncurry's survival before the coming of the railway, organizing camel trains which carried the ore to Normanton whence it was shipped to Europe – a role now largely forgotten.

Practicalities

The highway runs through town as **McIlwraith Street** in the east, and **Ramsay Street** in the west. Most services – the usual banks, supermarket, half-dozen bars and a post office – are along Ramsay or the grid of streets immediately north. Cloncurry's **train station** is a couple of kilometres southeast of the centre, while **buses** drop off along Ramsay – you can buy **tickets** for either at Cloncurry Agencies, 45 Ramsay St (ⓣ07/4742 1107). The best **campsite**, *Gilbert Park Tourist Village* (ⓣ07/4742 2300; camping $15, cabins ❸), is on the eastern edge of town off McIlwraith and has decent cabins. Otherwise, seek **accommodation** at the central *Wagon Wheel Motel* (ⓣ07/4742 1866; ❸) on Ramsay Street, founded in 1867 with both older pub rooms and a new motel block, or the trendily eco-conscious *Gidgee Inn* (ⓣ07/4742 1599, ⓦwww.gidgeeinn.com.au; ❺) on McIlwraith Street, built from recycled timber and rammed earth. The latter also has a good **restaurant**, specializing in steak and seafood. The bars have counter meals, and *Cuppa's*, a café on Ramsay Street, is cool, spacious, and serves up strong coffee and good-value food. For **entertainment**, there's an open-air cinema one block north of Ramsay on Scarr Street, which screens films once or twice a week.

Moving on, the highway, buses and trains continue west for 118km to Mount Isa, while the Burke Developmental Road heads 380km north past forests of anthills and kapok trees to Normanton, via the one-pub settlement of **Quamby** (which also has races and an underwear-throwing competition in May), and the **Burke and Wills Roadhouse**. Aside from being a welcome break in the journey, with fuel pumps, a bar and canteen selling drinks, sandwiches and burgers, the roadhouse also marks the turning west on a sealed road to Gregory Downs, gateway to the oasis of Lawn Hill Gorge.

Onwards to Mount Isa: Mary Kathleen

The rough country between Cloncurry and Mount Isa is evidence of ancient upheavals which shattered the landscape and created the region's extensive mineral deposits. While the highway continues safely to Mount Isa past the **Burke and Wills monument** and the Kalkadoon/Mitakoodi **tribal boundary** at Corella Creek, forays into the bush will uncover remains of less fortunate mining settlements. About halfway to Mount Isa, a short and steadily crumbling road north to **MARY KATHLEEN** is marked with a small plaque. By all accounts, **uranium** was found here by accident when a car broke down; while waiting for help the driver and his friends tried fossicking and found ore. The two-street town was built in 1956 and completely dismantled in 1982 when export restrictions halted mining. Since then, once-manicured lawns have run riot, and an occasional bougainvillea and an unkempt row of casuarinas tangling along the access road are the only signs that there were gardens here – in a few years it will all have gone. About a kilometre past the old town the road becomes a dirt track and splits; a kilometre along the right fork a bumpy uphill track leads to the terraces of the open-cast mine, now reminiscent of a flooded Greek amphitheatre. On a cloudy day you can be sure that the alarming blue-green colour of the water is not simply a reflection of the sky. Locals maintain it's safe to swim here though, and some even claim health benefits.

Mount Isa and around

As the only place of consequence for 700km in any direction, the ugly smoke-stacks, concrete paving and sterile hills at **MOUNT ISA** assume oasis-like qualities on arrival. Though the novelty might have worn off by the time you've had a cold drink in an air-conditioned bar, the city has a few points to savour before heading on. There's evidence of the area's **Aboriginal heritage**, a couple of unusual **museums**, tours of the local mines, Australia's **largest rodeo** every August and simply the fascinating situation and the community it has fostered.

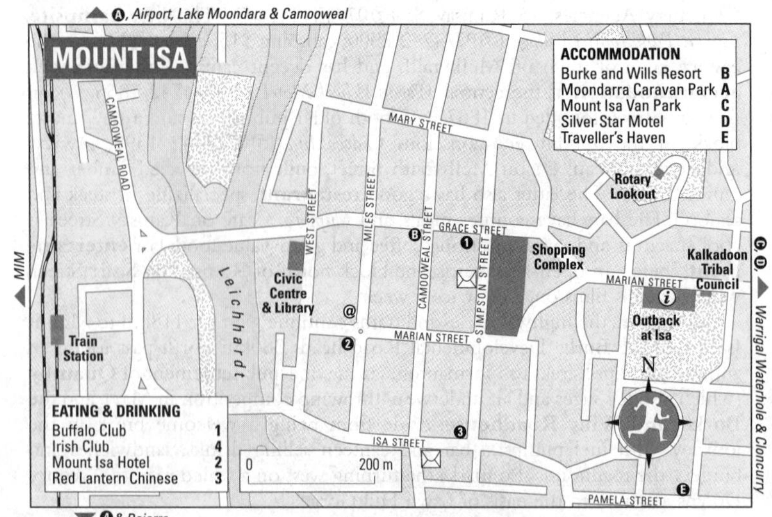

△ Mount Isa Rodeo

The largest city in the world in terms of surface area – its administrative boundaries stretch halfway to Cloncurry – Mount Isa sits astride a wealth of zinc, silver, lead and copper, and owes its existence to these reserves and the need for a staging post for interstate travellers. The city's founding father was **John Miles**, who discovered ore in 1923, established **Mount Isa Mines** (MIM) the next year and began commercial mining in 1925. Originally a settlement of canvas and scrap wood, the city enjoyed a forty-year boom under the hegemony of MIM, until the late 1980s saw a decline in profits. Developments such as the Hilton Mine, north of the city, keep business ticking over, but mines further afield – as at Cloncurry – tend to be staffed by workers who live on the east coast and fly in for their shifts, staying on site until they take their money home, completely bypassing the Isa.

Arrival and information

With its two huge chimneys illuminated at night – the Rotary lookout on Hilary Street gives a good view – **MIM** is the city's major landmark, west of the often dry **Leichhardt River**. The Barkly Highway runs through town as Marian and Grace streets, with the city centre immediately south of the latter between Simpson and West streets; the highway then crosses the river and joins the Camooweal road in front of MIM. **Buses** pull in at the **Outback at Isa** Centre on central Marian Street; **trains** terminate at the station in front of MIM; and the **airport** is 7km to the north, where taxis meet arrivals. The excellent **tourist office** is located in the Outback At Isa complex (daily 8.30am–5pm; ⓣ07/4749 1555, ⓦwww.outbackatisa.com.au) and can make all tour bookings.

Accommodation

There's a good range of accommodation scattered all over Mount Isa, catering to most budgets.

Burke and Wills Resort ⓣ07/4743 8000. Upmarket and central motel on the corner of Grace and Camooweal streets. ❺

Moondarra Caravan Park ⓣ07/4743 9780. Four kilometres north of the city off Camooweal Rd, and close to a creek that draws plenty of local birdlife. The cabins are nothing special, but the shady, picturesque location compensates. Camping $15, cabins ❷

Mount Isa Van Park ⓣ07/4743 3252, ⓦwww.mtisacaravanpark.com.au. Situated on the eastern side of town just off Marian St, this is a well-kept campsite with pretty white-and-red cabins and a children's play area. Camping $19, cabins ❸

Silver Star Motel ⓣ07/4743 3466. East of centre, on the corner of Marian St and Doughan Terrace. Good facilities and a tree-lined pool, a welcome feature in this climate. ❹

Traveller's Haven ⓣ07/4743 0313, ⓦwww.users.bigpond.net.au/travellershaven. Hostel on the corner of Spence and Pamela streets – it's cool, quiet, has a pool and staff can pick you up from the train and bus stations. Dorms $22, doubles ❷

The City

All the city's main attractions are handily grouped together in the **Outback At Isa Centre** (above for opening hours). The history of the region is explored in the **Isa Experience Gallery** ($10): the ground floor consists of a series of informative multimedia displays examining early prehistoric life, indigenous culture and the development of Mount Isa as a centre of mining activity; while the theatre on the upper level shows a surprisingly moving film focusing on the personalities who helped to build the city's multinational community over the years. The adjacent **Riversleigh Fossils Centre** ($10) gives an excellent insight into how paleontologists working at the Riversleigh Fossil Site (see p.537) have discovered an incredible record of the marsupial and mammalian evolution and environmental change that occurred between ten thousand and twenty million years ago. Imaginative, life-sized dioramas and an informative video recreate the region at a time when it was a lush wetland,

MIM

The **Mount Isa Mines** complex is a land of trundling yellow mine-trucks, mountains of slag, intense activity and miles of noisy vibrating pipelines. Copper, silver, lead and zinc deposits are mined almost 2km down by a workforce of 1200; the rock is roughly crushed and hoisted to the surface before undergoing a second crushing, grinding and washing in flotation tanks, to separate ore from waste. Zinc is sold as it is, copper is smelted into ingots and transported to Townsville for refining, while four-ton ingots of lead and silver mix are sent to England for the few ounces of silver to be separated. **Power** for the mines and the entire region comes from MIM's own plant, and any surplus is sold to the state grid.

populated by ancestral platypus and koalas, giant snakes and emus, carnivorous kangaroos and the enigmatic "thingadonta". You can also visit the **laboratory** (guided tours daily at 10am & 1pm) out the back, where fossils are being prepared by soaking boulders collected at Riversleigh in weak acid, dissolving the rock but leaving bones, beaks and teeth intact.

Mount Isa's working mines are no longer accessible to the general public. However, you can still get a fairly vivid taste of what the mines are like by taking the **Hard Times Underground Mine Tour** ($45; not suitable for children under 7). Accompanied by an actual miner, visitors are equipped with full protective gear, including hard-helmet and torch, before descending into the 1.2km of tunnels that make up the specially constructed mine.

Eating and drinking

Mount Isa boasts inhabitants of over fifty nationalities, many of whom have their own **clubs** with **restaurants** and **bars**. The best is probably the central and flashy *Buffalo Club*, on the corner of Grace and Simpson streets. Known to one and all as "The Buffs", it hosts an **Oktoberfest** and has a comfy, heavily air-conditioned bar, and a bistro serving the best steaks in town. The other mainstay, the *Irish Club* on Buckley Avenue, 2km south of the centre, gets targeted for weekend-night bands and inexpensive food; both places offer **courtesy buses** to and from accommodation. Hotels are the alternatives – the bulky *Mount Isa Hotel*, on the corner of Marian and Miles streets, sets the standard for cheap lunch-time specials, or try the *Red Lantern Chinese*, on the corner of Simpson and Isa streets.

Listings

Airlines Qantas (☎ 13 13 13) fly daily to Brisbane; Macair (🌐 www.macair.com.au) fly daily to Brisbane and Townsville as well as operating services to numerous towns in the region.
Bus Greyhound Australia (☎ 13 14 99, 🌐 www.greyhound.com.au) cover routes to Townsville, Tennant Creek and Brisbane. The tourist office can make bookings.
Car rental Avis, Marian St (and at the airport) ☎ 07/4743 3733; Four Wheel Drive Hire Service, Simpson St (☎ 07/4743 3962, 🌐 www.4wdhire.com.au), charge $150 per day for their 4WDs and also rent out camping gear ($300 per week for two people); Thrifty, cnr of Patricia and Miles streets ☎ 07/4743 2911.
Hospitals 30 Camooweal St ☎ 07/4744 4444; Georgina Medical Centre, 71 Camooweal St ☎ 07/4743 1488.
Internet Back of Mount Isa newsagent at 25 Miles St; $5.50 an hour.
Pharmacy Corner Pharmacy, cnr Marian and Miles streets.
Police 7 Isa St ☎ 07/4744 1111.
Post office For poste restante, use the Isa St branch (☎ 07/4743 2454); there's another office on Simpson St opposite the shopping complex.

Taxi ⓣ07/4743 2333.
Tours Campbell's, located at the Outback at Isa Centre (ⓣ07/4743 2006, ⓦwww.campbellstravel.com.au) run day-tours to local mines ($22), as well as three-day safaris to Lawn Hill Gorge (April–Oct; $660).

Trains Queensland Rail operate a twice-weekly service back to Townsville. For information and bookings call ⓣ13 16 17, or check ⓦwww.qr.com.au.

Kalkadoon country

The scrub around Mount Isa is thick with abandoned mines, waterholes and Aboriginal sites; to explore the area you need your own vehicle – check at the tourist office for the latest road conditions. The city marks the centre of territory belonging to the **Kalkadoons**, a tribe often compared with the Zulus for their fierce opposition to white invasion in the nineteenth century. After hounding squatters for ten years with guerrilla tactics, they were decimated in a pitched battle with an army of local settlers and Native Mounted Police near **Kajabbi** in 1884 – Kalkadoon bones littered the battleground for years.

Numerous sites around Mount Isa attest to the Kalkadoons' abilities in toolmaking and painting, and it's worth checking out their Tribal Council office (Mon–Fri 9am–5pm; ⓣ07/4749 3838), next to the Outback at Isa Centre on Marian Street, and talking to the staff. Bear in mind that many local sites have been vandalized and you might find the council evasive.

Warrigal Waterhole, Poison Hole and Lake Moondarra

You need high clearance or great care to reach **Warrigal Waterhole**: drive 7km towards Cloncurry from the Outback at Isa Centre, turn south through the gate and bear left along a very rough track to reach a parking area 3.4km later, from where you walk past "ripple rocks" to the waterhole. One red figure with strange hair outlined in yellow on the left seems to have escaped damage but not so other figures and symbols, which have melted to ochre smears. The waterhole itself is hemmed in by sheltering rocks, which makes for a cool retreat from the sun.

A flooded open-cut mine, **Poison Hole**'s name comes from the surreal appearance of the water, coloured green by copper – it's actually safe to swim in, however. Tracks there change each year, but the hole is about ten minutes from the highway, and the turn-off should be roughly 25km east of the city towards Cloncurry; look for signs spray-painted on the road. **Lake Moondarra**, 20km along on a good road (follow the signs from the highway heading towards Camooweal), is less offensively toned, and packed out with windsurfers and boats at weekends. During the week it's nearly deserted and other animals are attracted to the water – goannas, wallabies and flocks of pelicans. Beyond the dam wall at the north end of the lake, the unexpectedly green and shady **Warrina Park** is the unlikely home of peacocks and apostle birds.

Camooweal and Boodjamulla National Park

West of Mount Isa, the **Barkly Highway** (and buses) continues to Camooweal and the NT, passing routes to **Boodjamulla National Park** on the way. The park has two sections: **Riversleigh** – a huge fossil site – and the oasis of **Lawn Hill Gorge**; if you're making for either, ensure you have a campsite booked (see p.538) and check the latest road conditions (ⓣ1300 130 595, ⓦwww.racq.com.au). The route via Riversleigh is sometimes 4WD-only or closed, but the Lawn Hill road via the **Gregory Downs** roadhouse is fine for most cars if it's dry. Wherever you're driving, **fuel up**; from Mount Isa it's two hundred monotonous kilometres to Camooweal and the fringes of the black-soil Barkly Tablelands, and at least twice that to Boodjamulla.

Camooweal

There's no way to avoid **CAMOOWEAL** but you might wish there were – the township's atmosphere of lazy aggression is exacerbated by a total lack of charm. The highway from Mount Isa forms the main street, built in 1944 by American servicemen whose names are painted on a rock at the edge of town. You'll find a roadhouse, mechanic, general store (and Westpac Bank agent), post office and hotel – a risky place for a last drink in Queensland. The store's old decor is worth a peek, and murals at the *Camooweal Roadhouse* (ⓣ07/4748 2155; camping $5.50 per person, cabins ❸) should raise a chuckle. Otherwise, fuel up and move on.

Heading on from Camooweal there's a track north to Lawn Hill via Riversleigh (see p.537), while 200km south is **Urandangie** and a 650-kilometre 4WD "short cut", across to Alice Springs. To the west, it's a mere ten minutes' drive to the cattle grid separating Queensland from the NT's time zone and better roads; the next fuel along this route is at the Barkly Homestead, 275km away.

Gregory Downs and Boodjamulla National Park

Hidden from the rest of the world by the Constance Range and a hot ocean of bleached grass, the red sandstone walls and splash of tropical greenery at **Boodjamulla National Park** seem outrageously extravagant. There's little warning of this change in scenery; within moments, a land which barely supports scattered herds of cattle is exchanged for palm forests and creeks teeming with wildlife. There are two sections to the park, **Riversleigh Fossil Site** and **Lawn Hill Gorge**, connected to each other by a seventy-kilometre track (sometimes closed or 4WD-only). Most people base themselves at the gorge, which has the easiest access and the best facilities and scenery, though it's definitely worth making a trip to Riversleigh.

For Lawn Hill Gorge, routes from Cloncurry, Camooweal and Burketown all converge at **GREGORY DOWNS**, a tiny community of just nine inhabitants, whose roadhouse acts as a pub and general store, and undertakes mechanical repairs; each May Day weekend, there's a wild **canoe race** down the Gregory River. From here, the gorge is 76km west along a decent gravel road, via the controversial **Century Zinc Mine**, where work was halted when local Aboriginal groups claimed traditional ownership of the region. After several years of negotiations, they finally accepted a substantial payment for use of the land and the mine reopened. While the situation has exacerbated the frustration felt by mining companies and farmers over the legal ambiguities surrounding the 1992 Mabo Decision (see Contexts), it's evidence that the wishes of Aboriginal communities are now being taken far more seriously.

Riversleigh Fossil Site

Around 110km north of Camooweal, **Riversleigh Fossil Site** was once cloaked in rainforest supporting many ancestral forms of Australian fauna. The road from Camooweal to Riversleigh crosses the Gregory River three times around **Riversleigh Fossil Site**, which is why you need a 4WD on this route. The crossings are a foretaste of Lawn Hill – sudden patches of shady green and cool air in an otherwise hostile landscape. You can **camp** nearby at **Miyumba bush camp**, run by the National Parks (open March–Oct only; Ⓦwww.epa.qld.gov.au; $4.50).

The **fossil finds** here cover a period from twenty million to just ten thousand years ago, a staggering range for a single site, and one which details the transitional period from Australia's climatic heyday to its current parched state. Riversleigh may ultimately produce a fossil record of evolutionary change for an entire ecosystem, but don't expect to see much *in situ* as the fossils are trapped in limestone boulders which have to be carefully blasted out and treated with acid to release their contents. A roadside shelter houses a map of the landscape with fossil sites indicated on a rock outcrop nearby where, with some diligence, you can find bones and teeth protruding from the stones.

Lawn Hill Gorge

When **Lawn Hill Creek** started carving its forty-metre-deep gorge the region was still a tropical wetland, but as the climate began to dry out, vegetation retreated to a handful of moist, isolated pockets. Animals were drawn to creeks and waterholes and people followed the game – middens and art detail an **Aboriginal culture** at least seventeen thousand years old. The National Parks **campsite** (tank water, showers, toilets) occupies a tamed edge of the creek at the mouth of the gorge and is booked solid between Easter and October (bookings on Ⓣ13 13 04 or Ⓦwww.epa.qld.gov.au; $4.50). Alternative accommodation is at the pleasant *Adel's Grove* (Ⓣ07/4748 5502, Ⓦwww.adelsgrove.com.au; camping $10, safari tent cabins with meals ❹), a Savannah Guides (see p.540) post 5km from the gorge, run by Barry Kubala, an expert on the gorge's vegetation.

Canoes are an excellent way of exploring the gorge from the inside (you can rent them for $10 an hour at *Adel's Grove*). An easy hour's paddle over calm green water takes you from the National Parks campsite between the stark, vertical cliffs of the **Middle Gorge** to **Indari Falls**, an excellent swimming spot with a ramp so you can carry your gear down. Beyond here the creek relaxes, alternating between calm ponds and slack channels choked with vegetation, before slowing to a trickle under the rock faces of the **Upper Gorge**. You'll certainly see plenty of birds – egrets, bitterns and kites – though **freshwater crocodiles** are hard to spot. Since visitor numbers have increased, this timid reptile has retreated to the **Lower Gorge**, a sluggish tract edged in water lilies and forest where goannas lounge during the day and rare purple-crowned fairy wrens forage in pandanus leaves. The rocks along the banks of the Lower Gorge – reached on a short walking track from the campsite – are daubed with designs relating to the **Dingo Dreaming**, a reminder of the sanctity of the gorge to the Waanyi people.

In the creek itself are turtles, shockingly large catfish, and sharp-eyed **archer fish** that spit jets of water at insects above the surface. Just how isolated all this is becomes clear from the flat top of the **Island Stack**, a twenty-minute walk from the camp. A pre-dawn hike up the steep sides gives you a commanding view of the sun creeping into the gorge, highlighting orange walls against green palm-tops, which hug the river through a flat, undernourished country.

The Gulf of Carpentaria

The great savannahs of the **Gulf of Carpentaria** were described in 1623 by the Dutch explorer Jan Carstensz as being full of hostile tribes – not surprising, since he'd spent his time here kidnapping and shooting any Aborigines he saw. The Gulf was ignored for centuries thereafter, except by Indonesians gathering sea slugs to sell to the Chinese. Interest in its potential however, was stirred in 1841 by **John Lort Stokes**, a lieutenant on the *Beagle* (which had been graced by a young Charles Darwin on an earlier voyage), who absurdly described the coast as "Plains of Promise":

A vast boundless plain lay before us, here and there dotted with woodland isles . . . I could discover the rudiments of future prosperity and ample justification of the name which I had bestowed upon them.

It took Burke and Wills' awful 1861 trek to discover that the "woodland isles" were deficient in nutrients and that the black soil became a quagmire during the wet season. Too awkward to develop, the Gulf hung in limbo as settlements sprang up, staggered on for a while, then disappeared – even today few places could be described as thriving communities. Not that this should put you off visiting – with few real destinations but plenty to see, the Gulf is a perfect destination for those who just like to travel. On the way, and only half a day's drive from Cairns, the awesome lava tubes at **Undara** shouldn't be missed, while further afield there are **gemstones** to be fossicked, the coast's birdlife and exciting **barramundi fishing** to enjoy, and the Gulf's sheer remoteness to savour.

The main route through the region is along the sealed, 580-kilometre-long **Gulf Developmental Road** west off the Atherton Tablelands, covered three times weekly from Cairns by Trans North **buses** (a subsidiary of Greyhound) who continue north of Normanton to Karumba. If you want to travel further afield you'll need either your own vehicle, to take a **safari** from Cairns (see box on p.465), or make use of one of the region's two rustic **railways** (see box below). Be warned that wet-season **flooding** (possible

Gulf trains

Two unconnected, anachronistic **railways** still operate in the Gulf region, mostly as tourist attractions.

The **Savannahlander** (Ⓣ4053 6848, Ⓦwww.savannahlander.com.au) runs every Wednesday morning from Cairns to Almaden on the Chillagoe road, where it overnights before continuing via Mount Surprise and Einasleigh to Forsayth, arriving Thursday afternoon. Friday morning it leaves Forsayth for Mount Surprise, arriving back in Cairns on Saturday evening. You spend the snail's-pace journey being hauled over rickety bridges in carriages with corrugated-iron ceilings and wooden dunnies – a pastiche of Outback iconography. The trip costs from $172 each way including one night's accommodation (various **packages** can also be booked online), and you'll need to bring extra for hotel accommodation and meals.

The **Gulflander**, run by Queensland Rail (Ⓣ07/4036 9250, Ⓦwww.traveltrain.com.au), runs once a week each way along an isolated stretch of line between Croydon and Normanton, a journey that takes a mere four hours. The train departs Croydon at 8.30am on Thursday and Normanton 8.30am on Wednesday ($52 each way).

from Dec–April) can cut main roads and isolate areas of the Gulf for weeks at a time, and that you shouldn't venture far off-road without a four-wheel-drive vehicle at any time.

Visitors to the Gulf need to be reasonably **self-sufficient**, as there are few banks and accommodation is limited for the most part to campsites or pricey motels. For **information** before you go, contact *Gulf Savannah Development* at 74 Abbott St, Cairns (Ⓣ07/4031 1631, Ⓦwww.gulf-savannah.com.au), which offers brochures and advice, though doesn't make bookings. Many of the regional reserves are managed by the **Savannah Guides** (Ⓣ08/8985 3890, Ⓦwww.savannah-guides.com.au), a private ranger organization voted the best of its type in the world, which runs campsites with guides to show you around. On a more alarming note, you might also come face to face with the Gulf's two **crocodile** species – take care.

Undara Lava Tubes

The **Undara Lava Tubes** are astounding, massive subterranean tunnels running in broken chambers for up to 35km beneath the scrub – most weren't even discovered until the 1980s. They were created 190,000 years ago after lava flowing from the now-extinct **Undara volcano** followed rivers and gullies as it snaked northwest towards the Gulf. Away from the cone, the surface of these lava rivers hardened, forming insulating tubes which kept the lava inside in a liquid state and allowed it to run until the tubes were drained. Today, thick vegetation and soil have completely covered the tubes, and they'd still be undiscovered if some of their ceilings hadn't collapsed, creating a way in. These **entrance caves** are decked in rubble and remnant pockets of thick prehistoric vegetation quite out of place among the dry scrub on the surface. Tool sites around the cave mouths show that local Aboriginal groups knew of their existence, though there's no evidence that they ever ventured in.

Once **inside**, the scale of the 52 tubes is overpowering. Up to 19m high, their glazed walls bear evidence of the terrible forces that created them – coil patterns and ledges formed by cooling lava, whirlpools where lava forged its way through rock from other flows, and "stalactites" made when solidifying lava dribbled from the ceiling. Some end in lakes, while others are blocked by lava plugs. Animal tracks in the dust indicate the regular passage of kangaroos, snakes and invertebrates, and seasonally you'll encounter twittering colonies of bats clinging to the ceiling, but the overall scale of the tubes tends to deaden any sounds or signs of life.

Practicalities

Run by Savannah Guides, Undara is 130km from the Atherton Tablelands on **Yarramulla Station**, which lies 16km south of the Gulf Developmental Road – buses will drop you off at the junction and the *Lodge* will pick you up if forewarned. **Accommodation**, bar and restaurant at the *Lava Lodge* (Ⓣ07/4097 1411, Ⓦwww.undara.com.au; safari tents $20 per person, cabins ④) are set in eleven restored railway carriages brought over from Mareeba and set up amongst a thin wattle forest – an eccentric but comfortable idea. Their swimming pool is an almost essential place to spend time during summer.

Access to the lava tunnels is only allowed on a Savannah Guides–led **tour** booked at the *Lodge* ($37 for a 2hr introduction, $67 half-day, $105 full day), which takes you through some of the tubes and delivers an intimate rundown on local geology, flora, fauna and history. There are also plenty of good self-guided walks to make through woodland and up to lookout points in the low hills above the *Lava Lodge*.

Mount Surprise, Georgetown and around

MOUNT SURPRISE, 40km north of Undara, reputedly takes its name from the shock of the local Aborigines when they first saw whites. Aside from being a stop for the *Savannahlander* **train** on its weekly return leg to Cairns, there's little more here than a service station, *Mount Surprise Hotel* (ⓣ07/4062 3118; ❸) and *Mount Surprise Tourist Park and Motel* (ⓣ07/4062 3153; camping $15, motel rooms ❹), which has a **gem shop** and plenty of **information**. The area's main attraction lies a bumpy 40km north at **O'Briens Creek Topaz Field** (check on road conditions at ⓦwww.racq.com.au or call ⓣ1300 130 595), where you can camp at a waterhole known as **the Oasis**, and organize a fossicking trip, although you will need a fossicker's licence first (available from *Mount Surprise Tourist Park*). You might find a handful of topaz in a couple of hours and while it's not very valuable, there's pleasure in the hunt and it's beautiful when cut. **Moving on** from Mount Surprise, buses continue west to Georgetown, while the train heads south to Einasleigh and then Forsayth.

Beyond Mount Surprise the Gulf Developmental Road, which is the worst in all Queensland for stray cattle, crosses **the Wall**, where expanding gases in a blocked subterranean lava-tube forced the ground above it up 20m into a long ridge. After 25km, there's a turning south for a forty-kilometre detour to **EINASLEIGH**, an ordinary handful of weatherboard and iron houses made memorable by the huge, delicious evening meals served at the *Central Hotel* (ⓣ07/4062 5222; ❸), and summer dips in Einasleigh Creek's deep **basalt gorge**. If you don't have your own vehicle (and you might need 4WD after rain), the *Savannahlander* **train** also passes this way.

Back on the Normanton road about 90km west of Mount Surprise, **GEORGETOWN** is a diminutive place, home to the *Midway Caravan Park* (ⓣ07/4062 1219; camping $12, cabins ❸), and the rather plusher, pink *La Tara Resort Motel* (ⓣ07/4062 1190; ❹), along with a couple of shops and **hotels** (*Wenaru* has the best meals). The area around Georgetown has a reputation as somewhere to fossick for **gold nuggets** – for information on likely places to try, head for **TerrEstrial** on Low Street (daily: April–Sept 8am–5pm; Oct–March 8.30am–4.30pm; exhibition $10; ⓣ07/4062 1485), which acts as both **tourist office** and home to the Ted Elliott Mineral Collection, an impressive display of precious stones. **Buses** stop on the highway at the BP fuel station, and then continue west to Croydon.

Forty kilometres south of Georgetown down a decent gravel road is **FORSAYTH**, terminus for the *Savannahlander* **train** and home to the *Goldfields Hotel* (ⓣ07/4062 5374; ❺ including dinner). It's also the last place to stock up before heading into the bush to two unusual locations. Two hours south in a 4WD through the scrub, the basic camp at **Agate Creek** (ⓣ07/4062 5335; Easter–Oct) caters to agate hunters who scour the creek banks after each wet season for these semiprecious stones and rate this the best site in the world. This may be a matter of opinion but the colours, ranging from honey through to delicate blue, justify the time spent grubbing around with a pick looking for them. **Cobbold Gorge**, at Robinhood Station (Easter–Oct), 50km south of Forsayth on a passable dirt road, is a starkly attractive oasis inhabited by freshwater crocodiles and crayfish and surrounded by baking-hot sandstone country. Book **accommodation** here in advance at *Cobbold Camping Village* (ⓣ07/4062 5470, ⓦwww.cobboldgorge.com.au; camping $6.50 per person, cabins ❹), which also organizes **tours** ($40–110), including a 4WD trip around the station, fossicking for agates, lunch, and a scout up the kilometre-long gorge in a motorized punt – an excellent way to experience a very remote corner of the Outback.

Croydon

CROYDON, 150km west of Georgetown along the Normanton road, was the site of Queensland's **last major goldrush** after two station hands found nuggets in a fence-post hole in 1885. For a brief period the region received the attention it had always craved: within five years the **railway** was built and lucky miners whooped it up at Croydon's 36 hotels, before chaotic management brought operations to a close in 1900. Today, despite rumours of a new gold strike near town, the place is pretty sedate, with most buildings predating 1920. The *Club Hotel* (the last of the 36 to survive), the general store and the restored old courthouse all have their original fittings and offer directions to other scattered relics. If you're tempted to stay, the *Club Hotel* (Ⓣ07/4745 6184; ❷) has **rooms**, or you can pitch a tent at *Croydon Gold Van Park* (Ⓣ07/4745 6238; $10) on the Georgetown side of town.

Moving on, buses and the main road plough on to Normanton, 154km west, as does the **Gulflander train**, which departs from the station on Helen Street (see box on p.539). When the rails and sleepers were unloaded at Normanton's wharves in the nineteenth century they were meant to form the first stage of a line to Cloncurry, but this was redirected to Croydon when gold was found – at the height of the gold rush the service carried two hundred passengers a week.

Normanton

Founded on the banks of the Norman River in 1868, **NORMANTON** was the Gulf's main port, connected to the Croydon goldfield by rail and Cloncurry's copper mines by camel train, though today the town lacks the air of faded splendour one might expect. Set in gritty, flat country, Normanton's fortunes declined along with regional mineral deposits and today there's only a thin collection of stores and service stations, a bank and post office, with shop awnings and a handful of trees providing scant shade. A worthy survivor of former times is the **Burns Philp Store**, whose timber shell, built in the 1880s, covers almost an acre and remains upright (if empty) despite the attentions of over a century's worth of termites.

Barramundi fishing is beginning to brighten the area's prospects; you can set this up with Norman River Cruises (Ⓣ07/4745 1347), who also run **croc-spotting tours**. Normanton's **accommodation** prospects include campsites and motel rooms at the *Gulfland Motel* (Ⓣ07/4745 1290, Ⓦwww.gulflandmotel.com.au; camping $15, rooms ❹), under the sign of the "Big Barra" at the south entrance to the town, or at Normanton's lurid *Purple Pub* (Ⓣ07/4745 1324, Ⓕ4745 1626; ❹). This is also a good place to **eat**, with a beer garden and tasty char-grilled steaks and fish. The town's other two hotels, the *Albion* and *Middle Pub*, are pretty raw watering-holes.

Moving on, Karumba lies north, covered by the **bus**; Cloncurry is 400km south via the Burke and Wills Roadhouse; Burketown is a dusty trip west; and the **train** runs once a week east to Croydon.

Karumba

Reached from Normanton across 70km of cracked, burning saltpan, patrolled by saurus cranes and jabiru storks, **KARUMBA**'s tidy gardens are, given the setting, ridiculously suburban. Set near the mouth of the Norman River and once an airforce base for **Catalina flying boats** moving between Brisbane and Singapore, today the town mostly survives on prawn trawling and fishing, though a major landmark are the huge **sheds** storing slurry from the Century

Zinc Mine near Lawn Hill Gorge; the slurry is fed through pipes to Karumba, then shipped overseas for refining. Declining stocks of barramundi in the Gulf have inspired the opening of the **Barramundi Discovery Centre** (daily 1–4.30pm; $4), 2km from town along the river, which raises fish for release into the wild. One thing that will probably register is that there are few Aborigines in town – they shun the area, as many died in a tribal battle nearby.

Karumba comprises **two areas** – central Karumba itself, and Karumba Point, a couple of kilometres downstream near the estuary. **Central Karumba** is along Yappar Street on the Norman River's south bank, with a supermarket, the *Karumba Café* (serving good barraburgers) and a post office. For **accommodation** here, the *Gulf Country Van Park* (Ⓣ07/4745 9148; camping $12, cabins ③) has a shady campsite, while *Matilda's End* (Ⓣ07/4747 6500, Ⓦwww.matildasend.com.au; ③) has tidy units. There's also the *Karumba Lodge* (Ⓣ07/4745 9121; ④), which started life as the airforce mess – the ramp that runs alongside the lodge down to the river was where the Catalina aircraft berthed. The *Lodge* has two **bars** – the ordinary *Suave Bar* and the infamous **Animal Bar**, which you should probably avoid unless you're extremely serious about drinking and don't mind occasional bouts of hand-to-hand combat. **Karumba Point** overlooks mudflats and mangroves along the river mouth and has a pool, campsites, and a twice-weekly free fish barbecue at the *Karumba Point Tourist Park* (Ⓣ07/4745 9306; camping $12, cabins ②). For outstanding sunsets, meals and ice-cold beer, head to the riverside *Sunset Tavern*.

To spot crocodile and birds, or catch something for the pot, contact Kerry D (Ⓣ07/4745 9275) or Katheryn M Fishing Charters (Ⓣ07/4745 9449). If you have your own tackle, Pilot's Rest Boat Hire (Ⓣ07/4745 9024) rents out four-metre-long tinnies from $50 for a half-day.

Buses terminate opposite the *Sunset Tavern* on Palmer Street at Karumba Point, and head back to Cairns three times a week.

Burketown and on to the Territory

Set on the Albert River some 230km west of Normanton, via the site of Burke and Wills' northernmost camp near the Bynoe River, **BURKETOWN** balances on the dusty frontier between grassland and the Gulf's thirty-kilometre-deep, unfriendly coastal flats. Styled Queensland's "Barramundi Capital" after the delicious sports-fish, it has a huge road-maintenance depot employing most of its 235 inhabitants. Despite lukewarm fame for providing background to Nevil Shute's *A Town Like Alice*, there's little beyond the welcoming and historic *Burketown Pub* (Ⓣ07/4745 5104; units ④), *Burketown Caravan Park* (Ⓣ07/4745 5118, Ⓦwww.burketowncaravanpark.com.au; cabins ③), a **hot artesian spring**, a store, a couple of fuel pumps and a post office. Accommodation spots can organize barra fishing, or head 16km west to *Escott Barra Lodge* (Ⓣ07/4748 5577, Ⓕ4748 5649; units ⑤), where you can also go riding, mustering, or tour one of the Gulf's precarious cattle stations. There's a restaurant and bar at the *Lodge*, but no store.

The Hell's Gate Track

The best road from Burketown heads south for about 120km to Gregory Downs and routes to Lawn Hill and Cloncurry. If you're serious about fishing and have a 4WD however, head 170km west from Burketown via the Aboriginal community at **Doomadgee**, to the **Hell's Gate Roadhouse**, 50km from the NT (Ⓣ07/4745 8258, Ⓦwww.hellsgateroadhouse.com.au; camping $6, rooms ④). Besides supplying fresh provisions, fuel and accommodation, the roadhouse is a Savannah Guide station, and organizes short **tours** of the area ($30). A good place to set yourself up for **fishing** is at Massacre Inlet, reached from *Wollogorang Station* (Ⓣ08/8975 9944;

❻) on the Territory border; they'll supply you with a $12 fishing permit as well as camping, motel rooms, meals, beer and the last fuel before Borroloola. Giant anthills, pandanus-frilled waterholes and irregular tides are the rewards – and the area is stacked with wildlife, including saltwater crocodiles.

The road on from Hell's Gate improves inside the Territory and once there you shouldn't have any trouble reaching **Borroloola**, 266km down the track.

Travel details

Trains

Barcaldine to: Emerald (2 per week; 6hr); Longreach (2 per week; 2hr); Rockhampton (2 per week; 10hr).
Cairns to: Almaden (weekly; 6hr 30min); Forsayth (weekly; 2 days).
Charleville to: Brisbane (2 per week; 17hr); Mitchell (2 per week; 3hr 30min); Roma (2 per week; 5hr); Toowoomba (2 per week; 11hr 30min).
Charters Towers to: Cloncurry (2 per week; 13hr 30min); Hughenden (2 per week; 4hr 30min); Mount Isa (2 per week; 18hr); Richmond (2 per week; 7hr); Townsville (2 per week; 3hr).
Cloncurry to: Charters Towers (2 per week; 13hr); Hughenden (2 per week; 8hr 30min); Mount Isa (2 per week; 4hr 30min); Richmond (2 per week; 6hr); Townsville (2 per week; 16hr).
Croydon to: Normanton (weekly; 4hr).
Emerald to: Barcaldine (2 per week; 6hr 45min); Longreach (2 per week; 9hr); Rockhampton (2 per week; 4hr).
Forsayth to: Cairns (weekly; 2 days); Mount Surprise (weekly; 5hr 15min).
Hughenden to: Charters Towers (2 per week; 5hr); Cloncurry (2 per week; 9hr); Mount Isa (2 per week; 13hr); Richmond (2 per week; 2hr 15min); Townsville (2 per week; 8hr).
Longreach to: Barcaldine (2 per week; 2hr); Emerald (2 per week; 8hr 30min); Rockhampton (2 per week; 12hr 30min).
Mitchell to: Brisbane (2 per week; 13hr 30min); Charleville (2 per week; 4hr); Roma (2 per week; 2hr); Toowoomba (2 per week; 10hr).
Mount Isa to: Charters Towers (2 per week; 17hr 30min); Cloncurry (2 per week; 4hr); Hughenden (2 per week; 13hr); Richmond (2 per week; 10hr 30min); Townsville (2 per week; 22hr).
Mount Surprise to: Cairns (weekly; 11hr).
Normanton to: Croydon (weekly; 4hr).
Richmond to: Charters Towers (2 per week; 7hr); Cloncurry (2 per week; 6hr 15min); Hughenden (2 per week; 2hr 20min); Mount Isa (2 per week; 13hr); Townsville (2 per week; 8hr 30min).
Roma to: Brisbane (2 per week; 12hr); Charleville (2 per week; 5hr 30min); Mitchell (2 per week; 2hr); Toowoomba (2 per week; 7hr 30min).
Toowoomba to: Brisbane (2 per week; 4hr); Charleville (2 per week; 12hr 30min); Mitchell (2 per week; 9hr); Roma (2 per week; 7hr).

Buses

Barcaldine to: Blackall (1 daily; 2hr); Brisbane (1 daily; 16hr 30min); Charleville (1 daily; 5hr 30min); Cloncurry (1 daily; 8hr); Longreach (1 daily; 1hr 15min); Mitchell (1 daily; 7hr 30min); Mount Isa (1 daily; 10hr 30min); Rockhampton (2 per week; 7hr 30min); Roma (1 daily; 8hr 30min); Toowoomba (1 daily; 14hr 30min); Winton (1 daily; 3hr).
Charleville to: Barcaldine (1 daily; 5hr 30min); Blackall (1 daily; 4hr 10min); Brisbane (2 daily; 11hr); Cloncurry (1 daily; 13hr); Longreach (1 daily; 6hr 30min); Mount Isa (2 daily; 15hr); Roma (2 daily; 3hr 15min); Toowoomba (2 daily; 8hr); Winton (1 daily; 8hr 30min).
Charters Towers to: Camooweal (5 weekly; 13hr); Cloncurry (1 daily; 8hr); Hughenden (1 daily; 3hr); Mount Isa (1 daily; 10hr); Richmond (1 daily; 5hr); Townsville (1 daily; 1hr 40min).
Cloncurry to: Barcaldine (1 daily; 7hr); Camooweal (5 weekly; 5hr); Hughenden (1 daily; 5hr 30min); Mount Isa (2 daily; 1hr 30min); Richmond (1 daily; 3hr 30min); Townsville (1 daily; 10hr).
Emerald to: Anakie (2 per week; 35min); Barcaldine (2 per week; 4hr); Dingo (1 daily; 1hr 30min); Longreach (2 per week; 5hr); Mackay (1 daily; 5hr 30min); Rockhampton (1 daily; 3hr 30min).
Longreach to: Barcaldine (1 daily; 1hr 15min); Blackall (1 daily; 3hr 15min); Brisbane (1 daily; 17hr 30min); Charleville (1 daily; 6hr 30min); Cloncurry (1 daily; 6hr 30min); Dingo (2 per week; 7hr); Emerald (2 per week; 5hr); Mitchell (1 daily; 9hr); Mount Isa (1 daily; 8hr 30min); Rockhampton (2 per week; 9hr); Roma (1 daily; 10hr); Toowoomba (1 daily; 15hr); Winton (1 daily; 2hr).
Mitchell to: Barcaldine (1 daily; 8hr); Blackall (1 daily; 6hr); Brisbane (2 daily; 7hr 45min); Charleville (2 daily; 2hr 15min); Cloncurry (1 daily;

15hr); Longreach (1 daily; 9hr); Mount Isa (1 daily; 17hr); Roma (2 daily; 1hr); Toowoomba (2 daily; 6hr); Winton (1 daily; 9hr).

Mount Isa to: Barcaldine (1 daily; 10hr); Blackall (1 daily; 11hr); Brisbane (1 daily; 26hr); Charleville (1 daily; 15hr); Charters Towers (1 daily; 10hr 30min); Cloncurry (2 daily; 1hr 30min); Hughenden (1 daily; 7hr 30min); Longreach (1 daily; 8hr 30min); Mitchell (1 daily; 17hr); Richmond (1 daily; 5hr 30min); Roma (1 daily; 18hr); Toowoomba (1 daily; 24hr); Townsville (1 daily; 12hr); Winton (1 daily; 6hr).

Richmond to: Charters Towers (1 daily; 5hr); Cloncurry (1 daily; 3hr); Hughenden (1 daily; 1hr 20min); Mount Isa (1 daily; 5hr 30min); Townsville (1 daily; 6hr 30min).

Roma to: Barcaldine (1 daily; 8hr 30min); Blackall (1 daily; 7hr); Brisbane (2 daily; 8hr); Charleville (1 daily; 3hr 15min); Cloncurry (1 daily; 16hr); Longreach (1 daily; 10hr); Mitchell (2 daily; 1hr); Mount Isa (1 daily; 18hr 30min); Toowoomba (2 daily; 5hr); Winton (1 daily; 12hr).

Stanthorpe to: Brisbane (1 daily; 5hr); Toowoomba (2 daily; 2hr 30min); Warwick (2 daily; 40min).

Toowoomba to: Barcaldine (1 daily; 13hr 30min); Blackall (1 daily; 12hr); Brisbane (8 daily; 1hr 50min); Charleville (2 daily; 8hr); Cloncurry (1 daily; 21hr); Kingaroy (6 weekly; 3hr); Longreach (1 daily; 15hr); Mitchell (2 daily; 6hr); Mount Isa (1 daily; 23hr); Roma (2 daily; 5hr); Stanthorpe (2 daily; 2hr 30min); Surfers Paradise (2 daily; 3hr); Warwick (2 daily; 3hr); Winton (1 daily; 18hr 30min).

Warwick to: Brisbane (2 daily; 3hr); Stanthorpe (2 daily; 40min); Toowoomba (2 daily; 3hr).

Winton to: Barcaldine (1 daily; 3hr); Blackall (1 daily; 5hr 10min); Brisbane (1 daily; 19hr 30min); Charleville (1 daily; 9hr 30min); Cloncurry (1 daily; 3hr 30min); Longreach (1 daily; 2hr); Mitchell (1 daily; 11hr); Mount Isa (1 daily; 6hr); Roma (1 daily; 12hr); Toowoomba (1 daily; 17hr).

Flights

Emerald to: Brisbane (2 daily; 2hr); Cairns (1–2 daily; 6hr 40min); Mackay (5 weekly; 5hr); Maroochydore (1 daily; 4hr 35min); Rockhampton (1–2 daily except Sun; 4hr); Townsville (1 daily except Sat; 4hr).

Longreach to: Brisbane (1 daily; 2hr 25min); Roma (5 weekly; 2hr).

Mount Isa to: Brisbane (1–2 daily; 2hr 15min); Burketown (weekly; 1hr 35min); Cairns (1–2 daily; 5hr 20min); Mackay (1 daily except Sun; 8hr); Mornington Island (5 weekly; 1hr 50min); Rockhampton (1–2 daily; 4hr); Townsville (1–3 daily; 2hr).

Roma to: Brisbane (1–2 daily; 1hr 10min); Longreach (4 per week; 2hr).

Winton to: Townsville (2 per week; 1hr 25min).

Northern Territory

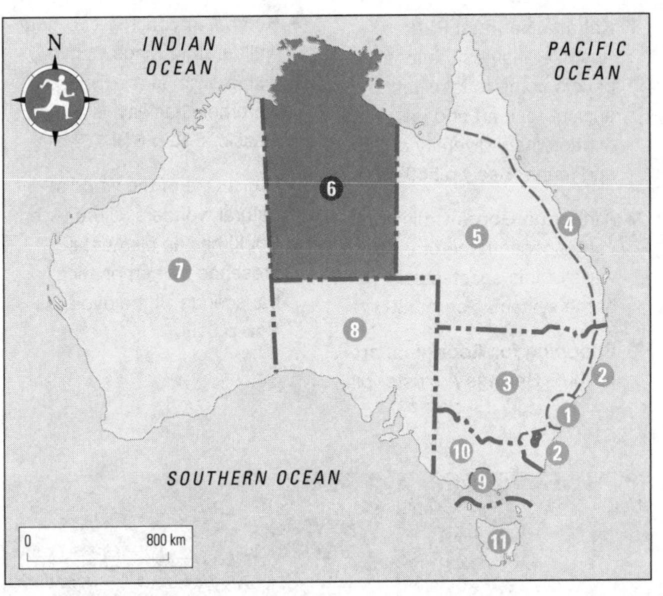

CHAPTER 6

Highlights

* **Aboriginal culture** You won't get all the answers, but the Territory is the best place to ask. See p.552
* **Top End crocs** The Mary River Wetlands have the highest concentration of crocodiles in Australia. See p.565
* **Kakadu National Park** Australia's largest national park is home to fascinating ancient rock art and an extraordinary diversity of flora and fauna. See pp.566–574
* **Katherine Gorge** Cruise or canoe beneath the orange walls of this spectacular gorge system. See p.580
* **Shopping for Aboriginal art in Alice Springs** A cluster of galleries in and around Todd Mall make finding a special souvenir easy. See p.601
* **Four-wheel driving in the Red Centre** Hop into your 4WD and explore the network of dirt tracks that radiate outwards from Alice Springs. See p.612
* **Kings Canyon** The two-hour walk around Kings Canyon, with a swim in a secluded waterhole halfway, is a classic. See p.615
* **Uluru** One of the world's natural wonders, Uluru (Ayers Rock) has an elemental presence that emphatically transcends all the hype. See p.618

△ Saltwater crocodile

6

Northern Territory

For the majority of Australians the **Northern Territory** – usually known as "the Territory", or simply "NT" – embodies the antithesis of the country's cushy suburban rim. The name itself conjures up a distant, frontier province – and, to an extent, this is still the case. Only around one percent of Australians inhabit an area covering a fifth of the continent, which partly explains why the Territory has never achieved full statehood. Territorians play up the extremes of climate, distance and isolation that mould their temperaments and accentuate their tough, maverick image as outsiders in a land of "southerners". The Territory attracts those wanting to escape their past, and it's a place where people ask few questions: most people were born elsewhere and that Australian institution, the "character", is in his element here, propping up the bars and bolstering the more palatable myths of the Territory's frontier history. The real "Crocodile Dundee" (see p.585) met his end here, and episodes like regular croc attacks and highway psycho killers help augment the Territory's untamed, Outback mystique.

The Territory's boundaries include some of Australia's oldest sites of Aboriginal occupation and some of the last regions to be colonized by Europeans. **Darwin**, the Territory's capital, is a prospering tropical town, while travellers from around the world flock to explore the **Top End** (as tropical NT is known), primarily **Kakadu National Park**'s wildlife, waterways and Aboriginal art sites. Adjacent **Arnhem Land**, to the east, is also Aboriginal land – and out of bounds to casual visitors, although many tours now visit this never-colonized wilderness of scattered communities. Heading south you arrive at **Katherine**, where the main attraction is the nearby gorges within the **Nitmiluk National Park**.

By the time you reach **Tennant Creek**, 650km south of Katherine, you've left the interminable light woodland of the Top End and have begun to pass pastoral tablelands on the way to the central deserts surrounding **Alice Springs**. By no means the dusty Outback town many expect, Alice Springs makes an excellent base to explore the region's natural wonders, of which that famous monolith, **Uluru** – or **Ayers Rock** – 450km to the southwest, is but one of many. This is one of the best areas to learn about the Aborigines of the Western Desert, among the last to come into contact with European settlers and the most studied by anthropologists.

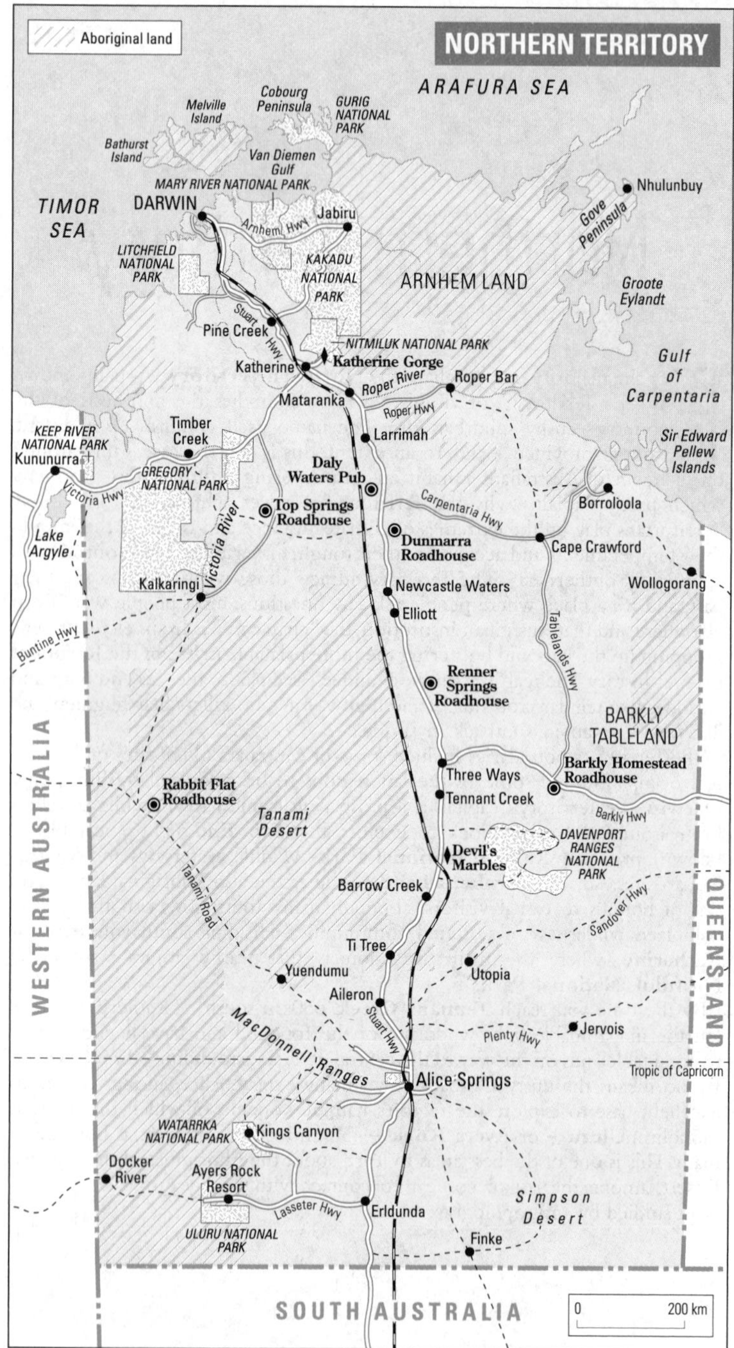
NORTHERN TERRITORY
Aboriginal land
ARAFURA SEA
TIMOR SEA
Melville Island
Bathurst Island
Cobourg Peninsula
GURIG NATIONAL PARK
Van Diemen Gulf
MARY RIVER NATIONAL PARK
DARWIN
Jabiru
Arnhem Hwy
LITCHFIELD NATIONAL PARK
KAKADU NATIONAL PARK
ARNHEM LAND
Nhulunbuy
Gove Peninsula
Groote Eylandt
Gulf of Carpentaria
Stuart Hwy
Pine Creek
NITMILUK NATIONAL PARK
Katherine Gorge
Katherine
Roper River
Roper Bar
Mataranka
Roper Hwy
Larrimah
Timber Creek
KEEP RIVER NATIONAL PARK
Kununurra
GREGORY NATIONAL PARK
Victoria Hwy
Sir Edward Pellew Islands
Daly Waters Pub
Borroloola
Carpentaria Hwy
Top Springs Roadhouse
Dunmarra Roadhouse
Cape Crawford
Lake Argyle
Victoria River
Wollogorang
Kalkaringi
Newcastle Waters
Elliott
Buntine Hwy
Tablelands Hwy
Renner Springs Roadhouse
BARKLY TABLELAND
WESTERN AUSTRALIA
Three Ways
Barkly Homestead Roadhouse
Rabbit Flat Roadhouse
Tennant Creek
Tanami Desert
Barkly Hwy
DAVENPORT RANGES NATIONAL PARK
Devil's Marbles
Tanami Road
Barrow Creek
Sandover Hwy
QUEENSLAND
Ti Tree
Utopia
Yuendumu
Aileron
MacDonnell Ranges
Stuart Hwy
Plenty Hwy
Jervois
Tropic of Capricorn
Alice Springs
WATARRKA NATIONAL PARK
Kings Canyon
Docker River
Ayers Rock Resort
Lasseter Hwy
Erldunda
Simpson Desert
ULURU NATIONAL PARK
Finke
SOUTH AUSTRALIA
0
200 km

Darwin and the Top End

Darwin, the Territory's capital, lies midway along Australia's convoluted northern coast. The majority of tourists come up here to visit nearby **Kakadu** and **Litchfield national parks**, continue their Australian circuit or maybe fly on to Indonesia. However, whilst the city possesses little to detain short-term visitors, there are a few attractions worth seeking out and plenty more within half a day's drive. The **Mary River National Park** offers a chance to explore a croc-infested wetland environment not accessible in Kakadu, while to the east, little-known and never colonized **Arnhem Land** is slowly opening up to tourism. In the southwest, the **Daly River** region comprises small Aboriginal communities and riverside fishing haunts.

Darwin and around

In spite of its history and languid tropical torpor, Darwin manages to feel young, vibrant and even cosmopolitan, a mood that's illustrated as easily by an evening on thronging Mitchell Street as it is joining the fitness fanatics you'll see cycling, hiking and jogging through the lush waterfront suburbs. The fact that Darwin is an ocean city isn't always fully appreciated – to make sure you do, head out to Stoke's Hill Wharf, Cullen and Fannie bays and East Point, and perhaps take a sunset cruise.

Some history

Setting up a colonial settlement on Australia's remote northern shores was never going to be easy, and it took four abortive attempts in various locations over a period of 45 years before **DARWIN** (originally called Palmerston) was finally established in 1869 by the new South Australian state keen to exploit its recently acquired "northern territory". The early colonists' aim was to pre-empt foreign occupation and create a trading post – a "new Singapore" for the British Empire.

Things got off to a promising start with the arrival in 1872 of the **Overland Telegraph Line (OTL)**, following the route pioneered by explorer **John McDouall Stuart** in 1862, that finally linked Australia with the rest of the world. **Gold** was discovered at Pine Creek while pylons were being erected for the OTL, prompting a goldrush and the construction of a southbound railway. After the goldrush ran its course, a cyclone flattened the depressed town in 1897, but by 1911, when Darwin adopted its present name, the rough-and-ready frontier outpost had grown into a small government centre, servicing the mines and properties of the Top End. Yet even by 1937, after being razed by a second cyclone, the town had a population of just 1500.

The first boom came with World War II after **Japanese air raids** destroyed Darwin once again at a cost of hundreds of lives, though this information was suppressed at the time, as was news of systematic looting by the army. The fear of invasion and an urgent need to get troops to the war zone led to the swift construction of the **Stuart Highway**, the first reliable land-link between Darwin and the rest of the country.

Three decades of guarded postwar prosperity followed until Christmas Day, 1974, when **Cyclone Tracy** devastated Darwin. Fortunately a low tide limited

Aborigines in the Northern Territory

Over a quarter of the Territory's inhabitants are Aborigines, a far higher proportion than anywhere else in Australia. Most modern maps show that half of the Territory is now **"Aboriginal land"**, commercially unviable and returned to nominal Aboriginal control following protracted land claims. This uniquely Territorian demography is the result of a formerly sympathetic federal government's cooperation with the politically powerful Land Councils within the NT, established following the Land Rights Act of 1976. Excepting the national parks, most Aboriginal land is out of bounds to visitors without a permit or invitation, although some transecting roads are exempt.

Most Aborigines live in Outback **communities**, or occasionally in very remote **outstations**: small satellite communities supporting a couple of families. While outstations replicate a nomadic, pre-Contact social group, the communities have been less successful, mixing clans who may have been enemies for eons.

Although snazzy interpretive centres in the national parks tend to concentrate on the eco-trendy bond with nature, the truth is that Aboriginal society in the Territory and elsewhere in the north is imploding. The Territory is Australia's murder capital, chiefly led by men whose self-esteem as family providers and custodians of the law (or even once poorly paid but respected stockmen) has been eliminated. The fact that Aboriginal men make up a disproportionately high percentage of the prison population is not solely due to widely assumed racism – although such attitudes may have driven them there in the first place. Furthermore, the conditions in which many Aboriginal people now live, along with their health, is worse than in many developing nations.

You will be reminded of these thorny and complex issues as you encounter the depressing spectacle of the Aboriginal fringe-dwellers staggering around, most conspicuously in Katherine and Alice Springs. Alienated from the affluent white society that busies itself around them, these people are the casualties of the clash of cultures which, in the Territory, is still within living memory. This chasm between two different cultures is actually far greater than most visitors realize. The failure of assimilation – the naive policy of the 1950s and 1960s – has been followed by the current failure of self-determination, while talk of reconciliation or even land rights is merely symbolic and does little to improve actual living conditions.

Yet looking at the galleries of Alice Springs and the droning forests of didgeridoos, it would appear that Aboriginal **culture** is thriving. Some communities are inviting

storm surges and no more than 66 people lost their lives, but Tracy marked the end of old Darwin, psychologically as well as architecturally. The city was hastily and functionally rebuilt, but for many residents this was the last straw, and having been evacuated, they never returned.

With the help of the tourist boom kicked off by Kakadu's exposure in the film *Crocodile Dundee* (as well as continuing development along Mitchell Street, including a proposed crocodile park), Darwin is trying to shake off its bland feel of a "company town". Since the mid-1990s, Darwin has been making a concerted effort to take itself seriously as Australia's commercial "gateway" into Asia and has attracted budget air-carriers such as Tiger Airways and Jetstar, which has resulted in greater tourist numbers. Mining continues to flourish and economic prospects were boosted still further by the completion in record time of the long-proposed **Darwin rail link** with Alice Springs in early 2004.

Day-trips from Darwin include the popular Litchfield Park (see p.577) as well as the Aboriginal-owned Bathurst and Melville islands, a thirty-minute flight from town. Crocodylus Park, on the edge of Darwin, or the Darwin Crocodile Farm, south of town, make a good day out when combined with the

The great outdoors

The popular image of Australia as a brown desert surrounded by countless picture-postcard beaches has appeal, but gives only a very partial description of this vast island continent. Snow-covered mountains, inland lakes, wild rivers and deep gorges, lush pastures, magnificent forests – both temperate and tropical – and immense underground caves add much more variety, and the Australian love of the outdoor life has ensured a host of different ways to enjoy them.

▲ Ningaloo Reef, Western Australia

The coast

Most Australians live within a couple of hours of the ocean, and beach culture is part of the Australian way of life. The 35,000km of coast (nearer 60,000km if you include all the islands) have an abundance of beaches that, to the visitor's eye, can seem almost improbably perfect, with vast stretches of brilliant white sands, caressed by deep blue seas under cloudless skies. From the geometric curve of temperate **Wineglass Bay** (Tas) to the cosmopolitan bustle of **Byron Bay** (NSW), the choice seems endless – and the country's disproportionately small population means that you'll likely have the sun, sea and surf as your only companions, on beaches so idyllic that they'd be crowded anywhere else in the world.

Other areas of the coast have a more active appeal. Victoria's **Great Ocean Road** is an inspiring drive (or a wonderful walk) past spectacular towering columns of rock, sculpted by the ocean and standing like off-shore sentinels in defiance of the pounding waves. Whether snorkelling with whale sharks at **Ningaloo Reef** (WA), diving in the **Great Barrier Reef** (Qld), surfing at **Bells Beach** (Vic) or fishing (pretty much anywhere), a lot of Australian life is lived in, on or near the ocean – just remember to follow the locals' lead and "slip, slap and slop".

▼ Fishing in Western Australia

Forest and mountains

Despite the fact that most of Australia is flat, the **Great Dividing Range**, which runs roughly parallel to the eastern coast, is the fourth-longest mountain range in the world. The area around the country's highest peak, **Mount Kosciuszko** (2228m) in the **Snowy Mountains** (NSW), offers the full gamut of winter alpine activities, from skiing to snow-tubing, but elsewhere much of the Range is covered with lush forests that provide spectacular bushwalking country. In the popular **Blue Mountains** (NSW), also renowned for its rock-climbing and caving, the roads and towns are on top of the escarpment, so you look down into immense canyons of dense forest. It's a genuine "land that time forgot" – near here, the dinosaur-contemporary **Wollemi pine** was discovered just ten years ago, a tree previously believed to be extinct for more than two million years.

Equally ancient are the magnificent trees of Tasmania's **Tarkine** forests, the second-largest temperate rainforest in the world and host to no fewer than 56 threatened and endangered species. At the other end of the country, the **Daintree** rainforest (Qld) shelters the largest range of plants and animals on earth.

▲ The Daintree, Queensland

National parks

Nearly ten percent of Australia's great outdoors is protected within national parks, many of them – such as **Kakadu** (NT), a vast area of natural beauty and Aboriginal rock art dating back tens of thousands of years – significant enough to be listed as World Heritage Sites. The **Tasmanian wilderness** is one of the largest conservation reserves in Australia, and the sixty-five-kilometre **Overland Track** from **Cradle Mountain** to **Lake St Clair** one of the world's great walks. Other equally spectacular parks include **Karajini** (WA), astonishing for its wild flowers, gorges and red dust, and the **Flinders Ranges** (SA), renowned for the great bowl of **Wilpena Pound** and as the start of the **Heysen Trail**, a punishing twelve-hundred-kilometre walk.

▲ Cradle Mountain, Tasmania

▲ Cattle herding in the Outback

The Outback

The **Outback** – everything west of the Great Dividing Range – is the essence of Australia, where the myths, facts and uncertainties of Australian identity interweave with the uncompromising harshness, scale and beauty of this ancient land. Covering an area almost as big as Europe, there is a lot of Outback to enjoy, with the ever-popular **Uluru (Ayer's Rock)** and the nearby underground town of **Coober Pedy** must-see destinations. Lasting memories, however, are likely to be of countless scrubby bushes, termite mounds and eucalypts, and the life-line of an empty road that points across a flat vastness to the shimmering haze where intense red finally yields to saturated blue.

Either in your own vehicle or as part of a tour, **driving** is the best way to experience the Outback. You can also travel by **train** from Adelaide to Darwin on the Ghan Railway, but some places, such as the beehive-shaped Bungle Bungles (WA), are best seen from the **air**, while others, particularly the Red Centre, are appreciated more **on foot**.

▼ Dirt track leading into the Outback

responsible tour operators to visit their settlements, or are setting up their own operations, so allowing you to experience something of their current and former way of life. However, even in the Territory Aborigines no longer live in or off the bush, although hunting and gathering is still a pastime to supplement conventional food sources.

Despite the often bleak realities, for those interested in getting to the heart of the enigmatic Australian wilderness, the Northern Territory offers enriching and memorable travel, providing an introduction to a land that has sustained a fascinating and complex culture for at least sixty thousand years.

Aboriginal tours

The term **"Aboriginal tour"**, while seeming to offer the promise of a privileged insight into the culture of indigenous Australians, can be misleading. Some tours will simply be focused on Aborigines and their culture, some will be offered by white-managed agencies but led by Aboriginal people (sometimes coerced into the role of guide), and some will be run by Aboriginal-owned organizations. Tours can often be no more than an opportunity for the operator to charge tourists over the odds to learn Aboriginal secrets and laws. Yet this secrecy, which was one of the pillars that supported traditional Aboriginal society, is exactly that, and what you learn on a tour can be a very watered-down version of the truth, from people reluctant to give away closely guarded customs.

As a tourist, meeting Aboriginal people by chance and getting to know them is difficult or takes some nerve, especially as Aboriginal land is, for the most part, out of bounds: meaningful contact with Aborigines for the short-term visitor is therefore unlikely. Many Aborigines are weary of endless questions, well-meaning though they are, and an entirely different strategy in social dealings renders most exchanges awkward and superficial. In many cases then, it is from a knowledgeable and sympathetic non-Aboriginal guide (as well as from older, pre-PC-era books on the subject) that you can learn more about Aboriginal life and culture than which berries make good eating.

The message here is that you should not expect the earth by hopping onto an Aboriginal tour. In most cases it will only scrape the surface of a complex and arcane way of life, an experience that cannot easily be bought across a travel desk.

Territory Wildlife Park (see p.577). To appreciate Kakadu, you'll need more than a day; for tours there, see p.561.

Arrival and information

Darwin airport is 12km northeast of the city centre; a **shuttle bus** service (Ⓣ08/8981 5066 or 1800 358 945; $9.50) meets international flights and drops off passengers at all major hotels and the **Transit Centre** behind 69 Mitchell Street; a **taxi** (Ⓣ13 10 08) to town from the airport costs about $30.

Given the proximity of Indonesia, Darwin is the cheapest place from which to leave Australia (see "Listings", p.563, for details). On the other hand, Darwin is a long way from anywhere in Australia – the bus journey from Townsville, in Queensland, takes a gruelling two-and-a-half days, including a 20hr layover in Tennant Creek; coming direct from Sydney, Melbourne or Perth, you're much better off flying. **Interstate buses** also arrive at the Transit Centre, where you can make reservations for onward journeys. Trains arrive at the forlorn **Darwin Passenger Rail Terminal** 20km from town, south of Berrimah, on Tuesday afternoons, heading back on the two-day journey to Adelaide on Wednesday

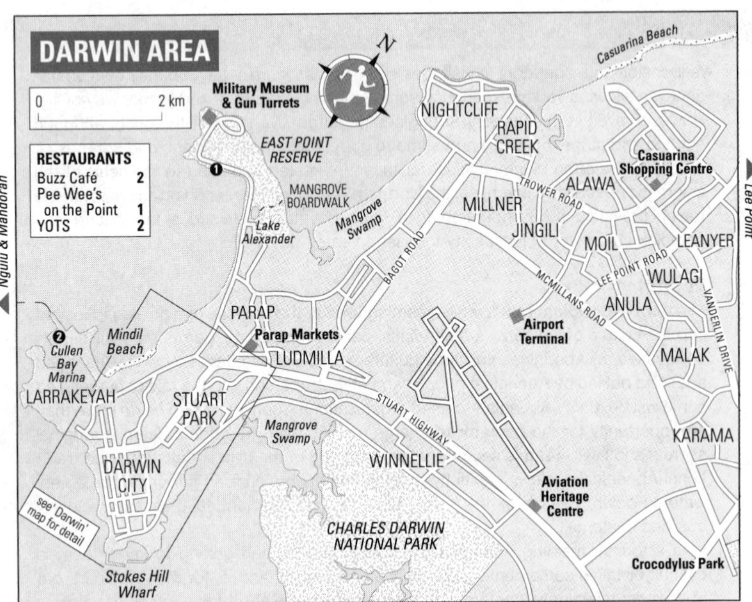

mornings, though in peak season (May, June & July) this service also runs on Saturday mornings. A shuttle bus ($9) ferries passengers between the Transit Centre and the rail terminal.

Five minutes' walk up from the Mitchell Street Transit Centre, the **visitors information centre** (Mon–Fri 9am–5pm, Sat 9am–3pm, Sun 10am–3pm; ⓣ1300 138 886, ⓦwww.tourismtopend.com.au) has plenty of material on national parks throughout the NT – if you're planning to visit the Mary River Wetlands try and pick up the relevant *Discovery Trails* brochure here. Note that local rental cars booked through the centre can come with unlimited kilometres (albeit at a higher rate), a deal that may not be available if you approach the rental agency direct. The free glossies, *This Week in Darwin* and the better *Destination Darwin and the Top End*, can be picked up all around town – they're mostly rose-tinted advertorials, but are handy for their **maps**, including bus routes.

City transport

The city's inexpensive **bus service** can deliver you to most corners of Darwin. Services operate daily from around 7am to 8pm, with some routes running until 11pm on Friday and Saturday. The **bus terminal** (ⓣ08/8924 7666) is on Harry Chan Avenue, at the bottom of Cavenagh Street, with a major **interchange** at the Casuarina shopping centre in the northern suburbs. A "Tourcard", offering unlimited travel (1–7 days; $5–25), is available at both places. Buses leaving the city for the suburbs head out along Cavenagh Street, running out as far as Palmerston, and come back in along Mitchell and Smith streets.

Most hostels and some hotels rent out **bicycles** for around $20 a day. Although Darwin is flat, it's also perennially hot and humid, so East Point Reserve, 8km from the centre, is about as far as you'd want to ride for fun. A

Top End weather

There is a certain amount of misunderstanding about the **tropical climate** of the Top End, usually summed up as the hot and humid "Dry" and the hotter and very humid "Wet". Give or take a couple of weeks either way, this is the pattern: the **Dry** begins in April when rains stop and humidity decreases – although this always remains high in the maritime tropics, whatever the season. It may take a couple of months for vehicular access to be restored to all far-flung tracks, but the bush is at its greenest, while engorged waterfalls pound the base of the escarpments. From April until October skies are generally cloud-free, with daily temperatures reliably peaking in the low thirties centigrade, though June and July nights might cool down to 10°C – sheer agony for seasoned Top Enders but bliss for unacclimatized tourists.

From October until the end of the year temperatures and humidity begin to rise: the dreaded **Build Up**. Clouds accumulate to discharge brief showers, and it's a time of year when the weak-willed or insufficiently drunk can flip out and go "troppo" as the unbearable tensions of heat, humidity and dysfunctional air-con push them over the edge. Around November storms can still be frustratingly dry but often give rise to spectacular lightning shows (Darwin is the world's most lightning-prone city). While rain showers become longer and more frequent towards Christmas – the onset of the **Wet** – access on sealed roads is rarely a problem.

Only when the actual **monsoon** commences at the turn of the year do the daily afternoon storms quickly rejuvenate and then saturate the land. This daily cycle lasts for at least two months and is much more tolerable than you might expect, with a daily thunderous downpour cooling things off from the mid- to the low-thirties. Along with Queensland's Cape York, Darwin's proximity to the equator gives it a true monsoon. Two hundred kilometres south the rains are lighter, though a Wet is experienced along the coast as far southwest as Derby, WA, and Townsville on the north Queensland coast.

Coming in from the west, **cyclones**, sometimes just a week apart, occur most commonly at either end of the Wet and can dump 30cm of rain in as many hours, with winds of 100kph and gusts twice that speed. Frequent updates on the erratic path and intensity of these tropical depressions are given on national and state radio, so that most people are fully prepared if and when a storm actually hits. Some fizzle out or head back out to sea; others can intensify and zigzag across the land, as nearly every community between Exmouth, WA (1999), and Darwin (1974) has found to its cost.

"twist and go" **scooter** is much more entertaining; you can rent them from next to the YHA (Ⓣ0418 892 885, Ⓦwww.scoota.com.au). To rent a 50cc moped ($50 per day; no passengers) and 150cc bike (from $80 per day; passenger allowed) you'll need to show a driver's license. A few local **car rental** outfits do battle along Mitchell and Smith streets, with prices starting from as little as $35 a day for an economy car, plus mileage (see "Listings" on p.562, for more). **Taxis** work out at about $1.50/km and there are plenty cruising around: either hail one on the street or call Ⓣ13 10 08.

Accommodation

Darwin has plentiful **accommodation** ranging from luxury hotels to backpackers', and most of it's conveniently central. Rates in the town's apartments and more expensive hotels can drop by half from **late September through to March**, and even hostels drop a couple of dollars from their rates, especially for longer stays: ring around or check the websites before making a reservation during this period.

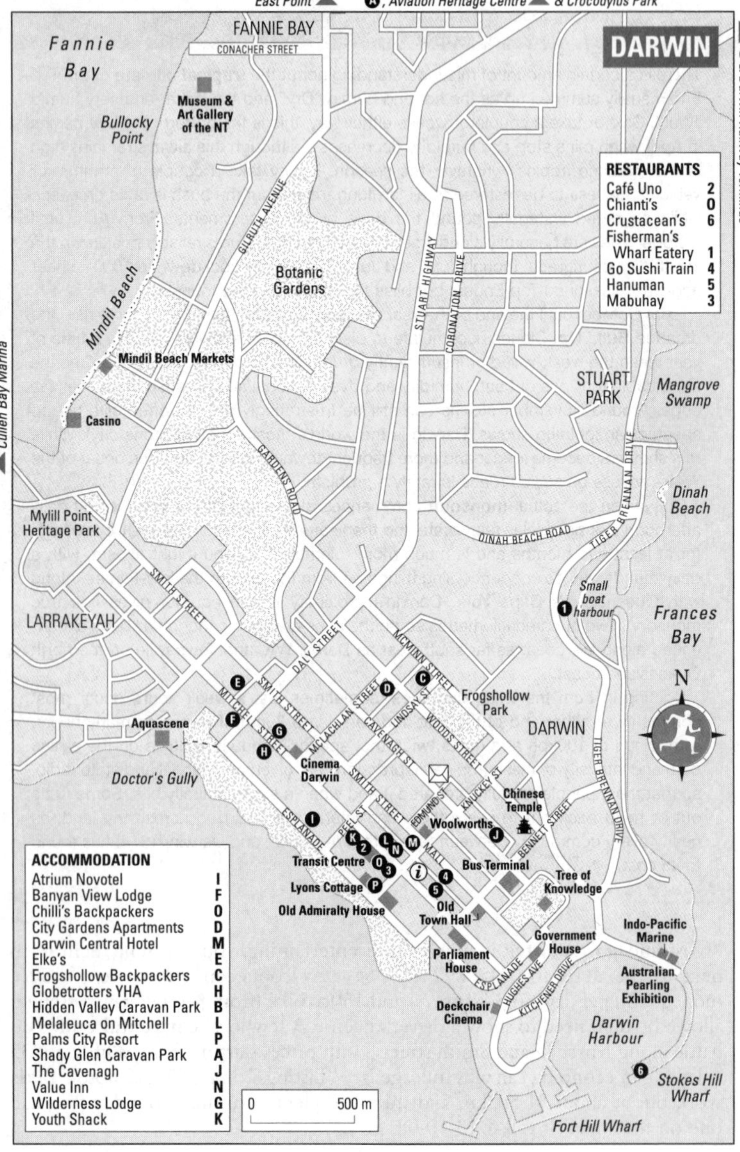

Hotels, motels and apartments

Most **hotels** and **motels** are right in the city centre, with the more prestigious examples found along the Esplanade offering views of the bay. If you're looking for self-catering accommodation, there are a couple of **apartment-hotels** in the centre, but for the most part they're further out.

Atrium Novotel 100 Esplanade ⓣ08/8941 0755, ⓦwww.novoteldarwin.com.au. Upmarket hotel along the Esplanade with a foliage-draped atrium, bars, restaurants, a gym and pool as well as sea views and the popular *Zest* restaurant. ❻–❽

City Gardens Apartments 93 Woods St ⓣ08/8941 2888 or 1800 891 138, ⓦwww.citygardensapts.com.au. Modern, spacious and centrally located family units with a pool, two minutes' walk from Frogshollow Park, five minutes from town. ❻

Darwin Central Hotel Knuckey St ⓣ08/8944 9000, ⓦwww.darwincentral.com.au. Luxury high-rise modern hotel right by the Mall with large rooms, a choice of restaurants and bars. Great off-season rates. ❼

Palms City Resort 64 Esplanade, corner of Knuckey St ⓣ08/8982 9200, ⓦwww.citypalms.com. Set in its own mini-jungle in a good location at the city end of the Esplanade. Accommodation is a block of motel rooms (basic or deluxe) or in a few detached duplex villas with some a/c facilities and a deck. There's also a small pool. Breakfast from $15. ❺–❼

Value Inn 50 Mitchell St ⓣ08/8981 4733, ⓦwww.valueinn.com.au. No-frills motel with small en-suite rooms (TV, a/c and fridge) that sleep up to three – a real squeeze, but it's in a great location, there's a pool and guests have access to *Melaleuca*'s facilities. ❺

Backpackers' and budget accommodation

Compared to the East Coast, you pay more for less in most of Darwin's **backpackers'**, and staff aren't always the cream of the hospitality industry (it's a Territory thing). Some places offer to pay for your airport shuttle if you book two nights or more, and as some backpackers' are owned by tour operators, staff may try to sell you tours whether you're interested or not. Many turn on the air-con (where available) only at night; without air-con a big, quiet fan is essential (and in fact can be preferable to noisy a/c units). Every backpackers' features a tour desk and Internet facilities, but don't get too excited about offers of a "free breakfast": in most cases it's usually Z-brand tea or coffee, plus dried milk, bread and jam.

Banyan View Lodge 119 Mitchell St ⓣ08/8981 8644. At the quiet end of Mitchell Street, this YWCA (it accepts single males too) has spick-and-span dorms, doubles and twin rooms with fridge and a/c (some rooms have fans) with mostly shared bathrooms. There's a large garden, a pool and free Internet – the only downside is a lack of lounge area. Parking available. Four-bed dorms from $25, rooms ❸–❹

The Cavenagh 12 Cavenagh St ⓣ08/8941 6383 or 1300 851 198, ⓦwww.thecavenagh.com. Converted motel built around a good-sized swimming pool with a popular café-bar and deck out front and a big kitchen. All dorms ($22–27) have bathrooms and some have TVs and fridges. Rooms are modern and functional but some don't have windows. ❺

Chilli's Backpackers 69A Mitchell St ⓣ08/8980 5800 or 1800 351 313, ⓦwww.chillis.com.au. The town's original YHA, with airy decks where you can eat, chat or sunbake by the spas. It's very central, attracts a lively crowd and enjoys use of the *Youth Shack*'s facilities. Dorms (4, 6 or 8 beds) $22, rooms ❷–❸

Elke's 112 Mitchell St ⓣ08/8981 8399 or 1800 808 365, ⓦwww.elkesbackpackers.com.au. Set in an old tropical house opposite the *Banyan View Lodge*, popular *Elke's* has plainly functional rooms and staff are friendly. There's a shady pool and garden area with off-street parking. Small four-bed dorms $29, rooms ❸

Frogshollow Backpackers 27 Lindsay St ⓣ08/8941 2600 or 1800 068 686, ⓦwww.frogs-hollow.com.au. A little out of town, *Frogshollow* is a purpose-built but cramped and ramshackle place with a small kitchen and pool. Dorms $22–26, rooms ❷–❸

Globetrotters YHA 97 Mitchell St ⓣ08/8981 5385 or 1800 800 798, ⓦwww.yha.com.au. The YHA relocated to this shabby ex-motel but it has a long way to go to achieve the group standards. Pool, bar, tiny kitchen and tour booking office. Dorms (4, 6 or 8 beds) $20–25, rooms ❸

Melaleuca on Mitchell 52 Mitchell St ⓣ08/8941 7800 or 1300 723 437, ⓦwww.momdarwin.com. This enormous and impressive-looking 400-bed "backpackers hotel resort" lifts the processing of Darwin backpackers to a new level. Accommodation is in dorms (4 or 6 beds), doubles, triples and quads, while facilities include a flashy sundeck, pool, waterfall, and a bar with huge TV screen – though it's all rather soulless. Swipe-card security tracks your every move, and there's also off-street parking and a women-only floor. Dorms $23, rooms ❸–❹

Wilderness Lodge 88 Mitchell St ⓣ08/8981 8363 or 1800 068 886, ⓦwww.wildlodge.com.au. Cheap 'n' cheerful and close to town, set in a small, old building midway along Mitchell St with a good-sized pool, shady back lot and a rather cramped kitchen. Dorms from $25, rooms ❸

Youth Shack 69 Mitchell St ⓣ08/8923 9790, ⓦwww.youthshack.com.au. Well-designed backpackers' right by the Transit Centre (though it's now overshadowed by the snazzy new *Melaleuca* over the road), with a spacious dining area overlooking the pool. Dorms $25, budget rooms ❸, e-nsuite rooms ❹

Camping and caravan parks

The following places are near the Stuart Highway in Winnellie, between 7km and 10km from the centre, a rather godforsaken light-industrial suburb, lying along the southern edge of the airport. Buses #5 and #8 both run here from the central bus terminal.

Hidden Valley Caravan Park 25 Hidden Valley Road, Berrimah ⓣ08/8947 1422, ⓦwww.hvtp.com.au. Lush caravan park offering powered ($28) and tent sites ($22) as well as bargain bunkhouse rooms ($35) and a range of self-catering units (❸–❺), plus a pool, kiosk and Internet access.

Shady Glen Caravan Park cnr Farrell Crescent and Stuart Highway ⓣ08/ 8984 3330 or 1800 662 253, ⓦwww.shadyglen.com.au. Suffering a little at the hands of newer options like *Hidden Valley*, *Shady Glen* is a little closer to town and offers camping ($12.50), budget rooms ($45) and a/c cabins (❹). Pool, kiosk, kitchen and Internet access on site.

The City

Present-day Darwin spreads north from the end of a stubby peninsula where the settlement was originally established on the lands of the Larrakeyah Aborigines. Over the years, suburbs have sprung up across the flat, mangrove-fringed headland, but for the visitor most of the action lies between the Wharf Precinct and East Point, 9km to the north. Repeated destruction from cyclones, air raids and termites has put paid to much of Darwin's old architecture, giving the town centre a modern, functional feel. Away from the bars and shops of Mitchell Street, there's a handful of interesting sights, while beaches and tropical vegetation offer a healthy slice of the great outdoors within the city limits.

If you don't mind the humidity, the city's attractions can all be reached on foot. Alternatively you could rent a car or scooter, or take the **Tour Tub** minibus (daily 9am–4pm; day-ticket $30; ⓣ08/8985 6322), a fun way to see most of the places detailed below. It departs on the hour from Smith Street Mall, on Knuckey Street, and you can hop on and off as you please.

The City Centre

The city's shopping centre is **Smith Street Mall**. Kids love the walk-through fountain near the century-old **Hotel Victoria**, once Darwin's answer to a Wild West saloon, though it has now been subsumed by modern development so you'll hardly notice it's there. On and around the Mall, several art galleries and gift shops sell pearls, croc-skin products, classy Aboriginal crafts and tacky Australiana.

Other old buildings are found further south along Smith Street as you cross Bennett Street: the **Old Town Hall**, built in 1883, was demolished by Cyclone Tracy, but its ruins are occasionally used as the location for outdoor performances by the theatre group based in the stone building, **Brown's Mart**, opposite. In the park behind Brown's Mart (opposite Darwin City Council) is a huge banyan tree known as the **Tree of Knowledge**, marking the location of the former Chinatown, destroyed during the raids of World War II. At the beginning of the last century the industrious Chinese outnumbered Europeans three-to-one in the Top End, and were involved in everything from building the Pine Creek railroad to running market gardens. Backtracking up Bennett Street to Woods Street you'll find the ornate **Chinese Temple** (daily 8am–4pm; free) and **museum** (April–Oct Wed–Mon 10am–2pm; free). The still-working temple is another post-Tracy restoration, employing the altar and statues from the 1887 original.

Walking back through the Mall, a left turn down Knuckey Street and over Mitchell Street leads to the Esplanade. On the left corner is the former **Admiralty House** (Mon–Sat 10am–5pm; free), a tropical 1920s house elevated on stilts that's managed to survive cyclones and air raids. Opposite is **Lyons Cottage** (daily 10am–4pm; free), a stone bungalow dating from the same decade, which hosts changing photographic displays of early Territorian history. Back on Mitchell Street near the Transit Centre, the **Mitchell Street Tourist Precinct** is home to a welcome cluster of outdoor bars and cafés with occasional street entertainment.

The lawns along the **Esplanade** make for a pleasant stroll, looking over the harbour. Walking north along the Esplanade you'll end up at Daly Street, and the end of the Stuart Highway; from here it's a straight 3000-kilometre run to Port Augusta in South Australia. Otherwise, a left turn down Doctor's Gully leads to the ever-popular **Aquascene** (ⓣ08/8981 7837, ⓦwww.aquascene.com.au for tide-dependent opening hours; $8), where at high tide scores of catfish, mullet and metre-long milkfish come in to be hand-fed on stale bread (supplied free). Heading in the opposite direction brings you to the modern white **Parliament House** (daily 8am–6pm; free; free 90min tours available Sat 9am & 11am), at the southern end of the Esplanade, from where pathways along the shore lead to the Wharf Precinct.

The Wharf Precinct

At the southern end of town, **Stokes Hill Wharf** has become the focus of a lively tourist precinct with a couple of souvenir shops and a food court with quayside seating. If you want to enjoy the wharf from a different perspective, take a **sunset boat tour** on a traditional pearl-lugger such as *Streeter* (ⓣ0423 522 423; $50 including snacks; BYO) or *Cape Adieu* (ⓣ08/8942 2011; $78 including dinner; BYO), both of which depart for three-hour cruises daily at 5pm.

Also well worth a visit is the live coral display at **Indo-Pacific Marine** (daily: May–Oct 9am–5pm; Nov–April 9am–2pm; $18; ⓣ08/8981 1294, ⓦwww.indopacific.com.au), where the regular, informative talks will set you straight about corals – the Timor Sea north of Darwin is one of the world's richest and most diverse coral environments, though they're obscured from view by the tidal silt which feeds them. Night shows (Wed, Fri & Sun 7pm; $80) focus on nocturnal coral life followed by a four-course seafood dinner and then more coral – this time to observe fluorescing species. In the same building, the **Australian Pearling Exhibition** (daily 10am–5pm; $6.60; ⓣ08/8999 6573) is a similarly imaginative display, describing Darwin's role in northwestern Australia's still-booming pearling industry. Round the other side of the harbour, a stairway up the cliff just past the Oil Storage Tunnels (on the Tour Tub itinerary, but about as interesting as they sound) leads up to a viewing point and to **Government House**, built in 1883 after the original residence was devoured by white ants. Though much restored, it's a good example of an elegant, tropical building, parts of which are open to the public (daily 9am–4pm; guided tours 9am & 11am Wed & Sat during the Dry, Sat-only in the Wet).

Cullen Bay Marina and the Fannie Bay museums

Walking north about 2km along the full length of Smith Street will bring you to a small roundabout and a sign pointing down to Cullen Bay Marina. Right by the roundabout you'll notice the so-called **Mylill Point Heritage Park**, a couple of pre-Tracy tropical houses, while down in **Cullen Bay Marina** itself you'll find some good restaurants (see opposite) with an attractive waterside setting. You can also take **boat trips** from Cullen Bay; the *Spirit of Darwin* (Ⓣ08/8981 3781; $33) is a cheap option, but for something a little more memorable, try the pearl lugger *Anniki* (Ⓣ08/8941 4000; $50) – both have licensed bars.

From the marina roundabout it's a short hop north to the extensive **Botanic Gardens** (daily 7am–7pm; free). A further kilometre north brings you to the excellent **Museum and Art Gallery of the NT** (Mon–Fri 9am–5pm, Sat & Sun 10am–5pm; free) on Conacher Street overlooking Fannie Bay. The museum features an absorbing display of Aboriginal art by the Tiwi people of Bathurst and Melville islands, as well as Top End bark paintings and works from the central deserts in pointillist style. Elsewhere there are stuffed examples of everything that flies, swims and hops, skips or jumps in the Territory, while the maritime section comprises a massive boat-shed housing various craft such as pearl luggers, Indonesian *praus*, Polynesian outriggers and the simplest of bark canoes. There's also an imaginatively designed exhibition commemorating Darwin's destruction by Cyclone Tracy, with a chilling film of the aftermath.

On to East Point

Continuing north, the main road (served by buses #4 and #6) curves right, while East Point Road continues straight up, entering **East Point Reserve**, an area of bushland home to around two thousand wallabies. A kilometre from the turn-off you pass **Lake Alexander**, a recreational saltwater lake suitable for year-round swimming.

The road ends at the **Military Museum** (daily 9.30am–5pm; $10) and **gun turrets**. Darwin was repeatedly bombed by the Japanese from 1942; at the time, news of both the air raids and the thirty thousand enemy troops massed on Timor was suppressed. The museum commemorates these events with a short video and some rather staid displays of uniforms, medals and other wartime memorabilia, while in the grounds a collection of aircraft engines and associated hardware quietly rusts away. **East Point** itself is also a good spot to observe the striking hues of Darwin's multichrome sunsets; if driving, watch out for the wallabies on the way back.

Aviation Heritage Centre and Crocodylus Park

Set in a hangar off the Stuart Highway, on the southeastern edge of the airport, the nonprofit **Aviation Heritage Centre** (daily 9am–5pm; $12; Ⓣ08/8947 2145, Ⓦwww.darwinsairwar.com.au; bus #5 or #8) is dominated by the huge bulk of a B52 bomber on loan from the US Air Force and describes the engaging story of civil and military aviation in the region.

Further down the Stuart Highway, taking a left at the Berrimah traffic lights leads you to the crocodile research facility and farm of **Crocodylus Park** (daily 9am–5pm; tours 10am, noon, 2pm & 3.30pm; $25; bus #5) on McMillans Road. You can get within kissing distance of a three-metre man-eater; these usually dormant reptiles are coaxed into action during daily feeding sessions that coincide with tours led by guides. There's also an absorbing museum giving you the lowdown on our reptilian friends.

Eating

There are plenty of good-quality options for every budget in Darwin. The climate makes it likely that **seafood** will have been frozen, and so might as well be from

Tours from Darwin to the Top End

For most visitors, Darwin is simply a convenient base for trips into the surrounding countryside. **Kakadu** is the obvious draw, but **Litchfield Park** is nearer and has several easily accessible swimming holes. Litchfield remains a popular day-trip, while most Kakadu tour operators offer two- to five-day tours, including possible excursions into **Arnhem Land** or a return via Litchfield.

Note that the Territory and especially the Top End has not always attracted the cream of **tour guides** – budget operators used to try to outdo one another with dangerous practices designed to make tours more exciting and memorable. This trend came to a tragic end when a well-established guide led a group into a croc-filled billabong in Kakadu one night in 2002, resulting in the death of one woman. Although proper training of guides has since been introduced, standards still vary.

Connections ⓣ1800 077 251, ⓦwww.connections.travel. Very professional outfit operating tours all over Australia. A wide range of camping and hotel tours are on offer and Top End tours range from two days in Kakadu ($410) to week-long trips ($1355).

Kakadu Dreams 50 Mitchell St ⓣ08/8981 3266, ⓦwww.kakadudreams.com.au. Low-cost full-on fun and games in packed 4WDs. "No oldies allowed." Two-day tours from $340.

Odyssey Tours and Safaris 50 Mitchell St ⓣ1800 891 190, ⓦwww.odysaf.com.au. Safari-tented or motel-based tours across the Top End and the Kimberley for those who don't want to rough it. Three-day Kakadu tours ($895 in a lodge) as well as five-day and one-week see-it-all trips from Manyallaluk, south of Katherine, to Katherine Gorge, Litchfield and Kakadu ($1495–1995).

Top End Escapes ⓣ1300 736 892, ⓦwww.topendescapes.com.au. Offers a mix of tours ranging from Darwin day-trips ($49) to longer trips that can be broken up to allow hop-on, hop-off access to Top End sights (weekly passes from $399).

Unique Indigenous Land Tours ⓣ08/8928 0022, ⓦwww.uniqueindigtours.com.au. One-day Litchfield tours ($154) and one- or two-day Kakadu tours with Aboriginal guides from $231.

Wilderness 4WD Adventures ⓣ08/8941 2161, ⓦwww.wildernessadventures.com.au. Competitively priced tours (2–5 days; $465–765) through Kakadu and Litchfield, with plenty of fun and action. The longer tours are a better deal.

Cape Cod as from the Timor Sea. That said, anglers are drawn to the Top End hoping to catch **barramundi**, an overrated "fighting fish"; **snapper** (aka Red Emperor) is much more flavoursome. Besides the places listed below, Mindil Beach and the other markets offer a plethora of delectable possibilities (see p.563). There are also a varied range of inexpensive takeaways alongside the water at the end of Stokes Hill Wharf – a great option for a sunset drink and dinner.

City centre and the wharf area

Café Uno Mitchell St Tourist Precinct. Nice Italian café serving dinners for around $20; there's a cocktail bar at the back. Daily 7.30am–late.

Chianti's Mitchell Centre, Mitchell St. Another quality Italian joint; the house salad, penne carbonara and *ravioli funghi* (all $15–17) are especially popular. Daily 7am–late.

Crustacean's Stokes Hill Wharf ⓣ08/8981 8658. Set apart from the takeaway hoi-polloi at the end of the pier, this place serves a gourmet selection of dishes such as local scallops, saffron ginger mussels and prawn and bacon penne (mains $25). Thurs–Sun 11.30am–2pm, daily from 6pm.

Fisherman's Wharf Eatery Fisherman's Wharf, Frances Bay Drive. Out of the centre, this long-established Darwinians' getaway does cheap seafood and chips ($7.50). Mon–Sat 8.30am–8.30pm, Sun 10.30am–8.30pm.

Go Sushi Train Mitchell St. All your rolled-up Japanese favourites plus vegetable *udon* ($10), prawn *tempura* ($17), Asahi beer and *sake*. Mon–Sat 10.30am–3pm & 5.30–9pm.

Hanuman 28 Mitchell St ☎08/8941 3500. One of Darwin's best restaurants, serving Indian, Nonya and Thai dishes such as barramundi *pongali* in yellow curry sauce ($24), *madras* lamb ($21) and Hanuman oysters with lemongrass, sweet basil, ginger, chilli and coriander. Mon–Fri noon–2pm & daily from 6.30pm.

Mabuhay 34–35 Mitchell St. The name means "hello" in Tagalog, and a welcoming place it is, serving a range of tasty Filipino, Indonesian and Malaysian dishes including pork *adobo* and *nasi goreng*. Mon–Sat 11.30am–10pm, Sun 6–10pm.

Zest Atrium *Novotel*, 100 Esplanade (☎08/8941 0755). *Zest* is a stylish yet relaxed restaurant serving tasty modern Australian cuisine in the *Novotel*'s tropically landscaped atrium. Dishes incorporate bush game and seafood and are surprisingly affordable. Daily 11.30am–late.

Cullen Bay, Fannie Bay and East Point

Buzz Café Marina Blvd, Cullen Bay. Popular quayside café with a range of dishes including sandwiches, pies and burgers, as well as Asian fare such as jungle curry ($28.50) and Thai reef fish ($35.50). Mon–Fri 11am–late, Sat & Sun 9am–late.

Pee Wee's on the Point East Point Road ☎08/8981 6868. Set on an outdoor terrace in the bush, with great views over Fannie Bay, *Pee Wee's* features a daily-changing starter menu and an interesting range of fusion mains such as crispy roasted duck on Shoxing greens ($36). Daily 5pm–late.

YOTS Marina Blvd, Cullen Bay. A great Greek restaurant in a lovely setting, overlooking the marina. For starters try eggplant spring rolls ($14.50) or some dips, followed by Greco barramundi ($29.50). Nov–May Tues–Sun 6pm–late; June–Oct Tues–Sun 7.30am–late.

Drinking and nightlife

Darwin's alcohol consumption is notorious, with **beer** being knocked back at around 230 litres per year per person – fifty percent more than in the rest of Australia (although consumption of soft drinks is also well above the national average). However, if that's not your scene there are a few other options, including the chance to enjoy a movie under the stars.

Pubs and bars

Mitchell Street is the venue for most of Darwin's drinking and live-music scene. Unless otherwise mentioned all of the places listed below are open from 11am until midnight and until 2am on the weekends.

The Cavenagh Cavenagh St. Affectionately known as the "Cav", this place attracts a young and up-for-it crowd and sometimes hosts some offbeat live music.

Ducks Nuts 76 Mitchell St. *Ducks* feels sophisticated during the day but loosens up in the evenings to feature live music (Thurs–Sun, from 9.30pm). The popular *Tzars Vodka Bar* is also on site.

The Fox Mitchell St. Opposite the *Ducks Nuts*, the *Fox* is a popular British-style pub where it's standing room only come weekend evenings.

Hotel Victoria 27 Smith St. Mall. The *Vic* remains Darwin's most popular pick-up joint, and offers nightly drinks and meal deals.

Lizards Bar and Grill cnr of Mitchell and Daly St. There are four drinking venues to choose from in the *Top End Hotel* and *Lizards* is the most salubrious of them; features DJs from 10pm.

Lost Arc 89 Mitchell St. *Lost Arc* is a tacky club with aspirations of grandeur; nevertheless it's open later than most places (9pm–4am) and hosts nightly live acts ranging from local bands to international DJs.

Shenannigans 69 Mitchell St. This enduringly popular Irish pub often has live music and seems to strike the right chord with travellers and locals alike – it serves Guinness and is always busy.

The Tap Mitchell St. Opposite the Transit Centre, *The Tap* is a good place for a quiet drink with plenty of outdoor seating, hearty and well-priced snacks and wireless Internet connection.

Throb 64 Smith St. Darwin's best-known gay club, *Throb* has nightly DJs and regular themed nights. Open Thurs–Sun from 10pm.

Wisdom Mitchell St. This upscale bar has over 50 beers on offer and challenges you to try them all (hopefully not in one night) to get your name inscribed on the "Wall of Wisdom".

Entertainment

For something a little more cultured than a beer, the Darwin Entertainment Centre at 93 Mitchell St (☎08/8980 3366) hosts various acts from musicals to intimate revues. Opposite the Entertainment Centre, the five-screen **Cinema Darwin** has cheap tickets on Tuesdays, or, for an alternative to mainstream films, the open-air **Deckchair Cinema**, on the Esplanade below Parliament House (☎08/8981 0700, Ⓦwww.deckchaircinema.com; $13; closed Nov–March), shows a mix of homegrown, art-house and cult classic movies.

Festivals and events

The onset of the Dry season sees an upsurge in activity as the city shakes off the languor of the Wet. As well as agricultural shows, rodeos and racing, August's **Festival of Darwin** stages bands, plays, cabaret, movies and workshops all around the city. Some time between June and September the famous **Beer Can Regatta** takes place on Mindil Beach in Fannie Bay – wacky boat races in sea craft made entirely from beer cans. A genuine manifestation of Territorian eccentricity, interest has picked up after a few slow years, but it's not the alcohol-fuelled celebration it used to be.

Markets

Every Thursday and Sunday night from 5.30pm (May–Oct only) **Mindil Beach Markets** attracts locals who park, unpack their eskies and garden furniture, and settle in for the sunset. It's an unmissable event: a mouthwatering array of sizzling food stalls from all corners of the earth (mostly Asia) tantalizes your nostrils, while stalls selling New Age remedies and handicrafts and performers add to the atmosphere. It's a three-kilometre walk from town through the Botanic Gardens, or a short ride on a #4 or #6 bus from the city centre; alternatively, a minibus service runs to and from most accommodation ($2.50 each way).

Parap's Saturday-morning market, on Parap Road (bus #6), or **Rapid Creek market**, off Trower Road on Sunday mornings (bus #6 or #10), are good year-round substitutes, with a smaller food selection, old books and knick-knacks.

Listings

Airlines The Flight Centre (☎1300 727 706) in the Mitchell Centre can organize overseas flights and visits to Bali and the Palau Islands.
Banks All major banks are located in or near Smith St Mall.
Bookshops Readback Book Exchange has a branch on the Mall near Star Arcade.
Buses Greyhound Australia, Transit Centre, behind 69 Mitchell St ☎08/8981 8100.
Camping equipment The NT General Store, 42 Cavenagh St, has everything you need for going out into the bush, from a new pair of Blunnies to mozzie nets, eskies, potties and billies.
Car and campervan rental Advance, 86 Mitchell St ☎1800 002 227; Britz 4WDs and campervans, 17 Bombing Rd ☎1800 331 454, Ⓦwww.britz.com; Europcar, 77 Cavenagh St ☎08/9841 0300; Thrifty Rental Cars, 64 Stuart Highway ☎1800 891 125 (they also have an office at the *Value Inn* in Mitchell St); Traveller's Auto Barn, 13 Daly St ☎1800 674 374, Ⓦwww.travellers-autobarn.com.
Consulates Indonesia, 20 Harry Chan Ave (Mon–Fri 9am–1pm & 2–4.30pm; ☎08/8941 0048).
Hospital Royal Darwin Hospital, Rocklands Drive, Casuarina ☎08/8922 8888.
Internet access Most of the hostels have Internet access, or there's Global Gossip on the corner of Mitchell and Knuckey sts ($4/hr). Wireless Internet is accessible along Mitchell Street as far as *Shenannigans*.
Permits for Aboriginal Land Northern Land Council, PO Box 42921, Casuarina 0811 ☎08/8920 5100, Ⓦwww.nlc.org.au.

Pharmacy Amcal, next to the Woolworths between Smith and Cavenagh sts (Ⓣ08/8981 8522) is open until 8pm on weekdays.

Police Mitchell Centre, end of Knuckey St Ⓣ08/8901 0200.

Post office 48 Cavenagh St, cnr Edmunds St.

Supermarket Coles, in the Mitchell Precinct, is open 24hr; Woolworths on Cavenagh St is open till midnight.

Swimming The nearest decent-sized pool is at Ross Smith Ave, Parap (Ⓣ08/8981 2662); take bus #4 or #10 from the city centre. Or try Lake Alexander at East Point.

Vaccinations If you're travelling on to Southeast Asia and need vaccinations, call in advance to book appointments at all of the following: Carpentaria Medical Centre, 13 Cavenagh St (Ⓣ08/8981 4233); Cavenagh Medical Centre, 50 Woods St (Ⓣ08/8981 8566); International Immunisation Clinic, 43 Cavenagh St (Ⓣ08/8981 7492).

Bathurst and Melville islands

Around six thousand years ago, rising sea levels created **Bathurst and Melville islands**, 80km north of Darwin. Home of the **Tiwi** Aborigines, the islands are often collectively known as the Tiwi Islands. Differing significantly from mainland Aborigines, with whom they had only limited contact until the nineteenth century, the Tiwi people's hostility towards all intruders hastened the failure of **Fort Dundas**, Britain's first north Australian outpost (on Melville Island), which lasted just five years until 1829. The Tiwi word for white men, *murantani* or "hot, red face", probably originates from this time.

In just two generations, since a Belgian missionary cautiously established the present-day town of **NGUIU** in 1912 on Bathurst, the Tiwi have moved from a hunter-gatherer lifestyle to a commodity-based economy with much less difficulty than mainland Aborigines, though still not without social upheavals – alcoholism, drug addiction and suicide are all major problems, although these fail to get a mention in the utopian view presented by tours to the islands. **Tours** are the only way to see the islands: *Tiwi Tours* (Ⓣ1300 721 365, Ⓦwww.aussieadventure.com.au) will fly you over in thirty minutes for a day-trip ($310, including return flight and permit, but not a pick-up to the airport). High-speed ferry from Cullen Bay (Ⓣ08/8941 1991; from $219 plus $16 Land Council permit) takes two hours to cross Van Diemen Gulf to Nguiu. Either way, it's all a bit of a shopping trip, inspecting Tiwi art-and-craft outlets, although lunch at Taracumbie Waterfall and a visit to an overgrown burial ground, where lopsided crosses mingle with carved *pukamani* burial poles, makes the trip worthwhile. At around $564, the **overnight tours** are much better value: you'll get the exciting chance to go food-gathering with local Tiwi, either offshore or through the bush.

East along the Arnhem Highway

The **Arnhem Highway**, which runs east towards Kakadu, parts company with the main southbound Stuart Highway 10km beyond Howard Springs. Passing agricultural stations, farms and Humpdy Doo on the way east you'll see the turn-off to **Fogg Dam Conservation Reserve**. Originally established in the late 1950s as an experimental rice- and cotton-growing area that was to transform the Territory's economy, for various "operational" reasons, not least the passing birds which munched their way through the crops, the whole scheme was a flop. Since then the dam has become more successful as a bird sanctuary, and driving across the barrage you'll easily spot jacanas, egrets and geese, and maybe even one or two of the countless pythons who feed on the water rats, goannas and wallabies. Being the first bit of wetland on the arid drive out of Darwin, it's restful on the eyes, and all the more pleasant if you follow the 3.6km boardwalk into the adjacent woodland or to the lagoon itself.

Back on the highway you'll spot the distinctive observation platform of the **Windows on the Wetlands Visitors Centre** (daily 7.30am–7.30pm), which overlooks the Adelaide River flood plain from the top of Beatrice Hill. On the top floor you can play with interactive displays describing the surrounding ecology. Unfortunately, the reality is, in the words of one ranger, a "window on the weedlands", since the floodplain has been infested by a "giant sensitive plant", one of many exotic plants that proliferate and choke out all other plant life and fish life, a problem nearby Kakadu also struggles with.

Adelaide River jumping crocs

Seeing crocodiles in their natural habitat is one of the Top End's undoubted highlights, but at the **Adelaide River Crossing**, 64km east of Darwin, you can go one better and join a **jumping crocodile cruise**. You'll have seen at least two other croc-jumping outfits along the road en route, but the *Adelaide River Queen* ($34 for a 1hr cruise; up to 4 times daily; check times on Ⓣ08/8988 8144, Ⓦwww.jumpingcrocodilecruises.com.au) is the original, involving enticing the river's numerous salties to surge out of the water and grab bits of boney offal on a string, making it easy and safe to snap great photographs. Sea eagles also sometimes swoop in to snatch the meat from the crocs' maws and, whatever your thoughts on the methods or wisdom of encouraging crocodiles to jump 2m out of the water, they are an amazing spectacle.

The Mary River

Continuing along the Arnhem Highway, you'll pass some huge cathedral **termite mounds** on the south side of the road, a popular tour-bus photo stop. Twelve kilometres past the *Bark Hut Inn* roadhouse (camping), the **Jim Jim Road** leads southeast to Cooinda in Kakadu. Another 6km further along the Arnhem Highway, the Point Stuart Road turns north into the **Mary River Park**, ending at the point on Chambers Bay where the explorer Stuart was carried lame and blind to reach the sea in 1862. And it was here that legendary bushman Tom Cole made his living for a while, shooting crocs and buffalo, a tough life described with wry stoicism in his book, *Riding the Wildman Plains* – and where Rod Ansell (see p.585) briefly ran Melaleuca station.

The Mary River's attractions won't be giving Kakadu too much to worry about, but it does offer a rare chance to explore a wetland environment away from the crowds and get as close as you dare to some huge crocs. Try to find a copy of the *Mary River Wetlands* brochure/map in the "Discovery Trails" series produced by the visitors centre in Darwin.

A sealed section turns off from the highway to reach another turn-off on the left for the Wildman Ranger Station (Ⓣ08/8978 8986), and **Couzens Lookout**, a basic campsite overlooking the river. Nearby **Rockhole** is a popular place to put a boat in for some barra fishing. From this point you can either backtrack to the main Point Stuart Road or follow the 32km 4WD **Wildman Track**, which rejoins Point Stuart Road further north. It's a great drive along a little-used trail amidst hopping marsupials, flocks of birds, huge termite mounds and, if you're observant, some crocs cruising among the lilies at Connellan Lagoon. With skilled driving a high-clearance 2WD will make it; if you're in a tall rental 4WD, beware of scratching the vehicle on overhanging trees. From Connellan Lagoon the Wildman Track gets sandier before it rejoins the Wildman Lodge Road (though the old lodge is closed), though a new riverside resort is under construction on the same site.

Further up Point Stuart Road is a turn-off for *Point Stuart Wilderness Lodge* (☎08/8978 8914), the only non-camping option in the area with a pool, bar and restaurant, plus four-share budget rooms (❹) and smart en-suite motel rooms with big bathrooms (❺). They also run wildlife cruises from Rockhole (call for times and prices) and can arrange four-person boats at **Shady Camp** ($120/90 per half-day for a large/small boat) where a barrage separates the Mary River's fresh water from the tidal reach of the open sea. These habitats seem to suit a whole lot of local crocs, and by hiring a boat you're guaranteed to see several of these grisly reptiles lolling on the banks of either side of the barrage, as well as countless birds, including beautiful Jabiru storks.

Kakadu National Park

Some 150km east of Darwin lies the World Heritage site, **KAKADU NATIONAL PARK**. The park derives its name from the Bininj/Mungguy people, the area's traditional owners who jointly manage the park with the

Crocodiles and swimming in Kakadu

Two distinct types of crocodile inhabit the Top End. Bashful **Johnston** or **freshwater** crocodiles ("freshies") grow up to 3m in length, and are almost exclusively fish-eaters, living in freshwater rivers and billabongs. Unique to Australia, and distinguishable by their narrow snouts and neat rows of spiky teeth, they look relatively benign and are considered harmless to man.

Estuarine, or **saltwater**, crocodiles ("salties") can live in both salt and fresh water and are the world's biggest reptiles. Once fully mature (up to 6m long and 1000kg in weight), they have no natural predators other than each other and have been known to take buffaloes trapped in the mud. Their broad, powerful snouts and gnarled jaw line have changed little since the time of the dinosaurs – only then, salties were four times bigger. They are opportunistic hunters, catching their prey in sudden, short bursts of speed and then resuming their customary inactivity for days if not weeks at a time. Apart from the jumping crocs at Adelaide River, most you'll see will be basking on mudbanks or cooling off underwater.

Aborigines have lived alongside crocodiles, and eaten them or their eggs, for thousands of years, but in the early twentieth century crocodiles were hunted close to extinction – either for sport, as vermin, or for their skin. Legislation reversed this trend in the late 1960s, and the Top End is now seeing the return of the big crocs.

Human fatalities due to **croc attacks** are surprisingly rare, but in October 2002 a Kakadu tour guide ignored warning signs and led his group for a midnight dip in Sandy Billabong, near Nourlangie Rock – a spot which was well known for its resident salties. The timing could not have been worse: crocs are most active at night, and this was also the breeding season when males become aggressive. The inevitable happened and a German woman was killed by a 4.5-metre saltie (which was harpooned by rangers early next morning with the body still in its jaws). It's become the latest story in every tour guide's repertoire, with the formerly ignored billabong now featured on many tour itineraries.

The park authorities responded by **warning against swimming** in **all** of the park's waterholes – even those that were formerly considered safe or kept croc-free during the Dry season. Some visitors ignore this advice and swim at Gubara, Maguk, Jim Jim Falls plunge pool, Gunlom and Jarrangbarnmi (Koolpin Gorge). There have been no incidents to date at any of these places, but obviously you swim at your own risk.

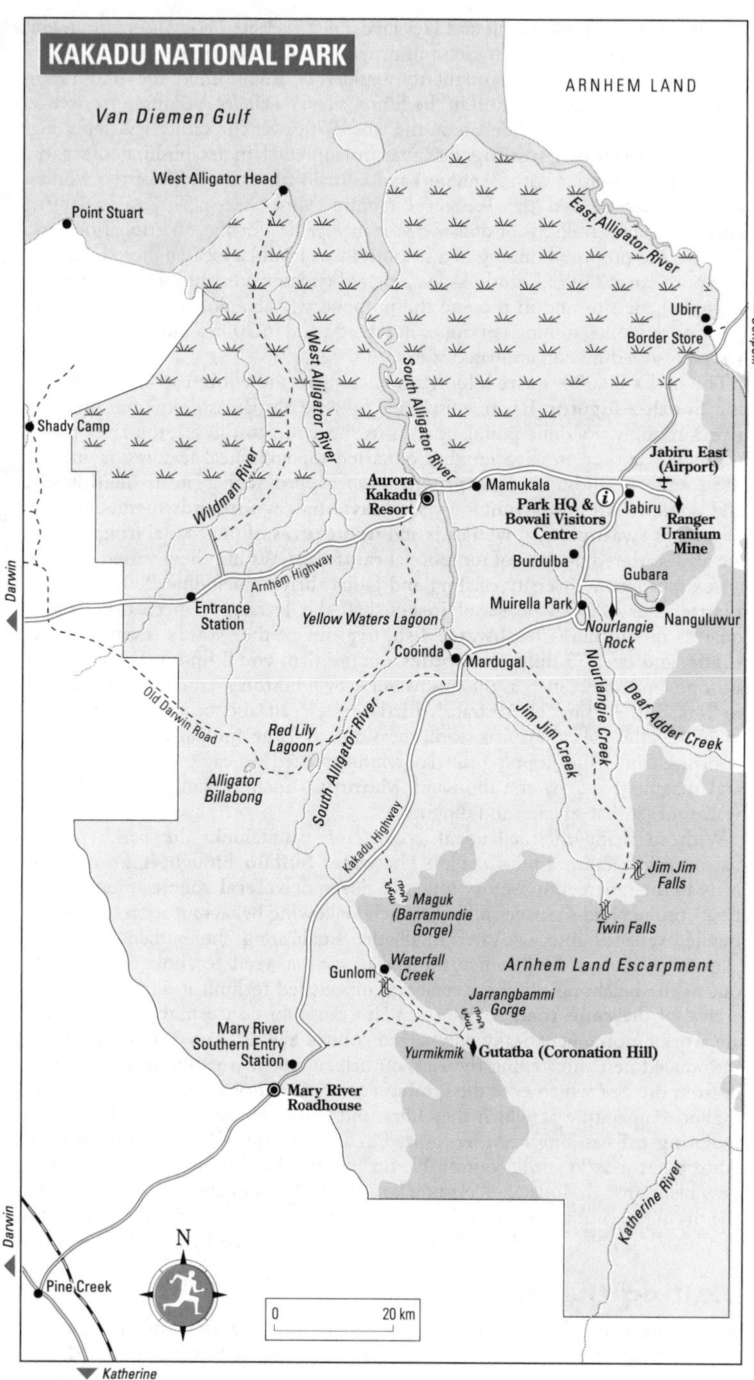
KAKADU NATIONAL PARK
ARNHEM LAND
Van Diemen Gulf
West Alligator Head
Point Stuart
East Alligator River
Ubirr
Border Store
Oenpelli
West Alligator River
South Alligator River
Shady Camp
Wildman River
Jabiru East (Airport)
Aurora Kakadu Resort
Mamukala
Park HQ & Bowali Visitors Centre
Jabiru
Ranger Uranium Mine
Burdulba
Gubara
Arnhem Highway
Darwin
Entrance Station
Muirella Park
Nanguluwur
Yellow Waters Lagoon
Nourlangie Rock
Cooinda
Mardugal
Nourlangie Creek
Deaf Adder Creek
Old Darwin Road
Jim Jim Creek
Red Lily Lagoon
South Alligator River
Alligator Billabong
Kakadu Highway
Jim Jim Falls
Maguk (Barramundie Gorge)
Twin Falls
Waterfall Creek
Arnhem Land Escarpment
Gunlom
Jarrangbammi Gorge
Mary River Southern Entry Station
Yurmikmik
Gutatba (Coronation Hill)
Mary River Roadhouse
Katherine River
N
Darwin
Pine Creek
0
20 km
Katherine

Department of Environment and Heritage. Their website (Ⓦ www.environment.gov.au/parks/kakadu) is a mine of information about the park.

Kakadu was originally brought to worldwide attention in the mid-1980s when it was used as a location in the film *Crocodile Dundee* – though previously, it was the environmental debate in the late 1970s over the rather less appealing subject of **uranium mining** that was instrumental in establishing the park. Areas on the border with Arnhem Land contain fifteen percent of the world's known reserves, and the Ranger Uranium Mine (see p.571), near Jabiru, currently yields millions of dollars a year in royalties for the traditional owners. In 1998 the proposed mining of a second site at Jabiluka located close to Ubirr, one of the park's most beautiful spots, created widespread controversy. Protestors occupied the site, and in the end the proposal was abandoned. In spite of this positive outcome, mining continues in Kakadu and in 2005 a number of miners were poisoned by contaminated water.

The park's 20,000 square kilometres encompass the entire catchment area of the **South Alligator River**, misnamed by an early British explorer after the river's prolific crocodile population. In its short run to the sea, the river passes through – and creates – a number of varied topographical features: ravines in the southern sandstone **escarpment**, itself topped with plateau **heathlands**, and downstream more commonly seen **savannah woodlands** merge into the paperbark **swamps**, tidal **wetlands** and **mangroves** of the coastal fringe. There are also scattered pockets of monsoonal **rainforest**. Within these varied habitats an extraordinary diversity of flora and fauna thrives, including 2000 different **plants**, over 10,000 species of **insect**, half the Territory's species of **frog**, a quarter of Australia's **freshwater fish**, five out of the world's seven types of **turtle**, and over 75 different **reptiles** – more than you'll find in the whole of Europe (and some, such as the freshwater – or Johnston – crocodile, are unique to Kakadu). A third of Australia's **bird** species can also be spied in Kakadu, including the elegant Jabiru stork, the similarly large brolga, with its curious courting dance, lily-hopping jacanas, white-breasted sea eagles, as well as galahs and magpie geese by the thousand. **Mammals** include kangaroos, wallabies, wallaroos, 26 bat species, and dingoes.

With so many interdependent ecosystems, maintaining the park's natural balance has become a full-time job. The **water buffalo**, brought in from Timor early in the nineteenth century (one of a dozen or so **feral species** found in the park), proliferated so successfully that their wallowing behaviour soon turned the fragile wetlands into saltwater mudbaths. Eradicating the buffalos, however, allowed their main food source, the *salvinia molesta* weed, to choke all other life out of the billabongs until a weevil was introduced to limit it. The long-feared arrival of the **cane toad** in 2002 was also cause for concern, though scientists are working on a genetically engineered control. Yellow crazy ants are the latest introduced pest threatening the Kakadu habitat, but it is exotic **grasses** blown in from the east which pose the greatest ecological threat to the park, due to the higher temperature at which they burn and so the greater damage they cause. **Burning off** has long been recognized as a technique of land management by Aborigines who lit small, controllable fires as an aid to hunting and to stimulate new plant growth. Today, rangers imitate age-old Aboriginal practice, burning off the drying speargrass during June to preclude catastrophic fires at the end of the Dry, when the desiccated countryside could be devastated by a wildfire.

Visiting the park

It must be stressed that Australia's largest national park is a difficult place to appreciate in one short visit. Access to the park's diverse features is limited, and

Ancient rock art

Up to five thousand **Aboriginal art sites** cover the walls of Kakadu's caves and sheltered outcrops, ranging in age from just thirty years old to over twenty thousand. Most of them are inaccessible to visitors, and many are still of spiritual significance to the three hundred or so Gagudju and other language groups who live in the park. The paintings include a variety of styles, from handprints to detailed cross-hatched depictions of animals and fish from the rich **Estuarine period** of six thousand years ago. At this time, rising sea levels are thought to have submerged the land bridge by which Aborigines crossed into Australia. It's not unusual to see paintings from successive eras on one wall. **Contact period** images of seventeenth-century Macassar fishing *praus* and larger European schooners might be superimposed (a common feature of petroglyphs worldwide) over depictions of ancient and bizarre spirit-beings. Though partially understood at best and only really known by the individual artist, Kakadu's rock art provides a fascinating record of a culture that has been present in the Top End for over sixty thousand years.

those expecting to find the bush humming with wildlife will be disappointed, especially if they stick to the two main sealed highways. Furthermore, at the most popular times of year for visitors, Kakadu is much **drier** than might be imagined, and most of the wildlife is active only during the early morning, in the evening or at night. Early-morning drives or walks along dirt tracks will certainly increase wildlife-spotting opportunities. The danger from crocodiles and the need to keep certain important Aboriginal sites secret – not to mention the harsh terrain and climate – mean that the wetlands and, especially, the most interesting escarpment country are difficult to fully value, though it is something that is becoming easier in adjacent Arnhem Land (see p.574).

Although Kakadu's Aborigines distinguish six **seasons** throughout the year, to most people it's either the Wet, with up to 1600mm (just over five feet) of torrential rainfall between December and March, or the Dry, an almost complete drought. The **dry-season months** of June, July and August are the most popular times to visit the park, with acceptable humidity and temperatures and fairly conspicuous wildlife. Towards the end of the Dry, birdlife congregates around the shrinking waterholes, while November's rising temperatures and epic electrical storms – known as the Build Up – herald the onset of the Wet. To see Kakadu during the **Wet** or the early Dry is, some say, to see it at its best. Water is everywhere and, while some sights are inaccessible and the wildlife dispersed, the land possesses the kind of verdant splendour that people often expect, but fail to find, in the most-visited months.

Getting there and information

The **Arnhem Highway** leaves the Stuart Highway 43km south of Darwin, after which it's a fairly dull 210km drive to the Park HQ near Jabiru, past the entrance station (where they should give you a visitors' guide with a map). From Jabiru the sealed **Kakadu Highway** heads southwest through to Pine Creek on the Stuart Highway (an alternative entry point into the park if approaching from the south), passing Cooinda, pretty much the heart of the park. The unsealed **Old Darwin Road** (also known as **Old Jim Jim**) starts 12km east of the *Bark Hut Inn* on the Arnhem Highway, but is passable for robust 2WD cars in dry conditions, and is a good alternative to slogging the full length of the Arnhem Highway. On the way you're bound to see some wildlife at Alligator Billabong and Red Lily Lagoon before joining the Kakadu Highway near Cooinda, 100km further on.

There are **buses** into the park: Greyhound Australia operates a service between Darwin, Jabiru and Cooinda every day except Thursday and Saturday. However, trying to see the park using only a bus pass may leave you frustrated. To make the most of using the bus, take a **day-tour** out of Jabiru or Cooinda, although this can take some planning. Alternatively you could take a tour from Darwin or Katherine (see p.561 & p.581). If you'd prefer to **rent** a car, this can be arranged through the Thrifty office at the *Gagudju Crocodile Hotel* in Jabiru (ⓣ08/8979 2552). The **map** you're given when you enter the park is handy, but details only the most popular areas; for the whole picture the HEMA 1:400,000 *Kakadu National Park* map is best.

At the eastern edge of the park, near the junction of the Arnhem and Kakadu highways, lies the **Park Headquarters and Bowali Visitors Centre** (daily 8am–5pm; ⓣ08/8938 1120). A *What's On* pamphlet lists details of **Dry-season ranger-led walks** at many of the sites covered below, and a programme of **evening slide-shows** at the caravan parks and resorts. An innovative walk-through **exhibition** takes you through a condensed Kakadu habitat, passing snakes and under a croc's belly. A café and gift shop round off the facilities.

Accommodation

Within Kakadu, most of the accommodation is at **Cooinda** or **Jabiru**. There are also a dozen free basic camping areas in the park, some accessible only along rough tracks where a 4WD is best. There are also five better-equipped camping areas ($5.40pp) at **Mardugal** near Cooinda, **Muirella Park** near Nourlangie Rock, **Merl** at Ubirr, **Garnamarr** near Jim Jim Falls and at **Gunlom**. In the Wet season some of the camping areas may not be open, while in the Dry booking ahead at the Park HQ is advisable.

Aurora Kakadu Resort Arnhem Hwy, 2.5km west of South Alligator Bridge ⓣ08/8979 0166, ⓔkakadu@aurora-resorts.com.au. Attractively landscaped resort with café, restaurant, and central pool area visited by birds and wallabies. There are pricey motel rooms (7) plus spacious en-suite motel rooms with a pair of bunk beds plus balcony or deck (4). Camping also available ($10–16pp).

Gagudju Crocodile Holiday Inn Jabiru ⓣ08/8979 2800, ⓦwww.gagudju-dreaming.com. Overpriced crocodile-shaped hotel, but nothing to sniff at if it's part of your package. 7

Gagudju Lodge Cooinda ⓣ08/8979 0145, ⓦwww.gagudju-dreaming.com. Near Yellow Waters and Warradjan Cultural Centre, but unless you're camping (powered sites $30, unpowered $15), the worst budget choice in the park with pricey dorms ($32) and no kitchen to speak of. There are also comfortable, well-equipped motel units (8).

Lake View Park Lakeside Drive, Jabiru ⓣ08/8979 3144, ⓦwww.lakeviewkakadu.com.au. The best-value place on this side of the park, with a range of options including camping ($30). Has mesh-walled "bush bungalows" (4), with a double bed and bunk bed, plus fridge, tea and coffee, and (external) private bathroom and shared BBQ area – though they are closely packed and noise carries through the mesh walls. The a/c and fanned double/twin rooms (5) around a communal kitchen and lounge area are quieter, though bathrooms are shared. There are also fully equipped s/c cabins sleeping four, with external private bathrooms (6).

Around the park

Seeing the **rock art** at Ubirr or Nourlangie Rock, taking a **cruise** at Guluyambi or Yellow Waters and checking out the Bowali Visitors Centre or Warradjan Cultural Centre will give you a taste of the park, and can just about be fitted into a day. However, you can easily spend a week visiting all the spots detailed below, ideally followed by a return visit six months later to observe the seasonal changes. All the places below are reached off the **Kakadu Highway**. Unless indicated, all roads below are sealed and so accessible to rental 2WDs.

East along the Arnhem Highway

Soon after the entry station, a turn-off heads north 80km to **West Alligator Head**, currently the only place in Kakadu where you can get to the sea (via an increasingly rough track; allow at least two hours). The main attraction of the drive is the good chance it offers of seeing plenty of wildlife, especially early in the morning. In the Dry a regular 2WD can easily get to the two no-frills campsites (see below) along the Wildman River; if you want to get all the way to the coast (basic camping, so be prepared) you'll need a higher-clearance 2WD or a 4WD.

On the way up you pass turn-offs to two **free campsites** on the Wildman River at **Two Mile Hole** (12km from the highway and slightly the nicer of the two) and **Four Mile Hole** (38km from the highway), but given that there are no toilets, little shade and a river full of crocs, there's not a whole lot to recommend them. Continuing north, about 60km from the Arnhem Highway you emerge onto a treeless flood plain for a kilometre or two. On re-entering the woodland the track narrows to two rough and corrugated ruts that can become quite bottom-numbing for the last 20km to West Alligator Head. It ends at the ruins of a former fish-processing plant (where there are some toilets). Straight ahead you can camp on **Pocock's Beach**. Combing the beach is fun here, as jumping fish flutter across the water, but wander among the mangroves and eventually a croc will come cruising towards you. You'll find a bit more shade (but not much else) 4km further on at **Middle Beach**, a shallow, kilometre-wide bay, nice enough to walk along, but inevitably unsafe to swim in without sniper support. There's room for a couple of tents but no facilities.

Jabiru and the Ranger Uranium Mine

JABIRU, a couple of kilometres east of the Park HQ, is a company town, originally built to serve Kakadu's uranium-mining leases before the park was established. Of the four mine leases in the park (and another in Arnhem Land) only one or two are operating at present. As a result, Jabiru is less than half-full of mine workers and park employees. There's a **tour booking centre** (☎08/8979 2548), a small **supermarket**, a takeaway, bakery, post office and Westpac bank, all located in the **shopping plaza**. You'll also find a **health clinic** (☎08/8979 2018) and a swimming pool (daily 9am–7pm; $3).

Kakadu Air (☎1800 089 113) operates out of the airport (6km east of Jabiru), offering thirty-minute **scenic flights** along the escarpment and wetlands (from $80; 20min helicopter rides from $145). From Kakadu Air's office you can also take a one-hour tour of **Ranger Uranium Mine**. However, the mine consists of nothing more than a pit, pipelines and mysterious-looking buildings where the ore is processed, while the tour itself is largely a public-relations exercise.

Ubirr and the Guluyambi Cruise

The rock galleries at **Ubirr** (Dry season 8.30am–sunset; Wet season 2pm–sunset), 43km north of the Park HQ, illustrate the rich food resources of the wetlands. Fish, lizards, marsupials and the now-extinct Tasmanian tiger (or thylacine) are depicted, as well as stick-like Mimi spirits, ancestral beings said to inhabit cracks in the rock and not unlike the "Bradshaw" or Gwoin Gwoin figures found in the Kimberley. A short diversion from the rock-art trail brings you to the **Lookout** which offers one of the park's most beautiful views across the East Alligator River to the rocky outcrops of Arnhem Land. To escape the crowds the six-kilometre return **Sandstone and River Walk** along the East Alligator River is one of the few longish walks in the park.

Near the start of the Sandstone and River Walk you can take the **Guluyambi Cruise** ($50; 2hr 30min; daily; ☎1800 089 113) along the East

Bushwalking in Kakadu

One of Kakadu's biggest disappointments is the lack of long-distance walking trails. A leaflet at the Park HQ lists twenty marked trails in the park, but most are short **nature trails**. Only the twelve-kilometre **Barrk Walk** – a three-hour trek (the sign claiming "allow 6–8 hours" can exist solely to put people off) through Nourlangie Rock's backcountry – offers any challenge: a half-hour slog up the rock which you then cross, descend and circumnavigate. The trail is marked, should not be undertaken lightly, and is best done in the cool of early morning. No less energetic is the little-advertised two-hour walk up to the top of **Jim Jim Falls** for fine views across the escarpment.

In the often-overlooked southwest of the park near Gunlom, the **Yurmikmik** area on the edge of the escarpment offers a similar challenge in the unmarked **Motor Car Creek Walk** (11km) and **Motor Car and Kurrundie Creek Circle Walk** (14km; overnight stop recommended). Ask for the **Yurmikmik Park Notes** at the visitors centre. You're more than likely to have the track to yourself.

Alligator River. A local Aboriginal guide takes you upstream to view the towering escarpment and rock paintings while demonstrating some canny bush trickery and even gives you a chance to set foot, briefly, on Arnhem Land. The combination of Aboriginal insight and dramatic scenery makes it an enjoyable (if not necessarily superior) alternative to the better-known Yellow Waters option out of Cooinda (see p.574).

Nourlangie Rock Area

Nourlangie Rock, Kakadu's most accessible and most visited site, is 31km south of the Park HQ. It includes the **Anbangbang Rock Shelter**, where the dry ground preserves evidence of occupation stretching back twenty thousand years; dimples on boulders show where ochre was ground and then mixed with blood for painting. The **Anbangbang Gallery**, nearby, depicts the dramatic figures of Nabulwinjbulwinj, Namarrgon (the Lightning Man) and his wife Barrkinj. Unusually vivid, they were in fact repainted (a traditional and sometimes ritual practice) in the 1960s over similar but faded designs. The **Lookout** over the Arnhem Land escarpment, traditionally recognized as the home of Namarrgon, is also the beginning of the twelve-kilometre **Barrk Walk** (see box above). Other places in the Nourlangie Rock area, all signposted and marked in the *Visitors' Guide* which you should have been given when you arrived in the park, include **Nanguluwur**, a less popular but fascinating art site 1.5km from the Nourlangie car park, which includes images from the Contact period when Aborigines first encountered explorers and settlers. **Nawulandja Lookout** has views onto the imposing hulk of Nourlangie Rock itself, which looms over **Anbangbang Billabong**, a *Crocodile Dundee* location. During the Dry, a 2.5km track around circles the billabong.

Gubara, or Burdulba Springs, 13km along an unsealed track off the Nourlangie road, comprises a string of small pools along a palm-shaded creek, itself a hot forty-minute walk from the car park, but you can take a dip at the end of it (see box, p.566).

Jim Jim Falls and Twin Falls

Although over 100km south of Park HQ and ending along a slow bumpy track, these two falls are definitely worth visiting. Allow two hours for the 60km drive from the Kakadu Highway or take a day-trip with an operator: *Gagudju Lodge's*

△ Painting of Nabulwinjbulwinj, Nourlangie Rock Area

(Ⓣ08/8979 0145) full-day Kakadu Gorge and Waterfall Tour costs $165 and operates from Jabiru or Cooinda. The road there passes the *Garnamarr* campsite and a barrier which blocks access to the road between 8.30pm and 6.30am.

Jim Jim Falls plunge 150m straight off the escarpment and are best viewed from a plane in the Wet or in the early Dry as soon as the road reopens – they stop flowing later. A rocky, one-kilometre trail leads alongside the large pool (swimming at own risk; see box, p.566) to the base of the falls, while another track leads to the top of the cliffs, though it's quite a slog – ask at the Bowali Visitors Centre near Jabiru (see p.571).

Twin Falls is a bumpy, sandy ten-kilometre drive from Jim Jim and involves crossing Jim Jim Creek, for which you'll definitely require a 4WD. The bottom of the creek has been cobbled, but it's subsiding and should be driven across slowly. From the Twin Falls car park you must pay around $10 (the exact figure varies) to be ferried up the gorge and traipse along a boardwalk to the plunge pool (no swimming). As an alternative there's a 3km walk up to the top of Twin

Falls: once up here you can overlook the falls and swim in pools up to 2km upstream (but see box, p.566).

Yellow Waters and the Warradjan Aboriginal Cultural Centre

As Jim Jim Creek begins meandering into the flood plains close to the Cooinda resort, 50km southwest of Jabiru, it forms the inland lagoon of **Yellow Waters**. From the car park here, a short walk leads along the edge of the billabong from where popular **cruises** (6 daily; book in advance on ☎08/8979 0145) weave through the lushly vegetated waterways. The early-morning cruise (2hr; $55) catches the lagoon and wildlife at their best: heat-of-the-day tours are thirty minutes shorter and ten dollars cheaper.

The turtle-shaped **Warradjan Aboriginal Cultural Centre** (daily 9am–5pm), on the Cooinda access road, offers unusually designed interpretive displays on the culture and lore of the local Aborigines, together with an arts and crafts shop. Interesting though it is, it has to be said that the display is not particularly effective at communicating its message and, unless you have some previous understanding of Aboriginal culture, you've forgotten much of what you've seen soon after leaving.

Maguk, Gunlom and other beauty spots

Robust 2WD cars can manage the twelve-kilometre corrugated track from the Kakadu Highway to **Maguk** (also known as Barramundie Gorge), which leaves the highway 57km southwest of Cooinda. A path leads from the car park, along the creek to the large pool (swim at own risk; see box, p.566). The pool is possibly still the home of a once-harassed freshie; for its sake rather than yours, keep away from the left bank. The top of the waterfall and more rock pools can be reached by clambering up the tree roots to the right of the falls.

Gunlom (also known as Waterfall Creek) is another *Crocodile Dundee* location, on a ridged track 36km off the Kakadu Highway, close to the park's southwestern exit. Although the falls don't flow all year, it's a lovely paperbark-shaded place (swim at own risk; see box, p.566), and as you can camp here it's well worth the diversion if entering or leaving via Pine Creek (if your car can take it). The steep path to the top of the falls reveals still more pools (again, swim at own risk).

A right turn at the junction that leads to Gunlom follows on through Koolpin Creek to a locked gate and the **Koolpin** – or **Jarrangbarnmi** – **Gorge**. The key is available ($50 deposit) from the Mary River Roadhouse (☎08/8975 4564) on the Pine Creek road, but you must also get a permit from the Bowali visitors centre which limits the number of visitors to forty vehicles per day. The track to the gorge crosses the creek again and requires 4WD. You can camp here or follow the escarpment on foot to the northwest for 3km to the narrow chasm of **Freezing Gorge** which, you'll be pleased to discover, lives up to its name. Five kilometres past the locked gate is Gutatba, a picnic site on the South Alligator River. Also known as Coronation Hill, this is the site of a former uranium mine: to local Jawoyn Aborigines this area is traditionally "Sickness Country", suggesting that even in its natural state, uranium, along with other toxic minerals found in the area, has proved harmful to human health.

Arnhem Land

ARNHEM LAND is geographically the continuation of Kakadu eastwards to the Gulf of Carpentaria, but without the infrastructure and picnic areas. Never colonized and too rough to graze, it was designated an Aboriginal reserve in 1931 and has remained in Aboriginal hands since that time. In 1963 the Yirrkala of northwestern Arnhem Land appealed against the proposed mining of bauxite on their land. It was the first such protest of its kind, and included the presentation of sacred artefacts as well as a petition in the form of a bark painting to the government in Canberra. Although it didn't help in this particular case, their actions brought the issue of Aboriginal land rights to the public eye and paved the way for subsequent successful land claims in the Territory.

Except for two places, independent tourists are not allowed to visit Arnhem Land without an invitation, and, by and large, the twelve thousand Aborigines who live here prefer it that way. Little disturbed for over forty thousand years, Arnhem Land, like Kakadu, holds thousands of rock-art sites and burial grounds. In recent years, the mystique of this "forbidden land" has proved a profitable source of income for Arnhem Land's more accessible communities, and **tours**, particularly to the areas adjacent to Kakadu, are now offered in partnership with some operators. Prices reflect this exclusivity. Davidson's Arnhem Land Safaris (ⓣ08/8927 5240, ⓦwww.arnhemland-safaris.com) offer tours in the Mount Borradaile area from $500 a day with flights from Darwin, while Lord's Kakadu (ⓣ08/8948 2200, ⓦwww.lords-safaris.com) runs a day-trip into Arnhem Land from the Border Store in Kakadu for around $189. Despite the expense, a visit here, even for one day, is a special experience: with its intangible allure, amazing rock galleries and unique sites, you'll capture the sense of an ancient, untamed land that an over-managed national park can never imitate.

The only major settlement is **NHULUNBUY**, also known as **Gove**, in the northeast corner, a distant mining town of little appeal. Independent travellers are now allowed to make an unescorted day-visit directly to the Injalak Arts and Crafts store (Mon–Fri 8am–5pm, also June–Sept Sat 8am–noon; ⓣ08/8979 0190, ⓦwww.injalak.com) in the town of **OENPELLI** (or Gunbalanya), 15km over the East Alligator River crossing at the Border Store near Ubirr. A $12 permit must be obtained from the Northern Land Council (NLC; Jabiru ⓣ08/8979 2847, Darwin ⓣ08/8920 5100; ⓦwww.nlc.org.au), which usually takes ten days. At the store you'll have a chance to buy locally made items and watch them being made; it might also be possible to see the rock art on nearby Injalak Hill.

NLC permits are also issued to drive to Smith Point on the **Cobourg Peninsula**. Most visitors here are fishermen, and without a boat it's a long rough drive for comparatively little reward.

Along the Stuart Highway

From Darwin, the **Stuart Highway** passes old mining outposts and overgrown, but still commemorated, World War II airstrips. Along its length are a number of attractions that can be visited either as excursions from Darwin or as diversions on the journey to Katherine, 320km to the south. Don't expect to get to any of the places off the highway without organizing local transport.

Darwin Crocodile Farm

South of the Arnhem Highway turn-off, 40km from Darwin, is the **Darwin Crocodile Farm** (daily 9am–4pm; $10), where crocodiles are studied, and also bred for their skins and meat (as they also are at Crocodylus Park near Darwin; see p.560). The lucky ones get scarred at an early age, rendering themselves unsuitable for conversion into handbags, and become breeding stock instead. Rogue crocs

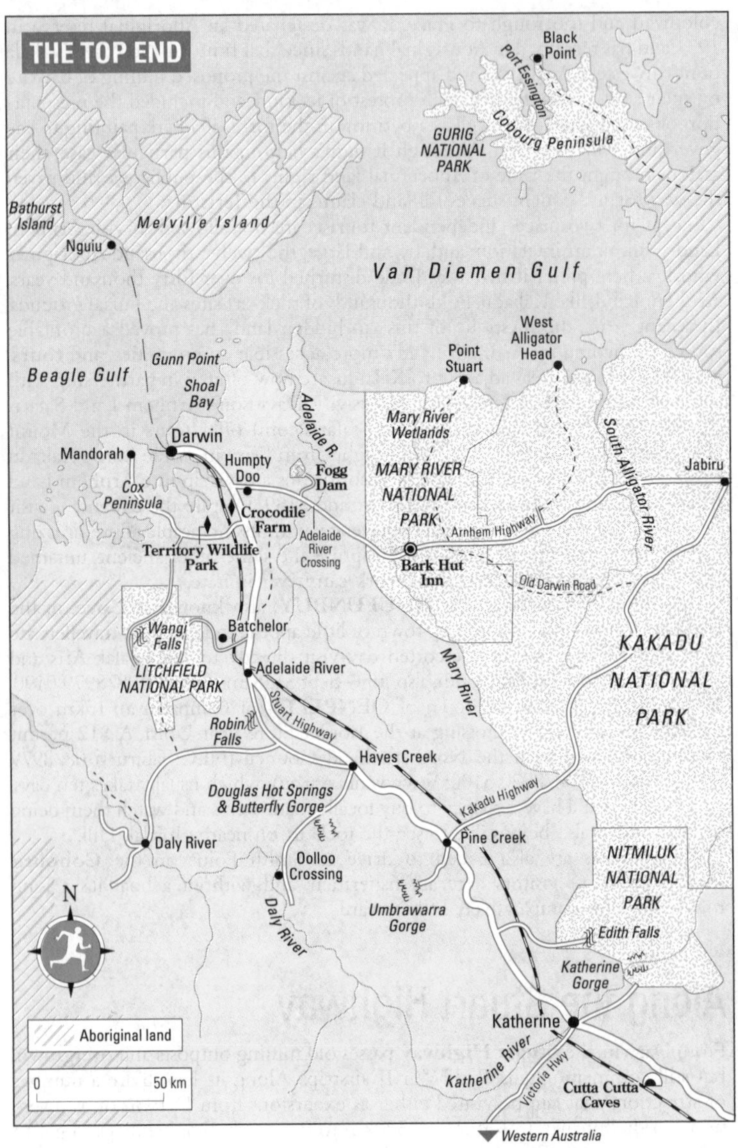

who turn nasty and harass local communities, as well as the sixty-odd crocs caught annually in the traps around Darwin Harbour, are also relocated here.

Souvenirs (including photo opportunities to cradle baby salties) and croc burgers are available at the shop, and **guided tours** set off on the hour, when some of the eight thousand crocodiles and alligators also get fed. It's worth trying to catch the main feeding time (Mon–Fri 2pm, Sat & Sun noon & 2pm), since it's one of the few occasions when the crocs actually move.

Territory Wildlife Park and termite mounds

Eight kilometres further south down the highway, the turning west to the Cox Peninsula leads to the **Territory Wildlife Park** (daily 8.30am–6pm, last admission 4pm; $20), where you can spend a happy couple of hours wandering through a variety of Territorian habitats, including walk-in aviaries, nocturnal houses and walk-through aquariums. The entry fee – worth every cent – includes free rides on the circulating train, saving trudging along the four-kilometre roadway.

Twenty kilometres west before the Cox Peninsula road veers north to Mandorah there's a turning onto the northern approach track to Litchfield National Park (see below). Crossing through the usually dry Finniss River, this road passes fields of **termite mounds**, a combination of fluted "cathedral" mounds, up to 4m high, and so-called "magnetic" or "meridian" mounds. Not often seen in the same vicinity, both designs are made of digested grass and are designed to create a regulated internal temperature. Magnetic mounds are always aligned along the polar axis and were once thought to be in tune with the earth's magnetic field. In fact, they're arranged so as to present a knife edge to the full heat of the midday sun, thus maintaining the habitat at a termite-preferred 30°C; you can feel the temperature difference by touching either side of the mound.

Litchfield National Park

"Kaka-don't, Litchfield-do" is an over-simplified quip expressing many people's preference for **LITCHFIELD NATIONAL PARK** over its better-known neighbour. Situated 100km south of Darwin, and roughly 16km west of the Stuart Highway, it encompasses the Tabletop Range, a spring-fringed plateau from which gush several permanent and easily accessible **waterfalls**. The whole park is a popular and enjoyable destination, free of restrictions, long drives, the need for 4WDs and intangible expectations. It's also largely free of crocodiles so you can splash around to your heart's content.

If you're driving to Litchfield straight from Kakadu along the Arnhem Highway, the **Marrakai Track**, a smooth dirt road just after the Corroboree Park Roadhouse, cuts 50km off the sealed route. Alternatively, if you're coming directly from Darwin you can enter the park from the north, passing the Territory Wildlife Park (40km of gravel road) and exit via Batchelor to the east or, with a 4WD, leave to the south via the Reynolds River Track passing some of the park's less visited waterfalls. For details of **organized tours**, which are the only way to see the park without your own transport, see box, p.561.

Batchelor

BATCHELOR – 8km west of the Stuart Highway – was originally built to serve the postwar rush to mine uranium at nearby Rum Jungle. In the early 1970s, when large-scale mining ceased, the establishment of Litchfield gave the town a new lease of life. The town's only sight of note is a replica of the Gothic **Karlstein Castle**, next to the police station, built by a homesick Czech immigrant. There's no admission fee to enter the park, but no visitors centre either, so get all the **information** you need (including a map) from the Parks and Wildlife Commission (P&WC) offices in Batchelor (☎08/8976 0282) or at the visitors centre in Darwin. They also have information on extended **bushwalks** in Litchfield if you want to do more than hop from one waterfall to the next. There are several **caravan parks** in and around Batchelor, but camping in the park is generally more appealing and convenient; though choose your time and place carefully, especially at weekends, when Litchfield is popular. The *Batchelor Resort* (☎08/8976 0123) on Rum Jungle Road holds a caravan park (powered sites $29, tent sites $12pp) and *Best Western* motel rooms (❻), whilst 12km down the road towards the national park, the *Banyan Tree* (☎08/8976 0330) is a friendly, if ramshackle place with cheap camping (powered sites $18.50, unpowered $8.50pp) and cabins with free breakfasts and wireless Internet connection. There's also a small pool and a tasty Thai restaurant.

Along Litchfield Park Road

Heading into the park from Batchelor you'll pass black-soil plains dotted with grey, tombstone-like termite mounds. The first chance for a splash is at the **Buley Rock Holes**, a string of easily accessible rock pools with basic camping nearby. Both the road and a 2.5km trail follow the Buley Creek to **Florence Falls**. A lookout surveys the twin twenty-metre falls from above, where a convoluted stairway drops right down to the shady plunge pool where you can swim year-round.

Back on the Litchfield Park Road (the main sealed road in the park linking all the most visited spots), a turn-off south leads to the **Lost City**, a jumble of unusually weathered sandstone columns. Back on the main park road the uninteresting Tabletop Swamp is followed soon after by **Tolmer Falls**, probably the park's most photogenic waterfall, though you can only view it from the cliffs opposite due to the resident rare orange horseshoe bats. Look carefully above the chute and you'll notice a natural rock arch bridging the falls. From the clifftop lookout, a half-hour walk leads back to the car park via the pools at the top of the falls, passing examples of ancient cycads (see p.451) on the way. From **Green Ant Creek** a 1hr return walk leads through pockets of rainforest to the top of the **Tjaetaba Falls**, with a pool to cool off in right on the lip of the cascade.

Packed out at weekends and during school holidays, **Wangi Falls**, on the west side of the park, has easy access past tree-shaded lawns and a café to a large plunge pool. Near the base of the left-hand cascade is a sun-warmed natural spa, but note the multilingual signs warning of the risk of drowning (the pool closes in the Wet when abnormal undertows develop and crocs can lurk). A trail leads through a rainforest boardwalk up over the falls and down the other side via a **lookout** – a good way to work off lunch.

The road leads north from Wangi out of the park to the rather grandly named **Litchfield Tourist Precinct**; basically a pair of caravan parks that can be quieter than those in the park, as well as being better equipped and less congested. *Litchfield Campground* (☎08/8978 2077; half-board in safari tents $85pp) is a base for **helicopter flights** over the park's falls (from $89) and also has the log-cabin *Monsoon Café* which serves snacks and home-style meals. You can also join twice-daily **billabong cruises** on the Reynolds River here (☎08/8978 2330). If you have your own equipment, a kilometre along a dirt road the *Wangi Tourist Park* (aka *Litchfield Safari Camp* ☎08/8978 2185; powered sites $25, unpowered $8pp) is a cheaper and more basic option, but also has cabins (❹).

You re-enter the park (without really knowing you left it) near **Walker Creek**, where there's a string of rock pools to wallow in and, upstream, eight secluded creekside **campsites** with room for just one or two tents; they can only be reached on foot (a walk of up to 2km). When paying their fees, campers are supposed to write on a board to indicate that they have occupied one of the sites, but no one seems to bother, so it may be worth seeing if there's one free before you lug in all your overnight gear. As in other parts of Litchfield, avoid weekends – it'll be packed out.

Southern Litchfield: the Reynolds River Track

Near Green Ant Creek, the **Reynolds River Track** leads 44km south out of the park to the sealed Daly River Road. A half-metre-deep creek crossing near the start of the track discourages 2WDs from continuing, and if you want to get right through to Daly River you'll definitely need 4WD for the sandy section before Surprise Creek Falls, and some steep drops into possibly deep creek crossings. The track itself is appealing, passing many huge termite mounds and burnt or recovering woodland, depending on the last bushfire, though the speed humps along its entire length can get annoying.

A few kilometres after the start of the track there is a turning left to the abandoned **Blyth Homestead**, adding some token historic interest to the park. Back on the main track you soon reach the turn-off leading a couple of kilometres to **Tjaynera Falls** campground (also known as Sandy Creek). From the campground car park it's a 1.7km walk to the falls above a large plunge pool. Nice though it is to strip off and dive in, the pool only gets the sun in the afternoon and there's virtually no room here to spread out in comfort. At the Tjaynera turn-off, on the main track, a sign warns that your 4WD may need a raised air-intake to cross the Reynolds River, 6km further on, though in the late Dry the crossing is no drama. **Surprise Creek Falls** (camping), about 20km further on, are the highlight along the track. A short walk from the campsite car park leads to the sunny plunge pool and, tucked away on the rocks above, two perfectly positioned ten-metre-wide spa pools overlooking the whole scene. From this point it's about a twenty-minute drive over a few more speed humps to the junction with the Daly River Road.

Adelaide River and around

Established during the construction of the Overland Telegraph Line, the town of **ADELAIDE RIVER** was the supply head for Darwin's defence during World War II and consequently suffered sporadic Japanese bombing. Today the town, 110km south of Darwin, provides little more than a lunch-stop along the Stuart Highway, unless you want to visit the town's **war cemetery**, where many of the victims of the air raids are buried. Officially, 243 people died as a result of the eighteen months of Japanese bombing, which began in February 1942, but the cemetery has twice as many graves. The *Mobil Roadhouse* has **camping**, as does the *Adelaide River Inn* (Ⓣ08/8976 7047) along with rooms (❸) and a **restaurant**.

Just south of town, the old highway forks west along a rolling 75km scenic drive before rejoining the main road at *Hayes Creek* roadhouse. After the first 17km on this route you'll come to the turn-off for **Robin Falls**, a pretty little cascade reached after a ten-minute scramble up the creek bed from the car park. Seventeen kilometres south of Robin Falls turn-off, a road leads to **Daly River** community (passing a southern entrance into Litchfield Park; 4WD only), a dead-end favoured by barra fishermen; beyond is Aboriginal land.

Pine Creek and around

Site of the Territory's first goldrush, **PINE CREEK**, 230km from Darwin, is one of the Territory's oldest towns and has managed to hang onto an unreconstructed charm despite (or perhaps because of) its low tourist status. Gold was discovered here while digging holes for the Overland Telegraph Line pylons in 1871, and fools rushed in, hoping to pan their way to fortune. Unfortunately the gold was in the rock, not the riverbeds, requiring laborious crushing with heavy stamp batteries, which, for most prospectors, was too much like hard work for unpredictable returns. The subsequent labour shortage was solved by importing Chinese workers who kept the progressively poorer-quality ore coming for a few more years until fears of Asian dominance led to their being banned from the Territory in 1888. Ah Toys general store on Main Terrace is still run by the descendants of its original Chinese owner.

Around the town, the various time-worn buildings, such as the 1889 **Old Playford Hotel** and **Old Bakery**, may lead you to contemplate the crucial role of corrugated iron, or "galvo", in the colonial pioneering process. The **Miners Park**, at the northern end of town, displays crude mining hardware from over a century ago, and there's a **museum** (Mon–Fri 1–5pm; $2.20) on Railway Terrace, near the police station, and an old locomotive at the old train station itself. For **accommodation**, the *Lazy Lizard Caravan Park* – where there's also a pub and a pool – the *Pine Creek Digger's Motel and Laundromat* (☎08/8976 1442; ④) on Main Street, and the *Pine Creek Hotel* (☎08/8976 1288; $95) round the corner opposite the BP petrol station, are the main contenders. If you want **to eat**, choose between the pub and *Mayse's Café* next door.

From Pine Creek it's 200km along the sealed **Kakadu Highway** to Jabiru, in the heart of Kakadu National Park, passing the majority of the park's highlights on the way. Down the Stuart Highway, 91km south of Pine Creek, a turn-off leads 20km east to **Edith Falls** (Leliyn). Like Wangi in Litchfield, Edith Falls is popular on weekends with a kiosk and small waterfall at the back of the large pool. To get away from the recreational throng you can walk round to the secluded upper pools, on to Sweetwater Pool (9km return) or indeed all the way to Katherine Gorge along a 66-kilometre trail (see p.583).

Katherine to Alice Springs

An obligatory stopover (at least for a couple of days) for visitors to the Top End, **Katherine** is a small but rapidly growing regional centre on the southern banks of the Katherine River. It's just 30km to **Katherine Gorge**, the town's primary tourist attraction and itself part of the larger **Nitmiluk National Park**.

West of Katherine, the **Victoria Highway** leads for 500km west to the WA border, passing Timber Creek and the entrance to **Gregory National Park** on the way. South of town is a vast touristic no-man's-land all the way to Alice Springs. A dip in **Mataranka**'s thermal pool and a couple of "bush pubs" are the highlights of the 670km to **Tennant Creek**. South of Tennant Creek, only the rotund boulders of the **Devil's Marbles** brighten the string of roadhouses along the Stuart Highway, which rolls on for just over 500km to Alice Springs.

Katherine

Traditionally home of the Jawoyn and Dagoman people, the **Katherine River** area must have been a sight for explorer John McDouall Stuart's sore eyes as he struggled north in 1862. Having got this far, he named the river after a benefactor's daughter, Catherine, and within ten years the completion of the Overland

Telegraph Line (OTL) encouraged European settlement, as drovers and prospectors converged on the first reliable water north of the Davenport Ranges. In 1926 a railway from Darwin finally spanned the river and "Kath-rhyne", as die-hard locals still call the town of **KATHERINE**, became established on its present site. It's essentially a "one-street" town, though in January 1998 that street found itself under two metres of water when two cyclones dumped a Wet-season's worth of rain over southern Arnhem Land – a crocodile was spotted cruising lazily past the semi-submerged Woolworths.

The town and around

The Stuart Highway becomes **Katherine Terrace**, the main street, as it passes through town. Along it lie most of the shops and services, including a big Woolworths, as well as several Aboriginal art galleries giving Katherine a compact and unexpectedly busy feel. If you're not just doing the gorge and shooting through, the town is also a good place to pick up **casual work** on the stations and market gardens surrounding it.

If you want the full story on the town head 3km up Giles Street to the **Katherine Museum** (Mon–Fri 10am–4pm, Sat 10am–1pm, Sun 2–5pm; $5), just before the original town site at Knotts Crossing, where a few original OTL pylons still remain upright. Inside are displays relating to Katherine's colonial history, including early medical instruments and a biplane from the time when the building did duty as a Flying Doctor base.

Some 27km south of town lie the **Cutta Cutta Caves**, with guided tours (hourly 9–11am & 1–3pm; $13.50; ⓣ08/8972 1940) of the Limestone Cave and Cutta Cutta. These caves display subterranean karst features, as diverse as they are delicate. Cutta Cutta is the more visually impressive and is also the home of the rare orange horseshoe bat and rather alarming stalactite-climbing brown snakes.

Practicalities

The **train station** is a few kilometres west off the Victoria Highway, from where a **taxi** (ⓣ08/8972 1777 or 8972 1999) to Katherine costs about $20. All buses arrive at the **Transit Centre**, at the south end of Katherine Terrace, next to the 24-hour *BP Roadhouse*. Katherine is a busy interchange for buses, with at least one daily arrival or departure for Darwin, Kununurra (WA) and Alice Springs. Just over the road you'll find the **tourist information centre** (March–Oct daily 8.30am–5pm; Nov–Feb Mon–Fri 8.30am–5pm, Sat & Sun 9am–2pm; ⓣ08/8972 2650 or 1800 653 142, ⓦwww.krta.com.au), with shelves groaning with leaflets. For more detailed information on Nitmiluk, Gregory and Keep River national parks call in at the **Parks and Wildlife Commission**

Tours from Katherine

Gecko Canoe Tours ⓣ08/8972 2224 or 1800 634 319, ⓦwww.geckocanoeing.com.au. One- to seven-day canoeing trips on the Katherine River system downstream of town for around $200 per day. Suitable for beginners, and in many ways far more satisfying than the rather crowded Katherine Gorge.

Manyallaluk ⓣ08/8972 2224. Long-established Aboriginal culture tours now operated by Gecko (see above); a fun day out with didgeridoo-playing, painting, spear-throwing, fire-lighting and bushtucker, all for $165 (or $125 self-drive).

Travelnorth ⓣ08/8971 9999, ⓦwww.travelnorth.com.au. Katherine to Darwin over three days for $569–699 (depending on accommodation type), visiting all the sights.

(☎08/8973 8888) on Giles Street, just over a kilometre from town, past O'Shea Terrace. There's fast **Internet access** at the Katherine Art Gallery opposite Woolworths on Katherine Terrace, at the *Didj Café* round the corner, and in the library on the main street. To **rent a car** call Thrifty (☎08/8972 3183 or 13 61 39) or Hertz Rent-A-Car (☎08/8971 1111, Ⓦwww.hertznt.com). **Bikes** can be rented from the backpackers' or the bike shop on the main street in town.

Accommodation and eating

There's a decent range of places to stay, though the town centre can get rowdy late at night. The tourist information centre provides a list and current prices of all the town's accommodation; the best options – and both backpackers' – are detailed below. There are also at least four caravan parks around town with en-suite cabins (from ❺). **Eating out** in Katherine is nothing to get excited about. The *Terrace Cafe* in the Woolworths Shopping Centre is a popular spot for a daytime snack; in the evening your best bet is a bar meal in a hotel/pub or the *All Seasons* restaurant on the Stuart Highway.

Backpackers

Cocos 21 First St ☎08/8971 2889, Ⓦwww.21firstst.com. Ramshackle, but relaxed and friendly, *Cocos* has just a few four-bed dorm rooms and is popular with cyclists. There's a small kitchen and a washing machine and you can pitch tents at the back of the property. There's also a good gallery and didgeridoo shop next door. Dorms $22pp, tents $11.

Kookaburra Palm Court Backpackers Cnr Giles and Third sts ☎08/8972 2722 or 1800 626 722, Ⓦwww.travelnorth.com.au. Old motel with a cramped kitchen and small pool. Dorms are mostly four-bed with fridge and en suite. Free breakfast. Dorms from $22, rooms ❷ and self-contained units ❸

Motels

All Seasons Katherine Stuart Highway ☎08/8972 1744, Ⓦwww.allseasons.com.au. Katherine's best motel, located four kilometres south of town and set back from the road (so you're guaranteed a good night's sleep). Also has a pool, bar and restaurant. ❹

Beagle Motor Inn 2 Fourth St ☎08/8972 3998. The best choice in town for a basic, inexpensive motel room. Pool, spa and laundry facilities. ❸

Paraway Motel Cnr O'Shea and First sts ☎08/8972 2644. The most comfortable motel in the town centre. ❹

Nitmiluk National Park

The central attraction of the **Nitmiluk National Park** is the magnificent twelve-kilometre **Katherine Gorge**, carved by the Katherine River through the Arnhem Land plateau. Often described as thirteen gorges, it is in fact one continuous cleft, turning left and right along fault lines and separated during the Dry season by rock bars. The spectacle of the river, hemmed in by orange cliffs, makes for a wonderful **cruise** or canoe trip and, unlike Kakadu, Nitmiluk also welcomes bushwalkers along its many marked **trails**. The only **accommodation** is at the pleasant, shady campsite (powered sites $24, unpowered $9.50pp) near the visitors centre, which is a popular spot with wallabies.

Nitmiluk Tours (☎1300 146 743) operates **shuttle buses** along the sealed road between Katherine and the gorge for $24 return. Once at the gorge the **Park Visitors Centre** (March–Nov daily 8am–7pm) has interpretive displays on the park's features from the local Jawoyn Aborigines' perspective (they own the park), and provides maps and further information on the trails, including the *Guide to Nitmiluk National Park* ($6.55) with topographical walking maps. It also includes a restaurant, gallery and a model of the gorge system which puts it all in perspective. As you sit on the terrace overlooking the river below, consider that in January 1998 you would have been under a metre of water.

If you want to do an extended **bushwalk** you'll have to register with the rangers. Trails include the 66-kilometre **Jatbula Trail** to Edith Falls, in the park's northwestern corner, for which you'll need at least three days, a minimum of two people and a $50 returnable deposit.

Exploring Katherine Gorge

Buses from Katherine terminate at the canoe ramp and jetty. Tickets for cruises are sold at the visitors centre. There is also safe swimming – you'll be pleased to know that saltwater crocs are virtually unknown in the gorge. While waiting for a cruise, you might want to take the steep, nine-hundred-metre walk leading from the jetty to the superb Baruwei clifftop **lookout** up the river.

Cruises ply the gorge in a series of boats. **Nitmiluk Tours** (☎1300 146 743) offer somewhat rushed two-hour cruises to the second gorge for $45, a four-hour cruise to the third gorge (the limit during the Wet season, when a more powerful jet boat is brought in) for $65, and an eight-hour "safari", which includes some rock-hopping that demands secure footwear, for around $106. The relaxed safari cruise includes a barbecue lunch, refreshments, plenty of time for swimming and a peep at the sixth gorge; it gets away from the rather busy downstream sections and is highly recommended. Nitmiluk Tours also arrange exhilarating **helicopter flights** up the gorge from as little as $75pp for eight minutes.

Canoeing up the gorge is an option for the more energetic, but don't expect to paddle up to the "thirteenth" in a day; canoeing is hard work for unaccustomed arms and shoulders, especially against the breeze which wafts down the gorge. Nitmiluk Tours rent solo canoes (available at 8am and 1pm) for $49 a day, $44.50 per half-day, or $98 overnight – add about fifty percent for two-person canoes (easier to control and a shared load for beginners) – waterproof containers are included. You'll need to put down a deposit of $20–60 and overnight trips also require a permit ($3.30) available on site. Alternatively, put your own canoe on the river for a small fee payable at the visitors centre. Expect long sections of canoe-carrying over boulders and successively shorter sections

△ Katherine Gorge

of water as you progress up the gorges. Those determined to reach the thirteenth gorge (which, scenically speaking, is not really worthwhile) will find it easier to leave their canoe at the fifth and swim/walk the last couple of kilometres.

The first permissible overnight **campsite** is *Smith's Rock* in the fifth gorge (or anywhere upstream from there) – this is regarded as a fair day's paddling and portaging. Canoeing is best done early in the Dry season, when small waterfalls run off cliff walls and the water level is still high enough to reduce the length of the walking sections.

The Victoria Highway to Western Australia

The **Victoria Highway** stretches for 510km southwest of Katherine to Kununurra in Western Australia. South of the highway, between Gregory and Keep River national parks, is the legendary Victoria River Downs (VRD) station, once the country's biggest cattle station and the base of Australia's biggest heli-mustering outfit, which pursues the daredevil practice of mustering widely dispersed stock with single-seater helicopters.

After passing through **Timber Creek**, the best spot for a pit stop on the long journey west, the Victoria Highway enters a picturesque spur of the remote and wild **Gregory National Park**, around 150km from Katherine, where, with the right equipment and transportation, you can do a walk or a spot of bush camping. More accessible and also worth a diversion is the **Keep River National Park**, just before the Western Australia border.

Timber Creek

Although little more than a pair of roadhouses-cum-bars with adjacent campsites, **TIMBER CREEK**, 300km west of Katherine, makes a welcome break on the long run to Kununurra. In 1856, the explorer Augustus Gregory's ship ran aground on the Victoria River and forced to make repairs, Timber Creek was born, an inland port to serve the vast pastoral properties then being established throughout the region. This remote outpost was soon the scene of bitter disputes between Aborigines and the settlers, and in 1885 a **police station** was set up at Timber Creek, staffed by two policemen and an Aboriginal tracker whose task was to patrol an area the size of Tasmania.

The **museum** (Mon–Fri 10am–noon; $3), housed in a previous police station west of the town, features the usual display of miscellaneous pioneering relics, dragged out of the surrounding undergrowth or abandoned homesteads and used to illustrate a pithy historical commentary about the region. On a different note, the town has the easternmost examples of the curious, bottle-trunked **boab trees**, similar to Africa's baobabs; according to Aboriginal mythology, the boab was a once-arrogant tree which was turned upside down to teach it a lesson in humility (interestingly, West African tribes subscribe to a similar myth to account for their baobabs).

Practicalities

Tourist information is dispensed from the Victoria River Cruise office between the two roadhouses (daily 8am–4.30pm; ⓣ08/8975 0850, ⓦwww.victoriarivercruise.com). Inside you'll find one of the finest selections of "croco-bilia" north of the 26th parallel. Of special note is a rubber "Rude

Croc" – squeeze one and see. A four-hour afternoon **boat tour** (daily 4pm; $70) runs 40km down the Victoria River, on which you'll undoubtedly see some real reptiles, arriving back for sunset on the crags.

Accommodation and **fuel** can be found at the *Timber Creek Hotel* (☎08/8975 0772), incorporating the *Gunamu Tourist Park* which has camping (powered sites $18.50, unpowered $6.50pp), cabins (❷–❸) and motel rooms (❹). The hotel also offers a daily croc feeding session during the dry season at 5pm which takes place from a bridge at the back of the property. The *Wayside Inn* (☎08/8975 0732; ❸–❹) also has rooms – the cheaper ones have shared bathrooms. **Eating** options include whatever's going on at either of the two roadhouses or what you can dig up at the store.

Gregory National Park

Gregory National Park, the Territory's second-largest park, is most easily reached via the Victoria Highway, 11km east of Timber Creek. Carved out from unviable pastoral leases, the park exhibits sandstone escarpments and limestone hills covered in light woodland. Because of its remoteness and rough terrain, it can only be explored in a suitable **4WD vehicle**, and it's a good idea to call at the **P&WC** office in Timber Creek (turn right just before Watch Creek, west of town; ☎08/8975 0888) to study the large map and get information about conditions.

Conventional cars with good clearance and up for a hammering can get as far as **Limestone Gorge**, on a corrugated track 47km south of the highway. Here

Life and death of the real Crocodile Dundee

The survival story of **Rod Ansell** and his subsequent media exposure are generally agreed to be the inspiration for the character of Mick "Croc" Dundee in the popular 1980s films which portrayed a tough bushman as a "fish out of water" in the big city. In 1977, Ansell, then 27 years old, claimed he became marooned when his boat was overturned while fishing at the mouth of the Victoria River, northwest of Timber Creek. With just one oar he paddled a spare dinghy up the Fitzmaurice River to fresh water and survived for seven weeks using the bush skills he'd been brought up with. Living on a diet of feral cattle, berries and sharks, Ansell and his two bull terriers were found, emaciated but coherent, seven weeks later by stockmen. He played down his ordeal but the tale grew legs and, as in the film, a journalist, Rachel Percy, tracked him down and publicized his story in a TV documentary and later in a slim book, *To Fight the Wild*. Sensing an opportunity, Ansell hit the TV chat-show circuit, where his story inspired the comedian Paul Hogan to co-write *Crocodile Dundee*. The film came out in 1985 and was a worldwide hit, helping to put Australia's Outback on the map.

Following the success of the film, Ansell took on a station near Shady Camp on the Mary River, but his tourist plans were foiled when he was barred from using the "Crocodile Dundee" epithet and his entire stock was subsequently shot as part of a bovine disease-eradication programme. Under financial pressure, he lost his station and was later charged with assault and cattle stealing in Arnhem Land. Embittered by his own failure compared with the success of the film, Ansell broke up with his family and became a speed-addled recluse living near Roper Bar. In August 1999, weighing less than seven stone and in the grip of drug-induced paranoia, he shot at strangers near Berry Springs who he thought had kidnapped his sons, before shooting dead a policeman on the Stuart Highway. A shoot-out ensued, and when reinforcements arrived Ansell came out of hiding, firing, and was himself shot dead. Kate Finlayson's 2003 book *A Lot of Croc* describes a semi-fictionalized search to unravel the Rod Ansell story and, on the way, describes many definitively Territorian and politically-incorrect characters, encounters and situations.

you'll find a short walking trail looping up onto the surrounding escarpment, a croc-free billabong and a campsite. The stockyards and old homestead at Bullita, along with the ranger at Bullita Ranger Station (☎08/8975 0833), are another 9km south of the Limestone Gorge turn-off where there's a phone to self-register. The seventy-kilometre **Bullita Stockroute** loops back northwards, crossing a couple of rivers and crawling over some extremely rocky terrain which will chew up your tyres. This takes a full day and scenically it's not worth it, although **camping** is permitted at designated spots along the way.

Alternatively, 4WDs can choose to leave the park south along the **Humbert River Track** – another rocky drive (allow at least six hours for the 112km to the park's eastern boundary), from where you can head east along station tracks. For another route continue circuitously south to the **Buntine Highway** and Kalkaringi via the **Broadarrow** or **Wickham tracks**. Both the stockroute and this route are **one-way** only from Bullita, and are closed from December to March.

Keep River National Park and the WA border

West of Timber Creek, the land flattens out into the evocatively named **Whirlwind Plains**, where the East and West Baines rivers frequently cut the Victoria Highway in the Wet. **Keep River National Park** lies just before the Western Australia border, 185km from Timber Creek. Accessible to all vehicles, it's an easily explored area of dissected sandstone ridges, shallow gorges and Aboriginal art sites, the best of which is **Nganalam**, 24km from the park entrance. Marked trails start from the two **campsites** in the park, and the ranger station (☎08/9167 8827), 3km from the highway, supplies details on longer walks and other attractions.

By now you can hardly have failed to get the message that Western Australia does not want any infested Territorian livestock, produce or honey. The intensively irrigated agricultural area around Kununurra is hoping to remain free from pests found elsewhere in Australia, so eat up your offending foodstuffs before the border or throw them away. If you're not sure what to get rid of, the guys at the checkpoint will put you right; the regulations are not as severe as they seem. Note too that **WA time** is an hour and thirty minutes behind the Territory. At the **border**, Kununurra (see p.712) is just 40km away.

South to Alice Springs

The 1100km south from Katherine, down the "**Track**" (as the Stuart Highway is known) to Alice Springs, are something of a **no-man's-land** for travellers – a sparsely populated, flat, arid plain rolling all the way from the Top End's big rivers to the waterholes of the Red Centre.

West of the Track, the vast Aboriginal lands of the Warlpiri and neighbouring groups occupy just about the entire **Tanami Desert**, while to the east are the grasslands of the **Barkly Tableland**, a declining pastoral region extending north to the seldom-visited coast of the **Gulf of Carpentaria**. The town of **Tennant Creek**, just over halfway, is an anticlimactic break to a journey; car drivers tend to press on down the Track before something breaks or wears out. The landscape as seen from the Stuart Highway encourages a kind of agoraphobic urgency (or just plain boredom), while the mind repetitively churns over such imponderables as "Just how many anthills *are* there in the Northern Territory?"

Mataranka and the Roper River Region

MATARANKA – just over 100km from Katherine – is a small town, the capital of the repeatedly hyped "Never Never" country named after Jeannie Gunn's 1908 novel of a pioneering woman's life, *We of the Never Never*, set in the region. Site of reviled Administrator John Gilruth's planned Northern Territory capital, today the town is practically eclipsed by the nearby **Mataranka Homestead** resort, which lures in buses and passing tourists. South of town the **Elsey National Park road** leads to the often-overlooked freshwater wetlands of the **Roper River**.

There's not much to the town itself, but as you come in a sign leads to the **Bitter Springs** enclave of Elsey National Park, where you can swim in the same lukewarm, minty blue mineral waters which fill the Mataranka thermal pool (see below).

All **accommodation**, along with the supermarket, roadhouses, museum, café and craft shop, is lined up along **Roper Terrace**, the main highway, with a couple of new places on the Bitter Springs road. The *Shell* roadhouse has basic rooms and cabins (④), whilst the *Mataranka Hotel* has motel rooms (②–③) and is linked to the *Old Elsey Roadside Inn* pub. There are better cabins at *Mataranka Cabins* (ⓣ08/8975 4838, ⓦwww.matarankacabins.bigpondhosting.com; ④) just a couple of hundred metres from the Bitter Springs pool, where they also have powered ($22) and unpowered sites ($18) by the river. Just a few hundred metres off the Stuart Highway, *Territory Manor* (ⓣ08/8975 4516; $23) is another camping option on the Bitter Springs road, and they also have motel rooms (④) and a pool.

Mataranka Homestead

Mataranka Homestead, 6km from town (ⓣ08/8975 4544 or 1800 754 544, ⓔmatarankahomestead@bigpond.com.au), was established by Gilruth to raise sheep and horses and is now a bush resort. The palm-shaded **thermal pool**, actually in Elsey National Park but seemingly part of the resort, is the only attraction here: it's free, always open, teeming with people and the water is a pleasant 34°C. The resort has a **bar** and **bistro**, and free nightly entertainment (April–Sept only) as well as a tour-booking service. **Accommodation** includes rooms and self-catering cabins (⑤), motel rooms (③), a backpackers' (budget beds $17) and a campsite (powered sites $22, unpowered $9pp). Overland **buses** stop at the homestead, which is signposted south of Mataranka.

Elsey National Park and the Roper River and Highway

A twelve-kilometre road into **Elsey National Park** (turn off just before the homestead) leads to a more secluded **campsite** with less of a holiday-camp atmosphere, offering canoe rental and swimming in the (almost croc-free) upper Roper River, as well as a small kiosk.

The **Roper River** itself is barely developed, yet it's as scenic as the wetlands of Kakadu. **Cruises** operate along the Roper wetlands in the dry season (ⓣ0427 754 804; from 4pm to sunset; $30). You'll be able to explore the river's so-called **Pandanus Avenue** and some "*African Queen*" – type channels into the beautiful **Red Lily Lagoon**, the most extensive freshwater wetlands in the Territory.

A couple of kilometres south of Mataranka, the **Roper Highway** leads east for 185km (the bitumen ends at around 140km) to the remote community store at **ROPER BAR** with self-catering cabins (③) and a campsite. If you've got this far, you're probably heading for **Borroloola**, 380km away (see p.589), a corrugated track that is passable in the Dry for regular cars in good shape.

Down the Track to Three Ways

LARRIMAH, 72km south of Mataranka, was where the old Darwin railway terminated until 1976 when it closed for good following Cyclone Tracy. Up until then, it had been a busy road–rail terminus, receiving goods brought up from Alice Springs. Now it's just a fuel stop on the highway with a bit more history than most. The *Larrimah Hotel* is a typical **bush pub**, full of eccentricity and historic memorabilia (for more of the same check out the free dusty museum just across the way); you can **camp** here (powered sites $15, unpowered $5pp) or take one of the hotel's inexpensive basic rooms (❷).

Another 89km south brings you to the **Daly Waters Pub**, situated 3km off the highway. Having held a "gallon licence" since 1893, it's laden with memorabilia, including money and women's underwear pinned to the walls: you're welcome to contribute. During the 1930s, when Qantas's Singapore flights refuelled here, world-class aviators used to pop in for a pint, and these days tourists come to marvel at the nutty quaintness of it all and buy the famous tea towels. If you fancy a break there's camping (powered sites $18, unpowered $5pp) and a range of **rooms** (❷–❸) and cabins on offer (❹).

Just beyond here, the **Carpentaria Highway** (technically the circumnational Highway 1) heads off east to Borroloola, 414km away (see opposite); the turn-off is at the *Hi Way Inn Roadhouse* (open 24hr). There's another turn-off further down the Track, just before *Dunmarra Roadhouse*, where the **Buchanan Highway** heads west to *Top Springs Roadhouse* (185km) and ultimately, if you turn off south, Halls Creek in Western Australia (see p.709) along almost 800km of mostly unsealed road.

Further down the Track, **NEWCASTLE WATERS** can't seem to make up its mind whether it's a historic droving township wanting to encourage tourists or a semi-abandoned ghost town. It's of little interest today except to nostalgic drovers.

Further south, **ELLIOTT** is little more than a string of roadhouses with cheap **camping** at the *Mobil Roadhouse* (powered sites $15, unpowered $10) and slightly better facilities at the *Midland Caravan Park* (☎08/8969 2037; powered sites $21.50, unpowered $8pp, cabins ❸), which is also the local post office. The *Elliott Hotel* (☎08/8969 2069; ❸) has simple **rooms** whilst the *Ampol Roadhouse* (☎08/8969 2018; ❹) offers slightly better quality. There are a few shops serving the Jingili Aboriginal communities at either end of town, but apart from filling up with fuel or a counter meal at the pub, there's no reason to stop.

As you leave town to the south, the trees which have hidden the horizon for days recede into shrubs and soon disappear altogether as you approach the deserts of Central Australia. **Renner Springs** is another bush hotel with its insides plastered with eccentric knick-knacks and offers rooms (❹), camping (powered sites $22.50, unpowered $7.50) and Internet access.

On the way to **THREE WAYS** (with its roadhouse open 24hr) watch out for the turn-off to a rocky profile of Churchill's Head and also the **Attack Creek Memorial** – where explorer Stuart was repelled by Aborigines on one of his expeditions. At Three Ways, the **Barkly Highway** heads east to Camooweal, Mount Isa and eventually Townsville, all in Queensland; 210km in you'll hit the *Barkly Homestead* (6am–1am), a better-than-average roadhouse with all the usual services. From Three Ways, Tennant Creek (see p.590) is just 26km down the road.

Cape Crawford, Borroloola and the Tablelands Highway

Cape Crawford is nothing more than a highway junction with the *Heartbreak Hotel* roadhouse (☎08/8975 9928; camping $8pp, rooms ❸). From the roadhouse the single-width **Tablelands Highway** offers a bitumen alternative to the Gulf route, leading to western Queensland via the *Barkly Homestead* roadhouse.

Borroloola

Situated on the croc-infested **McArthur River**, **BORROLOOLA** has had a colourful history which reads like an exaggerated version of the familiar boom, bust and dribble pattern of so many Outback towns. The explorers Leichhardt and Gregory came this way in the mid-nineteenth century, reporting good pasture, and the cattle followed in droves. By the early 1880s, when Tennant Creek and Katherine were still just shacks on the Overland Telegraph Line, the settlement was a wild outpost that even the missionaries avoided. Ships that formerly supplied the OTL came upriver with provisions for the hard-living drovers, who were helping stock the pastoral leases right across the north of Australia.

Borroloola was proclaimed, or "gazetted", in 1885 and a new police station was established in an attempt to control the town's lawless urges. The end came when today's Barkly Highway became the favoured stock route, and by 1900 just a handful of Europeans remained in "The 'Loo". With their passing the four local Aboriginal groups comprising the Yanyuwa have reclaimed the town and surrounding land, which now serves their communities.

The only original building to have survived the punch-ups, white ants and cyclones is the **Old Police Station**, now a museum (Mon–Fri 10am–4pm; free). With Borroloola's exceptional history (see box, below), the museum couldn't fail to be fascinating. Read, for example, E. Gaunt's hair-raising account of *The Birth of Borroloola*, recalling the sporadic insanity of the early days; it seems the toxic home-brew known as "Come Hither", whose label showed a red-eyed Lucifer beckoning malevolently, was to blame. Not surprisingly, the coverage of local Aboriginal history is lightweight. All this history may tickle your fancy but don't be misled: Borroloola is a rough and depressing Aboriginal welfare town of interest only to those needing fuel and a feed on the coastal Gulf route.

There are a couple of basic **campsites** along the main road (cabins ❸–❺) and rooms in the pub (❺) which from the outside looks about as inviting as a detention centre. By road, Borroloola is easily accessible along the **Carpentaria Highway**, via the *Heartbreak Hotel* at Cape Crawford. Depending on who you ask, the **dirt road** to **Wollogorang** roadhouse and Hell's Gate in Queensland (see p.543) is either terrible or not bad, but it's bound to be an adventure.

The classics library and hermits of Borroloola

There are a number of more or less unlikely explanations for Borroloola's improbable **classics library**, including one which starts with a bored policeman's request for reading matter to New York's Carnegie Foundation. In truth, it was a gradual acquisition of nearly two thousand literary classics by the town's McArthur Institute at the beginning of the twentieth century. Termites tucked into the library, a cyclone destroyed the remains and only a handful of books survived, many in "private collections", gathering what must be enormous overdue fees.

In 1963 a boyish David Attenborough made a TV documentary about three **hermits** who had chosen to retreat to the 'Loo. Jack Mulholland came across as a slightly jaded recluse when pressed about "loneliness and… women", and the reputedly aristocratic "Mad Fiddler" was too deranged to face the camera, but **Roger Jose** was, and looked like, the real thing. Having devoured the library ahead of the ants, he lived in a water tank with his Aboriginal wife and was a humane if eccentric "bush philosopher" who once observed that "a man's riches are the fewness of his needs". He is buried at the end of the airstrip in Borroloola.

Tennant Creek

Visitors expect to be disappointed by **TENNANT CREEK**, 26km south of Three Ways junction, and indeed its appeal to tourists is not immediately apparent. Hang around, however, and you'll discover an unpretentious Outback town, defying stagnation and hoping for prosperity.

John McDouall Stuart came through in the early 1860s, followed by the Overland Telegraph Line ten years later. Pastoralists and prospectors arrived from the south and east, and in 1933 Tennant Creek was the site of the last major **goldrush** in Australia. This was the time of gritty "gougers", such as Jack Noble and partner Bill Weaber (with one eye between them), who defied the Depression by pegging some of the town's most productive claims. Today mining corporations use modern methods to exploit marginal deposits, but the main business in Tennant these days is looking after the health, education and other needs of the region's Aboriginal communities.

Arrival and information

Tennant Creek is 504km from Alice Springs and 664km from Katherine. The **airport** is about 3km from the centre, at the end of Davidson Street, and the **train station** is by the highway 5km south of town, though the train only stops if someone has a ticket for Tennant – getting off you'll feel like Spencer Tracy in the opening scene of *Bad Day at Black Rock*. The new train service has not been so good for the town as most people now shoot through to Darwin, some transporting their cars on the train. On Paterson Street (the town's main street, essentially the Stuart Highway) you'll find the 24-hour *BP Roadhouse* where interstate **buses** pull in – both north- and south- bound buses come through at around 3am, which also doesn't encourage stopovers. Paterson Street also holds **Internet** access at *Switch* next to the Transit Centre and the *Top of the Town* **café** next to that. The helpful **visitors information centre** is out at Battery Hill (daily 9am–5pm; ⓣ08/8962 1281 or 1800 500 879, ⓦwww.barklytourism.com.au), 1.5km east along Peko Road.

Accommodation

There are motels at each end of town and one in the middle, but they occasionally fill up with contract workers if there is some exploration activity going on.

El Dorado Motor Inn Paterson St North ⓣ08/8962 2402. Motel at the north end of town with a licensed restaurant and nice pool area. ❹

Safari Lodge Motel and Backpackers Davidson St ⓣ08/8962 2207, ⓔsafari@swtch.com.au. Functional motel right in the town centre, with budget rooms (❷) and dorms ($20) also available. ❹

Tennant Creek Caravan Park Next to the Shell service station, Paterson St ⓣ08/8962 2325, ⓦwww.users.bigpond.com/tennantcreek. One of three caravan parks in town, this one has good deals for camping (powered sites $23, unpowered $9pp), backpackers' bunkhouse doubles (❷) and roomy cabins (❷–❸).

Tennant Creek Tourist's Rest Leichhardt St ⓣ08/8962 2719, ⓦwww.touristrest.com.au. A time-worn row of two- and three-bed rooms with an authentic lived-in "Tennant" feel, plus a pool, free breakfasts and pick-ups off the bus. Also organizes fossicking and Devil's Marbles tours (see opposite). Dorms $20, rooms ❷

The Town and around

In town, the Tuxworth and Fullworth **museum** (daily 3.30–5.30pm; donation), across the road from the *Memorial Club*, minutely details the history of Tennant Creek, using a chronological time scale starting from the year 0 "AS" (After Stuart). If you're heading to the visitors centre at **Battery Hill** you might as well take the sixty-minute tour of the mine site (up to 4 daily; $20), which includes an entertaining stroll through a specially-built show mine. On site there's also a museum (daily 9am–5pm; $5) detailing the region's social history and a collection of international minerals, as well as the chance to check out the old stamp battery. The scale of the 1930s goldrush was not insignificant; for a year the equivalent of nearly a million dollars of gold came out of Tennant Creek each day.

Back in town, the recently built Nyinkka Nyunyu **Arts and Cultural Centre** (May–Sept Mon–Fri 9am–5pm, Sat & Sun 10am–2pm; Oct–March Mon–Fri 9am–5pm; Ⓦwww.nyinkkanyunyu.com.au; $10), at the south end of Paterson Street, is similar in concept to the better-known cultural centres at Uluru and Kakadu. This one comes without the baggage of those glamorous locations, and instead gives a more rounded picture of a real community. Historical events are displayed in mini-dioramas alongside looped films of Warumungu talking about their experiences, as well as artefacts, bushtucker lore and some indifferent paintings. Particularly interesting is the story of the twenty-year land claim against an initially obstructive NT administration, which had only just gained self-government itself and was not yet disposed to giving large chunks of the Territory away.

Without your own vehicle, that's about it, although a couple of kilometres north of town is an old **telegraph station**, restored as a historic exhibit (contact visitors centre for opening times). If you've come down the Track and not seen an OTL station yet, here's your chance.

Eating and drinking

You won't be surprised to hear that the Michelin **food guide** has overlooked Tennant Creek yet again. Your options are the *Top of the Town* café near the Transit Centre, which is open for daytime meals, *Woks Up* Chinese in the Sporties Club on Ambrose Street which runs off Peko Road, or you can sign in as a guest at the *Memorial Club* on Schmidt Street for an $18 feed and have a quiet drink afterwards.

Dedicated **drinkers** are well looked after, as the town boasts around thirteen licences and two pubs. Like a lot of pubs in Outback towns, front bars can be intimidating, while the carpeted back bars are for games of pool and benign socializing. *Goldfields*, on Paterson Street, has a cleared front bar where you can get a good swing at your neighbour without breaking any of the fittings; the back bar is the place to take your mum for a sherry. Over the road, the *Tennant Creek Hotel* also has a back bar for a quiet drink.

Towards Alice Springs and the Centre

If you're feeling a bit "Top Ended" then the 505km from Tennant to Alice Springs offers some respite as the land opens out into the subtle hues of the central deserts. Unless you have a 4WD, only the Devil's Marbles are worth breaking the journey for, and if you've not got your own transport then they can be visited on a day-tour from Tennant Creek with Devil's Marbles Tours (Ⓣ0418 891 711; $75, 2 people minimum).

Eighty-seven kilometres from town, a sign points east towards the **Davenport Ranges National Park**. Here a track runs 160km east along the north side of the ranges before looping back west along the rougher but scenically more interesting southern side, passing a couple of waterholes, station homesteads and outstations on the way – a chance to see something of central NT other than the Stuart Highway. Ideally using a 4WD, you can expect to do the standard loop with an overnight camp and emerge about 100km further on down the Track. If you're interested, get a leaflet and map from Tennant Creek's visitor centre. Fuel and provisions are available at Kurundi and Murray Downs station stores on the way (both are on or near the main track).

South to Ti Tree

Right by the highway about 100km south of Tennant Creek, the **Devil's Marbles** (basic camping) are a genuine geological oddity, a scattering of huge rounded boulders thought by the local Warumungu Aborigines to be the eggs of the Rainbow Serpent. They're well worth a look as any excuse for a break is welcome around these parts. A short drive south of the Marbles is **WAUCHOPE** (pronounced "Walkup"), with its old roadhouse/pub which has a motel (❸), budget rooms (❷), dorms ($20), camping (powered sites $18, unpowered $7pp) and a restaurant. **WYCLIFFE WELL Holiday Park**, a little further south, has the largest range of beer in Australia and the apparent chance of UFO sightings (see box, below). On site there's camping (powered sites $25, unpowered $20), a range of rooms (❷–❺), Internet access and a sorry collection of wildlife in the so-called animal sanctuary.

BARROW CREEK, 60km further on, has one of the oldest roadhouses on the Track, originally a telegraph station. The old pub is as characterful as they come along the Track, with walls daubed in coarse humour and foreign bank notes (a "bush bank"), as well as old rooms (❸) and free camping out back.

Barrow Creek is also remembered as the site of the Barrow Creek Massacre in 1874, when a local clan was all but wiped out in reprisal for the killing of the two men whose graves are in the forecourt. Fifty-four years later, the last of the Territory's massacres took place at Coniston, 100km to the southwest, when up to a hundred Aboriginal men, women and children were killed by a policeman following the death of a dingo trapper.

At **TI TREE**, an Aboriginal community close to the middle of the continent, a couple of galleries sell keenly priced artefacts and paintings produced by the local Anmatjera and communities further afield, though as all over the Territory the quantity of indigenous art seems now to be in inverse proportion to its quality. After another 59km, the **AILERON** roadhouse has camping (powered sites $15) and rooms (❹) and is the last fuel stop before Alice Springs.

The Plenty Highway and Tanami Road

Heading towards Alice Springs, the land finally begins to crumple as you near the MacDonnell Ranges. The **Plenty** and **Sandover highways**, which run off the Stuart Highway 66km south of Aileron, head northeast towards Queensland

Area 51 – Down Under

For decades there have been apparent sightings of UFOs in the skies over Wycliffe Well. While the roadhouse has capitalized on this to the full with some kitsch "alien-obilia" and a space ship on the forecourt, scores of newspaper articles in the restaurant attest to the regular sightings of UFOs, if not necessarily bug-eyed ETs. The location has certain parallels with Nevada's Area 51, a sparsely populated semi-desert, and the shady goings-on at the Pine Gap US military base near Alice Springs are just 400km to the south. Of course that's no distance at all for the latest remote orbiters fitted with the new-generation plasma drives. Rationalizations of the sightings include that they are merely "glowing birds" or the "Min Min Light" (see p.526). Whatever the truth is, it would be unfair to suggest that Wycliffe Well's global selection of over three hundred beers has any connection with the phenomenon, but it gives you something to do while you watch the skies and wait.

through the scenic Harts and Jervois ranges. Both are passable with sound, well-equipped conventional cars – the Plenty (which becomes the Donohue Highway in Queensland) is generally the busier and better maintained. If you're heading down to Birdsville or Winton this way (both in Queensland), the Donohue Highway shortcut down to Boulia isn't half as bad as maps suggest.

Twenty kilometres north of Alice Springs, the **Tanami Road** leads 1040km northwest to Halls Creek in Western Australia. The track is a dirt freeway up to the Granites mines just before the WA border, from where things can get a little rough and sandy. If you're heading from Alice Springs to the Bungles (see p.710), the Tanami is quicker than the bitumen via Katherine, but pretty boring (although of course you need 4WD to get into the Bungles). The longest section without fuel is the 322km from Yuendumu to **Rabbit Flat** roadhouse (closed Tues–Thurs), with the next section to Billiluna station in WA nearly as long at 292km. You can also pop into the art gallery at the Aboriginal community of **Balgo Hills**, which sometimes has fuel, 31km south of the Tanami (the turn-off is about 88km on the WA side of the track); their garish and splodgy school of dot paintings is highly distinctive.

Before embarking on either route, it's worth checking out the condition of the tracks; phone Emergency Services in Alice Springs (Ⓣ08/8951 6686) or the Main Roads Dept, Halls Creek (Ⓣ08/9168 6007); you can also check out up-to-date road conditions of desert tracks at Ⓦwww.exploreoz.com. Although they shouldn't be considered time-saving short cuts, the Plenty and Tanami tracks are both perfectly feasible in a tough, well-equipped 2WD vehicle.

Alice Springs and the Red Centre

Set at what is just about the geographical centre of the continent, **Alice Springs** has a population of just 28,000, yet is still the largest settlement in the Australian interior. A modern and compact town in the midst of the MacDonnell Ranges, it makes an excellent base from which to explore the surrounding countryside.

The **Red Centre**, a marketing term coined to describe the area to the south, west and east of Alice Springs, is a historically rich and scenically spectacular region. It includes the lands inhabited by the "Anangu", the tourist-friendly epithet for the Aborigines from the Uluru region. Notwithstanding massacres as late as 1928, the **Aborigines of the central deserts** were fortunate in being among the last to come into contact with white settlers, by which time the exterminations of the nineteenth century had passed their peak and anthropologists like Ted Strehlow were hurrying to record a "dying race". As a result of this, their traditional way of life was well documented, though their isolation is also said to have made their adjustment to modern life more difficult than Aborigines of the northern coast, who had contact with foreigners even before European colonization.

Ayers Rock – or **Uluru** – is Australia's most famous and most visited natural spectacle, and still the primary reason why most people come to the Centre. At first sight, even jaded "seen-it-all" cynics will find it hard to take their eyes away from its awesome bulk. But there's much more in the Centre than just the Rock, and it's rare in Outback Australia to find such a large region crammed with so many worthwhile and accessible places of interest. The **West MacDonnells**, a series of rugged ridges cut at intervals by slender chasms or huge gorges, start right on Alice Springs's doorstep. In the other direction, the **Eastern MacDonnells** are less visited but no less appealing, with the remote tracks of the **Simpson Desert** to the south attracting the intrepid. To the west, **Palm Valley**, now linked to **Kings Canyon** via a good dirt road, can add a few days to a trip which, including the Rock, makes for probably the most memorable tour in the Outback. While most of these places certainly don't need a 4WD vehicle to get to, there are a few enjoyable and easy off-road tracks that can be fun in a rented 4WD; they're detailed in the box, p.612.

When to go and what to take

The aridity of the Centre results in seasonal extremes of temperature that are best avoided, if at all possible. In the midwinter months of July and August the air is lovely and clear, although **freezing nights**, especially around Uluru, are not uncommon. But there's no escaping the **summer heat**: in December and January the temperature may have reached 40°C by 10am and won't drop below 30°C all night. The transitional seasons of autumn (April–June) and spring (Sept & Oct) are the best times to explore the region in comfort.

Rain is a rare and wonderful thing in the Centre. Whenever you visit, a sudden storm may temporarily transform the desert into a garden of wild flowers as well as cut off access along even the main roads, though as a rule it is **midsummer storms** which bring the most rain.

Out here a **wide-brimmed hat** is not so much a fashion accessory as a life saver, keeping your head and face in permanent shadow. All but the shortest of walks will also require a **water bottle** and loose, long-sleeved clothing plus lashings of **sun block** on any exposed skin. Australia's many venomous but rarely seen snakes and, more relevantly, rocky tracks and the carpet of prickly spinifex grass that covers a fifth of the continent, make a pair of **covered shoes or boots** the final precaution to safe and comfortable tramping around the Centre.

Alice Springs and around

Most visitors are surprised by the modern appearance of **ALICE SPRINGS**. The bright, clear desert air gives the Outback town and its people a charge that you don't get in the languid, tropical north. In Alice Springs, the shopping centre is actually in the middle of town and not in some distant suburb, and so allusions to Nevil Shute's flyblown *A Town Like Alice Springs*, or even Robyn Davidson's ockersome observations in *Tracks*, have long been obsolete.

The area has been inhabited for at least thirty thousand years by Aranda Aborigines, who moved between reliable water sources along the MacDonnell Ranges. But, as elsewhere in the Territory, it was only the Overland Telegraph Line's arrival in the 1870s that led to a permanent settlement here. Following **John McDouall Stuart**'s exploratory journeys through the area in the early 1860s, it was the visionary **Charles Todd**, then South Australia's Superintendent

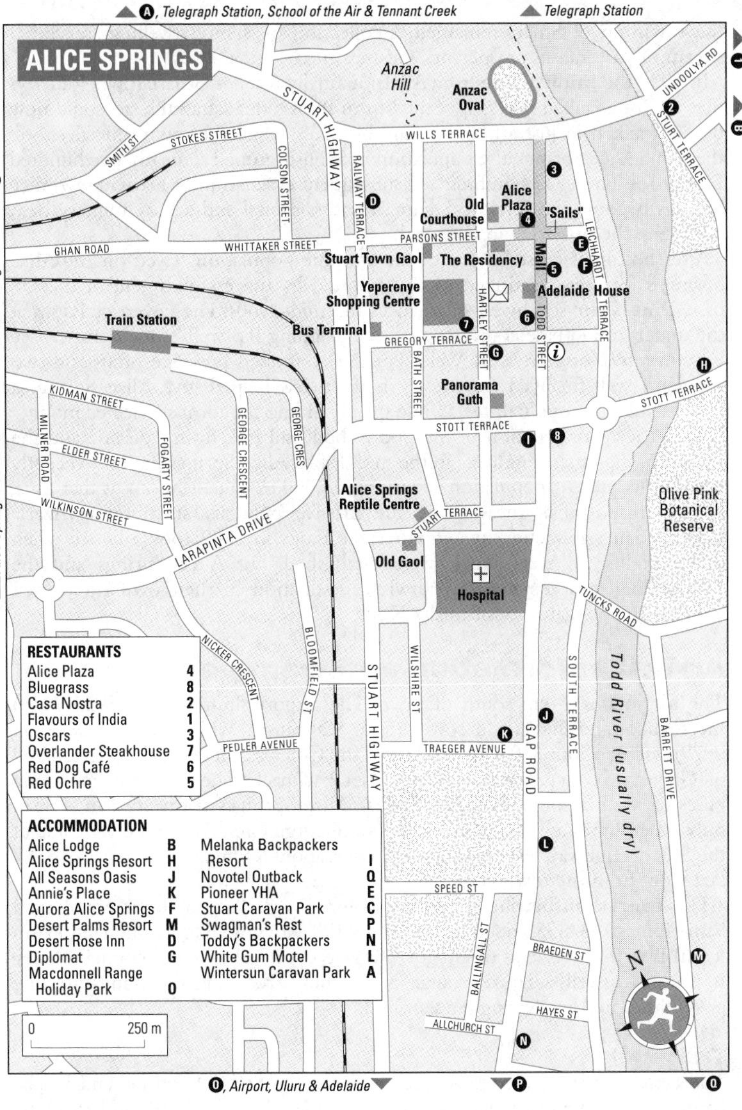

of Telegraphs, who saw the need to link Australia with the rest of the empire. The town's river and its tributary carry his name, and the "spring" (actually a billabong) and town that of his wife, Alice.

With repeater stations needed every 250km from Adelaide to Darwin to boost the OTL signal, the billabong north of today's town was chosen at the spot at which to erect the necessary buildings. When a spurious ruby rush led on to the discovery of gold at Arltunga in the Eastern MacDonnells, **Stuart Town** (the town's seldom-used official name in its early years) became a jumping-off point for the long slog to the riches out east. Arltunga's goldrush fizzled out, but the township of Stuart remained, a collection of shanty dwellings serving a stream of pastoralists, prospectors and missionaries.

In 1929 the **railway line** from Adelaide finally reached Stuart Town. Journeys that had once taken weeks by camel from the Oodnadatta railhead could now be undertaken in just a few days and by 1933, when the town officially took the name Alice Springs, the population had mushroomed to nearly five hundred Europeans. The 1942 bombing and subsequent evacuation of Darwin saw Alice Springs become the Territory's administrative capital and a busy military base, supplying the war zone in the north.

After hostilities ceased, some of the wartime population stayed on and Alice Springs's fortunes continued to rise, boosted by the establishment of the US base, **Pine Gap**, southwest of town in the mid-1960s. The covert activities at the underground base conjure up many intriguing Roswell-esque theories (see box on p.592 or search the Web), but the continued presence of around two thousand well-financed Americans in town has helped give Alice Springs a purposeful, cosmopolitan feel, while greatly aiding the local service economy.

With the reconstruction of the poorly built rail link from Adelaide and the sealing of the Stuart Highway in the mid-1980s, Alice Springs has only recently attained its present population of around 28,000. A tourist boom at that time, helped in no small measure by the massive publicity surrounding Azaria Chamberlain's abduction by a dingo at the Rock in 1980, took a knock when direct flights to Ayers Rock were established, but Alice Springs and the surrounding area remain a worthwhile destination in their own right, even without the obligatory visit to the Rock.

Arrival, information and transport

The **airport** is 14km south of town. The airport shuttle (ⓣ08/8953 0310) meets incoming flights and costs $15, or $28 return, while a taxi (ⓣ08/8953 0979) will be about $30. **Buses** arrive at the Coles Complex at the western end of Gregory Terrace. Some of the keener backpacker hostels meet incoming buses (as well as some incoming flights). Alice Springs's **train station** – open only when trains are due to arrive – is on George Crescent on the west side of the Stuart Highway, just off Larapinta Drive, about a fifteen-minute walk (or $7 taxi ride) from the town centre.

The **tourist information office** (Mon–Fri 8.30am–5.30pm, Sat & Sun 9am–4pm; ⓣ08/8952 5800 or 1800 645 199, ⓦwww.centralaustraliantourism.com) is at the river end of Gregory Terrace by the library and council offices. It features a well-organized range of brochures detailing the mind-boggling possibilities in Alice Springs and around.

Transport

The centre occupies a compact area between the Stuart Highway and Leichhardt Terrace, along the dry Todd River, bordered to the north and south by Wills Terrace and Stott Terrace respectively. Bisecting this rectangle is **Todd Mall**, once the main street, now a relaxing pedestrian thoroughfare lined with alfresco cafés, galleries and souvenir outlets.

The town's sights are scattered, but you can still get around them all in a couple of days on foot. An alternative is to use the green-and-yellow **Alice Springs Wanderer** (ⓣ08/8952 2111; day-ticket $38), a hop-on hop-off bus service with commentary which visits most of the places of interest every seventy minutes. The Yepereneye Shopping Centre, on Hartley Street, is the terminus for the **suburban bus** network; it's best to check bus times before you set out (timetables are available from the tourist office or the Civic Centre on Todd Street). Of the four main routes, #1 West and #4 South are the most useful. Otherwise your best bet is to rent a **car** (see "Listings", p.602) or a **bicycle** from any of the hostels (around $25 a day). There's an enjoyable seventeen-kilometre partly **paved cycle track** through the bush to Simpson's Gap, starting at Flynn's Grave, 7km along Larapinta Drive, west of the town centre.

Accommodation

Most places in Alice Springs (except the campsites) are either in the town centre area or along Todd Street and its southern continuation, **Gap Road** – a twenty-minute walk from the Mall which some find off-putting late at night. Booking ahead is advisable during the winter school holidays (June & July) or during special events like the Masters Cup in October. Note that the price codes given for self-contained apartments are for a unit sleeping from four and six people; they often work out a better deal than a motel and are certainly more spacious. One day someone will invest in a purpose-built **backpackers'**, but for the moment you get what you pay for from the selection of generally lacklustre converted motels listed below.

Motels and hotels

Alice Springs Resort 34 Stott Terrace ⓣ08/8951 4545 or 1300 134 044, ⓦwww.voyages.com.au. Just over the river but not too far away, this plush four-star has all mod cons and the gourmand's *Barra-on-Todd* restaurant. ❻

All Seasons Oasis 10 Gap Rd ⓣ08/8952 1444, ⓦwww.accorhotels.com.au. Nicely laid-out motel with landscaped pool area, comfortable, spacious rooms and a good bar-restaurant. ❺

Aurora Alice Springs 11 Leichhardt Terrace ⓣ08/8950 6666, ⓦwww.aurora-resorts.com.au. About as central as they get and better than it looks, with covered parking, in-house movies and the adjacent *Red Ochre Grill* on the Mall. ❹

Desert Palms Resort 74 Barrett Drive ⓣ08/8952 5977 or 1800 678 037, ⓦwww.desertpalms.com.au. Rows of semi-detached cabins in a palm-tree setting just over the river, with well-equipped kitchens and a pool. ❺

Desert Rose Inn 15 Railway Terrace ⓣ08/8952 1411, ⓦwww.desertroseinn.com.au. Central budget motel with cooking facilities in some rooms, backpacker twins (❷), a BBQ area and off-street parking. ❹

Diplomat 15 Gregory Terrace, cnr of Hartley St ⓣ08/8952 8977. Right in town, a large four-star motel popular with coach groups with a better than average *Keller's* restaurant. ❺

Novotel Outback Stephens Rd ⓣ08/8952 6100 or 1300 656 565, ⓦwww.accorhotels.com.au. Tucked under the MacDonnell Ranges on the edge of town, this spacious and well-equipped modern four-star hotel comes with a gym, pool and *Ainslie's* restaurant. ❺–❻

Swagman's Rest 67–69 Gap Rd ⓣ08/8953 1333 or 1800 089 612, ⓦwww.theswagmansrest.com.au. Nothing fancy, but a good-value, fully self-contained option; sleeps up to six people. ❹

White Gum Motel 17 Gap Rd ⓣ08/8952 5144, ⓦwww.whitegum.com.au. A notch below the *Swagman's*, this place has seen better days, but has the nearest self-contained motel units to the town centre. ❹

Backpackers

Alice Springs Lodge 4 Mueller St ⓣ08/8953 1975 or 1800 351 925, ⓦwww.Alice Springslodge.com.au. A converted house, not a motel, set in a quiet, residential street on the east side of the river, all which makes for a mellow atmosphere. Nearer to the centre than it feels, there's a shady garden area and pool. Various aged caravans in the back cater for twins and doubles, but the tiny kitchen gets quickly crowded. Eight-share dorms $20, four-share dorms $24, rooms ❸

Annie's Place 4 Traeger Ave ⓣ08/8952 1545 or 1800 359 089, ⓦwww.anniesplace.com.au. Converted motel which has had great word-of-mouth thanks to the adjacent bar and cheap meals, but the kitchen is poor and the hard sell on its own Mulga Tours is infamous. Eight-share dorms ($18) share fridge and a bathroom, rooms (some with private en-suite) ❸

Melanka Backpackers Resort 94 Todd St ⓣ08/8952 4744 or 1800 815 066, ⓦwww.melanka.com.au. This huge complex based round a shabby motel is popular with backpackers tours and enjoys a good location. *Melanka Party Bar* next door rages till 4am and there's a cheap cafeteria, pool and even beach volleyball, but as usual the kitchen is neglected. The once-notorious four-bed dorms are now threes, but even then the 8-beds appear spacious in comparison. All dorms $20, small twin rooms with fridge ❸

Pioneer YHA Todd River–end of Parsons St ⓣ08/8952 8855, ⓔAlice Springspioneer@yhant.org.au. It may be a "matronly" Y, but apart from a lack of parking (don't park by the river), this is still one of the best actually in town; a central but surprisingly quiet converted walk-in cinema which layout-wise, works a lot better than some ex-motels. Four-bed air-con dorms $27.50, sixes for $25.50, eights for $23.50, plus a pool and a kitchen big enough to cope. Rooms ❸–❹

Toddy's Backpackers 39–41 Gap Rd ⓣ08/8952 1322, ⓦwww.toddys.com.au. Large converted motel with cheap mixed, four- and six-bed dorms, standard rooms plus motel rooms with bath, kitchen facilities and DVD players. There's also cheap beer and nightly BBQs. Free light breakfasts and shuttle/pick-ups make up for the twenty-minute walk to the town centre. Dorms, six-bed $18 (with en-suite $19), four-bed $20. ❸

Caravan parks

Macdonnell Range Holiday Park Palm Place ⓣ08/8952 6111. Camping (powered sites $33, unpowered $29) and cabins in a leafy setting on the south edge of town with all mod-cons. Cabins ❹–❺

Stuart Caravan Park Opposite Araluen Centre, Larapinta Drive ⓣ08/8952 2547, ⓦwww.stuartcaravanpark.com.au. The most central caravan park, about 2km west of town, with regular camping and powered sites ($27). Cabins ❸

Wintersun Caravan Park Stuart Highway, 3km north of town ⓣ08/8952 4080. Regular camping ($11pp) and powered sites ($26). Cabins ❹

The Town

Start your tour of town by nipping up to **Anzac Hill** (off Wills Terrace) for a great view over Alice Springs to the Heavitree Ranges beyond. In town, on Parsons Street is the Old Courthouse and across the street is the Residency (Mon–Fri 9am–4pm, Sat 10am–4pm; free), a neat period dwelling which is a tangible symbol of the brief independence Central Australia once had from the Northern Territory. A bit further down Parsons Street comes the **Stuart Town Gaol**, Alice Springs's oldest building, dating from 1909.

From the "Sails" awning, a short stroll down the mall will take you past **Adelaide House** (March–Nov Mon–Fri 10am–4pm, Sat 10am–noon; $4), an ingenious convection-cooled building designed by the Reverend John Flynn, founder of the Royal Flying Doctor Service (RFDS). Adelaide House was the first hospital in Central Australia, and also the site of Flynn's and Alf Treager's innovative radio experiments using portable, pedal-generated electricity. Inside you'll come across early medical and RFDS memorabilia. Next door to Adelaide House is the **John Flynn Memorial Church**.

Half a kilometre southwest of Adelaide House, the **Alice Springs Reptile Centre** (daily 9.30am–5pm; $12; ⓣ08/8952 8900, ⓦwww.reptilecentre.com.au) at 9 Stuart Terrace is also definitely worth an hour or so of your time and highlights the countless reptiles which inhabit this part of the country, along with species from the rest of Australia. Deadly snakes such as the inland Taipan vie for your attention alongside less fearsome, but equally fascinating reptiles such as the comedic thorny devils. All of the enclosures are informatively and amusingly captioned and there are also grisly feeding displays and more playful shows where you'll have the opportunity to handle lizards and even a giant olive python. Opposite the Reptile Centre at 2 Stuart Terrace, the **Old Gaol** (March–Nov daily 10am–5pm; $6.50; ⓣ08/8952 9006) was operational until 1996 and is now home to the National Pioneer Women's Hall of Fame, a stirring photographic exhibit detailing the achievements of women such as Olive Pink.

When you've had enough of artefacts and memorabilia, head out to the **Olive Pink Botanical Reserve** (daily 10am–6pm; donation), just across the causeway on Tuncks Road. Olive Pink was a passionate defender of Aboriginal rights long before the issue became fashionable. Like T.G.H. Strehlow, with whom she briefly worked, Pink practised a kind of fanatical "inverted eugenics", working solely for the welfare and preservation of "full-blood" tribal Aborigines and their lore, while dismissing those of mixed blood as a lost cause. She also found time to collect native flora from the surrounding lands, all of which can be seen neatly labelled along pathways winding up through the reserve. Displays in the **visitors centre** (daily 10am–4pm) next to the car park explain the various strategies the plants use to survive in the desert.

The Telegraph Station and School of the Air

The old **Telegraph Station** (daily 8am–5pm, picnic grounds until 9pm; $7) is tucked in the hills just to the north of town. Fully restored and accessible along a three-kilometre riverside walk from Wills Terrace (or off the Stuart Highway, 4km north of town), the historic reserve – situated right by the pool from which the town derives its name – faithfully re-creates the settlement's earliest years. There are free and informative thirty-minute **tours** further detailing pioneering life at the telegraph station. All in all, it's a pleasant place to while away a quiet afternoon, with the surrounding picnic area giving a taste of the Outback on the edge of a city. The station is also the starting point of the **Larapinta Trail** bushwalk to Standley Chasm in the Western MacDonnells (see p.605).

On the other side of the Stuart Highway is the **School of the Air** (Mon–Sat 8.30am–4.30pm, Sun 1.30–4.30pm; closed during school holidays; $6.50), at 80 Head St. Explanatory sessions are offered every thirty minutes on this famous Outback institution, through which children living on remote stations are taught over the radio. It's mostly visited by overseas schoolchildren and teachers. From town, take bus #3 and alight at stop 5 or 11.

Along Larapinta Drive to the Alice Springs Desert Park

Larapinta Drive heads out through the western suburbs to the **Alice Springs Cultural Precinct** (daily 10am–5pm; $9), some 2km from the town. The walk to the precinct isn't too bad, but check out the bus service if you're continuing to the Alice Springs Desert Park.

The precinct has brought together some of Alice Springs's best attractions and is well worth the entry fee. The **Araluen Centre for Arts and Entertainment**, for example, is the focal point for the performing arts in the region with a 500-seat theatre, cinema, and art galleries that always have something on that is worth checking out. The **Central Australian Aviation Museum**, located in the Old Connellan Hangar, houses many of the aircraft in which Outback plane travel was pioneered and has a special memorial to the "Coffee Royale Incident" of 1929, in which rescuers searching for missing aviator Charles Kingsford-Smith perished in the northern Tanami Desert. Kingsford-Smith was accused of cynically staging the crash for publicity purposes, though this was never proved; the memorial poignantly displays the wreckage of the long-lost *Kookaburra* used in the search.

The **Museum of Central Australia** contains local fauna, including the largest known bird that ever lived and an impressive display of locally found meteorites. In the same building the **Strehlow Research Centre** commemorates the life and work of T.G.H. Strehlow. Around the corner on Memorial Drive is the **Alice Springs Memorial Cemetery**, which includes the graves of pioneer aviator Eddie Connellan, artist Albert Namatjira and the reburied remains of the legendary, luckless prospector Harold Lasseter (see p.623), after whom the town's casino is rather ironically named.

Continuing from the precinct on Larapinta Drive you will come to one of Alice Springs's premier attractions, the **Alice Springs Desert Park** (daily

7.30am–6pm; $20). Set right beneath the ranges topped by Mount Gillen, the park is an example of a thoughtful and imaginative design displaying various natural environments of the Territory. Allow at least two hours to fully appreciate the centre's ecology. Shown on the hour, the twenty-minute film is actually a little over-portentous, and the real highlight, after you've wandered through various aviaries and creek, sand-dune and woodland habitats, is the large **nocturnal house** where the Territory's varied, but rarely seen, fauna can be seen scurrying around in fake moonlight. The park succeeds in blurring the boundary between the surrounding bush and the fenced interior – there's as much birdlife darting about outside the aviaries as in, and now the park is beginning to grow into itself it's better than ever.

Eating, drinking and nightlife

The **eating** opportunities in Alice Springs aren't at all bad. Todd Mall is lined with **cafés** with outdoor seating, and the **pubs** (see below) do counter meals for around $10. Besides the places listed below, the *Barra on Todd* at the *Alice Springs Resort* hotel and *Ainslie's* at the *Novotel* on Stephens Road are both very good.

Cafés and snack bars

Alice Springs Plaza Todd Mall. Food halls with Asian-inspired lunches and sandwiches.

Red Dog Café Todd Mall, south end. Along with the place next door, a good spot for breakfast croissants and early morning people-watching.

Restaurants

Bluegrass cnr Stott Terrace and Todd St. Old colonial building hung with Aboriginal art makes *Bluegrass* one of the few places in town with some individual character and one of Alice Springs's most popular restaurants. Starters include a prawn and veg tempura with sweet soy and ginger or spicy *calamari*, both for $14. Mains include a baby barramundi baked with dill and hollandaise sauce with prawns, avocados and potatoes for $28; a kangaroo steak for $26 has much more flavour. Good vegetarian selection too. Wed–Mon 6–9pm.

Casa Nostra Undoolya Rd. Just over the river from Wills Terrace, a traditional *ristorante* that's a little slice of wood-fired Sicily serving pizzas and the usual pastas with a variety of sauces for under $20. BYO and takeaway. Daily from 5pm.

Flavours of India 20 Undoolya Rd ⓣ08/8952 3721. All your favourite Indian dishes in a licensed restaurant. Chicken tikka or lamb pasanda from $16 and a good selection of vegetarian mains from $13. Daily from 5.30pm.

Oscars Todd Mall Cinema Complex. Among the better of the two or three modern Italian restaurants in the Mall, try seafood risotto for $27 or roast pumpkin salad for $16, but watch out for the cheap WA wines. Mon–Fri 11.30am–9pm, Sat & Sun 9am–9pm.

Overlander Steakhouse 72 Hartley St ⓣ08/8952 2159, ⓦwww.overlanders.com.au. Long-established Alice Springs favourite with tourists: the Drovers Blowout serves a selection of Territorian meats on one plate for $60, along with a host of other kingsize options, including delicious barramundi ($29.50), but there are some veggie options too. Daily 6pm till late.

Red Ochre Todd Mall ⓣ08/8952 9614. The *Red Ochre* has a pleasant patio to watch the world wander by along Todd Mall whilst enjoying a kangaroo and bacon burger ($13.50) and maybe a glass of Australian wine. There's also a modern, air-conditioned interior and other dishes to try include pitta wraps (from $12.50), or the breakfast buffet ($16.50) which should set you up nicely for a day of sightseeing.

Drinking, nightlife and entertainment

Like the surrounding desert, night-time Alice Springs initially appears lifeless. However, something can be found going on somewhere most nights, particularly in the latter half of the week. The daily *Centralian Advocate* carries details of what's going on.

The *Todd Tavern*, at the top of Todd Mall, is the town's landmark **drinking** spot, complete with "unofficial" segregated bars. Thursday night at the enduringly popular *Bojangles Saloon* on Todd Street is all action. *Sean's Irish Sibin* on Bath Street is a quieter option, while homesick Brits can head for the *Firkin and Hound*, on Hartley Street, a British theme pub that shows just what can be done with a multi-level car park and a little imagination. If nothing else tempts you, there's always the **cinema** at the top of Todd Mall, with cheap nights on Tuesday. Check the programme at the **Araluen Centre for Arts and Entertainment** (Ⓣ08/8952 5022) on Larapinta Drive: you'll usually find a worthwhile play, film or concert. And if you're feeling lucky, *Lasseters Hotel Casino* on Barrett Drive along the river's east bank can accommodate you – but not in thongs and a tatty singlet.

Events

The more energetic activities tend to occur in the cooler months, starting with the **Bangtail Muster** on the first Monday in May, followed by May's **Heritage Week** celebrating Alice Springs's history, a colourful and irreverent parade of silliness. The **Camel Cup races** in mid-July are Australia's biggest camel race meeting, ending in a huge fireworks display. The string of **rodeos** along the Track hits Alice Springs in late August, while the town's most famous event, the wacky **Henley-on-Todd Regatta** kicks off in August or September (Ⓦwww.henleyontodd.com.au). Bottomless boats (or, to be honest, any contraption) are run down the dry riverbed; needless to say, the event is heavily insured against the Todd actually flowing. There's also a rather uninspiring **market** every second Sunday in the mall.

Shopping for Aboriginal art

Alice Springs has become the country's foremost centre for **Aboriginal art and crafts**, and Todd Mall is full of galleries. Most distinctive are the **dot paintings**, which derive from temporary sand paintings once used to pass on sacred knowledge during ceremonies. The first dot paintings on canvas were produced in the early 1970s at Papunya, northwest of Alice Springs, under the encouragement of a local teacher, Geoff Bardon. What was intended as a kind of constructive graffiti for youngsters was actually taken up by the elders and has since blossomed into one of the more positive aspects of Aboriginal self-determination as well as a highly lucrative industry.

△ Tribal elder playing a didgeridoo

Clifford Possum and Billy Stockman were among the earliest of the Papunya artists to find fame, but they've since been superseded by astute, commercially minded painters from communities throughout the central desert, the most successful of whom have experimented with innovative abstract and minimalist styles in their bid to woo international collectors. Alice Springs's burgeoning number of art dealers and gallery owners have fanned the market, encouraging their top artists to churn out countless variations of their most marketable designs, supplying them with materials and studio space and even subbing them thousands of dollars when funds run low.

Some of the most sought-after **modernists** working in the Alice Springs area include sisters Gloria and Kathleen Petyarre, and Barbara Weir (daughter of the recently deceased Minnie Pwerle), who all come from the famously productive Utopia community 270km northeast of Alice Springs; Papunya artist George Tjungurrayi; the Pintupi Walala Tjapaltjarri, who only encountered white people for the first time in 1984 when he and his family emerged from the Gibson Desert; Kathleen Wallace of Santa Teresa's Keringke Arts Centre; and Alice Springs–based Margaret Turner, daughter of Clifford Possum. Most of these artists are represented by more than one of Alice Springs's top five galleries, and it only takes a few hours' browsing to become familiar with their idiosyncratic styles; their best works can sell for tens of thousands of dollars.

Of the two dozen **outlets for Aboriginal art** in Alice Springs, the most serious, and expensive, include the Aboriginal co-operative Papunya Tula Artists, at 63 Todd Mall (Ⓦwww.papunyatula.com.au); the Mbantua Gallery, at 71 Gregory Terrace (Ⓦwww.mbantua.com.au), which has an upstairs museum (Mon–Fri 9am–5pm, Sat 9.30am–4pm, Sun 1–4pm; $4.40) housing works by Albert Namatjira and Minnie Pwerle; and Gallery Gondwana, 43 Todd Mall (Ⓦwww.gallerygondwana.com.au), which specializes in Warlpiri and Pintupi arts. All of these are fun to browse even if you can't afford to buy. Reputable cheaper art shops on Todd Mall, where prices start at around $40, include Red Sand, Desert Art Gallery, and the Australian Aboriginal Dreamtime Gallery. Another place offering mediocre but inexpensive paintings and didgeridoos is The House of Oz, opposite *Melanka Backpackers Resort*. The more you spend, the more chance there is of making a deal, with free overseas postage and insurance usually offered at the bigger places. If you're heading north, there are galleries at Ti Tree (see p.592) and Tennant Creek (p.590) too, though Alice Springs has the best pieces and widest choice.

The better galleries supply labels of **authenticity** with each artwork to assure buyers they're getting the genuine article (some small, cheap pictures are produced in Indonesia and are identifiable both by their vague labels, stating "inspired by Aboriginal art", and a lack of the flaws that characterize genuine Aboriginal-produced canvases). Whatever style of painting you buy, at whatever price, it will definitely not hold the key to a dreaming or sacred site. Despite what some gallery owners might say, there is no such thing as a dreaming painting, though the male artists who own a particular dreaming may choose to present an interpretation that is appropriate for public consumption. Traditionally, women never paint dreamings, but are said to get inspiration from aerial landscapes, bushtucker and body painting.

Listings

Camping supplies Barbeques Galore on the corner of Whittaker and Colsen sts, or Lone Dingo on Todd Mall.

Car rental Outback Rentals (Ⓣ08/8952 1405 or 1800 652 133), at 78 Todd St opposite the council offices, has mopeds and Suzuki 4WD jeeps, as well

Buying and playing a didgeridoo

Didgeridoos, the simple wooden instruments whose eerie drone perfectly evokes the mysteries of Aboriginal Australia, have become phenomenally popular souvenirs, and even a New Age musical cult to some. Authentic didges are created from termite-hollowed branches of stringybark, woollybark and bloodwood trees which are indigenous from the Gulf to the Kimberley. Most commonly they are associated with Arnhem Land, where they were introduced around 2000 years ago and are properly called *yidaka* or *molo* by the Yolngu people of that region. "Didgeridoo" is an Anglicized name relating to the sound produced.

Minuscule, bamboo and even painted pocket didges have found their way onto the market (anything under $100 has probably been drilled out in Bali), but a real didge is a natural tube of wood with a rough interior. Painted versions haven't necessarily got any symbolic meaning; plain ones can look less tacky and are cheaper. Branches being what they are, every didge is different but, if you're considering playing it rather than hanging it over the fireplace, aim for one around 1.3m in length with a 30–40mm diameter mouthpiece. Beeswax is often used to bring an oversize didge's mouthpiece down to an operable size, but a didge with a body of the right diameter and without wax can feel nicer to use. The bend doesn't affect the sound but the length, tapering and wall thickness (ideally around 10mm) does. Avoid cumbersome, thick-walled items which get in the way of your face and sound flat.

You'll be surprised that making the right sound instead of an embarrassing raspberry will take only a few minutes of persistence; the key is to hum while letting your pressed lips flap, or vibrate, with the right pressure behind them – it's easier using the side of your mouth. The tricky bit – beyond the ability of most uninitiates – is to master circular breathing; this entails refilling your lungs through your nose while maintaining the sound from your lips with air squeezed from your cheeks. A good way to get your head round this concept is to blow or "squirt" bubbles into a glass of water with a straw, while simultaneously inhaling through the nose. Unless you get the hang of circular breathing you'll be limited to making the same lung's worth of droning again and again.

Most outlets that sell didges also sell tapes and CDs and inexpensive "how to" booklets which offer hints on the mysteries of circular breathing and how to emit advanced sounds using your vocal chords.

The Sounds of Starlight show in Todd Mall (April–Nov Tues, Fri & Sat 8pm; $25; ⓣ08/8953 0826, ⓦwww.soundsofstarlight.com) features Alice Springs didge impresario Andrew Langford and friends, and gives you a good chance to hear what can be done with a didge as well as being an entertaining night out. You'll also be given a free lesson afterwards, if you choose.

And finally, remember that there is nothing magical about a didgeridoo; it's your lips that make the sound, which resonates through the tube – any tube. A length of grey 40mm PVC pipe from a hardware store may not have the same cachet or eerie timbre but produces a similar sound at around $5 a metre.

as special deals, as does Thrifty (ⓣ08/8952 9999), on the corner of Hartley St and Stott Terrace. For 4WDs, Britz/Maui (ⓣ1800 331 454) is on the Stuart Highway north of Alice Springs and has fully equipped Toyota Bushcampers sleeping two inside, or Adventurers sleeping four in two roof tents, as well as regular campervans.

Hospital Gap Rd ⓣ08/8951 7777.

Internet access Try the library on Gregory Terrace (one hour per day limit when busy); Adventchanet on Todd Mall; Outback Internet on the opposite corner (very cheap and open on Sun, but with old equipment); or the JPC computer shop in the Coles complex off Bath St.

Maps The Map Shop, Alice Springs Plaza, first floor (ⓣ08/8951 5393), for detailed maps of the Centre.

Permits for Aboriginal Land Central Land Council, 33 North Stuart Highway, PO Box 3321, Alice Springs 0871 ⓣ08/8951 6320, ⓦwww.clc.org.au. Blank forms and subsequent permits can be faxed. For the WA section of the Great Central Rd (see p.623) get your permit from the Ngaanyatjarra Council, 58 Head St, next to *Sammy's Pizza* ⓣ08/8950 1711, ⓦwww.ngaanyatjarra.org.au.

Police Parsons St ⓣ08/8951 8888.

Post office Hartley St ⓣ08/8952 1020.

Sights south of Alice Springs

Several sites of interest are located beyond **Heavitree Gap**, a couple of kilometres south of town. The museum and camel farm described below are within range of the #4 bus, which terminates at the **Old Timers Folk Museum** (April–Nov daily 2–4pm; $2), just off the Stuart Highway, and features yet another display of pioneering memorabilia. The remainder are easily reached by bike, or on the Alice Springs Wanderer bus route.

Tours from Alice Springs

A large number of **tour operators** offer adventure, cultural or historic tours throughout the area. Just about every hotel and backpackers' offers a tour-booking service, though be aware that not all of the latter do so impartially. Alternatively, you can try any of a number of travel shops that specialize in selling tours; there are a few around the corners of Todd Street and Gregory Terrace. Though Uluru can be visited in a long day, the average tour is two to three days with a visit to Kings Canyon included and costs from as little as $300, though the $25 Uluru park entry fee isn't always included.

Austour ⓣ1800 335 009, ⓦwww.austourl.com.au. Daily one-day bus trips to Uluru (from $190) and two-day visits including Kings Canyon (from $350 in a tent or from $430 accommodated).

Australasian Jet ⓣ08/8953 1444, ⓦwww.ausjet.com.au. Scenic flights around Alice Springs and the MacDonnells (from $95) or further afield to Uluru and Kata Tjuta (from $595).

Ballooning Downunder ⓣ1800 801 601, ⓦwww.ballooningdownunder.com.au; **Outback Ballooning** ⓣ08/8952 8273 or 1800 809 790, ⓦwww.outbackballooning.com.au; **Spinifex Ballooning** ⓣ08/8953 4800 or 1800 677 893, ⓦwww.spinifexballooning.com.au. Alice Springs is Australia's ballooning capital and any of these three operators will take you up, up and away – and back down to a champagne breakfast (from $210 for a 30min flight, or $310 for an hour). Don't wear your best clothes.

Connections ⓣ1800 077 251, ⓦwww.connections.travel. Professional operation offering two- to five-day camping and accommodated tours through the West MacDonnells, to Kings Canyon and Uluru using comfortable minibuses. As is often the case, the longer tours are the best value.

Frontier Camel Tours ⓣ08/8950 3030, ⓦwww.ananguwaai.com.au. One-hour camel rides down the Todd River plus breakfast or dinner ($110–165), or short rides (from $10).

Mulga Tours ⓣ08/8952 1545 or 1800 359 089, ⓦwww.mulgas.com.au. Cheap ($250 plus entry fees) and cheerful three-day Rock tours sleeping in swags.

Outback Experience ⓣ08/8953 2666, ⓦwww.outbackexperience.com.au. Four-wheel-drive day-trips to Chambers Pillar, Rainbow Valley and other spots in the northern Simpson for around $150.

Outback Quad Adventures ⓣ08/8953 0697, ⓦwww.oqa.com.au. Fun quad-bike rides on a cattle station close to town using automatic machines: all you have to do is turn the throttle and steer (from $109 for an hour's ride). Dress for extreme dust. There's another quad operation at Kings Creek Station (p.614).

Wayoutback ⓣ08/8952 4324 or 1300 551 510, ⓦwww.wayoutback.com.au. Popular three- to five-day Rock and Canyon tours packed into a Troopcarrier (around $150 a day).

A few kilometres down the Ross Highway you'll find the **Frontier Camel Farm** (daily 8am–5pm; $10), which offers short rides on camels, plus a camel and cameleering museum. Back down the Stuart Highway just before the airport, about 10km south of town, the **Ghan Preservation Society** (April–Nov daily 9am–5pm; Dec–March Mon–Fri 9am–1pm; $8) at MacDonnell Siding features a converted old train station housing a **museum** of Alice Springs's early rail years, and is also involved in the refurbishment of old Ghan locomotives and rolling stock, which are used for train rides (Sun 11am; $25; ⓣ08/8955 5047) along a short section of track. Next door, the **National Transport Hall of Fame** (daily 9am–5pm; $6) features a collection of old cars, trucks and motorbikes, including a cute red Fiat Tipo, something called the "Mulga Express" (not your average touring Kingswood) as well as the original 8WD road train that used to slog up to Darwin during the 1930s at a hot and noisy 30kph.

The MacDonnell Ranges

The **MacDonnell Ranges** are among the longest of the parallel ridge systems that corrugate the Centre's landscape. Their east–west axis, passing right through Alice Springs, is broken in many places by gaps carved through the ranges during better-watered epochs. It is these striking ruptures, along with the grandeur and colours of the rugged landscape – particularly west of Alice Springs – which make a few days spent in the MacDonnells so worthwhile. The expansive **West MacDonnell Ranges National Park** is best appreciated with at least one overnight stay at any of the campsites mentioned below, while the often-overlooked **Eastern MacDonnells** have a more compact, intimate feel and are a better bet if your time is limited. Both can be visited as part of a tour (see box, opposite) or with your own vehicle. Although some tracks are unsealed, 4WD vehicles are mostly unnecessary. However, because most rental companies don't like you driving conventional cars on corrugated tracks, you may end up renting one. If you do, then make the most of its all-terrain capabilities; check out the box on pp.612–613, as well as the **off-road driving advice** in Basics (p.40).

A better way still to get in touch with the West MacDonnells is to do part of the **Larapinta Trail**, a long-distance footpath following the ranges that starts at the Telegraph Station north of Alice Springs and ends 223km to the west on the 1347-metre summit of Mount Sonder. The walk is divided into around a dozen sections, but these do not necessarily delineate a day's walk. Trailside water tanks are situated no more than two days' walk or 30km apart. As a rule, the more impressive but also more arduous sections are nearer town. Section 2 from Simpson's Gap to Jay Creek is 25km long – an overnight stop is advised, while the next section is a short but hard 14km to Standley Chasm with 350m of climbing. See Alice Springs's tourist information office for latest details or print off the whole trail guide with maps from the PWCNT website (ⓦwww.nt.gov.au/nreta/parks/; look under "Walks, Talks and Trails").

The West MacDonnell Ranges and Finke Gorge national parks

The **route** described below follows an anticlockwise loop out along Larapinta Drive and then Namatjira Drive to *Glen Helen Resort*, from where a 110-kilometre part-dirt road brings you past Gosses Bluff to the turn-off for Palm Valley,

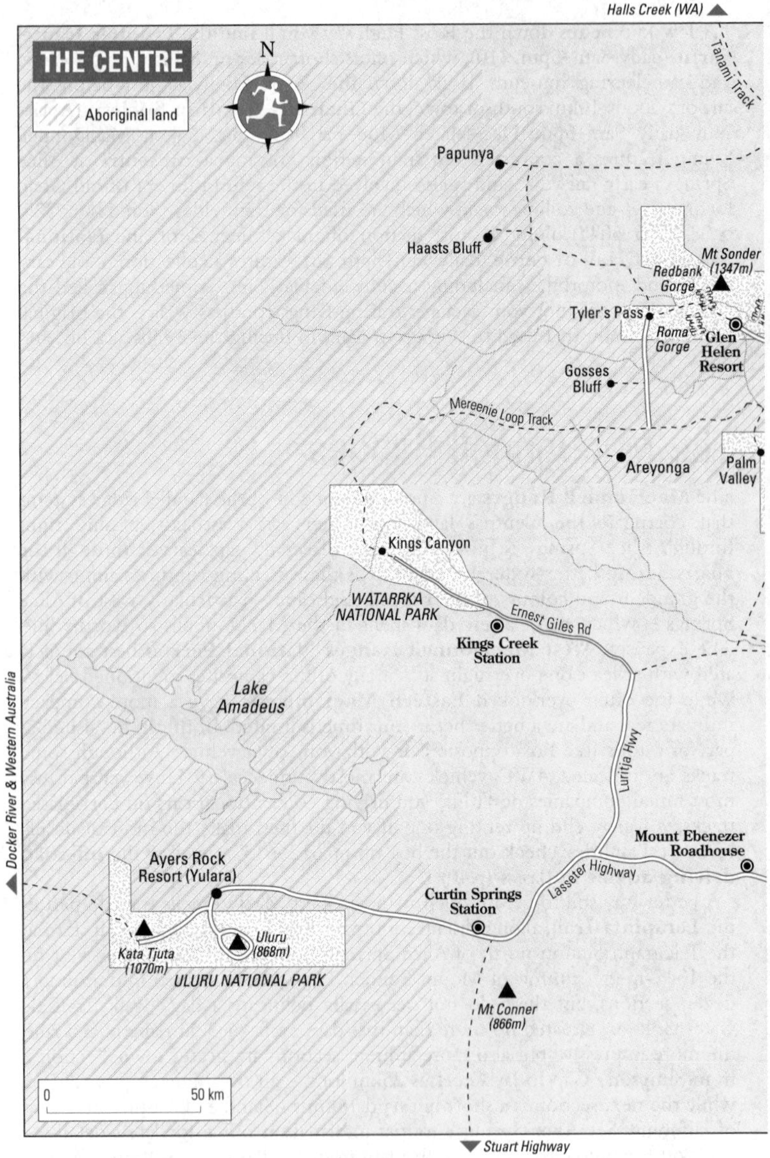

Hermannsburg and back to Alice Springs – a total distance of 370km. The track passes through **Aboriginal land** on its return section, but no permit is required (unless stated), providing you keep to the road and camp at designated sites.

About 8km from town is a turning to **Simpsons Gap** (gates open daily 8am–8pm), the nearest and most popular of the West MacDonnells' gaps, where a white, sandy riverbed lined with red and ghost gums leads up to a small pool. Agile rock wallabies live on the cliffs and there's a **visitors centre** and

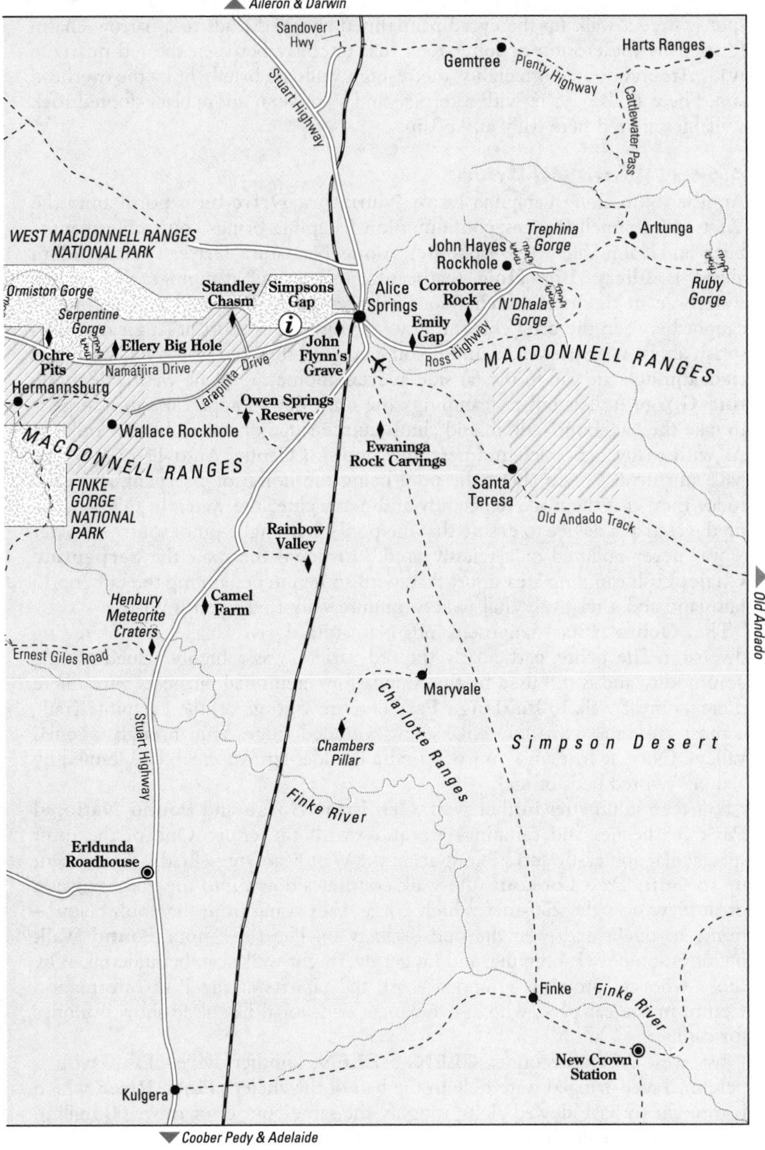

barbecues, as well as a seventeen-kilometre cycle track leading back to town. The first stage of the **Larapinta Trail** ends here – a 24-kilometre walk from the Telegraph Station in Alice Springs.

Further along Larapinta Drive are the **Twin Ghost Gums**, immortalized in Albert Namatjira's definitive painting of the Centralian landscape; just beyond is a turn-off north to **Standley Chasm** (daily 8am–6pm; $6), 50km from Alice Springs. Situated on Iwupataka Aboriginal land, this is another very popular spot, where a walk up the cycad palm–lined riverbed leads to a narrow chasm formed by the erosion of softer rock that once lay between the red-quartzite walls. Around noon, both eighty-metre-high walls are briefly lit by the overhead sun. There is also a café with a terrace and a souvenir shop; black-footed rock wallabies are fed here daily at 9.30am.

Along Namatjira Drive

Another 6km along Larapinta Drive, **Namatjira Drive** turns north amid the West MacDonnell Ranges; continuing on Larapinta brings you to Hermannsburg and Palm Valley (see opposite). Along Namatjira Drive, a scenic 42km ahead is **Ellery Big Hole** (barbecues, toilets and camping), the biggest waterhole in the area, which floods a large gap in the ranges. Nevertheless, caught between the brief ebb and flow of visiting bus tours, it's a great spot to splash about with the ducks, and if you can stand the cold water you can swim right through the gap to the far side. Eleven kilometres to the west is **Serpentine Gorge** (toilets but no camping): the only way to appreciate this gorge is to take the half-hour walk in and climb up the ridge on the right to a lookout. As with many concealed and perennial pools in Central Australia, the Aranda have nurtured a myth about the pool being the home of a serpent, and even today they visit the place reluctantly and never enter the water. In this way, the myth acted as a device to ensure that the pool – a drought-proof source of water – was never polluted or carelessly used. Just down the road, the **Serpentine Chalet** bush camping area is just that, with some pitches among the rather arid bushland and a relatively dull twenty-minute walk to a silted-up dam.

The **Ochre Pits**, signposted off Namatjira Drive, make an interesting diversion. The ochre, particularly the red variety, was a highly valued trading commodity and is still used by the Aranda for ceremonial purposes. From here there's a great walk to **Inarlanga Pass** (a narrow gorge on the Larapinta Trail), a most enjoyable two-hour hike along rounded ridges and through wooded valleys. Once at Inarlanga you will find a boulder-strewn creek bed framed by acutely twisted beds of rock.

Fourteen kilometres further west, **Ormiston Gorge** and **Pound National Park** (barbecues and camping) are also worth the effort. One of the most spectacular and easily accessible spots in the West MacDonnells, the short ascent up to **Gum Tree Lookout** (the walk continues down into the gorge) gives a great view over the 250-metre-high gorge walls rising from the pools below – home to ducks and even the odd black swan. The three-hour **Pound Walk** includes some rock-hopping, and longer overnight walks can be undertaken by those who are properly equipped – ask the rangers at the Park Information Centre in the car park, who also organize occasional free slide-show evenings for campers.

Just west of Ormiston is **GLEN HELEN**, another wide chasm with a perennial reed-fringed waterhole in the bed of the ancient **Finke River**, which is thought to have flowed along roughly the same course for over 100 million years and which, on the rare occasions when it does flow, can reach as far as Lake Eyre in South Australia. *Glen Helen Resort* (ⓣ08/8956 7489, ⓦwww.glenhelen.com.au; four-share bunkhouse $80, rooms ❻) has fuel, camping space (powered sites $25, unpowered $10pp) and accommodation and is a lovely place to spend a comfortable night out in the West MacDonnells, with a good restaurant and frequent live music in the bar. Helicopter flights over the nearby sites cost from $50. If you're heading towards Kings Canyon along the **Mereenie Loop Track** (see p.612), you're supposed to get your permit here ($2.20) though they're seldom checked. Make sure you have fuel for at least 250km.

Roma Gorge, Redbank Gorge and Gosses Bluff

Beyond Glen Helen the bitumen ends, but the natural spectacles continue. If you intend to complete the loop, it's about 107km to Hermannsburg (part-sealed), and another 126km east along Larapinta Drive to Alice Springs. Providing you stay on the road, it's easily done by 2WD vehicles at a sensible pace in dry conditions.

Shortly after leaving Glen Helen you'll reach a lookout to the distant **Mount Sonder**, well worth getting to early in the morning. The mountain, said to be a pregnant woman laying on her back, is featured in many of Albert Namatjira's best-known paintings. **Redbank Gorge** turn-off is 20km from Glen Helen; continue a further 8km to reach the car park. On the way you'll pass the *Woodland* and more exposed *Ridgetop* **campsites**. From the car park a strenuous eight-hour return hike leads to the summit of Mount Sonder, though most visitors settle for the twenty-minute hike to Redbank Gorge itself. The narrowest cleft in the West MacDonnells, Redbank is never warmed by direct sunlight and, anytime outside the height of summer, exploring its freezing string of rock pools is for wetsuit-clad adventurers only.

The turn-off for **Roma Gorge** is a few kilometres on from the Redbank turn-off. The small gorge is 10.5km and only about 25 minutes from the road (4WD clearance needed), despite what the sign indicates. From the basic **campsite**, a short walk leads to the gorge, where you'll have little difficulty spotting the scores of obscure **engravings** on the rocks; the well-known concentric circles are here, as well as feather-like depictions also found at Ndala Gorge (see p.611).

Seventeen kilometres from the Redbank turn-off, you keep straight on for **Tyler's Pass**, passing the Haasts Bluff and Papunya turn-off to your right (these tracks eventually lead north to the Tanami Track); from the pass, the road is sealed as far as the Hermannsburg track. The road can be rough until you're over the pass, from where a short ascent to the radio mast gives a great view of **Gosses Bluff**. Further down the track, you join a sealed road from which a turn-off (not 4WD as stated) leads to the interior of this extraordinary two-kilometre-wide crater, created by a comet impact 140 million years ago. Inside, the majority of the crater (known to the Western Aranda as *Tnorula*) comprises a fenced-off ceremonial site where male miscreants once paid the penalty for sexual indiscretions. The interior of the crater is rather less satisfying than the view from outside, or the even better view from above. A good way to appreciate the wonder of it all is to scramble up to the rim; there's no path, though it's less steep on the outside slope.

South of the bluff, you reach the Hermannsburg–Mereenie Loop junction and you're back on the dirt. Left leads to Palm Valley, Hermannsburg and Alice Springs; right to Kings Canyon and close encounters of the corrugated kind (see p.615).

Finke Gorge National Park and the road back to Alice Springs

The popularity of **FINKE GORGE NATIONAL PARK** is founded on its prehistoric cycads and unique red cabbage palms that have survived in the park's sheltered **Palm Valley** for over ten thousand years. Despite the difficult 4WD road leading to the valley, it's on every tour's itinerary, though it doesn't quite live up to the hype. The pleasant forty-minute loop walk is the valley's highlight; visiting the rest of the park requires a 4WD vehicle and seems to be discouraged, as does the route along the Finke riverbed from Hermannsburg (see box, p.610). On the way in or out of the valley, you can climb up to the once-sacred **Initiation Rock**, giving a fine view over the Amphitheatre, a cirque of sandstone cliffs. The park has barbecues, toilets, solar-heated showers and camping.

HERMANNSBURG was originally a Lutheran mission established in the 1870s, making it among the oldest communities in the Centre. Unusually, you are able to visit the town, or more specifically the **Historic Precinct** (daily 9am–4pm; $6), which features the original mission buildings converted into tearooms and an art gallery. Albert Namatjira and Theodore Strehlow were both born here (see box, below). There is also a supermarket and fuel (cash only), but no accommodation.

Back towards Alice Springs, you'll pass the **Albert Namatjira Memorial** before reaching the small community of **Wallace Rockhole**, where there are one-hour tours (Ⓣ08/8956 7415; $10) of nearby Aboriginal petroglyphs, as well as a shop, fuel and camping.

The Eastern MacDonnells and the northern Simpson Desert

Heading out of Alice Springs through the **Heavitree Gap** and along the Ross Highway you soon reach **Emily Gap**, Alice Springs's nearest waterhole, 10km from town. This is one of the most significant Aranda sacred sites, the start of the Caterpillar Dreaming trail. There are some interesting stylized depictions of the caterpillars on the far side of a pool that is worth wading through; you'll see the same image at **Jessie Gap**, a little further east. **Corroborree Rock**, 45km east of Alice Springs, is an unusual, fin-like outcrop of limestone with an altar-like platform and two crevices piercing the fin. The rock was once a repository for sacred objects and a site of initiation ceremonies, or *corroborees*, and is now roped off.

Albert Namatjira

Born on the Hermannsburg Lutheran mission in 1902, Albert Namatjira was the first of the Hermannsburg mission's much-copied school of **landscape watercolourists**. Although lacking much painting experience, Namatjira assisted Rex Battarbee on his painting expeditions through the Central Australian deserts in the 1930s during which his talent soon became obvious to Battarbee, who later became Namatjira's agent. Like all NT Aborigines at that time, Namatjira was forbidden to buy alcohol, stay overnight in Alice Springs or leave the Territory without permission, but at the insistence of southern do-gooders – and against his wishes – he was the first Aborigine to be awarded **Australian citizenship**, in 1956. This meant he could travel without limitations, but needed a permit to visit his own family on Aboriginal reserves, while the house in Alice Springs he longed for was denied him for fear of the entourage he might have attracted. Following the success of his first exhibition in the south, which sold out in three days, he became a reluctant celebrity, compelled to pay taxes on his relatively huge earnings, which were further depleted by the "share-it-all" kinship laws that still hamper successful Aboriginal artists today. A shy and modest man, much respected for his earnestness and generosity, he died in 1959 following a sordid conviction and short imprisonment for supplying alcohol to fellow Aborigines.

Critics could never make up their minds about his work, but his popular appeal was undoubted: exhibitions in the southern cities, which he rarely attended, persistently sold out within hours of opening, and today his paintings remain among the most valuable examples of Australia's artistic preoccupation with its landscape.

John Hayes Rockhole and Trephina Gorge

John Hayes Rockhole and Trephina Gorge, by far the most satisfying of the accessible destinations in the Eastern MacDonnells, are just 80km from Alice Springs. Both offer superb scenery and a selection of enjoyable walks, and there's a four-hour ridge walk linking the two. **John Hayes Rockhole** (limited camping space), reached along a rocky four-kilometre track requiring a high-clearance vehicle, is a series of pools linked by (usually dry) waterfalls along a canyon. The ninety-minute "Chain of Pools" walk takes you to the top of the gorge and down through the pools – an ideal way to get hot, but with plenty of opportunities to cool off. Alternatively, the lower pools are accessible from the car park.

Trephina Gorge, perhaps the most impressive spot in the eastern part of the range, is a beautiful, sheer-sided sandy gorge whose rich red walls support slender, white-barked ghost gums and a small pool, while huge river red gums grow in the bed. There's a pleasant **campsite** and two enjoyable walks (the "Gorge" and "Panorama", both taking about 30min).

Arltunga and N'Dhala Gorge

Five kilometres beyond Trephina Gorge, a turning northeast leads a corrugated 33km to **ARLTUNGA**, the site of Central Australia's first goldrush. The road here may still be long overdue for a grading, but a whole heap of money was spent on restoring the ghost town and providing it with a fancy **visitors centre** (daily 8am–4.30pm; ⓣ08/8951 8211). All the place needs now is some visitors – even the "loneliest pub in the scrub" (which served grub) has closed down. Arltunga's story began in the 1890s, in the midst of the country's first economic depression, when gold was discovered by the miners originally drawn to the garnets at Ruby Gap (see p.612). Over the next fifteen years, they regularly pushed barrows the 600km from Oodnadatta railhead, groping in desperate conditions for pitiful returns. Arltunga was never a particularly rich field and remains yet another abandoned testament to pioneering optimism. With a 4WD it's possible to continue on to Ruby Gap or north over the ranges to the Plenty Highway (see 4WD box, p.612).

Carrying on along the Ross Highway leads to the defunct Ross River Homestead and a right turn for an eleven-kilometre 4WD track to **N'Dhala Gorge**. On the way in you have a chance to appreciate the immense geological forces that have shaped the MacDonnell Ranges, warping formerly horizontal beds by ninety degrees or more. The gorge itself is home to various **Aboriginal rock engravings** representing aspects of the Caterpillar Dreaming, with which other sites in the East MacDonnells are also associated; the tall feather-like symbol (also found at Ruby Gorge) is said to represent the stages of a newly hatched moth taking flight.

About 4km before you arrive at N'Dhala, a track to the left (signposted with the "Explorer Territory" logo) leads for a pleasant 13km south through a valley and over a couple of sandy river crossings to a less interesting station access track, which joins the Ross Highway just before Jessie Gap.

Ruby Gap and Glen Annie Gorge

From Arltunga, it's a fairly rough four-wheel drive out to Ruby Gap and Glen Annie Gorge (see box, p.612–613), both of them beautiful and wild places. Back in 1885, the explorer Lindsay discovered "rubies" while in the process of digging for water, thereby initiating the customary rush for what turned out to be worthless garnets. Crossing the sandy Hale riverbed leads into **Ruby Gap**

Some 4WD tracks in the Centre

While most us have little need to own a heavy, fuel-guzzling 4WD, renting one for a few days of off-road driving is fun and can get you to some beautiful corners of the central deserts. Below are some **4WD-only** routes close to Alice Springs, which could all be linked into a memorable week in the dirt. Remember that 4WD vehicles are not invincible: when driven carelessly they can easily get stuck, become uncontrollable or damaged. They can also make a mess of the terrain if driven off main tracks; avoid wheel spins and tearing up vegetated ground, which takes years to recover. Finally, make sure the outfit you're renting from understands and approves your proposed 4WD itinerary and, at the very least, read the advice and carry the gear recommended in Basics, p.40. Ask at Alice Springs's tourist office for the *4×4 Guide* booklet, which details other routes in the area. One problem with renting is that you're rarely supplied with any recovery gear; even a tow strap or second spare tyre have to be prised out of rental companies or must be rented as an extra item. Although most of the rental 4WDs are in good shape, it's in your own interest to make sure you are appropriately equipped, especially for travelling in remote areas. For recommended 4WD rental agents, see the "Listings" for Alice Springs on p.603.

Mereenie Loop Track

The main appeal of the Mereenie, linking the West MacDonnells with Kings Canyon (around 200km, allow 3–4hr), is that it avoids backtracking on the usual "Canyon and Rock" tour. However, scenically from the junction west of Palm Valley it's nothing special and the corrugations west of Areyonga can be fearsome. A further irritation is that, according to the mandatory permit issued either at Glen Helen or Kings Canyon, you're not allowed to stop, let alone camp, except for one so-so lookout just before the descent to the *Kings Canyon Resort*.

Finke River Route

With a day to spare and minimal experience with a 4WD, following the Finke riverbed from **Hermannsburg** down to the **Ernest Giles Road** offers an adventurous alternative to the highway and also saves some backtracking from Kings Canyon. Rewards include stark gorge scenery, a reliable waterhole and the likelihood that you'll have it all to yourself. Before you set off, seek out the ranger at Palm Valley (☎08/8956 7401) who'll fill you in on the state of the track and provide a handy **map** that clarifies all the junctions. When on the route follow the small signs for "Kings Canyon".

The hundred-kilometre track starts immediately south of Hermannsburg. After 10km of corrugated road you descend into the riverbed. From now on it's slow driving along a pair of sandy or pebbly ruts – you should deflate your tyres to at least 25psi/1.7bar and keep in the ruts to minimize the risk of getting stuck. The sole designated campsite is at **Boggy Hole**, much nicer than it sounds and around two hours (28.5km) from Hermannsburg. The campsite looks out from beneath river red gums to permanent reed-fringed waterholes, best seen at dawn as the sunlight creeps across the gorge and the ponds are alive with birdlife.

Beyond Boggy Hole, the track crisscrosses rather than follows the riverbed before the roller-coaster ride to the Giles Road across some low dunes thinly wooded with desert oaks – beware of oncoming traffic on blind crests. Boggy Hole to the Giles Road is 65km, so allow three hours. If you fancy taking the direct route to the Ernest

and then **Glen Annie Gorge** (no facilities except camping). At the end of the day, even with the flies handing over to the mozzies, it's one of the most tranquil places you'll find in Central Australia.

Giles Road from the Tempe Downs station track, keep straight over the dunes just after a salt pan instead of turning sharply east; subsequent dunes can be avoided but the Palmer River crossing can be very sandy and may require further tyre deflation. Back on the road, keep speeds down until you can reflate your tyres.

Arltunga to Ruby Gap

Ask the ranger at the **Arltunga Visitors Centre** (☎08/8951 8211), 101km east of Alice Springs, for the latest track conditions for this scenic, if bumpy, 53-kilometre drive (allow 2hr) through the ranges. It includes some steep creek crossings until you reach the sandy riverbed of the Hale and the **Ruby Gap Nature Park**. From here, keep to the sandy ruts and inch carefully over the rocks for 7km to **Glen Annie Gorge**, a dead-end with maroon cliffs, bright green reeds and off-white sand.

Cattlewater Pass and the Harts Ranges

A less difficult track heads north from Arltunga past Claraville station and up over the Harts Ranges through the **Cattlewater Pass** to the Plenty Highway, 67km or three hours from Arltunga. It's a worthwhile and no less scenic way of returning to Alice Springs from Ruby Gap via a different route and you're bound to see some hopping marsupials along the way. Once you reach the Plenty Highway it's an easy dirt road via Gemtree to the Stuart Highway and Alice Springs, 150km away.

The Finke and Old Andado tracks

More ambitious than the above is the 550-kilometre loop into the fringes of the Simpson Desert along the **Finke** and **Old Andado tracks**, which diverge at Alice Springs's airport and meet at the community of Finke. At the airport, the Finke Track is also known as the **Old Ghan Heritage Trail**, as it follows the route of the old railway all the way past Oodnadatta to Port Augusta in South Australia. On the way, you'll pass stands of desert oak and may well see some feral camels, descendants of the original beasts led by Afghan cameleers before the Ghan train reached Alice Springs in 1928. It passes Ewaninga Rock Carvings but before Maryvale detours east to the ruins of Rodinga sidings. The section from Rodinga to Finke is the best part of this route, either on the embankments of the actual railway or on the rougher track alongside it, passing other sidings with interpretive boards on the history of this pioneering overland route. As you near Finke, the red sand ridges create some sandy passages, after which you cross the sandy Finke River itself and enter the community (fuel).

After Finke, the nature of the route changes as you traverse overgrazed plains to New Crown station; you may prefer to call it a day here and turn west from Finke to Kulgera on the Stuart Highway. To complete the loop via Andado, head east, recrossing the broad Finke, and follow the denuded pasturelands past Andado homestead and on to the ramshackle but still occupied *Old Andado* homestead, set between two dune ridges (camping $9pp; ☎08/8956 0812). North of here the track remains easy but gets bleaker still as the sand ridges thin out. After a while, the ranges of the East MacDonnells rise from the horizon and bring you back into vegetated and then wooded country for the rough, final 150km past Santa Teresa community and the airport close to town.

The Old South Road and the northern Simpson Desert

Just 14km out of Alice Springs, shortly after the airport turn-off, a sign indicates "Chambers Pillar (4WD)". This is the **Old South Road**, which follows the abandoned course of the Ghan and original Overland Telegraph Line to Adelaide, 1550km away; these days, the sandy route has become part of the Old

Ghan Heritage Trail, which takes adventurous four-wheel drivers all the way to South Australia (see also box, pp.612–613).

Ordinary cars can easily cover the 35km to **Ewaninga Rock Carvings**, a jumble of rocks by a small claypan (a dried-up pool). This sacred Aboriginal site is part of the Rain Dreaming, but we're told the meaning of the symbols is too dangerous to reveal.

Heading on past the store at **MARYVALE** (shop and fuel), you'll need a 4WD vehicle and to be in the mood for a thorough shaking if you want to get across the Charlotte Ranges and subsequent sand ridges all the way to **Chambers Pillar** (camping), a historic dead-end, 165km from Alice Springs. Named by Stuart after one of his benefactors (who had natural features named after him and his family all the way to the Arafura Sea), the eighty-metre-high sandstone pillar was used as a landmark by early overlanders heading up from the railhead at Oodnadatta, in South Australia. The plinth is carved with their names as well as those of many others, and can be seen from the platform at the pillar's base. If you don't fancy renting your own vehicle, Outback Experience in Alice Springs (see box, p.604) has full-day tours to this area that include Chambers Pillar.

South to Kings Canyon

Kings Canyon is 320km southwest of Alice Springs, of which the hundred-kilometre section from the Stuart Highway turn-off towards Stockyard Homestead/Wallara is unsealed. From Stockyard, it's bitumen all the way to the Watarrka National Park, which envelops Kings Canyon. If you're heading straight down the track from Alice Springs there's an increasingly barren run of nearly 700km to Coober Pedy (itself no oasis; see p.798) in South Australia.

Most **tours** of two days or more departing from Alice Springs include Kings Canyon on their see-it-all itineraries, providing the easiest and cheapest way to enjoy the canyon. There are daily **bus services** from Alice Springs to Kings Canyon with Greyhound Australia, or from Ayers Rock Resort with AAT Kings.

The Stuart Highway to Kings Canyon

Around 76km along the Stuart Highway from Alice Springs, the turn-off to **Rainbow Valley** (basic camping) follows a twenty-kilometre dirt track (the very last bit may be sandy), to the "valley", actually a much-photographed outcrop set behind claypans that are said to produce rainbows following rain. More commonly, sunset catches the red-stained walls spectacularly and it's a wild place to spend the night, best followed in the morning by a climb up the crag.

You soon reach the Ernest Giles Road, where you turn off right for Kings Canyon; note that the first 100km are unsealed and in poor condition. Not far along this track there's another turn-off, to **Henbury Meteorite Craters**. The extraterrestrial shower that caused these twelve depressions, from 2m to 180m in diameter, may have occurred in the last twenty thousand years, given that one of the Aranda's names for the place translates as "sun walk fire devil rock". A walk with interpretive signs winds among the craters, long since picked clean of any unearthly fragments. There is camping, barbecues and toilets.

The bone-shaking Ernest Giles Road heads west from here, joining the sealed Luritja Highway linking Ayers Rock Resort to Kings Canyon. The bitumen road continues west, past **Kings Creek station** (Ⓣ08/8956 7474, Ⓦwww.kingscreekstation.com.au), 35km from the canyon. Unlike most other pastoral properties in Australia, Kings Creek has taken to rounding up and raising the feral camels that other station owners regard as vermin. As meat, they fetch the same price as cattle, but as racing camels sold to Arabia they are worth six times as much. There are various activities at Kings Creek, including quad rides (from $63), Harley rides (from $25), helicopter flights over the canyon or beyond (from $210), and, of course, camel rides at sunrise or sunset ($50). You'll also find a well-equipped campsite (powered sites $33, unpowered $14pp), a pool, fuel, Internet access and a shop/café, though the "canvas cabin" accommodation – a row of heavy-duty two-person tents baking in the sun – is expensive at $63 per person. Camp with your own gear or head for the better-value lodge at *Kings Canyon Resort* (see below).

Kings Canyon (Watarrka National Park)

As you cross the boundary of the **Watarrka National Park**, you'll see the turning to **Kathleen Springs**, a sacred Aboriginal waterhole that is an easy twenty-minute stroll away. It was once used to corral livestock and is now a good place to catch sight of colourful birdlife.

Another twenty minutes down the road is **KINGS CANYON** itself. The big attraction here is the two-hour, six-kilometre **Rim Walk** up and around the canyon, one of the Centre's best hikes. **Early morning** is the most popular time to enjoy the walk, and for a couple of hours from sunrise, visitors swarm out from the car park along the track – if you don't mind missing the sunrise, you might have the place to yourself in the afternoon. Undertaken in the now mandatory clockwise direction, the walk starts with a well-constructed stepped ascent (the toughest part of the walk), after which the trail leads through a maze of sandstone domes, known as the **Lost City**, where interpretive boards fill you in on the geology and botany. Don't miss the excursion to the vertiginous **Cotterill Lookout** overlooking the dramatic **southern wall**, with its curious "hieroglyphic" weathering patterns. Back on the signed track you soon clamber down into a palm-filled chasm known as the **Garden of Eden**, bridged by an impressive array of staircases. Coming up the far side, there's an easily missed detour downstream to a shady **pool** where you can swim. The highlight of the walk, looking out from the throat of the canyon above a (usually) dry waterfall, is just a minute beyond, accessible either by wading knee-deep for a few steps round the right bank of the pool (or simply swimming across). Peering from the brink you get a perfectly framed **view** of the sunlit south wall and the canyon below. Returning to the staircase, the walk comes to the very edge of the south wall and then descends gently to the car park. For a different perspective, the easy two-kilometre return walk along the canyon bottom is also worthwhile.

There have been some long-overdue improvements in facilities at the park (including a kiosk), but there is still no camping at Kings Canyon itself, although you can camp elsewhere in the park with a ranger's permit. Ten kilometres past the canyon, the *Kings Canyon Resort* (Ⓣ08/8956 7442, Ⓦwww.voyages.com.au) is a small resort with grassy **camping** (powered sites $29, unpowered $13pp), a pool and plenty of cooking and ablutions facilities. There's also an upgraded lodge featuring four-bed bunkhouses (sleeping up to six; $39pp) with TV and a fridge and, at long last, a much-improved kitchen area. Over the road, the **hotel** (❼–❽) offers privacy and great views but if you don't want to spend this much you can get a whole lodge room to yourself for around $150. For something **to eat**, the service station has a pricey shop (daily 7am–7pm), while the daytime café next door (10am–3pm) serves pizzas, sandwiches, salads and chips and also has Internet access. In the evening, the grill next to the bar (6–9pm) has main courses from around $30, or try the $45 buffet at *Carmichaels*

Restaurant (5.30–10am & 6–9pm) at the hotel over the road – actually a great deal when you clock the mouthwatering spread on offer.

Uluru–Kata Tjuta National Park and Ayers Rock Resort

Uluru–Kata Tjuta National Park encompasses **Uluru** (the Anangu name for **Ayers Rock**) and **Kata Tjuta** (or the **Olgas**). The park is the most visited single site in Australia and if you're wondering whether all the hype is worth it, then the answer is, emphatically, yes. The Rock, its textures, colours and not least its elemental presence, is without question one of the world's natural wonders. Overt commercialization has been controlled within the park, designated by UNESCO in 1987 a World Heritage Site, and other tourists can be avoided if you steer clear of the area and walks at the base of the climb.

Kata Tjuta (meaning "Many Heads") lies 45km west from the park entry station. A cluster of rounded domes divided by narrow chasms and valleys, it is geologically quite distinct from Uluru. Public access is limited to the "Valley of the Winds" walk; none of the domes, including Mount Olga, actually 200m higher than Uluru, can be climbed.

You can't camp in the park, nor can you go anywhere other than Uluru and Kata Tjuta or the Cultural Centre and the few roads and paths linking them, which can explain why some popular spots get crowded. Instead the **Ayers Rock Resort**, part of the settlement of Yulara, just outside the park, takes care of all tourists' needs.

Getting there

It's 210km from Alice Springs to **ERLDUNDA**, a busy roadhouse on the Stuart Highway, from where the **Lasseter Highway** heads to Ayers Rock Resort, 247km to the west. After 56km is *Mount Ebenezer Roadhouse* and later the turning for the **Luritja Highway**, which leads 167km up to Kings Canyon.

The next thing to catch your eye will be the flat-topped mesa of **Mount Conner**, sometimes mistaken for Uluru. *Curtin Springs Station* (☎08/8956 2906), 11km west of Mount Conner offers the last normal-priced accommodation

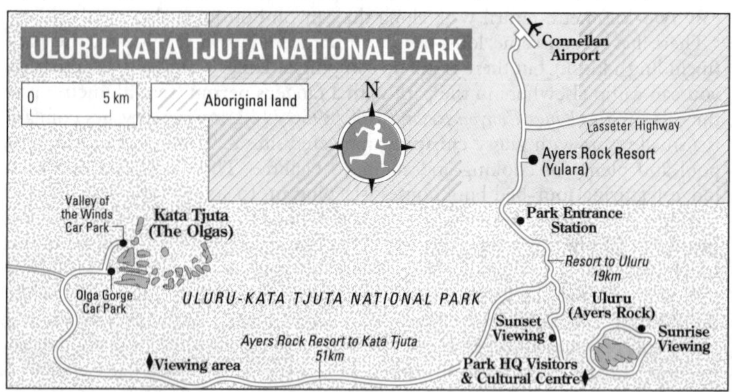

before Ayers Rock Resort (dustbowl camping free with $2 charge for showers; rooms ❸–❺). There's also a reasonably priced restaurant (daily 7am–2pm and 6.30–8.30pm), fuel and a bar, plus 4WD tours to Mount Conner ($50–175). You-know-what is now only 80km away.

Ayers Rock Resort (Yulara)

The purpose-built **AYERS ROCK RESORT** (aka Yulara) is far from the eyesore it could have been. Low-impact, environmentally aware design were not just buzz words, the resort was actually ahead of its time when it was built between 1983 and 1990, keeping building heights below the adjacent landscape, desalinating bore water (and recycling some of it to keep the gardens fresh), and using solar-powered electricity. Over the years, it has aged well, helped along by occasional refurbishments and carefully considered extensions.

Practicalities

All the town's facilities branch off a central ring road called Yulara Drive, around which a **free bus** circulates (10.30am–6pm & 6.30pm–midnight; every 20min). Within this ring is a duned area crisscrossed with tracks and a couple of **lookouts**, scanning the Rock and Kata Tjuta on the horizon. In the **Shopping Square**, the hub of the resort, off the north side of Yulara Drive, you'll find a post office, supermarket (daily 8am–9pm), newsagent and an ANZ **bank** (Mon–Thurs 9.30am–4pm, Fri 9.30am–5pm) with an ATM, as well as cafés and restaurants. Apart from hotel bars, the only alcohol outlet is the **bottle shop** at the *Outback Pioneer Lodge*, where you'll also find the only **laundry**. There's also the all-important **Tours and Information Centre** (daily 8am–8.30pm; ⓣ08/8957 7524) where you can rent a car and book everything that's going – see the box, p.619, for some ideas. You'll also find coin-operated **Internet access** here for a phenomenal $18 per hour. In case of emergencies, there's a Flying Doctor **Medical Centre** (Mon–Fri 9am–noon & 2–5pm; ⓣ08/8956 2286), as well as fire and police stations near the campground on Yulara Drive.

Buses will either drop you off at your chosen accommodation, where you'll be given a town map, or at the Shopping Square. All incoming **flights** to Connellan Airport, 6km from town, are met by a free shuttle bus, or there are private shuttles (ⓣ08/8956 2152) for $10pp. The main Uluru–Kata Tjuta Cultural Centre (see p.619) is located within the park, but just as worthwhile is the **visitors information centre** (daily 9am–5pm; ⓣ08/8957 7377), tucked out of the way between the Shopping Square and the *Desert Gardens Hotel*. In here you'll find absorbing visual displays on the geology, ecology and Anangu connections with Uluru. The centre is well worth an hour's browse and much more broadly informative than the Cultural Centre in the park – if you want more detailed information, there are audio-guides available in four languages for $2.

Accommodation

The cost of accommodation at Ayers Rock Resort will come as a shock – two or three times what you would pay in Alice Springs for the same standard of room, and even in summer prices only drop by less than ten percent. But as visitor numbers continue to grow, you're advised to **book ahead** unless camping or visiting in midsummer, because the constant flow of tour groups from all over the world fills out the hotels quickly, and even the campground overflows at times. All accommodation is operated by the Sydney-based Voyages group who own Ayers Rock Resort (ⓣ1300 134 044, ⓔreservations@voyages.com.au). To ring the actual hotels, call ⓣ08/8957 7888 (or ⓣ08/8956 2055,

Ⓔcampground@voyages.com.au for the campground). All the places below are situated off Yulara Drive, and none is more than fifteen minutes' walk from the Shopping Square.

Ayers Rock Campground Offers electric BBQs, a small shop and swimming pool and does its best to keep the sites grassy for tents, with camping at $14.50pp. As well as powered van sites ($34), the campground also has a few air-con cabins that sleep six, with fully-equipped kitchens and TV ($150) – if you don't mind sharing bathroom facilities, these are almost a good deal.

Desert Gardens Hotel Four-star hotel with a floral theme and well-appointed studio rooms ($448), which actually measure up pretty well compared to the *Lost Camel* and certainly the *Outback Pioneer Lodge*.

Emu Walk Apartments Apartments with fully equipped kitchens, a lounge and a balcony, close to the Shopping Square and with either one small bedroom ($448) or two bedrooms and a balcony ($540).

Longitude 131° At $1980 per night and with a minimum two-night stay, you won't be turning up here off-the-cuff. In fact, you couldn't even if you tried, as this bank of super-luxury tented modules is hidden among the dunes with no signed access from the resort. Each is individually themed after a Centralian pioneer and has a direct view of the Rock. Meals are eaten communally in the central *Dune House* and all tours and other activities are thrown in. Realistically, you're likely to enjoy your room so much you may want to skip the tour programme, or stay an extra day or two.

Lost Camel Hotel Right behind the Shopping Square, pitched as a trendy boutique hotel, the *Lost Camel* features small one-bedroom units sleeping three at a pinch; with en-suite bathrooms and music centres but no TV, all set around an attractively tiled courtyard with a heated pool ($404). The foyer has soft furnishings, a large TV screen and a small bar.

Outback Pioneer Lodge Most distant from the Shopping Square but with its own dining options and a bottle shop. Beds in the twenty-bed dorms (a record in the NT) go for $33 (also a record); more acceptable mixed four-bed dorms go for $41. The cheapest rooms ($180) are small and plain budget options with two bunk-beds and a/c, TV, fridge, tea and coffee; the same unit with a bathroom costs $206. There are also conventional en-suite motel rooms with all the usuals (from $404).

Sails in the Desert Hotel Until recently the resort's flagship, with à la carte restaurants and galleries. It's still the favoured choice of upmarket package-tour operators, who are probably paying a lot less than the $548 rack rate for a standard room.

Eating and drinking

Listed below are the resort's more moderately priced eating options. For the half-dozen, à la carte, expense-be-damned alternatives, head to the restaurants, grills and bars at the *Sails in the Desert* or *Desert Gardens* hotels.

Geckos Shopping Square. Mediterranean-style restaurant serving wood-fired pizzas, pastas, seafood and steak, for around $15–30. Open 10.30am–10pm.

Outback Pioneer Lodge Yulara Drive. The kiosk (11am–9pm) has various offerings, including fish and chips or burgers from around $7, as cheap a feed as you'll get here. Another good deal is the cook-your-own BBQ (6–9.30pm) for around $16–20 including unlimited salad (note that they may insist on covered shoes). Opposite the pool is the *Bough House Restaurant* with an all-you-could-ever-want-to-eat buffet with countless meats, fish, salads and wobbling desserts for around $40 a head. A wheelbarrow ride back to your room is extra.

Takeaway Shopping Square. Sandwich bar, with an ice creamery nearby, too. Open 8am–5pm.

Uluru–Kata Tjuta National Park

Even with our bus tours and our fully automatic cameras and our cries of "Oh, wow!", we still couldn't belittle it. I had come expecting nothing much, but by the power of the thing itself I had, like some ancient tribesman wandering through the desert and confronting the phenomenon [sunset on Uluru], been turned into a worshipper. Nobody was more surprised than I.

Geoff Nicholson, *Day Trips to the Desert*

The entry fee for **ULURU–KATA TJUTA NATIONAL PARK** (daily from one hour before dawn to one hour after dusk; $25, under-16s free) allows unlimited access for up to three days, though it's easily extendable if you ask. Besides the two major sites of Uluru and Kata Tjuta the park incorporates the closed Aboriginal community of Mutujulu, near the base of the Rock, once site of the original pre-Yulara tourist resort.

The **Uluru–Kata Tjuta Cultural Centre** (daily: April–Oct 7.30am–5.30pm; Nov–March 7am–6pm; ⓣ08/8956 1128), situated 1km before the Rock, opened in 1995, on the tenth anniversary of the so-called "hand back" of Uluru to its traditional owners. The centre also houses a café, souvenir shop and two galleries, and all together you'd want to allow yourself at least an hour to look around. As in the Kakadu equivalent at Cooinda, the strikingly innovative design doesn't conceal the fact that you're getting a sanitized and superficial coverage of Aboriginal life which will leave you saturated with the usual Dreamtime myths, affirmations of land care and bushtucker know-how.

Otherwise, leaflets are available at the information desk on the park's geology, flora and fauna, as well as informative *Park Notes* on various topics and issues: the park is also home to over 400 species of plants, 25 native mammals, 178 different birds and no less than 72 species of reptiles, and away from the two

Uluru National Park: tours from Ayers Rock Resort

All tours can be booked at your hotel desk or at the **Tours and Information Centre** in the Shopping Square, but note that most do not include the $25 park entry fee. **Car rentals** can also be booked at the Tours and Information Centre or directly from Hertz (ⓣ08/8956 2244), Avis (ⓣ08/8956 2266) and Thrifty (ⓣ08/8956 2030) for around $100 a day, including 100km free mileage.

Anangu Tours ⓣ08/8950 3030, ⓦwww.ananguwaai.com.au. Unchallenging cultural tours expanding on Dreamtime myths and bushtucker know-how along the Liru, Kuniya and Mala walks at Uluru, led by a local Aboriginal guide and an interpreter from around $75 (self-drive $58) for a 3.5hr tour with pick-ups. Unfortunately, the advertised "small groups" can consist of up to 35 people and the tours do not visit exclusive areas, so your tour can get invaded by other groups and curious individuals.

Ayers Rock Helicopters ⓣ08/8956 2077. Fifteen-minute helicopter rides over the Rock from $105, with longer options as far as Kings Canyon and Lake Amadeus salt lake for $590.

Discovery Ecotours ⓣ08/8956 2563, ⓦwww.ecotours.com.au. Small group tours around Uluru and Kata Tjuta with local experts from $82. For $113 the Uluru Walk circling the Rock is particularly informative, covering both scientific and cultural aspects – perhaps the best tour in the park. The Spirit of Uluru (same price) covers a similar area but is vehicle-based. Both tours include breakfast. Also has afternoon tours (3–4hr, including walks) to Kata Tjuta and Mount Conner from around $80 to $227 with dinner. Discovery also operates Night Sky shows ($33) which detail the often stunning stars of the desert skies.

Scenic Flights ⓣ08/8956 2345, ⓦwww.ayersrockflights.com.au. Scenic flights (40 min; $149) over Uluru and Kata Tjuta, or add Kings Canyon and Lake Amadeus for $370 (2hr).

Uluru Camel Tours ⓣ08/8950 3030, ⓦwww.ananguwaai.com.au. Operated by Anangu Tours (see above), sunrise and sunset camel rides are on offer from $60.

Uluru Express ⓣ08/8956 2152. Not really a tour but a small minibus that shuttles you from your accommodation to the Rock or the Olgas (from $35/$40 for a sunrise/sunset trip to $140 for a three-day pass, including park entry fee).

Uluru Motorcycle Tours ⓣ08/8956 2019. Pillion rides round the Rock on the back of a Harley-Davidson. Passengers from $155, two-hour rental from $275.

rocks features subtly diverse habitats from spinifex-covered sand hills to desert oak woodlands. Around the back, the two galleries sell arts and crafts from local artisans, though if you are looking for a painting, the best selection is in Alice Springs. It's possible to walk the two kilometres from the Cultural Centre to the base of the climb along the **Liru path**.

Uluru

It is thought that Aboriginal people arrived at the Rock about 20,000 years ago, having occupied the Centre around 10,000 years earlier. These days **Uluru** straddles the ancestral lands of the people who still speak Yankunytjatjara and Pitjantjatjara dialects of what is called the Western Desert Language (the most used and, area-wise, most extensive Aboriginal language). They survived in this semi-arid environment in small mobile groups, moving from one waterhole to another. Water was their most valued resource, and so any site like Uluru or Kata Tjuta which had permanent waterholes and attracted game was of vital practical – and therefore religious – significance.

The first European to set eyes on Uluru was the explorer Ernest Giles, in 1872, but it was William Gosse who followed his Afghan guide up the Rock and so completed the first ascent by a European a year later, naming it **Ayers Rock** after a South Australian politician. With white settlement of the Centre came relocation of its occupants from their traditional lands to enable pastoralists' stock to deplete the fragile desert environment.

In 1958 the national park was excised from what was then an Aboriginal reserve and it wasn't long before tour operators succeeded in having most of the people who lived in the park relocated to a new community at Docker River (Kaltukatjarra), 300km to the west, close to the WA border. By the early 1970s the tourist facilities in the park were failing to cope and the purpose-built resort of Yulara was conceived and completed within a decade. At the same time the traditional custodians of Uluru began to protest about the desecration of their sacred sites by tourists, who at that time could roam anywhere. After a long land claim the park was subsequently returned with much flourish to the Yankunytjatjara and Pitjantjatjara people in 1985. Reclaimed, the site was initially unchanged under Aboriginal ownership, since it was a condition of hand-back that the park was leased straight back to the Department of Environment and Heritage who administer the park. Tourism continued unaffected but since that time, changes assisted by Aboriginal input have manifested themselves with characteristic subtlety, guiding the park's development. These days up to 550,000 tourists visit the relatively small park every year and, as most come in buses or tour groups, the place can sometimes feel crowded.

Anangu mythology

Uluru, Kata Tjuta and the surrounding desert are bound to a culture whose holistic cosmology sees the People – *anangu* – as having the Land and the Law – *tjukurpa* – as their central tenet of belief. A little confusingly, *tjukurpa* can also refer to the Time of Creation or Dreamtime. *Uluru* is actually the name of one of the many temporary waterholes near the summit. The *tjukurpa* seeks to provide its adherents with a connection with the past and a moral code by which to live and behave correctly, but in Aboriginal society these stories (which can sound simplistic when related to tourists) acquire more complex meanings as an individual's level of knowledge increases with successive initiations.

While Uluru is a key intersection along many "dreaming trails" (or "Songlines", as Bruce Chatwin's book described them) – principally those of the **Mala** (hare wallaby), **Liru** (poisonous snake), **Kuniya** (python) and

Kurpany (monster dog) – it is not, as one often reads, the pre-eminent shrine to which Aborigines flocked like pilgrims from around the country. A muddy waterhole 200km away may be as significant. Uluru was once important to the Anangu as a reliable source of water and food as well as one of many landmarks incorporating ceremonial and burial sites along the trails created by the Anangu's Dreamtime ancestors. You can get a fuller version of these myths in the Cultural Centre or by joining an Anangu Tour.

Geology

The reason Uluru rises so dramatically from the surrounding plain is because it is a **monolith** – that is, a single piece of rock. With few cracks to be exploited by weathering, and the layers of very hard, coarse-grained **sandstone** (or arkose) tilted to a near-vertical plane, the Rock successfully resists the denudation of the landscape surrounding it. If one can visualize the tilted layers of rock, then Uluru is like a cut loaf, its strata pushed up to near-vertical slices so that from one side you look at the flat ends (the classic, steep-sided sunset profile). Elsewhere the separate vertical layers or slices are clearly evident as eroded grooves – the pronounced fluting and chasms along the Rock's southeast and northwest flanks. Brief, but spectacular, waterfalls stream down these channels following storms. In places, the surface of the monolith has peeled or worn away, producing bizarre features and many caves, mostly out of bounds but some accessible on the Kantju Gorge walk left of the car park by the start of the climb. The striking orangey-red hue, enhanced by the rising and setting sun, is merely superficial, the result of oxidation ("rusting") of the normally grey sandstone which can be seen in these caves.

Up and around Uluru

You can appreciate Uluru in any number of ways on various tours but to climb or not to climb... that is the question. "Anangu don't climb" is the oft-repeated message found at the base of the climb, along with the plea that "Anangu feel sad" when someone hurts themselves or dies on the Rock. That said, the Anangu have exclusive access to many more culturally significant sites along the base of the Rock than the summit climb.

Regardless of Anangu sentiment, many visitors to the Rock do attempt the hour-long **climb** to the summit, but make no mistake, if you do decide to climb it will be the greatest exertion you will undertake during your visit to Australia. Probably a third who try give up and, on average, one tourist a year dies, usually from a heart attack, with scores more needing rescuing. If you slip or collapse you'll roll straight back to the car park. But with a firmly attached hat, plenty of water, secure footwear and frequent rests, you'll safely attain the end of the chain from where the gradient eases off considerably and continues up and down gullies to the **summit**, often a windy spot, especially in the morning. Most people hang around only long enough for their legs to de-jellify and then climb back down; the daunting view into the car park can cause some freak outs. But the summit plateau is quite an interesting place. Gnarled trees survive in wind-scooped gullies and, while obviously maintaining caution near the edges, it's satisfying to explore the area away from the throng before they put signs up forbidding it. And in case you're wondering, yes mobile phones do work on the summit.

If you're at all unfit or are nervous about heights and exposed places, do not attempt the climb. These days the climb is regularly closed during high winds or by 8am if the temperature that day is expected to exceed 36°C, a precaution which often leads to disappointment amongst visitors. **Weather** statistics suggest that from September to December and in March you have a fifty percent chance of finding the climb closed due to winds, with April, August and, oddly enough January and February a ninety percent chance of the climb being open. Summer in fact is not as hot as you might think, with only six weeks above 40°C between October and April. At this time most of the average annual 300mm of rain falls in the park, though this figure is extremely variable and can be three times more or less in any year. Daily weather forecasts are posted in the resort's accommodation and information centres and in the park's Cultural Centre.

Far less strenuous, no less satisfying and certainly more in keeping with the spirit of the place are the **walks** one can take along the base of the rock. At the very least, the five-minute walk from the car park to **Mutitjulu**, a perennial pool, low-grade art site and scene of epic ancestral clashes, is recommended as long as you hit it between the waves of visiting tour groups. In the other direction from the base of the climb, the two-kilometre walk to **Kantju Gorge** (also known as the Mala Walk) is even better, passing unusually eroded caves, more rock art as well as pools shaded by groves of desert oaks, ending at the huge cliff above Kantju Gorge itself. Best of all is combining this with the nine-kilometre walk **around the Rock**, which takes an easy three hours, including time for nosing about. It offers a closer look at some Anangu sites (though most are closed – heed any warning notices) as well as a chance to appreciate the extraordinary textural variations and surface features you'll have noticed if driving round the rock. Remember though to take water, hat and appropriate footwear.

Kata Tjuta

The "Many Heads", as **Kata Tjuta** – or the **Olgas** – translates from the local Aboriginal language, are situated 51km from the resort or Uluru. This remarkable formation may have once been a monolith ten times the size of Uluru, but has since been carved by eons of weathering into 36 "monstrous domes", to use Giles' words, each smooth, rounded mass divided by slender chasms or broader valleys. The composition of Kata Tjuta – markedly different from Uluru's fine-grained rock – can be clearly seen in the massive, sometimes sheared, boulders set in a **conglomerate** of sandstone cement. Access to this fascinating maze is unfortunately limited to just two walks, in part because of earlier problems with over-ambitious tourists. Furthermore, the east of Kata Tjuta is said to be a site sacred to Anangu men and so is not accessible to the public.

The first of the permitted walks, the **Olga Gorge Walk**, is a rather pointless one-kilometre stroll into the dead-end chasm flanking Mount Olga (which, at 1070m, is the highest point in the massif). Better by far is the **Valley of the Winds Walk**, a seven-kilometre loop trail which takes about two hours, or the five-kilometre "there and back" walk to a **pass** between two domes. This is as much as

△ Wild camels at Kata Tjuta

you can see of Kata Tjuta's interior without a permit. It's worth knowing that the large tour buses tend to visit the Rock in the early morning and Kata Tjuta in the afternoon. By reversing this trend you might succeed in avoiding the worst of the crowds and enjoy either of these magical places in reasonable solitude.

The Great Central Road

From Kata Tjuta the **Great Central Road** leads west over 1100km to Laverton, 350km northeast of Kalgoorlie. The track is also known as the "Warburton Road" or, to tourism-marketing types, the "Outback Highway", and in 2004 commitments were again made to seal the road, so providing an all-weather link from southern WA to Ayers Rock and beyond. Until that happens, though, it's unsealed but in fairly good condition.

Two **permits** are needed to travel the Great Central Road, both free and easily obtained in Alice Springs or in Perth. The first is issued by the Central Land Council (CLC) in Alice Springs overnight (or possibly while you wait); the second comes over the counter at the Ngaanyatjarra Council, which covers most of the WA section (for addresses see "Listings", p.603 – or, if coming from Perth, p.640). No one checks permits and so not everyone bothers with them, though showing the CLC permit at the entrance to Uluru national park allows non-stop transit through the park without paying the entry fee. Even once you're out of the park, both permits are for a **direct transit only**. Technically you're not supposed to stop anywhere along the way and only camp at the designated campsites next to roadhouses, but there are enough side tracks along the way to enable you to get out of sight without carving up the dense bush in a 4WD – definitely not acceptable.

As long as you don't get caught in a storm, a 4WD isn't necessary on the Great Central Road, but the usual precautions for driving on remote dirt roads should be taken: take more than enough fuel (note unleaded petrol restrictions), spare tyres and water, especially in summer, when it's not advisable to tackle this route alone in an old banger. Filling up at Yulara, the greatest diesel range needed is around 350km, while for modern vehicles specifically requiring unleaded petrol, it's a rather daunting 816km to **Tjukayirla roadhouse**. The restricted availability of petrol exists to curb the epidemic of petrol-sniffing which has claimed many lives in remote Aboriginal communities. Opal is a non-stupefying unleaded petrol substitute available at the Warakunna and Warburton roadhouses which works fine in most vehicles designed to use unleaded. Fuel prices are around 25 percent higher than in Alice Springs.

Along the road

Scenically the first half of the route is more interesting, passing **Lasseters Cave** in the Petermann Ranges where the prospector **Harold Lasseter** sheltered with an Aboriginal family in 1931 after his camels bolted. He died trying to get to the Olgas and the location of the now legendary gold claim he had pegged went with him. Soon after, a dense woodland of desert oaks spreads across the valley leading to the forlorn community of **DOCKER RIVER** (or **Kaltukatjara**; store), 240km from Yulara (basic camping 2km down the road). Ten kilometres later you reach the WA border with the Rawlinson Ranges to the north and soon another nice stand of desert oaks.

Next up is **WARAKURNA (Giles)** community, where there's camping ($10–12pp) plus budget and self-contained motel rooms (☎08/8956 7344; ❷–❺), as well as a store, Opal and diesel. West from here the land flattens all the way to **WARBURTON**, more or less halfway between Yulara and Laverton, where there's a roadhouse (Ⓣ08/8956 7656), Opal and diesel, a store in the roadhouse and a campground round the back with budget and motel rooms (❷–❺). Just past the roadhouse is the Ngaanyatjarra shire office with a café and **gallery** which is well worth a look (some local paintings are also on show at the Kalgoorlie's Mining Hall of Fame, see p.671). From Warburton the 255km to **Tjukayirla roadhouse** (unleaded petrol and diesel, plus camping and rooms for $30pp and $50pp respectively) and the following 320 kilometres to **LAVERTON** look very much like each other, especially if you're concentrating mainly on not joining the countless roadside wrecks. Laverton itself is not an overly noteworthy spot to rejoin civilization – if you have it in you, **LEONORA** is just another 134km down the road.

Travel details

Trains

In peak season (May, June & July) the service between Alice Springs and Darwin runs twice-weekly in both directions.
Alice Springs to: Adelaide (Thurs & Sun; 24hr); Darwin (Mon & Thurs; 24hr); Port Augusta (Thurs & Sun; 17hr; change for Sydney or Perth).
Darwin to: Alice Springs (Wed & Sat; 23hr) and on to Adelaide (51hr).

Buses

Alice Springs to: Adelaide (1 daily; 20hr); Darwin (1 daily; 22hr); Katherine (1 daily; 17hr; change here for WA); Tennant Creek/Three Ways Roadhouse (1 daily; 7hr; change at Tennant Creek for Queensland destinations); Yulara (1 daily; 5hr).
Darwin to: Alice Springs (1 daily; 22hr); Katherine (1 daily; 4hr; change for WA); Tennant Creek/Three Ways Roadhouse (1 daily; 14hr).
Katherine to: Alice Springs (1 daily; 17hr); Darwin (1 daily; 4hr); Kununurra (1 daily; 6hr 30min); Tennant Creek/Three Ways Roadhouse (1 daily; 10hr).
Tennant Creek to: Alice Springs (1 daily; 7hr); Darwin (1 daily; 14hr); Katherine (1 daily; 10hr); Townsville (1 daily; 20hr).

Domestic flights

Alice Springs to: Adelaide (1–2 daily; 3hr); Brisbane (1–2 daily; 3hr); Darwin (1–2 daily; 2hr); Melbourne (1–2 daily; 3hr); Sydney (1–2 daily; 3hr); Yulara (1–2 daily; 40min).
Darwin to: Adelaide (5 weekly; 4hr 30min); Alice Springs (1–2 daily; 2hr); Brisbane (2–3 daily; 4hr); Broome (1 daily; 2hr); Cairns (1 daily; 3hr); Perth (1 daily; 4hr 30min).
Yulara (Ayers Rock) to: Alice Springs (1–2 daily; 40min); Brisbane (1 daily; 4hr); Melbourne (1 daily; 4hr); Perth (3–5 weekly; 4hr 30min); Sydney (1–2 daily; 4hr 30min).

International flights

Darwin to: Brunei (2 weekly); Denpasar, Bali (3 weekly); Kuala Lumpur, Malaysia (1 direct weekly, or change at Singapore); Kupang and Dili, East Timor (4 weekly); Singapore (2 daily).

7

Western Australia

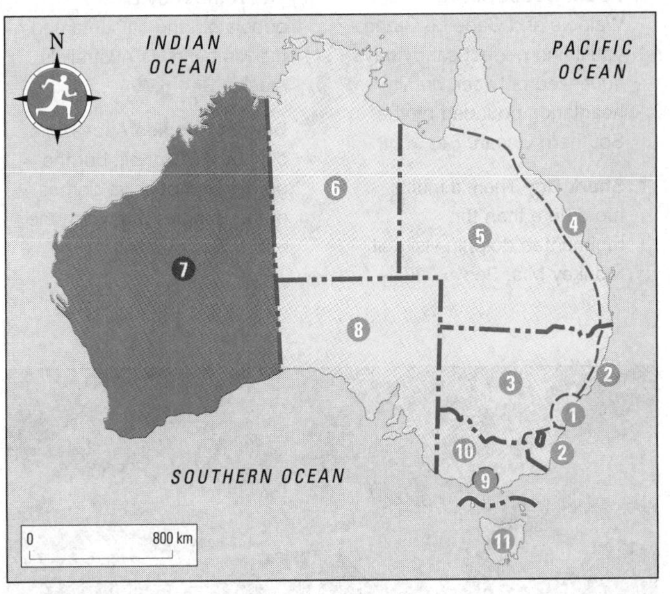

CHAPTER 7

Highlights

* **Fremantle** Eclectic, authentic and alive – worth more than the usual day-trip. See p.640

* **Tall Timber Country** Hike or cycle forest tracks, paddle the Blackwood River or drive among magnificent karri forests. See p.657

* **South Coast** Between Walpole and Cape Le Grand you'll find perfect sandy bays squeezed between granite headlands pounded by the Southern Ocean. See p.661

* **Shark Bay** There's much more here than the regimented dolphin visits at Monkey Mia. See p.680

* **Ningaloo Reef** "A barrier reef without the barriers". See p.684

* **Karijini National Park** Test your mettle exploring the banded chasms of the Hamersley Ranges. See p.694

* **The Kimberley** Barely populated and still untamed, the Kimberley is Australia's Alaska. See p.706

* **Bungle Bungles** Accessible only by 4WD or air, but the gorges and beehive domes of the Bungles are worth the effort. See p.710

△ A helicopter flying over Kimberley

7

Western Australia

Western Australia (WA) covers a third of the Australian continent; almost the size of India, yet with less than half a percent of that country's population. Conscious of its isolation from the more populous eastern states or indeed anywhere else, WA is ironically the most suburban of Australian states: almost all of its 1.9 million inhabitants live within 200km of Perth and most of the rest live in communities strung along the coastline.

Perth itself retains the leisure-oriented vitality of a young city, while the port of **Fremantle** resonates with a largely European charm. South of Perth, the wooded hills and trickling streams of the **southwest** support the state's expanding wine-growing and holiday-making area, and the giant **eucalyptus forests** around **Pemberton** further ripen a land fed by generous winter rains. East of the forests is the state's intensively farmed **wheat belt**, an interminable man-made prairie struggling against the saline soils it has created. Along the Southern Ocean's stunning storm-washed coastline, **Albany** is the primary settlement, part summer holiday, part retirement resort; the dramatic granite peaks of the **Stirling Ranges** just visible from its hilltops are among the most botanically diverse habitats on the planet. Further east, past **Esperance** on the edge of the Great Australian Bight, is the **Nullarbor Plain**, while inland are the Eastern Goldfields around **Kalgoorlie**, the only inland town of any size and sole survivor of the century-old mineral boom on which WA's prosperity is still firmly based.

While the temperate southwest of WA has been tamed by colonization, the north of the state is where you'll discover the raw appeal of the **Outback**. The virtually unpopulated inland deserts are blanketed with spinifex and support remote Aboriginal and mining communities, while the west coast's winds abate once you venture into the tropics north of **Shark Bay**, home of the amicable dolphins at **Monkey Mia**. From here, the mineral-rich **Pilbara** region fills the state's northwest shoulder with the dramatic gorges of the **Karijini National Park** at its core. Visitors also home in on the submarine spectacle of the easily accessible **Ningaloo Reef**, surrounding the North West Cape's beaches – some consider it superior to Queensland's Barrier Reef.

Northeast of the Pilbara, **Broome**, once the world's pearling capital, is indeed a jewel in the cyclone-swept coastline of the rugged "Nor'west", and an ideal preliminary to the **Kimberley**'s wilderness and hard-won cattle country. Cut off in the wet season, the Kimberley is regarded as Australia's last frontier, its convoluted and barely accessible coasts washed by huge tides and occupied only by secluded pearling operations, a handful of Aboriginal communities and crocodiles. On the way to the Northern Territory border is

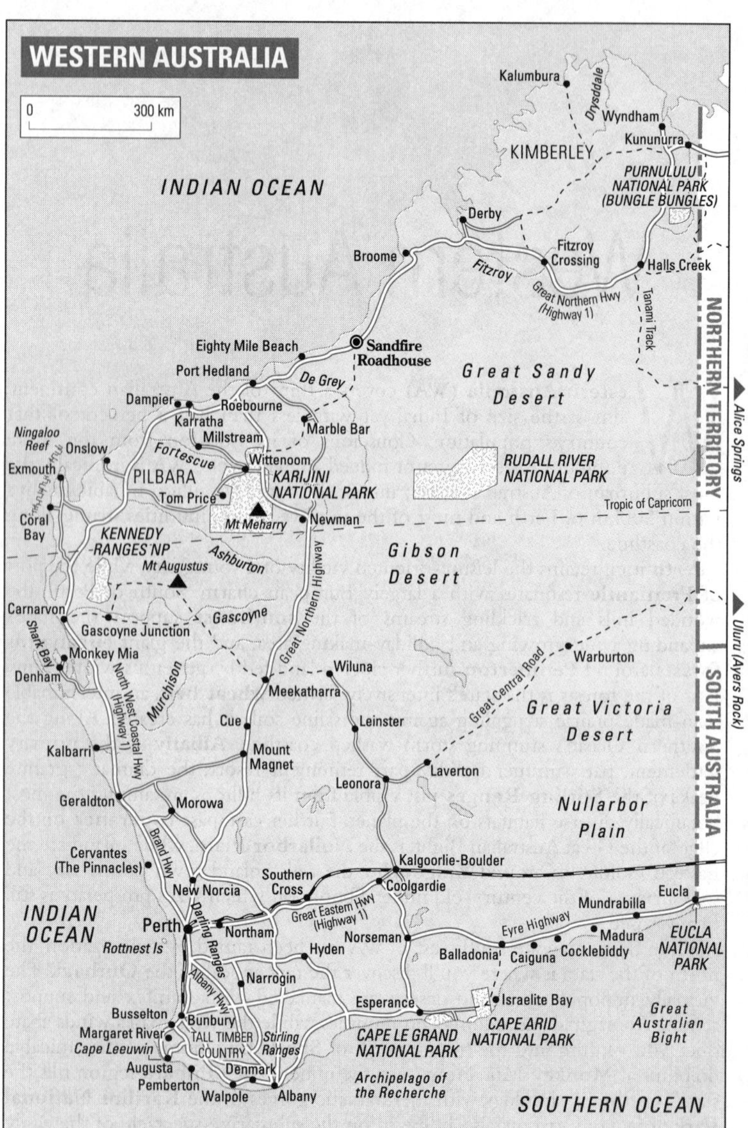

the surreal enigma of the World Heritage–listed **Bungle Bungles** – one of WA's greatest natural wonders.

Travellers never fail to underestimate the **massive distances** in WA, which is half the size of the USA. If you hope to explore any significant part of the state's million and a half square kilometres, and in particular the remote Northwest, your own **vehicle** is essential, although you'll get to the most interesting places by combining local **tours** with buses. Either way, WA offers an essential mix of Outback grandeur, albeit more dispersed than elsewhere, and continues to attract tourists keen to break away from "the East", as the rest of Australia is known in these parts.

WA's **climate** is a seasonal mix of temperate, arid and tropical. **Winters** are cool in the south and wet in the southwest corner, while at this time the far north basks in daily temperatures of around 30°C, with no rain and tolerable humidity: this is the tropical dry season. Come the **summer**, the enervating wet season or "Wet" (from December to March) washes out the north while the rest of the state, particularly inland areas, crackles in the mid-40s°C heat. The southern coast is the only retreat for the heat-struck; the southwest coast is cooled by dependable afternoon sea breezes, known in Perth as the "Fremantle Doctor".

WA is eight hours ahead of GMT, one and a half hours behind the Northern Territory and South Australia and two hours behind the other eastern states. From October to mid-March **time differences** increase by an hour, as New South Wales, Victoria, Tasmania, ACT and South Australia adopt daylight saving.

Some history

Aborigines had lived all over WA for around twenty thousand years by the time the seventeenth-century traders of the **Dutch East India Company** – and possibly the **Portuguese** before them – began wrecking themselves on the west coast in their quest for the valuable spices of the East Indies. A Dutch mariner, **Dirk Hartog**, was among the first of these and in 1616 he left an inscribed pewter plate on the island off Shark Bay that now bears his name. Recent evidence was also found hereabouts to suggest that the **French** claimed the whole continent just a few years before Cook. For the next two hundred years, however, WA's barren and waterless fringes remained – commercially at least – uninspiring to European colonists.

France's continued interest in Australia's southwest corner at the beginning of the nineteenth century brought a legacy of Francophone coastal features, and led the **British** to hastily claim the unknown western part of the continent in 1826. **Fredrickstown** (Albany) was established on the south coast in that year and the **Swan River Colony**, today's Perth, two years later. This **new colony** initially rejected convict labour and so struggled desperately in its early years, but it had the familiar effect on an Aboriginal population that was at best misunderstood and at worst annihilated. Aborigines and their lands were cleared for agriculture: these days black faces are rarely seen south of Perth.

Economic problems continued for the settlers until stalwart explorers in the mid-nineteenth century opened up the country's interior, leading to the goldrushes of the 1890s which propelled the colony into autonomous statehood in less than a decade. This **autonomy**, and growing antipathy towards the eastern states led to a move to secede from the federation in the depressed 1930s, when WA felt the rest of the country was dragging it down. However, following World War II the whole of white Australia – and especially WA – began to thrive, making money first from wool and later from huge iron ore and off-shore gas discoveries that continue to form the basis of the state's wealth and today account for a quarter of the nation's entire economy. Meanwhile, most of WA's forty thousand Aborigines continue to live in squalid and remote communities, as if in another country.

Perth and the South

South of the **Great Eastern Highway**, which joins **Perth** to **Kalgoorlie**, is the most climatically benign portion of WA, something you can only appreciate if you've spent much time up north. It supports intensive agriculture and coastal resorts, with all points eventually connected to Perth, the modern expression of the state's wealth. East of the state capital, the **Darling Ranges** offer a number of appealing day-trip destinations, while south of Perth, the **Margaret River Region**'s verdant landscape is especially attractive, supporting orchards, wineries and numerous holiday hideaways in the giant karri forests around **Pemberton**. Both **Albany** and **Esperance** are engaging resort towns on the Southern Ocean's rugged coastline, where sea breezes take the edge off the summertime heat. They make ideal bases for exploration of their adjacent national parks, while the dreary **Wheatlands**, north of the coast, is a region to pass through rather than head for. **Kalgoorlie**, at the still-thriving heart of the **Eastern Goldfields**, is a colourful caricature of an Outback mining town and certainly deserves a stop if you're travelling east.

National parks entry fees, walking times and school holidays

DEC (the government Department of Environment and Conservation) maintains WA's parks and also levies an entry fee or "pass" to the most-visited national parks in WA. The prices of the various passes are listed below. Throughout this chapter those DEC parks that require an entry fee have the phrase "DEC fee" placed in brackets after their names. You can obtain a pass from the entry station (often unattended), local DEC offices and some visitor information centres. The DEC website (Ⓦwww.dec.wa.gov.au) contains details of all passes, as well as useful information about WA's national parks.

Day Pass $10 per car, $5 per motorbike. For any number of WA parks visited on that day; useful in the Southwest.

Annual Local Park Pass $20 per vehicle; gives unlimited access to parks in a given area for a year.

Holiday Pass $35 per vehicle; allows entry into all WA parks for four weeks.

Annual All Parks Pass $75 per vehicle; allows entry into all WA parks for a year.

Walking times

Right across the state (if not the entire country) signs for short walking trails consistently exaggerate a suggested duration time to the point where it dissuades many from even trying. Experience has shown that you can comfortably halve the indicated times and still factor in a picnic and a siesta. Where shown, the chapter gives actual walking times: the minimum time it takes to complete the walk at a normal pace without stops.

School holiday dates in southern WA

Summer: mid-December to the end of January

Easter: middle two weeks of April

Winter: middle two weeks of July

Spring: first two weeks in October

Perth

Although its absence of urban grime creates a favorable first impression, after visiting the other major Australian capitals it's hard to get too worked up – favorably or otherwise – about the sprawling suburban spread of **PERTH**. Western Australia's modern hub is home to nearly 1.5 million people and has a reputation for sunshine and an easy-going lifestyle – after work, people often go sailing, swimming or fire up a barbie on the south shore of the Swan River, which forms a broad lagoon ideal for recreation and sport. It's partly because of this contented detachment from the rest of the country (the city's on Western Standard Time, two hours behind the east coast), and partly because the original settlement sites of Fremantle and Guildford are now located 20km to either side, that central Perth lacks the charisma which makes a great city something more than just a clutch of skyscrapers and sweeping freeways.

The state's wave of mineral prosperity saw Perth change quickly in the 1980s and considering its modest population, development continues today – seemingly for development's sake. The city centre is essentially an uncovered shopping mall with museums, galleries and an adjacent Central Business District (CBD), but oddly fails to integrate the riverside frontage that's left to the joggers, cyclists and gulls. **Northbridge** is the tourist restaurant and club district just north of the city centre; otherwise imitate the weekending locals and head for the hills, the beaches, the south shore of the river, the western suburbs of Leederville, Subiaco and Cottesloe, or last but not least the port of Fremantle, 20km southwest.

Arrival and information

Perth's **international airport** (Ⓣ13 12 23) is 16km east of the city centre and the busier **domestic** terminal a few kilometres closer. **Shuttle buses** (international $15, domestic $12; Ⓣ08/9277 7958) meet arrivals at both airports and take you to your accommodation; don't let them influence your preference if you have one. Poorly signposted, but directly opposite the Qantas domestic terminal, you can also catch a green Transperth bus #37 straight to the city (Mon–Fri 5.31am–11pm, Sat 7am–11pm, Sun 9am–7pm; $3.20), at least every twenty minutes during the day, but slowing at night. Otherwise, a trip by **taxi** to or from the international airport will take thirty minutes and cost around $30, less from the domestic terminal. An airport shuttle runs to **Fremantle** (from $30 one way; Ⓣ08/9335 1614, Ⓦwww.fremantleairportshuttle.com.au) once every hour.

Interstate **trains** and **buses** as well as Transwa (formerly Transco) buses serving rural WA use the **East Perth Rail and Bus Terminal**, three train stops east of the city central Transperth **Perth train station** on Wellington Street. Near the latter you will find the **Wellington Street Bus Station** for suburban services, and to confuse matters further there is also the **Esplanade Bus Station** on Mill Street by the Perth Conference Centre.

The main **visitor information centre (**Mon–Thurs 8am–6pm, Fri 8am–7pm, Sat 9.30am–4.30pm, Sun noon–4.30pm); Ⓣ1300 361 351 or 1800 812 808, Ⓦwww.westernaustralia.net), just across the road from the Transperth station in Forrest Chase precinct, has numerous free city guides and maps, tour information and statewide promotional videos. An alternative is the **Travellers' Club Tour and Information Centre** (Mon–Fri 9am–5.30pm, Sat 10am–4pm; Ⓣ08/9226 0660, Ⓦwww.travellersclub.com.au), down the road opposite the bus station at 555 Wellington St, with an information service for backpackers

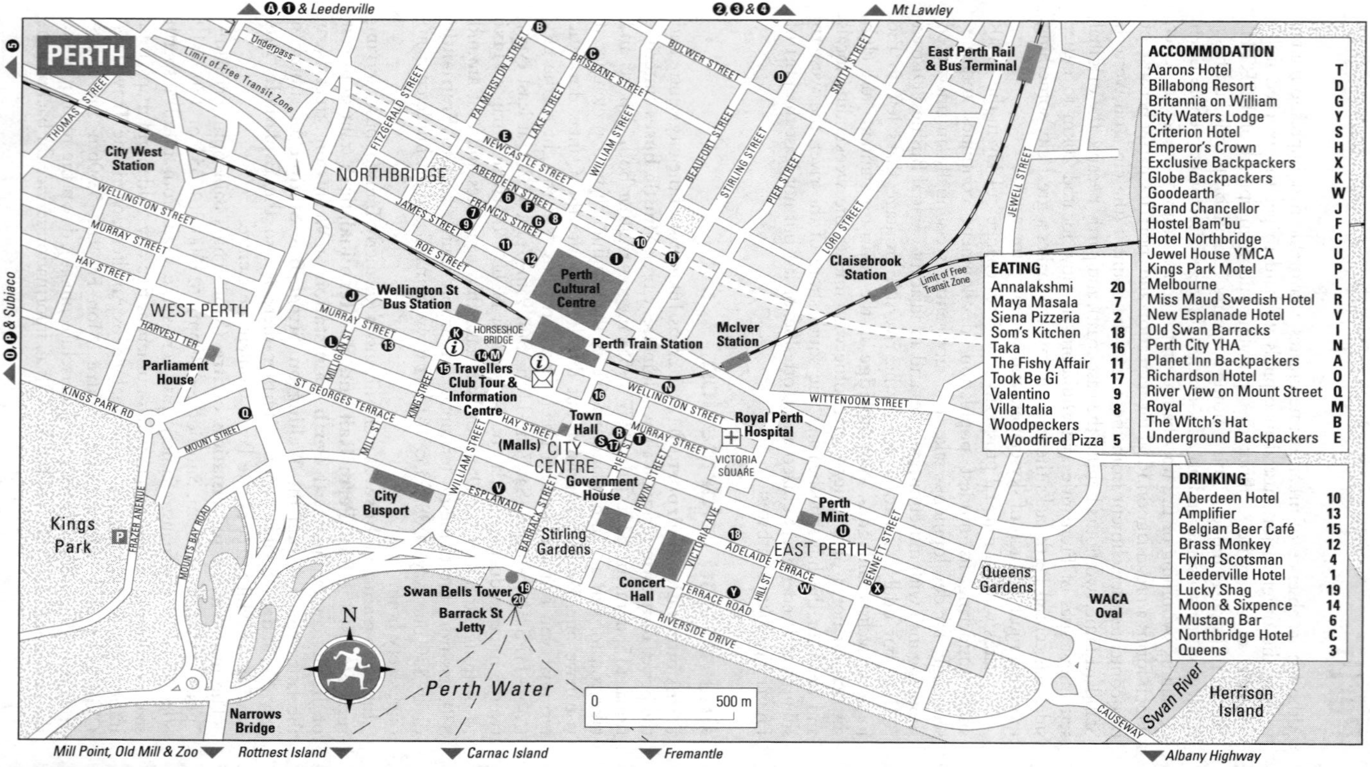

PERTH
A, 1 & Leederville
2, 3 & 4
Mt Lawley
5
O, P & Subiaco
Mill Point, Old Mill & Zoo
Rottnest Island
Carnac Island
Fremantle
Albany Highway
ACCOMMODATION
Aarons Hotel T
Billabong Resort D
Britannia on William G
City Waters Lodge Y
Criterion Hotel S
Emperor's Crown H
Exclusive Backpackers X
Globe Backpackers K
Goodearth W
Grand Chancellor J
Hostel Bam'bu F
Hotel Northbridge C
Jewel House YMCA U
Kings Park Motel P
Melbourne L
Miss Maud Swedish Hotel R
New Esplanade Hotel V
Old Swan Barracks I
Perth City YHA N
Planet Inn Backpackers A
Richardson Hotel O
River View on Mount Street Q
Royal M
The Witch's Hat B
Underground Backpackers E
EATING
Annalakshmi 20
Maya Masala 7
Siena Pizzeria 2
Som's Kitchen 18
Taka 16
The Fishy Affair 11
Took Be Gi 17
Valentino 9
Villa Italia 8
Woodpeckers Woodfired Pizza 5
DRINKING
Aberdeen Hotel 10
Amplifier 13
Belgian Beer Café 15
Brass Monkey 12
Flying Scotsman 4
Leederville Hotel 1
Lucky Shag 19
Moon & Sixpence 14
Mustang Bar 6
Northbridge Hotel C
Queens 3
East Perth Rail & Bus Terminal
City West Station
NORTHBRIDGE
WEST PERTH
CITY CENTRE
EAST PERTH
Wellington St Bus Station
Perth Cultural Centre
Perth Train Station
McIver Station
Claisebrook Station
Parliament House
Travellers Club Tour & Information Centre
Horseshoe Bridge
Town Hall
(Malls)
Royal Perth Hospital
Victoria Square
Government House
City Busport
Stirling Gardens
Concert Hall
Perth Mint
Queens Gardens
WACA Oval
Kings Park
Swan Bells Tower
Barrack St Jetty
Perth Water
Narrows Bridge
Swan River
Herrison Island
Limit of Free Transit Zone
Underpass
Thomas Street
Wellington Street
Murray Street
Hay Street
Harvest Ter
Kings Park Rd
Mount Street
Frazer Avenue
Mounts Bay Road
Fitzgerald Street
Palmerston Street
Lake Street
Newcastle Street
Aberdeen Street
James Street
Francis Street
Roe Street
William Street
Brisbane Street
Bulwer Street
Beaufort Street
Stirling Street
Pier Street
Smith Street
Lord Street
Jewell Street
Milligan St
King Street
St Georges Terrace
Mill St
Esplanade
Barrack Street
Irwin Street
Victoria Ave
Adelaide Terrace
Terrace Road
Hill St
Bennett Street
Wittenoom Street
Riverside Drive
Causeway
N
0 500 m

△ Perth at night: a view from Kings Park

and budget travellers as well as inexpensive **Internet** access and notice boards for work and car sales.

City transport

Transperth, Perth's efficient and inexpensive **suburban transport** network, has frequent **trains** to Fremantle and the northern, eastern and southern suburbs of Joondalup, Midland, Armadale and Mandurah, plus a fleet of **buses** filling in the gaps. The city centre has two suburban **bus stations**, one on Wellington Street (information office Mon–Fri 7.30am–5.30pm, Sat 8am–1pm; ⓣ13 62 13), next to the central train station, and the Esplanade Bus Station (information office Mon–Fri 7.30am–6.30pm, Sat 10am–2pm, Sun noon–4pm; ⓣ13 62 13) ten minutes' walk south at the bottom of Mill Street which caters mostly for services south of the river. Any southbound bus crossing the railway line at Horseshoe Bridge near the Wellington Street bus station goes to the Esplanade Bus Station.

Outside the **Free Transit Zone** (see box, p.634), Perth is divided into eight concentric zones – zones 1 and 2 (tickets $3.20) are the most useful to visitors, incorporating Fremantle, the northern beaches and Midland. **Tickets** are available from bus conductors or vending machines at all (mostly unstaffed) stations; they are valid for up to two hours' (some for 1hr 30min) unlimited travel within the specified zones on Transperth buses, trains and the ferry to South Perth from Barrack Street Jetty. All-zone day-passes ($7.70) and ten-trip MultiRiders (from $17.85) are also available from certain newsagents.

Perth has a far-reaching network of **cycle lanes**, which spread out to the suburbs and can make cycling a pleasant and viable option; the government agency Bikewest (ⓣ08/9216 8000) or the Bicycle Transportation Alliance (ⓣ08/9420 7210, ⓦwww.btawa.org.au) can provide more information.

Accommodation

There's a full range of **accommodation** around the centre of Perth, much of it – from backpackers' hostels to hotels and apartments – inexpensive and

Free transport in central Perth: the FTZ

Both of Perth's central bus stations, as well as the local train stations one stop on either side of the main Wellington Street train station, are within the Free Transit Zone, or FTZ. Most buses passing through the FTZ offer free travel within it, as do the snazzy "CAT" (Central Area Transit) buses serving the city centre. You can board the buses at special CAT stops to take you along two circular CAT routes with a third route, the Yellow CAT running up and down Wellington Street to East Perth; press a button and a voice tells you when the next bus is due. The Blue CAT runs from Barrack Street Jetty along the Foreshore and up Mounts Bay Road to Barrack Street and Aberdeen Street and then down William Street and over Horseshoe Bridge back to the river, while the Red CAT runs east to west along St Georges Terrace, the non-pedestrianized part of Hay Street and Wellington Street. All routes run from Mon to Thurs 7am to 6pm, Fri 7am to 1am, Sat 8.30am to 1am and Sun 10am to 5pm, with intervals of fifteen minutes at the most.

conveniently close to, or even right in, the city centre. Self-contained apartments can be great value for groups of four or more. The nearest campsites are 7km from the city. Booking ahead for hotels and apartments is advisable if you want to stay at the first place on your list.

Hotels and self-contained apartments

Aarons Hotel 70 Pier St ⓣ08/9325 2133, ⓦwww.aaronsperth.com.au. Standard mid-range hotel in a great location in the CBD, close to bars and restaurants. 4

City Waters Lodge 118 Terrace Rd ⓣ08/9325 1556, ⓦwww.citywaters.com.au. Small one- and two-bedroom apartments close to the river in a nice location, ten minutes' walk from the centre. 4

Criterion Hotel 560 Hay St ⓣ08/9325 5155 or 1800 245 155, ⓦwww.criterion-hotel-perth.com.au. Popular modernized Grand-era hotel on the east side of central Hay St; rooms are on the small side but there's an in-house Italian restaurant and English-style theme pub. Internet access and some secure parking. Booking essential. 4

Goodearth 195 Adelaide Terrace ⓣ08/9492 7777, ⓦwww.goodearthhotel.com.au. Large hotel close to the centre with a clean, contemporary look, views to the river and a range of good-value rooms, all with kitchenettes. 4

Grand Chancellor 707 Wellington St ⓣ08/9327 7000 or 1800 999 144. Central four-star providing spacious rooms with mini-bar and in-house movies, as well as a gym, sauna and roof-top pool. 6

Hotel Northbridge 210 Lake St ⓣ08/9328 5254, ⓦwww.hotelnorthbridge.com.au. Appealingly refurbished traditional hotel at the top end of Northbridge, which has good-value four-star rooms with a spa in all and some budget options. Off-street parking and three-bar pub below. 3–5

Jewel House YMCA 180 Goderich St ⓣ08/9325 8488, ⓦwww.ymcajewellhouse.com. Simple, clean and cheap in a pleasant part of the city. Rooms have shared facilities with fan and heater – some have TV and fridge. Popular with students who don't like hostels. 2

Kings Park Motel 255 Thomas St, Subiaco ⓣ08/9381 0000, ⓦwww.kingsparkmotel.com.au. Good-value modern motel with spas in some rooms, five minutes from the city, on the edge of Kings Park and close to Subiaco shops and restaurants. 4

Melbourne Cnr Hay and Milligan sts ⓣ08/9320 3333, ⓦwww.melbournehotel.com.au. Small, heritage-listed Federation-era boutique hotel at the west end of Hay St. Well-equipped rooms with in-house movies, cable TV, Internet access, a café/bar and 24hr reception. Breakfast included. 6

Miss Maud Swedish Hotel 97 Murray St ⓣ08/9325 3900, ⓦwww.missmaud.com.au. Cute and comfy rooms with a Swedish/Alpine flavour equipped with large plasma screens, not to forget the spectacular smorgasbord breakfast included. Great location. 5

New Esplanade Hotel 18 The Esplanade ⓣ08/9325 2000, ⓦwww.newesplanade.com.au. Small mid-level hotel, located close to the water (most rooms have water views), that's a good option if you want to be close to everything. 4

Richardson Hotel 32 Richardson St ⓣ08/9217 8888, ⓦwww.therichardson.com.au. Perth's newest and best five-star boutique hotel has all the trimmings you'd expect, including top-class spa and massage facilities, and an excellent French restaurant. ❽

River View on Mount Street 42 Mount St ⓣ08/9321 8963, ⓕ9322 5956. Comfortable, well-equipped units with kitchens, between the city centre and Kings Park, on a beautiful street dotted with luxurious apartments. ❹

Royal Cnr Wellington and William sts ⓣ & ⓕ08/9324 1510, ⓦwww.royalhotelperth.com.au. A tidy hotel with mostly shared facilities and with some big rooms that are better and less expensive than the *Wentworth Plaza* next door. ❸

Backpackers'

The majority of Perth's backpackers' are located in Northbridge, where a variety of converted hotels and houses have been turned into sociable dens for working holiday-makers and travellers. As a rule, the further from central Northbridge the better the accommodation offered, including the new breed of "flashpacker" hostels that resemble facilities you'd expect in a four-star hotel.

Northbridge does not have free on-street daytime parking, but off-street parking is available at some accommodation and this is indicated in the reviews; there are plenty of inexpensive central car parks. The keener establishments meet incoming trains and buses at East Perth Rail and Bus Station and will also collect you for free from the airports, though some may insist on a two-night minimum stay for this.

Northbridge and City Centre

Britannia on William 253 William St ⓣ08/9227 6000, ⓦwww.perthbritannia.com.au. Huge, three-storey warren in the heart of Northbridge, a stone's throw from the clubs and cafés but also affected by the noise of late-night revels and early morning garbage collection. Improvements include new bathrooms, which has made it a better option. 24hr reception, no parking. Eight- or six-share dorms $19–21, four-share $24, rooms ❸

Emperor's Crown 85 Stirling St ⓣ08/9227 1400 or 1800 991 553, ⓦwww.emperorscrown.com.au. Outstanding a/c "flashbacker" hostel, with a clean, modern interior, plasma-screen TV/DVD, Internet, a fully equipped kitchen fit for cooking and an adjacent café. Standard six- or four-bed dorms at $24 and several double ❹ or triple ❹ configurations, some with en suite and private rooms, with TV/DVD and fridges. Limited parking.

Globe Backpackers 553–561 Wellington St ⓣ08/9321 4080, ⓦwww.globebackpackers.com.au. Right next to Travellers Club Tour and Information Centre and as central as they come, with good security, a small kitchen, sociable outdoor eating area and big TV rooms. Six- and four-bed dorms cost $24–27, with the unusual luxury of private (as opposed to communal) bathrooms. Free breakfast and cheap Internet access. ❷

Hostel Bam'bu 75 Aberdeen St ⓣ08/9328 1211, ⓦwww.bambu.net.au. Once a disused warehouse, this very distinctive hostel is themed on a southern Colombian resort that the owner/adventurer Dave fell in love with. Spacious throughout (the bathrooms are huge) with a great lounge bar, where DJs often come and spin. Limited parking. Eight- to four-bed dorms $22–24, rooms ❸

Old Swan Barracks 2–8 Francis St ⓣ08/9428 0000, ⓦwww.theoldswanbarracks.com. As the name suggests, its draw card is its grand and historic old stone building (built in1896). Other than that, the rooms are standard, but everything else, including the lounge and dining areas are huge. Parking available. Dorms start at $21, rooms ❸

Perth City YHA 300 Wellington St ⓣ08/9287 3333, ⓦwww.yha.com.au. One of the new wave of "flashbacker" hostels sweeping the country located in a magnificent Art-Deco building close to everything. Classy design and facilities with first-rate kitchen, lounges, bathrooms and everything in between, but the train line next door means earplugs are needed. Booking essential. Secure parking available for $10 a night. Four-bed dorms ($24) and twin/doubles ❸

Along Newcastle Street

Planet Inn Backpackers 496 Newcastle St ⓣ08/9227 9969, ⓦwww.planetinn.com.au. The detached houses that make up this popular backpackers' are a bit far out of the centre, but there's a bar, mini-shop, and free breakfast. More outdoor space than most and some parking. Eight- to six-share dorms from $16, rooms ❷

Underground Backpackers 268 Newcastle St ⓣ08/9228 3755, ⓦwww.undergroundbackpackers.com.au. Friendly backpackers', formerly a pub. There's a spacious foyer and a newer block at the back by the pool, which makes up for some windowless rooms. Free breakfast, bar with great nightly specials, cheap Internet access, a/c rooms, a video lounge and 24hr reception. Ten-share dorms $20, six-share $22 and four-share $24. Rooms for ❸ or $5 more with TV.

North of Newcastle Street

Billabong Resort 381 Beaufort St ⓣ08/9328 7720, ⓦwww.billabongresort.com.au. Not as central as others (1km north of CBD) but this resort has been a favourite for years. The four-bed ($24) and eight-bed ($21) dorms all have an attached bathroom, while downstairs there's an appealing pool area. Just about every possible service is on offer, short of tucking you in at night. Free breakfast, plenty of parking and close to Mt Lawley shops. Rooms ❸

The Witch's Hat 148 Palmerston St ⓣ08/9228 4228 or 1800 818 358, ⓦwww.witchs-hat.com. Exceptionally well-managed hostel located in a distinctive heritage building in a residential area northeast of central Northbridge with nice communal BBQ area, a few small doubles and some parking. A real home-away-from-home feel, with tour service and happy employees. Eight-, six- and four-bed dorms (some female-only) all at $24, rooms ❸

East of the Centre

Exclusive Backpackers 158 Adelaide Terrace ⓣ08/9221 9991, ⓦwww.exclusivebackpackers.com. An attractive jarrah-wood interior, balcony and spacious dorms give this hostel a touch of class and homely feel, which is why many travellers loyally return. Off-street parking and a nice café next door supplement the rather inadequate kitchen. Five-bed dorms from $22 and comfortable twins or doubles ❸

Caravan parks

Central 34 Central Ave, 7km east of Perth ⓣ08/9277 1704, ⓦwww.perthcentral.com.au. Located in Ascot, by the domestic airport, a ten-minute drive to the city. Cabins ❹

Scarborough Starhaven 18 Pearl Parade ⓣ08/9341 1770, ⓦwww.starhaven.com.au. Situated in a popular beach suburb, a 35min bus ride from the centre. On-site vans ❹

The City

The compact and walkable **central area** of Perth, from Wellington Street down to St Georges Terrace, and bounded vaguely by Hill Street to the east and Milligan Street to the west, is an easy-to-negotiate grid. Much of your time will be spent exploring the links between **Hay Street** and **Murray Street**, both of which are pedestrianized between William and Barrack streets and connected by numerous, glittering arcades. William Street runs north over the railway at **Horseshoe Bridge** and on into the restaurants and bars of Northbridge, while Barrack Street runs south to the **Barrack Street Jetty** on Perth Water, site of the millennial **Swan Bells Tower** (daily 10am–4.30pm; $10; ⓦwww.swanbells.com.au). The distinctive tower houses the 280-year-old bells of London's St Martin-in-the-Fields Church, presented to WA on the 1988 bicentenary. Perth Water is a lagoon on the **Swan River** formed by the bridged **Narrows** and popular with windsurfers, sailors and jet-skiers. From the jetty, a Transperth ferry (Sept–April 6.50am–9.15pm; May–Aug 6.50am–7.24pm) regularly crosses the Narrows to Mends Street Jetty on the south shore, while tourist ferries ply the river upstream to the Swan Valley wineries and downstream to Fremantle and **Rottnest Island** (see box, p.646).

Museums and old buildings

Situated just over the railway tracks in Northbridge, at the end of James Street, the **Perth Cultural Centre** comprises the **Art Gallery of Western Australia** (daily 10am–5pm; ⓦwww.artgallery.wa.gov.au; donation) and the state **museum** (daily 9.30am–5pm; donation), as well as the state library. The gallery's constantly changing displays include Aboriginal art, and other contemporary and classic works by Western Australian artists. There's always something worth seeing, the air conditioning is blissful in summer, and the free guided tours are very informative. The museum – part of the same complex – includes a floor devoted to Aboriginal culture, plus exhibitions of vintage cars, stuffed marsupials, meteorites, a diorama of a swamp and a reconstruction of an old jail.

Perth's surviving colonial-era buildings are so embedded in the modern infrastructure that they hold little interest. One exception is the **Perth Mint** (Mon–Fri 9am–5pm, Sat & Sun 9am–1pm; $9.90; ⓦwww.perthmint.com.au), on the corner of Hill and Hay streets. Operating from its original 1899 base, Australia's principal specialist mint still trades in precious metals in bar or coin form and displays some large-scale replicas of gold nuggets and alluring 400-ounce ingots. Admission gives visitors a chance to observe hourly gold-pouring as well as minting operations in the refurbished foundry, along with a guided tour.

Other than that, the **Old Mill** (daily 10am–4pm; $4; Transperth ferry from Barrack Street Jetty), situated at Mill Point, south of the Narrows and in the shadow of the Kwinana Freeway bridge, is an early building that has managed to retain its charm. A quaint, fairy-tale relic, the mill ground the colony's first flour and now houses a collection of pioneering bull-carts and period artefacts in its attractive grounds.

Kings Park

The mostly wild, five-square-kilometre expanse of **Kings Park** is situated 2km west of the centre down Mount Street (bus #37 from St Georges Terrace). Created with great foresight in 1872, the park remains one of Perth's most popular recreational areas, along with the river. There's a trail leading through the native bushland, a botanic and aromatic garden, playgrounds, picnic areas, an elevated walkway through the trees and free guided tours and maps offered by the **information centre** (daily 9.30am–4pm; ⓣ08/9480 3600, ⓦwww.bgpa.wa.gov.au) next to the car park. The Aspects of Kings Park (daily 9am–5pm) shop located next door houses art by local artists including textiles, ceramics, visual art, jewellery and printed works.

Eating and drinking

Northbridge, especially around James and Lake streets, is the heart of Perth's tourist café and restaurant scene, with over forty establishments crammed into a square kilometre. Except for Sundays and Mondays, the area is very busy in the evenings, as people wander from place to place, eating and drinking until late. Places in the city centre are also worth a look.

To eat well and inexpensively in Perth, stick to **Italian** and **Asian** places; these two cuisines cater for ninety percent of eateries and dominate the **food courts**, where you can easily get a decent meal for as little as $10. In Northbridge, food courts include the primarily Asian *Shang Hai* on James Street, while in the city you'll find *Metro* and the cosmopolitan *Carillon* off Hay Street Mall. At the other end of the scale, some of the better seafood restaurants may cost you $30 or more per head – still great value if you've come from Europe.

It's also worth exploring options elsewhere, such as the strip of restaurants along Beaufort Street in Mount Lawley, north of Northbridge, lively Leederville to the west, Subiaco on the west side of Kings Park or **Fremantle** (see p.640). All are fun places to dine without the congested, frenetic feel of Northbridge. A good local website with restaurant reviews can be found at ⓦwww.eatingwa.com.au.

Annalakshmi Jetty no. 4, Barrack St, just south of CBD. Named after the Hindu goddess of food, this truly excellent Indian vegetarian restaurant has volunteer chefs (mostly grandmothers) that come to share their secret recipes. Uniquely there are no prices – you merely pay what you feel like. Excellent in every way. Tues–Sun noon–2pm & 6.30–9.30pm.

The Fishy Affair 132 James St, Northbridge ⓣ08/9328 3939, ⓦwww.fishyaffair.com.au. One of Northbridge's longest established restaurants known for their huge seafood platter from $39 per person. Tues–Sun 11.30am–3pm & 5.30pm–late.

Maya Masala Cnr Lake and Francis sts, Northbridge ⓣ08/9328 5655. One of Perth's most popular Indian restaurants with *masala dosa* from $12, seafood *thali* for $17 and curries from $16. Tues–Sun 11.30am–2.30pm & 5.30pm–late.

Siena Pizzeria 500 Beaufort St, Mt Lawley ⓣ08/9227 6991, ⓦwww.sienas.com.au. Deservedly busy restaurant with mouthwatering, wood-fired pizzas for around $16 and all your other Italian favourites such as veal and *calamari* for around $22. Daily 5.30pm–late, plus Wed–Sun noon–3pm, Sat & Sun breakfast 7.30–10.30am.

Som's Kitchen 240 Adelaide Terrace, CBD. Tiny, family-run Thai restaurant that fills up nightly with students ordering an assortment of curries with nothing over $8. Mon–Fri 11am–2pm, 6–8pm.

Taka Cnr Barrack & Wellington sts, CBD. Popular student/backpacker haunt where set-meal sushi portions are huge and under $10. Mon–Sat 11am–9pm, Sun 11am–5pm.

Took Be Gi Pier St, CBD. The entire Korean student population would head home if this wasn't here. Specializes in steamboats (where patrons share a bowl of ingredients over a flame in the middle of the table) but their hot and spicy soups are always a winner, and the prices (around $13 for mains) are great value for money. Go with a group and get there early to guarantee a seat. BYO. Wed–Mon 11am–11pm.

Valentino Cnr Lake and James sts, Northbridge. Italian restaurant with lunch specials, wood-fired pizzas and pastas for around $13, as well as a good range of cakes. Mon–Fri 7am–late, Sat 8am–late.

Villa Italia Cnr Aberdeen and William sts, Northbridge. Jazzy Italian café with a similar range of food as *Valentino*. Mon–Fri 7am–late, Sat 8am–late.

Woodpeckers Woodfired Pizza 372 Hay St, Subiaco ⓣ08/9388 1122. Gourmet pizza and pasta from around $15. Daily 6pm–late.

Entertainment and nightlife

As with food, **Northbridge** is the focal point of after-dark action, with plenty of **pubs**, **bars** and teeming **dance clubs** concealed in improbable buildings. In view of Perth's famed isolation, a night in Northbridge is the hottest spot for thousands of kilometres in any direction – but there are also some lively bars in the city and inner suburbs. ⓦwww.thehappiesthour.com.au is a humorous search engine that lists the areas best drink specials. Late at night however, Northbridge can have an edge to it that some might find intimidating and many locals avoid the place these days. Perth's nightlife centres around alcohol and although the city is attempting to curb antisocial carousing and promote responsible behaviour, there's little chance of this with so many pubs and bars offering **free beer**, happy hours and other value-added incentives to tempt you.

The free weekly *X Press* newspaper available outside various central outlets has comprehensive **listings** on what's going on and who's playing where, or check out the entertainment section of Thursday's *West Australian* newspaper. For the lowdown on the **gay and lesbian scene**, see "Listings".

Pubs and bars

Aberdeen Hotel 84 Aberdeen St, Northbridge. Ever-popular meeting place in Northbridge, with a long-established gay night on Sun.

Amplifier 383–393 Murray St, City. Excellent late-night bar and one of Perth's best live-music venues. Drinks specials on Fridays drag in the punters from all corners.

Belgian Beer Café 347 Murray St, City. An upmarket feel with nice wooden interior, and for beer lovers the $14 tasting tray is a lesson in quality brewing.

Brass Monkey Cnr William and James sts, Northbridge. Enduringly popular pub with a good atmosphere in the heart of Northbridge. Live entertainment and a range of local beers.

Flying Scotsman 639 Beaufort St, Mount Lawley. Well-known student hang-out, with cover bands, drink specials and cheap meals on a nightly basis.

Leederville Hotel Oxford St, cnr of Newcastle St, Leederville. The Sun sessions are all the rage but you need to dress up a bit (no thongs, singlets etc). Mainstream bands and DJs.

Lucky Shag Barrack St Jetty, just south of CBD. The unbeatable beer garden looking over the Swan River is reason enough to come here, especially at sunset.
Moon & Sixpence 300 Murray St, CBD. Popular English theme pub in the city centre, with tables out the front to watch the city workers go by.
Mustang Bar 46 Lake St, Northbridge. Big-screen sports with free pool, cheap food, competitions and karaoke make this a favourite among partying backpackers.
Northbridge Hotel 198 Brisbane St, Northbridge. Quiet piano lounge and restaurant which does good breakfasts. Livelier public bar with Internet facilities.
Queens 520 Beaufort St, Mt Lawley. One of Perth's best bars, away from the Northbridge mania with a great atmosphere, locally brewed beers and a good restaurant for Sun morning breakfasts.

Cinemas and theatres

Most of Perth's mainstream **cinemas** are located in the arcades off Hay and Murray streets in the city centre. Tuesday nights are cheap, with matinees also discounted at some places. Art-house cinemas close to the centre include Cinema Paradiso, in the Galleria complex on James Street. A little further out are the Art Deco–style Astor, at Mount Lawley on the corner of Beaufort and Walcott streets and the Luna on Oxford Street, Leederville, both a fifteen-minute walk west of Northbridge.

Any out-of-the-ordinary **shows** that visit Perth tend to set the city astir and are advertised and patronized heavily. The *Burwood International Resort and Casino* (Ⓣ08/9362 7777, Ⓦwww.burswood.com.au), just over the Causeway, southeast of the centre, is a do-it-all leisure complex comprising a five-star hotel, numerous restaurants and a huge dome hosting all sorts of sporting and show-business events. Otherwise try the Perth Concert Hall on St Georges Terrace (Ⓣ08/9231 9900, Ⓦwww.perthconcerthall.com.au) or Her Majesty's Theatre (Ⓣ08/9322 2929) on the corner of King and Hay streets.

Listings

Airline Skywest Ⓣ1300 660 088, Ⓦwww.skywest.com.au. Flights to Albany, Broome, Carnarvon, Esperance, Exmouth, Geraldton, Goldfields, Kalbarri, Karratha, Kununurra, Monkey Mia and Port Hedland.
Buses Greyhound Australia (Ⓦwww.greyhound.com.au) goes up along the coast to Darwin daily, less frequently to Port Hedland via Newman on the inland route; Integrity Coach Lines (Ⓣ08/9226 1399 or 1800 226 339, Ⓦwww.integritycoachlines.com.au) heads north via the Great Northern Highway to Port Headland (Thurs); South West Coach Lines (Ⓣ08/9324 2333, Ⓦwww.southwestcoachlines.com.au) has daily services to the Margaret River region as far as Augusta; and Transwa (Ⓣ1300 662 205, Ⓦwww.transwa.wa.gov.au) operates daily bus services as far as Esperance and, less frequently, north to Kalbarri and Meekatharra via Mullewa. They also do a four-week Southern Discovery Pass for around $155.
Car purchase For used vehicles, backpackers' notice boards and the many Internet cafés and travel shops like Travellers Club on 535 Wellington St are best for private sales. Try to avoid buying non-WA-registered vehicles in WA as the change of ownership requires an inspection in the state of origin, or a local inspection prior to registration on WA plates, which might entail expensive repairs. Buying and running WA-plated cars within the state is simple as there is no annual roadworthy or change-of-ownership inspection; all you do is renew the annual vehicle-registration document, aka "rego".
Car rental Travellers Auto Barn, 365 Newcastle St, Northbridge (Ⓣ9228 9500, Ⓦwww.travellers-autobarn.com), is well respected and has offices throughout the country. Prices start around $35 a day. For **scooter rental** go to Scootaround, 127 Hill St, East Perth (Ⓣ08/9325 5100), or Modomio, 14 (rear) Norfolk St, Fremantle (Ⓣ08/9433 2377, Ⓦwww.modomio.com.au).
Cycle hire About Bike Hire, Causeway Car Park, Riverside Drive. Mon–Sat 10am–5pm, Sun 9am–5pm Ⓣ08/9221 2665, Ⓦwww.rideaway.com.au, or available from most backpackers' from $30 a day.
Gay and lesbian Perth The quickest way to plug into the scene is to pick up the weekly community paper *Out in Perth* (Ⓦwww.outinperth.com) and the monthly *Women Out West* (Ⓦwww.womenoutwest.com.au), both free from Cinema Paradiso on James St or the Arcane Bookshop, 212 William St, Northbridge (Ⓣ08/9328 5073).

Hospitals Royal Perth, Victoria Square ⓣ08/9224 2244; Fremantle, Alma St ⓣ08/9242 5544.
Maps Perth Map Centre, 900 Hay St (ⓣ08/9322 5733), has a full range of topographic and touring maps.
Motoring associations RACWA, 228 Adelaide Terrace (ⓣ08/9421 4444), offers a complete range of services, as well as maps.
Permits for Aboriginal Land Aboriginal Affairs Department, 197 St Georges Terrace ⓣ08/9235 8000, ⓦwww.dia.wa.gov.au/Land/Permits/.
Police 2 Adelaide Terrace ⓣ08/9222 111 or 13 14 44 for non-urgent calls.
Post office Forrest Chase, opposite the train station. Mail collection service.
Taxis Call Swan Taxis on ⓣ13 13 30.
Trains The Indian-Pacific rail service (ⓣ13 21 47, ⓦwww.trainways.com.au) leaves on Wed and Sun, getting to Sydney or Melbourne two days later, and there are great deals like half-price backpackers/ overseas concessions and the six-month Great Southern Rail Pass ($690, conc. $590; for full details see p.36). Check their website for latest prices, but over very long distances a flight becomes better value with the savings in travel time. Transwa also has daily rail services south to Bunbury and twice on weekdays to Kalgoorlie. Both Transwa and Indian-Pacific have offices at the Wellington St Bus Station.

Around Perth

For excursions beyond central Perth, the port of **Fremantle**, at the mouth of the Swan River, should not be overlooked, nor should a trip over to **Rottnest Island**, an eighty-minute ferry ride from the city or half that from Fremantle. Perth's **beaches** form a near-unbroken line north of Fremantle, just a short train or bus ride from the centre, while with your own vehicle you can escape to wineries of the **Upper Swan Valley** and the **national parks** northeast of Perth, atop the **Darling Ranges**, which run parallel to the coast. Patchily forested hills, just half an hour's drive east of the city, the Ranges offer a network of cool, scenic drives and marked walking trails among the jarrah woodlands. Further afield, **Toodyay** and **New Norcia** can make a satisfying day-trip with a tour or in a rented car, as can visits to the old colonial settlement of **York**.

Fremantle

Although long since merged into the metropolitan area's suburban sprawl, Perth's port of **FREMANTLE** – "Freo" – retains a character that the city centre of Perth lacks. It's small enough to keep its energy focused, with a real working harbour instead of a fake marina, and it has an eclectic, arty ambience without too many upmarket pretensions. The various buildings in the historic precinct that have been taken over by Notre Dame University also give the town a youthful, vibrant feeling.

Much of the convict-built dock, dating from the 1890s, was spruced up before the 1987 Americas Cup yacht race for an eagerly anticipated tourist boom that never quite materialized. Before the makeover Freo was as rough as any port – the period hotels were then "bloodhouses" full of brawling sailors – but today the town attracts a "latte and deck shoes" weekend crowd to its famed **markets** (worth planning your visit around) and the "cappuccino strip", as café-lined **South Terrace** is known. It's also worth noting that in the heat of summer Fremantle is often a breezy 5°C cooler than Perth, a mere 25 minutes away by train.

Arrival and information

Fremantle Station is located at the top end of Market Street, five minutes' walk north of the town centre. **Buses** (routes #102–106 and #151 from Perth's Esplanade Busport) also stop here; local **taxis** can be called on ⓣ08/9335 3944. **Ferries** to Rottnest and Perth leave from the wharfside B Shed (behind the E

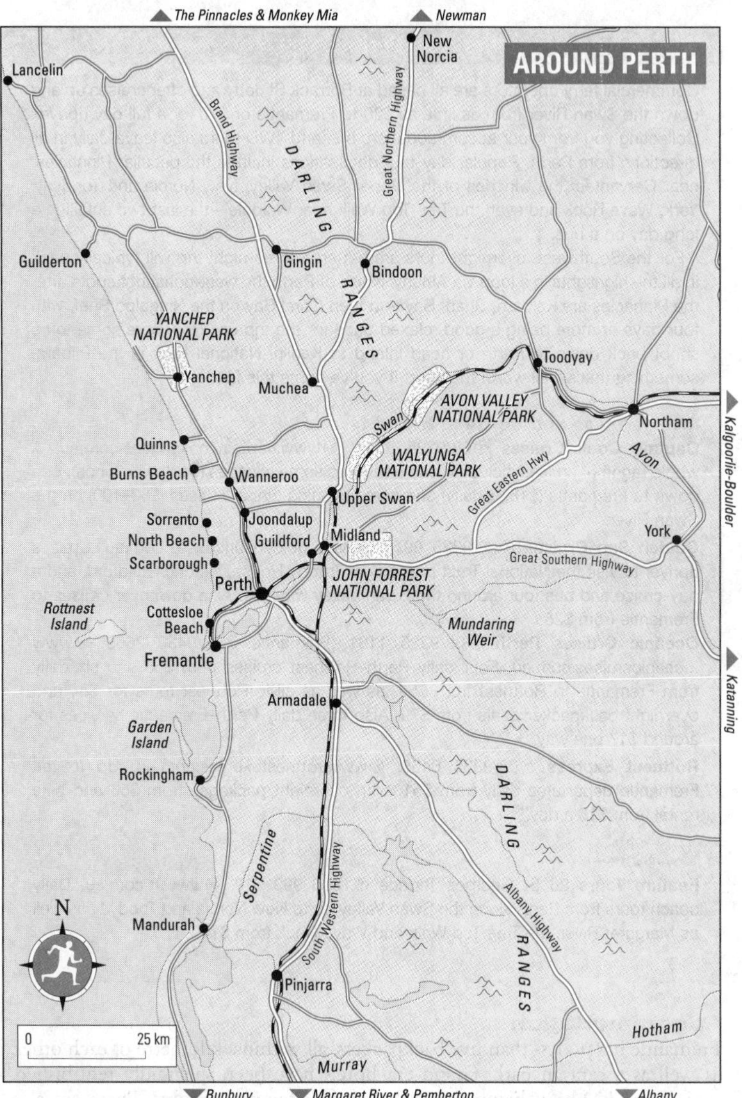

Shed), which is ten minutes' walk from the station along Phillimore Street (see box on p.642 for details and prices). The orange **Fremantle CAT** (Mon–Fri 7.30am–6.30pm, Sat & Sun 10am–6.30pm) is a free bus service which runs roughly every ten minutes along a figure-of-eight route that covers all places in the description below. You could also consider hopping aboard the **Fremantle Tram**, which offers informative commentaries on its various tours (daily 10am–4pm; hourly; from $20), and departs from outside the Town Hall on Kings Square. There's a small **visitor information centre** in the Town Hall on Kings Square (Mon–Fri 9am–5pm, Sat 10am–3pm, Sun 11.30am–2.30pm; ⓣ08/9431 7878, ⓦwww.fremantlewa.com.au).

River cruises and tours from Perth

Commercial ferry operators are all based at Barrack St Jetty and offer cruises up and down the Swan River from as little as $20 to Fremantle or $70 for a full day upriver. Collecting you from your accommodation, bus and 4WD tours also leave daily in all directions from Perth. Popular day-tour destinations include the peculiar Pinnacles, near Cervantes, the wineries of the Upper Swan Valley, New Norcia and Toodyay, York, Wave Rock and even the Tree Top Walk near Walpole – the last two entailing a long day on a bus.

For the Southwest, overnight tours are better: a three-night trip will typically pack in all the highlights in a loop via Albany. North of Perth the west-coast hot spots after the Pinnacles are Kalbarri, Shark Bay and then Coral Bay on the Ningaloo Reef, with four days or more being a good relaxed pace for the trip up. From here some tours shoot back down to Perth or head inland to Karijini National Park in the Pilbara, something that's well worth the effort if you've come this far north.

River cruises and Rottnest Island ferries

Captain Cook Cruises ⓣ08/9325 3341, ⓦwww.captaincookcruises.com.au. A whole range of cruises including one upriver to some wineries ($125 with lunch), one down to Fremantle ($18; 3 daily) and some evening dinner cruises ($80–100) on the Swan River.

Golden Sun Cruises ⓣ08/9325 9916, ⓦwww.goldensuncruises.com.au. Cruises upriver to visit the National Trust property at Tranby House, historic Guildford, and a day-cruise and bus tour around the Swan Valley wineries. Also downriver cruises to Fremantle from $25.

Oceanic Cruises Perth ⓣ08/9325 1191, Fremantle ⓣ08/9430 2666, ⓦwww.oceaniccruises.com.au. Four daily Perth–Rottnest cruises from $65 and six daily from Fremantle to Rottnest from $56, as well as all-in Rottnest tours for $84 and overnight backpacker deals from $79. Also three daily Perth–Fremantle services for around $17 one way.

Rottnest Express ⓣ08/9335 6406, ⓦwww.rottnestexpress.com.au. Up to ten Fremantle departures daily from $51, with overnight packages from $56 and bike rental from $18 a day.

Day-tours

Feature Tours 26 St Georges Terrace ⓣ1800 999 819, ⓦwww.ft.com.au. Daily coach tours from Perth along the Swan Valley up to New Norcia and Toodyay as well as Margaret River, the Tree Top Walk and Wave Rock from $140–175.

Accommodation

Fremantle has no less than five backpackers' all within a kilometre of each other, as well as a caravan park. Grand-era hotels have been splendidly refurbished, their only drawback being shared bathrooms for most rooms. There are also plenty of B&Bs in and around the centre and keep in mind that accommodation should be booked in advance all year round.

100 Hubble 100 Hubble St, East Fremantle ⓣ08/9339 8080 ⓦwww.100hubble.com. Crazy, wonderful, hippy, eco-friendly abode where rooms (one is an old train carriage) are decked out in a mishmash of bric-a-brac, plants and a whole lot of love. Breakfast included in price. ❺–❻

Fremantle Village Caravan Park Cnr Cockburn and Rockingham rds, South Fremantle ⓣ08/9430 4866, ⓦwww.fremantlevillage.com.au. The nearest campsite to the centre of town. On-site vans and cabins ❸

Norfolk Hotel 47 South Terrace ⓣ08/9335 5405, ⓦwww.norfolkhotel.com.au. Centrally located pub accommodation with mostly en-suite rooms plus a few budget options, all with a kettle and a fridge. The rooms are quiet despite bands

Western Travel Bug ⓣ08/9204 4600 or 1800 627 488, ⓦwww.travelbug.com.au. Pinnacles, Wave Rock and Margaret River for around $135, all with plenty of activities.

Swan Valley wine tours

Various operators run **bus and boat tours** of the valley from Perth, among them Swan Valley Tours (ⓣ08/9299 8667, ⓦwww.svtours.com.au; $80), Captain Cook Cruises (see opposite), who run a daily wine cruise from Barrack St Jetty in Perth for around $125 including lunch, and Out and About Wine Tours (ⓣ08/9377 3376, ⓦwww.outandabouttours.com.au), who have group day-tours every day except Mon including a three-course lunch, for $79.

Overnight tours

All Terrain Safaris ⓣ08/9295 6680 or 1800 633 456, ⓦwww.allterrain.com.au. Runs up the coast from $120 a day to Coral Bay, as well as Karijini and from Broome right into the northern Kimberley and the Bungles to Kakadu.

Easyrider Backpacker Tours 224 William St, Northbridge ⓣ08/9227 0824, ⓦwww.easyridertours.com.au. Hop on and off the yellow bus, with tickets valid from three days up to six months as far as Darwin via Coral Bay, Karijini and Broome, or over to Kalgoorlie, Esperance and Albany from as little as $70 per day plus food and lodging. Discounts available when booked online.

Planet Perth Tours ⓣ08/9225 6622, ⓦwww.planettours.com.au. Accommodated tours into the Southwest and five- to seven-day trips up to Exmouth and Broome from around $130 a day.

Red Earth Safaris ⓣ08/9279 9011 or 1800 501 968, ⓦwww.redearthsafaris.com.au. Mon departures for one-week coastal trips up to Exmouth and back ($735/599 with YHA VIP card).

Westernxposure 179 William St, Northbridge ⓣ08/9244 1200, ⓦwww.westernxposure.com.au. Four-day Monkey Mia trips, three-day Southwest tours or ten-day jaunts via Exmouth and Karijini to Broome. Around $135 a day.

Surf tours

Lancelin Beach Surf School ⓣ1800 198 121, ⓦwww.surfschool.com.au. Picks you up early from Perth for up to four days, at around $95 a day with wetsuits, accommodation and food included.

Wedge Island Surf Co ⓣ08/9336 6773, ⓦwww.wedgeislandsurfco.com.au. Day-trips to Lancelin or a two-day tour to Wedge Island (in 4WD), including overnight camp for $249.

playing most nights in the basement. Parking available. ❸

Old Fire Station Backpackers 18 Phillimore St ⓣ08/9430 5454, ⓦwww.old-firestation.net. Two minutes from the station, this large sprawling hostel has a huge common room, great outdoor cinema area, women-only lounge and dorms, and discount food from the Indian restaurant downstairs. Yes, there is an old fireman's pole but it's rarely used. Four- to twelve-bed dorms from $20, rooms ❸

Pirates Backpackers 11 Essex St ⓣ & ⓕ08/9335 6635, ⓦwww.piratesbackpackers.com. Very sociable backpackers', in a nice quiet location close to the parks and water, with a happy, friendly vibe throughout. Small enough to make you feel you're not one of the mob, but can be too cramped for some. The relaxing outdoor area fills up with people every night. Dorms from $23, rooms ❸

Rosie O'Gradys 23 William St ⓣ08/9335 1645, ⓦwww.rosieogradys.com.au. Great old pub, right in the centre of town, that has simple rooms (some en suite). Can get noisy when bands play downstairs on weekends. ❸–❹

Sundancer Backpacker Resort 80 High St ⓣ08/9336 6080 or 1800 061 144, ⓦwww.sundancer-resort.com.au. Fremantle's designated party hostel. Huge, slightly impersonal, with an outdoor pool, beer garden and bar with various drink specials. Congested ten-bed dorms $21, four-bed $23 and rooms ❸

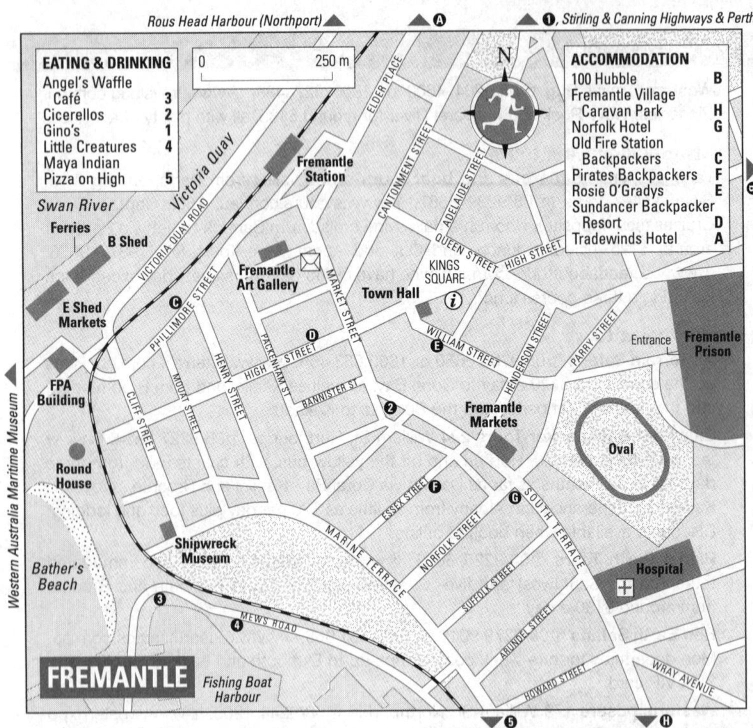

Tradewinds Hotel 59 Canning Highway ⓣ08/9339 8188, ⓦwww.tradewindshotel.com.au. Good-looking, Federation-era hotel with well-equipped, self-catering apartments, close to the river and 2km from the centre. ❺

The Town

Exploring Fremantle on foot, with plenty of streetside café breaks, is the most agreeable way of visiting the town's compactly grouped sights. If you want to tick off all of them, start your appraisal on the relatively dull east side before moving down to the ocean to end up at the Fishing Boat Harbour, ready for a sunset seafood dinner.

Kick off with the hillside enclosure of **Fremantle Prison** (daily 10am–5pm; $16; ⓦwww.fremantleprison.com), whose entrance is on The Terrace, on the west side of the compound. Built by convicts in 1855, soon after the struggling colony found it couldn't do without their labour, the complex was only decommissioned in 1991. The high admission charge is offset by free tours (every 30min) of the prison buildings, sometimes guided by ex-wardens.

Not far from the prison are the more cheerful **Fremantle Markets** (Fri 9am–9pm, Sat 9am–5pm, Sun & Mon 10am–5pm; ⓦwww.fremantlemarkets.com.au), on the corner of Henderson Street and South Terrace. A real locals' market, it's well worth a browse for some fresh food, unusual souvenirs from the many arts-and-crafts stalls, or New Age accessories. Moving down **South Terrace**, Fremantle's main street, you can rest your aching feet in one of the many inviting alfresco **cafés** that lend the town a distinctive Mediterranean atmosphere.

Suitably recaffeinated, head towards the "**West End**", as the old shipping office and freight district of Freo is known. A left-turn down the High Street will lead you past various arts-and-crafts galleries and knick-knack shops to the **Round House** (daily 10am–3pm; donation), the state's oldest building and original gaol, which boasts fine views back down into town and out to sea.

From here you can't miss the striking building housing the **Western Australian Maritime Museum** on Victoria Quay (daily 9.30am–5pm; $10 or $15 with submarine *Ovens*, free every second Tues of the month; Ⓦ www.museum.wa.gov.au/maritime). The museum, with architectural overtones of the Sydney Opera House (though they don't like to admit it), features several galleries covering just about every nautical aspect of WA. Pride of place goes to the glossy-hulled *Australia II* yacht that won the America's Cup several times; alongside is the rather more weather-beaten *Parry Endeavour* belonging to many-times world circumnavigator John Sanders. Other highlights range from the very first Indonesian *prau* seized in WA for illegal fishing, right down to a boy's canoe made from a folded sheet of galvo. There are also displays on fishing, whaling, pearling and trade across the Indian Ocean. The **submarine** *Ovens* is round the back (same times; $8 or $15 with main museum entry; free tours every half-hour 10am–3.30pm).

Outside the Fremantle Port Authority building at the end of Phillimore Street, there's a statue to C.Y. O'Connor, who masterminded the rebuilding of the docks in the 1890s, as well as the construction of the vital water pipeline to Kalgoorlie. Nearby, where the Rottnest ferries berth, the **E Shed markets** (Fri 10am–9pm, Sat & Sun 10am–5pm) hold a food hall and a similar range of stalls to the better-known Fremantle Markets. The **Fremantle Motor Museum** (daily 9.30am–5pm; $9.50; Ⓦ www.fremantlemotormuseum.net) is in the B Shed opposite. Part of the York Motor Museum's collection, it houses a range of classic machines from the very first single-cylinder three-wheeled "automobile" built by Benz in 1886 to cars raced by the likes of Stirling Moss as well as a few Harleys, new and old.

Fremantle's original maritime museum, the **Shipwreck Museum** (daily 9.30am–5pm; donation), is on Cliff Street. The centrepiece is the *Batavia*, the Dutch East Indiaman wrecked off present-day Geraldton in 1629. As well as the ship's reconstructed stern, the exhibit includes the stone portico bound for the Dutch East India Company's unfinished fort at Batavia (modern-day Jakarta) and numerous corroded artefacts, together with a fascinating film about the extraordinary drama of the wrecking (and subsequent salvage) of the ship. The rest of the museum has collections from other Dutch vessels which regularly struck Australia's west coast on their way to the East Indies. Coming out of the Shipwreck Museum you find yourself on the grassy esplanade facing the numerous seafood restaurants on **Fishing Boat Harbour** – see "Eating", below.

Eating

Seafood restaurants overlook the Swan River or jut out into the Fishing Boat Harbour along Mews Road, while in town, South Terrace and its adjacent streets are lined with predominantly **Italian** or **Asian** cafés and restaurants, all adding to Freo's distinctive, fun atmosphere. At the **Food Halls** (Thurs–Sun noon–9pm) on Henderson Street, next to the Markets, you'll find an array of global cuisines, but mostly Asian "pop foods".

Angel's Waffle Café 24 Essex St. Great breakfasts served all day (around $13), including huge waffles and crêpes that bring the locals back again and again. Also has free WiFi. Sun–Thurs 8am–6pm, Fri & Sat 8am–9pm.

Cicerellos Fishermans Wharf, 44 Mews Rd. Hugely popular restaurant that serves fish and chips right on the harbour. Platters are a good deal if there are a few of you, or go for a "Catch of the Day" or a "Seafood Tray" for around $15. Daily 8am–late.

Gino's 1 South Terrace. Like *Cicerellos*, a Fremantle institution. This enduringly well-liked and unpretentious sidewalk café serves great coffee and cakes, as well as your traditional range of pasta with sauces from $15. Daily 8am–late.

Little Creatures 40 Mews Rd, Fishing Boat Harbour ⓣ08/9430 5555, ⓦwww.littlecreatures.com.au. Sit amidst towering vats of fermenting pale ale in this old aircraft hangar, as the restaurant serves up wood-fired pizzas with inventive toppings such as harissa lamb or Atlantic salmon for around $20. Choose one of their four excellent beers and sit outside overlooking the water. Bliss. Mon–Fri 10am–midnight, Sat & Sun 9am–midnight.

Maya Indian 75 Market St. A Fremantle institution for over ten years and widely regarded as the best Indian restaurant in the state. Prices aren't on the cheap side (mains around $20), but the standard of food is exemplary; waiters will recommend the perfect accompanying wines. Takeaway available. Tues–Sun dinner from 6pm, plus Fri lunch from noon. Closed Mon.

Pizza on High 33 High St. A favourite with those on a budget in search of decent Italian pizza and pasta, with all-you-can-eat dinners for $14.50. Mon–Fri 11am–3pm, Wed–Sat 5.30pm–late.

Drinking and entertainment

Like the town itself, entertainment in Fremantle is generally a laid-back, easy-going affair, which at the same time produces a creative and diverse scene. Some of the country's eminent bands like the John Butler Trio and Eskimo Joe started out in Freo's pubs. The *Sail & Anchor* at 64 South Terrace is the town's main watering hole, serving a variety of "boutique" **beers** (a trend which originated in Fremantle) such as "Chill Beer" which makes your mouth hot and in need for more. The *Left Bank Bar & Café*, at 15 Riverside Rd in East Freo is a beautifully renovated nineteenth-century house and a popular spot, usually packed on sunny weekends.

Bars with **live music** include *Rosie O'Grady's* at 23 William St, the intimate basement at the *Norfolk Hotel* and the rowdy *Newport Hotel*, 2 South Terrace. The *Market Bar* in the market often has bands playing throughout the day as well. Just over the river, *Mojos Bar* at 237 Queen Victoria St is good for original music in a café-bar setting, or try the *Swan Basement* at the *Swan* hotel down the road at no. 201. *Metropolis*, 52 South Terrace, is Fremantle's gigantic **nightclub**, offering a choice of bars and dance floors, while the *Fly By Night*, at the prison end of Queen Street, is a musicians' co-op airing local talent and makes an enjoyable, smoke-free change from pub venues.

Fremantle has no less than four **cinemas**, on Essex Street, William Street, Collie Street and Adelaide Street, all with cut-price tickets on Tuesdays and for some matinees.

Rottnest Island

Eighteen kilometres offshore, west of Fremantle, **Rottnest Island** was so named by seventeenth-century Dutch mariners who mistook its unique, indigenous **quokkas**, beaver-like marsupials, for rats. Today, following an ignominious period as a brutal Aboriginal penal colony in the nineteenth century, Rottnest is a popular holiday destination, easily accessible from Perth or Fremantle by ferry and – at the very least – makes for a fun day out.

The island, inevitably abbreviated to "Rotto", is 11km long and less than half as wide, with one settlement, the main resort, stretching along the sheltered Thompson Bay on the east side. West of the settlement, a low heathland of salt lakes meets a coastline of clear, scalloped bays, small beaches and offshore reefs ending at the "West End", as the seaward "tail" of the island is known. Although well attuned to the demands of its 400,000+ annual visitors, Rotto gets packed out during school summer holidays (for dates see p.77), especially around New Year when accommodation can be hard to find. Motorized traffic on the island is virtually nonexistent, a real treat that makes **cycling** from bay to sparkling bay the best way to appreciate Rotto. Besides riding around the island, you can take a **train ride** up to Oliver Hill (3 trips daily; 2hr; $11.80), or get underwater with the help of the Dive Shop (daily 7.30am–6pm; ⓣ08/9292 5111, ⓦwww.rottnestdiving.com.au), which organizes **dive trips** and rents out everything from snorkels and fins to full scuba-diving equipment. The diving and snorkelling off Rotto's beautiful coves are unlike anywhere on the adjacent mainland and a couple of days spent here, especially midweek when it's less busy, are well worth the excursion from Perth. Of interest is the Little Salmon Bay Snorkel Trail, where underwater plaques describe the surroundings. The *Underwater Explorer* (ⓣ0400 202 340, ⓦwww.underwaterexplorer.com.au) is a glass-bottomed boat that operates a reef-and-wreck tour (Sept–May; $22; 45min) for those who don't want to get wet.

Practicalities

There are at least three **ferry** operators that service Rotto from the B Shed in Fremantle and Perth's Barrack Street Jetty. Prices have stabilized at around $50 day-return from Freo and $65 from Perth (see box, p.642, for details). The trip from Perth takes about eighty minutes and less than half that from Fremantle, so to make the most of your day aim to board at the latter. You can also **fly** to Rotto in twenty minutes from Jandakot airport, about 20km south of Perth, with the Rottnest Air Taxi (ⓣ1800 500 006, ⓦwww.rottnest.de; from $80) among others. Rottnest Airport is a fifteen-minute walk from the settlement.

Ferries arrive at the jetty in Thompson Bay right in front of the island's **visitor information centre** (daily 7am–5pm; ⓣ08/9372 9732, ⓦwww.rottneestisland.com), which has maps and bus timetables and also serves as a **post office**. Daily two-hour **bus tours** depart from the bus stop behind the visitor information centre at varying times throughout the day ($24.30). There is also the more-or-less half-hourly Bayseeker **bus service** (Oct–April daily 9am–5pm; $7.50 day-ticket) which takes you to the island's bays as far as the isthmus, Narrow Neck, 3km from the West End. Also behind the visitor information centre is the Salt Store building, which is where the Rottnest Voluntary Guides begin free daily walking tours at 11am. Around the corner is the small museum (daily 10.45am–3.30pm, donation) holding displays representing the island's wildlife, geology and history. The **bike-rental** building (daily 9am–1pm & 2–5pm; from $20 per day; ⓣ08/9292 5105) is behind the *Quokka Arms Hotel*, a couple of minutes south of the visitor information centre.

Accommodation is found along Thompson, Longreach and Geordie bays, all adjacent to each other at the developed northeast end of the island and linked by the Bayseeker bus service. The central reservations number for accommodation is ⓣ08/9432 9111 or email ⓔreservations@rottnestisland.com; note that prices drop about twenty per cent in winter. A small YHA-associate **hostel** (ⓣ08/9372 9780, ⓔrottnest@yhawa.com.au; booking essential; dorms $24) is located in Kingstown Barracks at the southeastern end of Thompson Bay, 1km from the shops. Nearby, the *Rottnest Lodge Resort* (ⓣ08/9292 5161, ⓕ9292 5158; ❻) is a former prison converted into first-class motel units. The historic *Quokka Arms Hotel* (ⓣ08/9292 5011, ⓔquokkaarms@rottnestisland.com; ❻), a five-minute walk from the visitor information centre, has eighteen comfortable rooms, four with sea views. **Camping** is available just behind the settlement (ⓣ08/9432 9111). Tents and mattresses can be rented (❶), or there are four- and six-bed self-contained cabins (❸). Camping is not permitted anywhere else on the island. The settlement has undergone somewhat of a boom in recent years, and there are many eating options, including a, for better or worse, *Red Rooster* and a *Subway*. The *Quokka Arms Hotel* makes a good gourmet pizza and sipping a beer on one of their tables beside the sea is particularly relaxing.

Perth's beaches

Perth's closest beaches extend along the **Sunset Coast**, 30km of near-unbroken sand and coastal suburbs stretching north of the Swan River, bordered by the Indian Ocean and cooled by afternoon sea breezes. There are also inshore beaches well worth a look along the **Swan River** at Crawley, Nedlands, Peppermint Grove and Mosman Bay on the north shore, and Como, Canning Bridge and Applecross on the south shore, and which are calm and safe for children.

Cottesloe Beach, 7km north of Fremantle, is the most popular city beach, with safe swimming. There are ice-cream vendors, cafés and watercraft-rental outlets aplenty, all just a ten-minute walk from Cottesloe train station. Two kilometres north of here, **Swanbourne Free Beach** – cut off by army land in both directions but accessible from the road – has nude bathing. North of **Scarborough Beach**, itself another favoured venue 6km north of Swanbourne, the surf and currents are more suited to wave-riding and experienced swimmers, though with fewer beachside facilities, crowds are reduced. Bus #400 leaves from Perth's Wellington Street Bus Station for the 35-minute journey.

New Norcia and Toodyay

One of WA's most unusual architectural sights is **NEW NORCIA**, a monastic community dating from the nineteenth century, 130km northeast of Perth on the Great Northern Highway. This unexpected collection of Spanish-style buildings, bizarrely out of place in the Australian bush, is part of a community founded by Benedictine monks in 1846 with the aim of converting the local Aborigines to Christianity. Nowadays the community is a much-visited tourist attraction.

The community has a roadhouse with a restaurant, a **visitor information centre** (daily 9.30am–4.30pm; ⓣ08/9654 8056) and a **museum and art gallery** (daily 9am–4.30pm; $10) that explains the Benedictines' motivation in coming here and displays a fine collection of religious art. The visitor information centre also runs two-hour **tours** of the town leaving at 11am and 1.30pm ($14.50). The **rooms** in the *New Norcia Hotel* (ⓣ08/9654 8034, ⓦwww.newnorcia.wa.edu.au; ④) don't quite match the building's grand exterior, but they still offer an old-fashioned treat. The two-kilometre New Norcia **heritage trail** begins here and takes you on a circuit past the community's impressive buildings.

The two most ornate buildings, on either side of the cemetery, are **St Gertrude's Residence for Girls** and **St Ildephonsus's for Boys** (both open only to tour groups), the latter with striking Moorish minarets. Among other buildings, you can also visit the **Flour Mills** (arrange with visitor information centre) and the Abbey Church (open daily; mass times Sunday 7.30am & 9am) – both relatively ordinary in comparison. You'll find the wood-fired **bread** made at the mills in Perth's best restaurants and at the retail outlet at 163 Scarborough Beach Rd, Mount Lawley.

Several bus-tour companies offer **day-trips** from Perth to New Norcia (see box, pp.642–643), which is otherwise served only three times a week by Transwa's rural bus service.

Toodyay

The old town of **TOODYAY**, set among the wooded hills of the Avon Valley, 85km northwest of Perth, makes an agreeable diversion on the way to – or from – New Norcia. The town was founded in 1836, making it one of the earliest inland settlements of the Swan River Colony, and a few buildings survive from that era. The **visitor information centre** (Mon–Sat 9am–5pm, Sun 10am–5pm; ⓣ08/9574 2435, ⓦwww.toodyay.com) is situated by the station behind **Connor's Mill** on Stirling Terrace, the town's main road. The mill houses a **museum** ($2.50), as does the **Old Newcastle Gaol** just over the rails on Clinton Street (Mon–Fri 10am–3pm, Sat & Sun 10am–4pm; $2.50). Other historic buildings include the riverside **St Stephen's Church**, opposite the mill, as well as the former Mechanics' Institute – now the **library** – on Stirling Terrace.

Guildford and the Swan Valley

North of the town of **GUILDFORD**, a thirty-minute drive northeast of Perth, is the **Upper Swan Valley** – WA's oldest wine-growing region. It makes for a pleasant day's **wine-tasting**, although the wines produced here reputedly don't match those of the Margaret River region, which themselves are not considered Australia's finest. **Guildford** itself is a historic town dating back to the earliest years of the colony, with several Federation-era grand hotels to admire. Guildford Village Potters, at 22 Meadow St, acts as the town's **visitor information centre** (daily 9am–4pm; ⓦwww.swanvalley.com.au). If you're heading up into the valley, pick up the *Swan Valley Wineries* guide from here, which details the area's attractions and its three dozen or so wineries.

The Swan Valley Drive

Heading north from Guildford Village Potters, a clearly marked thirty-kilometre drive follows the west side of the river. Turning left down Banera Road will bring you to **Pinelli Wines** on Bennett Road (Mon–Fri 9am–6pm, Sat 9am–5pm, Sun 10am–5pm; ⓣ08/9279 6818), which offers two-litre flagons of decent table wine for around $15. Further up Route 203, the **Little River Winery & Café** (daily 10am–5.30pm) is a small, independent winery with some award-winning wines and a pleasant café in which to enjoy them.

Driving down the valley's east side, several more wineries tempt you in: **Talijancich Wines** (Sun–Fri 10am–5pm), produces a rich muscat, while **Houghton's**, on Dale Road (daily 10am–5pm; ⓦwww.haughton-wines.com.au), is the area's biggest and most diverse producer of wines, with an art gallery, excellent café and tended lawns on which to contemplate your tastings. The route returns to Guildford via Midland and thence to Perth, passing the Toodyay Road, which winds up into the Darling Ranges. For Swan Valley tours, see p.643.

York

Stranded in the Avon Valley, 97km from Perth via the Great Southern Highway, **YORK** looks like a film set for an Australian western. The town is the state's most complete pioneering settlement, filled with attractive and well-preserved early architecture. The commercial centre of the Avon Valley until the railway – and with it the Great Eastern Highway – bypassed it 30km to the north, York is now an agricultural centre but also plays a historic role as a venerable museum of ornate nineteenth-century public buildings, coaching inns and churches. Be warned though: this inland region regularly bakes at 40°C in mid-summer.

The **Old York Gaol & Courthouse** (daily 10am–4pm; $5) on Avon Terrace harks back to the town's pioneer history while the **York Motor Museum** (daily

9.30am–4pm; $8.50), opposite the visitor information centre on Avon Terrace, capitalizes on York's antiquarian charisma with a large collection of vintage and classic vehicles – from a hundred-year-old single-cylinder tricycle to Ossie Cranston's 1936 Ford V8 racer. At the north end of the terrace are the **Sandalwood Yards**, where the perfumed wood – once prolific in WA and highly prized in the Orient – was stored during York's heyday. Near here you can take a walk down to the wobbly **suspension bridge** spanning the generally sluggish Avon River and take a look at the 1854 **Holy Trinity Church**, with its modern stained-glass designs by Robert Juniper, one of WA's foremost artists.

Practicalities

York's **visitor information centre** (daily 9am–5pm; ⓣ08/9641 1301, ⓦwww.yorkwa.org) is at 105 Avon Terrace, the main road on which most of York's fine old buildings are located. A **town map** and information sheet is available here, which locates and briefly describes all of these structures as well as listing places to stay and eat. The *Castle Hotel* (ⓣ08/9641 1007, ⓦwww.castlehotel.com.au; ④) has a splendid old charm, and there are several B&Bs in and around town; ask at the visitor information centre or check out their website.

The Southwest

The region south of Perth and west of the Albany Highway, known as **the Southwest**, is the temperate corner of the continent, where the cool Southern and warm Indian oceans meet to drop heavy winter rains. North of **Bunbury**, 180km from Perth, lies a knot of industrial installations and satellite or retirement towns such as Rockingham and Mandurah: suburbs which offer little of interest to the visitor compared to what's ahead. South of Bunbury things improve greatly. The **Margaret River region**, WA's most popular holiday destination, is famed for its wineries and surf. **Tall Timber Country**, situated to the southeast, encompasses towns set amid the remnants of the giant karri forests and offers a chance to experience one of the world's last stands of temperate old-growth forest.

At its best in spring and outside school holidays (dates on p.77), the Southwest's lush bucolic scenery is all the more appealing in that it can be enjoyed without donning a hat, water bottle and sunblock while swatting away flies and avoiding the crowds, an experience augmented by several commendably untacky **galleries** and **woodcraft studios** displaying the work of local artisans, from boardroom tables to salad tongs – and at prices (even with overseas shipping) that are worth consideration.

There is also better-quality, and more varied **accommodation** in this region than the rest of the state put together and, backpackers' apart, the recommendations given below barely scratch the surface. Make the most of the visitor information centres, and their invaluable sources of places to stay.

South West Coach Lines (ⓦwww.southwestcoachlines.com.au) serves Augusta via Margaret River and Busselton and Bunbury, as well as Collie, Donnybrook, Bridgetown and Manjimup. Transwa (ⓦwww.transwa.gov.au) has a similar provincial **bus** service as well as 28-day unlimited-travel **bus passes** for around $155, but the best way to get about is with a **car**, making use of Perth's inexpensive rental agencies. Expect to cover at least 2000km in a typical week's tour as far as Albany and note that some attractions and scenic drives take in unsealed roads, which are probably not permitted in your rental contract.

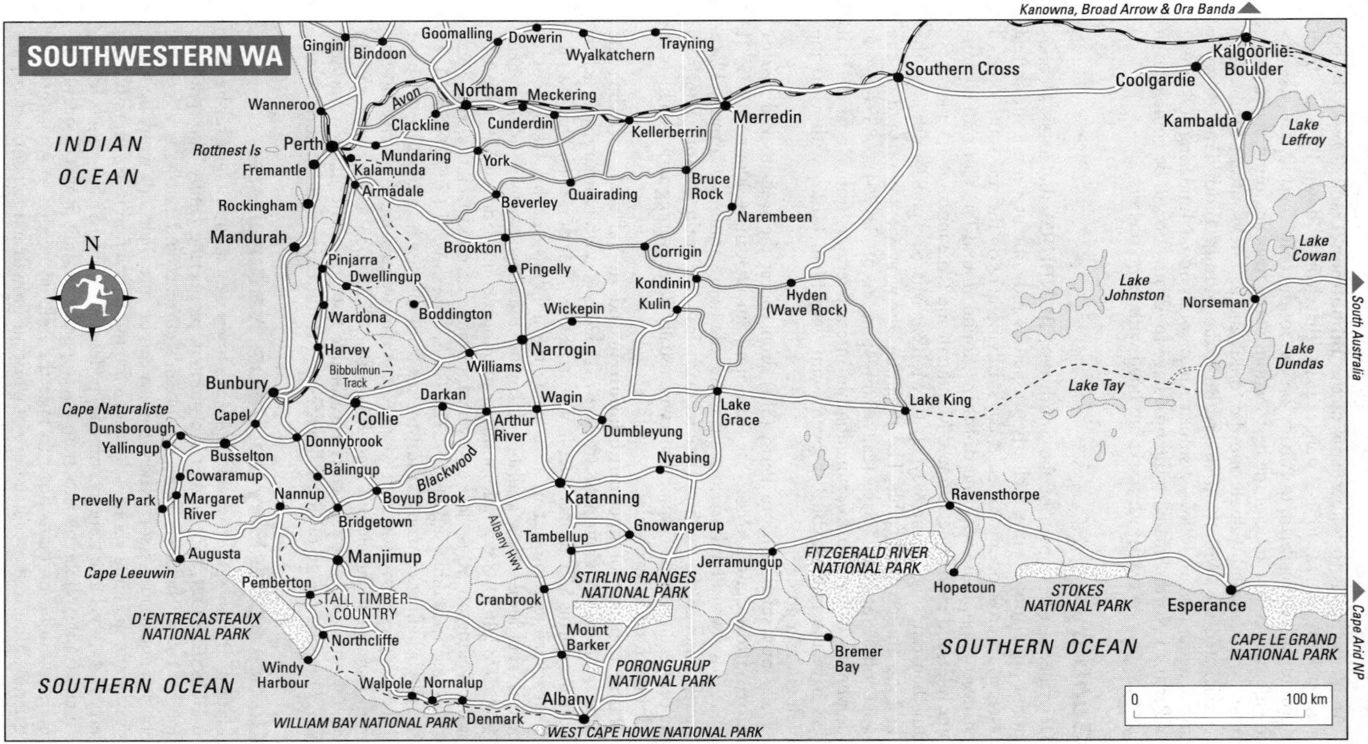

SOUTHWESTERN WA
Kanowna, Broad Arrow & Ora Banda
South Australia
Cape Arid NP
INDIAN OCEAN
SOUTHERN OCEAN
SOUTHERN OCEAN
N
Gingin
Bindoon
Goomalling
Dowerin
Wyalkatchern
Trayning
Southern Cross
Coolgardie
Kalgoorlie-Boulder
Kambalda
Lake Leffroy
Wanneroo
Avon
Northam
Meckering
Merredin
Clackline
Cunderdin
Kellerberrin
Rottnest Is
Perth
Mundaring
Kalamunda
York
Fremantle
Armadale
Beverley
Quairading
Bruce Rock
Narembeen
Rockingham
Mandurah
Brookton
Corrigin
Lake Cowan
Pinjarra
Dwellingup
Pingelly
Kondinin
Hyden (Wave Rock)
Lake Johnston
Norseman
Wardona
Boddington
Wickepin
Kulin
Harvey
Bibbulmun Track
Williams
Narrogin
Lake Dundas
Bunbury
Darkan
Wagin
Lake Grace
Lake King
Lake Tay
Cape Naturaliste
Capel
Collie
Arthur River
Dumbleyung
Dunsborough
Yallingup
Busselton
Donnybrook
Balingup
Blackwood
Nyabing
Cowaramup
Prevelly Park
Margaret River
Nannup
Boyup Brook
Katanning
Ravensthorpe
Bridgetown
Gnowangerup
Tambellup
Albany Hwy
Augusta
Manjimup
Jerramungup
FITZGERALD RIVER NATIONAL PARK
Cape Leeuwin
Pemberton
STIRLING RANGES NATIONAL PARK
Hopetoun
STOKES NATIONAL PARK
Esperance
TALL TIMBER COUNTRY
Cranbrook
D'ENTRECASTEAUX NATIONAL PARK
Northcliffe
Mount Barker
Bremer Bay
CAPE LE GRAND NATIONAL PARK
Windy Harbour
Walpole
Nornalup
PORONGURUP NATIONAL PARK
Albany
WILLIAM BAY NATIONAL PARK
Denmark
WEST CAPE HOWE NATIONAL PARK
0
100 km

An alternative is to follow parts of the **Bibbulmun Track** (Ⓦwww.bibbulmuntrack.org.au), a long-distance path that winds down 963km from Kalamunda, east of Perth, to Albany on the south coast. The full trek takes six to eight weeks, but some of the best sections of the track are found between the coastal inlets around Walpole and the forests and pastures south of Bunbury.

Designated the "Mountain Bikers' Bib", the **Munda Biddi Trail** (Ⓦwww.mundabiddi.org.au) follows a similar route; south from Mundaring, 40km east of Perth, to Northcliffe, with the final stage to Albany soon to be completed in the next year or two. Both tracks are lined with camp shelters.

Bunbury

Described as the capital of the Southwest, **BUNBURY**, the state's second-largest population centre, is clearly prosperous and content, yet not the sort of place you'd cross oceans to see. A day's dallying here on the way south offers a chance to commune with the **dolphins** (found around The Cut on Leschenault Inlet, and in the inlets around Mandurah and Rockingham). It's a lot more fun than traipsing all the way up to Monkey Mia (see p.682), although the sightings are less predictable. The Dolphin Discovery Centre, situated on the beach off Koombana Drive (daily 8am–4pm; $6; Ⓣ08/9791 3088, Ⓦwww.dolphindiscovery.com.au), runs dolphin-interactive tours from a boat ($37); if you have the money, you can even swim with them ($125) with a marine biologist as a guide.

Daily **bus services** from Perth (3hr) drop you at the well-stocked **visitor information centre** (Mon–Sat 9am–5pm, Sun 9.30am–4.30pm; Ⓣ08/9721 7922, Ⓦwww.visitbunbury.com.au) in the old train station on Carmody Place. Shuttle buses to the town operate regularly from the **train station**, 3km from the centre, during the day and otherwise usually meet evening arrivals. The train from Perth takes two hours.

There is plenty of **accommodation** in and around town including the *Wander Inn* at 16 Clifton St (Ⓣ08/9721 3242, Ⓦwww.bunburybackpackers.com.au; dorms $25, rooms ❸), off Victoria Street, the main road. This is a nice backpackers' to hang out in after seeing the dolphins, and has bikes, boogie-boards and local tours available. Likewise the clean *Dolphin Retreat YHA* (Ⓣ08/9782 4690, Ⓦwww.dolphinretreatbunbury.com.au; dorms $20, rooms ❷) at 14 Wellington St, is close to everything and has good facilities. For ocean views and incredible sunsets try *The Fawlty Towers Motel* (Ⓣ08/9721 24 27, Ⓔfawltyby@iinet.com.au, ❹) just metres from the beach at 205 Ocean Drive, three minutes' drive south of town – if you're wondering, they have no staff from Barcelona. The elegant *Rose Hotel* (Ⓣ08/9721 4533, Ⓦwww.therose.com.au; ❺) on Victoria Street boasts a reasonable restaurant with meals for around $15. There are plenty of sidewalk **cafés** and **restaurants** along Victoria Street.

Geographe Bay to Cape Naturaliste

South of Bunbury, the Bussell Highway curves west around **Geographe Bay** to **BUSSELTON**, named after a prominent pioneering family. The sprawling holiday town, sheltered from the ocean's currents and swells, is a popular "bucket and spade" resort where parents can be sure their kids won't be swept away while splashing about. The town's foremost attraction is its famously long **jetty** (Ⓦwww.busseltonjetty.com.au; pedestrian access $2.50) right by the Fantasy Castle. While the jetty train has stopped operating (it was damaging the pier), optimistic residents hope to raise the millions needed to strengthen the structure. With well over a century of maritime growth and soft corals adorning the 2km-long jetty's supports, the **underwater observatory** (daily 8am–5pm; $20) paints a vibrant picture of aquatic activity 8m below the surface.

Out of town the highway turns south towards Margaret River, though continuing west brings you to the small resort town of **DUNSBOROUGH**, 21km from Busselton. The well-equipped visitor information centre (daily 9am–5pm) is located at the Dunsborough Park Shopping Centre which is visible as you enter the town from the north, and offers free accommodation- and tour-booking services. In the middle of town and 100m from the water the *Dunsborough Beach Lodge* (Ⓣ08/9756 7144, Ⓦwww.dunsboroughbeachlodge.com.au; dorms $20, rooms ❸) at 13 Dunn Bay Rd is recommended for their cleanliness, service and great balcony with ocean views, where people congregate at night. Even closer to the water, the *YHA Dunsborough Beachouse* (Ⓣ08/9755 3107, Ⓦwww.dunsboroughbeachouse.com.au; dorms $22, rooms ❸), 2km southeast of town (get off the bus at Quindalup), has a very relaxed surfer vibe. A step up in quality is the *Dunsborough Motel* (Ⓣ08/9756 7711, Ⓦwww.dunsboroughmotel.com.au; ❹), at 50 Dunn Bay Rd, in the heart of town; but for those who want real quality, *Newberry Manor* (Ⓣ08/9756 7542, Ⓦwww.newberrymanor.com.au; ❼), 16 Newberry Rd, has three luxurious suites for those needing a pampering. For a good meal, the Dunsborough Bakery in the Centrepoint Shopping Centre, has been serving up a fantastic variety of pies since 1941, while the town's only pub, the *Three Bears Bar*, on the corner of Caves Road and Seymour Boulevard, has the usual pub grub and hosts live music acts passing through. With its sheltered position and minimal tides, Geographe Bay is ideal for **diving** – all the more so since the scuttling of the old *Swan* warship in 1997 in 30m of water (see p.67). Cape Dive, 222 Naturaliste Terrace, Dunsborough (Ⓣ08/9756 8778, Ⓦwww.capedive.com), visits this and other dive sites in the bay (around $70). Surfboard hire is available at Yahoo Surfboards (Ⓣ08/9756 8336), on the corner of Clark and Naturaliste Terrace, for $30 a day.

Cape Naturaliste itself, 14km northwest of the resort, is the less impressive of the two capes that define the Margaret River region. Its truncated **lighthouse** (Mon & Wed–Sun 9.30am–4.30pm; $5) is open for inspection, and along the way there are turn-offs to secluded beaches and coves.

Along Caves Road to Margaret River and Cape Leeuwin

South of Dunsborough you head into the **Margaret River region** proper, characterized by caves, wineries, choice restaurants and snug hideaways all interspersed with woodcraft galleries, glass-blowing studios, potteries – and lots of fellow tourists. There's plenty to see, do, taste and spend your money on here, but the region tends to dominate people's idea of the Southwest – delve a little deeper and you'll find plenty more out there.

Passing **Ngilgi Cave** you come to the turn-off for **YALLINGUP**, a small seaside resort with a lovely clean beach, populated by surfers bobbing around waiting for the big one. **Caves Road** leads south from here, passing the Gunyulgup Gallery (daily 10am–5pm; Ⓦwww.gunyulgupgalleries.com.au), which has a particularly fine selection of pottery, glass, paintings and furniture by local artisans, and a lovely restaurant overlooking a lake. *Yallingup Forest Resort* (Ⓣ08/9755 2550, Ⓦwww.yallingupforestresort.com.au; ❻) on Hemsley Road, off Caves Road, is good for an extended stay, offering large, self-contained chalets sleeping four, a pool and tennis court. *Caves House Hotel* (Ⓣ08/9755 2131, Ⓦwww.caveshouse.com.au; ❺) is an inviting lodge dating from the 1930s, in the middle of town on Yallingup Beach Road.

Back on Caves Road a right turn leads, after 3km, to **Canal Rocks**, where the waves relentlessly pound the pink-granite outcrops into curious, scalloped forms. Further south are more turn-offs to the winery at **Abbey Vale Estate** (daily 10am–5pm) and **Bootleg Brewery** (daily 10am–4.30pm; Ⓦwww.bootlegbrewery.com.au), which cheekily claims to be "a beer oasis in a desert of wine". Lager lovers should try the award-winning *Raging Bull* and *Wills Pils* brews; those intent on visiting some of the four-score wineries (and breweries) in the region should pick up the *Margaret River Regional Vineyard Guide* or the *Regional Map and Guide* from the Margaret River visitor information centre. With a new winery said to be opening somewhere in Australia every three days, you can rest assured that the choice is getting greater year by year.

Further down Caves Road you come to the crossroads leading 5km inland to the Margaret River township, while a right turn takes you to the oceanside resort of **PREVELLY PARK**, close to the estuary of the Margaret River. The Greek **Chapel of St John** will catch your eye: a memorial to the Preveli Monastery on Crete which sheltered Allied soldiers, Australians among them, in World War II. The turning opposite leads down to the blustery Prevelly beach where November's annual Margaret River Classic **surfing** championships are held.

Back at the chapel, the road continues down into the **resort**, where a boom in sea-view property over the last few years has seen private houses outnumber holiday chalets and caravan parks. With a better location than most, the spacious and well-equipped *Surfpoint Resort*, on Reidle Drive (Ⓣ08/9757 1777 or 1800 071 777, Ⓦwww.surfpoint.com.au; dorms $22, en-suite rooms ❹), is the best backpackers' in the region and does free pick-ups from Margaret River if you call ahead.

Margaret River

The **wine-lovers'** resort town of **MARGARET RIVER** and the surrounding region has been adopted by Perthian gastronomes as their weekend retreat from the urban rat-race. Shared with a mix of docile holiday-makers, partying wave-riders and tourists drawn in by the hype, this buzzing but increasingly expensive town is handy for shopping (supermarket open till 9pm), eating out and browsing for crafty knick-knacks, though you may not want to stay here if it's rural bliss you're seeking.

Practicalities

The **visitor information centre** (daily 9am–5pm; Ⓣ08/9757 2911, Ⓦwww.margaretriver.com), at the downhill end of the main road, embodies the swish, self-confident ethos of its preferred clientele, and can book you straight into accommodation and wineries, and also onto tours. Transwa and South West **buses** visit daily from Perth, while local-guided wine-tasting **tours** (which also include breweries) with outfits like Cheers (Ⓣ08/9757 2270, Ⓦwww.cheerstours.com.au) cost from around $65 including BBQ lunch. Bushtucker Tours (Ⓣ08/9757 1084, Ⓦwww.bushtuckertours.com; $70) offer just that from a canoe at the river mouth on Prevelly Beach, and the Margaret River Surf School (Ⓣ08/9757 1111, Ⓦwww.margaretriversurfschool.com) offers daily two-hour lessons for $45 or a three-day course for around $110.

Accommodation

Apart from the two main backpackers', the range of **accommodation** is daunting, with scores of options in the immediate vicinity. The woodland settings out of town are the ones to go for; the visitor information centre has a big portfolio full of ideas.

Innetown Backpackers 93 Bussell Hwy ⓣ1800 244 115, ⓦwww.Innetown.com. Just 100m from the main shopping strip, this super-friendly, slightly cramped hostel is mostly full of backpackers working in the area. Has a great outdoor BBQ area for socializing at night. Dorms $25, rooms ❸

Isaacs Ridge 62 Orchid Ramble ⓣ08/9758 8860. Just minutes from the beach, but set in bush land, these spacious cottages (can sleep 4) are great value and come with everything including fully-equipped kitchen, huge bedrooms and nice outdoor decking. ❻

Margaret River Hotel 139 Bussell Hwy ⓣ08/9757 2655, ⓦwww.margaretriverhotel.com.au. Large country pub–style accommodation right in the heart of town, which offers reasonably priced en-suite economy rooms. ❹

Margaret River Lodge 220 Railway Terrace, ⓣ08/9757 9532, ⓦwww.mrlodge.com.au. Huge property with a vast array of rooms that can hold over 100 people. A pool, volleyball court and other facilities keeps them entertained, as the location, 1.5 km southeast of town, is a bit residential. ❹

Redgate Beach Escape 14 Redgate Rd, ⓣ08/9757 6677, ⓦwww.redgatebeachescape.com.au. A ten-minute drive southwest of town. Four contemporary two-bedroom chalets stand on a hill overlooking the water with exquisite views of the surrounding landscape offering arguably, the best accommodation in the area. ❼

Riverview Tourist Park 8 Wilmott Ave ⓣ1300 666 105, ⓦwww.riverviewcabin.com. Good option with tidy cabins (some en suite) set on a picturesque location on the river, just 800m from town. ❸

Eating and drinking

The countryside surrounding Margaret River is dotted with charming **restaurants**, often attached to wineries, galleries or lodges. In town, and all situated along the main road, the best places to eat include *Goodfellas* (daily 6pm–late) for wood-fired pizzas, the *Margaret River Hotel*, which has cheap backpacker specials on Tuesdays, or *Wild Thyme* (Mon–Fri 7.30am–5pm, Sat & Sun 8.30am–3.30pm), just off the main road on Willmott Avenue, with their hearty breakfasts, gourmet wraps, panini and pies. *VAT 107* is the town's premier gourmet restaurant for local seafood dishes or you can join the young crowd at *Settlers*, the town's main pub, which puts on live music in summer.

Augusta and Cape Leeuwin

Five kilometres southwest of Margaret River, on Boodjidup Road, one of the more interesting attractions vying for your attention is **Eagles Heritage** (daily 10am–5pm; $10; ⓦwww.eaglesheritage.com.au), a fascinating collection of birds of prey. Aviaries house huge wedge-tail and white-breasted sea eagles, peregrine falcons and a selection of owls.

Rejoining Caves Road, having passed the turning for the **Leeuwin Winery** (daily 10am–4.30pm; ⓦwww.leeuwinestate.com.au) with its art gallery and restaurant, you head south into the silvery-barked **karri forest**. It's a magnificent sight and one well worth taking some time to appreciate, if you're not planning to visit Pemberton. Down the road are Mammoth and Lake caves (see box, p.656), where the steam trickling out of the latter's subterranean lake springs up on **Cowup Bay** beach, 4km from the cave entrance along a dirt road, and with a campsite on the way. Back on Caves Road, Boranup Drive takes an off-road detour through the **Boranup Forest**, a great place for biking and riding, while Boranup Gallery (ⓣ08/9757 7585, ⓦwww.boranupgallery.com) sells local art and gorgeous **furniture** made from local timbers.

South of the forest, the Brockman Highway leads 90km east to Nannup, while continuing 3km south down Caves Road brings you to a turn-off to the old timber port of **Hamelin Bay**, which has a couple of shipwrecks that are ideal for snorkellers and scuba divers. The *Hamelin Bay Caravan Park* (ⓣ08/9758 5540, ⓦwww.mronline.com.au/accom/hamelin/bookings.htm; cabins ❸) is beachside, and also offers bikes for rent.

Passing **Jewel Cave**, the Bussell Highway takes you 8km further to the small town of **AUGUSTA**, on the estuary of the Blackwood River – WA's oldest settlement after Albany and Perth. Little remains from those days, although the **museum** (daily: May–Aug 10am–noon; Sept–April 10am–noon, 2–4pm; $3) on Blackwood Avenue, the main road, retains some old relics and is more absorbing than you might expect. The **visitor information centre** (daily 9am–5pm; ⓣ08/9758 0166, ⓦwww.augusta-wa.com.au) is on Ellis Street. On Blackwood Avenue, the *Augusta Motel* (ⓣ08/9758 1944, ⓕ9758 1227; ❹) has great river views, as well as backpackers' dorms from $22. On the same road, the pristine *Baywatch Manor* (ⓣ08/9758 1290, ⓦwww.baywatchmanor.com.au), offers quality backpackers' accommodation for $22, self-contained chalets (❹) and also rents bikes and canoes. *Doonbanks Caravan Park* (ⓣ08/9758 1517, ⓔdoonbanks@westnet.com.au; on-site vans ❷, cabins ❷) is further up the road, and there are two more caravan parks south of town. On the main road you can **eat** at the *Augusta Bakery & Café* (open to 4pm daily) which has a nice outdoor deck, or at the *Augusta Hotel* for reasonable dinners and a cold beer.

Cape Leeuwin, 9km south of town, is probably why you've come this far, and it's worth the journey, with its bleak, windswept "land's end" feel in this corner of Australia, especially on a mean and moody day. A Dutch captain named the cape after his ship in 1622, and Matthew Flinders began the onerous task of mapping Australia's coast right here, at the bottom left corner, in 1851. From the top of the still-working **lighthouse** (daily 8.45am–5pm; tours every 45min; $10), built in 1895, you can contemplate your position – halfway between the equator and the Antarctic coast. There is also a café on the premises, which is ok for a coffee, but the standard of food is better in town. Nearby, an

Margaret River caves

A band of limestone passing through the cape has created some 350 caves around Margaret River, four of which are open to the public. Most involve guided tours to avoid damage and accidents, with relatively high entrance fees and shuffling crowds rather detracting from the cavernous spectacle. Nevertheless, a visit to the region would be incomplete without seeing at least one. All are humid and include some long, stepped ascents, with temperatures around 17°C. Tours are less frequent from May to August – for more details about all except Ngilgi Cave, enquire at the visitor information centre in either Margaret River or Augusta. The Cave Works Interpretive Centre at Lake Cave (daily 9am–5pm; free with cave ticket; ⓣ08/9757 7411) sells a Grand Tour pass for $44 (valid for 7 days), which includes entry to Lake, Jewel and Mammoth caves; it also offers special discount options to visit all the caves except Ngilgi.

Jewel Cave (daily 9.30am–4pm; 7–12 tours per day, 1hr; $17). The best cave, featuring extraordinary and fragile formations such as five-metre "helictites" (delicate, straw-like formations) protected by breeze-proof doors. Also includes a two-hour tour of Moodyne Cave (see below).

Lake Cave (daily 9.30am–4pm; 7–12 tours per day, 45min; $17). A collapsed cavern, overgrown with huge karri trees, marks the impressive entrance to the cave, where a unique "suspended table" hangs over the subterranean lake. The cave is also the site of the Cave Works Interpretive Centre (see above), dealing with all things speleological.

Mammoth Cave (daily 9am–4pm; self-guiding; $17). Large cavern and easy access, with some bones and fossils of extinct creatures inside; it would really be your last choice.

Moondyne Cave (daily 2pm; $20, equipment supplied, maximum 10 people). A mildly adventurous and less rushed excursion with some belly crawling, although you won't miss any amazing features by not taking the tour. Enclosed footwear is compulsory.

Ngilgi Cave (daily 9.30am–4.30pm; $17). Not visited on the cave tours but with plenty of nooks to explore and delicate features to admire.

old water wheel, originally constructed for the lighthouse builders and now petrified in salt, is a well-known landmark.

Hikers may want to consider the 140km Cape Leeuwin to Cape Naturaliste **coastal walk**, though the less adventurous can tackle its five sections individually. The DEC office in Busselton (ⓣ08/9752 1677) has detailed information on this, while the Cape Leeuwin lighthouse store has maps and advice.

Tall Timber Country

Sandwiched between the popular tourist areas of the Margaret River region and Albany's dramatic coast, the forests of the so-called **Tall Timber Country** are some of WA's greatest sights. Along with the sinuous **Blackwood River** (ideal for sedate canoeing, especially downstream of Nannup; see p.658), the

△ Karri trees

highlight of the region is the brooding, primeval majesty of the **karri forests**, famed not as much for their arboreal gimmicks – of which the "climb-if-you-dare" **Gloucester Tree** near Pemberton is the best known – as for the raw, elemental nature of the unique forest environment. Since the practice of literally tearing down or "clear-felling" the irreplaceable ancient forests was greatly reduced in 2001 (see box, below), logging towns like Pemberton and Manjimup are adjusting to an economy based around sustainable tree plantations and tourism. Check out Ⓦwww.southernforests.com.au for further details on this area as far as Walpole.

The Blackwood River Valley and south

The northern part of the forest country is watered by the **Blackwood River** and divided by scenic roads that link the riverside mill towns. Though once a notoriously insular loggers' town which in the late hippy era earned comparisons with New South Wales' Nimbin, these days **NANNUP**, 60km southeast of Busselton, is an idyllic settlement of wooden cabins nestling quietly among wooded hills. The **visitor information centre** (daily 9am–5pm; Ⓣ08/9756 1211, Ⓦwww.nannupwa.com.au), on Brockman Street, has a portfolio of local **accommodation**. Nannup Telecentre (daily 10am–5pm) opposite has Internet access ($5/hr).

Set in a glorious garden, the wonderfully peaceful *Black Cockatoo Traveller's Retreat* on Grange Road (Ⓣ08/9756 1035, Ⓦwww.blackcockatoo.nannup.net; dorms $21, rooms ❷) has no Internet or TV, bikes or tour desk, but it does have an Indian teepee. On the hill behind the *Cockatoo* is the smart and child-free B&B, *Holberry House* (Ⓣ08/9756 1276, Ⓦwww.holberryhouse.com; ❺), while lost among the jarrah 6km northwest of town, the *Nannup Bush Cabins* (Ⓣ08/9756 1170, Ⓔbonica@wn.com.au; ❹) are enchantingly situated hideaways. In the centre of town the century-old *Nannup Hotel* (Ⓣ08/9756 1080, Ⓔnannuphotel.com.au; rooms ❸) is a real Aussie pub, offering private rooms with shared facilities and a lodge for groups of six or more. The *Blackwood Café* opens all day for big breakfasts and great burgers served in a nice garden

Logging in Tall Timber Country

After a century and a half, the controversial logging of the Southwest's irreplaceable old-growth forest officially came to an end in 2001. Public debate over logging, and the sell-off of old-growth forests by DEC (the government department which also looks after WA's parks) to logging mills had grown ever more intense throughout the 1990s. Campaigners criticized DEC's sell-off as a display of mind-boggling environmental short-sightedness, pointing out that the ancient trees of old-growth forest predate colonization, and support a complex ecological system. As you explore the area along scenic drives you may assume the forest looks healthy and dense, but at times you're travelling in a 200m tree-lined corridor, outside of which lies an area still devastated by old-growth clear-felling. Quick to capitalize on a vote-winning issue, Labor won the 2001 state election by promising to outlaw the logging of old-growth forests. Some backtracking followed and loopholes remain, but since that time the recession predicted in the logging industry has not materialized, and fast-growing plantations of blue gum trees (aka Tasmanian oak) have been found to offer a viable future to sustainable plantation logging in WA. Today the Forest Product Commission – Western Australia's trading enterprise – is continuing to focus on plantations, working with local governments, private landholders and communities to try to augment the attractiveness of tree farming. Debate continues as to how best to address the effect of tree farming on the land: issues such as farming communities, blending monocultures with bushland areas, accessing water and changing weather patterns dominate.

setting, or there's the *Mulberry Café* (Tues–Sun 10am–4pm, 6pm–late) up the road for something fancier.

If not walking, then a great way to enjoy the region is in a **canoe**. Blackwood Canoeing (08/9756 1209, blackwoodrivercanoeing@wn.com.au) have their own bush camp and offer self-guided one- to three-day **trips** on the lower Blackwood River, starting 27km south of town, from $35 a day. Nannys (08/9756 1252), located 12km west of town, offers a more casual half-day canoe trip for $20. River levels vary with the seasons, making the overnight trips easier in the summer months.

From Nannup, a **scenic drive** winds 41km along the river to unremarkable Balingup, while the tree-lined Brockman Highway heads east 46km to **BRIDGETOWN**, a busy mill town with a large **visitor information centre** (Mon–Fri 10am–5pm, Sat 10am–3pm, Sun 10am–1pm; 08/9761 1740, www.bridgetown.com.au) on Hampton Street. The town itself doesn't warrant much of a stay; however, the quirky *Horti Towers* (daily 10am–5pm except Wed; 08/761 2216) is well worth a breather for a light lunch or Devonshire tea. Next to the rail crossing, it's a huge property dotted with an intriguing array of bric-a-brac, garden nurseries, and tranquil tables at which to sit.

Thirty-seven kilometres south of Bridgetown, **MANJIMUP** is the region's commercial centre, handy for shopping and other services but, apart from a visit to the **Timber Park** – which celebrates the local timber industry – behind the **visitor information centre** (both daily 9am–5pm) on Rose Street, it has little appeal. Graphite Road is a picturesque forest drive heading west 22km to **One Tree Bridge** and – after another couple of kilometres – to the magnificent **Four Aces**, a quartet of huge 350-year-old karri trees standing in a row. With a detailed map it's possible to spend all day driving around these gravelly, winding logging roads, and should you head south to Pemberton along the surfaced road you'll pass a turn-off to the **Diamond Tree**, where you can climb a fifty-metre lookout tree for free.

Pemberton and around

Though there may be quainter towns in the region, **PEMBERTON** is the most central base for Tall Timber touring. The **visitor information centre** (daily 9am–5pm; 08/9776 1133, www.pembertontourist.com.au) halfway up the hill on Brockman Street, where you can pick up the *Pemberton–Northcliffe* map and guide ($1), as well as information on **horse riding**, **canoe** and **bike rental**, local **tours** and maps of **day-hikes** in the area, including part of the Bibbulmun Track. Behind here, the interactive Karri Forest Discovery Centre (daily 9am–5pm; donation) replicates the forest environment, giving a detailed explanation of the area's fauna and wildlife.

On Dickinson Street, Fine Woodcraft is one of the best craft galleries in the Southwest with everything you see, including the building itself, made from old-growth timber, either reclaimed or rejected by the mills. A fun way of enjoying the surrounding forest is to take the **tram** (08/9776 1322, www.pemtram.com.au; from $18) from Pemberton to Warren Bridge (2 daily; 1hr 45min return). The diesel tram rattles noisily along the old logging railway, over rustic timber bridges spanning tiny creeks, and visits the **Cascades**, a local beauty spot also accessible by road. There's also a weekend **steam train** service ($24) that operates outside of the summer months up to Eastbrook Sidings, north of town.

The region's single most popular attraction is the **Gloucester Tree** (DEC fee; see box, p.630), situated 3km southeast of town. At 61m, it's the world's tallest fire-lookout tree and its platform is accessible by climbing a terrifying spiral of horizontal stakes. Only a small proportion of people actually climb to the platform – these being people with courage to spare and no fear of heights.

The surrounding countryside is crisscrossed with peaceful walking trails and enchanting forest drives venturing deep into the karri woodlands. From **Beedelup National Park**, on the Vasse Highway 20km west of town, there's a short walk to a wobbly suspension bridge over **Beedelup Falls**, while the drive through the native karri forests of the **Warren National Park**, 10km southwest of town, will leave you in awe of these huge trees. The specially signed 86km **Karri Forest Explorer** is a scenic drive that winds past many of the above attractions on a mixture of dirt and sealed roads. Otherwise, Pemberton Hiking and Canoeing (ⓣ08/9776 1559, ⓔpemhike@wn.com.au) or Pemberton Discovery Tours (ⓣ08/9776 0484, ⓦwww.pembertondicoverytours.com.au) can take you out for a day-trip to see the sites mentioned above (including the D'Entrecasteaux dunes – see below) or the popular half-day wine tour.

As for **accommodation**, the centrally located *Pemberton Backpackers* (ⓣ08/9776 1105, ⓦwww.pembertonbackpackers.com.au; dorms $22, rooms ③) right by the bus stop, has comfy doubles and a self-contained cottage (③). A great option, also in town, is the *Old Picture Theatre* (ⓣ08/9776 0258, ⓦwww.oldpicturetheatre.com.au; ⑤). Built in 1929 to entertain the townspeople, it is now lavishly renovated offering the best choice in town: sleeping up to seven people, their *Adyar Cottage* is a happy combination of luxury and value for money. Just out of town, the surrounding countryside abounds with tranquil self-contained woodland retreats, like the working farm, *Pump Hill* (ⓣ08/9776 1379, ⓦwww.pumphill.com.au; ④–⑤), or *Treenbrook Cottages* (ⓣ08/9776 1638, ⓦwww.treenbrook.com.au; ⑤), with open fireplaces and nestled amongst the trees, 5km west. The central **caravan park** (ⓣ08/9776 1300, ⓦwww.pembertonpark.com.au) has cabins and five-bed cottages from ③ while there are a number of DEC-approved **campsites** in the surrounding forests. For a meal, the *Pemberton Hotel* serves huge portions of the usual pub fare for around $17 for mains (daily lunch and dinner). For the local delicacies, trout or marron (freshwater crayfish), try the restaurant at the *Eagle Springs Marron Farm*, signposted just north of town. The real highlight is *Jarrah Jacks Brewery* (ⓦwww.jarrahjacks.com.au), five minutes north of town, which burst on the scene with six world-class beers and gourmet meals to match (Mon–Fri 9am–5pm, Sat & Sun 9am–6pm).

Northcliffe and D'Entrecasteaux National Park

Some 30km south of Pemberton, **NORTHCLIFFE** is a small, untouristy logging town. The *Northcliff Hotel* (ⓣ08/9776 7089; ②) has typical pub-style rooms with shared facilities, while the *Bibbullmun Break Motel* (ⓣ08/9776 6060, ⓦwww.bibbullmunbreakmotel.com; ④) is for those who want the creature comforts. To the southwest a long spread of coastal heathland and inland dunes make up the mostly inaccessible **D'Entrecasteaux National Park**. Driving south of Northcliffe you emerge from the forest and onto the heathland, passing a short, steep walk up the 187m Mount Chudalup for views of the Southern Ocean breaking against Sandy Island, 30km south of Northcliffe, just off **WINDY HARBOUR**. The tidy and seemingly deserted settlement has about fifteen permanent residents, one shop at the campsite and a few dozen weatherboard holiday homes. As long as you're suitably equipped, a grassy **campsite** (ⓣ08/9776 8398; no dogs allowed) in the centre of the hamlet makes an inviting stopover. West of the main bay you can walk to a broader, slightly more sheltered beach, also accessible from a car park off Old Lighthouse Road, a dead end that leads west out of the settlement. From here it's possible to walk the 2km up the clifftop to **Point D'Entrecasteaux**, where a platform hangs out over the pounding surf below. You can also reach the Point in your car by following the Salmon Beach turn-off just before Windy Harbour. **Salmon Beach** itself is a wild, exposed strand below Point D'Entrecasteaux, facing the prevailing south-westerlies and therefore good for a hair-tussling stroll.

Albany and the southern coast

Alternating sheltered bays and rounded granite headlands make up the southern coast, or "Great Southern", around Albany. As elsewhere in the Southwest, the temperate climate and changeable weather create a rural antipodean–English idyll unknown in the rest of WA. Site of the region's original settlement, nowadays it's an appealing area of wineries, craft galleries and tasteful restaurants.

Albany, 410km from Perth, is an agricultural centre and holiday destination, while **Denmark**, 54km to the west, is a twee, arty hamlet. **Walpole**'s bays and tingle forests mark the western limit of the southern coast. An hour's drive north of Albany lie the burgeoning wine-making region of Mount Barker and the mountainous **Porongurup** and **Stirling Ranges national parks**.

Perth's radial **bus services** to the main centres run on a frequent basis, but moving around by bus requires some planning to avoid inconvenient delays. Transwa buses depart from Perth for Albany at least daily, either directly down the Albany Highway (6hr) or four times a week via Bunbury and twice weekly via Pemberton (8hr). If you don't want to go on **tours** (see pp.642–643), then **car rental**, or shared lifts, are the best option for getting around.

Albany and around

In 1826, two years before the establishment of the Swan River Colony, the British sent Major Lockyer and a team of hopeful colonists to settle the strategic **Princess Royal Harbour** (Ⓦ www.forts.albany.wa.gov.au). It was a hasty pre-emptive response to French exploration of Australia's Southwest, and the small colony, originally called Fredrickstown, was allowed to grow at a natural pace – thus avoiding the vicissitudes of "Swan River Mania" that plagued Perth in the 1880s, when thousands of starry-eyed settlers poured into the riverside shanty town. Prior to the building of Fremantle Harbour in the 1890s, **ALBANY**'s huge natural harbour was a key port on the route between England and Botany Bay; a coaling station in the age of steamers. It was also the last of Australia that many Anzacs saw on their way to Gallipoli in 1914.

Now serving the southern farming belt, Albany has also become the centre of one of the Southwest's main holiday areas. Factors such as proximity to Perth, moderate summer temperatures, a surfeit of natural splendour and historical kudos all combine to make an agreeable and genuine destination, largely bereft of bogus tourist traps.

Arrival, information and accommodation

Transwa **buses** arrive near the old train station on Lower Stirling Terrace, the location of the particularly clued-up **visitor information centre** (daily 9am–5.30pm; Ⓣ 08/9841 1088 or 1800 644 088, Ⓦ www.albanytourist.com.au), which dispenses a handy local and regional **map**. Loves Bus Service (timetables at the visitor information centre, or Ⓣ 08/9841 1211) provides in-town **public transport**: the #301 route between York Street, the town's main road, and Middleton Beach/Emu Point is particularly useful (Mon–Fri 9am–3pm, Sat 9.15–11am). For **car rental** try King Sound Vehicle Hire at 6 Sanford Rd

(Ⓣ08/9841 1211, Ⓦwww.kingsoundcars.com). Note that Albany can only be reached from Esperance (see p.687) on Tuesdays, Fridays and Saturdays and that buses leave from Albany to Esperance on Monday and Thursday.

Several **guesthouses** and **B&Bs** are situated along Stirling Terrace near the harbour; there are also highway-side motels and self-contained units in the Middleton Bay area, 3km east of the centre. In the countryside, you can stay on working farms or in a number of cosy cottages. The visitor information centre has a detailed photographic portfolio of the town's accommodation options. Note that prices drop by fifty percent in winter, especially for apartments.

Motels, backpackers' and guesthouses

Albany Backpackers cnr Stirling Terrace and Spencer St Ⓣ08/9841 8848, Ⓦwww.albanybackpackers.com.au. One of Albany's oldest buildings: a warren of corridors and rooms with murals at every turn, plenty of amenities, lots of space and a good atmosphere. Breakfast and free Internet for a few minutes; coffee, one beer and cake every evening is included in price. Dorms $25, rooms ❸

Bayview YHA 49 Duke St Ⓣ08/9842 3388, Ⓔalbanyyha@westnet.com.au. Old wooden building, five minutes from the centre, with dorms, twins, BBQs and some parking. Dorms $20, rooms ❸

Discovery Inn 9 Middleton Rd Ⓣ08/9842 5535, Ⓦwww.discoveryinn.com.au. Close to Middleton Beach, this place has a chilled-out beach-house vibe, and breakfast is included. Dorms $25, rooms ❸

Frederickstown Motel cnr Frederick and Spence sts Ⓣ08/9841 1600 or 1800 808 544, Ⓦwww.albanyis.com.au/fredmtl. Good-value rooms close to the town centre and shops, with an acceptable restaurant. ❹

Vancouver House 86 Stirling Terrace Ⓣ08/9842 1071, Ⓦwww.vancouverhousebnb.com.au. Charming nineteenth-century guesthouse converted into a B&B with excellent service and huge breakfasts. Set in a great location; most rooms are en suite, with some looking onto the harbour. ❹

Caravan parks

Emu Beach Emu Point, 7km from the town centre Ⓣ08/9844 1147, Ⓦwww.emubeach.com. Not a bad spot to stay for a few days. Amenities include trampolines and mini-golf. On-site vans ❸, cabins ❹

Middleton Beach 28 Flinders Parade, Middleton Beach Ⓣ08/9841 3593, Ⓦwww.holidayalbany.com.au. Right on the weekend-posing drag and the sometimes windy beach. Cabins and on-site vans ❸

The town and around

Albany's attractions are spread between the Foreshore – where the original settlers set up camp – the calm beaches around **Middleton Beach** and Emu Point on the still waters of Oyster Harbour. Some 40km east round the harbour is the idyllic nature reserve at **Two Peoples Bay**, while the natural spectacles and attractions on the **Torndirrup Peninsula**, 20km southwest of town, along Frenchman's Bay Road, are also well worth a look.

On the **Foreshore** there's a replica of the *Amity* (daily 9am–4pm; entrance free, guided tour $7), the brig that landed its sixty-odd settlers here on Boxing Day 1826, after six months at sea. Nearby stands the **Old Gaol** (daily 10am–4.30pm; $4), the earliest surviving relic of European colonization right across Australia and the **Albany Residency Museum** (daily 10am–5pm; donation), which has meticulous displays of the town's maritime history, a section on Aboriginal bush medicines and an educational see-and-touch gallery for children upstairs.

Closer to Middleton Beach, the curious tower on top of **Mount Melville Lookout**, off Serpentine Road, is colloquially known as "the spark plug". One of two lookouts in Albany, this one offers the better seaward vista. From here, backtrack to York Street, turn left and head 2km down Middleton Road to the **Old Farm**, Strawberry Hill (daily 10am–4pm; $5; closed June), tucked behind modern houses in its own enchanting gardens. Reminiscent of an English cottage, the farm (WA's first) provided the settlers with locally grown produce, while the building itself (built in 1836) once housed the visiting Governor Stirling. Devonshire tea is available to take full advantage of the historic landscape.

Middleton Beach itself is dominated by Albany's upmarket *Esplanade Hotel*, and the town's main beach. From the beach, head up Marine Drive and turn right towards **Mount Clarence Lookout**, with its Anzac memorial and, on a clear day, a view as far as the Stirling Ranges, 80km to the north. On the way down you pass the **Princess Royal Fortress** (daily 9am–5pm; $4), an impressively restored naval installation dating from the end of the nineteenth century.

Eating

Albany shares the rest of the Southwest's laudable preoccupation with quality eating; several independent **restaurants** offer far better grub than the fast-food franchises or dreary motel dining rooms.

Dylans on the terrace 82 Stirling St. Popular café that rarely has an empty seat at breakfast time; the locals like it for lunch and dinner too. Daily 7am–late.

Leonardo's Ristorante 166 Stirling Terrace West. Award-winning restaurant considered to be the best Italian in town, with a selection of delicious pizzas and pastas. BYO. Wed–Sun 6.30pm–late.

Rookleys cnr Peels Place and York St. Deli-style café with outdoor seating that has good focaccias (around $10) and decent coffee. Mon–Sat 9am–5pm (summer), 9am–3pm (winter).

Rustlers Steak House 63 Frederick St. If you like meat, this is the place: T-bones for $29 or sizzling chicken pesto for $27. Has a reasonable veggie selection too. Daily 5pm–late.

The Squid Shack Boat Ramp, Emu Point. The freshest seafood in a nice setting by the water. As the name suggests, squid is their speciality. Daily 10am–7.30pm.

Tangle Head 72 Stirling St. New, stylish brewery/restaurant that makes excellent gourmet pizzas (around $15) and has a variety of beers, including the popular "harbourside lager". There are also brewery tours (Wed & Sat; 2pm). Daily 11am–late.

Listings

Bus Transwa ⓣ13 10 53 or call into their office, inside the visitor information centre.

DEC 120 Albany Hwy (Mon–Fri 9am–5pm; ⓣ08/9841 7133). Information and passes for local national parks (see box, p.630).

Diving AlbanyDive.com (ⓣ08/9842 6886, ⓦwww.albanydive.com), on the cnr of York St and Stirling Terrace, goes to local dive sites (year-round visibility apart from a couple of weeks in January) from $150 with full gear rental. Popular wrecks include the HMAS *Perth* that was scuttled in 2001, and the older *Cheyne III* whaler, on nearby Michaelmas Island.

Fishing Blueback Charters (ⓣ08/9841 1320, ⓔblueback@bigpond.com). Full-day's charter in the hope of catching the big one is $150 per person, which includes all equipment and food.

Post office cnr Grey and York sts ⓣ08/9841 1811.

Taxis ⓣ08/9844 4444.

Tours and cruises Sail-A-Way (ⓣ0409 107 180) offers a three-hour catamaran sunset cruise and whale watching in King George Sound – when in season (June–Oct) – from $55. Escape Tours (ⓣ08/9844 1945) has full-day and half-day minibus tours around the region from $65. Silver Star Cruises (ⓣ08/9842 9876, ⓦwww.whales.com.au) can take you whale watching (June–Oct) in King George Sound for around $65.

Torndirrup National Park and Whaleworld

Frenchman's Bay Road leads onto a peninsula incorporating the **Torndirrup National Park** (DEC fees; see box, p.630), 20km southwest of town, where there are a number of beaches, lookouts and other natural attractions. Passing various B&Bs, craft outlets and the **Wind Farm** with its ridge-top boardwalk, the turn-off to **the Gap** and **Natural Bridge** is the first attraction worth a visit. Note that this area has claimed several lives: people die not just by slipping or getting blown into the sea but also as a result of **king waves** – huge waves that are indistinguishable in the swell. As you return to the car park, the sandy arc of **Cable Beach** on the right will catch your eye: a path leads down to the sloping granite shoreline from where – if the tide and the winds are right – you can get onto the beach itself.

Most tourists and tours visit the attractions above, but out of the summer season many places further along on the peninsula will be less crowded: check out the view from Stony Hill as well as at tiny Misery Beach. Nearby, a track goes up a kilometre through a tunnel of shrubs to the summit of **Isthmus Hill**, in spring passing several varieties of orchids on the way; there's even one growing inside a stone shelter on the summit. A bracing half-day **walk** leads from the summit, culminating at Bald Head on the very tip of the Flinders Peninsula.

Frenchman's Bay Road ends its orbit of the Princess Royal Harbour at sheltered **Frenchman's Bay** on the Torndirrup peninsula. Just before, you'll have passed the turn-off to **Whaleworld** (daily 9am–5pm; $18; free tours on the hour 10am–4pm; Ⓦwww.whaleworld.org), site of Australia's last whaling station, which closed in 1978. The facility has been imaginatively developed into a world-class museum dedicated to the world's biggest creatures, once hunted to near extinction. The informative half-hour **tours** explain Australia's role in ending the hunting, though not before sharing the grisly details of the process of dismembering and boiling down the blubber and bones of a whale, and displaying the actual machinery that once did the job. Don't miss having a look around the towering *Cheyne IV* whale chaser beached right in the middle of the complex.

Along the southern coast

An hour's drive west of Albany, **West Cape Howe National Park** is a coastal wilderness best suited to exploration by 4WD, while **William Bay National Park**, 15km west of Denmark, has many inviting coves accessible to regular vehicles. A few kilometres before Walpole, the **Valley of the Giants** is home to the much-imitated **Tree Top Walk** and marks the edge of the giant tingle tree country. Transwa buses run on Monday and Friday between Albany and Perth (via Bunbury; 6hr), but you won't see much this way – renting a car or arranging a lift is a better bet.

Denmark and William Bay National Park

DENMARK, set on the river of the same name, is a cute little country town and a great spot to enjoy lunch, wander around some galleries, take a stroll or boat up the river. By the coast, the big lagoon of Wilson Inlet can turn an unappealing tannin colour if the moving sand bar happens to plug the lagoon's narrow mouth to the sea. Just outside the mouth of the lagoon is **Ocean Beach** (accessible via Ocean Beach Rd on the west edge of town), with a spectacular view across the broad Ratcliffe Bay – here the swells sweep in to create ideal **surfing** conditions for learners. South Coast Surfing (Ⓣ08/9848 2057 or 0401 349 854) run one-to-one lessons (2hr; $50) or group sessions from one to three days (2hr per day, includes gear rental; $90).

Denmark's **visitor information centre** (daily 9am–5pm; Ⓣ08/9848 2055), on the corner of Ocean Beach Road and South Coast Highway, houses the world's largest barometer (12m) and can advise you on the array of **places to stay** in the vicinity and will book on your behalf. They also offer a free comprehensive guide to the area, as well as the *Wine Lovers' Guide to Denmark* brochure, which lists over twenty local wineries. Keep heading along the highway towards the river, and you can't miss the *Traveller's Inn* (Ⓣ08/9848 1700, Ⓦwww.denmarkaccommodation.com.au; rooms ❸, dorms $25), a clean, well-run place with Internet access. The small *Blue Wren Travellers' Rest YHA* (Ⓣ08/9848 3300,

Ⓦwww.bluewren.batcave.net; dorms $21, rooms ❷) nearby is another good option, and has a more homely feel. For great value, the *Denmark Luxury Apartments* (Ⓣ08/9848 2055; ❺) behind the shops on Strickland Street can sleep up to five, and have balconies with riverside views. If you want to be close to the sea, *Denmark Waterfront Motel and Cottages* (Ⓣ08/9848 1147, Ⓦwww.denmarkwaterfront.com.au), on Inlet Drive, is an idyllic hideaway on the water with motel-style accommodation (❸) and great-value studios (❹). Check their website for specials.

Excellent organic restaurants dot the town: *McSweeney's* (Mon–Fri 7.30am–4.30pm) is great for breakfasts and lunches, and the tiny *Indigo Indian* (dinner Thurs–Sun), serves the best Indian cuisine this side of Fremantle. Both are located on Strickland Street (the latter as part of a food mall).

From Denmark town you can head west to the **William Bay National Park**, through the hills along **Shadforth Scenic Drive**, passing the **wineries** of West Cape Howe and Howard Park. Once at William Bay you'll find **Green Pool** cove, one of the prettiest spots along the coast, with Madfish Bay and Waterfall Bay further west also worth a visit.

The Valley of the Giants' Tree Top Walk and Walpole

About 40km west of Denmark you can turn south to **Peaceful Bay**, a pleasant lunch stop with a caravan park and chalets. The forest of massive tingle and karri trees that make up the **Valley of the Giants** is known for its **Tree Top Walk** (daily 9am–4.15pm; $8), an amazingly engineered 600m walkway (accessible to wheelchairs), which sways on half a dozen pylons among the crowns of the karri trees, 40m above the ground. To gain a better impression of the surrounding forest, take the **Ancient Empire Walkway** that winds through the forest floor (same hours as above).

Back on the coastal highway, you pass through **NORNALUP**, which has a good roadside restaurant, with a riverside park and chalets nearby (Ⓣ08/9840 1107, Ⓦwww.valleyofthegiants.com.au/nornalupriversidechalets; ❹). You can take the track 6km west of town to the lovely Conspicuous Beach. **WALPOLE**, 10km from Nornalup, is the hub of many scenic drives to more towering forests, oceanic lookouts and sheltered inlets. There's a **visitor information centre** on the main road (Mon–Fri 9am–5pm, Sat & Sun 9am–4pm; Ⓣ08/9840 1111, Ⓦwww.walpole.southernforests.com.au) and a couple of **caravan parks** on the Walpole and Nornalup inlets. For a more comfortable stay try *Hideaway Cottage* (Ⓣ08/9840 1138; ❹), 10km north of town, or the *Walpole Motel* (Ⓣ08/9840 1023, Ⓔalpolehotelmotel@bigpond.com.au; ❸) in the centre. Backpackers head for the *Tingle All Over YHA* (Ⓣ08/9840 1041, Ⓔtingleallover2000@yahoo.com.au; five-bed dorms $20, rooms ❸); situated at the west end of town, it owns one of the biggest chess sets in the southern hemisphere (the pieces are around 2ft high). On Pier Street, *Walpole Lodge* (Ⓣ08/9840 1244, Ⓦwww.walpolelodge.com.au; dorms $20, rooms ❷) has a very chilled atmosphere.

West of Walpole the **South Western Highway** starts its scenic run northwest – through more colossal forests – to Northcliffe (100km) and Pemberton (138km) at the heart of the Tall Timber Country.

The Porongurups and the Stirling Ranges

North of Albany lie the ancient granite highlands of the Porongurups and the impressive thousand-metre-high Stirling Ranges, 40km and 80km from Albany respectively. Both have been designated **national parks**; the DEC office in Albany provides further information and maps.

Porongurup National Park

The granite hills comprising the **Porongurup National Park** (DEC fees; see box, p.630) are often described as "among the oldest rocks on earth" and encompass a dozen wooded peaks, whose protruding bald summits are over 600m high. The fifteen-kilometre-long ridge catches coastal moisture to support its isle of karri forests, thereby leaving the loftier Stirlings to the north dry and treeless.

Once at the park, most people are happy to do no more than take the five-minute stroll to **Tree in a Rock**, a natural oddity near the park's northern entrance. However, if you want to get your teeth into a good walk, head up the marked trail to **Devil's Slide** (671m) and return via Nancy and Hayward peaks; the full route warrants at least half a day. **Balancing Rock**, at the eastern end of the park, can be reached in 45 minutes from the car park, with a cage on the exposed outcrop of Castle Rock providing safe viewing.

The Stirling Range National Park

Taking the Chester Pass Road north towards the looming **Stirling Range National Park** (DEC fees; see box, p.630), the distinctive profile of Bluff Knoll will, if you're lucky, emerge from the cloudbanks often obscuring its summit. Avid hillwalkers could spend a few days "peakbagging" here and come away well-satisfied; the Stirlings are WA's best – if not only – mountain-walking area, with as many as five peaks over 1000m. Be aware, however, that the area can experience blizzards as late as October. **Bluff Knoll** (1073m), the park's highest and most popular ascent, has a well-built path involving a three-hour-return slog. Like much of the area, the floral biodiversity in the Range is exceptional.

The unsealed 45km Stirling Range **scenic drive** winds amid the peaks to Red Gum Pass in the west, where you can turn around and go back the same way (with superior views). Halfway along the drive **Talyuberup** (800m) is a short, steep ascent, with great vistas at the top, while **Toolbrunup** (1052m), accessed by a track next to the park campsite (see below) is a short, steep three-hour trip, with some exposed scrambling near the summit. Many other **trails** wander between the peaks and link up into overnight walks. Before heading off through the bush discuss your plans with the **park ranger** (ⓣ08/9827 9230 or 9827 9278) at his residence next to the *Moingup Springs* **campsite** off Chester Pass Road. With a lack of showers, the campsite is basic; more comfortable options are the *Stirling Range Retreat* (ⓣ08/9827 9229, ⓦwww.stirlingrange.com.au; cabins ❸, four-bed chalets ❸), just outside the park's northern boundary, opposite the Bluff Knoll turn-off. There's a café here, whose owners can fill you in on wild-flower locales; they also sell DEC park passes. Mount *Trio Park* campsite (ⓣ08/9827 9270, ⓦwww.mounttrio.com.au) is on the park's south side on Salt River Road, with inexpensive tent sites, a campers' kitchen and showers; 10km north of the Bluff Knoll turn-off is *The Lily* (ⓣ08/9827 9205, ⓦwww.thelily.com.au; ❺), which offers a touch of Holland in the middle of nowhere. Look for the sixteenth-century replica windmill (that used to grind flour), and prepare yourself for incredibly good food, quaint Dutch, cottages and Dutch bicycle-riding owners.

Esperance and the south coast

Esperance, 721km southeast of Perth, is at the western end of the **Archipelago of the Recherche**. Both town and archipelago were named after the French ships that visited the area in the late eighteenth century, and whose persistent interest in the region precipitated the hasty colonization of WA by the edgy British. The archipelago's string of haze-softened granite isles, bobbing in the inky blue Southern Ocean, presents an almost surreal seascape common to coasts washed by cold currents. The mild summer weather (rarely exceeding 30°C), fishing opportunities and surrounding national parks ensure the town is a popular destination for heat-sensitive holiday-makers.

Around 50km southeast of Esperance is the **Cape Le Grand National Park**, on the edge of the Great Australian Bight. Care should be taken all along this coastline, as unpredictable **king waves** frequently sweep the unwary away from exposed, rocky shores.

You can get to Esperance from Kalgoorlie with Transwa's **bus service** (3 weekly; 5hr) or direct from Perth on the *Spirit of Esperance* bus service (6 weekly; 10hr). Buses leave from Albany to Esperance on Monday and Thursday.

Esperance and around

The town of **ESPERANCE** prospered briefly as a supply port during the heyday of the Eastern Goldfields, and was revived after World War II when its salty soils were made fertile with the simple addition of certain missing trace elements. Now an established farming and holiday centre, the town lacks the charm promised by its name, but makes an ideal base from which to explore the south coast's dazzling beaches and storm-washed headlands.

Dempster Street is the town's main road, where you'll find the arts-and-crafts vending cabins known as the **Museum Village**. Nearby on James Street, the actual **museum** (daily 1.30–4.30pm; $4) is a surprisingly good repository of local memorabilia and is very proud of its Skylab satellite display: it disintegrated over Esperance in 1979 and NASA was reputedly fined $400 for littering.

Besides a walk along the Norfolk pine–lined esplanade and a round of mini-golf or go-karting, there's not much to do in Esperance, so it's best to rent a bike or car and head out along the 36km **scenic loop** west of town. Travelling clockwise, you'll come first to the **Rotary Lookout** surveying the captivating seascape. You'll spot the **windfarm** on the way to **Twilight Beach**, an idyllic and sheltered spot that's much prettier than the town's more exposed beaches. From here settle in for more windswept grandeur (and a free nudist beach) at **Observation Point Lookout**, before the road turns inland towards **Pink Lake**. This is one of many lakes between here and Merredin, sometimes so-coloured by salt-tolerant algae, whose seafaring cousins give the coastline its enchanting turquoise hue.

The hundred or so islands of the romantically named Archipelago of the Recherche – known as the **Bay of Isles** – around Esperance are chiefly occupied by seals, feral goats and multitudes of seabirds. Dolphins may also be spotted offshore and Southern Right whales are commonly observed migrating to the Antarctic in spring. Mackenzies Island Cruises, 71 The Esplanade (Ⓣ08/9071 5757, Ⓦwww.woodyisland.com.au), offers daily trips with the possibility of overnight stays in comfortable huts on **Woody Island** (summer only).

Practicalities

Transwa **buses** stop in the town centre, with **taxis** available on Ⓣ08/9071 1782. The **visitor information centre** (Mon, Tues, Thurs 9am–5pm, Wed & Fri 8am–5pm, Sat 9am–4pm, Sun 9am–2pm; Ⓣ08/9071 2330, Ⓦwww.visitesperance.com) is in the Museum Village on Dempster Street and there is a

shopping centre on Andrew Street, over the roundabout. The DEC office, at 92 Dempster St (Ⓣ08/9071 3733), provides information and passes for the national parks around Esperance. **Bicycles** can be rented from the visitor information centre or along the Esplanade. For **car rental**, try Hollywood Hire (Ⓣ08/9071 3144) or Avis (Ⓣ08/9071 3998). Esperance Diving and Fishing, 56 The Esplanade (Ⓣ08/9071 5111, Ⓦwww.esperancedivingandfishing.com.au), run **dive** charters and courses, while Kepa Kurl (Ⓣ08/9072 1688, Ⓦwww.kepakurl.com.au) offer a series of tours, including an interesting insight into the indigenous Noongar people and their relationship to the land.

For an incredible **meal** head to *Loose Goose* (Ⓣ08/9071 2320, open daily for dinner) at 9A Andrew St, which serves up sublime fresh seafood. The raw scallops ($15), in particular, are indescribable. A few metres away the Turkish Bakery (daily 8am–8pm) prepares excellent pies and traditional dips, perfect for lunches on the beach.

Accommodation

Although the self-contained units around town will almost certainly be booked out during school holiday periods (see p.77), there are a number of **other options** – especially given that air conditioning is rarely necessary in Esperance. There are also at least three caravan parks in and around town.

Blue Waters Lodge YHA Goldfields Rd Ⓣ08/9071 1040, Ⓔesperance@yhawa.com.au. Sprawling former hospital situated right on the bay, with pick-ups, bikes and possibly the largest hostel kitchen in the southern hemisphere. Can get inundated with school groups. Dorms $20, rooms ②

Captain Huon Motel 5 The Esplanade Ⓣ08/9071 2383, Ⓦwww.captainhuonmotel.com.au. Charming, small motel with some self-catering units and bike rental. Breakfast included. ④–⑤

Esperance B&B By the Sea 34 Stewart St Ⓣ08/9071 5640, Ⓦwww.esperancebb.com. As the name suggests, great panoramic views of the sea and a comfy, homely feel makes this one of the best options in town. ⑤

Esperance Guesthouse 23 Daphne St Ⓣ08/9071 3396, Ⓦwww.esperanceguesthouse.com.au. Small, family-run place with a good communal room, and a backyard to chat over an open fire. Very chilled out. Price includes breakfast with home-made bread. Bike and surf hire available. Dorms $25, rooms ②.

The Jetty Resort 1 The Esplanade Ⓣ08/90713333, Ⓦwww.thejettyresort.com.au. Well-appointed, two-storey motel with ocean views and swimming pool. ④

Old Hospital Motel William St Ⓣ08/9071 3587, Ⓔoldesp@emerge.net.au. With its tasteful decor, this boutique establishment offers an antidote to motel sterility. ④

Cape Le Grand National Park

Once in Esperance, a visit to **Cape Le Grand National Park** (DEC fee; see box, p.630) is well worth the expense of renting a car or taking a tour; it's essentially a climb up a hill and a beach-hop – but on a good day they're the kind of beaches you want to roll up and take home with you. Once in the park, the climb to the summit of **Frenchman's Peak** (262m) is not as hard as it looks, and warrants the half-hour's exertion if you have a sturdy pair of shoes. The secret of its distinctive, hooked summit is an unexpected hole that frames an impressive view out to sea. Soon after the Frenchman's Peak turn-off, a track leads to **Hellfire Bay** – sheltered coves don't come any more perfect than this. From here you can take a tough, three-hour walk northwest to **Le Grand Beach** (limited camping), which is also accessible in a 4WD from Wylie Bay at the end of Bandy Creek Road if the tide is right. There is also a less demanding two-hour trek east to **Thistle Cove**, from where an easier trail leads to the broad arc of **Lucky Bay** further east (camping and water), with more sheltered swimming and wonderful hues of ocean colours. **Rossiter Bay**, another 6km east from here, is distinctly unimpressive by comparison.

The Eastern Goldfields

Six hundred kilometres east of Perth, at the end of the **Great Eastern Highway**, are the **Eastern Goldfields**. In the late nineteenth century, gold was found in what still remains one of the world's richest gold-producing regions. Lack of fresh water made life very hard for the early prospectors, driven by a national economic depression into miserable living conditions, disease and, in most cases, premature graves. Nevertheless, boom towns of thousands, boasting grand public buildings, several hotels and a vast periphery of hovels, would spring up and collapse in the time it took to extract any ore.

In 1892 the railway from Perth reached the town of **Southern Cross**, just as big finds turned the rush into a national stampede. This huge influx of people accentuated the water shortage, until the visionary engineer C.Y. O'Connor oversaw the construction of a 556km **pipeline** from Mundaring Weir, in the hills above Perth, to Kalgoorlie in 1903. Around this time many of the smaller gold towns were already in decline, but the Goldfields' wealth and boost in population finally gave WA the economic autonomy it sought in its claim for statehood in 1901.

In the years preceding the goldrush, the area was briefly one of the world's richest sources of **sandalwood**, an aromatic wood greatly prized throughout Asia as joss sticks, and still a staple in modern perfumery. Supplies in the Pacific had become exhausted, so by 1880 the fragrant wood was WA's second-largest exportable commodity after wool. Exacerbating the inevitable over-cutting was the goldrush's demand for timber to prop up shafts, or to fire the pre-pipeline water desalinators. Today the region is a pit-scarred and prematurely desertified landscape, dotted with the scavenged vestiges of past settlements, while at its core the **Super Pit** gold mine in Kalgoorlie gets wider and deeper year by year.

Moribund **Coolgardie** may have been the original goldrush settlement, but the Goldfields are now centred around the twinned towns of **Kalgoorlie–Boulder**. A thriving, energetic hub, Kalgoorlie is Australia's richest town after Canberra. Even if you're not planning to pass through the Goldfields, there's enough to see in Kalgoorlie to make a couple of days excursion from Perth worthwhile – if for nothing else than the novelty of riding on the new "high speed" **Prospector**, the daily six-hour rail link between Perth and Kalgoorlie. **Buses** depart with similar regularity, taking about eight hours.

Coolgardie

Not quite dilapidated and abandoned enough to carry the name "ghost mining town", **COOLGARDIE** is more of a museum to itself, a town which – at its peak – had twenty-three hotels, three breweries and six newspapers serving a population ten times greater than its present twelve hundred. Arthur Bayley cranked the gold fever up when he arrived into Southern Cross – then the easternmost extent of the rush – in 1892 with nearly sixteen kilos of gold. The ensuing wave of prospectors started within hours – ten thousand men rushed out of Southern Cross, culminating in a fourfold increase in WA's population by the end of the century.

The imposing **Wardens Court Building** on Bayley Street is a good point from which to start an appraisal of Coolgardie's numerous boom-time relics. The building houses the **visitors information centre** (Mon–Fri 10am–5pm, Sat & Sun 10am–4pm; ⓣ08/9026 6090) and one of the most extensive provincial **museums** in WA (9am–noon, 12.30–4pm; $3.50). The grand upper floors

Wave Rock

WA's best-known natural oddity is Wave Rock (www.waverock.com.au; $7 per car), 3km from the tiny farming settlement of Hyden, at the eastern edge of the Wheatlands prairie. At 15m high and 110m long, the formation resembles a breaking wave, an impression enhanced by the vertical water stains running down the overhanging face.

At the base of the rock a marked twenty-minute trail leads to another outcrop, Hippo's Yawn, while 21km from Wave Rock, on the way to Southern Cross, Bates Cave features Aboriginal hand paintings.

Be aware that accommodation hereabouts is overpriced, including the *Wave Rock Caravan Park* (08/9880 5022; chalets ④), 5km east of town, and the *Hyden Wave Rock Hotel* on Lynch Street (08/9880 5052; ⑥). The shopping village has a range of eateries, such as the *Wave Rock Bush Bakehouse* (Mon–Fri 6.30am–3pm, Sat 6.30am–noon), which sells freshly baked pastries and bread.

are filled with a comprehensive collection of bottles and glassware dating back to 300 BC; the rest of the museum warrants a prolonged browse, giving you a sense of the dramatic effect the goldrush had on the area.

Outside the museum is an index to the 155 **historic markers** set around the town, and directly opposite you can't miss the junk comprising **Ben Prior's Open-Air Museum** (free). Half a kilometre up Hunt Street, at the end of McKenzie Street, **Warden Finnerty's House** (daily except Wed 11am–4pm; $3) is the finely restored 1895 residence of the man whose unenviable job it was to set the ground rules for mining at the height of the rush. Accommodation and places to eat are in town but a far better range is available at Kalgoorlie, 40km down the road.

Kalgoorlie-Boulder

Whichever way you approach **Kalgoorlie** – the bustling gold capital of Australia: officially twinned, municipally merged but still fervently distinct from **Boulder** (see opposite) – it comes as a surprise after hundreds of kilometres of desolation. The conurbation possesses the idiosyncratic quality of places like Coober Pedy (see p.798) or Las Vegas. All three blithely disregard their isolation and bleak surroundings, so devoted is their attention to the pursuit of earthly riches – which, in Kalgoorlie's case, is **gold**.

Kalgoorlie

In 1893 **Paddy Hannan** (then 53 years old) and his mates, Tom Flannigan and Dan O'Shea, brought renewed meaning to the expression "the luck of the Irish" when a lame horse forced them to camp by the tree which still stands at the top of Egan Street in **KALGOORLIE**. With their instincts highly attuned after eight months of prospecting around Coolgardie, they soon found gold all around them, and as the first on the scene enjoyed the unusually easy pickings of surface gold. Ten years later, when the desperately needed water pipeline finally gushed into the Mount Charlotte Reservoir, Kalgoorlie was already the established heart of WA's rapidly growing mineral-based prosperity. As sole survivor of the original rush, and revitalized by the 1960s nickel boom, Kalgoorlie has benefited from new technology that has largely dispensed with slow and dangerous underground mining. Instead, the fabulously rich "**Golden Mile**" reef east of town, near Boulder, is being excavated around the clock to create the vast, open-cast "Super Pit", which is still going strong and being expanded every day.

Proud of its history and continued prosperity, Kalgoorlie is one of the most parochial towns in Australia – a country that's full of them. Despite the encroachment of a suburban "shopping mall" lifestyle, "Kal" is first and foremost a "Working Man's Town" of twelve-hour, seven-day shifts, a testament to the ethos of hard work and hard play that flourished in Australia's Anglo-Celtic heyday. A pub without a half-dressed barmaid (known in WA as "skimpies") is the exception and in the sniggeringly louche red-light district of Hay Street, three of the infamous "tin shack" brothels remain conspicuously in business.

Start your tour of the town by taking a walk up to the top of Hannan Street to the bright red head-frame. This is the impressive entrance to the **Museum of the Goldfields** (daily 10am–4.30pm; donation), right next to the spot where Paddy and his crew found their first, auspicious nuggets. Inside is a display of Goldfields artefacts and history, with the very stuff that keeps the town going viewable in the basement vault. Aboriginal history and the sandalwood industry are also covered in this excellent summary of the area, and there's a lookout over the town from the top of the red head-frame.

Hannan Street itself is one of Kalgoorlie's finest sights, with its superbly restored **Federation-era architecture**, imposing public buildings and numerous flamboyant hotel facades. You're welcome to inspect the grandiose interior of the **town hall** (Mon–Fri 8.30am–5pm), with its splendid hall and less impressive art gallery. It's only when you stop to reflect that this is a remote, century-old town in the Western Australia desert that the stunning wealth of the still-continuing boom years is brought home to you. Outside the hall, a replica of a bronze **statue** of Paddy himself invites you to drink from his chrome-nozzled waterbag – the much vandalized original is now safely in the Mining Hall of Fame.

If it's merely your curiosity that's drawn you to Hay Street then *Langtrees 181* at no. 181 has found a novel and very successful way of perking up business in the quiet daylight hours – by offering **brothel tours** (daily 1pm, 3pm, 6pm; 1hr; $35). Although prostitution is illegal in WA, Kalgoorlie's "special needs" see a local policy of containment and toleration. This sordid industry is made slightly more palatable by the official ban on male control – investment benefits the entrepreneurial "madames" only. The tour leads you through the dozen or so themed rooms (some of which are more popular than others) while relating some of the not-so-lighthearted history of prostitution in WA, and answering all the questions you dare to ask.

Boulder and the Mining Hall of Fame

BOULDER, 5km south of Kalgoorlie, is much quieter and smaller than its twin – a place to visit rather than stay in. It was originally set up as a separate settlement to serve the Golden Mile but Boulder's heyday passed as Kalgoorlie's suburbs slowly expanded around it. Boulder has a similar collection of grand old buildings that – as in Kal – have received a face-lift, along with the pubs.

Just north of Kalgoorlie are a couple more unmissable attractions: the **Mining Hall of Fame** (daily 9am–4.30pm; $24, surface only $17; Ⓦ www.mininghall.com) is an old mine site transformed into a museum and mining theme-park. Inside you can have a crack at gold panning or take a guided underground tour, led by former miners. This is probably as long as you'd want to spend down a mine – especially after the brief demonstration of the pneumatic "air leg" drill. Back above ground, the Hall of Fame building has a comprehensive display of rocks and minerals, as well as Aboriginal art from the Warburton region. The Prospectors Gallery is also fascinating.

Practicalities

Goldfields Express (Ⓣ1800 620 440, Ⓦwww.goldrushtours.com.au) buses arrive at Forrest Street in Kalgoorlie, opposite the **train station** (Transwa; Ⓣ08/9021 2923). **Taxis** (Ⓣ13 10 08) meet the daily trains, which are no quicker than buses. Kalgoorlie's **visitor information centre** (Mon–Fri 8.30am–5pm, Sat & Sun 9am–5pm; Ⓣ08/9021 1966, Ⓦwww.kalgoorlie.com) is part of the Town Hall, on the corner of Hannan & Wilson streets, in the centre of town, and gives out informative maps pinpointing Kal's dispersed attractions. There's an Internet café on Hannan Street and a post office up the road at 204 Hannan St.

A local **bus service** operates between Kalgoorlie and Boulder every 25 minutes (Mon–Sat 8am–6pm; $2), with timetables available from Kalgoorlie's visitor information centre. **Car rental** is expensive, though Halfpenny Rentals, 544 Hannan St (Ⓣ08/9021 1804), try to live up to their name by offering slightly better rates. Goldfields express also offer an entertaining ninety-minute "History and Heritage" tour ($30).

Accommodation

The town gets busy with business travellers using the motels, and with holiday-makers in the winter school holidays, so it's best to check room availability in advance. The many splendid hotel facades along Hannan Street deteriorate inside, but they all offer inexpensive rooms with either shared or en-suite facilities. There are also several caravan parks around town with vans and cabins for around ❸.

All Seasons Kalgoorlie 45 Egan St Ⓣ1300 65 65 65, Ⓦwww.allseasons.com.au. Good option for the business traveller and those wanting a bit more comfort. Has everything you'd expect for the price and rooms have nice balconies looking over the town. ❺

Kalgoorlie Backpackers 166 Hay St Ⓣ08/9091 1482, Ⓦwww.kalgoorlie.com/kalbackpackers/. Former brothel close to the centre with a big kitchen, dorms and twins as well as a pool and bikes. Dorms $19, rooms ❷

Midas Motel 409 Hannan St Ⓣ08/9021 3088, Ⓦwww.midasmotel.com.au. Motel with nightclub, pool and self-catering rooms within walking distance to the station and main part of town. ❺

Palace Hotel 137 Hannan St Ⓣ08/9021 2788, Ⓦwww.palacehotel.com.au. Beautiful old building in a perfect location with an assortment of small rooms; those on the balcony are slightly more expensive. Free WiFi in lounge downstairs. Men-only singles ❷, twins/doubles ❸

YHA Gold Dust Backpackers 192 Hay St Ⓣ08/9091 3737, Ⓦwww.yha.com.au. Purpose-built hostel with a/c, pool, free bikes, Internet and pick-ups. Dorms $20, rooms ❷

York Hotel 259 Hannan St Ⓣ08/9021 2337. Probably the best-looking facade on Hannan St. Shared bathrooms; rates include breakfast. ❸

Eating and drinking

Starting at the cheap end, treat yourself to a good old **counter meal** at the *Star and Garter* pub at 197 Hannan St. At the top of the same street at no. 71, *Top End Thai* has been bringing in the miners and tourists alike for over 25 years, and is open from 6pm daily – their three-course deal is especially good value. Close by at 90 Egan St, trendy *Saltimbocca* serves up the town's best Italian cuisine. At the other end of town, at 418 Hannan St, *Akudjura* restaurant offers seafood and steaks in a classy setting for around $25–30. For most locals, Kal's **nightlife** revolves around scantily-clad pub barmaids laying on beer jugs all down Hannan Street, so if you can't beat them, join them; otherwise there is a **cinema** complex on Oswald Street, halfway to Boulder.

The Goldfields Highway

North of Kalgoorlie, there are a number of mining and Aboriginal communities along the 726km stretch up to Meekatharra, itself halfway up the Great

Northern Highway. Scenically the route hasn't got much to commend it, but it's useful if you're heading northeast to Alice via the Great Central Road (see p.673), or if you want to get from the Eyre Highway to northern WA in a hurry, avoiding Perth. Most of the so-called **ghost towns** in this area – especially the ones closer to Kalgoorlie – are merely foundations of long-gone buildings, as all abandoned structures and materials were scavenged for reuse elsewhere. Nevertheless, the **Golden Quest Discovery Trail** self-guides tourists through the region as far as Leonora and Laverton – ask for the free map and guide at Kalgoorlie's visitor information centre.

Though it once boasted twelve thousand residents, two breweries and an hourly train to Kalgoorlie, you can give the rubble remains of **Kanowna** a miss. Even the two ghost towns of **BROAD ARROW** and **ORA BANDA** (respectively 38km and 66km from Kalgoorlie) have only a "bush pub" each to show for themselves. Broad Arrow is just a couple of dilapidated shacks and a **pub** popular with weekending Kal-Boulderians. At **Kookynie**, a short distance off the highway, is another bush pub, the *Grand Hotel* (❹), standing alone in the dust.

LEONORA, 237km north of Kalgoorlie, is a sprightly century-old mining town – a "one-horse" version of Kalgoorlie that survives with a Federation-era main street and a couple of hotels (❹). Just south of town is the reconstructed **Gwalia** ghost town – an evocative scattering of galvo hovels, a general store and a museum (daily 10am–4pm; Ⓦwww.gwalia.org.au/museum; $5) at the top of the hill.

A sealed road branches northeast to **Laverton**, from where the long, straightforward **Great Central Road** leads around 1100km to Yulara, NT (see p.673 for a full description). Back on the road to Meekatharra, **LEINSTER** is a bizarrely suburban-looking company town, with a supermarket and a motel (❹), while **Wiluna**, 175km north of Leinster (hotel ❷) is the polar opposite – a century-old settlement that's now an Aboriginal welfare ghost-town of quite intimidating desolation: fuelling up is the only reason you'd want to stop here. From Wiluna the extensive, unmaintained **Gunbarrel Highway** winds east towards the NT border, while the **Canning Stock Route** runs northeast across the Great Sandy Desert for 1900km to Halls Creek; both routes are most definitely 4WD expeditions. The last 180km from Wiluna to Meekatharra is a gravel road.

The Eyre Highway to South Australia

South of Kalgoorlie the Great Eastern Highway runs 190km to Norseman, at the western end of the **Eyre Highway**. The highway is named after the explorer John Eyre, who crossed the southern edge of the continent in 1841, a gruelling five-month trek that would have cost him his life but for some Aborigines who helped him locate water. Eyre crawled into Albany on his last legs but set the route for future crossings, the telegraph lines and the highway.

NORSEMAN was named after a prospector's horse that kicked up a large nugget in 1894 – a genuine case of lucky horseshoes. A bronze effigy of the nag now stands proudly on the corner of Roberts and Ramsay streets. Arrivals from South Australia may be eager to pick up their "I've crossed the Nullarbor" certificate from the **visitor information centre** (daily 9am–5pm; Ⓣ08/9039 1071) on Roberts Street. The *Railway Hotel/Motel* (Ⓣ08/9039 0003, Ⓦwww.therailwayatnorseman.com.au) has decent budget rooms (❷) and en-suite rooms (❹); it also serves up good pub meals. If you've come from the east and are in a quandary about which route to take to Perth, consider nipping up to Kal but then return south and head west along the coast.

If you're heading back east on the Eyre Highway, it's about 730km to the South Australian border and another 480km from there to Ceduna, where the bleak **Nullarbor** section ends, though that still leaves 800km before you reach Adelaide – a drive of notorious monotony. Although the longest stretch without fuel is only around 200km, do not underestimate the rigours of the journey in your own vehicle. Carry reserves of fuel and water, take rests every two or three hours and beware of kangaroos and other wildlife, especially between dusk and dawn. There are no banks between Norseman and Ceduna, and both towns have a quarantine checkpoint where a large range of prohibited animal and vegetable goods must be discarded.

BALLADONIA, 193km east from Norseman, has a hotel, *Balladonia Hotel* (ⓣ08/9039 3453, ⓔballadonia@bigpond.com; ❹), as well as an adjacent caravan park. Some 200km of virtually dead-straight road further along, you reach **CAIGUNA**, equipped with a motel and caravan park (ⓣ08/9039 3459; on-site vans ❸, motel units ❹), and **COCKLEBIDDY**, another 66km further on (motel ❹; ⓣ08/9039 3403). The place to stay in **MADURA**, 92km east of Cocklebiddy – and halfway between Perth and Adelaide if you're still counting – is the *Madura Pass Oasis Motel* (ⓣ08/9039 3464; ❹), while **MUNDRABILLA**, 116km further on and where you rise up into the actual Nullarbor plain, has a combined motel and campsite, the *Mundrabilla Motor Hotel* (ⓣ08/9039 3465; ❸).

EUCLA, just 12km from the border, was re-established up on the escarpment after sand dunes exposed by overgrazing engulfed the original settlement by the sea. Only 4km away, the old telegraph and weather station are still visible above the sands, an eerie sight well worth a look. South of town is the **Eucla National Park** (DEC fee; see box, p.630), where the coastal cliffs can be seen extending east for 200km along the coast of South Australia. For accommodation, Eucla has a caravan park (bunkhouse ❶, on-site vans ❷), the *Eucla Amber Motor Hotel* (ⓣ08/9039 3468; ❹), or right on the border, there's the *Border Village* (ⓣ08/9039 3474; ❸). For the South Australian section of this route, see p.795.

From Perth to Kununurra

The 4400km haul up Highway 1 along Western Australia's arching coastline from Perth to Broome, across the Kimberley and on to Darwin in the Northern Territory, is one of Australia's great road journeys. Even without detours, it's a huge, transcontinental trek between the country's two most isolated capitals, fringing the barely inhabited desert that separates them.

If any single trip across Australia benefits from independent mobility, it's this one: a car enables you to explore intimately and linger indefinitely. While some days in WA's **Northwest** will be punctuated by nothing more than road trains, road kill and roadhouses, there are several places where the climate, scenery and ambience may collectively conspire to subdue your road fever for a few days. If you're interested in discovering the wayside attractions, allow at least three to four weeks for the journey right through to Darwin. Otherwise, a fortnight will whizz you through the highlights; anything less and you may as well fly.

The route is sealed all the way, but a glance at any map clearly shows the long distances between roadhouses, let alone settlements. Your vehicle should be in sound condition, particularly the tyres and the cooling system, both of which will be working hard in the heat of the Northwest. If you undertake the trip between January and March, expect very high temperatures as well as storms or even **cyclones**, with associated flooding and disruption. Following damage, roads and bridges on Highway 1 are repaired amazingly quickly, but if rain persists, back roads can be closed for weeks.

If you don't have a car, the rigid schedules and butt-numbing sectors of long-distance **bus** travel require certain equanimity. Greyhound Australia offers a range of **regional passes** up the coast to Exmouth, Broome and Darwin while Integrity Coachlines covers the inland route to Port Hedland once a week in each direction. It should be noted that by doing the journey *from* Perth, schedules generally match connections to places off the highway with little delay. In the opposite direction, you are travelling "against the flow" of the timetable and can expect long waits unless heading directly back to Perth.

Up the coast to Broome

Ironically, nowhere along the 2400km drive to Broome will you glimpse vistas of frothing surf breaking temptingly onto golden beaches. The highway takes a more sheltered inland route with access to the ocean limited by private land, not to mention the sheer impenetrability of some of the terrain. Beach-camping your way up a deserted coast will more likely turn out to be bush camping, but there are just about enough attractions to make up for this, including the spooky **Pinnacles** near Cervantes, the idyllic resort of **Kalbarri**, and the **Shark Bay Peninsula**, with its friendly dolphins. Further north, the **Ningaloo Reef** running down the North West Cape should not be missed.

The Brand Highway

Travelling the **Brand Highway** (as Highway 1 is initially known), there's an obligatory detour to view the remarkable Pinnacles in **Nambung National Park** (DEC fee $10 per vehicle; no camping; see box, p.630), 250km from Perth and 70km west off the highway. A young crayfishing town, beaten by strong winds in summer, **CERVANTES** is the closest overnight stop. The *Pinnacles Caravan Park* at 35 Aragon St (ⓣ08/0652 7060; $20/$25 unpowered/powered) caters to campers and also has cabins (❸) on site. *Cervantes Lodge*, incorporating *Pinnacles Beach Backpackers* (dorms $25, rooms ❸–❹), at 91 Seville St (ⓣ08/9652 7377 or freecall 1800 245 232, ⓦwww.cervanteslodge.com.au), has kitchen and barbecue facilities, laundry, TV/DVD lounge and Internet access and has deservedly been commended as Western Australia's best hostel three times. The *Best Western Cervantes Pinnacles Motel* (ⓣ08/9652 7145, ⓦwww.bestwestern.com.au/pinnacles; ❺) has blandly functional rooms, a pool and the *Anchor Restaurant and Café* which serves passable, if pricey pasta. Other places to eat include the *Pinnacle Country Café* next to the Liberty service station, which serves tasty fish and chips, or the Ronsard Bay *Tavern*. Near the *Tavern* on Cadiz Street you'll find the General Store, post office, Internet access and the visitors information centre (Mon–Fri 9am–5pm, Sat & Sun 10am–4pm; ⓣ08/9652 7700). Turquoise Coast Enviro Tours (ⓣ08/9652 7047, ⓦwww.pinnacletours.info) run three-hour walking trips through the Pinnacles at 8am and 5 or 6pm (depending on sunset time) which leave from the information centre and cost $40.

In the park, there's access to the ocean at **Kangaroo Point** and **Hangover Bay**, but the **Pinnacles** are the main attraction: a spread of limestone columns

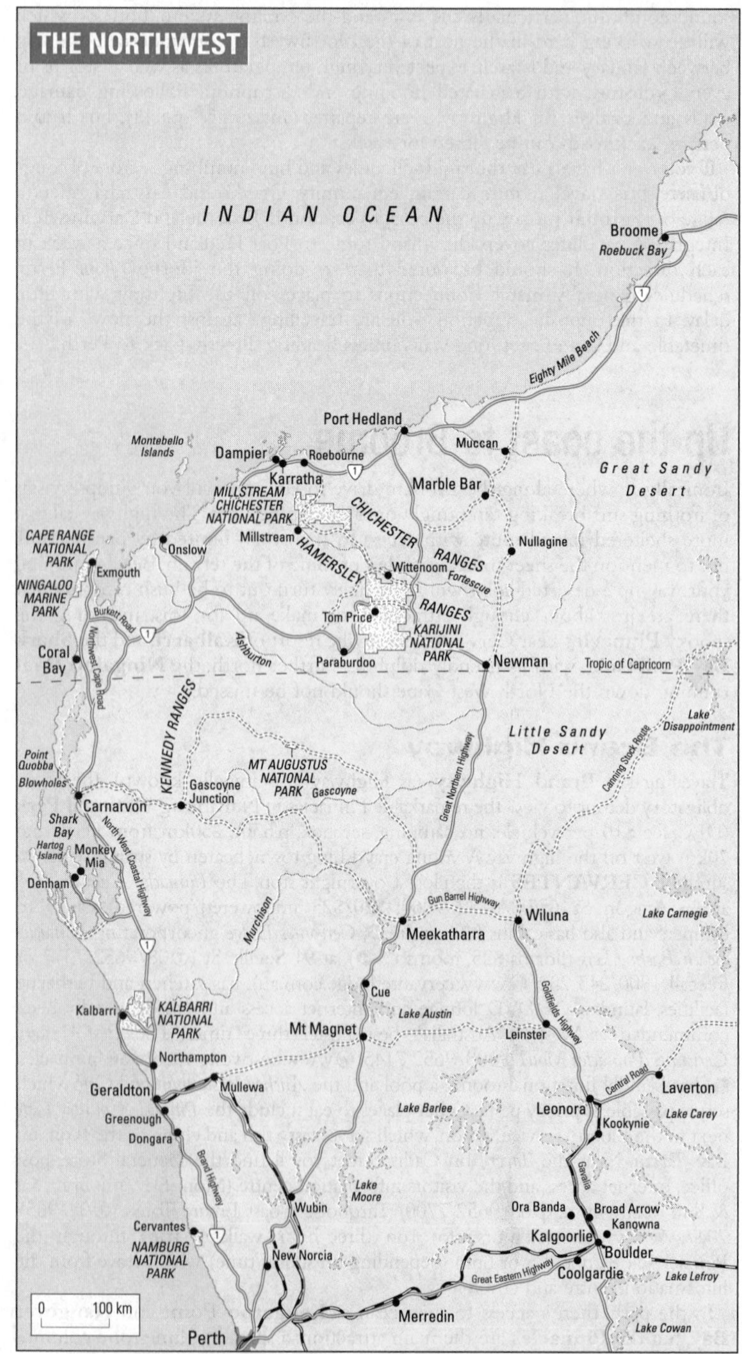
THE NORTHWEST
INDIAN OCEAN
Broome
Roebuck Bay
Eighty Mile Beach
Port Hedland
Montebello Islands
Dampier
Roebourne
Karratha
Muccan
Great Sandy Desert
Marble Bar
MILLSTREAM CHICHESTER NATIONAL PARK
CHICHESTER RANGES
Millstream
HAMERSLEY RANGES
CAPE RANGE NATIONAL PARK
Onslow
Nullagine
Exmouth
Wittenoom
Fortescue
NINGALOO MARINE PARK
Burkett Road
Tom Price
Northwest Cape Road
KARIJINI NATIONAL PARK
Coral Bay
Ashburton
Paraburdoo
Newman
Tropic of Capricorn
KENNEDY RANGES
Lake Disappointment
Little Sandy Desert
Point Quobba
Blowholes
MT AUGUSTUS NATIONAL PARK
Great Northern Highway
Canning Stock Route
Gascoyne Junction
Gascoyne
Carnarvon
Shark Bay
North West Coastal Highway
Hartog Island
Monkey Mia
Denham
Murchison
Gun Barrel Highway
Wiluna
Lake Carnegie
Meekatharra
Goldfields Highway
Cue
Kalbarri
KALBARRI NATIONAL PARK
Lake Austin
Mt Magnet
Leinster
Northampton
Central Road
Laverton
Geraldton
Mullewa
Lake Barlee
Leonora
Lake Carey
Greenough
Kookynie
Dongara
Brand Highway
Gavalia
Lake Moore
Wubin
Ora Banda
Broad Arrow
Kanowna
Cervantes
Kalgoorlie
NAMBURG NATIONAL PARK
New Norcia
Boulder
Great Eastern Highway
Coolgardie
Lake Lefroy
0
100 km
Merredin
Perth
Lake Cowan

up to 3m high which were originally formed underground and have since been exhumed from the sands, like a terracotta army, by the perennial southwesterlies. A three-kilometre drive winds among them, but however lazy you're feeling, you'll find it hard not to park up and wander around this eerie expanse, sometimes enhanced by a "mist" of fine, windblown sand. Most day-tours from Perth arrive around noon, missing the evening sun's long shadows, which add still further to the Pinnacles' photogenic qualities.

After the Pinnacles there's really very little of interest until you get to the fishing town of **Dongara**, 150km north of Cervantes, with its fine Moreton Bay fig trees, and 40km later the tiny coastal resort of **GREENOUGH**, and its unusually well-restored nineteenth-century **Historical Hamlet** (daily 10am–4pm; $5; ⓣ08/9926 1084). Up the road you'll notice Greenough's strange **leaning trees** – some bent almost flat against the ground by the prevailing salt-laden winds – as well as the imposing, three-storey bulk of **Clinch's Mill**, the **Pioneer Cemetery** and the **Pioneer Museum** (daily except Fri 10am–4pm; $4.50; ⓣ08/9926 1058), which records the area's heritage.

Geraldton

Situated in the middle of the **Batavia Coast**, 420km north of Perth, **GERALDTON** is a crayfishing, mining and pastoral centre. It's the state's second-largest city and development has given it more the feel of a busy Perth suburb than a country town.

On Cathedral Drive, the honey-coloured **St Francis Xavier Cathedral** was completed in 1938, the crowning glory of architect John Hawes' career (tours Mon 10am & Fri 2pm; free). If you're sufficiently impressed, ask at the visitors information centre (see below) about the **John Hawes Heritage Trail**, which leads you around some of his other works: you'll find half a dozen examples of his unique Romanesque-Byzantine architectural style in the vicinity of the cathedral. Check out the **Maritime Museum** (Mon–Sat 10am–4pm, Sun 1–5pm; donation) on Marine Terrace, by the yellow submarine, which focuses on the *Batavia* tragedy (see p.644), off the Houtman Abrolhos Islands (see below), as well as the contemporary crayfishing industry.

△ The Pinnacles

Geraldton is the departure point for flights to the Houtman Abrolhos Islands, 100km offshore, and the cause of many a historic shipwreck. The 122 islands, spread over more than 100km, are renowned for their warm waters which allow both temperate and tropical marine life to thrive. You can reach the islands by boat or a short flight, but there is no accommodation on the Abrolhos. Day-trips ($175–220) involve a scenic flight while the more expensive options include a nature walk and some snorkelling – the visitors information centre can help you arrange a visit.

Practicalities

The visitors information centre, in the Bill Sewell Complex (Mon–Fri 9am–5pm, Sat & Sun 10am–4pm; ⓣ08/9921 3999, ⓦwww.geraldtontourist.com.au) on Chapman Road, 2km north of town, will happily sort out all accommodation bookings. Greyhound Australia services arrive here daily and Transwa buses alight at the old train station, just down the road. For **places to stay**, there's *Batavia Backpackers,* behind the visitors information centre (ⓣ08/9964 3001, ⓔgeraldtonbackpackers@hotmail.com; dorms $20, rooms ❷), and *Foreshore Backpackers*, 172 Marine Terrace (ⓣ08/9921 3275, ⓔforeshorebp@hotmail .com; three- to four-bed dorms $20, rooms ❷). Alternatively, motels include *Best Western*, *Comfort Inn* and *Mercure* chains, among others (❺). Recommended **restaurants** are the *Boatshed* at 357 Marine Terrace, which serves decent seafood, as does *Skeetas* at 101 Foreshore Rd.

Kalbarri and around

About 70km north of Geraldton, your curiosity may be aroused by a sign for the **Hutt River Principality**, a caravan park and old pastoral property that comes and goes as a goofy tourist attraction after it "ceded" from the Australian Commonwealth many years ago on an arcane legal technicality. The principality issues its own postage and passport stamps and has a chapel featuring religious paintings.

Situated on the mouth of the Murchison River nearly 600km north of Perth and 66km off Highway 1, **KALBARRI** is one of the best of the west coast's resorts. With the dramatic scenery of Kalbarri National Park on its doorstep, few resorts can boast such an ideal location, together with good, inexpensive accommodation and a host of activities.

The area's history holds a few wonders of its own. In the 1920s a stockman discovered the remains of a **castaway's camp** on the clifftops north of Kalbarri and subsequent excavation revealed the wreck of the Dutch trader, *Zuytdorp*, at the base of the cliff, but no human remains. The fate of the survivors had been a three-hundred-year-old mystery until the diagnosis of the rare Ellis van Creveld Syndrome (endemic in the seventeenth-century Netherlands) among local children of Aboriginal descent suggested that some of the *Zuytdorp*'s castaways survived long enough to pass the gene on to the Aborigines of the area.

Arrival and information

Greyhound Australia **buses** from Perth drop passengers at Binnu, a little before the Kalbarri turn-off on Highway 1, to be met by a shuttle bus on Monday, Wednesday and Friday only. Transwa buses from Perth arrive at the visitors centre at 5pm. The visitors information centre (daily 9am–5pm; ⓣ08/9937 1104 or 1800 639 468, ⓦwww.kalbarriwa.info) is in the Allen Centre on Grey Street; many local activities and tours can be booked here. The small **shopping centre** on Porter Street includes a bakery, supermarket and **post office**, with bank agencies and ATMs at various outlets around town. There's Internet access at a number of places around town, including the Traveller's Book Exchange on Grey Street. Suzuki **4WD Jeeps** can be rented from *Kalbarri Backpackers*.

Accommodation

In the school holidays (see p.77) when Kalbarri is packed out, most holiday units insist on a minimum one-week's booking.

Anchorage Caravan Park Anchorage Lane ⓣ08/9937 1181. A ten-minute walk from town, the *Anchorage* enjoys good views over the river and has a decent-sized pool. Powered sites are $21.

Kalbarri Backpackers 2 Mortimer St ⓣ08/9937 1430, ⓔkalbarribackpackers@wn.com.au. Spacious and tidy, the mixed dorms are $25 and double rooms are $44. This large resort is a little bland but has a big pool, sauna, tennis court and two restaurants, the *Zutydorp* and *Jake's* (see p.679) ❺

Kalbarri Palm Resort 8 Porter St ⓣ08/9937 2333 or 1800 819 029, ⓦwww.kalbarripalmresort.com.au. Good-value sizeable rooms with pool and tennis courts. ❺

Kalbarri Seafront Villas 108 Grey St ⓣ08/9937 1025, ⓦwww.kalbarriseafrontvillas.com.au. Offers well-equipped units, a few with ocean views. ❻

Kalbarri Sunsea Villas 38 Grey St ⓣ08/9937 1187, ⓦwww.kalbarrisunseavillas.com. Although ugly from the outside, these units are spacious and well-equipped and some have sea views. There's also a pool. ❺

Murchison Park Grey St ⓣ08/9937 1005. A well-shaded and central caravan park opposite the beach, although it can get a little crowded. Cabins are $65–85, while powered camp sites are $24.

The town and around

For those not content to laze on **Chinaman's Beach** all day, there are plenty of active pursuits on offer. An easy way to get yourself moving is to take a **cruise** up the Murchison River with Kalbarri Wilderness Cruises (ⓣ08/9937 2259) or rent all sorts of **watercraft** on the Foreshore from Kalbarri Boat Hire & Canoe Safaris (ⓣ08/9937 1245). They can also take you up the lower Murchison to Gregory's Rock for a morning's canoeing, with a traditional bush breakfast on the way, for $60. For a saltwater experience, Kalbarri Sports and Dive (ⓣ08/9937 1126) can organize **dives** while the *Reef Walker* (ⓣ08/9937 1356) sets off on a variety of coastal cruises ($35 for a one-hour sunset cruise or $175 for a half-day fishing trip).

Big River Ranch, 4km inland from Kalbarri (ⓣ08/9937 1214; pick-ups available), runs very popular **horse-riding** trips for both beginners and the experienced; the two-hour morning or afternoon rides ($60) through the river, along the beach and back again, are extremely worthwhile. **Scenic flights** with Kalbarri Air Charter (ⓣ08/9937 1130; enquire at the gift shop at 28 Grey St) start from just $45 for the short but spectacular Coastal Cliffs run, and go up to $180 for the Grand Tour or $205 for a five-hour visit to Monkey Mia.

Eating and drinking

Don't leave Kalbarri without checking out *Finlay's Fish BBQ* (daily 11.30am–2pm & 5.30–8.30pm; ⓣ08/9937 1260) on Magee Crescent. With Captain Finlay's fresh fish, salad and damper for $12, and an unusual setting in an old ice works (plus occasional fireside ballads), *Finlay's* is a treat on a balmy night.

All the other **restaurants** can seem rather conventional by comparison; the marine-themed *Zuytdorp* (daily 5.30–9pm) at the *Kalbarri Beach Resort* is worth a try, with a $25 smorgasbord, while in the same place, *Jake's* is less formal. The *Black Rock Cafe* (daily 10am–8pm), on Grey Street, has views and seafood lunches, as does the *Grass Tree* (Thurs–Tues 10am–late; ⓣ08/9937 2288) a little further along, which also offers good Asian dishes. For a cheap, quick and simple meal, the *Jetty Seafood Shack* (daily 11am–2.30pm & 5–8pm, closed Sat lunch) near the *Anchorage Caravan Park* has delicious fish and chips. There's also a good health-food café inside the shopping centre. Of the two **pubs**, the *Kalbarri Hotel* on Grey Street is where the locals hang out, while the livelier *Gilgai Tavern* on Porter Street also serves decent meals.

Kalbarri National Park

Kalbarri National Park (DEC fee $10 per vehicle; see box, p.630), which surrounds the town, has two popular attractions: the **coastal gorges** created by lesser creeks, a few kilometres south of Kalbarri and just about within cycling range, and the serpentine **river gorge** of the upper Murchison River, reached off the Ajana road east of town. Kalbarri Coach Tours (ⓣ08/9937 1161, ⓦwww.kalbarricoachtours.com.au) visit both areas several times a week for around $50 each.

The **coastal gorges** are accessible by tracks and short walks off the Kalbarri to Northampton Road. **Red Bluff** is the prominent butte overlooking Jakes Corner, where there's good surfing, and the site of some barely discernible, prehistoric crustacean fossils. **Rainbow Valley** has some intriguing features exposed by weathering, as well as a coastal walk up to **Mushroom Rock**, and is the most interesting part of the coastline. Pot Alley is another lookout and Eagle Gorge has a tiny secluded beach, but the view from the cliffs above **Natural Bridge** (at 16km, the furthest from town) gives the impression that you are indeed perched on the edge of a vast continent.

Eleven kilometres east of Kalbarri on the Ajana Road, a corrugated track turns north for 25km to the **river gorge** along the Murchison River, where at a junction you can go a few kilometres further north to **the Loop**, or south to **Z Bend**. It's possible to walk round the Loop (a horseshoe bend in the Murchison River) in about two hours although this may be prolonged by the abundance of swimming opportunities, birdlife and the odd, mean-looking feral pig; the walk is best undertaken early in the morning. Z Bend is the most dramatic lookout over the Murchison River far below, accessible down a steep track. You can abseil, rap jump and climb up Z Bend's cliff; enquire at *Kalbarri Backpackers'* or the visitors information centre for all activities – no experience is necessary. Back on the Ajana road, heading inland for 30km from the Loop turn-off, Hawks Head and Ross Graham Lookout, both a few kilometres off the road, are less impressive but worth stopping for a break on the way out of Kalbarri if you're driving.

It's possible to **walk** from Z Bend to the Loop over a couple of days and from Ross Graham Lookout to the Loop in four days, but both are demanding treks so consult the **park ranger** (ⓣ08/9937 1140) first.

Shark Bay

Shark Bay is the name given to the two prongs of land and their corresponding lagoons that comprise Australia's westernmost point, forming a roughly W-shaped coastline. **Denham**, the only settlement, is on the west side of the Peron Peninsula, while at **Monkey Mia Dolphin Resort**, on the sheltered east side of the peninsula, a family of dolphins has been coming in almost daily to meet people for nearly fifty years. Shark Bay's location at the confluence of three climatic zones (desert, tropical and temperate) has earned it a World Heritage listing as a remarkable **ecological habitat**. The shallow aquamarine waters here hold the largest seagrass banks in the world that support a significant proportion of the planet's dugong population while the region is also home to six of Australia's most endangered species including the banded-hare wallaby and the

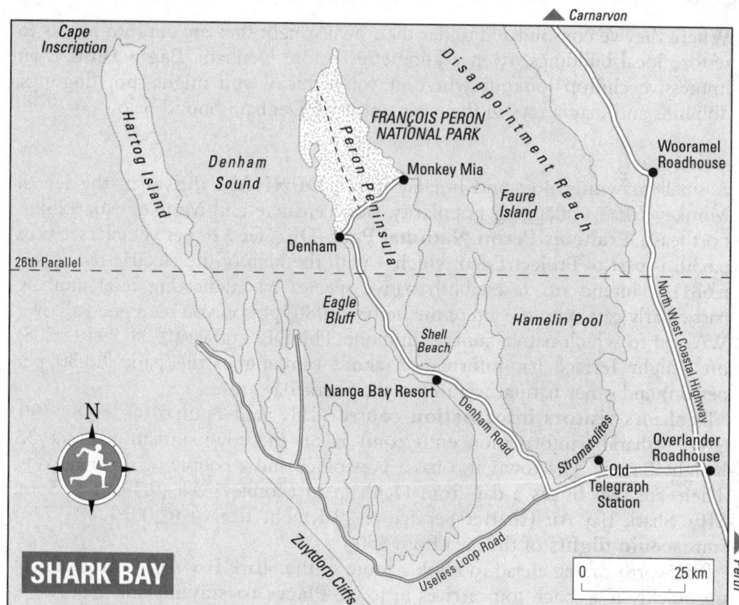

western barred bandicoot – however, these facts tend to be overshadowed by the dolphins. It's worth noting that dolphins also "interact", albeit less reliably, at Rockingham, Mandurah and Bunbury south of Perth.

Greyhound Australia **buses** run to Monkey Mia from Perth on Monday, Wednesday and Friday (12hr) and stop at *Overlander Roadhouse* where they are met by shuttle services on to Denham and Monkey Mia: if you plan to visit, make sure your bus pass includes this connection.

The road to Monkey Mia

It's 150km to Monkey Mia from the *Overlander Roadhouse*, a drive that's much like the rest of the coastline in this area – a dull, dense mulga scrub punctuated with some unusual sights along the way. Twenty-eight kilometres west of the *Overlander*, a road leads 5km north to the **Old Telegraph Station** caravan park (Ⓣ08/9942 5905; no drinking water; powered sites $15, donga cabins $15 per person) and **Hamelin Pool**. The Pool is home to an unusual community of **stromatolites**, colonies of sediment-trapping algae which are direct descendants of the earth's earliest life forms, dating back over three billion years. It is their ancestors we can thank for diligently oxygenating the earth's atmosphere, which eventually led to more complex life forms. Viewed from a platform, the 3000-year-old examples in Hamelin Pool flourish because no potential predator can handle the pool's hyper-saline water. The *Old Telegraph Station* has a pet "stromie" in a tank that can look more interesting than the actual colony unless the tide is right out.

Continuing on the main road towards Denham, you'll pass *Nanga Bay Resort* (Ⓣ08/9948 3992, Ⓔnangabay@wn.com.au; dorms $15, rooms ❺), with cabins and dorms in various formats; it's a popular fishing base but otherwise uninspiring. Across the isthmus – now spanned by an electric fence, which emits a recording of barking dogs (an attempt to scare feral animals off the peninsula) – is **Shell Beach**, composed of millions of tiny shells, several metres deep.

Where they've consolidated under their own weight they are cut into blocks to restore local buildings. Twenty kilometres before Denham, **Eagle Bluff** is an impressive clifftop lookout where, if you're lucky, you might spot dugongs, dolphins and manta rays in the clear waters of Denham Sound below.

Denham

A small prawning port and holiday resort, **DENHAM** thrives in the lee of Monkey Mia's unflagging popularity. Between here and Monkey Mia (25km northeast), **François Peron National Park** (DEC fee $10 per vehicle; see box, p.630) is part of Project Eden which – with the help of the electric fence (see p.681) – intends to re-establish native species by eradicating feral animals, particularly cats, with the aid of the herbal "1080" poison you see signed all over WA and to which native fauna is immune. The DEC office (ⓣ08/9948 1208) on Knight Terrace has information about camping in the park ($6.50 per person) and other natural features in the Shark Bay area.

Denham's **visitors information centre** (daily 9am–6pm; ⓣ08/9948 1590, ⓦwww.sharkbayinformationcentre.com) is on the town's main road at 33 Knight Terrace. The town also has a post office and a couple of supermarkets. There are two **buses** a day from Denham to Monkey Mia (9.30am & 5pm; $10). Shark Bay Air Charter Service at 29 Knight Terrace (ⓣ08/9948 1773) runs **scenic flights** of the area from $50.

It is worth calling ahead to book a room in the Shark Bay region as it can fill up quickly if a coach tour arrives in town. **Places to stay** include *Bay Lodge*, 113 Knight Terrace (ⓣ08/9948 1278, ⓦwww.baylodge.info; dorm $22, rooms ❸–❹), and the *Tradewinds Holiday Village* (ⓣ08/9948 1222; ❹–❺), with units that sleep up to six people. The *Heritage Resort* (ⓣ08/9948 1133, ⓦwww.sharkbay.com.au; ❻), on the corner of Durlacher Street, is the town's finest, and has a very pleasant, friendly bar and restaurant. Of the three **caravan parks** in town, the *Shark Bay Caravan Park*, 4 Spaven Way (ⓣ08/9948 1387, ⓦwww.sbvan.com; powered site $22, cabins ❸–❹), is your best bet and has a big pool.

The only notable **restaurant**, apart from the one in the *Heritage Resort*, is the *Old Pearler* (daily 11.30am–1.30pm & 6–8.30pm; ⓣ08/9948 1373) opposite, which is built from shell block and has an attractive maritime interior. It serves fresh local seafood for around $40 a head. Other than that, there are a couple of cafés, a pizza bar and a bakery along Knight Terrace. Note that fresh **water** is very precious in the Shark Bay area: salty bore water is used as much as possible but locally desalinated public drinking water is available at the tap just as you come into Denham after the information board.

Monkey Mia

After all the hype, you might be surprised to find that **Monkey Mia** ($9 per person) is nothing more than a busy caravan park and a jetty by a pretty beach, overlooking the inauspiciously named Disappointment Reach. It is here that scores of day-trippers flock to witness the almost daily **dolphin** visits (usually for three feeds between 8am and 1pm and most reliably in winter). An intriguing video in the **Dolphin Information Centre** (daily 7.30am–4pm; ⓣ08/9948 1366) explains how the entirely unprompted interaction began in the 1960s. Much of what has been learned about dolphins has been gleaned from studies of Monkey Mia's regular troupe of visitors, each one known by name, and numbering between three and six females and their third-generation progeny.

Unfortunately, for both dolphins and tourists, the place has become a victim of its massive popularity: the dolphins' repeated visits and their spontaneous familiarity seem to take a toll on their breeding patterns. Calves lack immunity to human infections in their early weeks and are kept away from visitors, and juniors aren't fed until they have learned to hunt for themselves. However, if you push into the right spot you can get a close-up shot of a dolphin – the first feed tends to attract the most tourists, although the later visits are less predictable. If you want to get more involved, volunteer at the information centre for periods from four days to up to two weeks: as well as feeding and monitoring the dolphins more mundane duties include keeping the centre spick and span.

It's possible to take a spin around the bay in one of the two catamarans berthed at the jetty, the best being the stripped-down *Shotover* with **cruises** starting from $39 an hour – just turn up, and hop on. With luck, you'll see plenty of marine life (including prancing dolphins and docile dugongs). If you'd rather go it alone there are glass-bottomed boats ($30), pedal-boats ($30) and kayaks ($10) for hire by the hour on the beach. You can also arrange dives from Monkey Mia, but the shallow depth of the bay makes snorkelling a more worthwhile experience – contact Powerdive (T08/9948 3031) at the resort (see below). For those preferring dry land there are short camel safaris which can be arranged from the visitors centre.

The *Monkey Mia Dolphin Resort* (T08/9948 1320 or 1800 653 611, Wwww.monkeymia.com.au), right on the beach, is the only place to stay. The resort has a range of accommodation options including beachfront (6) and garden villas (5), budget rooms (3), dormitories ($22–25) and camping facilities: grassed sites for tents are $10 and sand sites for caravans and campervans are $27. There's also a pool, spa, tennis court, bar, restaurant, Internet access and a small shop with basic groceries.

Carnarvon and around

A centre for prawning fleets and the sheep stations of the Upper Gascoyne region, tropical **CARNARVON**, 900km from Perth, also supports a large agricultural zone, thanks to the superficially dry Gascoyne River's retrievable subterranean water. Unfortunately, the town continues to battle against a reputation for drink-related violence and crime and it's one of the few places between Perth and Katherine, in the NT, where you'll regularly see police cars on the prowl.

There's little in town to detain a passing traveller anyway, but a couple of diversions up the coast can make a fun day out. Six kilometres east of Carnarvon a bridge crosses the riverbed, passing the 65°C thermal well of Bibbawarra Bore and joins the sealed Blowholes Road, which leads to the **Blowholes** at Point Quobba, 65km from town. On all but the calmest days, incoming waves compress air through vents in the low cliff and erupt like geysers up to 20m into the air, a sight and sound well worth the detour. A couple of kilometres to the south is a basic campsite (no water) with sheltered snorkelling in the bay. Heading north past occasional tracks down to shell-lined beaches, you cross a private road linking the Dampier Saltworks at Lake MacLeod with the jetty at Cape Cuvier. Just north of the cape is the wreck of the *Korean Star*, beached here during a cyclone in 1988.

Practicalities

Carnarvon's ever-hopeful **visitors information centre** (Mon–Fri 9am–5pm, Sat 9am–noon; T08/9941 1146) is on the corner of Robinson Street and Camel Lane. **Buses** also arrive here, and the **post office** is just opposite. **Accommodation** in town includes the *Gateway Motel* at 379 Robinson St (T08/9941 1532, Wwww.carnarvonmotel.com.au; 4) and the *Hospitality Inn*

(Ⓣ08/9941 1600, Ⓦwww.hospitalityinnscarnarvon.com.au; ❺) on West Street. The only hostel, *Carnarvon Backpackers*, on the foreshore, left at the end of Robinson Street (Ⓣ08/9941 1095; dorms $20; doubles ❷), is as good as you'd expect for this small town. There are no fewer than seven **caravan parks** close to town catering for itinerant workers, and caravanners seeking the winter sun.

The North West Cape

Back on Highway 1, 140km north of Carnarvon, is the *Minilya Roadhouse* (daily 7am–9pm), from where a turning 6km later leads to the **North West Cape**. This hot, arid and often windy spike of land is notable for the 250-kilometre **Ningaloo Reef** that fringes its western edge, never more than 7km offshore and in places accessible right from the beach; "WA's barrier reef without the barriers" as some call it. **Exmouth** is the main settlement on the cape, located near its tip and growing year by year. However, the tiny resort of **Coral Bay**, 100km from the *Minilya*, is not only more convenient and pleasant, but the easiest place from which to view the reef. **Buses** leave from Carnarvon every morning, stopping at Minilya where you can connect with shuttles to Coral Bay and Exmouth.

Coral Bay

CORAL BAY is 12km west off the road to Exmouth and – school holidays excepted (see p.77) – can be a lovely spot from which to enjoy the reef. It's the idyllic beach resort many expect to find along the west coast, and here you can enjoy all the activities offered at Exmouth, but within walking distance of the sea. Hot salty bore water and a lack of available land have held back large-scale development and the resort remains little more than a couple of caravan parks and motels with mini–shopping centres and other services. A desalination plant, power station, wind turbines and a new boat ramp are all scheduled for completion by 2008, but it remains to be seen if these developments will alter Coral Bay's low-key tourist scene. **Internet** access is widely available and there are **ATMs** in town, though it's worth noting that there is no official **visitors information centre** here; the many places displaying the familiar blue-and-white "i" logo are run – like almost everything else in Coral Bay – by one of the two business interests which between them own the resort. There is however, a DEC Hut (Ⓣ08/9948 5131), towards the end of the road, which can provide information on the region's parks and wildlife.

All the **accommodation** and associated services are a few hundred metres apart along the resort's only road. On your right as you enter town is the *Ningaloo Club* backpackers' (Ⓣ08/9948 5100, Ⓦwww.ningalooclub.com; four- to ten-bed dorms $22–25, rooms ❸), which has a big kitchen and games area, a small pool and nightly movies. The club also runs its own reef tours. Down the road on the left, the *Bayview Coral Bay* (Ⓣ08/9385 6655, Ⓦwww.coralbaywa.com) forms a large resort with shady powered sites for caravans and campervans ($26), various configurations of cabins, en-suite chalets, motel-type rooms and fully equipped self-contained villas (❹–❼). Next door, the more upmarket *Peoples' Park Caravan Village* (Ⓣ08/9942 5933, Ⓦwww.peoplesparkcoralbay.com) offers powered sites for $29, or motel-style cabins (❻). Note that if you arrive after 6pm the boom gate will be down and you won't be able to get in – call in advance to arrange entry. Also on site are a supermarket, **fuel** and *Fins* restaurant, which offers **Internet** access, serves good coffee, and serves tasty goldband snapper. Situated at the end of the road, the *Ningaloo Reef Resort* (Ⓣ08/9942 5934, Ⓦwww.ningalooreefresort.com.au) has comfortable rooms in the *Coral Bay Hotel* (❺–❽), with a **bar**. *Shades* restaurant

Ningaloo marine-spotters' calendar

Manta rays – all year, Coral Bay
Coral spawning – March to April
Whale watching – June to October
Turtle hatching – January to March
Whale sharks – April to July
Turtle nesting – November to January

serves good seafood and also has a popular takeaway, all by a grassed pool area with a great view over the bay.

Several **glass-bottomed boats** operate cruises over the reef, some of which also include snorkelling. Trips cost from $29 to $40 depending on duration, and times depend on the tides. Snorkelling gear is included in the price and can be kept for the rest of the day. The recommended longer trips take you snorkelling on the more impressive outer reef, as well as visiting the Manta rays around the headland where you'll see an amazing variety of fish, and soft and hard coral. Other **activities** at Coral Bay include catamaran cruises, resort dives or full PADI courses, scenic flights, sea kayaking, fishing trips and quad-bike tours. You can arrange all of these activities at your place of accommodation or with either Coral Bay Adventures (Ⓣ08/9942 5955, Ⓦwww.coralbayadventures.com.au) or Coastal Adventure Tours (Ⓣ08/9948 5190, Ⓦwww.coralbaytours.co.au) in the shopping centre next to *Ningaloo Club*. But even without all this activity and expenditure, you can still enjoy yourself just strolling up and down the beach, watching the dazzling white swell break over the reef.

Exmouth

Back on the North West Cape Road on the way up to Exmouth, you pass Burkett Road, which cuts 150km from the journey if you're coming from the north. Turning north towards Exmouth, two roads lead up onto the emerging **Cape Range**: the Charles Knife Road climbs precipitously to the top of the range, 311m above sea level. From here it's possible to walk to the head of Shothole Canyon (allow 2hr), also accessible by car off the Exmouth road, though this is a far less dramatic introduction to the range.

△ Spotting whale sharks, Ningaloo Reef

EXMOUTH was built in 1967 to serve a former US Navy Communications Station and has since become a tourist base for visits to the Cape Range National Park and Ningaloo Marine Park. A high proportion of cloud-free days make the town a popular winter resort, with tourist numbers increasing as the wonders of the Ningaloo Reef become more widely known. Though far from being a west-coast Cairns, diving and fishing charters, as well as marine wildlife-spotting tours (see box, p.685) and other recreational activities all vie for attention. Unlike Cairns, however, the ocean is a couple of kilometres away (a necessary cyclone precaution), although recent developments at the marina, a couple of kilometres south of town, enjoy sea frontage. The nearest place to see the reef is off Bundegi Beach (see opposite), but the best of the **reef** and **beaches** are 50km away on the west side of the Cape.

Practicalities

Buses stop outside the **visitors information centre** (Mon–Fri 9am–5pm, Sat & Sun 9am–1pm; ⓣ08/9949 1176, ⓦwww.exmouthwa.com.au) on the main Murat road opposite *Winstons/Ningaloo Caravan Resort*. Here, you can try to get your head around the range of offshore charters and tours offered. Note that if you are coming up to swim with the whale sharks, you can expect to pay at least $300 a day for the privilege and will need both to be here at the right time of year (see box, p.685) and have time to wait around for whale sightings.

The town centre is based around the apex of Maidstone Crescent; turn left at the Caltex fuel station. Here you'll find banks and the post office, supermarket and a couple of cafés. **Internet access** is offered by most of the hostels, along with wireless connection by What Scooters on Murat Road (450 metres left out of the visitors information centre). In peak season (April–Nov), a **bus** runs daily to Coral Bay and back (ⓣ08/9949 4623; $75 one way). Ningaloo Reef Bus (ⓣ1800 999 941) operates a daily service at 8.30am that runs round the Cape as far as the Turquoise Bay ($20 return) and returns at 2.45pm, which gives you a few hours to snorkel and relax on the beach – snorkels can be hired for $5 on the bus. To make the most of this place you'll need some sort of transport: **cars** can be rented from Allens Car Hire, 24 Nimitz St (ⓣ08/9949 2403, ⓔalscarhire@bigpond.com), and from What Scooters at 102 Murat Rd, (ⓣ08/9949 4748, ⓦwww.whatscooters.com.au) who also have scooters for hire and can organize scooter trips. Exmouth Camper Hire (ⓣ08/9949 4050, ⓦwww.exmouthcamperhire.com.au) has campervans for use in the Exmouth and Coral Bay area.

There are tons of trips you can take from Exmouth and it's easy to pass a few weeks here exploring the fabulous landscapes and wildlife. Tours can be booked through the visitors information centre, at most accommodation options and from the operators themselves. A worthwhile nightly trip is run by the *Ningaloo Reef Retreat* (see opposite) to see turtles laying eggs (ⓣ08/9949 1776; Dec–Feb; $25, all proceeds go to the Ningaloo Turtle Programme). What Scooters (see above) offers day scooter tours of the Cape Range National Park ($120, includes meals; bring your driving license). The Ningaloo Reef is a diver's paradise with the Muiron Islands a favourite: the recommended Ningaloo Reef Dreaming (ⓣ08/9949 4777, ⓦwww.ningaloodreaming.com) offers three dives ($150–175, depending on the dive sites) as well as PADI and Divemaster courses, and they also run the much-touted whale-shark swimming tours ($330). There are also snorkelling trips, or if you don't want to get into the water, glass-bottom boat rides and fishing trips. And if you fancy viewing the region from the air, Norwest Airwork (ⓣ08/9949 2888) offers scenic plane trips ($195 for three people).

When it comes to **eating** there are the usual takeaways and a Chinese restaurant in the shopping centre. Other favourites include *Whalers Café* on Kennedy Street which presents Asian dishes, or for something a little smarter, *Manta Ray* in the *Novotel* does good seafood and Mediterranean cuisine from $30. The *Potshot Hotel* accommodates the town's main **pub**, whilst *Grace's Tavern* is opposite the *Exmouth Cape Holiday Park*, south of the town centre.

Accommodation

Exmouth Cape Holiday Park (Exmouth Backpackers) 3 Truscott Crescent ⓣ08/9949 1101 or 1800 621 101, ⓦwww.aspenparks.com.au. Some 2km south of town on the corner of Murat Road, this place is in the process of modernizing and improving the site. The park has spacious caravan berths, along with rows of prefab cabins ($75 or $80 en suite) with fitted kitchens, and some dorms ($24). Tours, cruises, dives and car rental available, and the site also has a small pool and BBQ area.

Lighthouse Caravan Park Vlamingh Head ⓣ08/9949 1478; about 16km north of town at the tip of the Cape. Basic cabins (3), en-suite bungalows (4) and fully featured "lookout chalets" (6) on the hillside. Powered sites ($18) and camping ($13) are also available. The owners are friendly and there's a pool, tennis court, small shop and fuel on site.

Ningaloo Caravan Holiday Resort Murat Rd, ⓣ08/9949 2377, ⓦwww.exmouthresort.com. A spacious and well-ordered campsite with shaded powered ($32) and unpowered ($24) sites, studios (5) and chalets (5), this resort has good facilities including a pool. **Winston's Backpackers** is also on site and has a small block of four-bed dorms ($25), and budget rooms (3).

Ningaloo Lodge Off Maidstone Crescent ⓣ08/9949 4949, ⓦwww.ningaloolodge.com.au. Centrally located hotel resort with well-equipped and good-value en-suite rooms, a kitchen and a pool. 4

Ninglaoo Reef Retreat Yardie Creek Rd, Cape Range National Park ⓣ08/9949 1776, ⓦwww.ningalooreefretreat.com. An hour's drive from Exmouth, the eco-friendly retreat's luxuriously appointed tents look straight out onto the ocean and guests all chip in to cook meals from the camp's recipe book. From $235 for a swag to $640 for a twin tent and the price includes everything from snorkelling on the beach, kayaking, guided activities and all meals. You need to bring any other snacks, soft drinks or alcohol you might want whilst here. There are only a small number of tents, so call in advance to book.

Novotel Ningalo Resort Madaffari Drive ⓣ08/9949 0000, ⓦwww.novotel.com. By far the most upmarket option in Exmouth, the *Novotel* is simply but elegantly decked out in earthy tones and is the only place to stay in Exmouth where you can actually see the ocean from your room and walk out on to a beach. The resort focuses on the stylish central pool and also has a first-rate restaurant, *Manta Ray* (see above). All the rooms are tastefully furnished and have comfortable beds, large balconies, state-of-the-art audiovisual equipment and large bathrooms. The two bedroom bungalows also come with kitchen facilities and outdoor spas. The only downsides are the distance from town and – until the resort is fully landscaped and the rest of the marina is developed – the construction site appearance of the area, although you won't notice this once inside. 8

Potshot Hotel Resort Murat Rd ⓣ08/9949 1200, ⓦwww.potshotresort.com. The town's main motel with restaurants, bottleshop, Internet and a pool. Offers budget motel rooms (4), plusher rooms (5) and apartments (6–7). **Excape Backpackers'** ⓦwww.exmouthbackpackers.com) is also on site and has small but en-suite dorms ($24), en-suite twins and doubles (3) and a basic kitchen.

Cape Range and Ningaloo parks

These parks are adjacent land- and sea-conservation areas on the western edge of the North West Cape: to explore them from Exmouth you need either a vehicle, or to join one of the many tours sold around town. The proximity of the continental shelf is what gives the **Ningaloo Marine Park** such a stunning variety of marine life: over 500 species of fish and 250 species of coral have been recorded here which – among other things – is what attracts migrating whales and whale sharks. Heading north out of town for 14km past the navy base, **Bundegi Beach**, just after the turn-off for Cape Range National Park, and set right below the huge antennae – is nicer than the town beaches; you can see a dark platform of **coral** just a couple of hundred metres offshore, so bring a snorkel; there are glass-bottomed coral-viewing boats here too.

Backtracking to the turn-off for **Cape Range National Park** (DEC fee $10; see box, p.630), you pass a turn for the wreck of the *Mildura*, which clipped the reef in 1907 during a cyclone. There's also a fine **lookout** from Vlamingh Head lighthouse, from where you can see the **Muiron Islands** to the northeast (popular with turtles and diving charters). Moving from here on south it's essentially a coastal drive past several deserted beaches, lagoons, creeks and small campsites ($6.50 per person – book ahead at the park entrance or at the DEC office in Exmouth, 22 Nimitz St ⓣ08/9949 1676). For snorkelling, the reef comes close again at the south point of **Turquoise Bay** where the wind and current tend to drift you north across the bay – stay clear of the sand bar as the currents are stronger here. Oyster Stacks, just to the south, is an alternative snorkelling venue best visited around high tide (ask at the visitors information centre for tide times), but you can pick pretty much any turn-off to enjoy a pristine beach and probably spot a few emus along the way.

DEC's Milyering **visitors centre** (daily 10am–4pm), 52km from Exmouth, is a solar-powered complex with videos and displays on the local ecology, and helpful staff. Another 30km past more bays and campsites brings you to **Yardie Creek**, a steep-walled canyon just a kilometre from the ocean. This is as far south as 2WDs can safely get in the park, but the walk up along the gorge's cliffs is worth the effort. From here 4WDs can continue south through the park past Ningaloo Homestead, enjoying beach camping or picnics all the way to Coral Bay, a drive that takes about a day – leave at low tide and reduce your tyre pressure.

To Dampier and Karratha

Back on the North West Coastal Highway, it's over 500km from Carnarvon to the industrial twin towns of Dampier and Karratha, with just three roadhouses along the way. At *Nanutarra Roadhouse* (daily 6.30am–10pm; rooms ❹) a sealed road heads east via the pristine company towns of **Paraburdoo** and **Tom Price** (70km dirt road or 131km sealed) and on to the fabulous Karijini National Park (see p.694). Further up the highway a road leads north 80km to the cyclone-battered **ONSLOW**, one of the Northwest's original settlements on the mouth of the Ashburton River, but now bypassed by the highway and most travellers too. The new town is east of the old settlement and has a visitors information centre (April–Oct Mon–Sat 9am–4pm, Sun 10am–2pm; ⓣ08/9184 6644) and a few places to stay, including the beachside *Onslow Mackerel Motel* (ⓣ08/9184 6586; ❺) and the *Ocean View Caravan Park* (ⓣ08/9184 6053; powered sites $25, cabins ❸). Shell-laden Sunrise and Sunset beaches are both within walking distance of the town centre. Onslow is also the departure point for trips to the Mackerel Islands, 22km offshore: Thevenard Island is a small coral atoll fringed by good beaches and has accommodation in the form of *Club Thevenard* (ⓣ08/9184 6444, ⓦwww.mackerelislands.com.au), a converted mining camp that has rooms ($110pp including all meals), or beachside bungalows (❼) sleeping up to five. Nearby Direction Island gives the chance for some real solitude as there's only one chalet on the entire island ($2000). You can arrange transport to the islands by boat from Onslow (45min) on Wednesdays and Saturdays for $80.

The two young towns of **DAMPIER** and **KARRATHA** make up the Northwest's biggest industrial conurbation and population centre. Dampier was initially the export facility for Hamersley Iron's iron-ore mines at Tom Price, Paraburdoo and Marandoo, which are linked by a 350-kilometre railway.

Karratha was established in 1968 when space ran out around Dampier and both grew dramatically when the **North West Shelf Natural Gas Project** got underway in the early 1980s. The project collects gas from offshore platforms 135km northwest of Dampier, from where it's piped 1500km to Perth or liquefied locally (LNG) for export to Japan and China. Offshore, on the Montebello Islands, the British experimented with hydrogen bombs in the 1950s, before tests moved down to Maralinga in South Australia.

While useful for shopping centres, car repairs, accommodation and 24-hour fuel at the Caltex, the two towns have precious little to detain the passing traveller. Karratha's **visitors information centre** is on Karratha Road (Mon–Fri 9am–5pm, Sat 9am–noon; ⓣ08/9144 4600, ⓔmanager@tourist.karratha.com), the access road off the Coastal Highway if approaching from the east. Of some interest are the **Aboriginal engravings** on the Burrup Peninsula on the northeastern outskirts of Dampier and several examples can also be seen at Deep Gorge, 1.1km before Hearson's Cove, where there's also good swimming at high tide.

There are several pricey, business-oriented **motels** in Karratha such as the *Best Western* (ⓣ08/9143 9888; ❻–❼) on Warambie Road, or shabbier lodgings at *Karratha Backpackers*, 110 Welland Way (ⓣ08/9144 4904; dorms $22, rooms ❸). If you're on a budget you'd be better at one of the caravan parks like *Pilbara Holiday Park* (ⓣ1800 451 855; powered sites $38, unpowered $28, rooms ❺) on Rosemary Road. **Internet** facilities are available at the hostel, the town library or in the shopping centres.

Roebourne, Cossack and Point Samson

Established in 1864 and once the capital of the Northwest, **ROEBOURNE**, 40km east of Karratha, is the oldest surviving settlement between Port Gregory (near Kalbarri) and Darwin, though these days the town is mainly a centre for the Aboriginal population displaced by the pastoral settlement of the Northwest. The sturdy **Old Gaol** now houses the **visitors information centre** (Mon–Fri 9am–4pm, Sat & Sun 9am–3pm; ⓣ08/9182 1060) and **museum** (same hours; donation). Other nineteenth-century institutional buildings are dotted around the town. There's a caravan park (ⓣ08/9182 1063; powered sites $24, tent sites $14 and rooms ❹) on De Grey Street, at the town's east end, but there are better options in Karratha or Cossack.

In Roebourne, a turn-off north leads a few kilometres to Wickham, Point Samson (see p.690), and passes another turn right to **COSSACK**, the small seaport which begat the town of Roebourne, and well worth a visit. All early settlers to the Northwest came through Cossack – pastoralists, pearlers and prospectors heading for the goldfields of the East Pilbara. The first stone building, the post office, was built in 1884, replacing the original tin and timber buildings that used to be chained to the ground to weather the cyclones. But at the end of the nineteenth century, the inlet by the quay began silting up and the harbour was moved to nearby Point Samson until Port Hedland's became pre-eminent. By the 1940s Cossack was abandoned, its tramlines to Roebourne uprooted for scrap.

What's left of this historic "ghost port" has been finely restored, with interpretive signs filling you in on the origins and history of the place. The **courthouse**, with its museum of the settlement (for opening times ask at the café, next door; donation), is the most impressive building, both inside and out, while the former post and telegraph office is now a small art gallery (same access arrangements as for the courthouse; see above) displaying some fine local work. Cheap rooms are available at the well looked after *Cossack Budget Accommodation*

(ⓣ08/9182 1190; ③) and there's a café, next door in the old police barracks. Perseverance Street leads to the restored nineteenth-century **cemeteries**, both Christian and Asian, where the ages and occupations on the graves show how tough life here once was. The road continues on to **Settler's Beach**, a vast expanse of mudflat at low tide, where the pioneers came ashore before the quay was built. The original cast-iron lighthouse on **Jarman Island** is accessible by tour boat if visitor numbers and tides converge; ask at the café or the backpackers'.

Beyond Robe River Iron's oddly anachronistic company town of **Wickham** (handy for facilities and services, and there's a drive-in cinema), **POINT SAMSON** is a fishing port and a popular retirement and "wintering" centre. East of town is **Honeymoon Cove**, which has good swimming at high tide. Those weary of roadhouse meat-pies will relish the **seafood** with a view at the *Trawlers Tavern* first-floor restaurant (daily 6–10pm), or from the pricier *Moby's Kitchen* takeaway on the ground floor (daily 11am–2pm & 5–9pm). **Places to stay** include deluxe chalets at the *Point Samson Resort*, 56 Samson Rd (ⓣ08/9187 1052; ⑦), which also runs **boat charters**, or the small *Solveig Caravan Park* (ⓣ08/9187 1414; powered sites $25) next to the *Trawlers Tavern*.

Millstream-Chichester National Park

Little more than a scenic drive and an inland oasis of palms and pools along the Fortescue River, the **Millstream–Chichester National Park** (DEC fee $10; see box, p.630), about 100km south of Karratha or Roebourne, is only worth a visit if you're coming or going from the Hamersley Ranges (a long fuel stage). Access from the north breaks off the coastal highway between Roebourne and Whim Creek, passing Pyramid Homestead soon after. Looking back north from the many lookouts in the park, atop the **Chichester Ranges**, you'll see why the homestead is so named; the view across this ancient Pilbara landscape is stirring and timeless.

Just inside the park, **Python Pool** is a striking waterhole backed with black and orange cliffs, where the silence is cut by the shriek of birds. From this photo-worthy point it's a sixty-kilometre run south to **MILLSTREAM**, 150km from Roebourne and 183km from Wittenoom, where an old homestead has been converted into an unusually good **visitors information centre** (daily 8am–5pm; ⓣ08/9184 5144). A display predictably describes the rustic bliss of the Yinjibarndi Aborigines of Ngarrari (Millstream), but omits to mention that they were all cleared out by pastoralists. **Chunderwarriner Pool**, a short walk from the homestead, is a lily-dappled pool surrounded by palm trees. The date palms introduced by Afghan cameleers in the mid-nineteenth century have overrun the indigenous Millstream palm, though this does not detract from the unexpectedly luxuriant scene. Black flying foxes hang from the palm fronds, and Millstream is also a haven for dragonflies and damselflies: 22 species have been recorded here. Walking trails up to 7km long follow the palm- and paperbark-lined Fortescue River to Crossing and Deep Reach pools, where you can **camp**.

Port Hedland and on to Broome

Whichever way you approach **PORT HEDLAND**, 1650km north of Perth via the inland Great Northern Highway, you'll spot the dazzlingly white stockpile of industrial salt at the Dampier Salt Works. It's particularly striking as red iron-ore dust coats everything else in the old town and port; even the pigeons are "enrouged". Port Hedland is set on an island surrounded by mangroves and sludge. If you're travelling by bus, hopping off at Port Hedland will give you a chance to get to Karijini gorges. The detached suburb of South Hedland was the preferred residential area but these days is wracked by alcohol-fuelled brawls and antisocial behaviour.

The visitors information centre (see below) runs a couple of tours if there is enough interest. The town tour sees scant numbers, whilst the ninety-minute tour of the **BHP loading facility** (Mon, Wed, Fri 10.30am; $24) where ships load up with 250,000 tons of iron ore at a time, operates if there are more than eight people booked. In a bid to supply the huge demand in China, the port is busier than ever – exacerbating the dust problems for residents. Should you find yourself here in the wet season, whale- and turtle-watching tours are organized by the visitors information centre, with fishing, diving charters and harbour cruises available all year.

Practicalities

The **visitors information centre**, where long distance **buses** stop, is on Wedge Street (Mon–Fri 9am–4pm, Sat 10am–2pm; ⓣ08/9173 1711, ⓔphtbinfo@norcom.net.au). The **post office** is opposite, as are most banks. Most places to stay are located to the south, out of the dust zone and include motels such as the *Best Western Hospitality Inn* (ⓣ08/9173 1044, ⓦwww.hospitalityinnporthedland.com; ❺) on Webster Street and the *All Seasons* (ⓣ08/9173 1511; ❼–❽), on the highway opposite the airport. There are less expensive options at the *Port Hedland Caravan Park* (ⓣ08/9172 2525; powered sites $28, unpowered $22, cabins ❸–❺) on the highway, and at *Cooke Point Caravan Park* (ⓣ08/9173 1271; powered sites $33, rooms ❻), on Athol Street by the ocean, 8km from town.

Iron-ore dust can't do much for the taste buds, judging by Port Hedland's eateries. Good **restaurants** are confined to the motels. *Katz*, opposite the visitors information centre on Wedge Street, is roadhouse-grade mush. For evening entertainment you'll be pleased to hear that the *Pier Hotel* on the Esplanade no longer has the highest pub death-rate in Australia and – as one local put it – at least you can see a punch coming, which is more than can be said for drinking holes in South Hedland. There are **Internet facilities** at the visitors information centre.

Port Hedland to Broome

The six-hundred-kilometre drive northeast from Port Hedland to Broome is one of world-class boredom, a dreary plain of spinifex and mulga marking the northern edge of the Great Sandy Desert. Halfway to Broome, the *Sandfire Roadhouse* (daily 6am–10pm; powered sites $10 per person, rooms ❹) provides a welcome fuel stop before the 286-kilometre stretch to the *Roebuck Roadhouse* (daily 6am–10pm).

Despite your proximity to the ocean, beach access is only possible at the promisingly named **Eighty Mile Beach**. There's not much to do at the caravan park there (ⓣ08/9176 5941; shop, fuel; cabins ❸), ten corrugated kilometres off the highway, but a drive along the beach at low tide is always exhilarating.

If you're coming south from Broome and heading for Karijini, there's an interesting dirt-road alternative that bypasses Port Hedland. One hundred kilometres after Sandfire turn south onto the sandy Borehole Road, climb into the ranges at Shay Gap and then cross the De Grey River near Muccan station (ask at Sandfire if it's running deep). From here work your way through to **Marble Bar**, 270km south of Sandfire, where you'll find motels and fuel. After Marble Bar, head southwest to Hillside station and then west to Woodstock Community, where you soon rejoin the sealed road heading down to the

The strike that never ended

In 2002 a sculpture was unveiled in Port Hedland's Leak Park to commemorate the Aboriginal stockmen's strike of the 1940s. It acknowledged that Australia's once-legendary pastoral wealth was built on the backs of the Aboriginal people, on whose land and free or cheap labour it depended. Even John Forrest, WA's turn-of-the-twentieth-century premier, pastoralist and former explorer, conceded that "Many of us could not be in the position we are today without native labour on our stations."

By the 1940s Australia was producing a sixth of the world's mutton and a quarter of its wool. In the Northwest, two million sheep grazed vast tracts of meagre land into the dustbowls of today, a marginal enterprise made economical by the low wages for black stockmen – barely $2 a week. The archaic Native Administration Act of the time protected the interests of rural industry by hampering mobility of the Aboriginal population and sanctioning low or nonexistent pay for black workers.

Around this time Don McLeod, a white prospector, encouraged Clancy McKenna and Dooley Binbin to defy their conditions. After several years of painstaking preparation, eight hundred black workers simultaneously walked off their stations in the Port Hedland/Nullagine region on May 1, 1946. Police were instructed to harass the two camps established near Port Hedland and east of Marble Bar, and arrested McKenna and Binbin for communist subversion. Postwar food coupons were withheld, so the strikers returned to traditional ways of feeding and trading amongst themselves. Port Hedland was at this time a small town with an "official" (white) population of just 150 and a "mob" of 400 strikers down the road. Jittery police arrested a visiting mediator, Padre Hodge, for being "within five miles of a congregation of natives", adding further support to the strike, coverage of which was largely censored from the national press.

In 1949 things came to a head, and a station-to-station march was organized, calling all remaining workers to join the strike. Arrest for such defiance was certain, and the strikers cheerfully offered to fill up the jail at Marble Bar and others throughout the Northwest. Only when the Seamen's Union banned the handling of "slave station" wool did the government hastily concede to McLeod's proposals – though they swiftly reneged on the deal. All through the 1950s, McLeod employed and assisted the strikers in mining ventures around Marble Bar, until the big mining companies began taking an interest in the Pilbara's mineral wealth and pushed them off their claims. The strikers never returned to the stations, demonstrating black assertion long before the 1960s civil-rights campaigning in the USA, or the indigenous Australian land claims of the 1970s.

Munjina Roadhouse, 250km from Marble Bar and 42km from Wittenoom. You only save 20km, but it's a lovely, if lonely, drive through the ochre ranges of the East Pilbara.

Inland to the Pilbara

About a thousand kilometres north of Perth are the ancient, mineral-rich highlands of the **Pilbara**, an area which includes Mount Meharry, at 1249m the highest point in WA. The world's richest surface deposits of **iron ore** were developed here in the 1950s by Lang Hancock (see p.671) and rich discoveries continue to be made as private railroads cart the ore to the coast for shipping to Japan's – and lately China's – steel-hungry industries. Surrounding the huge open-cast mine sites are vast and arid pastoral properties, recovering from or surrendering to the early over-grazing, while in the centre of this region sits the grandeur of the **Karijini National Park**, which boasts some of WA's most spectacular natural scenery.

The Great Northern Highway

Apart from the passage through the Hamersley Ranges north of Newman, scenically there's little to commend the **Great Northern Highway**'s 1600-kilometre inland section from Perth to Port Hedland – most people shoot through in two long days. But like the famed Nullarbor, the monotony can have its own fascination as you pass from the wooded farmlands northward into ever more marginal sheep country, until the only viable commodity is the mineral riches below ground. Soon after New Norcia on the still narrow Great Northern Highway you'll encounter **road trains**, the iconic Outback transporters. North of Wubin they're made up into full-length trains up to 55m long, and run around the clock serving the Pilbara and the northwest coastal ports.

Unless you fancy overnighting in often-unhygienic roadside parking areas (ear plugs may help), note that **motels** and **hotels** can be up to 260km apart and are not especially the pick of the crop. Integrity **buses** (ⓣ08/9926 1339; ⓦwww.integritycoachlines.com.au) make the 22-hour journey between Perth and Port Hedland once a week.

Among the half-dozen surviving towns along this inland route, semi-abandoned **CUE**, 650km north of Perth, retains some character from the goldrush era and, if nothing else, is a good place to stretch your legs. The **visitors information centre** on Robinson Road has displays on the town's history and details on nearby sites, including the Aboriginal rock paintings at **Walga Rock**, a few kilometres west of town. A night in the spacious jarrah interior of the *Queen of the Murchison Guest House* (ⓣ08/9963 1625; ❺), on the main road, beats any anodyne motel. The old building still echoes with the ghosts that presaged the town's decline following World War II.

North of Cue the landscape outruns the south's rain-bearing fronts; claypans and scrub replace the trees and bloated or desiccated remains of roadkill proliferate. **MEEKATHARRA**, 115km north of Cue, is a mining and pastoral centre (though this makes it sound grander than it is), with a couple of century-old **hotels** like the *Royal Mail* on the main road (ⓣ08/9981 1148; ❹). The *Auski Inland Motel* (ⓣ08/9981 1433; ❺) is more salubrious, or you can listen to shunting road trains all night at the caravan park behind the Ampol service station. From Meekatharra, it's 180km of dirt east to forlorn Wiluna, then another 600km of dull bitumen south to Kalgoorlie–Boulder, while to the west Carnarvon (itself no paradise) lies at the end of a good seven-hundred-kilometre dirt road. Continuing north from Meekatharra on the Great Northern Highway, you'll see a road sign marking the **26th parallel**, welcoming you to the fabled "Nor'west", and clumps of the spiky spinifex grass which carpet Australia's interior deserts begin to appear.

NEWMAN, 350km north of "Meeka", is a company town built to serve what is now the world's largest open-cut iron-ore mine. Besides stocking up at the Woolworths supermarket, the **mine tours** (Mon–Sat 8.30am & 10.30am; 1hr 30min; long-sleeved shirt, trousers and enclosed shoes necessary; $20), departing from the **visitors information centre** (daily 8am–5pm; ⓣ08/9175 2888, ⓦwww.newman-wa.org) on Newman Drive are the only other reason you'd want to stop here. The tours clearly demonstrate the scale and astonishing simplicity of the operation, as **Mount Whaleback** is gradually turned inside out and shipped to the Far East. The town has a pair of **motels** (❺) with bunkhouses (❸) and two **caravan parks** (dorms $28, en-suite cabins ❹).

Marble Bar

From Newman, a dirt road leads north for 300km through the scenic East Pilbara to **NULLAGINE** and **MARBLE BAR**. The latter (now linked to Port Hedland by a sealed road) was notorious for being Australia's hottest town, in 1923–24 clocking up 160 days over 38°C. This is the sole reason many visitors come to "the Bar", misnamed after a colourful bar of jasper by the Coolingan River 5km south of town. For an overnight stay, there's a **caravan park**, a **motel** (ⓣ08/9176 1166; ④) and the town's famed, windowless *Ironclad Hotel* (ⓣ08/9176 1066; ④) – a good place to get some drinking done or, if you're a "sheila", be stared at.

Karijini National Park

The **Karijini National Park** (DEC fee $10; see box on p.630) is WA's second largest park, with a vast unvisited section to the south, separated by the BHP Yandicoogina mine railway. Apart from the impressive gorges, it's the distinctive blend of crooked, white-trunked snappy gums sprouting from the ox-blood red rock, over a carpet of pale green spinifex, which makes the eastern Pilbara more resplendent than the better-known Kimberley, especially in July and August (also the busiest months). Most of the roads in the park are dirt, but barring cyclone-related storms in late summer, the park remains accessible throughout the year.

The **gorges** themselves cut through the north-facing escarpment of the Hamersley Ranges and can be broadly divided into three groups: those in the east near the visitors information centre; the central "Four Gorges" area; and those in the far west. All offer **spectacular views** as well as short walks through their interiors. Some of these (detailed in the *Pilbara Walks* book available from DEC offices or the visitors information centre; $16) develop into challenging **canyoneering adventures** with immersions or swims through cold pools; not forbidden, but not encouraged without supervision. Take heed of the "Trail Risk [beyond this point]" **warning signs** in some of the gorges, and better still take advantage of adventure tours and their guides' experience. If heading past the signs you must **inform a ranger** of your plans (via the campground host's radios or the visitors information centre) and report your safe return. Accidents occur regularly and fatalities are not uncommon; rangers are rarely seen. Currently the park lacks well-signposted day-walks; you're either gazing down from lookouts or acting out Indiana Jones fantasies far below, although there's talk of long-distance walks being developed in the next few years.

If you're driving through the park, note that **distances** can be deceptive; a full tour of all the gorges can involve a drive of over 250km. The nearest fuel and accommodation points are *Munjina Roadhouse* in the east (120km from the central gorges) or Tom Price in the west (84km). Most travellers without vehicles pick up tours (see box, opposite) in Port Hedland, Tom Price or Karratha.

The visitors centre and the eastern gorges

On the east side of the park, around 36km from the turn-off on the Great Northern Highway is the **visitors centre** (daily 9am–5pm; ⓣ08/9189 8121). Constructed in massive iron plate, it symbolizes both the riches of the Pilbara and, from above, a goanna or *bungarra* lizard of the local Banijima Aboriginal people. Inside, exhibits include some pioneering-era relics and captivating posters of the gorges as well as an "Aboriginal care-of-the-land" display – a subject that is not actually pursued or explained anywhere else in the park. It's the selective view adopted by many national parks to underline their preferred eco-message while leaving visitors clueless as to the bigger picture of Australian indigenous culture.

Tours of the Karijini

Make sure you enquire about the nature of these tours: the two outfits below offer adventurous outings, depending on interest. Note too that if they are responsible, large groups of ten or more should have more than one guide for exploring deep into the gorge interiors.

Lestok Tours (Ⓣ08/9189 2032, Ⓦwww.lestoktours.com.au). Operates out of Tom Price and offers scenic day-tours to all the gorge lookouts for $130, with lunch.

Pilbara Gorge Tours (Ⓣ08/9188 1534, Ⓦwww.pilbaragorgetours.com.au). Another outfit running out of Tom Price, Pilbara has ten-hour day-tours that offer a glimpse at Karijini's highlights for $130, including morning tea and lunch.

Ten kilometres before the visitors information centre you'll have passed the **Dales Gorge** area, which has basic **camping** (toilets; gas barbecues) and is popular with caravanners. Here, the idyllic Fortescue Falls make a great lookout or a place to swim. With half a day to spare, a visit to the falls can be combined with a great six-kilometre walk to Fern Pool and Circular Pool beyond, with plenty of water to cool off in along the way. If you're still feeling energetic you can explore further up or down Dales Gorge.

The Four Gorges area

Just west of the visitors information centre, Bunjima Drive turns to gravel and soon you reach a turn-off leading north to **Kalamina Gorge**, with easy walks along its bed. Though pretty enough, Kalamina can be given a miss if you don't have much time. Back on Bunjima Drive, the next turn-off leads to an impressive lookout onto the tiered amphitheatre of **Joffre Falls** (usually just a trickle). The top of the "falls" can be easily reached and crossed along a spinifex-fringed path.

The dirt road winds on to end at **Knox Gorge** car park with another dramatic lookout platform nearby. Though not signposted, to the left of the notice board a narrow path leads through the spinifex for about a kilometre to a still more dramatic view into Red Gorge 100m below, near its confluence with Knox Gorge (beware of loose edges). Back at the car park, a loose rubbly track leads down into Knox Gorge itself. Just upstream is a pretty pool, while heading downstream through pools or along ledges, the gorge suddenly narrows at a warning sign (allow 30min from the car park). Progress from here on becomes awkward and ends at the exhilarating (to say the least) "Knox Slide", which is itself immediately followed by the potentially more dangerous 5m "Knox Jump" into a shallow pool. From here you can hop into the green waters of Red Gorge. However, the Slide and what follows should not be undertaken without equipment or the know-how to get back up the Slide (using rope ladders); wet suits, other flotation aids and the commitment to swim up Red Gorge through cold pools of a depth up to 300m to Junction Pool are essential (allow an hour from the Slide).

Back on Bunjima Drive, the next turning north passes the privately run *Savannah Campground* (showers and gas barbecues available). The road ends at a car park on the spur between Hancock and Weano gorges. From here it's a short walk to **Oxer's Lookout**, which surveys the dramatic confluence of four gorges. Straight ahead is **Red Gorge**, which runs on into Wittenoom Gorge and Wittenoom itself. Returning from Oxer's Lookout on the Hancock Gorge (south) side of the spur is a more impressive viewing platform, which looks straight down to the mouth of Hancock Gorge as it runs into Junction Pool with its stand of tall cadjiput trees.

Back again from this viewing platform, and on the north side of the spur, steps drop down into **Weano Gorge** that, for most visitors, ends after a fifteen-minute walk along the bed of the gorge at **Handrail Pool**. If you're prepared to get wet and wild you can drop down into the pool and carry on carefully downstream, along narrow chasms and ledges, ending at a point where Weano Gorge falls 25m into Junction Pool. This is an exhilarating but not overly dangerous way of appreciating the full drama of Weano Gorge – best undertaken with the guidance of a tour guide.

From the car park, the descent into **Hancock Gorge** – ending at a metal ladder – is no less impressive, as you enter a magical realm of banded iron walls washed smooth by passing floods. The warning signs start at **Kermit's Pool** (1hr return) from where some very tricky moves and slippery descents lead all the way down to **Junction Pool**. Unless led by tour guides, few visitors get to this point, where the former Miracle Mile used to lead up the cliff into the mouth of Weano Gorge. Tour operators are no longer permitted to go up the cliff (and so complete the true "Miracle Mile") though it must be said that, apart from one exposed step, the ascent of Weano cliff is technically much easier than some moves on the descent into Hancock. Following recent misadventures, the approved way out of Junction Pool is either back up Hancock, or up the freezing pools of Joffre Gorge to the first scree slope on the left, which leads 1.5km cross-country back to the Knox Gorge car park (a long way from Oxer's Lookout area where you may have started). From Junction Pool it's also possible to swim and walk all the way down Red Gorge, past Knox Gorge entrance at the Slide and out of the park into Wittenoom Gorge and eventually into Wittenoom itself (allow a day and, if they ask, don't expect the blessing of the park rangers who toe the state line on Wittenoom; see opposite).

Mount Bruce, the western gorges and Tom Price

From the Four Gorges, Bunjima Drive continues across the roof of the Pilbara to rejoin the sealed road between Tom Price in the west and the Great Northern Highway in the east. Overlooking the junction is **Mount Bruce**, at 1235m WA's second-highest peak and climbable along a six-kilometre path from where you can survey the Marandoo mine.

Depending on where you're going, it's now quite a detour to visit **Hamersley Gorge**, just outside the northwestern corner of the park, 48km west of Wittenoom and about 80km northeast of Tom Price. Should you make the effort you'll find its spa-like pool and unique, acutely folded beds of blue-grey and orange rock: a bit of exploring up- and downstream could easily fill a day here. Just east of the Hamersley Gorge turn-off, the dirt road leading to Wittenoom passes through **Rio Tinto Gorge**, which bears an extraordinary resemblance to a box-canyon film set from 1950s westerns.

Given the pariah status of Wittenoom (see opposite), **TOM PRICE**, on the east side of the park, is the government-approved base for exploring Karijini. The **visitors information centre** (Mon–Fri 9.30am–3.30pm, Sat 9am–noon; ⓣ08/9188 1112, ⓦwww.tompricewa.com.au) on Central Road has **Internet access** and organizes daily ninety-minute **tours** ($19) of Hamersley Iron's mine, time of departure dependent on when, and how many, people turn up. Accommodation is limited to the *Tom Price Hotel Motel* (ⓣ08/9189 1101; ❺) on Central Road or the *Tourist Park* (ⓣ08/9189 1515) below Mount Nameless on the Nanutarra Road (powered sites $27, unpowered $22, backpacker dorms $29, en-suite cabins ❹). Although it's not on the bus route, the town has all the services you'd expect, including the *Millstream Café* near the **supermarket**.

Wittenoom and Wittenoom Gorge

At each end of **WITTENOOM**, warning signs proclaim the possible health hazard incurred by setting foot in the town as a result of the asbestos mining carried out here up to 1966. It's estimated that one in ten ex-miners and former inhabitants have died of diseases associated with inhaling asbestos dust, so nowadays, for legal reasons, the sole public call-box is situated just outside the town's limits – to be on the safe side.

In its natural state **blue asbestos** (or crocidolite) is a harmless and unusual fibrous mineral, readily found in the Yampire and upper Wittenoom gorges; it's only the **dust** produced during milling operations that can be lethal. Unfortunately, tailings from the mill were once used to make "sandpits" for the town's children, leaving all residents at the time susceptible to a virulent form of lung cancer. These days, resurfacing has long been completed and, unless you're burrowing into what's left of the tailings in Wittenoom Gorge, the town's air is no more harmful than most urban centres or indeed, active open-cut mines. Nevertheless the WA government has long been committed to shutting down Wittenoom, and have even deleted it from some maps and other information sources.

Partly because of its tragic history and partly due to its spectacular setting, the remainder of the town possesses an intangible ambience like few other places in WA. In the 1950s it was the biggest settlement in the Northwest – today the empty lots and roaming kangaroos speak of a ghost town not prepared to die just yet.

Once a week the Perth to Port Hedland **bus** stops at the Wittenoom visitors information centre. As far as services in town go, there's a **post office** at the Gem Shop (daily 8am–5pm; ⓣ08/9189 7096) on Sixth Avenue, which also dispenses basic groceries as well as a highly recommended **sketch map** of the national park. If you're planning to stay a few days bring what you need.

There are two **places to stay** in Wittenoom, neither fancy but both cheap. *Wittenoom Holiday Homes* (ⓣ08/9189 7096; enquire at the Gem Shop) have furnished three-bedroom houses for rent ($25 per person) or there's the charmingly basic *Wittenoom Guest House* (ⓣ08/9189 7060; dorms $15, rooms ❷), the green bungalow by the "church" with camping in the well-kept garden or car park. The *Guest House* is the sort of place you'll come for a night, but be so relaxed you might find yourself staying a week.

Wittenoom itself is at the mouth of **Wittenoom Gorge**, with Cathedral Pool on the left and Town Pool on the right, both around 6km south of town. At the end of the sealed road 5km further on are the foundations of the so-called Settlement, the former asbestos mining offices razed in 2003 as part of the clean-up operation; the same fate has befallen the ageing mill nearby, which may still be surrounded by the potentially lethal blue-grey tailings.

From the Settlement, it's possible to trek up to the impressive entrance of **Red Gorge** (2hr), and then walk and swim for another hour or so to **Junction Pool** (see opposite); all in all a hard day's adventuring.

Broome and around

"Slip into Broometime" used to be a well-worn local aphorism that still captures the tropical charm of **BROOME**, an ever more popular and – for the Northwest – uncharacteristically classy town with a population of fifteen thousand, which clings to a peninsula hanging over Roebuck Bay. William Dampier, the English buccaneer-explorer, passed through in 1699 while on the run from an irate Spanish flotilla, and 160 years later the local Aborigines repelled an early fleet of prospective pastoralists. Easily collected pearl shell heaped along Eighty Mile Beach led to the northwestern "**Pearl Rush**" of the 1880s, initially enabled by enslaved Aborigines. Later indentured workers from Asia sought the shell in ever-greater depths below the waves, boosted by the invention of hard-hat diving apparatus. Broome originated as a camp on sheltered Roebuck Bay where the pearl luggers "laid up" during the cyclone

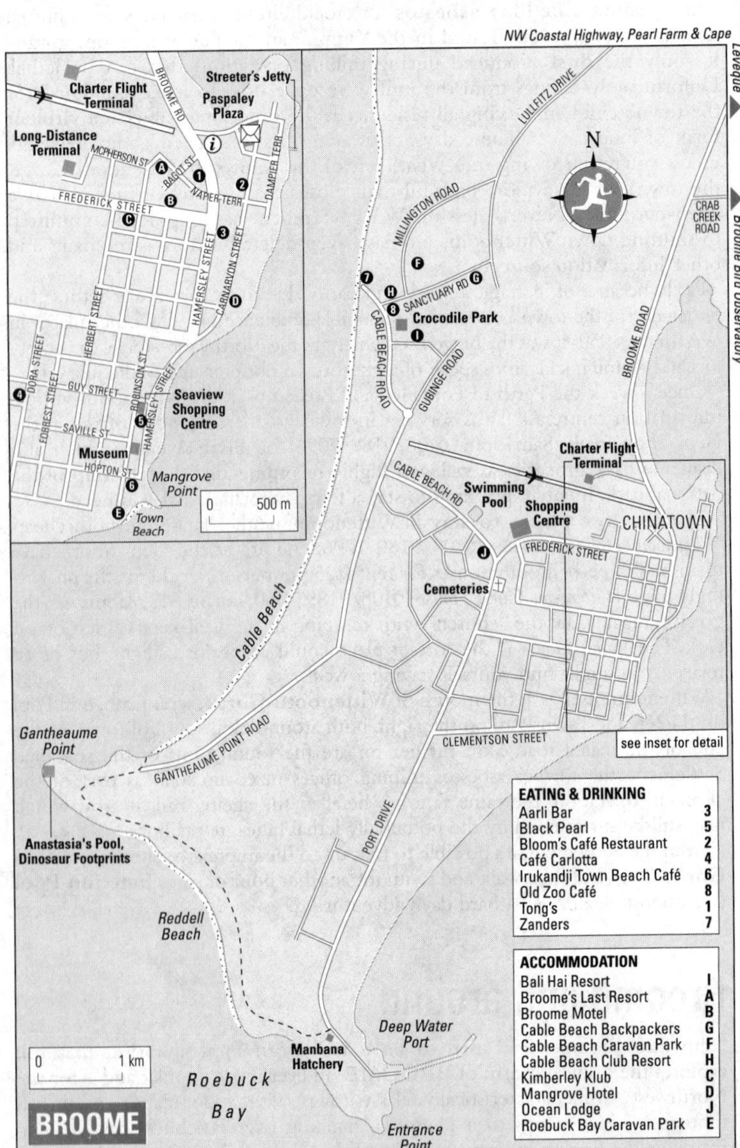

season. After a violent and raucous beginning common to many frontier towns of that era (see Borroloola, p.544), the port finally achieved prosperity which lasted until the outbreak of World War I.

It was actually the nacre-lined oyster shells, or **mother-of-pearl**, rather than extremely rare pearls themselves, which brought fortune to the town. By 1910, eighty percent of the world's pearl shell – used in the manufacture of buttons and cutlery handles amongst other things – came from Broome, by which time a rich ethnic mix and a rigidly racially stratified "plantation" society had developed. "Chinatown" teemed with riotous Kupangers, Filipinos and "Malays" (Southeast Asians) crewing for the predominantly Japanese divers – a boiling pot collectively termed "Saltwater Cowboys" in a well-known album by local musicians, the Pigram Brothers. Each season one in five divers died, several more became paralyzed and, as Broome's cemeteries steadily filled, only one shell in five thousand produced a perfect example of the silvery pearls unique to this area – a fascinating story vividly told in John Bailey's book *The White Divers of Broome*.

Stagnation followed both world wars, after which the wily Japanese – masters in the secret art of pearl culturing – returned and invested in the pearl-farming ventures around Broome's well-suited coastal habitat. Things improved with the sealing of the coastal highway from Perth in the early 1980s and the philanthropic interest of the English businessman Alistair McAlpine, who fell for Broome and subsequently kicked off its latter-day reinvention. He led the old town's tasteful development and refurbishment that capitalized on its oriental and pearling mystique. This rich history is enhanced by the sweeping expanse of **Cable Beach**, **Gantheaume Point**'s paprika-red outcrops and the Indian Ocean's breathtaking shade of turquoise. New beach resorts and housing developments are springing up and, combined with the nearby Kimberley's "frontier" appeal, both aspiring lotus-eaters and visitors alike continue to be drawn in: Broome's prosperity looks set to continue.

Arrival and information

Greyhound **buses** stop at Carnarvon Road, where minibuses and taxis meet arrivals. The interstate **airport terminal** on McPherson Street is central, being less than 1km west of Chinatown and a short walk to the two main backpackers' and a motel. The clued-up staff at the **visitors information centre** (Mon–Fri 8am–5pm, Sat & Sun 8.30am–4pm; ⓣ08/9192 2222, ⓦwww.broomevisitorcentre.com.au) hand out local guides and town maps to help you find your way around the initially confusing layout of Broome. The town's **bus service** (ⓦwww.broomebus.com.au; $3 per ride, Multirider tickets from $14 for 5 rides) runs between Chinatown and the end of Cable Beach Road from around 7am to 6pm, via most of Broome's accommodation centres. It's now supplemented by the Nightrider service (ⓦwww.broomenightrider.com) that runs nightly from 6.30pm until just after midnight from April to December ($3.50 per ride, Night Pass $6). For taxis and car, scooter and bike rentals, see "Listings".

Accommodation

Most of the **hotels** are in the southern part of town with the **backpackers'** located in and around Chinatown. Self-contained apartments are available in resort compounds just off Cable Beach Road. These **resorts** can be good value if there's a group of you, though some don't have restaurants or bars. Prices are relatively expensive up here, but if you're stuck down south in winter and want to make a visit, it's possible to pick up package holidays to Broome aimed at the domestic market; ask at any travel agent. The southern winter is high season here, at which time you'll be advised to book ahead, although many Europeans escaping their winter blues turn up in Broome's hot and humid season when they can expect prices lower than those listed below. There are six main **caravan parks** in town, the best of which are listed below.

Hotels and resorts

Bali Hai Resort 6 Murray Rd, Cable Beach ⓣ08/9191 3100 or 1800 807 061, ⓦwww.balihairesort.com. Sumptuous and spacious luxury self-catering studios and two-bedroom apartments, furnished Balinese-style with outdoor shower and patio, all set around a shady pool. Ten percent reduction for three nights or more. ⑧

Broome Motel Frederick St ⓣ08/9192 7775, ⓦwww.broomemotel.com.au. Set among tropical herbage, this is Broome's best-value motel, with comfortable rooms and a small pool. A short walk from the airport and Chinatown; good summertime reductions. ⑤

Cable Beach Club Resort Cable Beach Rd ⓣ08/9192 0400, ⓦwww.cablebeachclub.com. Established by Alistair McAlpine (see p.699) and now owned by the Hawaiian group, this is one of Broome's best places to stay with large, elegant rooms and suites ($969–1566), and some older bungalows. Rooms are set in attractive Oriental-style gardens and have verandas, some of which enjoy ocean views. Service is friendly and attentive and there are a couple of good restaurants and two pools. ⑧

Mangrove Hotel Carnarvon St ⓣ08/9192 1303 or 1800 094 818, ⓦwww.mangrovehotel.com.au. Very comfortable hotel, 5min from Chinatown and in a great position on a rise overlooking Roebuck Bay. The spacious terrace incorporating the *Tides* garden restaurant is a popular spot to view the "Staircase to the Moon"; see opposite. ⑦

Ocean Lodge Cnr of Frederick St and Cable Beach Rd ⓣ08/9192 7700 or 1800 600 603, ⓦwww.oceanlodge.com.au. An average motel, part of the *Budget* chain, located halfway between Cable Beach and Chinatown, opposite the town pool and bus stop, and near the shopping centre. Rooms are in several blocks, all s/c and including stoves. Set around a central pool. ⑤

Backpackers' and caravan parks

Broome's Last Resort Bagot St ⓣ08/9193 5000, ⓦwww.broomeslastresort.com.au. Broome's original purpose-built backpackers' – close to a cinema and the visitors information centre – looks a bit cramped these days. There's a small landscaped pool, bar, bikes and coin-operated a/c. Dorms from $19, rooms ③

Cable Beach Backpackers End of Sanctuary Rd ⓣ08/9193 5511 or 1800 655 011, ⓦwww.cablebeachbackpackers.com. Laid-back and spacious place away from the sometimes noisy central Broome alternatives. Has a pool, hammocks, bar, and big kitchen, as well as town shuttle bus and bus/airport pick-ups. Dorms ($20) are fanned and mostly four-bed, with a few doubles. ③

Cable Beach Caravan Park Millington Rd ⓣ08/9192 2066. One of Cable Beach's three caravan parks, 2km from the beach with self-catering cabins (⑤) and powered sites ($30).

Kimberley Klub Frederick St ⓣ08/9192 3233 or 1800 004 345, ⓦwww.kimberleyklub.com. One of the best-designed backpackers' around: a purpose-built mini-resort that ticks all the boxes, although some dorms suffer from their proximity to late-night chatterboxes (dorms near the laundry are quieter). Roomy and breezy layout with volleyball, pool, bar, Internet access and fans, with coin-operated a/c in the six-bed dorms and rooms. Ten-bed dorms from $25, rooms ④

Roebuck Bay Caravan Park 91 Walcott St ⓣ08/9192 1366, ⓔroebuckbaycp@broomewn.com.au. The best-located caravan park in town, right next to the small beach and Seaview Shopping Centre. From April to September, camping is available in the adjacent mango field with kitchen, on-site vans (③), tent sites $11, powered sites $25–30.

The town and around

Broome originally flourished around the old port area known as **Chinatown**, a misnomer as people from several, mostly Asian, cultures once lived here. This old quarter has seen much reconstruction of original buildings with street signs in several languages and payphones topped with jaunty pagoda roofs. Trendy boutiques and cafés occupy most of the buildings; Sun Pictures (see "Nightlife and events") on Carnarvon Street opened in 1916, which makes it as old as

Hollywood itself. During the daytime you can take a tour (10.30am & 1pm; $5) around the virtually unchanged interior and see photographs showing the segregated seating order of the bad old days. At the end of the street is the **post office** and the Paspaley Plaza **shopping centre** (supermarket open till midnight). A right turn leads to the renovated Streeter's Jetty, which runs into the mangroves off the end of Dampier Terrace. Conscious of the street's heritage, several **pearl dealers** have shops here, where you'll also find **Pearl Luggers** (daily 9am–5pm), a free exposition of Broome's pearling heritage, with a couple of dry-docked luggers and informative one-hour tours (3 daily; $18.50). **Johnny Chi Lane** runs between Dampier and Carnarvon streets; like much of Chinatown, these days it's mostly full of boutiques and the odd art gallery, though historical plaques fill you in on the events which begat Broome right where you stand, over 120 years ago.

Back down Napier Terrace past the Male Oval, a left onto Hamersley Street at the Shell garage takes you past the 1888 telegraph office and to the **courthouse** on the corner of Frederick Street, where there are Sunday-morning **markets** – a good place to pick up prints of Broome's photogenic environs. Hamersley Street leads to what was the rich end of the old town, where masters and merchants once lived in splendid, airy bungalows such as **Captain Gregory's House**, now *Matso's Brewery* near the junction with Carnarvon Street. Next door, *Matso's Store* (daily 10am–5pm) displays local artwork and is a trendy and shady spot for an alfresco lunch.

Following the road round, along the edge of Roebuck Bay, you'll come to the former Customs House which holds the local **museum** (June–Oct Mon–Fri 10am–4pm, Sat & Sun 10am–1pm; Nov–May daily 10am–1pm; $3). Naturally focusing on the town's maritime traditions, and with a pleasing "junk shop" appearance, it could easily occupy an hour or two and really deserves a better venue. Round the back of the museum, the old **Pioneer Cemetery** overlooks **Town Beach**, the nearest to the town centre. From the jetty, very low tides reveal a lot of mud and the remains of Dutch seaplanes bombed by the Japanese in 1942. This is also one vantage point for observing the "**Staircase to the Moon**", the somewhat overrated reflections of the full moon rising over the

△ A seaplane trip to Horizontal Waterfall

Tours around Broome

Although just hanging out in Broome can be satisfying, the resort's growing popularity means that there's no shortage of things to do. Broome Day Tours (☎08/9192 1068) organize four-and-a-half-hour historic tours around the town (daily; $90), as do Pearl Town Tours (daily 8.15am; ☎08/9192 6948; $90), which end with a free cocktail at *Matso's Brewery*. Kujurta Buru Aboriginal Tours offer fun and informative three-hour cultural tours around Broome (☎08/9192 2660; $66). Four outfits: Ships of the Desert, Broome Camel Safaris, Cable Beach Camel Safaris and Red Sun Camels (all bookable via the visitors information centre) offer sunset camel rides along Cable Beach (from $40). At the other end of the beach, you can go sea-kayaking around Gantheaume Point with Broome Adventure Company (April–Nov up to twice daily; ☎1300 665 888, Ⓦwww.broomeadventurecompany.com.au; $65). Tours are undemanding, using stable "sit-on-top" kayaks with no experience required.

There are few better places to watch the sunset than at sea on a traditional craft such as the *Intombi* (☎08/9192 7321; 2pm–dusk, fully licensed bar: $99) or the *Pindan*, a schooner built by its skipper (☎08/9192 3836; $65; plus snacks, BYO alcohol 3pm–dusk). If none of that takes your fancy there are jaunts on Harley trikes, helicopters, hovercraft, motorized hang-gliders and hot-air balloons, and that's just "h": the full alphabet of activities is available at the visitors information centre.

Broome is well-positioned for scenic flights across the spectacular west Kimberley coast, which is otherwise only accessible by sea (and even then with difficulty due to the extreme tides). The Buccaneer Archipelago and the extraordinary spectacle of the Horizontal Waterfall, where the huge tides tear back and forth through narrow openings into sea-flooded valleys, are the highlights. Horizontal Falls Adventure Tours (☎08/9192 2885, Ⓦwww.horizontalfalls.com.au; $495) offer half-day flights in a high-wing seaplane that lands in Turtle Bay from where a small powerboat will take you through the lesser rapids – a rare chance to see this far-flung corner of Australia from the air and sea.

Further afield

Luxury cruise boats pass along the convoluted inlets of the north Kimberley coast, but with some craft featuring à la carte menus and helidecks for incoming guests, prices will be as spectacular as the coastline. One-day bus excursions include visits to Windjana Gorge and Tunnel Creek ($225) or Geikie Gorge ($260) with Australian Pinnacle Tours (☎08/9192 8080, Ⓦwww.pinnacletours.com.au). Their buses are thoughtfully equipped with movies as it's a hefty 800km trip. Or you can do all three places in two days with Kimberley Wild Expeditions (☎08/9193 7778, Ⓦwww.kimberleywild.com; from $429). Both the above outfits also do one- to three-day visits up to Cape Leveque, from $239 for the 470km round trip.

Between Broome and Kununurra, interstate buses run overnight so you won't see much of the Kimberley countryside – all the more reason to take an eastbound tour to Kununurra along the unsealed Gibb River Road (GRR; see p.714) instead. Outfits that are based in, or pass through Broome include Kimberley Wild (see above), who offer a four-day Kimberley Gorges Tour between April and November which takes in the GRR from $849. Between May and October, All Terrain Safaris (☎1800 633 456, Ⓦwww.allterrainsafaris.com.au) run seven- to twelve-day camping tours right across the GRR, including the remote Mitchell Plateau as well as the Bungles, costing around $150 a day (longer tours continue to Darwin). Australian Adventure Travel (☎1800 621 625, Ⓦwww.safaris.net.au) do a five-day GRR trip in a big, comfy bus, ending up in Kununurra, for $965.

mud flats, which occur at very low tides a few nights a month between March and October. You can observe the same phenomenon at many places along the northwestern coast such as Port Hedland or Cossack, but Broome capitalizes on it with nightly markets. Dates and precise times can be obtained from the visitors information centre or at your accommodation.

Broome Port, Gantheaume Point and Cable Beach

The outskirts of Broome offer a number of interesting attractions, and a full day could be spent cycling along the following route, which ends at Cable Beach, 6km from town on the ocean side of the peninsula. Alternatively you can take the bus or rent a car, or better still, a scooter.

Heading down Frederick Street past the main Broome Boulevard **shopping centre** (8am–8pm) and the Cable Beach turning, you'll get to Broome's old **cemeteries**, which filled quickly during the pearling years. The Japanese section's enigmatic headstones (refurbished by a philanthropic countryman) testify to the hundreds of lives lost in the hazardous collection of mother-of-pearl, mostly due to "the bends", although the 1908 cyclone took the lives of over 150 men – five percent of the workforce at that time. The Chinese cemetery next door is less well cared for, and the Muslim and Aboriginal graveyards at the back are barely distinguishable, though the latter group's enslavement prior to the hard-hat era contributed greatly to Broome's early pearling boom. It's a story touched on at **Manbana aquaculture hatchery** (tours April–Sept Mon–Sat 10am & 1.30pm; $19; ⓣ08/9192 3844), on Murakami Road near the end of Port Drive. The trochus shell hatchery (real shell buttons are back in vogue) has coral viewing aquariums and barramundi feeding, and also gives an insight into the maritime cultures of the local Yawuru and Bardi people, who for millennia traded pearl shell right across Australia, as far away as current-day NSW.

The turn off Port Drive continues to **Reddell Beach** on the Roebuck Bay side of the peninsula. Tides permitting, you can walk right along the shore, past the outcrops weathered by cyclones, to **Gantheaume Point**, where the dark red sandstone formations contrast sharply with the pearly white expanse of Cable Beach and pastel blue ocean stretching northwards. The old **lighthouse** is now a beacon, but the pool built by the former keeper for his disabled wife, Anastasia, remains among the tidal rocks. A cast of some 120-million-year-old **dinosaur footprints** is set in the rocks – the originals are out to sea and visible at very low tides. In 1996 more dinosaur footprints were found on Aboriginal land north of Cable Beach, but were hewn from the rock by international fossil thieves.

Named after the nineteenth-century telegraph cable which came ashore here, **Cable Beach** extends for an immaculate 22km north of Gantheaume Point to Willie Creek. Regular 2WD cars can get to the beach just before Gantheaume Point (where sea-kayaking and some cruises commence – see "Tours" box, opposite) – to drive along the beach itself a 4WD is recommended. To the north, below *Zanders* restaurant is the "children's" part of the beach (ie no cars, dogs or nudity). Windsurfers and sailboards are available on the beach during the season, and lately they've taken to corralling swimmers into a 100m band of shore patrolled by a lifeguard. This is very comforting, but restrictive enough to drive you into the nude-sunbathing area north of the rocks where cars (ideally 4WD) are also allowed, all the way up to Willie Creek.

Broome is regarded as the westernmost limit of saltwater **crocodiles**; there's the odd sighting at the end of the Wet. The **Broome Crocodile Park** (April–Oct Mon–Sat 11am–5pm, Sun 2–5pm; guided feeding tours at 11am & 4.15pm; $15), on Cable Beach Road, can show you scores of these gruesome beasts at close quarters, including one-eyed Willie who was shot and eventually trapped in Willie Creek a few years ago.

The rich mudflats around Roebuck Bay are visited by thousands of migratory shore birds in late March – a third of Australia's species have been seen here. The **Broome Bird Observatory** (ⓣ08/9193 5600, ⓦwww.broomebirdobservatory.com; day entry $5, 1hr to full-day tours from $15 to $120, times dependent on tides and season) is 25km north from town, with the last 15km accessible only by 4WD – call in advance to arrange a pick-up from Broome ($35 return). The Observatory welcomes day- and overnight visitors and accommodation includes camping ($11 per person), bunks from $40 and self-contained chalets (❹).

Eating and entertainment

Gastronomically, Broome might almost be a trendy suburb of Perth; the cafés and restaurants are the best selection for a thousand kilometres or more, so make the most of it. Contrary to expectations, but as in metropolitan Australia, the town's best cuisine tends to be Mediterranean rather than Oriental.

Aarli Bar Hamersley St, cnr of Frederick St. Wood-fired pizzas and tapas, with fresh fish the speciality; check out the blackboard. Threadfin salmon, mangrove jack and, if you're lucky, coral trout make a change from the ubiquitous barramundi. Outdoor seating available. Daily 8am–late.

Black Pearl Seaview Shopping Centre, 63 Robinson St ⓣ08/9192 1779; BYO. Pleasant and airy restaurant with outdoor seating that has views across to the sea. The European cuisine and seafood are reasonably priced; the filet mignon is especially recommended. Daily 7am–9pm.

Bloom's Café Restaurant Carnarvon St, Chinatown ⓣ08/9192 7606. Popular café with a fan-cooled jarrah interior, sandwiches, meals, and the best big breakfast in town. Daily 7.30am–late.

Café Carlotta Jones Place off Dora St, opposite Saville St; BYO. With wood-fired pizzas, risotto and pasta, this is one of Broome's most popular eateries, so book ahead. Daily except Sun 5.30pm–late.

Irukandji Town Beach Café Town Beach, south end of Hamersley St. Popular spot for a relaxing and tasty Sun morning breakfast. Daily 8am–11.30am, noon–2pm & 6pm–late.

Old Zoo Café Challenor Drive, behind the Crocodile Park, Cable Beach. Far and away your best bet out on Cable Beach. Among the many mouthwatering dishes, the steak with prawn sauce is the one to go for. 7am–late.

Tong's Napier Terrace. May have missed out on the McAlpine makeover but said to be the best Chinese in town. Wed–Mon 5.30–9.30pm.

Zanders Cable Beach ⓣ08/9193 5090, ⓦwww.zanders.com.au. An open, airy and modern place with ocean views, serving a range of European and seafood dishes, with good pizzas. Daily 8am–late.

Nightlife and events

Broome's lively **pub** is the *Roebuck Bay Hotel* on Napier Terrace, with two bars, a club (*Oasis*) and an eatery (*Cheffy's*), live entertainment and happy hours. The least rough of the two bars is the *Pearlers' Rest*. The *Divers' Camp Tavern* at Cable Beach is another popular spot and sometimes stages bands. The only other **nightclub** is the *Nippon Inn* on Dampier Terrace which draws in the backpackers. If you prefer **real ale** to tinned lager, pay a visit to the Broome Brewery at *Matso's Store and Brewery* at the end of Hamersley Street, where all sorts of local fermentations await you.

Sun Pictures' **walk-in cinema** in Chinatown is a uniquely "Broomtime experience": watch the latest movies while mosquitoes nibble your ankles and the odd light aircraft comes in low across the screen. The town also has a conventional indoor twin-screen on the corner of Weld Street behind *McDonalds*.

The visitors information centre has information on various events, such as the **Broome Arts and Music Festival** (**BAMF**; usually held between April and June). However, the big one is the week-long **Shinju Matsuri** in August or September, which attracts people from all over the country. The town celebrates its ethnic diversity, and the pearl that created it, finishing up with a huge fireworks display. Broome can get packed out for the Shinju, so unless you want to end up camping at the Bird Observatory, book your accommodation in advance. Other notable events include the races, which are held in May and June. Exact dates for all events and festivals can be found at the visitors information centre.

Listings

Bicycle and scooter rental Broome Cycles is next to the Shell garage in Chinatown and also outside the zoo on Cable Beach; bike rental costs from $24 per day. Broome Car Rentals (see below) also hire scooters from $35 a day. Driver's licence required.
Bookshop Kimberley's Books on Napier Terrace in Chinatown, near the *Roebuck Bay Hotel*, and Woody's Book Exchange in Johnny Chi Lane.
Buses Greyhound Australia (ⓣ13 14 99 or 08/9192 7578, ⓦwww.greyhound.com.au) buses stop at Broome daily on its Darwin to Perth run. Book at the visitors information centre.
Car rental Besides the big names with offices at the airport (and who may offer relocation deals), Broome Discount Hire (ⓣ08/9192 3100) at the airport delivers cars to your accommodation from $50 a day with 75km free mileage. Broome Car Rentals (ⓣ08/9192 2110, ⓦwww.broomebroome.com.au), next to the Shell on Hamersley St, does local runabouts with 50km free from $58 a day, up to full-size 4WD Land Cruisers for Cape Leveque or the Kimberley from $148.
Hospital Robinson St ⓣ08/9194 2222.
Internet Telecentre in Chinatown at 40 Dampier Terrace; Internet Café, next to *McDonalds* on Hamersley St, and most of the hostels.
Police ⓣ08/9194 0200.
Taxis ⓣ08/9192 1133 or 1800 880 330.

Willie Creek Pearl Farm

About 10km east of Broome, almost opposite the turn-off south for the Bird Observatory, a road leads north to the Aboriginal lands of the Dampier Peninsula, ending at Cape Leveque (see p.706). Thirty-eight kilometres north from Broome a turn-off from this road leads to the **Willie Creek Pearl Farm** (ⓣ08/9193 6000, ⓦwww.williecreekpearls.com.au; several tours daily with courtesy pick-ups in town $65, self-drive option $32.50, pre-booking essential), a popular day-tour from Broome. With the main showroom based on the banks of Willie Creek, most of the operation, which involves regularly cleaning and turning a quarter of a million shells by hand, has now moved offshore for security reasons. On arrival you get a very comprehensive presentation of the entire pearl-farming process, information that was given up by the Japanese only half a century ago. A boat tour in the creek follows, which inspects racks of seeded oysters that hang for two years at a time, building up layers of pearlescent nacre as they feed off the tidal nutrients. This process takes half the normal time, and these local oysters are very large, making Willie Creek pearls among the finest and biggest in the world, a success story that has kick-started other pearling ventures all the way from Shark Bay to Darwin.

Exploring the Dampier Peninsula

Access to the isolated **beaches** on the southwest side of the Dampier Peninsula and north of Broome is possible off the Cape Leveque road, about 10km north of the junction with the sealed highway or 20km from Broome. Some day-tours come here from Broome and camping is possible, although you ought to be well prepared as there are no facilities whatsoever. The first of the beaches is **Barred Creek**, reached via a **sandy section** where most 2WDs get stuck. A few kilometres north up the coast is **Quondong Point**, overlooking the low red cliffs and a white rocky beach below. **Price Point**, after another 14km, is considered the pick of the points. Continue a few hundred metres past its signed turn-off and you'll find a ramp giving easy access to the beach and numerous coves below. From here it's around 40km back to the Cape Leveque road or 60km back to Broome.

Unless you don't mind giving your car a hammering, your best bet is to arm yourself with a solidly built 4WD rental, or to join a tour for the corrugated two-hundred-kilometre track all the way to **Cape Leveque**. With miles of pristine and **deserted beaches** and basic accommodation, this area is slowly opening up to low-key ecotourism. Note that if visiting any of the Aboriginal communities on the Cape you must **book your accommodation** in advance; free camping is not allowed and you should not wander uninvited into residential areas.

The Aboriginal community of **Beagle Bay** (fuel and store Mon–Fri; ⓣ08/9192 4913; entry $5) is 125km from Broome. The highlight here is the **Sacred Heart Church**, built by German missionaries in 1918, a beautiful building with an unusual altar decorated with mother-of-pearl. After Beagle Bay the track to Cape Leveque gets narrower and sandier and you'll reach the turn-off leading after 33km to **Middle Lagoon** (no fuel; ⓣ08/9192 4002, ⓦwww.ibizwa.com/natureshideaway; entry $8), a lovely white-sand cove with camping, beach shelters (❷), partially equipped four-bed cabins (❺) and a six-bed self-contained cabin (❻). The bay offers sheltered swimming and good snorkelling. Up the road another 20km or so is the community of **Lombadina/Djarindjin** (no camping; fuel Mon–Fri; ⓣ08/9192 4936, ⓦwww.lombadina.com; entry $5), where you'll find well-equipped backpacker-style accommodation (❷), four-bed self-contained units (❺) and 4WD access to the beach over banks of soft sand (follow the signs). The wide shallow bay before you is again ideal for safe swimming.

A stay at the very popular *Kooljaman Resort* right at the tip of **Cape Leveque** (ⓣ08/9192 4970, ⓦwww.kooljaman.com.au; powered campsites $37, cabins ❺, safari tents ❼) is the reason why you've endured the last 211km. You'll find *Dinkas* **restaurant** and a small kiosk selling basic provisions. Situated right on the "sunrise" beach, the paperbark **cabins** and **beach shelters** (basically shade, a windbreak and a barbecue) are the pick of the accommodation – the fancier four-berth tents are up the hill. Come well-prepared however, as despite the prices, *Kooljaman* is no upmarket wilderness experience.

From *Kooljaman* you can rent a dinghy, try fishing, mud-crabbing, fishing and bushtucker **tours** and cruises to the old mission buildings on nearby Sunday Island. Ask at the resort for information.

The Kimberley

A region of tablelands, tropical woodland, big rivers and gorges about the size of Poland, the **Kimberley** is often romantically described as Australia's last frontier. It's a wilderness dotted with dormant or barely viable cattle stations, isolated Aboriginal communities and, increasingly, vast tracts of Aboriginal land, all capped with a ragged, tide-swept coastline inhabited chiefly by crocodiles, secluded pearling operations and a couple of exclusive, fly-in getaways.

With the difficulty of running cattle in a region wracked by floods or bushfires and subject to land claims, many stations have turned to tourism, though even this is not without its setbacks; one week of cyclonic rain washed out two properties in early 2002, and in 2005 winds of 280kph devastated *Faraway Bay* (see p.715) on the north coast. Even the full exploitation of minerals known to exist on the region's Mitchell plateau is made uneconomical by the climate and location; this alone indicates the Kimberley's remoteness.

The region holds many examples of the enigmatic Wandjina-style rock paintings, which depict rows of mouthless beings with owl-like heads and the slender Bradshaw figures, thought to be much older. When the dry season sets

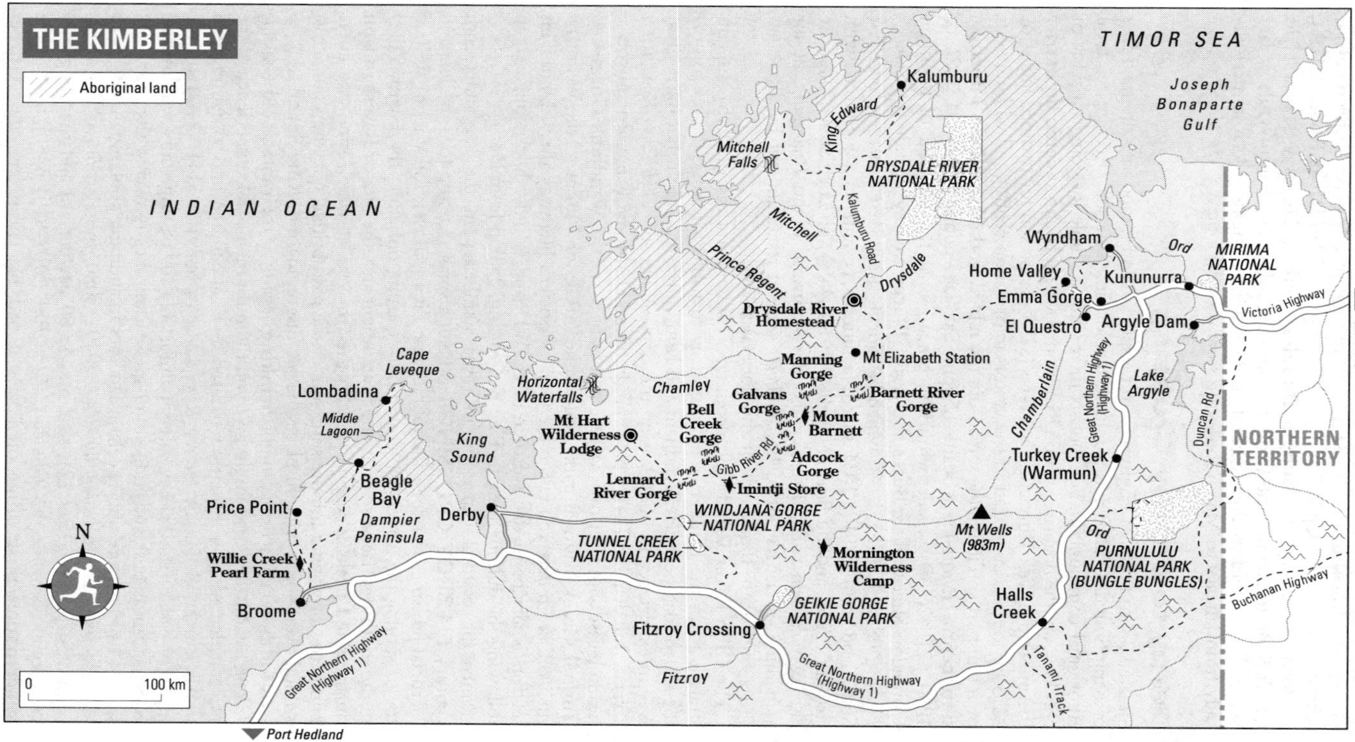

THE KIMBERLEY

Aboriginal land

TIMOR SEA

Joseph Bonaparte Gulf

INDIAN OCEAN

Katherine

NORTHERN TERRITORY

MIRIMA NATIONAL PARK

Victoria Highway

Buchanan Highway

Duncan Rd

Ord

Kununurra

Argyle Dam

Lake Argyle

Wyndham

Home Valley

Emma Gorge

El Questro

Great Northern Highway (Highway 1)

Chamberlain

Turkey Creek (Warmun)

PURNULULU NATIONAL PARK (BUNGLE BUNGLES)

Tanami Track

Halls Creek

Mt Wells (983m)

Kalumburu

DRYSDALE RIVER NATIONAL PARK

Drysdale

Kalumburu Road

King Edward

Mitchell Falls

Mitchell

Prince Regent

Drysdale River Homestead

Mt Elizabeth Station

Barnett River Gorge

Manning Gorge

Mount Barnett

Galvans Gorge

Adcock Gorge

Gibb River Rd

Imintji Store

Mornington Wilderness Camp

GEIKIE GORGE NATIONAL PARK

Great Northern Highway (Highway 1)

Fitzroy Crossing

Fitzroy

Chamley

Bell Creek Gorge

WINDJANA GORGE NATIONAL PARK

Lennard River Gorge

TUNNEL CREEK NATIONAL PARK

Mt Hart Wilderness Lodge

Horizontal Waterfalls

King Sound

Derby

Cape Leveque

Lombadina

Middle Lagoon

Beagle Bay

Dampier Peninsula

Great Northern Highway (Highway 1)

Price Point

Willie Creek Pearl Farm

Broome

Port Hedland

N

0 100 km

in around April, **tours** of the Kimberley resume, mainly between Broome and Kununurra (see boxes, p.702 and p.713) along the **Gibb River Road (GRR)**, or down to the popular **Bungle Bungles**, south of Highway 1, near Halls Creek. June to August, the coolest months, are the best time to visit; by late September the heat is already building up and even Highway 1 closes periodically from January to March following storms or cyclones.

Derby to Fitzroy Crossing

Situated 36km north of Highway 1, on a spur of land jutting into the mud flats of King Sound, **DERBY** is a mineral exploration base and a centre for local Aboriginal communities. For tourists there's not a whole lot going on short of checking out the boab-tree prison 8km from town, or taking a **scenic flight** over the impressive West Kimberley coastline ($255 per person for two passengers or $215 for four passengers; ask at the visitors information centre), and without your own transport you'll find the spread-out town hard work. The **visitors information centre** (Mon–Fri 8.30am–4.30pm, Sat 9am–noon; ⓣ08/9191 1426 or 1800 621 426, ⓦwww.derbytourism.com.au) is at the top end of town on Clarendon Street, where **buses** also arrive. **Places to stay** include the *Spinifex Hotel* (ⓣ08/9191 1233; ❷–❸) which has dorms ($20); *West Kimberley Lodge* at 7 Sutherland St (ⓣ08/9191 1031; shared facilities ❸, en suite ❹), a guesthouse with shared facilities, and the *Boab Inn* (ⓣ08/9191 1044; ❺) on Loch Street. There are also two caravan parks. There's a good **restaurant** at the *Boab Inn*, but for something special it's got to be the *Point* seafood restaurant out by the wharf (Tues–Sun 10am–10pm), which also does takeaways.

The **Gibb River Road** (full account, p.714) starts just east of Derby and cuts straight across the Kimberley, passing many turn-offs for gorges before joining the sealed road between Wyndham and Kununurra, 667km further on. A great way to experience the GRR is on the hop-on, hop-off *Gibb River Road River Express* (full details p.714), which runs between Derby and Kununurra. If you're heading east with your own vehicle and want to see the **Windjana Gorge** and **Tunnel Creek** national parks, follow the GRR for 119km to the Windjana turn-off. From here you rejoin the Great Northern Highway after 123km. This section is alright in dry weather in a 2WD and is only 30km longer than following the dull highway to Fitzroy Crossing, 256km from Derby.

Since the pastoral expansion into the Kimberley in the late nineteenth century, **FITZROY CROSSING** has been a small rest stop for travellers and a crucial crossing over the still-troublesome Fitzroy River. Today it's a "welfare town" serving the Aboriginal communities strung out along the Fitzroy Valley to the southwest. Because of its large catchment area, the Fitzroy River's run-off during flood peaks is second only to the Amazon, at which time two cubic kilometres of water a minute surge under the road bridge, spreading out across a flood plain 40km wide in places, before disgorging into King Sound.

As for the town, a Friday-night **drinking** session at the century-old *Crossing Inn* on Skuthorpe Road might give you the most memorable experience of the place, its having been brightly repainted by local children into something of a tourist attraction. The *Fitzroy River Lodge* (ⓣ08/9191 5141; ❻–❽), on the highway east of the bridge, caters comfortably for passing tours with **motel rooms**, canvas bushland lodges and grassy campsites (powered sites $27, tent sites $11 per person) and excellent facilities including a pool, restaurants, a bar and Internet. The *Crossing Inn* (ⓣ08/9191 5080; motel rooms ❺) also has campsites (powered sites $21, tent sites $8.50 per person) and the obligatory counter meals, while the *Tarunda Caravan Park* (ⓣ08/9191 5330), next to the **supermarket/post office** on Forrest Road, has cheap tent sites ($10 per person, powered sites $23) and pricier cabins (❺). The **visitors information centre** (daily 8am–4.30pm; ⓣ08/9191 5355, ⓔfxtourism@sdwk.wa.gov.au) is on Flynn Drive, by the roadhouse, and can give you the lowdown on tours to the nearby national parks described below.

The Devonian Reef national parks

During the Devonian era, 350 million years ago, a large barrier reef grew around the then-submerged Kimberley plateau. The limestone remnants of this reef are today exposed in the national parks of **Geikie Gorge**, **Tunnel Creek** and, most spectacularly, **Windjana Gorge** (DEC fees apply for all; see box, p.630), sometimes misleadingly labelled the "West Kimberley", but of which they are just a dramatic and easily accessible fraction. All three parks are closed from December to April.

Geikie Gorge National Park

Eighteen kilometres upstream from Fitzroy Crossing, the river has carved out the five-kilometre **Geikie Gorge** through the exposed reef, best seen by **boat** with Darngku Heritage Cruises (ⓣ08/9191 5552; 2–4hr; $55–140). Watermarks on the gorge's walls clearly show how high the river can rise, while below the surface harmless freshwater crocodiles jostle with freshwater-adapted stingrays and sawfish. Walking trails lead along the forested western banks, which are strategically dotted with picnic sites, barbecues and campsites.

Tunnel Creek and Windjana Gorge national parks

Going back along the highway, 42km west of Fitzroy Crossing, a dirt road turns north to follow the Napier Range (as the reef is known here) to **Tunnel Creek National Park** (no camping), 105km from Fitzroy Crossing. Here, Tunnel Creek has burrowed its way under the range, creating a 750-metre tunnel hung with bats and who-knows-what in the pools. Although the collapsed roof illuminates the cavern halfway, the wade through the progressively deeper and colder water to the other end still takes some nerve – you'll need a torch and shoes that you don't mind getting soaked.

The most impressive remainders of the reef are the towering ramparts of **Windjana Gorge** (camping), 135km from Fitzroy Crossing and 140km from Derby. A walking trail leads through a limestone crevice into a wide gorge splitting the Napier Range, lined with paperbark and Leichhardt trees. Freshwater crocodiles share the pools with various birds and can be seen sunning themselves in the afternoons.

Halls Creek and around

Further down the Great Northern Highway, **HALLS CREEK** is 288km east of Fitzroy Crossing. The goldrush of 1885 took place in the hills 17km south of town, and in less than four years a thousand prospectors succeeded in exhausting the area's potential, before stampeding off to Kalgoorlie. Today, new gold and diamond mines are opening up, even if for most the town is just another stop on the highway.

The **visitors information centre** (May–Sept daily 8.30am–4.30pm; ⓣ08/9168 6262, ⓔvisitors@hcshire.wa.gov.au) has a café and is in the middle of town. **Internet** access is available next door in the library. For somewhere to **stay**, the *Halls Creek Caravan Park* (ⓣ08/9168 6169), on Roberta Avenue, has camp sites (powered sites $11 per person, unpowered $9.50 per person), grim single cabins ($22) and more spacious on-site vans (❷). The *Kimberley Hotel*

(Ⓣ08/9168 6101 or 1800 355 228, Ⓦwww.kimberleyaccommodation.com.au), opposite the caravan park, has budget rooms (❹) and better corporate (❺) and deluxe rooms (❻). It also has a pool and the only **pub** in town. The *Best Western Halls Creek Motel* on Duncan Road (Ⓣ08/9168 6001, Ⓦwww.bestwestern.com.au/hallscreek; ❺–❻) is another option if the *Kimberley* is full.

The gold-bearing hills to the southeast offer a few attractions for those with their own transport. Six kilometres south of town, **China Wall** is a block-like outcrop of quartzite rising from the hillside, which, from a distance, resembles China's Great Wall. **Caroline Pool**, 9km further south, can be a bit fetid for swimming but **Palm Springs**, about 25km further on, is well worth a splash although you're better off spending the night by **Sawpit Gorge**, a couple of kilometres further on; all bar the final creek crossing just before the gorge are manageable in a 2WD during the dry season, although a 4WD makes life easier.

Purnululu National Park (Bungle Bungles)

The spectacular **Bungle Bungles** massif, seldom referred to by its official name, the **Purnululu National Park** (closed Jan–March; DEC fee $10 – see box, p.630), is one of Australia's greatest natural wonders and in 2003 earned prestigious UNESCO World Heritage listing alongside the Pyramids, the Grand Canyon and the Great Barrier Reef. A couple of days spent exploring its chasms and gorges is well worth the effort and expense. Though visited by Europeans a century earlier, the Bungles were brought to prominence in the early 1980s and have quickly attracted a mystique matching that of Ayers Rock. Due to the fragile nature of the banded rock domes as well as the difficulty in patrolling the remote park, road access from the Great Northern Highway is limited to 4WDs. The park was acquired in a severely over-grazed state (like much of the Northwest) but over the years DEC has worked hard to revive the soil and replace feral animals with indigenous wildlife. Note that the Bungles are always **hot**, with temperatures of 40°C possible in early September, so make sure you carry water and wear a hat on the longer walks.

The geology of the Bungles

The weathered, beehive-like domes of the Bungles are a most unusual sight, exhibiting alternating sedimentary strata of iron oxide (orange) and cyanobacteria (grey-green or black), which itself forms a fragile crust over the sometimes powdery interior. The theory is that over millennia, sediments were deposited from two differing sources, creating interchanging strata with varying mineral characteristics. The darker bands are marginally more porous (water bearing) and so support the lichen-like cyanobacteria – incidentally another name used for the stromatolite formations found at Shark Bay (see p.681).

You'll also notice the rocks on the higher, north side of the massif are conglomerate (stones set in a sand cement) and are actually older than the southern domes which were deposited on top of them. The whole range has tilted to the south over time, exposing the older conglomerate.

Meanwhile, back on the south side, the maze of chasms dividing each "bungle" is being put down to an impact structure recently discovered on the roof of the plateau. At some stage a meteor is thought to have struck with such force that it sent fracture lines down through the rocks below. Over time the smashed upper strata have eroded, exposing the splintered layers which were subsequently weathered into the well-known domes. The fact that there are "mini-bungle" formations elsewhere in the Kimberley, as well as the proven tilting of the massif and the current fashion for explaining epochal cataclysms with meteor strikes, makes this dramatic concept a little hard to swallow.

The **fly-drive tours** available from Kununurra (see box, p.713), which involve flying to the park's airstrip and then being driven around in a 4WD, offer the best of both worlds. However, the thirty-minute doorless **helicopter** flights (turn up at the airstrip or call ☎08/9168 1811; $265) available in the park are permitted to fly much lower – if you've ever wanted to fly in a chopper you won't be disappointed. Helicopter flights are also available from Turkey Creek (see below).

From the highway it's a fun, 53-kilometre (two-hour) 4WD ride through station land to the **visitors centre** and entry station (April–Nov daily 8am–4.30pm; ☎08/9168 7300). Take it easy as the track is narrow and hilly, and expect oncoming traffic in the morning. From the entry station you can head to either of the two basic campsites on the north or south side of the park. **Kurrajong Camp** is the north site, 10km from the entry station and gives access to **Echidna Chasm**, a one-hour return walk into a slender chasm nearly a kilometre long and half as high. At times the cleft is less than half a metre wide and each time you think it's over, another chink opens up and you head further into the rock. **Frog Hole** (30min return) is a wider chasm, with a seasonal pool at the end, while **Mini Palms** is a longer walk along a creek bed to a palm-filled amphitheatre and then on over collapsed boulders to a viewing platform with a gorge below. At any point on these walks you can look up and see palms clinging to the rock walls hundreds of metres above you; the scale of the clefts is emphasized when you realize the palms can be up to 20m high.

Wilardi Camp, on the south side of the park, is a better laid out campsite, 25km from the entry station with access to the classic Bungle vistas. From the main car park, the short **Domes Walk** leads you among some bungles on the way to the half-hour walk into **Cathedral Gorge**, a huge overhanging amphitheatre with a seasonal pool whose rippled reflections flicker across the roof above.

Piccaninny Gorge is a tough, thirty-kilometre overnight walk for which you'll need to register and carry **large quantities of water**. Most people are understandably put off but it's quite possible to walk the seven kilometres along the creek to the **Elbow** and back in a day, following the creek. The rest of the park is currently inaccessible, the northeast being the ancestral burial grounds of the Djaru and Gidja people.

On to Wyndham

Halfway between Halls Creek and Kununurra is the roadhouse at **TURKEY CREEK** (dorms $20, motel rooms ❹, s/c units ❺) next to the Warmun community, where a **helicopter** offers 45-minute flights (☎08/9168 7337; $265–415 depending on the number of passengers) into the Bungles. Compared to the open helicopters used in the park, the faster, enclosed machine is a less exhilarating way of seeing the domes. Opposite the roadhouse, the Aboriginal Gidja Culture Centre displays the art of, and books on, the original occupants of the region; there is also **Internet** access.

From Turkey Creek the road continues directly north, passing a roadhouse and the Argyle Diamond Mine (tours from Kununurra; see box p.713), source of most of the world's industrial diamonds. The scenery hereabouts takes on a rugged turn (especially at sunset) as you pass the Ragged and Carr Boyd ranges to the junction with the Victoria Highway. At the junction, Kununurra is 46km to the east and Wyndham 51km northwest.

Strung out in three built-up areas along the muddy banks of the Cambridge Gulf, **WYNDHAM** was the port established to serve the brief goldrush at Halls Creek. The town was then well-positioned to process and export East Kimberley beef until the meat works closed in 1985; these days the West Kimberley's only port ticks over quietly serving local Aboriginal people. At the top of the town is the **Crocodile Farm** (May–Nov daily 8.30am–4pm; feeding time 11am; $16; ⓣ08/9161 1124). If you haven't been to one yet, here is your chance, but give the paltry crocodile sandwiches a miss. The biggest "salties" (see p.566) make the in-house Komodo Dragon look rather lame, while the pens packed with crocodile hatchings draped over each other could go so far as to be deigned hideously cute. You get a good aerial view of the farm and a whole lot more from the **Five Rivers Lookout** at the top of the 335-metre Bastion Ranges, overlooking the town on the east side. With the tide out you'll see the intricate web of creeks feeding into the muddy delta and the Cambridge Gulf.

The **visitors information centre** (daily 6am–6pm; ⓣ08/9161 1281) is on the Great Northern Highway, and you can **camp** at the *Wyndham Caravan Park* (ⓣ08/9161 1064; powered sites $14 per person, rooms ③) on Baker Street. The *Gulf Breeze Guest House* (ⓣ08/9161 1401; ③) in the old post office on O'Donnell Street is more of a long-termers' haunt. Opposite the *Gulf Breeze*, the *Wyndham Town Hotel* (ⓣ08/9161 1003, ⓔwyndham@bigpond.com; ⑤) is as good as it gets and has the town's one **restaurant** – nothing special but better than gnawing on your shoe.

Kununurra and the Ord River

KUNUNURRA is the Kimberley's youngest town, built in the early 1960s to serve the **Ord River Irrigation Project**, fed by Lake Kununurra. The Diversion Dam Wall, an impressive sight as you come in from the west, created this lake, essentially the bloated Ord River. Fifty kilometres upstream is a bigger dam, known as the Argyle Dam Wall, built in 1971 to ensure a year-round flow to the project, which has created **Lake Argyle**, the world's largest man-made body of water. Easy-to-produce sugar cane has become the most viable crop, backed up by the more labour-intensive watermelons and other farmed produce which offer steady opportunities for menial **work**; see the backpackers' notice boards. Enhanced by the copious amounts of nearby fresh water which lends itself to recreational use, Kununurra escapes the listless feel of the older Kimberley towns.

A couple of kilometres east of town is **Hidden Valley** or Mirima National Park (DEC fee; see box on p.630), where a road leads into a narrow valley of "mini-bungles" and terminates with some short trails – you couldn't ask for a better walking area so close to town. Another popular spot is **Ivanhoe Crossing**, 13km north of town on the Ord River. Officially, the ford is closed to vehicles and you wouldn't want to try crossing it in anything less than a hefty 4WD. Downstream is saltwater crocodile country although some locals fish and bathe by the banks – just the sort of habitual behaviour "salties" go for. **Valentines Pool**, **Black Rock Falls** and **Middle Springs** are other waterholes on the far side of the Crossing (also accessible off the Wyndham highway), though all three get pretty soupy towards the end of the dry season.

Triple J Tours (ⓣ08/9168 2682, ⓦwww.triplejtours.net.au) offers speedy cruises (from $125) up **Lake Kununurra** to Argyle Dam, as do the long-established Lake Argyle Cruises (ⓣ08/9168 7687, ⓦwww.lakeargylecruises.com) who have **boat trips** (2–6 hours; around $25 an hour) to search out wallaby caves, Jabirus and other birds, as well as freshwater crocodiles. The *BBQ Boat* (ⓣ08/9168 1718) does a slower-paced three-hour sunset cruise ($67 including dinner) around Lily Creek Lagoon, where you'll see crocodiles, fish, turtles and trees full of bats, which all take to the air in a dramatic sky-darkening mass just after sunset. The lagoon is a great place to rent a canoe for a bit of exploring among the pandanus reeds; ask about rentals at the visitors information centre

Regional tours from Kununurra

Although prices are as high per day as anywhere in Australia, Kununurra is the best base from which to visit the Bungles as well as the Kimberley. *Kununurra Backpackers'* (ⓣ1800 641 998) offers two- to three-day Bungles trips from around $150 a day. East Kimberley Tours (ⓣ08/9168 2213 or 1800 682 213, ⓦwww.eastkimberleytours.com.au) has a range of options including fly-in, fly-out one-day Bungles tours ($495). Slingair (ⓣ1800 095 500) visits the diamond mine in a day, along with a large range of other flight options, from $175. Alligator Air (ⓣ1800 632 533) has two-hour Bungles flights in high-wing aircraft for around $230 (no minimum numbers). Their four-and-a-half hour "The Works" flight ($495) includes a stop on the Mitchell Plateau and is one of the best scenic flights over the Kimberley, but needs a minimum of four passengers; call in advance.

or Go Wild Adventure Tours (ⓣ0409 456 643 or 1300 663 369, ⓦwww.gowild.com.au), who lay on one- to three-day self-guided canoeing trips down the Ord River from $150 to $200 per person.

Practicalities

The **visitors information centre** (Mon–Fri 8am–5pm, Sat & Sun 9am–4pm; ⓣ08/9168 1177, ⓦwww.kununurratourism.com) on Coolibah Drive has displays and videos on the area's many attractions, and details of all the tours that you can take there. You'll find a **telecentre** next door and a perennially warm **swimming pool** ($3) over the road. The **post office** is also on Coolibah Drive. **Buses** arrive outside the BP **24-hour roadhouse**, passing through daily for Katherine, Darwin and Broome.

The only recommended **backpackers'** in town are the recently remodelled *Kimberley Croc* (ⓣ08/9168 2702 or 1300 136 702, ⓦwww.kimberleycroc.com.au; dorms from $22, twins and doubles ❸) on Konkerberry Drive, close to the pub and supermarket with a shaded pool and terrace, and *Kununurra Backpackers'* (ⓣ08/9169 1998 or 1800 641 998, ⓦwww.adventure.kimberley.net.au; dorms from $22, doubles ❷) on 24 Nutwood Crescent. The *Backpackers'* is made up of a couple of converted houses and a nice garden, and is in a quiet backstreet ten minutes' walk from town. It also has a small pool, TV room and a farm-workers' annexe. Of the town's six **caravan parks**, the *Town* (ⓣ08/9168 1763; powered sites $28, cabins ❺), on Bloodwood Drive, is the most central, while the *Kona* (ⓣ08/9168 1031; powered sites $28, cabins ❹), right by Lake Kununurra, is 5km west of town. The *Mercure Inn* (ⓣ08/9168 1455 or 1300 656 565; ❻), on the highway, is the town's best **motel**; you could also try the cheaper *Hotel Kununurra* (ⓣ08/9168 0400, ⓦwww.kimberleyaccommodation.com.au; budget rooms ❸, premium rooms ❻) on Messmate Way.

Places to eat include *Valentine's* (daily 5–10pm) on Papuana Street for pizzas, and the bistro at *Gulliver's Tavern* that gets the occasional band in the picking season.

Lake Argyle

When the **Argyle Dam** was completed in 1972, the Ord River managed to fill **Lake Argyle** in just one wet season; along with the neighbouring Victoria and the Fitzroy, these rivers account for a third of Australia's freshwater run-off and plans are often mooted to pipe it south where it's needed. Creating the lake was an engineer's dream: only a small defile needed damming to back up a shallow lake covering up to two thousand square kilometres. Since that time the fish population has grown over the years to support commercial fishing, as well as numerous birds and crocodiles, both estuarine and freshwater. When the lake was proposed, the Durack family's Argyle Homestead was moved to its present site, 2km from the tourist village (see below), and is now a **museum** (May–Oct daily 7am–4pm; $3) of early pioneering life in the Kimberley, as described in Mary Durack's droving classic, *Kings in Grass Castles*. For lake cruises, see p.713.

The Gibb River Road

On the way to Wyndham you pass the start of the mostly unsealed **Gibb River Road** (or **GRR**) with its attendant warning sign. Originally built to transport beef out of the Kimberley to Wyndham and Derby, it cuts through the region's heart, offering a vivid slice of this vast and rugged expanse. At around 670km to Derby, it's 230km shorter than the Great Northern Highway, but although the people have mistaken it as so, the "Gibb" is no short cut. The hammering from the route's notorious corrugations depends partly on the quality of your suspension (letting some air out of the tyres helps greatly) but it's rare to get across without something breaking or falling off. Punctures are common (many stations can do repairs) and roll-overs are not that rare either. Heed the advice on off-highway driving on p.42.

Although as a scenic drive it's very satisfying, the attractions that make this route even more interesting – homesteads, gorges and their pools – are off the GRR and some are accessible only to robust, high-clearance vehicles, although unless stated a 4WD is not necessary in the places listed below. At times when your vehicle is vibrating so much it's drifting across the track, you may wonder if the trip is worth it. To absorb the experience it's best to plan to stop for a couple of days somewhere along the road at some of the places listed below; after all, you'll probably only be here once. Derby visitors information centre (see p.708) produces a comprehensive and annually updated *Travellers Guide* to the GRR ($4), including accommodation prices, which is also available at other visitors information centres. Distances given in brackets below are to destinations off the GRR.

If you're traversing the GRR west to east and want to spare your car the full ordeal, turn back at Manning Gorge and head down to the highway via Windjana Gorge, as the best GRR gorges are in the western half. **Tours** are available from Broome (see p.702) and Kununurra (see box, p.713). The hop-on, hop-off **Gibb River Road Express** bus service (Ⓣ08/9169 1880, Ⓦwww.gibbriverbus.com.au; $260) runs during the Dry (May–Oct) between Kununurra and Derby in about twelve hours, while dropping you off and picking you up at many of the points listed below. Some enterprising **cyclists** are already using the service as a way of missing out or reducing the gruelling corrugation transits, while exploring the side tracks; it's possible the service may offer mountain-bike packages on future runs. The problem is that without transport, getting to all but the nearest gorges and homesteads is quite a trek off the GRR (let alone carting provisions), although some stations will do pre-arranged pick-ups. Even then, doing the GRR in a day on the Express is surprisingly satisfying; the big-windowed bus gives great views and, with the driver's commentary, you'll be able to appreciate the great landscape a whole lot more without your teeth clenched and knuckles clamped around the wheel of your own vehicle.

The Karunjie Track

If you're starting the GRR from Wyndham consider taking the **Karunjie–King River Track**, which starts just out of town (follow signs for King

River and *Drovers Rest*). The track is on El Questro station land and is more varied than the easternmost section of the GRR which you bypass, but you'll need a 4WD to get through the deep bull dust as you near the Gibb at the Pentecost River crossing, 85km from Wyndham – allow about three hours.

The track starts by heading out across a causeway to follow the King River, crossing it (it's usually dry) 30km from Wyndham by a Boab Prison Tree, once used to detain Aborigine prisoners in transit. Here the track divides: the left intercepts the GRR east of the Emma Gorge turn-off and the right leads west slowly round to the Cockburn Ranges, at one point crossing smooth, hardened mud flats before the going gets rough again as the track nears the Pentecost River. There are some washed-out sections and deep patches of bull dust that need to be churned through slowly. You join the GRR at the Pentecost crossing about 57km west of the Great Northern Highway.

The Northern Kimberley

Though a common destination in the dry season, the Northern Kimberley is a remote region where a well-equipped 4WD is essential. You'll find the Kalumburu Road junction 250km along the GRR, with a store and fuel at *Drysdale River Homestead* (59km; April–Nov daily 8am–noon & 1–5pm; ⓣ08/9161 4326, ⓦwww.drysdaleriver.com.au; units ④), which also offers cheap camping, a bar, meals and scenic flights over some remote northwest Kimberley waterfalls. The main attraction near here is the beautiful, four-tiered Mitchell Falls, 240km off the GRR and 70km west off the Kalumburu Road; turn off at the King Edward River (camping, see below). This once remote spot is getting less so by the year and is now a national park (DEC fees apply, see p.630) with basic camping. There are also "exclusive" campsites at King Edward River and at Mitchell Falls car park run by APT/Kimberley Wilderness Adventures (June–Oct; ⓦwww.kimberleywilderness.com.au; half-board $120 per person) and used on their tours. From the Mitchell Falls car park it's a three-kilometre walk northwest to the falls themselves (passing Little and Big Merten's Falls on the way) where a helicopter stands by (ⓣ08/9161 4512) to offer scenic flights in season from around $150. Just before you arrive at Mitchell Falls there's a turn-off to Surveyors Pool and Walsh Point (extremely rough, allow 3hr), right on the coast from where you may want to pre-arrange a pick-up to *Kimberley Coastal Camp* (see below) on the other side of the bay.

Kalumburu (276km; ⓣ08/9161 4300; $40 vehicle permit) is an Aboriginal community with the languorous feel of a dispersed African village, where ancient cars lie rusting and palms flap and sway in the tropical breeze. Buy your one-week vehicle permit on arrival from the community office (if there's anyone there); you'll also need to get another (free) permit in advance from the Department of Indigenous Affairs (most easily obtained online at ⓦwww.dia.wa.gov.au or from Broome, Derby or the Kununurra visitors information centres). As well as being able to get (expensive) fuel and basics from the store here, you can visit a mission set up in the nineteenth century by Benedictine monks. North of town along sandy tracks, there are basic campsites at pretty *McGowans Beach* (22km) and *Honeymoon Beach* (26km), the latter situated on a small bay and the better of the two, though lately a site at *Pago* has opened up too.

There are a couple of other accommodation options on the otherwise unpopulated Kimberley coast: exclusive, all-inclusive resorts like the *Kimberley Coastal Camp* (ⓦwww.kimberleycoastalcamp.com.au) southwest of Kalumburu, or *Faraway Bay* (ⓦwww.farawaybay.com.au) to the east, costing at least $800 a day and only accessible by air or sea.

The eastern Gibb River Road

The GRR proper starts halfway between Wyndham and Kununurra. The scenically impressive 250-kilometre eastern section up to the Kalumburu junction crosses many ranges and is crossed in turn by big rivers, the first of these being the King River, 17km from the sealed highway. Eight kilometres further is the turn-off for the plush mini-resort at *Emma Gorge* (2km; ⓣ08/9161 4388; part of *El Questro Wilderness Park*; tented cabins ⑦), a manicured bush-camp of tented cabins with a restaurant, bar and pool. It's popular with coach parties, and there's a thirty-minute walk along Emma Creek to the fern-draped **gorge**, which is worth the entry fee. Better still if you're fit is the "Emma Dreaming Trail" which ascends the cliffs of the Cockburn Ranges behind Emma Gorge, passing pools and rock-art sites on the way.

Further down the GRR is the turn-off for the station homestead or "township" of **El Questro Wilderness Park** (16km; ⓣ08/9169 4318, ⓦwww.elquestro.com.au; $12.50 day-use for all of *ELQ*; details from the reservations office in the Kununurra visitors information centre ⓣ08/9168 1777). Uniformed "rangers" will guide or point out all sorts of activities, including heli-fishing and gorge cruises as well as various walks, gorges, rock-art sites and drives over much of the million-acre property. They've spent a huge amount of money on making *ELQ* into a "see-it-all-here" private national park and for some it may come across as a bit too commercialized compared to the other, more authentic station-stays out here. Although you can do full-day tours from Kununurra for $185, it's much better to visit with your own vehicle (ideally a 4WD) and make the most of your day-pass; the drive up to **El Questro Gorge** is recommended, as is Explosion Gorge. Affordable accommodation in *ELQ* includes secluded camping ($15 per person; some with distant washing facilities and so more suited to campervans), more central camping at the *Black Cockatoo* site, or en-suite bungalows (⑧). There's also a bar, shop, fuel and restaurant.

From the *El Questro* turn-off, the Cockburn Ranges' cliffs lead you to the shallow but broad **Pentecost River** crossing. Eight kilometres on is *Home Valley Station* (1km; ⓣ08/9161 4322, ⓦwww.homevalley.com.au), a friendly, relaxed alternative to corporate *El Questro*, based around a breezy barn-like homestead that's more like the real thing, and boasting great sunset views across the Pentecost to the Cockburn Ranges. As well as camping ($15 per person), there are comfortable rooms for $80 per person including breakfast, eco-tents for $95 per person, a pool, and an ever-growing network of 4WD tracks and walking trails to fishing spots.

The track rattles away beneath your wheels for about 70km until *Ellenbrae Station* (5km; ⓣ08/9161 4325, ⓔellenbrae3@bigpond.com; meals available; camping $10 per person, bungalows $100), another million-acre property that's not had a cattle muster for years. The campground amenities area, like the main homestead itself, follow an "organic" open-plan design in stone and wood, a treat if you have it to yourself. Self-guide tour maps are available.

Kalumburu Road junction to Derby

After the Kalumburu Road junction, the turn-offs from the GRR to accessible gorges and waterholes increase. About 50km from the junction is a turn north to *Mount Elizabeth* (30km; ⓣ08/9191 4644; camping $14 per person, three-course meals for $50), with half-day tours of the property available for $88. Another 10km down the GRR is **Barnett River Gorge** (5km; basic camping), nothing too spectacular but with a couple of places where you can camp for free and swim in a billabong. Twenty kilometres after that is the *Mount Barnett*

Roadhouse (April–Oct daily 7am–5pm; Nov–March Mon–Sat 8am–noon & 2–4pm; ⓣ08/9191 7007), from where you can drive the 7km to the *Manning Gorge* (if the road is open), which has basic camping and the opportunity to walk to the even nicer, multi-tiered **Upper Manning Gorge**. Further down the GRR both **Galvans** (700m) and **Adcock** (5km) gorges are less impressive by comparison.

Beverley Springs Station (ⓣ08/9191 4646; camping with gorge access $15, en-suite rondaval bungalows $150 per person half-board) is now open for visitors, 55km north off the GRR. Theoretically it's one of the few GRR stations from where you can get to the sea at Walcott Inlet, although the track has been closed for the last three years, and if you can get here, swimming here is not advisable.

Back on the GRR, a long 95km detour south brings you to *Mornington Wilderness Camp* (ⓣ08/9191 7406 or 1800 631 946, ⓦwww.australianwildlife.org), a former station that, like *Mount Hart* (see below), has been bought out by a conservation organization. Expect a few creek crossings in the final 15km after *Glenroy Homestead*. Washed out by the rain in 2002, the rebuilt *Mornington* now includes airy en-suite safari tents (full-board $180) and creekside camping as well as a bar and restaurant. From the camp, you can access two impressive gorges on the Fitzroy River: **Sir John Gorge** (14km; 30min) has broad pools ideal for swimming and exploring upstream leads you to even greater grandeur. To appreciate **Dimond Gorge** (23km; 1hr) you'll have to rent a canoe from the homestead ($60 per day) to paddle downstream beyond the sheer walls.

Back on the GRR just after Saddlers Creek is *Imintji Safari Camp*, run by APT/Kimberley Wilderness Adventures but open to passers-by (ⓣ1800 675 222; half-board safari tents $120 per person). The **Imintji Store** (ⓣ08/9191 5761), just down the road, stocks fuel, ice, and a good supply of groceries, as well as carrying out basic vehicle repairs. Seven kilometres further on is the access track north to **Bell Creek Gorge** in the *King Leopold Conservation Park* (30km; vehicle entry fee, camping at two locations). Well worth some extra corrugations, this is the loveliest gorge along the GRR, and is now very popular. Twenty-three kilometres further down the Gibb, on the far side of the King Leopold Ranges, is **Lennard River Gorge** (8km; last 3km 4WD), a dramatic cleft carved through tiers of tilted rock. Even in a 4WD you may find it quicker and certainly easier to walk the last two kilometres, which, unless they've been recently repaired, are very rough in parts.

A few kilometres on down the GRR is the turning north for *Mount Hart Wilderness Lodge* (50km; ⓣ08/9191 4645, ⓦwww.mthart.com.au; half-board $180 per person, lunch included if you stay more than one night; no camping or day-visits). You need to book ahead but you can call from the Imintji Store or use the lodge's private radio at the GRR turn-off. The former homestead has been cultivated into a cosy shaded retreat with a bar, comfortable indoor areas and a waterhole, and has private gorges to explore a few kilometres away. Scenic flights and helicopters use the lodge's airstrip to stop for lunch (and are available to visitors), but at other times it could be all yours.

Back on the GRR once more, you wind your way through the impressive **King Leopard Ranges** and soon come to the **Napier Ranges**, which are composed of the Devonian Reef, and where a rock-chiselled profile of Queen Victoria's head is evident as you pass through the gap. Nine kilometres from here a turn leads southeast to Windjana Gorge National Park (21km) and Fitzroy Crossing (165km). The last 62km to Derby is a sealed avenue of portly boab trees.

Travel details

Trains

Perth to: Adelaide/Sydney (2 weekly; Adelaide 50hr, Sydney 60hr); Bunbury (2–3 daily; 2hr); Kalgoorlie (1–2 daily; 6hr).

Buses

Kalgoorlie to: Adelaide (1 daily; 36hr); Esperance (3 weekly; 5hr); Leonora (2 weekly; 11hr); Perth (daily; 8hr).
Perth to: Adelaide (1 daily; 35hr); Albany (3 daily; from 6hr); Augusta (6 weekly; 6hr); Broome (daily; 33hr); Bunbury (1–2 daily; 2hr); Carnarvon (daily; 13hr); Coral Bay (6 weekly; 16hr); Dampier–Karratha (5 weekly; 21hr); Darwin (daily; 59hr); Derby (daily; 36hr); Esperance (4 weekly; 10hr); Exmouth (6 weekly; 18hr); Fitzroy Crossing (daily; 40hr); Geraldton (2 daily; 6hr–8hr 30min); Halls Creek (daily; 43hr); Hyden (for Wave Rock; 2 weekly; 5hr); Kalbarri (daily; 8hr 30min–9hr); Kalgoorlie (daily; 8hr); Karratha (1 daily; 22hr); Kununurra (daily; 48hr); Margaret River (3 daily; 5hr); Meekatharra (1 weekly; 10hr); Monkey Mia (3 weekly; 13hr); Newman (1 weekly; 16hr); Port Hedland (8 weekly; 22–26hr).

Flights

Perth to: Adelaide (6 daily; 4hr 15min); Alice Springs (5 weekly; 4hr); Ayers Rock Resort (3 weekly; 3hr 45min); Brisbane (3 weekly; 6hr 15min); Broome (1–2 daily; 2hr 30min); Carnarvon (3 weekly; 2hr); Darwin (1 daily; 6hr 15min); Esperance (2 daily; 1hr 50min); Exmouth (11 weekly; 1hr 45min–2hr 45min); Geraldton (2–5 daily; 1hr 5min); Kalbarri (3 weekly; 1hr 15min); Kalgoorlie (1 daily; 1hr); Kununurra (3 weekly; 3hr 15min–4hr 15min); Melbourne (12 daily; 5hr 15min); Monkey Mia (2 weekly; 1hr 50min); Newman (2 weekly; 1hr 45min–2hr 25min); Port Hedland (3 weekly; 2hr 5min); Sydney (12 daily; 6hr); Tom Price (1 daily; 2hr).

South Australia

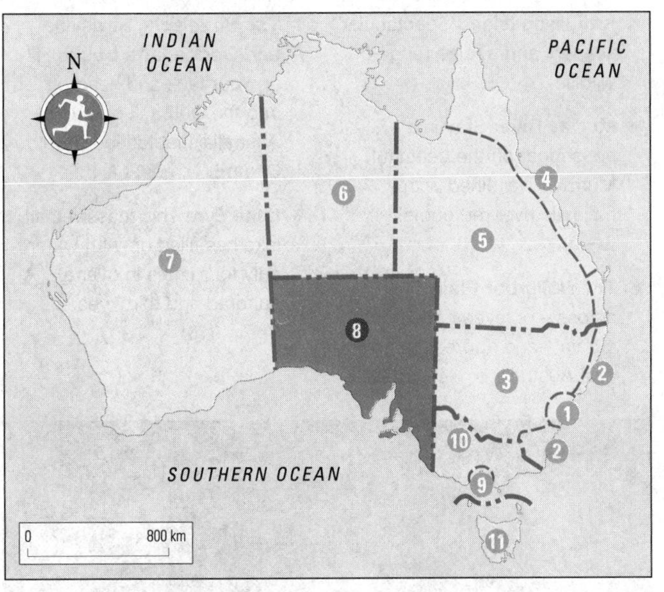

CHAPTER 8

Highlights

* **Adelaide Festival of Arts** The country's best-known and most innovative arts festival. See p.741
* **Barossa Valley** A popular day-trip from Adelaide, the Barossa Valley is home to some of Australia's finest wineries. See p.751
* **Kangaroo Island** Spectacular scenery and a huge range of wildlife. See p.765
* **Murray River** Stay in a houseboat on the beautiful Murray River, lined with majestic river red gums. See p.782
* **The Nullarbor Plain** Drive across – or, even better, catch a train – and appreciate how vast Australia is. See p.795
* **Coober Pedy** The inhabitants of scorching Coober Pedy live underground to escape the heat of summer. See p.798
* **Wilpena Pound** The main attraction of the Flinders Ranges National Park is the huge natural basin of Wilpena Pound. See p.804
* **The Strzelecki, Birdsville and Oodnadatta tracks** Fill up your tank and head off into the Outback on one of Australia's fabled journeys. See p.808, p.808 & p.811
* **Lake Eyre** This massive salt lake has filled up with water only four times in over a hundred and thirty years. See p.810

△ Church, Coober Pedy

8

South Australia

South Australia, the driest state of the driest continent, is split into two very distinct halves. The long-settled southern part, watered by the **Murray River**, and with **Adelaide** as its cosmopolitan centre, enjoys a Mediterranean climate that makes it tremendously fertile and has been thoroughly tamed. The northern half, arid and depopulated, most definitely has not and as you head further north the temperature hots up to such an extreme that by **Coober Pedy** people live underground to escape the searing summer temperatures.

Most of southeastern South Australia lies within three hours' drive of Adelaide. Food and especially **wine** are among its chief pleasures: this is prime grape-growing and wine-making country. As well as wineries the **Fleurieu Peninsula**, just south of Adelaide, has a string of fine beaches, while nearby **Kangaroo Island** is a great place to see Australian wildlife at its unfettered best. Facing Adelaide across the Investigator Strait, the **Yorke Peninsula** is primarily an agricultural area, preserving a little copper-mining history and offering great fishing. The superb wineries of the **Barossa Valley**, originally settled by German immigrants in the nineteenth century, are only an hour northeast from Adelaide on the **Sturt Highway**, the main road to Sydney. This crosses the Murray River at Blanchetown and follows the fertile Riverland region to the New South Wales border.

Following the southeast coast along the **Princes Highway**, you can head towards Melbourne via the extensive coastal Coorong lagoon system and enjoyable seaside towns such as Robe, before exiting the state at **Mount Gambier**, with its crater lakes. The inland trawl via the **Dukes Highway** is faster but far less interesting. Heading north from Adelaide, there are old copper-mining towns to explore at **Kapunda** and **Burra**, the area known as the mid-north, which also encompasses the **Clare Valley**, a quieter, more down-to-earth wine centre than the Barossa Valley.

In contrast with the gentle and cultured southeast, the remainder of South Australia – with the exception of the relatively refined **Eyre Peninsula** and its strikingly scenic west coast – is unremittingly harsh **desert**, a naked country of vast horizons, salt lakes, glazed gibber plains and ancient mountain ranges. Although it's tempting to scud over the forbidding distances quickly, you'll miss the essence of this introspective and subtle landscape by hurrying. For every predictable, monotonous highway there's a dirt alternative, which may be physically draining but enables you to get closer to this precarious environment. The folded red rocks of the central **Flinders Ranges** and Coober Pedy's post-apocalyptic scenery are on most agendas and could be worked into a sizeable circuit, but overall the Outback lacks any real destinations. Making the most of the journey is what counts here

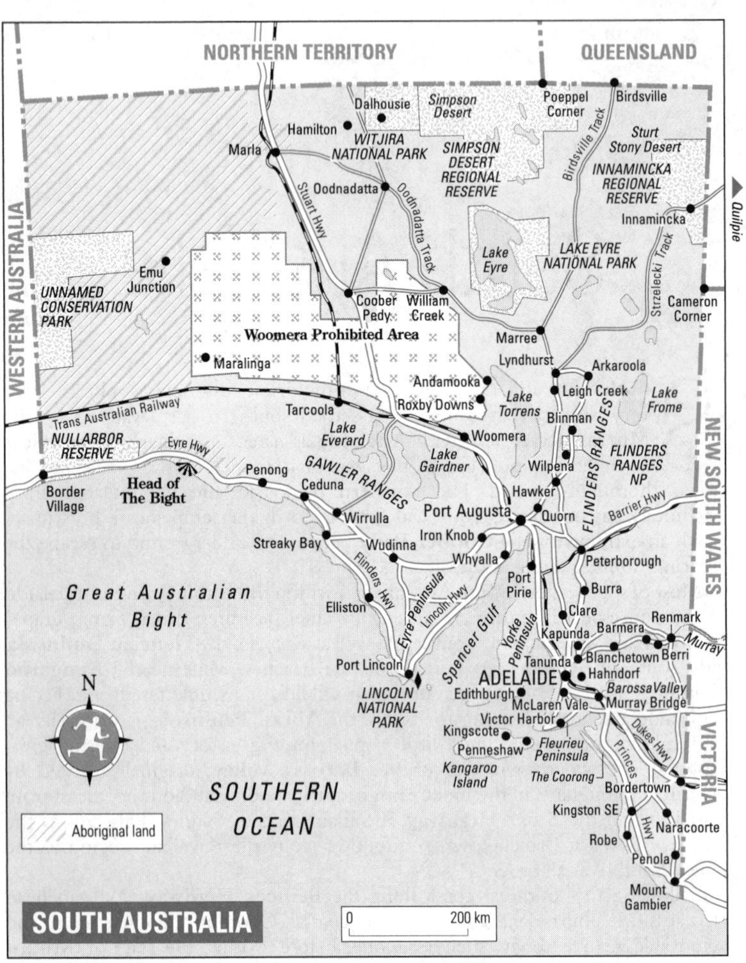

though – the fabled routes to **Oodnadatta, Birdsville** and **Innamincka** are still real adventures, and not necessarily only for 4WDs.

Rail and **road** routes converge in Adelaide before the long cross-country hauls west to Perth via Port Augusta on the Indian Pacific, or north to Alice Springs and Darwin on the Ghan – both ranking as two of Australia's great train journeys.

Some history

The coast of South Australia was first explored by the **Dutch** in 1627. In 1792 the French explorer Bruni d'Entrecasteaux sailed along the Great Australian Bight before heading to southern Tasmania, and in 1802 the Englishman Matthew Flinders thoroughly charted the coast. The most important expedition, though – and the one which led to the foundation of a colony here – was **Captain Charles Sturt**'s 1830 navigation of the Murray River, from its source in New South Wales to its mouth in South Australia. In 1836, **Governor John**

Hindmarsh landed at Holdfast Bay – now the Adelaide beachside suburb of Glenelg – with the first settlers, and the next year Colonel William Light planned the spacious, attractive city of Adelaide, with broad streets and plenty of parks and squares.

Early problems caused by the harsh, dry climate and financial incompetence (the colony went bankrupt in 1841) were eased by the discovery of substantial reserves of **copper**. The population of Adelaide boomed over the following decades, while the state's tradition of civil and religious **libertarianism** which was guaranteed to the early settlers continued; in 1894, South Australia's women were the first in the world to be permitted to stand for parliament and the second in the world to gain the vote (after New Zealand). The depressions and recessions of the interwar period hit South Australia hard, but the situation eased following World War II when new immigrants arrived, boosting industry and injecting fresh life into the state.

The 1970s were the decade of **Don Dunstan**: the flamboyant Labor Premier was an enlightened reformer who had a strong sense of social justice, abolishing capital punishment, outlawing racial discrimination and decriminalizing homosexuality. The state has been a duller place since his retirement in 1979, and a poorer one since the recession started to bite at the end of the 1980s.

Economic woes and political arguments have affected the public image of the state since, much to the chagrin of South Australians themselves, who feel that their state's attractions are being unfairly eclipsed by the lure of other Australian destinations, although in recent years South Australia's economic growth has caught up with the rest of the country.

When South Australia was first settled by Europeans in 1836, it was home to as many as fifty distinct **Aboriginal groups**, with a population estimated at fifteen thousand. Three distinct cultural regions existed: the Western Desert, the Central Lakes, and the Murray and southeast region. It was the people of the comparatively well-watered southeast who felt the full impact of white settlement, those who survived being shunted onto missions controlled by the government. Some Aboriginal people have clung tenaciously to their way of life in the Western Desert, where they have gained title to some of their land, but most now live south of Port Augusta, many in Adelaide.

Adelaide and around

ADELAIDE is always thought of as a gracious city and an easy place to live in, although despite a population of around one million and a veneer of sophistication, it still has the feel of an overgrown country town. It's a pretty place, laid out on either side of the **Torrens River**, ringed with a green belt of parks and set against the rolling hills of the **Mount Lofty Ranges**. During the hot, dry summer the parklands are kept green by irrigation from the waters of the Murray River, on which the city depends, though there's always a sense that the rawness of the Outback is waiting to take over.

The original occupants of the Adelaide plains were the **Kaurna people**, whose traditional way of life was destroyed within twenty years of European settlement. After a long struggle with Governor John Hindmarsh, who wanted to build around a harbour, the colony's surveyor-general, Colonel William Light, got his wish for an inland city with a strong connection to the river, formed around wide and spacious avenues and squares.

Postwar **immigration** provided the final element missing from Light's plan: the human one. **Italians** now make up the city's biggest non-Anglo cultural group, and in the summers, Mediterranean-style alfresco eating and drinking lend the city a vaguely European air. Not surprisingly, one of Adelaide's chief delights is its **food and wine**, with South Australian vintages in every cellar, and restaurants and cafés as varied as those in Sydney and Melbourne, only much cheaper.

Adelaide may not be an obvious destination in itself, but its free-and-easy lifestyle and liberal traditions make it a great place for a relaxed break on your way up to the Northern Territory or across to Western Australia.

Arrival

Buses from out of town, including the airport bus, will drop you off at the basic **Central Bus Station** on Franklin Street. The new **airport**, 7km southwest from the centre, is modern and well-equipped and has a currency exchange, car rental desks and information booth. It's serviced by the Skylink **airport bus** (daily 6.15am–9.45pm; 1–2 departures hourly; $5 coming from the airport, $7.50 return; hotel pick-ups available, contact ⓣ08/8332 0528, ⓦwww.skylinkadelaide.com), which will drop you off at most city accommodation on request and do a little sightseeing along the way. The bus also stops at Victoria Square, North Terrace, and Central Bus Station as well as at the **Keswick Interstate Train Terminal**, about 1km southwest of the centre, from where it costs $4.00 to the city or airport.

You can also catch a train from the airport into **Adelaide Train Station**, situated on North Terrace in the city centre; walk across the terminal to the suburban platform. A **taxi** from the airport costs around $17 to either the city or the beachside suburb of Glenelg; taxis to the city from the interstate train terminal charge about $10.

Information

The first stop for information is the **South Australian Travel Centre,** at 18 King William St between Rundle Mall and North Terrace (Mon–Fri 8.30am–5pm, Sat & Sun 9am–2pm; ⓣ1300 655 276, ⓦwww.southaustralia.com). This large, modern office has helpful staff and masses of general information, including excellent free touring guides plus maps of Adelaide and the state. You can also purchase a discount booklet if you plan to do a lot of sightseeing. Just around the corner on Rundle Mall itself is the **Rundle Mall Visitor Information Centre** (Mon–Thurs 10am–5pm, Fri 10am–8pm, Sat 10am–3pm, Sun 11am–4pm; ⓣ08/8203 7611, ⓦwww.southaustralia.com), a smaller version of the above.

Opposite the bus station at 110 Franklin St, the bright pink **Backpacker Transit and Travel Centre** (daily 9am–6pm; ⓣ08/8410 3000) can provide free maps and book all domestic tours; there's also a good notice-board and Internet access ($3 for 1hr).

City transport

The city centre is compact and flat, making walking an easy option, but if the heat becomes too much there are also two **free buses**. The **Bee Line** (#99B) runs from Victoria Square via King William Street, North Terrace and the Adelaide Train Station to Hindley Street, then back again. Services run every five minutes during the week (Mon–Thurs 8am–6pm, Fri 8am–9.30pm) and every fifteen on Saturdays (10am–5pm). The **City Loop Bus** (#99C, same times; every 15min) takes in all the city's major cultural and commercial centres, beginning at Adelaide Train Station.

To explore further out of the city centre, you'll need to use the integrated **Adelaide Metro system**, which comprises buses, suburban trains and one tramline from the city to Glenelg. Metro buses and trains run until about 11.30pm, with reduced services at night and on Sundays, while the **Wandering Star** night-bus service operates Fridays and Saturdays (12.30–5am; $6). The **O-Bahn** is a fast-track bus which runs on concrete tracks through scenic Torrens Linear Park, between the city (Grenfell St) and Tea Tree Plaza in Modbury, 12km northeast. Four suburban train lines run from Adelaide train station, west to Grange and Outer Harbour and south to Noarlunga and Belair. The **tram** to seaside Glenelg (every 15–20min; 30min; $2.30–3.80, depending on the time of day) leaves from Victoria Square.

Information on all of the above services as well as free timetables can be found at **Adelaide Metro Info Centre**, on the corner of King William and Currie streets (Mon–Fri 8am–6pm, Sat 9am–5pm, Sun 11am–4pm; Ⓦwww.adelaidemetro.com.au); staff also sell tickets and hand out copies of *The Metroguide*, a free information booklet including a handy map of the system. You can also get transport information on Ⓣ08/8210 1000 (daily 7am–8pm).

Tickets for the Metro system come in single-trip, multi-trip and day-trip permutations, and can be used on buses, trains and the tram; if you need to use more than one form of transport for a single journey, one ticket will suffice. Single tickets range in price from $2.30 to $3.80, depending on the time of day, and are valid for two hours. You can buy single-journey tickets from machines on board trains, buses and trams, as well as from train-station ticket offices and the Adelaide Metro Info Centre. Other types of ticket, including the day-trip ticket ($7.20), can be bought from the Adelaide Metro Info Centre, train stations, post offices and some newsagents – look for the Metroticket sign.

Cycling is a popular and excellent alternative to public transport: the wide streets and level surfaces make riding a breeze, and there are several good cycling routes – including the Torrens Linear Park track, which weaves along the river from the sea at Westbeach to the hills at Athelston. Bike SA has an overview of all cycling routes and **maps**; they also rent out bikes (see "Listings", p.744).

Accommodation

Adelaide has loads of **hostels**, and competition keeps prices low. Hostels outside the centre will pick you up from the bus or train station if you phone ahead (several also send minibuses to scout for custom), and some hostels will even come to the airport if you call in advance.

There are cheap **hotel** rooms on Hindley Street, Adelaide's nightclub area and red-light district; it's pretty tame, though some women may find it threatening. The swankiest accommodation is along **North Terrace**. The only time you

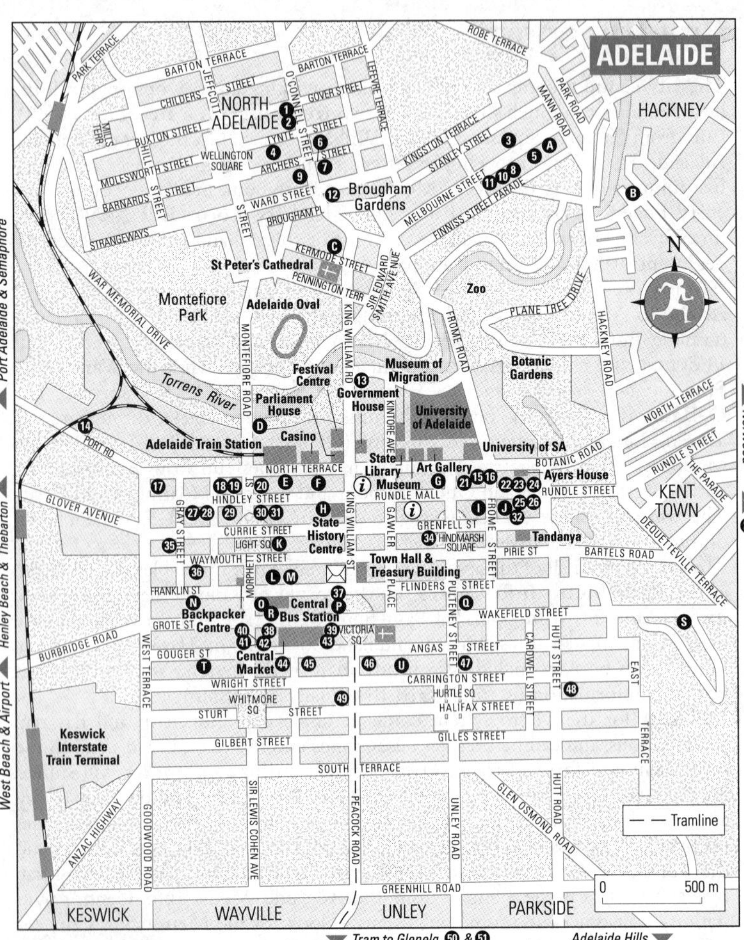

ACCOMMODATION

Adelaide Backpackers Inn	U
Adelaide Caravan Park	B
Adelaide Central YHA	K
Adelaide Meridien	A
Annie's Place	N
Austral Hotel	I
Backpack Oz	Q
Cannon Street Backpackers	L
Director's Studios	T
Franklin Central Apartments	M
Greenways Apartments	C
Holiday Backpackers	R
Majestic Roof Garden Hotel	J
Mercure Grosvenor	E
Metropolitan Hotel	P
Nomads Tatts Inner City	H
Norwood Apartments	S
Oaks Horizons	D
Richmond Hotel	G
Stamford Plaza Adelaide	F
Sunnys	O

EATING & DRINKING

Al Fresco Gelateria & Pasticceria	23
Amalfi Pizzeria Ristorante	15
Apothecary 1878	20
Archer Hotel	6
Bunca at the Austral	I
Café Paradiso	51
Caffe Buongiorno	33
Cargo Club	28
Church	21
Chuy's	9
Cibo	12
Citrus	48
Cowley's	37
Crown and Sceptre	46
The Daniel O'Connell	4
Earl of Aberdeen	47
Edinburgh Castle Hotel	35
Elephant Walk	5
Enigma	29
Eros Ouzeri	25
Exeter Hotel	22
Gaucho's	44
Governor Hindmarch	14
Grace Emily	36
The Grange	39
HQ	17
Jasmin	34
Jerusalem	30
Jolleys Boathouse	13
Kings Head Hotel	49
Kwik Stix	7
Marcellina	27
Mars Bar	41
The Melting Pot	50
Mesa Lunga	40
Monsoon	10
Oostende	32
Oxford Hotel	2
Rhino Room	16
Royal Oak Hotel	1
Sato	8
Scoozi	24
Star of Siam	45
Supermild	19
The Store	11
T-chow	38
Tempo	31
Universal Wine Bar	26
Worldsend	18
Ying Chow	42
Zambracca	3
Zuma	43

may have difficulty finding accommodation is during March, when the annual **Womadelaide** festival and the **Arts Festival** (even years only) attract throngs of visitors – book ahead. Rooms also fill up quickly at weekends, especially at the more popular hostels around the Central Bus Station on Franklin Street and adjacent Waymouth Street.

The seaside suburb of **Glenelg** and the nearby beach resorts (see p.728), about half an hour away from Adelaide by public transport, are good alternatives to the city centre, with plenty of self-catering apartments and one of Adelaide's liveliest hostels.

City centre

Hotels, motels and pubs

Austral Hotel 205 Rundle St ⓣ08/8223 4660, ⓦwww.theaustral.com. Basic rooms in one of Adelaide's best pubs on this "arty" street. There are bands or DJs nearly every night, so it can be noisy. ③

Director's Studios 259 Gouger St ⓣ08/8213 2500 or 1800 882 601, ⓦwww.savillesuites.com.au. A five-minute walk to Chinatown and the Central Market, this modern, good-value hotel has well-furnished self-catering studios and standard rooms. 24-hour reception and free parking. ④

Franklin Central Apartments 36 Franklin St, cnr of Betham St ⓣ08/8221 7050, ⓦwww.franklinapartments.com.au. Fully serviced one-, two- and three-bedroom apartments in a central location, ideal for business or extended stays. ⑥

Majestic Roof Garden Hotel 55 Frome St ⓣ08/8100 4499, ⓦwww.majestichotels.com.au. High-standard and fashionable place offering 120 very well appointed suites at surprisingly affordable rates. Facilities include room service, gym and Internet access. ⑥

Mercure Grosvenor 125 North Terrace ⓣ08/8407 8888 or 1800 888 222, ⓔre1@mercuregrosvenorhotel.com.au. Dating from 1918, this genteel establishment offers spacious, modern en-suite rooms with a/c, plus 24-hour room service, a gym and sauna, bar and bistro and parking. ⑥

Metropolitan Hotel 46 Grote St ⓣ08/8231 5471, ⓕ8231 0633. Rather tacky locals' pub offering good-value meals and basic clean rooms upstairs at bargain prices. ②

Oaks Horizons 104 North Terrace ⓣ08/8210 8000, ⓕ8210 8001, ⓦwww.theoaksgroup.com.au. Surprisingly reasonably priced self-catering apartments, all with balcony. Chic minimalist interiors and great city or river views from the top apartments. Facilities include pool, spa and gym. ⑥

Richmond Hotel 128 Rundle Mall ⓣ08/8223 4044, ⓕ8232 2290, ⓦwww.hotelrichmond.com.au. The pick of the lot, with a huge terrace overlooking Rundle Mall, this trendy hotel offers all mod cons plus a great restaurant in a relaxing atmosphere. ⑥

Stamford Plaza Adelaide 150 North Terrace ⓣ08/8461 1111, ⓦwww.stamford.com.au. This central, high-rise luxury five-star hotel has everything you'd expect: swimming pool, sauna, three restaurants, room service and views of the Festival Centre. Cheaper weekend packages are available. There's also a beachside equivalent, the *Stamford Grand Hotel*, at Glenelg. ⑦

Hostels

Adelaide Backpackers Inn 112 Carrington St ⓣ08/8223 6635 or 1800 247 725, ⓦwww.adelaidebackpackersinn.net.au. Shabby place in a converted pub, with a friendly ambience and helpful staff. Generous breakfast thrown in and free apple pie in the evening. Internet access available. Reception doubles as a travel agency and sells bus and train tickets. Dorms $22.

Adelaide Central YHA 135 Waymouth St ⓣ08/8414 3010, ⓦwww.yha.com.au. Modern, rather ugly but extremely efficient youth hostel with over two hundred beds in the heart of the city – don't expect a lively atmosphere though. There are also well-equipped kitchens, a large laundry room, lockers, a travel centre and Internet access next door. Some off-street parking spaces can be reserved. Dorms $23–25, rooms ③

Annie's Place 239 Franklin St ⓣ08/8212 2668, ⓦwww.anniesplace.com.au. Welcoming, family-owned hostel in a beautifully restored Victorian house with a country-style kitchen and breakfast room, small bar and cozy, plant-filled courtyard. Four-, six- and ten-bed dorms are available as well as immaculate doubles. Courtesy pick-up, free night tour and hearty continental breakfast included. Dorms $20, rooms ③

Backpack Oz 144 Wakefield St, cnr Pulteney St ⓣ & ⓕ8223 3551, ⓦwww.backpackoz.com.au. Converted from a nineteenth-century hotel, this low-key hostel has light, spacious rooms, dorms (four-, six- and ten-bed) and a guesthouse just across the street. There's a comfortable common room downstairs, plus a laundry and a small kitchen. Pick-ups from bus, train and airport, and tour bookings available. Dorms $20–22, rooms 3

Cannon Street Backpackers 110 Franklin St ⓣ08/8410 1218, ⓦwww.cannonst.com.au. One of the best hostels in town, this huge, warehouse-style place has a cool, young feel and is very clean and well run. The big and colourful foyer has a travel centre, Internet access and a funky licensed bar with the cheapest beer in town. Free light breakfast included as well as free apple pie in the evening, cheap day-membership at the gym around the corner, and spa if you've booked a double. Dorms $19–22, rooms 3

Holiday Backpackers 128 Grote St ⓣ08/8231 0639. Certainly shouldn't be your first pick but definitely the cheapest hostel in the centre of town, near Central Market and Chinatown, and with a friendly owner. A large percentage of the guests are Asian, hence the free rice for breakfast. Dorms $16, rooms 2

Nomads Tatts Inner City 1st Floor, 17 Hindley St ⓣ08/8231 3225. Small, centrally located hostel above a Heritage–listed hotel. A bit noisy, but it has good facilities, including a sunny veranda overlooking the main street, and a well-equipped kitchen. A renovation was planned at the time of writing, so call ahead. Dorms $20–22, rooms 3

Sunny's 139 Franklin St ⓣ08/8231 2430 or 1800 631 391, ⓦwww.sunnys.com.au. A friendly place in an old house next to the bus station. Facilities include a pool table, sound system, TV and video, and train, bus and plane tickets are sold and tours booked. There's cheap Internet access too, plus off-street parking. Rates include tea, coffee and a pancake breakfast. Dorms $22, rooms 2

North Adelaide and Kent Town

Adelaide Meridien 21 Melbourne St, North Adelaide ⓣ08/8267 3033, ⓦwww.adelaidemeridien.com.au. Located on fashionable Melbourne St, this modern brick building is actually an eyesore and the 1980s decor is rather dated. Creature comforts include a sauna, spa and outdoor pool. 7

Greenways Apartments 41–45 King William Rd, North Adelaide ⓣ08/8267 5903. One-, two- and three-bedroom fully furnished self-catering units, in an excellent location. Also good for long-term accommodation. 4

Norwood Apartments 7 Wakefield St, Kent Town ⓣ08/8338 6555, ⓕ8336 4555, ⓦwww.norwoodapartments.com.au. Five self-contained two-person units, each containing kitchen facilities, washing machine, TV, video and CD player. Good value and convenient location. 4

Beach suburbs

Glenelg Beach Hostel 1–7 Moseley St, Glenelg ⓣ08/8376 0007 or 1800 066 422, ⓦwww.glenelgbeachhostel.com.au. Award-winning hostel near the beach, located in a beautiful building with high ceilings and veranda. Lots of doubles as well as five- to six-bed dorms (no bunks). The lively common area downstairs has a trendy bar open to the public, with occasional live music. Both the abundant daily breakfast and BBQ on Sun are free. Dorms $25, rooms 3

Glenelg Jetty Hotel 28 Jetty Rd, Glenelg ⓣ08/8294 4377, ⓕ8295 4412. When all other options have failed, this is the place to go and join the blue-rinse brigade at the pokies. Friendly, homely pub accommodation popular with country people visiting the city. Rooms haven't been refurbished for decades so don't expect any luxury, and earplugs are a must as it can be extremely noisy. 4

Meleden Villa 268 Seaview Rd, Henley Beach ⓣ08/8235 0577, ⓦwww.meledenvilla.com. Good-value B&B one street back from the beach, in a lovely old two-storey building with a pool and outdoor terrace. Downstairs rooms share a bathroom, while upstairs rooms, with balconies and sea views, are en suite. 4

Oaks Plaza Pier Hotel 16 Holdfast Promenade ⓣ08/8350 6688, ⓦwww.theoaksgroup.com.au. The most recent development on the foreshore, this is quite the grandest hotel in Glenelg. Suites come with private balconies affording unspoilt ocean views, the sleek, modern rooms have all the comforts you'd expect at these prices, and facilities include a pool, gym, spa and sauna. 7

Taft Motor Inn 18 Moseley St, Glenelg ⓣ08/8376 1233, ⓦwww.taftmotorinn.com.au. Well-equipped motel units and spacious one- and two-bedroom self-catering apartments near the beach; all have a/c, a microwave and TV. The decor has had a recent upgrade but is still fairly colourless. Good for families, with a playground, garden, swimming pool (and toddler pool), and baby-sitting. 5

Camping and caravan parks

Adelaide Beachfront Tourist Park 349 Military Rd, Semaphore ⓣ08/8449 7726 or 1800 810 140, ⓦwww.adelaidebeachfront.com.au. A pleasant location with swimming pool, recreation room, playground and a free shuttle-bus service to West Lakes Mall and Ethelton train station. Book ahead in summer. Cabins ❹

Adelaide Caravan Park Bruton St, Hackney, on the Torrens River 2km northeast of the centre ⓣ08/8363 1566, ⓦwww.adelaidecaravanpark.com.au. The most central option, right on the Torrens Linear Park cycling route, reachable by bus #281 or #282 from North Terrace, or on foot through parkland and along the river. Cabins and two-bed holiday units ❹, villas with spas ❺

Adelaide Shores Caravan Park Military Rd, West Beach ⓣ08/8355 7320, ⓦwww.adelaideshores.com.au. Beach-front setting with a heated pool, barbecues and a nearby golf course. Take bus #276 or #278 from Currie St. Cabins and on-site vans ❸

The City

Adelaide's city centre is laid out on a strict grid plan surrounded by parkland: at the heart of the grid is **Victoria Square**, and each city quarter is centred on its own smaller square. **North Terrace** is the cultural precinct, home to the city's major museums, two universities and the state library. **Hindley Street** is the liveliest in town, and the focus of the city's nightlife, while **Rundle Mall**, its continuation, is the main shopping area; **Rundle Street**, further east, is home to the city's arty café strip. West of Victoria Square between **Grote** and **Gouger** streets is the lively **Central Market** and the small **Chinatown**. The **Torrens River** flows to the north of North Terrace, with the Botanic Gardens and zoo set on its south bank. Three main roads cross the river to the distinctive colonial architecture and café culture of **North Adelaide**.

Adelaide suffered numerous economic setbacks and built up its wealth slowly, and its well-preserved **Victorian architecture** has a reassuring permanence quite unlike the over-the-top style of 1850s Melbourne, with its grandiose municipal buildings funded by easy goldrush money. The bourgeois solidity of Adelaide's streets is enhanced by the fact that virtually every building, public or domestic, is made of **stone**, whether sandstone, bluestone, South Australian freestone or slate.

The Botanic Gardens and Ayers House

There's really only one place to start your tour, and that's tree-lined **North Terrace**, a long heritage streetscape perfect for exploring on foot. At its eastern extremity is the main entrance to the **Botanic Gardens** (Mon–Fri 7.15am–dusk, Sat & Sun 9am–dusk; free guided tours operate daily from the restaurant by the main lake at 10.30am; ⓦwww.botanicgardens.sa.gov.au). Opened in 1857, the lovely gardens boast ponds, fountains, wisteria arbours, statues and heritage buildings just like a classic English-style garden, but with plenty of native trees too. The elegant glass-and-wrought-iron **Palm House**, completed in 1877, was based on a similar building in Germany and used to display tropical plant species, a role now taken over by the stunning **Bicentennial Conservatory** (daily 10am–4pm, summer until 5pm; $4.50). This, the largest glasshouse in Australia, houses a complete tropical rainforest environment with its own computer-controlled cloud-making system. Other attractions include a fragrant herb garden, a rose garden and **Simpson House**, a pleasantly cool thatched hut containing palms and ferns beside a stream. The **information centre** (daily noon–4pm) is located in the centre of the park and has a shop selling books on botany and gardening, plus other souvenirs and a lovely café next door.

Heading away from the gardens on North Terrace, the first notable building you come to is the National Trust–owned **Ayers House** (Tues–Fri 10am–4pm, Sat & Sun 1–4pm; $8). Home to the politician **Henry Ayers**, who was premier of South Australia seven times between 1855 and 1897 and after whom the Rock was named, it began as a small brick dwelling in 1845 – the fine bluestone mansion you now see is the result of thirty years of extensions. Inside, it's elaborately decorated in late nineteenth-century style, with portraits of the Ayers family.

The universities and the Art Gallery of South Australia

Between Frome Road and Kintore Avenue, a whole block of North Terrace is occupied by the **University of Adelaide**, and the art gallery, museum and state library. The University of Adelaide, the city's oldest, was established in 1874 and began to admit women right from its founding – another example of South Australia's advanced social thinking. The grounds are pleasant to stroll through: along North Terrace are **Bonython Hall**, built in 1936 in a vaguely medieval style, and **Elder Hall**, an early twentieth-century Gothic-Florentine design now occupied by the **Conservatorium of Music** (concerts Fri 1.10pm; $6; ⓣ08/8303 5925, ⓦwww.music.adelaide.edu.au).

Overbearing Victorian busts of the upright founders of Adelaide line the strip between Bonython Hall and Kintore Avenue until you reach the **Art Gallery of South Australia**, established in 1881 (daily 10am–5pm; daily guided tours 11am & 2pm; free; ⓦwww.artgallery.sa.gov.au). The gallery has an impressive collection of **Aboriginal art**, including many nontraditional works with overtly political content; major works by the **Western Desert school** of Aboriginal artists are on permanent display in Gallery 7. There's a fine selection of colonial art, too, and it's interesting to trace the development of Australian art from its European-inspired beginnings up to the point where the influence of the local light, colours and landscape began to take over. The collection of twentieth-century Australian art has some good stuff – Sidney Nolan, Margaret Preston, Grace Cossington-Smith – but a lot of dross too. There's also a large collection of twentieth-century **British art**, including paintings by Roger Fry and Vanessa Bell (Virginia Woolf's sister). The gallery has a good bookshop and coffee shop too.

The South Australian Museum, State Library and Migration Museum

Next to the art gallery, a huge whale skeleton guards the entrance to the **South Australian Museum** (daily 10am–5pm; tours Mon–Fri 11am, Sat & Sun 2 & 3pm; free; ⓦwww.samuseum.sa.gov.au). The museum's east wing houses the engrossing **Australian Aboriginal Cultures Gallery** (40min guided tours Wed–Sun; $10; book at the museum shop or on ⓣ08/8207 7370), home to the world's largest collection of Aboriginal artefacts. Amongst the exhibits are a 10,000-year-old boomerang and the *Yanardilyi (Cockatoo Creek) Jukurrpa*, a huge painting by a collection of artists from across the continent recalling four important dreaming stories.

The west wing focuses on **natural history** and **geology**, including an extensive collection of minerals from around the world. There's also a permanent exhibition on local geologist **Sir Douglas Mawson** (1882–1958), who was commissioned by the museum to explore much of Australia in the early 1900s and who undertook the historic Australasian Antarctic Expedition in 1911.

Some of the animals he brought back from this expedition are still on display, along with others from around Australia. The **fossil gallery** includes a skeleton of *Diprotodon*, the largest marsupial ever to walk the earth, plus the Normandy Nugget (at the east wing entrance on the ground floor), the second-largest gold nugget in the world, weighing 26kg. For those wishing to gain a more comprehensive understanding of the museum's treasures, the **Science Centre** (Mon–Fri 10am–4pm) holds the museum archives (booking essential: ⓣ08/8207 7500) as well as the entire Douglas Mawson Collection.

Next door to the museum, on the corner of Kintore Avenue, the 1884 **State Library** (Mon–Wed 10am–8pm, Thurs & Fri 10am–6pm, Sat & Sun 10am–5pm; ⓣ08/8207 7250, ⓦwww.slsa.sa.gov.au) has everything from archives to newspaper- and magazine-reading rooms and free Internet access. It also holds the **Bradman Collection** (daily 10am–5pm; free), Sir Donald Bradman's personal collection of cricket memorabilia, including his own memoirs of the infamous Bodyline series with England. A large screen shows interviews and footage of his finest moments.

Around the corner on Kintore Avenue is the **Migration Museum** (Mon–Fri 10am–5pm, Sat & Sun 1–5pm; free; ⓦwww.history.sa.gov.au), which takes you on a journey from port to settlement in the company of South Australia's settlers, through innovative, interactive displays and reconstructions – the "White Australia Walk" has a push-button questionnaire giving you the red, green or amber light for immigration under the guidelines of the **White Australia policy**, which was in force from 1901 to 1958.

The government buildings and arts spaces

Continue west along North Terrace, past the War Memorial, to reach **Government House**, Adelaide's oldest public building, completed in 1855: every governor except the first has lived here. Across King William Road, two parliament houses, the old and the new, compete for space. The current **Parliament House**, begun in 1889, wasn't finished until 1939 because of a dispute over a dome, and while there's still no dome (and only half a coat of arms), it's a stately building all the same, with a facade of marble columns. Alongside is the modest **Old Parliament House** (closed to the public), built between 1855 and 1876.

On the corner of North Terrace and Morphett Street, the **Lion Arts Centre** is home to theatres, bars, a cinema, galleries and the **Experimental Art Foundation**, which houses artists' studios upstairs and provocative exhibitions in the gallery downstairs (gallery Tues–Fri 11am–5pm, Sat 2–5pm). A short stroll south of here on Morphett Street, the **Jam Factory Craft and Design Centre** (Mon–Fri 9am–5.30pm, Sat 10am–5pm, Sun 1–5pm; ⓦwww.jamfactory.com.au) displays beautiful objects (all of them for sale) made of leather, glass, wood and clay. A blue-metal spiral staircase leads to a viewing platform above the **glass-blowing** centre (demonstrations Mon–Fri 9am–4pm, Sat & Sun 10am–4pm). A block west of here is the latest addition to Adelaide's contemporary art scene, the **Light Square Gallery** (Mon–Fri 10am–5pm; free) in the basement of the Roma Mitchell Arts Education Centre on Light Square. The focus here is on techno art and the digital age.

Along the Torrens River

The **Torrens River** meanders between central Adelaide and North Adelaide, surrounded by parklands. Between Parliament House and the river is the **Festival Centre**, two geometric constructions of concrete, steel and smoked glass, in a concrete arena scattered with abstract 1970s civic sculpture. The main

△ The Festival Centre, Adelaide

auditorium, the **Festival Theatre** (Ⓦ www.adelaidefestivalcentre.com.au), has the largest stage in the southern hemisphere, hosting opera, ballet and various concerts; the foyer is often the venue for **free Sunday-afternoon concerts**. The smaller Playhouse Theatre is the drama theatre, while the Space Theatre is used for cabaret and stand-up comedy.

A short walk across **Elder Park** is the river, with its large fountain and black swans. **Popeye Cruises** leave from here for the zoo (Mon–Fri 1–3pm hourly,

Sat & Sun 11am–5pm every 20min; more frequent during holidays; $5 one way, $9 return), and you can also rent paddleboats ($10 per 30min). Nearby, the green shed at **Jolleys Boathouse**, across King William Road, is an Adelaide institution, housing a restaurant (see p.739) and a cheaper kiosk, both with river views.

The most pleasant way to get to **Adelaide Zoo**, whose main entrance is on Frome Road (daily 9.30am–5pm; free guided walks at 11am & 2pm; $18, children $10; call ⊕08/8267 3255 for feeding times and keeper talks, ⓦwww.adelaidezoo.com.au), is to follow the river, either by boat (see opposite) or on foot, a fifteen-minute stroll. Alternatively, walk from the **Botanic Gardens** through Botanic Park, entering through the children's zoo entrance on Plane Tree Drive, or take bus #271 or #273 from Grenfell or Currie streets. Opened in 1883, the country's second-oldest zoo (after Melbourne's) is full of century-old European and native trees, including a huge **Moreton Bay fig**, and grounds full of picnic tables. The Victorian architecture here is well preserved, and a few classic examples of the old-fashioned animal houses have survived, such as the **Elephant House**, built in 1900 in the style of an Indian temple. The zoo is best known for its extensive collection of **native birds**, with two large walk-through aviaries, while the Southeast Asian Rainforest exhibit has naturalistic settings that are home to sixteen animal species, including the endangered Malaysian tapir.

King William Street and Victoria Square

The city's main thoroughfare, **King William Street**, is lined with imposing civic buildings and always crowded with traffic. Look out for the **Edmund Wright House** at no. 59, whose elaborate Renaissance-style facade is one of Adelaide's most flamboyant. Inside the building, the **State History Centre** (Mon–Fri 9am–4.30pm) sometimes hosts free travelling exhibitions. On the other side of the street a couple of blocks south, the **Town Hall** (1866) is another of Edmund Wright's Italianate designs. The **General Post Office**, on the corner of Franklin Street, is yet another portentous Victorian edifice, this time with a central clock-tower: look inside at the main hall with its decorative roof lantern framed by opaque skylights. Opposite, on the corner of Flinders Street, the **Old Treasury Building** retains its beautiful facade, although it now houses apartments.

Halfway down King William Street lies pleasant **Victoria Square**, a favourite Aboriginal meeting place and home to the **Catholic Cathedral of St Francis Xavier** (1856) and the imposing **Supreme Court**, on the corner of Gouger Street. Just to the west, the covered **Central Market** (Tues 7am–5.30pm, Thurs 11am–5.30pm, Fri 7am–9pm, Sat 7am–3pm) has been a well-loved feature of Adelaide for over a hundred years. Here you can find delectable European and Asian produce in a riot of smelly stalls and lively banter, as well as heaps of shops (open Mon–Sat), cafés, sushi and noodle bars and restaurants. Nearby Gouger and Grote streets also have good options for a meal or a coffee.

Rundle Mall and Rundle Street

The main shopping area in the central business district is the pedestrianized **Rundle Mall**, which manages to be bustling yet relaxed, enhanced by trees, benches, alfresco cafés, fruit and flower stalls, and usually a busker or two. The two main shopping centres are the **Myer Centre**, with over 120 speciality stores over five floors, and the **Adelaide Central Plaza**, dominated by the upmarket **David Jones** department store and a fantastic foodmart in the basement. Towards the east end of the mall is the decorative **Adelaide Arcade** and the **Regent Theatre**. By night, Rundle Mall is eerily deserted, a strange contrast to Hindley and Rundle streets on either side, which really come to life after dark.

Rundle Street was once the home of Adelaide's wholesale fruit and vegetable market, but was later appropriated by the alternative and arty, and by university students from the nearby campuses on North Terrace. It's now home to over fifty **cafés** and **restaurants**, many of them alfresco, several slick wine bars and two of the best pubs in town (*The Austral* and *The Exeter*, see p.741). The disused **Adelaide Fruit and Produce Exchange** (1903) is worth a peek: it's a classically Edwardian building built of red brick, with curved archways decorated with yellow plaster friezes of fruit, vegetables and wheat. The facade has remained, but the interior has been transformed into pricey apartments.

Tandanya: the National Aboriginal Cultural Institute

Tandanya, the **National Aboriginal Cultural Institute**, is situated opposite the classic old market buildings at 253 Grenfell St (daily 10am–5pm; $5; ⓣ08/8224 3200, ⓦwww.tandanya.com.au). The centre is managed by Aboriginal people, and its main focus is the visual arts, with temporary exhibitions of national significance and a permanent display of work called the "Desert Dream", created by Aboriginal communities from the Northern Territory. Displays cover Dreamtime stories, history and contemporary Aboriginal writing, while political paintings confront black deaths in custody and other issues. There's also a 160-seat theatre for live performances, with daily **didgeridoo** or **dance performances** held at noon.

North Adelaide

North Adelaide, a ten-minute walk from the city centre, makes for an enjoyable stroll past stately mansions and small, bluestone cottages, or a good pub crawl around the many old hotels. There are three ways of getting there. The best walking route to North Adelaide is up King William Road past the Festival Centre (nearly every bus from outside the Festival Centre also goes this way). From Elder Park you cross the pretty 1874 **Adelaide Bridge** over the river to Cresswell Gardens, home of the **Adelaide Oval** cricket ground (guided tour April–Sept Mon–Fri 10am; Oct–March Tues & Thurs 2pm except match days; 2hr; $10), which has a small museum of cricketing memorabilia (Tues & Thurs 10am–1pm; $2) and affords superb views of **St Peter's Cathedral** (daily 9.15am–4pm; free guided tours Wed 11am & Sun 2.30pm) on Pennington Terrace. This Anglican cathedral was built in 1869 in the French Gothic-Revival style, with an entrance suggestive of Notre-Dame in Paris. The *Cathedral Hotel* opposite, built in 1850, is Adelaide's second-oldest hotel. At the top of King William Road, the peaceful and shady **Brougham Gardens** boast palm trees set against the backdrop of the Adelaide Hills. If you continue straight up, you'll come to North Adelaide's main commercial strip, **O'Connell Street**, whose restaurant scene rivals that of Rundle Street.

The district's best range of early **colonial architecture** lies a block west of here along **Jeffcott Street**. Just south of here in Montefiore Park is **Light's Vision**, a bronze statue of Colonel William Light pointing proudly to the city he designed. On Jeffcott Street itself is the neo-Gothic 1890 mansion **Carclew**, with its round turret, and the **Lutheran Theological College**, a fine bluestone and red-brick building with a clock tower and cast-iron decoration. Halfway up the street, on peaceful **Wellington Square**, lies the pretty 1851 *Wellington*

Hotel, complete with its original wooden balcony. Turning into tree-lined **Gover Street** you'll find rows of simple bluestone cottages; in contrast, **Barton Terrace West**, two blocks north, has grand homes facing parklands.

East of O'Connell Street is **Melbourne Street** (buses #207, #208 or #209 from King William Street, and #271 or #273 from Currie and Grenfell streets), an **upmarket strip** of cafés, antique stores, restaurants, designer clothing boutiques and speciality shops. The **Banana Room**, at no. 125, is probably the best retro-chic clothes store in Australia, with an immaculate range of designer dresses from the 1920s through to the 1950s. Don't expect bargains – most things are over $100 – but it's fascinating to browse.

The suburbs

Adelaide's **suburbs** spread a long way, and though they remain little visited, some of the inner suburbs – such as **Norwood** and **Thebarton** – have plenty of local character, inexpensive restaurants and out-of-the-ordinary shopping that's worth venturing out of the city centre for. West of the city lies a string of beaches, from **Henley** via **Glenelg** to **Brighton**, sheltered by the Gulf St Vincent. Further north, **Port Adelaide** has some excellent museums to set off its dockside atmosphere.

Norwood, Thebarton and Unley

Norwood, just east of the city, has two interesting streets: **Magill Road** (bus #106 from Grenfell or Currie streets), with its concentration of antique shops, and **The Parade** (bus #122–125 from Grenfell or Currie streets), a lively shopping strip with some great cafés, pubs and bookshops. The small **Orange Lane Market** (Sat & Sun 10am–5pm), at the corner of Edward Street and The Parade, is a sedate place to browse among secondhand and new clothes, books and bric-a-brac, or eat at Asian food stalls.

In **Thebarton**, west of the city, the lively **Brickworks Market** (Fri–Sun 9am–5pm; bus #110–113 from Grenfell or Currie sts) spreads out from the 1912 Brickworks Kilns at 36 South Rd. There are plaza shops and indoor and outdoor stalls, mostly selling new clothes, and it's always busy with buskers and crowds of people.

Immediately south of the city, **Unley Road** (buses #190–199 from King William St) is known for its antique shops and expensive boutiques. The parallel King William Road at Hyde Park (bus #203 from King William St) is shaded by lots of trees, plants and vine-covered awnings, and has some good cafés to relax in.

Port Adelaide and Torrens Island

The unfortunate early settlers had to wade through mud when they arrived at Port Misery, but thanks to William Light's visionary flair, **Port Adelaide** became the primary gateway to the state. Established not far from Port Misery in 1840, by 1870 it was a substantial shipping area with solid stone warehouses, wharves and a host of pubs. The area bounded by Nelson, St Vincent and Todd streets and McLaren Parade is a well-preserved nineteenth-century streetscape; several ships' chandlers and shipping agents show that it's still a living port, a fact confirmed by the many corner pubs (with pretty decorative iron-lace balconies) still in business.

The tourist office, near the waterfront on the corner of Commercial Road and St Vincent Street (daily 9am–5pm; ⓣ08/8405 6560), provides up-to-date details of attractions and information about local history. To get here, take a **train** from Adelaide Train Station or bus #151 (Mon–Sat daytime only) or #153 (evenings and Sun) from North Terrace.

The best day to visit is Sunday or public-holiday Mondays, when the **Fishermen's Wharf Markets** (9am–5pm) take over a large waterfront warehouse on Queens Wharf and several **cruises** are available on the water. The market (mainly bric-a-brac) adds some life to the waterfront, but the once-varied food stalls are now dominated by purveyors of meat pies and steak sandwiches. Outside is the quaint metal **lighthouse** (Mon–Fri 10am–2pm, Sun 10am–5pm) dating from 1869, which can be visited as part of a trip to the South Australian Maritime Museum (see below), as can the museum's two floating vessels moored 300m away, the steam tug *Yelta* and the coastal trader *Nelcebee*.

The pick of Port Adelaide's several museums is the **South Australian Maritime Museum**, located in the old Bond Store on Lipson Street (daily 10am–5pm; $8.50; ⓦwww.history.sa.gov.au), with both temporary and permanent exhibitions emphasizing the connection South Australia has with the sea. Further along Lipson Street, the **National Railway Museum** (daily 10am–5pm; $10; ⓦwww.natrailmuseum.org.au) is a trainspotter's delight, with a collection of over twenty steam and diesel locomotives. A free train ride runs on demand.

A few kilometres north of Port Adelaide is **Torrens Island**. Apart from a lively fresh fish and produce market on Sunday (6am–1pm), its main attraction is its intricate **mangrove forests**. This tranquil habitat rich in marine life can be explored on foot on the **St Kilda Mangrove Trail** (Mon–Fri 10am–4pm, Sat & Sun 10am–5pm; $6.90; booking essential on ⓣ08/8280 8172), which has an interpretive centre and a 1.7-kilometre boardwalk for self-guided tours; or by **kayak** with Blue Water Sea Kayaking (self-guided tour $35 for 2hr; booking essential; ⓣ08/8295 8812, ⓦwww.adventurekayak.com.au), giving the chance to spot Port River dolphins along the way.

Semaphore to Henley Beach

On the coast just east of Port Adelaide, **Semaphore**, with its picturesque jetty and fine old buildings, was important as the site of Adelaide's signal station from 1856 until the mid-1930s, before becoming a desirable holiday spot. Its current incarnation is as a popular **lesbian area** (see box, p.743), with several gay- and lesbian-run cafés and a pub on **Semaphore Road**, a charming street running at right angles to the beach, with awnings, stained-glass shop and café windows, and an old-fashioned cinema. In the summer a steam train runs once a month from Semaphore Jetty to **Fort Glanville** at 359 Military Rd (Sept–May every third Sun 1–5pm; $5.50), the only complete example of the many forts built in Australia in the mid-nineteenth century, when fear of Russian invasion reached hysterical heights after the Crimean War. To get to Semaphore by public transport, take a bus to Port Adelaide (see p.735), then catch bus #333.

About 8km south of Semaphore, **Grange** is a charming beachside suburb, with a row of Victorian terraced houses facing the sands and a popular pier with an upmarket kiosk. Take bus #110 from Grenfell Street (30min) or a Grange line train (20min). The next beach along is atmospheric **Henley Beach**, where the focus is **Henley Square**, opposite the long wooden pier. The square is lined with classic Federation-style buildings housing several popular restaurants and cafés (Mon–Sat bus #137, Sun #130, both 20min from Currie St; #286 or #287 from North Terrace, 35min).

Glenelg and Brighton

The most popular and easily accessible of the city's beaches is at **Glenelg**, 11km southwest of the city. You can get here by tram from Victoria Square (30min), or take bus #167 or #168 from Currie or Grenfell streets. Glenelg was the site of the landing of **Governor John Hindmarsh** and the first colonists on Holdfast Bay; the **Old Gum Tree** where he read the proclamation establishing the government of the colony still stands on McFarlane Street, and there's a re-enactment here every year on Proclamation Day (Dec 28).

Nowadays, Glenelg is busy even in the off-season. **Jetty Road**, the main drag, is crowded with places to eat (for the obligatory seaside fish and chips, *Bay Fish Shop* at no. 27 is the best) and there's lots of **accommodation** (see p.728). The tram terminates at **Moseley Square**, with its elegant town hall and clock tower. At the opposite corner, the original *Victorian Pier Hotel*, now part of the imposing seafront *Stamford Grand Hotel*, is crowded with drinkers on Sunday, when Glenelg is at its most vibrant. From Moseley Square, the jetty juts out into the bay, and in summer the beach on either side is crowded with people swimming in the calm waters; it's also a popular windsurfing spot year-round.

Facing the shore, **Glenelg Tourist Information** (Mon–Fri 9.30am–4.30pm, Sat 9.30am–3pm, Sun 10am–2pm; ⓣ08/8294 5833, ⓦwww.holdfast.sa.gov.au) can help book accommodation, tours and rental cars; there's also a 24-hour touch-screen information terminal outside. Next door, **Beach Hire** (ⓣ08/8294 1477) rents out deck chairs, umbrellas, surf skis, body-boards and snorkel sets. Rollerblading and cycling are other popular activities in Glenelg, with a **bike track** south of the square – you can rent cruisers and tandem bikes from Beach Hire for around $35 per day.

South of Glenelg, **Brighton** has an old-fashioned, sleepy air, dominated by the stone **Arch of Remembrance**, flanked by palm trees, which stands in front of the long jetty. Running inland from the beach, **Jetty Road** has a string of appealing one- and two-storey buildings shaded with awnings that contain an assortment of art, craft and secondhand stores, and two popular alfresco cafés: *A Cafe Etc* and *Horta's*. Brighton can be reached by train from Adelaide (25min) or bus #265 from Grote Street. For beaches further south, see p.758.

Eating

Adelaide has roughly one restaurant for every thirty people, so not surprisingly **eating out** is a local obsession, and it's wonderfully inexpensive compared to Sydney or Melbourne. One of the city's most popular places for a meal out is **Gouger Street** – many of the restaurants here have outdoor tables and are at their busiest on Friday night, when the nearby Central Market stays open until 9pm. **Moonta Street**, right next to Central Market, is the home of Adelaide's small **Chinatown**, and has several Chinese restaurants and supermarkets, while the excellent **food plaza** off Moonta Street (Mon 11am–2.30pm, Tues–Thurs 11am–4pm, Fri 11am–9pm) serves Vietnamese, Indian, Singaporean, Thai, Chinese and Malaysian food. **Hutt Street**, on the eastern edge of the city, has a string of fine Italian eateries and is a good place to go for breakfast. Café society is based around **Rundle Street** in the centre, and **O'Connell Street** and the decidedly chic **Melbourne Street** in North Adelaide. Finally, eating in pubs doesn't just mean the usual steak and salad bar but covers the whole spectrum, from some of the best contemporary Australian food in town to bargain specials in several pubs along **King William Street**.

Thanks to the state's liberal licensing laws most cafés are **licensed**, with South Australian wine featuring heavily.

City centre

Cafés

Al Fresco Gelateria & Pasticceria 260 Rundle St. Packed every night, the young Italian community have made it their own; this is the place to people-watch and be seen, while treating yourself to great coffee, biscotti, delicious home-made *gelati* and focaccia. Daily 6.30am until late.

Citrus 199 Hutt St. One of several Italian diners on this leafy street, *Citrus* benefits from a secluded outdoor eating area and serves one of the best breakfasts in town. Mon–Sat breakfast, lunch & dinner, Sun breakfast & lunch.

Cowley's Franklin St. An Adelaide institution; this mobile pie-cart takes up its position each night outside the GPO and is famous for its pie floaters. Mon–Thurs & Sun 6pm–1am, Fri & Sat 6pm–3.30am.

Jerusalem 131B Hindley St. Dimly lit Lebanese BYO that serves fresh and tasty Middle Eastern dishes. Daily noon until midnight.

Marcellina 273 Hindley St. This all-night pizza, steak and pasta bar is always full of people who have spilled out from the area's clubs and pubs. The pizzas are among the best in town, and deliveries are also available (☎08/8211 7560). Daily 11am until late.

Scoozi 272 Rundle St. A few doors east of *Al Fresco*, this popular licensed café does great Italian food – try the excellent wood-fired pizzas for lunch or dinner.

Tempo 91 Hindley St. Italian breakfasts and traditional trattoria-style cooking in the Art-Deco foyer of a former cinema. The daily specials board is worth checking out, as is the modern wine list. Mon–Fri from 8am–9.30pm.

Zuma 56 Gouger St. Locals flock here for the huge breakfasts, big salads, and filo parcels, bruschetta, focaccia and quiche baked on the premises. Mon–Thurs 7am–6pm, Fri 7am–10pm, Sat 7–4am.

Pubs and wine bars

Bunca at the Austral Hotel 205 Rundle St. The old beer garden here has been transformed into a funky venue with an industrial feel. Main dishes like butter chicken curry or spinach lasagne go for around $16, and the extensive wine list is sourced from boutique wineries. Daily lunch & dinner.

Earl of Aberdeen 316 Pulteney St, Hindmarsh Square. Set in a gazebo full of greenery, this place serves huge portions of moderately priced, imaginatively cooked pasta, steak, fish and kangaroo. Attentive service too. Open daily from noon until late.

Kings Head Hotel 357 King William St. Wide selection of wines by the glass and inexpensive meals like Thai green curry or simple burgers or steaks. Tasteful interior with plush seats and a dark wooden floor. The rear of the pub doubles as a disco on Fri. Tues–Sun lunch & dinner.

Oostende Ebenezer Place, off Rundle St. Busy Belgian café with loads of different Belgian beers (bottled and on tap) and typical dishes like *waterzooi* (soup with fish and potatoes) and Belgian waffles. A proven concept worldwide. Daily noon until late.

Universal Wine Bar 258 Rundle St ☎08/8232 5000. Stylish place that aims to educate people about wines, either South Australian or Italian. Superb Italian cooking with an Australian twist – try their home-made sun-dried tomatoes or mouthwatering Marron fish in season. Live jazz on Wed. Tues–Sun lunch & dinner.

Restaurants

Amalfi Pizzeria Ristorante 29 Frome St ☎08/8223 1948. Upbeat, jazzy and young with a variety of moderately priced vegetarian dishes, innovative pasta sauces and some traditional ones with a hot edge. Crowded, and open very late. Closed Sat lunch & Sun.

Eros Ouzeri 275–277 Rundle St ☎08/8223 4022. Greek *meze*-style dining with a smart and airy setting in a renovated old building with high Baroque ceilings. Abundant lunch menu with traditional dishes like *saganaki, souvlaki* and *moussaka*, while the attached café serves Greek pastries and coffee. Daily noon until late.

Gaucho's 91 Gouger St ☎08/8231 2299. If you're after red meat, this Argentinean place serves some of the best steaks in town – just name your weight. Licensed and BYO. Closed Sat & Sun lunch.

The Grange *Adelaide Hilton*, 233 Victoria Square ☎08/8217 2000. European-style fine dining prepared by one of Australia's best chefs, Cheong Liew, who brings an Asian angle to already adventurous dishes. Very expensive. Tues–Sat dinner; closed Dec & Jan.

Jasmin 31 Hindmarsh Square ☎08/8223 7837. Highly regarded North Indian restaurant. The menu may not be overly adventurous, but the cooking is impeccable – try the magnificent beef *vindaloo*, or check for daily specials. Thurs & Fri lunch, Tues–Sat dinner.

Jolleys Boathouse Jolleys Lane, off Victoria Drive next to City Bridge ☎08/8223 2891. Converted boathouse serving mouthwatering but pricey contemporary Australian cuisine. A popular venue for Sun lunch. Closed Sun night.

Mesa Lunga Cnr Morphett and Gouger sts ☎08/8410 7617. The hottest place in town for the Adelaide in-crowd serves everything from Spanish tapas to Italian *osso buco* in an überhip environment. Don't go here if you're looking for privacy; as the name suggests everyone eats from long tables and the place can get noisy. Lunch & dinner Tues–Sun, tapas until 11pm and pizzas until midnight.

Star of Siam 67 Gouger St ☎08/8231 3527. Extremely popular, award-winning Thai restaurant with a superb, reasonably priced menu, including a good range of vegetarian dishes. Mon–Fri lunch, Mon–Sat dinner.

T-chow 68 Moonta St ☎08/8410 1413. Huge, popular and reasonably cheap Chinese restaurant serving Teochew regional specialities such as tender duck, shark's-fin soup and green-peppercorn chicken, plus quick noodle lunches for $6. Voted best Chinese restaurant by the *Advertiser* in 2006.

Ying Chow 114 Gouger St ☎08/8211 7998. Unpretentious and always crowded place, serving inexpensive Northern Chinese cuisine including specialities such as aniseed-tea duck or scallops cooked with coriander and Chinese thyme. Vegetarians can enjoy delicious dishes such as bean curd with Chinese chutney. Licensed and BYO. Lunch Fri only, dinner nightly.

North Adelaide, Norwood and Unley

Cafés

Café Paradiso 150 King William Rd, Hyde Park, near Unley. A long-established Italian favourite, with great coffee and biscotti plus alfresco dining out front. Daily 7.30am–10pm.

Caffe Buongiorno 145 The Parade, Norwood. Large, always lively café serving a wide variety of Italian food and drink which reaches a crowded and noisy crescendo on Sun night. Daily 8–1am or later.

Elephant Walk 76 Melbourne St, North Adelaide. Lively but intimate coffee and late-night snack place, with small private lounge areas divided by carved wooden elephants and bamboo screens. Daily 8pm until late.

Oxford Hotel 101 O'Connell St, North Adelaide. Recently refurbished into a groovy pub with flaming red walls and a stainless-steel kitchen. The upgrade has also upgraded the price, with mains averaging between $10 and $22. Daily lunch, dinner Mon–Sat.

The Store Level 1, 157 Melbourne St, North Adelaide This corner location attracts a trendy, young clientele, has plenty of outdoor tables, and offers interesting breakfast and lunch menus. Daily 7am–7pm.

Restaurants

Chuy's 33–35 O'Connell St, North Adelaide ☎08/8267 3188. Cheap lunch specials and original Thai mains costing between $12 and $16, in a trendy if sober atmosphere. Licensed and BYO. Daily lunch and dinner; takeaway also available.

Cibo 10 O'Connell St, North Adelaide ☎08/8267 2444. Wood-fired pizzas, innovative pasta dishes and expensive Italian classics given a modern makeover using local ingredients. Can get very crowded at lunchtime. Daily 5.30–9pm & Sun–Fri noon–2.30pm.

Kwik Stix 42 O'Connell St, North Adelaide ☎08/8239 2023. Spacious modern Asian restaurant with good-value meals, including excellent chargrilled and sizzling dishes from Vietnam, Korea and Malaysia. Daily noon–2.30pm & 5–10pm.

The Melting Pot 160 King William Rd, Hyde Park, near Unley ☎08/8373 2044. One of the best modern French restaurants in Adelaide, with fantastic veal, spiced duck and seasonal fish, plus good wines and champagnes. Tues–Sat dinner; lunch in adjoining café.

Monsoon 135 Melbourne St, North Adelaide ☎08/8267 3822. Slick white interior in this fully licensed Indian restaurant for Adelaide's finest. Large selection of vegetarian dishes as well as different kinds of *naan* breads. Specializes in Indian sweets. Also BYO. Daily lunch & dinner.

Sato 131 Melbourne St, North Adelaide ☎08/8267 3381. Japanese restaurant with plenty of choice in sushi, sashimi and tempura dishes. BYO and licensed. Tues–Sun dinner.

Zambracca 94–98 Melbourne St, North Adelaide ☎08/8239 1345. A lively, licensed bistro crowded with Adelaide's smart set and dishing up superb, moderately priced Mediterranean food in spacious surroundings. Daily 8am until late.

Beach suburbs

Cafés

Sarah's 85 Dale St, Port Adelaide ⓣ08/8341 2103. Probably the best vegetarian café in Adelaide. Without any menus, diners are asked to place their trust in chef Stuart Gifford's capable hands – disappointment is unlikely. Tues–Sat lunch, Thurs–Sat dinner.

Stamford Grand Hotel The Foreshore, Glenelg ⓣ08/8375 0622. There are several good cafés and places to eat in this hotel, including the excellent *Rickshaw's* café, divided by an open kitchen where you watch the chefs at work: one side serves a variety of spicy Asian dishes and the other side is a coffee bar. There's also a more upmarket contemporary restaurant, *The Promenade*, with great sea views.

Restaurants

Estias Henley Square, Henley Beach ⓣ08/8353 2875. Fun seaside place for casual dining on Greek *meze* amongst playful, modern decor with reproduction classical sculptures and columns supporting the bar. Also serves more substantial, moderately priced dishes such as *moussaka*, and daily specials. Licensed and BYO. Lunch & dinner Tues–Sun.

Europa at the bay 12–14 Jetty Rd, Glenelg. Trendy restaurant and espresso bar with a stylish brown interior. The menu is not adventurous but includes a good selection of risottos and pastas. *The* place to have a *piccolo nero* coffee in the morning, and just as good as any pick on the rather commercial Moseley Square.

Lido On the Marina Pier Promenade, Glenelg. A bit of an outsider on the trendy promenade, but it does offer the best sea views and reasonably priced Mediterranean-style restaurant right on the water. Daily lunch & dinner.

Salt Holdfast Shores Marina, Glenelg. Modern-designed restaurant and wine bar in an exclusive location, serving tapas and cocktails to the hip and trendy. The oysters are fresh from Coffin Bay, and DJs on Sun funk up the evening. Open daily.

Nightlife and entertainment

Adelaide may appear dead at night, but there's actually quite a lot going on – bands, clubs, film and theatre – if you know where to look. The best place to find out **what's on** is *The Guide*, which comes with Thursday's *Advertiser* and has film and theatre listings and reviews. There's also a thriving **press**: top of the culture stakes is *The Adelaide Review*, a highbrow monthly covering the visual and performing arts, dance, film, literature, history, wine and food, available from bookshops such as Imprints on Hindley Street, museums, galleries and just about everywhere else. At the more populist end of the scale, *Rip It Up* is a gig listings magazine out every Thursday, with film, theatre, club and music reviews and interviews; *db Magazine*, in the same vein, is published every two weeks on Wednesdays – both can be picked up at record stores such as B# Records, 240 Rundle St, and Muses, 112–118 Rundle Mall. B# Records also sells tickets for underground events around town, but most big music events can be booked through Bass (ⓣ13 12 46, ⓦwww.bass.net.au).

At night, the two spots to head for are **Rundle Street**, which boasts the most fashionable pubs and bars, and the more mainstream and rather sleazy **Hindley Street**, where you'll find several funky clubs and live-music venues east of Morphett Street catering for the nearby university crowd. For something a bit different, try the **Adelaide Casino** (open 24hr daily; neat dress required) near the train station, complete with stunning domed marble entrance, glitzy gaming rooms and jaw-dropping Austrian crystal chandeliers.

Pubs and bars

Apothecary 1878 118 Hindley St. Multi-level wine bar housed in a nineteenth-century pharmacy, one of the coolest venues in town. Tasty Italian bar snacks and decent cocktails add to the allure. Tues–Thurs & Sat from 4pm until late, Fri noon until late.

The Adelaide Festival of Arts and Womadelaide

The huge Adelaide Festival of Arts (@www.adelaidefestival.org.au), which takes over the city for three weeks from late February to mid-March in even-numbered years, attracts an extraordinary range of international and Australian theatre companies, performers, musicians, writers and artists. An avant-garde Fringe has grown up around the main festival, which for many people is more exciting than the main event. The official festival began in 1960 and has been based at the purpose-built Festival Centre (see p.731) since 1973. In addition, free outdoor concerts, opera and films are held outside the Festival Centre and at various other locations during the period, while other venues around town host an Artists' Week, Writers' Week and a small film festival.

The Fringe Festival (@www.adelaidefringe.com.au) begins with a wild street parade on Rundle Street a week before the main festival, and events are held at venues all over town, with bands, cabaret and comedy at the *Fringe Club*, plus free outdoor shows and activities, while full use is made of the 24-hour licensing laws. Advance programmes for both the main and the fringe festival and further information is available from the offices of Tourism South Australia, or from all Bass outlets.

The Womadelaide (@www.womadelaide.com.au) world-music weekend began in 1992 as part of the Arts Festival but has now developed its own separate identity, attracting over thirty thousand people annually. Held in early March in the Botanic Park – with four stages, two workshop areas, multicultural food stalls and visual arts – it's a great place to hear some of Australia's local talent, with a broad selection of Aboriginal musicians as well as internationally acclaimed contemporary and traditional artists from around the world. The full weekend (Fri night–Sun night) costs $168, but day- and session-passes are also available. Tickets are available from Bass (Ⓣ13 12 46, @www.bass.net.au).

Archer Hotel 60 O'Connell St, North Adelaide. This recently renovated pub now has chic retro decor, with a good range of Aussie beers on the ground floor and a cocktail bar upstairs. It's a good lunch venue too.

Austral Hotel 205 Rundle St Ⓣ08/8223 4660. More consciously arty and music-oriented than the *Exeter* (see opposite), the *Austral* is frequented by students for the independent local bands (Fri & Sat nights) and DJs (Tues–Thurs & Sun nights). DJs are free, as is most of the music – when there's a cover charge, it's around $5. Fri & Sat open until 3am.

The Daniel O'Connell 165 Tynte St, North Adelaide Ⓣ08/8267 4032. Huge Irish pub with a lovely beer garden set around an old pepper-tree plus a large restaurant. Live bands – sometimes Irish folk musicians – play on Fri and Sat nights, when the place is heaving.

Exeter Hotel 246 Rundle St Ⓣ08/8223 2623. This spacious old pub with an iron-lace balcony is a long-established hangout for Adelaide's artists, writers and students, yet remains totally unpretentious. Good lunches served, and music nightly.

Grace Emily 232 Waymouth St Ⓣ08/8231 5500. Relaxed atmosphere, a young, alternative crowd and a range of local acts to suit everyone. Nightly until late.

Worldsend 208 Hindley St Ⓣ08/8231 9137. Large, multifunctional pub popular with the nearby university crowd and boasting two bars, a restaurant, cocktail bar, lounge, beer garden, and live music at weekends. Licensed till 4am.

Clubs, comedy and live music

Cargo Club 213 Hindley St Ⓣ08/8231 2327. Laid-back club featuring live jazz, spoken word, cabaret, soul, Latin, African and reggae acts plus local and international DJs. The decor is a mix of classic cool and trendy design, and there's something on most nights.

Church 9 Synagogue Place, off Rundle St Ⓣ08/8223 4233. This industrial-chic club venue in a converted temple is the enduring focus for Adelaide's rave scene, with local and international DJs. Wed–Sat 9pm–5am.

Crown and Sceptre 308 King William St Ⓣ08/8212 4159, @www.sceptre.com.au. A Heritage–listed pub that's been groovified into one of Adelaide's best venues, complete with sparkly bar stools, cozy couches in the intimate band area and a busy espresso machine. Local bands and DJ's Tues–Fri & Sun (usually free); Sat is club night (until 5am; around $5).

Enigma 173 Hindley St ⓣ08/8212 2313. Hip venue for the alternative university crowd. The small bar spills out into the street at weekends, and there's either funk or live grunge music upstairs. Wed–Sat until late.

Governor Hindmarsh 59 Port Rd, Hindmarsh ⓣ08/8340 0744, ⓦwww.thegov.com.au. The Gov, as this Adelaide institution is affectionately known, is one of Adelaide's leading live venues and hosts a broad range of live music and cabaret, with gigs from Tues to Sat at 8pm.

HQ 1 North Terrace ⓣ08/7221 1245, ⓦwww.hqcomplex.com.au. By far the largest venue in Adelaide, with 70s tunes (Wed), live music (Thurs & Fri) and better known DJ's on Sat.

Rhino Room Upstairs at 13 Frome St ⓣ08/8227 1611. Underground club venue with an intimate lounge atmosphere: come casual or get glammed up, no one cares, though the regular clientele may make you feel as if you've barged into a private party. Comedy Wed & Fri and live music Fri & Sat. Wed 7.30–11pm, Fri 7.30pm–2am, Sat 9pm–3am. Standard charge $6.

Royal Oak Hotel 123 O'Connell St, North Adelaide ⓣ08/8267 2488, ⓦwww.royaloakhotel.com.au. Popular North Adelaide bar and restaurant with arty decor and a young crowd. Live music (Tues & Sun), jazz (Wed) and DJs (Thurs and Fri).

Supermild 182 Hindley St West ⓣ08/8212 9000. One of the best clubs in town, with a laid-back atmosphere, chilled tunes and good cocktails. Wed 9pm–1am, Thurs 9pm–3am, Fri & Sat 9pm–5am, Sun 9pm–midnight.

Gay and lesbian nightspots

Edinburgh Castle Hotel 233 Currie St ⓣ08/8410 1211. Friendly gay- and lesbian-only venue with a dance floor from Thurs to Sun plus jukebox, bistro, beer garden and drag shows on Sun Mon–Sat 11am–late, Sun 2pm–late.

Mars Bar 122 Gouger St ⓣ08/8231 9639. This Adelaide institution has been around for years and hosts drag acts for a big, friendly mixed crowd. Wed–Sat 9pm–late.

Film

Adelaide's reputation as a city of festivals was further enhanced with the inaugural **Adelaide Film Festival** in 2003, held in odd-numbered years and running for two weeks from late February to early March. Booking ahead is advisable (ⓣ08/8271 1029, ⓦwww.adelaidefilmfestival.org). As well as several city and suburban mainstream film complexes, Adelaide now has four arthouse/retro cinemas. The main **discount day** for mainstream cinemas is Tuesday. In the summer, you can watch films outdoors at the **Moonlight Cinema** in the Botanic Gardens ($14; ⓣ1300 551 908, ⓦwww.moonlight.com.au); bookshops around town also have programmes.

Capri 141 Goodwood Rd, Goodwood ⓣ08/8272 1177. Alternative and arty films complete with pre-show Wurlitzer organ on Tues, Fri and Sat evenings. Take the tram to Glenelg to get here.

Chelsea 275 Kensington Rd, Kensington Park ⓣ08/8431 5080. The latest releases and a "crying room" for parents and babies.

Mercury Cinema Lion Arts Centre, 13 Morphett St ⓣ08/8410 1934, ⓦwww.mercurycinema.org.au. A great arthouse cinema showing shorts and foreign films.

Nova Cinema 251 Rundle St ⓣ08/8223 6333. Arts cinema complex with three screens; substantial backpacker discounts are available with the relevant card.

Odeon Star Cinema 65 Semaphore Rd, Semaphore ⓣ08/8341 5988. Quaint local beachside cinema showing mainstream films.

Palace East End 274 Rundle St ⓣ08/8232 3434. Alternative venue showing foreign-language and arthouse films plus other new releases. Discounts for backpackers.

Trak Cinemas 375 Greenhill Rd, Toorak Gardens ⓣ08/8332 8020. Good alternative cinema with two screens. Bus #145 from North Terrace to stop 10.

Gay and lesbian Adelaide

South Australia was the first state to legalize gay sex and remains one of the most tolerant of lesbian and gay lifestyles, although Adelaide's gay scene remains more modest than Sydney's or Melbourne's. Apart from the city's more mainstream annual festivals, there are a few strictly gay and lesbian fiestas. The biggest and best is Feast (ⓣ08/8231 2155, ⓦwww.feast.org.au), launched in 1997, which runs for three weeks in November. Events include theatre, music, visual art, literature, dance cabaret and historical walks, plus a Gay and Lesbian Film Festival at the Mercury Cinema (see opposite). The festival culminates in Picnic in the Park, an outdoor celebration in the parklands that surround central Adelaide which includes a very camp dog-show. Earlier in the year, June's Stonewall Celebrations are less flamboyant, featuring serious talks and exhibitions in a number of venues. A popular male gay hangout is Pulteney 431 Sauna, 431 Pulteney St (Mon & Tues 7pm–1am, Sun, Wed & Thurs noon–1am, Fri & Sat noon–3am; ⓣ08/8223 7506), with a spa, sauna, steam room, pool and snack bar.

To find out where the action is, pick up a copy of *Blaze* or check out "Listings" opposite.

Useful organizations and publications

Blaze 213 Franklin St ⓦwww.blazemedia.com.au. Fortnightly gay and lesbian newspaper with news, features and listings. Free from venues and bookshops. *Blaze* also publishes the handy free *Lesbian & Gay Adelaide Map*.

Darling House Gay and Lesbian Community Library 64 Fullarton Rd, Norwood. Fiction, non-fiction and newspapers. Mon–Fri 9am–5pm.

Liberation Monthly newsletter for lesbians – good for contacts and local events.

Murphy Sisters Bookshop 240 The Parade, Norwood. Gay/lesbian bookshop with a handy notice board. Wed–Sat only.

Parkside Travel 70 Glen Osmond Rd, Parkside ⓣ08/8274 1222 or 1800 888 501. Gay-owned and-operated company offering hotel reservations, information and travel services.

Theatre and the performing arts

Out of festival time, mainstream theatre, ballet, opera, contemporary dance, comedy and cabaret continue to thrive at the **Festival Centre** (see p.731). Classical concerts are held at the **Adelaide Town Hall** (usually performed by the Adelaide Symphony Orchestra) and at **Elder Hall** in the Conservatorium of Music on North Terrace. The **Lion Theatre**, on the corner of Morphett Street and North Terrace, is the main venue of the Lion Arts Centre with interstate performers, jazz bands and comedy line-ups (ⓣ08/8218 8400), while **Theatre 62**, 145 Burbridge Rd, offers two venues under one roof with pantomime, a theatre-restaurant and experimental productions (ⓣ08/8234 0838). Almost anything that's on can be booked through Bass (ⓣ13 12 46, ⓦwww.bass.net.au).

Shopping

You can find most things you'll need in **Rundle Mall** (see p.734), which has three department stores, plus a handy Woolworths at no. 86 with a small supermarket attached. There's also a Coles supermarket at 21 Grote St (open daily), next to the Central Market. For alternative fashion, **Rundle Street** and, particularly, Miss Gladys Sym Choon at no. 235 is the place to go. For **retro** clothing visit Naked at no. 238, Irving Baby, 33 Twin St, off Rundle Mall, or The Banana Room (see p.735). For **Aboriginal arts** and crafts try Tandanya (see p.734) or the Otherway Centre at 185 Pirie St. B# Records, at 240 Rundle St, and Krypton Discs, at 34 Jetty Rd, Glenelg, are both good for music.

There are several good **bookshops** around the city: the excellent Unibooks, at Adelaide University, provides an excuse to nose around the university; Angus & Robertsons, 138 Rundle Mall, is a large mainstream store; while the huge Borders, in Rundle Mall, has an excellent range of international newspapers and magazines plus an in-store café. Adelaide Booksellers, at 6A Rundle Mall, sells good secondhand titles, as does O'Connell's Bookshop at 62 Hindley St – they also buy or exchange books.

Markets include Central Market, Orange Lane Market, Brickworks Market, Port Adelaide Market and Torrens Island Fish and Produce Market (see p.733, 735, 735, 736 & 734). **Shopping hours** are generally Monday to Saturday 9am to 5 or 6pm, with late-night shopping until 9pm on Friday in the city and Thursday in the suburbs, plus Sunday trading (11am–5pm) in the city only.

Listings

Airlines Air New Zealand ⓣ13 24 76; Alitalia ⓣ08/8306 8363; British Airways ⓣ08/8238 2138; Garuda ⓣ1300 365 330; Japan Airlines ⓣ08/8212 2555; Lufthansa ⓣ1300 655 727; Malaysia Airlines ⓣ13 26 27; Qantas ⓣ08/8407 2233; Singapore Airlines ⓣ08/8203 0800.

American Express Shop 32, City Centre, Rundle Mall (Mon–Fri 9am–5pm, Sat 9am–noon; ⓣ1300 13 90 60).

Banks and foreign exchange All the major banks are located on King William St. Exchange services are available at the international airport, at American Express (see above) and at Travelex, 45 Grenfell St (Mon–Fri 9am–5pm; ⓣ1800 637 642). Outside these hours, the casino (see p.740) or international hotels on North Terrace can help, but obviously the exchange rates will be poor.

Bikes and bike rental Flinders Camping, 187 Rundle St (ⓣ08/8223 1913), rents bikes for $20 per day and offers weekly rates; Linear Park Mountain Bike Hire at Elder Park (ⓣ08/8223 6271), situated near a section of the River Torrens Linear Park bike track, rents bikes by the hour or day at competitive prices; Bike SA, 46 Hurtle Square (ⓣ08/8232 2644), is a nonprofit cycling organization providing information and cycling maps and organizing regular touring trips. They offer free bikes for the first two hours and charge $6 per hour thereafter; they also have a pick-up point at *Cannon Street Backpackers*.

Camping equipment and rental Rundle St is the place: for rental, try Flinders Camping at no. 187 (ⓣ08/8223 1913); they are also the only place in town that repairs backpacks. Paddy Pallin at no. 228 sells a range of high-quality gear, plus maps, or there's the Scout Outdoor Centre at no. 192.

Canoe rental and tours Adelaide Canoe Works, 74 Daws Rd, Edwardstown (ⓣ08/8277 8422), offer a range of courses and expeditions as well as very reasonably priced canoe and kayak hire.

Car rental Avis (ⓣ13 63 33), Hertz (ⓣ13 26 07) and Thrifty (ⓣ08/8211 8788) have desks at the airport. Otherwise, small and friendly Access, 60 Frome St (ⓣ08/8359 3200 or 1800 812 580), does free airport deliveries; they also rent out sports cars. Other options include Action (ⓣ08/8352 7044) or Excel (ⓣ1300 551 164). Older, cheaper cars can be obtained from Cut Price Car Rentals (ⓣ08/8443 7788), which also does one-way rentals and buy-backs, or Rent-a-Bug (ⓣ08/8234 0911). Britz Campervan, Car and 4WD Rentals (ⓣ08/8234 4701 or 1800 331 454) have a full range of campervans for hire.

Disabled travellers Disability Information and Resource Centre, 195 Gilles St ⓣ08/8236 9555.

Environment and conservation The Conservation Council of South Australia, 120 Wakefield St (ⓣ08/8223 5155), is a good place to find out what's going on. The Wilderness Society has its campaign office at 118 King William St (ⓣ08/8231 6586) and a shop in Victoria Square Arcade, Victoria Square (ⓣ08/8231 0625).

Hospital Royal Adelaide Hospital, North Terrace ⓣ08/8222 4000; Dental Hospital, Frome Rd ⓣ08/8222 8222.

Internet access There's limited-time free access at the State Library (see p.731; book in advance), and cheap access at iNet Zone, 42 Grote St ($5 per hour). Most of the backpackers places have Internet access for guests as well.

Laundries Adelaide Launderette, 152 Sturt St (daily 7am–9.30pm; service washes Mon–Fri 9am–5pm).

Left luggage Adelaide Train Station has 24-hour lockers. There are also facilities at the Central Bus Station with Premier Stateliner ($2 per 24hr) and Greyhound Australia (from $6 per 24hr).
Maps The Map Shop, 16A Peel St, between Hindley and Currie streets, has the largest range of local and state maps. If you're a member of an affiliated overseas automobile association, you can get free regional maps and advice on road conditions from the Royal Automobile Association, 55 Hindmarsh Square (☎08/8202 4600, www.raa.net).
Medical centre City Centre Medical Clinic, 77 Gilbert Place ☎08/8212 3226.
Motorbike rental Show & Go Motorcycles, 236 Brighton Rd, Somerton Park ☎08/8376 0333.
Newspapers The *Advertiser* is very provincial and doesn't have good coverage of national and international news, but is useful on Thurs for entertainment listings, and Wed and Sat for classifieds if you're looking for a car or other travel equipment. Alternatively, Melbourne's *The Age* is widely available. The best place to buy foreign and interstate newspapers is Rundle Arcade Newsagency, off Gawler Place, or Borders in Rundle Mall.
Pharmacy Midnight Pharmacy, 13 West Terrace (Mon–Sat 7am–midnight, Sun 9am–midnight). In Glenelg try Stephens Pharmacy, on the corner of Jetty Rd and Gordon St (daily 8.30am–10pm).
Police For emergencies call ☎000.
Post office GPO, 141 King William St, cnr Franklin St (Mon–Fri 8am–6pm, Sat 8.30am–noon); for poste restante use Adelaide GPO, SA 5000.
Swimming pool Adelaide City Swim, 235 Flinders St (Mon 6am–8.30pm, Sat 7.30am–2pm, Sun 8.30am–12.30pm; $10 per hour). Adelaide Aquatic Centre, corner of Jeffcott Rd and Fitzroy Terrace, North Adelaide (Mon–Sat 5am–10pm, Sun 7am–8pm; swimming $5.90), is an indoor centre with pool, gym, sauna and spa; take bus #231 from North Terrace.
Taxis There's a taxi rank on the corner of Pulteney and Rundle streets, otherwise call Adelaide Independent (☎13 22 11), Suburban Taxi Service (☎13 10 08), or Yellow Cabs (☎13 22 27).
Telephones Rundle Mall has lots of phones, including ones that take credit cards. For peace and quiet, try the Phone Room in the GPO.

Tours from Adelaide

There are a huge number of tour companies operating out of Adelaide, offering everything from leisurely day-trips to hard-core camping excursions.

Adelaide Explorer City Sights Tour ☎1300 655 276. This hop-on hop-off tour covers the city, Glenelg and West Beach, with daily departures from the Travel Centre, 18 King William St, at 9.05am, 10.30am & 1.30pm (3hr; $30).
Camp Wild Adventures ☎08/8132 1333, www.campwild.com.au. Offers an adventurous 4WD camping tour to Kangaroo Island (three days; $395 all inclusive), and another tour to Alice Springs via the Flinders Ranges (seven days; $825 all inclusive).
Gray Line (☎1300 858 687, www.grayline.com), **Premier Day Tours** (☎08/8415 5566, www.premierstateliner.com.au) and **Adelaide Sightseeing** (☎08/8413 6199, www.adelaidesightseeing.com.au) all head for the Barossa Valley (see p.751), Kangaroo Island (see p.765) and the Fleurieu Peninsula (see p.758), and can also arrange trips further afield to the Murray River, or the Coorong and Flinders ranges.
Groovy Grape Getaways ☎1800 661 177, www.groovygrape.com.au. For something different to the Barossa, try this small-group day-tour which stops at Gumeracha's giant rocking horse, the Whispering Wall near Lyndoch, and four large wineries, and includes a barbecue lunch – it's particularly popular with backpackers ($69).
Heading Bush 4WD Adventures ☎08/8356 5501, www.headingbush.com. Operates an epic ten-seater camping tour to Alice Springs, taking in Flinders Ranges, Coober Pedy, the Simpson Desert and Uluru (ten days; $1495).
Prime Mini Tours ☎1300 667 650, www.primeminitours.com. Runs a fairly sedate minibus tour from Adelaide with a similar itinerary to Groovy Grape, including a three-course sit-down lunch ($67).
Wayward Bus 115 Waymouth St ☎08/8410 8833 or 1800 882 823, www.waywardbus.com.au. Adelaide is the home base for this excellent company, which does good one-way, small-group tours from Adelaide to Melbourne (or vice versa) via the scenic coastal route (three and a half days; $345 including breakfast, lunch and hostel accommodation). They also run one-way tours to Alice Springs taking in the Clare Valley, Flinders Ranges, Oodnadatta Track, Lake Eyre, Coober Pedy, Uluru, Kata Tjuta and Kings Canyon (eight days; $895 all inclusive).

Travel agents Adelaide YHA Travel, 135 Waymouth St ⓣ08/8414 3000; City Centre Travel, 75 King William St ⓣ08/8221 5044; Flight Centre, 186 Rundle St ⓣ08/8227 0404; Jetset, 23 Leigh St, off Hindley St ⓣ08/8231 2422; Peregrine Travel, upstairs at 192 Rundle St ⓣ08/8223 5905; STA Travel, 235 Rundle St ⓣ08/8223 2426; Thor Adventure Travel, upstairs at 228 Rundle St ⓣ08/8232 3071.

Work Information on work rights is available from the Department of Immigration and Multicultural Affairs (ⓣ13 18 81, ⓦwww.immi.gov.au/employers). Unemployment is high in Adelaide itself, but it's a good place to find out about casual fruit-picking work in the Riverland. Hostels can help with finding work, and often provide a source of employment for young travellers.

Moving on from Adelaide

For **domestic flights** from Adelaide, Air South (ⓣ08/8234 4988, ⓦwww.airsouth.com.au) flies to Kangaroo Island; Jetstar (ⓣ13 15 38, ⓦwww.jetstar.com.au) flies to the Gold Coast, Melbourne and Hobart; O'Connor Airlines (ⓣ08/8723 0666, ⓦwww.oconnor-airlines.com.au) flies to Port Augusta, Whyalla and Mount Gambier; Regional Express (ⓣ13 17 13, ⓦwww.rex.com.au) serves Broken Hill, Ceduna, Mount Gambier, Port Lincoln, Whyalla, Coober Pedy, Olympic Dam and Kangaroo Island; and Virgin Blue (ⓣ13 67 89, ⓦwww.virginblue.com.au) flies to major cities countrywide.

The *State Guide*, available from the South Australian Travel Centre (see p.724), has route maps and timetables for all of South Australia's bus routes. Most **long-distance buses** leave from the Central Bus Station on Franklin Street. Greyhound Australia (ⓣ1300 4739 46863) has a nationwide service that includes Alice Springs in its destinations, while Firefly Express (ⓣ1300 730 740, ⓦwww.fireflyexpress.com.au) runs to Melbourne and Sydney. V/Line (ⓣ08/8231 7620 or 13 61 96, ⓦwww.vline.com.au) also runs to Melbourne from Adelaide and Mount Gambier.

State services are dominated by Premier Stateliner Coach Service (ⓣ08/8415 5555, ⓦwww.premierstateliner.com.au), which goes to the Riverland, Whyalla, Port Lincoln, Ceduna, Woomera, Roxby Downs and Olympic Dam, the Yorke and Fleurieu peninsulas and to Mount Gambier either inland or along the coast. Other local operators include the Barossa Coach Service (ⓣ08/8564 3022), which stops at the main towns in the Barossa Valley en route to Angaston; the Yorke Peninsula Passenger Service (ⓣ1800 625 099), which runs from Adelaide to Yorketown down the east coast via Ardrossan, Port Vincent and Edithburgh, and down the centre via Maitland and Minlaton; the Mid North Passenger Service (ⓣ08/8823 2375) via the Clare Valley and/or Burra to Peterborough; and the Murray Bridge Passenger Service (ⓣ08/8532 2633) to Pinnaroo via Murray Bridge and to Murray Bridge via Mannum and Meningie. Tickets can be purchased at the Central Bus Station. The **Bus Booking Centre** at Station Arcade, 52 Hindley St (ⓣ08/8212 5200), can arrange travel on any bus service.

There are three options for onward **train** travel – The *Overlander* to Melbourne, the *Ghan* to Darwin via Alice Springs and the *Indian Pacific*, which runs east to Sydney and west to Perth. Tickets can be booked through the Great Southern Railway Travel Pty (ⓣ13 21 47, ⓦwww.gsr.com.au), which produces a glossy brochure with current timetables.

Around Adelaide

Escaping Adelaide for a day or two is easy and enjoyable, with a tempting range of beaches, hills and wineries to choose from. Closest at hand are the **Adelaide Hills**, southeast of the city, which are popular for weekend outings and have numerous small national and conservation parks that are great for walking. To the south, the **Fleurieu Peninsula** extends towards Cape Jervis and has plenty of fine beaches and several small wineries.

If wine is your priority, though, head for the **Barossa Valley**, Australia's premier wine-producing region, with over fifty excellent wineries within 50km of Adelaide. The valley is easily visited in a day from the city, but is also a great place to stop over and unwind. The **Yorke Peninsula**, across the gulf from Adelaide, is far less known, though many locals holiday here: as well as beaches, it's home to the remains of an old copper-mining industry and an excellent national park.

The Adelaide Hills

The beautiful **Adelaide Hills** are the section of the **Mount Lofty Ranges** that run closest to the city, just thirty minutes' drive away, and largely accessible by train and the Transit Plus bus service (ⓣ08/8339 7544); several tours heading for the Fleurieu Peninsula also take in the area. Many people have set up home in the hills to take advantage of the cooler air, and there are some grand old summer houses here. The **Heysen Trail** long-distance walk from Cape Jervis to Parachilna Gorge cuts across the hills, with four quaint YHA hostels along it; most are run on a limited-access basis and you'll have to pick the key up first from the Adelaide office at 135 Waymouth St (ⓣ08/8414 3010). The **Adelaide Hills Visitors Information Centre** in Hahndorf (see p.749) is a good source of information about the area, and can also make accommodation bookings.

Leaving the city by Glen Osmond Road you join the **South Eastern Freeway**, the main road to Melbourne – there's an old tollhouse not far out of the city at Urrbrae and several fine old coaching hotels such as the *Crafers Inn*. At **CRAFERS** itself you can leave the freeway for the scenic Summit Road, which runs along the top of the hills, past the western side of the extensive **Mount Lofty Botanic Gardens** (Mon–Fri 8.30am–4pm, Sat & Sun 10am–5pm) to the **Mount Lofty Lookout** (710m), the highest point of the range. There's an **information centre** here (daily 9am–5pm; ⓣ08/8370 1054, ⓦwww.environment.sa.gov.au) with fantastic views and a café-restaurant and bar. Transit Plus buses #863, #864, #865 and #866 run from Adelaide's Central Bus Station or Currie Street to Crafers, and bus #823 from Crafers will take you up the hill, from where you can access the eastern side of the Botanic Gardens.

The turn-off to **Cleland Wildlife Park** (daily 9.30am–5pm; $13.50; ⓦwww.cleland.sa.gov.au) is the first on the left after the lookout. Here you can cuddle a koala and see other Australian fauna in enclosures, and there are several good walking trails through native bush leading from the park into the surrounding Cleland Conservation Area. You can get up here as part of a tour with Gray Line ($41; ⓣ1300 858 687, ⓦwww.grayline.com), Adelaide Sightseeing ($48; ⓣ08/8413 6199, ⓦwww.adelaidesightseeing.com.au) or Premier Day Tours ($48; ⓣ08/8415 5566, ⓦwww.premierstateliner.com.au).

The **Morialta Conservation Park**, to the north, is easily reached by taking the #105 bus (35min) from Grenfell Street in the city centre, which goes right into the park along the scenic Morialta Falls Road; from the entrance it's a two-kilometre bushwalk into the park to a lovely waterfall. By car you can

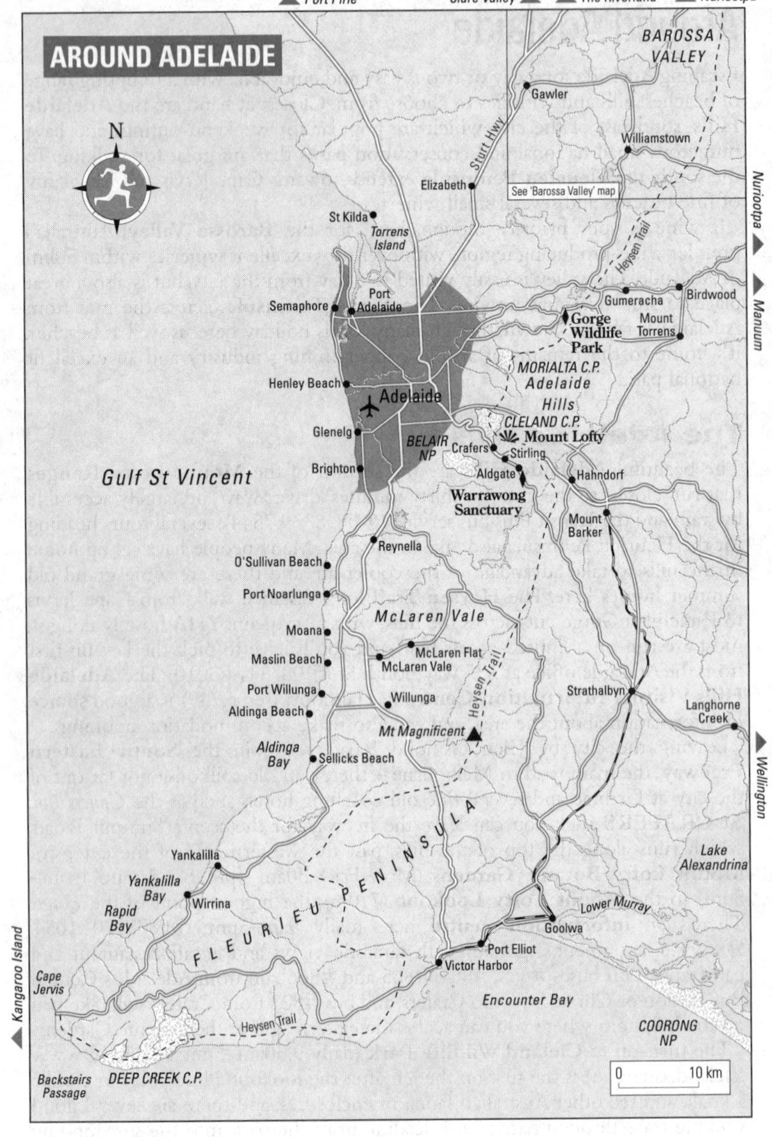

approach the park along the equally impressive Norton Summit Road; the *Scenic Hotel*, clinging to the side of the hill at Norton Summit, is a great place to stop for a drink.

South of Crafers, virtually in the southern suburbs of Adelaide, is **Belair National Park** (daily 8am till sunset; $2.90, or $7 per car; Ⓦ www.belair.sa.gov.au). Getting there is half the pleasure – you take a suburban train from Adelaide Train Station (35min), which winds upwards through tunnels and valleys with

Wineries and B&Bs in the hills

Less than thirty minutes' drive from the city, the Adelaide Hills' wineries may not be as famous as those in the neighbouring Barossa Valley, but they are gaining popularity and are definitely worth checking out. The cool-weather (this is the coolest wine-growing region on mainland Australia) contributes to wonderful Sauvignon Blancs and fresh Chardonnays and you can even expect a superb cool-weather Shiraz. *Hahndorf Hill Winery* at 10 Pains Rd in Hahndorf (daily 10am–5pm; ⓦwww.hahndorfhillwinery.com.au) makes an award-winning Sauvignon Blanc and a rosé made of rare German grapes; it's also great for lunch overlooking the valley. The more commercial *Nepenthe* winery on Jones Road (daily 10am–4pm, ⓦwww.nepenthe.com.au) has vast vineyards with everything from hand-picked Riesling to a Pinot Noir. Apart from being an excellent winery, *Petaluma Bridgewater Mill*, located in a 1860 mill at Mount Barker Road in Bridgewater (daily 10am–5pm; ⓦwww.bridgewatermill.com.au), has won prizes its restaurant and is well worth a visit.

B&Bs are plentiful in the hills, but don't come cheap. Adelaide Hills Country Cottages (ⓦwww.ahcc.com.au) lists a number of excellent B&Bs in and around Oakbank; alternatively, the South Australia B&B and Farmstay (ⓦwww.bandbfsa.com.au) has a useful brochure of places to stay, available from the South Australian Travel Centre in Adelaide (see p.724). One of the best places is *Apple Tree Cottage*, in Oakbank to the east (ⓣ08/8388 4193, ⓦwww.ahcc.com.au; ⑦), a self-contained 1860 cottage beside an idyllic lake. In Aldgate, *Cladich Pavilions* are luxurious modern apartments set in native bushland (ⓣ08/8339 8248, ⓦwww.cladichpavilions.com; ⑥), while for train enthusiasts, the 1880s *Mount Lofty Railway Station* (ⓣ08/8339 7400, ⓦwww.mlrs.com.au; ④) in Mount Lofty has been converted into a sociable B&B.

views of Adelaide and Gulf St Vincent. From Belair station, steps lead to the valley and the grassy recreation grounds and kiosk. With its joggers, tennis courts, man-made lake, hedge maze and **Old Government House** (open to visitors Sun 12.30–4pm), a residence built in 1859 as a summer retreat for the governor, this seems more like a garden than a national park, though there are also some more secluded bush trails through gum forests.

The **Warrawong Sanctuary**, southeast of Belair National Park on Stock Road, reached by Sturt Valley Road, Heather Road and Longwood Road, was set up in the late 1960s as a sustainable conservation model to halt the loss of Australian wildlife. Guided **bushwalks** starting at dawn or sunset ($20; bookings essential; ⓣ08/8370 9197, ⓦwww.warrawong.com) offer the opportunity to spot the sanctuary's mostly nocturnal animals in their natural habitat, including several endangered species such as bettongs and potoroos (both from the marsupial family) as well as the elusive platypus. The sanctuary also has a licensed **restaurant** as well as **accommodation** in air-conditioned, en-suite tent-cabins ($100 per person including dusk tour, dinner and breakfast). From Wednesday to Sunday they have shows with birds of prey (11am & 2pm; $7.40). There's no public transport or tours to Warrawong, but Transit Plus bus #866 goes to Stirling, where you can get a taxi for the remaining 5km.

Hahndorf

HAHNDORF, 28km southeast of the city, is the most touristy destination in the hills, and is always crowded at weekends. There are frequent Transit Plus bus services here from Central Bus Station (40min). Founded in 1839, it's Australia's oldest **German settlement** and still has the look of a nineteenth-century village. The Bavarian-style restaurants and coffee houses, crafts, antique and gift shops are thoroughly commercial, but it's still enjoyable, especially in autumn when the chestnuts and elms lining the main street have turned golden.

The **Hahndorf Academy** (Mon–Sat 10am–5pm, 4pm in winter; free) is a working artist's studio with a small collection of photographs, prints, displays and well-written interpretive boards that shed light on the lives of early German settlers, plus a few sketches by the town's most famous resident and one of Australia's best-known artists, **Hans Heysen**, who settled here in 1908. There's a more comprehensive collection of Heysen's paintings on display at his old home, **The Cedars**, about 2.5km northwest of the village off Ambleside Road (Tues–Sun 10am–4pm; Sept–May guided tours 11am, 1pm & 3pm, June–Aug 11am & 2pm; $10 studio and house, shop and garden free).

The **Adelaide Hills Visitors Information Centre**, 41 Main St (June–Aug Mon–Fri 9.30am–4.30pm, Sat & Sun 10am–4pm; Sept–May Mon–Fri 9am–5pm, Sat & Sun 10am–4pm; ⓣ08/8388 1185 or 1800 353 323, ⓦwww.visitadelaidehills.com.au), has lots of information on B&Bs and other **accommodation** in the hills (no charge for bookings) and can provide information about the entire area, though you won't need much help in the village itself – there's basically just one street and all the buildings have blue plaques recounting their history.

For a glass of authentic locally brewed pilsner, head for the lovely wooden bar at the *German Arms Hotel*, which has a log fire and photos of old Hahndorf, a reasonably priced bistro, and a more expensive **restaurant**. There are dozens of other places to eat – try *Muggletons General Store* on Main Street (open for lunch) where you can also buy delicious home-made jams and chutneys. The **German Cake Shop**, near the visitor information centre, just off the main street on Pine Avenue (daily 8.30am–5.30pm), is a crowded bakery and coffee shop where the speciality is *bienenstich*, a yeast cake topped with honey and almonds and filled with cream, butter and custard. Cheese lovers should not miss Udder Delight at 91A Main St, a shop specializing in goats' cheese. This is also the departure point for the cheese and wine trail; for $15 you can pick up an eski filled with cheese and follow your own wine route through the hills. Behind the cheese shop is a gorgeous but pricey **B&B** (ⓣ08/8388 1588; ❻–❼).

Torrens River Gorge

Further north in the upper valley, the 27-kilometre **Gorge Scenic Drive** beside the Torrens River Gorge is one of the loveliest areas in the Adelaide Hills, but you'll need your own car to get there: take the Gorge Road off the A11 from Adelaide, a few kilometres past the suburb of Campbelltown. Fourteen kilometres along this road is the **Gorge Wildlife Park** (daily 9am–5pm; koala cuddling 11.30am, 1.30pm & 3.30pm; $12; ⓦwww.gorgewildlifepark.com.au), a private park with mainly native birds and animals housed in walk-through enclosures. A few kilometres past the park, at Cudlee Creek, the Gorge Scenic Drive turns southeast away from the river and passes through picturesque valleys and vineyards to Mount Torrens. If you want to stick with the river, turn north before Cudlee Creek towards the Chain of Ponds, where the road connects after a few kilometres to the equally stunning Torrens Valley Scenic Drive.

GUMERACHA, the first town east of here, is home to **The Toy Factory**, 389 Birdwood Rd (daily 9am–5pm; ⓦwww.thetoyfactory.com.au), which sells wooden toys, games and puzzles and has a tacky eighteen-metre-high rocking horse which children (and adults) can climb up for good views of the countryside. At the eastern end of the Torrens Valley Scenic Drive is **BIRDWOOD** and the **National Motor Museum** on Shannon Street (daily 9am–5pm; $9; ⓦwww.history.sa.gov.au), Australia's largest collection of veteran, vintage and classic cars, trucks and motorcycles.

The Barossa Valley

The **Barossa Valley**, only an hour's drive from Adelaide, produces internationally acclaimed wines and is the largest premium wine producer in Australia. Small stone **Lutheran churches** dot the valley, which was settled in the 1840s by German Lutherans fleeing from religious persecution: by 1847 over 2500 German immigrants had arrived and after the 1848 revolution more poured in. German continued to be spoken in the area until World War I, when the language was frowned upon and German place names were changed by an act of parliament. The towns, however – most notably Tanunda – remain thoroughly German in character, even without the large doses of tourist hype, and the valley is well worth visiting for the **vineyards**, wineries, bakeries and butcher's shops, where old German recipes have been handed down through generations. With up to eight hundred thousand visitors per annum, the valley can seem thoroughly touristy and traffic-laden if you whizz through it quickly, but the peaceful back roads are more interesting, with a number of small, family-owned wineries to explore.

The first vines were planted in 1847 at the Orlando vineyards, an estate which is still a big producer. There are now over fifty **wineries** with cellar doors, from multinationals to tiny specialists. Because of the variety of soil and climate, the Barossa seems able to produce a wide range of wine types of consistently high

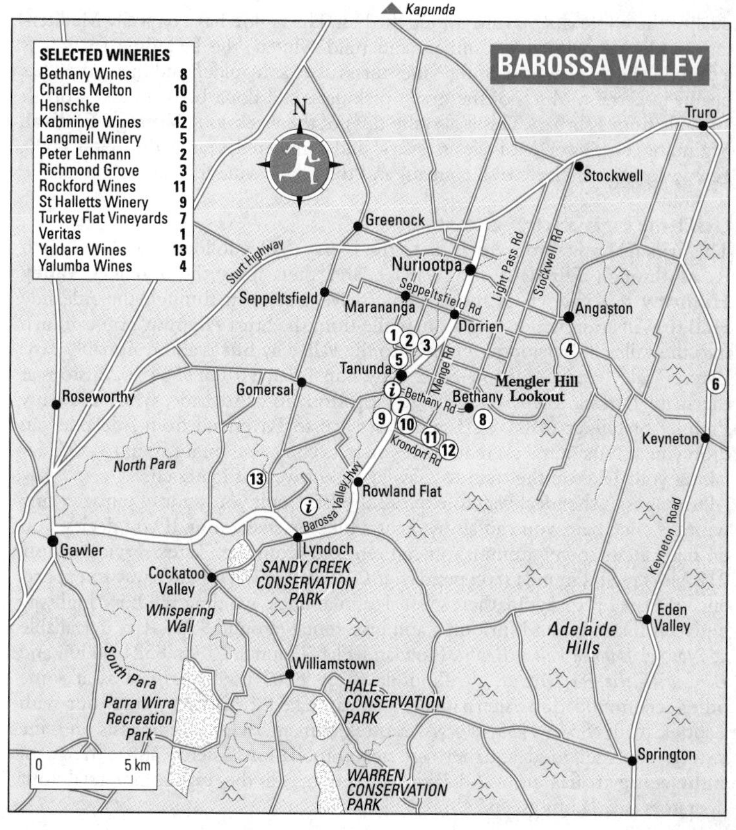

Wine-tasting tips

Smaller wineries tend to have more charm and intrinsic interest than the larger commercial operators and it's here you'll often get to talk personally to the winemaker. Groups are welcomed by most wineries but are encouraged to book, although some wineries are too small to accommodate them. A few charge an entry fee, but for this expect extra staff and a more personalized tasting experience. You're under no obligation to buy any wine, but coming away with a few of your favourite taste sensations of the day – often only available at the cellar door – and a few fruity adjectives to describe them is part of the fun.

For a novice, wine tasting can be an intimidating experience. On entering the tasting area (or cellar door) you'll be shown a list of wines that may be tasted, divided into reds and whites, all of which are printed in the order that the winemaker considers best on the palate. Unless you know what you're doing, it's not acceptable to alter this order, though by all means concentrate on red or white if you prefer. To get the full taste, sniff the wine first to appreciate the aroma or bouquet, and then take a sip, rolling it around on your tongue before swallowing; there's usually a spittoon if you don't want to swallow. Don't be shy about discussing the wines with the person serving – their purpose is to dispense chat and wisdom, and even wine snobs are down-to-earth Australians at heart.

quality; the white rieslings are among the best. The region has a typically Mediterranean climate, with dry summers and mild winters; the best time to visit is autumn (March–May), when the vines turn russet and golden and the harvest has begun in earnest. Much of the grape-picking is still done by hand and work is available from February. This is also the time of the week-long **Vintage Festival**, beginning on Easter Monday in every odd-numbered year (Ⓣ08/8563 0600, Ⓦwww.barossavintagefestival.com.au) and the oldest wine festival in Australia.

Getting around the valley

The principal route from Adelaide to the Barossa Valley follows the Main North Road through Elizabeth and Gawler, and then joins the **Barossa Valley Highway** to Lyndoch. A more scenic drive takes you through the Adelaide Hills to Williamstown or Angaston, while from the Sturt Highway you can turn into the valley at Nuriootpa. Getting to the valley by **bus** is also reasonably easy: Barossa Valley Coaches (Mon–Sat 2 daily, Sun 1 daily; Ⓣ08/8564 3022) stops at the main Barossa towns en route to Angaston from Adelaide, while the daily Premier Stateliner (Ⓣ08/8415 5555) service to Riverland from Adelaide can drop you at Nuriootpa on request. If you're cycling, you might want to consider taking your bike on the train to Gawler, 14km west of Lyndoch.

Driving isn't the ideal way to explore the Barossa if you want to enjoy tasting wines – once here, you can always rent a bike or take a tour. If you decide you do need a **car** to get around, you can rent one from the Caltex service station, 212 Murray St, Tanunda ($65 per day; Ⓣ08/8563 2677). A better way to experience the area is to **cycle**; there's a sealed bike track avoiding the busy highway between Tanunda and Nuriootpa and bike rental (around $30 a day) is available at *Novotel Barossa Valley Resort*, Rowland Flat, Tanunda (Ⓣ08/8524 0000), and *Barossa Secrets*, 91 Murray St, Tanunda (Ⓣ08/8563 0665), as well as at some other accommodation. Alternatively, you can take a two-day cycling tour with Ecotrek (Ⓣ08/8346 4155, Ⓦwww.ecotrek.com.au), with an emphasis on wine tasting, gourmet food and heritage accommodation. There's also a range of **sightseeing tours** from Adelaide offered by all the big commercial tour operators (see "Listings", p.745).

△ Penfolds Winery, Barossa Valley

Lyndoch and around

"A beautiful place, good land, plenty of grass and its general appearance open with some patches of wood and many kangaroos," reported Colonel William Light in 1837 on first sighting the **LYNDOCH** area. Settled in 1839, it's one of the oldest towns in South Australia, and although vineyards were established from the outset, the primary activity until 1896 was the growing of wheat, when someone had the bright idea of converting a flour mill into a winery.

Today there are ten wineries in the immediate Lyndoch area, from some of the smallest to one of the largest in the Barossa, all still family-owned. **Kies Family Wineries** on Barossa Valley Way provides free informal tourist information

Barossa wineries

It's hard to choose between so many wineries, as almost all of them are worth a look. However, this selection should start you off.

Bethany Wines Bethany Rd, Bethany Ⓦwww.bethany.com.au. A hillside winery set in an old quarry, with views over Bethany Village; five generations of the Schrapel family have grown grapes here. The ports are worth trying, especially the unusual white variety. Mon–Sat 10am–5pm, Sun 1–5pm.

Charles Melton Krondorf Rd, Tanunda Ⓦwww.charlesmeltonwines.com.au. Small, friendly winery concentrating on a limited range of full-bodied reds that sell out fast. Informal tasting area in a wooden shed, where you sit at a long wooden table, with the door open to the vineyards and a friendly dog at your feet. Daily 11am–5pm.

Henschke Moculta Rd, Keyneton, 14km southeast of Angaston Ⓦwww.henschke.com.au. Fifth-generation winemakers, the Henschke family's wines have won many international prizes. It's located in a peaceful setting off the beaten track and you'll need to ring the bell to rouse the amiable staff and start tasting. Mon–Fri 9am–4.30pm, Sat 9am–noon.

Kabminye Wines Krondorf Rd, Tanunda Ⓦwww.kabminye.com. Relatively new family-run winery with a modern restaurant serving authentic Barossa food in a loungey atmosphere, and an art gallery upstairs. Best known for their rare combination of Mataro, Carignan, Cinsaut and Black Frontignac grapes in their red Schliebs Block wine. Daily 11am–5pm.

Langmeil Winery Langmeil Rd, near Tanunda Ⓦwww.langmeilwinery.com.au. This was the original Langmeil village, built in the 1840s; the little vineyard you can see from the tasting area was planted in 1846. Prints of nineteenth-century photos on the walls document the local wine industry. With a slow and thoughtful approach to tasting, and a small range, you really get to know the wines – try the very peppery Grenache. Daily 10.30am–4.30pm.

Peter Lehmann Para Rd, near Tanunda Ⓦwww.peterlehmannwines.com. Another pleasant spot for a bit of tasting or a picnic, in a homestead with vine-entwined verandas surrounded by flowerbeds, gum trees and palms, overlooking a lawn leading down to the Para River. Lehmann is as well known for his art collection as for his red wines, whose labels feature paintings by South Australian artists displayed here. Mon–Fri 9.30am–5pm, Sat & Sun 10.30am–4.30pm.

Richmond Grove Para Rd, near Tanunda Ⓦwww.richmondgrovewines.com. Large, historic winery sourcing grapes from around the Barossa and from other premier wine-growing areas in Australia – good if you want to compare the different regional characteristics of Australian wine. There's a lovely picnic area alongside the North Para River. Daily 10.30am–4.30pm.

Rockford Wines Krondorf Rd, Tanunda. No-nonsense approach and big unfussy wines by Robert O'Callahan, produced using old-fashioned techniques and including a good Basket Press Shiraz and an amazing fizzy Black Shiraz at around $50 a bottle. Mon–Sat 11am–5pm.

St Halletts Winery St Hallett's Rd, Tanunda Ⓦwww.sthallet.com.au. Medium-size, quality producer whose star wine is Old Block Shiraz, sourced from vines eighty to a hundred years old, with an intense flavour and a velvety softness. Daily 10am–5pm.

Turkey Flat Vineyards Bethany Rd, Tanunda Ⓦwww.turkeyflat.com.au. Named after the bush turkeys that used to wander here, this vineyard has the second-oldest Shiraz grapes of the valley, planted 158 years ago. Also famous for their rosé. Daily 11am–5pm.

Veritas Cnr Stelzer and Seppeltsfield roads, near Tanunda Ⓦwww.veritaswinery.com. Established in the 1950s and known for its Hungarian-style wines, this family operation is a good place to come during harvest, around April, with tastings and sales in an unpretentious shed. Mon–Fri 10am–4.30pm, Sat & Sun 11am–4pm.

Yaldara Wines Gomersal Rd, Lyndoch Ⓦwww.yaldara.com.au. The ruins of a nineteenth-century flour mill have been transformed into a Baroque-style chateau complete with wine cellar and café. Daily 9.30am–5pm.

Yalumba Wines Eden Valley Rd, Angaston Ⓦwww.yalumba.com. Largest and oldest family-operated Barossa winery, established in 1849, set in a lovely building and gardens. Daily 10am–5pm.

(daily 9.30am–4.30pm; ⓣ08/8524 4110); their wine-tasting cellars (same hours) are in the same building.

Eight kilometres southwest of Lyndoch, off Yettie Road, is the Whispering Wall, a retaining wall for the Barossa Reservoir; it's shaped in such a way that words spoken on one side of the reservoir can be heard plainly on the opposite side 140m away. To the northeast, four kilometres along the Barossa Valley Highway, the village of **ROWLAND FLAT** is dominated by the **Orlando Winery** complex, the oldest winery in the valley and home of some of Australia's best-known wines, sold under the **Jacob's Creek** label. Johann Gramp planted the first commercial vines at nearby Jacob's Creek in 1847, and forty years later his son expanded the winery and moved it to Rowland Flat. The **Jacob's Creek Visitor's Centre**, located on the banks of Jacob's Creek itself, has a tasting centre and restaurant with a gallery that includes information on production techniques and the history of the area (daily 10am–5pm).

Four kilometres north of Rowland Flat, the peaceful **Krondorf Road/ Hallet Valley** area runs east of the Barossa Valley Highway, with three charming wineries – Rockford, St Hallets and Charles Melton – each with its own philosophy of wine making and tasting. Next to St Hallets Winery you can watch skilled coopers at work at the **Keg Factory** on St Hallet Road (Mon–Sat 8am–4.30pm, Sun 10am–4.30pm); the huge stainless-steel fermentation tanks you'll see around the valley aren't suitable for all wines, many of which still need to be aged in wood to impart flavour.

Parallel to Krondorf Road to the north, Bethany Road runs east off the Barossa Valley Highway to **BETHANY**, the first German settlement in the Barossa. The land is still laid out in the eighteenth-century Hufendorf style, with long, narrow farming strips stretching out behind the cottages, and the creek running through each property. Pretty gardens set off the old stone cottages, which remain well cared for. At dusk each Saturday the bell tolls at **Herberge Christi Church**, keeping up a tradition to mark the end of the working week, and Bethany – without even a pub or shop – retains its peaceful, rural village feel.

Tanunda and around

TANUNDA is the Barossa's most quintessentially German town. The tree-lined main drag, **Murray Street**, boasts several old and beautiful buildings and proclaims its pedigree with German music wafting out of small wooden kegs above the shops. There's a more authentic atmosphere in the narrow streets on the western side of town, towards the river. Here, **Goat Square** was the site of the first town market and is bordered by the original cottages; the early market is re-enacted during the Vintage Festival (see p.752). Many wineries dot the town, the largest concentration being along **Para Road**, beside the Para River, including Stanley Brothers, Peter Lehmann, Richmond Grove, Langmeil and Veritas, all of which can be visited in the course of a pleasant stroll along the road and river.

For a good introduction to the region, head for the **Barossa Tourism Centre**, 66–68 Murray St (Mon–Fri 9am–5pm, Sat & Sun 10am–4pm; wine centre daily 10am–4pm; $2; ⓣ08/8563 0600 or 1300 852 982, ⓦwww.barossa.com). The low-key Barossa Valley **Historical Museum**, 47 Murray St (Mon–Fri 10am–5pm, Sat & Sun 10am–4pm; $2), crams local history into a small quaint building which it shares with an antiques shop.

Three kilometres out of town, **Norm's Coolies**, at "Breezy Gully" off Gomersal Road (Mon, Wed & Sat 2pm; $10, children $4; ⓣ08/8563 2198), could only be in Australia: 28 sheepdogs are put through their paces by Norm and a herd of sheep. Note that the dogs are not allowed to perform when the temperature exceeds thirty degrees. **Mengler's Hill Lookout**, east of Tanunda along Basedow Road and then the Mengler's Hill Road Scenic Drive, provides an unmatched view of the valley and its vineyards: there's a **sculpture garden** with white marble sculptures on the slopes below, and at night you can see the lights of Adelaide.

Seppeltsfield, off the highway 4km northwest of Tanunda, must be, visually at least, the most spectacular of the wineries (tastings Mon–Fri 10am–5pm, Sat & Sun 11am–5pm). During the Great Depression the Seppelt family paid their workers in food to plant an avenue of date palms from Marananga to Seppeltsfield; on a hill halfway along the palm-lined avenue stands the Seppelt **family mausoleum**, resting place of the male members of the family. The estate itself was founded in 1851 when Joseph Seppelt, a wealthy merchant, arrived from Silesia with his workers: he turned to wine making when his tobacco crop failed, establishing the largest winery in the colony, with everything from a port-maturation cellar to a distillery, vinegar factory and brandy bond store. All have been preserved in their original condition, and can be seen on a **tour** (daily 11.30am, 1.30pm & 3.30pm; $10).

Nuriootpa, Angaston and Springton

Just 7km from Tanunda, **NURIOOTPA** is the valley's commercial centre: as the place where local Aborigines gathered to barter, it takes its name from the word for "meeting place". It's not the most attractive of towns, dominated as it is by **Penfolds**, the Barossa's largest winery, which churns out mass-produced wines made with grapes from across South Australia. The finest building here is **Coulthard House**, a gracious, two-storey edifice commissioned by the area's first settler, William Coulthard. The town grew around his red-gum slab hotel, now the site of the *Vine Inn* community hotel. Together with the community store, this finances many developments in the town, such as the excellent **swimming** centre in Coulthard Reserve, by the shady, gum-lined North Para River.

ANGASTON, southeast of Nuriootpa, is a pretty little town situated in the Barossa Ranges, an area of predominantly grazing land, red gums and rolling hills, although a few of the Barossa's oldest winemakers have been here for more than a century. This is the side of the Barossa that attracted the British pioneers, including George Fife Angas, the Scotsman after whom the town is named. The **Collingrove Homestead** (guided tours only Mon–Fri 1–4.30pm, Sat & Sun noon–4.30pm; $10; Ⓦwww.collingrovehomestead.com.au), 6km from town on Eden Valley Road, was one of his homes. Now owned by the National Trust, it's surrounded by lush gardens. Angas also lived at nearby Lindsay Park, now the private **Lindsay Park Stud**, Australia's leading racehorse breeding and training complex.

The major attraction at **SPRINGTON**, 20km south of Angaston, is the **Herbig family tree**, a hollowed-out gum tree in which a pioneer German couple lived for five years from 1855; they began their married life in the tree and had two of their sixteen children in it. Inevitably, Springton's old buildings have undergone the "boutique-ing" process: the blacksmith's is now a winery, and the old post office has been transformed into an arts and crafts gallery.

Barossa accommodation

There's comfortable **accommodation** in B&Bs and caravan parks throughout the valley, and you shouldn't have a problem finding somewhere to stay. As every town has a decent hotel or motel along the main road, the selection below mainly focuses on tucked-away B&Bs scattering the area.

Barossa Brauhaus Hotel 41 Murray St, Angaston Ⓣ08/8564 2014. Good-value basic rooms and cheap singles in a centrally located pub first licensed in 1849. Light breakfast included. No ensuite. ❸

Barossa Doubles Dvine Barossa Valley Highway, 1.5km south of Nuriootpa Ⓣ & Ⓕ08/8562 2260, Ⓦwww.doublesdvine.com.au. A comfortable, friendly, family-run B&B set in vineyards, with large, secluded rooms and a swimming pool for summer. Bike rental available. Rooms ❷, self-contained cottage ❸

Blickinstal Vineyard retreat Rifle Range Rd, Tanunda ⓣ08/8563 2716. Great views over the valley from this peacefully set B&B nestled into the foothills of the Barossa. All units are self-contained, two of them studio-style and two split-level. Four-course breakfast and afternoon tea included. ❺–❻

Caithness Manor 12 Hill St, Angaston ⓣ08/8564 2761, ⓦwww.caithness.com.au. A former girls' grammar school whose lower storey has been transformed into a gracious guesthouse run by a friendly family. There's a sitting room complete with open fires, plus a swimming pool and spa. Each of the two spacious guest rooms has its own bathroom and antique furnishings. Gourmet breakfast included. ❻

Langmeil Cottages Langmeil Rd, Tanunda ⓣ08/8563 2987, ⓦwww.langmeilcottages.com. German-style stone cottage with cooking facilities, peaceful setting, spa and a resort-style pool. Extras include champagne on arrival, breakfast provisions, free bicycles, heated pool and laundry facilities. Friendly owners. ❺

Lawley Farm Krondorf Rd, south of Tanunda ⓣ08/8563 2141, ⓦwww.lawleyfarm.com.au. Restored stone cottages shaded by pepper-trees, on a quiet road within walking distance of the best wineries. A full breakfast (included in room rates) is served in the farmhouse kitchen, and there's a hot spa in the garden. ❻

Peppers The Louise Seppeltsfield Rd, Marananga ⓣ08/8562 2722, ⓦwww.peppers.com.au/thelouise. Absolutely top of the bill if you are willing to spend a few bucks. The luxurious rooms, with private terrace, have all the mod cons you can imagine. The most expensive suites have outdoor showers but the cheaper ones are actually a lot larger. ❽

Seppeltsfield Vineyard Cottage Gerald Roberts Rd, Seppeltsfield ⓣ08/ 8563 4059, ⓦwww.seppeltsfieldvineyardcottage.com.au. It doesn't get more exclusive than this, with an entire German settler's cottage just for one couple. Enjoy great views over the valley from your French-style bathtub. This award-winning B&B does require a two-night minimum stay though. ❽

Tanunda Caravan and Tourist Park Murray St, Tanunda ⓣ08/8563 2784, ⓦwww.tanundacaravantouristpark.com.au. Set in parkland among beautiful waratah trees. On-site vans ❷, cabins ❸

Tanunda Hotel 51 Murray St, Tanunda ⓣ08/8563 2030 or 8563 2165, ⓦwww.tanundapub.com. Built from local stone and marble in 1845, with Edwardian additions and decor inside. All rooms have TV, a/c, fridge, tea and coffee; some are en suite. ❸–❹

Vine Inn Hotel Motel 14 Murray St, Nuriootpa ⓣ08/8562 2133, ⓦwww.vineinn.com.au. Spacious, modern motel-style units with a/c and queen-size beds; continental breakfast included and there's a spa and heated pool. ❺

Barossa eating and drinking

There are excellent **restaurants** throughout the valley, as well as plenty of picnic spots and barbecue areas. Make the most of the restaurants at the wineries, as they usually offer value for money in a picturesque setting.

1918 Bistro and Grill 94 Murray St, Tanunda ⓣ08/8563 0405. Expensive but good fresh food using local ingredients cooked with a Mediterranean twist. Eat outside on the wide, plant-shaded veranda, or inside the beautiful old house, built in 1918, with a variety of nooks and corners for intimate dining. Local wines or BYO. Daily lunch & dinner.

Alfresco at Junipers 33 Murray St, Angaston ⓣ08/ 8564 3277. Open seven days a week for breakfast, lunch and dinner. Australian cuisine with Mediterranean influences in a lovely leafy garden.

Appellation Seppeltsfield Rd, Marananga ⓣ08/8562 4144. Fresh seasonal products and a menu that changes every night in this pricey restaurant next to *Peppers The Louise*. Contemporary minimalistic interior attracts the hotshots of the area. Expensive.

Barossa Wurst Haus and Bakery 86A Murray St, Tanunda. Specializing in traditional Barossa *Mettwurst* (German sausage), this delicatessen offers cheap but very tasty food and good cappuccino. Daily 7.30am–5pm.

Harvesters Café 29D Murray St, Nuriootpa ⓣ08/8562 1348. Spacious, contemporary-style café with a nice courtyard serving great cooked breakfasts, home-made soups and a variety of vegetarian dishes. Tues–Sun 9am–5.30pm.

Lyndoch Bakery & Restaurant Barossa Valley Highway, Lyndoch. The best German bakery in the Barossa. The adjoining licensed restaurant serves hearty, moderately priced traditional dishes. Daily 11am–2.30pm & 6pm until late.

Salters Saltram Winery, Nuriootpa Rd, Angaston ⓣ08/8561 0200. Elegant bistro serving modern Australian–Italian cuisine, all freshly, deliciously prepared and reasonably priced. The attached nineteenth-century winery specializes in full-bodied reds – try them at the cellar door before eating. Open daily for lunch, dinner Fri & Sat. Book ahead in summer.

Vintners Bar and Grill Cnr Stockwell and Nuriootpa rds, Angaston ⓣ08/8564 2488. A winemakers' hangout with expensive Mediterranean-style regional produce on the menu and a suitably impressive wine list. The decor is a mix of cool contemporary plus old stone walls, fireplaces and wooden beams, and there's a vine-covered courtyard for warm days. Open daily for lunch, dinner Mon–Sat.

Zinfandel Tea Rooms 58 Murray St, Tanunda. Popular place for hot, cooked breakfasts, German and Australian dishes for lunch and delicious strudels and cakes. You can sit inside the cozy cottage or out on the veranda. Daily 8.30am–5pm.

The Fleurieu Peninsula

The **Fleurieu Peninsula** (ⓦwww.fleurieupeninsula.com.au), thirty minutes south of Adelaide by car, is bounded by Gulf St Vincent to the west and the Southern Ocean to the south, the two connected by the Backstairs Passage at **Cape Jervis** (where ferries leave for Kangaroo Island, see p.765). There are fine beaches on both coasts and more wineries inland in the rolling **McLaren Vales**. It's a pleasantly undeveloped area, where many of the towns were settled from the 1830s, and there's a lot of colonial architecture, much of it now housing restaurants or B&Bs.

For a round trip, leave the city via the Adelaide Hills and cut down through Mount Barker to well-preserved Strathalbyn and Goolwa on the south coast, before circling round through Victor Harbor, Yankalilla, Willunga and McLaren Vale. The peninsula is a good place to **cycle** – in addition to its roads it has two sealed bike paths: the 24-kilometre **Encounter Bikeway** (see box, p.761) follows the coast from Goolwa to just beyond Victor Harbor; and another shorter path runs between Willunga and McLaren Vale. For walkers, the **Heysen Trail** starts at the southern tip of the peninsula at Cape Jervis and winds its way across the hilly countryside north to the Adelaide Hills and beyond. Although the trail is meant for long-distance walking, there are a number of well-signposted short walks along the way, including the 3.5-kilometre **Deep Creek Waterfall Trail**, just east of Cape Jervis with its wild coastal scenery. The Heysen Trail also passes through the Mount Magnificent Conservation Park, which contains a number of shorter walks offering excellent panoramic views.

If you're relying on **public transport**, Premier Stateliner (ⓣ08/8415 5555) makes four trips daily from Adelaide to Goolwa via McLaren Vale, Willunga, Victor Harbor and Port Elliot. There's also a sporadic service provided by the *Southern Encounter* and *Highlander* **steam trains** (occasionally replaced by a diesel locomotive) which chug from Mount Barker to Victor Harbor and Strathalbyn respectively (first Sun of month June–Nov; ⓣ1300 655 991, ⓦwww.steamranger.org.au). Adelaide Sightseeing Tours run **tours** of the area (Wed & Sat; $79; ⓣ08/8413 6199, ⓦwww.adelaidesightseeing.com.au), visiting Goolwa, Victor Harbor and McLaren Vale and connecting with Coorong Pelican cruises from Goolwa, with optional overnight stays at Victor Harbor to see the penguins returning to Granite Island.

The McLaren Vales

The wineries of the **McLaren Vales**, in the northwest of the peninsula, are virtually in Adelaide, as the suburban fringes of the city now push right up to **REYNELLA**, where the first vineyards were planted in 1838. Among the earliest was Hardy's Reynella Winery on Reynell Road (daily 10am–4.30pm), where the tasting room occupies the original ironstone and brick building, set in botanical gardens. There are several other wineries in Reynella, but the largest concentration – often in bush settings only an hour's drive from Adelaide – is around the small town of **McLAREN VALE**, which has about fifty wineries, mostly small and family run. Since the 1960s there has been a trend for grape growers to switch from supplying winemakers to producing their own wine, and there's a swath of "boutique" wineries here as a result. More recently, the area has gained a reputation for its **olives**, and a number of shops have opened for tastings and sales. The Olive Grove (daily 9am–5pm), opposite the D'Arenberg winery, is the best, with excellent olives, oils, pestos and other sauces.

McLaren Vale itself is a "boutique" town, with many B&Bs and restaurants catering for the wine-buff weekend crowd.

Practicalities

Information on the area's wineries can be found at the **McLaren Vale and Fleurieu Visitor Centre** on Main Road, about 2km from the centre (daily 10am–5pm; ⓣ08/8323 9944, ⓦwww.mclarenvale.info), and the staff can also book **accommodation**. Among the town's B&Bs are the historic *Claddagh Cottage*, Lot 8, Caffrey St (ⓣ08/8323 9806; ❺), within walking distance of the town centre and *Southern Vales*, 13 Chalk Hill Rd (ⓣ08/8323 8144; ❻), a bit larger and with vineyard views. If you have a **tent** the *Lakeside Caravan Park*, Field Street (ⓣ08/8323 9255, ⓦwww.mclarenvale.net; on-site vans ❷, cabins ❸), is your best bet, with a pool, tennis and volleyball in a scenic setting.

Most places to **eat** in town are fairly fancy, and many wineries also have restaurants attached. For a more relaxed lunch, try *Blessed Cheese* at 150 Main Rd, where aside from the divine dairy products, you can sample locally-grown olives and great coffee. This is also the pick-up point for your cheese hamper to explore the cheese and wine trail (ⓦwww.cheeseandwinetrails.com.au), taking you past several wineries where you can taste matching wines. The

McLaren Vale wineries

Listed below are half a dozen favourites from a wide choice of excellent wineries.

Chapel Hill Chapel Hill Rd, McLaren Vale, adjacent to the Onkaparinga Gorge ⓦwww.chapelhillwine.com.au. A small but very civilized winery in an old stone chapel with nice views over the vineyards. Daily noon–5pm.

D'Arenberg Osborn Rd, McLaren Vale ⓦwww.darenberg.com.au. A family winery set up in 1928, well known for its prize-winning reds. The first-rate restaurant is a good stop for lunch. Daily 10am–5pm.

Hoffmann's Ingoldby Rd, McLaren Flat ⓦwww.hoffmannwine.com.au One of the smaller wineries with five labels to choose from, only available through the cellar door or by mail order. A great place to sit in a peaceful setting and chat about wines with the friendly owners. Cellar door daily 11am–5pm, lunch Fri–Mon.

Kay's Amery Vineyards Kays Rd, McLaren Vale ⓦwww.kaybrotherswines.com. A wonderful family winery established in 1890; old photos of the family and the area cover the oak casks containing port. It's renowned for its Block 6 Shiraz from vines planted in 1892, though it sells out quickly. Also has a picnic area set amid towering gum trees. Mon–Fri 9am–5pm, Sat & Sun noon–5pm.

Samuel's Gorge Cnr Chaffey and Chapel rds, McLaren Vale ⓦwww.gorge.com.au. The smallest winery, located in an 1853 homestead with a Jamaican-born winemaker who won't discuss wines with you without a glass himself. His Shiraz is one of the most outstanding in the region, and there's also an unusual Tempranillo. Fri–Mon 11am–5pm.

Scarpantoni Scarpantoni Drive, McLaren Flat ⓦwww.sparpantoni-wines.com.au. Small, prize-winning winery run by an Italian family, with a contemporary cellar more akin to a city wine bar. Mon–Fri 9am–5pm, Sat & Sun 11am–5pm.

Wira Wira McMurtie Rd, McLaren Vale ⓦwww.wirrawirra.com. A large, classic ironstone building provides the setting for an impressive range of reds, whites and award-winning tawny ports, not forgetting the fortified Shiraz. Mon–Sat 10am–5pm, Sun 11am–5pm.

award-winning *Magnum Bistro* in the *Hotel McLaren*, 208 Main Rd (ⓣ08/8323 8208), has delicious main courses, all reasonably priced. Across the road at no. 201, the stylish *Oscar's* serves pizzas and Mediterranean salads. Restaurants include *The Barn*, on the corner of Main and Chalk Hill roads (ⓣ08/8323 8618), where you can dine on moderately-priced contemporary cuisine accompanied by local wines. On the corner of McMurtie Road, in the direction of Willunga, the award-winning *Salopian Inn* (ⓣ08/8323 8769; Fri & Sat lunch, dinner daily except Tues & Sun) is set in an atmospheric 1851 stone inn with a seasonally varying menu.

Gulf St Vincent beaches

A series of superb swimming beaches, often known as the **wine coast**, runs along the Gulf St Vincent shore roughly parallel to the McLaren Vales, from **O'Sullivan Beach** down to **Sellicks Beach**. All are easily accessible from Adelaide on public transport: take the train from Adelaide to Noarlunga Centre and bus #750 or #751 to the various beaches.

PORT NOARLUNGA is the main town, surrounded by steep cliffs and sand hills. Its jetty is popular with anglers and with wetsuit-clad teenagers who dive-bomb from it; at low tide a natural reef is exposed. Lifesavers patrol the local beaches, and you can rent surf and snorkelling gear at Ocean Graffix Surf and Skate Centre, 21 Salt Fleet Point. **Moana**, two beaches south, has fairly tame surf that's perfect for novices. The southern end of **Maslins Beach**, south again, broke new ground by becoming Australia's first legal nude beach in 1975. The wide, isolated beach is reached by a long, steep walking track down the colourful cliffs from the Tait Road car park, deterring all but the committed naturalist. **Port Willunga**, the next stop down, offers interesting diving around the wreck of the *Star of Greece*, while just further south is Aldinga Beach, reached by the daily Adelaide–Cape Jervis Public Coach Service. From here there's a connecting bus to Sellicks Beach where, if you have your own car, you can drive along 6km of firm sand.

The coastal region south of here is more rugged, although there are some nice secluded beaches as well as the popular Heritage–listed sand dunes at **NORMANVILLE**. You can camp here at *Normanville Beach Caravan Park* (ⓣ08/8558 2038, ⓦwww.normanvillebeach.net.au; en-suite cabins ❸). A few kilometres inland, the **Yankalilla Bay and Beyond Visitor Information Centre**, 104 Main Rd (Mon–Fri 9am–5pm, Sat & Sun 10am–4pm; ⓣ08/8558 2999, ⓦwww.yankalilla.sa.gov.au), has a complete list of caravan parks and B&Bs along the gulf as well as information on diving. A bit further down the coast, the basic campsite (ⓣ08/8598 4139; $5) at unspoilt **Rapid Bay** is a good base if you want to go underwater exploring and try to spot the rare **Leafy Sea Dragon**. Ferries for Kangaroo Island (see p.765) depart from Cape Jervis at the end of Main South Road.

Victor Harbor

The old resort of **VICTOR HARBOR**, on Encounter Bay, is experiencing a resurgence in its fortunes, thanks principally to whales and penguins. In the 1830s there were three whaling stations here, hunting **southern right whales**, which came to Encounter Bay to mate and breed between June and September, heading close to shore, where they became easy targets. Not surprisingly, their numbers began to decline, and by 1930 they had been hunted almost to extinction. Half a century later there were signs of recovery: in 1991, forty were spotted in the bay and eighty thousand people flocked to see them, while in 1998, sixteen females stayed in the bay to calf, and a dozen humpback whales

The Encounter Bikeway

The Encounter Bikeway follows a scenic 24-kilometre stretch of coast between Victor Harbor and Goolwa. Parts of the route are on-road and slightly inland, but mostly it follows the coastline and is for cyclists and walkers only. The return trip can be completed comfortably in a day; the most scenic – and hilliest – section is between Dump Beach in Victor Harbor and the town of Port Elliot. Mountain-bike rental is available at Victor Harbor Cycle, 73 Victoria St, Victor Harbor ($20 per day; ⓣ08/8552 1417) or at the *Whalers Inn*, 121 Franklin Parade, Victor Harbor (from $30 per day; ⓣ08/8552 4400). Unfortunately, there's no bike rental available in Goolwa and none offer a drop-off service for one-way journeys, but on Sundays you can take your bike on the *Cockle Train* (see below) between Victor Harbor and Goolwa and cycle back.

were also spotted. In 2006 over 250 sightings of calves have been reported enjoying the calm waters.

A Heritage-listed former railway goods shed on Railway Terrace now houses the **South Australian Whale Centre** (daily 11am–4.30pm; $6; ⓦwww.sawhalecentre.com.au), with excellent interpretive displays, exhibits and screenings on whaling and the natural history of whales, dolphins and the marine environment. The centre also acts as a monitoring station, locating and tracking whales, and confirming sightings, most likely in June, July or August. Two-hour **whale cruises** depart from Granite Island in season (daily June–Sept; $60; ⓣ08/8552 7000).

As well as whales, **Little Penguins** come to nest, roost and moult on **Granite Island**, which is linked to the esplanade by a narrow causeway. At dusk they come back from feeding – this is the best time to see them, on one of the ranger-led **penguin walks** run by Granite Island Nature Park (daily at dusk; 1hr; $12.50; booking essential on ⓣ08/8552 7555, ⓦwww.graniteisland.com.au). Before exploring the island you can visit the **Penguin Interpretive Centre**, which houses an audiovisual holographic display with a 3D park ranger giving the lowdown on daily penguin life (daily 12.30–3.30pm plus an hour before the start of the walk). You can walk across the six-hundred-metre causeway to the island at any time, or take a traditional holiday ride with the **Victor Harbor Horse Tram** (daily 10am–4pm, longer in summer depending on demand; $7 return).

Other local attractions include the **Cockle Train**, a Sunday steam train (sometimes diesel-hauled) which runs on the otherwise disused line along the coast to Goolwa via Port Elliot and back (Sun & daily during school holidays; $24 return; ⓦwww.steamranger.org.au). If you're travelling with restless children, **Greenhills Adventure Park** on Waggon Road, alongside the Hindmarsh River (daily 10am–5pm, 6pm in summer; $22 adult, $17 child; ⓣ08/8552 5999, ⓦwww.greenhills.com.au), has activities from canoeing to waterslides, while the **Urimbirra Wildlife Experience** (daily 9am–6pm; $9, child $4.50), 5km north of Victor Harbor on Adelaide Road, is an open-range park with native animals from all over the continent.

Practicalities

For further information on the area, head for the **Victor Harbor Tourist Information Centre** next to the causeway (daily 9am–5pm; ⓣ08/8552 5738, ⓦwww.tourismvictorharbor.com.au); in the same building, **Top Choice Travel Booking Centre** (ⓣ1800 088 552, ⓦwww.topchoicetravel.com.au) can book accommodation and tours. The best **place to stay** is the *Anchorage*, 21 Flinders Parade (ⓣ08/8552 5970,

ⓦwww.anchorageseafronthotel.com; ❸), a lovingly restored beachfront guesthouse with en-suite and spa facilities.

Good places to **eat and drink** abound; those listed below are some of the best.

Café Bavaria 11 Albert Place. A gleaming venue with delicious fresh-baked German cakes and savouries at reasonable prices. Open daily.

Hooked on Victor Shop 1–3, The Esplanade. Upmarket place with everything from pasta to oysters in a contemporary setting. Lunch & dinner Tues–Sun.

Hotel Crown The Esplanade. The best place to drink, with cheap bar meals, streetside tables, and bands and DJs on weekends.

Nino's 16 Albert Place. The place to be if you're after Italian food, where you can plough into some generous portions of pasta and home-made *gelati*.

Ocean Grill 21 Flinders Parade at the *Anchorage* hotel. Superb seafood in this lively city-style café, which has an eclectic menu but slow service. Open daily.

Victor Harbor Fish Shop 20 Ocean St. For excellent fish and chips, this place is hard to beat ,although the interior doesn't make for intimate dining.

Port Elliot

PORT ELLIOT, just 5km east of Victor Harbor, is a pleasant little town with some good coastal walks along the cliffs at Freeman Knob and an attractive sandy beach with safe swimming at **Horseshoe Bay**. Campers can enjoy the beachside setting at the award-winning *Port Elliot Caravan & Tourist Park* (ⓣ08/8554 2134, ⓦwww.portelliotcaravanpark.com.au; cabins ❹, cottages ❺–❻). A more pleasant though pricier option is the *Trafalgar House*, a lovely 1890 brick house, where you can stay in the English-style maids' cottage (ⓣ08/8554 3888, ⓦwww.trafalgarhouse.com.au; ❺–❻).

Expect a queue for the mouthwatering pastries and pies of *Port Elliot Bakery* on 31 North Terrace, a great spot for **lunch**. For a superb (if expensive) meal overlooking the bay, head for the *Flying Fish Café* on The Foreshore. From here you can explore the coastal Encounter Bikeway (see box, opposite), or learn how to surf at nearby Middleton; for experienced surfers, Waitpinga Parsons and Chiton offer more thrills. Boards, wetsuits and fins can be rented from Southern Surf, 36 North Terrace (ⓣ08/8554 2375).

Goolwa

GOOLWA lies 14km east of Port Elliot, and 12km upstream from the ever-shifting sand bar at the mouth of the Murray River. Boaties love its position adjacent to vast **Lake Alexandrina**, yet with easy access to the **Coorong** (see p.772) and the ocean. Although it's so close to the coast, Goolwa feels like a real river town, and it thrived in the days of the Murray paddle-steamer trade, when it was the steamers' final offloading port – a rip-roaring place with almost a hundred taverns and the biggest police station in South Australia. The railways brought the good times to an end, and today only a few reminders of the era remain along Railway Terrace, with its old buildings painted in Federation colours.

Steam trains make a comeback on Sundays, however, when the **Cockle Train** heads along the coast to Victor Harbor and back (see p.760), and the **Southern Encounter** runs from Mount Barker in the Adelaide Hills to Goolwa via Strathalbyn and on to Port Elliot (see above) and Victor Harbor. There are also frequent **coaches** from Adelaide to Goolwa run by Premier Stateliner (Mon–Fri 4 daily, Sat 2 daily, Sun 1 daily; ⓣ08/8414 5555). Overlooking the wharf beside the Hindmarsh bridge is **Signal Point Interpretive Centre** (daily 9am–5pm; $5.50), housing an innovative exhibition telling the story of the Murray and its river trade. The centre also contains a small souvenir shop and café, as well as the helpful **Goolwa Tourist Information Centre** (daily 10am–5pm; ⓣ08/8555 3488, ⓦwww.visitalexandrina.com), which can book local river tours and accommodation.

Cruises from Goolwa

Cruises to the mouth of the Murray and as far as Coorong National Park (see p.772) leave from the end of the wharf. Spirit of the Coorong Cruises (Ⓣ08/8555 2203, Ⓦwww.coorongcruises.com.au) run two trips: the Discovery Cruise goes to the dune-covered Younghusband Peninsula, where passengers can alight and walk to the Southern Ocean (Mon & Thurs, also Tues & Sat Oct–May; 4hr; $74, or $135 from Adelaide), while the Adventure Cruise consists of a 30-kilometre trip right into the national park (Wed, also Sun June–Sept; 6hr; $88, or $145 from Adelaide).

For **B&Bs**, *Cottages of Goolwa* (Ⓣ08/8555 5880, Ⓦwww.cottagesofgoolwa.com) has a selection of self-catering cottages, including *Joseph's* (❻), a luxurious historic option near the centre of town. The *PS Federal* on Barrage Road (Ⓣ08/8362 6229; minimum two-night stay; ❻) started life as a working paddle-steamer in 1902 and now provides comfortable, self-contained accommodation. *Riverport Motel*, on Noble Avenue 3km northeast of Goolwa (Ⓣ08/8555 5033, Ⓕ8555 5022; ❹), has motel units in a quiet setting beside the Lower Murray River, plus a pool, tennis court, bar and inexpensive dining room. Alternatively, try the *Corio Hotel* on Railway Terrace (Ⓣ08/8555 2011, Ⓕ8555 1109; ❸), which is also a popular **eating place**, along with the *Whistlestop Café* on Hays Street and *Café Lime* just across the road, a trendy lime-green joint with great espressos and takeaways. Campers can head for *Goolwa Caravan Park*, Noble Avenue (Ⓣ08/8555 2737, Ⓕ8555 1095, Ⓦwww.goolwacaravanpark.com.au; cabins ❸).

Strathalbyn

The pretty town of **STRATHALBYN** sits quietly amongst rolling hills about 25km north of Goolwa and an hours' drive southeast of Adelaide. Settled in 1839 by Scottish immigrants, the historic town is the market centre for the surrounding farming community, but is also renowned for its antique shops, Heritage–listed buildings and serene atmosphere. Strathalbyn comes alive during its irregular but well-publicized horse-racing meetings and for a few traditional **festivals**: an antiques fair held in the third week of August, and an agricultural show and duck race in October or November. For a self-guided walking brochure of the town, head to the **Strathalbyn Tourist Information Centre**, at the Old Railway Station on South Terrace (daily 9am–5pm; Ⓣ08/8536 3212).

The best of the town's many **B&Bs** is the *Watervilla*, 2 Mill St (Ⓣ08/8536 4099, Ⓔwatervillahouse@triplei.net.au; ❺), a beautiful 1840s cottage overlooking landscaped gardens and the River Angas Park. Alternatively, the historic *Victoria Hotel* has quality motel rooms and a reasonable bistro (Ⓣ08/8536 2202, Ⓕ8536 2469, Ⓔdougkate@senet.com.au; ❺). For **eating**, *Café Ruffino*, on the High Street, serves excellent home-made pastries and cakes, while *Jack's Bakery*, on the other side of the street, has excellent coffee and an interesting gourmet menu. The only regular **public transport** is from Adelaide on Transit bus #843 via Adelaide Hills (Mon–Fri only); alternatively, if your timing's right, the *Southern Encounter* and *Highlander* steam trains chug in from Mount Barker and Goolwa on selected Sundays (see opposite).

The Yorke Peninsula

The **Yorke Peninsula** was almost the last section of the Australian coastline to be mapped by Matthew Flinders in 1802. Flat plains stretch out to the sea, so extensively cleared for farming that only tiny areas of original vegetation remain – in the Innes National Park at the very tip of the peninsula and in a couple of conservation parks. Much is made of the northern peninsula's **Cornish heritage**, but the miners from Cornwall who flocked to the area when **copper** was discovered in 1859 have left behind little but their names and the ubiquitous Cornish pasty. The three towns of the Copper Triangle or "**Little Cornwall**" – Kadina, Wallaroo and Moonta – make the most of it at the Kernewek Lowender (Cornish Festival), held over the long weekend in May of odd-numbered years, though in fact the mining boom ended more than seventy years ago, and they've been plain country towns ever since.

Just two hours' drive from Adelaide, the peninsula offers a peaceful weekend break as well as good **fishing**. The east-coast ports of Ardrossan, Port Vincent and Edithburgh on the Gulf St Vincent were visited first by ketches and schooners, and later by steamers transporting wheat and barley to England; now, the remaining jetties are used by anglers. They're all pleasant to visit, but **EDITHBURGH** offers the most facilities – once a substantial salt-production town and grain port, it still has a few fine old buildings and a long jetty. There's also a tidal swimming pool set in a rocky cove, and from Troubridge Hill you can see across to the Fleurieu Peninsula and the offshore **Troubridge Island Conservation Park**, with its 1850s iron lighthouse, migrating seabirds and **Little Penguin population**: guided tours are available (on demand only; 2hr; $35; ⓣ08/8852 6290). **Accommodation** is available here in the lighthouse-keeper's cottage, which sleeps up to ten and a minimum of four – if you stay here you'll have the whole island to yourself, but it doesn't come cheap (arrange through the tour guide; minimum two-night stay; ❻).

In Edithburgh itself, more affordable accommodation options include foreshore motel units and comfortable two-bedroom apartments at *The Anchorage Motel and Holiday Units*, 25 O'Halloran Parade (ⓣ08/8852 6262, ⓕ8852 6147; holiday units and rooms ❸–❹), and *Edithburgh Caravan Park* (ⓣ08/8852 6056, ⓦwww.edithburghcaravanpark.com) further along the foreshore, which has vans (❷) and en-suite cabins (❸). There are also motel units at the back of the *Troubridge Hotel* on Main Street (ⓣ08/8852 6013, ⓕ8852 6323; ❹). Across the road, the 1878 *Edithburgh Hotel* is the best place for **meals**, including oysters.

At the tip of the peninsula lies the **Innes National Park**, with its contrasting coastline of rough cliffs, sweeps of beach and sand dunes, and its interior of mallee scrub. The park is untouched except for the ruins of the gypsum-mining town of **Inneston**, near **Stenhouse Bay**. The **visitor centre** (ⓣ08/8854 3200) in the park sells entry permits ($7 per car) and **camping permits** (an extra $4–12 per car depending on which campsite you choose) and offers facilities such as hot showers. The main camping area is at **Pondalowie Bay**, which has some of the best **surf** in the state; there are several other good surfing spots around the park and north towards Corny Point. Other more sheltered coves and bays are good for **snorkelling**, with shallow reef areas of colourful marine life, while on land you might see emus, western grey kangaroos, pygmy possums and mallee fowl. The **NPWS** also operates five self-contained lodges around Inneston (ⓣ08/8854 3200, ⓕ8854 3299; ❶–❻).

Premier Stateliner (ⓣ08/8415 5555) has a daily **bus service** from Adelaide to Moonta, via Kadina and Wallaroo. The Yorke Peninsula Passenger Service (ⓣ08/8391 2977) runs from Adelaide to Yorketown, alternating daily between the east coast via Ardrossan, Port Vincent and Edithburgh and the centre via Maitland and Minlaton. There's no transport to Innes National Park. For more information, visit ⓦwww.yorkepeninsula.com.au.

Kangaroo Island

As you head towards **Cape Jervis** along the west coast of the Fleurieu Peninsula, **KANGAROO ISLAND**, only 13km offshore, first appears behind a vale of rolling hills. Once you're on the island, its size and lack of development – there's only one person for every square kilometre – leave a strong impression. This is actually Australia's third-largest island (after Tasmania and Melville Island, north of Darwin), with 450km of quite spectacular and wild coastline, and so takes some time to explore. To see all the island's unusual geological features and **wildlife** habitats, you'll need at least three days, though most people only visit the major attractions on the south coast – Seal Bay, Little Sahara, Remarkable Rocks and Flinders Chase National Park.

Although the island is promoted as South Australia's premier destination for tourism, it's still very unspoilt; only in the peak holiday period (Christmas to the end of Jan, when most of the accommodation is booked up) does it feel busy. Once out of the island's few small towns, there's little sign of human presence to break the long, straight stretches of road as they run through undulating fields, dense gum forests or mallee scrub. There's often a strong wind off the Southern Ocean, so bring something warm whatever the season, and take care when **swimming** – there are strong rips on many of the beaches. Safe swimming spots include Hog Bay and Antechamber Bay, both near Penneshaw; Emu Bay, northwest of Kingscote; Stokes Bay, further west; and Vivonne Bay, on the south side of the island.

A third of Kangaroo Island is protected in some form, and is consequently one of the best place in Australia for **wildlife spotting**; there's an astonishing range of animals here, largely untroubled by disease or natural predators. When Matthew Flinders first sighted the island in 1802, "black substances" seen on shore in the twilight turned out to be **kangaroos**, prolific and easily hunted; they still abound though, as do wallabies. **Koalas** were introduced at Flinders Chase National Park in 1923 as a conservation measure. They have remained free of chlamydia, which is common in the mainland population, and have spread so widely that they are killing off many of the gum trees – calls for culling in the mid-1990s caused national controversy, so fertility control and relocation to other parts of Australia are being tried instead. Other animals found here include echidnas, platypuses, Little Penguins, fur seals, sea lions and, in passing, southern right whales. The island is also home to over two hundred other kinds of **birds**, as well as snakes, some of them poisonous.

Wild pigs and feral goats, the descendants of those left here by early seafarers, can also be found, while a pure strain of **Ligurian bees** brought by early settlers now forms the basis of a local honey industry. There are also over a million **sheep** on the island, most of them merino, and a sheep dairy here makes delicious cheeses. The latest local craze is for **marron farming**, with about 140 licensed producers of the freshwater crustacean, a bit like a cross between a lobster and a yabbie. Other diverse new industries include abalone farming, oyster and mussel production, olive-oil pressing and the revival of eucalyptus-oil distilling.

Getting to the island

The ridiculously expensive Kangaroo Island Sealink **ferries** ply across the Backstairs Passage from Cape Jervis to Penneshaw – often a rough journey, though mercifully short. Two large vehicle ferries make the journey at least three times daily, and up to seven times during peak holiday periods, taking about forty minutes to cross: buses connect the service with Adelaide twice daily ($78 ferry return, $118 including bus from Adelaide, cars $158, motorbikes $50, bikes $11; ⓣ13 13 01, ⓦwww.sealink.com.au). At Penneshaw, connecting Sealink buses run to American River ($10 one way) and Kingscote ($13), though they need to be booked in advance on the same number.

In addition, it's worth checking out various cheap **packages**, including accommodation and tours or car rental, often with special backpacker rates. At one end of the scale, Adelaide Sightseeing does a whirlwind $218 one-day coach tour leaving Adelaide at 6.45am and returning at 10.40pm, but it's pretty exhausting. Camp Wild Adventures (ⓣ08/8132 1333 or 1800 444 321, ⓦwww.campwild.com.au) has an excellent, more laid-back two-day 4WD tour from Adelaide, camping overnight in a secluded spot on the southern coast ($320 per person). The Wayward Bus's two-day tour from Adelaide also takes advantage of an overnight stop near the Flinders Chase National Park, giving more time for viewing the spectacular sights there ($355 per person, or $385 to upgrade from dorm to twin or double room; ⓣ08/8410 8833, ⓦwww.waywardbus.com.au).

It takes thirty minutes to **fly** to Kingscote Airport (actually closer to Cygnet River) on Kangaroo Island from Adelaide – costs vary, starting from $120 for a return ticket. There's a bus to Kingscote for about $10 with Airport Shuttle Services (ⓣ08/8553 2390).

Getting around, tours and activities

There's no public transport on the island, so without a tour or your own vehicle, hiring a car is pretty much essential. There are two **car rental** firms; it's best to book ahead to be sure of getting a vehicle and ensure you'll be met with it off the ferry or plane. Budget Rent a Car has an office at Penneshaw Ferry Terminal ($72–127 per day; ⓣ08/8553 3133), or you could try Kangaroo Island Rental/Hertz in Kingscote, on the corner of Franklin Street and Telegraph Road ($77 per day or $470 per week, $180 per day for 4WD; ⓣ08/8553 2390 or 1800 088 296, ⓦwww.hertz.com.au). Both have a desk at the airport.

Roads to most major attractions are bitumen-sealed, including the scenic eighty-kilometre **South Coast Road** from Cygnet River to the Flinders Chase National Park, Remarkable Rocks and Admirals Arch. The main drag is the **Playford Highway**, running from Kingscote through Cygnet River and Parndana to the western tip of the island at Cape Borda; the last part of the highway along the northern edge of Flinders Chase National Park is not sealed and can be rough. At the eastern end of the highway, sealed roads feed off to the airport, Emu Bay, American River and Penneshaw. Most other roads are constructed of ironstone rubble on red dirt and can be very dangerous; the recommended speed on these roads is 60kph. Driving at night on all roads is best avoided due to the high risk of collision with kangaroos and wallabies; you'll see animal remains alongside the road at depressingly short intervals – most are hit by speeding trucks. Cars have far less protection from impact and insurance excesses are often a mandatory $2000 for animal collision. The main roads are all good for **cycling** – you can rent bikes at most accommodation or at KI Cycling Adventures ($35 per day; ⓣ0412 860 034).

Most people opt to visit the island on a **tour**, which can be good value if bought as part of a package (see p.745). There are several small-group tour companies based on the island: Exceptional Kangaroo Island in Kingscote (ⓣ08/8553 9119, ⓦwww.adventurecharters.com.au), led by an ex-park ranger, offers 4WD tours with an emphasis on fine food, wine and accommodation as well as nature. There are also a couple of dive-tour operators: Kangaroo Island Diving Safaris

(Ⓣ08/8559 3225, Ⓦwww.kidivingsafaris.com), based at Telhawk Farm on the north coast, offers diving charters and residential dive courses with special backpacker rates; and K.I. Diving on Beach Crescent, American River (Ⓣ08/8553 1072, Ⓦwww.kidiving.com), offers a three-day residential scuba course and certification ($425), as well as a half-day Discover Scuba course ($89).

Information and park entrance fees

Many of the national or conservation parks on the island charge entry fees and extras for guided tours. However, a one-year **Island Pass** ($44.50 per person) covers virtually all these costs (except for camping and the night-time penguin tours from Penneshaw and Kingscote; see p.769 & p.768), and is worth it if you're here for a while. The entry fees and tour prices quoted in the following accounts apply only if you don't have a pass – add up the cost of what you want to see and work out which is cheaper. Passes can be bought from the parks themselves or from the NPWS office on Dauncey Street, Kingscote (Mon–Fri 8.45am–5pm; Ⓣ08/8553 2381, Ⓦwww.parks.sa.gov.au); this office can also arrange camping permits and cottage accommodation in most of the national parks around the island. Passes can also be purchased from the **Kangaroo Island Gateway Visitor Information Centre**, at the edge of Penneshaw on the main road to Kingscote (Mon–Fri 9am–5pm, Sat & Sun 10am–4pm; Ⓣ08/8553 1185, Ⓦwww.tourkangarooisland.com.au), which also has an interpretive display on the island's history, geology and ecology, and dispenses free maps.

The island

Coming by boat, you'll arrive at Kangaroo Island's eastern end, either at the small settlement of **Penneshaw**, with its Little Penguin colony, or **Kingscote**, a little further west, the island's administrative centre and South Australia's second-oldest colonial settlement, though little remains to show for it. Between Penneshaw and Kingscote, sheltered **American River** is another good base. The airport is situated near **Cygnet River**, a quiet spot inland from Kingscote. From here, the Playford Highway and South Coast Road branch out to traverse the island, entering **Flinders Chase National Park** from the north and south respectively. The national park and surrounding wilderness protection area cover the entire western end of the island.

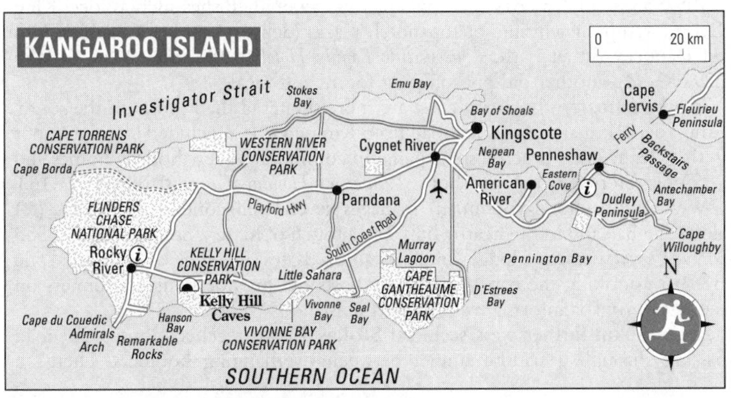

The rugged **south coast** provides more wildlife spotting and fine scenery: running west to east you can visit the aptly named **Remarkable Rocks** and **Admirals Arch**, both within the national park; go bushwalking in Hanson Bay; tour the limestone caves of Kelly Hill; camp at Vivonne Bay Conservation Park; play Lawrence of Arabia among the impressive sand dunes of Little Sahara; or roam amongst sea lions at Seal Bay. The quieter **north coast** has a series of sheltered beaches, including Emu Bay and Stokes Bay, and wild coastal cliff walks around Scotts Cove.

Kingscote and the north coast

With banks, shops, Internet access, a hospital, library and the only high school, **KINGSCOTE** is the island's main town. The coast here has been the scene of several shipwrecks – interpretive boards on the foreshore provide details. For more history, you can walk north along the Esplanade to the **Reeves Point Historic Site**, where boards commemorate the South Australia Company's first landing of settlers in July 1836, before they headed off to establish nearby Adelaide. The settlement never numbered more than three hundred people, and folded in 1839. Less than a kilometre up the hill above, on Seaview Road, is **Hope Cottage Folk Museum** (daily 1–4pm, Sat only in Aug; $5), the restored 1859 home of a pioneering family.

Kingscote has a small colony of **Little Penguins** that were transported from Penneshaw during the building of the boardwalk there; they aren't as impressive in numbers as Penneshaw's, and are best seen on the guided ranger talks that leave from the **Marine Centre** on the wharf (April–Sept 7.30pm & 8.30pm; Oct–March 8.30pm & 9.30pm; $5; ⓣ08/8553 3112). There's also pelican feeding around the Fisherman's Jetty, with a small talk about their habits and habitat (daily 5pm; $2).

Upmarket motel **accommodation** with sea views is found at *Wisteria Lodge*, Cygnet Road (ⓣ08/8553 2707, ⓦwww.wisterialodgeki.com; ❻). For the budget-conscious there's the *Kangaroo Island Central Lodge*, 19 Murray St (ⓣ08/8553 2787; dorms $22, rooms ❷–❸), which has large clean dorms, a kitchen and common room. *Nepean Bay Caravan Park* (ⓣ & ⓕ08/8553 2394, ⓦwww.kingscotetouristpark.com.au; cabins ❸) at Brownlow Beach, 3km away, is the only place for campers.

Established in 1907, the waterfront *Ozone Hotel* (ⓣ08/8553 2011 or 1800 083 133, ⓦwww.ozonehotel.com; ❺) is a local institution with comfortable rooms and a lively dining area. The best **restaurant** in town is *Bella* on Dauncey Street (ⓣ08/8553 0400), a cozy space where you can enjoy dishes such as local King George tempura whiting, or top-notch pizzas (delivery service available). Also on Dauncey Street is the *Queenscliffe Family Hotel* (ⓣ08/8553 2254, ⓕ8553 2291; ❸–❹), another old pub offering rooms and meals.

The **beaches** on the north coast are more sheltered than those on the south. Emu Bay, 21km along a sealed road from Kingscote, is a secluded and quiet spot with a clean, sandy beach, a small penguin community, a few holiday homes and a couple of B&Bs, but no shops. *Wintersun Holiday Units* (ⓣ08/8553 5163, ⓦwww.emubayholidays.com.au) manages several self-contained cottages (❹) along the bay and in the nearby hills. For a touch of luxury, *Seascape* (ⓣ08/8553 5199, ⓦwww.seascapelodge.com.au; ❼) on Bates Road is a boutique-style B&B overlooking the bay. The friendly hosts can provide gourmet dinners on request as well as informative tours of the island.

About 30km further west, secluded **Stokes Bay** is reached along a dirt road passing through a natural tunnel between overhanging boulders. There's a delightful, calm rock pool – a perfect semicircle of rounded black stones which conveniently provides protection from the dangerous rip in the bay. Outside the tunnel, the *Rockpool Café* (daily 9am–5pm summer only; ⓣ08/8559 2277) looks after the beachfront campsites and also sells milk and bread to campers.

Penneshaw and around

It's a 45-minute drive on a sealed road from Kingscote to **PENNESHAW**, set on low, penguin-inhabited cliffs. This is a popular base, with comfortable accommodation and plenty of places to eat. Penneshaw's crescent of sandy beach at Hog Bay curves from the rocks below the wharf, where the ferries come in, around to a wooded headland. The bay provides safe **swimming** and even a shady shelter on the sand. Above, there's a grassy picnic reserve with barbecues and the **Penguin Interpretive Centre** (check opening hours with tourist office). Penneshaw Penguin Tours (daily: winter 7.30pm & 8.30pm; summer 8.30pm & 9.30pm; $9; ⓣ08/8553 1103) provide an excellent informative commentary on the antics of the **Little Penguins** from the centre at dusk. This is the time they return from feeding in the unpolluted sea and cross the beach at Hog Bay to their cliffside burrows – a specially lit boardwalk provides a rookery viewing area.

Antechamber Bay, 10km southeast of Penneshaw, also has good, safe swimming. If you drive or cycle a further 10km along the unsealed dusty road you'll come to **Cape Willoughby Lighthouse**, at the eastern end of the island. Guided tours are offered by the NPWS (daily 11.30am, 12.30pm & 2pm; summer, spring and autumn also at 3.15pm & 4pm; $11.50; ⓔcape.willoughby@saugov.sa.gov.au), and you can even stay in the sandstone homes of the original keepers (see below). You'll find more safe swimming at **American Beach**, southwest of Penneshaw along the scenic road that hugs Eastern Cove.

The **Dudley Peninsula**, on which Penneshaw stands, is attached to the rest of the island by a narrow neck of sand; at the isthmus 511 steps lead up to **Mount Thisby** (Prospect Hill), a 99-metre hill of sand with views across to the mainland, to Hungry Beach, Pelican Lagoon and American River on the island's north coast, and in the opposite direction to Pennington Bay.

Penneshaw practicalities

Penneshaw's Sealink office is at 7 North Terrace (daily 8am–5.45pm; ⓣ08/8553 1122). There's no bank, but the **post office** (Mon–Fri 9am–5pm, Sat 9am–11pm) acts as an agent, and there's EFTPOS at Grimshaw's, the town's **general store** opposite the hotel (daily 8am–7pm, summer until 8pm). Penneshaw's **accommodation** options include the comfortable *Kangaroo Island YHA*, 33 Middle Terrace (ⓣ08/8553 1344, ⓦwww.yha.com.au; dorms $25, rooms ❸). The upmarket alternative is the friendly *Kangaroo Island Seafront Hotel* (ⓣ08/8553 1028, ⓦwww.seafront.com.au; ❺), set in landscaped gardens with motel-style rooms and fully equipped cabins, plus a heated pool, spa, sauna and tennis court, bar and restaurant. You can also stay in the two lighthouse-keepers' cottages at **Cape Willoughby** (ⓣ08/8559 7235, ⓔkiparksaccom@saugov.sa.gov.au; BYO linen; ❺).

The best **restaurant** in town is *Sorrento's* in the *Seafront Hotel*, specializing in seafood, steaks and local wines. The nearby *Fish* (Sept–June daily 4.30pm–8.30pm) is a neat black-and-white-tiled establishment cooking up a wonderful array of locally caught produce such as lobster, marron, whiting and oysters. The tin-roofed bungalow of the *Penneshaw Hotel* is a small and friendly place to drink, with a veranda overlooking the water.

American River

Facing Penneshaw across Eastern Cove, **AMERICAN RIVER** is actually a sheltered bay where many small fishing boats moor, aiming to catch some of its abundant whiting. It's a peaceful place to stay, with a concentration of accommodation along the hilly shoreline and a general store. Boats can be chartered for local **fishing and sailing** from the kiosk at American River Rendezvous (ⓣ08/8553 7150) or direct from Cooinda Charter Services (ⓣ & ⓕ08/8553 7063).

For **accommodation**, *Matthew Flinders Terraces* (ⓣ08/8553 7100, ⓦwww.matthewflindersterraces.com.au; ❻) is a beautifully situated motel with pool and spa, or try the *Wanderers Rest* (ⓣ08/8553 7140, ⓦwww.wanderersrest.com.au; ❼), an upmarket B&B with a quality seafood restaurant. Holiday units include the budget *Casuarina Coastal Units* (ⓣ08/8553 7020; ❸) and the more expensive *Ulonga Lodge* (ⓣ & ⓕ08/8553 7171, ⓦwww.ulonga.com.au; ❹), which also has a café.

The south coast

There are several conservation parks strung out along the exposed south coast. The largest is **Cape Gantheaume**, an area of low mallee scrub supporting prolific birdlife around **Murray Lagoon**, the largest freshwater lagoon on the island. The adjacent **Seal Bay Conservation Park** is home to almost six hundred sea lions, the third-largest breeding population in Australia. They are unusually tolerant of humans and you can walk quietly among the colony on the beach at **Seal Bay** when accompanied by a national park guide (daily 9am–5.15pm in holidays, all other times until 4.15pm; $13.50, sunset tour $31; ⓣ08/8559 4207), or take a stroll on the boardwalk ($9.50).

Vivonne Bay, with its long, sandy beach and bush setting, is a great place to camp. There's a **beachside campsite** ($10) with toilets, water and barbecues, and a well-stocked store and bottle shop 1km away on the main South Coast Road. It's safe to swim near the jetty or boat ramp or in the Harriet River, but the bay itself has a dangerous undertow. Between Seal Bay and Vivonne Bay, **Little Sahara** comprises 15km of perfect white-sand dunes rising unexpectedly out of mallee scrub.

The main features of the **Kelly Hill Conservation Park** are the **Kelly Hill Caves**, extensive limestone cave formations (NPWS guided tours daily 10am–4.15pm; $11.50). The tour explores only the largest cave – not the usual damp, bat-filled cavern, but very dry, with a constant temperature of 16°C. The NPWS runs **adventure caving tours** of three other caves at 2.15pm daily ($28.50; ⓣ08/8559 7231 for details and booking). The eighteen-kilometre return **Hanson Bay Trail** runs from the caves to the sea, passing freshwater lagoons and dune systems: allow at least eight hours, or longer if you'll be tempted to stop for a swim. *Hanson Bay Sanctuary Homestead* (ⓣ08/8559 7344, ⓦwww.hansonbay.com.au; minimum three-night stay; ❹), just west of the Kelly Hill Conservation Park, is situated in a lovely secluded spot surrounded by bushland with excellent walking trails.

Flinders Chase National Park

Flinders Chase National Park, Kangaroo Island's largest, occupies the entire western end of the island. It became a park as early as 1919, and in the 1920s and 1930s koalas, platypuses and Cape Barren geese from the Bass Strait islands were introduced. The land is mainly low-lying mallee forest, with occasional patches of taller sugar-gum trees. The **Flinders Chase Visitors Centre** (daily 9am–5pm; park entry fee $7.50 per person; ⓣ08/8559 7235, ⓔflinders.chase@saugov.sa.gov.au) is surrounded by open grasslands where large numbers of kangaroos and

△ Koalas, Kangaroo Island

wallabies graze. Koala signs lead to a glade of trees where you can see the creatures swaying overhead, within binocular range. Follow the **Platypus Waterhole Walk** for 3km to a platypus-viewing area, but be warned that to get a glimpse of the creatures requires endless patience. The winding sealed road through the park will take you to its most spectacular features: the huge, weirdly shaped, rust-coloured **Remarkable Rocks** on Kirkpatrick Point, and the impressive natural formation of **Admirals Arch**, where hundreds of New Zealand fur seals bask around the rocks. At the northern corner of the park, you can go on a guided tour of the 1858 **Cape Borda Lighthouse** (daily 11.30am, 12.30pm & 2pm; summer, spring and autumn also at 3.15pm & 4pm; $11.50; ⓣ08/8559 3257).

The main **camping** area is at Rocky River, or there are various **cottages** (❺) throughout the park – bookable through the Flinders Chase Visitors Centre – and several other good places to stay along the South Coast Road just outside the park. *Kangaroo Island Wilderness Resort* (ⓣ08/8559 7275, ⓦwww.kiwr.com; ❻) has large wood cabins set amidst bushland, plus an excellent restaurant – at dusk you can watch the nocturnal animals coming out to feed. Nearby, the *Western KI Caravan Park* (ⓣ08/8559 7201, ⓦwww.westernki.com.au; cabins ❹–❺) is set in an expansive wildlife reserve, where you can camp under the tall gum trees and try to spot koala bears. By staying at this end of the island you'll also see the spectacular coastal sights at their best – particularly Remarkable Rocks, which turn a deep orange with the setting and rising sun.

The southeast

Most travellers en route between Adelaide and Melbourne pass through southeast South Australia as quickly as possible. From Tailem Bend, just beyond

Murray Bridge some 85km out of Adelaide, three highways branch out. The northernmost, the **Mallee Highway**, is the quintessential road to nowhere, leading through the sleepy settlements of Lameroo and Pinnaroo to the insignificant town of Ouyen in Victoria's mallee country (see p.937). The second, the **Dukes Highway**, offers a fast and boring route to Melbourne via the South Australian mallee scrub and farming towns of **Keith** and **Bordertown**, before continuing in Victoria as the Western Highway across the monotonous Wimmera (see p.937). It is, however, well worth breaking your journey to visit the **Coonawarra** and **Naracoorte**, in between the Dukes Highway and the coastal route: the former is a tiny wine-producing area that makes some of the country's finest **red wine**; the latter is a fair-sized town with a freshwater lagoon system that attracts prolific birdlife, and a conservation park with impressive World Heritage–listed caves.

The third option, the **Princes Highway** (Highway 1), is much less direct but far more interesting. It follows the extensive coastal lagoon system of the **Coorong** to **Kingston SE**, and then runs a short way inland to the lake craters of **Mount Gambier** before crossing into Victoria. There's another possible route on this last stretch – the **Southern Ports Highway** – which sticks closer to the coast, plus a potential detour along the Riddoch Highway into the scenic Coonawarra wine region.

Premier Stateliner (Ⓣ08/8415 5555) **buses** serve two routes between Adelaide and Mount Gambier, one inland via Keith, Bordertown, Naracoorte, Coonawarra and Penola; the other along the coast via Meningie, Kingston SE, Robe and Millicent. The NPWS free newspaper, *The Tatler*, gives practical details relating to the southeastern coastal parks – pick up the latest copy from the Adelaide office (see p.724), or regional offices en route. Further information can be found at the regional visitor information website (Ⓦwww.thelimestonecoast.com).

Coorong National Park

From Tailem Bend, the Princes Highway skirts Lake Alexandrina and the freshwater Lake Albert before passing the edge of the **Coorong National Park**. The coastal saline lagoon system of the Coorong (from the Aboriginal "Karangk", meaning long neck) is separated from the sea for over 100km by the high sand dunes of the **Younghusband Peninsula**. This is the state's most prolific **pelican breeding ground**, and an excellent place to observe these awkward yet graceful birds – there's a shelter with seating and a telescope focused on the small islands where some birds breed at Jacks Point, 3km north of Policemans Point on the Princes Highway. If you don't have your own transport, you can get to the park on a **cruise** from Goolwa (see box, p.763).

There are several designated **camping areas** with shelters, barbecues, toilets, running water (but no showers) and marked **walking trails**. The Coorong is also good for beach camping: with a permit (see below) you can camp anywhere along the beach, but cars must be parked in designated places and you must bring your own drinking water, which can be collected outside the seldom-manned **Salt Creek NPWS ranger station** on the edge of the park. Information, camping permits ($4 per car) and maps of the park and campsites can be obtained at the **national park headquarters** at 32–34 Princes Highway, Meningie (Mon–Wed 9am–5pm; Ⓣ08/8575 1200), the Meningie Information

Centre, 14 Princes Highway, in the old town hall (daily 9am–5pm; ⓣ08/8575 1770), and most petrol stations on the way to the park.

There are **caravan parks** at Long Point, Parnka Point, Gemini Downs and 42-Mile Crossing – the only land access to the Younghusband Peninsula. If you're passing by, park your car at the 42-Mile Crossing information area and walk 1km along a sandy 4WD track for great views of the sand dunes and the wild Southern Ocean. This track runs alongside the beach all the way up the peninsula to Barkers Knoll and down to Kingston SE, with camping along the way. If you want to stay in more comfort, there are plenty of motels at the popular, if dull, fishing centre of **Meningie**, by Lake Albert.

Camp Coorong, run by the Ngarrindjeri Lands and Progress Association, is 10km south of Meningie. This cultural centre attempts to explain the heritage and culture of the **Ngarrindjeri Aborigines**, once one of the largest groups in South Australia, occupying the land around the Coorong and the lower Murray River and lakes. There's a fascinating museum (Mon–Fri 10am–5pm; donation), and you can camp here or in the nearby bush reserve ($5 per group) or stay in the well-fitted-out cabins (booking required on ⓣ08/8575 1557, ⓦwww.ngarrindjeri.com; ❸). A few kilometres further south is the Ngarrindjeri-owned *Coorong Wilderness Lodge*, designed in the shape of a fish (ⓣ08/8575 6001, ⓦwww.cooronglodge.com; camping $10 per car, en-suite cabin ❸). The **restaurant** serves indigenous meals (booking essential), and if you want to learn more about Ngarrindjeri culture, the owners offer short tours, plus a comprehensive three-day wilderness and cultural tour.

Southern Ports Highway: Kingston to Robe

KINGSTON South East (SE), on Lacepede Bay, is the first town past the Coorong: here the Princes Highway turns inland, while the Southern Ports Highway continues along the coast before rejoining the main road at Millicent. As the **Big Lobster** on the highway in Kingston suggests, the town has an important lobster industry: you can buy them freshly cooked at Lacepede Seafood by the jetty (daily 9am–6pm) for around $49 a kilo.

Lobsters apart, you're better off continuing down the coast. **ROBE**, on the south side of Guichen Bay, 44km from Kingston, was one of South Australia's first settlements, established as a deep-water port in 1847. After 1857, over sixteen thousand Chinese landed here and walked to the goldfields, 400km away, to avoid the poll tax levied in Victoria. As trade declined and the highway bypassed the town, Robe managed to maintain both dignity and a low-key charm, and during the busy summer period the population of less than eight hundred expands to over eleven thousand. Summer is also the season for Robe's other major industry, **crayfishing**.

Robe practicalities

Tourist information is available inside the library on the corner of Smiley and Victoria streets (Mon–Fri 9am–5pm, Sat & Sun 10am–4pm; ⓣ08/8768 2465, ⓦwww.robe.sa.gov.au); they also have walking and driving maps, and free, limited-time Internet access. Premier Stateliner **buses** pass through on their way from Adelaide to Mount Gambier, while Wayward Bus calls in en route to Melbourne.

Accommodation

There are dozens of places to **stay**, most of which double up as places to eat.

Bushland Cabins Nora Criena Rd ⓣ08/8768 2386. Southeast of the centre with walking trails into the surrounding bush, including a one-kilometre cliff-top track into Robe. Dorms $20–22, cabins ❸

Caledonian Inn 1 Victoria St ⓣ08/8768 2029, ⓦwww.caledonian.com.au. The charming, ivy-covered building was first licensed in 1858 and wouldn't look out of place in an English village – it offers B&B accommodation upstairs or in homely cottages with sea views, and serves excellent food. Rooms ❹, cottages ❻

Guichen Bay Motel 42 Victoria St ⓣ08/8768 2001, ⓦwww.gbmotel.com.au. This place offers good-value, spacious rooms, some with kitchenette, as well as the licensed *Cottage Restaurant*, which has special crayfish dishes in season (booking advised). ❹

Lakeside Manor Backpackers 22 Main Rd ⓣ08/8768 1995 or 1800 155 350, ⓦwww.lakesidemanorbackpackers.com.au. Pick of the town for backpackers is the brand new *Lodge*, with spacious old-English-style dorms and an impressive library. Free Internet access and bike hire is included. Dorms $24, double ❸

Robe Hotel Mundy Terrace ⓣ08/8768 2077, ⓦwww.robehotel.com.au. An old stone beachfront hotel, with en-suite motel-style rooms with views and spa units; the downstairs bars serve good bistro meals. ❹

Sea Vu Caravan Park 1 Squire Drive ⓣ08/8768 2273, ⓦwww.robeseavu.com. Family-run and one of the four caravan parks close to town, with a swimming beach right next door. Cabins ❹

Eating

For **meals**, *The Gallerie*, 2 Victoria St, serves modern breakfasts, lunches and dinners and a decent selection of wines in the adjacent wine bar. *Robe Seafood and Takeaway*, 21 Victoria St, provides the ubiquitous fish and chips, while for self-caterers, Foodland Supermarket, opposite the Ampol petrol station, is open daily 7.30am–7pm.

Beyond Robe

Between Robe and Beachport are four lakes: for part of the way you can take the Nora Criena Drive through **Little Dip Conservation Park**, 14km of coastal dune systems. The drive provides views of Lake Eliza and Lake St Clair before returning to Southern Ports Highway and the former whaling port of **BEACHPORT**, which boasts one of the longest jetties in Australia and many lobster-fishing boats at anchor on Rivoli Bay. Beachport has plenty of **accommodation** but the pick of the town is *Bompas*, overlooking the bay at 3 Railway Terrace (ⓣ08/8735 8333, ⓦwww.bompas.com.au; dorms $27.50, en-suite rooms ❹), with a pleasant restaurant serving modern Australian dishes. The helpful **Visitor Information Centre** on Millicent Road (Mon–Fri 9am–5pm, Sat & Sun 10am–1pm, summer Sat & Sun until 4pm; ⓣ08/8735 8029, ⓦwww.wattlerange.sa.gov.au) can give you more information on the region.

Continuing south on Southern Ports Highway, there are several turn-offs to **Canunda National Park**, which has giant sand dunes, signposted coastal walking trails, an abundance of birdlife and camping facilities ($4 per vehicle; honesty box). The best place to explore the park from is **SOUTHEND** but there's also access to the park near the rather ordinary town of **MILLICENT**, 15km to the south, which has its own **Visitor Information Centre**, 1 Mt Gambier Rd (Mon–Fri 9am–5pm, Sat & Sun 10am–4pm; ⓣ08/8733 0904), and plenty of accommodation. The Southern Ports Highway rejoins the Princes Highway at Millicent.

Mount Gambier and around

Set close to the border with Victoria, **MOUNT GAMBIER** is the south-east's commercial centre. The small city sprawls up the slopes of an extinct volcano whose three craters – each with its own lake surrounded by heavily wooded slopes and filled from underground waterways – are perfect for subterranean diving.

The **Blue Lake** is the largest of the three, up to 70m deep and 5km in circumference. From November to March it's a stunning cobalt blue, reverting to duller grey in the colder months. There are lookout spots and a **scenic drive** around the lake, and guided tours are offered by Aquifer Tours (daily on the hour: Feb–May & Sept–Oct 9am–2pm; June–Aug 9am–noon; Nov–Jan 9am–5pm, Twilight Tour 7pm; 45min; $7; ⓣ08/8723 1199). The second-largest crater holds Valley Lake and a **Wildlife Park** (daily 7am–dusk; free), where indigenous animals range free amid native flora; there are also lookouts, walking trails and boardwalks.

West of the city centre, on Jubilee Highway West, is the extensive complex of underground caverns at **Engelbrecht Cave** (guided tours hourly 10am–3pm, check times in winter with tourist office; 45min; $6). You can dive here in limestone waterways under the city, though you'll need a CDAA (Cave Divers Association of Australia) qualification to tackle these dark and dangerous waters. Contact the Department for Environment and Heritage at 11 Helen St (ⓣ08/8735 1114, ⓦwww.environment.sa.gov.au/parks) for further information.

The centrepiece of Mount Gambier itself is **Cave Gardens**, a shady park surrounding a deep limestone cavern with steps leading some way down; the stream running into it eventually filters into the Blue Lake. Fronting the park is the former Town Hall and the **Riddoch Art Gallery** (Tues–Fri 10am–5pm, Sat 11am–3pm; free) whose focus is the impressive Rodney Gooch collection of Aboriginal art from the Utopia region of the Northern Territory.

The CDAA issues permits for snorkelling in the crystal-clear waters of **Piccaninnie Ponds Conservation Park** and **Ewans Pond Conservation Park**, both south of Mount Gambier near Port Macdonnell. At Piccaninnie Ponds, a deep chasm with white limestone walls contains clear water that is filtered underground from the Blue Lake – it takes five hundred years to get here. East of the city is Umpherston Sinkhole (open access), also known as the **Sunken Garden** since it contains Victorian-era terraced gardens – they are floodlit at night when possums come out to feed.

Practicalities

For more information on Mount Gambier's attractions, head for the excellent **Lady Nelson Victory and Discovery Centre**, on Jubilee Highway East (daily 9am–5pm; exhibition $12; ⓣ08/8724 9750, ⓦwww.mountgambiertourism.com.au), where the ecology, geology and history of Mount Gambier are explored from Aboriginal and European perspectives. They also have free limited-time Internet access.

Mount Gambier has heaps of **places to stay**, with motels lining the highway either side of town – the pick of them is the *Barn Motel & Apartments*, on Nelson Road (ⓣ08/8726 8366, ⓦwww.barnmotel.com; motel ❸–❹, apartments ❺). Aside from these, *The Jail*, on Margaret Street (ⓣ08/8723 0032, ⓦwww.jailbackpackers.com; dorms $22), was built in 1866 and is now a Heritage-listed building. The last inmates left in 1995 and you can stay in the original cells behind locked doors (the solitary loo in the corner is referred to as in-suite instead of en-suite). There's also a bar, laundry facilities and Internet access and the owner has a couple of cuddly alpacas in the garden. Centrally located at 2 Commercial St West, *The G Hotel* (Ⓣ08/8725 0611, Ⓦwww.mountgambierhotel.com.au; ④) is the plushest of the lot in town, with large well-priced rooms and a trendy retro bar downstairs with live music and DJs on weekends, as well as a contemporary restaurant.

Dining options are plentiful – pick of the bunch is the unassuming-looking *Sage and Muntries*, Commercial Street West, serving up fine modern Australian cuisine (closed Sun). Alternatively, try the modern *Anno Domani* at 17 Commercial St West, a split-level restaurant serving seafood risottos and lots of varieties of strong coffee. Classic Italian pizza and pasta can be found at the award-winning *Caffè Belgiorno* on Percy Street, with the town's cinema next door in the Oatmill Building.

Heading on to Melbourne from Mount Gambier, V/Line (Ⓣ13 61 96) has a daily **bus** service via Portland, Warrnambool, Geelong and Ballarat.

The Coonawarra wine region

Directly north of Mount Gambier, the Riddoch Highway heads through the low-key and pretty **Coonawarra wine region**, and past some World Heritage–listed caves at **Naracoorte**, eventually linking up with the Dukes Highway at Keith. Most wineries are located on a ninety-kilometre stretch of highway between **Penola** and Padthaway – the region is renowned for the quality of its reds, which have been compared to those of Bordeaux. The soil and drainage is ideal, classic Terra Rossa over limestone, and the climate is perfect – as the weather is not really variable from year to year, the wines are consistently good. Premier Stateliner (Ⓣ08/8415 5555) stops daily at Penola and Naracoorte on its Adelaide-to-Mount Gambier inland service, while Penola Coonawarra Tour Service (Ⓣ08/8737 2779) offers restaurant transfers and winery tours around the area.

Coonawarra wineries

There are twenty Coonawarra wineries that do tastings (most open Mon–Fri 9am–5pm, Sat & Sun 10am–4pm); for more information visit the Coonawarra Wine Association website at Ⓦwww.coonawarra.org. A few favourites (arranged in order as if you were driving north along the Riddoch Highway from Penola towards Coonawarra Township) include *Hollick Wines* (Ⓦwww.hollick.com), once a tiny 1870s wood-and-stone slab cottage, now a modern winery with trendy restaurant attached; Balnaves (Ⓦwww.balnaves.com.au), with its innovative architecture; Leconfield (Ⓦwww.leconfieldwines.com), with very well-regarded Cabernet Sauvignons; and Zema Estate (Ⓦwww.zema.com.au), a small family-run winery with Italian roots. Wynns Coonawarra Estate (Ⓦwww.wynns.com.au), west of the Riddoch Highway on Memorial Drive at Coonawarra Township, is Coonawarra's longest-established (1896) and best-known winery. Continuing back on the Riddoch Highway towards Padthaway, the down-to-earth Redman family winery (Ⓦwww.redman.com.au) has been making red wine for generations. Beyond Redman, the modern winery complex of Rymill (Ⓦwww.rymill.com.au), attractively located on Clayfield Road west of the Riddoch Highway, includes a glass-walled tasting area overlooking the vineyards, and platforms upstairs for viewing the testing lab.

Penola and around

Twenty-two kilometres north of Mount Gambier, **PENOLA**, gateway to the Coonawarra wine region, is a simple but dignified country town with well-preserved nineteenth-century architecture. For information, head for **Penola Coonawarra Visitor Centre** in the historic **John Riddoch Centre** (Mon–Fri 9am–5pm, Sat & Sun 10am–5pm; ⓣ08/8737 2855, ⓦwww.wattlerange.sa.gov.au), which houses a display of this pioneer of Coonawarra's vineyards, and hands out the free *Historic Penola and Coonawarra* map with details of the region's wineries.

Beside the 1857 Cobb & Co booking office, **St Joseph's Catholic Church** looks like something out of an Italian village, a world away from the very modern **Mary MacKillop Interpretative Centre** (daily 10am–4pm; $3.50; ⓣ08/8737 2092) next door. Sister Mary MacKillop (1842–1909) was Penola's most famous resident, and Australia's first would-be saint – in 1995 Pope John Paul II pronounced her "Blessed", the last stage before full sainthood. MacKillop set up a school, created her own teaching method and, with Father Julian Tennyson Woods, co-founded the Sisters of St Joseph of the Sacred Heart, a charitable teaching order that spread throughout Australia and New Zealand. Dramatic episodes of alleged disobedience and excommunication give her story a certain oomph – there's an informative display in the centre, with Barbie-doll lookalike "nuns on the run" and dressed-up dummies in the original school room. Across the fields stand the National Trust–listed cottages of **Petticoat Lane**, where many of Mary's poverty-stricken students lived.

The focus of the town is the friendly, National Trust–listed *Heyward's Royal Oak Hotel*, 31 Church St (ⓣ08/8737 2322, ⓦwww.heywardshotel.com.au; ④), with four-poster doubles and some twin rooms. *Penola Caravan Park* on South Terrace (ⓣ08/8737 2381) has good-value en-suite cabins (③). An odd sight amongst the rather traditional architecture of Penola is *Must* at 126 Church St (ⓣ08/8737 3444, ⓦwww.mustatcoonawarra.com.au; ⑥), a brand-new B&B complex with outstanding self-contained units and all the mod cons you can imagine, including free broadband Internet and plasma TV screens.

The best place to **eat** is *Heyward's Royal Oak Hotel*, which has a beautiful beer garden and an excellent bistro. Otherwise head for the nearby **wineries** for a superb lunch overlooking the vineyards.

Coonawarra Township

There isn't much to **COONAWARRA TOWNSHIP**, a settlement developed to house and service the adjacent Wynns Coonawarra Estate (see box opposite), but it does make a good base if you're touring local vineyards. Cottage **accommodation** here includes *Coonawarra Country Cottages* (ⓣ08/8737 2683, ⓦwww.coonawarracountrycottages.com.au; ⑤), a quaint tin-roofed bungalow just around the corner from the old Coonawarra school, now *Red Fingers* restaurant (ⓣ08/8736 3006; closed Tues). Just out of town on the Riddoch Highway is the upmarket motel complex *Chardonnay Lodge* (ⓣ08/8736 3309, ⓦwww.chardonnaylodge.com.au; ⑥), set amongst lawns and rose gardens, with a swimming pool and an attached café-restaurant.

Naracoorte Caves

Midway between Penola and Padthaway, the **Naracoorte Caves Conservation Park** protects a World Heritage–listed system of limestone caves. Your first point of call should be the **Wonambi Fossil Centre** (daily 9am–5pm, summer until sunset; ⓣ08/8762 2340), which gives an insight into the area's archeological significance – important fossils of extinct Pleistocene megafauna, including giant kangaroos and wombats, were discovered here in the Victoria Fossil Cave in 1969. A walking trail from here leads to another notable feature, the **Bat Centre**, the only place in the world where you can watch bats inside a cave with the help of infrared remote-control cameras.

The caves themselves are spread out over the conservation park: **Alexandra Cave** has the prettiest limestone formations (tours daily 9.30am & 1.30pm; 30min; ⓣ08/8762 2340), while **Victoria Fossil Cave**, not surprisingly, is popular for its fossils (daily 10.15am & 2.15pm; 1hr; ⓣ08/8762 2340). You can guide yourself through the **Wet Cave** (daily 9am & 5pm; ⓣ08/8762 2340), named after the very wet chamber at its deepest part; an automatic lighting system switches on as you walk through. **Admission fees** are $11.50 for one cave, $18.50 for two, $25.50 for three or $32.50 for all four of the show caves. There are also **adventure caving** tours in several other caves (2hr novice tours $28.50; 3hr advanced tours $51.50; overalls can be rented for $5, lights and helmets supplied; ⓣ08/8762 2340).

You can **camp** within the park ($19 per car), where facilities include powered sites, hot showers and a free laundry, or stay in dorms at *Wirreanda Bunkhouse* (ⓣ08/8762 2340; $14.50). More appealing is the rural tranquillity at *Cave Park Cabins* (ⓣ08/8762 0696, ⓕ8762 3180; ❸–❹), only 1.5km from the caves. For **meals**, the licensed *Bent Wing Cafe* by the Fossil Centre is surprisingly sophisticated, dishing up everything from Greek salads to chargrilled kangaroo fillets with native-plum chutney.

On the highway 12km west of the caves, the town of **NARACOORTE** is a small regional centre with a supermarket (open daily) and several places to **eat** and **stay**. *Naracoorte Hotel Motel*, 73 Ormerod St (ⓣ08/8762 2400, ⓦwww.naracoortehotel.com.au; ❸), has motel rooms and cheap meals; while the relaxed *Naracoorte Backpackers* (ⓣ08/8762 3835, ⓦwww.naracoortebackpackers.com.au; dorms $20) can take you to the caves and has 24-hour Internet access. A ten-minute walk north of town at 81 Park Terrace, *Naracoorte Holiday Park* (ⓣ08/8762 2128, ⓦwww.naracoorteholidaypark.com.au; cabins ❸) is set in a shady spot by a creek, close to a swimming lake.

The Riverland

The **Riverland** is the name given to the long irrigated strip on either side of the **Murray River** as it meanders for 300km from Blanchetown to Renmark near the Victorian border. The Riverland's deep red-orange alluvial soil – helped by extensive irrigation – is very fertile, making the area the state's major supplier of oranges, stone fruit and grapes. Fruit stalls along the roadsides add to the impression of a year-long harvest, and if you're after **fruit-picking** work it's an excellent place to start; contact the Harvest Labour Office on Riverview Drive in Berri (ⓣ08/8582 9307). The area is also Australia's major **wine-producing** region, though the high-tech wineries here mainly make mass-produced wines for casks and export. Many are open to visitors, but their scale and commercialism make them less enjoyable than those in other wine regions.

The **Sturt Highway**, the major route between Adelaide and Sydney, passes straight through the Riverland. Premier Stateliner runs a twice-daily **bus** service along the highway from Adelaide to Renmark via Blanchetown, Waikerie, Barmera and Berri, and also goes daily (except Sat) to Loxton. Between Waikerie and Renmark all the towns feel pretty much the same, with a raw edge, little charm or sophistication, and a yobbo culture (most apparent on drunken Fri nights).

Blanchetown to Waikerie

BLANCHETOWN, 130km east of Adelaide, is the first Riverland town and the starting point of the Murray's lock and weir system, which helps maintain the river at a constant height between the town and Wentworth in New South Wales. Eleven kilometres west of town, **Brookfield Conservation Park**, a gift to South Australia from the Chicago Zoological Society, is home to the endangered **southern hairy-nosed wombat**; the creatures also thrive at nearby *Portee Station* (ⓣ08/8540 5211, ⓦwww.portee.com.au; ❺), a two-hundred-square-kilometre sheep-grazing property where you can stay in the 1873 riverfront homestead. They run a range of tours (call for details) including river trips in a small boat to look at the prolific birdlife, and a 4WD station tour where you'll see wombats close up.

Following the river from Blanchetown, it's 36km directly north to **MORGAN**, one of the most attractive of the Riverland towns. At the height of the river trade between 1880 and 1915 Morgan was one of South Australia's busiest river ports, transferring wool from New South Wales and Victoria onto trains bound for Adelaide; parts of its mainly red-gum and jarrah river-wharf remain intact. You can wander through the riverfront park, past the old train station and the station-master's building, now a **museum** (tours by appointment; ⓣ08/8540 2130), and up onto the wharves overlooking moored houseboats on the river to bushland beyond. The well-preserved nineteenth-century streetscape of Railway Terrace, the main street, sits above the old railway line and wharf, dominated by the huge Landseer shipping warehouse. There's standard accommodation in two adjacent old pubs: the *Terminus Hotel* (ⓣ08/8540 2006; ❸) and the *Commercial* (ⓣ08/8540 2107; ❷); a more comfortable option is the *Morgan Colonial Motel*, 1 Federal St (ⓣ08/8540 2277, ⓔmorganmotel@bigpond.com; ❹). You can also stay at the *Morgan Riverside Caravan Park* (ⓣ08/8540 2207, ⓔmorgancp@riverland.net.au; cabins ❹), in a great spot right in town by the river.

From Morgan the river takes a sharp bend east, meandering south to **WAIKERIE**; it's 32km from Morgan to Waikerie on a riverside road, with a free ferry crossing at Cadell. A less attractive drive from Blanchetown bypasses the river loop, reaching Waikerie by heading 42km northeast along the Sturt Highway. Waikerie is at the heart of the largest citrus-growing area in Australia; the first thing you notice is a huge complex owned by **Nippy's** that takes up both sides of a street, allegedly the largest fruit-packing house in the southern hemisphere. A good base for fruit-picking work is *Nomads-on-Murray* (ⓣ08/8583 0211 or 1800 665 166; dorms $22, rooms ❷), on the Sturt Highway about 30km east of Waikerie.

Loxton and around

Some 35km east of Waikerie, the Murray makes another large loop away from the Sturt highway, bypassing **Barmera** and twisting instead through

LOXTON and **Berri**. Leaving the highway at Kingston-on-Murray, you pass the **Moorook Game Reserve**, a large swamp fringed with river red-gums and home to many waterbirds. In Loxton itself, the **Tourist & Art Centre**, at Bookpurnong Terrace (Mon–Fri 9am–5pm, Sat 9.30am–12.30pm, Sun 1–4pm; ⓣ08/8584 7919, ⓦwww.loxtontourism.com.au), acts as an agent for Stateliner and can fill you in on local attractions such as the riverside **Loxton Historical Village** (Mon–Fri 10am–4pm, Sat & Sun 10am–5pm; $8; ⓦwww.loxtonhistoricalvillage.com.au), a replica of an early twentieth-century Riverland town.

Altogether more compelling is the **Katarapko Game Reserve**, opposite Loxton where Katarapko Creek and the Murray have cut deep channels and lagoons, creating an island. Access from Loxton is by water only – perfect for canoeing and observing birdlife; to camp, you need a permit from the NPWS, 28 Vaughan Terrace, Berri (ⓣ08/8595 2111). *Loxton Riverfront Caravan Park*, Packard Bend (ⓣ08/8584 7862, ⓦwww.lrcp.com.au; cabins ❸), is a peaceful spot opposite the game reserve, with canoes for rent ($11 per hour, $55 per day).

The plushest place to **stay** in town is the *Loxton Hotel-Motel*, East Terrace (ⓣ08/8584 7266, ⓦwww.loxtonhotel.com.au; ❹), where you can also get good bistro **meals** (daily noon–2pm & 6–8pm). Alternatively, the slightly shabby *Harvest Trail Lodge* (ⓣ08/8584 5646, ⓦwww.harvesttrail.com; dorms $26.40) has small dorms and can help you find fruit-picking work.

Barmera and Herons Bend Reserve

If you haven't followed the river to Loxton, **BARMERA**, on the shores of Lake Bonney, is the next major stopping point along the highway. At **Pelican Point**, on the lake's western shore, there's an official **nudist beach** (and a nearby nudist resort with camping and on-site vans ❷; ⓣ08/8588 7366, bookings essential), while every June, the **South Australian Country Music Festival** and Awards are held in the lovely old Bonney Theatre. For more about the music awards, and tourist information in general, contact the **Barmera Visitor Information Centre**, Barwell Avenue (Mon–Fri 9am–5.15pm, Sat 9am–noon, Sun 10am–1pm; ⓣ08/8588 2289, ⓦwww.berribarmera.sa.gov.au).

The best bet for fully clothed **accommodation** is the *Barmera Lake Resort Motel*, Lakeside Drive (ⓣ08/8588 2555, ⓔlakeresort@riverland.net.au; ❺), overlooking the lake with a pool, laundry, games room, barbecue and *Cafe Mudz*, a bright and attractive café/wine bar serving Australian country-style breakfasts, lunches and evening meals. The extensive *Lake Bonney Holiday Park* is close by on Lakeside Drive (ⓣ08/8588 2234; cabins & cottages ❸), superbly located next to the lake and great for kids. There's a YHA hostel at 6 Dice St (ⓣ08/8588 3007, ⓔbackpack@riverland.net.au; dorms $25), but it mainly accommodates seasonal workers so check availability before turning up.

At the time of writing, the government was considering closing off Lake Bonney's supply from the Murray river, to help battle the drought in the region; of course, the government could count on fierce resistance by the community, as the drying up of the lake would have a disastrous impact on the economy of Barmera.

Just under 20km from town towards Morgan, you pass a bend in the river dubbed **Overland Corner**, the former crossing point for the overland cattle trade heading to New South Wales. Opened here in 1859, the restful and delightfully isolated *Overland Corner Hotel* (ⓣ08/8588 7021, ⓔochotel@dodo.com.au; ❸–❹ including continental breakfast) serves food and has basic, old-fashioned accommodation – look too at the flood level from the incredible

1956 flood, practically up to the roof. You can camp and bushwalk in the adjacent **Herons Bend Reserve**, where an eight-kilometre trail (around 3hr) takes you past old Aboriginal campsites; a pamphlet detailing sites on the walk is available from the pub.

Berri

The Big Orange sets the scene in **BERRI**, announcing the fact that this is the town where the trademark orange juice comes from, and many travellers are drawn here between October and April by the prospect of fruit-picking work. The river is the main attraction, of course, with scenic river walks above coloured sandstone cliffs. You can also climb up the **Big Orange** for a good view of the Riverland, or watch the juice itself being produced in vast quantities at Berri Ltd on the Old Sturt Highway (ⓣ08/8582 3321). For more information, head for the **tourist office** on Riverview Drive (Mon–Fri 9am–5.30pm, Sat & Sun 10am–4pm; ⓣ08/8582 5511, ⓦwww.berribarmera.sa.gov.au).

△ Paddle steamer on the Murray River

The Murray River

The Murray River is Australia's Mississippi – or so the American author Mark Twain declared when he saw it in the early 1900s. It's a fraction of the size of the American river, admittedly, but in a country of seasonal, intermittent streams it counts as a major river and, like the Mississippi, the Murray helped open up a new continent. Fed by melting snow from the Snowy Mountains, and by the Murrumbidgee and Darling rivers, the Murray flows through the arid plains, reaching the Southern Ocean southwest of Adelaide near Goolwa. With the Darling and its tributaries, it makes up one of the biggest and longest watercourses in the world, giving life to Australia's most important agricultural region, the Murray–Darling basin. For much of its length it also forms the border between New South Wales and Victoria, slowing as it reaches South Australia, where it meanders through extensive alluvial plains and irrigation areas. Almost half of South Australia's water comes from the Murray; even far-off Woomera in the Outback relies on it.

Historically, the Riverland was densely populated by various Aboriginal peoples who navigated the river in bark canoes, the bark being cut from river red-gums in a single perfect piece – many trees along the river still bear the scars. The Ngarrindjeri people's Dreamtime story of the river's creation explains how Ngurunderi travelled down the Murray, looking for his runaway wives. The Murray was then just a small stream, but, as Ngurunderi searched, a giant Murray cod surged ahead of him, widening the river with swipes of its tail. Ngurunderi tried to spear the fish, which he chased to the ocean, and the thrashing cod carved out the pattern of the Murray River during the chase.

The explorers Hume and Hovell came across the Murray at Albury in 1824. In 1830 Sturt and Mitchell navigated the Murray and Darling in a whale boat, Sturt naming it after the then Secretary of State for the Colonies (coincidentally, Murrundi was the Aboriginal name for part of the river). Their exploration opened up the interior, and from 1838 the Murray was followed as a stock route by "overlanders" taking sheep and cattle to newly established Adelaide. In 1853 the first paddle-steamer, the *Mary Ann*, was launched near Mannum. Goods were transported far inland, while wool was carried to market. River transport reached its peak in the 1870s, but by the mid-1930s it was virtually finished, thanks to the superior speed of the railways.

Seeing the river

The best way to appreciate the beauty of the Murray – lined with majestic river red-gums and towering cliffs that reveal the area's colourful soils – is to get out on the water. Several old paddle-steamers and a variety of other craft still cruise the Murray for pleasure – try the *Murray Princess* (three-night wetlands cruise $724 per person, four-night outback cruise $942 per person, seven-night Murraylands and wildlife cruise $1520 per person; ⓣ08/9206 1122, ⓦwww.captaincook.com.au), based at Mannum, an hour's drive east of Adelaide (or take the Murray Bridge Passenger Service; Mon–Fri 1 daily; ⓣ08/8532 2633). Other cruises from Mannum include sporadic trips on the paddle steamer *Marion* (book at Mannum Tourist Information Centre, 67 Randell St; ⓣ08/8569 1303), and regular outings on the MV *Proud Mary* (morning tea cruises Mon 11am; 1hr 15min; two-, three- and five-night cruises also available; book at Mannum Tourist Information Centre or on ⓣ08/8231 9472, ⓦwww.proudmary.com.au).

Renting a houseboat is a relaxing and enjoyable way to see the river. All you need is a driving licence, and the cost isn't astronomical if you get a group of people together and avoid the peak holiday seasons. A week in an eight-berth houseboat out of season should cost around $1250, in a four-berth $950. The South Australian Tourism Commission (ⓣ1300 655 276, ⓦwww.southaustralia.com) has pamphlets giving costs and facilities and can also book for you; alternatively, contact the Houseboat Hirers Association (ⓣ08/8231 8466, ⓦwww.houseboat-centre.com.au).

A more hands-on way to explore the wetlands and creek systems is in a canoe, while the flat country, short distances between towns and dry climate are perfect for cycling – bikes can be rented at various hostels along the way.

In terms of places to **stay** in town, the *Berri Resort Hotel*, Riverview Drive (☎08/8582 1411, Ⓦwww.berriresorthotel.com; ⑤), is a huge riverfront hotel with a swimming pool, tennis courts, good food and a café with great river views. The excellent *Berri Backpackers* (☎08/8582 3144; dorms $25, rooms ②), 1km out of town towards Barmera on the Old Sturt Highway opposite the *Berri Club*, is the place to stay if you're fruit-picking, but is popular, so book ahead. Amenities include free bikes, Internet access, a sauna, swimming pool, gym, tennis and volleyball courts, plus two Balinese-style tree houses. The well-equipped *Berri Riverside Caravan Park* (☎08/8582 3723, Ⓦwww.berricaravanpark.com.au; on-site vans ②, en-suite cabins ③) at the eastern end of Riveride Drive has a pool, barbecue area, and a few doubles and bunk beds.

For **food**, *Primo* at 1 Worman St is a good Aussie-style Italian restaurant open daily for lunch and dinner, while the *Mallee Fowl* restaurant, on the Sturt Highway 4km west of Berri (lunch & dinner Thurs–Sat) serves excellent barbecue-style meals in a busy and characterful setting full of Australiana.

Renmark

RENMARK, on a bend of the Murray 254km from Adelaide, is the last major town before the New South Wales border. As with the other Riverland towns, the main attraction of Renmark is the river and its surrounding wetlands, and there's not a great deal to see in the town apart from **Olivewood**, an interesting National Trust property on the corner of Renmark Avenue and 21st Street (Mon 10am–4pm, Tues 2–4pm, Thurs–Sun 10am–4pm; $4). The former home of the Chaffey brothers, the Canadians who pioneered the irrigation and settlement of the Murray region, a palm-lined drive leads through a citrus orchard and olive trees to the house, which is a strange hybrid of Canadian log cabin and Australian lean-to. The attached museum is the usual hotchpotch of local memorabilia, unrelated to the Chaffeys or their ambitious irrigation project. The **Chaffey Theatre** on 18th Street (☎08/8586 1800) has an impressive performing-arts centre hosting amateur and professional plays, films and concerts.

The riverfront **Renmark Paringa Visitor Centre** on Murray Avenue (Mon–Fri 9am–5pm, Sat 9am–4pm, Sun 10am–4pm; ☎08/8586 6704) can book **river cruises**. The PS *Industry* – one of the few wood-fuelled paddle-steamers left on the Murray – is moored outside and cruises once a month (1hr 30min; $17; contact the visitor centre for times and bookings). Other cruises are run by Renmark River Cruises, which offers trips aboard the *Big River Rambler* (Tues–Thurs & Sat 2pm, Sun 11am; 2hr; $30; ☎08/8595 1862); the vessel leaves from Renmark wharf and heads upstream for 7km past colourful river cliffs. Riverland Leisure Canoe Tours (☎08/8588 2053, Ⓦwww.riverlandcanoes.com.au) rents out **kayaks** for $30 per day or two-person **canoes** for $40 per day, and arranges day and overnight guided tours.

The obvious place to **stay** in Renmark is the landmark *Renmark Hotel/Motel* (☎08/8586 6755, Ⓦwww.renmarkhotel.com.au; ④), overlooking the river. Built in 1897 and given its facade in the 1930s, the hotel has been thoroughly modernized and has a large bistro, outdoor swimming pool and spa. The *Renmark Riverfront Caravan Park*, on Patey Drive 2km east of town (☎08/8586 6315, Ⓦwww.big4renmark.com.au; en-suite cabins ④), has an idyllic setting along 1km of riverfront and luxurious villas overlooking the river or the lagoon-style pool. An authentic Italian hangout is *Café Sorelle*, with home-made lasagne and focaccias, or for Chinese, try *The Golden Palace*, 114 Renmark Ave (both closed Mon).

The mid-north

Stretching north of Adelaide up to Port Augusta and the south Flinders Ranges is the fertile agricultural region known as the **mid-north**. The gateway to the region is the town of **Kapunda**, 16km northwest of Nuriootpa in the Barossa Valley (see below), which became the country's first mining town when copper was discovered here in 1842. Kapunda can also be reached as a short detour from the **Barrier Highway** en route to Broken Hill in New South Wales, a route that continues through the larger mining town of **Burra**, and close to Peterborough, the self-proclaimed "frontier to the Outback". The centre of the mid-north's wine area, **Clare**, is 45km southwest of Burra on the Main North Road, the alternative route to Port Augusta. Heading north to Port Augusta on **Highway 1** for the Northern Territory or Western Australia, you'll pass through the ugly lead-smelting city of Port Pirie, and from there on to the south **Flinders Ranges.**

Getting around the area by **bus** is problematic – while most of the major towns have transport links to Adelaide, there are virtually no buses between towns, however close they might be. The Mid North Passenger Service (Ⓣ08/8823 2375; Mon & Fri only) from Adelaide takes in Burra, Peterborough and the main Clare Valley settlements. In addition, the Barossa to Adelaide Passenger Service (Ⓣ08/8564 3022) has a weekday service from Gawler – which can be reached by train – to Kapunda. All interstate buses to Darwin or Perth take Highway 1 through Port Pirie.

Kapunda and Burra

At the beginning of the 1840s South Australia was in serious economic trouble, until the discovery of **copper** at Kapunda in 1842 rescued the young colony and put it at the forefront of Australia's mining boom. The early finds at **Kapunda** were, however, soon overshadowed by those at **Burra**, 65km north: the Burra "**Monster Mine**" was the largest in Australia until 1860, creating fabulous wealth and attracting huge numbers of Cornish miners. The boom ended as suddenly as it began, as resources were exhausted – mining finished at Burra in 1877 and Kapunda in 1878.

Heading to **KAPUNDA** from the Barossa, the landscape changes as vineyards are replaced by crops and grazing sheep. As you come into town, you're greeted by a colossal sculpture of a Cornish miner entitled *Map Kernow* – "Son of Cornwall". A place that once had its own daily newspaper, eleven hotels and a busy train station is now a rural service town, pleasantly undeveloped and with many old buildings decorated with locally designed and manufactured iron lacework.

If you have your own transport, you can follow a ten-kilometre **heritage trail** that takes in the ruins of the Kapunda mine, with panoramic views from the mine chimney lookout; details are available from the **Kapunda Information Centre** on Hill Street (Mon–Fri 9am–5pm, Sat & Sun 10am–4pm; Ⓣ08/8566 2902, Ⓦwww.kapundatourism.com.au). On the same street, the **Kapunda Museum** (daily 1–4pm; $5; Ⓣ08/8566 2286) depicts the history of the town and, occupies the mammoth Romanesque-style former Baptist church. The best time to come to Kapunda is during the **Celtic festival**, held on the weekend before Easter, when Celtic music, bush and folk bands feature at the four pubs.

For **accommodation**, there's the colonial-style B&B *Ford House*, 80 Main St (Ⓣ & Ⓕ08/8566 2280; ④), or the *Sir John Franklin Hotel* on the same road (Ⓣ08/8566 3233; ③), with simple, clean rooms and popular for inexpensive meals. Campers are catered for at *Kapunda Tourist and Leisure Park* on Montefiore Street (Ⓣ08/8556 2094, Ⓦwww.kapundatouristpark.com; cabins ③).

Burra

In 1851 the mine at **BURRA** was producing five percent of the world's copper, but when the mines closed in 1877, it became a service centre for the surrounding farming community, and nowadays takes advantage of its mining heritage to attract visitors. Plenty of money has been spent restoring and beautifying the place (even to the extent of topping up pretty, gum-shaded **Burra Creek** to ensure that it's always flowing), and the town's well-preserved stone architecture, shady tree-lined streets, great country pubs and upmarket home stores, art-and-craft and antiques shops, make it a popular weekend escape between March and November, before it gets too hot. The creek divides the town in two: the mine is in the north, while the southern section has the shopping centre, based around **Market Square**, where you'll also find the **Burra Visitors Centre** (daily 9am–5pm; Ⓣ08/8892 2154, Ⓦwww.visitburra.com). Its main function is to issue the Burra Passport Key to people driving the eleven-kilometre **heritage trail** ($15 per person, plus $10 deposit); the key gives you access to eight sites en route, and for an extra $10 you gain entry to all four museums (see below).

Heading north along Market Street you come to the **Burra Monster Mine** site, where there are extensive remains and interpretive walking trails, as well as the **Morphetts Enginehouse Museum** (daily 11–1pm; $5). Continuing north, the **Bon Accord Mine Complex** on Linkson Street (daily 2–4pm; $5) was a short-lived failure compared to its hugely successful neighbour; there's a scale model of the monster mine and a shaft and mining relics on view. Other key-pass places in the northern section of the town include the **old police lock-up and stables**, **Redruth Gaol**, and **Hampton**, a now-deserted private township in the style of an English village. Back in the main part of the town, the pass gets you entry to the **Unicorn Brewery Cellars** (1873) and the two fascinating remaining miners' dugouts: by 1851, because of a housing shortage nearly two thousand people were living in homes clawed out of the soft clay along Burra Creek. There are two further museums: the **Market Square Museum** (daily 11am–1pm; donation) was a general store, post office and home from 1880 to 1920, while the **Malowen Lowarth Museum cottages** on Kingston Street (daily tours at 9am & 10am, book at the visitors centre, also open for groups; $5) are decorated in 1860s style.

You can **stay** in other miners' cottages in Paxton Square, all overseen by the office in the former Methodist chapel at the end of the row (Ⓣ08/8892 2622, Ⓕ8892 2508; ④). There are 32 in all, although on weekends from mid-March to October they get quickly booked out by Adelaidians on short winter breaks. It can get very cold in the winter, but the cottages have fireplaces (free wood provided) and plenty of blankets, as well as modern kitchens; breakfast is available at the office. Other accommodation in town includes the tree-surrounded *Burra Motor Inn*, Market Street (Ⓣ08/8892 2777; ④), with contemporary rooms backing onto a creek, an indoor swimming pool and a well-priced restaurant. If you have a tent you could try the *Burra Caravan Park*, Bridge Terrace (Ⓣ08/8892 2442; on-site vans ①), in a pretty spot beside the creek, a couple of minutes' walk from the shops.

The *Burra Hotel*, 5 Market St, does excellent **meals**, but if you're in the mood for a real treat head for *White Cedars Café*. A bit of an oddity in town, this Indonesian café offers authentic Balinese cuisine and great banana pancakes for breakfast. The chef might even perform a traditional Balinese dance if asked kindly.

The Clare Valley

The wine industry in the **Clare Valley**, west of the Barrier Highway between Kapunda and Burra, was pioneered by Jesuit priests at **Sevenhill** in the 1850s. There's no tourist overkill here: bus trips are not encouraged, and because it's a small area with just over **thirty wineries**, you can learn a lot about the local styles of wine (the valley is especially recognized for its fine Rieslings). You'll often get personal treatment too, with the winemaker presiding at the cellar door. In the cool uplands of the **North Mount Lofty Ranges**, Clare Valley is really a series of gum-fringed ridges and valleys running roughly 30km north from **Auburn** to the main township of **Clare**, on either side of Main North Road. Huge sheep runs were established here in the nineteenth century and the area, which is prime merino land, still has a pastoral feel; several stations can be visited. There are also beautiful old villages and some well-preserved mansions, plenty of charming B&B accommodation and some superb restaurants attached to wineries. The big event of the year is the **Clare Valley Gourmet Weekend**, held in May at local wineries.

Between Clare and Auburn, the old railway line has been transformed into the **Riesling Trail**, a 27-kilometre cycling path; to cycle one way takes about two hours. Mountain bikes can be rented from Clare Valley Cycle Hire, 32 Victoria Rd, Clare ($25 per day; ⓣ08/8842 2782), which will deliver to anywhere in the valley.

Auburn to Watervale

Heading north through the valley the first settlement you come to is the small village of **AUBURN**, 120km from Adelaide, which began life as a halfway resting point for wagons carrying copper ore from Burra to Port Adelaide. The *Rising Sun Hotel* (ⓣ08/8849 2015, ⓔrising@capri.net.au; ❹ including breakfast), first licensed in 1850, is one of many great pubs in the valley. It has small bedrooms in the hotel and mews-style accommodation in old stone stables, as well as a very affordable modern Australian menu and an appropriately long wine list. A more luxurious place to stay is *Dennis Cottage* (ⓣ08/8277 8177, ⓦwww.denniscottage.com.au; ❼), which has a spa, as well as paraphernalia associated with C.J. Dennis, the popular poet who was born here in 1876. *Cygnets*, on Main North Road (ⓣ08/8849 2030, ⓔcygnetsatauburn@bigpond.com; ❻), is a contemporary dining/guesthouse combination and the departure point for the cheese and wine trail (ⓦwww.cheeseandwinetrail.com.au). There are two small wineries nearby: Grossets (Wed–Sun 10am–5pm) and Mount Horrocks (Sat & Sun 10am–5pm).

The next small village is **LEASINGHAM**, where you can camp or stay at *Leasingham Village Caravan & Cabins* (ⓣ08/8843 0136; cabins ❸), a popular place for **grape-pickers** from March to May. You can taste **wines** nearby at **Tim Gramp Wines** (Sat & Sun 11am–4pm, ⓦwww.timgrampwines.com.au). There are four small wineries at **WATERVALE**, 2km north: of them, **Crabtree of Watervale**, North Terrace (Mon–Sat 11am–5pm; ⓦwww.crabtreewines.com.au), is one of the most enjoyable in the valley.

Mintaro

From Leasingham, you can turn off east to **MINTARO**, a village whose tree-lined streets and cottages are beautifully preserved from the 1850s, when it was a resting place for bullock teams travelling from the Burra copper mines. There's no general store or petrol supply here; the emphasis is on upmarket cottage accommodation, popular with Adelaide weekenders. The focus of the village is the *Magpie and Stump Hotel*, which is particularly lively on Sunday afternoons. Opposite, at **Reilly's Wines** (daily 10am–4pm; Ⓦwww.reillyswines.com), housed in an 1856 Irish bootmaker's building, you can taste vintages produced since 1994 from Watervale grapes; the **restaurant** here serves Italian food for lunch (Ⓣ08/8843 9013) and can also book accommodation in the nearby *Mintaro Pay Office Cottages* (❺). *Mintaro Mews*, on Burra Street (Ⓣ08/8843 9001, Ⓕ8843 9002; ❺), has upmarket B&B accommodation with an indoor heated pool and spa; Saturday nights are package-only ($120 per person), including a four-course meal in the atmospheric restaurant.

Southeast of the town lies the Georgian-style **Martindale Hall** (Mon–Fri 11am–4pm, Sat & Sun noon–4pm; $7; Ⓣ08/8843 9088, Ⓦwww.martindalehall.com; ❼ including breakfast), the mansion featured in the 1975 film *Picnic at Hanging Rock*. For $195 per person you can stay overnight and enjoy a four-course meal, cooked breakfast and the full run of the place – it's freezing in winter though.

Heading northwest from Mintaro to Sevenhill (see below) takes you through the rolling hills of the Polish Hill River area. About 8km along, **Paulett Wines** (daily 10am–5pm; Ⓦwww.paulettwines.com.au) has fabulous views, its veranda overlooking the "river" – a dry creek for eleven months of the year.

Sevenhill and the Spring Gully Conservation Park

The village of **SEVENHILL** is home to the valley's oldest winery, **Sevenhill Cellars**, on College Road (Mon–Fri 9am–5pm, Sat & Sun 10am–5pm; Ⓦwww.sevenhillcellars.com.au). This is still run by a religious order and mainly makes sacramental wine, though the brothers have diversified into table wines, sweet sherry and port, doing everything from growing the grapes to bottling. The sandstone building has a tasting room with lots of character and history, and there's an old Catholic church in the grounds. Nearby, on College Road, *Thorn Park Country House* (Ⓣ08/8843 4304, Ⓦwww.thornpark.com.au; ❽) occupies an 1850 stone and slate building in a gorgeous setting; it offers B&B and a beautifully indulgent dinner for an extra $85 per person. *Sevenhill Hotel*, on Main North Road, is a classic country pub serving popular inexpensive **meals** (daily except Sun).

To the west of Main North Road, **Spring Gully Conservation Park** has the last remnant of red stringybark forest in South Australia. There are steep gullies, waterfalls, wildlife and, in spring, lovely wild flowers; free camping is allowed outside the fire-ban season (usually early Dec–late April). Nearby, attached to boutique wineries signposted from Sevenhill, are two excellent **restaurants** serving gourmet meals made from deliciously fresh local produce, at moderate prices. **Eldredge Wines**, Spring Gully Road (tastings daily 11am–5pm; lunch Thurs–Sun; restaurant bookings Ⓣ08/8842 3086, Ⓦwww.eldredge.com.au), is located in a small farmhouse fronting a dam; **Skillogalee Winery** (daily 10am–5pm; lunch bookings advised; Ⓣ08/8843 4311, Ⓦwww.skillogalee.com) occupies a wonderful spot set against the backdrop of a clunking windmill, bushclad hill and vineyards, with meals and tastings by the fire in the 1850s cottage or on the veranda.

Clare

CLARE itself is a surprisingly ordinary town, with few concessions to the weekend visitors who pour in from Adelaide: it consists primarily of Main North Road, and virtually everything is closed on Sunday. The **tourist office**, right next to the caravan park at the corner of Main North and Spring Gully roads (Mon–Fri 9am–5pm, Sat 10am–4pm, Sun 11am–5pm; ⓣ08/8842 2131, ⓦwww.clarevalley.com.au), provides an excellent free visitors guide and can book accommodation and restaurants. **Wineries** around town include **Knappstein Wines**, 2 Pioneer Ave (Mon–Fri 9am–5pm, Sat 11am–5pm, Sun 11am–4pm; ⓦwww.knappsteinwines.com.au), an ivy-covered sandstone building with a veranda and an open log fire in winter; **Jim Barry**, a friendly, family-run place on Main North Road (Mon–Fri 9am–5pm, Sat & Sun 9am–4pm; ⓦwww.jimbarry.com); and **Leasingham**, 7 Dominic St (Mon–Fri 8.30am–5pm, Sat & Sun 10am–4pm; ⓦwww.leasingham-wines.com.au), a large commercial winery established in 1893.

Some local sheep stations are open for tours, and **farmstays** are also available: pick of the bunch is *Bungaree Station* (ⓣ08/8842 2677, ⓦwww.bungareestation.com.au; BYO air-bed & bedding; shearers' quarters $22, B&B cottages ❸), a working merino station 12km north of Clare on Main North Road; one of the oldest and largest properties in the district, it has its own church as well as a swimming pool. *Geralka Rural Farm* (ⓣ08/8845 8081, ⓕ8845 8073; on-site vans ❶, units ❸) is a sheep and cereal property 25km north of Clare which offers weekend farm activity tours aimed at families (Sat, Sun & daily during school holidays 1.30pm, or by appointment; 2hr; $8, children $4).

For **accommodation**, take advantage of the numerous B&Bs scattered around the valley; get the tourist office to make a booking for you. Otherwise head for one of the hotels along Main North Road: 2.5km south of the centre at no. 74, with a beautiful view overlooking the hills and surprisingly good value for money, is *Clare Valley Motel* (ⓣ08/8842 2799, ⓦwww.sunrez.com.au; ❹); the *Clare Central Motel* is at the north end of town at no. 325 (ⓣ08/8842 2277, ⓕ8842 3563; ❺) – both have pools. You can camp 4km south of town at *Clare Caravan Park* on Main North Road (ⓣ08/8842 2724, ⓦwww.clare-caravan-park.com.au; en-suite cabins ❸), which also has a swimming pool. For lunch, make the most of what the wineries have to offer as it's generally of higher standard than what the pubs in town will serve you.

Port Pirie

From Clare, the Main North Road heads to Jamestown, 65km north. To the west, a road branches off towards Crystal Brook, where there's a hikers' lodge at Bowman Park providing basic overnight shelter for hikers on the Heysen Trail. From here it's not far up Highway 1 to **PORT PIRIE**, the fourth-largest urban centre in South Australia. An ugly industrial city, its skyline is dominated by smelters' chimneys: as the nearest seaport to Broken Hill, the lead and zinc smelting industry here dates back to the discovery of the rich vein of lead-silver-zinc found there in 1883. The **Port Pirie Tourist Office and Arts Centre**, on Mary Elie Street (Mon–Fri 9am–5pm, Sat 9am–4pm, Sun 10am–4pm; ⓣ08/8633 8700 or 1800 000 424, ⓦwww.pirie.sa.gov.au), has interpretive brochures and self-guided walking tours of the town if you're interested in **historic buildings** and the smelting industry. If not, there's little else to keep you here. Beyond Port Pirie, Telowie Gorge and Mount Remarkable National Park, in the southern stretches of the Flinders Ranges (see p.803), are within easy reach.

Outback South Australia

. . . a country such as I firmly believe has no parallel on earth's surface.

The explorer Charles Sturt, 1844

Leaving behind the civilized south, the wild and vast expanses of South Australia's **Outback** can take some adjusting to. With little in the way of obvious destinations, the experience is the thing – few areas of the planet feel quite so isolated or hostile to human habitation. All routes radiate from **Port Augusta**, the commercial centre for the far north, and though buses cover the highways, elsewhere you'll need to have your own transport or take a tour. To the west, the Eyre Highway runs 950km to the border of Western Australia; the journey can be broken by taking a detour around the coast of the **Eyre Peninsula**, which has fine, sandy beaches and excellent fishing. Once past **Ceduna**, on the eastern edge of the **Nullarbor Plain**, there's little beyond you and the desert. The Indian Pacific **train** traverses the Nullarbor further inland, through even more extreme desolation. To the north, the Stuart Highway and New Ghan rail line link Port Augusta with the Northern Territory through 890km of progressively drier scenery, where regular markers along the roadside record the distance covered, as well as how far there is to go. Prohibited zones surround much of the highway, though about the only places you'd want to leave it anyway are at **Woomera** and the opal-mining town of **Coober Pedy**, with its unusual underground dwellings; both lie outside the military areas and the boundaries of Aboriginal land.

All other roads north follow the route taken by the legendary but now defunct Old Ghan to the country towns of **Quorn** and **Hawker**, where routes diverge. To the northeast lie the **Flinders Ranges**, a series of spectacularly beautiful gorges and geological curiosities, most famous of which is **Wilpena Pound**. Continuing northeast will take you along the **Strzelecki Track** to **Innamincka** and beyond to Queensland. Heading due north takes you to **Marree**, at the head of the **Birdsville** and **Oodnadatta** tracks. Travel beyond Marree is not for the faint-hearted, but worth the effort for those wishing to experience the eerie silence and emptiness of **Lake Eyre** and the sheer isolation of the Dalhousie Hot Springs and the Simpson Desert.

A **Desert Parks Pass** is required for legal entry into Innamincka Regional Reserve, Lake Eyre National Park, Witjira National Park and the Simpson Desert: $95 per vehicle allows unlimited access and use of campsites for twelve months, with copies of the detailed *NPWS Desert Parks Handbook* and Westprint Heritage Maps' surveys thrown in. Passes are available from agencies throughout the north, or by post from the Port Augusta **NPWS** at 9 Mackay St (☎08/8648 5300).

To find out about **road conditions** in these regions, call ☎1300 361 033. Many roadhouses and fuel pumps have EFTPOS facilities. **Water** is vital: with few exceptions, lakes and waterways are dry or highly saline, and most Outback deaths are related to dehydration or heatstroke – bikers seem particularly prone. As always, stay with your vehicle if you break down. Summer temperatures can be lethally hot, and winters pleasant during the day and subzero at night; rain can fall at any time of year, but is most likely to do so between January and May.

RAA road **maps** are good but lack topographical information, so if you're spending any time in the north, pick up the excellent Westprint Heritage maps and the cluttered Landsmap *Outback: Central and South Australia*. The **South Australia Tourist Association** issues a road map of the Flinders Ranges, but it's inadequate for walking; hikers traversing the Flinders on the **Heysen Trail** need topographic maps of each section and advice from the nearest NPWS office. Conditions of minor roads are so variable that maps seldom do more than indicate the surface type; local police and roadhouses will have current information.

Port Augusta and the west

How you see **Port Augusta** depends on where you've come from. Arriving from the Outback, the town's trees, shops and hotels can be a real thrill, but compared with the southeast of the state, it's pretty basic. However, being a transport hub has saved the town from destitution, and recent developments have made the foreshore area with its city beach more attractive. While you're deciding where to head next, there are a few things to see in town and some good **bushwalking** country around Mount Remarkable, at the tail end of the Flinders Ranges.

The direct route west from Port Augusta, the Eyre Highway, begins its daunting journey towards Western Australia across the top of the Eyre Peninsula, but going this way you'll see virtually nothing. An alternative route detours around the peninsula's coastline (via the Lincoln and Flinders highways) before rejoining the highway at Ceduna on the brink of the Nullarbor Plain, while the **rail** line parallels the coast some 100km inland.

Port Augusta

Unkindly dubbed "Porta Gutter" by Adelaide's smart set, who paint dire pictures of a town rife with petty crime, **PORT AUGUSTA** sits at the tip of the Spencer Gulf and on the edge of everywhere else. Despite the name, the docks closed long ago and more recent employment mainstays such as the power station and railways were drastically scaled down during the 1980s – the former rail buildings have been converted to Employment Service offices.

During summer, you should make the most of the **swimming beach** at the end of Young Street or at the foreshore to escape the dust and heat – the old wooden pile crossing, now a footbridge, and a hundred-year-old jetty, all that remains of the port, make good perches for fishing and there are barbecue facilities available. The chief source of information is the **Wadlata Outback Centre** at 41 Flinders Terrace (Mon–Fri 9am–5.30pm, Sat & Sun 10am–4pm; ⓣ08/8641 0793, ⓦwww.wadlata.sa.gov.au). This has a very helpful **visitor information centre**, an attractive café and an interesting permanent exhibition ($9.95). Audiovisual technology, didgeridoo loudspeakers and a giant model of Akurra, the Dreamtime snake, are deployed to explain Aboriginal bushcraft and Flinders Ranges' creation myths, while geological and mining displays give a scientific perspective. You can also book a wide variety of **tours** from the centre including plane trips, fishing expeditions, 4WD tours and even golf. Internet access is available here ($5 for 30min).

The **Homestead Park Pioneer Museum**, east of the town centre on Elsie Street (daily 9am–4pm; $2.50), is centred around a log-built sheep station building. The 135-year-old homestead has been moved 100km from Yudnapinna and is filled with period furnishings, heaps of farm and railway machinery, plus animals, birds and a photographic museum in a vintage railway carriage.

Flanking the north side of town on the Stuart Highway is the ambitious **Australian Arid Lands Botanic Garden** (Mon–Fri 9am–5pm, Sat & Sun

10am–4pm; free entry, but it's worth taking the 1hr guided tour for $5.95, winter 11am, summer 9.30am), a showcase and research centre for regional and international desert flora. The rain-gathering, solar-powered information centre, shop and café underline the ideals of the garden as an ongoing ecological project.

Practicalities

The centre of town overlooks the east side of the **Spencer Gulf**, more like a river where it divides the town. The **airport** (⊕08/8642 3100) is down Caroona Road, 5km west of the centre – taxis travel into the centre (⊕08/8642 4466). The **bus** terminal, serving Greyhound from Adelaide to Alice Springs and Stateliner from Adelaide to Whyalla and Ceduna, is at 21 Mackay St (all services ⊕08/8642 5055), while **trains** from Sydney, Perth and Darwin pull in at Stirling Road (⊕08/8642 6699). Shops, banks and the post office are clustered along narrow **Commercial Road**. If you need maps and information beyond what's available at the Outback Centre, try the helpful **NPWS** at 9 Mackay St (⊕08/8648 5300) for park maps, info and permits; if you're a member, the RAA, at 7 Caroona Rd (⊕08/8642 2576), provides very good road maps. **Cars** can be rented from Budget, at 14 Young St (⊕08/8642 6040).

The friendly *Flinders Hotel*, 39 Commercial Rd (⊕08/8642 2544; dorms $22, rooms ❸), is your best bet for budget **accommodation**. Alternatively, there are several motels, such as the comfortable *Poinsettia*, 24 Burgoyne St (⊕08/8642 2411; ❸), along the highway just across the gulf. The town's closest **campsites** are nearby, including the *Shoreline Caravan Park* at the end of Gardiner Avenue (⊕08/8642 2965; cabins ❸) and the *Big 4 Holiday Park* at the junction of the Eyre and Stuart highways (⊕08/8642 6455, Ⓦwww.aspenparks.com.au; cabins ❸).

Hotels are the place for **meals** and **entertainment**, but opening hours are vague and often depend on demand, which can be almost nonexistent during the week. The *Transcontinental*, Port Augusta's weekly rag, will have details of anything happening around town. You'll find a few cafés for lunch and snacks along Commercial Road, while *Barnacle Bill's*, on Victoria Parade 3km southeast of the town centre, has pretty good value **seafood** and all the salad you can eat. The central *Commonwealth Hotel* on Commercial Road does decent food at weekends, while the *Hotel Augusta*, by the Westside Beach, serves meals with a fine view of sand, mangroves and the distant Flinders Ranges.

Mount Remarkable National Park

Mount Remarkable National Park lies in two sections, encircled by a ring road that starts 45km southeast of Port Augusta and runs via Wilmington, **Melrose** and Port Germein. The larger western slice contains **Mambray Creek** and **Mount Cavern**, and connecting tracks run from them to **Alligator Gorge**; **Mount Remarkable** and sections of the Heysen Trail rise to the east behind Melrose. If time is short, there are easy walks in Alligator Gorge, while the Mount Cavern circuit is considerably harder – both make good day-trips from Port Augusta. The only **campsite** with facilities is at Mambray Creek, but bushcamping is allowed elsewhere with permission from the NPWS (⊕08/8634 7068); you should also consult them in hot weather, as the park may be completely closed if there's a high risk of fire. Stateliner **buses** go daily to Mambray Creek, and three times weekly to Wilmington and Melrose.

Alligator Gorge, Melrose and Mount Remarkable

The eleven-kilometre dirt road from Wilmington to **Alligator Gorge** ($7 per car) ends at a picnic area perched on a spur above two bush campsites at Teal and Eaglehawk dams. Stairs descend into the gorge, with several **walking** options once you reach the gorge floor, including a three-hour circuit north to the ranger's office past the rippled Terraces (the remains of a fossilized lake shore), or an hour-long trek south along the creek through a tight red canyon alive with frog calls, moss gardens and echoes (this section sometimes gets flooded, though there are usually enough stepping stones to avoid wet feet). For longer hikes down to Mambray Creek you'll need maps and approval from the NPWS.

Nearby, the quiet former copper-mining town of **MELROSE** has two hotels and a pleasant creekside **caravan park** (Ⓣ08/8666 2060; dorms $15, cabins ❷). **B&B** is available at *Bluey Blundstone's Blacksmith Shop* (Ⓣ08/8666 2173; ❹), carefully restored to its original 1865 condition. When the proprietor isn't producing decorative wrought-ironwork he serves cakes in a coffee shop at the back of the forge. The unremarkable summit of **Mount Remarkable** can be reached in three hours via the Heysen Trail, starting a couple of kilometres north of town from the showground.

Telowie Gorge, Mambray Creek and Mount Cavern

The small and appealing **Telowie Conservation Park** lies to the south off the Port Germein to Murray Town road. A very short path leads between the gorge walls, but unless you're properly equipped for a long hike over to Wirrabara Forest and the Heysen Trail, you'll get more of a flavour of the area by **camping** along the creek and looking for rare wallabies at dawn and dusk.

The access track to **Mambray Creek** is east off the highway, halfway between Port Germein and the Wilmington road. Here you'll find a **campsite** (with water and toilets) and the national park headquarters. Mambray Creek is the start of some serious walks, either into the north part of the park along the **Battery Track** and **Alligator Creek**, or on the tough but shorter **Mount Cavern circuit**, which follows the path anticlockwise along the Black Range, giving spectacular views. The descent runs down a loose stone slope held together by grasstrees, before entering cool woodland at Mambray Creek Gorge, where you might be able to get close to large groups of emus.

The Eyre Peninsula

Far from the rigours of the true Outback, and long appreciated by Adelaidians as an antidote to city stress, the Eyre Peninsula's broad triangle is protected by the **Gawler Ranges** from the arid climate further north. The area began to be farmed in the 1880s, fishing communities sprang up at regular intervals and iron ore, discovered around 1900, is still mined around **Whyalla**. The detour around the coast passes imposing scenery and superlative **surfing** and **beach fishing**, especially where the Great Australian Bight's elemental weather hammers into the western shore – a chance to give your senses a workout before dealing with the Nullarbor's deadening horizons.

Stateliner **buses** from Port Augusta run either across the top of the peninsula to Ceduna, or via Whyalla down the east coast to Port Lincoln at the southern tip – you'll need your own transport to tackle the western side. Major **car** rental companies have outlets at both Whyalla and Port Lincoln which, if time is limited, are only fifty minutes by **air** from Adelaide. For general information on the peninsula, check Ⓦwww.tep.com.au.

Whyalla and the east coast

First visible an hour from Port Augusta as a smudge of grey over Long Sleep Plain, **WHYALLA**, the state's second most important city and headquarters of its **heavy industry**, isn't the prettiest of places. **One Steel** has its massive steelworks here (tours Mon, Wed & Fri 9.30am; 2hr; $17; book through the information centre) and tankers queue offshore to fill up at Santos' oil and gas refinery. Until it closed in 1978, the shipyard produced a few famous **vessels**, the first being the *Whyalla*, which now guards the northern entrance to town. The accompanying **information centre and maritime museum** (daily 10am–4pm; $8 including ship tour; Ⓣ08/8645 8900, Ⓦwww.whyalla.com) is largely occupied by a huge model of the oil refinery, as well as displays of shipping history. From the southwest, Whyalla presents a much greener aspect - at the junction of Broadbent Terrace and Playford Avenue an old aerodrome site has been landscaped into a series of ponds to recycle stormwater.

The highway curves through the old town under the name of Darling Terrace; you'll find a **post office**, **banks**, a **bus station**, hotels and shops around the junction with Forsyth and Patterson streets, all periodically covered in harmless red fallout from the steelworks' mysterious pellet plant.

Accommodation options include the *Foreshore Caravan Park* on Broadbent Terrace (Ⓣ08/8645 7474, Ⓦwww.bestonparks.com.au; cabins ❸) and *Whyalla Foreshore Motor Inn* on Watson Terrace (Ⓣ08/8645 8877, Ⓦwww.whyallaforeshore.com.au; ❺), both a ten-minute walk from the centre along a surprisingly attractive beach, with Hummock Hill mercifully obscuring the view of the steelworks; people and pelicans find good fishing off the jetty. Otherwise, try your luck at one of the **hotels**: *Spencer* on Forsyth Street (Ⓣ08/8645 8411; ❷) has rooms, good food and weekend music. For **food**, seafood at *Spaggs*, 26 Patterson St, makes a welcome change from counter meals; after eating, walk past the rows of fifty-year-old workers' homes to the top of Hummock Hill for a view of the industrial complexes by night.

Beyond Whyalla, the **east coast** is an unassuming string of sheltered beaches and villages nestled beneath towering grain silos, the sort of places you could drive through without a second glance or else get waylaid beachcombing for a week. **COWELL** is known for its whiting and as the world's largest source of black "nephrite" jade, though not much of it is in evidence, since it's largely exported rough. Arno Bay, Port Neill and the larger Tumby Bay all boast clean, quiet beaches, good fishing and a range of accommodation.

Port Lincoln

A tuna port and resort town built on a hillside above Boston Bay, **PORT LINCOLN** has the busiest atmosphere of anywhere on the peninsula. The town's harbour is dotted with trawlers, and the main seafront streets of Tasman Terrace and Liverpool Street are full of eateries and far-from-genteel taverns. There's a **tourist office** here too (daily 9am–5pm; Ⓣ08/8683 3544 or 1300 788 378, Ⓦwww.visitportlincoln.net), between the post office and shopping mall; Stateliner **buses** (Ⓣ08/8415 5555) terminate a couple of streets away on Darling Terrace.

Most of Port Lincoln's **attractions** are underwater. You can get bait and tackle from any service station and **fish** off the town jetty, or for heavier game fishing contact Sea Charters (ⓣ08/8682 2425), which can also take you on a **cruise** to Dangerous Reef for spotting seals, birdlife and sharks. The seas off Lincoln were once rated as the best place in the world to see **great white sharks** – footage for *Jaws* was filmed here – but trawling and hunting since the mid-1970s have placed this little-understood fish on the endangered species list. If this doesn't put you off **diving** – or if you just need advice on good places to fish or arrange a boat charter – contact Got One at 80 Tasman Terrace (ⓣ08/8683 0021). **Porter Bay**, until recently a swamp just south of town, has been transformed into a marina which has drawn many of the boats and some of the life away from the old town. The development includes a large, modern **leisure centre** (Mon–Fri 6am–9pm, Sat, Sun & holidays 9am–6pm; ⓣ08/8682 3833, ⓦwww.leisurecentre.net.au).

Entering Port Lincoln from the north, the Lincoln Highway (which later becomes Tasman Terrace and then London Street) affords splendid views of Boston Bay and presents you with myriad motel **accommodation** options, such as the luxurious *Limani Motel* (ⓣ08/8682 2200, ⓦwww.limanihotel.com.au; ❺). At the highway's far end lie the terraced tent sites of *Port Lincoln Tourist Park* (ⓣ08/8621 4444, ⓦwww.portlincolnaccommodation.com; cabins ❸).

Around Port Lincoln

Lincoln National Park, just south of Port Lincoln, covers a rough peninsula of sandy coves, steep cliffs and mallee scrub, which is home to the discreet rock parrot. The NPWS at 75 Liverpool St in Port Lincoln (ⓣ08/8688 3111) can supply maps and advice on road conditions. There's similar scenery 32km south at **Whalers Way**, a privately-owned stretch of road for which you'll need to collect a permit and key from the tourist office in Port Lincoln ($25, plus $10 key deposit); the name derives from the whaling station which once operated at Cape Wiles – relics are stacked up around the gate. The power of the Southern Ocean is memorably demonstrated at **Cape Carnot**, in the southern section of the park, where giant waves and frosty blue surf force their way through blowholes which sigh as they erupt in sync with the swell.

The picturesque setting of the town of **COFFIN BAY** is worth a look, though perhaps not during school holidays, when the caravan park (ⓣ08/8685 4170; on-site vans ❷, cabins ❸) and abundant holiday cottages are full to bursting. A stroll along the coastal "Oyster Walk" takes you past the original fishermen's shacks, now mostly summer houses, and reveals a wealth of bird and plant life – a taste of the national park to the west.

Coffin Bay National Park, an hour's drive west from Port Lincoln, comprises a landscape of dunes and salt marsh, mostly accessible only by 4WD, though parts are open to other types of vehicle – consult the NPWS in Port Lincoln before visiting. You'll be rewarded by isolation, sand sculptures at Sensation and Mullalong beaches, and the quality of the fishing. Semicircular stone walls on the northern shore are **Aboriginal fish traps** – fish were chased in at high tide and then the gaps in the side blocked with nets as the water receded. If you don't have your own 4WD, Great Australian Bight Safaris (ⓣ08/8682 2750, ⓦwww.greatsafaris.com.au) offers various day-trips ($60–150), as well as longer camping and fishing adventures.

The west coast

To catch the best of the west coast and the townships along the way, you'll need to detour off the main road between Coffin Bay and Ceduna. The region's coastal communities are an unlikely mix of conservative farmers and "alternative" surfies who come to ride the endless succession of strong, hundred-metre-long crests rolling into Waterloo Bay at **ELLISTON**, one of the state's most highly regarded **surf beaches**. Bold murals at the Community Hall between the café and campsite address local themes – including a long-suppressed incident when Aboriginal people were driven over the cliffs.

North of Elliston just before Venus Bay, rocks have been hollowed by the sea to form the **Talia Caves**, but the lengthy beach is more compelling, though camping is prohibited. To the north again, if you turn to the coast about 20km north of Port Kenny, you pass the strangely flared **Murphy's Haystacks**, a group of low granite monoliths that look like giant mushrooms. Pushing on to **Point Labatt** brings you to mainland Australia's only colony of fur seals – binoculars or a telephoto lens help to distinguish mother seals teaching pups to swim from the torpid, bulkier males basking on the rocks. Then it's back to the highway at **Streaky Bay** – the only place on the west coast that has a real centre – and then to drier country as you approach Ceduna and the Nullarbor.

The Eyre Highway and Gawler Ranges

Taking the **Eyre Highway** directly across the top of the peninsula from Port Augusta ensures an easy crossing to Ceduna, speeding past the mines at **Iron Knob** and dry scrub populated by green ring-necked parrots. Unusual geology appears around Wudinna in the form of isolated granite mounds (inselbergs) of various shapes and sizes. The largest, **Mount Wudinna**, 10km to the northeast of town, is the largest monolith in South Australia, while 30km southwest lies **Ucontichie Hill**, whose curved natural formations include a **wave rock** similar to Hyden's in Western Australia (see p.670).

Iron Knob is the start of forays along dirt tracks into the **Gawler Ranges**, before you rejoin the highway at Wirrulla. While you might not need a 4WD, it's a remote area that requires advance preparation and advice from the NPWS. The ranges are low, rounded volcanic ridges coloured orange by dust, with occasional speckled boulders poking through a thin grass cover, and it's worth frightening the sheep and pink Major Mitchell cockatoos by walking up one of the peaks for a closer look. *Mount Ive Homestead* (Ⓣ08/8648 1817, Ⓦwww.mtive.com.au; ❷–❸), 135km west of Iron Knob and right in the heart of the Ranges, has fuel, information and **accommodation** in basic rooms, plus camping space, but don't turn up unannounced. The track into the ranges passes **Lake Gairdner**, largest of the Gawler's **salt lakes**, with the ruins of Pondanna Homestead on a lonely plain at its southern end.

Ceduna and the Nullarbor Plain

You know where you are in **CEDUNA**: all the shops from camping store to supermarket are unambiguously named and a large signpost in the centre gives distances to everywhere between Perth and Port Augusta. Despite being small enough to walk around in twenty minutes, there's no lack of **caravan parks**, **banks** or **service stations**. Stateliner **buses** pass through town on their way from Adelaide to Port Augusta. It's a punishing 1200km west from here to the next town of any note, so this is the place to fill up the tank – not surprisingly competition for your custom is fierce, with almost every brand of fuel on offer.

The *Foreshore Van Park* on South Terrace (Ⓣ08/8625 2290, Ⓦwww.cedunaforeshorecaravanpark.com.au; cabins ❸) and the *Ceduna Foreshore Hotel-Motel* on O'Loughlin Terrace (Ⓣ08/8625 2008 or 1800 655 300, Ⓦwww.ceduna.bestwestern.com.au; ❹) are right next to the jetty – you can fish for whiting on the turn of the high tide. Before your early-morning start call in at the **tourist office** on Poynton Street (Mon–Fri 9am–5.30pm, Sat & Sun 9am–5pm; Ⓣ08/8625 2780, Ⓦwww.ceduna.net) and the NPWS on McKenzie Street (Ⓣ08/8625 3144) for the latest on the Nullarbor's attractions. Incidentally, it almost never rains on the plain, and there's always a charge for **water**, which has to be distilled from underground reserves – so carry your own.

The Nullarbor Plain

Nullarbor may not be strictly correct Latin for "treeless", but it's an apt description of the plain which stretches flat and infertile for over 1200km across the Great Australian Bight. Taking the **train** brings you closer to the dead heart than the **road** does, which allows some breaks in the monotony of the journey to scan the sea for southern right whales and visit at least one Aboriginal site. From Ceduna to the Western Australian border it's 480km, which you can easily cover in under five hours if you want; Dalíesque fridges standing along the highway in the early stages of the drive are actually makeshift mailboxes for remote properties.

The last chance to catch some **waves** is at **Cactus Beach/Point Sinclair** south of **Penong**, though its popularity took a dive after a surfer was killed by a great white here in 2000. Even for non-surfies it's worth the drive through white dunes, green shrubbery and blue lagoons to watch the extraordinary wave formations; there's a **campsite** with firewood provided (but no drinking water) and a basic store (daily 12.30–2pm). In Penong itself, **accommodation** is provided by the *Penong Hotel* (Ⓣ08/8625 1050; ❷) and *Penong Caravan Park* (Ⓣ08/8625 1111, Ⓔoatsfarm@bigpond.com; cabins ❸). There's also a general store and post office with EFTPOS (Mon–Fri 8am–5.30pm, Sat & Sun 9am–1pm).

Two hours beyond Penong you arrive at **Yalata Community**, settled by the Maralinga peoples cleared off their ancestral land by the British atomic bomb tests at Maralinga in the 1950s. At the roadhouse and White Well ranger station (Ⓣ08/8625 2780) you can obtain permits to cross community borders and reach the **Head of the Bight**, the best place to see whales when they migrate

△ Road sign, Nullarbor Plain

up here between June and October. The Head is a stirring setting, where powdery dunes rise to absurdly melodramatic cliffs over just a couple of kilometres – you can't help feeling that this is how early cartographers must have envisaged the edge of the world. Twenty minutes away is the *Nullarbor Roadhouse* (☎08/8625 6271; ④), which has budget **beds**, motel rooms and a campsite, and is the last place to get fuel before Border Village. The famous triple yellow sign on the highway warning of camels, wombats and kangaroos marks the beginning of the run, which has absolutely no trees. Ironically, rabbits – no longer controlled by farmers now that the area is a national park – have almost crowded out the wombats.

Curiously enough for a land with minimal rainfall, the Nullarbor is undermined by partially flooded limestone **caverns**. From the outside, **Koonalda Cave** (just north of the *Nullarbor Roadhouse*) is a large hole with recently planted fruit trees growing in the mouth; inside, a tremendously deep network of tunnels leads to an underground lake, the shafts grooved by fingers being dragged over their soft walls. Although the patterns are clearly deliberate, their meaning is unknown. The cave is closed off to protect the engravings, but the Ceduna NPWS (see opposite) might be able to arrange a visit.

Border Village is just another roadhouse (☎08/9039 3474; ④) with a natty fibreglass kangaroo in the car park – certainly the largest one between here and Antarctica. **Eucla** (see p.674) and the rest of the Nullarbor lie 16km over the border in Western Australia on a noticeably worse road and in a considerably earlier time zone.

The Stuart Highway: Woomera and beyond

Heading north of Port Augusta along the Stuart Highway, the first place of any consequence is **WOOMERA**, an uncharismatic but well-appointed barracks town two hours beyond Port Augusta. The town has had a fair share of negative publicity because of its harsh **detention centre**, which used to house political asylum seekers while their cases were being decided, before public pressure brought its closure in 2003. In fact, the whole town was closed to the public until 1982, as it sits at the southeast corner of a five-hundred-kilometre corridor known locally as "the Range", ominously highlighted on maps as **Woomera Prohibited Area**.

Don't expect to find out why at the **tourist office** (daily: March–Nov 9am–5pm; Dec–Feb 10am–2pm; ☎08/8673 7042) or the mostly military Heritage Centre (same hours; $5), both at the crossroads of Dewrang and Banool avenues. Models, rocket-relics and plenty of pictures detail the European Launcher Development Organisation's unsuccessful efforts to launch satellites here in the 1960s, but the reasons for the creation of the Prohibited Area – weapons testing and the British-run 1950s **atomic bomb tests**, contaminated dust from which is still being scraped up and vitrified – are not mentioned. For a first-hand account, read

Len Beadell's *Outback Highways*, cheerful tales of the bomb tests and the construction of "some sort of rocket range – or something" by the chief engineer.

There are two places to **stay**: the modern *Eldo Hotel* on Kotara Crescent (ⓣ08/8673 7867, ⓦwww.eldohotel.com.au; ❹), which also provides **meals** and booze on the huge veranda overlooking the Outback; and the welcoming *Woomera Travellers Village* on Wirruna Avenue (ⓣ08/8673 7800, ⓦwww.woomera.com; ❸) – **camping** on the lawn is preferable to the beds in the dreary ex-barracks. The **shopping centre** has banks and other facilities, while next door *The Oasis* houses a small leisure centre with a café, bar and bowling alley. Greyhound Australia **buses** travelling on the Stuart Highway don't go into Woomera but will drop you off at the roadhouse at Pimba, 7km away; Stateliner services call into the town, however.

Roxby Downs, Andamooka and Lake Torrens

Instead of returning to the highway, you might want to carry on past Woomera to the strangest two companion towns in Australia. The first, **ROXBY DOWNS**, 80km away, is completely modern, a service centre built in 1986 for miners working the copper, gold, silver and uranium deposits at the nearby **Olympic Dam Mine** (bookings essential on ⓣ08/8671 2001; donation). The friendly **Roxby Downs Cultural Precinct** on the main street (daily 9am–5pm; ⓣ08/8671 2001, ⓦwww.roxbydowns.com), has local information and a café. You can get as far as Olympic Dam and Port Augusta with Stateliner **buses**.

Another thirty minutes on along an unsurfaced road lies **ANDAMOOKA**, an opal-mining shantytown of block and scrap-iron construction whose red-earth high street becomes a river after rain. The soil proved to be too loose for the underground homes which became *de rigueur* at Coober Pedy (see below), but mud lean-tos, built in the 1930s, are still standing opposite the post office. **Facilities** include fuel, a supermarket, the *Tuckerbox Restaurant* (daily 11am until late), two hotel-motels, two campsites, and the Opal Creek Showroom, which distributes maps and advice. If you fancy your luck "noodling", head to **German Gully**; opals here are more strongly coloured than those at Coober Pedy, but few have been found for years.

Another thirty-minute 4WD ride away is **Lake Torrens**, a sickle-shaped salt lake related to the Acraman meteorite (see box, p.804) which gets popular with birdwatchers in wet years. The lake is also renowned in paleontological circles for traces of the 630-million-year-old **Ediacaran fauna**, the earliest-known evidence of animal life anywhere on the planet, first found in Australia and possibly wiped out by the meteorite. Delicate fossil impressions of jellyfish and obscure organisms are preserved in layered rock; the South Australian Museum in Adelaide has an extensive selection, but rarely issues directions to the site, which has been plundered by collectors since its discovery in 1946 by the geologist Reg Sprigg.

Coober Pedy

COOBER PEDY is the most enduring symbol of the harshness of Australia's Outback and the determination of those who live there. It's a place where the

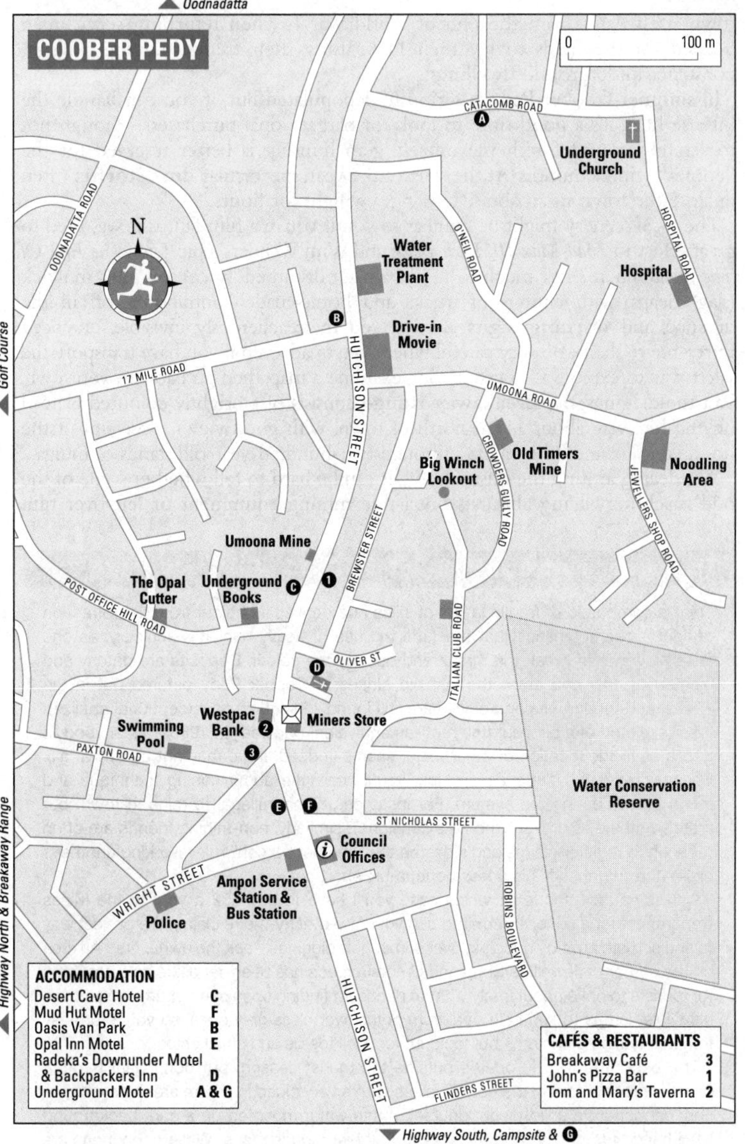

terrain and temperatures are so extreme that homes – and even churches – have been built underground, yet which has managed to attract thousands of opal prospectors. In a virtually waterless desert 380km from Woomera, and considerably further from anywhere else, the most remarkable thing about the town – whose name stems from an Aboriginal phrase meaning "white man's burrow" – is that it exists at all. **Opal** was discovered by William Hutchison on a gold-prospecting expedition to the Stuart Range in February 1915, and the town itself dates from the end of World War I, when returning servicemen headed for the fields to try their luck, using their trench-digging skills to construct underground dwellings.

In summer Coober Pedy is seriously depopulated but, if you can handle the intense heat, it's a good time to look for bargain opal purchases – though not to scratch around for them yourself: gem hunting is better reserved for the "cooler" winter months. At the start of the year, spectacular **dust storms** often enclose the town in an abrasive orange twilight for hours.

The local scenery might be familiar to you if you're a film fan, as it was used to great effect in *Mad Max III*, *Pitch Black* and Wim Wenders' epic *Until The End Of The World*. There's not much to it, just a plain disturbed by conical pink mullock (slag) heaps, with clusters of trucks and home-made contraptions off in the distance, and **warning signs** alerting you to treacherously invisible, unfenced thirty-metre shafts. Be very careful where you tread: even if you have transport, the safest way to explore is to take a tour, examine a map, then go back on your own. Past the diggings, the **Breakaway Range** consists of a brightly coloured plateau off the highway about 11km north of town, with good views, close-ups of the hostile terrain, and bushwalking through two-hundred-year-old stands of mulga.

Wandering around the dusty streets, it can be hard to tell whether some of the odd machinery lying about is bona-fide mining equipment or left-over film

Finding and buying an opal

Opal is composed of fragile layers of silica and derives its colour from the refraction of light – characteristics that preclude the use of heavy mining machinery, as one false blow would break the matrix and destroy the colour. Deposits are patchy and located by trial and error: the last big strikes at Coober Pedy petered out in the 1970s, and though bits and pieces are still found – including an exceptional opalized fossil skeleton of a pliosaur (the reptilian equivalent of a seal) in 1983 – it's anybody's guess as to the location of other major seams (indeed, there may not be any at all). Because so much depends on luck, you'll hear little about mining technique and more about beating the system. For instance, it's now illegal to mine in town, but there's nothing to prevent "home extensions"; similarly, non-mining friends are often roped in to register claims and sidestep the "one per person" rule. Working another's claim (the "night shift") is a less honourable short cut.

Unless you're serious (in which case you'll have to pay $52 a year to the Mines Department for a Miner's Permit to peg your fifty-by-fifty-metre claim), the easiest way to find something is by noodling over someone's diggings – ask the owner first. An area on the corner of Jewellers Shop and Umoona roads has been set aside as a safe area for tourists to poke about freely without danger of finding open mine-shafts. Miners use ultraviolet lamps to separate opal from potch (worthless grey opal), so you're unlikely to find anything stunning – but look out for shell fossils and small chips.

The best time to buy opal is outside the tourist season, but don't deal through grizzled prospectors in the hotels unless you're very clued in. There are three categories: cabochon, a solid piece; doublet, a thin wafer mounted on a dark background to enhance the colour; and triplet, a doublet with quartz lens. While cabochons are the most expensive and triplets the least valuable, it takes some experience to price accurately within each category, as size, clarity, strength of colour, brightness and personal aesthetics all contribute. With about fifty dealers in town, it's up to you to find the right stone; reputable sources give full written guarantees. One of the best is The Opal Cutter on Post Office Hill Road (Ⓣ08/8672 3086, Ⓦwww.opalcutter.com.au), where the proprietors will tell you all you need to know about the precious stones and you can watch opals being cut on the premises.

props. The **Big Winch Lookout** in the centre gives a grandstand view of the mix of low houses and hills pocked with ventilation shafts. The welded metal "tree" up here was assembled before any real ones grew in the area, though in the last few years there have been some attempts to encourage greenery with recycled waste-water. For more on mining, there are several mine displays and museums in town: try **Old Timers Mine**, Crowders Gully Road (ⓣ08/8672 5555, ⓦwww.oldtimersmine.com $10), or **Umoona** on Hutchison Street (ⓣ08/8672 5288, ⓦwww.umoonaopalmine.com.au; entrance free, tours $10). There are numerous **tours** on offer, all of which feature a town drive, a spot of noodling and a visit to an underground home – which you might find embarrassingly like visiting a zoo. One of the best is Radeka's four-hour tour ($50; ⓣ08/8672 5223), which includes a look at the Breakaway Range. Alternatively, book through your accommodation.

Coober Pedy has lately achieved a bit of a reputation for **violence**, which is perhaps not surprising given its extreme climate and the fact that most people have access to explosives. However, signs warning "no parking unless your car is dynamite-proof" are really for amusement value only, and visitors are unlikely to be the object of any discord.

Practicalities

Just about everything you'll need in Coober Pedy lies around the five-hundred-metre strip between the *Opal Inn Hotel* and the water-treatment plant on **Hutchison Street** (also known as Main Street), which leads north off the highway. Greyhound Australia **buses** (ⓣ13 20 30) drop you off at the Ampol service station. From the **airport** you may be able to get a lift with one of the hostel buses that meet most flights, or make an advance reservation to ensure that someone meets you.

The **tourist office** on Hutchison Street (Mon–Fri 8.30am–5pm, Sat & Sun 10am–1pm; ⓣ1800 637 076, ⓦwww.opalcapitaloftheworld.com.au), opposite the Ampol service station, is a mine of local information. Underground Books (ⓣ08/8672 5558), on Post Office Hill Road opposite the Mobil service station, is a good alternative source – it stocks packs of local sketch maps which are a useful back-up to road maps. The Miners Store supermarket on Hutchison Street (ⓣ08/8672 5051) is also the **post office** and Commonwealth **bank** agent (there's a Westpac branch opposite). The **hospital** is on Hospital Road, at the north end of town (ⓣ08/8672 5009), and there's a **pharmacy** at the Medical Centre in the middle of Hutchison Street. Everyone shops on Thursday, as fresh meat and veggies arrive in a refrigerated lorry on Wednesday night and are scarce by the weekend. The **swimming pool** at the school on Paxton Road gives a welcome chance to cool down; check the opening hours at the tourist office.

Accommodation

Coober Pedy relies heavily on tourist income, so finding **lodgings** shouldn't be a problem. To some people, the idea of sleeping underground is disturbing but, while not all accommodation is subterranean, it's worth spending at least one night in naturally cooled tunnels for the experience.

Desert Cave Hotel Hutchison St ⓣ08/8672 5688 or 1800 088 521, ⓦwww.desertcave.com.au. This place offers a choice of below- or above-ground four-star accommodation. There's a swimming pool, and scenic flights, tours and car rental can be arranged. ❻

Mud Hut Motel Next to the council offices ⓣ08/8672 3003 or 1800 646 962, ⓦwww.mudhutmotel.com.au. The bare, rammed-earth construction of this well-furnished motel gives a flavour of the subterranean without losing out on daylight. ❺

Oasis Van Park Opposite the water-treatment plant, Hutchison St ⓣ08/8672 5169, ⓔbig4cooberpedy@bigpond.com. Spacious, air-conditioned cabins as well as camping facilities. Cabin rooms ❷

Opal Inn Motel Hutchison St ⓣ08/8672 5054 or 1800 088 523, ⓦwww.opalinn.com.au. A standard motel block behind the hotel of the same name. Facilities include bar, bottle shop and tour bookings. ❹

Radeka's Downunder Motel and Backpackers Inn Oliver St ⓣ08/8672 5223 or 1800 633 891, ⓦwww.radekadownunder.com.au. The best budget option in town. There are snaking tunnels downstairs with alcoves holding from two to six beds – though it can be a long trek upstairs to the well-appointed kitchen and toilets – and a bar and pool table provide evening entertainment. Dorms $22, motel rooms ❹

Riba's Caravan Park and Underground Camping William Creek Rd ⓣ08/8672 5614, ⓦwww.camp-underground.com.au. Don't miss the unique opportunity of pitching a tent beneath the earth's surface.

Underground Motel Catacomb Rd ⓣ08/8672 5324 or 1800 622 979, ⓦwww.theundergroundmotel.com.au. Clean, tiled rooms with views over the desert from the front porch. Breakfast included. ❹

Eating and drinking

Restaurants in town are scarce but good value and portions are huge – beware of over-ordering. As Coober Pedy has a large Greek population your best bet would be the popular *Tom and Mary's Taverna* on the main road, serving large portions of authentic, good-value Greek food as well as pizzas – don't be put off by the rather bare interior, the food is marvellous. Otherwise head for the nearby *John's Pizza Bar*, a popular pizza and fast-food joint, or *Breakaway Café*, with a pleasant covered terrace, both on the main road.

The town lacks decent **watering holes** so make the best of the bar in your accommodation. The drive-in **cinema** on Hutchison Street shows a double bill most Saturday nights.

Beyond Coober Pedy

The Stuart Highway ploughs 350km north from Coober Pedy to the state border. From **Marla** township (where there's a shop, post office and Commonwealth Bank at the roadhouse) you could head east to Oodnadatta across the **Painted Desert** at Arkaringa Hills, a larger version of the Breakaway Range, or 35km west into Aboriginal land to the state's newest opal strike at Mintabie – seek permission from Marla's police (ⓣ08/8670 7006). If you want to get to **Oodnadatta** and don't have your own vehicle, the direct two-hundred-kilometre dirt road from Coober Pedy across the pan of Giddi-Gidna (the **Moon Plain**) is covered by the **mail run**, and you should be able to cadge a lift (ⓣ1800 069 911, ⓦwww.desertdiversity.com; $165). The service departs from Underground Books in Coober Pedy on a roughly twelve-hour triangular route to William Creek and Oodnadatta every Monday at 9am (anticlockwise) and Thursday (clockwise); this is the only public transport in the area.

Australia's hottest 4WD journey has to be west from Coober Pedy to the **atomic bomb sites** at **Emu Junction**: concrete slabs cap pits where contaminated equipment lies buried, and sand fused into sheets of glass by the blasts covers the ground – the area is still highly radioactive and you'd be advised to pass through quickly. Beyond lies the virgin **Unnamed Conservation Park** and routes across the sand dunes and Aboriginal land to the **Great Central Road** in Western Australia (see p.673). The NPWS at 11 McKenzie St in Ceduna (ⓣ08/8625 3144) supplies practical details and permits to 4WD convoys only.

The Flinders Ranges and northeast

If you're heading north from Port Augusta but want to avoid the Stuart Highway, an adventurous alternative route leads up to the spectacular **Flinders Ranges National Park** passing the quaint villages of **Quorn** and **Hawker** on the way. From the off-the-beaten-track settlement of **Blinman** in the **Northern Flinders**, the route continues down the isolated **Strzelecki Track** and beyond to the far-flung settlements of **Maree** and **Innamincka**.

Quorn and around

The first stop between Port Augusta and the Flinders Ranges National Park is 50km northeast at **QUORN**, whose stone buildings and village atmosphere offer a last taste of the pastoral south before the austerities of the Outback set in. Best known for the **Pichi Richi railway**, the sole operational section of the old Ghan, Quorn was a major rail centre until the line was re-routed through Port Augusta in the 1950s. Enthusiasts restored the service twenty years later and started taking passengers on a two-hour return haul to Woolshed Flats through the **Pichi Richi Pass** – whose name has been variously attributed to a medicinal herb or an Aboriginal word for "gorge". Punctuated by a break at Woolshed Flats for a cream tea, it makes a relaxing and mildly scenic journey. Trains run only on a few weekends and holidays between April and October; call ahead to check and book (ⓣ08/8658 6598 or 1800 440 101, ⓦwww.prr.org.au). More regular **public transport** includes Wayward Bus to Coober Pedy and Adelaide or Gulf Getaways (ⓣ08/8642 6827) to Wilpena Pound and Port Augusta. First Street and the block between it and Railway Terrace contain a few arts-and-crafts and secondhand shops to poke about in.

The **tourist office** is at 3 Seventh St (daily 9am–5pm; ⓣ08/8648 6419, ⓦwww.flindersranges.com) and can supply you with heaps of information on the entire region. *The Austral* at 16 Railway Terrace (ⓣ08/8648 6017, ⓦwww.australinn.com; ③) is the most agreeable **hotel** in town, with a good-value restaurant and modern deluxe rooms. They can also book scenic flights and camel rides in the area. A slightly cheaper option is the *Transcontinental Hotel* next door (ⓣ08/8648 6076; ③), with an easy-going crowd of truckies and drovers from the north for company. The **caravan park** in Quorn (ⓣ & ⓕ08/8648 6206; cabins ③) may not be overly luxurious but is very environmentally conscious, using vinegar instead of detergents to clean. The main road through town is Railway Terrace, where you'll find the town's post office and hotels, which all do good-value **meals** but are quite strict about serving times.

Around Quorn

There's good local bushwalking off the back road to Hawker along a string of ridges and cliffs, outrunners from the main body of the central Flinders Ranges, 100km north. Closest to Quorn is **Dutchmans Stern**, a solid day's hike for the reasonably fit from the car park to various lookouts. Less-dedicated walkers will find **Warren**, **Buckaringa** and **Middle gorges** an easier proposition. Buckaringa's steep face is the most reliable place in the ranges to see the rare and ravishingly pretty **yellow-footed rock wallaby**, with its bushy, ringed tail and yellow paws – climb to the top at around 4pm and sit quietly until they appear. Closer to Hawker, it's also worth taking in the well-preserved remains of **Kanyaka Homestead**, abandoned after a drought in the 1880s, and **Yourambulla Cave**, which has some unusual charcoal symbols in a high overhang, reached by a ladder. Both are signposted from the road.

HAWKER itself, some 100km from Port Augusta, is somewhere to fuel up, make use of the last banks and shops, have a meal at the *Old Ghan Restaurant* or organize a flight over the Flinders through *Hawker Caravan Park* at the Wilpena exit (ⓣ08/8648 4006, ⓦwww.hawkerbig4holidaypark.com.au; ❸–❹). Once in Hawker, only reachable with Gulf Getaways from Wilpena Pound or Port Augusta, you'll have to decide whether to press on into the Flinders Ranges and the northeast or continue following the former Ghan line north towards Marree; the bitumen on the latter route extends past the Leigh Creek coalfields to Lyndhurst, at the start of the Strzelecki Track.

Flinders Ranges National Park

The procession of glowing red mountains at **Flinders Ranges National Park**, folded and crumpled with age, produces some of the Outback's most spectacular and timeless scenery, rising from flat scrub to form abrupt escarpments, gorges and the famous elevated basin of **Wilpena Pound**. The hard contrast between sky and ranges is softened by native cypresses and river red-gums, and in spring the plains are burnished by **wild flowers** of all colours and you'll see more kangaroos than you can count. Bushwalkers, photographers and painters flock here in their hundreds, but with a system of graded **walking tracks** ranging from a few minutes' length to several days – not to mention roads of varying quality – the park is busy without being crowded. Most tracks lead into Wilpena Pound, though you can also pick up the Heysen Trail and follow it north from Wilpena for a couple of days around the ABC Range to **Aroona Ruins** on the northern edge of the park.

Nestling up against the edge of Wilpena Pound, **WILPENA** is a good place to orient yourself: it has a motel, campsite, gas, diesel and petrol pumps and an overpriced store.

The Acraman meteorite

In the mid-1980s a band of red earth from 600-million-year-old deposits in the Flinders Ranges was bafflingly identified as coming from the Gawler Ranges, 400km away. Investigations and satellite mapping suggested that 35-kilometre-wide Lake Acraman in the Gawler Ranges was an eroded meteorite crater, while Lake Gairdner and fragmented saltpans (such as Lake Torrens, see p.798) further east were set in ripples caused by the force of the strike. Estimates suggest that to have created such a crater the meteorite must have been 4km across; the mystery band in the Flinders Ranges was dust settling after impact. Though there is fossil evidence of animal life prior to this event – notably the *Ediacaran fauna* – recent research indicates that the Acraman meteorite may well have killed it all. It's certainly true that the ancestors of almost all species living today evolved after this impact.

Flinders Dreaming and geology

The almost tangible spirit of the Flinders Ranges is reflected in the wealth of Adnyamathanha ("hill people") legends associated with them. Perhaps more obvious here than anywhere else in Australia is the connection between landscapes and Dreamtime stories, which recount how scenery was created by animal or human action – though, as Dreamtime spirits took several forms, this distinction is often blurred. A central character is Akurra, a gigantic maned serpent (or serpents) who guards waterholes and formed the Flinders' contours by wriggling north to drink dry the huge salt lakes of Frome and Callabonna. You may well prefer the Aboriginal legends to the complexities of geology illustrated on boards placed at intervals along the Brachina Gorge track, which explain how movements of the "Adelaide Geosyncline" brought about the changes in scenery over hundreds of millions of years.

Practicalities

The **tourist office** (daily: 8.30am–5pm in summer; 8am–6pm in winter; ⓣ08/8648 0048) is situated at the end of the bitumen where the main routes start into Wilpena Pound. Wayward Bus **coaches** will get you as far as Adelaide and Alice Springs from here; Gulf Getaways services Port Augusta twice a week.

In Wilpena, *Wilpena Pound Resort* (ⓣ08/8648 0004 or 1800 805 802, ⓦwww.wilpenapound.com.au; ❻) provides comfortable but expensive **accommodation**; there's a good restaurant, however, and the pool is a welcoming change after a long hike. Four-wheel-drive tours and flights can also be arranged here, which is a good option if you don't have a lot of time and still wish to grasp the vastness of the pound. If you have a tent, the adjacent *Wilpena Campsite* (ⓣ08/8648 0004) is wooded and well equipped, and has standing tent accommodation.

Wilder places further into the park to set up camp for a few days include the national park campsites at **Bunyeroo** and **Brachina Gorge** in the west, **Trezona** and **Oraparinna** in the centre, and **Wilkawillana Gorge** in the extreme northeast, all accessible on unsealed roads. Even the more formal **lodgings** tend to be basic: for a longer stay you might consider renting a holiday cottage, which can be a bargain during the summer – Flinders Ranges Accommodation Booking Service (ⓣ1800 777 880, ⓦwww.frabs.com.au) offers a range of cabins (❷–❺) in the region. Other places to stay are dotted around the park: about 20km back towards Hawker, *Rawnsley Park* (ⓣ08/8648 0030, ⓦwww.rawnsleypark.com.au; cabins ❹, plus tent spaces) is beautifully located below Rawnsley Bluff and offers mountain-bike rental and 4WD trips; *Willow Springs* (ⓣ08/8648 6282, ⓦwww.frabs.com.au/willowsprings.htm; ❹), 17km north of Wilpena before the Wilkawillana Gorge junction, is a working sheep station with blockhouse dormitories and cottage.

The Wilpena tourist office offers booklets, maps and the latest information on routes; you're required to log out and back with them on any walk exceeding three hours. Realistically, hiking is restricted to the cooler winter months between May and October, as scant shade and reflective rocks raise summer temperatures above 40°C. Don't underestimate conditions for even short excursions: you'll need good footwear, a hat, sunscreen and **water** – at least half a litre per hour is recommended. **Camping out**, a waterproof tent, groundmat and fuel stove are essential, and note that the **weather** is very changeable; wind-driven rain can be a menace along the ridges and heavy downpours can make tracks dangerous.

Wilpena Pound

Wilpena Pound's two major hiking destinations are **St Mary's Peak** on the rim, and **Edowie Gorge** inside the pound – from Wilpena, allow nine hours for Edowie Gorge and eight hours for St Mary's (both return trips). Alternatively, an **overnight** trip through the pound allows you to see all its major attractions. Leave the peak until last and head off across the pound's flat, grassy bowl to the remains of **Hill's Homestead** – further evidence of the region's unsuitability for farming – then follow the track northwest to **Cooinda Camp**, about two hours from Wilpena. Assuming you left early enough, there's time to pitch a tent and spend the rest of the day following the creek upstream past **Malloga Falls** to **Glenora Falls** and views into Edowie Gorge before heading back to Cooinda. Next morning it's a steep climb to **Tanderra Saddle** below the peak, followed by the last burst up to the summit of St Mary's Peak itself. The effort is rewarded by unequalled views west to Lake Torrens and north along the length of the ABC Ranges towards Parachilna; on exceptional mornings the peak stands proud of low cloud inside the pound. The direct descent from the saddle back to Wilpena is initially steep, but shouldn't take more than three hours.

Shorter routes from Wilpena lead up **Mount Ohlssen Bagge** (a not-too-tiring four hours) and **Wangara Lookout** (2hr) for lower vistas of the pound floor, and southwest across the pound to **Bridle Gap** (6hr) following the Heysen Trail's red markers. Things to look out for are euro wallabies, emus and parrots inside the pound, and cauliflower-shaped fossil **stromatolites** – algal corals – on the Mount Ohlssen Bagge route, similar to those still living at Hamelin Pool in Western Australia (see p.681).

Arkaroo Rock, Sacred Canyon and nearby gorges

Two **Aboriginal galleries** worth seeing (although erosion and touching has damaged the paintings) are Arkaroo Rock and Sacred Canyon, both a short drive from Wilpena. **Arkaroo** is back off the main road towards Rawnsley Park and involves an hour's walk up the outside of Wilpena Pound to see mesh-protected rockfaces covered in symbols relating to an initiation ceremony and the pound's formation, some dating back six thousand years. Snake patterns depict St Mary's Peak as the head of a male Akurra coiled round the pound. To reach **Sacred Canyon**, briefly take the road from Wilpena into the north of the park, past the **Cazneaux Tree** – a river red-gum made famous by Harold Cazneaux's prize-winning 1930 photograph *Spirit of Endurance* – before turning right and following a bumpy track to its end. Rock-hop up the narrow, shattered gorge to clusters of painted swirls covered in a sooty patina and clearer engraved emu prints and geometric patterns; the best examples are around the second cascade.

The main road through the park heads straight out to Blinman, but another track detours to **Bunyeroo and Brachina gorges** on the western limits. The gorges make good campsites: you have to walk into Bunyeroo but the track passes through Brachina on its way to the surfaced Hawker-to-Marree road. If you're pressing directly on to the Northern Flinders, you can avoid Blinman by turning right off the main road about 20km from Wilpena, heading to **Wirrealpa Homestead**.

The Northern Flinders

The Wilpena–Blinman road passes through a low group of hills, thin in timber but still swarming with wallabies, emus and galahs. **BLINMAN** comprises a few houses with well-tended gardens, three fuel pumps, and a hotel (Ⓣ08/8648 4867, Ⓦwww.blinmanhotel.com.au; ❹) with log fires, games room, pool and campsite. The main track winds west through beautiful Parachilna Gorge, in the middle of which you could stay at *Angorichina Tourist Village* (Ⓣ08/8648 4842; on-site vans ❶–❷), which also has a campsite. The track meets the Hawker–Marree road at **Parachilna**, where there's great bushtucker and rooms at the *Prairie Hotel* (Ⓣ08/8648 4844, Ⓦwww.prairiehotel.com.au; ❺).

According to the Adnyamathanha, **coal** was made by Yoolayoola the kingfisher man, who built fires at **Leigh Creek**, halfway between Hawker and Marree. Today, 2.6 million tonnes of it are scooped out of the ground annually to be sent by rail and burnt at the power station in Port Augusta. At a car park just off the road you can climb around an old dragline crane and look over the edge of an open-cast mine; there are **free tours** daily (Ⓣ08/8675 2723). Coal-workers live either in the well-planned modern township of **Leigh Creek South** or at more traditional **Copley**, where *Tulloch's Bush Bakery* does a very civilized cappuccino and quandong pie. Fuel and camping sites are available at both towns.

The route into the Northern Flinders lies east, joining up with the direct road from Wilpena and then running north to the **Gammon Ranges National Park** and Arkaroola. Arkaroola marks the limit of **public transport** in the area, running its own connection to meet the Stateliner bus at Hawker on Monday and Friday; you really need your own vehicle to explore properly though.

Chambers Gorge and Big Moro

On the road to the Gammon Ranges are the remote and little-visited sites of Chambers Gorge and Big Moro, worth every groan and twang of your vehicle springs for their stark beauty and Aboriginal significance. The ten-kilometre access track east into **Chambers Gorge** (28km after Wirrealpa) is decidedly dodgy after rain when you'll need a 4WD, but at other times 2WD vehicles should – with care – reach the natural campsite at the foot of **Mount Chambers**, within twenty minutes' walk of the gorge mouth. In a Dreamtime story, Yuduyudulya, the Fairy Wren spirit, threw a boomerang which split Mount Chambers' eastern end and then circled back to form the crown. An indistinct left fork before the gorge leads to a dense gallery of **pecked engravings**; most are circles, though a goanna stands out clearly on the right, facing the main body of art. Chambers Gorge itself is huge and silent, the broad stony entrance guarded by high, perpendicular cliffs and brilliant green waterholes that would take days to explore properly.

Big Moro is sacred to the Adnyamathanha as the residence of an Akurra (the Dreamtime snake). The creek trickles through a crumbling gorge into two clear green pools, while limestone outcrops on the south side conceal miniature caves. The gorge lies west down an exceptionally tortuous fifteen-kilometre 4WD track opposite **Wertaloona Homestead**, 60km from the Mount Chambers junction. Pay attention to any signs and leave the three gates as you found them.

The Gammon Ranges

Arid and bald, the **Gammon Ranges** are the Flinders' last fling, a vicious flurry of compressed folds plunging abruptly onto the northern plains. Balcanoona is the NPWS headquarters for the otherwise undeveloped **Gammon Ranges**

National Park, a thick band of sandstone cliffs. There are two ways to experience the area: either carry on to Arkaroola (outside the park), or take the road west across the park through **Italowie Gorge** to Copley on the Hawker–Marree road. The steep red walls of the gorge are home to iga – native orange trees which symbolize the Adnyamathanha. There are **bush campsites** here and shearers' quarters at **Balcanoona** (book through the Wilpina NPWS ⓣ08/8648 0049; ❸).

On the northern edge of the park, **Arkaroola Wilderness Sanctuary** is a private wildlife sanctuary and **resort** (ⓣ08/8648 4848, ⓦwww.arkaroola.com.au; ❹), with a restaurant, caravan park and swimming pool. Scene of Australia's most recent volcanic activity, the area is a geologist's dream: **Paralana Hot Springs** (two hours away by 4WD) bubble out radioactive radon gas, and walks into the shattered hills surrounding the resort turn up fossils and semiprecious minerals. According to Aboriginal legend, the springs mark the site where a Dreamtime warrior extinguished his firestick after using it to kill a rival. The area is so rugged that conventional mining isn't really a profitable venture – drilling rigs are airlifted in, then ferried around on the lower half of a Chieftain tank. The resort's **Ridgetop Tour** ($98 per person) brings you closest to the heart of the scenery: four hair-raising hours in an open 4WD (wear something warm) following precipitous contours to **Sillers Lookout** and views east to the shimmering salt lakes of **Frome** and **Callabonna**. Remains of the hippopotamus-sized marsupial *Diprotodon* have been found at Callabonna. It survived well into Aboriginal times, but died out as the climate changed after the last Ice Age.

Some vehicles (with either high clearance or very careful drivers) can continue directly north to join the **Strzelecki Track** at Mount Hopeless, a little under half the distance to Innamincka. If you're unsure, the track can also be reached via Lyndhurst on the Hawker–Marree road, but this involves a three-hundred-kilometre detour from Arkaroola.

The Strzelecki Track

The 460-kilometre **Strzelecki Track** between Lyndhurst and Innamincka was pioneered in 1870 by **Harry Redford**, better known as Captain Starlight, who stole a thousand cattle from a property near Longreach in Queensland and drove them south across the Strzelecki Desert and down to Adelaide for more on Redford). Later used for more orthodox purposes, the track had a reputation as one of the roughest stock routes in the country, a serious obstacle for transport. Much of its epic nature has since been flattened, along with the road surface, by companies draining the **Moomba gas and oil fields**, and it's negotiable in any sound vehicle when dry.

Start at Lyndhurst by filling the tank – the next **fuel** is at the other end – and heading off around the northern tip of the Flinders Ranges; once past them, the journey becomes flat and pretty dull. Around the 105-kilometre mark you cross the 4850-kilometre-long **Dog Fence** (or Great Dingo Fence), designed to keep dingoes away from southern flocks, which stretches from the Nullarbor Plain east into New South Wales. Although its value is debatable, you do frequently see desiccated canine corpses poisoned by "1080" bait lying nearby. The road from Arkaroola connects within sight of **Mount Hopeless** (a pathetic hill, appropriately named); the next place to stop and perhaps camp is at the hot outflow from **Montecollina Bore**, 30km on. From here the scenery improves slightly as the road runs between dunes, and it's hard to resist leaving footprints along one of the pristine red crests.

At **Strzelecki Crossing** there's a choice of routes: you could abandon the track and head east to where Queensland, New South Wales and South Australia meet at **Cameron Corner**, where there's a store with fuel, a campsite (Ⓣ08/8091 3872; $5 per car, fee donated to the Royal Flying Doctors Service) and a small bar; alternatively, you could continue to Innamincka either via Moomba or by following the direct but less-frequented **Old Strzelecki Track**. Cameron Corner and the old track are 4WD only, and all of the routes are crossed by straight **seismic test lines** which run off to dead ends in the bush – you risk becoming permanently lost if you accidentally follow one, so take care. **Moomba**'s jumble of pipes and lick of flame are sometimes marked as a township on maps but, though visible from the road, the refinery is closed to the public. Within an hour you've crossed into the **Innamincka Regional Reserve** and are approaching Innamincka's charms.

Innamincka

Cooper Creek, which runs through Innamincka, is best known for the misadventures of explorers Burke and Wills, who ended their tragic 1861 expedition by dying here (see box, p.514). **INNAMINCKA** was later founded on much the same spot as a customs house to collect taxes on stock being moved between Queensland and South Australia. Never more than a handful of buildings, it found fame mainly because John Flynn's Flying Doctor Service ran a mission here and because the hotel piled up decades of empties into a legendary 180-metre-long bottle dump before the town was abandoned in 1952. Lately, however, recreational four-wheel driving has led to a renaissance. The new *Innimincka Hotel* (Ⓣ & Ⓕ08/8675 9901; ④) has weekend barbecues, a video jukebox and impromptu dance sessions on Friday and Saturday nights, while the *Innamincka Trading Post* (Ⓣ08/8675 9900) has a couple of comfortable **cabins** (④), and stocks provisions and fuel. The mission was rebuilt in 1994 as a **museum** (for opening hours ask at the *Trading Post*), and there's a solar-powered telephone and spotless shower block opposite. Pelicans, parrots and inquisitive dingoes will be your companions if you camp out for free along the creek.

It only takes an hour to look around the museum and hunt for evidence of the bottle dump before you're ready for other distractions – you can take your pick from taking a walk, **fishing** for yellowbelly, bream and catfish, swimming in the creek, or renting a canoe from the hotel or the *Trading Post*. With a vehicle you could strike out 20km west to **Wills' grave** or 8km east to where **Burke** was buried (both bodies were removed to Adelaide in 1862). Another 8km beyond Burke's cairn is **Cullyamurra waterhole**, the largest permanent body of water in central Australia, and a footpath to rock engravings of crosses, rainbow patterns and bird tracks. With a 4WD you can also tackle the 110-kilometre track north to the shallow **Coongie Lakes**, where you can swim and watch the abundant birdlife. An hour's drive east of Innamincka along a rather poor track is Queensland, the Dig Tree and a fuelless route to Quilpie (see p.514).

The far north: Marree and beyond

MARREE is a collection of tattered houses which somehow outlived the old Ghan's demise in 1980, leaving carriages to rust on sidings and rails to be used for tethering posts outside the hotel. Although it was first a camel depot, then a staging post for the overland telegraph line, and finally the point where the rail line skirted northwest around **Lake Eyre**, today all traffic comes by road and is bound for the **Birdsville Track** into Queensland or the **Oodnadatta Track**, which follows the former train route to Oodnadatta and beyond into the Northern Territory or **Simpson Desert**.

Accommodation is limited to the hotel on the main street (ⓣ08/8675 8344; ③), which is also good for lunch or dinner, and the caravan park run by the *Oasis Café* (ⓣ08/8675 8352; cabins ③), a fairly well-stocked shop, fuel and fast-food outlet which was originally the telegraph relay station. The General Store (ⓣ08/8675 8360), across the railway track towards Oodnadatta, doubles as a Commonwealth Bank agent and post office with fuel and EFTPOS. If it's open, visit the **Arabana Community Centre**, whose friendly staff will explain the uses of different types of boomerang.

Lake Eyre

Lake Eyre is a massive and eerily desolate salt lake caught between the Simpson and Strzelecki deserts in a region where the annual evaporation rate is thirty times greater than the rainfall. Most years a little water trickles into the lake from its million-square-kilometre catchment area, which extends well into central Queensland and the Northern Territory, but floods have filled the basin only four times since white settlement of the region – most dramatically in 1974, when the lake expanded to a length of 140km. A hypnotic, glaring **salt crust** usually covers the southern bays, creating a mysterious landscape whose harsh surrounds are paved by shiny gibber stones and walled by red dunes – in 1964 the crust was thick enough to be used as a range for Donald Campbell's successful crack at the world land-speed record. Some **wildlife** also manages to get by in the incredible emptiness. The resident Lake Eyre dragon is a diminutive, spotted grey lizard often seen skimming over the crust, and the rare flooding attracts dense flocks of birds, wakes the plump water-holding frog from hibernation and causes plants to burst into colour.

While you can **fly** over the lake (ⓣ08/8670 7962, ⓦwww.wrightsair.com.au; $180), only 4WDs can reach the shore 95km north of Marree, though the track to the campsite at a gum-shaded waterhole, just over halfway at **Muloorina Homestead**, is good. Timber at the lake is sparse and protected, which means that there's little shade and no firewood. There's no one to help you if something goes wrong, so don't drive on the lake's crust – should you fall through, it's impossible to extricate your vehicle from the grey slush below. This isn't a place to wander off to unprepared, but if you wish to grasp the vastness and emptiness of the state, don't miss it.

The Birdsville Track

Assuming there's been no rain, the 520-kilometre **Birdsville Track** is no obstacle to careful drivers during the winter: the biggest problem is getting caught in dried wheel ruts and being pulled off the road. Tearing north from Marree, the distant tips of the Flinders Ranges dip below the horizon behind, leaving you on a bare plain with the road as the only feature. Look for the **MV Tom Brennan**, a vessel donated to the area in 1949 to ferry stock around during floods, but now bearing an absurd resemblance to a large grey bathtub. Before the halfway house at Mungeranie Gap, a scenic variation is offered by the **Natterannie Sandhills** (150km), once a severe obstacle which has now been graded by digging out the soft sand and replacing it with clay. The **Mungeranie roadhouse** (Ⓣ08/8675 8317; ③) provides the only services on the track (fuel, beds and snacks). In a 4WD you can head west from the roadhouse to **Kalamurina campsite** near Cowarie Homestead (58km) for the thrill of desert fishing on Warburton Creek.

Back on the track, a windmill at **Mirra Mitta bore** (37km from the roadhouse) draws piping-hot water out of the ground beside long-abandoned buildings; the water smells of tar and drains into cooler pools, providing somewhere to camp. By now you're crossing the polished gibber lands of the **Sturt Stony Desert**, and it's worth going for a walk to feel the cold wind and watch the dunes dancing in the heat haze away to the west. The low edge of **Coonchera Dune** to the right of the track (190km from the roadhouse) marks the start of a run along the mudpans between the sandhills; look for desert plants and dingoes. In two more hours you should be pulling up outside the Birdsville pub (see p.516).

The Oodnadatta Track

The road from **Marree** to **Oodnadatta** is the most interesting of the three famous Outback tracks, mainly because abandoned sidings and fettlers' cottages from the old Ghan provide frequent excuses to get out of the car and explore. Disintegrating sleepers lie by the roadside along parts of the route, otherwise embankments and rickety bridges are all that remain of the line. As with the roads to Birdsville and Innamincka, with care, any sound vehicle can drive the route in dry winter weather.

About 100km into the journey, near **Curdimurka ruins**, the road runs within sight of **Lake Eyre South**, giving a flavour of its bigger sister if you can't get out there. Twenty-five kilometres later, a short track south ends below three conical hills – two of which have hot, bubbling **mound springs** at the top, created when water escaping from the artesian basin deposits heaps of mud and minerals. The perfectly symmetrical **Blanche Cup** looks out across a plain – stripped of every shred of greenery by rabbits and cattle – to **Hamilton Hill**, an extinct spring, while further south the **Bubbler** gurgles a verdant stream into the desert where it evaporates after a couple of hundred metres. Important to the Arabana, these springs were used by Sturt in the 1850s and later by the telegraph and rail depots, but tapping the artesian basin for bore water has greatly reduced their flow.

One of these bores is not far up the road at **Coward Springs** (open daily 9am–5pm; $1), where a corroded pipe spilling into ponds has created an artificial environment of grasses and palms behind a **campsite** (Ⓣ08/8675 8336, Ⓦwww.cowardsprings.com.au; $8) with toilet blocks and showers built from sleepers. One of the old railway buildings is now a display centre. **WILLIAM**

CREEK, 75km further, has a resident population of just ten – and is a source of fuel, camping and relaxation in the **hotel** (Ⓣ08/8670 7880, Ⓦwww.williamcreekhotel.net.au; ❸). Bar, walls and ceiling are heavily decorated with cards and photographs of 4WD disasters, and it also serves as a hangout for stockmen from **Anna Creek Station**, the world's largest cattle property, covering an area the size of Belgium. A solar-powered phone outside faces the battered remains of a Black Arrow **missile** dragged off the Woomera Range, just a few minutes' drive away. Off-road drivers can take a seventy-kilometre track from here to Lake Eyre's western shore; in the other direction is a more passable road to Coober Pedy, though there's almost nothing to see on the way except **Lake Cadibarrawirracanna**, a salt lake with permanent water and birdlife at the halfway mark.

After William Creek the track gets rougher, crossing sand dunes and then moving into stony country cut by frequent creeks – shallow for most of the year. Hardy mulgas line the banks, their soft yellow blooms giving off a distinctive acrid scent. On the last stretch to Oodnadatta, look out for a sight of the extraordinary red and black crescent petals of **Sturt's desert pea**, the state emblem, growing by the roadside.

Oodnadatta

Unless you stay long enough to meet some locals, you'll probably feel that, like Marree, **OODNADATTA** survived the Ghan's closure with little to show for it. A few logically arranged but untidy streets lacking atmosphere or purpose, Oodnadatta was founded as a railhead in 1890, and mail and baggage for further north had to make do with camel trains from here until the line to Alice Springs was completed in 1928. Now that has gone, the town has become a base for the Aranda community – utnadata ("mulga blossom") is the Aranda name for a local waterway – and 4WD crews heading into the Simpson Desert. After rain you'll even need a 4WD for the last slippery kilometre into town, past the racecourse. If your visit coincides with the **race weekend** in May, helicopters will be circling the track on the left, trying to dry it out, and the town will be deserted, so stop at the track, buy a pass and join in. With neat clothes and some sort of tie, you'll even get into the "formal" ball afterwards.

You can camp at the **Pink Roadhouse** (Ⓣ08/8670 7822, Ⓦwww.pinkroadhouse.com.au), unless the relative luxury of a bed at the *Transcontinental Hotel* appeals (Ⓣ08/8670 7804; ❹). The roadhouse acts as a store, bank and café (home of the famous Oodnaburger), and sells detailed sketch maps of the area. The hotel holds the key to the **Railway Museum** opposite, where you'll find a strangely timeless photographic record of the town – scenes are hard to date because so little seems to have changed. Stock up with provisions and then check the Transport SA hotline (Ⓣ1300 361 033) for road conditions and fuel supplies if you plan to head north towards Dalhousie Springs and the Simpson Desert (4WD only), or west to the Stuart Highway at Coober Pedy or Marla.

The Simpson Desert and Dalhousie Hot Springs

Apart from the track out to the Stuart Highway, the area north of Oodnadatta is strictly for 4WDs, with **Dalhousie Hot Springs** in the Witjira National Park a worthwhile destination, or the **Simpson Desert** for the ultimate

△ Sand dunes at sunrise, Simpson Desert

challenge. The route directly north, towards Finke and the Northern Territory, is relatively good as far as **Hamilton Homestead** (110km), though Fogarty's Claypan, around halfway, might present a sticky problem. From Hamilton the direct route east to Dalhousie Springs, shown on some maps, is now closed; take the longer route via **Eringa ruins** (160km) and **Bloods Creek bore** on the edge of **Witjira National Park**.

From Bloods Creek you can detour 30km northeast to **Mount Dare Hotel** (fuel, accommodation, food and provisions; Ⓣ08/8670 7835, Ⓦwww.mtdare.com.au; ④). In winter the homestead is busy with groups of 4WDs arriving from or departing for the desert crossing; it's at least 550km to the next fuel stop at Birdsville in Queensland.

Dalhousie Hot Springs

From the homestead it's a rough and bleak drive southeast to **Dalhousie Hot Springs**. The explorer Giles passed through this way in the 1870s, before the artesian basin had been extensively tapped by pastoralists, and described the scene:

> **The ground we had been traversing abruptly disappeared, and we found ourselves on the brink of limestone cliffs. . . From the foot of these stretched an almost illimitable expanse of – welcome sight – waving green reeds, with large pools of water at intervals, and dotted with island cones topped with reeds or acacia bushes.**

Though reeds and water are less abundant today, Giles' account still rings true. The collection of over one hundred **mound springs** form Arabian-like oases, an impression enhanced by the green circle of date palms clustered around many of the pools. The largest spring, next to the **campsite** (which has showers and toilets), is cool enough to swim in and hot enough to unkink your back. What survives of the vegetation simmers with birdlife: budgerigars, galahs and the eye-catching purple, blue and red fairy wren. As nothing flows into the springs, the presence of **fish** – some, like the Dalhousie hardyhead, unique to the system – has prompted a variety of improbable explanations. One theory is that fish eggs were swept up in dust storms and later fell with rain at Dalhousie,

The Simpson Desert crossing

Crossing the approximately 550km of steep north–south dunes through the Simpson Desert between Dalhousie in South Australia and Birdsville in Queensland is the ultimate challenge for any off-roader. In June, 4WD groups are joined by bikes attempting to complete the punishing Simpson Desert Cycling Classic. In winter, a steady stream of vehicles moves from west to east (the easier direction since the dunes' eastern slopes are steeper and harder to climb), but there's no help along the way, so don't underestimate the difficulties. Convoys need to include at least one skilled mechanic and, apart from the usual spares, a long-handled shovel and a strong tow-rope. While keeping weight to a minimum, you'll also need more than adequate food and water (six litres a day per person), and of course fuel – around a hundred litres of diesel if you take the shortest route, or two hundred litres of petrol. Dune-ascent techniques start with reducing tyre pressures to around 15psi to increase traction; select the gear and build up revs before starting. Don't attempt a gear change on the way up, and beware of oncoming vehicles on blind dune crests. If you don't make it over, slide down and try again; lighter vehicles may end up towing overburdened trucks. If all else fails, detours bypass many dunes.

The most testing, direct route follows the French Line, with the Rig Road detouring around the worst section but adding substantial distance (and fuel requirements) to the crossing. The enjoyment is mostly in the driving, though there's more than sand to look at: trees and shrubs grow in stabilized areas and at dusk you'll find dune crests patrolled by reptiles, birds, small mammals and insects. Photographers can take advantage of clear skies at night to make timed exposures of the stars circling the heavens. Purni Bore, 70km from Dalhousie, is another uncapped spout (though this may change with growing concerns over diminished ground water), where birdlife and reeds fringe a 27°C pool; camping facilities here include a shower and toilet. A post battling to stay above shifting sand at Poeppel Corner (269km) marks the junction of Queensland, South Australia and the Northern Territory; salt lakes here vary in their water content and sometimes have to be skirted around. After the corner the dunes become higher but further apart, separated by claypans covered in mulga and grassland; you'll have to negotiate some of Eyre Creek's channels too, which can be very muddy. Big Red, the last dune, is also the tallest; once over this it's a clear 41-kilometre run to Birdsville.

A large area of the Simpson Desert outside the Witjira National Park and the Simpson Desert Conservation Park is now a Regional Reserve under the control of the NPWS, from whom you should seek advice and a Desert Parks Pass before setting out. Contact the NPWS at Port Augusta (☎1800 816 078).

but it's more likely that fish were brought in during an ancient deluge or that the population survives from when the area was an inland sea.

While the main springs area is flat and trampled by years of abuse from campers and cars – stay on the marked paths here to avoid causing further erosion – trudging out to other groups over the salt and samphire-bush flats armed with a packed lunch and camera gives you an idea of what Giles was describing, and a good overview of the region from the top of well-formed, overgrown mounds. More views can be had from the stony hills to the west, and from **Dalhousie Homestead**, 16km south of the springs along the Pedirka road. The homestead was abandoned after the Ghan line was laid down, and today the stone walls, undermined by rabbit burrows, are gradually falling apart in the extreme climate.

Travel details

Trains

For all trains contact Great Southern Railway ⓣ13 21 47, ⓦwww.gsr.com.au.

Adelaide to: Alice Springs (Ghan, 2 weekly; 20hr); Darwin (Ghan, 1 per week; 47hr); Melbourne (Overlander, 4 per week; 12hr 30min); Perth (Indian Pacific, 2 per week; 38hr); Sydney (1 per week, 23hr; Indian Pacific, 2 per week; 26hr).

Buses

Further details of bus services can be found at ⓦwww.bussa.com.au.

Adelaide to: Alice Springs (1 daily; 18hr 30min); Barossa Valley (1–2 daily; 1hr 30min); Broken Hill (3 per week; 7hr); Ceduna (1 daily; 12hr); Clare (1 daily; 2hr 15min); Coober Pedy (1 daily; 10hr 30min); Goolwa (1–4 daily; 1hr 55min); Loxton (1 daily except Sat; 3hr 30min); McLaren Vale (1–3 daily; 50min); Melbourne (6 daily; 9hr 30min–14hr); Mount Gambier (1–3 daily; 6hr); Port Augusta (4–6 daily; 6hr); Port Lincoln (1–2 daily; 10hr); Renmark (2 daily; 4hr); Sydney (3 daily; 21–24hr); Victor Harbor (1–4 daily; 1hr 30min); Whyalla (3–6 daily; 5hr); Woomera (1 daily; 6hr); Yorke Peninsula (1–2 daily; 3–4hr).

Ceduna to: Adelaide (1 daily; 9hr 30min); Port Augusta (1 daily; 5hr); Port Pirie (1 daily; 5hr 30min).

Coober Pedy to: Adelaide (1 daily; 11hr); Alice Springs (1 daily; 7hr); Port Augusta (1 daily; 6hr 10min).

Port Augusta to: Adelaide (3–5 daily; 4hr 15min); Alice Springs (1 daily; 14hr); Ceduna (1 daily; 5hr); Coober Pedy (1 daily; 6hr 10min); Mambray Creek (for Mount Remarkable; 3–5 daily; 1hr); Marla (1 daily; 10hr); Port Lincoln (2 daily; 4hr 30min); Quorn (3 per week; 40min); Roxby Downs (1 daily except Sat; 3hr); Whyalla (3–4 daily; 50min); Woomera (1 daily except Sat; 2hr).

Port Lincoln to: Adelaide (1 daily; 10hr); Port Augusta (1 daily; 4hr 30min); Whyalla (1 daily; 3hr 30min).

Flights

Adelaide to: Alice Springs (1 daily; 2hr); Brisbane (6–8 daily; 4hr); Broken Hill (1–3 daily; 1hr 40min); Cairns (1 daily; 4hr); Canberra (1–3 daily; 3hr 10min); Ceduna (1–2 daily; 1hr 30min); Coober Pedy (1 daily except Sat; 1hr 30min); Darwin (2 daily; 5hr); Kangaroo Island (4–5 daily; 30min); Melbourne (11–12 daily; 1hr); Perth (4–6 daily; 5hr); Port Augusta (2 daily Mon–Fri; 1hr); Port Lincoln (5–7 daily; 30min); Sydney (9 daily; 2hr 10min); Whyalla (2–4 daily; 45min).

Ceduna to: Adelaide (1–2 daily; 1hr 20min).

Coober Pedy to: Adelaide (1 daily except Sat; 2hr).

Port Lincoln to: Adelaide (6–7 daily; 45min).

Melbourne and around

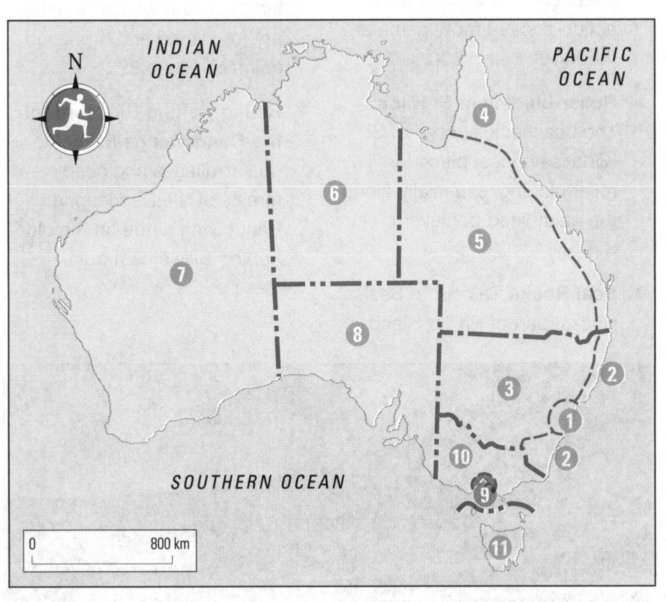

CHAPTER 9 Highlights

* **Chinatown** The low-rise, narrow streets of Melbourne's Chinatown haven't changed much since the nineteenth century, when a goldrush brought every corner of the world to this cosmopolitan city. See p.834

* **Aussie Rules match at the MCG** Join the cheering Melbourne crowds for an action-packed footy game at the MCG. See p.838

* **Roller-blading in St Kilda** The beachside suburb of St Kilda is an ideal place for roller-blading, especially along the palm-lined boulevard. See p.848

* **Seal Rocks** Sail out to Seal Rocks, part of Phillip Island Reserve, to see the largest known colony of Australian fur seals. See p.879

* **Yarra Valley** Victoria's answer to South Australia's Barossa Valley boasts pretty scenery and some great wineries. See pp.881–883

* **Healesville Sanctuary** Visit the beautifully located bushland zoo and wildlife sanctuary for injured and orphaned animals. See p.882

* **Riding Puffing Billy through the Dandenongs** Enjoy the quaint villages and shady forests of the Dandenong Range with a ride on the old *Puffing Billy* steam train. See p.883

△ Melbourne Cricket Ground

Melbourne and around

MELBOURNE is Australia's second-largest city, with a population of 3.7 million, around half a million less than Sydney. Rivalry between the two cities – in every sphere from cricket to business – is on an almost childish level. In purely monetary terms, Sydney is clearly in the ascendancy, having stolen a march on Melbourne as the nation's financial centre. However, as Melburnians never tire of pointing out, they have the incredible good fortune to inhabit what is often described as "one of the world's most liveable cities", and while Melbourne may lack a truly stunning natural setting or in-your-face sights, its subtle charms grow on all who spend time here, making it an undeniably pleasant place to live, and enjoyable to visit, too.

In many ways, Melbourne is the most European of all Australian cities: magnificent landscaped gardens and parks provide green spaces near the centre, while beneath the skyscrapers of the Central Business District (CBD), an understorey of solid, Victorian-era facades ranged along tree-lined boulevards present the city on a more human scale. The European influence is perhaps most obvious in winter, as trams rattle past warm cafés and bookshops, and promenaders dress stylishly against the chill. Not that Europe has supplied the city's only influences: large-scale immigration since World War II has shaken up the city's formerly self-absorbed, parochial WASP mindset for good. Whole villages have come here from Lebanon, Turkey, Vietnam and all over Europe, most especially from Greece, furnishing the well-worn statistic that Melbourne is the third-largest Greek city behind Athens and Thessaloniki. Not surprisingly, the immigrant blend has transformed the city into a **foodie mecca**, where tucking into a different cuisine each night – or new hybrids of East, West and South – is one of the great treats.

Melbourne's strong claim to being the nation's **cultural capital** is well founded: laced with a healthy dash of counterculture, the city's artistic life flourishes, culminating in the highbrow Melbourne International Arts Festival for two weeks in October, and its slightly more offbeat (and shoestring) cousin, the Fringe Festival. The city also takes pride in its leading role in Australian literary life, based around the Writers' Festival in August. Throughout the year, there are heavyweight seasons of classical music and theatre, a wacky array of small galleries, and enough art-house movies to last a lifetime. **Sport** too, especially Australian Rules Football, is almost a religion here, while the Melbourne Cup in November is a public holiday, celebrated with gusto.

Melbourne is an excellent base for day-trips out into the surrounding countryside. Closest to Melbourne are the quaint villages of the eucalypt-covered **Dandenong Ranges**, while the scenic **Yarra Valley**, in the northeast, is Victoria's answer to South Australia's Barossa Valley, and one of many wine-producing areas around Melbourne. To the south, huge **Port Phillip Bay** is encircled by the arms of the Bellarine and Mornington peninsulas. **Mornington Peninsula** offers more opportunity for wine tasting, and in addition to bucolic scenery there are beaches galore, the windswept ones facing the sea popular with surfers, while the placid waters of the bay are good for swimming and messing about in boats. **Geelong** and most of the **Bellarine Peninsula** are maybe not quite so captivating, but Queenscliff near the narrow entrance to Port Phillip Bay, with its beautiful, refurbished grand hotels, is a stylish (and expensive) weekend getaway.

Melbourne boasts a reasonably cool **climate** (although January and February are prone to barbaric hot spells when temperatures can climb into the forties with the threat of bushfires which may close off certain areas to the public).

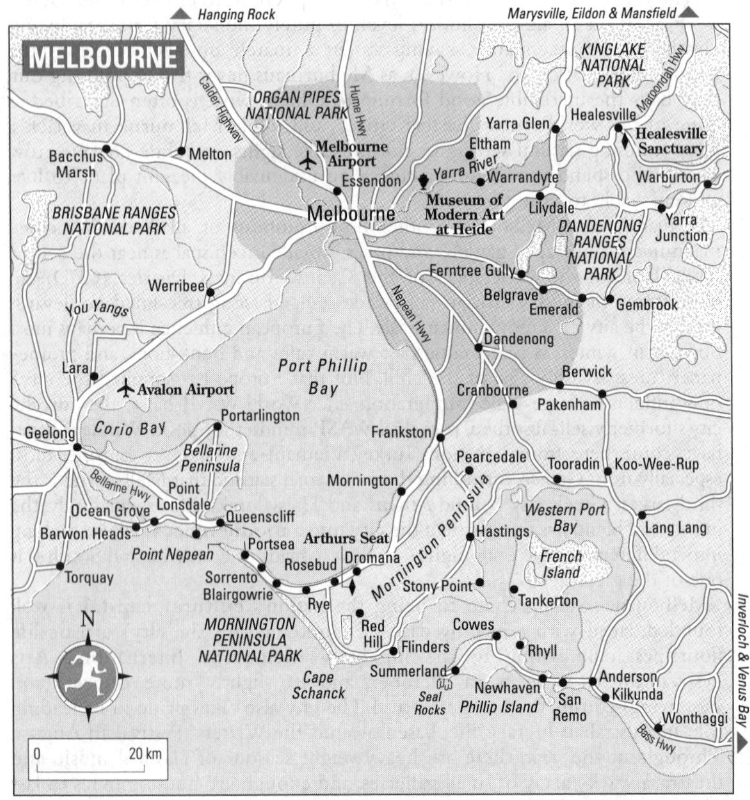

Arrival and information

Melbourne's Tullamarine Airport is 22km northwest of the city; the **Skybus Super Shuttle** (every 15min 6am–9.30pm, every 30min 9.30pm–1am and 5–6am, hourly 1–5am; $15 one way, $24 return, valid one year; ⓣ03/9670 7992; on-line ticket booking ⓦwww.skybus.com.au) will take you to Southern Cross station on Spencer Street on the west side of the city. A complimentary minibus service (Mon–Fri 6am–10pm, Sat & Sun 7.30am–6pm) picks up passengers from the coach terminal and drops them off at hotels in the city centre and the adjacent suburbs of Carlton, East Melbourne and South Melbourne. Travelling time between Melbourne Airport and the coach terminal is about thirty minutes. A taxi from Melbourne Airport costs around $37 to the city centre, $47 to St Kilda. Jetstar Airways, a budget subsidiary of Qantas, operates a limited number of **domestic flights** from **Avalon Airport**, located just off the Princes Freeway, 55km southwest of Melbourne. Transport is provided by **Sunbus** (ⓣ03/9689 6888; $18 one way), which meets all arriving Jetstar flights and drops off passengers at Spencer Street, and takes about 45 minutes, depending on traffic.

Greyhound Australia, V/Line and Firefly buses now all arrive at the **Southern Cross Station Coach Terminal**. Some hostels pick up from Southern Cross Station, as well as from the Tasmanian **ferry terminal** located about 4km southwest of the city centre at Station Pier in Port Melbourne. The terminal is served by the #109 **tram** to Collins Street in the CBD.

Information

The **Melbourne Visitor Centre**, housed underneath Federation Square, directly opposite Flinders Street (daily 9am–6pm; ⓣ03/9658 9658, ⓦwww.thatsmelbourne.com.au), has brochures and maps galore about Melbourne and the rest of the state, in particular the pocket-sized *Melbourne Walks* series is probably the most useful: each one describes a themed, self-guided walk (1hr 30min–2hr 30min) around the city and has a good reference map. There's also information on public transport and major events, and a tour and accommodation booking service (same hours; ⓣ03/9650 3663). Available at the centre is the discount sightseeing card, See Melbourne & Beyond Smartvisit Card (also sold online at ⓦwww.seemelbournecard.com), which provides free admission to more than fifty attractions in and around Melbourne and costs $65 for one day, $99 for two days, $129 for three days and $199 for seven days. It's well worth the expense if you intend doing some serious sightseeing. A free **Greeter Service** matches up visitors with local volunteers for half a day (starting at 10am), giving them an unparalleled insider's view of the city – book at least three days in advance (ⓣ03/9658 9658, ⓔgreeter@melbourne.vic.gov.au). **Information Victoria**, at 356 Collins St (Mon–Fri 8.30am–5pm; ⓣ1300 366 356), has books and other publications on topics related to the state as well as the city's largest range of local maps; it also has a notice board of city events. **Tourism Victoria** (daily 8am–6pm; ⓣ13 28 42, ⓦwww.visitvictoria.com) is a phone and Internet service providing information on attractions, accommodation and upcoming events.

Volunteers in red uniforms – so-called **City Ambassadors** – roam the CBD between Elizabeth, Russell, La Trobe and Flinders streets (Mon–Fri 10am–4pm, Sat 11am–2pm). They'll try to assist with all kinds of tourist enquiries, and at the very least can point you in the right direction. There's also a **Visitor Information Booth** in the middle of Bourke Street Mall (Mon–Sat 9am–5pm, Sun 10am–5pm). Alternative sources of information include the **DSE Information Centre**, 8 Nicholson St, East Melbourne, run by the Department of Sustainability and Environment (Mon–Fri 8.30am–5.30pm; ⓣ03/9637 8325,

Ⓦwww.dse.vic.gov.au), and **Parks Victoria** (phone and Internet information service only: Ⓣ13 19 63, Ⓦwww.parkweb.vic.gov.au). Both dispense information about national parks and conservation areas in Victoria. Another good resource is the **National Trust** office, Tasma Terrace, 6 Parliament Place (Mon–Fri 9am–5pm; Ⓣ03/9654 4711, Ⓦwww.nattrust.com.au), which sells several historical walking-tour guides. *Melway*, available from all newsagents, is the city's best **street directory** and a good online option can be found at Ⓦwww.zoomin.com.au.

City transport

Melbourne has an efficient public-transport system of trams, trains and buses, called **Metlink**. Unless you're going on a day-trip to the outer suburbs, you can get anywhere you need to, including St Kilda and Williamstown, on **a zone 1 ticket** ($3.20); this is valid for two hours (or all evening if bought after 7pm) and can be used for multiple trips on trams, buses and trains within zone 1. A **day-ticket** ($6.10 for zone 1; $9.70 for zones 1 and 2; $12.60 for zones 1–3) is better value if you're making a few trips in zone 1, or if you are planning a trip to the outer suburbs. For longer stays, a **weekly ticket** ($26.70 for zone 1; $45.20 for zones 1 and 2; $54 for zones 1–3) is an even better bargain. On Sundays, the Sunday Saver Metcard (just $2.50) entitles the bearer to travel on zones 1, 2 and 3 for the entire day, but tickets must be purchased at ticket windows at stations and are not available through ticket machines. The **City Saver Metcard** ($2.30) is valid for a single trip on a tram or bus or between two stations in the City Saver area (the CBD and adjacent areas). Transfers between bus, tram and train are not possible with this card.

You'll need to **validate** your ticket by machine every time you board a new vehicle. Two-hour and day-tickets are available from **vending machines** on board trams and at train stations. Those on trams accept coins only, but change is given. You can't buy tickets from the tram driver. The reverse applies on buses: there are no vending machines, so buy your ticket from the driver (exact change preferred). Major train stations have staffed ticket offices; other stations are equipped with coins-only vending machines. You can also buy Met Tickets and get travel advice at the Melbourne Visitor Centre at Federation Square, the MetShop at the Melbourne Town Hall on the corner of Swanston and Little

Melbourne's vintage trams

Some of Melbourne's trams are vintage wooden vehicles dating back as far as the 1930s (though none is quite as old as the system, which dates from 1885). Vintage **City Circle trams** (free) run in a loop along Flinders, Spring, Nicholson, La Trobe and Spencer streets (daily except Christmas Day and Good Friday every 10min 10am–6pm, Nov–March Thurs–Sat until 9pm). The **Colonial Tramcar Restaurant** (Ⓣ03/9696 4000, Ⓦwww.tramrestaurant.com.au) is a converted 1927 tram offering traditional silver- and white-linen restaurant service as you trundle around Melbourne. The service starts at Normanby Road near the Crown Casino, South Melbourne; the restaurant (nonsmoking) offers a three-course early dinner (daily 5.45–7.15pm; $66) and a five-course dinner (daily 8.35–11.30pm; $110 Fri & Sat, $99 Mon–Thurs & Sun), plus a four-course lunch (daily 1–3pm; $71.50). All drinks are included. You'll need to reserve at least two to three weeks ahead, or up to three or four months in advance for Friday and Saturday evenings

Collins streets, and at other shops, including most newsagents, a few milk bars and pharmacies – look for the flag with the Metcard logo.

Train and tram services operate Monday to Saturday from 5am until midnight, and Sunday from 8am until 11pm, supplemented in the early hours of Saturday and Sunday by **NightRider buses** (every hour 12.30–4.30am; $6), which head from the City Square (in front of the *Westin Hotel* on Swanston Street to the outer suburbs of Frankston, Dandenong, Belgrave, Lilydale, Eltham, Epping, Craigieburn, St Albans, Werribee and Melton ($8.20), more or less in the same direction as the suburban train routes. Each bus has an onboard mobile phone, on which the driver can book a taxi to meet you at a bus stop (free call), or you can call a friend ($1) to meet you. The buses also operate during big events such as New Year's Eve and the Melbourne Grand Prix. For further information, call metlink (daily 6am–10pm; ⓣ13 16 38). For a range of public-transport information including timetables and disability services, visit ⓦwww.metlinkmelbourne.com.au.

Trams

Melbourne's **trams** give the city a distinctive character and provide a pleasant, environmentally friendly way of getting around: the **City Circle** (see box, opposite) is particularly convenient, and free. Trams run down the centre of the road, and stops are signposted (the "Central Melbourne" map, overleaf shows the main routes in the centre); they often have central islands where you can wait: remember to keep an eye out for trams when crossing the road. Some trams can be boarded only at the front; others also have access via middle and rear doors.

Trains

Trains are the fastest way to reach distant suburbs. An underground loop system feeding into seventeen suburban lines connects the city centre's five train stations: **Southern Cross**, which also serves as the station for interstate and country trains; **Flagstaff**, on the corner of La Trobe and William streets; **Melbourne Central**, on the corner of Swanston and La Trobe streets; **Parliament**, on Spring Street; and **Flinders Street**, the main suburban station. Bikes

Driving and cycling in Melbourne

Driving in Melbourne requires some care, mainly because of the trams. You can overtake a tram only on the left and must stop and wait behind it while passengers get on and off, as they step directly into the road (though there's no need to stop if there's a central pedestrian island). A peculiar rule has developed to accommodate trams at major intersections in the city centre: when turning right, you pull over to the left-hand lane and wait for the lights to change to amber before turning – a so-called "hook turn". Signs overhead indicate when this rule applies.

Cyclists should also watch out for tram lines – tyres can easily get wedged in them. This apart, Melbourne is perfect for cycling and you'll be in good company as it's a popular way of getting around. The friendly staff at **Bicycle Victoria** on Level 10, 446 Collins St (Mon–Fri 9am–5pm; ⓣ03/8636 8888), can assist with practical information; their website ⓦwww.bv.com.au has a list of organized bike-rides in Victoria and interstate. The useful *Discovering Victoria's Bike Paths* ($24.95) is available at Bicycle Victoria or at newsagents. See "Listings", p.867, for **bike rental**. A good way of getting a handle on Melbourne is joining one of the guided, 3.5-hour cycling tours run by **Real Melbourne Bike Tours** (ⓣ0417 339 203, ⓦwww.byohouse.com.au/biketours; $80 everything included; bookings necessary). They operate daily on demand and include a refreshment stop for coffee and cake.

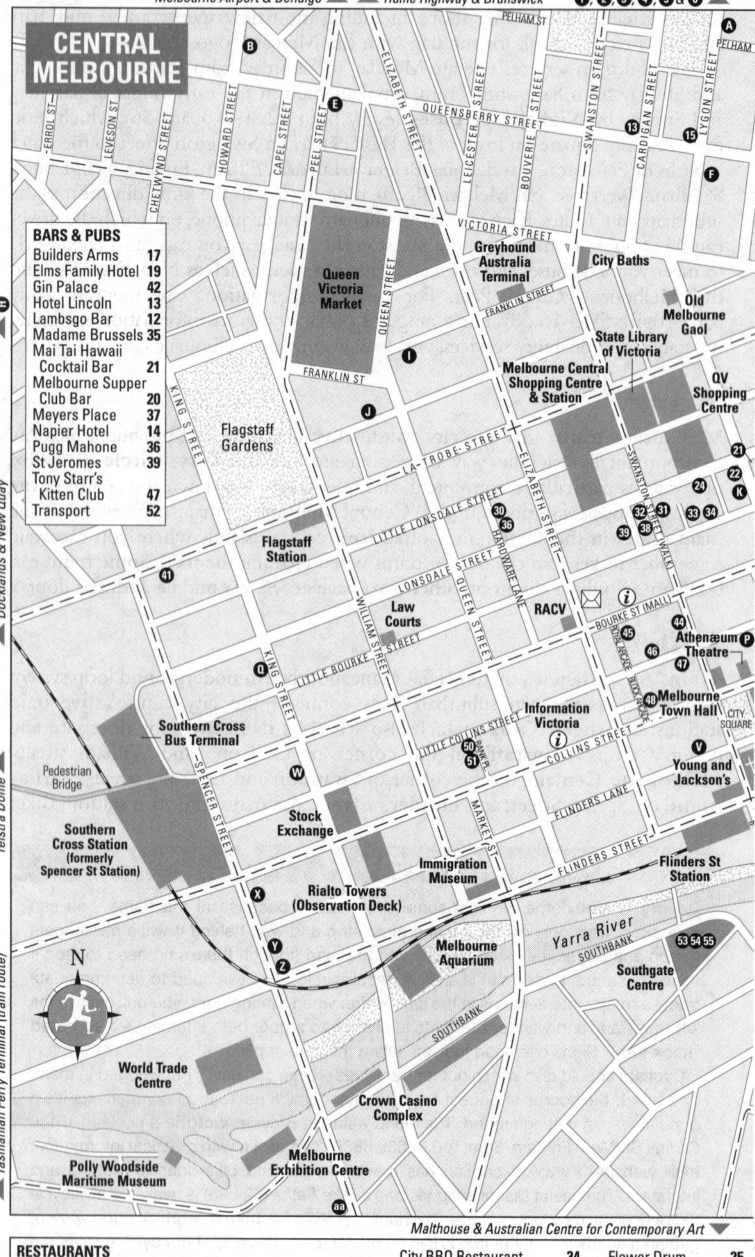

RESTAURANTS

Arcadia	16	Blue Train Café	54	City BBQ Restaurant	34	Flower Drum	25
Babka Bakery Cafe	7	Brunetti	3	Cookie	31	Gigi Sushi Bar	32
Bar Lourinha	40	Camy Shanghai Dumpling and Noodle Restaurant	33	Crossways Food for Life	44	Grossi Florentino	27
BearBrass	53	China Bar	22	eat drink bento	30	Hofbrauhaus	26
Big Harvest	1			Empress of China	23	Jimmy Watson's	4
				ezard at the Adelphi	49	Ladro	18

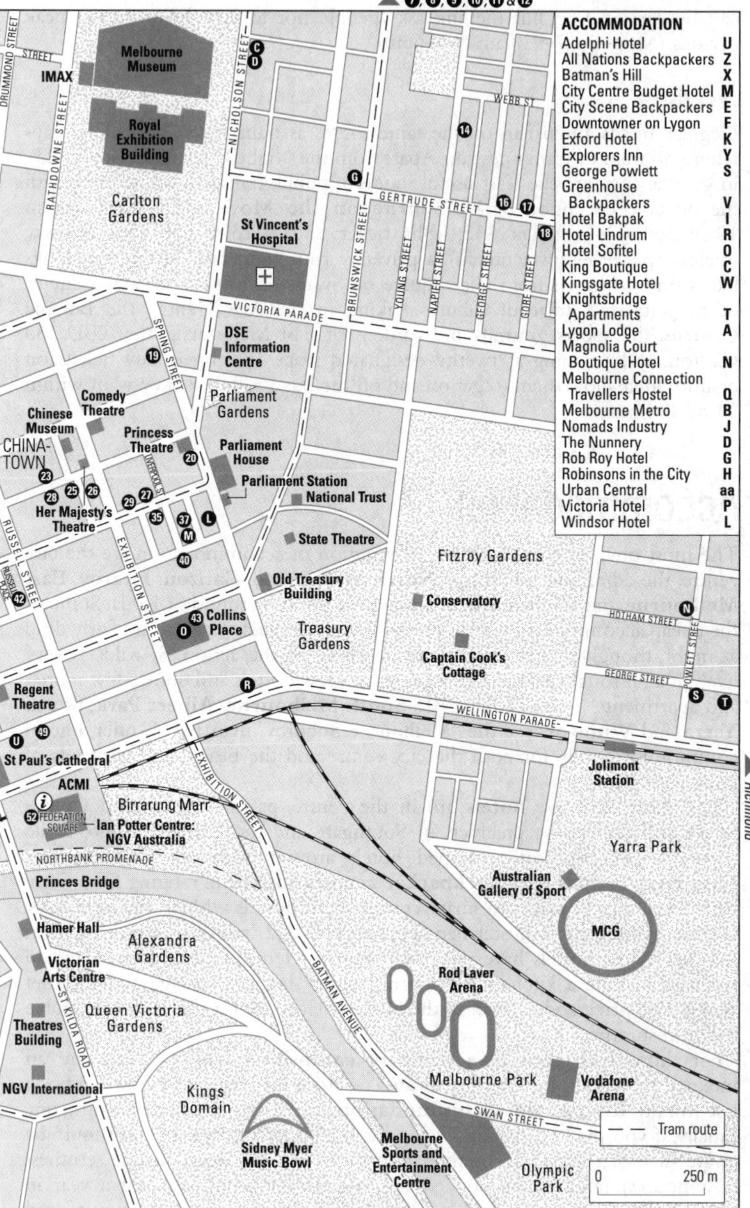

Shrine of Remembrance, Royal Botanic Gardens, Government House & Observatory Gate

Lambs on Brunswick	11	Syracuse	51	Vue De Monde	50	**CAFÉS**			
Mario's	8	Thai Thani	9	Walter's Wine Bar	55	Cafe La	43	Medallion Cafe & Cakes	24
Mekong	38	Three, One, Two	2	William Angliss College	41	Hopetoun Tea Rooms	48	Pellegrini's Espresso Bar	29
Shakahari	5	Tiamo 1	6			Koko Black Shop	45		
Shark Fin House	28	Toto's Pizza House	15			Laurent Patisserie	46		
		The Vegie Bar	10						

can be carried free, but metlink asks people not to take bikes during peak periods (Mon–Fri 7–9.30am & 4–6pm).

Buses

Regular **buses** often run on the same routes as trams, as well as filling gaps where no train or tram lines run. Apart from the NightRider buses (see p.823), in general they are the least useful mode of public transport for visitors, with the possible exception of **Melbourne on the Move** (daily every 30min 10am–3pm; 24hr ticket $32; 48hr ticket $50; ⓣ1300 558 686, ⓦwww.melbourneonthemove.com.au), a privately run "tram bus" (a bus that looks like a tram). It starts from City Square on Swanston Street and does a circuit of the city and adjacent suburbs, taking in the Arts Centre, the Botanic Gardens, the sports grounds and gardens of East Melbourne, the CBD and Carlton, and stopping at twenty designated stops. Passengers buy tickets on board which allow them to get on and off the bus as often as they want within 24 or 48 hours.

Accommodation

The most obvious areas with a concentration of accommodation are the city centre, the adjoining suburbs of **North Melbourne**, **Carlton**, **Fitzroy**, **East Melbourne** and **Richmond**, and down by the bay around St Kilda. Some of the cheap accommodation areas on the fringes of the city centre are fairly dead at night, though they're within easy reach of all the action. St Kilda is very lively, if a bit rough around the edges, with a few hostels and quite a few motels and apartments. South of the CBD, **South Melbourne**, **Albert Park**, **South Yarra** and **Windsor** (see the "Melbourne Suburbs" map, p.844) offer a good compromise, handy for both the city centre and the beach, and with lots of good eating options.

The most exclusive **hotels** are in the centre, particularly around Collins Street and the leisure precincts of Southgate and the Crown Casino, while there's a collection of revamped hotels around Southern Cross Station. Melbourne has plenty of **backpacker accommodation**, ranging from fairly basic, even scruffy places to smart, custom-built hostels with all the mod cons. During winter, most hostel beds cost around $22, rising to around $28 in summer. Most hostels have separate dorms for females on request. Standard facilities include a kitchen, TV room, laundry, luggage storage and Internet access. The price codes given in the listings below are for the cheapest double room in summer.

For those with their own transport, **campsite** cabins and vans are an inexpensive option but they are located far from the city centre. You can book last-minute **discounted accommodation** in the city at ⓦwww.wotif.com. Finally, if you plan on staying during the big **sporting events** you should be aware that virtually all accommodation (from five-star hotels to the scruffiest doss houses) tends to be booked out, usually for months, if not a year in advance. This applies particularly to the Australian Open Tennis in January and the Grand Prix (first or second weekend in March); other events and times to avoid or pre-book long in advance are the Melbourne Cup (first Tuesday in November and the preceding weekend) and the AFL Grand Final (second-last Saturday in September).

City centre

Hotels and motels

Adelphi Hotel 187 Flinders Lane ⓣ03/9650 7555, ⓦwww.adelphi.com.au. Stylish hotel with a striking exterior and a sparse, ultramodern interior design that extends to the large guestrooms, all topped with a glass-bottomed pool that looks over the street. ❼

Batman's Hill 623 Collins St ⓣ03/9614 6344, ⓦwww.batmanshill.com. An elegant Edwardian exterior belies a functional and modern interior. The wide range of facilities includes bars, a restaurant and 24hr room service, and it's handy for Southern Cross station, Telstra Dome, Docklands and the Casino Entertainment Complex just south of the river. ❺

Explorers Inn 16 Spencer St ⓣ03/9621 3333 or 1800 816 168, ⓦwww.explorersinn.com.au. Renamed and redecorated medium-price hotel. Its lobby and café-bar decorated in groovy colours front pleasant if somewhat plain en-suite rooms. Internet access. ❺

Hotel Lindrum 26 Flinders St ⓣ03/9668 1199, ⓦwww.hotellindrum.com.au. Named after Australia's most famous billiard-player Walter Lindrum (the billiard room has one of his original tables), this luxurious hotel has a boutique feel about it, attracting those who want more personal attention and service. Rooms are designed with rich wood furnishings and the comfort you would expect for the price. ❼–❽

Hotel Sofitel 25 Collins St ⓣ03/9653 0000 or 1300 656 565, ⓦwww.sofitelmelbourne.com.au. An I.M. Pei–designed hotel, set on the top floors of a fifty-storey building, with marvellous views across Melbourne and surrounds, gloriously comfortable rooms and a good spread of cafés and restaurants, including the airy and reasonably cheap *Cafe La* (see p.852). ❽

Kingsgate Hotel 131 King St ⓣ03/9629 4171 or 1300 734 171, ⓦwww.kingsgatehotel.com.au. Huge, renovated old private hotel. En-suite rooms with colour TV, heating and air-con are good value; there are also inexpensive no-frills budget rooms with shared facilities and a few rooms for small groups or families (up to four beds). Facilities include a laundry, Internet access, a pleasant TV lounge and a bar and café (but no kitchen). Breakfast available. ❸–❹

Robinsons in the City 405 Spencer St West Melbourne ⓣ03/ 9329 2552, ⓦwww.robinsonsinthecity.com.au. Relatively unknown, tiny boutique hotel with just six luxuriously spacious double rooms. Located in a former bakery built in the 1850s, the service is immaculate, giving it a B&B-type feel. Perfect for those looking for a personal touch in the middle of town. ❻–❼

Victoria Hotel 215 Little Collins St ⓣ03/9653 0441 or 1800 331 147, ⓦwww.victoriahotel.com.au. Huge refurbished hotel in an unbeatable central location, with its own café, bar, a pool and sauna, and a wide range of rooms; the cheapest ones have shared facilities. Undercover parking available ($10 per day). ❸–❺

Windsor Hotel 103 Spring St ⓣ03/9633 6000 or 1800 033 100, ⓦwww.thewindsor.com.au. A Melbourne landmark. This luxurious Victorian-era hotel has 180 spacious, lavishly decorated rooms and suites. ❽

Budget hotels and hostels

All Nations Backpackers 2 Spencer St, at the corner of Flinders St ⓣ03/9620 1022 or 1800 222 238, ⓦwww.allnations.com.au. Big, rambling hostel that doesn't look like much from the outside and isn't much better inside, though an in-house employment agency and a great bar with free beer on arrival seem to keep the guests happy. There's 24hr reception and good security. Pick-up from airports 5.15–1.30am; use courtesy phone at the airport. Rates include a light breakfast. Dorms (4–10 beds) $25–30, rooms ❹

City Centre Budget Hotel 22–30 Little Collins St ⓣ03/9654 5401, ⓦwww.citycentrebudgethotel.com.au. Good option for those on a budget that want their own rooms (shared bathrooms), but still have the facilities a hostel offers. The timber-floored rooms are nicely designed, and there is a great rooftop garden. Free wireless Internet and full tour-booking service is also available. ❹

Exford Hotel 199 Russell St ⓣ03/9663 2697, ⓦwww.exfordhotel.com.au. Secure, clean and good-value hostel set in an extremely central position in the middle of Chinatown above a refurbished pub, with friendly and helpful staff and the usual amenities, plus a tiny sundeck with BBQ. Accommodation is in two- to four-bed dorms, twins and doubles. Dorms $22–26, rooms ❸

Greenhouse Backpackers 228 Flinders Lane ⓣ03/9639 6400 or 1800 249 207, ⓦwww.friendlygroup.com.au. Clean and very friendly place in a superb sixth-floor location amidst the characterful alleys and laneways of Melbourne's CBD. Sleeping is in spacious dorms (4–6 beds), or in singles and doubles. The big kitchen is well equipped with lots of cookers and plenty of storage space. In addition, there's a lounge, a big TV room, pool table, and a pleasant rooftop garden with

BBQ. Staff can assist with finding work. A travel desk is located on the ground floor. Rates include breakfast and 30min Internet access per day. Dorms $27–30, rooms ❸

Hotel Bakpak 167 Franklin St ⓣ03/9329 7525 or 1800 645 200, ⓦwww.bakpakgroup.com. Around six hundred beds in a converted former school building brightened up with colour-coordinated paintwork, carpets and polished timber floors. In-house facilities include an employment agency, travel shop, café, cellar bar and a small cinema with free screenings plus Internet access. All dorms (4–12 beds) have fans and lockers; female dorms available on request. There are also some spartan singles and doubles. Free pick-ups from bus terminals and airport between 6am and 8pm. Rates include light breakfast. Dorms $24–30, rooms ❸

Melbourne Connection Travellers Hostel 205 King St ⓣ03/9642 4464, ⓦwww.melbourneconnection.com. Convenient location close to Southern Cross station and Queen Victoria Market. A small, clean hostel – the polished wooden floor-boards in the corridor are a nice touch – with TV-lounge and Internet room in the basement and a smallish but well-equipped kitchen on the ground floor. Rates include breakfast. Dorms (❹–❽ beds) $24–27, rooms ❸

Nomads Industry 196 A'Beckett St ⓣ03/9328 4383, ⓦwww.nomadsindustry.com. One of the new breed of "flashbacker" hostels, this spotless and incredibly social place has an array of decent-sized rooms (some en suite) and very helpful staff. Facilities include kitchen, laundry, rooftop garden and a great bar downstairs with excellent happy hours, beer garden and pool table which is just as popular with the locals. Free dinner each night is also included in the price. Dorms $24–32, rooms ❹

Urban Central 334 City Rd Southbank ⓣ03/9693 3700, ⓦwww.urbancentral.com.au. Huge, recently built hostel on the city's edge, with singles, doubles and four-bed dorms. Can be a bit impersonal due to the size but it is clean, well managed, and has a good tour information desk and funky bar downstairs. Price includes free daily breakfast and rice/pasta for meals. Free airport pick-up if staying for more than three nights. Dorms $27, rooms ❹

North Melbourne, Carlton and Fitzroy

City Scene Backpackers 361 Queensberry St ⓣ03/9348 9525, ⓦwww.cityscene.com.au. Small friendly hostel next to Melbourne's premier soccer pub; the rooms and dorms (4 beds) come with heating and air-con; rates include breakfast. Ring for airport pick-up. Dorms $19, rooms ❷

Downtowner on Lygon 66 Lygon St, Carlton ⓣ03/9663 5555 or 1800 800 130, ⓦwww.downtowner.com.au. Attractively refurbished rooms with all mod cons (some with spa) in the heart of Carlton. Undercover parking. ❻

King Boutique 122 Nicholson St, Fitzroy ⓣ03/9417 1113, ⓦwww.kingaccomm.com.au. This heritage-listed mansion built in 1867 is a prime example of the wealth that existed during the goldrush period. The timber-floored, three double rooms are stylishly designed yet still stay true to the elegance of the time. A real gem ideally positioned on the border of Fitzroy and Carlton. ❺–❻

Lygon Lodge 220 Lygon St, Carlton ⓣ03/9663 6633, ⓦwww.lygonlodge.com.au. Good motel in central Carlton with attractive rooms, some with small kitchenette. Undercover car parking. ❺

Melbourne Metro YHA 78 Howard St, off Victoria St ⓣ03/9329 8599, ⓦwww.yha.com.au. An easy ten-minute walk from the bus terminal, this huge modern hostel – really more like a smart hotel – has family, double/twin and single rooms, with or without en suite, plus dorms (4–8 beds), and a host of other amenities: 24hr kitchen, rooftop garden with BBQ, Internet lounge, bicycle hire, car parking, plus a licensed cafeteria, currency exchange and an in-house travel agent. Skybus drops off and picks up here every half-hour. Dorms $26–30, rooms ❸

The Nunnery 116 Nicholson St, Fitzroy ⓣ03/9419 8637 or 1800 032 635, ⓦwww.nunnery.com.au; take #96 tram from Bourke St. The hostel section here has rather crammed dorms (4–12 beds), but the atmosphere is busy and friendly; there's also a big, cosy TV lounge, a kitchen and Internet access. The much more spacious guesthouse section next door has private rooms with shared facilities, plus a kitchen and lounge. Brunswick Street cafés and pubs are close to hand. Breakfast included. Dorms $26–30, hostel rooms ❸–❹, guesthouse rooms ❺

Rob Roy Hotel 51 Brunswick St, Fitzroy ⓣ03/9419 7180, ⓦwww.therobroyhotel.com.au. The quintessential Fitzroy experience. *Rob Roy Hotel* is one the best live-music venues in Melbourne, and the small hostel upstairs is the prime place to stay to experience the nearby nightlife. Popular with touring bands, the rooms are clean yet small, and the comfy lounge is a prime place to meet other travellers. Naturally it can get a bit noisy at night, being above a band room. Dorms $25, rooms ❸

East Melbourne

George Powlett Powlett St, cnr George St ⓣ03/9419 9488, ⓦwww.georgepowlett.com.au. Motel-style units off two central courtyards in a central location. Kitchenette with microwave and fridge, plus parking available. ❹

Knightsbridge Apartments 101 George St ⓣ03/9419 1333, ⓦwww.knightsbridgeapartments.com.au. Bright, serviced self-catering studio and two-bedroom apartments 1km from the centre, on a quiet street running off the east side of Fitzroy Gardens. Laundry and off-street parking. Excellent value. ❺

Magnolia Court Boutique Hotel 101 Powlett St ⓣ03/9419 4222, ⓦwww.magnolia-court.com.au. Elegant hotel in a quiet street, but within walking distance of Fitzroy Gardens, the CBD, MCG and Melbourne Park. Very tastefully furnished rooms with all facilities in two older, lovingly restored buildings as well as a new annexe. Breakfast available. ❺–❼

Richmond

Amora Hotel Riverwalk 649 Bridge Rd ⓣ03/9246 1200, ⓦwww.amorahotels.com.au. Close to the city, but a world away when you are looking at the peaceful rustic setting of the Yarra River from the riverview rooms. Has good-value packages which include full buffet breakfasts. ❺–❻

Freeman Lodge 153 Hoddle St ⓣ03/8430 2978, ⓦwww.freemanlodge.com.au. Renovated, clean budget guesthouse that has a funky sharehouse feel, with well-equipped rooms and dorms (maximum 4 beds) for a very low price. It's just around the corner from West Richmond station, within walking distance of Bridge Rd. Dorms $20, rooms ❷

Richmond Hill Hotel 353 Church St (between Bridge Rd and Swan St) ⓣ03/9428 6501 or 1800 801 618, ⓦwww.richmondhillhotel.com.au. Set in a stately Victorian mansion in a pretty garden, with spacious and cosy dining and sitting rooms. The guesthouse section offers B&B rooms with en-suite or shared facilities; the budget section has small, very clean dorms and good-value singles and twins (bunks), all with shared facilities and a kitchen. Tram #75 or #48 from Spencer St or Flinders St. Dorms $24, budget rooms ❸, guest-house rooms ❹–❺

Albert Park, Middle Park, South Yarra and Windsor

The Beach Accommodation 97 Beaconsfield Parade, Albert Park ⓣ03/9690 4642, ⓦwww.thebeachaccommodation.com.au. Pleasant dorms, twins and doubles above a pub, everything completely refurbished, in a hard-to-beat location opposite a tram stop, overlooking the beach and handy for the Tasmanian ferry. Price includes all-you-can-eat breakfast. Take tram #1 from Swanston St to South Melbourne Beach. Dorms from $21, rooms ❷–❸

Chapel Street Backpackers 22 Chapel St, Windsor ⓣ03/9533 6855, ⓦwww.csbackpackers.com.au. Friendly hostel at the southern, quieter end of Chapel St, with very clean and comfy en-suite dorms (4–6 beds) and doubles. Small outdoor courtyard with BBQ. Opposite Windsor station (Sandringham line). Continental breakfast included. Dorms $28, rooms ❷–❸

College Lawn Hotel 36 Greville St, Windsor ⓣ03/9510 6057, ⓦwww.collegelawnhotel.com.au. Simple, good-value backpacker accommodation above a great pub at the less-noisy end of Greville Street. Small kitchen. Dorms $18, rooms ❸

The Como 630 Chapel St, South Yarra ⓣ03/9825 2222 or 1800 033 400. Very upmarket accommodation with spacious suites in unusually bold colours and with all the amenities you'd expect in a five-star hotel, including indoor heated pool, sauna, spa, gym, valet parking, restaurant and a jazz bar. ❽

Gunn Island Brew Bar 102 Canterbury Rd, cnr Armstrong St, Middle Park ⓣ03/9690 1882, ⓦwww.gunnisland.com.au. Inexpensive dorms and simple but pleasant rooms with shared facilities above a refurbished pub-cum-brewery, in a great location between beach and city. Take tram #96 from Spencer St. Close to the Aquatic Centre, beach, and lots of restaurants and delis. Dorms $20, rooms ❷

St Kilda

Annies B&B 93 Park St, St Kilda West ⓣ03/9534 8705, ⓦwww.anniesbedandbreakfast.com.au. Small, family-run B&B in a renovated Edwardian house with a courtyard garden and BBQ facilities. Guests can use the front lounge with an open fireplace and TV/DVD player. Rooms have en-suite or private bathroom. ❺

Gay and lesbian accommodation

For further accommodation possibilities other than those listed below, ring Gay Share (☎03/9691 2290), which arranges house shares for gays and lesbians, or visit Ⓦwww.gayshare.com.au.

169 Drummond Street 169 Drummond St, Carlton ☎03/9663 3081, Ⓦwww.169drummond.com.au. Nonsmoking B&B in a refurbished Victorian terrace house with en-suite rooms. ❺

California Motel 138 Barkers Rd, Hawthorn ☎03/9818 0281 or 1800 331 166, Ⓦwww.californiamotel.com.au. Gay-friendly motel accommodation close to the city; parking available. Take tram #109 or #42 from Collins St. ❼

Heathville House 171 Aitken St, Williamstown ☎03/9397 5959, Ⓔheath@jeack.com.au. B&B in a pretty weatherboard house. Nonsmoking. ❻

Laird Hotel 149 Gipps St, Abbotsford ☎03/9417 2109, Ⓦwww.lairdhotel.com. Good-value rustic rooms and a self-contained cottage situated close to everything in one of Melbourne's oldest hotels (1847). Rooms ❹–❺, cottage ❻

Opium Den 176 Hoddle St, Collingwood ☎03/9417 2696, Ⓦwww.opiumden.com.au. Small nightspot has good-value, pub-style rooms with a touch of velvet opulence. Shared bathrooms. Price includes breakfast. ❸

Base 17 Carlisle St, St Kilda ☎03/8598 6222, Ⓦwww.basebackpackers.com. A swish, custom-built hostel with minimalist decor, bright colours and unusual features, such as the sunken fish-tank spanning the breezy common-room (behind the reception area) like a covered stream. All dorms (great girls-only dorms) and rooms are en suite, scrupulously clean, with air-con and drawers big enough to accommodate a backpack underneath the dorm beds. Other facilities include fast Internet access, a travel desk and a pleasant bar for drinks, budget meals and entertainment. Dorms $24–32, rooms ❷

Boutique Hotel Tolarno 42 Fitzroy St ☎03/9537 0200, Ⓦwww.hoteltolarno.com.au. Pleasant, small and incredibly funky hotel in a restored building located right in the thick of things. Rooms, with en-suite bathrooms, polished-timber floors and all mod cons, are good value. ❺

Cooee on St Kilda 333 St Kilda Rd ☎03/9537 3777, Ⓦwww.cooeeonstkilda.com. Recently opened hostel that has good, clean facilities, and a host of organized activities. The super large kitchen and courtyard is where travellers tend to swap stories. Has good-value BBQ dinners (Saturday) and roasts (Sunday) for $5. Free airport pick-up when staying over 3 nights. Dorms $24–$30, rooms ❹

Easystay Bayside 63 Fitzroy St ☎03/9525 3833 or 1300 301 730, Ⓦwww.easystay.com.au. Good, secure budget motel well situated for all the action and within a ten-minute walk of the beach. If you want quiet, book one of the units facing the car park out the back (which is locked at night). ❹

The Prince 2 Acland St ☎03/9536 1111, Ⓦwww.theprince.com.au. This boutique hotel is one of Melbourne's most elegant places to lay your head. The minimalistic bedrooms come with TVs and DVD players, Bose stereo radios, and a data connection for modem and fax. Other facilities include a day-spa and relaxation centre, the elegant *Circa* restaurant (see p.857), the *Mink Bar* (see p.861), and a club/band room. ❽

Ritz Backpackers 169B Fitzroy St ☎03/9525 3501, Ⓦwww.ritzbackpackers.com. If you like beer and continuously love to party, then this is the place for you. Ideally located in the heart of Fitzroy St (right next door to a popular pub), the rooms are simple and not as fancy as others, but most come for the social scene. Has a ladies-only section with private kitchen and bathroom for added privacy, and free pancake breakfast each morning which can help the hangovers. Dorms from $19, rooms ❷

Camping and caravan parks

There are no campsites anywhere close to the centre; the nearest is the *Melbourne Big 4 Holiday Park*.

Crystal Brook Holiday Centre Cnr Anderson's Creek and Warrandyte roads, East Doncaster ⓣ03/9844 3637, ⓦwww.crystalbrook.net.au. Modern campsite and holiday park with tennis courts and a pool, 21km northeast of the city centre (20min via the Eastern Freeway). On-site vans and cabins ❸–❹

Melbourne Big 4 Holiday Park 265 Elizabeth St, Coburg East ⓣ03/9354 3533 or 1800 802 678, ⓦwww.melbournebig4holidaypark.com.au. Shady park 10km north of the city, with kitchen and a swimming pool. Take bus #526 to the city (daytime only, no service Sun). Cabins ❸

The City

Melbourne is a city of few sights but plenty of lifestyle, and you'll get to know the city just as well by sitting over a coffee or strolling in the park as by traipsing around museums or attractions. At the heart of the city lies the **Central Business District (CBD)**, bounded by La Trobe, Spring, Flinders and Spencer streets, dotted with fine public buildings and lots of shops. Sights include the ghoulish **Old Melbourne Gaol**, just north of La Trobe Street, and the Immigration Museum in the Old Customs House, dedicated to Victoria's immigration history. The CBD is surrounded by gardens on all sides (save the downtown west): few cities have so much green space so close to the centre. To the north of the CBD a wander through lively, century-old **Queen Victoria Market** will repay both serious shoppers and people-watchers, while the **Melbourne Museum** in tranquil Carlton Gardens draws on the latest technology to give an insight into Australia's flora, fauna and culture. In the east, the CBD rubs up against Eastern Hill, home to **Parliament House** and other government buildings as well as the landscaped **Fitzroy Gardens**, from where it's a short walk to the venerable **Melbourne Cricket Ground (MCG)**, a must for sports fans.

Bordering the south side of the CBD, the muddy and, in former decades much-maligned **Yarra River** lies at the centre of the massive developments which have transformed the face of the city, with new high-rises still popping up like mushrooms. The shift towards the Yarra River kicked off in the mid-1990s with the waterfront development of **Southgate**, **Crown Casino** and the **Melbourne Exhibition Centre**. Federation Square on the north bank of the Yarra River opposite Flinders Street station is considered the centre of the city; its adjacent park, Birrarung Marr, links Federation Square with the sports arenas further east. Continuing south of the river, the **Victorian Arts Centre** forms a cultural strip on one side of St Kilda Road, while on the other, Government House and the impressive Shrine of Remembrance front the soothing **Royal Botanic Gardens**.

Federation Square and around

The huge, orange-and-brown **Flinders Street station**, the city's main suburban railway station, lies sandwiched between the southern edge of the CBD and the Yarra. "Under the clocks" – its entrance with a row of clocks detailing the times of all train departures – is still a traditional Melbourne meeting place. This famous old city landmark is faced by **Federation Square** (or "Fed Square", as it's generally known), which occupies an entire block between Flinders Street and the Yarra River, and provides Melbourne with a single, central unifying focus it had always previously lacked. It has become a popular after-work drinking spot, with the **Plaza** at its core, and it is here crowds gather to check out one of the many events staged throughout the month, including short art films, live music and dance parties. Rising up from St Kilda Road in a gentle incline, the Plaza narrows into a horseshoe-shape where it is hemmed in by buildings including the Ian Potter Centre, one of Melbourne's most interesting art museums (see p.832), and the Alfred Deakin Building, which houses the Australian Centre for the Moving Image; there are also numerous cafés and restaurants. The underground Melbourne Visitor Centre (see "Information", p.821) is located at the north-western end of the Plaza, directly across from Flinders Street station.

On the north side of the Plaza, the **Australian Centre for the Moving Image** (daily 10am–6pm; free; Ⓦwww.acmi.net.au) is devoted to exploring the moving image in all its forms: film, television, games, art and new media. Worth checking out is the Screen Gallery, an underground exhibition space spanning the entire length of Federation Square, and featuring changing exhibitions of screen-based art; and Memory Grid on the ground floor, which displays film work by independent filmmakers, students and participants in ACMI workshops (daily 10am–6pm; free). Two state-of-the-art cinemas screen themed programmes and host film festivals and events. Group tours can be arranged and give a lot of background information on architectural and technological aspects of ACMI and Federation Square (by appointment; $12; Ⓣ03/8663 2200, Ⓔtours@acmi.net.au).

Ian Potter Centre: NGV Australia

Walk from Flinders Street through the **Atrium** – a unique passageway of glass, steel and zinc – or from the Plaza through the similarly narrow **Crossbar** to reach the home of the National Gallery of Victoria's collection of Australian art, the **Ian Potter Centre: NGV Australia** (Tues-Thurs 10am–5pm, Fri 10am–9pm, Sat & Sun 10am–6pm; free, except for special exhibitions; Ⓦwww.ngv.vic.gov.au), named in honour of Sir Ian Potter (1902–94), a local financier, philanthropist and patron of the arts. Occupying three floors, the centre showcases one of the best collections of Australian art in the country, with some seventy thousand works, of which about 1800 are usually on display (exhibits are rotated regularly). Traditional and contemporary indigenous art is displayed in four galleries on the ground floor; historic and modern Australian collections are housed on the second floor; while the galleries on the third floor are reserved for special temporary exhibitions. The artworks are complemented by interactive videos, which feature an overview of artists' works, with biographies and interviews.

The building itself is as much a work of art as its exhibits, constructed from two overlapping wings forming a slightly crooked X and offering constantly shifting views, with glimpses of the Yarra and the parklands through the glass walls in the southern part of the building. The best way to get a handle on the collection, as well as the building, is to participate in a **free guided tour** (daily at 11am and 2pm).

Galleries 1–4 on the ground floor give an excellent overview of the art produced in Australia's **indigenous communities**, showcasing works in both traditional and contemporary styles. Traditional art is represented by carved and painted figures from Maningrida, masks from Torres Straits Islands, Pukumani poles from the Tiwi Islands north of Darwin, the Wandjina paintings from the north of Western Australia and bark paintings from Yirrkala and other places in Arnhem Land. One of the highlights is undoubtedly *Big Yam Dreaming* (1995), an enormous canvas by Emily Kam Kngwarray (c.1910–96) showing tangled, spidery webs of white against a black background, representing the pencil yam that grows along the creek banks at the artist's birthplace northeast of Alice Springs. In her brief career – she didn't take up painting until she was in her mid-70s – Emily produced a staggering three thousand-plus works, transcending the Western Desert–style dot paintings and developing a uniquely personal style, which, seemingly abstract and vibrantly coloured, is sometimes reminiscent of late Monet or Jackson Pollock.

On the second floor, galleries 5–11 contain paintings, sculptures, drawings, photographs and decorative arts from the mid-nineteenth century to the 1980s displayed in chronological order. One leitmotif is the harsh beauty of the Australian landscape, and (European) peoples' place in it. The early **colonial paintings** – with works by artists such as John Glover, Henry Burn, Frederick McCubbin and Tom Roberts – are particularly interesting, showing European artists struggling to come to terms with an alien land, as well as offering pictorial records of the growth of new cities and the lives of immigrants and pioneers.

Highlights of the twentieth-century collection include paintings by Albert Tucker, Russell Drysdale, John Perceval and, especially, **Sidney Nolan** (1917–92). Dissatisfied with his Eurocentric art training at Prahran Technical College, Nolan strived to express the Australian experience in a fresh style, exploring new ways of seeing and painting the nation's landscapes, as in his *Wimmera* painting of the 1940s. Nolan also showed a unique interest in the histories of convicts, explorers and bushrangers, resulting in pictures such as his well-known *Ned Kelly* series (1946–48). Another highlight is the gallery dedicated to the overwhelming *Pilbara* collection of Fred Williams, painted in 1979 in the Pilbara region of Western Australia.

The CBD

Seen from across the river, Melbourne's **Central Business District** presents a spectacular modern skyline; on close inspection, however, what you notice are the florid nineteenth-century facades, grandiose survivors of the great days of the goldrushes and after. The former Royal Mint on William Street near Flagstaff Gardens is one of the finest examples, but the main concentrations are south on **Collins Street** and along **Spring Street** to the east. At the centre of the CBD, trams jolt through the busy but somewhat tired-looking **Bourke Street Mall**. A stone's throw from these central thoroughfares, narrow lanes, squares and arcades with quaint, hole-in-the-wall cafés, small restaurants, shops and boutiques add a cosy and intimate feel to the city.

Collins Street

North of Fed Square, **Collins Street** is *the* smart Melbourne address, becoming increasingly exclusive as you climb the hill from the Spencer Street end. At the western end of Collins Street the Stock Exchange squares up to the Rialto Building opposite, an Italianate-Gothic complex built in the 1890s which now houses the luxury *Meridien* hotel. The massive **Rialto Towers** is Melbourne's tallest structure, the reflective surface of its twin towers lending the skyline a bit of oomph. On clear days, especially at around dusk, a trip up to the **Melbourne Observation Deck** on the 55th floor is a must (daily 10am–late; $13.50; Ⓦwww.melbournedeck.com.au). There's a licensed café on the deck, and the admission fee includes the use of binoculars, and a twenty-minute film at the Rialto Vision Theatre at street level that highlights the best parts of Melbourne and Victoria. Nearby, at no. 333, the former **Commercial Bank of Australia** has a particularly sumptuous interior, with a domed banking chamber and awesome barrel-vaulted vestibule which you're welcome to admire during business hours.

Further up Collins Street, beyond the worthwhile diversion down William Street to the Immigration Museum in the Old Customs House (see p.834), shops become the focus of attention. The 1890s **Block Arcade**, at nos. 282–284, is one of Melbourne's grandest shopping centres, its name appropriately taken from the tradition of "doing the block" – promenading around the city's fashionable shopping lanes. Restored in 1988, the L-shaped arcade sports a mosaic-tiled floor, ornate columns and mouldings, and a glass-domed roof. **Australia on Collins** is a modern alternative next door with an upmarket food court and adjacent licensed restaurants and bars in its basement. Beyond this, on the corner of Collins and Swanston streets, the Neoclassical Melbourne **Town Hall** squats on City Square, a beleaguered space that never achieved its intended purpose: to provide Melbourne with a focal point. There is, however, an unmissable landmark on the south side of the square: the splendid **St Paul's Cathedral**, built in the 1880s to a Gothic-Revival design by English architect William Butterfield (who never actually visited Australia). Across from the cathedral on Swanston Street, the restored *Young and Jackson's Hotel* is now protected by the National Trust, not for any intrinsic beauty but as a showcase for a work of art which has become a Melbourne icon: **Chloe**, a full-length nude which now reclines upstairs in *Chloe's Bar and Bistro*. Exhibited by the French painter Jules Lefebvre at the Paris Salon of 1875, it was sent to an international exhibition in Melbourne in 1881 and has been here ever since.

Back on Collins Street, the pompous **Athenaeum Theatre** next to the Town Hall is an important ingredient in the rising streetscape leading up past **Scots Church**, whose Gothic-Revival design merits a peek, though it's famous mainly as the place where Dame Nellie Melba first sang in the choir. Further up, beyond expensive boutiques and souvenir shops, Collins Place and the towering **Hotel Sofitel** next door dominate the upper part of Collins Street. The (male) toilet of *Cafe* on the 35th floor of the *Sofitel* is known as the "loo with a view", but the view from the tables by the window isn't bad, either. Opposite, overshadowed by the *Sofitel* tower, stands one of the last bastions of Australian male chauvinism: the very staid, men-only **Melbourne Club**.

The Immigration Museum

At the corner of Flinders and William streets, just off the western stretch of Collins Street, the **Immigration Museum** (daily 10am–5pm; $6; Ⓦwww.immigration.museum.vic.gov.au) is dedicated to one of the central themes of Australian history. Housed in the beautifully restored Old Customs House, the museum builds a vivid picture of immigration history and personal stories using the spoken word, music, moving images, light effects and interactive screens, evoking the experiences of being a migrant on a square-rigger in the 1840s, a passenger on a steamship at the beginning of the twentieth century, or a postwar refugee from Europe. In the **Tribute Garden**, the outdoor centrepiece of the museum, a film of water flows over polished granite on which are engraved the names of migrants to Victoria, symbolizing the passage over the seas to reach these faraway shores. The names of all the Koorie people living in Victoria prior to white settlement are listed separately at the entrance to the garden.

Bourke Street and Chinatown

Bourke Street Mall extends west from Swanston Street to Elizabeth Street. After a fire gutted most of its interior in 2003, the Melbourne **General Post Office**, an imposing Victorian-era building at the corner of Elizabeth Street and Bourke Street, was restored, and reopened late 2004 as a light and airy shopping complex for high-end designer clothes and upmarket eateries. Running off Bourke Street Mall, the lovely **Royal Arcade** is Melbourne's oldest (1839), paved with black and white marble and lit by huge fanlight windows. A clock on which two two-metre giants, Gog and Magog, strike the hours adds a welcome hint of the grotesque. As you climb the hill east of here, Bourke Street keeps up the interest, with several cafés and bars that put out pavement tables at night – including *Pellegrini's*, Melbourne's first espresso bar and still buzzing – as well as late-opening book and record stores.

North of Bourke Street, and running parallel to it, is Little Bourke Street, with the majestic **Law Courts** by William Street at the western end, and Chinatown in the east between Exhibition and Swanston streets. Australia's oldest continuous Chinese settlement, Melbourne's **Chinatown** began with a few boarding-houses in the 1850s (when the goldrushes attracted Chinese people in droves, many from the Pearl River Delta near Hong Kong) and grew as the gold began to run out and Chinese fortune-seekers headed back to the city. Today the area still has a low-rise, narrow-laned, nineteenth-century character, and it's packed with restaurants and stores. The **Chinese Museum**, in an old warehouse on Cohen Place (daily 10am–5pm; $7.50; Ⓦwww.chinesemuseum.com.au), is concerned particularly with the Chinese role in the foundation and development of Melbourne. The museum organizes the **Chinatown Heritage Walk**, a two-hour guided tour of the building and Chinatown (hours vary depending on bookings; $18 or $34 including lunch; Ⓣ03/9662 2888). The walk requires a minimum of fifteen people, but for one or two people it's still worth ringing as the museum might be able to slot you in with a larger group.

QV and the State Library of Victoria

North of the Chinese Museum rises the latest bulk development to change the structure and feel of the CBD: **QV** (Queen Victoria Village), which takes in almost the entire block between Russell, Lonsdale, Swanston and La Trobe streets, and is named after the Queen Victoria Women's Hospital which occupied this site from 1896 until the late 1980s. It now houses a shopping complex with a gym, supermarket, restaurants and bars. The building itself is an irregularly formed structure crisscrossed by open-air lanes and passageways with floor-to-ceiling glass walls. The basement houses a busy supermarket and a homeware chainstore, while the levels above offer a diverse range of shops, eateries and bars. The lanes themselves are dedicated to high-end fashion.

Aussie Rules aficionados may want to fork out the rather steep admission fee for the **AFL Hall of Fame and Sensation** (daily 9am–5pm; $17.50; Ⓦwww.aflhalloffame.com.au), located at the QV, where visitors step into the imaginary shoes of a footy player and follow his journey through the build-up of Grand Final week, culminating in the finale on Saturday. For footy novices there's the **Australia's Own Game Theatre** on the ground floor where a short film explains the rules and the history of Australian Rules football (same hours; free admission). To the western edge of QV, along Swanston Street, is the **State Library of Victoria** (Mon–Thurs 10am–9pm & Fri–Sun 10am–6pm; closed public holidays; Ⓦwww.slv.vic.gov.au) which has free wireless Internet. The building, dating from 1856, is a splendid example of Victorian architecture, and houses the state's largest research and reference library accessible to the public. The interior has been painstakingly refurbished and is well worth a visit, in particular the Cowen Gallery with a permanent display of paintings illustrating the changing look of Melbourne, the La Trobe Reading Room with its imposing domed roof and the Dome Gallery dedicated to the history of Victoria. Also worth a mention is the **Chess Collection**; with almost 12,000 chess-related items it is reputedly one of the largest public collections in the world. You can play here, too.

Opposite the State Library is the refurbished **Melbourne Central** shopping complex mirroring the QV concept of alleys and passageways lined with cafés, sushi bars and boutiques. On its top levels are several high-class restaurants, a gym and a new cinema complex.

Old Melbourne Gaol

The **Old Melbourne Gaol** (daily 9.30am–5pm; $12.50; Ⓦwww.nattrust.com.au), on Russell Street, a block north of the State Library, is one of the most fascinating sights in the CBD. It's certainly the most popular, largely because Australian folk hero and bushranger **Ned Kelly** was hanged here in 1880 – the site of his execution, the beam from which he was hanged and his death mask are all on display (for more on Ned Kelly's exploits, see p.959), as is assorted armour worn by the Kelly Gang. The "Hangman's Night Tour" (Mon, Wed, Fri, Sat & Sun: April–Oct 7.30pm, Nov–March 8.30pm; $25; advance bookings required with Ticketek Ⓣ13 28 49) uses the spooky atmosphere of the prison to full effect.

The bluestone prison was built in stages from 1841 to 1864 – the goldrushes of the 1850s caused such a surge in lawlessness that it kept having to be expanded. A mix of condemned men, remand and short-sentence prisoners, women and "lunatics" (often, in fact, drunks) were housed here; long-term prisoners languished in hulks moored at Williamstown, or at the Pentridge Stockade. Much has been demolished since the jail was closed in 1923, but the entrance and boundary walls at least survive, and it's worth walking round the building to take a look at the formidable arched brick portal on Franklin Street.

The gruesome collection of **death masks** on show in the tiny cells bears witness to the nineteenth-century obsession with phrenology, a wobbly branch of science which studied how people's characters were related to the size and shape of their skulls. Accompanying the masks are compelling case histories of the murderers and their victims. Most fascinating are the women: Martha Needle, who poisoned her husband and daughters (among others) with arsenic, and young Martha Knorr, the notorious "baby farmer", who advertised herself as a "kind motherly person, willing to adopt a child". After receiving a few dollars per child, she killed and buried them in her backyard. The jail serves up other macabre memorabilia, including a scaffold still in working order, various nooses, and a triangle where malcontents were strapped to receive lashes of the cat-o'-nine-tails. Perhaps the ultimate rite of passage for visitors is the "Art of Hanging", an interpretive display that's part educational tool and part setting for a medieval snuff-movie.

Queen Victoria Market

Opened in the 1870s, **Queen Victoria Market** (Tues & Thurs 6am–2pm, Fri 6am–6pm, Sat 6am–3pm, Sun 9am–4pm; Ⓦwww.qvm.com.au) remains one of the best loved of Melbourne's institutions. Its collection of huge, open-sided sheds and high-roofed decorative halls is fronted along Victoria Street by restored shops, their original awnings held up with decorative iron posts. Although undeniably quaint and tourist-friendly, the market is a boisterous, down-to-earth affair where you can buy practically anything from new and secondhand clothes to fresh fish at bargain prices. Stallholders and shoppers seem just as diverse as the goods on offer: Vietnamese, Italian and Greek greengrocers pile their colourful produce high and vie for your attention, while the huge variety of deliciously smelly cheeses effortlessly draws customers to the old-fashioned deli hall. Saturday morning marks a weekly social ritual as Melbourne's foodies turn out for their groceries, while Sunday is for clothing and shoe shopping. The guided **Foodies Tour** (10am Tues, Thurs, Fri & Sat; $28 including food sampling, bookings essential) takes in all the culinary delights of the market, while the action-packed Night Market (every Wed night in summer 5.30pm–10pm) has music stages, bars and over thirty stalls providing on-site cuisine from around the world. The market also runs regular day, evening and weekend cooking classes. For programmes and tour bookings call ⓣ03/9320 5822; details of the Cooking School programme are shown on the market's website.

△ Fresh produce at Queen Victoria Market

Carlton Gardens and Melbourne Museum

At the CBD's northeast corner is **Carlton Gardens**, home to one of Melbourne's most significant historic landmarks – the **Royal Exhibition Building**. It was built by David Mitchell (father of Dame Nellie Melba) for the International Exhibition of 1880 and visited by 1.5 million people. In later years this is where Australia's first parliament sat in 1901, and the Victorian State Parliament from 1901–27. It was also used as a sporting venue for the 1956 Melbourne Olympics. The magnificent Neoclassical edifice, with its soaring dome and huge entrance portal, is the only substantially intact example in the world of a Great Hall from a major exhibition; its scale and grandeur reflect the values and aspirations attached to industrialization, so much so that in 2004 Carlton Gardens and the Royal Exhibition Building were inscribed on the UNESCO World Heritage List. One-hour tours of the building leave daily at 2pm (ⓣ13 11 02; $5) from the Melbourne Museum next door.

Melbourne Museum (daily 10am–5pm; $6; ⓦwww.melbourne.museum.vic.gov.au) is an ultramodern, state-of-the-art museum, which makes a dramatic contrast to its nineteenth-century neighbour, with its geometric forms, vibrant colours, immense blade-like roof and a greenhouse accommodating a lush fern gully flanked by a canopy of tall forest trees. The museum, which also houses a 400-seat amphitheatre, touring hall for major exhibitions and a shop, has been designed with the multimedia generation in mind – glass-covered display cabinets are few and far between; instead, there's a greater emphasis on digital culture with exhibition spaces exploring the way science and technology are shaping the future.

Highlights include the **Science and Life Gallery**, which explores the plants and animals inhabiting the southern lands and seas; **Bunjilaka**, the Museum's Aboriginal Centre, showcasing an extraordinary collection of Aboriginal culture from Victoria and further afield (curving for 30m at the entrance is *Wurreka*, a wall of zinc panels etched with Aboriginal artefacts, shells, plants and fish); and the **Australia Gallery**, focusing on the history of Melbourne and Victoria, and featuring the legendary racehorse Phar Lap (reputedly Australia's most popular museum exhibit) and the kitchen set from the TV show *Neighbours*. Also of interest are the Evolution Gallery, which looks at the earth's history and holds an assortment of dinosaur casts, and the Children's Museum, where the exhibition gallery, "Big Box", is built in the shape of a giant, tiled cube painted in brightly coloured squares. One of the most striking exhibits is the **Forest Gallery**, a living, breathing indoor rainforest containing over 8000 plants from more than 120 species, including 25-metre-tall gums, as well as birds, insects, snakes, lizards and fish. Also part of the museum, the **IMAX Melbourne** boasts one of the world's biggest movie screens. Up to seven different IMAX films (daily on the hour 10am–10pm; $18, 3D films $22.50; ⓣ03/9663 5454, ⓦwww.imax.com.au) are projected each day; for some you need to don special liquid-crystal glasses for 3D action.

Parliament House and around

The Eastern Hill area beyond Spring Street has many fine public buildings, centred around **Parliament House**. Erected in stages between 1856 and 1930, the parliament buildings (guided tours on non-sitting days Mon–Fri on the hour between 10am, noon, 2pm, 3pm & 3.45pm; free; ⓣ03/9651 8568) have a theatrical presence, with a facade of giant Doric columns rising from a high flight of steps, and landscaped gardens either side. Just below, the Old Treasury Building from 1857 and adjacent State Government office, facing the beautiful Treasury Gardens, are equally imposing. The **Gold Treasury Museum** in the Old Treasury features an audiovisual presentation, *Built on Gold*, shown in the old gold-vaults deep in the basement (Mon–Fri 9am–5pm, Sat, Sun & public holidays 10am–4pm; $8.50; ⓦwww.citymuseummelbourne.org), which illustrates the impact of the Victorian goldrushes on the fledgling colony. A permanent exhibition on the social and architectural history of Melbourne shares the ground floor with temporary shows.

East of Parliament House, the broad acres of **Fitzroy Gardens** run a close second to Carlton Gardens as a getaway from the CBD. Originally laid out in the shape of the Union Jack flag, the park's paths still just about conform to the original pattern, though the formal style has been fetchingly abandoned in between. The flowers, statuary and fountains are best appreciated on weekdays, as at the weekend you'll spend most of your time dodging the video cameras of wedding parties. The gardens' much-touted main attraction is really only for kitsch nostalgists: **Captain Cook's Cottage** (daily: April–Oct 9am–5pm; Nov–March 9am–5.30pm; $4) was the supposed home of Captain James Cook, the English navigator who explored the southern hemisphere in three great voyages and first "discovered" the east coast of Australia. Otherwise, there are attractive flower displays at the **Conservatory** (daily 7am–5pm; free).

The MCG and around

East of Birrarung Park lies **Yarra Park**, containing the hallowed **Melbourne Cricket Ground (MCG)** – also easily reached by tram along Wellington Parade or train to Jolimont station. Hosting state and international cricket matches and some of the top Aussie Rules football games, the 'G', as it is affectionately referred to, is one of sportsmad Melburnians' best-loved icons. Home to the Melbourne Cricket Club since 1853, the complex became the

River and bay cruises

Most cruises ply the **Yarra River** and the upper reaches of Port Phillip Bay (called Hobsons Bay) between St Kilda and Williamstown at the mouth of the Yarra (see p.840). A cruise on the western suburbs' **Maribyrnong River** reveals a side of Melbourne tourists don't usually get to see, and contrary to local (eastern suburbs) prejudices it is not all factory yards and oil-storage containers either.

The main departure points in the city for cruises along the Yarra River are **Northbank Promenade**, at the southern end of Federation Square (sometimes still referred to as Princes Walk), **Southgate** and, further west, **Williamstown**. All cruises run weather permitting; in the cooler months (May–Sept) the last scheduled departures of the day may be cancelled.

Melbourne River Cruises (ⓦwww.melbcruises.com.au) depart five to six times daily from Northbank Promenade near Princes Bridge. Tickets are available at the blue kiosks there or at Southgate, or call ⓣ03/8610 2600. The Scenic River Garden Cruise (1hr 15min; $19.80) heads upriver past South Yarra and Richmond to Herring Island. The Port and Docklands Cruise (1hr 15min; $19.80) runs downriver past Crown Casino and Melbourne Exhibition Centre to the Westgate Bridge. Combined up- and downriver cruises cost $33.80. In addition, cruises to Williamstown and back (approx 1hr 15min; $28) leave daily every hour (10.30am–2.30pm, in the cooler months 10.30am, 12.30pm and 2.30pm – enquire at the office).

City River Cruises (ⓣ03/9650 2214, ⓦwww.cityrivercruises.com.au) operate similar Yarra cruises for a marginally cheaper price. Buy tickets at the orange kiosk near the departure point at Northbank Promenade or on board. There are four departures daily between 10am and 2.30pm; additional departure in summer at 4pm.

Williamstown Bay and River Cruises (ⓣ03/9682 9555, ⓦwww.williamstownferries.com.au) ply the lower section of the Yarra between Williamstown and Southgate in the west of the city. Departures from Southgate daily every half-hour between 9.30am and 5pm, from Williamstown one hour later ($13.80, or $23.80 return). The company also runs six ferry services per day from St Kilda Pier to Williamstown on Saturdays, Sundays and public holidays, departing hourly between 11.30am and 4.30pm and from Gem Pier in Williamstown between 11am and 4pm ($8, or $15 return; tickets can be bought at the white ticket box at Southgate or from pier attendants and on board).

Maribyrnong Cruises (ⓣ03/9689 6431, ⓦwww.blackbirdcruises.com.au). Cruises depart from Wingfield Street and land at Footscray. The Maribyrnong River Cruise passes Flemington Racecourse, Footscray Park and various other parklands to Essendon and shows the tranquil and pretty side of the supposedly drab Western suburbs (2hr; departs Tues, Thurs, Sat & Sun 1 pm; $14), while the Port of Melbourne Cruise takes in the industrial aspects of the lower Maribyrnong and Yarra rivers plus the Docklands development (1hr; departs Tues, Thurs, Sat & Sun at 4pm; $7). Take the train to Footscray station (Sydenham/Werribee line) or take bus #219 from the city to Sunshine, and get off at bus stop 17.

Penguin Waters Cruises (ⓣ03/9386 8488, ⓦwww.penguinwaters.com.au). Departs from berth 1, Southgate, for a sunset cruise (2 hr, $55; includes BBQ dinner and wine) along the Yarra to a structure in Port Phillip Bay, 4km from the mouth of the Yarra, where penguins come ashore. As this is the only cruise vessel permitted to visit the penguin colony and the exact location isn't publicized, you can see them without the crowds that congregate on Phillip Island (see p.877).

centrepiece of the 1956 Olympic Games after it had been completely reconstructed – only the historic members' stand survived. Fifty years later, a new members' stand has just been completed, pushing the ground's capacity to over 100,000. **MCG City**, a new development in the northeast that is currently being built after many delays, will eventually house galleries and exhibition spaces including the **Australian Gallery of Sport and Olympic Exhibition**, the **Australian Cricket Hall of Fame**, the **Sport Australia Hall of Fame** and the **Aussie Rules Exhibition**. One-hour tours of the ground (hourly 10am–3pm; no tours on event days; $14.50; Ⓦwww.mcg.org.au) offer the chance to visit the players' changing rooms, coaches' boxes and cricket viewing areas and whatever is currently accessible.

From the MCG, three pedestrian bridges over Brunton Avenue lead to **Melbourne Park**, home to a further cluster of sporting venues. Rod Laver Arena and Vodafone Arena in Melbourne Park are the home of the Australian Open tennis championship in January – the latter can seat up to 10,500 people and has a retractable roof and moveable seating that allows for fully enclosed or open-air events such as cycling, tennis, basketball and concerts. On the other side of Swan Street lies the **Melbourne Sports and Entertainment Centre**, or "Glasshouse", as it's known locally; next door, Olympic Park is where the Melbourne Storm rugby-league team play their matches and the Lexus Centre next to this is the new training home for the Collingwood AFL Club.

Birrarung Marr

Melbourne's newest park, **Birrarung Marr**, forms a green link between the sports precinct of Melbourne Park and Federation Square, giving striking views of the city skyline, the sports arenas, river and parklands. Created from land previously used by railway lines, a swimming pool and a road, it now consists of grassy slopes, intersected by a long **footbridge** that crosses the entire park from the southeast to the northwest. The footbridge starts at a small, artificially created wetland area in the southeast by the river called the **Billabong** and leads over Red Gum Gully to the park's centrepiece, the **Federation Bells**, a collection of 39 bells ranging in size from a small handbell to one weighing a ton, created to commemorate the Centenary of Federation in 2001. The bells are computer-controlled and normally ring every day from 8am to 9.10am, 12.30pm to 1.30pm and 5pm to 6pm.

The Yarra River and Southgate

Despite its nondescript appearance, the muddy **Yarra River** was – and still is – an important part of the Melbourne scene. Traditionally home to the city docks, tidal movements of up to two metres meant frequent flooding, a problem only partly solved by artificially straightening the river and building up its banks – this also had the incidental benefit of reserving tracts of low-lying land as recreational space, which are now pleasingly crisscrossed by paths and cycle tracks. Four **bridges** cross the river from the CBD: Spencer Street Bridge at the end of Spencer Street; Kings Bridge on King Street; Queens Bridge, not quite at the end of Queen Street; and Princes Bridge, which carries Swanston Street across. There's also a pedestrian bridge from the bank below Flinders Street station to the Southgate Centre. The best way to see the Yarra is on a cruise – see the box on p.839.

On the south side of Princes Bridge you can **rent bikes** to explore the river banks (see "Listings", p.866); on fine weekends, especially, the Yarra comes to life, with people messing about in boats, cycling and strolling. Southgate, immediately west of Princes Bridge, is an upmarket shopping complex with lots of smart cafés, restaurants, bars and a huge food court with very popular outdoor tables; at lunchtime and weekends it's very hard to find a table, even indoors.

The Crown Casino, Docklands and Telstra Dome

Providing the Yarra's unavoidable focal point, the **Crown Casino** is Australia's largest gambling and entertainment venue, stretching across 600m of riverfront west of Southgate between Queens Bridge and Spencer Street Bridge. Next door, the **Melbourne Exhibition Centre** (known locally as "Jeff's Shed", a reference to Jeff Kennett, the former state premier behind its construction) is a whimsical example of the city's dynamic new architectural style: facing the river is an immense 450-metre-long glass wall, while the street entrance has an awning resembling a ski jump propped up by wafer-thin pylons. At the time of writing the interesting **Maritime Museum** was closed for extensive renovations (due to open in late 2008). It holds the *Polly Woodside* (enquiries Ⓔpolly@nattrust.com.au), a small, barque-rigged sailing ship, built in Belfast in 1885 for the South American coal trade and retired only in 1968, when it was the last deep-water sailing vessel in Australia still afloat.

Opposite the Crown Casino, on the corner of Queenwharf Road and King Street, is the **Melbourne Aquarium** (daily: Jan 9.30am–9pm; Feb–Dec 9.30am–6pm; $24; Ⓦwww.melbourneaquarium.com.au). Resembling a giant fish-and-chip shop, the aquarium harbours thousands of creatures from the Southern Ocean. Part of it is taken up by the Oceanarium tank, which rests seven metres below the Yarra, holding over two million litres of water and containing 3200 animals from 150 species (there are over 550 species, or 4000 creatures, in the aquarium in total), as well as a sting-ray-filled beach with a wave machine and a fish bowl turned inside out where you can stand in a glass room surrounded by shark-filled water. The curved, four-storey building also houses a hands-on learning centre where children get a fish-eye view of life underwater, "Ride the Dive" platforms that simulate an underwater roller-coaster, lecture halls, an amphitheatre, cafés, shop and a restaurant.

Further downstream lies the **old dock area**, which is very slowly transforming into a large-scale commercial, residential and leisure development as part of the **Docklands project**. Of all the city's new developments, this is likely to have the biggest impact on the look and feel of Melbourne: if all goes to plan, in around ten years an entire new city district will stand by the waterfront here. For the time being, a few of the apartment buildings have sprouted up although Melbournians have been slow to purchase or rent them. The relatively nice restaurant promenade seems a bit sterile but is a good place to sit in the warmer months and watch those watching you. Squat in the middle of it all sits another of Melbourne's giant sporting venues, **Telstra Dome**, a 54,000-seater venue for AFL, cricket, domestic and international soccer and rugby union matches, as well as concerts by big-name artists. A wide pedestrian footbridge crosses the railway tracks at Southern Cross station, connecting Telstra Dome and the Docklands district-in-the-making with Spencer Street and the older part of the city.

Victorian Arts Centre

The **Victorian Arts Centre** (Ⓦwww.theartscentre.com.au), on St Kilda Road, comprises Hamer Hall, the Theatres Building and the Sidney Myer Music Bowl, an open-air venue across St Kilda Road in Kings Domain (see p.842). At the top of the Theatres Building is a 162-metre-tall **spire** whose curved lower sections are meant to evoke the flowing folds of a ballerina's skirt; the mast at its peak turns an iridescent blue at night. A **guided tour** of Hamer Hall and the Theatres Building provides an insight into the history of the buildings and gives an overview of the architecture and design (Mon–Sat noon & 2.30pm; $11), while the **backstage tour** ventures behind the curtains, taking in the dressing rooms and costumes (Sun 12.15pm; $13.50, ticket from Theatres Building foyer). There are visual arts collections and other exhibits on display in the small **George Adams Gallery** and the basement of the Theatres Building (Mon–Sat 7am–late, Sat 9am–late, Sun 10am–till after last show; free).

The bluestone building next to the Theatres Building is home to the **National Gallery of Victoria (NGV)**, Australia's oldest public art museum. After extensive refurbishments it was reopened in late 2003 and the gallery now houses a collection of international works under the name **NGV: International** (daily 10am–5pm, closed Mon; free, except for temporary exhibitions; Ⓦwww.ngv.vic.gov.au), having moved its Australian collection to its new domicile on Federation Square. Features such as the **Waterwall** at the entrance – a water curtain flowing down a glass wall twenty metres wide and six metres high – and the **Great Hall** on the ground floor, with a beautiful stained-glass ceiling, have been retained, and there's access to the landscaped **Sculpture Garden** via the Great Hall. In addition, individual galleries on the four levels were redesigned, and the overall exhibition space increased. The ground floor contains three large rooms for temporary exhibitions plus galleries dedicated to Oceanic Art, Pre-Columbian, Egyptian and Near Eastern, as well as Greek and Roman Antiquities. Level 1 has rooms displaying European paintings and sculpture from the fourteenth to the seventeenth century. Level 2 comprises paintings, sculpture and decorative arts from the seventeenth to the mid-twentieth centuries: the Flemish and Dutch masters, including the Rembrandt Cabinet, being some of the highlights here, while the contemporary era is represented using installations and photos on level 3. There's also a pleasant *Garden Restaurant* (Tues–Fri 10am–5pm, Sat & Sun 11am–6pm, closed Mon) located in the Sculpture Garden. NGV has a regular programme of floor talks, lectures, discussion groups, films and other activities – check out the gallery's *What's On* flyer or its website for details.

Further south, on Sturt Street, next to the Malthouse Theatre, the **Australian Centre for Contemporary Art** (**ACCA**; daily 11am–6pm; free) has consistently challenging exhibitions of contemporary international and Australian art.

On Sunday between 10am and 6pm the stalls of a good **arts and crafts market** line the pavement outside the Victorian Arts Centre, extending onto the footpath under the Princes Bridge.

Kings Domain

Across St Kilda Road from the National Gallery of Victoria, the grassy open parkland of **Kings Domain** encompasses the **Sidney Myer Music Bowl**, which serves as an outdoor music arena for the Victorian Arts Centre. South of the Bowl, and behind imposing iron gates with stone pillars and a British coat of arms, you can glimpse the flag flying over **Government House**, the ivory mansion of the governor of Victoria, set in extensive grounds. The National Trust runs **guided tours** of the house (Mon & Wed; closed Dec 16–Jan 25 Ⓣ03/9654 4711; $15), the highlight being the state ballroom, which occupies the entire south wing and includes a velvet-hung canopied throne, brocade-covered benches, ornate plasterwork and three huge crystal chandeliers.

Further south, on Dallas Brooke Drive, La Trobe's Cottage (included in tour) has been re-erected as a memorial to Lieutenant-Governor La Trobe, who lived in this tiny house throughout his term of office (1839–54). The whole thing was sent over from England in prefabricated form, and makes a telling contrast to the later governor's residence. Inside there are interesting displays on La Trobe and the early days of the colony.

The Shrine of Remembrance, in formal grounds in the southwestern corner of the Domain, was completed in 1934. It's a rather Orwellian monument, apparently half-Roman temple, half-Aztec pyramid, given further chill when a mechanical-sounding voice booms out and calls you in to see the symbolic light inside. The shrine is designed so that at 11am on Remembrance Day (Nov 11) a ray of sunlight strikes the memorial stone inside – an effect that's simulated every half-hour.

Royal Botanic Gardens

The **Royal Botanic Gardens** (daily: May–Aug 7.30am–5.30pm; April, Sept & Oct 7.30am–6pm; Nov–March 7.30am–8.30pm; free; Ⓦwww.rbg.vic.gov.au) on Dallas Brooke Drive contain twelve thousand different plant species and over fifty thousand individual plants, as well as native wildlife such as cockatoos and kookaburras, in an extensive landscaped setting. Melbourne's much-maligned climate is perfect for horticulture: cool enough for temperate trees and flowers to flourish, warm enough for palms and other subtropical species, and wet enough for anything else. The bright and airy **visitors centre** (daily 9am–5pm) at Observatory Gate on Birdwood Avenue has displays, maps and brochures and is the best place to start your wanderings.

Highlights include the **herb garden**, comprising part of the medicinal garden established in 1880; the **fern gully**, a lovely walk through shady ferns, with cooling mists of water on a hot summer's day; the large ornamental **lake** full of ducks, black swans and eels; and various **hothouses** where exotic cacti and fascinating plants such as the Venus flytrap thrive. The *Observatory Gate Café* next to the visitors centre has indoor and outdoor sitting under sun sails and sells coffee, scrumptious cakes and sandwiches as well as light meals. The *Terrace Tearooms and Reception Centre* (daily 10am–4pm) by the lake is licensed and serves meals, or there's a snackbar next door. On summer evenings, plays are often performed in the gardens. Cinema buffs can also swap popcorn for picnic baskets each year from mid-December to mid-March when art-house, cult and classic films are projected onto a big outdoor screen at the Moonlight Cinema ($16 or $14 online; recorded info on Ⓣ1900 933 899, or visit Ⓦwww.moonlight.com.au). Enter at D Gate on Birdwood Avenue; films start at sunset. Don't forget to take an extra layer of clothing, a rug and, most importantly, insect repellent. Every second Saturday on the month, the "Gardens Market" (9am–2pm; Ⓦwww.marketsinthegarden.com.au) is held, where one hundred stallholders sell plants, art, gourmet food and other items.

Guided walks (bookings essential; Ⓣ03/9252 2300) start at the visitors centre: the Gardens Discovery Walk (Sun–Fri 11am & 2pm; $4.50) gives a fine introduction to the history and horticultural diversity of the gardens; and the Aboriginal Heritage Walk (Thurs & second Sun of month 11am–12.30pm; $15.50) explores the traditional uses of plants for foods, medicine, tools and ceremonies. The painstakingly restored **Observatory Gate** complex, a group of Italianate buildings (originally built 1861–63) next door to the visitors centre can be visited on a self-guided tour (Mon & Fri–Sun 9am–4pm), or join a "Night Sky Experience tour" from the centre (Tues 7.30–9pm; during daylight-saving time 9–10.30pm; $15.50).

Melbourne suburbs

Far more than in the city centre, it's in Melbourne's **inner suburbs** that you'll really get a feel for what life here is really all about. Many have quite distinct characters, whether as ethnic enclaves or self-styled artists' communities. What's more, all can easily be reached by a pleasurable tram ride from the centre. Browsing through markets and shops, cruising across Hobsons Bay, sampling the world's foods and, of course, sipping espresso are the primary attractions of the suburbs. Café society finds its home to the north among the alternative galleries and secondhand shops of **Fitzroy**, while the Italian cafés on Lygon Street in nearby **Carlton** fuelled the Beat Generation

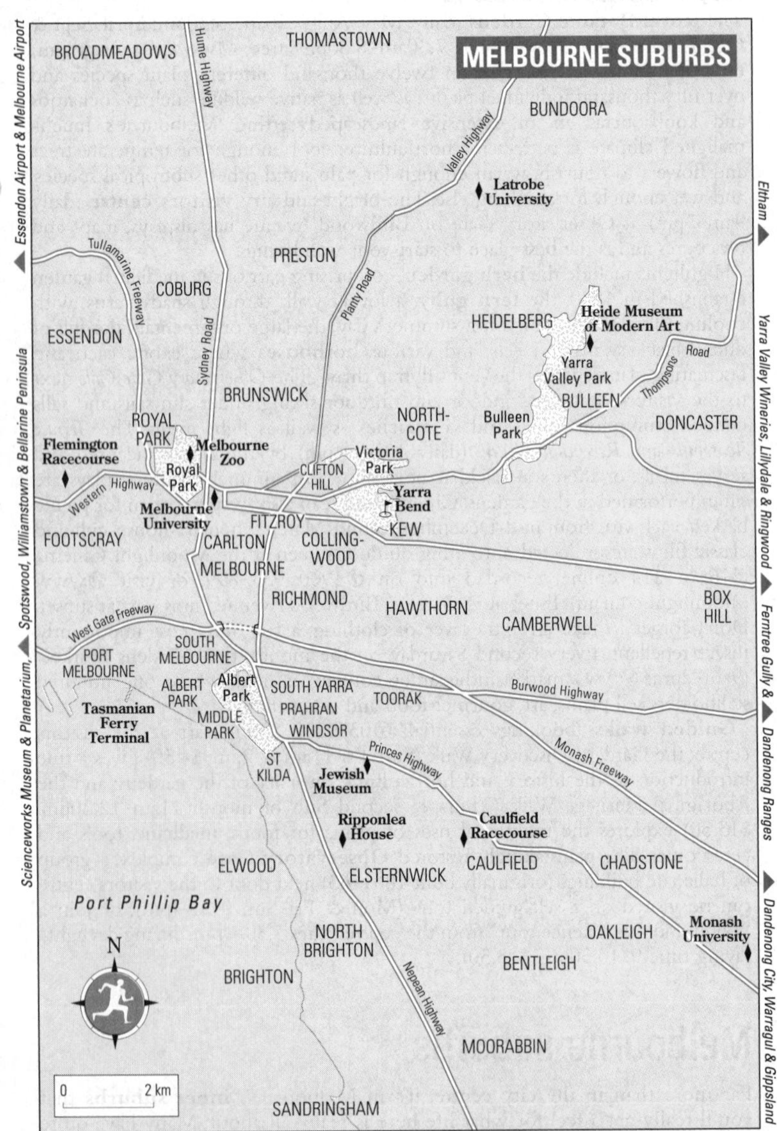

with espresso, though boutiques now far outnumber bookshops. Grungy **Richmond**, to the east, can claim both Vietnamese and Greek enclaves, and a diverse music scene in its many pubs. South of the river is the place to shop until you drop, whether at wealthy **South Yarra**, self-consciously groovy **Prahran** or snobby **Toorak**. To the south, **St Kilda** has the advantage of a beachside location to go with its trendy but raucous nightlife. To firm up your itinerary with something more concrete, make for the well-designed Zoo in Carlton, or Scienceworks, a hugely enjoyable interactive museum in Spotswood. Also of interest is the Heide Museum of Modern Art in Bulleen and, a bit further along in the same direction, Eltham, with its artists' colony of Montsalvat.

Carlton

Carlton lies just north of the city (tram #1, #3 or #5 from Swanston Street) but, with its university presence and its long-established Italian restaurant scene, it could be a million miles away. **Lygon Street** is the centre of the action, and it was here, in the 1950s, that espresso bars were really introduced to Melbourne; exotic spots such as the *Caffe Sport*, *La Gina*, *University Caffe* and *Toto's* (which claims to have introduced pizza to Australia) had an unconventional allure in staid Anglo-Melbourne, and the local intelligentsia soon made the street their second home. Victorian terraced houses provided cheap living, and this became the first of the city's "alternative" suburbs. These days Carlton is no longer bohemian; its residents are older and wealthier, and Lygon Street has gone definitively upmarket, though the smart fashion shops still jostle with bookshops, excellent ethnic restaurants and cafés like **TIAMO1** (see p.854).

Lygon Street itself is the obvious place to explore, but the elegant architecture also spreads eastwards to Drummond Street and, flanking Carlton Gardens, Rathdowne and Nicholson streets. Running along the western side of the university, Royal Parade gives onto Royal Park, with its memorial to the explorers Burke and Wills (see box p.514), from where it's a short walk through the park to the zoo.

Melbourne Zoo

When it opened in 1862, **Melbourne Zoo** (daily 9am–5pm; $22; Mon–Sat tram #55 from William Street, Sun tram #68 from Elizabeth Street, or train from Flinders Street station to Royal Park on the Upfield line; Ⓦwww.zoo.org.au) was the first in Australia. Some of its original features are still in evidence, including Australian and foreign trees, and landscaped gardens, but the animals have been rehoused in more natural conditions. The Australian area contains a central lake with waterbirds, open enclosures for koalas and other animals, and a bushland setting where you can walk among emus, kangaroos and wallabies. Strolling along the boardwalks of the **Great Flight Aviary** (daily 10.30am–4.30pm) you'll come across areas of rainforest, wetland, and a scrub area with a huge gum tree where many birds nest. The dark **Platypus House** (daily 9.30am–4.30pm) is also worth a look, since the mammals are notoriously difficult to see in the wild – even here there's no guarantee you'll be lucky. **Butterfly House** (weekdays 9.30am–4.30pm, Sat & Sun 9.30am–5pm), a steamy tropical hothouse with hundreds of colourful Australian butterflies flitting about, is also highly enjoyable. In summer, the zoo stays open until 9.30pm on selected nights (usually weekends) for its "Zoo Twilights" music programme, which hosts live bands playing on the central lawn.

Fitzroy and Collingwood

In the 1970s, **Fitzroy** took over from Carlton as the home of the city's artistic community, and every year at the end of September, the colourful Fringe Parade and a street party on Brunswick Street usher in the **Fringe Festival**, the alternative scene's answer to the highbrow Melbourne International Arts Festival. The **International Comedy Festival** (April) and the **Next Wave Festival** (May, even-numbered years), two other notable arts events, also take place mainly in Fitzroy. The district's focus is **Brunswick Street** (tram #11 from Collins St), especially between Gertrude Street, home to Turkish takeaways, and Johnston Street, with its lively Spanish bars. In the shadow of Housing Commission tower-blocks, welfare agencies and charity shops rub shoulders with funky secondhand clothes and junk shops, ethnic supermarkets and restaurants, cafés full of students and equally grungy artists, writers and musicians, and thriving bookshops that stay open late and are often as crowded as the many bars and music pubs. Most of the rough old hotels have been done up to match the prevailing mood: the *Provincial* is a good example, with its distressed paint-job and deli/café/bar inside. Some great pubs have remained untouched down the side streets, however, such as the *Napier Hotel* at 210 Napier St opposite the imposing but hidden-away Fitzroy Town Hall, and *The Standard* at 293 Fitzroy St which, many say, has Melbourne's best beer-garden.

Fitzroy's fringe art leanings are reflected in wacky "street installations" such as mosaic chairs, and sculptures like *Mr Poetry*. The eye-catching wrought-iron gate at the entrance to the Fitzroy Nursery at 390 Brunswick St, with its fairy-tale motif, sets the theme for the Artists Garden above the nursery, which exhibits sculptures and other decorative items for garden use. Fitzroy also boasts the unique but overpriced Rose Street **Artists Market** (Oct–May Sat 11am–5pm) at 60 Rose St where fashion designers, painters, photographers, ceramicists, sculptors and other artists sell their work. The **Fitzroy Pool**, in the north of the suburb on the corner of Young and Cecil streets, is a summer meeting place where people occasionally swim between posing sessions.

While not as trendy as Brunswick Street, the partly shabby **Smith Street** (tram #86 from Bourke St), which forms the boundary between Fitzroy and Collingwood to the east, is forever catching up, but you'll still find quite a few charity shops, ethnic butchers and cheap supermarkets which the New Age bookshops, quirky little cafés and revamped pubs haven't managed to relegate to the edge. **Collingwood** and the adjacent suburb of Abbotsford have a large **gay** population, with a clutch of gay bars and clubs, particularly on Peel and Glasshouse streets.

South Yarra, Toorak, Prahran and Windsor

South of the river, the suburbs of **South Yarra**, **Prahran** and, to the east, Toorak, are home to the city's biggest **shopping** area, both grungy and upmarket. **Chapel Street** is the main drag: in South Yarra it extends for a Golden Mile of trendy shopping and *very* chic cafés; heading south beyond Commercial Road through Prahran and Windsor the stereotypically glossy streetscape takes on a refreshingly chequered, ruddier appearance. Crossing Chapel Street at right angles in South Yarra, Toorak Road boasts equally ritzy designer boutiques and, if that's possible, becomes even more exclusive east of Grange Road, as it enters Toorak, a suburb synonymous with wealth. **Trams** #5, #6 and #72 from Swanston Street will get you from the city centre to Chapel Street.

South Yarra and Toorak

The **South Yarra** stretch of **Chapel Street** is awash with boutiques and speciality shops, bistro bars full of beautiful people and cooler-than-thou nightclubs.

Amongst the wall-to-wall chic, it's worth making a beeline for the **Jam Factory** shopping complex, named after its former incarnation, as well as **Como Historic House and Gardens**, overlooking the river from Lechlade Avenue in South Yarra (daily 10am–5pm; $11). This elegant white mansion, a mixture of Regency and Italianate architectural styles, is a good example of the town houses built by wealthy nineteenth-century landowners. The admission fee includes a one-hour tour of the house; the last tour departs at 4pm. To reach the house, walk east along Toorak Road from Chapel Street, and then north on Williams Road; from the city centre, take tram #8 from Swanston Street.

Toorak has never been short of a bean: when Melbourne was founded, the wealthy built their stately homes here on the high bank of the Yarra, leaving the flood-prone lower ground for the poor; in addition, many European Jews who made good after arriving penniless in Australia celebrated their new wealth by moving to Toorak in the 1950s and 1960s. There's little to see or do in the suburb: the hilly, tree-lined streets are full of huge mansions in extensive private gardens, while so-called Toorak Village is stuffed with wickedly expensive designer boutiques.

Prahran and Windsor

Beyond Commercial Road in **Prahran** proper, Chapel Street still focuses on fashion, but in a more street-smart vein, becoming progressively more downmarket as it heads south. Landmarks include **Prahran Market** (Tues & Thurs dawn–5pm, Fri & Sat dawn–6pm), round the corner on Commercial Road, an excellent though expensive food emporium (fish, meat, fruit, vegetables and delicatessen) plus cafés and a few clothes shops. **Chapel Street Bazaar**, on the western side of Chapel Street, has good secondhand clothes, Art Deco jewellery, furniture and bric-a-brac. Just opposite, tucked away in Little Chapel Street, a lane off Chapel Street, **Chapel off Chapel** provides a venue for an eclectic mix of theatre performances, music and art exhibitions. Heading a further 100m south along Chapel Street brings you to **Greville Street**, in the heart of Prahran, which has taken over from Chapel Street as the corridor of cutting-edge cool, with retro and designer boutiques, music outlets, bookshops, and groovy bars and restaurants. Things really hot up over the weekend, and every Sunday the small **Greville Street Market** has arts, crafts and secondhand clothes and jewellery on the corner of Gratton Street in Gratton Gardens (noon–5pm).

As Chapel Street crosses High Street the suburb changes to **Windsor** and becomes more interestingly ethnic. Discount furniture and household-appliance shops sit cheek by jowl with inexpensive Asian noodle bars, organic produce shops and up-and-coming café-bars. Busy Dandenong Road marks the boundary of Windsor and **St Kilda East**. Just across Dandenong Road on Chapel Street lies the **Astor Theatre**, a beautifully decorated cinema in an Art Nouveau building.

Prahran and Windsor can be reached by train; take the Sandringham train and get off at Prahran or Windsor station, or by tram; all trams leave from Swanston Street and run along St Kilda Road, turning left at some point: #72 turns left into Commercial Road, #6 turns left at High Street, #5 and #64 turn left into Dandenong Road; get off at the corner of these roads and Chapel Street.

South Melbourne and Albert Park

If it's the bay you're heading for, then St Kilda is the obvious destination; the quickest and most interesting way there is on the #96 tram from Bourke or Spencer streets, which runs on a light-rail track via South Melbourne and Albert

Park, past the Aquatic Centre with its five swimming pools (see "Listings", p.866). **South Melbourne**'s focus is the **South Melbourne Market** on the corner of Coventry and Cecil streets (Wed, Sat & Sun 8am–4pm, Fri 8am–6pm), an old-fashioned, value-for-money place where you can browse stalls selling everything from fruit and vegetables to clothes and continental delicacies. Opposite here, a number of cafés and upmarket retail stores line **Coventry Street**; at no. 399, three portable iron houses, prefabricated residences constructed in England and shipped to Melbourne during the goldrush, have been preserved by the National Trust. At the other end of Coventry Street, **Clarendon Street** is South Melbourne's main shopping precinct, and a fine example of a nineteenth-century streetscape, with original Victorian awnings overhanging numerous cafés, clothing shops and restaurants.

Exclusive **Albert Park** has the feel of a small village, with many lovely old terraced houses and Dundas Place, a shopping centre of mouthwatering delis and bakeries. In the shadow of the St Kilda Road office buildings lies Albert Park itself, the home of the Australian Grand Prix (held in March).

St Kilda and around

The former seaside resort of **St Kilda** has an air of shabby gentility, which enhances its current schizophrenic reputation as a sophisticated yet seedy suburb, largely residential but blessed with a raging nightlife. Running from St Kilda Road down to the Esplanade, **Fitzroy Street** is Melbourne's red-light district – usually pretty tame, though late at night not a comfortable place for women alone – and epitomizes this split personality, since it's lined with dozens of thoroughly pretentious cafés and bars from which to gawp at the strip's goings-on. On weekend nights these and others throughout St Kilda are filled to overflowing with a style-conscious but fun crowd. During the day there's a very different feel, especially on **Acland Street**, with its wonderful continental cake-shops and bakeries.

On Sunday, the **St Kilda Arts and Craft Market** (10am–4pm) lines the waterfront on Upper Esplanade. Going there is part of the ritual that includes taking a look at the beach, feeding your face, ambling into a few shops and listening to a busker.

St Kilda's most famous icon, **Luna Park** (Easter to Sept Sat & Sun 11am–6pm; Oct to Easter Fri 7–11pm, Sat 11am–11pm, Sun 11am–6pm; also Mon–Thurs 11am–6pm & Fri 11am–11pm on school and public holidays; Ⓦwww.lunapark.com.au), is located on the Esplanade, entered through the huge, laughing clown's face of "Mr Moon". Despite a couple of new attractions, there's nothing very high-tech about this 1912 amusement park: the Scenic Railway – the world's oldest operating roller-coaster – runs along wooden trestles and the Ghost Train wouldn't spook a toddler – but then that's half the fun. Wandering around is free, but you pay $7 for individual rides, or $35.95 for a day's unlimited rides. You can sit under the palm trees of **O'Donnell Gardens** next door, or nearby **St Kilda Botanical Gardens**, and eat your Acland Street goodies. The **beachfront** is a popular weekend promenade all year round, with separate cycling and walking paths stretching down to Elwood and Brighton, and a long pier thrusting out into the bay. Near the base of the pier is the botched redevelopment of a historic site, the **St Kilda Sea Baths**, which dates back to 1931, a heroically bad mix of shopping complex and function centre with a Moorish twist.

On Saturday, Sunday and public holidays, boat trips from the pier across Hobsons Bay to Williamstown (see box, p.839) give lovely views of St Kilda and the city.

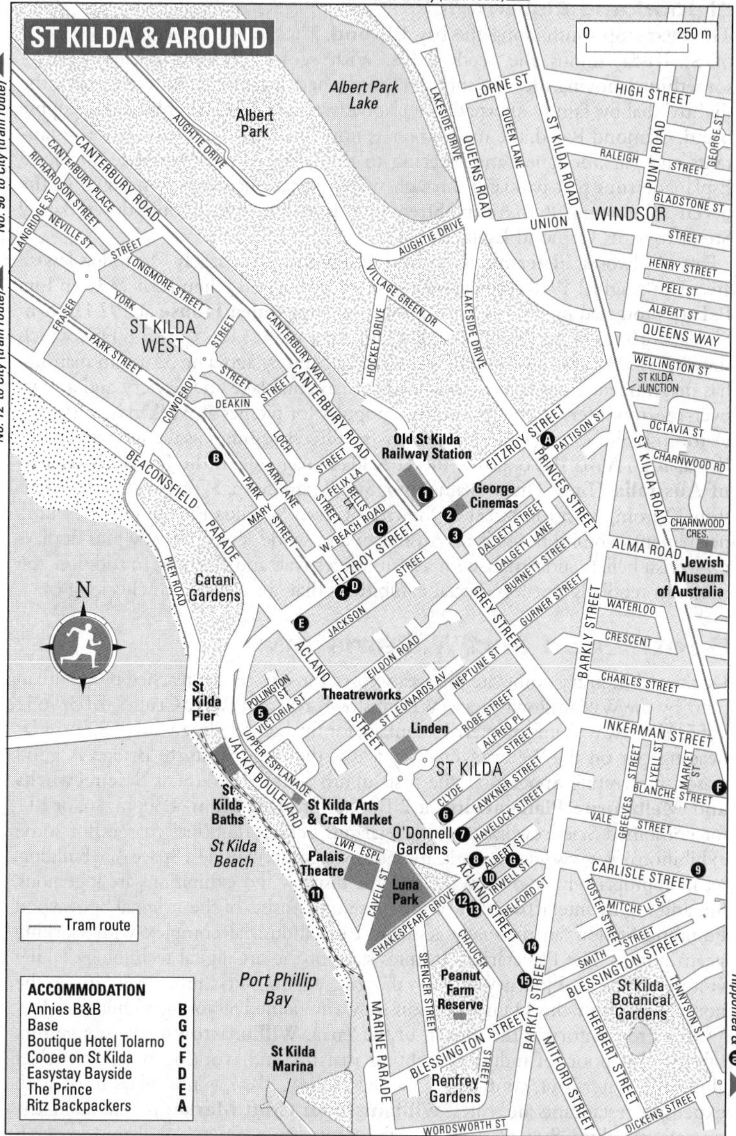

RESTAURANTS & CAFÉS				BARS & CLUBS	
Bala's	12	Le Bon Continental Cake Shop	13	Dog's Bar	6
Big Mouth	14	Renix	7	Elephant and Wheelbarrow	A
Café Tarrango	18	Stokehouse	11	The Esplanade Hotel	5
Circa, the Prince	E	Termini	1	The George Public Bar	2
Galleon Cafe	8	The Espy Kitchen	5	Mink Bar	E
Glicks	16	Topolinos	4	The Prince Public Bar	E
Jerry's Milk Bar	17	Turtle Cafe	19	St Kilda Army and Navy Club	10
La Roche Café	15	Wall Two 80	9	Traffik	3

Elwood and Elsternwick

The next stop south along the bay, **Elwood**, is a smaller, less colourful version of St Kilda, minus the seedy edge. With scores of high-salaried twenty-somethings moving into the suburb's refurbished apartments in recent years, the slightly shabby, faintly alternative feel of Elwood has been replaced by yuppie bland. Ormond Road, the main street, is now lined with expensive café-restaurants and bars, designed and catering to the tastes of their clientele. Ormond Esplanade runs past parkland through which occasional paths run down to the beach. Take tram #96 to Acland Street in St Kilda, then walk south down Barkly Street towards Ormond Esplanade.

East of Elwood, **Elsternwick** (train to Ripponlea) is a largely Orthodox Jewish area. The original 1918 fittings and facade of Brinsmead Chemist at 73 Glen Eira Rd are protected by the National Trust, as is **Ripponlea House** at 192 Hotham St (daily 10am–5pm, closed Mondays during winter; $12; ⓣ9523 6095), which shows how Melbourne's wealthy elite lived a century ago. The 33-room mansion has magnificent gardens, complete with ornamental lake and fernery, and a way-over-the-top interior. The grounds are popular for picnics at weekends, when the tearoom is also open (11am–4pm). Ten- to fifteen-minutes' walk away in East St Kilda, at 26 Alma Rd opposite the St Kilda Synagogue, is the **Jewish Museum of Australia** (Tues–Thurs 10am–4pm, Sun 11am–5pm; $7; tram #3 or #67 to stop 32 from Swanston Street in the city or from St Kilda Road). The museum's permanent exhibitions focus on Australian and world Jewish history, plus displays on Jewish beliefs and rituals, with a focus on festivals and customs. In addition, the museum regularly puts on special exhibitions that are well worth checking out.

Spotswood and Williamstown

Docks and industry dominate the area west of the city centre, reached by suburban train, by the Williamstown ferry (Williamstown Bay and River Cruises ⓣ03/9682 9555, ⓦwww.williamstownferries.com.au; for further details see box, p.839), or by heading out on the Westgate Freeway across the huge Westgate Bridge. A good reason for visiting Spotswood, the first suburb across the Yarra, is **Scienceworks and Melbourne Planetarium**, at 2 Booker St (daily 10am–4.30pm; $6, or $11 for combined Scienceworks and Planetarium ticket; additional charges for some exhibitions; ⓦwww.scienceworks.museum.vic.gov.au). Inside a Space Age building, set in appropriately desolate wasteland, the displays and exhibitions are ingenious, fun and highly interactive. Part of the museum consists of the original Spotswood Pumping Station, an unusually aesthetic early industrial complex with working steam pumps. The Planetarium features state-of-the-art digital technology, taking visitors on a virtual journey through the galaxy (Mon–Fri 2pm, Sat & Sun on the hour 11am–3pm; the 11am and noon shows are aimed at younger children).

On a promontory at the mouth of the Yarra, **Williamstown** is a strange mix of rich and poor: of industry, yachting marinas and working port. The street along the waterfront, confusingly named Nelson Place, is nowadays lined with expensive restaurants and cafés. **Williamstown Craft Market** is held along the waterfront (third Sun of each month, 10am–4pm; ⓦwww.williamstowncraftmarket.com.au). The most enjoyable way to get to Williamstown is by ferry from St Kilda or from Southgate in the city (both with Williamstown Bay and River Cruises; for details, see the box, p.839).

Bulleen and Eltham

Further afield in the northeastern suburbs lie two further attractions: the Heide Museum of Modern Art in **Bulleen** and Montsalvat in **Eltham** – you could make a day of it and visit them en route to the Yarra Valley wineries and the Healesville Sanctuary (see p.882).

The **Heide Museum of Modern Art** (Tues–Fri 10am–5pm, Sat & Sun noon–5pm; $12; ⓣ03/9850 1500, ⓦwww.heide.com.au) on Templestowe Road in Bulleen was the home of Melbourne art patrons **John Reed** (1901–81) and **Sunday Reed** (1905–81), who in the mid-1930s purchased what was then a derelict dairy farm on the banks of the meandering Yarra River. During the following decades the Reeds fostered and nurtured the talents of young unknown artists and played a central role in the emergence of Australian art movements such as the Angry Penguins, the Antipodeans and the Annandale Realists; the painters Sidney Nolan, John Perceval, Albert Tucker and Arthur Boyd were all members of the artistic circle at Heide at one time or another. The **Heide I Gallery** is set in the farmhouse where the Reeds lived from 1934 until 1967. The gallery exhibits pieces from the museum's extensive collection of paintings and other works purchased by the Reeds over four decades, including works by famous Australian artists of the mid- to late twentieth century, including Nolan, Perceval and Boyd. Exhibits change every six months. In mid-2006 and at a cost of $3 million, two new galleries, an education centre, an outdoor sculpture area and restoration of Heide II (the latter house of John and Sunday built in the mid-1960s) were completed. The most prominent addition is the Albert & Barbara Tucker Gallery (Heide III) which features over 200 artworks from Albert's personal collection. There is also an excellent licensed café (Tues–Fri 11am–4pm, Sat & Sun 11am–5pm) which serves gourmet produce and local wine, including fantastic hamper packs (from $38, must be prepaid 24 hours in advance) which can be enjoyed in the lovely gardens. The museum is located 14km from the city centre; take the suburban train to Heidelberg station (Eltham line) then bus #291 to Templestowe Road (frequent services).

Eltham, a bushy suburb further northeast, about 24km from the city, is known as a centre for **arts and crafts**. Its reputation was established in 1935 when the charismatic painter and architect Justus Jorgensen moved to what was then a separate town and founded **Montsalvat**, a European-style artists' colony. Built with the help of his students and followers, the colony's eclectic design was inspired by medieval European buildings with wonderful quirky results; Jorgensen died before it was completed and it has deliberately been left unfinished. He did, however, live long enough to see his community thrive, and to oversee the completion of the mud-brick Great Hall, whose influence is evident in other mud-brick buildings around Eltham. Today Montsalvat, a two-kilometre walk from Eltham station, contains a gallery and is still home to a colony of painters and craftspeople (gallery open daily 9am–5pm; $10; ⓦwww.montsalvat.com.au).

Eating and drinking

Melbourne is Australia's premier city for **eating out**. Sydney may be more style-conscious and Adelaide comparatively cheaper, but Melbourne has the best food and the widest choice of it – and almost all of it is exceptionally good value. In the **city centre**, Greek cafés line Lonsdale Street between Swanston and Russell streets, while Little Bourke Street is the home of Chinatown. Lygon Street, in inner-city **Carlton**, is just one of many places across the city with a concentration of Italian restaurants. Nearby, Brunswick Street in Fitzroy and Smith Street in neighbouring **Collingwood** both have a huge variety of international cuisines as well as trendy bars and cafés. Indeed, Fitzroy and **St Kilda**, another gastronomically mixed bag, are the centres of bar and café society; St Kilda also has great restaurants, bakeries and delis, as does Jewish **Balaclava** (aka St Kilda East). In **Richmond**, Greek restaurants fill Swan Street while further north Vietnamese places dominate Victoria Street. In March each year, the city celebrates all this culinary diversity with a **Food and Wine Festival**, with food-themed street parties in the city's various different ethnic areas.

A lot of licensed restaurants still allow you to bring your own drink, though check first. It is worth noting, however, that most places only allow you to bring in wine, which usually incurs a corkage fee ($1–2 per person to $5–10 per bottle. If you're going to be around for a while, *The Age Cheap Eats in Melbourne*, and its more upmarket companion, *The Age Good Food Guide*, are worthwhile investments.

City centre

You can still find the odd old-fashioned **coffee lounge** in the city – the type of place where you can get a milky cappuccino and grilled cheese on toast – but stylish **cafés** with smarter decor and more diverse menus now set the scene. In the department stores, both the Myer and David Jones **food halls** are excellent for upmarket picnic ingredients, while the QV complex on Lonsdale Street has several good eating places.

Cafés

Cafe La 35th floor, *Hotel Sofitel*, cnr Collins and Exhibition sts ☎03/9653 7744. The café with the best views in Melbourne, including the incredible view from the toilet. Open daily for breakfast, lunch, dinner and afternoon teas.

Hopetoun Tea Rooms Block Arcade, 282 Collins St ☎03/9650 2777. Tea, scones and delicious cakes have been served in these elegant surroundings for more than one hundred years, but newfangled delicacies such as focaccia with pesto sauce have now wheedled their way onto the menu. Prices are moderate. Mon–Thurs 9am–5pm, Fri 9am–6pm, Sat 10am–3.30pm.

Koko Black Shop 4 Royal Arcade, 335 Bourke St. A chocoholic's paradise where they can watch in awe as the melted chocolate is poured into the moulds before their eyes. Makes the best hot chocolate in town. Mon–Thurs 9am–6pm, Fri 9am–8.30pm, Sat 9.30–6pm, Sun 10am–5.30pm.

Laurent Patisserie 306 Little Collins St (between Collins and Elizabeth sts). Mouthwatering breads, cakes and pastries, as well as filled baguettes, croissants, soups for lunch. Licensed. Mon–Sat 8am–6pm, Sun 9am–5pm.

Medallion Cafe & Cakes 209 Lonsdale St. Popular Greek café, once shabby, now with an over-the-top, disco-style interior, but still serving authentic, cheap food. Daily 8am until late (3am Fri & Sat).

Pellegrini's Espresso Bar 66 Bourke St. Melbourne's first espresso bar, and still an institution, with classic 1950s interior and great cheap pasta. Mon–Sat 8am–11.30pm, Sun noon–8pm.

Restaurants

Bar Lourinha 37 Little Collins St ☎03/9663 7890. It might look like a secluded wine bar, but it's the tapas people come for. Dishes can be seen being made in the open kitchen (range from $7–$16) such as chargrilled baby squid or porkbelly with coriander salad. Mon–Wed noon–11pm, Thurs & Fri noon–1am, Sat 4pm–1am.

Cookie Level 1, 252 Swanston St ☎03/9663 7660. The place is a trendy nightspot as well as a restaurant; there are DJs every night. The restaurant serves moderately priced nibbles, salads and full meals, Asian-style, in an upstairs, roomy, modernized former Victorian dining hall. Licensed. Daily noon–11pm; bar until 3am.

Crossways Food for Life 123 Swanston St ☎03/9650 2939. Dirt-cheap, Indian-style vegetarian food prepared by Hare Krishnas (some practising their vows of silence). Mon–Sat 11.30am–2.30pm.

eat drink bento 115 Hardware Lane ☎03/9642 1136. This busy lunchspot serves bento boxes with contents such as sashimi, Peking duck pancakes and nori rolls, and is also open for dinner Thurs & Fri until 10pm. Licensed.

ezard at the Adelphi 187 Flinders Lane ☎03/9639 6811. This hip, dimly lit place is one of Melbourne's coolest eateries, with a tasty range of

East-meets-West favourites. Expensive, with mains $40+. Licensed. Mon–Fri noon–2.30pm & 6–10.30pm, Sat 6–10.30pm.

Gigi Sushi Bar 237 Swanston St. Popular with the nearby RMIT students, the sushi rolls here are larger than similar outlets around town but just as cheap ($2). Get a seat outside on the footpath before others do. 10.30am–10pm daily.

Grossi Florentino 80 Bourke St ☎03/9662 1811. A Melbourne institution. Choose between the cellar café-grill-restaurant, serving inexpensive, home-style pasta dishes, drinks and good coffee, and the very pricey, elegant Italian–French restaurant upstairs. Licensed. Mon–Sat 7.30–1am, upstairs restaurant Mon–Fri lunch and dinner, Sat dinner only.

Mekong 241 Swanston St. One of many small Vietnamese cafés in the city specializing in *pho* (beef or chicken noodle soup). Excellent-value food (dishes about $6), but packed at lunchtime. Mon–Sat 9am–10pm, Sun 10am–10pm.

Southgate Across the river from Flinders Street station. With fine views of the river and the city skyline, this centre is a very popular place to dine and drink – advance booking is essential for the restaurants on Friday and Saturday nights. Some of the best places are *BearBrass* (☎03/9682 3799), lively, popular beer garden and restaurant; *The Blue Train Café* (☎03/9696 0111), forever noisy and buzzy, which attracts a young, hip crowd and serves drinks and tasty, inexpensive light meals; and the more upmarket *Walter's Wine Bar* (☎03/9690 9211).

Syracuse 23 Bank Place ☎03/9670 1777. Mouth-watering tapas (served from 3pm) and lamb and leek sausages, along with fantastic cheeses, *panforte* and coffee. There's also an extensive wine list, a good selection of cigars and seductive atmosphere. Mains start at $28. Licensed. Mon–Fri 7.30am–11pm, Sat 6–11pm.

Vue De Monde 430 Little Collins St ☎03/9691 3888. Regarded as one of the country's best restaurants, young chef Shannon Bennett has blended fine French cuisine with contemporary imagination. It's not cheap (although a 2-course lunch deal is a steal at $55) but you would struggle to find better anywhere. Also excellent value is the lunch box that can be purchased next door at *Café Vue*. Tues–Fri noon–2pm & 6.30–9.30pm, Sat 6.30–9.30pm.

William Angliss College La Trobe St ☎03/9606 2111. Owned by a catering college, this cheap restaurant aims to dish up fine food and service, and usually succeeds, though occasional hiccups may occur. Bookings essential.

Chinatown

Yum cha (elsewhere known as dim sum, a series of small delicacies served from trolleys) is available at lunchtime almost everywhere; on Sunday it's a crowded ritual.

Camy Shanghai Dumpling and Noodle Restaurant Tattersalls Lane, between Little Bourke and Lonsdale sts, close to Swanston St ☎03/9663 8555. An extremely cheap, partly self-service place, dishing up very simple but delicious dumplings and noodles. No alcohol. Daily 11am–10pm.

China Bar 235 Russell St ☎03/9639 1633. Cheap chain with lots of Malaysian-Chinese noodle or rice fast-food classics such as won ton soup, *char kway teow* (fried rice noodles), *nasi lemak* (coconut rice); plus assorted claypot dishes and desserts. BYO. Other branches at 747 Swanston St, Carlton, and 500 Chapel St, South Yarra. Mains start at $12. Sun–Thurs 11am–5pm, Fri & Sat 11am–6pm.

City BBQ Restaurant 178 Little Bourke St ☎03/9663 2311. Known around the area for their value-for-money duck dishes (see them hanging in the window). Service can be a bit rushed but that's because they are always busy. Daily 11am–11pm.

Empress of China 120–122 Little Bourke St ☎03/9663 1883. Expensive but good value, with lots of lesser-known dishes on offer. Licensed. Closed Sat lunchtime.

Flower Drum 17 Market Lane, between Bourke and Little Bourke sts ☎03/9662 3655. Outstanding Cantonese cuisine, including exquisite seafood and fish, an extensive wine list, excellent service and luxurious ambience. Naturally, this all comes at a price: expect to pay at least $70 per person for three courses. Licensed. Mon–Sat noon–3pm & 6–10pm, Sun 6–10pm.

Hofbrauhaus 18 Market Lane ☎03/9663 3361. If you're not in the mood for Asian food, head here for large servings of Bavarian fare, including whopping schnitzels and fatty sausages. Help it all down with some German beer on tap, because the other patrons will be. Also provides knee-slapping entertainment on some nights. Mains $18–$30.

Shark Fin House 131 Little Bourke St ☎03/9663 1555. Converted warehouse with three storeys devoted to about fifty kinds of *yum cha*. Very busy at lunchtime, especially at weekends. There's another branch at 50–52 Little Bourke St (☎03/9662 2681). Moderate–expensive. Licensed and BYO. Daily noon–3pm (Sat from 11.30am, Sun from 11am) & 5.30pm–1.30am.

Carlton and North Melbourne

Lygon Street, between Grattan and Elgin streets, is mainly wall-to-wall Italian pizza and pasta restaurants spilling out on the footpath, and on most evenings all but the most resolute looking passers-by are accosted by their touts. *Really* good restaurants are few and far between here, and cheap Asian noodle-bars, catering to the large number of Asian students at Melbourne Uni and the RMIT, are cropping up every month. To the southwest of Carlton, North Melbourne harbours an excellent Balinese restaurant.

Big Harvest 151 Elgin St ⓣ03/9348 0066. Super-small shop with only one communal table that only fits about 6 people, but this place is all about quality food (they specialize in catering). Great range of specials on the board with a Middle-Eastern slant and coffee that rivals those nearby. Mon–Fri 7.30am–5pm.

Brunetti 198–204 Faraday St ⓣ03/9347 2801. An array of display cases filled with a mouthwatering selection of chocolates, pastries, biscuits and cakes, plus coffee. Licensed restaurant next door. Sun–Thurs 6am–11pm, Fri & Sat 6am–midnight.

Jimmy Watson's 333 Lygon St ⓣ03/9347 3985. The strengths of this Lygon Street icon are its very good bar meals (modern Australian cuisine) in convivial, atmospheric surroundings, and a super wine list. Moderate prices. Licensed. Mon 10.30am–6pm, Tues–Sat 10.30am–late.

Shakahari 201–203 Faraday St ⓣ03/9347 3848. Excellent and imaginative Asian-influenced vegetarian food at moderate prices. Licensed. Mon–Sat noon–3pm & 6.30–9.30pm (Fri & Sat until 10pm).

Tiamo 1 303 Lygon St ⓣ03/9347 5759. One-time beatnik hangout and still popular with students, with layers of browning 1950s posters and a good-value blackboard menu. Next door is its sibling,

Three, One, Two 312 Drummond St ⓣ03/9347 3312. Melbourne's most exciting new restaurant is the dream of renowned chef Andrew McConnell as he redefines modern Australian cuisine. The Degustatian Menu is a great option to sample what the whole country is talking about (8 courses $95). Bookings essential. Open for lunch Fri–Sun, dinner Tues–Sat.

Toto's Pizza House 101 Lygon St ⓣ03/9347 1630. Melbourne's first pizzeria, dating from the 1950s – cheap, cheerful and noisy. Licensed. Daily 11am–11pm.

△ Outdoor dining on Lygon Street

Fitzroy and Collingwood

Adjacent Fitzroy and Collingwood probably have the widest choice of cuisines in the city, and are good places to finish off a night on the town, as there's always lots going on.

Brunswick Street

Babka Bakery Cafe 358 Brunswick St ☎03/9416 0091. A deservedly popular place: the home-made bread and cakes are divine, and dishes from the changing blackboard menu are equally enticing. Try Russian blintzes for breakfast or *borscht* (a tangy, beetroot-based soup) and sourdough bread for lunch. Moderate. Licensed and BYO. Tues–Sun 7am–7pm.

Lambs on Brunswick 314 Brunswick St ☎9415 7365. It might look the less appealing of all the nearby *souva* shops, but this old-timer does great kebabs ($7) and a lamb pizza that's perfect after all those beers. Open 11am–late daily.

Mario's 303 Brunswick St ☎03/9417 3343. European-style café where you can eat breakfast, lunch and dinner or just have a coffee or a drink. Dauntingly smart staff and decor, but not expensive or dressy. The clientele is an interesting mixture of poseurs, celebrities and scruffs. Daily 11am–11pm.

Thai Thani 293 Brunswick St ☎03/9419 6463. One of Melbourne's best Thai restaurants, on two crowded levels, with moderate prices. Licensed and BYO (wine only). Daily 6–11pm.

The Vegie Bar 380 Brunswick St ☎03/9417 6935. Cheap, popular and hip (rather than hippie) place with simple, fresh vegetarian and vegan food. Licensed and BYO (wine only). Daily 11am–10pm.

Gertrude Street

Arcadia 193 Gertrude St ☎03/9416 1055. Favourite local hangout with great-portioned hearty fare such as pastas and curries including popular vegetarian options. Try to get a seat in the outside courtyard. Tues–Sun 10am–11pm.

Ladro 224 Gertrude St ☎03/9415 7575. Sensational yet simple authentic Italian-style pizzas that have won over thousands throughout the city. Booking is essential but takeaway available. Pizzas from $14. Wed–Sun 6pm–late.

Johnston Street and Smith Street

Café Dreams 147 Johnston St ☎03/486 9988. Known only to a few Turkish taxi-drivers, this no-frills restaurant has great kebabs, dips and pizza. A real find. Open Mon–Sat from 5pm.

Gluttony – It's a Sin 278 Smith St ☎03/9416 0336. Good cakes, cooked breakfasts and meals. Popular with locals. Licensed and BYO. Tues–Sat 9.30am–11pm, Sun 9am–6pm.

Soul Food Cafe 273 Smith St ☎03/9419 2949. Comfortable cafeteria-style vegetarian café with wooden trestle tables. Mon–Thurs 8am–9pm, Fri–Sun 9am–6pm.

Richmond and Abbotsford

Swan Street, running from Church Street towards Wattle Park, is home to Greek restaurants, while **Victoria Street**, separating Richmond from Abbotsford, is lined with Vietnamese supermarkets, clothes shops and dozens of cheap, authentic restaurants.

Fenix 680–682 Victoria St, Richmond ☎03/9427 8500. Great views over the Yarra, especially in summer on the deck. As for the food, you can dive into steak, fish and steamed pudding, all of it decently priced and well presented. Mon–Fri 9am–11pm, Sat & Sun 8am–11pm.

Minh Minh 94 Victoria St, Richmond ☎03/9427 7891. Good, cheap Indochinese food (Vietnamese, Laotian and Thai dishes) served in surroundings that are a little bit more stylish than most on this street. BYO. Mon & Tues 4–10pm, Wed, Thurs & Sun from 11.30am, Fri & Sat 11.30am–11pm.

Pacific Seafood BBQ House 240 Victoria St, Abbotsford ☎03/9427 8225. The duck here is a particular favourite, though if that's not your taste go to the tanks and pick which fish to devour. Great ambience and reasonable prices. Sun–Thurs 10.30am–10.30pm, Fri & Sat 10am–11.30pm.

Vlado's 61 Bridge Rd, Richmond ☎03/9428 5833. Vegetarians don't bother. This 50-year-old steakhouse, where you pick the cut of meat you want from passing waiters, isn't easy on the waistline or the wallet but is always delicious. Set-price 4-course menu is $74. Open lunch Sun–Fri, dinner Mon–Sat.

South Yarra and Windsor

Botanical Hotel 169 Domain Rd, South Yarra ⓣ03/9820 7800. Premier gastro-pub with flair that serves excellent breakfast, lunch and dinners. Nearly always full and a popular nightspot as well with a very deep wine list. Daily 7am–11pm.
Caffe e Cucina 581 Chapel St, South Yarra ⓣ03/9827 4139. Still one of Melbourne's coolest eating spots, attracting a smart clientele and dishing up fantastic pasta. Licensed. Mon–Sat 7am–midnight.
Falafel House 196 Toorak Rd, South Yarra ⓣ03/9827 6236. Middle-Eastern takeaway, perfect after pubbing or clubbing. Daily 9–5am.
Globe Cafe 218 Chapel St, Windsor ⓣ03/9510 8693. Serves breakfast all day, and has great cakes and bread made on premises. Moderate. Licensed. Mon–Thurs 8.30am–10pm, Fri 8.30am–late, Sat & Sun 9am–late.
Lucky Coq 179 Chapel St, Windsor ⓣ03/9525 1288. Renovated pub that has a grungy, bohemian-type feel. Serves excellent gourmet pizzas for just $4 (noon–2pm weekdays) and around $8 at other times. Open 11.30–2.20am, making it the prime destination for partygoers.
New Wind 106 Chapel St, Windsor ⓣ03/9827 1888. Pleasant Vietnamese–Thai bar-restaurant; lunch is particularly good value. BYO. Mon–Fri 11.30am–late, Sat & Sun 5pm–late.
Orange 126 Chapel St, Windsor ⓣ03/9529 1644. Epitomizes the grunge-chic of the Windsor end of Chapel St. Great place to chill out; they serve breakfast all day, light meals for lunch and more substantial fare for dinner, or relax with a cocktail or two until the wee hours. Great garden out the back. Licensed. Mon & Tues 7am–6pm, Wed–Fri & Sun until 2am, Sat until 3am.
Patersons Cakes & Café 117 Chapel St, Windsor ⓣ03/9510 8541. The long-established, renowned cake and pastry shop now also runs a good café on the premises. Mon–Fri 9.30am–5pm, Sat till 4pm.

South Melbourne, Albert Park and Port Melbourne

The night-time scene in these suburbs is rather low-key, but there are cafés and delicatessens aplenty dishing up a mouthwatering selection of food during the day.

Andrew's Hamburgers 144 Bridport St, Albert Park ⓣ03/9690 2126. Much-loved and extremely low-key hamburger shop which serves them big, fatty and with all the trimmings. Prices around $6.50.
Bell's Hotel & Brewery 157 Moray St, South Melbourne ⓣ03/ 9690 4511. Typical pub with good chicken parmas, burgers and the usual fare, but most people come for their exceptional, award-winning homebrews. Open for lunch and dinner daily.
Cafe Sweethearts 263 Coventry St, South Melbourne ⓣ03/9690 6752. Good for breakfast, and also has numerous (and some very exotic-sounding) varieties of sandwiches. Mon–Fri 7am–3pm, Sat & Sun 8am–3pm.
Dundas & Faussett Cnr Dundas Place and Faussett St, Albert Park ⓣ03/9645 5155. One of the many swish cafés in the heart of the Albert Park village. Mon–Fri 7am–6pm, Sun & Sat 8am–6pm.
Feedings at Readings 253 Bay St, Port Melbourne ⓣ03/9681 9255. An irresistible bookshop with a café – browse, and read the first pages of your newly acquired book on the café terrace, perched a few steps above Bay Street. Licensed. Mon–Thurs 8am–7pm, Fri 8am–9pm, Sat 8am–6pm, Sun 9am–8pm.
Misuzu's 7 Victoria Ave, Albert Park ⓣ03/9699 9022. Pleasant Japanese eatery and very modestly priced given the location. Open daily for lunch and dinner. Daily noon–3pm & 5.30–10pm.
Montague Park Foodstore & Café 406 Park St ⓣ03/9682 9680. Delicious dishes and desserts to take away or eat in – it's particularly pleasant in summer when tables are set out on the footpath. Mon–Fri 7.30–5pm, Sat & Sun 8am–4pm.

St Kilda

This suburb's café scene and nightlife revolve around **Acland Street** and **Fitzroy Street**. While the former is good for browsing in shops, for late breakfast and for pigging out on cakes, the latter, especially the block from Grey Street to the waterfront, arguably has the edge on vibrant nightlife.

Bala's 1D Shakespeare Grove, just off Acland St near Luna Park ☎03/9534 6116. Excellent, cheap Asian takeaway food, including lassis and lots of stir-fried dishes with ultra-fresh ingredients. There are a few tables if you want to eat in, though it gets very busy at lunch and dinner. Mon–Sat noon–10.30pm, Sun 10am–9.30pm.

Big Mouth 201 Barkly St ☎03/9534 4611. A great spot for people-watching. The café downstairs is open for breakfast and light meals from 10am until late, while the upstairs restaurant (modern Australian cuisine) is open Monday to Friday 5pm–1am, Saturday 11am–late, and Sunday 10.30am till late. Licensed.

Circa, the Prince 2 Acland St ☎03/9536 1122. Part of *The Prince* establishment (see *Mink Bar* and *Prince Public Bar*), this is still one of Melbourne's best spots for fine dining, boasting a magnificently theatrical fit-out and excellent food and wine. Licensed. Tues–Thurs & Sat 6–11.30pm, Fri & Sun noon–3pm & 6–11.30pm.

The Espy Kitchen, at the Esplanade Hotel, 11 Upper Esplanade ☎03/9534 0211. Decent pub-style food, especially their burgers ($10 with a half-pint on Mondays). Mon–Fri 5–10pm, Sat & Sun from noon.

Galleon Cafe 9 Carlisle St ☎03/9534 8934. Breakfast, served until 4pm, is the big attraction in this retro-style café, which is especially popular at weekends. Licensed and BYO. Mon–Fri 9am–11pm, Sat & Sun 8.30am–11pm.

La Roche Café 185 Acland St ☎03/9534 1472. Popular and unpretentious eatery that has a rustic and jovial feel. The tables that spill onto the street are taken early in the day so get in fast and sample their signature dish – lamb roasting on the spit. Open daily for lunch and dinner.

Le Bon Continental Cake Shop 93 Acland St ☎03/9534 3785. Fifty-year-old store, that never fails to tempt the hundreds of passers-by with their array of delicious Mediterranean-influenced cakes and pastries.Daily 8am–midnight.

Renix 60 Acland St ☎03/9534 7346. Great little place known for their gourmet pizzas, especially the "fat-free pizza" ("well almost" the menu says). Has a "Polish night" on Mondays serving traditional meals and music, which is popular. An array of vodkas are on offer to wash down the meals. Open 5pm–midnight daily.

Stokehouse 30 Jacka Blvd ☎03/9525 5555. Right by the beach (it gets packed in warm weather), this restaurant has two sections: a very affordable downstairs section with lots of unusual pizzas and pastas, fantastic cakes, coffee and wines; and a pricier upstairs section with superb views of the bay and excellent Italian-inspired food. Licensed. Downstairs open Mon–Sat 11–1am, Sun 10–1am, upstairs daily noon–2.30pm & 6–10pm.

Topolinos 87 Fitzroy St, St Kilda ☎03/9534 4856. A dimly lit, noisy and smoky St Kilda institution, which churns out cheap pizzas, generous portions of pasta and good cocktails until very late. Licensed. Mon–Thurs noon–3am, Fri–Sun noon–6am.

Elwood and Balaclava

Elwood's Ormond Street sports wall-to-wall trendy cafés, whereas **Balaclava**, along Carlisle Street, is catching up, but still manages to retain a bit of its old migrant atmosphere.

Cafe Tarrango 15 Ormond Rd, Elwood ☎03/9531 7151. Indian-run café, with delicious organic, biodynamic vegetarian food at cheap prices, though there's not much atmosphere. Licensed and BYO. Mon 5–11pm, Tues–Sun 10am–11pm.

Glicks 330A Carlisle St, Balaclava ☎03/9527 2198. Friendly bakery renowned for bagels and traditional Jewish savouries: try the *kreplach*, *latkes* or gefilte fish. Mon–Thurs & Sun 5.30am–9pm, Fri 5am–5pm, Sat 9.30pm–12.30am.

Jerry's Milk Bar 345 Barkly St, Elwood ☎03/9531 3078. Cornershop milkbar-cum-café brimming with old-fashioned trappings and locals who come for the cheap delicious soups, pasta and risotto. Winter Mon–Sat 7.30am–7.30pm, Sun 8am–6pm; summer Mon–Thurs till 9pm.

Turtle Cafe 34 Glenhuntly Rd, Elwood ☎03/9525 6952. Relaxed, old-corner café that attracts a faithful crowd for breakfast and light meals and snacks including bagels, focaccia, soups and salads, all at moderate prices. Daily 7am–6pm.

Wall Two 80 280 Carlisle St (rear), Balaclava ☎03/9539 8280. Simple hole-in-the-wall café that has become the coffee lifeline for those that can find it. Daily 6.30am–6pm.

Nightlife and entertainment

Melbourne has a rich arts and music scene, and there's always plenty to do in the evening. To find out **what's on**, check out *The Age* on Friday, when the newspaper publishes the fairly small entertainment guide, "EG". *Melbourne Events* is a handy free monthly guide to all sorts of happenings, available at tourist information outlets. Also check out the great free magazines *Beat* (Ⓦwww.beatmag.com.au) and *Inpress*, which you can pick up at most record shops, cinemas and cafés. For those on a budget looking for the best food and drink specials try the witty Ⓦwww.thehappiesthour.com.

Annual **festivals** further enliven the scene: the **Melbourne International Arts Festival** (Ⓦwww.melbournefestival.com.au) in October presents a selection of visual and performing arts, opera, and features individual performers from Australia and overseas, as well as a host of free events at Federation Square and other places around the city. The more innovative and cutting-edge **Melbourne Fringe Festival** (Ⓦwww.melbournefringe.com.au) starts in late September and overlaps a few days with the Melbourne Festival, while the **Melbourne Writers' Festival** (Ⓦwww.mwf.com.au) takes place in late August. The heavily promoted **Moomba Festival**, held in March, has a more commercial, "fun for the masses" approach, featuring events such as firework displays and dragon-boat races on the banks of the Yarra River in Alexandra Gardens. Three music festivals take place in the first half of the year: the **Melbourne Music Festival** in February, one of the largest Australian festivals of contemporary music; the **Brunswick Music Festival** in the third week of March, concentrating on folk and world music; and the **Umbria Jazz Festival** (formerly known as the Melbourne Jazz Festival) which runs for eleven days in early May at various venues around the city centre and inner suburbs. The **Next Wave Festival**, held over two weeks in the second half of May, celebrates Victoria's young artists, writers and musicians.

Tickets for most venues can be booked through Ticketmaster7 (Ⓣ13 61 00, Ⓦwww.ticketmaster7.com) or Ticketek (Ⓣ13 28 49, Ⓦwww.ticketek.com.au); both take credit-card bookings only. You can buy tickets half-price on the day of performance from Half Tix at Melbourne Town Hall (Mon 10am–2pm, Tues–Thurs 11am–6pm, Fri 11am–6.30pm, Sat 10am–4pm; cash only; Ⓣ03/9654 9420, Ⓦwww.halftixmelbourne.com).

Bars and pubs

Melbourne's fondness for a drink or three is reflected in its abundance of excellent **bars and pubs** – from places so obscure and cutting-edge you'll only know they exist by word of mouth to large establishments catering to broader and louder tastes. The push to revive Melbourne's once-staid CBD has seen many older watering-holes transformed into lively, youth-oriented venues, while cheap bar licences have meant that new spots are popping up each week. In addition, the relaxing of Melbourne's once-draconian licensing laws has produced enlightened opening hours, meaning that it's now possible to drink from noon until dawn. A number of drinking places are also listed under "Live music", below.

City centre

Elms Family Hotel 269 Spring St. Somebody dropped a country pub in the middle of the CBD. A real bet on the races and have a few cold beers kind of pub, where getting dressed in more than a T-shirt is frowned upon. The food prices are stuck in the 1980s (big steak sandwich for $6.50) and there is a nice little heated beer-garden.

Gin Palace 190 Little Collins St (entry via Russell Place). Glamorous subterranean joint with an upmarket drinks-list specializing in cocktails – not cheap, but delicious and generous. Yummy food and good lounge music, too.
Madame Brussels Level 3, 59 Bourke St. Feels like something out of a David Lynch film, with fake grass and tacky outdoor banana-lounges – and that's inside. Outside, the fantastic beer-garden patio looks through to the city spires. Cocktails come in jugs.
Mai Tai Hawaii Cocktail Bar 234 Russell St. It may feel like a time warp back to the 1980s, but this place, a section of a Thai restaurant, is so completely daggy it just has to be cool. Tasty cocktails complete the picture.
Melbourne Supper Club Bar Level 1,161 Spring St. Lounge bar with comfy couches that manages to be elegant and laid-back at the same time. Cocktails range from affordable to expensive and there's an extensive wine list; a range of tasty snacks such as veal meatballs or polenta cakes will keep the hunger at bay.
Meyers Place 20 Meyers Place, off Bourke St. This swish, dimly-lit hole-in-the wall bar has proved a massive hit with those in the know and Melbourne's trendy office-workers.
Pugg Mahone 106–112 Hardware St. Another Irish theme-pub, with a great party atmosphere of office workers and backpackers, especially on Friday and Monday nights. Great happy hours as well.
St Jeromes 7 Caledonian Lane. Hard to find but that's the appeal. Dark little entrance leads to a great little outside area which is a converted lane. Longneck beers are only $7 so expect to see fewer business types, more artists and students. Home to the excellent St Jeromes Laneway Festival in February.
Tony Starr's Kitten Club 267 Little Collins St. Sleek and stylish interior tricked out with slightly oriental furnishings, conducive to lolling on comfy sofas and ottomans while cradling a cocktail and nibbling on Asian-inspired food from the grill.
Transport Federation Square. This new watering-hole takes the zinc metal-jigsaw theme of its surroundings as its own decorative leitmotif and is a good spot either for after-work drinks or to finish off a night out. The windows of the airy ground-level pub look out on to St Kilda Rd – a great place for people-watching. The top-floor lounge bar and restaurant, *Taxi*, features a Japanese-inspired menu.

Carlton and Fitzroy

Builders Arms 211 Gertrude St, Fitzroy. Groovy pub with guest DJs on weekends and the occasional weekday. Laid-back and unpretentious atmosphere with great outdoor setting in the street.
Hotel Lincoln 91 Cardigan St, Carlton. Revamped pub where you can order inexpensive dishes from a blackboard menu in the dining room and wines by the glass from an excellent wine list.
Lambsgo Bar 135 Greeves St, Fitzroy. Inside this unassuming bluestone cottage is a beer-lover's dream, with over 100 local and imported varieties to choose from. Dark and cosy, with quirky amusement machines and art on the walls, it's a cult favourite of the locals in the know.
Napier Hotel 210 Napier, Fitzroy. Old-school Fitzroy pub that is always busy due to the relaxed surroundings and incredibly enormous meal portions. Try if you dare to finish their Bogan Burger (includes chicken schnitzel, steak, egg, potato cake, beetroot, huge wedges and salad) or just sit in their small, relaxing beer garden.

Richmond and South Yarra

Belgian Beer Café 557 St Kilda Rd, Windsor. A rare find in St Kilda Road's sterile office territory: a European-style beer hall in a historic bluestone building set back from the street. Convivial and comfortable in a rustic sort of way but definitely not downmarket. Unusual Belgian beers on tap and a food menu featuring well-prepared, solid European fare. Great beer garden in summer. Only drawback: prices are rather steep.
Bridie O'Reilly's 462 Chapel St, South Yarra. Irish-themed pub incongruously housed in an old church and saved from terminal tackiness by the pleasant front patio. Has meals and plenty of memorabilia from the Emerald Isle. Can get raucous on weekends, but it's fun if you're desperate for a Guinness or British beer.
Der Raum 438 Church St, Richmond. German for "the space", this is actually a small, groovy cocktail bar – the martinis, in particular, are well worth crossing town for.
Great Britain 477 Church St, Richmond. Excellent pub that is hugely popular with the university-student brigade. Has an array of funky couches and chairs, and a brand-new beer garden for those long, hot nights. Ask for their famous homebrewed beer on tap called PISS (light beer is called PISS WEAK), which goes down a treat.

St Kilda

Dog's Bar 54 Acland St. Chic setting attracting a dedicated clientele. The wine list is terrific (although there's a surprisingly small range of beers) and there's great tucker like bangers and mash, steak, pizza, pasta and chips.
Elephant and Wheelbarrow 169 Fitzroy St. Corny English theme-pub that is enormously popular with

backpackers looking for love and good times. Has cover bands playing on the weekend and special events during the week (such as Meet the Cast of *Neighbours* on Mondays). Good seating outside on the road.

The Esplanade Hotel 11 Upper Esplanade. Famous for its beachside views, this hotel is the epicentre of St Kilda's drinking scene and shouldn't be missed. Bands play every night and there are inexpensive meals from *The Espy Kitchen* at the rear, plus pool tables and pinball machines.

The George Public Bar 127 Fitzroy St. Very cool underground bar with an upbeat design. Favoured by locals, it has a large range of beers on tap, plus a pool table and free live music on Saturday afternoons. The service is friendly and the kitchen is open until late each night, serving a wide range of snacks and good-value meals. Table seats outside.

Gay and lesbian Melbourne

Melbourne's gay and lesbian scene may not be as in-your-face as Sydney's, but it's almost as big, and is also less ghettoized than in Sydney. Fitzroy, Collingwood and Carlton, north of the river, and St Kilda, South Yarra and Prahran, to the south, boast a strong **gay** presence; Fitzroy, Northcote and Clifton Hill are the city's recognized stomping grounds for **lesbians**. There are two free gay and lesbian **papers**: *Bnews* (Ⓦwww.bnews.net.au) and *MCV* (*Melbourne Community Voice*; Ⓦwww.mcv.com.au), both published weekly.

Big **events** are mostly organized by the ALSO (Alternative LifeStyle Organisation) Foundation, including one over the Australia Day weekend at the end of January: **Red Raw Resurrection**. The scene's annual highlight, however, is the fabulous **Midsumma Festival** (late Jan to early Feb; Ⓣ03/9415 9819, Ⓦwww.midsumma.org.au). Already in its 17th year, Midsumma provides an umbrella for a wide range of sporting, artistic and theatrical events. The Queen's Birthday public holiday in June is the time for the **Winterdaze** party, while Melbourne Show Day in September is marked by the **Show Off** dance party.

Organizations, support groups, bookshops and radio station

ALSO Foundation 1st Floor, 6 Claremont St, South Yarra Ⓣ03/9827 4999, Ⓦwww.also.org.au. Organizes events and publishes the *ALSO Directory*, free from community outlets, which lists everything from gay vets to lesbian psychologists.

Beat Books 157 Commercial Rd, Prahran Ⓣ03/9827 8748. Gay bookshop with a large range of magazines, books, sex toys and leather goods.

Gay and Lesbian Switchboard Ⓣ03/9827 8544 or 1800 631 493 (Mon, Tues, Thurs & Fri 6–10pm, Wed 2–10pm) for counselling, referral and information.

Joy 94.9 FM Ⓣ03/9699 2949, Ⓦwww.joy.org.au. Gay and lesbian radio station, with 24hr music ranging from classical to R&B and world music, plus news and updates about the arts and club scene.

Hares and Hyenas 135 Commercial Rd, Prahran Ⓣ03/9824 0110. Gay and lesbian bookshop.

Cafés and meeting places

Globe Cafe 218 Chapel St, Prahran Ⓣ03/9510 869. Good choice for a well-deserved treat after a hard morning's browsing on Chapel St. Mon–Wed 8.30am–11pm, Thurs & Fri 8am–midnight, Sat & Sun 9am–late.

Ice Café Bar 30 Cato St, Prahran Ⓣ03/9510 8788. Popular gay and lesbian meeting place in a small lane off Commercial Rd, opposite Prahran Market. Breakfasts are served daily until 4pm, with an extensive breakfast menu to choose from, plus light meals (pasta, risotto) and cocktails. Cheap–moderate. Daily 8am–late.

Jackie O 204 Barkly St, St Kilda Ⓣ03/9537 0377. Comfy, atmospheric surroundings complemented by relaxed service and value-for-money food. Daily 7.30–1am.

See also p.830 for gay- and lesbian-friendly places to stay and p.863 for gay and lesbian club-nights.

△ *The Prince Public Bar*, St Kilda

Mink Bar At *The Prince*, 2B Acland St, St Kilda. Refurbished hotel-bar-restaurant complex, this subterranean vodka-bar has back-lit refrigerated shelves stacked high with an astonishing array of Russian, Polish, Swedish, Finnish, Lithuanian and – gulp – Japanese vodka. A great place for convivial quaffing and mellowing.

The Prince Public Bar 29 Fitzroy St, St Kilda. Defiantly local and no-frills, the downstairs public bar of *The Prince* (see p.830 and *Circa, The Prince*) has an air of stubborn resistance in the face of St Kilda's freewheeling gentrification. Frequented in equal parts by colourful local identities and desperadoes, it's not for the faint-hearted.

St Kilda Army and Navy Club 88 Acland St. In an area where pretentiousness is rife, it doesn't come any more down to earth than this. After signing in at the door, the many locals who spend more time here than their own home, are happy to swap stories and tell you about the good old days. Drink prices are the cheapest in the area, and they occasionally have live bands.

Traffik 16 Grey St. Dedicated backpacker-bar that packs them in due to its late closing time (5am) and ridiculously cheap happy-hours ($2 pints).

Live music

Melbourne has a thriving **band** scene, and just about every pub puts on some sort of music – often free – at some time during the week. Grungy Richmond has a big concentration of **music pubs**, and Fitzroy and St Kilda are also worthy areas to head to for a range of live music. Note the line between bars, music pubs and clubs is getting increasingly blurred; the pubs listed below are also good places for a drink and always have at least two bars, so you can escape the din if you want to. Most clubs have a **cover charge** of between $5 and $10. Some backpacker hostels give vouchers for reduced or free admission to a rapidly changing array of venues, or you can pick up the passes in music shops such as Gaslight at 85 Bourke St.

Free **listings** magazines such as *Beat*, *Inpress* or *Zebra* are good sources of information about the local music scene, while local FM stations Triple R (102.7) and PBS (106.7) air alternative music and tell you what's on and where.

City centre and the northern suburbs

Bar Open 317 Brunswick St, Fitzroy. The beauty of this place is that you never know what you're going to get. Comedy, acoustic folk, funk, or visual performances are just some of the things you might encounter. With comfy couches dotted over the two floors, it's a perfect place to see what Fitzroy music is all about. Totally unpretentious.
Bennetts Lane 25 Bennetts Lane, off Little Lonsdale St in the CBD, between Exhibition and Russell sts. One of Melbourne's most interesting jazz venues, now expanded to include a larger back room to complement the original cramped, 1950s-style cellar.
The Curry Family Hotel 289 Wellington St, Collingwood. Also appropriately known as the "Gem", this long-standing pub has recently changed hands, and the new owners have done wonders, bringing in free nightly blues, folk and jazz performances. The comfy restaurant area also serves one of the city's best chicken parmas.
Ding Dong Lounge 18 Market Lane, City. Small and busy place that plays host to jazz musicians, tribute bands and DJs.
Empress Hotel 714 Nicholson St, North Fitzroy. Lots of bands play here, the bar meals are big, if somewhat unsophisticated, and there's a great beer garden.
Pony Club 68 Little Collins St, CBD. You wouldn't expect to find a gritty rock'n'roll bar deep in the heart of Melbourne's business district, but that's what the *Pony Club* truly is. With a 7am closing time on weekends (5am on weeknights), this is where the people come who don't have to get up next morning, to immerse themselves in all things rock. Also has one of the tiniest men's toilets in the country.
The Rainbow 27 St David St, Fitzroy. Mellow atmosphere, interesting crowd and decor in an intimate bar with free music – R&B, funk and fusion – every night.
The Tote 71 Johnston St, Collingwood. A Melbourne institution for those that like their music loud and raw. Every night of the week you're guaranteed to witness bands plying their trade in the dark and dingy band-room where rock was born to thrive. With a nice beer garden (including BBQ), colourful characters and good happy hours (6–8pm weekdays), it's easy to see why many consider this Melbourne's best place to hear music.

Richmond and the southern suburbs

Corner Hotel 57 Swan St, Richmond. Big-name, alternative independent bands often play here from overseas. Also has a great beer garden on the roof.
The Esplanade Hotel 11 Upper Esplanade, St Kilda. The "Espy" is the soul of St Kilda and of Melbourne's eclectic band scene (huge bouncers make it look rougher than it actually is), hosting an interesting nightly line-up of bands in the front bar (free) and *Gershwin Room* (small admission charge).
The Greyhound 1 Brighton Rd, St Kilda. Old-fashioned pub with cosy band-room playing live music most nights of the week.
The Prince Band Room At *The Prince*, 2 Acland St, St Kilda. Part of the refurbished *Prince* complex, this is another St Kilda icon which has undergone a facelift to fit in with the smart cafés and restaurants at this end of Fitzroy St. Upstairs late-night venue with good bands.

Clubs

Altitude Bar Bullens Lane (near the corner of Bourke and Russell sts), City. Trance and progressive house.
Brazen Lounge 169 Exhibition St, City. Spread over two storeys. The programme spans a wide range from indie/alternative, Brit pop, goth, house, R&B and funk.
Chasers 386 Chapel St, South Yarra. Remains popular after many years and has a good sound and lighting system.
Club Odeon Crown Casino Entertainment Complex, south of the Yarra. Has a cabaret-type feel and tends to get full in the early hours of the morning.
Metro 20 Bourke St, City. Huge old theatre on three floors with eight bars and three dance-floors, all very lavish. Expect an enormous queue of spivved-up kids on Friday night.
Monsoons Russell St, City. Upmarket club at the *Grand Hyatt*: *daFunk Club* for R&B, funk and soul.
Revolver 229 Chapel St, Prahran. Live music in the bandroom most weekends, while every night (Sundays from 7am) in the lounge room DJs spin electronic beats, reggae and dub sounds.
Twister Lower Esplanade, St Kilda. Huge club at the back of the Palace Theatre that packs mostly university students in with its array of mainstream dance hits and retro music.
Viper Room 373 Chapel St, Prahran. Popular spot with Melbourne's dancing crowd.

Gay and lesbian venues and club nights

Diva Bar 153 Commercial Rd, South Yarra. Cocktail and dance bar with a mixed crowd. Open Wed–Sun.
DT's Hotel 164 Church St, Richmond. Mixed crowd and popular pool competitions. Open Wed–Sun.
Laird Hotel 149 Gipps St, Collingwood. Well-equipped men-only venue, with two bars, DJs, a beer garden and games room; popular with the leather crowd. Open daily; cheap drinks until 10pm.
The Market 143 Commercial Rd, South Yarra. Excellent dance club with weekly menu of top-notch drag shows, karaoke nights and talent quests. No cover charge. Open Thurs–Sun.
The Peel 113 Wellington St (corner of Peel St), Collingwood. Dance floor, music videos and shows, drawing a large and appreciative crowd, mainly men. Open Wed–Sun.
Salon Kitty 399A High St, Northcote. Intimate lounge bar for women. Open Thurs–Sun.
Templebar Precinct 98 Smith St, Collingwood. New restaurant/bar that has a super entertaining "spag and drag" night ($10 for beer, spaghetti and drag show on Wednesdays).
Xchange Hotel 119 Commercial Rd, South Yarra. Mainly men. Open daily.

Comedy

Melbourne is the comedy capital of Australia, home of the madcap Doug Anthony All Stars, Wogs Out of Work and comedians from TV shows such as *The Big Gig* and *The Comedy Company*. The highlight of the comedy year is the **Melbourne International Comedy Festival** (Ⓦwww.comedyfestival.com.au) in April, based at the Town Hall in Swanston Street, with performances at several other venues around town. As well as local and interstate acts, you're likely to see some of the best stand-up comedians from overseas. For one-off performances and other venues, check out the "EG" supplement to *The Age* on Fridays.

Comedy Club @ Athenaeum Theatre 188 Collins St, City ⓣ03/9650 1500 . Slick, cabaret-style space, which features largely mainstream comedians.
The Comics Lounge 26 Erroll St, North Melbourne. Comedy shows seven days a week; all formats from stand-up to cabaret. Tues & Wed nights host stand-up comedy newcomers. Pre-show dinner available Wed–Sat.
Dirty Reitop's Dirty Secrets 80 Smith St, Collingwood. Excellent cavern-like basement that is perfect for intimate comedy. Tuesday nights from 8.30pm and only $3 entry.
The Esplanade Hotel 11 Upper Esplanade, St Kilda. Stand-up shows each Tuesday and Sunday from 8pm.

Theatre

Melbourne offers a rich array of dramatic productions, from fringe to mainstream, with venues everywhere. Watch out for **outdoor performances** in summer, including alfresco Shakespeare and shows for children in the Royal Botanic Gardens from December until the end of February (ⓣ03/9650 1500 for details; credit-card bookings with Ticketmaster7 ⓣ1300 136 166).

Athenaeum Theatre 188 Collins St, City ⓣ03/9650 1500. One of numerous small Victorian theatre buildings in the city, hosting guest performances – mainly plays and concerts.
Comedy Theatre 240 Exhibition St, City ⓣ03/9209 9000. Not a comedy venue, but a small theatre hosting events similar to the Athenaeum.
Her Majesty's Theatre 219 Exhibition St, City ⓣ03/9663 3211. Lavish musicals in a fabulously ornate old theatre.
La Mama 205 Faraday St, Carlton ⓣ03/9347 6142. Plays by new writers, as well as poetry and play readings.
Malthouse 113 Sturt St, South Melbourne ⓣ03/9685 5111. A renovated malthouse containing two venues – the Beckett Theatre and the larger Merlyn Theatre – hosting guest performances, opera, dance, concerts and readings. The resident Playbox company produces contemporary Australian plays.
Playhouse Theatre Victorian Arts Centre, 100 St Kilda Rd ⓣ03/9281 8000. Mainstream productions, mainly from the Melbourne Theatre Company.
Princess Theatre 163 Spring St, City ⓣ03/9299 9500. Small but lavish old-fashioned theatre which stages musicals and mainstream plays.

Regent Theatre 191 Collins St, near City Square, City ⓣ03/9299 9500. This lovingly restored old theatre puts on productions of big-name musicals.

Theatreworks 14 Acland St, St Kilda ⓣ03/9534 4879. Ground-breaking new Australian plays.

Classical music, opera and dance

The **Melbourne Symphony Orchestra** has a season from February to December based at Hamer Hall and the Melbourne Town Hall, while the **State Orchestra of Victoria** performs less regularly at Hamer Hall, often playing works by Australian composers. If you can't afford the ticket prices – expect to pay $40–80 for classical music performances, $70–150 for opera – you can listen to the Symphony Orchestra concerts on Tuesday at 7pm on Radio 3MBS (103.5FM).

Her Majesty's Theatre 219 Exhibition St, City ⓣ03/9663 3211. Occasionally hosts some of the great foreign ballet companies.

Malthouse Studio Victorian Arts Centre, 100 St Kilda Rd ⓣ03/9281 8000. Modern dance and plays.

Hamer Hall Victorian Arts Centre, 100 St Kilda Rd ⓣ03/9281 8000. Big-name concerts.

State Theatre Victorian Arts Centre, 100 St Kilda Rd ⓣ03/9281 8000. Venue for the Victoria State Opera and the Australian Ballet Company.

Film

The Crown Casino and Melbourne Central have a number of **cinemas** showing blockbuster movies (cheap tickets available on Tuesdays). In summer, watching a film under the stars at the Moonlight Cinema in the Botanic Gardens (see p.843) or at the Cinema at the Bowl (Sidney Myer Music Bowl) nearby can be a real treat (details from local press; bookings through Ticketmaster7 ⓣ13 61 00). The city's independent cinemas screen less obviously commercial US films and foreign-language films; these cinemas tend to offer discounts on Monday. The **Melbourne International Film Festival** in July (ⓦwww.melbournefilmfestival.com.au) has been going for over forty years, based at a number of cinemas around the city. The much younger Melbourne Underground Film Festival (ⓦwww.muff.com.au) held in July continues to grow in popularity at an enormous rate.

ACMI Federation Square ⓣ03/8663 2583, ⓦwww.acmi.net.au. Film-buff's cinema; often shows Australian movies.

Astor Theatre Cnr of Chapel St and Dandenong Rd, St Kilda ⓣ03/9510 1414, ⓦwww.astor-theatre.com. Classic and cult movie double bills in a beautiful Art Deco cinema.

Cinema Nova Lygon Court Plaza, 380 Lygon St, Carlton ⓣ03/9347 5331, ⓦwww.cinemanova.com.au. A rabbit warren of small, recently refurbished and comfortable cinemas showing the latest Hollywood releases, as well as art-house movies. Cheap-day Monday.

Como Gaslight Gardens, cnr of Toorak Rd and Chapel St, South Yarra ⓣ03/9827 7533, ⓦwww.palacefilms.com.au. Belongs to the Palace Cinemas chain, which shows latest releases of Hollywood movies as well as art-house films.

IMAX Theatre Melbourne Museum complex, Rathdowne St, Carlton ⓣ03/9663 5454, ⓦwww.imax.com.au. Part of the Melbourne Museum complex (see p.837), with kitsch interiors and awesome technology, including a gigantic screen and film reels so big they require a forklift to move them. Shows both 2D and 3D films, usually lasting from 45min to 1hr, mostly documentaries on inaccessible places or anything involving a Tyrannosaurus Rex.

Kino Dendy 45 Collins St, City ⓣ03/9650 2100, ⓦwww.kinodendy.com.au. In the Collins Place atrium, with several cafés and bars in the complex.

Westgarth Theatre 89 High St, Northcote ⓣ03/9482 2001. Sadly the old girl was recently renovated turning the historic cinema hall into four separate screens. Still showcases independent films; however, it doesn't quite seem the same.

Shopping

Melbourne's big two **department stores**, David Jones and Myer, are located off the Bourke Street Mall. **Shopping hours** are generally Monday to Friday 9am to 5.30pm, with late-night shopping till 7pm on Thursday and Friday evenings; many places also open at weekends from noon to 5pm.

Clothes

Some good, middle-of-the-road Australian brand names are Chelsea Girl, Country Road, David Lawrence, Jag, Rivers, Sportsgirl and Witchery. Dangerfield sells modern, funky clothes and great accessories. At the higher end of fashion look out for designer names such as Alanna Hill, Lisa Ho, Carla Zampatti and Saba. Some streets or precincts have clusters of shops of a particular type, making it possible to go clothes hunting by district.

Bridge Road, Richmond (between Punt Road and Church Street). This is Melbourne's inner-city bargain district: lots of factory outlets, clothes and shoe shops selling seconds, samples and end-of-season stock.

Brunswick St, Fitzroy Interspersed with cafés, bars and "cutting edge" hairstylists you'll find lots of small, groovy clothes boutiques and accessories shops – great for unusual hats, costume jewellery and "lifestyle" bric-a-brac: unusually shaped wall clocks or whatever is the latest craze in interior decor.

Chapel St: South Yarra, Prahran and Windsor Many upmarket fashion outlets at the northern (South Yarra) end, getting progressively less expensive, younger and grungier towards Prahran and Windsor in the south.

City Arcades and Lanes Lots of boutiques and small shops, selling designer brands and unusual fashion and shoes, are tucked away in the laneways of the two city blocks bordered by Flinders, Swanston, Bourke and Elizabeth streets.

Elizabeth St, City At the upper end between La Trobe and Franklin streets there are a few big shops selling samples and seconds (look out for Jump or Sportscraft labels).

GPO Centre, corner of Bourke St and Elizabeth St, City This grand, magnificently restored Victorian building is now home to high-fashion outlets.

Greville St, Prahran (off Chapel St). A few big-name clearing centres.

Hardware St and Little Bourke St, City Lots of shops selling travel clothing and equipment. The place to head for if you want to kit yourself out for your skiing, hiking or rafting trip.

Lygon St, Carlton Mainly lined with cafés and restaurants, but there are also a few good shoe shops and fashion retail outlets, most of them at the northern end between Grattan and Elgin streets.

QV, City The latest city development with boutiques clustered in the "lanes" running from Russell St towards Swanston St, selling high-fashion designer labels.

Smith Street, Collingwood/Fitzroy Has a number of secondhand clothing stores as well as backpacker stores and footwear wholesalers.

Books

Academic and General Bookshop 259 Swanston St, City. Secondhand bookshop selling a wide range of topics.

Angus & Robertson cnr of Bourke and Elizabeth streets, with other branches at 35 Swanston St, and 379 Collins St; all in the City. Mainstream bookshop.

Black Mask Books 78 Toorak Rd, South Yarra. Specializes in mystery and crime.

Book Affair 200–202 Elgin St, Carlton. Very good secondhand bookshop, particularly for novels.

Books for Cooks 233 Gertrude St, Fitzroy. Australia's largest range of cookbooks and related titles.

Border's, Jam Factory 500 Chapel St, South Yarra, also at Lygon Court Plaza, Lygon St, Carlton. Huge American chainstore with a superb range. Both branches have a café.

Brunswick Street Bookstore 305 Brunswick St, Fitzroy. Good independent bookseller with occasional launches and readings.

Chronicles 91 Fitzroy St, St Kilda. Small, well-stocked independent bookseller.

Collins Booksellers 86 Bourke St. Mainstream bookshop with large range.

Grub Street Bookshop 379 Brunswick St, Fitzroy. Secondhand and antiquarian books.

Hill of Content Bookshop 86 Bourke St, City. Very small but very well-stocked.
Kill City 226 Chapel St, Prahran. Small bookshop specializing in mystery and crime.
Map Land 372 Little Bourke St, City. Good stock of maps and travel books.
Readers Feast Midtown Plaza, cnr of Bourke and Swanston streets, City. Big mainstream bookstore.
Readings Books & Music 309 Lygon St, Carlton, also at 253 Bay St, Port Melbourne. This independent bookshop is one of Melbourne's best. Both stores have pleasant cafés.
Traveller's Bookstore 294 Smith St, Collingwood. Speciality bookstore that has a wide range of travel writing and guides. The store also doubles as a travel agent and staff are always helpful.

Music

Basement Discs 24 Block Place, off Little Collins St, City. Great range of jazz and world music.
Blue Moon Records 54 Johnston St, Fitzroy. Specializes in world music, particularly Latin and Spanish.
Border's, Jam Factory See p.847. Large American bookstore with a big CD department.
Cosmos Books and Music 112 Acland St, St Kilda. Small music department, with a good selection of CDs; classical, jazz and world music.
Discurio 113 Hardware Lane, City. Classical music, jazz, blues and folk.
The Last Record Store 304 Smith St, Collingwood. Good range of local artists.
Metropolis Music Store Level 3, 252 Swanston St. Sells a good range of local and imported titles, some of which are very hard to come by.
Readings Books & Music See above. Very good CD department.
Rhythm and Soul Records 128 Greville St, Prahran. Funk, electronic, trance and techno grooves.
Missing Links 405 Bourke St, City. Melbourne's premier alternative music store and ticket-seller to gigs around town.

Markets

Abbotsford Convent Farmers Market Good number of stalls selling mostly organic produce in a fantastic setting on the banks of the Yarra River. The Collingwood Children's Farm is next door and is a great intermission. 8am–1pm, 4th Saturday of every month.
Camberwell Market Station St, Camberwell. Large flea market with lots of good secondhand clothes stalls, books, records, bric-a-brac, and plenty of food vans and cafés. Sun 7am–3pm; take the train to Camberwell.
Federation Square Book Market New and secondhand books are sold in The Atrium at Federation Square every Sunday 11am–4pm.
Gaslight Night Market Held on the premises of the Queen Victoria Market. A lovely market with stalls selling unusual (and good) food, spices, deli items and gifts. Wed 5.30–10pm; end of November until end of February.
Prahran Market Commercial Rd, Prahran. Fresh produce market. Tues & Thurs dawn–5pm, Fri & Sat dawn–6pm.
Queen Victoria Market Probably the best loved of Melbourne's fresh produce markets. A huge range of products is available and the deli section is well worth visiting. Turns into a general clothes market on Sundays with only the fruit and veg section open also. Tues & Thurs 6am–2pm, Fri 6am–6pm, Sat 6am–3pm, Sun 9am–4pm; ⓦ www.qvm.com.au.
Royal Botanical Gardens Market Limited to 100 stalls; sells a variety of art, food and plants in a great setting. Every 2nd Saturday of the month. 9am–2pm.
South Melbourne Market Cecil St, South Melbourne. Fresh produce market with an array of junk food as well. Wed 8am–2pm, Fri 8am–6pm, Sat & Sun 8am–4pm.
St Kilda Arts and Crafts Market A Melbourne institution and particularly nice in warm weather: retreat to the beach afterwards or to one of the cafés in Fitzroy or Acland streets. Sun 9am–4pm, longer in summer.
Telstra Dome Concourse Market A new market selling arts and crafts. Sun 9am–4pm.
Victorian Arts Centre Crafts Market Good crafts market on the footpath alongside the Arts Centre, extending to the underpass towards Southgate. Sun 9am–4pm; in summer 10am–6pm.

Listings

Airlines (domestic) Jetstar ⓣ03/8341 4901, ⓦwww.jetstar.com.au; Qantas ⓣ13 13 13, ⓦwww. qantas.com.au; Virgin Blue ⓣ13 67 89, ⓦwww.virginblue.com.au.

Airlines (international) Alitalia ⓣ03/9920 3799; British Airways ⓣ03/8696 2633; Garuda Indonesia ⓣ1300 365 330; Japan Airlines ⓣ03/8662 8333; KLM ⓣ1300 303 747; Lauda Air ⓣ1800 642 438; Malaysia Airlines ⓣ13 26 27; Qantas ⓣ13 13 13; Singapore Airlines ⓣ13 10 11; Thai Airways ⓣ1300 651 960; United Airlines ⓣ13 17 77.

American Express 233 Collins St and 360 Collins St (Mon–Fri 9am–5pm, Sat 10am–1pm).

Banks and foreign exchange All major banks can be found on Collins St. Standard banking hours are generally Mon–Fri 9.30am–4pm (Fri until 5pm), although some branches of Westpac/Bank of Melbourne, including the one at 142 Elizabeth St, are open on Saturday (9am–noon). Most banks have 24-hour ATMs, which accept a variety of cash, credit and debit cards. Branches of Travelex are at 233 Collins St, 136 Exhibition St and 261 Bourke St (Mon–Fri 9am–5.30pm, Sat 10am–3pm). There are Thomas Cook desks at Arrivals at the international terminal of Melbourne Airport.

Bike rental Hire a Bicycle, riverside next to Princess Bridge (daily 10am–5pm, weather permitting; ⓣ0417 339 203, ⓦwww.byohouse.com.au/biketours) has basic bicycles, mountain bikes and tandems ($15–17/2hr, or $35 per day; helmets, locks, maps and backpacks are provided). The owner also runs a three and a half hour Real Melbourne Bike Tour ($50 incl. bike hire, and coffee and cakes in Lygon St). In St Kilda, try the helpful St Kilda Cycles, 11 Carlisle St (Mon–Fri 9am–6pm, Sat 9am–5pm, Sun 10am–4pm; ⓣ03/9534 3074, ⓦwww.stkildacycles.com.au; full day $25, or $18 per half-day after 1pm).

Consulates Canada, Level 50, 101 Collins St, City ⓣ03/96539674; UK, Level 17, 90 Collins St ⓣ03/9652 1600; USA, 553 St Kilda Rd ⓣ03/9526 5900.

Disabled travellers Paraquad Victoria, 208 Wellington St, Collingwood ⓣ03/9415 1200, ⓦwww.paraquad.asn.au. Assistance is available at metropolitan, suburban, country and interstate stations, while relevant information for people with disabilities can be obtained by calling metlink on ⓣ13 16 38. Buses are progressively being replaced with low-floor wheelchair-accessible models; however, passengers in wheelchairs still need to contact local bus operators for information. The Melbourne City Council produces a free mobility map of the CBD showing accessible routes and toilets in the city, available from the front desk of the Melbourne Town Hall. For wheelchair-accessible taxis, call Central Booking Service ⓣ1300 364 050. TADAS (Travellers Aid Disability Access Service), at Level 2, 169 Swanston St, near Bourke St Mall (Mon–Fri 9am–5pm, Sat & Sun 11am–4pm; ⓣ03/9654 7690), provides personal care and various services, including wheelchair rental; to get to the lifts, enter via alcove 2 shops south of Bourke St Mall.

Diving Underwater Victoria – Dive Industry Victoria Association (ⓣ1800 816 151, ⓦwww.underwatervictoria.com.au) has a list of members in the Greater Melbourne area who rent equipment, organize diving trips and offer dive courses.

Emergency ⓣ000 for fire, police or ambulance.

Employment Backpackers Resource Centre, at *Hotel Bakpak* (Mon–Fri 9am–5pm, Sat 9am–1pm; ⓣ03/9329 7525, ⓦwww.bakpak.com). Traveller's Work Centre at the *Coffee Palace*, 24 Grey St, St Kilda (ⓣ03/9534 2003; Mon–Sat 10am–6pm). In addition Traveller's Contact Point (see "Travellers aid centre", below) has a notice board.

Environment and conservation Australian Trust for Conservation Volunteers ⓣ03/9326 8250 or 1800 032 501, ⓦwww.atcv.com.au; Department of Sustainability and Environment (DSE) Information Centre, 8 Nicholson St, East Melbourne ⓣ03/9637 8325, ⓦwww.dse.vic.gov.au; Parks Victoria telephone information service ⓣ13 19 63; Wilderness Society Shop, 247 Flinders Lane ⓣ03/9639 5455. The Melbourne Visitor Centre at Federation Square has a range of brochures on national parks.

Flat-hunting and sharing Check the Saturday edition of *The Age*, as well as the notice boards of hostels and cafés along Brunswick St in Fitzroy, the *Galleon Café* at 9 Carlisle St in St Kilda, Readings Books and Music, 309 Lygon St in Carlton, and at Traveller's Contact Point (see p.870).

Hospitals and medical centres Alfred Hospital, Commercial Rd, Prahran ⓣ03/9276 2000; Royal Children's Hospital, Flemington Rd, Parkville ⓣ03/9345 5522; Royal Melbourne Hospital, Grattan St, Parkville ⓣ03/9342 7000; and St Vincent's Hospital, Victoria Parade, Fitzroy ⓣ03/92882211. Melbourne Sexual Health Centre, 580 Swanston St, Carlton (ⓣ03/9347 0244 or 1800 032 017) offers a free service. For vaccinations, anti-malaria tablets and first-aid kits contact the Travel Doctor (TMVC), 2nd Floor, 393 Little Bourke St ⓣ03/9602 5788, ⓦwww.tmvc.com.au.

Internet access There are plenty of cybercafés throughout Melbourne with most charging between $3–7 per hour. Most backpacker hostels also have Internet access. Alternatively, in the City try the

Tours from Melbourne

Melbourne can be used as a base for a wide variety of **tours** to the interior of Victoria or along the coast. Popular destinations are the Yarra Valley, the Great Ocean Road, the Grampians and the Penguin Parade at Phillip Island; sadly, only one operator offers walking tours of the gorgeous "Prom" (Wilson's Promontory). Given the distances, **day-trips** to all these destinations (except the Yarra Valley and Phillip Island) would be far too rushed. To get more than the most superficial impression, it is advisable to choose one of the **two-** to **four-day** excursions offered by various operators. The Great Ocean Road and the Grampians can also be visited on a one-way tour between Melbourne and Adelaide. Some of the smaller outfits do not operate during the winter months.

Adventure Tours Australia ⓣ1300 654 604, ⓦwww.adventuretours.com.au. A South Australia–based safari-tour operator who has expanded enormously in the last few years. They do runs along the west coast from Perth to Darwin, Darwin to Adelaide and along the top of Australia from Darwin to Cairns and have Tasmania "stitched up". They also do a three-day one-way tour from Melbourne to Adelaide via the Great Ocean Road and the Grampians departing 2–3 times a week ($345). All the major sights are visited and there is a hop-on, hop-off option with accommodation upgrades possible.

Autopia Tours ⓣ03/9419 8878 or 1800 000 507, ⓦwww.autopiatours.com.au. Long-established outfit running popular day-trips by minibus along the Great Ocean Road ($95), to Phillip Island ($99) and the Grampians ($90), plus a combined tour to the Great Ocean Road and the Grampians (3 days; $170). They also offer one-way tours between Melbourne and Adelaide via the Great Ocean Road and the Grampians (3 days; $345), and between Melbourne and Sydney via the Snowy Mountains and Canberra (3–4 days; $395). Max. 22 people; prices include meals and accommodation.

Bunyip Bushwalking Tours ⓣ03/9531 0840, ⓦwww.bunyiptour.com. Nature-focused tours with – as their name implies – lots of bushwalking, mainly to Wilson's Promontory National Park (1–3 days; $110–195). For the longer trips you need to be reasonably fit and able to carry a pack with your own tent and supplies. The one- and two-day tours can be combined with the Phillip Island Penguin Parade on the way back to Melbourne. A two-day tour to the Grampians departs every Saturday ($170), and there are two departures midweek for a trip to the Great Ocean Road and the forests and waterfalls of the Otways ($175). Very small groups.

Echidna Walkabout ⓣ03/9646 8249, ⓦwww.echidnawalkabout.com.au. Long-running upmarket ecotour operator, with very small groups and enthusiastic, extremely know-ledgeable guides, focusing on native wildlife. The Savannah Walkabout day-tour ($160)

huge Central Internet Café, 279 La Trobe St (daily 9am–1am); Global Gossip, 440 Elizabeth St (Mon–Fri 9am–10.30pm, Sat 10am–10.30pm, Sun 11am–10pm); Internet Café, 429 Elizabeth St (Mon–Sat 10am–6pm, closed Sun); and Traveller's Contact Point, see p.870; in St Kilda: Hubway Internet Café, 9 Grey St (daily 9.30am–11pm), and at World Wide Wash at 361 Brunswick St, Fitzroy (daily 9.30am–10pm).

Laundries Almost all of the hostels and hotels have their own laundry. Commercial self-serve coin laundries include Melbourne City Dry Cleaners, 244 Russell St, corner of Lonsdale St (Mon–Fri 7am–6.30pm, Sat 9am–8.30pm); World Wide Wash at 381 Brunswick St, Fitzroy (daily 9.30am–10pm); The Soap Opera Laundry & Cafe, 128 Bridport St, Albert Park (Mon–Fri 7.30am–7.30pm, Sat 8am–6pm, Sun 10am–6pm); and Blessington Street Launderette, 22 Blessington St, St Kilda (daily 7.30am–9pm).

Left luggage and luggage forwarding Most hostels and many hotels store luggage; hostels usually don't charge an extra fee for this service. Southern Cross station has lockers (daily 6am–10pm; $8 for medium locker; emptied nightly as does Flinders Street station (8am–8pm; $8 for medium locker). Traveller's Contact Point (see p.870) stores luggage, forwards it and/or sends it home.

Library The Redmond Barry Reading Room at the State Library of Victoria, 328 Swanston St (Mon–Thurs 10am–9pm, Fri–Sun 10am–6pm), has current Australian and overseas magazines; the Newspaper Room has Australian and overseas papers.

goes to Serendip Sanctuary and the You Yangs, southwest of Melbourne, while longer trips head along the Great Ocean Road and to remoter parts of East Gippsland, and include bushwalks. Accommodation is in B&Bs or very comfortable camps ($900).

Eco Platypus Tours ⓣ1800 819 091, ⓦwww.ecoplatypustours.com. One very long day-trip along the Great Ocean Road, going as far as Loch Ard Gorge and staying at the Twelve Apostles for the sunset. The return trip is along the faster inland route via Colac ($90, but cheaper if more than three people book at the same time).

Go West ⓣ1300 736 551, ⓦwww.gowest.com.au. This family-run tour company offers day-trips, primarily aimed for the backpacker market, on a 21-seater minibus travelling the Great Ocean Road ($70) and to Phillip Island ($70); tours are very good value, entertaining and informative.

Groovy Grape ⓣ1800 661 177, ⓦwww.groovygrape.com.au. One-way tour specialist offering regular trips between Melbourne and Adelaide via the Great Ocean Road and the Grampians (3 days; $325). In Adelaide you can join their day-tour to the Barossa Valley ($69) and their one-way tour to Alice Springs (7 days; $825). Max. 20 people.

Melbourne's Best Tours ⓣ1300 130 550, ⓦwww.melbournetours.com.au. More conventional half-day and full-day tours in a small (21-seater) luxury coach to various destinations including Mornington Peninsula ($138), Phillip Island and the Dandenongs ($158).

Oz Experience ⓣ1300 300 028, ⓦwww.ozexperience.com.au. One-way trips from Melbourne to Adelaide and from Melbourne to Sydney are integral to this (almost) Australia-wide network backpacker bus-company. Primarily attracts a very young, party crowd but a switch in their format to shorter day-long itineraries and more emphasis on hands-on activities such as surfing, hiking, mountain biking, might change this.

Phillip Island Penguin Tours ⓣ03/9629 5888, ⓦwww.penguinislandtour.com.au. As the name suggests, it focuses solely on day-trips to see penguins ($99) and does it well with good minibuses equipped with DVD players.

Wayward Bus ⓣ1300 653 510, ⓦwww.waywardbus.com.au. Long-established one-way specialist, their regular tours follow the coast all the way between Melbourne and Adelaide, running via the Great Ocean Road, Mount Gambier and The Coorong (3–4 days; $345 for hostel bed; $460 twin share). In Adelaide, you can join their Kangaroo Island tour or their trip to all the natural attractions of the Red Centre and the Northern Territory's Top End. Max. 21 people.

Motorbikes The northern end of Elizabeth Street in the city centre has a string of motorbike shops. Garner's Motorcycles, 179 Peel St, North Melbourne (ⓣ03/9326 8676, ⓦwww.garnersmotorcycles.com.au), does rentals and may sell secondhand machines with buy-back deals.

Newspapers Melbourne's *The Age* is one of Australia's better papers; the pulpy *Herald Sun* is the city's only other daily known mostly for sport coverage. Foreign newspapers can be perused at the State Library (see opposite).

Pharmacies Australian Unity Pharmacy, 286 Little Bourke St, next to the Myer department store (Mon–Wed 9am–5.45pm, Thurs 9am–6.30pm, Fri 9am–9pm, Sat 10am–5pm; Mulqueeny's Pharmacy, cnr Swanston and Collins streets, opposite the Town Hall (Mon–Fri 8am–8pm, Sat 9am–6pm, Sun 11am–6pm).

Police Melbourne East City Police Station, 226 Flinders Lane ⓣ03/9650 7077; emergency ⓣ000.

Post office The GPO retail shop is located at 250 Elizabeth St (Mon–Fri 8.30am–5.30pm, including the poste-restante counter). Other post offices are open Mon–Fri 9am–5pm. For voicemail and mail forwarding, contact Traveller's Contact Point (see "Travellers aid centre", below).

RACV The RACV outlet in the city is at 422 Little Collins St; it has good maps of Melbourne, Victoria, and the rest of Australia (discounted for RACV members and members of affiliated overseas motoring associations; ⓦwww.racv.com.au). RACV also books accommodation listed in its guides and package holidays; members get special rates.

Skiing AUSKI Ski Hiring & Information Centre, 9–11 Hardware Lane ⓣ03/9670 1412, can advise on skiing conditions at Baw Baw, Buffalo, Mount Hotham, Buller, Falls Creek and at Thredbo in NSW.

Swimming pools City Baths, cnr of Swanston and Franklin streets (Mon–Thurs 6am–10pm, Fri 6am–8.30pm, Sat & Sun 8am–6pm; $4.70 for a swim, $9.90 including the sauna and spa, $18 for use of gym, pool, sauna and spa; ⓣ03/9663 5888), has a 30-metre heated indoor pool for swimming, plus a pool for water-aerobics and a gym. In the state-of-the-art Melbourne Sports & Aquatic Centre, Aughtie Drive, off Albert Park Rd in Albert Park, there's a choice between a wave pool, a 50-metre pool, a dive pool, a 25-metre lap pool, a 20-metre multi-purpose pool and a toddler area, plus a giant curling waterslide, spa, sauna and steam rooms (Mon–Fri 6am–10pm, 50-metre pool Mon–Fri 5.30am–8pm, Sat & Sun 7am–8pm; admission $5.90 or $9.70 including use of spa, sauna and steam room; ⓣ03/9926 1555, ⓦwww.msac.com.au). Take tram #112 from Collins St or #96 from Bourke St in the city.

Taxis Taxi rank on Swanston St outside Flinders Street station, and plenty to flag down. Call Yellow Cabs ⓣ13 22 27; Embassy Taxis ⓣ13 17 55; or Silver Top ⓣ13 10 08.

Telephones Melbourne has an abundance of public telephones and there are a plethora of discount phone-cards around (such as ezycom, Unidial, iprimus and Green Card), which can be used in any payphone for dirt-cheap international calls (as low as 1–3¢ per minute to the UK) and are sold in lots of shops, as well as Internet cafés and some backpacker hostels. Read the fine print before buying – watch out for flagfall billing in units of 3min or more, and a too-short expiry date. Don't make an overseas call using a public phone without a card, as it is ridiculously expensive.

Transport For information on trams, suburban buses and trains, call metlink ⓣ13 16 38 (6am–10pm daily).

Travel agents For flight bookings: Flight Centre (ⓣ13 18 66), 19 Bourke St and Shop 2, 250 Flinders St (ⓣ9663 6266), plus many branches throughout the city; STA Travel (ⓣ13 47 82, ⓦwww.statravel.com.au), 394 Little Collins St, City, and 144 Acland St, St Kilda, plus other branches throughout the city; Student Flights (ⓣ1800 046 462, ⓦwww.studentflights .com.au), many branches, including Shop 4, 250 Flinders St or 357 Little Bourke St. Travel agent: Backpackers World, Shop 1, 250 Flinders St (Mon–Fri 9am–6pm, Sat 10am–4pm; ⓣ03/9654 8477); Peter Pan Adventure Travel, 415 Elizabeth St (ⓣ1800 886 590); Traveller's Contact Point (see below); YHA Travel, 83 Hardware Lane (ⓣ03/9670 9611, ⓦwww.yha.com.au).

Travellers aid centre 2nd Floor, 169 Swanston St (Mon–Fri 9am–5pm; ⓣ03/9654 2600). As well as information there's also a café serving budget meals, nappy-changing facilities, showers (for a fee), toilets, lounge rooms, lockers, wheelchairs for rent and assistance for disabled and frail persons. Traveller's Contact Point, Level 1, 361 Little Bourke St (Mon–Fri 9am–5.30pm Sat 9am–12.30pm; ⓣ03/9642 2911, ⓦwww.travellers.com.au), sells backpacker discount cards, WWOOF memberships and has an employment notice board.

Moving on from Melbourne

Three **bus** services operate from Melbourne: V/Line buses (daily 7am–9pm; ⓣ13 61 96, ⓦwww.vlinepassenger.com.au), Firefly (reservations daily 7am–8.30pm; ⓣ1300/730 740, ⓦwww.fireflyexpress.com.au), and Greyhound Australia buses (reservation desk daily 6.30am–10.30pm; ⓣ13 20 30, ⓦwww.greyhound.com.au), all of which have terminals at Southern Cross station. For up-to-date **train** information, Southern Cross station has a staffed information desk with all V/Line train (and bus) timetables and there is also a V/Line booking desk (6am–10pm; ⓣ13 61 96). If you're travelling with a bicycle, come at least thirty minutes earlier to book it on the train. Suburban train information is available from metlink (see above). The **ferry** from Melbourne to Devonport in Tasmania, run by the *Spirit of Tasmania I* and *II*, takes ten hours. There's a nightly departure from Station Pier, Port Melbourne, at 9pm, plus additional departures at 9am (daily from mid-Dec to mid-Jan). The cheapest one-way fares range from $96 off-peak to $160 peak. The fare for standard cars and campervans is normally $69; for motorbikes the cost is $45. Reservations with TT Line ⓣ13 20 10, ⓦwww.spiritoftasmania.com.au. To get to Station Pier take tram #109 from Collins Street in the City.

Finally, many **car rental** and campervan companies offer one-way rental (see listings below). Two used-car companies who offer cheaper rates are Rent-A-Bomb (☎13 15 53) and Ugly Duckling in St Kilda (☎03/9525 4010 or 1800 335 908).

Car rental companies

Apex ☎03/9330 3877
Ascot ☎13 24 94
Avis ☎13 63 33
Budget ☎13 27 27
Hertz ☎1300 132 607
Network ☎1800 736 825
Thrifty ☎1300 367 227
Travellers Auto Barn ☎1800 647 374

Campervan companies

Apollo Motorhomes ☎1800 777 779
Backpacker Campervan Rentals ☎03/8379 8768
Britz ☎1800 331 454
Kea Campers Australia ☎1800 252 555
Maui ☎1300 363 800
NQ Australia Rentals ☎1800 079 529
Wicked Campers ☎1800 246 869

Around Melbourne

There are many possible day-trips out of Melbourne, mainly around the shores of the huge **Port Phillip Bay**, encircled by the arms of the Bellarine and Mornington peninsulas. The **Mornington Peninsula** on the east side has farmland and wineries on gently rolling hills and is home to some of the city's most popular beaches and surfing spots, packed on summer weekends. **Western Port Bay**, beyond the peninsula, encloses two fascinating islands – little-known **French Island**, much of whose wildlife is protected by a national park, and **Phillip Island**, whose nightly "Penguin Parade", when masses of Little penguins waddle ashore each night, is among Australia's biggest tourist attractions. The **Bellarine Peninsula** and the western side of Port Phillip Bay are less exciting, but they do give access to the west coast and the Great Ocean Road. A regular ferry service operates from Phillip Island and French Island to the Mornington Peninsula and from here on to the Bellarine Peninsula, making it possible to visit these places in one big loop before continuing along the Great Ocean Road, thus bypassing the need to backtrack to Melbourne. Even without your own car it is a doable travel option but not one that gets much publicity in Melbourne.

Inland to the east, the **Yarra Valley** and the **Dandenong Ranges** offer beautiful countryside, wine tasting and bushwalking.

The Mornington Peninsula

The **Mornington Peninsula** curves right around Port Phillip Bay, culminating in Point Nepean, well to the southwest of Melbourne. The shoreline facing the bay is beach-bum territory, though the well-heeled denizens of **Sorrento** and **Portsea**, at the tip of the peninsula, might well resent that tag. On the largely straight, ocean-facing coast, **Mornington Peninsula National Park** encompasses some fine seascapes, with several walking trails marked out. The western side of the peninsula facing the shallow waters of **Western Port Bay** (and French and Phillip islands) has a much quieter, rural feel. Heading north from the pleasant township of **Flinders** the coastline of rocky cliffs flattens out to sandy beaches, while north of **Stony Point** are mudflats and saltmarshes lined by white mangroves; not particularly visually appealing but an internationally recognized and protected habitat for migratory waterbirds. Further inland, the area around **Arthurs Seat** and **Red Hill** is probably the most scenic: a bucolic landscape of rolling hills, orchards and paddocks. This is also where the bulk of the peninsula's 200 or so **vineyards** are located. They produce superb, if pricey, Pinot Noir and Shiraz wines, as well as good whites. As in the Yarra Valley, good restaurants, especially winery restaurants, have proliferated on the peninsula in recent years, some of them in truly spectacular settings. Two of the best are *Crittenden at Dromana*, Harrison's Road, Dromana (Ⓣ03/5987 3800, Ⓦwww.crittendenwines.com.au), which serves light lunches daily; and *Max's at Red Hill*, 52 Red Hill–Shoreham Road, Red Hill (Ⓣ03/5931 0177), which has views over the hills and Western Port Bay; they serve lunches daily and dinners during the summer (Nov to Easter Thurs–Sat from 6pm). You could also try the equally scenic *Montalto Vineyard and Olive Grove*, 33 Shoreham Rd, Red Hill South (Ⓣ03/5989 8412, Ⓦwww.maxsatredhillestate.com.au), open for lunches daily and dinner Friday and Saturday. For more details, see the *Peninsula Wine Country Annual*, published by the Mornington Peninsula Vignerons Association, or *Wine Regions of Victoria*, available at tourist information centres. If you're in the mood for a beer instead, the Red Hill Brewery at 88 Shoreham Rd, Red Hill South (Ⓣ03/5989 2959, Ⓦwww.redhillbrewery.com.au) has an excellent range straight from the vat and serves up complimentary food to accompany it.

As well as the beaches, the peninsula's **community markets**, selling local produce and crafts, attract many city dwellers: most are monthly affairs, so there's usually one every weekend. One of the biggest and best is the Red Hill Community Market, held on the first Saturday of every month (Sept–May 8am–1pm), at Red Hill Recreation Reserve, Arthurs Seat Road, 10km east of Dromana; others include the Farmers Market at Dromana Estate, 555 Old Mooroduc Rd, Tuerong, every fourth Saturday (year-round 8am–1pm); Balnarring Racecourse Market at Colaart Road, Balnarring, on the third Saturday of every month (Nov–April 8am–1pm); the Mornington Racecourse Market (year-round every second Sunday 9am–2pm) at Racecourse Road, Mornington; and the Sunday Market at the Dromana Drive-in Cinema (year-round 7am–1pm) on the Bittern–Dromana Road, just off the Mornington Peninsula Freeway.

You can get to the peninsula by **public transport** from Melbourne to Frankston and from there to the main beach resorts and towns along the Nepean Highway on the northern side, but for a sightseeing trip taking in wineries, beaches and Arthurs Seat you'll need your own vehicle. Take a metlink train to Frankston and change there for Stony Point, or connect with a Portsea Passenger Service bus #788 from Frankston to Sorrento, stopping at the Peninsula Searoad Ferry terminal ($8.40) and Portsea ($8.70; for timetable information call Ⓣ1800 115 666). From Sorrento there's a community bus to Dromana via Blairgowrie, Rye and Rosebud (4 daily Mon–Fri), but no transport to Arthurs Seat. The *Bayplay Adventure Lodge* (see opposite) in Blairgowrie runs a **transfer service** to and from Melbourne or Frankston once daily, picking up passengers early in the morning for various dive excursions, sea-kayaking tours or other activities in the area, before returning them to Frankston or Melbourne in the evening (Ⓣ03/5988 0188; Melbourne $30, 4 people minimum, Frankston $20 one way).

The western coast

The peninsula starts at suburban **Frankston**, 40km from central Melbourne. From here on down, the western coast, flanked by the Nepean Highway,

Food and drink

Australia is a country that takes dining seriously. Yet it makes it fun, too. The wealth of local produce – fresh seafood, exotic meat, delicious fruit and some of the finest New World wines – means that you could easily spend your days moving from café brunch to late "Mod Oz" lunch. Just remember to leave room for the ubiquitous "barbie" on the beach.

Fish and seafood

Surrounded by the bountiful Pacific Ocean and crisscrossed by some mighty rivers, it's little wonder that Australia's **fish** and **seafood** is exceptional. The country's waters make rich pickings for restaurants, which serve up everything from Northern Territory **barramundi** to **Moreton Bay bugs** and from Queensland **reef fish** to **Sydney rock oysters**, some of the best in the world. **Marron** and **yabbies** (types of freshwater crayfish) are farmed in many places throughout the country, Tasmanian **Atlantic salmon** is raised in cold southern waters, and **tuna** from South Australia and **rock lobsters** from Western Australia are also world class. All of these, and much more, go under the hammer at **Sydney Fish Market**, the largest of its kind in the Southern Hemisphere, which auctions over 100 species daily.

▲ Sydney Fish Market

Only in Australia

You're unlikely to find these typical, sometimes quirky foods anywhere else in the world.

Lamingtons Small cake squares dipped in chocolate icing and rolled in coconut.

Pavlova A marshmallow-textured meringue dessert served with whipped cream and fresh fruit. New Zealanders argue that they actually created it – not that any Australian really believes that.

Anzac biscuits These oatmeal biscuits may have been developed as care-package treats for Australian and New Zealand Army Corps (ANZAC) soldiers in the World War I. Their chewy texture and distinctive caramel flavour has kept them popular for generations.

Pie floaters Definitely an acquired taste, these meat pies are submerged in mushy peas and topped with tomato sauce. Available from roadside stalls in Adelaide (SA), they are great favourites for late-night diners.

▲ Pepper Tree Winery, Hunter Valley

Wine and beer

Despite being a relatively new **wine**-producing country, Australia has earned worldwide respect for its fine yet affordable vintages, producing all styles including sparkling wines. Restaurant wine lists usually have selections from several states: **Margaret River** in Western Australia, for instance, is noted for its Cabernet Sauvignon, and New South Wales' **Hunter Valley** for its Sémillons. If you want a full-blooded red wine, go for Cabernet Sauvignons from **Coonawarra** in South Australia. The **Yarra Valley** and **Mornington Peninsula**, both in Victoria, are known for their Pinot Noirs and Chardonnay, while superb Shiraz comes from South Australia's **Barossa Valley**.

Beer is always popular, with boutique as well as major breweries across the country producing quality ales and lagers. Each state has its own brand and fiercely supportive fans, so it's XXXX (pronounced "four-ex") in Queensland, Swan and Emu in Western Australia, Coopers in South Australia, Cascade and Boags in Tasmania, Tooheys in New South Wales, and Carlton and VB in Victoria. Just don't walk into a pub and ask for Fosters – despite its prevalence outside of the country, it's nowhere near as popular in Australia itself.

BYO

In a restaurant, **BYO**, or **Bring Your Own**, means diners may, literally, bring their own wine to enjoy with their meal. Some establishments add "wine only" after BYO, but the understanding is generally that you may not bring spirits or beer. A small corkage fee is usually charged, either per bottle or per head.

Coffee

The increased appreciation of **espresso coffee** has resulted in a wealth of cafés throughout Australia. Melbourne (Vic), in particular, takes its beans seriously and prides itself on the high standard of its cafés though, naturally, Sydney-siders would say theirs are better. Most state capital cities and many country towns have cafés that serve fine coffee, often with outdoor dining.

▲ Melbourne is a good place to try Mod Oz cuisine

"Mod Oz" cuisine

Guides may list **Modern Australian** or "**Mod Oz**" when describing a restaurant's cuisine, and yet no one's come up with an exact definition. "Modern" is doubtless meant to distinguish current cuisine from "old-fashioned" Australian cooking in which "meat and three veg" once featured. Many countries have made a definite impact on this country's dining and cooking. Migrants from Greece and Eastern Europe have settled in Melbourne, while Sydney is now home to many people from Asia and the Middle East. Most chefs and restaurateurs seem to agree that a combination of **Mediterranean** and **Asian** styles of cooking techniques and local ingredients has come together in recipes that often are unique to Australia. Some Sydney restaurants now choose to call their cuisine **Contemporary**, which is perhaps a better description in this multicultural country.

▼ Emu farm

Bushtucker

Before whites settled the continent, indigenous Aborigines subsisted on tubers and roots, seeds, and wild game such as emu, goanna and kangaroo, as well as large white larvae called witchetty grubs. This food became known as "**bushtucker**", "tucker" meaning food. Until about twenty years ago, it was illegal to sell or serve kangaroo or emu anywhere outside of South Australia, but following legislation that allowed their consumption in other states, dishes featuring kangaroo, crocodile or emu are now readily available on most menus, with a few restaurants, even serving only indigenous foods.

sports beach after beach, all crowded and traffic-snarled in summer. Twelve kilometres beyond Frankston, the fishing port of **Mornington** preserves some fine old buildings along Mornington Esplanade; there's a produce and craft market on Main Street every Wednesday. Five kilometres further on, near Mount Martha, **Briars Park** (daily 9am–5pm; $4.70) comprises an 1850s homestead complete with a collection of furniture and memorabilia given to the owner by Napoleon Bonaparte, and an enclosed wildlife reserve with woodlands and extensive wetlands (daily 9am–5pm; closed during total fire bans; free). The **visitors centre** near the homestead has an audiovisual display giving you an overview of how the affluent upper crust lived in early pioneering days, as well as a rundown on the present-day facilities of the park. Two walkways through the woodlands start near the visitors centre; the adjacent **wetlands** are visited by more than fifty species of waterbirds, which can be observed at close distance from two bird-hides, accessible via a boardwalk from the visitor information centre.

Inland from Dromana, where seaside development begins in earnest, the granite outcrop of **Arthurs Seat State Park** rises 305m, providing breathtaking views of Port Phillip Bay. At the time of writing the Arthurs Seat Chairlift was closed and for sale after recent safety issues but in the meantime you can drive up the winding road. At the summit, **Arthurs Seat Maze** (daily 10am–6pm; Ⓦwww.arthursseatmaze.com.au; $13) combines four landscaped mazes with theme gardens, a sculpture park and a children's animal farm, and offers lots of family-oriented activities and a good restaurant. Alternatively, you can have a drink or a bite at the nearby revamped *Arthurs Seat Hotel*, with live jazz on Sunday afternoons.

Sorrento

Beyond Arthurs Seat, the peninsula arcs and narrows: the sands around Sorrento and Portsea offer a choice between the rugged surf of the ocean ("back" beaches) or the calmer waters of the bay ("front" beaches). With some of the most expensive real estate outside the Melbourne CBD, **SORRENTO** is the traditional haunt of the city's rich during the "season" from Boxing Day to Easter. Well-heeled outsiders also make it their playground in January and on summer weekends, flocking here to swim, surf and dive at the bay and ocean beaches. Exploring beautiful rock formations and low-tide pools, and swimming with bottlenose dolphins add to the attraction. The smell of money is everywhere – in the wide, tree-lined residential streets, the clifftop mansions boasting million-dollar views, and the town-centre cafés, restaurants, galleries and antique shops, running along Ocean Road down to the beach.

Sullivan Bay, 3km southeast, was in 1803 the site of the first white attempt to settle in what is now Victoria; the settlers struggled here for four months before giving up and moving on to what is now Tasmania. One of the convicts in the expedition was the infamous William Buckley who, having escaped, was adopted by the local Aborigines and lived with them for 32 years. When the "wild white man" was seen again by settlers he could scarcely remember how to speak English; his survival against all odds has been immortalized in the phrase "Buckley's chance". You can walk along the cliffs and around the pioneer cemetery; there's a signposted turn-off from the main road.

Swimming with dolphins and seals is one of Port Phillip Bay's prime attractions. Operators include the environmentally-conscious Polperro Dolphin Swims (Ⓣ03/5988 8437 or 0428 174 160, Ⓦwww.polperro.com.au), which takes the smallest groups, and Moonraker (Ⓣ03/5984 421, Ⓦwww.moonrakercharters.com.au). Both run, weather permitting, 3–4 hour trips twice daily during the season (Sept/Oct to April/May) for roughly the same prices: $99 for swimmers, including wetsuit and snorkelling equipment and $44 for sightseers. The *Bayplay Adventure Lodge* in Blairgowrie (see below) doubles as a PADI **dive resort** and offers dive courses (all levels): as well as a wide range of leisure dives for novices and experienced divers, they also run a guided sea-kayaking trip along the coast to Portsea (daily 4hr; $75). On most days dolphins come to frolic around the boats and often seals and penguins can be sighted. They also provide a free booking service for all kinds of other outdoor activities around the peninsula including horse riding and surfing lessons.

Practicalities

A reliable **car and passenger ferry** service operated by Peninsula Searoad (☎03/5258 3244, Ⓦwww.searoad.com.au) runs across the mouth of the bay from Sorrento to Queenscliff on the Bellarine Peninsula all year round (hourly 7am–6pm, Boxing Day to end of daylight savings until 7pm). One-way fares for pedestrians are $9, while standard cars are $52–59 (depending on the season) for 2 passengers plus $6 for each additional passenger. Motorbikes plus a rider are $24–28. No advance bookings are necessary but cars should be at the terminal thirty to forty-five minutes prior to departure.

Accommodation

Bayplay Adventure Lodge 46 Canterbury Jetty Rd, Blairgowrie ☎03/5988 0188, Ⓦwww.bayplay.com.au. Comfortable budget accommodation in a bushland setting near the beach, with a self-catering kitchen, free bicycles, Internet access and camping space. The lodge is also a PADI dive resort (see above) and offers daily transfers from and to Melbourne (see opposite). The Frankston–Portsea bus (#39) stops just out front. Dorms $25, rooms ③

Carmel of Sorrento 142 Ocean Beach Rd, Sorrento ☎03/5984 3512, Ⓦwww.carmelofsorrento.com.au. Charming, sandstone B&B (nonsmoking) smack in the middle of town. ⑥

Hotel Sorrento 5 Hotham Rd, Sorrento ☎03/5984 2206, Ⓦwww.hotelsorrento.com.au. A charming, 1871 limestone hotel located in a secluded spot on a hill above the jetty. Try to stay in their "Heritage Suites" with sea views. ⑤–⑥

Sorrento Beach Motel 780 Melbourne Rd, Sorrento ☎03/5984 1356, Ⓦwww.sorrentobeachmotel.com.au. Mid-level, well-managed yet quirky motel where the outside of each room looks like an old bathing house. ④–⑥

Sorrento Hostel YHA 3 Miranda St, Sorrento ☎03/5984 4323, Ⓔsorrento@yhavic.org.au. Cosy place run by a friendly couple, with small dorms (some en suite), doubles and twin rooms, and stacks of local information. Dorms $30, rooms ④

Eating and drinking

As is to be expected in this posh part of the peninsula, most eating places tend to be on the pricey side but some come with great water-views as a bonus. In winter, a lot of eateries have restricted opening times or are only open at weekends.

The Baths 3278 Point Nepean Rd, Sorrento. Best location in Sorrento but with high prices. The little fish-and-chip shop around the side is a more affordable option. Open daily 9am–late.

Continental Hotel 21 Ocean Beach Rd, Sorrento ☎03/5984 2201. This venerable old-timer has a good café with a range of Mornington Peninsula wines on its wine list, plus live music and a disco at weekends. Tues–Thurs 9am–4.30pm, Fri–Mon 9am–11pm.

Hotel Sorrento 5 Hotham Rd ☎03/5984 2206. It has a casual hotel-bar and a restaurant whose menu features seafood dishes, wood-fired gourmet pizzas, steaks and similarly conventional fare – the prime attraction is the view across the Bay.

Shells Café 95 Ocean Beach Rd, Sorrento ☎03/5984 5133. This light-filled, breezy café serves good coffee and cakes plus the standard café fare, and is a prime spot for people-watching. Popular spot for surfers. 8am–5pm daily.

Smokehouse Pizza Kitchen 182 Ocean Beach Rd ⓣ03/5984 1246. Since 1992 this place has been dishing up some of the best pizzas this side of Melbourne. Takeaway available. Daily noon–late.

Spargo's 113 Ocean Beach Rd ⓣ03/5984 3177. Big, sometimes chaotic café with nice outdoor seating in which to get stuck into their excellent wine list and seafood specials. Open for breakfast, lunch and dinner daily.

Stringers Store 2–8 Beach Rd. Part gourmet supermarket, part great café that serves up the best continental breakfasts in town. 8am–5pm daily.

Portsea and Point Nepean

PORTSEA, just beyond Sorrento, is a mecca for divers, with excellent dives of up to 40m off Port Phillip Heads; trips operate from the pier throughout the summer and there are a couple of good dive shops. Portsea Front Beach, on the bay by the pier, is wall-to-wall beautiful people, as is Shelley Beach, which also attracts playful dolphins. On the other shore, Portsea Ocean Beach has excellent surfing, and a hang-gliding pad on a rock formation known as London Bridge. Back on the bay side, the extensive lawns of *Portsea Hotel*, a hugely popular drinking spot which features bands at weekends, overlook the beach.

The tip of the peninsula, with its fortifications, quarantine station and former army base is now privately operated under the name **Park at Point Nepean**, part of a patchwork of parks sprinkled over the southern end of the peninsula, collectively known as Mornington Peninsula National Park. The visitor centre and a car park are 1km west of Portsea (daily 9am–5pm; ⓣ03/5984 4276). Because of its fragile sandy environment, visitor numbers are limited, so if you want to visit on weekends and during school holidays it's advisable to book. Entrance to this part of the national park costs $7.60. To get to **Point Nepean**, 6km from the visitor centre, you can either rent a bike ($15 for 4hr) or board the Transporter "train" – actually a few carriages pulled by a tractor ($12 one way, $15 return; these fares include the park admission fee). The Transporter departs from the visitor centre hourly between 9.30am and 12.30pm and at 2pm and 3pm. Alternatively, you can drive to Gunners car park, 2.5km into the park, and walk the rest of the way to Point Nepean.

The Transporter runs to the fortifications at Point Nepean, with four optional drop-offs for walks: the first, the **Walter Pisterman Heritage Walk** (1km), leads through coastal vegetation to the Port Phillip Bay shoreline; the second (1km) leads to the top of Cheviot Hill, where you can look across to Queenscliff, then continues to **Cheviot Beach** where on December 17, 1967, **Harold Holt**, Australia's then prime minister, went for a swim in the rough surf of Bass Strait and disappeared, presumed drowned: his body was never found. The third walk, the **Fort Pearce and Eagle's Nest Heritage Trail** (2km), crosses through defence fortifications. A fourth walk takes you around **Fort Nepean**, right at the tip of the peninsula. Built at the same time as Fort Queenscliff opposite to protect wealthy post-goldrush Melbourne from the imagined threat of Russian invasion, the fort comprises two subterranean levels, whose tunnels lead down to the Engine House at water level.

South and east coast

The rest of Mornington Peninsula National Park, which spreads along the ocean coast, is freely open to the public. An enjoyable two-day walk (27km) runs from London Bridge along the coast to **Cape Schanck**, site of an 1859 lighthouse. Here walkways lead down to the sea along a narrow neck of land, providing magnificent coastal views. The three **lighthouse-keeper's cottages** offer the most scenic accommodation on the peninsula (ⓣ0500 527 891,

Ⓦwww.austpacinns.com.au; ❹–❺), each with a cosy lounge and kitchen. There's a small maritime museum ($8) at the lighthouse, which is open daily for tours at half-hour intervals (10am–5pm; $10).

The nearby **Bushrangers Bay Nature Walk** (6km; 2hr) heads from the cape to Main Creek, beginning as a leisurely walk along the clifftop, then leading down to a wild beach facing Elephant Rock. More energetic activities in this part of the peninsula include **horse rides** along Gunnamatta Beach or through bushland, organized by the Gunnamatta Equestrian Centre, Trueman's Rd, Rye (Ⓣ03/5988 6755, Ⓦwww.gunnamatta.com.au), and **surfing** lessons, offered by the East Coast Surf School at various spots near Point Leo (daily year-round; all levels $40 for 90min, equipment provided).

For a decent place **to stay**, the pleasant village of Flinders has a good B&B; *Samburu*, Eastern Grey Rise, off Meakins Rd, 14km west of Flinders (Ⓣ03/5989 0093, Ⓦwww.samburu.com.au; ❺), has a guest wing in the main farmhouse and a separate studio with great views. A cheaper option is the shady *Flinders Caravanpark* (Ⓣ03/5989 0458), which has tent sites and cabins (❸–❹).

Set in bushland 15km southeast of Frankston, near the northern end of Westernport Bay, **Pearcedale Conservation Park**, at 55 Tyabb-Tooradin Rd (Wed–Sun noon–5pm; $9; Ⓣ03/5978 7935, Ⓦwww.moonlit-sanctuary.com) is home to lots of kangaroos, wallabies, emus and waterbirds. However, the park's emphasis is on rare nocturnal Australian animals, so it's well worth coming late in the day to take part in their guided **Moonlit Sanctuary tour** (90min; $19.50; reservations essential). Starting at dusk, this tour offers the chance to see rare nocturnal Australian creatures such as eastern quolls, eastern bettongs, pademelons, gliders and tawny frogmouths in bushland enclosures. If you really want to get close to the animals, following this tour is The Feed Out Tour ($33, reservations essential), where you accompany the guide and help feed the animals.

French Island

FRENCH ISLAND, on the eastern side of the Mornington Peninsula, is well off the beaten track. A former prison farm, about two-thirds of the island is a national park, with the remaining third used as farmland. The island is renowned for its rich **wildlife**, especially birds of prey, and a flourishing koala colony. Virtually vehicle-free, it's a great place to cycle, an activity which is encouraged, with all walking tracks open to bikes. The French Island Tourist Association runs a telephone information service on Ⓣ03/5985 5730.

Places to stay include *McLeod Eco Farm and Historic Prison* (Ⓣ03/5678 0155; ❸), where you can sleep in former prison cells converted into twins with bunk beds, or in the former officers' quarters with queen-sized beds; all have shared facilities. The farm is surrounded by national park and has 8km of beach frontage; the very reasonable rates include organic meals and transfer from the ferry jetty 29km away. Also in the national park is the small and basic *Fairhaven Campground* which has a pit toilet and tank water, but no showers. Camping is free, but must be booked in advance – two weeks ahead is advised during the summer school holidays and at Easter; at other times booking one or two days in advance will suffice (Ⓣ03/5986 8987 or 13 19 63). Near the jetty, the small *Tortoise Head Guesthouse* (Ⓣ03/5980 1234, Ⓦwww.tortoisehead.net; ❺) offers B&B accommodation in guest rooms with shared facilities and four en-suite cabins with water views. Moderately priced lunches and dinners are also available. *French Island B&B* is a cottage with two bedrooms, operated by the general store, 2.5km from the jetty (ⓣ03/5980 1209, ⓦwww.frenchislandbandb.com.au; ⑤), who also provide well-priced lunches and dinners. The *Bayview Chicory Kiln Tea Room* (10km from the jetty) has a private campsite with toilets and shower. In addition, scrumptious lunches and Devonshire teas are served here.

Inter Island Ferries (ⓣ03/9585 5730, ⓦwww.interislandferries.com.au) connects the Mornington Peninsula with French Island and Phillip Island (see below), departing from **Stony Point**, on the eastern side of the Mornington Peninsula to **Tankerton jetty** on French Island (daily 8.30am & 4.15pm, noon Tues, Thurs, Sat & Sun, also 10am Sat & Sun; $20 return plus $8 per bicycle). To get to Stony Point from Melbourne, take the Frankston train from Flinders Street station and a bus to Stony Point.

For a brief visit to French Island, it's best to book one of the afternoon tours covering the island's natural attractions and the historic prison. The **French Island Bus Tour** ($20 including Devonshire tea; ⓣ03/5980 1241, ⓦwww.frenchisland tours.com.au) operated by Lois Airs from the *Bayview Chicory Kiln Tea Rooms*, runs on Tuesdays, Thursdays and Sundays, and during school holidays also on Saturday. Alternatively, **French Island Eco Tours** ($30; ⓣ1300 307 054, ⓦwww.french islandecotours.com.au) runs tours on Thursday and Sunday with a two-course lunch available for $10 at *McLeod Eco Farm*, made from their organic produce. For both, take the Inter Island Ferry from Stony Point at noon to Tankerton jetty; the tours meet the ferry and drop off at the jetty at the end of the tour.

Phillip Island

The hugely popular holiday destination of **PHILLIP ISLAND** is famous above all for the nightly roosting of hundreds of Little penguins at Summerland Beach – the so-called **Penguin Parade** – but the island also boasts some dramatic coastline, plenty of surfing (for more information, call the Phillip Island Surf Report on ⓣ1902 243 082), fine swimming beaches, and a couple of well-organized wildlife parks. It is also home to the Australian Motorcycle Grand Prix in September which is why the History of Motorsport Museum is located on the island (daily 9am–7pm; ⓣ03/5952 9400, ⓦwww.phillipisland circuit.com.au; $13.50), featuring snapshots and memorabilia of the crazy exploits and heroics of Australia's early racers. **Cowes**, on the sheltered bay side, is the main town and a lively and attractive place to stay. Other, smaller, communities worth a visit are **Rhyll**, to the east, and **Ventnor**, just west of Cowes.

A daily **V/Line bus** to Cowes departs from Melbourne's Southern Cross station at 3.50pm, but there's no public transport on the island itself, so it can be tricky getting around and to the Penguin Parade, over 10km from Cowes. Joining a **tour** solves the transport problem. A few operators specializing in small groups (up to 20 people) run day-tours of the island from Melbourne that include the Penguin Parade at dusk; the going rate is $85 including dinner and all entrance fees (see box, p.869 for a list of tour operators).

If you're **driving**, head southeast from Melbourne on the Princes Highway to Dandenong, then follow the South Gippsland Highway to Lang Lang and from there the Bass Highway to Anderson where the road heads directly west to San Remo and the bridge across to the island, a drive of approximately three hours in total. The scenic lookout about 3km before San Remo is worth stopping at, for fantastic views of Western Port Bay and the surrounding countryside. **SAN REMO** itself has lots of motels, a picturesque fishing fleet by its wharf and a co-operative selling fresh fish and crayfish. **NEWHAVEN**, the first settlement you come to after crossing the bridge, has a large tourist information centre (daily 9am–5pm; ⓣ1300 366 422, ⓦwww.visitbasscoast.com), where you can book accommodation, pick up a free map and buy tickets for the Penguin Parade ($17.40), Churchill Island ($9), the Koala Conservation Centre ($9.20), or a combined ticket for all three ($32), as well as ferry cruises. **Churchill Island** (daily 10am–5pm; $9), 1km north of town, is mostly occupied by a working farm. A leisurely walk leads around the small island (2hr) from the Churchill Island Visitor Centre, with views of the unspoilt coastline; the visitor centre has a café, and nearby there's a historic homestead and a cottage in English-style gardens, surrounded by ancient moonah trees which are home to abundant birdlife.

Phillip Island Reserve and the Penguin Parade

The **Phillip Island Reserve** includes all the public land on the **Summerland Peninsula**, the narrow tip of land at the island's western extremity. The reason for the reserve is the **Little penguin**, smallest of the penguins, which is found only in southern Australian waters and whose largest colony breeds at Summerland Beach (around 2000 penguins in the parade area, and 20,000 on the island altogether). The **Penguin Parade** (nightly after dusk; $17.40; ⓣ03/5956 8300, ⓦwww.penguins.org.au) sounds horribly commercial – and with four thousand visitors a night at the busiest time of the year (around Christmas, January and Easter, when bookings are essential), it can hardly fail to be. Spectators sit in concrete-stepped stadiums looking down onto a floodlit beach, with taped narrations in Japanese, Taiwanese and English. But don't be too hard on it: ecological disaster would ensue if the penguins weren't managed properly, and visitors would still flock here, harming the birds and eroding the sand dunes. As it is, all the money made goes back into research and looking after the penguins, and into facilities such as the excellent **Penguin Parade Visitor Centre** (open from 10am; admission included in the parade ticket): the "Penguin Experience" here is a simulated underwater scene of the hazards of a penguin's life, and there are also interactive displays, videos and even nesting boxes to which penguins have access from the outside, where you can

△ Phillip Island penguins

watch the chicks. To escape the majority of the crowds, you can choose the "Penguin Sky Box" option ($40) – an exclusive, elevated viewing-tower with a ranger on hand to answer questions.

The parade itself manages to transcend the setting in any case, as the penguins come pouring onto the beach, waddling comically once they leave the water. They start arriving soon after dark; fifty minutes later the floodlights are switched off and it's all over, at which time (or before) you can move on to the extensive boardwalks over their burrows, with diffused lighting at regular intervals enabling you to watch their antics for hours after the parade finishes – they're active most of the night. If you want to avoid the worst of the crowds, the quietest time to observe them is during the cold and windy winter (you'll need water- or windproof clothing at any time of year). Remember too that you can see Little penguins close to St Kilda Pier in Melbourne and at many other beaches in southern and southeastern Australia, perhaps not in such large numbers, but with far fewer onlookers.

The Nobbies and Seal Rocks

At the tip of the Summerland Peninsula is **Point Grant**, where **The Nobbies**, two huge rock-stacks, are linked to the island at low tide by a wave-cut platform of basalt, affording views across to Cape Schanck on the Mornington Peninsula. From the Point, a boardwalk leads across spongy greenery – vibrant in summer with purple and yellow flowers – along the rounded clifftops to a lookout over a blowhole. This is a wild spot, with views along the rugged southern coastline towards Cape Woolamai, a granite headland at the eastern end of the island. From September to April you may see muttonbirds (shearwaters) here – they arrive in September to breed and head for the same burrows each year, after an incredible flight from the Bering Strait in the Arctic Circle. Further off Point Grant, **Seal Rocks** are two rocky islets with the largest known colony of Australian fur seals, estimated to number around 16,000. It's possible to see seals here all year round, though their numbers peak during the breeding season between late October and December. **Cruises** to Seal Rocks are available from Cowes (see p.880).

Phillip Island Wildlife Park, the Koala Conservation Centre and Rhyll Inlet Boardwalk

Two further parks and a mangrove boardwalk complete Phillip Island's rich collection of wildlife attractions. **Phillip Island Wildlife Park**, on Thompson Avenue just 1km south of Cowes (daily 10am–5pm; $11), provides a shady sanctuary for Australian animals: beautiful pure-bred dingoes, Tasmanian devils, fat and dozy wombats, as well as an aviary and a koala reserve. There are also freely ranging emus, Cape Barren geese, wallabies, eastern grey kangaroos and pademelons.

The **Koala Conservation Centre**, on Phillip Island Tourist Road between Newhaven and Cowes (daily 10am–5.30pm; $9.20), aims to keep the koala habitat as natural as possible while still giving people a close view. A treetop walk through a part of the bushland park allows visitors to observe these marsupials at close range. At 4pm the rangers provide fresh gum leaves – a very popular photo opportunity. You can learn about koalas in the excellent interpretive centre.

The Conservation Hill Lookout, just off the Cowes–Rhyll Road further north, provides a good view of the **Rhyll Inlet**, a significant roosting and feeding ground for migratory wading birds which come from as far as Siberia. A **boardwalk** starting at the car park takes visitors into the middle of the inlet, a landscape of mangroves, saltmarshes and mudflats. Unlike most other places on the island, the fishing village of **RHYLL** has managed to retain a sleepy charm. There are a couple of cafés and a tavern on the foreshore, with splendid views of the tranquil, shallow waters of Western Port Bay and the South Gippsland coast.

Cowes and around

Phillip Island's main town, **COWES**, situated at the centre of the north coast, is busy, touristy and even somewhat tacky, though the sandy bays are sheltered enough for good swimming and there are several decent places to eat and stay around **The Esplanade**, a lively strip facing the jetty. From November to April, Wildlife Coast Cruises – confusingly still referred to by its old name Bayconnections (ⓣ03/5952 3501, ⓦwww.bayconnections.com.au) – offers various **cruises** from the jetty, the best being the trip to Seal Rocks (2hr 30min; $45) to see the Australian fur seals close up.

Inter Island Ferries (see p.877) run transfers between Stony Point and Cowes and French Island (depart Stony Point daily 8.30am & 5pm, also noon Tues, Thurs, Sat & Sun: $9, bikes $4), and from Cowes (daily at 9.10am & 5.25pm, also 12.40pm Tues, Thurs, Sat & Sun; one way).

Accommodation

Out of season you shouldn't have any trouble finding somewhere **to stay**, but during the peak Christmas to Easter season accommodation nearly doubles in price and some places require weekly bookings. The Phillip Island tourist information centre in Newhaven handles accommodation bookings for the island.

Amaroo Park Cnr Church and Osborne sts ⓣ03/5952 2548, ⓦwww.amaroopark.com. Accommodation comprises a good YHA hostel and a caravan park; facilities include a convivial bar, heated swimming pool, cheap meals and bike rental. They also run tours of the island. Dorms $28, rooms ❸

The Castle – Villa by the Sea 7–9 Steele St ⓣ03/5952 1228. Delightful boutique hotel in a pleasant and quiet location just around the corner from the Esplanade. Great restaurant as well. ❼

Cliff Top 1 Marlin St, Smiths Beach ⓣ03/5952 1033, ⓦwww.clifftop.com.au. Stunning views over the water are what make this the island's best accommodation option. The seven rooms are named after explorers and offer everything for a perfect romantic getaway. ❼–❽

Coachman Motel 51 Chapel St ⓣ03/5952 1098, ⓦwww.coachmotel.com.au. Luxurious town house with motel units and suites. Facilities include a heated pool and spa for communal use. Rooms from ❹

Kaloha Holiday Resort Cnr Chapel and Steele sts ⓣ03/5952 2179, ⓦwww.kaloha.com.au. Motel units with cooking facilities, plus cabins, camping sites and facilities for on-site vans. Located in shady grounds giving onto a quiet swimming beach. ❸

Seahorse Motel 29–31 Chapel St ⓣ03/5952 2003, ⓦwww.seahorsemotel.com.au. An above-average, centrally located motel. ❸

Spice Island 1A Hill St, Sunderland Bay ⓣ03/5956 7557, ⓦwww.spiceisland.com.au. Three luxurious studio buildings set on rolling hills in a quiet part of the island. With a spa, LCD TV and five star amenities, it offers excellent value for money. ❻

Eating and drinking

Carmichael's Restaurant Level 1, 17 The Esplanade ⓣ03/5952 1300. Stylish place serving breakfast, lunch and dinner (mains $25–32), with views from the wide balcony over the water. 9am–11pm daily.

Chicory 115 Thomas Ave, ⓣ03/5952 2655. Pricey, but offers excellent modern Australian cuisine using local produce (especially their Phillip Island eye fillet $34). Lunch on weekends, dinner daily except Wednesday.

Flynns Inn 72 Chapel St ⓣ03/5952 1800. Homely Irish pub which serves the usual fare such as beef & Guinness pie and Irish stew. Great place to go on cold nights. Tues–Sun 6pm–late.

Foreshore Tavern Beach St, Rhyll ☎03/5952 1300. A small, homely pub only a ten-minute drive away from the hustle and bustle of Cowes. The bistro serves great meals and the selection of wines is good too. Lunch and dinner daily; closed Mon and Tues in winter.

Harry's on the Esplanade Shop 5, 17 The Esplanade ☎03/5952 6226. Excellent seafood with a European slant served up in a nice setting. Tues–Sun 11am–late.

Isola di Capri 2 Thompson Ave, Cowes ☎03/5952 2435. Friendly, moderately priced, Italian restaurant at the corner of the Esplanade.

The Jetty The Esplanade ☎03/5952 2060. Relaxed restaurant specializing in fresh local seafood. Licensed.

The Yarra Valley and the Dandenongs

Northeast of Melbourne, the **Yarra Valley** stretches out towards the foothills of the Great Dividing Range, with **Yarra Glen** and **Healesville** the targets for excursions into the wine country and the superb forest scenery beyond. To the east, and still within the suburban limits, the cool **Dandenong Range** is as pretty as anywhere in Australia, with quaint villages, fine old houses, beautiful flowering gardens and shady forests of eucalypts and tree ferns.

To get to all these destinations and to have a good look round, you really need your own vehicle. From Monday to Saturday it's possible, although not exactly easy, to see the Dandenongs by **public transport** – for further details, enquire at metlink (☎13 16 38) in Melbourne. Trains run via Ferntree Gully to Belgrave, starting point of the **Puffing Billy** steam train (see p.883). **Bus #694** runs from Belgrave via Mount Dandenong Tourist Road to Olinda township in the Dandenong Ranges. **Bus #688** runs from Olinda via the northern part of Mount Dandenong Tourist Road to Croydon railway station, where you can catch a Met train back to Melbourne. **Healesville** comes within the orbit of the suburban transport system: take a train from Melbourne to Lilydale and then bus #685 (to visit the Healesville Sanctuary, it's best to take the daily bus departing from Lilydale). There's a daily V/Line service from Melbourne to **Eildon** via Healesville and Marysville; the V/Line service to **Mansfield** passes through Lilydale and Yarra Glen daily (for further information, call V/Line on ☎13 61 96). There are local buses from Belgrave to **Emerald**.

The Yarra Valley

Just half an hour's drive from Melbourne, the **Yarra Valley** is home to around thirty of Victoria's best small **wineries**. The combination of good wine and fine food is really taking off in the valley, and in recent years quite a few winery restaurants have made a name for themselves in culinary circles. Wine country starts in outer suburbia north of the Maroondah Highway just before Lilydale (turn-offs are signposted). North of Lilydale, you can check out wineries (again, all signposted) along or near three routes – the Warburton Highway to the east, the Maroondah Highway to Healesville, and the Melba Highway, heading north past Yarra Glen. The brochure *Wineries of the Yarra Valley* contains a complete list of all local wineries and a map. Even better is the detailed booklet *Wine Regions of Victoria* – both are available at tourist information centres. If you intend to take a few swigs (and can't find a teetotal driver) it's best to join a **winery tour**: Backpacker Winery Tours (☎03/9877 8333, Ⓦwww.backpackerwinerytours.com.au) picks up from four locations in central Melbourne, as well as one in North Melbourne and one in St Kilda, visiting four wineries in the Yarra Valley ($95 including transport, tastings, a good restaurant lunch and a food platter in the afternoon).

The following are just a few of the wineries and restaurants in the Yarra Valley worth a visit. **Yering Station** (daily 10am–6pm; Ⓦwww.yering.com, Ⓣ03/9730 0100), 32 Melba Highway, just south of Yarra Glen, is located on the site of the first vineyard planted in the area in 1838 (the cellar door operates from the original brick building) and has a glass-walled restaurant offering views across the valley, plus a wine bar and a shop selling regional produce. The grounds also host the lively **Yarra Valley Farmers' Market** (every third Sunday of the month 10am–2pm), selling fruit and vegetables, and other valley produce such as smoked trout, honey and jams. On the same property is the **Chateau Yering Historic House Hotel**. For real comfort and luxury, wine and dine at the hotel's more casual *Café Sweetwater* or the very posh *Eleonore's Restaurant*, then sink into a four-poster bed in one of the period-style rooms (Ⓣ03/9237 3333, Ⓦwww.chateauyering.com.au; ❻). The **Yarra Valley Dairy** (daily 10.30am–5pm; Ⓦwww.yvd.com.au) at McMeikans Road, just south of Yering station, sells gourmet cheeses and serves tasty lunches. **De Bortoli** (bookings for the restaurant advisable on Ⓣ03/5965 2271; Ⓦwww.debortoli.com.au) occupies an unbeatable location at Pinnacle Lane, off the Melba Highway at Dixon's Creek north of Yarra Glen, with views over gently rolling hills. This was one of the first places in the valley to offer gourmet food along with its wine – both cuisine and decor betray Italian influences.

Domaine Chandon (Ⓣ03/9738 9200, Ⓦwww.domainechandon.com.au), on the Maroondah Highway near the town of Coldstream, produces fine *méthode champenoise* sparkling wine, which you can sample ($7–9 per glass) in a modern, bright and airy tastings-room with brilliant views. Free thirty-minute tours depart hourly from 11am to 4pm. **Eyton on Yarra** (Ⓣ03/5962 2119) winery and restaurant, further up towards Healesville at the corner of Maroondah Highway and Hill Road, is known for its sparkling Pinot Chardonnay and specializes in locally produced food. There are four more wineries off the Warburton Highway, including **Yarra Burn** (Ⓣ03/5967 1428, Ⓦwww.yarraburn.com.au) on Settlement Road at Yarra Junction; the restaurant here serves hearty Australian country cuisine (lunches daily; dinner Fri & Sat), and B&B accommodation is available in the homestead.

From Yarra Junction it's not far to **WARBURTON**, a pretty, old-fashioned town on the Upper Yarra River, and starting point for the **Upper Yarra Track**, which follows old timber tram and vehicle tracks upstream for over 80km. The track can be covered as a series of short walks or as a continuous five- to seven-day trek, finishing in the **Baw Baw National Park**, where it joins the Alpine Walking Track. For more information contact the DSE Information Centre in Melbourne (Ⓣ03/9637 8325) or the telephone information service run by Parks Victoria (Ⓣ13 19 63).

Wineries apart, **YARRA GLEN** also boasts the splendidly restored *Grand Hotel* (Ⓣ03/9730 1230, Ⓦwww.yarraglengrand.com.au; ❺) with very comfy en-suite rooms and suites, some of them with antique furniture and balconies, plus a café-bar, a bistro for moderately priced lunches and dinners (both open daily) and a more upmarket restaurant (Thurs–Sat from 6.30pm and Sun 11.30am–2pm) and, not far away on the Melba Highway, the National Trust **Gulf Station** (Ⓣ03/9730 1286; Wed–Sun & public holidays 10am–4pm; $8), a collection of ten 1850s slab farm-buildings set in a large area of farmland.

Healesville and beyond

HEALESVILLE is a small, pleasant town nestled in the foothills of the Great Dividing Range; there's a **visitor information centre** in the old courthouse building at the southern end of town, just off the Maroondah Highway (daily

10am–5pm). The town's main attraction is the renowned **Healesville Sanctuary** (daily 9am–5pm; $22; ⓣ03/5957 2800, ⓦwww.zoo.org.au), a bushland zoo with more than 200 species of Australian animals and a refuge for injured and orphaned animals, some of which are subsequently returned to the wild; those that stay join the sanctuary's programmes for education and the breeding of endangered species. It's a fascinating place in a beautiful setting, with a stream running through park-like grounds, dense with gum trees and cool ferns, and 3km of walking tracks. Many of the animals are in enclosures, but there are paddocks of emus, wallabies and kangaroos you can stroll through. The informative "meet the keeper" presentations are worth joining, especially the one featuring the birds of prey (noon & 2.30pm, weather permitting).

Continuing north on the Maroondah Highway over the Black Spur and Dom Dom Saddle towards Alexandra, the scenery becomes progressively more attractive. The **Maroondah Reservoir Lookout**, just off the highway 3km north of Healesville, is worth a brief stop, with picturesque views across the forest-fringed dam, and popular **picnic grounds** and **gardens** in the park on the southwest side of the reservoir. Soon after the reservoir, the highway meanders along bush-clad mountain slopes and enters luxuriant wet eucalypt forest with incredibly tall mountain ash, moss-covered myrtle beech, manna gum, gurgling creeks and waterfalls. The **Fernshaw Reserve and Picnic Ground** is a good place to stop and view the scenery. After the Dom Dom Saddle, 509m above sea level and 16km past Healesville, the highway descends towards Narbethong, where it enters drier country. Three kilometres past Narbethong there's a worthwhile detour down a turn-off to scenic **MARYSVILLE** (ⓦwww.marysvilletourism.com), 9km off the highway. The village nestles in the foothills of the Great Dividing Range, with **Lake Mountain** (1400m), a very popular area for cross-country skiing and tobogganing, 20km further west. In summer, Marysville makes an excellent base for **bushwalking**, being surrounded by forests with many waterfalls. The best-known, **Steavensons Falls**, can be reached from the village by a walking trail or by road and is floodlit at night until 11pm. Just out of Marysville, the unsealed **Lady Talbot Forest Drive** turns off the Lake Mountain road and then winds 46km through the forest, past picnic areas and walking tracks (suitable for conventional vehicles, though after heavy rainfall it's best to check in Marysville for road conditions). Return to Marysville via the Buxton Road, or turn right and head north to Buxton, where you rejoin the highway. Further up, the Maroondah Highway passes the drier **Cathedral Range State Park**: west of the road here the mighty sandstone cliffs of Cathedral Mountain rise almost vertically behind the paddocks, overlooking the Acheron Valley.

The Dandenongs

As in the Blue Mountains of New South Wales, the **Dandenong** hills are enveloped in a blue haze rising from forests of gum trees which cover much of the area. Rain ensures the area stays cool and lush, while fine old houses and gardens add to the scenery. Easy bushwalks in the **Dandenong Ranges National Park** start from Ferntree Gully, accessible by train or by car via the Burwood Highway. A pleasant way to enjoy the forests and fern gullies is to take a ride on the **Puffing Billy** steam train (ⓣ03/9754 6800, ⓦwww.puffingbilly.com.au), which runs for 13km from the Puffing Billy station in Belgrave to Lakeside ($31.50 return) on Lake Emerald, stopping at Menzies Creek and Emerald: one train a day continues a further 9km from Lake Emerald to Gembrook ($43.50 return). The Puffing Billy station is a short, signposted walk from **Belgrave** station (suburban trains). The train has run more or less continuously since the early twentieth century, though its operation now depends on dedicated volunteers; on total-fire-ban days, diesel locomotives are used. Timetables vary seasonally but there are generally several services daily until late afternoon.

Just outside Emerald, man-made **Emerald Lake** has paddle-boats to rent and a swimming pool, as well as trails through bushland which continue into the nearby state reserve. *Emerald Backpackers*, 2 Lakeview Court (Ⓣ03/5968 4086, Ⓦwww.emeraldbackpackers.com.au; dorms $20, rooms ❷) caters mainly for people seeking farm work; the owners have local contacts. On weekdays and Saturday morning, bus #695 runs from the Belgrave train station to Emerald.

Geelong and the Bellarine Peninsula

Heading west towards Geelong – for the Bellarine Peninsula and Great Ocean Road – it's just a short detour off the Princes Freeway to **WERRIBEE**, home to the restored **Mansion at Werribee Park** (Mon–Fri 10am–5pm daily; $12.50; Ⓣ13 19 63, Ⓦwww.werribeepark.com.au), located on K Road. Built in 1874–77 by Scottish squatters Thomas and Andrew Chirnside, who struck it rich on the back of sheep, the sixty-room mansion is the largest private residence in Victoria. Guides in period costume show you around the ornate homestead and the Victorian-era gardens; alternatively, free audioguides are available at the entrance. The grand sandstone building is surrounded by ten hectares of formal gardens, including the **Victoria State Rose Garden** (free admission), which is at its best between November and April when the five thousand rose bushes are in bloom. Beyond the gardens are the extensive grounds of **Victoria's Open Range Zoo** (daily 9am–5pm; $22; Ⓣ03/9731 9600, Ⓦwww.zoo.org.au) where giraffes, cheetahs, rhinoceroses, hippopotamuses, monkeys, as well as kangaroos and emus, roam in large open enclosures. A fifty-minute **safari bus**, included in the admission price, takes visitors through the property (bus departs every 50min 10.30am–3.40pm). **Werribee Park Shuttle**, a private bus service, provides transport to Werribee Park (mansion and zoo) from Melbourne, departing from the Victorian Arts Centre, St Kilda Road, at 9.30am ($30.80 return; advance booking required on Ⓣ03/9748 5094; Ⓦwww.werribeeparkshuttle.com.au). Southeast of here is the **Shadowfax Winery** (Ⓦwww.shadowfax.com.au), an impressive box-like structure that offers cellar-door sales (Sat & Sun from 10am), glimpses of the wine-making process and gourmet food.

Continuing along the freeway, you can detour west again through Little River to the **You Yangs**, small but rugged volcanic peaks which rise sharply out of the surrounding plains. Scramble to the top of the highest, **Flinders Peak** (348m), and you're rewarded with fine views of Geelong and Port Phillip Bay. The You Yangs, as well as the nearby **Brisbane Ranges**, are excellent places for spotting kangaroos, wallabies, koalas and possums at dusk. Alternatively, you can observe kangaroos, wallabies and emus, as well as numerous waterbirds, in their natural habitat at the little-known **Serendip Sanctuary**, 20km north of Geelong at 100 Windermere Rd, Lara (daily 10am–4pm; free; Ⓣ03/5282 1584), which occupies a square kilometre of bush, marsh and wetlands. A refuge for threatened birds of the Western Plains of Victoria, the sanctuary is renowned for its captive breeding programme of brolgas, magpie geese and Australian bustards.

Geelong

Approaching **GEELONG** via its industrial outskirts, you can be forgiven for wanting to zip past the bland mélange of fast-food outlets, petrol stations and suburban housing to the beckoning seaside attractions of the Bellarine Peninsula and the Great Ocean Road beyond. However, Geelong has made a big effort to shed its rust-bucket image, mainly by revamping the waterfront it had previously turned its back on, and while still not warranting an extended stay, the city centre is a pleasant enough place to do some exploring, combined with a lunch stop.

The **National Wool Museum** (Mon–Fri 9.30am–5pm, Sat & Sun 1–5pm; $7.30), housed in the Geelong Wool Exchange, a National Trust–listed building at the corner of Brougham and Moorabool streets, is worth a visit. The well-set-up exhibition concentrates on the social history of the wool industry, with reconstructions of typical shearers' quarters and a millworker's 1920s cottage; wool is still auctioned off thirty days a year on the top floor of the exchange. Many of the town's best Victorian buildings are on **Little Malop Street**, including the elegant **Geelong Art Gallery** (Mon–Fri 10am–5pm, Sat & Sun 1–5pm; free, but donation appreciated; Ⓦwww.geelonggallery.org.au), which has an extensive collection of paintings by nineteenth-century Australian artists such as Tom Roberts and Frederick McCubbin, plus twentieth-century Australian paintings, sculpture and decorative arts. From Little Malop Street and Malop Street, Moorabool Street leads down to **Corio Bay** and the waterfront, with its renovated promenades, rotunda, fountains and lovely nineteenth-century carousel featuring over thirty sculpted wooden horses. There's a swimming enclosure at Eastern Beach. Notable waterfront eating places include the large **Cunningham Pier**. Nestled among the lawns and trees of Eastern Park around ten minutes' walk from the city centre are Geelong's **Botanic Gardens** (Mon–Fri 7.30am–5pm, Sat & Sun 7am–7pm; free). The entrance is through the latest addition to the gardens, the 21st Century Garden, which specializes in resilient native and exotic, dry-climate plants. Beyond this are the historic gardens: begun in the late 1850s they boast lawns, rare trees, a fernery and conservatory, fountains and sculptures, as well as the small *Tea House* (daily 11am–4pm).

On the way to Torquay, **Narana Creations** (Mon–Fri 9am–5pm, Sat 10am–4pm; free; Ⓦwww.narana.com.au), an Aboriginal arts, crafts and cultural centre at 410 Torquay Rd (Surfcoast Highway) in Grovedale is worth a brief stop. Paintings and various arts and crafts are sold here, and visitors can sometimes listen to Dreamtime stories or didgeridoo playing.

Practicalities

In addition to the **visitor information centre** (daily 9am–5pm; Ⓣ1800 620 888, Ⓦwww.visitgeelong.org) at the Wool Museum, there's a helpful **tourist information stall** (Mon–Sat 9am–5pm) in the Market Square Shopping Centre at the corner of Moorabool and Malop streets. Both provide lots of brochures and free maps. The main **shopping** strip is along Malop Street.

To check out what's going on, pick up a copy of the free **listings magazine** *Forte*, available at music shops, and sometimes also at the visitor information centre. It covers the whole of southwest Victoria, and also has information on surfing, diving and other activities.

To get to the Bellarine Peninsula from Geelong, take a McHarry's Buslines **bus** (Ⓣ03/5223 2111, Ⓦwww.mcharrys.com.au) from the Busport on Brougham Street (next to the Wool Museum) for Ocean Grove and Barwon Heads, Point Lonsdale via Queenscliff, St Leonards via Portarlington, and Grovedale via Torquay.

Accommodation

The Colonial Lodge Motel Fyans St, about 2km south of the city centre Ⓣ03/5223 2266. Reasonably priced motel units. ③

Irish Murphys 30 Aberdeen St, Geelong West Ⓣ03/5221 4335, Ⓦwww.irishmurphys.com. Backpacker accommodation above a popular traveller's pub; dorms from $20, rooms ❸

The National Hotel 191 Moorabool St, Geelong ⓣ03/ 5229 1211, ⓦwww.nationalhotel.com.au. Mega-sociable hostel that has a relaxed vibe. Rooms are a bit on the small side but guests will be spending most of their time in the excellent pub downstairs anyway. Dorms $22.

Riverglen Holiday Park Barrabool Road, Belmont ⓣ03/5243 5505, ⓕ5243 4760. Good caravan-park on the south bank of the Barwon River, with shady tent-sites and timber cottages. ❹

The Sphinx 2 Thompson St, North Geelong. ⓣ03/5278 2911 ⓦwww.sphinxhotel.com.au. Bizarre and extremely corny entertainment complex that has really overdone it with the Egyptian motif. Rooms are fine and good for the price though. Look for the huge Sphinx out the front. ❹

Sundowner Geelong 13 The Esplanade ⓣ03/5222 3499, ⓦwww.sundownermotorinns.com.au. Upmarket accommodation with water views, a restaurant and bar, sauna and a pool. ❺

Eating

Barwon Club Hotel 509 Moorabool St, South Geelong ⓣ03/5221 4584. Geelong's most popular band-venue and pub also serves up tasty grub (mains around $20) which you can tuck into on the outdoor tables. Open for lunch Mon–Fri, dinner daily.

Beach House Restaurant Eastern Beach Reserve ⓣ03/5221 8322. The café downstairs (open Mon–Sun from 9am; closed evenings) serves breakfast all day as well as other cheap fare, while the upmarket restaurant upstairs (Thurs–Sat from 6pm; also Sun lunch) offers eclectic East-meets-West cuisine. Great views, especially from the restaurant. Mains around $28. Licensed.

The Bended Elbow 69 Yarra St, Geelong ⓣ03/5229 4477. English-themed pub which has good-portioned lunch specials for $8 every day. At night the place fills up with people in search of a pint. Daily 11.30–late.

Fishermen's Pier Seafood Restaurant Bay end of Yarra St ⓣ03/5222 4100. Fish and seafood prepared in a range of styles, from Thai to Tuscan. Expensive. Licensed. Daily 11.30am–2.30pm & 5.30–9.30pm.

Irrewarra Sourdough Shop & Café 10 James St. Outlet of bakery based in Colac in the Otways. Sells their range of outstanding breads, and serves delicious breakfasts and light lunches in the café section. Licensed. Moderate. Mon–Fri 7.30am–3.30pm.

Giuseppe's Café 149 Parkington, Geelong West ⓣ03/5223 2187. When the locals crave good Italian cuisine, they head here. Mains under $20. Tues–Sun 11am–10pm.

Tonic 5 James St ⓣ03/5229 8899. This restau-rant-bar just around the corner from Little Malop St goes for cool, minimalist chic. The menu has a bit of everything: Cajun chicken salad, risotto, linguini, beef rendang, crispy lime-battered fish, all available either as an entree or main course. Moderate. Licensed. Mon–Sat lunch and dinner.

Wharf Shed Cafe 15 Eastern Beach Rd ⓣ03/5221 6645. Popular café-restaurant in a converted boatshed in Geelong's waterfront precinct that feeds cakes, pizzas and fish-and-chips to the masses coming here on a sunny weekend. Licensed. Mon–Fri 11am–late, Sat & Sun from 9am. Upstairs is the upmarket (and much pricier) *Le Parisien Restaurant* (ⓣ03/5229 3110), open for lunch and dinner daily.

Queenscliff and around

From Geelong, the Bellarine Highway runs 31km southeast to **QUEENSCLIFF** through flat and not particularly scenic grazing country. Queenscliff is essentially a quiet fishing village on Swan Bay – with several quaint cottages on Fishermens Flat – which became a favourite holiday resort for Melbourne's wealthy elite in the nineteenth century, then fell out of favour, and has only recently begun to enjoy something of a revival as a popular place for a weekend away or a Sunday drive. Queenscliff's position near the narrow entrance to Port Phillip Bay made it strategically important: a **fort** here faces the one at Point Nepean. Now the home of the Australian Army Command and Staff College, the fort and its museum can be visited on guided tours (Sat & Sun 1pm & 3pm; $4.40).

Full details of other things to do are available from the Queenscliff **Visitor Information Centre**, 55 Hesse St (daily 9am–5pm; ⓣ1300 884 843, ⓦwww.queenscliff.org). During school holidays and in summer, **Queenscliff**

Historical Tours (Ⓣ03/5258 3403) rents out bicycles ($20 per half-day), as well as providing a map and audioguide to the town; you can either pick up a bike near the pier at the end of Symonds Road, or have it delivered to your accommodation. Other activities include kayaking ($30 for 2hr; Ⓣ03/5258 2166; rentals from the marina at 2 Larkin Parade) along the coast or further offshore; diving among wrecks and marine life with the **Queenscliff Dive Centre** (Ⓣ03/5258 1188, Ⓦwww.divequeenscliff.com.au); and a cruise with **Sea All Dolphin Swims** (4hr; $115; twice daily in January, varying rest of the year; Ⓣ03/5258 3889, Ⓦwww.dolphinswims.com.au) visiting a seal colony, a gannet rookery and the chance to swim with dolphins in Port Phillip Bay.

Among the attractions is the **Queenscliff Maritime Museum**, Weerona Parade (Mon–Fri 10.30am–4.30pm, Sat & Sun 1.30–4.30pm; $5; Ⓣ03/5258 3440), which concentrates on the many shipwrecks caused by The Rip, a fierce current about 1km wide between Point Lonsdale and Point Nepean. Outside, a tiny fisherman's cottage is set up as it would have been in 1870, and there's a shed where an Italian fisherman painted, in naive style, all the ships he'd seen pass through from 1895 to 1947 (imaginatively including the *Titanic*). Next door, the **Marine Discovery Centre** has a small aquarium stocked with local marine life (daily 10am–4pm during school holidays, other times by appointment; $5; Ⓣ03/5258 3344, Ⓦwww.dse.vic.gov.au/mafri/discovery); it also organizes a range of activities, mainly during the summer holidays, such as marine-biology cruises, rock-pool rambles and snorkelling tours. Every Sunday, the **Bellarine Peninsula Railway** operates steam trips from the old Queenscliff Railway Station to Drysdale, 20km northwest (11.15am & 2.45pm; $18 return; Ⓣ03/5258 2069, Ⓦwww.bpr.org.au).

The **Queenscliff Music Festival** (Ⓦwww.qmf.net.au), held annually on the last weekend of November, features an eclectic mix of Australian contemporary music (folk, blues, world music, fusion) and draws ever-growing crowds.

Practicalities

Grand **Victorian-era hotels** are a popular choice for the romantics when staying in Queenscliff. The best options are the *Vue Grand*, 46 Hesse St (Ⓣ03/5258 1544, Ⓦwww.vuegrand.com.au; ❼–❽), which has a Spanish-style exterior and a fabulously ornate Victorian interior with a very expensive restaurant; while the refined *Queenscliff Hotel*, 16 Gellibrand St (Ⓣ03/5258 1066, Ⓦwww.queenscliffhotel.com.au; ❻–❽), is considered the best of all. For a bit more personal attention the *Lathamstowe Guesthouse*, 44 Gellibrand St (Ⓣ03/5258 4110; ❻ including breakfast), oozes luxury and is set in a heritage-listed mansion dating back to 1883. **Budget alternatives** include the *Queenscliff Dive Centre Lodge* (Ⓣ03/5258 1188, Ⓦwww.divequeenscliff.com.au; dorms $27–35, rooms ❷–❸) which has good facilities including a sociable lounge with open fire place or the *Queenscliff Inn YHA*, 59 Hesse St (Ⓣ03/5258 3737, Ⓔqueenscliff@yhavic.org.au; dorms $23, rooms ❹), which is a pleasant Victorian B&B guesthouse – the single rooms (❷) are particularly good value. *Beacon Resort Holiday Park & Motel*, 78 Bellarine Highway (Ⓣ03/5258 1133, Ⓦwww.beaconresort.com.au), has tent sites, cabins (❹), holiday units, motel rooms (❺) and a heated pool.

Among the town's **eating places**, the best fish-and-chips are at *Queenscliff Fish and Chips*, 77 Hesse St, while *Café Cliffe*, 25 Hesse St, serves locally produced wines by the glass and light lunches in a pleasant, Tuscan-style courtyard (Mon–Fri 11am–4pm, Sat & Sun 10am–4pm). Great value can be found at the *Ripview Bar & Bistro* (daily noon–2pm, 6–8pm) situated on the first floor of the Bowling Club at 118 Hesse St, which has two-course lunches for under $9. *Harry's*, a renowned old-timer, is located on the balcony of the

Esplanade Hotel with great sea views at 2 Gellibrand St, and has a good wine list in addition to expensive, but excellent seafood (daily noon–3pm, 6.30pm–late; closed Tues–Thurs in winter; ⓣ03/5258 3750). Even pricier options include the gorgeous restaurants at the *Vue Grand* (lunch and dinner daily) and the *Queenscliff Hotel* (lunch daily, dinner Wed–Sat). The latter also has a cheaper courtyard restaurant. All are licensed.

Ferries run from Queenscliff across the mouth of Port Phillip Bay to Sorrento (see p.873).

Point Lonsdale and Portarlington

From Queenscliff it's about 5km to peaceful **Point Lonsdale**, whose most noticeable feature is its magnificent 1902 lighthouse, 120m high and visible for 30km out to sea. Below the lighthouse, on the edge of the bluff, is "Buckley's Cave" where William Buckley is thought to have lived at some stage during his thirty-year sojourn with the Aborigines. At **PORTARLINGTON**, which sits on Port Phillip Bay about 14km north of Queenscliff, there's a beautifully preserved steam-powered flourmill (Wed, Sat & Sun noon–4pm; $3; ⓣ03/5259 3847), four storeys of solid stone, owned by the National Trust.

Travel details

Trains

Melbourne to: Adelaide (3 weekly; 10hr); Alice Springs (2 weekly; 36hr); Ballarat (15–19 daily; 1hr 20min); Bendigo (12–20 daily; 1hr 45min); Geelong (15–28 daily; 1hr); Perth (2 weekly; 60hr); Sydney via Albury (2 daily; 11hr); Warrnambool (3 daily; 3hr 15min).

Buses

Melbourne to: Adelaide (4 daily; 10hr); Brisbane (1 daily; 23hr); Sydney via Bega (1 daily; 17hr); Sydney via Canberra (4–5 daily; 12–14hr).

Ferries

Melbourne to: Devonport, Tasmania (1–2 daily; 10hr).

Flights

Qantas flies from **Melbourne** to: Adelaide (9–12 daily; 1hr 20min); Alice Springs (3 daily; 2hr 50min direct); Ayers Rock Resort (3 daily; 3hr 30min); Brisbane (12–15 daily; 2hr 5min); Cairns (5–7 daily; 3hr 20min direct); Canberra (6–9 daily; 1hr 5min); Darwin (3 daily; 4–5hr with one stopover); Hobart (2 daily; 1hr 10min); Launceston (2–3 daily; 1hr 20min); Mackay (3 daily; 4hr 15min with one stopover); Perth (6–7 daily; 4hr 10min); Rockhampton (5–6 daily; 3hr 30min with one stopover); Sydney (20–27 daily; 1hr 20min); Townsville (4–5 daily; 5hr with one stopover).

Jetstar flies from **Melbourne Tullamarine** to: Cairns (1 daily; 3hr 20min); Gold Coast (6–7 daily; 2hr); Hamilton Island (1 daily; 2hr 55min); Hobart (4 daily; 1hr 10min); Launceston (3–4 daily; 1hr); Newcastle (2 daily; 1hr 25min); Sunshine Coast (2 daily; 2hr 10min); and from **Melbourne Avalon** (near Geelong) to: Adelaide (1 daily; 1hr 20min); Brisbane (2 daily; 2hr); Sydney (6–7 daily; 1hr 15min).

Virgin Blue flies from **Melbourne** to: Adelaide (8–11 daily; 1hr 15min); Brisbane (7–9 daily; 2hr); Cairns (3–4 daily; 3hr 20min with one stopover); Canberra (4 daily; 1hr); Darwin (1 daily; 7hr with one stopover); Coffs Harbour (2 daily; 3hr 50min with one stopover); Gold Coast (7–9 daily; 2hr); Hobart (4 daily; 1hr 10min); Launceston (4 daily; 1hr); Mackay (3 daily; 4hr 10min with one stopover); Perth (4 daily; 4hr 15min); Sydney (18–23 daily; 1hr 20min); Townsville (6 daily; 6hr 30min with one stopover).

10

Victoria

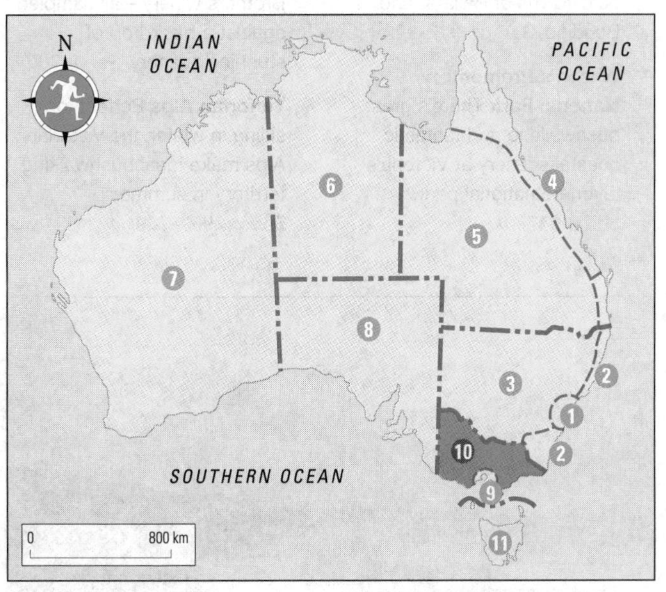
N
INDIAN OCEAN
PACIFIC OCEAN
SOUTHERN OCEAN
1
2
2
3
4
5
6
7
8
9
10
11
0
800 km

CHAPTER 10

Highlights

* **Great Ocean Road** Wait until the sun is down and the crowds are gone and watch the fairy penguins come out to play at the Twelve Apostles. See pp.894–912

* **Goldfields** Mining memorabilia and grandiose architecture grace the old gold-towns of Ballarat and Bendigo. See pp.912–929

* **Wilson's Promontory National Park** There's great bushwalking and fantastic coastal scenery at Victoria's favourite national park. See p.947

* **Ned Kelly Country** Follow in the steps of Australia's most famous bush outlaw, in the historic towns that dot the northeast. See p.957

* **Milawa Gourmet Trail** Excellent local produce washed down with great wines from the Brown Brothers winery – all sampled against a backdrop of stunning scenery. See p.960

* **Victorian Alps** Perfect for skiing in winter, the Victorian Alps make ideal bushwalking territory in summer. See pp.963–969

△ The Twelve Apostles

Victoria

Australia's second-smallest state, **Victoria** is the most densely populated and industrialized, and has a wide variety of attractions packed into a small area. Although you're never too far from civilization, there are plenty of opportunities to sample the state's wilder days when it was a centre for **gold prospectors** and **bushrangers**. All routes in the state radiate from **Melbourne**, and no point is much more than seven hours' drive away. Yet, all most visitors see of Victoria apart from its cultured capital is the **Great Ocean Road**, a winding 280km of spectacular coastal scenery. Others may venture to the idyllic **Wilsons Promontory National Park** (the "Prom"), a couple of hours away on the coast of the mainly dairy region of **Gippsland**, or to the **Goldfields**, where the nineteenth-century goldrushes left their mark in the grandiose architecture of old mining-towns such as **Ballarat** and **Bendigo**.

There is, however, a great deal more to the state. Marking the end of the Great Dividing Range, the massive sandstone ranges of the **Grampians**, with their Aboriginal rock paintings and dazzling array of springtime flora, rise from the monotonous wheatfields of the **Wimmera** region and the wool country of the western district. To the north of the Grampians is the wide, flat region of the Mallee – scrub, sand dunes and dry lakes heading to the **Murray River**, where Mildura is an irrigated oasis supporting orchards and vineyards. In complete contrast, the **Victorian Alps** in the northeast of the state have several winter **ski slopes**, high country that provides perfect bushwalking and horse-riding territory in summer. In the foothills and plains below, where bushranger **Ned Kelly** once roamed, are some of Victoria's finest wineries (wine buffs should pick up a copy of the excellent hundred-page brochure, *Wine Regions of Victoria*, available from the visitor information centre in Melbourne and other towns). Beach culture is alive and well on this **coastline** with some of the best **surfing** in Australia.

The only real drawback is the frequently cursed **climate**. Winter is mild, and the occasional heatwaves in summer are mercifully limited to a few days at most (though they can create bushfires that last for weeks), but the problem is that of unpredictability. Cool, rainy "English" weather can descend in any season, and spring and autumn days can be immoderately hot. But even this can be turned to advantage: as the local saying goes, if you don't like the weather, just wait ten minutes and it'll change.

Public transport, by road and rail, is with **V/Line** and subsidiary country bus lines. However, using your own vehicle is definitely a more convenient option, as train and bus services are fairly infrequent and quite a few places can be reached only with difficulty, if at all.

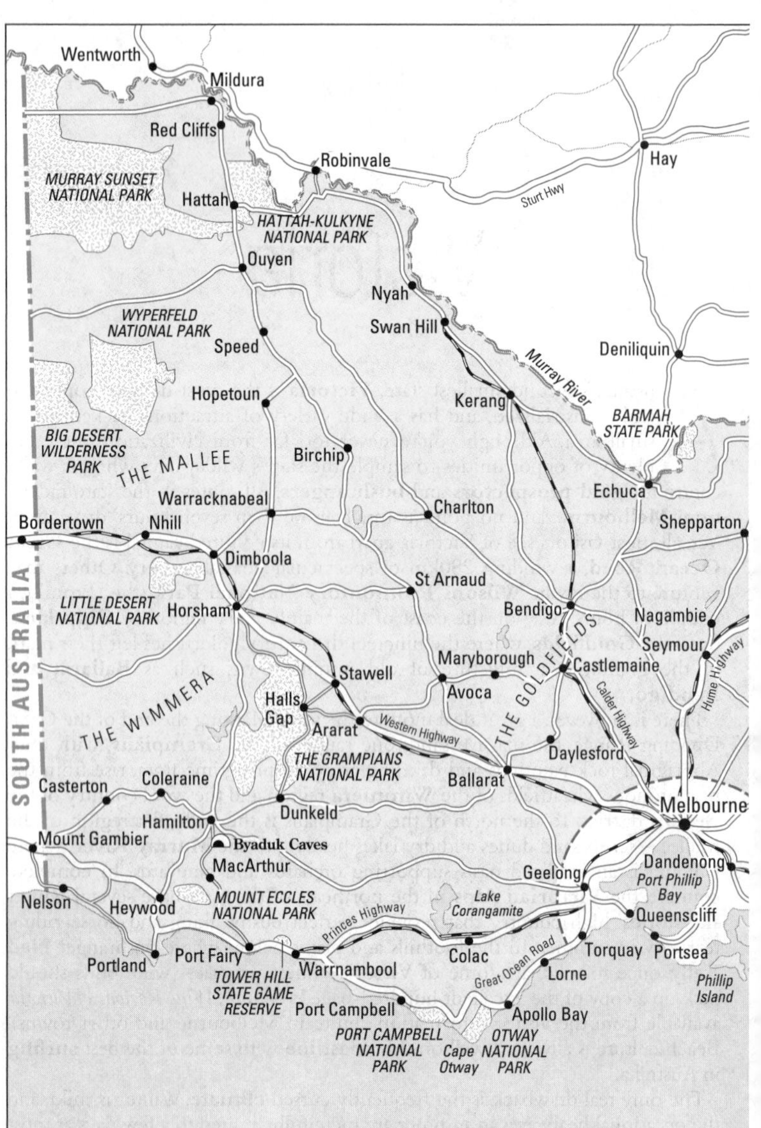

Some history

Semi-nomadic **Koories** have lived in this region for at least forty thousand years establishing semi-permanent settlements such as those of circular stone houses and fish traps found at Lake Condah in western Victoria. For the colonists, however, Victoria did not get off to an auspicious start: there was an unsuccessful attempt at settlement in the **Port Phillip Bay** area in 1803 but Van Diemen's Land (Tasmania) across the Bass Strait was deemed more suitable.

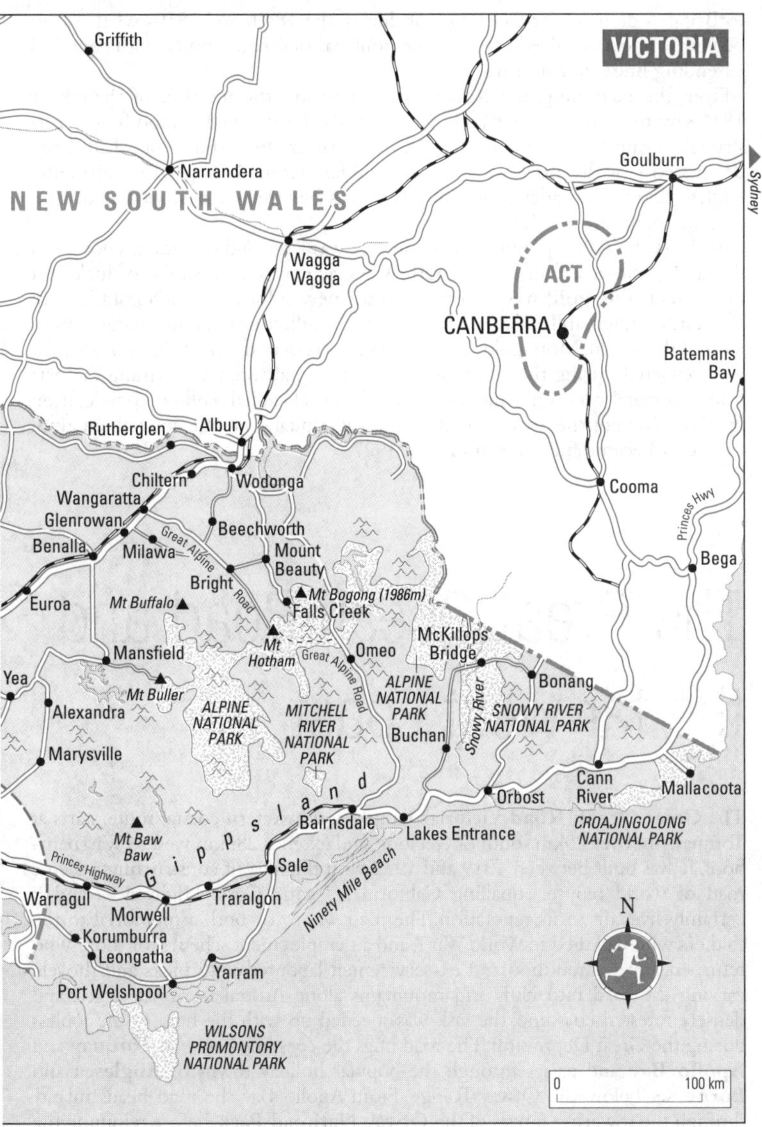

It was in fact from Launceston that Port Phillip Bay was eventually settled, in 1834; other Tasmanians soon followed and **Melbourne** was established. This occupation was in defiance of a British government edict forbidding settlement in the territory, then part of New South Wales, but **squatting** had already begun the previous year when Edward Henty arrived with his stock to establish the first white settlement at **Portland** on the southwest coast. A pattern was created of land-hungry settlers – generally already men of means – responding to Britain's demand for wool, so that during the 1840s and 1850s what was to become Victoria evolved into a prosperous pastoral community with squatters extending huge grazing runs.

From the beginning, the Koories fought against the invasion of their land: 1836 saw the start of the **Black War**, as it has been called, a bloody guerrilla struggle against the settlers. By 1850, however, the Aborigines had been decimated – by disease as well as war – and felt defeated, too, by the apparently endless flood of invaders; their population is believed to have declined from around 15,500 to just 2300.

By 1851 the white population of the area was large and confident enough to demand separation from New South Wales, achieved, by a stroke of luck, just nine days before **gold** was discovered in the new colony. The rich goldfields of Ballarat, Bendigo and Castlemaine brought an influx of hopeful migrants from around the world. More gold came from Victoria over the next thirty years than was extracted during the celebrated California goldrush, transforming Victoria from a pastoral backwater into Australia's financial capital. Following federation in 1901, Melbourne was even the political capital – a title it retained until Canberra became fully operational in 1927.

The Great Ocean Road and the far west coast

The **Great Ocean Road**, Victoria's famous southwestern coastal route, starts at Torquay, just over 20km south of Geelong, and extends 285km west to Warrnambool. It was built between 1919 and 1932 with the idea of constructing a scenic road of world repute, equalling California's Pacific Coast Highway – and it certainly lives up to its reputation. The road was to be both a memorial to the soldiers who had died in World War I, and an employment scheme for those who returned. Over three thousand ex-servicemen laboured with picks and shovels, carving the road into cliffs and mountains along Australia's most rugged and densely forested coastline; the task was speeded up with the help of the jobless during the Great Depression. The road hugs the coastline between **Torquay** and **Apollo Bay** and passes through the popular holiday towns of **Anglesea** and **Lorne**, set below the Otway Range. From Apollo Bay the road heads inland, through the towering forests of the **Otway National Park**, before rejoining the coast at Princetown to wind along the shore for the entire length of the **Port Campbell National Park**. This stretch from Moonlight Head to Port Fairy, sometimes referred to as the "Shipwreck Coast", is the most spectacular – there are two hundred known shipwrecks here, victims of the imprecise navigation tools of the mid-nineteenth century, the rough Southern Ocean and dramatic rock formations such as the **Twelve Apostles**, which sit out to sea beyond the rugged cliffs. Information on all the villages and sights on the Great Ocean Road can be found on the area's website, Ⓦ www.greatoceanroad.org.

From **Warrnambool**, the small regional centre where the Great Ocean Road ends, the Princes Highway continues along the coast, through quaint seaside **Port Fairy** and industrial **Portland**, before turning inland for the final stretch to the South Australian border.

Transport

If you don't have your own car, you might want to consider one-way **car rental**, usually available from the big-name companies in Melbourne. There are plenty of parking spots where you can pull over and admire the view, but with narrow roads, steep cliffs and incessant hairpin bends drivers need to keep their eyes glued to the road. In summer the road is filled with **cyclists**, and although the routes are exhilarating they are really only suitable for the experienced and adventurous.

V/Line (Ⓣ13 61 96, Ⓦwww.vline.com.au) has a "Great Ocean Road" **bus** service from Geelong to Apollo Bay, calling at Torquay, Anglesea, Lorne and points in between. There is also a **train** service from Melbourne to Warrnambool with connecting buses to Port Fairy, Portland and Heywood and on to Mount Gambier in South Australia (1 daily). From Warrnambool you can also return to Melbourne on the inland road, or go north to Ballarat. See "Travel details" at the end of the chapter for more info.

Tours

One-way tours between Melbourne and Adelaide, via the Great Ocean Road, are a good way to take in the scenery. The backpackers' busline Oz Experience (Ⓣ1300 300 028, Ⓦwww.ozexperience.com) currently covers this route in three days, taking in the Great Ocean Road and the Grampians ($240, transport only). Wayward Bus (Ⓣ1300 653 510, Ⓦwww.waywardbus.com.au) sticks to the coast all the way to the Coorong in South Australia on its three-and-a-half-day tour (from $345, including hostel accommodation, breakfasts and lunches). The small and friendly Groovy Grape covers the Great Ocean Road–Grampians route in an all-inclusive three-day tour (Ⓣ1800 661 177, Ⓦwww.groovygrape.com.au; $325).

A few other reliable tour operators do one- or two-day **round-trips** from Melbourne to the Great Ocean Road, some with an extra Grampians option and/or possible transfer to Adelaide – see the box on pp.868–869.

Hiking

Walking and hiking enthusiasts can choose between two magnificent **walking tracks** along the coast: the **Great Ocean Walk** (Ⓦwww.greatoceanwalk.com.au; see also p.902), a 91-kilometre track from Apollo Bay to Glenample Homestead (near Princetown); and the long-established **Great Southwest Walk** (Ⓦwww.greatsouthwestwalk.com), a superb 250-kilometre circuit starting from just outside Portland. Further sources of information include Parks Victoria (Ⓣ13 19 63, Ⓦwww.parkweb.vic.gov.au) and the DSE Information Centre, 8 Nicholson St, East Melbourne (Ⓣ03/9637 8325, Ⓦwww.dse.vic.gov.au).

Torquay

TORQUAY is the centre of **surf culture** on Victoria's "surf coast" and two local beaches, **Jan Juc** and **Bells Beach**, are solidly entrenched in Australian surfing mythology. If you're not here for the waves, then there's not really a lot

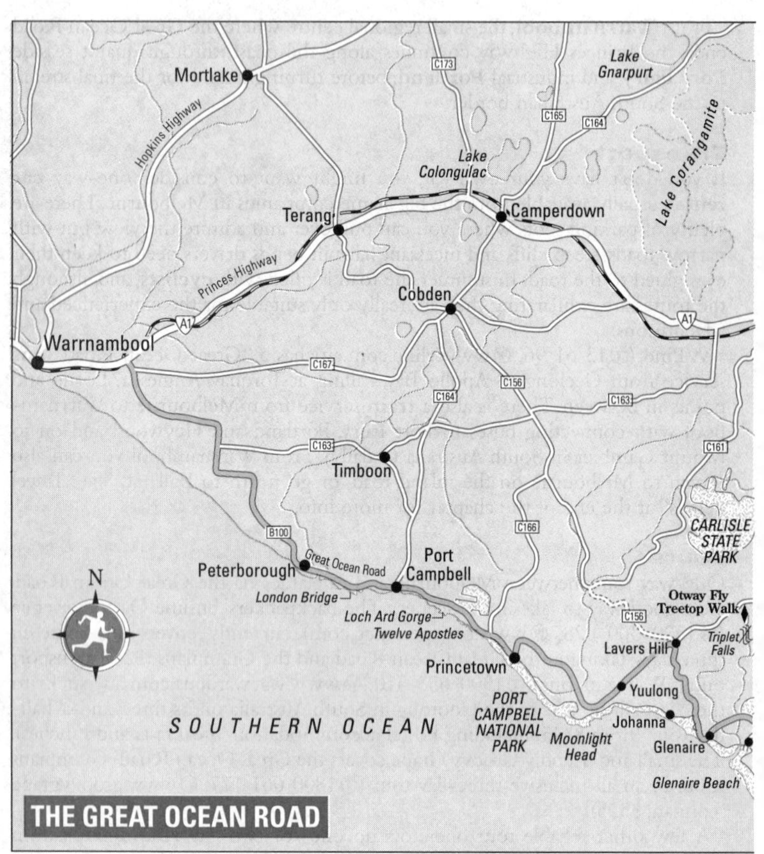

happening: in hot weather the place is boisterously alive, but out of season it's somnolent and low-key. The big event here is the Rip Curl Pro Classic, held at Bells Beach at Easter, which draws national and international contestants and thousands of spectators (call Surf Victoria on ⓣ03/5261 2907 or see ⓦwww.ripcurl.com/ripcurlpro/ for details). Local **buses** run between Geelong and Torquay via Jan Juc – McHarry's Buslines (ⓣ03/5223 2111, ⓦwww.mcharrys.com.au) has details.

As you come into Torquay along the Great Ocean Road you'll see the **Surf City Plaza** shopping centre on your right, one of the best places in town to rent and buy surf gear. The **Surfworld Museum** at the rear of the plaza (daily 9am–5pm; $8.50; ⓦwww.surfworld.org.au) features a wave-making machine, interactive videos that explain how waves are created, and displays about the history of surfing. The museum doubles as the **Torquay Visitor Information Centre** (ⓣ03/5261 4606), handing out a few leaflets and brochures. The **Mary Elliott Pottery**, 80 Surfcoast Highway (open daily; ⓣ03/ 5261 3310), is worth a look; it supplies tourist information as well. Turning left from the Great Ocean Road towards the beach, there's another cluster of shops, supermarkets and cafés around Gilbert Street.

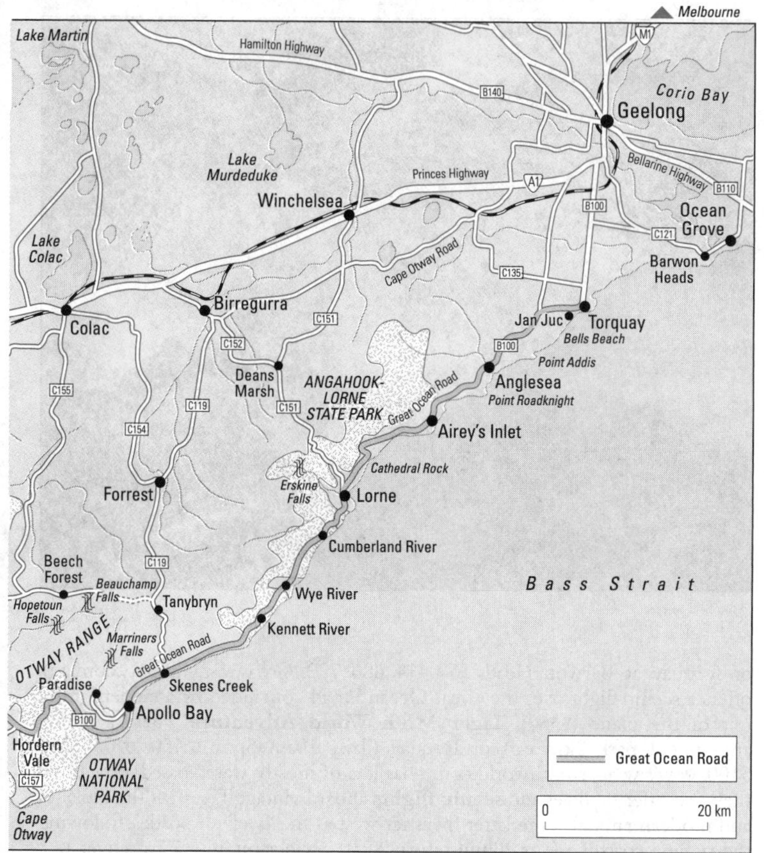

A grassy public reserve shaded by huge Norfolk pines (with electric barbecues and picnic tables) runs along rocky **Fisherman's Beach** and **Front Beach**. The **Surf Beach** (or "back beach"), south of Cosy Corner (a headland separating Front and Surf beaches), is backed by rugged cliffs and takes a full belting from the Southern Ocean; it's patrolled in summer. **Jan Juc**, just south of Surf Beach across Torquay Golf Club, is also patrolled in season and has better swimming and surfing. The **South Coast Walk** to Aireys Inlet via Anglesea begins from here (25km; 8hr); the stretch to **Bells Beach** is a one-hour, three-kilometre walk.

Practicalities

Go Ride a Wave (Ⓣ1300 132 441, Ⓦwww.gorideawave.com.au), a long-established outdoors-activities company based in neighbouring Anglesea with an outlet in Bell Street, Torquay, offers **surfing lessons** (2hr/$60 or packages; gear included) as well as **sea-kayaking** instruction and trips exploring the coastline. The Westcoast Surfing School runs surfing classes in Torquay and Anglesea (2hr/$50 or packages; gear included Ⓣ03/5261 2241, Ⓦwww.westcoastsurfschool.com). If you feel like taking to the air, **Skydive City**, east

△ Surfing at Bells Beach, Torquay

of Torquay at Barwon Heads (ⓣ0414 686 722, ⓦwww.skydivecity.com.au), offers a scenic flight over the Great Ocean Road concluded by a tandem jump out of the plane ($360). **Tiger Moth World Adventure Park**, a family amusement park 3km east of Torquay (daily 10am–5pm; $9.50; ⓣ03/5261 5100, ⓦwww.tigermothworld.com), has lots of mostly water-based attractions; they also offer skydives and **scenic flights** aboard vintage Tiger Moths, biplanes and modern aircraft – the latter fly as far west as the Twelve Apostles, following the rugged coastline (1hr 20min return, $250 per person, min 2 passengers).

Accommodation

Anita's Guesthouse Cottage and Cabins 17 Anderson St ⓣ03/5261 4732, ⓦwww.torquaycottage.com.au. Budget cabins with shared facilities, as well as more upmarket rooms with en-suite bathrooms and a self-contained cottage with two bedrooms. Budget cabins ❸, en-suite rooms and cottage ❹–❺

Bells Beach Backpackers 51–53 Surfcoast Highway ⓣ03/5261 7070, ⓦwww.bellsbeachbackpackers.com.au. Close to Surf City Plaza and painted with beach-house murals, this place is hard to miss. The small, clean and well-run hostel has dorms and a double, a nice backyard for BBQs and volleyball, plus Internet access, bikes, boards and wetsuits for hire. Unsurprisingly, it's very popular – book at least a week in advance, earlier in Jan. Dorms $20–25, rooms ❸

Grossmans Country Cottages Ashmore Road ⓣ03/ 5261 2656. Excellent-value, fully equipped cottages positioned on rolling hills, five minutes out of town. Has a real country-farm feel to it, making it perfect for those who want a bit of space. Each cottage can sleep five people, and some have sea views. Owners also run a luxury spa centre on the premises that guests can use. ❹

Surf City Motel 35 The Esplanade ⓣ03/5261 3492, ⓦwww.surfcitymotel.com.au Super location right across from the beach, but rooms are a little dated and prices are on the high side. Does come with a spa bath, heated pool and BBQ area. ❹–❻

Torquay Hotel 36 Bell St ⓣ03/5261 2001, ⓦwww.torquayhotel.com.au. Very centrally located option, with good bistro fodder and live bands at the weekend too. Rooms are ok, but you are really paying for the location. ❺

Torquay Foreshore Caravan Park Bell St ⓣ03/ 5261 2496, ⓦwww.gorcc.com.au/torquay-caravan-park/. Situated right next to the beach, and close to the shops, this huge park has an array of accommodation options, from powered sites to standard and deluxe cabins. Popular with students in the summer months. ❸–❻

Eating and drinking

Bells Beach Hotel 3 Stuart Ave. Popular with beach-goers, this friendly local pub serves up excellent traditional pub food (huge burger $16). Open 9am–late, seven days a week.
Growlers 23 The Esplanade ⓣ03/ 5246 1397. Despite the sophisticated cuisine (mains around $20), this place has a laid-back beach vibe due to the Californian bungalow it occupies across from the water. Open Wed–Fri noon–late, Sat–Sun 10am–late.
Moby 41 The Esplanade. Former run-down beach cottage, which has transformed into a great café serving tasty organic food (around $8–15). A local favourite. Daily 7am–5pm (hours extended in summer).
Sandbah 21 Gilbert St. This large and airy place is one of the nicest cafés on this street; they serve tasty breakfasts, cakes and lunches. Open 7.30am–6pm.
Scandinavian Ice Cream Company 34 Bell St. Great ice cream option near the beach, where surfers come at the end of the day. Open daily.

Anglesea and Aireys Inlet

On the way to Anglesea from Torquay, you can make a short but worthwhile detour to **Point Addis**; turn left just beyond Bells Beach. The road goes right out to the headland car park where you look down on the waves crashing onto the point. Steps lead down to an even better vantage point, with surf heaving below you and Bells Beach stretching to the northwest. Just before the headland, there's another car park from where an access track leads to the **Point Addis Koori Cultural Walk**. Interpretive signs along this one-kilometre trail point out the use of plants and other aspects of the traditional lifestyle of the Wathaurong clan who inhabited the Geelong region.

ANGLESEA itself is a pleasant place for a holiday, with the Anglesea River running through to the sea, and picnic grounds along its banks; its main claim to fame is a large population of **kangaroos**, which graze on the golf course. Despite tourist development, the beach has managed to retain its sand dunes and untouched aspect. Children can swim safely here, as the surf is fairly gentle, but the waves are high and powerful enough for body-surfers to enjoy. The small *Anglesea Backpackers Hostel* on 40 Noble St (ⓣ03/5263 2664, ⓦwww.home.iprimus.com.au/angleseabackpacker; dorms $23, room ❸), located between the river and the golf course, has two six-bed dorms and an en-suite double. Internet access is also available ($5 per hour). A great place to unwind is the friendly *Rivergums B&B* (ⓣ03/5263 3066, ⓦwww.greatoceanroad.org/rivergums; ❹) at 10 Bingley Parade, along the river. There are two self-contained apartments (one with private access to the *Anglesea Hotel*). The local's favourite **café** is *Furios* at 95 Great Ocean Rd, where they serve breakfast, lunch and dinner with an Italian slant seven days a week. Two companies organize surfing and kayaking lessons here; see p.897.

From Anglesea the road goes inland for a few kilometres through scrubby bush. Beyond, a pretty white lighthouse with a red cap overlooks the small town of **AIREYS INLET**, where there's a general store, a café and craft shop near the lighthouse in what used to be the former lightkeeper's stables (7 Federal St; daily 9am–5pm). The horse-riding outfit Blazing Saddles operates rides through the Angahook Lorne State Park: beach rides and pony rides for kids (ⓣ03/5289 7322 or 0418 528 647, ⓦwww.blazingsaddlestrailrides.com). For **accommodation** try *Aireys Inlet Caravan Park* on the Great Ocean Rd (ⓣ03/5289 6230, ⓦwww.aicp.com.au; cabins ❸–❺) or *Split Point Cottages* at 40 Hopkins St (ⓣ03/5289 6566, ⓦwww.splitpointcottages.com.au; ❺–❻), which features accommodation in four mud-brick cottages with two bedrooms. *Airey's by the*

Light, 2 Federal St, on the way to the lighthouse (ⓣ03/5289 6134, ⓦwww.greatplacestostay.com.au/aireys/default.asp; ❻), is a very upmarket B&B with private decks and sea views that you will never forget.

Lorne and around

Picturesquely set at the foot of the heavily forested **Otway Range**, on the banks of the Erskine River, **LORNE** has long been the premier holiday town of the Great Ocean Road. Only two hours' drive from the city, it's hugely popular with Melbourne weekenders who relish its well-established café society and whiff of 1960s counterculture overlaid on an essentially middle-class 1930s resort. To complete the picture, the **Angahook–Lorne State Park** (see p.902), with its walking tracks, plunging falls and fern gullies, surrounds the town.

About a thousand people live in Lorne, but from Christmas until the end of January twenty thousand more pour in; if you arrive unannounced, you'll have no hope of finding even a camping spot. The **Falls Festival** (ⓦwww.fallsfestival.com) on New Year's Eve is celebrated with a big rock concert that attracts droves of teenagers, followed eight days later by the Mountain to Surf Run and one day later by the highlight of the peak season, the **Pier to Pub Swim**. It is said to be the largest blue-water swimming event in the world and attracts as many as four thousand competitors who race the 1200m from Lorne Pier to the main beach. The atmosphere surrounding these events is a lot of fun, but generally Lorne is much more enjoyable when it's less crowded, which means avoiding weekends and the peak summer season.

The town's beachfront is enlivened by the restored *Grand Pacific Hotel* with its 1870s facade, on a headland at the western end, and the modern, pink, terraced *Cumberland Resort*. Between the street and the beach is a foreshore with trampolines and a pool. The **surf beach** itself is one of the safest in Victoria, protected from the Southern Ocean by two headlands, but in summer it gets very crowded.

Practicalities

Lorne's **tourist office**, at 144 Mountjoy Parade (daily 9am–5pm; ⓣ03/5289 1152 or 1300 614 219, ⓦwww.visitsurfcoast.com.au), is very helpful and has a good stock of leaflets packed with local information. Mocean Surfboards on Mountjoy Parade (daily 9.30am–5.30pm; ⓣ03/5289 1011) rents out quality surf- and boogie-boards and wetsuits. Other services, such as banks, a post office and shops, are clustered primarily along Mountjoy Parade and parallel Smith Street.

Accommodation

Most accommodation is in the upper price bracket, and in December and January the majority rent by the week, with even B&Bs insisting on a three- or four-night minimum stay. To keep costs down, contact the Lorne Foreshore Committee, Ocean Road by Erskine Bridge (ⓣ03/5289 1382, ⓦwww.lorneforeshore.asn.au), which runs four **caravan parks** in the vicinity.

Cumberland Apartments 150 Mountjoy Parade ⓣ03/ 5289 2400, ⓦwww.cumberland.com.au. Luxurious, fully equipped apartments set right on the beach, many with private balconies overlooking the water. Facilities include gym, tennis and squash courts, indoor-swimming pool, and surfboard and mountain-bike hire. ❼–❽

Erskine Falls Cottages Cora-Lynn Court, off Erskine Falls Rd, 4.5km north of town ⓣ03/5289 2666, ⓦwww.lornecottages.com.au. Spacious timber cottages (1–3 bedrooms) and units in the hills near Erskine Falls, with views of the ocean, big verandas, fireplaces, a pool, a tennis court and a licensed café. ❺

Erskine River Backpackers 4 Mountjoy Parade ⓣ03/ 5289 1496. Located above the *Ba Bu Lu Restaurant* (see below), this ramshackle beach house can get hot in summer and dorms are on the small side. However, with its friendly atmosphere, great location and excellent balcony, many will forget its weaknesses. Dorms $22.

Grand Pacific Hotel 268 Mountjoy Parade, opposite the pier at Point Grey ⓣ03/5289 1609, ⓦwww.grandpacific.com.au. The restored and refurbished Victorian lives up to its name: it has great views over Loutit Bay from the dining room and the bar, and rooms have old-world charm but all the mod cons. It's worth shelling out a bit more for a room with sea views. Hotel rooms ❹, apartments ❻

Great Ocean Road Backpackers YHA 10 Erskine Ave ⓣ03/5289 1809, ⓔlorne@yhavic.org. This excellent, attractive hostel shares the grounds with *Great Ocean Road Cottages* (see below). The hostel section comprises two large timber cottages with balconies, and there's free use of laundry, bicycles and boogie-boards. Dorm bed $20, rooms ❸

Great Ocean Road Cottages 3 Erskine Ave ⓣ03/5289 1070, ⓦwww.greatoceanroadcottages.com. Well-designed, comfortable, self-catering cottages in a lovely forest setting beside the Erskine River, just minutes from the main strip. ❺

Lorne Hotel Mountjoy Parade ⓣ03/5289 1409, ⓦwww.lornehotel.com.au. Super-central pub that has nice enough rooms, but can get noisy on weekends. Some rooms have ocean views with balconies and spa. ❺

Eating, drinking and entertainment

There are great places to **eat** and **drink** everywhere in town – but they charge Melbourne prices and then some. Most licensed places allow you to BYO wine but charge a hefty corkage fee. The Lorne Theatre, 78 Mountjoy Parade (ⓣ03/5289 1272, ⓦwww.greatoceanroadcinemas.com.au), screens films all week during summer and in the school holidays.

Andrew's Chicken Joint 134 Mountjoy Parade. Licensed takeaway known for cooking up burgers and souvlakis at affordable prices. Where the surfers come to refuel. Open daily.

The Arab 94 Mountjoy Parade ⓣ03/ 5289 1435. An original beatnik hangout, which opened two weeks before the Olympic Games in 1956 and has been going strong ever since. It now sports minimalist decor and is still good for daytime snacks and fancier meals at night. Licensed and BYO wine. Daily 8.30am–late.

Ba Ba Lu Bar and Restaurant 6A Mountjoy Parade. Nice joint at the quieter eastern end of town with a great outdoor area. The restaurant follows a Spanish–Latin American theme with tapas and mains such as *gambas a la plancha* (chargrilled prawns in a sherry sauce). There's also a good range of breakfasts and cheaper lunch items. Licensed and BYO. Daily 8.30–1am.

Beach Buns Bakery Shop 2/32 Mountjoy Parade. The place to come to buy straight-out-of-the-oven pies, pastries and snacks for the beach. Also makes gourmet sandwiches for those looking to take a picnic lunch. Open daily.

Kosta's 48 Mountjoy Parade. A popular, Greek-style bar and eating place, serving up good seafood as well as grilled meats. Often has music in the evenings. Licensed or BYO wine. Daily 9–1am; closed July.

The Lorne Deck 1 William St. The real highlight of this place isn't the modern and reasonably priced menu, but the great sun-deck that looks over the town towards the water. A great place to hang out and watch the sunset. Daily 11am–late.

Lorne Hotel 176 Mountjoy Parade. Best pub meals in town ($14–25), plus a dining room and a sensational beer garden overlooking the ocean and live music on Fri and Sat. Daily noon–9pm.

Lorne Pier Seafood Restaurant ⓣ03/5289 1119. Pricier than the average fish-and-chips shop but this well-known seafood restaurant is worth it for the setting alone. Licensed and BYO. Daily 6–9.30pm, longer in summer.

Qdos Allenvale Rd ⓣ03/5289 1989. Tucked away in the eucalypt-clad hills above Lorne, this art gallery-cum-café serves light lunches, dinners and tasty home-made cakes and coffee in a relaxed atmosphere. Bookings advisable. Mon & Fri–Sun 9am–5pm, summer 9am–late.

Angahook-Lorne State Park

Angahook–Lorne State Park extends along some 50km of coastline, from Aireys Inlet to Kennett River. Pockets of temperate rainforest, towering blue-gum forests, cliffs and waterfalls characterize the Lorne section of the park, south of the Erskine River. The **Erskine Falls**, one of the most popular attractions, drop 30m into a fern-fringed pool – you can reach them along a winding eight-kilometre road that ends with a short descent on a very steep but sealed section. From the car park the falls are a few minutes' walk through majestic trees and tall umbrella ferns; another 150m takes you down to the quiet, rocky Erskine River. It's also possible to walk through the bush from Lorne to the falls (7.5km one way; 4hr), starting from the *Erskine River Caravan Park* (one of the four caravan parks run by the Lorne Foreshore Committee) next to the bridge over the Erskine River, just off the Great Ocean Road and following the river; after 1km you'll pass the Sanctuary, a natural rock amphitheatre, then Splitter Falls and Straw Falls, before reaching Erskine Falls.

Closer to Lorne, **Teddy's Lookout**, in Queens Park, is either a quick drive from the Great Ocean Road (up Otway Street, turn left at the roundabout into George Street), or a three-kilometre walk along the same streets; just follow the signposts. You end up high above the sea, with a view of the St George River below and the Great Ocean Road curving around the cliffs.

Apollo Bay and the Otway Ranges

Between Lorne and Apollo Bay wooded hills fall away steeply into the ocean. If you can, stop for lunch and take advantage of the stunning ocean views at *Rookery Nook Hotel* (ⓣ03/5289 0240, ⓦwww.wyepub.com.au) in the sleepy hamlet of **Wye River**. It also has rooms (④) in case you find it hard to leave. **APOLLO BAY** itself enjoys a picturesque setting between pounding surf and gently rounded green hills. **Fishing** – commercial and recreational – is the main activity here. If you're interested in doing a bit yourself, enquire at Apollo Bay Fishing and Adventure Tours (ⓣ03/5237 7888, ⓦwww.apollobayfishing.com.au), which offers fishing trips, seal watching and scenic boat cruises. The town has an enjoyably alternative feel – a lot of artists and musicians live here and both local pubs often have music at weekends. The weekly Foreshore Market (Sat 8.30am–4.30pm) is well worth a browse and showcases locally produced arts and crafts as well as fresh produce. The annual Apollo Bay Music Festival takes place over a weekend in mid-March and features jazz, rock, blues and country, plus many workshops (information and bookings ⓣ03/5237 6761, ⓦwww.apollobaymusicfestival.com). For information on local activities, head for the Great Ocean Road Visitor Information Centre on the foreshore at the eastern end of town (daily 9am–5pm; ⓣ03/5237 6529), which has very helpful staff who can book accommodation.

Practicalities

Apollo Bay marks the start of the **Great Ocean Walk**, a 91-kilometre track through forests and some of the state's most stunning coastal scenery. Note that sections of the track become impassable at high tide and in rough weather so make sure you register with the Apollo Bay Visitor Information Centre which provides updates on its condition as well as any other information. If you're a **cycling** enthusiast enquire about mountain-bike tours run by Otway Expeditions that go from the "rainforest to the beach" (ⓣ0419 007 586; $55). **Flying** seems to be rather popular here, too: the Wingsports Flight Academy, in Evans Court (ⓣ0419 378 616, ⓦwww.wingsports.com.au), offers courses in hang-gliding and para-gliding and allows those with no prior experience to fly with a fully qualified pilot along the coast in a powered hang-glider. Twelve Apostles Aerial Adventures (ⓣ03/5237 7370, ⓦwww.tigermothworld.com) and Apollo Bay Aviation (ⓣ04/07 306 065, ⓦwww.apollobayaviation.com.au), both at the Apollo Bay airfield south of town, do scenic flights to a variety of destinations, including nearby Cape Otway and the Twelve Apostles ($130–180 per person for 45 mins, depending on size of group), and as far afield as King Island, Tasmania. Sunroad Tours picks up people from their accommodation and takes them to view **glow-worms** on a private property (ⓣ03/5237 6080, ⓦwww.greatoceanroad.com.au/glowwormtours; 90min; $30) while Otway Eco Tours operates out of the Otway town of Forrest, 37km northwest of Apollo Bay, and runs **canoe trips** in the densely forested hinterland to see platypus and glow-worms (ⓣ03/5236 6345, ⓦwww.platypustours.net.au; 2–6 people; 3.5–4hr; $85). For other sightseeing **tours** (4WD or normal vehicle) enquire at the Visitor Information Centre.

Accommodation

Numerous **accommodation** options can be found in the area, many of them picturesquely located in the hills and valleys surrounding the town – a scenic location is the **Barham River Valley** 8km west of town that has places in a lush rainforest setting. Apollo Bay's main street is lined with **motels**, most of them rather drab affairs dating from the 1970s.

There are several **caravan parks**, the closest to town being the *Waratah Caravan Park* at 7 Noel St (ⓣ03/5237 6562, ⓕ03/5237 7700; cabins ❸–❹). Both the *Pisces Caravan Resort*, 2km north of the town centre (ⓣ03/5237 6749, ⓔpiscespark@hotkey.net.au; ❹), and the *Marengo Holiday Park* on Marengo Crescent in secluded surroundings on the foreshore (ⓣ03/5237 6162, ⓦwww.marengopark.com.au; ❸–❺), have cabins, some with en-suite facilities.

Apollo Bay Backpackers 47 Montrose Ave ⓣ0419 340 362, ⓦwww.apollobaybackpackers.com.au. Small house that has a very chilled "beach bum" vibe. Has Internet access, BBQ in the backyard and nice tables at the front for socializing. Dorms $20, rooms ❷

Eco Beach YHA 5 Pascoe St ⓣ03/5237 7899, ⓔapollobay@yhavic.org.au. Easily the state's best budget-accommodation option. This million-dollar property has incredible facilities including a great sundeck looking towards the sea, and state-of-the-art kitchen and lounge rooms. Those not acquainted with such extravagance may want to stay here indefinitely. Dorms $28, rooms ❸

Marriner's Falls Cottages 1090 Barham River Rd, Barham River Valley ⓣ03/5237 7494, ⓦwww.marrinersfalls.com.au. Spacious and cosy cottages, built on a hillside, with spa, open fire, balconies and great views, but no TV. ❻

A Room with a View 280 Sunnyside Rd, Wongarra ⓣ03/5237 0218, ⓦwww.roomwithaview.com.au. Cozy, aptly named B&B accommodation, 14km east of town, with magnificent views of green rolling hills and the ocean, and gourmet breakfasts to set you up for the day. ❻

Sandpiper Motel 3 Murray St ⓣ03/5237 6732, ⓦwww.sandpiper.net.au. Only 50 metres from the beach, these new stylish apartments (some with ocean views) offer a luxurious setting in the middle of everything. Also has broadband. ❺

Skenes Creek Lodge Motel 61 Great Ocean Rd, Skenes Creek ⓣ03/5237 6918, ⓕ5237 6329. Good budget motel in a garden setting above the main road, with restaurant and ocean views. ❸–❺

Surfside Backpackers Cnr of Great Ocean Rd and Gambier St ⓣ1800 357 263, ⓔsurfbakpak@greatoceanroad.org. A friendly place with small dorms and cheap doubles in a scenic location on a hill at the western side of town looking over the water. Facilities include disabled access, outdoor BBQs and a large vinyl collection. Dorms $17–20, rooms ❷

Eating

In town, the **eating** places are strung along the Great Ocean Road. To buy freshly caught seafood, go to the Fishermen's Co-op at the harbour (Mon–Thurs 9.30am–4.30pm, Fri until 5pm, Sat & Sun 10am–3pm).

Apollo Bay Hotel 95 Great Ocean Rd ⓣ03/5237 6470. Great pub that offers very good bistro meals ($12 plus) with an excellent beer garden that looks towards the water.

Be Bep 4A Hardy St ⓣ03/5237 6766. Very good Thai–Vietnamese cuisine at average prices (mains $11–16). Takeaway available. Dinner daily.

Bend Café 3225 Great Ocean Rd ⓣ03/5237 9287. Halfway to Lavers Hill, this makes the perfect stop to take in the charming rural setting. Food is sourced from local producers. Open daily for breakfast, lunch and dinner.

Buffs Bistro 51 Great Ocean Rd. This reliable old-timer serves light snacks, seafood and pasta. Daily 11am–late.

Chris's Beacon Point Restaurant 2km up Skenes Creek Road, Skenes Creek ⓣ03/5237 6411. The renowned restaurant in the hills above Skenes Creek features Mediterranean cuisine with a Greek accent and specializes in seafood – but it doesn't come cheap (mains $30–36). Noon–2.30pm, 6pm–late daily.

Nautigals Buzz Bar 55 Great Ocean Rd. Has healthy breakfasts, light lunches and dinners and when the sun sets, the backpackers come out to play with mid-priced cocktails and occasional live music. 8am–late daily.

Tanybryn Tea House and Gallery on the corner of Skenes Creek and Wild Dog roads ⓣ03/5237 6271. Worth the fifteen-minute drive from Apollo Bay township for its well-stocked craft shop, café and fine panorama (10am–5pm; closed July to mid-Sept).

Otway National Park

From Apollo Bay, the Great Ocean Road soon enters **Otway National Park**, curving and bending upwards through temperate rainforest and offering occasional glimpses of cleared hilltops and grazing sheep in the distance. From Maits Rest car-park, 17km west of Apollo Bay, you can take an easy stroll through a lovely fern gully, which gives a feel of the dense rainforest that once covered the entire Otway Ranges. A little further down the road, towards Lavers Hill, you'll see a turn-off to the **Cape Otway Lighthouse**, 14km away on a sealed road, where there's a small café (daily 10am–5pm) and pleasant accommodation in two refurbished lighthouse-keepers' residences, simply but tastefully decorated and fully equipped (ⓣ03/5237 9240, ⓦwww.lightstation.com; ❻). You can visit the lighthouse (daily 9am–5pm; $10) or join a guided tour (usually 11am, 2, 3 & 4pm daily; no extra fee). Three kilometres north of Cape Otway, the turn-off to Blanket Bay is a good location for spotting koalas.

The only **caravan park** actually within the national park is *Bimbi Park* (ⓣ03/5237 9246, ⓦwww.bimbipark.com.au; cabins ❷–❸), about halfway along the road to the lighthouse. The facilities and some of the cabins are quite basic but the setting is gorgeous – on a small farm with paddocks surrounded by bushland – and the caravan park offers excellent **horse-riding** excursions, including a ride to Station Beach (1hr 30min; $50), a three-kilometre-long stretch of sand with freshwater springs and waterfalls.

Back on the Great Ocean Road, you momentarily return to the ocean at **Castle Cove**, a good lookout-point across green, undulating dairy country. As you turn inland again, stepped hills rise sharply from the road as it passes turn-offs to **Johanna**, one of Victoria's best-known surf beaches, and winds up towards **LAVERS HILL**, the highest point in the Otway Ranges. The tiny town has two good cafés: *Gardenside Manor* (9am–5pm daily) and *Blackwood Gully Tea Rooms* (11am–5pm daily); both serve light snacks and Devonshire teas daily. There's motel accommodation at the *Otway Junction Motor Inn* (ⓣ03/5237 3295; ❹) and a small, cosy cottage at Fauna Australia Wildlife Retreat, a privately run Australian wildlife sanctuary – they also offer guided tours and serve refreshments (Ⓣ03/5237 3234, Ⓦwww.faunaaustralia.com.au; ❻).

Before continuing west, it's worth taking a detour to the **Otway Fly Treetop Walk**, about ten to fifteen minutes' drive east of Lavers Hill (daily 9am–5pm; $19.50; Ⓦwww.otwayfly.com) – just follow the road signs. A 600m steel-trussed walkway here allows you to walk through temperate rainforest at canopy level, 20–25m above the ground. The Otway Fly Visitor Centre on top of the hill, 300m from the beginning of the walkway, has a good licensed café and a souvenir shop.

The Shipwreck Coast

The 130-kilometre stretch of coast between lonely, windswept Moonlight Head and Port Fairy is known as the **Shipwreck Coast**; it takes in the Twelve Apostles – something of an icon of the Great Ocean Road – and other well-known coastal formations such as Loch Ard Gorge and London Bridge. Most of the coast is protected within Otway National Park and **Port Campbell National Park**. At least 180 ships have come to grief in the coast's treacherous waters, and the **Historic Shipwreck Trail**, which links the sites of dozens of wrecks with informative plaques and signed walking-paths, runs between Moonlight Head and Port Fairy. A brochure about the trail is available at all the visitor information centres in the region.

At the tiny hamlet of Princetown, *The 13th Apostle* (Ⓣ03/5598 8062, Ⓦwww.users.bigpond.com/the13thapostle; dorm beds $19–23, rooms ❸), a modern, purpose-built hostel, provides pleasant and clean budget accommodation. A general store and pub are across the road.

The Twelve Apostles and Loch Ard Gorge

The most awe-inspiring formations on the coast are the **Twelve Apostles** – gigantic limestone pillars, some rising 65m out of the ocean, which retreat in rows as stark reminders of the power of the sea (the cliff faces erode at a rate of about 2cm a year). The (unstaffed) Twelve Apostles Centre at the car park on the northern side of the road provides clean toilet facilities and welcome shelter from the rain and bone-chilling winds blowing off the Southern Ocean. It features wall-length panels of sailcloth with scripted poems about the Shipwreck Coast's awesome, dangerous beauty. Covered walkways lead through a tunnel under the road to the lookout points and a short walk along the clifftop. Sunset here (summer around 9pm, winter around 5.45pm) is a popular time for photographers and, unfortunately, crowds. Wait ten minutes or so after dusk, however, when the tourists have jumped back on their coaches and left, and you'll be treated to another fantastic spectacle, as hordes of fairy penguins waddle onto the shore in droves.

Next stop is underrated **Loch Ard Gorge**, where a small network of clifftop walks and a staircase leading down to a beach give you the chance to view the fantastic rock formations all around. It was here that the *Loch Ard*, an iron-hulled square rig, hit a reef and foundered while transporting immigrants from England to Melbourne in the spring of 1878. Of 53 people on board, only two survived: Eva Carmichael and Tom Pearce, both in their late teens. They were swept into a long gorge that had a narrow entrance, high walls and small beach, and Tom dragged Eva into a cave in the western wall of the gorge before going for help. A walkway leads down to the beach, covered with delicate pink kelp, and you can scramble over craggy rocks to the cave where Eva sheltered, now a nesting site for small birds. The Loch Ard cemetery, where the ship's passengers and crew are buried, is on the clifftop overlooking the gorge. As you drive further, you pass more scenic points, with resonant names such as the Blowhole and the Thundercave, before reaching Port Campbell.

For a bird's-eye view of all this, take a helicopter ride with one of two companies in the area: PremiAIR Helicopter Services operate from the Twelve Apostles Centre (ⓣ03/5598 8266), while 12 Apostles Helicopters are found on the Great Ocean Road near Loch Ard Gorge, just east of Port Campbell (ⓣ03/5598 6161, ⓦwww.12ah.com).

Port Campbell and around

PORT CAMPBELL is a small settlement on the edge of the Port Campbell National Park, and the main base for those visiting the Twelve Apostles. The **Port Campbell Information Centre** on Morris Street (daily 9am–5pm; ⓣ03/5598 6089 or 1300 137 255, ⓦwww.visit12apostles.com) has displays and information about the area and its national parks, and can also book accommodation. Ask here too about the **Port Campbell Discovery Walk** (90min), which will take you along a clifftop to a viewpoint above Two Mile Bay.

Port Campbell **beach** is a small sandy curve, safe for swimming and patrolled in season – the town climbs the hill behind the beach.

If you're really fascinated by shipwrecks, Port Campbell Boat Charters at the Mobil Petrol Station at 32 Lord St (ⓣ03/5598 6366), offers **diving** to some wreck sites ($50), fishing trips (3hr $70, 5hr $90, 8hr $150) and can rent out snorkelling or diving gear to those who want to go it alone.

Practicalities

The town itself is a pleasant place to while away an evening, and with two hostels in town, **accommodation** needn't be expensive. In summer and for long weekends, however, it's advisable to book far ahead. The *Port Campbell Hostel* (ⓣ03/5598 6305, ⓦwww.portcambellhostel.com.au; dorms $25, rooms and cabins ❸) on Tregea Street is a pleasant, well-run place with a good kitchen, a spacious common room and TV lounge, Internet access, bright dorms, double/twin rooms and two cabins. In comparison, *Ocean House Backpackers* (ⓣ03/5598 6942; dorm bed from $20) may have a great location facing the water on Lord Street but the old house is rather dark and somewhat cramped. This hostel is operated by the Port Campbell National Park Cabin & Camping Park on Morris Street (ⓣ03/5598 6492, ⓔcampinport@datafast.net.au); small groups are possibly better off booking into one of their beachside cabins (❹). The *Loch Ard Motor Inn* (ⓣ03/ 5598 6433, ⓦwww.loachardmotorinn.com.au; ❹–❺) is in a prime position opposite the beach, and most of their simple yet comfortable rooms have personal patios facing the water. Rooms also have wireless Internet. Moving more upmarket, the *Sea Foam Villas* (ⓣ03/5598 6413, ⓦwww.seafoamvillas.com; ❻) at no. 14 are well equipped with private balconies with sea views.

Port Campbell offers plenty of choices for **eating** places, all close to each other on Lord Street. For regular Aussie fare or a late-night drink (they close when the last person leaves), go to the good-quality bistro at the *Port Campbell Hotel* (daily lunch and dinner). The simply titled *Take-Away* opposite the foreshore is a favourite with surfers needing their fish-and-chip fix, while *Nico's Pizza and Pasta* (noon–2.30pm, 6–8pm) opposite serves pancakes, egg breakfasts and a huge variety of pizzas. *Waves* (8am–late daily; mains from $18.50; booking advised on ⓣ03/5598 6111) at no. 29 is considered the best place in town serving reliably good breakfasts, lunch and dinner.

Port Campbell's expensive **general store** (daily: winter 8am–6pm; summer 7am–7pm) also has a bottle shop and an EFTPOS system that takes every type of card; it also functions as the post office and newsagent.

London Bridge, the Grotto and Timboon

Tourists could once walk across the double-arched rock formation known as **London Bridge**, a short distance west of Port Campbell, to the outer end facing the sea. In mid-January 1990, however, the outer span collapsed and fell into the sea, minutes after two very lucky people had crossed it – they were eventually rescued from the far limestone cliff by helicopter. As fate would have it, the couple were conducting an extramarital affair, and fled from the waiting media as soon as the helicopter arrived. Another good place to stop, just before Peterborough, is the **Grotto**, where a path leads from the clifftop to a rock pool beneath an archway.

Moving on, you pass through undulating dairy country on the last stretch of the Great Ocean Road from Peterborough, on Curdies Inlet, to Warrnambool.

Warrnambool and around

Coming into **WARRNAMBOOL** on the Great Ocean Road you see the city's more pleasant aspects: its lovely coastal setting, with **Allansford Cheeseworld** (Mon–Fri 8.30am–5pm, Sat 8.30am–4pm, Sun 10am–4pm; Ⓦwww.cheeseworld.com.au) indicating that this is the centre of rich **dairy country**. As well as selling cheese, it has tastings, a café serving teas and light meals, and a local history museum. However, if you approach Warrnambool from the northeast along the Princes Highway, you'll pass car lots, motels and an ugly factory belching smoke.

Lady Bay, where Warrnambool is sheltered, was first used by sealers and whalers in the early nineteenth century and was permanently settled from about 1839. **Southern right whales**, hunted almost to extinction, have begun to return in the last decade. Every year between June and September, female whales come to the waters off Logans Beach to calve. Often the whales swim very close to the shore and can be viewed from a specially constructed platform at Logans Beach.

The perils of shipping in the treacherous waters of the Shipwreck Coast are the theme at **Flagstaff Hill** at 23 Merri St (daily 9am–5pm; Ⓦwww.flagstaffhill.com; $15.50). The extensive grounds feature a recreated nineteenth-century coastal village, arranged around the original fort, erected in 1887 when the fear of a Russian invasion was widespread in Australia. Entry is via the building housing the visitor information centre, an upmarket restaurant, a souvenir shop plus a theatre and gallery. Flagstaff Hill's *pièce de résistance*, however, is the multi-million-dollar sound and laser show **Shipwrecked** ($25; 70min, book at least a day in advance; Ⓣ1800 556 111). Screened nightly after dusk (sometimes a second screening will commence after it if the first show is booked out early), it recounts the story of the Loch Ard disaster (see p.905).

Warrnambool has a bustling downtown, with a major shopping centre on Liebig Street, several galleries and museums, and some fine old churches. Perhaps the best of the sights is the **Warrnambool Art Gallery** on Liebig Street (Mon–Fri 10am–5pm, Sat & Sun noon–5pm; free), a fine provincial gallery with collections of Western District colonial paintings and contemporary Australian prints. The Botanic Gardens on Botanic Road, designed in 1877 by William Guilfoyle, then director of the Melbourne **Botanic Gardens**, are also worth visiting if you have some spare time.

Practicalities

The well-organized **Warrnambool Visitor Information Centre** (daily 9am–5pm; ⓣ03/5559 4620 or 1800 637 725, ⓦwww.warrnamboolinfo.com.au) is part of the Flagstaff Hill complex at 23 Merri St. **Internet** access is available at Southern IT, 190 Timor St (ⓣ03/5561 4087). Dive Inn (ⓣ03/5561 6108, ⓦwww.diveinn.com.au) do whale-watching cruises, scenic tours ($35/hr), **fishing and diving charters** as well as dive courses (PADI open water, 4 days, about $400); for **horse rides** along the beach contact Rundell's Mahogany Trail Rides (ⓣ03/5529 2303, ⓦwww.rundellshr.com.au about $50/2hr).

Accommodation

Girt By Sea B&B 52 Banyan St ⓣ03/5561 3162, ⓦwww.girtbyseabandb.com.au. Three tastefully furnished bedrooms with their own bathroom in a restored historic house (built 1856). Convenient location between the town centre and the beach. ⑤

Hotel Warrnambool Cnr of Koroit and Kepler sts ⓣ03/5562 2377, ⓔozone1@hotkey.net.au. Upmarket, refurbished place offering good B&B pub accommodation in the town centre; particularly good value for single travellers. Their British breakfasts are a good start to the day. ③

Lady Bay Apartments 2 Petrobe Rd ⓣ03/5562 1662, ⓦwww.ladybayapartments.com.au. Recently built, located on the foreshore, these self-contained apartments have views towards the sea. Also has an outdoor, heated swimming pool. ⑤

Warrnambool Beach Backpackers 17 Stanley St ⓣ03/5562 4874, ⓦwww.beachbackpackers. The best backpacker hostel in town, less than a 5min walk from the beach. It has comfy dorms with lockers (phone ahead for a female dorm) and doubles, some with en-suite, and a licensed bar and Internet access. Guests are picked up from the bus stop or train station in town on request. Dorms $22, en-suite rooms ③

Warrnambool Surfside Holiday Park Pertobe Rd, opposite Lake Pertobe ⓣ03/5559 4700, ⓦwww.surfsidepark.com.au. Self-contained one- to three-bedroom cottages and cabins as well as camping right on the beach. ④–⑥

Whale Bay B&B 17 Stanley St ⓣ03/5562 2204. Modern designed accommodation with panoramic views of the coastline from all of the bedrooms. A good choice in whale-watching season (May–Aug). ⑤

Eating, drinking and nightlife

There are plenty of good places to **eat** and **drink**, most of them on Liebig Street. Out of town, two eating places near the water are worth seeking out: the licensed *Fishsails Café* near the southern end of Pertobe Street at the breakwater (a branch of the *Fishtales Café* on Liebig Street), and *Proudfoots on the River* at 2 Simpson St, in a refurbished historic boathouse on the Hopkins River, with tearooms, a smoke-free bistro and a tavern bar. In terms of **nightlife** the *Whalers Inn* at the corner of Liebig and Timor Streets, is popular and has a nightclub next door (*Club 59*) that is open until 3am. Across the road at 62 Liebig St is the *Seanchai Irish Pub* that fills up on weekends and, nearby, the *Loft* at no. 56 is the town's best music venue with nightly performances.

Beach Babylon 72 Liebig St. Pleasant place for pizza and pasta or just a glass of wine. Open daily from 6pm. Mains start at $21.

Black Olive Bar Restaurant & Café *Hotel Grand*, 158 Liebig St ⓣ03/5561 6106. The dinner menu features Mediterranean-inspired dishes and there's a good wine list. Open daily noon–late.

China City 132 Koroit St. It may be average Chinese food but at least there's lots of it. All you can eat buffet 11am–2.45pm ($6.20), 5–9.30pm ($7.90) that attracts backpackers like flies. Open daily.

Mack's Snacks 77 Liebig St. Open since 1948 and still operated by the same family, this US-style diner (booth seating) is always popular, serving up great burgers ($6), wraps ($8), and an assortment of cakes and biscuits. Open breakfast, lunch and dinner daily.

Pippies by the Bay 23 Merri St ⓣ03/5561 2188. Located next to the tourist office at Flagstaff Hill, its main attraction is the views over Flagstaff Hill Maritime Village (see p.907) and Lady Bay. Enquire about dinner and show packages for the *Shipwrecked* programme. 10am to late Mon–Fri, 9am to late Sat & Sun.

Puds Pantry and Deli 60 Kepler St. Excellent home-made bread and pastries, as well as soups, pasta and curries to take away or eat in. Closed Sun.

Port Fairy

PORT FAIRY, the next stop along the coast, was once an early port and whaling centre but is now a quaint crayfishing and tourist town with a busy jetty, a harbour full of yachts, and over fifty National Trust–listed buildings. Heavy southern breakers roll into the surrounding beaches, and on **Griffiths Island**, poised between the ocean and Port Fairy Bay, there's a **muttonbird** rookery with a specially constructed lookout where, between September and April, you can watch the birds roost at dusk. For a historic small town, it's quite a happening place, hosting numerous events. In summer the four-week-long **Moyneyana Festival** focuses on outdoor activities – with events such as a raft race on the Moyne River – reaching its climax with the Moyneyana New Year's Eve procession. At Easter the annual Queenscliff to Port Fairy yacht race ends here, with a huge party. **Music** is big too, with the Spring Music Festival in mid-October concentrating on classical music, with a bit of opera and jazz thrown in for good measure, and the huge **Port Fairy Folk Festival** over the Labour Day long weekend in March, which takes over the entire town, with Australian and overseas acts playing world, roots and acoustic music. Tickets are sold in early November, and usually sell out in two to three hours. For more information and festival bookings contact the **visitor information centre**, on Bank Street (daily 9am–5pm; ⓣ03/5568 2682, ⓦwww.port-fairy.com). The centre also produces an excellent 20¢ map of the Port Fairy Heritage Walk, which takes you on a route around town to admire the many fine buildings. The **History Centre**, in the old courthouse on Gipps Street by the river (Wed, Sat & Sun 2–5pm, daily during holidays; $3), displays costumes, historic photographs, shipwreck relics and other items relating to the town's pioneer history. Other activities and attractions include the excellent links-style golf course (ⓦwww.portfairygolf.com.au) which has awe-inspiring views over the sea.

Practicalities

With its village-like atmosphere and variety of excellent **accommodation** options, as well as good pubs, tearooms and restaurants, Port Fairy makes a good place to break your journey between Melbourne and Adelaide.

The *Port Fairy YHA*, at 8 Cox St (ⓣ03/5568 2468, ⓦwww.portfairyhostel.com.au; dorm bed $19, rooms ❸), is a well-run and super-friendly hostel in a lovely old house right in the town centre. They also have wireless and broadband Internet access. The *Comfort Inn* at 22 Sackville St (ⓣ03/5568 1082, ⓦwww.seacombehouse.com.au; ❸–❻), is one of many National Trust–listed buildings in the town, with cheaper hotel rooms including excellent-value singles, gorgeous but pricey modern motel units and historic cottages. There are also a number of B&Bs, but those on the Moyne River in quaint colonial cottages are the best. Amongst them *The Douglas on the River*, at 85 Gipps St (ⓣ03/5668 1016, ⓦwww.portfairyabed.com; ❺–❻), is a family-run gem with some rooms set right on the river. The *Moorings Riverside Apartment* (ⓣ03/5561 4690, ⓔjhutson@optusnet.com.au; ❹), at 69A Gipps St, is a beautiful house with deluxe amenities, sleeping up to six people and even has its own fishing and boat jetty. Full details of all cottages and B&Bs, and of Port Fairy's six caravan parks, can be obtained from the visitor information centre.

One of the best places for a **drink** and a feed is the *Caledonian Inn* ("The Stump"), on the corner of Bank and James streets, which is open to 1am most nights of the week – it's the oldest continually licensed pub in Victoria (since 1844). In Sackville Street, *Rebecca's* at no. 70 does breakfasts, light lunches, cakes and good coffee, while around the corner are a few more eateries including *Portofino on Bank*, 26 Bank St (daily 5pm till late; ⓣ03/5568 2251), renowned throughout the district with its fusion of Middle Eastern and Australian cuisine. Not to be missed is the *Time and Tide Café* (9.30am–5pm daily; ⓣ03/5568 2134, closed Tues) which has stunning views right on the beach, 5 minutes out of town at 21 Thistle Place. The simple yet delicious delicatessen-style menu complements the setting.

Portland to Nelson

PORTLAND, the last stop on the Victoria coast going west on the Princes Highway, is an important industrial and fishing port. Portland likes to describe itself as the "Birthplace of Victoria". Indeed, there are quite a few historic buildings, but unlike Port Fairy, they don't add up to form a coherent, captivating townscape. **Nelson**, a friendly fishing village further west, or **Port Fairy** make for more atmospheric overnight stops on the coast route between Melbourne and Adelaide. The rugged coastal scenery to the southwest around Cape Nelson and Cape Bridgewater, however, is not to be missed.

Portland

If you want to learn what makes Portland tick, the comprehensive tour of the port and the **aluminium smelter** at Point Danger, 5km from the foreshore, is well worth taking (departs Mon, Wed & Fri from Visitor Information Centre; 2hr 30min–3hr; free but reservations necessary ⓣ1800 035 567). Back in town, the small **Maritime Discovery Centre** (daily 9am–5pm; $5.50) extends to the back of the information centre (see opposite) on the foreshore down from Bentinck Street. Its centrepiece is a life-sized model of a 5.7-metre great white shark, caught eight miles west of Cape Bridgewater in 1982. There is also a motley assemblage of boat-building tools, memorabilia, photos and marine wildlife information – but strangely, nothing of note on the Koori people who had lived in the region for a long time prior to white settlement.

A restored and modified vintage **cable tram** (daily 10am–4pm; ⓦwww.portlandcabletrams.com.au; $12) transports sightseers along the foreshore on a round trip of 7.5km, from the depot at Henty Park past the **Powerhouse Vintage Car Museum** (daily 1–4pm weekdays, 10am–4pm weekends; $5) to **Fawthrop Lagoon** (home to pelicans), then back through the **Botanic Gardens**. Alternatively, you can follow the Historic Buildings Trail (the visitor information centre has a brochure) which starts at the former Customs House in Cliff Street (near the southern end of Bentinck Street) and takes in some of the two hundred nineteenth-century buildings in Portland.

Out of town, along the coast to the southwest around craggy **Cape Nelson** and stormy **Cape Bridgewater** (the highest coastal cliffs in Victoria), the scenery is stunning, including caves, blowholes, a petrified forest, and the beach at **Bridgewater Bay**, which extends in a wide, sandy arc from one cape to the other. The best way to explore these features is along the walking tracks that start from the car park signposted left off the road to Cape Bridgewater. Bring good walking shoes – the volcanic rocks can be very sharp – and food and drink. **Seal Point** at Cape Bridgewater is home to about 850 **fur seals**. Seals by the Sea run tours (45min) where you can interact with these social creatures (ⓣ03/5526 7247; $28). Tickets can also be purchased at the *Beach Café and*

Information Centre (ⓣ03/5526 7155) at Bridgewater Bay. The licensed café is open daily for breakfast and lunch, also Friday and Saturday for dinner.

Practicalities

The excellent **visitor information centre** (which is shaped like an anchor), part of the Maritime Discovery Centre (daily 9am–5pm; ⓣ03/5523 2671 or 1800 035 567), has tourist pamphlets and maps galore, and the staff are happy to advise on local attractions, driving routes and the Great Southwest Walk which begins and ends in Portland. Internet access is available at 67 Bentinck St (9am–5pm daily; $6 an hour).

There is a wide range of **accommodation** in Portland. At the more affordable end and with a prime location is the *Gordon Hotel* (ⓣ03/552 31121, ⓔgordonhotel@hotkey.net.au ❸), across from the water at 63 Bentinck St. This huge pub has simple rooms with shared facilities and the price includes a light breakfast; ask for a room with sea views. For a bit of history try *Annesley House* (ⓣ03/55211434, ⓦwww.annesleyhouse.com.au; ❹) at 60 Julia St, which blends simple charm with modern amenities. The *Clifftop Accommodation B&B*, 13 Clifton Court (ⓣ03/5523 5100, ⓦwww.portland.au.com; ❺–❻), is within walking distance to the main drag of town and has three spacious, light-filled rooms with en suite and balconies overlooking Portland Bay; one room also has cooking facilities. The *Clock by the Bay Apartments* (ⓣ03/5523 4777, ⓦwww.clockbythebay.com.au; ❺–❻), on the corner of Cliff and Bentinck Streets, was once Portland's post office and has luxurious rooms looking over the bay.

At the southern end of the esplanade (Bentinck Street) is a cluster of **eating** options from where you can look out over the water and across to the busy port. Two notable ones are the very reasonably priced *Sully's Café and Wine Bar* (Tues–Sat 9am–late, Sun & Mon 10am–4pm) at no. 55, and at no.79, *Kokopelli's* (Sun–Thurs 8.30am–11pm, Fri & Sat 8.30–1am), a cool juice-bar and café serving tapas, lunches and dinners. The *Gordon Hotel* serves good pub food (noon–1.30pm & 6–8pm daily) and has bands on the weekends, but for a bit of class try *Sandilands* set in a 1950s Georgian mansion (ⓣ03/5523 3319) at 33 Percy St, known for their seafood. Glenelg Adventure Services at 67 Bentinck St (ⓣ03/5523 7646, ⓦwww.g-adventures.com.au) can kit you out for the Great Southwest Walk and other activities in the region; they sell camping accessories and all sorts of gear, as well as bikes and canoes.

Lower Glenelg National Park and Nelson

From Portland, the Princes Highway makes its uneventful way, via Heywood, to Mount Gambier in South Australia. After 120km it crosses the **Glenelg River** (which has its source in the Grampians) at Dartmoor, a popular point to begin a four-day canoeing trip down to the river's mouth at Nelson; ask about canoe rental at the Nelson Parks & Visitor Information Centre (see p.912). For most of the journey, the clear blue river flows through the unspoilt **Lower Glenelg National Park** in a sixty-kilometre gorge cut through limestone. The **Princess Margaret Rose Cave** (daily 40min guided tours at 10am, 11am, noon, then hourly from 1.30pm to 4.30pm; $11; ⓣ08/8738 4171), a huge chamber of actively growing stalactites and stalagmites, is the main cave in the system and the only one which is open to the public. It lies beside the river as it loops round by the South Australian border. It can be reached by canoe, car (unsealed roads from both sides of the border lead to the caves) or on a cruise from Nelson (see below).

NELSON, at the end of the coastal road and virtually on the Victoria/South Australia border, is well worth an overnight stay. A peaceful, friendly little hamlet, it feels caught in a time warp, and there's little to do but wander along the coast, read on the beach, and **fish** or **canoe** on the Glenelg. Nelson Boat & Canoe Hire on Kellet Street (daily 8.30am–6pm; ⓣ08/8738 4048, ⓦwww.nelsonboatandcanoehire.com.au) rent out canoes and kayaks. They also sell bait; but you'll need a fishing licence, obtained from the Nelson Kiosk (daily 8am–6pm; ⓣ08/8738 4220), the local service general store and post office. Fishing shelters line the river. Glenelg River Cruises on Old Bridge Road operates **cruises** to the Princess Margaret Rose Caves (daily in peak season, other times Sat & Sun and on some weekdays; departs 1pm; 4hr; $22.50; ⓣ08/8738 4191).

The **Nelson Parks & Visitor Information Centre** (daily 9am–5pm; ⓣ08/8738 4051) is signposted just off Leake Street; it also covers the Discovery Bay Coastal Park, which protects the shoreline almost all the way from Portland to the border. Here you can get camping permits for this and the Lower Glenelg National Park (book in advance in peak season) and information on walks and activities. They also have Internet access ($6 an hour).

If you're **staying overnight**, the best option is the charming *Nelson Cottage* (ⓣ08/8738 4161, ⓦwww.nelsoncottage.bigpondhosting.com; ④) which has comfortable rooms with shared facilities in an old police station dating from the early 1880s. The *Beach Road B&B* (ⓣ08/738424; ④), indeed on Beach Road, is very good value, located on the bottom floor of a private house set on the water's edge. The *Pinehaven Motel* on Main Road (ⓣ08/8738 4041; ③) is a basic motel owned by the petrol station next door. Rooms are small but clean. The *Kywong Caravan Park* on North Nelson Road (ⓣ08/8738 4174, ⓦwww.kywongcp.com) has cheap cabins (②) 1km north of town. The fantastic *Nelson Hotel* is a true country pub, and has excellent fresh **seafood** and huge steaks. The only other places in town are the Kiosk, which sells sandwiches and the usual junk food, and the petrol station on the main road which doubles as a fish-and-chip shop.

Central Victoria: the Goldfields

Central Victoria is classic Victoria: a rich pastoral district, chilly and green in winter and parched a brownish yellow in summer. Two grand provincial cities, **Ballarat** and **Bendigo**, whose fine buildings were funded by gold, draw large numbers of visitors, while, by contrast, the area's other centres such as **Maryborough** and **Castlemaine**, once prosperous gold-towns in their own right, now seem too small for their extravagant architecture.

There's fairly good **transport** from Melbourne with regular V/Line trains and buses to Bendigo, Ballarat and the other major centres in the Goldfields, and a few local buses fill some gaps. However, as elsewhere in the state, your own transport is a big advantage. The easiest way to tour is to follow the **Goldfields**

The goldrushes

The California goldrushes of the 1840s captured the popular imagination around the world with tales of the huge fortunes to be made gold-prospecting, and it wasn't long until Australia's first goldrush took place – near Bathurst in New South Wales in 1851. Victoria had been a separate colony for only nine days when gold was found at Clunes on July 10, 1851; the **goldrush** began in earnest when rich deposits were found in Ballarat nine months later. The richest goldfields ever known soon opened at Bendigo, and thousands poured into Victoria from around the world. In the golden decade of the 1850s, Victoria's population increased from eighty thousand to half a million, half of whom remained permanently in the state. The British and Irish made up a large proportion of the new population, but over forty thousand Chinese came to make their fortune too, along with experienced American gold-seekers and other nationalities such as Russians, Finns and Filipinos. Ex-convicts and native-born Australians also poured in, leaving other colonies short of workers; even respectable policemen deserted their posts to become "diggers", and doctors, lawyers and prostitutes crowded into the haphazard new towns in their wake.

In the beginning, the fortune-seekers panned the creeks and rivers searching for **alluvial gold**, constantly moving on at the news of another find. But gold was also deep within the earth, where ancient riverbeds had been buried by volcanoes; in Ballarat in 1852 the first **shafts** were dug, and because the work was unsafe and arduous, the men joined in bands of eight or ten, usually grouped by nationality, working a common claim. For deep mining, diggers stayed in one place for months or years, and the major workings rapidly became stable communities with banks, shops, hotels, churches and theatres, evolving more gradually, on the back of income from gold, into grandiose towns.

Tourist Route, whose chocolate-brown signs are marked by a distinctive circled capital G. The route links the major cities and towns – Bendigo, Castlemaine, Ballarat, Ararat and Stawell – with many smaller places in between.

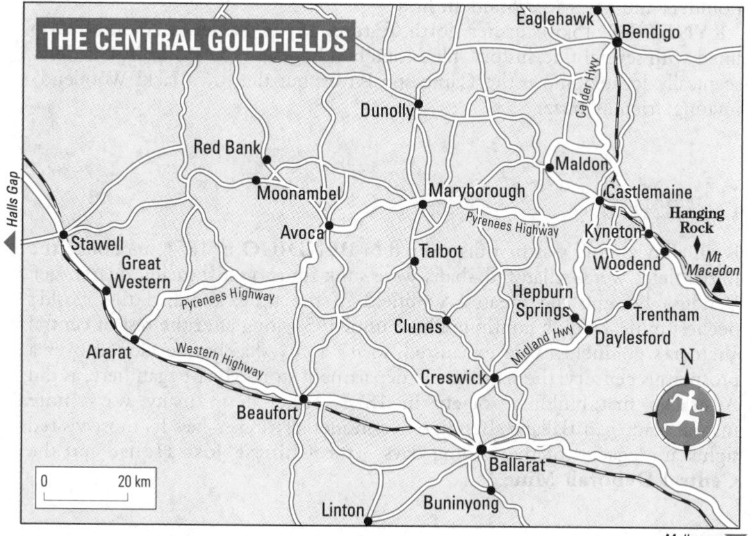

Towards the Goldfields: the Calder Highway

Though you could take the Western Freeway or the train directly to Ballarat, the route along the **CALDER HIGHWAY** towards Bendigo, 150km northwest of Melbourne, is much more interesting. The railway to Bendigo, which continues to Swan Hill, follows the same route, calling at the main towns.

At Diggers Rest, 22km from Melbourne on the highway, a short detour to the east will take you to the tiny **Organ Pipes National Park** (Mon–Fri 8.30am–4.30pm, Sat & Sun & public holidays until 6pm; ⓣ03/9390 1082), designated a national park for its outstanding geological interest. The rock formations here form a series of basalt columns, created by lava cooling in an ancient riverbed, and rising up to 20m above Jacksons Creek. The park can be explored along walking tracks and has picnic areas with tables. Back on the highway you'll come to **Gisborne**, 50km from Melbourne, developed as a coaching town for travellers on their way to the Bendigo and Castlemaine goldfields; it's dominated by **Mount Macedon**, an extinct thousand-metre volcano.

Fifteen kilometres or so from Gisborne, **Woodend** is a friendly, buzzing place with antique shops and cafés lined up along the main street, and also the jumping-off point for the **Hanging Rock Reserve**, 6km northeast (daily 8am–6pm; ⓦwww.hangingrock.info; $8 per car). The rock became famous because of the eerie 1975 film *Picnic at Hanging Rock* (directed by Peter Weir who went on to direct *Dead Poets Society* and *The Truman Show*), about a group of schoolgirls who mysteriously go missing here after a picnic – a story which many people falsely believed to be true. More about that story, as well as scientific information about the geological history of the rock, can be gleaned from the displays in the Hanging Rock Discovery Centre at its base; adjacent to it is a licensed café and a gift shop. You can walk around the base of the rock or climb to the summit with its massive boulders and crags in around an hour.

KYNETON, 15km further north, features **Piper Street**, a colourful strip lined with several fine, historic bluestone buildings and the **Botanic Gardens**, scenically located above the Campaspe River; but the town lacks Woodend's inviting, friendly buzz.

Bendigo

Rich alluvial gold was first discovered in **BENDIGO** in 1851, and, once the initial fields were exhausted, shafts were sunk into a gold-bearing quartz reef. Bendigo became the greatest goldfield of the time, and had the world's deepest mine. Mining continued here until 1954, long after the rest of central Victoria's goldfields were exhausted, so it's a city that has developed over a prosperous century: the nationwide department store Myer began here, as did Australia's first building society in 1858. Although in many ways more magnificent than Ballarat, Bendigo is considerably lower-key. Its most visited sights are legacies of the mining days – the **Chinese Joss House** and the **Central Deborah Mine**.

Arrival, information and transport

Bendigo Airport Service provides a link to Melbourne's Tullamarine Airport (3 daily; $35 one way; booking essential on ⓣ03/5447 9006, ⓦwww.bendigoairportservice.com.au). V/Line trains and buses arrive at the train station on Railway Place, just south of the CBD, while Greyhound Australia buses stop at the Caltex service station in Golden Square, at the corner of High and Oak streets.

The **visitor information centre** on Pall Mall (daily 9am–5pm; ⓣ1800 813 153, ⓦwww.bendigotourism.com) has a free accommodation-booking service and provides lots of brochures and maps, including the free *Bendigo Visitor Guide*, complete with walking map. Wanting to give Bendigo a sophisticated air reminiscent of London, the newly prosperous citizens called its central crossroads **Charing Cross**. Mitchell Street leads south to the **train station** and High Street (the Calder Highway) is the main exit west out of the city. The other important street is Hargreaves, parallel to Pall Mall one block south, with its impressive town hall and a revamped shopping mall. A good way to get an overall impression of the place is to take the **Vintage Talking Tram Tour** (daily 9.30am–4.30pm; departures on the half-hour, from the Central Deborah Goldmine; 1hr; $12.50). The tram tour ticket includes entrance to the **Bendigo Tram Museum**, located on Hargreaves Street at the opposite end of the route. Internet access is available at 70 Pall Mall (Mon–Fri 10am–5pm).

Accommodation

In terms of atmosphere and style, the **B&B guesthouses** and **cottages** throughout Bendigo and the whole goldfields area are a much better option than the average, somewhat sterile, motel room.

Barclay on View Motor Inn 181 View St, ⓣ03/5443 9388, ⓦwww.barclayonview.com. Excellent location across the road from the cricket ground and with gym, spa and sauna facilities this is one of the better motel options around town. ④

Bendigo YHA 33 Creek St South ⓣ03/5443 7680, ⓔbendigo@yhavic.org.au. Ultra-casual hostel right

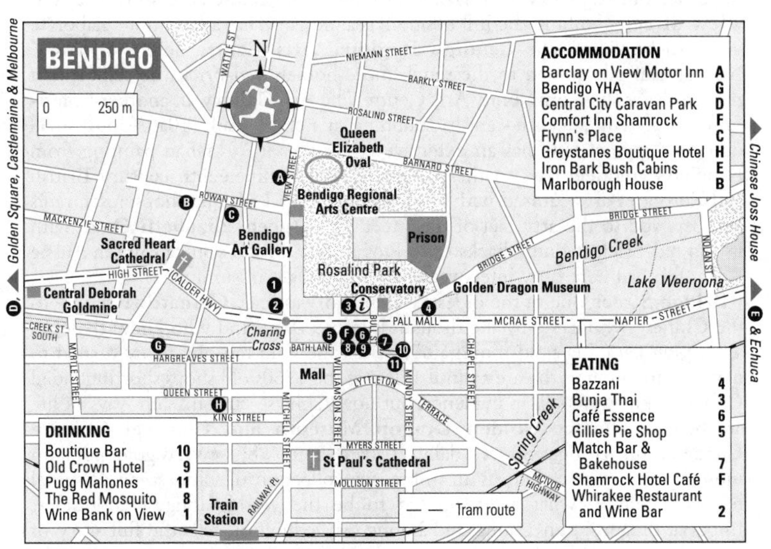

10

VICTORIA | Bendigo

in the centre of town with dorms ($21), and two twin and two family rooms. Open fire in the lounge, and Internet access. Rooms ❷

Central City Caravan Park 362 High St, Golden Square ⓣ03/5443 6937, ⓦwww.centralcitycaravanpark.com.au. Small caravan park with modern amenities block and a pool. Handy location 2.5 km southwest of the CBD; plus there's a bus stop to town just outside. En-suite cabins ❸

Comfort Inn Shamrock Cnr of Pall Mall and Williamson St ⓣ03/5443 0333, ⓦwww.shamrockbendigo.com.au. Fabulous Victorian hotel that has a wide range of accommodation, from budget-priced rooms to executive suites. ❹–❻

Flynn's Place 104 Short St ⓣ03/5444 0001, ⓦwww.flynnsplace.com.au. Two stylish self-contained apartments with all the latest nick-nacks including broadband access and wide-screen TVs.

Greystanes Boutique Hotel 57 Queen St ⓣ03/5442 2466, ⓦwww.greystanesmanor.com.au. Centrally located, beautifully appointed rooms in an elegant Victorian mansion with separate bar/lounge and open fires. ❻

Iron Bark Bush Cabins Watson St ⓣ03/5448 3344. Self-contained cabins, also available on a share basis for backpackers (bed $20), in a bushland setting a few kilometres out of town. Linen is supplied and there are cooking facilities and a licensed bar. Activity options include horse riding (trail rides from $30/hr) and a water slide ($8 for 10 rides). ❷

Marlborough House 115 Wattle St ⓣ03/5441 4142, ⓦwww.marlboroughhouse.com.au. B&B in a goldrush-era mansion near Sacred Heart Cathedral, with stained-glass windows, marble fireplaces and a covered balcony. ❹

The City

At the heart of Bendigo is the vast **Rosalind Park**, and three important religious buildings constructed with money from gold-digging – All Saints Church, St Paul's Cathedral and **Sacred Heart Cathedral**. Local Catholics imported stonemasons from Italy and England, and their craftsmanship can be seen in the design and details of Sacred Heart, begun in 1897 in English Gothic style. The interior has beautiful woodcarvings of the Twelve Apostles, and the crypt is the burial place of local bishops (daily 9am–5pm).

Many of Bendigo's finest goldrush buildings are along **Pall Mall**, including the law courts (1896) and the ornate Italianate (1887) edifice which now houses the visitor information centre – neither of which would seem out of place in a capital city. The amazingly decorative **Shamrock Hotel** stands opposite, four storeys of Victorian gold-boom architecture at its most extreme. **View Street**, climbing the hill beside Rosalind Park, has a few more elaborate goldrush buildings. The **Bendigo Regional Arts Centre** here is a massive Neoclassical pile, joined to the much more homely red-brick fire station that now serves as the Community Arts Centre. The **Art Gallery**, in another beautifully restored nineteenth-century building at no. 42 (daily 10am–5pm; small donation appreciated), has an extensive collection of Australian painting from Bendigo's goldfield days to the present, as well as nineteenth-century British and European art acquired with all that gold. Several antique shops, restaurants and bars add to the arty feel of the street. The **Queen Elizabeth Oval**, with its old red-brick stadium, backs onto Rosalind Park, and you can watch Aussie Rules football here on winter weekends and cricket in summer.

Bridge Street, one of the oldest in Bendigo, was once **Chinatown**, home to the Chinese who came by the thousands in the 1850s and who knew Bendigo as *dai gum san* ("big gold mountain"); when the gold ran out, many turned to market gardening in the area. Until as late as the 1960s old shops sporting faded Chinese signs were still in evidence, but now Chinese customs and ways of life are best seen in the **Golden Dragon Museum and Classical Chinese Gardens** on Bridge Street (daily 9.30am–5pm; $8; ⓦwww.goldendragonmuseum.org), where there is an impressive collection of Chinese processional regalia including what are supposed to be the world's longest and oldest Imperial dragons, Sun Loong and Loong. An exhibition tells the full story of

Bendigo's Chinese community since the days of the goldrush, whilst the attached gardens feature a temple to the goddess Kuan Yin. The National Trust-operated **Joss House**, on Finn Street in North Bendigo (ⓣ03/5442 1685; daily 10am–4pm; $3), was built by the Chinese in the 1860s and is the oldest Chinese temple still in use in Australia. The route to the shrine passes man-made Lake Weeroona, whose picnic grounds are the setting for the lovely *Boardwalk Restaurant & Café* (daily 7am till late; ⓣ03/5443 9855) in an old Chinese teahouse. To get to the Joss House, take bus #7 (approximately hourly Mon–Fri).

The Central Deborah Goldmine

The **Central Deborah Goldmine**, at the corner of Violet Street and the Calder Highway (daily 9.30am–5pm; ⓦwww.central-deborah.com), was the last mine in the Central Goldfields to close. While exploring the area above ground is free, it's worth taking the sixty-minute underground **Mine Experience Tour** (6 times daily 10.10am–4pm; 11 times daily during school holidays; $18.90) if you've never been down in a mine; everybody is issued with a reassuring hard hat, complete with torch and generator. You go down to a depth of 60m in a lift, which takes 85 seconds – it would take thirty minutes to reach the bottom of some of the deepest shafts. The further down you go the hotter it gets, but at 60m it's quite warm and airless, dripping with water and muddy underfoot. If you want to scramble around the mine a bit longer, climb ladders, perhaps operate a drill, you can join a longer **Underground Adventure** which also includes a meal (tours depart 9.30am, noon & 2pm; $58). For bookings, call ⓣ03/5443 8322 or see the website.

Eating, drinking and nightlife

The town offers a fairly good choice when it comes to eating and drinking, and there's plenty of student-influenced nightlife during term time. Several pubs have **bands** playing on Friday and Saturday nights, including the *Old Crown Hotel* at 238 Hargreaves St and *Pugg Mahones* on the corner of Bull and Hargreaves Streets which also has a good beer garden. The try-hard trendy crowd head next door to the *Boutique Bar* but those in the know go to the *Wine Bank on View* at 45 View St, which is located in a fantastic old building and has a great wine and tapas selection. For beer-lovers, the *Rifle Brigade Hotel* at 137 View St, a brewery pub with good food, has four homebrew beers on tap and a wrought-iron veranda. Night owls head to *The Red Mosquito*, a nightclub where the music doesn't stop until 4am on Fridays and 5am on Saturdays.

Bazzani Howard Place ⓣ03/5441 3777. Cozy restaurant at the end of the mall, renowned state-wide for the interesting, aesthetic and downright tasty dishes on the menu. Licensed. Daily noon–late.

Bunja Thai 32 Pall Mall. Set in a grand 1880s bank building, this Thai restaurant is a local favourite with delicious banquet menus (starting at $40 per person). Also known for their freshly brewed coffee. Tues–Thurs 10am–10.30pm, Fri & Sat 8.30am–10.30pm, Sun 8.30am–3.30pm. The Colonial Gallery featuring works by local artists is also on the premises.

Café Essence 53 Bull St. Popular café known for their breakfasts and the great second-floor veranda that offers the perfect outlook for the start of the day. Breakfast and lunch daily.

Gillies Pie Shop Cnr Hargreaves Mall & Williamson St. A Bendigo institution that is known Australia-wide. Come and watch through the windows as they make and bake their myriad assortment of pies and pasties. Daily 10am–6pm.

Match Bar & Bakehouse 58 Bull St. Stylish café-restaurant with lots of pasta, focaccia and pizza. Dinner daily; lunch daily except Sat.

Shamrock Hotel Café Cnr Pall Mall and Williamson St. This café-restaurant in the lovely, refurbished former public bar serves good breakfasts (home-baked bread) and has interesting, mainly modern Australian cuisine for lunch and dinner. Open daily.

Whirakee Restaurant and Wine Bar 17 View Point ⓣ03/5441 5557. Now an old-timer, but still serving outstanding modern cuisine, with an excellent wine list. Lunch Wed–Fri, dinner Tues–Sat.

Castlemaine and around

CASTLEMAINE, 39 km southwest of Bendigo, is at the centre of the area once known as the Mount Alexander Goldfields. Between 1851 and 1861, when its gullies were among the richest in the world, 105,000kg of gold were found here (modest quantities are still found at Wattle Gully mine at nearby Chewton, the oldest working gold mine in Australia). Castlemaine became the headquarters of the Government Camp for the area in 1852, and its impressive buildings were built during the following ten years. With no deep mines to sustain it, however, the town has developed little since then. Some 19km northwest of Castlemaine lies the quaint, small historic town of **Maldon**.

Information and accommodation

The very helpful **Castlemaine Visitor Information Centre** is in the Market Building on Mostyn Street (daily 9am–5pm; ⓣ03/5470 6200 or 1800 171 888, ⓦwww.maldoncastlemaine.com) and can arrange **accommodation** in the area. Internet access is available at 155 Barker St (9.30am–5pm daily).

Campbell St Motor Lodge 33 Campbell St, ⓣ03/5472 2377, ⓦwww.campbellstlodge.com.au. Motel-style rooms in a historic National Trust–listed house in the centre of town. ④

Castlemaine Gardens Caravan Park Doran Avenue ⓣ03/5472 1125, ⓦwww.castlemainegardenscaravanpark.com. Just out of the town centre, but next to the open-air swimming pool and Botanic Gardens, it offers simple but clean cabins. ③

Claremont Coach-House Burnett Rd ⓣ03/5472 2281. Fully self-contained double-storey stone cottage built in 1857, 3km north of the CBD near the Botanic Gardens. ⑤

Empyre Boutique Hotel 68 Mostyn St ⓣ03/5472 5166, ⓦwww.empyre.com.au. Newly opened luxury accommodation in the heart of town that has embraced the history of the area in its design and has instantly become the town's best accommodation option. ⑦

Ken and Chris' B&B 25 Johnstone St ⓣ03/5472 5292, ⓔkenchris@castlemaine.net. Quaint self-contained cottage with spa bath, wireless Internet and even a BBQ in your own private courtyard. ⑤

The Town

The town's finest building is the **Old Castlemaine Market** on Mostyn Street, a wonderfully over-the-top piece of Neoclassical architecture. The **Theatre Royal** on Hargreaves Street, one of the oldest theatres in Australia, is also quite magnificent; it's said that when the famous Lola Montez performed here, miners threw nuggets of gold at her in appreciation. It's now a **cinema** (ⓣ03/5472 1196, ⓦwww.theatreroyal.info) incorporating a cabaret-style section and a licensed bistro downstairs, and more traditional movie-house seating upstairs. Theatre groups and live bands sometimes perform here, and there's even a sporadic disco.

Another unusual attraction, a short distance from the centre, is **Buda**, at 42 Hunter St (Wed–Sat noon–5pm, Sun 10am–5pm; $5 for garden, $9 for house and garden; ⓦwww.budacastlemaine.org), a gracious nineteenth-century home and garden originally built in 1861 by a retired Baptist missionary in the style of an Indian villa. It was added to by its subsequent owner Ernest Leviny, a Hungarian silversmith, in the 1890s. The house and gardens give an insight into the good life enjoyed in the goldrush days, and much work by Leviny and his family is on display, including carved-wood hangings, embroidery, and the family's art and silverware collection. The **Castlemaine Art Gallery and Museum** on Lyttleton Street (Mon–Fri 10am–5pm, Sat & Sun noon–5pm; $4, ⓦwww.castlemainegallery.com) is also worth a visit. It specializes in Australian photographs and paintings, featuring many works by the Heidelberg School, notably Frederick McCubbin and Tom Roberts. Partly because of the big **Castlemaine State Festival** which takes place over ten days in early April in odd-numbered years, this is quite an arty place, and there are several other galleries around town. In odd-numbered years lots of gardens in the Castlemaine district open their doors to visitors during the **Festival of Gardens**, which takes place during the Melbourne Cup week in November.

If you're here on a Saturday, trek the 2km out along the Melbourne Road to **Wesley Hill Market**, a giant flea market selling local produce and crafts (7.30am–1pm).

Eating and drinking

Food in Castlemaine is excellent, with a wide variety of places to choose from.

Capones 50 Hargreaves St. A local favourite for those in need of huge if somewhat standard pizzas, in a comfy setting that resembles a tavern.

Empyre Hotel 113 Mostyn St. New hotel/ restaurant that has hit the ground running, becoming the town's best culinary option with sophisticated dining and delicious food for breakfast, lunch and dinner.

Railway Hotel 65 Gingell St. Traditional country-style pub, with locals sitting at the bar, and happy patrons in the bistro eating pub favourites such as chicken parma and steaks. Daily lunch; dinner Wed–Sat.

Saff's 64 Mostyn St. Considered the best café in town, and not just because of the food. Hosts special night-time events including recitals and poetry readings. Daily breakfast & lunch; dinner Thurs, Fri and Sat.

Tog's Place 58 Lyttleton St ⓣ03/5470 5090. Good café-style food in a peaceful setting, with sunny courtyard for warmer days. Bookings recommended.

Maldon

MALDON, closely surrounded by low hills, is a tiny, peaceful town of quirky shops and a few B&Bs, a popular weekend getaway where you can simply relax and unwind. Gold was found here in 1853 and the rich, deep alluvial reefs were mined until 1926. The main shopping street largely preserves its original appearance, with single-storey shopfronts shaded by awnings and decorated with iron-lace work. Some accommodation options are popping up above these shops. Apart from the town's shops, cafés and architecture, there aren't many other points of interest, though you can take an underground tour at the stunning candlelit **Carman's Tunnel Goldmine**, off Parkin's Reef Road, 3km south of town (Sat, Sun, school & public holidays; tours depart every 30min between 1.30–4pm; 25min; $5).

During the long weekend before the Melbourne Cup (first weekend of November), things get a bit busier than usual as people head to town for the four-day **Maldon Folk Festival** (ⓦwww.maldonfolkfestival.com; weekend tickets $95, day tickets $30). Since its inception in 1973 the event has steadily grown, and apart from traditional folk, it also features blues, bluegrass and world music as well as some theatre and dance. The main performance space is at the Tarrangower Reserve at the base of Mount Tarrangower, just out of town, but throughout the weekend there are also lots of things happening in town itself where you can listen for free.

Practicalities

Castlemaine Bus Lines run services from Castelmaine to Maldon (timetables and info available at Ⓦwww.castlemainebuslines.com.au). Return buses leave from Maldon post office to connect with trains back to Melbourne. The *Victorian Goldfields Railway*, a tourist **steam train** (or diesel locomotive on days of total fire ban) runs between Maldon and Castlemaine (Sun, also Wed & Sat during school holidays and more frequently during the summer holidays; single trip $18; Ⓦwww.vgr.com.au).

For information on the town, check with the **Maldon Visitor Information Centre** in the Shire Gardens, High Street (daily 9am–5pm; Ⓣ03/5475 2966, Ⓦwww.maldoncastlemaine.com).

Places to **stay** include the authentic *Beehive* (Ⓣ03/5475 1300; ❹), a two-level bluestone apartment with modern luxuries situated over an antique store at 72A Main St. Nearby at no. 58 is the 98-year-old *Maldon Hotel* (Ⓣ03/5475 2231; ❸), which has eight rooms with shared facilities, and includes use of the fantastic balcony overlooking the streetscape. The *Heritage Cottages*, 25 Adair St (Ⓣ03/5475 1094, Ⓦwww.heritagecottages.com.au; ❼), has a selection of ten historical cottages, most with period furnishings and open fires.

Eating places include *Café Maldon* (8am–5pm daily) at 52 Main St and *Berryman's Café* in an old bowling alley at 30 Main St. McArthur's Coffee & Books, further up at no. 43, has a very pleasant courtyard and also sells new and secondhand books (Wed–Sun 9am–5pm). The quirky *Gourmet Yabbies Café* at 46 Main St (daily 11am–6pm, closed Tues) sells the unique "yabbie pie" which tastes a lot better than it sounds. The *Penny School Gallery Café* (daily 10am–5pm) further out at 11 Church St is a delightful place for coffee, lunch or afternoon tea, after checking out the current exhibition at the gallery. A good place for a beer is the 150-year-old *Kangaroo Hotel*, opposite the tourist office, which has a cozy beer-garden.

Maryborough and around

When Mark Twain visited **MARYBOROUGH**, 47km west of Castlemaine on the Pyrenees Highway, he described it as "a train station with a town attached". Nowadays it's a rather dull country place, interesting only for remnants of goldrush architecture far too pompous for this quiet setting. The grandiose, renovated **Maryborough Railway Station** houses an **Antiques Emporium** and an excellent café (closed Tues, dinner available Fri & Sat). At the heart of town, the Civic Centre is a classic nineteenth-century square with an elegant post office and gracious town hall and courthouse. For more information and accommodation bookings, turn to the **Maryborough Information Centre**, corner of Nolan and Alma streets, just behind High Street (daily 9am–5pm; Ⓣ1800 356 511, Ⓦwww.visitmaryborough.com.au).

Twenty-one kilometres north of Maryborough is **DUNOLLY**, an attractive town filled with many distinctive old buildings and with kurrajong trees lining the main street. The *Royal Hotel* is a good place to stop for lunch with most bar meals under $10. The goldfields here produced more nuggets than any in Australia, including the largest ever found: the 65-kilogram "Welcome Stranger" nugget, found in 1869 by two Cornish miners just 3cm below the surface as they were working around the roots of a tree, and valued at £10,000. Fourteen kilometres south of Maryborough, **TALBOT** is a tiny settlement consisting of little more than a pub and a corner store. It's hard to believe now that the town once had 56 hotels and a population of 33,000. Every third Sunday of the month, people congregate here to buy fresh produce at the **Talbot Farmers Market** (10am–2pm).

Daylesford and Hepburn Springs

The attractive, hilly country around Daylesford and Hepburn Springs is known as the "spa centre of Australia", with a hundred **mineral springs** within a fifty-kilometre radius. Daylesford grew from the Jim Crow gold diggings of 1851, but the large Swiss-Italian population here quickly realized the value of the water from the mineral springs, which had been bottled since 1850. People have been taking the waters at Hepburn Springs for almost as long – the spa complex was built in 1895. V/Line has a direct bus service from Melbourne to Daylesford (Mon–Sat 2 daily, Sun 1 daily). Alternatively (Mon–Fri), you can take a train from Melbourne to Ballarat and then transfer to a bus departing Ballarat in the early afternoon. This is the V/Line **bus service** between Geelong and Bendigo via Ballarat, Daylesford and Castlemaine. For enquiries and bookings, phone ⓣ13 61 96 or go to ⓦwww.vline.com.au.

Daylesford

The town of **DAYLESFORD**, a popular weekend retreat for Melburnians, has a New Age, alternative atmosphere, with a large gay community. As a result, the town has several gay-friendly guesthouses, and on the second weekend in March it is the venue for **ChillOut**, Australia's largest rural gay and lesbian festival, featuring a street parade, music and cabaret, dance parties and a carnival at Victoria Park.

Daylesford's well-preserved Victorian and Edwardian streets rise up the side of Wombat Hill, where you'll find the Botanical Gardens, between Hill Street and Central Springs Road, whose lookout tower has panoramic views. Not far away, on the corner of Daly and Hill streets, is the **Convent Gallery** (daily 10am–5pm; ⓦwww.conventgallery.com.au; $4.50), a rambling former convent that now has seven galleries selling high-quality arts, crafts and antiques, and a café and a bar. There's a great Sunday market (8am–2pm) just nearby, on the main road to Castlemaine. The town has "healing centres" aplenty; the spectrum of services ranges from natural therapies to the more esoteric, such as tarot readings – enquire at the visitor centre about a list.

Lake Daylesford, a short distance south from the town centre on Vincent Street, is the location of the Central Springs Reserve, which has several walking tracks and old-fashioned water pumps from which you can drink the mineral springs. The **Lake Daylesford Book Barn** here (open daily 10am–5pm) is a picturesquely situated bookshop, with an extensive range of secondhand books. The charming *Boathouse Café* (9–11am & noon–4pm daily, dinner Sat & Sun; ⓣ03/5348 1387) has lakeside dining, as well as dinghies, canoes and paddle-boats for rent. With your own transport there are two more options further afield: the **Lavandula Swiss Italian Farm** (daily 10.30am–5.30pm; ⓦwww.lavandula.com.au; $3.50) in nearby Shepherds Flat, 5km north of Hepburn Springs, where you can walk among the historic stone farmhouses, in the extensive gardens and lavender fields, and then have lunch or coffee and cake at *La Trattoria*, the farm's renowned Italian restaurant (ⓣ03/5476 4393); and **Tuki trout farm** (ⓣ03/5345 6233, ⓦwww.tuki.com.au) in Smeaton, 23km west of Daylesford via Creswick, where you can catch your own lunch and have it boned and cooked for you while you wait. They also have quaint cottage accommodation (⑤–⑥), some with spas.

Practicalities

The Daylesford **Visitor Information Centre**, servicing the whole area, is at 98 Vincent St in Daylesford (daily 9am–5pm; ⓣ03/5321 6123, ⓦwww.visitdaylesford.com); it has loads of brochures for the many places offering bed and breakfast and a board listing the vacancies at weekends, when places tend to fill up. Internet access is also available.

Accommodation

You must book well in advance if you want **to stay** in Daylesford at the weekend. Bookings are handled by Daylesford Accommodation Booking Service (ⓣ03/5348 1448, ⓦwww.dabs.com.au), or try Daylesford Getaways (ⓣ03/5348 4422, ⓦwww.dayget.com.au).

35 Hill Street ⓣ03/5348 3878, ⓔjoanvdf@netconnect.com.au. Early Victorian brick cottage just below the Botanical Gardens, much loved for its casual, friendly attitude. ④

Daylesford Caravan Park Ballan Rd ⓣ03/5348 3821. Nice parkland setting close to the lake with fully-contained cabins. ③

Daylesford Hotel 2 Burke Square ⓣ03/5348 2335, ⓦwww.daylesfordhotel.com.au. Simple rooms in a simple pub with shared facilities, but you can't get more central and the price is right. ②

The Lake House King St ⓣ03/5348 3329, ⓦwww.lakehouse.com.au. The town's premier accommodation and culinary option continues to add to its collection of awards each year. The waterfront rooms and suites are a stone's throw from the lake and take in the essence of Daylesford. ⑦–⑧

Royal Hotel Cnr of Vincent and Albert sts ⓣ03/5348 2205. Refurbished Victorian pub with ten pleasant, centrally heated rooms with en-suite facilities, some with spa bath. B&B ④

Wildwood YHA 42 Main Rd, Hepburn Springs ⓣ03/5348 4435, ⓔdaylesford@yhavic.org.au. A small and lovely renovated guesthouse with a homely kitchen and a deck overlooking a great garden area. If you're arriving by bus, phone ahead for a pick-up. Booking is essential anyway just to let them know you are coming. Dorm bed from $22, rooms ③

Eating and drinking

In such a gay-friendly place you can expect the local bars and eateries to be gay friendly, too.

Breakfast and Beer 117 Vincent St. Don't get the name confused and order cereal with lashings of VB. They specialize in great hearty breakfasts and at more socially acceptable hours, offer a huge list of international beers with pizza and wraps thrown in. Thurs–Sun 8.30–late.

Cliffy's Emporium 30 Raglan St. In a town of good cafés, this delightful deli-café/wine bar rates a special mention for food and atmosphere. Mon–Thurs 9.30am–4pm, Fridays till late.

D'bar Restaurant Club Lounge 74 Vincent St. Dine on scrumptious Mediterranean food in the first-floor wine bar (Fri–Sun), listen to live jazz on Fri nights, or check out the DJs from 10pm on Sat.

Frangos & Frangos Restaurant/Koukla Café Both at 82 Vincent St ⓣ03/5348 2363. The café serves excellent breakfasts and slightly simpler and cheaper lunches and dinners than the fine restaurant; in both the food is Mediterranean inspired. Café open Mon & Tues 8am–4pm, Wed–Sun 8am–late; restaurant Mon & Tues 4pm–late, Fri & Sat 11am–late, Sun 11am–5pm.

Lake House King Street near the lake ⓣ03/5348 3329. Multi-award-winning restaurant that is regarded as one of the state's best .The cooking style is very sophisticated modern Australian and there is a strong emphasis on using seasonal local produce. The lunch special ($35 for two courses plus wine) is a winner. Daily 8–11am, noon–5pm & 7pm–late.

Mercato 32 Raglan St. New on the scene targeting those who enjoy high-quality Italian-inspired cuisine using local ingredients. Main meals start at $30. Complimentary wine tasting every Fri. Sun noon–3pm, Tues–Fri 6pm–late.

Pastry King Café 60 Vincent St. For the last seventy years this place has been baking up great pies, muffins and other delicacies perfect for picnic lunches by the lake.

Sweet Decadence at Locantro 87 Vincent St. Chocolates, coffee and cake served up in an old building full of character. Daily 9.30–5.30pm, dinner Fri & Sat.

Hepburn Springs

HEPBURN SPRINGS is not really a town at all, but a collection of guesthouses and a wonderful Art-Deco **resort hotel** in a green, hilly and peaceful spot only 4km north of Daylesford. From the bus stop, walk through the shady Soldiers Memorial Park to the Mineral Springs Reserve, where you can taste three kinds of mineral water from old pumps and take advantage of the pool, spa and massage facilities at the ultra-posh **Hepburn Spa Resort** (Sun–Fri 10am–6pm, Sat 9am–7pm; ⓣ03/5348 2034, ⓦwww.hepburnspa.com.au). Bookings must be made at least three (preferably six) weeks in advance, especially for weekends.

Practicalities

The recently renovated and super-fancy *Peppers Springs Retreat* at the corner of Main Road and Tenth Street (ⓣ03/5348 2202, ⓦwww.peppers.com.au; ❼–❽) is a classic 1930s Art-Deco resort with tastefully renovated en-suite rooms. Tasty meals are available in the bar, and there's a more expensive restaurant on the premises. *Dudley House*, at 101 Main Rd (ⓣ03/5348 3033, ⓦusers.netconnect.com.au/~dudley/; ❺, weekends ❻), is a lovely Federation-style weatherboard house with bed and breakfast and a fine restaurant. At the budget end of the scale is *Continental House*, 9 Lone Pine Ave (ⓣ03/5348 2005, ⓦwww.continentalhouse.com.au; ❷), a vegan retreat that offers basic accommodation, yoga classes and massages on request. The rambling house is located in a lovely garden setting on a hill above the Mineral Springs Reserve. In addition to small dorms (bed $30) and simple twins/doubles ($70, BYO linen for all) there's a kitchen and several lounge rooms; a café offers vegan banquets on Saturday night ($25).

A few **eating** places can be found along Main Street. The newest and the best place to relax is *The Red Star Café* at 115 Main Rd (daily 8am–5pm, dinner Fri & Sat), which is a casual, communal-type café with a wide range of pasta and salad dishes. For traditional Thai food go to *Jasmine Thai* across the road at no. 114 (dinner daily except Tues; ⓣ03/5348 1163). The *Art Nouveau Palais* at no. 111 (ⓦwww.thepalais.com.au) is a restaurant and bar (Wed–Sat eve) with an adjacent ballroom that's used for dance classes and as an entertainment venue – quite a few top-notch names from the Melbourne music scene and further afield perform here. Further down the road, *The Old Hepburn Hotel* at no. 236 is good for a drink in the beer garden or for tasty pub grub (dinner Tues–Sun). They also have live bands on Sunday afternoons.

Ballarat

BALLARAT is a grandiose provincial city that makes a memorable first impression, especially if approaching from the west, via the Western Highway, along **Avenue of Honour**. Lined on either side with over 22km of trees and dedicated to soldiers who fought in World War I, it ends at the massive **Arch of Victory**, through which you drive to enter Sturt Street and the city. Over a quarter of all **gold** found in Victoria came from Ballarat's fantastically rich reef mines before they were exhausted in 1918. Nowadays, in addition to the more obvious tourist attractions – especially Sovereign Hill – and fine **architecture**,

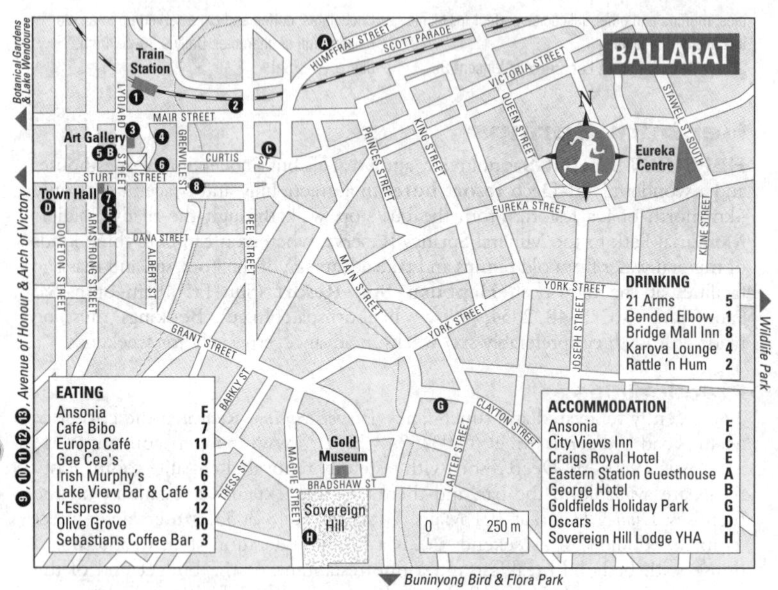

the town is interesting in its own right, with a fairly large student population that gives the city a somewhat vibrant character and reasonably active nightlife.

Information and transport

The **Ballarat Visitor Information Centre**, located in the Eureka Centre on the corner of Rodier and Eureka streets (daily 9am–5pm; Ⓣ1800 446 633, Ⓦwww.ballarat.com), has free **information** and maps of the town and can make accommodation bookings. There is also a more central information office at the Town Hall on Sturt Street (Mon–Fri 9am–5pm). Public **transport** in Ballarat and surrounding areas is handled by Davis Buslines (Ⓣ03/5331 7777); they charge a flat two-hour fare.

Accommodation

There's an abundance of **accommodation** in all price ranges in Ballarat, from hostels to grand hotels, so you shouldn't have a problem finding a room to suit. Bear in mind that many places will be more expensive at weekends.

Ansonia 32 Lydiard St Ⓣ03/5332 4678, Ⓦwww.ansonia.com.au. Lovely boutique hotel in the historic precinct, with restaurant, library and guest lounge. ❺–❻

City Views Inn 101 Curtis Ⓣ03/5329 2777, Ⓦwww.cityviewsballarat.com. New on the scene but good value for money with classy rooms, indoor pool and wireless Internet in an excellent location. ❺

Craigs Royal Hotel 10 Lydiard St South Ⓣ03/5331 1377 or 1800 648 051, Ⓦwww.craigsroyal.com. The accommodation at this grand Victorian-era hotel ranges from traditional pub rooms to luxurious suites – go for the wonderful two-level North Tower if your budget will allow it. ❻–❽

Eastern Station Guesthouse 81 Humffray St Ⓣ03/5338 8722, Ⓦwww.ballarat.com/easternstation.htm. Reasonably priced comfortable doubles with shared kitchen and bathroom facilities. ❸

George Hotel 27 Lydiard St Ⓣ03/5333 4866, Ⓦwww.georgehotelballarat.com.au. Three-storey 1850s hotel with colonial-style decor, an inexpensive bistro and rooms, some with four-poster beds. ❸ including breakfast

The Eureka Stockade

The **Eureka Rebellion** is one of the most celebrated events of Australian history and generally regarded as the only act of white armed rebellion the country has seen – however, some historians argue that Aborigines were involved in it as well. It was provoked by conditions in the goldfields, where diggers had to pay exorbitantly for their right to prospect for gold (as much as thirty shillings a month), without receiving in return any right to vote or to have any chance of a permanent right to the land they worked. The administration at Ballarat was particularly repressive, and in November 1854 local diggers formed the **Ballarat Reform League**, demanding full civic rights and the abolition of the licence fee, and proclaiming that "the people are the only legitimate source of power". At the end of the month a group of two hundred diggers gathered inside a **stockade** of logs, hastily flung together, and determined to resist further arrests for non-possession of a licence. They were attacked at dawn on December 3 by police and troops; thirty died inside, and five members of the government forces also lost their lives.

The movement was not a failure, however: the diggers had aroused widespread sympathy, and in 1855 licences were abolished, to be replaced by an annual **Miner's Right** which carried the right to vote and to enclose land. The leader of the rebellion, the Irishman Peter Lalor, eventually became a member of parliament.

The **Eureka Flag**, with its white cross and five white stars on a blue background, has become a symbol of the Left – and indeed of almost any protest movement: shearers raised it in strikes during the 1890s; wharfies used it before World War II in their bid to stop pig-iron being sent to Japan; and today the flag is flown by a growing number of Australians who support the country's transformation to a republic. On a deeper level, all sorts of claims are made for the Eureka Rebellion's pivotal role in forming the Australian nation and psyche. The diggers are held up as a classic example of the Australian (male) ethos of mateship and anti-authoritarianism, while the goldrush in general is credited with overthrowing the hierarchical colonial order, as servants rushed to make their fortune, leaving their masters and mistresses to fend for themselves.

Goldfields Holiday Park 108 Clayton St ⓣ03/5332 7888 or 1800 632 237, ⓦwww.ballaratgoldfields.com.au. Well located, right next to Sovereign Hill, this place has good facilities for campers, including a kitchen. Cabins ③

Oscars 18 Doveton St ⓣ03/5331 1451, ⓦwww.oscarshotel.com.au. Recently renovated hotel and restaurant with 13 luxurious rooms targeted at the picky business-traveller market. ⑦

Sovereign Hill Lodge YHA Magpie St ⓣ03/5333 3409, ⓔballarat@yhavic.org.au. This small hostel – part of a motel as well as part of Sovereign Hill theme park – has four rooms, a kitchen/dining area and a bar on site. Dorms from $22, rooms ③, B&B in motel rooms ⑤

The City

Sturt and Victoria streets terminate on either side of the Bridge Mall, the central shopping area at the base of quaint **Bakery Hill** with its old shopfronts. Southeast of the city centre, Eureka Street runs off Main Street towards the site of the **Eureka Stockade**, with several museums and antique shops along the way. Main Street becomes Ballarat–Buninyong Road, and six blocks down is crossed by Bradshaw Street, where you'll find Sovereign Hill, the recreated gold town. Northwest of the centre, approached via Sturt Street, are the **Botanical Gardens** and Lake Wendouree, which at the time of writing was completely dry due to the fierce drought that has been affecting the area for years.

The city centre

The most complete **nineteenth-century streetscape** is probably along Lydiard Street, which runs from the centre up past the train station; there are several two-storey terraced shopfronts, with verandas and decorative iron-lace work, mostly dating from the mid- to late nineteenth century. The former **Mining Exchange** (1888) has been renovated to its former splendour, and the architecture of Her Majesty's Theatre (1875) also proclaims its goldrush-era heyday. The **Ballarat Fine Art Gallery** at 40 Lydiard St (daily 10.30am–5pm; free guided tours Wed-Sun 2pm; $5; Ⓦwww.balgal.com), another superb building, is the oldest provincial art gallery in Australia, established in 1884. The original, frayed **Eureka Flag** (see box, p.925) is on display here in a purpose-built space, with subdued lighting to protect the precious relic. The gallery's extensive collection is particularly strong on colonial and Heidelberg School paintings; displayed alongside are the watercolours of S.T. Gill, a self-taught artist who painted scenes of goldrush days in Ballarat. In another part of the gallery is a reconstruction of the drawing room of the famous Lindsay family (whose best-known members are the artist Norman and the writer Jack), from nearby Creswick, complete with several of their paintings. The new wing of the gallery, a striking structure with a curved zinc roof and a glass-encased staircase, extends out to former Camp Street, now renamed Alfred Deakin Place, and stands cheek by jowl with an 1880s red-brick building, a police station in its previous incarnation and now the *Gallery Café*. Walking from the Art Gallery along Lydiard Street to Sturt Street you'll see more nineteenth-century goldrush architecture: check out the imposing Classical-Revival **town hall** on Sturt Street, which dominates the centre of the city.

There are still over forty **hotels** in Ballarat – survivors of the hundreds that once watered the thirsty diggers. Some of the finest are on Lydiard Street: Craig's *Royal Hotel* at no. 10 and the *George Hotel* at no. 27 are an integral part of Ballarat's architectural heritage. Sadly, during the 1970s, the council forced most of the old pubs to pull down their verandas on the grounds that they were unsafe, so very few survive in their original form. One that does is attached to the Golden City Hotel (now known as *Gee Cee's*), 427 Sturt St, which took the council to the Supreme Court to save its magnificent wide veranda with original cast-iron decoration.

The Botanical Gardens

The **Botanical Gardens**, laid out in 1858, cover about half a square kilometre alongside Lake Wendouree, just to the northwest of the city centre (#16 bus from Sturt Street, near the Myer department store). Begonias grow so well in Ballarat that a Begonia Festival runs for ten days in March. The Conservatory at the Botanic Gardens, an impressive glasshouse whose design was inspired by origami, is used to showcase them, and other floral displays, throughout the year (conservatory daily 9am–5pm; free).

Other highlights are the **Avenue of Big Trees**, with a California redwood among its monsters, and the classical statuary, donated by rich gold-miners, scattered about the gardens. Pride of place goes to *Benzoni's Flight from Pompeii*, housed in the Statuary Pavilion. Along Prime Minister Avenue you can see a bust of every prime minister of Australia.

Eureka and York streets

As you head east of the centre towards Eureka Street and the Eureka Stockade (bus #8 from outside the ANZ Bank on Sturt St), take a look at the unique shop facades on Main Street. The site of the Eureka Stockade is preserved in Eureka Gardens – to commemorate and honour the influential uprising (see

△ Panning for gold at Sovereign Hill

box, p.925), the **Eureka Centre** (daily 9am–4.30pm; $8; ⓦ www.eurekaballarat.com) was built on the western edge, on the corner of Eureka Street; its exhibits give detailed background information on the historic rebellion. Outside the centre, the big blue-and-white Eureka sail, shaped like a mining wind sail, is a Ballarat landmark.

Parallel to Eureka Street is York Street, where you'll find the **Ballarat Wildlife Park**, on the corner of Fussell Street (daily 9am–5.30pm; $19.50; ⓣ03/5333 5933, ⓦwww.wildlifepark.com.au); which has kangaroos, as well as enclosures with wombats, Tasmanian devils, koalas, nonvenomous and venomous snakes and crocodiles. There's an emphasis on getting up close to the cuddlier animals and having your photo taken, and there are daily guided tours at noon. Feeding times are also worth attending (weekends, daily during the school holidays: between noon & 3pm).

Sovereign Hill and the Gold Museum

The recreated gold-mining township of **Sovereign Hill** is located 1.5km southeast of the city centre, on Bradshaw Street (bus #9 from outside the ANZ Bank on Sturt Street; daily 10am–5pm; $33.50 also includes admission to the Gold Museum; ⓣ03/5331 1944, ⓦwww.sovereignhill.com.au). Seventy buildings and shops here are modelled on those that lined Ballarat's main street in the 1850s, with a cast of characters wandering about in the dress of the period. The township was planned around an actual mine-shaft from the 1880s, where guided underground tours are available. There are diggings where you can learn how to pan for gold (and perhaps get a small memento) and a mining museum filled with steam-operated machinery. Sovereign Hill puts on a spectacular outdoor **sound-and-light show**, "Blood on the Southern Cross" (nightly; 1hr 30min; $41, or joint ticket for show and Sovereign Hill, or for dinner and show, $69; bookings essential on ⓣ03/5333 5777) which makes use of the whole panorama of Sovereign Hill to tell the story of the Eureka Stockade.

Opposite Sovereign Hill, the **Gold Museum** (daily 9.30am–5.20pm, in summer until 6pm; $8.20 if not going to Sovereign Hill) offers a good overview of the recreated settlement. It has an outstanding display of real gold, and a large collection of coins that are arranged in displays exploring the history and uses of gold. The museum also has a small Eureka display which details life on the goldfields and explains the conditions that provoked the Eureka Stockade. Central to the display is a large painting of the rebellion by George Browning, a mid-nineteenth-century artist: it's interesting to see quite a few black faces portrayed in the stockade, which is generally labelled as the only white armed uprising to have taken place in Australia.

Ballarat Bird World

The delightful, privately-run **Ballarat Bird World** (daily 10am–5pm; $10; ⓣ03/5341 3843, ⓦwww.ballaratbirdworld.com.au) at 408 Eddy Ave, Mount Helen, 7km south of Ballarat, is worth a detour. It has ten acres of landscaped bushland gardens, complete with a small rainforest and a waterfall, and about 150 parrots and cockatoos from Australia, Asia, Africa and South America, some of which were bred here.

Eating and drinking

For its size, Ballarat has an astonishing number and variety of **eating places**, ranging from European coffee-bars established by postwar immigrants to upmarket gourmet restaurants, not to forget more than forty pubs.

Ansonia 32 Lydiard St ⓣ03/5332 4678. Restaurant in a refurbished building that also houses a swish boutique hotel. The eclectic cuisine has influences from the Mediterranean to Southeast Asia. Licensed; open daily for breakfast, lunch and dinner (book for dinner).

Bended Elbow 120 Lydiard St. The place to go when in need of a beer, with over 20 varieties on tap. Popular with students and local football teams on weekends. Open daily.

Café Bibo 205 Sturt St. The kind of retro-style diner you might expect to see in the US. Watch the cook as he toils away cooking up delicious breakfasts. Prices around $15. Open daily for breakfast, lunch and dinner.

Gee Cee's 427 Sturt St. The outside tables may be hot property, but it's still worth the wait to taste items from this very popular gastro-pub. Mains from $16. Open daily for lunch and dinner.

Europa Café 411 Sturt St. A pleasant café serving good coffee, cakes and breads, and light meals. Mon–Wed & Sun 9am–6pm, Thurs–Sat 9am until late.

Irish Murphy's 36 Sturt St. Big food at small prices, decent beer and frequent live music with minimal Irish kitsch combine to make this bar one of the most popular in town. Open lunch and dinner daily.

Lake View Bar & Café 22 Wendouree Parade. The lake may have disappeared but that hasn't stopped people coming to sample the breakfasts, coffee and desserts on offer here; there is also an à la carte menu for full meals. Open daily from 7am till late.

L'Espresso 417 Sturt St. European-style, hip place for coffee and eclectic breakfasts; the mains are good too, and very moderately priced. Daily 6.30am–6pm, also Thurs–Sun 6.30pm until late.

Olive Grove 1303 Sturt St. Excellent delicatessen with a wide range of fresh produce that is a favourite with Ballarat's students. Worth the extra walk to get here. 8.30am–7pm daily.

Sebastian's Coffee Bar 58 Lydiard St North. Café-bar with cool minimalist decor opposite the Regent Multiplex cinemas. Open daily from 11am.

Entertainment and nightlife

Thanks to a burgeoning number of students – about twenty thousand are enrolled at the University of Ballarat – the city has a lively **music** and **club** scene; for up-to-date information about what's on, check *The Courier* on Thursday. The bustling *21 Arms* at 21 Armstrong St, Ballarat North, is open until 5am and has four main areas ranging from a sofa lounge to the frenetic "*Shed*". *Rattle 'n Hum* at 49 Mair St is another mainstay of the Ballarat club scene. Popular bands from Melbourne and around the country play at the *Karova Lounge* (Ⓦwww.karovalounge.com), corner of Field and Camp Streets and *The Bridge Mall Inn* (locally known as *The Rat*) showcases **live bands** six nights a week.

The elaborate Victorian-era Her Majesty's Theatre, at 17 Lydiard St (Ⓣ03/5333 5800), stages all types of touring **productions**, and the Regent has a three-screen **cinema** on the same street at no. 49 (Ⓣ03/5331 1399).

Western Victoria and the Mallee

Several roads run west from the goldfields to the South Australia border through the seemingly endless wheatfields of the **Wimmera**. To the west of the farming centre of **Ararat** is the major attraction of the area, the **Grampians National Park**, the southwestern tail-end of the Great Dividing Range. Stawell and Horsham – the latter regarded as the capital of the Wimmera – are good places to base yourself, but **Halls Gap**, in a valley and surrounded by national park, is even better. North of Horsham is the wide, flat **Mallee** with its twisted mallee scrub, sand dunes and dry lakes. This region, with several state and national parks, extends from **Wyperfeld National Park** in the south, right up to Mildura's irrigated oasis on the Murray River. South of the Grampians is sheep country; following the Hamilton Highway from Geelong you'll end up at **Hamilton**, the major town and wool capital of the western district, also accessible via **Dunkeld** on the southern edge of the Grampians.

V/Line (Ⓣ13 61 96, Ⓦwww.vline.com.au) has a **bus service** from Ballarat to Hamilton via Dunkeld and from Warrnambool to Hamilton. The Grampians Link consists of a **train service** from Melbourne to Ballarat and a connecting bus to Halls Gap, via Ararat and Stawell. The Daylink connection (train from Melbourne to Bendigo, and from there a connecting bus via Horsham and Dimboola to Adelaide) departs Melbourne daily in the morning. Greyhound Australia and Firefly buses to Adelaide travel the Western Highway via Ballarat, Ararat, Stawell, Horsham, Dimboola and Nhill.

Ararat

ARARAT, some 90km west from Ballarat, is still very much a goldfields town, with an overabundance of grandiose Victorian architecture and a main street laid out to show off the best profiles of the nearby mountains: **Mount Ararat** in the west and the **Pyrenees Range** with **Mount Cole** in the east. The town was founded in 1857, when a group of seven hundred hopeful Chinese from Guangdong province in southern China, making the slow trudge from the South Australian ports to the central Victorian goldfields, stumbled across a fabulously rich, shallow alluvial goldfield, the **Canton Lead**. The new multi-million-dollar **Gum San Chinese Heritage Centre** (daily 10am–4.30pm; $8; Ⓦwww.gumsan.com.au) pays homage to the fact that Ararat is the only town in Australia founded by the Chinese. It was designed by a Melbourne architect of Chinese origin and is a recreation of a two-storey southern Chinese temple set in a traditional Chinese garden. The exhibits recount the tale of the founding of the city and familiarize Western visitors with aspects of Chinese culture.

These days Ararat is the commercial centre for a sheep farming and wine-producing area; local **wineries** include the Montara Winery, 3km south along the Chalamabar Road (Ⓦwww.montara.com.au; Mon–Sat 10am–5pm, Sun noon–4pm), and Mount Langi Ghiran on Vine Road north of Buangor (Mon–Fri 9am–5pm, Sat & Sun noon–5pm; Ⓦwww.langi.com.au), renowned for its superb whites and reds; turn north from the Western Highway towards Warrak.

The **visitor information centre** is located on High Street near the train station, parallel to the town's main thoroughfare, Barkly Street (Mon–Fri 9am–5pm; Ⓣ03/5355 0281 or 1800 657 158, Ⓦwww.visitararat.com.au). It provides information on the Grampians and can book accommodation in the area and has Internet access. The **Langi Morgala Museum** (Tues 10–3pm, Sat & Sun 1–4pm; $5) occupies an old brick building banded with bluestone at the base and around the huge arched windows and doors. Along with the usual pioneering displays, there's an important collection of Aboriginal artefacts. A guided tour at **J Ward** further north across the railway tracks at Girdlestone Street (Mon–Sat at 10am, 11am, 1pm & 2pm; additional tours on Sun and school holidays from 11am to 3pm; $10; Ⓦwww.jward.ararat.net.au), gives a chilling insight into one of the darker aspects of the area's social history. The 1859 building started out as a prison, but from the late 1880s it operated as a high-security ward of the Ararat Lunatic Asylum; criminally insane men were incarcerated here, in appalling conditions that were at the time considered acceptable. J Ward itself was closed as late as 1991.

Practicalities

A cheap **accommodation** option can be found at the *Shire Hall Hotel* (Ⓣ03/5352 1280, Ⓦwww.shirehallhotel.com.au; ❷) at 240 Barkly St, which has shared facilities in a building erected in 1860. A more comfortable option is the very good value *Orchid City Motor Inn* (Ⓣ03/5352 1341, Ⓦwww.araratorchidcitymotorinn.com.au; ❹), located at 96 High St, opposite the train station. It has fully renovated, spacious rooms with kitchens and cable TV. Those in need of luxury and serenity should head to the *Links Retreat* (Ⓣ0419 438 948, Ⓦwww.linksretreat.com.au; ❺), a cosy wooden house with full amenities, situated in woodland close to the Chalambar Golf Course at 139 Golf Links Rd.

For **food**, head for Barkly Street, where you'll find a supermarket, a bakery and a few good cafés. *Vines Café & Bar* at no. 74 has good breakfasts, light meals and lots of local wines by the glass and is open daily 9am–6pm, Friday and Saturday also 6.30pm–late. *Sicilian's Café-Bar-Restaurant* at no. 102 serves good pizza and pasta, open Monday to Wednesday 11.30am–9.30pm, Thursdat to Saturday till late. For bar meals the slightly upmarket *Hippo Café and Bar* at no. 157 is popular with locals having a night out, but head to the *Rex Hotel* at 129 Barkly St or the *Blue Duck Hotel* at no. 257 if you want traditional pub grub or a late-night beer. A good-value option is the bistro at the *Ararat RSL Club*, 74 High St, which serves inexpensive meals daily (10am–10pm).

Stawell

STAWELL (pronounced "stall") is most famous for the **Stawell Gift**, a sprint race offering big prize-money ($40,000 to the winner) that has been held here every Easter since 1877. It's also the closest major town to the Grampians and the departure point for the bus to Halls Gap. The helpful **Stawell & Grampians Visitor Information Centre** is at 52 Western Highway (Ⓣ1800 330 080; 9am–5pm daily) and has a detailed brochure, *The Cultural Heritage Trail*, listing all the notable buildings and landmarks from the mid-to late 1800s. The **Stawell Gift Hall of Fame** on Main Street (Mon–Fri 9–11am or by appointment; $2; Ⓣ03/5358 1326) charts the history of the race itself. The *Town Hall Hotel* at 62 Main Rd (built in 1873) is a good place to stop for a meal or a beer (lunch noon–2pm, dinner 6–9pm).

The Grampians and around

Rising from the flat plains of western Victoria's wheat and grazing districts, the sandstone ranges of the **GRAMPIANS**, with their weirdly formed rocky outcrops and stark ridges, seem doubly spectacular. In addition to their scenic splendour, in the **Grampians National Park (Gariwerd)** you'll find a dazzling array of **flora**, with a spring and early summer bonanza of wild flowers; a wealth of **Aboriginal rock art**; an impressive **Aboriginal Cultural Centre**; waterfalls and lakes; and over fifty **bushwalks** along 150km of well-marked tracks. There are also several hundred kilometres of road, from sealed highway to rough track, on which you can make exciting **scenic drives** and **4WD** tours.

The **best times to come** are in autumn, or in spring and early summer when the waterfalls are in full flow and the wild flowers are blooming (although there'll always be something in flower no matter when you come). Between June and August it rains heavily and can get extremely cold; at that time many tracks are closed to avoid erosion. Summers are very hot, with a scarcity of water and the ever-present threat of bushfires. If you're undertaking extended walks in summer, carry a portable radio to get the latest information on the fire risk: on **total fire ban days** no exposed flames – not even that from a portable gas stove – are allowed.

Halls Gap

HALLS GAP, 26km from Stawell, on the eastern fringes of the Grampians, is the only settlement actually surrounded by national park. Its setting is gorgeous, in the long flat strip of the Fyans Valley surrounded by the soaring bush and rock of the Wonderland, Mount Difficult and Mount William ranges; koalas are frequently seen in the surrounding trees. Packed with accommodation and other facilities catering to park visitors, this is the obvious place to base yourself, especially if you don't have your own transport.

Information and activities

The friendly staff at the **Halls Gap Visitor Information Centre** on Grampians Road next to the Mobil service station book accommodation, tours and activities as well as having an ATM (daily 9am–5pm; ⓣ03/5356 4616 or 1800 065 599). A few companies offer introductory climbing and abseiling; the going rate is about $60 for half a day and $110 for a full day.

Absolute Outdoors Grampians Shop 4, Stoney Creek Stores ⓣ03/5356 4556, ⓦwww.absoluteoutdoors.com.au. In addition to climbing/abseiling tours, also offer canoeing and kayaking trips, guided nature and night-time spotlight walks as well as mountain-bike tours; they sell outdoor gear and rent mountain bikes too ($40/day).

GMAC (Grampians Mountain Adventure Company ⓣ03/5383 9218 or 0427 747 047, ⓦwww.grampiansadventure.com.au. Trained and accredited by the Australian Mountain Climbers Association; they also operate at Mt Arapiles and can cater for advanced levels.

The Grampians Horse Riding Centre Brimpaen in the Wartook Valley on the northwestern side of the Grampians ⓣ03/5383 9255, ⓦwww.grampianshorseriding.com.au. Trail rides through the bush twice a day (2hr; $65).

Grampians Scenic Flights ⓣ03/5357 3234. Offers 40-min flights giving the definitive overview of the mountain range. $170 for three-passenger aircraft, $270 for five.

Hangin' Out in the Grampians ⓣ03/5356 4535 or 0407 684 831, ⓦwww.hanginout.com.au. Casual climbing tours start at $65 (4 hours), and rise to $90 for full-day tours that include abseiling.

Accommodation

Although Halls Gap has lots of **accommodation** of every kind, during school holidays, particularly in January and at Easter, you'll need to book in advance. Note that many places will insist on long stays, and prices rise at weekends.

A permit is required for the **campsites** in the national park, which must be obtained at the National Park Centre at Brambuk (see opposite). After hours you fill in a form and put your money into the box outside the centre. The fee is $11 per site per day. **Bushcamping** is allowed in the park, except in the Wonderland Range and within 100m of a dam, river or creek, or within 50m of a road; but the staff at the National Park Centre will want to be informed about where and when you are going to pitch your tent.

Hostels

Asses Ears Wilderness Lodge RMB 7351 Schmidt Road, Brimpaen ⓣ03/5383 9215, ⓦwww.assesearslodge.com.au. Great backpacker accommodation in timber cabins in a quiet location in the Wartook Valley on the northwestern side of the Grampians. There's a licensed bar, inexpensive restaurant, a swimming pool and a pool table, and you can hire mountain bikes ($20/day). The owners drop people off for hikes and organize loads of activities. Rates include continental breakfast and linen. Dorms $22–25, cabin ❸

Brambuk Backpackers Grampians Rd ⓣ03/5356 4609, ⓔbramback@netconnect.com.au. Great lounge area with open fireplace, but the dorm rooms are dated. Ask for a bed in the newer part of the hostel – the older section has been in need of a spruce-up for years. Has broadband and wireless Internet. Rates include light breakfast. Dorms $24, rooms ❷

Grampians YHA Eco Hostel Grampians Rd ⓣ03/5356 4544, ⓔgrampians@yhavic.org.au. Hostel built according to environmentally friendly principles, recycling waste water and using solar electricity and wood-heating stoves. It has excellent facilities, including Internet access and spotless same-sex dorms. Dorms $24, rooms ❸

Neds Beds 2 Heath St, Halls Gap ⓣ03/5356 4516, ⓦwww.grampiansbackpackers.com.au. The recent addition of two new buildings (each includes lounge, kitchen and rooms) out the back, have improved things remarkably for this old-timer. The central location near the shops, a BBQ area and outdoor veranda are pluses. Rates include light breakfast. Dorms $23, double ❸

Tim's Place Grampians Rd, Halls Gap ⓣ03/5356 4288, ⓦwww.timsplace.com.au. Friendly small hostel with a lovely, homey feel. There are dorms in the main house, and decent studio apartments out the back. Rates include continental breakfast. Extras include cheap Internet access ($2/hr) and free use of mountain bikes. Dorms $22, rooms ❸

Hotels and apartments

Glengarriff Halls Gap Townhouses 194 Grampians Road, Halls Gap ⓣ5358 5332, ⓦwww.hallsgaptownhouses.com.au. Three luxurious two-storey apartments designed to exploit the natural light and scenery. Has BBQ, spa and elegant furnishings. Only 800 metres from the main shops. ❻

Grand Canyon Motel Less than 1km north of Halls Gap on Grampians Rd ⓣ03/5356 4280, ⓦwww.grandcanyonmotel.com.au. Simple and cheap motel accommodation in a good location – good value for the price. ❸

Mountain Grand Boutique Hotel Grampians Rd, Halls Gap ⓣ03/5356 4232, ⓦwww.mountaingrand.com.au. This elegant, refurbished 1930s-style guesthouse has comfortable en-suite rooms, some with spa. There's also a good licensed restaurant on the first floor. ❺

Caravan parks

Halls Gap Caravan Park ⓣ03/5356 4251, ⓦwww.hallsgapcaravanpark.com.au. Right opposite the shopping centre and so a bit noisy, but it's well equipped, and at the start of many walks. Cabins ❹, on-site vans ❸

Lakeside Caravan Park ⓣ03/5356 4281, ⓦwww.hallsgaplakeside.com.au. 4km out of town on the banks of Lake Bellfield, another good option. Cabins ❸

Brambuk the National Park and Cultural Centre

Just over 2km south of Halls Gap along the Grampians Road (also known as the Dunkeld Road or the Dunkeld–Halls Gap Road) is **Brambuk the National Park and Cultural Centre**, the best place to start your visit. It consists of two separate buildings: the first one (daily 9am–5pm; ⓣ5361 4000, ⓦwww.parkweb.vic.gov.au) mainly dispenses information on the national park and sells guide books and maps; don't miss the display and videos that trace the development of the Grampians over four hundred million years. There is also a restaurant/café with average food and Internet access ($6 an hour).

Located behind this building is the original **Aboriginal Cultural Centre** (daily 9am–5pm; ⓣ03/5356 4381, ⓦwww.brambuk.com.au) opened in 1989. With its undulating red-ochre tin roof it blends in wonderfully with the backdrop of bush and rocky ridge; its design incorporates many symbolic features that are important to the five Koorie communities who own and manage the centre. A small exhibition inside features a poignant photographic

Rock art in the Grampians

It's estimated that **Koorie** Aborigines lived in the area known to them as **Gariwerd** at least five thousand years ago. The area offered such rich food sources that the Koories didn't have to spend all their time hunting and food-gathering, and could therefore devote themselves to religious and cultural activities. Evidence of this survives in **rock paintings**, which are executed in a linear style, usually in a single colour (either red or white), but sometimes done by handprints or stencils. You can visit some of the rock shelters where Aborigines camped and painted on the sandstone walls, although many more are off-limits. In the northern Grampians one of the best is **Gulgurn Manja** (also known as Flat Rock), 5km south of the Western Highway near the *Hollow Mountain* campsite; from Flat Rock Road it's a signposted fifteen-minute walk. The name means "hands of young people", as many of the handprints here were done by children. In the southern Grampians is **Billimina**, a fifteen-minute walk above the *Buandik* campsite; it's an impressive rock overhang with clearly discernible, quite animated, red stick figures.

history of the area's orginal inhabitants, while downstairs the Gariwerd Dreaming Theatre features presentations on the region's creation story and natural history (shows run from 10am–4.30pm; $5).

There are short rock-art tours from the centre, as well as half- and full-day walks to other Aboriginal art sites in the national park. All tours are on demand only, must be booked at least 24hr in advance, and require a minimum of four people.

Bushwalks and scenic drives

The National Park Centre at Brambuk hands out masses of free leaflets, walking guides and more detailed topographic maps; the easy-to-use *Southern Walks*, *Northern Walks* and *Wonderland Walks* ($3.30 each) are good all-rounders and handy for short walks. Although most walking tracks are clearly defined and well signposted, it's a good idea to buy *Vicmap*, or the walking maps published by Parks Victoria, and carry a compass if you're planning an overnight trek.

△ The Balconies, Grampians National Park

In January 2006, the Mount Lubra **fires** swept through the Grampians National Park, affecting over half of it. While most of the popular walking tracks and sites have been reopened to the public, at the time of writing some were still undergoing repairs as Parks Victoria takes the opportunity to improve tourist infrastructure. For more information about what is currently closed, go to Ⓦwww.parkweb.vic.gov.au or contact the Brambuk National Park and Cultural Centre on Ⓣ03/5361 4000.

Before beginning an extended walk, call into the centre and register. Some **walks** start from the campsite at Halls Gap, while others branch off the Victory and Grampian roads, making them difficult to get to without a car.

You can **drive** on roads through the park to major points and then get out and walk. The most popular section for visitors is the **Wonderland Range**, immediately to the west of Halls Gap. From the Halls Gap campsite you can head directly to **Venus Baths** (1.2km return). **The Pinnacle**, the most popular lookout in the Grampians, is usually accessed from the Wonderland Car Park (just off Mount Victory Rd; the turn-off is signposted). The 4.2km return walk is easy, except for the slightly trickier Grand Canyon section where a series of steel ladders must be negotiated – as long as you wear sturdy shoes, are reasonably fit and don't suffer from vertigo, you'll be fine. **Delleys Dell** is another Wonderland walk (5km), through canopies of tree ferns: start at the Delleys Dell car park at the *Rosea Campground* (the turn-off from Mount Victory Rd is signposted). The other major features in the Grampians are the Balconies, Mackenzie Falls and Zumstein, all accessible via the Mount Victory Road northwest of Halls Gap. The walk to the **Balconies** (1.6km return), formerly known as the **Jaws of Death**, begins from the Reed Lookout car park (the turn-off is signposted) and goes for about ten minutes through a stand of lichen-covered tea trees until you have reached the lookout over the Victoria Valley and towards the Balconies. The much photographed, weird rock formation consists of one ledge above another, forming the image of a reptile's elongated, open jaw.

At **Zumstein** (5km east on Mount Victory Road) there's a picnic area and car park where western grey kangaroos stand passively, waiting for food. They're tame enough to pet, but can be a serious nuisance when you get out your food; don't encourage them by feeding them. A three-kilometre walk runs along the Mackenzie River Gorge from here to the base of **Mackenzie Falls**, which you can also reach more directly from Mount Victory Road. There's parking above the falls, and it's a short but strenuous walk to the base.

If you're reasonably fit, consider tackling the walk to the peak of Mount William (1168m; 3.5km return), the highest point in the park. This starts from the Mount William Road car park, for which you turn off 16km south of Halls Gap. More challenging overnight walks include one to the Major Mitchell Plateau, starting from the same car park but involving a difficult five-hundred-metre climb to the plateau, and the Mount Difficult walk, which starts from Rose Gap and goes across a large, undulating, rocky plateau.

Eating, drinking and entertainment

Halls Gap's main **eating** options are located in the Stoney Creek complex, but around the area are some good country-style pubs worthy of a beer and a feed. For entertainment, there's **live jazz** at the *Mountain Grand*: Saturday mornings (10am–1pm) at the *Café Grand* downstairs, and Saturday evenings from 7pm at their *Balconies Restaurant* upstairs. An alternative **film festival** comes to town at the beginning of November, and there's a jazz festival in mid-February.

Balconies Restaurant ⓣ03/5356 440. Situated above the *Mountain Grand Guesthouse*, it offers elegant dining with reasonably priced good-quality meals and wine. Open for dinner daily.

Black Panther Café and Bar Stoney Creek complex. Good breakfasts and lunch; licensed and BYO. Daily 9am–5pm.

Flying Emu Café Stoney Creek complex. The place to go in between meals for cakes, snacks and something light. Daily 8.30am–4.30pm.

Halls Gap Hotel & Family Bistro 1km out of town on Stawell Road. Serves decent pub meals, but people mostly come here for the views from the balcony looking towards the mountains. Lunch & dinner daily.

Halls Gap Tavern 300 metres south of the shops on Lot 5, Dunkeld Road. The closest pub option in town, which is fine for a cold beer and a hearty steak. Daily 4–10pm.

Kookaburra Restaurant Grampians Rd. ⓣ03/5356 4222. Dependable bistro-style dishes – including baked duckling, kangaroo filet and home-made ice cream. Lighter pasta and salad dishes are also available. Lunch Sat & Sun, dinner Tues–Sun.

Quarry Restaurant Stoney Creek complex. ⓣ03/5356 4955 Popular spot in a pleasant setting with big windows facing a small reserve. It has an extensive wine list and every Thursday night their "Aussie Bush Tucker Menu" packs them in. Daily 7.30–10.30am, Fri, Sat & Sun noon–2pm & 6–9pm.

Hamilton

Three highways converge at **HAMILTON**, a civilized little city where you can see the Grampians from the edge of the main street. Its main claim to fame is that it's the "Wool Capital of the World" – about six million sheep within a 80km radius yield about ten percent of the world's wool production. The only reason you're likely to be here is if you're passing through, though there's a few things to distract you and the friendly **Hamilton Visitor Information Centre** on Lonsdale Street (daily 9am–5pm; ⓣ03/5572 3746 or 1800 807 056; ⓦwww.sthgrampians.vic.gov.au/tourism) can book accommodation if you decide to stay.

The most worthwhile of the town's five museums and galleries is the **Hamilton Art Gallery**, on Brown Street (Mon–Fri 10am–5pm, Sat 10am–noon & 2–5pm, Sun 2–5pm; donation), one of the finest provincial art galleries in the state. Its collection of eighteenth-century watercolours of English pastoral scenes by Paul Sandby is the largest outside Britain. Also in the town centre, but of marginal interest, is the **Hamilton History Centre** (2–5pm; closed Sat), located in the Mechanics Institute Building at 43 Gray St. East of town, on the Ballarat Road, is the **Sir Reginald Ansett Transport Museum** (daily 10am–4pm; $4), charting the history of the now-defunct Ansett flight network which began here, while **The Big Woolbales** (daily 9.30am–4pm) on Coleraine Road contain a small exhibition telling you about the wool industry of the Western district.

Practicalities

Hamilton features a wide variety of **accommodation**. Budget travellers can stay at the simple yet central *Commercial Hotel* (ⓣ03/5572 4119; ❷) at 145 Thompson St, which has shared facilities, or the pleasantly located *Lake Hamilton Caravan Park*, 10 Ballarat Rd (ⓣ & ⓕ03/5572 3855, ⓦwww.lakehamilton.com.au; cabins ❸). On the same road at no. 142 is the luxurious *Quality Inn Grange Burn* (ⓣ & ⓕ03/5572 5755; ❺–❻), which is one of the better places to stay in town.

The *Darriwill Farm Restaurant and Café* at 99 Brown St is a town favourite and has an array of products you can buy and take with you, or you can stay and order a variety of gourmet options (breakfast and lunch Mon to Sat, dinner Thurs Fri and Sat).

The Wimmera

The **Wimmera**, dry and hot, relies heavily on irrigation water from the Grampians for its vast wheatfields; before irrigation and the invention of the stump jump plough, the area was little more than mallee scrub, similar to the lands beyond **Warracknabeal**, the northernmost wheat-growing centre.

HORSHAM, capital of the wheatfields, makes a good stop-off point en route to Adelaide; it has an idyllic picnic spot, complete with barbecues, by the Wimmera River. There's little else to detain you, though the Grampians National Park (see p.931) is within striking distance to the southeast, and **Mount Arapiles**, 40km west, is one of the most important **rock-climbing** centres in Australia – if you're interested contact The Climbing Company in Natimuk (Ⓣ1800 357 035), which can also organize **abseiling**. The **Horsham Visitor Information Centre**, at 20 O'Callaghan Parade (daily 9am–5pm; Ⓣ03/5382 1832 or 1800 633 218, Ⓦwww.horshamvic.com.au), books both accommodation and tours. One central, cheap **place to stay** is the *White Hart Hotel*, 55 Firebrace St (Ⓣ03/5382 1231; rooms with shared facilities ❸), which is the best of the pub accommodation around town. The best-value meals in town can be found at the *Horsham Sports and Community Club* which has two course lunches for under $9 (noon–2pm daily), while *Café Bagdad* (11am–late, except Sunday) at 48 Wilson St has a very local, slightly arty alternative feel and serves espresso, cakes and ice cream, as well as big portions of cheap soups, salads and focaccias for under $10.

The Mallee

The Mallee, the most sparsely populated area of Victoria, begins north of Warracknabeal, from where the **Henty Highway** heads up to join the Sunraysia Highway and forge its way to Mildura, on the border with New South Wales. You really need your own transport to see anything; the only **public transport** is the small Henty Highway Coach that runs between Horsham and Mildura and mainly carries freight (departs Horsham BP service station Tues & Thurs at 9.15am and Fri at 5.45pm; Mildura train station Mon, Wed & Fri at 7.45am; 6hr; $62; Ⓣ03/5023 5658). Along the way are small dusty towns such as Brim, Bealah and **HOPETOUN** ("Gateway to the Mallee"). Here the *Bon Bon Café* at 74 Austin St is a nice little place with surprisingly good food to break up the journey.

Fifty kilometres west of Hopetoun is **Wyperfeld National Park**, which at 3500 square kilometres is Victoria's third largest. Bushcamping is not allowed in the park but a sealed road leads from Hopetoun via Yampeet to the *Wonga Campground*, where there's shady camping ($13 per site per night, max 6 people; payable by self-registration) and a picnic area with water and toilets.

Beyond Hopetoun, the Henty Highway merges into the Sunraysia Highway. Heading north on the Sunraysia, you pass **SPEED** and **OUYEN**, which don't warrant much time. Heading west on the Mallee Highway, the access track to the picturesque **pink salt lakes** of the **Murray–Sunset (Yanga–Nyawi) National Park** leads north from Linga. Continuing north on the Calder Highway from Ouyen, you pass the **Hattah–Kulkyne National Park**, just east of the highway; the park consists of dry mallee scrub, native woodland, and a lakes system lined with gums. Lake Hattah is reached by turning off the highway at Hattah, 34km north of Ouyen, onto the Hattah–Robinvale Road. From Hattah it's less than 70km to Mildura and the Murray River.

The Murray region

From its source close to Mount Kosciuszko high in the Australian Alps, the **Murray River** forms the border between Victoria and New South Wales until it crosses into South Australia (someone got a ruler out for the rest of the border to the coast), and although the actual watercourse is in New South Wales, the Victoria bank is far more interesting and more populous. After the entire length was navigated in 1836, the river became the route along which cattle were driven from New South Wales to the newly established town of Adelaide, and later in the century there was a thriving paddle-steamer trade on the lower reaches of the river, based at Wentworth on the New South Wales side (see p.327). In 1864, **Echuca** was linked by railway to Melbourne, stimulating the river trade in the upper reaches, and thus became a major inland port, the furthest extent of the navigable river. At the height of the paddle-steamer era, **Mildura** was still a run-down, rabbit-infested cattle station, but in 1887 the Chaffey brothers instituted irrigation projects that now support dairy farms, vineyards, vegetable farms and citrus orchards throughout northwestern Victoria. Between Mildura and Echuca, **Swan Hill** marks the transition to sheep, cattle and wheat country; the **Pioneer Settlement** here explores the extraordinarily hard lives of the early settlers. Above Echuca the Murray loses much of its magic as it flows through the more settled northeast.

Nowadays **paddle steamers** cruise for leisure, and are the best way to enjoy the river and admire magnificent **river red gums** lining its banks, as well as the huge array of birds and other wildlife that the Murray sustains. Renting a houseboat is also a relaxing (if expensive) way to travel.

Mildura and around

MILDURA has a mirage-like aura, its vineyards and orange orchards standing out from a hot, dry landscape. To the southwest is the evocatively named **Sunset Country**, with nothing but gnarled mallee scrub, red sand and pink salt lakes

Murray River red gums

The magnificent **red gum forests** of the Murray River floodplains are one of the major draws of the Murray River region, with evocative photographs gracing the pages of most tourist brochures. However, while these hardy trees are well adapted to the irregular cycles of drought and flood typical in Australia, human demand for water has created conditions of near-permanent drought they seem unable to cope with. In November 2004, a government report revealed that 75 percent of all red gums along the Murray are stressed, dying or dead. The cause is salinity and a lack of water, exacerbated by a four-year natural drought. The infrequently released environmental flows are not sufficient to flush out the saline build-up and supply the trees with the water they need, and though the state and federal governments have agreed to let an additional 500 billion litres flow through the Murray, critics say this is just a third of what the river and the floodplains need in order to be moderately healthy. Time seems to be running out and, as the trees play a crucial part in maintaining the health of the river system, Australia stands to lose more than just an iconic landscape.

(reached via Linga on the Mallee Highway). Mildura makes a good winter getaway, but summer can be stiflingly hot and it's best to avoid the area at this time if you can.

Deakin Avenue runs northwest through town to the river, with 7th Street and the train station facing the parklands that run along the river. Like any self-respecting small city, Mildura has a couple of malls, one running parallel to Deakin Avenue between 8th and 9th street town at Deakin Avenue and 15th Street. The **Mildura Visitor Information** s, and another, smaller one out of **and Booking Centre** is situated in the state-of-the-art Alfred Deakin Centre at Deakin Avenue and 12th Street (Mon–Fri 9am–5.30pm, Sat & Sun 9am–5pm; ⓣ03/5018 8380 or 1800 039 043, ⓦwww.visitmildura.com.au), which also houses a pool ($4.90) and gym, a decent café and a modern library, where you can check your email ($2/30min). The visitor centre will book accommodation and supply free town maps: they also have particularly good information on the Murray–Sunset (Yanga–Nyawi) and Hattah–Kulkyne national parks.

Down on the river the seventy-year-old **Mildura Weir** system, designed to provide stable pools for irrigation and to enable navigation throughout the year, makes a pleasant place to while away an hour or so. Alternatively, wander down to the **Mildura Arts Centre**, 199 Cureton Ave (daily 10am–5pm; gallery $3; ⓦwww.milduraarts.net.au;), which consists of the historic home **Rio Vista**, the Mildura Regional Art Gallery, a theatre and a sculpture park. Rio Vista was built in 1891 for William Chaffey, who lived here with his first and second wives (both called Hattie Schell, the second the niece of the first) until he died in 1926. It's a lovely house, though rather ill-suited to the climate, and inside are various displays about the Chaffeys and the development of Mildura. The art gallery's most important piece is *Woman Combing Her Hair at the Bath*, a pastel by Edgar Degas; it also has some excellent sculpture by Australian artists.

Cruises, tours and activities

The best **short river cruise** is on the PS *Melbourne* (daily 10.50am & 1.50pm; 2hr 10min; $24; ⓣ03/5023 2200), Mildura's only genuinely steam-driven paddle steamer. Built in 1912, it still has its original boiler and engine. The same company runs *Paddleboat Rothbury*, built in 1881 and in its day the fastest steamboat on the river; it's now been converted to diesel and takes people on cruises to local attractions, such as the Thursday cruise to Trentham Estate Winery ($50 including lunch and wine tasting).

Away from the river, the most outstanding natural attraction is **Mungo National Park** (see p.327), 110km across the border in New South Wales. It's visited by tour operators from Mildura who charge about $80 a head: Junction Tours (ⓣ03/5027 4309 or 0408 596 438, ⓦwww.junctiontours.com.au) and Jumbunna Walkabout Tours (ⓣ03/5024 3406).

Koorie tour operators belonging to the Barkindji people also lend their perspective on the park with Harry Nanya Tours, based just over the border in Wentworth (Mon–Sat; ⓣ03/5027 2076). They also do tours around Mildura, to Wentworth, and to other attractions and national parks in the surrounding area.

Mildura Ballooning (ⓣ03/5024 6848, ⓦwww.milduraballooning.com.au) arranges **hot-air balloon flights** daily, weather permitting, for $260 per person for a 3hr 30min flight, including breakfast. Rainy days can be passed at the **Deakin Cinema Complex** at 98 Deakin Ave, while a back-to-nature alternative to the swimming pool on Deakin Avenue is available at the sandy **swimming beach** at Chaffey Bend. There are lifeguards in summer, but take local advice and beware of dangerous currents.

Practicalities

Mildura is 555km from Melbourne, about as far as you can go in this small state; right on the border of New South Wales, and a little over 100km from South Australia, it's ideally located for **onward transport** to either. Buses on the Sturt Highway, the major route between **Adelaide** and **Sydney**, pass through several times daily. From Melbourne, there's also a V/Line train–bus connection via Bendigo or Swan Hill at least twice daily. **Broken Hill**, north up Silver City Highway, can be reached by bus via Wentworth (departing Mildura train station Mon, Wed & Fri 9am; 4hr; book at the visitor information centre). In terms of **local transport**, Coomealla Buslines runs a service across the river to Wentworth via Buronga (see p.942), while the very regular Sunraysia Buslines (ⓣ03/5023 0274) services the centre from 7th to 15th streets, and to suburban areas further to the east and west, and to the south as far as Red Cliffs. Alternatively, you can **rent a car** from, among others, Budget at 7th Street and Etiwanda Avenue (ⓣ03/5021 4442).

Mildura has a good reputation as a place to find **fruit-picking work**, though the only guaranteed time is in February, when the grape harvest takes place. Unfortunately, this is also the time when the heat is most intense. If you think you can handle it, come around the end of January, the beginning of the eight-week season. Otherwise, there's a chance of picking up work during the citrus harvest in June and August, and possibly vine pruning. For details, call in at MADEC Jobs Australia/ Mildura Harvest Labour Office, 97–99 Lime Ave (Mon–Fri 7am–7pm; ⓣ03/5022 1797), or contact the National Harvest Labour Hotline (ⓣ1800 062 332, ⓦwww.jobsearch.gov.au/harvesttrail). Most of the town's backpacker hostels have contacts with a wide range of employers, will find a job for you, assist with the paperwork and provide transport to and from work.

Accommodation

Mildura has lots of reasonably priced **accommodation**, and an ever-increasing number of hostels to cater to the hordes of hard-up backpackers who drift here looking for work. If you are staying longer, ask the hostel for their weekly rates – they come much cheaper. There are also a number of houseboats based in Mildura or across the river in Buronga or Wentworth. Ring the visitor information centre for information and bookings.

Apex Riverbeach Holiday Park Cureton Ave ⓣ03/5023 6879, ⓦwww/apexriverbeach.com.au. Nestled within the gum trees along the river bank, but still close to the main shops, the fully contained one- and two-bedroom cabins offer good value in a picturesque setting. ❷–❸

Mildura Grand Hotel 7th St, opposite the train station ⓣ03/5023 0511, ⓦwww.milduragrand hotel.com. Restored hotel, complete with ballroom, renowned gourmet restaurant, games room, spa, sauna and outdoor swimming pool. The sparsely decorated rooms range from basic to luxurious, with breakfast included. ❹–❼

Mildura City Backpackers 50 Lemon Ave ⓣ5022 7922, ⓦwww.milduracitybackpackers .com.au. Sociable and homely house close to the centre of town, which has a good blend of workers and travellers passing through. The couches on the patio are a nightly event. Dorms $22; rooms ❷

Mildura International Backpackers 5 Cedar Ave ⓣ03/5021 0133, ⓔmildrabp@vic.ozland.net .au. Work-oriented hostel with recreation area, cable TV and laundry. The operators have work contacts, do all the paperwork required and organize transport too. Rooms are twin-, three- and four-bedded. Only weekly stays accepted; $120 per person per week.

Mildura Stopover 29 Lemon Ave ⓣ03/5021 1980, ⓦwww.stopover.com.au. Despite the name, this place mostly houses long-term workers who want a clean place to stay with good facilities, including a sunny courtyard with BBQ. Doesn't have the party atmosphere of the other hostels. Dorms $20, rooms ❷

Riverboat Bungalow 27 Chaffey Ave ⓣ03/5021 5315, ⓦwww.riverboatbungalow.com. The 1891 house is a work-and-play-oriented place with work registry, Internet access, cable TV and a swimming pool in a large backyard near the river. Dorms $22, rooms ❷

Riverview B&B 115 7th St ☎03/5023 8975. Two rooms with en-suite in a 1950s-style house overlooking the river in a central location. ❹

Houseboats

Adventure Houseboats Buronga ☎03/5023 4787, ⓦwww.adventure.ozland.net.au. Self-contained houseboats with laundry, CD player, TV and BBQ. Expect to pay from $400 off-peak for a 2-berth boat for 3 nights.

B&B on a boat ☎03/ 50221510, ⓦwww.acaciaboats.com.au. Probably no better way to experience the Murray River then to live on it for a few days. Houseboats are air-conditioned, fully equipped and can accommodate up to 6 people. Full breakfast is included (but you have to cook it). ❺ plus $35 per extra adult.

Eating

Healthy food abounds in Mildura's **cafés** and **restaurants**, most of which are clustered on Langtree Avenue, just south of the mall. If you have your own transport, you can make an enjoyable outing to buy fruit and vegetables from surrounding farms. Otherwise, there are three excellent supermarkets, including a 24-hour Coles, surrounding Langtree Mall.

27 Deakin Stefano's Good Food Store, Caffè and Bakery 27 Deakin Ave. Owned by celebrity chef Stefano de Pieri, this is just one of his shrines to food that serves delicious breakfasts, lunches, coffee, cakes and bread as well as gourmet grocery items. Mon–Sat 8am–3pm, Sun 9am–3pm.

Avoca Paddle Boat ☎03/5022 1444. Another Stefano restaurant with impeccable food and atmosphere, located in an old steamer on the river built in the 1870s, sunk in the 1930s and fully renovated in the 1970s. Meals start at $14, open Wed–Sun for lunch and dinner. Bookings recommended.

Hudak's Bakery Café 139 8th St & opposite Mildura Centre Plaza, 15th St. Good continental breads, pies, focaccias and cakes, with great seating on the outdoor balcony. Daily 7am–6pm.

Mildura Grand Hotel *The Grand*, as it's known, incorporates four eateries. Tucked away in the cellar is its crowning glory, *Stefano's* (dinner Mon–Sat; bookings essential ☎03/5023 0511). There's no menu but the Northern Italian banquets (about $80 for 5 courses) are excellent. The other options include: *Dining Room One*, a bistro featuring Mediterranean cuisine; the *New Spanish Grill*, where you order your choice of grilled meat, side dishes and wine at the bar; and the *Grand Pizza Café and Wine Bar* for pasta and wood-fired pizzas.

Mildura RSL Cnr Madden Ave & 10th St. Has good-portioned $6.90 lunch specials every day, but the dinner menu is much more expensive.

Restaurant Rendezvous 34 Langtree Ave ☎03/5023 1571. Cheap lunches and other meals served in the bistro. There's also an upmarket restaurant, as well as a bar and courtyard seating. Lunch Mon–Fri, dinner Mon–Sat.

Nightlife

Mildura's **nightlife** may not be the world's greatest, but there's enough to keep you occupied. The *Mildura Brewery* at 20 Langtree Ave offers incredibly good beer straight from the giant vats visible from the tables. *O'Malley's Irish Tavern* at 46 Deakin Ave is a barnlike venue that fills up on weekends and occasionally has cover bands, whereas *Settlers* at 110 8th St has a more student/backpacker-type vibe with daily drink specials and poker nights, karaoke etc. Another good place for a drink and where the locals like to go is the *Sandbar* (nightly till 1am) at 43 Langtree Ave, with an excellent courtyard and live music on weekends.

Around Mildura

The easiest excursion from Mildura is to **RED CLIFFS**, some 15km south, with its vineyards and tree-lined streets. The huge **Lindemans Karadoc Winery** (daily 10am–4.30pm; ⓦwww.lindemans.com.au) is one of the largest **wineries** in Australia, where fifty thousand tonnes of grapes are crushed every year. The range of wines for tasting is extensive, prices are very reasonable and there's a café serving light lunches, coffee and cake (Mon–Fri 10am–3pm).

Across the Murray from Mildura at **BURONGA** (actually in NSW but more readily accessible from the Victoria side of the river), is the **BRL Hardy wine company** (Mon–Fri 10am–4pm, Sat 10.30am–4pm, Sun noon–4pm; ⓣ03/5018 9907), the largest cask winery in New South Wales, their most famous brand being Stanley Wines – you can taste the wine here or just pose for photos in front of the big wine cask outside. On a much smaller scale, **Trentham Estate Winery**, 10km down the Sturt Highway in an idyllic setting overlooking the river, has cellar-door sales (daily 9.30am–5pm); and an upmarket restaurant (lunch Tues–Sun; ⓣ03/5024 8888, ⓦwww.trenthamestate.com.au).

Swan Hill and around

As you approach **SWAN HILL**, the landscape changes – this is cattle and sheep country, with wheatfields further north. The Murray here is shallow and tricky to navigate, so there's not much river traffic. Swan Hill is a service centre for the pastoral industry and has a typically solid, conservative atmosphere. Surprisingly, it's quite a multicultural place, having ten percent of Victoria's Aboriginal population, and a large Italian community. The Pioneer Settlement is undoubtedly Swan Hill's main attraction, but while you're here, you could also visit the **Swan Hill Regional Art Gallery** (Tues–Fri 10am–5pm, Sat & Sun 11am–5pm; entry by donation; free guided tour Sun 1.30pm; ⓦwww.swanhill.vic.gov.au/gallery), which specializes in folk and Aboriginal art. The town's swimming pool on Monash Drive has several pools and a waterslide (Nov–March daily 11am–7pm; open for morning laps Mon, Wed & Fri 6–8am; $3.50). Next to the train station you can't miss the fake thirteen-metre Murray Cod (built for a film), which doesn't really serve a purpose, but amuses tourists who pass by.

Pioneer Settlement

Swan Hill's **Pioneer Settlement**, a reconstruction of a pioneering community at Horseshoe Bend about 1km south of the train station, was the first of its kind in Australia and is still one of the best (Tues-Sun plus Mon on school holidays 9.30am–4pm; $20.50; combination ticket for settlement, sound-and-light show and *Pyap* Cruise $41.50; ⓦwww.pioneersettlement.com.au).

In the settlement's streets many of the **shops** are functional – the baker, the printer, the haberdashery and the porcelain-doll shop – with assistants dressed in vaguely period costume. Generally, though, it's low-key and peaceful: buildings such as the barber's shop and the stock and station agents are open for you to wander around undisturbed. You can go on rides around the settlement in a 1924 Dodge or a horse-drawn carriage. In the evening, the **sound-and-light show** (nightly from dusk; $15.50) is strikingly effective.

The settlement is situated on the banks of the Marraboor River, a branch of the Murray, and a wooden bridge spans the river to Pental Island, which has an assortment of native flora and fauna. Otherwise, an old **paddle steamer**, the *Pyap*, cruises from the settlement upriver past Murray Downs every day at 10.30am and 2.30pm (1hr; $15.50), while the *Kookaburra* offers a longer luncheon cruise (ⓦwww.swanhillrivercruises.info; 1hr 30min; $38), departing at 12.30pm (Tues & Thurs–Sun).

Practicalities

The **Swan Hill Visitor Information Centre**, across the road from the train station, on the corner of McCrae and Curlewis streets (daily 9am–5pm; ⓣ03/5032 3033 or 1800 625 373, ⓦwww.swanhillonline.com), has a free map of the town giving detailed information on local attractions; it also sells tickets for the Pioneer Settlement, its sound-and-light show and the MV *Kookaburra* and PS *Pyap* cruises. **Parks Victoria** at 324 Campbell St (Mon–Fri 8.30am–5pm; ⓣ03/5033 1290) can provide you with information on camping in the nearby Nyah and Vinefera state forests.

There's a strip of **motels**, all with swimming pools, along Campbell Street, where almost all the town's facilities are located. The most luxurious of the lot is the *Sundowner Swan Hill Resort* at no. 405 (ⓣ1800 034 220, ⓦwww.sundownermotorinns.com.au; ❺) which has an indoor and outdoor pool and spa, gym and other sports facilities. The *Paddle Steamer Motel* on the Murray Valley Highway, 3km south of the centre, has very good facilities and is much cheaper (ⓣ03/5032 2151, ⓦwww.paddlesteamermotel.com.au; ❸). Also good value and much closer to the centre is *Jacaranda Holiday Units* at 179 Curlewis St (ⓣ03/5032 9077, ⓦwww.jaracandaholidayunits.com.au; ❸–❹). *The Riverside* at 1 Monash Drive (ⓣ03/5032 1494, ⓦwww.swanhillriverside.com.au; cabins ❸–❺) is a good, centrally located **caravan park** right on the riverfront.

Swan Hill **restaurants** still demonstrate an Italian culinary influence. *Bartalotta's Hot Bread*, at 178 Campbell St, is always busy and makes huge sandwiches, while *Spoons* at no. 387 is a licensed deli serving up a variety of gourmet foods. The best restaurant is *Quo Vadis* (open from 5pm daily), an authentic pizzeria at 255 Campbell St that serves mammoth portions of pasta (from $14), yet *Java Spice* at 17 Beveridge St (lunch Thurs, Fri & Sun; dinner daily except Mon) is also very good, serving spicy Thai cuisine in a great outdoor setting. A nice place for a cheap meal and a beer with the locals is the *R.S.L. Club* at 138 Curlewis St (daily lunch and dinner).

Echuca and around

ECHUCA, a lively and progressive place, is the most easily accessible river town from Melbourne – it's only three hours or so by bus or car, making it a popular

River cruises

A wide choice of **cruises with paddle steamers** is on offer, departing from berths just beyond the old wharf, best approached from High Street. One-hour port cruises are available on the PS *Alexander Arbuthnot*, PS *Pevensey* and the PS *Adelaide*; the latter, built in 1866, is the oldest wooden-hulled paddle steamer still operating in the world (about $19/hr; for all of them call ⓣ03/5482 4248). Other boats offering one-hour cruises are PS *Pride of the Murray* and PS *Canberra* (for both call ⓣ03/5482 5244). The PS *Emmylou*, a wood-fired paddle steamer, has a variety of cruises (ⓣ03/5480 2237, ⓦwww.emmylou.com.au), while the MV *Mary Ann* (ⓣ03/5480 2200, ⓦwww.maryann.com.au) does lunch cruises (12.30pm; 1.5hr; $40) and dinner cruises (7pm; from $55). Kingfisher Cruises (ⓣ03/5480 1839, ⓦwww.kingerfishercruises.com.au) offers a two-hour eco-cruise (Mon, Wed, Thurs, Sat & Sun, plus other days during busy times; $25) through the Barmah wetlands some 30km upstream of the Murray, which contain the world's largest single stand of river red gums.

weekend getaway. Echuca became the largest inland port in Australia after the railway line connected it with Melbourne in 1864. The **Port of Echuca**, a popular tourist attraction where stores, pubs and businesses have been preserved, gives a good insight into the period. When the **missions** began to close in the 1930s, many Aboriginal families migrated to the Echuca area. Since they weren't made welcome in the towns, the migrants were forced to live on the fringes in badly constructed, flood-prone housing, just close enough to be able to get to work and school. Women commonly worked in the canneries and hospitals, and the men packed fruit, sheared sheep and did other labouring jobs.

Arrival and information

The **tourist information centre**, 2 Heygarth St (daily 8am–5pm; ⓣ03/5480 7555 or 1800 804 446, ⓦwww.echucamoama.com), sells tickets to the port complex and for cruises, books accommodation and is an agent for V/Line and Countrylink bus tickets. V/Line runs up to six services between Melbourne and Echuca (train–bus and one direct train); there is also one daily connection with Sydney via Albury, and two to Adelaide (one direct, one via Bendigo). Internet access is available at the Tangled Garden Bookshop at 495 High St (9am–5pm Mon–Fri, 9am–5pm Sat, 11am–4pm Sun).

Accommodation

As well as the **accommodation** options listed below, ask at the tourist office about the many houseboats available to rent in the area.

The Clocktower 234 Anstruther St ⓣ03/5482 1932, ⓦwww.clocktowerapartments.com.au. Luxurious apartments and suites set in a fully renovated post office built in 1879, in the centre of town. ❻

Echuca Caravan Park Crofton St, Victoria Park ⓣ03/5482 2157, ⓦwww.echucacaravanpark.com.au. A well-equipped caravan park right on the riverfront. Cabins ❸

Echuca Gardens YHA 103 Mitchell St ⓣ03/5480 6522 (8–10am & 5–10pm), ⓔechuca@yhavic.org.au. Budget accommodation in a restored Victorian worker's cottage – cozy atmosphere, but the dorms are cramped and tiny. The location on the edge of the Banyule Forest is very scenic though, and it's a ten-minute walk through red gums to sandy river beaches where it's safe to swim on the inner bends. Dorms $25, rooms ❷

Nomads Oasis Backpackers 410–424 High St ⓣ03/5480 7866, ⓔnomads@river.net.au. Centrally located, air-conditioned dorms as well as twins/doubles at an affordable price. There's a small kitchen and courtyard, and the owner has employment contacts and can provide transport to places of work. Dorms $25, rooms ❷

Shamrock Hotel 579 High St ⓣ03/5482 1036, ⓔshamrockechuca@bigpond.com. Grand old pub in the old port district offering basic but cheap rooms with shared facilities. It can get loud on weekends when it turns into a drinking hole. ❸

Steam Packet Inn Cnr of Leslie St and Murray Esplanade ⓣ03/5482 3411, ⓦwww.steampacketinn.com.au. A National Trust–listed B&B with super-friendly service, offering traditionally decorated rooms in the heart of the old port area. ❺ includes big breakfast

The Town

The **Port of Echuca** is where most people head to, with its massive wharves and collection of old buildings several cruises ply along the river from here. The town itself, however, is not too touristy, and has retained much of its charm. There are two principal streets: High Street, the former main street, leads to Murray Esplanade and the wharf, and is the centre of tourist activity, with lots of cafés and boutiquey shops, while Hare Street, the present-day main street, is lined with more commercial buildings.

To enter the old wharf area, dubbed the **Historic Wharf** (daily 9am–5pm; ⓦwww.portofechuca.org.au), you'll need to pay an $11.50 entrance fee.

Alternatively, you can combine a tour with a cruise on the *Pevensey* or the *Alexander Arbuthnot* (see box, p.943) for $24.50. The **Star Hotel** was first licensed in 1867 and is a typical pioneer pub, a tiny one-storey building with a tin roof and veranda. As the river trade declined, the *Star* was delicensed (in 1897), along with many of the other 79 hotels in town. Drinking on the premises became illegal, so the loyal clientele dug a tunnel to the street through which they could escape at the first hint of a police raid – you can examine this, along with the cellar and a small museum.

The magnificent red-gum **wharf** was a quarter of a mile long in its prime and is still fairly extensive. Three landing platforms at different levels allowed unloading, even during times of flooding, and there are wonderful views from the top, high over a bend in the river. At the lowest level, several **old paddle steamers** are moored, including the *Pevensey*, a 1911 cargo boat which you can wander aboard. In the wharf cargo-shed there's a scale model of the working port and a ten-minute audiovisual presentation.

Back outside the wharf complex, along Murray Esplanade opposite Hopwood Gardens, is the **Bridge Hotel**, opened in 1858 but delicensed in 1916. It was built by the founder of Echuca, Henry Hopwood, an ex-convict who also started a punt service across the Murray. The story goes that if the pub wasn't doing well he'd close the ferry down for a few hours, leaving prospective passengers with little else to do but drink.

Another unique (if not alcoholic) attraction is the **Great Aussie Beer Shed** (9.30am–5pm weekends; ⓣ03/5480 6904, ⓦwww.greataussiebeershed.com.au; $8.50) at 377 Mary Ann Rd, which features over 16,000 types of beer can.

Eating, drinking and nightlife

With hungry Melburnians to feed, there's no shortage of decent **eating places**. The small and friendly *American Hotel* is a good place to head for a **drink**; while the *Harvest Hotel*, 183 Hare St, draws a youngish crowd and plays host to live bands at weekends, as does the *Shamrock Hotel* at 579 High St, which has the best beer garden in town. The OPT Entertainment Complex at 273 Hare St has a restaurant, bar and pool tables (Wed–Sat 5pm–2am); the nightclub is open Friday and Saturday nights till 4am. The Paramount Cinemas & Performing Arts Centre at 392 High St has an auditorium and four cinemas with state-of-the-art facilities (ⓣ03/5482 3399, ⓦwww.echucaparamount.com). If you happen to be around in mid-February, look out for the **Jazz, Food and Wine Weekend**.

Echuca's workers' **clubs** serve very cheap meals and drinks, presumably as an incentive to get you to their gambling machines – non-members can sign in as visitors. There are more clubs across the river in Moama.

Beechworth Bakery 513 High St. A branch of the original, very successful bakery from Beechworth; they sell a variety of breads baked in a wood-fired oven, sandwiches, pastries and other snacks, and there's a sun deck which is a good spot for breakfast or lunch. Daily 6am–6pm.

Bridge Hotel Hopwood Place. Coffee shop, bar and restaurant in the historic port area; good coffee, cakes and desserts, light lunches and mainly traditional Aussie dishes in the restaurant. Open daily for breakfast, lunch and dinner; the bar is open daily 7.30–1am, Sun till 11.30pm.

Fish in a flash 602 High St. Excellent array of fresh seafood including some of the best battered tiger prawns this side of Melbourne. Open daily.

Leftbank Café & Restaurant 551 High St. Housed in an old bank built in 1862, this recently opened restaurant offers modern Australian cuisine in a refined setting. Tues–Sat 6pm–late, Wed–Sun noon–3pm, Sun also 8am–noon.

Oscar W's Wharfside Murray Esplanade ⓣ03/5482 5133. This restaurant serves excellent, superbly presented food to match the scenic setting next to the old Echuca Wharf, overlooking the Murray River. The moderately expensive cuisine is Mediterranean-inspired "mod Oz". Service can be poor when the place is full though. Licensed. Bookings essential. Open daily 11am–late.

Wistaria Tearooms High St, opposite the *Shamrock Hotel*, or enter from the port. Lovely Victorian house where you can get breakfast and light meals, coffee and cakes. Licensed. Daily 8am–6pm.

Around Echuca

Thirty kilometres southeast of Echuca, Kyabram's main attraction is **Kyabram Fauna Park** (daily 9.30am–5.30pm; $12; Ⓦwww.kyabramfaunaparkcom.au), a community-owned wildlife park divided into grassland for free-ranging kangaroos, wallabies, emus and other animals, and a huge wetland area. You can wander around the grassland area and through several aviaries; a two-storey observation tower affords views of the more than eighty species of native birdlife. Diamond pythons, tiger snakes, crocodiles and other not-so-pleasant creatures can be viewed from a safe distance at the Reptile House.

BARMAH, some 30km upstream on the Murray, is most easily reached by crossing into NSW at Echuca and heading north on the Cobb Highway, then turning east. This small river town is associated with red-gum milling, and with sleeper-cutting in the early railway days. The *Barmah Caravan Park* (Ⓣ03/5869 3225, Ⓦwww.barmahcaravanpark.com.au; ❶–❸) has a great site on the banks of the river among red gums, with a small, sandy beach for swimming and a few cabins. **Barmah State Park**, 10km out of town, has Australia's largest stands of **river red gum**, some of them 40m tall and five hundred years old. The forest runs along the Murray for over 100km and stands in an extensive flood plain – **canoeing** among the trees at flood time (July–Nov) is a magical experience; you can arrange transport and rent canoes from Echuca Boat and Canoe Hire (Ⓣ03/5480 6208, Ⓦwww.echucaboatcanoehire.com). During the wet season more than two hundred species of waterbird come here, and there's plenty of other wildlife; you might even see brumbies (wild horses). When it's dry you can use several well-established walking tracks: the place was of special significance to the local Yorta Yorta Aborigines and you can still see fish traps, middens and scars on trees where the bark was used for canoes.

Yorta Yorta culture and lore are explained in the park's **Dharnya Centre** (daily 10.30am–4pm; Ⓣ03/5869 3302), which also has archeological information and artefacts. A **cruise** in the MV *Kingfisher* leaves from the bridge near the centre (see box, p.943) – a flat-bottomed boat that glides over Barmah Lake and through stands of red gum. Bushcamping is permitted in the park; contact Parks Victoria (Ⓣ13 19 63) for details.

Gippsland

GIPPSLAND stretches southeast of Melbourne from Western Port Bay to the New South Wales border, between the Great Dividing Range and Bass Strait. Green and well watered, it's been the centre of Victoria's dairy industry since the 1880s. South Gippsland has Victoria's most popular national park, **Wilsons Promontory**, or "The Prom", a hook-shaped landmass jutting out into the strait, with some superb scenery and fascinating bushwalks. In the east, around the **Gippsland Lakes** and **Ninety Mile Beach**, the region is beautifully untouched and just beyond Orbost–Marlo the unspoilt coastline of the **Croajingolong National Park** – with its rocky capes, high sand dunes and endless sandy beaches – stretches to the New South Wales border.

Transport

Having your own **car** is essential for getting off the highway to really experience the region's diverse highlights and to get to the unspoilt bush campsites on the coast. The Princes Highway itself is a very boring drive, particularly the stretch from the Latrobe Valley to Bairnsdale, but after Orbost the highway becomes more scenic as it goes through the tall, dense eucalypt forests of Far East Gippsland. If you don't have a car, you might want to consider travelling with Oz Experience, the **backpacker bus** company that covers the Sydney–Melbourne route in five days, via Phillip Island, Gippsland, the Snowy Mountains and Canberra.

V/Line **trains** run from Melbourne to Bairnsdale, basically following the Princes Highway through South Gippsland. From Bairnsdale, **buses** leave for Orbost, stopping at Lakes Entrance. The Sapphire Coast Link is a daily train–bus connection between Melbourne and Narooma on the south coast of New South Wales: take the train to Bairnsdale, then a connecting bus along the Princes Highway via Lakes Entrance, Orbost, Cann River and Genoa. Similarly, the Capital Link train/bus service heads to Canberra via Bairnsdale on Monday, Thursday and Saturday around midday, returning from Canberra Tuesday, Friday and Sunday mornings. Bookings for all the above should be made through V/Line (Ⓣ13 61 96, Ⓦwww.vline.com.au). Premier Motor Service (Ⓣ13 34 10, Ⓦwww.premierms.com.au), an NSW-based coach company, runs a daily service from Melbourne to Sydney along the coast but it's not very convenient if you want to get off at stops in East Gippsland: the bus leaves Melbourne at 5.45pm Sunday to Friday, and gets to Lakes Entrance and Cann River in the early hours of the morning.

Wilsons Promontory

WILSONS PROMONTORY, or "The Prom", the most southerly part of the Australian mainland, was once joined by a land bridge to Tasmania. Its barbed hook juts out into Bass Strait, with a rocky coastline interspersed with sheltered sandy bays and coves; the coastal scenery is made even more stunning by the backdrop of granite ranges. It's understandably Victoria's most popular **national park**, and though the main campsite gets totally packed in summer, there are plenty of walking tracks and opportunities for bushcamping, and the park's big enough to allow you to escape the crowds. You can swim at several of the beaches and even **surf**: The Prom Surf School, based at Tidal River, operates courses in summer, for all ages and abilities, with all equipment provided (Ⓣ03/5680 8512, Ⓔpeck@pocketmail.com.au).

Arrival and information

There's no public transport to Wilsons Promontory, so if you don't want to hire a car, you can take the evening V/Line bus from Dandenong to Yarram and get off at **FOSTER** on the South Gippsland Highway, from where the Foster Taxi Service transports people to the national park and back (Ⓣ03/5682 2188; $85–90 one way for max 5 people). For an overnight stay at Foster, try the motel units at the *Wilsons Promontory Motel* at 26 Station St (Ⓣ03/5682 2055, Ⓕ5682 1064; ④).

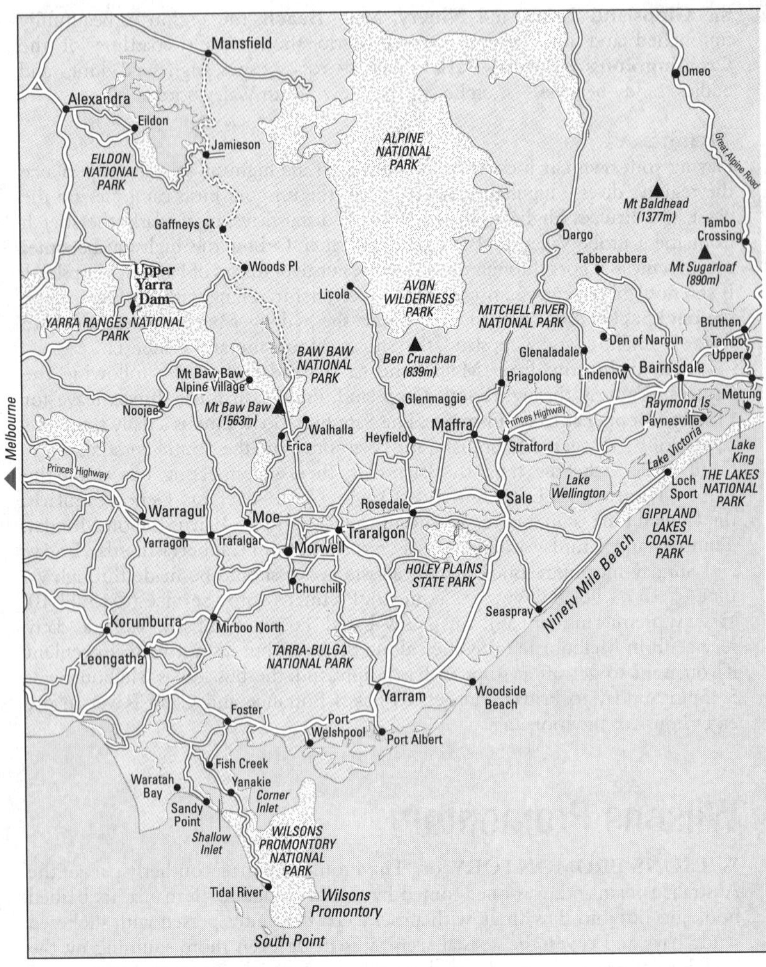

Melbourne-based eco-tour operator Bunyip Bushwalking Tours (ⓣ03/9531 0840, ⓦwww.bunyiptours.com) is a long-established Prom specialist. Their two-day Bushwalking Tour ($225; Mon, Wed & Fri) can be combined with the penguin parade on Phillip Island; they also do a three-day and a four-day Coastal Circuit Hike (from $195; weekly). All food and camping gear is provided; sleeping bags and backpacks can be rented.

With your own vehicle, the easiest way to get here from Melbourne is to follow the **South Gippsland Highway** to Meeniyan, where you turn right onto Route 189 which takes you all the way to the park entrance. Once you get into the park, it's 30km to **Tidal River** on a good sealed road. At the entrance you pay $9.90 per car per day, or $15.60 for two consecutive days – if you stay overnight, this is deducted from the cost. The **information centre** (daily 8.30am–4.30pm; ⓣ03/5680 9555 or 1800 350 552, ⓦwww.parkweb.vic.gov.au)

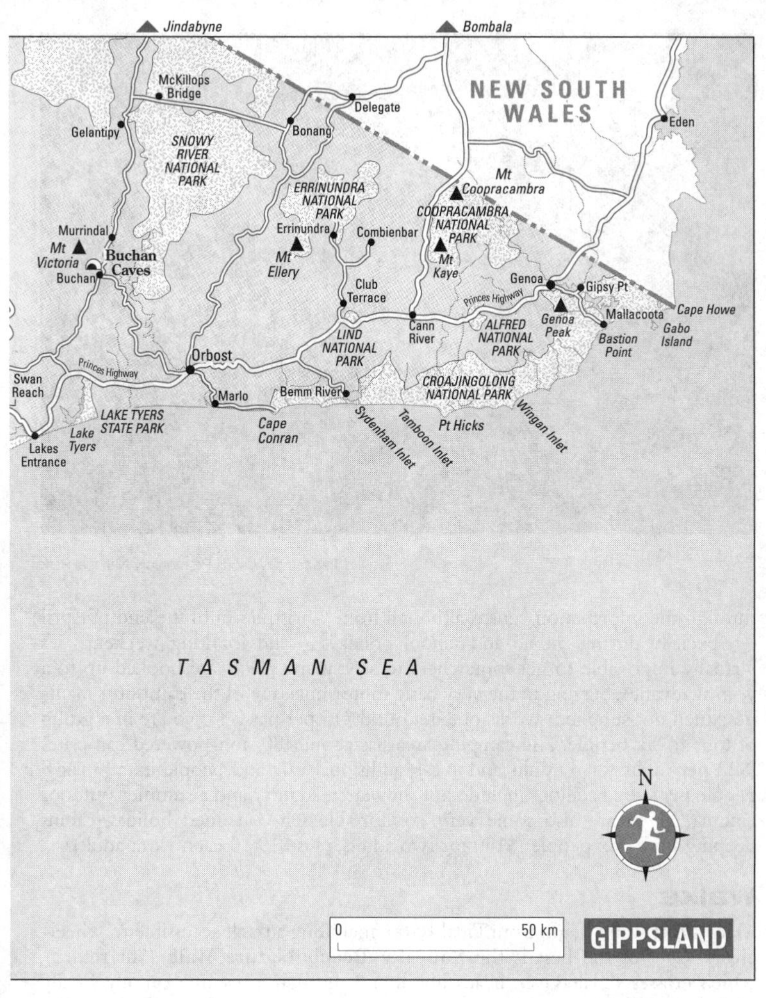

at Tidal River is an obvious first stop. They have plenty of information, though not all of it is on display, so ask: the small booklet *Discovering the Prom on Foot* ($14.95) is invaluable if you're attempting any of the overnight **walks**.

Accommodation

Detailed information on all sorts of **accommodation** close to Wilsons Promontory is available from Ⓦwww.promaccom.com.au. If you have a car, you could try for backpacker accommodation run by the *Sandy Point Café & Restaurant* in the small fishing and holiday village of Sandy Point (Ⓣ03/5684 1448, Ⓦwww.sandypointcafe.com; ❷).

Tidal River, situated by a small river on Norman Bay, is the national park's main camping and accommodation centre, with a general store including a pricey supermarket, takeaway food and fuel. Accommodation is arranged

△ Tree ferns, Wilsons Promontory National Park

through the information centre, although from Christmas until the end of April – especially during public and school holidays – and for long weekends it's virtually impossible to get somewhere to stay; many places are booked up to a year in advance. Staying in the very basic motor huts (use of the campsite's facilities; linen not supplied) works out at around $15 per person if you're in a group of four to six people. The camping area has about 480 non-powered campsites ($22 per night for 3 adults and 1 car; additional cars and people extra; max 8 people per site). Facilities include hot showers, a laundry and a summer outdoor cinema. There are also some very comfortable self-contained holiday cabins sleeping up to six people ($150 for two adults, plus $19.10 each extra adult).

Walks

Many short walks begin from Tidal River, including a track accessible to wheelchairs. One of the best is the **Squeaky Beach Nature Walk** (1hr return), which crosses Tidal River, heads uphill and through a tea-tree canopy, finally ending on a beach of pure quartz sand that is indeed squeaky underfoot. **The Lilly Pilly Gully Nature Walk** (3hr return) is very rewarding, as it affords an excellent overview of the diverse vegetation of "the Prom", from low-growing shrubs to heathland to open eucalypt forest, as well as scenic views. The walk starts at the Lilly Pilly Gully car park near Tidal River, follows a small valley and returns to the car park along the slopes of Mount Bishop. For **overnight camping** ($6.20 per person per night), you need to obtain a **permit** from the information centre at Tidal River (see p.949), as there is a restriction on the number of people allowed on the campsites.

The tracks in the southern section of the park are well defined and not too difficult; the campsites here have pit toilets and fresh water. The most popular walk is the two- to three-day (37km) **Sealers Cove–Refuge Cove–Waterloo Bay** route, beginning and ending at the Mount Oberon car park. During summer holidays and at long weekends between November and the end of April, the tracks become extremely busy, so book well in advance or show up early. The remote north of the park is only suitable for experienced, properly equipped bushwalkers; there are no facilities (except for pit toilets at Tin Mine Cove) and limited fresh water.

The Gippsland Lakes region

The **Gippsland Lakes**, Australia's largest system of inland waterways, are fed by the waters of the Mitchell, Nicholson and Tambo rivers, and are separated from the sea by Ninety Mile Beach. East of Yarram, the beach stretches long and straight towards **Lakes Entrance**, the tacky focal point of the area and one of Victoria's most popular holiday spots, with the foothills of the high country within easy reach to the north.

Sale

SALE, at the junction of the South Gippsland Highway and the Princes Highway, is a good point from which to head off to explore the coastal park and Ninety Mile Beach. From Seaspray, 35km south, a coastal road hugs the shore for 20km to Golden Beach, from where a scenic drive heads through the Gippsland Lakes Coastal Park to Loch Sport; here you're faced with the enviable dilemma of lakes on one side and ocean beaches with good surfing on the other. An unsealed road then continues on to Sperm Whale Head in the Lakes National Park. Sale's **tourist information centre** (daily 9am–5pm; ⓣ1800 677 520, ⓦwww.tourismwellington.com.au), as you come into town from the west on the Princes Highway, can provide you with all the details. They have Internet access ($3/15 min) and can also give information about the **Bataluk Cultural Trail**, which starts in Sale and links sites of cultural and spiritual significance to the Gunai people, the original inhabitants of the Gippsland coast.

If you'd like to get friendly with the locals, opt for a stay off the beaten track at the small *Cambrai Backpackers* at 117 Johnston St in **Maffra**, a small dairy-farming town, 20km off the Princes Highway in the foothills of the Great Dividing Range. Located in a lovely, refurbished building right in the town centre, the hostel has dorms (8 beds) and doubles, a communal kitchen, comfy lounge and licensed bar. The owners pick up from the bus stop (pre-book), arrange walks in the high country and have work contacts (ⓣ1800 101 113, ⓦwww.maffra.net.au/hostel/; dorms $25, rooms ❸).

Bairnsdale and around

BAIRNSDALE is the next major town on the highway east of Sale and serves as another departure point for the lakes to the south. The efficient staff at the **tourist office** on Main Street (daily 9am–5pm; ⓣ03/5152 3444, ⓦwww.egipps.vic.gov.au/tourism/index.htm) will provide all the local information you'll need. A small exhibition at the **Krowathunkoolong Keeping Place**, parallel to the Princes Highway at 37–53 Dalmahoy St, explains the history of the Gunai people (Mon–Fri 9am–noon & 1–5pm; ⓣ03/5152 1891; $3.50).

For budget **accommodation** in Bairnsdale itself, try the *Grand Terminus Hotel* at 98 McLeod St (ⓣ03/5152 4040; ❷) or the *Bairnsdale Holiday Park* (ⓣ03/5152 4066, ⓦwww.bairnsdaleholidaypark.com; cabins ❸, units ❹) just west of the town at 139 Princess Highway. A gorgeous – if pricey – alternative is the luxurious *Lake Gallery B&B* (ⓣ03/5156 0448, ⓦwww.lakegallerybedandbreakfast.com; ❻) in **Paynesville**, 16km south of Bairnsdale, which has two designer-decorated guest suites at the water's edge and its own jetty.

A short ferry-ride away across the McMillan Straits from Paynesville is **Raymond Island** which, with its prolific birdlife, kangaroos and koalas, is an idyllic place to stay. The Raymond Island Ferry runs roughly every half-hour throughout the day (Mon–Thurs 7am–10.30pm, Fri & Sat 7am–midnight, Sun 8am–11pm; cars $7 return, foot passengers free). Accommodation options on the island are *Currawong Cottage*, 27 Currawong Close, ⓣ03/5156 7226; ⑤), which sleeps up to four people, or a couple of two-bedroom flats at *Swan Cove Holiday Flats*, 390 Centre Rd (ⓣ03/5156 6716; ③).

Forty-five kilometres northwest of Bairnsdale is another site on the Bataluk Cultural Trail, the **Den of Nargun** in the **Mitchell River National Park**. According to a Gunai legend, the small cave here was inhabited by a large female creature, a nargun, who would abduct people who wandered off on their own. As the Den of Nargun was a special place for Gunai women and may have been used for initiation ceremonies, the story served the purpose of keeping unauthorized people away. The cave is located in a small, beautiful valley; follow the loop track from the park picnic area via a lookout to the Mitchell River (30min), then take the track along Woolshed Creek to the cave and climb up the steep path back to the starting point (40min).

Lakes Entrance

LAKES ENTRANCE is named after the entrance to the Gippsland Lakes. A sandy barrier between the Gippsland Lakes and the sea formed about six thousand years ago, when first seen by white men in the 1840s the outlet was a seasonal, intermittent gap, unsuitable for reliable trade. In 1889 the present stable entrance was opened 6km east of the old one: the artificial entrance effectively cuts off the town's access to the length of **Ninety Mile Beach**.

As you might expect from the area's popularity, Lakes Entrance is a big, rather tawdry, tourist town, with loads of motels at either end of town as you enter from the highway. There are all sorts of attractions aimed at keeping holidaying children happy – from Fun Park to minigolf – on the Esplanade, which fronts onto an arm of Lake King. The **Griffiths Sea Shell Museum** at 125 Esplanade (daily 9am–5pm; $5; ⓣ03/5155 1538), with its rather off-putting 1950s-style facade, has a huge collection of shells and marine life, as well as an aquarium containing an intriguing assortment of fish from the Gippsland Lakes. Lakes Entrance is also a big **fishing port**: the Fishermans Cooperative Wharf has a viewing platform where you can watch the catch being unloaded, as well as a tantalizing fish shop.

Beaches are obviously the big attraction here. Lakes Entrance Surf Beach, a substantial stretch of white sand patrolled in season by surf lifesavers, can be reached via a footbridge across the lake to Hummocks Reserve. A stand on the beach side of the footbridge hires canoes, paddleboats, aquabikes and catamarans. Of the many **lake cruises** on offer, one of the most popular is the trip from the *Club Hotel* jetty at the western end of town, up North Arm to the Wyanga Park Winery (ⓣ03/5155 1508, ⓦwww.wyangapark.com.au) – the most famous local winery – on the fringe of the Colquhoun Forest, in the winery's own boat, the *Corque* (daily lunch cruise $45, Fri & Sat dinner cruise $70, Sun brunch cruise $30; book at Lakes Entrance Visitor Centre, or through the winery). Other waterside activities are three-hour **fishing** trips with Mulloway Fishing Charters (ⓣ0427 943 154, ⓔmulloway3@hotmail.com; $40).

Practicalities

Lakes Entrance Tourist Information (daily 9am–5pm; ⓣ1800 637 060), on the Esplanade, provides local advice and tickets for cruises on the lakes, and can also book accommodation, a useful service in summer when the place gets very crowded. There is Internet access at 10 Myer St (Mon–Fri 9am–5.30pm, Sat 10am–3pm, Sun 10am–2pm; $7 an hour).

Accommodation

Deja Vu Out of town at 17 Clara St ⓣ03/5155 4330, ⓦwww.dejavu.com.au. A rather special B&B in a pleasant location, with spacious en-suite rooms as well as separate 1- and 2-bedroom cottages overlooking the waterway of North Arm. ❻–❼

Goat and Goose B&B 16 Gay St ⓣ03/5155 3079, ⓦwww.goatandgoose.com. Recommended B&B in a timber house on a hill at the western end of town. There are great ocean views from the balconies, and three of the four suites come with a spa. Breakfast is huge and scrumptious, and, to top it all off, guests get a tour of Lakes Entrance in the owner's Rolls Royce. ❺

Kalimna Woods Kalimna Jetty Rd ⓣ03/5155 1957, ⓦwww.kilimnawoods.com.au. Fully self-contained timber cottages in a nice bush setting, some with spas and log fires. ❹–❺

Lakes Waterfront Motel & Cottages 10 Princess Highway ⓣ03/5155 2841, ⓔlwfmotel@netspace.net.au. The motel rooms are just average, but the self-contained cottages (hold 3 people) on the water's edge offer excellent value. Also has pool and cable TV. Rooms, cottages ❹

Riviera Backpackers YHA 5 Clarkes Rd ⓣ03/5155 2444, ⓔlakesentrance@yhavic.org.au. In the east end of town, this is a friendly place situated close to a beautiful stretch of lake. It has dorms and good en-suite rooms, a large kitchen/common room, Internet access, a laundry and a small pool with spa. Dorms $18.50, rooms ❷

Waters Edge Holiday Park 623 Esplanade ⓣ03/5155 1914, ⓦwww.watersedgeholidaypark.com.au. Popular option with great amenities such as two pools, games room, playground and modern holiday units. ❸–❹

Eating

Ferryman's Seafood Café Situated on the water by Myer St in a 40-year-old ferry, it offers surprisingly well priced seafood in a setting you'd think would be more expensive. Lunch noon–3pm, dinner 6pm–late; daily.

Henry's Wine Café Wyanga Park Winery ⓣ03/5155 1508. 3km from town, it offers excellent cuisine sourced from local producers. Daily 10am–4pm, dinner Fri–Sat.

Lakes Entrance Bowls Club Cnr of Rowe and Bulmer St. Perhaps not trendy, but you can't go wrong with the generous portions at very cheap prices ($7 lunches). Daily lunch and dinner.

L'Ocean Fish & Chips 19 Myer St. Fantastic fresh seafood place that, despite its modest exterior, has become an institution. Located just off the Esplanade, they serve gluten-free and wheat-free batter. Daily 11am–8pm.

Tres Amigos Mexican 521 Myer St. A backpacker/surfer favourite since 1977, dishing out cheap Mexican fare. Takeaway available. Daily dinner.

Metung

If the commercialism of Lakes Entrance turns you off, head for the more refined charms of **METUNG**, a pretty, upmarket boating and holidaying village just 10km west along the shoreline. To get here, take the highway towards Bairnsdale, then turn south on the side road at Swan Reach. There is a new tourism information office at 50 Metung Rd (9am–5pm daily; ⓣ03/ 5156 2969) which books accommodation and hires out boats.

A good **accommodation** option is *McMillans of Metung* (ⓣ03/5156 2283, ⓦwww.mcmillansofmetung.com.au; ❻–❼), at 155 Metung Rd, which has very comfortable, fully equipped cottages of different sizes in a garden setting, with a solar-heated pool, tennis court and a private jetty. For a taste of history *Clovelly House* at 5 Essington Close (ⓣ03/5156 2428, ⓦwww.clovellybedandbreakfast.com; ❻–❼) was one of the first residencies built in the area in 1881, and is perched high above the town. *The Moorings at Metung*, 28 Main Rd (ⓣ03/5156 2750, ⓦwww.themoorings.com.au; ❺–❻), are luxury apartments with sun decks and BBQs overlooking Bancroft Bay; their bistro menu offers everything from champagne brunch to coffee and cake. Cheaper is the *Metung Hotel* (ⓣ03/5156 2206, ⓦwww.metunghotel.com.au; ❹), which also offers food (noon–2pm & 6–8.30pm daily) and a fantastic outdoor table area on the water. The newest and best **restaurant** in town is the *Kings Cove Club* (part of the new golf-course development; Fri & Sat 6–9pm; ⓣ03/5156 2927) on Kings Cove Boulevard, serving modern seafood in a chic setting. The pleasant BYO *Little Mariners Café* at 57 Metung Rd serves breakfast, light meals and local seafood daily, while *Ninas* at no. 51 is a tiny café that serves great jaffles ($4) and other light meals.

Buchan and the Snowy River Loop

Nowa Nowa is the inauspiciously named town where you turn north off the Princes Highway for the small town of **BUCHAN**, in the foothills of the Victorian Alps, and take a satisfying loop through the Snowy River National Park. Buchan boasts over six hundred **caves**, the most famous of which – the Royal Cave and the Fairy Cave – can be seen on **guided tours** (daily: April–Sept 11am, 1pm & 3pm; Oct–March 10am, 11.15am, 1pm, 2.15pm & 3.30pm; $12.50; booking advised on ⓣ03/5162 1900). In the extensive park surrounding the caves there's an icy, spring-fed swimming pool, a playground, walking tracks and a campsite, plus lots of wildlife.

On the north bank of the Buchan River in the town is *Buchan Lodge* (ⓣ03/5155 9421, ⓦwww.buchanlodge.com; ❶), a smallish backpackers **hostel** with dorms, a country-style kitchen, laundry, log fire in winter, BBQ and a nice outdoor garden. The owner will advise about activities in the area, including caving, trail riding and rafting. If you need more than a dorm bed, the *Buchan Valley Log Cabins* (ⓣ03/5155 9494, ⓦwww.buchanlogcabins.com.au; ❹), 16 Gelantipy Rd, consists of a series of spacious two-bedroom cabins with full amenities in a garden setting. For good pub grub head to the *Caves Hotel* (lunch Wed–Sun, dinner Tues–Sun) or the *Café Caves* across the road for their kangaroo pie.

The road continues north from Buchan through hilly country, following the Murrindal River and slowly winding its way up to the plateau of the Australian Alps. The sealed road ends at Wulgumerang, just before the turn-off to McKillops Bridge. You can continue straight up to Jindabyne in the Snowy Mountains of New South Wales – a spectacular drive – but about two-thirds of the road is unsealed and can be rough; check conditions before setting out.

Snowy River National Park

Turning right at Wulgumerang, about 55km north of Buchan, enables you to make a scenic, yet at certain times terrifying, arc through part of the **Snowy River National Park**, following the road towards Bonang (check road conditions in advance, as this is an unsealed road that can deteriorate badly in adverse weather conditions). **Little River Falls** are well worth a stop on this stretch: a short walk leads from the car park past snow gums to a lookout with breathtaking views of Little River Gorge and the falls. Equally stunning is the view from the second lookout from the top of the northeastern cliff-face of **Little River Gorge** (about 10min from the car park).

Further on, you descend to the valley of the Snowy River, which you cross at **McKillops Bridge**, set in the landscape that inspired "Banjo" Paterson's famous ballad, *The Man from Snowy River*. The river's sandy banks are a favourite swimming spot, and are also the place to set out on a **rafting** trip through deep gorges, caves, raging rapids and tranquil pools. Snowy River Expeditions offers good-value river expeditions, as well as rafting, abseiling, rock-climbing, horse riding ($30/hr) and wild caving adventures ($85). They also run *Karoonda Park*

(Ⓣ03/5155 0220, Ⓦwww.karoondapark.com; dorms $24, rooms ❸), a small country **hostel** situated on a beef and sheep farm in Gelantipy. Oz Experience buses pass through Gelantipy.

Bonang to Orbost

The road through the Snowy River National Park continues until it meets the Bonang–Orbost road. The general store at **BONANG**, a former goldrush town, sells takeaway food, groceries and fuel, and has some information about the area.

The winding road down from the plateau to the coast, still mostly unsealed, leads past the **Errinundra National Park**, which protects magnificent wetland eucalypt forests containing giant, centuries-old specimens, as well as Victoria's largest surviving stand of **rainforest**. At **Errinundra Saddle**, in the heart of the park, there's a delightful picnic area and a self-guided boardwalk through the forest (about 40min). Take special care while driving, as all the roads in the area are heavily used by logging trucks.

The road from Bonang eventually leads to the old-fashioned town of **ORBOST**, on the Princes Highway where it crosses the Snowy River. The **Orbost Visitors Centre** at 39 Nicholson St (daily 9am–5pm; Ⓣ03/5154 2424) books accommodation and tours. There's a tranquil picnic spot opposite the *Snowy River Orbost Camp Park* (Ⓣ03/5154 1097; cabins; ❸), on the corner of Lochiel and Nicholson streets, with huge gums lining one bank and cows roaming the paddocks on the other. The *Orbost Club Hotel* (Ⓣ03/5154 1003; ❸) at 63 Nicholson St has cheap rooms with shared bathrooms, and offers unusually good Chinese food. *A lovely little lunch* at 125a Nicholson St is appropriately titled.

Mallacoota and around

MALLACOOTA is an unspoilt village in a gorgeous location surrounded by Croajingolong National Park, on the lake system of the **Mallacoota Inlet**. During the summer and Easter holidays the tranquil place turns into a bustling holiday resort. It's approached via Genoa, 47km east from Cann River along the Princes Highway. About 10km from Genoa, a turn-off to the left leads to **Gipsy Point**, an idyllic spot near the confluence of the Genoa and Wallagaraugh rivers on the upper reaches of the Mallacoota Inlet.

The very helpful Mallacoota Information Centre is situated on the main wharf (open 10am–5pm daily; Ⓣ03/5158 0800) and gives advice on accommodation and attractions around town. You can go on bushwalks and explore the beautiful waterways of the Mallacoota Inlet (Bottom Lake and Top Lake) on your own by renting a boat or canoe from Mallacoota Hire Boats (Ⓣ03/5158 0704, Ⓔhireboats@mallacoota.com) located 200 metres to the left of the information centre. The **Parks Victoria office**, on the corner of Allan and Buckland drives (daily 9.30am–3.30pm; Ⓣ03/5158 0219, Ⓦwww.parkweb.vic.gov.au), has details of secluded camping spots and local bushwalks, and provides fishing licenses. There is Internet access available at 64 Maurice Ave

During the summer, Mallacoota, although seemingly remote, teems with holiday-makers. The population of just over a thousand trebles again for the Easter **Festival of the Great Southern Ocean**, which includes music, theatre and comedy, a community market, and fascinating sand sculptures.

The **Parks Victoria ranger office**, on the Princes Highway in Cann River (Mon–Fri 9am–noon & 12.30–3.30pm; ⓣ03/5158 6351), can provide information on the nearby **Croajingolong National Park**, which begins southeast of the town at Sydenham Inlet and continues for 100km along the coast to the state border. A three-day **bushwalking safari** run by OzStyle Adventures (ⓣ1800 000 824, ⓦwww.ozstyle.net.au) is a good option without roughing it too much: the tour leaves every Thursday ($625; includes a tour of Point Hicks Lighthouse and gourmet catering; minimum 6 people or 4 people during NSW and VIC school holidays). Or you can choose to go it alone and stay in the lighthouse-keeper's cottage (entire cottage $255 for 6 people) or a bungalow (sleeps two; ❹) at *Point Hicks* (ⓣ03/5158 4268, ⓦwww.pointhicks.com.au).

Practicalities

Several good **guesthouses** are located in and around Mallacoota.

Adobe Flats 17 Karbeethong Ave ⓣ03/5158 0329, ⓦwww.adobeholidayflats.com.au. Spacious self-contained mud-brick apartments on a former chicken farm. Popular with couples. ❸–❹

Karbeethong Lodge 16 Schnapper Point Drive ⓣ03/5158 0411, ⓦwww.karbeethonglodge.com.au. A renovated, old-style weatherboard guesthouse with singles and doubles, most en suite. Has a nice country feel to it. ❹

Mallacoota Foreshore Caravan Park ⓣ03/5158 0300, ⓔcamppark@bigpond.net.au. Great location, just metres from the water. Easily the best place in town to pitch a tent. Their office also offers good advice about where the fish are biting. ❷

Mallacoota Hotel 51 Maurice Ave ⓣ03/5158 0455, ⓔinncoota@bigpond.net.au. Very central on the main shopping strip; offers accommodation in motel units and cheap dorms ($22–24) in a separate building out the back. ❹

Wave Oasis 36 Vista Drive ⓣ03/5158 0995, ⓦwww.thewaveoasis.com.au. One of the best options in town, with extremely comfortable apartments and great views of the surrounding inlet. ❻

Eating

Choices for **food** are very limited although the standard is high. The *Croajingolong Café* (daily 8.30am–3pm) on Allan Drive serves brunch, light meals and good coffee, while the bakery next door is the pride of the town, selling award-winning pies. The *Tide Restaurant & Cocktail Bar* on Maurice Avenue is the best place in town for dinner, sometimes having **live music**; otherwise, counter meals and cold beer are served at the *Mallacoota Hotel*, where there's live music every night in January. A summer cinema operates at the Mallacoota Community Centre, Allen Drive.

Gipsy Point accommodation

Gipsy Point, about 20km northwest, has another good accommodation option, *Gipsy Point Lakeside Luxury Apartments*, set in a garden by the Wallagaraugh River (ⓣ03/5158 8200 or 1800 688 200, ⓦwww.gipsy.com.au; ❻–❼), with attractive apartments, some with spa, and a heated pool. The *Gipsy Point Lodge*, nearby on MacDonald Street, has rooms (dinner, bed and breakfast) and cottages (ⓣ1800 063 556, ⓦwww.gipsypoint.com; rooms ❻, cottages ❺), with free use of canoes and rowboats; bird-watching and bushwalking excursions can be arranged. Closer to Genoa are the *Coopracambra Cottages* (ⓣ03/5158 0802, ⓦwww.mallacoota.com/coopracambra; ❸), which offer excellent value, and a great choice for those wanting a bit of space.

The northeast

The **Hume Highway**, the direct route between Melbourne and Sydney, cuts straight through Victoria's northeast – an area that has become known as **Ned Kelly Country**. **Benalla** and **Glenrowan** (where he was finally seized after a bloody shoot-out) all have traces of the masked bushranger's activities, with Glenrowan wholeheartedly cashing in on his fame. Further north **Wangarrata** is a sizeable town known for its jazz festival and lively nightlife. **Rutherglen**, right up against the state border, is Victoria's oldest established wine-producing region while the tiny **Chiltern** is a sleepy town nearby, where not much has changed in the last 150 years. Heading east, the picturesque **Beechworth** is rich in history and increases in popularity every year with beautiful streetscapes, haunting attractions and famous bakery. **Bushwalking** and **mountain biking** in the Alpine region are most easily organized through outdoor tour operators such as the South Australia–based Ecotrek Bogong Jack Adventures (Ⓣ08/8383 7198, Ⓦwww.ecotrek.com.au).

V/Line runs several **train and bus routes** through the northeast. For bookings and up-to-date timetables call Ⓣ13 61 96 or go to Ⓦwww.vline.com.au.

The Hume Highway and Kelly Country

SEYMOUR is the first major stop on the Hume Highway out of Melbourne; an important train interchange, it's an uninspiring place for the visitor but the nearby **Tahbilk Winery** (Mon–Fri 9am–5pm, Sat & Sun 11am–5pm; Ⓦwww.tahbilk.com.au), 6km southwest, is worth exploring. The oldest continually operating winery and vineyard in Victoria; it opened in 1860, and its Shiraz and Marsanne vines have seen more than 140 harvests. The whitewashed buildings have been well preserved and there are extensive grounds to wander around.

Ninety-two kilometres northeast of Seymour, **BENALLA** is a civilized town on the lake of the same name, formed by the Broken River which runs through town and occasionally floods it. There's a rose festival held here every November, which transforms the town's picnic spots and gardens. The helpful **Benalla Visitor Information Centre**, 14 Mair St (daily 9am–5pm; Ⓣ03/5762 1749), has lots of pamphlets and information on the region, and can also book accommodation. In the same building, the **Costume and Pioneer Museum** (Ⓦwww.benallamuseum.org; $3) displays a collection of women's dresses from the 1920s, ball gowns and male fashion from the late eighteenth century until

Fruit picking in the Goulburn Valley

The rich plains of the **Goulburn Valley**, running through Seymour, Nagambie and Shepparton, yield much **fruit**, and it's a popular area for backpackers looking for **seasonal work**. The small city of **Shepparton** is the operations centre for the SPC and Ardmona canned-fruit companies, with peaches, pears, apples and plums tinned and exported worldwide. The Greater Shepparton Visitor Information Centre can point you in the right direction regarding **fruit-picking work**. They are located beside Victoria Park Lake in the south of town, at 534 Wyndham St on the Goulburn Valley Highway (daily 9am–5pm; Ⓣ1800 808 839, Ⓦwww.shepparton.vic.gov.au).

the early twentieth century, and also a range of Ned Kelly relics, including the green silk cummerbund he was awarded as a child for saving a friend from drowning, and which he proudly wore when captured. The **Benalla Art Gallery**, in a lovely setting across the lake (daily 10am–5pm; free), has a fine collection of early twentieth-century and contemporary Australian art.

If you want to stay, the well-equipped *Trekker's Rest*, 1km out of town on the Kilfeera Road (Ⓣ03/5762 3535, Ⓦwww.trekkersrest.com.au; ❷–❸) has cheap rooms and en-suite apartments, all with heating and air conditioning. Close to the train station the *North Eastern Hotel* (Ⓣ5762 3252, Ⓦwww.northeasternhotel.com; ❸) is an atmospheric old pub with a great lounge that has four simple guest rooms with en-suites and a pool. For something to eat during the day, there's the *Gallery Café* in a serene location at the Art Gallery by the lake (licensed; daily 10am–4pm), or in town, *Hides Bakery* at 111 Bridge St has been preparing excellent pies, salads and sandwiches since 1929. The *Benalla Health Food Shop* (Mon–Fri 9am–5pm, Sat 9am–1pm) at 67 Nunn St has excellent sandwiches and reasonable breakfasts, and for dinner *Café Raffety's*, 55 Nunn St (Ⓣ03/5762 4066), where a blackboard menu features daily specials.Further up on the price scale, *Georgina's*, 100 Bridge St (lunch Thurs & Fri, dinner Mon–Sat; Ⓣ03/5762 1334), is the best option for excellent contemporary Australian cuisine.

Glenrowan and Kelly's last stand

GLENROWAN, 29km on from Benalla, was the site of the Kelly Gang's last stand and you're never allowed to forget it. A gigantic effigy of Ned Kelly, in full iron-armour regalia, greets you as you enter town, and there are lots of other tawdry attractions along the highway, such as the Last Stand Show (daily 9.30am–4.30pm; every half-hour; 40min; $16; Ⓣ03/5766 2367), a "computerized animated theatre" using dummies shuffling around on cue to dramatize the story of the siege – your money's better spent elsewhere. The last stand itself took place in Siege Street near the train station. Along the rail lines north of town, a small stone monument marks the spot where Kelly forced railworkers to rip up a section of the track, to try to derail the trainful of troopers he had lured to the town – though visitors are asked to stay away, as the site is dangerous. Overlooking the town to the west is Mount Glenrowan, which the bushrangers used as a lookout.

More interesting and far better value than the Last Stand Show is Kate's Cottage and Ned Kelly Memorial (daily 9am–5.30pm; $4.50), a replica of the Kelly home. With its bare earth floor, bark roof and newspaper-lined walls, it speaks volumes of the deprivation that drove the family to crime. An evocative audiotape narrates Ned's story from childhood and is interspersed with folk songs inspired by his life. The original homestead, 9km west along Kelly Gap Road, is now nothing more than rubble and a brick chimney.

Wangaratta

The town of **WANGARATTA**, at the junction of the Ovens and King rivers, 16km from Glenrowan, is a convenient overnight stop between Sydney and Melbourne, but there are few reasons to linger unless you're here for the famous four-day **Wangaratta Festival of Jazz** (Ⓣ1800 803 944, Ⓦwww.wangaratta-jazz.org.au). Beginning on the Friday prior to the Melbourne Cup (the last weekend in Oct or the first weekend in Nov), this is one of the premier jazz events in the country, attracting national stars and international legends. The highway on either side of "Wang" is lined with motels, and the staff at the new

The Ned Kelly story

Even before **Ned Kelly** became widely known, folklore and ballads were popularizing the free-ranging bush outlaws as potent symbols of freedom and resistance to authority. Born in 1855, Ned Kelly was the son of an alcoholic rustler and a mother who sold illicit liquor. By the time he was eleven he was already in constant trouble with the police, who considered the whole family troublemakers; constables in the area were instructed to "endeavour, whenever the Kellys commit any paltry crime, to bring them to justice . . . the object [is] to take their prestige away from them".

Ned became the accomplice of the established bushranger **Harry Power**, and by his mid-teens had a string of warrants to his name. Ned's brother, Dan, was also wanted by the police – hearing that he had turned up at his mother's, a policeman set out, drunk and without a warrant, to arrest him. A scuffle ensued and the unsteady constable fell to the floor, hitting his head and allowing Dan to escape. The following day warrants were issued for the arrest of Ned (who was in New South Wales at the time) and Dan for attempted murder; their mother was sentenced to three years' imprisonment.

From this point on, the **Kelly gang**'s crime spree accelerated and, following the death of three constables in a shoot-out at Stringybark Creek, the biggest manhunt in Australia's history began, with a £1000 reward offered for the gang's apprehension. On December 9, 1878, they robbed the bank at Euroa, taking £2000, before moving on to Jerilderie in New South Wales, where another bank was robbed and Kelly penned the famous **Jerilderie Letter**, describing the "big, ugly, fat-necked, wombat-headed, big-bellied, magpie-legged, narrow-hipped, splay-footed sons of Irish bailiffs or English landlords which is better known as Officers of Justice or Victoria Police" who had forced him onto the wrong side of the law.

After a year on the run, the gang formulated a grand plan: they executed Aaron Sherritt, a police informer, in Sebastopol, thus attracting a trainbound posse from nearby Beechworth. This train was intended to be derailed at Glenrowan with as much bloodshed as possible before the gang moved on to rob the bank at Benalla and barter hostages for the release of Kelly's mother. In the event, having already sabotaged the tracks, the gang commandeered the Glenrowan Inn and, in a moment of drunken candour, Kelly detailed his ambush to a schoolteacher who escaped, managing to save the special train. As the armed troopers approached the inn, the gang donned the home-made iron armour that has since become their motif. In the ensuing gunfight Kelly's comrades were either killed or committed suicide as the inn was torched, while Ned himself was taken alive, tried by the same judge who had incarcerated his mother, and sentenced to hang.

Public sympathies lay strongly with Ned Kelly, and a crowd of five thousand gathered outside Melbourne Gaol on November 11, 1880, for his execution, believing that the 25-year-old bushranger would "die game". True to form, his last words are said to have been "Such is life".

△ Ned Kelly statue, Glenrowan

The Milawa Gourmet Region

The high-country area of Victoria – and in particular the small town of **MILAWA**, 15km southeast of Wangaratta on the Snow Road – is renowned amongst foodies for the excellent quality of its locally produced food and wine, so much so that it has been dubbed the **Milawa Gourmet Region** (Ⓦwww.milawagourmet.com), and even the most urban Melburnians have been known to make the two-hour trip just to stock up on dinner-party supplies.

If it's a tipple of something special you're after, try a tour of the **Brown Brothers Winery** (daily 9am–5pm; Ⓣ03/5720 5500, Ⓦwww.brown-brothers.com.au), situated about 2km from Milawa and clearly signposted; there's also a great café-restaurant here, the *Epicurean Centre* (daily 11am–3pm; Ⓣ03/5720 5540), which specializes in complementing Brown Brothers wines with unusual local foods. Back in the town, there's the **Milawa Cheese Factory** (daily 9am–5pm; Ⓣ03/5727 3589) on Factory Road, where you'll find award-winning cheeses and another excellent restaurant. At the crossroads nearby, **Milawa Mustards** (10am–5pm) offers seventeen home-made seed varieties, while on the Snow Road, **Whitehead's Mead** (daily 9am–5pm) sells a variety of meads made from Australian honey, a wide array of sticky, sweet honeys that put commercial brands to shame, candles and other honey products. The **Olive Shop** (Mon 10am–4pm, Thurs–Sun 10am–5pm) has locally grown olives and extra virgin olive oil. On the same road, **King River Café** (Wed–Sun 10am–late; Ⓣ03/5727 3461, Ⓦwww.kingrivercafe.com.au) is a popular eatery specializing in local wines and good food – the cakes and coffee are excellent, too.

Wangaratta Tourist Information, 100 Murphy St (daily 9am–5pm; Ⓣ1800 801 065), can book local tours and accommodation and give out stacks of leaflets about the area. They also have fast Internet access for $2 per 30 minutes.

There's a vast range of **accommodation** in town. Good choices include the *Pinsent Hotel* (Ⓣ5721 2183; ❸) at 20 Reid St, a renovated country pub-cum-bistro with reasonable double rooms, and the modern *Parkview Sundowner*, 56 Ryley St (Ⓣ03/5721 5655, Ⓦwww.parkviewmotorinn.com.au; ❹), which has wifi, cable and free videos for **food**, *Scribbler's Café* (Mon–Sat 8am–5.30pm, Sun from 9am) at 66 Reid St, serves good cakes and lunchtime fodder, as does the *Yipee Bean Café* (10am–5pm Mon–Fri, 10am–3pm Sat) at 76 Ovens St. For dinner, great-value food and drinks can be found at the *Wangarrata RSL* on Victoria Parade (open lunch and dinner daily) while the *Indian Tandoor Restaurant* (5–11pm daily) at 54 Ryley St packs them in most nights. For those seeking nightlife, the *Grand Central* at 80 Murphy St and the *Riva Bar* at 40 Faithful St fill up on weekends. Out of town, the *Boorhaman Hotel*, a small country pub with an award-winning **microbrewery**, is worth a detour: they serve hearty country tucker, washed down with a lager, dark ale, or wheat beer produced by its Buffalo Brewery. It's on Boorhaman Road, 16km north of Wangaratta towards the Murray Valley Highway – call Ⓣ03/5726 9215 for further directions.

Beechworth

Thirty-five kilometres east of Wangaratta, off the Ovens Highway (also known as the Great Alpine Road), is **BEECHWORTH**, once the centre of the rich **Ovens gold-mining region**. Sited picturesquely in the foothills of the Victorian Alps, the entire town has been acknowledged by the National Trust as being of historic significance, and the town and surrounding area have been designated a **Historic Park** by the Department of Sustainability and Environment. The **visitor information centre** is located in the fine, old shire office at 103 Ford St (daily

9am–5pm; ⓣ1300 366 321, ⓦwww.beechworthonline.com.au), and can book accommodation and tours as well as provide you with pamphlets on places of interest, including the Gorge Scenic Drive (see below). There is expensive Internet access at the *Green Gekko* at 78 Ford St ($6 for 15mins).

As is true in so many other towns in the northeast, Beechworth is rich in **Ned Kelly** history. The **government buildings** on Ford Street house the imposing HM Training Prison, where he and his mother were incarcerated, and the **courthouse** (daily 9am–5pm; $5) where his trial was held. Opposite, underneath the town hall, is the grim cell where he was imprisoned as a teenager (daily 10am–4pm; free). Other sights of interest in town include the **Burke Museum** on Loch Street (daily 10am–5pm; $5), dedicated to the explorer Robert O'Hara Burke, one-time superintendent of police in Beechworth, who perished with William John Wills on their historic journey from Melbourne to the Gulf of Carpentaria (see box on p.514).

The five-kilometre, one-way route of the **Gorge Scenic Drive** begins at Sydney Road and ends at Bridge Street, along the western edge of the town. It includes the famous Spring and Reid creeks, which supported eight thousand diggers in 1852, and an old storehouse for blasting powder known as the powder magazine, as well as natural features such as Flat Rock, Telegraph Rock and Woolshed Falls.

Practicalities

V/Line has a **bus service** from Wangaratta to Beechworth and an additional service to Bright via Beechworth. Call V/Line on ⓣ13 61 96 or consult ⓦwww.vline.com.au for the latest information. During school terms Beechworth Buslines has a service twice daily (ⓣ03/5728 2182; Mon–Fri) from Beechworth to Albury and Wodonga.

Accommodation

Armour Inn Motel 1 Camp St ⓣ03/5728 1466, ⓦwww.armour-motor-inn.com.au. Central, comfortable rooms, with pool and cable TV. ❺

Freeman on Ford 97 Ford St ⓣ03/5728 2371, ⓦwww.freemononford.com.au. Best option in town for those who can afford it. Has five beautifully decorated rooms in traditional Victorian style right in the heart of town. ❻

Old Priory Priory Lane St ⓣ03/5728 1024, ⓦwww.oldpriory.com.au. Reasonably priced singles are the real drawing card to this historic B&B. If you want peace and quiet, it's best to come at the weekend, when the school groups have gone. ❸

Rose Cottage 42 Camp St ⓣ03/5750 1069, ⓦwww.hotkey.net.au/~rose-cot/. Central, good-value B&B with equal doses of history and elegance. ❹

Tanswell's Commercial Hotel 50 Ford St ⓣ03/5728 1480. Beautiful old building on the town's main strip that offers traditional pub accommodation with reasonable double rooms (shared facilities). Has a somewhat haunted feel to it, which some may enjoy. ❸

Eating

For **food**, try the *Beechworth Bakery*, 27 Camp St (daily 6am–7pm). It's famous all over Australia for its delicious pies, bread, cakes and pastries, and on sunny days you can have breakfast on the balcony. Just starting to become famous is the *Bridge Road Brewery* situated in an old coach-house behind the *Tanswell Commercial Hotel*, which churns out a variety of fantastic ales and food to match (Mon–Sat 11am–5pm, Sun noon–11pm). The *Green Gekko* (9am–5pm daily) at 78 Ford St is a great little café with an excellent garden area out the back, serving big breakfasts and gluten-free Thai-influenced lunches. The stately *Bank Restaurant*, in the Bank of Australia building at 86 Ford St (licensed; daily from 6pm; Sat & Sun 9.30am–noon; ⓣ03/5728 2223) offers à la carte dining with a contempory Australian menu.

Chiltern

CHILTERN, a sleepy former gold-mining centre with a well-preserved, mid-nineteenth-century streetscape, lies just off the Hume Highway about 40km from Wangaratta. There is a small community-run tourism centre at 30 Main Rd (daily 9.30–4.30pm; ⓣ03/5726 1611) which stocks the *Chiltern Touring Guide* brochure, explaining the nearby local landmarks and history of the area. For refreshment, the *Telegraph Hotel* (daily lunch and dinner) on Conness Street serves up cheap pub grub for around $10, yet most head across the road to the *Mulberry Tree Tearooms*, which also offers pleasant B&B accommodation (ⓣ03/5726 1277; ❹).

Rutherglen

RUTHERGLEN, 18km west of Chiltern and 32km west of Wodonga on the Murray River Highway, is at the heart of Victoria's oldest wine-producing region, renowned for its excellent fortified wines, Rutherglen Muscat and Tokay. Nineteen **wineries** are situated in the area, most of them third- or fourth-generation establishments with cellars full of character. The weather partly accounts for the quality of Rutherglen's fortified wines: the long, mild autumns allow the grapes to stay on the vines for longer, producing higher levels of sugar in the fruit. All the wineries are open for free tastings and cellar-door sales (Mon–Sat 10am–5pm; Sun hours differ from place to place).

The **Wine Experience Centre** at 57 Main St (daily 9am–5pm; ⓣ1800 622 871) is local history museum, shop, café and visitor information centre all in one – it has informative displays about the goldrush and agricultural history of the district, including wine making. The shop sells local wines and arts and crafts, and there are stacks of brochures, including the informative *Rutherglen Touring Guide and Map* published by the wine makers of Rutherglen. They also rent mountain bikes ($30/day). On the Queen's Birthday weekend in June the town hosts the **Winery Walkabout** – one of Australia's biggest wine-tasting festivals, when the new season's releases are presented to the public. Another festive event, the **Tastes of Rutherglen**, is held over the Victorian Labour Day weekend in mid-March, and sees some of the best local restaurants guest-starring at the wineries.

Practicalities

Rutherglen is a popular weekend getaway from Melbourne, so **accommodation** can be hard to find at that time; during the week you'll have no problem. Right in the centre of town, you can't miss the 150-year-old *Victoria Hotel* at 90 Main St (ⓣ03/6032 8610; ❸) which has standard doubles, some with en suite. A more modern option is the *Poachers Paradise Hotel Motel*, 97 Murray St (ⓣ02/6032 7373, ⓦwww.poachersparadise.com.au; ❹), with ten motel units with air conditioning and the usual mod cons; two with a spa bath are tucked away behind the 1860s hotel, whose bistro serves breakfast and hearty pub grub for lunch and dinner daily. *The Walkabout Motel*, Murray Valley Highway (ⓣ02/6032 9572, ⓦwww.walkaboutmotel.com.au; ❹), offers similar standards. If you can afford it, the *Avine* (ⓣ0409414356, ⓦwww.avine.com.au; ❻–❼), a beautifully restored home from the 1950s nestled within landscaped gardens, is considered one of the best options in town.

Parker Pies (open daily for lunch and dinner) at 88 Main St is an award-winning bakery and licensed **café** serving a myriad of excellent pies, while *Tuileries Restaurant* (ⓣ03/6032 9033; from 6.30pm daily) on Drummond Street has an excellent range of local wines and highly recommended Australian cuisine. For a great beer head to the *Bintara Brewery* (11am–6pm daily) on Drummond Street, where for $10 you can sample all their beers with some light snacks thrown in.

The Victorian Alps

The **VICTORIAN ALPS**, the southern extension of the Great Dividing Range, bear little resemblance to their European counterparts; they're too gentle, too rounded, and above all too low to offer really great **skiing**. Nonetheless in July and August there is usually plenty of snow, and the resorts are packed out. Most people come here for the downhill skiing, though the **cross-country skiing**, which is rapidly growing in popularity, is excellent: **Lake Mountain**, 21km from Marysville, is the region's premier cross-country destination. **Snowboarding** was first encouraged at Mount Hotham and is now firmly established everywhere. **Falls Creek, Mount Hotham** and **Mount Buller** are the largest and most commercial skiing areas, particularly the last which is within easy reach of Melbourne; smaller resorts such as **Mount Baw Baw** are more suited to beginners.

In summer, when the wild flowers are in bloom, the alps are ideal **bushwalking** territory with most of the high mountains (and the ski resorts) contained within the vast **Alpine National Park**. The most famous of the walks is the four-hundred-kilometre **Alpine Trail**, which begins in Baw Baw National Park, near Walhalla in Gippsland, and follows the ridges all the way to Mount Kosciuszko in the Snowy Mountains of New South Wales. If you are doing any serious bushwalking, you'll need to be properly equipped. Water can be hard to find, and the weather can change suddenly and unexpectedly: even in summer it can get freezing cold up here, especially at night. After prolonged dry spells, **bushfires** can also pose a very real threat, as was the case in 2003 and early 2007 when roads were blocked off, while bushland and farms were burnt.

Mansfield and **Bright** are good bases for exploration of the Alps, and are great places to unwind. In summer the ski resorts can be ugly and only half the facilities are open, but there are often great bargains to be had on rooms. If you're **driving**, you'll need snow chains in winter (they're compulsory in many parts), and you should heed local advice before venturing off the main roads.

Mansfield and Merrijig

MANSFIELD is located at the junction of the Maroondah and Midland highways, just a few kilometres north of Lake Eildon, 140km east of Seymour and 63km south of Benalla. As the main approach to Mount Buller, it's a lively place with good pubs, restaurants and a cinema. The annual highlight is the **Mountain High Country Festival** in early November, which begins the weekend prior to the Melbourne Cup; activities include a picnic race known as the "Melbourne Cup of the Bush". In the middle of April hundreds of hot-air-balloon pilots flock here for the three-day **Mansfield Balloon Festival**.

V/Line has a year-round bus service from Melbourne to Mansfield. Call V/Line on ⓣ13 61 96 or consult ⓦwww.vline.com.au for the latest information. The helpful **Mansfield Visitor Information Centre** on the Maroondah Highway (daily 9am–5pm; ⓣ03/5775 1464 or 1800 060 686 for accommodation bookings, ⓦwww.mansfield-mtbuller.com.au), has complete information on all sights and activities, including skiing and walks in the surrounding country. Out of the snow season, you have a choice of horse riding, hiking, climbing, abseiling, hang-gliding, rafting, canoeing or 4WD tours. Among the many local outfits are Stirling Experience (Ⓣ03/5775 3541, Ⓦwww.stirling.au.com) and Alpine 4WD Tours (Ⓣ03/5777 3709) for 4WD tours around Mount Buller (see below) and Mount Stirling.

The *Alzburg Inn Resort*, 39 Malcolm St (Ⓣ1800 033 023, Ⓦwww.alzburg.com.au; ❸–❺), is a resort **hotel** with all mod cons, popular with skiers, while the neat and friendly *Mansfield Traveller's Lodge*, 116 High St (Ⓣ03/5775 1800, Ⓦwww.mansfieldtravellodge.com; dorm bed $23, rooms ❹), has motel rooms and a good backpackers' **hostel** in a separate building next door. For a bit of old-world charm the *Tavistock House* (Ⓣ03/5775 1024, Ⓦwww.tavistockhouse.com.au; ❺) at the corner of High and Highett streets, is a fully renovated, colonial-style house in the centre of town. Directly across the road is the *Delatite Hotel* (Ⓣ03/5775 2004, Ⓦwww.mansfieldonline.com.au/delatitehotel.html; ❸), a true country pub with clean rooms, some with en-suite.

Merrijig

The small town of **MERRIJIG**, a little under halfway to Mount Buller from Mansfield, is largely responsible for the great number of **riding** outfits in the area. The breathtaking high-country scenery nearby was used as the location for the 1982 film *The Man from Snowy River*, and visitors have been trying to live out their fantasies ever since. If you want to combine riding with lodge **accommodation**, try *Merrijig Lodge and Trail Rides*, Mount Buller Road (Ⓣ03/5777 5590, Ⓦwww.merrijiglodge.com.au; ❷). The *Willawong Bed & Breakfast and Cottage* at Lot 12, Mount Buller Road, Merrijig (Ⓣ03/5777 5750, Ⓦwww.willawongbnb.com.au; B&B ❹, cottage ❺) offers Bavarian-style accommodation in a gorgeous wooden house and a separate cottage in a lovely garden at the foot of the Alps.

Mount Buller

To reach **MOUNT BULLER ALPINE VILLAGE**, 48km from Mansfield, you ascend gradually upwards on the smooth, sealed Summit Road. With 7000 beds, 24 modern ski-lifts and 80km of runs, the village has the greatest capacity of any Australian ski-resort. In **winter**, during the ski season, Mansfield Mt Buller High Country Reservations books **accommodation** and dispenses **information** about all things snow-related (Ⓣ1800 039 049, Ⓦwww.mtbuller.com.au); in summer, call the Mansfield Visitor Information Centre on Ⓣ03/5775 1464 or Ⓦwww.mansfield-mtbuller.com.au. Most accommodation options also have **restaurants** on the premises, otherwise the Village Square has some decent options, though with inflated prices.

Accommodation

Andres at Buller Hotel Cobbler Lane Ⓣ03/5777 6966, Ⓦwww.andresatbuller.com. The first B&B built in the area is still the best, mirroring the kind of accommodation you'd more likely see in the French Alps (Andre's home country). Every luxury is awarded including stunning views, but it comes at a price. Open all year round. ❽

Arlberg Hotel 53 Summit Rd Ⓣ03/5777 6260, Ⓦwww.arlberg.com.au. Huge property with variety of rooms and six- to eight-bed self-contained apartments. Also has variety of restaurants for most budgets. Summer ❻, winter ❼

Duck Inn 18 Goal Post Rd Ⓣ03/5777 6326, Ⓦwww.duckinnmtbuller.com. Cosy boutique hotel that has regular rooms as well as lodge-style accommodation with bunk beds. Cooked breakfast included in price. Also has an excellent restaurant on the premises (*Drakes*). Rooms ❺, lodge ❸

Monash Alpine Lodge 84 Stirling Rd Ⓣ03/5777 6577, Ⓦwww.sport.monash.edu.au/alpine-lodge.html. Operated by Monash University (but anyone can stay), this two-storey wooden lodge has standard facilities with slightly cramped dorms, kitchen and a good living area. Open Jun–Sept. Dorms $60.

Skiing practicalities

The official start of the **ski season** is the Queen's Birthday long weekend in June (though there may not be enough snow cover until August), lasting through to October. Day-trip or weekend **packages** are the best way to go, and are far cheaper than trying to do it yourself. The best value for money are trips organized by the *Alzburg Inn Resort* at Mansfield (ⓣ1800 033 023, ⓦwww.alzburg.com.au). The day-tours leave Melbourne at 4am and arrive at Mount Buller at about 9am, giving the opportunity for a full day's skiing ($150, including entrance fees, a limited lift pass and a two-hour beginner's ski lesson or, for more advanced skiers, an Unlimited Day Lift Ticket); the 2 days/1 night package includes accommodation at the *Alzburg Inn* (from $230). It's also worth checking out the area around Hardware Street in Melbourne, where such companies as Auski at no. 9 (ⓣ03/9670 1412), and Mountain Designs at 373 Little Bourke St (ⓣ03/9670 3354) can advise on skiing conditions at the resorts, and sell or rent equipment.

During the snow season, an entry fee of $20–30 per car applies, depending on the resort. For **weather** and snow conditions, call the **Victorian Snow Reports Line** (ⓣ1902 240 523; 55c per min). For accommodation, phone the central reservation hotlines of each mountain resort. The free *Australian Alpine News* is available at the visitor information centre in Melbourne as well as in the Alpine region. As a rough guide to **costs**, a lift ticket at Mount Buller is $92 per day, while **lessons** cost $88 for beginners (1-day limited lift and a 2hr lesson) and $124 for lower intermediate (1-day lift and a 3hr lesson). Full equipment rental is about $65 per day.

During the season, Mansfield–Mount Buller Bus Lines, 133 High St, Mansfield (ⓣ03/5775 2606, ⓦwwww.buslines.com.au/mmbl/), operates a **ski transport service** to Mount Buller eight times a day. In Bright, Adina Ski Hire, 15 Ireland St (ⓣ03/5755 1177, ⓦwww.adina.com.au), and Bright Ski Centre, 22 Ireland St (ⓣ03/5755 1093, ⓦwww.brightskicentre.com.au), rent out skiing and snowboarding equipment, offer package deals including off-mountain accommodation and transport to Mount Hotham, and have up-to-date snow reports and information on road conditions. There's no transport to Mount Buffalo.

YHA Lodge The Avenue ⓣ03/5777 6181, ⓔmountbuller@yhavic.org.au. Unbeatable location right in the centre of the village, which has dorm rooms, large living areas and suitable kitchen. Open June–August; dorms $58. Advance booking (available from May 1) is essential. Enquire about transport, accommodation and ski/snowboard hire packages.

Bright

BRIGHT is at the centre of the picturesque Ovens Valley, between Mount Buffalo and Mount Beauty about 75km southeast of Wangaratta on the Ovens Highway. It began life as a gold-mining town in the 1850s and today still has a faintly elegant air, with tall European trees lining the main street and filling the parks. A clear stream flows through Centennial Park, opposite the tourist information centre, and in autumn the glorious colours of the changing leaves make for a very un-Australian scene.

As the ski fields of Mount Hotham, Mount Buffalo and Falls Creek are less than an hour's drive away, the town is popular as a **ski base** in winter. In summer **outdoor activities** are on offer – such as paragliding, hang-gliding, bushwalking, horse riding and cycling. Alpine Paragliding, 6 Ireland St (ⓣ03/5755 1753, ⓦwww.alpineparagliding.com), organizes tandem flights for novices, and introductory and full courses leading to a licence. You could also take to the air in a powered hang-glider from Bright Micro-Lights (ⓣ03/5750 1555) located at 22a Ashwood Ave or with the Eagle School of Micro-Lighting and Hang Gliding

(Ⓣ03/5750 1174, Ⓦwww.eagleschool.com.au), which also does very enjoyable instructor-accompanied tandem flights.

For a change of pace, visit **Boynton's Winery Café** (daily 10am–5pm; Ⓣ03/5756 2730, Ⓦwww.boynton.com.au), 10km northwest of Bright at Porepunkah, on the northeast slopes of the Ovens River Valley. Enjoy the spectacular views of Mount Buffalo while sampling a house wine – they specialize in cool-climate wines. In the summer months they open a café with Mediterranean-inspired cuisine. Alternatively, head south to nearby **Wandiligong**, a beautiful village entirely owned by the National Trust, where you'll find the *Wandiligong Café* and **maze** (Wed–Sun 10am–5pm; Ⓦwww.wandimaze.com.au; $7). The hedge maze itself is a lot of fun but the café, serving salads, freshly squeezed juices and home-made treats, and set in a tranquil garden at the end of a six-kilometre bushwalk from Bright, is a truly wonderful find.

Practicalities

V/Line operates a **bus** service to Bright from Wangaratta. Bright Tourist Information Centre, at 119 Gavan St (daily 9am–5pm; Ⓣ03/5755 2275), has information on what's happening around town and also books accommodation. There's also an excellent Internet café in the same building.

To **get around**, you can rent a mountain bike from Cyclepath, 74 Gavan St (Ⓣ03/5750 1442, Ⓦwww.cyclepath.com.au; from $24 a day) – which also operates biking tours. The new **Alpine Visitor Information Centre** in **Myrtleford** dispenses all sorts of information about the entire Alpine region from Wangaratta to Gippsland and books accommodation too (daily 9am–5pm; Ⓣ1800 991 044); next door the *Alpine Enoteca*, a wine bar-café-restaurant, showcases regional produce and is open daily from 9am, Thursday to Sunday until late; for bookings phone Ⓣ03/5752 1155.

Accommodation

Alpine Hotel 7 Anderson St Ⓣ03/5755 1366. Charming century-old place which is the focal point of town, with a rowdy bar, good-value bistro meals and excellent breakfasts; the back bar has bands on Fri night, and outside there's a sunny beer garden. ❸

Bright Hikers Backpackers 4 Ireland St Ⓣ03/5750 1244, Ⓦwww.brighthikers.com.au. One of the best budget places to stay, right in the centre of town. Its wide range of facilities includes a games room, Internet, and a great lounge and balcony where travellers like to socialize. Dorms $25, rooms ❸

The Buckland McCormacks Lane, Buckland Valley Ⓣ03/5755 2280, Ⓦwww.thebuckland.com.au. Situated 12km out of town, this eco-oasis has four studio houses with first-class amenities in a completely relaxing rural setting. Not cheap, but popular with the weekend getaway crowd. ❼

Coach House Inn 100 Gavan St Ⓣ1800 813 992, Ⓦwww.coachhousebright.com.au. Medium-priced motel opposite the tourism office that has spacious rooms and a bit of character. Great communal BBQ gazebo area. ❹

Elm Lodge Holiday Motel 2 Wood St Ⓣ1800 245 845, Ⓕ03/5755 2206. Good-value and centrally located motel with a beautiful garden and a pool. Evening meals available. ❹

Eucalypt Mist B&B 125A Delany Ave. Ⓣ03/5755 1336. Charming and comfortable house nestled amongst the trees teaming with birdlife, where getting privacy is not a problem. ❺

Riverside Holiday Park 4–10 Toorak Rd Ⓣ03/5755 1118, Ⓦwww.riversideholidaypark.com.au. Great riverside location in the heart of town, that offers good-value cabins and holiday units that sleep up to 4 people. Also has wireless Internet coverage through the park. Cabins and units ❹

Eating

Bright Brewery Great Alpine Rd (next to tourism office). New kid on the block that is attracting the crowds with their multi-award-winning beers, a well-priced menu (around $15 for mains) and relaxed outdoor setting. Daily noon–9pm.

Riverdeck Cafe Behind tourism office. Sells great deli sandwiches and hearty breakfast with a good outdoor area looking towards the river. Daily 9am–5pm.

Sasha's of Bright 2D Anderson St ⓣ03/5750 1711. The Czech owner and chef cooks mainly hearty Central European fare (around $30 for mains), and does it well. This is the place to come for Hungarian goulash, smoked pork neck with sauerkraut or crispy skinned duck. Daily 6pm–late; licensed.

Simone's 98 Gavan St ⓣ03/5755 2266. One of the top Italian restaurants in Victoria; given the quality of the cooking the prices are very reasonable. Tues–Sat 6.30pm–late.

Sweet Retreat 12A Barnard St. Strangely this place sells the best coffee in town, despite primarily being a chocolate shop. Mon–Thurs 9.30am–5.30pm, Fri–Sun 9.30am–9.30pm.

Tin Dog Café & Pizzeria 94 Gavan St. Casual family restaurant known for their gourmet pizzas. Wed–Mon 6pm–late.

Mount Hotham and Dinner Plain

Heading southeast out of Bright on the Great Alpine Road, it's 18km to **HARRIETVILLE**, tucked just below **Mount Hotham** and Mount Feathertop. Originally a gold-mining town, it's now a pretty little village of wide, tree-lined streets, and is also a popular skiing base: there are outlets to rent skis and chains, a seasonal shuttle-bus service up to the resorts, and several places to stay and eat. Beyond Harrietville, it's a steep ascent to Mount Hotham in the Alpine National Park, the "powder snow capital of Australia". Because this is the state's highest ski area, the snow here can be marginally less sticky than elsewhere. **Dinner Plain**, a resort village 8km from the summit and about 1500m above sea level, has much more of a cosy, alpine-village feel – complete with architect-designed timber houses that are meant to resemble cattlemen's mountain huts – than the somewhat unsightly Hotham resort. With 15km of groomed cross-country trails around the village and an 11km trail leading to Mount Hotham, Dinner Plain is really the domain of cross-country skiers, but a regular shuttle-bus ferries downhill skiers to Mount Hotham. Victorian **snowboarding** started at Hotham so there are lots of special facilities here, equipment rental and lessons. During the ski season, tractor-driven carts ferry you around the village and to the start of cross-country trails and skiing areas

△ Skiing on Mount Hotham, Victorian Alps

(all day until late; free), and helicopter shuttle-flights in winter link Mount Hotham with Falls Creek, only a few minutes away by air (about $99 return) where you can ski or snowboard on the same lift pass. Following the establishment of a fully fledged airport at Horsehair Plain, 20km south of Mount Hotham where seventy-seater jets from Melbourne and Sydney can land, it's now easier than ever to get to Hotham and surrounding areas.

A few centres handle bookings for the mainly lodge-style **accommodation**: Mount Hotham Reservation Centre (ⓣ1800 354 555, ⓦwww.hotham.com.au); Alpine Accommodation (ⓣ1800 246 462, ⓦwww.skihotham.com.au); and Dinner Plain Central Reservations (ⓣ1800 670 019, ⓦwww.dinnerplain.com). For general information about Dinner Plain, go to ⓦwww.visitdinnerplain.com.

Falls Creek

Thirty kilometres east of Bright, in the Upper Kiewa Valley, the town of **Mount Beauty** lies at the base of the state's highest peak, Mount Bogong (1986m). **FALLS CREEK**, 32km further along, on the edge of the Bogong High Plains, has a much more villagey feel than its sister resort at Mount Hotham, despite being Victoria's largest alpine resort. It also has probably Victoria's **best skiing**, with the largest snow-making system in Victoria to supplement any shortage of the real stuff, a wide variety of downhill pistes, and good cross-country trails. **Snowboarding** is really big here, too, and in addition there are rides on snowmobiles and snowbikes and a tube park for snowtubing. For **accommodation** bookings and information, contact Falls Creek Central Reservations (ⓣ1800 033 079, ⓦwww.fallscreek.com.au) or ask at the **Mount Beauty Visitor Information Centre** (daily 9am–5pm; ⓣ1800 808 277, ⓦwww.mtbeauty.com) on the Kiewa Valley Highway in the town. The budget-conscious would do best to stay in Mount Beauty and travel to Falls Creek for their skiing: enquire about packages at the Mount Beauty Accommodation Service (ⓣ03/5754 1267). Accommodation options in the valley include *Mountain Creek Motel* in Tawonga (ⓣ03/5754 4247, ⓦwww.mountainreekmotel.com; motel units ❹); the wonderful *Braeview B&B* in Mount Beauty (ⓣ03/5754 4746, ⓦwww.braeview.com.au; ❺), which has two luxurious guest rooms, one self-contained studio apartment and a separate cottage, all in an established garden setting; and the super-fancy *Svarmisk Resort and Spa* (ⓣ03/5754 4544, ⓦwww.svarmisk.com.au; ❽), which is pure decadence if you have the money.

Many of the pubs, **restaurants** and lodges in Falls Creek stay open in summer: some of the best are *The Man Hotel* (Tues–Sun 5pm–late), a cosy pub with great gourmet pizzas on Telemark Street, and the *Milch Café Wine Bar* (daily noon–8pm) on Schuss Street.

Horse riding and other activities

Apart from **bushwalks**, nature lovers can join Alpine Nature Rambles for informative short walks, studying the alpine flora (ⓣ03/5758 3492, ⓦwww.rambles.com.au). Bogong Horseback Adventures (ⓣ03/5754 4849, ⓦwww.bogonghorse.com.au), a very professional and experienced **horse-riding** operator based on a farm, specializes in three- to seven-day **packhorse** tours across the high plains which they run from December until the end of April (from $900 per person). They also run two-hour ($70), three-hour ($80) and day-rides ($160 including lunch) through the Kiewa Valley and the lower levels of the Alpine National Park.

Another horse-riding outfit, Packer's High Country Trail Rides (ⓣ03/5159 7241, ⓦwww.dinnerplaintrailrides.com), operates from the small hamlet of

Anglers Rest, further south towards Omeo. Their rides range from one and a half hours ($80) to overnight treks (from $990), and they also offer cheap lodge accommodation and a cottage (④) at their farm, *The Willows*.

As for **festivals**, the entire village of Falls Creek, plus visitors, get together to celebrate "A Taste of Falls Creek" in mid-January.

Mount Buffalo National Park

Six kilometres northwest of Bright, back along the Ovens Highway, you can turn off into **Mount Buffalo National Park** ($9.90 per car in summer, $14.10 in winter), which encompasses a huge plateau around Mount Buffalo, and has a number of beautiful walking tracks. In early 2007, fire raced through the area, destroying a number of lodges and chalets and effectively closing the park. While it has since reopened, at the time of writing there was no "roofed" accommodation or eating places available. The best option is to consult the Bright tourist office on ⓣ03/5755 5159 or the Park Office on ⓣ03/5755 1466 for latest developments. Meanwhile, you can **camp** at Lake Catani in the summer months (Nov–April; booking essential on ⓣ03/5755 1466, or through Parks Victoria on ⓣ13 19 63).

Mount Baw Baw

The ski village at **MOUNT BAW BAW** near the edge of the Baw Baw National Park, is considerably south of all the resorts and is, strictly speaking, in Gippsland. It's a quiet little place, commanding magnificent views south over much of Gippsland and consisting mainly of private lodges (reservations on ⓣ1800 629 578). Otherwise, try the *Cascades Apartments* (ⓣ1800 229 229, ⓦwww.ski.com.au/cascadeapartments; ⑥) which can sleep up to ten people. The entry fee is $9.90 per vehicle per day. There are five ski lifts here, and a lift day-pass costs about $69, a much more reasonable price than at other resorts. As at Mount Buffalo, the ski runs are mainly for beginners and intermediates. In addition to downhill skiing and snowboarding, you can ski cross-country on 10km of groomed trails and snowtube at the Frantic Frog Super Tube Park. For more on Mount Baw Baw, see ⓦwww.mountbawbaw.com.au.

Transport to and from the mountain has improved, though it's still far from ideal: in winter, Jindivick Charter & Tours (ⓣ03/5628 5447 or 0428 285 286) provides a bus service on Fridays and Mondays from Warragul Station (65km south) to the resort ($45 return); they also run a luggage transport service from the day car-park to the lodges ($15). If you drive yourself, access is via Noojee, 48km west of Mount Baw Baw. You get there from Melbourne either on the northeastern route via Lilydale and Yarra Junction, or on the Princes Highway via Dandenong and Pakenham, turning off at Drouin. The road between Nojee and the resort is narrow, steep and winding. To make matters worse, there are lots of logging trucks thundering along, so take care.

Travel details

V/Line monopolizes transport within Victoria, with a comprehensive combination of train and bus services; Melbourne, Ballarat and Geelong (see p.884) are the main interchanges. Following are the main V/Line Victorian services; local buses are detailed in the text. Timetables are subject to frequent change – call V/Line on ⓣ13 61 96 or consult ⓦwww.vline.com.au for the latest information.

Trains

Melbourne to: Albury (5 daily; 3hr–3hr 40min); Bairnsdale (3 daily; 3hr 10min); 2hr–2hr 30min); Ballarat (15–19 daily; 1hr 30min); Benalla (5 daily; Bendigo (12–20 daily; 2hr); Castlemaine (12–20 daily; 1hr 35min); Colac (1–3 daily; 1hr 50min); Echuca (Fri & Sun 1 daily; 3hr 20min); Geelong (15–28 daily; 1hr); Sale (2–3 daily; 2hr 45min); Shepparton (2–3 daily; 2hr 15min); Swan Hill (2 daily; 4hr 10min); Wangaratta (5 daily; 2hr 30min–3hr); Warrnambool (1–3 daily; 3hr 10min).

Buses

Apollo Bay to: Geelong (2–3 daily; 2hr 30min); Lorne (2–3 daily; 1hr); Port Campbell (Mon, Wed, Fri only; 1hr 55min); Torquay (2–3 daily; 2hr); Twelve Apostles (Mon, Wed, Fri only; 1hr 25min); Warrnambool (Wed, Thurs, Fri only; 3hr 20min).
Bairnsdale to: Canberra (Capital Link 3 weekly; 6hr 30min) via Lakes Entrance (30min), Orbost (1hr 15min), Narooma/NSW (Sapphire Coast Link daily; 6hr) via Lakes Entrance (30min) and Orbost (1hr 15min).
Ballarat to: Bendigo (5 weekly; 2hr); Castlemaine (5 weekly; 1hr 30min); Daylesford (5 weekly; 45min); Geelong (3 daily; 1hr 25min); Hamilton (1–2 daily; 2hr 20min); Horsham (1–2 daily; 2hr 20min); Mildura (6 weekly; 7hr 35min); Mount Gambier (5 weekly; 3hr 30min); Warrnambool (5 weekly; 3hr).
Beechworth to: Bright (1–3 daily; 1hr); Wangaratta (1–4 daily; 30min).
Bendigo to: Echuca (2–3 daily; 1hr 20min); Geelong (5 weekly; 3hr 55min); Horsham (daily; 3hr 15min); Mildura (2 daily; 5hr 30min); Swan Hill (2 daily; 3hr 5min).
Bright to: Beechworth (1–2 daily; 1hr); Wangaratta (1–2 daily; 1hr 25min).
Castlemaine to: Ballarat (5 weekly; 1hr 30min); Maryborough (2–4 daily; 55min).
Echuca to: Albury (1–2 daily; 4hr 30min); Bendigo (2–3 daily; 1hr 20min); Melbourne (6–8 daily; 3hr); Mildura (4 weekly; 5hr 55min); Rutherglen (4 weekly; 3hr 40min–4hr 30min); Shepparton (4 weekly; 2hr 5min); Swan Hill (daily; 2hr 20min).
Foster (closest to Wilson's Promontory NP) to: Melbourne (daily; 2hr 40min).
Geelong to: Apollo Bay (2–3 daily; 2hr 55min) via Ballarat (2–4 daily; 1hr 25min); Ballarat (5 weekly 1hr 30min); Bendigo (5 weekly; 4hr); Daylesford (5 weekly; 2hr 15min); Castlemaine (5 weekly; 3hr); Lorne (2–3 daily; 1hr 50min); Maryborough (4 weekly; 3hr 5min); Mildura (6 weekly; 9hr); Torquay (2–3 daily; 45min); Warrnambool (Coastlink via Apollo Bay; Fri only; 7hr).
Halls Gap (Grampians) to: Stawell (1 daily; 35min).
Hamilton to: Ballarat (1–2 daily; 2hr 20min); Warrnambool (1–2 daily except Sat; 1hr 35min).
Horsham to: Ararat (3–4 daily; 1hr 35min); Ballarat (1–2 daily; 2hr 20min); Stawell (3–4 daily; 1hr 10min).
Lakes Entrance to: Bairnsdale (1–3 daily; 35min); Canberra (Capital Link 3 weekly; 6hr) via Orbost (45min) and Cann River (2hr 15min); Narooma/NSW (Sapphire Coast Link daily; 5hr 35min) via Orbost and Cann River.
Mansfield to: Melbourne (2 daily; 3hr); Mount Buller (snow season only; 6–8 daily; 1hr).
Maryborough to: Ballarat (6 weekly; 1hr); Castlemaine (1–4 daily; 55min).
Mildura to: Bendigo (1–2 daily; 5hr 30min); Ballarat (6 weekly; 7hr 40min); Geelong (6 weekly; 9hr); Swan Hill (1–3 daily; 2hr 30min–3hr).
Mount Beauty to: Wangaratta (3 weekly; 2hr 40min).
Mount Buller to: Mansfield (snow season only; 8 daily; 1hr).
Portland to: Mount Gambier (1–2 daily; 1hr 35min); Port Fairy (1–3 daily; 1hr); Warrnambool (1–3 daily; 1hr 30min).
Shepparton to: Albury (1–3 daily; 2hr 20min–3hr); Melbourne (1–2 daily; 3hr).
Stawell to: Ballarat (5 weekly; 1hr 40min); Halls Gap (Grampians; 1 daily; 35min); Horsham (3–4 daily; 1hr 10min).
Swan Hill to: Albury (1–2 daily; 5hr 45min–6hr 20min); Bendigo (1–3 daily; 2hr 40min); Echuca (1–2 daily; 2hr 20min); Mildura (1–2 daily; 2hr 30min–3hr).
Wangaratta to: Beechworth (2–3 daily; 30min); Bendigo (3 weekly; 3hr); Mount Beauty (2 weekly; 2hr 30min) via Bright (1hr 35min); Rutherglen (1 daily; 30min).
Warrnambool to: Apollo Bay (Mon, Wed, Fri only; 3hr 10min); Ballarat (5 weekly; 2hr 55min); Geelong (3 weekly; 7hr); Hamilton (1–2 daily except Sat; 1hr 40min); Mount Gambier (1–2 daily; 3hr); Port Fairy (1–4 daily; 40min); Portland (1–3 daily; 1hr 30min).

Flights

Mildura to: Melbourne (4–8 daily; 1hr 10min).
Portland to: Melbourne (1–3 daily; 40min).

Tasmania

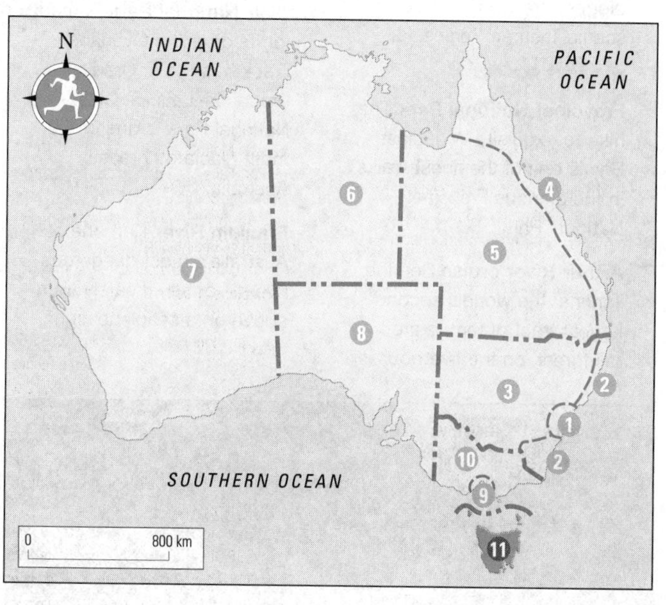
N
INDIAN OCEAN
PACIFIC OCEAN
SOUTHERN OCEAN
0
800 km
1
2
3
4
5
6
7
8
9
10
11

CHAPTER 11 Highlights

* **Salamanca Market** Lined with old stone warehouses and characterful old pubs, Hobart's Salamanca Place comes alive for its colourful open-air Saturday market. See p.989

* **Port Arthur** The infamous old penal settlement is the biggest draw on the wild, scenic Tasman Peninsula. See p.1011

* **Freycinet National Park** The hike to exquisite Wineglass Bay is one of the finest walks in the glorious Freycinet National Park. See p.1016

* **Arthur River cruise** See the Tarkine, the world's second-largest tract of temperate rainforest, on the five-hour Arthur River cruise. See p.1057

* **Gordon River cruise** A cruise up the dark, brown Gordon River is the best way to get a glimpse of the World Heritage–listed wilderness. See p.1065

* **Cradle Mountain–Lake St Clair National Park** Famed for its gruelling Overland Track bushwalk, Cradle Mountain–Lake St Clair National Park is one of the most glaciated areas in Australia. See p.1068–1072

* **Franklin River** Raft one of Australia's most dangerous rivers – or see it safely from above on a seaplane flight. See p.1071

△ Port Arthur

11

Tasmania

There's an otherworldly quality to **TASMANIA**, with its gothic landscape of rain clouds and brooding mountains. This was a prison island whose name, Van Diemen's Land, was so redolent with horror that when convict transport ended in 1852 it was immediately changed. Yet the island has another, friendlier side to it, too, with distances comprehensible to a European traveller – it's roughly the size of Ireland – and resonant echoes of England: cream teas, old-fashioned B&Bs and amiable, homespun people. In winter, when the grass is green, the gentle and cultivated midlands, with their rolling hills, dry stone walls and old stone villages, are reminiscent of England's West Country. Town names, too, invariably invoke the British Isles – Perth, Swansea, Brighton and Somerset among them. It's a "mainlander's" joke that Tasmania is twenty years behind, and it's true that in some ways it is very old-fashioned, a trait that is by turn charming and frustrating. However, things are changing fast: with the rise of its cool-climate wine industry, foodie accolades for its superb local produce used in a newly sophisticated café and restaurant scene, booming real estate and immigration, and cheaper and more frequent ferries and flights creating an increase in new and luxurious accommodation.

Tasmania is the closest point in Australia to the Antarctic Circle, and the west coast is windswept, wet and savage, bearing the full brunt of the Roaring Forties – and Australia's **whale-stranding** hot-spot. The southwest has wild rivers, impassable temperate rainforests, buttongrass plains, and glacially carved mountains and tarns that together form a vast World Heritage Area, crossed only by the Lyell Highway, providing some of the world's best wilderness walking and rafting. With forty percent of the island protected in parks and reserves, it's still one of the cleanest places on earth: a wilderness walk, breathing the fresh air and drinking freely from tannin-stained streams, is a genuinely bucolic experience.

A north–south axis divides the settled areas, with the two major cities, **Hobart**, the capital, in the south, and **Launceston** in the north. The **northwest coast**, facing the mainland across the Bass Strait, is the most densely populated region, the site of Tasmania's two smaller cities, **Devonport** (where the Bass Strait ferries dock) and **Burnie**. Tasmania's **central plateau**, with its thousands of lakes, is sparsely populated, mainly by weekenders in fishing shacks. The sheltered **east coast** is the place to go for sun and watersports activities; set against a backdrop of bush-clad hills, it has plenty of deserted beaches and is safe for swimming.

It rarely gets above 25°C in Tasmania, even at the height of summer, and the **weather** is notoriously changeable, particularly in the uplands, where it can sleet and snow at any time of year; the most stable month is February. Winter

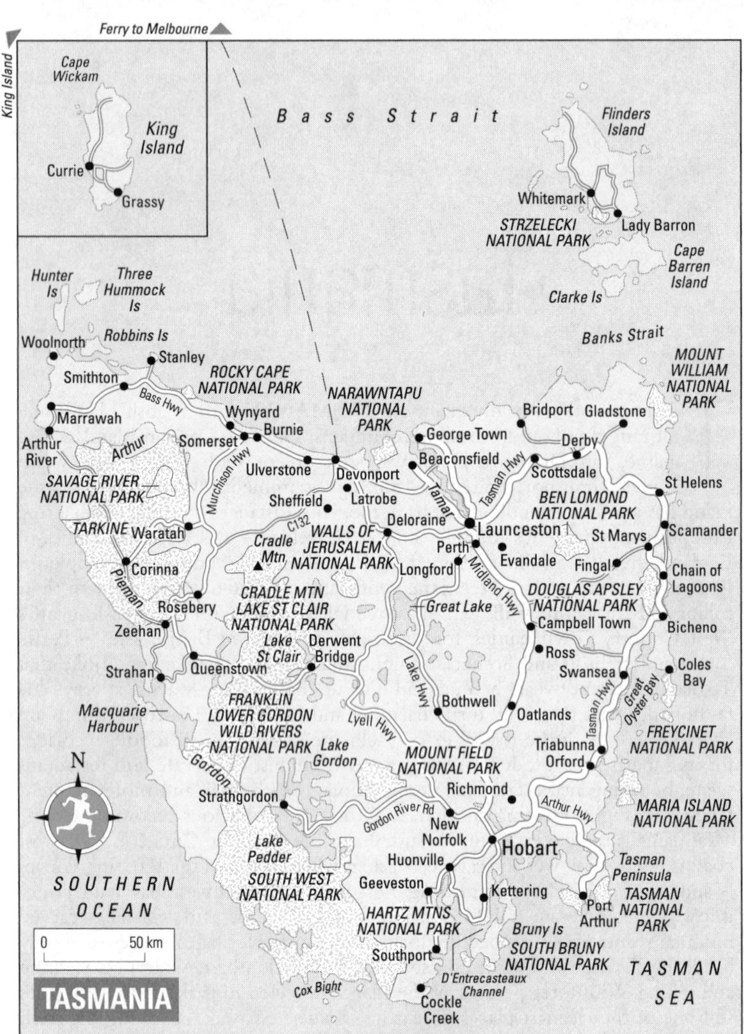

(June–Aug) is a cold time to visit unless you choose the more temperate east coast; wilderness walks are best left to the most experienced and well equipped at this time of year.

Some history

The Dutch navigator **Abel Tasman** sighted the west coast of the island in 1642. Landing a party on its east coast, he named it **Van Diemen's Land** in honour of the governor of the Dutch East Indies. Early maps show it connected to the mainland, and several eighteenth-century French and British navigators, including Bruny d'Entrecasteaux, William Bligh and James Cook – who claimed it for the British – did not prove otherwise. Matthew Flinders' discovery of the **Bass Strait** in 1798 reduced the journey to Sydney by a week. In 1803, after Nicholas Baudin's French expedition had been observed around the island's southern waters, it was decided to establish a second **colony** in Australia and Lieutenant David Bowen was dispatched to Van Diemen's Land, settling with a group of convicts on the banks of the Derwent River at Risdon Cove. In the same year, Lieutenant-Colonel John Collins set out from England with another group to settle the Port Phillip district of what would become Victoria; after a few months they gave up and crossed the Bass Strait to join Bowen's group. **Hobart Town** was founded in 1804 and the first **penal settlement** opened at Macquarie Harbour (Strahan) in 1821, followed by Maria Island and Port Arthur; they were mainly for those who had committed further offences while still prisoners on the mainland. Van Diemen's Land, with its harsh conditions and repressive, violent regime, became part of British folklore as a place of terror, a prison-island hell. Collins was Lieutenant-Governor of Van Diemen's Land until his death in 1810, but it is Lieutenant-Governor **George Arthur** (1824–36) who has the more prominent position in the island's history. His ideas were an influence on the prison settlement at Port Arthur and he was in charge at the time of the **Black Line**, the organized white militia used against the Aboriginal population.

Tasmania did not experience the postwar industrialization and immigration that transformed the mainland. A small and isolated state, it remains predominantly Anglo-Saxon in character, with an insular, often conservative, population. Its **natural resources** include forests and water, and the mountainous terrain and fast-flowing rivers meant that hydroelectricity schemes began early here, under the auspices of the Hydro Electricity Commission (HEC). The flooding of **Lake Pedder** in 1972 led to the formation of the **Wilderness Society**, a conservation organization whose successful **Franklin Blockade** in 1982 saved one of Tasmania's last wild rivers and spawned the Tasmanian Green Party, led by the famous environmental activist **Dr Bob Brown**. Often-bitter controversy over the best balance between conservation and exploitation of its natural resources still divides the state's population between "greenies" and "traditionalists", with both major political parties (Liberal Party and Australian Labour Party) supporting the practice of clearfelling areas of old growth forests (followed by incineration of the remnants and poisoning of grazing wildlife). Most wood taken from Tasmania's forests ends up as woodchips for export to Japanese paper manufacturers, with Tasmania the only state in Australia that woodchips its rainforests. Ongoing conservationist campaigns are aimed at stopping old-growth logging in the **Styx Valley** (p.1008) and the **Blue Tier** (p.1021) and preventing a pulp mill being built in the north of the state.

Tasmanian practicalities

Although it's small in Australian terms, make sure you give yourself enough time to see Tasmania; if you want to see only its cities, you need no more than a few days, but to get a flavour of the countryside – the great outdoors is the real reason to come here – a couple of weeks or longer is necessary. The Tasmanian Travel and Information Centre in Hobart (Ⓣ1300 655 145, Ⓦwww.tastravel.com.au) can provide **information** and also book all transport, tours and accommodation; their free information paper, *Tasmanian Travelways* (Ⓦwww.travelways.com.au), is extremely useful, filled with detailed, comprehensive information on accommodation, attractions, bus timetables, car rental, adventure tours and national parks. It can also be picked up at local tourist offices in Tasmania. For general tourist information, check out the government-funded Tourism Tasmania site Ⓦwww.discovertasmania.com.au. Available for purchase at tourist offices is the **See Tasmania Card** (3-day $149, 7-day $209, 10-day

The Aboriginal peoples of Tasmania

The attempted genocide of the **Aboriginal peoples of Tasmania** is one of the most tragic episodes of recent history. Ironically, if it were not for American and British sealers and whalers who had operated from the shores of Van Diemen's Land since 1793, abducting Aboriginal women and taking them to the Furneaux Islands in the Bass Strait as their slaves and mistresses, the Tasmanian Aborigines would have disappeared without trace. Until recently, it was stated in schoolbooks that the last Aboriginal Tasmanian was **Truganini**, who died at Oyster Cove, south of Hobart, in 1876. However, a strong Aboriginal movement has grown up in Tasmania in the last thirty years.

The Aboriginal people of Tasmania appear to have been **racially distinct** from those of the mainland, although many of their beliefs and rituals were similar. About twelve thousand years ago, the thawing of the last Ice Age brought rising ocean levels, which separated these people from the mainland and caused their genetic isolation; it's thought that on the mainland new cultures probably entered ten thousand years ago. This isolation was also evident in **cultural development**: they couldn't make fire but kept alight smouldering fire-sticks; their weapons were simpler – they didn't have boomerangs; and although seafood was a main source of food, eating scaly fish was taboo. In **appearance**, the men were startling, wearing their hair in long ringlets smeared with grease and red ochre, while women wore theirs closely shaved. To keep out the cold, they coated their bodies with a mixture of animal fat, ochre and charcoal; women often wore a kangaroo-skin cloak. Men decorated their bodies with linear scar patterns on their abdomens, arms and shoulders. Their **art** consisted of rock carvings of geometric designs, still to be seen in areas on the west and northwest coasts.

When the first **white settlement** was established in the early years of the nineteenth century there were reckoned to be about five thousand Aboriginal people in Tasmania, divided into nine main **tribes**. A tribe consisted of bands of forty to fifty people who lived in adjoining territory, shared the same language and culture, socialized, intermarried and – crucially – fought wars against other tribes. They also traded such items as stone tools, ochre and shell necklaces, and bands moved peaceably across neighbouring tribes' territory along well-defined routes at different times of the year to share resources: the inland Big River tribe, for example, would journey to the coast for sealing. Once they realized the white settlers were not going to "share" their resources

$279; Ⓦwww.seetasmaniacard.com), a passcard that provides entry to sixty tourist attractions.

It's easy to find **Internet access** in Tasmania, as many towns have a state-government-funded Online Access Centre. The Tasmanian Communities Online website (Ⓦwww.tco.asn.au) gives locations of all the 64 centres as well as access to town sites, often useful sources of information on local attractions and businesses.

Getting there

With so many airline companies offering competitive fares from the mainland to Tasmania, and the ferry company now with two ships running between Melbourne and Devonport, it's cheaper and easier to get to Tassie than it's ever been.

By ferry

If you've bought a car to travel around Australia, you'll naturally choose to go by ship, and it's also the most romantic way to arrive. From the long-established Port Melbourne departure point, it's a potentially rough, ten-hour trip across the Bass Strait on the TT Line *Spirit of Tasmania* **ferries** to Devonport (daily Port Melbourne and Devonport departing 9pm, arriving 7am; also day sailings daily mid-December

in this traditional exchange economy but were instead stealing the land, the nomadic people displayed a determination to defend it – by force, if necessary. Confrontation was inevitable, and by the 1820s the white population was in a frenzy of fear – though for every settler who died, twenty Aborigines met a similar fate. In 1828, Governor Arthur declared martial law, expelling all Aboriginal people from the settled districts and giving settlers what was, in practice, a licence to shoot on sight. Alarmed by these events, the British government planned to round up the remaining Aborigines and confine them to **Bruny Island**, south of Hobart Town. In 1830, a mass militia of three thousand settlers formed an armed human barrier, the **Black Line**, which was to sweep across the island, clearing Aborigines before them, in preparation for "resettlement".

The line failed; but unfortunately the final tactic was "divide and rule", in which the Aboriginal people themselves, with their superb tracking skills, were enlisted to help ensnare their tribal enemies. The 135 Aborigines who survived the Black Line were moved in 1834 to a makeshift settlement on Flinders Island. Within four years most of these people died of disease, or as a result of harsh conditions. In 1837, the 47 survivors were transferred to their final settlement at Oyster Cove, near Hobart, where – no longer a threat – they were often dressed up and paraded on official engagements. The skeleton of the last survivor, "Queen" Truganini, originally from Bruny Island, was displayed in the Tasmanian Museum until 1976, when her remains were finally cremated and scattered in the D'Entrecasteaux Channel, according to her final wishes.

The descendents of the original Aboriginal Tasmanians were given a voice with the establishment of the **Tasmanian Aboriginal Centre (TAC)** in the 1970s. The TAC's push for land rights has included the handing over of Wybalenna in Flinders Island and, in 2005, of the whole of Cape Barren Island, to its south. In the 1981 census, 2700 Tasmanians ticked the Aboriginal box; 16,000 did so in 2001. But this huge increase of people proclaiming Aboriginal heritage has ironically not pleased the TAC, whose sympathies lie with the long-documented and distinct Bass Strait communities. Many of those now identifying themselves as Aboriginal are from mainland Tasmania, but of these only descendents of Aborigines such as Fanny Cochrane (see p.988) and Dolly Dalrymple can produce documents that trace a genealogy back to the time of white settlement.

to mid-January departing 9am, arriving 7pm; bookings ⓣ13 20 10, enquiries ⓣ1800 634 906, ⓦwww.spiritoftasmania.com.au). Peak fares operate mid-December to late January, shoulder fares late January to April and September to mid-December, and off-peak fares May to September. On board, there are restaurants, bars and entertainment, and you can choose to sit up on reclining cruise seats (one way $123–160) or take a private en-suite cabin (pricier with portholes), ranging from basic twins (one way per person: $225–275) and four-bunk cabins ($202–230) to luxury cabins ($310–398). Meals are extra.

Book in advance in summer, especially if you want to take a vehicle: cars less than 2m in length cost (one way) $69, bike/motorbikes cost $7/$45. Cheaper Apex return fares (21-day advance purchase) are available.

By air

Prices are very competitive for **flights** to Tasmania from the mainland with Virgin Blue (ⓣ13 67 89, ⓦwww.virginblue.com.au), with direct flights from Melbourne and Sydney to Hobart or Launceston, and from Adelaide to Hobart. Check the website for "Happy Hour" specials (noon–1pm AEST) and other deals. Qantas' budget arm Jetstar (ⓣ13 15 38, ⓦwww.jetstar.com.au) has direct flights from Melbourne, Sydney and Brisbane to Hobart and Launceston – a typical fare is Melbourne to Launceston one way at $200, though check website for specials – while Rex Airlines (Ⓦwww.rex.com.au) fly from Melbourne to Burnie, as well as from Melbourne to King Island; for other flights to King and Flinders islands, see p.1041.

Qantas itself (Ⓣ13 13 13, Ⓦwww.qantas.com.au) also has pricier (more comfortable) direct flights from Melbourne and Sydney to Hobart, while QantasLink flies between Devonport and Melbourne. **Fly-drive packages**, which include accommodation, can be particularly good deals; ask at travel agents.

Getting around

With the vagaries of the public-transport bus system and the difficulties of using it to get to all those out-of-the-way wilderness places that make Tasmania so attractive as a destination, the trend for travellers in the last few years is to hire a car, or for the more intrepid to motorbike or cycle. There are several good-value **tours** aimed at independent travellers that will get you off the beaten track, and any number of **adventure expeditions** will provide transport from the cities as part of the deal (major tour and expedition operators are detailed in the box on opposite).

By bus

Six local **bus companies** and two charter services (detailed in the box below) reach most destinations on the island. You cannot use a mainland bus-pass with

Bus operators

Bicheno Coach Service Ⓣ03/6257 0293. Runs between Coles Bay and Bicheno, and also offers airport transfers.

Hobart Coaches Ⓣ03/6233 4232, Ⓦwww.hobartcoaches.com.au. Heads north out of Hobart to Richmond and New Norfolk, and south to Kingston, Snug, Kettering, Woodbridge and Cygnet.

Manion's Coaches Ⓣ03/6383 1221. Launceston to Rosevears, Beaconsfield and Beauty Point.

Maxwell's Ⓣ03/6492 1431. Provides a charter service, based on a minimum of four passengers, from Devonport and Launceston to and around the Cradle Mountain–Lake St Clair area and the Walls of Jerusalem National Park.

Tasmanian Tour Company Ⓣ1300 659878, Ⓦwww.tasmaniantourcompany.com.au. Bushwalking charter service from Devonport to Cradle Mountain, Frenchmans Cap and Walls of Jerusalem.

"Tasmania's Own" Redline Coaches Ⓣ03/6336 1446 or 1300 360 000, Ⓦwww.tasredline.com.au. The island's largest operator, referred to in the rest of the text as "Redline", offers frequent scheduled services between Hobart and Launceston via the east coast or direct via the Midland Highway, from Devonport to Hobart via Deloraine and Launceston, and along the northwest coast from Devonport to Burnie and on to Smithton and Stanley.

TassieLink Ⓣ03/6230 8900 or 1300 300 520, Ⓦwww.tassielink.com.au. Specializes in scheduled regional transport year-round and bushwalkers' "Wilderness Link" services for the South Coast Track and the Mount Anne Circuit from November to the end of March. Scheduled services run from Hobart to Devonport and Launceston; Hobart to Strahan via Lake St Clair and Queenstown; Hobart to Port Arthur; Hobart south to Dover; Hobart up the east coast to St Helens; Launceston to Bicheno on the east coast via St Marys; and Launceston to Strahan via Devonport, Cradle Mountain and Queenstown. Charters available on request.

any of these, and services are limited, often not running at weekends, especially on the east and west coasts; in winter and spring, services are even further reduced.

Buying a local **bus pass** can be one way of cutting costs, but study timetables carefully before you buy. Redline's **Tassie Pass** comes in 7-, 10-, 14- and 21-day versions ($135/$160/$185/$219) starting from the first day of use. TassieLink's **Explorer Bus Pass** has several formats: a seven-day pass valid for travel over ten days $172, ten-day for fifteen days $205, fourteen-day for twenty days $237, 21-day for 30 days $280. A YHA or VIP membership will give you substantial savings on all bus tickets and tours (see Basics, p.51).

By car and by bike

Renting a car is a sensible option, considering the vagaries of the transport system. Local operators offer reasonable weekly rates including basic insurance (see "Listings" in city accounts); as Tasmania is such a small island, kilometres are usually unlimited, and you don't need a lot of petrol. Though distances seem short compared to the mainland, roads are often winding and mostly two-laned – there are few freeways, except some short stretches on the outskirts of large cities – so **driving** can be slow and tiring. At dusk and night time, you have to be especially careful of animals darting in front of your car, as evidenced by the high number of dead native animals you'll see by the roadsides, and huge log trucks are unpleasant and sometimes scary road company. But with relatively few cars, it's easy to relax and enjoy the scenery, also making **cycling** an attractive option, especially in summer, and on the flatter midlands and east-coast routes (otherwise, plenty of gruelling hills will keep you in shape). Several operators in Hobart, Launceston and Devonport rent bikes for touring.

National parks and bushwalking

All **national parks** in Tasmania charge daily (24hr) **entry fees**, often on an honour system, of $10 per pedestrian or cyclist, or $20 per vehicle (including

Major tour and expedition operators

Another way to get around the island is by taking a **tour**. The excellent Under Down Under Tours (☎03/6362 2237 or 1800 064 726, Ⓦwww.underdownunder.com.au) is a small-group ecotourist outfit aimed at independent-minded travellers. Trips usually depart Launceston or Devonport and include bushwalking and wildlife spotting, hostel accommodation (which can be upgraded), and some but not all breakfasts and lunches. Their five-day tour ($645) does a loop of the island including Cradle Mountain and the Freycinet Peninsula, while their two-day Tarkine tour ($275) of the northwest includes the Arthur River cruise. Both can be combined into a seven-day trip ($745). Another five-day tour focuses on the wild west coast ($625). The "Bloomin Lot" eight-day ($925) or nine-day ($950) versions can be treated as a tour pass with the components done at your leisure.

The operators listed below offer trips and treks Tasmania-wide, detailed in the text.

Bottom Bits Bus ☎03/6234 5093 or 1800 777 103, Ⓦwww.bottombitsbus.com.au.
Craclair Tours ☎03/6339 4488, Ⓦwww.southcom.com.au/~craclair.
Island Cycle Tours ☎03/6234 4591 or 1300 880 334, Ⓦwww.islandcycletours.com.
Rafting Tasmania ☎03/6239 1080, Ⓦwww.raftingtasmania.com.
Roaring 40s Ocean Kayaking ☎03/6267 5000, Ⓦwww.roaring40skayaking.com.au.
Tasmanian Expeditions ☎1300 666 856 or 03/6339 3999, Ⓦwww.tas-ex.com.
Tiger Trails ☎03/6234 3931, Ⓦwww.tasmaniawalks.com.

up to eight passengers); if you plan to go bush for longer periods, then a **Parks Pass** will be better value. On offer are a two-month holiday pass (person, cyclist or motorcyclist $30, vehicle $50) or an annual pass for longer-stayers (car $42 for one park, $84 for all parks); camping fees are not included (though many sites are free anyway). Tasmania's wilderness has always attracted thousands of **bushwalkers**, and many of the churned-up tracks are gradually being boardwalked; keeping to set paths to avoid further erosion is just one of the national park's guidelines, available in a leaflet *Minimal Impact Walking* from the **Tasmania Parks and Wildlife Service**, 134 Macquarie St, Hobart (Ⓣ03/6233 2270, Ⓦwww.parks.tas.gov.au). This, and all free walking and rafting notes referred to in this chapter, can be downloaded from their website. Detailed topographic **Tasmaps** ($9.10 each) of major walking tracks are available at the Service Tasmania shop at the same address and in all main towns (for locations Ⓣ1300 135 513 or Ⓦwww.servicetas.gov.au). It must be emphasized that walking in the wilderness can be dangerous if you're ill prepared: never go by yourself and always register your plans with a park ranger or inform others of your intentions. The downloadable brochure *Essential Bushwalking Guide and Trip Planner* gives information about the clothing and equipment needed in these parks, where the weather can change rapidly – even on a warm summer day hail, sleet or snow can suddenly descend in the highlands, and walkers who have disregarded warnings have died of hypothermia. As a minimum, you'll need wet-weather gear, thermal clothing, walking boots, a sturdy tent, warm sleeping bag, a fuel cooking stove, maps and a compass (which you should know how to use). Gear can be rented from outdoor shops in Hobart, Launceston and Devonport.

Festivals and events

The **Ten Days on the Island** festival is Tasmania's international arts festival, held biennially in March/April in venues around Tasmania (Ⓣ03/6233 5700, Ⓦwww.tendaysontheisland.org). The big music events are the **Cygnet Folk Festival** (see p.1000) and the rock **Falls Festival** (Ⓦwww.fallsfestival.com), held over the New Year at Marion Bay (shuttle bus provided from Hobart). On the sports front, the biggest deal is the finale of the **Sydney–Hobart yacht race** (see p.946), while **Targa Tasmania** is a car rally for GT and sports cars that takes over 2000km of the state's bitumen roads for six days in April or May of each year (Ⓦwww.targa.org.au).

Hobart and the east

From Lake St Clair in central Tasmania, the **Derwent River** flows past **Mount Field National Park**, Tasmania's oldest and most popular national park, through well-preserved **New Norfolk**, and towards Hobart, Tasmania's capital. Here, the river estuary widens to form a fine harbour before flowing into the waters of **Storm Bay** and out to the Tasman Sea. **Hobart** is Australia's most southerly city, battered by winter winds roaring, and surrounded by a jagged coastline. The hook-shaped **South Arm**, at the entrance to Storm Bay, is echoed on a larger scale by the **Tasman Peninsula**, with its infamous convict settlement at **Port Arthur**. To the south, the two tenuously connected halves of **Bruny Island** protect the waters of the **D'Entrecasteaux Channel**. On the mainland opposite Bruny Island is the fertile and cultivated **Huon Valley**, but as you head further south the coastline becomes increasingly wild: there are caves and thermal springs, the **Hartz Mountains National Park** inland, and the **Picton River**, where there's good rafting. The last settlement in this direction is **Cockle Creek**, the starting point for the South Coast Track, which takes you towards the South West National Park (see pp.1074–1077), the great mass of wilderness forming Tasmania's southwest corner.

North of Hobart, the **east coast** of Tasmania is the tamest and most temperate part of the island, providing a popular cycling route past numerous sandy and deserted beaches and some lovely national parks. The **Tasman Highway** follows this coastline from Hobart to Launceston, heading inland through the northeast at **St Helens**, the east coast's largest town. The northeast corner is virtually unpopulated, and the **Mount William National Park** here is a haven for the Forrester kangaroo. Inland are some old tin-mining towns, and superb rainforest remnants and mountain scenery at **Weldborough Pass**, beyond which you pass through rich agricultural and forestry country to Launceston.

Hobart

HOBART is small but beautifully sited, and approaching it from any direction is exhilarating: speeding across the expressway on the Tasman Bridge over the wide expanse of the Derwent River, or swooping down the Southern Outlet with hills, harbour, docks and houses spread out below. The green- and red-tin-roofed timber houses climb up the lower slopes of Mount Wellington, snow-topped for two or three months of the year, and look down on the expansive harbour. It's a city focused on the water: the centre is only a few minutes' walk from the waterfront, where fresh seafood can be bought directly from fishing boats in Sullivans Cove, and yachties hang out at old dockside pubs or head for fish and chips served from the punts moored in Constitution Dock. South of Constitution Dock is Salamanca Place, a well-preserved streetscape of waterfront stone warehouses, which is the site of a famous Saturday market, a Hobart highlight. Yacht races and regattas are held throughout the year, while at weekends the water is alive with boats; you can choose any type of craft for a harbour cruise – perfect in the summer when it's dry and not too hot. In winter, though, the wind roars in from the Antarctic and temperatures drop to 5°C and below.

Australia's second-oldest city, after Sydney, Hobart has managed to escape the worst excesses of developers, and its early architectural heritage is remarkably well preserved – more so than any other antipodean city. There's a wealth of colonial Georgian **architecture**, with more than ninety buildings classified by the National Trust, sixty of which are on Macquarie and Davey streets. **Battery Point**, a village of workers' cottages and grand houses set in narrow, irregular streets, has hardly changed in the last 150 years.

Some history

In 1803, **Lieutenant John Bowen** led a party of 24 convicts from Sydney to settle on the eastern shores of the Derwent River at Risdon Cove. A year later, **Lieutenant-Colonel David Collins** arrived, with about three hundred convicts, a contingent of marines to guard them, and thirty or more free

HOBART

Royal Tasmanian Botanical Gardens & A

C

North Hobart & New Town

E, F, 1, 2, 3, North Hobart & New Town

N

13

Cascade Brewery, Mt Wellington & South Hobart

Ferry to Bellerive

S, Sandy Bay & Wrest Point Casino

18, Short Beach & Marina

Queens Domain

GLEBE

Penitentiary Chapel & Criminal Courts

Olympic Pool

Hobart Bus Terminal (TassieLink)

Theatre Royal

Gasworks

Federation Concert Hall

Centre for the Arts

State Library

YHA Office

Bank Arcade

Mall

Tasmanian Museum & Art Gallery

Victoria Dock

Town Hall

Constitution Dock

St David's Cathedral

Franklin Square

Maritime Museum of Tasmania

Sullivans Cove

Elizabeth Street Pier

NPWS

Watermans Dock

Brooke Street Pier

Parliament House

Murray Street Pier

Princes Wharf

St Davids Park

Salamanca Arts Centre

Battery Point

Transit Centre (Redline)

Kelly's Steps

Salamanca Square

Princes Park

BATTERY POINT

Arthurs Circus

Anglesea Barracks

Narryna Folk Museum

St George's Church

Scott Street, Patrick Street, Edward St, Upper Domain Road, Lower Domain Road, Tasman Highway, Brooker Avenue, Campbell Street, Sackville St, Brisbane Street, Argyle Street, Liverpool Street, Melville Street, Bathurst Street, Elizabeth Street, Criterion St, Hunter St, Murray Street, Watchorn St, Wharf, Goulburn St, Harrington Street, Collins Street, Macquarie St, Davey Street, Despard St, Morrison St, Franklin, Victoria St, Salamanca Place, Castray Esplanade, Barrack Street, Sandy Bay Road, Montpellier Retreat, Stowell Ave, Kelly St, South Street, Runnymede St, Hampden Road, James St, Molle Street, Francis St, Secheron Road, Mona St, Waterloo Crescent, Colville Street, Clarke Avenue, Albuera Street, Byron Street, Dewitt Street, Cromwell Street, Crelin Street, St Georges Terrace, Bath Street, Quayle Street, Napoleon Street

0 250 m

N

EATING & DRINKING

Annapurna	2
Criterion Street Cafe	6
Da Angelo Ristorante	14
Drifters Internet Cafe	11
Gondwana	16
Jackman & McRoss	15
Kaos Cafe and Lounge Bar	1
La Cuisine	4
Macquarie Street Foodstore	13
Mures Fish Centre	7
Prosser's on the Beach	18
Retro Café	10
Shipwright's Arms Hotel	17
Shu Yuan	5
Sirens	9
Sugo	12
Tandoor & Curry House	8
Vanidol's	3

ACCOMMODATION

Adelphi Court YHA	C
Astor Private Hotel	M
Central City Backpackers	I
Colville Cottage	P
Crelin Lodge	R
Customs House Hotel	L
Graham Court Apartments	F
Grand Chancellor	I
Hadley's Hotel	J
Henry Jones Art Hotel	H
The Lodge on Elizabeth	E
New Sydney Hotel	G
The Pickled Frog Backpackers	N
Prince of Wales	O
St Ives Hotel Apartments	Q
Somerset on the Pier	K
Theatre Royal Hotel	D
Treasure Island Caravan Park	A
Wellington Lodge	B
Wrest Point Hotel	S

settlers including women and children, and founded Hobart Town on Sullivans Cove, 10km below the original settlement and on the opposite shore. Collins went on to serve as lieutenant-governor of the colony for ten years. For the first two years, food was scarce, and settlers had to hunt local game, creating an early culture based on guns that was later to have terrible effects on the Aboriginal population. The fine deep-water port helped make the town prosperous, and a merchant class became wealthy through whaling, shipbuilding and the transport of crops and wool. The period between the late 1820s and the 1840s was a golden age for building, with the government architect **John Lee Archer** and the convict **James Blackburn** responsible for some of Hobart's finest buildings.

Arrival, information and city transport

Hobart **airport** is 17km northeast of the city. Redline's **Airporter Shuttle Bus** ($12 one way, $20 return; bookings ⓣ0419 383 462 or 0419 382 240), meets all flights, dropping off at central accommodation, as well as north to New Town and south to Sandy Bay. A **taxi** into the city centre costs around $30. Redline **coaches** arrive at the **Transit Centre**, 199 Collins St (ⓣ1300 360 000; left-luggage $1.50 per item per day; their airport service also drops off and picks up here). TassieLink disembarks at the **Hobart Bus Terminal**, 64 Brisbane St (ⓣ1300 300 520), where there's a free short-term left-luggage service for passengers (or $10 per bag for several days if you are going on a bushwalk) and a cafeteria.

Information

The first stop for general information is the **Tasmanian Travel and Information Centre** at 20 Davey St, corner of Elizabeth Street (Mon–Fri 8.30am–5.30pm, Sat & Sun 9am–5pm; ⓣ1300 655 145 or 03/6230 8233), though it functions mainly as a travel, car-rental and accommodation-booking agency. The **National Trust Shop**, in the Penitentiary Chapel at the corner of Brisbane and Campbell streets (Mon–Fri 10am–2.30pm; ⓣ03/6231 0911), displays charts detailing the bewildering range of listed buildings. On a more natural note, the **Tasmanian Environment Centre**, 102 Bathurst St (Mon–Fri 9am–5pm; ⓣ03/6234 5566, ⓦwww.sustainablelivingtasmania.org.au), is a relaxed resource space with lots of books about Tassie's flora and fauna, and animals and information on environmental events. For **bushwalking information** and a full range of Tasmaps, head for the Service Tasmania Shop at 134 Macquarie St (Mon–Fri 8.15am–5.30pm; ⓣ1300 135 513). The Parks and Wildlife Service has an unmanned desk (same hours and number) here with information sheets or phone ⓣ6233 6191 to talk to a parks officer for advice; other general and bushwalking maps are stocked at the Tasmanian Map Centre, 100 Elizabeth St (ⓣ03/6231 9043).

City transport

Hobart's public-transport system, the **Hobart Metro** (information ⓣ13 2201, ⓦwww.metrotas.com.au), is useful for getting to less-central accommodation and some more distant points of interest. The Metroshop, inside the GPO on Elizabeth Street, sells Metro Tens (a pack of ten tickets giving a twenty percent saving) and provides timetables, as do several newsagents; the area outside the GPO – Elizabeth Street, Franklin Square and Macquarie Street – is the bus interchange. The handy yellow-painted **Busy Bee bus** does a circuit from Franklin Square through Battery Point and up Sandy Bay Road to the casino and back again. Single **tickets** cost from $1.70 (valid 1hr 30min); off-peak day-rover passes are $4.40. Captain Fell's Historic Ferries (see p.987) offer a morning and evening commuter **ferry** to Bellerive on the eastern shore (Mon–Fri 7.50am & 5.25pm from Sullivans Cove, 8.15am & 5.40pm from Bellerive; $4; 20min), while the cute Hobart Yellow Water Cab (Ⓣ0407 036 268) has an on-call service (9am–8pm) from only $10.You can hail a **taxi** on the street, or there are taxi stands around the city; the major one is outside the Town Hall on Elizabeth Street.

Accommodation

There's plenty of **accommodation** in Hobart, but during the peak season from Boxing Day and throughout the first week of January, when the yachties hit town, prices shoot up and places can be hard to find. City and dockside **hotels** are the best option for clean, affordable private accommodation, and there are an increasing number of **hostels**; in the summer, student rooms are available for extended stays at Jane Franklin Hall in South Hobart (Ⓣ03/6223 2000). Battery Point is full of (sometimes pricey) **B&Bs**, and the area has several good self-catering holiday **apartments**, with costs comparable to a motel. Most **motels** are situated in Sandy Bay, about 3km south of the centre, or along the Brooker Highway, but B&Bs and guesthouses tend to offer better value.

Hotels and motels

Astor Private Hotel 157 Macquarie St Ⓣ03/6234 6611, Ⓦwww.astorprivatehotel.com.au. Central, old-fashioned, family-run hotel established in the 1920s. All rooms share bathrooms; rates include breakfast. The elegant *Astor Grill* at street level specializes in fine Tasmanian beef and seafood. 4

Customs House Hotel Cnr Murray and Morrison streets, opposite Watermans Dock Ⓣ03/6234 6645, Ⓦwww.customshousehotel.com. Established in 1846, this waterfront pub opposite Parliament House has been stylishly modernized; accommodation is now all en suite, and excellent value for the location. The pub bistro is well regarded and it's a lively drinking spot. 4, waterfront 5

Grand Chancellor 1 Davey St Ⓣ03/6235 4535 or 1800 753 379, Ⓦwww.hgchobart.com.au. Ugly exterior but occupying a great waterfront spot. Facilities include two restaurants, two bars and a health club. 5–8

Hadley's Hotel 34 Murray St Ⓣ03/6223 4355 or 1800 131 689, Ⓦwww.hadleyshotel.com.au. National Trust–listed hotel close to the waterfront, with an old-fashioned feel but modern facilities; in-house restaurant, café, bistro and bar. Room service, 24hr reception and free parking. 7–8

Henry Jones Art Hotel 25 Hunter St Ⓣ03/6210 7700, Ⓦwww.thehenryjones.com. Combining the ambience of a nineteenth-century waterfront stone warehouse and jam factory with a five-star luxury hotel-cum-contemporary art gallery, this is the place to stay in Hobart. Elegant touches include timber furnishings, sandstone walls, sensuous lighting, huge beds draped in vibrant silks, stunning opaque bathrooms, art by Tasmanian artists, LCD flat-screen TVs and DVDs. There's dining at the hotel's *Steam Packet Restaurant*, and the adjacent *IXL Bar* is very New York. 8

Prince of Wales 55 Hampden Rd, Battery Point Ⓣ03/6223 6355, Ⓦwww.princeofwaleshotel.net.au Ugly modern pub but in a great heritage location, with good motel-style rooms (but no phones), which either have views of the water or of Mount Wellington. Bathrooms all have tubs. Light breakfast in the bistro is included in the rate. Guest laundry and parking. 5

Theatre Royal Hotel 31 Campbell St Ⓣ03/6234 6925, Ⓦwww.theatreroyalhotel.com. A basic hotel, but in a good position across from the Theatre Royal, with plain but presentable rooms, some en suite; some singles available, and light breakfast included. Excellent bar and bistro downstairs. 5

Wrest Point Hotel 410 Sandy Bay Rd, Sandy Bay Ⓣ03/6225 0112, Ⓦwww.wrestpoint.com.au. Attached to the casino, this upmarket hotel has riverside rooms. Heated indoor pool, sauna and 24hr room service. Luxury tower or cheaper motel section. 6–8

B&Bs and guesthouses

Colville Cottage 32 Mona St, Battery Point Ⓣ03/6223 6968, Ⓦwww.colvillecottage.com.au. Peaceful, Victorian weatherboard B&B, with en-suite rooms and a pleasant garden. 6

The Lodge on Elizabeth 249 Elizabeth St, cnr Warwick St ⓣ03/6231 3830, ⓦwww.thelodge.com.au. Delightful guesthouse in an elegant National Trust–listed 1829 mansion; guest lounge with fireplace, games and complimentary port. All rooms en suite, some with spa. Also offers a self-contained cottage with spa (min two nights). Light buffet breakfast included. ❺–❻, cottage ❻

Wellington Lodge 7 Scott St, Glebe ⓣ03/6231 0614, ⓦwww.wwt.com.au/wellingtonlodge. A Victorian-era weatherboard B&B (cooked breakfast served) classified by the National Trust, close to Queens Domain and the city centre, and with a pretty rose garden. All rooms either en suite or with own private bathroom nearby. ❹–❺

Hostels and budget accommodation

Adelphi Court YHA 17 Stoke St, New Town ⓣ03/6228 4829, ⓔadelphi@yhatas.org.au. Modern, motel-like hostel and guesthouse arranged around a courtyard, on a quiet suburban street, with the usual facilities. Far from the city (2.5km north), and a 10min walk to North Hobart's restaurant strip, but with plenty of parking. Bus #15 or #16 from Argyle Street, or #25–42, #100 or #105–128 from Elizabeth Street. Dorms $21–24, rooms ❸

Central City Backpackers 2nd Floor, 138 Collins St, entrance off Imperial Arcade ⓣ03/6224 2404 or 1800 811 507, ⓦwww.centralbackpackers.com.au. One of Hobart's best hostels, in the spacious quarters of a once grand hotel. Friendly, efficient management. All dorms (three- to eight-bed, no bunks), singles ($49), twins and doubles are heated; linen rental extra. Well-set-up kitchen, pleasant dining area, TV and games rooms, Internet access and bike rental. No parking. Dorms $22–26, rooms ❸

Narrara Backpackers 88 Goulburn St ⓣ03/6231 3191, ⓦwww.narrarabackpackers.com. Attractive old house turned into a friendly, secure hostel, with an amiable live-in manager. The common room has pretty leadlight windows, a big table and comfy sofas, and there's a decent, well-equipped kitchen. Dorms, triples, twins and doubles are all very clean. Free Internet access. Off-street parking, and bike rental. Dorms $19, rooms ❷

New Sydney Hotel 87 Bathurst St ⓣ03/6234 4516, ⓦwww.newsydneyhotel.com. Clean, central and small backpackers' above a pub with kitchen facilities and guest lounge, plus Internet access. Always lively, though noisy bands play downstairs six nights, and budget pub meals are available. Parking $2 per day. Dorms $20, rooms ❷

The Pickled Frog Backpackers 281 Liverpool St ⓣ03/6234 7977, ⓦwww.thepickledfrog.com. Large hostel with young staff and a lively feel. The extensive communal area includes a bar/café selling cheap beers and meals, comfortable sofas, booths, pool table, wood fire, Internet access and industrial kitchen. Simple, clean dorms (four- to eight-bed) and rooms; all have sinks and heating, though no storage. Light breakfast and linen included, bedding extra. Bike rental. Parking available. Dorms $22, rooms ❸

Caravan parks and self-catering apartments

Crelin Lodge 1 Crelin St, Battery Point ⓣ03/6223 1777, ⓦwww.colvillecottage.com.au Pleasant apartments with up to five beds, on a great perch in Battery Point. Most have views down the river. ❺

Graham Court Apartments 15 Pirie St, New Town ⓣ03/6278 1333, ⓦwww.grahamcourt.com.au. Comfortable, well-equipped one- to three-bedroom self-contained apartments set in a pleasant garden, but 2.5km north of the city centre. Disabled access. ❹–❺

St Ives Hotel Apartments 67 St Georges Terrace, off Sandy Bay Rd, Battery Point ⓣ03/6224 1044, ⓦwww.stivesmotel.com.au. Two-level two-bedroom apartments with full kitchen, TV/dining room, bathrooms with tubs, and neutral decor. Others – on four floors – are like standard motel rooms, but with full kitchen. All have balconies with water views; luggage-lift only. Rooms ❹, apartments ❺–❻

Somerset on the Pier Elizabeth St Pier ⓣ03/6220 6600 or 1800 766 377, ⓦwww.somersetonthepier.com. Waterfront apartment hotel – gorgeous split-level, spacious and light-flooded studio and one-bedroom apartments. Some have balconies, all have kitchen and laundry, and there's a gym and sauna. ❼–❽

Treasure Island Caravan Park 671 Main Rd, Berriedale ⓣ03/6249 2379. Large park 14km northwest of the city centre on the banks of the Derwent River; camp kitchen and pool. Vans ❷, en-suite cabins ❸

The City

Hobart is small and easy to find your way around, with the streets arranged in a grid pattern running southeast towards **Sullivans Cove**. You can walk anywhere in the city centre, which is mostly flat, although surrounded by some steep hills. The civic centre is **Franklin Square**, bounded by **Macquarie** and

△ View of Mount Wellington from Elizabeth Street Pier

Davey streets, which between them have a concentration of listed buildings. The main shopping area is **Elizabeth Street Mall**, roughly in the centre of the **CBD** (the City Business District); Elizabeth Street slopes down from **North Hobart**, known for its many fine restaurants, to the Elizabeth Street Pier on **Franklin Wharf**. Here, at the harbour, fishing boats and yachts are moored, and cruises leave from Brooke Street Pier. **Salamanca Place**, with its row of Georgian warehouses and famous weekly **market**, is on the waterfront on the south side of the cove; a steep climb up Kelly's Steps brings you to **Battery Point**, to the south. Following the Derwent River around from Battery Point, you reach salubrious **Sandy Bay**, with its casino and Royal Yacht Club. To the north of the centre are the parklands of the **Queens Domain**, with the **Royal Botanical Gardens** along the waterfront; from the Domain, the **Tasman Bridge** crosses the river to the residential eastern shore.

There are relatively few sights in Hobart other than the streets themselves, but these are enough to keep you wandering around for hours, stopping at a few museums and parks along the way. While walking through the city, it's worth glancing up occasionally to observe the **street signs**; the streets are often named after important local figures and the signs bear portraits and biographies. Around the docks area, and in Battery Point, interpretive boards point out historic and architectural features. Get self-guided walking maps from the Travel and Information Centre or go on one of the good historical walking tours (see p.983).

Franklin Square and around

Set within a fountain in leafy **Franklin Square** is an imposing statue of Sir John Franklin, governor of Van Diemen's Land between 1837 and 1843, and later posthumously famous as an Arctic explorer – his ill-fated 1845 expedition discovered the Northwest Passage. From the square, where a giant chess-set gets plenty of use, you can walk south past many of the fine old buildings on Davey Street to **St Davids Park**, at the corner of Murray and Macquarie streets, originally the graveyard of St Davids Cathedral but converted to a park in the early twentieth century. It's a quiet spot containing some important monuments,

Harbour cruises

Captain Fell's Historic Ferries Brooke Street Pier ⓣ03/6223 5893, ⓦwww.captainfellshistoricferries.com.au. A range of particularly good-value harbour cruises on the MV *Emmalisa*, all of which include meals of some kind ($17–30). Also combined double-decker bus and harbour cruise (return leg) Cadbury's tour $50; departs Mon–Fri 10am or noon; includes lunch and wine.

The Cruise Company Brooke Street Pier ⓣ03/6234 9294. Their Cadbury's Cruise heads upriver on a ferry to the chocolate factory at Claremont (Mon–Fri 10am; 4hr; $50 includes factory tour).

Navigators Brooke Street Pier ⓣ03/6223 1914, 03/6224 0033 or 1300 134 561, ⓦwww.navigators.net.au. Two historic boats and two state-of-the-art catamarans run a variety of coastal and harbour cruises. Short cruises start from $22; a trip to Moorilla Estate Winery costs $35. The trip to Port Arthur travels along the stunning, rugged coastline on the MV *Marana*, a 25-metre fast catamaran (departs 8am Wed, Fri & Sun, no service June–Sept; 2hr 30min cruising, 3hr 30min at Port Arthur; site entry fee and return coach to Hobart leaving at 4pm included, plus morning tea; $150, without return coach $70).

Wild Thing Adventures ⓣ03/6224 2021, ⓦwww.wildthingadventures.com.au. Options for harbour and coastal cruises priced from $25 to $165 on a Ferrari-red powerboat include a tour of Moorilla Estate Winery and a Monday-only circumnavigation of Bruny Island (Oct–April; dress warmly whatever the weather).

Lady Nelson Elizabeth Street Pier ⓣ03/6234 3348, ⓦwww.ladynelson.org.au. This replica of the brig in which Matthew Flinders made his exploratory journeys is a sail-training vessel, but also offers bargain pleasure-trips most weekends year-round (call for times; 1hr 30min; $10).

The Peppermint Bay Cruise Brooke Street Pier ⓣ1300 137 919, ⓦwww.hobartcruises.com.au. Spectacular cruise on a luxury catamaran (May–Sept Mon, Wed & Fri–Sun 11.30am; Oct–April daily noon; from $78; gourmet-platter lunch included): south along the Derwent River and the D'Entrecasteaux Channel past Bruny Island to Woodbridge where there's a shore excursion to the stylish *Peppermint Bay Hotel*.

among them a huge memorial to the first governor, David Collins. Other gravestones have been removed and set into two undulating sandstone walls at the bottom of the park.

Tasmanian Museum and Art Gallery and around

Just north of Franklin Square is the excellent **Tasmanian Museum and Art Gallery** at 40 Macquarie St (daily 10am–5pm; free but charge for some special exhibitions; free fifty-minute guided tours Wed–Sun 2.30pm; ⓦwww.tmag.tas.gov.au). The collection is, as the building's name suggests, a mixed bag. Much space is devoted to exploring Tasmania's tragic history, dwelling on penal cruelty, near genocide and the extinction of animal species.

As you enter, video-loop footage shows the last known **Tasmanian tiger** (**thylacine**), which died in captivity in Hobart Zoo in 1936. In 2003, in a collaborative purchase with Launceston's Queen Victoria Museum and Federal Hotels in Strahan, the museum acquired a unique, eight-skinned **thylacine rug** made in the late 1890s, which the three take turns exhibiting. The peculiar, flesh-eating, dog-like marsupial, which had a rigid tail, stripes and a backwards-opening pouch, was hunted out of existence by farming families fearful for their stock and encouraged by the 1888-to-1909 bounty on the creature's head (2184 were paid) – although unconfirmed thylacine sightings still occur. A project by Sydney's Australian Museum to resurrect the species using DNA from pickled specimens was restarted in May 2005. A stuffed example is part of the unexciting taxidermy exhibition in the rest of the room, but the life-sized reconstructions in an adjacent room of the Pleistocene-era **megafauna**, giant marsupials that once roamed Australia, are far more riveting.

On the next level above, the **Tasmanian Aboriginal room** displays cultural artefacts of the island's indigenous people, including some examples of the kind of exquisite shell necklaces that would have adorned "Queen" Truganini, reputed to be the last Aboriginal Tasmanian. The display gives a comprehensive account of the Aboriginal people, from their tragic near-extermination to recent events involving land-rights campaigns. Particularly poignant is the recording of the voice of **Fanny Cochrane** (1834–1905) singing traditional songs; it is she who was probably the last full-blooded Aboriginal Tasmanian rather than Truganini, as the myth relates.

The adjacent **art gallery** section has a display of colonial art featuring several 1830s and 1840s portraits of the well-known "final" Aborigines, including Manalargenna and Truganini, by artists such as **Benjamin Duterrau** and **Thomas Bock**, as well as superb landscape paintings of Tasmania by the nineteenth-century artists **John Glover** and **W.C. Piguenit**. There's also an excellent section on **convicts**: if you can't get to the convict ruins at Port Arthur or Richmond Gaol, this display will convince you of the brutality of the regime. At ground level, adjacent to the decent museum café, is a great **Children's Discovery Room**, and you can take some air at the café's pleasant outdoor courtyard.

Opposite the museum, the modest **Maritime Museum of Tasmania** (daily 9am–5pm; $6; Ⓦwww.maritimetas.org), in the red-brick Carnegie Building on the corner of Argyle and Davey streets, houses memorabilia, photographs and exhibits dominated by models of boats – the most impressive is a third-scale model of an open whaling boat. Arranged thematically, it provides an excellent introduction to the history of Hobart as a maritime city.

North of Macquarie Street

There are several worthwhile sights along the straight streets that run north of Macquarie Street (running alongside Franklin Square), particularly Murray and Campbell streets. Three blocks northwest of Macquarie Street, on Murray Street at the corner of Bathurst Street, the **State Library** (Mon–Thurs 9.30am–6pm, Fri 9.30am–8pm, Sat 9.30am–12.30pm; Ⓦwww.statelibrary.tas.gov.au) holds the **Allport Library and Museum of Fine Arts** (Mon–Fri 9.30am–5pm, last Sat of month 9.30am–2.30pm, and in Jan Sat 9.30am–12.30pm; free), the Allport family's private collection of eighteenth- and nineteenth-century furnishings, ceramics, silver and glass, paintings, prints and rare books relating to Australia and the Pacific, made as a bequest to the library in 1965. *Zest*, the great little contemporary café at ground level, does good sushi.

The **Theatre Royal**, on Campbell Street at the corner of Sackville Street, is Australia's oldest surviving theatre, built in 1837. It has an intimate interior decorated in Regency style, best seen while attending a performance; otherwise, the staff might let you in for a peek. Further up, at the corner of Brisbane Street, the **Penitentiary Chapel and Criminal Courts** (daily tours except Aug 10am, 11.30am, 1pm & 2.30pm; 1hr; $8; Ⓣ03/6231 0911) comprise a complex of early buildings with two courtrooms, underground tunnels and cells. There's also a rather spooky ghost tour (nightly 8pm or 8.30pm depending on season; $10; 1hr; bookings essential on Ⓣ0417 361 392).

The waterfront

The focus of **Sullivans Cove** is busy **Franklin Wharf**, the first commercial centre of Hobart, where merchants erected large warehouses as the colony grew wealthier. In the 1830s, Hobart was one of the world's great whaling centres, and to cater for the growing volume of shipping, the New Wharf – **Princes Wharf** – was built, featuring a row of handsome sandstone warehouses on Salamanca Place. As the new wharf became the focus of port activity, the old wharf developed into an industrial centre of flour mills and factories. Part of the Henry Jones Jam Factory, between Victoria and Macquarie docks on Hunter Street, is now the **Centre for the Arts**, the University of Tasmania's art school. Beyond the original facade in a courtyard there are several large pieces of sculpture and the high-tech face of the art school. Inside, the **Sir James Plimsoll Gallery** (daily noon–5pm when there is an exhibition; free) has several shows a year featuring the work of contemporary Tasmanian artists. The rest of the old jam factory has been redeveloped and extended into a complex made up of the luxury *Henry Jones Art Hotel*, with a restaurant, bar, and art galleries featuring Aboriginal art, and wood and furniture design. On the waterfront near the hotel, look out for the several sculptures and a plaque commemorating the links between Hobart and Antarctica, from the first 1840 expedition of the evocatively named *Erebus and Terror* under Captain Ross. Beyond this is the renovated old **Gasworks** on Macquarie Street in the former red-light slum district of **Old Wapping**. Its restored stone buildings are pleasant enough, but the slick shops, restaurants and enterprises within – many are part of chains – try too hard to attract tourists. Opposite is the **Federation Concert Hall** (see p.996), attached to the *Grand Chancellor* hotel and home to the Tasmanian Symphony Orchestra. The brass-clad building, opened in 2000, is oval-shaped, in keeping with the original gas cylinder in the old gasworks, and its acoustics are supposedly the best in Australia.

The old docks along Franklin Wharf are also thriving: at **Victoria Dock**, lobster boats are moored; at **Constitution Dock**, boats sell fresh and cooked seafood and alongside is the Mures Fish Centre, a two-level complex of restaurants and cafés. The stylish development on Elizabeth Street Pier has a slew of trendy bars, eateries and luxury hotel-apartments, while Murray Street Pier has been jazzed up with several restaurants. From Brooke Street Pier and Watermans Dock, any number of **cruises** depart (see box on p.987).

On **Salamanca Place**, the old warehouses, shipping offices and storerooms are now full of arts-and-crafts galleries, speciality shops and cafés, interspersed with characterful waterfront pubs. At the end of Salamanca Place, on Castray Esplanade, the old silos have been converted into upmarket apartments. Salamanca Place comes alive for the open-air **Salamanca Market** (Sat 8am–3pm), an event with an alternative feel and wonderful local food, including colourful fruit and vegetable stands, and buskers; stalls focus on local crafts, particularly woodwork using distinctive Tasmanian timber (often recycled), and there's lots of bric-a-brac and secondhand books and clothes. Several of the narrow lanes and arcades in the area are worth exploring – with shops devoted to books and secondhand clothes and crafts – as is the **Salamanca Arts Centre**, a former jam-canning factory that's now home to a diverse range of arts-based organizations. Downstairs, the Peacock Theatre is the performance venue, and there are several galleries (daily 10am–5pm); upstairs, emerging contemporary artists show at the Long Gallery, with smaller displays in Sidespace.

Through the Arts Centre, Woobies Lane leads to lively **Salamanca Square**, a large public square with a fountain at its centre. The square is filled with cafés, restaurants and bars with outside seating, and some interesting shops, including the Hobart Bookshop, which has a big Tasmania-related section.

A **guided walk** explores Sullivans Cove and Salamanca Place, starting from outside the Travel and Information Centre (daily 10am; 1.30hr; $25; bookings ⓣ03/6230 8233).

Battery Point

Kelly's Steps lead up from Salamanca Place to **Battery Point**, a district with an enduring village atmosphere. With the building of the new wharf in the 1830s, a working-class community grew up behind Salamanca Place; it takes its name from the battery of guns that were once sited on present-day **Princes Park**, protecting the harbour below. The area was first home to small cottages for waterfront workmen and, later, fine merchants' houses: the old pubs, with names such as the *Shipwright's Arms* and *Whalers Return*, leave no doubt about the nature of the population. Narrow streets, closely packed cottages, the flower-filled green of **Arthurs Circus** and the "corner-store" nature of the shops enhance the nineteenth-century village feel.

There's a particular concentration of early buildings on De Witt and Cromwell streets. **St George's Church**, on Cromwell, is the joint work of John Lee Archer (responsible for the nave, completed in 1838) and James Blackburn (the tower, added in 1847), the early colony's two best-known architects. **Hampden Road** has more fine nineteenth-century mansions, including one at no. 103 known as "Narryna" (Tues–Fri 10.30am–5pm, Sat & Sun 2–5pm; $6), a house museum furnished with period Georgian antiques.

Queens Domain and Royal Tasmanian Botanical Gardens

The **Queens Domain**, just north of the city centre, is a sparse, bush-covered hill traversed by walking and jogging tracks but positioned between two very busy highways. At the base of the hill on the Derwent, where the trees suddenly become lush and green, are the **Royal Tasmanian Botanical Gardens** (daily 8am–4.45pm), a formal collection of flower displays and orderly trees. Pick up a leaflet outlining the features of the gardens at any entrance, or from the **Botanical Discovery Centre** at the main entrance on the west side of the park (daily 10am–4.30pm, until 5pm Sept–April; free), where you'll find interactive games and exhibits as well as the **information centre**, café and restaurant. It's easy enough to walk to the Domain, following Davey Street or Liverpool Street from the city centre, but the gardens are quite far inside the grounds: from the city centre to the gardens should take you about thirty minutes. Bus #17 or any of the many buses to the Eastern Shore will drop you at Government House, in the centre of the Domain near the gardens, but there's no transport back.

Around the harbour

The estuary of the **Derwent River** is the deepest (and second-busiest) natural port in Australia. Just north of the Queens Domain, at **Cornelian Bay** in **New Town**, you'll find cute fishing shacks and the well-regarded *Cornelian Bay Boat House Restaurant* (ⓣ03/6228 9289), which also has a kiosk for coffees. A bike track runs here from the end of the Queens Domain below the Aquatic Centre (see p.998). Heading upstream, the scenery becomes increasingly industrial, with a huge zinc-processing plant, but by Berriedale the setting is more unspoilt. Here, the **Moorilla Estate Winery**, off Main Road, has gorgeous river views from its landscaped grounds. Established in

1958, it's one of Tasmania's oldest wineries; you can taste some of its fine cool-climate wines, eat lunch in its wonderful restaurant (bookings ⓣ02/6277 9900, ⓦwww.moorilla.com.au) or stay in the five-star chalets ($350), adorned with artefacts from the Moorilla Museum, scheduled to reopen to the public some time in 2008. Beyond Berriedale lies Claremont and the riverfront **Cadbury's Factory**, dating from 1921, on Cadburys Road. The understandably popular factory tours include lots of chocolate tasting (every 30min Mon–Fri 8am–2.30pm; 2hr; $12.50; booking essential on ⓣ03/6249 0333); from the city centre, take bus #37, #38 or #39 direct to the factory. Alternatively, you can cruise here (see box, p.987.)

The eastern side of the river is more residential, and looking across you'll see swelling, bush-clad hills with a modest line of homes below. The **Tasman Bridge** connects the eastern shore with the city: it was put out of action for over two years from January 1975, when the 20,000-tonne tanker *Lake Illawarra*, heading for the zinc-smelting works, crashed into it and destroyed two pylons. The ship is still at the bottom of the river, with its cargo of zinc concentrate, as are the bodies of the twelve unfortunate people on board.

The **Kangaroo Bluff Battery** at Bellerive, on the eastern shore – along with its counterparts at Sandy Bay (Alexandra Battery) and Battery Point (Mona Street Battery) – was erected in response to a Russian scare in the late nineteenth century, but it never saw active service. **Bellerive**, which you can reach by ferry from Brooke Street Pier (see p.987), has a long, sandy beach at the Esplanade; some swim from it, although the water is somewhat polluted. The beach suburb is host to international test cricket at the modern **Bellerive Oval** on Derwent Street (details on ⓣ03/6211 4000). There's cleaner water and surf beaches across the promontory from Bellerive at **Opossum Bay** (bus #296 or #300), while **Seven Mile Beach**, on Frederick Henry Bay, offers calmer swimming (bus #292 or #293). Ten kilometres north of Bellerive is **Risdon Cove**, site of the first European settlement of Van Diemen's Land; interpretive boards explain its early history (bus #267, #269 or #270).

Sandy Bay

Leafy, well-heeled **Sandy Bay**, a suburb just south of Battery Point, is home to a busy shopping centre on Sandy Bay Road. Near the shops, the Royal Yacht Club (where visitors can take a drink) fronts a marina, beside a beach and waterfront park. Further around the bay is the **Wrest Point Casino** on Sandy Bay Road; an incongruous 1970s high-rise, the casino strives hard to be glamorous, but a rather downmarket tone is set by swarms of tour groups wearing name tags. More glamorous is the annual weekend **Sandy Bay Regatta** in January, when yachts are moored all around Sandy Bay's marinas, the river is filled with boats, and a funfair is held on the waterfront. At weekends throughout the year, too, hundreds of yachts are out on the water. Several buses go to Sandy Bay from the city centre, among them the yellow Busy Bee bus, and buses #52–56 and #60, #61 and #94.

Taroona to Kingston

South of the centre, what are defined as Hobart's suburbs terminate at beachside Kingston, reached speedily after 13km on the inland **Southern Outlet** or by a scenic, winding coastal drive via Sandy Bay Road and the **Channel Highway**. En route, at **Taroona**, 10km south of Hobart, the 48-metre-high **Shot Tower** (ⓣ03/6227 8885; daily 9am–5pm; $4.50), built in 1870 to make lead shot, gives wonderful views of Hobart and the Derwent Estuary. **Kingston** is a residential suburb with wide, sandy **Kingston Beach**, which is 1km down Beach Road from the large and busy shopping centre. As all sea craft coming into Hobart have to go past the sheltered beach, it's a particularly good place to catch the end of the Sydney–Hobart yacht race. On the Esplanade, there's a cluster of accommodation, including the homely *Kingston Beach Motel* (ⓣ03/6229 8969; all units with kitchenettes; ❹), a pub – the *Beachside Hotel* – serving good bistro meals (plus bands Thurs & Fri nights), and a nearby café, the recommended *Citrus Moon*, at 23 Beach Rd (daily 9/10am–5pm, Fri till 9pm). Heading south on the Channel Highway, the historical display at Australia's **Antarctic Division Headquarters** (Mon–Fri 9am–5pm; free), on the town's southern edge, can fill you in on Antarctic exploration; there's also a decent canteen. To get to Taroona, take bus #60 or #61; bus #61 continues on to Kingston; bus #67, #70 and #80 services Kingston.

Inland to Mount Wellington and Mount Nelson

Heading inland, the route southwest towards Mount Wellington via Davey and Macquarie streets takes you through **South Hobart**, on to Cascade Road and past the pretty **Cascade Gardens** and the nearby **Cascades Female Factory Historic Site** on Degraves Street. The sandstone walls here are all that remain of a prison built in 1827 to house recidivist convict women who were set to work washing and sewing; fascinating interpretive boards tell their story. It's free to visit, though the fudge factory and café beside it (daily 8am–4pm) offer guided tours to fund site conservation (Mon–Fri 9.30am plus Dec 26 to Easter Mon–Fri 2pm, Sat & Sun 9.30am; $10; 1hr 15min; bookings ⓣ03/6233 1559, ⓦwww.femalefactory.com.au). Beyond Cascade Gardens, at 140 Cascade Rd, the magnificent seven-storey **Cascade Brewery** is the oldest in Australia, still using traditional methods and taking advantage of the pure spring water that cascades – of course – down Mount Wellington. **Tours** (daily 9.30am, 10am, 1.30pm & 2pm; 2hr; $18; bookings essential on ⓣ03/6221 8300) are pretty active – there are 220 stairs – but you're rewarded with up to three glasses of draught beer at the end in the brewer's recently renovated original residence. The small **museum** of brewing paraphernalia (Mon–Fri 9.15am–4pm; free) includes a few childhood pictures of the Hollywood actor Errol Flynn, who was brought up in the South Hobart area. If you miss the tour, you can visit the souvenir shop and museum and have a drink at the bar or in the beer garden. Take bus #43, #44, #46, #47 or #49 to the brewery. Alternatively, you can walk or cycle all the way to Cascades Gardens and past the Female Factory Historic Site along the pathway following the peaceful **Hobart Rivulet** (platypus are often seen here), starting from just behind the Village Cinema on Collins Street near the corner with Molle Street.

In any image of Hobart, **Mount Wellington** (1270m) is always looming in the background, sometimes snow-covered. Access is up winding Huon Road lined with houses as far as **Fern Tree**, from where Pillinger Drive turns into the steep and winding Pinnacle Road to the summit; the nineteen-kilometre drive provides several lookout points. Near the bottom of a walking route that goes right up the mountain (via Fernglade Track, Pinnacle Track and Zig Zag Track; 13km; 2hr 45min one way; detailed in *Mount Wellington Walks*, $4 from Service Tasmania outlets), the *Fern Tree Tavern* offers teas, meals and views. There are picnic grounds with barbecues, shelters, toilets and information boards at the beginning of the track at Fern Tree, and about halfway up at **The Springs**. Pure, drinkable water cascades from rocks as you climb and the thick bush begins to gradually thin; by the top it's bare and rocky. Here, the stone **Pinnacle**

Observatory Shelter (daily 8am–6pm) has details of the magnificent panorama of the city and harbour spread before you, which includes vast tracts of bush and grass plains, and views to Bruny Island to the south and as far as Maria Island to the north; there are toilets but no refreshments available at the top. Metro buses #48 or #49 run to Fern Tree, or the Mount Wellington Shuttle Bus Service can get you to the summit (Mon–Fri 9.30am, noon & 2.30pm, Sat & Sun 9.30am & 1.30pm; $25; 2hr tour includes 30min on top; ⓣ0417 341 804), leaving from the Travel and Information Centre (see p.983), or picking up from accommodation. Island Cycle Tours' three-hour trip includes a visit to the summit, and then a twenty-kilometre downhill mountain-bike ride to Salamanca Place (9.30am & 1.30pm city pick-ups; $65 includes drink and snack; see p.979).

The views are also terrific from the Old Signal Station on **Mount Nelson** (340m) above Sandy Bay. The station was established in 1811 to announce the appearance of ships in Storm Bay and the D'Entrecasteaux Channel; the signalman's residence has been converted into tearooms (daily 9.30am–4.30pm), from where you get a panorama of the city below. To get to Mount Nelson, take bus #57 or #58.

Eating and drinking

Hobart's fare can't compare with the mainland cities' ethnically eclectic range of cuisines, but its dining scene is increasingly cosmopolitan; the greatest diversity of restaurants and cafés is found along the Elizabeth Street strip in North Hobart, including Turkish, Indian, Sudanese and Mexican. In the city centre, there's a concentration of inexpensive ethnic eateries on Harrington Street between Collins and Liverpool streets, and then around the Liverpool Street corner – African, Middle Eastern and the like. Superlative **seafood** can be had throughout the city, but especially in the restaurants by Victoria Dock and Elizabeth Street Pier, and from the permanently moored punts selling fresh and cooked fish and seafood in Constitution Dock. On Saturdays, the fresh produce and food stalls at **Salamanca Market** are excellent.

Cafés, pubs, bars and takeaways

Criterion Street Cafe 10 Criterion St. The pavement tables outside this relaxed, cosmopolitan café take in appealing Criterion Street, with its organic foodstore and retro clothes stores. The Spanish omelette and the gourmet bacon sandwich are both very popular for breakfast, and lunchtime blackboard specials include soup, salad, risotto or savoury cheesecake and lots of vegetarian options; nothing on main menu over $12.50. Divine cakes and coffee, too. Mon–Fri 7.30am–5pm, Sat 8.30am–3pm.

Drifters Internet Cafe 33 Salamanca Place, off Montpellier Retreat. Cosy, long nook of a café, its walls covered with Errol Flynn paraphernalia. Soups, toasted sandwiches and nachos all come under $9. Lots of computers with Internet access ($1 per 10min, $5 per hour). Mon–Sat 10am–7pm, Sun 11am–7pm.

Jackman & McRoss 57–59 Hampden Rd, Battery Point and 32 Cross St, New Town. Two stylish eat-in bakeries, both serving excellent pastries and savouries such as gourmet baguettes and rolls. Mon–Fri 7.30am–6pm, Sat & Sun 7.30am–5pm.

Kaos Cafe and Lounge Bar 237 Elizabeth St, North Hobart. Trendy, gay-friendly late-night coffee spot, with groovy music and magazines to read. Focaccia, real fruit muffins and cakes, plus delicious all-day breakfast. Now licensed, *Kaos* has its own very funky bar room, *Soak*, with plenty of relaxing lounge space, and on Fri and Sat nights there's a club atmosphere, with DJs spinning until the late hours. Mon–Thurs noon–midnight, Fri & Sat noon–2/3am.

La Cuisine 85 Bathurst St. Café-patisserie serving excellent French-style pastries and mounds of delicious, healthy salads. Mon–Fri 7am–5pm, Sat 8am–1.30pm.

Macquarie Street Foodstore 356 Macquarie St, South Hobart. For those en route to the Cascade Brewery or Mount Wellington, this colourful laid-back café, close to the Hobart Rivulet, is an essential stop for its legendary breakfast – big portions, free-range eggs, and huge and fluffy pancakes – served until 3pm. Mon–Fri 7.30am–6pm, Sat & Sun 8.30am–5pm. Licensed.

Retro Café 31 Salamanca Place. Relaxed, light and airy place serving the best espresso in town, plus wonderful breakfasts. Often full of politicians from the nearby State Parliament and other high-flyers meeting over coffee midweek. Outside tables popular on market day (Sat). A good place to find out what's on – notices and flyers cover one wall. Mon–Sat 8am–6pm, Sun 8.30am–6pm.

Shipwright's Arms Hotel Cnr Colville and Trumpeter streets, Battery Point. Old pub, popular with the yachtie crowd. Dishes up a legendary fresh seafood platter.

Shu Yuan Bank Arcade, 64 Liverpool St. This tiny vibrant place, little more than a takeaway, packs in the customers – many Asian – eager for its delicious vegetarian food from a Taiwan-trained chef who morphs mushrooms, gluten and tofu into delicious, filling creations (a lunch special of three dishes on rice costs $8.50). Also fresh fruit drinks. Mon–Sat 10am–3.30pm.

Sugo Shop 9, Salamanca Square. Trendy café, with a dramatic red interior and big glass windows giving a view of the action-packed square. Despite appearances, it's not at all expensive. The Italian-styled coffee and food is excellent, and includes gourmet pizza (from $13), focaccia, salads, pasta and risotto. Breakfast, served until 11.30am, costs up to $12.50. Mon–Fri 8.30am–4.30pm, Sat & Sun 9am–4.30pm.

Restaurants and bistros

Annapurna 305 Elizabeth St, North Hobart ☎03/6236 9500. Popular, casual restaurant serving North and South Indian food. Great masala dosas plus curry-and-rice lunch specials for under $10. BYO. Closed lunch Sat & Sun.

Da Angelo Ristorante 47 Hampden Rd, Battery Point ☎03/6223 7011. A great village spot for an upmarket, tasty Italian meal including gourmet pizzas; generous portions and good service. Licensed and BYO. Dinner Mon–Sat.

Fish 349 349 Elizabeth St, North Hobart ☎03/6234 7788. A minimalist, modern fish café – order your food at the counter and find a seat. The food is cheap and terrific ($10–24). Open daily for lunch and dinner. Licensed.

Gondwana Cnr Hampden Rd and Francis St, Battery Point ☎03/6224 9900. In an old cottage with village views, *Gondwana* is one of Hobart's best restaurants; the creative and innovative cuisine – mains $26–33 – is sourced from quality fresh, local ingredients. Tasmanian wines available by the glass. Lunch Wed–Fri, dinner (bookings essential) Mon–Sat. Closed public holidays.

Mures Fish Centre Victoria Dock. Set among yachts and fishing boats, this two-level food centre houses three restaurants, a fishmonger, a bakery (great scallop pies) and a café. *Mures Upper Deck* (☎03/6231 1999) is an upmarket restaurant that has lovely harbour views; *Mures Lower Deck* (☎03/6231 2121) has bistro food, with cheaper prices; *Orizuru* (☎03/6231 1790; closed Sun) serves authentic sushi – their salmon is delicious – and is Hobart's best Japanese option.

Prosser's on the Beach Long Point Beach Rd, Sandy Bay ☎03/6225 2276. In a relaxing spot in extensive Long Beach Reserve on Little Sandy Bay overlooking the Derwent River, this is Hobart's – and probably Tasmania's – best contemporary seafood restaurant utilizing superb local fresh fish. Asian-influenced dishes vie with simple fish fillets on mash. Prices are very reasonable, with mains around $28–32. Licensed. Lunch Wed–Fri, dinner Mon–Sat from 6pm. Bookings essential.

Sirens 6 Victoria St ☎03/6234 2634. Upmarket vegetarian/vegan restaurant serving subtle Middle Eastern/North African–inspired food in a lovely plant-filled, high-ceilinged space that's a cross between Gothic and the Ottoman Empire. Licensed. Mon–Sat from 5.30pm.

Tandoor & Curry House 101 Harrington St ☎03/6234 6905. Good, authentic Indian eatery serving all the favourites and accompaniments with mains around $14. Licensed. Closed Sat & Sun lunch.

Vanidol's 353 Elizabeth St, North Hobart ☎03/6234 9307. A popular veteran, this casual, affordable place serves Thai, Indian and Indonesian food. BYO. Dinner Tues–Sun.

Entertainment and nightlife

A lively **nightlife**, though on a small scale, is centred around the waterfront. The focal point is *Knopwood's Retreat* (see opposite), which attracts a large crowd on Friday and Saturday nights, and has a popular nightclub upstairs. The more conservative *Wrest Point Casino*, at 410 Sandy Bay Rd in Sandy Bay, is open late every night for gambling, drinking and dancing (☎03/6225 0112; casino Mon–Thurs & Sun 2pm–2am, Fri & Sat 2pm–3am; *Regine's* nightclub Wed–Sun 10pm–4am).

To find out **what's on**, check the gig guide in Thursday's *Mercury*, or pop into *Aroma Records*, 323 Elizabeth St, North Hobart, which has lots of flyers and info plus a great little café; a local website, Ⓦwww.dwarf.com.au, also details the live-music scene. Tasmania is too small to lure many touring bands, so the ones that play the pubs are mainly local. There's free **live music** in the courtyard at Salamanca Place on Friday evenings (5.30–7.30pm). Also see *Trout Bar* (p.996) and *Customs House Hotel* (overleaf, p.984). For more compelling gigs, keep an eye on what's happening at the University of Tasmania campus at Sandy Bay (Ⓣ03/6220 2861). **Concerts** are staged by the Tasmanian Symphony Orchestra at the Federation Concert Hall and by the Tasmanian Conservatorium of Music at the Conservatorium (5–7 Sandy Bay Rd; Ⓣ03/6226 7306) or in churches around town. Most **tickets** can be booked via Centretainment, at 132 Liverpool St (Ⓣ03/6234 5998).

Bars, clubs and live music

Bar Celona 24 Salamanca Square. Renovated sandstone warehouse turned into a slick and spacious café (by day) and bar on two levels. The light lunches (from $8.50 to $15) can also be eaten at tables on the square. On Fri and Sat nights DJs play laid-back lounge music on the mezzanine level (9pm–12.30am). Daily 9am–midnight, till 1am Fri & Sat.

Isobar 11 Franklin Wharf. Young and packed, the *Isobar* (Wed 5pm–midnight, Fri 6pm–2am, Sat 7pm–2am) is a weekend favourite with live music on Fri and Sat; Wed attracts a student crowd. At *The Club* upstairs (Fri & Sat 10pm–5am; Fri $5, Sat $7 or free before 11pm; happy hour 11pm to midnight) DJs play commercial dance on the main floor and there's also an R&B room and the quieter *Back Bar*.

Knopwood's Retreat 39 Salamanca Place. A favourite with students, yachties and just about everyone else, this pub has a relaxed, coffee parlour/bar feel, with plenty of magazines and newspapers, plus outside tables. Lunch served

Gay and lesbian Hobart

Acts of male homosexuality were still a criminal offence in Tasmania until 1997. Founded in 1988, the **Tasmanian Gay and Lesbian Rights Group (TGLRG)** put persistent pressure on the government. Led by spokesperson **Rodney Croome**, their rally cry "We're here, we're queer, and we're not going to the mainland" certainly shook up conservative Tasmania; thousands signed the petition to urge the reform of the law. The federal government and the UN Human Rights Commission also pressed for change, and Tasmania's Upper House finally cracked, changing the law on May 1, 1997. Ironically, Tasmania now has Australia's best legislation to protect gay and lesbian rights: it's the only state that allows same-sex couples to officially register their relationship to access the same rights as married couples under Tasmanian law.

The TGLRG can be contacted on Ⓣ03/6224 3556 or check Ⓦwww.tglrg.org. Working It Out (Ⓣ03/6231 1200, Ⓦwww.workingitout.org.au) is a state-funded gay and lesbian support and health agency, and there's a social and support group Gay and Lesbian Community Centre (GLC Inc). GLC Inc publishes a monthly newsletter, *CentreLines*, which is sold from the TGLRG stall at Salamanca Market and details events and occasional dance parties around town that they organize, details of which are available on their recorded **Gay Information Line** (Ⓣ03/6234 8179, Ⓦwww.glctas.org). A comprehensive **Tasmanian Gay and Lesbian Vistor's Guide** can be dowloaded from Ⓦwww.discovertasmania.com.au. *GAY TAS*, a fold-out gay and lesbian visitor guide, is available from tourist offices. *The Trade Hotel*, 24 Barrack St, is popular for its Saturday-night DJs (free) and so is the monthly **gay and lesbian club night**, La La Land Bar & Club at *Halo*, 37A Elizabeth Street Mall, on the first Saturday of the month (10pm–5am; $10; Ⓣ0408 328 456 to check details). Other gay-friendly places are *Kaos*, a café and cocktail lounge, *T-42°*, a restaurant, and the nightclub *Syrup*.

Mon–Fri; open until 1am on Fri, when the pavement outside is packed.

The Lark Distillery 14 Davey St. A handy spot to recharge, with pavement tables overlooking Mawson Place. A range of spirits made on the premises can be tasted for free (the single malt whisky has a $4 charge). Also a huge range of whiskys, and an all-Tasmanian wine list. Cheese platters to snack on (and soup in winter). Live folk music on Fri evenings (5.30–8pm; free). A cocktail bar operates nightly except Fri from 6pm to 2am. Mon–Thurs & Sun 10–2am, Fri 9am–10pm.

New Sydney Hotel 87 Bathurst St (☎03/6234 4516). Hobart's Irish pub, featuring live music nightly except Mon – from traditional Irish to blues and folk. Twelve beers on tap, including Guinness, and decent pub meals (no lunch Sun).

Queen's Head Cafe & Wine Bar 400 Elizabeth St, North Hobart ☎03/6234 4670. Colourful, spacious and casual venue hosting free live music nightly except Sun (from 8.30pm Mon–Thurs, 9.30pm Fri & Sat), from pub rock to reggae and jazz. Lunch menu ranges from a $5 soup to a $17 chargrilled steak, while dinner includes a $12.50 roast of the day and more meaty mains, including half a kilo of rib-eye steak for $22.

Republic Bar & Café 299 Elizabeth St ☎03/6234 6954. Laid-back lounge atmosphere, funky decor and free music, usually blues and jazz, six nights a week (except Mon); attracts a good crowd, including plenty of students. Excellent meals, too, with lots of seafood on the menu.

Rockerfeller's 11 Morrison St ☎03/ 6234 3490. Gay-friendly bar-restaurant. A fun atmosphere and a contemporary Australian menu, plus cocktails. Lunch Mon–Fri, dinner nightly. Live jazz Sun night.

Syrup 39 Salamanca Place ☎03/6224 8249. Often hosting international guest DJs, this trendy club is on two levels above *Knopwood's*. Different nights and different floors have changing sounds and themes: anything from Sixties theme nights, techno, house, drum'n'bass, and 1980s retro, to live disco and funk. Open from 9pm Thurs, 8pm Fri & Sat (until 6am) and with live bands on Sat afternoon 3pm to 6pm. Cover charge around $7.

T-42° Elizabeth Street Pier ☎03/6224 7742. Stylish lounge bar in a great waterfront location – some tables on the pier – attracting a cross-section of trendies and young professionals. Half the place is an eating area serving well-priced modern Australian–style meals at lunch and dinner (mains from $18). A good place to try Tasmanian wines, with many available by the glass. Daily 11.30–1.30am.

Telegraph Hotel 19 Morrison St ☎03/6234 6254. No cover charge and very popular with the young after-work crowd and, possibly thanks to there being no cover charge, the university's students. DJ (Wed–Fri) and live band on Sat, plus tapas on Thurs & Fri.

Trout Bar and Cafe *Eagle Hawk Inn*, Elizabeth St, cnr Federal St, North Hobart ☎03/6236 9777. Relaxed pub which feels more like an arty café. Small menu of pasta, salads, steaks, chicken and Asian curries. Music, often jazz or blues, usually free (or around $7), Thurs to Sun nights in a friendly, chatty atmosphere. Lunch Wed–Fri, Sun brunch 11am–3pm, dinner nightly.

Film, theatre, concerts and cabaret

Federation Concert Hall 1 Davey St, bookings ☎1800 001 190. Home to the Tasmanian Symphony Orchestra, with regular concerts.

The Playhouse Theatre 106 Bathurst St ☎03/6234 1536. The Hobart Repertory Theatre Society, an amateur not-for-profit group established in 1926, puts on at least five plays a year here plus a popular Christmas panto. Premises are also rented out to travelling shows.

Salamanca Arts Centre 77 Salamanca Place ☎03/6234 8414. Base of several performance companies, including the Terrapin Puppet Theatre, which puts on touring shows – including a puppet picnic at the end of Dec in St David's Park. Puppeteers are welcome to come in and look around. Specializing in contemporary works, the Peacock Theatre hosts performances by various local theatre companies.

State Cinema 375 Elizabeth St, North Hobart ☎03/6234 6318, Ⓦwww.statecinema.com.au. Art-house and foreign films; reduced ticket prices Wed ($10). Licensed bar.

Theatre Royal 29 Campbell St ☎03/6233 2299, Ⓦwww.theatreroyal.webcentral.com.au. This lovely old place (see p.988) is not too expensive or stuffy, offering a broad spectrum of entertainment from comedy nights to serious drama. Tickets from $17.

Village Cinema Centre 181 Collins St ☎03/6234 7288, Ⓦwww.villagecinemas.com.au. Seven screens showing mainstream new releases; discount day is Tues.

Festivals and events

Hobart's premier event is the last part of the **Sydney–Hobart yacht race** (see also p.61). The two hundred or so yachts, which leave Sydney on December 26, arrive in Hobart around December 29, making for a lively New Year's Eve waterfront party complete with fireworks. The race coincides with the fortnight-long **Hobart Summer Festival** (Dec 27 to Jan 9; more information via Ⓦwww.hobartsummerfestival.com.au), focused on waterfront Sullivans Cove. The major event is **The Taste of Tasmania** (daily 11am–11pm, Dec 28–Jan 3), a gourmet food-fest promoting Tasmanian food, wine and beer, held at Princes Wharf. The main festival features outdoor concerts in St David's Park (the kids' one is free), a circus, symphony concerts, children's theatre in the Botanical Gardens, the 1km Pier-to-Pier River Swim, a Tasmanian film festival, buskers, and night-time gallery openings. The **Australian Wooden Boat Festival** runs over three days in early February in odd-numbered years, marked by a host of boats moored around the docks; activities include theatrical and musical performances and boat-building courses (Ⓣ03/6231 6407, Ⓦwww.australian woodenboatfestival.com.au).

The week-long **Hobart Fringe Festival** in mid-February has visual arts, film and performance components (Ⓦwww.hobartfringe.org; many events free). The whole city shuts down on October 24 during the **Royal Hobart Show** (Oct 23–26), an agricultural festival.

Listings

Airlines Jet Star Ⓣ13 15 38, Ⓦwww.jetstar.com.au; Par Avion Wilderness Tours, Cambridge Airport Ⓣ03/6248 5390, Ⓦwww.paravion.com.au; Airlines of Tasmania Ⓣ1800 144 460, Ⓦwww.airtasmania.com.au; Qantas Ⓣ13 13 13, or their travel centre at 130 Collins St; Tasair, Cambridge Airport Ⓣ03/6427 9777 or 1800 062 900, Ⓦwww.tasair.com.au; Virgin Blue Ⓣ13 67 89, Ⓦwww.virginblue.com.au; King Island Airways, Ⓣ03/9580 3777, Ⓦwww.kingislandair.com.au.

American Express 74A Liverpool St Ⓣ03/6234 3711.

Banks Branches of all major banks are on Elizabeth Street.

Bike rental and tours Several hostels rent bikes as do Island Cycle Tours (see p.979). Derwent Bike Hire (Ⓣ03/6234 2910, Ⓦwww.derwntbikehire.com); $7 per hour, $20 per day, $90 per week) rents mountain bikes at the beginning of the bike track to Cornelian Bay, by the Cenotaph in the Regatta Grounds.

Bookshops Ellison and Hawker Bookshop, 90 Liverpool St, has an excellent travel section upstairs. Fullers Bookshop, 140 Collins St, and The Hobart Bookshop, 22 Salamanca Square, are Hobart's two best literary bookstores; Fullers has its own café. For a fine range of secondhand books, try Rapid Eye Books, 36–38 Sandy Bay Rd, Battery Point.

Bus companies "Tasmania's Own" Redline Coaches, Hobart Transit Centre, 199 Collins St Ⓣ1300 360 000; TassieLink, Hobart Bus Terminal, 64 Brisbane St Ⓣ1300 300 520.

Campervan rental Tasmanian Campervan Hire, Cambridge Airport (Ⓣ03/6248 9623 or 1800 807 119, Ⓦwww.tascamper.com), from $80 per day off-peak to $110 in summer, minimum five-day rental.

Camping and outdoor equipment There is a concentration of camping-gear shops on Elizabeth St near Bathurst St, including a big range at Jolly Swagman Camping World, 107 Elizabeth St; Paddy Pallin, 119 Elizabeth St, has quality outdoor equipment, and provides bushwalking information; Mountain Creek Great Outdoors Centre, 75–77 Bathurst St Ⓣ03/6234 4395, has a big selection, from cheap to top of the range, and also rents out gear.

Car rental Autorent-Hertz, at the airport and 122 Harrington St (Ⓣ03/6237 1111 or 1800 030 222, Ⓦwww.autorent.com.au), also has campervans; and Avis, at the airport (Ⓣ03/6248 5424), have similar rates; Lo-Cost Auto Rent, at the airport and at 225 Liverpool St (Ⓣ03/6231 0550 or 1800 647 060, Ⓦwww.locostautorent.com), has older cars plus newer models; Devil Campervans (Ⓣ03/6248 4493, Ⓦwww.devilcampervans.com.au), from $50 per day minimum 5 days rental (mention Rough Guide for $10 discount). Rent-A-Bug, 105 Murray St (Ⓣ03/6231 0300, Ⓦwww.rentabug.com.au), has low-priced VW Beetles.

Disabled travellers The Commonwealth Carelink Centre (Ⓣ1800 052 222) and the Aged and Disability Care Information Service, 181 Elizabeth St (Ⓣ03/6228 5799, Ⓦwww.adcis.org.au), are excellent sources of information, providing free mobility maps of Hobart. Hobart City Council produces a free *Hobart CBD Mobility Map*, available from their HQ on the corner of Elizabeth and Davey

sts (☎03/6238 2711).City Cabs (☎131 008 or 03 6274 3103) has specially adapted vehicles.
Diving The Dive Shop, 67A Argyle St (☎03/6234 3428), hires equipment and runs PADI certification courses.
Environment To find out about or to volunteer for environmental conservation programmes, the Wilderness Society's campaign office is at 130 Davey St (☎03/6224 1550, Ⓦwww.wilderness.org.au/tas); its shop is at 33 Salamanca Place.
Hospitals Royal Hobart Hospital, 48 Liverpool St ☎03/6222 8308.
Internet access There's paid access at the State Library (see p.988; free for Australian residents, $5.50 per 30min for overseas visitors) but the best rates are at hostels ($2–3 per hour) and at Drifters Internet Café ($5 per hour; also cheap phone cards for calling overseas.
Laundry 12 Salamanca Square is a combined café/laundry.
Pharmacy Macquarie Pharmacy, 180 Macquarie St (daily 8am–10pm; ☎03/6223 2339); North Hobart Pharmacy, 360–362 Elizabeth St (daily 8am–10pm; ☎03/6234 1136).
Post office GPO, cnr Elizabeth and Macquarie Sts (Mon–Fri 8am–6pm). Poste restante: Hobart GPO, TAS 7000.
Swimming pool Hobart Aquatic Centre (☎03/6222 6999), cnr Liverpool St and Davies Ave (Mon–Fri 6am–10pm, Sat & Sun 8am–6pm; $5.00). Heated swim centre with waterslides and bubble-jets. Also gym and fitness centre.
Taxis City Cabs ☎13 10 08; Combined Services ☎13 22 27.
Tours Tigerline (☎03/6272 6611, Ⓦwww.tigerline.com.au) runs large-group bus tours: their Hobart City Centre and Mount Wellington Tour covers the city, the dock area, Battery Point, Mount Wellington and the Royal Botanical Gardens (Tues & Thurs 2pm, Sun 9.00am; 3hr; $51). Tigerline also offers day-trips to Mt Field National Park, Port Arthur, Richmond, Tahune Forest AirWalk and Bruny Island. The best tour to Bruny Island is with Bruny Island Ventures (book through Tigerline), which does a small-group day-tour led by a knowledgeable guide (8.30am, returning 5.30pm; $145 including meals). The Bottom Bits Bus (see p.979) offers a range of great small-group tours from Hobart (all $99), including Port Arthur and the Tasman Peninsula, Bruny Island and Mount Field National Park, Mount Wellington and the Tahune Forest AirWalk, and Freycinet National Park.
Women Women Tasmania, 140 Macquarie St (☎03/6233 2208, Ⓦwww.women.tas.gov.au), provides information services. Hobart Women's Health Centre, 25 Lefroy St, North Hobart ☎03/6231 3212, Ⓦwww.hwhc.com.au.
YHA Tasmania Head Office, 28 Criterion St ☎03/6234 9617, Ⓦwww.yha.com.au (Mon–Fri 9am–5pm).

Around Hobart

Picturesque channels, orchards and islands define the landscape south of Hobart. The D'Entrecasteaux Channel region and the Huon Valley form Tasmania's premier **fruit-growing** district, which once exported millions of apples to England; when the UK joined the European Community in the 1970s, however, two-thirds of the apple orchards were abandoned. The region is also heavily forested, and around **Geeveston** magnificent woodlands are still logged. **Hartz Mountains National Park** and the **Picton River** are easily accessible to the west of Geeveston and you can get wonderful views of both, and of old-growth forests, from the **Tahune Forest AirWalk**. As you head down the coast, caves and thermal springs are all accessible en route to **Cockle Creek**, the southernmost point you can drive to in Australia, with foot access along a track into the South West National Park. Offshore, across the D'Entrecasteaux Channel from **Kettering**, **Bruny Island** – Truganini's birthplace – has deserted beaches and coastal bushwalks. To the north, you can head inland to **New Norfolk** and on to **Mount Field National Park**, while to the east lies historic **Richmond** and, on the Tasman Peninsula, the old penal settlement at **Port Arthur**.

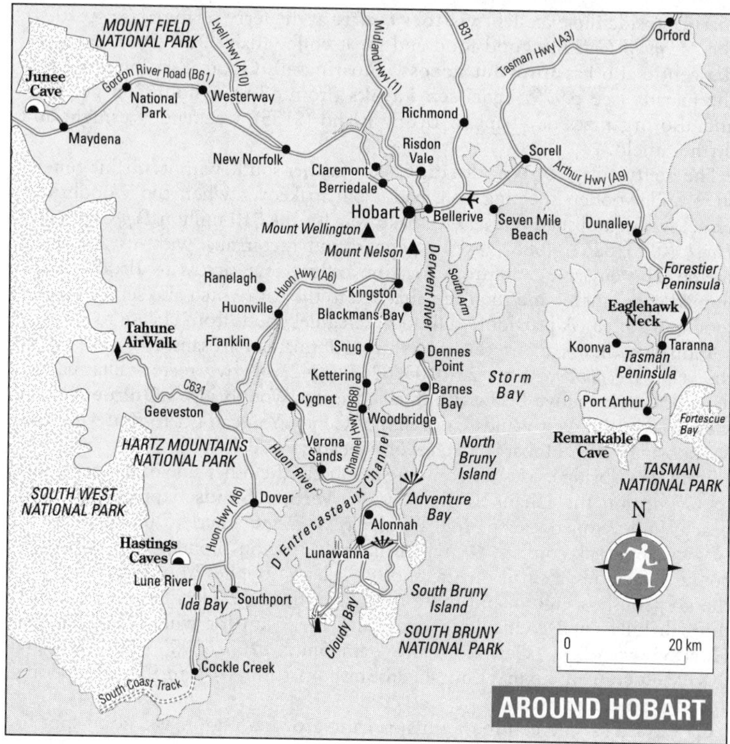

South: the D'Entrecasteaux Channel, Huon Valley and beyond

The **Channel Highway** (B68) hugs the coastline south from Hobart and makes a lovely drive around the shores of the **Huon Peninsula**, circling back alongside the Huon River to Huonville. Heading to Huonville directly, it's a much shorter 37km on the **Huon Highway** (A6), which then heads south for 64km, terminating at Southport. An excellent free fold-out guide map, *The Huon Trail*, is available from tourist offices; it outlines the **Huon Discovery Trail**, a series of signs and interpretive boards detailing points of interest off the Channel and Huon highways.

The Channel Highway

On the Channel Highway beyond Taroona and Kingston (see p.991), **KETTERING**, 34km south of Hobart, is a thriving fishing port, with an attractive marina. It's from Kettering that you catch the ferry for Bruny Island (see p.1004). The unpretentious *Oyster Cove Inn* (Ⓣ03/6267 4446; rooms share bathroom; B&B ❸–❹) is right on the water, not far from the ferry terminal, and has fantastic views from its restaurant, and a quirky sculpture-cum-beer garden; it specializes in seafood and local produce. More upmarket, *Herons Rise Vineyard* on Saddle Road (Ⓣ03/6267 4339, Ⓦwww.heronsrise.com.au; ❺) has luxury self-contained cabins gazing across the marina. Inside the excellent **visitors centre** at the ferry terminal (see p.1004), the *Mermaid Café* has good food and great coffee (daily 9am–5pm; licensed); the centre also has **Internet access**. Roaring 40s Ocean Kayaking, based at the marina (see p.979), rents **sea kayaks** (from $20 per hour, $55 per day), and also organizes day-trips to Bruny Island ($155), weekend overnight and further afield.

The pretty village of **Woodbridge**, 4km further south, with its quaint general store and wooden meeting hall, had a big makeover when the Woodbridge Hotel was demolished in 2003 to make way for the $10 million *Peppermint Bay Hotel* (ⓣ03/6267 4088, ⓦwww.peppermintbay.com.au) with its fine-food theme. The enviable waterfront location offers views across to Bruny in the upmarket restaurant and the deck attached to the bar (which also serves simpler food and coffee). A providore sells local Channel goods from cheese to smoked salmon, and there's an art gallery featuring Tasmanian artisans. You can **stay** in the *Old Woodbridge Rectory* (ⓣ03/6267 4742, ⓦwww.rectory.alltasmanian.com; ④), an attractive B&B with disabled access. Woodbridge's **Online Access Centre** is at the West Winds Community Centre. You can get to Kettering and Woodbridge with Hobart Coaches on weekdays (2 daily).

From Woodbridge, you can continue around to the other side of the peninsula to Cygnet on the Channel Highway via **Verona Sands**, a pretty, sheltered beach, undeveloped except for the *Applejack Resort Motel* (ⓣ03/6297 8177, ⓦwww.applejack.com.au; ④), which has tidy, spacious holiday units with full cooking facilities; a small on-site shop sells basic supplies. You could also take the gorgeously scenic inland route to Cygnet from Woodbridge on the C627 through hilly, rural countryside, detouring after 5km for wine tastings at the **Hartzview Wine Centre** (daily 9am–5pm; ⓣ03/6295 1623, ⓦwww.hartzview.com.au; luxury three-bedroom homestead ⑥), a further 2km along a well-graded dirt road.

CYGNET, at the centre of a major fruit-growing region, is a good spot to look for **fruit-picking work** in the busy apple-harvest season (March–May), but there's also the chance of finding strawberry – (Nov–May) or blueberry-picking work (Dec–Feb) at other times. The town itself is very pleasant, backed by bush-covered hills; the appearance is sweetly old-fashioned but the town has an alternative cultural scene, the focus of which is the elegant *Lotus Eaters* (Mon & Thurs–Sun 8am–5pm), whose simple wholesome meals include a couple of vegetarian choices; it also does great coffee and cakes. Nearby, the *fire bird bakehouse* serves woodfired pizzas (Thurs–Sat from 6pm). The more traditional, cosy *School House Coffee Shop* across the road does great scones, while all three pubs offer counter meals. You can also **stay** in clean rooms at the *Cygnet Hotel* (ⓣ03/6295 1267; ②) or camp at the *Cygnet Holiday Park*, both on Mary Street (ⓣ03/6295 1869). Two kilometres south out of town, right on the water, is the tranquil *Cygnet Bay Waterfront Retreat*, at Crooked Point (ⓣ03/6295 0980, ⓦwww.cygnetbay.com.au; ⑤). *Nomads Huon Valley Backpackers*, at 4 Sandhill Rd just off the Channel Highway, 4km north at Cradoc (ⓣ03/6295 1551, ⓦwww.nomadsworld.com; dorms $25, rooms, some en suite ②–③; pick-ups available if arranged in advance), on several rural acres, with river views, has all the necessary contacts for fruit-picking work. The weekend-long **Cygnet Folk Festival** (ⓦwww.cygnetfolkfestival.org; around $75 for the weekend; tickets through Centretainment), established in 1982, is the state's major folk, world and roots music event, and takes over the town in early January. Hobart Coaches (see p.978) runs a limited service from Hobart to Cygnet (Mon, Tues & Fri 5.15pm, Thurs 9am & 3.10pm).

The Huon Highway: Huonville and around

The commercial centre of **HUONVILLE** is the focus of the region's apple industry, and another place where the prospect of finding work in the apple-harvest season (March–May) is good; it's also known for its delicious Huon Valley mushrooms. Once a rather redneck place, the town has developed a more alternative and upmarket edge, suited to its picturesque position on the Huon River. The handy **Parks and Wildlife Service information centre** and shop at 24 Main Rd (Mon–Fri 9am–4.30pm; ⓣ03/6264 8460) has information on all parks and reserves, and sells park passes, books, maps, and some walking gear. There's also a community-based drop-in **Environment Centre** at 17 Wilmot Rd (daily 9am–5pm; ⓣ03/6264 1286), northwest of the roundabout near the Parks shop. There's a decent eat-in bakery, *Banjo's*, opposite at no. 8 (daily 6am–6pm), or real café culture at *Cafe Moto* in the same building as the Environment Centre (daily 8am–6pm). Another good place to **eat** is *Huon Manor Bistro* (ⓣ03/6264 1311; Mon–Sat noon–2.30pm & 6–8pm), a cosy, reasonably priced restaurant-cum-bar in a big Federation-style riverfront homestead, just by the bridge into town.

There are several options available to go for a ride on the river at Huonville with Huon River Cruises (ⓣ03/6264 1838, ⓦwww.huonjet.com), based at the **Huonville Visitor Information Centre** (daily 9am–5pm; same phone; Internet access $2 per 30min) on The Esplanade, as the Channel Highway is called coming into town from Cygnet. Huonville's **Online Access Centre** is at 23 Wilmot Rd. TassieLink runs a service from Hobart to Huonville.

At **GROVE**, 6km back towards Hobart on the Huon Highway (A6), the **Apple Heritage Museum** (daily 9am–5pm; $3) celebrates the local produce. The museum is surprisingly interesting, with hundreds of varieties of apples when in harvest season (March–May) and assorted apple paraphernalia from what was once a huge export industry.

Three kilometres northwest of Huonville via Wilmot Road, the picturesque hamlet of **RANELAGH** is home to the lauded *Matilda's of Ranelagh* at 44 Louisa St (ⓣ03/6264 3493; ❻), a B&B in an 1850 National Trust–listed mansion within English-style gardens with a characterful outhouse on the grounds. Just out of Ranelagh, the sleek vineyard-set winery/restaurant, *Home Hill*, at 38 Nairn St (wine tasting daily 10am–5pm; lunch Wed–Sun, dinner Fri & Sat, morning and afternoon tea daily; Sun lunch bookings essential ⓣ03/6264 1200), has a stunning backdrop of the peaks of Sleeping Beauty.

Southwest beyond Huonville, the road follows the west bank of the Huon for 8km to **FRANKLIN**, a bucolic community dating from 1839 with several fine old buildings and cute weatherboard homes facing the river and set against green hills. Franklin's chief attraction is the **Wooden Boat School**, where you can observe students (who come from around the world for the unique 18-month course) learning traditional wooden-boat building and restoration (daily 9.30am–5pm; $5.50; ⓦwww.woodenboatschool.com). You can **stay** in the colonial-era *Franklin Lodge* (ⓣ03/6266 3506, ⓦwww.franklinlodge.com.au; ❺) or in self-catering accommodation such as the friendly hilltop *Kay Creek Cottage* (ⓣ03/6266 3524, ⓦwww.kaycreekcottage.com; ❺ includes breakfast provisions). There's a varied modern menu at the waterfront *Petty Sessions Gourmet Cafe* (daily 10am–5pm plus dinner Fri–Sun; licensed). In the evening, offerings at the well-regarded *Franklin Grill* include fresh Bruny Island oysters (dinner Wed–Sun; ⓣ03/6266 3645; licensed & BYO) or try *Franklin Woodfired Pizza* (from 5pm Mon–Fri, from 4pm Sat & Sun). *Tasmanian Seafood*, opposite the fire station, does tasty fish and chips, delicious tempura Huon Valley mushrooms and sweet-potato cakes.

Geeveston and around

Two huge upright logs serve as the entrance to sleepy and solid **GEEVESTON**, a traditional logging town 18km south of Franklin and in the heart of the Southern Forest. Confrontation between conservationists and the timber industry here led to the so-called "Battle of Farmhouse Creek" in 1986, a dispute won by the conservationists, after which some of the forests were awarded World Heritage listing. The Forestry Commission was awarded millions of dollars in compensation, to be used on special forestry projects, one of which is the **Forest and Heritage Centre** in the town hall on Church Street (daily 9am–5pm; ⓣ03/6297 1836, ⓦwww.forestandheritagecentre.com.au; free), which also has a **visitor information centre**. Displays explain how the Southern Forests grow, and look at the history of logging in the area – including the Farmhouse Creek dispute. There's also a gallery of local woodwork and a woodturner in residence (lessons are available). A related Forestry Tasmania project, the Tahune Forest AirWalk (see below), is 26km southwest along the now-sealed Arve Road. En route to the must-see AirWalk, on the drive along Arve Road, several boardwalks have been constructed through magnificent swamp gum and eucalypt forests – they're detailed on the free leaflet that's handed out.

Twenty-four kilometres southwest along Arve Road is the rugged **Hartz Mountains National Park**, with its glacial lakes, rainforests and alpine moorlands; a day-walk map is available from the Forest and Heritage Centre. From Arve Road, a stony, unsealed track winds up for 12km, with several stopping-off points; 2km from the end of the track is a very short walk to Waratah Lookout with great views over the Huon Valley and the Southern Forests. Another walk (4km) heads off to the sometimes-snowcapped Hartz Peak (1255m); most of the trail is boardwalked, but parts are wet and boggy underfoot and there's the potential for fog to settle and icy winds and snow to sweep in at any time – recommended for well-prepared walkers only.

The **Picton River** skirts the Hartz Mountains from its source deep in the South West National Park; with its bouncy rapids, intermittent gentle sections and magnificent wilderness scenery, it's a popular, short (and affordable) **rafting** alternative to the Franklin River. Rafting Tasmania (see p.979) runs year-round day-trips from Hobart for $115. The river continues towards the **Tahune Forest Reserve**, at the junction with the Huon River, just north of Hartz Mountains National Park. Here, the impressive $4.5 million **Tahune Forest AirWalk and Visitor Centre** (daily 9am–5pm; $17; ⓣ03/6297 0068, ⓦwww.tasforestrytourism.com.au) was opened in 2001. The 597-metre-long, steel-framed walkway is supported by twelve towers and suspended 25–48m in the air at the level of the tree canopy of the surrounding old-growth forest and, thrillingly, above the confluence of the rivers, with magnificent views across to the Hartz Mountains. For more thrills, the latest addition is the **Eagle Glide**, an aerial cable that whizzes you individually across the forest for an extra $33. Below, the riverside Huon Pine boardwalk provides an easy twenty-minute return stroll to huge and ancient Huon Pines. The visitor centre has a Forestry Tasmania interpretive display, while the attached licensed café focuses on local gourmet products. If you're picnicking, there are great shelters with roaring fires and gas barbecues for even the wildest day; camping is also allowed here.

You can **stay** at the *Geeveston Forest House*, a cottage hostel on the edge of town at 24 Arve Rd (ⓣ03/6297 1804, ⓦwww.geevestonforesthouse.com; dorms $20, room ❷). TassieLink has a Hobart–Geeveston service (five daily Mon–Fri, one daily Sat and Sun) and operates a day-tour to the AirWalk (depart 9am; $99).

Dover and around

DOVER, 21km from Geeveston, is an attractive fishing village on a large bay, **Port Esperance**, fed by the Esperance River. There are trees everywhere, and lush hills surround the village, backed by the clear, virtually triangular, outline of **Adamsons Peak** (1226m), snowcapped in winter. Boats moor off a jetty in the bay, where two tiny tree-covered islets are silhouetted against the sky at dusk.

The hub of Dover is the *Dover Hotel*, on the Huon Highway (ⓣ03/6298 1210, ⓦwww.doverhotel.com; rooms ❸, motel units for 4 ❹), beside an apple orchard and rolling fields, with an old-fashioned dining room overlooking the water. Southern Wilderness Eco Adventure Tours (ⓣ03/6297 6368, ⓦwww.tasglow-wormadventure.com.au) offers a popular Glow Worm Adventure Caving Trip (4hr; $65) departing from the hotel. The *Dover Beachside Tourist Park* on Kent Beach Road (ⓣ03/6298 1301; vans ❷, cabins ❸–❹) is scenically sited near the jetty, beside a creek. Back up towards Geeveston, 12km north near picturesque Police Point, *Huon Charm* (ⓣ03/6297 6314, ⓦwww.huoncharm.com; ❹) consists of two waterfront cottages and a houseboat and is a more secluded alternative. Six kilometres south along the highway at **Strathblane** is the truly marvellous *Far South Wilderness Lodge and Backpackers* (ⓣ03/6298 1922, ⓦwww.farsouthwilderness.com.au; ❸; camping also available; TassieLink will drop off outside) sitting right on an inlet of the Esperance River in eighty acres of unspoilt forest. Activities include a nightly campfire, guided walks, mountain biking ($10 half-day; $15 full day) and kayak hire ($15/hr; $45/day). A great place to eat in Dover itself is the excellent *Dover Woodfired Pizza* (daily 4–10pm; BYO), with wall-length windows looking down to the water; it's near the **Online Access Centre**. Although you can find fuel and supplies 20km south at **Southport** (the last place to get either), there's more choice and better value in Dover. TassieLink runs a service to Dover (Mon–Fri 1–2 daily plus extra services Dec–April).

Thirty-one kilometres from Dover are the Hastings Caves, in the foothills of Adamsons Peak, with the **Thermal Springs State Reserve** en route. The small, shallow and rather tepid springs, ranging from 20–30°C, are no great shakes, but the setting is lush and there are several walks in the grounds and also a pleasant café and visitor centre (ⓣ03/6298 3209 ⓦwww.parks.tas.gov.au; $5 or cave ticket includes pool entry). Tickets to visit **Hastings Caves**, a few kilometres further on from the springs, must be bought from here: Newdegate Cave, the best, is open daily for tours (hourly 11am–3pm, with extra tours Oct–March; 45min; $22); it's always wet and cold inside, so bring something warm to wear. Bottom Bits Bus does a tour to Hastings Cave from Hobart (see p.979).

Cockle Creek

Beyond Ida Bay, the unsurfaced Cockle Creek Road takes you past picturesque sheltered bays and coastal forests, where wild flowers bloom in summer, to **COCKLE CREEK** on the lovely **Recherche Bay** (pronounced "research" by locals), so named because it was here that the French expedition under **Bruny D'Entrecasteaux**, sent to look for the missing La Pérouse expedition (see "Sydney", p.154), set up temporarily for four weeks in 1792 and again in 1793. As well as the important botanical research carried out by naturalist Labilladière, a garden was established and cordial meetings with the Aboriginal people were recorded.

The only provision at the small settlement clustered around the Recherche Bay Community Centre is an emergency phone. Beyond, there are lots of free camping spots along the shore (one-month limit), as well as caravans inhabited semi-permanently by mainly fishing-obsessed retirees after the abundant crayfish, cockles and fish in the bay. Pit toilets and water are the only facilities. The wooden bridge across Cockle Creek leads to the **South West National Park** where an interpretive board outside the intermittently-staffed office (to speak to a ranger, contact Huonville NPWS ⓣ03/6264 8460; see p.1001) provides a fascinating history from Aboriginal, French, whaling and other perspectives. There's a five-minute walk to a waterfront bronze sculpture of a baby southern right whale and from here the easy Fishers Point walk takes you around the coast (4km round trip; up to 2hr), but the most popular walk is the muddy but boardwalked first part of the **South Coast Track** to the beach at South Cape Bay and back (4hr return; moderate difficulty); the entire length of the track is for the very experienced only, but this portion gives you a small taste (see p.1076 for details of the whole walk). TassieLink has a "Wilderness Link" service to Cockle Creek from November to April.

Bruny Island

For beautiful lonely beaches and shorter coastal walks, one of the best places in Tasmania is **Bruny Island**. Almost two distinct islands joined by a narrow isthmus (where you can sometimes see Little penguins from a specially constructed viewing platform), it's roughly 71km from end to end and has a population of only four hundred. The cost of taking a car across on the ferry deters casual visitors, so the island is never very full. The ferry from Kettering goes to substantially rural North Bruny, although most of the settlements, and places to stay and eat, are on South Bruny – the more scenic half, with its state forests and reserves.

Getting there, information and getting around

The **ferry from Kettering** (see p.999) sails at least nine times daily (Mon–Sat 6.35am–6.30pm, till 7.30pm Fri, Sun 7.45am–6.30pm; 20min; ⓣ03/6273 6725 for times; $25 per car return or $30 public holidays, motorbikes $12.50, bikes $3.50, foot passengers free). The **Bruny D'Entrecasteaux Visitor Centre** at

△ Bruny Island

the Kettering ferry terminal on Ferry Road off the Channel Highway (daily 9am–5pm; ⓣ03/6267 4494, ⓦwww.tasmaniaholiday.com or www.brunyisland.net) books island accommodation, much of which is in self-catering cottages (stock up on groceries and petrol in Kingston – p.991 – as island prices are high and choice limited). It's best to book before going over, especially on the weekend when it's a popular getaway. The centre can also supply you with **information** on the island, including a good free fold-out map. As there is no public transport on the island, you'll need your own car or bike to get around unless you come on the excellent small-group day-tour from Hobart with Bruny Island Ventures (see p.998), or Bruny Island Charters, which does very popular three-hour **wildlife cruises** exploring the south, around Fluted Cape, following the spectacular cliff line, to a seal colony. If you're lucky you'll see dolphins and maybe even a southern right whale, as well as the abundant birdlife in the area (Oct–April daily except Sat 11am from the jetty at Adventure Bay; $95; ⓣ03/6293 1465, ⓦwww.brunycharters.com.au). They also offer the cruise as part of a return trip from Hobart (Hobart pick-up 8am, returning 5/5.30pm; $155 including lunch).

If you're driving or riding yourself, be aware that many of the island's roads are unsealed – even the stretch of speedy highway will suddenly become a dusty unsealed road for kilometres at a time. Petrol is only available at Dennes Point, Adventure Bay, Alonnah and Lunawanna. Hobart Coaches operates services from Hobart to Kettering that connect with a couple of the ferries (see p.978).

Around the island

There's no town at **Roberts Point**, where the ferry docks on the north of the island, just a phone box, some public toilets, a post box and, in the summer, a stall selling cherries. The main settlement on **North Bruny** is **DENNES POINT** at the northern extreme of the island, which has a general store (petrol sold) and attached café, and a jetty. This is a popular spot for weekend getaway "shacks" for Hobart citizens fond of fishing. A detour off this route, 3km off the main road along an unsealed road, is the secluded settlement of **Barnes Bay**, where pretty Shelter Cove was the first "Black station" to be established for the forced resettlement of Aboriginal people (see box, p.976). There's a small jetty which is a peaceful spot to contemplate the boats bobbing in the cove, and a pebbly beach, but no facilities – though you can **stay** here in the two-bedroom, very stylish *Bruny Beach House* (ⓣ03/5243 8486, ⓦwww.brunybeachhouse.com; ⑤).

At the northern end of the isthmus connecting the two islands, the **Neck Game Reserve** (free) acts as a sanctuary for Little penguins and muttonbirds who inhabit rookeries in the sand dunes here. A wooden boardwalk (with stairs) descends over the burrows to the beach and an interpretive board provides information on the birds, best sighted between September and February as they return to their burrows after dusk. Atop the tallest sand dune here, reached by a high wooden stairway, is a small monument to **Truganini** (the "last" Tasmanian Aborigine, who was born here as one of the 70-strong Nuenonne band of the South East tribe), and you can take in superb views of the southern part of the island, where three former reserves have been turned into **South Bruny National Park**. You can see the Fluted Cape State Reserve region to the east of Adventure Bay; here, a steep climb to the top of the Cape (2hr 30min return) offers still better views. The Labillardière State Reserve area occupies the western "hook" of South Bruny Island; a winding, bumpy road leads to the **Cape Bruny Lighthouse** (guided tours by arrangement $8; ⓣ03/6298 3114), built in 1836 and manned until 1996; beyond this a seven-hour walking trail explores the peninsula. East of the hook, across **Cloudy Bay**, is the final chunk of the national park, with its great sweep of surf beach. You can do a spot of bushcamping here (pit toilet only, no water), and at Neck Beach about 1.5km from the isthmus viewing point (pit toilet, water, shelter with barbecue). For considerably more comfort, there's the secluded, self-catering beachfront *Cloudy Bay Cabin* (ⓣ03/6293 1171; ❺), powered by solar energy and gas. You can also stay just north of Cloudy Bay in the comfortable self-contained cottage at *Inala* (ⓣ03/6293 1217, ⓦwww.inalabruny.com.au; ❻), which doubles as the base for Inala Nature Tours (half-day to extended customized trips) run by a qualified biologist.

ADVENTURE BAY is the main settlement on the east coast of South Bruny, and the principal tourist centre strung along Adventure Bay Road. You can swim from the beautiful sandy sweep of beach, and there's a general store (petrol sold) with an ATM, and several accommodation choices. The **Bligh Museum of Pacific Discovery** (daily 10am–5pm; $4) charts Bruny's links with early explorers and seafarers (including Abel Tasman, Tobias Furneaux, James Cook, William Bligh, Bruny D'Entrecasteux and naturalist Labillardière, and Nicolas Baudin), for whom it provided a safe refuge after the arduous journey across the Southern Ocean, and the museum displays maps, documents, paintings and artefacts relating to landings here. *The Penguin Café* (daily 10am–5pm plus dinner Sat; ⓣ03/6293 1352; licensed & BYO) does tasty casseroles, vegetarian dishes, gourmet burgers, yummy cakes and real coffee. A good place to stay nearby is the three-bedroom *Lumeah*, a comfortable homestead on Quiet Corner (ⓣ03/6293 1265, ⓦwww.lumeah-island.com.au; ❺), with an outside spa and pretty garden. You can camp next to the beach at the *Captain James Cook Caravan Park* (ⓣ03/6293 1128, ⓦwww.capcookolkid.com.au; vans ❷, cabins ❹), which is closer to the shops but less attractive than the tree-filled *Adventure Bay Holiday Village* (ⓣ03/6293 1270, ⓦwww.adventurebayholidayvillage.com.au; dorms $20, vans ❶, cabins ❸, cottages ❹), a couple of kilometres further along, with the pleasant *Bay Café* and the island's only **hostel** accommodation. Just north of town, *Morella Island Retreats* (ⓣ03/6293 1131, ⓦwww.morella-island.com.au; ❻–❼) has several secluded, individual retreat cabins in their 25 acres of gardens; their *Hothouse Café* (bookings essential after 5.30pm) offers exotic dining in a hothouse amongst peacocks and parrots, surrounded by an abundant vegetable garden, with panoramic views across Neck Beach and all the way to Mount Wellington.

On the west coast, along the D'Entrecasteaux Channel, **ALONNAH** is the main settlement. As well as a general store and post office here (petrol sold) on Bruny Main Road, you'll find the *Hotel Bruny* (ⓣ03/6293 1148; basic motel-style units ❸) next door; though it's unattractive, it has uninterrupted water views and offers good-value counter meals, and has the island's only bottle shop. Bruny Island's **Online Access Centre** is nearby on School Road. Near the settlement, *The Tree House* (ⓣ03/5255 5147, ⓦwww.thetreehouse.com.au; ❻) is a gorgeous all-wood, open-plan studio apartment (sleeps up to four) with wonderful water views.

Five kilometres south at **LUNAWANNA**, the Mangana Store (daily 8am–6/7pm) sells petrol, groceries and hamburgers; the bakery next door bakes pizzas (Thurs only). You can stay at the excellent, well-maintained two-bedroom *Bruny Island Explorer Cottages* on Light House Road overlooking Daniels Bay (ⓣ03/6293 1271, ⓦwww.brunyisland.com; ❺); cottages have wood combustion fires and facilities include a communal laundry. From Lunawanna, it's a scenic drive south to Cloudy Bay.

New Norfolk, Mount Field National Park and Maydena

Heading inland from Hobart through the Derwent Valley towards Mount Field National Park, the A10 hugs the Derwent River for the 50km to the well-preserved colonial buildings of **NEW NORFOLK**. It was to here that the original settlers of Norfolk Island (see p.296) were moved between 1806 and 1814. The sizeable town has been at the centre of the hop-growing industry for 150 years, and there are still oast houses in the surrounding hop fields. The broad stretch of the Derwent here is clean, beautiful and swimmable, disturbed only by thrillseekers in jet boats: Devil Jet runs high-speed rides through the rapids (daily 9am–4pm, on the hour; 30min; $55 per person, minimum two people; ⓣ03/6261 3460), leaving from the Esplanade. The river-facing *Bush Inn* at 49 Montagu St, the main road, claims to be Australia's oldest continuously licensed **hotel** (ⓣ03/6261 2011; ❸), and with its stained wooden floorboards, huge stone fireplaces and a small ballroom with chandeliers and piano, it's a lovely place to stay, as is the antique-furnished *Old Colony Inn*, a simple, whitewashed building on the same street at no. 21 (ⓣ03/6261 2731; ❹). From New Norfolk, you can visit the **Salmon Ponds** (daily 9am–5pm; $5.50), 18km west on the Glenora Road in Plenty; established in 1864, this is Australia's oldest trout hatchery, set in beautiful formal gardens, with six display ponds and a restaurant.

Hobart Coaches has eight **buses** on weekdays from Hobart to New Norfolk and three on Saturday; the buses leave from Metro Hobart's Elizabeth Street terminus. TassieLink also runs to New Norfolk (five weekly) on their scheduled year-round service to Queenstown. New Norfolk's **Online Access Centre** is on Charles Street.

Mount Field National Park

It's 37km through pretty rolling countryside full of hop fields from New Norfolk to **Mount Field National Park**, a high alpine area with tarns created by glacial activity where, in winter, there's enough snow to create a small ski field. At the base, the magnificent stands of **swamp gum** (the tallest species of eucalypt and the tallest hardwood in the world), along with the many **waterfalls**, help make this Tasmania's most popular park. Most people come here to see the impressive **Russell Falls**, which cascades in two levels. It's close to the park entrance and can be reached on an easy thirty-minute circuit walk. Longer walks continue on to **Horseshoe Falls** (1hr) and **Lady Barron Falls** (3hr return). The best short walk is the **Tall Trees Track** (1hr 30min), where huge swamp gums dominate; the largest date back to the early nineteenth century.

To get away from the tour-group mob, several shorter walks leave from various spots along the Lake Dobson Road, which leads high up to **Lake Dobson**, 16km into the park in the area of the alpine moorlands and glacial lakes. From the lake car-park, you can go on plenty of longer walks, including treks along the tarn shelf that take several days, with huts to stay in along the way. The walk to **Twilight Tarn**, with its historic hut, is one of the most rewarding (4hr return), or you can continue on for the full tarn-shelf circuit (6hr return). A shorter option is the **Pandani Grove Nature Walk** (with an accompanying leaflet available from the ranger station – see below), a forty-minute circuit of the lake, including a section of tall **pandanus** – the striking heath plant which, with its crown of long fronds, looks like a semitropical palm. You'll need your own transport to reach these higher walks, or you could come with the small-group Bottom Bits Bus (see p.979) from Hobart on a Mount Field day-trip which includes a walk around Lake Dobson ($99). Tigerline (see p.998) also operates day-tours from Hobart, visiting the Salmon Ponds (see p.1007) en route and allowing several hours to explore the park ($110 including morning tea).

Park practicalities

For information on the walks, to register for overnight hikes and to talk to the ranger, drop in to the **Mount Field Ranger Station** at the entrance to the park (daily 9am–4pm; ⓣ03/6288 1149), a complex also housing a café, shop and interpretive centre. An excellent range of free pamphlets details the natural environment alongside several of the walks in the park. There's also information here about walks in the South West National Park, several of which can be started from Scotts Peak Road, which runs off the Gordon River Road to the west of Mount Field. If you want to stay in the vicinity, head for the tiny settlement of **NATIONAL PARK** on Maydena Road, a ten-minute walk from the park, where there's basic ground-floor **pub** accommodation at the friendly *National Park Hotel* (ⓣ03/6288 1103; ❸ including breakfast), with popular **meals**. The nearest fuel is 7km further on at Westerway. Just outside the entrance to the park are spacious 1950s-style self-contained units at *Russell Falls Holiday Cottages* (ⓣ03/6288 1198; ❹), while within the park itself there's a well-equipped campsite near the entrance. Cabins (ⓣ03/6288 1149; ❶) at Lake Dobson (1000m elevation) make an excellent base from which to explore the alpine regions of the park.

Maydena and around

Nearby **Junee Cave State Reserve** is prime platypus-spotting territory; to get there head 11km southwest to **MAYDENA**, then right onto the narrow, winding Junee Road for 3.5km. A ten-minute walk from the reserve entrance through lush rainforest will bring you to **Junee Cave**, popular with cave divers. In Maydena, you can stay right on the Tyenna River at the recommended *Giants' Table* in newly renovated self-contained cottages (ⓣ03/6288 2293, ⓦwww.giantstable.com.au; ❺); their à la carte restaurant serves delicious fresh-baked **meals**, with plenty for vegetarians. A nearby lake has a resident population of platypuses. Maydena's **Online Access Centre** is in the Maydena Kindergarten on Holmes Street.

Out of Maydena, the **Styx Valley** is known as the "**Valley of the Giants**" after its huge swamp gum (*eucalyptus regnans*) – some of which are over 95 metres tall, five metres wide at the base and over 400 years old – in a large remnant of old-growth forest that's suffered damage from logging activities. There has been a long-running conservationist campaign aimed at protecting 150 square kilometres of this forest as the Styx Valley of the Giants National Park. Contact the Wilderness Society (p.998) for campaign details and to get hold of a self-guided-drive leaflet.

Richmond

RICHMOND, on the Coal River about 25km north of Hobart and surrounded by undulating countryside scattered with wineries, is one of the oldest and best-preserved towns in Australia. Settlers received land grants in the area not long after the fledgling colony had been set up in 1803, and in 1824 Lieutenant-Governor Sorell founded the town, on the route between Hobart and the east coast. Soon, traffic to the new penal settlement at Port Arthur began to pass through, and Richmond's strategic location made it an important military post and convict station when Richmond Gaol was built in 1825; by the 1830s it was the third-largest town in Tasmania. In 1872, however, the

Sorell Causeway was opened, bypassing Richmond, which became a rural community with little incentive for change or development. Most of the approximately fifty buildings – plain and functional stone dwellings – date from the 1830s and 1840s, and many are now used as galleries, craft shops, cafés, restaurants and guesthouses; the gorgeous village green is still intact. A free leaflet and map, *Let's Talk About Richmond*, is available at the gaol and details the buildings. Attractions along Bridge Street include the wooden **Richmond Maze** (daily 9am–5pm; $6.50) and the **Old Hobart Town Model Village** (daily 9am–5pm; $10), a large-scale outdoor model of Hobart in the 1820s.

Richmond's most authentic drawing-card, however, is the sandstone, slate-roofed **Richmond Gaol** (daily 9am–5pm; $5.50), an intact example of an early prison. The prison's function was mostly to house prisoners in transit or those awaiting trial, and to accommodate convict road gangs working in the district; the east wing was designed to hold female convicts, who could not be accommodated at Port Arthur. Informative signs explain the various features of the gaol, which now seems incongruously pretty, set around a leafy central square. Richmond also has the distinction of having both Australia's oldest Roman Catholic church – that of **St John**, which dates in part from 1837 – and its oldest bridge. The graceful, arched stone **Richmond Bridge** was constructed in 1823 under harsh conditions using convict labour; legend says that it's haunted by the ghost of the brutal flagellator, George Grover, who was beaten to death by the convicts and thrown into the river during its construction.

Practicalities

Hobart Coaches runs four **bus** services a day from Hobart (Mon–Fri; buses leave from Metro Hobart's Elizabeth Street terminus) and TassieLink also drops off on their Hobart to Swansea service (1 daily Mon–Fri during term time; Tues, Thurs & Sat only during school holidays). The Richmond Tourist Bus (Ⓣ0408 341 804; $25) departs the tourist centre in Hobart twice daily (9.15am & 12.20pm) and leaves Richmond at 12.50pm & 3.50pm. The **Online Access Centre** is on Torrens Street. One of the best **places to stay** is *Prospect House* (Ⓣ03/6260 2207, Ⓦwww.prospect-house.com.au; ⑥), a Georgian country mansion set in extensive landscaped grounds, with its own well-regarded licensed restaurant open for dinner; it's on your left as you come into town on Cambridge Road. The central and pretty *Richmond Arms Hotel*, 42 Bridge St (Ⓣ03/6260 2109; ④–⑤), has characterful, self-catering accommodation in its converted mid-nineteenth-century stone stables. The hotel serves affordable meals, or there's the cheaper *Richmond Cabin and Tourist Park*, on Middle Tea Tree Road on the outskirts of town (Ⓣ03/6260 2192; vans ②, cabins ③), with shady grounds for camping and an indoor heated pool.

For **food**, there's an upmarket café-restaurant in the *Richmond Wine Centre*, 27 Bridge St, in an old weatherboard cottage set in pretty gardens with outside tables (Ⓣ03/6260 2619; lunch daily, dinner Wed–Sat), where just about everything served is Tasmanian, including the wine. The award-winning Swiss-run *Richmond Bakery* on Edward Street, just off Bridge Street, has an attached café; you can eat in the courtyard or take away to picnic tables on the village green.

The Forestier and Tasman peninsulas

The fastest route from Hobart to the **Tasman Peninsula** heads northeast along the Tasman Highway and then across the **Sorell Causeway** to the small town of **Sorell**, your last chance for shopping and banking; on the huge expanse of

Pittwater, windsurfers are out in force on a sunny day. From Sorell, the Arthur Highway heads 34km southeast to **Dunalley** (fuel available), where a bridge crosses the narrow isthmus to the **Forestier Peninsula**. The bridge regularly opens to let boats through, which can cause delays. Once across, it's a further 42km to the infamous **Eaglehawk Neck**, the narrow point connecting the two peninsulas, once guarded by vicious dogs that in effect turned the Tasman Peninsula into a kind of prison island. Of the substantial military station here, only one building survives, the timber **Officers Quarters** dating from 1832. The NPWS have turned it into a fascinating mini-museum, which provides a useful overview of Tasmanian history as well as detailing the site, and there's an entertaining eight-minute sound-and-silhouette diorama which tells the story of the infamous bushranger **Martin Cash**'s swimming escape from Eaglehawk Neck. Entry is free and the museum stays open as long as the nearby Officers Mess General Store, where there's an ATM, café and takeaway.

Eaglehawk Neck Backpackers (☎03/6250 3248; dorms $14), at 94 Old Jetty, 1km west of the Arthur Highway on the Forestier Peninsula side of Eaglehawk Neck, is the perfect **place to stay** to explore the area – friendly, nonsmoking and green (in both senses of the word). Bikes are loaned (for a small donation) and there are canoes, too. For a great deal more luxury, plus fantastic views and European hospitality, try the nearby *Osprey Lodge Beachfront Bed and Breakfast* at 14 Osprey Rd off Pirates Bay Drive (☎03/6250 3629; ❻). A good place for something to **eat** is the *Eaglehawk Café*, on the Arthur Highway near the turn-off to the blowhole (daily: summer 9am–8pm; winter 9am–5pm; licensed &

Exploring the Tasman Peninsula

While Port Arthur, at the very bottom of the Tasman Peninsula, is the major attraction, the hardly developed peninsula has several good **bushwalks**, and some truly impressive rock formations on the rough ocean side. Some of the finest coastal features are around Eaglehawk Neck: just to the north, there's the **Tessellated Pavement**, onto which you can climb down at low tide; and to the south, off the highway, the fierce **Blowhole**, the huge **Tasman Arch**, and the **Devils Kitchen**, a sheer rock cleft into which the sea surges. Much of this area was proclaimed the **Tasman National Park** (☎03/6250 3497, ⓦwww.parks.tas.gov.au) in 1999; the **Tasman Trail** is an exhilarating 16km coastal walk starting from the Devils Kitchen and ending at **Fortescue Bay**, which has a good camping area (otherwise, the bay is 12km down a dirt road east off the Arthur Highway). Download walking notes for the Tasman Trail on the NPWS website (see p.979). South of Port Arthur, several walking tracks begin from **Remarkable Cave**: to Crescent Bay (5hr return), Mount Brown (5hr return) and Maingon Blowhole (3hr return).

The Eaglehawk Dive Centre, 178 Pirates Bay Drive (☎03/6250 3566, ⓦwww.eaglehawkdive.com.au), offers **dive-boat charters** (equipment included) at low rates to caves, shipwrecks, kelp forests and nearby seal colonies with an underwater visibility of 15–30m. A glorious way to see the towering 190-metre cliffs and surging sea-caves in southern Tasman Peninsula is from the water with Tasman Sea Charters (☎1300 554 049, ⓦwww.tasmanseacharters.com; daily 10.30am; 3hr; $95; max 30), which hug the coast for over 50km. The commentary on geology is fantastic, but also expect to see and learn about giant kelp, jellyfish, sea eagles, the seals on Tasman Island and, if you're lucky, dolphins and even whales. Book in advance if possible, and if the morning trip is full yhey'll usually offer one in the afternoon. If you're interested in any other **outdoor activities**, Hire it with Dennis (☎0427/362 789) can deliver canoes, kayaks, dinghies, fishing lines, tents, sleeping bags and bicycles to the area, including Port Arthur.

BYO), overlooking Norfolk Bay; the food is tasty and reasonably priced, utilizing local produce with a menu ranging from filled baguettes and platters of local produce to home-made pies (rabbit, venison, seafood), plus coffee and yummy cakes. At the blowhole car park, a cut-above-the-usual snack van (daily Oct–April) sells local oysters and seafood, crayfish pies, ice cream and strawberries, as well as hot drinks.

Southwest of Eaglehawk Neck at the small settlement of **Koonya**, **Cascades Historic Site** is a well-preserved 1840s Probation Station that has been owned by a farming family for five generations and is now converted into self-catering cottages, most with open fires and one with a spa (*Cascades Colonial Accommodation*; ⓣ03/6250 3873, ⓦwww.cascadescolonial.com.au; ❺–❼). The peaceful, rural site has a half-hour waterfront walk. The TassieLink Port Arthur service can drop you off near either accommodation.

Port Arthur

The most unceasing labour is to be extracted from the convicts . . . and the most harassing vigilance over them is to be observed.

Governor Arthur

PORT ARTHUR was chosen as the site for a **prison settlement** in September 1830, as a place of secondary punishment for convicts who had committed serious crimes in New South Wales or Van Diemen's Land itself, men who were seen to have no redeeming features and were treated accordingly. The first 150 convicts worked like slaves to establish a timber industry in the wooded surroundings of the "natural penitentiary" of the Tasman Peninsula, with narrow Eaglehawk Neck guarded by dogs. The regime was never a subtle one: **Governor George Arthur**, responsible for all the convicts in Van Diemen's Land, believed that a convict's "whole fate should be ... the very last degree of misery consistent with humanity". Gradually, Port Arthur became a self-supporting industrial centre: the timber industry grew into shipbuilding, there was brickmaking and shoemaking, wheat-growing, and even a flour mill. There was also a separate prison for boys – "the thiefs prison" – at **Point Puer**, where the inmates were taught trades. From the 1840s until transport of convicts ceased in 1853, the penal settlement grew steadily, the early timber constructions later replaced by brick and stone buildings. The lives of the labouring convicts contrasted sharply with those of the prison officers and their families, who had their ornamental gardens, drama club, library and cricket fields. The years after transport ended were in many ways more horrific than those that preceded them, as physical beatings were replaced by psychological punishment. In 1852, the **Model Prison**, based on the spoked-wheel design of Pentonville Prison in London, opened. Here, prisoners could be kept in tiny cells in complete isolation and absolute silence; they were referred to by numbers rather than names, and wore hoods whenever they left their cells. The prison continued to operate until 1877, by now incorporating its own **mental asylum** full of ex-convicts, as well as a geriatric home for ex-convict paupers. The excellent **interpretive centre**, housed in the new visitors centre (daily 9am–5pm), provides much more detail on the prison's sad history through artefacts and texts, and there's more fascinating information in the older museum, housed in what was the asylum.

In 1870, Port Arthur was popularized by Marcus Clarke's romantic tragedy, *For the Term of His Natural Life*. The public became fascinated by its buildings and the tragedy behind them, and soon after the prison closed, guided tours were offered by the same crumbling men who had been wrecked by the regime. In the 1890s the town around the prison was devastated by bushfires that left most buildings in ruins. A major conservation and restoration project began in the 1970s and today the **Port Arthur Historic Site** covers a huge area (Ⓣ03/1800 659 daily 8.30am–7pm; office 8.30am–11pm; $25 for a 48hr pass – $12 after 4.30pm – including 40min guided tour and 30min harbour cruise; for an extra $3 the pass lasts two years). The ticket-office area houses a visitor information centre (Ⓣ03/6251 2371, Ⓦwww.portarthur.org.au). There's a cruise on the *MV Marana* to explore the boys' prison at Point Puer (2hr; $10; daily except Aug) and another to the **Isle of the Dead** (1hr; $10; daily except Aug), Port Arthur's cemetery from 1833 to 1877, where you can view the resting places of 1100 convicts, asylum inmates, paupers and free men; the same company also runs a longer two-and-a-half-hour Tasman Island Wilderness Cruise (subject to demand and weather) from here to see the island's sheer cliffs and its sea birds and fur seals (Ⓣ03/6224 0033, Ⓦwww.portarthurcruises.com.au; Mon 8am, also Thurs 26 Dec–May, no service Aug; $65).

The Port Arthur Historic Site houses more than sixty buildings, some of which – like the poignant **prison chapel** – are furnished and restored. Others, like the ivy-covered **church**, are picturesque ruins set in a landscape of green lawns, shady trees and paths sloping down to the cove. The beautiful setting makes it look more like a serene, old-world university campus than a prison, and indeed, the benign feeling of the place seems to have a capacity to absorb tragedy: another horrific chapter in Port Arthur's history occurred in April 1996, when the massacre of 35 tourists and local people by a lone gunman made international headlines. The café where most of the people were killed has been partially dismantled and a memorial has been built – a garden and reflecting pool laid out around the remaining walls. Visitors are requested to act sensitively and not ask the staff about the tragedy.

If you're staying overnight in Port Arthur, join the nightly lantern-lit **Historic Ghost Tour** (1hr 30min; $17; bookings on Ⓣ03/6251 2310), which features lovingly researched and hauntingly retold tales of the settlement's past as you wander through the ruins.

Practicalities

If you don't have your own transport, and want to get to Port Arthur from Hobart on a **regular bus**, you'll usually have to stay overnight. TassieLink has a single afternoon service (Mon–Fri during school terms; Mon, Wed & Fri school holidays), stopping en route at Eaglehawk Neck, Koonya and other places on the Tasman and Forestier peninsulas. However, there are plenty of **bus tours** that sample some of the Tasman Peninsula sights along the way. The best is the small-group Bottom Bits Bus ($110; see box, p.979), which also takes in peninsula walks and sights and the night-time ghost tour. Navigator Cruises also offers a pricey but spectacular cruise from Hobart (see box on p.987) with an optional return coach-trip.

There are various **places to stay** on the outskirts of Port Arthur. The *Comfort Inn Port Arthur* (Ⓣ03/6250 2101, Ⓦwww.portarthur-inn.com.au; ❺), overlooking the ruined church, is a pleasant place, with a bar open to the public – the only place nearby to drink – and reasonable counter meals. A little more expensive, the spacious *Port Arthur Villas* (Ⓣ03/6250 2239, Ⓦwww.portarthurvillas.com.au; ❺) has the amenities of a motel and kitchens in the units. Both are just across the road from the site on Safety Cove Road. Otherwise, there are bunkhouse rooms and camping (including an excellent enclosed camp-kitchen) at the tree-filled *Port Arthur Caravan and Cabin Park* at Garden Point (Ⓣ03/6250 2340, Ⓦwww.portarthurcaravan-cabinpark.com.au; dorms $16, en-suite cabins ❹).

Within the Port Arthur Historic Site, in the visitors centre, you can **eat** by day at the cafeteria-style *Port Café* (daily 9am–5pm) or spend more at the good *Felons Restaurant* at night (dinner only) or the *Museum Tea Rooms* in the old asylum; all three are licensed. In **Taranna**, 10km before Port Arthur on the A9, it's hard to miss the blue-and-yellow-painted *The Mussel Boys Café* (daily; licensed), which serves fresh seafood done superbly – try the mussels in a dill coconut broth. Though you can come in for coffee and cake, it's really restaurant food and prices ($15–24); for a more relaxed atmosphere, sit outside on the veranda and enjoy the water views.

The east coast: the Tasman Highway

For much of its length along the sunny **east coast**, the **Tasman Highway** gently rises and falls through grazing land and bush-covered hills. In summer there's something of an unspoilt Mediterranean feel about this stretch, with its long white beaches, blue water stretching to a cloudless sky, scenic backdrop of hills, and a thriving local fishing industry. Because the east coast is sheltered from the prevailing westerly winds and is washed by warm offshore currents, it has one of the most temperate climates in Australia. This, and the mainly safe swimming beaches, mean that it's a popular destination for Tasmanians in the school holidays – prices go up and accommodation is scarce from Christmas to the middle of February. Even so, it's still relatively undeveloped and peaceful; there are four national parks, which include a whole island – **Maria Island** – and an entire peninsula – the glorious **Freycinet National Park**. The only blight on the landscape is the huge and controversial export **woodchip mill** at Point Home, one of four in Tasmania near Triabunna, which can be seen from the ferry to Maria Island.

The east coast is also Tasmania's best **cycling route**: it's relatively flat, and the winter climate is mild enough to tackle it in colder months, too. Distances between towns are reasonable, and there's a string of youth hostels so you don't need to camp. **St Helens** is the largest town on the east coast, with a population of just over a thousand; situated on **Georges Bay**, it makes a good base to explore the northeast corner and **Mount William National Park**. The oldest town, **Swansea**, lies sheltered in **Great Oyster Bay**, facing the Freycinet Peninsula. To the north, the small fishing town of **Bicheno** offers fantastic diving, and it's a convenient place from which to visit both the Freycinet National Park (and its tiny settlement of **Coles Bay**) and the **Douglas Apsley National Park** inland. The highway detours inland at **St Marys**, although there's a more recently built road that allows you to follow the coast and enjoy spectacular views without having to tackle any hills.

Because the east coast is not heavily populated, **banking facilities** are rather inadequate, while small settlements have post offices that are also Commonwealth Bank agents. EFTPOS facilities are widely available in shops and service stations, but it's important to make sure you always have enough cash.

Transport services offered by Redline and TassieLink don't run to daily schedules, with big transport gaps on weekends – another good reason to cycle or drive – and various local bus services may need to be interchanged to get from one place to another. If you don't fancy getting stuck somewhere for a couple of days, check timetables carefully. **From Hobart**, TassieLink goes to Orford, Triabunna, Swansea, Bicheno, Scamander and St Helens via the Coles Bay turn-off for Freycinet National Park (1 daily Wed, Fri & Sun). **From Launceston**,

Redline has services to the Coles Bay turn-off and Bicheno via towns along the Midlands Highway (1 daily Mon–Fri) and to Scottsdale (2 daily Mon–Fri, 1 daily Sun); TassieLink has a route to Bicheno via St Marys (1 daily Fri & Sun). Three local bus companies also operate: Stan's (ⓣ03/6356 1662) between Scottsdale and Bridport; Broadby's (ⓣ03/6376 3488) between St Helens and Derby via Pyengana and Winnaleah; and the Bicheno Coach Service (ⓣ03/6257 0293) takes you to Coles Bay and the Freycinet National Park.

Maria Island National Park

As the Tasman Highway meets the sea at **ORFORD**, a small holiday resort on the estuary of the Prosser River, you get your first views across to **Maria Island**. The entire island, 15km off the east coast, is a national park, uninhabited save for its ranger. Its wide tracks are ideal for mountain biking, an activity encouraged here – because no other vehicles are allowed, you can ride in perfect safety (bike hire is available at Triabunna). The island's coastal road has no gradient, but inland there are a few hills to climb. **Birdlife** is prolific, with over 130 species; it's the only national park containing all eleven of the state's endemic bird species. The old airstrip is covered with Cape Barren geese, which you'll see if you walk to the **fossil cliffs**, a twenty-minute stroll from Darlington.

The ferry (see below) lands at **DARLINGTON**, where the structures of the former **penal settlement** (dating from 1825 and later a probation station until 1850) still stand, including the commissariat store with its visitor information boards, the convict barn, the cemetery, the mill house and the penitentiary. The penitentiary is now an atmospheric **bunkhouse** ($22 per unit, sleeping six, or $8.80 per person in the "backpackers" bunkhouse); the basic units have wood stoves, table and chairs, and bunks with mattresses, but you'll need to bring your own cooking equipment and bedding. The units are often booked up well in advance, so call the ranger before turning up. The **campsite** here ($4.40 per person) is the island's best, with a public phone, toilets, fireplaces, cold-water taps and tank water for drinking. As there is little water elsewhere on the island, free-range camping is best done at **Frenchs Farm** or the more picturesque **Encampment Cove**, two campsites with a rainwater supply and fireplaces.

You can take many short **walks** on the island, as well as longer bushwalks (though watch out for cyclists); a range of free pamphlets is available from the ranger's office at Darlington (Mon–Fri 4.30–5pm; ⓣ03/6257 1420, ⓦwww.parks.tas.gov.au). With a couple of days to spare, you can walk past the narrow isthmus to the rarely visited **southern end** of the island, which has unspoilt forests and secluded beaches. As there's no water here, be sure to bring supplies with you. The Maria Island Walk $1699; max 8; ⓣ03/6227 8800, ⓦwww.mariaislandwalk.com.au) is a four-day guided walk skirting 25km of the coastline and staying in very comfortable wilderness camps and the late nineteenth-century house of failed entrepreneur Diego Bernacchi in Darlington, with three-course gourmet meals each night.

Getting there: Triabunna

The **ferry** to Maria Island (Mon–Fri 9.30am, Sat & Sun 9.30am & 1.30pm; 12.30pm & 4pm; extra trips Dec–April, reduced service May–July; confirm bookings and departures on ⓣ03/6227 8900; 40min; return $25, bikes and kayaks $3) leaves from **TRIABUNA**, reached by TassieLink from Hobart, Bicheno or St Helens. As well as the ferry fare, a $10 park entry fee is applicable in addition to camping fees – if you have a car pass, bring the receipt. It's not advisable to do Maria as a day-trip, as given the ferry times, you won't be able to really appreciate the walks, with probably just enough time to take in the convict ruins and the fossil cliffs.

The **visitor information centre** on the Esplanade in Triabunna (ⓣ03/6257 4772) provides details on the island. Triabunna's **Online Access Centre** is on the corner of Vicary and Melbourne streets. A good base for day- and overnight trips to Maria Island is the friendly, relaxing and cosy *The Udder Backpackers YHA* on Spencer Street, 1km west of Triabunna (ⓣ03/6257 3439; dorms $20, rooms ❷). Popular with cyclists, it's located on a peaceful farm, where fresh organic fruit, vegetables, herbs and other foods are sold cheaply to guests; and there's also a takeaway liquor licence. Camping equipment can be hired to take over to Maria Island. You can rent bikes to take over from On-Ya-Bike Bike Hire, 5 Vicary St (ⓣ03/6257 4086; $20 half-day, $33 per day). East Coast Eco Tours (ⓣ03/6257 3453) offers **boat trips** to local seal colonies and you might see dolphins, whales and sea eagles along the way.

Swansea

On a sunny day, the fifty-kilometre drive north from Triabunna to **SWANSEA** is spectacularly beautiful with brilliant white beaches, the intense aquamarine of Great Oyster Bay and views across to the Freycinet Peninsula, where the pink contours of the Hazards Mountains shimmer in the distance. One of Tasmania's oldest settlements, Swansea is an administrative centre, fishing port and seaside resort, with well-preserved architecture dating from the 1830s to the 1880s. The focus of town has always been **Morris's General Store**, on Franklin Street, run by seven generations of the family since 1868. Swansea's past can be revisited at the **Glamorgan War Memorial Museum and Community Centre** (Mon–Sat 9am–5pm; $3), also on Franklin Street, and at the impressive collection in the restored **Swansea Bark Mill**, 96 Tasman Highway (daily 9am–6pm; $10), once used to produce leather-tanning agents from native blackwattle bark. Swansea's **Online Access Centre** is on Franklin Street.

A *YHA* was opening in late 2007, but at the time of writing **accommodation** options include the *Swansea Motor Inn*, at 1 Franklin St (ⓣ03/6257 8102; ❸–❹), a waterfront red-brick motel and a bistro; *Freycinet Waters*, at 16 Franklin St (ⓣ03/6257 8080, ⓦwww.freycinetwaters.com.au; ❹–❺), a light, refreshingly uncluttered seaside B&B in the old post-office building where each en-suite room has its own private veranda overlooking the bay; and the nearby *Tubby and Padman*, at no. 20 (ⓣ03/6257 8901, ⓦwww.tubbyandpadman.com.au; ❺), in an 1840s colonial homestead with a huge front veranda and contemporary-style self-contained units out back. Another B&B option is the gay-friendly *Meredith House*, 15 Noyes St (ⓣ03/6257 8119, ⓦwww.meredith-house.com.au; en suite ❻), an antique-filled guesthouse on a hill with views over the bay. On the waterfront are two **caravan parks** with excellent facilities: *Swansea Holiday Park* on Shaw Street, opposite the Old Bark Mill (ⓣ03/6257 8177; cabins ❸), and the friendly *Kenmore Caravan Park*, 2 Bridge St (ⓣ03/6257 8148; vans ❷, cabins ❸).

As for **food**, Swansea has a fair selection. There's a very smart restaurant specializing in seafood and game in the atmospheric 1846 *Schouten House*, 1 Waterloo Rd (dinner nightly; ⓣ03/6257 8564), with alfresco dining in summer. *The Ugly Duck Out*, 2 Franklin St (ⓣ03/6257 8850; open May–Nov 11.30am–9pm; Dec–April 8.30am–9pm), is a licensed restaurant and takeaway with a wide-ranging menu of fish, grills, burgers and salads made from organic ingredients. *Kabuki By the Sea* is a fine Japanese restaurant 12km south on the Tasman Highway with stunning views (open daily for morning and afternoon tea and lunch; dinner: May–Nov Fri & Sat, Dec–April Tues–Sat; ⓣ03/6257 8588); it also has some guest cottages (❺).

The Freycinet Peninsula

Heading for Coles Bay and **Freycinet National Park**, you turn off the Tasman Highway 33km north of Swansea, following the Coles Bay Road. The drive from Swansea onwards is winding, with fantastic views of rural countryside contrasted with dramatic mountain- and sea-scapes. After about 8km along Coles Bay Road, you can turn left down a side road (3km unsealed) to the **Friendly Beaches**, part of the national park, taking in a length of unspoilt shoreline backed by eucalypt forest. If you're **cycling**, you can cut 40km from your journey by riding along Nine Mile Beach Road, at the end of which a ferry (book the night before on ⓣ03/6257 0239; $15; no service May–Sept) crosses the Swan River to **SWANWICK**, about 6km northwest of Coles Bay.

COLES BAY, on the north edge of the Freycinet National Park, is a sheltered inlet with fishing boats moored in the deep-blue water, all set against the striking backdrop of **The Hazards**, three pink-granite peaks – Amos, Dove and Mayson – rising straight from the sea. Since the 1930s, the hamlet of Coles Bay has been the base for the park, and for fishing and recreation, but is now best known in Australia as the first town to ban the use of plastic shopping bags. There are numerous fishing shacks and **holiday houses** available to rent: call Freycinet Rentals (ⓣ03/6257 0320). Just 3.5km west of Coles Bay, *The Edge of the Bay* (ⓣ03/6257 0102, ⓦwww.edgeofthebay.com.au; cottages ❻, suites ❼) has secluded, self-catering two-bedroom cottages set in bushland, or elegant Japanese-style suites with water views; there are minimum stays depending on season. There's also a restaurant and bar (dinner nightly). The *Iluka Holiday Centre*, in a great spot on the Esplanade across from Muirs Beach (ⓣ03/6257 0115 or 1800 786 512, ⓦwww.ilukaholidaycentre.com.au; dorms $20, rooms ❷, vans ❷, units ❸–❹), has a wide variety of accommodation, including a **YHA hostel** section. Nearby is a small supermarket, a tavern with bistro meals and the outstanding *Freycinet Café & Bakery* (daily 8am–7pm), an eat-in bakery selling European-style breads, pastries, pizza from 5pm, and decent coffee. One kilometre from the *Iluka Holiday Centre*, overlooking The Hazards, supplies of all sorts are available at the **general store**, Coles Bay Trading, on Garnet Avenue (daily 8am–6pm, until 7pm Dec 26 to end Feb; ⓣ03/6257 0109), which also serves as the post office, service station and official tourist **information centre**; you can book accommodation, buy park passes, rent bikes ($11 half-day, $17 full day) and use the public phones. Its coffee shop has great views of The Hazards. Next door you can get a wonderful seafood dinner at *Madge Malloy's* (dinner Tues–Sat; licensed; ⓣ03/6257 0399). For more information, check out the excellent website ⓦwww.freycinetcolesbay.com.

Redline and TassieLink drop off 31km away from Coles Bay, at the turn-off on the Tasman Highway, connecting with the Bicheno Coach Service to Coles Bay (up to 3 daily; booking for off-peak times on ⓣ03/6257 0293), which can also take you right to the start of the walking tracks.

Freycinet National Park

The **national park office** (daily 9am–5pm; ⓣ03/6256 7000) is just 1km from Coles Bay, and sells maps and booklets on day-walks and has an interpretive display on the park. From here, the gravelled, disabled-access Great Oyster Bay path leads down to the beach (10min return). Opposite the centre, the powered national-park **campsite**, with water and toilets but no showers, is in

△ Wineglass Bay

a sheltered location among bush and dunes behind Richardsons Beach; it's packed in holiday season, when you'll need to book well in advance through the park office. At the other end of Richardsons Beach, *Freycinet Lodge* (☎03/6257 0101, Ⓦwww.freycinetlodge.com.au; ❽) has wooden cabins spread through bushland and offers guided bushwalks and other activities; there's a bistro and a more upmarket restaurant with fabulous views overlooking the bay, both open all day and available to non-guests, and a tennis court. You can also stay at the basic *Coles Bay YHA* (no hot water) in the park itself, but only if you've booked in advance through the Hobart YHA office (see p.985; dorms $10, rooms ❷); it's very popular during the summer months and Easter.

Tracks into the park begin at the **Walking Track Car Park**, a further 4km from the office. **Water** is scarce, so you must carry all you'll need, although the ranger can advise if there are any streams where the water is safe to drink. The shorter walks are well marked: the strenuous, gravelly walk up to the lookout to exquisite **Wineglass Bay**, with its perfect curve of white beach, is where most walkers head, and many continue on down to the beach itself (2.6km return to the lookout, 1–2hr; 5km return to the beach, 2hr 30min to 3hr 30min). The 27-kilometre **peninsula circuit** is a wonderful walk (10hr), best done over two days; it makes a good practice run for the big southwest hikes. There's a **campsite** at **Cooks Beach**, with a pit toilet, water tank, and a rough hut where you can stay.

Schouten Island, off the tip of the peninsula, is part of the national park: it's perfect for really secluded camping, as you're quite likely to have it all to yourself. Freycinet Sea Cruises, in Coles Bay (☎03/6257 0355, Ⓦwww.freycinetseacharters.com), will drop you off here for around $75 per person return. They also offer cruises around the island (daily; 2hr 30min; $75) and to Wineglass Bay (daily 9am; 4hr; $110), one of which includes a walk on The Hazards (Mon–Fri 9am; $150), or you could charter the boat for a day-trip that could take in a walk on the island and a visit to a nearby seal colony. There are campsites with pit toilet, a hut and two water tanks at **Moreys Bay**, and the creek at **Crocketts Bay** has reliable upstream water. Although there are no proper tracks on the island, walking is easy.

Freycinet Adventures (ⓣ03/6257 0500, ⓦwww.freycinetadventures.com.au) offers three-hour sea-kayaking tours on Coles Bay (8.30am and a sunset trip; $90), which can be extended to include overnight camping in the national park. All Four Adventure (ⓣ03/6257 0018, ⓦwww.all4adventure.com.au) offers all-terrain-vehicle tours of the park.

Bicheno

Halfway up the east coast, **BICHENO** (pronounced "bish-eno"), sheltered in **Waubs Bay**, is a busy crayfishing and abalone port. The same conditions that make Bicheno ideal for fishing also make it a perfect spot for diving. Don't let the unattractive inland town centre on the Tasman Highway put you off; it has a beautiful bay setting and there's lots to do.

The 3.5km, one-way **Bicheno Foreshore Footway** runs from Redbill Point (reached via Gordon Street off the Tasman Highway at the western edge of town) and follows several points, bays and beaches, with views of **Governor Island Marine Nature Reserve**, and past the Blowhole. The usually clear waters are rich with a variety of marine life, and the reserve has spectacular large caves and extraordinary vertical rockfaces with swim-throughs and drop-offs. Bicheno Dive Centre, opposite the Sea Life Centre at 2 Scuba Court (ⓣ03/6375 1138), offers dive courses and rents out gear. One of the most popular activities in Bicheno are the evening tours to a local **penguin rookery** with Bicheno Penguin Tours (ⓣ03/6375 1333; nightly; $20). The French-owned Le Frog Trike Rides (ⓣ03/6375 1777) runs a range of fun and thrilling three-wheeler tours, from $12 for a 10- to 15-minute ride to $170 for a two-hour ride to the Elephant Pass. Bicheno Glass Bottom Boats (ⓣ03/6375 1294) offers forty-minute, **glass-bottom-boat tours** of the marine reserve ($15). The **Sea Life Centre** (daily 9am–5pm; $6.50), on the Tasman Highway, has a rather dingy aquarium but an excellent seafood restaurant (daily 9am–9pm; dinner bookings ⓣ03/6375 1121). Bicheno's Online Access Centre is at The Oval, Burgess Street.

With a wide choice of **accommodation**, Bicheno makes a pleasant stopover. You can camp at the *East Coast Holiday Park* at 4 Champ St (ⓣ03/6375 1999; vans ❶–❷, cabins ❸, apartments ❷–❸) or stay at the small, tidy and well-equipped *Bicheno Backpackers*, 11 Morrison St (ⓣ03/6375 1651, ⓦwww.bichenobackpackers.com; dorms $21). For something really special, head for the *Bicheno Hideaway*, at 179 Harveys Farm Rd (ⓣ03/6375 1312, ⓦwww.bichenohideaway.com; ❹–❺), 3km south of Bicheno, where uniquely designed oceanfront self-contained chalets are set on six acres of natural bushland teeming with wildlife. Other options include the central *Beachfront Family Resort*, on the Tasman Highway (ⓣ03/6375 1111; ❹), which has a swimming pool, and the *Bicheno Gaol Cottages*, on the corner of James and Burgess streets (ⓣ03/6375 1430; ❺), with accommodation in the old prison and its converted stables. **Food**, too, is good in Bicheno. The formal *Cyrano French Restaurant*, at 77 Burgess St (dinner nightly; mains $20–24; ⓣ03/6375 1137), is in the classic French vein, while the *Beachfront Tavern*, on the Tasman Highway, has the best counter meals: big servings and a great salad bar. The eat-in *Freycinet Bakery* (daily 8am–4pm) next to the post office is an excellent café, while across the grassy traffic island the *Cod Rock Cafe* cooks up fresh fish and other seafood (daily 10am–8pm). To sample some gourmet Tasmanian products, head for *Mary Harvey's Restaurant* in the gardens of the Bicheno Gaol Cottages (ⓣ/03 6375 1866; lunch & dinner daily Dec–April, dinner only Sept–June).

The Bicheno Coach Service (ⓣ03/6357 0293) to Freycinet National Park leaves from the *Bicheno Takeaway* at 52 Burgess St.

The Douglas Apsley National Park to St Marys

Just 4km north of Bicheno on the Tasman Highway there's a turn-off to the **Douglas Apsley National Park**. Proclaimed in 1990, it's the location of the state's only remaining large dry sclerophyll forest. Because of the temperate weather of the east coast, the park's two-day walk, the **Leeaberra Track** – undertaken north to south – is a good one at any time of the year. Although facilities are being improved, this is a low-maintenance, untouristy park, so be prepared for basic bushcamping; get hold of the *Douglas Apsley Map and Notes* ($10).

Thirty kilometres north of Bicheno, just past Chain of Lagoons, the coastal Tasman Highway continues north to **St Helens**; turn off to the left for a spectacular climb with views of the surrounding coastline on a detour inland to St Marys, 17km away. You can stop at the dramatic **Elephant Pass** for pancakes, views and atmosphere at the *Mount Elephant Pancake Barn* (daily 8am–6pm), though the menu prices are high.

From Elephant Pass the road heads on to **ST MARYS**, a picturesque little Fingal Valley town surrounded by state forest and waterfalls best viewed from the 832-metre peak of logging-threatened **South Sister**, accessed 6km up unsealed and winding German Town Road. The place has a quiet, old-fashioned feel to it, but an alternative edge focused around the licensed *Escape Tasmanian Wilderness Café Gallery* at 21 Main St (ⓣ03/6372 2444; dinner Wed–Sat 9am–5pm; all-day breakfast and excellent coffee), with a pool table and regular live music and film screenings; and the fantastic little *Purple Possum Wholefoods Café* in the health-food store (closed Sun) around the corner on Storey Street. The best place to stay is magical *Seaview Farm* (ⓣ03/6372 2341, or 0417 382 876, ⓦwww.seaviewfarm.com.au), 8km uphill on German Town Road; the hilltop position gives panoramic South Sister and sea views. There's hostel accommodation in a comfortable cottage that has a big eat-in kitchen and cosy lounge with a wood stove, and the "dorms" are pretty rooms with beds not bunks (dorms $24, with linen and towel $27); or choose private accommodation in a row of en-suite rooms (❸) with veranda access providing fabulous views. You can arrange a pick-up in advance if you don't have your own transport. St Marys' **Online Access Centre** is at 23B Main St. There are **bank services** in the post office at no. 36.

St Helens and the Bay of Fires

Heading downhill back to the coast, **ST HELENS** is the largest town on the east coast and the last before the Tasman Highway turns inland. It's situated on **Georges Bay**, a long, narrow bay with two encircling arms, and the surrounding coastline holds plenty of interest. Local **information** is available from the **St Helens History Room**, at 55 Cecilia St opposite the post office ($2; ⓣ03/6376 1744), which details the area's mining history in the nearby Blue Tier (see p.1021) and provides maps and walk information. With a new resort hotel, new cinema, loads of great cafés, a health-food store and even a vintage clothes store, St Helens is fast changing from a sleepy backwater, as the impressive beauty of the nearby Bay of Fires becomes more widely known and real estate prices rocket.

The southern arm of Georges Bay is the site of **St Helens Point Recreation Area**, where there's a large lagoon – Diana's Basin – which the highway skirts as it enters town. On the ocean side the **Peron sand dunes** stretch for several kilometres, and at the point there's good surfing at **Beer Barrel Beach**.

Binalong Bay, 10km north of Georges Bay, is another popular surf spot (with a strong current, so beware); there's safer swimming in the large lagoon tucked behind, where people boat and water-ski. Binalong is the southern end of the mesmerizingly beautiful **Bay of Fires** (named for the many fires explorer Tobias Furneaux saw in 1773), where the beach of bright sugary sand stretches for over 30km to Eddystone Point. Binalong Bay is an easy bike ride away from St Helens (hire bikes at the *YHA*), with only a couple of small climbs. From Binalong Bay, you can walk in around two hours along the beach to **Cosy Corner**; however, unless you want to walk back again you need to arrange to be picked up or go on a tour. There's accommodation, a shop and petrol, and you can **camp** here, as well as further along at Grants Lagoon in the **Bay of Fires Coastal Reserve** which stretches for 13km north alongside the partly sealed coastal drive to the scenic spot known as The Gardens.

To get to the lower half of **Mount William National Park** at the northern end of the Bay of Fires, take the road running inland north for 54km from St Helens to the pink-granite tower of the Eddystone Lighthouse. The northern end of the park is reached via Gladstone, by taking an unsealed track to **Great Musselroe Bay**, where there's a free basic **campsite**. There are no real tracks within the park itself, but plenty of beach and headland walking, and lots of Forrester kangaroos. **Bay of Fires Walk** leads a superb four-day guided coastal walk along the Bay of Fires and through Mount William National Park (Ⓣ03/6331 2006, Ⓦwww.bayoffires.com.au; $1750); packs and waterproof jackets are provided and accommodation is in luxury "ecotents" and a superbly designed ecolodge 40m above the sea with stunning views up and down the coast.

St Helens practicalities

There's a good range of **accommodation** to choose from in town. The *St Helens YHA*, at 5 Cameron St (Ⓣ03/6376 1661; dorms $18, rooms 2; bike hire $10 day, boards $5), is very homely and clean with friendly owners: expect a peaceful atmosphere with books, magazines, games and a wood stove to chat around; a self-contained flat is also available (❹). Across the road, *Dohertys* (Ⓣ03/6376 1999, Ⓦwww.dohertyhotels.com.au; ❻–❼) provides a sophisticated edge to the town, with the well-patronized *Deck on the Bay* café-bistro (daily 11am–9.30pm), pricier *Ocean View Restaurant* (daily breakfast & dinner), and the *Lobby Bar*. Among the numerous B&Bs, the best value is *Artnor Lodge*, at 71 Cecilia St (Ⓣ03/6376 1234; ❷, en suite ❸). *The Bayside Inn*, at 2 Cecilia St (Ⓣ03/6376 1466; all rooms en suite ❸–❹), is a modern waterfront hotel/motel with a restaurant, pool and drive-in bottle shop. However, staying at Binalong Bay is much more scenic and relaxing, and there's plenty of choice, including the self-contained *Binalong Bungalows* (Ⓣ03/6376 8368; ❸) and the upmarket B&B *Bed in the Treetops* (Ⓣ03/6376 1318, Ⓦwww.bedinthetreetops.com.au; ❻–❼) at 124 and 701 Binalong Bay Rd respectively. *Fidlers on the Bay*, facing Georges Bay at 2 Jason St (Ⓣ03/6376 2444; daily 11am to late), is a highly regarded **café-restaurant** serving delicious local seafood and grills with a great Tasmanian wine list. For excellent coffee and a great menu featuring local organic produce, head for the cute *Milk Bar Café* at 57B Cecilia St (Mon–Sat 9am–5pm). Next door the reasonably priced *Wok Stop* (lunch Mon–Fri, dinner Mon–Sat) does curries, wok-fried noodles and fresh juices. The **Forum Cinema** (Ⓣ03/6376 1000) shows films Friday to Sunday, plus there's a funky café-bar with couches, art exhibitions, live music on Friday nights, and an eclectic affordable menu. St Helens' bank is Westpac, at 41 Cecilia St, and its **Online Access Centre** is in the library at no. 61.

St Helens to Scottsdale: the Tasman Highway

From St Helens, the **Tasman Highway (A3)** cuts across the northeast highlands towards Launceston, 170km away. This is mostly dairy country, although there's the odd patch of surviving rainforest and the remnants of a tin-mining industry, based around the **Blue Tier**, a mountain plateau that experienced a mining boom in the 1870s. Many **ghost towns** were left after the mines finally closed in the 1950s.

Twenty-six kilometres northwest of St Helens on the A3 is the turn-off south for **PYENGANA** (1km) and St Columba Falls (a further 4km). In Pyengana it's worth touring **Healey's Pyengana Cheese Factory** (daily 9am–5pm; free), where you can watch the stuff being made (except Fri & Sat) and buy all the ingredients for a picnic at the falls, or have something to eat at the new café here. Further along, the one-storey *St Columba Falls Hotel* (Ⓣ03/6373 6121) – the "Pub in the Paddock" – looks like a farmhouse; it's a real country local, serving huge steaks (from $18.50), and you can also **stay** here in cute tidy rooms with peaceful rural views (❸) and buy drinks for the two resident pigs. At the end of the road (the last bit on dirt) is the **Columba Falls State Reserve**, an area of cool, temperate rainforest. The 1km return walk to the viewing platform at the base of **St Columba Falls** is easy, passing through a forest of man ferns and under a canopy of sassafras and myrtle. At 90m, the falls are among the highest in Tasmania, pouring with tremendous force over the cliffs – truly thunderous in winter.

Back on the A3 approaching the Blue Tier, **Goshen** is the first of the ghost towns, little more than an old school and the ruins of the *Oxford Arms Inn*. A little further on is the turn-off for **Goulds Country**, with the remaining buildings – all wooden – of what was once a town. Head through Goulds Country and past the site of another abandoned mining town, Lottah, and take the steep, unsealed Poimena Road to the site of Poimena. En route, there's "Hands Off The Blue Tiers" notices and other signs of the fierce environmental campaign against logging of the area (Ⓦwww.bluetier.org), one of the few remaining old-growth forests left in the northeast. The boardwalked twenty-minute circuit **Goblin Forest Walk** (wheelchair accessible) provides fascinating interpretive boards that help to imagine the town once here. There's also a thirty-minute walk to the 810-metre-high Blue Tier Summit, Mount Poimena, for views right across the northeast to the coast, and several other signposted walks taking between two to six hours. Get details on Blue Tier walks at St Helens History Room (see p.1019).

Returning to the Tasman Highway, the Weldborough Pass (595m) is probably the most beautiful part of the drive, with views across the valleys to the sea; it's worth taking the twenty-minute walk through the **Weldborough Pass Scenic Reserve**, predominately myrtle forest with man ferns and occasional tall blackwoods. **WELDBOROUGH** itself, once the centre of a Chinese mining community, now consists of the isolated, characterful *Weldborough Hotel* (Ⓣ03/6354 2223; ❷), where you can get a **meal** (Mon–Sat) and a basic share-bathroom pub **room** for the night; there's also a campsite.

DERBY, on the Ringarooma River, was made prosperous by the profitable Briseis Tin Mine between 1876 and 1952. The **Derby Tin Mine Centre** (daily 10am–3pm; $4.50; Ⓣ/03 6354 2262) is now the only sign of development in a town that's been closing down since the 1950s: it has some interesting relics connected with the Chinese miners. **SCOTTSDALE**, 99km from St Helens, is a large, pleasantly situated town servicing the agricultural and forestry industries of the northeast. The **Scottsdale Forest EcoCentre**, on the outskirts of town at 88 King St (daily 9am–5pm; free) is yet another Forestry Tasmania public-relations exercise; the unique, energy-smart building looks like a headless Dalek that has landed and half-sunk into the ground. Inside, an "eco-walk" winds up the circular building, putting the local forest and forestry industry into historical and ecological context, and there's a pleasant café (daily 9am–5pm) and a **visitor information centre** (Ⓣ03/6352 6520). Scottsdale has good facilities, including a Westpac bank at 21 King St, supermarkets, the bustling *Cottage Bakery* at 9 Victoria St, with a fresh sandwich bar and real coffee (closed Sun), and an **Online Access Centre** in the library at 51 King St. The classic Victorian-era *Beulah of Scottsdale*, 9 King St, set amongst flowery gardens, has attic bedrooms with mountain views, and a guest lounge and dining room (Ⓣ03/ 6352 3723; B&B ❻). There are some beautiful areas to visit nearby, including Ralph Falls in the Mount Victoria Forest Reserve and Evercreech Forest Reserve – get details from the EcoCentre, or Pepper Bush Peaks 4WD Adventure Tours (Ⓣ03/6352 2263, Ⓦwww.pepperbush.com.au; Launceston pick-ups) can take you off-road to visit some of these places. Tours include fine food and wine and range from a nocturnal wildlife tour with BBQ ($115) to a full day tour ($275).

Twenty-one kilometres northwest, the fishing town and holiday spot of **BRIDPORT** has several places to **stay** including the modern, purpose-built *Bridport Seaside Lodge YHA Backpackers*, at 47 Main St (Ⓣ03/6356 1585, Ⓔbridportseasidelodge@hotmail.com; dorms $19, rooms ❷) right on the river estuary. There's camping at *Bridport Caravan Park* (Ⓣ03/6356 1227; sites only), which stretches for about a kilometre along Anderson Bay. The **beaches** in the area are lovely, especially the wide, sandy expanse where the Bird River flows among sand dunes and into the sea. *Bridport Seafoods* (daily 10am–7pm), attached to the fish-processing plant on Main Street, does excellent sit-down meals.

North and central Tasmania and the Bass Strait

The **north** of Tasmania is rich and settled agricultural country, and the fertile soil of the **Tamar Valley** in particular made this a prosperous area during the early colonial period. Thirty kilometres inland at the confluence of the Tamar and the North and South Esk rivers, **Launceston** quickly grew as a port and city; gracious early houses and well-preserved villages are still found around the area. Also settled early, due to its fine and open land, was the mostly flat, gently undulating **midlands** area between Launceston and Hobart; the **Midland Highway** more or less follows the old coaching route between the two cities. With its stone walls, hedgerows, haystacks, and small villages and towns, this rural stretch from the Tamar Valley to Hobart is softly appealing but not particularly exciting. In contrast, the area around **Deloraine**, 45km west of Launceston, is spectacular: the early colonial town is surrounded by rich farmland and dramatically located in hilly country below the crest of the **Great Western Tiers** – a Mecca for bushwalkers. From Deloraine, the **Lake Highway** heads steeply south up over the Western Tiers and on to the **Central Plateau**, a sparsely populated, lake-filled region dominated by the **Great Lake** and its fishing shacks.

Lying off the northern coast, in Bass Strait, are two islands worth visiting for their bushwalks and historic associations: **Flinders Island** in the northeast, largest of the Furneaux Islands, and **King Island** to the far northwest, part of the Hunter Island group. Both are reached by plane, with flights from Victoria or Tasmania.

Launceston and around

LAUNCESTON is dominated by the **Tamar River**, and approaching from the north along the Tamar Highway, zooming through haystack-filled countryside, it's a lovely sight, with grand Victorian houses nestling on hills above the banks. Approaching from the south on the dreary Southern Outlet, however, gives a slightly more accurate picture of the dull but worthy provincial town. With a population of around 98,000, the "northern capital" is Tasmania's second largest city.

As the third-oldest city in Australia, first settled in 1804, Launceston has hung on to disappointingly little of its elegant colonial Georgian architecture. What the city does have in abundance are many fine examples of colonial **Victorian architecture**: the 1870s and 1880s were prosperous times for Launceston, years of mineral exploration spurred on by the mainland goldrush, and a number of massive, dignified public buildings date from this boom period.

Launceston's real attractions, though, are its natural assets. It's situated at the confluence of the narrow **North Esk** and **South Esk rivers**, with the breathtaking **Cataract Gorge**, where the South Esk has carved its way through rock to reach the Tamar River, only fifteen minutes' walk from the centre. Yachts and outboard motors ply the 50km of river, and the surrounding countryside of the **Tamar Valley**, with its wineries, strawberry farms and lavender plantations is idyllic. Beyond the eastern suburbs bush-covered hills fold back into the distance to **Ben Lomond**, a popular winter skiing destination just an hour's drive away.

Arrival, information and city transport

Launceston Airport is 20km south of the city, near the town of Evandale. The **Airport Shuttle Bus** (Ⓣ0500 512 009) meets most flights and drops off at accommodation for $11. A **taxi** costs about $30,or you could **rent a car** – the main car companies have desks at the airport, or see "Listings", p.1031.

Long-distance **buses** arrive in the city centre at the **Cornwall Square Transit Centre**, on the corner of Cimitiere and St Johns streets, where both Redline (Ⓣ1300 360 000) and TassieLink (Ⓣ1300 300 520) have ticket offices; Redline has left-luggage (Ⓣ/03 6336 1446; $1.50 per bag till closing time) and there is a café plus tourist information. If driving, note that most streets operate on a **one-way system** and the length of Cameron Street is interrupted by Civic Square, and Brisbane Street by the Mall.

Information

For **information**, your first stop should be the **Tasmanian Travel and Information Centre**, on the corner of St John and Cimitiere streets (Mon–Fri 9am–5pm, Sat 9am–3pm, Sun 9am–noon; ⓣ03/6336 3133 or 1800 651 827, ⓦwww.discoverlaunceston.com), which can also arrange car rental and book accommodation and travel tickets.

City transport

Launceston is very compact and most accommodation is within walking distance of the city centre, although **public transport** (the MTT) is useful for a couple of scattered attractions and some outlying accommodation (buses run until 6.15pm Mon–Thurs, 10pm Fri & Sat; restricted services Sun). The **MTT bus interchange** (information ⓣ13 22 01, ⓦwww.metrotas.com.au), where all buses arrive and depart, is on St John Street, on either side of the **Brisbane Street Mall**. Single fares are inexpensive, but it may be worth buying a Day Rover ($4.20) for unlimited off-peak travel (buy on board) or a ten-trip ticket (from $13.60; buy at any one of twenty or so Metrofare ticket agents, including Teagues Newsagency, opposite the post office).

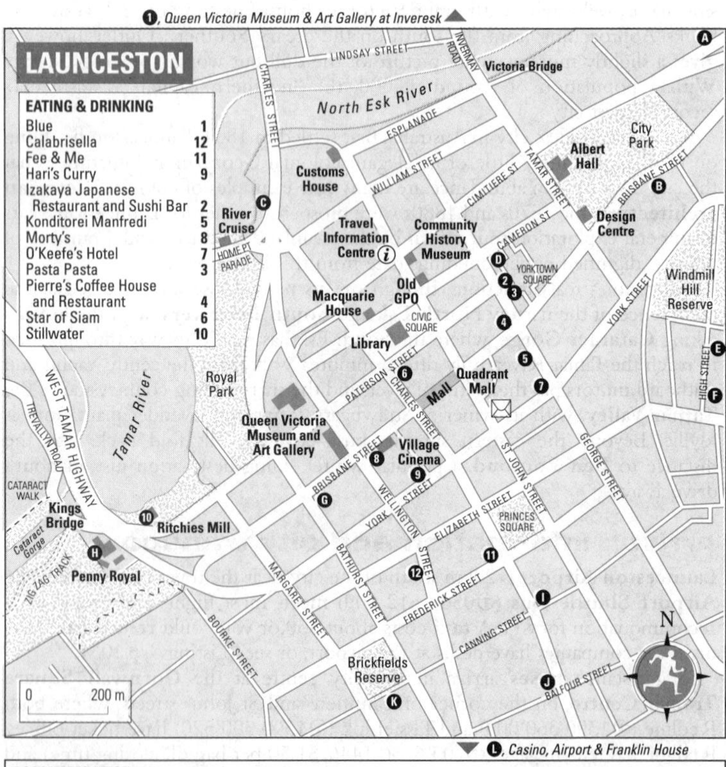

ACCOMMODATION

Ashton Gate	F	Irish Murphy's Backpackers	G	Sandors on the Park	B
Batman Fawkner Inn	D	Launceston Backpackers	K	Sportsman's Hall Hotel	J
The Edwardian	I	Penny Royal Watermill Motel and Village Apartments	H	Treasure Island Caravan Park	L
Glebe Cottages	A	Peppers Seaport Hotel	C		
Hatherley House	E				

Accommodation

Accommodation in Launceston is very good value, though rates can hike up in the busy December-to-February period and **hostel** beds can be scarce then. A tragic fire at the *YHA* hostel on New Year's Eve 2004 led to its closure; contact the YHA office in Hobart (see p.985) for the latest details of any new hostel. There's a concentration of **motels** along Brisbane Street and an abundance of **B&Bs** and self-catering accommodation.

Hotels, motels, B&Bs and self-catering

Ashton Gate 32 High St ⓣ03/6331 6180, ⓦwww.view.com.au/ashtongate. Classified by the National Trust, this weatherboard B&B has been taking guests for over forty years. Bedrooms are large and light; all are en suite, with TV and hot drinks. ❺–❻

Batman Fawkner Inn 35–39 Cameron St ⓣ03/6331 7222. This pleasant pub, established in 1822, offers bargain, single en-suite rooms with TV and phone ($45); larger, more attractive rooms have similar facilities. Light breakfast included. There's an Italian restaurant and bar meals, and a nightclub open on Fri & Sat nights, which makes it a bit noisy – better to stay here midweek. ❹

The Edwardian 229 Charles St ⓣ03/6334 7771, ⓦwww.theedwardian.com.au. Lovely, two-storey red-brick Edwardian house near Princes Square, with self-contained self-catering suites. Breakfast provisions provided. Handy for the supermarket. No children. ❹–❺

Glebe Cottages 14A Cimitiere St ⓣ0500 500 581, ⓦwww.glebecottages.com.au. Good-value, spacious two- and three-bedroom self-contained cottages, in a convenient location near City Park, though they prefer longer-term stays. ❺

Hatherley House 43 High St ⓣ03/6334 7727, ⓦwww.hatherleyhouse.com.au. Voted one of the top eighty new hotels by *Condé Nast Traveller*, this gorgeous 1830s colonial mansion set in extensive English-style gardens (views stretch off to Ben Lomond) combines original architectural features, tapestries, carvings and sculptures from India, Africa and the Orient with contemporary design and five-star luxury. Scrumptious breakfast served on the veranda, in the library café-bar or out in the garden. ❼–❽

Penny Royal Watermill Motel and Village Apartments 145–147 Paterson St ⓣ03/6331 6699, ⓔpennyroyal@leisureinns.com.au. Built in 1840, this motel has a comfortable old-world charm, while the more modern self-contained apartments are spacious and reasonably priced. Close to the city centre and a short walk to the gorge and Cliff Grounds. Rooms ❹, apartments ❻–❽

Peppers Seaport Hotel 28 Seaport Boulevard ⓣ03/6345 3333, ⓦwww.peppers.com.au. This brand-new resort has finally given Launceston a waterfont-lifestyle focus, with its cluster of bars, cafés and restaurants. In the hotel itself, rooms are very stylish, with natural wood furnishings and luxury fabrics. Spacious suites feature fully equipped kitchen and laundry. Most rooms have water views, but don't bother shelling out to stay here for a "city view" room – they provide a very unattractive road vista. ❼–❽

Sandors on the Park 3 Brisbane St ⓣ03/6331 2055 or 1800 030 140. The best of a bunch of motels on this strip overlooking City Park – but not the most expensive – and just a short walk from the centre. Friendly professional service; guest laundry. Its bistro-style *Monkey Bar Café* opens noon–10.30pm. ❹

Sportsman's Hall Hotel 252 Charles St ⓣ03/6331 3968. Pleasant pub with well-furnished, comfortable rooms (shared bathrooms). Breakfast included. Excellent, café-style bistro downstairs serving up very reasonably priced meals. ❸–❹

Hostels and caravan parks

Irish Murphy's Backpackers 211 Brisbane St ⓣ03/6331 4440, ⓦwww.irishmurphys.com.au. Hostel accommodation above a lively, centrally located pub. Facilities include TV lounge and a fully equipped kitchen but no laundry. Bedding $3 extra for dorms. Dorms $17, rooms ❷

Launceston Backpackers 103 Canning St ⓣ03/6334 2327, ⓦwww.launcestonbackpackers.com.au. Launceston's best hostel is in a cheerfully painted, clean, two-storey mansion with an adjoining modern annexe. Well run without being regimental, the friendly much-travelled managers maintain a secure atmosphere. Good communal facilities include Internet access. Dorms come in three-, four- and six-bed varieties (sheet hire $2, blanket 50¢), single rooms are available ($40), and some of the doubles (bedding included) have en suites. Tours and bus tickets booked. reserve ahead in summer. Dorms $18–20, rooms ❷–❸

Treasure Island Caravan Park 94 Glen Dhu St, South Launceston, 2km south of the centre

ⓣ03/6344 2600. A small park, sloping up a hillside and looking right over a noisy freeway. Hard, uneven ground; crowded in summer. Camp kitchen with TV. Bus #21 or #24 to Wellington Street (stop 8). Vans ❷, en-suite cabins ❸

The City

The **Brisbane Street Mall** marks the centre of the city, which is arranged in a typical grid pattern around it. **Brisbane Street**, with the mall as its focus, is the main shopping precinct. The city is small and easy to get around, but if you want some background information, join Launceston Historic Walks (departs Mon–Fri 10am; 1hr 15min; $15; bookings ⓣ03/6331 3679) outside the Travel and Information Centre on the corner of St John and Cimitiere streets.

City Park and the old wharf area

City Park (daily 8am–5pm), with its entrance of impressive wrought-iron gates on Tamar Street, is a real treasure. Established in the 1820s, the impression of a formally organized, very English park is reinforced by the **John Hart Conservatory**, full of flowers and ferns, and by the wrought-iron drinking fountain erected here for Queen Victoria's Diamond Jubilee in 1897. Referred to by the locals as "Monkey Park", it's the closest thing Launceston has to a zoo: its Japanese macaques (over twenty of them), romp around their small, moat-surrounded island.

Within City Park, on the corner of Tamar and Brisbane streets, is the **Design Centre of Tasmania** (daily 9.30am–5.30pm), established in 1976 to support and encourage Tasmanian designers. In a state that's always been perceived by the mainland as lagging behind, it's a source of pride that Tasmanian designers helped furnish the New Parliament House in Canberra. The Design Centre is now the home of the **Tasmanian Wood Design Collection** ($2.20), which showcases Tasmanian woodcrafts of some of these superb local designers, wood-workers and furniture-makers using native Tasmanian woods. Prices are beyond the range of most visitors, but the centre is also one of the best places to buy more portable **craft** items, such as woodwork, leatherwork and jewellery.

The wharves on the North Esk River have disappeared, but the massive Neoclassical **Customs House** is still there on The Esplanade, just east of the Charles Street Bridge. The **old wharf area**, around William Street and the Esplanade, has several interesting industrial buildings, including the 1881, still-operational **J. Boag & Son** brewery. Its popular brewery tours start in the **Boag's Centre For Beer Lovers**, opposite at 39 William St, which includes a **museum** (Mon–Fri 8.45am–4.30pm; free) and gift shop, and finish with a small tasting of four beers. (Bookings essential on ⓣ03/6332 6300 or ⓦwww.boags.com.au).

The North Bank and Heritage Forest

Opposite the Esplanade, reached by Victoria Bridge from Tamar Street, and then a boardwalk along the river, is the **Queen Victoria Museum and Art Gallery at Inveresk** (daily 10am–5pm; free but charges for touring exhibitions; ⓦwww.qvmag.tas.gov.au), part of a multimillion-dollar redevelopment of the complex of old railway yards here. Opened in late 2001, the building's interior – two-thirds of which is home to the University of Tasmania's **Academy of Arts** – has an incredible sense of space. The art gallery is well worth visiting for its "Aspects of Tasmanian Art" exhibition, which notably contains landscapes by the nineteenth-century painter W.C. Piguenit, and "Strings Across Time – Tasmanian Aboriginal Shell Necklaces", which displays beautiful examples of the ancient women's art, including recent examples from the tradition of Cape Barren Islanders. From the art gallery you walk through to the former **Railway Workshops**, now transformed into a social history museum; the history of railways in Tasmania is hardly compelling stuff (though the Playzone for kids is great), but the walkway through the old Blacksmith Shop, complete with soundscape of machinery and voices, is eerie, and the exhibition on migration to the state, based on personal stories, gives a different angle on contemporary Tasmania. The sedate licensed café in the Railway Workshops has part of its seating in an old train carriage.

The railway-yards site spans a large expanse of riverfront land dubbed by the council as the **Northbank Experience**. It includes the Tasmanian Conservation Workshops, the Exhibition Centre and the York Park Sports and Entertainment Centre (see p.1030), which has finally brought live AFL football to Launceston. Still to come is a visitor information centre and a clutch of cafés, restaurants and stores. The boardwalk to the art gallery continues along the North Esk River to **Heritage Forest**, parkland with walking, bike-riding and horse-riding trails.

Civic Square and around

Shady, grassy **Civic Square**, closed to traffic, does convey a tidy spirit of civic-mindedness. Here, **Macquarie House** was built as a warehouse in 1830 for Henry Reed, a wealthy merchant. **Cameron Street** was one of the first streets laid out after the city's settlement in 1806, and the stretch from Civic Square to Wellington Street is an almost perfectly preserved nineteenth-century streetscape, including the imposing Supreme Court building and, opposite, a row of fine Victorian red-brick terraced houses adorned with beautiful wrought-iron work.

South of Civic Square is the main shopping thoroughfare, the pedestrianized **Brisbane Street Mall**, a modest precinct taking up one small city block. Just off here is the arc of the **Quadrant Mall**, bounded by Brisbane and St John streets, with several lanes and an arcade leading from it. Gourlay's Sweet Shop here is a Launceston institution – for something really local, try the leatherwood honey drops. East of Quadrant Mall and one block north along George Street, **The Old Umbrella Shop** at no. 60 is a **National Trust information centre** (Mon–Fri 9am–5pm, Sat 9am–noon; ⓣ03/6331 9248) housed in an 1860s Tasmanian blackwood-lined shop.

The Queen Victoria Museum and Art Gallery

The **Queen Victoria Museum and Art Gallery**, on Wellington Street (daily 10am–5pm; free but charges for touring exhibitions; ⓦwww.qvmag.tas.gov.au), was opened in 1891 to mark half a century of Queen Victoria's reign. Its most valued possession is the Chinese joss house from Weldborough (see p.1021), constructed in the 1870s by Chinese workers introduced to the east-coast tin mines to provide cheap labour. Elsewhere, other permanent **museum** exhibitions include: a history of mining in Tasmania; displays about the state's fauna, with big sections on the Tasmanian tiger and the Tasmanian devil; accounts of the geology of Launceston and the local area; a **Planetarium** (Tues–Fri 3pm, Sat 2pm & 3pm; $5); and the "Discovery Plus" room, containing microscopes and specimen trays, as well as a display of live spiders and puzzles to play with. The art **gallery** section includes traditional and contemporary Aboriginal works, and decorative arts including costumes, textiles and ceramics, but most of the collection has moved to the Inveresk site. The *Queen Vic Café* is one of the best in Launceston.

Royal Park to Ritchies Mill Arts Centre

Behind the museum, and across Bathurst Street, **Royal Park** has extensive formal parklands running down to the Tamar River; there's even a croquet lawn here, if you were in any doubt about its English lineage. Between Royal Park and Cataract Gorge is a concentrated tourist area. **Ritchies Mill Arts Centre**, at 2 Bridge Rd on the Tamar River, has been converted from a nineteenth-century flour mill and millers' cottage and now contains two galleries and an alfresco café, *Stillwater*.

To the north of the park, the excellent **Tamar River Cruises** (Ⓣ03/6334 9900, Ⓦwww.tamarrivercruises.com.au) depart from Home Point, at the end of Home Point Parade, and head along the Tamar and into the mouth of beautiful Cataract Gorge, allowing a close-up view of the Launceston Yacht Club, as well as the wealthy suburb of **Trevallyn**, filled with classic Victorian mansions strung along the tree-covered hillside (daily: Sept–May hourly 9.30am–3.30pm; June & Aug hourly 11.30am–1.30pm; 50min; $15). A longer trip continues north up the Tamar as far as the Rosevears vineyards (see p.1033; Mon–Sat 3pm; 2.5hr; $48 including afternoon tea). Nearby, the **Old Launceston Seaport** on Seaport Boulevard is a clutch of lively new waterfront cafés, bars and restaurants around the *Peppers Seaport Hotel*, a great spot with views over the yachts in the marina to the Trevallyn hillside.

Cataract Gorge and beyond

Few cities have such a magnificent natural feature within fifteen minutes' walk of the centre as Launceston. For a beautiful view of **Cataract Gorge**, turn left out of Penny Royal World and walk to the decorative wrought-iron 1863 **Kings Bridge**, which has a span of 60m. From the bridge the cliffs rise almost vertically from the smooth water of the South Esk River as it empties into the Tamar. The natural spectacle is even more dramatic when floodlit after dusk.

The **Zig Zag track** (25min one way) is the more strenuous of the two walking routes along the gorge. The rock-stepped path shrouded by bush is

△ Kings Bridge

satisfyingly secluded. The track runs steeply along the top of the gorge, from Kings Bridge to the **First Basin**, a large, deep canyon worn away by the river and filled with water. Across the Kings Bridge is the easier but busier **Cataract Walk** (40min one way), which begins by the small tollhouse; the stroll is suitable for wheelchairs, and offers spectacular views of the gorge. From the trail, you'll see people canoeing, abseiling and even jumping off the cliffs into the water; Tasmania Expeditions offers abseiling trips here (see "Tours", p.1031).

The Cataract Walk leads to the gardens of the **Cliff Grounds**, on the shady northern side of the gorge – genteel, English-style gardens with parading peacocks and arranged around a lovely 1896 rotunda, they make for a startling contrast with the gorge's wild beauty. *The Gorge Restaurant* (Ⓣ03/6331 3330; closed Mon) in the grounds has stunning views over the First Basin; less expensive cream teas are served from the kiosk. If you enter the grounds from the First Basin end (where there's a car park; or take bus #51B), you'll find an enormous, unattractive **swimming pool**, built mainly to discourage people from swimming in the basin itself, where some have died.

To get across the First Basin to the Cliff Grounds, the **Launceston Basin Chair Lift** (daily 9am–4.30pm weather permitting; $8.50; Ⓣ/03 6331 5915) takes an exhilarating six minutes to cover 457m – it's supposed to have the longest single span (308m) of any chair lift in the world. The views are wonderful, but if you're afraid of heights you might want to cross on foot via the **Basin Walk** directly underneath, although this route is impassable when the river is in flood. The other alternative, the narrow **Alexandra Suspension Bridge**, called the "swinging bridge" by locals, is even shakier when crowded with joggers.

A track starting from the Alexandra Suspension Bridge follows the river through unspoilt bush to the narrower **Second Basin** and the disused **Duck Reach Power Station** (90min return). From the station you could continue a bit further to the large **Trevallyn State Recreation Area** (daily 8am–dusk; no camping), on the South Esk River, and the **Trevallyn Dam**, 6km west of the city centre. To reach the area by road, go via the suburb of Trevallyn, following Reatta Road. In the recreation area at Aquatic Point, there's an **information centre**, summer canoe and windsurf boards rental, a playground, toilets and barbecues. The rest of the reserve consists of open eucalypt forest, with marked bushwalks and nature trails shared with horse riders.

Eating

Eating out in Launceston is a predominantly Anglo-Saxon affair, with **pubs** in particular offering decent meals. However, there are also a few excellent **cafés** and the odd ethnic place, and a new level of choice and sophistication at the Old Launceston Seaport surrounding *Peppers Seaport Hotel* (see p.1025). Options include the popular and very casual *Fish 'n' Chips* where you can sit at outside tables, the trendy *Mud Bar and Restaurant*, the rowdier *Dockside Cafe Winebar*, plus *Cube*, a funky little café, and *Porthole*, a more traditional café-patisserie.

Blue Inveresk Railyards, off Invermay Rd. This café/bar, in a round and sunny former powerhouse, is a young, lively art-college hangout. Classic, café meals for under $10, plus more substantial mains up to $20; also gourmet pizzas and $5.50 tapas menu to go with a drink. Outside tables prove very popular for the excellent weekend breakfast. Ambient DJs spin Fri night (from 7pm) and Sun afternoons (2–5pm). Licensed. Mon–Sat from 8.30am (dinner Mon–Sat), Sun 8am–3pm.

Calabrisella 56 Wellington St Ⓣ03/6331 1958. A crowded, noisy, atmospheric and affordable Italian restaurant. BYO. Dinner nightly except Tues.

Fee & Me 190 Charles St Ⓣ03/6331 3195. Award-winning restaurant serving up expensive regional cuisine with an international flavour. Licensed. Dinner Mon–Sat.

Hari's Curry 152 York St ⓣ03/6331 6466. Very cheap, well-recommended Indian eatery – average main is $8.50 and there's nothing over $20. BYO. Dinner daily.

Izakaya Japanese Restaurant and Sushi Bar Yorktown Square ⓣ03/6334 2620. This excellent, long-established place serves all the favourite Japanese dishes: *ramen*, sushi, tempura, *bento*, though noodles are available lunchtime only. Mains average $15. Licensed (sake) and BYO. Lunch Wed–Fri, dinner Tues–Sun.

Konditorei Manfredi 106 George St. German cakes and pastries accompanied by delicious coffee; also a full menu of contemporary meals served on the smart upper level with its polished wood floors, licensed bar and outside courtyard. There's a sandwich bar for healthy takeaways. Mon–Sat 8.30am–5.30pm.

Morty's Cnr Brisbane and Wellington streets. Popular foodcourt near the cinema, with lots of Asian kitchens including Thai and Chinese. Also fish and chips, pancakes, and a juice bar. Licensed. Daily 10am–9.30pm.

O'Keefe's Hotel 124 George St. Tasty pub meals, including a big range of international dishes such as curries and seafood are on offer, and there are cheap $9 lunch specials.

Pasta Pasta 75 George St. You can fill up here on freshly made pasta ($9–14) with delicious and inventive as well as traditional sauces. There's plenty of choice for vegetarians, too, such as roasted vegetables in a Napoli sauce, or pesto with pumpkin and pine nuts. Takeaway prices are substantially cheaper. Mon–Sat 10.30am–7.30pm, Thurs–Sat to 8.30pm.

Pierre's Coffee House and Restaurant 88 George St ⓣ03/6331 6835. Established in the 1950s by a French immigrant, *Pierre's* has the feel of a classic café-bistro. There's great coffee, fabulous hot chocolate, gorgeous cakes, and Tasmanian wines by the glass. Mon–Thurs 10am–9pm, Fri 10am–10pm, Sat 10am–2pm & 6pm–10pm.

Star of Siam Cnr Charles and Paterson streets ⓣ03/6331 2786. Launceston's favourite Thai restaurant, worth booking on weekends. Mains average around $16. Licensed and BYO. Lunch Tues–Fri, dinner nightly.

Stillwater Ritchies Mill Arts Centre, Paterson St ⓣ03/6331 4153. Very popular riverside café/restaurant and wine bar (with an extensive local wine list) with a great atmosphere. During the day, it's an alfresco café, with generous all-day breakfasts and board specials, while at night the menu is more upscale. Licensed and BYO. Daily 10am to late (book for dinner).

Entertainment and nightlife

The *Examiner*, based in Launceston, is the newspaper for the north of Tasmania – Thursday's entertainment section details weekly events. The **Princess Theatre**, 57 Brisbane St (ⓣ03/6323 3666), stages regular drama, opera, ballet and concerts, usually touring from interstate. Behind the theatre, the Earl Arts Centre, 10 Earl St (ⓣ03/6334 5579), has fringe theatre productions, while the **Silverdome**, out of town on the Bass Highway at Prospect (ⓣ03/6344 9988), is the venue for major exhibitions as well as entertainment and sports events. Hugely popular AFL football matches are held in **York Park Sports and Entertainment Centre** just near the Inveresk development (details and bookings ⓦwww.aflintasmania.com), and you can gamble at the **Country Club Casino**, 9km out of town, off the Bass Highway at Prospect Vale (daily noon–1am, Fri & Sat until 4am; bus #61, #64, #65; ⓣ03/6335 5777). The only **cinema**, the four-screen Village 4, at 163 Brisbane St (ⓣ03/6331 5066), shows mainstream films. Check the Gay Information Line (see p.995) for the latest details on the gay scene in Launceston.

Pubs, bars and clubs

Irish Murphy's 211 Brisbane St. Spirited Irish pub with Guinness on tap, live music (Wed–Sun) and pub meals.

Launceston Saloon 191 Charles St ⓣ03/6331 7355. Always packed-out on event nights with a young student crowd. The huge main *Saloon Bar* has several plasma screens, local bands (Wed nights) and irregular interstate and international band events, and DJ nights on Wed, Fri and Sat (9.30pm–5/6am; free) when the mezzanine-level becomes a karaoke bar. Big-screen TV and typical pub food served in the *Sports Bar* and the *Saloon Bar*.

Royal Oak Hotel 14 Brisbane St ☎03/6331 5346. Popular, genial watering hole with live blues and jazz Thurs to Sat nights. Crowded bistro serves Greek dishes as well as counter meals (mains $12–18). Mon–Sat until midnight, Sun until 10pm.
Royal on George 90 George St ☎03/6331 2526. Renovated glass-fronted, light and colourful pub with an emphasis on food (from 8.30am for breakfast). A modern café-style menu – gourmet sandwiches and salads, pasta and risotto, plus classic but meaty mains. Live rock, jazz or acoustic music Fri and Sat. Mon–Thurs & Sun until midnight, Fri & Sat to 3am.
Star Bar Café 113 Charles St ☎03/6331 6111. Sophisticated bar with slick, modern decor and pavement tables; brasserie-style Mediterranean food available. Daily 11am until late.

Listings

Banks and foreign exchange Commonwealth Bank, 97 Brisbane St; Travelex, 98 St John St (Mon–Fri 9am–5.30pm, Sat 10am–1pm).
Bike rental Bike Hire Tasmania, 83 George St ☎0400 256 588, Ⓦwww.bikehiretasmania.com rents city and touring bikes for $45 day, $252 per week.
Books Fullers Bookshop, 93 St John St.
Camping equipment A good option for renting or buying gear is Allgoods, with stores at 71–79 York St and 60 Elizabeth St. Paddy Pallin, 110 George St, focuses on the top end of the market and sells a wide range of freeze-dried foods, guidebooks and maps.
Car rental Europcar, airport and 112 George St (☎03/6331 8200 or 1800 030 118), also has 4WDs. Autorent-Hertz, airport and 58 Paterson St (☎03/6335 1111), also has campervans. For cheaper rates try: Economy Car Rentals, 27 William St (☎03/6334 3299), or Lo-Cost Auto Rent, 80 Tamar St (☎03/6334 6202).
Hospital Launceston General, Charles St ☎03/6332 7111.
Internet access Launceston's Online Access Centre is on the ground floor of the State Library, Civic Square.
Motorbike rental Tasmanian Motorcycle Hire, 17 Coachmans Rd, Evandale (☎03/6391 9139, Ⓦwww.tasmotorcyclehire.com.au; from $115 per day, helmets included).
Pharmacy Amcal Centre Pharmacy, 84 Brisbane St (daily 9am–10pm; ☎03/6331 7777).
Post office 111 St John St, Launceston, TAS 7250. ☎13 13 18.
Swimming The Launceston Swimming Centre, Windmill Hill Reserve (Mon–Fri 6am–7pm, Sat & Sun 9am–7pm except April to Oct daily from 11am; $3.20). Aquarius Roman Baths, 127–133 George St (☎03/6331 2255), is a self-indulgent, opulent complex of therapeutic warm, hot and cold baths, sauna, steam rooms, gym, massage and solarium (Mon–Fri 9am–9pm, Sat & Sun 9am–6pm; admission to baths and saunas $26 or $44 per couple).
Taxis Taxi ranks are on George St between Brisbane and Paterson sts, on St John St outside Princes Square. Central Cabs ☎13 10 08; Taxis Combined ☎13 22 27.
Tours Coach Tram Tour Company (☎03/6336 3133) offers city-sights tours ($26; 3hr; Jan–April daily 10am & 2pm; May–Dec 10am) leaving from the Gateway centre. Tigerline (☎01300 653 633) has a programme of big commercial coach tours: Launceston city sights and Cataract Gorge (3hr; $51); and Cradle Mountain tour (full day $127), which gives 3hr 30min at the park. Tiger Wilderness Tours has the most interesting day-trips (☎03/6394 3212, Ⓦwww.tigerwilderness.com.au) including Tamar Valley Eco Tour, with an afternoon of four short walks (half-day; $60); Cradle Mountain including Mole Creek caves and Sheffield, and a walk around Dove Lake (full day $100); Meander Falls Remote Walk, including a six-hour return walk and lunch (full day $120). Tasmanian Expeditions (see p.979) lead rock-climbing at Cataract Gorge (half-day $100, full day $180) and canoeing, as well as longer trekking, cycling and rafting tours.

Around Launceston

Before launching yourself into the beauty of the Tamar Valley, there are several fine Georgian farming estates and mansions around the well-preserved towns of **Evandale** and **Longford**, just twenty-odd kilometres south of Launceston. If you're here in winter, you might consider joining the ski crowd who descend upon **Ben Lomond National Park**, southeast of Launceston; out of season, this is fine bushwalking country.

Evandale and Longford

Though no public transport runs to **EVANDALE**, 20km southeast of Launceston, this National Trust–classified town from the 1830s rewards a visit, particularly for its long-running Sunday market. At the **Evandale Tourism and History Centre** on High Street (daily 9am–4pm; ⓣ03/6391 8128), pick up a $2.20 *Heritage Walk* brochure. Otherwise, the map opposite the popular eat-in *Ingleside Bakery* (licensed), in restored 1867 council chambers, also on High Street, points out notable features – many of the old buildings bear descriptive plaques. The **Clarendon Arms Hotel**, on nearby Russell Street (ⓣ03/6391 8181; ❷), was built in 1847 on the site of the former convict station; its mural-covered interior depicts the early history of Tasmania. The **Evandale Market**, held in Falls Park on Logan Road (Sun 8am–2pm), attracts large crowds to its varied hundred-odd stalls, which include local organic produce. Once a year in late February, Evandale hosts the three-day-long **National Penny Farthing Championships** as part of its Village Fair; the races using the old bikes are quite a sight. Eight kilometres south of Evandale via the C416 and the C418 is the National Trust–owned **Clarendon Homestead** on the banks of the South Esk River (daily 10am–5pm, to 4pm June–Aug; $10.00), a grand white Neo-classical-style country house built in 1838 for a wealthy wool-grower and furnished in Georgian style; it's worth coming just for the lovely conservatory tearooms at the front.

Australia's oldest continually running **racecourse** was established in 1847 at **LONGFORD**, 20km southwest of Launceston. It's a country classic, with the big event the New Year's Day Longford Cup. On the outskirts of town, along Woolmers Lane (C521), **Brickendon Estate** (Tues–Sun 9.30am–5.30pm; closed July & Aug; $12.00; ⓣ03/6391 1251) was set up from land granted to William Archer in 1824; fascinatingly, it's still run by Archers as a working sheep property. Generations of the family saw fit to preserve the early architecture and walking into the farm compound with its huge Dutch-style wooden barns is like setting foot into the film *The Girl With the Pearl Earring*. This ramshackle appeal is the setting for **accommodation** in absolutely charming old estate cottages (❺). William's brother Thomas Archer established his estate **Woolmers** (ⓣ03/6391 2230, ⓦwww.woolmers.com.au) in 1819 – just a few kilometres further along the hawthorn-hedgerow-lined Woolmers Lane – which lasted through six generations of Archers until 1994. The original Georgian bungalow with its dark warren of rooms still stands, as does the impressive Italianate villa that was adjoined in 1843. A guided **tour** of the house, with its grand dining room still set up as it was for a royal visit in 1868, is fascinating as much for the interiors as for the family story (daily 10am, 11am, 12.30pm, 2pm & 3.30pm; $18 includes Rose Garden). It's a scenic spot too, perched above the Macquarie River with views across the Great Western Tiers. The **National Rose Garden** (self-guided tour of grounds and garden $12), with over 4000 rose plants, has been set up in former orchards.

Ben Lomond National Park

The plateau of the **Ben Lomond Range**, over 1300m high and 84 square kilometres in area, lies entirely within **Ben Lomond National Park**, 50km southeast of Launceston. A small ski village sits below **Legges Tor** (1572m), the second-highest point in Tasmania, and can be reached in an hour from Launceston; above it the bumpy outline of the range's steep cliffs dominates the horizon. The **ski season** runs from mid-July to the end of September, and **accommodation** is limited to the *Ben Lomond Creek Inn* (ⓣ03/6372 2444; bunk rooms ❹, half-board rooms ❽), which is usually booked out at weekends.

However, the region's accessibility means there's no real need to stay. **Meals** are available at the inn, or there's fast food from the ski-resort kiosk.

An all-day pass on the **ski lifts** costs around $40 (more details at Ⓦwww.ski.com.au/resorts/benlomond). Some ski rental is available on the mountain but there's a better range at Launceston Sports Centre, 88A George St (Ⓣ03/6331 4777). The Travel and Information Centre (see p.1024) can advise on ski packages and the **bus service** from Launceston which operates during the season. If you're driving, be warned that the final 20km to the ski village is unsealed and the last leg, **Jacobs Ladder**, is very steep, with hairpin bends, sheer drops and no safety barriers. You must carry wheel chains, which can be rented from the snowline. Otherwise, you can park just before the Ladder and take the **shuttle bus**. Outside the ski season, all services cease and the businesses close down, but the scenery and the alpine vegetation are magnificent enough to lure **bushwalkers**. There's a 12.5-kilometre track from *Carr Villa*, on the slopes of Ben Lomond, to Legges Tor. Bush **camping** is permitted anywhere in the national park, but *Carr Villa* is an informal camping area with a pit toilet. For more information, contact the ranger (Ⓣ03/6230 8233).

The Tamar Valley

To the north of Launceston is the beautiful **Tamar Valley**, where, for 64km, the tidal waters wind through orchards, vineyards, strawberry farms, lavender plantations, forested hills and grazing land. Only the Batman Bridge, near Deviot, and the APPM Wood Mill and Bell Bay Power Station, near the river's mouth, spoil the idyllic scenery.

West of the Tamar

The West Tamar Highway (A7) follows the line of the Tamar River from Launceston to Beauty Point and **Brady's Lookout State Reserve** provides magnificent views of the Tamar Valley and Ben Lomond; you can see as far as Low Head, 34km away. Rather than head straight along the highway, it's worth detouring for a stretch through **ROSEVEARS**, on a picturesque sweep of road along the riverbanks that's popular with cyclists. In the village itself you can have a drink in the 1831 *Rosevears Taverne*. A few kilometres west of Rosevears is **Notley Gorge State Reserve**, a beautiful fern gorge with a number of walking tracks, reached by turning west off the highway at Legana. Back on the highway, **EXETER** has the useful **Tamar Visitor Centre** (daily 9am–5pm; Ⓣ1800 637 989, Ⓦwww.tamarvalley.com.au), an Online Access Centre on Main Road, and the excellent *Exeter Bakery*. Further north, **BEACONSFIELD** was once at the centre of Tasmania's former gold-mining area, and the mining ruins are still visible; two former mine buildings house the interesting, interactive **Grubb Shaft Gold & Heritage Museum** (daily 10am–4pm; $9).

At gorgeous **Beauty Point**, the fascinating **Seahorse World** at Inspection Head Wharf (tours 9.30am–3.30pm, every 30min; $18; 45min–1hr; Ⓦwww.seahorseworld.com.au) is the world's only commercial seahorse farm. By successfully harvesting the difficult-to-breed creatures for aquariums and the Chinese market, the farm is helping save those in the oceans from further depletion. The **Australian Maritime College (AMC)**, established in Beauty Point in 1978, has developed the interpretive material at the farm, and there is also an interesting display about the AMC on the top floor, beside a café with wonderful water views. There are more curious creatures next door in the

Platypus House (daily 9am–4pm; Ⓦwww.platypushouse.com.au; guided one-hour tour $18); platypus are elusive in the wild but you can catch a glimpse here (also Tasmanian frogs, butterflies and lizards). The AMC lends Beauty Point bags of atmosphere, with a big busy training ship moored at the marina by the *Beauty Point Hotel*. From the jetty here, the **Shuttlefish Ferry** crosses the Tamar to George Town (2–4 daily except Tues; $10 one way, $18 return; 20 min; 2hr, $30 cruise to Low Head daily except Tues 11am; bookings essential Ⓣ03/6383 4479). The faded motel units at the *Beauty Point Hotel* (Ⓣ03/6383 4363, Ⓦwww.beautypointhotel.com.au; ❸) have fantastic river views. The pub itself is more upmarket, with tables outside on the water and views from the dining room, which has an excellent menu featuring a wide range of seafood. For somewhere really special to stay, *Pomona* (Ⓣ03/6383 4073, Ⓦwww.pomonabandb.com.au), just across the road on a rise above the river, has B&B accommodation (❺) in a charming Federation-style house with great views from the veranda-cum-breakfast nook, or luxurious, timber self-catering cottages (❻ includes breakfast hamper).

East of the Tamar: George Town and Low Head

Leaving Launceston and heading north along the East Tamar Highway, it's only a few minutes before you're zooming through scenic countryside, passing through Dilston where cows graze in paddocks at the base of bush-covered hills. After Hillwood and its famous strawberry farm, you're headed for the port of **GEORGE TOWN**, one of the oldest towns in Australia, where Colonel Paterson landed in 1804 to begin settlement of northern Tasmania. The **George Town Visitor Information Centre** is on Main Road on the way into town (daily 10am–4pm; Ⓣ03/6382 1700); George Town's **Online Access Centre** is on Macquarie Street.

Despite its history, George Town isn't particularly compelling, with only one colonial building to look at, **The Grove**, an elegant stone Georgian mansion at 25 Cimitiere St (daily 10am–5pm; $6.50). More appealing is **LOW HEAD**, 5km north, with 24 National Trust–listed buildings, whitewashed cottages and rambling houses, all set amid extensive parkland. The original convict-built **Pilot Station** now houses a **museum** (daily 9am–5pm; $5; Ⓦwww.lhhp.com.au), which has a display of maritime memorabilia. There's also a **Little penguin colony** at Low Head; guided tours are offered each evening at sunset (1hr; $15; bookings on Ⓣ0418 361 860, Ⓦwww.penguintours.lowhead.com). Diving options and cruises to a nearby **fur seal colony** on Tenth Island are also on offer with Seal and Sea Adventure Tours (3 hours; $120; bookings Ⓣ0419 357 028, Ⓦwww.sealandsea.com). You can catch a ferry to Beauty Point from George Town with the Shuttlefish Ferry (see above).

George Town **accommodation** includes the *George Town Heritage Hotel*, at 77 Macquarie St (Ⓣ03/6382 2655; ❹), the oldest pub in town but with few discernible traces of its early nineteenth-century roots. On the warfront, the pretty wooden *Pier Hotel*, at 5 Elizabeth St (Ⓣ03/6382 1300; rooms ❺, apartments ❻), has rooms upstairs in the old part, modern motel-style rooms on the waterfront, and self-catering units; the **food** here is good, from pasta to Asian curries. Opposite, at 4 Elizabeth St, is the *Traveller's Lodge* (Ⓣ03/6382 3261; dorms $19, rooms ❷), a backpackers' in a pretty 1870 home, with a clean, modern interior.

In Low Head, you can stay in heritage-style cottage accommodation at the *Pilot Station* (see above; Ⓣ03/6382 1143; ❹), and at *Belfont Cottages*, at 178 Low Head

Rd (Ⓣ03/6382 1399; ❺, with breakfast provisions supplied), or **camp** at *Low Head Caravan Park*, 136 Low Head Rd (Ⓣ03/6382 1573; vans ❷, cabins ❸).

Around George Town: the Pipers River wine region

Heading east of George Town, a pleasant day can be spent exploring the **vineyards** around the **Pipers River area**, which produce distinctly flavoured, crisp and fresh cool-climate wines. The *Tamar Valley Wine Route* brochure, available from the information centres in Launceston (p.1024) and Exeter (see p.1033), covers 21 vineyards in the Tamar Valley and Pipers Brook area (virtually all open daily 10am–5pm) and offering free tastings. One of the best known is **Pipers Brook Vineyard** (now part of Kreglinger), on the sealed C818, 2km off the B82. Established in 1974, the winery is housed in a modern, architect-designed complex, with self-guided tours. It also has a café and vine-covered courtyard. Nearby, also on the C818, lake-fronted **Janz** makes premium champagne; there's information on the wine-making process in the interpretive centre. The friendly, small-scale **Delamere Vineyard**, on the B82, specializes in Pinot Noir and Chardonnay. Valleybrook and Tiger Wilderness run wine tours from Launceston (see "Tours", p.1031).

The Midland Highway

The **Midland Highway** is a fast three-hour route between Hobart and Launceston, more or less following the old coaching road (look for signs to the "Heritage Highway"), although you'll have to detour if you want to visit some of the towns on the way. Redline has several daily **bus** services between Hobart and Launceston, stopping at the major midland towns.

Campbell Town and Ross

Beyond **CAMPBELL TOWN** – a rather plain community originally settled by Scots but the Midlands' major centre – you drive south through sheep-grazing countryside, eventually turning off the highway to **ROSS**, 2km east. Also settled by Scots, this has a very secluded, rural feel; elm trees line the main Church Street, creating a beautiful avenue, while paddocks with grazing sheep stretch alongside. Old stone buildings along the idyllic street are well preserved, including the characterful sandstone *Man O'Ross Hotel*. From the grounds of St John's Church of England, one of the town's three pretty churches, there are views of the Macquarie River, spanned by the sandstone **Ross Bridge**, designed by John Lee Archer and built by convicts in 1836; the intricate stone carvings on its three arches earned the convict stonemason a free pardon. A melancholy walk in the other direction from the church leads down to the original Ross burial ground and past the site of the **Female Factory**, actually a prison, where women convicts were held before being sent to properties as assigned servants. You can **stay** in several of the old cottages dotted about town: *Colonial Cottages of Ross* (Ⓣ03/6381 5354, ❺–❻ including breakfast provisions) has five to choose from. The *Man O'Ross Hotel* (Ⓣ03/6381 5445, Ⓦwww.manoross.com.au; ❸ including breakfast) has several intimate rooms in which to **eat or drink**, and shared-bathroom accommodation upstairs. There's **camping** at the pleasant *Ross Caravan Park* on Bridge Street (Ⓣ03/6381 5224; cabins ❶–❷). Two recommended **cafés** face each other across the main street: the cosy *Bakery Tea Rooms* and the more contemporary-style *That Place In Ross*, next door to the new Gourmet Chocolate Factory. The Tasmanian Wool Centre on Church Street (daily 9am–5pm; Ⓦ www.taswoolcentre.com.au, Ⓣ 03/6381 5466) acts as an **information centre** and also houses a wool exhibition and history museum (entry by donation) and has **Internet access**.

Oatlands

Back on the Midland Highway, it's 88km south from Ross to **OATLANDS**, which has Australia's greatest concentration of colonial **Georgian buildings**: 140 in two square kilometres, most built by convicts. Many are now occupied by antique and bric-a-brac shops, B&Bs and guesthouses. The most striking edifice is the **Callington Mill** and its outbuildings; the partly restored windmill was built in 1837 and remained in operation until 1892. From the top there are fine views of the town and the surrounding countryside; ask to go up to the adjacent **Dolls At The Mill** (daily 10am-4pm; $2), an extensive doll collection in the old mill residence. The best way to see the town is to go on one of Peter Fielding's guided **heritage walks** (Ⓣ 03/6254 1135; $5), which visit several other buildings, including the Old Gaol and courthouse. Contact him to arrange a spooky evening **ghost tour** ($10).

For **food**, the cosy *Blossom's Georgian Tea Rooms*, 116 High St (Ⓣ 03/6254 1516), serves scones and light lunches. The **Central Tasmania Tourism Centre**, 85 High St (daily 9am–5pm; Ⓣ 03/6254 1212), can book **accommodation** from the many colonial-style B&Bs in the town; a good choice is the central *Oatlands Lodge*, at 92 High St (Ⓣ 03/6254 1444; 5). Oatlands' **Online Access Centre** is in the library at 68 High St.

The Great Western Tiers and Central Plateau

Deloraine, on the **Meander River**, is nestled in a valley of rich farmland dominated by **Quamby Bluff** (1256m) and the **Great Western Tiers**, where the Central Plateau drops abruptly to the surrounding plains. On the Bass Highway, it's roughly equidistant from Devonport (51km) and Launceston (48km). From Deloraine the **Lake Highway** begins, rising up over the Western Tiers to the Central Plateau, with its thousands of lakes. To the west of Deloraine are the extensive **cave systems** around **Mole Creek**, while **Walls of Jerusalem National Park** is accessed from **Western Creek**, 32km southwest of Deloraine.

Deloraine and around

DELORAINE is a delightful hilly town, often shrouded in mist, even on summer mornings, and divided into two parts by the bubbling **Meander River**. Although the area was settled by Europeans in the 1830s, Deloraine didn't really begin to develop until after 1846, and today it's a National Trust–classified town. **West Parade** follows the river, facing the park; at no. 17 the Georgian **Bonney's Inn** dates from 1830 and is the town's oldest remaining building (now a B&B; see p.1038). At the next block, Westbury Place rises up steeply from West Parade; if you climb the hill you'll reach the tall spire-dominated **St Mark's Church**, built in 1860, and there's a scenic **lookout** that gives a panoramic view over the town and the Western Tiers to the south. Deloraine has a café culture, plenty of secondhand and antique shops, and a small, alternative arts-and-crafts scene, witnessed regularly at the **market** on the first Saturday of every month across the river opposite the *Apex Caravan Park*, and at the annual **Tasmanian Craft Fair**, a huge event held over four days in early November.

Close to prime **bushwalking** areas in the Western Tiers, Deloraine is an established base for walkers. Popular tracks are the short walk to **Alum Cliffs**, overlooking the Mersey River Gorge (40min return), signposted on the road between Mole Creek and Chudleigh; a difficult walk to **Quamby Bluff**, renowned for its myrtle rainforest (6.5km; 6hr; beginning at Brodies Road, off the Lake Highway); the track to **Liffey Falls** (8km; 3hr; beginning at the picnic ground 5km west of the tiny community of Liffey), and the day-walk to **Meander Falls** through the Meander Forest Reserve, about 25km south of Deloraine, reached via the small settlement of Meander and Meander Falls Road (10km; 6–7hr; beginning from the picnic ground; Tiger Wilderness Tours

△ Tasmanian Devil

does an excellent tour from Launceston – see p.1031). There's a walker registration and information booth at the Meander Falls car park. A free leaflet issued by Forestry Tasmania, *Visiting the Great Western Tiers*, has a map of the Meander Forest Reserve and tracks; you can pick it up from the Deloraine information centre (see opposite).

The western end of the Great Western Tiers overlooks **MOLE CREEK**, 24km west of Deloraine. Here, you can get up close to some Tasmanian devils at the **Trowunna Wildlife Park** (daily 9am–5pm; $16; ⓦwww.trowunna.com.au), or buy delicious local honey from **Stephens Leatherwood Honey Factory** (Mon–Fri 8am–5pm). Surrounding the town, the **Mole Creek Karst National Park** has a network of over two hundred underground caves. About 14km west of Mole Creek are two rather spectacular ones: **Marakoopa Cave**, with huge caverns, streams, pools and glow worms (daily hourly from 10am–4pm; 50–80min; $15); and 6km further west the smaller but more richly decorative **King Solomons Cave**, with stalactites and stalagmites (daily 10.30am, 11.30am, 12.30pm, 2.30pm, 3.30pm & 4.30pm; 40–60min; $15). Wild Cave Tours (ⓣ03/6367 8142, ⓦwww.wildcavetours.com) offers excellent $85 half-day and $170 full-day caving tours of the Mole Creek caves, underground streams and subterranean systems. Places to **stay** in Mole Creek range from an excellent campsite (ⓣ03/6363 1150) to the congenial **Mole Creek Guest House** (ⓣ03/6363 1399, ⓦwww.molecreekgh.com.au; ⑤), with its own restaurant and tourist information.

Deloraine practicalities

The two major **bus** companies both make regular stops in Deloraine. Redline stops daily on its Launceston–Devonport service, and its Launceston–Deloraine service which continues on to Mole Creek once daily on weekdays; and TassieLink on its Launceston–Queenstown service (Tues/Thurs and Sat); TassieLink is based at *Sullivans Restaurant*, at 17 West Parade. The depot for Redline is the **Great Western Tiers Visitor Information Centre**, at 98 Emu Bay Rd (daily 9am–5pm; ⓣ03/6362 3471, ⓦwww.greatwesterntiers.org.au). The centre has maps, details on walking times and conditions, and makes free accommodation bookings; it is housed in an old inn with an attached folk museum ($7), which features a series of vast, woven silk wall-hangings, made by the local community. The **Online Access Centre** is behind the library at 21 West Parade.

Operators leading **outdoor activities** in the area include Jahadi Indigenous Experiences (ⓣ03/6363 6172, ⓦwww.jahadi.com.au; 4WD tours) and the Tasmanian Fly Fishing School (ⓣ03/6362 3441, ⓦwww.tasmanianflyfishing.com.au).

There's a wide range of **accommodation** choices in Deloraine. The popular, clean and well-run *Highview Lodge YHA Hostel*, at 8 Blake St (ⓣ03/6362 2996, ⓔbodach@microtech.com.au; dorms $20, rooms ②; bike rental available), set on a hill commanding unparalleled views of Quamby Bluff, is about a ten-minute walk from the information centre. In the centre of town, the big old *Deloraine Hotel* faces the river on the corner of Emu Bay Road and Barrack Street, and has shared-bathroom and en-suite rooms upstairs (ⓣ03/6362 2022; ③). Just across Barrack Street, a more upmarket choice is the *Georgian Bonney's Inn*, at 17 West Parade (ⓣ03/6362 2974, ⓦwww.bonneys-inn.com; ⑤), which has spacious suites. A good motel on the outskirts of town is *Mountain View Country Inn*, 144 Emu Bay Rd (ⓣ03/6362 2633; ④), where the row of units affords great Tiers views. *Bonney's Farm*, off Weetah Road, 4km northwest of Deloraine (ⓣ03/6362 2122; ④), has a guesthouse (B&B) and self-contained two- or three-bed units. The exquisite French-influenced guesthouse/restaurant *Calstock*, on the Lake Highway just outside Deloraine (☎03/6362 2642, Ⓦwww.calstock.net; ❼–❽), serves country-style meals created from local organic ingredients. You can **camp** at the riverside *Apex Caravan Park*, 51 West Parade (☎03/6362 2345).

In Deloraine, there are plenty of informal **places to eat** on the main street, Emu Bay Road. The pick of the lot is the *Deloraine Deli* at no. 36 (Mon–Fri 9am–5pm, Sat 9am–2.30pm), a combination deli-counter and tearoom with meals under $11 and great coffee. The best pub meals can be found at the *Deloraine Hotel*.

Walls of Jerusalem National Park

The **Walls of Jerusalem National Park** is on the western side of the Central Plateau, a series of five mountain peaks that enclose a central basin, an isolated area noted for its lakes, pencil pines and the biblical names of its various features. The best time to visit is November through to April; people have died of exposure here, so make sure you're well prepared. You'll need the *Walls of Jerusalem National Park Map and Notes* ($9.10; see p.979).

As the Walls of Jerusalem is the only national park in Tasmania that you can't drive into, the walk in begins outside the park boundaries. From King Solomons Cave (see opposite), head south, following the Mersey River and the unsealed road east of Lake Rowallan; the car park is at Howells Bluff. You walk through wilderness into the park, which is isolated and lacking even basic facilities, without a ranger (although rangers do patrol). However, the track is well kept, with boardwalks laid down over boggy areas, and there's plenty of clean water to drink from the streams and lakes. The few small leaky huts are really for emergencies only. If you just want to walk into the park to the central basin (through **Herods Gate**, with views of Barn Bluff and Cradle Mountain to the northwest), set up camp and then walk back; it's a 14km return hike, which takes seven or eight hours altogether, going at a steady pace over two days. The walk begins with a steep climb then levels out on the plateau. There are numerous routes to the various peaks and lakes – from **Damascus Gate** you get stunning views of Cradle Mountain–Lake St Clair National Park immediately west – and an experienced, well-equipped walker could spend a couple of days here. **Organized walks** are provided by the recommended Tiger Trails, with a four-day expedition ($899), and Tasmanian Expeditions (see p.979), who offer a six-day circuit walk ($1290; Oct–April). Maxwell's (☎03/64921431) operates on demand from Devonport ($180 1–4 people; $45 per person, 5 or more people) and Launceston ($240/$60).

The Central Plateau

At its northern and eastern edges, the **Central Plateau** is rimmed by the long crest of the Great Western Tiers (1440m). At over a thousand metres above sea level, the plateau is often covered in frost and subject to sleet and snowstorms in winter. The **Great Lake** lies on the plateau about 8km from the escarpment, and only 40km from Deloraine, along the Lake Highway that continues to **BOTHWELL**, the plateau's only town, ending at Melton Mowbray, where it joins the Midland Highway. The major lakes can be reached from roads leading off the Lake Highway. To the west, between Cradle Mountain–Lake St Clair National Park and below the Walls of Jerusalem National Park, is the inaccessible "Land of Three Thousand Lakes".

The Central Plateau has few inhabitants – only around eight hundred live here year-long – but it's full of **fishing shacks**, and on a fine weekend the population sometimes swells to 25,000. It's also the base for the **Hydro Electricity Commission (HEC)**: the countless high-altitude lakes are used as water storage for the generation of electricity. Several temporary HEC villages set up for hydroelectric workers have been transformed into lodge-style accommodation. One is the *Bronte Park Highland Village* (Ⓣ03/6289 1126, Ⓦwww.bronteparkhighlandvillage.com.au; dorms $20, cabins ❹, lodge ❹, spa cottages ❻), which also has a campsite, EFTPOS facilities, a dining room and bar, a store selling groceries and fuel, and is ideally situated for **Lake St Clair** (25km; see p.1070) and nearby **Lake Big Jim**, popular trout-fishing spots. Ausprey Tours (Ⓣ03/6330 2612, Ⓦwww.gotroutfishtasmania.com.au) offers **fly-fishing tuition**.

To reach the *Bronte Park Highland Village*, take the bone-shattering Marlborough Highway (B11), which runs southwest off the Lake Highway as it curves around the bottom of the lake to Miena. TassieLink drops off at the *Bronte Park* turn-off on the Lyell Highway on their Hobart–Queenstown scheduled service.

The Bass Strait Islands

Located in the rough waters of the Bass Strait, battered by the Roaring Forties, are two groups of islands: the Hunter group, dominated by **King Island** off the northwest tip of Tasmania, and the Furneaux group, the largest of which is **Flinders Island**, lying just beyond the northeast corner of the state. In the nineteenth century, sealers roamed the Bass Strait, but the two main islands now consist of low-key rural communities, while several tall lighthouses, and many shipwrecks offshore are testimony to the turbulence of the sea at King Island.

You can go by **ship** to Flinders Island from Bridport (see p.1022) on the northeast coast of Tasmania: Southern Shipping Co Mon, Tues; departure times depend on tides; Ⓣ03/6356 3333, Ⓦwww.southernshipping.com.au) operates a car and passenger ferry. Car costs are prohibitive, but the return passenger fare of $96.10) is good value if you can put up with a possibly rough, eight-hour trip. Book at least four weeks in advance. **Airlines of Tasmania** (Ⓣ03/6359 2312 or 1800 144 460, Ⓦwww.airtasmania.com.au) flies to Flinders Island from Moorabbin Airport, just outside of Melbourne (one way $202), and from Launceston (one way $150). Tasmania's regional airline, Tasair (Ⓣ03/6248 5088 or 1800 062 900, Ⓦwww.tasair.com.au), flies daily to King Island from Burnie and Devonport ($192.50 one way) with connecting Tasair flights from Hobart; Regional Express (REX; Ⓣ13 17 13, Ⓦwww.rex.com.au) flies from Melbourne Tullamarine daily ($114 one way).

King Island

King Island, smaller but more heavily populated than Flinders Island, is chiefly known for its rich dairy produce, with crayfish and kelp and wind farming as secondary industries. Green, low and windswept, it can't offer anything like Flinders Island's dramatic landscape, nor its history, though it did witness around sixty **shipwrecks** between 1801 and 1995, and there are several working lighthouses – **Cape Wickham Lighthouse** in the north is the tallest in the southern hemisphere. Many of the wreck sites can be dived with King Island Dive Charters (Ⓣ03/6461 1133, Ⓦwww.kingislanddivecharter.com.au).

The island's main town is **CURRIE**, which has a simple museum (daily 2–4pm, closed July & Aug; donation suggested), and the bleak village of **GRASSY**, on the eastern side of the island, may experience a revival with the reopening of the tungsten mine that sustained its economy for 73 years from 1917. The best thing about King Island is the food, with free-range lamb and pork and local beef and wallaby, as well as seafood and delicious creamy milk, which you can drink unpasteurized while on the island – a rare treat. Indeed, top of the list of things to do on the island is a visit to the **King Island Dairy** (Mon–Fri 8am–5pm, Sun 12.30–4pm), 8km north of Currie, for free tastings of the rich local dairy produce; the brie and the thick cream in particular have legendary gourmet status around Australia. The island's **kelp factory** is near Currie's golf course; the bull kelp is gathered from the surrounding shores and left to dry outside the factory on racks – you'll see it as you pass by. Once dry, the kelp is milled into granules and shipped to Scotland to be processed into alginates, used as a gelling agent in literally thousands of products ranging from toothpaste to ice cream.

Practicalities

King Island Coach Tours, 95 Main St, Currie (Ⓣ03/6462 1138 or 1800 647 702), does pre-booked **airport transfers** to Currie, which is less than 10km away ($20 for 1–4 passengers), and Grassy. They also run various coach, bushwalking and wildlife **tours**; the best is the short evening tour to see the **Little penguin** community at Grassy (Mon & Thurs; $40). Otherwise, to **get around**, Cheapa Island Car Rentals (Ⓣ03/6462 1603) and King Island Car Rental (Ⓣ03/6462 1282 or 1800 777 282) both do airport drop-offs. The Trend, 26 Edward St, Currie provides **tourist information** (daily 8.30am–6.30pm; Ⓣ03/6462 1360) or you can contact **King Island Tourism Inc** (Ⓣ1800 645 014, Ⓦwww.kingisland.org.au).

The most obvious **places to stay** are around Currie. *King Island Gem Accommodation* (Ⓣ03/6462 1260 or 1800 647 702, Ⓦwww.kingislandgem.com.au; airport pick-up included) incorporates several styles and standards on North Road, 1.5km from town: *Devils Gap Retreat* have two delightful cottages full of art works by the exuberant Caroline Kininmonth in a bracing seafront location (Ⓣ/03 6462 1180; ❺), and there are also *A-Frame Holiday Homes* (❺), *King Island Cosy Cabins* (❹) or **camping** at *Bass Caravan Park* (vans ❷). Right in the centre, *Parers Hotel* (Ⓣ03/6462 1633, Ⓔparers@kingisland.net.au; ❺) has en-suite, motel-style rooms and serves excellent meals in its bistro. Near the golf course, there's the immaculate *Wave Watcher Holiday Units*, 18 Beach Rd (Ⓣ & Ⓕ03/6462 1517; ❻). Nearby, the rooms at *Boomerang By the Sea* (Ⓣ03/6462 1288, Ⓦwww.bythesea.com.au; ❺) have immediate sea views – even better from the motel's glass-walled restaurant. Back in town, *King Island Bakery* makes delicious, gourmet-status pies – including crayfish and King Island beef – and hand-made breads, while *Nautilus Coffee Lounge* is Currie's best café. There's a supermarket (open daily), a bottle shop, a Westpac bank with an ATM, and an Online Access Centre at 5 George St.

Flinders Island

With a population of just 800 (nearly half of which are absentee landowners), **FLINDERS ISLAND** is nonetheless the largest of 52 named islands that make up the Furneaux group, first mapped by Tobias Furneaux in 1770. The islands became a base for seal hunters, who slaughtered seals in their tens of thousands and, so legend goes, lured many ships to their demise for a spot of piracy. Ironically, these rough men provided a vital link in the continuing survival of the

Tasmanian Aboriginal people, by abducting women to work for them on the islands. When sealing ended, the Aboriginal communities survived by **muttonbird harvesting**, a seasonal industry that continues today with land-rights claims in 1995 giving title to several outlying, though unoccupied, islands. In 2005, there was a further breakthrough when Tasmania's Legislative Council approved the handover of Aboriginal-occupied Cape Barren Island (population 75) and Clarke Island (population six), with the land to be managed by the Cape Barren Island Aboriginal Association.

Flinders Island itself played a large part in the tragedy of the Tasmanian Aboriginal people; between 1831 and 1834 the remnants of the Tasmanian tribes were persuaded or forced to accept relocation here. Settled at windswept **Wybalenna** on the west coast of the island, the Aborigines were without adequate food and shelter, and were forcibly Christianized, as their culture was expunged and their numbers dwindled. All that remains of the period of enforced Aboriginal settlement is the **chapel**, built in 1838 at Wybalenna, and the cemetery where only the white graves bear headstones. Of the 135 tribespeople who were sent here, only 47 were still alive when the settlement was abandoned in 1847 and moved to Oyster Cove, near Hobart. The chapel has been restored by the National Trust, but the Aboriginal people of Flinders Island succeeded with their land-rights claim on Wybalenna, which was handed over in early 1999, and it is now up to them to decide how they'll run it. Due to political infighting, it's presently abandoned but can be visited.

There's a walk to Settlement Point from Wybalenna, where a viewing platform looks over an extensive **muttonbird** rookery – the sight and sound of hundreds of thousands of birds flying to the nesting islands each evening at dusk during the breeding season (Oct to late March) is extraordinary. The only commercial muttonbirding done by Aboriginal people now, however, is on Great Dog Island; in the grounds of **Emita Museum** just a few kilometres northwest of Wybalenna (Sat & Sun: summer 1–5pm; rest of year 1–4pm; $4; ⓣ/03 6359 2010), there's a replica of a typical **muttonbirding shed**, with its floor lined with tussock grass. Inside, shell necklaces made by the Aboriginal people of Cape Barren Island are displayed, and there are exhibits relating to sealing and shipwrecks.

History aside, isolated Flinders Island is very much a Mecca for **bushwalkers** and **rock-climbers**. Only about half of the island is cultivated, and you can walk its entire length in about six days – you can arrange with Flinders Island Adventures to have food and water delivered en route – on the partially signposted north–south **Flinders Trail**, a route designed to provide a sampling of the various terrains. The best-known walk, however, is to the distinctive summit of **Mount Strzelecki**, named after the Polish count, explorer and scientist who climbed it in 1842. The climb to the top starts about 10km south of Whitemark, signposted on Trousers Point Road – look out for a brown national-park sign – the peak is in the **Strzelecki National Park** in the southwest corner (ranger ⓣ03/6359 2217). Though navigation is easy, it's a strenuous walk – about 5km return (3–5hr). The wind can be fierce at the summit, and mists roll in, so take something wind- and waterproof. **Trousers Point** itself, also in the park, is a good introduction to the delights of the island's deserted beaches. The site, with its fine, white sand and rust-coloured rock formations, is particularly spectacular, with Mount Strzelecki rising up behind the granite headland; there's a free camping area here, with a composting toilet, water tank and bins. Nearby, the *Healing Dreams Retreat* (ⓣ03/6359 4588, ⓦwww.healingdreams.com.au; ⑥) with its retreat and day-spa programmes, is a sign of the direction Flinders is heading. The **Flinders Island Ecology Trail** is a circuit designed to be followed in a car, with five stopping-points where interpretive material is provided. The Trail can be related to the excellent *Furneaux Ecological Notebook* ($7) available at the information office (see below). **Walkers Lookout**, in the Darling Range, is a good starting-point, offering the best panorama of Flinders and the surrounding islands, with signs pointing out all the landmarks; the other four points on the route highlight bird habitats. You can see the endemic protected **Cape Barren goose** everywhere and likewise the island's wombats.

Practicalities

There are two main bases on Flinders Island: **WHITEMARK**, the administrative centre on the west coast, and **LADY BARRON** in the south, the main fishing area and deep-water port, more picturesque but with few facilities. The post office (ⓣ03/6359 2020) in Whitemark houses the island's only **bank** – Westpac (Mon–Thurs 10am–2.30pm, Fri 10am–4/5pm) – with EFTPOS, but no ATM facilities. Whitemark's IGA **supermarket**, known locally as Walkers (ⓣ03/6359 2010, ⓔwalkers@vision.net.au; closed Sat afternoon and all Sun, but advance phone or email grocery orders delivered to accommodation), is opposite the pub. Look out for the locally made soaps and facial products for sale. The Lady Barron Multistore, tucked away on Henwood Street, is hard to find: head uphill from the pub. It has EFTPOS and a post office plus petrol and is open daily. As there's no public transport, the best option is to **rent a car** and arrange to pick it up at the airport on arrival. Prices are quite reasonable with *Flinders Island Cabin Park* (ⓣ03/6359 2188), who also have mountain bikes for hire, or Bowman Lees Car Hire (ⓣ03/6359 2388). Unfortunately there's no 4WD hire, though most of the roads are unsealed.

For general inquiries and **information** on activities such as cruises, scuba diving, fishing, birdwatching and scenic flights, and walking and climbing guides to the island, head for the Area Marketing and Development Office, as you come into Whitemark on Lagoon Road (Mon–Fri 8.15am–5pm; ⓣ1800 994 477, ⓦwww.flindersislandonline.com.au). *Flinders Island Naturally*, a free visitors' guide with map, can be picked up here and at Tasmanian Travel Centres before you arrive on the island. Flinders Island's **Online Access Centre** is just opposite. Of the island's many available **tours**, one which comes very highly recommended is the good-value boat trip to observe the mutton-birds return to their nests at dusk with Flinders Island Adventures (Oct–March; 2hr 30min–3hr; $30 per person; ⓣ03/6359 4507, ⓦwww.flindersisland.com.au) with the extremely knowledgable Luddingtons. They also offer several other half- or full-day trips, including cruises to the outer islands, fishing and diving trips and 4WD tours.

There's a **campsite** with water and showers (ⓣ03/6359 8560) and a shop at topaz-fossicking Killiecrankie Bay in the northwest of the island – or you can camp for free at the coastal reserves, or on any crown land as long as it's 500m from the road: designated sites are at Allports Beach, Lillies Beach, North East River and Trousers Point, and all have toilets and fireplaces, though only the last has water and a gas barbecue. You can also camp in more comfort a few kilometres out of Whitemark, near the airport, in pleasant sheltered grounds at the *Flinders Island Cabin Park* on Bluff Road (ⓣ03/6359 2188; ❸), with tasteful, spacious and mostly en-suite cabins. In Whitemark itself, you can **stay** at the *Interstate Hotel* in the centre of town (ⓣ03/6359 2114; B&B ❸–❹), which has some en-suite rooms and serves huge throwback-to-another-era meals in the popular bistro (except Sun); it also offers showers and laundry facilities to non-residents. The *Flinders Island Bakery* (closed Sun) has alfresco tables; delicious local wallaby and red-wine pies are part of its repertoire and there's real coffee. Otherwise, apart from the pub (above), try the *Flinders Island Sports Club* at the end of the Esplanade for a reasonable meal in pleasant surroundings. In Lady Barron, the *Furneaux Tavern*, overlooking Adelaide Bay on the dramatic Franklin Sound, has spacious and attractive cabin-style motel units set in pretty native gardens (Ⓣ03/6359 3521; ❹). Meals are served here in the upmarket *Shearwater Restaurant*, much Flinders Island's best **place to eat**, or there are simple bar meals in the convivial public bar. You could also try the excellent cabins with beautiful views at *Partridge Farm*, a ten-minute drive from Lady Barron at the end of the road to Badger Corner (Ⓣ03/6359 3554; ❺).

The West

The wild **west coast**, densely forested and battered by the rough Southern Ocean and the Roaring Forties, its shores strewn with huge dead trees washed down from the southwest's many rivers, would probably still be uninhabited if it weren't for the **logging** and **mining** industries. The western half of Tasmania is untamed, except for the rich beef, dairy and vegetable-growing land along the northwest coast. This part of the island is very densely populated (by Tasmanian standards), and the **Bass Highway**, which skirts the northwest coast, passes through two unattractive industrial cities, **Devonport** and **Burnie**. **Rocky Cape National Park** and the town of **Stanley** (originally built by the Van Diemen's Land Company – VDL – which still owns the northwest corner of the state) are the most interesting places for visitors.

Just south of Stanley the highway turns inland to **Smithton**, marking the beginning of a thickly forested region and a logging heartland. The Bass Highway ends at the tiny settlement of **Marrawah**, on the west coast (popular with surfers), where it meets the **Western Explorer** road, which runs south to sleepy **Arthur River** and then through the Arthur Pieman Protected Area to **Corinna**, where the road heads east via Savage River and Waratah onto the A10 (Murchison Highway). Alternatively, you can continue southwards, taking a barge (the "Fatman") across the Pieman River and then heading on to Zeehan (on the C249) and **Strahan** (on the B27), on the vast **Macquarie Harbour**. To reach Strahan on sealed roads, you have to go back to Marrawah and then to Somerset on the northwest coast, from where the Murchison Highway heads south through a copper- and lead-mining backwater. On the way you pass **Queenstown**, which has been subject to an ecological disaster; its surrounding rainforest has been destroyed, and in its place are bare and chalky hills.

Strahan sits on the edge of the **southwest wilderness**, an area of rugged coastlines, wild rivers, open plains, thick rainforest and spectacular peaks – the wettest part of Australia after the tropical lowlands of north Queensland. It's mostly inaccessible, except to very experienced and well-prepared bushwalkers, but **cruises** leave from Strahan to go up the **Gordon River**, offering a glimpse of its magnificent scenery. Some years ago, a plan to dam the Gordon River below the point where it joins the **Franklin River** put Strahan at the centre of a struggle between environmentalists and the state government. Eventually the federal government stepped in, and, following a landmark High Court ruling in 1983, the whole of the southwest – including the **South West National Park**, the **Franklin Lower Gordon Wild Rivers National Park** and the adjoining heavily glaciated **Cradle Mountain–Lake St Clair National Park** – became a vast, protected UNESCO World Heritage Area, occupying twenty percent of the state's land area. From Queenstown, en route to Hobart, the **Lyell Highway** provides limited access to the mainly inaccessible Franklin Lower Gordon park, and to Lake St Clair at **Derwent Bridge**.

The northwest coast

A succession of Tasmania's larger towns dot the conservative, agricultural **northwest coast**, including the cities of **Devonport** and **Burnie**, and the smaller community of older **Stanley**, on a peninsula jutting into the Bass Strait. The **Bass Highway**, which connects them, becomes spectacularly beautiful beyond Wynyard, passing Table Cape, Boat Harbour Beach and Rocky Cape National Park, though it skirts the very northwest tip (privately owned by the Van Diemen's Land Company). At the end of the highway is **Marrawah**, from where you can head to Arthur River for a cruise. Redline runs daily services from Devonport to Burnie, and from Burnie to Smithton, stopping at all towns along the Bass Highway; there is no public transport to Marrawah or Arthur River.

Devonport and around

The industrial port of **DEVONPORT**, which in 1959 replaced Launceston as the terminal of the **Bass Strait ferry**, the *Spirit of Tasmania*, is not the most inspiring first point of contact with Tasmania. As the ship makes its slow progress up the Mersey River, you might almost think you're arriving at a 1950s English seaport, but for the tin-roofed weatherboard bungalows, the brittle quality of the light, the bush-covered hills to the east and a *McDonald's* on the waterfront. As a jumping-off point for Cradle Mountain, the Overland Track and the rugged west coast, Devonport has developed a significant tourism infrastructure – car-rental companies, bus companies, camping stores and backpacking information – and though it's hardly a destination in itself, it makes a good **base** for trips into the surrounding countryside.

Arrival and information

Thousands of people arrive in Devonport on the *Spirit of Tasmania* **Bass Strait ferries** (see p.976) from Melbourne and Sydney; the ferries dock at the terminal in East Devonport, just across the Mersey River from the city centre. As the boats have their own tourist information and booking centre, you might have made all your arrangements on board. If not, there are company representatives and car-hire desks in the terminal, and you can buy bus passes and tickets here. Most passengers head immediately for the waiting Redline and TassieLink **express buses** to Launceston and Hobart. Other bus routes leave from the depots in town (see "Buses", p.978). If you decide to stay, you can get to the city centre by walking north for a short distance to the bottom of Murray Street, where the ferry *Torquay* crosses the river (on demand Mon–Sat 7.45am–6pm; $2.50, bikes $0.50).

Devonport Airport is 10km east of the city; taxis into Devonport cost about $20 and it's a good idea to pre-book (Taxis Combined ⓣ03/6424 1431). In town, staff at the **Tasmanian Travel and Information Centre**, 92 Formby

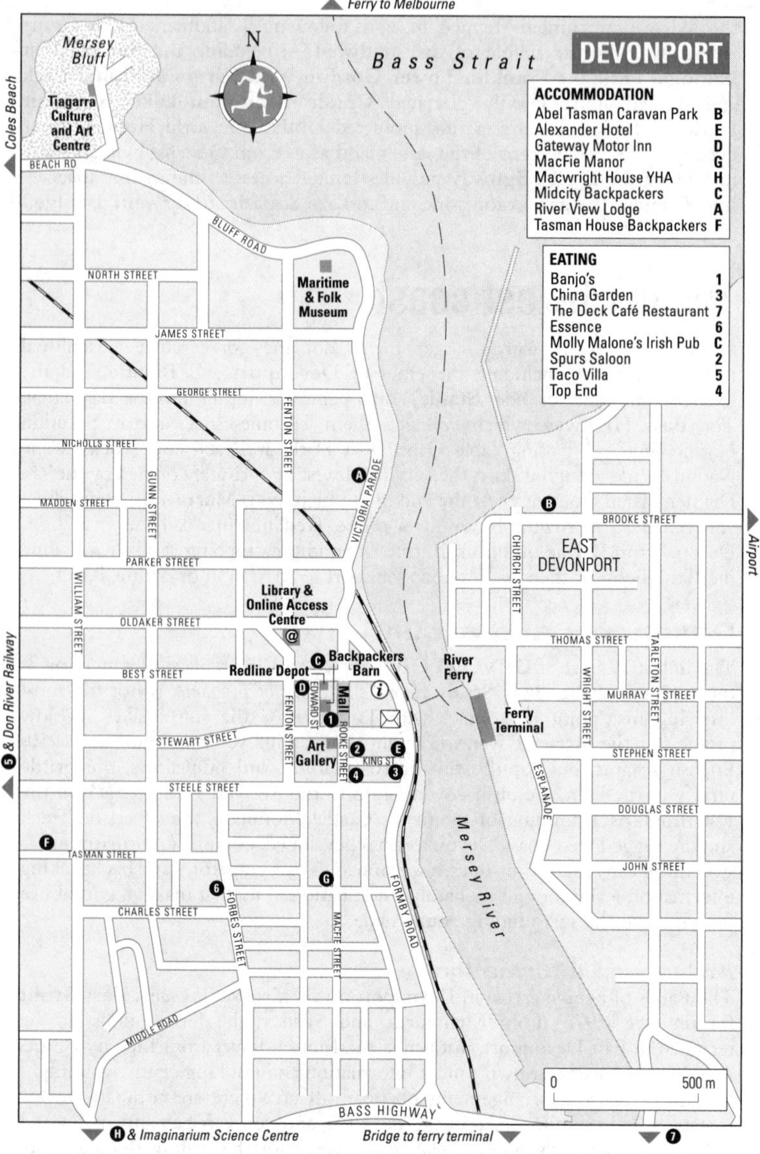

Rd (daily 7.30am–5pm and until 9pm when day-sailings arrive; ⓣ03/6424 4466), book accommodation, tours and travel including car hire, sell bus passes, National Park passes, YHA membership, See Tasmania cards, fishing licences, and maps and specialist guides. For a full range of Tasmaps, bushwalking tips and local knowledge of the area visit the excellent **Backpackers Barn**, 10–12 Edward St (Mon–Sat 9am–6pm; ⓣ03/6424 3628, ⓦwww.backpackersbarn.com.au), which specializes in planning itineraries, booking bushwalking transport charters and tours to Cradle Mountain and other destinations with the in-house Tasmanian Tour Company (Ⓣ01300 659878, Ⓦwww.tasmaniantourcompany.com.au), and renting and selling equipment for bushwalkers; it also offers travellers a day-room, showers ($2) and huge lockers ($1 per day, $5 per week) and there's a great organic café, *Rosehip*. The huge Allgoods, at 6 Formby Rd (Ⓣ03/6424 7099; closed Sun), sells gear, too. The Redline depot is opposite Backpackers Barn; TassieLink leaves from the tourist information centre, which sells tickets for both. Devonport's **Online Access Centre** is at the library at 21 Oldaker St.

Accommodation

Devonport has plenty of **accommodation**, mainly intended for ferry passengers. Hotels, motels and B&Bs take advantage of the summer trade to raise their prices.

Abel Tasman Caravan Park 6 Wright St, East Devonport Ⓣ03/6427 8794. Campsites on East Devonport Beach, just a short walk from the ferry terminal. Vans ❷, cabins ❸

Alexander Hotel 78 Formby Rd Ⓣ03/6424 2252. Neat, well-furnished, shared bathrooms, all with sinks and some with views of the port. TV room, plus tea and coffee room; light breakfast served in the dining room, and other meals available in the good pub bistro. ❷

Gateway Motor Inn 16 Fenton St Ⓣ03/6424 4922. Quiet and centrally located, Devonport's best hotel offers views over the port and river mouth. Rooms are spacious and tastefully decorated. Bar, restaurant and room service. ❺

MacFie Manor 44 MacFie St Ⓣ03/6424 1719. A rambling, two-storey, early twentieth-century B&B that has distant views of the water from its wrought-iron balcony. ❹–❺

Macwright House YHA 115 Middle Rd Ⓣ03/6424 5696. A large, barracks-like hostel with loads of rules and regulations. More than half an hour's walk from the city centre and not close to any shops, but the local Mersey Bus will get you from the city on weekdays. Dorms $15, rooms ❶

Midcity Backpackers Above *Molly Malone's Irish Pub*, 34 Best St Ⓣ03/6424 1898, Ⓔmollymalones@vantagegroup.com.au. Convenient backpackers' accommodation, with four-bed dorms and comfortable rooms – some en suite – well away from the noise of the Irish theme-pub downstairs. Good facilities and security. Dorms $16, rooms ❷

River View Lodge 18 Victoria Parade Ⓣ03/6424 7357. A waterfront guesthouse with a convivial atmosphere. Serves generous cooked breakfasts. Some en-suite rooms but most share bathroom. ❸–❹

Tasman House Backpackers 169 Steele St Ⓣ03/6423 2335, Ⓦwww.tasmanhouse.com. Hostel in a large, former nurses' residence. Mostly well-furnished twins, a couple of en-suite doubles and some dorms. Affordable tours available to places such as Cradle Mountain. Fifteen minutes' walk from the city centre, but free pick-ups on request. Dorms $16, rooms ❷–❸

The City

Central Devonport is bounded by the Mersey to the east; Formby Road runs alongside it, while Stewart Street, at right angles, is dominated by a view of the bulky *Spirit of Tasmania* ferries when they're in port, and sometimes other colourful freighters. The **Devonport Art Gallery** at 45 Stewart St (Mon–Sat 10am–5pm, Sun 2–5pm; free) is a converted church with changing exhibitions and a small permanent collection of Tasmanian ceramics. The city centre caters well to departing tourists in need of last-minute souvenirs, with big-name chain stores on **Rooke Street Mall** and tasteful gift-shops on Stewart Street.

The **Devonport Maritime and Folk Museum**, north of the city centre at 47 Victoria Parade, near the river's mouth (Tues–Sun 10am–4pm; $3), has an extensive display of model ships ranging from sailing vessels to modern passenger ferries. The **Imaginarium Science Centre**, 19–23 MacFie St, near the *YHA*, is Tasmania's hands-on science discovery centre (Mon–Thurs 10am–4pm, Sat & Sun noon–5pm; $8; Ⓣ03/6423 1466). The only really compelling place to visit, though, is the **Tiagarra Tasmanian Aboriginal Culture and Art Centre** (ⓣ03/6424 8250; daily 9am–5pm; $3.80), located at the dramatic **Mersey Bluff**, 1.5km northwest of the Maritime and Folk Museum, near the end of Bluff Road. The centre has preserved around 270 Aboriginal rock engravings (eleven of which are on show), and a **Display Centre** provides generalized (and rather rushed) taped background information on how the Tasmanian Aborigines lived.

The **Don River Railway**, using steam or diesel locomotives, runs excursions from Don Recreation Ground, west of town, along the Don River to the popular surfing spot of **Coles Beach** (hourly 10am–4pm; 30min; $10 return; ⓣ03/6424 6335).

Eating, drinking and nightlife

Banjo's Rooke Street Mall. One of a Tasmanian chain of early opening, eat-in bakeries offering inexpensive fresh-baked goods and unlimited tea and coffee. Daily 6am–6pm.

China Garden 33 King St ⓣ03/6424 4148. Popular Cantonese restaurant with $7.50 lunch specials. Licensed.

The Deck Café Restaurant 188–190 Tarleton St, East Devonport ⓣ03/6427 7188. Devonport's city-style waterfront hangout: you can relax on sofas with a coffee and cake, come for Sun breakfast or have a beer outside watching the boats come in. By day, there's sushi, pasta and risotto ($12.50–18.50), pizzas and gourmet sandwiches ($8.50). Lunch until 5pm segues into the pricier dinner menu, from a Tasmanian seafood plate ($26.50) to prime sirloin steaks. Fully licensed bar. Mon–Sat 10.30am until late, Sun 8.30am until late.

Essence 28 Forbes St ⓣ03/6424 6431. This big, old charming house offers the best of Tasmanian produce – traditional European stand-bys of venison, lamb, beef, trout, turkey and duck feature – with a contemporary edge. The crisp-skinned confit of duck is always popular. Mains around $24. You can just come in for a drink in the *Lounge Bar*, where several Tasmanian wines are available by the glass. Lunch Tues–Fri, dinner Tues–Sat.

Molly Malone's Irish Pub 34 Best St. Characterful and extensive Irish theme-pub with a great bistro. Lots of meaty pub favourites – including a roast of the day for $10 – and fish as well as vegetarian choices.

Spurs Saloon 18 King St ⓣ03/6424 7851. *Warehouse Niteclub* attached. Also a venue for touring bands. Wed–Sun 5pm–late.

Taco Villa Kempling St. Good Mexican food. BYO. Dinner Tues–Sun.

Top End 12 Rooke St. This light contemporary café has comfy sofas, magazines, a big spread of healthy food under glass counters and a fresh juice bar. Good coffee, pots of tea including chai, and yummy cakes. Vegetarian choices include curry samosas served with salad for $7.50. Licensed. Mon–Sat 7am–6pm.

Listings

Bookshop Angus & Robertson Bookworld, 43 Rooke St ⓣ03/6424 2022.

Buses Redline and TassieLink both have ticket desks at the ferry terminal. Redline's depot is at 9 Edward St (ⓣ1300 360 000; left luggage $1 per item); TassieLink (ⓣ1300 300 520) services leave from the tourist office at 92 Formby Rd. Backpackers Barn (see p.1046) is the booking office and collecting point for Tasmanian Tour Companies on-demand bushwalking charter service to Cradle Mountain, Frenchmans Cap and Walls of Jerusalem. Also the similar Maxwells

The Tasmanian Trail

The **Tasmanian Trail** is a 480-kilometre multipurpose recreational trail extending from Devonport on the north coast to Dover on the south coast. Created by connecting forestry roads, fire trails and country roads (often going through small towns) and at times traversing private land, it's primarily used for mountain biking and horseriding. For more details, consult ⓦwww.parks.tas.gov.au/recreaton/tstrail.html; or the *Tasmanian Trail Guidebook* is available from tourist offices and bookshops for $22.

charter service is based in nearby Wilmot (☎03/6492 1431).

Car rental Firms located at the airport and ferry terminal include Autorent-Hertz ☎03/6424 1013, Avis Tasmania ☎03/6427 9797 and Budget ☎03/6427 0650; among cheaper alternatives are Lo-Cost Auto Rent ☎03/6424 9922, Ⓦwww.locostautorent.com and the popular Rent-A-Bug ☎03/6427 9304, Ⓦwww.rentabug.com.au, both on Murray St by the ferry terminal, East Devonport.

Cinema C-Max Cinemas, 5–7 Best St (☎03/6240 2111), is a four-screen cinema complex.

Post office Cnr Stewart St and Formby Rd, TAS 7310.

Taxi Taxis Combined ☎03/6424 1431.

Around Devonport

East of Devonport are some particularly rewarding spots on the **Rubicon River estuary**, where you'll find the seaside resort of **PORT SORELL**, roughly 19km from Devonport and across the river from the Narawntapu National Park (see overleaf). You can **stay** here in a self-catering three-bedroom solar-heated house at *Heron on Earth Organic Farm* (☎03/6428 6144, Ⓦwww.herononearth.com; ❸), which lends out canoes for you to paddle across to the national park, and also bikes. More luxurious accommodation is provided 4km northeast at **HAWLEY BEACH**, at the well-regarded, rather grand Victorian-era *Hawley House* (☎03/6428 6221, Ⓦwww.hawleyhousetas.com; ❻), which has a fine restaurant and its own vineyard producing Chardonnay and Pinot Noir. From Hawley Beach there's a 10km-return walk to Point Sorell.

To reach the western edge of the **Narawntapu National Park** (formerly Asbestos Range National Park), on the east side of the Rubicon River estuary, it's a meandering, 40km drive from Devonport. The remote park is worth the trip – particularly at dusk – for the chance to spot some wildlife: introduced **Forrester kangaroos** come down to feed at **Bakers Beach** at that time, and it's the best place in Tasmania to see **wombats**. The park is renowned for its occasional spectacular storms, accompanied by strong winds roaring along the beach. There's a self-registering **campsite** here, for which you pay a small fee (ranger ☎03/6428 6277), and the beach is good for swimming, and for oyster hunting from the rocks at low tide. You'll need your own transport to get out here.

The quirky town of **LATROBE**, just 5km south of Devonport, has put itself firmly on the map with the latest addition to Australia's list of "Big Things", a **Big Platypus** plonked on top of the *Lucas Hotel* at 45 Gilbert St. Inside, the **Platypus Experience** ($5) gives the lowdown on the platypus lifestyle, creatures you can often see at dusk at Kings Creek right by the hotel and in other spots near the town – the "experience" gives you the details, but the pub also has a **tourist information centre** that hands out free maps. Further along the street at no.139, **Reliquaire** is a vast and extraordinary toy–novelty shop hybrid that would probably even astonish in a big city.

SHEFFIELD, 30km south of Devonport, is a popular stop en route to Cradle Mountain. The cute, old-fashioned town, set amongst farmland made fertile by red volcanic soils, is situated near the base of Mount Roland (1231m) which provides a scenic backdrop. The town's rural economy was ailing when the community decided to reinvent itself through the medium of visual art; since the mid-1980s over thirty **murals** in various styles have been painted by several local artists, showing the history and folklore of the town. Next to the post office, the very efficient council-run **Sheffield Visitor Information Centre** (daily 9am–5pm; ☎03/6491 1036) hands out a free pamphlet detailing the history of the murals project and a self-guided walking tour, which should take about an hour. They also book accommodation for free and offer Internet access; the **Online Access Centre** itself is in the high school on Henry Street.

The best **eating** option in town is *Coffee on Main*, 43 Main St (☎03/6491 1893; BYO; Wed–Sun from 11am–5pm, which offers fair-trade organic coffee made by trained baristas, inexpensive gourmet sandwiches and salads by day, and, on Fridays and Saturdays dinner mains ($14–$28) from fresh local produce by the European-trained chef-owner.

Sixteen kilometres southwest of Sheffield at **GOWRIE PARK** at the base of **Mount Roland**, you can **stay** at *Mount Roland Budget Backpacker Rooms* (☎03/6491 1385; dorms $20), which has bunk-style quarters as well as the en-suite *Gowrie Park Wilderness Cabins* (❸). It makes a good base for walks up and around the summit (2hr return), which provide great views of Cradle Mountain. At the other end of the scale, *Eagles Nest Retreat* (Ⓦwww.eaglesnestretreat.com.au; ❽) has a quirky individualism in its opulence and provides an unsurpassed view of Mount Roland.

You can get to Sheffield and Gowrie Park with TassieLink on their scheduled Launceston–Queenstown service via Cradle Mountain (3 weekly).

Ulverstone to Burnie

Redline buses follow the unremarkable coast from Devonport west to industrial Burnie, stopping at Ulverstone and Penguin. **ULVERSTONE**, 20km west of Devonport where the **Leven River** flows into the sea, is a popular family holiday centre with unpolluted **beaches**. A population of Little penguins comes to breed on the beach here between September and April, and Penguin Point Twilight Tours takes small groups from the *Ulverstone Waterfront Inn* out at dusk (2–3hr; $15; bookings ☎03/6425 1599). More remarkable, Todd Walsh takes groups to see the **giant freshwater crayfish**, a threatened species that can grow up to several kilograms and lives only in the northern flowing rivers of Tasmania. This unique tour is by arrangement and must be booked (☎03/6425 5302 or 0439 693377). The town's **accommodation** possibilities include the pleasant, two-storey *Ocean View Heritage B&B* at 1 Victoria St (☎03/6425 5401; ❺), and the splendid 1903 red-brick *Furners Hotel* at 42 Reibey St (☎03/6425 1488; en-suite B&B ❹), the latter complete with carved blackwood staircase and bistro; or you can **camp** at the waterfront *Ulverstone Caravan Park*, 1km east of the centre (☎03/6425 2624; vans ❷, cabins and units ❸). The best **place to eat** is the riverside *Pedro's* on Wharf Road (☎03/6425 6663), the perfect spot for a seafood restaurant, with one of Tassie's most rated fish-and-chips shops attached. You can pick up free maps and information from the volunteer-run **Ulverstone Visitor Information Centre**, behind the post office (9am–5pm all year except Christmas; ☎03/6425 2839).

In the picturesque hop-growing countryside just under 25km south of Ulverstone, the **Gunns Plains Caves** (hourly tours daily 10am–4pm; 50min; $10; ☎03/ 6429 1388), part of the **Gunns Plains State Reserve**, are worth visiting for their remarkable limestone formations which, when lit from behind, glow a succulent red. A permanent stream feeds an underground lake, and platypuses and possums enjoy the cool temperatures.

The best route west from Ulverstone follows the old Bass Highway (Penguin Road) along the coastline, passing the Three Sisters and Goat Islands bird sanctuaries, Penguin Point where Little penguins roost, and a beautiful array of flowers as you come into **PENGUIN** itself, 12km along the highway. The eye-catching, neatly tended little town has three safe swimming beaches and a strong café culture. Cute blue-and-white penguin-shaped garbage bins line the beach-front main street, culminating in the two-metre-high **Big Penguin** in the foreshore park. The **Visitor Information Centre** (Mon–Fri 9am–4pm, Sat & Sun 9am–12.30pm; ☎03/6437 1421) can provide more details about things to do in the area including twilight penguin trips (1hr30min; ⓣ03/6437 2590; $12). Worth a visit in its own right, the *Groovy Penguin* (closed Mon & Tues; dinner available Fri night) is a fantastically colourful, cluttered and alternative-feel café with young and friendly owners – filling fare includes lentil burgers and lasagne. When it's closed, try the upmarket *Madsen Café,* in a former bank, with stylish bed-and-breakfast **accommodation** upstairs (ⓣ03/6437 2588, ⓦwww.themadsen.com; ❻). Five kilometres south outside town, there are walking trails in the **Dial Range State Forest**.

BURNIE, on Emu Bay 15km west of Penguin, is an industrial and paper-manufacturing centre and container port, and Tasmania's third-largest city with a population of nearly 20,000. The port, with its controversial pile of export woodchips and nearby paper mill, is unattractive but the city is situated amid rich farmland and beautiful rocky coves, and tourism is now being actively developed. The Redline depot is at 117 Wilson St and TassieLink departs from outside the **Tasmanian Travel and Information Centre** at the Civic Square precinct, off Little Alexander Street (Mon–Fri 8am–5pm, Sat & Sun 10am–4pm; ⓣ03/6434 6111). The Civic Centre on Wilmot Street is home to both the **Pioneer Village Museum**, with its reconstructed early twentieth-century street (Mon–Fri 9am–5pm; $6), and the **Burnie Regional Art Gallery** (Tues–Fri 10.30am–5pm, Sat & Sun 1.30–4.30pm; free). In complete contrast to the region's industrial base, the large-scale **Australian Paper Mill**, check out the wonderful community-based, nonprofit **Creative Paper Mill**, on Old Surrey Road (C112), 100m off the Bass Highway on the eastern side of Burnie (Nov–April daily 9am–4pm; tours 10am, noon & 2.30pm; 35–40min; $10; ⓣ03/6430 7717, ⓦwww.creativepapertas.com.au). The paper here is handmade and there's a product showroom, plus an art gallery. Three kilometres further along Old Surry Road, **Lactos** is a prize-winning speciality **cheese factory** (tastings Mon–Fri 9am–5pm, Sat & Sun 10am–4pm; free), where you can sample and buy blends and variations of European cheeses, and also buy lunch. Forking off Old Surrey Road just after the Creative Paper Mill, and just 1km from the city centre, **Fernglade** is a **platypus reserve** on a peaceful, forested stretch of the Emu River. The platypuses are easy to spot, particularly at dawn and after dusk. Burnie also has a free **penguin interpretive centre**, reached via a 1km boardwalk from the town centre; the long, thin building is open to the Little penguins who, lit by infrared light, can be observed through windows via a periscope-style mirrored tunnel; the best time to view the penguins is after dusk between September and April. Conservationist William Walker (ⓣ03/6435 7205) runs nature-based interpretive tours, visiting Fernglade and the penguins and other local points of interest, and specializing in day-walks with local gourmet food.

There's plenty of **accommodation**, should you decide to stay in Burnie; the information centre does free bookings. The *Burnie Holiday Caravan Park*, 253 Bass Highway, at Cooee on the pleasant, non-industrial side of town towards Wynyard (ⓣ03/6431 1925; vans ❷, cabins ❸, motel ❹), has something to suit everyone with the attached *Ocean View Motel*, cabins, a **YHA hostel** section (dorms $18) and a campground. For more character, *Glen Osborne House*, at 9 Aileen Crescent (ⓣ03/6431 9866; ❻), is a stylish Victorian-era B&B with en-suite rooms and a lovely garden of lawns, roses and fruit trees. **Food** choices include the veteran Italian, *Rialto Gallery*, at 46 Wilmot St (BYO; ⓣ03/6431 7718), and the licensed *Café Europa*, at the corner of Cattley and Wilson streets (Tues–Sun), a cosmopolitan hangout, with some Greek Cypriot offerings on the Mediterranean menu (also good-value toasted Turkish sandwiches, snacks and lots of different kinds of coffee). The Metro Cinema, at the corner of

Marine Terrace and Wilmot Streets (Ⓣ03/6431 5000, Ⓦwww.metrocinemas.com.au), is the entertainment focus. Burnie's **Online Access Centre** is at 2 Spring St.

Wynyard and around

WYNYARD, another 19km along the old Bass Highway from Burnie, snuggles into the lush pasturelands between the **Inglis River** and the sea. The wharf area, with its fishing boats and fresh fish shop, is just off bustling Goldie Street – the main street that parallels the river. There are over 12km of riverside walking tracks, starting from the riverfront park on the corner of Goldie and Hogg streets. It's an easy 3km walk to **Fossil Bluff** where layers of sedimentary rock containing fossilized seashells can easily be examined at low tide, and the beach itself has good views of the 170-metre seaface of **Table Cape**. A drive up to the **lookout** on Table Cape will reward you with magnificent views of the coast and hinterland, particularly pretty when the cape's **tulip fields** are in bloom around October.

Wynyard may well be the first place you see in Tasmania, since "Burnie" **airport** is actually just a five-minute stroll from the town centre. You can **rent a car** at the airport with Autorent-Hertz (Ⓣ03/6442 4444), Avis (Ⓣ03/6442 2512) or Budget (Ⓣ03/6442 1777). The Burnie Air-Bus connects the airport with Burnie ($30:00; Ⓣ0439 322 466). MTT **public transport buses** connect Wynyard with Burnie, departing from 38 Jackson St. Redline calls at Gale's Auto Service, 28 Saunders St (Ⓣ03/6442 2205), en route from Burnie to Smithton via the turn-offs to Table Cape, Boat Harbour Beach and Rocky Cape.

Wynyard Tourist Information, behind the intersection of Jackson and Dodgin streets (daily 9am–5pm; Ⓣ03/6443 8330), has information on local activities and **accommodation**. There's camping at *Beach Retreat Tourist Park*, at 30B Old Bass Highway on the way out of town to Burnie (Ⓣ03/6442 1998; budget rooms ❶, vans ❷, cabins ❸). However, the best place to stay is *The Waterfront Wynyard*, 1 Goldie St (Ⓣ03/6442 2351; ❹), in a fantastic riverfront spot right by the wharf. The very cute motel rooms are equipped with everything from satellite TV to DVD players, and the on-site café-restaurant (where the included light breakfast is served) is the best in town: couches, a river-view terrace, great coffee and cake served daily from 8am, and a pub-competitive restaurant at night (from $15 roast of the day to seafood curries). The takeaway fish-and-chip shop on the wharf is good, or try the tacky-looking *Buckaneers Restaurant*, at 4 Inglis St (Ⓣ03/6442 4104), which does excellent takeaway fresh fish and seafood. Wynyard's **Online Access Centre** is at 21 Saunders St.

Boat Harbour Beach and Sister Beach

Eleven kilometres west of Wynyard, a turn-off from the Bass Highway winds down to **Boat Harbour Beach**, the prettiest on the northwest coast, with pale-blue water, white sand and very gentle waves. It's perfect for **diving**, too; equipment can be rented from the Scuba Centre at 62 Bass Highway in Wynyard (Ⓣ03/6442 2247), which also organizes excursions. *Jolly Rogers on the Beach* is a licensed café-restaurant right on the beach with tables out front; the kiosk does takeaways and rents **boogie-boards** and **wave skis**. Attractive Sisters Beach, closer to Rocky Cape, is much less developed (and there are no building works going on); you can stay at *Birdland Holiday Cottages*, 7 Banksia Ave (Ⓣ03/6445 1471; ❹), set in forest. Back on the highway the Boat Harbour Store has petrol and a post office.

Rocky Cape (Tangdimmaa) National Park

Stretching for a mere 12km along the coast, from Sisters Beach to Rocky Cape, are the rugged hills and cliffs of **Rocky Cape (Tangdimmaa) National Park**, Tasmania's smallest national park, created in 1967 for the purpose of preserving some remarkable **Aboriginal archeological** finds. The mainly quartzite hills are pockmarked with caves, of which the two major ones, North Cave and South Cave, contain huge shell middens, bones and stone tools dating back as far as eight thousand years, when the sea was several fathoms below its current level.

Rocky Cape is now managed in consultation with the Tasmanian Aboriginal Land Council, and visitors are no longer allowed to enter the caves, although it's okay to reach the entrances. To reach North Cave it's a fifteen-minute walk there and back from the road, reached by driving 5km into the park and taking the left fork at the lighthouse – most people prefer just to walk along the various easy tracks. It takes seven hours to traverse the whole length of the park; there's no water, no toilets, and camping is not allowed. Rocky pools, safe swimming beaches and picnic areas are scattered along the route, while in spring and summer there's a profusion of wild flowers on the scrubby heathland, including some unique native orchids. At dusk you may see wallabies, echidnas and various species of bird. Back on the highway, the *Rocky Cape Tavern* (Ⓣ03/6443 4110) has camping and there's a petrol station nearby.

Stanley

It's a 31km drive from the Rocky Cape turn-off west along the Bass Highway (A2) to the fishing village of **STANLEY**, the original 1826 headquarters of the **Van Diemen's Land Company** and the first settlement in northwest Tasmania; the scenic coastal drive hugging the coast is marred only by the industrial scene at Port Latta. About 5km beyond here, a turn-off leads 27km south on the C225 to the must-see **Dip Falls Big Tree**, a gigantic eucalypt measuring 17m at its base and thought to be over 400 years old.

Back on the highway, long before you arrive at Stanley, 6km off the Bass Highway, you'll see your first view of **The Nut**, described by Matthew Flinders as a "cliffy round lump in form resembling a Christmas cake" that rises directly out of the ocean to a height of nearly 150m. **Circular Head**, as it's officially called (the name also for the surrounding municipality), is thought to be a volcanic plug, with the softer sediments around it having eroded away. The town itself is on a small, foot-shaped peninsula right at the base of The Nut, perched high above Sawyer Bay and Tallows Beach.

Information and tours

For tourist **information**, accommodation bookings and Internet access visit the Stanley Visitor Centre on the way into Stanley at 45 Main Rd (Mon–Fri 9.30am–5.30pm, Sat & Sun 10am–4pm; Ⓣ03/6458 1330); it also serves as the Redline **bus depot** and sells bus tickets – Stanley is reached on the route between Burnie and Smithton (Mon–Fri daily either way). The General Store is below the town centre on Wharf Road and has an ATM, while the newsagents' towards the end of Church Street also has supplies and is an ANZ bank agent; there are more banking facilities a few doors up at the post office.

Stanley-based Wilderness to West Coast Tours (Ⓣ03/6458 2038, Ⓦwww.wildernesstasmania.com) offers a dusk platypus-viewing tour (2hr; $35) and a penguin tour (1hr; $15; both tours combined $45). The "Tarkine Discovery Tour" 4WD tour explores the northwest tip, through farm country, temperate rainforest, gum forests and button-grass plains (6hr; $198); a longer version also visits the wild west coast (8.5hr; $249; both include morning tea and gourmet lunch). Stanley Seal Cruises on Wharf Road will take you to view the populous colony of the rare **Australian fur seal**, weather permitting (daily 10am; also April–June 3pm; $44; ⓣ0419 550 134).

Accommodation

Stanley is packed with holiday **accommodation**. In keeping with its historic ambience, Stanley has many "colonial" **B&Bs**, which are actually self-contained cottages with breakfast provisions supplied.

Beachside Retreat West Inlet Main Road ⓣ03/6458 1350, ⓦwww.beachsideretreat.com. Two and a half kilometres south of the town centre, some of the stunning designer cabins here have fantastic Nut views framed by huge porthole and picture windows, and there's access to a private beach. ❻

Dovecote Motel 1km along Dovecote Road ⓣ03/6458 1300, ⓦwww.dovecote.com.au. There are some of the best views of the Nut, across the green fields of the Dovecote Estate, from the *Dovecote*'s spacious, well-appointed units (some self-catering); facilities include a bar and a restaurant. ❹–❺

Old Cable Station West Beach Rd, north of town, beyond Highfield House ⓣ03/6458 1312, ⓔcablestation@westnet.com.au. Once linking Tasmania with the mainland via King Island, this peaceful retreat is surrounded by a pretty flower-filled garden and has views stretching across fields to water. Choose from a spacious three-bedroom cottage, or two stylish en-suite rooms. Rooms ❺, cottage ❻

Palm Tree Spa Cottage 48 Alexander Terrace ⓣ1800 222 397. There are gorgeous Sawyer Bay views from the front veranda of this charming, weatherboard self-contained house nestled under The Nut. The same management have several other excellent options, including *Abbeys Spa Cottage*, nearby at no. 34 (❺), and the modern, tiny but tidy and very good-value *Pol & Pen Holiday Chalets* close to Godfrey's Beach on Pearse Street (❸).

Stanley Cabin and Tourist Park and Stanley YHA Wharf Road ⓣ03/6458 1266. In a great waterfront location opposite Marine Park, near the fishing-wharf action and overlooking Tallows Beach with the general store nearby. The youth hostel is perennially popular. There's also the option to camp. Dorms $24, rooms ❷, cabins ❸–❹

Stanley Hotel Church Street ⓣ03/6458 1161. The rooms at this sprawling, three-storey old pub are brightly painted and quite smart, but still have good single rates ($40). Rooms ❸, en suite ❹

The Town

Stanley's main street, **Church Street**, runs below the foot of The Nut, and its restaurants and crafts shops – check out the contemporary wood designs in Stanley Artworks Studio Gallery near the post office – are high enough above the beach, wharves and the rest of the town to command excellent views. Although it's worthwhile doing the strenuous ten- to twenty-minute walk up the grassy **Nut** itself, you can get to the top more comfortably by means of an exhilarating **chairlift**, reached via the ramp opposite the post office (daily 9.30am–5pm, weather permitting; call ⓣ03/6458 1286 to check; no one-way tickets sold, $9 return). The licensed *Nut Rock Café*, next door to the chairlift, has fantastic views and decent coffee. A 2km circuit walk around the windy **Nut State Reserve** at the top affords views over the town and port, and southeast as far as Table Cape. Directly below is the exquisitely deserted **Godfrey's Beach** to the north, with its calm and translucent blue waters. Green Hills Road runs north alongside the beach and winds uphill to the original headquarters of the Van Diemen's Land Company, 2km north of the town, with superb views over Half Moon Bay. Though the rooms themselves of the **Highfield Historic Site** (daily 10am–4pm; $9) are bare of artefacts, the interpretive boards provide a fascinating and honest history of the VDL Company and the Northwest, with lots from the Aboriginal perspective.

Below Church Street and Alexander Terrace, the foreshore area spreads alongside Wharf Road, with the curve of **Tallows Beach** stretching for kilometres southeast and the busy fishing-port area, the marina full of colourful boats, to the west. By Marine Park, the slate-roofed **Van Diemen's Land Company Store** (now a B&B) was designed in 1844 by John Lee Archer, whose work can be seen notably in Hobart. From the nearby **port area**, at low tide, you can see the remnants of a 1923 **shipwreck**, a victim of the "furies" of the Bass Strait. On Fisherman's Dock, **Stanley Seaquarium** (daily 10am–4pm; $8) is full of creatures hauled up by fishermen. At feeding times, the Port Jackson and gummy sharks get so excitable they dance – it's a revelation that sharks can be so cute. The hands-on rockpool is fantastic, with sea stars, sea cucumbers and lots of shy hermit crabs in shells.

Eating

There's a good choice of **places to eat** within Stanley itself. *Hurseys Seafoods*, next to Marine Park on Wharf Road, is considered to be one of the best fish-and-chip shops in Tasmania. Inside are huge holding tanks from which you select live fish (around twenty kinds) and crayfish. Nearby at 15 Wharf Rd, *Stanleys on the Bay* is a well-regarded seafood and steak restaurant (Ⓣ03/6458 1404; dinner Mon–Sat; closed July & Aug). Back on Church Street, the *Stanley Hotel* serves fresh seafood and other delicious pub fare in its lively lounge bar bistro with terrace dining and views; and the *Touchwood Coffee Shop* has expansive views from inside and outside tables, the best coffee in Stanley, seafood from octopus salad ($14.50) to crayfish rolls ($15.50), toasted sandwiches, and yummy biscuits, muffins and cakes.

Smithton and around

The only way to see Tasmania's rugged northwest tip, which remains under the control of the Van Diemen's Land Company, is by tour. Tours to **Woolnorth**, the original VDL cattle and sheep property, depart from the rather unattractive rural-industrial town of **SMITHTON**, 22km west of Stanley, at the mouth of the Duck River. The full-day **tour** to Woolnorth (daily; $110 including morning tea and lunch at the board table of the 1970s-built Directors Lodge) take in **Cape Grim** (see box p.1056), where the air carried thousands of kilometres across the Great Southern Ocean by the Roaring Forties is reputed to be the cleanest in the world – it's the site of Australia's baseline air-monitoring station, the most sophisticated in a worldwide network, and Australia's largest **wind farm** taking advantage of these gusting winds. A couple of kilometres east of Cape Grim, you can stand at the point where Bass Strait meets the Southern Ocean and walk along the spectacular, rugged coastline.

What Smithton lacks in aesthetics it makes up for by its usefulness as a service centre, with supermarkets, fuel and banking facilities and an **Online Access Centre** on Nelson Street; the Redline **depot** is at 27 Victoria St. The resort-like *Tall Timbers Hotel Motel* on Scotchtown Road (Ⓣ03/6452 2755, Ⓦwww.talltimbershotel.com.au; ❺–❻), built from local timbers, has a vast and popular **bistro** and motel or self-catering **accommodation** and offers excellent 4WD tours. South of Smithton, ten **forestry reserves**, ranging from rainforests to blackwood swamps and giant eucalypt forests, are all accessible from a circular route, via Kanunnah Bridge and Taytea Bridge on the C218 (90km return). **Julius River Forest Reserve** and the **Milkshakes Hills Forest Reserve** are the most rewarding. Forestry Tasmania, at the corner of Nelson and Smith streets (Ⓣ03/6452 1317), provides maps and route information.

The Van Diemen's Land Company

. . . how is it that an absentee owner across the world got this magnificent and empty country without having paid one glass bead?

Cassandra Pybus

The **Van Diemen's Land Company (VDL)** was the brainchild of a group of prominent and well-connected individuals, who in 1824 managed to obtain by Royal Charter 250,000 acres of the mainly thickly forested, unexplored northwest corner of Tasmania. Their plan was to create their own source of fine wool in the colonies, which could be relied upon even if Europe was subject to political upheaval; the *Tranmere* arrived at Circular Head in 1826, with the personnel, livestock, supplies and equipment to create the township of Stanley.

The first flocks were grazed at Woolnorth on Cape Grim, a plateau of tussock grass and trees that might have been made for the purpose but, in fact, was prime Aboriginal hunting land. When hunting parties began to take the precious sheep, whites killed Aborigines in retaliation, and a vindictive cycle of killings began. The most tragic incident (a version of events denied by Woolnorth) was supposed to have occurred around 1826 or 1827: a group of Aboriginal men, seeking revenge for the rape of their women, speared a shepherd and herded one hundred sheep over the cliff edge. These deaths were ruthlessly avenged when a group of thirty unarmed Aborigines, hunting for muttonbirds near the same spot, were killed by shepherds and their bodies thrown over the cliff (now euphemistically called "Suicide Bay"). Ultimately, the Aboriginal people of the northwest were systematically hunted down: the last group, middle-aged parents and their five sons, were captured by sealers near the Arthur River in 1842 after the VDL's chief agent offered a £50 reward.

In the 1840s the company changed its emphasis from wool production to the sale and lease of its land, and it now holds just a fifth of its original land. Still registered on the London Stock Exchange, it is the only remaining company in the world operating under a Royal Charter; its major shareholder, who bought 87.5 per cent of the shares in 1993, is a New Zealand–based agribusiness in Dunedin.

Marrawah

From Smithton the Bass Highway cuts across the northwest corner to the rich farming settlement of **MARRAWAH** on the west coast. Thirty kilometres along the way, Forestry Tasmania have come up with a startling public-relations exercise: a Visitor Centre at the grumpily named **Dismal Swamp** (daily 10am–4pm; $20; ⓣ03/6456 7199), where a 110-metre slide (children must be over 8 years old) can whiz you down to the blackwood sinkhole, where a trail through the swamp includes mazes and art installations. The centre makes a good stopping point, with really good coffee at the smart attached café. Marrawah itself has a general store/café with a post office and **petrol**, and the *Marrawah Tavern* serves plain but filling meals. **Greenpoint Beach**, which has been voted one of the three best **surfing** beaches in Australia, is 2km west from Marrawah and has a small **camping area** as well as the stylish *Ann Bay Cabins* (ⓣ03/6457 1361; ❹). There's also excellent, spacious self-contained **accommodation** at *Glendonald Cottage* on the Arthur River Road, 3km south of Marrawah (ⓣ03/6457 1191; ❹); the owner, Geoff King, is a passionate conservationist who is working to regenerate the coastal land and preserve its Aboriginal sites. Geoff knows a lot about natural, local and Aboriginal history and his Kings Run Wildlife Tours include fascinating nocturnal viewings of **Tasmanian devils** in the wild ($75; one hour before sunset until midnight; ⓦwww.kingsrun.com.au).

The curve of Ann Bay here is shrouded by the hump of **Mount Cameron West** to the north. Three kilometres north of this bluff, at the end of a long exposed beach, is the most complex Aboriginal art site in Tasmania, now known as **Preminghana Indigenous Protected Area**: rock carvings of geometric or nonfigurative forms cover slabs of rock at the base of a cliff. Access is now restricted to a lookout.

Arthur River and the Arthur Pieman Protected Area

Just over 20km south of Marrawah, the scattering of holiday homes at **ARTHUR RIVER** marks the start of one of the Tasmanian coast's last great wilderness areas, where mighty trees that have been washed down the Frankland and Arthur rivers have crashed against the windswept shoreline. At one time the entire west coast looked like this, but the progressive damming of its rivers has left the **Arthur Pieman Protected Area**, part of the Tarkine, as a unique reminder, complete with a spectacular array of birdlife, such as black cockatoos, Tasmanian rosellas, orange-bellied parrots, black jays, wedge-tail eagles, pied heron and azure kingfishers. Trees on the steep banks of the never-logged river include myrtle, sassafras, celery-top pines and laurels, and there are giant tree ferns. From Gardiners Point – "**The Edge of the World**" – on the south side of the river mouth, the next land west is South America; it's a great vantage point to gaze on

The Tarkine

The Tarkine, covering 377,000 hectares in northwest Tasmania, was named after the Tarkiner band of Aboriginal people who once roved here. It's Tasmania's largest unprotected wilderness area – stretching from the wild west coast to Murchison Highway in the east and from the Arthur River in the north to the Pieman River in the south – though conservationists have been pushing for a Tarkine National Park since the 1960s and the area was recommended for UNESCO's World Heritage list in the 1990s. Of its 240,000 hectares of forest, seventy per cent constitutes Australia's largest tract of temperate rainforest, second only in global significance to tracts in British Columbia. This "forgotten wilderness" of giant myrtle forests, wild rivers and bare granite mountains is the sort of place where the Tasmanian tiger, long thought extinct, might still be roaming. Tasmania's forests were a key issue in the 2004 Australian federal election, with 73,000 hectares (mostly rainforest) of the Tarkine receiving protection from forestry – an outcome described by the Wilderness Society as "outstanding".

Dubbed by conservationists as "The Road to Nowhere", the Western Explorer road through the Tarkine, from Arthur River all the way south to Zeehan, was constructed hastily and finished in 1996. A year before, an incredibly vast and ancient Huon pine was found in the area, as big as a city block and thought to date from around 8000 BC. Pick up the *Western Explorer Travel Guide* pamphlet – issued by the Department of Infrastructure, Energy and Resources and available in information centres – and remember that the road is rough and Marrawah is the last fuel stop before Zeehan. Alternatively, the Tarkine National Coalition, based in Burnie (ⓣ03/6431 2373, ⓦwww.tarkine.org), produces guides to three self-drive Tarkine routes that don't involve the Western Explorer; these can be downloaded from their website. Tigs Trails (see box p.979) specializes in Tarkine tours; they do two six-day walking expeditions through giant myrtle forests and next to waterfalls ($1299), seven days on the battered west coast via Corinna and the Pieman River Cruise (ex-Launceston or Burnie; $1649) or a vehicle-based tour ($1649).

the battered coastline. It's obviously dangerous to swim here, due to extremely wild conditions and occasional freak waves – even walking along the beach can be an obstacle course, but it's possible to walk 9km to Sundown Point (arrange a pick-up vehicle or allow a full day to do the return walk.)

As you come into the settlement on the sealed Arthur River Road, get the latest information on conditions (and camping permits) from the Parks and Wildlife office here (daily 9am–5pm; ⓣ03/6457 1225). Opposite, the Arthur

△ Giant myrtle trees, The Tarkine

River Store (daily 7.30am–8pm; ⓣ03/6457 1207) sells supplies and tickets for the Arthur River Cruise, and books **accommodation**. Also on Gardiner Street is the spacious *Ocean View Holiday Cottage* (ⓣ03/6457 1100; ❸–❹), right on the river mouth with stunning views, and the excellent but smaller *Sunset Holiday Villas* opposite (ⓣ03/6457 1197; ❹). **Camping** at Arthur River is a truly pleasurable experience, with facilities that range from the fully serviced *Peppermint Campground* near the base office, to secluded areas among shady trees in the dips and hollows behind the dunes, equipped merely with water taps.

If you want to get out on the river, take a **cruise** (see below) or contact Arthur River Canoe & Boat Hire (ⓣ03/6457 1312), which has canoes and boats available for rent.

The Arthur River Cruise

Perhaps the biggest attraction of the entire northwest coast is the excellent five-hour **Arthur River Cruise** on the MV *George Robinson* (daily 10am, returning 3pm, enquire about summer evening cruises; no trips June to beginning Sept; $74; bookings ⓣ03/6457 1158, ⓦwww.arthurrivercruises.com; they will leave with only one person), which sails 14km upriver to the confluence of the Arthur and Frankland rivers at Turks Landing. The slow trip enables you to take in the tranquillity of the river and experience the transition from coastal scrub woodland to the edge of **The Tarkine** – the second-largest tract of temperate rainforest found anywhere in the world; en route you cruise past a white-breasted sea eagles' nest, and see the enormous mating pair being fed. Morning tea on the boat includes rum-spiked hot chocolate if you're up to it. Before a barbecue lunch (with wine) in a clearing, there's an informative half-hour guided bushwalk, where you'll learn about the rainforest species. The incredibly friendly crew even entertain with bush poetry on the trip back.

The A10 route to the west coast

From Somerset, a suburb of Burnie on the shores of Emu Bay, the A10 (called the Murchison Highway between here and the Zeehan turn-off) heads to **Queenstown**, in the heart of Tasmania's west-coast mining area. This major route to the west coast is relatively recent; prior to 1932 the coast was accessible only by sea. Following the highway, after 10km you pass **YOLLA**, a picturesque little town surrounded by rich farming country; you can get fuel here. A few kilometres past the Tewkesbury turn-off, the rural landscape ends and the road rises and winds through temperate rainforest to the **Hellyer Gorge State Reserve**. A walk leads through spicy ferns and dense myrtle forest to the Hellyer River and back on a wide and easy track (20min return).

West to Waratah and the Pieman River

Tiny, windswept **WARATAH**, set in mountain heathland 8km off the A10, reached its peak in the early twentieth century after thirty years of tin mining at **Mount Bischoff**, when it was linked to Burnie by the **Emu Bay Railway**, built to facilitate access to the silver fields of Zeehan and Rosebery. Though the mine closed in 1935, Waratah is still a miners' town, with recent mining developments at the Que River. Little more than a scattered collection of scruffy weatherboard cottages, it's a pretty soulless place, but you can stop off for a **meal** at the big old pub on the hill and get **petrol**. Beyond Waratah, the last fuel stop on the road is the former mining town of **Savage River**, 45km along the B23.

The beautiful, unspoilt **Pieman River**, within the **Pieman River State Reserve**, is reached from the old gold-mining settlement of **CORINNA** on an unsealed road (C247) 26km south of Savage River. It's hard to believe that 2500 people once occupied what is now just a few shacks surrounded by dense bush. Corinna even had its own port, despite the difficulties of getting through the narrow **Pieman Heads** from the coastline. The river here is too dangerous for swimming, with an average drop of nearly 20m from the banks. The reserve used to be a logging area and it still holds one of the biggest stands of remaining Huon pine – saved because the water here was too deep to allow a dam to be built. New owners have renovated the township and there are plenty of **accommodation** options at their new *Corinna Wilderness Experience* (ⓣ03/6446 1170, ⓦwww.corinna.com.au; ❻) including four original miners' cottages (one- and two-bedroom), an old pub (with singles and doubles) and original-style one-bedroom cottages with comfy queen beds. There's also a **campsite** (no showers; $10), while a general store sells basic grocery items. You can take a cruise on the river, all the way to the west coast, on the renovated Huon-pine MV *Arcadia II* (daily 10.30am; 4hr; $70 including morning tea, $7.50 extra with picnic lunch; bookings on ⓣ03/6446 1170 advisable). From its deck you can see Huon pine, leatherwood and pandanus ferns among the temperate rainforest of the river's north bank; the drier southern bank has mainly brown stringybark eucalypts. The trip allows you an hour to wander on your own along the wild west coast, or you can link up with Pieman Head Adventure Tours (book through ⓣ03/6446 1170) for a 4WD excursion to Granville Harbour (6hr; $150, $170 with BBQ lunch).

A barge (the "Fatman") can take you across the Pieman River from here (daily 9am–7pm; $20 car, $10 bike), to continue on the C249 to Zeehan, and then on the B27 to Strahan.

South to Zeehan

Back on the A10, there's no fuel until tiny **TULLAH**, 40km south of Waratah. Fourteen kilometres further on, after crossing forest-covered **Mount Black**, the comparatively large zinc-mining town of **ROSEBERY** is a good place to stock up on supplies, with an ANZ bank (Mon, Tues & Fri 9.30am–noon, Wed 2–4pm) and an ATM outside the newsagents'. The comfortable motel-style B&B **accommodation** at *Mount Black Lodge* right next to the mine on Hospital Road (ⓣ03/6473 1039, ⓦwww.mountblacklodge.com; also licensed restaurant; ❹), attracts bushwalkers and can organize photographic tours: the town is hemmed in by looming mounts Black, Read (often recording Tasmania's highest daily rainfall) and Murchison, and there's also a fine walk to the 113-metre **Montezuma Falls** (3hr return), 8km south of the town.

From Rosebery, it's 23km to the turn-off to **ZEEHAN**, 6km southwest off the A10. The town became prosperous from the silver-lead mines that opened in the 1880s, and at its height boasted a population of eight thousand. However, the mines had already begun to fail by 1908, and the town was not to see a revival until the 1970s, when the Renison Bell tin mines were opened. Several boom-period buildings are still standing, including the elaborate facade of the **Gaiety Theatre**, once Australia's largest theatre, where Lola Montez once trod the boards. The outstanding **West Coast Pioneer Memorial Museum** on Main Street (daily 8.30am–5pm; $10; ⓣ03/6471 6225) has displays on mining history and its own café. **Accommodation** is expensive, as Zeehan catches

Strahan's overflow, and includes the *Heemskirk Motor Inn* (ⓣ03/6471 6107; ❹), and basic pub rooms at the *Hotel Cecil* on Main Street (ⓣ03/6471 6221; ❸), where you can get decent counter meals. The *Mount Zeehan Retreat Bed and Breakfast* provides evening meals on request (ⓣ03/6471 6424; no en suites; B&B ❹). By far the cheapest option is the friendly *Treasure Island Caravan Park*, nicely situated 1km from the centre on Hurst Street (ⓣ03/6471 6633; vans ❷, cabins ❸). The ANZ **bank** has restricted opening hours (Mon & Tues 2–4pm, Wed 9.30am–noon, Thurs 9.30am–4pm & Fri 2–4pm), but there's an ATM at Vickers General Store on the main street.

From Zeehan it's possible to go straight to Strahan (47km) on a sealed road (B27), bypassing Queenstown and visiting the Henty Dunes (see p.1066) en route; or you could head back to the A10 (called the Zeehan Highway until Queenstown) and reach Strahan via Queenstown, another 32km along the highway. You can get to Rosebery and Zeehan on TassieLink's scheduled Launceston–Queenstown service via Cradle Mountain (3 weekly).

Queenstown

QUEENSTOWN is worth a visit, but not for reasons you might expect. Its infamous "**lunar landscape**" is chilling evidence of the devastation that single-minded commercial exploitation can wreak in such a sensitive environment. If you approach the town from Strahan you're confronted by the hideously ugly **copper mine**; from Hobart, the road winds down to the town around bare, reddish-brown rock.

Queenstown has been a mining centre since 1883, when gold was discovered at Mount Lyell, and it looks like a typical mining town, with its identical, pokey tin-roofed weatherboard houses. In 1893 the Mount Lyell Mining and Railway Company was formed and began to mine copper at Mount Lyell. The weird-looking mountains here, chalky white and almost totally devoid of vegetation, are the result of a lethal combination of tree-felling, sulphur, fire and rainfall. Since the smelters closed in 1969 there has been some regrowth on the lower slopes, but it's estimated that the damage already done has had an impact that will last some four or five hundred years. In late 1994 the Mount Lyell mine closed down, but the lease was taken over in 1995 by **Copper Mines of Tasmania**. Tailings from the mine are now dumped into a multimillion-dollar dam instead of the town's **Queen River**, where aquatic life is beginning to return. The Queen eventually flows into the **King River**, and its moonscaped banks all the way to the delta near Strahan attest to the lasting and wide-ranging environmental damage of the past century. Underground **tours** of the Mount Lyell mine are offered by Douggies Mine Tours, based at the *Empire Hotel*, below (daily 10am & 1pm; 2hr 30min; $58; ⓣ0407 049 612).

Next door to the mine is the **Parks and Wildlife Service office** (ⓣ03/6471 2511), the base for the Franklin Lower Gordon Wild Rivers National Park and the place to pick up the department's rafting and bushwalking guidelines. **Tourist information** is available from the reception desk of the **Galley Museum** housed in the old *Imperial Hotel* on Driffield Street, two blocks from the railway station (ⓣ03/6471 1483; Mon–Fri 10am–5pm, Sat & Sun 12.30–6pm; $4), whose extensive old photographic displays focus on west-coast life. Queenstown's **Online Access Centre** is nearby on the same street.

If you're **staying** in Queenstown, try the *Empire Hotel*, at 2 Orr St (ⓣ03/6471 1699, ⓔempirehotel@tassienet.au; rooms ❷, en suite ❸), a lovely, old-fashioned building noted for its National Trust–listed blackwood staircase; it has a good range of reasonably priced rooms and several budget singles

The West Coast Wilderness Railway

In 2002 the opening of the 35km **West Coast Wilderness Railway** between Queens-town and Strahan fulfilled the $30-million redevelopment of the old **Abt Railway**, which included the restoration or replacement of forty bridges and recreation of stations and associated buildings. Two of the four surviving locomotives from 1963 were restored and each carriage – replicas of old timber and brass models – was designed using different Tasmanian woods. The original railway was completed in 1896 to connect the Mount Lyell Mining Company in Queenstown with the port of Teepookana for the transport of copper ore, and in 1899 the line was extended to Regatta Point in Strahan. The railway closed in 1963, when it became more economical to transport by road, but years of lobbying finally led to the federal government financing its redevelopment. Reconstruction took three years; the original workers took six months less to hand-cut through the rugged rainforest terrain, struggling in the harsh, wet conditions. In fact, mining heritage is the main thrust of this trip and the informative commentary concentrates on it. The "wilderness" is something of a disappointing misnomer, though – at least for half of the journey the line follows slowly alongside the sadly polluted King River, its banks rusty from mine tailings and lined with tree stumps. Most people take the trip from Strahan: from Dubbil Barril, as the train climbs over 200m up a 1:16 rack gradient using the restored rack-and-pinion track (a system invented by the Swiss engineer Dr Roman Abt), there are stunning gorge views and the train is immersed in up-close rainforest scenery. However, coming into Queenstown, the vision alongside the tracks is a shocking contrast – a shanty town of tin shacks and dilapidated wooden houses.

Trains leave from Queenstown at the reconstructed station on Driffield Street, opposite the *Empire Hotel*, and at Strahan from the original station at Regatta Point (see p.1066). There's a daily service in both directions, both of which provide a one-hour lunchstop at Dubbil Barril (packed lunch included) where there's a rainforest walk that takes five minutes. The train from Queenstown stops at the reconstructed historic settlement of Lynchford for half an hour for morning tea and a try at gold panning; the Lower Landing morning-tea stop from Strahan is on the unscenic polluted King River and includes a lame, mass honey-tasting exercise. Trains are hauled by steam between Queenstown and Dubbil Barril and diesel between here and Strahan. You can choose to go one way from either Strahan or Queenstown with a coach return (with a 30min break in Queenstown or 1hr 30min in Strahan), or return from Dubbil Barril. The best return option is from Queenstown, as you avoid the ravaged river, enjoy a thrilling ascent and descent, get the steam train and a more enjoyable morning-tea stop; the Strahan return trip is best avoided (departs Queenstown 10am & 3pm, departs Strahan 10.15am & 3.15pm; one way 4hr, return 5hr; $99 one way, $185 premier class, includes light lunch; extra $15 for 45min return coach; bookings necessary ⓣ1800 420 155).

($50), plus good-value meals in the heritage dining-room. *Mountain View Holiday Lodge*, at 1 Penghana Rd (ⓣ03/6471 1163; dorms $15, motel units ❸), across the river from the town centre, has been converted from the mine's single-men's lodgings. For something special, *Penghana*, on The Esplanade at no. 32, provides B&B-style accommodation in an imposing stately mansion set in rainforest overlooking Queenstown (ⓣ03/6471 2560, ⓦwww.view.com.au/penghana; B&B ❻). There are **banking** facilities at the Commonwealth Bank on Orr Street (closed noon–1pm), which has an ATM, and ANZ banking and an ATM at the Railway Express General Store on the same street. From Queenstown you can drive to Strahan on the B24 (42km), which starts as a steep, winding road through bare hills, or you continue along the A10 (called the Lyell Highway from Queenstown to Hobart) 88km east to the first fuel at Derwent Bridge, surrounded by the World Heritage Area.

Strahan and around

STRAHAN, the only town and port on the west coast, sits in the huge **Macquarie Harbour** (over six times the size of Sydney's harbour), site of **Sarah Island**, a harsh, secondary convict settlement in use between 1822 and 1830, which can be visited on a Gordon River cruise (see box p.1065). The entrance to Macquarie Harbour, named **Hells Gates** by arriving convicts, is only 80m wide. **Huon pine**, perfect for shipbuilding, grows abundantly in the area – logging and boatbuilding became convicts' trades. After 1830 the timber continued to attract loggers, but it wasn't until 1882 that Strahan began life as a port for the nearby copper and lead fields. Although it was Tasmania's third-largest port in 1900, its unreliability led to closure by 1970 and the population dwindled to three hundred. It's now a small fishing village for abalone, crayfish and shark, and commercial fish-farming of rainbow trout and Atlantic salmon, though the main industry is tourism. The basing of the **Franklin Blockade** campaign here in 1982 shook up the town and brought the international media here for two months. **Cruises** on the **Gordon River** had already been running before this event, but the declaration of a **World Heritage Area** has meant that busloads of tourists now regularly descend upon Strahan to see the river, creating a hectic atmosphere while they're boarding and disembarking. The West Coast Wilderness Railway (see box, opposite) was added to the list of attractions in 2003. Federal Resorts owns both the railway and Gordon River Cruises, and much of the central accommodation and the pub; in the summer, at least, Strahan has ceased to seem "real", but there's no doubt that it's a beautiful town and the surrounding natural attractions are totally compelling.

Transport and services

The place to make enquiries and bookings for TassieLink **bus** services is West Coast Visitor Information and Booking Centre (see p.1064). There's a scheduled service from Launceston and Devonport via Cradle Mountain (3 weekly), connecting with a Queenstown–Strahan service (5 weekly), which connects with the service to Hobart via Lake St Clair. The Strahan Supermarket, 1km up the hill overlooking the centre on Reid Street (Mon–Fri 7.30am–7pm, Sat & Sun 8am–6pm), has EFTPOS facilities and is a Westpac **bank** agent; otherwise, there's an ANZ **ATM** outside *Banjos Bakery* on The Esplanade. At The Esplanade's far end, the old Customs House contains the **post office** (also a Commonwealth Bank agent), and there is a **Parks and Wildlife office** (Mon–Fri 9am–5pm; ⓣ03/6471 7122), where park passes are available, and an **Online Access Centre**.

Accommodation

If you've got your own transport to get there, you can **camp** for free at Ocean Beach and Henty Dunes (see p.1066); there are no facilities, but free hot showers can be had in town in the toilet block opposite the post office. **Accommodation** is expensive and gets booked up in the summer; to be safe, book ahead or bring a tent – otherwise you might have to head back to Zeehan or Queenstown. The West Coast Visitor Information and Booking Centre has a free accommodation-booking service. For something different, you can also stay onboard *West Coast Yacht* (see p.1066; also enquire about their comfortable self-contained holiday units *The Crays* (❻).

Cosy Cabins Strahan Backpackers Harvey St ⓣ03/6472 6211. Located beside a bush-lined stream with its own resident platypus, this modern hostel has spacious rooms and common kitchens, eating areas and a lounge. Well-cared-for timber bedroom cabins (double or twin), share the hostel bathrooms and kitchens. Also a self-contained unit sleeping four (4). It's 1km from the centre but TassieLink buses drop off. Dorms $30, rooms 2, cabins 3

Cosy Cabins Strahan Seaside The Esplanade ⓣ03/6471 7239. Well-positioned camping and cabins near the foreshore. Vans 2, cabins 3–4

Franklin Manor The Esplanade ⓣ03/6471 7311, ⓦwww.franklinmanor.com.au. Sedate and elegant two-storey weatherboard B&B, surrounded by trees and flowers. The interior is attractively decorated and lovingly maintained; classical music plays in the guest lounge, always filled with fresh flowers, and there's a classy restaurant run by an award-winning French chef (and co-owner). 5–7

Gordon Gateway Chalet Grining St, Regatta Point ⓣ03/6471 7165, ⓦwww.gordongateway.com.au. Peaceful harbourfront spot in over two acres of gardens looking across to the town and its fishing boats. Spacious studios with kitchenettes; gas BBQ site in the gardens. 5

Risby Cove The Esplanade ⓣ03/6471 7572, ⓦwww.risby.com.au. An old sawmill, fully renovated using corrugated iron and Huon pine salvaged from the harbour, now houses upmarket one- and two-bedroom accommodation suites with kitchenette area. There's an on-site restaurant/café, gallery, and even a digital film theatre (nightly 7pm; $9.50). 5–6

Strahan Colonial Cottages 7 Reid St ⓣ03/6471 7019. Three beautifully renovated and well-equipped cottages, one a renovated church. 6

The Strahan Village The Esplanade ⓣ03/6471 7160 or 1800 628 286, ⓦwww.strahanvillage.com.au. Among the various styles of Federal Hotels and Resorts' upmarket accommodation (all en suite) clustered along and above The Esplanade, best positioned are the spacious "Terrace" rooms above the renovated 1930s *Hamers Hotel*, with private balcony access looking right over the boats (6). There are a variety of "Village" units (6) along the Esplanade, some of which look like cute cottages, but they're really only motel rooms. The most expensive "Hilltop" (7–8) rooms command great views from the hill above, with the buffet-style *Macquarie Restaurant and Bar* also taking in the sights. The cheapest "Hilltop Garden View" rooms are tucked behind (5). 5–8

Wheelhouse Apartments 4 Frazer St ⓣ03/6471 7777, ⓦwww.wheelhouseapartments.com.au. These unique two-storey apartments, with abundant use of local timbers and a stylish maritime theme, sit on the edge of a cliff above the harbour. Slanted wall-to-ceiling windows in the downstairs living room give a prow-of-a-ship feel and awesome views. Upstairs, there are less spectacular vistas from the spa in the master bedroom and from the second bedroom. Full kitchen and laundry in both apartments. 8

The Town

Your first stop should be the innovative wooden-and-iron **West Coast Visitor Information and Booking Centre**, on The Esplanade (daily: Oct–March 10am–6pm, till 9pm Jan; April–Sept 11am–6pm; 24hr ticket $2; ⓣ03/6472 6800, ⓔwcvibcs@westcoast.tas.gov.au), whose exterior design aims to echo the area's boatbuilding and timber industries. The interior features a waterfall, and a huge glass wall providing views of the harbour. The centre sets out its exhibits in a provocative and challenging way, under seven main themes: the Aborigines, convicts, logging, ecology, economy, wilderness and conflict. You can enter the foyer free of charge to pick up leaflets and information and take advantage of the Internet access. Outside, an **amphitheatre** is the early-evening venue for an entertaining two-man show, *The Ship That Never Was*, which retells – in slapstick audience-participation vein – the true story of an 1834 convict escape from Sarah Island (daily 5.30pm plus 8.30pm performance in Jan; $15.00).

Adjacent to the visitor centre the **Strahan Woodworks**, in a large, corrugated-iron shed (daily 8am–5pm), sells well-designed and crafted woodwork; you're also welcome to roam around Morrison's Saw Mill next door, and watch the Tasmanian timbers being processed. Also worth a visit is the **Forestry Tasmania Office**, next to *Hamers* pub (Mon–Fri 9am–5pm; ⓣ03/6472 6000),

Cruising the Gordon River

The **Gordon River** is deep, its waters dark from the tannin leaching out of buttongrass plains – even the tap water in Strahan is brown (though perfectly fine to drink). Cruise boats used to travel as far as the landing at Sir John Falls, 30km upriver, but the speed at which the boats had to go was causing the riverbanks to erode – and they now travel only the 14km to **Heritage Landing**, where there's a chance to see a section of real **rainforest**: a boardwalk above the rainforest floor allows you to get close without disturbing anything. Trunks and branches of ancient myrtles and **Huon pines** provide homes for mosses, lichens and liverworts on their bark, and ferns and fungi grow from the trunks – even the dead trees support some forms of life, however lowly. The wet and swampy conditions are ideal for Huon pines, a threatened tree species found only in Tasmania: they're the second-oldest living things on earth after the bristlecone pines of western North America, with some trees found to be more than ten thousand years old. The massive pines, which may reach a height of 40m, can grow from seed but more often regenerate vegetatively, putting down roots where fallen branches touch the soil. The vast tree at the landing, reckoned to be around 2000 years old, split in two during 1997 – one half fell to the ground – but the trunk won't rot for up to one hundred years as it contains methyl eugenol oil which slows fungal growth. The oil content of the wood helps explain why it was so highly sought after as one of the few green Tasmanian timbers that floats: Huon pine logs were floated down to the boom camp and there fashioned into huge rafts to be rowed across Macquarie Harbour.

Two operators offer **river cruises**; both visit Sarah Island and make a thirty-minute stop at Heritage Landing. Gordon River Cruises have pre-designated seats, but there are floor-to-ceiling windows and you can move freely out on deck; to make the most of the experience on World Heritage Cruises, turn up early to bag a good seat. But for both, bring water- and windproof gear so you can brave the prow of the boat – much the most exhilarating spot when you whizz through Macquarie Heads (**Hells Gates**). Owned by Federal Resorts, **Gordon River Cruises** has one boat, the high-tech new *Jane Franklin II* (cruise departs 8.30am, returns 2pm, Nov–April extra cruise departs 2.45pm, returns 8pm; includes 1hr at Sarah Island; buffet lunch included, bow-atrium seat $85, window seats $110, upper-deck seats including smorgasboard lunch, snacks and drinks $180; ⓣ03/6471 4300 or 1800 420 555, ⓦwww.puretasmania.com.au). Their booking office is located on the waterfront in a spacious complex, the Strahan Activity Booking Centre, where there's a photographic display of Strahan's history and interpretive material relating to the unique thylacine rug (see p.987), which is exhibited in Strahan over the summer; the rug is displayed at 3.30pm with an accompanying talk (free). **World Heritage Cruises**, the local family-owned and-operated company with two day-trip boats (the *Wanderer II* and *Sorcha*), offers a slightly cheaper cruise, with a one-hour tour of the prison settlement Sarah Island, led by an actor telling convict tales (daily 9am–3pm; $85 (discounts available for early booking); snacks and $15 buffet meal available on board; licensed; ⓣ03/6471 7174, ⓦwww.worldheritagecruises.com.au). They also offer a similar afternoon cruise in summer (Jan–March 3–8.30pm; $85), and a shorter morning cruise in the warmer months that doesn't stop at Sarah Island (Oct–April; 9am–2pm; $80). Their brand-new *Discovery*, a 33-metre small ship launched at the end of 2004, takes 24 passengers for three-day two-night luxury cruises on the Gordon River (overnight moored at Heritage Landing) and Macquarie Harbour (overnight moored at Sarah Island), with shore and kayaking excursions ($1995).

which has an amazing window display featuring a Huon pine log transforming itself into the bow of a boat; inside you can pick up leaflets describing the trees in the area, as well as other information.

The 1.7km **Strahan Historic Foreshore Walkway** is a pleasant gravel track following the shore of the harbour around to **Regatta Point** and its 1899 train station from where the **West Coast Wilderness Railway** (see p.1062) leaves; self-guided-walk maps are available from the tourist office. En route you pass the **People's Park**, from where you can take the rainforest walk to **Hogarth Falls** (40min; 2km return).

Eating and drinking

On The Esplanade, *Hamers Hotel*, is the focus of the town's social life, in the public bar at least, which is always a lively place for a **drink**; next door *Hamers Bar & Grill* is a fine bistro which serves up a varied selection of seafood, pasta, grills and curries (mains around $16) in a bustling atmosphere. Alongside, *Banjo's Bakehouse* (daily 6am–8/9pm) has outside water-facing tables and does surprisingly good coffee to go with the pastries and the (pricey) cooked breakfasts (it also serves pizzas after 6pm). Just off The Esplanade on Harold Street, the *Strahan Central Café* is a city-style café with views over the water from the outdoor deck and excellent coffee but restricted hours (daily noon–4pm). Across the bay, Strahan's best restaurant is the dining room of the stylish *Franklin Manor* (see p.1064), where you can sample the best of modern Australian cuisine with an emphasis on fresh produce. Risby Cove (see p.1064) has waterfront café-restaurant (daily 10am through to dinner) where the contemporary Australian food has a good reputation and isn't too pricey.

Around Strahan

Six kilometres east of town, **Ocean Beach** is, at 30km, the longest beach in Tasmania but the wild waters are not safe to swim in. Come at dusk to observe the marvellous sunsets and to watch – from November to February – the migratory **muttonbirds** roost. It's an 11km drive on a gravel road, south off the road to Ocean Beach, to **Macquarie Heads** (Hells Gates). The extensive thirty-metre-high **Henty Dunes**, 12km north of town on the Zeehan Road (B27), are also worth seeing; two fun ways to experience them are by (see below) or by hiring sandboards from The Shack (Ⓣ03/6471 7396; $30 per 4hr). You can **camp** for free at the picnic area or in other clearings, and campfires are allowed. The **Teepookana Plateau** has an awe-inspiring stand of ancient Huon pines (some nearly 2000 years old) visited via an elevated walkway which leads to a viewing tower offering 360-degree forest, mountain and harbour views; the only way to reach it and the namesake King River railway port ghost-town is by tour (see opposite).

To get around, you can rent **mountain bikes** from Risby Cove (see p.1064); (half-day $10, full day $20). 4 Wheeler Bikes offers popular guided four-wheel motorbike **tours** of Henty Sand Dunes (40min; $40; bookings essential Ⓣ03/6471 7622 or 0419 508 175) and longer tours to Teepookana. In addition to the Gordon River cruises (see box, p.1065) there's a wide choice of water-based tours. West Coast Yacht Charters, on The Esplanade (Ⓣ03/6471 7422, Ⓦwww.tasadventures.com/wcyc), runs evening **crayfish dinner sails** on Macquarie Harbour on a sixty-metre ketch, *Stormbreaker* (daily 6–8.30pm except May–Aug; $70 including dinner, $80 with crayfish when it's in season) and longer cruises up the Gordon River (leaving 6pm overnight to Sir John Falls for morning Franklin rafter pick-up; $190 includes accommodation on boat, breakfast and lunch; overnight Gordon River cruise to Sarah Island and Heritage Landing $320 including all meals, two nights $420); you can even stay on board the ketch for a waterborne B&B experience ($40 per person). With Wild Rivers Jet, who have an office on The Esplanade (Ⓣ03/6471 7396), you can blast up the already devastated **King River**, just south of Strahan (50min; $65), but a better option is the combined jet boat–4WD trip to the Teepookana Plateau (11am daily; 1hr 45min; $78). Strahan Marine Charters (ⓣ0418 135 983) offers private fishing or sightseeing tours.

Wilderness Air, on Strahan Wharf, runs spectacular **seaplane flights** over Macquarie Harbour and the wilderness area (daily from 9am; 1hr 20min; $159; bookings ⓣ03/6471 7280, ⓦwww.tassie.net.au/~wildair/), providing the unforgettable image of the smooth dark ribbon of the pristine Franklin River easing through dense forest. The highlight of the trip is the dramatic landing at **Sir John Falls Landing**, further upriver than the cruise boats can reach. They also have longer flights for viewing the rugged scenery around Frenchmans Cap ($184). Seair Adventure Charters (ⓣ03/6471 7718, ⓦwww.adventureflights.com.au) offers **helicopter flights** over Hells Gates and Macquarie Harbour ($105; 15min), and the Teepookana Forest, which includes a landing and walk to see the old-growth Huon pine (1hr; $169).

The World Heritage Area

If we can revise our attitudes towards the land under our feet; if we can accept a role of steward, and depart from the role of conqueror; if we can accept the view that man and nature are inseparable parts of the unified whole – then Tasmania can be a shining beacon in a dull, uniform, and largely artificial world.

Olegas Truchanas, conservationist, 1971

It's the lure of the **wilderness** that attracts a certain type of traveller to Tasmania, to commune with nature at its most unspoilt. The state's vast wilderness areas of the South West National Park, Franklin Lower Gordon Wild Rivers National Park and the adjacent Cradle Mountain–Lake St Clair National Park make up the **World Heritage Area**, recognized by UNESCO.

The future of the parks could have been very different had it not been for the bitterly fought battle waged by the environmentalists in the 1980s. In 1972 the flooding of the beautiful and unique **Lake Pedder** led to the formation, in 1976, of the **Wilderness Society**, which began a relentless campaign against the next plan for the southwest by the Hydro Electricity Commission (HEC), which was to build a huge dam on the Lower Gordon River that would efface Tasmania's last wild river, the Franklin. Pro-HEC forces included the then Tasmanian Premier Robin Gray. Years of protests and campaigns ensued, but in 1981 the whole southwest area was proposed for the World Heritage List. The **Franklin Blockade**, organized by the Wilderness Society and led by **Dr Bob Brown**, began on December 14, 1982, the day the southwest officially joined the list – a fact the Tasmanian government was choosing to ignore.

For two months, blockaders from all over Australia travelled upriver from their base in Strahan to put themselves in front of the bulldozers at the site, in non-violent protest. The **blockade** attracted international attention, notably when the British botanist David Bellamy joined in the protest and was among the twelve hundred or so arrested for trespassing. During the course of the campaign, Bob Hawke's Labor government was voted in, and in March 1983, following a trailblazing High Court ruling, the federal government forbade further work by the HEC. Though the blockade itself had failed to stop the preparatory work on the dam, it had changed, or at least challenged, the opinion of many Australians.

Cradle Mountain–Lake St Clair National Park

This must be a national park for the people for all time. It is magnificent, and people must know about it and enjoy it.

Gustave Weindorfer, botanist and mountaineer, 1910

Cradle Mountain–Lake St Clair National Park is Tasmania's best known, its northern **Cradle Mountain** end easily accessible from Devonport, Deloraine or Launceston, and its southern **Lake St Clair** end from Derwent Bridge on the Lyell Highway between Queenstown and Hobart. A popular route from Devonport is via Sheffield (see p.1142) on the B14, then the C132 via Wilmot, and for the final stretch to Cradle Valley, the C136. One of the most glaciated areas in Australia, with many lakes and tarns, the park covers some of Tasmania's highest land, with craggy mountain peaks such as **Mount Ossa** (1617m), the state's highest point. At its northern end, **Dove Lake**, backed by the jagged outline of Cradle Mountain, is a breathtaking sight, and at the park's southern end, Lake St Clair is the country's deepest freshwater lake at over 200m, occupying a basin gouged out by two glaciers. Between Cradle Mountain and Lake St Clair, the eighty-kilometre **Overland Track** attracts walkers from all over the world, and is the best way to take in the stunning scenery – spread over five or more mud- and leech-filled days of physical, albeit exhilarating, exhaustion. However, you can do just part of the walk, or make several other satisfying day-walks around Cradle Mountain or Lake St Clair.

Transport to the park

TassieLink services both ends of the national park on two year-round **scheduled routes**, while The Overland Track summer service provides more frequent transport from November until the end of April. A scheduled service from Launceston and Devonport to Queenstown goes via Cradle Mountain (3 weekly; connecting with a Queenstown to Strahan service), while the scheduled Hobart–Strahan service takes the Lyell Highway to Lake St Clair (5 weekly). A daily Launceston to Cradle Mountain summer service runs via Deloraine, Sheffield and Devonport. A Hobart to Lake St Clair summer service via Mount Field National Park runs daily. You can also try Maxwell's Coaches charter service (Ⓣ03/6492 1431), which connects Devonport and Launceston to Lake St Clair ($70), and Launceston and Devonport to Cradle Mountain ($40).

Cradle Mountain

At **Cradle Mountain**, the impressive, modern **Cradle Mountain Visitor Centre** (daily 8am–5pm, later in summer; Ⓣ03/6492 1133) provides information on the many day-walks available in this area of the park, and acts as a registration point for the Overland Track (see box opposite); it's worth buying the *Cradle Mountain Day Walks – Map & Notes* ($4) for more information. You can start here with a gentle ten-minute boardwalk circuit through rainforest and overlooking **Pencil Pine Falls**, ideal for wheelchairs or strollers. There's also the "Enchanted Walk" that follows the creek through rainforest to *Cradle Mountain Lodge* (1km one way; 20min). Five kilometres into the park from the visitor centre, **Waldheim** ("Forest Home" in German) is the King Billy pine chalet built by the Austrian–Australian **Gustave Weindorfer** in 1912, and now a museum (open 24hr; free) devoted to the man who loved this wilderness area and helped to have it declared a national park; a fifteen-minute forest walk from the hut shows examples of ancient King Billy pine. Near the hut, there's a cosy

The Overland Track

In summer and autumn, around forty people a day depart Cradle Mountain to walk the **Overland Track**, probably Australia's greatest extended bushwalk: 80km, unbroken by roads and passing through buttongrass plains, fields of wild flowers, and forests of deciduous beech, Tasmanian myrtle, pandanus and King Billy pine, with side-walks leading to views of waterfalls and lakes and starting points for climbs of the various mountain peaks. Much of the track is frequently repaired boardwalk but you'll still end up ankle-deep in mud. Along the route are six basic coal-stove- or gas-heated huts (not for cooking – bring your own stove), with composting toilets outside. There's no guarantee there'll be space, so you should carry a good tent; a warm sleeping bag is essential even in the heated huts in summer.

The direct walk generally takes six days – five, if you catch a boat from Narcissus Hut across Lake St Clair; if you want to go on some of the side-walks, allow eight to ten days. On average, most walkers go for six to eight days. You should take enough food and fuel for the duration of your walk, plus extra supplies in case you have an accident or bad weather sets in; there's always plenty of unpolluted fresh water to drink from streams. Around eight thousand people walk the track each year; most people come between November and April, but the best time is during February and March when the weather has stabilized, though it's bound to rain at some point, and may even snow. The track is at its most crowded from Christmas to the end of January. Because of overloading of the track during peak periods, a Web-based booking system (Ⓦwww.overlandtrack.com.au) for departure dates applies between November and the end of April, and a fee of $150 per person in addition to the park entry fee will be applicable. Most people walk north to south, which is more downhill than up, and this will be the obligatory route direction between November and April. The rest of the year you can register at either end in the **national park offices** (see p.1070 and below), where you receive an obligatory briefing and have your gear checked to make sure it's sufficient. The office sells last-minute camping gear and supplies: fuel stoves, meths, water bottles, trowels, warm hats and gloves. The *Cradle Mountain–Lake St Clair Map and Notes 1:100,000* ($9.10) is an essential purchase, and *The Overland Track – A Walker's Notebook* ($13.75) is a handy reference. Once you end up at Derwent Bridge (see p.1070), exhausted and covered in mud, you can use the hot showers at the campsite, for which there's a small charge.

The logistics of doing a one-way walk are smoothed by a couple of operators: Maxwell's Coaches (see above) and the Tasmanian Tour Company (see p.1047) can do **transfers** to get you back to your car, while TassieLink has special Overland Track fares that include transfers from Launceston to Cradle Mountain, and then back from Lake St Clair to Launceston ($118) or Hobart ($113) or Devonport ($95) or any two combinations. They can provide baggage transfer for an extra charge. **Guided tours** are available, the best offered by Craclair Tours (Ⓣ03/6339 4488 Oct–April; 8 days $1950, 10 days $2250; see p.1069); you'll still have to camp (except for comfortable cabin accommodation at the start) and carry a ten-kilo pack. The easiest option is to go on a guided walk staying along the track at *Cradle Huts*, **private lodges** with hot showers, beds and delicious meals (6 days $2350 full board departing and returning Launceston; Ⓣ03/6331 2006, Ⓦwww.cradlehuts.com.au). Several operators combine Cradle Mountain with Walls of Jerusalem (see p.1039).

heated day-shelter where you can also picnic. There's a **shuttle bus** from the airstrip outside *Cradle Mountain Wilderness Cafe* (see p.1070) and the Visitor Centre to Dove Lake, 2.5km on from Waldheim (Oct to mid-May daily 8am–7pm; every 15min summer Ⓦwww.mcdermotts.com.au); the bus is included in the park entry fee (see above). Though you can still drive to the **Dove Lake car park**, in summer it's often full by 9am and the bus is the best alternative.

The Dove Lake circuit (2–3hr) is an easy all-weather walk around the shore of the lake, or a popular, but steep and strenuous, day-walk from here to the summit of **Cradle Mountain** (6hr return; get advice from the ranger first). If you're feeling lazy, you can opt for a **helicopter scenic flight** (weather permitting) over the area with Cradle Mountain Helicopters ($190, min 4 people; 50min; landing at Fury Gorge with 20min on the ground; ⓣ03/6492 1132, ⓦwww.adventureflights.com.au), which is based by the *Cradle Wilderness Café* (see below). Further on from the café, at *Cradle Mountain Chateau* (see below), the highly recommended nine-room **Wilderness Gallery** (daily 10am–5pm; $5, free for guests) features landscape photography – of Tasmania, Antarctica and the Pacific – from well-known and emerging local and international nature photographers, including the late, great Tasmanian, **Peter Dombrovskis**.

Just on the edge of the national park, and within walking distance of the visitor centre, the wonderful *Cradle Mountain Lodge* (ⓣ03/6492 1303, ⓦwww.cradlemountainlodge.com.au; cabins ❼) is the focus for **accommodation**, eating and drinking; it's definitely worth considering staying here as a treat after finishing the Overland Track. Scattered through the bush around the lodge are 86 luxurious serviced timber cabins, all with log or gas fires and bathrooms (no cooking facilities). At the lodge itself, guest facilities include lounges and the Waldheim Alpine Spa, with outdoor hot tub, cold plunge pool, steam room and a sauna, plus numerous massage treatments. Less self-indulgent options are a slideshow about the area, a night-time wildlife documentary, and a 45-minute walk. Other guided walks into the national park are available daily, ranging from $10 to $28. Non-guests can book in to eat at the classy **restaurant** (the buffet-style breakfast is well worth the cost – $24.95 full buffet and is included in the guest rate), or drop in to eat or drink at the cosy tavern **bar**. You can rent **bicycles** from the lodge ($15 half-day), and there's a boutique selling snacks and gifts. In the national park, there are eight basic self-catering **huts** (❸; linen extra $5.50 per person) at Waldheim (see above), which sleep four to eight people with generator electricity, pot-bellied stoves, and a shared amenities block – these are looked after by the National Park Visitor Centre (ⓣ03/6492 1303). There's more accommodation at the cute *Cradle Mountain Highlander Cabins*, 1.5km from the park entrance on Cradle Mountain Road (ⓣ03/6492 1116, ⓦwww.cradlehighlander.com.au; ❺–❻). The newer *Cradle Mountain Wilderness Village*, next door, has a more antiseptic feel (ⓣ03/6492 1018, ⓦwww.cradlevillage.com.au; self-catering cabins ❻). Its licensed fast-food/bistro-style *Cradle Wilderness Café* also sells petrol and diesel (daily 8.30am–8pm, to 10.30pm in summer). *Cradle Mountain Tourist Park* (ⓣ03/6492 1395, ⓦwww.cosycabins.com/cradle), another half-kilometre back along Cradle Mountain Road, has a **campsite** with camp kitchen, a **YHA hostel**, the *Cradle Mountain Backpackers* in three heated bunkhouses (dorms $25, rising to $30 in summer), and some basic huts (❸), plus well-set-up cabins sleeping up to six (❹). The campsite has a small **shop** and is linked to the lodge in summer by a shuttle bus. A little further on is the four-star *Cradle Mountain Chateau* (ⓣ03/6492 1404 or 1800 130 002, ⓦwww.federalresorts.com.au; ❼–❽), which has ground-floor rooms in two adjoining guest-wings, casual and upmarket restaurants, a bar serving snacks, a billiard room, tour desk, and an impressive photographic gallery directly opposite (see above).

Lake St Clair and Derwent Bridge

Outside peak walking months, you can register to walk the Overland Track in the opposite direction at the ranger station at **CYNTHIA BAY** on **Lake St Clair** (daily 8am–5pm; ⓣ03/6289 1115), which houses an informative

Rafting on the Franklin

One of the most rugged and inaccessible areas left on earth, the surrounds of the **Franklin River** can't really be seen on foot – few tracks lead through this twisted, tangled and wet rainforest. **Rafting** is the only way to explore the river and even this is possible only between December and early April. The Franklin is reached by rafting down the Collingwood River from the Lyell Highway, 49km west of Derwent Bridge. The full trip takes eight to fourteen days, ending at the Gordon River, where rafters head finally to Strahan by West Coast Yacht Charter (see p.1066) or seaplane with Wilderness Air (see p.1067) from Sir John Falls Camp.

One of the most dangerous Australian rivers to raft, with average **rapids** of grades 3 to 4 – and up to grade 6 in places – the Franklin requires an expedition leader with great skill and experience (though even guides have died in the rapids). It's also very remote, and in the event of an accident help can be days away. Despite this, the river's haunting isolation is part of the attraction for most visitors. The weather, too, can be harsh – and the water is cold. It's inadvisable to attempt the trip **independently** unless everyone in the party has white-water experience and the group leader has made a previous Franklin River trip; groups are required to have at least two rafts and to stay in contact with the **ranger** at Queenstown. Bear in mind that there's nowhere to rent rafting equipment in Tasmania. The **tour operators** don't require you to be experienced – just fit, with lots of stamina and courage. Prices are high, but this is an experience of a lifetime, with the seaplane flight back to Strahan usually included in the price. Water By Nature (Ⓣ0408 242 941 or 1800 111 142, Ⓦwww.franklinrivertasmania.com) offer a five-day ($1540) on the Lower Franklin, a seven-day trip on the Upper Franklin at $1840, or ten-day rafting the full navigable length of the river ($2460). The seven- and ten-day trips include a day-walk to Frenchmans Cap (see opposite), while the five- and ten-day trips include a seaplane flight return to Strahan. Trips are also offered by Rafting Tasmania and Tasmanian Expeditions.

The sketchy *Franklin River Rafting Notesheets* are available free from the Queenstown Ranger Station, PO Box 21, Queenstown, TAS 7467 (Ⓣ03/6471 2511). There are **campsites** all along the Franklin, but most have room for only two or three tents.

The route

From the **Collingwood River**, it takes about three days to raft to the **Frenchmans Cap Track**. This is the **Upper Franklin**, alpine country with vegetation adapted to survive snow and icy winds. Watch out for two endemic pines, the Huon pine and celery-top pine. There are lots of intermediate rapids along this stretch and a deep quartzite ravine and large, still pool at Irenabyss.

The **Middle Franklin** is a mixture of pools, deep ravines and wild rapids as the river makes a 50km detour around Frenchmans Cap. Dramatic limestone cliffs overhang the **Lower Franklin**, which involves a tranquil paddle through dense myrtle beech forests with flowering leatherwoods overhead. The best raftable white-water is here at Newlands Cascades. It's a short distance to **Kutikina Caves** and **Deena-reena**; only rafters can gain access to these Aboriginal caves.

interpretive centre and an attractive bistro restaurant with views over the lake. Short and long **walks** around Lake St Clair are detailed on a board in the centre. You can go on a **cruise** on the MV *Idaclair*, which will drop you off at Narcissus Hut to begin the Overland Track from the southern end, or you can walk back to the centre (5–6hr); alternatively, get off at Echo Point and return on a three-hour bushwalk (summer: Cynthia Bay 9am, 12.30pm & 3pm; Narcissus Hut 9.30am, 1pm & 3.30pm; round trip 1hr 30min; to Echo Point $17; to Narcissus Hut $22 one way, $27 return). Tickets (bookings essential) are sold at the restaurant, where you can enquire about renting dinghies with outboard motors, canoes and kayaks.

The restaurant also takes bookings for **accommodation**. *Lakeside St Clair Wilderness Holidays* (Ⓣ03/6289 1137, Ⓦwww.view.com.au/lakeside; ⑥) has several expensive lodges, and also a backpackers' lodge (dorms $25–30). Compared to Cradle Mountain, the **campsite** here is poor – there's no kitchen and there's even a fee ($0.50 per 6min) to use the showers (though this is handy if you've come all muddy off the Overland Track, as you're welcome to wash here). For supplies (and takeaway alcohol), you have to go to **DERWENT BRIDGE**, 5km away on the Lyell Highway, served by Maxwell's Coaches (Ⓣ03/6289 1125), whose $10 shuttle service runs on demand. At Derwent Bridge you can stay at the well-appointed self-catering *Derwent Bridge Chalets* (Ⓣ03/6289 1000, Ⓦwww.derwent-bridge.com; B&B ⑤–⑥), a couple of which are luxurious spa versions, where you'll be greeted by a welcoming fire, complimentary port and a friendly, considerate host; cheaper motel-style units, with limited kitchen facilities, are also available. The focus of the small community is the atmospheric pub, the *Derwent Bridge Wilderness Hotel* (Ⓣ03/6289 1144; ④), with its huge brick fireplace and high-ceilinged wood-raftered interior and generous, good-value bistro meals. You can stay in old-fashioned, lodge-style accommodation (some rooms en suite) or very basic hostel rooms (dorms $23; no kitchen) out back. Derwent Bridge is close to **Lake King William**, equivalent in size to Lake St Clair and popular with anglers. A must-see is the phenomenal **Wall** on Lyell Highway as you enter Derwent Bridge from the south (9am–5pm; $7.50). This work-in-progress by artist Greg Duncan is a frieze carved in Huon pine **depicting rural life**, each panel some 3m in height. The ten-year project, started in 2005, will eventually be 100m in length.

Franklin Lower Gordon Wild Rivers National Park

The **Franklin Lower Gordon Wild Rivers National Park** was declared in June 1980 and by 1982 had been included with the adjoining parks on the World Heritage List. The park exists for its own sake more than anything, most of it being virtually inaccessible. You can cruise up the Gordon, or fly over it, but the really adventurous can explore by **rafting the Franklin** (see box on p.1071) and walking the **Frenchmans Cap Track**, both accessible from the **Lyell Highway**, which extends from Strahan to Hobart and runs through the park between Queenstown and Derwent Bridge. Plenty of short **walks** also lead from the highway to rainforest, rivers and lookouts.

The **Franklin River** is one of the great rivers of Australia, and the only major wild-river system in Tasmania that's not been dammed. It flows for 120km from the Cheyne Range to the majestic **Gordon River**, from an altitude of 1400m down to almost sea level. Swollen by the storms of the Roaring Forties and fed by many other rivers, it can at times become a raging torrent as it passes through ancient heaths, deep gorges and rainforests. The discovery in 1981 of stone tools in the **Kutikina Cave** on the Lower Franklin proved that during the last Ice Age southwest Tasmania was the most southerly point of human occupation on earth.

A **seaplane** from Strahan flies over the national park (see p.1067), and from it you can see the confluence of the two rivers – the planned site of the ill-fated dam – surrounded by thick forest, much of it impenetrable and probably never traversed by humans. The Gordon appears wide and slow compared to the narrow, winding Franklin.

Along the Lyell Highway (A10)

Heading east from Queenstown, the Lyell Highway (A10) enters the Franklin Lower Gordon Wild Rivers National Park, reaching Nelson River bridge after 4km, from where **Nelson Falls** is an easy twenty-minute return walk through temperate rainforest. From here, the road begins to wind and rise up to **Collingwood River**, the starting point for raft or canoe trips down the Franklin (see box p.1071), with some basic camping facilities.

In fine weather, the white-quartzite dome of Frenchmans Cap, looking a little like snow, can be seen from the highway. For a more spectacular viewpoint that takes in the Franklin River Valley, **Donaghy's Hill Wilderness Lookout Walk** begins further along the highway on the right. Walk from the parking area along the old road to the top of the hill, where a sign marks the beginning of the forty-minute return track. Further along the highway, the **walking track to Frenchmans Cap** (see below) begins with a fifteen-minute stroll to the suspension bridge over the river. Continuing on the Lyell, you have another opportunity to see the Franklin on a ten-minute **Nature Trail**, at a point where the river is tranquil, as it flows around large boulders; there's also a longer 25-minute circuit. At the start of the trail there's a picnic area and a wooden shelter with an **interpretive board** about the river. Beyond this point, open button-grass plains take over, huge uninhabited expanses fringed with trees. This is **Wombat Glen**, which looks as though it's been cleared into grazing country until you step out into it and discover its bog-like nature.

At the foot of **Mount Arrowsmith**, the highway begins to ascend, winding around the mountain's southern side above the U-shaped glacial Surprise Valley. The **Surprise Valley Lookout** offers a good view of the valley and, across to the southwest, another excellent aspect of Frenchmans Cap. Continuing down, you come to King William Saddle, another fine lookout point with views of the **King William Range** to the south and **Mount Rufus** to the north.

The Frenchmans Cap Track

The most prominent mountain peak in the Franklin Lower Gordon Wild Rivers National Park is the white-quartzite dome of **Frenchmans Cap** (1446m). Its southeast face has a sheer five-hundred-metre cliff and from its summit there are uninterrupted views of Mount Ossa in the Cradle Mountain–Lake St Clair National Park, Federation Peak, Macquarie Harbour and, on a fine day, the whole of the southwest wilderness. It takes three to five days to do the 54-kilometre return trip to the summit, best done between December and March, though of the seven hundred who walk the track each year, only six hundred do so between these months. Frenchmans Cap is much more demanding than the relatively straightforward Overland Track, as it has some very steep extended climbs and sections of mud, and should be attempted only by skilled bushwalkers – preferably with experience of other Tasmanian walks. The weather is temperamental: it rains frequently, and it can snow even in summer. Beyond Barron Pass, the track is above 900m and at any time of the year is subject to high winds, mist, rain, hail and snowfalls.

The track begins at the Lyell Highway, 55km from Queenstown, served by TassieLink's scheduled Hobart–Queenstown service (5 weekly), or you can charter Maxwell's Coaches (Ⓣ03/6492 1431) for $65 from Lake St Clair. A fifteen-minute walk from the road brings you to the suspension bridge across the river for the start of the walk. Record your plans in the registration book here and again in the logbook at the two huts at Lake Vera and Lake Tahune that provide basic **accommodation** (though this is usually full and you must bring tents and stoves with you); Frenchmans Cap is a proclaimed "Fuel Stove Only Area". There are composting toilets at both huts and plenty of camping spots along the way; water along the track is safe to drink. From the Franklin River to Lake Vera the well-defined track crosses plains and foothills, then becomes steep and rough as it climbs to Barron Pass – where there are magnificent views – becoming easier again on the way to Lake Tahune, close to the cliffs of Frenchmans Cap. From here it's a steep 1km walk to the summit, before returning the same way.

For further **information**, get the free *Frenchmans Cap Track Bushwalker Notes* and the *Frenchmans Cap Map and Notes* ($9.10); or contact the Queenstown Ranger Station (Ⓣ03/6471 2511). Craclair Tours (see p.1069), organizes five-day guided treks (ex-Launceston $1150), and Tasmanian Expeditions offers a five-day trip (see p.979; ex-Launceston; Dec–March; $1150).

The South West National Park

Tasmania's **South West National Park** is an area of contrast: arrow-sharp, crested ranges of white quartzite cut across buttongrass plains. The isolation, rough terrain and unpredictable weather, even in summer – the southwest has more than two hundred days of rain a year – means that this is an area for experienced bushwalkers only. Being able to use a compass and read a map are important, but so is a tolerance for trudging through deep mud and swampy buttongrass while heavily laden with supplies and plagued by leeches.

The map *South Coast Walks* ($9.10) covers the southern gateways to the World Heritage Area: Cockle Creek through Port Davey to Scotts Peak, as well as Moonlight Ridge and South West Cape, including notes on track conditions, weather and campsites. For the rest of the area you'll need to purchase Tasmap topographic **maps**.

Two airlines operate **flights** into the national park from Cambridge aerodrome, 15km from Hobart. **Par Avion** (Ⓣ03/6248 5390, Ⓦwww.paravion.com.au) offers a charter service to Melaleuca, weather permitting (45min; $155 one way, $290 return); you can register your walk at the airstrip. They also offer a combined scenic flight and boat trip on Melaleuca Inlet (4hr; $170) or Bathurst Harbour (full day; $275 including lunch. Roaring 40s Ocean Kayaking (see p.979) offers amazing **kayaking expeditions**: you're flown in to Melaleuca and then spend six days camping and kayaking on Port Davey and Bathurst Harbour ($2250; shorter 3-day trip $1525). **TasAir** (Ⓣ03/6248 5088, Ⓦwww.tasair.com.au) flies to Melaleuca or Cox Bight (both $176 one way, $330 return, min 2 passengers), which can cut out the trudge from Melaleuca, and also offers joyrides over the whole of the World Heritage Area from Hobart for

The flooding of Lake Pedder

To Senator Bob Brown, Tasmania's foremost Green activist, **Lake Pedder** "was one of the most gently beautiful places on the planet". The glacial lake, in the Frankland Range in Tasmania's southwest, had an area of 9.7 square kilometres until 1972, when it and the surrounding valleys were flooded as part of a huge hydroelectric scheme, creating a reservoir covering a massive 240 square kilometres and reached by the Lake Gordon Road via Maydena. Before then, the lake was so inaccessible that it could only be visited by foot or by light aircraft, which used to land on the perfect sand of the lake beach. In late 1994, a scientist revealed that, beneath the water, the sandy beach remained; in 1995, divers filmed underwater, revealing the still-visible impressions of light-aircraft tyre tracks. Certain scientists and conservationists, backed by the Wilderness Society, believe if Lake Pedder were drained it would revert to its former state, though it might take up to thirty years.

$243 (2hr 30min, includes a landing and refreshment at Cox Bight). If you're planning an extended walk, you can arrange for either airline to drop food supplies for you ($4.40 per kilo).

Unless you're flying in, or beginning a walk at **Cockle Creek**, south of Hobart, access to the South West National Park is via the **Gordon River Road**, which passes to the south of Mount Field National Park. The ranger for this (northern) end of South West National Park is based at Mount Field (see p.1007) and you should drop in or call to ask about conditions and to check that you're adequately prepared. The good sealed road heads through state forest and the South West Conservation Area, where the amazing craggy landforms of the **Frankland Range** loom above and signposts helpfully point out the names of the features, and past the drowned **Lake Pedder** (see box opposite) and the Gordon Dam's power station. The Hydro Tasmania–run Gordon Dam Visitors Information Centre is at the end of Gordon River Road, above the dam (Nov–April daily 10am–5pm; May–Oct daily 11am–3pm; ⓣ03/6280 1134). The Gordon Dam lookout here is breathtaking, and if you're after a thrill you can abseil down it with Aardvark Adventures (ⓣ03/6273 7722, ⓦwww.aardvarkadventures.com.au; 4–5hr; $170) who will meet you at the site.

You can **stay** at Lake Pedder at the refurbished *Lake Pedder Chalet* (ⓣ03/6280 1166; shared-bathroom or en-suite rooms ❷–❹), a former staff house for the HEC that has lake views; facilities include a bar and bistro. Alternatively there are a number of free **campsites** in the area: just down the road on the shore of Lake Pedder, *Ted's Beach* has a shelter shed, electric barbecues, water and toilets; and there are two more campgrounds at Scotts Peak at the southern end of Lake Pedder, where the Port Davey walk begins (see p.1076). TassieLink runs a "Wilderness Link" service to Scotts Peak and to Condominium Creek (Mount Anne) from Hobart, via Mount Field (Nov–April).

Western Arthurs Traverse and Federation Peak

The most spectacular bushwalk in Tasmania, only 20km in length and 5km in width, **Western Arthurs Traverse** takes in 25 major peaks and 30 lakes. The last glacial period gouged into this range, leaving sharp quartzite ridges, craggy towers and impressive cliffs, and carving cirque valleys that are now filled by dark, tannin-stained lakes, surrounded by contrasting buttongrass plains. Violent storms, mists and continuous rain can plague the route in summer since it's in the direct path of the Roaring Forties. Crossing these ranges makes for a superb but difficult walk, taking between nine and twelve days, and camping areas are limited. Though there's no man-made track, the route, starting at Scotts Peak Road, is not difficult to follow; it involves scrambling over roots and branches and making short descents and ascents into gullies and cliff lines, and you'll need to use a rope at some point.

The **Eastern Arthur Range** is the location of the major goal for intrepid southwest walkers – **Federation Peak**, often considered the most challenging in Australia, with its steep, almost perfectly triangular outline rising starkly above the surrounding rugged peaks and ridges. It was named by a surveyor in 1901, the year of federation, when most of the major landmarks in the southwest were still unvisited; in fact, the peak was not successfully scaled until 1949, its thick scrub, forests and cliffs having kept walkers at bay. Although the walk is now easier since the terrain has been "broken in", each year many walkers are turned back by the worst weather in Tasmania, and one person has died tackling the route. All the ascents are extremely difficult, and most parties take between seven and ten days to reach the peak and return; minor rock-climbing is required to get to the summit. The walk begins at the same point as the Port Davey Track.

Mount Anne Circuit

The highest peak in the southwest, **Mount Anne** (1423m) is part of a small range capped with red dolerite – a contrast to the surrounding white quartzite. Views from the summit are spectacular in fine weather, but even in summer the route is very exposed and prone to bad weather. It's suitable only for experienced walkers carrying a safety rope. The three- to four-day walk begins 20km along Scotts Peak Road at Condominium Creek (where there are basic camping facilities) and ends 9km south at Red Tape Creek; a car shuttle might be advisable, or you can be picked up and dropped off from Hobart with TassieLink's "Wilderness Link" service (Nov–April).

Port Davey Track

Going straight through the heart of the World Heritage Area, from Scotts Peak Dam south to Melaleuca (where you fly out; see p.1075), is the little-used 70km **Port Davey Track**, a wet, muddy four- to five-day trek over buttongrass plains, with views of rugged mountain ranges along the way. It's less interesting than some of the other walks in the area and most groups combine it with the South Coast Track for a ten- to sixteen-day wilderness experience, which requires a drop-off of food supplies. This combined walk is often called the **South West Track**. TassieLink offers a "Wilderness Link" (Nov–April) service to Scotts Peak.

South Coast Track

The **South Coast Track** is known for its magnificent **beaches** and spectacular coastal scenery of Aboriginal **middens**, rainforest and buttongrass ridges. At 85km, it's one of the longest tracks in the South West National Park – a six- to eight-day moderate-to-difficult walk, usually done from Melaleuca east to Cockle Creek. Since the route is mostly along the coast, the climate is milder than in many parts of the World Heritage Area but there is exposure to cold southerly winds and frequent rain; also, while crossing the exposed Ironbound Range (900m), even in summer it can sleet or snow. Elsewhere, you do need to plough through sections of mud. There are no huts along the way, except at the Melaleuca airstrip. Around a thousand people do the walk each year, 75 percent of them between December and March. The best **approach** is to fly direct to Cox Bight with TasAir, cutting out the boring buttongrass-plains walk from Melaleuca, then head for Cockle Creek where TassieLink provides a "Wilderness Link" (Nov–April) service to Hobart. Alternatively, you can begin at Cockle Creek and fly out at Melaleuca with TasAir or Par Avion, or arrange for extra food supplies to be flown in at Melaleuca and continue along the Port Davey Track across the water, using the rowboats provided.

Tasmanian Expeditions (see p.979) runs an extended **organized walk** of the South Coast Track (Nov–March; $1990). You need to be very fit for the nine-day trip, as each party member (maximum of ten) carries a share of the food and tents, a weight of 18–20kg. They also offer a 16-day trip ($3200), which combines the South Coast Track with the Port Davey Track, above.

South West Cape

The granite South West Cape juts out for 3km into the wild Southern Ocean. **Walking** is fairly easy here, though the rough unmarked tracks across open countryside require sound navigation, and some high, windy ridges have to be crossed. All routes start and end at Melaleuca or Cox Bight but there are a variety of ways to the cape and beyond, taking in different beaches and bays. Depending on which you choose, a simple route will take from three to seven days, and the full circuit between six and nine. Because of the growing popularity of the walks, they may be overcrowded in the summer months.

Travel details

Between Tasmania and the mainland states

Ferries

Spirit of Tasmania Bass Strait ferry from Port Melbourne to Devonport (1–2 daily; 10hr).

Flights

Mainly through Sydney's Mascot or Melbourne's Tullamarine airports, with smaller companies operating from Essendon and Moorabbin airports, on the fringes of Melbourne.

Flinders Island to: Launceston (2–4 daily; 45min); Melbourne (Moorabbin 4 weekly; 50min).

King Island to: Burnie (3 daily Mon–Fri, 2 daily Sat & Sun; 45min); Devonport (4 daily Mon–Fri, 2 daily Sat & Sun; 45min); Melbourne (Tullamarine 5 weekly; 45min).

Melbourne to: Burnie (4 daily; 1hr); Devonport (4 daily; 1hr); Flinders Island (Essendon 4 weekly; 50min); Hobart (10 daily; 1hr); King Island (Tullamarine 5 weekly; 45min); Launceston (10 daily; 1hr).

Sydney to: Hobart (4–7 daily; 2hr 20min); Launceston (1–3 daily; 2hr 35min).

Transport on the island

Buses – scheduled services

Burnie to: Smithton via the northwest coast (1–3 daily Mon–Sat, 1 daily Sun; 1hr 30min).

Deloraine to: Devonport (3 daily; 40min); Hobart (2–4 daily; 4hr); Launceston (3–5 daily; 45min).

Devonport to: Burnie (3–6 daily; 50min); Cradle Mountain (3 weekly; 2hr 15min); Deloraine (3 daily; 40min); Hobart (2–4 daily; 5hr 30min); Launceston (3–5 daily; 1hr 30min); Queenstown (3 weekly; 7hr).

Hobart to: Bicheno (3–6 weekly; 4hr); Burnie (3–6 daily; 4hr 45min); Cygnet (3 on Thurs, 1 daily rest of week; 55min); Deloraine (2–4 daily; 4hr); Devonport (2–4 daily; 5hr 30min); Dover (2 daily Mon–Fri; 55min); Geeveston (4 daily Mon–Fri, 1 daily Sun; 1hr 15min); Kettering (Mon–Fri 4 daily; 40min); Lake St Clair (4 weekly; 3hr); Launceston (3–7 daily; 2hr 30min); New Norfolk (1–7 daily; 30min); Port Arthur (2 daily Mon–Fri; 2hr); Queenstown via New Norfolk, Lake St Clair and Frenchmans Cap with connections to Strahan (5 weekly; 7hr 45min); Richmond (5 daily Mon–Fri; 25min); St Helens (1–2 daily except Sat; 3hr); St Marys (1–2 daily except Sat; 3hr); Swansea (1–2 daily except Sat; 2hr 30min–3hr 30min).

Launceston to: Bicheno (3 daily except Sat; 2hr 40min); Burnie (3–6 daily; 3hr); Cradle Mountain (3 weekly; 4hr); Deloraine (2–5 daily; 45min); Derby (1–2 daily except Sat; 2hr 40min); Devonport (3–5 daily; 1hr 30min); Hobart (3–7 daily; 2hr 30min); Mole Creek (1 daily Mon–Fri; 1hr 30min); Queenstown (3 weekly; 7hr); St Helens via St Marys (1 daily except Sat; 2hr 45min).

Queenstown to: Strahan (5 weekly; 45min).

Scottsdale to: Bridport (2 daily Mon–Fri; 30min).

Ferries

Beauty Point to: George Town (2–3 daily Mon–Sat, 2 daily Sun; 15–20min).

Bridport to: Flinders Island (1 weekly; 8hr).

Kettering to: Bruny Island (10–11 daily Mon–Sat, 8 daily Sun; 20min).

Triabunna to: Maria Island (1–2 daily; 45min).

Contexts

Contexts

History

The first European settlers saw Australia as *terra nullius* – empty land – on the principle that Aborigines didn't "use" the country in an agricultural sense, a belief that remained uncontested in law until 1992. However, decades of archeological work, the reports of early settlers and oral tradition have established that humans had occupied Australia for a minimum of forty thousand years – evidence that Aboriginal peoples shaped, controlled and used their environment as surely as any farmer. Even so, it's difficult for visitors to form an idea of pre-colonial times, as two centuries of European rule shattered traditional Aboriginal life, and evidence of those earlier times mostly consists of cryptic art sites and legends – though if you're lucky enough to get beyond the tourist image, you'll realize that Aboriginal culture, though being redefined, is far from confined to the past. The very simplified outline of Aboriginal history below is intended mainly as a background to accounts given in the Guide, followed by a fuller description of the years since European colonization.

From Gondwana to the Dreamtime

After the break-up of the supercontinent **Gondwana** into India, Africa, South America, Australasia and Antarctica, Australia moved away from the South Pole, reaching its current geographical location about fifteen million years ago. Though the mainland was periodically joined to New Guinea and Tasmania, there was never a land link with the rest of Asia, and the country developed a unique fauna. Most notably marsupials, or pouched mammals, became common, but a whole range of giant animals – the megafauna – also flourished, along with widespread rainforests, until about fifty thousand years ago. Subsequent Ice Ages dried out the climate; by six thousand years ago the seas had stabilized at their present levels and Australia's environment was much as it appears today: an arid centre with a relatively fertile eastern seaboard. **Humans** had been in Australia long before then of course, most likely taking advantage of low sea levels to cross the Timor Trough into northern Australia, or island-hop from Indonesia onto what is now the Cape York Peninsula via New Guinea. Exactly when this happened, how many times it happened and what the colonists did next are debatable. There's no direct evidence for either distinct or continuous migrations from Asia, but since the earliest dated sites are found in the south of Australia, it seems reasonable to believe that human occupation goes back further than scientists' current estimate of forty thousand years. The oldest known remains from central Australia are only 22,000 years old, so it's also fairly plausible that initial colonization occurred around the coast, followed by later exploration of the interior – though it's just as likely that corrosive rainforests, which covered the centre until about twenty thousand years ago, obliterated all trace of earlier human habitation. When the European settlers arrived, the **thylacine** (Tasmanian tiger) had disappeared from the Australian mainland but still lived in Tasmania, while the dingo, a descendant of the domesticated dogs introduced to Australia by Aborigines, was prevalent on the mainland but unknown in Tasmania. This indicates that there was a further influx of people and **dogs** more recently than twelve thousand years ago, after rising sea levels had separated Tasmania and it had become an island. The earliest inhabitants used crude **stone implements**, gradually replaced by a more refined technology based around lighter tools, **boomerangs**, and the use of core stones to flake "blanks", which were then fashioned into spearheads, knives and scrapers. As only certain types of stone were suitable for the process, tribes living further away from quarries had to trade with those living near them. **Trade networks** for rock, **ochre** (a red clay used for ceremonial purposes) and other products – shells and even wood for canoes – eventually stretched from New Guinea to the heart of the continent, following river systems away from the coast. **Rock art**, preserved in an ancient engraved tradition, and other more recent painted styles seem to indicate that cultural links also travelled along these trade routes – similar symbols and styles are found in widely separated regions.

It's probable that the disappearance of the megafauna was accelerated by Aboriginal hunting, but the most dramatic change wrought by the original Australians was the controlled use of **fire** to clear areas of forest. Burning promoted new growth and encouraged game, indirectly expanding grassland and favouring certain plants – cycads, grasstrees, banksias and eucalypts – which evolved fire-reliant seeds and growth patterns. But while the Aborigines modified the environment for their own ends, their belief that land, wildlife and people were an interdependent whole engendered a sympathy for natural processes, and maintained a balance between the population and natural resources. Tribes were organized and related according to complex kinship systems, reflected in the three hundred different **languages** known to exist at that time. Legends about the mythical **Dreamtime**, when creative forces shaped the landscape, provided verbal maps of tribal territory and linked natural features to the actions of these Dreamtime ancestors, who often had both human and animal forms. This spiritual and practical attachment to tribal areas was expedient in terms of use of resources, but was the weak point in maintaining a culture after white dispossession: separated from the lands they related to, legends lost their meaning, and the people their sense of identity.

The first Europeans

Prior to the sixteenth century, the only regular visitors to Australia were the **Malays**, who established seasonal camps while fishing the northern coasts for trepang, a sea slug, to sell to the Chinese. In Europe, the globe had been carved up between Spain and Portugal in 1494 under the auspices of Pope Alexander VI at the **Treaty of Tordesillas**, and all maritime nations subsequently kept their nautical charts secret, to protect their discoveries. It's possible, therefore, that the inquisitive **Portuguese** knew of **Terra Australis**, the Great Southern Land, soon after founding their colony in East Timor in 1516.

But while the precise date of "discovery" is contentious, it is clear that various nations were making forays into the area: the **Dutch** in 1605 and 1623, who were appalled by the harsh climate and inhabitants of Outback Queensland, and the **Spanish** in 1606, who were looking for both plunder and pagans to convert to Catholicism. The latter, guided by **Luis Vaes de Torres**, blithely navigated the strait between New Guinea and Cape York as if they knew it was there. As Torres hailed from Portugal it is indeed likely that he knew where he was; there's evidence that the Portuguese had **mapped** a large portion of Australia's northern coastline as early as 1536.

Later in the seventeenth century, the Dutch navigators **Dirk Hartog**, **Van Diemen** and **Abel Tasman** added to maps of the east and north coasts, but eventually discarded "New Holland" as a barren, worthless country. British interest was first stirred in 1697 by **William Dampier**, a buccaneer who wrote popular accounts of his visit to Western Australia. However, it wasn't until the British captured the Spanish port of Manila, in the Philippines, in 1762, that detailed maps of Australia's coast fell into their hands; it took them only six more years to assemble an expedition to locate the continent. Sailing in 1768 on the *Endeavour*, **Captain James Cook** headed to Tahiti, then proceeded to map New Zealand's coastline before sailing west in 1770 to search for the Great Southern Land – unsure whether this was New Holland or an as yet undiscovered landmass.

The British sighted the continent in April 1770 and sailed north from Cape Everard to **Botany Bay**, where Cook commented on the Aborigines' initial indifference to seeing the *Endeavour*. When a party of forty sailors attempted to land, however, two Aborigines attacked them with spears; the British drove them off with musket fire. Continuing on up the Queensland coast, the British passed Moreton Bay and Fraser Island before entering the treacherous passages of the Great Barrier Reef where, on June 11, the *Endeavour* ran aground off Cape Tribulation. Cook managed to beach the ship safely at the mouth of the Endeavour River (present-day Cooktown), where the expedition set up camp while the ship was repaired.

Contact between Aborigines and whites during the following six weeks was tinged with a mistrust that never quite erupted into serious confrontation, and Cook took the opportunity to make notes in which he tempered romanticism for the "noble savage" with the sharp observation that European and Aboriginal values were mutually incomprehensible. The expedition was intrigued by some of Australia's wildlife, but otherwise unimpressed with the country, and were glad to sail onwards on August 5. With imposing skill, Cook successfully managed to navigate the rest of the reef, finally claiming possession of the country – which he named **New South Wales** – for King George III on August 21, at Possession Island in the Torres Strait, before sailing off to Timor.

Convicts

The expedition's reports didn't arouse much enthusiasm in London however, and the disdainful attitude towards the Great Southern Land matched the opinion voiced by the Dutch more than a century before. However, after the loss of its American colonies after the **American War of Independence** in 1783, Britain was deprived of a handy location to offload convicted criminals. They were temporarily housed in prison ships or "hulks", moored around the country, while the government tried to solve the problem. **Sir Joseph Banks**, botanist on the *Endeavour*, advocated Botany Bay as an ideal location for a **penal colony** that could soon become self-sufficient. The government agreed (perhaps also inspired by the political advantages of gaining a foothold in the Pacific), and in 1787 the **First Fleet**, packed with over seven hundred convicts, set sail for Australia on eleven ships, under the command of **Captain Arthur Phillip**. Reaching Botany Bay in January 1788, Phillip deemed it unsuitable for his purposes and instead founded the settlement at **Sydney Cove**, on Port Jackson's fine natural harbour.

The early years at Sydney were not promising: the colonists suffered erratic weather and starvation, Aboriginal hostility, soil that was too hard to plough, and timber so tough it dented their axes. In 1790, supplies ran so low that a third of the population had to be transferred to a new colony on **Norfolk Island**, 1500 kilometres northeast. Even so, in the same year Britain dispatched a second fleet with a thousand more convicts – 267 of whom died en route. To ease the situation, Phillip granted packages of farmland to marines and former convicts before he returned to Britain in 1792. The first **free settlers** arrived the following year, and Britain's preoccupation with the French Revolutionary Wars meant a reduction in the number of convicts being transported to the colony, thus allowing a period of consolidation.

Meanwhile, **John Macarthur** manipulated the temporary governor into allowing his **New South Wales Corps**, which had replaced the marines as the governor's strong arm, to exercise considerable power in the colony. This was temporarily curtailed in 1800 by **Philip King**, who also slowed an illicit rum trade, encouraged new settlements, and speeded production by allowing convicts to work for wages. Macarthur was forced out of the corps into the wool industry, importing Australia's first **sheep** from South Africa. He continued to stir up trouble though, which culminated in the **Rum Rebellion** of 1808, when merchant and pastoral factions, supported by the military, ousted **Governor William Bligh**. Britain finally took notice of the colony's anarchic state and appointed the firm-handed **Colonel Lachlan Macquarie**, backed by the 73rd Regiment, as Bligh's replacement in 1810. Macquarie settled the various disputes – Macarthur had fled to Britain a year earlier – and brought eleven years of disciplined progress to the colony.

Labelled the "Father of Australia", for his vision of a country that could rise above its convict origins, Macquarie implemented enlightened policies towards former convicts or **emancipists**, enrolling them in public offices. He also attempted to educate, rather than exterminate, Aboriginal people and was the driving force behind New South Wales becoming a productive, self-sufficient colony. But he offended the landowner **squatters**, who were concerned that emancipists were being granted too many favours, and also those who regarded the colony solely as a place of punishment. In fact, conditions had improved so much that by 1819 New South Wales had become the major destination for voluntary emigrants from Britain.

In 1821 Macquarie was replaced as governor, and his successor, Sir Thomas Brisbane, was instructed to segregate, not integrate, convicts. To this end, when New South Wales officially graduated from being a penal settlement to a new British colony in 1823, convicts were used to colonize newly explored regions – Western Australia, Tasmania and Queensland – as far away from Sydney's free settlers as possible.

Explorers

Matthew Flinders had already circumnavigated the mainland in 1803 (and suggested the name "**Australia**") in his leaky vessel, the *Investigator*, and with the colony firmly established, expeditions began pushing inland from Sydney. In 1823, John Oxley, the Surveyor General, having previously explored newly discovered pastoral land west of the Blue Mountains, chose the **Brisbane River** in Queensland as the site of a new penal colony, thus opening up the fertile Darling Downs to future settlement. Meanwhile, townships were being founded elsewhere around the coast, eventually leading to the creation of **separate colonies** to add to that of Van Diemen's Land (Tasmania), settled in

1803 to ward off French exploration: Albany and Fremantle on the west coast were established in 1827 and 1829 respectively, followed by the Yarra River (Melbourne, Victoria) in 1835, and Adelaide (South Australia) in 1836.

But it was the possibilities of the **interior** – which some maintained concealed a vast inland sea – which captured the imagination of the government and squatters. Setting out from Adelaide in 1844, **Charles Sturt** was the first to attempt to cross the centre. Forced to camp for six months at a desert waterhole, where the heat melted the lead in his pencils and unthreaded screws from equipment, he managed to reach the aptly named Sturt's Stony Desert before scurvy forced him back to Adelaide. At the same time, **Ludwig Leichhardt**, a Prussian doctor, had more luck in his crossing between the Darling Downs and Port Essington, near Darwin, which he accomplished in fourteen months. Unlike Sturt, Leichhardt found plenty of potential farmland and returned a hero. He vanished in 1848 however, while again attempting to cross the continent. In the same year, the ill-fated **Kennedy** expedition managed the trek from Tully to Cape York in northern Queensland, but with the loss of most of the party – Kennedy included – as a result of poor planning, starvation and attack by Aborigines. Similarly, **Burke and Wills**' successful 1860 south-to-north traverse between Melbourne and the Gulf of Carpentaria in Queensland was marred by the death of the expedition leaders upon their return south, owing to bad organization and a series of unfortunate errors (see box, p.514 for the full story of their trek). Finally, Australia's centre was located by **John MacDouall Stuart** in 1860, who subsequently managed a safe return journey to Adelaide from the north coast the following year. Hopes of finding an inland sea were quashed, and the harsh reality of a dry, largely infertile interior began to dawn on developers.

Aboriginal response

British advances had been repulsed from the very first year of the colony's foundation; Governor Phillip reporting that "the natives now attack any straggler they meet unarmed". Forced off their traditional hunting grounds, which were taken by the settlers for agriculture or grazing, the Aborigines began stealing crops and spearing cattle. Response from the British was brutal; the relatively liberal Lieutenant-Governor George Arthur ordered a sweep of Tasmania in 1830, to round up all Aboriginal people and herd them into **reserves**, a symbolic attempt to clear "the uncivilized" from the paths of progress (see box, pp.976–977). More direct action, such as the **Myall Creek Massacre** in 1838 (see box, p.336), when 28 Aborigines were roped together and butchered by graziers, created public outcry, but similar "**dispersals**" became commonplace wherever indigenous people resisted white intrusion. More insidious methods, such as poisoning waterholes or lacing gifts of flour with arsenic, were also employed by pastoralists angered over stock losses.

The Aboriginal people were not a single, unified society, and the British exploited existing divisions by creating the notorious **Native Mounted Police**, an Aboriginal force that aided and abetted the extermination of rival groups. By the 1890s, citing a perversion of Darwinian theory which held that Aboriginal people were less evolved than whites and so doomed to extinction, most states had followed Tasmania's example of "**protectionism**", relocating Aborigines into reserves which were frequently a long way from their traditional lands – in Queensland, for instance, Rockhampton Aborigines were moved to Fraser Island, 500km away.

Gold

The discovery of **gold** in 1851 by Edward Hargraves, fresh from the California fields, had a dramatic bearing on Australia's future. The first major strikes in New South Wales and Victoria brought an immediate rush of hopeful miners from Sydney and Melbourne and, once the news spread overseas, from the USA and Britain. The British government, realizing the absurdity of spending taxes on shipping criminals to a land of gold when there were plenty of people willing to pay for their passage, finally **ended transportation** in 1853. Gold also opened up Australia's interior far more thoroughly than explorers had done; as returns petered out in one area, prospectors moved on into uncharted regions to find more. Western Australia and Queensland (which was saved from bankruptcy by the discovery of gold in 1867) experienced booms up until 1900 and, although mining initially followed in the path of pastoral expansion, the rushes began to attract settlements and markets into previously uncultivated regions.

A new "level society", based on a work-and-mateship ethic, evolved on the goldfields, where education had little bearing on an ability to endure hard work and spartan living conditions. Yet the **diggers** were all too aware of their poor social and political rights. At the end of 1854, frustrations over mining licences erupted at **Eureka** (see box, p.925), on the outskirts of Ballarat in Victoria, where miners built a stockade and ended up being charged by mounted police. Twenty-two of the miners were killed in the event, which is commonly regarded as a turning point in Australian history. The surviving rebels – put on trial for high treason – were vindicated, and rights, including the vote, were granted to miners. The Victorian goldfields also saw **racial tensions** directed against a new minority, the Chinese, who first arrived there during the 1850s. Disheartened by diminishing returns and infuriated by the Chinese ability to find gold in abandoned claims, diggers stormed a Chinese camp at **Lambing Flat** in 1861. Troops had to be sent in to stop the riots, but the ringleaders were later acquitted by an all-white jury. Throughout the country, goldfields became centres of **nationalism** (despite the fact that the Chinese improved life by running stores and market gardens in mining towns), peaking in Queensland in the 1880s, where the flames were fanned by the importation of **Solomon Islanders** to work on sugar plantations. Ostensibly to prevent slavery, but politically driven by recession and growing white unemployment, the government forced the repatriation of Islanders, taxed the Chinese out of the country, and passed the 1901 Immigration Act – also known as the **White Australia policy** – which greatly restricted non-European immigration.

Federation and war

Central government was first mooted in 1842, but new states were not keen to return to the control by New South Wales, lose interstate customs duties, or share the new-found mineral wealth which had consolidated separation in the first place. But by the end of the century they began to see advantages to **Federation**, not least as a way to control indentured labour and present a united front against French, German and Russian expansion in the Pacific. A decade of wrangling by the states, to ensure equal representation irrespective of population, saw the formation of a High Court and a two-tier parliamentary system consisting of a House of Representatives and Senate, presided over by a Prime Minister. Each state would have its own premier, and Britain would be represented by a Governor-General. Approved by Queen Victoria shortly before her death, the **Commonwealth of Australia** came into being on January 1, 1901.

It's notable that the Immigration Act (see opposite) was the first piece of legislation to be passed by the new parliament, and reflected the nationalist drive behind federation. Though the intent was to create an Australia largely of European – and preferably British – descent, the policy also sowed the seeds for Australian independence from the "Mother Country". The first pull away came as early as 1912, when the **Commonwealth Bank** opened; Australia was trying to become less financially reliant on Britain. Centred entirely on white interests, the White Australia policy ensured that Aboriginal people were not included in the national census, nor were they allowed to vote, until 1967. The new government did, however, give white **women** the vote in 1902, and the Australian Labor Party, which had grown out of the economic recession and union battles with the government during the 1890s, established the concept of a **minimum wage** in 1907.

Defence had also been a positive force behind federation. But even though the war between Japan and Russia in 1904 had highlighted the need to build its own defence force, Australia was largely unprepared for the outbreak of hostilities in Europe a decade later, owning little more than a navy made up of secondhand British ships. Promising to support Britain to "the last man and the last shilling", there was a patriotic rush to enlist in the army, and an opportunistic occupation of German New Guinea by Australian forces. Surprisingly, the issue of compulsory conscription, raised by **Prime Minister Billy Hughes**, was twice defeated in referendums during World War I.

From the Australian perspective, the most important stage of the war occurred when Turkey gave its support to Germany in 1915. **Winston Churchill** formulated a plan to defend British shipping in the Dardanelles by occupying the **Gallipoli Peninsula**, and diverted Australian infantry bound for Europe. Between April and December 1915, wave after wave of Australian troops were mown down below Turkish gun emplacements, as they attempted to take control of the peninsula. By the end of the year, it became clear that Gallipoli was not going to fall, and the survivors were evacuated to fight on the Western Front. The long-term effect of the slaughter was the first serious questioning of Anglo-Australian relations: should Australia have committed and sacrificed so much to defend a (geographically) distant country's interests? Conversely, Gallipoli, as Australia's debut on the world stage, is still to this day treated as a symbol of national identity and pride.

1918–39

After World War I, the Nationalist Party joined forces with the **Country Party**, to assume government under the paternalistic and fiercely anti-socialist guidance of **Earle Page** and **Stanley Bruce**. The Country Party was formed as a result of the widening divisions between the growing urban population and farmers, who felt isolated and unrepresented politically. Under the coalition, pastoral industries were subsidized by overseas borrowing, allowing them to compete internationally, and technology began to close the gap between the city and the Outback. Radio and aviation developments saw the birth of **Qantas** – the Queensland and Northern Territory Aerial Service – and the

Royal Flying Doctor Service in Queensland's remote west. Development also occurred in the cities: work started on the Sydney Harbour Bridge, and the new Commonwealth capital, **Canberra**, was completed.

On the social front, the USA stopped mass immigration in 1921, deflecting a flood of people from depressed **Southern Europe** to Australia, which the government countered by encouraging British immigrants with assisted passages. While progressive in some areas – a dole was proposed for the unemployed, the sick, pensioners and mothers – the government overreacted to opposition, as exemplified by their response to the **seamen and dockers' strike** of 1928. Citing the arch-villain, "communism", as being behind the dispute, they attempted to stretch the scope of the Immigration Act to allow action to be taken against disturbances that were politically motivated. However, the implication that the law could be altered against anyone who disagreed with the government contributed to the downfall of Bruce and Page the following year. The themes of their rule, however – differences between rural and urban societies, questions of Australian identity, union disputes, and the effects of heavy borrowing to create artificially high living standards, unsupported by Australia's actual capabilities – are issues that are still relevant today.

As the **Great Depression** set in during the early 1930s, Australia faced the collapse of its economic and political systems, with all the parties divided. Pressed for a loan, the Bank of England forced a restructuring of the Australian economy. Adding to national embarrassment, politics and sports became blurred during the 1932 "**body-line**" cricket series: the loan was made virtually conditional on the Australian cricket authorities dropping their allegations that British bowlers were deliberately trying to injure Australian batsmen during the tour.

Meanwhile, worries about communism were succeeded by concern about the rise of fascism, as Mussolini and Hitler took power in Europe and Japanese forces invaded Manchuria – the **Tanaka memorial** in 1927 actually cited Australia as a target for future conquest by Japan. Although displaying a certain ambivalence towards fascism, Australia assisted the immigration of refugees from central Europe, and – after a prolonged union battle – halted iron exports to Japan. When Prime Minister Joseph Lyons died in office, **Robert Menzies**, a firm supporter of British notions of civilization, was elected to the post, in time to side with Britain as hostilities were declared against Hitler in September 1939.

World War II and after

As happened in World War I, Australia developed its identity getting involved on a global scale in World War II, but this time without Britain's involvement. Menzies' United Australia Party barely lasted long enough to form diplomatic ties with the USA – in case Germany overran Europe – before internal divisions saw the government crumble, replaced by **John Curtin** and his Labor Party in 1941.

Curtin, concerned about Australia's vulnerability after the Japanese attack on Pearl Harbor, made the radical decision of shifting the country's commitment in the war from defending Britain and Europe to fighting off an invasion of Australia from Asia. After the **fall of Singapore** in 1942 and the capture of sixteen thousand Australian troops, Curtin succeeded in ordering the immediate recall of Australians fighting in the Middle East, despite opposition from Churchill, who wanted them for the Burma campaign. In February, the Japanese unexpectedly bombed Darwin, launched submarine raids against Sydney and

Newcastle, and invaded New Guinea. Feeling abandoned and betrayed by Britain, Curtin appealed to the USA, who quickly adopted Australia as a base for coordinating Pacific operations under **General Douglas MacArthur**. Meanwhile, Australian troops in New Guinea halted Japanese advances along the **Kokoda trail** at Milne Bay, while the Australian and US navies slowed down the Japanese fleet in the **Battle of the Coral Sea** – which, thanks to modern cannons, was notable as the first naval engagement in which the two sides never even saw each other.

Australia came out of World War II realizing that geographically, the country was closer to Asia than Europe, that it could not count on Britain to help in a crisis (Churchill had been ready to sacrifice Australian territory to protect British interests elsewhere), and that it was able to form political alliances independent of the mother country. From this point on, Australia began to look to the USA and the Pacific, in addition to Britain, for direction. Another consequence of the war was that immigration was speeded up, fuelled by Australia's recent vulnerability. Under the slogan "Populate or Perish", the government reintroduced assisted passages from Britain – the "ten-pound-poms" – and also accepted substantial numbers of European refugees. Even Torres Strait Islanders, previously banned from settling on the mainland, were allowed to move onto Cape York in northern Queensland.

With international right-wing extremism laid low by the war, the old fear of **communism** returned. When North Korea, backed by the Chinese, invaded South Korea in 1950, Australia, led by a revitalized Menzies and his new Liberal Party, was the first country after the USA to commit troops to counter communist forces. Menzies also sent soldiers and pilots to Malaya (as it was known at the time), where communist rebels had been fighting the British colonial administration almost since the end of World War II, under the anti-communist SEATO (Southeast Asia Treaty Organization) banner. At home, he opened up central Australia to British **atomic bomb tests** in the 1950s, because – echoing the beliefs of the first European colonists – "nobody lived there". A number of Aborigines were moved to reserves but others – along with the British troops involved in the tests – suffered the effects of fallout and had their traditional lands rendered uninhabitable for the foreseeable future. Wrangles with the British government over compensation, and the clearing of the test sites at **Maralinga** and **Emu Junction** were finally settled in 1993.

Menzies was still in control when the USA became involved in **Vietnam**, and with conflict in Malaya all but over, Australia volunteered "advisers" to Vietnamese republican forces in 1962. Once fighting became entrenched, the government introduced conscription and – bowing to the wishes of the American president **Lyndon B. Johnson** – sent a battalion of soldiers into the fray in 1965, events that immediately split the country. Menzies quit politics the following year, succeeded by his protégé **Harold Holt**, who, rallying under the catchphrase "All the way with LBJ", willingly increased Australia's participation in the Vietnamese conflict. But as the war dragged on, world opinion shifted to seeing the matter as a civil struggle, rather than as a fight between democratic and communist ideologies, and in 1970 the government began scaling down its involvement. In the meantime, Aboriginal people were finally granted **civil rights** in 1967, and Holt mysteriously disappeared while swimming in the sea off the coast of Victoria, leaving the Liberals in turmoil and paving the way for a Labor win under **Gough Whitlam** in 1972.

Whitlam's three years in office had far-reaching effects: he ended national service and participation in Vietnam, granted independence to **Papua New Guinea**, recognized the People's Republic of China, and instituted free health care and higher education systems. In doing so however, he alienated the mostly conservative Senate, and when the government attempted to finance mining interests with an illicit overseas loan in 1975, the opposition prevented the Senate from functioning. In an unprecedented move, the **Governor-General John Kerr** (until then, a largely decorative representative of the Crown overseeing Australian affairs) dismissed the government – a move that shocked many into questioning the validity of Britain's hold on Australia – and called an election, which Labor lost. In contrast, the following eight years were uneventful, culminating in the return of Labor in 1983 under the charismatic **Bob Hawke**, a former trade-union leader. Labor's subsequent thirteen years and record four terms in office, which produced surprisingly little lasting legislation, were suddenly brought to a close by the arrogant antics of Hawke's successor and former treasurer, **Paul Keating**. He was already widely unpopular for his scornful rhetoric and general lack of concern for the country's woes – particularly the effects of a massive foreign debt and crippling drought in eastern Australia – when news of a secret military agreement with Indonesia created a public backlash, resulting in a landslide victory for the **Liberal-National coalition**, led by **John Howard**, in 1996.

Current events

Previously dismissed by many as an ineffectual character, Howard's performance in office soon showed that his critics had underestimated his tenacity and consummate political skills, honed by 22 years in federal politics. In particular, his talent to quickly grasp any opportunity to rally (potentially flagging) support, thereby detracting from problems and scandals in his own government, combined with a superb sense of timing and, arguably, sheer good luck, enabled him to turn many potentially dangerous situations around in his favour.

By 1998, Howard's political position was so secure that the coalition managed to be re-elected on what some considered a suicidal platform of **tax reform** through the implementation of a **GST**, or Goods and Services Tax. When Howard's prospects of winning the next election were slipping away in mid-2001, due to the unfavourable effects of this tax reform on farmers, many small businesses and consumers, he successfully turned the country's attention to the ongoing issue of **refugees**, playing on the time-honoured Australian fear of being "swamped" by hordes of immigrants. His political status was strengthened; the government's popularity soared, and the tribulations of the GST and the not-so-perfect shape of the economy were all but forgotten. The terrorist attacks on September 11 did nothing to assuage xenophobic fears and, buoyed by his good ratings in the opinion polls, Howard called a federal election for November 10. Predictably, it was a comfortable win for his coalition, and the opposition Labor Party was further diminished.

A year later, Australia's possible involvement in the US- and UK-led war on Iraq dominated the headlines. The carnage of the **car bomb in Kuta, Bali**, on October 12, 2002 – terrorist action targeted at Westerners but in particular, some argued, Australians – added urgency to the debate.

Defying public opinion, Howard vociferously supported the war in Iraq, UN-backed or not, and subsequently joined the "coalition of the willing" in the military attack on Iraq. In contrast to the government's emphatic rhetorical support, Australia's physical contribution to the war was actually quite small – two thousand troops, plus some warships and aircraft.

The domestic arena

When in 2004 it finally transpired that Saddam Hussein's arsenal of weapons of mass destruction, and the immediate threat it posed to international security, was a furphy, it failed to cause a public backlash in Australia. In his speech calling the election for October 9, 2004, Howard deftly sidestepped a debate about his government's sincerity, by saying voters had to decide whom they most trusted to look after Australia and its economic future. By pointing out that in eight and a half years the coalition government had delivered a strong and robust economy, and by warning that interest rates would be higher under a Labor government, Howard played on another kind of fear – the "hip-pocket nerve". From then on, foreign affairs, in particular complex and sensitive topics like Iraq and national security, were practically off the radar screen and the election campaign was fought mainly on the theme of economic management, a tactic that paid off handsomely for Howard. At the federal elections in October 2004, the Liberals scored a resounding victory and Howard was elected Prime Minister for the fourth time. By December 2004, he had become **Australia's second-longest serving Prime Minister**, surpassed only by Menzies' eighteen years in office. In addition, from July 2005 the Liberal Party held the absolute majority (39 of 76 of seats) in the Senate, enabling it to push through a raft of previously blocked legislation, notably in the area of industrial relations.

By 2007, after eleven years at the helm, John Howard had influenced and shaped Australian culture and society according to his conservative world-view to an extent almost unimaginable back in 1996. Underpinned by an ongoing resources boom, the Australian economy seemed in very good shape, with China's and India's ravenous demands for Australian minerals and metal ore boosting the price of its commodity exports. However, closer inspection revealed a much less rosy picture. Australia had been running a **trade deficit** for almost five years and the volume of Australian exports had not increased significantly. While high commodity prices had reduced the deficit from $25 billion at the end of 2005 to $12 billion by February 2007, improvements were hampered by increased consumer spending on imports and by the worst drought on record. Hitherto, the Howard government had denounced global warming as scientifically unsound scaremongering; any measures to deal with it, including ratifying the **Kyoto Protocol** and putting a cap on Australia's (abysmally high) emission levels, were rejected on the grounds that they would impact negatively on the Australian economy and jeopardize Australia's living standards. However, the dire warnings contained in the 2007 IPCC reports on climate change could not be so easily dismissed, given the unprecedented length and severity of the drought and, by then, the almost annual occurrence of widespread ferocious bushfires in Australia. In April 2007, the Howard government announced there was a water crisis and proposed the establishment of a **national water management scheme**, while steadfastly maintaining the jury was still out on the link between the increased frequency of bushfires, the drought and climate change. This continuing denial seemed so short-sighted to State Premiers that they decided to establish their own **carbon trading system** if the Federal government failed to do so.

With a federal election due towards the end of 2007, **climate change**, or at the very least, the undeniable realities of drought and water-shortages, are topics that will not go away. Add to that the country's other urgent issues with long-term implications – the inadequate state of the infrastructure (rail, roads, ports, telecommunications and vocational training) and the uncertain future of Australia's energy supply – and it is clear that the current Liberal government will have a harder time than in previous election campaigns to convince voters of its merits. Stacked against them are two further contentious issues: an exit strategy for the war in Iraq and, in the domestic arena, the topic of **industrial relations**. One year on, public support for the "Work Choices" legislation, passed in March 2006, was very low, with many employees feeling that, in terms of remuneration, working conditions and job security, they were worse off than before.

Having been rendered ineffectual by years of constant leadership struggles, the Australian Labor Party entered into the election year energized and revitalized under the leadership of **Kevin Rudd**. A former diplomat, bureaucrat and business consultant, Rudd has a reputation of being very determined, a consummate negotiator and a sharp and shrewd politician. His somewhat intellectual demeanour is at odds with Howard's favoured common-man persona, but in the first months of 2007 Rudd consistently increased his ratings in the opinion polls as preferred Prime Minister despite numerous attempts by his political opponents to discredit him – which says as much about the need of the electorate for a change as about Rudd's skills as a political campaigner.

Foreign policy

Looking beyond its shores, for most of the twentieth century Australia faced **Asia** with ambiguity, seeing it partly as a strategic threat, partly as an economic opportunity. The example of Japan is symptomatic: in the 1930s, Japan had become Australia's second-largest trading partner but during the 1940s Australia had to fight off an impending Japanese invasion. By the 1970s, with the White Australia policy coming to an end, Whitlam initiated a policy shift towards greater engagement with its neighbours in the region, which continued under the Fraser government and was intensified by the Hawke-Keating governments in the 1980s and early 1990s. This stance was based on the pragmatic recognition of Australia's economic interests, and led to an often appallingly conciliatory attitude to some Asian countries' more dubious actions against each other, as well as a pitifully weak response to regional human-rights abuses. As was the case with most of his other political visions, Keating was unable to sell his orientation towards Asia to the general Australian public. The ubiquitous catchphrase of the 1990s: **"Australia is part of Asia"** confused and alienated voters. Howard capitalized on that during his first successful election campaign of 1996, with the recurring reproach that Keating was "obsessed with Asia" and out of touch with what ordinary Australians felt. The "part of Asia" notion did not wash with the countries in the area, either. Australia, with its predominantly white population and strong cultural and political ties to the Anglophone Western world (and a prime minister given to arrogant remarks and schoolmasterly lectures) would not be accepted as "Asian". Australia's most outspoken critic was Malaysia, under the rule of Dr Mahatir Mohamad (himself no stranger to schoolmasterly lectures), who continually vetoed Australia's attempts to join ASEAN, the regional trading bloc. The rough-hewn right-wing outbursts by **Pauline Hanson** and the (short-lived) rise of her **One Nation** party in 1996, which capitalized on widespread dissatisfaction with the major political groups, did nothing to enhance Australian credibility in the region.

From his first days in office, Howard's statements and actions in public signalled a backing off, if not complete reversal, from his predecessors' Asia policy. There was his refusal to distance himself emphatically from Pauline Hanson's spiteful, xenophobic – and, in particular, anti-Asian – utterances. In 1996, during his first state visit to Indonesia as Australian prime minister, he stated that Australia did not have to choose between geography and history.

While Australia was geographically close to Asia and would eagerly pursue closer economic and security ties in the region, it did not want to be identified as an Asian nation. It would maintain its own culture and traditions, including a security alliance with the US and close ties to Europe.

The Australian-led UN intervention in the civil war in East Timor in 1999, instigated by pro-Indonesian militia, and covertly by members of the Indonesian armed forces, put a stop to the massacre and helped the emerging new nation stand on its own feet. Not surprisingly, Australia's relationship to Indonesia deteriorated badly as a result. Short of condoning a ruthless and murderous grab for power, it is hard to see how upsetting the sensibilities of Indonesians could have been completely avoided in this instance. However, subsequent noises about Australia taking a more proactive role in maintaining regional security, and playing the role of America's deputy sheriff, added fuel to the fire and caused a furore across the entire region. Forging closer links with the US always has been the highest priority of the Howard government. Australia's participation in the war on Iraq and the signing of the Free Trade Agreement between Australia and the US are two examples of the importance attributed to the alliance with America.

Engagement with Asia, however – while much more low-key – has never been taken totally off the agenda. Australia's role in delivering aid to Indonesia's Aceh province, the region worst hit by the **tsunami** on Boxing Day 2004, went a long way towards creating goodwill in the region, and counteracting Australia's "bullyboy" image. In December 2005, Australia participated in the inaugural meeting of the **East Asia Summit (EAS)** in Kuala Lumpur. The EAS was founded in the hope of establishing a first step towards a united East Asian Community but as old regional rivalries flared up at the first two meetings it remains doubtful whether it will amount to more than another talkfest. But ever the pragmatist, Howard recognized there may be economic and strategic opportunities for Australia in these developments, and quietly readjusted his foreign policy. Should Kevin Rudd become prime minister after the federal elections at the end of 2007 the pendulum may well swing back towards a more substantial engagement with Australia's northern neighbours, though not at the expense of good US–Australia relations. At the very least, what can be expected is effective interaction, based on a deeper understanding and familiarity with that part of the world – Rudd is a fluent Mandarin speaker and spent some time in China as a diplomat and a business consultant for Australian firms.

Aboriginal rights

In the domestic arena, there were some advances under Labor in the field of **Aboriginal rights**. An ineffectual inquiry into Aboriginal deaths in custody was overshadowed in June 1992, when the High Court handed down the landmark **Mabo Decision**, legally overturning the concept of *terra nullius*. Eddie Mabo's claim, set around Murray Island (Mer) in the Torres Strait, was granted, and the Merriam were acknowledged as traditional landowners. This decision led to the passing of the Native Title Act of 1993, after extensive discussions with indigenous representatives. Next came the **Wik Decision** in December 1996, which stated that native title and pastoral leases could coexist over the same area. The new Howard government initiated an alarmist debate about its implications, and triggered something of a public backlash against Aborigines. Support for One Nation increased as the party exploited people's fears to the hilt, contributing to Australia's racist image overseas. The government refused to negotiate with indigenous representatives who had sought to bring forward constructive proposals. In 1998, it introduced amendments to the Wik Decision, which wound back indigenous rights under the Native Title Act, whilst enhancing the rights of landholders and developers.

While Mabo and Wik had an effect in some instances – such as the handing back of the **Silver Plains** property on Queensland's Cape York to its traditional owners in 2000 – few similar land claims are likely to succeed. A **Native Title Tribunal** has been set up to consider each case, but given former resettlement policies, claimants have an uphill struggle as they need to prove constant association with the land in question since white occupation. Nonetheless, a growing acknowledgement that Aboriginal people were in fact the land's original inhabitants, and the perception that they will eventually be re-enfranchised, has seen mining companies, farmers, and notably – and ironically, given its past record – the Queensland government ignoring the political and legal wrangles and making private land-use agreements with, or handovers to, local communities. In this sense, Mabo and Wik have confirmed that Aboriginal people have land rights, despite the best efforts of the Howard government to undermine these.

Australia's indigenous peoples

White Australians have grouped the country's indigenous peoples under the term Aborigines, but are now coming to recognize many separate cultures as diverse but interrelated as those of Europe.

Today, these cultures include urbanized **Koorie** communities in Sydney and Melbourne, semi-nomadic groups such as the **Pintupi** living in the western deserts, and the **Yolngu** people of eastern Arnhem Land, an area never colonized by settlers. If there is any thread linking these groups, it is the island continent they inhabit and, particularly in the north, the worsening state of health, education and opportunities they experience, despite the apparent revitalization of Aboriginal culture.

Colonization

From 1788, the estimated 750,000 indigenous people of Australia were gradually dispossessed of their lands and livelihoods by the British colonists who failed to recognize them as legitimate inhabitants. Australia was annexed to the British Empire on the basis that it was *terra nullius*, or uninhabited wasteland. This legal fiction persisted until the High Court judged in the 1992 **Mabo** case that native title to land still existed in Australia unless it had been extinguished by statute or by some use of the land that was inconsistent with the continuation of native use and ownership. The **Wik Decision** of 1996 went a step further, acknowledging that native title continues to exist on pastoral leases, though with the proviso that "pastoral interest will prevail over native title rights, wherever the two conflict" (for more on the Mabo and Wik decisions, see "History", p.1081).

Upon deciding that the country was unoccupied, successive waves of new settlers hastened to make it so. Violent conflicts between indigenous and recently arrived Australians resulted in the decimation of Aboriginal groups. The most widely known of these conflicts was the **unofficial war** waged against Tasmania's Aboriginal peoples, which resulted in the near-destruction of indigenous Tasmanians (see also box on pp.976–977). Historians estimate that twenty thousand Aborigines may have died in these mostly unrecorded battles. Measuring the impact of colonization on the indigenous population has been hampered by a lack of information about conditions prior to colonization, as well as the failure of successive governments to record indigenous people as part of the population until the 1960s.

Australia's geographical isolation meant that the introduction of European **diseases** was also a powerful agent in decimating the indigenous populations. Whole populations were wiped out by smallpox and malaria epidemics, and the diaries from the First Fleet record the rapid destruction from smallpox of the Aboriginal camps in the Sydney hinterland within a few years of the establishment of the colony. Those who didn't die fled the area, unwittingly infecting neighbouring groups as they went. When Governor Hunter made the first exploratory expedition to western New South Wales in the 1820s, he recorded evidence of prior smallpox epidemics among Aboriginal groups who had not previously come into contact with European settlers. The lack of immunity to these introduced diseases was exacerbated by the trauma of dispossession, the lack of availability of – or access to – traditional food and water supplies, and the unhygienic consequences of being required to wear European-style clothing.

The **interruption of traditional food and water supplies** became progressively worse through the nineteenth and twentieth centuries as the pastoral industry expanded across rural Australia, and vast areas were stripped of vegetation to provide for grazing land. Grazing animals competed with local animals for food, drained established water sources and dug up the flora on the soil surface with their hooves, contributing to erosion and salinity and so creating dustbowls. Other European animals, originally introduced to make the countryside seem more like "home", rapidly multiplied and have now become ubiquitous throughout Australia. Foxes, and especially cats, have been blamed for the near extinction of small mammals and birds throughout arid Australia. Rabbit populations expanded to fill the niche the mammals vacated, and their destructive grazing habits have contributed to the increasing desertification of Australia's rangelands. Aboriginal people in central Australia have witnessed this ecological disaster within the last sixty years, and have lamented the loss of many animal species that once sustained them.

Australia's Aboriginal peoples have also been subjected to various forms of **incarceration**, ranging from prisons to apartheid-style reserves. Much of this systematic imprisonment was instigated between 1890 and 1950 as an official policy of **protection**, in response to the devastating impact of colonization. Missionaries and other well-meaning people believed that Aborigines were a dying race, and that it was a Christian duty to provide for them in their passing. Parliamentary records of the time reveal a harsher mentality. Aborigines were often viewed as a weak and degenerate people who exposed white settlers to physical and moral turpitude. For the wellbeing of Aborigines and settlers alike, state governments enacted legislation to appoint official **Protectors of Aborigines**, established reserves in rural areas and removed Aboriginal people to them. In some parts of Australia these reserves were established on traditional lands, allowing people to continue to live relatively undisturbed. Elsewhere, notably Queensland, people were forcibly removed from their home areas and relocated in reserves throughout the state. Families were broken up and the ties with the land and religion shattered. The so-called protectors had autonomy over those in their ward. For example, Aboriginal people required permits to marry or to move from one reserve to another, or were forced into indentured or simply slave labour to be paid in flour or tobacco. This treatment persisted in some areas until the late 1960s.

Aboriginal people are still ridiculously over-represented in Australia's prison population. In 1991, the situation led to a **Royal Commission into Aboriginal Deaths in Custody**, which reported to the Federal Parliament. It called for wide-ranging changes in police and judicial practice, and substantial changes to social programmes aimed at improving the lot of Aboriginal peoples in the areas of justice, health, education, economics and empowerment. But despite considerable government lip-service to the recommendations of the Royal Commission, it has not resulted in any substantial change to incarceration rates.

Since the 1920s, Aboriginal children fathered by Europeans but born to black mothers were removed and put into state institutions or with white foster parents as part of a policy of **assimilation**. The practice of "taking the children away" began in Victoria in 1886 and continued until 1969, and still haunts the lives of many Aboriginal Australians, now known as the **Stolen Generation**, who have lost contact with their natal families and their culture, and whose plight was depicted in the 2002 film *Rabbit-Proof Fence*. But despite the policy being the subject of a major government inquiry in 1997, and the subsequent media attention since the release of its report, the people are yet to receive an official national **apology**.

Revitalization

The **revitalization** of Aboriginal people and their culture effectively began in 1967, when a constitutional referendum overwhelmingly endorsed the rights of indigenous Australians as voting citizens, and gave the federal government the power to legislate for Aboriginal people. Prior to this referendum, Aboriginal people had the status of wards of each of the states. The referendum ushered in a new era of **self-determination** for Aboriginal people, evidenced by the establishment of the first Ministry for Aboriginal Affairs in the Whitlam Labor Government of 1972–75. After more than a hundred years of agitation, **land rights** were accorded to Aboriginal groups in the Northern Territory in 1976 under federal legislation. Since then, other states have legislated to vest title over various pieces of state-owned land to their traditional Aboriginal owners. All the mainland states and territories now have provisions for Aboriginal land rights. Throughout the 1970s and 1980s successive federal governments set up various representative bodies, including the notorious **Aboriginal and Torres Strait Islanders Commission** (**ATSIC**: 1990–2004). This statutory authority gave elected Aboriginal representatives effective control over many of the federal funding programmes directed at Aboriginal organizations and communities. Substantial funds were directed towards training for employment and improved health education. Running at around two billion dollars per annum, this should have seen Aboriginal people thriving right across Australia. The reality was far different: corruption, nepotism and flawed or hare-brained projects all helped bring about ATSIC's abolition in 2004 and a return to greater federal government control (see "The future", overleaf).

Along with ownership of land and some control over funding came opportunities for economic self-sufficiency and expansion previously unavailable to Aboriginal groups. In many parts of the country, this allowed Aborigines to buy the cattle stations on which they had worked without wages for many years. In central Australia, Aboriginal enterprises include TV and radio stations, transport companies, small airlines, publishing companies, tourist businesses and joint-venture mining operations.

Cooperative agreements with the Australian Nature Conservation Agency have led to Aboriginal ownership and joint management of two of Australia's most important conservation reserves, **Uluru–Kata Tjuta** and **Kakadu** national parks in the Northern Territory. These arrangements recognize that Aboriginal owners retain an enormous understanding about the ecology of their traditional lands that can be of great assistance in the development of land-management plans.

Citizenship and its problems

Despite these successes, Australia's indigenous peoples are struggling against considerable disadvantages. Along with citizenship in 1967 came a new-found unemployability (few station owners were willing to pay black workers the same wage as white people) along with the legal right to purchase **alcohol**, a disastrous combination. Institutionalized welfarism has compounded feelings of futility as well as shame towards one's Aboriginal origins, and substance abuse is heavily implicated in the destructive spiral often observed by visitors to Outback towns (and some inner-city areas). The negative repercussions are evident in sickness and death, violence and despair, exclusion from education and meaningful employment, as well as families and communities in disarray. The vast over-representation of Aboriginal people in the criminal-justice system is directly attributable to alcohol. **Poor health** continues to reduce substantially the life expectancy of Aborigines. About seventy percent of indigenous Australians die before they turn 65 (compared with a bit over twenty percent for other Australians), Aboriginal infant mortality is two to three times higher than for white babies and the death rate from diabetes is eight times higher. As with most areas of social service, health services for Aboriginal peoples have been the province of white professionals until very recently; an essential focus of the new strategy is to empower Aboriginal people by giving resources to them directly.

On the **positive** side, many families and communities are confronting the problems that alcohol is causing. Between them they are putting pressure on problem drinkers to limit their drinking, and are now able to implement new laws to reduce the damage alcohol is doing to the people around them.

The future

The process of **reconciliation** with its "rights"-based approach, as initiated by the Labor government under Keating, always has been anathema to Prime Minister John Howard. As he saw it, "symbolic measures" such as an apology or a treaty were an insult to the present generation of non-Aboriginal people who were not responsible for past mistakes, and did nothing to address problems in Aboriginal communities such as alcoholism, appalling health and lack of access to education. Upon his re-election in 1998, "**practical reconciliation**" was the new catchphrase and essentially meant the delivery of welfare services through mainstream programmes. Consistent with this approach, he steadfastly refused to give a formal apology, ignoring the widespread popular movement to that effect in 1999 and 2000. His government promised $63 million over four years of funding for counselling and "link-up" services for those who had been removed from their families. By 2004, only a small amount of the package had been spent.

In the same year, the Howard government abolished ATSIC and its service delivery arm ATSIS. The new "whole of government" approach meant the responsibility for the delivery of indigenous programmes was to be shared by several government departments. A new, complex bureaucratic structure full of Orwellian acronyms emerged: the **Office of Indigenous Policy Coordination (OIPC)**, which, in addition to coordinating programmes, also provides advice to a Ministerial Task Force on Indigenous Affairs and the **National Indigenous Council (NIC)**. The latter consists of fourteen hand-picked indigenous advisers, who meet four times a year and whose function is to advise the government on the future direction of policies and programmes that will impact on every facet of Aboriginal lives. "**Mutual obligation**" and "**shared responsibility**" were the new buzzwords, a rhetoric that seemed to align with

Noel Pearson, the Aboriginal lawyer and community leader from the Cape York Peninsula, whose aim is to replace social welfare with social enterprise. On Cape York, he embarked on a community-based social-renewal project, which includes having payments of benefits invested in enterprise activity rather than as an individual welfare cheque, with each individual and family making a commitment to contributing as well as receiving.

Now, Aboriginal communities had to enter into **Shared Responsibility Agreements (SRA)** with government departments, committing to behavioural change or similar actions in exchange for funding for specified community infrastructure needs. The first SRA released in December 2004 was with Mulan, a remote community in Western Australia. The government agreed to install a petrol bowser, and in return the community agreed to make sure their children showered daily and looked after other health issues. In several places, including Wadeye in the Northern Territory, there was a "no school, no pool" agreement: in return for a swimming pool, kids had to attend school. In most cases, these SRAs were reported to be successful. School attendance rates were up and chronic ear, eye and skin infections that afflict Aboriginal children seemed to be alleviated by the chlorine in the water. At first glance, it seemed a common-sense approach – no more wasting of money by a corrupt organization rife with nepotism, no more "one size fits all" solutions. However, although the inefficient ATSIC had been disbanded, a new, confusing and very costly bureaucratic structure had taken its place, one that distributes funds on a seemingly ad-hoc basis and with no mechanisms in place to check if and how its "mutual obligation" is fulfilled.

This belief in the validity of "big picture" issues like the constitutional recognition of the rights of indigenous people, Native Title, the right to self-determination, however currently unfashionable, was echoed by **Megan Davis**, a young Aboriginal lawyer specializing in international law and human rights, in an interview with Radio National in March 2006. "I've no doubt that ten years down the track these Shared Responsibility Agreements, this nonsense where Aboriginal people have to enter into agreements with the state that no other Australian citizen has to enter into, will be chalked up to another crappy failed experiment on behalf of the federal government," she said. "I have no doubt that the resolution of this issue is Australians taking a good look at their public institutions, about the constitutional arrangements between Aboriginal people and the state, and that's the only way forward. And they can call it wishy washy, they can call it café latte, or whatever the hell they want, but that's the answer."

Flora and fauna

Despite forty thousand years of human pressure and manipulation, accelerated in the last two centuries by the effects of introduced species, Australia's ecology and wildlife remain among the most distinctive on earth. Nonetheless, they are also some of the most endangered: in the last two hundred years, more native mammals have become extinct here than on any other continent, and land clearing – particularly in Queensland – kills an estimated 7.5 million birds a year, bringing several species to the edge of extinction.

Australians love to tell stories about the **dangers** the bush holds for the inexperienced traveller (see the "Health" section of Basics, pp.44–47, for general advice on coping with hazardous wildlife). In reality, fearsome "drop bears" lurking in gums, fallen tree trunks that turn out to be giant snakes, bloodthirsty wild pigs and other rampaging terrors are mostly confined to hotel bars, the product of suburban paranoia laced with a surprising naivety about the great outdoors. Apart from a couple of avoidable exceptions, there's little to fear from Australia's wildlife, and if you spend any time in the bush, you'll undoubtedly end up far better informed than the yarn-spinners. For more on the dangers Down Under, see the "Australian Wildlife" colour section.

Marsupials and monotremes

In the years after the demise of the dinosaurs, Australia split away from the rest of the world, and the animals here evolved along different lines to anywhere else. As placental mammals gained the ascendency in South America, Africa, Europe and Asia, it was the marsupials and monotremes that took over in Australia, alongside the megafauna (see box opposite). These orders may not be exclusive to Australia (they're also found in New Guinea and South America), but it's here they reached their greatest diversity and numbers.

Marsupials are mammals that give birth to a partially formed embryo, which itself then develops in a **pouch** on the mother; this allows a higher breeding rate in good years. Easiest to find because they actively seek out people, **ringtail** and **brushtail possums** are common in suburbs and campsites, and often hard to avoid if they think there's a chance of getting some food. With a little persistence, you should encounter one of the several species of related **glider possums** on the edges of forests at dusk. **Kangaroos** and **wallabies** are the Australian answer to deer and antelope, and range from tiny, solitary rainforest species to the gregarious two-metre-tall red kangaroo of the central plains – watching these creatures bouncing effortlessly across the landscape is an extraordinary sight. The arboreal, eucalyptus-chewing **koalas** and tubby, ground-dwelling **wombats** are smaller, less active and more sensitive to disturbance; this has made them more elusive, and has placed them on the endangered list as their habitat is cleared. Carnivorous marsupials are mostly shrew-sized today (though a lion equivalent probably survived into Aboriginal times, and fossils of meat-eating kangaroos have been found); two of the largest are spotted native cats or **quolls**, and Tasmania's indigenous **Tasmanian devil**, a terrier-sized scavenger.

Platypuses and echidnas are the only **monotremes**, egg-laying mammals that suckle their young through specialized pores. Once considered a stage in the

Ancient Australian wildlife

Australia has a **fossil record** that makes up in range what it lacks in quantity. Imprints of invertebrates from South Australia's **Ediacaran fauna**, dated to over 600 million years, are the oldest evidence of animal life in the world. On a larger scale, footprints and remains of several **dinosaur** species have been uncovered, and **opalized marine fossils** are unique to the country. Perhaps most intriguing is evidence of the **megafauna** – giant wildlife which included the twenty-metre-long, constricting snake montypythonides, flightless birds bigger than an ostrich, a rhino-sized wombat, carnivorous kangaroos, and thylacaleo, a marsupial lion – which flourished until about thirty thousand years ago, overlapping with Aboriginal occupation. Climatic changes were probably responsible for their demise, but humans definitely wiped out the **thylacine**, a dog-like marsupial with an oversized head, which vanished from the mainland after the introduction of dingoes but survived in Tasmania until 1936 – the year it received government protection.

evolution of placental mammals, they're now recognized as a specialized branch of the family. Neither is particularly rare, but being nocturnal, shy and, in the case of the platypus, aquatic, makes them difficult to find. Ant-eating **echidnas** resemble a long-nosed, thick-spined hedgehog or small porcupine, and are found countrywide; **platypuses** are confined to the eastern ranges and look like a blend of duck and otter, having a grey, rubbery bill, webbed feet, short fur, and a poison spur on males. This combination seemed too implausible to nineteenth-century biologists, who initially denounced stuffed specimens as a hoax, assembled from pieces of other animals.

Introduced fauna

Of the **introduced mammals**, **dingoes** are descended from dogs, introduced to Australia by Aboriginal people in the last twelve thousand years. To keep them away from flocks, graziers built "vermin fences", which were finally connected by the Australian government to form a 5400-kilometre-long, continuous fence, allegedly the world's longest. The **Dingo Fence** stretches from South Australia into northwest Queensland and down again to New South Wales. **Camels** have also become acclimatized to Australia since their introduction in the 1840s; they are doing so well in the central deserts that they are becoming a pest. Australia is the only place where dromedaries still occur in the wild, and they are regularly exported to the Middle East. The blight that **hoofed mammals** – horses, cows, sheep and goats – have perpetrated on Australia's fragile fauna is horrendous. Much of the country has been prematurely desertified by their eating habits, abrasive hooves and demand for water; once extracted from below ground, it is not replenished, which alters the mineral balance and kills remaining plant life. The damage caused by **rabbits** is equally pervasive, especially in the semi-desert areas where their cyclic population explosions can strip every shred of plant life from fragile dune systems. In an attempt to control the problem, the myxoma virus was introduced in the Fifties, and although a large part of the rabbit population was initially wiped out, the rabbits eventually developed a resistance and their numbers increased again in the following decades. Since 1996, another viral disease affecting the European rabbit, the rabbit calicivirus disease (RCD), has been released all over Australia, resulting in a dramatic reduction of rabbit numbers. It remains to be seen, however, whether the unsuccessful story of the myxoma virus will be repeated.

Feral **cats**, which hunt for sport as well as necessity, are currently one of the greatest threats to indigenous fauna, primarily small marsupials and birds. An introduced amphibian, however, has turned out to be the most insidious and rapacious invader of all. The highly poisonous **cane toads**, brought in to combat a plague of greyback beetles, have no natural enemies and for thirty years have been on a relentless march from the north Queensland sugar-cane fields, southwards along the coast and across northern Australia. In 2004, they invaded the lush Top End floodplains, which have more wildlife per square kilometre than the richest parts of Africa, Asia and the Americas. For more on the cane toad, see box, p.459 and the "Australian wildlife" colour section.

Reptiles, birds, bats and marine life

Australian **reptiles** come in all shapes and sizes. In the tropical parts of the country, the pale lizards you see wriggling across the ceiling on Velcro-like pads are **geckos**, and you'll find fatter, sluggish **skinks** – such as the stumpy blue-tongued lizard – everywhere. Other widespread species are **frill-necked lizards**, known for fanning out their necks and running on their hind legs when frightened, and the ubiquitous **goanna** family, which includes the monstrous perentie, third-largest lizard in the world. In central Australia, look out for the extraordinary **thorny devil** or moloch, an animal that seems part rock, part rosebush.

Crocodiles are confined to the tropics and come in two types. The shy, inoffensive **freshwater crocodile** grows to around 3m in length and feeds on fish and frogs. The larger, bulkier, and misleadingly named saltwater or **estuarine crocodile** can grow to 7m, ranges far inland (often in freshwater), and is the only Australian animal that constitutes an active threat to humans. Highly evolved predators, they should be given a very wide berth (see box, p.566 for specific precautions to take while in crocodile country). Despite their bad press, **snakes** are generally timid and pose far less of a problem, even though Australia has everything from constricting pythons through to three-quarters of the world's most venomous species.

With a climate that extends from temperate zones well into the tropics, Australia's **birdlife** is prolific and varied. Small **penguins** and **albatrosses** live along the south coast, while **riflebirds**, related to New Guinea's birds of paradise, and the **cassowary**, a colourful version of the ostrich, live in the tropical rainforests. The drabber **emu** prefers drier plains further west. Among the birds of prey, the countrywide **wedge-tail eagle** and the coastal **white-bellied sea eagle** are most impressive in their size. Both share their environment with the stately grey **brolga**, an Australian crane, and the even larger **jabiru stork**, with its chisel beak and pied plumage. **Parrots**, arguably the country's most spectacular birds, come in over forty varieties, and no matter if they're flocks of green budgerigars, outrageously coloured rainbow lorikeets or white sulphur-crested cockatoos, they'll deafen you with their noisy song. Equally raucous are **kookaburras**, giant kingfishers found near permanent water. The quieter **tawny frogmouth**, an incredibly camouflaged cousin of the nightjar, has one of the most disgruntled expressions ever seen on a bird.

Huge colonies of **bats**, of orange, ghost and horseshoe varieties, congregate in caves and fill entire trees all over Australia. The **fruit bat**, or flying fox, is especially common in the tropics, where evenings can be spent watching colonies of the one-metre-winged monsters heading out from their daytime roosts on feeding expeditions.

In addition to what you'll see on the Barrier Reef (covered in the Coastal Queensland chapter), **whales**, **turtles**, **dolphins**, **seals** and **dugongs** (sea cows) are part of the country's marine life, with humpback southern right whales recently making a welcome return to the coasts after being hunted close to extinction.

Flora

Australia's most distinctive and widespread **trees** are those that developed a **dependence on fire**. Some, like the seemingly limitless varieties of **eucalypts** or gum trees, need extreme heat to burst open button-shaped pods and release their seeds, and encourage fires by annually shedding bark and leaves, depositing a thick layer of tinder on the forest floor. Other shrubs with similar habits are **banksias**, **grevillias** and **bottlebrushes**, with their distinctive bushy flowers and spiky seed-pods, while those prehistoric survivors, palm-like **cycads** and **grasstrees**, similarly depend on regular conflagrations to promote new growth. For thousands of years, Aborigines used controlled burn-offs to make the land more suitable for hunting, thereby possibly enhancing these fire-reliant traits.

Despite the country having extensive arid regions, there is no native equivalent to the cactus, although the dry, spiky **spinifex**, or porcupine grass, the succulent **samphire** with its curiously jointed stem, and the aptly named **saltbush** come closest in their ability to survive extreme temperatures. After a rain, smaller desert plants rush to bloom and seed, covering the ground in a spectacular blanket of colour, a phenomenon for which Australia's Outback regions are well known.

On a larger scale, the Outback is dotted with stands of hardy **mulgas** and **wattles**, which superficially resemble scrawny eucalypts but have different leaf structures, as well as scattered groups of bloated, spindly-branched **bottle trees**, whose sweet, pulpy and moisture-laden cores can be used as emergency stock feed in drought conditions. The similar but far larger **boab**, found in the Kimberley and northeastern Northern Territory, is thought to be an invader from East Africa. **Mallee scrub** is unique to the southeastern Outback, where clearing of these tangled, bush-sized eucalypts for grazing has endangered both scrub and those animals which rely on it – the mound-building **mallee fowl** being the best known.

Mangrove swamps, found along the tropical and subtropical coasts, are tidal zones of thick grey mud and mangrove trees, whose interlocked, aerial roots make an effective barrier to exploration. They've suffered extensive clearing for development, and it wasn't until recently that their importance to the estuarine life-cycle won them limited government protection; Aboriginal people have always found them a rich source of animal and plant products.

Rainforest once covered much of the continent, but today only a small portion of its former abundance survives. Nevertheless, you'll find pockets everywhere, from Tasmania's richly verdant wilderness to the monsoonal examples of northern Queensland and the Top End in the Northern Territory. Trees grow to gigantic heights, as they compete with each other for light, supporting themselves in the poor soil with aerial or buttressed roots. The extraordinary **banyan** and **Moreton Bay fig** trees are fine examples of the two types. They support a huge number of plant species, with tangled **vines** in the lower reaches, and **orchids**, **elkhorns** and other epiphytes using larger plants as roosts. **Palms** and **tree ferns**, with their giant, delicately curled fronds, are found in more open forest, where there's regular water.

Some forest types illustrate the extent of Australia's prehistoric flora. **Antarctic beech** or *Nothafagus*, found south of Brisbane as well as in South America, along with native pines and **kauri** from Queensland, which also occur in New Zealand (the similarly-named Western Australian **karri** is also huge but unrelated), are all relict evidence of the prehistoric supercontinent, Gondwana. Other "living fossils" include primitive marine **stromatolites** – algae corals – still found around Shark Bay, Western Australia, and in fossilized form in the central deserts.

As long as you don't eat them or fall onto the pricklier versions, most Australian plants are harmless – though in rainforests you'd want to avoid entanglement with spiky **lawyer cane** or wait-awhile vine (though it doesn't look like it, this is a climbing palm). Also watch out for the large, pale-green, heart-shaped leaves of the **stinging tree**, a scraggly "regrowth" plant found on the margins of cleared tropical rainforest. Even a casual brush delivers an agonizing and prolonged sting; if you're planning on bushwalking in the tropics, learn to recognize and avoid this plant.

Australian film

All visitors to Australia these days will be aware of the popularity and respect for the Australian film industry since the early 1970s. It is generally agreed (with deference to a 1900 Salvation Army promo, *Stations of the Cross*) that *The Story of the Kelly Gang*, made by Charles Tait in 1906, was the world's first feature-length film. Australians' well-known antagonism towards figures of authority soon led to a hugely popular series of bushranger movies, eventually to be banned in 1912 by the New South Wales police on the grounds that their unsympathetic portrayal in these pictures was corrupting youngsters.

This **early heyday** of Australian film-making predated that of Hollywood and persisted with the production of various World War I morale boosters, despite the creation of a distribution duopoly (known as the "combine") that showed little interest in independent Australian films outside its control. With the ending of the war and its many cinematic testaments to the heroic disaster of Gallipoli, Australian silent cinema reached a creative peak. **Raymond Longford** was Australia's Spielberg of silents at this time, and his 1919 production of *The Sentimental Bloke* and its sequel, *Ginger Mick*, a year later, were popular and notably naturalist dramas about a woman's taming of her larrikin husband's proclivities. Along with the already established contempt for authority, Longford's films featured a distrust of sophistication and formality and, even then, the mythic spell of "the bush" began to make its mark on Australian productions.

Hollywood domination

The combine gradually squeezed the life from Australian cinema, which continued to decline as the powerful Hollywood studios got into their stride and entered the Golden Age of talkies. In 1933 the mildly reformed wild boy from Tasmania, **Errol Flynn**, starred in his first feature film, *In the Wake of the Bounty*, directed by **Charles Chauvel**, a leading figure in Australian film-making until the late 1950s.

During World War II there was a return to newsreels and documentaries, with the legendary cameraman, Damien Parer, earning **Australia's first Oscar** for his account of the fighting in New Guinea (*Kokoda Front Line*, 1942). Following the war, however, Hollywood's global domination of cinema was unassailed, and Australian cinema just about perished. Nevertheless, **Chips Rafferty** turned up as Australia's answer to John Wayne, appearing in an unremarkable series of formula films, such as the scenically superb epic of bovine migration, *The Overlanders* (1946).

In the 1950s the British Ealing Studios and the American MGM set up production companies in Australia, turning out the odd Outback drama which was watered down for international consumption (but not success). This era produced few notable Australian films other than Cecil Holmes' return to the bushranger format in *Captain Thunderbolt* (1953), and his similarly leftist study of mateship, *Three In One* (1957). Chauvel's remarkable *Jedda, the Uncivilized* (1955) was more unusual in that it tackled the tricky issue of an Aboriginal girl's white upbringing, sexual temptation and subsequent abduction back to tribal life, where a tragic death inevitably awaited her. If there is one subject Australian cinema still has difficulty in dealing with (the New Wave having finally come to grips with women as individuals), it is that of the Aborigines.

Australia was by now nothing more than an exotic, marsupial-speckled location for "**kangaroo westerns**" and other dramas where British and American actors could exercise their skills. In 1959 Stanley Kramer directed *On the Beach*, Nevil Shute's post-nuclear apocalypse drama, with Ava Gardner, Gregory Peck and Fred Astaire tiptoeing through the fallout. A year later Fred Zinnemann directed Deborah Kerr and Robert Mitchum in *The Sundowners*, an affectionate classic of Outback itinerant labour.

The New Wave

The birth of the **New Wave** was a response to the burgeoning counterculture of the late 1960s. Among the many notable reforms of Gough Whitlam's Labor government was support for the long-neglected arts. Film-makers in particular were given a shot in the arm with the introduction of extremely generous grants to more than cover the cost of production. While in its early years this financial support helped produce some of the crassest male-fantasy "sex romps" ever seen (Tim Burstall's 1973 *Alvin Purple* and Terry Bourke's *Plugg* are matchlessly dire), the opening of the **Australian Film School** in 1973 allowed genuine talents such as Gillian Armstrong, Bruce Beresford and Paul Cox to flourish.

Two years later, the **Australian Film Commission** evolved from previous similar organizations to help produce and market Australian films, and although the grants have been regularly reduced ever since, their introduction kick-started the moribund industry so that there presently exists a diverse pool of directors and technicians to keep things going.

Peter Weir's unsettlingly eerie *Picnic at Hanging Rock* (1975) remains an early jewel, and the decade ended with further acclaim for his *Gallipoli*, Phillip Noyce's extraordinary *Newsfront* and Gillian Armstrong's first feature, *My Brilliant Career*. Auspicious futures were launched for Armstrong, and actors Sam Neill, Judy Davis and Mel Gibson, whose post-apocalyptic *Mad Max* trilogy saw a gradual stylistic evolution to suit the huge American market.

Australian cinema of the 1980s and 1990s was perhaps most exceptional for establishing a number of **women directors** and **producers** and providing a handful of strong women's roles. Inevitably, only the mainstream hits, such as the uplifting *Strictly Ballroom* and *Death in Brunswick*, achieved wide overseas release, while many equally fine "small" films remained largely unseen. It is these quirky, uniquely Australian films of which the rejuvenated industry can be most proud. The prestige of numerous and consistent awards at the Cannes Film Festival and others proved that Australia's long-established cinematographic heritage, more than any other art form, helped rid the country of its former philistine reputation. Confident and uncompromising films such as *Malcolm*, *Celia*, *Sweetie* and *The Year My Voice Broke* were just a few that complemented their better-known siblings. 1994 saw a media-led "renaissance" in Australian film: Stephan Elliott's sartorially outrageous *The Adventures of Priscilla, Queen of the Desert* was the country's biggest box-office success up to that time and won international acclaim, while P.J. Hogan's wonderful *Muriel's Wedding* perfectly encapsulated the indigenous film-making idiom and proved that Australia still could make financially viable and idiosyncratic films. By 1996, however, Australian film critics had grown weary of the trend in making "quirky, offbeat romances", such as Shirley Barratt's *Love Serenade* and Emma-Kate Croghan's 1996 Cannes hit *Love and Other Catastrophes*, although few would have much to complain about with Scott Hicks' globally acclaimed *Shine*.

In the new millennium

At the start of the new millenium, young writer-directors focused on **crime stories**, often blackly comic, such as Gregor Jordan's first feature, the Sydney-set *Two Hands* (1999), which launched the career of Heath Ledger; Scott Roberts' *The Hard Word* (2002), with Guy Pearce and Rachel Griffiths; and Andrew Dominik's more graphic *Chopper* (2000), based on the autobiography of the very scary "Chopper" Read. Another trend has been towards telling **Aboriginal stories**: Rolf de Heer's *The Tracker* (2002) and Phillip Noyce's *Rabbit-Proof Fence* (2002) both look back critically to the attitudes and atrocities of the 1920s and 1930s (respectively), dealing with the difficult subject matter of massacres (de Heer) and the "Stolen Generation" (Noyce). Two films portray indigenous life in Arnhem Land from very different perspectives: Stephen Johnson's *Yolgnu Boy* (2001) confronts contemporary indigenous adolescent experience, including graphic scenes of petrol sniffing, while the humorous storytelling in de Heer's *Ten Canoes* (2006), beautifully photographed in the Arafura Swamp, transcends cultural barriers, appealing in equal measure to the local Yolgnu audience and Western tastes.

Some contemporary Australian films, such as the high-finance thriller *The Bank* by Robert Connolly (2001), starring American-based Anthony LaPaglia, could be set and told in any Western country, whereas films such as *Rabbit-Proof Fence*, Ray Lawrence's bleak but brilliant *Lantana* and Cate Shortland's melancholic *Somersault* show a distinctly Australian sensibility and landscape without exoticism, kitsch suburbia or cute and quirky characters, and reveal a new level of profundity and maturity in Australian cinema.

As the Liberal government slashed funding to the Australian Film Commission and Film Finance Corporation, Australia's phenomenally successful **actors** now work mostly overseas where the pay, recognition and opportunities are much greater. These actors include Oscar-winners Russell Crowe (*Gladiator* and *Master and Commander*), Nicole Kidman (*Moulin Rouge* and *The Hours*) and Geoffrey Rush (*Shine* and *Quills*), and other major actors such as Judy Davis (*Naked Lunch* and *Celebrity*), Mel Gibson (*Braveheart* and *The Patriot*), Rachel Griffiths (*Blow* and the TV series *Six Feet Under*), Toni Collette (*The Sixth Sense* and *Little Miss Sunshine*), Cate Blanchett (*The Aviator*, *The Lord of the Rings*, *Babel*), Sam Neill (*The Piano* and *Jurassic Park*), Anthony LaPaglia (*29th St* and *Lowdown*), Guy Pearce (*L.A. Confidential* and *Memento*), Richard Roxburgh (*Mission Impossible II* and *Moulin Rouge*), Hugh Jackman (*Kate & Leopold* and *Swordfish*), David Wenham (*Moulin Rouge* and *The Lord of the Rings*), Heath Ledger (*10 Things I Hate About You* and *Brokeback Mountain*), Rose Byrne (*I Capture the Castle* and *Troy*) and Naomi Watts (*Mulholland Drive* and *The Assassination of Richard Nixon*). These actors do occasionally return home to star in films such as Gregor Jordan's 2003 *Ned Kelly* (featuring Geoffrey Rush, Naomi Watts and Heath Ledger), but this won't necessarily attract the locals. Australian films usually have short runs at home: in 2004, box-office receipts were a record AUS$907.2 million yet Australian films made up only 1.3 percent of that; 2006 was a slightly more successful year with takings of AUS$866.6 million and 4.6 percent of that from Australian films.

However, a low Australian dollar, skilled crews and Sydney's Fox Studios (see p.138), which opened in 1998, have attracted major productions such as *Dark City*, *The Matrix* trilogy, *Mission Impossible II*, *Star Wars Episode II* and *III*, *Superman Returns*, *Moulin Rouge* and *The Quiet American* to Australia.

Films to watch out for

While you'd be lucky to catch all the recommendations below on the big screen (although keep an eye on the programmes of art-house, or repertory, cinemas in the major cities), many of the titles can be found in video-rental stores.

Humour, black comedy and satire

The Adventures of Priscilla, Queen of the Desert (Stephan Elliott, 1994). A queer romp across the Outback, prying into some musty corners of Australian social life along the way.

Babakiueria (Julian Pringler, 1988). A culture-reversing spoof beginning with Aborigines invading Australia during a roadside barbie and continuing with an anthropological-style study of white Australia. Rare, but well worth the search.

The Castle (Rob Sitch, 1997). A family's struggle to defend their home in the face of a trinity of suburban horrors: toxic-waste dumps, overhead power-lines and airport developers.

Death in Brunswick (John Ruane, 1990). A black comedy about the misfortunes of a hapless dishwasher who becomes embroiled in a gangland killing.

The Hard Word (Scott Roberts, 2002). Three bank-robbing brothers (one played by Guy Pearce) are in cahoots with corrupt cops and a crooked lawyer. Their target: $100 million in cash held by Melbourne Cup bookies. Double-and-triple crossing has them on the run from everyone. Also stars Rachel Griffiths.

Kenny (Clayton Jacobson, 2006). The eponymous hero is a plumber, owner of a Portaloo business – expect lots of lavatory humour – whose family and ex-wife give him a hard time. A heart-warming "mockumentary" of the quintessential decent Aussie bloke.

Malcolm (Nadia Tass, 1985). A charming, offbeat comedy about a slow-witted tram driver in Melbourne.

Muriel's Wedding (P.J. Hogan, 1994). Kleptomaniac frump Muriel wastes away in an Abba-and-confetti dreamworld until ex-schoolchum Rhonda masterminds Muriel's escape from her awful family and ghastly seaside suburb of Porpoise Spit. Great performances.

Adolescent and misfit romance

Better Than Sex (Jonathan Teplitzky, 2000). Josh, played by David Wenham (*The Boys*), has only three days left until he goes back to London, so a one-night, after-party fling with Cin (*Susie Porter, Mullet*) shouldn't hold any complications. A very sexy, warm and hilarious romantic comedy.

Flirting (John Duigan, 1989). This sequel to *The Year My Voice Broke* follows a young boy's adventures in

Hot spots for film buffs and soap groupies

The majestic scenery of the Northern Territory has featured in many films. **Kakadu National Park** provided the setting for many of the scenes in *Crocodile Dundee*: familiar spots are possibly Anbangbang Billabong (see p.572) and Waterfall Creek (see p.574). *We of the Never Never* was set in the **Mataranka** region, which, predictably, has been rechristened "Never Never" country (see p.587).

Desolation and Outback grandeur have a stranglehold on the science-fiction and post-apocalyptic genres. Locations for *Mad Max II* include the **Silverton** area of New South Wales (see p.353); as his parting shot, Mel Gibson upscuttled the semi-trailer on the nearby **Mundi Mundi Plains**. In nearby **Broken Hill**, scenes from *The Adventures of Priscilla, Queen of the Desert* were filmed at the kitsch *Mario's Palace Hotel* (see p.348). In South Australia, the pockmarked scenery of **Coober Pedy** (see p.798) has found favour with many film-makers, including Wim Wenders, who made his epic *Until the End of the World* here, while the lunar-like landscape was also an invaluable element in creating the atmosphere of *Mad Max III*. And that Outback pub in *Crocodile Dundee* was none other than the *Walkabout Creek Hotel*, at **McKinlay** in Queensland (see p.526).

More lush surroundings have also caught the imagination: in Victoria, the eponymous **Hanging Rock** (see p.914), which featured in *Picnic at Hanging Rock*, is within striking distance of **Woodend** (though the imposing mansion-school is actually in South Australia, the visitable Martindale Hall in the Clare Valley – see p.786).

The production of big-budget international films at Fox Studios in **Sydney** has provided locals with many location-spotting opportunities: *Mission Impossible II* provided the best haul, including scenes filmed at the **Bare Island** fortifications (see p.154). The soapy teenage angst and surfie bonhomie of *Home and Away* has long revolved around **Palm Beach** in Sydney's northern beaches (see p.153), with the **Barrenjoey Lighthouse** and headland regularly in shot. **Melbourne** is famous for being the filming location of *Home and Away*'s competitor, the veteran soap *Neighbours*; Ramsay Street, Erinsborough, is actually Pin Oak Court in Vermont South, while the cool international-hit TV series, *The Secret Life of Us* was filmed around St Kilda.

boarding school. Superior coming-of-age film.

Lonely Hearts (Paul Cox, 1981). Following the death of his mother, 50-year-old Peter buys a new toupee and joins a dating agency. A sensitive portrayal of the ensuing, at times awkward, relationship. Other Paul Cox features include *Man of Flowers*, *My First Wife* and *Cactus*.

Looking for Alibrandi (Kate Woods, 2000). Light yet surprisingly layered story of a teenage Sydney girl dealing with suicide, high school, new love and immigrant cultural identity.

Mullet (David Caesar, 2001). A slow-motion plot set in a New South Wales south-coast fishing town where nothing happens until a mysterious prodigal son (Ben Mendelsohn) returns to mixed receptions from his family, former friends and fiancée.

Somersault (Cate Shortland, 2004). Having been caught pashing with her mother's no-hoper boyfriend, 16-year-old Heidi runs away from home and winds up in wintery Jindabyne in the snowfields of southern New South Wales. She tries to cobble together a new life there, but her strong sensuality, coupled with emotional fragility, gets her into new trouble. Sensitive portrait of adolescent female sexuality.

Strictly Ballroom (Baz Luhrmann, 1991). Mismatched dancers who, together, dare to defy the prescribed routines. A feel-good hit at Cannes and the box office, and the first feature from the highly successful director of *Moulin Rouge* (2001).

Urban dysfunctionals

The Boys (Rowan Woods, 1998). This tense drama follows Brett, played by rising star David Wenham (*Better Than Sex*) as an ex-prisoner who terrorizes his dysfunctional family and coerces his unemployed brothers into a violent crime.

Careful, He Might Hear You (Carl Shultz, 1982). An absorbing tug-of-love drama set in 1930s Sydney.

Chopper (Andrew Dominik, 2000). Eric Bana brilliantly plays notorious, nihilistic Melbourne criminal Mark "Chopper" Read who ruthlessly dominates prison inmates and underworld associates alike. Based on Read's autobiography.

The Devil's Playground (Fred Schepisi, 1975). Burgeoning sexuality oozes between pupils and their tutors in a Catholic seminary.

Head On (Ana Kokkinos, 1998). Unemployed Ari (Alex Dimitriades) escapes living with his strict Greek parents by spending a hectic 24 hours nightclubbing, drug taking and graphically exploring his homosexuality.

Lantana (Ray Lawrence, 2001). A sometimes bleak but thought-provoking tale of trust and secrecy in marriage, set in Sydney. Coincidences and consequences bind lives of strangers together in ways that are as twisting, tangled and tough as the Australian plant that provides the film's title. The strong cast includes Geoffrey Rush and Anthony LaPaglia.

The Last Days of Chez Nous (Gillian Armstrong, 1991). A middle-aged woman slowly loses her grip on her marriage and family.

Romper Stomper (Geoffrey Wright, 1991). A bleak and pointless account of the violent disintegration of a gang of Melbourne skinheads, notable only as Russell Crowe's big-screen debut.

Sweetie (Jane Campion, 1988). Part black comedy, part bleakly disturbing portrait of a bizarre suburban family.

Ockerdom

The Adventures of Barry McKenzie (Bruce Beresford, 1972). Ultra-ocker comes to England to teach the "pommie sheilas about real men". Ironically, Barry Humphries' satire got beer-spurting ovations from the very people he despised and also set Beresford back a couple of years.

Crocodile Dundee (Peter Faiman, 1985). The acceptable side of genial, dinky-di ockerdom saw Paul Hogan sell Australian bush mystique to the mainstream and put Kakadu National Park firmly on the tourist agenda. Enjoyable once, but don't bother with the sequels.

Wake in Fright aka Outback (Ted Kotcheff, 1970). A horrifying gem in its uncut, 114min version; a real *Deliverance* Down Under. A coast-bound teacher blows his fare in Outback Hicksville and his life slowly degenerates into a brutal, beer-sodden nightmare.

Gritty and defiant women

Celia (Ann Turner, 1988). A wonderful allegory that mixes a 1950s rabbit-eradication programme with a communist witch-hunt. Stubborn Celia is determined to keep her bunny.

Dance Me to My Song (Rolf de Heer, 1998). A unique and moving film written by and starring cerebral-palsy-sufferer Heather Rose as she is abused by her carer and falls in love.

The Getting of Wisdom (Bruce Beresford, 1977). Spirited Laura rejects the polite sensibilities and snobbery of an Edwardian boarding school.

My Brilliant Career (Gillian Armstrong, 1978). An early feminist questions and defies the expectations of 1890s Victoria.

Puberty Blues (Bruce Beresford, 1981). Two teenage beach girls refuse to accept their pushchair-and-shopping-trolley destiny.

We of the Never Never (Igor Auzins, 1981). A good-looking version of Jeannie Gunn's autobiographical classic of early twentieth-century station life in the Top End.

Men in rugged circumstances

The Dish (Rob Sitch, 2000). Light-hearted take on how Australia saved NASA during the broadcasting of the 1969 Apollo 11 moon landing from New South Wales' Parkes Space Observatory (see p.311), and an aside on how the country's technological skills are often overlooked. Starring Sam Neill.

Gallipoli (Peter Weir, 1980). A deservedly classic buddy movie in which a young Mel Gibson strikingly evokes the Anzacs' cheery idealism and the tragedy of their slaughter.

The Last of the Knucklemen (Tim Burstall, 1978). Tensions build up in a remote Outback mine and explode in bare-fisted punch-ups.

The Man from Snowy River (George Miller, 1981). Men, horses and the land from A.B. ("Banjo") Paterson's seminal and dearly loved poem caught the overseas' imagination. A modern kangaroo western.

Plains of Heaven (Ian Pringle, 1982). A spookily atmospheric story of two weathermen in a remote meteorological station slowly losing their minds.

Sunday Too Far Away (Ken Hannam, 1973). A simple tale of macho shearers' rivalries in Outback South Australia.

Outback nightmares

Cunnamulla (Dennis O'Rourke, 2000). Controversial documentary of malaise in an isolated Outback town, 800km west of Brisbane, shot in a laconic style befitting Queensland, and featuring inhabitants' own stories of teen sex and hopelessness, frontier redneckery, racial tension, social dysfunction, and desperate longings for escape to distant cities.

Evil Angels (*A Cry in the Dark*) (Fred Schepisi, 1987). A dramatic retelling of the Azaria Chamberlain story; Ayers Rock (Uluru) and dingoes will never seem quite the same again.

Picnic at Hanging Rock (Peter Weir, 1975). A richly layered tale about the disappearance of a party of schoolgirls and its traumatic aftermath.

Razorback (Russell Mulcahy, 1984). Dark comedy exploiting urban paranoia of the Outback and featuring a remote township, a gigantic, psychotic wild pig, and some bloodthirsty nutters who run the local abattoir.

Walkabout (Nicolas Roeg, 1971). Following their deranged father's suicide during a bush picnic, two children wander through the wilderness until an Aboriginal boy guides them back to civilization.

Wolf Creek (Greg McLean, 2005). Three backpackers are stuck in the desert at nightfall, hundreds of miles from anywhere, when their car won't start. Luckily, help is at hand in the person of Mick Taylor, an affable truck driver who offers to tow them to his place down the road to fix the car. Or so the backpackers think... Relentless, terrifying, nightmare Outback slasher movie inspired by the (real) Milat backpacker murders of the 1990s.

About Aboriginal people

The Chant of Jimmie Blacksmith (Fred Schepisi, 1977). Set in the 1800s, when a mixed-race boy is forced onto the wrong side of the law. Based on the novel by Thomas Keneally.

Dead Heart (Brian Brown, 1996). A long-overdue and regrettably overlooked thriller, set on an Aboriginal community near Alice Springs. Bravely gets its teeth into some juicy political and social issues.

The Fringe Dwellers (Bruce Beresford, 1985). An aspiring daughter persuades her family to move from the bush into a suburban white neighbourhood, with expected results.

Jedda, the Uncivilized (Charles Chauvel, 1955). An orphaned Aboriginal girl brought up by a "civilized" white family cannot resist her "tribal" urges when she is semi-voluntarily abducted by a black outlaw.

Manganinnie (John Honey, 1980). Set during the time of the "black drives" of 1830s Tasmania, a young Aboriginal girl gets separated from her family and meets a white girl in similar straits.

Rabbit-Proof Fence (Phillip Noyce, 2002). Very moving film, with beautiful cinematography, set in 1930s Western Australia and based on a true "Stolen Generation" story. Three girls, daughters of absent white fathers – construction workers of the fence itself – and black mothers, are taken from their families according to the policy of the all-powerful A.O. Neville, Chief Protector of Aborigines (Kenneth Branagh) to a settlement at Moore River, but manage to escape. The girls – Outback-cast unknowns giving emotive, natural performances – make their way over 2000km home following the fence, pursued by a tracker (David Gulpilil).

Ten Canoes (Rolf de Heer, 2005). A goose-egg-hunting expedition in the Arafura Wetlands in Arnhem Land in tribal times: Dayindi (played by Jamie Gulpilil, son of David Gulpilil) fancies one of the wives of his older brothers – a threat to tribal law. To teach him a lesson, the older brother tells him a parable from the mythical past. The story weaves back and forth between the two timelines, with the dreamtime events in colour, the goose-egg hunting in black and white. This beautifully photographed and humorously narrated film (voice-over by David Gulpilil) has a timeless appeal that transcends cultures. It is the result of close co-operation between de Heer, David Gulpilil and the Arnhem Land community of Ramingining.

The Tracker (Rolf de Heer, 2002). Set in 1922, this is something of a fable told in an experimental way. Each character is a type: "The Fanatic", a police officer who will stop at nothing including cold-blooded massacre, leads "The Tracker" (the film is a star vehicle for David Gulpilil), "The Follower" (a young, green policeman), and "The Veteran", all in search of "The Accused", an indigenous man wanted for a white woman's murder. Violent massacre scenes are replaced by landscape paintings but with a painful soundtrack, while songs (performed by Aboriginal musician Archie Roach) and narration mostly convey the themes, creating a disturbing impression.

Yolgnu Boy (Stephen Johnson, 2001). In Yolgnu country in Arnhem Land, Lorrpu, Milika and Bortj have always been an inseparable trio. But when adolescence hits, 15-year-old Bortj's petrol-sniffing rampages land him in jail; as Lorrpu and Milika become tribally initiated, Bortj finds himself outside his own culture and unable to become a man, and friendships and loyalties are tested. When the three embark on a – beautifully shot – 500-kilometre overland trek to Darwin, living off the land, distress gives way to joy ... until they hit the city.

Portents of doom

Cane Toads: an Unnatural History (Mark Lewis, 1988). A very eccentric, original and amusing documentary about the mixed feelings Queensland's poisonous amphibians arouse and the real threat they may pose to Australia's ecology.

The Last Wave (Peter Weir, 1977). An eerie chiller about a lawyer defending an Aborigine accused of murder – and the powerful, elemental forces his people control.

Mad Max II (George Miller, 1981). The best of the trilogy, set in a near future where loner Max protects an oil-producing community from fuel-starved crazies. Great machinery and stunts.

Australian music

For a geographically isolated, sparsely inhabited island with a tiny market for its own recorded music, Australia has, with ever more assurance, shouldered its way in to occupy a distinguished place in the international pop-music hierarchy. In contrast with its fifty-year rock-music heritage, the country's Aboriginal music boasts a creative presence of thousands of years. With a strong influence on contemporary Australian music, its importance in the ongoing reconciliation between black and white Australia can hardly be overstated.

Rock music

The story of Australian contemporary music closely parallels that of Britain and the US – rock'n'roll arrived in the 1950s, and each decade since has offered up its own revolutionary shift in the popular-music landscape. Given the ubiquitous nature of Western popular culture, this is hardly surprising. Less predictable, however, has been the impact of Australian music on the global music scene, beginning in the 1970s with AC/DC, continuing in the 1980s with Midnight Oil and INXS, through to the more recent Silverchair, The Vines and Jet.

The early years

Australia's very first rock star emerged in 1957 in the form of a lean, throaty, stage-strutting powerhouse named **Johnny O'Keefe**. All snake-hips and sex appeal, "The Wild One", as he became known, was one of the few early rock performers who could very nearly out-Elvis Elvis. Concert footage of his live performances is largely taken up by shots of women screaming, passing out and being carried from concert venues by sweaty police and exhausted security people. O'Keefe discovered early on that all the big players in the industry – performers, managers, promoters and record companies – were expert manipulators, and he quickly set about becoming one himself: legend has it that he bullied his way into his first recording contract by calling a press conference and announcing that the deal was done, guessing correctly that the publicity would leave the record company no option but to sign him.

Johnny O'Keefe was, to Australians, the embodiment of the defiant new brand of music that was then sweeping the world. He was to become synonymous with 1960s TV programmes that showcased Australian rock'n'roll talent, even as his own recording efforts were gradually swamped by the peace-love-hair movement of the time. O'Keefe remained a presence on television and radio until his death of a heart attack in 1978, aged just 43. In keeping with the requirements of rock god-dom, his last years were characterized by a series of breakdowns, bouts of depression and problems with alcohol. His rendition of the classic crowd-anthem **Shout** (1959) remains, to this day, an integral part of early rock'n'roll's global legacy.

Surviving the Sixties

In company with the rest of the world, Australian music rode out the 1960s hanging onto the coat-tails of the massive British rock invasion. Overwhelmed by the omnipresent Beatles and Rolling Stones, Australia was to produce little ground-breaking rock music beyond the efforts of Billy Thorpe and the Aztecs, The Easybeats and Russell Morris, each of whom left behind a signature song forever embedded in the Australian psyche, and still played on commercial radio today: *Most People I Know (Think that I'm Crazy)* – Billy Thorpe and the Aztecs (1968); *Friday on My Mind* – The Easybeats (1966); *The Real Thing* – Russell Morris (1969).

The Seekers, however, were operating well clear of the crowded rock-music mainstream, creating their own musical niche by building three-part harmonies around chords strummed on acoustic guitars, the two male voices cushioning the pristine power of lead vocalist Judith Durham. Songs such as *If I Had a Hammer* (1965) might sound like hippie anthems today, but The Seekers' brand of idealism appealed to millions of record-buyers, and several successful comeback tours show that their popularity has barely waned.

It was in 1967, though, that millions of Australians witnessed the decade's most significant music-industry event – and not a single one of them even knew it. A young man named **Johnny Farnham** had appeared on television, performing a cute but innocuous ditty entitled *Sadie (the Cleaning Lady)* (1967). Good-looking and with a superb voice, as well as charming beyond his years, Farnham endeared himself immediately to Australian audiences; it was a promising debut, but nobody could have predicted how far he'd go. His name shortened these days to John, Farnham is now into his fifth decade as a performer, and continues to shift with apparently effortless ease between roles as rock star, stage-musical lead and TV personality. From 1982 to 1986 he was a popular frontman for the hugely successful Little River Band (having replaced Glen Shorrock), but it was in 1987 that his career peaked, with the release of his album *Whispering Jack*, which sold millions of copies worldwide, driven, appropriately enough, by the success of the single *You're the Voice* (1987).

Livin' in the Seventies

Having emerged from the shadows of the 1960s, Australian music began to find a voice of its own in the mid-1970s. For no obvious reason, **Glam Rock** was a phenomenon Australian bands not only embraced, but excelled at. Sherbet and **Skyhooks** pulled off the satin-jumpsuits-and-crazy-make-up combo with singular style. The "Mighty Hooks" were at all times the cheekier and sexier of the two. Singer "Shirley" Strachan famously performed in only a pair of tight satin trousers with a large, bright-red hand painted over the crotch; the other band-members were equally indulgent of their penchants for self-expression.

Top ten great Oz rock albums

1) *Livin' in the Seventies* Skyhooks. Mushroom Records, 1974.
2) *Howzat!* Sherbet. Sherbet Records, 1976.
3) *Goodbye Tiger* Richard Clapton. Infinity Records, 1977.
4) *Back in Black* AC/DC. Albert Records, 1980.
5) *East* Cold Chisel. WEA, 1980.
6) *Business As Usual* Men At Work. CBS, 1981.
7) *Kick* INXS. WEA, 1987.
8) *Diesel and Dust* Midnight Oil. CBS, 1987.
9) *Songs From the South: Paul Kelly's Greatest Hits* Paul Kelly. Mushroom Records, 1997.
10) *Highly Evolved* The Vines. Capitol Records, 2002.

There was no sacrifice of substance for style, however, with the band recording several of Australia's finest and most enduring pop songs, including such irresistible numbers as *You Just Like Me 'cause I'm Good in Bed* (1974), *Horror Movie* (1974), *Ego (Is Not a Dirty Word)* (1975), and *Women in Uniform* (1978).

Sherbet seemed almost serious by comparison, doing without the make-up and looking as though they only wore the satin pants, silly shoes and poncy scarves because that was what fashion dictated. It was a highly accomplished band no matter what they were wearing, and led by virtuoso pop vocalist Daryl Braithwaite, they recorded several standout tracks, including *Child's Play* (1976), *Howzat!* (1976), *High Rolling* (1977) and *Summer Love* (1975). Although both bands flirted with overseas success, touring the US (and subsequently expressing bitterness at not having cracked the big time), history has conferred upon them the honour of having kicked open the rock-music establishment's door, on behalf of an Australian music fraternity that had simply been waiting around for someone to show them "we're just as good as those bands from overseas".

Proof perhaps of the depth of talent concentrated in these two bands is the continued presence of individual members in Australian music and media today. Trivia buffs can still track down various Skyhooks alumni: former guitarist Red Symons is now a Melbourne radio announcer and is regularly cast as the villain on some of TV's nastier game shows, while Greg Macainsh is in high demand still as a bass player and songwriter; former lead singer Graeme "Shirley" Strachan was tragically killed in a helicopter crash in 2001, having enjoyed almost twenty years as a popular TV presenter. Stalwarts of Sherbet likewise have soldiered on: Daryl Braithwaite, the lead singer, is now a successful solo performer; and Garth Porter, former keyboardist, has gone on to assume the unlikely mantle of producer/guru for many of Australia's top country-music performers.

But even as Glam Rock was fading from cool to kitsch, a clannish group of young Scottish immigrants were beginning to play their own version of Chuck Berry–inspired blues-rock, only three times as loud and with heavily distorted guitars. **AC/DC** not only had the skills, the songs and the "muscle" to back it all up, they also boasted two figures who were destined to become universal icons of rock'n'roll rebellion: guitarist Angus Young's delinquent-schoolboy persona had to share the adulation of wannabe rock rebels with singer Bon Scott, who was possessed not only of a genuine, self-destructive, live-hard-die-young ethos, but also sported the most mischievous grin ever seen in tandem with a microphone. It's unlikely anyone besides Bon could have delivered songs such as *Highway to Hell* (1979), *Whole Lotta Rosie* (1978), and *Dirty Deeds...Done Dirt Cheap* (1976) with the required sass to make them acceptable in a 1970s commercial market.

True to form, Bon died a rock-star's death in London in 1980, poisoned by alcohol in the back seat of a car. It was, ironically, smack in the middle of a golden age for Australian music, when, during the period 1977–83, bands Men at Work, Midnight Oil, Cold Chisel, INXS, Air Supply and Little River Band were lining up right alongside AC/DC to take the pop-music world by storm.

Oz music grows up

Even as AC/DC managed – in the space of a year following Bon's death – to recruit a new singer (Brian Johnston), settle permanently into life in Britain, and record the most acclaimed and successful heavy-rock album of all time, *Back in Black* (1980), bands back in Australia suddenly found that the world was interested in them, too. **Little River Band**'s sound was so West Coast USA that commercial success in North America had long seemed inevitable; **Air Supply**, meanwhile, had the sort of stranglehold on the American easy listening love-song market to which Michael Bolton was perhaps, even then, beginning to aspire. More surprising was the impact made by **Men at Work**, a band whose well-crafted songs were invariably, if unfashionably, punctuated by arresting melodies played on a flute, and whose style came to be described as "white reggae". They announced their arrival in 1981 with the ska-ish *Who Can It Be Now?*, followed by *The Land Down Under*, both of which bombarded radio airwaves and shifted by the million.

During this period, Midnight Oil, Cold Chisel and INXS stayed closer to home, recognizing perhaps that their styles were less easily translatable from an Australian to a global audience. It is surely no coincidence that among these bands (all highly accomplished, and equally revered at home) the least identifiably "Australian" act – **INXS** – was the first to experience worldwide fame and fortune, when in 1987 their album *Kick* plundered the US charts. (This wave of success held tragic implications for singer Michael Hutchence; he would struggle to make the transition from rock star to rock superstar, suffering depression until his death by suicide in 1997.) Of the other two, most needs to be said about the band that had the biggest impact at home, and the least impact abroad – Cold Chisel. If the period three years either side of 1980 was to be remembered as the grand era of Oz "pub rock", then Chisel was the band that owned it, lock, stock and smoking barrel.

From Chisel to The Church

Formed in Adelaide in 1975, **Cold Chisel** was, like every great band from the Rolling Stones to U2, greater than the sum of its parts. Steve Prestwich (drums) and Phil Small (bass) made a compact and classy rhythm team, variously casting light and shadow about the more illustrious members of the group. Ian Moss's blues-rock guitar virtuosity and awesome soul voice made him a natural star on any stage, in lethal combination with lead singer Jimmy Barnes, Australia's self-styled wild man of rock and working-class hero. A great band must have great songs, and these were duly delivered by the immensely tall and serious man at the piano, **Don Walker**, arguably Australia's greatest songwriter.

Among hundreds of examples of Don Walker's craftsmanship in capturing the times/places/people/events poignant to Australians, *Khe Sanh* (1978) – a treatise on the Australian experience of surviving the war in Vietnam – remains a work without peer, while *Star Hotel* (1980) encapsulates, in three verses and a chorus, the mood and events of September 19, 1979, when, in the working-class steel-town of Newcastle, police came to close down the city's main pub-rock venue, *The Star Hotel*, only to find themselves confronted by an angry crowd spoiling for a fight. Police cars were overturned and set alight in the course of a civil disturbance that echoed convict rebellions of two centuries earlier. The hotel was finally closed down, but the punters had made their point – and Chisel weren't going to let the police forget it.

Cold Chisel not only recorded the boozy summer nights, the trips up the coast, the girls, the fights, the pubs, the streets, the cities and towns, they sang it all back to the faithful in sweaty pubs and heaving stadiums night after night. When they called it a day in 1984, Chisel were Australia's greatest-ever rock band, bar none. "Mossy" and "Barnesy" went on to fame and fortune as solo performers, but the band's long-awaited return did not come until 1998, when they released their first studio album in fourteen years, *The Last Wave of Summer*; predictably, though, it failed to capture the power of the band in its heyday.

During this period, **Midnight Oil** by no means played second fiddle to Cold Chisel; rather, they had a different agenda, and their commitment and energy in delivering it live were never in question. Always highly political (lead singer Peter Garrett narrowly missed out on a Senate seat while he was leader of Australia's Nuclear Disarmament Party), "the Oils" brought Aboriginal land rights into the forum of pop culture, even as their uncompromising album *Diesel and Dust* (1987) brought them worldwide success. Twenty-five-year veterans with fourteen albums to their credit (and often bracketed by critics with bands like Queen and U2 as the most powerful live act in the world), Midnight Oil's rage against the machine ended in 2002, with Peter Garrett leaving the band in order to resume his political career. In 2004, he was elected Labor member for Kingsford Smith, and stands on committees for indigenous people's affairs and the arts.

Among the distinguished musicians of the 1970s and 1980s, two songwriters stand (alongside Don Walker) above the rest as chroniclers of their culture and environment: **Richard Clapton** and **Paul Kelly**. Clapton's 1977 album *Goodbye Tiger* is unmatched as a celebration of the very fact of life in Australia – riding the city tram, searching for the perfect wave, soaking up the streetscapes of Oxford Street and Kings Cross. Paul Kelly is a more contemporary presence, and his songs go unerringly to the heart of the matter: *Have You Ever Seen Sydney from a 727 at Night?* (1985), *From St Kilda to Kings Cross* (1985) and *Adelaide* (1985) capture their respective subjects better than any photograph, while his ode to *Bradman* (1987) – written in homage to Australia's greatest Test cricket batsman Sir Donald Bradman ("The Don"), is the stuff of a true bard.

However, in order to appreciate the depth and diversity of Australian music as it reached **maturity**, one needs to take a stroll out to the fringes. With a well-established canon of "major" Australian bands now in place, others were finding looser creative environments in which to operate. The Triffids, The Birthday Party (with star alumnus Nick Cave), The Church and the Go-Betweens seemed tied to weirder and more eclectic influences (such as The Velvet Underground, David Bowie and Bob Dylan) than their "mainstream" counterparts. Although musically diverse, they held several characteristics in common: their songs seemed more poetic, or just more sensitive to light and shade; they were also far less commercially successful in Australia, yet all made a big impact in Britain and Europe. Among all of these, The Church alone continue to record and tour from various bases in Europe, while Nick Cave enjoys a position of enormous respect within the international music industry, thanks to several well-received albums with his current band The Bad Seeds. Australia could boast, too, a white-hot outfit schooled in the nasty traditions of 1970s British punk: The Saints. Although known for their Sex Pistols-ish two-minute thrash exercises, The Saints were nevertheless real musicians, and survivors Ed Kuepper and Chris Bailey – still singing with an incarnation of the band – continue to record and perform songs of the highest quality.

The Nineties and beyond...

Strangest perhaps of all the facets of Australia's music industry has been its propensity for throwing up **TV soap stars** who mutated into pop stars. At last count, there were no less than five ex-*Neighbours* cast members at large within the music industry: Kylie Minogue, Danii Minogue, Natalie Imbruglia, Holly Valance and Delta Goodrem. Australians have never known what to make of this, but both Natalie Imbruglia and Kylie Minogue have earned their stripes by recording fine pop albums; Holly Valance, meanwhile, has been widely dismissed as just another in a long line of soft-porn pop wannabes.

The roaring success of these soap-star singers goes some way to explaining the listlessness that afflicted the music community during the late 1980s to early 1990s. It seemed the moment **Kylie** was formally adopted by an adoring British public, Australian musicians breathed a collective sigh of relief, and got straight back to work. You Am I, The Whitlams, Powderfinger and The Cruel Sea had always been likely to show the way by writing and recording with passion and originality. By the mid-1990s, quality Australian bands were once again jostling for position in local and overseas markets, this time led by three scruffy-looking, 15-year-old schoolboys.

In 1994, Newcastle high-school trio Innocent Criminals sent a demo tape to radio station Triple J in response to a band competition, the prize for which was use of the station's recording facilities. The song, *Tomorrow*, had the Seattle grunge sound all over it, and an awesome rock vocal performance from singer/guitarist Daniel Johns. He didn't sound like a 15-year-old, although the band's written entry should have given some kind of clue; their "twenty-five-words-or-less" were written in green felt marker-pen on yellow cardboard: "We're not rap or hip-hop, we're rock and we love to play." *Tomorrow* arrived atop the Australian singles charts where it stayed for several weeks, and with the band renamed **Silverchair**, their 1995 album *frogstomp* took them into league – and onto a stage – with grunge giants such as Pearl Jam and Soundgarden, even as the three "boys" were negotiating their last year of high school. Subsequent Silverchair albums *Freak Show* (1997), *Neon Ballroom* (1999) and *Diorama* (2002) all met with solid sales and critical approval. Having fought the twin ravages of anorexia and a crippling bout of arthritis, Daniel Johns took a break from the band to write and record with prominent Aussie DJ Paul Mac, a brief hiatus that is well and truly over – the band's latest album, *Young Modern* (2007), is the most successful one of their career.

Not to be left out of the latest shift in the music biz, Australia has recently seen the emergence of two groups of precocious young rockers – The Vines and Jet. Having tapped into the retro-rock mood that reared its head in 2002 with bands like The Strokes, The White Stripes and The Hives (each of which mined the raw and rampant sound of The Who, The Stooges and The Ramones), **The Vines** exploded onto the world scene with such a rush that they scored both a recording deal and a hit album (*Highly Evolved*, 2002) after having played only a handful of live shows. Since then, beset by on-stage dramas and rumours of a split, their second album *Winning Days* (2004), received mixed reviews, while their third, *Vision Valley* (2006), fared little better; however, impressive live performances in early 2007 hint at brighter things to come. **Jet** soared into the hearts and minds of young rock fans, most notably in the UK, with their absurdly catchy guitar riffs and the kind of hard-living rock attitude that no doubt makes bands such as the Rolling Stones, Led Zeppelin and the Black Crowes (all influences emblazoned on Jet's leather-jacketed sleeves) fairly weep with pride. The album *Get Born* (2003) spent more than a year tearing up the charts worldwide, largely on the strength of the single *Are You Gonna Be My Girl?*, a success that has not quite been matched by the band's second album *Shine On* (2006).

Australian rock music looks set to continue punching well above its weight. From Jet and other rock outfits Powderfinger and Wolfmother to the thrashier Jebediah and The Living End, stylish and witty The Avalanches, and the rock/techno crossover work of Regurgitator, the latest array of talent is dizzying.

Aboriginal music

Aboriginal music is an increasingly powerful and invigorating seam in the fabric of world music. Its instruments and rhythms have a strong influence on contemporary Australian music, and there's probably no better example of the musical crossing of cultural boundaries than in the story of Australia's most recognizable instrument, the didgeridoo. Known also as a *yidaki*, or simply a "didge", this hollowed-out tree branch, when blown into, produces a resonant hum that can be punctuated by imitations of animal and bird noises. Its sound is uniquely evocative of the Australian landscape.

The big surprise for many visitors to Australia is the sheer **diversity** of Aboriginal music. From the big rock sound of the Warumpi Band, and the heartfelt guitar ballads of Archie Roach, to the cruisey island reggae of Saltwater and the echoes of an ancient culture in the work of Nabarlek (who sing mostly in their own language), there is no way of pigeonholing the music. The hottest new indigenous talent to hit the radio airwaves is Yilila, a band whose music – an energetic mix of pulsing didge, screaming guitar solos and funky bass – is based on the story of *Dhumbala* or Red Flag, which chronicles their ancestors' centuries-old relationship with Indonesian traders.

It's no problem to see Aboriginal bands playing live, doing everything from metal to hip-hop and performing in all parts of the country, but there's really no better way to immerse yourself than by attending an indigenous music festival.

Festivals

Biggest of all the festivals is the **Barunga Sports & Cultural Festival**, which showcases up to forty bands, along with team sports, traditional dance, spear-throwing and didge-playing competitions. It's held at Barunga Community, 80km south of Katherine in the NT, over the Queen's Birthday holiday weekend in June (campsites with facilities are available); for information, phone the Barunga Community direct on ⓣ08/8971 2427. Also in the Top End, the Milingimbi community's **Gattjirrk Cultural Festival** is purely a music event and, being harder to get to than Barunga, gets fewer white visitors. Dates for this one are hard to nail down, although it's always held sometime mid-year, on Milingimbi Island in the Crocodile archipelago. There are flights from Darwin, otherwise you need permission from the Northern Land Council (Darwin Head Office ⓣ08/8920 5100, ⓦwww.nlc.org.au) to drive across Arnhem Land to Ramingining to catch a barge. Traditional music and dance are featured, along with gospel bands and lots of Arnhem Land rock.

The **Laura Dance Festival** (ⓦwww.laurafestival.tv), held every odd-numbered year in far north Queensland (next one is 2009), attracts high-profile performers like the Warumpi Band and Christine Anu, plus all the local Murri bands. Held in June, there are usually quite a few backpackers and hippies about, as well as the local Murri community. It's about three hours' drive (on sealed roads) north from Cairns to Laura, a small town 60km west of Cooktown. The vibrant **Festival of the Dreaming** (ⓦwww.thedreamingfestival.com) takes place each June near the town of Woodford, northwest of Brisbane. Begun in 2006, this major four-day event features a strong line-up of musical talent alongside other cultural events.

Otherwise, another intriguing possibility on the west coast is the **Stompem Ground Festival**. First staged in Broome, Western Australia, in 1992, it drew on the strong and highly independent Aboriginal communities of the Kimberley region, attracting singers, dancers and bands into the incomparable beauty of Western Australia's far north, and is finally establishing itself on the Broome annual events calendar (Sept/Oct; ⓦwww.kimberleytourism.com) and is well worth checking out. Even if you find yourself stranded in the Big Smoke, you need not miss out; if you're in **Sydney** over summer, there's no better place to be on the Australia Day holiday (January 26) than at "Survival", Waverley Oval, Bondi. This festival began as a highly political event, deliberately juxtaposed with the Australia Day festivities that mark the arrival of the First Fleet of "white invaders". It continues as a celebration of the survival of indigenous people and cultures in the face of white oppression, and draws many of the biggest names in indigenous music.

Artists

Most of the **bands** mentioned above have work available on CD, while other outstanding artists whose albums are widely available include Yothu Yindi, No Fixed Address, Tiddas, Kev Carmody and Coloured Stone. Compilation albums are worth looking into also, particularly those that cover a wide range of styles: *Meinmuk: Music from the Top End* (1996) and *Culture: Music from Black Australia* (2000) are Triple J compilations that showcase both the quality and diversity of Aboriginal music – from rock, reggae and rap to gospel and metal. CAAMA (Central Australian Aboriginal Media Association) is an excellent source for the latest indigenous CDs and videos, all of which are available online at ⓦwww.caama.com.au.

Books

Australian writing came into its own in the 1890s, when a strong nationalistic movement, leading up to eventual federation in 1901, produced writers such as Henry Lawson and the balladeer A.B. "Banjo" Paterson, who romanticized the bush and glorified the mateship ethos, while outstanding women writers, such as Miles Franklin and Barbara Baynton, gave a feminine slant to the bush tale and set the trend for a strong female authorship. In the twentieth and twenty-first centuries, Australian novelists came to be recognized in the international arena: Patrick White was awarded a Nobel Prize in 1973, Peter Carey won the Booker Prize in 1988 and again in 2001, and Kate Grenville scored the 2001 Orange Prize for Fiction. Other writers who have made a name for themselves within Australia, such as David Malouf, Julia Leigh, Tim Winton (twice nominated for the Booker Prize), Thomas Keneally, Richard Flanagan, Chloe Hooper and Robyn Davidson have aroused curiosity further afield. Literary journals such as *Meanjin*, *Southerly*, *Westerly* and *Heat* provide a forum and exposure for short fiction, essays, reviews and new and established writers. The big prizes in Australian fiction include the Vogel Prize for the best unpublished novel written by an author under the age of 35, and the country's most coveted literary prize, the Miles Franklin Award.

Many of the best books by Australian writers or about Australia are not available overseas, so you may be surprised at the range of local titles available in Australian **bookshops**. A good website to check is that of Gleebooks (ⓦwww.gleebooks.com.au), one of Australia's best literary booksellers, with a whole host of recent reviews; you can also order books online, to be posted overseas.

Travel and travel guides

Peter Carey *30 Days in Sydney: a wildly distorted account*. Part of Bloomsbury Publishers' "The Writer and the City" project, where "some of the finest writers of our time reveal the secrets of a city they know best". Based in New York, famous Australian writer Carey set himself a thirty-day time frame and gave it its aforementioned subtitle to defuse ideas that it might be a comprehensive guide. As he hangs out with old friends, it is their lives, the tales they tell and the often nostalgic trips around Sydney that form the basis of this vivid city portrait.

Bruce Chatwin *Songlines*. A semifictional account of an exploration into Aboriginal nomadism and mythology that turns out to be one of the more readable expositions of this complex subject, though often pretentious.

Sean Condon *Sean and David's Long Drive*. Australia's answer to Kerouac's *On the Road*, with humour in overdrive: Melbourne-based Condon and his friend David are fully fledged city dwellers when they set off on a tour around their own country, to come face to face with the dangers of crocs, tour guides and fellow travellers.

Robyn Davidson *Tracks*. A compelling account of a young woman's journey across the Australian desert, accompanied only by four camels and a dog. Davidson manages to break out of the heroic-traveller mould to write with compassion and honesty of the people she meets in the Outback and the doubts, dangers and loneliness she faces on her way. A classic of its kind.

Larry Habegger (ed) *Traveller's Tales Australia*. Excerpts and essays from some of the world's best travel writers – Bruce Chatwin, Tim Cahill, Jan Morris, Tony Horwitz, Pico Iyer and Paul Theroux – as well as new talents.

Tony Horwitz *One for the Road*. Married to an Australian, Pulitzer Prize–winning American author Horwitz comes to live in Sydney, but pines for adventure and sets off to hitchhike through the Outback. Along the way he encounters colourful characters from Aborigines to jackeroos, and hard-drinking men in a multitude of bush pubs. A comical yet highly perceptive account.

Howard Jacobson *In the Land of Oz*. Jacobson focuses his lucidly sarcastic observations on a round-Australia trip in the late 1980s that gets rather too close to some home truths for most Australians' tastes.

Mark McCrum *No Worries*. Knowing nothing of the country except the usual clichés, McCrum arrives in 1990s Australia and makes his way around by plane, train, thumb and Greyhound, meeting a surprising cast of characters along the way. As he travels, the stereotypes give way to an insightful picture of modern Australia.

Ruth Park *Ruth Park's Sydney*. Prolific novelist Park's 1973 guide to the city was fully revised and expanded in 1999. A perfect walking companion, full of personal insights, anecdotes and literary quotations.

Nicholas Shakespeare *In Tasmania*. During the seven years writing and researching a biography of Bruce Chatwin, British writer Shakespeare spent time in Australia following in his footsteps. Lured to Tasmania as one of the few remote places Chatwin had *never* been to, Shakespeare now lives there six months of the year. Discovery of a cache of letters written by the black sheep of the family revealed a Tasmanian connection: ancestor – and colourful villain – Anthony Fenn Kemp. Researching his family history, Shakespeare found living Tasmanian relatives on his mother's side: two elderly spinsters who'd only once left their farm. A brilliantly Chatwinesque book, where historical tales weave in with the writer's own experiences.

Alice Thomson *The Singing Line*. The great-great-granddaughter of Alice Todd, the woman after whom Alice Springs was named, retraces her ancestor's journey to central Australia. Nice change from the usual male-centric view of the early pioneers.

Mark Whittaker and Amy Willesee *The Road to Mount Buggery: a Journey through the Curiously Named Places of Australia*. Australia certainly has some unfortunate, banal and obscure place-names, which Mark and Amy seek out on their journey, from Lake Disappointment to Cape Catastrophe. This entertaining, well-informed travelogue gives the fascinating stories behind the names.

Autobiography and biography

Julia Blackburn *Daisy Bates in the Desert*. For almost thirty years from 1913, Daisy Bates was Kabbarli, "the white-skinned grandmother", to the Aboriginal people with whom she lived in the desert. Blackburn's beautifully written biography interweaves fiction with fact to conjure up the life of one of Australia's most eccentric and misunderstood women.

Jill Ker Conway *The Road from Coorain*. Conway's childhood, on a drought-stricken Outback station during the 1940s, is movingly told, as is her battle to establish herself as a young historian in sexist, provincial 1950s Australia.

Robert Drewe *The Shark Net.* Accomplished novelist and journalist, Drewe has written a transfixing memoir of his boyhood and youth in Perth which segues into a literary true-crime story. Against a vividly drawn 1950s middle-class backdrop, Drewe shows how one man's random killing spree struck fear into the 'burbs of sunny, friendly and seemingly innocent Perth.

Albert Facey *A Fortunate Life.* A hugely popular autobiography of a battler, tracing his progress from a bush orphanage to Gallipoli, through the Depression, another war and beyond.

Barry Hill *Broken Song: T.G.H. Strehlow and Aboriginal Possession.* As a child growing up on the Hermannsburg Mission in Central Australia, Strehlow had learnt the Aranda (Arrente) language. In 1932, the anthropologist began collecting Aranda songs, myths and tjurunga (sacred objects); his book *Songs of Central Australia* may have saved the Aranda language from extinction, and he was the first to really value the spirituality of Aboriginal religion. Resented by other anthropologists for his unique insight and access, Strehlow's was a fascinating career that ended in disgrace.

Eddie Mabo and Noel Loos *Edward Koiko Mabo: His Life and Struggle for Land Rights.* Mabo spent much of his life fighting for the autonomy of Torres Strait Islanders and in the process overthrew the concept of *terra nullius*, making his name a household word in Australia. Long interviews with the late black hero form the basis of this book and affectionately reveal the man behind the name.

David Malouf *12 Edmondstone Street.* An evocative autobiography-in-snatches of one of Australia's finest literary novelists, describing, in loving detail, the eponymous house in Brisbane where Malouf was born, life in the Tuscan village where he lives for part of each year, and his first visit to India.

Leah Purcell *Black Chicks Talking.* In an effort to overcome Aboriginal stereotypes, indigenous actor and writer Purcell gives insight into the lives of contemporary black women with this collection of lively, lengthy interviews, conducted with nine young females (all under 35), including the first Aboriginal Miss Australia (and now politician) Kathryn Hay, dancer Frances Rings, and actor Deborah Mailman.

Hazel Rowley *Christina Stead: a Biography.* Stead (1902–83) has been acclaimed as Australia's greatest novelist. After spending years in Paris, London and New York with her American husband, she returned to Australia in her old age.

Society and culture

Richard Baker *Land is Life: From Bush to Town – the Story of the Yanyuwa People.* The Yanyuwa people inhabited the Gulf of Carpentaria before the Europeans arrived, but most now live in the town of Borroloola, 750km southeast of Darwin. Historian Baker, assigned a "skin" in the Yanyuwa kinship system, gathered the people's oral history and produced this fascinating story told from the Yanyuwa point of view and time.

Geoffrey Blainey *Triumph of the Nomads.* A fascinating account portraying Aboriginal people as masters and not victims of their environment. One of the best books on the subject.

Peter and Gibson Dunbar-Hall *Deadly Sounds Deadly Places.*

Comprehensive guide to contemporary Aboriginal music in Australia, from Archie Roach to Yothu Yindi; includes a handy discography.

Monica Furlong *Flight of the Kingfisher: a Journey among Kukatja Aborigines*. Furlong lived among the Aboriginal people of the Great Sandy Desert; this is her account of Kukatja perceptions and spiritual beliefs.

Roslynn Haynes *Seeking the Centre: the Australian Desert in Literature, Art and Film*. The geographical and metaphorical impact of the desert on Australian culture is explored in this illustrated book, as is the connection Aboriginal people have with the desert.

David Headon *North of the Ten Commandments*. An anthology of Northern Territory writings from all perspectives and sources – an excellent literary souvenir for anyone who falls for the charms of Australia's "one percent" territory.

Donald Horne *The Lucky Country*. This seminal analysis of Australian society, written in 1976, has yet to be matched and is still often quoted.

Peter Singer and Tom Gregg *How Ethical is Australia? An Examination of Australia's Record as a Global Citizen*. Australian Peter Singer, world-renowned philosopher and professor of bioethics at Princeton University, teams up with Tom Gregg to examine Australia's policies on foreign aid, the United Nations, overseas trade, the environment and refugees.

History and politics

Robyn Annear *Nothing But Gold: the Diggers of 1852*. With an eye for interestingly obscure details and managing to convey a sense of irony without becoming cynical, this is a wonderfully readable account of the goldrushes of the nineteenth century, a period in Australia's history which perhaps did more than any other to shape the country's national character.

Len Beadell *Outback Highways*. Extracts from Len Beadell's half-dozen books, cheerfully recounting his life in the central Australian deserts as a surveyor, and his involvement in the construction of Woomera and the atomic bomb test sites.

John Birmingham *Leviathan: the unauthorised biography of Sydney*. Birmingham's tome casts a contemporary eye over the dark side of Sydney's history, from nauseating accounts of Rocks' slum life and the 1900 plague outbreak, through the 1970s traumas of Vietnamese boat people (now Sydney residents) to scandals of police corruption.

Manning Clark *A Short History of Australia*. A condensed version of this leading historian's multi-volume tome, focusing on dreary successions of political administrations over two centuries, and cynically concluding with the "Age of Ruins".

Inga Clendinnen *Dancing With Strangers*. Empathetic, almost poetically written account of the interaction of the British and the Aborigines (whom Clendinnen calls "Australians") in the five years after the arrival of the First Fleet.

Ann Curthoys *Freedom Ride: A Freedom Rider Remembers*. History professor Curthoys was one of the busload of young, idealistic white university students who accompanied Aboriginal activist Charles Perkins (only 29 himself) on his revolutionary trip through northern NSW in 1965, to look at Aboriginal living conditions and root out and protest against racial discrimination.

David Day *Claiming a Continent: a New History of Australia*. Award-winning, general and easily readable history, concluding in 2000. The possession, dispossession and ownership of the land – and thus issues of race – are central to Day's narrative. Excellent recommended reading of recent texts at the end of each chapter will take you further.

Colin Dyer *The French Explorers and the Aboriginal Australians*. From Bruny d'Entrecasteaux's (1793) to Nicolas Baudin's (1802) expeditions, the French explorers and on-board scientists kept detailed journals which provide a wealth of information on Aboriginal Australians, particularly those of Tasmania who d'Entrecastaux noted "seem to offer the most perfect image of pristine society". Dyer provides engaging access to much recently translated material.

Bruce Elder *Blood on the Wattle: Massacres and Maltreatment of Aboriginal Australians Since 1788*. A heart-rending account of the horrors inflicted on the continent's indigenous peoples, covering infamous nineteenth-century massacres as well as more recent mid-twentieth-century scandals of the "Stolen Generation" children.

Tim Flannery (ed) *Watkin Trench 1788*. One of the most vivid accounts of early Sydney was written by a twenty-something captain of the marines, Watkin Trench, who arrived with the First Fleet. Trench's humanity and youthful curiosity shine through as he brings alive the characters who peopled the early settlement, such as the Aboriginal Bennelong.

Robert Hughes *The Fatal Shore*. A minutely detailed epic of the origins of transportation and the brutal beginnings of white Australia.

Dianne Johnson *Lighting the Way: Reconciliation Stories*. Twenty-four very personal stories, written in a simple, engaging style, show Aboriginal and non-Aboriginal Australians working with each other, from community artworks to political activism. Positive and inspiring.

Mark McKenna *Looking for Blackfellas Point: an Australian History of Place*. This prize-winning book uncovers the uneasy history of Aboriginals and European settlers on the far south coast of NSW and widens its scope to the enduring meaning of land to both Aboriginal and white Australians.

Alan Moorehead *Cooper's Creek*. A historian's dramatic retelling of the ill-fated Burke and Wills expedition that set out in 1860 to make the first south-to-north crossing of the continent. A classic of exploration.

Sarah Murgatroyd *The Dig Tree: the Story of Burke and Wills*. Murgatroyd's recent retelling of the Burke and Wills story is gripping and immaculately researched – she journeyed along the route, and utilized the latest scientific and historical evidence, complemented by maps, photos and paintings.

Rosemary Neill *White Out: How Politics is Killing Black Australia*. Outspoken book which asserts that the rhetoric of self-determination and empowerment excuses the wider society from doing anything to reduce the disparity between black and white Australian populations. Busting taboos about indigenous affairs, Neill criticizes idealogies of both Left and Right.

Cassandra Pybus *Community of Thieves*. Attempting to reconcile past and future, fourth-generation Tasmanian Pybus provides a deeply felt account of the near-annihilation of the island's Aboriginal people.

Henry Reynolds *The Other Side of the Frontier* and *The Law of the Land*. A revisionist historian demonstrates that Aboriginal resistance to colonial invasion was both considerable and organized. *The Whispering in Our Hearts* is a history of those settler Australians who, troubled by the treatment of Aboriginal people, spoke out and took political action. *Why Weren't We Told?* is his most personal, an autobiographical journey showing how he, like many generations of Australians, imbibed a distorted, idealized Australian history, and describing his path to becoming an Aboriginal-history specialist; includes a moving story about his friendship with Eddie Mabo.

Portia Robinson *The Women of Botany Bay*. The result of painstaking research into the records of every female transported from Britain and Ireland between 1787 and 1828, as well as the wives of convicts who settled in Australia, Robinson tells with conviction and passion who these women really were.

Eric Rolls *Sojourners and Citizens* and *Flowers and the Wide Sea*. The first and second volumes of farmer-turned-historian Rolls' fascinatingly detailed history of the Chinese in Australia.

Anne Summers *Damned Whores and God's Police*. Stereotypical images of women in Australian society are explored in this ground-breaking reappraisal of Australian history from a feminist point of view.

Linda Weiss, Elizabeth Thurbon and John Mathews *How to Kill a Country: Australia's Devastating Trade Deal with the United States*. Australia's leading policy analysts examine the recent Free Trade Agreement with the United States, arguing that Australia's interests and identity will be damaged by the quest for a "special relationship".

Keith Windschuttle *The Fabrication of Aboriginal History. Volume One. Van Diemens Land 1803–1847*. According to Windschuttle, the genocide of the original Tasmanians is a "fabrication" of revisionist historians who did not do their research properly and deliberately misconstrued evidence to support a political agenda. Windschuttle asserts that the original Tasmanians never owned their land, as they had no concept of possession, that their attacks on the settlers could not be interpreted as resistance and that in any case, only 120 were killed. Windschuttle does not always follow his own criteria in his work, as critics have since pointed out (notably also in his subsequent book, *The Australia Policy*) but what is truly astounding is his utter lack of empathy.

Ecology and environment

Tim Flannery *The Future Eaters*. Paleontologist and environmental commentator Flannery poses that as the first human beings migrated down to Australasia, the Aborigines, Maoris and other Polynesian peoples changed the region's flora and fauna in startling ways, and began consuming the resources needed for their own future; the Europeans made an even greater impact on the environment, continuing this "future eating" of natural resources.

Tim Flannery *The Weather Makers: The History and Future Impact of Climate Change*. Written in Flannery's usual easy and engaging style, this book represents scientific journalism at its best – where it painstakingly traces the history of climate change and climate science – but suggested solutions neglect the necessary change of social and economic structures, focusing mainly on how individuals can reduce their carbon emissions.

Josephine Flood *The Riches of Ancient Australia*. An indispensable and lavish guide to Australia's most famous landforms and sites. The same author's *Archaeology of the Dreamtime* provides background on the development of Aboriginal society.

Drew Hutton and Libby Connors *A History of the Australian Environmental Movement*. Written by a husband-and-wife team, Queensland academics and prominent in Green politics, this well-balanced book charts the progress of conservation attempts from 1860 to modern protests.

Peter Latz *Bushfires and Bushtucker: Aboriginal Plant Use in Central Australia*. Handbook with photos, published by an Aboriginal-owned press.

Ann Moyal *Platypus: the Extraordinary Story of How a Curious Creature Baffled the World*. When British and French naturalists were first introduced to the platypus, they were flummoxed: Was it bird, reptile or mammal? And did it really lay eggs? Moyal, a science historian, provides a captivating look at the platypus – and Australian nature – through European eyes.

Tim Murray (ed) *Archeology of Australia*. The last thirty-odd years have seen many ground-breaking discoveries in Australian archeology, with three sites in particular of great significance: Kakadu in the Northern Territory, Lake Mungo in NSW, and South West Tasmania; a range of specialists contribute essays on the subject.

David Owen *Thylacine: the Tragic Tale of the Tasmanian Tiger*. Hunted to extinction, the last known Tasmanian tiger died in Beaumaris Zoo in Hobart in 1936. But unconfirmed sightings continue: "The longer the thylacine stays dead, the greater the interest it arouses," writes Owen of the marsupial predator's now-mythic status. Packed with fascinating facts and stories.

Mary White *The Greening of Gondwana*. Classic work on the evolution of Australia's flora and geography.

James Woodford *The Wollemi Pine: the Incredible Discovery of a Living Fossil from the Age of the Dinosaurs*. The award-winning environment writer at the *Sydney Morning Herald* tells the story of the 1994 discovery in Wollemi wilderness near Sydney. *The Secret Life of Wombats* begins as a fascinating account of the "wombat boy", a schoolboy so curious to find out about how wombats lived he crawled into their burrows. In *The Dog Fence: a Journey through the Heart of the Continent* Woodford travels the 5400-kilometre length of the fence built to keep livestock safe from dingoes.

Contemporary fiction

Thea Astley *The Multiple Effects of Rainshadow*. On an Aboriginal island reserve in 1930, a white woman dies in childbirth, and her husband goes on a shotgun-and-dynamite rampage. The novel traces the effects over the years on eight characters who witnessed the violent events, ultimately exploring the brutality and racism in Australian life.

Murray Bail *Eucalyptus*. Beautifully written novel with a fairytale-like plot: NSW farmer, Holland, has planted nearly every type of eucalyptus tree on his land. When his extraordinarily beautiful daughter Ellen is old enough to marry, he sets up a challenge for her legion of potential suitors, to name each tree.

John Birmingham *He Died with A Felafel in His Hand*. A collection of squalid and very funny tales emerging from the once-dissolute author's experience of flat-sharing hell in Brisbane.

Anson Cameron *Tin Toys*. The Aboriginal "Stolen Generation" issue explored through the tale of Hunter Carolyn, an unintentional artist who can change skin colour at will.

Peter Carey *Bliss*. Carey's first and perhaps best novel is the story of a Sydney ad executive who drops out to New Age NSW. Other novels by Carey to look out for include his two Booker Prize–winners *Oscar and Lucinda* and *The True History of the Kelly Gang*, about the bushranger Ned Kelly. Also worth a read are his bizarre short stories, *The Fat Man in History*, with which he launched his career, and his latest novel *Theft. A Love Story*, an equally bizarre *tour de force* and a take on the international art world.

Robert Drewe *The Savage Crows*. A writer, whose own life is falling apart in a cockroach-ridden Sydney of the 1970s, sets out to discover the grim truth behind Tasmania's "final solution".

Richard Flanagan *Death of a River Guide*. Narrator, environmentalist Aljaz Cosini, goes over his life and that of his family and forebears as he lies drowning in the Franklin River. Thoughtful writings about Tasmanian landscape, place, migration and the significance of history are the hallmark of Flanagan's novels. His nineteenth-century-set *Gould's Book of Fish: a Novel in Twelve Fish* delves into Tasmania's past as the brutal penal settlement of Van Diemen's Land.

Tom Gilling *Miles McGinty*. Nineteenth-century Sydney comes alive in this riotous, entertaining love story of Miles, who becomes a levitator's assistant and begins to float on air, and Isabel, who wants to fly.

Peter Goldsworthy *Three Dog Night*. It takes three dogs to keep a person warm on a desert night, an allusion to the love triangle which emerges when psychiatrist Martin Blackman returns to Adelaide after a decade in London with his new, much-loved wife, and visits his oldest friend, the difficult Felix, a once-brilliant surgeon dying of terminal cancer. Felix is an initiated man who has lived with Aborigines in the Central Australian desert; when Lucy accompanies him there, Martin must confront his insecurities.

Kate Grenville *The Idea of Perfection*, set in the tiny, fictional NSW town of Karakarook, and about two unlikely characters who fall in love, won the 2001 Orange Prize for Fiction. *The Secret River* was short-listed for the Man Booker Prize in 2006 and won the Commonwealth Writers Prize. This historical novel explores the uneasy terrain of early white contact with Aborigines, telling the story of freed convict William Thornhill taking up land in the Hawkesbury with his family.

Chloe Hooper *A Child's Book of True Crime*. With a claustrophobic Tasmanian setting, this perverse, chilling novel is narrated by a young primary-school teacher having an affair with the married father of her smartest pupil. His writer-wife's true-crime book, about a love triangle that disintegrates into murder, leads the anxious teacher into imagining a child's-classic-Australian-literature-style version, with characters such as Kitty Koala and Wally Wombat.

Linda Jaivin *Eat Me*. Billed as an "erotic feast", this novel opens with a memorable fruit-squeezing scene (and this is only the shopping) as three trendy Sydney women (fashion editor, academic and writer) swap stories of sexual exploits.

Douglas Kennedy *The Dead Heart.* A best-selling comic thriller made into a film; an itinerant American journalist gets abducted by man-eating hillbillies in Outback Australia.

Julia Leigh *The Hunter.* Intriguing, internationally acclaimed first novel about the rediscovery and subsequent hunt of the Tasmanian tiger; a faceless biotech company after thylacine DNA plays the bad guy.

David Malouf *The Conversations at Curlow Creek.* One of Australia's most important contemporary writers charts the developing relationship between two Irishmen the night before a hanging; one is the officer appointed to supervise the execution and the other the outlaw facing his death. *Remembering Babylon* is the moving story of a British cabin boy in the 1840s who, cast ashore, lives for sixteen years amongst the Aboriginal people of far north Queensland, and finally re-enters the British colonial world.

Andrew McGahan *The White Earth.* Set in Queensland's Darling Downs wheatfields; it's 1992, and the Mabo land-rights case fills the news. After the death of his father, 8-year-old William and his unstable mother are invited to live on his ageing uncle's Kuran station, which has been his life's obsession to own. William, forced to prove himself worthy of inheritance, is drawn into his discontented uncle's White League. Questions of Aboriginal dispossession and white belonging reverberate. The polemical tone of *Underground* (2006), a dystopian novel with a somewhat far-fetched plotline, set in a not too distant future in totalitarian Australia, raised the ire of neo-conservative reviewers.

Alex Miller *Journey to the Stone Country.* A betrayed wife leaves her middle-class Melbourne existence and returns to tropical North Queensland, setting out on a journey with a childhood Aboriginal acquaintance into the stone country which is his tribe's remote heartland. However, dark secrets from the lives of their grandparents threaten what future they may have together.

Elliot Perlman *Seven Types of Ambiguity.* The chain of events, secrets and lies stretching back a decade that lead to Simon Heywood kidnapping his ex-girlfriend's son are related by seven different narrators. Probing middle-class anxiety in a consumeristic, market-driven society, Perlman's conscience-driven writing can be moralistic at times, but at its best is clever and insightful, providing an intense social portrait of contemporary Melbourne, from Toorak to St Kilda.

Janette Turner *Hospital Oyster.* Disquieting novel set in the literally off-the-map, opal-mining, one-pub Queensland town of Inner Maroo, whose inhabitants are either rough-as-guts mining people, or religious fundamentalists.

Tim Winton *Cloudstreet.* A wonderful, faintly magical saga about the mixed fortunes of two families who end up sharing a house in postwar Perth. His novel *Dirt Music* provides a wonderful evocation of the Western Australian landscape with a compelling narrative and was short-listed for the 2002 Booker Prize. *The Turning*, a collection of seventeen linked short stories set in a fictitious Western Australian coastal town, won the 2005 NSW Premier's Literary Award.

Danielle Wood *The Alphabet of Light and Dark.* Set evocatively on Bruny Island, in melancholy Tasmanian-Gothic vein. Like the main character Essie, Wood's great-great grandfather was superintendent of the Cape Bruny Lighthouse. Essie returns from Western Australia to the lighthouse after her grandfather's death to write her family history and becomes immersed in her ancestors' tragedies.

Alexis Wright *Carpentaria*. Childhood memories and stories that her Waanyi grandmother told her flowed into Wright's novel about the Gulf country – in title, subject and scope, reminiscent of Xavier Herbert's classic *Capricornia*, but from an Aboriginal point of view. Shortlisted for the Miles Franklin 2007.

Australian classics

Barbara Baynton *Bush Studies*. A collection of nineteenth-century bush stories written from the female perspective.

Rolf Boldrewood *Robbery Under Arms*. The story of Captain Starlight, a notorious bushranger and rustler around the Queensland borders.

Marcus Clarke *For the Term of His Natural Life*. Written in 1870 in somewhat overblown prose, this romantic tragedy is based on actual events in Tasmania's once-notorious prison settlement.

Miles Franklin *My Brilliant Career*. A novel about a spirited young girl in early twentieth-century Victoria who refuses to conform.

May Gibbs *Snugglepot and Cuddlepie*. A timeless children's favourite: the illustrated adventures of two little creatures who live inside gumnuts.

Xavier Herbert *Capricornia*. An indignant and allegorical saga of the brutal and haphazard settlement of the land of Capricornia (tropical Northern Territory thinly disguised).

George Johnston *My Brother Jack*. The first in a disturbing trilogy set in Melbourne suburbia between the wars, which develops into a semi-fictional attempt to dissipate the guilt Johnston felt at being disillusioned with, and finally leaving, his native land.

Thomas Keneally *The Chant of Jimmie Blacksmith*. A prize-winning novel that delves deep into the psyche of an Aboriginal outlaw, tracing his inexorable descent into murder and crime. Sickening, brutal and compelling.

Henry Lawson Ballads, poems and stories from Australia's best-loved chronicler come in a wide array of collections. A few to seek out are: *Henry Lawson Bush Ballads*, *Henry Lawson Favourites* and *While the Billy Boils – Poetry*.

Norman Lindsay *The Magic Pudding*. A whimsical tale of some very strange men and their grumpy, flavour-changing and endless pudding; a children's classic with very adult humour.

Ruth Park *The Harp in the South*. First published in 1948, this first book in a trilogy is a well-loved tale of inner-Sydney slum life in 1940s Surry Hills. The spirited Darcy family's battle against poverty provides memorable characters.

A.B. ("Banjo") Paterson Australia's most famous bush balladeer, author of *Waltzing Matilda* and *The Man from Snowy River*, who helped romanticize the bush's mystique. Some of the many titles published include *Banjo Paterson's Favourites* and *Man from Snowy River and Other Verses*.

Henry Handel Richardson *The Getting of Wisdom*. A gangly country girl's experience of a snobby boarding school in early twentieth-century Melbourne; like Miles Franklin (see above), Richardson was actually a female writer.

Nevil Shute *A Town Like Alice*. A wartime romance that tells of

a woman's bravery, endurance and enterprise, both in the Malayan jungle and in the Australian Outback where she strives to create the town of the title.

Christina Stead *For Love Alone*. Set largely around Sydney Harbour, where the late author grew up, this novel follows the obsessive Teresa Hawkins, a poor but artistic girl from a large, unconventional family, who scrounges and saves to head for London and love.

Randolph Stow *The Merry-go-round in the Sea*. An endearing tale of a young boy growing up in rural Western Australia during World War II.

Kylie Tennant *Ride on Stranger*. First published in 1943, this is a humorous portrait of Sydney between the two world wars, seen through the eyes of newcomer Shannon Hicks.

Patrick White Considered dense and symbolic – even visionary (though some claim misogynistic) – White's novels can be heavy going, but try and plough through *Voss*, *A Fringe of Leaves* or *The Twyborn Affair*, the latter a contemporary exploration of ambiguous sexuality.

Aboriginal writing

Faith Bandler *Welour, My Brother*. A novel by a well-known black activist describing a boy's early life in Queensland, and the tensions of a racially mixed community.

John Muk Muk Burke *Bridge of Triangles*. Powerful, landscape-driven images in this tale of a mixed-race child growing up unable to associate with either side of his heritage, but refusing to accept the downward spiral into despair and alcoholism adopted by those around him.

Evelyn Crawford *Over My Tracks*. Told to Chris Walsh, this oral autobiography is the story of a formidable woman, from her 1930s childhood among the red sandhills of Yantabulla, through her Outback struggles as a mother of fourteen children, to her tireless work, late in life, with Aboriginal students, combating prejudice with education.

Nene Gare *The Fringe Dwellers*. A story of an Aboriginal family on the edge of town and society.

Ruby Langford *Don't Take Your Love to Town*. An autobiography demonstrating a black woman's courage and humour in the face of tragedy and poverty lived out in northern NSW and the inner city of Sydney.

Sally Morgan *My Place*. A widely acclaimed and best-selling account of a Western Australian woman's discovery of her black roots.

David Mowaljarlai and Jutta Malnic *Yorro Yorro*. Starry-eyed photographer Malnic's musings while recording sacred Wandjina sites in the west Kimberley and, more interestingly, Mowaljarlai's account of his upbringing and Ngarinyin tribal lore.

Mudrooroo *Wildcat Falling*. The first novel to be published (in 1965) by an Aboriginal writer, under the name Colin Johnson, this is the story of a black teenage delinquent coming of age in the 1950s. *Doctor Wooreddy's Prescription for Enduring the Ending of the World* details the attempted annihilation of the Tasmanian Aborigines. Mudrooroo's three latest novels – *The Kwinkan* (1995), *The Undying* (1998) and *Underground* (1999) – are part of his magic-realist Master of Ghost Dreaming series.

Oodgeroo Noonuccal *My People*. A collection of verse by an established campaigning poet (previously known as Kath Walker).

Paddy Roe *Gularabulu*. Stories from the west Kimberley, both traditional myths and tales of a much more recent origin.

Kim Scott *Benang*. Infuriated at reading the words of A.O. Neville, Protector of Aborigines in Western Australia in the 1930s, who planned to "breed out" Aborigines from Australia, author Scott wrote this powerful tale of Nyoongar history using Neville's own themes to overturn his elitist arguments.

Archie Weller *The Day of the Dog*. Weller's violent first novel came out in an angry burst after being released, at 23, from incarceration in Broome jail. The protagonist, in a similar situation, is pressured back into a criminal world by his Aboriginal peers and by police harassment. Searing pace and forceful writing. His second novel, *Land of the Golden Clouds*, is an epic science-fiction fantasy, set 3000 years in the future, which portrays an Australia devastated by a nuclear holocaust and populated by warring tribes.

Specialist and wildlife guides

Jack Absalom *Safe Outback Travel*. The bible for Outback driving and camping, full of sensible precautions and handy tips for preparation and repair.

John Chapman and Monica Chapman *Bushwalking in Australia*. The fourth edition of this bushwalking bible, meticulously updated in 2003, has detailed notes for 25 of the best bushwalks Australia-wide, accompanied by colour topographic maps and photographs. The Chapmans also publish several other excellent walking guides, including the indispensable *South West Tasmania*.

David Clark *Big Things*. From the Big Banana to the Big Lobster, Clark provides a comprehensive guide to Australia's kitsch icons.

Catherine de Courcey and John Johnson *River Tracks: Exploring Australian Rivers*. A practical and up-to-date motoring guide to six river journeys, providing lots of insider insight and history too.

The Great Barrier Reef A *Reader's Digest* complete rundown on the Reef, lucid and lavishly illustrated. Available in coffee-table format and in a slighter, more portable, edited edition.

James Halliday *Australian Wine Companion*. Released every year, the venerable Halliday provides not only an authoritative guide to the best wines but to the wineries themselves – with over 1865 wineries in the 2005 edition, making it a great accompaniment when visiting any of Australia's wine regions.

Huon Hooke and Ralph Kyte-Powell *The Penguin Good Australian Wine Guide*. Released every year in Australia, this is a handy book for a wine buff to buy on the ground, with the best wines and prices detailed to help navigate you around the bottle shop.

Tim Low *Bush Tucker: Australia's Wild Food Harvest* and *Wild Food Plants of Australia*. Guides to the bountiful supply of bushtucker that was once the mainstay of the Aboriginal diet; the latter is pocket-sized and contains clear photographs of over 180 plants, describing their uses.

Greg Pritchard *Climbing Australia: the Essential Guide*. Comprehensive guide for rock-climbers. Covers everything from the major climbing sites to the best websites, with easy-to-understand route descriptions.

Peter and Pat Slater *Field Guide to Australian Birds*. Pocket-sized, and the easiest to use of the many available guides to Australian birds.

Tyrone T. Thomas Regional bushwalking guides by local publisher Michelle Anderson Publishing. A series of ten local guides, from *50 Walks in North Queensland* to *120 Walks in Tasmania*, which make excellent trail companions.

Mark Warren *Atlas of Australian Surfing*. A comprehensive guide to riding the best of Australia's waves.

Nicola Wells et al *Cycling Australia*. Published in 2001, thirty-five popular cycling routes are described, from day-rides to extended trips, with accompanying maps.

Australian English

The colourful variant of Australian English, or strine (which is how "Australian" is pronounced with a very heavy Australian accent), has its origins in the archaic cockney and Irish of the colony's early convicts as well as the adoption of words from the many Aboriginal languages. For such a vast country, the accent barely varies to the untutored ear; from Tasmania to the northwest you'll find little variation in the national drawl, with its curious, interrogative ending to sentences – although Queenslanders are noted for their slow delivery. One of the most consistent tendencies of strine is to abbreviate words and then stick an "-o" or, more commonly, an "-ie" on the end: as in "bring your cozzie to the barbie this arvo" (bring your swimming costume to the barbecue this afternoon). This informality extends to the frequent use of "bloody", "bugger" and "bastard", the latter two used affectionately. Attempting to abuse someone by calling them a bastard will most likely end up in an offer of a beer. There's also an endearing tendency to genderize inanimate objects as, for example, "she's buggered, mate" (your inanimate object is beyond repair) or "do 'im up nice and tight" (be certain that your inanimate object is well affixed).

The popularity of dire Australian TV soap operas has seen strine spread overseas, much as Americanisms have pervaded the English-speaking world. Popular strinisms such as "hang a U-ey" (make a U-turn) and the versatile and agreeable "no worries" are now commonly used outside Australia.

The country has its own excellent *Macquarie Dictionary*, the latest edition of which is the ultimate authority on the current state of Australian English. Also worth consulting are *The Dinkum Dictionary: The Origins of Australian Words* by Susan Butler, and *Word Map* by Kel Richards, a dictionary of Australian regionalisms. What follows is our own essential list.

Akubra Wide-brimmed felt hat; a brand name.
Anzac Australia and New Zealand Army Corps; every town has a memorial to Anzac casualties from both world wars.
Arvo Afternoon.
Back o'Bourke Outback.
Banana bender Resident of Queensland.
Barbie Barbecue.
Battler Someone who struggles to make a living, as in "little Aussie battler".
Beaut! or **You beauty!** Exclamation of delight.
Beg yours? Excuse me, say again?
Beyond the Black Stump Outback; back of beyond.
Billabong Waterhole in dry riverbed.
Billy Cooking pot.
Bitumen Sealed road as opposed to dirt road.
Blowies Blow flies.
Bludger Someone who does not pull their weight, or a scrounger – as in "dole bludger".
Blue Fight; also a red-haired person.
Blundstones Leather, elastic-sided workmen's boots, now also a fashion item in some circles. Often shortened to "blundies".
Bonzer Good, a good thing.
Bottle shop Off-licence or liquor store.
Brumby Feral horse.
Buckley's No chance; as in "hasn't got a Buckley's".
Bugs Moreton Bay bug – type of crayfish indigenous to southern Queensland.

Bunyip Monster of Aboriginal legend; bogeyman.
Burl Give it a go; as in "give it a burl".
Bush Unsettled country area.
Bushranger Runaway convict; nineteenth-century outlaw.
Bushwhacker Someone lacking in social graces, a hick.
BYO Bring your own. Restaurant which allows you to bring your own alcohol.
Chook Chicken.
Chunder Vomit.
Cocky Small farmer; cow cocky, dairy farmer.
To come the raw prawn To try and deceive or make a fool of someone.
Coo-eee! Aboriginal long-distance greeting, now widely adopted as a kind of "yoo hoo!"
Corroboree Aboriginal ceremony.
Cozzies Bathers, swimmers, togs; swimming costume.
Crim Criminal.
Crook Sick or broken.
Crow eater Resident of South Australia.
Cut lunch Sandwiches.
Dag Nerd
Daggy Unattractive.
Daks or **strides** Trousers/pants.
Dam A man-made body of water or reservoir; not just the dam itself.
Damper Soda bread cooked in a pot on embers.
Dekko To look at; as in "take a dekko at this".
Deli Delicatessen, corner shop or sandwich bar.
Derro Derelict or destitute person.
Didgeridoo Droning musical instrument made from a termite-hollowed branch.
Digger Old-timer, especially an old soldier.
Dill Idiot.
Dilly bag Aboriginal carry-all made of bark, or woven or rigged twine.
Dinkum True, genuine, honest.
Disposal store Store that sells used army and navy equipment, plus camping gear.
Dob in To tell on someone; as in "she dobbed him in".
Drizabone Voluminous waxed cotton raincoat, originally designed for horse riding; a brand name.
Drongo Fool.
Drover Cowboy or station hand.
Dunny Outside pit toilet.
Esky Portable, insulated box to keep food or beer cold.
Fair dinkum or **dinky di** Honestly, truly.
Fossick To search for gold or gems in abandoned diggings.
Furphy A rumour or false story.
Galah Noisy or garrulous person; after the bird.
Galvo Corrugated iron.
Garbo Garbage or refuse collector.
G'day Hello, hi.
Gibber Rock or boulder.
Give away To give up or resign; as in "I used to be a garbo but I gave it away".
Grog Alcoholic drink, usually beer.
Gub, gubbah Aboriginal terms for a white person.
Gutless wonder Coward.
Hoon A yob, delinquent.
Humpy Temporary shelter used by Aborigines and early pioneers.
Jackeroo Male station-hand.
Jilleroo Female station-hand.
Joey Baby kangaroo still in the pouch (also, less familiarly, a baby koala).
Koorie Collective name for Aboriginal people from southeastern Australia.
Larrikin Mischievous youth.
Lay by Practice of putting a deposit on goods until they can be fully paid for.
Lollies Sweets or candy.
Manchester Linen goods.
Mate A sworn friend, as essential as beer to the Australian stereotype.

Mexicans Residents of New South Wales and Victoria.
Milk bar Corner shop, and often a small café.
Moleskins Strong cotton trousers worn by bushmen.
Never Never Outback, wilderness.
New Australian Recent immigrants; often a euphemism for Australians of non-British descent.
No worries That's OK; It doesn't matter; Don't mention it.
Ocker Uncultivated Australian male.
Op shop Short for "Opportunity Shop"; a charity shop/thrift store.
Outback Remote, unsettled regions of Australia.
Paddock Field.
Panel van Van with no rear windows and front seating only.
Pashing Kissing or snogging, often in the back of a panel van.
Perve To leer or act as a voyeur; as in "What are you perving at?"
Piss Beer.
Piss head Drunkard.
Pissed Drunk.
Pokies One-armed bandits; gambling machines.
Pommie or **Pom** Person of English descent – not necessarily abusive.
Rapt Very pleased, delighted.
Ratbag An eccentric person; also a term of mild abuse.
Ratshit or **shithouse** How you feel after a night on the piss.
Rego Vehicle registration document.
Ridji didge The real thing or genuine article.
Ripper! Rather old-fashioned exclamation of enthusiasm.
Rollies Roll-up cigarettes.
Root Vulgar term for sexual congress.
Rooted To be very tired or to be beyond repair; as in "she's rooted, mate" – your [car] is irreparable.
Ropable Furious to the point of requiring restraint.
Rouseabout An unskilled labourer in a shearing shed.
Sandgroper Resident of Western Australia.
She'll be right or **she'll be apples** Everything will work out fine.
Shoot through To pass through or leave hurriedly.
Shout To pay for someone, or to buy a round of drinks; as in "it's your shout, mate".
Sickie To take a day off work due to (sometimes alleged) illness; as in "to pull a sickie".
Singlet Sleeveless cotton vest. The archetypal Australian singlet, in navy, is produced by Bonds.
Skivvy Polo neck.
Slab 24-can carton of beer.
Smoko Tea break.
Snag Sausage.
Speedo Famous Australian brand of athletic swimming costume; speedos (or sluggos) commonly refers to men's swimming briefs, as opposed to swimming trunks.
Spunk Attractive or sexy person of either gender; as in "what a spunk!" Can also be used as an adjective: spunky.
Squatter Historical term for early settlers who took up public land as their own.
Station Very large pastoral property or ranch.
Sticky beak Nosy person, or to be nosy; as in "let's have a sticky beak".
Stockman Cowboy or station hand.
Stubby Small bottle of beer.
Swag Large bedroll, or one's belongings.
Tall poppy Someone who excels or is eminent. "Cutting down tall poppies" is to bring overachievers back to earth – a national pastime.
Thongs Flip-flops or sandals.
Throw a wobbly Lose your temper.
Tinnie Can of beer, or a small aluminium boat.

Ute Short for "utility" vehicle; pick-up truck.
Wacko! Exclamation of enthusiasm.
Walkabout Temporary migration undertaken by Aborigines; also has the wider meaning of a journey.
Gone walkabout To go missing.
Warm fuzzies Feeling of contentment.
Waxhead Surfer.
Weatherboard Wooden house.
Whinger Someone who complains – allegedly common among Poms.
Wog Derogatory description for those of Mediterranean descent.
Wowser Killjoy.
Yabber To talk or chat.
Yabbie Freshwater crayfish.
Yakka Work, as in "hard yakka".
Yobbo Uncouth person.

Small print and Index

A Rough Guide to Rough Guides

Published in 1982, the first Rough Guide – to Greece – was a student scheme that became a publishing phenomenon. Mark Ellingham, a recent graduate in English from Bristol University, had been traveling in Greece the previous summer and couldn't find the right guidebook. With a small group of friends he wrote his own guide, combining a highly contemporary, journalistic style with a thoroughly practical approach to travelers' needs.

The immediate success of the book spawned a series that rapidly covered dozens of destinations. And, in addition to impecunious backpackers, Rough Guides soon acquired a much broader and older readership that relished the guides' wit and inquisitiveness as much as their enthusiastic, critical approach and value-for-money ethos.

These days, Rough Guides include recommendations from shoestring to luxury and cover more than 200 destinations around the globe, including almost every country in the Americas and Europe, more than half of Africa and most of Asia and Australasia. Our ever-growing team of authors and photographers is spread all over the world, particularly in Europe, the USA and Australia.

In the early 1990s, Rough Guides branched out of travel, with the publication of Rough Guides to World Music, Classical Music and the Internet. All three have become benchmark titles in their fields, spearheading the publication of a wide range of books under the Rough Guide name.

Including the travel series, Rough Guides now number more than 350 titles, covering: phrasebooks, waterproof maps, music guides from Opera to Heavy Metal, reference works as diverse as Conspiracy Theories and Shakespeare, and popular culture books from iPods to Poker. Rough Guides also produce a series of more than 120 World Music CDs in partnership with World Music Network.

Visit www.roughguides.com to see our latest publications.

Rough Guide travel images are available for commercial licensing at www.roughguidespictures.com

Rough Guide credits

Text editor: Nikki Birrell, Keith Drew, Helen Marsden, Andy Turner & Lucy White
Layout: Jessica Subramanian
Cartography: Rajesh Mishra, Maxine Repath
Picture editor: Nicole Newman
Production: Aimee Hampson
Proofreader: Diane Margolis
Cover design: Chloë Roberts
Photographer: Helena Smith, Karen Trist
Editorial: **London** Kate Berens, Claire Saunders, Ruth Blackmore, Polly Thomas, Alison Murchie, Karoline Densley, Edward Aves, Alice Park, Sarah Eno, Jo Kirby, Samantha Cook, James Smart, Natasha Foges, Roísín Cameron, Emma Traynor, Emma Gibbs, Joe Staines, Duncan Clark, Peter Buckley, Matthew Milton, Tracy Hopkins, Ruth Tidball; **New York** Andrew Rosenberg, Steven Horak, AnneLise Sorensen, Amy Hegarty, April Isaacs, Ella Steim, Anna Owens, Joseph Petta, Sean Mahoney; **Delhi** Madhavi Singh, Karen D'Souza
Design & Pictures: **London** Scott Stickland, Dan May, Diana Jarvis, Mark Thomas, Jj Luck, Sarah Cummins; **Delhi** Umesh Aggarwal, Ajay Verma, Ankur Guha, Pradeep Thapliyal, Sachin Tanwar, Anita Singh, Nikhil Agarwal
Production: Vicky Baldwin
Cartography: **London** Ed Wright, Katie Lloyd-Jones; **Delhi** Jai Prakash Mishra, Rajesh Chhibber, Ashutosh Bharti, Animesh Pathak, Jasbir Sandhu, Karobi Gogoi, Amod Singh, Alakananda Bhattacharya, Swati Handoo
Online: **New York** Jennifer Gold, Kristin Mingrone; **Delhi** Manik Chauhan, Narender Kumar, Rakesh Kumar, Amit Verma, Rahul Kumar, Ganesh Sharma, Debojit Borah
Marketing & Publicity: **London** Liz Statham, Niki Hanmer, Louise Maher, Jess Carter, Vanessa Godden, Vivienne Watton, Anna Paynton, Rachel Sprackett; **New York** Geoff Colquitt, Megan Kennedy, Katy Ball; **Delhi** Reem Khokhar
Manager India: Punita Singh
Series Editor: Mark Ellingham
Reference Director: Andrew Lockett
Publishing Coordinator: Helen Phillips
Publishing Director: Martin Dunford
Commercial Manager: Gino Magnotta
Managing Director: John Duhigg

Publishing information

This eighth edition published September 2007 by **Rough Guides Ltd**,
80 Strand, London WC2R 0RL
345 Hudson St, 4th Floor,
New York, NY 10014, USA
14 Local Shopping Centre, Panchsheel Park,
New Delhi 110017, India
Distributed by the Penguin Group
Penguin Books Ltd,
80 Strand, London WC2R 0RL
Penguin Group (USA)
375 Hudson Street, NY 10014, USA
Penguin Group (Australia)
250 Camberwell Road, Camberwell,
Victoria 3124, Australia
Penguin Books Canada Ltd,
10 Alcorn Avenue, Toronto, Ontario,
Canada M4V 1E4
Penguin Group (NZ)
67 Apollo Drive, Mairangi Bay, Auckland 1310,
New Zealand
Cover concept by Peter Dyer.

Typeset in Bembo and Helvetica to an original design by Henry Iles.

Printed in Italy by LegoPrint S.p.A

1160pp includes index

A catalogue record for this book is available from the British Library

ISBN: 978-1-84353-857-8

1 3 5 7 9 8 6 4 2

Help us update

We've gone to a lot of effort to ensure that the eighth edition of **The Rough Guide to Australia** is accurate and up to date. However, things change – places get "discovered", opening hours are notoriously fickle, restaurants and rooms raise prices or lower standards. If you feel we've got it wrong or left something out, we'd like to know, and if you can remember the address, the price, the time, the phone number, so much the better. We'll credit all contributions, and send a copy of the next edition (or any other Rough Guide if you prefer) for the best letters. Everyone who writes to us and isn't already a subscriber will receive a copy of our full-color thrice-yearly newsletter. Please mark letters: **"Rough Guide Australia Update"** and send to: Rough Guides, 80 Strand, London WC2R 0RL, or Rough Guides, 345 Hudson St, 4th Floor, New York, NY 10014. Or send an email to **mail@roughguides.com**
Have your questions answered and tell others about your trip at
www.roughguides.atinfopop.com

Acknowledgements

Chris Canty Thomas Redmond in Wangaratta, Daniel Lowther in Geelong, Blair Kelly in Fremantle, Tim Stafford and Nathan Malin in Perth.

Tim Dub Keith Drew, Margo Daly and the many Tasmanians who ensured that travelling the state was so entertaining and pleasurable.

Simon Foster Annett Forman in Exmouth, Gwen & Steph, Broome Visitors Centre, Katherine Visitors Centre, Roddy at Tennant Creek Visitors Centre, Bec Goodwin at Ayers Rock Tours and Information Centre, Travellers Auto Barn and the YHA.

Helen Marsden The YHAs of NSW for all the bike hire, and the guys at *Bello YHA* for being so friendly and trusting me with their car. Also Ginny Retmock on Lord Howe Island, Britz for the campervan and Matt for cooking me so many dinners and not complaining (much) about all the 2am finishes.

Suzanne Morton-Taylor Jovanka Ristich of the South Australian Tourist Board for her help with travel arrangements and Collin & Cynthia and Vito Romano for their hospitality in the Barossa and in Adelaide. Special thanks to my editor Helen Marsden for being sharp as a knife, and Stimp for surviving the harshness of the Outback.

Ian Osborn As ever, to Sia, Tieri, Patrick and Safaira who helped with opinions and accompanied me in my travels. Also, to a childhood friend Bridget, found again by pure chance in Kings Cross, and to whom I am indebted for her insight into the more sophisticated side of Sydney's nightlife.

Readers' letters

Thanks to all the readers who have taken the time to write in with comments and suggestions (and apologies if we've inadvertently omitted or misspelt anyone's name):

Keith Bartlett, Robert Battersby, Elias Baumgarten, Natasha Brewins, Colin Brosnan, Sarah-Jane Brooks, Isla Campbell, Andy Fraser, Wim & Dorothy Helderman, John Hupp, Fiona Hutcheon, Suzanne Kelly, Sara Kendall, Leo Lacey, John McCabe, Nicola Milsom, Sally Neil, Clive Paul, Ann Sacra, Heidi van Spaandonk, Joe Sproats, Pete & Trisch Thornton, Chelsea Webber, Jill Wookey, Vivian Wu.

Photo credits

All photos © Rough Guides except the following:

Introduction

Noosa Triathlon © Jonathan Wood/Getty Images
Great Barrier Reef © John W Banagan/Getty
Ulysses butterfly © Nicole Duplaix/National Geographic/Getty
Luna Park, Sydney © Nicole Newman
Twelve Apostles, Victoria © Doug Pearson/JAI/Corbis
Camp breakfast in the Outback © Bill Bachman/Alamy
Sunset over Yellow Waters in Arnhem Land © Penny Tweedie/CORBIS
Aboriginal art bark painting © Ken Welsh/Alamy

Things not to miss

1 Whitehaven Beach on Whitsunday Island © David Lawrence/CORBIS
2 The Blue Mountains © Dallas and John Heaton/Free Agents Limited/Corbis
3 Coober Pedy © Alessandro Gandolfi/photolibrary
4 Beer Can Regatta © Mark Crummy/Tourism NT
5 Skiing Thredbo © John William Banagan/Getty
6 Humpback whale © Daniel Bayer/AFP/Getty Images
7 Cradle Mountain–Lake St Clair National Park © Ted Mead/photolibrary
8 Melbourne Cup © Robert Cianflone/Getty Images
9 Scuba divers swimming over coral fish © Jeff Hunter/Getty
10 Aboriginal woman and a witchetty grub © Suzy Bennett/Alamy
11 Lake McKenzie, Fraser Island © Alamy
13 Rafting on the Franklin River © Tasmania Tourism Tasmania
14 Fighting sea lions on Kangaroo Island © Woody Stock/Alamy
16 Kakadu © John William Banagan/Getty
17 Saltwater crocodile © Dave Watts/naturepl .com
18 Katherine Gorge © Hemis /Alamy
19 Houseboat on the Murray River © imagebroker/Alamy
20 Termite mounds, Northern Territory © John William Banagan/Getty
21 Barossa Valley © Gary Lewis/photolibrary
23 The Kimberley © Simon Grosset/Alamy
24 Sydney Gay and Lesbian Mardi Gras © Will Burgess/Reuters/Corbis
25 Kings Canyon © Cephas Picture Library/Alamy
26 Wilpena Pound © Alamy
28 Mutawintji National Park © Dave G. Houser/Corbis
29 Lake Eyre © Nicholas Pitt/Alamy
30 Laura Dance Festival © Alamy
31 Carnarvon Gorge © Terry Whittaker/Alamy
32 Karijini National Park © Getty
33 Great Ocean Road © David Wall/Alamy
34 Valley of the Giants © Warwick Kent/photolibrary
35 Symposium of Sculptures, Broken Hill © Marco Brivio/Alamy
36 4WD in the Bungle Bungles © Theo Allofs/CORBIS
37 Bondi Beach, Sydney © Nicole Newman
38 Wilsons Promontory National Park © Ern Mainka/Alamy
39 Atherton Tablelands © Papa Kay/Alamy
40 Uluru © Jeremy Woodhouse/Getty

Food and drink colour section

Barbeque on Coogee Beach © Ian Waldie/Getty Images
Lobster for sale © David Hancock/Alamy
Lamingtons © Worldwide Picture Library/Alamy
Shiraz sign in the Pepper Tree Winery, Hunter Valley © Tim Graham/Corbis
Cafés and restaurants at Block Place in Melbourne © David Wall/Alamy
Emu farming © Helene Rogers/Alamy

The great outdoors colour section

Gordon River, Wild Rivers National Park, Tasmania © Ted Mead/phtolibrary
Ningaloo Reef, Ningaloo Marine Park © Doug Pearson/JAI/Corbis
Fisherman on pier near Busselton © Robert Garvey/Corbis
Daintree National Park © Getty
Cradle Mountain National Park, Tasmania © Ted Mead/photolibrary
Australian cowgirl herding cattle © Joseph J. Scherschel / national Gepgraphic/ Getty
The Gunbarrel Highway, Outback Western Australia © Machteld Baljet & Marcel Hoevenaars/Alamy

Wildlife colour section

Blue-winged kookaburra © James Hager/ Getty Images/Robert Harding
Echidna © Staffan Widstrand/CORBIS
Common wombat © Getty Images/Altrendo
Redback Spider © Ian Waldie / Getty
Great white shark © Tim Davis/CORBIS
Cane toad © Jack Picone / Alamy
Flock of rose-breasted cockatoos © Martin Harvey/CORBIS

Black and whites

p.86 Sydney Harbour Bridge and the Opera House © Nicole Newman
p.97 Centrepoint and the Monorail © Ian Osborn
p.126 Darling Harbour © Sergio Pitamitz/Robert Harding
p.149 Surfer, Sydney © Nicole Newman

p.187 Pittwater and Ku-ring-gai Chase National Park © David Messent
p.196 Lindemans Winery, Hunter Valley © Ian Osborn
p.209 The Three Sisters in the Blue Mountains © Gavin Hellier/Robert Harding
p.226 Lord Howe Island Tourism ©
p.237 Australian War Memorial © Paul A. Souders/CORBIS
p.253 Snowy Mountains © David Bigwood/Alamy
p.272 Big Banana, Coffs Harbour © James Davis; Eye Ubiquitous/CORBIS
p.284 Michael Franti, East Coast International Blues & Roots Festival, Byron Bay © James Green/Getty
p.292 Masked booby © Dave Watts/Alamy
p.304 Bald Rock © Kevin Lang/Alamy
p.326 Murray River © Robert Cianflone/Getty Images
p.330 Slim Dusty © Peter Lorimer/epa/Corbis
p.349 Old mining equipment in Broken Hill © Dave G. Houser/Corbis
p.358 Sailing the Whitsunday islands in Whitehaven Bay © Picpics/Alamy
p.378 Castlemaine-Perkins (XXXX) brewery © Scott Stickland
p.384 Q1 Tower view of Surfers Paradise © Scott Stickland
p.399 Crocodile Hunter Steve Irwin, Australia Zoo © Vera Devai/epa/Corbis
p.410 Fraser Island © Ian Osborn
p.415 Bundaberg Rum © photolibrary
p.429 Duck-billed platypus, Eungella National Park © blickwinkel/Alamy
p.447 Magnetic Island © Panoramic Images/ Getty Images
p.469 Great Barrier Reef © Yann Arthus-Bertrand/ CORBIS
p.483 Daintree River, Daintree National Park © Tim Graham/Getty
p.500 Canoeists in Lawn Hill National Park © Bill Bachman/Alamy
p.510 Palms and ferns in Carnarvon Gorge © Geoff Higgins/photolibrary
p.520 Yellow sapphire, Rubyvale Gem Gallery © Doug Steley/Alamy
p.533 Bull-riding at Mount Isa © Sindre Ellingsen/ Alamy
p.548 Saltwater crocodile © Phillipa Lawson /naturepl.com
p.573 Nabulwinjbulwinj at Nourlangie site © Archivo Iconografico, S.A./CORBIS
p.583 Waterfall, Katherine Gorge © Michael S. Yamashita/CORBIS
p.601 Tribal elder playing a didgeridoo © Doug Steley/Alamy
p.622 Feral camels at The Olgas, Uluru–Kata Tjuta National Park © Tim Wimborne/Reuters/ Corbis
p.626 Bungle Bungles © Robert Garvey/Corbis
p.633 Perth © Gavin Hellier/Robert Harding
p.657 Karri Forest © Bill Bachman/Alamy
p.677 The Pinnacles© Rob Blakers/photolibrary
p.685 Whale shark at Ningaloo Reef © Jeffrey L. Rotman/CORBIS
p.701 Seaplane trip to Horizontal Waterfalls, The Kimberley © Robert Garvey/Corbis
p.720 Coober Pedy © Roland Liptak/Alamy
p.732 Festival Centre Adelaide © Jon Arnold Images/Alamy
p.753 Barossa Valley © Doug Pearson/JAI/Corbis
p.771 Koalas, Kangaroo Island © Steve Bloom Images/Alamy
p.781 Paddle Steamer on the Murray River © Peter M. Wilson/Alamy
p.796 Animal road signs, Nullarbor Plain © Bill Bachman/Alamy
p.813 Sand dunes at sunrise, Simpson Desert © Ted Mead/photolibrary
p.878 Phillip Island penguins © photolibrary
p.890 The Twelve Apostles © James Osmond/ Alamy
p.898 Rip Curl Pro Surfing Contest, Bells Beach © ASP/Pierre Tostee/Reuters/Corbis
p.927 Panning for gold, Sovereign Hill, Ballarat © Bill Bachman/Alamy
p.934 The Balconies rock formation, Grampions NP © Julie Mowbray/Alamy
p.950 Tree ferns, Wilsons Promontory National Park © Peter Fakler/Alamy
p.959 Ned Kelly Statue © Jon Arnold Image /Alamy
p.967 Mount Hotham, The Victorian Alps © Stuart Hannagan/Getty
p.972 Port Arthur © Alamy
p.986 View of Mount Wellington from Elizabeth Pier, Hobart © Nicole Newman
p.1004 Tasman Head, Bruny Island © Ian Osborn
p.1017 Aerial view of Wineglass Bay © Yann Arthus-Bertrand/CORBIS
p.1028 Kings Bridge, Cataract Gorge, Launceston © Nicole Newman
p.1037 Tasmanian Devil © Ian Waldie/Getty Images
p.1058 Giant myrtle trees, Tarkine © Rob Blakers/ photolibrary

Index

Map entries are in colour.

C

INDEX

D

E

F

INDEX

G

H

INDEX

I

J

K

L

INDEX

M

INDEX

N

O

P

Q

R

S

INDEX

T

U

V

W

Y

Z

INDEX

Map symbols

maps are listed in the full index using coloured text

State/territorial boundary	Metro station
Chapter division boundary	Bus/taxi stop
Main road	Point of interest
Minor road	Internet access
Unpaved road	Information office
Pedestrianized street (town maps)	Post office
Steps	Hospital
Path/track	Parking
Railway	Garden
Ferry route	Golf course
River	Chinese temple
Mountain peak	Campsite
Mountain range	Accommodation
Gorge	Restaurant
Rock	Building
Reef	Church/cathedral
Viewpoint	Aboriginal land
Waterfall	Prohibited area
Cave	Beach
Conservation hut	Cemetery
Lighthouse	Marsh
Airport	Park
Airfield	Salt lake